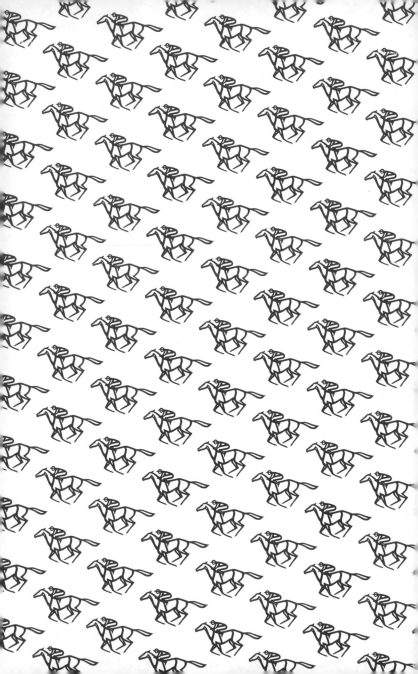

RACEHORSES
OF 1990

A Timeform Publication

Price £65.00

A Timeform Publication

Compiled and produced under the direction of
Reg Griffin

by members of the Timeform Organisation

G. Greetham, B.A., G. F. Walton, Dip.A.D. (Directors), J. D. Newton, B.A. (Editor-in-Chief), D. P. Adams (Editor), R. J. C. Austen, B.A., G. Crowther, G. J. Cunningham, LL.B., P. R. Entwistle, B.Sc., W. Hughes, G. M. Johnstone, P. A. Muncaster, B.Sc., G. J. North, B.Sc. and C. S. Williams.

© **Portway Press Limited 1991**

ISBN 0 900599 52 9

CONTENTS

AGE, WEIGHT & DISTANCE TABLE

Timeform's scale of weight-for-age for the flat

Dist	Age	Jan		Feb		Mar		Apr		May		June	
		1-16	17-31	1-16	17-28	1-16	17-31	1-16	17-30	1-16	17-31	1-16	17-30
5f	4	10-0	10-0	10-0	10-0	10-0	10-0	10-0	10-0	10-0	10-0	10-0	10-0
	3	9-5	9-5	9-6	9-7	9-7	9-8	9-8	9-9	9-9	9-10	9-10	9-11
	2						8-0	8-1	8-3	8-4	8-5	8-6	8-7
6f	4	10-0	10-0	10-0	10-0	10-0	10-0	10-0	10-0	10-0	10-0	10-0	10-0
	3	9-2	9-3	9-4	9-5	9-5	9-6	9-7	9-7	9-8	9-9	9-9	9-9
	2									8-0	8-2	8-3	8-4
7f	4	9-13	9-13	10-0	10-0	10-0	10-0	10-0	10-0	10-0	10-0	10-0	10-0
	3	9-0	9-1	9-2	9-3	9-4	9-4	9-5	9-6	9-6	9-7	9-8	9-8
	2											7-13	8-1
1m	4	9-13	9-13	9-13	9-13	10-0	10-0	10-0	10-0	10-0	10-0	10-0	10-0
	3	8-12	8-13	9-0	9-1	9-2	9-2	9-3	9-4	9-5	9-5	9-6	9-7
	2												
9f	4	9-12	9-12	9-12	9-13	9-13	9-13	9-13	10-0	10-0	10-0	10-0	10-0
	3	8-10	8-11	8-12	8-13	9-0	9-1	9-2	9-2	9-3	9-4	9-5	9-5
	2												
1¼m	4	9-11	9-12	9-12	9-12	9-13	9-13	9-13	9-13	9-13	10-0	10-0	10-0
	3	8-8	8-9	8-10	8-11	8-12	8-13	9-0	9-1	9-2	9-2	9-3	9-4
	2												
11f	4	9-10	9-11	9-11	9-12	9-12	9-12	9-13	9-13	9-13	9-13	9-13	10-0
	3	8-6	8-7	8-8	8-9	8-10	8-11	8-12	8-13	9-0	9-1	9-2	9-2
1½m	4	9-10	9-10	9-10	9-11	9-11	9-12	9-12	9-12	9-13	9-13	9-13	9-13
	3	8-4	8-5	8-6	8-7	8-8	8-9	8-10	8-11	8-12	8-13	9-0	9-1
13f	4	9-9	9-9	9-10	9-10	9-11	9-11	9-11	9-12	9-12	9-12	9-13	9-13
	3	8-2	8-3	8-4	8-5	8-7	8-8	8-9	8-10	8-11	8-12	8-13	9-0
1¾m	4	9-8	9-8	9-9	9-9	9-10	9-10	9-11	9-11	9-12	9-12	9-12	9-13
	3	8-0	8-2	8-3	8-4	8-5	8-6	8-7	8-8	8-9	8-10	8-11	8-12
15f	4	9-7	9-8	9-8	9-9	9-9	9-10	9-10	9-11	9-11	9-11	9-12	9-12
	3	7-13	8-0	8-1	8-2	8-4	8-5	8-6	8-7	8-8	8-9	8-10	8-11
2m	4	9-6	9-7	9-7	9-8	9-9	9-9	9-10	9-10	9-11	9-11	9-11	9-12
	3	7-11	7-12	7-13	8-1	8-2	8-3	8-4	8-5	8-6	8-7	8-8	8-9
2¼m	4	9-5	9-5	9-6	9-7	9-7	9-8	9-9	9-9	9-10	9-10	9-11	9-11
	3	7-8	7-9	7-11	7-12	7-13	8-0	8-2	8-3	8-4	8-5	8-6	8-7
2½m	4	9-3	9-4	9-5	9-6	9-6	9-7	9-7	9-8	9-9	9-9	9-10	9-10
	3	7-5	7-7	7-8	7-9	7-11	7-12	7-13	8-1	8-2	8-3	8-4	8-5

For 5-y-o's and older, use 10-0 in all cases
Race distances in the above tables are shown only at 1 furlong intervals.
For races over odd distances, the nearest distance shown in the table should be used:
thus for races of 1m to 1m 109 yards, use the table weights for 1m;
for 1m 110 yards to 1m 219 yards use the 9f table

AGE, WEIGHT & DISTANCE TABLE

Timeform's scale of weight-for-age for the flat

Dist	Age	July		Aug		Sept		Oct		Nov		Dec	
		1-16	17-31	1-16	17-31	1-16	17-30	1-16	17-31	1-16	17-30	1-16	17-31
5f	4	10-0	10-0	10-0	10-0	10-0	10-0	10-0	10-0	10-0	10-0	10-0	10-0
	3	9-11	9-12	9-12	9-12	9-13	9-13	9-13	9-13	10-0	10-0	10-0	10-0
	2	8-8	8-9	8-10	8-11	8-12	8-13	9-0	9-1	9-2	9-2	9-3	9-4
6f	4	10-0	10-0	10-0	10-0	10-0	10-0	10-0	10-0	10-0	10-0	10-0	10-0
	3	9-10	9-10	9-11	9-11	9-12	9-12	9-12	9-13	9-13	9-13	9-13	10-0
	2	8-5	8-6	8-7	8-8	8-9	8-10	8-11	8-12	8-13	9-0	9-1	9-2
7f	4	10-0	10-0	10-0	10-0	10-0	10-0	10-0	10-0	10-0	10-0	10-0	10-0
	3	9-9	9-9	9-10	9-10	9-11	9-11	9-11	9-12	9-12	9-12	9-13	9-13
	2	8-2	8-3	8-4	8-5	8-6	8 7		8-9	8-10	8-11	8-12	8-13	9-0
1m	4	10-0	10-0	10-0	10-0	10-0	10-0	10-0	10-0	10-0	10-0	10-0	10-0
	3	9-7	9-8	9-8	9-9	9-9	9-10	9-10	9-11	9-11	9-12	9-12	9-12
	2			8-2	8-3	8-4	8-5	8-6	8-7	8-8	8-9	8-10	8-11
9f	4	10-0	10-0	10-0	10-0	10-0	10-0	10-0	10-0	10-0	10-0	10-0	10-0
	3	9-6	9-7	9-7	9-8	9-8	9-9	9-9	9-10	9-10	9-11	9-11	9-12
	2					8-1	8-3	8-4	8 5	8-6	8-7	8-8	8-9
1¼m	4	10-0	10-0	10-0	10-0	10-0	10-0	10-0	10-0	10-0	10-0	10-0	10-0
	3	9-5	9-5	9-6	9-7	9-7	9-8	9-8	9-9	9-9	9-10	9-10	9-11
	2							8-1	8-2	8-4	8-5	8-6	8-7
11f	4	10-0	10-0	10-0	10-0	10-0	10-0	10-0	10-0	10-0	10-0	10-0	10-0
	3	9-3	9-4	9-5	9-5	9-6	9-7	9-7	9-8	9-8	9-9	9-9	9-10
1½m	4	10-0	10-0	10-0	10-0	10-0	10-0	10-0	10-0	10-0	10-0	10-0	10-0
	3	9-2	9-2	9-3	9-4	9-5	9-5	9-6	9-7	9-7	9-8	9-9	9-9
13f	4	9-13	9-13	10-0	10-0	10-0	10-0	10-0	10-0	10-0	10-0	10-0	10-0
	3	9-0	9-1	9-2	9-3	9-4	9-4	9-5	9-6	9-6	9-7	9-8	9-8
1¾m	4	9-13	9-13	9-13	10-0	10-0	10-0	10-0	10-0	10-0	10-0	10-0	10-0
	3	8-13	9-0	9-1	9-2	9-3	9-3	9-4	9-5	9-5	9-6	9-7	9-7
15f	4	9-12	9-13	9-13	9-13	9-13	10-0	10-0	10-0	10-0	10-0	10-0	10-0
	3	8-12	8-13	9-0	9-1	9-1	9-2	9-3	9-4	9-4	9-5	9-6	9-6
2m	4	9-12	9-12	9-13	9-13	9-13	9-13	10-0	10-0	10-0	10-0	10-0	10-0
	3	8-10	8-11	8-12	8-13	9-0	9-1	9-2	9-3	9-3	9-4	9-5	9-5
2¼m	4	9-11	9-12	9-12	9-12	9-13	9-13	9-13	9-13	10-0	10-0	10-0	10-0
	3	8-8	8-9	8-10	8-11	8-12	8-13	9-0	9-1	9-2	9-2	9-3	9-4
2½m	4	9-10	9-11	9-11	9-12	9-12	9-13	9-13	9-13	9-13	9-13	10-0	10-0
	3	8-6	8-7	8-8	8-9	8-10	8-11	8-12	8-13	9-0	9-1	9-2	9-3

For 5-y-o's and older, use 10-0 in all cases
Race distances in the above tables are shown only at 1 furlong intervals.
For races over odd distances, the nearest distance shown in the table should be used:
thus for races of 1m to 1m 109 yards, use the table weights for 1m;
for 1m 110 yards to 1m 219 yards use the 9f table

5

The Sporting Life

The
runner
to follow
since
1859

THAT'S WHY IT'S
RACING'S GREATEST DAILY

FOREWORD

"Racehorses of 1990" deals individually, in alphabetical sequence, with every horse that ran under Jockey Club Rules (including on the all-weather tracks) in 1990, plus a number of foreign-trained horses that did not race here. For each of these horses is given (1) its age, colour and sex, (2) its breeding, (3) a form summary giving details of all its performances during the past two seasons, (4) a rating of its merit, (5) a commentary upon its racing or general characteristics as a racehorse, with some suggestions, perhaps, regarding its prospects for 1991 and (6) the name of the trainer in whose charge it was on the last occasion it ran. For each two-year-old the foaling date is also given.

The book is published with a twofold purpose. Firstly, the book is intended to have permanent value as a review of the exploits and achievements of the more notable of our thoroughbreds in 1990. Thus, while the commentaries upon the vast majority of the horses are, of necessity, in note form, the best horses are more critically examined, and the short essays upon them are illustrated by half-tone portraits and photographs of the finishes of some of the races in which they were successful; and secondly, the book is designed to provide data for practical use in analysing the racing programmes from day to day, and instructions as to its use in that capacity will be found in the Explanatory Notes.

The attention of foreign buyers of British bloodstock, and others who are concerned with Timeform Ratings as a measure of absolute racing class in terms of a standard scale, is drawn to the section headed "The Level of the Ratings" in the Explanatory Notes.

February, 1991

INDEX TO PHOTOGRAPHS

PORTRAITS & SNAPSHOTS

8

9

Jahafil	2 b.c.	Rainbow Quest– River Spey (Mill Reef)	*W. W. Rouch & Co*	447
Jimmy Barnie	2 ch.c.	Local Suitor– Sharper Still (Sharpen Up)	*Rex Coleman*	452
Kartajana	3 b.f.	Shernazar–Karamita (Shantung)	*John Crofts*	469
Knight of Mercy	4 b.g.	Aragon–Little Mercy (No Mercy)	*W. W. Rouch & Co*	483
Kooyonga	2 ch.f.	Persian Bold–Angjuli (Northfields)	*Jacqueline O'Brien*	486
Kostroma	4 b.f.	Caerleon–Katie May (Busted)	*Jacqueline O'Brien*	487
Legal Case	4 b.c.	Alleged–Maryinsky (Northern Dancer)	*John Crofts*	502
Linamix	3 gr.c.	Mendez–Lunadix (Breton)	*John Crofts*	510
Line Engaged	2 b.c.	Phone Trick– Quick Nurse (Dr Fager)	*W. W. Rouch & Co*	512
Lord Florey	3 b.c.	Blushing Groom– Remedia (Dr Fager)	*John Crofts*	520
Lord of The Field	3 b.c.	Jalmood–Star Face (African Sky)	*John Crofts*	521
Louve Bleue	3 b.f.	Irish River–Lupe (Primera)	*John Crofts*	523
Lugana Beach	4 br.c.	Tumble Wind– Safe Haven (Blakeney)	*W. W. Rouch & Co*	529
Lycius	2 ch.c.	Mr Prospector–Lypatia (Lyphard)	*P. Bertrand*	532
Madiriya	3 ch.f.	Diesis–Majanada (Tap On Wood)	*John Crofts*	543
Majmu	2 b.f.	Al Nasr– Affirmative Fable (Affirmed)	*John Crofts*	549
Malvernico	2 b.c.	Nordico– Malvern Beauty (Shirley Heights)	*Jacqueline O'Brien*	552
Markofdistinction	4 br.c.	Known Fact–Ghislaine (Icecapade)	*John Crofts*	561
Missionary Ridge	3 ch.c.	Caerleon–Shellshock (Salvo)	*Rex Coleman*	584
Moon Cactus	3 b.f.	Kris–Lady Moon (Mill Reef)	*Camilla Russell*	595
Mujaazif	2 b.c.	Alydar–Miss Snowflake (Snow Sporting)	*John Crofts*	603
Mujadil	2 b.c.	Storm Bird– Vallee Secrete (Secretariat)	*John Crofts*	606
Mujtahid	2 ch.c.	Woodman–Mesmerize (Mill Reef)	*John Crofts*	609
Mukaddamah	2 b.c.	Storm Bird–Tash (Never Bend)	*W. W. Rouch & Co*	611
Nazoo	2 b.f.	Nijinsky–La Dame du Lac (Round Table)	*Jacqueline O'Brien*	627
Negligent	3 gr.f.	Ahonoora–Negligence (Roan Rocket)	*Rex Coleman*	629
Night-Shirt	3 b.g.	Night Shift–Vestina (Run The Gantlet)	*John Crofts*	634
Northern Goddess	3 b.f.	Night Shift–Hearten (Hittite Glory)	*Fiona Vigors*	641
Norwich	3 b.c.	Top Ville–Dame Julian (Blakeney)	*Rex Coleman*	645
Old Vic	4 b.c.	Sadler's Wells–Cockade (Derring-Do)	*John Crofts*	652

10

11

RACE PHOTOGRAPHS

13

Gold Seal Oaks (Epsom)	John Crofts	193
Goodwood Cup (Goodwood)	John Crofts	527
Gordon Richards EBF Stakes (Sandown)	John Crofts	255
Gordon Stakes (Goodwood)	John Crofts	466
GPA National Stakes (the Curragh)	Caroline Norris	386
Grand Prix de Paris Louis Vuitton (Longchamp)	John Crofts	809
Grand Prix de Saint-Cloud (Saint-Cloud)	P. Bertrand	435
Gran Premio d'Italia-Trofeo Saima (Milan)	Perrucci	222
Great Voltigeur Stakes (York)	Ed Byrne	98
Grosser Preis der Berliner Bank (Dusseldorf)	K-J. Tuchel	416
Grosser Preis von Baden (Baden-Baden)	K-J. Tuchel	593
Hanson Coronation Cup (Epsom)	John Crofts	434
Hardwicke Stakes (Ascot)	John Crofts	70
Harry Rosebery Challenge Trophy (Ayr)	A. Russell	386
Heinz '57' Phoenix Stakes (Phoenix Park)	Caroline Norris	539
Hillsdown Cherry Hinton Stakes (Newmarket)	John Crofts	173
Homeowners Sprint (Handicap) (York)	John Crofts	526
Hoover Cumberland Lodge Stakes (Ascot)	A. Russell	420
Hue-Williams Stakes (Newbury)	John Crofts	946
James Seymour Stakes (Newmarket)	John Crofts	881
Jefferson Smurfit Memorial Irish St Leger (the Curragh)	Caroline Norris	416
Jersey Stakes (Ascot)	John Crofts	791
Jimmy Heal Memorial Trophy Nursery (Brighton)	Ed Byrne	389
Jockey Club Cup (Newmarket)	A. Russell	364
John Smith's Magnet Cup (York)	Tony Edenden	286
Juddmonte International Stakes (York)	A. Russell	431
Juddmonte Lockinge Stakes (Newbury)	John Crofts	786
Keeneland Nunthorpe Stakes (York)	A. Russell	226
Kerridge Computers Trophy Handicap (Newbury)	John Crofts	58
Kildangan Stud Irish Oaks (the Curragh)	Ed Byrne	484
King Edward VII Stakes (Ascot)	A. Russell	712
King George Stakes (Goodwood)	John Crofts	62
King George VI and Queen Elizabeth Diamond Stakes (Ascot)	John Crofts	97
King's Stand Stakes (Ascot)	John Crofts	225
Kiveton Park Stakes (Doncaster)	A. Russell	368
Kosset Yorkshire Cup (York)	John Crofts	126
Krug Diadem Stakes (Ascot)	A. Russell	766
Ladbroke Chester Cup (Handicap) (Chester)	A. Russell	956
Ladbroke European Free Handicap (Newmarket)	John Crofts	54
Ladbrokes (Ayr) Gold Cup (Ayr)	A. Russell	307
Ladbroke Sprint Cup (Haydock)	A. Russell	227
Lancashire Oaks (Haydock)	A. Russell	683
Lanes End John Porter EBF Stakes (Newbury)	John Crofts	136
Lanson Champagne Vintage Stakes (Goodwood)	John Crofts	610
Laurent-Perrier Champagne Stakes (Doncaster)	A. Russell	115
Leslie And Godwin Spitfire Handicap (Goodwood)	John Crofts	472
'Mail On Sunday' Three-Year-Old Series Handicap Final (Newmarket)	John Crofts	147
Man o'War Stakes (Belmont Park)	NYRA Photo	236
Mappin & Webb Henry II EBF Stakes (Sandown)	John Crofts	917
Marley Roof Tile Oaks Trial (Lingfield)	George Selwyn	730
May Hill Stakes (Doncaster)	A. Russell	548
Michael Sobell Handicap (York)	A. Russell	628
Molecomb Stakes (Goodwood)	John Crofts	693
Moyglare Stud Stakes (the Curragh)	Caroline Norris	153
Nell Gwyn Stakes (Newmarket)	Sport And General	388
Newcastle 'Brown Ale' Northumberland Plate (Handicap Sweepstakes) (Newcastle)	A. Russell	40
Newgate Stud Middle Park Stakes (Newmarket)	John Crofts	531
N.M. Financial Predominate Stakes (Goodwood)	John Crofts	738
Norfolk Stakes (Ascot)	John Crofts	511
Offa's Dyke Maiden Fillies Stakes (Chepstow)	Ed Byrne	579
Oh So Sharp Stakes (Newmarket)	John Crofts	221
'Pacemaker Update' Lowther Stakes (York)	John Crofts	655
Palace House Stakes (Newmarket)	A. Russell	887
Phil Bull Trophy (Pontefract)	Fotosport (Racing)	26

14

Philip Cornes Houghton Stakes (Newmarket)	*A. Russell*	458
Philip Cornes Nickel Alloys Handicap(Ayr)	*A. Russell*	998
Philip Cornes Nickel Alloys Nursery Handicap	*John Crofts*	218
(Newmarket)		
Phoenix Champion Stakes (Phoenix Park)	*Ed Byrne*	276
Prince of Wales's Stakes (Ascot)	*John Crofts*	87
Princess of Wales's Stakes (Newmarket)	*John Crofts*	805
Princess Royal Stakes (Ascot)	*John Crofts*	623
Prix Daphnis (Evry)	*P. Bertrand*	149
Prix d'Arenberg (Longchamp)	*P. Bertrand*	253
Prix de Diane Hermes (Chantilly)	*P. Bertrand*	730
Prix de la Foret (Longchamp)	*John Crofts*	822
Prix de la Salamandre (Longchamp)	*P. Bertrand*	391
Prix de Malleret (Longchamp)	*John Crofts*	581
Prix de Ris Orangis (Evry)	*P. Bertrand*	766
Prix des Aigles (Longchamp)	*John Crofts*	564
Prix d'Ispahan (Longchamp)	*P. Bertrand*	203
Prix Djebel (Maisons-Laffitte)	*John Crofts*	535
Prix du Cadran (Longchamp)	*John Crofts*	571
Prix du Conseil de Paris (Longchamp)	*P. Bertrand*	669
Prix du Gros Chene (Chantilly)	*P. Bertrand*	620
Prix du Haras de Fresnay-le-Buffard	*P. Bertrand*	710
Jacques le Marois (Deauville)		
Prix du Jockey-Club Lancia (Chantilly)	*John Crofts*	802
Prix Eugene Adam (Saint-Cloud)	*P. Bertrand*	222
Prix Ganay (Longchamp)	*P. Bertrand*	202
Prix Jean Prat (Longchamp)	*P. Bertrand*	709
Prix Lupin (Longchamp)	*John Crofts*	284
Prix Marcel Boussac (Longchamp)	*P. Bertrand*	825
Prix Maurice de Gheest (Deauville)	*P. Bertrand*	232
Prix Minerve (Evry)	*P. Bertrand*	980
Prix Morny Agence Francaise (Deauville)	*George Selwyn*	390
Prix Niel (Longchamp)	*P. Bertrand*	285
Prix Royal-Oak (Longchamp)	*P. Bertrand*	426
Prix Saint-Alary (Longchamp)	*John Crofts*	32
Prix Thomas Bryon (Saint-Cloud)	*P. Bertrand*	293
Prix Vermeille (Longchamp)	*P. Bertrand*	796
Queen Alexandra Stakes (Ascot)	*A. Russell*	744
Queen Anne Stakes (Ascot)	*A. Russell*	559
Queen Elizabeth II Stakes (Ascot)	*John Crofts*	560
Queen Mary Stakes (Ascot)	*John Crofts*	657
Queen Mother's Cup (Lady Amateur Riders) (York)	*A. Russell*	622
Racecall Gold Trophy (Redcar)	*A. Russell*	178
Racing Post Trophy (Doncaster)	*A. Russell*	679
Ribblesdale Stakes (Ascot)	*John Crofts*	395
Rokeby Farms Mill Reef Stakes (Newbury)	*John Crofts*	934
Rothmans International (Woodbine)	*Michael Burns*	323
Royal Hong Kong Jockey Club Trophy (Handicap)	*George Selwyn*	119
(Sandown)		
Royal Hunt Cup (Ascot)	*John Crofts*	697
Royal Lodge William Hill Stakes (Ascot)	*A. Russell*	602
Schweppes Golden Mile (Goodwood)	*John Crofts*	555
Scottish Classic (Ayr)	*A. Russell*	414
Scottish Equitable Gimcrack Stakes (York)	*A. Russell*	608
Scottish Equitable Richmond Stakes (Goodwood)	*John Crofts*	538
Sea World EBF Pretty Polly Stakes (the Curragh)	*Caroline Norris*	332
Shadwell Estates Firth of Clyde Stakes (Ayr)	*A. Russell*	423
Shadwell Stud Cheshire Oaks (Chester)	*John Crofts*	682
Shernazar EBF Curragh Stakes(the Curragh)	*Caroline Norris*	551
Soham House Stakes (Newmarket)	*John Crofts*	695
Spindrifter Sprint Stakes (Pontefract)	*A. Russell*	935
State of New York Stakes (Belmont Park)	*Ed Byrne*	746
St James's Palace Stakes (Ascot)	*John Crofts*	839
St Leger Stakes (Doncaster)	*A. Russell*	865
Strathclyde Stakes (Ayr)	*A. Russell*	256
St Simon Stakes (Newbury)	*John Crofts*	262
Stud Lite L.A. Lager Stakes (Handicap) (Ascot)	*A. Russell*	697
Sussex Stakes (Goodwood)	*John Crofts*	247

Tattersalls Cheveley Park Stakes (Newmarket)	*John Crofts*	154
Tattersalls Musidora Stakes (York)	*A. Russell*	429
Tattersalls Tiffany Highflyer Stakes (Newmarket)	*John Crofts*	315
Tattersalls Tiffany Yorkshire Fillies Stakes (Doncaster)	*John Crofts*	626
Three Chimneys Dewhurst Stakes (Newmarket)	*John Crofts*	337
Tia Maria March Stakes (Goodwood)	*John Crofts*	755
Timeform Futurity (Pontefract)	*A. Russell*	936
Timeform Nursery Handicap (Pontefract)	*A. Russell*	371
Tote Cesarewitch (Handicap) (Newmarket)	*A. Russell*	955
Tote Ebor Handicap (York)	*A. Russell*	328
Tote Gold Trophy (Handicap) (Goodwood)	*John Crofts*	108
Tote-Portland Handicap (Doncaster)	*A. Russell*	524
Troy Stakes (Doncaster)	*John Crofts*	507
Turf Classic (Belmont Park)	*NYRA Photo*	143
Van Geest Criterion Stakes (Newmarket)	*John Crofts*	760
Vodafone Nassau Stakes (Goodwood)	*W. Everett*	467
Walmac International Geoffrey Freer Stakes (Newbury)	*John Crofts*	168
Waterford Foods EBF Phoenix Flying Five (Phoenix Park)	*Caroline Norris*	124
Westminster-Motor (Taxi) Insurance City And Suburban Handicap (Epsom)	*George Selwyn*	885
William Hill Cambridgeshire Handicap (Newmarket)	*John Crofts*	754
William Hill Dante Stakes (York)	*A. Russell*	801
William Hill Lincoln Handicap (Doncaster)	*John Crofts*	292
William Hill November Handicap (Doncaster)	*A. Russell*	77
William Hill Stewards' Cup (Handicap) (Goodwood)	*John Crofts*	482
William Hill Trophy (Handicap) (York)	*A. Russell*	472
Windsor Castle Stakes (Ascot)	*A. Russell*	343
Wokingham Stakes (Handicap) (Ascot)	*A. Russell*	481
Wynyard Classic Northumberland Sprint Trophy (Handicap) (Newcastle)	*A. Russell*	910

EXPLANATORY NOTES

To assess the prospects of any horse in a race it is necessary to know two things about him: first, how good he is; and second, what sort of horse he is. In this book the merit of each horse is expressed in the form of a *rating* (printed on the right) and the *racing character* of the horse is given in the commentary.

TIMEFORM RATINGS

The Timeform Rating of a horse is simply the merit of the horse expressed in pounds and is arrived at by careful examination of its running against other horses. We maintain a "running" handicap of all horses in training throughout the season, or, to be strictly accurate, two handicaps, one for horses aged three years and over, and one for two-year-olds.

THE LEVEL OF THE RATINGS

At the close of each season all the horses that have raced are re-handicapped from scratch, and each horse's rating is revised. It is also necessary to adjust the general level of the handicap, so that all the ratings are kept at the same standard level from year to year. Left to itself, the general level of the ratings, in each succeeding issue of Timeform, tends to rise steadily. For technical reasons it is desirable to allow it to do so during the season: but, in winter, when the complete re-handicap is done, the ratings must, of course, be put back on their proper level again.

This explains why, in this book, the ratings are in general, different from those in the final issue of the 1990 Timeform series.

RATINGS AND WEIGHT-FOR-AGE

These matters, however, are by the way. What concerns the reader is that he has, in the ratings in this book, a universal handicap embracing all the horses in training it is possible to weigh up, ranging from tip-top classic performers, with ratings from 130 to 145, down to the meanest selling platers, rated around the 20 mark. What we now have to explain is the practical use of these ratings in the business of weighing up a race.

Before doing so, it is important to mention that all ratings are at weight-for-age, so that equal ratings mean horses of equal merit: perhaps it would be clearer if we said that the universal rating handicap is really not a single handicap, but four handicaps side by side: one for 2-y-o's, one for 3-y-o's, one for 4-y-o's and one for older horses. Thus, a 3-y-o rated, for argument's sake, at 117 is deemed to be identical in point of "merit" with a 4-y-o also rated at 117: but for them to have equal chances in, say, a mile race in May, the 3-y-o would need to be receiving 9 lb from the 4-y-o, which is the weight difference specified by the Age, Weight and Distance Tables on pages 4 and 5.

USING THE RATINGS

In using Timeform Ratings with a view to discovering which horses in any race have the best chances at the weights, we have two distinct cases, according to whether the horses taking part are of the same age or of different ages. Here is the procedure in each case:-

A. Horses of the Same Age

If the horses all carry the same weight there are no adjustments to be made, and the horses with the highest ratings have the best chances. If the horses carry different weights, jot down their ratings, and to the rating of each horse add one point for every pound the horse is set to carry less than 10 st, or subtract one point for every pound he has to carry more than 10 st. When the ratings have been adjusted in this way the highest resultant figure indicates the horse with the best chance at the weights.

Example (any distance: any week of the season)

2 Good Girl (9-6)	....	Rating 119	add 8	127
2 Paulinus (9-4)	....	Rating 113	add 10	123
2 Abilene (8-11)	....	Rating 107	add 17	124
2 Bob's Joy (8-7)	....	Rating 108	add 21	129
2 Time Warp (8-2)	....	Rating 100	add 26	126
2 Eagle Eye (7-7)	....	Rating 92	add 35	127

Bob's Joy (129) has the best chance; Good Girl (127) and Eagle Eye (127) are the next best.

B. Horses of Different Ages

Take no notice of the weight any horse receives from any other. Instead, consult the Age, Weight and Distance Table on the page facing the front cover. Treat each horse separately, and compare the weight it has to carry with the weight prescribed for it in the table, according to the age of the horse, the distance of the race and the month of the year. Then, add one point to the rating for each pound the horse has to carry less than the weight given in the table: or, subtract one point from the rating for every pound he has to carry more than the weight prescribed by the table. The highest resultant figure indicates the horse most favoured by the weights.

Example (1½ miles on June 30th)

(Table Weights: 5-y-o 10-0; 4-y-o 9-13; 3-y-o 9-1)

6 Nimitz (10-2)	....	Rating 115	subtract 2 .	113
4 Red Devil (9-9)	....	Rating 114	add 4	118
6 Sweet Cindy (9-5).	...	Rating 115	add 9	124
3 Jailhouse (9-2)	....	Rating 120	subtract 1 .	119
4 Haakon (8-11)	....	Rating 101	add 16	117
3 Fine Strike (8-7)	....	Rating 108	add 8	116

Sweet Cindy (124) has the best chance at the weights, with 5 lb in hand of Jailhouse.

JOCKEYSHIP AND APPRENTICE ALLOWANCES

There is just one further point that arises in evaluating the chances of the horse on the basis of their ratings: the question of jockeyship in general, and apprentice allowances in particular. The allowance which may be claimed by an apprentice is given to enable apprentices to obtain race-riding experience against experienced jockeys. For the purposes of rating calculations it should, in general, be assumed that the allowance the apprentice is able to claim (3 lb, 5 lb, or 7 lb) is nullified by his or her inexperience. Therefore, the *weight adjustments to the ratings should be calculated on the weight allotted by the handicapper, or determined by the conditions of the race,* and no extra addition should be made to a rating because the horse's rider claims an apprentice allowance.

The above is the general routine procedure. But of course there is no reason why the quality of jockeyship should not be taken into account in assessing the chances of horses in a race. Quite the contrary. Nobody would question that the jockeyship of a first-class rider is worth a pound or two, and occasionally an apprentice comes along who is riding quite as well as the average jockey long before losing the right to claim. Once the age and weight adjustments have been made to the ratings, small additional allowances may, at the discretion of the reader, be made for these matters of jockeyship. Please note, though, that if a horse is regularly ridden by a claiming apprentice, the fact will have been taken account of when its previous performances have been assessed by our handicappers.

WEIGHING UP A RACE

The ratings tell you which horses in a particular race are most favoured by the weights; but complete analysis demands that the racing character of each horse, as set out in the commentary upon it, is also studied carefully to see if there is any reason why the horse might be expected not to run up to its rating. It counts for little that a horse is thrown in at the weights if it has no pretensions whatever to staying the distance, or is unable to act on the prevailing going.

These two matters, suitability of distance and going, are no doubt the most important points to be considered. But there are others. For example, the ability of a horse to accommodate himself to the conformation of the track. Then there is the matter of pace versus stamina: as between two stayers of equal merit, racing over a distance suitable to both, firm going, or a small field with the prospect of a slowly-run race, would favour the one with the better pace and acceleration, whereas dead or soft going, or a big field with the prospect of a strong gallop throughout the race, would favour the sounder stayer. There is also the matter of temperament and behaviour at the start: nobody would be in a hurry to take a short price about a horse with whom it is always an even chance whether he will consent to race or not.

A few minutes spent checking up on these matters in the commentaries upon the horses concerned will sometimes put a very different complexion on a race from that which is put upon it by the ratings alone. We repeat, therefore, that the correct way to use Timeform, or this annual volume, in the analysis of individual races is, first to use the ratings to discover which horses are most favoured by the weights, and second, to check through the comments on the horse to discover what factors other than weight might also affect the outcome of the race.

Incidentally, in setting out the various characteristics, requirements and peculiarities of each horse in the commentary upon him, we have always expressed ourselves in as critical a manner as possible, endeavouring to say just as much, and no whit more than the facts seem to warrant. Where there are clear indications, and definite conclusions can be drawn with fair certainty, we have drawn them: if it is a matter of probability or possibility we have put it that way, being careful not to say the one when we mean the other; and where real conclusions are not to be drawn, we have been content to state the facts. Furthermore, when we say that a horse *may not* be suited by hard going, we do not expect the reader to treat it as though we had said that the horse *is not* suited by hard going. In short, both in our thinking and in the setting out of our views we have aimed at precision.

THE FORM SUMMARIES

The form summary enclosed in the brackets shows for each individual horse the distance, the state of the going and where the horse finished in each of its races on the flat during the last two seasons. Performances are in chronological sequence, the earliest being given first.

The distance of each race is given in furlongs, fractional distances being expressed in the decimal notation to the nearest tenth of a furlong. Races on an all-weather surface are prefixed by letter 'a'.

The going is symbolised as follows: h = hard or very firm; f = firm (turf) or fast (all-weather); m = fairly good, or on the firm side of good; g = good (turf) or standard (all-weather); d = dead, or on the soft side of good; s = soft, sticky or holding (turf) or slow (all-weather); v = heavy, very heavy or very holding.

Placings are indicated, up to sixth place, by the use of superior figures, an asterisk being used to denote a win.

Thus [1989 NR 1990 10s* 12f^3 11.7g a11g^2] signifies that the horse was unraced in 1989. He ran four times in 1990, winning over 10 furlongs on soft going first time out, finishing third over twelve furlongs on firm going next time out, unplaced, not in the first six, over 11.7 furlongs on good going, and then second over eleven furlongs on standard going on an all-weather track.

Included in the pedigree details are the highest Timeform Annual ratings during their racing careers of the sires, dams and sires of dams of all horses, where the information is available.

Where sale prices are given F denotes the price in guineas sold as a foal, Y the price in guineas sold as a yearling. The prefix IR denotes Irish guineas.

THE RATING SYMBOLS

The following symbols, attached to the ratings, are to be interpreted as stated:-

p   the horse is likely to make more than normal progress and to improve on his rating.

P   there is convincing evidence, or, to say the least, a very strong presumption that the horse is capable of form much better than he has so far displayed.

+   the horse may be rather better than we have rated him.

d   the horse appears to have deteriorated, and might no longer be capable of running to the rating given.

§   a horse of somewhat unsatisfactory temperament; one who may give his running on occasions, but cannot be relied upon to do so.

§§   an arrant rogue or thorough jade; so temperamentally unsatisfactory as to be not worth a rating.

?   the use of a query without a rating implies that although the horse has form, his merit is impossible to assess with confidence. If used in conjunction with a rating this symbol implies that the rating is based upon inadequate or unsatisfactory data, or that the rating is suspect.

CURRAGH BLOODSTOCK AGENCY

Presenting Golden Moments of 1990

SAUMAREZ
by Rainbow Quest
out of Fiesta Fun

Winner of Prix de l'Arc de Triomphe (Gr.1), Grand Prix de Paris Louis Vuitton (Gr.1). The CBA privately purchased Saumarez as a 3-y-o on behalf of Emmanuel de Seroux's Narvick International, prior to being transferred to Nicholas Clement's stable where he established himself as Champion European 3-y-o (at 11f+).

BELMEZ
by El Gran Senor
out of Grace Note

Winner of the King George VI And Queen Elizabeth Diamond Stakes (Gr.1). The CBA privately purchased his dam GRACE NOTE as a 3-y-o on behalf of Darley Stud Management. Belmez is her first foal.

"SERVICING THE NEEDS OF THE BLOODSTOCK INDUSTRY"

22

RACEHORSES OF 1990

AAHSAYLAD 4 b.c. Ardross 134–Madam Slaney 92 (Prince Tenderfoot (USA) **76**
126) [1989 11f 11s 12g 12g⁴ 11g³ 1990 12f⁵ 14g* 16g³ 17.6m⁴ 14g⁶ 13g* 13g³ 13f*
14.8m³ 14m³ 13d*ᵗ 14d⁴ 15v³ 15d⁴] big, good-topped colt: modest handicapper:
winner at Carlisle and Ayr (3 times) as 4-y-o, beating One For The Pot gamely in a
close finish to Bogside Cup in September for final success: best at 13f to 2m: acts on
any going: often apprentice ridden: genuine and most consistent. *F. H. Lee.*

AARDVARK 4 ch.g. On Your Mark 125–Vaguely Jade (Corvaro (USA) 122) [1989 **74**
7g 8.5d 8m* 8m* 8.2g³ 8h* 8g⁴ᵈⁱˢ 8m 8f⁵ 8m⁶ 8g² 7m 9g 11g⁵ 10g 1990 8f³ 8h⁶ 8g
8m⁴ 8.2s 8g 8.5g 9f⁴ 10m² 10.6d² 10.2m* 8.2m* 10.6d² 10f³ 8g³ 8f² 8g⁵ 8d 8g 10d⁴]
lengthy gelding: modest handicapper: successful at Newcastle in August and
Nottingham early following month: effective at 1m to 1¼m: seems unsuited by soft
going, acts on any other: effective with and without visor: suitable mount for
inexperienced rider: tough. *R. M. Whitaker.*

ABBEY GREEN 2 ch.c. (Mar 19) Gabitat 119–Getaway Girl 63 (Capistrano 120) **—**
[1990 5m] 2,000F, 4,700Y: workmanlike colt: fourth reported foal: brother to 3-y-o
Escape Talk, 5f and 7f winner at 2 yrs, and half-brother to a winner abroad: dam
stayed 13f: tailed off in maiden at Warwick in April. *C. J. Hill.*

ABDICATE (IRE) 2 ch.f. (Feb 5) Be My Guest (USA) 126–Crown Godiva 83 **66 p**
(Godswalk (USA) 130) [1990 7g] 94,000Y: close-coupled filly: second foal: closely
related to Irish 3-y-o 7f winner Cambrina (by El Gran Senor): dam 1m winner, is
half-sister to What A Guest (by Be My Guest) and Infantry: green, around 7 lengths
ninth of 20, held up after slow start then fading from over 1f out, to Campestral in
maiden at Newmarket: should improve. *L. M. Cumani.*

ABEL PROSPECT (USA) 3 b.c. Mr Prospector (USA)–Able Money (USA) **89**
(Distinctive (USA)) [1989 7g 1990 10f* 12f* 12f 12f4] leggy, quite attractive colt:
moderate walker: odds on, made all in maiden (hung right last 3f) at Brighton and
minor event at Thirsk in April: first run for 3 months, improved form when fourth of
6 in handicap at Goodwood in August: should stay further: yet to race on a soft
surface. *G. Harwood.*

ABERFOYLE (IRE) 2 b.g. (Apr 14) Vision (USA)–Princess John (Run The **58**
Gantlet (USA)) [1990 5m 6g 6m⁴ 7m 6m 7d a8g a6g a8g⁴] IR 6,500F, 3,600Y: leggy
gelding: moderate walker: poor mover: third foal: half-brother to Irish 3-y-o Miss
Gantlet (by Lomond), 5f winner at 2 yrs: dam maiden: plating-class maiden: easily
best effort final appearance: ran moderately in sellers fourth and sixth outings:
suited by 1m: twice blinkered: races keenly. *M. Johnston.*

ABIGAIL'S DREAM 3 gr.f. Kalaglow 132–Moss Pink (USA) (Levmoss 133) **63**
[1989 6m a8g a6g³ 1990 a8g² a10g* a10g⁴ a7g⁴ 8m 9m² 10m⁶ 9f* 10m⁴ 10f⁵]
lightly-made filly: quite modest performer: won claimers at Lingfield in January and
Wolverhampton (made all) in August: appeared to run extremely well in Chepstow
handicap penultimate start: stays 1¼m well: acts on firm going: apprentice ridden
last 4 outings: sold out of A. Lee's stable 1,750 gns Ascot April Sales after fifth. *D.
Burchell.*

ABIGAILS PORTRAIT 4 ch.f. Absalom 128–Corr Lady (Lorenzaccio 130) **43 §**
[1989 7g 6f² 6h³ 1990 a5g⁵ a5g⁴ a7g 5f 6g 8.2g³ 7m] sparely-made, angular filly: has
a round action: quite modest form at best in maidens: looked temperamentally
unsatisfactory second and third (visored then and next time) outings: twice refused
to enter stalls: in foal to Good Times. *M. P. Naughton.*

ABLE JET (USA) 2 br.c. (May 13) Northjet 136–Princess Nicketti (USA) (Tom 80
Rolfe) [1990 6g⁶ 6g⁵ 6m⁴ 5d² 5d⁴ 5f³ 5f* 5m⁵ 5.3h³ 7f 6m 5f⁴ 5f⁴ 5m³ 5m⁶ 5s* 5d
5g] $10,000Y: robust, attractive colt: poor mover: fourth foal: half-brother to a minor
winner in North America: dam minor winner as 2-y-o: improved performer: won
maiden at Folkestone in July and minor event (by 4 lengths) at Ayr in October: best
at 5f: acts on any going: twice blinkered: trained first 5 appearances by W.
O'Gorman: game and genuine. *Mrs N. Macauley.*

ABLE JUMBO 3 b.g. Norwick (USA) 120–Bourges (FR) (Luthier 126) [1989 NR —
1990 8.2s a11g⁵ 10f] leggy, dipped-backed gelding: sixth living foal: half-brother to
several winners here and abroad, including 1¼m winner Mitner (by Vilgora) and 6f
winner Indian Set (by Windjammer): dam placed over hurdles at 3 yrs in France:
bandaged, behind in minor event and maidens. *Mrs N. Macauley.*

ABLE LASSIE 2 gr.f. (Mar 10) Grey Desire 115–Clairwood (Final Straw 127) 57
[1990 5f⁴ 6f⁵ 7g² 6g* 6m⁴ 6m⁴ 7m 7f² 8.2s²] smallish, angular filly: moderate
mover: second foal: dam lightly raced: fairly useful plater: won claimer at Hamilton
in July: stays 1m: acts on any going. *E. Weymes.*

ABLE MAC (USA) 2 ch.c. (May 17) Red Ryder (USA)–Amber Amethyst (USA) 56
(Staff Writer (USA)) [1990 5.8f³ 7f⁴ 5m 6m 5s a6g⁶ a5g⁶] $11,000Y: lengthy colt:
brother to 3 winners in North America, including 8.5f Illinois Oaks winner Amber
Ryder, and half-brother to another: dam won at up to 9f: sire unraced brother to Mr
Prospector: plating-class maiden: easily best effort second outing: ran poorly last 4
starts, mulish to post on first of them: suited by 7f: twice blinkered: sweating and
edgy fifth appearance: trained first 3 starts by W. O'Gorman. *Mrs N. Macauley.*

ABLE PLAYER (USA) 3 b. or br.g. Solford (USA) 127–Grecian Snow (CAN) 62
(Snow Knight 125) [1989 6g 6f 8g⁴ a7g* a8g 1990 a7g³ a8g² a8g 7m⁶ 9m 12.2m⁵
8.5d 8g² 9m* 8h² 10f a8g 8m] leggy, quite good-topped gelding: quite modest
handicapper: won at York in July: worth another try at 1¼m: acts on hard ground:
claimed out of Mrs N. Macauley's stable £9,000 on sixth outing. *C. W. Thornton.*

ABLE ROCKET (USA) 3 b.g. Shimatoree (USA)–Fast Ride (FR) (Sicambre 53
135) [1989 7g a7g² a6g 1990 a6g⁵ a7g³ a8g³ a8g⁴ 7f 10f 6m 7.5f⁵ 7m a8g]
good-topped gelding: plating-class maiden: best at 1m: acts on firm going: raced too
freely and swished tail when blinkered second outing: sometimes on toes: sold out
of Mrs N. Macauley's stable 575 gns Ascot October Sales after ninth start. *D.
Morrill.*

ABLE SUSAN 2 b.f. (May 7) Formidable (USA) 125–Susanna (USA) 81§ 73 p
(Nijinsky (CAN) 138) [1990 6m⁴ 7f⁴ 7d*] angular filly: has a roundish action: sixth
foal: half-sister to 3-y-o Totham (by Shernazar) and 2 other winners, including
useful 7f and 1¼m winner Sue Grundy (by Grundy): dam placed 5 times over 1m but
disappointing, is daughter of 1000 Guineas winner Full Dress II: won maiden at
Catterick in October by a length from Sunny Davies: will stay 1m: will improve
further. *G. Wragg.*

ABLE VALE 4 b.f. Formidable (USA) 125–Valeur (Val de Loir 133) [1989 7s 7m 51
7m⁴ 8m⁶ 10g⁵ 1990 12.5f* 12f³] close-coupled, deep-girthed filly: won seller
(bought in 4,500 gns) at Wolverhampton in April, clear 5f out: suited by 1½m: acts
on firm ground: keen sort, suited by forcing tactics: also successful over hurdles in
spring. *R. J. Holder.*

ABOM SWIFT 2 gr.c. (May 12) Absalom 128–Swift Return 79 (Double Form 130) 82
[1990 5g⁶ 5m³ 5.8h*] 12,000F, 21,000Y, 14,000 2-y-o: workmanlike, good-
quartered colt: has a quick action: third foal: half-brother to a winner abroad by
Music Boy: dam 2-y-o 6f winner, is half-sister to smart Skyliner: fair performer:
rallied to win nursery at Bath in August: better suited by 6f than 5f. *I. Campbell.*

ABOU MINJAL (MOR) 4 ch.g. Asandre (FR)–Honeyou (MOR) (Honey Hot 41
(FR)) [1989 8s 12f 12m 17.1f³ 1990 14g⁴] Moroccan-bred gelding: poor handicapper:
stays 17f: bandaged only outing (April) at 4 yrs. *G. Lewis.*

ABRIGO 3 b.c. Aragon 118–Poshteen 86 (Royal Smoke 113) [1989 6g 1990 7m 6f³ —
a5g] plating-class form: 6½ lengths last of 3 to impressive Emtyaaz in minor contest
at Lingfield in July, easily best effort as 3-y-o: faced very stiff task in handicap
following month: stays 6f. *O. O'Neill.*

ABSAAR (USA) 3 b.f. Alleged (USA) 138–My Nord (USA) (Vent du Nord) [1989 76
NR 1990 14g² 11m* 11.7m²] IR 340,000Y: lengthy, angular filly: has round action:
tenth foal: half-sister to 8 winners, notably Grand Prix de Paris and Melbourne Cup
winner At Talaq (by Roberto) and Grade 1 8.5f and 9f winner Annoconnor (by
Nureyev): dam won 2 sprint claiming races: won maiden at Redcar in July, making

most: lacked turn of foot, and would have been well suited by return to 1¾m +: retired and visits Polish Precedent. *A. C. Stewart.*

ABSALOUI 2 gr.f. (Feb 29) Absalom 128–Agreloui 59 (Tower Walk 130) [1990 64 5f³ 6g 5f² 5.3h⁴ 5m⁵ 5v*] 8,800Y: leggy, workmanlike filly: third reported living foal: dam lightly-raced maiden from family of Sing Sing and Burglar: quite modest performer: won maiden auction at Chester in October: should stay 6f: looks ideally suited by plenty of give. *W. G. M. Turner.*

ABSENT FOREVER 2 ro.g. (Mar 24) Absalom 128–Strawberry Fields 66 59 (Song 132) [1990 5d⁵ 5f⁵] 10,500Y: lengthy, good-topped gelding: has plenty of scope: fourth reported foal: brother to 3-y-o 6f winner Solomon's Nephew, half-brother to 1987 2-y-o 7f seller winner Lynsdale Boy and 1m seller winner Fille de Fraise (both by Mr Fluorocarbon): dam ran only at 2 yrs, winning 6f seller: favourite, around 5 lengths fifth of 13 to Orient Air in maiden at Catterick in September: very backward on debut: will be better suited by 6f. *K. M. Brassey.*

ABSENT LOVER 9 ch.m. Nearly A Hand 115–Straight Avenue 62 (Royal 58 Avenue 123) [1989 10.2g 1990 10.8m² 10.2m² 12d⁴ 10m⁴ 10.2f 10m] workmanlike mare: poor mover: quite modest handicapper: stays 1½m: probably not suited by firm going, acts on any other: bandaged first 2 starts: sometimes misses the break. *F. J. Yardley.*

ABSO 2 b.g. (Mar 8) Absalom 128–Classical Vintage 80 (Stradavinsky 122) [1990 60 5f 5m⁶ 6g a7g³ a7g] strong, lengthy gelding: third foal: dam 2-y-o 5f winner: quite modest maiden: best effort penultimate start: ran as if something amiss final outing: stays 7f: unseated rider to post second outing, off course 6 months after. *R. Hannon.*

ABSOLATUM 3 ro.c. Absalom 128–Omnia 80 (Hill Clown (USA)) [1989 NR 1990 — 8g 8m 9m 10m 12m⁴ 12m 10f] 12,000Y: big, workmanlike colt: half-brother to 5 winners, notably smart 1982 2-y-o 6f and 7f winner All Systems Go and fairly useful 1m winner First of All (both by Bay Express): dam won over 1½m: no worthwhile form in first half of season, including in handicaps: visored last 6 outings: sold to join J. Thomas 1,700 gns Ascot September Sales. *P. Howling.*

ABSOLUTELY HUMMING 4 ch.g. Absalom 128–Hum 69 (Crooner 119) 51 [1989 5m 6f 5g 5f4 8f² 8.3m a7g 1990 a8g⁶ a7g⁶ a7g⁴ 8m⁵ 7f] lengthy, good-quartered gelding: fair winner as 2-y-o: well below his best early in 1990: bandaged and taken down early, didn't find great deal in selling handicap final outing: probably stays 1m: acts on firm and dead going: blinkered once at 3 yrs and last 3 starts. *D. A. Wilson.*

ABSOLUTELY RIGHT 2 ch.c. (May 6) Absalom 128–Sun Worshipper (Sun 62 Prince 128) [1990 5.8m 5f4 6m 8g³ 9g³ 7s] 9,000Y, 14,000 2-y-o: sturdy colt: has scope: has a quick action: third reported foal: dam unraced half-sister to smart 6f and 7f performer Columnist: quite modest maiden: stays 9f: seems to act on any going. *S. Dow.*

ABSOLUTE STEAL 4 ro.f. Absalom 128–Thorganby Victory 82 (Burglar 128) — [1989 7d 6m⁴ 8.2f⁵ 8m 8g* 8h⁴ 7m 8f⁵ 1990 7.5m 8g] workmanlike filly: winning plater as 3-y-o: needed both her races in 1990, tailed off in second: stays 1m: acts on hard ground. *C. Tinkler.*

ABSOLUTION 6 gr.h. Absalom 128–Great Grey Niece 74 (Great Nephew 126) 92 [1989 5f* 5f³ 5f² 5g⁴ 6m⁶ 5g³ 5m³ 5m³ 6f 5g* 5g⁵ 1990 5m 5d 5g³ 5m 5m 5m⁵ 6m 5m* 5g² 6g 5g 5.6g] workmanlike, good-quartered horse: moderate walker and mover: fairly useful handicapper: returned to his best when winning £8,000 contest at Haydock in August for second successive year: ran poorly in Tote-Portland at Doncaster final outing: best at 5f: acts on any going: has won for apprentice: blinkered seventh to eleventh starts and once at 4 yrs. *D. W. Chapman.*

ABSONAL 3 gr.c. Absalom 128–Aldbury Girl 79 (Galivanter 131) [1989 5s⁴ 5d³ 94 5g⁵ 1990 6g⁶ 6g* 6m⁴ 6m 7m² 7m* 8m* 8m* 8m⁶ 8g 8g 7m 8m 8g] strong, good-topped colt: fairly useful handicapper: progressed very well when justifying favouritism at Windsor in May and Sandown, Kempton and Newmarket (£19,100 Food Brokers Trophy) in July: generally below form after: suited by 1m: acts on good to firm going: ran fairly well when edgy penultimate start. *R. Hannon.*

ABSTEMIOUS 2 gr.f. (Apr 12) Absalom 128–Kilttaley 74 (Tower Walk 130) 33 [1990 5g⁶ 5f⁶] 5,200Y: smallish, close-coupled filly: second foal: dam stayed 1m: poor form in maiden auction and seller early in season. *R. J. Holder.*

ABSTONE LAD 3 b.g. Blazing Saddles (AUS)–Abbey Rose 84 (Lorenzaccio — 130) [1989 5m⁴ 6g 6m⁴ 7g 1990 8.2g] leggy gelding: poor maiden. *A. W. Jones.*

ABS (USA) 3 b.c. Nureyev (USA) 131–Reyah 83 (Young Generation 129) [1989 **103**
7g³ 7g* 7g⁵ 1990 8.2m² 8.5d⁶ 8d 8.5m⁶ 8m* 8m³ 8g 8g² 8m³] small, stocky colt:
has a fluent action: useful handicapper: clearly best efforts at Newcastle, making all
in July and second in October: stays 1m: acts on good to firm going, probably
unsuited by dead: usually sets or races up with pace: to join David Hayes in
Australia. *H. Thomson Jones.*

ACCEPTED DATE 3 ch.g. Cure The Blues (USA)–Ivor's Date (USA) (Sir Ivor —
135) [1989 NR 1990 10m4] tall gelding: fifth foal: half-brother to Irish 1¾m winner
Jaiyaash and fairly useful juvenile hurdler Ivors Guest (both by Be My Guest): dam
French maiden: 40/1 and green, soundly beaten in 5-runner maiden at Pontefract in
August: sold 2,300 gns Doncaster September Sales. *Mrs J. R. Ramsden.*

ACCESS CRUISE (USA) 3 ch.g. Wajima (USA)–Lady of Meadowlane (USA) —
(Pancho Jay (USA)) [1989 8m 1990 10g⁶ 12m⁶ 14g] tall, sparely-made gelding:
moderate walker and mover: modest form at best: may well prove best short of
1¼m: keen sort, wore crossed noseband final start (June): subsequently gelded. *R.
Boss.*

ACCESS FLYER (IRE) 2 b.c. (Mar 15) Reasonable (FR) 119–Fenland Queen **73**
(King's Troop 118) [1990 7f4 7g 10s a8g*] IR 6,000F, 12,500Y: good-bodied,
workmanlike colt: has plenty of scope: poor mover: half-brother to several winners,
including fairly useful 1977 2-y-o Fosteridge (by St Chad) and quite modest 1m
winner Taylors Queen (by Tender King): dam unraced half-sister to high-class
miler Belmont Bay: won 12-runner maiden at Lingfield by 5 lengths from Rainstone:
best previous effort on debut: suited by 1m. *R. Boss.*

ACCESS HOLIDAYS 2 ch.c. (Apr 24) Faustus (USA) 118–Lardana 65 (Burglar **74**
128) [1990 6g² 5d* a6g* a6g²] 22,000Y: leggy colt: eighth reported living foal:
half-brother to modest sprinter The Mechanic (by Lochnager) and a winner in
Scandinavia: dam 9f winner: modest performer: won maiden at Redcar by ½ length
and claimer at Lingfield, staying on strongly having disputed lead, by 1½ lengths:
stays 6f. *R. Boss.*

ACCESSOFHORNCHURCH 4 ch.g. Coquelin (USA) 121–The Saltings (FR) —
(Morston (FR) 125) [1989 10d⁵ 7m4 8f 7s 1990 10.2m 7m 7f⁶ 8m⁶ 8f 7f 8m] tall, leggy
gelding: modest handicapper at one time: well below his best as 4-y-o, though did
show a little on occasions: probably stays 1m: acts on any going: blinkered and got
loose at start once at 3 yrs: sold 1,600 gns Doncaster November Sales. *E. H. Owen
jun.*

ACCESS SKI 3 b.c. Bustino 136–Crimson Lake (FR) 71 (Mill Reef (USA) 141) **96**
[1989 7m³ 8f² 8m³ 1990 12.5f² 10m² 12d² 15.3m* 13.3m⁶ 18.4f² 16.2f² 18m* 15d4
16m 18d] close-coupled, robust colt: easy mover: fairly useful performer: won
maiden at Wolverhampton in May and minor event at Pontefract in September: well
beaten last 3 starts, in Cesarewitch at Newmarket on final one: suited by test of
stamina and top-of-the-ground: genuine. *R. Boss.*

*Phil Bull Trophy, Pontefract—Regal Reform can't peg back Access Ski
in this annual long-distance event*

ACCESS SUN   3 b.g. Pharly (FR) 130–Princesse du Seine (FR) (Val de Loir 133)   —
[1989 8m⁵ 8m* 10g² 1990 11g⁶ 16m 8h⁶ 12g⁶] leggy, quite attractive gelding: fairly
useful as 2-y-o: behind in varied events in 1990, making running first 3 starts then
stiff task on final one, first for 3 months: should stay 1½m: trained until after third
start by R. Boss: winning hurdler. *J. S. King.*

ACCESS SUPREME   2 b.c. (Apr 27) Law Society (USA) 130–Honeypot Lane 91   72 p
(Silly Season 127) [1990 10.2s4] 20,000Y: leggy, sparely-made colt: looks weak:
ninth foal: half-brother to 3 winners, including quite useful 1½m winner Hymettus
(by Blakeney): dam middle-distance winner, is half-sister to good middle-distance
performer Bedtime: over 9 lengths fourth of 15, held up then staying on under firm
hand riding, to Persian Halo in minor event at Doncaster in November: will stay
1½m: sure to improve. *R. Boss.*

ACCESS TRAVEL   4 b.c. Auction Ring (USA) 123–Lady Tippins (USA) 83 (Star   95 §
de Naskra (USA)) [1989 6g³ 6g³ 5m³ 6m⁵ 5f 6m 5g³ 1990 6f³ 5f 6f² 7m⁴ 5m 5m 5m
5g4] small, sturdy colt: poor mover in slow paces: one-time useful sprinter: below
his best as 4-y-o, mainly in listed contests: best form at 5f on a sound surface: best in
blinkers: carries head high: not an easy ride or one to trust. *R. Boss.*

ACCOLADE (IRE)   2 b.c. (Apr 21) Auction Ring (USA) 123–Age of Elegance   87
(Troy 137) [1990 5f³ 6g* 7.3m² 7g² 7m³ 7d] IR 200,000Y: strong-quartered,
attractive colt: has scope: second foal: half-brother to 3-y-o Sheer Precocity (by
Precocious), 6f (at 2 yrs) and 7.6f winner: dam French 11f and 1½m winner, is
half-sister to Elegant Air: fair performer: made all in Nottingham maiden in May:
ran well when placed after in £6,300 event at Newbury and minor races at
Nottingham and Goodwood: will be suited by 1m: possibly unsuited by a soft surface:
sold 26,000 gns Newmarket December Sales. *H. R. A. Cecil.*

ACHELOUS   3 b.c. Dominion 123–Siren Sound (Manado 130) [1989 NR 1990   70
8.2m 9m 12.2d² a11g*] medium-sized colt: fourth foal: half-brother to fairly useful
1986 2-y-o 5f winner Echoing (by Formidable): dam from family of Time Charter:
favourite, made all in claimer (claimed to join J. Glover £11,600) at Southwell in
November: moved badly to post second start: stays 1½m: trained first 3 outings by J.
Fanshawe. *T. D. Barron.*

ACHNAHUAIGH   6 ch.m. Known Fact (USA) 135–Djimbaran Bay (Le   —
Levanstell 122) [1989 11.7d 10.2h⁵ 8g 1990 8g 8f 8.3m 8h 7m 8f] lengthy mare: bad
plater: probably stays 1¼m: acts on hard and dead going: pulls hard. *J. M. Bradley.*

ACKERS WOOD   2 b.g. (Mar 31) Castle Keep 121–Gloria Maremmana (King   —
Emperor (USA)) [1990 8.2d4] half-brother to several winners, including 7f to 1¼m
performer Emperor Hotfoot (by Hotfoot) and 1½m winner Hot Girl (by Hot Grove):
dam won at 2 yrs in Italy: tailed off in 4-runner minor event at Haydock in
September. *R. F. Johnson Houghton.*

ACONITUM   9 b.g. Fair Season 120–The Yellow Girl 102 (Yellow God 129) [1989   §§
8s 9v² 9f 8f5 8m* a8g a7g a10g⁴ a11g⁵ 1990 a11g⁴ a10g³ a8g⁵ a12g 9f 9f 8g] strong
gelding: carries plenty of condition: thoroughly unreliable handicapper: sold to join
R. Marvin's stable 850 gns after final outing: stays 11f: probably acts on any going:
visored twice, blinkered sixth outing: has refused to race and proved reluctant to do
so on many other occasions: one to leave well alone. *J. R. Jenkins.*

ACQUA NOIR   3 ch.c. Kings Lake (USA) 133–Late Sally 101 (Sallust 134) [1989   55
NR 1990 a8g a5g⁶ a6g 7.5d² 7g⁶ 8.3m* 8.3m⁴ 8m² 8m 10d 11.5g a12g a8g] IR
38,000Y: sparely-made colt: first foal: dam, Irish sprinter who probably stayed 7f, is
half-sister to prolifically successful 1980 2-y-o Spindrifter: plating-class handicapper: won at Windsor in July: stays 1m: acts on good to firm ground and dead:
visored final start, blinkered previous eight. *R. J. Williams.*

ACQUISITION   3 b.c. Petorius 117–Steady The Buffs 62 (Balidar 133) [1989 NR   59
1990 8.2g 8g²] 6,200F, 20,000Y: quite good-topped colt: third foal: half-brother to
useful 6f (at 2 yrs) to 8.5f winner Aldbourne (by Alzao): dam stayed 1¼m: 33/1 and
bit backward, about 10 lengths third of 14 to disqualified Line of Vision in maiden at
Carlisle in April, staying on well: should stay further. *M. A. Jarvis.*

ACROSS THE BAY   3 ch.g. Krayyan 117–Siofra Beag (Steel Heart 128) [1989   78 §
5s² 5g4 5.3m* 6f² 6g² 6m³ 5f5 6f² 5m 6g 5m³ 5m⁴ 6v 1990 6g 6f 5f³ 6f² 6m⁵ 7.6m
5m 5d] close-coupled gelding: carries condition: moderate walker and mover: fair
performer: stays 6f: acts on firm going, ran poorly on heavy: took little interest for
7-lb claimer last 2 starts: often on toes: not one to rely on: gelded after final start. *S.
Dow.*

ACROW LINE   5 b.g. Capricorn Line 111–Miss Acrow (Comedy Star (USA) 121)   —
[1989 10.2h 12m 10g³ 13.1h³ 14m* 14m 12m 1990 10m 12m 17.1f 12f 15.3f4] stocky

gelding: well beaten since winning handicap at Salisbury (apprentice ridden) as 4-y-o: suited by 1¾m: possibly unsuited by firm going: often sweats. *J. C. Fox.*

ACROW LORD 3 b.g. Milford 119–Miss Acrow (Comedy Star (USA) 121) [1989 **76** 8m 8g 1990 12.5f⁴ 11.7g 15.3m⁴ 12.2g² 12m⁴ 11.5f² 11m² 14m⁴ 11m²] close-coupled, quite good-bodied gelding: modest maiden: second in handicaps: seems suited by 1½m: acts on firm ground: joined M. Pipe and gelded. *W. Jarvis.*

ACTEUR FRANCAIS (USA) 2 b.c. (Mar 15) Al Nasr (FR) 126–Kilmona **106** (USA) 121 (Bold Bidder (USA)) [1990 7.5g* 6d³ 8m³] fourth foal: half-brother to French 1m and 11f winner Pandia (by Affirmed) and a winner in North America: dam French 9f winner, is half-sister to smart 1973 French 2-y-o Dancer's Prince: won maiden at Deauville in August by 1½ lengths: third afterwards to Hector Protector in Prix Morny Agence Francaise on same course and to Beau Sultan in Prix La Rochette at Longchamp in September: will stay 1¼m: acts on good to firm ground and dead. *A. Fabre, France.*

ACTIVE MOVEMENT 2 ch.f. (Feb 17) Music Boy 124–Royal Agnes 71 (Royal **36** § Palace 131) [1990 5m² 5m⁶ 5g⁵ 7.5g 7m 6m] 9,000F, 13,500Y: smallish, workmanlike filly: moderate mover: fourth reported foal: half-sister to 1m and 1¼m winner Dancing Days (by Glenstal): dam 1¾m winner, is half-sister to smart 1982 2-y-o All Systems Go: ungenerous plater: blinkered third to fifth starts: sold 1,400 gns Doncaster August Sales. *Mrs J. R. Ramsden.*

ACT OF DIPLOMACY (USA) 2 b.c. (Mar 2) Northern Prospect (USA)– **90** Faithful Diplomacy (USA) (Diplomat Way) [1990 6m* 7f* 7g⁵ 7g 6g⁴ 7d] IR 78,000Y: close-coupled, quite good-topped colt: fluent mover: half-brother to several winners here and in USA, including 1¼m winner Dusty Diplomacy (by Run Dusty Run), as well as successful hurdler State Diplomacy (by State Dinner): dam 1m winner: fairly useful performer: successful in July in maiden at Newmarket and minor event at Doncaster: blinkered and edgy, fourth of 7 to Time Gentlemen in Rokeby Farms Mill Reef Stakes at Newbury in September, easily best subsequent effort: poorly drawn in Cartier Million at Phoenix Park final outing: stays 7f: acts well on firm ground: possibly hasn't ideal attitude. *R. W. Armstrong.*

ACTRESS 4 b.f. Known Fact (USA) 135–Tin Tessa 87 (Martinmas 128) [1989 6s³ **59** 6d 8g 7f* 7m* 8f³ 7g⁵ 7m 1990 7g 7g 5m⁵ 6m] good-bodied, angular filly: modest handicapper in 1989: generally well below form as 4-y-o: stays 1m: acts on any going: blinkered third outing: sold 1,200 gns Newmarket December Sales. *J. Wharton.*

ADAMIK (USA) 3 b.c. L'Emigrant (USA) 129–Tountinna (USA) (Caro 133) **97** [1989 NR 1990 8g² 8g² 9g² 8m* 11.7m² 10m² 10s³] $30,000Y: good-topped, attractive colt: has scope: has a free, rather round action: moderate walker: third foal: half-brother to a winner in USA by Nodouble: dam unraced half-sister to Fappiano: useful form: won maiden at Pontefract in July: contested minor events after, good second at Windsor and Nottingham: will prove best at 1½m + : acts on good to firm ground: sold 84,000 gns Newmarket Autumn Sales. *H. R. A. Cecil.*

ADANAR (USA) 3 gr.g. Irish River (FR) 131–Adjanada 108 (Nishapour (FR) 125) — [1989 5f³ 6m⁵ a8g a7g 1990 8m 10f 8.3m 10f 6d] compact gelding: plater: behind in handicaps as 3-y-o: stays 1m: blinkered second start: trained until after then by R. Hannon: sold out of I. Campbell's stable 1,000 gns Newmarket September Sales after fourth: resold to join J. Thomas 2,600 gns Doncaster October Sales. *M. C. Chapman.*

ADDISON'S BLADE 3 b.g. Pas de Seul 133–Addison's Jubilee 73 (Sparkler **88** 130) [1989 5f⁵ 5m* 5f² 5g 6g⁴ 6m⁶ 6m 6g 7d⁶ 1990 5f³ 5f⁶ 6m 6g² 6d] compact gelding: carries condition: poor mover: fairly useful performer: easily best efforts as 3-y-o (not seen out after July) when placed in handicaps at Doncaster and Ripon: suited by 6f: acts on firm ground: inconsistent. *M. Johnston.*

ADELINE LYNN 4 ch.f. What A Guest 119–Grande Promesse (FR) (Sea Hawk **63** II 131) [1989 10d 1990 10g⁶ 12f² 12.2m] sturdy ex-Irish filly: poor mover: sister to a winner in Spain and a winner over hurdles and half-sister to 3 other winners abroad: dam won over 10.5f in France: runner-up in maiden at Clonmel in June: tailed off in similar event at Catterick month later: won selling hurdle in December: trained until after second start by D. Murphy. *N. Tinkler.*

ADEVA 2 gr.f. (Apr 10) Bustino 136–Faakirah (Dragonara Palace (USA) 115) [1990 **72** 7m* 7g 6m² 7g² a7g² a8g] lengthy, light-framed filly: first foal: dam unraced sister to smart 2-y-o sprinter Crime of Passion: won 14-runner seller (bought in 15,500 gns) at Newmarket impressively by 6 lengths: second in nurseries after, running well when beaten short head by Scottish Castle at Lingfield on penultimate start. stays 7f. *J. W. Hills.*

ADJACENT (IRE) 2 ch.f. (Mar 1) Doulab (USA) 115–Near The Door (USA) **61** p (Stage Door Johnny) [1990 6m3] IR 32,000Y: angular filly: first foal: dam (ran once in Ireland) from good family: 7 lengths third of 12, keeping on steadily not knocked about, to Gracebridge in maiden at Nottingham in August: should improve. *B. W. Hills.*

ADMINISTER 2 b.f. (Feb 4) Damister (USA) 123–Apply 87 (Kings Lake (USA) — p 133) [1990 7g] angular, sparely-made filly: first foal: dam 1¼m and 1½m winner, is daughter of very useful middle-distance filly Alia: bit backward, in touch over 4f in 15-runner minor event (moved moderately down) at Newbury in September: should improve. *R. Charlton.*

ADMIRAL BYNG (FR) 3 ch.c. Caerleon (USA) 132–Pig Tail 98 (Habitat 134) **96** [1989 7g 7d4 1990 10f* 14m2 12f2 12m] workmanlike colt: moderate walker and mover: fairly useful performer: won maiden at Nottingham in May: well backed but on toes and sweating, ran poorly in minor event at Newmarket final start: unlikely to stay beyond 1¾m: acts on firm going: usually makes the running: sold to join M. Charles 7,600 gns Newmarket Autumn Sales. *H. R. A. Cecil.*

ADMIRALTY WAY 4 b.g. Petorius 117–Captive Flower 99 (Manacle 123) [1989 **82** d 7g* 7g3 7g5 6m4 7f5 8.2m 9f4 8.2d4 8s 7f2 8g a8g* a7g3 1990 8f4 7.5m 10.4d* 10f 9m 12.3m5 16f5 10.6d] leggy, quite attractive gelding: 20/1 and apprentice ridden at overweight, won strongly-run handicap at Chester in May, easily best run of year: bolted to post seventh intended start: stays 1¼m: acts on firm and dead going: has been tried in blinkers and visor: has sweated: has pulled hard, looked reluctant, and is not one to rely on. *M. O'Neill.*

ADORING MAN 5 b.g. Taufan (USA) 119–Adorit 76 (Habat 127) [1989 a10g a12g **38** 1990 a12g a8g a8g3] attractive gelding: moderate mover: fair maiden at best at 2 yrs: third at Southwell in March: stays 1m: best effort on firm going: blinkered last 2 starts: wears bandages. *A. Bailey.*

ADVANCE TO GO 3 ch.f. Horage 124–La Bellilotte (Ridan (USA)) [1989 5s5 **32** 5d2 5g4 5m 1990 a5g5 a5g3 6d 6d a6g] lengthy filly: moderate mover: poor maiden: off course 8 months after second start and showed little after: acts on dead going: bandaged near-hind third start: sometimes sweating. *J. Wharton.*

ADVIE BRIDGE 3 ch.f. High Line 125–Marypark 93 (Charlottown 127) [1989 **90** § 8g* 8.2g3 1990 12m2 12m 11.5g] angular filly: fairly useful performance when short-head second in minor event at Newmarket in August, drifting left: never able to challenge in listed race at York then swerved and unseated rider leaving stalls in Sandown minor event: should prove suited by forcing tactics at 1½m, and will stay further: clearly not one to trust. *H. R. A. Cecil.*

ADWICK PARK 2 b.c. (May 1) Blazing Saddles (AUS)–Ana Gabriella (USA) **95** (Master Derby (USA)) [1990 5m4 5g5 6g5 7m2 7d2 7.5f3 7f* 7f* 7g 7f4 7f* 6g* 6d] 4,200Y: robust, good-quartered colt: fourth foal: half-brother to 3-y-o Magic Ana (by Magic Mirror), successful at 7f (in seller at 2 yrs in France) and 6f, and fairly useful 7f (at 2 yrs) and 1m winner Burkan (by Star Appeal): dam ran once: fairly useful performer: made all or most in maiden auction and nursery at Thirsk in August and autumn nurseries at Catterick and York: effective at 6f and 7f: seems unsuited by softish ground: often ridden by girl apprentice, but easily better form for stronger handling: suited by forcing tactics. *T. D. Barron.*

AELLOPOUS 2 b.f. (Feb 12) Kris 135–Graecia Magna (USA) 109 (Private **73** Account (USA)) [1990 6m4 8g] leggy, quite good-topped filly: has scope: second foal: sister to useful 3-y-o middle-distance performer Akamantis, 1m winner at 2 yrs: dam won at 7f and 1½m: about 10 lengths fourth of 8 to impressive Island Universe in £9,600 maiden at Ascot: below that form in similar event at Yarmouth later in October: should be suited by at least 1m. *G. Harwood.*

AFAFF (USA) 3 b.f. Nijinsky (CAN) 138–Continual (USA) (Damascus (USA)) — [1989 6g 1990 8f3] lengthy, good-quartered filly: keen walker: sixth foal: sister to 2000 Guineas winner Shadeed and half-sister to 2 winners, including 9f winner Basoof (by Believe It): dam, successful at 6f and 7f, is sister to Tuerta, the dam of Kentucky Derby and Belmont Stakes winner Swale: bit backward, 8 lengths third of 6, weakening quickly approaching final 1f, to Circus Feathers in maiden at Warwick in May: went down well: bred to stay 1¼m. *M. R. Stoute.*

AFFAIR OF HONOUR (IRE) 2 ch.c. Ahonoora 122–Good Relations **60** (Be My Guest (USA) 126) [1990 5g3 5m 5d5 7h* 7m2] 31,000Y: strong colt: has a round action: third foal: half-brother to 3-y-o Trojan Relation (by Trojan Fen) and

1m winner Tacoma Heights (by Taufan): dam Irish 7f and 1½m winner, is half-sister to Montekin: modest performer: won 4-runner nursery at Brighton by a short head: good second, clear, in similar event at Yarmouth later in month: will stay 1m. *P. F. I. Cole.*

AFFIE   2 b.f. (Apr 18) Afzal 83–Watch Her Go (Beldale Flutter (USA) 130) [1990   **34** a6g a6g 8m 5.8d a5g⁶ a6g] small, lengthy filly: moderate mover: first foal: dam ran once at 2 yrs: seems of little account: trained first 5 starts by B. Preece. *R. T. Juckes.*

AFFIRMATION   3 b.f. Tina's Pet 121–Affirmative 96 (Derring-Do 131) [1989   **75** 5g* 1990 7m⁶ 7m⁶ 8m 8g 10g⁶ 10m* 10d5] workmanlike filly: modest handicapper: faced stiff tasks then won at Redcar in October: better at 1¼m than shorter: acts on good to firm ground and dead. *J. W. Hills.*

AFFORDABLE   2 b.g. (Apr 21) Formidable (USA) 125–Ophrys 90 (Nonoalco   **73** § (USA) 131) [1990 5f⁴ 5m³ 6m² 5m² 6g² 5g⁶ 6m³ 7m] 31,000Y: strong, good-quartered, sprint type: has a quick action: third foal: dam 2-y-o 7f winner from family of Persepolis, Vayrann and Valiyar: modest maiden: stays 6f: tends to hang, and find nothing off bridle: ran badly when blinkered: trained by Mrs L. Piggott on debut: ungenuine, and is one to avoid. *W. Carter.*

AFKAR   3 gr.g. Mouktar 129–Afeefa (Lyphard (USA) 132) [1989 NR 1990 10m²   **103** 10g* 12g² 12s³] rangy, rather angular gelding: fourth foal: half-brother to useful 1¼m winner Afriyd (by Darshaan) and quite useful but untrustworthy Afshoun (by Nishapour), later winner in USA: dam unraced daughter of half-sister to Val de Loir and Valoris: landed odds in maiden at Leicester in May: progressive form after, again held up, in King George V Stakes Handicap at Royal Ascot and Old Newton Cup Handicap (hung badly right, July) at Haydock: stays 1½m: acts on soft going. *M. R. Stoute.*

AFRICAN AFFAIR   5 br.g. Be My Native (USA) 122–Moment of Weakness 76   **—** § (Pieces of Eight 128) [1989 10d 9f 9f⁶ 10m³ 11f⁵ 10f³ 12f² 12f³ 8.5m³ 11g³ 10.2g 10f 1990 11d] neat gelding: poor walker: irresolute plater: stays 1½m: acts on firm going. *R. M. Whitaker.*

AFRICAN CHIMES   3 b.c. Kampala 120–Rynville (Ballymore 123) [1989 8g   **67** 1990 8m 12.2m² 12f³ 8g 10m⁶ 8g 10m³ a8g a10g² a10g*] leggy, angular colt: has round action: quite modest form in varied company: 7/4 on, won 9-runner claimer (claimed to join W. O'Gorman £6,000) at Lingfield in December by 6 lengths: stays 1½m: acts on firm ground. *P. F. I. Cole.*

AFRICAN GUEST   3 b.g. What A Guest 119–Kalaya (Tanerko 134) [1989 5s² 5v   **46** 5.3m⁵ 6h 5.8h⁴ 1990 8m 7d a6g a11g a12g³ a14g] quite attractive gelding: plating-class maiden: third in claimer at Southwell in December, making most and best effort for some time: stays 1½m: acts on soft ground: sweating third start. *Capt. J. Wilson.*

AFRICAN SAFARI   6 b.g. Daring March 116–African Berry 84 (African Sky 124)   **—** [1989 6f³ 6f² 6m 6g 6f 7g 6g a6g⁶ 1990 a7g a10g 7f⁴ 6g] tall gelding: has a round action: poor handicapper: stays 7.6f: best on a sound surface: blinkered twice: often sweats: sold to join Mrs S. Smith's stable 4,300 gns Ascot May Sales: won valuable 3-runner novice chase at Ascot in November. *P. D. Cundell.*

AFRICAN SPIRIT   6 b.g. African Sky 124–Relic Spirit (Relic) [1989 7.6m 7f⁴ 8f⁵   **57** 8m⁴ 8.5g⁵ 8f³ 7g³ 7g² 7m 8d 8g 10g⁴ 1990 a8g² a8g⁴ 8.2s⁴ 10.4g 10.6d 8g] good-topped gelding: carries plenty of condition: poor mover: quite modest handicapper: off course 5 months after third outing and never a threat last 3: has seemed to stay 1¼m: acts on any going: blinkered once: has swished tail. *R. M. Whitaker.*

AFTER THE SUN (USA)   2 b.f. (Feb 22) Storm Bird (CAN) 134–Encorelle   **110** (FR) (Arctic Tern (USA) 126) [1990 6.5g⁴ 7.5g² 8s* 8g⁴ 8g²] third foal: half-sister to a minor winner in North America by Clever Trick: dam unraced sister to Escaline: won 20-runner maiden at Maisons-Laffitte in September by 3 lengths: over 3 lengths fourth of 9 to Shadayid in Prix Marcel Boussac and neck second of 8 to Masslama in Prix des Reservoirs at Longchamp in October: will stay 1¼m: has raced only on easy ground. *F. Boutin, France.*

AFWAJ (USA)   4 ch.c. Caro 133–Just A Kick (USA) (Olympiad King (USA)) [1989   **107** 10g 8m³ 8f³ 7f* 7m* 7.6f⁵ 7f² 6m* 6m⁶ 6g⁴ 1990 6g⁵ 6m* 6g⁴ 6m² 6g 6m 5f⁵ 5g 6m] rather leggy, good-topped colt: moderate walker: easy mover: useful sprinter on his day: won £7,800 handicap under 10-0 at Newmarket in May: best efforts after when in frame (edging left) in Duke of York Stakes and listed event at Lingfield and fifth to Argentum in King George Stakes at Goodwood: effective at 5f and 6f: suited by sound surface: sent to race in USA. *J. L. Dunlop.*

AGAINST THE FLOW 3 ch.f. Salmon Leap (USA) 131–Tricky Tracey (Form- —
idable (USA) 125) [1989 7s 1990 8m] rather sparely-made filly: last in maidens. *J. D.
Czerpak.*

AGALEION (FR) 3 ch.c. Esprit du Nord (USA) 126–Algaselle (FR) (Timmy Lad 81
130) [1989 7g⁴ 8g⁵ 1990 12m² 11.5m⁵ 12g 10g] big, sparely-made colt: good mover:
fair maiden: tired final 1f and headed on post at Newmarket in April: behind in
pattern events at Lingfield, Rome and Naples: may prove as effective over 1¼m as
1½m: bandaged behind first 2 starts when trained by P. Kelleway. *R. Giovanale,
Italy.*

AGEETEE 2 ch.c. (Apr 30) Tina's Pet 121–Woolcana 71 (Some Hand 119) [1990 87
5g 6m⁵ 6m 5m⁴ 6m³ 7f² 6g* 6s] big, lengthy colt: has plenty of scope: shows knee
action: seventh foal: half-brother to 3 winners, including modest 7f winner Pullover
(by Windjammer): dam 5f winner: fair performer: made all, showing much improved
form, in maiden at Folkestone in October: seems unsuited by very soft ground.
Andrew Turnell.

AGENT BLEU (FR) 3 b.c. Vacarme (USA) 121–Acoma 121 (Rheffic 129) [1989 118
NR 1990 9g² 10f* 10.5d* 10g⁵ 9.2g⁶ 10d² 10g³ 9.7g*] half-brother to French 1½m
winner Axianne (by Mill Reef) and French 11f to 15f winner Action de Graces (by
Northern Baby): dam, half-sister to Ashmore, won over 1¼m and 1½m in France
from only 3 starts: successful at Longchamp in maiden and listed race in April and
Ciga Prix Dollar (pulled hard, led final ½f to beat Pirate Army a length) in October:
stays 10.5f: yet to race on soft going, acts on any other: smart. *E. Lellouche, France.*

A GENTLEMAN TWO 4 b.c. All Systems Go 119–Solar Honey 77 (Roi Soleil 59
125) [1989 NR 1990 7m 9f 6m⁴ 6g 7g* 8m² 8f⁵ 8.5f³ 7.5g⁴] lengthy colt: carries
plenty of condition: moderate mover: second reported foal: dam 5f winner at 2 yrs:
won claimer at Ayr in July: ran well when placed in seller (odds on) at same course
and claimer at Beverley: stays 1m: won claiming hurdle in November. *G. M. Moore.*

AGE OF MIRACLES 3 b.g. Simply Great (FR) 122–Single Gal 97 (Mansingh 90
(USA) 120) [1989 6f⁴ 6m³ 6g⁶ 6f 6m³ 8m* 8m 1990 8.2f 7d 8m a8g 8m 9m³ 12g⁶ 10d*
10m* 10m] leggy, rather close-coupled gelding: fairly useful handicapper: won at
Ayr then Ascot (£9,200 event, week later) in September: looking tremendously
well, well below-form favourite in £8,400 contest at Newmarket shortly after: stays
1¼m: acts on good to firm ground and dead. *C. A. Cyzer.*

AGE OF ROMANCE 3 b.f. Chukaroo 103–Eastern Romance 73 (Sahib 114) —
[1989 6g 1990 a11g 7g³ 8g] tall, leggy filly: staying-on third in seller at Catterick in
June: should stay further than 7f. *J. M. Bradley.*

AGHAADIR (USA) 2 b.c. (Apr 26) Private Account (USA)–Kris Kris (USA) 95 p
(Hoist The Flag (USA)) [1990 7g*] $350,000Y: half-brother to 3 winners, including
Grade 3 9f winner Laser Lane (by The Minstrel): dam never ran: 10/1 and ridden by
5-lb claimer, impressive winner of 17-runner maiden at Salisbury in October,
quickening clear 1½f out and running on strongly to beat Turbofan 8 lengths: will
stay at least 1¼m: sure to win more races. *J. H. M. Gosden.*

AGHNIYAH (USA) 2 ch.f. (Apr 7) Lyphard (USA) 132–Goodbye Shelley (FR) 76 ?
116 (Home Guard (USA) 129) [1990 6d 7g* 7m⁵ 8f⁴ 8d] small, workmanlike filly:
fourth foal: half-sister to a winner in USA by Halo: dam won from 7f to 1m, and is
half-sister to Heighlin: comfortable winner of maiden at Wolverhampton in July: ran
well after when fourth, hampered considerably final furlong, in nursery at Bath:
stays 1m: acts on firm and dead going: sometimes gives trouble in preliminaries. *P.
T. Walwyn.*

AGNES DODD 3 b.f. Homing 130–Mosso 81 (Ercolano (USA) 118) [1989 6g 1090 —
a7g4] compact, workmanlike filly: 20/1 and ridden by 7-lb claimer, never-nearer
fourth of 9 in claimer at Southwell in August: sold 1,650 gns Newmarket Autumn
Sales. *J. A. R. Toller.*

AHD (USA) 3 b.c. Linkage (USA)–Old Gypsy (USA) (Olden Times) [1989 6g³ 94
6m⁶ 6f* 7g² 7m⁴ 7g 8d 7g 1990 10g 8m³ 8g⁶ 9m* 8m² 8g⁴ 7d² 8m⁵ 9m² 10m]
$135,000Y: small colt: half-brother to smart 6f and 1¼m winner Zinzara (by Stage
Door Johnny) and 3 minor winners in USA: dam stakes winner at up to 1m: sire high
class at up to 9.5f: fairly useful performer in Ireland, winning minor event at
Tipperary in May: never dangerous in veteran jockeys race at Ascot final start:
stays 9f: acts on good to firm ground and dead: wears blinkers: sold 29,000 gns
Newmarket Autumn Sales. *K. Prendergast, Ireland.*

AHEAD 3 b.f. Shirley Heights 130–Ghislaine (USA) 71 (Icecapade (USA)) [1989 113
7g 1990 12f* 12d⁵ 12d 12m² 12m³ 12g⁴] big, rangy, good sort: made all to land odds in
minor event at Salisbury in May: made most in Gold Seal Oaks at Epsom next start:

in frame in listed race at Newmarket, Princess Royal Stakes at Ascot and Long Island Handicap at Belmont Park in the autumn: stays 1½m: yet to race on soft going, probably acts on any other. *G. Harwood.*

AHSANTA SANA   4 b.g. Nicholas Bill 125–Dancing Valerina 61 (Comedy Star (USA) 121) [1989 7g⁴ 7g 7f 6m 6m 6m 6s³ 6s 6s* 1990 10s] leggy, close-coupled gelding: fair form as 2-y-o: gave trouble going down, never dangerous in May handicap only outing on flat as 4-y-o: best form at sprint distances on soft going: sold 1,800 gns Doncaster June Sales: winning selling hurdler in September: resold 3,000 gns Ascot October Sales. *Mrs J. R. Ramsden.*   —

AIGUE   4 b.f. High Top 131–Cecilia Bianchi (FR) (Petingo 135) [1989 NR 1990 8m* 9g 8g*] lengthy filly: carries condition: successful at Yarmouth in maiden (33/1 on only second start) in September and minor event (beating Rakeen a length) in October: not disgraced in Newmarket listed race in between: will stay 1¼m. *G. Wragg.*   96 p

AILEEN'S JOY   3 b. or br.c. Runnett 125–Originality (Godswalk (USA) 130) [1989 8.2d 1990 8g 8g 6m 8.2v] compact colt: well beaten in maidens and claimer. *R. F. Fisher.*   —

AILORT   3 b.f. Ardross 134–Forres (Thatch (USA) 136) [1989 NR 1990 12m⁴ 12f⁴ 12.5m 12m⁵ 12.2d* 12.4s² a14g] smallish filly: moderate mover: fifth foal: half-sister to fairly useful 1985 2-y-o 5f winner Loch Hourn (by Alias Smith), later successful in Hong Kong: dam never ran: modest performer: won claimer at Catterick in October: always tailed off in handicap final outing: should stay further than 1½m: acts on good to firm and soft going: ran poorly for 7-lb claimer: sold out of H. Cecil's stable 3,200 gns Newmarket December Sales after penultimate outing. *N. Tinkler.*   73

AIMAAM (USA)   2 b.c. (Feb 6) Danzig (USA)–Lucky Lucky Lucky (USA) (Chieftain II) [1990 6m* 7m* 8m⁴] well-made, good sort: second foal: closely related to temperamental maiden Alfarqad (by Northern Dancer): dam high-class filly, successful from 7f to 9f: fair performer: comfortable winner of maiden at Salisbury in June and slowly-run minor event (green and idled) at York in July: favourite, found little in listed race won by Selkirk at Goodwood in September. *J. L. Dunlop.*   86

AINT 'ARF HOT   3 b.f. Electric 126–Hot Ember 75 (Hot Spark 126) [1989 NR 1990 6m 8m a7g 8.5f a12g] 3,800Y: rather angular filly: fifth foal: half-sister to fairly useful 1988 2-y-o sprinter Blue Bell Music (by Music Boy) and to a winning selling hurdler: dam won at 6f: probably of little account: sold out of G. Blum's stable 1,100 gns Doncaster June Sales after second start. *Miss G. M. Rees.*   —

AIN'TLIFELIKETHAT   3 gr.c. Godswalk (USA) 130–Blue Alicia (Wolver Hollow 126) [1989 NR 1990 a8g⁶ a8g⁶ a6g 6m 7m 8.2g 8.2m 7g 6g* 7g* 7m* 7f⁶ 8m 7m* 8h⁴ 6m 7m 7d] IR 3,100F, 28,000Y: workmanlike, good-quartered colt: third foal (previous 2 by Junius): dam ran several times: quite modest handicapper: successful at Hamilton and Ayr (twice) in space of 8 days in July then at Newmarket in August: stays 1m: acts on hard ground, possibly unsuited by dead: visored (below form) final outing, blinkered previous 9: has been bandaged: best with waiting tactics: sold 12,000 gns Newmarket Autumn Sales. *A. Bailey.*   60

AIR DANCER   2 b.f. (Apr 25) Teenoso (USA) 135–Lasani (FR) (Appiani II 128) [1990 5m] workmanlike filly: moderate walker: fifth foal: half-sister to poor and headstrong maiden Proposal (by Sharpo): dam French 1m to 10.5f winner: very slowly away and always behind in maiden at York in May: has joined C. Austin. *C. E. Brittain.*   —

AIR DE RIEN   3 b.f. Elegant Air 119–On The Tiles (Thatch 136) [1989 6s³ 6g 8g 7d 8g* 7v³ 1990 8d³ 10.5g* 10g* 10.5d³ 12g⁶ 10g⁴ 12m⁵] 5,000Y: first foal: dam   120

Prix Saint-Alary, Longchamp—
bargain-buy Air de Rien wins from Louve Bleue

Jacques Beres' "Air de Rien"

lightly-raced Irish 1¼m winner: won nursery at Saint-Cloud then Prix Penelope at Saint-Cloud and Prix Saint-Alary at Longchamp in spring as 3-y-o: best efforts in Prix de Diane Hermes at Chantilly (promoted from fourth) and Prix Vermeille (under 2 lengths behind Salsabil) at Longchamp fourth and final starts: stays 1½m: acts on good to firm ground and dead: smart. *Mme M. Bollack-Badel, France.*

AIREDALE (USA) 3 b.g. Dixieland Band (USA)–Good Hart (USA) (Creme Dela Creme) [1989 7m 8f 8g 1990 8f 10f* 10.6f³ 12.3g 12g] good-topped, angular gelding: quite modest handicapper: favourite, won at Folkestone in May: suited by 1¼m: acts on firm going: should prove best on a galloping track: has worn tongue strap: gelded after final start (July). *W. J. Haggas.* **59**

AIRE VALLEY LAD 3 b.c. The Brianstan 128–Rojael (Mansingh 120) [1989 5s 5d 5f 7m 6m⁵ a7g a8g 1990 6g 6f 8g 8g 8g 10m 9g 6f² 7.5g] lengthy, sparely-made colt: has a quick action: poor plater: second in ladies event at Thirsk in August: stays 1m: acts on firm going: often sweating and edgy: sometimes ridden by 7-lb claimer: blinkered 4 starts including when unseating rider and bolting on intended eighth. *R. Bastiman.* **35**

AIR MUSIC (FR) 3 b.c. Fabulous Dancer (USA) 126–Santa Musica (Luthier 126) [1989 7g 7m⁴ 8g² 8m³ 1990 8f² 9g 12m³ 12g⁵ 10f³ 10d] rather leggy, attractive colt: very useful form when third in King Edward VII Stakes at Royal Ascot and fifth in Grand Prix de Saint-Cloud: made most in Newmarket maiden then ran poorly in Group 2 event at Deauville last 2 starts: suited by 1½m: probably acts on firm going. *C. E. Brittain.* **110 ?**

AIR NYMPH 3 b.f. Elegant Air 119–Elfinaria 79 (Song 132) [1989 5m³ 5g⁶ 5m 6f 1990 6g⁵ 6f² 6g⁵ 6s⁶ a6g⁵ a8g a8g⁴ a7g³] strong, robust filly: carries condition: moderate mover: quite modest maiden: stays 1m: acts on firm going: visored fifth and sixth starts, blinkered final 2 at 2 yrs. *C. C. Elsey.* **65**

AIR OF ELEGANCE 2 b.f. (Apr 4) Elegant Air 119–Mighty Fly 117 (Comedy **70** p Star (USA) 121) [1990 7m⁴ 7m⁴] rather leggy, workmanlike filly with scope: moderate mover: fourth foal: half-sister to 3-y-o 11.5f winner West With The Wind (by Glint of Gold) and 1m and 9f winner Riptide and 13f winner Skimming (both by Mill Reef): dam won Lincoln Handicap and Royal Hunt Cup: fourth in maidens at Sandown (slowly away, not unduly knocked about) in August and Salisbury (got poor run then stayed on strongly last 1½f in moderately-run race) following month: will stay at least 1¼m: sure to improve. *I. A. Balding.*

AIR TIME 2 gr.c. (Mar 26) Good Times (ITY)–Ville Air 85 (Town Crier 119) [1990 **76** 6f⁵ 7m⁴ 7m³ 8d 7s⁶] 1,600Y, 5,000 2-y-o: tall, good-bodied colt: has scope: quite good mover: first foal: dam won over 6f at 2 yrs on only start, is out of a 1½m and 13f winner: modest maiden: should stay 1m: seems unsuited by a soft surface: blinkered third and fourth starts. *P. Mitchell.*

AISLABY DAYS (IRE) 2 b.f. (Apr 29) King of Clubs 124–Sharply (Sharpman **55** 124) [1990 6g² 6f*] IR 3,300Y, 1,000 2-y-o: neat, strong filly: moderate walker: has a roundish action: second foal: dam Irish 4-y-o 1¼m winner: well backed, won seller (sold to join T. Barron 9,800 gns) at Thirsk in June: will stay 7f. *J. L. Harris.*

AITCH N'BEE 7 ch.g. Northfields (USA)–Hot Case 92 (Upper Case (USA)) **86** [1989 7.5d³ a8g 1990 a7g* a7g² a7g² a7g* a7g* 8.2d⁴ 7g] small, strong gelding: in tremendous form in summer handicaps at Southwell, beating Hackforth a length in £7,600 event in August for last of 3 successes: ran poorly final outing: stays 1m: best form on all-weather nowadays: visored first outing at 6 yrs, blinkered second: usually apprentice ridden: has sweated. *Lady Herries.*

AJAAYEB (USA) 3 b.c. Shadeed (USA) 135–Connie Knows (USA) (Buckpasser) — [1989 NR 1990 10.1g³] $200,000Y: rather leggy, attractive colt: fifth foal: closely related to 1988 2-y-o 7f and 1989 U.S. winner Connie's Gift (by Nijinsky) and half-brother to a winner in USA by Sir Ivor: dam, winner at up to 7f, is half-sister to good colt Sportin' Life (by Nijinsky) and to the dam of Local Suitor: 15¾ lengths third of 15 in minor event at Windsor in April, travelling well long way and not knocked about: sold only 7,600 gns Newmarket Autumn Sales. *M. R. Stoute.*

AJALITA 4 ch.f. Move Off 112–Citrine 77 (Meldrum 112) [1989 12g 10m⁴ 10g⁴ — 11.5m⁶ 10m⁴ 12s³ 12g⁴ 16f⁵ 1990 15.5f 10f 10g³] leggy, lengthy filly: disappointing maiden: stays 1½m: acts on soft going, probably not at best on top-of-the-ground: blinkered final start: winning selling hurdler in June. *M. J. Ryan.*

AJANAC 6 br.g. Known Fact (USA) 135–Majan 67 (Brigadier Gerard 144) [1989 **100** 6f⁴ 6f 6m 6m² 6s³ 1990 6m 6m 6m 6g 8m* 7m³ 8m³] rather angular gelding: good mover: useful performer: won moderately-run minor event at Leicester in September by ½ length from Azadeh: creditable third in handicap (pulled hard early) at Newmarket and minor race (didn't find great deal) at Chepstow: stays 1m: acts on any going: below form in blinkers and visor: sweating fourth and final (also edgy) outings. *R. Charlton.*

AJJAJ 5 b.h. Habitat 134–Cassy's Pet 89 (Sing Sing 134) [1989 5g 6f⁶ 1990 a8g a8g — a11g a6g a6g 9f 7.5m] good-bodied, quite attractive horse: winning sprint handicapper in first half of 1988: has lost his form completely: sometimes blinkered: has sweated and worn bandages: sold 800 gns Doncaster June Sales. *Ronald Thompson.*

AKAMANTIS 3 b.f. Kris 135–Graecia Magna (USA) 109 (Private Account (USA)) **97** [1989 8f* 7m² 1990 10m³ 12d⁵ 10.1m² 9m² 10.1g³ 9m⁴ 10g³ 10g³] big, strong filly: useful performer: mostly ran creditably as 3-y-o, in listed races won by Song of Sixpence at Windsor and Va Toujours at York fifth and sixth starts: best short of 1½m: acts on firm going: tends to be edgy: often sweating. *G. Harwood.*

AKAROA 3 ch.c. Kalaglow 132–St Isadora (Lyphard (USA) 132) [1989 7g 1990 **88** 10g³ 12f⁶ 10.5m² a12g² 10.6d⁴ a12g*] leggy, lengthy colt: fair performer: 15/8 on, comfortably won 8-runner maiden at Southwell in November: second to Emperor Fountain in listed race at York in June: stays 1½m: acts on good to firm going. *W. Jarvis.*

AKDAM (USA) 5 b.h. Arctic Tern (USA) 126–Dancers Countess (USA) **101** (Northern Dancer) [1989 10m 10m 10.2g⁵ 1990 12.3d 9g* 9m* 10m² 9m* 8m* 10m*] big, strong, close-coupled horse: moderate mover: in tremendous heart in summer, successful 4 times at Kempton (first 2 ladies races) and in £6,600 1m ladies event (caught close home by disqualified If Memory Serves) at Ascot: odds on, not at his best when winning claimer (claimed to race in Saudi Arabia £42,101) final outing: stays 1¼m: acts on good to firm and dead going: useful. *R. F. Johnson Houghton.*

AKEEM (USA) 2 b.c. (Apr 4) Skywalker (USA)–Kankam (ARG) (Minera 102) **113**
[1990 7s3 a8g* 8v2] sturdy, quite attractive colt: half-brother to a minor winner in
North America by Riverman: dam won 10 races in Argentina, and was leading 2-y-o
filly there: sire won Breeders' Cup Classic: short-head second of 16 to Steamer
Duck in Gran Criterium at Milan in November: earlier made all in maiden at
Lingfield: will stay 1¼m: acts well on heavy going: very useful. *J. H. M. Gosden.*

AKID (USA) 4 ch.c. Secreto (USA) 128–Raise The Bridge (USA) (Raise A Cup —
(USA)) [1989 6v2 1990 6m 8g] sturdy, good-topped colt: useful as 2-y-o: extremely
lightly raced subsequently and well beaten in handicaps in 1990: should stay beyond
7f. *D. H. Topley.*

AKIMBO 3 ch.c. Bold Lad (IRE) 133–Western Gem 86 (Sheshoon 132) [1989 8v **92**
1990 8.5g* 8m* 10s3 8v3 8g 9f2 10m 8m 8g] well-made colt: successful twice from 3
starts at Cagnes-sur-Mer early in year: off course nearly 5 months after fourth
outing, best effort after when good eighth of 16 in £8,400 handicap at Newmarket
seventh start: showed little on final one: will be suited by return to 1¼m: acts on
good to firm and heavy going: fairly useful. *C. R. Nelson.*

AKKAZAO (IRE) 2 b. or br.f. (Jan 24) Alzao (USA) 117–Akka (Malacate (USA) **94** ?
131) [1990 5f2 6m2 6d4 5d3 6m4 6m6] workmanlike filly: third foal: sister to a winner
in Scandinavia: dam thrice-raced daughter of half-sister to Sir Wimborne and Lady
Capulet: just over a length sixth of 9, ridden along at halfway and keeping on well, to
Only Yours in 'Pacemaker Update' Lowther Stakes at York in August, easily best
effort: better suited by 6f than 5f: raced very freely when blinkered fifth outing. *W.
Carter.*

ALAMIRA (USA) 2 ch.f. (Feb 28) Affirmed (USA)–Manchester Miss (USA) **76**
(Groton) [1990 8m3 7.3s5] $190,000Y: tall, sparely-made filly: has a roundish action:
half-sister to 3 winners, including Auntie Betty (by Faraway Son), graded
stakes-placed winner at up to 9f: dam minor winner at 3 yrs: shaped well when third
to Glowing Ardour in maiden at Chepstow, leading 1½f out and looking likely to win
then green and no extra close home: 11 lengths fifth of 6, pushed along at halfway
and soon losing touch, to Shaima in listed event at Newbury 2 months later: should
stay 1¼m. *P. F. I. Cole.*

ALAMSHAH (IRE) 2 b.c. (May 16) Lashkari 128–Alannya (FR) (Relko 136) **49**
[1990 7m 8.2s3] compact colt: half-brother to several winners, including disqualified
Oaks winner Aliysa (by Darshaan) and French 9f winner Aliyoun (by Kalamoun),
subsequently useful winner at up to 1½m in USA: dam smart 1m winner in France: 9
lengths third of 13, staying on, to Magic Secret in maiden at Hamilton in September:
ridden by girl apprentice, gave trouble stalls on debut: will be well suited by 1¼m +:
sold to join Pat Mitchell's stable 6,200 gns Doncaster October Sales. *M. R. Stoute.*

AL ANBA (USA) 3 b.f. Lear Fan (USA) 130–Dacquoise (USA) (Lyphard (USA) **80**
132) [1989 7m2 7m2 6m2 1990 7m 10f8f* 8m6 10m*] sturdy filly: has a fluent action:
won handicaps at Leicester in July and Newmarket (moderately-run £12,200 event,
wandered under pressure) in August: best efforts at 1¼m: yet to race on an easy
surface. *G. A. Huffer.*

ALAOUI 8 ch.g. Al Sirat (USA)–Sunny Sunset (Sunny Way 120) [1989 NR 1990 —
a14g3] workmanlike gelding: half-brother to several winning Irish chasers/point-to-
pointers: dam unraced sister to useful stayer Sun Lion: 12 lengths third of 9 to Off
The Record in maiden at Southwell in June: sold 25,000 gns Doncaster August
Sales: winning hurdler/chaser: dead. *Mrs S. Oliver.*

AL ASOOF (USA) 5 gr.g. Shareef Dancer (USA) 135–Jet Quick (USA) —
(Determine) [1989 NR 1990 16.2m 14s 16g] sturdy gelding: moderate mover: quite
modest maiden at best: bandaged, well beaten in handicaps at 5 yrs: stays 1½m:
needs give in the ground: fairly useful hurdler. *M. E. D. Francis.*

AL BADETO 3 b.f. Hays 120–Atedaun (Ahonoora 122) [1989 5d2 6m 6g3 6m3 6m **52**
6m 5s 1990 6m 6m3 7m2 8g6 8.2g 6h 7m6 6d2 6d 6s a6g] lengthy, rather
sparely-made filly: plating-class maiden: stays 7f: acts on good to firm ground and
dead: blinkered tenth start, visored sixth at 2 yrs: has found little: inconsistent. *J.
Norton.*

ALBADR (USA) 5 ch.h. Arctic Tern (USA) 126–Spring Tour (USA) (Ack Ack **110**
(USA)) [1989 13.3f* 12v4 1990 12g2 13.4d3 14g4 12.5g4 12m6 12g 10d] big, strong,
workmanlike horse: suffered stress fracture of off-fore as 3-y-o: very useful
performer: ran creditably when placed in John Porter EBF Stakes at Newbury and
slowly-run Ormonde EBF Stakes at Chester in spring and when fourth to Robetet
in Grand Prix de Deauville Lancel on fourth outing: tailed off next time in
Cumberland Lodge Stakes at Ascot, acted as pacemaker last 2 outings: stays 13.4f:

possibly needs give in the ground nowadays (not at his best on heavy): sold 25,000 gns Newmarket December Sales. *R. W. Armstrong.*

AL BATAL (USA) 3 ch.c. Blushing Groom (FR) 131–Salpinx (USA) 123 — (Northern Dancer) [1989 7g 1990 10m 10g 10m] close-coupled colt: quite modest form at best in maidens: showed nothing last 2 starts, wearing tongue strap on final one, in June: bred to be suited by middle distances. *J. L. Dunlop.*

ALBERT 3 b.c. Kings Lake (USA) 133–Darine 114 (Nonoalco (USA) 131) [1989 **65** 6s* 8s 1990 10.6s 12g 12.3g⁵ 13d 12v 15d] good-bodied colt: shows a round action: never dangerous in handicaps since winning minor event at Ayr as 2-y-o, staying on having been set lot to do when good fifth of 19 at Ripon in August: stays 1½m: acts on soft going. *C. W. Thornton.*

ALBERTA HENRIETTA 3 ch.f. Tickled Pink 114–Queens Pearl (Queen's — Hussar 124) [1989 NR 1990 7g⁵ 6g 6g⁵ 7.5m 6d] sturdy filly: has round action: third foal: dam of no account: well beaten, in handicap (pulled hard) and claimer last 2 starts: trained by M. Bell first three. *K. R. Burke.*

ALBERT HENRY 6 ch.h. Tickled Pink 114–Queens Pearl (Queen's Hussar 124) **49** [1989 6d 5s⁶ 5m⁶ 1990 6s a6g⁴ 5g] small, strong, workmanlike horse: modest winner early as 4-y-o: showed he retained some ability in spring handicaps on last 2 outings (sweating final one) in 1990: best at 5f: possibly suited by an easy surface nowadays: flashed tail and looked none too keen in blinkers. *M. Bell.*

ALBERTS TREASURE 2 b.g. (Apr 25) Sweet Monday 122–Dancing Amber — (Broxted 120) [1990 5g a7g] fourth reported foal: dam tailed off in novice hurdle: behind in maiden at Carlisle and seller at Southwell. *M. W. Ellerby.*

ALBERT'S WAY OUT 4 ch.g. Camden Town 125–Grunhilde 54 (Mountain Call **47** 125) [1989 6s 8g 7g 10g⁶ 8f⁴ 7.6h 9m 1990 a8g 8m⁶ 9f 10f² 11.7g³ 11.5m 10.1m 11.7m 10.1m] rather leggy, short-backed gelding: moderate mover: plating-class handicapper: lost his form after fifth outing: suited by middle distances: best form on a sound surface: visored 4 times, including eighth start: bandaged final one. *S. Dow.*

ALCANDANCE 3 b.f. Alzao (USA) 117–Dancing Sun (Will Somers 114§) [1989 **71** 5m³ 5f⁴ 5m⁴ 6g⁴ 6v⁵ 7g 1990 5m³ 6m* 6m 5.8m³ 6h 6m⁴ 6s] close-coupled, sturdy filly: modest handicapper: favourite, won at Goodwood in May: unlikely to stay beyond 6f: acts on good to firm ground and heavy: tends to be on toes. *C. James.*

ALCANDO 4 b.f. Alzao (USA) 117–Kaniz (Darius 129) [1989 7m³ 8f⁴ 10m² 12g⁶ **106** 10g* 10g 1990 10m³ 10m⁶ 10g² 10f⁵ 9f] small, compact filly: useful performer: creditable second of 7, making her ground up quickly 3f out, to Husyan in Scottish Classic at Ayr in July: ran poorly when blinkered next outing, then beat only one in Beverly D Stakes at Arlington: suited by 1¼m: acts on firm and dead going: usually held up: genuine. *C. James.*

ALCHIEA 3 b.f. Alzao (USA) 117–Dancing Lass (King Emperor (USA)) [1989 5m⁴ — 6m⁶ 6h² 1990 7m 9g 8f 7f⁵ 6h 5m 7m 6m 5.8d] small, sturdy filly: quite modest maiden as 2-y-o: well below form in handicaps: best effort at 6f on hard ground: blinkered fourth and fifth outings. *C. James.*

ALDAHE 5 ch.g. Dalsaan 125–Alanood 85 (Northfields (USA)) [1989 6g 6g 7m 6g **66** 8g 7f 8m 5g³ 6g⁶ 5m⁶ 1990 a8g² a7g* 8f³ 7m² 8.2s³ 8f⁵ 7m² 8h 6g a7g³ 8.2g⁵ 7g⁶ 6g 8m⁴ 6m⁶ 7.5m* 7m 8g 7d⁴] sparely-made gelding: usually dull in coat: has a round action: quite modest handicapper: won at Southwell in March (was in very good form early in year) and Beverley in September: stays 1m: acts on any going: best form without blinkers: often hangs but went well for 5-lb claimer at Beverley: claimed out of T. Craig's stable £5,900 fourteenth start. *B. R. Millman.*

AL DAMOUR (USA) 3 b.c. Lypheor 118–Visual Effects (USA) (Silent Screen **68** (USA)) [1989 7m 8g⁵ 1990 10.2f⁵ 11.7g 12f⁵] sturdy colt: has a round action: modest maiden: probably stays 1½m: yet to race on a soft surface: has joined C. Broad. *L. M. Cumani.*

ALDBOURNE 4 b.f. Alzao (USA) 117–Steady The Buffs 62 (Balidar 133) [1989 **106** 7g² 8g³ 8m² 8f⁶ 1990 8m* 8m⁶ 7g² 8f⁵ 8.5f* 8.5s² 10s² 10g] tall, rather angular filly: moderate walker and mover: very useful performer: successful in 3-runner listed event at Sandown (making all) in May and Budweiser Breeders' Cup Handicap at Atlantic City in August: beaten head in Grade 3 event at Belmont Park and 5 lengths by Ruby Tiger in Grade 2 E P Taylor Stakes at Woodbine next 2 outings: stays 1¼m: acts on any going: sometimes on toes: game and consistent. *R. Guest.*

ALDERHEY (USA) 3 b.c. Blushing Groom (FR) 131–Native Nurse (USA) **75**
(Graustark) [1989 8m 1990 10g³ 10.1m⁵] lengthy, angular colt: modest form: should
have stayed 1½m: dead. *M. R. Stoute.*

ALDINO 7 ch.g. Artaius (USA) 129–Allotria 86 (Red God 128§) [1989 12s³ 14g² —
12g⁵ 1990 12m] fair handicapper: bit backward, shaped well in amateurs event at
Ascot in October: stays 1¾m: yet to race on firm going, acts on any other: best in
blinkers or visor: smart hurdler, winner twice in autumn. *O. Sherwood.*

ALDWICK COLONNADE 3 ch.f. Kind of Hush 118–Money Supply (Brigadier **62**
Gerard 144) [1989 6g 1990 8m 8.2g 10f³ 10f³ 13.1h⁴ 8g* 9g⁵ 8m⁶ 8g 8m⁴ 8d⁴ 8m*
8g⁵] workmanlike filly: moderate walker and mover: quite modest performer: won
claimer at Goodwood in June and handicap at Wolverhampton in October: suited by
1m: acts on firm and dead ground. *M. D. I. Usher.*

ALEXANDRA FAIR (USA) 2 b. or br.f. (Apr 12) Green Dancer (USA) 132– **104**
Mira Irish Key (USA) (Irish Castle (USA)) [1990 8g* 8g 9v] $44,000Y: fourth foal:
half-sister to 2 winners in North America, including 3-y-o Puffy Doodle (by
Northjet), graded-stakes placed winner at up to 7f in 1989: dam minor winner at 3
yrs, is half-sister to Grand Criterium winner Femme Elite: won newcomers race at
Longchamp in September by ¾ length: under 5 lengths seventh of 9 to Shadayid in
Prix Marcel Boussac there following month: will stay 1¼m. *D. Smaga, France.*

ALEXANDRA KATRINE 4 b.f. Precocious 126–Sipapu 90 (Targowice (USA) — §
130) [1989 5f⁵ 5f² 5h³ 6m² 6m³ 6f 5g 5f⁵ 5f³ 6f³ 6m 6g² 7g a6g³ a7g a6g⁶ 1990 6g a6g
5.1m a6g 5g 6g] strong, good-quartered filly: moderate mover: maiden handicapper:
stays 6f: acts on hard and dead going: blinkered twice, visored once: trained until
after reappearance by F. J. Houghton: ungenuine. *M. H. Tompkins.*

ALFAARES (USA) 2 b. or br.c. (Feb 16) Danzig (USA)–Palm Reader (USA) (Sir **78**
Ivor 135) [1990 6m² 7m⁶] $925,000Y: strong, good-bodied colt: powerful galloper,
with a very round action: first foal: dam winner at up to 1¼m, from family of
Caerleon: ½-length second of 7, slowly away, green, good headway to challenge
final 1½f, to Buster in minor event at Nottingham in September: 8 lengths sixth of
18, racing keenly, unable to quicken from 2f out then eased, to Environment Friend
in maiden at Newmarket following month: probably stays 7f. *Major W. R. Hern.*

ALFA VITA 4 ch.f. Absalom 128–Aruba 77 (Amber Rama (USA) 133) [1989 6m — §
6f⁶ 7g a8g 1990 7f] smallish, sturdy filly: no worthwhile form, including in seller:
wearing tongue strap, reluctant to race and always tailed off in Wolverhampton
handicap in April: sold out of C. Brittain's stable 1,100 gns Ascot February Sales. *D.
R. Tucker.*

ALFEREZ 3 gr.g. Petong 126–Sarah's Venture 70 (Averof 123) [1989 7f 7g 1990 —
8f] workmanlike gelding: well beaten in maidens. *M. McCormack.*

AL FROLIC 3 b.c. Alzao (USA) 117–Fun Frolic (Sexton Blake 126) [1989 5v 6m 6f **62**
7g⁴ 1990 10d 7.9m 8m⁶ 7m² 8.5m 8g 9g⁴ 8.2g 8d³ 9.1s] IR 14,000Y: close-coupled,
quite good-topped colt: first foal: dam, placed over 7f and 1¼m (3 times) in Ireland,
is half-sister to a leading 2-y-o in Japan: quite modest ex-Irish maiden: in frame in
handicaps at Galway and Phoenix Park then minor event at Edinburgh: stays 9f: acts
on good to firm and dead going: trained until after eighth start by E. O'Grady. *P.
Monteith.*

ALFUJAIRAH 3 ch.c. Diesis 133–Soluce 98 (Junius (USA) 124) [1989 5f² 6f³ 6f³ **97** +
1990 8d* 7g] sturdy, lengthy colt: much improved form when making all in good
style in handicap at Newbury in April: badly hampered early on in £20,000 handicap
following month: stays 1m well: goes well on a soft surface: found little second start
at 2 yrs. *J. Gosden.*

ALGAIHABANE (USA) 4 b.g. Roberto (USA) 131–Sassabunda 108 (Sassafras —
(FR) 133) [1989 11f³ 14g³ 14f² 13.6f³ 12.4g 1990 a13g⁵ 14.8m 14m 16.2g⁶ 12m⁴ 16m
16f⁴ 16m] close-coupled, rather finely-made gelding: good mover with a light, easy
action: modest maiden at best: stays 2m: acts on firm going: blinkered final start at 3
yrs: bandaged off-fore last 2 outings. *Miss A. J. Whitfield.*

ALHAJRAS (USA) 3 b.c. Northern Dancer–Call Me Goddess (USA) (Prince —
John) [1989 NR 1990 10.5g] $1,600,000Y: attractive colt: closely related to a winner
in USA by Northern Jove and half-brother to 4 winners, notably very smart French
7.5f to 10.5f winner Smuggly and very useful 7f and 11f winner Asl (both by Caro):
dam stakes-placed winner at up to 1m out of CCA Oaks winner Marshua: 10/1 and
burly, slowly away and always behind in 12-runner maiden at York in October. *J. L.
Dunlop.*

ALHAWRAH (USA) 3 b.f. Danzig (USA)–Khwlah (USA) 99 (Best Turn (USA)) **68**
[1989 5g⁵ 1990 7m² 7m 7h⁴] tall, rather leggy filly: second in minor event at

Kempton: well behind in maidens at Yarmouth (hampered early) and Brighton (blinkered) later in summer: should stay 1m. *H. Thomson Jones.*

ALIBI WARNING 3 b.g. Belfort (FR) 89–Carymara (FR) (Dankaro (FR) 131) —
[1989 5g 5d⁴ 6m⁴ 7.5f 7f⁵ 6m⁴ 7m³ 7m² 7m⁵ 8.5f⁶ 6g 1990 8.2m 8d] tall, good-topped gelding: moderate walker: plater: faced stiff tasks in summer as 3-y-o, blinkered and front rank 6f final start: should prove ideally suited by return to shorter: blinkered then visored last 2 starts at 2 yrs: sold 1,300 gns Doncaster November Sales. *J. Berry.*

ALICANTE 3 b.c. Alzao (USA) 117–Safe And Happy (Tudor Melody 129) [1989   63
7m⁵ 7g⁵ 7m⁶ 8m⁵ 9g⁴ 8f³ 8g 1990 8f⁵ 12.3f 10g 7f 8g² 8m⁶ 8f⁴ 10.2f4 7.6g³ 8.2g 8m²
7f⁴ 8f² 9g⁶ a8g] small, close-coupled colt: quite modest maiden: best form at 1m: acts on firm going: ran moderately in blinkers: has run well for 7-lb claimer: tends to edge left, and has looked none too keen: trained until after third start by R. Guest, next 10 by Pat Mitchell: winning hurdler. *P. A. Blockley.*

ALIDIVA 3 b.f. Chief Singer 131–Alligatrix (USA) 111 (Alleged (USA) 138) [1989 105
6g* 1990 8g* 10m⁵ 7m* 8g⁴] close-coupled filly: won £8,800 event (odds on) at Kempton in April and listed race (beat Filia Ardross 2½ lengths) at Goodwood in July: favourite, modest fourth in listed race at Sandown in August: best form over 7f: useful. *H. R. A. Cecil.*

ALIM (CAN) 3 gr.c. The Minstrel (CAN) 135–Jiving Queen (CAN) (Drone) [1989   63
7g⁵ 8g² 8m⁴ 1990 10.2f4 12m⁶ a11g⁴ 12g 10.8g] leggy, quite good-topped colt: quite modest maiden: below form after reappearance, racing too freely in handicap final outing: stayed 1¼m: acted on firm ground: dead. *B. Hanbury.*

A LITTLE HOT 3 gr.f. Petong 126–Hot Money 50 (Mummy's Pet 125) [1989 NR   —
1990 5g⁴ 5g⁴ 6m 6d 6d 8d] 7,400F, 10,000Y: leggy filly: closely related to quite modest 5f winner Robrob (by Mansingh) and half-sister to 2 winners abroad, including Italian 5f to 7f winner Nonna Pepa (by Monsanto): dam 3-y-o 6f winner: quite modest form at best: never dangerous in claimer (blinkered) and selling handicaps last 3 starts: should stay at least 6f: sometimes slowly away. *J. P. Hudson.*

A LITTLE PRECIOUS 4 b.g. Precocious 126–The Silver Darling 75 (John   71
Splendid 116) [1989 6s² 6v* 6d 7g 6g 1990 6m⁴ 6m³ 7m 7.6g 7m⁶ 7g 8d 6g² 6m²
7g] strong, close-coupled, attractive gelding: poor mover: modest handicapper: effective at 6f to 7f: yet to race on firm going, acts on any other: sweating second and third starts: ran well for lady rider on penultimate. *J. R. Bostock.*

ALJANAN 3 b.c. Pitskelly 122–Charley's Aunt 80 (Will Somers 114§) [1989 5f⁵   61
5m² 6m⁶ 6v 6g⁵ 6g⁶ 6g 1990 8f 7m* 7m⁵ 6f⁵ 8m² 10.6v] rather leggy, unfurnished colt: quite modest performer: dropped to sellers when winning at Doncaster (no bid) in May and second at Carlisle (claimed out of M. Johnston's stable £6,230) in June: needs further than 6f, and stays 1m (in need of race over 10.6f): acts on any going: blinkered second outing at 2 yrs: has raced freely. *R. F. Fisher.*

ALJARIH (USA) 4 b.c. Nijinsky (CAN) 138–Love Words (USA) (Gallant Romeo   91
(USA)) [1989 8m² 7f4 10.6g* 11v 1990 10m 10.4d³ 10g⁴ 10m³ 12m⁶ 10f* 10f² 10f*]
strong, good-bodied colt: carries lot of condition: has a rather round action: fairly useful handicapper: won at Newmarket in August and Chepstow following month: stays 10.6f: acts on firm and soft going: heavily bandaged seventh start: consistent: sold 24,000 gns Newmarket Autumn Sales. *H. Thomson Jones.*

AL-KHAGOOLA (IRE) 2 b.f. (May 14) Coquelin (USA) 121–Demeter 83 (Silly   48
Season 127) [1990 5g⁶ 5f⁵ 6m⁵ 5f⁵ 7m] IR 2,100F: smallish, angular filly: keen walker: has a round action: half-sister to useful 5f to 7f performer Mother Earth (by Jukebox) and 1½m winner Gilt Star (by Star Appeal): dam 7f winner as 2-y-o: poor form in maidens and claimer: should stay 7f. *J. L. Spearing.*

AL KHOBAR (USA) 3 b.c. Our Native (USA)–Blazing Grace (USA) (Cannon-   79
ade (USA)) [1989 8g 1990 10f* 12g² 10.1g] leggy, quite good-topped colt: moderate walker: won 5-runner maiden at Beverley in March, keeping on well despite flashing tail: easily better effort in minor events after when second at Carlisle, wandering under pressure: may prove suited by forcing tactics over 1¼m: sweating final start: sold 12,500 gns Newmarket Autumn Sales. *P. F. I. Cole.*

ALKILONG 3 b.g. Longleat (USA) 109–Alkion (Fordham (USA) 117) [1989 6f⁶   —
a6g 1990 10f] compact gelding: poor mover: soundly beaten in maidens and claimer: sold 1,350 gns Ascot April Sales. *R. Simpson.*

ALKUWAH 2 b.f. (Mar 1) Sure Blade (USA) 128–Buthayna 85 (Habitat 134) [1990   —
7m 7m] big, good-topped filly: has plenty of scope: first foal: dam placed at 6f, is half-sister to Reach and daughter of Lingfield Oaks Trial winner Gift Wrapped:

backward and green, slowly away and always behind in autumn maidens at Newmarket and Leicester: sold 1,400 gns Newmarket December Sales. *J. L. Dunlop.*

ALLAYAALI 2 b.f. (Mar 18) Dunbeath (USA) 127–Walladah (USA) 71 (Northern — Dancer) [1990 6g] good-topped filly: third foal: dam second 3 times at 1¼m, is closely related to very smart filly Beaudelaire and daughter of very smart winner at up to 1m Bitty Girl: backward, no show in maiden at Newbury in August: sold 1,100 gns Newmarket December Sales. *P. T. Walwyn.*

ALLAZZAZ 4 ch.c. Mill Reef (USA) 141–Polavera (FR) (Versailles II) [1989 6g6 — 1990 10.1g 10m 11.5m 11.5m] rather leggy, sparely-made colt: of little account: sold out of D. O'Donnell's stable 2,000 gns Ascot April Sales before reappearance: resold 950 gns Ascot November Sales. *M. J. Haynes.*

ALLEGRA 3 b. or br.f. Niniski (USA) 125–Alruccaba 83 (Crystal Palace (FR) 132) 73 [1989 NR 1990 11.5g4 a12g* 11f4] 5,000Y: sparely-made filly: first foal: dam, 6f winner, raced only at 2 yrs: favourite, comfortably won maiden at Southwell in July: fair fourth of 7, never able to challenge, in handicap at Redcar following month: stays 1½m. *J. H. M. Gosden.*

ALLEZ MILADY (USA) 3 b.f. Tom Rolfe–Why Me Lord (USA) (Bold 52 Reasoning (USA)) [1989 NR 1990 10f3] leggy, rather angular filly: eighth reported foal: sister to very smart 1m (at 2 yrs) to 1½m winner Allez Milord and half-sister to 3 winners in USA: dam 5f winner in USA: 6/5 on, 4 lengths third of 10 to Black Sapphire in maiden at Salisbury in May, held up taking keen hold then staying on at one pace: should be suited by 1½m. *G. Harwood.*

ALLEZ-OOPS 3 ch.f. Moulin 103–Ever So Cool (FR) (Never Say Die 137) [1989 65 7f2 8g2 8.2g5 8.2g5 1990 12s3 10.2m 13.8m 10.2m* 8m* 10.6s6 10f4 12m4 10m] smallish, sturdy filly: dropped in class then returned to form when winning claimers at Doncaster in June, claimed out of J. FitzGerald's stable £8,000 when easy winner on first occasion: below form after, rather running in snatches for 7-lb claimer final start: best form at up to 1¼m: acts on good to firm ground, possibly unsuited by soft. *A. Smith.*

ALL FIRED UP 3 b.f. Song 132–Honey Pot 111 (Hotfoot 126) [1989 5g* 5m2 6g 69 1990 6f* 6m4 7d 5m2 5m6 6m 5f4 5m2 5m 5d 5d 5g2 5g5] rather leggy, unfurnished filly: modest performer: 2/1 on, won minor event at Brighton in April: best efforts when second in handicap then claimers: stays 6f: acts on firm going, seems unsuited by dead: edgy sixth (also sweating) and eleventh starts: blinkered last 7: sold 6,000 gns Newmarket Autumn Sales. *R. J. R. Williams.*

ALL GREEK TO ME (IRE) 2 b.g. (May 15) Trojan Fen 118–Do We Know 47 p (Derrylin 115) [1990 7v4] fourth live foal: half-brother to a winner in Spain by Pharly: dam thrice-raced half-sister to high-class 1¼m horse Rarity: around 14 lengths fourth of 11, staying on well after very slow start, to Beachy Head in maiden at Ayr in October: sure to improve. *C. W. Thornton.*

ALLINSON'S MATE (IRE) 2 b.c. (Feb 28) Fayruz 116–Piney Pass (Persian 96 Bold 123) [1990 5f2 5m2 5m* 5m* 6f2 6m2 6m] 28,000Y: small, robust colt: carries plenty of condition: moderate mover: third foal: half-brother to modest 1989 2-y-o 5f and 6f winner Mountview and fair 1988 2-y-o 7f winner Woosie (both by Montekin): dam Irish 2-y-o 8.5f winner: fairly useful colt: won maiden at Catterick in May and nursery at York in July: ran poorly in Ascot nursery on final outing: better form at 6f than 5f: good mount for an apprentice. *T. D. Barron.*

ALL IS REVEALED 8 b.g. Welsh Pageant 132–Senorita Rugby (USA) 86 74 (Forward Pass) [1989 NR 1990 16g 16d 16m2 14g 16.2m* 18m6] big, rangy gelding: modest handicapper: won at Goodwood in May: ran moderately when favourite later in month: suited by a test of stamina and a sound surface: goes well with forcing tactics: best visored: has run well when sweating. *D. T. Thom.*

ALL NIGHT DELI 3 b.g. Night Shift (USA)–Tzarina (USA) (Gallant Romeo — (USA)) [1989 6f 7m 6g4 7m3 1990 6m 6m 10.4g4 8g] compact, workmanlike gelding: quite modest maiden at 2 yrs: stays 7f: visored second outing at 2 yrs: ran well when sweating final one: sold 950 gns Doncaster September Sales. *E. H. Owen jun.*

ALLSORTS 3 br.c. Noalto 120–Cheri Berry 87 (Air Trooper 115) [1989 NR 1990 — 8f] 500Y: lengthy, plain colt: third foal: dam sprint handicapper: 20/1, backward and green, tailed off in claimer at Salisbury in May. *W. G. R. Wightman.*

ALL THE KING'S MEN (IRE) 2 b.c. (Jan 31) Alzao (USA) 117–Hill's Realm 94 (USA) (Key To The Kingdom (USA)) [1990 8s2 8v* 9v2] IR 12,000F, 17,500Y: good-topped colt: has plenty of scope: fourth foal: brother to fairly useful 1988 2-y-o 7f winner Cooks Gorse and half-brother to 1987 Irish 2-y-o 7f winner Rathal (by Taufan): dam stayed 6f: fairly useful form: won listed race at Milan in November:

narrowly beaten other starts, by Il Corsair in similar event at same track later in month: will stay 1¼m. *P. F. I. Cole.*

ALLURE 3 b.f. Bustino 136–Albany 120 (Pall Mall 132) [1989 NR 1990 10f⁵ 10g⁶ 10.2f a8g 10m] neat, good-quartered filly: poor walker: closely related to smart stayer Buttress (by Busted) and half-sister to several winners, including smart middle-distance performer Dukedom (by Connaught): dam, daughter of high-class stayer Almeria, was smart at 1¼m: little worthwhile form in varied company: claimed out of W. Hastings-Bass' stable £8,100 in seller (visored) on debut. *D. Burchell.*

ALL WELCOME 3 b.g. Be My Guest (USA) 126–Pepi Image (USA) 111   **64** (National) [1989 8d 1990 8f4 10m 10s 8.2m³ 10m³ 9g 8m² 10.4d] angular gelding: poor mover: modest maiden: best efforts at 1m on top-of-the-ground: blinkered fourth to sixth (slowly away in apprentice race) starts: sold to join G. Moore 8,000 gns Newmarket Autumn Sales. *J. R. Fanshawe.*

ALMAASEH (IRE) 2 b.f. (Feb 10) Dancing Brave (USA) 140–Al Bahathri (USA)   **63 p** 123 (Blushing Groom (FR) 131) [1990 6m⁵] second foal: half-sister to 3-y-o Hasbah (by Kris), very useful but inconsistent 7f and 1m winner: dam won Lowther Stakes and Irish 1000 Guineas: favourite, around 4 lengths fifth of 6, leading over 4f, losing place then keeping on, to Possessive Dancer in maiden at Newmarket in November: sure to improve. *H. Thomson Jones.*

ALMAGHRIB 3 b.c. Red Sunset 120–Another Match (Sovereign Path 125) [1989   **73** 6f⁶ 6m² 6m³ 6m² 6m 6g³ 1990 7m³ 8g⁵ 8g⁶ 8d 8m⁴ 10g 10f³ 10f² 10.2g³ 10g 10.4d] workmanlike colt: modest handicapper: worth a try at 1½m: acts on firm ground, possibly unsuited by dead: blinkered final outing at 2 yrs: sold 12,500 gns New-market Autumn Sales. *R. Hannon.*

AL MAHEB (USA) 4 b.c. Riverman (USA) 131–Une Amazone (USA) **117** (Youth (USA) 135) [1989 8g 8g 10m* 10f² 13.3m* 1990 12m⁵ 13.3m* 16m* 15g* 18g* 16m4]

The standard of the big handicaps in Britain has, in general, declined considerably in the last thirty years and their status has been kept deliberately low since the introduction of official pattern races in 1971: handicaps are excluded from the pattern, shortsightedly, as we've written before. Handicaps can not only attract greater public interest than weight-for-age races, they can also be a better guide to horses' merit. The Northumberland Plate, the Ebor and the Cesarewitch—the year's three most valuable staying handicaps—are three that no longer carry the same prestige as they did in days of old. The winners of the Northumberland Plate, Ebor and Cesarewitch in the 'fifties had an average Timeform rating of 112, 118 and 114,

Newcastle Brown Ale Northumberland Plate (Handicap Sweepstakes), Newcastle—
Al Maheb is the third of Carson's six winners on the day's card;
Dance Spectrum and Holy Zeal follow them home

Doncaster Cup—Al Maheb, in his owner's second colours,
continues on the upgrade and beats Teamster (left) and Regal Reform

respectively, compared to 91, 113 and 90 in the 'eighties. Yet the story isn't one of utter decline. In terms of prize-money the three handicaps haven't lost any ground to the Gold Cup, Goodwood Cup and Doncaster Cup, thanks largely to sponsorship. The Cesarewitch winner's purse has, in fact, grown almost twice as much as any of the three Cup races, and in the latest season success in the Cesarewitch earned almost as much as the Doncaster Cup and Goodwood Cup winners put together. Furthermore, the Northumberland Plate and Cesarewitch winners of 1990 were the best for some time, and the former, Al Maheb, who progressed throughout the season and won four of his six races, ranks alongside the likes of Sweet Story (1965), Piaco (1966), Tug of War (1977 and 1978) and Karadar (1984). Al Maheb, penalised 3 lb for his success in a five-runner handicap at Newbury earlier in June, carried joint-second top weight of 8-11 at Newcastle, with Chester Cup winner Travelling Light, in receipt of 13 lb from Per Quod. Dance Spectrum, a well-backed favourite to continue Harwood's fine record in the race, set a modest pace until Cossack Guard went on after three furlongs. Al Maheb still had a fair bit to do three furlongs from home having been unable to hold his place when the tempo quickened approaching the home straight, then made up his ground impressively to join Holy Zeal and Dance Spectrum at the distance and ran on well to beat Dance Spectrum by a length and a half and Holy Zeal a further three quarters of a length. Both winner and runner-up were to figure among the top stayers by the end of the season. Northumberland Plate day, incidentally, was a red-letter day for Al Maheb's rider Willie Carson who partnered six winners on the seven-race card; only Gordon Richards at Chepstow in 1933 and Alec Russell at Bogside in 1957 have 'gone through the card' in Britain, both on a six-race programme.

Piaco and Karadar had won the Doncaster Cup the year before their Newcastle victories. Al Maheb did things the other way round and went to Doncaster after justifying favouritism in the Prix Kergorlay at Deauville where he had the French three-year-olds Ethan Frome and Ozal in second and third. The field for the Doncaster Cup was probably the strongest for a long-distance race in Britain all year and contained the Goodwood Cup first and second, Lucky Moon and Ecran, the Gold Cup winner Ashal and the Henry II Stakes winner Teamster. Ashal set too strong a gallop for his own good and dropped away in the final quarter of a mile together with Dance Spectrum, who followed him into the straight, and it was Al Maheb, Teamster

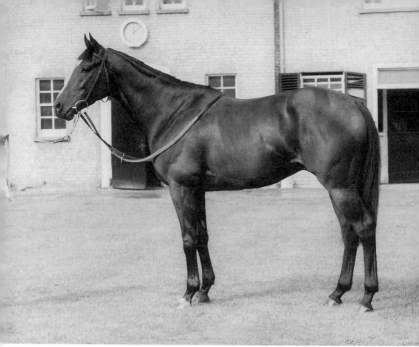

Hamdan Al-Maktoum's "Al Maheb"

and Regal Reform who came from off the pace to dominate matters in the closing stages. Al Maheb had travelled smoothly from the outset, quickened a couple of lengths clear under two furlongs out and was always going to repel the late surge of Teamster. A neck separated them on the line with Regal Reform, clear of the others, two and a half lengths back in third. Al Maheb ran once more, finishing a disappointing fourth to Great Marquess in the Jockey Club Cup at Newmarket. It was reported over a week later that he had thrown a splint on his off-fore, and the following month that he was to continue his career in Australia.

		Never Bend	Nasrullah
	Riverman (USA)	(b 1960)	Lalun
	(b 1969)	River Lady	Prince John
Al Maheb (USA)		(b 1963)	Nile Lily
(b.c. 1986)		Youth	Ack Ack
	Une Amazone (USA)	(b 1973)	Gazala II
	(b 1978)	Galoubinka	Tamerlane
		(b 1967)	Rhenane

There's plenty of stamina on the distaff side of Al Maheb's pedigree. His dam Une Amazone is an unraced half-sister to the Prix Royal-Oak winner Henri Le Balafre and the listed winner Grandcourt, third in the Prix Vicomtesse Vigier and Prix de Barbeville. Une Amazone, who produced two winners in France before Al Maheb, is a daughter of the Prix du Jockey-Club winner Youth and mile winner Galoubinka, herself a half-sister to the Prix du Jockey-Club and Grand Prix de Paris winner Rheffic and daughter of an unraced half-sister to Bella Paola, who won the One Thousand Guineas, Oaks and Champion Stakes. Al Maheb's sire Riverman, whose majority of winners in Britain and Ireland have come at distances up to a mile and a quarter, is also sire of Gold River, whose successes include the Prix Royal-Oak and Prix du Cadran as well as the Prix de l'Arc de Triomphe. The game and consistent Al Maheb is a small, attractive colt who carries plenty of condition. He has yet to race on a soft surface. *A. C. Stewart.*

AL MANHAL (IRE) 2 ch.c. (Apr 11) Glint of Gold 128–Hossvend (Malinowski — (USA) 123) [1990 6m 7f 8m] 10,000F, 7,000 2-y-o: smallish, good-quartered colt: third foal: dam once-raced half-sister to To-Agori-Mou: bit backward, little worthwhile form in claimer and maiden auctions: retained by trainer 2,400 gns Newmarket Autumn Sales. *R. Hollinshead.*

ALMARAI (USA) 3 b.f. Vaguely Noble 140–Waterbuck (USA) (The Axe II 115) 73 [1989 NR 1990 10g 8m3 10m2 10m3 10m2] \$140,000Y, resold \$400,000Y: rather leggy, workmanlike filly: seventh reported foal: half-sister to several winners, including Irish 1m winner Tetradrachm (by Royal And Regal) and minor 1984 U.S. 2-y-o stakes winner Amorphous (by Sir Wiggle): dam 2-y-o 5f winner is sister to very smart American winner at up to 9f Al Hattab: modest maiden: may well have been better suited to 1½m: set pace last 3 starts: to visit Green Desert. *A. C. Stewart.*

ALMASA 2 b.f. (Apr 14) Faustus (USA) 118–Superfrost 49 (Tickled Pink 114) 83 [1990 5m4 5f4 5m6 6m2 6g* 5f 7g 6g5 7m4 6m2 7f3 6f* 5g2 6m6 6m3 6d] sparely-made filly: poor mover: first foal: dam 1m seller winner: fair performer: won claimer at Leicester in June and minor event at Lingfield in August: probably best short of 7f: possibly unsuited by a soft surface: unseated rider seventh outing: tends to drift right: tough, game and genuine. *J. C. Fox.*

ALMENDARES (USA) 2 b.c. (Apr 1) Tsunami Sleu (USA)–Marquessa de Sade 101 (USA) (Le Fabuleux 133) [1990 8g* 8g3 9g6] second foal: dam showed only a little ability in North America: useful French colt: won maiden at Clairefontaine in August by 8 lengths: over 2 lengths third of 8 in listed race at Evry following month, over 5 lengths sixth of 12 to Pistolet Bleu in Prix de Conde at Longchamp in October: will stay 1¼m. *J. E. Hammond, France.*

ALMOOJID 4 b.c. Sadler's Wells (USA) 132–Irish Bird (USA) (Sea Bird II 145) 69 [1989 10g5 10g5 12g3 10g 1990 11.5m3] rangy ex-Irish colt: closely related to top-class middle-distance performer Assert (by Be My Guest) and half-brother to 4 winners, notably Irish St Leger winner Eurobird (by Ela-Mana-Mou) and Prix du Jockey-Club winner Bikala (by Kalamoun): dam, French 11f winner, is half-sister to Irish Derby winner Irish Ball: 25/1, backward and sweating, close staying-on third of 10 in maiden at Lingfield in June: will stay beyond 1½m: blinkered last 2 outings at 3 yrs: bought out of D. Weld's stable 6,600 gns Newmarket Autumn (1989) Sales. *J. H. Baker.*

ALMOST A PRINCESS 2 b.f. (Jan 23) Alleging (USA) 120–Rabab (Thatching 68 131) [1990 7m 8m4 7g 8d] leggy filly: first foal: dam lightly-raced daughter of Be Merry, useful at up to 13f: modest maiden: should stay at least 1¼m. *R. Simpson.*

ALMOST BLUE 4 ch.g. Ballacashtal (CAN)–Blue Garter 70 (Targowice (USA) 93 130) [1989 5m 5f6 5m4 5g2 5m4 5m4 5g5 5g 1990 5m6 5g2 5m 5m6 5m 6m 5.6g 6d 5m 5m2 5d 5g] lengthy, deep-girthed gelding: moderate mover: quite useful on his day: ran well when second in valuable handicaps won by Lucedeo at York and Sloe Berry, edging right, at Ascot: speedy, best at 5f: acts on good to firm and soft going: blinkered fourth and seventh starts: usually taken down early and very quietly: inconsistent. *J. Berry.*

ALMUHIT 2 b. or br.f. (May 3) Doulab (USA) 115–Silojoka 95 (Home Guard — (USA) 129) [1990 6g] fifth foal: half-sister to quite moderate middle-distance winner Yamrah (by Milford): dam sprinting daughter of half-sister to very smart Golden Horus: backward, soon struggling in maiden at Kempton in September: sold 2,200 gns Newmarket Autumn Sales. *C. J. Benstead.*

ALMUINJJID (USA) 3 ch.c. Blushing Groom (FR) 131–Herb Wine (USA) (Full — Pocket (USA)) [1989 8.2d* 10g 1990 9m6 12.3m6] sturdy, attractive colt: won maiden at Haydock as 2-y-o: easily better effort facing stiff tasks in summer handicaps in 1990 at Sandown: hanging right and carrying head high: stays 9f: sent to USA. *H. Thomson Jones.*

ALNAAB (USA) 2 b. or br.c. (Apr 17) Mr Prospector (USA)–Hail Maggie (USA) 111 (Hail To Reason) [1990 7m 7m2 7f* 7m* 7g2] \$200,000Y: quite attractive colt: has scope: closely related to fairly useful 1984 2-y-o 7f winner Sabona (by Exclusive Native), later high class at up to 1m in USA, and half-brother to fair 3-y-o 11.5f winner Ruddy Cheek (by Blushing Groom) and a minor winner in USA: dam once-raced sister to Trillion, dam of Triptych: very useful performer, successful at Goodwood in maiden and minor event in August: very good ½-length second of 9 to Radwell in Imry Solario Stakes at Sandown final start, leading over 1f out and rallying really well despite hanging right: will stay 1m: progressing well. *J. L. Dunlop.*

ALNASRIC PETE (USA) 4 b.c. Al Nasr (FR) 126–Stylish Pleasure (USA) 72 (What A Pleasure (USA)) [1989 8s 12f 9f² 9m⁶ 1990 9g 10g 7.6m 6g⁶ 10m 12g⁶ 8g² 8m* 8g 7g⁴ a8g* a8g⁴ a8g a8g*] rather leggy, good-topped colt: carries condition: has a round action: became very disappointing, but after joining present trainer was in fine heart: won handicaps at Leicester in October and Southwell (amateur events) in November and December, leading on bridle first 2 occasions: suited by around 1m: acts on firm going: found nothing when blinkered third start: occasionally bandaged: takes keen hold, and best held up as long as possible: trained until after reappearance by G. Harwood: sold out of R. Smyth's stable 2,000 gns Ascot July Sales after fifth outing. *D. A. Wilson.*

ALO EZ 4 b.f. Alzao (USA) 117–Azina (USA) (Canonero II (USA)) [1989 6m* 7f 95 ? 6m⁵ 6m* 6g⁴ 1990 6m 6m⁶ 6m] neat, good-quartered filly: won strongly-run races at Newmarket for handicap (25/1) and listed race (50/1) as 3-y-o: showed she retained plenty of ability in face of stiff task when sixth in latest running of latter event in August: still backward, out of her depth final outing: suited by 6f: best efforts on top-of-the-ground: occasionally sweats. *J. Pearce.*

ALOSAILI 3 ch.c. Kris 135–Vaison La Romaine 100 (Arctic Tern (USA) 126) 77 [1989 NR 1990 12m 10.1m³ 10.4m³ 8m⁵] 50,000Y: lengthy, rather angular colt: has a round action: first foal: dam placed at around 7f here at 2 yrs later at 7.5f in France: modest maiden: refused to settle third start, well-beaten favourite on final one: suited by 1¼m: sold 10,000 gns Newmarket Autumn Sales. *M. A. Jarvis.*

ALPHABEL 4 b.c. Bellypha 130–Absolute (FR) (Luthier 126) [1989 10.1m* 110 10.6g² 12m* 12f² 13.3g³ 14.6s 1990 9m 12f* 12g* 14m² 10.6m² 12m³ 10d⁵ 10g⁶] big, strong colt: moderate walker and mover: very useful performer: won 4-runner listed contest (slowly run) at Newmarket in June: far superior to only rival in minor event at Thirsk previous outing: third in Group 3 races at Haydock (promoted a place behind Defensive Play) and Ascot (outpaced 3f out) fifth and sixth starts: probably stays 1¾m: acts on firm ground, apparently unsuited by soft surface: visored seventh start: ran moderately when sweating and on toes on reappearance: often edges left: sent to join D. Hayes in Australia. *A. C. Stewart.*

ALPHA HELIX 7 b.g. Double Form 130–Daidis 66 (Welsh Pageant 132) [1989 — 13.8d 12d* 13.8d* 12g* 12m⁵ 13f* 12g³ 13m³ 13g³ 12.3m 14m² 15g³ 13.6f⁶ 1990 12g⁵ 13g 13m⁴ 13f⁵] deep-girthed gelding: not a good walker or mover: won 4 handicaps in 1989: little form as 7-y-o, and seemed to return to his temperamental ways on third outing: stays 15f: yet to show his form on soft going, acts on any other: has worn blinkers, visored nowadays: best held up. *J. S. Wilson.*

ALPHA RASCAL (USA) 2 b.f. (Mar 17) Alphabatim (USA) 126–Rascal Rascal 71 (USA) (Ack Ack (USA)) [1990 7m a8g* a8g²] leggy filly: has scope: third foal: half-sister to winners in USA by Raise A Native and Miswaki: dam successful (at up to 9f) in 4 of 8 races, including in minor stakes: won 10-runner maiden at Southwell readily by 1½ lengths from Richmond: 8 lengths second of 11 to Smiling Sun in nursery at Lingfield later in November: will stay 1¼m: bandaged on debut. *J. H. M. Gosden.*

ALPINE TROOPER 3 ch.c. Burslem 123–Alpina 83 (King's Troop 118) [1989 — NR 1990 12m] IR 3,000Y: half-brother to several winners here and abroad: dam won over 1m: difficult at stalls, took keen hold and weakened over 2f out in claimer at Goodwood in June. *B. Stevens.*

ALQWANI (USA) 2 b.f. (Mar 5) Mr Prospector (USA)–Dire (USA) (Roberto 83 (USA) 131) [1990 6m² 6m* 6m⁶ 6m⁵ 8d⁵ 8d] $700,000Y: rangy, attractive filly: has scope: first foal: dam minor winner at up to 1¼m, is half-sister to Bellotto (by Mr Prospector): fair performer: won maiden at Goodwood in June: good running-on fifth of 17 to Glenorthern in nursery at Goodwood in October: suited by 1m: acts on good to firm ground and dead. *J. L. Dunlop.*

ALRAYED (USA) 2 b.c. (Feb 25) Alydar (USA)–Life's Magic (USA) (Cox's — p Ridge (USA)) [1990 8m] second foal: dam champion 1984 3-y-o filly, won 8 of her 32 races, at 6f to 1¼m: favourite, niggled along at halfway and dropped away 3f out in minor event at Newmarket in November: went down well: should do better. *Major W. R. Hern.*

ALREEF 4 b.g. Wassl 125–Joey (FR) 110 (Salvo 129) [1989 10g* 10.6m* 1990   **72**
10m² 10m⁵ 12m 11.5m 10m⁵ 10m³ 10m 10.6d³ 10g³] sparely-made, rather
dipped-backed gelding: quite modest handicapper: stays 10.6f: acts on good to firm
and dead going (probably unsuited by very soft): blinkered or visored last 4 starts at
2 yrs: has won for amateur: won over hurdles in December. *T. Thomson Jones.*

ALRIYAAH 3 b.f. Shareef Dancer (USA) 135–Sharpina (Sharpen Up 127) [1989   **—**
5f² 5f* 5.8f⁵ 5m 1990 6g 6m⁶ 6g] lengthy filly: modest winner at 2 yrs: well beaten in
minor event and handicap company since, weakening quickly and eased as 3-y-o:
bred to stay much further: blinkered (went very freely to post) final start: sold
13,000 gns Newmarket July Sales. *A. A. Scott.*

ALSAAMER (USA) 3 ch.c. Megaturn (USA)–Regal Nip (USA) (Raja Baba   **66**
(USA)) [1989 7m⁴ 8g⁵ 8g a8g² 1990 10m⁶ 11m² 10.6f⁴ a11g* 12m⁴ 13.3m 12.3g 10.6s]
lengthy, robust colt: good mover: quite modest performer: won maiden at Southwell
in May: fair fourth in apprentice handicap (visored) at York, easily best subsequent
effort: should stay 1½m: acts on good to firm ground: ran well in blinkers final start
at 2 yrs, moderately (edgy) sixth in 1990. *S. G. Norton.*

ALSAAYBAH (USA) 2 b.f. (May 10) Diesis 133–Secretarial Queen (USA)   **73 p**
(Secretariat (USA)) [1990 7m*] leggy filly: seventh foal: half-sister to several
winners worldwide, including useful 1m and 1¼m winner Thameen (by Roberto):
dam was at up to 1m: better for race and bandaged off-hind, won maiden at Chepstow
in October by a neck from Ryewater Dream, good headway 2f out and running on
well under considerate handling: will stay 1¼m: sure to improve. *J. L. Dunlop.*

AL SABAK (IRE) 2 ch.c. (Mar 17) Commanche Run 133–Sea Swallow (FR) 90   **54**
(Dan Cupid 132) [1990 6f⁴ 7g 8m 7.6v⁴ a8g] 32,000F, IR 26,000Y: half-brother to
numerous winners, including fairly useful 1983 2-y-o 6f and 7f winner Optimism Flamed (by
Ahonoora) and 1m/1¼m performer Optimism Flamed (by Malinowski): dam 1¼m
winner: plating-class maiden: will be suited by a good test of stamina: acts on
top-of-the-ground and heavy: suitable mount for apprentice. *R. Hollinshead.*

AL SHANY 4 ch.f. Burslem 123–Paradise Regained 41 (North Stoke 130) [1989   **59**
6m⁴ 7g⁵ 7m² 6m 7g 1990 a7g⁵ a7g⁴ 9f 10v 10f⁵ 8m 9f² 10m⁵ 10m 9m 10f² 10f⁶ 10m³
10f² 9m⁴ a10g³ a12g²] close-coupled, angular filly: tends to look dull in coat: quite
modest performer: stays 1½m: acts on firm and dead going: blinkered fifth and sixth
(also hooded) outings: often wears tongue strap: has started slowly. *W. Carter.*

AL SHAREEF 5 b.g. Shareef Dancer (USA) 135–Tarpoon (USA) (Vaguely Noble   **59**
140) [1989 NR 1990 a12g a10g⁵ 9s* 10v² 9s] quite attractive gelding: has a round
action: first form when winning maiden claimer at Hamilton by 7 lengths, wandering
in front: ran well when second in apprentice handicap at Ayr later in April: stays
1¼m: seems to need the mud: has worn bandage on near-hind. *D. Burchell.*

ALSHEEN 3 br.f. Alzao (USA) 117–Miss Olympus (Sir Gaylord) [1989 7m 6d 1990   **—**
8g 10f⁶ 10m 12h⁵ 12m] strong filly: carries condition: has a quick action: plating-
class form: stays 1¼m: blinkered last 2 starts. *K. M. Brassey.*

AL SKEET (USA) 4 b.g. L'Emigrant (USA) 129–Processional (USA) (Reviewer   **— §**
(USA)) [1989 8d⁶ 9f 9f² 10f³ 12m³ 12m 1990 8m 11.7g 9g²] lengthy, quite attractive
gelding: fair handicapper at one time: well beaten as 4-y-o, in amateurs race (taken
down early) first outing: stays 1½m: acts on any going: ran poorly in blinkers:
carries head high under pressure and is probably irresolute. *B. J. Wise.*

ALTAIA (FR) 3 gr.f. Sicyos (USA) 126–Haloom (Artaius (USA) 129) [1989 6m⁶   **85**
7g 7f³ 1990 7.6d² 7m* 7.3m* 8g⁵ 7m 7g³ 7m 7.3g 6m 6d³] leggy, workmanlike filly:
fair handicapper: won at Thirsk (£6,900 event) in May and Newbury in June:
effective at 6f and 7f: acts on good to firm ground and dead: usually makes the
running. *W. J. Haggas.*

ALTERMEERA 2 br.g. (Feb 14) Noalto 120–Mac's Melody (Wollow 132) [1990   **77 p**
7g³] fifth foal: dam ran once at 2 yrs: kept on well when 2¾ lengths third of 13 to
Eastern Magic in maiden at Salisbury in October: will stay 1m. *Mrs Barbara Waring.*

ALTOBELLI 6 b.g. Northern Treat (USA)–Imagination (FR) (Dancer's Image   **54**
(USA)) [1989 7v 7g 8f⁶ 7m⁶ 7f 7.6f 10h 10f⁴ 12m* 12f 1990 a13g² a12g⁵ a12g* a12g²
a16g* a13g⁴ 12f⁶ 14f a12g a12g³ a12g⁵ a12g³ a13g⁵ a13g* a12g a16g] leggy,
good-topped gelding: plating-class handicapper: won at Lingfield twice early in year
and once in December: stays 2m: acts on any going: blinkered twice: suitable mount
for apprentice: changed hands 2,500 gns Ascot July Sales: inconsistent. *P. Mitchell.*

ALTON BAY 2 b.g. (Apr 6) Al Nasr (FR) 126–Dabbiana (CAN) (Fappiano (USA))   **84**
[1990 6m⁴ 6g⁵ 7f* 7m⁴ 7m 7m] 92,000Y: leggy, close-coupled gelding: first foal:
dam winner at around 7f in USA: fair performer: comfortable winner of maiden at
Brighton in July: will stay 1m: none too consistent. *A. A. Scott.*

AL-TORFANAN 6 b.g. Taufan (USA) 119–Powder Box (Faberge II 121) [1989 8g **61** 7s 7g² 7m⁶ 7.6f³ 8h* 7g 8h* 8f 7.6m⁴ 8m 7.6f⁴ 8h 8f 8f 1990 a8g a8g* a7g 8f 8m 7.6m 7h² 8h⁴ 7g 7f* 8m⁵ 8f⁴ 8f 7.6m³ 8.3m² 7m⁶ 8f³ 7f⁵ 7f⁵ 7g 10f⁶] leggy, good-topped gelding: carries plenty of condition: has a round action: quite modest handicapper: won at Lingfield in February and Brighton in June: suited by 7f to 1m: goes particularly well on top-of-the-ground: usually visored: best racing up with pace: goes very well on switchback tracks: sold 7,000 gns Doncaster November Sales. *P. Howling.*

ALWATHBA (USA) 3 b.f. Lyphard (USA) 132–D'Arqueangel (USA) (Raise A **99** Native) [1989 6g* 1990 7m⁵ 6g⁴ 10m 8g² 7m³] sturdy filly: won Blue Seal Stakes at Ascot as 2-y-o: easily best effort in 1990 when second of 8 to Arpero in listed race at Sandown, keeping on well: suited by 1m: possibly needs give in the ground. *L. M. Cumani.*

ALWAYS ALEX 3 b.f. Final Straw 127–Two High 89 (High Top 131) [1989 6m* **—** 1990 8m 8g 8g] smallish, workmanlike filly: plating-class performer: won seller at Goodwood as 2-y-o: backed at long odds, easily best effort in 1990 in handicap at Sandown (first run for 5 months) second start: will probably stay beyond 1m. *Mrs Barbara Waring.*

ALWAYS ALLIED (IRE) 2 b.g. (Mar 15) Dalsaan 125–Novesia (Sir Gaylord) **84** [1990 a7g² 7m³ 7d² 8m⁴ 7f 7s²] IR 4,200F, 5,000Y: fifth foal: dam won in Italy: fair maiden: good staying-on second to Scottish Castle in nursery at Doncaster final start: will stay 1¼m: acts on good to firm ground and soft. *N. A. Graham.*

ALWAYS FRIENDLY 2 ch.f. (Apr 30) High Line 125–Wise Speculation (USA) **75 p** (Mr Prospector (USA)) [1990 7m] 6,200Y: workmanlike filly: third foal: half-sister to a winner in Sweden by Persian Bold: dam ran 3 times: green, around 5 lengths seventh of 18, keeping on steadily having been slowly away, to Noble Destiny in maiden at Leicester in October: sure to improve. *H. Candy.*

ALWAYS NATIVE (USA) 9 b. or br.g. Our Native (USA)–Mountain Memory **—** (USA) (Groton) [1989 10s 8v 12m 6f 5m⁶ 12f 5f 8f 1990 5m 7g 5m 8.5g 7f 5m 8m] workmanlike gelding: of no account: has sweated profusely: has run tubed. *G. P. Kelly.*

ALWAYS READY 4 b.g. Tyrnavos 129–Merchantmens Girl 58 (Klairon 131) **—** [1989 5s* 5s 5s 5g 5m 5m 5g⁵ 5d a6g 1990 5g 5g 7m 5s] strong, good-bodied gelding: carries plenty of condition: won handicap at Leicester in spring as 3-y-o: no worthwhile form in 1990, needing race final outing, first for nearly 5 months: should stay 6f: acts on soft going: usually visored or blinkered: trained until after third outing by J. Holt. *J. Balding.*

ALWAYS REMEMBER 3 b.c. Town And Country 124–Try To Remember **—** (Music Boy 124) [1989 NR 1990 8g 12.2f⁵ 11.7m⁶ 12m] rangy colt: has a round action: first foal: dam, fairly useful hurdler, was maiden plater on Flat, in frame over 1m: no worthwhile form, showing signs of ability when sixth in Windsor minor event: tailed off facing very stiff task in handicap: hung markedly left second start, and may well prove suited by an easy surface. *J. A. R. Toller.*

ALWAYS TAKE PROFIT 4 ch.g. Noalto 120–Pour Moi 73 (Bay Express 132) **—** [1989 12s 10f⁵ 12m 8m 1990 a13g⁶] leggy, shallow-girthed gelding: poor maiden: form only over 7f on a soft surface as 2-y-o: blinkered, sweating and edgy final start that season: wears crossed noseband: sold 740 gns Doncaster March Sales. *C. N. Allen.*

ALWAYS TREASURE 4 b.f. Lochnager 132–Rosinka 62 (Raga Navarro (ITY) **35 §** 119) [1989 5s⁶ 5g 5m 5m 5m⁵ 5f 8f⁵ 6g⁵ 6g 1990 a5g a5g⁴ a5g² a5g 5g 5g³ a5g 5m] lengthy, workmanlike filly: poor maiden: stays 6f: has looked unenthusiastic. *J. Balding.*

ALYANAABI (USA) 3 ch.f. Roberto (USA) 131–Fair (CHI) (Madara) [1989 NR **74** 1990 8m⁵ 10m 8g⁴ 10.2f³ 12.5m⁴ 12f⁵ 10g*] $250,000Y: rather leggy, unfurnished filly: half-sister to fairly useful miler My Noble Lord (by Northern Baby) and to several other winners, including stakes winner at up to 9f Fairly Regal (by Viceregal): dam won 7 times in Chile: modest form: 20/1-winner of handicap at Folkestone in October: best at 1¼m: acts on firm going: sold 18,000 gns Newmarket December Sales. *P. T. Walwyn.*

ALYSUNSET (USA) 2 ch.f. (Mar 19) Alydar (USA)–Northern Sunset (North- **73 p** fields (USA)) [1990 8.5m*] $550,000Y: half-sister to several winners, including very smart French middle-distance colt Norberto (by Roberto) and smart 9f and 1¼m winner Lac Quimet (by Pleasant Colony): dam Irish 6f and 7f winner: odds on, won 11-runner maiden, apparently easily, at Galway in August by a length: wasn't seen out again. *J. S. Bolger, Ireland.*

ALZAMINA 4 b.f. Alzao (USA) 117–Timinala 58 (Mansingh (USA) 120) [1989 6m 6f⁴ 7g 7m⁶ 7m⁶ 7m 1990 a6g⁴] leggy, sparely-made filly: quite modest form at best: has run in sellers: suited by 6f: acts on firm and dead going: tends to get on toes. *J. White.* —

AMADORA 4 b.f. Beldale Flutter (USA) 130–Zerbinetta 96 (Henry The Seventh 125) [1989 8g⁴ 8f a8g² 1990 10g 10g⁴ a11g 9f⁴ 10g²] leggy, angular filly: poor walker: moderate mover: modest maiden: stays 1¼m: acts on firm going: bandaged off-fore at 2 yrs, sometimes off-hind at 4 yrs: sold to join M. Pipe's stable 7,800 gns Newmarket Autumn Sales. *J. L. Dunlop.* 69

AMANA RIVER (USA) 3 ch.f. Raise A Cup (USA)–Barada (USA) (Damascus (USA)) [1989 5m* 1990 8f* 8m 8m³ 8f⁵ 7m] quite attractive filly: has a powerful, round action: won handicap at Ripon in April: ran well when third in similar event at Goodwood, poorly after: should stay further: visored fourth start: sometimes bandaged behind. *J. Gosden.* 77

AMANDHLA (IRE) 2 ch.c. (Apr 1) Red Sunset 120–Paradise Bird 94 (Sallust 134) [1990 5v 5f⁵ 5d⁴ 6f² 6f 5m⁴ 6g⁶ 6m⁴ 7d⁴] 12,500Y: rather leggy, close-coupled colt: moderate walker: fifth foal: half-brother to fairly useful 1989 2-y-o 5f winner Drayton Special (by Lyphard's Special) and 2 winners (at up to 9f) in Ireland by Sandhurst Prince: dam 2-y-o 6f winner: modest maiden: easily best efforts in nurseries on fourth and sixth starts, ridden by lady jockey most other starts: stays 6f: best form on good to firm ground: sold 8,000 gns Newmarket Autumn Sales. *N. Tinkler.* 73 d

AMATHUS GLORY 3 b.f. Mummy's Pet 125–Copt Hall Realm 85 (Realm 129) [1989 5f² 5m* 5f 5g³ 1990 6m 5f 8g 10g] good-topped filly: has a round action: modest winner at 2 yrs: well beaten in 1990, including in handicaps: not certain to stay beyond 5f: has run well when sweating: edgy on reappearance. *P. J. Makin.* —

AMAZAKE 3 ch.g. Rousillon (USA) 133–Kesarini (USA) 87 (Singh (USA)) [1989 6g⁴ 7g 8d³ 1990 8m 8.5g⁵ 10g 8m² 10.4g⁶ a8g⁵ 10m 10.6v⁶ a11g] close-coupled, angular gelding: modest maiden at 2 yrs: below form in 1990, staying-on second in seller at Leicester: should stay beyond 1m: acts on dead going: blinkered 3 times: trained until after fourth start by A. Stewart. *C. Dwyer.* 46

AMBASSADOR ROYALE (IRE) 2 gr.c. (Apr 24) Pennine Walk 120–Hayati 94 (Hotfoot 126) [1990 7g⁴ 7m 7f⁵ 8m⁵ 7.3g² 7m] 13,000F, 52,000Y: well-made colt: has scope: second foal: half-brother to smart middle-distance 3-y-o Ruby Tiger (by Ahonoora): dam 7f and 1¼m winner: modest maiden: blinkered, good second in nursery at Newbury in September: ran poorly in blinkers only subsequent start: should be as effective at 1m as 7f. *P. F. I. Cole.* 72

AMBER MILL 2 b.f. (Mar 14) Doulab (USA) 115–Millaine 69 (Formidable (USA) 125) [1990 5m² 5f² 5g² 5m* 6f* 5g⁶ 5m³ 6d] lengthy, quite good-topped filly: has scope: second foal: half-sister to a winner in Italy: dam stayed 1½m: modest performer: won maiden at Doncaster in June and nursery at Goodwood in August: better at 6f than 5f: best form on firm ground: hung left and carried head high second start. *J. Berry.* 79

AMBER NECTAR 4 ch.c. Sallust 134–Curtana (Sharp Edge 123) [1989 6f* 6m 5.8m² 6f* 6m* 6g⁵ 7g 1990 6f 6m 6f 6m 6m 6f² 6h³ 7f² 7f⁵ 7m⁴ 7f³ 7.6m 8f] workmanlike, deep-girthed colt: quite modest handicapper: stays 7f: acts on hard going: often claimer ridden: tends to sweat: has joined M. McNeill. *L. J. Holt.* 63

AMBROSE 3 b.g. Ile de Bourbon (USA) 133–Curtana (Sharp Edge 123) [1989 8m⁶ 8m² 10g³ 8g⁰ 1990 10m² 10.4d⁵ 10m² 12g³ 12m* 10g² 12m⁵ 12m⁴ 13.3g⁵] lengthy, workmanlike gelding: has scope: fairly useful performer: won maiden at York in September: ran very well in £71,300 handicap at Ascot seventh start: suited by waiting tactics in strongly-run race at 1½m: acts on good to firm ground and dead: blinkered (hung left) final start at 2 yrs: changed hands 38,000 gns Newmarket Autumn Sales. *R. F. Johnson Houghton.* 97

AMBUSCADE (USA) 4 ch.g. Roberto (USA) 131–Gurkhas Band (USA) (Lurullah) [1989 NR 1990 8m⁵ 12m 16.2f² 14s⁴ 20m 16g⁶ 15g⁵ 16m² 18g⁵ 14m⁶] lengthy gelding: fluent mover: modest maiden: ran moderately in blinkers last 2 outings, not finding much off bridle first of them: seems to stay 2m and act on any going: successful hurdler in 1989/90. *G. M. Moore.* 75 d

AMELIANNE (FR) 4 b.f. Bustino 136–My Candy 81 (Lorenzaccio 130) [1989 12f³ 12m* 14f* 14f⁶ 12m 1990 14f⁴ 13.3m⁴ 12g* 16m 12f 12m² 12m 12g* 12m² 12g⁴] lengthy, angular filly: useful handicapper: won at Goodwood in June and Salisbury in 98

47

October: good second to Roll A Dollar in £7,600 event at Newmarket penultimate outing: effective at 1½m and 1¾m: acts on firm going: has won when sweating: sold 30,000 gns Newmarket Autumn Sales: game. *D. R. C. Elsworth.*

AMENABLE 5 b.g. Kampala 120–Kirin (Tyrant (USA)) [1989 7g² 8s³ 8m 7.6m 84 7f* 7.6f⁶ 1990 7g a8g³ a8g³ a7g*] sturdy, compact gelding: fair handicapper: favourite, stayed on to lead last strides when winning at Southwell in December: stays 1m: acts on any going. *T. D. Barron.*

AMERICAN CONNEXION 3 ch.c. Tender King 123–Chieftain Girl (USA) 66 (Chieftain II) [1989 6m 6g² 8g³ 7g 6v 1990 8d 9f 7m⁶ 8.3f⁶ 10m⁵ 8d 10s³ a10g⁴] workmanlike colt: quite modest maiden: in frame at Lingfield late in season, travelling strongly 1m before finding nothing (blinkered and on toes) on second occasion: suited by 1¼m: acts on good to firm ground and soft: temperament under suspicion. *J. Sutcliffe.*

AMERICAN HERO 2 ch.c. (Apr 12) Persian Bold 123–American Winter (USA) 55 (Lyphard (USA) 132) [1990 7g⁶ 7m] IR 25,000Y: tall, leggy colt: third foal: half-brother to 1988 Irish 2-y-o 1m winner Classic Pleasure (by Shirley Heights): dam, 7f winner, is out of half-sister to top-class filly and broodmare Fanfreluche: plating-class form in maidens, drifting right and carrying head awkwardly final start: sold 7,400 gns Newmarket Autumn Sales. *M. R. Stoute.*

AMERICAN STANDARD (NZ) 3 br.c. Babaroom (USA)–Minimal (NZ) — (Minuit) [1989 NR 1990 10.1m⁶ 12.2f] rather sparely-made New Zealand-bred colt: behind in minor event (green and edgy) and maiden: winning hurdler. *J. R. Jenkins.*

AMERINDIAN 3 b.f. Commanche Run 133–Supremely Royal (Crowned Prince 84 (USA) 128) [1989 NR 1990 10m* 12m³ 12d⁵] 155,000Y: rather leggy, useful-looking filly: moderate walker: closely related to quite modest stayer Elegant Monarch (by Ardross) and half-sister to several winners, including 6f to 1m winner Capricorn Belle (by Nonoalco) and 6f to 10.2f winner Royal Invitation (by Be My Guest): dam poor maiden from top American family: won maiden at Newbury in July, hanging left 4f out and leading inside last: better effort in handicaps (still bit green) next time: stays 1½m. *L. Cumani.*

AMETHYSTINE (USA) 4 ch.f. Barachois (CAN)–Amathus (Song 132) [1989 65 6s 6v 8d 7f 8f⁵ 7m 7m³ 7m³ 9f* 8h² 10h⁴ᵈⁱˢ 8.3m 7m 7s 1990 8m² 8m² 7f⁵ 7.6m³ 10m 9m 5.8f⁴ 7f* 8m* 8h³ 6h³ 7f 6m] sparely-made, angular filly: quite modest handicapper: won at Brighton in June and Bath (apprentice ridden) in July: finds 6f on sharp side and stays 9f: goes very well on top-of-the-ground: usually on toes. *R. J. Hodges.*

AMIDON REVE 2 ch.c. (Apr 24) Starch Reduced 112–Reno's Dream (Rupert — Bear 105) [1990 7m] lengthy colt: first reported foal: dam bad plater stayed 7f: bit backward, no show in autumn maiden at Chepstow. *B. Palling.*

AMIENS 3 ch.g. Noalto 120–Two Stroke (Malicious) [1989 NR 1990 8.3f⁴ 8m 62 10m²] fourth foal: half-brother to lightly-raced fair 5f winner Catalani and quite useful 1986 2-y-o 5f winner Vivaldi (both by Music Boy): dam poor half-sister to very useful French 1¼m winner Aberdeen Park: quite modest form in frame in minor event at Windsor and maiden at Redcar: stays 1¼m: sold 15,500 gns Newmarket Autumn Sales. *W. Jarvis.*

AMIGO MENOR 4 ch.g. Whistling Deer 117–Chive (St Chad 120) [1989 6f⁴ 6m⁴ 94 7.2g 6f⁴ 6g⁶ 6m 6f 6d 6g 1990 6f 6m 6m* 6m⁵ 6d² 6m³ 6m² 6d 5m 6m² 6s* 6s⁵] leggy, lengthy colt: quite useful handicapper: won at Lingfield (making virtually all) in May and Newbury (£8,100 event) in October: ran very well when placed in Wokingham Stakes at Royal Ascot, Stewards' Cup at Goodwood and £15,700 event at Goodwood fifth to seventh outings: best racing up with pace over 6f: acts on any going: best blinkered: sweating and edgy final outing (ran creditably). *K. M. Brassey.*

AMIGOS 2 ch.g. (Apr 28) Nordance (USA)–Hi Gorgeous (Hello Gorgeous (USA) ? 128) [1990 7m² 7d⁶] 2,200F, 14,000 2-y-o: second foal: dam unraced: 3½ lengths second of 14 to Marcham in maiden at Goodwood in September: favourite, modest sixth in maiden auction there following month: will stay 1m: possibly unsuited by a soft surface. *P. Mitchell.*

AMIRA T' SAHRRA 3 b.f. Little Wolf 127–Mummy's Whistler (Mummy's Pet — 125) [1989 7g 6g 1990 a7g 8.2g] poor maiden. *W. W. Haigh.*

AMOOD POINT 3 ch.g. Jalmood (USA) 126–Nice Point (Sharpen Up 127) [1989 — p 8.2g 1990 8.5g 9.1s⁵] lengthy, rather sparely-made gelding: some promise in maidens and minor event, off course over 5 months after reappearance: should stay beyond 1m: may well be capable of better. *J. Etherington.*

AMOUR DU SOIR (USA) 3 b.c. L'Emigrant (USA) 129–Evening Kiss (USA) **71**
(Saggy) [1989 5f² 5f³ 1990 5h² 5m² 5g⁶ 5f⁴ 5.8h* 5m 5.8f] rather leggy,
useful-looking colt: has a roundish action: modest sprinter: evens, won maiden at
Bath in July: below form in claimer and handicap after: acts on hard ground: seems
highly strung: sold out of Sir Mark Prescott's stable 8,400 gns Newmarket
September Sales after sixth start. *R. Lee.*

AMPHOTERIC VENTURE 5 ch.h. Sparkler 130–Covenant 75 (Good Bond —
122) [1989 a7g 1990 a11g] sturdy, good-topped horse: has a quick action: poor
maiden: bred to stay at least 1m: sold 1,000 gns Doncaster January Sales. *K. A.
Morgan.*

AMPNEY BOY 3 b.g. Ampney Prince 96–Mellarney (Meldrum 112) [1989 NR —
1990 13.8f⁵ 12.2d] second reported foal: dam bad plater at 2 yrs: tailed off in claimers
at Catterick. *R. M. Whitaker.*

AMRON 3 b.g. Bold Owl 101–Sweet Minuet (Setay 105) [1989 5v* 5g⁵ 5s⁶ 5s⁵ **53**
a6g³ 1990 5s 5f 5g 6g a7g² 6m* 6g* 6g 6m⁵ 6f³ a6g⁴ a7g⁴ 6m 6g 6d] sparely-made
gelding: plating-class handicapper: won at Carlisle and Ayr (apprentices, led post) in
June: creditable fourth at Southwell: should stay 1m: acts on any going except
possibly firm: suitable mount for 7-lb claimer: blinkered second start: gelded after
final one. *J. Berry.*

AMY'S STAR 4 b.f. Touch Boy 109–Keep Believing (Sweet Revenge 129) [1989 —
8g 1990 8.5m 7d a8g] lengthy, lightly-made filly: moderate mover: behind in
maidens: pulled hard and saddle slipped on reappearance. *P. Wigham.*

ANAGRAM (USA) 2 ch.f. (Apr 13) Shahrastani (USA) 135–Troyanna 109 (Troy —
137) [1990 8g] fair sort: third foal: half-sister to 1989 2-y-o 7f winner Aquatic and
1¼m and 1¾m winner Trojan River (both by Riverman): dam, 7f winner at 2 yrs and
fourth in Irish Oaks, is out of half-sister to very smart 1963 American 2-y-o Traffic:
close up almost 6f in maiden at Pontefract in October: sold 7,000 gns Newmarket
Autumn Sales. *M. R. Stoute.*

ANATROCCOLO 3 b.f. Ile de Bourbon (USA) 133–Art Deco (Artaius (USA) **59**
129) [1989 6g a7g* 1990 7f³ 10.2f⁶ 8g 10g] unfurnished filly: quite modest
performer: won maiden at Lingfield as 2-y-o: visored and edgy, pulled hard then
good headway until hanging right and weakening approaching final 1f in handicap
final start in 1990: stays 1m: acts on firm going: sweating third outing. *C. A. Horgan.*

ANBAK (USA) 5 ch.g. Riverman (USA) 131–Virgin (FR) 114 (Zeddaan 130) [1989 —
NR 1990 a11g] leggy, angular gelding: has a long stride: little sign of ability: visored
only start at 5 yrs: sold 1,250 gns Ascot May Sales. *M. B. James.*

ANCIENT CITY 3 gr.g. Persepolis (FR) 127–Fair Melys (FR) 81 (Welsh Pageant **61**
132) [1989 6g a7g 1990 10f³ 10.2f⁶ 8m 10f⁵ 7d⁵] angular gelding: disappointing
maiden: stays 10.2f: acts on firm going: blinkered (raced freely) third outing: edged
left and looked none too keen for 7-lb claimer on reappearance: gelded after third
start. *G. Wragg.*

ANDERSON ROSE 2 b.f. (Jan 19) Kind of Hush 118–Fille de Bourbon 71 (Ile de **41**
Bourbon (USA) 133) [1990 7s a7g a8g a8g⁵ a7g a6g a8g] 750Y: close-coupled filly:
has a round action: third foal: half-sister to unraced mare in Italy by Carwhite: dam placed
over 7f and 1m: poor maiden: probably stays 1m. *M. C. Chapman.*

ANDERTON'S LOT (IRE) 2 b.c. (Apr 11) Stalker 121–Tell The Truth —
(Monseigneur (USA) 127) [1990 5f⁶ a6g 8g] IR 3,500F, 2,500Y, 3,200 2-y-o: leggy,
workmanlike colt: poor walker: third reported foal: half-brother to 7f and 1m seller
winner Highland Tale (by Crofter): dam never ran: well beaten in maidens. *A. W.
Jones.*

ANDORRA 8 gr.g. Godswalk (USA) 130–Lady Sioux (USA) 86 (Apalachee (USA) **67**
137) [1989 NR 1990 12.3f³ 18.4d³] strong, workmanlike gelding: won Newcastle
maiden in July, 1988: having only third race on flat since, good third to impressive
Travelling Light in Ladbroke Chester Cup (Handicap) in May: not seen out again:
stays 2¼m: best runs on soft surface: bandaged on reappearance. *J. G. FitzGerald.*

ANDRASSY (IRE) 2 ch.c. (Mar 25) Ahonoora 122–Anna Matrushka (Mill Reef **83** p
(USA) 141) [1990 6m*] medium-sized, well-made colt: first foal: dam unraced
daughter of champion German filly Anna Paola: favourite, won 4-runner maiden at
Ascot in September by 3½ lengths from Lucknam Dreamer, leading 2f out and
drawing clear steadily final furlong: will stay 1m: sure to improve. *L. M. Cumani.*

ANDRATH (IRE) 2 b.c. (Feb 26) Commanche Run 133–Rathvindon 93 (Realm **90**
129) [1990 7m⁵ 7f⁴ 7m] 29,000F, 32,000Y: strong, good-bodied, attractive colt: has
plenty of scope: fifth foal: half-brother to Irish 5f winner Queen Share (by Main

Reef) and a winner in USA: dam 5f winner, is half-sister to useful French 1¼m winner Interdit: fairly useful form, unable to quicken from over 1f out and beaten over 6 lengths, behind Mukaddamah in Lanson Champagne Vintage Stakes at Goodwood and Flying Brave in Tattersalls Tiffany Highflyer Stakes at Newmarket final 2 starts: will stay 1m: should win a race. *C. E. Brittain.*

ANDRELOT   3 b.c. Caerleon (USA) 132–Seminar 113 (Don (ITY) 123) [1989 6m 6m⁵ 8.2f 1990 10g 11.7m 14g² 14m] leggy colt: quite modest form: staying-on second in handicap at Salisbury in August, carrying head awkwardly: suited by 1¾m: probably best with give in the ground: blinkered and sweating second start at 2 yrs. *Mrs J. Pitman.*   **60**

ANDREW'S FIRST   3 br.g. Tender King 123–Dame Kelly (Pitskelly 122) [1989 7f⁵ 7f⁵ 8.2f 10.6d² 8g a8g* a8g* 1990 9f 10.2s⁴ a12g* a11g³ a12g² a11g*] leggy, rather sparely-made gelding: claimer ridden, showed improved form when winning 4 claimers at Southwell: not seen out until October as 3-y-o: should prove better at 1½m than shorter: blinkered last 2 outings. *T. D. Barron.*   **74**

ANDROBOTE (FR)   4 ch.g. The Wonder (FR) 129–Andromeda (FR) (Dankaro (FR) 131) [1989 8g 12.3d⁶ 12m⁵ 12m 16.5g⁵ 16.2g⁶ 19g* 1990 14g⁶ 16.2m³] rangy gelding: showed much improved form when winning minor event at Goodwood (100/1, apprentice ridden) in autumn as 3-y-o: fair third to All Is Revealed in handicap at same course (scratched to post) in May: well suited by test of stamina: best efforts on an easy surface. *R. Curtis.*   **64**

ANFIELD SALLY   4 b.f. Anfield 117–Bargain Line 68 (Porto Bello 118) [1989 8g 7d⁶ 7m 7.5m 8s 10g a11g 1990 8.2s² 8f⁴ 8m³ 8f² 9m³ 8f⁴ 10m² a12g* 12m a11g⁶ 10m² 12m⁴] rather leggy filly: fair plater: landed odds at Southwell (bought in 4,800 gns) in August: ran well in blinkers previous 2 and last 2 outings: stays 1½m: acts on any going: visored once at 3 yrs: has worn bandages. *J. G. FitzGerald.*   **46**

ANGEL BRIGHT   4 ch.f. Krayyan 117–Godhood 86 (Green God 128) [1989 7m² 7m³ 8s³ 8.2m² 9g⁵ 10d² 1990 10.2f² 10m⁵ 10.2m 11m 9m 10f³ a8g² 10.6d 10g] leggy, angular filly: still a maiden: effective at 1m to 1¼m: acts on any going: sometimes sweats: trained until after fifth start by E. Eldin. *C. Weedon.*   **66**

ANGEL FALLING   2 b.f. (Apr 17) Scottish Reel 123–Autumn Gift 65 (Martinmas 128) [1990 5m³ 6m 6s³ 6m⁴ 8d a8g⁶ a7g] 2,800F: leggy, angular filly: moderate mover: second living foal: half-sister to plating-class 1½m winner Brilliant Future (by Welsh Saint): dam stayed well on flat and over hurdles: poor maiden: ran moderately on all-weather last 2 starts: should be suited by much further than 6f: acts well on soft ground. *E. H. Owen jun.*   **46**

ANGEL FALLS (USA)   3 b.c. Nijinsky (CAN) 138–Angel Island (USA) (Cougar (CHI)) [1989 NR 1990 12g 10.5m⁵] rangy, attractive colt: has a markedly round action: seventh foal: half-brother to 5 winners, notably good-class Sharrood (by Caro), best up to 1¼m here and later stakes winner in USA: dam very smart 2-y-o in USA, successful in 7f graded stakes: well beaten in maidens at Newbury (bit coltish) and York: sold 5,500 gns Newmarket Autumn Sales. *R. Charlton.*   **—**

ANGELICA PARK   4 b.f. Simply Great (FR) 122–Rosana Park 83 (Music Boy 124) [1989 9f 8.2d⁴ 8.2g⁶ 10g⁵ a11g 1990 8f 12.5g³ a12g⁶ 12m* 14m⁴ 12m 14g 17.6g* 14.6d⁶] stocky filly: little form: 4-y-o except when winning claimers at Newmarket (making all) in August and Wolverhampton in October: stays well: best form on sound surface: hung left second start. *J. Wharton.*   **57**

ANGELO'S DOUBLE (IRE)   2 b.c. (Feb 8) M Double M (USA)–Bebe Altesse (GER) (Alpenkonig (GER)) [1990 a7g² 7g] IR 33,000Y: strong, workmanlike colt: has plenty of scope: has a roundish action: second known foal: half-brother to modest 1989 2-y-o 6f winner Saltessa (by Thatching): dam, winner in Germany, is out of good German mare Bebe Girl: sire won from 6f to 9f: around 10 lengths eighth of 21, well clear of other 2 who raced on his (possibly disadvantageous) side, to Balaat in maiden at Newbury in August: second to Panikin in similar event at Southwell on debut: should improve. *J. H. M. Gosden.*   **64 p**

ANGEL TRAIN (IRE)   2 ch.f. (Mar 29) Burslem 123–Senama (FR) (Sanctus II 132) [1990 5m⁴ 5m* 5g² 6g* 5m 7g⁴ 6m 7d³ a8g² a7g³ a7g a7g⁴ a8g] IR 2,000F, 8,000Y: angular filly: very poor mover: half-sister to minor winners in France by Sassafras and Hard Fought: dam French 1¼m winner: useful plater, successful at Leicester (retained 10,000 gns) in April and Warwick (retained 7,800 gns) in June: very good second of 18 to Sarsta Grai in claimer at Southwell, best subsequent effort: trained first 9 outings by T. Thomson Jones: rather inconsistent. *J. Parkes.*   **59**

50

ANGLICE (USA) 2 b. or br.f. (Mar 30) Doulab (USA) 115–Light Angle (USA) 75 **61**
(Angle Light (USA)) [1990 5f* 5m² 5m 6m³ 5m 6d 7g] $20,000Y, 7,400 2-y-o: small,
good-topped filly: first foal: dam probably best at 5f: quite modest performer: won
maiden auction at Bath in June: worthwhile form since only when placed: stays 6f:
blinkered fourth and fifth outings: sold 4,600 gns Newmarket Autumn Sales. *M. A.
Jarvis.*

ANGLOINTERNATIONAL 3 b.f. Millfontaine 114–Brigadiers Nurse **53**
(Brigadier Gerard 144) [1989 5f³ 5.8h⁶ 5f 5.8h* 6f⁴ 5m² 6g² 6g 7g 1990 a6g a7g³
a7g* a6g⁴ a7g⁶ 7m 6f⁵] compact filly: poor performer: won 4-runner handicap
(ridden by 7-lb claimer) at Southwell in February: stays 7f: blinkered once at 2 yrs:
below form when sweating: sold 2,800 gns Newmarket July Sales. *R. W. Stubbs.*

ANISESNO 3 ch.f. Mansingh (USA) 120–Missive (FR) 55 (Bold Lad (USA)) [1989 **—**
NR 1990 6m 10m] small, sparely-made filly: fourth foal: dam, from good family,
showed only poor form: behind in sellers, swerving right leaving stalls in apprentice
event on debut. *L. J. Codd.*

ANJIZ (USA) 2 b.c. (Feb 23) Nureyev (USA) 131–Prayers'n Promises **104** +
(USA) (Foolish Pleasure (USA)) [1990 6m* 6m* 6m* 7d⁶]
    Tests on Anjiz failed to find any reason for his dismal showing in the
Three Chimneys Dewhurst Stakes at Newmarket. A sturdy, good-quartered
colt of some quality, unbeaten in three races and held in high regard by his
trainer, the normally-placid Anjiz was unusually on the jog and sweating
beforehand, drifted in the betting and finished distressed after trailing
throughout. It's quite possible, of course, that the rain-softened ground
wasn't in Anjiz's favour—all his previous runs had been on good to firm—but
it's at least as likely that something was physically amiss, and it would be
foolish to dismiss him out of hand in stronger company than he's beaten so far.

Maktoum Al-Maktoum's "Anjiz"

Certainly, at Ripon in August, in the three-runner BonusPrint Champion Two-Year-Old Trophy, Anjiz looked a smart prospect, quickening four lengths clear of the useful pair Big Blow and Timeless Times before being eased a length and a half; and in his two previous races, a maiden at Newbury and the four-runner Veuve Cliquot Champagne Stakes at Salisbury, he'd hardly been tested in winning by a length and a half and two and a half respectively. While Anjiz had something to find on form to take a hand in the Dewhurst he was going on well enough to anticipate his doing so. If all's well with him—he was reportedly working satisfactorily again late in the year—it's probable that he'll put his Dewhurst running behind him as a three-year-old.

			Northern Dancer	Nearctic
Anjiz (USA)	Nureyev (USA)		(b 1961)	Natalma
(b.c. Feb 23, 1988)	(b 1977)		Special	Forli
			(b 1969)	Thong
	Prayers'n Promises (USA)		Foolish Pleasure	What A Pleasure
	(b 1978)		(b 1972)	Fool-Me-Not
			Luiana	My Babu
			(ch 1963)	Banquet Bell

Up to the Dewhurst, Anjiz had appeared to have a greatly more relaxed disposition than either of his close relatives Nabeel Dancer (by Northern Dancer), a smart if rather temperamental sprinter, and the headstrong maiden Stormy Praise (by Storm Bird). Interestingly, their dam Prayers'n Promises, whose fifth foal Anjiz is, spent most of the later part of her career running over sprint distances after winning Grade 1 events over six and seven furlongs and being placed in similar races over a mile as a two-year-old. Prayers'n Promises is a half-sister to several winners, notably the Kentucky Derby and Preakness Stakes winner Little Current, as well as the ex-British graded stakes-placed Water Dance. Their dam Luiana never ran but is well related, being a half-sister to another Kentucky Derby winner in Chateaugay. Anjiz doesn't have any pretensions to staying middle distances; he should stay seven furlongs though, even if he gives the impression that he's likely to prove best at five or six. Anjiz acts well on top-of-the-ground—conditions, incidentally, which suited the now-retired Nabeel Dancer ideally. *A. A. Scott.*

ANKARA'S PRINCESS (USA)   3 ch.f. Ankara (USA) 106–Tales of Long Ago (USA) (Raise A Cup (USA)) [1989 5g* 5m* 5s6 6g 1990 5d3 6m 5m5 6m3 7g 6f6 6d 7d] workmanlike filly: moderate walker and mover: modest handicapper: won twice at Chester as 2-y-o: third at Chester and Newmarket, best efforts in 1990: stays 6f: acts on good to firm ground and soft. *R. Hollinshead.*   **73**

ANNABELLE ROYALE   4 b.c. Anfield 117–France (Milesian 125) [1989 8.2s4 6s2 8d2 7.5f 8m 8.2f* 10g 8.2f5 8g3 8.2m4 8m5 7g5 8.2f* 7m2 7.6f* 9g 8.2g 1990 10f3 9g 8f5 10.2m5 7.6m* 8m5 7m* 7g5 7.6f4 7.6m 7f* 7f* 7m* 10m2 8m 6m4 7m] small, strong, lengthy colt: carries condition: moderate mover: fair handicapper: won at Lingfield in May, June (making all) and August and twice at Yarmouth also in August: effective at 6f to 1¼m: goes particularly well on top-of-the-ground: has worn bandages: has won when sweating: genuine. *Mrs N. Macauley.*   **81**

ANNAF (USA)   4 b.c. Topsider (USA)–Kawkeb (USA) 72 (Vaguely Noble 140) [1989 10.1g5 10.8m* 9f3 1990 10f3 10f] rather leggy, angular colt: moderate walker and mover: quite useful winner as 3-y-o: tending to carry head awkwardly, no chance with Shellac in 5-runner minor event at Pontefract in April: harshly treated and still carrying condition, well beaten in Newmarket handicap over 3 weeks later: should stay beyond 11f: acts on any going: refused to enter stalls once at 3 yrs. *H. Thomson Jones.*   **93 ?**

ANNA KARIETTA   3 ch.f. Precocious 126–Karietta (Wollow 132) [1989 NR 1990 7m 7m4 6m 7m* 7g2 6m*] small, quite attractive filly: first foal: dam, French provincial 11.5f winner, is half-sister to very useful middle-distance performer Karelia out of half-sister to high-class sprinter Full Out: progressive form, winning maiden at Lingfield in August and £8,400 handicap at Newmarket in October: effective at 6f and 7f. *H. Candy.*   **82**

ANNA PETROVNA (FR)   3 b.f. Wassl 125–Anna Paola (GER) (Prince Ippi (GER)) [1989 7m5 8f2 1990 9m3 8.5g3 10.2m* 10m6 10f2 12m2 10g2 10.5g* 10d6] leggy, sparely-made filly: fairly useful handicapper: won at Doncaster in May and York (best effort) in October: probably stays 1½m: acts on firm going, seems unsuited by dead: takes keen hold and tends to edge left: none too easy a ride: consistent. *J. L. Dunlop.*

ANNELI ROSE 3 gr.f. Superlative 118–Red Rose Bowl (Dragonara Palace **56** (USA) 115) [1989 NR 1990 6f a6g a8g⁴ a7g⁶ a6g² a6g*] third foal: half-sister to lightly-raced Flowery (by Kind of Hush) and smart sprinter Gallic League (by Welsh Saint): dam, winner over 7f at 2 yrs in Ireland, is half-sister to Cesarewitch winner Private Audition: improved form to make all in claimer at Lingfield in December: best form at 6f: blinkered last 2 starts. *P. F. I. Cole.*

ANODYNE (USA) 3 b.g. Riverman (USA) 131–Tongue Tied Muse (USA) (Stage **93** Door Johnny) [1989 NR 1990 7.2d* 8d* 7.6v³] $285,000Y: tall, attractive gelding: third reported foal: dam, winner at 3 yrs in France, is half-sister to high-class stakes winner at up to 1m Equanimity, useful hurdler Son of Ivor and dam of Enchantment: not seen out until late-September, winning maiden (edgy) at Haydock and handicap (week later) at Goodwood: favourite, well-beaten third of 13 in £9,700 handicap at Chester: sold 45,000 gns Newmarket Autumn Sales, probably to race in Italy. *R. Charlton.*

ANONOALTO 2 br.c. (Mar 12) Noalto 120–No Can Tell (USA) (Clev Er Tell **73** (USA)) [1990 5f² 5s 5m² 5g⁴ 6d² 5f² 5g⁵ 5m⁶ 5g* 5m* 5m] 3,200 2-y-o: lengthy colt: first foal: dam maiden out of half-sister to dam of Dibidale: much improved ex-plater: made all in claimer at Beverley and nursery at Sandown in August: gave impression something possibly amiss final start: suited by 5f: well beaten on soft ground: visored twice, blinkered final 3 outings: trained on debut by K. Brassey: sold 5,200 gns Newmarket Autumn Sales. *R. W. Stubbs.*

ANOTHER BOB (USA) 2 b.c. (Mar 22) Roberto (USA) 131–Spicy Stuff (USA) **91** p (Reviewer (USA)) [1990 8m² 8s*] $23,000Y, resold $50,000Y: tall, quite good-topped colt: has plenty of scope: fourth reported foal: half-brother to 2 minor winners: dam won at up to 9f at 4 yrs: second favourite, won 14-runner minor event at Newbury in October by short head from All The King's Men, ridden along over 3f out and quickening only gradually: will be better suited by 1¼m+: likely to do better. *M. A. Jarvis.*

ANOTHER EARL (USA) 6 ch.g. Belted Earl (USA) 122–Aloran (USA) (Prince **58** John) [1989 8m³ 8m 8m a8g 1990 a8g² a10g 8.2d] lengthy, robust gelding: ½-length second in handicap at Southwell in January, only worthwhile form for long time: off course 9 months before final outing (bandaged), tailed off): stays 1m: acts on heavy going: blinkered twice at 4 yrs and last 4 starts. *B. Smart.*

ANOTHER LANE 3 b.f. Tina's Pet 121–Spinner 59 (Blue Cashmere 129) [1989 — 5g⁴ 5m* 5m⁵ 1990 5g] smallish, sturdy, sprint type: moderate mover: has faced stiff tasks since winning minor event at Thirsk as 2-y-o, in £11,600 handicap in August on only start in 1990. *R. M. Whitaker.*

ANOTHER MARCH 4 b.g. Marching On 101–River Sirene (Another River 89) — § [1989 6d⁴ 6m 7f 6h⁵ 6f² 7f⁵ 6m² 7f⁶ 6g 6g a7g⁶ a6g 1990 a8g] leggy gelding: has a round action: modest handicapper at best: below form last 5 starts, twice looking hard ride: effective at 6f and 7f: acts on firm and dead going: blinkered once: sometimes sweating and edgy: not one to rely on. *T. D. Barron.*

ANOTHER MARQUESSA 3 b.f. Beldale Flutter (USA) 130–Marquessa — d'Howfen 93 (Pitcairn 126) [1989 5m⁴ 6f² 6g⁵ 7g 1990 11m 9.1m a7g 11m 6m] tall, leggy, unfurnished filly: easy mover: plating-class form at 2 yrs, none in 1990: bred to stay quite well but races keenly. *F. H. Lee.*

ANOTHER NICK 4 ch.g. Nicholas Bill 125–Another Move 69 (Farm Walk 111) — [1989 14d 15s⁴ 12d 1990 13v] tall, lengthy, sparely-made gelding: showed promise first 2 outings as 3-y-o: soundly beaten in Ayr handicap in April. *J. M. Jefferson.*

ANOTHER RHYTHM 6 b.g. Music Boy 124–Just You Wait (Nonoalco (USA) — § 131) [1989 5f³ 5f 6g 5g 5f² 5f 1990 a6g] big, lengthy gelding: runner-up in seller as 5-y-o: unlikely to stay beyond 6f: best on a sound surface: visored once: often taken down early or very steadily: highly strung: not genuine. *J. R. Jenkins.*

ANSHAN 3 ch.c. Persian Bold 123–Lady Zi (Manado 130) [1989 7g⁵ 7f* **119** 8m* 7g³ 7g³ 1990 7m* 8f³ 10.5g³ 8m 7d* 7m² 9f³]
The race for the Ladbroke European Free Handicap at Newmarket in April went to Anshan, who made most and finished strongly to beat Osario by a length and a half. The Free Handicap is nowadays seldom as significant a classic trial as it used to be: Privy Councillor (1962) and Mrs McArdy (1977) were the last winners to go on to win their Guineas. In 1990 none of the top

twenty-eight in the original handicap stood their ground; the highest-weighted acceptor was Anshan himself, allotted 8-8 behind Machiavellian's 9-7 after a first season which had seen him finish third in the Cartier Million and the Three Chimneys Dewhurst Stakes on his last two outings. Nevertheless, Anshan's performance was sufficiently encouraging for him to start second favourite in similar conditions for the General Accident Two Thousand Guineas at 6/1, and he acquitted himself very well in coming third to Tirol, beaten four lengths. Smartly away, he tracked the pacemaker, going strongly, went to the front three out and remained there until outpaced by Tirol and Machiavellian approaching the final furlong. When pressed by Rock City in the closing stages he rallied, giving the impression he'd get further.

Anshan's breeding also suggested he'd get further. His test at a longer distance when even money in the William Hill Dante Stakes at York later in May proved inconclusive, but persuaded connections to go for the St James's Palace Stakes rather than the Derby or the Grand Prix de Paris. To tell the truth Anshan didn't shape like a top-class horse in the Dante; on the other hand he had some sort of excuse in that Karinga Bay took him on for the lead early, and more than three furlongs went very quickly by before he could be given a breather. Under pressure three furlongs out, he found no extra inside the last and was beaten a length and a half and the same into third behind Sanglamore and Karinga Bay. Anshan disappointed at Royal Ascot, sweating up beforehand and racing with little zest. He wasn't seen out again until October, when, on softish going for the first time, he made all in the seven-furlong City Of Portsmouth Supreme Stakes at Goodwood. The value of his beating Palace Street comfortably in that Group 3 race was more problematical than the value of his two-and-a-half-length second of eight to Sally Rous in the Jameson Irish Whiskey Challenge Stakes at Newmarket later in the month. The latter showed him very nearly back to his best, allowing a pound or two for a stumble going into the Dip which cost him the chance of finishing closer to the winner, and he earned a shot at the nine-furlong Hollywood Derby in California in November. The race attracted a good field, and Anshan did every bit as well as could be expected of him in finishing third of twelve behind the Breeders' Cup Mile second Itsallgreektome and the Foret winner Septieme Ciel, beaten a head and two lengths after being prominent throughout.

Anshan's dam Lady Zi won over a mile and a half in France and her one previous foal, Freeway of Love (by High Top), has won over that distance in Italy. So there is a basis for arguing that, on breeding, Anshan may stay further than nine furlongs. The second dam Exbury Grace never ran, the third dam Your Grace II ran only a little. Exbury Grace is also grandam of the promising sire No Pass No Sale, who got the 1985 Poule d'Essai des Poulains

Ladbroke European Free Handicap, Newmarket—Anshan (second left) makes virtually all; Osario (third left) and Book The Band (rails) fill the places

		Bold Lad	Bold Ruler
	Persian Bold	(b 1964)	Barn Pride
	(br 1975)	Relkarunner	Relko
Anshan		(b or br 1968)	Running Blue
(ch.c. 1987)		Manado	Captain's Gig
	Lady Zi	(b 1973)	Slipstream
	(b 1980)	Exbury Grace	Exbury
		(br 1970)	Your Grace II

on a disqualification; Your Grace II was a daughter of the 1950 Prix de Diane winner Aglae Grace and a half-sister to the 1962 Arc winner Soltikoff. Anshan, a big, leggy, quite good-topped colt, acts on firm going and also, though regarded at one time by connections as a top-of-the-ground horse, on dead. He will race on in the States as a four-year-old, based in C. Whittingham's stable. *J. Gosden.*

ANSTEY BOY 5 gr.g. Decoy Boy 129–Miss Twiggy 80 (Tycoon II) [1989 10s 8s6 8.3m5 7g4 8g4 a10g 1990 8f] small gelding: moderate mover: poor maiden: stays 1m: goes well with a bit of give in the ground: visored once at 3 yrs. *C. N. Allen.* —

ANTAGONIST 3 b.c. Aragon 118–Princess Story 64 (Prince de Galles 125) [1989 NR 1990 8g 7m6 7m 10g2 8m6 7f] 6,400F, 4,500Y: leggy, good-topped colt: eighth foal: half-brother to several winners, including 6f winner Aquarian Prince (by Mansingh) and 1¼m and 1½m winner Kiki Star (by Some Hand): dam, successful in sellers at around 1m, is daughter of sister to Compensation: confirmed earlier promise when second in handicap at Lingfield: ran fairly well next start: blinkered, poorly drawn on final one (July): stays 1¼m. *B. R. Millman.* **60**

ANTE UP (IRE) 2 b.c. (May 1) Sharpen Up 127–Petillante (USA) (Riverman (USA) 131) [1990 7d6] 82,000Y: tall, close-coupled, shallow-girthed colt: looks weak: first foal: dam won at up to 9f: around 6 lengths sixth of 11, steadied stalls and keeping on well near finish, to Junk Bond in quite valuable event at Newmarket in October: should improve, and win a race. *L. M. Cumani.* **76 p**

ANTHONY LORETTO 5 b.g. Mummy's Game 120–Miss Silly (Silly Season 127) [1989 7g4 7.6f4 7f3 7f 7m2 7g 6m5 6d6 6g* 6v* 1990 6m 6s4 6m3 6m 6d3 6g5 6m] smallish, good-quartered gelding: moderate walker: fair handicapper: not seen out after July: effective at 6f and 7f: acts on any going: has worn crossed noseband: usually taken early or steadily to post: consistent. *Lord John FitzGerald.* **78**

ANTIQUE ANDY 3 br.g. Mansingh (USA) 120–Spanish Bold 78 (Tower Walk 130) [1989 5m 1990 a7g4 a6g5 8g5 7g 10m5 10.1m 5.8h5] neat, strong gelding: carries condition: poor maiden: probably stays 1¼m: blinkered final start: sold to join R. Brotherton 2,100 gns Ascot October Sales and gelded. *D. J. G. Murray-Smith.* —

ANTIQUE MAN 3 b.g. Sayyaf 121–Firey Ann 80 (Firestreak 125) [1989 5g 5d6 1990 9m5 7g3 7m2 6g5 7g2 5g3 6f4 8.3g6 6m6 11.7f4] lengthy, workmanlike gelding: good walker: smart plater: stays 7f: acts on good to firm ground: has run well for 7-lb claimer: found little fourth outing: trained until after seventh by J. Berry. *D. Burchell.* **55**

ANTISAAR (USA) 3 b.c. Northern Dancer–Detroit (FR) 131 (Riverman (USA) 131) [1989 NR 1990 10s3 10g* 10g* 10d* 12m2 12g] **121 p**

French racing's most successful jockey-trainer partnership in the last three years has been ended by the recruitment of Steve Cauthen to ride Sheikh Mohammed's horses in 1991, including those in Fabre's stable; Asmussen will go freelance. While Fabre and Asmussen enjoyed phenomenal success together, France's biggest prize, the Prix de l'Arc de Triomphe, eluded them as a pair. The stable had entries in the latest Arc, as usual. By all accounts, from mid-September opinion differed as to their best prospect in the race, Asmussen declaring that the lightly-raced and progressive Antisaar 'has improved pounds and pounds and will appreciate the easing in the ground' while Fabre just preferred In The Wings—'the Arc is an easier race for four-year-olds and older horses because they are so mature'. Asmussen stuck to his guns to the end, and having made the wrong choice generously conceded afterwards: 'Antisaar may still be a little tender'.

Prior to the Arc, Antisaar had had only five runs, none of them in a Group 1 event, and had first stepped onto a racecourse in April when he came third in a Longchamp maiden. By October he'd improved a great deal. A win in another

Longchamp maiden in late-May was followed by victories at Saint-Cloud, in the listed Prix Ronde de Nuit by a short head, and at Deauville where he beat subsequent Prix Dollar winner Agent Bleu by a length in a ten-strong field for the Group 2 Prix Guillaume d'Ornano. Then Antisaar produced a performance which brought him into the Arc reckoning. Stepped up to a mile and a half Antisaar made Epervier Bleu, generally regarded as France's top three-year-old middle-distance colt, pull out all the stops in a moderately-run Prix Niel at Longchamp; battling on extremely gamely in the straight, just failing by a head and giving the clear impression that the Arc, insofar as it was certain to be run at a much stronger pace, would suit him even better. Antisaar started at 37/10 in the Arc coupled with Belmez and In The Wings, and finished behind both in eleventh-of-twenty-one position. He never looked dangerous. Held up and still with plenty to do turning into the straight, he was just beginning to struggle when receiving a bad bump from the back-pedalling Ile de Nisky which effectively ended his chance. Interestingly, In The Wings also finished eleventh in his first Arc having had none too good a run; and as Antisaar is to remain in training he should get the second chance his stable-companion did. Given his inexperience, Antisaar should have plenty of improvement in him as a four-year-old.

		Nearctic	Nearco
	Northern Dancer	(br 1954)	Lady Angela
	(b 1961)	Natalma	Native Dancer
Antisaar (USA)		(b 1957)	Almahmoud
(b.c. 1987)		Riverman	Never Bend
	Detroit (FR)	(b 1969)	River Lady
	(b or br 1977)	Derna	Sunny Boy III
		(b 1961)	Miss Barberie

Antisaar fetched 2,450,000 dollars as a yearling at the Keeneland July Selected Sale. By Northern Dancer out of Arc de Triomphe winner Detroit, he has an exceptional pedigree. Antisaar is the fourth foal of Detroit. The second and third, also by Northern Dancer, managed only one win between them, the colt Nordic Legend finishing fifth in a two-year-old maiden at Phoenix Park when trained by Vincent O'Brien before being sent back to the States. But her first foal turned out all right. He was the smart Lake Erie (by Kings Lake), one of the most improved horses in training as a four-year-old in 1987, winning six times, including in the St Simon Stakes. Detroit herself is a half-sister to numerous winners, notably the Cheveley Park winner Durtal, dam of dual Gold Cup winner Gildoran. Antisaar's grandam Derna II was placed from ten to thirteen furlongs in France and came from quite a stout family. The close-coupled, good-quartered Antisaar should prove well suited by a strongly-run mile and a half. He acts on good to firm ground and dead. *A. Fabre, France.*

ANTOINETTE JANE 3 b.f. Ile de Bourbon (USA) 133–Hability (Habitat 134) — [1989 7g* 7m⁴ 10g 1990 8d 7.6m⁴] rather dipped-backed, good-quartered filly: has a quick action: fair fourth of 7 in handicap at Lingfield in May: appears not to stay 1¼m: acts on good to firm ground, probably unsuited by dead. *G. Harwood.*

ANVARI 3 b.c. Persian Bold 123–Anne Stuart (FR) (Bolkonski 134) [1989 NR **111** 1990 10m 10m* 10m* 12m 10f³ 10d] 68,000F: leggy, quite attractive colt: third foal: half-brother to useful 1988 2-y-o 1m winner Star Shareef (by Shareef Dancer): dam, French 1m winner, is half-sister to good French colt Arokar: led inside final 1f to win £7,400 event at Newmarket and Group 2 Derrinstown Stud EBF Derby Trial at Leopardstown in May: 3 lengths third to Missionary Ridge in Gallinule Stakes at the Curragh: well beaten in Prix du Jockey-Club at Chantilly and Champion Stakes (edgy on first run for 3 months) at Newmarket: should stay 1½m: very useful. *C. E. Brittain.*

ANXIOUS TIMES (USA) 2 b.f. (May 1) Fast Topaze (USA) 128–Maxencia **80** (FR) (Tennyson (FR) 124) [1990 6f⁵ 7f* 6m⁶ 7m⁶ 6m 6m* 7m] rather leggy, close-coupled filly: fluent mover: sixth foal: half-sister to several winners, including smart 1986 French 2-y-o stayer Magistros (by Carwhite): dam French maiden half-sister to smart 1985 French staying 2-y-o Manetho: fair performer: won maiden at Yarmouth in August and nursery at Folkestone in October: sweating, raced alone (probably led 5f) in nursery at Newmarket on final start: probably better suited by 6f than 7f: sometimes edgy. *N. A. Callaghan.*

ANYTIME ANYWHERE 3 b. or br.f. Daring March 116–Martini Time 90 **65** (Ardoon 124) [1989 5g⁵ 5s³ 5d² 5d⁵ 5f⁵ 5f* 5m* 1990 5f⁴ 5d* 5m⁴ 5g 5g 5d

Sheikh Mohammed's "Anvari"

5g] smallish, good-quartered filly: keen walker: has quick action: quite modest handicapper: lost her form after making all in £7,400 event at Chester in May: will prove best at 5f: has won on firm (not best form) and dead going: sold 2,500 gns Doncaster November Sales. *Mrs G. R. Reveley.*

APACHE PRINCE 3 gr.g. Red Sunset 120–Maxi Girl (My Swanee 122) [1989   **81**
7m 8m 8g 1990 12.2m⁶ 14g 14m⁴ 13m* 16m* 18g* 16.2m² 16f² 18g²] rangy gelding: good walker and mover: fair handicapper: won at Ayr (maiden claimer) in July and at Redcar and Ripon in August: suited by thorough test of stamina: acts on firm ground: tends to idle: consistent. *D. Morley.*

APOLLO KING 4 b.g. Indian King (USA) 128–Mehudenna 77 (Ribero 126) [1989   **55**
8d⁶ 8g 8g² 10m 10g⁴ 11m⁴ 11.7m⁴ 11f² 10g⁴ 10f² 12m⁶ 1990 a12g²] leggy, rather close-coupled, angular gelding: plating-class handicapper: odds-on second of 9 in maiden at Lingfield in January: stays 1½m: acts on firm and dead going: not discredited when sweating: winning hurdler twice in autumn. *P. Mitchell.*

APPAREL 3 ch.f. Absalom 128–Anoda (FR) (Amber Rama (USA) 133) [1989 5g³   **37**
5v 5d⁵ 5m⁵ 5f⁵ 5f³ 7f⁶ 7f⁵ 5m 6g 5m 6g 1990 5f 5f⁵ 5s⁵ 5s 6g³ 6f⁴ 6g 6g 7m⁴ 6m⁵ 6g⁵ 7m] small, very sparely-made filly: poor walker and moderate mover: poor maiden: stays 7f: best on a sound surface: sold 930 gns Doncaster October Sales. *M. Brittain.*

APPEAL FOR HELP 5 br.h. Star Appeal 133–Sovereign Help 98 (Sovereign   **— §**
Lord 120) [1989 5s 5g 1990 a6g 5s 5m] small, sturdy horse: of little account and is temperamentally unsatisfactory: refused to race second outing: blinkered (sweating and edgy) on reappearance at 4 yrs. *J. L. Spearing.*

APPELANIA 3 b.f. Star Appeal 133–Penna Bianca (My Swallow 134) [1989 7m   **77**
8m⁵ 7.3v 1990 8g* 8g* 8.2f 8d⁵ 10g⁶ 8d 10.2s] strong, workmanlike filly: good mover: won maiden at Carlisle in April and moderately-run handicap at York in May: well below form in handicaps after: stays 1m well: seems unsuited by extremes of going. *M. H. Tompkins.*

Kerridge Computers Trophy Handicap, Newbury—
Applecross and Clare Court finish well clear of the rest

APPLECROSS 3 b.f. Glint of Gold 128–Rynechra 102 (Blakeney 126) [1989 NR **117**
1990 12.5m* 10g* 12.2g² 13.3m* 14.6g² 12m²] sparely-made, angular filly: fine
mover: first foal: dam, unraced at 2 yrs, won twice over 1½m and stayed 1¾m well:
successful in minor events at Wolverhampton in May and Nottingham in June and in
£11,500 handicap at Newbury in July: smart performances behind Madame Dubois in
A F Budge Park Hill Stakes at Doncaster and Narwala in Princess Royal Stakes at
Ascot last 2 starts: gives impression suited by 1¾m. *H. R. A. Cecil.*

APPLETON LE MOOR 3 b.f. Marching On 101–Lady Mede 74 (Runnymede —
123) [1989 NR 1990 5g 7.5f] compact filly: fourth foal: dam sprint maiden: tailed off in
maiden and claimer. *M. W. Ellerby.*

APPLIANCEOFSCIENCE 3 b.g. Bairn (USA) 126–Moonlight Serenade 66 **63**
(Crooner 119) [1989 6m³ 6f³ 6m³ 7g 1990 8d 7m 8f 10g² 10f⁶ 10m⁴ 10d 10g² 10.5g*
12m] workmanlike gelding: moderate walker: quite modest handicapper: favourite,
won selling event (bought in 9,000 gns) at York in October: ran poorly in apprentice
race later in month: stays 1¼m: acts on good to firm ground: has sweated, including
at York when also on toes: inconsistent: sold to join G. Moore 11,000 gns Newmarket Autumn Sales. *D. W. P. Arbuthnot.*

APPROACH THE BENCH (IRE) 2 b.c. (Feb 13) Law Society (USA) **101**
130–Arguing 71 (Pharly (FR) 130) [1990 7g³ 7g* 6.3g² 6d² 8d* 10s] IR 24,000Y:
second foal: dam, 13.8f winner later successful in Italy, is half-sister to Washington
International winner Argument: useful colt: successful in listed event and
Juddmonte EBF Beresford Stakes (by a short head from Roger Ramjet) at the
Curragh: ¾-length second to Sir Harry Hardman in valuable restricted race at the
Curragh in October on fourth start: last of 9 in Criterium de Saint-Cloud in
November: should stay 1¼m: acts on dead going. *J. E. Mulhern, Ireland.*

A PRAYER FOR WINGS 6 gr.g. Godswalk (USA) 130–Late Swallow (My **113**
Swallow 134) [1989 5s* 6f² 6.3g* 6g³ 7g⁵ 1990 6m³ 6m²] tall, rather leggy gelding:
smart sprinter: first past the post in EBF Greenlands Stakes at the Curragh in May,
beating Duck And Dive a neck, but demoted for bumping runner-up over 1f out:

suited by 6f: acts on any going: looked difficult ride when tried in blinkers: has started slowly, including on reappearance. *J. Sutcliffe.*

APRES HUIT   3 b.f. Day Is Done 115–Ma Minti 62 (Mummy's Pet 125) [1989 5v⁵   **66 d**
1990 a6g² a5g* a5g² a6g² 5f² 5f 5f* 5.8f⁶ a5g 5.3h 5m³ a7g 5.8f 10.8f 6g a6g a5g] sparely-made filly: moderate mover: quite modest performer who lost her form: made all in claimer at Southwell in January and seller (bought out of Mrs N. Macauley's stable 8,600 gns) at Bath in May: claimed out of D. Wintle's stable £6,015 after seller fourteenth outing: best efforts over 5f on firm ground: occasionally sweating and edgy: tends to hang. *Mrs N. Macauley.*

APRIL CRACKER   3 b.f. Cragador 110–Chanita (Averof 123) [1989 6f 7g² 8.2f   **33**
1990 8g 10m 12m 7m 8m⁶ 7f 8f⁴ 8f 6f 6g 8.2v 10m³ 10d] workmanlike, good-quartered filly: has a round action: poor plater: stays 1¼m: probably acts on firm going: blinkered nowadays, has been visored: occasionally sweating: bandaged at 2 yrs: retained 1,500 gns Newmarket September Sales. *G. H. Eden.*

APSIMORE   3 ch.f. Touching Wood (USA) 127–Balgreggan (Hallez (FR) 131)   **67**
[1989 NR 1990 12f³ 13.3m⁶ 10.1m 13.1m 14g 12f² 14m³] 17,000Y: sturdy filly: moderate mover: half-sister to several winners, including useful 6f to 1m winner Sailor's Song (by Song) and sprinters Manton Dan (by Tower Walk) and Street Market (by Porto Bello): dam twice-raced half-sister to smart stayer Golden Love: form only in maiden (ran in snatches) at Salisbury and 20-runner handicap (staying on strongly from rear) at Nottingham last 2 outings: stays 1¾m: visored fifth and sixth starts. *G. B. Balding.*

AQUAINTED   5 b.m. Known Fact (USA) 135–Gay Trinket 72 (Grey Sovereign   —
128§) [1989 7d⁴ 7d⁶ 7f 8m 7g⁴ 6f a8g 1990 a8g a7g 8g 9g 8m] leggy, rather sparely-made mare: moderate mover: no longer of much account. *M. Brittain.*

ARABAT   3 b.c. Habitat 134–Kalamac (FR) (Kalamoun 129) [1989 NR 1990 7g³   **79**
7m² 8m* 7.2d* 8g] robust, attractive colt: third reported living foal: brother to fairly useful 1986 2-y-o 5f winner Propensity, once-raced at 3 yrs, and half-brother to French 5.5f (at 2 yrs) and 13f winner Kalidancer (by Far North): dam 2-y-o 5f and 6f winner who showed quite useful form at up to 1m at 3 yrs: fair form: comfortably landed odds in 7.2f maiden at Haydock in September: later awarded similar event at Pontefract: faced stiff task and not given hard race in handicap final outing: may prove best at 7f: sold to join K. McCauley 36,000 gns Newmarket Autumn Sales. *L. M. Cumani.*

ARABIAN BOLD (IRE)   2 br.c. (Apr 7) Persian Bold 123–Bodham 88 (Bustino   **74 p**
136) [1990 7m³] IR 25,000Y: leggy, attractive colt: fifth foal: half-brother to fairly useful 1¼m winner Barsham (by Be My Guest) and a winner in France by Kalaglow: dam 1½m and 13.3f winner, is out of half-sister to Blakeney and Morston: 4 lengths third of 11, keeping on one pace, to Democratic in maiden at Leicester in September: will stay at least 1¼m: sure to improve. *W. J. Haggas.*

ARABIAN KING   2 b.c. (Mar 21) Sayf El Arab (USA) 127–New Edition 72 (Great   **68**
Nephew 126) [1990 6d² 6g³] 4,400Y: workmanlike colt: first foal: dam, 5f winner at 2 yrs, appeared to stay 7f: quite modest form, staying on, in autumn maidens at Ayr and Nottingham. *M. Brittain.*

ARABIAN SILENCE   3 ch.c. Sayf El Arab (USA) 127–Silent Prayer 58   **71**
(Queen's Hussar 124) [1989 6m 6m⁴ 7m⁶ 7g 7m² 8g⁴ 8g² 1990 10g 8m 10g⁵ 11m⁶ 11.7m² 11.7m 12g 12g] big, strong colt: turns off-fore in: modest maiden: made most when good second at Windsor in June, clearly best effort in handicaps: stays 11.7f: acts on good to firm ground: has joined D. Gandolfo. *R. Hannon.*

ARABIAN STAR   3 ch.c. Sayf El Arab (USA) 127–Tahoume (FR) (Faristan 123)   **38**
[1989 5f⁵ 6m 8f 8.2s 1990 9s 11m⁵ 8.5d⁴ 10g] strong, compact colt: poor maiden: may prove ideally suited by around 1m: acts on good to firm ground and dead: blinkered as 3-y-o, except second start: sometimes bandaged: sold 3,300 gns Newmarket July Sales. *J. G. FitzGerald.*

ARABIAN SULTAN   3 b.c. Muscatite 122–Church Bay 76 (Reliance II 137)   —
[1989 NR 1990 10.1m⁶ 10.1m⁵ 12.2f⁶ 10m 10g] IR 4,600F, 11,500Y, 4,600 3-y-o: small, close-coupled colt: half-brother to several winners here and abroad, including Hymn of Harlech (by Welsh Chanter), successful from 5f to 1m, and 1m winner Bright Aisle (by Don): dam showed ability at 2 yrs: well beaten, including in selling handicap: blinkered fourth start: unruly at stalls time before. *J. White.*

ARAGANT MAN   3 b.g. Aragon 118–Cuillin Gael (Scottish Rifle 127) [1989 7g   —
1990 12f 12h] tall, leggy gelding: well beaten, in seller final outing: unruly in preliminaries. *B. Stevens.*

Andrew Heffernan's "Archway"

ARAGON COURT 2 b.c. (Feb 1) Aragon 118–Balatina 85 (Balidar 133) [1990 6m 7m] good-topped colt: fourth foal: half-brother to 3-y-o 1m and 1¼m winner Latin Leap and 1988 2-y-o 6f seller winner Casbatina (both by Castle Keep) and 6f winner Count Me Out (by Vaigly Great): dam sprinter: soundly beaten in maidens at Kempton (when trained by R. Hoad) in July and Warwick (slowly away) 3 months later. *J. Pearce.* —

ARAK (USA) 2 b.c. (Apr 7) Clever Trick (USA)–Twilight Flight (USA) (Quack (USA)) [1990 8.2d²] $77,000Y: rather leggy, quite attractive colt: fourth reported foal: half-brother to a winner by Tilt Up: dam unraced half-sister to Cornwallis winner Hadif (by Clever Trick) and good 1985 American 2-y-o filly Silent Account: 4 lengths second of 15, making most, to Hip To Time in minor event at Nottingham in October: showed a fluent action: sure to improve, and win a race. *R. W. Armstrong.* **76** p

ARALDO BLU (IRE) 2 b.c. (Apr 22) Heraldiste (USA) 121–Lisahunny (Pitskelly 122) [1990 5f 6d 5v² 5d²] IR 5,600Y: neat, strong colt: fifth foal: half-brother to Irish middle-distance winner Desert Gale (by Taufan): dam Irish 5f winner: much improved form on final 2 starts, in seller at Ayr and claimer at Edinburgh: should stay 6f: acts well on a soft surface. *W. J. Pearce.* **63**

ARANY 3 b.c. Precocious 126–Bellagio 68 (Busted 134) [1989 5d⁶ 6m⁵ 6g³ 6s 6g⁴ 6d* 1990 6g⁴ 6m 7d⁵ 6m 7f 8.5m² 8f⁵ 11s 8d* 9m] lengthy, quite attractive colt: has a round action: fairly useful handicapper: made all in minor event at Ayr in September: 16/1, prominent over 6f in Cambridgeshire at Newmarket 15 days later: stays 1m well: should prove best on an easy surface: blinkered fourth outing. *M. H. Tompkins.* **99**

ARBITRAGEUR 3 ro.g. Ile de Bourbon (USA) 133–Jenny Diver (USA) (Hatchet Man (USA)) [1989 6m* 7m³ 7m 6f 1990 8.2f 8.5d 9m 6m 8m 10.4v⁶] lengthy gelding: shows knee action: has shown little since modest winner at 2 yrs: should stay 1m: —

blinkered, edgy and sweating third start: sold out of E. Owen's stable 2,800 gns Doncaster September Sales after fifth. *M. B. James.*

ARBOR VITAE 3 b.g. Dominion 123–Plain Tree 71 (Wolver Hollow 126) [1989 NR 1990 8m 10m 7.6d 7m⁵ 10m* 10m² 12m³] 27,000Y: workmanlike gelding: keen walker: fifth foal: half-brother to useful sprinter Plain Fact (by Known Fact) and a winner in Belgium: dam, 7f winner, is half-sister to good French middle-distance stayer Djakao and daughter of half-sister to Shantung: modest form: won claimer at Nottingham in September: claimed to join M. Pipe £18,002 when fair third in similar event at Newmarket: probably stays 1½m. *D. Morley.* **73**

ARBORY STREET 5 b.g. Anfield 117–Melvin (Quiet Fling (USA) 124) [1989 8s* 1990 8f 8.2s 10.6f⁶ 10m 10d 8f⁶ 10m⁶ 13g⁶ 10m] lengthy gelding: poor mover: well backed, won selling handicap at Leicester in spring as 4-y-o: later broke bone in off-fore: below form in handicaps (including selling) in 1990: should stay 1¼m: acts on soft going. *Mrs J. R. Ramsden.* **—**

ARCHWAY (IRE) 2 ch.c. (Feb 23) Thatching 131–Rose of Jericho (USA) (Alleged (USA) 138) [1990 6d*] IR 50,000Y: first foal: dam, unraced, is out of half-sister to high-class 1m to 1½m winner Critique: odds on, won 18-runner maiden at Naas in November by a length: apparently very highly regarded. *M. V. O'Brien, Ireland.* **80 p**

ARC LAMP 4 b.g. Caerleon (USA) 132–Dazzling Light 116 (Silly Season 127) [1989 5m a6g⁴ a6g 1990 a6g a6g 5g 7m] workmanlike, angular gelding: fair winner as 2-y-o: no subsequent worthwhile form, including in seller: bred to stay further than 5f: trained first 3 starts by C. Spares. *H. J. Collingridge.* **—**

ARCTIC HEIGHTS (USA) 3 ch.c. Arctic Tern (USA) 126–Dols Jaminque (USA) (Kennedy Road (CAN)) [1989 6f⁶ 7m⁵ 1990 10f⁵ 10g 7g 10f² a10g* 10m 12f² 11.7m 11.5m⁵ 10h] tall, leggy colt: quite modest handicapper: won at Lingfield in May: stays 1½m: acts on firm going: blinkered last 8 outings, except when ran fairly well in visor once: may be temperamentally unsatisfactory. *G. Lewis.* **62**

ARDEARNED 3 b.f. Ardross 134–Divine Penny 65 (Divine Gift 127) [1989 NR 1990 8m 8m 10m 10.1g 14g 15.3g 12f² 11.7g 11m 12g 12d] leggy, good-topped filly: moderate mover: fifth reported foal: half-sister to 1¼m and 1½m winner Divine Charger (by Treboro) and modest stayer Pour Encourager (by Kind of Hush): dam, placed in sellers at up to 1¼m, later won 5 times in Hong Kong: worthwhile form only when second in selling handicap at Brighton in July: stays 1½m: acts on firm going: blinkered last 3 outings: sometimes bandaged: sold 1,700 gns Ascot November Sales. *G. Lewis.* **35**

ARDENT GROOM (IRE) 2 ch.c. (Apr 21) Coquelin (USA) 121–Arminiya (Roan Rocket 128) [1990 a7g 7m⁵ 7d 7d a7g] IR 5,000F, 4,000 2-y-o: dipped-backed colt: half-brother to 4 winners here and abroad, including fair 1984 2-y-o 6f winner Armorad (by Red Alert) and 1½m winner Arifa (by Wolver Hollow): dam French 10.5f winner: poor maiden: had very stiff task when ridden by claimer in nurseries on last 2 starts. *T. M. Jones.* **36**

ARDLUI 3 b.c. Lomond (USA) 128–Rocket Alert 110 (Red Alert 127) [1989 8m⁴ 1990 10f* 10g² 12g⁴ 10.6s*] well-made colt: moderate walker: won maiden (odds on) at Folkestone in March and amateurs handicap (blinkered and showing improved form) at Haydock in June: didn't look easy ride in between: should stay 1½m: acts on any going: will prove best on a galloping track: sold 52,000 gns Newmarket July Sales. *G. Harwood.* **95**

ARDNAMURCHAN 3 b.f. Ardross 134–Starlite Night (USA) 105 (Star de Naskra (USA)) [1989 NR 1990 10g 10.2f 12g] IR 4,700Y: quite good-topped filly: first foal: dam 7f winner: no sign of ability in maidens. *D. R. C. Elsworth.* **—**

ARDOUR 4 b.g. Ardross 134–Evita 111 (Reform 132) [1989 10g 10m⁵ 10.2h² 1990 10.2f] angular gelding: quite modest form at best: stays 1¼m. *M. C. Pipe.* **—**

ARDROSS BEST 4 ch.g. Ardross 134–Do Your Best 89 (Try My Best (USA) 130) [1989 10f 8.2m⁶ 1990 8.2s⁶ 8m 9f⁴ 12m a10g] lengthy, good-quartered gelding: has a light, easy action: lightly-raced maiden: may prove best short of 1½m: sold out of M. Jarvis' stable 4,000 gns Ascot June Sales and gelded after third start. *F. J. O'Mahony.* **—**

AREA CODE 6 gr.h. Blakeney 126–Fayreela (Zeddaan 130) [1989 17.4s⁴ 16m a14g⁴ 1990 16.5d] leggy, sparely-made horse: fair handicapper at his best, but has deteriorated: backward, tailed off only outing at 6 yrs: suited by test of stamina and give in the ground (unsuited by heavy going): usually blinkered: won novice hurdle in November. *J. H. Johnson.* **—**

ARETHUSA LEISURE 3 gr.f. Homing 130–Birch Creek (Carwhite 127) [1989 — 5m³ 5m⁴ 1990 6f 7m] lengthy filly: quite modest maiden: soundly beaten in minor event and handicap in the spring: dead. *M. J. Fetherston-Godley.*

AREYOUREAL 2 b.f. (Mar 13) Prince Sabo 123–Adduce (USA) (Alleged (USA) — 138) [1990 6g 6m⁶ 6d] 21,000Y: quite good-topped filly: second foal: half-sister to Italian St Leger third Capo Speranza (by Star Appeal): dam stayed 1¼m, is half-sister to 2 good winners at up to 1¼m: no worthwhile form in maidens: trained first 2 starts by P. Felgate, off course 3 months after. *C. Tinkler.*

ARGAKIOS 3 b.c. Busted 134–Salamina 106 (Welsh Pageant 132) [1989 NR 1990 **88** 12m⁵ 12m² 12m 12g⁴] leggy, lengthy, quite attractive colt: moderate mover: fifth foal: half-brother to 4 middle-distance winners, including high-class 1¼m horse Ile de Chypre (by Ile de Bourbon) and fair 10.5f to 1½m winner Halkopous (by Beldale Flutter): dam 5f to 1m winner: fairly useful maiden: best effort second at Pontefract: bit fitted incorrectly and run should be ignored next start: will be suited by 1¾m +: sold 12,500 gns Newmarket Autumn Sales. *G. Harwood.*

ARGENTUM 3 br.c. Aragon 118–Silver Berry (Lorenzaccio 130) [1989 5f* 6m⁵ **116** 6f* 5m* 6g 1990 5m* 5d 5f* 5m⁴ 6m⁶] small, good-quartered colt: carries condition: smart performer: won minor event at Kempton in May and King George Stakes, held up then coming with steady run to lead inside final 1f and beat Blyton Lad and Dancing Music 1½ lengths, at Goodwood in August: ridden along at halfway and never able to challenge in Keeneland Nunthorpe Stakes at York and Krug Diadem Stakes at Ascot after, fair 7½ lengths fourth to Dayjur at York: best form over 5f, though has won at 6f: needs top-of-the-ground: tends to get on edge: reportedly returned lame final start. *L. J. Holt.*

ARIAL STAR 3 b.c. High Line 125–Premiere Danseuse 72 (Saritamer (USA) **83** 130) [1989 NR 1990 9m⁴ 10.6s⁵ 10.1m³ 11.7m* 12m² 14g⁶ 12.3g³ 12g⁴ 10m⁶] 32,000Y, IR 50,000Y: good-topped colt, with scope: moderate mover: brother to 1986 2-y-o 7f winner Bracorina and half-brother to a winner in Italy: dam, 7f winner, is half-sister to useful sprinters Glenturret and Rollahead: fair handicapper: won at Windsor in July despite not handling bends: will prove ideally suited to strongly-run 1½m: acts on good to firm ground: trained first 3 starts by R. J. R. Williams: has joined J. FitzGerald. *A. A. Scott.*

ARIBIE 4 b. or br.f. Konigsstuhl (GER)–Arita (FR) (Kronzeuge) [1989 9f 12.2m⁵ **52** 10m⁴ 8m 12f⁶ 9g 10v 1990 a11g 10.8m² 10f⁴ 9g* 10f⁶ 10.6s 8m] plain filly: has round action: plating-class handicapper: won at Wolverhampton in May: flashed tail under pressure next outing, ran as though something badly amiss final one, first for 4 months: stays 10.8f: acts on firm and dead going: trained until after penultimate outing by P. Leach. *R. E. Peacock.*

ARISTOCRATIC PETER (USA) 3 b.c. Sir Ivor 135–Glimmer Glass (USA) **57** (The Axe II 115) [1989 7g 7g 1990 10.1g 12g 12f.1f 11.7h³ 7f a7g²] good-topped colt: has quick action: worthwhile form only when placed in maiden claimer at Bath, leading 1¼m, and handicap at Lingfield, staying on: may be ideally suited by 1¼m: blinkered last 3 starts: trained until after fourth by G. Harwood. *R. V. Smyth.*

ARITA 3 b.f. Never So Bold 135–Exotic (Jaazeiro (USA) 127) [1989 5f* 5.3f* 1990 — 5m] dipped-backed filly: fair winner of maiden at Beverley and minor event at Brighton as 2-y-o: bit backward, moved moderately down and soon behind in June handicap on only start in 1990: will be better suited by 6f. *R. W. Armstrong.*

King George Stakes, Goodwood—
Argentum has the firm ground in his favour and makes the most of his opportunity;
Blyton Lad (No. 5) and Dancing Music (No. 11) dead-heat for second

ARMAITI   2 b.f. (Apr 2) Sayf El Arab (USA) 127–Almitra (Targowice (USA) 130)   72
[1990 6g 7m] lengthy, dipped-backed filly: fourth foal: half-sister to fairly useful 5f
winner Bay Hero (by Bay Express): dam Irish 9f winner out of smart 7f to 1¼m
winner Donna Cressida: around 6 lengths eighth of 18, edging right and one pace, in
maiden at Leicester in October: green on debut. *C. James.*

ARMED FORCE   3 b.g. Shernazar 131–Skittish (USA) 73 (Far North (CAN) 120)   —
[1989 NR 1990 10m a12g⁵ 10d 11.5g⁶ 12m 16s] 3,600Y: tall, plain gelding: third foal:
dam thrice-raced 1½m winner: no worthwhile form, including in handicaps: may
well prove suited by test of stamina. *C. A. Cyzer.*

ARMORY SHOW (FR)   3 b.g. Mille Balles (FR) 124–Bamburi 93 (Ragusa 137)   —
[1989 8m 1990 12.2m 12h⁶ 12m 15g] smallish, workmanlike gelding: little form in
maiden and sellers. *J. G. FitzGerald.*

ARMY OF STARS   5 b.h. Posse (USA) 130–Starawak 68 (Star Appeal 133) [1989   90
8s³ 8f³ 8f 8g 8f 8g 10.2g* 12g² 10.6s* 1990 10f³ 10f³ 12f⁴ 10m 10.5m 12m⁵ 8g 10m⁶
10.4v⁴ 12s²] tall, useful-looking horse: usually takes the eye: moderate mover:
fairly useful handicapper: good second to Azzaam in 24-runner William Hill
November Handicap at Doncaster: needs further than 1m nowadays and stays 1½m:
acts on any going except seemingly heavy: blinkered once: bandaged behind third
and fifth outings: usually races up with pace. *C. E. Brittain.*

AROGOTO   2 b.c. (Apr 23) Ahonoora 122–Tikanova (USA) (Northern Dancer)   — p
[1990 6m⁶] well-made colt: good walker: first foal: dam unraced daughter of Cairn
Rouge: green, 13 lengths sixth of 12 to Bold Bostonian in maiden at Salisbury in
August, no extra and not knocked about last 2f: looked sure to do better, but not
seen out again. *R. Charlton.*

AROKAT (USA)   2 gr.c. (Mar 1) Caro 133–Katsura (USA) (Northern Dancer)   90 p
[1990 7g³ 7g²] compact, workmanlike colt: fifth foal: half-brother to fairly
useful 3-y-o middle-distance performer Katzina (by Cox's Ridge), 7f winner at 2 yrs,
7f and 1½m winner Rambushka (by Roberto) and a winner in North America: dam
Irish 7f and 1½m winner, is out of sister to very smart middle-distance filly
Trillionaire: long odds on following promising run, won maiden at Chester (by 6
lengths) in August: well-backed second favourite, 4 lengths second of 5, ridden
along 2f out and one pace, to Bog Trotter in Laurent-Perrier Champagne Stakes at
Doncaster month later: will stay 1¼m. *B. W. Hills.*

AROMATIC   3 b.c. Known Fact (USA) 135–Mint 100 (Meadow Mint (USA) 120)   106
[1989 7g⁶ 7m* 8f* 8g 8g 1990 7f 12g 10f* 10f² 10f² 10m³ 8m] well-made colt: has a
free, round action: useful handicapper: won at Lingfield in July: ran well at
Goodwood (£31,600 event, sweating), Newmarket and Yarmouth next 3 starts,
moderately in £11,100 contest (blinkered, on toes) at Ascot on final one: on toes,
slowly away when intended pacemaker in Ever Ready Derby: stays 1¼m: acts on
firm going: to join Bobby Frankel in USA. *G. Harwood.*

AROUSAL   3 br.f. Rousillon (USA) 133–Model Girl (FR) (Lyphard (USA) 132)   109
[1989 6g³ 6f* 7s* 8m⁴ 1990 8m* 8f² 8d 8g⁶] rangy, rather unfurnished filly: won
4-runner minor event at Newcastle in June: 2½ lengths second of 5 to odds-on
Chimes of Freedom in Child Stakes at Newmarket, then ran poorly in Prix d'Astarte
at Deauville and minor event (edgy, raced too freely) at Newbury: should stay bit
further: acts on any going: has worn crossed noseband: goes well with forcing
tactics. *Major W. R. Hern.*

ARPERO   3 b.f. Persian Bold 123–Arvel (Thatching 131) [1989 7f* 7m⁰ 8m³ 1990   107
7m⁴ 8h⁴ 8m² 8g* 8g⁶ 10m⁶] strong, workmanlike filly: shows a round action:
useful performer: won apprentice race at Lingfield in May, 2-runner minor event at
Carlisle in July and listed race (ran on really well to beat Alwathba 3½ lengths) at
Sandown in August: below form in listed race at Doncaster and Group 2 contest at
Newmarket last 2 starts: will prove best with strong pace at 1m, doesn't stay 1¼m:
possibly ideally suited by some give in the ground. *Sir Mark Prescott.*

ARRACK PRINCESS   2 b.f. (Mar 15) Precocious 126–Petrary 67 (Petingo 135)   38
[1990 5d 5g⁵ 5m⁵ 5g] small, close-coupled filly: fifth foal: half-sister to modest 7f
winner Petrify (by Air Trooper) and 6f and 8.2f winner Reyah (by Young
Generation): dam won over 5f at 3 yrs and stayed at least 7f: moderate plater. *M. W.
Easterby.*

ARRASTRA   2 b.f. (Apr 16) Bustino 136–Island Mill 79 (Mill Reef (USA) 141)   — p
[1990 7m] second foal: half-sister to quite modest maiden Victoria Mill (by Free
State): dam suited by a test of stamina, is out of 1973 Cambridgeshire winner
Siliciana: behind in maiden at Goodwood in September: should do better. *I. A.
Balding.*

George Stubbs Stakes, Newmarket—progressive Arzanni beats the Cesarewitch winner

ARRIVEZ DEUX   2 ch.f. (May 16) Reach 122–Apair (Red Slipper 126) [1990 5m 50 §
5m⁴ 5f³ 6m* 6g⁵ 7.5f 6m⁵ a7g 5m 6m 5g] 5,000Y: leggy, rather angular filly: has a
quick action: half-sister to 1m seller winner Wolfie (by Wolverlife) and a winner
abroad: dam Irish middle-distance winner: plating-class performer at best: won
seller (bought in 8,400 gns) at Warwick in May: will stay at least 1m: blinkered sixth
start: rather temperamental, and is one to treat with caution: sold 780 gns Doncaster October Sales. *J. Wharton.*

ARROW DANCER   4 b.g. Gorytus (USA) 132–Rose And Honey (Amber Rama   —
(USA) 133) [1989 8d⁴ 7m⁴ 8f⁶ 8f⁶ a8g⁵ 1990 a10g a10g a13g] lengthy gelding: modest
maiden at best: below form in Lingfield handicaps early in year: stays 1m: acts on
good to firm and dead going: blinkered twice: has joined J. J. O'Neill. *R. J. O'Sullivan.*

ART FORM (USA)   3 b.c. Little Current (USA)–Christi Dawn (USA) (Grey   78 ?
Dawn II 132) [1989 NR 1990 12m 10f 12m³ 14m 16.2d a14g* 18g² 17.4d 16m 16m⁶]
4,000Y: tall, angular colt: has a round action: half-brother to 2 winners in North
America: dam never ran: sire won Preakness and Belmont Stakes: modest
handicapper: improved form in August when winning at Southwell then short-head
second in moderately-run race at Ripon: ridden by 7-lb claimer, fair sixth at
Warwick, clearly best subsequent effort: suited by test of stamina: seems to need a
sound surface: reluctant to race turning into back straight at Haydock fifth outing.
C. A. Cyzer.

ARTHURS STONE   4 ch.g. Kings Lake (USA) 133–Two Rock 70 (Mill Reef   —
(USA) 141) [1989 12.2m* 16.2g 12f 13.8g⁶ 12m 12s² 12.5f³ 10.6s* 1990 8.2s 13v 12g
11m⁶ 11g³ 10.6s] quite modest winner as 3-y-o: below his best in 1990, though
showed a little in claimer (visored) and amateurs handicap fourth and fifth outings:
stays 1½m: acts on any going: sometimes bandaged: sold to join O. Brennan's stable
3,000 gns Ascot September Sales: inconsistent. *J. S. Wilson.*

ARTIC ENVOY (USA)   4 ch.c. Arctic Tern (USA) 126–Eternity (FR) (Luthier   108
126) [1989 12s* 12m² 12f 15g 12g² 12m⁴ 1990 12f² 12g⁶ 12m³ 12g* 12g³ 12m⁶ 12g³
14s] leggy, angular colt: keen walker: has a rather round action: won Group 3
Premio Ellington at Rome in May: third in General Accident Jockey Club Stakes at
Newmarket, Gran Premio di Milano and Grosser Preis der Berliner Bank (5½
lengths behind Ibn Bey) at Dusseldorf: well beaten in Group 3 race at Rome final
outing, first for nearly 4 months: suited by 1½m: acts on any going except possibly
heavy: useful. *P. A. Kelleway.*

ARTURIAN   2 b.c. (Mar 4) Vaigly Great 127–Aspark (Sparkler 130) [1990 5g³ 5d³   83
5f⁴ 6f³ 6f⁵ 5m² 5f² 5g⁴ 5m* 5f³ 5g² 5m⁴ 6s⁶ 5d⁴] 6,800Y: lengthy colt: keen walker:
has a quick action: first foal: dam little form: fair performer: comfortable winner of

nursery at Wolverhampton in August: best form at 5f: best in blinkers, and when held up: has given trouble at stalls: consistent. *R. F. Johnson Houghton.*

ARYLH (USA) 2 b.f. (Mar 13) Lyphard (USA) 132–Riviere Enchantee (FR) 83 p (Riverman (USA) 131) [1990 6m² 6d*] rather angular filly: half-sister to a winner in USA by Spruce Needles: dam unraced half-sister to smart French miler Lypheor out of smart French sprinter Klaizia: odds on, made all in maiden at Leicester in October in good style by 5 lengths from Katy's Pet: will be better suited by 7f: sure to improve further, and win more races. *A. C. Stewart.*

ARZANNI 3 gr.c. Darshaan 133–Astara 83 (Nishapour (FR) 125) [1989 NR 1990 110 10m⁴ 10m* 10.1m* 12g² 12m* 12m 16m*] big, lengthy, quite attractive colt: moderate mover: second foal: dam, 7f and 8.5f winner, is half-sister to Prix de Diane winner Crepellana: progressed very well, winning maiden at Chepstow and minor event at Windsor in July, £14,800 handicap at York in September and listed event (led under 2f out and ran on well to beat Trainglot 3 lengths) at Newmarket in November: stays 2m: takes time to quicken: changed hands before penultimate race. *L. M. Cumani.*

AS ALWAYS (IRE) 2 ch.f. (Feb 20) Hatim (USA) 121–Red Magic (Red God 59 128§) [1990 6m 6f³ 6m 6d 8m] 13,500Y: good-topped filly: has plenty of scope: easy mover: fourth living foal: half-sister to 1985 2-y-o 6f winner D'Artigny (by Dalsaan): dam lightly-raced sister to smart 1970 Irish 2-y-o Supernatural: quite modest maiden: well supported in nurseries final 2 starts: should stay beyond 6f: possibly unsuited by dead ground. *G. Lewis.*

ASBAAB 5 b.g. Young Generation 129–The Yellow Girl 102 (Yellow God 129) 41 § [1989 8g 8s⁵ 9f 7m³ 7m³ 10g³ 8.3m³ 7f 9m 9g 7g 8g a8g² a7g 1990 a8g 8f 8m⁶ a10g³ 8m⁵ 8g⁵ 8.2v 8m] good-bodied gelding: carries plenty of condition: moderate mover: only poor nowadays: tailed off last 2 outings: effective at 7f and probably stays 1¼m: not at his best on firm ground: has had tongue tied down: trained until after sixth outing by B. McMath: not genuine: sold privately 800 gns Ascot December Sales. *I. Campbell.*

AS D'EBOLI (FR) 3 b.c. What A Guest 119–Ana d'Eboli (FR) (King of The 74 Castle (USA)) [1989 5m⁴ 6f⁴ 6m⁶ 8m⁶ 10g 1990 12.2m* 12.3f² 12m³ 16.2s⁴ 12f³ 16.2d³ 12.4f² 14m] sturdy colt: carries condition: moderate mover: modest handicapper: won maiden at Catterick in March: ran poorly at York final start: probably stays 2m and acts on any going: blinkered last 2 starts at 2 yrs: sometimes on toes: winning hurdler. *J. G. FitzGerald.*

ASHAL 4 b.c. Touching Wood (USA) 127–Johara (USA) 92 (Exclusive 114 Native (USA)) [1989 14f² 16f* 16f* 14g* 1990 14f² 16m* 20d* 20f⁵ 18g⁵ 16m³]
Time is up for the Cup races in their traditional form, or so it seems. Jockey Club policy—or rather the lack of it—has led to the virtual destruction of long-distance racing in Britain to the point where, according to a consultative paper on extended distance races issued by the Race Planning Committee in the latest season, too many top owners and trainers now regard the Cup races as unsuitable targets for top-class horses. Champion trainer Henry Cecil—who has saddled five Gold Cup winners since 1979—went on record in the latest season as saying 'If horses haven't got enough speed to win over two miles they shouldn't be winning Group 1 races'. Cecil's views coincide with those of other eloquent and influential trainers, including John Dunlop—'these marathons serve no useful purpose'—who has been campaigning in recent years for the distances of the Cup races to be shortened. In October came the news that the Stewards of the Jockey Club had accepted a unanimous recommendation from the Flat-Race Pattern Committee that the distance of the Gold Cup and the Goodwood Cup should be reduced by half a mile, making them two-mile tests. The Ascot Trustees and the Goodwood executive were both consulted. Goodwood, which shortened the Goodwood Cup by a furlong in 1990, told the Stewards that it would be prepared to stage the Goodwood Cup over two miles 'provided this went hand-in-hand with a much larger prize-money allocation from the turf authorities for the whole Cup-race series'; at the time of writing, the Ascot Trustees had still to agree to the distance reduction (the pressure to do so included a warning from the Jockey Club that the Gold Cup's Group 1 status might otherwise have to be reviewed). The third leg of the so-called stayers' triple crown, the Doncaster Cup, is set to remain a two-and-a-quarter-mile

Gold Cup, Ascot—Ashal holds on bravely in miserable conditions

race, partly because there is no suitable place for a two-mile start at Doncaster.

The Cup races make up almost the whole racing programme for the top out-and-out stayers and reducing the distance of the Gold Cup and the Goodwood Cup will leave them with only two worthwhile non-handicaps to aim at, the Doncaster Cup and the Queen Alexandra Stakes, which is run over two and three quarter miles at Royal Ascot and would become a listed race under the new proposals. Meagre rations indeed! Why? Shouldn't a fair and proper programme of racing over long distances include a series for both two-mile and two-and-a-half-mile horses? The Race Planning Committee defends the shortening of the Gold Cup and Goodwood Cup by arguing that the stayers' championship should be decided at a distance which is 'at the mid-point of the stayers' range rather than at its extremity'. The reformers also believe that the size and quality of the fields for the Cup races would be improved by a distance reduction. However, there is precious little evidence to support that notion. The Group 3 Jockey Club Cup over two miles at Newmarket attracts about the same number of runners (thirty in the last five years) as its Goodwood (twenty-seven runners) and Doncaster (twenty-nine runners) counterparts and the quality of the field is barely any different. Over the last five years the Gold Cup has attracted more runners (fifty-one) than some other pattern races at the Royal meeting open to older horses including the Queen Anne Stakes (thirty-six), the Prince of Wales's Stakes (thirty-nine) and the Hardwicke Stakes (thirty-three). A full programme of races over two miles is as desirable as one over extreme distances but it should not have been considered a replacement. Existing two-mile races such as the Henry II Stakes at Sandown in May and the Lonsdale Stakes at York's August meeting would have been ideal for elevation in status and value, and would have provided a more balanced programme of racing at distances beyond a mile and a half. Apart from savaging the Cup races, the Race Planning Committee's consultative paper had much to commend it. Plans to introduce graduation races over a mile and three quarters, some valuable staying maiden events

66

and three or four more good staying handicaps, are praiseworthy; they will provide welcome additional opportunities for horses that need a distance of ground to show their true merit, alleviating a problem that has been obvious for many years. Better late than never.

There were eleven runners for the latest edition of the Gold Cup, though whether the field was worthy of a race of Group 1 status was open to argument. The 1988 and 1989 winner Sadeem was the only horse in the field who had previously gained a Group 1 success. The Prix du Cadran (French Gold Cup) form was represented by the second, third and fourth in that race, Cossack Guard, Turgeon and Thethingaboutitis, the first- and last-named both trained in Britain and no better than useful on the balance of their form. The 1989 Doncaster Cup and Jockey Club Cup winner Weld was also in the line-up, having his first run as a four-year-old after proving difficult to train on the prevailing firm ground; and the Irish St Leger runner-up Tyrone Bridge, transferred to Pipe before the start of the latest season, was another who had looked a potential Gold Cup winner as a three-year-old. But the short-priced favourite on the day was the much improved Teamster, winner in May of the Insulpak Sagaro Stakes at Ascot (from Thethingaboutitis and Cossack Guard) and the Mappin And Webb Henry II Stakes at Sandown (from Mountain Kingdom and Chelsea Girl, both of whom were in the Gold Cup field). Many a true stayer is slow to mature and such was Ashal, who started fifth favourite at 14/1 behind Teamster (13/8), Sadeem and Weld (both 5/1) and Tyrone Bridge (7/1). Raced once at two, Ashal made only four appearances as a three-year-old, all of them at Redcar (in an interview after the Gold Cup his trainer criticised the limited opportunities for maturing three-year-old stayers in the second half of the season). Ashal won his last three races most impressively and looked just the sort to train on into a smart stayer. He was seen out twice in the latest season before the Gold Cup, running Sadeem to a neck in receipt of 10 lb in a minor event at Salisbury and then winning the Group 3 Oleander-Rennen over two miles at Baden-Baden from Dance Spectrum, a stable-companion of Sadeem. Rain changed the going at Royal Ascot from firm overnight to good to soft by the time the Gold Cup was run, conditions which counted against Sadeem, for one, and contributed to the race being the thorough test of stamina it should be. The strong-galloping Ashal revelled in the conditions; he was in front forcing the pace a long way out and gamely kept up the gallop after being sent for home in earnest approaching the home turn. None of his rivals got in a serious challenge in the straight, Tyrone Bridge staying on best to be beaten four lengths, with The- thingaboutitis, coming from behind, a further length and a half away in third, a short head in front of Teamster, with Turgeon two lengths back in fifth. Nothing else finished within thirty lengths of the first five, Sadeem and Weld trailing in eighth and tenth respectively. Ashal never showed the same form again—perhaps his very hard race left its mark—and if he's to join the select few who have won the Gold Cup in successive years he'll need to perform a good deal better than he did in his three subsequent races, in all of which he was penalized 7 lb for his Gold Cup victory. He was trounced in the Goodwood Cup (running unaccountably badly when tried in blinkers) and then managed only fifth behind Al Maheb after making the running for a long way in the Doncaster Cup, in which Teamster, the Queen Alexandra Stakes winner Regal Reform and Chelsea Girl also finished ahead of him. Ashal ran his best race after the Gold Cup when third to Great Marquess and Dance Spectrum in the Jockey Club Cup, in which Al Maheb, Regal Reform and Teamster were down the field.

		Touching Wood (USA) (b 1979)	Roberto (b 1969)	Hail To Reason
				Bramalea
Ashal			Mandera (b 1970)	Vaguely Noble
(b.c. 1986)				Foolish One
		Johara (USA) (b 1979)	Exclusive Native (ch 1965)	Raise A Native
				Exclusive
			Never Linger (b or br 1973)	Never Bend
				Quick Flight

The leggy, quite attractive Ashal (who looked tremendously well at Ascot) is a grand mover with a long, raking stride, ideally suited to galloping courses like Ascot, Doncaster and Newmarket but slightly less so to

Hamdan Al-Maktoum's "Ashal"

Goodwood which, with its turns and gradients, is essentially a sharp track favouring the handy type rather than the long-striding horse. Stamina was the strong suit of Ashal's sire Touching Wood who won both the St Leger and the Irish St Leger after finishing second, still a maiden, to Golden Fleece in the Derby. Touching Wood was retired to Dalham Hall Stud at the end of his three-year-old days at a fee of 7,000 guineas (live foal) but his fortunes soon waned and he is now at stud in New Zealand. Like Touching Wood, Ashal's dam Johara was also trained by Thomson Jones who saddled her to win the six-furlong Virginia Water Stakes at Ascot on her debut. Johara didn't fulfil that promise and was unplaced in her three other races, including the International Fillies Stakes over a mile at Kempton on her only outing as a three-year-old. Thomson Jones also trained Johara's two other winners, the Tap On Wood colt Kashshaf (successful over a mile and a quarter as a three-year-old) and the Doulab filly Yanabee (who won a six-furlong maiden event at Thirsk as a two-year-old before being exported to Italy where she has also been successful). Ashal has yet to race on very soft going but acts on any other. He has worn a tongue strap but didn't do so on his last four starts. *H. Thomson Jones.*

ASH AMOUR 3 gr.f. Hotfoot 126–Loving Doll 72 (Godswalk (USA) 130) [1989 **46** 7m 1990 7g 8g[5] 10f 10f[3] 10f[2] 9g 10m[3] 10d* 10g[3] a12g[6] a13g] sparely-made filly: poor performer: won selling handicap (no bid) at Nottingham in October: below form on all-weather but shapes as though probably stays 1½m: acts on good to firm ground and dead: below form when blinkered fifth and sixth starts: has carried head high and hung badly left. *R. J. R. Williams.*

ASHDOWN 3 ch.f. Pharly (FR) 130–Ash Ridge (USA) 93 (Bold Reason) [1989 NR **—** 1990 7m[6] a8g[4] a8g] workmanlike filly: fourth foal: half-sister to Irish 12.8f winner Live Ash (by Electric): dam 6f winner at 2 yrs later suited by 1¼m, is daughter of

Favoletta: well beaten in maidens, awkward at stalls final outing: should be suited by further. *N. A. Graham.*

ASHDREN 3 b.c. Lochnager 132–Stellaris (Star Appeal 133) [1989 6g 6f 6g* 1990   90
7g* 8.5m 7f² 7g² 6m⁶ 7m⁵ 7d² 7m 7d] angular, plain colt: fairly useful handicapper: won at Edinburgh in June: ran very well at York and Ayr (led over 1f out then hung badly left and caught post) sixth and seventh starts, moderately in £71,900 contest at Ascot and £9,600 event at Redcar after: best efforts at 7f: acts on firm and dead ground: swishes tail. *A. Harrison.*

ASHGROVE CHERRY 2 b.f. (Mar 17) Creetown 123–Aldington Cherry (Legal   56
Eagle 126) [1990 6m 5f⁵ 5g⁴ 5m] leggy, good-topped filly: third foal: dam unraced: plating-class maiden: continually flashed tail second start: should stay 6f. *B. A. McMahon.*

ASHLEY WILDE 2 ch.f. (Mar 25) Night Shift (USA)–Opalescent 71 (Gulf Pearl   —
117) [1990 6g 5s⁶] 4,500Y: rather leggy, workmanlike filly: half-sister to 5f winner The Singing Man (by Mansingh) and a winner in Denmark: dam third over 5f from 2 starts at 2 yrs: green, well beaten in maiden auctions in autumn. *C. B. B. Booth.*

ASHTINA 5 b.g. Tina's Pet 121–Mrewa (Runnymede 123) [1989 5s* 5m 5f 5f 5g 6f   80 §
6f 6s 5m* 5m 1990 5m 5m 6d 5m 5g³ a6g* a7g⁵ a6g⁴] leggy, good-topped gelding: fair on his day: favourite, won 7-runner handicap at Lingfield in November, setting strong early gallop: best at sprint distances: acts on any going: blinkered once at 4 yrs: often gets on toes: thoroughly inconsistent, and not one to trust. *J. Sutcliffe.*

ASHWAQ (USA) 4 b.f. Robellino (USA) 127–Vexation (USA) (Vice Regent   —
(CAN)) [1989 10s³ 8d² 8m³ 8m⁵ 10d⁶ 1990 a8g 11s] lengthy, quite attractive filly: moderate walker and mover, with a quick action: modest maiden at best: well beaten both starts in spring: stayed 1¼m: acted on soft going, probably unsuited by top-of-the-ground: sweating and edgy final outing at 3 yrs: sold 12,500 gns Newmarket December Sales, in foal to Sharpo. *W. Hastings-Bass.*

ASITAPPENS 4 ch.g. Music Maestro 119–Dalchroy (Hotfoot 126) [1989 7m⁵   60
7m* 7.5m* 8m* 9m 7s 8.2d² 1990 10.2f 7.5m² 8m 7.5m³ 8.2f⁵ 9s 8m⁴ 7.6g⁶] compact gelding: quite modest handicapper: should prove best at up to 1m: acts on firm and dead going: blinkered last 2 outings: bandaged near-hind seventh start: gives impression best with strong handling. *M. H. Tompkins.*

ASK FLO-JO 2 b.f. (May 2) Rolfe (USA) 77–Cresta Leap 72 (Piaffer (USA) 113)   41
[1990 5g⁵ 6m⁶ 5g³ 6m 6d] leggy, unfurnished filly: first foal: dam maiden suited by 6f: poor maiden: off course nearly 5 months after third start. *M. P. Muggeridge.*

AS QUE TO (FR) 2 b.c. (Feb 11) No Pass No Sale 120–Charming Queen (FR) 110
(Habitat 134) [1990 7g² 6.5d* 7g 6.5d² 7.5d³] 460,000 francs (approx £42,600) Y: half-brother to several winners, including 1985 Hollywood Derby winner Charming Duke (by Iron Duke): dam French 2-y-o 5f winner: successful in minor event at Evry in July: better form when placed at Saint-Cloud in Prix Eclipse (head second to Crack Regiment) and Prix Thomas Bryon (over 6 lengths third to Exit To Nowhere) in October: will stay 1m. *E. Lellouche, France.*

ASSATIS (USA) 5 b.h. Topsider (USA)–Secret Asset (USA) (Graustark) 127
[1989 12f* 12g² 11.1m* 12m* 12f 1990 12m⁴ 12d* 12m³ 12m³ 13.3g⁴ 12g]
    Whereas the Hardwicke Stakes has tended to be rather uncompetitive in recent years, the latest field for the race looked outstanding by any standards. The French and Irish Derby winner Old Vic was making his long-awaited reappearance, opposed by the Prix de l'Arc de Triomphe winner Carroll House, the St Leger winner Michelozzo, Husyan, Charmer, Assatis and Ile de Nisky. Old Vic started at odds on, while two of his opponents, Assatis and Ile de Nisky started at 50/1. Assatis himself had been long odds on when winning the race the previous season but seemed up against it this time, especially as the going had turned softer than was regarded as ideal for him. In the event both Old Vic and Carroll House ran as though they needed the outing, Michelozzo disappointed, and the finish of a very strongly-run affair came to be dominated by the two rank outsiders. Well handled by stable-jockey Cochrane, who switched mounts when Cacoethes was withdrawn in the morning, Assatis moved up from the back entering the straight as the pacemakers began to flag, followed by Ile de Nisky. He went on from Old Vic just under two furlongs out, and from then on he was always getting the better of Ile de Nisky, the pair of them edging right but drawing right away from the rest. There was three quarters of a length in it at the line. Assatis extended

*Hardwicke Stakes, Ascot—50/1-shot Assatis wins the race for the second year running;
Ile de Nisky gives him most to do*

his list of fine performances over the Ascot course when he was returned
there for the King George VI and Queen Elizabeth Diamond Stakes the
following month. He excelled himself in finishing third of eleven to Belmez
and Old Vic, ridden this time by the Japanese Shibata, making ground steadily
in the straight, having been waited with, to go under by less than two lengths.

Assatis' failure to reproduce his best form in his race on each side of the
King George is explained by the absence of a good gallop in either of them. In
the circumstances it would have been prudent to have provided him with a
pacemaker, as Cacoethes usually was. The Princess of Wales's Stakes at
Newmarket in July developed into a sprint; Assatis, having been held up, was
therefore poorly placed when the race began in earnest and could keep on only
steadily to be nearest at the finish, just over three lengths third to Sapience
who'd dictated matters from the front. Assatis' lack of top-class finishing pace
was equally evident in the Walmac International Geoffrey Freer Stakes at
Newbury in August where he came fourth of five, 13/8 favourite, to Charmer.
He started at 30/1 for the Arc on his final racecourse appearance. Those odds
fairly represented his chance and he finished in mid-field behind Saumarez,
never dangerous, beaten just under ten lengths.

			Nearctic
		Northern Dancer	Natalma
	Topsider (USA)	(b 1961)	Round Table
	(b 1974)	Drumtop	Zonah
Assatis (USA)		(b 1966)	Ribot
(b.h. 1985)		Graustark	Flower Bowl
	Secret Asset (USA)	(ch 1963)	Buckpasser
	(b 1977)	Numbered Account	Intriguing
		(b 1969)	

Assatis' pedigree has been discussed at length in previous Annuals. His
three-year-old close relation Razeen (by Northern Dancer), unraced at two

70

years due to a wind problem, won three times in the first half of the latest season, including in the N M Financial Predominate Stakes at Goodwood, and was sent off favourite for the Derby. He ran poorly there and after finishing a creditable fifth in the Eclipse was sent to join Whittingham in the States. Another close relative Warrshan (also by Northern Dancer) had also been sent to join Whittingham late on as a three-year-old, raced twice at four years, failing to make the frame on each occasion, and has recently been returned to England to stand at the Lavington Stud. Assatis has been retired to stud in Japan. A tall, good-topped horse, a fluent mover with a slightly round stride, he never raced on soft ground, but acted on any other. As he showed often enough, a strongly-run race at a mile and a half suited him extremely well, and Ascot might have been designed for him. Though he went well for several different jockeys and styles he wasn't the easiest of rides. He tended to get worked up in the preliminaries, too, and had a habit of swishing his tail. *G. Harwood.*

ASSERTION 3 b.f. Assert 134–Yes Please 108 (Mount Hagen (FR) 127) [1989 **104** ? NR 1990 8g 10m⁶ 9m⁴ 10m⁵ 12g⁴ 12f³ 10g⁴ 12g* 12m³ 12g⁵ 16d] fourth foal: half-sister to maidens by Monteverdi and London Bells: dam 2-y-o 6f winner: won maiden at the Curragh in June: 50/1, made most and appeared to put up improved performance when narrowly-beaten third of 10 to Knight's Baroness in Kildangan Stud Irish Oaks at the Curragh: well beaten in Group 3 and listed contests there after: stays 1½m: acts on good to firm ground: sold 34,000 gns Newmarket December Sales. *K. Prendergast, Ireland.*

ASSIGNMENT 4 b.c. Known Fact (USA) 135–Sanctuary (Welsh Pageant 132) **78** [1989 8s⁶ 7h² 7f⁴ 8m⁵ 7h* 7m² 7d a8g³ 1990 8d 7g a7g³ a7g³ a6g*] strong, deep-girthed colt: modest handicapper: in good form late in year, winning 5-runner event at Lingfield in December: seems best at 6f nowadays: acts on any going: has

Peter Leon's "Assertion"

worn severe noseband, pulled hard for apprentice and found little: sold out of P. Cole's stable 4,000 gns Doncaster January Sales: resold 4,400 gns Ascot April Sales. *J. Ffitch-Heyes.*

ASTERIX 2 ch.c. (Mar 20) Prince Sabo 123–Gentle Gael 97 (Celtic Ash) [1990   **86** 6m³ 6m² 5.8f* 6g⁵ 6g] smallish, lengthy colt: moderate mover: half-brother to winners here and abroad, including useful sprinter Cree Song (by Song) and 1980 2-y-o 1m winner Crystal Gael (by Sparkler): dam winner from 5f to 1m, is sister to high-class Italian colt Hoche: fair performer: won maiden at Bath in July: out of depth afterwards: stays 6f. *C. C. Elsey.*

ASTLEY JACK 4 gr.g. Belfort (FR) 89–Brigado 87 (Brigadier Gerard 144) [1989   — 6s⁵ 6m a7g 1990 8f 10.8g 12m 10m] leggy gelding: little form, easily best effort at 6f on soft ground: sometimes bandaged: often sweats and gets on edge: bolted going down second intended outing: led and taken early to post afterwards: trained until after second start by K. White: very headstrong. *K. S. Bridgwater.*

ASTRABEE 5 b.g. Show-A-Leg 107–Manatay (Brilliant Blue) [1989 NR 1990 18f]   — leggy gelding: well beaten in varied events on flat: sweating only start at 5 yrs: winning hurdler. *R. F. Marvin.*

ASTRAL'S DELIGHT 2 gr.f. (Mar 11) Absalom 128–Astral Suite 82 (On Your   **52** Mark 125) [1990 5f* 5m 5.8h⁴ 6m 6d⁵ 8d] smallish, workmanlike filly: seventh foal: half-sister to several winners, including sprinter Cumbrian Express (by Bay Express) and 1m and 1½m winner Trouvere (by Free State): dam 6f and 7f winner: plating-class performer: won maiden at Bath in June: very stiff task at 1m: yet to race on soft ground, acts on any other. *J. Berry.*

ASTRID GILBERTO 3 b. or br.f. Runnett 125–Natasha 87 (Native Prince)   — [1989 6h⁴ 6m* 6f² 5m* 5m⁶ 1990 a7g 6f⁴ 6g 6m 6g 10m 8.2m a8g] lengthy, quite attractive filly: modest winner at 2 yrs: well beaten in handicaps and claimer in 1990, leading 5f penultimate (mulish at stalls) outing: stays 6f: visored fourth start: tends to flash tail. *B. Richmond.*

ASTRONOMER 4 b.g. Head For Heights 125–Diamonds In The Sky (African   — Sky 124) [1989 6s 5f⁴ 5f 5m⁶ 7.5f 7f⁴ 8.5f* 8m 8m⁴ 8g⁶ 8f⁴ 8f 8f⁶ 1990 8m⁵ 8f 8.5g 10f] workmanlike, good-topped gelding: won apprentice handicap at Beverley as 3-y-o: better at around 1m than shorter: acted on firm going: sometimes slowly away: took strong hold and best held up: dead. *F. H. Lee.*

ATALL ATALL 5 b.h. Kampala 120–Bint Africa 71 (African Sky 124) [1989 6v   **79** 5d³ 6.1f² 6f³ 6f³ 6f 6m³ 7.6m² 6f³ 6f² 6m⁵ 6m* 6m 6f 1990 6v³ 7.6d 6m³] rather leggy, attractive horse: not a good walker or mover: modest nowadays: ran creditably first and final (June, finished lame) outings in 1990: best form at 6f: acts on any going: visored once, tailed off when blinkered: often taken down quietly. *G. M. Moore.*

ATATURK (USA) 2 ch.g. (Feb 1) Ankara (USA) 106–Wattle It Be (USA) (Bold   **79** Commander (USA)) [1990 7f² 7m 8m³] close-coupled gelding: has a long stride: half-brother to numerous minor winners in North America: dam placed 3 times from 8 starts: sire useful 7f and 1¼m winner in Ireland later successful in Australia: sweating and on toes, under 3 lengths third of 16, wandering badly under 2f out then keeping on, in maiden at Redcar in October: will stay 1¼m. *J. Etherington.*

ATEAMBER 3 b.g. Hays 120–Princess Lamia (Home Guard (USA) 129) [1989 6m   — 8.2d 1990 a7g6] quite attractive gelding: soundly beaten in maidens and claimer: dead. *R. Bastiman.*

ATHENE NOCTUA 5 b.m. Aragon 118–Lady Lorelei 105 (Derring-Do 131)   **46** [1989 12f 12g⁶ 10.2f 10f 1990 10.6s*] leggy, light-framed mare: 33/1, first form since 3 yrs when winning 20-runner apprentice handicap in good style at Haydock in October: stays 10.6f: acts on any going. *B. A. McMahon.*

ATHENIAN KING 2 b.c. (Mar 20) Fairy King (USA)–To Oneiro 69 (Absalom   **79** 128) [1990 5f² 5f* 5d³ 5f⁵ a6g* 5g⁵ 5m⁵] smallish, well-made colt: moderate mover: third foal: half-brother to a winner in Norway by Mourtazam: dam 5f and 6f winner: modest performer: won maiden at Newcastle in April and minor event at Southwell in August: ran as though needed race final start, first for over 6 weeks: probably better suited by 6f than 5f: has given trouble at stalls. *C. Tinkler.*

ATHENS BY NIGHT (USA) 4 ch.f. London Bells (CAN) 109–Senorita   **60** Poquito 110 (Connaught 130) [1989 NR 1990 10.2f 12m⁵ 14.8f 12h² 12f³ 12f⁵] rather leggy, quite good-topped filly: moderate mover: quite modest maiden: suited by 1½m: sweating second start. *Miss A. J. Whitfield.*

ATHENS GATE (USA)   6 ch.g. Lydian (FR) 120–Pago Miss (USA) (Pago Pago)   —
[1989 7.6m² 8f⁵ 9m* 10.5f⁶ 9f 9g⁴ 1990 10m 8h] smallish, barely-made gelding:
moderate mover: fair winner as 5-y-o: ran poorly both outings in spring: best short
of 1¼m: probably unsuited by soft going, acts on any other: blinkered once: sold
3,400 gns Doncaster June Sales, resold 1,900 gns Ascot December Sales. N. Tinkler.

ATHLON   3 b.c. Kings Lake (USA) 133–Antilla 87 (Averof 123) [1989 8v 1990 6f⁵   63
7.2d³ 8g 8g⁶] leggy colt: quite modest maiden: should stay 1m: acts on dead ground:
visored (front rank 7f) final start. M. E. D. Francis.

ATLAAL   5 b.g. Shareef Dancer (USA) 135–Anna Paola (GER) (Prince Ippi (GER))   —
[1989 12g² 9g 10f⁰ 12f⁴] tall, good-topped, attractive gelding: has been operated on
for a soft palate: has a quick action: useful at his best: modest fourth of 5 to Charmer
in £13 000 race at Doncaster in March: stays 1½m: has given impression ill at ease
on firm going: smart hurdler. J. R. Jenkins.

ATLANTIC BEAUTY   2 ch.f. (Jun 1) Chaparly (FR)–Atlantic Princess (Four   —
Burrow 91) [1990 6m] sparely-made filly: fifth foal: half-sister to a winner in
Belgium: dam won from 1m to 1½m: bandaged and bit backward, slowly away and
soon tailed off in seller at Lingfield. J. A. Bennett.

ATLANTIC CEDAR   4 b.g. Touching Wood (USA) 127–Enchanted 116 (Song   —
132) [1989 11.7m 12h⁶ 12f 1990 11.5g 12g] compact, good-bodied gelding: lightly
raced and soundly beaten since 2 yrs: visored final outing. P. Hayward.

ATLANTIC CLEAR   3 b.g. Starch Reduced 112–Kathy King (Space King 115)   57
[1989 5s⁶ 5f³ 7g³ 6g⁵ 1990 6m 7f 7f³ a8g 8m] leggy, unfurnished gelding: has free,
rather round action: quite modest maiden: claimed to join I. Campbell £12,000 after
claimer final outing, in May: stays 7f: acts on firm going: has run creditably for
apprentice: gelded after final start. B. Palling.

ATLANTIC FLYER (USA)   2 b.f. (Apr 19) Storm Bird (CAN) 134–Euphrosyne   98
(USA) (Judger (USA)) [1990 5m 6m* 6g² 6m³ 7m³ 6.5g² 8m³] 44,000Y: leggy filly:
closely related to 3-y-o My Love (by Nijinsky), successful at 1m (at 2 yrs) and 10.6f,
and half-sister to Orpheus Island (by Blushing Groom), successful at up to 11f: dam
graded-stakes winner at up to 13f: fairly useful filly: first past post in maiden at
Chepstow and £10,600 event (beat Seductress on merit by 2 lengths, but was
demoted for edging left near finish) at Newmarket in June: good second to Nazoo in
Tattersalls Tiffany Yorkshire Stakes at Doncaster and third to Shamshir in Brent
Walker Fillies' Mile at Ascot final 2 starts: stays 1m. J. Sutcliffe.

ATLANTIC WAY   2 gr.f. (Mar 21) Bold Owl 101–Overseas 48 (Sea Hawk II 131)   —
[1990 5m⁶ 6m 6m⁵ a6g] 3,100Y: leggy filly: has a round action: half-sister to several
winners here and abroad, including 1986 2-y-o 6f winner Swallow Bay (by
Penmarric): dam poor maiden: little worthwhile form in varied events: threw rider
in paddock on second start. C. J. Hill.

ATOLL   3 b.f. Caerleon (USA) 132–Shirley Reef (Shirley Heights 130) [1989 7g* 115
7g² 1990 8v* 12d* 10.5d 12m²] attractive filly: smart performer: won Premio
Regina Elena at Rome in April and Oaks d'Italia (by short neck from Ruby Tiger) at
Milan in May: ran well in mid-division behind Rafha in Prix de Diane Hermes at
Chantilly and when second of 10, always close up and leading 2f out until close
home, to Knight's Baroness in Kildangan Stud Irish Oaks at the Curragh: stays
1½m: yet to race on firm ground, acts on any other. A. Renzoni, Italy.

AT PEACE   4 b.c. Habitat 134–Peace 113 (Klairon 131) [1989 8d³ 1990 a8g* 8.3m   81
7.2g² 8d 9m 10.2s⁶] robust colt: carries plenty of condition: fair performer: won
maiden at Lingfield in May: better efforts in handicaps third and fourth outings:
stays 1m: will probably prove best on an easy surface: visored fifth start: sold to join
J. White's stable 14,000 gns Newmarket Autumn Sales. R. Charlton.

ATTADALE   2 b.c. (Apr 30) Ardross 134–Marypark 93 (Charlottown 127) [1990   — p
10s] rangy colt, rather unfurnished: half-brother to several winners, including fairly
useful stayer Halba (by Habat) and useful pair Loch Seaforth (by Tyrnavos) and
Rynechra (by Blakeney): dam well suited by long distances: backward and green,
dropped away quickly 3f out in autumn maiden at Nottingham: showed a fluent
action: should improve. W. Jarvis.

ATTILA THE HONEY   5 b.m. Connaught 130–Kimbo (Golden Dipper 119)   —
[1989 10m 11f 10f 7g 1990 a12g⁶ a14g⁶] small, good-bodied mare: fair plater as 3-y-o:
lightly raced and no subsequent form: stays 1¼m: needs a soft
surface: blinkered once at 3 yrs: bandaged final outing. S. R. Bowring.

AUCTION DAY   3 b.g. Runnett 125–Valediction 71 (Town Crier 119) [1989 5m³   58
6g 6g² 6g 8f³ 8m² 8g 1990 8f² 12.5g³ 10m⁶ 8.2m⁴ 10.4g] leggy, rather sparely-made
gelding: moderate mover: quite modest maiden: ran creditably in handicaps first 4

73

starts, pulled hard in apprentice contest on final one: will prove best at up to 1¼m: yet to race on a soft surface. *F. Jordan.*

AUCTION NEWS 3 b.g. Auction Ring (USA) 123–Cestrefeld 94 (Capistrano 120) [1989 6f 6f⁵ 6m⁴ 6g⁶ 7g 1990 10m 13.3m 10.2f* 10m³ 12m 10m 12m⁶ a10g] useful-looking gelding: has a quick action: won apprentice handicap at Bath in July: pushed along in rear 5f out when creditable third in handicap at Sandown, easily best subsequent effort: should prove suited by 1½m: acts on firm going: blinkered sixth start: has joined D. Gandolfo. *R. Hannon.*   59

AUCTION TIME 7 br.g. Auction Ring (USA) 123–Autumn Flush 57 (Rustam 127) [1989 NR 1990 10.1g] good-bodied gelding: winning handicapper as 4-y-o: has run just twice on flat since: stays 1¼m: yet to race on firm going, acts on any other: sold 1,500 gns Ascot June Sales. *R. Akehurst.*   —

AUGHFAD 4 b.c. Millfontaine 114–Saulonika 94 (Saulingo 122) [1989 5s 6s⁶ 5f⁶ 6m³ 6m* 6f² 6m³ 5.8m⁶ 6f 6g a8g a7g 1990 a5g⁴ a5g* a6g³ a6g 6f² 6f 6m 6h⁴ 5f* 5g³ 5g² 6g² 6f 6m 6m⁵ 5m³ 5m 5d* 5m⁴ 5g* 5s] strong, workmanlike colt: usually looks well: poor mover: fair handicapper: won at Southwell in January, Folkestone in June and Goodwood and Newbury (holding off Cantoris by neck) in October: effective at 5f to 6f: acts on hard and dead going: effective with or without blinkers: visored last 5 starts. *T. Casey.*   83

AUGHTON RIDGE (IRE) 2 b.f. (Apr 7) Hatim (USA) 121–Vote Barolo (Nebbiolo 125) [1990 5s 7f⁶ 7g 8m 10.6s⁵] IR 5,200F, IR 4,100Y, 2,400 2-y-o: smallish, angular filly: carries condition: fourth foal: half-sister to Manuale Del Utente (by Montekin), 7f winner at 2 yrs: dam ran twice at 2 yrs: poor maiden: stays 1¼m: very edgy first 2 starts. *M. O'Neill.*   37

AUGUST CLIMB 3 b.g. Kings Lake (USA) 133–May Hill 124 (Hill Clown (USA)) [1989 NR 1990 8m⁶ 10.1g³ 11f] 58,000Y: rangy gelding: fourth living foal: half-brother to fairly useful 1¼m to 13f winner Picea (by Mummy's Pet): dam won Yorkshire Oaks and Park Hill Stakes: well backed following most promising debut, about 1½ lengths third of 24 to Treble Eight in minor event at Windsor in May: broke leg and destroyed at Redcar later in month. *B. W. Hills.*   89

AUGUST TWELFTH 2 b.c. (Jan 18) Full of Hope 125–Espanita 64 (Riboboy (USA) 124) [1990 8d 8m] quite attractive colt: second foal: dam maiden suited by 1½m: always behind in autumn maidens at Ayr and Redcar. *W. J. Pearce.*   —

AUNT AGATHA 3 b.f. Homeboy 114–Eridantini (Indigenous 121) [1989 NR 1990 7m 7g⁶ 7d] 3,200F: compact filly: has a long stride: half-sister to several winners, notably prolific sprint winner Offa's Mead (by Rathlin) and useful sprinter Perfect Timing (by Comedy Star): dam never ran: behind in maidens. *D. R. C. Elsworth.*   —

AUNT HESTER (IRE) 2 br.f. (Apr 11) Caerleon (USA) 132–Lady Hester (Native Prince) [1990 5m³ 5m* 5m 6m³ 6g 5f 5g 5v⁴] IR 44,000Y: smallish, good-quartered filly: moderate walker: closely related to smart French 1m and 9f performer L'Irresponsable (by Ile de Bourbon) and half-sister to several winners, including 5f winner Spoilt Son (by Mummy's Pet): dam Irish 5f and 6f winner, is granddaughter of excellent broodmare Zanzara: quite modest performer: won maiden at Sandown in April: better suited by 6f than 5f: acts on good to firm ground and heavy: blinkered final start. *M. Bell.*   68

AUNTIE CYCLONE (USA) 6 ch.m. Dust Commander (USA)–Dame du Moulin (USA) (Mill Reef (USA) 141) [1989 NR 1990 7g] robust, well-made mare: fair plater as 3-y-o: always behind in October handicap at Yarmouth, only subsequent outing: suited by 1m: used to act well on top-of-the-ground: has sweated: has been mounted on track: has been to stud. *W. Holden.*   —

AUROREUM 3 ch.c. Glenstal (USA) 118–Abelina (Thatch (USA) 136) [1989 NR 1990 6g 7d 6m³] IR 11,500F: good-topped colt: fourth foal: closely related to a winner in Spain by Try My Best: dam unraced sister to Thatching: 50/1 and carrying condition, first form in maidens when 2 lengths third of 8 to Illusory at Redcar in October, staying on well from rear: capable of better. *L. J. Holt.*   68 p

AUSHERRA (USA) 2 ch.f. (Jan 31) Diesis 133–Princess of Man 104 (Green God 128) [1990 6m* 7m² 8m] tall, attractive filly: has scope: good walker: half-sister to fairly useful 6f (at 2 yrs) and 1m winner Concorde Island (by Super Concorde) and 2 winners in USA: dam won Musidora Stakes: made virtually all in maiden at Kempton in May: good second of 5, rallying well, to Jaffa Line in £20,900 event at Goodwood over 3 months later: ran moderately in Brent Walker Fillies' Mile at Ascot: should stay 1m. *F. I. Cole.*   95

AUSTHORPE SUNSET 6 b.g. Majestic Maharaj 105–Kings Fillet (King's Bench 132) [1989 12g² 13f² 10m 1990 12f⁴ 16s] small, dipped-backed gelding: poor   33

handicapper: shaped as though retaining ability despite unsuitable conditions final outing, first for over 5 months: stays 13f: acts on firm going: slowly away on reappearance: trained until after then by Mrs R. Wharton: fair front-running hurdler. *M. D. Hammond.*

AUTHORSHIP (USA) 4 b. or br.g. Balzac (USA)–Piap (USA) (L'Aiglon (USA)) 40
[1989 8.5d 8.2s 8m 11.7m 8.3g 8g 1990 a13g³ 16m⁴ 14g 21.6m² 16.2g* 17.6m⁵ 14g 16m⁵] leggy gelding: poor form in handicaps: won at Beverley in May: stays extreme distances: winning hurdler. *W. J. Musson.*

AUTOBIRD (FR) 3 b.c. Procida (USA) 129–Star of The Stage (Nureyev (USA) 71
131) [1989 6f 6f² 7.3g 7f⁴ 7m a6g³ a6g⁶ 1990 a7g⁴ a5g² a6g² a6g* a5g* a6g* a5g a8g 5f⁵ 6f 6f³] leggy colt: modest performer: won maiden and claimer at Lingfield and 5f handicap at Southwell in February: effective at 5f and 6f: usually blinkered (wasn't when slowly away eighth outing): twice visored: suitable mount for apprentice: has run creditably when sweating and on toes: not seen out after April. *C. N. Allen.*

AUTO CONNECTION 4 b.f. Blushing Scribe (USA) 107–Smitten 72 (Run The 62
Gantlet (USA)) [1989 7f³ 8m⁶ 8f³ 10.2g⁵ 10g* 10m³ 10m⁵ 12g 1990 10m³ 10g² 12f²
10g⁶ 10f³ 8m⁴ 8.2d³ 8g⁵] leggy, lengthy filly: has a rather round action: quite modest handicapper: suited by 1¼m: acts on firm and dead going: blinkered fourth start: hung left when successful as 3-y-o: may need waiting tactics: trained until after fifth start by G. Huffer: consistent. *Miss J. Thorne.*

AUTONOMOUS 5 b.g. Milford 119–Mandrian 103 (Mandamus 120) [1989 10.2g — §
9f 10m 12.3m³ 16.5g* 15m⁴ 16.2m³ 16.5m⁴ 19f* 15.8g⁴ 16.2m⁴ 18m⁶ 15g a16g a14g³
1990 a14g³] lengthy gelding: carries condition: poor handicapper: stays 19f, at least in slowly-run race: acts on firm and dead going: visored twice, blinkered last 3 outings: has run well when sweating: sold 1,000 gns Doncaster September Sales: unreliable. *D. W. Chapman.*

AUTRE AMIE 3 ch.f. Blushing Scribe (USA) 107–Soho 63 (Camden Town 125) —
[1989 NR 1990 10.6s 10g 12.2m⁶ 8m 8f] 450F: leggy filly: first reported foal: dam lightly-raced daughter of Prix Morny and French 1000 Guineas winner Solitude: no form in maidens, claimer and handicaps: visored last 2 starts, sweating and slowly away on first occasion. *J. M. Jefferson.*

AUTUMNAL (IRE) 2 ch.f. (Feb 22) Fast Topaze (USA) 128–Awatef (Ela-Mana- 66
Mou 132) [1990 7m 7d] rather close-coupled filly: first foal: dam poor French maiden from good family: well backed, never able to challenge in maiden at Ayr: had shaped promisingly in moderately-run similar event at Salisbury earlier in September. *W. J. Haggas.*

AUTUMN MORNING 3 b.g. Elegant Air 119–Short And Sharp 88 (Sharpen Up —
127) [1989 7m 7.6m 7m 1990 10g 12m 14g] strong, rangy gelding: well beaten, in handicaps and claimer as 3-y-o: bred to stay 1¼m: visored final start. *T. M. Jones.*

AUTUMN VINE (USA) 3 ch.f. Desert Wine (USA)–Orange Leaf 100 (Thatch 70
(USA) 136) [1989 NR 1990 a7g 8g a7g* a8g⁵] $77,000Y: smallish, good-quartered filly: fourth foal: half-sister to a winnner in North America by Super Concorde: dam, 8.5f winner here later successful in USA, is half-sister to Jacinth: made all in maiden at Southwell: ridden by 7-lb claimer, led 6f in handicap (moved moderately down) there later in July: should stay 1m: sold 3,400 gns Newmarket Autumn Sales. *J. M. H. Gosden.*

AUVILLAR (USA) 2 br.c. (Feb 6) Temperence Hill (USA)–Exquisita (USA) —
(Cougar (CHI)) [1990 6m 6s 6f⁵] $35,000Y: compact colt: moderate walker: has a roundish action: second foal: dam ran 7 times: little worthwhile form in maidens: sweating final start: may well do better over 1m +. *J. W. Watts.*

AVERON 10 b.g. Averof 123–Reluctant Maid 94 (Relko 136) [1989 14.8s 1990 —
a16g⁵] tall, workmanlike gelding: lightly-raced handicapper: probably stays 1¾m: used to go particularly well on heavy going: blinkered once. *C. P. Wildman.*

AVE VALEQUE (USA) 2 ch.c. (Mar 28) Diesis 133–Hail Proudly (USA) 76
(Francis S) [1990 6g⁵ 6f² 6f² 6g 8d⁶ 7.6v] $200,000Y: sturdy, lengthy colt: half-brother to several winners, including prolific minor stakes performer Triocala (by Trijet): dam ran once: modest maiden: worth a try at 7f: acts on firm and dead (unsuited by heavy) ground: visored final 2 starts: finds little off bridle: sold to join Mrs N. Macauley 13,000 gns Doncaster November Sales. *M. R. Stoute.*

AVISHAYES (USA) 3 b.c. Al Nasr (FR) 126–Rose Goddess (Sassafras (FR) 67 §
135) [1989 NR 1990 10m⁴ 10g 10.1m 11.7m 11.7g 10m³ 12g 10g² 10.6s 10.2s]
$275,000Y: big, lengthy colt: somewhat unfurnished: moderate mover: fourth foal: brother to fair 1987 2-y-o 7f winner Shaybani and half-brother to smart 1986 2-y-o 6f to 1m winner Sanam (by Golden Act): dam unraced daughter of half-sister to Caro:

modest form when placed in claimers, carrying head high and to one side on second occasion: tailed off in apprentice handicap and seller afterwards: stays 1¼m: blinkered sixth to ninth starts: trained until after ninth by G. Harwood: ungenuine. *Mrs J. R. Ramsden.*

AVOCA HOLMES 3 ch.f. Be My Guest (USA) 126–Bid For Freedom (Run The 56 Gantlet (USA)) [1989 7m⁴ 7g 1990 10m³ 10.1g 11.5m⁶ 12f² 14d 12.5m⁴ a11g 12m² 12m] angular, sparely-made filly: quite modest maiden: worth another try over 1¾m: best efforts on top-of-the-ground: blinkered last 2 starts, pulling hard final one: sold 5,500 gns Newmarket Autumn Sales: rather inconsistent. *Lord John FitzGerald.*

AVONSIDE 3 b.f. Ile de Bourbon (USA) 133–Lady Abernant 90 (Abwah 118) — [1989 5d 6g 7g 7m⁵ 8.5f 8.2s⁴ 10.6d 7d 1990 10m 14g⁴ 12.2d⁴] leggy, sparely-made filly: has runout action: poor plater: out of depth in 1990: should stay well: acts on soft ground: visored 3 times at 2 yrs: sold 800 gns Doncaster October Sales. *J. H. Johnson.*

AVRA (FR) 3 gr.f. Mendez (FR) 128–Vague Bubble (USA) (Vaguely Noble 140) 65 [1989 NR 1990 10g² 10.1m⁵] 52,000Y: rather leggy, close-coupled filly: third foal: closely related to minor French 1m and 8.7f winner Tetrahedron (by Bellypha): dam unraced half-sister to Arctic Tern: quite modest form, taking keen hold, in maidens at Nottingham (moderately run) and Windsor in the summer. *H. R. A. Cecil.*

AVRO ANSON 2 b.c. (May 6) Ardross 134–Tremellick 87 (Mummy's Pet 125) 57 p [1990 8.2s] big, workmanlike colt: fifth foal: half-brother to 1¼m seller winner Cadenette (by Brigadier Gerard) and useful hurdler Lanhydrock (by Tower Walk): dam won 3 times over 5f: backward and green, 18 lengths seventh of 13, staying on, to Red Rainbow in maiden at Haydock in October: will stay at least 1¼m: should improve. *M. J. Camacho.*

AVUNCULAR 3 ch.g. Rousillon (USA) 133–Aunt Judy (Great Nephew 126) [1989 66 NR 1990 8g 10g 10f 10g³ 10m²] 62,000Y: strong, close-coupled gelding: second foal: half-brother to Island Mead (by Pharly), quite useful 7f winner at 2 yrs in 1988: dam well beaten daughter of Juliette Marny: visored, worthwhile form only when placed in handicaps at Nottingham and Lingfield in July: may be ideally suited by return to 1m: sold 8,200 gns Newmarket September Sales and subsequently gelded. *J. H. M. Gosden.*

AWAY FROM REALITY 2 ch.f. (Mar 1) Dreams To Reality (USA) 113– 55 Runaway Girl (FR) (Homeric 133) [1990 7g 8m] 2,600Y: strong, close-coupled filly: sixth reported foal: half-sister to plating-class 1988 1¼m winner Hasty Sarah (by Gone Native) and a winner in USA by Tachypous: dam never ran: plating-class form, never dangerous, in maidens at Kempton and Leicester. *G. A. Huffer.*

AWESOME POWER 4 b.g. Vision (USA)–Majestic Nurse 80 (On Your Mark 71 125) [1989 5v 6g 6f 7f³ 7m⁵ 7g* 7g 1990 7g 7.9m 8s 7.9m⁵ 7d 7g* 7v 7d 7g⁴ a8g²] ex-Irish gelding: half-brother to Irish 1987 2-y-o 1m winner Musical Nurse (by Ballad Rock): dam won Irish Cambridgeshire: won handicap at Galway in September: 10/1 from 5/1, made eye-catching British debut (not knocked about at any stage) when second in claimer at Lingfield (running subject to stewards inquiry, jockey and trainer fined £500) in December: stays 1m: has been tried in blinkers: trained until after ninth outing by M. Cunningham: inconsistent. *C. R. Nelson.*

AWKAS 5 b.g. Busted 134–Moreno (Varano) [1989 13.8d² 12d³ 12d³ 13m* 12m — 1990 12m 14m 12s 15.8d³] workmanlike, good-bodied gelding: moderate mover: modest handicapper at best: show as 5-y-o only on final outing, no extra final 2f: best form at around 1½m: acts on good to firm (though has looked ill at ease on it) and soft going. *G. M. Moore.*

AYAH (USA) 2 b.f. (May 23) Secreto (USA) 128–Native Nurse (USA) 74 p (Graustark) [1990 7g⁵] $400,000Y: leggy, workmanlike filly: closely related to 2 winners, notably Irish Oaks dead-heater Melodist (by The Minstrel) and half-sister to several other winners, best of them high-class middle-distance filly Love Sign (by Spanish Riddle): dam placed in USA: around 3 lengths fifth of 15, pulling hard then staying on, to Fragrant Hill in minor event at Newbury in September: bred to stay middle distances: sure to improve, and win a race. *M. R. Stoute.*

AYODESSA 3 b.f. Lochnager 132–Melody Song 74 (Saintly Song 128) [1989 5d⁶ 59 5d³ 5g² 5m² 5m* 5f³ 5f² 5g⁶ 5m⁴ 5g² 5g 1990 5m 5f⁵ 6m 5g 5g 5m⁶ a5g 5m⁴ 5f³ 6m 6m³ 5f 6g] good-topped filly: quite modest handicapper: ran as if something amiss final start: stays 6f: acts on firm going: twice blinkered, swerving left at start on first occasion: usually taken steadily down. *K. B. McCauley.*

AYR CLASSIC 2 b.f. (Mar 11) Local Suitor (USA) 128–Iyamski (USA) 86 (Baldski 74 (USA)) [1990 5v* 6g* 7f⁶ 6d] 24,000Y: rather angular filly: first foal: dam, 7f and 1m winner, half-sister to smart 1983 Canadian 2-y-o Concorde Prince: modest performer: made virtually all in maiden at Ayr in April and minor event at York in May: had very stiff task final outing, off course almost 3 months before penultimate one: should stay 7f. *J. S. Wilson.*

AYR RAIDER 3 ch.c. Claude Monet (USA) 121–Thimothea (FR) (Timmy My 72 Boy 125) [1989 6f* 6v 6g 1990 8m⁶ 7.2g 6d 7m⁵ 7m⁵ 7g] strong, workmanlike colt: not seen out until late-summer as 3-y-o, easily best efforts when fifth in handicaps at Redcar and Newmarket: worth another try at 1m: acts on firm going: visored last 2 starts. *J. S. Wilson.*

AZADEH (USA) 3 ch.f. Compliance (USA)–Mervat (USA) (Vaguely Noble 140) 98 [1989 8g* 1990 8m³ 8g² 8m² 8m 9f] angular, rather leggy, lengthy filly: fairly useful performer: off course 3½ months then second in moderately-run races for £8,200 handicap at Newbury and minor event at Leicester: behind in valuable handicaps at Ascot and Aqueduct, USA, on last 2 starts: should be suited by 1¼m. *G. Harwood.*

AZIM 3 b.c. Mummy's Pet 125–Dimant Blanche (USA) (Gummo (USA) 117) [1989 — NR 1990 6m 6m] quite attractive colt: has a markedly round action: first foal: dam 5f winner at 2 yrs: well beaten in minor event and maiden: sold 3,200 gns Newmarket July Sales. *A. A. Scott.*

AZUBAH 3 b.f. Castle Keep 121–Louisianalightning (Music Boy 124) [1989 5f³ 67 5m 6g 1990 7f⁶ 7g² 8m⁵ 7f* 8.5d⁵ 8f² 8f² 10m⁴ 10m³ 9g] lengthy, rather sparely-made filly: moderate walker: turns near-fore in: good mover: quite modest handicapper: made all at Carlisle in June: ridden by 7-lb claimer, ran well in 1¼m events at Ripon and Redcar: stays 1¼m: acts on firm going, seems unsuited by dead: often makes the running: winning hurdler. *G. M. Moore.*

AZUL BLUE 2 b.f. (Feb 24) Tina's Pet 121–Sailing Brig (Brigadier Gerard 144) — [1990 5f⁶ 5m 5g 6d 7m] 2,000F: strong, medium-sized filly: has a round action: second reported live foal: dam never ran: poor form in maidens and a claimer. *N. Bycroft.*

AZUREUS (IRE) 2 ch.c. (Mar 24) Horage 124–Effortless (Try My Best (USA) 86 130) [1990 6g² 7g⁵ 6m² 6s⁵ 6f* 7h² 7g⁵ 6d³ 6d 10.2s⁶] IR 6,500F, IR 16,500Y: strong, attractive colt: thrived physically: first foal: dam Irish 9f winner: much improved colt: made all in nursery at Ayr in July: ran very well in similar events next 3 starts: best at 6f or 7f: acts on hard and dead ground: suitable mount for apprentice: game and genuine. *J. S. Wilson.*

AZZAAM (USA) 3 ro.c. Chief's Crown (USA)–Princess Oola (USA) (Al 114 p Hattab (USA)) [1989 6m³ 7m³ 7g* 7m⁴ 7d* 1990 9g 10.2g⁶ 10m* 12s*]

Azzaam's performance in the William Hill November Handicap at Doncaster was one of the best in handicap company all season, rivalling Anshan's in the Ladbroke European Free Handicap at Newmarket back in the spring. He won what had appeared beforehand to be a wide-open contest by three and a half lengths from Army of Stars, having the other twenty-two runners strung out like washing. Azzaam, previously untried over the distance, was given a good, enterprising ride by Carson. Soon racing prominently, switched to the outside of the track down the back straight in search of better ground, he was sent on about a mile from home, and from over two furlongs out he never looked like being caught, ridden along with hands and heels. Azzaam had gone into the race an improving sort, more lightly raced than the majority of his rivals. Muscle trouble followed by the dry

William Hill November Handicap, Doncaster—Azzaam has them well strung out

summer hampered his training, and it was mid-August before he was able to reappear. He failed to make the frame in competitive handicaps on his first two starts, though giving the distinct impression that he still retained plenty of ability, then comfortably won a similar event at Newmarket in October. Azzaam will be in training as a four-year-old and, if all remains well with him, he may well improve enough to win in pattern company.

	Azzaam (USA) (ro.c. 1987)	

Chief's Crown (USA) (b 1982)	Danzig (b 1977)	Northern Dancer Pas de Nom
	Six Crowns (ch 1976)	Secretariat Chris Evert
Princess Oola (USA) (b 1978)	Al Hattab (ro 1966)	The Axe II Abyssinia
	Courtly Dee (b 1968)	Never Bend Tulle

Azzaam cost Hamdan Al-Maktoum 425,000 dollars at the Fasig-Tipton Saratoga Select Yearling Sale in August 1988. He's the third reported foal of Princess Oola, the dam of four winners now including Azzaam's close relative Balwa (by Danzig). Princess Oola, a minor eight-and-a-half-furlong stakes winner at four years, is a half-sister to the leading American filly Althea. A tall, close-coupled colt with a sharp action, Azzaam has won on good to firm ground but goes particularly well on soft. He stays a mile and a half well, and has won when sweating and a bit on edge. *J. L. Dunlop.*

B

BAATISH (USA) 2 b.c. (Feb 4) Slew O' Gold (USA)–Shukey (USA) (Key To **80** The Mint (USA)) [1990 5.1g³ 7m⁵ 8.2s² 8d*] $125,000Y: good-quartered colt: has scope: half-brother to 1985 2-y-o 7f winner Elwadhna (by Sir Ivor) and 2 winners in USA by Raise A Native: dam 1m stakes winner out of champion filly Shuvee: sweating and on edge, made all, showing improved form, in maiden at Edinburgh in October, beating Noble Society by 3 lengths: will stay 1¼m: acts on soft ground. *H. Thomson Jones.*

BABAROOMS PARADISE (NZ) 3 b.f. Babaroom (USA)–Our Paradise (NZ) — (Belmura 112) [1989 NR 1990 8f 12.5m⁴ 12m a12g⁶ 12h³] leggy New Zealand-bred filly: has round action: no worthwhile form on flat, including in claimer and handicap: winning claiming hurdler. *J. R. Jenkins.*

BABA'S LADY (NZ) 3 b.f. Babaroom (USA)–Windsor Lady (NZ) (Silver Dream — 107) [1989 NR 1990 12m 12m 10f 12.2f⁴] leggy, plain New Zealand-bred filly: has a round action: no worthwhile form on flat: may prove best short of 1½m: winning hurdler. *J. R. Jenkins.*

BABICOS 3 b.f. Free State 125–Chellaston Park 117 (Record Token 128) [1989 **55** NR 1990 6f³ 6f⁴ 7f⁶ 8m] 40,000Y: workmanlike filly: first foal: dam sprinter: plating-class maiden: stays 7f. *Sir Mark Prescott.*

BACHELOR BOY 2 b.g. (Apr 22) Ballacashtal (CAN)–Miss Solo (Runnymede **49** 123) [1990 6g 6d⁵ 6g 6d] leggy, close-coupled, sparely-made gelding: has a round action: seventh reported foal: half-brother to 7f to 9f handicapper Single (by Jellaby): dam poor plater: poor form in maidens. *W. G. R. Wightman.*

BACHELOR'S PET 4 b.g. Petorius 117–Smile For Me Diane (Sweet Revenge **43** 129) [1989 8g⁴ 7m² 7f a7g a10g³ 1990 a8g] sturdy, close-coupled gelding: plating-class handicapper at best: best form at up to 1m: acts on good to firm going: visored (swerved left stalls) once at 2 yrs, blinkered first 3 starts in 1989. *J. D. Thomas.*

BACK RAISE (USA) 3 ch.c. Raise A Man (USA)–Double Polite (USA) **49** (Nodouble (USA)) [1989 6s 7m 6g 1990 7f 9m 8f 8.2g³ 9m a8g] workmanlike colt: plating-class maiden: creditable staying-on third at Hamilton, best effort in handicaps as 3-y-o: hampered early when tailed off final outing, in July: should stay beyond 1m: seems to need some give in the ground. *S. G. Norton.*

BAJUN DOMINO 2 b.f. (May 10) Dominion 123–Ilfet 76 (Thatch (USA) 136) — [1990 6d] leggy filly: third foal: dam 2-y-o 5f winner out of half-sister to top-class 1971 French staying 2-y-o First Bloom: tailed off in autumn maiden at Lingfield: sold 800 gns Newmarket Autumn Sales. *N. A. Callaghan.*

Hamdan Al-Maktoum's "Balaat"

BAKER CONTRACT   5 ch.g. Roman Warrior 132–Toe Tapper 73 (Record Run   —
127) [1989 6f 5m 5h 6f 1990 a7g 5f 5m 7m] big, workmanlike gelding: no longer of
much account: blinkered once at 3 yrs: wears bandages. *J. M. Bradley.*

BAKILANI (FR)   3 b.c. Darshaan 133–Baykara (Direct Flight) [1989 10v 1990 105
11.5g² 12d* 12m²] third foal: half-brother to 2 French winners, including 4-y-o 1½m
winner Balasani (by Labus): dam, French 3-y-o 1m winner on only start, is out of
half-sister to smart French middle-distance stayer Budapest: won maiden at
Maisons-Laffitte in April: finished lame when 2 lengths second of 7 to Top Waltz in
Prix Hocquart at Longchamp and not seen out again. *A. de Royer-Dupré, France.*

BALAAT (USA)   2 b.c. (Mar 28) Northern Baby (CAN) 127–Bar J Gal (USA) (Key   95
To The Mint (USA)) [1990 6f² 7g* 8m² 7m²] leggy, rather angular colt: moderate
mover: third foal: closely related to quite modest Sail (by Topsider): dam second
over 6f in USA, is half-sister to French 1m winner and very useful American
middle-distance stayer Properantes: fairly useful performer: won maiden at
Newbury in August: runner-up after to Selkirk in listed race at Goodwood and
Kimbers in minor event at Ascot: will stay 1¼m: gives impression ill at ease on
top-of-the-ground. *P. T. Walwyn.*

BALANCED REALM (USA)   7 b.g. Lines of Power (USA)–Brown Hare   40
(USA) (Coursing) [1989 a7g 1990 a5g⁵ a7g⁵ a7g 10.8m 8m 6d a7g⁵ a6g 8f]
workmanlike gelding: poor maiden: should stay 1m: blinkered sixth to eighth
outings: wears bandages. *T. Casey.*

BALAO   4 ch.f. Mr Fluorocarbon 126–Bombay Duck 65 (Ballyciptic 122) [1989 7s   —
12.2d 10m⁶ 10f 1990 12m] leggy, close-coupled filly: plater: stays 1¼m: best efforts
on a sound surface. *R. Hollinshead.*

79

BALASANI (FR) 4 b.c. Labus (FR)–Baykara (Direct Flight) [1989 12v³ 12s* 8g   **58** ?
8m⁵ 1990 10f 11.7g 11.7g 14m⁴ 12m³ 14g⁵ 12m 11.5g] sturdy colt: carries plenty of
condition: quite modest form at best in handicaps as 4-y-o: stays 1¾m: blinkered
final outing: has found little, and is one to treat with caution. *J. R. Jenkins.*

BALDSKI BOY (USA) 2 b. or br.c. (May 2) Baldski (USA)–Starlet Annie   **60**
(USA) (Silent Screen (USA)) [1990 8m⁶ a8g⁶ a8g] medium-sized, plain colt: first
foal: dam, maiden, is half-sister to a Grade 1 winner at up to 13f in USA: shaped well
when keeping-on sixth of 13 to Orujo in maiden at Leicester on debut: below that
form on all-weather after, running poorly final start. *J. M. P. Eustace.*

BALIGAY 5 b.m. Balidar 133–Gaygo Lady 113 (Gay Fandango (USA) 132) [1989   **58**
7v 7f 8f 8m 7f³ 8f 8.3m 1990 9f 8m 7f² 7f⁴ 7.6g⁵ 7m* 6f* 6h⁴ 7m* 7m] lengthy,
workmanlike mare: moderate mover: quite modest handicapper: won at Chepstow
in July and August (making all) and Salisbury in between: probably best at 6f or 7f:
acts well on top-of-the-ground: usually blinkered: good mount for claimer. *R. J.
Hodges.*

BALIGH 3 b.c. Sadler's Wells (USA) 132–Santa's Sister (USA) 104 (Middle   **95**
Brother) [1989 8m⁴ 8g* 8g² 1990 12m 10m³ 10.2s²] rangy, attractive colt: won
3-runner maiden at York and second in Racing Post Trophy at Newcastle as 2-y-o:
not seen out until October in 1990, placed in minor events at Leicester and
Doncaster: will stay 1½m: acts on soft going: stays in training. *J. L. Dunlop.*

BALI LADY 3 b.f. Balidar 133–Silk's Suggestion (Shantung 132) [1989 6g⁴ 1990   **79**
7m² 7g⁵] lengthy filly: 33/1, caught eye finishing really well when beaten ½ length
by Rahaam in maiden (moved moderately down) at Newmarket in April: 10/1,
sweating and unimpressive in appearance, pulled hard and weakened quickly when
well-beaten last of 5 in £11,100 contest there following month: stays 7f well. *J. R.
Shaw.*

BALISHY 3 ch.f. Shy Groom (USA)–Bally 74 (Balidar 133) [1989 5f⁵ 5h* 6m⁶   **73** §
6m* 6f⁵ 6g⁴ 6f² 6f⁴ 1990 6f⁵ 7d² 8f 7f⁴ 6m² 5.8f² 6d] leggy, good-topped filly: shows
a round action: modest performer: second in claimer and handicap: stays 7f: acts on
firm and dead going: has hung and looked irresolute: not one to trust. *R. J. Holder.*

BALI SUNSET 4 b.f. Balidar 133–Orange Silk 68 (Moulton 128) [1989 6g* 6f⁴   **61**
6f⁴ 5g⁵ 8f⁵ 6g⁶ 6s 6m 1990 5g² 5m² 6m² 6g* 5d⁴ 6m 6m 6m 5m⁵ 5g 5d] lengthy,
workmanlike filly: has a rather round action: quite modest handicapper: generally
ran well in first half of season and won at Hamilton in June: effective at 5f and 6f: has
given impression is unsuited by firm ground: has run well for apprentice. *G. M.
Moore.*

BALI SURFER 2 ch.c. (Apr 24) Pharly (FR) 130–Miss Kuta Beach 91 (Bold Lad   **74**
(IRE) 133) [1990 6g 6f³ 8d 7f* 7v⁵] compact colt: third foal: dam 6f and 1¼m winner,
is half-sister to very useful 1m and 9f winner Bali Dancer: modest performer: made
all in maiden at Brighton in October: possibly suited by 7f: acts on firm ground, and
seems unsuited by soft: sold 13,000 gns Newmarket Autumn Sales. *G. Wragg.*

BALKAN LEADER 6 b.g. Balidar 133–Perfect Lady 85 (Sovereign Lord 120)   **65**
[1989 5m 5m* 5f* 5f² 5m⁴ 5m 5m* 5m² 5g⁶ 5.6g 5f⁵ 1990 5f⁶ 5g 5m 5s⁵] strong,
compact gelding: won 3 handicaps in 1989: below his best as 6-y-o, and not seen out
after May: best at 5f on a sound surface: usually blinkered: often apprentice ridden:
usually races up with pace: has worn a tongue strap: sold 1,500 gns Newmarket
Autumn Sales. *J. G. FitzGerald.*

BALLAD DANCER 5 ch.g. Ballad Rock 122–Manx Image (Dancer's Image   **32**
(USA)) [1989 5g⁶ 6v 11.7d⁶ 7.6m 6f 6g³ 6f 6f⁶ 6m 7g 6m 6d 8v⁶ 6g 1990 10.8m 8m
a7g⁴ a7g] angular, lengthy gelding: moderate mover: fair winner as 3-y-o, but has
deteriorated: best form at 6f or 7f: needs an easy surface: blinkered once at 4 yrs:
wore crossed noseband final outing: sometimes starts slowly: has joined E. Alston.
G. Price.

BALLAD TUNE 5 b.g. Ballad Rock 122–Haut Lafite (Tamerlane 128) [1989 NR   **—**
1990 6g 7f a6g a5g] seems no longer of much account: possibly temperamental. *S. R.
Bowring.*

BALLAFORT 5 b.m. Ballacashtal (CAN)–Fortune's Fancy 48 (Workboy 123)   **47** d
[1989 6f⁶ 6f5.8h 6f⁵ 6f⁴ 7f 6g⁵ 6m 6f² 6m⁶ 6g 1990 a7g 10m² 10.8m 8f² 7.6m⁶ 8h³ 7f²
6f 8m 6m 6g⁴ 6d⁵] big, workmanlike mare: easy mover: poor handicapper: finds 6f
on short side nowadays and stays 1¼m: acts on hard and dead going: blinkered and
visored once: bandaged tenth outing: often sweats and gets on toes: didn't find great
deal sixth start. *J. R. Bosley.*

BALLA LAD 3 b.c. Ballacashtal (CAN)–Limerick Lace (Pall Mall 132) [1989 7m —
a8g 1990 7.2d 10.6s] quite attractive colt: has a round action: well beaten in maidens
and apprentice handicap. *J. M. Bradley.*

BALLANTRAE 6 b.m. Creetown 123–Tecllyn 97 (Technion 96) [1989 NR 1990 23
a12g a13g² a12g a13g] sturdy, deep-girthed mare: moderate mover: bad maiden:
probably best short of 1½m: yet to race on soft going, acts on any other. *R. Voorspuy.*

BALLAROCK 4 b.f. Ballacashtal (CAN)–Rockery 91 (Track Spare 125) [1989 8s —
7.6m 7g 1990 8f 7f 6f 8f 10.1m] lengthy, workmanlike filly: carries condition:
moderate mover: of little account. *J. C. Fox.*

BALLASECRET 2 ch.f. (Mar 30) Ballacashtal (CAN)–Soft Secret (Most Secret 67
119) [1990 5m 6d a5g³ a5g³] 3,000Y: lengthy filly: third reported foal: dam winner in
Belgium: quite modest maiden: should stay 6f: has run well for 7-lb claimer. *R.
Dickin.*

BALLASTRAND 2 b.f. (May 17) Ballacashtal (CAN)–Tina's Magic (Carnival 43
Night) [1990 5f³dis 5f4 5.8f4 5f 6s 6d] leggy filly: has a markedly round action: fourth
foal: half-sister to 1988 2-y-o 5f winner Jomana (by Roman Warrior): dam won
novice selling hurdle: poor maiden: faced very stiff tasks in nurseries on final 2
starts. *J. C. Fox.*

BALLERINA ROSE 3 b.f. Dreams To Reality (USA) 113–Ragtime Rose —
(Ragstone 128) [1989 NR 1990 7m 7m 8g 6g] leggy filly: has a round action: third
foal: half-sister to fair 5f and 6f winner Supreme Rose (by Frimley Park) and 5-y-o 7f
winner Mel's Rose (by Anfield): dam ran 3 times: no show, including in handicap. *E.
A. Wheeler.*

BALLETA (USA) 3 b.f. Lyphard (USA) 132–Navajo Princess (USA) (Drone) 87
[1989 NR 1990 7g⁶ 10g² 10.6d 10g*] leggy, attractive filly: sixth reported foal: sister
to outstanding Dancing Brave: dam won 16 races in USA from 3 yrs to 5 yrs at up to
8.5f: favourite, won maiden at Newbury in October, always close up and tending to
idle: stays 1¼m: possibly unsuited by dead ground: wore tongue strap second start:
to be trained by R. McAnally in USA. *R. Charlton.*

BALLET CLASSIQUE (USA) 3 b.f. Sadler's Wells (USA) 132–Estaciones 84
(USA) (Sonny Fleet) [1989 NR 1990 10.5g² 11f² 11.5g² 12g² 11.5g³ 10.2g4 12m* 11g²
12s] $75,000Y: leggy, workmanlike filly: has a fluent, round action: half-sister to
Oaks third New Coins (by New Prospect) and useful stayer Kublai (by
Effervescing): dam won over 1m: fair performer: won maiden at Folkestone in
October: beaten head in listed race at Toulouse next start, long way in November
Handicap at Doncaster on final one: stays 1½m: seems unsuited by extremes of
going: lacks turn of foot. *B. Hanbury.*

BALLET RUSSE (USA) 3 b.f. Nijinsky (CAN) 138–Mariella (USA) 106 64
(Roberto (USA) 131) [1989 NR 1990 12g⁶ 12.2m³] $700,000Y: lengthy, good-
quartered filly: moderate walker and mover: first foal: dam, middle-distance stayer,
is half-sister to 2 very useful winners, including middle-distance filly Elect, and
daughter of Oaks winner Monade: 9/2, about 8 lengths third of 7 to Golden Treasury
in maiden at Catterick in July: will be suited by stiffer test of stamina and more
galloping track: retained by trainer 6,000 gns Newmarket December Sales.
L.Cumani.

BALLET TEACHER 2 b.f. (Feb 1) Lochnager 132–Tarte Aux Pommes 75 —
(Song 132) [1990 6g 5m 7.5g 6m 7f] 5,600Y: angular, workmanlike filly: sixth foal:
half-sister to 2 winning sprint platers by Record Token: dam sprinter: poor form in
maidens and sellers: probably doesn't stay 7f: trained first 4 starts by A. Robson:
sold 670 gns Doncaster October Sales. *D. Dutton.*

BALLYDURROW 13 ch.g. Doon 124–Even Tint (Even Money 121) [1989 12m* 52
12g 12h⁶ 10.6g5 12.3f³ 12.3m² 12m5 12m 12f² 13.6f5 12g a11g² 1990 a11g5] big, strong
gelding: fair handicapper at his best: acted on any going: held
up and suited by a strong pace: one-time smart hurdler: tough: dead. *R. F. Fisher.*

BALLY KNIGHT 4 b.g. Balidar 133–Silk's Suggestion (Shantung 132) [1989 67
8.2f 10g a6g a11g 1990 a12g⁶ a8g³ a10g³ a10g⁶ a8g 13g² 16.5m* 16.5g* 16.5f4
16.1m²] smallish, workmanlike gelding: easy winner of handicaps at Doncaster in
June: improved again in similar events at same course (hanging left) and Newmarket (apprentice ridden) later in summer: suited by 2m: acts on firm ground:
visored at 4 yrs on all-weather: sold to join J. White's stable 18,000 gns Newmarket
Autumn Sales. *J. R. Shaw.*

BALLYRAIN (USA) 2 ch.f. (Feb 21) Halo (USA)–Raise Rain (USA) (Raise A 73
Native) [1990 5m* 6m4 a6g² 6m] rather sparely-made, angular filly: second foal:
dam successful at up to 9f, is half-sister to top-class American filly Winning Colors:

modest performer: won maiden at Catterick in June: good second in minor event at Southwell: probably better suited by 6f than 5f and will stay 1m. *P. F. I. Cole.*

BALLY SONG 2 b.c. (May 19) Song 132–Ballyreef (Ballymore 123) [1990 7m 7m] — compact, workmanlike colt: second live foal: half-brother to 3-y-o Derry Reef (by Derrylin): dam poor granddaughter of Prix de Diane winner Belle Sicambre: prominent 4f in maiden at Chepstow in October: carrying condition and slowly away on debut. *R. Hannon.*

BALLYSTATE 2 ch.f. (Feb 9) Ballacashtal (CAN)–Brandenbourg 66 (Le 71 Levanstell 122) [1990 6m 7m 7m³ 9m²] rather angular filly: fifth reported foal: dam won over hurdles: modest maiden: better suited by 9f than 7f. *C. James.*

BALSMO 2 ch.c. (May 12) Absalom 128–Nyeri 104 (Saint Crespin III 132) [1990 5g 62 6m³ 6d 6m² 6m a8g⁵ a6g*] 5,000Y: sturdy, plain colt: brother to winning stayer Grey Gypsy and half-brother to several winners here and abroad, including useful 1986 2-y-o 6f winner White Mischief (by Dance In Time) and useful middle-distance stayer Greatham House (by Run The Gantlet): dam stayed 1½m: blinkered first time, won 12-runner claimer at Southwell after slow start by a short head from Continental Carl: second in Lingfield seller fourth outing: seems suited by 6f. *D. Haydn Jones.*

BALTHUS (USA) 7 b.g. Forli (ARG)–Keep Off 99 (Bold Lad (IRE) 133) [1989 8f — 10f 8f 10.2m⁴ 8m⁶ 1990 10.6m a11g] good-topped gelding: turns fore-feet in: poor walker and moderate mover: won Cambridgeshire Handicap at Newmarket as 4-y-o: little subsequent form: stayed 1¼m: probably unsuited by extremes of going: blinkered at Newmarket and 5 times after: occasionally sweated: sometimes swished tail, and reportedly suffered back trouble: retired. *J. A. Glover.*

BALUOD 3 ch.f. Doulab (USA) 115–June Darling (Junius (USA) 124) [1989 5m⁶ — 1990 5f⁶ 5m⁵ 6f 8.2g⁶ 7f] close-coupled filly: poor maiden: suited by 1m: dead. *G. Lewis.*

BALWA (USA) 2 b.f. (Mar 22) Danzig (USA)–Princess Oola (USA) (Al Hattab 89 (USA)) [1990 5g⁶ 5m* 5m* 5f 5m⁴ 5g] \$375,000Y: smallish, quite attractive filly: fourth reported foal: closely related to 3-y-o Azzaam (by Chief's Crown), successful from 7f (at 2 yrs) to 1½m, and winners by Mr Prospector (in USA) and Alydar: dam 8.5f stakes winner at 4 yrs, is half-sister to top American filly Althea: fairly useful filly: on toes, successful in maiden at York and Charles Heidsieck National Stakes at Sandown in May: creditable fourth to Malvernico in Group 3 event at the Curragh, easily best effort after. *A. A. Scott.*

BALZAON KNIGHT 3 b.g. Alzao (USA) 117–April Sal 65 (Sallust 134) [1989 6m 53 7g a6g a7g 1990 7g 8m 8g 10d³] rather sparely-made, angular gelding: plating-class maiden: not seen out until late-September as 3-y-o, best effort (4/1 from 14/1 and sweating) in claimer at Chepstow second start: blinkered in seller on final one: stays 1m: acts on good to firm going. *P. J. Makin.*

BANANA CUFFLINKS (USA) 4 b.c. Peterhof (USA) 116–Heather Bee — (USA) (Drone) [1989 7d 10.1m 14g 10m 7f² 7.6m 7m⁶ 9g 1990 7f] lengthy, attractive colt: has a fluent, rather round action: quite modest on his day: may well prove suited by 1m: acts on firm going: visored last 5 starts. *J. R. Shaw.*

BANBURY FLYER 2 b.g. (Apr 21) Mummy's Game 120–Haddon Anna 73 (Dragonara Palace (USA) 115) [1990 5m 6g 5g³ 5m* 5.8d⁴ 5d] leggy gelding: has a quick action: third foal: dam unraced granddaughter of very speedy Granville Greta: modest performer: won nursery at Wolverhampton in October: stays 6f: acts on good to firm ground and dead. *Miss A. L. M. King.*

BANCROFT 3 b.f. Kabour 80–Mrs Buzby 71 (Abwah 118) [1989 NR 1990 6d a6g — a8g] sturdy filly: poor mover: first living foal: dam 6f and 7f winner: well beaten in late-season claimers and maiden. *D. W. Chapman.*

BANDIT COUNTRY 3 b.g. Fairy King (USA)–Hillberry Corner 70 (Atan) [1989 — NR 1990 10.1g 10m 10m⁶] IR 7,000Y: smallish gelding: half-brother to several winners, including very useful 1978 French 2-y-o 5f and 7f winner Chrisfranol (by African Sky): dam 2-y-o 5f winner: never dangerous in varied events though showed ability when sixth in claimer at Newbury in June: may be worth a try over shorter: sold 900 gns Newmarket Autumn Sales. *M. E. D. Francis.*

BAND OF HOPE (USA) 3 ch.f. Dixieland Band (USA)–Reflection 111 (Mill 67 § Reef (USA) 141) [1989 7m 1990 8g⁵ 8g⁴ 8f 7.3m] workmanlike, rather plain filly: quite modest maiden, not seen out after June: best efforts over 1m with give in the ground: ran badly in visor last 2 outings: one to avoid. *I. A. Balding.*

BAND ON THE RUN 3 ch.c. Song 132–Sylvanette (FR) 70 (Silver Shark 129) **80**
[1989 5m5 5d4 6d6 1990 6m5 6m* 7g* 7.6f2 8m2 8.2m3 7.6g] rather angular,
good-topped colt: poor mover: fair performer: won apprentice race (made all) at
Pontefract and handicap at Ayr in June: stays 1m: acts on firm going. *B. A. McMahon.*

BANHAM COLLEGE 4 b.g. Tower Walk 130–Baby Flo 67 (Porto Bello 118) **51**
[1989 10m 1990 5m2 7m 5d] robust, rather dipped-backed gelding: moderate mover:
first form when slow-starting second of 20 in seller at Beverley: faced stiff tasks in
handicaps later in autumn: should be suited by further than 5f. *B. A. McMahon.*

BANKER MASON (USA) 4 b.c. Sadler's Wells (USA) 132–Alwah (USA) —
(Damascus (USA)) [1989 8.2s2 7d 6m 8g a10g2 a11g3 a10g* a10g4 1990 a12g 8.5f6 10f
12f a7g] smallish, sparely-made colt: has a rather round action: won maiden claimer
at Lingfield late on as 3-y-o: no form in first half of 1990: stays 1¼m: possibly
unsuited by firm ground, acts on any other: sold out of N. Callaghan's stable 7,000
gns Doncaster January Sales. *D. Yeoman.*

BANKROLL 3 b.g. Chief Singer 131–Very Nice (FR) (Green Dancer (USA) 132) **77**
[1989 7g 7m4 7m4 7.5f* 7g6 8m 1990 7m4 12.3d 8g 10g4 12m4 12d 9m4] tall,
workmanlike gelding: shows a round action: fair handicapper: good fourth in
apprentice race at Ascot fifth start: stays 1½m: acts on firm going, probably
unsuited by a soft surface. *C. A. Cyzer.*

BANKSY BOY (IRE) 2 ch.g. (Feb 27) Gorytus (USA) 132–Kampai (General **56**
Assembly (USA)) [1990 5f3 6g 6f6 6m 7f4 7g 10.6s 8d6] IR 10,500F, IR 50,000Y:
leggy, rather angular gelding: second foal: half-brother to Irish 3-y-o Dash of
Courage (by Final Straw), 7f winner at 2 yrs: dam ran 4 times in Ireland: moderate
plater: should stay beyond 7f: blinkered 5 times. *M. W. Easterby.*

BANK VIEW 5 ch.g. Crofter (USA) 124–Stony Ground (Relko 136) [1989 10.4m —
1990 12s] stocky, workmanlike gelding: poor mover: modest winner as 3-y-o: has
run just twice on flat since, needing only outing in 1990: should prove no effective at
1¼m as 1m: possibly needs an easy surface nowadays: has been tried in blinkers and
visor. tends to get on edge: much improved hurdler in 1989/90. *N. Tinkler.*

BANTEL BAMBINA 2 gr.f. (Mar 11) Bold Owl 101–Bantel Baby (Warpath 113) **41**
[1990 5g 7f 5m2 6m 5g3 5m3] plain filly: second foal: dam and grandam of no account:
poor maiden: should be suited by further than 5f: blinkered final start. *R. Allan.*

BANTEL BARONET 2 b.g. (Apr 3) Tickled Pink 114–Bantel Bouquet 46 (Red —
Regent 123) [1990 5d] 1,600Y: sturdy gelding: moderate walker: first foal: dam
sprint maiden at 2 yrs: backward and slowly away in seller at Catterick (moved badly
down) in July. *R. Allan.*

BANTON LOCH 3 br.g. Lochnager 132–Balgownie 43 (Prince Tenderfoot **55**
(USA) 126) [1989 6f 6g3 7v4 8g2 8d 1990 8.2s 8v 8g 7g3 7g 8.2d] lengthy,
good-topped gelding: plating-class maiden: third in handicap at Wolverhampton,
easily best effort as 3-y-o: stays 1m: best efforts on good ground. *C. Tinkler.*

BARACHOIS PRINCESS (USA) 3 b.f. Barachois (CAN)–Egregious (USA) **62**
(Barbizon) [1989 6m5 7m5 1990 8f3 8.2m4 10.4g 8g] workmanlike filly: moderate
mover: quite modest maiden: ran moderately in handicap final outing: suited by 1m:
acts on firm going. *R. Hollinshead.*

BARAKAT 3 b.f. Bustino 136–Rosia Bay 102 (High Top 131) [1989 NR 1990 10m3 **93**
12m3 11.5d2 14f* 14.6g* 16m5] 135,000Y: big, lengthy filly: sixth foal: half-sister to
very smart middle-distance performers Ibn Bey (by Mill Reef) and Roseate Tern (by
Blakeney) and 1984 2-y-o 5f winner Cerise Bouquet (by Mummy's Pet): dam, miler,
is half-sister to Teleprompter: won poor maiden at Yarmouth in July and £18,400
handicap (well backed, showing improved form) at Doncaster in September:
disappointing favourite for £7,700 handicap at Newmarket final start: stayed 1¾m:
seemed suited by an easy surface: visits Zilzal. *A. C. Stewart.*

BARAKISH 3 b.c. Mummy's Pet 125–Blissful Evening (Blakeney 126) [1989 6m **77** +
6g2 7g2 7v* 8g3 1990 7d3 7g6 10m] lengthy, attractive colt: fair handicapper:
unlucky-third at Chester in May: favourite, hampered early and one pace from 3f out
when fair sixth in £20,000 event at York week later: ran badly after lengthy absence
on only subsequent outing: stays 1m: needs give in the ground and acts well on
heavy: sold 12,000 gns Newmarket Autumn Sales. *M. R. Stoute.*

BARANYKA 3 b.f. Horage 124–Sister Jinks 88 (Irish Love 117) [1989 6m 7.5f3
7f* 7m 1990 8.5m 7m 7d] sparely-made filly: quite modest at best: has run
moderately since winning as 2-y-o, favourite for seller second start in 1990: stays
7.5f: has joined M. Wilkinson. *M. H. Tompkins.*

BARBARA'S CUTIE   2 ch.f. (May 26) Tina's Pet 121–Eucharis 41 (Tickled Pink   —
114) [1990 5m 5f⁶ 6m] good-quartered, close-coupled filly: first foal: dam, maiden,
stayed 1m: poor form in maiden and sellers: should prove better at 6f than 5f. *M.
Blanshard.*

BARBARY REEF (IRE)   2 b.g. (Apr 13) Sarab 123–Brown's Cay 71   46 p
(Formidable (USA) 125) [1990 6f 7f⁵ 6d] 2,000Y: strong gelding: third foal:
half-brother to 3-y-o 1¼m winner Superetta (by Superlative) and a winner in
Sweden: dam placed over 1m at 2 yrs, is half-sister to smart stayer Antler: 9 lengths
fifth of 16 to Time Line in maiden auction at Chepstow in September: off course
nearly 2 months after: looks sort to do better. *G. H. Eden.*

BARBEZIEUX   3 b.c. Petong 126–Merchantmens Girl 58 (Klairon 131) [1989 7g   55
5g 1990 a7g 5f* 6g 5d⁴ 5m⁶ 5f 5m 5f 5f 5d 5g 5m] strong, workmanlike colt:
moderate mover: plating-class handicapper: won at Leicester in March: best efforts
fourth (raced alone, ridden by 7-lb claimer) and fifth starts: ran poorly after: best at
5f: acts on firm and dead ground: sold 2,000 gns Ascot November Sales. *D. A.
Wilson.*

BARCHAM   3 b.g. Blakeney 126–La Pythie (FR) 89 (Filiberto (USA) 123) [1989   —
7g 7m* 7m 1990 10g 12.5g⁶ 12g 11.5m] leggy, quite good-topped gelding: quite
modest performer: stays 1½m: sweating and blinkered final start. *G. A. Pritchard-
Gordon.*

BARDOLPH (USA)   3 b.c. Golden Act (USA)–Love To Barbara (USA)   65
(Stevward) [1989 7.3g⁵ 7f⁴ 6h* a8g² 1990 12m⁶ 11.7m 11.5g 8d 8m⁵ 10g⁴] compact
colt: modest handicapper: stays 1½m: acts on hard ground: blinkered last 3 starts:
has run well for 7-lb claimer, and when sweating and edgy: bandaged behind final
start at 2 yrs. *P. F. I. Cole.*

BARELY BLACK   2 br.g. (Apr 10) Lidhame 109–Louisa Anne 73 (Mummy's Pet   —
125) [1990 6g 7f 5s] big, leggy gelding: fourth foal: half-brother to 1988 2-y-o 5f and
7f winner Nite Nite Louisa (by Night Shift) and a winner in Belgium: dam sprinter:
well beaten in varied company: backward first 2 starts. *J. S. Haldane.*

BARESI (IRE)   2 b.c. (Mar 23) Alzao (USA) 117–Hedwige (African Sky 124)   — p
[1990 6g] IR 24,000F, 110,000Y: half-brother to one-time useful 5f and 6f winner
Sylvan Tempest (by Strong Gale), fair over 1¼m, and a winner in Italy: dam ran
once: favourite, slowly away and never able to challenge in large-field autumn
maiden at Yarmouth: clearly thought capable of better. *H. R. A. Cecil.*

BARFORD LAD   3 b.g. Nicholas Bill 125–Grace Poole (Sallust 134) [1989 NR   82
1990 8m 8.2s² 10g⁶ 8g 8m 7g⁴ 10f² 8v 8d*] 15,000Y: good-topped gelding:
half-brother to 3 winners, including modest 1988 2-y-o 5.1f winner Ranweli Reef (by
Superlative) and 5f to 9f winner Olore Malle (by Camden Town): dam won at 1m to
1½m in Ireland: fair form: best effort winning handicap at Doncaster in October:
stays 1¼m: acts on any going, with possible exception of heavy: visored (pulled
hard) fifth outing: gelded after final one: below form when sweating and edgy. *G. A.
Huffer.*

BARICHSTE   2 ch.g. (Mar 1) Electric 126–Be Sharp 85 (Sharpen Up 127) [1990   51
6s⁵ 6f a7g³ 8.2d 8d] 1,900Y: leggy gelding: third living foal: brother to 3-y-o 1m
seller winner Lilly Camilly: dam 5f winner: plating-class maiden: probably stays 1m.
B. A. McMahon.

BARKERVILLE (USA)   2 b.c. (May 14) Mr Prospector (USA)–Euryanthe   88 p
(USA) (Nijinsky (CAN) 138) [1990 7m³] $1,200,000Y: tall, leggy, unfurnished colt:
has scope: half-brother to several winners, including smart 1982 2-y-o 6f and 1m
winner and French Oaks third Air Distingue (by Sir Ivor): dam unraced sister to
high-class middle-distance stayer Caucasus: co-favourite but green, ½-length
third of 18, headed soon after leading 1f out and keeping on really well without being
knocked about unduly, to Environment Friend in maiden at Newmarket in October:
will stay 1m: sure to improve, and win races. *M. R. Stoute.*

BARKSTON SINGER   3 b.f. Runnett 125–Miss Flirt (Welsh Pageant 132)   79 §
[1989 7f⁴ a8g² a8g* 1990 8.5g 7m⁵ 8d² 7f³ 8f 8.2d⁵ 8g] leggy, lightly-made filly: poor
walker: fair handicapper: stays 1m: acts on firm and dead going: ran poorly when
blinkered, tongue tied down and edgy final start: refused to enter stalls fourth
intended outing: mulish at them fifth: difficult ride, has looked temperamental and
isn't one to trust: has joined *J. L. Harris. I. Campbell.*

BARLEY MOW   4 b.g. Wolverlife 115–Ellette 105 (Le Levanstell 122) [1989 7m⁵   —
10m 10.1g 1990 a10g] fifth in maiden at Tipperary on debut at 3 yrs: well beaten
since, in maiden claimer at Lingfield in December: bandaged final start in 1989. *J.
White.*

BARNEY O'NEILL 4 gr.c Ballad Rock 122–Lapis Lazuli 84 (Zeddaan 130) 75
[1989 NR 1990 8.5g⁶ 8g 8g 6g⁶ 8m* 8h* 8f* 8m* 10.2m⁵ 8m 7g⁵ 8d] tall,
workmanlike colt: good walker: half-brother to 3 winners, notably smart 1m to 1¼m
winner Farioffa (by Hotfoot): dam 2-y-o 5f winner, is half-sister to smart Bas Bleu:
progressed very well in summer, winning claimer at Ayr, apprentice handicaps at
Carlisle and Thirsk and slowly-run handicap at Pontefract: effective at 7f and 1m:
acts well on top-of-the-ground: idles in front: changed hands 25,000 gns Doncaster
September Sales. *J. J. O'Neill.*

BARON CORVO (USA) 6 ch.g. Sir Ivor 135–A Medium Hello (USA) (Droll —
Role) [1989 NR 1990 17.4d 16.5d a14g] robust, round-barrelled gelding: moderate
mover: useful winner in 1987: tailed off in late-season handicaps: looked to finish
lame first of them: suited by a test of stamina. *K. B. McCauley.*

BARONESS GYMCRAK 3 b.f. Pharly (FR) 130–My Therape 112 (Jimmy 62 §
Reppin 131) [1989 6m 6m³ 6g⁴ 1990 5m² 6m 5g 5g² 5m⁴ 6m³ 5g⁵ 5m⁴ 7g⁶ a6g a6g⁵
5d] angular filly: moderate mover: quite modest sprint maiden: acts on good to firm
ground: has swished tail and appeared ungenerous: sold 6,400 gns Newmarket
Autumn Sales. *M. H. Easterby.*

BAROQUE ANGEL (IRE) 2 b.f. (Mar 3) Tate Gallery (USA) 117–Blues In —
The Night (Cure The Blues (USA)) [1990 6d] IR 9,000Y: first foal: dam French 9f
winner: well beaten in maiden at Folkestone in November. *D. A. Wilson.*

BARQAISH 3 br.g. Jalmood (USA) 126–Adeebah (USA) 94 (Damascus (USA)) 68
[1989 NR 1990 8.2g 10g⁴ 8m⁵ 10m⁶ 8g] leggy, quite good-topped gelding: has a quick
action: brother to fair 1988 2-y-o 7f winner Junuh and half-brother to 1½m
winner Jeewan (by Touching Wood): dam 2-y-o 5f winner: modest maiden: will be
suited by return to 1¼m: sold to join N. Ayliffe 7,200 gns Newmarket Autumn Sales.
R. W. Armstrong.

BARRICADE 3 b.g. Viking (USA)–Avebury Ring (Auction Ring (USA) 123) 48 ?
[1989 6m 6g 1990 a8g⁶ 9s⁵ 12.5g⁶ 15g* 15.3g 15d³] small gelding: plater: set modest
pace when winning at Edinburgh (bought in 6,400 gns) in June: well beaten
subsequently: stays 15f: sold to join J. Parkes 7,000 gns Doncaster August Sales. *C.
W. Thornton.*

BARRIES PET 2 gr.f. (May 1) Petong 126–Second Event 86 (Fine Blade (USA) 47
121) [1990 a7g a7g a8g⁵] fourth live foal: half-sister to a winner in Holland: dam 5f to
1½m winner, is out of half-sister to Irish 2000 Guineas winner Furry Glen: poor
maiden: apprentice ridden final start, best effort. *M. H. Tompkins.*

BARRISH 4 b.c. Wassl 125–Rowa 83§ (Great Nephew 126) [1989 8s⁴ 8.5g⁵ 10m 90
12f* 12.4g 12g⁶ 1990 12f* 18f2 14m³ 18.4d 16m³ 12d⁴ 12m* 12f² 14m* 12f⁴ 14g⁶ 12g²
13.3g⁶ 12m 12s] angular colt: fairly useful handicapper: had very good season,
winning at Doncaster in March, Newbury in June and Sandown (well-backed
favourite) in July: best form at up to 1¾m: acts on firm and dead going: often sweats
and gets on edge: genuine and consistent: a credit to his trainer. *R. Akehurst.*

BARRON'S BOY 2 b.g. (May 14) Track Barron (USA)–Baltic Leap (USA) 45
(Northern Dancer) [1990 6g a6g a7g 6d a5g] 6,000Y: rather angular gelding: first
foal: dam ran 6 times in North America, is from family of good American filly Sea
Saga, successful at up to 1¼m: poor form in varied events: had stiff tasks in
nurseries last 2 starts. *W. Carter.*

BARRYMORE 3 b.c. Robellino (USA) 127–Screenable (USA) (Silent Screen 87
(USA)) [1989 NR 1990 10g² 10.2g² 10.1m² 10.6d² 12m² 10f² 10f*] IR 42,000Y:
strong, angular colt: moderate mover: second foal: dam minor winner at around 1m
from good family: fairly useful form in maidens, leading close home to land odds at
Brighton in October: wandered under pressure then and hung left in
apprentice race time before: stays 1½m: acts on firm going: below best when set
pace. *L. Cumani.*

BARRYS GAMBLE 4 gr.c. Nishapour (FR) 125–Scoby Lass (Prominer 125) 99
[1989 6g 5g² 5f6 5f5 5m 5g 5f3 5m⁶ 5m 1990 5f* 5f² 5f 6m 5.6g 5m³ 5m 5m 5s]
robust, good-quartered colt: carries plenty of condition: moderate mover, with a
quick action: useful handicapper: comfortably justified favouritism at Doncaster in
March: never able to challenge last 3 outings, bit awkward at stalls and slowly away
when ridden by 7-lb claimer final one: best at 5f on top-of-the-ground: occasionally
blinkered. *T. Fairhurst.*

BARSAC 4 b.c. (Apr 23) Sulaafah (USA) 119–Counsel's Verdict (Firestreak 125) 34
[1990 6g 6g 6g 6m 6d⁶ 7d 6d] smallish, good-quartered colt: sixth foal: half-brother
to 3-y-o 6f winner Spanish Verdict (by King of Spain): dam of little account: bad
maiden: blinkered fifth and sixth starts. *M. D. I. Usher.*

BARSTOX BOY 5 b.g. Touch Boy 109–Siciliana 77 (Sicilian Prince 126) [1989 —
NR 1990 10d 7m] seems no longer of much account: blinkered twice: bandaged on
reappearance: reluctant to go down final outing. *L. J. Barratt.*

BARUD (IRE) 2 b.c. (Mar 9) Persian Bold 123–Pale Moon 58 (Jukebox 120) —
[1990 6g 6m 6d] IR 21,000F, 40,000Y: rather leggy, quite good-topped colt: fourth
foal: brother to Irish 1½m winner Mettle Moon and half-brother to 2 winners,
including 6f seller winner Saturn Man (by Dalsaan): dam stayed 1m, out of very
speedy Rose of Tralee: well beaten in autumn maidens. *C. J. Benstead.*

BASENITE 3 br.f. Mansingh (USA) 120–Iridium 78 (Linacre 133) [1989 6g6 1990 —
6f 8.5g] leggy, rather sparely-made filly: bit backward, no form in maidens and minor
event. *M. A. Jarvis.*

BASHAQ 4 b.c. Jalmood (USA) 126–Welwyn 92 (Welsh Saint 126) [1989 6s 8g 30
5.3h6 6f 7f* 6m 7m 7f6 1990 a7g a10g3 a10g5 9f5 8f4 7f 7.6m 10m 10f2 8h 8h 8f]
good-bodied colt: poor mover: poor handicapper: stays 1¼m: acts on firm going: ran
moderately when blinkered final outing: hung right when winning at 3 yrs: sold
1,450 gns Newmarket Autumn Sales: inconsistent. *C. J. Benstead.*

BASHFUL BOY 5 b.g. Jalmood (USA) 126–Sesta (Artaius (USA) 129) [1989 10v4 89
8m4 11.1m5 10m 1990 10d4 12d5 10m2 12s 10g3 10g2 10.5m6 11s4 10s*] big,
heavy-topped gelding: carries plenty of condition: good mover: quite useful
performer nowadays: reportedly broke blood vessel fourth outing: then ran
creditably in handicaps and claimer prior to winning quite valuable event in French
Provinces: stays 11f: acts on soft going, yet to race on firm. *W. Hastings-Bass.*

BASIC FUN 4 b.f. Teenoso (USA) 135–Sirenivo (USA) 113 (Sir Ivor 135) [1989 —
10s2 10f 10m5 11.7m6 14g4 15g 1990 11g 13g 12g] leggy, rather sparely-made filly:
modest maiden at best: no form on flat in 1990: probably stays 1¾m: unsuited by
top-of-the-ground: winning hurdler in 1989/90. *J. L. Spearing.*

BASIC THOUGHTS 3 b.f. Simply Great (FR) 122–Final Thought (Final Straw —
127) [1989 NR 1990 8m 10.1g a12g4 a10g4 a8g] 10,000Y: small, sturdy filly: first foal:
dam unraced half-sister to Middle Park winner Creag-An-Sgor: no worthwhile form,
including in handicap: should prove better at 1½m than shorter: sold to join Mrs A.
Knight 3,600 gns Doncaster November Sales. *P. T. Walwyn.*

BASTILLE DAY 3 ch.c. Persian Bold 123–Marie Antoinette (Habitat 134) [1989 105
7m* 7g 1990 8m6 12g 12.3g3] IR 52,000Y: compact colt: third foal: half-brother to
Irish 1½m winner Sea Shadow (by Hello Gorgeous): dam, Irish middle-distance
winner, is half-sister to Irish Derby winner Weavers' Hall: odds on, won maiden at
Fairyhouse as 2-y-o: beaten about 2½ lengths behind both Tirol in moderately-run
Irish 2000 Guineas at the Curragh and Nordic Region in Ulster Harp Derby
(blinkered) at Down Royal: unimpressive in coat and mulish, always behind in Ever
Ready Derby: should be suited by at least 1¼m. *T. Stack, Ireland.*

BASTIN (IRE) 2 ch.c. (Apr 3) Alzao (USA) 117–Benita 94 (Roan Rocket 128) 71
[1990 5g4 6f3 7g5 10.6s2 7d a8g5 a8g2] 24,000Y, IR 21,000Y: small colt: moderate
mover: half-brother to several winners, including fairly useful sprinter Red Rosie
(by Red Alert) and 1984 2-y-o 7f winner Maid of Arosa (by Baptism): dam sprinter:
quite modest maiden: stays 1¼m well: acts on soft going. *M. H. Tompkins.*

BATHSHEBA EVERDENE 2 gr.f. (Mar 12) Monsanto (FR) 121–Gill Breeze 34
(Farm Walk 111) [1990 6m 6m4 5.8h6 6d] 1,500Y: sparely-made, dipped-backed filly:
half-sister to several winners, including 7f performer Secret Gill (by Most Secret):
dam unraced: poor maiden: virtually pulled up third start (last for W. G. M. Turner)
and off course over 3 months afterwards. *R. Akehurst.*

BATON BOY 9 ch.g. Music Boy 124–Lobela 77 (Lorenzaccio 130) [1989 NR 1990 44
7f3 7m 5d 6s a6g6 a8g4 a7g 1990 a7g] lengthy, rather sparely-made gelding: usually dull
in coat: poor mover: one-time fair handicapper, but has deteriorated: winner in
Jersey in summer: effective over stiff 6f and stays 1m: probably acts on any going:
has run moderately in blinkers: occasionally bandaged behind. *J. S. Wainwright.*

BATRA (USA) 2 b.f. (Apr 17) Green Dancer (USA) 132–Avatar's Court (USA) 60
(Avatar (USA)) [1990 5f* 6m] $110,000Y: lengthy, unfurnished filly: has scope: third
foal: dam minor winner at around 6f at 2 yrs in USA: blinkered, won 3-runner maiden
at Haydock in May: favourite, broke blood vessel in minor event at Windsor nearly 2
months later: ridden by 7-lb claimer. *P. F. I. Cole.*

BATSHOOF 4 b.c. Sadler's Wells (USA) 132–Steel Habit (Habitat 134) 122
[1989 7s* 7d3 7.6m* 10.5m* 10m* 10.6g3 10.5f5 9m3 1990 10f* 10m3 10m*
10m* 10.5g3 10g4 10f4]

Batshoof has improved with every season, ending his first a maiden
having been placed behind some very promising juveniles, his second the

*Prince of Wales's Stakes, Ascot—a very close finish between Batshoof,
Relief Pitcher (left) and Terimon (right)*

winner of four races, two of them listed contests, and his third not far behind
the best over a mile and a quarter and a Royal Ascot winner to boot. One of
those who finished ahead of him as a two-year-old, Two Timing, went on to
take the Prince of Wales's Stakes the following year. Batshoof was made
favourite for the latest running of the race. He'd been in tremendous heart in
the spring and was unlucky not to arrive at Royal Ascot unbeaten as a
four-year-old, having won a minor event at Kempton and the Tattersalls EBF
Rogers Gold Cup (in effortless style from Pirate Army) at the Curragh, getting
a poor run when a close third to Dolpour in the Gordon Richards EBF Stakes
at Sandown in between. The firm conditions at Ascot, ideal for Batshoof, were
against Dolpour and Legal Case and it was Relief Pitcher and Terimon who
fought out the finish with Batshoof. Relief Pitcher was allowed to establish a
clear lead and still held a healthy advantage over Dolpour and Batshoof, his
closest pursuers, into the straight. Batshoof soon moved into second,
gradually closed the gap and forced his head in front in the last fifty yards
under particularly strong driving from Eddery. A short head separated
Batshoof and Relief Pitcher, with the fast-finishing Terimon also involved in
the photo-finish. Batshoof didn't get the chance to take on the three-year-olds
in the Eclipse for he wasn't even entered for the race, the aim being to bring
him out a fresh horse in the Juddmonte International Stakes at York. When he
did get the chance he wasn't up to beating the best. A well-backed favourite at
York, he didn't get much of a run on the rail but couldn't make any impression
on In The Groove and Elmaamul inside the final furlong, once more just
having enough in reserve to hold off Terimon. His trainer's view that
Batshoof was best after a rest, hard to agree with as the Prince of Wales's
Stakes was his fourth race in ten weeks, did receive some credence twelve
days later in the Phoenix Champion Stakes. The horse sweated and got more
on edge as the preliminaries went on, tended to carry his head a bit high under
pressure after pulling hard (in that respect he wasn't helped by the modest
gallop) and finished more than twice as far behind Elmaamul as he'd done at
York. The Phoenix Champion Stakes was Batshoof's last race in Europe and
when he next appeared on the track he was beaten just over two lengths into
fourth in the Grade 1 Budweiser International at Laurel Park when under the
care of Neil Drysdale.

That Batshoof remained a maiden at two and went on to show his best
form over a mile and a quarter was very much a departure from the norm for

Mr Muttar Salem's "Batshoof"

		Northern Dancer	Nearctic
	Sadler's Wells (USA)	(b 1961)	Natalma
	(b 1981)	Fairy Bridge	Bold Reason
Batshoof		(b 1975)	Special
(b.c. 1986)		Habitat	Sir Gaylord
	Steel Habit	(b 1966)	Little Hut
	(b 1979)	Ampulla	Crowned Prince
		(b 1974)	A 1

his family: precociousness and speed are in abundance there. His dam Steel Habit, twice a winner in Italy, is a sister to the very useful Irish 1982 two-year-old Ancestral, winner of the Railway Stakes at the Curragh and later a graded winner in USA. Their dam Ampulla, useful at two when successful in the Cherry Hinton Stakes, was one of numerous speedy animals produced by A1, most notable of the others the good-class sprinter of 1975 Steel Heart, the top Irish two-year-old filly of 1979 Smokey Lady and Chili Girl, runner-up in the Queen Mary Stakes and the dam of Chilibang. A1 was a half-sister to Taittinger, one of the best two-year-old fillies of 1956. The quick-actioned Batshoof, a good-topped, quite attractive colt, developed well physically and usually impressed in appearance. He acts particularly well on top-of-the-ground, although he did win on soft early as a three-year-old. Splendidly tough and consistent, he possesses a good turn of foot and in Britain was usually held up. *B. Hanbury.*

BATTLE OF FLOWERS 3 b.f. Shernazar 131 Valiant Cry (Town Crier 119) 63
[1989 NR 1990 8m 10g⁴ 7g³ 8g⁶ 7d⁴ 7m³] 62,000Y: unfurnished filly: has quick,
fluent action: fifth foal: half-sister to fairly useful Irish sprinter Mitsubishi Vision
(by Cure The Blues) and minor French middle-distance winner Tap The Line (by
Tap On Wood): dam won over 9f in French Provinces: modest maiden: worth
another try at 1¼m. *C. F. Wall.*

BATTLE ON 3 b.f. Blakeney 126–Perfect Picture (FR) 78 (Hopeful Venture 125) 58
[1989 NR 1990 11v⁴ 11g³ 10g* 12.4f⁵ 16.2g⁴ 12s 13v⁵] half-sister to quite useful 10.5f
winner Malvern Beauty (by Shirley Heights), the dam of useful Irish 2-y-o
Malvernico, and quite modest 1¾m and 2m winner Glowing Picture (by Kalaglow):
dam lightly-raced daughter of 1000 Guineas second Photo Flash: quite modest
performer: favourite, won claimer at Ayr in June: probably stays 2m: acts on firm
going, not soft: sold 16,000 gns Doncaster November Sales, reportedly to join J.
Bolger. *Miss S. E. Hall.*

BATTLERS GREEN (IRE) 2 b.g. (Feb 28) Hard Fought 125–Reparata 60
(Jukebox 120) [1990 7g 8.2m⁶ 8g⁴ 8.2d] IR 5,000F, 6,000Y: rather angular gelding:
half-brother to poor winning stayer Suivez Moi (by Pas de Seul) and winners in
Belgium and Italy: dam Irish 6f winner: quite modest maiden: had very stiff tasks
final 2 starts. *G. B. Balding.*

BATZUSHKA (USA) 3 b.c. Danzig (USA)–Nicole Mon Amour (USA) (Bold 111
Bidder) [1989 6f² 7.3g² 6m* 6m⁵ 6g⁶ 6f* 5m* 6m⁶ 1990 5m⁵ 5m 6m 8.5m* 8m⁵
8m* 8g³ 8g² 8g⁵ 7d⁴ 9g] neat, strong, good-bodied colt: won handicaps at Beverley
and Goodwood (£13,000 event) in July: ran particularly well in listed race
(strong-finishing second to Thakib) at Kempton and £11,900 handicap at Doncaster
eighth and ninth starts, below best in Group 3 event at Goodwood and listed race at
Newmarket after: best at around 1m: acts on firm going: blinkered last 3 starts at 2
yrs and first 2 in 1990: seems best with waiting tactics: very useful. *Mrs L. Piggott.*

BAWBEE 3 gr.f. Dunbeath (USA) 127–Fee 111 (Mandamus 120) [1989 8.2g⁵ 8g⁺ 91 §
1990 8g² 10m² 10f⁶ 11.7m³ 11.5g* 12g³ 12m 10m⁵] lengthy filly: won minor event at
Sandown in August by a head, leading on bridle over 2f out then vigorously driven
inside last: hung left and put head in air when good third in listed race at Doncaster:
stays 1½m: acts on firm going: blinkered last 2 starts, refusing to settle first
occasion: capable of fairly useful form, but ungenuine and a hard ride. *R. F. Johnson
Houghton.*

BAXTERGATE 7 b.g. Ahonoora 122–Khadija 69 (Habat 127) [1989 NR 1990 6m —
8.2v] lengthy, workmanlike gelding: has a round action: won 4 handicaps as 4-y-o:
well beaten in handicap and claimer in autumn: used to be suited by 7f or 1m:
probably acts on any going: visored once. *E. J. Alston.*

BAYBEEJAY 3 b.f. Buzzards Bay 128§–Peak Condition (Mountain Call 125) 43
[1989 8g a7g⁵ 1990 5m* 8m³ 10.2m⁵ 8.5g⁶ 8m 7g 8m⁶ 8m] lengthy, leggy filly:
poor maiden: seems best at around 1m on an easy surface: blinkered twice: sold to
join R. Brotherton 1,800 gns Ascot October Sales. *H. J. Collingridge.*

BAY CHIMES 3 b.f. Buzzards Bay 128§–Wrekin Belle (Dance In Time (CAN)) —
[1989 5f⁵ 7f 5f 5g 8.2s 1990 a5g 6s] small, sturdy filly: poor maiden: should prove
best at 5f. *J. Wharton.*

BAYFORD ENERGY 4 ch.g. Milford 119–Smiling 62 (Silly Season 127) [1989 42
12d⁴ 12f⁵ 10m 12.4g³ 16m³ 16.2f³ 18g 1990 a14g 16.2m⁶ 17m⁵ 21.6m⁴ 16.2g² 17.6m
16.2d 16.5m⁴ 15d* 15.8d² 16.2f* 16f 16g 16.2s 15.8d] rather leggy, workmanlike
gelding: moderate mover: won narrowly from small fields in handicaps at Edinburgh
(selling event, no bid) and Beverley in July: below form after, giving impression
something amiss next outing: should stay beyond 2m: acts on firm and dead ground:
visored once at 3 yrs and twice in 1990. *R. M. Whitaker.*

BAYLIS 3 b.c. Sadler's Wells (USA) 132–Noblanna (USA) 85 (Vaguely Noble 140) 102 +
[1989 NR 1990 8m⁶ 10.4d³ 12m³ 10.1m* 10.1m³ 10f³ 11.7m* 10.6g² 10g³ 12g*] IR
130,000Y: rather lengthy, attractive colt with plenty of scope: has round action: fifth
foal: closely related to poor 1987 2-y-o/winning hurdler Quai d'Orsay (by Be My
Guest) and half-brother to Irish 2-y-o 9f winner Roblanna (by Roberto): dam,
middle-distance winner, is half-sister to good middle-distance horse Anne's
Pretender and daughter of Prix Vermeille winner Anne La Douce: useful performer:
won Windsor minor events in June and August and Group 3 race at Belmont Park in
October: ran well in valuable handicaps at Haydock and Newbury eighth and ninth
starts: stays 1½m: acts on firm ground: genuine and consistent. *L. M. Cumani.*

BAYLORD PRINCE (IRE) 2 b.c. (Apr 22) Horage 124–Miss Moat (Dike 62
(USA)) [1990 6m 7m 6f⁴ 8f⁵ 10s⁶ a8g⁴] IR 11,200F, 13,000Y: lengthy, good-topped

colt: has scope: half-brother to several winners abroad, including French middle-distance performer Mister Moat (by Oats): dam 1m winner at 4 yrs in France: quite modest maiden: stays 1¼m. *W. Carter.*

BAY MEADOWS STAR 2 b.f. (Apr 23) Sharpo 132–Upper Caen (High Top 131) 60
[1990 6m⁴ 6g 5f 7f] 19,000Y: sparely-made filly: first live foal: dam unraced sister to very useful miler Miner's Lamp: quite modest maiden: blinkered, ran freely and tended to hang at Brighton final start: should stay 7f. *I. A. Balding.*

BAY MOUNTAIN 4 b.g. Tyrnavos 129–Just You Wait (Nonoalco (USA) 131) 40
[1989 10s 10g 1990 13v 10g 14m 6f² 6g³ 7g] tall, well-made gelding: shows knee action: poor handicapper: evidently much better suited by 6f than 1¼m + . *R. Curtis.*

BAYPHIA 2 ch.g. (Mar 20) Bay Express 132–Sophie Avenue (Guillaume Tell 46
(USA) 121) [1990 6h⁶ 6m⁶ 5m 6g 6d⁶] 3,500F, 6,600Y: quite good-topped gelding: has a quick action: third foal: brother to 3-y-o 8.2f winner Parking Bay: dam French 2-y-o 7f winner: poor maiden, best effort blinkered final start: will probably be better suited by 7f + : slowly away first 3 starts. *G. Lewis.*

BAY RUNNER 3 b.f. Bay Express 132–Foothold (Hotfoot 126) [1989 NR 1990 —
9m] lengthy, angular filly: fifth foal: sister to 4-y-o jumper Precious Lad and half-sister to modest 1986 2-y-o 6f winner Connaught Lad and a winner in Norway (both by Connaught): dam ran twice at 2 yrs: 25/1, slowly away when tailed off in claimer at Goodwood in August. *R. Akehurst.*

BAYSHAM (USA) 4 b.c. Raise A Native–Sunny Bay (USA) (Northern Bay 66
(USA)) [1989 10.6g 10.2f⁴ 1990 10.8m 8m 6f² 6m² 5m⁶ 6d² 6m³ 7f² 6g] tall, close-coupled colt: quite modest handicapper: still a maiden: needs further than 5f and stays 7f: acts on firm and dead going: wore tongue strap on reappearance: blinkered or visored last 3 outings. *B. R. Millman.*

BAY TIGER 2 b.c. (Apr 6) Bay Express 132–Perang's Niece 82 (High Award 119) 41 p
[1990 5v] third foal: dam stayed 1m: around 6 lengths seventh of 18, slowly away then one pace final 2f, in seller at Ayr in October: should improve. *W. Hastings-Bass.*

BAY TO STAY 3 b.c. Shareef Dancer (USA) 135–Costly Wave (FR) 117 (Caro —
133) [1989 NR 1990 10.1m 12m a12g] 40,000Y, 3,000 3-y-o: angular, workmanlike colt: closely related to useful Irish 7f and 1m winner Great Lakes (by Lomond), and half-brother to several winners, including very useful French 9f and 1¼m winner Swept Away (by Kris): dam French miler out of Oaks third Arctic Wave: probably of little account: twice bandaged: very edgy final start: sold 1,000 gns Ascot September Sales. *T. M. Jones.*

BAY TROUPER (IRE) 2 b.f. (Apr 22) Bay Express 132–Record Finish (Record 47
Token 128) [1990 5g 5m a6g⁴ a7g] IR 1,300F, IR 5,400Y: sturdy filly: first foal: dam unraced half-sister to sprinters Whipper In and Hotbee: bit backward on first run for nearly 3 months and ridden by 7-lb claimer, 9 lengths fourth of 10 to South Crofty in claimer at Lingfield in November. *M. Bell.*

BDOORE (IRE) 2 b.f. (Mar 4) Petoski 135–Princess Biddy 86 (Sun Prince 128) 62
[1990 7m⁶ 8m⁴] 38,000Y: rangy, well-made filly: has scope: half-sister to several winners, including 1986 2-y-o 6f winner Hydraulic Power (by Northfields) and 6f winner Fawley's Girl (by He Loves Me): dam stayed 7f, is half-sister to Royalty, Double Jump and Sunyboy: quite modest form in maidens: stays 1m. *M. A. Jarvis.*

BEACHOLME BOY (IRE) 2 b.g. (Apr 9) Dominion 123–Bronte (USA) 88 —
(Bold Forbes (USA)) [1990 7m 7f] 5,200Y, 1,000 2-y-o: leggy, angular gelding: looks weak: poor walker: second foal: half-brother to 3-y-o Native Suitor (by Local Suitor): dam 11f winner: soundly beaten in maiden auctions. *Miss G. M. Rees.*

BEACH PATROL (IRE) 2 b.c. (Mar 3) Thatching 131–Waveguide 76 (Double 55
Form 130) [1990 6f 7m] 33,000Y: angular colt: first foal: dam placed at 5f at 2 yrs is out of half-sister to Centro, dam of Nicholas Bill, Centroline and Centrocon, herself dam of Time Charter: sixteenth of 17 in Tattersalls Tiffany Highflyer Stakes at Newmarket in August: green on debut: sold 2,000 gns Newmarket Autumn Sales. *W. Jarvis.*

BEACHY GLEN 3 b.g. Glenstal (USA) 118–Ampersand (USA) 86 (Stop The 66
Music (USA)) [1989 5v⁴ 5d* 5f³ 6m³ 6m² 6d 6f³ 6f 1990 a6g⁴ 7f 6f 6f² 6f² 7m⁶ 6s* 7g³ 7m³ 6g* 6m 5m 6d 6g⁶ 6s 6d a7g⁶ a6g a7g] leggy gelding: quite modest performer: made virtually all to win handicap at Nottingham in May and seller (bought in 4,300 gns, gamely) at Hamilton in July: below form last 9 starts: suited by 6f: acts on any ground: usually visored nowadays, but wasn't fourteenth to sixteenth starts: sold 3,000 gns Doncaster November Sales. *C. Tinkler.*

BEACHY HEAD 2 gr.c. (Feb 25) Damister (USA) 123–No More Rosies 74 **78** p
(Warpath 113) [1990 7v*] 11,000F: first foal: dam 1¼m winner from 2 starts, is
half-sister to Derby third Mount Athos and smart sprinter John Splendid: won
maiden at Ayr in October by a neck, clear, from Crimson Cloud, staying on well to
lead near finish after slow start: sure to improve. *C. W. Thornton.*

BE A HONEY 2 ch.f. (Feb 7) Be My Guest (USA) 126–Reltop 72 (High Top 131) **84**
[1990 6.5g6 8.2v3] 48,000Y: rangy filly: half-sister to several winners, including
Chester Cup winner Just David (by Blakeney) and 1983 2-y-o 5.1f seller winner
Captiva (by Bay Express): dam won over 1½m: promising sixth of 17 in Tattersalls
Tiffany Yorkshire Stakes at Doncaster in September, slowly away then staying on
really well last 2f: favourite, around 10 lengths third of 14, keeping on, in minor
event at Haydock following month: will be suited by 1¼m + : sure to win a race. *N.
A. Graham.*

BEAN BOY 12 ch.g. Some Hand 119–Battling 75 (Pinza 137) [1989 10.2g 14s 12f* **47**
15.8m 1990 12.8g 10.6s 12.3g4 12g3 15.8d* 18g3 12f 16.2m4 15.8d6 15d6 16s4] sturdy,
workmanlike gelding: won for twelfth time on flat in handicap at Catterick in July:
below form after next outing: stays well: acts on any going: has worn blinkers:
excellent mount for inexperienced rider: a grand old campaigner. *M. H. Easterby.*

BEAN KING 4 gr.g. Ardross 134–Meanz Beanz (High Top 131) [1989 8s2 9.5g4 **101**
8g* 10.1m3 10.1m 11.7m6 10m3 10m6 a12g2 a12g* a14g2 1990 12m* 12d* 12f 10m6
12f 14g2 17.4d* 16d4] robust gelding: moderate mover: useful handicapper:
successful in early-summer events at York and Epsom (£22,400 race by 2 lengths
from Gaasid) and in £6,400 contest at Ayr in September: excellent second to
Further Flight in Tote Ebor at York: stays well: acts on good to firm and dead going:
genuine. *R. W. Armstrong.*

BEATLE SONG 2 b.f. (Apr 8) Song 132–Betyle (FR) (Hardicanute 130) [1990 **58**
5m5 5m2 6m6 5f2 a7g a5g5] good-quartered, workmanlike filly: has scope:
half-sister to a pattern-placed animal in Italy and a winner in Norway: dam unraced,
has been in Italy: quite modest maiden: pulled hard third start: should be suited by
further than 5f: sold out of I. Balding's stable 7,400 gns Newmarket Autumn Sales.
C. J. Hill.

BEAU BENZ 6 b.g. Camden Town 125–War Lass 100 (Whistler 129) [1989 10.2g **64**
10d 10.8d 10d* 12g 11.7m 10.4m 10.6s 1990 13v 12m* 12d4 10m5 12g3 a11g 12s6 10v2
11d3 12s2 a12g] rather leggy, good-topped gelding: carries plenty of condition: quite
modest handicapper: won at Carlisle in June by neck, leading on bridle over 1f out:
well-backed favourite, ran poorly on all-weather final outing: effective at 1¼m to
1½m: acts on any going except possibly firm: effective with or without blinkers or
visor: has started slowly: tends to carry head high: inconsistent. *M. H. Easterby.*

BEAUCADEAU 4 b.g. Alzao (USA) 117–Pretty Gift (Realm 129) [1989 6s2 6s4 **62**
5s* 6f6 5g3 5d 5s 5s a6g a6g 1990 a6g5 5g 6m 6d 6m 10m* a11g3 10.2f6 10f] leggy,
close-coupled gelding: moderate mover: won in seller (bought in 3,200 gns) at
Chepstow in July having started slowly: pulled hard and found little eighth start:
stays 1¼m: acts on good to firm and soft going: has worn blinkers (only once at 4
yrs): has sweated: sometimes taken down early: inconsistent. *K. M. Brassey.*

BEAUCHAMP EVE 3 ch.f. Jalmood (USA) 126–Buss 102 (Busted 134) [1989 —
NR 1990 10g] half-sister to fairly useful 1989 7f and 1¾m winner Beauchamp Dream
(by Castle Keep) and numerous other winners, including fairly useful 1m winner
Imperial Ace (by Derring-Do) and 17.6f winner Beauchamp Cactus (by Niniski): dam
game performer at up to 11f: always behind in maiden at Kempton in June: sold 1,800
gns Newmarket Autumn Sales. *J. L. Dunlop.*

BEAUCHAMP EXPRESS 3 b.g. Castle Keep 121–Jubilee 101 (Reform 132) **106**
[1989 NR 1990 11d6 12d3 12m5 15g4 12f4 15g5] rather angular gelding: fifth foal:
half-brother to 13.1f winner Beauchamp Crest (by Jalmood): dam won over 7f at 2
yrs: useful efforts in King Edward VII Stakes (set plenty to do) at Royal Ascot, Prix
Hubert de Chaudenay at Longchamp and Prix Kergorlay at Deauville (reportedly
finished lame) third, fourth and final outings: stays 15f: seems unsuited by very firm
ground, and moved down moderately fifth start: gelded after final one. *J. L. Dunlop.*

BEAUCHAMP FIZZ 2 ch.c. (Apr 26) Jalmood (USA) 126–Buss 102 (Busted **78**
134) [1990 7m5 7m2 8.2g] unfurnished colt: half-brother to numerous winners,
including fairly useful 1m performer Imperial Ace (by Derring-Do) and stayer
Beauchamp Cactus (by Niniski): dam game performer at up to 11f: second of 11,
staying on well unable to challenge, to Democratic in maiden at Leicester in
September: should be suited by 1m: possibly handicapped by soft surface. *J. L. Dunlop.*

BEAUCROFT 2 ch.c. (Apr 15) Crofthall 110–Patent Pending (Goldhill 125) [1990 — p
8.2s] well-grown, close-coupled colt: third foal: brother to temperamental 1988
2-y-o plater Foaminathemouth and to 3-y-o 7f winner Euro Galaxy: dam ran 3 times:
better for race, never placed to challenge or knocked about in maiden at Haydock in
October: should improve. *J. A. Glover.*

BEAU DADA (IRE) 2 b.f. (Feb 25) Pine Circle (USA)–Beauvoir (Artaius (USA) **66**
129) [1990 5m6 5g3 5g2 5.8m6 6f* 6m5 6m5 6m3] 7,200Y: neat, quite attractive filly:
third foal: dam French 1m winner, is half-sister to Sangue: sire stayed 1½m: quite
modest performer: ridden by 5-lb claimer, won maiden auction at Folkestone in
August: better suited by 6f than 5f: tends to get on edge: visored final 2 starts:
trained first 4 by S. Harris. *P. J. Makin.*

BEAUDENE 4 b.g. Song 132–Princess Tavi (Sea Hawk II 131) [1989 7f5 8m 8m —
10m 1990 14g 12m 18m6] workmanlike gelding: has a round action: poor maiden:
headstrong, and suited by much shorter than 2¼m: sweating and edgy on reappearance: wears crossed noseband. *J. Mackie.*

BEAUFORTS BRIGADE (IRE) 2 b.c. (Apr 25) Gorytus (USA) 132– —
Sparkling Air (Malinowski (USA) 123) [1990 a6g a7g 7g] IR 6,000F, 4,700Y: compact
colt: fourth foal: half-brother to 3-y-o 1m winner Salmon Sparkle and a winner in
Sweden (both by Salmon Leap): dam, unplaced in 5 starts in Ireland, is half-sister to
Sparkler: seems of little account: blinkered final 2 starts: sold 740 gns Newmarket
September Sales: resold 480 gns Doncaster October Sales. *W. Wilson.*

BEAU IDEAL 5 b.h. Brigadier Gerard 144–Princess Lieven (Royal Palace 131) —
[1989 14g 11f 10f6 13.3m3 11.5g* 12g 11v3 12g 1990 12g6 12m6 11.1m4 12f 12d3 16.2m6
10f6 8.3m] smallish horse: has a rather round action: quite modest handicapper:
much too free in blinkers last 2 outings: probably best at up to 1½m: acts on good to
firm and heavy going: occasionally sweats and gets on toes. *C. E. Brittain.*

BEAU JOHN (IRE) 2 b.c. (Feb 18) Le Johnstan 123–Flore (Dance In Time —
(CAN)) [1990 6s 7.5f 5m] IR 10,000Y: workmanlike colt: has a round action: first
foal: dam never ran: well beaten, in seller (blinkered) final start. *J. S. Wainwright.*

BEAUJOLAIS NOUVEAU 3 ch.g. Aragon 118–No Halo 74 (Aureole 132) **61**
[1989 5g 1990 8f 7g2 8f4 10g6 8m 10g2] workmanlike gelding: moderate mover: quite
modest performer: visored, very good second in claimer at Newmarket final start:
suited by 1¼m: possibly best with give in the ground. *M. R. Channon.*

BEAUMONT'S KEEP 4 b.c. Castle Keep 121–Powderhall 81 (Murrayfield 119) **54 §**
[1989 5.8m 5h 6m 5f6 5f3 6f2 5m6 1990 5g4 6m 6m 6g4 6m2 5m5 6m6 5m2 5m 5m*
5m 5f6 6f 5.8d6] good-topped colt: carries plenty of condition: moderate mover:
capable of quite modest form, but can't be trusted: won for only time when leading
virtually on line in apprentice handicap at Goodwood in August: stays 6f: acts on
firm and dead going: has gone freely to post: wore cheek-piece near-side eighth
outing (hung left): sold 5,400 gns Ascot November Sales. *L. J. Holt.*

BEAUMOOD 4 b.c. Jalmood (USA) 126–Falcon Berry (FR) (Bustino 136) [1989 **68**
10g4 10.6g5 10m5 10.6g6 12g5 13s* 12s2 13.3d 1990 12g5 12m6 12.2g* 12g 10m5 12g2
12d5 12m 12m6] neat colt: carries condition: modest handicapper: made all at
Warwick in July: stays 13f: seems suited by an easy surface: well suited by forcing
tactics: sold 7,200 gns Newmarket Autumn Sales. *M. A. Jarvis.*

BEAU NASH 6 b.g. Prince Tenderfoot (USA) 126–Dominica (GER) (Zank) [1989 **56**
12.4g* 12d5 12f 12g6 14g 12.4m2 13m6 12m 12.3m 13s 12.4g 1990 13.8m2 12.4f3 13.8m
14g 12.4m6] compact gelding: carries plenty of condition: has a quick action: quite
modest handicapper on his day: stays 1¾m: best form on a sound surface: blinkered
once at 4 yrs: suitable mount for inexperienced rider: inconsistent. *A. P. Stringer.*

BEAU QUEST 3 b.c. Rainbow Quest (USA) 134–Elegant Tern (USA) 102 (Sea **71**
Bird II 145) [1989 6m 7m4 8.5f 8f3 1990 12.3f* 12f2 12m5 16.2s3 12.3g4 12.5m5
12h2 12f6 14g 14d6 16d] small colt: has quick action: modest handicapper: won at
Ripon in April: suited by 1½m: probably acts on any going: ran creditably in blinkers
final start at 2 yrs: flashes tail: largely consistent. *R. Hollinshead.*

BEAU ROU 3 br.g. Rousillon (USA) 133–Beautiful Dawn (USA) (Grey Dawn II **64**
132) [1989 6d 1990 8g 8f 8m3 8.5g 10.2f* 11.7m5] big, useful-looking gelding:
has a quick action: won maiden claimer at Bath in June: suited by 1¼m: acts on firm
going: blinkered last 4 starts: carries head high: sold to join P. Hedger 12,500 gns
Newmarket July Sales and gelded. *D. R. C. Elsworth.*

BEAU SHER 7 b.h. Ile de Bourbon (USA) 133–Mai Pussy 91 (Realm 129) [1989 —
8g* 8d2 7g* 7.2s* 8g2 8.5g2 10f2 8g6 12s6 1990 8g] big horse: has a rather round
action: improved into smart performer as 6-y-o, second to Two Timing in Prince of
Wales's Stakes at Royal Ascot: reportedly badly struck into next outing, and below

form both subsequent starts: effective at 7f to 1¼m: acted on any going: sweated and ran too freely when tried in blinkers: splendidly tough and genuine: a credit to his trainer: to stand at Knockhouse Stud, Co. Waterford. *B. Hanbury.*

BEAU SULTAN (USA) 2 ch.c. (Feb 6) Bering (USA) 137–Devalois (FR) 117 **110**
(Nureyev (USA) 131) [1990 7.5g* 8m* 8g³] good-bodied French colt: powerful galloper: first foal: dam French 1m to 10.5f winner, later successful at 9f in graded company in USA, is half-sister to good French 1m to 1¼m colt Dunphy from good French family: successful in newcomers race at Deauville in August and Prix La Rochette (by a length from Eternity Star, finishing strongly having been pushed along early) at Longchamp in September: 5 lengths third of 5 to Hector Protector in Grand Criterium at Longchamp in October: will stay 1¼m: very useful. *Mme C. Head, France.*

BEAUTIFUL NINA 4 ch.f. Rabdan 129–Donna Sirena 72 (Julio Mariner 127) —
[1989 7f 8m 1990 a5g a7g 8m] leggy, close-coupled, plain filly: no sign of ability: sold 1,400 gns Doncaster June Sales. *G. Blum.*

BEAU VENTURE (USA) 2 ch.c. (Mar 31) Explodent (USA)–Old Westbury **93 ?**
(USA) (Francis S) [1990 6s 6m³ 5m 5m* 5.8d³ 5g* 5d] $27,000Y: leggy, quite good-topped colt: poor walker: moderate mover: half-brother to several minor winners in North America: dam claiming winner at up to 9f: won maiden at Beverley in September and nursery at Newmarket (showed greatly improved form) in November: keen sort, probably best at 5f: easily best form on good ground: sweated and ran as if something amiss on third outing: inconsistent. *F. H. Lee.*

BECKINGHAM BEN 6 gr.g. Workboy 123–Pickwood Sue 74 (Right Boy 137) **62**
[1989 5m⁶ 5m 5f⁶ 5f⁴ 5m⁶ 5f⁶ 6f³ 5m⁶ 5f² 5.1g² 5f 5g³ a5g 1990 a6g⁶ a5g⁵ a5g² a5g* 5m⁴ a5g 5g 5m a5g² a5g² 5m³] tall gelding: quite modest handicapper: won at Lingfield in February: ran very well back on all-weather when second twice at Southwell: suited by 5f: acts on firm and dead going: usually visored or blinkered: wore crossed noseband fifth to eighth starts, looking none too keen last of them: goes well with forcing tactics. *J. P. Leigh.*

BECKONING 2 b.c. (Apr 27) Bellypha 130–Courtesy Call (Northfields (USA)) **54 p**
[1990 7m 8.2d] sturdy colt: fourth foal: half-brother to 3-y-o 10.2f winner Royal Passion (by Ahonoora), modest 6f winner Courtoisie (by Thatching) and a winner over hurdles in Ireland: dam thrice-raced half-sister to smart 1976 2-y-o 5f performer Piney Ridge: green, lost place 2f out in maiden at Newmarket and minor event (better effort) at Nottingham in October: should do better. *J. M. P. Eustace.*

BECOCIOUS 3 b.g. Precocious 126–Baheejah (Northfields (USA)) [1989 5f³ 6m —
6m 6m⁵ 5m⁶ 6s 1990 7g 7g] strong, good-bodied gelding: had a quick action: plating-class maiden: showed nothing as 3-y-o: best form at 6f: blinkered or visored last 3 outings at 2 yrs: dead. *J. Etherington.*

BECQUEREL (USA) 4 ch.c. Sharpen Up 127–Marie Curie 96 (Exbury 138) **96**
[1989 8m* 8m⁴ 8f 1990 8f 8f* 8g⁶ 9m 7.6f] compact, attractive colt: quite useful handicapper: successful under 10-0 at Salisbury in May: ran moderately last 2 outings, and not seen out after July: dam 1¼m winner up over 1m: goes well on firm going: sweating third and fourth (also on edge) outings: often pulls hard: sold 23,000 gns Newmarket Autumn Sales. *R. Charlton.*

BEDOUIN PRINCE (USA) 3 b.c. Danzig (USA)–Regal Heiress 81 (English **54**
Prince 129) [1989 NR 1990 8m⁴ 8g 8.2m⁴ 10.1m 10g 8g 8m] $500,000Y: heavy-topped colt: poor walker and mover: fifth foal: half-brother to one-time fair middle-distance colt Royal Bequest (by Mill Reef): dam 1½m and 13f winner, is half-sister to Shirley Heights: form only in handicap at Leicester fifth start, making most: stays 1¼m: blinkered last 3 outings: sold to join J. L. Harris 4,000 gns Newmarket Autumn Sales. *A. A. Scott.*

BEE BEAT 2 ch.c. (Apr 20) Bairn (USA) 126–Thorny Rose 81 (Tap On Wood 130) **71**
[1990 6d² 7m 7g] rather unfurnished colt: first foal: dam 2-y-o 6f winner later suited by middle distances: modest maiden: easily best effort second at Goodwood in October: raced keenly next start: should stay 7f. *E. A. Wheeler.*

BEEBOB 2 b.f. (Mar 22) Norwick (USA) 120–Anzeige (GER) (Soderini 123) [1990 **62**
7m⁵ 7m⁴ 8.2v] half-sister to several winners here and abroad, including useful 7f winner Flower Bowl (by Homing): dam, German 1m winner, out of German Oaks runner-up Ankerette: quite modest maiden: apparently injured hind leg final start: should be better suited by 1m than 7f. *B. Hanbury.*

BEECHWOOD COTTAGE 7 ch.g. Malinowski (USA) 123–Drora (Busted **67**
134) [1989 6d 7m 8h 7h* 7m 7.6m 7m 7f² 7.6m 7m² 7m⁴ 6m 7d a7g* 1990 a8g⁴ a7g⁴ a10g² a8g² a10g⁴ a10g² a8g* a10g⁴ a8g³ a8g⁶ a8g³ a8g 7g³ 8f 8.2f 7m] small, sturdy

gelding: poor walker and mover: quite modest handicapper on his day: won at Lingfield in January: stays 1¼m: acts on any going: effective with or without blinkers: usually starts slowly and gets behind: a difficult ride, who goes well for tender handling: inconsistent. *A. Bailey.*

BEE HIVE HILL 2 ch.c. (Jun 2) Aragon 118–Sun Lamp 76 (Pall Mall 132) [1990 **62** 5f⁶ 5m 5m* 5f⁵ 5m a5g] 3,100F, 4,600Y: rangy colt: has scope: sixth living foal: brother to 4-y-o 6f winner Tophams and half-brother to sprint winner Velocidad (by Balidar): dam 7f winner: quite modest performer: first run for 3 months, won maiden at Catterick in August: ran moderately at Southwell: will stay 6f. *Ronald Thompson.*

BEEKMAN STREET 4 b.c. Jalmood (USA) 126–Plato's Retreat 73 (Brigadier **69** Gerard 144) [1989 8s 10.6s 11m⁴ 12.4m⁴ 14m* 14m⁴ 14f 16m² 17.4s² 16m⁴ 18g² 15g⁴ 1990 17.1f³ 14g³ 14m 18.8f⁵] leggy colt: modest handicapper: stays well: acts on any going: moved down moderately final outing (July): winning hurdler in April. *I. P. Wardle.*

BE FRESH 4 ch.c. Be My Guest (USA) 126–Fresh (High Top 131) [1989 8m⁵ 7m⁵ **105** 6g* 6g* 6v 6d 1990 6d 6f² 6m* 5g 6m] good-topped, attractive colt: useful sprinter: won £15,700 handicap at Goodwood in August under top weight comfortably by length, clear, from Amigo Menor: well beaten after in Doncaster all-aged listed race (favourite) and Krug Diadem Stakes at Ascot: should prove as effective at 5f as 6f: needs a sound surface. *L. M. Cumani.*

BEGUILED (IRE) 2 ch.f. (Mar 28) Be My Guest (USA) 126–Apple Peel 109 **54 p** (Pall Mall 132) [1990 7g] sister to very useful 6f to 8.5f winner Eve's Error and half-sister to several other winners, including fairly useful 6f and 7f winner Apple Rings (by Godswalk) and 11f and 13.3f winner Discord (by Niniski): dam 1m and 1¼m winner: over 10 lengths seventh of 13 to Eastern Magic in maiden at Salisbury in October, late headway having been slowly away and soon ridden along: sure to do better. *W. Hastings-Bass.*

BEHIND THE CLOCK 3 b.g. Sula Bula 109–Hale Lane 59 (Comedy Star — (USA) 121) [1989 6f 1990 a7g] no promise in minor event and maiden. *T. M. Jones.*

BELAFONTE 3 b.c. Derrylin 115–Ulla Laing 107 (Mummy's Pet 125) [1989 NR **71** 1990 10g 10g³ 12.3g³ 10.5m³ 10m⁴ 12m 12.2d⁵ 9s] 13,500Y: compact colt: first foal: dam 5f and 6f winner at 2 yrs stayed at least 7f: modest maiden: below form in claimers (visored) and handicap (blinkered) last 3 starts: stays 1½m: acts on good to firm ground: has run well for apprentice: sold 10,500 gns Doncaster November Sales. *D. Morley.*

BELARIUS 2 b.g. (May 17) Bellypha 130–Celebrity 101 (Troy 137) [1990 8g] — 40,000Y: lengthy, quite attractive gelding: first foal: dam 10.2f winner suited by 1½m, is daughter of Portland winner Matinee: very slowly away and soon pulled up (reportedly injured hock) in minor event at Wolverhampton in October. *W. Hastings-Bass.*

BELDINE 5 gr.g. Belfort (FR) 89–Royal Celandine (Royal Palace 131) [1989 NR **50** 1990 13g* 12g⁴ 12s] lengthy, angular gelding: easily landed gamble when making all in handicap at Hamilton (bandaged) in May: faced stiffish tasks in similar company afterwards: stays 13f: won selling hurdle in December. *P. Monteith.*

BELDONAYR 3 ch.f. Rabdan 129–Pearl Cove 63 (Town And Country 124) [1989 **51** 7m⁶ 7m 7g 1990 7.5f 8f³ 9f⁵ 10f² 8g 10g* 8.2m⁶] angular filly: had a round action: late plater: won at Ripon (bought in 4,100 gns) in July: suited by 1¼m: acted on firm going: visored last 2 starts: dead. *E. Weymes.*

BELFORT GIPSY 4 b.g. Belfort (FR) 89–Tringa (GER) (Kaiseradler) [1989 6d⁶ — 7s 6m⁵ 6m⁴ 8h⁶ 6g 6f³ 6g a7g 1990 a6g a6g 6f 6f 8m 6m] neat gelding: poor maiden: no form in 1990: suited by 6f and top-of-the-ground: blinkered or visored 6 times. *J. Norton.*

BELFORT PRINCE 3 b.g. Belfort (FR) 89–Turtle Dove (Gyr (USA) 131) [1989 **53** NR 1990 8f⁶ 7g⁵ 8m³ 10g 13.8d² 11g 12g] 8,000Y: leggy, shallow-girthed gelding: brother to quite modest maiden Dove Grey and half-brother to numerous winners by Warpath, including useful middle-distance stayer Path of Peace and out-and-out stayer Path's Sister: dam ran once: plating-class maiden: good second in handicap at Catterick: ran as if something amiss next start: stays 1¾m: acts on good to firm ground and dead: winning hurdler. *G. M. Moore.*

BELFORT RULER 3 gr.g. Belfort (FR) 89–Call Me Kate 72 (Firestreak 125) **78** [1989 5f⁴ 1990 5g² 6m* 6d 6m 6g⁶ 8.3m 6g 6m] close-coupled, workmanlike gelding: won minor event at Goodwood in May: ran fairly well in minor event (taken down very early) fifth start, poorly in handicaps and behind in German Group 3 event (seventh start): stays 6f: acts on good to firm ground: on toes fourth start. *B. Gubby.*

BELINDA'S BOY 3 b.g. Swing Easy (USA) 126–Queen of The Hills 72   33
(Connaught 130) [1989 5g⁴ 6m⁶ 6m⁶ 5g 5f 5g 5g⁴ 1990 5f 5v 6g 5g 5f 6f³ 6g 7m 8.3m
8f⁵ 8f] quite attractive gelding: moderate mover: plating-class maiden: best form at
5f on easy ground: blinkered third start, hooded next 3: sold 640 gns Newmarket
September Sales. *W. Carter.*

BELLA NOAL 4 b.f. Noalto 120–Nimble Fingers 64 (Burglar 128) [1989 12f 10g⁶   —
10f 1990 a10g⁵ a16g] workmanlike, plain filly: no worthwhile form in varied events:
dead. *W. T. Kemp.*

BELLA SEVILLE 6 gr.m. King of Spain 121–Tempered Wind (Fleece 114) [1989   71
6m 5m⁴ 5g⁶ 5f⁵ 5g⁶ 5f⁵ 5m* 5g 5m² 5d 5s² 5f* 5d⁴ 5d 1990 5m 5m 5d⁶ 5g² 5g* 5m
5f² 5g* 5m⁴ 5f³] lengthy mare: modest handicapper: better than ever in summer,
justifying favouritism at Ayr in June and July: best at 5f: acts on any going: best in
blinkers: often apprentice ridden, but not when successful: consistent. *T. D. Barron.*

BELL BOY 2 b.c. (May 9) Daring March 116–Belle Tower 69 (Tower Walk 130)   40
[1990 6m 5g³ 6m⁵ 5f] leggy colt: poor mover: first foal: dam 6f and 7f winner:
plating-class form: ran poorly in seller final start: probably suited by 5f. *R. V. Smyth.*

BELLE CHOSE 2 b.f. (Apr 9) Bairn (USA) 126–Dingle Belle 72 (Dominion 123)   54
[1990 5m 5g² 5g* 5d²] 9,000Y: workmanlike filly: active sort: third living foal:
half-sister to 1987 2-y-o 6f winner Snake Eye (by Tina's Pet) and poor Lady Bay (by
Balidar): dam 13.8f winner, is half-sister to very smart Town And Country:
plating-class performer: made all in seller (no bid) at Beverley in May: hung left and
raced on next outing: will be better suited by 6f: taken early to post final 3
(unruly stalls final 2) starts: sold 4,000 gns Newmarket July Sales. *M. H. Easterby.*

BELLE DANSEUSE 2 b.f. (Feb 2) Bellypha 130–Rengaine (FR) (Music Boy   44
124) [1990 6d⁶ 6f 6f 6g] 5,200Y: lengthy, good-quartered filly: first foal: dam French
8.5f and 11f winner: poor maiden. *M. Blanshard.*

BELLE DE MONT 4 b.f. Montekin 125–Magic Lady (Gala Performance (USA))   —
[1989 6m 8m 5f 6g 8.2g 1990 a6g 8m 8m 5g] sparely-made filly: of little account:
blinkered 4 times: wears bandages. *T. Kersey.*

BELLEFAN (IRE) 2 b.f. (Mar 14) Taufan (USA) 119–Bellinzona (Northfields   56
(USA)) [1990 a6g⁵ 7m⁵ 6d⁴ 6d] IR 15,000Y: rather leggy filly: third foal: half-sister
to Irish 7f winner Media Award (by Thatching): dam French 9.5f winner:
plating-class maiden: will probably prove better suited by 7f than 6f: below form on
dead ground. *M. Bell.*

BELLE OF STEEL 2 ch.f. (Apr 6) Official–Linpac Belle 70 (Steel Heart 128)   38
[1990 a6g 6g³ 7f⁶ 5g 5m] workmanlike filly: first foal: dam, best at 2 yrs, out of
staying mare: poor plater: best effort second start: quickly outpaced in non-selling
nursery at Wolverhampton on final start. *D. Haydn Jones.*

BELLEPHERON 7 b.h. Bellypha 130–Une Pavane (FR) (Caro 133) [1989 13.8d   — §
1990 12.2f6] lengthy, quite attractive horse: poor handicapper: stays 1½m: best form
on sound surface: sometimes has tongue tied down: unreliable. *W. Storey.*

BELLE PRIZE 3 gr.f. Belfort (FR) 89–Balance (GER) (Orsini 124) [1989 NR   —
1990 10.6d] half-sister to several winners in Germany: dam won in Germany: 50/1,
tailed off in maiden at Haydock in September. *K. White.*

BELLEROFONTE (IRE) 2 b.c. (Feb 22) Tate Gallery (USA) 117–Faapette   77
(Runnett 125) [1990 5f³ 5f* 6m² 6f³ 6m³ 6g 6m⁶ 5v] 9,400Y: small, sturdy colt: first
foal: dam Irish 2-y-o 1m winner: fair performer: won maiden at Thirsk in April:
better suited by 6f than 5f: seems unsuited by heavy ground: blinkered final 4 starts:
sold 11,800 gns Newmarket Autumn Sales. *Lord John FitzGerald.*

BELLING BELLING (IRE) 2 b.f. (Apr 5) Soughaan (USA) 111–Dame Ross 85   —
(Raga Navarro (ITY) 119) [1990 7g 7m 7m 10.6s] IR 6,400F, IR 7,500Y: workmanlike
filly: first foal: dam Irish 2-y-o 7f and 7.8f winner stayed 1¼m, is out of staying
half-sister to very smart Sweet Story: little worthwhile form, including in selling
nursery. *Dr J. D. Scargill.*

BELLTINA 2 b.f. (Jan 7) Belfort (FR) 89–Bacchantina (Gulf Pearl 117) [1990 5m⁴   41
5f⁶ 5f⁴ 5d⁴ a6g³ 7m³ 6g 6m⁵] small, good-quartered filly: sixth foal: dam poor plater:
modest plater: stays 7f: blinkered third to seventh (seemed reluctant to race) starts:
wandered and became unbalanced for 7-lb claimer final 2 outings. *B. W. Murray.*

BELL TURRET 3 b. or br.g. Beldale Flutter (USA) 130–Base Camp 80   55
(Derring-Do 131) [1989 7m³ 7g 8.2d 1990 7g 8.2f 5g 6f 8g² 10.1m* 10m² 11.7g 8g 10g]

good-topped gelding: improved form to win selling handicap (retained 9,800 gns) at Windsor in June by 8 lengths: below form last 3 outings, visored and well behind in claimer on final one: suited by 1¼m: acts on good to firm ground. *I. Campbell.*

BELLWICK   3 b.f. Norwick (USA) 120–Dusty Bluebell (Sky Gipsy 117) [1989 6f 6f⁵ 6m 6f 1990 8m 6m 8.3m 7h⁴ 7m 8f⁶ 7m] leggy, unfurnished filly: has a round action: poor plater: ran as if something amiss final outing: may prove suited by return to 6f: blinkered last 4 starts: often sweating. *J. W. Payne.*   —

BELMEZ (USA)   3 b.c. El Gran Senor (USA) 136–Grace Note (FR) 99 (Top **131** Ville 129) [1989 8g* 1990 11g* 12.3d* 12g³ 12m* 12g* 12g⁵ 12f]

For most of the year it was long odds against the sport's producing a more sensational come-back story than that of Belmez who was retired injured in May then won the King George VI and Queen Elizabeth Diamond Stakes in July. Those for whom Belmez might easily have remained as just one more in a long list of leading contenders for the Derby which failed to appear on race day, were instead sent scurrying for their Lazarus analogies and a shower of superlatives for the colt's trainer Henry Cecil after Belmez's rousing head-to-head with stable-companion Old Vic for Britain's most important middle-distance prize. That Belmez should be the sole three-year-old to take on his elders at Ascot and Old Vic the only one to make a fight of it with him, was an unlikely scenario, the proverbial privilege to watch, considering the chequered progress of both colts's final season. Just eleven weeks earlier the plan for Belmez had merely been 'to try to get him a job at stud somewhere' following a near-fore tendon injury sustained in the Dalham Chester Vase. How many stud owners must have raised their hands when nine days after that announcement the retirement prognosis had shifted to 'fifty-fifty'? Belmez was reported as having his first full workout two days later, then less than six weeks after that he was lining up for the Irish Derby. Following a ring-rusty third in that and his top-class performance in the King George, a place at stud needed no soliciting.

Dalham Chester Vase—the race attracts Belmez (left) and Quest For Fame

King George VI and Queen Elizabeth Diamond Stakes, Ascot—
stable-companions Belmez and Old Vic (rails) in a pulsating finish;
Assatis (right) beats his stable-companion Cacoethes (No. 2) for third

Encouraging as that run in Ireland was, the anticipation that surrounds the King George VI and Queen Elizabeth Diamond Stakes as a test of succeeding generations was in 1990 almost exclusively centred on the triple-classic winner Salsabil who had beaten Belmez four and three quarter lengths at the Curragh. Sadly, the watering at Ascot which trainer Harwood reportedly criticised as too extensive was not extensive enough for Salsabil's owner. Even without her, Belmez was still available in the morning at 12/1 sixth-favourite in a field of eleven. Besides on grounds of fitness, Cecil hoped for some improvement as a result of a near-side brush pricker (apparently the first time that he had used one) and Fulmar bridle, fitted to correct Belmez's tendency to hang left. With Cauthen not unnaturally siding once more with Old Vic, Belmez also had a new jockey in Kinane whose reputation as a man for the big occasion had burgeoned again after his classic successes on Tirol and Go And Go. He wore Sheikh Mohammed's third colours, the second going to Old Vic and the first to the Coronation Cup winner In The Wings who occupied the first two positions in the betting. Doubts existed about that pair's effectiveness on the good to firm ground and about the current form of two of the previous season's other leading three-year-olds Cacoethes (who'd lost narrowly to Nashwan in the 1989 running) and Legal Case. Without those four, the race looked a far from vintage edition, the rest comprising Cacoethes' pacemaker Limeburn, Lady Beaverbrook's pair Terimon and Charmer, the all-the-way Princess of Wales's Stakes winner Sapience, a progressive colt in Husyan, and Assatis whose outstanding record at Ascot was becoming expensive to ignore but whose jockey was the rather less well known Masato Shibata. Notable absentees and sizeable question marks then, but this was one ot the races of the season. It began, as had the Derby, with an element of farce when the pacemaker missed the break, and Old Vic was left to try and make all as he'd done so majestically at Chantilly and the Curragh over twelve months earlier. Sapience, then the redundant Limeburn, harried him for a long way but rounding the home turn it was Belmez who was Old Vic's nearest pursuer, two lengths down, with Cacoethes emerging best from scrimmaging caused by the weakening Limeburn, and Assatis, who'd come round the outside, just behind him. Only this quartet had a chance. Soon it came to rest between just two of them as Belmez joined Old Vic at the two-furlong marker. The younger colt seemed to have a clear edge at that stage but Old Vic would concede nothing, stretching to get back in front, and a stirring duel ensued with neither colt able to keep a true line but both running on with the utmost resolution under strong pressure. Belmez held on by a neck. Assatis was a length and a half further away in third, keeping on well, with Cacoethes another five back in fourth. Henry Cecil was winning a second

King George and Sheikh Mohammed his first, after the partnership had gone close with Oh So Sharp in 1985. Cecil's step-father Captain Boyd-Rochfort had trained Almeria and Doutelle to fill the minor places in 1958 and Barry Hills had done the same with Rheingold and Our Mirage in 1973 but this was the first time that a trainer had been responsible for both winner and runner-up, and it was only the second that an owner had had two horses placed, following the Queen's Boyd-Rochfort-trained duo who lost out to Ballymoss. Cecil was reported to be disappointed that the finishing order of his two in 1990 had not been the other way around!

So how would we remember Belmez if the injury sustained at Chester had been as serious as first thought? He'd surely earned some place in the history books as a Cecil-trained 50/1-winner when beating stable-companion Satin Wood first time out in a fast time for a two-year-old maiden at Newmarket, but although he kept his unbeaten record in the £6,900 Burghclere Stakes at Newbury and the Dalham Chester Vase, enthusiasm for him immediately after his win at Chester had become distinctly tempered. Emotions seldom run high about races with so small a field as that in which Belmez started at 13/8 on to beat the Horris Hill third Missionary Ridge, who'd disappointed in the Guardian Classic Trial, and the Newbury maiden-race winner Quest For Fame. A modest early gallop also failed to excite those searching for a classic trial of solid merit and Belmez struggled to win; having joined Quest For Fame on the final turn, he could never get more than a length in front, Cauthen having to administer some sharp slaps down Belmez's shoulder to try and prevent his hanging left. Belmez looked inexperienced and idle—much the same story as at Newbury. The *Sporting Life's* correspondent drew a parallel between Belmez's Derby backers (he was then second favourite) and those with 'money to burn' but while news of Belmez's retirement five days later effectively justified that observation, it also of course placed his workmanlike win in a rather better light, a light which became positively radiant, when Quest For Fame went on to win the Derby himself.

Ironically, Belmez turned out to be virtually the only one of Britain's top three-year-old colts left to contest anything from the increasingly enticing

Great Voltigeur Stakes, York—Belmez gives weight to Snurge

spread of big middle-distance races abroad at the back-end. Quest For Fame and Deploy weren't seen out after the Irish Derby, Sanglamore after the French. The Arc de Triomphe, Breeders' Cup Turf, Rothmans International and Japan Cup were all possible targets meanwhile for Belmez with the Great Voltigeur Stakes at York his one race in the interim. Though this wasn't going to be the exercise canter that Cecil's previous King George winner Reference Point enjoyed in 1987, a victory for Belmez still looked something of a formality in the Voltigeur's now-customary small field. Cecil, however, had earlier predicted that Belmez would 'never look impressive' and, for a 2/1-on shot, he certainly wasn't at York—except in his implacable tenacity. It was the 22/1-outsider Snurge, on only his second run of the year, who threatened a shock result and demanded everything of Belmez having caught him flat-footed over two furlongs out but, having looked beaten then, Belmez came back to win by a head. Ascot's short straight has witnessed some protracted battles for the King George, some of which clearly left their mark on the protagonists, and the possibility that Belmez might not have recovered after his exacting efforts there must have crossed some minds as he scraped home at York. However, a longer look revealed Karinga Bay, Blue Stag and Starstreak, who'd dominated the Gordon Stakes three weeks earlier, eight lengths adrift after a none too pressing early gallop. If there were still lingering doubts as to the merit of Belmez's performance in conceding 5 lb then hindsight, again, and Snurge removed them in the St Leger. Now to those prestige- and prize-money-loaded races in the autumn. After Old Vic's set-back, Belmez was to carry the stable's hopes in the Prix de l'Arc de Triomphe but he very nearly didn't make the field. Two days before the race (one after being supplemented for just over £30,000) he trod on a flint at exercise and bruised a foot, prompting another one of those 'fifty-fifty' prognoses. Belmez was allowed to take his chance, travelling to France on the morning of the race, but his four-and-three-quarter-length fifth to Saumarez, having held a good position, was below his best. Everything has to go right to win the Arc and in this instance it clearly didn't. His run when favourite for the Japan Cup at Tokyo in late-November needs even less excusing. The very firm ground may well be relevant to his performance but it's notoriously hard anyway to guarantee a horse's form so late in the season on the other side of the world and, for whatever reason, Belmez couldn't produce his, being unable to improve his position from the final turn and finishing seventh of the fifteen runners about five lengths behind the Australian winner Better Loosen Up. Belmez had reportedly taken the journey to Japan much better than that out of quarantine.

		Northern Dancer	Nearctic
	El Gran Senor (USA)	(b 1961)	Natalma
	(b 1981)	Sex Appeal	Buckpasser
Belmez (USA)		(ch 1970)	Best In Show
(b.c. 1987)		Top Ville	High Top
	Grace Note (FR)	(b 1976)	Sega Ville
	(b 1982)	Val de Grace	Val de Loir
		(b 1969)	Pearly Queen

Belmez is home bred from a family notable for its achievements over middle distances in France, including three winners of the Prix de Diane. Belmez's fifth dam Pearl Cap took the Pouliches, Jacques le Marois and Vermeille as well as the Diane before becoming the first filly to win the Arc de Triomphe in 1931 at the end of which she was hailed as 'undoubtedly the best filly seen on the French turf this century' by the *Bloodstock Breeders Review*. The 1966 Diane winner Fine Pearl was half-sister to Belmez's third dam Pearl Queen, and Lypharita who won the race in 1985 is out of a half-sister to Belmez's dam Grace Note. There are several other useful middle-distance performers in Grace Note's immediate family and she was one herself, winning a mile-and-a-quarter maiden at Chepstow and coming second to Kiliniski in the Lingfield Oaks Trial before disappointing in the Ribblesdale and Lancashire Oaks on her only two other starts. Trained by Ian Balding, she was prone to the same tendency to hang left as, for a long time, was her first foal Belmez. Grace Note's two-year-old of 1990 is the Irish-trained Sovereign Dancer colt Dowland who won a seven-furlong maiden at the Curragh and came third in the Beresford Stakes. After a short-lived colt by Shadeed, Grace

Note has foaled to Shadeed again and is now in foal to Darshaan. Belmez confirms El Gran Senor's ability to get runners in the top flight—some may have had doubts after Saratogan and Al Hareb—but increases the disappointment that the brilliant 1984 Guineas winner has had so few offspring to represent him; Belmez is one of only twenty-four live foals in his second crop though that's ten more than were produced in his first. An increase in the number of mares covered has resulted in an additional ten more foals again in his third crop but El Gran Senor's low fertility will presumably have had an adverse effect on the quality of mares visiting him. Belmez is in many ways the antithesis of his sire on the racecourse; he obviously didn't have anything like the same precocity and even the most ardent supporter would not claim that a turn of foot was his hallmark. Both El Gran Senor and Belmez displayed a phlegmatic attitude on the racecourse but whereas that helped make El Gran Senor the perfect ride, Belmez's jockey must have wished that the characteristic had been a little less pronounced. It soon became evident that Belmez would prove better at a mile and a half than shorter distances and suited by a strongly-run race at that trip. A moderate mover, he never raced on very soft ground and possibly didn't act on very firm. Fairly typically for the Northern Dancer line, Belmez is on the small side—but lengthy and attractive with it. He's to stand at the Queen's Wolferton Stud at a fee of £18,000 on October 1st terms. *H. R. A. Cecil.*

BELOVED VISITOR (USA) 2 b.f. (Feb 10) Miswaki (USA) 124–Abeesh 83
(USA) 77 (Nijinsky (CAN) 138) [1990 6m* 6g* 6m 7g³ 6d] rather leggy, quite attractive filly: second foal: half-sister to 3-y-o Tickle Touch (by Stop The Music), 7f winner at 2 yrs: dam lightly-raced middle-distance maiden: losing odds on, successful in 11-runner maiden at Leopardstown and 7-runner minor event (by 3 lengths, reportedly easing clear) at Naas: never better than mid-division in 13-runner Coventry Stakes at Royal Ascot, third start: seems to stay 7f. *J. S. Bolger, Ireland.*

BELSALAAMA (USA) 2 b.c. (Jan 28) Alydar (USA)–Softly (USA) (Solo 69 p
Landing (USA)) [1990 7m⁵ 7s 7s³] $300,000Y: unfurnished colt: half-brother to 4 winners, including quite useful 1982 2-y-o 7f winner The Quiet Don (by Caucasus): dam very useful sprinter at 2 yrs: quite modest form in maidens: caught eye not knocked about when remote third at Newcastle in November: likely to do better at 3 yrs over middle distances. *M. R. Stoute.*

BELTALONG 4 gr.f. Belfort (FR) 89–Gentian (Roan Rocket 128) [1989 9d 7.5d* —
10m 9f³ 10f² 12m* a12g 1990 a11g a14g 12.4s] leggy, angular filly: winning plater as 3-y-o: well beaten in autumn: best form over middle distances on top-of-the-ground: has won for claimer: bandaged last 3 starts at 3 yrs: sold 2,500 gns Ascot December Sales. *J. Wharton.*

BELTANE BOY 2 b.g. (Feb 21) Forzando 122–Travel Free (Be My Guest (USA) 53
126) [1990 5g 5g⁵ 5g³ 5m⁴ 5m] 4,200F, 5,800Y: smallish, rather sparely-made gelding: moderate mover: second foal: dam ran 3 times at 2 yrs: plating-class maiden at best: sold 680 gns Doncaster September Sales. *J. S. Wilson.*

BE MAGIC 2 ch.f. (May 12) Persian Bold 123–Be Sweet 117 (Reform 132) [1990 57
6m³ 5d⁶ 5g⁵ 8.2d] sparely-made, angular filly: seventh foal: half-sister to several winners, including useful 1984 2-y-o 7f and 1m winner Top Bee (by Shirley Heights) and 13.3f winner King Menelaos (by Ile de Bourbon): dam, half-sister to Royal Hive and Attica Meli, smart at up to 1½m: plating-class form: stays 1m: sold 7,400 gns Newmarket December Sales. *A. C. Stewart.*

BE MY BABY (IRE) 2 b.f. (Apr 3) Bairn (USA) 126–Sipapu 90 (Targowice 63
(USA) 130) [1990 a5g* 5m³ 5g³ 5m 6g² 6g 6d 5m² 6d] 4,400F, 10,500Y: lengthy, rather unfurnished filly: moderate mover: sixth foal: half-sister to irresolute 3-y-o Gotcher (by Jalmood), 6f winner at 2 yrs, and a winner in Norway: dam won at 6f and 7f: quite modest performer: won maiden at Lingfield in April: likely to prove better suited by 6f than 5f: has run well for 7-lb claimer: sold 7,500 gns Newmarket Autumn Sales. *N. A. Callaghan.*

BE MY CHIEF (USA) 3 b.c. Chief's Crown (USA)–Lady Be Mine (USA) 76 (Sir —
Ivor 135) [1989 6m* 6f* 7m* 7f* 7m* 8g* 1990 10g] strong, good-topped, attractive colt: has a powerful, slightly round action: leading 2-y-o of 1989 (rated 123), successful in maiden at Doncaster, Chesham Stakes at Royal Ascot, listed race at Newmarket, Imry Solario Stakes at Sandown, Lanson Champagne Vintage Stakes at Goodwood and Racing Post Trophy at Newcastle: reportedly unable to be trained on the firm ground in 1990, leading 7f and weakening quickly in Scottish Classic

(favourite) at Ayr on only start: should have stayed at least 1¼m: raced lazily: will stand at National Stud in 1991, fee £5,000 (Oct 1). *H. R. A. Cecil.*

BE MY RUNNER 4 b.g. Runnett 125–Ivorysguest (Be My Guest (USA) 126) **74** [1989 5s⁶ 6d³ 7g² 6m³ 6m⁶ 7g² 8m 7m* 7s² 8d² 1990 8g 8m³] leggy, quite attractive gelding: moderate mover: modest handicapper: third of 4 in £7,200 event won by Nayland at Newmarket in June: stays 1m: yet to race on firm going, acts on any other: below form in blinkers (edgy) seventh start at 3 yrs: has taken keen hold: consistent. *J. Sutcliffe.*

BEN ADHEM 8 b.g. Hotfoot 126–Heaven Chosen 91 (High Top 131) [1989 11v **86** 12d⁵ a12g⁴ 1990 10g 12d² 12d²] leggy, rather lightly-built gelding: has a rather round action: fair handicapper: stays 1½m: suited by give in the ground: has won for apprentice: occasionally on toes: none too consistent. *H. Candy.*

BENAZIR 3 b.f. High Top 131–Crusader's Dream 88 (St Paddy 133) [1989 7g⁴ **91** 1990 7g* 7g 8h³ 7d³ 7m⁵ 7f⁴ 7m² 7.6d⁴ 8m* 9m⁴] lengthy, good-topped filly: has plenty of scope: fairly useful performer: won maiden at Epsom in April and rallied well to dead-heat with Remthat Naser in minor contest at Leicester in October: ran well in Newmarket minor event final start: stays 9f: acts on hard and dead ground: keen sort. *W. Jarvis.*

BEN-ELEAZER 2 gr.c. (Feb 1) Electric 126 Elfinaria 79 (Song 132) [1990 7m — 8m] 4,400Y: angular, unfurnished colt: poor mover: eighth living foal: half-brother to 2 winners in Italy: dam sprinting half-sister to smart 7f and 1m performer Fair Season: well beaten in autumn maidens: taken out of stalls then refused to re-enter them intended debut: blinkered final start: temperamental. *J. D. Czerpak.*

BENNO 2 ch.c. (Mar 20) Chief Singer 131–Swan Ann 84 (My Swanee 122) [1990 **64** 5m⁶ 6g² 6d² 6g] 47,000Y: stocky colt: half-brother to 5 winners, including very smart sprinter Primo Dominie (by Dominion) and Salisbury 2000 Guineas Trial winner Poyle Crusher (by Sweet Revenge). dam 6f winner: quite modest form when runner-up in maidens at Nottingham and Catterick: ran poorly final start: will probably be better suited by 7f. *J. A. R. Toller.*

BENNY LEONARD 4 b.g. Henbit (USA) 130–Brenda (Sovereign Path 125) — [1989 10m 1990 12.5f] big, lengthy, good-quartered gelding: quite modest form as 2-y-o: tailed off in April claimer at Wolverhampton, only second subsequent outing: should stay at least 1¼m. *M. H. Tompkins.*

BENNYS SPECIAL 3 ch.g. Tower Walk 130–Needless 81 (Petingo 135) [1989 — NR 1990 a12g] 8,400Y: sixth foal: half-brother to useful middle-distance performer Telephone Man (by Record Token) and a winning hurdler: dam 1½m winner: no sign of ability in claimer at Lingfield in April. *E. Eldin.*

BEN ROYALE 3 b.g. King of Spain 121–Fille de General (Brigadier Gerard 144) — [1989 6g 8.2s⁶ 8.2g 1990 10v 9s 8m] workmanlike gelding: plating-class form: best effort over 1m on soft ground. *J. M. Jefferson.*

BEN'S BEAUTY 2 b.g. (Mar 4) Aragon 118–Aunt Charlotte 85 (Charlottown — 127) [1990 7.5g 6m 8g 6m] 1,000Y: leggy gelding: half-brother to several winners here and abroad, including fairly useful 1¼m to 1¾m winner Chiclet (by Formidable): dam stayed very well: well beaten, including in seller: twice unruly at stalls. *J. P. Smith.*

BEN'S BIRDIE 10 ch.g. Track Spare 125–Gold Topaz 76 (Goldhill 125) [1989 NR — 1990 13m 11 5g 15d 15 3g] smallish, plain gelding: won apprentice handicap as 8-y-o: no form in 1990: stayed 15f: best with plenty of give in the ground: occasionally wore blinkers: often sweated: dead. *C. N. Allen.*

BENZ BEST 4 gr.g. Busted 134–Howzat (Habat 127) [1989 12s⁵ 16d⁶ 12m³ 14f⁶ **62** 1990 10.2f 13s 12f⁶ 11f⁵ 10d² 10.2m⁵ 10m 8g 10m⁴ 10f² 10f⁵] sturdy, round-barrelled gelding: quite modest maiden: best at 1¼m: acts on firm and dead going: blinkered first and eighth outings: visored last 2: has started slowly. *M. H. Easterby.*

BENZINE (USA) 3 b.c. Secreto (USA) 128–Baby Diamonds (Habitat 134) [1989 **102** d 8m⁴ 8s³ 1990 2g² 11.5m² 12g 10f 10d 11s⁶ 8d³ 10.5g⁴ 12g³ᵈⁱˢ 10s] strong, stocky colt: carries condition: has a markedly round action: useful form when second in listed race at Epsom and to Rock Hopper in Group 3 event at Lingfield in the spring: subsequently contested 5 pattern events abroad and below best in frame in minor event and maidens: suited by 1½m, possibly not by extremes of going: may prove suited by more forcing tactics: changed hands before third outing and left P. Cole's stable afterwards: disappointing. *M. A. Jarvis.*

BERBERANA 3 b.f. Never So Bold 135–Ricura 83 (Hello Gorgeous (USA) 128) **65** [1989 6m* 6s 1990 6g⁶ 6m 6g⁵ 6g] leggy, workmanlike filly: quite modest performer: on toes and ran well in handicaps first 3 starts, poorly when blinkered-favourite for claimer in June: well worth a try over further: acts on good to firm ground, faced stiff task on soft. *J. W. Watts.*

BERCY (USA) 3 ch.g. Diesis 133–Bechamel (USA) 91 (Sauce Boat (USA)) [1989 — 6m⁵ 1990 10.6d] leggy gelding: no worthwhile form in minor event (sweating and coltish, tended to hang after slow start) and maiden (tailed off): sold 900 gns Newmarket Autumn Sales. *G. Harwood.*

BERILLON 3 b.c. Rousillon (USA) 133–Obertura (USA) 100 (Roberto (USA) 131) **105** [1989 8g 1990 10m* 11.7m 12m² 12m] rangy colt: won 3-runner £10,100 maiden at Ascot in July: clearly best other effort, putting up useful performance, when second of 13 to Down The Flag in £7,600 handicap at Newmarket, making most: suited by strong pace at 1½m, and will stay further: appeared unsuited by track at Windsor: to join Bobby Frankel in USA. *G. Harwood.*

BERKELEY HILL BOY 3 ch.g. Castle Keep 121–Brown Velvet 68 (Mansingh **53** (USA) 120) [1989 7f 6d 7g 1990 7m 8g 7g 7m 6f* 6f 6f 6g 6d] rangy gelding: won maiden at Brighton in August, making most and jinking right over 1f out: no comparable form: seems best at 6f: acts on firm going: blinkered last 6 outings: has wandered under pressure. *R. Akehurst.*

BERLIN BREAKOUT 2 b. or br.c. (Feb 19) Never So Bold 135–Rostova 91 — (Blakeney 126) [1990 6m⁶] quite attractive colt: second foal: dam middle-distance stayer: sixth of 10 to Act of Diplomacy in maiden at Newmarket in July: dead. *B. W. Hills.*

BERLIN WALL (IRE) 2 b. or br.c. (Feb 25) Thatching 131–Friedrichsruh (FR) — p (Dschingis Khan) [1990 6m] quite attractive colt: half-brother to smart 1¼m winner Blessed Event (by Kings Lake), 1½m winner Rhine Wine (by Home Guard) and a bumpers winner: dam won 11f German Oaks: hampered leaving stalls, soon behind and not knocked about in autumn maiden at Newmarket: looks sort to do better. *L. M. Cumani.*

BERMUDA LILY 3 br.f. Dunbeath (USA) 127–Lily Bank 73 (Young Generation — 129) [1989 5f 5m* 6g 5f 6g⁵ 6f⁵ 6d⁵ 1990 6g 6g 6f 6m 6f] angular, sparely-made filly: moderate walker and mover: modest winner at 2 yrs: below form in handicaps in 1990: stays 6f: acts on good to firm ground (out of her depth on dead): blinkered final start at 2 yrs: thrice bandaged behind. *R. Hannon.*

BERNSTEIN BETTE 4 b.f. Petong 126–Glenfield Portion 86 (Mummy's Pet **73** 125) [1989 6m* 6f3 6f4 6g² 6g² 6f4 7d 1990 6f 6m3 6s 6m* 6m3 6m 6m5 6m6 6m5 6m3 6d 6d] good-quartered filly: carries condition: modest handicapper: won at Redcar (on toes) in June: stays 6f well: probably acts on any going: has given trouble at stalls: retained by trainer 3,600 gns Newmarket December Sales. *P. S. Felgate.*

BERRY'S DREAM 3 b.f. Darshaan 133–Berrys Cay (USA) (The Minstrel **101** (CAN) 135) [1989 7.3v* 1990 10m5 10.5m4 12s4 11d²] leggy, quite attractive filly: won listed race at Newbury in October as 2-y-o: contested listed and pattern events in 1990, leading over 1¼m on first run for 2½ months when 1½ lengths second of 6 to Pirate Army in Doonside Cup at Ayr: very edgy when tailed off in Lancashire Oaks at Haydock time before: stays 11f: has given impression should prove best on an easy surface. *R. W. Armstrong.*

BERT DAVEY 3 b.g. Homing 130–Tea-Pot (Ragstone 128) [1989 NR 1990 12.5g] — 2,500Y: fourth foal: half-brother to winning hurdler Mr Dormouse (by Comedy Star) and modest 5-y-o 11f to 12.4f winner One For The Pot (by Nicholas Bill): dam out-and-out stayer: coltish and bit backward, moved poorly down when tailed off in claimer at Wolverhampton in July. *J. Pearce.*

BERTIE'S GIRL 3 b.f. Another Realm 118–Anner Amanda 57 (Mandamus 120) — [1989 NR 1990 12d] sixth foal: half-sister to a winning hurdler: dam, poor maiden on flat, successful in juvenile hurdles, is out of half-sister to top-class chaser Lochroe: 50/1, tailed off in maiden at Folkestone in November. *J. V. Redmond.*

BERTIE WOOSTER 7 ch.g. Homeboy 114–Peace of Mind 81 (Midsummer **94** Night II 117) [1989 7d 6g* 6f² 6f3 6m5 6m6 6m* 6s 6g 6v 1990 6f 6m3 6m 7g 6d5 7m 6m5 6m 6g* 6m² 6d² 5m 6d² 6s5] strong, compact gelding: moderate mover: quite useful handicapper: won £12,500 event at York in August by ½ length from Polar Bird: better efforts after when second to Masnun at same course, Final Shot in Ladbrokes (Ayr) Gold Cup and Reference Light in £8,400 race at Newmarket: suited by 6f: not at his best on soft going, acts on any other: has occasionally given trouble at start and sweated: effective with blinkers or without: usually gets behind: tough. *R. J. Holder.*

BESCABY BOY 4 b.g. Red Sunset 120–Charo (Mariacci (FR) 133) [1989 8.2s² 67
8g² 8.2s³ 8.2m² 10m⁵ 8g⁴ 8m* 8.2m* 8.3g⁵ 7s 1990 8.2m³ 10m 8g* 9f⁵ a8g⁵ 8m
8m⁶ 8m⁵ 8m⁶ 8d] strong, angular gelding: quite modest handicapper: tried to bite
eventual third well inside final 1f when winning at Ripon in July: suited by 1m: acts
on any going: blinkered 4 times at 2 yrs: has worn bandages, got on toes and given
trouble at stalls: winning hurdler in March. *J. Wharton.*

BESITO 3 b.f. Wassl 125–Field Day 87 (Northfields (USA)) [1989 7g 1990 7.6d⁴ 79
12m 16m* 14g 16f⁴ 16m³ 16d*] rather angular filly: good walker: moderate mover:
won maiden at Nottingham in August, leading post having wandered under
pressure, and handicap at Chester in October, showing improved form to beat
Glazerite by 25 lengths: suited by good test of stamina: clearly very well suited by
soft surface: trained until after second start by R. Hollinshead. *R. Simpson.*

BESSIE SURTEES 2 ch.f. (Apr 12) Mansingh (USA) 120–Stonebow Lady 52 44
(Windjammer (USA)) [1990 5m 6f²] 2,300Y: smallish, good-quartered filly:
half-sister to several poor animals: dam runner-up over 1m and 9f, is half-sister to
dam of Petong (by Mansingh): 3 lengths second of 11, staying on despite hanging
right, in maiden at Pontefract in July. *T. D. Barron.*

BESS POOL 2 ch.f. (Feb 26) Sayf El Arab (USA) 127–Bold Apple (Bold Lad (IRE) 61
133) [1990 5m³ 5g³ 6g 6m⁴ 6m⁶ 7f 6d* 6d] 4,200Y: sturdy filly: second foal:
half-sister to 3-y-o Lady Henrietta (by Aragon): dam half-sister to smart 6f and 1¼m
winner Sarania and to dam of Pennine Walk: blinkered first time, won selling
nursery (no bid) at Lingfield, showing much improved form, in October: raced on
disadvantageous part of track on final outing: will probably stay 7f: visored when
running poorly sixth start: sold 5,200 gns Newmarket Autumn Sales. *D. W. P.
Arbuthnot.*

BEST EFFORT 4 ch.g. Try My Best (USA) 130–Lunaria (USA) (Twist The Axe 58
(USA)) [1989 10.6g 11.5g⁵ 10m³ 12g 1990 12g 10f⁴ 8m⁴ 9s³ a11g] strong,
workmanlike gelding: quite modest maiden: stays 11.5f: acts on good to firm and soft
going: trained first 3 starts by R. Holder. *M. P. Naughton.*

BEST EMPEROR (USA) 4 gr.c. Secreto (USA) 128–Port Aransas (USA) 80 62 d
(Quack (USA)) [1989 NR 1990 11s³ 8v 12g 10g 12g 10m⁵] workmanlike colt: poor
mover: fourth foal: half-brother to a winner in North America by Sharpen Up: dam
winning stayer: worthwhile form only when third in maiden at Hamilton: ran too
freely in blinkers final outing: stays 11f: seems to need soft going: has had tongue
tied down: usually sweats away. *J. Mackie.*

BESTOW 3 br.f. Shirley Heights 130–Clandestina (USA) 98 (Secretariat (USA)) 76
[1989 6m⁶ 8g⁵ 1990 12.3g² 12.2d² 12.2m² 14f* 16m* 17.6f 18g⁴ a14g⁴] quite
attractive filly: good mover: modest performer: made virtually all to win maiden at
Yarmouth then led 6f out and battled on well to win handicap at Warwick, both in
August: may prove best at 2m: acts on firm and dead going. *B. W. Hills.*

BEST TIMES 3 br.g. Good Times (ITY)–Pretty Miss (So Blessed 130) [1989 NR 68
1990 10g⁴ 10.1m] rather leggy, angular gelding: third foal: half-brother to 7f and
1¼m winner Follow The Drum (by Daring March): dam once-raced half-sister to
useful 2-y-o Fair Parrot: fourth in maiden at Leicester in May: pulled up in minor
event following month: dead. *J. D. Bethell.*

BETHEL ORCHARD 5 b.m. Tyrnavos 129–Skysted (Busted 134) [1989 10.1m —
8.3m² 10f 14m 15.3m 1990 15.5f a14g] leggy, angular mare: poor maiden: effective at
1m and stays 11.7f: sold 820 gns Doncaster October Sales. *Dr J. D. Scargill.*

BET OLIVER 7 b.m. Kala Shikari 125–Lor Darnie 65 (Dumbarnie 125) [1989 NR —
1990 a7g a10g a6g a5g a6g a7g] compact mare: of little account: blinkered fourth and
fifth outings. *D. C. Jermy.*

BETONY (USA) 3 b.f. Majestic Light (USA)–Bethamane (USA) (Wajima (USA)) 81 p
[1989 NR 1990 12f*] lengthy filly: has scope: fifth foal: half-sister to a minor winner
in USA by Northern Baby and Irish bumper winner Merino Waltz (by Nijinsky): dam
unraced half-sister to smart 6f (at 2 yrs) to 10.6f winner Wassl Touch from excellent
family: 6/1 and very green, won 8-runner maiden at Salisbury in August by 8 lengths
from Apsimore, running on strongly under hand riding. *J. H. M. Gosden.*

BETWEEN THE SHEETS 5 b.g. Crooner 119–Miss Chianti (Royben 125) —
[1989 12s 15.8m⁴ 15.8m 18.8f⁴ 16.2f* a16g 1990 16m a13g] rangy gelding: poor
handicapper: won at Beverley as 4-y-o: tailed off both outings in autumn: stays 2m:
acts on firm going: has taken keen hold. *W. Carter.*

BETWEEN THE STICKS 3 gr.f. Pharly (FR) 130–Sandstream 72 (Sandford 80
Lad 133) [1989 5g* 5m* 5f² 5m⁴ 5f⁶ 6g³ 1990 6m 6f 6m³ 5m⁵ 6m⁵ a5g 5g 6d 5s]
smallish, rather sparely-made filly: fair performer: 40/1, good seventh of 28 to Final

Shot in Ayr Gold Cup penultimate start, ran poorly in Haydock minor event final one: stays 6f: acts on good to firm ground and dead: has run well for 7-lb claimer: swerved at stalls on reappearance. *M. H. Tompkins.*

BETWEEN TIME　3 gr.f. Elegant Air 119–Beveridge (USA) 86 (Spectacular Bid 　**63** (USA)) [1989 6f³ 6f² 6h* 7f² 6m² 7m 6s 1990 7.5m 8f 10g 7m⁵ 6m² 6f] rather sparely-made filly: quite modest handicapper: easily best 3-y-o effort when second at Ripon in August, short of room 2f out then running on strongly: co-favourite and on toes, slowly away and swished tail when always behind at Thirsk week later: probably stays 1m: acts on hard ground: possibly unsatisfactory. *P. Calver.*

BEX (USA)　4 ch.f. Explodent (USA)–Bay Street 114 (Grundy 137) [1989 8m* 10f³ 　— 10g* 10.5s* 1990 9m 10.5d 10m] useful-looking filly: progressive as 3-y-o, winning Prix de Flore at Saint-Cloud on final outing: well beaten in pattern events in 1990: should stay 1½m: goes well on soft ground, and possibly unsuited by firm. *R. W. Armstrong.*

BEYNOUNAH (IRE)　2 b.f. (Feb 12) Shareef Dancer (USA) 135–Rare Roberta 　**76** (USA) 118 (Roberto (USA) 131) [1990 6m⁶ 5g* 7g⁵ 7m] neat filly: fourth foal: half-sister to fair 1¼m winner Al Raja (by Kings Lake): dam 6f and 1m winner: modest performer: won maiden at Beverley in August: stays 7f: possibly suited by an easy surface. *B. Hanbury.*

BEYOND MOMBASA　3 br.f. Silly Prices 110–Elitist 72 (Keren 100) [1989 7m 　— 1990 10.6s 11g] compact filly: of little account. *N. Chamberlain.*

BEYOND OUR REACH　2 br.c. (Feb 20) Reach 122–Over Beyond 78 (Bold Lad 　**66** ? (IRE) 133) [1990 5f² 5s² 5f* 5f³ 5g⁵ 5m⁴ 6f² 5g* a8g⁵ a6g] 13,500Y: sturdy colt: moderate mover: half-brother to several winners here and abroad, including 11.5f winner and winning jumper Tebitto (by Derrylin): dam, placed at up to 9f in Ireland, is half-sister to good Italian winner Pipino: quite modest performer: successful in maiden at Ripon and nursery (making all and much better effort) at Hamilton: ran moderately on all-weather last 2 starts: should be at least as effective at 6f as 5f: possibly suited by an easy surface: sweated, and hung badly, seventh start: sold out of J. Berry's stable 5,900 gns Doncaster October Sales before ninth outing. *C. J. Hill.*

B GRADE　5 b.m. Lucky Wednesday 124–Hitravelscene (Mansingh (USA) 120) 　**53** [1989 7.5d 6g⁵ 6m 6g⁶ 7g 6g⁴ 6s² 6g 6g 5s 1990 6g a7g 6d 6d⁶ a7g a8g 6m 6s² 6d 6s² 6s 6s] leggy, plain mare: has a round action: quite modest handicapper on her day: suited by 7f or stiff 6f: best on an easy surface: often starts slowly: has got on toes, been mounted outside paddock and taken down early: looked none too keen fifth outing: not one to rely on. *J. Balding.*

B GREAT　2 ch.c. (Feb 3) Vaigly Great 127–Gunnard 62 (Gunner B 126) [1990 5g⁵ 　— 5g] 1,000 2-y-o: angular, workmanlike colt: fourth foal: half-brother to 3-y-o 11f winner Foot Soldier (by Hotfoot) and 1½m seller winner Innovator (by Relkino): dam won 1m and 1¼m sellers: no show in maidens in May. *Mrs P. A. Barker.*

BHARKAT　4 b.g. Beldale Flutter (USA) 130–Cienaga (Tarboosh (USA)) [1989 8g 　— 10.5g⁵ 1990 16.2g⁴] has a fluent action: lightly-raced maiden: bandaged off-hind, tailed-off last of 4 in amateurs handicap at Beverley in August: should be suited by 1½m +: winning hurdler in 1989/90. *J. Norton.*

BICKERMAN　7 b.h. Mummy's Pet 125–Merry Weather 69 (Will Somers 114§) 　— [1989 10.6d 10m⁶ 10m⁶ 1990 10m⁶ 10g] leggy, lightly-made horse: modest handicapper as 4-y-o: no subsequent worthwhile form on flat: stays 1¼m: acts on firm going: blinkered twice: has hung: winning hurdler in 1989/90. *J. L. Spearing.*

BIDDERS LOVE LANE　2 b.f. (May 5) Ring Bidder 88–Bundling Bed 69 　**48** (Welsh Pageant 132) [1990 5f⁶ 5f 5d* 6g 6m 5f⁶ 5g 5m⁶ 5g] small filly: has a quick action: first foal: dam 2-y-o 6f winner won 9f seller at 4 yrs: poor performer: made all in claimer at Beverley in May: should stay 6f: yet to race on soft going, acts on any other. *R. M. Whitaker.*

BID FOR ELEGANCE　2 b.f. (Mar 19) Nordance (USA)–Single Bid 68 (Auction 　**66** Ring (USA) 123) [1990 5m⁵ 6d² 5m² 7m⁴ 7m⁵] 12,500Y: angular filly: second foal: half-sister to 3-y-o One At A Time (by Music Boy): dam ran only at sprint distances: quite modest maiden: stays 7f: upset in stalls fourth outing. *R. Hannon.*

BID FOR STARDOM (IRE)　2 ch.c. (Apr 25) Fayruz 116–Windy Lady 　**59** (Whistling Wind 123) [1990 7m 7g 6d] 7,200Y: good-topped colt, with scope: half-brother to several winners, including 1¼m winner Al Khaled (by Lord Gayle) and 1985 2-y-o 5f winner Virgin Prince (by Prince Tenderfoot), later useful winner in Italy: dam lightly-raced Irish maiden: quite modest maiden: better suited by 7f than 6f. *R. Hannon.*

BIDING TIME   3 ro.f. Bellypha 130–Biding 97 (Habat 127) [1989 NR 1990 8f 8f **31** 10f 6f 6m⁵ 6m³ 5g 6g 6g 5g 6d] 45,000F: lengthy filly: moderate mover: fifth living foal: half-sister to a winner in Italy by Wassl: dam, from family of Bassenthwaite, won 2 of her 3 races over 5f at 2 yrs: poor form, best effort running-on third in handicap at Nottingham in June: visored and blinkered once. *J. Etherington.*

BID LATER   4 b.f. Auction Ring (USA) 123–Twenty Two (FR) 90 (Busted 134) **65** [1989 6f² 1990 6m³] quite attractive filly: placed in minor events at Folkestone in July, 1989, and Lingfield (bandaged, slowly away, tenderly handled behind long odds-on Rami) over 10 months later: should be suited by at least 1m. *Lord John FitzGerald.*

BIDWEAYA (USA)   3 b.f. Lear Fan (USA) 130–Sweet Snow (USA) (Lyphard **45** (USA) 132) [1989 NR 1990 8.2g⁴ 7g 8m 10g 8g 8m] 7,000Y: angular, sparely-made filly: first foal: dam French 10.5f winner out of Kentucky Oaks winner Sun And Snow: poor form: stays 8.2f. *G. A. Huffer.*

BIENNIAL (USA)   4 b.c. Lear Fan (USA) 130–Six Months Long (USA) **95** (Northern Dancer) [1989 10f* 10.1g* 10f* 10.1d⁶ 10g⁴ 1990 10g 11m³] good-topped, useful-looking colt: useful winner as 3-y-o, including of Extel Stakes at Goodwood: edgy, sweating slightly and wearing net muzzle to post, fair third in £7,900 handicap at Newbury in May, hanging left in front: stays 11f: acts on firm going, possibly unsuited by a soft surface: usually taken down early: sold to join M. Pipe's stable 9,600 gns Newmarket September Sales. *G. Harwood.*

BIFOCAL   3 b.g. Vision (USA)–Night Vision 100 (Yellow God 129) [1989 6m 6f⁶ **69 d** 6m 7.6m a8g⁴ 1990 a10g* a10g* a10g 12d⁶ 11.7m 10f⁴ 10f 10m⁴ 12m² 10m⁴ 14g 18d] tall, rangy gelding: has plenty of scope: quite modest performer: successful in January maiden and February handicap at Lingfield: ran well when in frame: stays 1½m: acts on firm going: has wandered under pressure: claimed out of R. Akehurst's stable £8,001 tenth outing. *P. J. Bevan.*

BIG BLOW   2 b.c. (Apr 20) Last Tycoon 131–Tuxford Hideaway 102 (Cawston's **93** Clown 113) [1990 6h* 6m⁵ 7m⁵ 6m² 8.2g² 7m*] 38,000Y: lengthy, quite attractive colt with scope: has quick action: first foal: dam sprinter: progressed really well after winning maiden at Brighton in May, making most and rallying well to win by ½ length from Hamadryad in minor event (sweating) at Ascot in September: effective at 7f and 1m: game and genuine. *M. J. Ryan.*

BIG CHIEF   5 b.g. Gorytus (USA) 132–Maybe So 90 (So Blessed 130) [1989 7.5g **—** 8g 6.5s 5g 6v² 1990 7m 8.2s 6f] angular, workmanlike gelding: modest maiden at best: stayed 7f: acted on heavy going: blinkered final outing: dead. *Miss L. C. Siddall.*

BIG DIAMOND (FR)   6 b.g. Bikala 134–Diathese (FR) (Diatome 132) [1989 NR **— p** 1990 8g 8.5d 8m⁴] tall, lengthy gelding: half-brother to 2 winners in France: dam, French 7f and 1¼m winner, is half-sister to high-class middle-distance performers Amadou and Kasteel: winner over hurdles in March: apprentice ridden and wearing net muzzle, never placed to challenge in maidens or 4-runner minor event in first half of year: gave impression capable of better. *I. Campbell.*

BIG ECK   3 b.g. Precocious 126–Dora's Rocket 69 (Roan Rocket 128) [1989 6g **45** 1990 a7g a5g 6m 5f 5s⁴ 5m⁴ 7m* 6g⁴ 8.2f³ 7f⁵ 7g² a8g 8.2g² 8.5d 9g 7g³ 8f⁵ 8.2m² 8f⁴ 9m³ 8m 8.2s] close-coupled, good-quartered gelding: poor handicapper: largely consistent after winning at Catterick in April: best at 7f to 9f: acts on firm going (bit below best on Fibresand) and possibly unsuited by dead: mostly blinkered: has run creditably for apprentice: has been bandaged: sold to J. Thomas 3,000 gns Doncaster October Sales. *M. Brittain.*

BIGHAYIR   3 gr.g. Petong 126–Nook (Julio Mariner 127) [1989 6g⁴ 9g² 9.5g 1990 **54** 8.5g 10m 12m 11.5f³ 10m* 11.7m] sturdy gelding: first foal: dam unraced half-sister to Forzando: in frame in Irish maidens at 2 yrs: form in 1990 only when placed in handicaps at Lingfield, winning 4-runner race in July: probably best at 1¼m: yet to race on a soft surface: blinkered last 3 starts and final one at 2 yrs: bought out of K. Prendergast's stable 3,100 gns Newmarket Autumn (1989) Sales. *B. R. Millman.*

BIG IDEA   3 ch.c. Sharpo 132–Wild Idea 116 (Silly Season 127) [1989 NR 1990 **46** a7g⁶ a8g⁴ 8m a8g] 15,500Y: leggy, good-topped colt: poor mover: half-brother to minor French 1¼m winner Brain Child (by Young Generation): dam French 7f to 9f winner: poor maiden: tailed off in apprentice event then faced very stiff task in handicap last 2 starts: should stay further: bandaged last 3 starts: wore eyeshield second and fourth. *Mrs L. Piggott.*

BIG SURPRISE   3 b.g. Comedy Star (USA) 121–Maxine's Here 52 (Copte (FR)) **44** [1989 5s⁵ 5g 6m⁵ 6m a8g³ a7g⁵ 1990 a11g* a8g³ a8g²] workmanlike gelding: poor walker: poor handicapper: led post in slowly-run 2-runner event at Southwell in January: twice ran well later in month: probably stays 11f: blinkered first 2 starts at 2 yrs. *J. Wharton.*

BIJOU RESIDENCE 2 b.f. (Jan 24) Bustino 136–Little Madam 66 (Habat 127) [1990 5g 5g⁴ 6m⁴ 6h⁵ 6g 6m³ 6f⁴ 7f⁵ a8g] smallish, good-bodied filly: shows knee action: third foal: half-sister to 1988 2-y-o 5f sellers winner Alo' Niko (by Mansingh): dam 5f winner: moderate plater: should be suited by 7f+: has been bandaged: trained until after penultimate outing by S. Dow. *B. R. Cambidge.* **49**

BIJOUX D'OR 2 b.c. (Mar 28) Cragador 110–Gold Spangle 97 (Klondyke Bill 125) [1990 6d 6f* 5g* 5f* 6f] 1,700Y: well-grown colt: moderate mover: half-brother to several winners, including fair 6f and 7f winner Kakisa (by Forlorn River) and sprint handicapper Ever Reckless (by Crever): dam 2-y-o 5f winner: fairly useful colt: successful in July in maiden auction at Pontefract and minor events there and at Hamilton: stayed 6f: broke leg in nursery at Newmarket, and destroyed. *R. Hollinshead.* **94**

BILIMBI 3 ch.f. Nicholas Bill 125–Scrub Oak 84 (Burglar 128) [1989 6f 1990 7f 7g⁶ 8.2g⁶ 9m⁶ 7g a8g 12.5g] angular filly: little form, including in sellers: sold out of J. W. Watts's stable 2,100 gns Doncaster June Sales after third start. *B. Preece.* —

BILLAN TARA 4 b.f. Nicholas Bill 125–Celtic Tara 71 (Welsh Saint 126) [1989 NR 1990 15g⁶ 12.3g 12.5g⁶ 13m a12g a12g 10.8m] leggy filly: poor mover: second foal: dam staying maiden on flat, successful over hurdles: well beaten in modest company, twice slowly away: sold 1,250 gns Ascot October Sales. *C. B. B. Booth.* —

BILLHEAD 4 b.g. Nicholas Bill 125–Time-Table 66 (Mansingh (USA) 120) [1989 10f³ 10.2g 10g⁵ 10m⁴ 10.2g 10f 10s⁶ 1990 a10g 15.3m⁵ 15.3f⁵] leggy gelding: fair maiden at best: well beaten, including in seller, last 6 starts: suited by 1¼m: acts on firm ground: often wears noseband and takes good hold. *B. Preece.* —

BILLIEWHO 3 b.f. Blue Cashmere 129–Petite Maman (Hittite Glory 125) [1989 NR 1990 8.2g] second live foal: half-sister to a bad animal: dam unraced: soundly beaten in apprentice maiden at Hamilton in May: sold 920 gns Doncaster September Sales. *C. Spares.* —

BILLION DOLLARBILL 2 ch.g. (May 8) Nicholas Bill 125–Rest Hill Dolly (Balinger 116) [1990 8g 8.2s 7g] close-coupled gelding: second foal: dam unraced half-sister to smart handicapper Pipedreamer: soundly beaten in autumn maidens, carrying condition first 2 starts. *T. M. Jones.* —

BILLION MELODY 8 b.g. Billion (USA) 113–Thistle 61 (Highland Melody 112) [1989 NR 1990 16.2m] workmanlike gelding: winning handicap hurdler: 50/1, never dangerous in maiden at Beverley in March. *A. W. Jones.* —

BILL MOON 4 ch.g. Nicholas Bill 125–Lunar Queen 96 (Queen's Hussar 124) [1989 8m 1990 11.5m 9g 7m⁴ 8m 7f* 7m 7m* 7g 6m³] leggy, quite attractive gelding: won amateur handicaps at Redcar (by 7 lengths, showing vast improvement) in August and Goodwood in September: stays 7f: acts well on top-of-the-ground. *P. J. Feilden.* **53**

BILLOW 3 br.f. Nicholas Bill 125–Time-Table 66 (Mansingh (USA) 120) [1989 NR 1990 10.2m 10g 15g 12m³] lengthy, sparely-made filly: fourth foal: sister to 4-y-o maiden Billhead: dam won over 6f: no worthwhile form in claimers: claimed out of J. W. Watts's stable £5,650 on second start: blinkered third, visored fourth: sold 2,100 gns Doncaster September Sales. *P. Monteith.* —

BILLSHA 4 b.f. Ahonoora 122–Sanjana (GER) (Priamos (GER)) [1989 8m⁶ 8m⁴ 8f⁴ a8g 1990 8m 10.6s 10g 10.2f 9m] rangy filly: fourth in minor event at Edinburgh second outing as 3-y-o: yet to reproduce that effort: winning hurdler in May. *B. R. Cambidge.* —

BILLY LOMOND (IRE) 2 b.c. (Apr 4) Lomond (USA) 128–Relko's Belle (FR) (Relko 136) [1990 6m⁵ 6d 7m⁴ 7m 7m 8m] 17,000F, 20,000Y: smallish, strong-quartered colt: carries condition: has a quick action: second foal: half-brother to a winner in Italy: dam French 11f winner: quite modest maiden: not knocked about in seller at Newmarket final outing: should stay 1m. *R. Hannon.* **64**

BILLY'S DANCER 7 ch.g. Piaffer (USA) 113–Hay-Hay 62 (Hook Money 124) [1989 8d a8g a8g 1990 8.2s 10m²] close-coupled, sparely-made gelding: poor mover: quite modest handicapper at best: showed he retained ability when second (ridden by 7-lb claimer) of 9 at Pontefract in July: stays 1¼m: yet to race on firm going, acts on any other: blinkered twice: has worn bandages. *W. Wilson.* **41**

BINGO BONGO 3 gr.f. Petong 126–Daring Display 85§ (Daring March 116) [1989 5m 6h³ 6m⁶ 6g 1990 6g³ 7f 10m⁴ 10m⁵ 7m 6m 8g 8m] rangy filly: plating-class **58** d maiden: ran poorly last 3 starts: may well prove best short of 1¼m: acts on hard ground: sold out of R. Smyth's stable 4,600 gns Ascot July Sales after sixth start: ungenuine. *D. Burchell.*

BIRDIE CHANCE 3 b.f. Dominion 123–Lucky Life (Green God 128) [1989 NR 1990 7f⁵ 6f 7m 8f⁶ 7f 8m⁵ 8.3m 12g 12d⁴ a12g a14g] small, sturdy filly: sixth foal: dam, Irish 1m winner, is half-sister to dam of Decent Fellow and Muscatite: plater: 25/1-fourth of 22 in handicap at Leicester, running on well from rear and only worthwhile form. *S. Dow.*   **41**

BIRDLESS GROVE 6 ch.m. Final Straw 127–Pilley Green 100 (Porto Bello 118) [1989 NR 1990 10f a8g a8g] angular, heavy-topped mare: no longer of much account: blinkered second outing. *J. P. Smith.*   **—**

BIRD OF PEACE (USA) 2 ch.f. (May 14) Sharpen Up 127–Timotara (USA) (Secretariat (USA)) [1990 7m 7m] 68,000Y: close-coupled filly: half-sister to 2 winners abroad: dam minor winner in USA, is from same family as Faustus: on toes, eye-catching tenth of 18 to Environment Friend in maiden at Newmarket in October, steadied start then keeping on really well under considerate ride: took keen hold and not knocked about when only moderate progress from 2f out in similar event at Chepstow later in month: likely to do better. *D. R. C. Elsworth.*   **53 p**

BIRD ON THE WING (IRE) 2 br.f. (Mar 6) Chief Singer 131–Seven Seas (FR) 76 (Riverman 131) [1990 7m6] 7,200Y: workmanlike filly: sixth foal: half-sister to 3-y-o 2m winner Royal Mazi (by Kings Lake) and 9f winner Soemba (by General Assembly): dam won at 7f and 11f: backward and green, 7 lengths sixth of 17 in maiden auction at Leicester in September: will improve. *C. James.*   **59 p**

BIRLING ASHES 2 gr.g. (Apr 24) Magic Mirror 105–Morning Miss 59 (Golden Dipper 119) [1990 5f⁵ 5s 5g⁴ 6g 6g⁶ 7.5d 6m 5m 5m 5f 7f⁴ 8f 7g a8g a8g] 4,000F, 5,200Y: small, angular gelding: sixth foal: brother to 3-y-o Conjurer, 5.8f and 1m winner at 2 yrs: dam lightly raced: poor form in varied events: stays 7f: best form on firm ground: blinkered twice, hooded once: inconsistent. *R. W. Stubbs.*   **47**

BIRMINGHAM'S PRIDE 4 br.f. Indian King (USA) 128–Cooliney Dancer (Dancer's Image (USA)) [1989 8.2s 8s⁶ 8.2s 8m⁴ 9f³ 10g² 9f⁴ 8h² 12f³ 10m³ 8.5m⁴ 11g⁶ 10f² 8.2f⁴ 9g⁴ 8.2f⁶ 9m 8.2d 10g³ 8g a8g 1990 a8g³ a11g⁵] strong, close-coupled filly: plating-class maiden: stays 1¼m: acts on firm ground, possibly unsuited by soft: finds little under pressure: one to treat with caution. *R. Hollinshead.*   **51 §**

BIRSTWITH (USA) 5 gr.h. Valdez (USA)–La Chaumiere (Thatch (USA) 136) [1989 8g⁴ 8d⁶ 8f 8.2g⁶ 9g 8g⁴ 1990 10f* 10m 10.4d 8.2m 8m³ 8.2d⁴ 10.2m⁴ 10.6d 8d 9f⁶] leggy, close-coupled, angular horse: modest handicapper: won at Ripon in April: stays 1¼m: acts on any going: has gone freely to post, and been taken down early. *C. W. C. Elsey.*   **73**

BIRTHDAY PARADE (USA) 3 b.f. Chief's Crown (USA)–Jubilous (USA) (Sir Ivor 135) [1989 6g 1990 8m⁴ 10g⁶ 8g⁴ 8m⁶] strong, attractive filly: has quick, rather round action: quite modest maiden: easily best effort in handicap at Ripon penultimate start: stays 1m: very mulish at stalls on reappearance. *H. R. A. Cecil.*   **67**

BIT OF A LARK 2 b.c. (Feb 15) Nomination 125–Straffan Girl (Sallust 134) [1990 6d 6m 5f* 5g³ 5m³ 5f* 5m* 5m] 7,200Y: strong, sturdy colt: has plenty of scope: second foal: half-brother to 1988 2-y-o 6f winner My Audrees (by Auction Ring): dam never ran: fair performer: successful in maiden auction at Beverley in July and minor events at Thirsk in September and Pontefract in October: sweating, had stiff task final start: likely to be as effective at 6f as 5f: suited by forcing tactics. *R. Hollinshead.*   **90**

BIT OF A LASS 4 br.f. Wassl 125–Idiot's Delight (USA) (Bold Ruler) [1989 9f⁶ 10.6m⁶ 12f 10m* 10.2f² 11g³ 12f 10m 10.2f⁴ a12g³ a12g⁶ 1990 a10g* a10g⁵ a10g 10m⁶ 10m] angular, sparely-made filly: poor handicapper: ridden by 7-lb claimer, won at Lingfield in January: no form after, and not seen out after May: suited by 1¼m: acts on firm going: usually bandaged behind on all-weather. *D. W. P. Arbuthnot.*   **53 d**

BLACK ARMORIAL 2 br.c. (Feb 18) Petong 126–Pattis Pet (Mummy's Pet 125) [1990 6g 7m³ 7g⁶ 7f* 7h³ 7h² 7m⁶ 8m⁴ 7m⁶] 10,000Y, 7,000 2-y-o: close-coupled colt: has a quick action: second foal: dam lightly-raced daughter of long-distance mare Blickling: modest performer: won maiden auction at Doncaster in July: stays 1m: visored final 3 starts: sold 13,500 gns Newmarket Autumn Sales. *M. Bell.*   **73**

BLACK COMEDY 7 b.h. Blakeney 126–Laughing Goddess 92 (Green God 128) [1989 10.8m⁶ 10f⁴ 10.2h 12.3m* 12.3g³ 10.6g⁴ 12m³ 12g 12m³ 12f 1990 a14g 10g 10m* 12d²] sturdy, compact horse: carries plenty of condition: moderate mover: quite modest handicapper: returned to form when winning at Pontefract in June: ran   **62**

creditably 2 days later: suited by strongly-run race at 1¼m and stays 1½m: acts on any going: visored twice: sometimes sweats: has worn crossed noseband: goes particularly well on turning track. *J. Mackie.*

BLACK FIGHTER (USA) 3 br.f. Secretariat (USA)–Faten (USA) (Northern 79
Dancer) [1989 7g 1990 10m 8f*dis 10m5dis 9g4dis 10.1g a10g] big, quite attractive filly: moderate mover: first past post in maiden at Kempton in May: beaten about 6 lengths in Lupe Stakes at Goodwood (best effort, wandered under pressure) and Wolverhampton minor event next 2 starts, long way in listed race (blinkered) and handicap after: stays 1¼m: acts on firm ground: tends to give trouble in preliminaries: disqualified second to fourth outings after positive test for steroid. *M. Moubarak.*

BLACK MARKETEER (NZ) 5 ch.g. Sir Tristram 115–Satina (NZ) (Monte- —
cello 102) [1989 9v 10f 9f2 12m 10m2 8g 1990 a7g 10d 8.2g 7.6m 8.2m 10.4g 8f] sparely-made, angular gelding: poor maiden: no form in 1990: blinkered once: sold 1,050 gns Doncaster October Sales: possibly temperamental. *D. W. Chapman.*

BLACK MONDAY 4 b.c. Busted 134–Lightning Legacy (USA) 78 (Super 95
Concorde (USA) 128) [1989 10.1m4 10.1m* 10.1m* 12f2 10f* 10g2 12m6 11v 1990 10g4 10m5 10.5m 12f* 12f2 12m3 12m4] strong, angular colt: carries plenty of condition: unimpressive mover: fairly useful handicapper: successful in £27,900 Tote Gold Trophy at Goodwood in August by 1½ lengths from Ivory Way: ran well in well-contested events afterwards: better suited by 1½m than shorter: acts on firm going, probably unsuited by heavy: probably best with strong handling: genuine and consistent. *L. M. Cumani.*

BLACK RUBY 2 br.g. (Apr 5) Green Ruby (USA) 104–Starboard (Stanford 121§) —
[1990 7f] 1,500Y: lengthy gelding: first foal: dam little worthwhile form: bit backward, slowly away and green in maiden auction at Thirsk in August. *C. Tinkler.*

BLACK SABBATH 5 b.h. Be My Guest (USA) 126–Merlins Charm (USA) 113 ?
(Bold Bidder) [1989 8g* 7g* 8g* 1990 a7g a7g 8.5g3] tall, rather leggy, useful-looking horse: winner 3 times in Belgium in spring as 4-y-o, including in listed event at Sterrebeek: never placed to challenge in claimers on all-weather early in 1990: withdrawn in November at Folkestone (failed to arrive in time) fourth intended outing: stays 1m. *Allan Smith, Belgium.*

BLACK SAPPHIRE 3 ch.g. Lomond (USA) 128–Star of India (General 78
Assembly (USA)) [1989 NR 1990 10m 10f* 10.8m* 11m2 12.3m5 12.3g 10m2 10.5g3] IR 180,000Y: lengthy, quite attractive gelding: moderate mover: first foal: dam, winner at 1¼m in Ireland, is half-sister to very smart French stayer El Badr: won maiden at Salisbury and handicap at Warwick in May: ran well most subsequent outings: will be suited by return to 1½m: acts on firm going: sold to M. Tompkins' stable 30,000 gns Newmarket Autumn Sales. *J. R. Fanshawe.*

BLACK THREE (IRE) 2 b.c. (May 4) Double Schwartz 128–Two's Company 58 p
(Sheshoon 132) [1990 7s] IR 32,000Y: quite attractive colt: good walker: half-brother to several winners, including fair 1½m handicapper Two High (by High Top) and modest stayer Baby's Smile (by Shirley Heights): dam useful French 6.5f and 1½m winner: better for race, around 14 lengths eighth of 22, progress at halfway and keeping on under considerate ride, to Desert Sun in maiden at Doncaster in October: sure to improve. *J. W. Hills.*

*Tote Gold Trophy (Handicap), Goodwood—Black Monday justifies favouritism;
the visored Ivory Way finishes strongly between Roll A Dollar (spotted cap)
and Barrish (rails) for second*

BLACKWATERFOOT 3 b.c. Kalaglow 132–Twelve O'Clock (Hardicanute — 130) [1989 NR 1990 10.6f³ 11.7f⁵ 10g⁵ a12g a10g] lengthy, angular colt: moderate mover: half-brother to several winners, including useful middle-distance stayer and very smart hurdler Asir (by High Top): dam, very useful French 2-y-o 6f winner, is half-sister to Irish Derby runner-up Lombardo: quite modest maiden: best effort on debut: gambled-on favourite in apprentice handicap final start: takes keen hold, and doesn't stay 1½m: flashed tail second start and hung left under pressure on third. *R. Boss.*

BLACKWELLS GALLERY (IRE) 2 ch.f. (Mar 28) Tate Gallery (USA) 58 117–Caelidh 98 (Silly Season 127) [1990 6m 5m 8m⁶ 8d] 10,000Y: rather leggy, sparely-made filly: has a quick action: fifth foal: half-sister to 4-y-o 1¼m and 11f winner Festive Falcon (by Sandhurst Prince) and to useful 1985 2-y-o 6f and 7f winner Resourceful Falcon (by Godswalk), later stayed 1¼m: dam, sister to Royal Lodge winner Adios, stayed 1m: plating-class maiden: appeared difficult ride final start: will stay 1¼m: possibly unsuited by dead ground. *R. Hannon.*

BLADE OF FORTUNE 2 b.g. (Mar 20) Beldale Flutter (USA) 130–Foil 'em 47 (USA) 88 (Blade (USA)) [1990 6g 5g⁵ 7g⁵ 7m 7g] leggy, rather unfurnished gelding: has scope: third foal: half-brother to fair 1m winner Coral Sword (by Main Reef) and 1988 2-y-o 7.5f winner Foilinski (by Niniski): dam won at 6f only start at 2 yrs but deteriorated: poor maiden: still carrying plenty of condition final 2 starts: headstrong. *F. H. Lee.*

BLAKENEYS GIFT 4 gr.g. Blakeney 126–Teleflora 89 (Princely Gift 137) 48 [1989 10.6s⁴ 10f⁵ 12m³ 12g⁴ 15g 1990 8m* 11.5m 12g⁶] leggy gelding: poor handicapper: 25/1-winner of 10-runner event (went down freely) at Carlisle: below form later in June: stays 1½m: acts on good to firm and soft going: has run creditably for apprentice and amateur: has joined B. Smart.*J. P. Hudson.*

BLAKE'S TREASURE 3 b.c. Mummy's Treasure 84 Andamooka (Rarity 129) 68 [1989 a8g* 1990 8m 8m³ 8f² 8.3m⁵ 8.2m² a8g] good-topped colt: ridden by 7-lb claimer, won maiden at Lingfield in December at 2 yrs: creditable second in handicaps at Bath and Nottingham, but flashed tail and looked reluctant in latter: well beaten facing stiffish task in £8,100 handicap in August, final start: not bred to stay much beyond 1m. *T. Thomson Jones.*

BLAKESWARE GOLD 4 ch.g. Vaigly Great 127–Presentable 60 (Sharpen Up — 127) [1989 10d 12m² 8m⁵ 10f* 12.2m 10f⁶ 10g* 9f³ 9f* 10.6d 10f³ 10f³ 1990 11f] angular, plain gelding: poor walker: moderate mover: useful winning plater as 3-y-o: ran as though in need of race only outing (May) in 1990: should stay beyond 1¼m: acts on firm going, probably unsuited by a soft surface: has sweated. *G. M. Moore.*

BLAZE O'GOLD (USA) 4 b.c. Slew O' Gold (USA)–Lady Be Mine (USA) 76 72 (Sir Ivor 135) [1989 10g² 1990 10.8m²] very big, strong colt: moderate walker: modest form: carrying condition, 6 lengths second of 16 to Rudjig in maiden at Warwick (had gash on off-hind quarter) in April: should stay 1½m. *H. R. A. Cecil.*

BLAZING BELLE 2 br.f. (Mar 12) Belfort (FR) 89–La Pepper 63 (Workboy 47 § 123) [1990 5f⁶ 5m⁶ 5.8h⁵ 7f⁴ 6g⁶ 6d⁵ a7g a6g2] 1,500Y: smallish, good-quartered filly: second reported foal: dam, plater, won over 1m at 2 yrs: poor maiden: looked thoroughly ungenuine sixth outing: whipped round for 7-lb claimer once before: stays 7f: best form on firm ground: thrice blinkered or visored: has worn bandages: one to be wary of. *M. D. I. Usher.*

BLAZING FEN 2 ch.c. (Mar 15) Myjinski (USA)–Clipeall 57 (Petitioner 83) 55 [1990 6m⁶ 6g 5f 7f 7d a8g⁴ a7g a7g a7g] neat colt: poor mover: first foal: dam 7f and 1m seller winner: fair plater: best effort in maidens at Southwell late in year: stays 1m: has run well for 7-lb claimer: carries head high, and has looked none too keen: trained first 3 outings by M. Tompkins: often bandaged. *Mrs N. Macauley.*

BLAZING HORSESHOE 2 br.f. (Feb 17) Blazing Saddles (AUS)–Martin- 36 Lavell Star 64 (Godswalk (USA) 130) [1990 5f 5m⁵ 5g 5g a6g 5f 6d 5d³ a5g] 900F, 1,100Y: compact, good-bodied filly: second foal: half-sister to poor 3-y-o Tuneful Charter (by Song): dam 6f winner from 2 starts at 2 yrs: poor maiden: blinkered last 2 starts: sweating penultimate. *N. Bycroft.*

BLAZING PEARL 2 b.f. (Feb 17) Blazing Saddles (AUS)–Ring of Pearl (Auction 57 d Ring (USA) 123) [1990 6f* 7f⁶ 6m 7g 6m 6m] 880F: small filly: moderate mover: first foal: dam ran 3 times at 2 yrs: won seller (bought in 6,000 gns) at Yarmouth in August: no comparable form, hampered in running twice: should stay 7f: sometimes slowly away. *Pat Mitchell.*

BLAZING SUNSET 3 ch.f. Blazing Saddles (AUS)–Krishnagar (Kris 135) [1989 50 d 5d⁴ 6m³ 6m⁶ 6m* 7g 5f³ 6f* a6g a7g a6g⁴ a8g 1990 a5g* a6g a6g⁴ 6d 5m 5g 6m⁵

5m⁵ 6m 6m 5.3f 6m 5m a6g⁶ a5g a7g⁶] workmanlike filly: has a round action: poor performer: little form after making all in handicap at Lingfield in January: stays 6f: acts on firm going: has run creditably when sweating, and for apprentice. *D. A. Wilson.*

BLAZONET (IRE)   2 b.g. (May 10) Heraldiste (USA) 121–Jillette (Fine Blade   —
(USA) 121) [1990 5g] IR 5,400Y: medium-sized gelding: ninth foal: half-brother to several winners, including 1¼m winner Egidia (by Welsh Saint): dam Irish 1½m winner: bit backward, slowly away and soon tailed off in maiden auction (went down well) at Epsom in April. *S. Dow.*

BLEU DE FRANCE (FR)   3 b.c. Crystal Glitters (USA) 127–Emeraldine (FR) **111**
(Tanerko 134) [1989 8d* 9d* 1990 10.5s⁴ 10.5g⁴ 8d³] half-brother to several winners, notably very smart French middle-distance stayer Galant Vert (by Luthier) and smart French 10.5f and 1½m winner Iris Noir (by Pharly): dam French 1½m winner: successful in maiden at Deauville and Prix Saint-Roman at Longchamp as 2-y-o: co-favourite for the Derby at time of reappearance but didn't win from 3 outings in the spring, in frame in Prix Greffulhe and Prix Lupin at Longchamp then Prix de la Jonchere at Saint-Cloud: possibly didn't stay 10.5f: died after colic attack in September. *J-M. Beguigne, France.*

BLIMPERS   2 gr.c. (May 31) Alias Smith (USA)–Melton Grange 70 (Song 132)   —
[1990 7g 6f 8g 6d⁶] compact colt: half-brother to plating-class 1988 2-y-o 5f winner Wasn't Me (by Wattlefield) and to a winner in Scandinavia: dam placed over 6f: well beaten in maidens and minor events: slowly away final outing. *E. H. Owen jun.*

BLIND SHOT   3 b.c. Kris 135–Shuteye 91 (Shirley Heights 130) [1989 NR 1990   —
9g 12m 16.5d⁵] 82,000Y: robust colt: moderate mover: second foal: half-brother to fair maiden Soporific (by Pharly): dam, 1m and 11.7f winner, is half-sister to high-class middle-distance gelding Bedtime: no worthwhile form in maidens then minor event (pulled hard): sold 3,100 gns Newmarket Autumn Sales. *J. R. Fanshawe.*

BLOW A KISS   3 b.f. Auction Ring (USA) 123–Follow Me Follow 92 (Wollow   —
132) [1989 6f² 1990 6f 6f⁵ 8.2g 8g] tall, quite good-topped filly: no worthwhile form (including in seller) and has shown signs of temperament: keen sort, unlikely to stay 1m: blinkered final start. *C. A. Cyzer.*

BLUE AEROPLANE   2 ch.c. (Mar 3) Reach 122–Shelton Song 60 (Song 132)   **98**
[1990 5m³ 6h* 7f² 6g*] 11,000Y: sturdy, angular colt: half-brother to several winners here and abroad, including quite modest 6f to 1m handicapper Master Driver (by Absalom): dam 5f winner at 4 yrs: progressive colt: comfortable winner of maiden auction at Brighton in August and nursery at Kempton (favourably drawn) in September: effective at 6f and 7f: strong-running type. *P. F. I. Cole.*

BLUE BELL RIBBONS   3 b.g. Music Boy 124–Ribbons of Blue 60 (Jimmy   —
Reppin 131) [1989 5d⁴ 5s 5m⁴ 5f⁴ 6g 6f 6m 8.5f 1990 a8g 6g 6g 10d a5g a8g] close-coupled gelding: shows a quick action: moderate plater at 2 yrs: no form in 1990: best form at 5f: tends to get on toes: blinkered fourth and fifth starts. *R. F. Marvin.*

BLUEBIRD LADY   5 ch.m. Thatching 131–Grankie (USA) (Nashua) [1989 9m⁶   **46**
6f² 5m³ 5m⁴ 6m³ 5f 5f⁵ 6f² 5m³ 6m⁵ 5.1g* 5.3f 5f⁶ 5m⁴ 1990 6m⁵ 6h⁶] angular, shallow-girthed mare: poor mover: winning handicapper in 1989: not seen out as 5-y-o after May: suited by 5f: yet to race on a soft surface: often blinkered or visored: has worn bandages: sold 3,500 gns Newmarket December Sales. *Mrs N. Macauley.*

BLUECHIPENTERPRISE   4 br.f. Blakeney 126–Hey Skip (USA) (Bold   —
Skipper (USA)) [1989 10m 1990 14f⁵ 13.3m⁵ 16g 17.6m 12d 12m] workmanlike filly: has a round action: well beaten in varied events. *L. G. Cottrell.*

BLUE CRANE (IRE)   2 b.f. (Feb 3) Never So Bold 135–Altara (GER) (Tarim)   **43**
[1990 6m⁶ 6m⁴ 6h³ 7f 7m⁴] 15,000Y: lengthy filly: has a quick action: third foal: half-sister to poor plater Andhra (by Indian King) and a winner in Italy: dam lightly-raced daughter of top German filly Alaria: poor maiden: blinkered and hung right final start: best efforts at 6f. *J. L. Dunlop.*

BLUE DAISY (USA)   2 gr.f. (Mar 15) Shahrastani (USA) 135–Blue Angel's   **91** p
Image (USA) (Ruritania) [1990 8d*] $110,000Y: half-sister to useful 1985 2-y-o sprinter Flyaway Bride (by Blushing Groom) and quite modest maiden Marlene's Days (by Olden Times): dam 6f winner, is half-sister to 2 good winners in Canada: evens, won 20-runner maiden at Leopardstown in October by a neck, 8 lengths clear: will stay at least 1¼m: sure to improve. *J. Oxx, Ireland.*

BLUE DISC   5 br.g. Disc Jockey 95–Kaotesse (Djakao (FR) 124) [1989 5d³ 7g²   **36**
7m 6f 8.3m 10g 1990 a6g⁴ a7g³ a8g⁴ 7f] workmanlike gelding: poor maiden: finds 5f

on short side and stays 1m: acts on any going: blinkered at 5 yrs: often sweats: possibly ungenuine. *J. R. Jenkins.*

BLUEFIELD BAY   3 br.c. Never So Bold 135–Bahamas Princess 89 (Sharpen Up 127) [1989 NR 1990 8m 8g⁴ 8g 8.2s⁵ 8g* 8g³ 10m] rangy, well-made colt with plenty of scope: has a quick action: third foal: half-brother to Irish 1¼m winner Firing Point (by Blakeney) and very useful 1986 2-y-o 5f winner Dominion Royale (by Dominion), later successful over 1m in USA: dam, half-sister to very useful 1m and 9f winner Miner's Lamp, won once over 5f at 2 yrs from only 2 starts: won handicap at Ripon in September: soon off bridle and tended to carry head high when creditable third at Doncaster, clearly better effort in similar events after: should stay 1¼m: blinkered final start. *R. W. Armstrong.*   89

BLUEFONTAINE   3 b.f. Rolfe (USA) 77–Annarise (Starch Reduced 112) [1989 NR 1990 a10g a6g 7f 10f 7m 7m 10m 12f 8m⁶ 10g] workmanlike filly: has a round action: fifth foal: dam, plating-class maiden, appeared to stay 1¼m: poor plater: bred to stay 1¼m: visored ninth start. *P. Howling.*   —

BLUE GUM   3 ch.g. Cure The Blues (USA)–Honey 79 (He Loves Me 120) [1989 NR 1990 a8g*] IR 29,000Y: useful-looking, rather unfurnished gelding: first foal: dam, placed twice at around 7f here as 2-y-o, won Italian 1000 Guineas: 6/1, easily won 13-runner maiden at Southwell in February by 6 lengths: gave trouble at stalls and was withdrawn intended debut, at 2 yrs. *W. Hastings-Bass.*   74 +

BLUE HABIT   3 b.f. Cure The Blues (USA)–Miss Habitat (Habitat 134) [1989 5m³ 5m⁵ 6m 5m 6g 8g 1990 7m 8m] leggy, light-framed filly: moderate mover: poor plater: should stay at least 6f: blinkered fifth outing. *P. A. Blockley.*   —

BLUEHAVEN FLYER   5 b.h. Cure The Blues (USA)–Home Bird (Ragusa 137) [1989 NR 1990 12f⁶] tall horse: poor maiden: blinkered once: winning hurdler twice in October. *W. Storey.*   —

BLUE ILLUSION   2 b.c. (Apr 29) Clever Trick (USA)–Bluebell 103 (Town Crier 119) [1990 5f⁶ 6g 7m³ 7g] 49,000Y: leggy, rather sparely-made colt: seventh foal: brother to fair 1m winner Mountain Bluebird, and half-brother to 4 other winners here and abroad, including modest 9f and 1¼m winner Speedwell (by Grundy): dam, out of half-sister to Queen's Hussar, ran only at 2 yrs when successful over 6f and 7.3f: modest maiden: better suited by 7f than shorter: possibly unsuited by an easy surface: sold 12,000 gns Newmarket Autumn Sales. *B. W. Hills.*   73

BLUELLA   3 b.f. Blue Cashmere 129–Set To Work (Workboy 123) [1989 5m 6g 5f 6m 1990 a7g 6g] lengthy, robust filly: no form, including in sellers. *J. S. Wainwright.*   —

BLUE MISCHIEF   4 ch.f. Precocious 126–Deep Blue Sea (Gulf Pearl 117) [1989 5d² 8.2g2 6f* 8m⁵ 5m 7g⁶ 6g² 6s 6s 5m² 1990 5f 5g 6m 5m⁵ 5d 7m⁵ 5d⁴ 7d⁶ 6s] strong, lengthy filly: carries plenty of condition: good walker: plating-class handicapper: ideally suited by 6f: seems unsuited by soft going, acts on any other. *R. Allan.*   50

BLUE RHYTHM   5 b.m. Blue Cashmere 129–Abalone (Abwah 118) [1989 7s* 6m* 6m 1990 a7g 6g] lengthy, workmanlike mare: moderate mover: difficult to train, but won handicaps on first 2 starts as 4-y-o: behind both starts in spring: stays 7f: acts on any going: visored once: wears bandages: retained by trainer 4,000 gns Newmarket Autumn Sales. *T. Thomson Jones.*   —

BLUE ROOM   3 b.f. Gorytus (USA) 132–Jokers High (USA) (Vaguely Noble 140) [1989 7g² 7f² 7g⁵ 7g a8g 1990 8f 8m 7m⁴ 7m 7m 7h* 7f* 7f² 7m 7g 7m] rather leggy, lengthy filly: moderate mover: modest performer: won seller (bought in 4,200 gns) at Brighton in July and claimer at Newmarket (leading halfway, by 7 lengths) in August: well out of depth final start, below form in handicaps previous 2: suited by 7f: acts on hard going: trained until after fifth start (sweating and edgy, ran moderately) by W. Brooks. *R. Akehurst.*   70

BLUES BALIDAR   2 ch.c. (May 14) Balidar 133–Kimble Blue 86 (Blue Refrain 121) [1990 6g] tall, workmanlike colt: first foal: dam 2-y-o 5f winner: hung left from start in maiden at Nottingham in September: moved poorly down. *J. L. Spearing.*   —

BLUES CLUB (USA)   2 b. or br.c. (Mar 15) Robellino (USA) 127–Brilliant Dancer (USA) (Dancer's Image (USA)) [1990 7g² 7m] $25,000Y: rangy colt: has scope: brother to Sudden Flame, successful at up to 9f, and half-brother to 4 winners: dam minor winner: green, promising ¾-length second of 11, slowly away and held up then staying on well, in maiden at Salisbury in October: favourite, weakened from 2f out and eased in similar event at Chepstow later in month: retained by trainer 12,000 gns Newmarket Autumn Sales. *R. Hannon.*   69 ?

111

BLUES INDIGO 5 b.m. Music Boy 124–Blueit (FR) 101 (Bold Lad (IRE) 133) **79**
[1989 6g 5m 5f 6m 5m² 5m² 5f 5g 1990 5g⁵ 5m] neat, good-quartered mare: fair on her day: creditable running-on fifth at Epsom, better effort in spring handicaps: speedy: best form on a sound surface: inconsistent. *J. Wharton.*

BLUE STAG 3 b.c. Sadler's Wells (USA) 132–Snow Day (FR) 123 (Reliance **121**
II 137) [1989 7m⁵ 10g* 1990 10.4d* 12g² 12g⁴ 12m³ 12g⁴]
'In a lot of Derbys you would have thought I was too far back but I wasn't worried because I knew half the field didn't stay.' It must have been a disappointment, however, for Blue Stag's jockey Asmussen to find that amongst the remaining half was Quest For Fame to whom Blue Stag, with only a handful of horses behind him, was at a disadvantage of some six lengths as the field rounded Tattenham Corner; at the post the margin between them was three lengths and Barry Hills had trained his fourth Derby runner-up following Rheingold, Hawaiian Sound and Glacial Storm. Blue Stag can't be called an unlucky loser, he wasn't closing in the last furlong, but one is bound to dwell on that performance, and any might-have-beens, as it was very much the zenith of his career in Europe. His Irish Derby fourth the following month was a creditable one, if marred by his hanging right when put under pressure, but below-par efforts followed in the Gordon Stakes at Goodwood where ground conditions were against him, and the Great Voltigeur Stakes at York where they were not. Blue Stag looked light in condition at York and found little when ridden along soon after the turn, flashing his tail when hit with the whip. He'd always struck us as a middle-distance stayer and the forcing ride he got at York should have worked in his favour, as should the easy ground. The race to bring back the best in him, if any could, was the St Leger but Blue Stag was withdrawn on the eve of the final classic following the announcement of Sangster's sale of half shares in him and eight other horses (including Distinctly North, Kostroma and Polar Bird) for 5,000,000 dollars and the decision of his new owner, a mystery Texan, not to run. Blue Stag was also left in the Irish St Leger until the final declaration stage as a precaution in case veterinary examination led to his sale falling through. All in all, then, it was a disappointing way for Blue Stag to leave the classic calculations he'd entered at Chester back in May where he provided his trainer with a ninth winner of the race, taking nearly all of the mile-and-a-quarter-plus to get to and pass the then Cecil-trained Saumarez (who gave 4 lb) for a game three-quarter-length victory. After Blue Stag's appearance at York in August and Saumarez's at Longchamp in October, that performance had taken on qualities of the chimera.

Dee Stakes, Chester—Blue Stag (left) wears down Saumarez

Mr R. E. Sangster's "Blue Stag"

Like the modest mile-and-a-half winner Snowkist (by The Minstrel), his dam's only previous reported foal, Blue Stag, though lengthy, is on the small side which helps explain why the bidding reached only 49,000 guineas before he was bought back at the Highflyer Yearling Sale. His pedigree suggested he'd have made a sum a good deal higher than that. Sadler's Wells' yearlings averaged about 188,000 guineas in 1988 and the dam Snow Day was a well-above-average racehorse, winning three races over ten and a half furlongs, including the Fille de l'Air and Royaumont, and running well in the Vermeille and Arc de Triomphe. She's the first and best offspring in the unraced Vindaria's sporadic and disappointing producing career but the third dam Heavenly Body has proved an influential broodmare with a high-class but ill-fated daughter in A Thousand Stars and other grandchildren such as Celestial Storm and Le Vague A L'Ame, the dam of River Memories. Heavenly Body was herself joint-second top-rated two-year-old of her sex in 1959 in the States and sister of the Kentucky Oaks winner Hidden Talent.

		Northern Dancer (b 1961)	Nearctic
	Sadler's Wells (USA) (b 1981)		Natalma
		Fairy Bridge (b 1975)	Bold Reason
Blue Stag			Special
(b.c. 1987)		Reliance II (b 1962)	Tantieme
	Snow Day (FR) (b 1978)		Relance III
		Vindaria (b 1974)	Roi Dagobert
			Heavenly Body

Blue Stag's prospects with Gary Jones in the USA aren't easy to gauge. Sangster was reported to have said that 'with a few months rest and a bit of sun on his back, I'm optimistic he will prove very useful on American tracks', and Jones certainly worked the oracle with Classic Fame and Quiet American, both of whom won big races in the United States in 1990 having raced in

Britain with rather less distinction in 1989. Blue Stag shapes as though stamina is his strong suit and American racing is dominated by competition at around a mile and a quarter, but the experience of some of our other runners there seems to show that this apparent dichotomy can be overcome by the end-to-end gallop usual in American races. Over whatever distance he's asked to race, we feel that Blue Stag, who has a short, scratchy action, will need an easy surface. *B. W. Hills.*

BLUE TAIL   2 gr.f. (Jan 26) Petong 126–Glyn Rhosyn (Welsh Saint 126) [1990 5f² **69** 5d⁴ 5f² a7g³] 12,500Y: sparely-made filly: has a light action: third foal: half-sister to 1988 2-y-o 6f winner Ipo (by Mummy's Game): dam poor maiden: modest maiden: may prove suited by 6f: best form on a soft surface: sweating and edgy second start. *P. J. Makin.*

BLUE VERYAN   3 b.f. Kalaglow 132–Head First 91 (Welsh Pageant 132) [1989 **74** p NR 1990 11.5g³ 15g* 14f*] leggy filly: half-sister to 2 modest winners, including 1½-mile winner Hello Steve (by Final Straw), and 2 winning hurdlers: dam 1½-mile winner out of smart Guillotina: 6/5 on, won claimers at Edinburgh and Yarmouth (easily, claimed to join M. Pipe £12,561) in July: stays 15f. *W. J. Haggas.*

BLUFF COVE   8 ch.g. Town Crier 119–Dolly Dickins 55 (Double-U-Jay 120) **70** [1989 NR 1990 18f³ 17m* 21.6m* 18m* 20m] sturdy, workmanlike gelding: carries condition: modest handicapper: justified favouritism on 3 occasions at Pontefract (has now won there 5 times) in first half of year: reportedly finished lame when tailed off in Ascot Stakes at Royal Ascot: suited by extreme test of stamina: unsuited by soft going, acts on any other: tends to idle in front: apprentice ridden: has won when sweating: very useful staying hurdler: tough and genuine. *R. Hollinshead.*

BLUISH (USA)   3 b.f. Alleged (USA) 138–Blue Command (USA) (Bold   — Commander (USA)) [1989 NR 1990 10.1m] 36,000Y: lengthy, leggy filly: tenth living foal: half-sister to fairly useful 1976 2-y-o 7.2f winner Gio (by Dictus) and 3 winners in USA, including smart 1980 2-y-o filly Carolina Command (by Gunflint): dam useful French middle-distance winner: very green, some late progress when well beaten in minor event at Windsor in June. *J. H. M. Gosden.*

BLUSHING BELLE   2 b.f. (Apr 12) Local Suitor (USA) 128–Shuteye 91 (Shirley **68** ? Heights 130) [1990 7m 8m⁶ 7m 8f 10.6s*] 5,800Y: unfurnished filly: has a very round action: third foal: half-sister to modest maiden Soporific (by Pharly): dam 1m and 11.7f winner, is half-sister to Bedtime: raced alone when winning selling nursery (bought in 5,200 gns) at Haydock by 6 lengths in October: suited by a test of stamina: acts well in the mud. *P. F. I. Cole.*

BLUSHING BLOOM   3 ch.f. Blushing Groom (USA) 131–Catherine's **73** Bet (USA) (Grey Dawn II 132) [1989 6g⁵ 1990 8f⁶ 8m*] rather sparely-made filly: moderate walker and mover: co-second favourite, improved form when winning 17-runner maiden at Yarmouth in June by short head, leading those in centre 2f out then overall close home: may well stay beyond 1m. *L. Cumani.*

BLUSHING POPEYE   3 ch.g. Blushing Scribe (USA) 107–Place In The Sun 48   — (Sun Prince 128) [1989 NR 1990 8m 10f 7m 8h⁶ 6m 6g] smallish gelding: moderate mover: third reported foal: dam plater placed at 1m: sixth in selling handicap at Brighton, only form: blinkered fifth outing: usually ridden by apprentice. *M. P. Muggeridge.*

BLUSHING RED   3 b.f. Jalmood (USA) 126–Mother Brown 103 (Candy Cane   — 125) [1989 6g 1990 8.2g 12m 13.8m a12g 11s 6g 11v] workmanlike, plain filly: moderate walker and mover: little sign of ability: bred to stay at least 1¼m: blinkered last 2 starts. *N. Bycroft.*

BLYTON LAD   4 b.g. Skyliner 117–Ballinacurra (King's Troop 118) [1989 8.5d **110** 6d³ 7f 6m⁶ 7f 5g* 6f² 5f* 5m³ 5m* 5g 6d² 1990 5f³ 5m⁴ 5m⁶ 5f² 5m 5m* 5d] big, rangy gelding: very useful sprinter: won listed event at Newmarket in October by ½ length from Tod: best efforts earlier in season when in frame in pattern races, wandering under pressure when second to Argentum in King George Stakes at Goodwood: effective at 5f and 6f: acts on firm and dead going: has sweated: often unruly in preliminaries, taken down early nowadays: withdrawn at start on intended reappearance and sixth outing (refused to enter stalls): reportedly to change stables. *J. Balding.*

BLYTON STAR (IRE)   2 b.g. (May 1) Horage 124–Saintly Angel 87 (So Blessed   — 130) [1990 5f 5m⁶] IR 12,500F, IR 8,800Y: sturdy gelding: moderate walker: half-brother to several winners, including fair 7f and 1m performer Brittania Bell (by Pitskelly) and useful 1983 sprinting 2-y-o African Abandon (by African Sky): dam lightly-raced 2-y-o 5f winner: green and edgy, under 10 lengths sixth of 13 to Sing 'n Swing in maiden auction at Pontefract in April. *J. Balding.*

BOBBY ON THE BANK 4 ch.g. Monsanto (FR) 121–Dewberry 68 (Bay **40** Express 132) [1989 9v* 10d5 8g 9f4 11f 10.6g 8.2g5 8.2g 8g 1990 10.6f4 8m6 9g 10f2 10d6 9g5 8h 10.4g2 10m* 10.6s] small, rather sparely-made gelding: moderate mover: poor handicapper: won selling event (bought in 4,400 gns) at Pontefract in September: stays 1¼m well: acts on any going: claimer ridden: looked none too keen sixth outing. *M. J. O'Neill.*

BOCAS ROSE 4 ch.f. Jalmood (USA) 126–Strathoykel 94 (Aberdeen 109) [1989 **98** 8f 8g4 7f4 8d 7m4 6m 1990 6g 6d4 6g 7m3 6m 6m2 6h2 6m 6g] smallish, sturdy filly: usually dull in coat: has a rather round action: fairly useful handicapper: good second to Knight of Mercy in Stewards' Cup at Goodwood on sixth outing: effective at 6f to 1m: particularly well suited by a sound surface. *R. Hannon.*

BODAMIST 3 b.c. Swing Easy (USA) 126–Diorina 91 (Manacle 123) [1989 6m6 **65** 6m* 6m2 7m 8g a7g 1990 6f 6m 6m* 6f2 6f6 6m2 8.2m] angular colt: quite modest sprinter: successful twice at Windsor, returning to form when winning handicap in July: second in handicap (wandering under pressure) and seller, easily best efforts after: acts on firm going: sold 2,400 gns Doncaster November Sales. *J. White.*

BODGE 3 b.f. Horage 124–The Flying Sputnik (Touch Paper 113) [1989 6m 7m3 **61** 7m 7m6 7g2 8m5 1990 8.2f6 10m2 12m 10m 10g3 11m2 12f] workmanlike filly: quite modest maiden: blinkered and edgy, good staying-on second in July handicap at Hamilton penultimate start, ridden along in rear 4f out: ran poorly in amateurs event following month: stays 11f: acts on firm going: also blinkered last 2 starts at 2 yrs, very edgy and below form on last of them: winning hurdler. *G. A. Pritchard-Gordon.*

BOG TROTTER (USA) 2 ch.c. (Apr 9) Irish River (FR) 131–Chaleur **113** (CAN) (Rouge Sang (USA) 116) [1990 7g3 7g* 7m2 7d2]

Back in 1982 Gorytus stamped himself a colt of abundant promise with a seven-length defeat of Salieri in the Acomb Stakes at York on his debut. Bog Trotter, a 33/1-chance, made his debut in the same race and, although he didn't create anywhere near the same impression as Gorytus, he did well, travelling as strongly as any for most of the way, pulling very hard under restraint in the early stages, and passing the post a clear third of eight behind the race-fit Sedair and Plan of Action. That performance suggested Bog Trotter would have no problem winning races, and soon after his trainer intimated that his next appearance might well be at the St Leger meeting. It was too, but instead of the original plan to run him in a six-furlong graduation event Bog Trotter was allowed to take his chance in the Group 2 Laurent-Perrier Champagne Stakes. It's rare a horse wins a race like the Champagne Stakes with only one previous run—only Gorytus and Gielgud had managed it in well over a decade—yet when Bog Trotter achieved the feat he was accorded far less publicity than might have been expected. To a certain extent the rather lukewarm reception was understandable. For a start the opposition he defeated was far from exceptional by Group 2 standards and several correspondents—with good reason as it turned out—centred much of

Laurent-Perrier Champagne Stakes, Doncaster—Bog Trotter keeps on really strongly

their copy around the lifeless performance of the ominously easy-to-back favourite Bravefoot. However, there was plenty to like about the way Bog Trotter took advantage of the opportunity which presented itself, and by the end of the season he'd proved himself close to the best British two-year-olds with a splendid effort in the Three Chimneys Dewhurst Stakes. Only five went to post for the Champagne Stakes. The unbeaten Bravefoot, despite numerous four-figure wagers, drifted from even money to 11/8 in the face of sustained support for Arokat, who went off at 15/8 having beaten a field of second-raters with a good deal in hand at Chester a fortnight earlier; Arokat's stable-companion Stone Mill was a 13/2 chance, with Bog Trotter on 8/1 and Peleng the outsider at 20/1. Those who'd supported Bravefoot knew a long way out that they wouldn't be collecting, but Bog Trotter, who looked tremendously well and was taken last and steadily to post, was always travelling strongly. As at York he took a really good hold in the early stages. He was never out of control, though, and after taking up the running from Peleng soon after halfway he quickened to put the whole field in trouble. Arokat was the only danger from the distance, but Bog Trotter soon put him in his place then galloped on with bags of enthusiasm to win by four lengths.

After such a convincing victory in a race that's thrown up many good horses in recent years, Bog Trotter's connections were entitled to start thinking about aiming high and plans to supplement him for the Dewhurst Stakes were announced almost immediately. Before that, Bog Trotter was beaten in a listed race, the Somerville Tattersalls Stakes over seven furlongs at Newmarket in early-October in which the conditions of the race forced him to concede 6 lb to each of his four opponents. At Doncaster the ground had been good and the gallop strong from end to end. This time none of the riders seemed particularly keen to press on, and after being held up Bog Trotter never really looked like getting his head in front, though he did keep on up the hill to finish runner-up behind the fast-improving Peter Davies. By this stage we'd seen enough of Bog Trotter to believe that attempting to conserve his energy until the closing stages of a race was counter-productive. Those closest to him evidently formed the same opinion, and allowing him to bowl along in front from the start in the Dewhurst—for which he went off 8/1 fourth favourite in a field of eight— almost paid a handsome dividend. For the third outing in a row Bog Trotter really took the eye in the paddock, and with three furlongs to run he was striding out over a length clear with most of the field off the bridle. He looked for all the world a winner when even further clear just under two out, but he couldn't quite sustain the effort inside the last and, faltering up the hill, found himself headed close home by the fast-finishing 50/1-shot Generous. It could be argued that Bog Trotter would just about have held on in the Dewhurst had his rider waited a bit longer in front, but having ventured the opinion that he'd benefit from forcing tactics beforehand we shan't seek to have it both ways. Even had he held on, the performance wouldn't have been that of a potential classic winner. We don't see him as one, but he's an admirable sort and should train on to run well in some important races at a slightly lower level.

		Riverman	Never Bend
Bog Trotter (USA) (ch.c. Apr 9, 1988)	Irish River (FR) (ch 1976)	(b 1969)	River Lady
		Irish Star (b 1960)	Klairon
			Botany Bay
	Chaleur (CAN) (b 1979)	Rouge Sang (b 1972)	Bold Bidder
			Red Damask
		Brief Attire (b 1962)	Menetrier
			Chorus Beauty

Bog Trotter, an angular, good-topped colt who thrived physically at two, was shrewdly bought as a yearling for 50,000 dollars at the Keeneland September Sale. His sire Irish River, who stands at Gainesway Farm in Kentucky, was a top-class racehorse, never beaten at a mile and the winner of seven Group 1 races in France during 1978 and 1979. Irish River hasn't enjoyed the same success as a stallion so far, but he's sired plenty of good horses including the Hardwicke Stakes winner Orban, the Prix Robert Papin and Prix Morny winner Seven Springs, the Ribblesdale winner Ballinderry and the Derby third Mashkour. Bog Trotter wasn't the only Irish River two-year-old to make a mark in the latest season. In France Exit To Nowhere

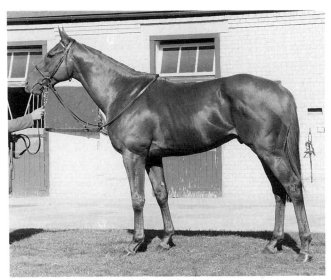

Mr B. Haggas' "Bog Trotter"

looked a colt with a very bright future when storming home in the Prix Thomas Bryon at Saint-Cloud, while another, River Traffic, reached the frame in the Prix de la Salamandre and ended the year with a successful trip to Washington for the Grade 3 Laurel Futurity. Although it isn't exceptional the female half of Bog Trotter's pedigree also has a fair bit to recommend it. His dam Chaleur was a fairly useful winner at up to a mile in North America and her three runners prior to Bog Trotter—by Private Account, Key To Content and Icecapade respectively—have all won races in varied company. Chaleur is by Rouge Sang, a very smart middle-distance performer at the age of four in England, France, Italy, Germany and the States. Her dam Brief Attire won eleven races without troubling the best, and at stud she's responsible for several other useful winners, among them the sprinter Gay Apparel, who's since become the dam of a couple of fast French horses in Cedrico and Bold Apparel. There's stamina as well as speed in this pedigree, but as far as we're concerned Bog Trotter needs to relax a good deal more in his races if he's to stay beyond a mile; and judged on his record at two that seems highly unlikely. *W. J. Haggas.*

BOLD AMBITION 3 b.c. Ela-Mana-Mou 132–Queen of The Dance (Dancer's Image (USA)) [1989 7g² 8m 1990 10.6f⁵ 10g⁴ 10.1g* 12m⁶ 8g⁶] good-bodied colt: fairly useful performer: made all in minor event at Windsor in August: needs forcing tactics at 1m and should stay 1½m: probably best with give in the ground: has joined D. Elsworth. *B. W. Hills.*   92

BOLD ANGEL 3 b.g. Lochnager 132–Lobela 77 (Lorenzaccio 130) [1989 5f 5d³ 6g⁴ 6g* 6d⁵ 6m³ 7m³ 1990 6f 7g 7m 6m 6d] strong, close-coupled gelding: carries condition: has a round action: modest handicapper: slowly away and soon outpaced when seventh of 11 at Newmarket fourth start, clearly best effort as 3-y-o: will be   72 suited by return to 7f: acts on good to firm ground and dead: blinkered final start: trained until after third by J. Wainwright. *M. Johnston.*

BOLD ANSWER 7 b.g. Bold Owl 101–Subtle Answer (Stephen George 102) — [1989 NR 1990 12.3g 16.5g⁶ 12f] winning plater here in 1986: in frame in middle-distance handicaps in Ireland following year: bandaged, tailed off in handicaps at 7 yrs. *Miss G. M. Rees.*

BOLD ARABELLA 2 b.f. (May 20) Never So Bold 135–Nativity (USA) 71 — p (Native Royalty (USA)) [1990 6f 6g] big, workmanlike filly: half-sister to several winners, including 1¼m winner Fearless Native (by Final Straw) and useful 6f and 7f winner Native Charmer (by Gay Fandango), later successful at up to 9f in USA: dam lightly-raced 2-y-o 5f winner: behind in maiden (prominent 4f) at Goodwood and minor event at Doncaster in August: sort to do better. *J. Berry.*

BOLD BOSTONIAN (FR) 2 b.c. (Feb 16) Never So Bold 135–Miss Boston 88 (FR) (River River (FR) 111) [1990 6m* 6g³ 7m³ 7.3g⁵] 19,500F, 25,000Y: workmanlike colt: good mover: first foal: dam French 5f winner at 2 yrs, stayed 1¼m: fairly useful colt: comfortable winner of maiden at Salisbury in August: creditable staying-on fifth of 9 to Sapieha in Vodafone Horris Hill Stakes at Newbury: will be suited by at least 1m. *H. Candy.*

BOLD-BRI 3 gr.f. Bold Owl 101–Bri-Ette 53 (Brittany) [1989 6g 7.5f 1990 7g⁶ 8g — 10m] workmanlike filly: poor plater. *Miss L. C. Siddall.*

BOLD CADET 5 b.g. Sandhurst Prince 128–Bold Lady (Persian Bold 123) [1989 — 10s² 10v² 8s⁴ 9g 10m⁶ 1990 a8g] ex-Irish gelding: sixth foal: half-brother to fairly useful 7f (at 2 yrs) and 1¼m winner Lavender Mist and French 10.5f winner Papermoon (both by Troy), very useful 1984 French staying 2-y-o Hello Bill (by Bellypha) and a winner in Morocco: dam won 3 times at up to 9f in France: second in handicaps at Leopardstown and Navan (apprentices) in spring as 4-y-o: always behind in Southwell claimer in January: stays 1¼m: acts on good to firm and heavy going: blinkered. *C. F. C. Jackson.*

BOLD CITIZEN 2 gr.g. (Mar 31) Never So Bold 135–Celestial City 97 — (Godswalk (USA) 130) [1990 8m 6m] 7,200Y: leggy, angular gelding: third living foal: half-brother to a winner in Italy: dam 2-y-o 5f winner: bandaged, in mid-division in 17-runner claimer at Leicester in October: slowly away and green on debut in seller: sold 1,100 gns Newmarket Autumn Sales. *A. N. Lee.*

BOLD COOKIE 2 b.f. (Mar 10) Never So Bold 135–Irish Cookie 80 (Try My 75 p Best (USA) 130) [1990 5g²] first foal: dam 6f and 7f winner, best at 4 yrs: promising second to Beynounah in maiden at Beverley in August, quickening 2f out then green and caught line: should improve, and win a modest race. *Miss S. E. Hall.*

BOLDDEN 8 b.h. Bold Lad (IRE) 133–Golden Keep 77 (Worden II 129) [1989 — 10.4m 8m 10m⁴ 8g⁶ 8h³ 1990 12.3f] strong, good-quartered horse: moderate mover: quite modest handicapper at best nowadays: ideally suited by 1¼m: needs a sound surface: ran creditably for apprentice final outing (July) at 7 yrs. *R. M. Whitaker.*

BOLD DISPLAY (USA) 3 b.f. Green Dancer (USA) 132–Worthyana (USA) — (Twice Worthy (USA)) [1989 NR 1990 10m⁵ 12f 7.6m 10d] $65,000Y: big, long-backed filly: fifth living foal: half-sister to 3 winners abroad, including prolific pair Penzance (by Hail The Pirates) and Grade 3 9f winner Balthazar B (by Nodouble): dam stakes-placed winner at up to 9f: plating-class maiden: well beaten after debut, in claimer (sweating) final start: sold 5,000 gns Newmarket December Sales. *D. J. G. Murray-Smith.*

BOLD DOUBLE 2 ch.c. (Feb 29) Never So Bold 135–Bold Flawless (USA) (Bold 89 Bidder) [1990 5d⁶ 5f* 5f⁴ 5m* 5m 6m³ 6m* 6g] 30,000Y: compact, good-quartered colt: has scope: fifth foal: half-brother to useful 1988 2-y-o 6f and 7f winner Life At The Top (by Habitat) and 1985 2-y-o 5f winner Sound Reasoning (by Known Fact): dam 1½m winner: fair performer: won maiden at Salisbury in May, minor event at Windsor in July and quite valuable nursery at Chepstow in August: best form at 6f: visored fourth and fifth starts: not particularly consistent. *C. R. Nelson.*

BOLD ELECT 2 b.c. (Apr 22) Electric 126–Famous Band (USA) (Banderilla 79 (USA)) [1990 6m⁵ 7.5m⁶ 7m 8g 8g⁵ 8g³] 18,500Y: sturdy, lengthy colt: carries condition: fifth foal: half-brother to 3-y-o 1½m winner Ambrose (by Ile de Bourbon), Irish 1m winner Famous Lad (by Bold Lad) and moderate 1986 2-y-o 5f winner Oriole Dancer (by Dance In Time): dam unraced granddaughter of good American filly Lalun, dam of Never Bend and Bold Reason: modest maiden: veered badly right and left final start: will stay middle distances: none too easy a ride. *P. Wigham.*

BOLD ENDEAVOUR　3 b.g. Try My Best (USA) 130–Explorelka (Relko 136)　—
[1989 5s 5s 5f 6m⁴ 6m 7m⁵ 8f⁵ 1990 a8g⁶ a8g³ 7m 12f 6m] quite attractive gelding:
has a quick action: quite modest maiden: well beaten as 3-y-o, including in seller:
stays 1m: tends to wander: blinkered third start: sold out of M. Fetherston-Godley's
stable 2,200 gns Ascot May Sales after fourth. *G. R. Oldroyd.*

BOLD FOX　4 b.c. Ballad Rock 122–Spadilla 59 (Javelot 124) [1989 10g* 9f*　**109**
10.2g⁴ 12d 1990 11m 12g* 12m² 10m* 10m⁵ 12f* 12g] tall, good-topped colt: good
walker: has a quick action: very useful performer: had fine season, winning
handicaps at Leicester in June, Sandown (caught Akdam final strides in £35,800
Royal Hong Kong Jockey Club Trophy) in July and Newmarket (moderately-run
£19,100 Brierley New Zealand Handicap gamely by ½ length from Black Monday) in
August: ran poorly in Group 3 event at the Curragh final outing: stays 1½m: acts on
firm ground, possibly unsuited by dead: genuine and consistent: sold only 20,000
gns Newmarket Autumn Sales. *G. Harwood.*

BOLD HABIBTI　3 b.f. Never So Bold 135–Cardinal Palace 85 (Royal Palace 131)　**75 p**
[1989 NR 1990 7m²] 5,000F, 25,000Y: third live foal: half-sister to 9f winner Sharp
Order (by Sharpo) and 12.4f winner Royal Penny (by Thatching), subsequently
successful in USA: dam won from 9.4f to 1½m: 14/1, 3½ lengths second of 9 to eased
Perfolia in maiden at Newmarket in November, travelling strongly much of way and
keeping on well: will stay 1m: sure to do better. *J. P. Hudson.*

BOLD HABIT　5 ch.g. Homing 130–Our Mother 95 (Bold Lad (IRE) 133) [1989　**75**
5f² 6g* 6m² 7g³ 6f 6m⁴ 7.6m 8f² 9f⁵ 10g⁴ a8g a7g* 1990 7m⁴ 8g⁵ 7m 7f³ 7g* 7f³ 7f⁵
7.5g 8g² 7.3g⁵ 7m³ 6g³ a8g³ a7g⁵ a7g*] sturdy, strong-quartered gelding: moderate
walker and mover: modest handicapper: won at Ayr (edging left) in July and
Lingfield (leading final strides) in November: best short of 1¼m: acts on firm and
dead going: blinkered once: sweating badly third outing: needs exaggerated waiting
tactics. *W. J. Pearce.*

BOLD HEART (IRE)　2 ch.c. (Mar 24) Pennine Walk 120–June Maid 56 (Junius　**74**
(USA) 124) [1990 5.1g⁴ 6g* 5m² 6m] 30,000Y: lengthy, unfurnished, dipped-backed
colt: second foal: half-brother to inconsistent 3-y-o Doulally (by Doulab), 6f seller
winner at 2 yrs: dam second over 7f at 3 yrs, is half-sister to very useful 6f and 1m
winner Magnetic Field: quite modest performer: won claimer at Goodwood in June:
well beaten in Group 3 event at Milan final outing: stays 6f. *A. A. Scott.*

Royal Hong Kong Jockey Club Trophy (Handicap), Sandown —
hard-ridden Bold Fox gets up from Akdam on the line

BOLD ILLUSION   12 ch.g. Grey Mirage 128–Savette (Frigid Aire) [1989 14.8s   —
12s 1990 12d] close-coupled, sparely-made gelding: lightly raced and well below his
best on flat nowadays, but did win over hurdles in 1989/90: stays 1¾m well: suited
by give in the ground and goes very well in the mud: best forcing pace: usually
apprentice ridden: taken down early only start in 1990: a grand old servant. *M. W.
Eckley.*

BOLD INTENTION   6 ch.g. Baptism 119–Fines Herbes (Tissot 131) [1989 NR   —
1990 9f] rather leggy gelding: quite modest winner as 3-y-o: bandaged, well beaten
in Ripon claimer in April, only subsequent outing: stays 9f: acts on firm going and is
possibly unsuited by soft: bought 1,000 gns Doncaster January Sales. *J. S.
Wainwright.*

BOLD LEZ   3 b.c. Never So Bold 135–Classy Nancy (USA) (Cutlass (USA)) [1989   90
6m 6g⁶ 6g³ 6d³ 1990 6g 6g² 5m* 6g 5m³ 5m* 5g² 6m 5m³ 5m] leggy colt: poor
mover: fairly useful handicapper: best efforts when clear-cut winner at Sandown in
May and July and when placed afterwards in well-contested events at York and
Ascot: possibly best over stiff 5f: yet to race on extremes of going: bandaged
near-fore second start, off-fore third: rather inconsistent. *M. J. Haynes.*

BOLD MERIT   3 b.c. Persian Bold 123–Basta 72 (Busted 134) [1989 NR 1990   55
10m 11.5g⁵ 11.5m⁴ 10m³ 12m² 10m] IR 56,000Y: tall colt with scope: blind in off-eye:
moderate mover: second foal: half-brother to 6f (at 2 yrs) and 1m winner Malibasta
(by Auction Ring): dam successful from 1¼m to 2¼m: plating-class maiden: ridden
by 7-lb apprentice when in frame in claimers, claimed out of D. Elsworth's stable
£6,000 at Newmarket penultimate start: well behind facing stiff task later in August:
stays 1½m. *B. J. McMath.*

BOLD NEPHEW   2 b.c. (Feb 6) Never So Bold 135–Cornelian 78 (Great   98
Nephew 126) [1990 6m* 6m³ 6f⁴ 6f⁶ 6m⁴] 47,000Y: leggy, useful-looking colt: has
scope: has a quick action: first foal: dam 1½m winner, is daughter of Jacinth: quite
useful colt: won maiden at Newbury in June: best subsequent efforts third to Mac's
Imp in Coventry Stakes at Royal Ascot and fourth, staying on, to Lycius in Newgate
Stud Middle Park Stakes at Newmarket: will be better suited by 7f: unsuited by firm
ground. *R. Hannon.*

BOLD PATRICK   3 b.c. Never So Bold 135–Baby's Smile 68 (Shirley Heights   —
130) [1989 8.2g³ 1990 8.2f 9m 11.7m 16m 12m] good-topped colt: not a good
walker: modest form when third in maiden as 2-y-o, none in handicaps: appears
suited by 1m: sold 840 gns Newmarket Autumn Sales. *M. Bell.*

BOLD PERFORMER   3 b.c. Bold Lad (IRE) 133–Miss St Cyr 86 (Brigadier   77
Gerard 144) [1989 7d* 1990 10s⁶ 10d³ 9m⁵ 10.2s⁴] sturdy colt: 33/1, led post in
Thirsk minor event as 2-y-o: not seen out until late-October in 1990, good
33/1-fourth of 17 to Rakeen in minor event at Doncaster: stays 1¼m: acts on soft
going, faced very stiff task on good to firm. *J. Wharton.*

BOLD RAB   3 ch.g. Rabdan 129–Herbary (USA) (Herbager 136) [1989 5m 6m 6f⁶   — §
1990 7f 7m 8.3g 7g 10. 1m] compact, quite attractive gelding: plater: has lost his form
and looks unsatisfactory: should stay beyond 6f. *J. White.*

*Goffs (C & G) Premier Handicap, the Curragh—
Bold Russian runs away with this valuable prize*

BOLD RELATIVE   3 ch.g. Superlative 118–Relko's Pride (Relko 136) [1989 NR   **54**
1990 6m⁵ 8.2g 8d⁶] 10,000Y: half-brother to 3 winners, including 1979 2-y-o 5f
winner Welsh Pride (by Welsh Saint): dam unraced half-sister to Bold Lad (IRE):
fifth of 13 in maiden at Carlisle, running on well after slow start: never dangerous in
similar event 3 months later, then well out of depth final start. *C. W. Thornton.*

BOLD REPUBLIC   4 gr.g. Nishapour (FR) 125–Gallant Believer (USA) (Gallant   **66** d
Romeo (USA)) [1989 8f³ 8g⁵ 10f⁴ 9m³ 10g* 10s 1990 a12g⁶ 12f 12f³ 12.3f⁶ 12f⁵ 12m⁴
12g* 12g 12m⁵ 12g⁵ 12g 13g⁵ 13.6d 16s] leggy, workmanlike gelding: quite modest
handicapper: won slowly run apprentice event at Leicester in May: below form
after, looking ungenuine twelfth outing then off course 3½ months: stays 1½m:
probably acts on any going: blinkered fourth outing: usually held up: not one to
trust: winning hurdler in December. *T. D. Barron.*

BOLD RESOLUTION (IRE)   2 b.c. (May 18) Shardari 134–Valmarine (FR)   —
(Val de Loir 133) [1990 7m 8m] 37,000F, 26,000Y: big colt: poor mover: half-brother
to 5 winners abroad, notably Valrant (by Tyrant), French 6f (at 2 yrs) and 1m winner,
including in listed company: dam 7f winner (at 2 yrs) in France: backward in autumn
maidens at Goodwood and Newmarket. *C. A. Cyzer.*

BOLD REX (FR)   8 b.g. Rex Magna (FR) 129–Lady Bold (Bold Lad (IRE) 133)   —
[1989 NR 1990 10.1g] strong, close-coupled gelding: moderate walker: fair
handicapper in 1986: bandaged and burly for Windsor claimer in April, only fourth
subsequent outing: best at 1½m: suited by soft surface. *R. J. Hodges.*

BOLD ROCKET   3 gr.g. Bold Owl 101–Marwick (Roan Rocket 128) [1989 NR   —
1990 7g 9g] 3,000Y, 6,200 2-y-o: neat gelding: first foal: dam ran once: bit backward,
never able to challenge in seller and maiden in June. *C. R. Beever.*

BOLD RUSSIAN   3 b.c. Persian Bold 123–Russian Ribbon (USA) 86 (Nijinsky   **114**
(CAN) 138) [1989 5m* 6g⁵ 6f⁴ 6g³ 8.2d⁶ 7g⁴ 1990 7m* 8g* 7f² 7f³ 8g²] quite

Sir Gordon White's "Bold Russian"

good-topped, attractive colt: won £6,200 handicap at Newmarket in April and IR £137,500 Goffs (C & G) Premier Handicap at the Curragh in May: easily best subsequent efforts when narrowly-beaten second to Sally Rous in Jersey Stakes at Royal Ascot and Kostroma in 1m EBF Desmond Stakes (tried to bite an opponent then bumped over 1f out) at the Curragh: will prove better at 1m than 7f: acts on firm going: smart. *B. W. Hills.*

BOLD SPARK 2 br.g. (May 5) Electric 126–Boldie 81 (Bold Lad (IRE) 133) [1990   **56** 5m[5] 6g 7g[3] 7m[2] a7g* 7f[6] 7m[5] a7g[4] 7f[2] 8m 8m[3] 8.2s[4] 10.6s[4] 7d[2]] sturdy gelding: good mover: third foal: half-brother to 7f winner Lord Patrick (by Formidable): dam won from 7f to 10.6f: fair plater: won at Southwell (retained 3,500 gns) in July: may prove best around 1m: acts on any going: effective with or without blinkers or visor: has sweated up: game and genuine. *J. Berry.*

BOLD STRANGER 5 br.h. Persian Bold 123–Lorna Doone (USA) (Tom Rolfe)   — [1989 16.2m[4] 20f[6] 16m[6] 12f[4] 13.4m[5] 14.6g 1990 20m] angular, workmanlike horse: poor mover: quite useful at his best, but became one to treat with caution as 4-y-o: backward, pulled up lame in Ascot Stakes (Handicap) at Royal Ascot: stayed 2m: best form on a sound surface: dead. *C. A. Austin.*

BOLD STREET BLUES 3 b.g. Bold Owl 101–Basin Street (Tudor Melody 129)   **68** [1989 6m 7.5f 7f[6] 7g[5] 7m[4] 8.2s* 8.2g[4] 8s[2] 8.2s[3] 1990 12f* 11v[3] 12.2m[3] 11m[2] 12.2m[3] 12.4m 13.8d[6] 15.3f* 15m 12.5g[3]] quite good-topped gelding: carries condition: has a markedly round action: quite modest performer: won claimer at Leicester in March and seller (bought in 6,500 gns) at Wolverhampton in September: claimed to join C. A. Smith £8,551 when good third in Wolverhampton seller final start: should be suited by return to further, uncertain to stay beyond 2m: acts on any going. *C. Tinkler.*

BOLGHERI 2 b.c. (May 2) Nicholas Bill 125–Barrie Baby 86 (Import 127) [1990   — 8.2m 8d 8g 8v] 12,000Y: workmanlike colt: has scope: second foal: dam 7f to 9f winner stayed 1¼m: poor maiden: will stay well: has joined E. Incisa. *N. Tinkler.*

BOLLIN GORGEOUS 4 b.f. Hello Gorgeous (USA) 128–Treberth 60 (Gay   — Fandango (USA) 132) [1989 6d[2] 8.2s 6g[3] 8m[4] 6g[5] 7m[4] 7g* 8f 8.2g 8g[5] 8g[3] a11g[6] 1990 11s] workmanlike filly: turns off-fore in: poor mover: won claimer as 3-y-o: ran poorly outing (April) in 1990: stays 1m: blinkered last 8 starts at 3 yrs: winning hurdler in 1989/90 with Miss S. Wilton. *C. R. Beever.*

BOLLIN MAGDALENE 2 b.f. (Apr 8) Teenoso (USA) 135–Klairlone 116   **55** (Klairon 131) [1990 6s[3] 6s[4] 7f 8v] 7,200Y: rather angular filly: moderate mover: sister to 1988 2-y-o 1m winner Staff Approved and half-sister to several winners, including Irish Heart (by Steel Heart), useful winner at up to 1¼m at 2 yrs here later stakes winner in North America: dam in frame in Irish 1000 Guineas and Irish Oaks: plating-class maiden: should stay 1m: acts on soft ground, possibly unsuited by firm. *M. H. Easterby.*

BOLLIN PATRICK 5 b.h. Sagaro 133–Bollin Charlotte 79 (Immortality) [1989   **82** 12g[3] 12s* 12f* 12m 12g 12m 12f 1990 12m 14s[3] 12m 12.2m[4]] strong, workmanlike horse: has a quick, rather round action: developed into quite a useful handicapper in spring as 4-y-o: best effort in 1990 always-prominent third at Haydock in June: stays 1¾m: possibly needs an easy surface nowadays. *M. H. Easterby.*

BOLLIN SHARON 2 b.f. (Mar 6) Nishapour (FR) 125–Royal Yacht (USA)   **42** (Riverman (USA) 131) [1990 5f[4] 6f 6f 5f 5m 5v] 4,000Y: leggy, rather unfurnished filly: has a quick action: third foal: half-sister to winners in Belgium and Sweden: dam placed at 7f, from family of high-class Traffic: poor maiden: should be suited by further than 5f: seems unsuited by heavy ground: visored third start: sold 1,100 gns Doncaster November Sales. *M. H. Easterby.*

BOLLIN WILLIAM 2 b.c. (May 11) Nicholas Bill 125–Bollin Charlotte 79   — p (Immortality) [1990 8g] big, close-coupled, good-topped colt: half-brother to 6 winners, including useful 6f to 9f winner Immortal Night (by Midsummer Night II) and middle-distance winners Bollin Palace (by Royal Palace) and Bollin Patrick (by Sagaro): dam miler: very green in maiden at Pontefract in October: looks sort to do better in time. *M. H. Easterby.*

BOLT 2 ch.g. (Apr 5) Precocious 126–Elope 68 (Jimmy Reppin 131) [1990 6s   **66** 5m[3] 6f[3] 8m[2] 8.2g 6d 8.2d[4] 6d[4] a8g[3]] lengthy, good-topped gelding: moderate mover: half-brother to 5f winner Pillowing (by Good Times): dam half-sister to Blushing Groom: quite modest maiden: ideally suited by 1m: acts on top-of-the-ground and dead going: visored sixth start: wore eyeshield final one: races keenly. *R. Boss.*

BOMBE SUPRISE (USA) 2 ch.f. (Mar 1) Arctic Tern (USA) 126–Dinner **60**
Surprise (USA) (Lyphard (USA) 132) [1990 8m* 8d] $30,000F: lengthy, shallow-
girthed filly: third foal: half-sister to a minor winner in USA by Overskate: dam
lightly-raced maiden: dead-heated with Salmino in maiden at Edinburgh in
September, running wide home bend: not discredited in nursery at Goodwood
following month: will stay 1¼m. *J. H. M. Gosden.*

BONANZA 3 ch.g. Glenstal (USA) 118–Forliana 75 (Forli (ARG)) [1989 NR 1990 **—**
8v 8g⁶ 7g 11m 13g 15g⁶] 9,000F: lengthy, attractive gelding: irresolute maiden on flat/winning hurdler, and
Myfor (by Be My Guest), irresolute maiden on flat/winning hurdler, and
half-brother to 1½m winner Fort Lino (by Bustino) and 1984 2-y-o 6f winner Major
Forum (by General Assembly): dam middle-distance winner: well beaten, blinkered
and making most in claimer final start: should be suited by further than 1m: winning
selling hurdler: sold Mrs G. Reveley 6,000 gns Doncaster November Sales. *C. W.
Thornton.*

BONDSTONE 3 b.c. Miller's Mate 116–Doumayna 79 (Kouban (FR)) [1989 7s* **99**
8.2g² 1990 10.1m² 10.8m² 12g*] small, close-coupled colt: contested minor events
as 3-y-o, ridden along 5f out when landing odds by ½ length from Kaher at Leicester
in July: operated on for split pastern later in month: looked very useful middle-
distance stayer in the making. *H. R. A. Cecil.*

BONNIE KATE 2 br.f. (Mar 16) Bold Owl 101–Piccadilly Rose 63 (Reform 132) **52**
[1990 5g⁵ 6g⁶ 7m² a7g³ 7m⁵] 3,700Y: neat filly: sister to modest 5f (at 2 yrs) and
1¼m winner Old Eros and half-sister to 5f and 6f winner Donovan Rose (by Song)
and 2 winners abroad: dam stayed 1½m: fair plater: blinkered, best effort in nursery
at Wolverhampton (wandered under pressure) final start: suited by 7f. *D. Haydn
Jones.*

BONNY ROSA 3 b.f. Dunbeath (USA) 127–Emmuska (USA) 68 (Roberto **51**
(USA) 131) [1989 8m 1990 10m⁶ 10g 11.5g 14m 11.5m³ 9f³ 9m 10d 12d] big, plain
filly: easy mover, with a long stride: plating-class maiden: ridden by 7-lb claimer,
easily best efforts when third in handicaps: stays 11.5f: acts on firm ground. *G. A.
Huffer.*

BONNY'S GAME 2 b.f. (Apr 2) Mummy's Game 120–Ribonny (FR) 33 (Fast **—**
Hilarious (USA)) [1990 6g] workmanlike filly: keen walker: first foal: closely
related to a plating-class maiden by Mummy's Pet: dam staying maiden, placed
over hurdles: bit backward and slowly away in maiden at Thirsk in August. *C. W. C.
Elsey.*

BOOKCASE 3 b.c. Siberian Express (USA) 125–Colourful (FR) (Gay Mecene **74**
(USA) 128) [1989 NR 1990 8m⁴ 9m* 10.2m² 12g 12g⁵ 13.3m⁴ 14g 12.5g³ 13.3g]
65,000Y: big, good-topped colt: first foal: dam French 2-y-o 5f winner is half-sister
to 2 good winners in France, including middle-distance performer First Prayer, and
daughter of high-class French staying 2-y-o First Bloom: modest form on his day,
winning maiden at Kempton in May and fourth in £11,500 handicap at Newbury in
July: probably stays 13f: didn't find much in blinkers third start, ran too freely in
them on final one: sometimes edgy: winning hurdler: may well be temperamentally
unsatisfactory. *D. R. C. Elsworth.*

BOOK THE BAND 3 ch.c. Be My Guest (USA) 126–Love Land (FR) **106**
(Kautokeino (FR)) [1989 6m² 6f* 6m² 7g³ 7g⁴ 1990 7m³ 8m⁴ 6m⁴ 8m⁵] strong,
lengthy, good sort: carries condition: useful performances in European Free
Handicap at Newmarket and Poule d'Essai des Poulains at Longchamp first 2
outings: 33/1 and looking very well, raced keenly in blinkers and readily outpaced
2½f out in St James's Palace Stakes at Royal Ascot final start: needs further than 6f,
and stays 1m: acts on firm going. *R. W. Armstrong.*

BOOMING (FR) 2 b.c. (Feb 4) Leading Counsel (USA) 122–Donche (FR) (Roi **114**
Dagobert 128) [1990 5g* 5.5g* 6g* 7g* 6.5g* 7g³ 8g* 7.5d⁵] 90,000 francs (approx
£8,300) Y: fourth foal: half-brother to 1986 French 2-y-o 5.5f winner Pibonson (by
River River): dam French 7f winner: successful in minor events at Evreux, Bernay,
Dieppe and Toulouse and listed events at Bordeaux and Vichy: 1½ lengths third of 7
to Hector Protector in Prix de la Salamandre at Longchamp in September: over 8
lengths fifth of 9 to Exit To Nowhere in Prix Thomas Bryon at Saint-Cloud in
October: stays 1m: apparently very useful. *R. Collet, France.*

BOOZY 3 b.f. Absalom 128–The High Dancer (High Line 125) [1989 5g² 5d⁵ 5f* **111**
5m* 6g 5f³ 5g⁴ 1990 5f² 5f³ 5f² 5d 5m² 5f 5g* 5g⁵] deep-girthed, workmanlike filly:
has a fluent action: very useful performer: made all to beat Tadwin ¾ length in
Waterford Foods EBF Phoenix Flying Five in September: below form in Prix de

Waterford Foods EBF Phoenix Flying Five, Phoenix Park —
Boozy (right) makes all from the hard-ridden Tadwin

l'Abbaye de Longchamp following month: suited by 5f: acts on firm going: makes the running: has run well sweating: game and consistent. *J. Berry.*

BORDER MATE (IRE) 2 b.f. (Feb 16) Be My Guest (USA) 126–Scots Lass 79 **69**
(Shirley Heights 130) [1990 7m³ 7g³] leggy filly: first foal: dam 13f winner: well backed, quite modest form in maidens at Yarmouth and Kempton: will be well suited by 1¼m +: can win a race. *L. M. Cumani.*

BORIS (USA) 2 b. or br.c. (Feb 21) Chief's Crown (USA)–Ivory Lady (USA) (Sir **69 p**
Ivor 135) [1990 7g²] leggy, attractive colt: second foal: dam minor winner at around 1m, is half-sister to very smart 1976 American 2-y-o Mrs Warren, Grade 1 winner at 6f and 7f: bit backward and green, 2 lengths second of 5 to Half A Tick in minor event at Chester in June: moved moderately down. *H. R. A. Cecil.*

BORN TO FLY (IRE) 2 b.f. (May 14) Last Tycoon 131–Chilblains 83 (Hotfoot **57**
126) [1990 6d⁶ 5m³ 5g 6.5g] 42,000Y: close-coupled filly: half-sister to 2 winners, including very speedy 1985 2-y-o Nashia (by Northern Guest): dam winner at 6f and 1m at 2 yrs, later won in Italy: well-backed favourite but edgy and still better for run, around 5½ lengths third in minor event at Chepstow in July, slowly away and soon ridden along then staying on well last 2f: stiff task final 2 (sweating and very edgy latter) outings: should be better suited by 6f + than 5f. *J. Sutcliffe.*

BORN WITH A VEIL 4 b.g. Thatching 131–Star Harbour 76 (St Paddy 133) **—**
[1989 5m 7f⁴ 9f⁶ a7g a8g 1990 8v 8.2g 7m 8g 7m 10.6d] leggy, rather angular gelding: fourth in maiden at Lingfield as 3-y-o: subsequently well beaten, mostly in handicaps in 1990: should stay 1m: blinkered then visored third and fourth outings. *D. Haydn Jones.*

BORUFUS 4 b.g. Sunley Builds 102–Song of Pride (Goldhills Pride 105) [1989 7g **—**
7g 6m⁴ 6f 6m 6m 1990 8m] sparely-made gelding: poor maiden: worth a try over 5f: often wears blinkers or visor: sweated final 3 starts at 3 yrs: usually wears crossed noseband. *R. Thompson.*

BOSAMBO (USA) 2 b.c. (Apr 27) Our Native (USA)–Grey Dawn Girl (USA) **64 p**
(Grey Dawn II 132) [1990 8g 8m⁴] $225,000Y: tall colt: easy mover: brother to good

124

6f to 9f winner Zoffany, later successful at 1½m in Grade 1 company in USA, and half-brother to several other winners: dam useful winner over 8.5f in North America: over 7 lengths fourth of 11, disputing lead over 6f and eased towards finish, to impressive Polish King in minor event at Newmarket in November: likely to improve again, and win a race. *G. Harwood.*

BOSTON BILL   3 ro.g. Magic Mirror 105–Barrow Girl (Dike (USA)) [1989 5f 6f   —
5m⁵ 6m 5m 1990 10g 7f 5.8h 5g 7m] light-framed gelding: moderate mover: poor on most form: showed none in 1990: blinkered once at 2 yrs: has worn bandages behind: sold 1,600 gns Ascot October Sales. *B. R. Millman.*

BOTTLES (USA)   3 b.c. North Pole (CAN) 96–Fooling Around (Jaazeiro (USA)   95
127) [1989 7g 1990 8m³ 8.5m³ 8f* 10g² 8m⁵ 10g⁴ 8f⁴ 9m⁴ 8m³ 10m² 9m 12.2d²
10d*] useful-looking colt: fluent mover: fairly useful handicapper: won at Pontefract (drifting left) in May and Redcar in October: stays 1½m: has won on firm going but best efforts on dead: has run well for 7-lb claimer. *G. A. Huffer.*

BOUGAINVILLEA   3 ch.f. Longleat (USA) 109–Diamante 83 (Sparkler 130)   35
[1989 5f 1990 7.5d 8m 5g⁴ 6m⁵ a5g 7.5g 7f 8.2s] small filly: plater: stays 6f: blinkered third and last 2 starts. *R. O'Leary.*

BOULES   4 gr.g. Petong 126–Placid Pet 65 (Mummy's Pet 125) [1989 6.5s² 7.5g
7s 6s* 1990 7g 6f 7g 6m 8g 7g6] strong, compact gelding: won minor event at Hamilton in autumn as 3-y-o: little worthwhile form in 1990, though showed signs of retaining ability final outing: should stay 7f: seems to need soft going: visored once at 3 yrs, blinkered fifth start. *L. G. Cottrell.*

BOULEVARD GIRL   5 b.m. Nicholas Bill 125–Gay Stampede (Lord Gayle   71
(USA) 124) [1989 14g 14f6 14g 14f 14m 16.2d 1990 14s⁵ 16.2d⁴ 15.3g6 a18g² 16g*
17.4d² 16g 18d 16.5d a16g⁵ a16g*] leggy mare: poor mover: modest handicapper:
won at Chester in August and Lingfield in December: stays 2¼m: acts on any going:
occasionally sweats: hung left third outing: has won for apprentice. *C. B. B. Booth.*

BOUNDER ROWE   3 b.g. Henbit (USA) 130–Arita (FR) (Kronzeuge) [1989 7g   48
7m 6f 1990 7g 8f 8h² 8h 6f6 16m³] rather leggy, quite attractive gelding: shows a quick, moderate action: moderate plater: second at Brighton, clearly best effort as 3-y-o: should stay 1¼m: acts on hard ground: blinkered third to fifth outings: twice bandaged: trained until after fifth start by D. Elsworth. *J. Ffitch-Heyes.*

BOURBON ROSE   4 b.f. Ile de Bourbon (USA) 133–Tantot 65 (Charlottown   —
127) [1989 8s 1990 11.7m 10m6] rangy, workmanlike filly: showed promise only outing as 3-y-o: always behind in minor events late in summer. *P. Leach.*

BOURBONVILLE (DEN)   3 b.f. Ile de Bourbon (USA) 133–Indoor Games   ?
(Habitat 134) [1989 7g 1990 8f⁵ 12g 12g⁴] leggy, unfurnished filly: trained by R. Guest, plating-class form in mid-division for 2-y-o maiden at Newmarket then well beaten in similar event at Warwick and Dansk Derby at Klampenborg: fourth in Swedish Oaks at Jagersro. *G. Jensen, Denmark.*

BOURNVILLE   4 b.f. Lochnager 132–Channing Girl 73 (Song 132) [1989 6s⁴ 7f   79
7m* 7g⁴ 7g⁵ 7g³ 7m⁵ 1990 7m 7g³ 7.6m* 8f 9m 7.6m 7g 8g] big, good-bodied filly: fair handicapper: favourably drawn, won £8,900 event at Lingfield in June: no subsequent worthwhile form: should stay 1m: acts on good to firm going: hung right second outing: visored last. *D. W. P. Arbuthnot.*

BOVVER BOY   2 b.c. (Mar 17) Doc Marten 104–Oh Well 61 (Sahib 114) [1990 6g   —
a7g 7f] 5,400F, 6,400Y, 4,100 2-y-o: smallish, sturdy colt: half-brother to several winners, including sprinter Jolic Courtisane (by Owen Dudley) and 1986 2-y-o 6f and 1m winner U-Bix Copy (by Absalom): dam stayed 1m: well beaten, including in seller: has had tongue tied down. *J. Mackie.*

BOWDEN BOY (IRE)   2 b.c. (May 6) Never So Bold 135–Glebehill 76   79
(Northfields (USA)) [1990 6f 6m² 6d³] 20,000Y: sixth live foal: half-brother to 4 winners, including 5f winner Java Jive (by Hotfoot) and 1m and 1¼m winner Alkinor Rex (by Welsh Pageant): dam 2-y-o 6f winner, is out of smart sprinter Pendlehill: fair maiden: slowly away on debut: will stay 1m: should win a race. *N. A. Callaghan.*

BOWMONT IMP   3 b.f. Import 127–Streets Ahead 67 (Ovid 95) [1989 NR 1990   —
8g 11g 8g⁵ 11m 12g 9f⁵] robust filly: keen walker: half-sister to several winners, including quite modest pair 11f to 17.1f winner Running Money and 7f winner Bills Ahead (both by Billion): dam 6f to 1½m winner: poor form in varied events, best effort second start: gave a lot of trouble at stalls and slowly away on debut: sold 1,000 gns Doncaster September Sales. *J. S. Haldane.*

BOXING DAY (FR)   3 b.c. Deep Roots 124–Flying Machine (Lightning 129)   113
[1989 8g* 8m* 8g* 1990 8d² 8d6 9g² 8d* 10d 9d⁴ 9g⁴ 8s6] 40,000 francs (approx

£3,700) Y: third foal: half-brother to maidens in France by Zino and Top Ville: dam French 9f and 1½m winner: unbeaten in autumn at 2 yrs, in minor event at Fontainebleau, seller (bought out of Mlle M. Geneste's stable approx £45,000) at Longchamp and listed race at Toulouse: contested only listed and pattern events in 1990, winning Prix de la Jonchere at Saint-Cloud in June by short head from Septieme Ciel: well-beaten seventh of 8 in Grand Prix de Paris at Longchamp: stays 9f: acts on good to firm ground and dead. *E. Lellouche, France.*

BOX OFFICE 3 ch.g. Taufan (USA) 119–Vera Van Fleet (Cracksman 111) [1989 NR 1990 10.6f 10m 12m 8m4 8.3m 10m5 8.2s 10g6] 4,000Y: tall gelding: moderate walker: fourth foal: half-brother to Irish 12.5f winner The East Anglian (by Sandhurst Prince), a winner in Italy and a winning hurdler: dam lightly-raced sister to dam of To-Agori-Mou: fair plater: should prove better at 1¼m than shorter: acts on good to firm going: sold to join J. Baker 4,800 gns Newmarket Autumn Sales. *C. A. Cyzer.*   **47**

BOXTOP 3 ch.f. Final Straw 127–Polly Packer 81 (Reform 132) [1989 NR 1990 11f6] sixth foal: half-sister to 3 winning stayers, notably useful 7-y-o Regal Reform (by Prince Tenderfoot): dam, daughter of very useful miler Vital Match, was second over 7f and 1m: remote last of 6 in maiden at Redcar: sold 1,000 gns Newmarket July Sales. *J. W. Watts.*   **—**

BOY EMPEROR 3 ch.c. Precocious 126–Much Too Risky 87 (Bustino 136) [1989 7g 8g4 1990 8.5m4 10d5 12.4m4 13g* 14m3 14.8m4 13d] tall, leggy, sparely-made colt: has a quick action: fair handicapper: favourite, always close up when winning at Ayr in July: set pace when running moderately last 2 starts: should prove suited by 13f+: sold 15,000 gns Newmarket Autumn Sales, probably to race in Italy. *M. R. Stoute.*   **83**

BOYS ROCKS 2 ch.c. (Jun 24) Lighter 111–Nelodor 69 (Nelcius 133) [1990 7m] tall, leggy colt: sixth reported living foal: half-brother to 1¼m seller winner Handsome Jinko (by Some Hand): dam winning hurdler: tailed off in maiden at Chepstow in October. *J. A. C. Edwards.*   **—**

BRAASHEE 4 b.c. Sadler's Wells (USA) 132–Krakow 85 (Malinowski (USA) 123) [1989 9g 10.1m2 12f2 10.1d* 13.3m* 12m* 10g 1990 13.4d* 14g* 13.4g3 14g3 15.5v*]   **118**

The decline of the St Leger has been the subject of many a debate in recent years and various proposals, such as increasing the prize-money, reducing the distance of the race, running it at a different time of the season and opening it up to older horses, have been suggested as the best ways of helping return the race to its former status. When compared to its Irish and

Kosset Yorkshire Cup, York—Braashee (right) holds on gamely from Sapience

French counterparts, however, the St Leger is positively blooming. The French race, the Prix Royal-Oak run at Longchamp in late-October, no longer merits its Group 1 status and the word 'classic' is a misnomer for a race whose last winner of genuine top quality was Ardross in 1981, the first older horse to be successful after the race was opened up in 1979; the Irish, by the way, lifted their age restriction four years later. The 1990 European Pattern Race book explains that the five major European racing countries each have an established standard (known as the pattern race rating) which a race should achieve to justify pattern status. For a Group 1 race the pattern race rating is 120 in Great Britain and France, 115 in Ireland and 110 in Italy and Germany. A pattern race rating is the average of the annual ratings achieved by a race over a five-year period, and the annual rating is the average of the official handicap rating of the first four horses to finish. By Timeform ratings (usually a few pounds higher than the official) the Prix Royal-Oak has achieved a pattern race rating of 117 over the last five years, compared to a St Leger rating of 123 and an Irish St Leger rating of 115. The latest running of the Prix Royal-Oak attracted a distinctly substandard field for a Group 1 race. The three-year-olds, in particular, were poorly represented, just as they had been in the Irish St Leger—none of the three in that race had won a pattern race beforehand and none finished in the first six. Of the five three-year-olds that ran in the Prix Royal-Oak, three had previously won a pattern event, arguably the best of them the King Edward VII Stakes winner Private Tender, well beaten on his latest two outings and not seen on the track for three months. The older contingent numbered six: accompanying the Yorkshire Cup winner and Irish St Leger third Braashee were the Grand Prix de Deauville winner Robertet; Turgeon, runner-up to Top Sunrise in the Royal-Oak the previous year; the disappointing 1989 St Leger winner Michelozzo; the useful five-year-old mare Indian Queen; and the dual bumpers winner Ruling. As often happens in races run under very testing conditions, none of those held up off the pace managed to launch a worthwhile challenge and it was Braashee and the front-running Indian Queen who had the race to themselves in the home straight. After a tremendous battle throughout the final furlong the pair dead-heated, six lengths clear of Turgeon and another two in front of Michelozzo. It was the first dead-heat in a French classic since that between Coronation and her pacemaker Galgala in the Poule d'Essai des Pouliches in 1949.

Braashee, a good-topped colt unraced at two, improved considerably late on as a three-year-old and started the latest season by winning from smallish fields in the Ormonde EBF Stakes and Kosset Yorkshire Cup. His ability to quicken counted for a lot in a slowly-run race at Chester and he held a three-length advantage over Michelozzo at the post. Just as the previous year's Ormonde winner Mountain Kingdom had done, Braashee justified favouritism at York. For a long way Braashee looked most unlikely to win and he was being pushed along at the back of the field three quarters of a mile from home. A lazy individual he may be, but he's game too; he responded to pressure and stayed on strongly to beat Sapience, who'd been travelling best of all three furlongs out, by three parts of a length. A jarred joint, which kept him off the track for the next three and a half months, meant Braashee had to miss the Hardwicke Stakes at Royal Ascot and connections were of the opinion that he still might not have been fully fit when third to Ibn Bey and Mr Pintips in the Jefferson Smurfit Memorial Irish St Leger at the Curragh.

		Northern Dancer	Nearctic
	Sadler's Wells (USA)	(b 1961)	Natalma
	(b 1981)	Fairy Bridge	Bold Reason
Braashee		(b 1975)	Special
(b.c. 1986)		Malinowski	Sir Ivor
	Krakow	(b 1973)	Best In Show
	(b 1980)	Fighting	Aggressor
		(b 1968)	Pelting

Braashee was knocked down to Dublin Bloodstock in 1987 for 170,000 guineas at the Tattersalls Highflyer Yearling Sale. His full brother, the unraced two-year-old Adam Smith, fetched four times that amount when the second-most expensive lot at the same sale two years later. Braashee comes from a highly successful family. His year-older half-sister Ghariba (by Final

Maktoum Al-Maktoum's "Braashee"

Straw), the first foal of the seven-furlong winner Krakow, won the Nell Gwyn Stakes and finished fourth in the One Thousand Guineas. Krakow is a daughter of the useful miler Fighting, whose several other winners include Leipzig, successful in listed company over a mile and runner-up in the Nell Gwyn; Stop The Fighting, successful three times at up to nine furlongs in Ireland as a three-year-old and later a graded-placed winner in North America; and Balilla, dam of the Gladness Stakes winner Careafolie and the Horris Hill winner Gouriev. Fighting was one of twelve winners, most of them useful, produced by Pelting. Among the others are the Cornwallis Stakes winner Splashing, dam of the Middle Park winner Bassenthwaite who's now at stud in New Zealand, and the Nell Gwyn third Glinting, dam of Hadeer and the 1990 four-year-old Night of Stars. The tough and consistent Braashee stays two miles; he won on good to firm going as a three-year-old, but raced solely on an easy surface in the latest season. He is to remain in the ownership of Maktoum Al-Maktoum in 1991, but in Australia with trainer David Hayes. Like Al Maheb, he could be the right type for the Melbourne Cup, won by the Al-Maktoum family in 1986 with At Talaq from the same stable. *A. C. Stewart.*

BRACKEN BAY 3 ro.f. All Systems Go 119–War Bird (Warpath 113) [1989 7g⁶ — 1990 8.5g 6m 8g a8g] sturdy filly: showed promise in seller at 2 yrs, none in 1990: bandaged penultimate start. *T. Kersey.*

BRACKEN BELLA 3 br.f. Gorytus (USA) 132–Habella 82 (Habitat 134) [1989 55 d 5d 6f⁵ 5m⁶ 7f³ 7g⁶ 7f⁶ 1990 7m² 7m⁴ 8g 7g 7h⁶ 10m 7m] smallish, sturdy filly: moderate mover: plating-class maiden: ran badly after second start, including in handicaps and seller: stays 7f: acts on firm going: sold to join S. Avery 1,200 gns Doncaster October Sales. *E. Weymes.*

BRADMORE'S CHUM   3 b.g. Commanche Run 133–Sweet Soprano 80 (High   —
Line 125) [1989 NR 1990 10m 10f] strong gelding: second foal: dam 7f and 11f winner
out of half-sister to smart Royal Hive and Attica Meli: bit backward, well beaten in
early-season maidens: subsequently gelded and joined M. Pipe. *G. Lewis.*

BRADMORE'S CLASSIC   3 ch.c. Jalmood (USA) 126–Water Pageant 58   35
(Welsh Pageant 132) [1989 6f 6f 6f5 6f 6m3 8g 6f6 7d3 1990 7f 8f 8.3g 8h3 8.5g 10.1m]
chunky colt: plater: form as 3-y-o only when staying-on third at Brighton: should
stay beyond 1m: yet to race on soft ground, acts on any other: highly strung and
races freely: blinkered 6 times, including at Brighton: sold to join B. McMath 2,800
gns Newmarket July Sales. *M. J. Haynes.*

BRAISWICK   4 b.f. King of Spain 121–Laughing Girl 110 (Sassafras (FR) 135) 118
[1989 8s* 11.3m* 12f5 12g4 10.6g* 10g* 10s* 1990 10m4 10g3 10g5] lengthy, quite
good-bodied filly: has a quick action: developed into very smart 3-y-o, successful in
Sun Chariot Stakes at Newmarket and E P Taylor Stakes at Woodbine final 2
outings: creditable third to Game Plan in Sea World EBF Pretty Polly Stakes at the
Curragh in June: below-par fifth in Scottish Classic at Ayr: best form at 1¼m with
give in the ground: game, genuine and consistent: a credit to her trainer: reportedly
strained suspensory and has been retired. *G. Wragg.*

BRAMBER   4 b.f. Castle Keep 121–Hartnell Dream (Grundy 137) [1989 7s 10f6   —
7f3 10g a7g5 1990 a8g] workmanlike, good-quartered filly: quite modest maiden at
best: bandaged and well backed, ran poorly in claimer in February: may prove suited
by 7f or 1m, though bred to stay further. *M. C. Pipe.*

BRAMDEAN   4 b.f. Niniski (USA) 125–Elizabethan 89 (Tudor Melody 129) [1989   50
12g3 12.5f5 10f 12g4 10m4 10v a10g3 a11g5 1990 11.1m 10g 12.3g4 12g 10d5 8g4 a10g*]
useful-looking filly: has a quick action: won for first time (previously considered
ungenuine) in handicap at Lingfield in November, still long way behind entering
straight then finishing strongly to lead line: stays 1½m: appears unsuited by
extremes of going. *P. T. Walwyn.*

BRANDON PRINCE (IRE)   2 b.c. (May 23) Shernazar 131–Chanson de Paris   56 p
(USA) (The Minstrel (CAN) 135) [1990 6g6 7m 8g] IR 27,000F, 17,500Y:
close-coupled colt: third foal: dam unraced daughter of Etoile de Paris, smart at up
to 1m and half-sister to Irish 2000 Guineas winner Northern Treasure: around 9
lengths seventh of 16, never dangerous and not knocked about, in maiden at
Kempton in September: will stay 1¼m +: may well do better. *I. A. Balding.*

BRANTFELL   2 b.c. (Apr 25) Say Primula 107–Jendor 82 (Condorcet (FR)) [1990   68 ?
5f 5f5 5m5 6v6] compact colt: good walker: first reported foal: dam 5f (at 2 yrs) and
1m (sellers) winner stayed 1½m: quite modest maiden: faced stiff task and hung left
on final outing: should be better suited by 6f than 5f. *D. H. Topley.*

BRASS MONKEY (USA)   2 ch.c. (Mar 11) It's Freezing (USA) 122–Josalee   58 p
(USA) (Jolie Jo (USA)) [1990 7m5] rangy, angular colt: first reported foal:
dam won 15 races at up to 9f, including in stakes: bit backward, around 12 lengths
eighth of 18, held up then staying on late, to Environment Friend in maiden at
Newmarket in October: sure to improve, particularly over further. *W. J. Haggas.*

BRAVEFOOT   2 b.c. (Feb 19) Dancing Brave (USA) 140–Swiftfoot 119   98 p
(Run The Gantlet (USA)) [1990 7m* 7m* 7g5]

With his languid deportment, tongue lolling out, the 11/8-favourite
Bravefoot was a cheerless sight as he trailed in over thirteen lengths last of
the five runners in the Laurent-Perrier Champagne Stakes at Doncaster in
September. Winner of his previous two races, including the Donnington
Castle Stakes at Newbury, and widely expected to make the transition to
pattern company, Bravefoot didn't take the eye beforehand, became the
subject of adverse rumour on the racecourse (so much so that he was eased
from evens despite attracting nearly £75,000 in recorded bets) and looked to
be in some distress virtually as soon as the stalls opened. Three furlongs out,
where he was labouring in last place, Bravefoot was a pale shadow of the horse
who'd travelled strongly in his races at Newmarket and Newbury; and
although he managed to stay in touch long enough to dispute fourth position
approaching the last furlong he wasn't persevered with any longer than was
necessary. After calling an inquiry and hearing evidence from, among others,
the betting intelligence officer and Bravefoot's connections, who reported
that the horse was listless beforehand and particularly subdued afterwards,
the Doncaster stewards referred the matter to the Jockey Club who called
in the police. Their investigations, which also covered the below-par

performance of the beaten Kiveton Park Stakes joint-favourite Norwich at the same meeting, revealed that both Bravefoot and Norwich had been drugged with the fast-acting tranquilizer acetylpromazine. Official confirmation that Bravefoot had been 'got at' evoked memories of the same stable's Gorytus, who was alleged to have been doped (although no proof ever came to light) before the 1982 William Hill Dewhurst Stakes, after which he never recaptured his form. Hopefully Bravefoot, as Norwich, will be none the worse for his experience. His name did appear among the acceptors for the Dewhurst in October but he wasn't seen out again.

Great interest had surrounded Bravefoot's debut at Newmarket two months earlier, for he was the first of Dancing Brave's sons or daughters to set foot on a racecourse in public. A sturdy colt, in appearance very like his half-brother Bannister, Bravefoot was favourite to make his first appearance a winning one and did so readily, taking up the running under two furlongs out and coming home three quarters of a length ahead of another newcomer Sea Level. Eleven days later Bravefoot reappeared in the Donnington Castle Stakes. Opposed by five, including the previous winners Self Expression and Les Animaux Nuages, Bravefoot confirmed that he was a very useful middle-distance prospect with a convincing, if rather lazy, half-length victory over Self Expression, quickening easily after a modest gallop then rallying well when challenged to be comfortably on top at the line. The manner of his victory suggested that Bravefoot was very much the type of horse who would have been well suited by the stronger gallop at Doncaster.

			Northern Dancer
	Dancing Brave (USA) (b 1983)	Lyphard (b 1969)	Goofed
		Navajo Princess (b 1974)	Drone
Bravefoot (GB) (b.c. Feb 19, 1988)			Olmec
	Swiftfoot (b 1979)	Run The Gantlet (b 1968)	Tom Rolfe
			First Feather
		Whitefoot (ch 1967)	Relko
			Mitraille

Bravefoot, a good walker and mover, is the fourth foal and third winner, following the fairly useful staying two-year-old Bannister (by Known Fact) and the three-year-old eleven-and-a-half-furlong winner Harefoot (by Rain

Lord Rotherwick's "Bravefoot"

bow Quest), from the Irish Oaks winner Swiftfoot. Swiftfoot was essentially a stayer, and would have been an interesting runner in the St Leger on the evidence of her comfortable victory in the Park Hill Stakes over the same course and distance. Plenty of Swiftfoot's relatives have stayed long distances—her close relation Reload and great-grandam Mitrailleuse, for example, both won the Park Hill Stakes as well, and most of Mitrailleuse's foals came into their own over a distance of ground—and Bravefoot will stay a mile and a half. He acts on good to firm ground. *Major W. R. Hern.*

BRAVE MELODY 4 b.c. Heroic Air 96–Kaymay 76 (Maystreak 118) [1989 6m **51** 6h³ 6f⁴ 5m 5m⁵ 5m² 5f⁵ 5f 6g 6s 1990 5m 5g 5d² 5m 5m³ a5g 5f⁶ 5m⁴ 5d*] compact colt: moderate mover: plating-class handicapper: won 20-runner event at Catterick in October: best at 5f: acts on hard and dead going: blinkered sixth outing: inconsistent. *Capt. J. Wilson.*

BRAVE MUSCATEER 3 ch.g. Muscatite 122–Amazing Gretts (Pitskelly 122) — [1989 6h⁶ 6g⁶ 5f³ 5f³ 6v 5g 1990 6g 5g 7m 8f⁶ 7g 6g] strong, quite good-topped gelding: quite modest form at 2 yrs but none in 1990, including in seller: likely to prove better at 6f than 5f: blinkered fourth outing: sold 850 gns Doncaster September Sales: doubtful temperamentally. *J. Etherington.*

BRAVE QUESTION (USA) 3 br.g. Cresta Rider (USA) 124–Marry Me (USA) — (Bold Reason) [1989 NR 1990 a12g 8m 9m 11.5g] $9,500Y: big, workmanlike gelding: fifth reported foal: dam, unplaced from 4 starts, is out of sister to Secretariat and half-sister to Sir Gaylord: well beaten in maiden, claimers then handicap. *B. J. Curley.*

BRAVO STAR (USA) 5 b.g. The Minstrel (CAN) 135–Stellarette (CAN) — §
(Tentam (USA)) [1989 12m 14f 12f 1990 18f] sturdy, close-coupled gelding: quite
modest maiden as 3-y-o: well beaten in subsequent handicaps, running moody race
and virtually pulled up only outing (visored) on flat in 1990: suited by 1½m: acts on
firm and dead going: blinkered 3 times: usually takes plenty of driving: sold 6,000
gns Ascot May Sales: best left alone. *P. Mitchell.*

BREAKERS AHEAD (USA) 2 ch.g. (Mar 28) Believe It (USA)–Emerald Reef — p
104 (Mill Reef (USA) 141) [1990 8g] fourth foal: dam disappointing sister to Diamond
Shoal and Glint of Gold, stayed 1¾m: backward, travelled quite smoothly until 3f out
then weakened noticeably in maiden at Kempton in September: will do better over
further. *I. A. Balding.*

BREAKFAST RIDE 2 ch.f. (Apr 14) Formidable (USA) 125–Beautiful Dawn 83
(USA) (Grey Dawn II 132) [1990 6m⁵ 6.5g 6d⁴ 6d] 42,000Y: sturdy, good-bodied
filly: good walker: fourth foal: half-sister to 7f winner Point House (by Diesis) and
3-y-o 10.2f winner Beau Rou (by Rousillon): dam won minor 6f stakes at 5 yrs: fair
form at best, seventh of 17, held up pulling hard then keeping on, in Tattersalls
Tiffany Yorkshire Stakes at Doncaster in September: edgy, raced much too freely
on unfavoured part of track at Nottingham on final outing: blinkered second and final
outings. *J. L. Dunlop.*

BREAK LOOSE 4 ch.f. Krayyan 117–Free Course 80 (Sandford Lad 133) [1989 50
5s 5d⁶ 6f 7g 6m 7g 7g³ 8.2f 6g 1990 7m 6m* 6g² 6d³ 6g³ 7g 5m⁴ 6f* 6m 5f 6g 6d]
lengthy filly: moderate mover: plating-class handicapper: made all at Catterick
(selling event, no bid) in June and Thirsk (racing on favoured stand rail) in August:
mostly ran moderately after, as though something amiss final outing: best at sprint
distances: acts on firm going, possibly unsuited by soft: usually blinkered or
visored: good mount for apprentice. *D. W. Chapman.*

BREAKOUT 6 ch.g. High Line 125–Wolverhants 79 (Wolver Hollow 126) [1989 —
a14g³ a14g⁴ a14g 1990 a12g] leggy, lightly-made gelding: has a fluent, rather round
action: fair winner as 4-y-o: well below his best at Southwell last 2 years, tailed-off
last of 18 in handicap in November: stays 17f: acts on firm and dead going: has won
for amateur: wears bandages. *J. L. Harris.*

BRECKENBROUGH LAD 3 b.c. Uncle Pokey 116–Fabulous Beauty 91 74
(Royal Avenue 123) [1989 6m 1990 8g³ 8m⁵ 10.2g 12d 10.6v⁴ 10v* 10.4d 12s³] leggy,
useful-looking colt: moderate mover: modest handicapper: improved form to win at
Ayr in October: soon struggling at Chester week later then fair third of 15, no extra
over 1f out, at Hamilton: possibly best at around 1¼m: best effort on heavy going. *T.
D. Barron.*

BREEZED WELL 4 b.c. Wolverlife 115–Precious Baby (African Sky 124) [1989 92
6m⁴ 7f⁶ 7m³ 6m 6m² 6m⁵ 6f⁶ 6m³ 8d 7g⁵ 7g* 6d a7g² a8g² 1990 a10g⁵ 8f 8g³ 7m
7.6d⁶ 8g³ 8m³ 7m³ 9m a7g⁶ a8g⁴ a10g³] smallish, sparely-made colt: usually looks
well: poor mover: fairly useful performer: ran very well in handicaps on all-weather
last 2 outings: stays 1¼m: acts on good to firm and dead going: blinkered once at 3
yrs: has won for 7-lb claimer. *C. N. Allen.*

BREEZY DAY 4 ch.f. Day Is Done 115–Bedouin Dancer 79 (Lorenzaccio 130) 69
[1989 6f² 5m² 5g* 7g⁴ 6m⁵ 1990 5d³ 5m 5s⁴ 5m] compact filly: modest performer:
ran poorly in claimer final outing: best at 5f: possibly needs give in the ground
nowadays. *B. A. McMahon.*

BREEZY SAILOR 4 ch.g. Tumble Wind (USA)–Bouganville (Gulf Pearl 117) —
[1989 5d 5f⁴ 6m 5m 6f 5g 6f a6g 1990 a7g 8m a8g] robust, good-quartered gelding:
very little form since 2 yrs: wore crossed noseband final outing: best form in
blinkers: visored once, best form in blinkers: won over hurdles in December. *R. Thompson.*

BREGUET 7 b.m. Rouser 118–Span (Pan II 130) [1989 12d 12f 12g² 15m³ 12f⁶ 12f⁶ 30
13s 15.8g⁴ 14g 1990 14g 12g 12m² 12.3g⁶ 12g⁶ 13m³ 12f 12m 17m⁵] small mare: poor
mover: poor maiden: probably doesn't stay 2m: seems to act on any going: often
bandaged: usually given too much to do. *Don Enrico Incisa.*

BRENDA FROM HUBY 2 ch.f. (May 18) Tina's Pet 121–Dominion Blue 66 —
(Dominion 123) [1990 5d⁶] 500F: angular, good-topped filly: second foal: closely
related to 3-y-o plater Domrun (by Runnett): dam 1¼m winner: backward and
slowly away in maiden (moved poorly down) at Chester in May. *B. C. Morgan.*

BRENDANS SUPERIOR 3 b.f. Hand of Hush 118–Waltham Terrace 50 —
(Auction Ring (USA) 123) [1989 NR 1990 9s⁵ 11v⁵ 11g⁵ 9s 7m 8m 9f] 2,500Y: lengthy
filly: fourth foal: half-sister to a winner in Belgium: dam maiden: poor maiden:
claimed out of W. Musson's stable £7,000 third outing: well beaten subsequently,
blinkered last 2 starts. *B. Preece.*

BRERA (IRE) 2 b.f. (Apr 3) Tate Gallery (USA) 117–Anoint (Connaught 130) 45 d
[1990 6g⁴ 6g 7m⁶ 6m a7g] 5,200Y: small, close-coupled filly: has knee action:
half-sister to 2 winners in France, including middle-distance performer Enlighted
(by Lightning), and a winner in Italy: dam (showed a little ability in France) is
half-sister to Sun Chariot winner Ranimer: poor maiden: should stay 7f: has twice
hung badly left: wore eyeshield final start. *Mrs L. Piggott.*

BRIC LANE (USA) 3 br.c. Arctic Tern (USA) 126–Spring Is Sprung (USA) —
(Herbager 136) [1989 8v 1990 11d 11.7f 11g a12g⁵] leggy, quite well-topped colt: no
worthwhile form in varied events but has shown signs of ability, staying-on fifth in
handicap at Southwell in August: favourite for similar event time before: should stay
middle distances: appeared unsuited (soon off bridle) by firm ground. *C. R. Nelson.*

BRIDAL DANCE (IRE) 2 ch.f. (Apr 18) Coquelin (USA) 121–Crosmieres (FR) 41
(Lyphard (USA) 132) [1990 6m 7m⁶ 6g 7g] IR 1,400F, 12,500Y: neat, strong filly:
sister to French 10.5f winner Poliguienne and half-sister to 3 winners here and in
France, including 1½m winner Pour L'Italie (by Posse): dam French maiden: poor
form in maidens and a nursery (faced stiff task). *R. Hannon.*

BRIDAL TOAST 3 b.c. Rousillon (USA) 133–Romantic Feeling 88 (Shirley 101
Heights 130) [1989 7m* 8m³ 1990 10.4d³ 10g* 8m² 10m⁴ 10.1g⁶] rangy, quite
good-topped colt: has a quick action: useful performer: sole rival broke leg in minor
event at Goodwood in June: ran creditably in minor contest at Newbury and listed
race at Phoenix Park next 2 starts: stays 1¼m: possibly best on top-of-the-ground,
seems unsuited by dead. *L. M. Cumani.*

BRIDGE BUILDER 2 b.c. (Apr 5) General Wade 93–Palmaria (Be Friendly 58
130) [1990 5f⁴ 5m* 5f⁵ 6m²] 2,100Y: good-quartered colt: has scope: fifth foal:
half-brother to 12.5f claimer winner My Swan Song (by Soul Singer): dam showed a
little ability at 2 yrs in Ireland: plating-class performer: won maiden auction at
Edinburgh in April: second in seller (claimed £7,350) at Windsor final start: ran as if
something amiss in between: better suited by 6f than 5f. *J. Berry.*

BRIDGE PLAYER 3 ch.f. The Noble Player (USA) 126–Auction Bridge 76 —
(Auction Ring (USA) 123) [1989 6f 6m⁵ 8.5m 8d³ 8d 10g² 7g 1990 12.5g 10d 10m] fifth
foal: half-sister to quite modest 1¼m winner Malmunster (by Lomond) and 2 other
winners, including untrustworthy 1½m winner Auction Fever (by Hello Gorgeous):
dam, 1m winner, is half-sister to Young Generation: form only when placed in
maiden and nursery in Ireland at 2 yrs: faced stiff task in August seller on sole
outing here: stays 1¼m: acts on dead ground: trained until after second start by T.
Stack. *D. Moffatt.*

BRIDGETTS SECURITY 4 b.f. Camden Town 125–Knight Security 86 —
(Swing Easy (USA) 126) [1989 NR 1990 a11g] sparely-made, shallow-girthed filly:
broke leg and died at Southwell in February. *Miss G. M. Rees.*

BRIERY FILLE 5 b.m. Sayyaf 121–Zeddera (FR) (Zeddaan 130) [1989 7v 7g 7f 59
7f⁵ 7m 8.2g 8m⁵ 7m³ 7g³ 7s 7g* 7m 8f* 8.2g⁵ a8g³ 1990 10.8m 10.1g 8.5g⁶ 10m² 10g
10m² 10f* 10g* 11.5g] lengthy, angular mare: won handicaps at Folkestone (first run
for 3½ months) and Lingfield in autumn: stays 1¼m: acts on firm going and probably
unsuited by soft: good mount for 7-lb claimer: below form when blinkered and
visored: trained until after sixth outing by I. Campbell. *A. Hide.*

BRIGADIER BILL 5 ch.g. Nicholas Bill 125–Sailing Brig (Brigadier Gerard 64
144) [1989 9f 10m³ 10f³ 10.2f² 11f 10.6d³ 1990 10m³ 11d² 9s⁴ a12g² a14g²] big,
angular gelding: quite modest maiden: ran well when placed in handicaps at 5 yrs,
but twice didn't find great deal off bridle: stays 1¾m: acts on any going: resolution
under suspicion. *Mrs G. R. Reveley.*

BRIGADIERS GLORY 4 ch.f. Castle Keep 121–Join The Club 67 (Dance In 59 d
Time (CAN)) [1989 8f 6g 1990 a11g² a11g* a12g 12f 10m 8f 8m 8m 8m⁶ 10.1m 8f⁶ 6g]
neat filly: won claimer (claimed out of B. McMahon's stable £7,551) at Southwell in
February: long way below that form after: saddle slipped and bolted to post eleventh
intended outing: pulls hard, but stays 11f: blinkered final outing: has got on edge:
taken down early nowadays: changed hands 2,600 gns Doncaster June Sales. *C. R.
Beever.*

BRIGGSCARE 4 b.g. Chief Singer 131–Magonis 74 (Blakeney 126) [1989 8s 10g 79
10m⁴ 10g⁴ 14f* 14m* 14m* 14m³ 14m⁴ 14g² 16m³ 1990 17m² 16f³ 14g⁵ 14s⁶ 16m
16.1f³ 14f* 14g 18.1m*] leggy gelding: fair handicapper: narrow winner from small
fields at Yarmouth in July and September: stays 2¼m: seems to act on any going:
looked unsatisfactory in blinkers third to fifth outings at 3 yrs: carries head high:
well suited by tender handling and waiting tactics: consistent. *W. Jarvis.*

BRIGGSMAID 2 b.f. (Feb 28) Elegant Air 119–Merry Yarn 64 (Aggressor 130)   —
[1990 7m] 5,200Y: half-sister to 3 winners, including useful middle-distance winner
Lamb's Tale (by March Past): dam won over 2m and is sister to top Australian
winner Raffindale: last of 16 in maiden at Newmarket in October. *J. M. P. Eustace.*

BRIGHT DANCER 5 ch.m. Move Off 112–Toadpool (Pongee 106) [1989 NR   — p
1990 a14g⁶] second foal: dam well beaten in novice hurdle: won novice hurdle
(wears crossed noseband) early in 1989/90: 20/1, slowly away, took keen hold and
weakened final 2f when sixth of 17 in claimer at Southwell in November: likely to
prove suited by shorter: should improve. *Mrs G. R. Reveley.*

BRIGHT RED 3 ch.c. Kris 135–Chiltern Red (Red God 128§) [1989 6g 6d 1990   58
7g³ 7m] short-backed colt: has a quick action: quite modest maiden: third of 11 at
Epsom, disputing lead 5f and only form: sweating, on toes and still bit backward only
subsequent outing, in May: may well stay 1m: sold to join H. Candy 2,800 gns Ascot
November Sales. *P. W. Harris.*

BRIGHT SAPPHIRE 4 b.g. Mummy's Pet 125–Bright Era 79 (Artaius (USA)   49
129) [1989 7s 8.5g⁵ 7m 8f 1990 a12g² a11g⁵] small, lightly-made gelding:
plating-class maiden: suited by 1½m: blinkered once: much improved hurdler in
autumn. *D. Burchell.*

BRIGHT START 3 ch.g. Precocious 126–Perma Fina 69 (Nonoalco (USA) 131)   —
[1989 NR 1990 a7g a7g] 5,000Y: compact gelding: half-brother to fairly useful 5f
winner Champion Joker (by Moorestyle) and 1¼m winner Non Permanent (by
Niniski): dam lightly raced: always behind in maidens at Southwell: dead. *W. W.
Haigh.*

BRIGTINA 2 b.g. (Apr 14) Tina's Pet 121–Bristle-Moss (Brigadier Gerard 144)   63
[1990 7.5d 7d⁵ 8m⁵ 7.5m⁵ 8f] 3,400Y: angular gelding: first foal: dam unraced: quite
modest maiden: likely to stay beyond 1m: well below form when blinkered final
outing. *B. W. Murray.*

BRISAS 3 ch.g. Vaigly Great 127–Legal Sound 85 (Legal Eagle 126) [1989 5g³ 5v⁶   79 ?
5f* 5m² 6m² 5m⁶ 5f⁴ 6m⁴ 5f* 5d* 5m 5m³ 5m³ 6g 6g 1990 5d⁵ 6f 5d 6f⁴ 5m⁵ 5m 5f⁵
5g 5d³ 5d 5m 5d 5m 5m] strong-quartered, attractive gelding: has a quick action: fair
at best as 3-y-o, third in handicap at Haydock in September: suited by 5f: acts on
firm going, possibly unsuited by heavy: blinkered: tends to be on toes: gelded after
final start: inconsistent, and out of sorts towards end of season. *T. Fairhurst.*

BRITTLE (USA) 4 ch.f. Diesis 133–Ashbrittle 101 (Great Nephew 126) [1989   —
10s³ 12f⁵ 7m 1990 8.2s 9m 7.5d] rather unfurnished filly: moderate walker: quite
modest maiden at best: little show in handicaps in first half of year: stayed 1¼m:
possibly unsuited by top-of-the-ground: sold 14,000 gns Newmarket December
Sales in foal to Night Shift. *N. A. Graham.*

BROAD APPEAL 2 ch.f. (May 20) Star Appeal 133–Cinderwench 95 (Crooner   59
119) [1990 5m³ 5f* 7g³ 7m³] angular filly: moderate mover: third foal: sister to 8.5f
to 1½m winner Planet Ash: dam won from 1m to 1½m: plating-class performer: won
seller (no bid) at Warwick in May: off course 3 months afterwards: will stay 1m. *M.
Bell.*

BROAD STORY (NZ) 3 b.c. Diesis 133–Broadway Hit (Hittite Glory 125) [1989   ?
6g⁶ 6.5g⁴ 8g⁴ 1990 5.5s* 8g⁴ 6g⁶ 6g³ 5g 8d a6g] IR 75,000Y: third foal: half-brother
to French 4-y-o 6f to 8.2f winner Theatreland (by Al Nasr): dam French 4-y-o 9f
winner out of Nell Gwyn Stakes and Yorkshire Oaks winner West Side Story:
ex-French handicapper: won minor event at Evry in March: not knocked about
under top weight in claimer at Southwell first outing here: bred to stay 1m: yet to
race on top-of-the-ground: trained until after penultimate start by A. Fabre. *P.
Calver.*

BROADWAY STAR 3 b.c. Alzao (USA) 117–Broadway Royal (Royal Match 117)   —
[1989 7m² 7f* 7m⁵ 7g⁵ 1990 8d 7.6m⁶ 12g 8g a8g] strong, deep-girthed, attractive
colt: moderate mover, with a roundish action: modest winner at 2 yrs, drifting right:
mostly well below form since, usually facing stiff tasks in 1990: blinkered, set strong
pace over 6f penultimate outing: should stay 1m. *M. Bell.*

BROCKETTE 2 ch.f. (Apr 13) Bustino 136–Explosiva (USA) 88§ (Explodent   109 p
(USA)) [1990 7m 8m* 7.3s² 8v*] rather angular filly: turns fore-feet in: sixth living
foal: sister to 1¾m winner Elplotino and half-sister to 1986 2-y-o 7f winner Stubble
Fire (by Thatch): dam 2-y-o 5f winner, was bad at start: won maiden at Leicester in
September and Premio Dormello (by 3 lengths) at Milan in November: 3 lengths
second to Shaima in listed event at Newbury in between: will be well suited by
1¼m + : acts well on heavy ground. *J. L. Dunlop.*

BROCKLEY HILL LASS (IRE) 2 b.f. (Mar 6) Alzao (USA) 117–Moorland   — p
Chant (Double Jump 131) [1990 7g] 54,000Y: half-sister to several winners,
including 1983 2-y-o 5f winner Handstand (by Thatching), later successful in USA:
dam won at 9f in France: backward and green, around 15 lengths fourteenth of 20,
losing position then keeping on, in maiden at Newmarket in November: moved
poorly down. *M. J. Ryan.*

BROCTUNE GREY 6 gr.m. Warpath 113–Hitesca 110 (Tesco Boy 121) [1989   69
14.6g 16.2d 12g² 14f⁵ 18h⁵ 16.5g² 14f² 16.1m² 17.6d⁴ 16m⁴ 18g⁴ 1990 12.3g 14m⁵
15d³ 16g 16f³ 18d⁵] angular, sparely-made mare: modest handicapper: ran well in
2¼m Tote Cesarewitch at Newmarket for last 2 years: needs extreme test of
stamina: yet to race on soft going, acts on any other except possibly hard: visored
(slowly away) fourth outing: has wandered, and is usually held up: useful hurdler.
Mrs G. R. Reveley.

BROMWICH BILL 5 b.g. Headin' Up–Bilbao 65 (Capistrano 120) [1989 6m   —
1990 6g] appears of little account: hung badly left last 2 outings. *L. J. Barratt.*

BRONZE BLADE 3 ch.g. Sunley Builds 102–Flyweight 69 (Salvo 129) [1989 NR   —
1990 12h⁵] leggy, unfurnished gelding: fourth foal: half-brother to 1m and 1¼m
winner True Weight (by True Song): dam fair hurdler: tailed off in 5-runner maiden
at Brighton in August. *M. Madgwick.*

BRONZE CROSS 5 b.g. Rontino 109–Make Your Mark (On Your Mark 125)   78
[1989 7d² 7s³ 6d⁵ 6f 7m 7.5f⁴ 7f 8f⁴ 8.5g⁶ 8g* 8.5m 8m 8.5f 7m⁵ 8g a7g² a7g⁶ a6g*
a6g⁵ 1990 a7g* a7g* a7g⁶ a7g* a6g⁵ a7g* a6g a7g* a7g] robust gelding: moderate
mover: in excellent form on all-weather early in year, winning claimers and
handicaps at Southwell and claimer at Lingfield: ideally needed further than 6f and
stayed 1m: particularly well suited by an easy surface: sometimes sweated: often
found nothing on turf: best handled tenderly, and went well for Alex Greaves:
changed hands 9,000 gns Ascot July Sales: dead. *T. D. Barron.*

BRONZE RUNNER 6 b. or ro.g. Gunner B 126–Petingalyn (Petingo 135) [1989   48
10g 12m 10m 12g⁴ 12f⁴ 14f 10m⁶ 16.5f⁴ 13.1h⁶ 1990 10f⁶ 10f⁵ 10.1g⁴ 10m* 10f⁴ 12h²
13.6g³ 10.2f² 10m² 12f³ 12m⁵ 10f⁴ 10.4g³ 10f⁴ 12f 10.2m²] leggy gelding: poor
mover: won selling handicap (bought in 5,200 gns) at Lingfield in May: ran
creditably in non-sellers most starts after: best at 1¼m: acts on any going: suitable
mount for inexperienced rider: usually blinkered or visored: consistent. *E. A.
Wheeler.*

BROOKFIELD BOY 3 b.c. Roscoe Blake 120–Forgets Image 87 (Florescence   —
120) [1989 NR 1990 7g 8g 10g] workmanlike colt: seventh foal: half-brother to 4
winners, including 9f and 13f winner Excavator Lady (by Most Secret): dam, winner
3 times over 1m, is half-sister to smart Millingdale Lily: no show, including in
sellers: blinkered final start. *G. M. Moore.*

BROOM ISLE 2 b.f. (Apr 14) Damister (USA) 123–Vynz Girl 82 (Tower Walk   74 p
130) [1990 7m³ 7m² 7f* 7f4] lengthy, quite good-topped filly: carries plenty of
condition: moderate mover: fourth reported foal: half-sister to winners in Denmark
and France: dam 1½m winner: progressive filly: landed odds in slowly-run maiden at
Ayr in July: will be suited by 1m. *J. W. Watts.*

BRORA ROSE (IRE) 2 b.f. (May 17) Drumalis 125–Run Swift (Run The   54
Gantlet (USA)) [1990 7g 7g a8g4] IR 5,200Y: leggy, close-coupled filly: sixth foal:
half-sister to 3-y-o Simply Swift (by Simply Great), Irish 1½m winner Boker-Tov
(by African Sky) and a winner over jumps: dam quite useful winner at up to 2m in
Ireland: plating-class form, staying on, in minor event at Newbury and maiden at
Folkestone on first 2 starts: well beaten on all-weather: will stay 1¼m. *J. D. Bethell.*

BROTHER RAY 3 b.c. Chief Singer 131–Havara 82 (African Sky 124) [1989 6g   65
6g 1990 a6g⁶ 6f 7f⁵ 7g* 7m* 7m] leggy, unfurnished colt: poor mover: quite modest
handicapper: successful in large fields at Warwick and Salisbury in June: 6/4 on,
soon off bridle and hung right as if something amiss following month: will stay
further: ridden by 7-lb claimer, slowly into stride first 2 outings. *J. Sutcliffe.*

BROUGHTINO 3 b.g. Sandhurst Prince 128–Modest Maiden (FR) (Bustino   44
136) [1989 6m 6s 1990 a7g 9s 8m 8.3m⁵ 7m³ 10d⁶ 10d 10g a12g] small, angular
gelding: carries little condition: poor walker and mover: plater: stays 1¼m: acts on
good to firm ground and dead: has run creditably for apprentice. *W. J. Musson.*

BROUGHTON BAY 3 b.c. Trojan Fen 118–Rose Noir (Floribunda 136) [1989   91
5d³ 5m* 5m* 5f4 6m³ 6g 1990 8v² 8g 8g* 6g² 8g 5g* 6g 5v] leggy colt: has a quick
action: fairly useful performer: very good second in minor event at Ayr: not
discredited in Premio Parioli at Rome next start then left W. Musson's stable,

winning at Milan in June and September: stays 1m: probably acts on any going: changed hands after reappearance. *L. D'Auria, Italy.*

BROUGHTON BLUES (IRE) 2 ch.c. (May 19) Tender King 123–Princess Galicia 82 (Welsh Pageant 132) [1990 6g² 7g5 7m 6d6 a8g a8g] sparely-made colt: third foal: half-brother to 1986 Irish 2-y-o 6f winner Pageant's Pride (by Sallust): dam, maiden, stayed 1m: fair plater: should stay 1m. *W. J. Musson.* **52**

BROUGHTON'S GOLD (IRE) 2 b.f. (Mar 8) Trojan Fen 118–Smash Hit (Roan Rocket 128) [1990 6d 6m] 8,400Y: lengthy, angular filly: half-sister to several winners here and abroad, including useful 1m to 1½m filly Jermaric (by Great Nephew) and very useful middle-distance filly Countess Eileen (by Sassafras): dam won over 6f in Ireland: showed signs of a little ability, not knocked about, in claimer at Goodwood and seller at Newmarket in autumn: will stay 1m. *W. J. Musson.* **—**

BROWN AS A BERRY (IRE) 2 b.c. (Jan 31) Glow (USA)–Sun Bed (Habitat 134) [1990 6d a7g4 a7g a7g6] IR 30,000Y: robust colt: first foal: dam Irish 2-y-o 5f winner: sire 7f to 9f winner: plating-class maiden: best effort debut: wore eyeshield last 3 starts. *Mrs L. Piggott.* **52**

BROWN CARPET 3 b. or br.g. Never So Bold 135–Geopelia 109 (Raffingora 130) [1989 5s6 5s² 6f4 5m² 6f 6f4 5m4 5f 6m 1990 5d 5m 7f 8m 11.5m 7g4 7m] smallish, workmanlike gelding: has a quick action: modest maiden at 2 yrs: little form in ladies race and handicaps in 1990: will be suited by return to 1m: acts on firm ground: blinkered 4 times: has been slowly away and carried head high: joined C. Horgan and gelded. *G. Lewis.* **—**

BROWN FAIRY (USA) 2 b.f. (Feb 14) Northern Baby (CAN) 127–Chepstow Vale (USA) 97 (Key To The Mint (USA)) [1990 5g² 6g² 6d 7f6 5g5 7g* 7f* 8m 8.2m 7g] $45,000Y: leggy filly: second foal: dam 2-y-o 5f and 6f winner stayed 1m: modest performer: won nurseries at Sandown (selling event, sold out of R. J. R. Williams' stable 13,500 gns) and Thirsk in September: should be suited by 1m: sweating and very edgy fifth appearance: sometimes gives trouble stalls. *Mrs N. Macauley.* **70**

BROWN PEPPER 4 b.g. Sharpo 132–Petrary 67 (Petingo 135) [1989 9s 7g 8g² 9s5 a8g 1990 a10g6] small, leggy gelding: modest form at best: stays 1m: acts on good to firm going. *S. Woodman.* **—**

BROWN RIFLE 10 bl.g. Scottish Rifle 127–Mother Brown 103 (Candy Cane 125) [1989 9v4 1990 a16g 11s 11s] angular, lightly-made gelding: lightly raced on flat nowadays: well beaten in handicaps and maiden at 10 yrs. *D. Burchell.* **—**

BRUNSWICK BLUE (IRE) 2 b.c. (May 8) Sarab 123–Lanata 64 (Charlottown 127) [1990 7m 7g 8g] 6,800Y: small, close-coupled colt: half-brother to several winners, including useful 6f and 10.2f winner Plaid (by Martinmas) and fairly useful 6f winner Land Ahoy (by Ahonoora): dam ran only at 2 yrs: never dangerous in maidens. *J. Sutcliffe.* **51**

BRUSH ASIDE (USA) 4 b.c. Alleged (USA) 138–Top Twig (High Perch 126) [1989 9g* 10g² 1990 12g* 12m5] **125**

Brush Aside's performance in the Lanes End John Porter EBF Stakes at Newbury in April deservedly received rave reviews: it was an outstanding front-running display, returning a timefigure of 1.10 fast (the equivalent of a 128 timerating), the best of the season over middle distances by an older horse. It's rare that the winner of such a race can be confidently called half a mile from home, as Brush Aside could. His superiority over his ten rivals was such that when he began to quicken clear early in the straight his rider Cauthen was the only jockey not having to resort to any kind of pressure.

Lanes End John Porter EBF Stakes, Newbury—Brush Aside is tremendously impressive

Most of those rivals had shown smart form, and while some—such as Ile de Nisky, Per Quod and Husyan—were making their seasonal reappearance, others—Shellac, Charmer, Artic Envoy and Jehol—had already had a run. The further Brush Aside went in the straight, the further he drew ahead, and he came home unchallenged eight lengths clear of Albadr who just held on to second from Charmer, the latter finishing strongly after being given too much to do. Significantly, Brush Aside started favourite. He'd had a big reputation for a long time, and early on as a three-year-old had seemed a very useful colt in the making (he was towards the head of the ante-post lists for the Derby until he pulled a muscle and jarred himself on his second and final outing in 1989). And on his Newbury showing Brush Aside looked a serious rival to stable-companion Old Vic for the top races over a mile and a half. Ironically, it was because connections wouldn't risk Old Vic on the firmish ground that Brush Aside took his place in the Jockey Club Stakes the following month. For the second year running his season was brought prematurely to an end because of an injury sustained at the Guineas meeting. He didn't impress on the way to post and, after making the running for over a mile, he quickly folded and trailed in a distant fifth of seven behind Roseate Tern. It transpired that he'd chipped a bone in his off-fore knee.

			Hoist The Flag	Tom Rolfe
		Alleged (USA)	(b 1968)	Wavy Navy
		(b 1974)	Princess Pout	Prince John
Brush Aside (USA)			(b 1966)	Determined Lady
(b.c. 1986)			High Perch	Alycidon
		Top Twig	(ch 1956)	Phaetonia
		(b 1967)	Kimpton Wood	Solonaway
			(b 1952)	Astrid Wood

Brush Aside did tremendously well physically from three to four. Colloquially, he looked a million dollars in every way at Newbury. He actually cost more than that as a yearling—1,100,000 dollars to be precise, at the Keeneland September Sale. From what his dam Top Twig achieved on the racecourse one would have been hard put to it to have foreseen how she would turn out as a broodmare. Last in maidens at Salisbury and Goodwood as a two-year-old, she was packed off to stud the following year and from her first three matings produced Twig (by Hul a Hul), Tip Moss and Twig Moss (both by Luthier), all good middle-distance winners in France, the last-named second in the Prix du Jockey-Club. Until Brush Aside came along she'd failed to produce another of that standard, although the thrice-raced Manal (also by Luthier) is the dam of the Lowther Stakes winner Muhbubh. The second dam Kimpton Wood, successful over six furlongs, is a daughter of the third dam of Levmoss, Le Moss and Sweet Mimosa. Dual-Arc winner Alleged, retired to take up stud duties in 1979, had classic winners Law Society, Leading Counsel, Midway Lady and Sir Harry Lewis amongst his third, fourth and fifth crops. Brush Aside's injuries have so far spoiled his chances of becoming as well established as them, but he may be able to return to the course again. A strong, lengthy, good sort who carries plenty of condition, he is better suited by a mile and a half than shorter and will stay further. He raced only on good ground until his final start—he may always be suited by some give in the ground. *H. R. A. Cecil.*

BRUSQUE (USA)   6 b.g. Assert 134–Cecelia (USA) (Royal Levee (USA)) [1989   **53**
11v[2] 12g[3] 10f 1990 12g 12g5 13g[5] 14g 16g[4] 16.2s[6] 18d 16s] compact gelding: quite
modest maiden: stays 2m: acts on heavy going: wears bandages. *Don Enrico Incisa.*

BRUTUS   6 ch.g. Junius (USA) 124–Orangery (Realm 129) [1989 5m 5m[3] 5m[4]   **51**
5m* 5m 6g 6m[2] 6m 5m 6g 7m[5] 7g 6f* 1990 6g[6] 6f 6f[4] 6m 6g] workmanlike gelding:
plating-class handicapper on his day: wearing brush pricker near-side, had stiff task
in claimer final outing, second in 2 days: best at up to 6f: acts on firm and dead going:
blinkered twice: often gets on edge: has won for apprentice: inconsistent. *Miss L. C. Siddall.*

BUBUBU   3 ch.f. Bairn (USA) 126–Calibina 101 (Caliban 123) [1989 NR 1990 5h   **49**
6m[4] 7m 5.3h[5]] 18,000Y: stocky filly: seventh foal: half-sister to several winners,
including sprinters Olympic Challenger (by Anfield) and King Charlemagne (by

Habat): dam won Steward's Cup and Wokingham: form only when fourth in minor event at Folkestone in July, leading 4f: edgy third start. *P. F. I. Cole.*

BUBULINA 3 b.f. Dunphy 124–Hi There 89 (High Top 131) [1989 7g³ 1990 10f² **63** 12f⁴ 8g] lengthy, good-bodied filly: quite modest maiden: worth another try at 1¼m: acts on firm going: swished tail repeatedly in paddock and awkward at stalls on reappearance. *Miss A. J. Whitfield.*

BUCARO BOY 2 br.g. (Apr 22) Mummy's Game 120–Izobia (Mansingh (USA) **68** 120) [1990 7m 7.5m⁶ 10s⁴] 4,300Y: compact, angular gelding: good walker: fourth live foal: closely related to unreliable sprint plater Firmly Attached (by Tina's Pet): dam ran 4 times: fourth to Walim in maiden at Nottingham in October: better suited by 1¼m than 7f: acts well on soft going. *W. G. M. Turner.*

BUCKLAND HAZE 4 b.f. Hays 120–Frensham (FR) 67 (Floribunda 136) [1989 — NR 1990 10.2f 11g] leggy filly: half-sister to 1980 2-y-o 5f winner Tough An Rough (by Saulingo) and a bumpers winner later successful over hurdles: dam's only sign of ability at 2 yrs: well beaten in maidens at Doncaster and Hamilton (claimer) in spring. *H. A. T. Whiting.*

BUCKLE KNIGHT (USA) 2 b. or br.c. (Mar 7) Spend A Buck (USA)–Knightly **69** Belle (USA) (Knightly Manner (USA)) [1990 6m 7g 7f⁵ 7g 8.2g] $52,000Y, resold $80,000Y: quite attractive colt: has scope: half-brother to several winners, notably Savy (by Tom Rolfe), stakes winner at up to 9f: dam, winner of 10 races, seemed best at around 1m: sire won Kentucky Derby: quite modest maiden: should stay 1m: blinkered final 2 outings: sold 1,600 gns Doncaster October Sales. *A. A. Scott.*

BUDGET 2 ch.g. (Feb 5) Bustino 136–Australia Fair (AUS) (Without Fear (FR)) — [1990 6m] leggy, angular gelding: fourth living foal: half-brother to a minor winner in Sweden: dam once-raced daughter of useful Australian middle-distance stayer Chulgin Princess: bit backward and on toes, tailed off in maiden at Newbury in October: moved freely to post: sold to D. W. Chapman 2,050 gns Ascot October Sales. *I. A. Balding.*

BUD'S BET (IRE) 2 b.c. (Apr 18) Reasonable (FR) 119–Pearl Creek (Gulf Pearl **46** 117) [1990 5f 6m² 6g⁴ 6m⁶ 6m 5m⁴ 5m⁵ 6m 6m 6d] IR 5,500F: compact colt: has a round action: dam twice raced half-sister to useful sprinter Queen of The Troops: poor maiden: better suited by 6f than 5f: has run well for 7-lb claimer. *L. J. Holt.*

BUFALINO (IRE) 2 b.c. (Feb 28) Nomination 125–Croglin Water (Monsanto **112** (FR) 121) [1990 5g* 5g* 5m² 5m⁵ 5g* 6d4] IR 8,200Y: first foal: dam lightly raced: useful performer: thrice successful at the Curragh, best effort when winning listed race (Heaven-Liegh-Grey, in receipt of 3 lb, over 10 lengths back in sixth) on penultimate outing by 2½ lengths from Inishdalla: over 2 lengths third (demoted) to Exhibition Cross in minor event at Phoenix Park in October: speedy, and probably better at 5f than 6f: possibly unsuited by a soft surface. *J. S. Bolger, Ireland.*

BUFFS EXPRESS 3 ch.f. Bay Express 132–Buff Beauty 92 (Mossborough 126) — [1989 6m 5.8m⁴ 6g 5m³ 6g 1990 6f⁶ 6m 11.5m 5m 7d 8m a6g a5g⁶] workmanlike filly: quite modest form at best: little in 1990, including in handicaps and claimer: best form over 5f: blinkered penultimate start: sold 4,300 gns Newmarket December Sales. *W. G. R. Wightman.*

BUILDMARK 4 ch.f. Longleat (USA) 109–Crescentia (Crepello 136) [1989 12s⁴ — 11v⁶ 7m⁶ 10.2f⁵ 10g² 1990 a10g] workmanlike filly: quite modest form when second in slowly-run claimer at Goodwood as 3-y-o: soundly beaten in Lingfield maiden in February: suited by 1¼m: unruly at stalls intended fourth start at 3 yrs. *W. G. M. Turner.*

BULLACE 3 ch.g. Bustino 136–Brush (Laser Light 118) [1989 7m 1990 10f² 10.8m **70** 11.5m⁵ 12m* 16.2d] rather unfurnished gelding: moderate mover: made all in claimer (claimed out of J. Dunlop's stable £15,115) at Goodwood in June: gelded after well beaten in handicap at Haydock 3 weeks later: should stay beyond 1½m: acts on good to firm ground: goes well with forcing tactics: changed hands 13,500 gns Ascot November Sales. *K. A. Morgan.*

BULLET PROOF (IRE) 2 ch.g. (Apr 28) Mazaad 106–Natija 70§ (Vitiges (FR) **49** 132) [1990 6g 7s a6g⁶ a7g⁶] 3,000Y: lengthy gelding: first foal: dam maiden stayed 1m: poor maiden: may well be better suited by 1m. *P. Howling.*

BULLI'S LAD 5 b.g. Bold Owl 101–Subtle Queen (Stephen George 102) [1989 — 11g 1990 10f 12f 13.8m⁵ 16m] angular, deep-bodied gelding: modest form as 2-y-o: well beaten after, in handicaps (including selling) in 1990: bandaged last 3 starts: dead. *W. Storey.*

BUMPTIOUS BOY 6 b.g. Neltino–Bellardita (Derring-Do 131) [1989 NR 1990 —
8m] sturdy gelding: winning hurdler in April: never-dangerous seventh of 20 in
amateurs race at Warwick following month: only outing on flat since 2 yrs. *A. J.
Wilson.*

BUNDLE OF LUCK 3 ch.f. Touching Wood (USA) 127–Best Offer 96 (Crepello 58 d
136) [1989 8f⁵ 9f⁴ a8g 1990 12g² 12m⁵ 12m 10g 10f⁴ 10f⁵] small, close-coupled filly:
has a long stride: quite modest maiden at best: ran moderately after reappearance,
in selling events last 2 starts: will stay well: best effort with give in the ground: on
toes second outing. *Lord John FitzGerald.*

BUNNYLOCH 6 b.m. Lochnager 132–Bunnycraft (The Go-Between 129) [1989 39 §
5f⁴ 5m 5m² 5f 5m² 5f⁶ 5f 7g⁶ 6m³ 5g² 6f 1990 a6g a5g⁶ a5g³ a6g a5g* a5g 5f 5.8f a5g
5g] rangy, angular mare: having fortieth race, won maiden at Southwell in February:
stays 6f: acts on firm and dead going: has worn blinkers and visor, but not for some
time: bandaged last 2 starts: not genuine. *K. T. Ivory.*

BUONARROTI 3 b.c. Ela-Mana-Mou 132–Amiel (Nonoalco (USA) 131) [1989 85
NR 1990 10m 14g³ 14g* 16.2d⁵ 16g² 17.4d] 38,000Y: big, strong colt with plenty of
scope: moderate walker: half-brother to 4-y-o Roosters Tipple (by Henbit) and a
good winner in USA by Manado: dam, winner in Italy, is sister to Noalcoholic: fair
performer: won 4-runner maiden at Redcar in June: ran well afterwards: will be
suited by thorough test of stamina: lacks turn of foot: may be worth a try in blinkers
or a visor: sold 23,000 gns Newmarket Autumn Sales. *H. R. A. Cecil.*

BURAN (USA) 3 ch.f. Blushing Groom (FR) 131–Born A Lady (USA) (Tentam 77
(USA)) [1989 7g 1990 8g⁶ 8m³ 8m* 9m³ 8g] small, stocky filly: modest performer:
won maiden at Kempton in July: not discredited in apprentice race next start, ran
moderately in handicap (sweating and edgy) on final one: will stay 1¼m: sold
150,000 gns Newmarket December Sales. *J. R. Fanshawe.*

BURCROFT 6 ch.g. Crofthall 110–Two's Up (Double Jump 131) [1989 12.3s 12d² —
12d⁴ 12g⁵ 16m 12g 12h 12m⁶ 12g⁴ 16.2f² 13s³ 17f 15s⁴ 13.6g⁴ a14g⁴ 1990 15v] leggy,
sparely-made gelding: moderate mover: plating-class handicapper: stays an easy
1¾m: well suited by an easy surface nowadays: has run well for apprentice:
effective with or without a visor. *R. M. Whitaker.*

BURDUR 2 b.c. (Mar 6) Bering 136–Mondialite (FR) (Habitat 134) [1990 8s] 70 p
rather leggy, workmanlike colt: first foal: dam French 6.5f winner, is half-sister to
smart French 1m to 1¼m performer Malaspina: around 10 lengths eighth of 14,
leading 6f then weakening quickly final furlong, to Another Bob in minor event at
Newbury in October: will improve, and win a race. *B. Hanbury.*

BURFORD (USA) 3 ch.c. Time For A Change (USA)–Windrush Lady (USA) 67
(Unconscious (USA)) [1989 7s² 7f 1990 8m⁴ 8g⁵ 8f* 8.5m] leggy colt: good mover:
quite modest performer: won handicap at Bath in June, running on well to lead
close home: ran moderately in similar event at Beverley week later, running wide
on turn and looking none too keen under strong pressure: stays 1m: acts on any
going: gets on toes: sold to join D. R. Tucker 30,000 gns Newmarket July Sales. *I. A.
Balding.*

BURGOYNE 4 b.g. Ardross 134–Love Match (USA) (Affiliate (USA)) [1989 54
12.2d* 11g* 1990 14m 12d 14.6g⁵ 17.4d 16g 13.8d 13.6d⁵] lengthy, angular gelding:
moderate mover: won 2 claimers as 3-y-o: failed to confirm 1990 promise of second
and third outings, though not entirely discredited final one: should prove effective at
2m +: sweated freely third start. *M. H. Easterby.*

BURN BRIDGE (USA) 4 b.c. Linkage (USA)–Your Nuts (USA) (Creme Dela — p
Creme) [1989 9f 10m 10.6m 10.6s 1990 a12g⁶ 10.6d 16.2s] small, lightly-made colt:
moderate mover: fair winner as 2-y-o: no worthwhile form for long time, but shaped
as though retaining ability last 2 outings, off course over 8 months before first of
them: likely to prove suited by shorter than 11f: acts on soft going: sold out of W.
Haggas' stable 5,200 gns Doncaster May Sales after reappearance. *M. D. Hammond.*

BURNDITCH GIRL 4 ch.f. Raga Navarro (ITY) 119–Queen of The Nile (Hittite —
Glory 125) [1989 8.2s* 10m 7f 1990 9s] compact filly: moderate mover: sweating,
won amateurs handicap at Haydock early as 3-y-o: lightly raced and no subsequent
form: should stay further than 1m: best form on an easy surface. *Mrs G. R. Reveley.*

BURNING BRIGHT 7 b.g. Star Appeal 133–Lead Me On (King's Troop 118) 40
[1989 16f² 16.5g 1990 17.6m 14m* 14m⁴ 17.1d] strong, compact gelding: easily best
effort for long time when winning handicap at Nottingham in June: unlucky next
outing: stays 2m: acts on firm going and probably unsuited by soft: blinkered twice:
sweated badly on reappearance at 6 yrs: often slowly away. *R. Curtis.*

BURRACOPPIN 3 b.g. Niniski (USA) 125–Favorite Prospect (USA) (Mr — p
Prospector (USA)) [1989 NR 1990 8.2m 10g⁴ 10.5g] 5,400Y: leggy, rather sparely-
made gelding: fifth foal: closely related to 6f to 1m winner Verdant Boy (by Green
Dancer) and 1½m winner Island Aspect (by Ile de Bourbon) and half-brother to
fairly useful 1½m winner Future Success (by Wassl): dam 3-y-o 6f stakes winner:
little sign of ability in maidens: moved poorly down on debut. *Mrs Barbara Waring.*

BURSANA 4 b.f. Burslem 123–Lady of Surana (Shirley Heights 130) [1989 10g³ 65 d
10s² 9.5g³ 10g⁴ 10s² 10g⁵ 12.3m 12.2m 12.3g⁴ 12m³ 12.3m² 11s³ 14m 1990 10d 12g
12m² 10g⁵ 12g 12.3g⁴ 13.6g⁵ 12.5g⁴ 10.4g 14g] sparely-made filly: poor mover: best
effort from 4 runs at Cagnes-sur-Mer early in year on third outing: failed to
recapture her form here: stays 1½m: acts on good to firm and soft going: sold 2,200
gns Doncaster November Sales. *C. B. B. Booth.*

BURSAR 3 b.f. Balliol 125–Trading 74 (Forlorn River 124) [1989 NR 1990 a7g a7g —
6g] workmanlike filly: has a round action: third foal: dam successful in 7 races from
1m to 1¾m: ridden by 7-lb claimer and backward, behind in maidens and claimer
(sweating). *W. Holden.*

BURSLEM BEAU 3 gr.g. Burslem 123–Divine Apsara (Godswalk (USA) 130) —
[1989 5g 5v 5d 5f* 5f³ 5g⁴ 5f 1990 5f⁶ 5f a7g⁶] quite good-topped, leggy gelding:
poor walker: quite modest winner at 2 yrs: off course 12 months then faced stiff
tasks in 1990, not discredited on reappearance: may be suited by return to 5f: acts on
firm ground, seems unsuited by soft: sometimes edgy: sold out of C. Tinkler's stable
8,800 gns Ascot May Sales: resold to join Miss S. Wilton 3,100 gns Newmarket
September Sales. *W. Carter.*

BURSLEM BELLE (IRE) 2 ch.f. (Apr 28) Burslem 123–Hy Carol (High Hat —
131) [1990 5s⁶ 5m 5g] IR 5,200F, 3,800Y: smallish, close-coupled filly: half-sister to
3 winners, including useful Irish middle-distance stayer Ramich John (by Kampala):
dam of little account: bit backward, soundly beaten, including in seller. *N. Tinkler.*

BURTONWOOD HARP 3 ch.g. Mandrake Major 122–Misty Arch (Starch 54 §
Reduced 112) [1989 5s 5f 5g⁴ 5g² 5g* 5f 6g a6g a5g 1990 5f³ 5g⁵ a5g⁵ 5m 5f] angular
gelding: plater: below form after reappearance: headstrong, and will prove best at
5f: acts on firm going: has looked a hard ride, and has worn a severe bridle: not one
to rely on. *M. H. Tompkins.*

BURWOOD LADY (IRE) 2 b.f. (Jan 30) Kafu 120–Cancaniere 86 (Hotfoot 126) —
[1990 5f 5g⁴ 5g⁵ 6m 5f 5m] IR 800Y: lengthy filly: has a quick action: closely related
to Irish 1986 2-y-o 5f winner Burkina (by African Sky) and half-sister to 3 winners in
Ireland or abroad: dam 2-y-o 1m winner, is half-sister to Gold Cup winner
Shangamuzo: poor plater: blinkered second run. *D. Haydn Jones.*

BUSH HILL 5 b.g. Beldale Flutter (USA) 130–Butosky 71 (Busted 134) [1989 65
12m 16f 14f² 13.3m 12m⁵ 12s 1990 12g⁵ 12f⁵ 12.8g⁴ 10d⁶ 16g² 16.2g²] leggy, rather
sparely-made gelding: has a rather round action: quite modest handicapper
nowadays: seems to stay 2m: ideally needs a sound surface: wore crossed noseband
first 4 starts: has hung: sold 23,000 gns Newmarket July Sales. *J. G. FitzGerald.*

BUSHY TAILED 2 b.c. (Feb 28) Teenoso (USA) 135–Bundu (FR) 88 (Habitat 70 p
134) [1990 8m³] third foal: half-brother to 1m winner Mbulwa (by Be My Guest):
dam 1¼m and 10.6f winner: better for race, 4 lengths third of 7, keeping on unable to
challenge, to Libk in maiden at Yarmouth in September: will stay at least 1¼m: will
improve. *G. Wragg.*

BUSINESS AS USUAL 2 b.c. (Apr 11) Domynsky 110–Pamora (Blast 125) 57
[1990 5.8h⁵ 6g 5.8m 7f 7m⁵ 6g* 6m 6d³ 6m⁶ 6d] 2,700Y, 5,000 2-y-o: small, rather
sparely-made colt: moderate mover: half-brother to 2 minor 2-y-o sprint winners:
dam twice-raced half-sister to Wokingham winner Ginnie's Pet: plating-class
performer: won seller (no bid) at Lingfield in August: suited by 6f: best form on an
easy surface: blinkered or visored final 5 starts. *Dr J. D. Scargill.*

BU-SOFYAN 6 b.g. Runnett 125–London Spin 86 (Derring-Do 131) [1989 6v 8m⁵ 71
7m 8h⁴ 7.6h³ 7m* 8f* 8h³ 7f³ 8f³ 8m a10g⁴ 1990 8f* 8f² 7h⁴ 8.3m 8g 9g] tall, rather
leggy gelding: quite modest handicapper: won at Salisbury in May: effective at 7f to
1m: acts on hard going and is possibly unsuited by soft. *M. Madgwick.*

BUSORM 10 ch.g. Bustino 136–Wrekinianne 96 (Reform 132) [1989 5g 5f 8m a11g —
a6g 1990 7.5m] no longer of any account. *M. C. Chapman.*

BUSTALA 3 ch.f. Bustino 136–B A Poundstretcher 82 (Laser Light 118) [1989 7g —
1990 10g 7m 8.2g 10f³ 7f] small, sparely-made filly: little sign of ability here,
including in sellers: blinkered final start: sold 2,000 gns Ascot September Sales,
afterwards placed over 1m and 11.5f in Norway. *A. N. Lee.*

BUSTED ROCK   5 b.h. Busted 134–Mexican Two Step (Gay Fandango (USA)   83
132) [1989 12h* 10.5f 10m⁶ 1990 12f 12.2m³ 10f⁶ 10m 12g* 12.3g³ 12m* 12f² 12m
12m⁵ 13.3g 12d² 12v] rangy, quite attractive horse: moderate mover: fair
handicapper: won at Goodwood and Doncaster in June: stays 1½m: acts on firm and
dead going: bandaged third and eighth outings: suited by waiting tactics and firm
handling. *Mrs L. Piggott.*

BUSTER   2 br.g. (Mar 7) Macmillion 110–Valsette (Anfield 117) [1990 5g* 5d 5m³   88
6f² 6m* 6g⁶] lengthy, sparely-made gelding: first foal: dam unraced half-sister to
useful 1981 2-y-o 5f winner Hampton Bay: fair performer: won maiden at Leicester
in June and minor event (rallied gamely) at Nottingham in September: hampered on
final outing: better suited by 6f than 5f: tends to wander: twice very edgy in
preliminaries, and virtually bolted to post second outing: usually taken early to post.
Mrs Barbara Waring.

BUSTER'S PAL   2 ro.c. (Apr 3) Scottish Reel 123–Tula Singh 66 (Mansingh   — p
(USA) 120) [1990 7f 8d 8g] 9,800F, 18,000Y: heavy-bodied colt: has scope:
half-brother to 3-y-o High Elegance (by Elegant Air) and 1984 2-y-o 5f winner Green
Spirit (by Dragonara Palace): dam, best at sprint distances, is sister to high-class
sprinter Petong: well beaten in maidens: bit backward first 2 starts: looks sort to do
better. *Denys Smith.*

BUTTER FINGERS   4 b.f. Cragador 110–Dairy Queen 76 (Queen's Hussar 124)   ?
[1989 8.5s* 7.5s* 7.5s* 1990 a10g 8g* 8g*] sparely-made filly: made all in
Folkestone seller as 2-y-o: favourite, seventh of 14 in handicap at Lingfield in
January: winner 5 times in Belgium in last 2 years, including twice over 1m in
March: blinkered in Britain. *John Mark Capitte, Belgium.*

BUZZARDS CREST   5 ch.g. Buzzards Bay 128§–Diamond Talk (Counsel 118)   —
[1989 8m 8m 10.6s 7g 1990 8.2f 12g a8g a14g] lengthy gelding: won maiden as 2-y-o:
lightly raced and little show subsequently: stays 7f: acts on soft going: bandaged on
all-weather. *H. J. Collingridge.*

BUZZARDS SON   4 b.g. Buzzards Bay 128§–Night Cap (SWE) (Hornbeam 130)   —
[1989 8d³ 8s⁴ 8g 7s⁴ 7m³ 6h 7m 7g a8g 1990 9g 8.3m] rangy gelding: has a round
action: quite modest maiden at best: hung in selling handicap (favourite) final
outing: stays 1m: acts on good to firm and soft going: blinkered once at 3 yrs: often
sweats. *F. Jordan.*

BYARDS LEAP   2 b.g. (Jan 10) Sulaafah (USA) 119–Roncastella (Royal Palace   51
131) [1990 5f 5m 5m⁴ 5m⁶ 7m 8.2s 6g⁶] 6,000F, 6,400Y: rather leggy, lengthy
gelding: moderate mover: half-brother to 1985 2-y-o 7f sellers winner Tommy
Topham (by Tyrnavos) and to a winner in Italy: dam, winner in Italy, is sister to
very useful sprinter Peterhof: plating-class form at best: pulled hard when visored
penultimate start: possibly best at around 6f. *Denys Smith.*

BY CHARTER   4 b.f. Shirley Heights 130–Time Charter 131 (Saritamer (USA)   98
130) [1989 11.3m² 1990 13.4d⁶ 12d5 12g³ 10.6m] rather unfurnished filly: has a quick
action: useful performer: form as 4-y-o only when 2¼ lengths third of 4 to Alphabel
in slowly-run listed contest at Newmarket in June: seems to stay 1½m: possibly
best on a sound surface: saddle slipped second start. *M. R. Stoute.*

BYE BYE BABY (FR)   2 b.f. (Feb 25) Baby Turk 120–Bustelda (FR) (Busted   51
134) [1990 6d⁵ 6g⁵ 7f⁴ 7g 7m⁶ a8g] 45,000 francs (approx £4,200) Y: rather
sparely-made, workmanlike filly: fifth foal: half-sister to 11.7f winner Esprit de
Femme (by Esprit du Nord) and Irish 1m winner Sakyko (by Sicyos): dam unraced
half-sister to good Italian colt Stifelius: plating-class maiden: should stay 1m. *S.
Dow.*

BY FAR (USA)   4 b.f. Far North (CAN) 120–Countess Babu (USA) (Bronze Babu)   —
[1989 7f⁵ 10.1g 8g⁵ a8g⁶ 1990 a12g a8g⁶ 10f 12.5m 12g⁶ 12d a12g] smallish,
close-coupled, sparely-made filly: quite modest form at best: seems to stay 1½m:
has raced freely: taken down early fifth and sixth starts. *O. O'Neill.*

BYKER LASS   3 b.f. Superlative 118–Golden Tern (FR) (Arctic Tern (USA) 126)   —
[1989 5f 6f 7m 7f 1990 8v 11g a8g 10f] leggy filly: seems of little account: blinkered
second start, visored after. *J. S. Wainwright.*

BYWELL LAD   5 ch.g. Mandrake Major 122–Juliette (Julio Mariner 127) [1989   49
12s² 15.5s* 13.8d5 1990 14g 16.2d 13.8d³ 16s⁴] rangy, angular gelding: plating-class
handicapper: stays 2m: acts on good to firm and soft going: often apprentice
ridden: tends to carry head high: best with waiting tactics in strongly-run race:
moody. *R. Curtis.*

BYZANTINE   2 b.g. (Jan 21) Damister (USA) 123–Rustle of Silk 67 (General   62
Assembly (USA)) [1990 6m 7m] leggy, quite good-topped gelding: second foal:

half-brother to 3-y-o 6f winner Craven (by Thatching): dam lightly-raced half-sister to very smart middle-distance horse Kirtling and daughter of Irish 1000 Guineas second Silky: plating-class form in York maiden and minor event: will stay 1m. *Miss S. E. Hall.*

C

CABBIE'S BOY 4 ch.g. Dublin Taxi–Petriva (Mummy's Pet 125) [1989 NR 1990 a8g] first foal: dam unraced: blinkered, slowly away and always behind in maiden at Southwell in March. *R. E. Barr.*   —

CABLELINK 3 ch.g. Horage 124–Night of Gladness 98 (Midsummer Night II 117) [1989 6f⁴ 1990 7d 6m⁶ 7m 9f⁴ 10m 10g⁶ 8d a14g] big, well-made gelding: has a quick action: no worthwhile form though showed signs of ability in seller sixth start, staying on from rear carrying head high: suited by 1¼m: blinkered fifth start. *K. B. McCauley.*   —

CABOCHON 3 b.g. Jalmood (USA) 126–Lightning Legacy (USA) 78 (Super Concorde (USA) 128) [1989 NR 1990 10m 12f 10.1g 10m⁵ 10g 14g* 16g³ 16.2s² 18d* 16s*] lengthy gelding: has a round action: second foal: half-brother to useful 1¼m to 1½m winner Black Monday (by Busted): dam, maiden, stayed 1m: in fine form in handicaps in the autumn, successful at Nottingham (twice) then Newcastle and comfortably justifying favouritism last 2 starts: stays well: goes well with plenty of give in the ground. *M. F. D. Morley.*   90

CABRA 4 ch.f. Red Sunset 120–Shangara (Credo 123) [1989 6d 7g 1990 10.2f 15.5f] good-quartered, workmanlike filly: moderate mover: no form, including in sellers: sold 1,200 gns Ascot May Sales. *C. A. Horgan.*   —

CACOETHES (USA) 4 b.c. Alydar (USA)–Careless Notion (USA) (Jester) [1989 10m* 12f* 12g³ 12f* 12m² 10.5f² 12g 1990 10m⁴ 12m⁴ 12m² 12f* 12g 12f³]   124

The size of the financial rewards available to those willing to travel halfway round the world and further was very well illustrated at the back-end of the season by the exploits of Cacoethes, whose trips to New York and Tokyo resulted in the first win by a British-trained horse in the Turf Classic in its fourteen-year history and a very narrow defeat in the Japan Cup, netting the equivalent of around £330,000. The five Grade 1 races run at Belmont Park on the first weekend in October were worth a total of 2,639,000 dollars, a figure higher than on any other weekend in North American racing except for the Breeders' Cup. Cacoethes' prize of 360,000 dollars for the Turf Classic bettered that of his stable-mate Defensive Play in the Man o' War Stakes, New York's second major turf race outside the Breeders' Cup series, by just over 75,000 dollars. Cacoethes' five opponents included the ex-British Alwuhush and the Canadian triple crown winner With Approval. Conditions were just right for Cacoethes, in the frame in the King George VI and Queen Elizabeth Diamond Stakes and the Hoover Cumberland Lodge Stakes at Ascot on his last two outings, and he was able to make almost all the running, galloping on relentlessly to withstand the challenges of Alwuhush and With Approval by a length and a half. His winning time lowered the previous best for the race set by John Henry in 1984 by a fifth of a second, and fell only the same fraction outside the track record held by Secretariat. Similar tactics failed to work as well in the Breeders' Cup Turf over course and distance three weeks later, and when With Approval swept by him into the straight Cacoethes dropped away tamely. The European challenge for the Japan Cup was a strong one, for also making the journey were the King George winner Belmez, who went off favourite, the Breeders' Cup Classic runner-up Ibn Bey, the Rothmans International winner French Glory and the Grand Prix d'Evry winner Ode. Against them were Alwuhush and the ex-Irish pair Petite Ile and Phantom Breeze representing the United States, Better Loosen Up and Stylish Century from Australia, and five from Japan. Having raced close up behind the leaders, Cacoethes burst clear two furlongs out and remained in front until collared in the final strides by Better Loosen Up and Ode, suffering a fate similar to another Harwood-trained runner Allez Milord, just beaten by Jupiter Island in 1986. Cacoethes again finished one and a half lengths ahead of

Turf Classic, Belmont Park—
right to left, Cacoethes, Alwuhush and With Approval

Alwuhush, the two divided by White Stone, the first of the home-trained quintet to cross the line.

The Japanese have been very successful in promoting and establishing the Japan Cup, in spite of obvious and difficult obstacles. Now, from small beginnings, they are a force on the world stage. Japanese buyers and their agents were very active at the sales in North America and Europe in 1990 and also snapped up several top young stallion prospects. The highest-priced lots at the Deauville Select Sale, the Fasig-Tipton Saratoga Sale in August, the Keeneland Selected Sale in July and the Newmarket Highflyer Sale were all bought, not by Arab interests, but on behalf of Japanese clients (the 840,000-guinea three-parts sister to Salsabil purchased at the Highflyer for Masaki Kobayashi, who won the Japanese Derby in 1990 with Ines Fujin, is due to start her career with Clive Brittain). The Japanese were particularly keen to buy top quality fillies for foundation mares and, in Britain, were on the lookout for the offspring of sons of Mill Reef—Shirley Heights and Reference Point to name two—possibly encouraged by the success of the Mill Reef stallion Mill George in Japan. For that reason, presumably, two of the last high-class sons of Mill Reef, Creator and Ibn Bey, were acquired to start their stallion careers in Japan in 1991. These last two are only part of a long list of colts who are to retire to stud there, along with Carroll House, Assatis, Markofdistinction, French Glory, dual Grade 1 winner Adjudicating, Sunday Silence no less, and Cacoethes who was bought after his sale to the Cardiff Stud in California fell through. Cacoethes is one of three top-class sons of the recently-deceased Alydar retiring to stud, the others, Criminal Type and Easy Goer, remaining in the States. Cacoethes is the eleventh foal of Careless Notion. Four of the previous ten were winners, notably Fabulous Notion (by Somethingfabulous), successful nine times including in the Grade 1 Santa

143

Lady Harrison's "Cacoethes"

		Raise A Native	Native Dancer
	Alydar (USA)	(ch 1961)	Raise You
	(ch 1975)	Sweet Tooth	On-And-On
Cacoethes (USA)		(b 1965)	Plum Cake
(b.c. 1986)		Jester	Tom Fool
	Careless Notion (USA)	(b 1955)	Golden Apple
	(b 1970)	Miss Uppity	Nasrullah
		(b 1956)	Nursery School

Susana Stakes over eight and a half furlongs. Careless Notion, successful over six furlongs at four, is one of a dozen winners foaled by Miss Uppity, a winner on four of her twenty-six starts. Cacoethes, a big, rangy colt, impressed in appearance and in the way he walked and moved in his faster paces. He was suited by a mile and a half and by top-of-the-ground. While he ultimately enjoyed a good season as a four-year-old, he will probably be remembered first and foremost for his great battle with Nashwan in the King George VI and Queen Elizabeth Diamond Stakes at three. *G. Harwood.*

CADEAU D'ARAGON 3 b.f. Aragon 118–Bold Gift 61 (Persian Bold 123) [1989 — NR 1990 8f 7d] 1,800F: close-coupled filly: second foal: half-sister to 7f and 1m seller winner Mrs Gates (by Good Times): dam, ran only at 2 yrs, stayed 7f: tailed off in claimer and seller. *R. J. Hodges.*

CADENCY 2 b.c. (May 4) Teenoso (USA) 135–Mullet 75 (Star Appeal 133) [1990 **68** p 7dʷᵒ 8d⁴] third foal: half-brother to 3-y-o 1½m to 13.6f winner Surcoat (by Bustino): dam 1¼m winner, is half-sister to very smart 7f to 13.3f winner Consol: walked over in private sweepstakes at Newmarket in October: 7 lengths fourth of 18 to El Dominio in maiden at Bath later in month: will stay well. *P. T. Walwyn.*

CADFORD BALARINA 3 ch.f. Adonijah 126–Jarama (Amber Rama (USA) 133) — [1989 5d 5d 5d⁵ 7f 6f² 7m⁵ 7f⁴ 6m 1990 8m⁵ 9m 8f 12.5g 8.2m 8f 10m] smallish, sparely-made filly: plater: easily best effort in claimer (claimed out of W. Turner's stable £4,500) on reappearance: evidently stays 1m. *K. S. Bridgwater.*

CAERDYDD (IRE) 2 ch.c. (Mar 2) Caerleon (USA) 132–Resooka (Godswalk **102** (USA) 130) [1990 6m 7m* 7g² 7m⁶] strong, compact colt: fourth living foal: brother to 1988 2-y-o 6f winner Gaijin and half-brother to fair 1986 2-y-o 6f winner Meadowbank (by Northfields): dam unraced daughter of Cheveley Park winner Sookera: useful performer: sweating, won maiden at Ascot in July: 1½ lengths second of 4, travelling strongly long way, to Heart of Darkness in Washington Singer Stakes at Newbury month later: hung right and found little when modest sixth of 8 in GPA National Stakes at the Curragh final start: has given impression may prove as effective at 6f as 7f. *B. W. Hills.*

CAERLESS WRITING 4 ch.f. Caerleon (USA) 132–Northern Script (USA) 95 **111** (Arts And Letters) [1989 9.5f* 12m⁵ 10g* 12g4 10g⁶ 10d³ 1990 10g² 10f*] second foal: dam miler: 20/1, ran excellent race when 1½ lengths second, hampered final 1f, to Game Plan in 10-runner Sea World EBF Pretty Polly Stakes at the Curragh in June: justified favouritism in valuable handicap at same course following month by neck and short head from Montefiore and Kostroma: suited by 1¼m: probably acts on any going. *J. S. Bolger, Ireland.*

CAERLINA (IRE) 2 b.f. (Apr 7) Caerleon (USA) 132–Dinalina (FR) (Top Ville **112** 129) [1990 5.5g* 6d³ 8g³ 8g2] first foal: dam French 2-y-o 1¼m winner: won maiden at Maisons-Laffitte in May: placed in pattern events at Longchamp in autumn on last 2 starts, length third to Magic Night in Prix d'Aumale and 2 lengths second of 9, running on well never dangerous, to Shadayid in Prix Marcel Boussac: will stay 1¼m: very useful. *J. de Roualle, France.*

CAERULIA 2 gr.f. (Apr 26) Absalom 128–Liberation 63 (Native Breeder) [1990 **51** 5g⁵ 5m 5f 7m⁶ 6f 5m² 6m 5s4 5d a5g] 6,000 2-y-o: smallish, good-quartered filly: half-sister to several winners, most at 2 yrs, including 1986 2-y-o 5f winner Bastillia (by Derrylin): dam twice-raced half-sister to good sprinter Tudor Grey: plating-class maiden: best efforts in claimers at Edinburgh: ran poorly in Redcar seller seventh start: suited by 5f: acts on top-of-the-ground and soft. *W. J. Pearce.*

CAESARS NIECE (IRE) 2 b.f. (May 17) Rhoman Rule (USA)–Great Dora **37** (Great Nephew 126) [1990 6h4 6f] IR 6,200Y: ninth foal: half-sister to 6f and 7f winner Takenhall (by Pitskelly): dam fairly useful in Italy: sire won from 7f to 9f: poor form in summer maiden auctions. *M. J. Fetherston-Godley.*

CAFFARELLI 3 b.c. Mummy's Pet 125–Klewraye (Lord Gayle (USA) 124) [1989 **78** 6f² 5m² 6g³ 1990 6m* 6g 6m³] small, rather sparely-made colt: good mover: modest performer: 5/4 on, very easy winner of maiden at Newcastle in March: good third in £6,800 event at Newmarket in May: may stay 7f: best efforts on top-of-the-ground. *R. Guest.*

CAGLIARI 3 ch.g. Dominion 123–Bedeni 100 (Parthia 132) [1989 8m 10g a8g — 1990 a10g 13.8m⁵] well beaten in varied events, claimers in 1990: sold out of R. J. R. Williams' stable 1,000 gns Doncaster February Sales after reappearance: resold 1,250 gns Doncaster October Sales. *M. Avison.*

CAIRNCASTLE 5 b.g. Ardross 134–Brookfield Miss 73 (Welsh Pageant 132) — [1989 16.1g² 19f 1990 16m4 14d6 16.5f6] close-coupled, sparely-made gelding: has a rather round action: modest form when 20/1-second of 7 in handicap at Newmarket as 4-y-o: very lightly raced and no subsequent form on flat: suited by 2m: acts on good to firm going: winning hurdler in August and October. *J. White.*

CAIRNHARROW 3 ch.g. Creetown 123–Suoic Hall (Gold Rod 129) [1989 NR — 1990 8.2g] 5,600Y: lengthy, angular gelding: sixth foal: half-brother to several winners, including milers Golden Game (by Mummy's Game) and Foolish Ways (by Comedy Star): dam unraced half-sister to top 1970 2-y-o filly Cawstons Pride: very slowly away when tailed off in claimer at Nottingham in April: moved poorly down: sold 1,400 gns Doncaster August Sales. *M. W. Easterby.*

CAITHNESS CLOUD 2 ch.c. (Mar 26) Lomond (USA) 128–Moonscape 87 **75 p** (Ribero 126) [1990 8.2d 8m²] 50,000Y: angular colt, rather unfurnished: half-brother to several winners, including very useful middle-distance stayer Lemhill (by He Loves Me) and useful 6f winner Luna Bid (by Auction Ring): dam staying half-sister to Derby fourths Moon Mountain and Great Wall: 2 lengths second of 11, losing place 3f out then staying on well, to impressive Polish King in minor event at Newmarket in November: very green on debut: will be much better suited by 1¼m +: sure to win a race. *M. A. Jarvis.*

CAJUN CURE 2 ch.f. (Mar 4) Glint of Gold 128–Blue Guitar 88 (Cure The Blues **50** (USA) [1990 7f* 7f³ 7h4] compact filly: first foal: dam suited by 1m, is half-sister to

Polished Silver, a smart winner over 7f and 1m at 2 yrs: won poorly-contested maiden at Yarmouth in July: tailed off in nursery (difficult stalls) at Brighton final start: will stay 1m: races keenly: sold 2,100 gns Newmarket December Sales. *D. Morley.*

CALABALI 3 b.f. Persian Bold 123–Bedfellow 104 (Crepello 136) [1989 8f 9f2 **40** 1990 9m 12m 12m3 12.5g 12f3 a11g 16.5m3 16f3 9f 12m3 12m3 10m 9f 12m4] tall, workmanlike filly: poor maiden: probably stays 1½m: acts on firm ground: has sweated and pulled hard: mounted on track final start: one paced: inconsistent. *R. Hollinshead.*

CALACHUCHI 3 b.f. Martinmas 128–Seleter (Hotfoot 126) [1989 6m 6m5 1990 **74** 7.5f* 8.5m* 8g2 8f 7.5f4 8h2 8.5f6 10.6g4 11s* 11d* 12.4s*] leggy filly: modest performer: successful in seller (no bid) at Beverley and claimers at Beverley, Hamilton, Redcar and Newcastle: better at 1½m than shorter: acts on any going: taken down early: very edgy on reappearance: genuine. *M. J. Camacho.*

CALAFURIA 4 b.f. Chief Singer 131–Cattarina Ginnasi (ITY) (Tierceron (ITY)) — [1989 8d 10.6g 8g 8s4 a8g 1990 7f 6f 6g] tall, leggy filly: poor maiden: has worn crossed noseband. *Don Enrico Incisa.*

CALAHONDA DAVE 3 gr.g. Song 132–Great Grey Niece 74 (Great Nephew **42** 126) [1989 6f3 7m2 6s 6g3 1990 a5g 5m 6g 7d 8m 6m 6g4 8.2g 6d 7v6 7d] leggy, close-coupled gelding: quite modest form at 2 yrs: on toes, best effort for some time on seventh start: blinkered last 2 starts, slowly away and tailed off on second: gives impression may prove best at 6f: best on a sound surface: sold 1,400 gns Doncaster October Sales. *D. W. Chapman.*

CALAHONDA SCRIBE 2 ch.g. (Mar 16) Blushing Scribe (USA) 107–Smitten — 72 (Run The Gantlet (USA)) [1990 6g] 7,000Y: leggy, shallow-girthed gelding: fourth foal: brother to 3-y-o 1½m seller winner The Healy and 1¼m winner Auto Connection: dam ran only at 2 yrs when placed at 6f and 7f: bit backward and slowly away in maiden at York in May. *N. Bycroft.*

CALAHONDA SONG 4 ch.g. Song 132–Obergurgl 69 (Warpath 113) [1989 7m — 6m 8.5f5 9f5 11f4 10g 8.5f 10.2g 10m5 1990 12m 10.6d] lengthy gelding: poor maiden: should prove best at up to 9f: acts on firm ground: blinkered and visored once at 3 yrs: sometimes takes strong hold. *J. Dooler.*

CALDAIRE (USA) 2 b.c. (Feb 19) Copelan (USA)–Rock Fever (USA) (Hawaii) **63** [1990 5f3 5f3] $110,000Y: good-quartered, quite attractive colt: half-brother to 3 winners here and in North America, including 1982 2-y-o 5f winner Centrust (by Mr Prospector): dam won at up to 1m, including in minor stakes: sire joint-best 2-y-o colt in USA in 1982: plating-class form in maidens at Nottingham and Bath when trained by A. Scott: sent to Italy and won over 5f at Milan in June. *O. Pessi, Italy.*

CALGARY REDEYE 3 gr.c. Kalaglow 132–River Call (FR) 103 (Riverman **75** (USA) 131) [1989 7g4 8.2g6 a8g* a8g5 1990 12f2 12m* 12m* 11.7m4 12m3 13d 16d6] small, dipped-backed colt: moderate walker: modest performer: favourite, won claimer (edged right) at Goodwood and handicap (pulled hard, bumped and awarded race) at Salisbury in June: probably stays 13f: acts on firm and dead going: blinkered last 6 starts: hung left and didn't look keen on fourth. *P. J. Makin.*

CALIBAIRN 2 ch.g. (Mar 9) Bairn (USA) 126–Calibina 101 (Caliban 123) [1990 **54** 6m 5f5 5f6 5.3f4 5m 6s a6g a5g4 a6g5] quite attractive gelding: eighth foal: brother to 3-y-o Bububu and half-brother to several winners, including sprinters Olympic Challenger (by Anfield) and King Charlemagne (by Habat): dam won Stewards' Cup and Wokingham Stakes: plating-class maiden: better form at 5f than 6f: blinkered last 6 outings: has twice reared in stalls: races keenly. *E. A. Wheeler.*

CALICON 4 ch.g. Connaught 130–Calgary 63 (Run The Gantlet (USA)) [1989 11s4 **86** 11.7d5 13.3m4 15s* 13.3d 1990 16d* 18.4d 16m5] lengthy, angular gelding: showed improved form when winning strongly-run handicap at Newbury in April, leading 3½f out and soon clear: not seen out after following month: suited by test of stamina: best efforts on soft surface: useful juvenile hurdler in 1989/90: none too consistent, and goes very well fresh. *I. A. Balding.*

CALIDORE BAY 2 b.f. (Mar 20) Bay Express 132–Calidore (Scottish Rifle 127) — [1990 5f 5d 5.3h6 5m] 1,150Y: workmanlike filly: fourth foal: dam ran 3 times: no form, including in sellers: thrice slowly away: bandaged off-hind first 3 starts. *R. W. Stubbs.*

CALL AT EIGHT (USA) 2 b.g. (Mar 20) Barachois (CAN)–Same Thyme **67** (USA) (Delaware Chief (USA)) [1990 5m4 5f4 6g3 6f4 7h4 7f 6g6 a6g2 a6g2] strong gelding: half-brother to winners in North America by Diamond Prospect and Strike

Gold: dam won at up to 9f: modest maiden: stays 7f: blinkered final 3 starts: (raced freely first time). *J. Etherington.*

CALL FOR ROONEY 2 b.c. (Apr 29) Music Maestro 119–Sally Bowles 87 — (Blakeney 126) [1990 8f] 1,000F: eighth foal: dam ran twice at 2 yrs: backward and green in maiden at Thirsk in September. *A. Harrison.*

CALLIPOLI (USA) 3 br.f. Green Dancer (USA) 132–Minstrelete (USA) (Round 81 Table) [1989 7f6 7g 1990 8.5m5 8g6 8g* 9g3 8g* 8.5m3 8.2d 8m 10m2 10.6v 9g*] close-coupled, rather sparely-made filly: fair handicapper: successful at Leicester in May and Ayr in June then at £19,600 'Mail On Sunday' Three-Year-Old Series Final at Newmarket in November: stays 1¼m: seems to need a sound surface. *Lord John FitzGerald.*

CALL RACECALL 3 b.g. Reasonable (FR) 119–Miel (Pall Mall 132) [1989 5m5 49 5d5 6g6 8g3 8m 8g 1990 a8g 9s6 10.2f6 12g3 14f6 13.8m6 12g 12d2] smallish, sturdy gelding: has a quick action: plating-class maiden: should stay beyond 1½m: acts on dead going: sold B. Palling 1,100 gns Doncaster November Sales. *C. W. Thornton.*

CALL TO ARMS 3 b.c. North Briton 67–Branitska (Mummy's Pet 125) [1989 104 6m* 5f4 7.5f* 7.3m2 7g2 6g2 1990 8g5 8m6 10m 8f 7m5 7g3 8m 7m] smallish, leggy colt: useful performer, usually highly tried: 66/1, best 3-y-o effort when 4 lengths third of 10 to Green Line Express in Kiveton Park Stakes at Doncaster: should stay 1m: needs give in the ground: bandaged on reappearance: on toes first 2 starts: sold 70,000 gns Newmarket Autumn Sales. *C. E. Brittain.*

CAL NORMA'S LADY (IRE) 2 ch.f. (May 7) Lyphard's Special (USA) 87 122–June Darling (Junius (USA) 124) [1990 6g* 6f* 7m* 7g4 8d 7s] IR 11,700F, 11,000Y: lengthy, rather sparely-made filly: second foal: dam never ran: fair performer: won seller (retained 8,000 gns) at Leicester and nurseries at Hamilton (ridden by 7-lb claimer) in July and Newmarket (hung badly left) in August: wandered next start, not knocked about on final 2: better suited by 7f than shorter: trained first 4 starts by J. S. Wilson. *M. W. Easterby.*

CALVANNE MISS 4 b.f. Martinmas 128–Blue Empress (Blue Cashmere 129) 62 [1989 5s 6g 5h 5m 6m2 6m6 7m 1990 5f* 6m2 7f2 6f5 5m* 5f3 5m 5f 5m4 5f 6g 5g2 6m* 5m*] leggy, sparely-made filly: quite modest handicapper: won at Chepstow in May (selling event, bought in 4,000 gns), July and October and Folkestone (apprentices) earlier in October: effective at 5f to 7f: acts on firm going, possibly unsuited by a soft surface: trained until after ninth outing by R. Hodges. *C. J. Hill.*

CALYMAR 4 gr.c. Bay Express 132–Tula Singh 66 (Mansingh (USA) 120) [1989 — NR 1990 10.2f] big, workmanlike colt: fifth foal: half-brother to 1984 2-y-o 5f winner Green Spirit (by Dragonara Palace): dam, best at sprint distances, is sister to high-class sprinter Petong: 50/1, slowly away and well beaten in 22-runner maiden at Doncaster in March. *J. A. Glover.*

CAMBO (USA) 4 b.c. Roberto (USA) 131–Cameo Shore (Mill Reef (USA) 141) 94 [1989 11s3 10s2 10g* 1990 10m 10.4d4 12m2 12s2 14g] close-coupled, good-quartered

'Mail On Sunday' Three-Year-Old Series Handicap Final, Newmarket— Callipoli holds on from Lucky Guest

colt: has a rather round action: ran well when in frame in handicaps at Chester, Newbury (awkward at stalls) and Haydock (making most when beaten length by Hateel in £22,700 event) in summer: sweating, raced keenly when well beaten in Tote Ebor at York: stays 1½m: acts on good to firm and soft going: sold to join M. Banks's stable 36,000 gns Newmarket Autumn Sales. *R. Charlton.*

CAMDEN KNIGHT 5 b.g. Camden Town 125–Motionless 109 (Midsummer **68** Night II 117) [1989 8g 8.5d⁴ 10.2g³ 12f³ 11m⁶ 14f 1990 11s⁴ 13v³ 12g* 13g³ 12m⁶ 12g 10.6d 11d⁶ 15v 12s] leggy, good-topped gelding: poor mover: modest handicapper on his day: won strongly-run event at Hamilton in May: edged left and demoted previous start: out of form last 5: stays 13f: goes particularly well with give in the ground: bandaged off-fore fifth start, in front on last: usually held up: winning hurdler in November: inconsistent. *N. Bycroft.*

CAMDEN'S RANSOM (USA) 3 b.c. Hostage (USA)–Camden Court (USA) **70** (Inverness Drive (USA)) [1989 6m 7f 1990 8m 10f³ 10m* 10m*] good-bodied colt: has a long stride: progressive form in handicaps in the spring, successful at Lingfield (edgy) and Leicester: should stay further: tends to edge under pressure. *M. J. Fetherston-Godley.*

CAMDEN WALK (IRE) 2 b.g. (May 9) Camden Town 125–Sky Valley 101 — (Skymaster 126) [1990 7.5m 8.2g] 3,100Y: leggy, close-coupled gelding: has a round action: half-brother to several winners, including Belgian 1000 Guineas second Hot Valley (by Hot Spark): dam sprinting half-sister to Owen Anthony: showed signs of ability in maiden auction at Beverley and seller at Nottingham in September: may do better. *C. Tinkler.*

CAMEO PERFORMANCE (USA) 3 b. or br.f. Be My Guest (USA) 126– **104** Nancy Chere (USA) (Gallant Man) [1989 7g³ 7m² 1990 10m* 11.3d⁴ 12d⁶ 12f* 10m⁵ 10.2m* 12g] lengthy, good-bodied filly: useful performer: won maiden at Sandown in April, slowly-run apprentice race at Chepstow in July and 4-runner listed race (caught Heart of Joy on post) at Newcastle in August: faced stiff task in Long Island Handicap at Belmont Park final start, a half-share in her reportedly sold to American interests: stays 1½m: acts on firm and dead going. *B. W. Hills.*

CAMERON PRIDE 2 br.g. (Apr 17) Kabour 80–Sandra's Sovereign (Workboy — 123) [1990 5s⁶ 5d 5m 7g 5m a8g] leggy, plain gelding: third foal: half-brother to 3-y-o Go Go Boy (by All Systems Go): dam of little account on flat, pulled up in a hurdle: of little account. *J. Dooler.*

CAMPAI 3 b.c. Try My Best (USA) 130–Musing 79 (Music Maestro 119) [1989 7g⁶ **74** 1990 10g 7.6d³ 7g⁵ 9m³ 8d a7g² a8g² 8f⁴ a8g² a8g² 12.3g⁴ a12g*] neat colt: capable of modest form: favourite, won maiden at Southwell in September: found little in moderately-run handicap time before: stays 1½m: acts on firm and dead going: blinkered fifth start: slowly away third. *R. W. Armstrong.*

CAMPESTRAL (USA) 2 b.f. (Jan 23) Alleged (USA) 138–Field Dancer 110 **83 p** (Northfields (USA)) [1990 7g*] leggy, unfurnished, angular filly: first foal: dam best around 1m, is out of Cheveley Park winner Sookera: 20/1 and green, won 20-runner maiden at Newmarket by 1½ lengths from Gravette in November, soon prominent, leading over 1f out and keeping on well: will stay at least 1¼m: sure to improve. *M. R. Stoute.*

CAMPO 5 b.g. Hill's Forecast 91–Shagra (Sallust 134) [1989 NR 1990 a8g a8g 10f — 8.2s 13.8m 16.2d] good-topped gelding: of little account. *D. W. Chapman.*

CANAAN VALLEY 2 ch.g. (Apr 8) Absalom 128–My Pink Parrot (Pirate King **75** 129) [1990 6g 6g2] 13,500Y: lengthy gelding: has plenty of scope: brother to a winner in Italy and half-brother to several other winners here, including fair 1978 2-y-o 5f winner Leo Vert (by Ballymoss): dam never ran: 2½ lengths second to Redden Burn in maiden at Ripon in June. *J. G. FitzGerald.*

CANADIAN GOLD (IRE) 2 b.g. (Jan 27) Coquelin (USA) 121–Bold Design **67** (Bold Lad (IRE) 133) [1990 a7g 8m³ 7.5m³ 7g] IR 3,200F, 10,000Y, 16,000 2-y-o: rather angular, good-quartered gelding: fifth foal: half-brother to some poor animals: dam ran twice: quite modest form in maiden auctions: blinkered, sweating and edgy when running far too freely final start: stays 1m. *J. G. FitzGerald.*

CANBRACK STYLE 3 b.f. Glenstal (USA) 118–Cottage Style 65 (Thatch (USA) **57** 136) [1989 8m 8g 1990 8g 6f³ 5m 8f⁴ 7f³ 7f⁵ 6g⁶] sturdy filly: plating-class maiden: easily best efforts over 7f. *W. A. Stephenson.*

CANDAVIA 3 b.f. Ardross 134–Sly Wink (Song 132) [1989 6m 8.2g 1990 12g 12m — 12m 12m a7g 8.2g] workmanlike, good-quartered filly: no sign of ability: blinkered final start. *M. D. I. Usher.*

CANDESCO 4 b.f. Blushing Scribe (USA) 107–Madame Mim 57 (Artaius (USA) **72**
129) [1989 8.2m 10d 1990 8v 8f a7g 8.2m a8g* 8m6 a8g a8g* 8.2v a7g2] strong,
close-coupled filly: successful at Southwell in handicap in August and claimer in
September: stayed on well final 1f when much-improved second in handicap there
final outing: will be ideally suited by return to 1m: easily best runs on all-weather. *B.*
A. McMahon.

CANDLE KING (IRE) 2 b.c. (Mar 28) Tender King 123–Candelaria (FR) **75**
(Touch Paper 113) [1990 5g4 6m* 7g2 6m 7.3g5 7m] IR 5,500F, 6,000Y: leggy,
sparely-made colt: keen walker: moderate mover: second live foal: dam showed
signs of a little ability in France: modest performer: won claimer at Leicester in
July: sweating, ran badly final outing: stays 7f: trained first 2 starts by B. McMahon.
M. J. Fetherston-Godley.

CANDY GLEN 3 b.c. Glenstal (USA) 118–Maiden Concert (Condorcet **120**
(FR)) [1989 5d* 5m* 6f3 7m* 6m 8s* 1990 8g4 8g* 10d4 9d* 8g5 8m2 8m 8v4
10s2 8v2]
     Somewhat unusually for a dual Group 1 winner, Candy Glen's reputation
is founded on his efforts in defeat. But then, two Group 1 victories could
hardly have gained less kudos here than those in the Gran Criterium and
Premio Parioli. Candy Glen was well worth his place in better Group 1 events
(only In The Groove contested more amongst the British-trained three-year-
olds) but came just short of that necessary to win one, while his Italian
successes, though carrying an official pattern rating 10 lb (at 110) below
British Group 1 races, still of course left him with a penalty to carry in Group 2
and Group 3. A 10-lb concession to the likes of Elmaamul, Raj Waki and Satin
Wood in the Easter Stakes on his reappearance quickly illustrated the sort of
tasks Candy Glen might have to face in Britain. It's a shame we didn't see
more of him here though, because in four outings in Italy and three in France,
in a season stretching from April to November, he proved one of the toughest
competitors around, ending the year with three runs on very soft ground in
the space of two weeks in which he showed himself better than ever with
seconds to Legal Case in the Premio Roma and Sikeston in the Premio
Vittorio di Capua. Candy Glen had first shown that sort of form in another
busy period in August on his fifth and sixth starts, leading over four furlongs
out but never threatening to get away in the Prix du Haras de Fresnay-le-
Buffard Jacques le Marois at Deauville, then never looking like catching
Shavian in the Beefeater Gin Celebration Mile at Goodwood, eventually
beaten just over two lengths in both.
     However, it's probably true to say that the races he was bought for, he
won. After the second of three wins in Britain as a two-year-old, Candy Glen
was purchased by Antonio Balzarini and ended that season with victory in

Prix Daphnis, Evry—Candy Glen picks up another prize abroad

Antonio Balzarini's "Candy Glen"

Italy's only Group 1 event for two-year-olds, the Gran Criterium at Milan, with the Parioli (Italian Two Thousand Guineas) his declared target for 1990. Whatever the wider status, financial or otherwise, of the Italian classics—the Parioli carried first prize money of about £78,000 compared to £106,000, £108,000 and £129,000 for its British, French and Irish equivalents—competition to be a successful owner in 1990 was fierce indeed. An Italian classic entry was almost as good an investment as any, such was the zeal with which Italian owners scoured the lists of foreign-trained runners who might carry their colours. The 1990 transfer season kicked off early when Candy Glen's owner acquired Victory Piper and Atoll from Barry Hills's stable and reached a frenzied climax in the days preceding the Derby Italiano by the end of which nine of the twenty-two runners, eight of them British-trained, had switched to Italian ownership. A week after Atoll had achieved her goal in the Premio Regina Elena, Candy Glen started 11/10 favourite for his, coupled with the same owner's Rotatori. Despite the late withdrawal of Curia Regis, for which his trainer was fined one million lire, British stables still mounted a four-strong challenge but after Daarik had flattered briefly in the straight it was left to two home-trained runners to fill the places behind Candy Glen, who won comfortably. Balzarini's hopes of a classic clean sweep, incidentally, were kept alight by Atoll in the Oaks d'Italia but fizzled out tamely with his Derby Italiano acquisitions Benzine and Shout And Sing. In marked contrast, Candy Glen and, for that matter, Atoll did very little to disappoint in the remainder of the season, the only real blemishes on Candy Glen's record coming with his seventh in the Queen Elizabeth II Stakes at Ascot, when he reportedly lost a shoe, and fourth in the Premio Ribot at Rome. In far less exalted company than that to which he was kept for most of the year, Candy Glen easily accounted for Eightsome and the disappointing Tarvisio in the nine-furlong Prix Daphnis at Evry in July.

		Northern Dancer	Nearctic
Candy Glen (b.c. 1987)	Glenstal (USA) (b 1980)	(b 1961)	Natalma
		Cloonlara	Sir Ivor
		(b 1974)	Fish-Bar
	Maiden Concert (ch 1981)	Condorcet	Luthier
		(b 1972)	Pan American
		Merdemain	Tamerlane
		(b 1960)	Damians

Candy Glen is the best representative of the National Stakes winner Glenstal. In the clutch of stallion prospects retired from Ballydoyle stables in 1983, Glenstal had as attractive a pedigree as any but his racecourse appearances were infrequent and some way inferior to those of Caerleon, Lomond and Solford. Glenstal's final start and only three-year-old success came in the Prix Daphnis. At IR 12,000 guineas, Candy Glen was about average for a yearling sold from Glenstal's third crop. His dam Maiden Concert ran only once but she's well enough related, being a half-sister to the dams of Irish One Thousand Guineas winner More So and Waterford Candelabra Stakes winner Obeah. Their dam Merdemain showed useful form at up to seven furlongs and is a half-sister to eleven other winners, including the very speedy pair Sixpence and Ballydam. Candy Glen has a two-year-old half-brother in the thrice-raced maiden Green's Van Goyen (by Lyphard's Special) and a yearling half-sister by Thatching. The well-made Candy Glen, a good mover, is at least as effective at a mile and a quarter as one mile and acts on any going. He's a credit to his trainer, for whom he was very much the stable star. *C. F. Wall.*

CANNON'S SPIRIT 3 gr.c. King Persian 107–Tinsel 95 (Right Boy 137) [1989 5s⁴ 5m 6f² 1990 6g⁶ a6g 6d 5m 6d] workmanlike colt: quite modest maiden, below form as 3-y-o: sprint bred: blinkered fourth start: has joined J. FitzGerald. *J. Berry.* —

CANNY CHRONICLE 2 b. or br.g. (May 10) Daring March 116–Laisser Aller (Sagaro 133) [1990 7m² 6m* 7f] 2,100F, 4,400Y: leggy gelding: third living foal: half-brother to 1½m winner Best of British (by Young Generation): dam minor 13f winner in France: comfortably landed odds in maiden auction at Hamilton in July: tended to hang and gave impression something amiss in Thirsk nursery 2 months later: stays 7f. *M. H. Tompkins.* 66

CANONESS 9 b.m. St Paddy 133–Sea Fable 51 (Typhoon 125) [1989 11.7d* 11.7m⁶ 10f⁶ 13.3m⁴ 12m 11.7m 10.2f 10.2f⁶ 12.2f² a12g 1990 11.7g⁶ 10m⁴ 12g* a12g³ a12g a13g⁶ a16g] small mare: poor handicapper: made all at Newbury in September: better suited by 1½m than 1¼m: acts on firm and dead going: sweated on reappearance: good mount for apprentice. *P. Hayward.* 45

CANTDONOWTRITE 3 gr.c. Belfort (FR) 89–Miss Tantan (Native Admiral (USA)) [1989 5d* 5g⁴ 6m⁵ 5m* 5g² 5s² 5g 1990 5v 5g⁵ 5g⁶ a5g⁶ 5f² 6m⁴ 5d⁶ 5g a6g] strong, workmanlike colt: modest winner at 2 yrs: best effort in 1990 in seller on sixth outing: well behind in handicaps last 2 starts, tubed on final one: best form at 5f: probably acts on any going: often edgy: tends to hang, and is not an easy ride: trained until after sixth outing by J. Berry. *B. Preece.* 52

CANTORIS 4 b.f. Song 132–Singing Witch 71 (Sing Sing 134) [1989 5f³ 6h² 5m² 6g⁴ 5.3f* 5m⁶ a6g 1990 5m⁶ 5f* 5m³ 5f² 6m 5g² 5f* 5m² 6d⁶ 5m⁶ 5.8h 6m 5m 5g⁴ 5m⁶ 5m³ 6m³ 5m* 5m³ 6d 5g² 5g⁴ 5s³] leggy, close-coupled filly: has a quick action: much improved handicapper, winner at Newcastle in April, Haydock in May and Ascot (£9,900 event by short head from Choir Practice) in September: ideally suited by 6f or stiff 5f: acts on any going: has run well for claimer: tremendously tough and consistent. *R. J. R. Williams.* 87

CANTY'S GOLD 4 b.f. Sonnen Gold 121–Canty Day 87 (Canadel II 126) [1989 8m 12.2m 1990 10.4g 15.3f 15d] leggy, angular filly: has a long stride: lightly raced and well behind in modest company since 2 yrs: blinkered once: sold out of J. J. O'Neill's stable 5,400 gns Doncaster May Sales before reappearance. *J. S. Wilson.* —

CANUTELL (FR) 2 b.f. (Feb 9) Persepolis (FR) 127–Dry Land 84 (Nonoalco (USA) 131) [1990 6f 6f⁶ 5m 5m] 5,800Y: fourth foal: half-sister to fair 1m winner River's Rising (by Mendez) and fairly useful 7f winner Trojan Desert (by Troy): dam —

CAP

5f winner, is granddaughter of very smart sprinter Lucasland: little worthwhile
form: blinkered in seller final start. *C. N. Williams.*

CAPA 10 ch.g. New Member 119–Poshteen 86 (Royal Smoke 113) [1989 16f³ 18g —
1990 14.8m] sturdy, plain gelding: poor handicapper: tailed off last 2 outings: stays
2¼m: possibly needs a sound surface: bandaged only start in 1990: one-time fairly
useful hurdler. *D. J. Wintle.*

CAPABILITY BROWN 3 b.g. Dominion 123–Tomfoolery 73 (Silly Season 127) **74**
[1989 8m³ 10g⁵ 1990 8.2s³ 8d⁶ 10m 10g² 12f³ 13.8f² 12m 13.8d] close-coupled
gelding: has a long, rather round action: modest maiden: hung left and found little
fifth outing: stays 13.8f: acts on firm ground: blinkered final start, visored previous
2: sold 13,000 gns Newmarket Autumn Sales: winning hurdler for M. Bradley. *D.
Morley.*

CAPE CRUSADE 3 b.g. Mufrij–Cape Farewell (Record Run 127) [1989 NR 1990 —
6f 7g] small gelding: first foal: dam novice hurdle winner out of useful
middle-distance filly Moving Isles: 100/1, no show in claimer and seller. *M. W.
Ellerby.*

CAPE PIGEON (USA) 5 ch.g. Storm Bird (CAN) 134–Someway Somehow **72 §**
(USA) (What Luck (USA)) [1989 7f 9.2f 7f³ 6m 6g³ 7f² 7f⁴ 7m² 1990 7g 7m 7m 7g⁴
8m⁴ 7m² 8g⁶ 8f³ 7m⁵ 8g⁶] big, strong, angular gelding: carries plenty of condition:
usually looks well: capable of modest form, but still a maiden: hung right and found
little sixth outing: probably best at 7f to 1m: acts on firm and dead going: visored
once at 3 yrs: not one to trust. *L. G. Cottrell.*

CAPITAL BOND (IRE) 2 b.c. (Feb 10) Hegemony 112–Have A Flutter **70**
(Auction Ring (USA) 123) [1990 5f⁶ 6m⁵ 6g³ 7m² 7m⁶ 8g 8m 7g] IR 11,500F,
32,000Y: smallish, quite attractive colt: keen walker: has a quick action: second foal:
half-brother to 1988 2-y-o 5f winner Done Better (by Dunphy): dam placed at 7f in
Ireland: modest maiden: best form at 6f and 7f: well below best in blinkers final
outing: looked awkward ride fourth start: sold 2,000 gns Doncaster November
Sales. *R. J. Holder.*

CAPITAL BUILDER 4 b.g. Pas de Seul 133–Double Touch (FR) (Nonoalco **30**
(USA) 131) [1989 8.5d 8.5g 8g 8f 7m⁴ 8g* 9f⁶ 11g 1990 8.2s 8v 8m 9s 8f 8m 7g⁶ 9g³
8.2m⁶] good-topped gelding: poor handicapper: stays 9f: acts on firm going,
probably unsuited by soft: blinkered second and last 3 outings. *I. Semple.*

CAPRAROLA (FR) 3 b.f. Bellypha 130–Olbia (Mill Reef (USA) 141) [1989 8s³ **113**
10d* 1990 10.5g⁴ 10.5d* 9.2g 10.5v⁴ 10.5v⁶] first foal: dam, French maiden, stayed
1m: won minor event at Saint-Cloud in December at 2 yrs and Prix Cleopatre (by
nose and 1½ lengths from Whitehaven and Colour Chart) at Maisons-Laffitte in
May: off course 5 months and below form in pattern events after: stays 10.5f: acts on
dead ground. *F. Boutin, France.*

CAPRICCIOSA (IRE) 2 b.f. (Mar 2) Alzao (USA) 117–Clanjingle **113 p**
(Tumble Wind (USA)) [1990 5g* 6m 6g* 6m* 6m*]
 Vincent O'Brien and his associates have been major buyers at the
sales down the years, their most recent notable big-money purchase being
Royal Academy—the most expensive yearling sold at public auction in 1988—
who proved himself in the July Cup and the Breeders' Cup Mile in the latest
season. However, the fact that most of O'Brien's time has been spent
operating at the upper end of the market doesn't mean he has lost his ability to
unearth a bargain at the lower end. Take Capricciosa. Apparently she was
spotted while her trainer was en route to view another yearling at Newmarket's October Sales in 1989. A bid of 27,000 guineas secured her—making
her one of the cheapest horses in the stable—and she's already repaid her
purchase price many times over with four wins from five starts, including in
the Moyglare Stud Stakes at the Curragh and the Tattersalls Cheveley Park
Stakes at Newmarket. Capricciosa was the first of the stable's two-year-olds
to set foot on a racecourse when she made her debut in a maiden race at the
Curragh in June. She was regarded as well forward and despite drifting from
5/2 to 9/2 in the market she won in convincing fashion, making all and forging
clear in the closing stages to beat Inishdalla by two and a half lengths.
Inishdalla had finished runner-up in a listed race on her debut so the form
looked quite useful. It was a long way removed from what's required to win
the Heinz '57' Phoenix Stakes, though, and in the face of a powerful challenge
from England Capricciosa and Inishdalla started at 5/1 and 12/1 respectively in

Moyglare Stud Stakes, the Curragh—
Capricciosa (right) is ridden along to hold off Inishdalla

a field of thirteen. Capricciosa beat only three home, in fact, but considering her inexperience and the fact she was poorly drawn she didn't fare at all badly, showing speed to track the principals for four furlongs only to find the effort taking its toll once Mac's Imp and Distinctly North went clear. Capricciosa's sights were lowered somewhat in the Group 3 EBF Debutante Stakes over the same course and distance later in August. Inishdalla, a good fifth in the Phoenix Stakes, was among the opposition again, but backers seemed confident Capricciosa would come out on top; so it proved, the 11/10 favourite making virtually all to beat Inishdalla by two lengths, the pair clear of the previously unbeaten Title Roll and Amparo. The Moyglare Stud Stakes was immediately put forward as Capricciosa's next objective. The race is Group 1, and during the last decade English trainers had won the race with Habibti, Minstrella and Chimes of Freedom, but for the latest renewal only the useful maiden Zigaura and the exposed minor winner Jameelaty made the journey. Among the Irish contingent, Isle of Glass looked an interesting contender following her easy win in a maiden at Phoenix Park a week earlier. However for the third time in four starts it was Inishdalla who caused Capricciosa most trouble. Capricciosa was soon breezing along in front again and looked capable of winning with something in hand with a furlong to run. Inishdalla and to a lesser extent Zigaura began to reduce the advantage soon after, but Capricciosa always looked like holding them off and passed the post three quarters of a length to the good with Zigaura half a length away in third.

In all probability Capricciosa needed only to reproduce her previous form to win the Moyglare. She needed to improve considerably to win a championship event like the Cheveley Park and did so in a race which led to considerable debate. Eleven faced the starter, including four supplementary entries, and the market was dominated by Divine Danse and Imperfect Circle. Divine Danse, the 9/4 favourite, was seeking to give Criquette Head her third success in the race following those of the subsequent Guineas winners Ma Biche and Ravinella; she looked a worthy favourite, too, following placed efforts in some of France's top two-year-old races and a convincing win in the Prix d'Arenberg at Longchamp; Imperfect Circle, who'd created a favourable

Tattersalls Cheveley Park Stakes, Newmarket—
Capricciosa again shows herself a tough and genuine filly,
as Imperfect Circle makes her pull out all the stops

impression in winning the Firth of Clyde Stakes at Ayr by four lengths, was a
5/2 chance; Capricciosa on 7/1; with Only Yours, the winner of a substandard
Lowther Stakes, and the once-raced maiden Sumonda bracketed on 9/1.
Capricciosa, who began to sweat up as the preliminaries progressed, showed
her customary dash to lead and put nearly all her opponents in trouble when
quickening a couple of lengths clear passing the two-furlong pole. Imperfect
Circle, checked against the far rail at around halfway, squeezed through to get
to her quarters with a furlong to run, but Capricciosa's willingness to battle
stood her in good stead up the hill and she kept pulling out extra under
pressure to win by three quarters of a length with Divine Danse two and a half
lengths away. Imperfect Circle would have finished a shade closer granted a
trouble-free passage, and Divine Danse looked desperately unlucky, as she
was able to quicken in fine style without being asked a serious question in the
final furlong after meeting all the trouble that was going. But to detract from
Capricciosa's hard-earned victory would be churlish. As on all her starts she
displayed an admirable attitude to the job, and her win in the Cheveley Park
gave the Irish their first two-year-old Group 1 success in Britain since Park
Appeal won the same race by four lengths back in 1984.

		Lyphard	Northern Dancer
Capricciosa (IRE) (b.f. Mar 2, 1988)	Alzao (USA) (b 1980)	(b 1969)	Goofed
		Lady Rebecca	Sir Ivor
		(b 1971)	Pocahontas II
	Clanjingle (b 1980)	Tumble Wind	Restless Wind
		(b 1964)	Easy Stages
		Fille Sifflante	Whistler
		(b 1965)	Polly Gilles

During the 'eighties three fillies completed the Moyglare Stud Stakes-
Cheveley Park double, namely Minstrella, Park Appeal and, another from
Ballydoyle, Woodstream. None of the three managed to win a single race in
her second season, and although it would be foolish to predict a similar fate for
Capricciosa we do have reservations about her prospects. First and foremost
her form as it stands falls short of what's required to make an impact at classic
level, and judged on her style of running she's far from certain to stay a mile in

Mr R. E. Sangster's "Capricciosa"

any case. There are plenty of opportunities to run at sprint distances outside handicaps, of course, but Capricciosa will be obliged to shoulder a penalty in all bar the best races and could find winning difficult. As we've already said, the sturdy, compact Capricciosa was sold for only 27,000 guineas as a yearling; she'd been sold as a foal for IR 8,000 guineas at Goffs. There's little to get excited about close up in the female side of her pedigree. Her dam Clanjingle, who finished placed a couple of times over five furlongs in Ireland, produced three foals prior to Capricciosa. The first, by Kafu, died, the second Hill's Halo (by Kampala) and the third Call Me Alice (a sister to Capricciosa) are moderate maidens; her two-year-old for 1991 is a colt by Anita's Prince, and her filly foal by Nordico was led out unsold at the latest Goffs November Premier Sale. Clanjingle's dam Fille Sifflante, a half-sister to the Queen Mary winner Grizel, showed far more temperament than ability during her racing career. She's bred several winners, though, including the useful handicapper Lion City, and her dam Polly Gilles comes from the same family as Pretty Polly. Capricciosa's sire Alzao, now resident at Coolmore, had another successful year with Aldbourne, Mirror Black, Va Toujours and a couple of useful performers in Italy advertising his prowess. Capricciosa's win at Newmarket allied to that of Pass The Peace in 1988 means he's now sired two Cheveley Park winners from only three crops to race—no mean feat for a stallion who began his career standing for just IR 4,000 guineas. *M. V. O'Brien, Ireland.*

CAPTAIN BROWN 3 b.g. Welsh Captain 113–Belinda Brown 83 (Legal Eagle **48**
126) [1989 a6g 1990 a6g a6g4 a7g5 a7g2 a5g4 a8g* a7g5] angular, lightly-made gelding: poor performer: apprentice ridden, won 3-runner claimer at Lingfield in February: better at 1m than shorter: slowly away fifth start: visored afterwards: sold 1,600 gns Doncaster March Sales: resold 750 gns Ascot May Sales. *T. D. Barron.*

CAPTAIN CHROME 3 b.g. Welsh Captain 113–Chrome Mag 63 (Prince de — Galles 125) [1989 5g⁶ 8f 7g 1990 a7g⁵ 12f a8g 8g 10m] leggy gelding: no worthwhile form on flat: winning selling hurdler. *K. S. Bridgwater.*

CAPTAIN FAWLEY 3 br.g. Petorius 117–Lady Fawley 86 (He Loves Me 120) — [1989 7g 6g 5g 1990 8g 8.2m 10m 10m] strong, useful-looking gelding: poor plater: worth a try back at 1m: wore net muzzle on reappearance: sometimes taken down early: sold 1,000 gns Newmarket Autumn Sales. *W. J. Musson.*

CAPTAIN KAGAR 2 b.g. (Mar 23) Ballacashtal (CAN)–Northern Hope (FR) 63 **39** (Fabulous Dancer (USA) 124) [1990 5f 5m 5s 5m 5f⁵ 5m⁶ 5m⁶] 2,300Y: sparely-made gelding: moderate walker: has a quick action: first foal: dam maiden on flat suited by 1¾m, won over hurdles: poor form, including in sellers: blinkered third start: inconsistent. *R. W. Stubbs.*

CAPTAIN MAVERICK (USA) 4 ch.c. Nureyev (USA) 131–Little Tobago — (USA) (Impressive (USA)) [1989 8v⁵ 10.2f 10f 1990 17.6g] big, leggy, lengthy colt: of little account: sold 730 gns Doncaster October Sales. *Ronald Thompson.*

CAPTAIN MAY 6 b.g. Welsh Captain 113–Maygo 57 (Maystreak 118) [1989 NR — 1990 a8g a8g] leggy, angular gelding: probably of little account: blinkered on reappearance. *R. E. Peacock.*

CAPTAIN MY CAPTAIN (IRE) 2 ch.c. (Mar 31) Flash of Steel 120–Amanzi **73 p** 94 (African Sky 124) [1990 7g 7g 7m⁴ 7m] IR 18,000F, 21,000Y: lengthy colt: has plenty of scope: second living foal: dam Irish 2-y-o 5f winner, is half-sister to very useful sprinter Touch Paper out of half-sister to Blue Wind: over 5 lengths fourth of 7, going on well and giving impression would have finished closer had run begun sooner, to Big Blow in minor event at Ascot in September: caught eye, never placed to challenge, in maidens other starts: will stay 1m: probably capable of better. *G. B. Balding.*

CAPTAIN'S BIDD 10 ch.g. Captain James 123–Muffet 75 (Matador 131) [1989 — 7d 6d² 6m⁶ 6f 5m* 6m 5f² 5m² 5f⁴ 5m³ 7f⁵ 5g² 5g⁵ 5m 5f³ 5.1g⁴ 5f* 5m 6g 5m* a6g* a5g⁶ 1990 6m 5m 5m⁶ 5m a5g a5g] sturdy, workmanlike gelding: carries plenty of condition: usually dull in coat: moderate mover: won 4 handicaps in modest company as 9-y-o: no worthwhile form in 1990: ideally suited by 5f: acts on any going: effective with or without blinkers or visor: ran poorly when sweating: good mount for apprentice. *R. Thompson.*

CARABALI DANCER 2 ch.c. (Apr 4) Ballacashtal (CAN)–Lillicara (FR) **43** (Caracolero (USA) 131) [1990 a7g 8.2d 8f] 4,500Y: lengthy colt: fifth foal: half-brother to 3 winners here and abroad, including 1988 2-y-o 5f winner Charm and 7f and 1m winner Rowlandsons Gems: dam never ran: poor maiden: taken down last and very quietly final outing. *D. T. Garraton.*

CARBISDALE 4 ch.g. Dunbeath (USA) 127–Kind Thoughts 71 (Kashmir II 125) — [1989 10m² 12.3m³ 14g 1990 a12g⁴] workmanlike gelding: has a round action: modest maiden: very much in need of race only outing at 4 yrs: suited by 1½m: winning hurdler in 1989/90. *E. Weymes.*

CARDEA CASTLE (IRE) 2 b.f. (Mar 23) Fayruz 116–Yamba (FR) (Amarko — (FR)) [1990 7d 9g] 5,000Y: third reported foal: dam French middle-distance winner: backward in maiden at Ayr and claimer at York in autumn. *C. B. B. Booth.*

CARDIFF ARMS 3 b.f. Another Realm 118–Gemgem 54 (Lochnager 132) [1989 **43** 5m⁵ 6m³ 6m 6f 6m 1990 7f 5f⁶ a5g 7g 6m⁵] small filly: poor maiden: suited by 6f: taken down early and took keen hold fourth start. *D. Haydn Jones.*

CARDINAL BIRD (USA) 3 b.c. Storm Bird (CAN) 134–Shawnee Creek (USA) — (Mr Prospector (USA)) [1989 NR 1990 8g 7mʷᵒ] $300,000Y: second foal: dam, stakes winner at up to 9f in USA, is half-sister to North Sider, Grade 1 winner at up to 1¼m in States: green and always struggling in maiden at Yarmouth in June: walked over in similar event at York following month: sold to join S. Mellor 9,600 gns Newmarket Autumn Sales. *J. Gosden.*

CARD TRICK 2 ch.f. (Feb 2) Good Times (ITY)–Double Shuffle 103 (Tachypous — 128) [1990 7m] fair sort: third foal: dam 1½m winner: always behind in autumn maiden at Newmarket. *G. A. Pritchard-Gordon.*

CAREER BAY 8 b.g. Orange Bay 131–Career (Hotfoot 126) [1989 12.2s 1990 18f — 16g⁵ 17.6m] lengthy gelding: poor handicapper: stays 2m: best form on an easy surface: blinkered last 2 outings. *D. Haydn Jones.*

CAREFREE TIMES 3 b.c. Good Times (ITY)–Danaka (FR) (Val de Loir 133) **71** [1989 NR 1990 9g⁶ 8.5g³ 8.2g² 11m* 12d 12g⁶ 10d] big, strong colt: has scope: seventh reported foal: half-brother to several winners, including 1986 2-y-o 7f winner Bills Henry (by In Fijar): dam, minor French 11f winner, is closely related to good middle-distance performer Val d'Aoste: modest performer: favourite, won 5-runner handicap at Edinburgh in August: found little in handicaps next 2 starts: may well be suited by 1¼m: probably needs a sound surface: bandaged near-hind final outing. *M. J. Camacho.*

CAREFUL DANCER   4 ch.f. Gorytus (USA) 132–Be Noble (Vaguely Noble 140)   —
[1989 NR 1990 7f4] angular filly: edgy, tailed-off last of 4 in August maiden (moved down moderately) at Redcar, only second outing. *E. Weymes.*

CAREFUL LAD   4 b.c. Precocious 126–Arenetta (Bold Lad (IRE) 133) [1989 6s5   —
6d2 7m* 6s3 1990 6m 7d 8m a8g 7g] sturdy, good-quartered colt: poor mover: winning plater in 1989: below form in handicaps and seller as 4-y-o: stays 7f: easily best effort on a soft surface: visored once at 3 yrs, blinkered final start: sold out of J. Hudson's stable 1,050 gns Ascot May Sales before reappearance. *J. White.*

CARELESS LOVE   2 b.f. (Apr 5) Top Ville 129–La Carlotta (USA) (J O Tobin   79
(USA) 130) [1990 7m 8g5] 27,000Y: leggy filly: second foal: dam, French 9.2f winner, is sister to very useful French 5f to 1m winner L'Orangerie out of half-sister to Irish River: 6 lengths fifth of 16 to Clare Heights in maiden at Yarmouth in October: slowly away on debut: will stay further. *Mrs L. Piggott.*

CARESS   2 gr.f. (Apr 8) Godswalk (USA) 130–Skelton 70 (Derrylin 115) [1990 5f3   84
5f3 5g* 5m2 6f4 5g 7m 5v5] 3,000F, 8,200Y: leggy filly: poor walker and mover: first foal: dam 2-y-o 7f and 8.2f sellers winner, is half-sister to very useful stayer Brief Bay: fair filly: made all in maiden at Wolverhampton in May: best form at 6f: seems unsuited by heavy ground: often bandaged: sold 10,000 gns Newmarket Autumn Sales. *Mrs N. Macauley.*

CARFIELD LAD (IRE)   2 br.c. (Apr 30) On Your Mark 125–June Lady (Junius   73 §
(USA) 124) [1990 5m3 5g2 5f* 6m4 5g2 5g2 5m3 5m6 5m] IR 3,800F, 8,200Y: compact colt: has a quick action: first foal: dam Irish maiden: modest performer: won median auction at Thirsk in June: hung throughout and looked ungenuine final outing: should stay 6f: blinkered seventh to ninth outings: one to be very wary of: sold 3,200 gns Newmarket Autumn Sales. *G. A. Pritchard-Gordon.*

CARIBBEAN KATIE   3 b.f. Valiyar 129–Heaven High (High Line 125) [1989   —
NR 1990 8m6 10g5] first foal: dam lightly raced and probably stayed 1½m, is granddaughter of smart 5f to 1¼m filly Pugnacity: beaten about 12 lengths in minor event (moved moderately down) at Newmarket and maiden (bandaged off-hind) at Beverley in August. *H. R. A. Cecil.*

CARIBBEAN PRINCE   2 ch.c. (Mar 24) Dara Monarch 128–My Ginny 83   —
(Palestine 133) [1990 8g 7m] 19,000Y: strong, workmanlike colt: half-brother to several winners, including one in Spain and winning stayer/fair hurdler Mariner's Dream (by Julio Mariner): dam 2-y-o 6f winner: always behind in autumn maidens at Kempton and Leicester (slowly away). *R. Hannon.*

CARISSIMA   2 b.f. (Feb 19) Kind of Hush 118–Divissima 62 (Music Boy 124)   45
[1990 5g4 6m 6m] 2,700F: strong, lengthy filly: first foal: dam 6f winner, is half-sister to very useful 1978 2-y-o sprinter Eyelet: poor maiden: seems unsuited by top-of-the-ground. *P. S. Felgate.*

CARJUJEN   6 b.g. Tumble Wind (USA)–Baldritta (FR) (Baldric II 131) [1989 10m   — §
12g 8m 10.8f4 8g 9g 1990 12g 8g 12g 16.2d5] close-coupled gelding: modest winner as 3-y-o: little subsequent sign of ability on flat: had very stiff tasks in autumn, virtually refusing to race second outing: stays 9f: acts on good to firm and dead going. *D. W. Browne.*

CARLINGFORD (USA)   4 ch.c. Irish Castle (USA)–Delta Sal (USA) (Delta   —
Judge) [1989 12f* 12f* 1990 8m 12f 12g 12m4] rangy colt: won King George V Stakes at Royal Ascot on final outing at 3 yrs: prominent until 2f out in Bessborough Stakes there in June: then off course 3 months and ran poorly last 2 starts: should stay beyond 1½m: used to act well on firm going: sold 12,500 gns Newmarket Autumn Sales. *G. Harwood.*

CARLITA (HOL)   4 ch.f. Shamaraan (FR)–Carmona (Track Spare 125) [1989 NR   —
1990 a12g] first known foal: dam won 6 times in Holland at 2 yrs and 3 yrs including Dutch 1000 Guineas and Dutch St Leger and is half-sister to Dutch triple crown winner Civano, very useful here as 4-y-o: tailed off in maiden at Lingfield in January. *R. Guest.*

CARLTON MOOR   3 gr.f. Mandrake Major 122–Greyburn 85 (Saintly Song 128)   —
[1989 6m 7d 1990 8.2v6 8d] quite good-topped filly: no worthwhile form, in claimers as 3-y-o: moved poorly down final start. *W. W. Haigh.*

CARMAGNOLE (USA) 4 b.c. Lypheor 118–La Bonzo (USA) (Miracle Hill) **84** d
[1989 10.8s* 12m² 12f² 17.1h² 13.1m* 14m⁵ 12mʷº 14g 12m* 12g⁵ 1990 12m² 12m⁵
12g 12m⁶ 12m] angular, quite attractive colt: fair handicapper: ran poorly last 3
outings: best short of 2m: acts on any going: blinkered fourth start: has won for
apprentice: goes well with forcing tactics: sold 11,000 gns Newmarket Autumn
Sales. *G. Harwood.*

CARMEN'S JOY 2 br.f. (Mar 12) Chief Singer 131–Bag Lady 86 (Be My Guest **72**
(USA) 126) [1990 a5g* 6g 6g⁴ 7.5f⁵ 6m⁵] 11,000Y: good-topped filly: has scope:
good mover: first foal: dam ungenuine maiden stayed 1m, is out of half-sister
to Malinowski, Gielgud and dam of El Gran Senor: modest filly: won maiden at
Southwell in May: went very keenly down and gave trouble stalls before running
poorly for 7-lb claimer final start: may prove best at short of 7.5f: sometimes slowly
away: seems rather temperamental. *Sir Mark Prescott.*

CARNBREA CUDDY (IRE) 2 ch.c. (Apr 21) King of Clubs 124–Mrs **82**
Tittlemouse (Nonoalco (USA) 131) [1990 6g 6g⁴ 7m 7m* 8g 8m² 8.2s] IR 13,500Y:
leggy, workmanlike colt: has scope: has a roundish action: third foal: brother to 1m
winner Solo Court: dam unraced half-sister to high-class miler Bairn: fair
performer: won nursery at Yarmouth in August: suited by 1m: acts well on good to
firm ground and seems unsuited by soft. *Dr J. D. Scargill.*

CARNIVAL BABY (USA) 2 ch.c. (May 10) Northern Baby (CAN) 127– **60** p
Carnival Princess (USA) (Prince John) [1990 7m⁶ 7s⁵] 52,000Y: leggy colt: closely
related to high-class 7f and 1m performer Salse (by Topsider) and half-brother to
3-y-o Dear Mimi (by Roberto) and a modest winner by Key To The Mint: dam minor
winner at 6f in USA, is half-sister to Italian Oaks winner Carnauba: quite modest
form in autumn maidens at Chepstow and Lingfield: may well do better. *M. R.
Stoute.*

CARN MAIRE 2 b.f. (Apr 16) Northern Prospect (USA)–Samsara (PER) (Golden **83**
Spur (USA)) [1990 6g³ 6g² 5m* 8f 6s² 5g⁶] 2,000F, 7,800Y: lengthy, leggy, angular
filly: has a rather round action: third foal: dam good winner in Peru: fair performer:
won maiden auction at Sandown in June: very good second to Russian Mink in
nursery at Newbury: suited by 6f: easily best form on soft ground. *R. V. Smyth.*

CAROLES CLOWN 4 gr.f. Another Realm 118–Show Business 72 (Auction — §
Ring (USA) 123) [1989 6s 6m 7f⁶ a8g⁶ a6g 1990 a6g a8g 12.5f 12m 12g⁵] leggy,
lightly-made filly: has a round action: plating-class winner at 2 yrs: very little
subsequent form on flat: should stay beyond 1m: visored once: looks a difficult ride,
and hasn't ideal attitude. *M. J. Haynes.*

CAROLES EXPRESS 2 ch.f. (Apr 21) Scottish Reel 123–Peregrine Falcon **66**
(Saulingo 122) [1990 5d⁴ 6d² 6d³] 5,400Y, 8,000 2-y-o: big, lengthy, filly: has a
moderate action: half-sister to Irish 9.5f winner Millennium Falcon (by Dunbeath)
and a prolific winner in Italy: dam half-sister to Bay Express, ran only at 2 yrs: quite
modest maiden: best effort second start: will stay 7f. *R. Akehurst.*

CAROLE'S KING (IRE) 2 b.c. (Feb 21) Kings Lake (USA) 133–Senane 86 **76**
(Vitiges (FR) 132) [1990 6m* 7.5f⁶ 6f⁵ 7f⁴ 8g³ 8g⁵ 8d³] 12,000F, 7,400Y:
good-bodied colt: moderate mover: third foal: half-brother to 1989 Irish 2-y-o 9f
winner Commanche Chief (by Commanche Run): dam 1m winner stayed 1½m,
possibly ungenuine, is out of top staying 2-y-o filly of 1978 Formulate: modest
performer: won maiden at Folkestone in July: ran well final 4 outings: will stay
1½m: acts on firm and dead ground: effective with or without blinkers. *W. Carter.*

CAROLS BELLE 7 ch.m. Ballymore 123–Love For Money 71 (Be Friendly 130) —
[1989 5f 8m 1990 a11g a8g] sparely-made mare: poor maiden: has worn blinkers. *C.
F. C. Jackson.*

CAROL'S TREASURE 6 b.h. Balidar 133–Really Sharp (Sharpen Up 127) **110**
[1989 5g³ 5f² 5f* 6f⁵ 5f 5g⁶ 5m* 5f³ 1990 5f* 5m⁵ 6m 5f 5m⁵ 5g⁶ 5m³ 6f] quite
attractive, good-quartered horse: good mover: very useful performer: first run for
nearly 9 months, won listed event at Haydock in April: struck into going down and
withdrawn next intended start: best efforts after in Keeneland Nunthorpe Stakes at
York and listed race won by Blyton Lad at Newmarket on fifth and seventh outings:
best at 5f: needed a sound surface: reportedly ran too freely when blinkered: best
held up: dead. *J. W. Hills.*

CAROMANDOO (IRE) 2 b.g. (May 2) Simply Great (FR) 122–Tanimara **75**
(Sassafras (FR) 135) [1990 6f⁴ a7g* 8g 7m* 7g³] IR 7,400Y: big, angular,
unfurnished gelding: half-brother to a winner in Italy by Nadjar: dam won in Italy:
modest performer: won maiden at Southwell in August and nursery at Yarmouth in
September: will probably stay 1¼m. *M. Bell.*

CAROMISH (USA) 3 br.f. Lyphard's Wish (FR) 124–Carom (USA) (Caro 133) 82
[1989 5s⁶ 6g 6m⁴ 7f² 6g* 6g* 7s* 6g 1990 7.3m 6m 6m⁶ 6m 7g 6d 6m 7g³ 7.6v⁴ a8g]
tall, rather leggy filly: fair handicapper: ran poorly (slowly away) at Southwell final
start: stays 7f: acts on good to firm ground and soft: seems best held up: not
particularly consistent. *M. D. I. Usher.*

CAROUSELLA 2 b.f. (Jan 27) Rousillon (USA) 133–Salchow 116 (Niniski (USA) 48 p
125) [1990 7m 8.2m 7m⁵] rather leggy, close-coupled filly: first foal: dam won at 7f
(at 2 yrs) and 12.3f and stayed 14.6f: plating-class form, giving impression capable of
better first 2 starts, in maidens and a minor event: will be better suited by 1¼m. *C.
E. Brittain.*

CARPE DIEM 5 b.m. Good Times (ITY)–Olympic Visualise 84 (Northfields —
(USA)) [1989 7s 7g⁵ 7.6f 6m 7m 7.6f⁴ 8.3m² 8m 1990 a7g a10g] medium-sized mare:
has a round action: poor maiden: stays 1m: yet to show her form on firm going, acts
on any other: blinkered final outing. *E. A. Wheeler.*

CARPET SLIPPERS 4 br.f. Daring March 116–Mollified 67 (Lombard (GER) 73
126) [1989 8m 12.5m³ 10.2f² 12f⁶ 10d 1990 14.8f⁵ 12g 11.7m³ 10m³ 10g* 10f* 12g
11.5g³ 12g 10d a10g⁶] leggy, lengthy filly: modest handicapper: successful twice at
Salisbury in August: ran moderately last 3 outings: should prove as effective at 1½m
as 1¼m: acts on firm going: ran creditably for lady fourth start. *J. D. Bethell.*

CARRIGANS GIRLS (IRE) 2 ch.f. (Mar 22) Fayruz 116–Very Seldom (Rarity —
129) [1990 a6g 7m a6g 6s] IR 3,000Y: rather unfurnished filly: has a round action:
second foal: half-sister to 1m winner Ruby Shoes (by Day Is Done): dam twice-raced
on flat here later placed over hurdles in Ireland: well beaten in maidens and a
claimer: blinkered final start. *W. Wilson.*

CARRINKY 2 gr.f. (Apr 13) Absalom 128–Nocturnal Bliss (Pyjama Hunt 126) — §
[1990 5m⁴ 6g] 12,000Y: sturdy filly: moderate mover: second foal: half-sister to 1989
winning 2-y-o sprint plater Ballet Bliss (by Balidar): dam ran twice: looked
thoroughly irresolute in maidens at Haydock (last of 4) and Ripon: sold 920 gns
Doncaster September Sales: one to leave alone. *J. Berry.*

CARROLL HOUSE 5 ch.h. Lord Gayle (USA) 124–Tuna 63 (Silver Shark 129) ?
[1989 10s³ 10m³ 12g* 12m⁵ 10g* 12g* 12f 1990 12d 12g⁴] good-topped, useful-
looking horse: moderate mover: improved considerably as 4-y-o: successful in Ciga
Prix de l'Arc de Triomphe at Longchamp having earlier won Princess of Wales's
Stakes at Newmarket and EBF Phoenix Champion Stakes: shaped as though
retaining much of his ability in Hardwicke Stakes at Royal Ascot (carrying deal of
condition) and Grand Prix de Saint-Cloud within 10 days in summer: stayed 1½m
well: well suited by easy surface and acted on heavy going: tremendously tough,
genuine and consistent: a credit to his trainer: reportedly struck into at Saint-Cloud,
and retired to stud in Japan. *M. A. Jarvis.*

CARROLLS MARC (IRE) 2 b.c. (Mar 28) Horage 124–Rare Find (Rarity 129) 71
[1990 6m 6s³ a7g³ a7g³ a7g*] IR 10,000F, 7,200Y: angular, medium-sized colt: poor
mover: half-brother to a winner in Spain and a winner over hurdles: dam Irish 2-y-o
7f winner: modest performer: won 11-runner claimer at Southwell by 2½ lengths in
December: will stay 1m. *M. H. Tompkins.*

CARRY ON CARY 4 b.g. Carriage Way 107–Greenhill Lass (Upper Case (USA)) —
[1989 8m² 8m² 10h² 8m⁴ 10f³ 1990 8m a10g a8g] leggy, sparely-made gelding:
moderate walker and mover: fair handicapper as 3-y-o: bandaged, well beaten all 3
outings in November: stays 1¼m: acts on any going. *R. W. Stubbs.*

CARTEL 3 b.c. Kris 135–Meis El-Reem 124 (Auction Ring (USA) 123) [1989 6m² 75
1990 6m³ 8m³ 6f4] close-coupled colt: moderate mover: modest maiden: favourite,
travelled well in lead over 4f then found little when well below form in apprentice
maiden final start, in July: should stay 1m. *A. A. Scott.*

CARVERALI (USA) 3 b.c. Roberto (USA) 131–Far Beyond (USA) (Nijinsky —
(CAN) 138) [1989 NR 1990 10g] $15,000F: very big colt: tenth foal: brother to a
minor winner at up to 9f at 4 yrs in USA and half-brother to 3 winners, including
Grade 3 8.5f winner Wings of Grace (by Key To The Mint) and the dam of smart 1989
U.S. 3-y-o Tricky Creek: dam 3-y-o winner in North America: green and burly,
about 13 lengths eleventh of 22 in maiden at Kempton in June. *G. Harwood.*

CASA BELLA 3 b.f. Belfort (FR) 89–Cassiar 84 (Connaught 130) [1989 NR 1990 47
8.5g 8.2m 8g 8.2m⁶ 8.5f⁴ 10.6d 8m⁴ 9g 10m⁶ 8.2v 11m² 12d] 2,400F, 7,500Y:
workmanlike filly: sister to 6f winner Persistent Bell and half-sister to a winner in
Mexico: dam 11.5f winner out of very speedy Fortune's Darling: plating-class form:
stays 11f: acts on firm going: blinkered eighth outing: ran well for 7-lb claimer (made
most) penultimate start. *J. G. FitzGerald.*

CASAMURRAE 3 b.f. Be My Guest (USA) 126–Loralane 86 (Habitat 134) [1989 **87** 7g⁴ 7g² 1990 8f² 8f* 8.5g² 8g⁴ 10g⁴ 10m 12.2d⁴ 12d* 16.5d²] leggy, angular filly: has a scratchy action: fair performer: won maiden at Newcastle in April and handicap (ridden along in rear over 4f out) at Leicester in October: good second in Doncaster handicap final start: stays 16.5f: yet to race on soft going, has form on any other: best on galloping track with strong handling. *G. Wragg.*

CASBATINA 4 b.f. Castle Keep 121–Balatina 85 (Balidar 133) [1989 8h 1990 8f **—** 8m 10.1g 7d] lengthy, angular, sparely-made filly: landed gamble in 6f seller as 2-y-o: lightly raced and no subsequent form: doesn't stay 1¼m: possibly unsuited by soft going: has worn bandage on off-hind: taken early or steadily to post. *J. Pearce.*

CASCADE 2 b.f. (Apr 21) Shirley Heights 130–Spin Turn (Homing 130) [1990 **—** 8.2m 8.2v] second foal: half-sister to a winner in Italy: dam unraced daughter of Oaks third The Dancer: never near leaders in autumn minor events at Nottingham and Haydock. *D. Morley.*

CASE FOR THE CROWN (USA) 3 b.f. Bates Motel (USA)–Crown The **70** Queen (USA) (Swaps) [1989 NR 1990 8m⁵ 8m³ 8m⁴ 9f 10.2s 7d a7g⁴] big, angular filly: eighth foal: half-sister to 5 winners in USA, notably Huggle Duggle (by Never Bend), stakes winner at up to 9f: dam stakes winner at up to 7f is half-sister to Kentucky Oaks winner Silent Beauty: modest form: stays 9f: acts on firm going: trained until after fourth start by A. Stewart. *B. J. Curley.*

CASE LAW 3 ch.c. Ahonoora 122–Travesty 63 (Reliance II 137) [1989 5g* 5s² **106** 5m² 5s 1990 a6g* 6f* 6g* 5d² 6g* 6f⁵ 6m⁶ a5g* 6g² 5.6g 6d] strong, good-bodied colt: usually looks well: poor mover: useful performer: won minor event at Lingfield, apprentice race at Ripon then handicaps at Newmarket (£19,600 Coral Bookmakers Handicap on fourth start) and Southwell: very good second in Group 3 event at Phoenix Park: first home on unfavoured far side in Portland Handicap at Doncaster then behind in Group 3 event at Maisons-Laffitte: stays 6f: has won on firm going, but best efforts with some give. *Sir Mark Prescott.*

CASESSA (USA) 3 gr.f. Caro 133–Bori (USA) (Quadrangle) [1989 NR 1990 **—** 8.5g²] seventh foal: half-sister to 3 winners in USA, notably Safe Play (by Sham), a high-class winner at up to 9f and dam of very smart 3-y-o 1¼m to 11f winner Defensive Play, and 2 winners here, notably 1000 Guineas winner Musical Bliss (by The Minstrel): dam placed at 3 yrs, from good family: placed once in minor company from 6 outings in USA at 2 yrs: 11/4, beaten 15 lengths by sole opponent 7/2-on Rudy's Fantasy in maiden at Beverley in August. *M. R. Stoute.*

CASHARII 3 ch.c. Ballacashtal (CAN)–Sister Rosarii (USA) (Properantes **—** (USA)) [1989 NR 1990 7f⁶] fourth foal: brother to 1988 2-y-o 5f seller winner Annother Sigwells, successful from 6f to 9f at 3 yrs in Italy: dam never ran: 20/1, about 6 lengths sixth of 9 to Iksab in maiden at Doncaster in March. *W. G. M. Turner.*

CASHMERE AMANDA 4 b.f. Blue Cashmere 129–Overide (Pitskelly 122) **—** [1989 NR 1990 7m⁵] lengthy filly: first reported foal: dam unraced: bit backward, never-dangerous fifth of 7 in claimer at Catterick in August: moved moderately down. *J. G. FitzGerald.*

CASH POINT 3 b.g. Sweet Monday 122–Kindling (Psidium 130) [1989 NR 1990 **63** 10.2g⁴ 9g⁴] big, workmanlike gelding: half-brother to 4 winners, including fairly useful 1¼m to 13f winner Timber Track (by Palm Track) and useful 7f to 1m winner Major Don (by Mandrake Major): dam ran only 3 times: bandaged and bit backward, over 6 lengths fourth of 7 to Scottish Jester at Ripon in July, second and better effort in maidens. *E. Weymes.*

CASHTAL DAZZLER 3 b.g. Ballacashtal (CAN)–Miss Meg 68 (John Splendid **86** 116) [1989 6m² 7m* 7f⁴ 7m³ 1990 8h⁵ 8m* 8.2f* 8g³ 8d 7.6f⁶ 8m² 8.2m 8m⁴ 10.6g] leggy gelding: good walker: has a quick action: fair handicapper: made most when successful at Thirsk and Haydock (£19,100 Tote Credit Silver Bowl) in May: easily best subsequent efforts when placed: stays 1m: acts on hard ground: game. *J. Berry.*

CASIENNE (IRE) 2 ch.f. (Feb 23) Doulab (USA) 115–Borshch (Bonne Noel 115) **55** [1990 5f⁵ 5.8h³ 8m 6m 8m 8.2d] sparely-made filly: fourth foal: dam lightly raced in Ireland, from family of Ardross: plating-class maiden: raced much too freely on final outing: stays 1m: blinkered final 3 outings. *R. J. Holder.*

CASPIAN BELUGA 2 b.g. (Apr 10) Persian Bold 123–Miss Thames 105 (Tower **58** Walk 130) [1990 6m² 7m² 7m] strong, close-coupled gelding: third foal: half-brother to fairly useful 6f winner Got Away (by Final Straw) and 3-y-o Tamise (by Dominion): dam useful at up to 1m: quite modest form when second, keeping on never able to challenge, in maidens at Newmarket and Yarmouth: bred to stay 1m. *M. R. Stoute.*

Mrs David Thompson's "Case Law"

CASPIAN GATES 6 b.g. Persian Bold 123–Galka 98 (Deep Diver 134) [1989 **63**
10s⁶ 10v 10d⁶ 10.8d⁴ 12m 11.5f* 12.4m* 14m² 12m 14m³ 12f* 12f² 13.8d 1990 10.8m
11.7g 12f⁵ 13.8m³ 14m² 11.5g³ 16m 14m⁵ 12f² 14m⁶ a12g] small, sturdy gelding:
carries plenty of condition: quite modest handicapper: ran badly on all-weather final
outing: stays 1¾m: suited by a sound surface: wore blinkers when trained in Ireland
and once at 5 yrs: often sweats. *A. N. Lee.*

CASPIAN GREY 2 gr.g. (Apr 1) Absalom 128–Sea Aura 89 (Roi Soleil 125) [1990 **78**
6m⁴ 6m* a7g⁶] 30,000Y: good-bodied gelding: fifth foal: half-brother to 3-y-o
Koracle Bay (by Kind of Hush), fair 6f winner at 2 yrs, and a winner in Norway by
Song: dam probably best at 7f: heavily-backed favourite, won 19-runner seller
(retained 12,000 gns) at Newmarket in October in very good style by 5 lengths from
Karim's Kid: well below that form in non-selling nursery at Lingfield following
month: may well stay 1m. *M. H. Tompkins.*

CASPIAN MIST 5 b.m. Remainder Man 126§–Bay Foulard (Shantung 132) [1989 **62**
10.2g² 12v* 10s⁴ 12f4 12m⁶ 12m² 11.5g⁵ 12f⁵ 11.7d⁵ 14f4 14g² 1990 14.8m² 16g⁵ 12f
12m⁴] big, good-bodied mare: moderate mover: fair winning handicapper as 4-y-o:
below her best in first half of 1990: should stay beyond 1¾m: acts on any going: has
run creditably when sweating and for apprentice: trained until after third outing by
G. Lewis. *Miss B. Sanders.*

CASSANOVA LAD 4 b.c. Swing Easy (USA) 126–Sallusteno 80 (Sallust 134) **—**
[1989 10f⁶ 1990 8f] leggy colt: soundly beaten in modest company: needed race only
outing at 4 yrs. *S. E. Kettlewell.*

161

CASSIBELLA 4 b.f. Red Sunset 120–Crane Beach (High Top 131) [1989 12.2d 10m 10.2f 8g 1990 10.2f 12.5f] small filly: useful plater as 2-y-o: no subsequent form: reluctant to race final start: often blinkered. *P. D. Evans.* —

CASTCAREAWAY (FR) 2 b.c. (Apr 28) Caerleon (USA) 132–Castaway (FR) **74** (Filiberto (USA) 123) [1990 6d 7m⁵ 7m⁵ 6g² 7s 7d 6g⁴ 8g a7g²] 220,000 francs (approx £20,400) Y: angular, good-quartered colt: moderate walker and mover: second living foal: dam poor maiden half-sister to very speedy Standaan: modest form in varied events, including second in Deauville seller and Lingfield nursery: will probably stay 1m: usually blinkered nowadays: trained first 5 outings by C. Brittain, next 3 by J. E. Hammond. *C. A. Austin.*

CASTEL VISCADO 3 b.c. Castle Keep 121–Myrtlegrove (Scottish Rifle 127) **52** [1989 a7g a8g 1990 a10g⁴ a10g⁵] form in maidens at Lingfield only on reappearance: may well stay beyond 1¼m: blinkered final start: sold 900 gns Ascot February Sales. *J. L. Dunlop.*

CASTLE BYTHAM 3 br.c. Goldhills Pride 105–Lucy Brotherton (Pieces of — Eight 128) [1989 8g 1990 8m] backward, behind in maiden at Leicester and seller (coltish and sweating) at Doncaster. *Miss P. Hall.*

CASTLE CAPERS 3 b.g. Castle Keep 121–Woodland Frolic (Hittite Glory 125) — [1989 NR 1990 12g 12d] second foal: half-brother to 1988 2-y-o 6f sellers winner Moor Frolicking (by Morston): dam unraced from family of Juliette Marny, Julio Mariner and Scintillate: well behind in late-season seller and maiden at Folkestone. *D. W. P. Arbuthnot.*

CASTLE CARY 4 gr.f. Castle Keep 121–Tibouchina 75 (Runnymede 123) [1989 **48** 5s² 6s 5.8m² 5f⁴ 5f 5g 5g 7.6m⁵ 6g 6g⁶ 7g 1990 6m 5g⁴ 5f⁵ 5m⁵ 6m³ 5m 6m 5m⁴ 6g 5m² 5g a5g⁶] workmanlike filly: carries condition: has a quick action: poor sprint maiden: acts on any going: sometimes bandaged off-hind: doesn't find much off bridle. *M. Blanshard.*

CASTLE CLOWN 5 ch.g. Castle Keep 121–Peteona 97 (Welsh Saint 126) [1989 **86** 10d² 10m* 11f 12g 1990 10g² 11m⁵ 11.5m³] tall, lengthy gelding: fair handicapper: not seen out after June: ideally suited by strongly-run race over 1¼m: yet to show his best form on extremes of going: usually wears visor. *Lady Herries.*

CASTLE COURAGEOUS 3 b.g. Castle Keep 121–Peteona 97 (Welsh Saint **90** 126) [1989 7s⁴ 7f³ 8g* 1990 8m⁶ 12m³ 12m 12m] leggy, angular gelding: good walker: fair performer: good 25/1-third of 10 in £7,300 event at Newbury in May, easily best effort in handicaps: stumbled 4f out at York on third outing: stays 1½m. *Lady Herries.*

CASTLE DANCE 4 b.f. Castle Keep 121–Coming Out (Fair Season 120) [1989 — 8d 8.5m⁶ 10.1m 10g 8m 13.3d 1990 10.6s 10g 16m] smallish, sparely-made filly: modest at best: little worthwhile form for long time: should stay beyond 1m: acts on good to firm and dead going: sold 1,000 gns Ascot September Sales. *G. B. Balding.*

CASTLE GALAH 3 b.f. Castle Keep 121–My Pink Parrot (Pirate King 129) — [1989 NR 1990 8m 7d a8g] tall, leggy filly: half-sister to several winners here and abroad, including fair 1978 2-y-o 5f winner Leo Vert (by Ballymoss): dam never ran: always behind in maidens and claimer. *S. Woodman.*

CASTLE MAID 3 b.f. Castle Keep 121–Village Lass (No Mercy 126) [1989 NR — 1990 7m 7m 6g 8m⁵] rangy, workmanlike filly: sixth foal: half-sister to modest 1m and 1¼m winner Sunapa's Owlet (by Derrylin): dam never ran: no worthwhile form in minor events and maiden. *L. G. Cottrell.*

CASTLE MERLIN 2 ch.c. (Apr 14) Scottish Reel 123–Aunt Winnie (Wolver **61** Hollow 126) [1990 7m a8g a7g a8g⁵] 3,100F, 4,000Y: leggy colt: half-brother to 6f seller winner Sing Galvo Sing (by Music Boy) and a winner abroad: dam poor maiden: plating-class maiden: ran creditably for apprentice final start: will be better suited by 1¼m. *R. J. Muddle.*

CASTLE ROCK 7 b.g. Shirley Heights 130–Fotheringay 101 (Right Royal V 135) — [1989 NR 1990 12f 12m⁶ 14g] big, rangy, angular gelding: has been operated on for a chipped knee: comfortable winner of seller only start at 5 yrs: sign of retaining ability only when sixth in Folkestone handicap: suited by 1½m: acts on dead going: takes keen hold, and has worn severe noseband. *Lady Herries.*

CASTLE SECRET 4 b.c. Castle Keep 121–Baffle 87 (Petingo 135) [1989 10s 12f **85 §** 12f4 12g* 14m* 16g² 1990 14s 16.2d* 16m 14m⁴ 16.2g³] quite attractive colt: moderate mover with a quick action: fair handicapper: won slowly-run £9,000 event at Ascot in June, coming back on bridle to lead 2f out, then edging left: looked ungenerous next 2 outings, coltish on last: stays 2m: possibly unsuited by soft going nowadays, acts on any other: blinkered last 2 starts: sold 14,000 gns Newmarket Autumn Sales: one to treat with caution. *J. L. Dunlop.*

CASTLE SERENADE 3 b.g. Castle Keep 121–Nusaro 68 (Sun Prince 128) [1989 NR 1990 12d] sixth reported foal: dam 2-y-o 5f winner: tailed off in maiden at Folkestone in November. *A. Moore.*

CASTORET 4 b.g. Jalmood (USA) 126–Blaskette 99 (Blast 125) [1989 8s³ 8f⁶ 87 10.1m⁶ 8d 1990 8g 8g⁶ 10s* a10g⁵] useful-looking gelding: showed much improved form when winning handicap at Lingfield in October easily by 6 lengths: needs testing conditions at 1¼m, and will be suited by further. *J. W. Hills.*

CASUAL FLASH (USA) 3 ch.c. Sharpen Up 127–Annie Edge 118 (Nebbiolo 74 125) [1989 7f⁵ 7g 1990 10f³ 10f⁴ 11.7m 16.5m² 16.2d* 16.2f⁵ 16.2g* 16g⁶ 16f 17.1m⁵ 14d⁵] leggy, sparely-made colt: has a round action: modest performer: won handicap at Haydock in July and 4-runner amateurs handicap at Beverley in August: well beaten in listed race at Baden-Baden and handicaps last 4 starts: uncertain to stay beyond 16.5f: yet to race on soft going, acts on any other. *I. A. Balding.*

CATBALLOU 3 b.f. Tina's Pet 121–Blue Brocade 91 (Reform 132) [1989 6g³ 1990 — 6m 6f⁶] angular filly: modest form when third at Newmarket, easily best effort in maidens: should have been suited by 7f: dead. *J. A. R. Toller.*

CATHEDRAL PEAK 6 b.g. Tyrnavos 129–Honeypot Lane 91 (Silly Season — 127) [1989 10f⁵ 10m 10m* 10m 12d 10f 10.6m 1990 10.2f] tall gelding: below his best since winning apprentice handicap at Kempton as 5-y-o: probably best at around 1¼m: acts on any going. *C. Spares.*

CATHERINE PARR (USA) 3 br.f. Riverman (USA) 131–Regal Exception 109 (USA) 126 (Ribot 142) [1989 6.5d³ 8g² 1990 10s⁵ 9g³ 8d³ 10g² 10g⁵ 8s⁴ 8s²] closely related to good-class middle-distance stayer Orban (by Irish River) and half-sister to several winners, including smart French 1m and 10.5f winner Twilight Hour (by Raise A Native): dam won Irish Oaks and was fourth in Arc: very useful performer but still a maiden: placed in Prix d'Astarte and Prix de Psyche at Deauville third and fourth starts: contested minor event at Maisons-Laffite penultimate one: stays 1¼m: acts on dead ground. *A. Fabre, France.*

CATHERINE'S LAD 2 b.c. (Mar 22) Nicholas Bill 125–Wellington Bear — (Dragonara Palace (USA) 115) [1990 6g] 10,500 2-y-o: good-topped colt: fourth foal: half-brother to 3-y-o Freddie's Star (by Tina's Pet), 7f winner at 2 yrs: dam never ran: backward and green, slowly away in maiden at Ripon in June. *A. W. Potts.*

CATHOS (FR) 5 b.g. Bellman (FR) 123–Charming Doll (Don (ITY) 123) [1989 77 10v⁶ 10d 13.3f⁶ 10.6s a10g 1990 a12g⁴ a16g² a13g* 12f 14g 14m 12g* 16m⁵ 16m⁵ 12f² 10m* 14m² 11.5m² 12f* 12.2f* 15.5f² 10.6d⁵ 11s 12s a16g a10g] leggy gelding: has a rather round action: modest handicapper: won at Lingfield in March, Carlisle (amateurs) in June and in ladies events at Pontefract in August and Brighton and Catterick (making all) in September: ran poorly last 4 outings: stays 2m: unsuited by soft going, acts on any other: has worn blinkers, but not for present trainer: often starts slowly: sweating and on toes sixth start: sold afterwards out of J. Old's stable 4,900 gns Ascot May Sales. *D. A. Wilson.*

CATIMINI 5 ch.g. Coquelin (USA) 121–Espadrille 81 (Hotfoot 126) [1989 10m 6f 36 9f 7g a6g 1990 a6g⁵ a8g⁶ a7g³ a7g a8g a7g] small, sparely-made gelding: showed signs of retaining ability in handicaps at Southwell in January: no form after, virtually pulled up (lame) final start: stays 7f: blinkered once at 3 yrs and last 4 starts: sold 720 gns Doncaster September Sales: may be unsatisfactory temperamentally. *D. W. Chapman.*

CATUNDRA (IRE) 2 ch.f. (Mar 18) Far North (CAN) 120–'tis A Kitten (USA) 70 p (Tisab (USA)) [1990 a7g*] 20,000Y: leggy, angular filly: fourth foal: half-sister to 3-y-o 7f winner Elemis (by Sir Ivor) and a winner in USA: dam winner at up to 9f, from good family: won maiden at Southwell in November by a short head, clear, from Pims Classic, tracking leader, outpaced 2f out then strong run to lead line: sure to improve. *W. Jarvis.*

CAUGHT UNAWARES 3 ch.g. Longleat (USA) 109–Mrs Cullumbine 60 (Silly 61 Season 127) [1989 6f² 6g³ 1990 8g⁴ 10.1m⁶ 8m 10f⁶ 10g⁴] leggy, angular gelding: quite modest maiden: stayed 1¼m: seemed best with give in the ground: trained until after penultimate start by S. Norton: dead. *J. R. Jenkins.*

CAUSLEY 5 br.g. Swing Easy (USA) 126–Four Lawns 77 (Forlorn River 124) 81 [1989 8.2m 7.5m⁶ 8f⁵ 8f 8.2g² 8.5m³ 8m⁵ 8.5g⁴ 10.6m 8.2d* 8.2g³ a8g* 1990 a8g⁴ 9f² 8m⁶ 8.2f³ 10d⁴ 8f² 8.2s 8g* 8.2s* 8m² 8.2f² 8.2d² 8m 7g³ 7d³ 8d] good-topped, workmanlike gelding: has a round action: fair handicapper: had fine season: won at Carlisle (making all) in June and Haydock week later: effective at 7f to 1m: acts on any going except possibly heavy: blinkered once at 4 yrs and seventh outing: good mount for inexperienced rider: suited by forcing tactics: has been mulish at stalls: tough and consistent. *B. A. McMahon.*

CAVALCANTI (USA) 4 b.g. Sir Ivor 135–Forelie 88 (Formidable (USA) 125) **85 ?** [1989 10f 1990 14f³ 10m 12.2d³ a12g] rangy, good sort: fair form at best: soon struggling in Southwell claimer final start: suited by further than 1½m: often bandaged near-hind: sold out of H. Cecil's stable 10,000 gns Newmarket Autumn Sales after third outing. *J. A. Glover.*

CAVALLA 3 b.f. The Brianstan 128–Bombay Duck 65 (Ballyciptic) [1989 9f² a8g³ **63** a8g³ 1990 a8g* a8g] strong, good-topped filly: won apprentice handicap at Southwell in January: always behind after slow start in handicap there 4½ months later: stayed 1m: got loose at stalls and withdrawn once at 2 yrs: dead. *R. Hollinshead.*

CAVEAT VENDOR 2 b.c. (May 26) Auction Ring (USA) 123–Star Court 102 **69 d** (Aureole 132) [1990 8f³ 8m³ 7d 7d] workmanlike colt: eighth foal: half-brother to several winners, including Ribblesdale winner Queen Midas (by Glint of Gold) and useful 1978 2-y-o 7f winner Etoile des Indes (by Kashmir II): dam 7f winner, is half-sister to Abwah and Owen Dudley: third in Thirsk maiden on debut: failed to reproduce that form: may well stay beyond 1m. *W. J. Pearce.*

CAXTON (USA) 3 b.c. Halo (USA)–Printing Press (USA) (In Reality) [1989 7f⁴ — 8m 1990 10f⁵ 10.2h⁶ 9g⁵ 10f 10.2f⁴] quite attractive colt: quite modest maiden: should stay beyond 9f: possibly unsuited by firm going nowadays: ran poorly in blinkers final start: has joined G. Moore. *I. A. Balding.*

CAYMAN BRAC (USA) 3 ch.c. Miswaki 124–Biting Wit 69 (Vitriolic) [1989 NR **60** 1990 6f⁶ 6m⁴ 6m 6f²] $55,000Y: neat, strong colt: fourth foal: half-brother to 2 minor winners: dam 5f winner bred to stay at least 1m, is closely related to 1000 Guineas winner Waterloo: quite modest maiden: not seen out after July. *H. R. A. Cecil.*

CAYMANIA 4 b.f. Wolver Hollow 126–Takachiho's Girl (Takachiho 111) [1989 — 10g 8m 1990 10g a12g] lengthy, workmanlike filly: little indication of ability. *P. Howling.*

CECILIANO (USA) 4 ch.c. Irish River (FR) 131–Derly (FR) (Lyphard (USA) **91** 132) [1989 12d* 12m 12f⁵ 12v 1990 12g³ 22d⁴ 16.1f⁶ a18g* 17.6g] big, rangy, heavy-topped colt: won handicap at Southwell in August: clear fourth to Regal Reform in Queen Alexandra Stakes at Royal Ascot: broke fetlock and put down at Haydock in September: appeared to stay extreme distances and to need an easy surface. *P. A. Kelleway.*

CEDRELA (USA) 2 ch.c. (Feb 7) Assert 134–Hot Princess 101 (Hot Spark 126) **74** [1990 6g⁴ 7f² 7f* 7m³ 7m] $65,000Y: rather leggy colt: first reported foal: dam Irish 5f to 7f winner later won in USA: modest performer: made all in maiden at Brighton (by 7 lengths) in August: will stay 1m: visored or blinkered final 4 starts: sold 17,500 gns Newmarket Autumn Sales. *W. J. Haggas.*

CEE-EN-CEE 6 b.g. Junius (USA) 124–Lady Red Rose 87 (Pitskelly 122) [1989 **64** 7.6f⁵ 5.8h 6f 6m* 6m⁵ 6g⁶ 6m* 6m² 5m² 6m 6m 6m⁴ 5d a6g⁶ 6m 6f³ 6m² 6m 7g 6m⁵ 6m² 6g² 5m⁴ 6f⁵ 7f³ 5m 6m 7m⁶ 5.8f* 7g* 6g 5m 7g] workmanlike gelding: has a round action: quite modest handicapper: successful in September at Bath and in very close finish to 18-runner event (apprentice ridden) at Kempton: faced stiff tasks last 3 outings: effective at 6f and 7f: acts particularly well on a sound surface: best in blinkers or visor. *M. McCourt.*

CEE-JAY-AY 3 gr.g. Free State 125–Raffinrula 75 (Raffingora 130) [1989 6m 5h² **75** 6h 7m⁴ 7.5f 8g⁶ 1990 9s 7m² 7g 7f² 8m 7g² 7m* 7.6m* 8f* a7g* 7m³ 7.6g⁶ 7d] smallish, workmanlike gelding: easy mover: modest performer: had excellent summer, successful in seller (no bid) at Warwick and handicaps at Chester (apprentices), Warwick and Southwell, coming from rear to lead post second and third occasions: stays 1m: acts on firm going: became rather unbalanced for 7-lb claimer eleventh start: usually slowly away. *J. Berry.*

CELERY SALT (USA) 2 ch.c. (May 6) Miswaki (USA) 124–Sea Flavour (Sea — Bird II 145) [1990 6f 6g] $55,000F, IR 32,000Y: compact colt: half-brother to several winners in France and Italy, including Derby Italiano third Sea's Valley (by Val de L'Orne): dam unraced half-sister to Enstone Spark: on toes, chased leaders around 4f and not knocked about at Goodwood in August, first and better effort in maidens. *J. L. Dunlop.*

CELESTIAL GUEST (USA) 3 b.c. Northjet 136–Tobira Celeste (USA) (Ribot **87** 142) [1989 8m 1990 10f³ 12f* 14m⁴ 12m] sturdy colt: has a fluent action: won maiden at Leicester in July, hanging right: appeared to run well when well-beaten last of 4 to

River God in Goodwood listed race, behind facing stiff task in £7,600 handicap at Newmarket: seems to stay 1¾m. *R. Guest.*

CELESTIAL SKY 2 ch.c. (Feb 29) Bairn (USA) 126–Angels Are Blue 73 **67 p** (Stanford 121§) [1990 5g⁶ 6m 5m⁵ 6g⁴ 7.3g⁴] 7,000F, 15,000Y: sturdy, workmanlike colt: carries condition: has scope: first foal: dam 5.8f winner, is half-sister to one-time smart sprinter Polykratis: ran well in nurseries final 2 starts: likely to prove as effective at 6f as 7f. *P. W. Harris.*

CELIBACY 3 b.f. Thatching 131–Une Folie (FR) 110 (Frere Basile (FR) 129) **71** [1989 NR 1990 7g 8f²] 15,500Y: leggy, angular filly: poor walker and mover: second foal: half-sister to lightly-raced French 4-y-o Petite Folie (by Salmon Leap): dam suited by 1½m: odds on, looked ill at ease on ground when second of 6, not handling bend well and edging left over 1f out, to Circus Feathers in maiden at Warwick in May: will be suited by further: sold to join N. Callaghan 2,000 gns Newmarket Autumn Sales. *H. R. A. Cecil.*

CELLATICA (USA) 3 ch.f. Sir Ivor 135–Sweetsider (USA) (Topsider (USA)) **67** [1989 6g 7s⁵ 8m 1990 8.2s 10f⁴ a12g² 12f⁶ 10.8m³] lengthy, rather angular filly: modest maiden: easily best efforts second and third starts: stays 1½m: acts on firm going. *M. McCormack.*

CELLYPH 3 gr.g. Bellypha 130–Such Style 80 (Sassafras (FR) 135) [1989 NR — 1990 8m 9m] 31,000Y: half-brother to 9f winner Chehana (by Posse), Irish middle-distance winner Black Tokk (by Blakeney) and a winner in Italy by Persepolis: dam, daughter of half-sister to Vaguely Noble, was placed over 1½m on only start: burly, tailed off at Newmarket in £6,700 maiden (very green to post, trained by R. Guest) and claimer 5 months later: sold 850 gns Newmarket Autumn Sales. *Lord John FitzGerald.*

CELTIC BHOY 4 b.g. Red Sunset 120–Nighty Night (Sassafras (FR) 135) [1989 **60** 10v⁵ 11.5f 12f 12m³ 12f* 13f* 14f⁵ 12f* 12g² 10f³ 12f⁴ 12f³ 1990 a13g* 14.8m⁶ a12g⁶ 12m³] strong, close-coupled gelding: carries condition: quite modest handicapper: won amateurs event at Lingfield in March: should stay 1¾m: acts on firm and dead going: slowly away on all-weather. *P. Mitchell.*

CELTIC CHIMES 6 ch.m. Celtic Cone 116–Dyna Bell 62 (Double Jump 131) — [1989 NR 1990 7m² 9m⁵] stocky mare: moderate mover: little sign of ability: blinkered on reappearance, visored and bandaged second outing. *A. W. Denson.*

CENTENARY STAR 5 b.g. Broadsword (USA) 104–Tina's Gold 66 (Goldhill **40** 125) [1989 12.2m 12.2g 16g⁵ 1990 a12g² 16m⁵ a14g⁶] leggy gelding: 33/1, first form ½-length second of 15 in handicap at Southwell in August: will be suited by extreme test of stamina: usually apprentice ridden: sold to join Mrs G. Reveley 6,000 gns Doncaster November Sales and later won over hurdles. *R. Hollinshead.*

CENTERLAND (USA) 3 ch.c. Green Forest (USA) 134–Pompoes (DEN) 117 **101** (Belmont (FR)) [1989 NR 1990 6m⁴ 6f* 7f* 6f* 6m* 6m⁴ 8g 5g³ 6m] lengthy, angular colt: moderate walker: sixth foal: half-brother to Three Generations (by Alydar), 7f and 1m winner in France later graded stakes placed at up to 8.5f, and Glittering Dawn (by Grey Dawn II), minor stakes winner at up to 9f: dam, outstanding 5.5f to 7f winner in Denmark and Sweden and later placed in good company in France, stayed 9f well: won maiden at Lingfield and minor events at Folkestone, Lingfield and Yarmouth in under 6 weeks in late-summer: in frame afterwards in listed race at Newmarket and £7,000 contest at Newbury: may prove ideally suited by 7f. useful. *M. Moubarak.*

CERTAIN CREATOR (USA) 3 b.c. Alleged (USA) 138–Producer (USA) 130 **79** (Nashua) [1989 NR 1990 12m⁵ 14g² a12g* 12g] 21,000Y: sturdy colt: turns off-fore in: half-brother to Irish 6f and 1¼m winner Dancing Goddess (by Nijinsky) and Irish sprint winner Music And Dance (by Northern Dancer), both useful: dam second in Irish Oaks but better at shorter distances and won Prix de la Foret and in USA: won maiden at Southwell in June by 8 lengths, making virtually all: well beaten in £15,000 handicap at Royal Ascot: stays 1½m well. *Lord John FitzGerald.*

CETONG 4 gr.g. Petong 126–My Cecilia 83 (Prevailing (USA)) [1989 6m⁴ 5.8m — 8.2m⁴ 6f⁵ 8m³ 5.8m⁴ 6f 6m 1990 a6g a7g 8f] angular, workmanlike gelding: quite modest handicapper as 3-y-o: ran poorly final outing (March) in 1990: stays 6f: yet to race on a soft surface: sometimes blinkered: has sweated, and tends to get on toes: wears bandages behind. *P. Calver.*

CHAD GREEN (IRE) 2 ch.c. (Apr 24) Coquelin (USA) 121–Tejah (Gay **40** Fandango (USA) 132) [1990 5m 5m⁵ 6g 6m⁵ 7m⁶ 5d a7g] IR 4,600F, IR 4,000Y: small, sturdy colt: second reported foal: dam closely related to Italian Derby winner

Tommy Way: plater: ran creditably when blinkered and sweating penultimate start. stays 6f. *J. D. Czerpak.*

CHAFF 3 b.c. Final Straw 127–Silky (USA) 112 (Nijinsky (CAN) 138) [1989 5m 7m 1990 7m 8m 8.2g] smallish, angular colt: shows a quick action: no worthwhile form, in July handicap final start: should stay 1m: sold to join D. Morris 1,200 gns Newmarket Autumn Sales. *G. Wragg.* —

CHAILEY 3 b.f. Little Wolf 127–Polygon (Tarboosh (USA)) [1989 NR 1990 12f 12f 12m 12d a14g] 2,000Y: big, close-coupled filly: half-sister to 1983 2-y-o 6f seller winner The Four Ays (by Kala Shikari) and a winning hurdler: dam winning hurdler: seems of little account: sold 1,700 gns Ascot November Sales. *M. Bell.*

CHAKALAK 2 b.c. (Mar 10) Damister (USA) 123–Wig And Gown (Mandamus 120) [1990 8m 7s6] 11,000Y: medium-sized, angular colt: moderate mover: half-brother to several winners, including useful stayers Halsbury (by Exbury) and Drumhead (by High Line) and useful 1976 2-y-o 6f winner Freight Forwarder (by Calpurnius), later successful jumper: dam unraced: soundly beaten in autumn maidens at Leicester (moved badly down) and Lingfield (late progress): will be much better suited by 1¼m: may do better. *S. Dow.* —

CHALKHILL BLUE 5 b.m. Dunphy 124–Lady Probus 70§ (Shantung 132) [1989 15.5s 8f 12.5f 1990 10m 10f] leggy mare: of little account: visored once: often sweats. *D. C. Jermy.* —

CHAMBROS 3 ch.g. Krayyan 117–Chilcombe (Morston (FR) 125) [1989 6m 6m2 6g 8.2f3 9g 8.2g5 1990 11.7g* 11m3 12m2 13.3m3] medium-sized gelding: moderate mover: fair performer: first past post in handicaps at Windsor in May and Salisbury (swerved left over 1f out, demoted for interference) in June: not entirely discredited in £11,500 handicap at Newbury in July final start: suited by 1½m: probably acts on firm going: has run creditably for 7-lb claimer: tends to wander under pressure. *J. W. Hills.* **80**

CHAMPAGNE CHARLIE 13 br.g. Charlottown 127–The Guzzler 69 (Behistoun 131) [1989 NR 1990 18g] plating-class staying handicapper as 7-y-o: 100/1, bandaged and apprentice ridden, behind in slowly-run race at Ripon, only subsequent outing on flat. *Mrs S. M. Austin.* —

CHAMPAGNE GOLD 3 ch.c. Bairn (USA) 126–Halkissimo 61 (Khalkis 127) [1989 5g2 5s* 5g* 6g* 6g* 6g2 6m5 8d* 1990 8g6 7.2f4 10.8m3 8m 9g 8d 12v] leggy, rather sparely-made colt: turns fore-feet out: has a quick, round action: rated 106 when winning listed race at Goodwood on final start at 2 yrs: didn't reproduce that in varied events in 1990: suited by 1m: acts on soft going, probably unsuited by top-of-the-ground: tends to be on toes: winning hurdler for J. McConnochie. *Denys Smith.* —

CHAMPION GIRL 4 b. or br.f. Blazing Saddles (AUS)–Mercy Cure 81 (No Mercy 126) [1989 5s 5s 5f 5m3 5m 5g6 5m 5.1f 5.1g a6g 1990 a6g3 a7g2 a6g4 a7g4 a6g a6g* a7g5 a7g6 a7g6 7f2 8f 7f 7h6 a7g 7m a7g 8f 6g 7g] workmanlike, sparely-made filly: moderate mover: won handicap at Southwell in February: ran moderately after second at Thirsk in April, once looking thoroughly ungenuine: stays 7f: acts on firm going: usually wears blinkers: has often sweated: sold 1,000 gns Newmarket Autumn Sales: best left alone. *A. Bailey.* **49 d**

CHANCE ALL (FR) 2 ch.f. (Apr 16) Glenstal (USA) 118–Auction Bridge 76 (Auction Ring (USA) 123) [1990 5m2 5m* 5m* 5m5 6d6] 9,000F, 13,000Y: lengthy, useful-looking filly: sixth foal: closely related to quite modest 1¼m winner Malmunster (by Lomond) and half-sister to 2 winners, including untrustworthy 1½m winner Auction Fever (by Hello Gorgeous): dam 1m winner, is half-sister to Young Generation: fair performer: won maiden auction (making all) at Windsor in July and nursery at Sandown in September: should stay 6f: possibly unsuited by dead ground: got loose at start, bolted and was withdrawn on intended debut. *C. F. Wall.* **88**

CHANCE REPORT 2 b.f. (Apr 22) Beldale Flutter (USA) 130–Report 'em (USA) 51 (Staff Writer (USA)) [1990 a5g5 5m4 5f5 5g 6m 5g 6v] 1,000Y: rather leggy filly: first foal: dam maiden form only at 6f: poor form in varied races: should prove suited by 6f+: best form on a sound surface. *F. H. Lee.* **49**

CHANDANNE 3 ch.f. Ballad Rock 122–Affirmation (FR) (Affirmed (USA)) [1989 5d4 5s3 5f4 6f 6g3 1990 6f 7f 5g2 6g5 5g5 6m 8.2m 8.3m3 9f5 8.3g5 10.8m a8g 7f 8.2s] sturdy, compact filly: moderate mover: moderate plater: well below form last 4 starts: stays 1m: acts on good to firm ground: has run creditably when edgy, moderately for apprentice. *T. Casey.* **43**

CHANDLERY (USA)   2 b. or br.c. (Mar 2) Woodman (USA) 126–Sail Loft 74   **78** p
(Shirley Heights 130) [1990 7m3] $190,000Y: strong, good sort: fourth foal: dam
maiden suited by 1½m, is half-sister to Julio Mariner, Juliette Marny and Scintillate:
heavily-backed favourite, over 6 lengths third of 16, unable to quicken from 2f out
and not knocked about unduly, to Sapieha in maiden at Newmarket in October:
showed a quick action: will stay at least 1¼m: sure to improve, and win races. *H. R.
A. Cecil.*

CHAN FU   5 b.g. Kafu 120–Chanrossa (High Top 131) [1989 12m5 14.8f6 1990   —
a10g] leggy, rather sparely-made gelding: has a round action: poor maiden: stays
1½m: acts on firm and dead going. *J. E. Long.*

CHANGE GUARD   4 b.f. Day Is Done 115–Mittens (Run The Gantlet (USA))   —
[1989 8g4 9f 10f5 1990 13.8m6 8f] leggy, angular filly: moderate mover: modest
maiden at 2 yrs: lightly raced and below form subsequently: stays 1m: acts on soft
going. *Roy Robinson.*

CHANNON HILL (IRE)   2 b.f. (Apr 29) Red Sunset 120–Sabura (Busted 134)   — p
[1990 7s] 1,500Y: leggy filly: half-sister to 1¼m seller winner Serious Business (by
Sallust) and a winner in Italy: dam Irish 5f winner: ridden by 7-lb claimer and on
toes, slowly away and never better than mid-division in 22-runner maiden at
Doncaster in October: can do better. *R. Hollinshead.*

CHANNOR   3 b.f. Norwick (USA) 120–Channing Girl 73 (Song 132) [1989 6g 8m   —
1990 10f 11.7h 8m 10f5] leggy filly: poor form, in selling handicap final start. *K. O.
Cunningham-Brown.*

CHANTRY BARTLE   4 ch.g. Say Primula 107–Sallametti (USA) 69 (Giacometti   **45**
130) [1989 7f 8.5f 8f 10f 12g2 12.5f* 12g6 1990 12g3 13.8m 12m6 12g5 12g6 16f3 15m*
16m3 16m5 15m3] sparely-made gelding: won handicap at Edinburgh in August:
stays 2m: acts on firm ground: ridden by claimer last 4 starts: winning hurdler in
September and October. *C. W. Thornton.*

CHAPALA   3 ch.f. Pharly (FR) 130–Amatrice (Appiani II 128) [1989 NR 1990 8.3f3   **85**
8m* 8g2 8m4 a10g] quite good-topped filly: seventh reported foal: half-sister to
useful Irish middle-distance filly Cienga (by Tarboosh) and fairly useful Irish 7f
winner Soluce (by Junius): dam won over 1½m in Ireland: favourite, won maiden at
Warwick in August: second in handicap (led over 2f out until post) at Sandown,
clearly best subsequent effort: should stay further than 1m. *A. C. Stewart.*

CHAPALIGHT   2 b. or br.f. (Apr 4) Chaparly (FR)–June Delight (Hickory   —
Dickory Dock) [1990 5m 8m] second reported living foal: dam unraced: sire French
middle-distance half-brother to Pharly: soundly beaten in minor event at Bath and
an apprentice seller at Warwick in autumn. *R. Curtis.*

CHAPEL CHIMES   4 b.f. Song 132–Lady Spey 55 (Sir Gaylord) [1989 8s4 9d3   —
12m a8g 10g a8g a10g6 1990 a14g5 a16g a13g5] angular, sparely-made filly: has a
round action: bad maiden: stays 1¼m: visored once at 3 yrs: sold 1,350 gns Ascot
April Sales. *P. J. Feilden.*

CHAPLINS CLUB (USA)   10 ch.g. Parade of Stars (USA)–Nautical Rose   **59**
(USA) (Henrijan) [1989 6.1f 6f 6f 6g2 6g4 6f 5g 6m2 6f 5m* 6s2 6m 6s5 6s3 1990 6f
6m5 6g6 6g 6g3 a6g 6m 6g 5d 7g 7d 8.2d 6s] small, strong gelding: one-time fairly
useful handicapper: should prove as effective at 7f as shorter: ideally suited by an
easy surface: best with strong handling: has hung and is blinkered off-side only: boot
covered up. *D. W. Chapman.*

CHAPMAN'S PEAK   3 b.g. Top Ville 129–Cape Race (USA) 88 (Northern   **64**
Dancer) [1989 8m2 8g a7g3 1990 13.3d3 12d2 12f4 8g] compact, quite attractive
gelding: modest maiden here: sent to race in Scandinavia, successful over 11f and
1½m on heavy going and second in Oslo Cup at Ovrevoll in September. *D. Morley.*

CHARACTER   2 ch.c. (Jan 30) Never So Bold 135–Ravaro 96 (Raga Navarro   **87** p
(ITY) 119) [1990 7g 7m2 8d*] IR 35,000Y: lengthy colt: has plenty of scope: first foal:
dam Irish stayer also useful hurdler: progressive colt: favourite, won 22-runner
maiden at Ayr comfortably by 2½ lengths from Matahif, leading 1f out and running
on well: will stay 1¼m: sent to race in California. *Mrs J. R. Ramsden.*

CHARBATTE (FR)   4 b.f. In Fijar (USA) 121–Evonsville (FR) (Val de Loir 133)   —
[1989 8m4 7m3 1990 8v 8g] big, leggy filly: fairly useful form in minor event at
Newmarket and listed race (didn't handle turn) at York as 3-y-o: ran poorly in
spring: stays 1m: seems unsuited by heavy going: gave trouble at stalls second
intended outing at 3 yrs: wears bandages. *M. Moubarak.*

CHARCOAL BURNER   5 br.g. Royal Match 117–Resist 55 (Reliance II 137)   **41** §
[1989 7m3 7f 7m4 8.2g 7g 7f* 7m 10.2f2 10f6 1990 10.8m 11.7f5 11.7g6 10m 8.2m4

Walmac International Geoffrey Freer Stakes, Newbury—
Charmer shows the best turn of foot in a slowly-run affair

7m² 8m 7f 8h² 7m³ 9g² 7m 10.2m] compact gelding: poor handicapper: effective at 7f and was staying on over 11.7f second outing: acts on hard going: seems best without visor: often pulls hard: has gone freely to post and been taken down early: not one to trust implicitly. *B. R. Millman.*

CHARDEN 4 b.g. Touching Wood (USA) 127–Fighting Lady 104 (Chebs Lad 120) **75**
[1989 10f⁶ 10.1m⁵ 10f² 14m² 11.7m⁶ 16m 1990 12m* 14m 12g 11.5m⁴ 14g 12g²] close-coupled, angular gelding: won for only time in handicap at Kempton in May: stays 1¾m: has raced only on sound surface: sold 9,000 gns Newmarket Autumn Sales: inconsistent. *D. R. C. Elsworth.*

CHARISMATIC LADY (IRE) 2 b.f. (Apr 9) Alzao (USA) 117–Chrism — **p**
(Baptism 119) [1990 7g] 200,000Y: leggy, quite good-topped filly: has scope: second foal: dam Irish maiden half-sister to Shining Finish and Bright Finish: bit backward and very green, slowly away and always behind in minor event at Goodwood in September: will improve. *D. R. C. Elsworth.*

CHARLAFRIVOLA 2 br.g. (Apr 6) Persian Bold 123–Tattle 61 (St Paddy 133) **72**
[1990 6g 7f4 6m² 6m⁵ 7f³ 8m 7m² 7m 7d4] 13,500Y: rather leggy gelding: moderate walker: has a quick action: fourth foal: half-brother to 3-y-o Undertones and a winner in Scandinavia (both by Song): dam lightly-raced sister to useful middle-distance performer King's General and from family of Espresso: quite modest maiden: should be suited by at least 1m: blinkered or visored final 3 starts: sometimes on toes: inconsistent. *F. H. Lee.*

CHARLES THE GREAT 3 b.g. Vaigly Great 127–Tin Tessa 87 (Martinmas —
128) [1989 6g a8g 1990 8g] strong, angular gelding: no sign of ability in maidens and claimer: sold 1,650 gns Doncaster September Sales. *J. Wharton.*

CHARLIE DICKINS 6 b.g. Free State 125–Time of Your Life (Mount Hagen —
(FR) 127) [1989 NR 1990 13v 14s] sturdy gelding: has a round action: plating-class maiden: never dangerous in handicaps in early-summer: possibly best short of 2m: acts on good to firm and soft going: none too genuine: winning hurdler in December. *S. Mellor.*

CHARLIE'S DARLING 2 b.f. (Mar 15) Homing 130–Kip's Sister (Cawston's **50**
Clown 113) [1990 5m 5m 6g* 6m a6g 7f 8m] 1,150Y: angular filly: poor mover: second

168

foal: dam unraced: 25/1-winner of seller (bought in 11,000 gns) at Nottingham in June: no other form: should stay 7f: bandaged on debut. *J. D. Czerpak.*

CHARLOTTE AUGUSTA (USA) 3 b.f. Chief's Crown (USA)–Noble Damsel **69** (USA) (Vaguely Noble 140) [1989 NR 1990 8m⁴ 10.6s³ 10f² 8.2m⁶] $200,000Y: leggy, angular filly: has a rather round action: second known foal: dam winner at up to 11f in USA out of smart 2-y-o sprinter Tender Camilla: modest maiden: stays 1¼m: acts on any going: slowly away final start: sold 5,200 gns Newmarket December Sales. *M. R. Stoute.*

CHARLYCIA 2 b.f. (May 24) Good Times (ITY)–Gallic Law 91 (Galivanter 131) **39** [1990 7m 7f a7g³ 7m a8g 8.5m⁵] 4,100Y: leggy, rather angular filly: sister to fair 1986 2-y-o 5f winner Gallic Times and half-sister to several winners, including useful sprinter Ferriby Hall (by Malicious): dam 2-y-o 7f winner: poor plater: stays 8.5f. *Mrs G. R. Reveley.*

CHARLY PHARLY (FR) 3 b.g. Pharly (FR) 130–Burnished (Formidable **51 ?** (USA) 125) [1989 NR 1990 11f²a8g 11m⁵ 10.6d* 10.2m 15d 12s 10.5g⁵ 10.2s] 13,000Y: good-topped, workmanlike gelding: third foal: half-brother to fair sprinters Chain Shot (by Pas de Seul) and The Kings Daughter (by Indian King): dam unraced half-sister to smart miler Hadeer: disappointed after winning moderately-run apprentice handicap (hung left) at Haydock in August: will stay 1½m: acts on dead ground: has been fitted with pricker on near-side. *F. H. Lee.*

CHARMER 5 b.h. Be My Guest (USA) 126–Take Your Mark (USA) (Round **116** Table) [1989 9g³ 8m² 10g⁵ 8g⁴ 1990 12f* 12g³ 10m³ 12d⁴ 12m² 12m 13.3g* 12g] well-made, attractive horse: poor walker: moderate mover: very smart at his best: won £13,800 event at Doncaster in March and slowly-run 5-runner Walmac International Geoffrey Freer Stakes at Newbury (by 2½ lengths from Sesame) in August: in frame in pattern and listed races in between, beaten ¾ length by Sapience in slowly-run Princess of Wales's Stakes at Newmarket: suited by 1½m+: acted on firm going, seemed not at his best on dead: visored once at 4 yrs: became coltish and mulish at stalls on occasions: sometimes ran in snatches: retired to Barton Stud, near Newmarket, fee £3,000 (Oct 1st). *C. E. Brittain.*

The Dowager Lady Beaverbrook's "Charmer"

CHARMING 3 ch.f. Glenstal (USA) 118–Threes A Charm (Nebbiolo 125) [1989 **83**
NR 1990 7g 7m* 8f³ 8m 7d⁶] 4,000F: smallish, rather angular filly: has a quick
action: third foal: dam unraced granddaughter of Mrs Moss: improved considerably
when 33/1-winner of minor event at Salisbury in June and third of 5 to Tafila in
£7,400 contest at Ayr: below form in minor contests after, particularly so fourth
start: suited by 1m: acts on firm going. *P. T. Walwyn.*

CHARMING GIFT 3 b.f. Petorius 117–Aubretia (USA) (Hatchet Man (USA)) **61**
[1989 NR 1990 7m 8g 8g² 8f⁴ 8s³ 7d a8g⁴] 6,600F, 10,500Y: useful-looking filly:
moderate mover: first foal: dam, 2-y-o 7f winner, is half-sister to useful staying
2-y-o Rockfest and daughter of half-sister to very smart Glen Strae: quite modest
maiden: below form last 2 starts, in handicap on first of them: stays 1m: acts on soft
going, off course over 3 months after looking ill at ease on firm. *R. J. R. Williams.*

CHARMING REPLY (IRE) 2 b.f. (Apr 7) Prince Tenderfoot (USA) 126– **—**
Breezy Answer (On Your Mark 125) [1990 5m] IR 17,500Y: workmanlike filly: sister
to a maiden in Italy and half-sister to several winners, including quite modest miler
The Great Match (by Runnett): dam unraced half-sister to dam of Roland Gardens:
bit backward, never-dangerous seventh of 10 in maiden auction at Sandown in June:
sold 2,200 gns Doncaster October Sales. *A. A. Scott.*

CHARM TIME 3 ch.g. Good Times (ITY)–Glamorous Girl (Caliban 123) [1989 **—**
7m 7v 8g⁶ 1990 9s 12.3f⁶] tall, rangy gelding: poor form in maidens: bit backward in
April handicaps: should stay at least 9f: sold 2,200 gns Doncaster October Sales. *T.
D. Barron.*

CHART CROSS 4 b.c. Millfontaine 114–Whichcombe 79 (Huntercombe 133) **50**
[1989 8.3m 8f⁴ 9f* 10m⁵ 10h⁵ 8.2f³ 9m 8g² a7g a7g⁶ 1990 8.2m 10.8g² 10g 8.3m 9f⁴
10.8m 8m] rather leggy, angular colt: plating-class handicapper: broke blood vessel
penultimate outing: stays 10.8f: acts on firm and dead going: has worn for apprentice.
K. S. Bridgwater.

CHARTERHOUSE RACER (IRE) 2 b.f. (Apr 28) Kafu 120–Swan River 70 **—**
(Roan Rocket 128) [1990 5d] IR 8,400Y: small, lightly-made filly: fourth foal:
half-sister to useful 6f (at 2 yrs) and 1m winner Alsahiba and Irish 9f winner Krismas
River (by Kris): dam, suited by 1¼m, is out of Park Hill winner Parmelia, herself
half-sister to St Paddy: slowly away and always behind in maiden at Redcar in
October. *G. A. Huffer.*

CHASE THE DOOR 5 b. or br.g. **87**
Red Sunset 120–Clonsella Lady (High
Top 131) [1989 NR 1990 7f 9m 8f* 8.3m⁴
8h* 8h* 8m 9m⁵] strong, good-bodied
gelding: carries condition: fair handicapper: won at Brighton in June and July
(hanging left) and Bath (making all) in
August: very good fifth of 40 to Risen
Moon in Cambridgeshire at Newmarket:
suited by 1m to 9f, forcing tactics and a
sound surface: best form in blinkers. *J.
Sutcliffe.*

*Brighton Summer
Challenge Cup (Handicap)—
Chase The Door (left) is hand-timed
inside the world record for a mile
as he narrowly beats
Sno Serenade*

CHATEAU DE BERNE (USA) 3 b.c. Fit To Fight (USA)–Liberally Laced **—**
(USA) (Silent Screen (USA)) [1989 7m 6d 1990 8f 7h⁴ 7.5d 10g 9m] rangy, rather
unfurnished colt: no worthwhile form, including in handicaps: blinkered final start:
sold 600 gns Ascot November Sales. *M. A. Jarvis.*

CHATEAUNEUF 3 b.c. Niniski (USA) 125–Valois (Lyphard (USA) 132) **64**
7g 1990 8g 10m⁵ 8g⁵ 12m⁵ 14g 14d 12d⁵ 12d³] rangy, useful-looking colt: has rather
round action: quite modest maiden: suited by 1½m: acts on good to firm and dead
going: blinkered (made most) seventh outing: subsequently sold out of B. Hills's
stable 13,000 gns Newmarket Autumn Sales: winning hurdler. *R. Akehurst.*

CHATHAM ISLAND 2 ch.g. (Feb 11) Jupiter Island 126–Floreal 68 (Form- **83**
idable (USA) 125) [1990 7m⁵ 7d] unfurnished gelding: looks weak: first foal: dam

ran twice at 2 yrs: around 3 lengths fifth of 18 \ lll,,g 6f, to Environment Friend in maiden at Newmarket: around 7 length \lll\ cllth of 11, steadied start and outpaced from over 2f out, to Junk Bond i, \ l\ l,,able minor event there later in October: will stay at least 1¼m. *C. E, R \lll\l,.*

CHATTERIS \ lll,. Shareef Dancer (USA) 135–Fenella 91 (Thatch (USA) 136)   **58**
[1989 11,,f \ll b,, 1990 a7g6 12.2m5 12m6 12f* 20m 12g] smallish, sturdy gelding: m,,ll,,l \l.. mover: quite modest handicapper: won at Brighton in June: sweating, \ll,gy and faced stiff task in 2½m Ascot Stakes at Royal Ascot: burly and not given hard race at Kempton over 3 months later: likely to prove best at 1½m to 1¾m: acts on any going. *M. Madgwick.*

CHECKPOINT CHARLIE   5 b.g. Artaius (USA) 129–Clouded Issue (Manado   **68**
130) [1989 11f 8m4 10m4 12m 1990 10m6 10g6 12f* 12m2 12g3 12s] useful-looking gelding: moderate mover: modest handicapper: won at Brighton in September: stays 1½m: needs a sound surface: good mount for inexperienced rider. *J. M. P. Eustace.*

CHEDZOY   2 ch.g. (Feb 20) Niniski (USA) 125–Pine (Supreme Sovereign 119)   **— p**
[1990 8m6] third foal: half-brother to 1¼m winner Firgrove (by Relkino) and modest middle-distance maiden Flying (by Head For Heights): dam ran twice: around 12 lengths sixth of 13, slowly away, in minor event at Bath in October: will stay well: should improve. *Major W. R. Hern.*

CHEEKY POT   2 b.c. (Mar 21) Petoski 135–Pato 90 (High Top 131) [1990 7g   **70**
7.5m4 6m 8m 8d* 8d5 8.2s] compact colt: poor mover: first foal: dam 7f (at 2 yrs) and 1¼m winner, is sister to one-time very smart sprinter Crews Hill: quite modest performer: won nursery at Ayr in September: stays 1m: acts well on dead going: has run well for 7-lb claimer: visored fifth and final starts. *M. J. Camacho.*

CHEERFUL CHARLIE   3 b.c. Roscoe Blake 120–Cereum (USA) 84 (Tudor   **—**
Grey 119) [1989 NR 1990 7.2d 7d a8g5] neat colt: sixth foal: half-brother to 3 winners, including fair 1980 2-y-o 6f winner Penshiel (by Comedy Star) and French 1m winner Moi Meisie (by Free State): dam won over 5f at 2 yrs: no worthwhile form in maidens, reluctant to go to post on debut. *B. A. McMahon.*

CHEERFUL NOTE   3 b.f. Cure The Blues (USA)–Strident Note 89 (The   **—**
Minstrel (CAN) 135) [1989 NR 1990 7g 10g6 10g 10g] rather angular filly: second foal: half-sister to lightly-raced 4-y-o Rowhedge (by Tolomeo): dam, maiden best at 2 yrs, is half-sister to Teenoso and Topsy: always behind in maidens and handicap in first half of season. *G. Wragg.*

CHEERFUL TIMES   7 b.g. Faraway Times (USA) 123–Chevulgan (Cheval 117)   **65 ?**
[1989 10f* 12m* 12g2 10.2f* 14f 1990 10g3 10.5m 10g 12.3g 12g 10.6d4 10.6v 8g5] good-topped gelding: usually looks well: poor walker: much improved as 6-y-o, winning 3 handicaps: below his best in 1990: stays 1½m: acts on any going: has worn bandages: has worn a visor, but better without: often apprentice ridden: occasionally reluctant at stalls: usually finds little off bridle, and well suited by extreme waiting tactics: winning hurdler in November. *B. A. McMahon.*

CHEERING   3 b.f. Chief Singer 131–Midaan (Sallust 134) [1989 NR 1990 7g 8f4]   **—**
25,000Y: close-coupled, deep-girthed filly: second foal: dam poor half-sister to smart 1979 French 2-y-o 6.5f and 1m winner Light of Realm: promoted fourth of 19 in maiden at Kempton in May, leading 6f: very green on debut: sold 920 gns Newmarket September Sales.*J. L. Dunlop.*

CHEERING NEWS   3 b.g. Shernazar 131–Florentink (USA) (The Minstrel   **103**
(CAN) 135) [1989 NR 1990 10g* 10g* 12m* 14f2] fifth foal: half-brother to fairly useful 1988 Irish 2-y-o 7f winner Guaranteed Bonus (by Darshaan) and a winner in USA by Hello Gorgeous: dam unraced daughter of smart American filly Gala Lil: successful in maiden at Phoenix Park and IR £8,650 contest at the Curragh in April and listed race (by 2 lengths from Thetford Forest, making all) at Leopardstown in June: 5 lengths second of 5 to Thetford Forest on same terms in listed Curragh Cup: subsequently gelded: seems best at 1½m: useful. *D. K. Weld, Ireland.*

CHELSEA GIRL   4 b.f. Pas de Seul 133–Buffy (French Beige 127) [1989 10m   **103 §**
12m* 12m* 12g2 14.8m3 14.6g* 14m 18g2 1990 14g4 16m3 20d 16.1f2 16.1m4 16g* 18g4 20g2 16m] leggy filly: moderate mover: useful stayer: won strongly-run 5-runner listed event at York in August by 6 lengths (flattered) from Tyrone Bridge, challenging tiring horses 2f out: in frame after in Doncaster Cup (bit mulish at stalls) and Ciga Prix Gladiateur at Longchamp: seems suited by a sound surface: gradually lost interest in the game, starting very slowly at York and next 2 outings, then virtually refusing to race final one: one to treat with caution: sold 49,000 gns Newmarket December Sales. *M. A. Jarvis.*

CHELSEA MORNING 2 b.c. (Mar 16) Sayf El Arab (USA) 127–Chezzy Girl   –
(Manor Farm Boy 114) [1990 5f⁴ 5m⁶] 2,000F, 1,000Y: leggy colt: has a quick action:
second foal: half-brother to plating-class 1989 2-y-o Absolute Madness (by
Absalom), subsequently winner abroad: dam, poor on flat, placed over hurdles:
tailed off in seller (4 ran) and minor event (blinkered) in spring. *N. Bycroft.*

CHELSWORTH 2 b.f. (Feb 12) Never So Bold 135–Ash Ridge (USA) 93 (Bold   **67**
Reason) [1990 6f⁵ 6m² 7m³] compact filly: good walker: fifth foal: half-sister to Irish
12.8f winner Live Ash (by Electric): dam 2-y-o 6f winner later suited by 1¼m, is
daughter of Favoletta: placed in maidens at Nottingham and Sandown (running on
well, never dangerous) in September: will stay 1m. *G. Wragg.*

CHEREN LADY 3 br.f. Comedy Star (USA) 121–Lilly Lee Lady (USA) (Shecky   –
Greene (USA)) [1989 7g 7d 1990 10.5m⁶ 12g 7.6d 10d] workmanlike filly: of little
account: blinkered last 2 starts. *R. Curtis.*

CHEROKEE MAID 3 b. or br.f. Anfield 117–Hopi 68 (The Brianstan 128) [1989   –
5d 5m² 6m 5m 1990 8f 10d] smallish, lengthy filly: moderate mover: poor plater:
trained on reappearance by R. Holder. *P. S. Felgate.*

CHERRY CROWN 3 gr.f. Uncle Pokey 116–Cherry Season 62 (Silly Season   **46**
127) [1989 6f 8m 10g 1990 10f⁶ 8m 8g⁶ 10m⁶ 10m⁶ 12m² 12g⁴ 10m 12d*] big, leggy
filly: moderate mover: plater: improved form to win 22-runner handicap (sold to join
M. Pipe 10,000 gns) at Leicester in October: suited by 1½m, seemingly by a soft
surface: on toes last 2 starts. *J. F. Bottomley.*

CHERRY DANCE 2 ch.f. (Feb 26) Nordance (USA)–Cherry Picking 85   **61**
(Queen's Hussar 124) [1990 5s² 5g³ 6g* 6v] 860Y: workmanlike filly: seventh
reported foal: dam middle-distance winner: won seller (changed hands 16,500 gns)
at York in August by a neck from My Alma, quickening well 2f out then idling and
edging left: slowly away and always behind in auction event at Ayr nearly 2 months
later: will be at least as effective at 7f: sold out of C. Thornton's stable 10,500 gns
Doncaster September Sales after third start. *D. W. Chapman.*

CHERRYWOOD LASS 2 br.f. (Mar 3) Belfort (FR) 89–Rainbow Vision 73   –
(Prince Tenderfoot (USA) 126) [1990 6m 6m 6d] smallish, angular filly: second foal:
dam 2-y-o 7f winner: no worthwhile form, but showed signs of ability in Goodwood
maiden (headway when bumped 2f out, then not knocked about) final start. *R.
Curtis.*

CHERRYWOOD SAM 6 ch.h. Dublin Taxi–Tollers Rose 53 (Some Hand 119)   –
[1989 5f 5f 1990 5m 5m 5m] angular horse: showed signs of retaining a little ability
second outing: stays 6f: acts on firm going: visored once, often blinkered. *R. Curtis.*

CHESHIRE NELL 2 b.f. (Mar 16) Absalom 128–Quenlyn (Welsh Pageant 132)   **53**
[1990 5g⁴ 5g² 6d 5m 5f³ 6m³ 6g 6m⁵] 10,000Y: leggy filly: sister to a winner in
Belgium and half-sister to 5f winner Roxby Melody (by Song): dam ran 3 times at 2
yrs: plating-class maiden: will stay 7f: taken down very steadily final 4 outings. *W.
Carter.*

CHESNUT TREE (USA) 2 b.f. (Jan 26) Shadeed (USA) 135–Expansive 111   **71 p**
(Exbury 138) [1990 7g⁵] leggy, unfurnished filly: half-sister to 3 winners, including
1½m winners Salient (by High Top) and Trying For Gold (by Northern Baby): dam,
sister to very smart Example, won Ribblesdale Stakes on last of 3 starts: 5 lengths
fifth of 20, staying on in eye-catching style having been green and niggled along, in
Campestral in maiden at Newmarket in November: sure to improve, particularly
over 1m + . *W. Hastings-Bass.*

CHESTER TERRACE 6 ch.g. Crofter (USA) 124–Persian Mourne (Mourne   **41**
126) [1989 10f³ 10.8m³ 10m 11.7m⁶ 1990 12.2m³ 12m] compact gelding: moderate
mover: poor handicapper: stays 1½m: probably acts on any going: winning hurdler
in late-October. *K. S. Bridgwater.*

CHEVELEY CHIEF 2 ch.g. (Feb 25) Chief Singer 131–Hawks Nest 66   **68**
(Moulton 128) [1990 6m⁵ 6f* 6m³ 6m⁵ 7m 7m] 4,200Y: fifth foal:
dam 6f winner: quite modest performer: won maiden at Redcar in May: stays 6f. *T.
Fairhurst.*

CHEVEUX MITCHELL 3 ch.c. Dunbeath (USA) 127–Hide Out (Habitat 134)   **82**
[1989 7f⁵ 7m 7m⁶ 7f* 9g 8f⁴ 7g 1990 7f⁵ 6g* 7m 7f⁵ 7m⁴ 7f* 7m 7m 6m⁴ 7m*
6m 7.6m* 7g⁴ 8m 8m] sturdy colt: fair handicapper: won at Kempton in April,
Folkestone in June, Salisbury in August and Lingfield in September, making all last
2 occasions: effective at 6f to 7.6f: acts on firm ground: visored last 6 starts:
sometimes bandaged behind: inconsistent. *M. R. Channon.*

CHEW IT OVER (IRE)   2 b.g. (Mar 13) Tautan (USA) 119–Stop The Cavalry   **63**
(Relko 136) [1990 7m 8.2s 7g⁶] 21,000Y: angular, workmanlike gelding: has a round
action: fourth foal: half-brother to winners abroad by Auction Ring and Try My Best:
dam never ran: 12 lengths sixth of 11, prominent over 4f, in mixed-aged event at
Newmarket in November, easily best effort. *M. A. Jarvis.*

CHEZ JARRASSE   3 b.c. Pharly (FR) 130–Miss Saint-Cloud 102 (Nonoalco   **77**
(USA) 131) [1989 6g 7m 1990 10m⁴ 10m 12m² 12g⁵ 12g* 12g 12s⁵] leggy, close-
coupled colt: modest performer: clearly best effort when winning handicap at
Kempton in September: should stay 1¾m: sold 8,400 gns Newmarket Autumn
Sales. *G. Wragg.*

CHIANINA   2 b.f. (Apr 12) Forzando 122–Cow Pastures (Homing 130) [1990   **—**
5m⁶] 11,000F, 12,500Y: good-topped filly: first foal: dam unraced daughter of useful
sprinter Pennycuick, and half-sister to Mummy's Pet, Arch Sculptor and Parsimony: odds on but green and edgy, over 12 lengths sixth of 7, finding little off
bridle and eased, rider giving impression something amiss, in maiden at Newbury
in June: evidently considered capable of better, but not seen out again. *A. A. Scott.*

CHIC ANTIQUE   6 ch.m. Rarity 129–What A Picture 80 (My Swanee 122) [1989   **42**
7h⁴ 6m² 5f* 6f² 5m 6f³ 6f 6f 1990 5g² 7f 5g³ 5.1f] workmanlike mare: has a quick
action: poor handicapper: best form at sprint distances: acts on firm going: blinkered
final outing: occasionally sweats and gets on toes: has won for apprentice. *P. J.
Makin.*

CHICARICA (USA)   2 b.f. (Jan 18) The Minstrel (CAN) 135–Little Lady   **102 p**
Luck (USA) (Jacinto) [1990 6d* 6d* 6m*]
  Firm ground reportedly kept Chicarica off the racecourse after the
Hillsdown Cherry Hinton Stakes at Newmarket in July. Plans to supplement
her for the Tattersalls Cheveley Park Stakes at the same course in October
were abandoned as the dry spell continued, and so she was retired for the
season unbeaten, still a supporting rather than a leading player. Chicarica
looks the sort to progress, though, and it's not beyond the realms of
possibility that she'll still force her way into the Guineas picture.
  The big, strong, rangy Chicarica, an early foal, resembled very much a
three-year-old at two and dwarfed her rivals in all her races, which began at
Leicester in June in a maiden event. Three years earlier the subsequent Oaks
winner Diminuendo had made a winning debut in the same race, and Chicarica
was no less impressive, belying her slightly backward condition and overcoming her obvious inexperience to win by six lengths, a margin which could
have easily been doubled had her rider so desired. Distance and ground were
identical for Chicarica's next race, the Chesham Stakes at Royal Ascot later in

*Hillsdown Cherry Hinton Stakes, Newmarket—
further promise from the well-built Chicarica (blaze),
who beats Zigaura (left), Atlantic Flyer and On Tiptoes (rails)*

the month, and Chicarica, who was favoured by the incongruous conditions of the race, which effectively treated her as a maiden, started odds on. There wasn't much doubt about the outcome from two furlongs out as Chicarica, who had travelled smoothly from the start, took up the running, and she ran on with great enthusiasm in the final stages to win by two lengths from Dominion Gold with the rest, led by Prodigal Blues, a length further away. Chicarica was kept to six furlongs for the Cherry Hinton. Six on good to firm ground at Newmarket is much more a test of speed than six on dead at Ascot, but Chicarica was quick enough to take on the Queen Mary winner On Tiptoes from the start before staying on much the better to account for the fast-finishing Ziguara and Atlantic Flyer by a length and a half and a short head respectively, in a time which broke the two-year-old record. For one who's bred to be suited by at least seven furlongs Chicarica's performance augured well for her prospects in the top fillies' races in the autumn, even on good to firm, and it was a pity she wasn't seen out again.

		Northern Dancer (b 1961)	Nearctic
	The Minstrel (CAN) (ch 1974)		Natalma
		Fleur (b 1964)	Victoria Park
Chicarica (USA) (b.f. Jan 18, 1988)			Flaming Page
		Jacinto (br 1962)	Bold Ruler
	Little Lady Luck (USA) (b 1976)		Cascade
		Harbor Wine (b 1969)	Herbager
			Bourbon Mist

A mile should suit Chicarica well at three, and there's some encouragement in her pedigree to suggest that she'll stay even further. Her sire The Minstrel, who had to be put down in 1990 after developing laminitis, won the Derby and the King George and has sired around fifty stakes winners, including such as L'Emigrant, Bakharoff, Musical Bliss, Melodist, and Treizieme; while her dam Little Lady Luck, who won over six furlongs as a three-year-old, has produced three other winners, including the middle-distance winners Tribal Mascot (by Our Native) and Queens Soldier (by L'Enjoleur). Little Lady Luck is a full sister to the good 1979 two-year-old Romeo Romani, who cut little ice on his only attempt beyond a mile here but subsequently won twice at up to a mile and a quarter in the States. Chicarica, who cost 500,000 dollars as a yearling, has already been entered for the Irish One Thousand Guineas. She'll need to improve considerably to hold her own at that level, but as we've said, she does look the type to progress. *J. H. M. Gosden.*

CHIC CAROLE   4 ch.f. Dalsaan 125–Valley of Diamonds 74 (Florescence 120)   — [1989 7s 8m 8.3d 10.6s⁶ 1990 a12g] leggy filly: of little account. *C. A. Dwyer.*

CHICO VALDEZ (USA)   6 ch.g. Valdez (USA)–Lypatia (FR) (Lyphard (USA)   — 132) [1989 12g 1990 10.2f 12f⁵ 12f a12g] close-coupled, rather sparely-made gelding: poor handicapper: stayed 1½m: acted on firm and dead going: often visored: winning hurdler/chaser: dead. *M. C. Chapman.*

CHIEF CELEBRITY (USA)   2 b.f. (Apr 29) Chief's Crown (USA)–My Nord   75 p (USA) (Vent du Nord) [1990 8d²] $400,000Y: close-coupled, angular filly: half-sister to numerous winners, including smart stayer At Talaq (by Roberto) and Grade 1 8.5f and 9f winner Annoconnor (by Nureyev): dam won 2 sprint claiming races: ½-length second of 13, ridden along 3f out and staying on strongly when checked inside final furlong, giving impression probably would have won otherwise, to Straldi in maiden at Leicester in November: will stay 1¼m: sure to improve and win a race. *M. R. Stoute.*

CHIEF DANCER   3 b.f. Chief Singer 131–Palumba 100 (Derring-Do 131) [1989   49 5d⁴ 1990 6f³ 6m⁶ 6g 7d] stocky filly: plating-class maiden: tailed off in handicap final outing: bred to stay further: best effort on good to firm ground. *M. W. Easterby.*

CHIEF ORNAMENT (USA)   2 b.f. (Mar 10) Chief's Crown (USA)–Embel-   57 p lished (USA) (Seattle Slew (USA)) [1990 6g4] leggy filly: fourth foal: half-sister to 3-y-o 1m winner Lord Charmer (by Our Native) and a winner by Grey Dawn: dam 6f winner in USA, is half-sister to champion U.S. 2-y-o filly Althea: odds on, 3 lengths last of 4, green throughout and no headway from 2f out, in maiden at Yarmouth in June: showed a quick action: should improve. *H. R. A. Cecil.*

CHIEFS BABU   2 ch.c. (Mar 5) Chief Singer 131–Nullah 71 (Riverman (USA)   51 131) [1990 6g 6g] 5,800Y, 27,000 2-y-o: quite good-topped colt: has scope: third foal:

dam, third over 1¼m on only start, is half-sister to smart Bolide: behind from halfway in autumn maidens at Newbury and Yarmouth. *B. Hanbury.*

CHIEFS KRAAL (NZ)   3 b.g. Babaroom (USA)–Sarahtello (NZ) (Saraceno 117)   **39** [1989 NR 1990 7g 8f 8m 10.2m 10.1m 10f3] compact New Zealand-bred gelding: third of 6 in seller at Folkestone in August, first form on flat: winning hurdler. *J. R. Jenkins.*

CHILDREY (USA)   3 ch.c. Chief's Crown (USA)–Batna (USA) (Cyane (USA))   **104** [1989 6g* 7g3 1990 7m2 7g5 6g6 6m2 7m* 7m6 7d3] lengthy, good-bodied, attractive colt: has a quick action: impresses in appearance: useful performer: ran well in smart company before justifying favouritism in apprentice event (drifted right) at Ascot in September: well beaten (stiff task) in Group 2 contest penultimate start, below form and didn't quicken as seemed likely (edged left) when narrowly-beaten favourite in minor event 12 days later: effective at 6f and 7f: acts on good to firm ground: wears net muzzle. *G. Harwood.*

CHILIBOY   3 gr.c. Precocious 126–Chili Girl 112 (Skymaster 126) [1989 6f5 6g   **89** 1990 6m* 6m3 6m3 6m 6m4 6m2 6d 6f2 5m* 5s] stocky colt: carries condition: chipped knee bone at 2 yrs: fairly useful sprinter: won maiden at Pontefract in April and handicap (making all far side) at Redcar in October: probably best at 5f on a sound surface: blinkered last 6 starts, hanging left under pressure first occasion. *J. L. Dunlop.*

CHILIPOUR   3 gr.g. Nishapour (FR) 125–Con Carni (Blakeney 126) [1989 6g 6g   **—** 8g 1990 6g 10f4 10.1m 11.7m] leggy, close-coupled gelding: has a free, round action: no form, including in handicap. *G. Lewis.*

CHIMAYO (IRE)   2 b.c. (Feb 14) Sure Blade (USA) 128–Seattle Siren (USA) 101   **83 p** (Seattle Slew (USA)) [1990 6g*] medium-sized, unfurnished colt: second live foal: half-brother to Irish 1¼m and 1¾m winner Distant Beat (by Touching Wood): dam 6f winner at 2 yrs, is half-sister to very smart middle-distance winner Pole Position: won maiden at Newmarket in October by 1½ lengths from Noelreac Julian, pushed along over 2f out then running on really well last ½f: showed a round action: will improve, particularly over 7f +. *B. W. Hills.*

CHIMES OF FREEDOM (USA)   3 ch.f. Private Account (USA)–Avi-   **121** ance 112 (Northfields (USA)) [1989 6f* 6m* 6g* 6g* 6m3 1990 7.3d4 8f* 8f* 8g]

For a short while in the summer Chimes of Freedom blossomed again into one of the best of her age and sex, adding the Coronation Stakes at Royal Ascot and the Child Stakes at Newmarket to her string of victories as a two-year-old. But the promise of those performances went unfulfilled. She was a beaten favourite in the Prix Jacques le Marois at Deauville next time, when standing in for Machiavellian, and in October she joined him on the retired list without a further run, having had just four outings in 1990. Evidently Chimes of Freedom's restricted appearances were chiefly a result of the prolonged dry weather. Her trainer told more than once of the difficulties he encountered in getting her right—'she'd become so disillusioned by the hard ground' in the spring and wouldn't work at all on the all-weather gallops at home. He attributed her lack-lustre fourth behind Salsabil in the Gainsborough Stud Fred Darling Stakes at Newbury in April to

Coronation Stakes, Ascot—Chimes of Freedom finds her form

these difficulties, and hoped conditions on the gallops would ease. However, looking at her racing record one is entitled to question whether the filly was as well suited by softish going (which she encountered for the only time in public at Newbury) as by firm. Her close third to Dead Certain on top-of-the-ground in the Cheveley Park Stakes was a very useful effort, and her victories on firm at Royal Ascot and Newmarket even better, of course.

Chimes of Freedom's defeat at Newbury put her out of the One Thousand Guineas, for which she'd been one of the ante-post favourites, and her return to the track in the Coronation Stakes seemed in some jeopardy until the eleventh hour because of the ground; but she took her chance despite no overnight rain and stormed home in tremendous style from a substandard field. She won by five lengths. Such a decisive margin could not be forecast for fourth favourite Chimes of Freedom as she turned into the straight third of seven behind long-time leader Hasbah and the pulling-double Heart of Joy, having been settled in mid-division not far off the pace. Pushed along vigorously, she improved past Heart of Joy to collar Hasbah inside the distance, and from there she really lengthened to draw right away, spreadeagling the field. The French challenger Mais Oui, a listed-race winner at Longchamp, ran as if out of her depth in finishing fourth. Chimes of Freedom had two fewer opponents in the Child Stakes three weeks later, and she started 6/4 on under a 6-lb penalty to beat Hasbah, Arousal, the four-year-old Aldbourne and Tabdea. She landed the odds by two and a half lengths from Arousal, again making her challenge with around two furlongs to go, leading under driving over a furlong out, then finishing well on top. However, as she pulled up she seemed to be moving short.

Chimes of Freedom's next race should have been the Sussex Stakes at Goodwood. Left in overnight in the hope of a thunderstorm, she was paid the compliment of being installed clear favourite by all the early-price layers. But connections refused to risk her on the firm, announcing that future running plans depended on the going. Machiavellian's unexpected defeat in the Prix Maurice de Gheest that weekend gave his owner's Chimes of Freedom another opportunity of a crack at the colts and older horses in the Marois. On good going she came seventh of ten to Priolo, no excuses as the race was run though later reports had it that the flight over hadn't gone smoothly. She was ideally placed and travelling as well as any entering the final three furlongs but soon came under the whip; this time her response to pressure was different from at Ascot and Newmarket, her effort gradually petering out. In going under by around six lengths she ran approximately a stone below her best.

			Damascus	Sword Dancer
	Private Account (USA)		(b 1964)	Kerala
Chimes of	(b 1976)		Numbered Account	Buckpasser
Freedom (USA)			(b 1969)	Intriguing
(ch.f. 1987)			Northfields	Northern Dancer
	Aviance		(ch 1968)	Little Hut
	(ch 1982)		Minnie Hauk	Sir Ivor
			(b 1975)	Best In Show

Chimes of Freedom's dam Aviance has made a flying start at stud: her second foal is the 1990 Cheveley Park runner-up Imperfect Circle (by Riverman). Aviance began her career with a win over seven furlongs but, like

Child Stakes, Newmarket — Chimes of Freedom beats Hasbah again; Arousal separates the pair

her offspring, had the speed to win at six as a two-year-old. She had four races as a three-year-old—coming a good, staying-on three lengths sixth to Oh So Sharp in the Guineas, disappointing in the Irish equivalent on her only outing on soft going, then being put back to sprinting, in which sphere she finished sixth to Never So Bold in the July Cup and William Hill Sprint Championship, showing up in both before being beaten around six lengths. More details of this excellent family are given in the essay on Chimes of Freedom in *Racehorses of 1989*.

Private Account tends to be an influence for stamina. Given that, and the way she got the mile in mid-season, a top-form Chimes of Freedom would have been an interesting candidate for races such as the Sun Chariot Stakes or the Champion Stakes; she might well have stayed a mile and a quarter. The leggy, good-topped Chimes of Freedom has a quick action. She showed her best form on firm going. *H. R. A. Cecil.*

CHINA CRISIS 3 b.f. Tina's Pet 121–Yellatown (Carnival Night) [1989 5m 5f⁴ 6f 6m⁶ 6f⁵ 7d 1990 a5g a7g a10g⁵] small, workmanlike filly: quite modest plater at 2 yrs: no form in non-selling handicaps and maiden claimer late on at 3 yrs: should stay 7f: seems unsuited by a soft surface. *P. Mitchell.* —

CHINA MOON 3 ch.f. Blushing Scribe (USA) 107–Derring Venture (Camden Town 125) [1989 7g⁴ 7f⁴ 7f 5f 5f³ 5d a6g³ a5g 1990 5g 7m 5f 6m 5f 5m² 5m 6d] leggy filly: plating-class maiden: easily best 3-y-o effort when 25/1-second in claimer at Sandown in September: best form at sprint distances: seems unsuited by a soft surface: usually edgy, has sweated: sold 820 gns Doncaster October Sales. *F. Durr.* 55

CHINA SKY   2 b.c. (May 10) Tina's Pet 121–Buy G's 60 (Blakeney 126) [1990 8.2s 8m a8g] rather sparely-made colt: second foal: half-brother to 1989 2-y-o 6f winner Scorpio Lady (by Vaigly Great): dam 12.2f winner: poor maiden. *C. N. Allen.* —

CHINA'S WAY (USA)   4 b. or br.f. Native Uproar (USA)–China Tea (USA) 95 (Round Table) [1989 8v⁶ 8g⁶ 7m⁶ 9g⁶ 12g² 10f⁴ 1990 12f⁵] leggy, angular filly: keen walker: plating-class maiden at best: suited by 1½m: possibly unsuited by extremes of going: sold to join M. Pipe's stable 3,200 gns Ascot May Sales. *Dr J. D. Scargill.* —

CHIN THE REF   2 ro.c. (Apr 28) Tina's Pet 121–Spanish Chestnut (Philip of Spain 126) [1990 a5g 6m⁴ 7f⁵] 2,100F, 2,400Y: leggy, quite good-topped colt: ninth foal: brother to 2 plating-class animals, closely related to temperamental 3-y-o Dontworryaboutit (by Aragon) and half-brother to 1980 2-y-o 5f winner Loddon Music (by Music Boy) and a winner abroad: dam poor plater: well beaten, including in seller. *J. D. Czerpak.* —

CHIPANDABIT   3 b.c. Mummy's Pet 125–Parlais 101 (Pardao 120) [1989 5g* 5m* 5f⁶ 6g³ 7g 5g 1990 5g 5d 5m 6m 6m] lengthy, leggy colt: good walker: modest winner at 2 yrs: faced stiffish tasks and little form in handicaps in 1990, twice sweating: stays 6f: sold 2,200 gns Newmarket Autumn Sales. *J. Sutcliffe.* —

CHIPAYA   2 b.f. (Mar 14) Northern Prospect (USA)–Flaming Rose (USA) **116** (Upper Nile (USA)) [1990 5m³ 5m⁵ 6d 6m* 6d* 6d*]

Did any horse make more improvement in such a short space of time in 1990 than Chipaya, who stormed away with the £100,000 Racecall Gold Trophy at Redcar in October, after which she entered the betting for the One Thousand Guineas, little more than a month after winning off the mark of a useful plater in a run-of-the-mill nursery at Nottingham? Chipaya was sent to Fanshawe's stable mid way through the summer, having run twice for Wall in maidens at Newmarket (where she finished third of five) in May and Nottingham in June. Her first outing for her new trainer, which came in a claimer at Haydock in September, was not an auspicious one: she reared up as the other runners set off, parted company with her rider and ended up beneath the stalls. This was the second time that Chipaya had given trouble at the start, and she had to pass a stalls test before contesting the Winthorpe Nursery at Nottingham later in the month. Running off what proved to be a benevolent mark of 70 she turned what had looked a competitive handicap into a one-horse affair, waited with travelling strongly, leading approaching the final furlong then drawing five lengths clear to win in a fast time. Chipaya was raised only 3 lb for that, and she followed up in a similar event over course and distance in October, forcibly underlining the handicapper's oversight with an even better display which had the runners strung out like jumpers.

The Racecall Gold Trophy, inaugurated in 1989, is rapidly becoming established as one of the most valuable, and popular, two-year-old races in the

Racecall Gold Trophy, Redcar—Chipaya's dramatic improvement continues; she has Distinctly North well beaten

Calendar. Nineteen participants contested the latest running, including the likes of Distinctly North and Vintage Only, first and third in the Flying Childers Stakes, the progressive Mill Reef runner-up Sylvan Breeze, and the Lowther winner Only Yours. On the day, confidence in the Carson-ridden Chipaya ran high and she was backed down to 7/1 second favourite behind Distinctly North. Dominating the race on what had been presumed to be the slower far side with Distinctly North, as Vintage Only and the useful Punch N'Run led the field down the stand side, Chipaya went to the front under two furlongs out, had the race in the bag soon afterwards, and increased her advantage in the closing stages as Distinctly North, who ran below his best on the dead ground, was eased. At the end of a smart performance Chipaya had five lengths to spare.

		Mr Prospector	Raise A Native
Chipaya (b.f. Mar 14, 1988)	Northern Prospect (USA) (b 1976)	(b 1970)	Gold Digger
		Sleek Dancer (b 1968)	Northern Dancer
			Victorine
	Flaming Rose (USA) (b 1982)	Upper Nile (b 1974)	Nijinsky
			Rosetta Stone
		Papamiento (ch 1973)	Blade
			Commemoration

There wasn't much of Chipaya as a two-year-old: she's a small, workmanlike filly, still rather unfurnished. She was bought for 13,500 guineas at Newmarket's October Yearling Sales. Her sire, Northern Prospect, a very useful sprinter in North America in the late-'seventies, may still be unfamiliar here, despite having sired the winners of over six hundred races worldwide, but the exploits of Act of Diplomacy, Prospective Ruler and Carn Maire, three other winning two-year-olds in the latest season, should also have ensured there'll be more of his offspring here in future. Chipaya's dam Flaming Rose, like her dam Papamiento and grandam Commemoration, ended her racecourse career still a maiden. Sold afterwards in foal for 90,000 dollars at Keeneland in November, 1987, and brought to Britain, since when she has had a foal by Rousillon and been barren to Jalmood, Flaming Rose has plenty to recommend her as a broodmare; she's a half-sister to Gwydion, a very smart sprinter for Cecil in the mid-'eighties, and, further removed, is related to the Grand Prix de Paris winner Armistice and the very smart American middle-distance colt Twice Worthy. Six furlongs to a mile will probably be Chipaya's range if she is able to return to the track at three. In December came the news that she would be confined to her box until the end of January, in order to rest an arthritic near-fore knee, and her chances of making the Guineas field are, at the time of writing, uncertain. Chipaya is particularly effective on a soft surface. *J. R. Fanshawe.*

CHIRONE (USA) 3 b.c. Lypheor 118–Distaff Magic (USA) (Fluorescent Light (USA)) [1989 7m5 8g* 8.2g* 8m5 1990 10f 10m 10.2g 10m3] neat, quite attractive colt: fairly useful winner at 2 yrs: first form in handicaps when creditable third in £8,300 event at Newmarket in October, not getting best of runs and shaping well but not unduly knocked about: stays 1¼m. *L. M. Cumani.* 93

CHIRRUP (FR) 3 b.f. Chief Singer 131–Bempton 57 (Blakeney 126) [1989 NR 1990 10.2g* 12m4 14 6g5 12m5 12s4] leggy, unfurnished filly: has a round action: seventh toal: half-sister to 4 winners, including useful 6-y-o middle-distance stayer Mr Pintips (by Kris) and Ribblesdale Stakes winner Gull Nook (by Mill Reef): dam, half-sister to Shirley Heights, was raced over 1m and 9f: won maiden at Doncaster in June: contested listed race then pattern events after, running well though never able to challenge in Princess Royal Stakes at Ascot and St Simon Stakes (blinkered and edgy, ran in snatches) at Newbury last 2 starts: should stay 1¾m: yet to race on firm going, acts on any other: sold 20,000 gns Newmarket December Sales. *J. L. Dunlop.* 102

CHLOES DIAMOND (IRE) 2 ch.f. (Feb 28) Heraldiste (USA) 121–Salique (Sallust 134) [1990 6f4 6m3 7s4] IR 18,000Y: unfurnished filly: fifth foal: half-sister to winning 3-y-o sprinter Indian Star (by Indian King) and 2 winners at up to 7f, including Simply Henry (by Simply Great): dam second over 7f in Ireland: quite modest maiden: should be suited by further than 6f. *C. B. B. Booth.* 67

CHLOE'S PET 3 ch.f. Local Suitor (USA) 128–Mischiefmaker 73 (Calpurnius 122) [1989 6m 6m 7f6 7f 1990 10f 10f 11.5m 14g 15.3g 15.5f] compact filly: poor walker: moderate mover: poor and of unsatisfactory temperament. *M. D. I. Usher.* — §

CHOBE RIVER 3 b.f. Dara Monarch 128–Fair Or Foul (Patch 129) [1989 NR 55 1990 9g⁴ 8g³ 10g⁶] 3,600F, 10,000Y: sturdy filly: third foal: half-sister to 1987 2-y-o 6f seller winner Play To Win (by Runnett): dam won over 1¼m at 2 yrs in Ireland: plating-class maiden: stays 1m: sold 2,500 gns Newmarket Autumn Sales. *D. Morley.*

CHOIR LEADER 3 b. or br.f. Chief Singer 131–View 88 (Shirley Heights 130) 78 [1989 NR 1990 7g⁴ 10.5g⁵ 8m⁴ 7m⁵ 8m² 8g³ 8g³ 9m² a8g³] tall, leggy filly: second foal: dam 6f and 1m winner: fair maiden: should be suited by 1¼m: blinkered, helped set strong pace fourth start: wore crossed noseband final one: ran creditably when sweating and edgy: claimed out of B. Hanbury's stable £10,112 penultimate start. *M. C. Pipe.*

CHOIR MASTER (CAN) 3 b.c. Assert 134–Choral Group (CAN) (Lord 91 Durham (CAN)) [1989 NR 1990 10.1g 10g³ 10.1m* 10f] IR 50,000Y: tall, lengthy colt with scope: fourth foal: half-brother to useful 1m winner Balakirev (by Nijinsky): dam joint top-rated Canadian filly at 2 yrs in 1981: made all in minor event at Windsor in June: ridden along 4f out then stayed on again until checked inside last in £8,000 handicap at Newmarket following month: will be suited by 1½m. *Major W. R. Hern.*

CHOIR PRACTICE 3 ch.c. Chief Singer 131–Good Try 92 (Good Bond 122) 87 [1989 NR 1990 8m 8f⁵ 7g⁴ 5m* 5m² 5m² 6d] 34,000Y: big, workmanlike colt: half-brother to several winners here and abroad, including quite useful 1984 2-y-o 6f winner Sergeant Gerard (by Brigadier Gerard): dam 2-y-o 5f winner: fair performer: won maiden at Warwick in August: best efforts in handicaps next 2 starts, always behind in similar contest (favourite and bandaged behind) final one: best form at 5f on top-of-the-ground. *H. Candy.*

CHORAL SUNDOWN 4 b.f. Night Shift (USA)–Choir (High Top 131) [1989 8d 75 d 8.5d* 8g³ 10f² 10.2g* 8m⁶ 10f² 12m⁶ 10.6d 9g* 9g 1990 8.5f² 8f 10.4d 10f⁶ 10.2m² 8m³ 10.5m 8g 9m 12g⁴ 10.4d 12s] stocky filly: carries condition: modest handicapper: trained until after seventh outing by C. W. C. Elsey, and below form afterwards: best form at up to 1¼m: yet to show her form on soft going, acts on any other: suitable mount for apprentice: reluctant at stalls eleventh start. *B. W. Murray.*

CHORUS BOY 5 br.g. Sonnen Gold 121–Toccata (Kythnos 126) [1989 10.2g 48 12.4g⁵ 9m 8v 8g³ 1990 8.2s⁵ 8f 10.6s⁶ 8g³ 8g⁴ 10f⁴ 10.6s 11d 9s⁶] tall, useful-looking gelding: has a rather round action: still a maiden: stays 1¼m: acts on any going: ideally needs strong handling. *E. Weymes.*

CHOTOMSKI 6 b.g. Busted 134–Crown Witness 95 (Crowned Prince (USA) 46 128) [1989 9v 8.5g 10g⁵ 1990 6m⁵ 7m⁴ 6m⁶ 7m⁶ 7g⁴ 6d 5f 7f] big, workmanlike gelding: poor maiden: possibly best at 7f: blinkered last 4 starts: dead. *M. W. Easterby.*

CHOUGH 2 br.g. (Mar 10) Green Ruby (USA) 104–Lochmar (Lochnager 132) 57 [1990 5f 6f² 5.3h 6g⁵ 6m⁴ 6d⁵] 2,000F: smallish, lengthy gelding: first foal: dam poor half-sister to smart French miler King James: plating-class maiden: will be suited by 7f. *C. R. Barwell.*

CHRISTIAN BOY 2 b.g. (Feb 9) Belfort (FR) 89–Harem Queen 66 (Prince 46 Regent (FR) 129) [1990 5f⁵ 5d⁶] 7,600Y: lengthy gelding: has scope: brother to 3 winners here and abroad, including 3-y-o Little Ripper, 6f and 7f winner at 2 yrs: dam half-sister to very smart 1976 2-y-o Avgerinos: poor form in maiden and minor event (slowly away) in May: sold 820 gns Doncaster September Sales. *J. Berry.*

CHRISTIAN LAD 2 gr.g. (May 21) Belfort (FR) 89–California Split (Sweet 71 Revenge 129) [1990 5m⁴ 5f* 5d³ 6m³ 6m² 6m² 6m⁵ 6d⁴ 5m⁴] 6,200Y: leggy, rather angular gelding: quite good mover: fifth foal: half-brother to 3-y-o 6f winner Miss Kellybell (by Kirchner) and 6f and 7f winner By Chance (by Le Johnstan): dam of no account: modest performer: wide-margin winner of early-season claimer at Newcastle: stays 6f: acts well on firm ground: blinkered penultimate start: tends to wander, and is a difficult ride. *J. Berry.*

CHRISTIAN SCHAD 8 b.g. Tumble Wind (USA)–Lorna Doone (USA) (Tom — Rolfe) [1989 NR 1990 12g⁶] strong, short-coupled, attractive gelding: useful handicapper at one time: backward, always behind in 8-runner event at Epsom in April, only race on flat after 1986: stayed 1m: ideally suited by plenty of give in the ground: dead. *O. O'Neill.*

CHRISTIAN SOLDIER 3 b.g. Tickled Pink 114–Super Princess 85 (Falcon 47 131) [1989 NR 1990 a7g a10g⁴ 10f 10g⁵ 13g⁴ 12.2g⁴ᵈⁱˢ 15.8m⁴] 1,650F, 4,300Y: workmanlike, good-quartered gelding: brother to quite modest 1987 2-y-o King's Falcon and half-brother to 4 sprint winners: dam won over 7f at 2 yrs and over hurdles: poor maiden. needs further than 1¼m: blinkered fifth (easily best effort) and sixth starts. *R. A. Bennett.*

CHRISTINE DAAE 4 b.f. Sadler's Wells (USA) 132–Chiltern Red (Red God 128§) [1989 NR 1990 10f6 10m4 8f4 8.5g4 11.5m5 9m6 10m*] strong, rangy filly: didn't have to be at her best to win maiden at Redcar in September, setting modest gallop: stays 1¼m: acts on firm going: looked unsuited by track at Lingfield fifth outing: often sweating and edgy. *P. W. Harris.* **74**

CHRISTMAS HOLLY 9 b.g. Blind Harbour 96–Holly Doon (Doon 124) [1989 NR 1990 a13g2 a14g2 a14g2 16m3 13.6d4] workmanlike gelding: poor handicapper: seems to stay 2m: acts on good to firm going and goes very well in the mud: suited by strong gallop: not resolute and needs holding up for as long as possible. *Mrs G. R. Reveley.* **43** §

CHRONOLOGICAL 4 b.g. Henbit (USA) 130–Forward Princess (USA) (Forward Pass) [1989 12.3d5 1990 13.8m5 16.5m4 17.6m 14g5 15.8g4 16.5g5 13m5 a12g a14g* a14g2 a16g3 a14g3] sparely-made, angular gelding: moderate walker and mover: easy 6-length winner of claimer at Southwell in November: again apprentice ridden in handicaps at same course after, soon well behind and nearest at finish last 2 outings: suited by good test of stamina: pulled hard in blinkers seventh outing. *M. H. Tompkins.* **66**

CHUCKLESTONE 7 b.g. Chukaroo 103–Czar's Diamond 66 (Queen's Hussar 124) [1989 16f5 14m4 15.3m4 16m* 16m* 16.1m3 17.6d5 16m6 16m5 1990 18f 16g6 16d4 18f5 17.1f* 17.1f2 16m3 17.6f2 17.6f3 16m 17.1m* 17.1d] neat gelding: has a free, rather round action: modest handicapper: won at Bath in June and October: tailed off there final outing: also winner over hurdles in summer: suited by good test of stamina: particularly well suited by top-of-the-ground: races up with pace: tailed off when visored: genuine. *J. S. King.* **72**

CHURCHILL EXPRESS 3 b.c. Full of Hope 125–Nello (USA) 85 (Charles Elliott (USA)) [1989 NR 1990 7m6 7m6 10m 10g4 12.2d6 10g a10g] IR 4,600Y: leggy colt: fifth foal: half-brother to a winner in Italy: dam 2-y-o 6f winner who became disappointing: quite modest maiden: best effort in claimer fourth start: may stay 1½m. *R. Akehurst.* **63** ?

CHURCH MELODY 2 b.c. (Mar 12) Song 132–Absaloute Service 96 (Absalom 128) [1990 7s 6d] 7,000F, 16,000Y: rangy colt: has scope: first foal: dam 2-y-o 5f winner: backward and green, always behind in late-season maidens at Doncaster. *R. W. Stubbs.* **—**

CHURCH MISSIONARY (USA) 3 b.f. Miswaki (USA) 124–Christchurch (FR) 88 (So Blessed 130) [1989 NR 1990 7g 10g2] lengthy, good-quartered filly: half-sister to several winners, including 1989 1¼m winner All Saints Day (by Miswaki), smart 6f to 10.5f winner Church Parade (by Queen's Hussar) and smart middle-distance stayer Castle Rising (by Blakeney): dam, 1½m winner, is half-sister to Highclere: 7/1 and carrying plenty of condition on first run for 6 months, 2 lengths second of 11 to Balleta in maiden at Newbury in October: may be capable of better. *W. Hastings-Bass.* **83**

CHURCH STAR 6 b.m. Cajun 120–Lady of Rathleek (Furry Glen 121) [1989 9v 1990 10m 7m] compact, good-bodied mare: ungenuine maiden: stays 1½m: wears bandages: has worn blinkers: visored and claimer ridden nowadays. *J. J. Bridger.* **—** §

CIBOURE 2 ch.f. (Apr 18) Norwick (USA) 120–Brandon Creek 79 (Be My Guest (USA) 126) [1990 5m 6m4 5g6 5f4 6m6 6h* 7h6 6m4 5.8h3 6m 6m* 6g5 7m3 7f5 6m] 7,200Y: leggy filly: fourth foal: half-sister to 1m winner Patience Creek and 1987 2-y-o 5f winner Hidden Creek (both by Mummy's Game) and 1986 2-y-o 1m seller winner Main Brand (by Main Reef): dam suited by 1½m: much improved filly: won claimer at Brighton in July and nursery at Lingfield (made all from favourable draw) in August: needs further than 5f and will stay 1m: visored fourth and fifth outings: suited by forcing tactics. *M. D. I. Usher.* **74**

CIELAMOUR (USA) 5 b.m. Conquistador Cielo (USA)–Nicole Mon Amour (USA) (Bold Bidder) [1989 8v* 7v3 9g 8g* 8g5 12s5 1990 10m* 8g* 12s* 10m* 10m 8f] leggy, close-coupled mare: powerful mover: useful performer: unbeaten first 4 starts in spring in handicaps at Leopardstown and the Curragh (Irish Lincolnshire Handicap under top weight), minor event (odds on) at Tipperary and listed contest at Phoenix Park: 50/1, never a threat in Royal Hunt Cup (Handicap) at Royal Ascot final outing: effective at 1m to 1½m: acted on any going: tough: retired in foal to Nordico. *J. S. Bolger, Ireland.* **105**

CINDEROSA (IRE) 2 b.f. (Apr 23) Kings Lake (USA) 133–Rosalita (USA) (Key To The Kingdom (USA)) [1990 6m3 6m4 8m 8f5 7g] IR 16,000Y: rather sparely-made **39**

filly: has a long, rather round stride: second foal: dam never ran: poor maiden: ran creditably in visor final start: stays 1m. *T. Thomson Jones.*

CIRCUIT RING 4 b.g. Electric 126–Brookfield Miss 73 (Welsh Pageant 132) **68** [1989 12.2m3 12.2g3 14d 12d5 1990 12f4 12.3d 12m6 13.8m4 16.2d* 16.5m2 16.5f2 19f* 16m4 16.2m3 16f6] workmanlike gelding: modest handicapper: won at Beverley in July and Redcar (slowly-run 4-runner event) in August: suited by 2m+: acts on firm and dead going: blinkered third outing, visored next 3 (twice mulish in preliminaries): sometimes taken down early. *P. Calver.*

CIRCUS FEATHERS 3 ch.f. Kris 135–Circus Plume 124 (High Top 131) [1989 **99** 7m 7f 1990 8f* 9g* 12m6] smallish, good-quartered filly: made most to win maiden at Warwick in May and minor event at Wolverhampton in June: 9 lengths sixth of 7 to Narwala in Princess Royal Stakes at Ascot, chasing leader 1¼m: suited by 1½m: acts on firm ground: game. *J. L. Dunlop.*

CIRCUS LIGHT 2 gr.c. (Jan 14) Kalaglow 132–Circus Plume 124 (High Top 131) **103 p** [1990 7m6 8.2m* 8m2] rangy colt: has scope: good mover, with long stride: second foal: half-brother to 3-y-o 1m and 9f winner Circus Feathers (by Kris): dam 7f winner at 2 yrs, won Oaks: edgy and mulish stalls, won maiden at Nottingham in September by 8 lengths from Matahif, soon leading, clear 2f out and running on strongly: heavily-backed favourite, beaten a neck by Sea Level in listed race at Ascot following month, travelling smoothly in lead then not finding as much off bridle as expected: will stay 1½m: coltish first 2 starts, on toes all 3: likely to improve further. *J. L. Dunlop.*

CIRCUS TAVERN 3 b.c. Mummy's Game 120–Swynford's Pride 95 (Rapid — River 127) [1989 NR 1990 6f] third living foal: half-brother to winning sprinter Viltash (by Tachypous): dam 5f winner at 2 yrs: tailed off in maiden at Chepstow in September. *M. C. Pipe.*

CITIDANCER 4 b.c. Lomond (USA) 128–Mrs McArdy 123 (Tribal Chief 125) **118** [1989 8d3 8d2 10g5 10m* 10g2 9g* 10s 1990 9m2 8m2 9.2g3 9m* 8m] strong, deep-bodied colt: carries plenty of condition: smart performer: first race for 3½ months and odds on, won 5-runner Glencairn EBF Stakes at Leopardstown in September, making virtually all: ran well in Earl of Sefton EBF Stakes at Newmarket (reportedly lost both front shoes), Trusthouse Forte Mile at Sandown and Prix d'Ispahan at Longchamp in spring: well beaten in Queen Elizabeth II Stakes at Ascot: effective at 1m to 1¼m: acts on good to firm and dead going. *H. R. A. Cecil.*

CITY BALLET (USA) 3 b.c. Nureyev (USA) 131–Balidaress (Balidar 133) [1989 — NR 1990 7g 8g] $460,000Y: compact colt: closely related to lightly-raced Balidarina (by Shareef Dancer) and half-brother to 6 winners, notably Irish Oaks winner Alydaress (by Alydar), Cheveley Park winner Park Appeal (by Ahonoora) and smart 6f to 1¼m filly Desirable (by Lord Gayle): dam won from 7f to 1¼m in Ireland: well beaten in maidens at York (heavily-backed favourite, tongue tied down and moved poorly to post) and Yarmouth (front rank 6f) in the summer. *J. Gosden.*

CITY FINAL 6 b.m. Final Straw 127–Paperchase (Brigadier Gerard 144) [1989 — NR 1990 8f 12.2m] lengthy mare: winning plater here in 1987: later winner in Jersey: bit backward, well beaten in selling and apprentice (tailed off) handicaps in autumn: stays 9f: unsuited by soft going, acts on any other: bought 2,700 gns Newmarket July Sales. *D. W. Chapman.*

CITY LINK PET 4 b.f. Tina's Pet 121–City Link Rose (Lochnager 132) [1989 5g **79** 1990 6g 5g 5g* 5g* 5m* 5m6 5m6 5m 5g* 6m5 5m 5.6g 5d 5g 5s] strong filly: moderate mover: reportedly fractured sesamoid at 2 yrs: much improved handicapper in summer, winning at Goodwood (twice in apprentice events) and Wolverhampton (making virtually all) in June and Newbury (racing alone stand side) in August: below form last 5 outings: suited by 5f: acts on good to firm going. *D. A. Wilson.*

CITYPLUMBJO 2 b.g. (Apr 30) Hotfoot 126–Vaula 49 (Henbit (USA) 130) [1990 **41** 6g 7m 7f 7g 7g] 10,000Y: rather leggy, lengthy gelding: first foal: dam won over 13f and 1½m at 4 yrs: poor maiden: very keen to post (pulled hard second time) first 2 outings: will be better suited by middle distances. *M. R. Channon.*

CITY SOLACE 2 b.c. (Mar 30) Last Tycoon 131–Sheeog 80 (Reform 132) [1990 **83** 5f* 5f* 5m6 6m3 6f 7g 7g 6m] 18,000Y: leggy, rather sparely-made colt: has a short, scratchy action: third foal: half-brother to 3-y-o Shanakee (by Wassl): dam 5f and 6f winner: fair performer: much improved after winning minor events at Folkestone in March and Salisbury in May: ran moderately (blinkered, on toes and went freely down) in nursery on final outing: probably better suited by 7f than 6f. *R. Hannon.*

CIXI 2 b.f. (Feb 19) Far Out East (USA)–Hasty Key (USA) (Key To The Mint **72** (USA)) [1990 7m⁵ 7m 7m⁵ 9g²] 11,500F, 6,000Y: sparely-made filly: shows knee action: third foal: half-sister to 3-y-o Cutting Note (by Diesis), 7f winner at 2 yrs, and to 1988 2-y-o 7f winner Hasty Vessel (by Raise A Cup): dam minor winner at up to 9f in USA: quite modest maiden: ran well when sweating final start: will be suited by 1¼m. *A. N. Lee.*

CLAIM HIGH (USA) 3 b.c. Alleged (USA) 138–Shine High (USA) (Tudor Grey — 119) [1989 NR 1990 11d 13.3m 12m] $45,000Y: lengthy, good-quartered colt: has scope: fourth foal: half-brother to 1988 American graded stakes-placed 2-y-o Shine Up (by Sharpen Up): dam, best at 5 yrs when dual 6f stakes winner, is half-sister to smart American cum Brave And Bold: showed signs of ability in Newbury maidens: last of 8 in claimer at Goodwood final start, first for 3 months: sold 1,500 gns Newmarket Autumn Sales. *G. Harwood.*

CLARE COURT 3 ch.f. Glint of Gold 128–Clare Bridge (USA) 107 (Little **89** Current (USA)) [1989 7f³ 7f² 8m* 1990 12g* 12.2g³ 13.3m² 14f⁶ 12m³ 14g* 13.3g²] unfurnished filly: fairly useful performer: won minor event at Carlisle in April and strongly-run handicap at Kempton in September: good second in £20,400 handicap at Newbury final start: will stay 2m: acts on firm ground, but best efforts on good: best up with pace: very game and genuine. *I. A. Balding.*

CLARE HEIGHTS 2 b.f. (May 8) Shirley Heights 130–Clare Island 108 **92 p** (Connaught 130) [1990 8g*] 26,000Y: fifth foal: half-sister to 7f winner Blade of Grass (by Kris), 1½m winner Island Lake (by Kalaglow) and middle-distance winner House of Commons (by General Assembly): dam half-sister to very smart 1½m horse Caliban, won Princess Elizabeth Stakes: 25/1 and green, won 16-runner maiden at Yarmouth in October by 1½ lengths from Sought Out, held up, ridden along 3f out then running on well to lead inside last 1f: will be well suited by further: sure to win more races. *J. R. Fanshawe.*

CLAREMONT BOY 2 b.c. (Feb 1) Another Realm 118–Lady Eton 106 (Le Dieu **61 p** d'Or 119) [1990 6g4] 7,800F, 11,000Y: strong colt: brother to 1988 2-y-o 6f and 7f seller winner Isobar, later a winning hurdler, and 1982 2-y-o 5f winner Paddock Princess (by Dragonara Palace): dam won over 5f and 6f at 2 yrs: carrying condition and coltish, over 8 lengths fourth of 14, keeping on well under considerate ride having run very green, to Mukaddamah in maiden at Nottingham in July: looked sure to improve, and win a similar event. *M. A. Jarvis.*

CLARE'S DELIGHT 5 b.m. Viking (USA)–Miss Inglewood 61 (Dike (USA)) **31** [1989 5d³ 6m 6m 6m 6g 6g 6f 6m a6g a6g 1990 8f 8v 8f 6g 6g4] small, light-framed mare: poor handicapper: stays 7f: acts on firm and dead going: often sweating and edgy: unseated rider leaving paddock third outing. *B. C. Morgan.*

CLARET (IRE) 2 b.c. (Feb 8) Rousillon (USA) 133–Consolation 95 (Troy 137) **80** [1990 7m³ 8g²] rangy, good sort: grand walker: second foal: dam 2-y-o 7f winner stayed 1½m, is half-sister to high-class middle-distance performer Morcon: favourite, fair form when placed in maidens at Leicester (tended to wander and carry head high) and Kempton (travelled strongly then faltered near line) in September: will stay 1¼m: should win a race. *Major W. R. Hern.*

CLARK STORE (FR) 2 gr.c. (Jan 3) Dom Pasquini (FR) 122–Comme Un **108** Garcon (FR) (Dom Racine (FR) 121) [1990 6d⁵ 6g⁵ 7g³ 8g4 0d² 10s⁶] first foal: dam ran 3 times at 2 yrs in France: useful French maiden: best effort ¾-length second of 4 to Pigeon Voyageur in Prix Saint-Roman at Longchamp in September: better subsequent effort in pattern races in Prix de Conde on same course in October: stays 9f: possibly unsuited by very soft ground. *B. Secly, France.*

CLASS ACT 4 b.g. Shirley Heights 130–Thespian 76 (Ile de Bourbon (USA) 133) **62** [1989 10m⁴ 10g 13.1h⁴ 12m² 12m⁵ 14f⁵ 14m 1990 12h* 14g4 16m² 16.2f² 13.8m* 16f² a14g] sturdy gelding: moderate mover: won 3-runner handicap at Brighton (making all) in May and apprentice claimer at Catterick (odds on, under hands and heels) in July: ran creditably most other starts at 4 yrs: stays 2m: acts on hard going: blinkered final outing: has swished tail: resolution under suspicion. *J. W. Hills.*

CLASS ADORNS 3 b.f. Sadler's Wells (USA) 132–Connaught Bridge 124 — (Connaught 130) [1989 NR 1990 11.5g⁵ 10.5g] strong, good-topped filly with scope: carries condition: fifth living foal: half-sister to 4 winners, including very useful 1986 French 2-y-o Conmaiche (by Kings Lake), later successful over middle distances, and 1½m to 1¾m winner Wassl Reef (by Mill Reef): dam high-class middle-distance performer: well beaten in late-season minor event at Lingfield and maiden at York. *P. W. Harris.*

CLASSIC ACCOUNT 2 ch.c. (Apr 7) Pharly (FR) 130–Money Supply — (Brigadier Gerard 144) [1990 7m 7s a8g] 13,500F, 7,000Y: workmanlike colt: third foal: half-brother to 1988 Irish 2-y-o 6.3f winner Roman Citizen (by Electric) and 1m winner Aldwick Colonnade (by Kind of Hush): dam unraced sister to very useful Irish 1m winner Senior Citizen: well beaten in maiden at Chepstow and Lingfield. *C. P. Wildman.*

CLASSIC COURT 2 b.c. (Apr 12) Lidhame 109–Cocoban (Targowice (USA) 130) **48** [1990 6f 8g 7f⁶ 7d⁶ 6s] IR 6,500Y: rather sparely-made colt: fifth foal: half-brother to Irish 1987 2-y-o 6f winner Daroban (by Formidable), middle-distance staying maiden Emperors Warrior (by High Line) and a winner abroad: dam won in Italy: modest plater: seems suited by 7f: acts on firm and dead ground: races freely. *M. Brittain.*

CLASSIC MINSTREL (USA) 2 b.c. (Mar 6) The Minstrel (CAN) 135–Bold **79 p** Caress 104 (Bold Lad (IRE) 133) [1990 7s*] IR 155,000Y: half-brother to 2 winners, including smart miler Homo Sapien (by Lord Gayle): dam Irish 7f winner from 3 starts, is sister to very useful filly Foiled Again: favourite, won 14-runner maiden at the Curragh in October by ¾ length: likely to do better. *M. V. O'Brien, Ireland.*

CLASSIC RING (IRE) 2 b.f. (May 3) Auction Ring (USA) 123–Classic Choice **50** (Patch 129) [1990 5g 5m⁵ 6g³ 6g³ 6d⁵ 7g⁵ 7m* 7f 6m 7m⁴ 7m³ a8g 8.5m² 8.2g³ 10.6s 7d] IR 6,200Y: leggy filly: has a roundish action: third foal: half-sister to French 3-y-o Jones Beach (by Sandhurst Prince), 7f winner at 2 yrs: dam unraced: fair plater: made all (no bid) at Catterick in July: ran badly on all-weather: stays 1m: seems unsuited by a soft surface: ideally suited by forcing tactics: trained first 4 starts by C. Allen: sold 1,000 gns Doncaster October Sales. *T. Fairhurst.*

CLASSICS PEARL (IRE) 2 gr.f. (Feb 27) Reasonable (FR) 119–Zanskar **49** (Godswalk (USA) 130) [1990 6m 6g⁵ 6m⁶ 6m⁶ 7f⁶ 6d 10.6s] IR 3,800Y: strong, stocky filly: moderate walker: fourth foal: half-sister to winning sprinter Iron King (by Tender King) and an ungenuine animal by Rusticaro: dam Irish 2-y-o 5f winner: poor maiden: stays 7f. *M. J. Haynes.*

CLASSIC STATEMENT 4 ch.c. Mill Reef (USA) 141–Lady Graustark (USA) **78** (Graustark) [1989 10.6g a10g 10g 1990 14g⁶ 14g 16.2m⁵ 18g⁵] leggy, quite attractive colt: fair handicapper: needs extreme test of stamina. *Mrs J. Pitman.*

CLASSIC SUITE 4 b.g. Ya Zaman (USA) 122–Lady Bidder (Auction Ring (USA) 123) [1989 8.2s* 9f 8m 8f⁵ 7f² 8.2f⁴ 8m* 8m 8.2d* 7s³ 8d 1990 8f 10v 8f⁵ 7.5d a8g a8g 10d⁶] lengthy, sparely-made gelding: moderate walker: poor mover: won 3 claimers as 3-y-o: well below his best in 1990: best form at about 1m: acts on any going. *R. M. Whitaker.*

CLASSIC VENTURE (IRE) 2 b.c. (Apr 3) Fairy King (USA)–Allorette 100 **78 p** (Ballymore 123) [1990 7d*] IR 62,000Y: third foal: half-brother to Irish 2m winner Sarah's Luck (by Sayyaf): dam Irish middle-distance stayer: favourite, won 16-runner maiden at the Curragh in October by 3 lengths: will stay 1¼m: sure to do better. *M. V. O'Brien, Ireland.*

CLAUDETTE 2 b.f. (Mar 5) Claude Monet (USA) 121–Miss Twights (Hopeful — Venture 125) [1990 6f 6f 6g 8.2g] 5,000Y: big, lengthy filly: has round action: half-sister to 4 minor winners abroad: dam twice-raced half-sister to smart miler Miracle: seems of little account: blinkered final outing: races slowly away. *F. J. Yardley.*

CLAUDIA MISS 3 b.f. Claude Monet (USA) 121–Palace Travel (High Top 131) **65** [1989 6g³ 7m⁵ 1990 8g⁶ 10.6s 8m² 8.2s⁴ 7g 7g⁵ 7f⁴ 7v*] workmanlike filly: poor mover: quite modest performer: won claimer at Ayr in October by a head, held up then plugging lead from 2f out: stays 1m: acts on any going, with possible exception of very firm: has often worn a crossed noseband. *W. W. Haigh.*

CLAY COUNTY 5 b.g. Sheer Grit 117–Make-Up 69 (Bleep-Bleep 134) [1989 **60** 12g⁵ 1990 11s⁴] leggy, quite good-topped gelding: has a round action: first form on flat when fourth of 18 in maiden at Hamilton in April: stays 11f: acts on soft going: likely to be suited by forcing tactics: winning hurdler, including in October. *R. Allan.*

CLAYSUUMAR 3 b.f. Montekin 125–Good Court (Takawalk II 125) [1989 5.3g³ — 5s⁴ 5f* 6f³ 7m 1990 8m 8f⁵ 8h⁴ 10.1g] lengthy, plain, sparely-made filly: plater: should stay 7f: acts on firm going: sold 2,700 gns Ascot June Sales. *R. Hannon.*

CLEAN AND POLISH 3 ch.g. Superlative 118–Greek Blessing 83 (So Blessed **39** 130) [1989 6m 6g 1990 7f 6m 5g 6h⁴ 6m 6m 7h] rangy, unfurnished gelding: moderate mover: form only when fourth in handicap at Brighton, hanging left 2f out: gambled on in seller there final start, in July: worth another try beyond 6f: blinkered sixth outing: has joined A. Denson. *G. Lewis.*

CLEAN UP 2 b.g. (Mar 1) Another Realm 118–Tudor Carnival (Last Fandango — 125) [1990 6m 7m⁴ 6m 6m a8g 8.5m 6d] 1,000F: strong, compact gelding: first foal: dam unraced: of little account: visored penultimate start. *N. Bycroft.*

CLEAR COMEDY (IRE) 2 br.f. (May 24) Jester 119–Clear Belle (Klairon 131) 65 [1990 7m 7g 6d⁶ a6g*] IR 8,000Y: workmanlike filly, rather unfurnished: half-sister to several winners here and abroad, including 1986 2-y-o 6f winner King Krimson (by Indian King) and useful Italian performer at up to 1m Laser Belle (by Laser Light): dam poor maiden: ridden by 5-lb claimer, won 8-runner maiden at Lingfield in December by a short head from Penando, showing much improved form. *R. Hannon.*

CLEAR IDEA (IRE) 2 ch.c. (Mar 11) Try My Best (USA) 130–Sloane Ranger 84 62 (Sharpen Up 127) [1990 8g⁴ 8g] IR 30,000Y: tall, quite attractive colt: fifth reported living foal: half-brother to 3-y-o Yarra Glen (by Known Fact) and 2 winners, including 6f to 1m winner Liffey Reef (by Main Reef): dam won at up to 1m: green, fourth to Jahafil in minor event at Sandown, every chance 2f out then not knocked about: took keen hold when well beaten in similar contest at Newbury later in September. *C. R. Nelson.*

CLEAR LEADER 2 ch.c. (Feb 2) Caerleon (USA) 132–Moulin Rapide (USA) 55 (Roberto (USA) 131) [1990 7m 8g 8.2s⁶ 10s 10.2s a7g] 13,000Y: rather unfurnished colt: first foal: dam daughter of Ribblesdale third Fenney Mill: plating-class maiden: should stay 1¼m: sold 1,400 gns Ascot November Sales. *R. F. Johnson Houghton.*

CLEAR LIGHT 3 ch.c. Exhibitioner 111–Beach Light 89 (Bustino 136) [1989 6f⁵ 78 6g⁴ 1990 7m 8g 8d* 10m 9m 10v⁵ 10g*] angular, useful-looking colt: modest performer: successful at Yarmouth in handicap in June and claimer (by 6 lengths) in October: no form in between, in Cambridgeshire Handicap (visored and sweating) at Newmarket fifth start: stays 1¼m well: acts on dead ground: has run well for 7-lb claimer: joined M. Pipe. *G. A. Huffer.*

CLEONTE 3 b.c. Dominion 123–Be Faithful 93 (Val de Loir 133) [1989 NR 1990 101 p 10m² 11f* 11.5m*] 37,000Y: well-made colt: closely related to fair 9f winner Top Wing and a winner in USA (both by High Top) and half-brother to 3 winners, including miler Onika (by Great Nephew): dam 2-y-o 7f winner, is half-sister to high-class sprinter Apollo Nine and to dam of Enstone Spark: successful in small fields for maiden at Redcar in May and minor event (went freely to post) at Lingfield in June: withdrawn lame before Haydock listed race (in July): stays 11f: may be capable of better. *L. Cumani.*

CLEVER CLAUDE 4 b.g. Cragador 110–La Mirabelle 92 (Princely Gift 137) 41 [1989 8g⁶ 7f 10h⁴ 11.7m 7m⁶ 1990 8.3m⁵] leggy, shallow-girthed gelding: modest form as 2-y-o: below his best since first outing in 1989: seems to stay 1m: blinkered first 2 starts as 3-y-o: has sweated and got on edge: winner of 2 selling hurdles early in 1990/1. *W. M. Perrin.*

CLIFTON CHAPEL 5 b.g. High Line 125–Britannia's Rule 108 (Blakeney 126) 76 [1989 16f³ 14m 12g 11v⁴ᵈⁱˢ 12d a14g³ a16g³ 1990 16.2s⁴ 18d³] rather angular gelding: keen walker: powerful mover: one-time useful performer: showed he retains plenty of ability in autumn, staying-on third to Trainglot in Tote Cesarewitch at Newmarket: stays very well: goes particularly well with plenty of give in the ground: slipped when blinkered: winning hurdler in March. *H. Candy.*

CLIFTON CHARLIE (USA) 2 b.c. (Mar 30) Crafty Prospector (USA)– 108 Illustrious Joanne (USA) (Illustrious) [1990 6g⁶ 5d* 5g³ 5m* 6m* 5m²] $45,000Y: lengthy colt: second foal: dam won 4 races at up to 9f: progressive colt: successful in maiden at Haydock in September and nurseries at Newmarket (making all to win readily on second occasion) within 3 days in October: very good second of 11 to Mujadil in Cornwallis Stakes at Ascot: effective at 5f and 6f: sometimes sweats: useful. *C. R. Nelson.*

CLIFTON HAMPDEN 2 b.c. (Feb 15) Blakeney 126–Red Ruby 113 (Tudor 65 p Melody 129) [1990 8d⁴] compact, rather sparely-made colt: brother to 1¾m winner Shingle Ridge and half-brother to several other winners, including useful 7f winner Entrancing (by Posse): dam, half-sister to smart sprinter Laser Light, was very useful miler: bit backward and very green, 10 lengths fourth of 8, losing place at halfway then staying on well, to Peking Opera in maiden at Leicester in October: will improve, particularly over 1¼m + . *Lady Herries.*

CLIPPERINA (USA) 2 b.f. (Mar 2) L'Emigrant (USA) 129–Wield (USA) 72 p (Judger (USA)) [1990 7g⁴] $75,000Y: tall, lengthy filly: has scope: sixth foal: sister to French 1989 2-y-o 7f winner Soleil d'Argent: dam unraced daughter of Special, dam also of Nureyev and grandam of Sadler's Wells and Tate Gallery: looking very

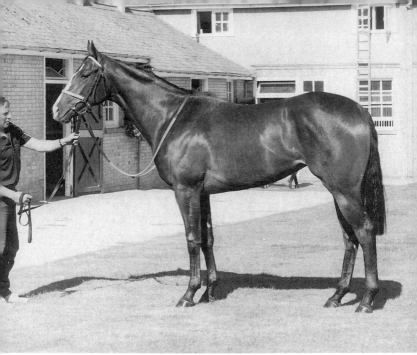

Mrs C. Pateras' "Cloche d'Or"

well, shaped promisingly when over 4 lengths fourth of 20, leading over 2f out until over 1f out and not knocked about when beaten, to Campestral in maiden at Newmarket in November: sure to improve, and win a race. *M. R. Stoute.*

CLIPPING   2 b.f. (Mar 28) Kris 135–Valkyrie 87 (Bold Lad (IRE) 133) [1990 6g³   **76** 6m³] rather unfurnished filly: has a quick action: third foal: sister to 1989 2-y-o 6f winner Flamberge and half-sister to 1987 2-y-o 6f to 1¼m winner Valentine (by Cure The Blues): dam half-sister to smart middle-distance performer Sabre Dance, ran only at 2 yrs, winning at 5f: favourite, never able to challenge in maidens won by Zonda at Newbury in August and Safa at Nottingham following month: will be suited by 1m or more. *H. R. A. Cecil.*

CLIVOLI (IRE)   2 b.c. (May 12) Muscatite 122–Miss Annie 73 (Scottish Rifle   — 127) [1990 6g⁵] 6,200 2-y-o: third foal: half-brother to moderate plater Joshykin (by Montekin): dam 7f and 1¾m winner: soundly-beaten last of 5 in maiden at Hamilton in June. *J. S. Wilson.*

CLOCHE D'OR   2 b.f. (Apr 25) Good Times (ITY)–Chrysicabana 88 (Home   **100** Guard (USA) 129) [1990 6m² 6g³ 7m³ 6m* 6m³ 6.5g⁵] lengthy, angular filly: has scope: third foal: sister to 3-y-o Krissos and half-sister to 1987 2-y-o 6f winner Dominion Treasure (by Dominion): dam 1¼m winner: useful filly: won 4-runner Princess Margaret Stakes at Ascot in July: creditable third, keeping on, to Only Yours in 'Pacemaker Update' Lowther Stakes at York following month: should be well suited by further than 6f: best form on good to firm ground. *C. E. Brittain.*

CLOCK GOLF   3 b.f. Mummy's Game 120–Stuff And Nonsense 86 (Crooner 119)   — [1989 6d 6g a6g⁴ a7g a8g³ 1990 a8g⁶ a10g⁴ a7g⁶ 8.3g] workmanlike, angular filly: quite modest maiden at 2 yrs well beaten early in 1990: suited by 1m: blinkered final

186

start at 2 yrs and first 2 (and hooded) at 3 yrs: sold out of F. J. Houghton's stable 1,300 gns Ascot February Sales after second: has joined J. Moore. *P. D. Cundell.*

CLOS DU BOIS (FR) 4 b.g. High Top 131–Our Shirley 84 (Shirley Heights 130) 52 [1989 10.1m5 12m3 12g3 a11g a8g 1990 11.5g 10d3 a11g] small, sparely-made gelding: form at 4 yrs only when third in seller at Folkestone in November: should stay 1½m: acts on good to firm and dead going: visored final start at 3 yrs: bandaged last 2 starts in 1990: winning hurdler. *Mrs N. Macauley.*

CLOSED SHOP 3 b.f. Auction Ring (USA) 123–Silent Sun 90 (Blakeney 126) — [1989 5d6 6m* 7m* 7m6 7f3 8g5 8f* 1990 8f 8g] neat filly: poor mover: quite modest winner at 2 yrs: suited by 1m: acted on firm ground: good mount for an apprentice: dead. *S. Dow.*

CLOSE FRIEND (IRE) 2 gr.c. (Feb 3) Law Society (USA) 130–Bellifontaine 59 p (FR) (Bellypha 130) [1990 7g] IR 62,000Y: deep-girthed colt: first foal: dam French 1m winner: green, beaten around 2 lengths, tenderly handled last 2f, when in mid-division for 17-runner minor event at Kempton in September: will stay 1¼m: capable of better. *B. W. Hills.*

CLOSE THE DEAL 2 ch.f. (Mar 30) Nicholas Bill 125–Cateryne (Ballymoss 51 136) [1990 6m 7.5f 6f2 7g5 7m2 10m4] 3,500Y: sparely-made filly: half-sister to 3 modest winners at up to 8.2f: dam ran once: plating-class maiden: stays 1¼m: sometimes sweats. *A. N. Lee.*

CLOUD BASE 4 br.g. Another Realm 118–A-Bye 116 (Abernant 142) [1989 7m — 5m 1990 a6g a5g] sparely-made gelding: no form, including in seller: blinkered on reappearance. *O. O'Neill.*

CLOUDED LAMP (USA) 3 b.c. Majestic Light (USA)–Unforetold (USA) 85 (Foolish Pleasure (USA)) [1989 NR 1990 8g 10.1m 7m4 7g4 9g 7f* 8.2d* 8d3] $350,000Y: good-topped colt: has plenty of scope: moderate mover: first foal: dam minor winner at up to 7f, is sister to Pleasure Cay, stakes winner at up to 9f: progressive form: won maiden at Catterick (slowly away) and moderately-run apprentice handicap at Haydock week later in September: stays 1m: acts on firm and dead ground: edged left behind horses fourth start: blinkered last 5: sold 15,500 gns Newmarket Autumn Sales. *J. Gosden.*

CLOUD FREE (USA) 3 ch.f. Conquistador Cielo (USA)–Pleasant Flight (USA) 56 + (Bold Ruler) [1989 NR 1990 12m4 12h2] $230,000Y: sturdy, good-topped filly: eleventh foal: half-sister to several winners, notably Grade 3 1½m winner Flittalong (by Herbager) and fair 1½m winner On A Cloud (by Val de L'Orne): dam, 2-y-o 6f winner, is sister to What A Pleasure and half-sister to leading filly Misty Morn: fourth in maiden at Beverley, looking sure to win once quickening clear over 2f out but weakening and caught close home: 11/10 favourite on first run for 3½ months, soundly beaten in similar event at Brighton. *G. Harwood.*

CLOVERMILL 2 b.f. (May 23) Sayf El Arab (USA) 127–Opinion 71 (Great 78 p Nephew 126) [1990 6m3] 1,100F, 7,000Y: sixth foal: half-sister to 3 winners, including fairly useful middle-distance handicapper Stratford Ponds (by High Top) and Kokoshka (by Alias Smith), successful at up to 2m in Ireland: dam 1½m winner, is half-sister to very useful stayer Kambalda: 4 lengths third of 19, disputing lead 4f and unable to quicken, to Shihama in maiden at Newmarket in November: will stay further: should improve. *H. Candy.*

CLWYD LODGE 3 b.g. Blakeney 126 High Carnaval (High Top 131) [1989 a7g 54 1990 a8g a10g 12.3d 14g3 16.2s 14m5 16f* 16m4 18.1m3 16m 16s2] sturdy gelding: moderate mover: plating-class handicapper: game winner at Redcar in July: will prove suited by thorough test of stamina: acts on any going: blinkered second start: sometimes sweating and edgy. *D. T. Thom.*

CLYRO 2 b.f. (Mar 25) Kind of Hush 118–Clear As Crystal 80 (Whitstead 125) 76 [1990 6m4 6m* 6f4 8d6 8m2] 400Y: angular filly: second foal: half-sister to 3-y-o 1½m winner Hot Rumour (by Hotfoot): dam 11.7f winner on only start: modest performer: won claimer at Chepstow in July: good second in nursery at Warwick later: much better suited by 1m than 6f: acts on firm and dead ground. *R. J. Holder.*

COBB GATE 2 b.c. (May 7) Creetown 123–Glazepta Final (Final Straw 127) — [1990 6m 6g5 7m] big, good-topped colt: first foal: dam of little account: seems of little account. *B. Stevens.*

COCKED HAT GIRL 3 ch.f. Ballacashtal (CAN)–Screen Goddess 65 (Caliban 37 123) [1989 5g6 5d6 6f5 6g5 6f2 6m6 7m6 6g 10.6d5 1990 8g a12g 10g 10m5 10m5 10.6v3 12.5m2 18d 12d a11g15] big, workmanlike filly: modest plater: stays 1½m: acts on any going: sometimes bandaged behind: has run well when on toes and sweating: blinkered 3 times at 2 yrs. *S. R. Bowring.*

COE 4 b. or br.g. Coquelin (USA) 121–Gully (Dike (USA)) [1989 8v⁵ 8m* 12f* 12f* —
12g 1990 10g] half-brother to a winner in Italy: dam won at up to 2m in Ireland:
trained by J. Oxx, won handicaps at Gowran Park, Mallow and Roscommon as 3-y-o:
needed race only outing in 1990: stays 1½m: acts on firm going: fairly useful hurdler,
successful in October. *R. Akehurst.*

COEURETTE 4 b.f. Nicholas Bill 125–Take To Heart 72 (Steel Heart 128) [1989 —
a12g a10g 1990 a14g] sparely-made filly: seems of little account: sold 725 gns Ascot
February Sales. *D. Burchell.*

COINAGE 7 gr.g. Owen Dudley 121–Grisbi 96 (Grey Sovereign 128§) [1989 16f⁵ —
1990 12h⁵ 16.2m 11.5m⁶ 12m 16m] big, rangy gelding: fairly useful performer in
1986: little subsequent worthwhile form on flat: used to be suited by a test of
stamina and top-of-the-ground: has run tubed: winning hurdler/novice chaser. *R. F.
Johnson Houghton.*

COINCIDENTAL 8 b.g. Persian Bold 123–Gentle Mulla (Sun Prince 128) [1989 56
7g 6f⁶ 7f 7m 7f² 7g 7f 8m³ 8g² 8.2m⁵ 8g⁵ 9.1f³ 8m³ 8f³ 8g 7.3m* 8g 7g 7g a7g³ 1990
a7g² a7g⁵ a8g 7g 8m a7g 8.3f³ 8.3m⁵ 8g 8f⁴ 7.5m a8g⁶ a7g] close-coupled,
workmanlike gelding: poor mover: quite modest handicapper: effective at 7f and
stays 9f: acts very well on top-of-the-ground and is unsuited by heavy: occasionally
bandaged: has worn a tongue strap: has gone freely to post: keen sort, usually
ridden up with pace. *D. Morris.*

COIN GAME (IRE) 2 b.f. (Apr 1) Dalsaan 125–Canhaar (Sparkler 130) [1990 7m —
7g] second foal: dam Irish 1½m winner: bit backward, never near leaders in autumn
maidens at Lingfield and Folkestone. *R. Hannon.*

COIR 'A' GHAILL 2 b.f. (Mar 28) Jalmood (USA) 126–Karsavina 89 (Silly 38
Season 127) [1990 6m 6f² 6g 7m] 6,000F, 1,900Y: leggy filly: half-sister to fairly
useful 1m and 9f winner The Shrew (by Relko) and 2 other winners: dam, runner-up
in Cherry Hinton, half-sister to very useful miler Boswellia and Triumph Hurdle
winner Peterhof: poor form, including in a seller. *R. V. Smyth.*

COLD BLOW 3 b.f. Posse (USA) 130–Warm Wind 84 (Tumble Wind (USA)) —
[1989 5g 6f 7m² 1990 10f⁴ 8f 8m⁴] sparely-made filly: maiden, quite modest form
when putting up easily best effort final start at 2 yrs: ran in seller final one in 1990:
worth another try over 1¼m: has given trouble in preliminaries. *M. J. Camacho.*

COLD MARBLE (USA) 5 b.g. Told (USA)–Coney Dell 77 (Ercolano (USA) 72
118) [1989 12d 12f² 12m⁶ 16m⁴ 16m⁴ 1990 12g⁴ 16m⁶ 14s 15m² 14.6d⁴] rather leggy,
workmanlike gelding: usually looks well: poor mover: modest handicapper: stays
2m: acts on firm and dead going: has won for apprentice: sold out of W. Haggas'
stable 15,500 gns Newmarket July Sales after fourth start. *D. R. Tucker.*

COLFAX LAD 3 br.c. Blue Cashmere 129–Silken Swift 83 (Saulingo 122) [1989 —
NR 1990 8.5m⁵ 8.2s 8f 12g] 4,400Y: leggy, sparely-made colt: sixth foal: half-brother
to 6f (at 2 yrs) to 17f winner Miss Pokey (by Uncle Pokey) and a winner in Norway by
Import: dam won over 7f and stayed 1¼m: no sign of ability in maiden events and
handicap: blinkered final start. *J. Parkes.*

COLFAX SAM 3 b.c. Norwick (USA) 120–Alwen (Blakeney 126) [1989 7.5f 7m⁵ —
6m 8.2f 1990 9m 10g 8f⁵] light-framed colt: moderate mover: poor maiden: twice
blinkered: has run wide into straight 3 times: sold 800 gns Ascot July Sales. *J.
Parkes.*

COLIN SELLER 3 ch.g. Noalto 120–Mallow 70 (Le Dieu d'Or 119) [1989 7m⁴ 57
6m 6f² 8f a6g² a7g⁴ a8g⁴ 1990 12f³ 12.3f 10.2m a12g 5m² 6f* a5g⁵ 6m 6g⁶ 5f²
5.1m⁶ 6g] good-topped, workmanlike gelding: has a quick action: quite modest
handicapper: made all at Yarmouth in July: ran badly in seller final start: may prove
ideally suited by 6f: goes well on firm going: blinkered fifth to ninth starts: has
joined P. Blockley. *R. Boss.*

COLLINS AVENUE (USA) 2 b.c. (Apr 2) Linkage (USA)–Trolling (USA) (Sir 76 p
Gaylord) [1990 6d²] $15,000Y: unfurnished colt: has a markedly round action:
half-brother to 2 winners by Coastal, one in minor stakes: dam minor winner from
family of Big Shuffle: sire high class at up to 9½f: looking really well but green, 2
lengths second of 18, bumping another when switched 2f out then running on in
great style, to Reshift in maiden at Doncaster in November: sure to improve,
particularly over further, and win a race. *B. W. Hills.*

COLNE STAR 2 br.f. (Apr 10) Primo Dominie 121–Broomstick Cottage (Habitat —
134) [1990 5g] 1,150Y: lengthy filly: first foal: dam never ran: backward and edgy,
slowly away and always behind in maiden at Wolverhampton in October: moved
poorly down: sold 1,800 gns Newmarket Autumn Sales. *E. Eldin.*

COLOMBIAN GOLD (IRE) 2 ch.c. (Apr 22) Red Sunset 120–Cafe Au Lait 97 85
(Espresso 122) [1990 6m⁵ 6f⁴ 7m⁴ 7f⁵ 8f*] 44,000Y: neat colt: brother to very useful
middle-distance performer Beeshi and half-brother to several other winners,
including useful 1¼m and 10.5f winner Chaumiere (by Thatching) and fairly useful
stayer Brando (by Busted): dam stayed 1½m: blinkered first time, won nursery at
Bath, showing improved form, in September: will stay 1¼m: a difficult ride: sold
13,000 gns Ascot October Sales. *R. Hannon.*

COLONEL CHINSTRAP 5 ch.g. Milford 119–Deep Blue Sea (Gulf Pearl 117) —
[1989 12g 12.5g⁶ 12m⁶ 12h⁴ 12g 10h³ 11g 12m* 1990 10f] lengthy gelding: moderate
mover: winning plater as 4-y-o: seemed ill at ease on track at Folkestone in March:
will stay beyond 1½m: acts on hard going: blinkered once: not the easiest of rides.
A. Moore.

COLONIAL LASS 3 ch.f. Saher 115–Colonial Line (USA) 75 (Plenty Old (USA)) —
[1989 NR 1990 5f 8h] fourth foal: half-sister to fairly useful 1m and 9f winner
Secretary of State (by Alzao): dam, best at 2 yrs, won over 5f at 3 yrs and 4 yrs:
behind in sellers at Bath and Brighton. *R. Simpson.*

COLONIAL LEGEND 2 ch.f. (Mar 3) Dominion 123–Dynamic Mistress 96 (No 40
Mercy 126) [1990 5m 5m² 5g a6g 6f 5m 5g 8m⁵ 7d 8g] small, workmanlikc filly:
half-sister to middle-distance plater Touch The Wind (by Windjammer): dam 2-y-o
5f winner: poor maiden: stays 1m: best form on good to firm ground: blinkered sixth
start: trained first 6 outings by J. Hills: inconsistent. *K. T. Ivory.*

COLONIAL SPIRIT 2 b. or br.c. (Mar 5) Primo Dominie 121–Persian Case 62
(Upper Case (USA)) [1990 6m³ 6f 7d³ 7g] 9,200F, 10,000Y: rather angular colt: sixth
living foal: half-brother to 3-y-o Persian Soldier (by Sandhurst Prince), 7f winner at
2 yrs, and 2 other winners, including 1987 2-y-o 7.5f winner Dissolution (by Henbit):
dam French 2-y-o 7.8f winner: quite modest maiden: gave impression something
amiss second outing: stays 7f. *J. M. P. Eustace.*

COLONNA (USA) 4 b.g. Run The Gantlet (USA)–Evolutionary (USA) (Silent 45
Screen (USA)) [1989 12f³ 14d 12.4g² 1990 a11g 14m⁶ 12.5f³ 17m⁴ 21.6m 16.2g 15.8g
15.3g a14g] close-coupled, quite good-topped gelding: moderate walker and mover:
poor form at best as 4-y-o: well beaten in handicaps last 5 outings: stays 17f:
blinkered on reappearance: sold out of C. Beever's stable 2,100 gns Doncaster June
Sales after eighth outing: winning hurdler in October. *J. L. Harris.*

COLORFAYRE 2 ch.f. (Jan 29) Tate Gallery (USA) 117–Independentia 68 59
(Home Guard (USA) 129) [1990 7m⁴ 7f³ 7m a6g³] third known foal: half-sister to a
winner in USA by London Bells: dam maiden stayed 1m, is granddaughter of
Musidora winner Jakomima: plating-class maiden: stays 7f. *L. J. Codd.*

COLORTAG 4 b.g. Runnett 125–Two's Company (Sheshoon 132) [1989 NR 1990 —
10f] rangy gelding: well tailed off having pulled hard in £4,000 contest at Kempton in
April, only second outing: reared stalls both starts. *Miss B. Sanders.*

COLOSSUS 2 ch.c. (Jan 20) Good Times (ITY)–Adrana 86 (Bold Lad (IRE) 133) — p
[1990 8s] lengthy, dipped-backed colt: second foal: dam 2-y-o 5f winner on only
start, is half-sister to Ardross: better for race, which leaders 4f then dropped away
quickly in minor event at Newbury in October. *C. E. Brittain.*

COLOUR CHART (USA) 3 b.f. Mr Prospector (USA)–Rainbow Connec- 122
tion (CAN) (Halo (USA)) [1989 8d* 1990 9d⁶ 10.5d³ 10.5d⁴ 10d⁵ 10g* 9.2g*]
The Ciga Prix de l'Opera on Arc day was run in a manner typical of races
over the round course at Longchamp, and had typical consequences. A dawdle
to the straight followed by a dash for the line resulted in a bunched finish,
twelve fillies within ten lengths of the winner, several of them unlucky or
apparently unlucky, others flattered or apparently thus. In the test of finishing
speed Colour Chart impressed enormously. Held up and last into the straight
except for Eddery's mount Taffeta And Tulle (who eventually came fifth of
fourteen after meeting all sorts of trouble), she made smooth headway to take
the lead over a furlong out and quickened on to lift the prize easily by two
lengths from the four-year-old Lady Winner. Although the results of such
races do tend to be among the more difficult to interpret, there's no doubt
Colour Chart is every bit as good as she looked. She'd already done enough to
prove it in the Prix de Diane Hermes at Chantilly back in June and more
recently in the Prix de la Nonette at Longchamp, finishing a half-length
second to Rafha in the former and winning by a length and a half and a length
from Spendomania and Cruising Height in the latter, on both occasions
showing an excellent turn of foot. The winner of a newcomers event at

Ciga Prix de l'Opera, Longchamp—
Colour Chart produces a fine turn of foot to win from Lady Winner and Tabdea

Longchamp on her only start as a two-year-old, she took another three races, until the Diane, to reveal her true ability. Colour Chart wasn't allowed to keep her clear second place in the Diane, for she'd interfered with Air de Rien when switched abruptly right to make a run well over a furlong out, and subsequently the stewards placed her behind Air de Rien in fourth, at the same time handing out a suspension to her jockey Asmussen which, added to a previous one, kept him out of Royal Ascot week. On her only outing between the Diane and the Nonette, Colour Chart was one of several good-class animals made to appear ordinary by Saumarez in the Grand Prix de Paris: she finished fifth, just over three lengths behind the second horse Priolo.

```
                              ┌Raise A Native  ┌Native Dancer
               ┌Mr Prospector (USA) │  (ch 1961)    │Raise You
               │  (b 1970)          └Gold Digger    │Nashua
Colour Chart (USA) ┤                   (b 1962)     └Sequence
   (b.f. 1987)  │Rainbow           ┌Halo           ┌Hail To Reason
               │Connection (CAN)  │  (b or br 1969) │Cosmah
               └  (b 1978)         └Hangin Round    ┌Stage Door Johnny
                                      (b 1970)      └Auburn's Pride
```

Colour Chart, the fourth foal of the twice-champion Canadian mare Rainbow Connection, was bought for 675,000 dollars as a foal at her breeder Hermitage Farm's dispersal sale. Previous matings had produced two runners, Zajal (by Seattle Slew) and Dance Spectrum (by Lyphard). Zajal won the Clarence House Stakes at Ascot in 1986; the following year he became disappointing in the USA after finishing well beaten in the Guardian Classic Trial and Poule d'Essai des Poulains, and ended up in Venezuela. Dance Spectrum, in contrast, has proved a really progressive sort and he developed into a smart stayer in the latest season. The next dam Hangin Round, who bred three other Grade 1 (Canadian) winners, was a daughter of a mare sold out of Major Hern's stable for export after winning over five furlongs at Manchester as a two-year-old. That mare Auburn's Pride traced back in two generations to Verdura, so came from one of the best families of Hern's patron L. B. Holliday, that of the very speedy Gratitude and Pharsalia, the Prix Vermeille winner Highest Hopes and the Cesarewitch winner Avon's Pride. *A. Fabre, France.*

COLOURIST 3 b.c. Petorius 117–Flaxen Hair (Thatch (USA) 136) [1989 6m³ 6g⁵ **91**
1990 6g 7f² 7.5g* 8g* 8d³ 8f 10g³ 9g⁴] compact colt: fairly useful handicapper: progressive form when justifying favouritism at Beverley and Ripon in May then third in Britannia Handicap at Royal Ascot: stays 1¼m: best efforts on an easy surface: has run creditably for apprentice: sold 34,000 gns Newmarket Autumn Sales, probably to race in Italy. *A. C. Stewart.*

COLOUR QUEST 2 ch.f. (Mar 20) Rainbow Quest (USA) 134–Formulate 119 **— p**
(Reform 132) [1990 7g⁶] compact, rather angular filly: seventh live foal: half-sister to 3-y-o 1¼m winner Game Plan (by Darshaan) and several winners here and abroad, including 15.8f winner Almarreekh (by Glint of Gold): dam top staying 2-y-o

filly of 1978, ran only twice afterwards: bit backward and green, over 9 lengths sixth of 9, slowly away, edging left 2f out and not knocked about, in maiden at Wolverhampton in July: will stay middle distances: should improve. *C. E. Brittain.*

COLOUR SCHEME 3 ch.g. Rainbow Quest (USA) 134–Much Pleasure 65 (Morston (FR) 125) [1989 NR 1990 7f 6f6 8f 10g 8f3 a8g* a8g* 8f5 a11g2 9s5 8m 12g a11g2 a12g4 a10g4] leggy, unfurnished gelding: seventh foal: half-brother to fair 6f (at 2 yrs) and 1m winner Rosie Potts (by Shareef Dancer) and very useful middle-distance performer Trakady (by Relkino): dam unraced half-sister to Hard Fought: quite modest handicapper: ridden by 7-lb claimer, won twice at Southwell in July: easily best subsequent efforts also on all-weather: suited by 1¼m + : claimed out of G. Lewis' stable £6,010 in Brighton seller fifth start. *J. R. Jenkins.*

COLOUR SERGEANT 2 br.c. (Mar 9) Green Desert (USA) 127–Tartan 79 p Pimpernel 109 (Blakeney 126) [1990 6g4 6g] strong, close-coupled colt: half-brother to prolific 3-y-o winning hurdler Hopscotch (by Dominion) and 3 winners, including fairly useful 1983 2-y-o 7f winner Elusive (by Little Current): dam, half-sister to Dunfermline, won May Hill and Galtres Stakes: carrying condition and green, 4 lengths fourth of 5 to Tiswa in minor event at Chester: last of 7, travelling well until 2f out in Rokeby Farms Mill Reef Stakes at Newbury later in September: looks sort to do better. *W. Hastings-Bass.*

COLSAN BOY 3 b.c. Remainder Man 126§–Wimbledon's Pet (Mummy's Pet 44 125) [1989 5m5 5m 6f4 6m 5f4 5d6 5m a6g 1990 a6g 6f* 5m3 7f 6h5 6m 6f] leggy, quite good-topped colt: poor walker: poor handicapper: won apprentice event at Folkestone in April: stays 7f: acts on firm and dead going: blinkered or visored 7 times, running poorly final start at 3 yrs. *M. D. I. Usher.*

COLVIN LAD 3 gr.g. Rusticaro (FR) 124–Twice Regal (Royal Prerogative 119) 43 [1989 6m6 6g 1990 a8g 11d4] leggy, good-topped gelding: poor maiden: stays 11f. *W. W. Haigh.*

COLWAY ANN 2 b.f. (Feb 4) Nomination 125–Sharp Run (Sharpen Up 127) 47 [1990 5f6 6d3 5f4 7f 6m 6v3 5s3] 4,800Y: close-coupled, unfurnished filly: second foal: dam never ran: plating-class maiden: hung left and looked ungenuine on fourth start: stays 6f: acts on any going: races keenly: withdrawn once after refusing to enter stalls: carries head high: rather temperamental. *A. P. Stringer.*

COLWAY CROWN (IRE) 2 b.c. (Feb 4) Wassl 125–Dignified Air (FR) 70 — (Wolver Hollow 126) [1990 8.2s 8m] workmanlike colt: moderate mover: third foal: half-brother to 3-y-o Sursas (by Chief Singer): dam 6f winner at 4 yrs, is out of half-sister to very smart Joking Apart: raced keenly and weakened quickly when headed in maidens at Haydock and Redcar in October. *A. P. Stringer.*

COLWAY DOMINION 2 ch.c. (Jan 22) Dominion 123–My Therape 112 (Jimmy 60 Reppin 131) [1990 5m* 6f5] 40,000Y: useful-looking colt: brother to very useful 1983 2-y-o 5f and 6f winner Domynsky, later stakes winner over middle distances in USA, and useful 6f winner Anodyne, and half-brother to several other winners, including smart 1¼m and 1½m winner Petrullo (by Electric): dam won 7 times at up to 1¼m: favourite, won maiden at Newcastle in June: favourite again, ran creditably in nursery at Ayr following month. *J. W. Watts.*

COLWAY PRINCE (IRE) 2 b.g. (Apr 29) Prince Tenderfoot (USA) 126–El — Cerrito (Tribal Chief 125) [1990 6f5 7v 7d] IR 10,500Y: workmanlike gelding: half-brother to 1987 2-y-o 6f winner Kings Crystal (by Persian Bold) and 2 winners abroad: dam, from good family, of little account in Ireland: backward, well beaten in maidens. *A. P. Stringer.*

COLWICK HALL LADY 3 b.f. Auction Ring (USA) 123–Dame Brisene (FR) — (Kashmir II 125) [1989 NR 1990 a8g] 1,750 2-y-o: seventh foal: half-sister to French 9.5f to 12.2f winner Brise Lame (by Miami Springs): dam, unplaced in France, is sister to Moulines, winner of Poule d'Essai des Poulains: sweating, last of 8 in maiden at Southwell in August. *H. A. T. Whiting.*

COMBINED EXERCISE 6 br.g. Daring March 116–Dualvi 91 (Dual 117) [1989 39 10.1m2 10f3 10m4 11.5f4 1990 10.8m5 10.1g4 10m 10h5] good-topped gelding: poor mover: modest at his best, now on the decline: best at up to 1¼m: acts on any going except possibly hard: often apprentice ridden: has looked none too enthusiastic. *R. Akehurst.*

COME AND STAY 3 ch.f. Be My Guest (USA) 126–Julip 99 (Track Spare 125) 54 § [1989 6g 1990 8g 8g 8g 8m] workmanlike filly: plating-class maiden: seemingly unlucky in slowly-run race on reappearance: below form after, in claimer (blinkered, edgy) final start: stays 1m: acts on firm going: pulled hard third start: sold 3,100 gns Newmarket July Sales: one to treat with caution. *J. W. Watts.*

COMEDIE FLEUR   2 b.f. (Apr 7) Martinmas 128–Welsh Flower (Welsh Saint   —
126) [1990 6f⁶ 5f 5m 5v] 2,200Y: unfurnished filly: fifth reported foal: half-sister to
fair 1m winner Flower of Tintern (by Free State): dam of no account: no worthwhile
form, including in seller: blinkered final start. *J. Balding.*

COMEDY FAIR   10 b.g. Comedy Star (USA) 121–Fair Saint 79 (Bleep-Bleep 134)   —
[1989 NR 1990 16d] winner over 1m and 1¼m as 3-y-o: well tailed off in celebrity
event at Sedgefield in November, only outing on flat since 1984: blinkered twice:
one-time quite useful hurdler, poor chaser nowadays. *P. A. Blockley.*

COMEDY RIVER   3 br.c. Comedy Star (USA) 121–Hopeful Waters 66 (Forlorn   65
River 124) [1989 5m² 6g 5f² 6g 5g 1990 6f⁵ 6f³ 5.8h⁴ 6f³ 5m³ 6f⁶ 7f³ 8m⁶ 6m⁴ 7d³
6d⁵ a10g2] leggy, rather sparely-made colt: moderate walker: has a roundish action:
quite modest maiden: good second in moderately-run claiming event at Lingfield:
seems to stay 1¼m: acts on firm and dead going: has run creditably when sweating
and on toes. *J. L. Spearing.*

COMEDY SAIL   6 b.g. Comedy Star (USA) 121–Set Sail 64 (Alpenkonig (GER))   —
[1989 15.5s⁴ 17f* 16m 15.5f⁴ 18h³ 16f* 16m 17.1f⁵ 1990 12m 15.8d] neat gelding: has
a quick action: won 2 handicaps in poor company as 5-y-o: well beaten last 4 outings:
stays 2¼m: best efforts on top-of-the-ground: often wears bandages: below his best
in blinkers. *S. Dow.*

COME HALLEY (FR)   4 b.g. Crystal Glitters (USA) 127–Edition Nouvelle (FR)   —
(New Chapter 106) [1989 10v* 12g 10f 9m⁵ 8m⁵ a8g 1990 a7g] sturdy gelding:
plating-class handicapper at best: blinkered, soundly beaten in claimer in March:
stays 1¼m: acts on heavy going: inconsistent: sold 1,600 gns Doncaster March
Sales. *Mrs A. Knight.*

COME HOME ALONE   2 ch.c. (Feb 22) Sayf El Arab (USA) 127–Apprila   69
(Bustino 136) [1990 6m⁵ 6m⁴ 7f⁵ a8g⁴ a8g² a7g⁴ a7g³] 5,800Y, 2,300 2-y-o: angular
colt: first foal: dam lightly-raced half-sister to winning sprinter Blessit: quite
modest maiden: best efforts on all-weather, running creditably final start: stays 1m.
R. Hannon.

COME HOME KINGSLEY   3 ch.g. Formidable (USA) 125–Pearl Wedding 83   47
(Gulf Pearl 117) [1989 6g 8.2d 1990 8.2g a11g⁶ 10g³ 10d* 11m⁴ 15d⁵ 10m⁴ 9m 10.8f⁶]
lengthy, rather angular gelding: plater: below form after winning apprentice event
(no bid) at Beverley in June: stays 1¼m: acts on dead ground: sweating first 2
outings, on toes final one: winning hurdler for P. Beaumont. *J. Berry.*

COME ON MY GIRL (IRE)   2 gr.f. (May 10) To-Agori-Mou 133–Travelin' Joan   87 p
(USA) (Al Hattab (USA)) [1990 7g³ 8g³] IR 4,500Y: sister to a maiden on flat and
over hurdles and half-sister to several winners abroad: dam minor winner in North
America: shaped well in large-field autumn maidens at Folkestone and Yarmouth:
will stay 1¼m: can win a race. *R. Boss.*

COME ON ROSI   3 b.f. Valiyar 129–Victory Kingdom (CAN) (Viceregal (CAN))   77
[1989 6g 6g 1990 6f* 6g 6s] strong, good sort: won 20-runner minor event at
Kempton in May, clear on unfavoured stand side (flashing tail) and leading close
home: ran poorly in handicaps, off course over 5 months in between: bred to stay
further: sweating final start: sold 19,500 gns Newmarket December Sales. *D. R. C.
Elsworth.*

COME TO GOOD   3 br.f. Swing Easy (USA) 126–Demta (Astec 128) [1989 NR   —
1990 8m⁵ a12g] plain filly: third live foal: dam won from 6f to 1¼m in France: showed
nothing in minor event (moved poorly down) and maiden. *M. P. Muggeridge.*

COME TO TERMS   4 gr.g. Welsh Term 126–Sparkling Time (USA) (Olden   79
Times) [1989 9d 11m² 12f³ 12f² 12f* 12.3g² 14m⁴ 12d⁶ 13s⁴ 14m 1990 a12g* a14g²]
leggy gelding: modest handicapper: won at Southwell in February: stays 1¾m: acts
on any going: usually held up. *T. D. Barron.*

COMHAIL (USA)   3 ch.f. Nodouble (USA)–Bronislava 68 (Nonoalco (USA) 131)   —
[1989 NR 1990 10g 12.4s⁵] $53,000Y, resold $80,000Y: leggy filly: second foal:
half-sister to minor stakes winner by Caro in USA: dam ran 3 times here as 2-y-o
later sent to USA, is half-sister to top-class 1½m filly Comtesse de Loir: no
worthwhile form in late-season maiden at Newbury and claimer at Newcastle. *W.
Jarvis.*

COMIC RELIEF   3 br.f. Comedy Star (USA) 121–Moberry 54 (Mossberry 97)   —
[1989 5f⁶ 5m⁵ 1990 7g 6m 6d 6g 8.2s 6d] sturdy filly: turns fore-feet in: poor maiden:
may be suited by return to further. *B. C. Morgan.*

COMINO GIRL   4 b.f. Indian King (USA) 128–Arab Art (Artaius (USA) 129)   40
[1989 10g 12s 12m 10h⁵ 10m⁴ 10f 9m 10g² a11g² a10g 1990 a11g³ a10g⁴ a11g* a13g⁴

COM

11.7m] small, sturdy filly: apprentice ridden, won claimer (claimed out of A. Hide's stable £6,505) at Southwell in February: ran poorly next outing (trained by Dr J. Scargill), then off course over 4 months and soon behind in handicap on return: stays 11f: usually blinkered: bandaged near-hind last 2 starts: sold 3,300 gns Newmarket July Sales, resold 2,000 gns Doncaster November Sales. *R. Akehurst.*

COMMANCHE GUEST (IRE) 2 b.c. (Feb 28) Commanche Run 133– 75 Canadian Guest 74 (Be My Guest (USA) 126) [1990 8m⁶ 7m³ 7s] IR 9,600Y: angular colt: first foal: dam maiden stayed 1m: around a length third of 14, leading over 1f out but not finding so much as seemed likely, in maiden at Chepstow in October: should stay at least 1m: possibly unsuited by soft ground. *R. Guest.*

COMMANCHE NATION 3 b.c. Commanche Run 133–Rally 88 (Relko 136) 66 [1989 10g 1990 10.8m⁴ a11g³] leggy colt: modest form in maidens here, clearly best effort on reappearance: sent to Scandinavia, successful over 1¾m at Taby in September. *Mrs L. Piggott.*

COMMANCHE RHYTHM 2 b.f. (Mar 7) Commanche Run 133–Hear My Song — 72 (Song 132) [1990 5m 5f⁶ 5m⁵ 5m 7.5d 7m a7g] 5,600F, 6,800Y: lengthy filly: half-sister to 3 winners abroad: dam raced here at 2 yrs before winning in Spain, is closely related to Captive Dream and half-sister to Pas de Seul: poor plater. *M. W. Easterby.*

COMMANCHERO 3 gr.g. Telsmoss 91–Count On Me 77 (No Mercy 126) [1989 — NR 1990 7f⁵ 5.8h] rather unfurnished gelding: fourth foal: brother to 4-y-o 5f to 7f winner Hard To Figure and half-brother to 7-y-o 5.8f to 8.3f winner Red River Boy (by Latest Model): dam stayed well: tailed-off last in minor event and maiden. *R. J. Hodges.*

COMMANCHE SONG 3 ch.f. Commanche Run 133–American Beauty 74 (Mill — Reef (USA) 141) [1989 7m 8s 8m⁶ 8g 1990 10.6f 12.2m 12h⁶] leggy, sparely-made filly: has a quick action: poor maiden: should stay beyond 1m: best effort on good to firm ground: led 6f when tailed off in blinkers second (bandaged off-hind) start. *J. S. Wilson.*

COMMANDING OFFICER 3 b.g. Be My Guest (USA) 126–Honeypot Lane — 91 (Silly Season 127) [1989 NR 1990 10.1m 10f 10m] 7,800Y: lengthy gelding: has plenty of scope: eighth foal: half-brother to 3 winners, including useful 1½m winner Hymettus (by Blakeney) and 1¼m winner Cathedral Peak (by Tyrnavos): dam, middle-distance winner, is half-sister to good middle-distance horse Bedtime: no sign of ability in maidens. *C. A. Cyzer.*

COMMAND PERFORMER 4 b.f. Comedy Star (USA) 121–Freely Given 69 84 (Petingo 135) [1989 7.6m² 8h* 8f² 10m⁴ 8g³ 9g⁶ 1990 8g 8h* 8m⁵ 8m⁴ 10f4 8m] tall, workmanlike filly: fair handicapper: won 4-runner event at Brighton in May: stays 1¼m: acts on hard and dead going: sold 16,000 gns Newmarket December Sales. *P. T. Walwyn.*

COMME CI COMME CA 4 ch.g. Buzzards Bay 128§–Morstons Maid 40 — (Morston (FR) 125) [1989 NR 1990 11m] lengthy gelding: moderate mover: second foal: dam plater suited by 1½m: bit backward, soundly beaten in maiden at Redcar in July. *B. Ellison.*

COMMENDABLE (IRE) 2 b.c. (Apr 27) Baillamont (USA) 124–Praise (FR) 95 p 116 (Hard To Beat 132) [1990 8g*] 34,000Y: lengthy, quite good-bodied colt: half-brother to several winners in France, notably one-time smart middle-distance winner Extol (by Green Dancer): dam smart 1¼m winner, is sister to good French middle-distance stayer Hard To Sing: green, won 7-runner maiden at York in October by a neck from Marcus Thorpe, niggled along early in straight, steady headway from 3f out and running on well despite tending to wander: will stay 1¼m: sure to improve. *G. Harwood.*

COMPOS MENTIS 3 b.g. Homeboy 114–Rhythm 64 (Bleep-Bleep 134) [1989 — 6m 7g⁴ 6m* 6g 8s 1990 8m 8.5g 11.7m 16m] smallish, angular gelding: quite modest winner of claimer at 2 yrs, below form after: stayed 7f: had been blinkered and visored: dead. *R. J. Holder.*

COMPUTER FOLLY 3 ch.c. Good Times (ITY)–Aiglon (HOL) (Shamaraan — (FR)) [1989 NR 1990 7m] colt: first reported foal: dam thrice-raced half-sister to top Dutch filly Libelle: 50/1, green to post, slowly away and always behind in Lingfield minor event: sold 1,100 gns Ascot September Sales. *M. J. Haynes.*

COMSTOCK 3 ch.g. Coquelin (USA) 121–Maura Paul (Bonne Noel 115) [1989 95 7.5f 7f² 7m* 7m³ 1990 10.6s⁶ 10g* 10m³ 12m* 12m] lengthy gelding: good mover: developed into fairly useful handicapper, winning at Newmarket in June and £8,100 contest (led briefly 2f out then again on post) at York in August: ran poorly in

£71,300 event at Ascot final start: will stay further: acts on good to firm ground: took keen hold on reappearance. *J. G. FitzGerald.*

COMTEC FLYER 2 ch.f. (May 2) Valiyar 129–Comtec Princess 73 (Gulf Pearl 117) [1990 a7g a8g] 2,600Y: fourth foal: sister to modest middle-distane stayer Qualitair Aviator and half-sister to 3-y-o Saskia's Hero (by Bairn) and 1988 2-y-o 5f seller winner Swynford Princess (by Raga Navarro): dam 1m to 1¼m winner: poor form in maiden (slowly away) at Lingfield and claimer at Southwell. *J. F. Bottomley.*

COMTE DU BOURG (FR) 3 b.c. Zino 127–Instancia (Le Fabuleux 133) [1989 **114** 9m³ 10v 1990 12v² 11g² 12d* 15g* 12s 15g⁴ 15.5v⁵] half-brother to 4 winners, notably 1¼m and 11f winner/good jumper Prince du Bourg (by Viceregal) and 10.5f and 1½m winner Duc du Bourg (by Bolkonski): dam French 10.5f winner: won Prix du Lys at Chantilly in June and Prix Hubert du Chaudenay at Longchamp in July: fair fifth of 11 to Braashee and Indian Queen in Prix Royal-Oak at Longchamp final start: stays 15f. *R. Touflan, France.*

CONAQUITA 4 ch.g. Celtic Cone 116–Late Decision (Alcide 136) [1989 NR 1990 — 10.1m] small gelding: first foal: dam never ran: bandaged, well beaten in minor event at Windsor in July. *B. Palling.*

CONCERT PITCH 11 ch.g. Royal Match 117–Ballychord (DEN) (Ballymoss **43** 136) [1989 8m⁴ 7f² 7.6h 7f⁴ 6f 7g 8m³ 7m⁵ 8f⁴ a8g² a7g a6g 1990 a8g⁵ a11g³ a8g² a8g⁵ a8g* a8g⁵ 8.2f⁴ 8f³ 8m⁶ 7f³ 7m² 7.6g 8g 7m 7g⁵ 6m] strong, dipped-backed, lengthy gelding: has a round action: won handicap at Southwell in February: best at 7f to 1m: acts on any going: has won in blinkers but has worn them only 3 times since 1983: good mount for inexperienced rider: tough. *B. Palling.*

CONDOVER FLYER 3 b.f. Krayyan 117–Messie (Linacre 133) [1989 NR 1990 — 9g 10g] IR 1,000F, IR 1,900Y: deep-girthed filly: sister to 5-y-o 7f and 1m winner Se-Aq and half-sister to 1980 2-y-o 5f seller winner Magaden (by Record Run): dam ran twice at 3 yrs in Ireland: no show in minor event and seller (bandaged off-hind): sold 1,100 gns Ascot July Sales. *F. Jordan.*

CONE LANE 4 ch.g. On Your Mark 125–Cee Beauty 74 (Ribero 126) [1989 7s⁶ **44** 6f⁵ 6g 7m³ 6m 6m 7h 7m 6m 12.2d 1990 7h* 7f] workmanlike gelding: 33/1, won for first time on flat when making all in 7-runner handicap at Brighton in May: ran moderately 2 weeks later: suited by 6f or easy 7f: acts on hard going: ran poorly in blinkers. *B. Gubby.*

CONEY ISLAND 2 ch.c. (Apr 4) Flash of Steel 120–Ever So 78 (Mummy's Pet **49** 125) [1990 6g 7g⁵ 7g⁶ 7f² 7g a8g³ 8.2s] 11,000F, IR 13,500Y: close-coupled colt: second foal: half-brother to 3-y-o 5f winner Ever So Artistic (by Claude Monet): dam 2-y-o 6f winner: fair plater: stays 1m: best form on a sound surface. *M. A. Jarvis.*

CONFEDERATE 4 ch.g. Mummy's Game 120–Shenandoah 85 (Mossborough — 126) [1989 NR 1990 a8g] lengthy gelding: plating-class form at best as 2-y-o: slowly away and never dangerous in Southwell maiden in March: sold 2,000 gns Ascot July Sales. *Mrs S. Oliver.*

CONFIDENCE 3 ch.f. Noalto 120–Orange Silk 68 (Moulton 128) [1989 5f³ 7.5f — 6g⁶ 6g 1990 6m] sturdy filly: plating-class form at 2 yrs: blinkered, front rank 3f in June seller only outing in 1990: stays 6f. *J. W. Watts.*

CONFUCIUS 3 b.g. Stanford 121§–Carrhae (Home Guard (USA) 129) [1989 5g⁵ — § 6d 5g 1990 6m 6g 7m 7.5d 6g⁶] tall gelding: quite modest form at 2 yrs, little in 1990: should stay 6f: seems to need a sound surface: bandaged on reappearance: has carried head rather high: blinkered and reluctant to race final start: sold 1,500 gns Newmarket July Sales: probably ungenuine. *W. J. Musson.*

CONJURER 3 gr.c. Magic Mirror 105–Morning Miss 59 (Golden Dipper 119) **65** [1989 6f³ 5.8h* 6g 6h⁵ 8m 7m³ a7g a7g³ a8g* 1990 a7g² a8g³ 8g⁵ 8f² 9f³] leggy, close-coupled colt: quite modest handicapper: not seen out after May: stays 9f: acts on firm ground: consistent. *R. Hannon.*

CONNABEE 6 b.g. Connaught 130–Sera Sera 88 (Hill Clown (USA)) [1989 NR — 1990 a12g a16g⁵] compact gelding: has a quick action: seemingly of little account. *S. Woodman.*

CONNEMARA CROFT (NZ) 3 b.f. Babaroom (USA)–Bally Irish (NZ) — (Ballybrit (NZ)) [1989 NR 1990 10m] New Zealand-bred filly: 33/1 and ridden by 7-lb claimer, tailed off in Goodwood claimer in September. *J. R. Jenkins.*

CONQUETE (IRE) 2 gr.f. (Apr 17) Godswalk (USA) 130–Day Dress (Ashmore **46** (FR) 125) [1990 7s a8g⁶ a7g] sparely-made filly: has a quick action: third foal: half-sister to temperamental 1988 2-y-o Pajons Shamal (by Tumble Wind), later successful in Belgium: dam never ran: poor form in maidens at Lingfield and Southwell. *C. C. Elsey.*

CONQUISTA 2 ch.f. (Jan 24) Aragon 118–Divine Fling (Imperial Fling (USA) 68 116) [1990 7m⁴ 7f 6g⁴ 7m⁵ 7g⁶ 8d⁴] 2,000F: leggy, workmanlike filly: first foal: dam poor maiden: quite modest maiden: stays 1m: acts on good to firm ground and dead: has run creditably for 7-lb claimer: sweating third outing: taken down early final one: consistent. *Lady Herries.*

CONSTANT DELIGHT 3 b.f. Never So Bold 135–Lady Constance 118 80 (Connaught 130) [1989 6g³ 1990 6m³ 6f 7m³ 9m* 9m⁶ 10m⁴ 9g] rather unfurnished filly: moderate walker and mover: fair handicapper: won at Sandown in June: ran moderately last 2 starts: should stay 1¼m. *M. R. Stoute.*

CONSTRUCTIVE (IRE) 2 ch.c. (Apr 11) Gorytus (USA) 132–Shirley's Joy 54 (Shirley Heights 130) [1990 5m 8m⁵ 6m a7g a7g³ a8g] IR 2,500Y: lengthy colt: third foal: dam, Irish 8.5f winner, is half-sister to very useful miler Eve's Error: quite modest maiden: beat effort penultimate outing: fifth in apprentice seller on second appearance: stays 1m: blinkered last 2 starts: trained by R. Hannon on debut: has been bandaged near-hind. *D. Morris.*

CONTACT KELVIN 8 br.g. Workboy 123–Take My Hand 49 (Precipice Wood — 123) [1989 12d 12g 1990 12g 13g 12m 12d] big, strong gelding: no form in handicaps for long time: blinkered final outing. *N. Bycroft.*

CONTINENTAL CARL (IRE) 2 b.c. (Jun 2) Two Punch (USA)–Lady Roberta 65 (USA) (Roberto (USA) 131) [1990 6g⁶ 5f* 5f 5m 6d 6m a7g a6g³ a6g² a6g³] 5,800Y: good-topped colt: half-brother to 3-y-o Hatari (by Assert) and 2 winners in North America, including listed-placed King Roberto (by Spectacular Bid): dam leading 3-y-o filly in Canada in 1980 when successful at up to 9f: sire by Mr Prospector: made all in 5-runner seller (no bid) at Folkestone in July: good second to Balsmo for 7-lb apprentice in claimer at Southwell: seems better suited by 6f than 5f: acts on firm and dead ground: wears blinkers or visor: keen sort: bolted to post third outing. *J. R. Jenkins.*

CONTRACT LAW (USA) 3 b.c. Lypheor 118–Permissible Tender (USA) (Al — Hattab (USA)) [1989 6m² 6f* 1990 8d⁴] medium-sized colt: second foal: dam winner at up to 9f out of half-sister to Law Society, Legal Bid and Strike Your Colors: suffered knee injury after winning Scottish Equitable Richmond Stakes at Goodwood impressively at 2 yrs: 8/1, 8¾ lengths last of 4 to Zoman in Group 2 event at Phoenix Park in July: should have proved best at up to 1m: retired to stand at Tally Ho Stud, Co. Westmeath, Ireland. *W. Jarvis.*

CONTRACTORS DREAM 2 b.g. (Jan 18) Librate 91–Opal Lady 64 (Averof — 123) [1990 a6g 8m] fifth foal: dam 6f winner: tailed off in sellers. *J. M. Bradley.*

CONVIVIAL 2 b.f. (Apr 16) Nordance (USA)–Rensaler (USA) (Stop The Music 81 (USA)) [1990 6m³ 6g²] rather leggy, sparely-made filly: modest walker: fourth foal: half-sister to 1989 2-y-o 6f winner Jovial (by Northern Jove), later graded-stakes winner in USA, and 1987 2-y-o 8.5f stakes winner Never Force (by Full Out): dam, winner at around 1m in USA, is half-sister to smart 1982 American 3-y-o Rose Bouquet and very useful 7f and 1m winner Shmaireekh: favourite, ran creditably, staying on, in maiden won by Crystal Path at Newmarket and minor event won by Triviality at York in October: will stay 7f: sure to win a race. *A. A. Scott.*

CONYGAR PARK 3 b.c. Mummy's Treasure 84–Whistling Girl 68 (Whistling — Wind 123) [1989 NR 1990 10s 10g 12d] 6,200Y: leggy colt: half-brother to very useful 1978 2-y-o sprinter General Atty (by Red Alert) and a winner in Belgium: dam appeared to stay 7f: backward, always behind in minor event, claimer and maiden. *R. Guest.*

COOLBANE BILLY 2 ch.g. (Jun 3) Nordance (USA)–Dawn's Dream (Sandford — Lad 133) [1990 5m⁵] fourth foal: half-brother to 6f and 7f winner Northern Commander (by Music Boy): dam lightly raced, won over 6f at 2 yrs: last of 5 in maiden at Catterick in July. *J. Berry.*

COOL CALCULATOR 2 br.g. (Feb 11) Seymour Hicks (FR) 125–Finlandaise 48 (FR) (Arctic Tern (USA) 126) [1990 a6g⁶ 6d 6g⁶ 7v] leggy gelding: third foal: brother to 1988 Irish 2-y-o 6f winner Ingmar and to a winner in Austria: dam French 9f and 1m winner: poor maiden: should stay 7f: sold 2,200 gns Doncaster October Sales. *J. Berry.*

COOL CHILI 2 gr.c. (Mar 12) Formidable (USA) 125–Chili Girl 112 (Skymaster 83 126) [1990 6s⁴ 6g² 6g³ 6f* 5m⁴] robust colt: has a roundish action: brother to quite modest maiden Eccolina and smart sprinter Chilibang and half-brother to several winners, including 3-y-o Chiliboy (by Precocious) and quite useful 6f and 7f winner

Hot Case (by Upper Case): dam sprinting half-sister to useful Steel Heart: fair performer: easy winner of nursery at Folkestone in July: well-backed favourite, ran creditably in similar event at Goodwood later in month: likely to prove better suited by 6f than 5f: blinkered final 2 starts: sold 27,000 gns Newmarket Autumn Sales. *J. L. Dunlop.*

COOL COQUELIN (IRE)   2 ch.f. (Mar 8) Coquelin (USA) 121–Cool Gales 85   **46** (Lord Gayle (USA) 124) [1990 5m⁵ 6m⁶ 5f⁵ 5.3h³ 5.1m⁶ 5f³ 5g a6g⁴ a6g] IR 4,000Y: small, plain filly: first foal: dam, maiden, probably stayed 1½m: moderate plater: stays 6f: acts on firm ground on turf, ran respectably on all-weather: inconsistent: tail flasher. *J. R. Jenkins.*

COOL DANCER   3 ch.f. Fabulous Dancer (USA) 124–Sarajill (High Line 125)   **58** [1989 8g 1990 14g 16f² a14g 17.1m] lengthy, rather plain filly: plating-class maiden: form only when second of 4 at Thirsk in July: stays 2m. *M. R. Stoute.*

COOL ENOUGH   9 ch.g. Welsh Captain 113–Sundrive (Status Seeker) [1989   **59** 7d⁴* 7m* 8h² 8.5m 8.2m⁴ 8f² 7g⁴ 8m 7.5m 7f³ 7m 7g³ 7m 8.2g ℓg⁶ 1990 7m³ 7.5m* 8f² 8f² 7.5m⁴ 7m² 7m 7g 8.2m⁵ 7g³ 8.5g 7m* 7m⁴ 7f⁴ 8m 6m³ 7f⁴ 7m 6s⁶] small, sturdy gelding: quite modest handicapper: successful at Beverley in March and Catterick in July: ideally suited by 7f to 1m: acts on any going: mostly apprentice ridden at 9 yrs: usually taken quietly to post: tough. *Mrs J. R. Ramsden.*

COOL PARADE (USA)   2 ch.c. (Mar 16) Listcapade (USA)–Yours Trudy (USA)   **67 p** (Star Envoy (USA)) [1990 8g 7s⁴] quite good-topped colt: half-brother to winners in North America by Castle Green and Plastic Surgeon: dam minor winner at up to 7f: sire seemed best at around 1¼m: around 13 lengths fourth of 15, first home on unfavoured stand side, in maiden at Newcastle in November: likely to improve again. *S. G. Norton.*

COOL RUN   5 b.m. Deep Run 119–Loyal And Regal 51 (Royal And Regal (USA))   **74** [1989 8h⁴ 8.2g 8g 10m* 8m⁴ 1990 12f⁴ 11m⁴ 10.6s 10g* 10m² 10f⁶ 12g² 12m 10.6g² 13.3g 10.5g² 10d⁵] leggy, quite good-topped mare: carries plenty of condition: moderate mover: won handicap at Ripon in June: improved afterwards, second to Anna Petrovna in similar race at York penultimate outing: unlikely to stay beyond 1½m: probably acts on any going: tough. *B. A. McMahon.*

COOLULAH   3 b.g. Dominion 123–Phoebe Ann 76 (Absalom 128) [1989 5f⁵ 7m 6d   **61** 6g a7g⁶ 1990 6m⁶ 5g* 6m² 6g 6m 5m⁴] medium-sized gelding: quite modest handicapper: won at Windsor in May, outpaced early on: ran very well final start: stays 6f: acts on good to firm ground: has hung left for apprentice: inconsistent: sold to join M. Pipe 6,000 gns Newmarket Autumn Sales. *H. Candy.*

COPFORD   3 b.c. Teenoso (USA) 135–Chalkey Road 100 (Relko 136) [1989 7m⁶   **78** 8m 1990 10m 14g⁵ 14m² 14d²] strong, lengthy colt: modest maiden: second in handicaps at Yarmouth: will stay 2m: acts on good to firm ground and dead: lacks turn of foot and may do better with more forcing tactics: sold 9,000 gns Newmarket Autumn Sales. *G. Wragg.*

COPPERBOTTOM   3 b.c. Night Shift (USA)–Crimson Damask (Windjammer   **61** (USA)) [1989 6m 6m² 6f⁴ 7m a7g⁴ 7g a7g² a6g⁴ a7g 1990 7g 7f6g 7m⁶ 7d⁴ 7f⁴ 5.8f⁵] leggy, good-topped colt: quite modest maiden: clearly best effort as 3-y-o in Epsom claimer fifth start: seems suited by 7f: acts on dead ground: sweating and edgy third start: has been bandaged behind: active sort: sold 6,200 gns Ascot July Sales. *R. V. Smyth.*

COPPER BURN   2 ch.f. (Feb 5) Electric 126–Divetta 72 (Ribero 126) [1990 7m*   **68** 7g 8.2d⁵] smallish, angular filly: fluent mover: fifth foal: sister to modest and unreliable maiden Power Crazy and half-sister to a winner abroad by Henbit: dam won over 6f and 1m: green, won claimer at Salisbury in September: ran well, keeping on, in nursery final start: will be suited by further. *J. R. Fanshawe.*

COPPERMILL LAD   7 ch.g. Ardoon 124–Felin Geri (Silly Season 127) [1989   **70** 5s⁶ 6v* 5s 6f⁵ 6m⁴ 6m⁶ 6s* 6s⁴ 6v 1990 5m 6d 6m 6m 6m 6m⁴ 6m 6d 6s³ 6s⁵] compact gelding: carries plenty of condition: has a round action: modest handicapper: suited by 6f: acts on any going: usually gets behind. *L. J. Holt.*

COPPER PLATING   2 b.c. (Apr 4) Rousillon (USA) 133–Etching 109 (Auction   **76** Ring (USA) 123) [1990 7m² 7m³] useful-looking colt: seventh foal: half-brother to fair 5f winner Inscription (by Posse), 1½m winner Sword Excalibur (by Kings Lake) and a winner in Germany: dam won from 7f to 1¼m: sweating, modest form in maidens at Salisbury and Sandown in July: will stay 1m. *P. W. Harris.*

COPPER RIVER   3 b.g. Glint of Gold 128–Carmelina 98 (Habitat 134) [1989 NR   **86** 1990 8g* 12f² 12f³] IR 3,000Y: lengthy gelding: moderate walker and mover: second foal: half-brother to Irish 1½m winner/winning hurdler Corvallina (by Corvaro):

dam French 7.5f and 1m winner: 25/1, won minor event at Carlisle in June: hung left when beaten 1½ lengths by long odds-on Onaway (sole opponent) in Pontefract minor event and 9 lengths behind Cameo Performance in slowly-run apprentice race at Chepstow following month: probably stays 1¼m. *R. Hollinshead.*

COPPER TOP 3 b.f. Longleat (USA) 109–Corn Rocket (Roan Rocket 128) [1989 5f³ 5h³ 5.1f* 5m 8m⁶ 5m 5m 1990 5m 8*og 8g 7.5f] small, sparely-made, angular filly: moderate walker: easily best effort when quite modest winner at 2 yrs: should stay 6f: acts on firm going: has won tongue strap: pulled too hard in blinkers second start: trained until after then by H. Collingridge. *G. R. Oldroyd.* —

COQUETA 5 ch.m. Coquelin (USA) 121–Clara Petacci (USA) (Crepello 136) [1989 8.2v⁵ 8d 7.6m 12h¹ 10m⁶ 1990 a12g³ a14g⁶] neat mare: has a quick action: retains a little ability: probably stays 1½m: acts on hard and dead going: blinkered once, visored last 4 outings: winning hurdler. *E. J. Alston.* 30

COR ANI 4 b.g. Crofter (USA) 124–Eyry 85 (Falcon 131) [1989 6m 6m⁵ 6f⁵ 7h 6m⁴ 6f² 5f⁵ 6m⁴ 6g⁴ 7s* 1990 6m] strong gelding: carries condition: winning handicapper in modest company as 3-y-o: needed race only outing (April) in 1990: suited to 7f: goes very well on soft ground: ran creditably in blinkers: inconsistent. *J. A. Glover.*

CORAL FLUTTER 3 b.f. Beldale Flutter (USA) 130–Countess Olivia 80 (Prince Tenderfoot (USA) 126) [1989 5f 5m⁴ 5f⁶ 1990 10g³ 8f² 8.2m⁵ a8g] lengthy, good-quartered filly: has a quickish action: quite modest maiden: stays 1¼m: acts on firm going: has run well when sweating and edgy: keen sort. *J. W. Payne.* 61

CORAL HARBOUR 8 ch.g. Bay Express 132–Coralivia (Le Levanstell 122) [1989 NR 1990 11.7f 17.1f⁶ 14.8f⁶] rangier angular gelding: poor handicapper: apprentice ridden, soundly beaten as 8-y-o: best form at around 1¼m: acts on good to firm going: blinkered twice: retained by trainer 2,400 gns Ascot October Sales. *A. Barrow.* —

CORCINA 2 gr.f. (Apr 17) Kalaglow 132–Feather Flower 74 (Relkino 131) [1990 6m⁴ a7g* 7g* 8g² 7.3g] 16,000Y: leggy, workmanlike filly: second foal: half-sister to a winner in Brazil: dam placed at 1¼m here before winning at 11.8f in France, is closely related to very smart middle-distance stayer Relay Race: fair performer: successful in maiden auction at Southwell in August and nursery at Chester in September: bit on toes and ran moderately in nursery on final outing: will stay 1¼m: races keenly. *M. Bell.* 85

CORDILLERO 4 b.g. Head For Heights 125–Petipa (FR) 115 (Habitat 134) [1989 9v 9m 12g⁴ 12g³ 12.8m³ 13.6m² 12m² 10d⁶ 1990 8f 7m 11.5m 10m* 12g* 10d] angular ex-Irish gelding: poor mover: fourth foal: half-brother to 2 winners, including Bustineto (by Bustino), successful over 7f in Ireland: dam very useful sprinter: won sellers (no bid) at Folkestone in October, making all in first, leading last strides in second: stays 13.6f: acts on good to firm going: blinkered final 5 outings at 3 yrs: sometimes bandaged. *A. Moore.* 62

CORINTHIAN GIRL 3 b.f. Welsh Captain 113–Combe Grove Lady (Simbir 130) [1989 6g a7g 1990 10f⁴ 8.2g 10m 8.3m 10f 10.8m³ 10m] leggy filly: moderate walker and mover: inconsistent plater: better at 1¼m than 1m: acts on firm going: visored fifth start, blinkered last 2: winning claiming hurdler. *R. Dickin.* 38

CORIO BAY 3 br.g. Blue Cashmere 129–Rushley Bay 87 (Crooner 119) [1989 6f 7f 7m 1990 8.2f 6m 8g 6f4 a6g 6m⁶] lengthy gelding: poor mover: poor maiden: stays 7f: acts on firm going: no show at Southwell. *D. Haydn Jones.* 47

CORLEY BOY 2 b.g. (Apr 27) Elegant Air 119–Corley Moor 97 (Habitat 134) [1990 7g 7m 8d] quite good-topped gelding: has scope: moderate mover: fifth foal: half-brother to fairly useful 1987 2-y-o 6f winner Topsy Moor (by High Top): dam 2-y-o 5f winner: always behind in autumn maidens: bit backward first 2 starts. *W. Hastings-Bass.* —

CORMAC'S 4 gr.g. Superlative 118–Tahoume (FR) (Faristan 123) [1989 8s 10f² 12f³ 9m a10g 1990 8f4 10m] tall, leggy, plain gelding: plater: stays 1½m: acts on firm ground. *A. Bailey.* —

CORMORANT CREEK 3 b.f. Gorytus (USA) 132–Quarry Wood 89 (Super Sam 124) [1989 1m⁶ 1990 8g 10.1m⁴ 10.4g* 10.6d 10.4d³ a10g³ a11g⁴] big, strong, rangy filly: modest form: won apprentice handicap at Chester in September, challenge delayed until inside final 1f, idling and edging left: easily best efforts when third in handicaps at same course and Lingfield: should stay 1½m: acts on dead going: sweating second start. *B. W. Hills.* 73

CORNCHARM 9 b.g. Thatch (USA) 136–Just Larking (USA) (Sea Bird II 145) —
[1989 5f4 6f 5f 1990 a6g a6g6] robust, compact gelding: moderate mover: modest at
best, but has deteriorated: best at 6f nowadays: acts on any going: has worn blinkers
and visor: sold 1,100 gns Ascot July Sales. *D. C. Jermy.*

CORN FUTURES 2 b.f. (May 28) Nomination 125–Hay Reef 72 (Mill Reef 78
(USA) 141) [1990 6g5 6g2 6d* 5d] compact filly: has a quick action: sixth foal:
half-sister to several winners, including fairly useful 1½m winner Legendary
Dancer (by Shareef Dancer) and 1983 2-y-o 5f winner Fluctuate (by Sharpen Up):
dam 1¼m winner, closely related to Wassl and half-sister to dam of Queen Mary
winner On Tiptoes: modest performer: won maiden at Chester in October: ran
creditably in nursery on final outing: stays 6f: races keenly. *R. F. Johnson Houghton.*

CORNISA 2 gr.f. (Apr 17) Dawn Johnny (USA) 90–Lallax 109 (Laxton 105) [1990 —
8.2m] first live foal: dam 7f (at 2 yrs) and 1¼m winner: slowly away and always
behind in minor event at Nottingham in September. *M. R. Leach.*

CORN LILY 4 ch.f. Aragon 118–Ixia 91 (I Say 125) [1989 10g 14f 11.7m4 12.3g 10f* 55
13.8g* 12.3m* 11g* 11s4 10.6m 11f2 12m* 1990 12m 12.8g6 13m5 12.2d2 11g2 11m5
12f2 12f* 10m* 12.3m2 12m6 12g 12m3 12m] tall, leggy filly: quite useful plater: won
at Thirsk (bought in 5,200 gns) and Nottingham (retained 16,000 gns) in August:
best efforts at up to 1½m: acts on firm and dead going: suited by forcing tactics:
genuine and consistent: sold to join Mrs G. Reveley's stable 13,500 gns Newmarket
Autumn Sales. *N. Tinkler.*

CORNWALL PRINCE 3 b.g. Taufan (USA) 119–Peach Stone (Mourne 126) 71
[1989 7g 1990 7g6 8.5m6 7f] leggy, workmanlike gelding: turns fore feet in: modest
maiden: easily best effort on reappearance: should stay 1m: changed hands 2,200
gns Newmarket September Sales: winning hurdler. *N. A. Callaghan.*

CORPORATE MEMBER 3 ch.g. Exhibitioner 111–Sciambola (Great Nephew 50
126) [1989 5g6 5v3 5d5 7g6 8.2s2 8m 8d 1990 9s3 11g2 8g 9g2 13g4 13m 12m4 12g]
tall, close-coupled, workmanlike gelding: moderate mover: plating-class maiden:
below form last 4 outings, mostly in claimers: stays 9f: acts on soft going: ran too
freely in visor fifth start: sold 4,600 gns Doncaster September Sales. *C. Tinkler.*

CORPORATE TYPE (IRE) 2 b.c. (Apr 17) Last Tycoon 131–Sherkraine 98 67
(Shergar 140) [1990 5m 6m5 7m 7h6 8g4 8.2g4 8m 7m2 a7g a7g5 a7g a8g] IR
48,000Y: medium-sized colt: has scope: first foal: dam Irish 2-y-o 6f winner is out of
Poule d'Essai des Pouliches winner Ukraine Girl: quite modest maiden: best effort
over 3 lengths second of 17 to Desert Splendour in nursery at Newmarket: below
form in similar events at Southwell after: effective at 7f and 1m: has carried head
high: has run well for a claimer: bought out of J. Sutcliffe's stable 10,000 gns
Newmarket Autumn Sales after eighth outing. *D. W. Chapman.*

CORREZE 2 b.f. (May 18) Stanford 121§–Our Mandy (Mansingh (USA) 120) [1990 —
7m a7g a6g] seventh foal: half-sister to 2 winning platers by Mandrake Major and 5f
seller winner Mandy's Love (by Tower Walk): dam of little account: soundly beaten
in maidens at Leicester (backward, bandaged behind) and Lingfield. *P. Howling.*

CORRIANNE 3 ch.f. Balidar 133–Serdarli (Miami Springs 121) [1989 NR 1990 7f —
8m 6f 7d 7.6g] angular, rather dipped-backed filly: first foal: dam placed at 1½m and
over hurdles: well beaten, including in seller: bandaged behind final start: sold 1,250
gns Doncaster June Sales. *R. Guest.*

CORRIENDO LIBRE 6 b.g. Tumble Wind (USA)–Bouganville (Gulf Pearl 117) —
[1989 NR 1990 11g 8m] sturdy ex-Irish gelding: second foal: dam won 3 times at up to
1½m in Ireland: won maiden at Mallow as 3-y-o: little subsequent form: stays 7f:
blinkered once at 4 yrs. *J. Parkes.*

CORRIN HILL 3 b.g. Petorius 117–Pete's Money (USA) (Caucasus (USA)) 60 §
[1989 5.3m4 5s2 6m3 6m* 7m 6m 6g2 6g5 7g6 a6g4 a7g3 a6g* a7g* 1990 a7g3 6m
6m 7m 6m 6m 6f* 7m 6f6 6m6 6m] useful-looking gelding: quite modest
handicapper: won at Yarmouth in August: stays 7f: acts on firm going: effective with
or without blinkers (has worn them last 8 starts): sometimes hangs, and flashes tail:
often comes from well behind, and did so at Yarmouth: sold 8,000 gns Newmarket
Autumn Sales and gelded: unsatisfactory. *N. A. Callaghan.*

CORRUPT (USA) 2 b.c. (Apr 10) Lear Fan (USA) 130–Nirvanita (FR) (Right 96
Royal V 135) [1990 7g* 7m4 7m2 7f5] 12,000Y, resold 36,000Y: tall, quite attractive
colt: shade unfurnished: shows knee action: half-brother to several winners in
France, including 1¼m to 12.5f winner Vaguely's Son (by Vaguely Noble): dam
unraced: fairly useful colt: comfortable winner of maiden at Newmarket: very good
second in nursery there later in June: ran poorly in Lanson Champagne Vintage
Stakes at Goodwood final start: will be better suited by 1m. *N. A. Callaghan.*

COU

CORSEE 3 ch.g. Song 132–Bundling (Petingo 135) [1989 5s 5d 6m² 1990 6m 5g] 46
lengthy, angular gelding: has a round action: poor maiden: faced stiff tasks in summer handicaps as 3-y-o, appearing to run well at first on sole final start: should be suited by return to 6f: acts on good to firm ground: wandered final start at 2 yrs. *M. W. Easterby.*

CORYPHEE 2 b.f. (Feb 25) Touching Wood (USA) 127–Dance In Rome 79 —
(Dance In Time (CAN)) [1990 8d a8g a8g] sturdy filly: has scope: sixth foal: half-sister to 3-y-o Dance Buster (by Bustino), two 2-y-o winners and 1¼m winner Dr Zeva (by Busted): dam ran only at 2 yrs, winning at 6f: slowly away when soundly beaten in maidens and claimers: blinkered final start. *Sir Mark Prescott.*

COSIMO (USA) 3 b.c. Lyphard's Wish (FR) 124–Vashti (USA) (Iron Ruler 86
(USA)) [1989 NR 1990 7d* 8m a8g3 10.6d2 8.2v2 10.4v a12g2 a12g* a12g5]
$25,000F: strong colt: moderate mover: third foal: half-brother to a minor winner in USA by Codex: dam unraced half-sister to high-class middle-distance performer Mutching: progressive form: won maiden at Catterick in July and claimer at Southwell in November: ridden by 7-lb claimer, ran very well final start: suited by 1½m: probably acts on heavy going: hung left fifth start: tailed off at Chester on sixth: trained until after fourth by J. Gosden. *P. A. Blockley.*

COSMIC DANCER 3 ch.g. Horage 124–Royal Cloak (Hardicanute 130) [1989 56
5m5 6m4 6f 6m4 6h 7.5m 8f 7g a6g a8g 1990 12f3 12.5g* 12m3 15.3g3 13m2 16f* 14m]
small, good-quartered gelding: moderate walker and mover: plating-class handicapper: won at Wolverhampton (selling, bought in 5,000 gns) in May and Lingfield in August: ran poorly final start: stays 2m: acts on good going: has joined A. Hide. *I. Campbell.*

COSMIC PRINCESS 3 b.f. Fairy King (USA)–Come True (FR) (Nasram II 125) 85
[1989 6g 7.3v2 1990 10.5g6 8.2m2 7m2 12m6 12m 10g 7d* 8m 7d* 6s] good-quartered, attractive filly: has a rather round action: fair performer on most form: made virtually all to win minor events at Ayr in September and Leicester in October: appeared to run very well when 3 lengths sixth in Irish Oaks on fourth start: well beaten in listed races eighth and final starts: may prove effective at up to 1¼m: possibly best on a soft surface: has taken keen hold. *M. A. Jarvis.*

COSSACK GUARD (USA) 4 br.c. Nureyev (USA) 131–Kilijaro 126 (African 106
Sky 124) [1989 9d5 10f2 12f3 12g6 12g* 14f6 13.3m2 12m 1990 14m5 16m3 20g2 20d6 16m6] compact, quite attractive colt: useful stayer: placed in moderately-run Insulpak Sagaro EBF Stakes (swished tail in paddock) at Ascot and Prix du Cadran (beaten 5 lengths by Mercalle) at Longchamp in spring: well beaten in Gold Cup at Royal Ascot next outing: best form on good surface: lacks turn of foot: sold 16,000 gns Newmarket December Sales. *C. E. Brittain.*

COSSACK NOIR 2 b.c. (Apr 23) Lidhame 109–Almeda 54 (Martinmas 128) 40 §
[1990 6g 6g 5v 7d6 7d] 4,600Y, 23,000 2-y-o: neat colt: second foal: dam 1m winner stayed 1½m: poor maiden: raced far too freely in blinkers final start: stays 7f: seems unsuited by heavy ground: bolted once in October, and was withdrawn: one to be wary of. *J. S. Wilson.*

COST EFFECTIVE 3 ch.g. Burslem 123–Perle's Fashion (Sallust 134) [1989 49
6f6 6m5 6g 1990 8f 10g 8g5 12m5 12.3g5 12f4 12g6 11m3 14g 12.5m5] narrow, angular gelding: plating-class maiden: stays 1½m: acts on firm going: bandaged near-fore on reappearance, all round next time: visored fifth start: lacks turn of foot. *N. Brittain.*

CO-TACK 5 ch.g. Connaught 130–Dulcidene 71 (Behistoun 131) [1989 12f 1990 —
17m] smallish gelding: has a round action: winning plater as 3-y-o: tailed off in handicap at Pontefract in April, only second subsequent outing on flat: stays 1¾m: acts on firm and dead going: sweated only start at 4 yrs: sold 3,000 gns Ascot July Sales. *A. P. Stringer.*

COTSWOLD COMEDY 3 b.f. Flying Tyke 90–Comedy Spring (Comedy Star —
(USA) 121) [1989 8.2g 8g 1990 10.1m6 12f 8.2m] workmanlike filly: thrice slowly away (reared stalls penultimate start) when well beaten in modest company. *R. Dickin.*

COTTON BLOSSOM (IRE) 2 ch.f. (Apr 20) On Your Mark 125–Valbona (FR) 42
(Abdos 134) [1990 5g 5d 5g 5m2 5f6] rather leggy filly: seventh living foal: half-sister to several winners in France, including useful middle-distance performer Vanann (by Kouban): dam never ran: poor maiden: will be better suited by 6f +: best effort on good to firm ground. *J. S. Wilson.*

COUNT BERTRAND 9 b.h. Brigadier Gerard 144–Gingerale (Golden Horus 51
123) [1989 10s 8.2f* 8f3 8.2g 8m 8m4 7.6m 8g 1990 7.5m 8.2m2 8g6 8f2 8.5f3 8m4 a8g5 a10g4] lengthy horse: poor handicapper: suited by 1m and top-of-the-ground:

199

ridden by 7-lb claimer and bandaged on all-weather: often starts slowly, gets well behind and is suited by strong gallop: goes well on a turning track: particularly well handled by J. Lowe: inconsistent. *W. Holden.*

COUNTESS BRUSSELS 2 ch.f. (Apr 25) Scottish Reel 123–Net Call 108 — (Song 132) [1990 5m 7m] 5,000Y, resold 8,500Y: workmanlike filly: has a round action: ninth foal: half-sister to fair 1m winner Dayajeer and fairly useful 6f and 7f winner Raabihah (both by Shirley Heights): dam seemed best at 6f: bit backward, always behind in maidens at Windsor (auction, slowly away) and Salisbury. *J. Sutcliffe.*

COUNTESS OF POLAND (USA) 2 b.f. (Mar 5) Danzig Connection 45 (USA)–Priceless Countess (USA) (Vaguely Noble 140) [1990 7f4 a6g4] workmanlike filly: second reported foal: half-sister to irresolute plating-class staying maiden Don Tristan (by Conquistador Cielo): dam, in frame at up to 12.5f in France, is half-sister to Allez France and daughter of top-class Priceless Gem: fourth of 10, soon ridden along, in maiden (wore eyeshield) at Southwell: well beaten when odds on for similar event in July: likely to prove suited by further than 6f: wears bandages. *Mrs L. Piggott.*

COUNT ME OUT 5 ch.g. Vaigly Great 127–Balatina 85 (Balidar 133) [1989 7g 6f 52 § 6f5 8.3g 6g 5m a6g 1990 a6g a7g* a6g a7g a7g6 a7g3 a7g3 5f3 6g 7.6m 7h a8g a6g a7g a5g4 a6g3] lengthy, plain gelding: poor mover: won handicap at Lingfield in January: stays 7f: acts on firm going: usually wears blinkers: often finds little, and is unreliable. *R. P. C. Hoad.*

COUNT MY BLESSINGS 5 b.g. Touching Wood (USA) 127–Topaz Too 78 59 (Sun Prince 128) [1989 12s 18.4m 18f4 17.1h3 16.5g 16f3 17f3 1990 20.4m3] neat, quite attractive gelding: usually looks well: moderate mover: quite modest handicapper: suited by test of stamina: best on a sound surface: blinkered twice at 3 yrs: not the easiest of rides: sold privately out of C. Wall's stable 7,800 gns Doncaster March Sales. *B. Ellison.*

COUNTRY COTTAGE (USA) 3 gr.f. Full Out (USA)–La Chaumiere (Thatch — (USA) 136) [1989 6f3 5f* 6m 1990 8m 6m 6f] leggy, quite attractive filly: quite modest winner at 2 yrs: well beaten in handicaps: collapsed at Ayr in July: bred to stay 7f: dead. *P. T. Walwyn.*

COURAGE-MON-BRAVE 2 gr.g. (Mar 22) Bold Owl 101–Bri-Ette (Brittany) 59 p [1990 7m 8g6] 12,000Y: compact gelding: has a round action: fourth foal: brother to 3-y-o Bold-Bri, 5f winner Mom Sally and 1988 2-y-o 6f winner Miss Ellie Pea: dam sister to useful sprinter Tinjar: around 9 lengths sixth of 12, staying on, in minor event at Wolverhampton in October: backward on debut: will improve again. *G. A. Pritchard-Gordon.*

COURT CHARMER 4 b.c. Enchantment 115–Abercourt 89 (Abernant 142) — [1989 6s 6g a6g 1990 a7g a12g a10g] workmanlike colt: of little account: blinkered at 4 yrs: sold 725 gns Ascot February Sales. *C. C. Elsey.*

COURT EQUERRY (IRE) 2 b.c. (Mar 7) King of Clubs 124–Perfect Guest 35 (What A Guest 119) [1990 6m 8m 10s] IR 10,000Y: small, close-coupled colt: moderate mover: first foal: dam unraced granddaughter of Sarah Siddons, dam of Seymour Hicks and Princess Pati: never dangerous in large fields of maidens and platers: visored final outing: sold 800 gns Newmarket Autumn Sales. *M. E. D. Francis.*

COURTESY TITLE (USA) 3 ch.c. Golden Act (USA)–Social Registry (USA) 93 (Raise A Native) [1989 5.8h5 7m2 7f* 8.2d3 8d4 8.5g 1990 8d2 7m2 7m5 8d] good-bodied colt: has a rather round action: fairly useful performer: below form after second start, in Britannia Handicap at Royal Ascot on final one: should prove better over 1m than 7f: yet to race on soft ground, acts on any other. *P. F. I. Cole.*

COURTING NEWMARKET 2 b.g. (May 1) Final Straw 127–Warm Wind 84 62 (Tumble Wind (USA)) [1990 6m a6g a6g 6m3] 2,200F, 9,000Y: leggy, good-topped gelding: moderate mover: third reported foal: half-brother to 3-y-o Cold Blow (by Posse): dam, 7f to 1¼m winner, is half-sister to Yorkshire Oaks winners Sally Brown and Untold: blinkered first time, 2 lengths third of 18, good speed long way, in nursery at Folkestone in October, first worthwhile form: wore eyeshield previous 2 outings: should stay beyond 6f. *Sir Mark Prescott.*

COUTURE INNOVATORS 3 b.c. Music Boy 124–Miss Couture 59 61 (Tamerlane 128) [1989 8v a7g 1990 10m 13.8m3 a14g* 16f2 14f6] sturdy, lengthy colt: carries condition: has a round action: quite modest handicapper: won at Southwell in July: led 1½m final outing, in August: stays 2m: acts on firm going. *P. J. Makin.*

COWORTH PARK 5 gr.g. Wolver Hollow 126–Sparkling Time (USA) (Olden — Times) [1989 NR 1990 16.2d⁶] second outing on flat, well-beaten sixth of 9 in minor event at Goodwood: winner over hurdles later in October. *P. Mitchell.*

COX CREEK 3 ch.g. Coquelin (USA) 121–Grande Maison (Crepello 136) [1989 65 NR 1990 7g⁴ 7m⁵ 7m⁵ 7m 7g 7m⁵ 7.6g 7m³ 7m 7.6m² 7.6d] IR 1,800F, 7,400 2-y-o: rangy gelding: seventh foal: dam, placed over 7f and 10.5f in France, is daughter to very speedy Obelisk: quite modest maiden: will stay 1m: probably best on top-of-the-ground: sometimes on toes: has run well for amateur: didn't handle descent at Epsom. *P. Mitchell.*

CRABBY BILL 3 br.g. Blakeney 126–Dancing Kathleen 53 (Green God 128) 62 [1989 NR 1990 10.1g 10m 10.1m a12g⁵ a13g⁵] unfurnished gelding: fourth reported living foal: dam out of half-sister to Irish 1000 Guineas winner Royal Danseuse: quite modest maiden: suited by 1½m. *Miss B. Sanders.*

CRACK 3 ch.c. High Line 125–Kiss 88 (Habitat 134) [1989 NR 1990 12g* 12m* 101 12m³ 14m³ 14g² 16.5d²] rangy, well-made colt with plenty of scope: has a powerful, markedly round action: fifth foal: half-brother to smart 11.5f to 14.6f winner Casey (by Caerleon) and a winner abroad: dam sprinting half-sister to very useful stayer Meistersinger: favourite, successful at Newmarket in apprentice maiden in June and amateurs event (odds on) in July: useful efforts in minor events and Goodwood listed race (fourth start) next 3 starts, well beaten by High Fountain in minor contest (9/4 on, looking very well) at Doncaster on final one: stays 1¾m well: acts on good to firm ground. *L. M. Cumani.*

CRACK REGIMENT (USA) 2 gr.c. (Apr 12) El Gran Senor (USA) 136– 115 Ancient Regime (USA) 123 (Olden Times (USA)) [1990 6d² 6d⁵ 6.5d² 6.5d* 7s²] 44,000Y: closely related to very smart sprinter La Grande Epoque (by Lyphard) and half-brother to 3-y-o Rami (by Riverman), successful at 6f and 7f: dam French sprinting sister to Cricket Ball: won Prix Eclipse at Saint-Cloud in October by a head from As Que To: earlier around 4 lengths fifth to Hector Protector in Prix Morny Agence Francaise at Deauville: 3 lengths second to Ganges in Criterium de Maisons-Laffitte on final start: will stay 1m: has raced only on a soft surface. *J. Fellows, France.*

CRAFT EXPRESS 4 b.g. Bay Express 132–Lydia Rose 68 (Mummy's Pet 125) 89 [1989 5g* 6d 5m⁵ 5f 5m 5g³ 5.6g* 5m³ 6v³ 1990 6v 5m 5m² 5g⁴ 6d 6g³ 6m⁶ 6m 5.6g 6d 5d² 6d 5m 6d] compact gelding: poor mover: fair handicapper: best over 6f or stiff 5f: acts on good to firm and heavy going: effective with or without blinkers: often hangs: none too consistent. *M. Johnston.*

CRAIGHALL (IRE) 2 b.c. (May 5) Mummy's Treasure 84–Make-Up (Bleep-Bleep 134) [1990 6g] IR 4,400Y: half-brother to a winner in Holland and a winner over hurdles: dam ran 3 times: slow-starting last of 11 in maiden auction at Hamilton in May. *P. Burgoyne.*

CRAIL HARBOUR 4 b.g. Don 128–Broccoli (Welsh Saint 126) [1989 8f³ 8m 70 1990 a7g a6g² a6g* a5g⁵ a6g⁶ a6g 6s² 6v 5g* 5g* 5g a5g⁵ a6g⁶ 6s⁶ 5d] angular, sparely-made gelding: progressed in handicaps, winning at Lingfield in January and Hamilton and Carlisle in May: suited by 6f or stiff 5f: acts on soft going. *M. Johnston.*

CRAKAFU 4 b.g. Kafu 120–Gayles Bambina 75 (Lord Gayle (USA) 124) [1989 6s⁴ 64 5g⁴ 5f³ 5m² 1990 6m² 5m* 6f 5m² a5g² 5g⁵ 5d* 5m³ 6f⁵] rather unfurnished gelding: quite modest handicapper: game winner at Warwick (making virtually all) in April and Catterick (well-backed favourite) in July: speedy, and best at 5f: acts on firm and dead going: blinkered eighth outing: often hangs. *M. H. Easterby.*

CRASH BANG WALLOP (IRE) 2 b.c. (May 20) Le Johnstan 123–Attendre — Moi (Saulingo 122) [1990 6g 6m 6m 8d] IR 1,500F, 3,000Y: rather leggy, unfurnished colt: third living foal: dam Irish maiden: little worthwhile form in maidens: off course 4 months before final start. *R. A. Bennett.*

CRASHLOCK 4 gr.f. Tyrnavos 129–Alicia Markova 64 (Habat 127) [1989 11g 12d — 12f⁶ 1990 12.5g] lengthy, angular filly: well beaten in maidens and sellers. *M. Brittain.*

CRAVEN 3 b.f. Thatching 131–Rustle of Silk 67 (General Assembly (USA)) [1989 69 7s 6g⁶ 1990 6f³ 8.2m³ 7f⁶ 6f* 7m] lengthy filly: quite modest performer: won 4-runner maiden at Redcar in August: likely to prove suited by forcing tactics over 6f: acts on firm ground: sold 1,600 gns Newmarket December Sales. *Miss S. E. Hall.*

CRAZY HORSE DANCER (USA) 2 b.g. (Apr 14) Barachois (CAN)–Why 66 Pass (USA) (Pass (USA)) [1990 5m⁵ 5f³ 5m⁴ 6g⁶] $30,000Y: good-quartered, workmanlike gelding: has plenty of scope: seventh foal: half-brother to several winners in North America, including Miss Enchanted (by Mount Hagen), successful at up to 9f: dam ran 3 times: quite modest maiden: on toes, ran moderately in nursery on final start: should be better suited by 6f than 5f. *J. Etherington.*

CRAZY RIVER   3 b.g. Vision (USA)–Etty 81 (Relko 136) [1989 8m⁴ 8g⁵ 8f⁶ 1990   **57** 12f⁵ 14m⁴ 16g² 17.1f⁴] workmanlike gelding: has a round action: quite modest maiden: lacks turn of foot, and needs thorough test of stamina: winning hurdler. *Mrs J. Pitman.*

CREAM AND GREEN   6 b.g. Welsh Chanter 124–Jumana (Windjammer (USA))   **— §** [1989 6s 7.5d⁶ 7g 6m a7g⁶ a7g⁵ 1990 a7g 6g 6d 6d] leggy, close-coupled, sparely-made gelding: plating-class handicapper on his day: best at 6f to 1m: suited by plenty of give in the ground: visored 3 times at 4 yrs: has raced very freely and often wears severe bridle: often slowly away: unreliable and not to be trusted. *K. White.*

CREAM SILK LADY (FR)   2 b.f. (Apr 8) Dancing Brave (USA) 140–Loveshine   **70 p** (USA) (Gallant Romeo (USA)) [1990 6f⁴] leggy filly: sixth foal: half-sister to French 7f and 9f winner Touching Love (by Touching Wood) and 12.2f winner Hug Me (by Shareef Dancer): dam 1m stakes winner, is half-sister to very smart sprinter/miler Clever Trick: well-backed 5/1-shot, over 6 lengths fourth of 6, green and unable to challenge, to Only Yours in maiden at Newmarket in July: will stay 1m: will improve. *A. A. Scott.*

CREATOR   4 ch.c. Mill Reef (USA) 141–Chalon 125 (Habitat 134) [1989   **126** 10s* 12m⁵ 10g³ 10m² 10g* 9.7m* 1990 10f* 10.5d* 9.2g* 10m⁶ 10d³ 9.7g⁴ 10f³]
      The Prix Ganay at Longchamp in April fell to Creator, the last-but-one foal of Mill Reef whose victory at 10/1 in the same race in 1972 was one of the most spectacularly impressive of modern times. Creator himself went into the Ganay with first-class credentials: he'd progressed well as a three-year-old, winning the Prix Guillaume d'Ornano at Deauville and the Ciga Prix Dollar at Longchamp on his last two outings, and had had three other Ganay runners—the Prix Vermeille winner Young Mother, Mansonnien and Emmson—behind him when accounting for Rainibik by three lengths in the Prix d'Harcourt at Longchamp on his reappearance three weeks earlier. Creator and the previous year's Arc favourite In The Wings were coupled on the French tote and started long odds on, while Ibn Bey, another son of Mill Reef, appeared to hold the best chance of the three British challengers. Ibn Bey quickened into the lead as the field entered the home straight, but Creator was still travelling smoothly just in behind him and after hitting the front over a furlong out went clear in excellent style. In The Wings stayed on well in the final stages but never got any closer than the two-and-a-half-length winning margin; Ibn Bey was the same distance away in third. The Prix Ganay has long been regarded as the most important middle-distance race in France restricted to four-year-olds and upwards, and the latest running clearly

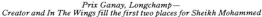

Prix Ganay, Longchamp —
Creator and In The Wings fill the first two places for Sheikh Mohammed

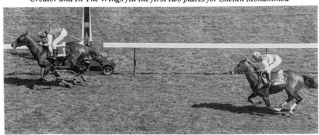

Prix d'Ispahan, Longchamp—Creator narrowly extends his winning sequence to five, ahead of Val des Bois, Citidancer, Louis Cyphre and Lady Winner

required a high-class performance to win, even though the second and third might have been at a disadvantage in that they were making their seasonal reappearance. The Prix d'Ispahan, run over two hundred and fifty metres less than the Ganay, looked to provide an easier opportunity for Creator and he was sent off a very warm favourite to extend his winning sequence to five; Val des Bois, unbeaten on two outings in the spring, and Ile de Chypre, coupled with his pacemaker Gold Minories, were the only others among the nine runners to start at shorter than 10/1. In the event Creator had to work harder than he'd done in the Ganay, but having been fourth into the straight never looked in much danger of defeat and held off Val des Bois and Citidancer, the last two into the straight, by half a length and a neck. Creator became the fourth in the last twenty years to complete the Prix Ganay/Ispahan double in the same season following Allez France, Sagace and Baillamont. Allez France and Sagace were outstanding racehorses; by now Creator had acquired a big reputation, but, like Baillamont, he failed to win again.

Creator's long run came to an end in an unexpected and disappointing manner in the Coral-Eclipse. Once again odds on, he seemed to resent being dropped out last and turned in a moody display, taking little interest early on, tending to hang for much of the straight and managing to pass only the 100/1-shot Call To Arms. Although he usually wore blinkers, we'd had little cause to suspect his temperament. Fabre was very critical of the ride his horse got from Asmussen, saying: 'You can't drop a horse out like that. He ought to have bustled him along to have got him in the race. Creator was ducking into the rail'. However, the trainer added that Creator had behaved in a similar way on his debut as a two-year-old when he took no interest in proceedings. He also told the stewards, who ordered a dope test, that travelling outside France for the first time might have been a factor. The horse reportedly returned home in perfect shape.

Creator was missing from the track for the next two and a half months and, although he ran creditably on three outings in the autumn, he never looked quite the horse that he'd been in the spring. Returned to Longchamp, he carried a penalty for his Group 1 successes in the Prix du Prince d'Orange and Ciga Prix Dollar and was beaten around two lengths by the subsequent Arc winner Saumarez and Agent Bleu, respectively. Creator ran in the Dollar in preference to the Arc. He missed another long-term target, the Dubai Champion Stakes, to run in the Grade 1 Budweiser International at Laurel Park where he finished one and a half lengths third to Fly Till Dawn, dividing Ode and Batshoof. Creator reportedly didn't handle the sharp turns and went particularly wide on the last bend, then rallied strongly but had no chance of catching the winner. Interestingly, Creator's defeat in the Prix Eugene Adam at Saint-Cloud as a three-year-old had been attributed to his failure to handle the left-hand turns. Longchamp's right-hand bends obviously didn't cause him any such problems.

Sheikh Mohammed's "Creator"

		Never Bend (b 1960)	Nasrullah Lalun
	Mill Reef (USA) (b 1968)	Milan Mill (b 1962)	Princequillo Virginia Water
Creator (ch.c. 1986)		Habitat (b 1966)	Sir Gaylord Little Hut
	Chalon (ch 1979)	Areola (ch 1968)	Kythnos Alive Alivo

Creator's dam Chalon was also high class. She won her first six races as a three-year-old, over seven furlongs and a mile, making all in the Coronation Stakes at Ascot and the Child Stakes at Newmarket. Her first living foal Sam Weller, like her trained by Cecil, was sold for just IR 1,500 guineas at the Goffs November Sales having run only once as a three-year-old. He's since won over hurdles, including at Bellewstown and Tipperary in 1990. Since Creator, Chalon has produced the unraced two-year-old filly Dandizette (by Danzig), a yearling filly by Ajdal and a colt foal by Sadler's Wells. Chalon was returned to Sadler's Wells in 1990. Chalon is a daughter of Areola, a game, genuine and very speedy two-year-old who won three times over five furlongs and met defeat only in the Queen Mary Stakes when a six-length second to Cawston's Pride. Areola, closely in-bred to Nasrullah, is the first foal and only important winner of Alive Alivo, who showed some form at two and none afterwards. Areola produced several winners besides Chalon, notably the smart Irish one-mile to mile-and-a-quarter winner Executive Perk (by Lord Gayle), a beaten favourite in the Irish Two Thousand Guineas. Creator, a short-backed colt, was suited by a mile and a quarter and acted on any going. He has been retired to stud in Japan. *A. Fabre, France.*

CREEAGER   8 b.g. Creetown 123–Teenager 71 (Never Say Die 137) [1989 10d⁵   **73**
10.2g 12f³ 12.8m a11g a14g⁵ a16g⁴ a14g⁶ 1990 12.3d⁶ 12m* 12m³ 14g* a12g⁴ 15.3g³

15g 16.5d⁵] lengthy, good-bodied gelding: carries plenty of condition: poor mover: modest handicapper: won comfortably at Thirsk in May and Yarmouth (apprentice ridden) in June: shaped well final outing, first for nearly 4 months: stays 2m: unsuited by soft going, acts on any other: has worn blinkers: best waited with. *J. Wharton.*

CREE BAY   11 b.g. Bay Express 132–Porsanger (USA) (Zeddaan 130) [1989 6m³ **39** 5m² 5f³ 5g⁵ 6g 5m 5d a6g 1990 a7g a8g³ a7g² a7g] keen walker: one-time useful sprinter, poor nowadays: placed in claimers at Lingfield early in year: acts on any going: has worn blinkers and a visor: often slowly away: suited by strong gallop and needs to be produced late: a difficult ride. *J. L. Spearing.*

CREEFLEUR   4 b.f. Creetown 123–Florence Mary 51 (Mandamus 120) [1989 6g² **37** 6s* 6g 6f 6g⁴ 7m 1990 6g 6g 8m 10.8g⁶ 8m⁴ 8.2m] workmanlike non-thoroughbred filly: poor handicapper: probably doesn't stay 10.8f: effective on good to firm going and soft going: ridden mostly by inexperienced claimer at 4 yrs. *K. M. Brassey.*

CRESELLY   3 b.f. Superlative 118–Gwiffina 87 (Welsh Saint 126) [1989 7m⁵ 7d⁵ **69** 1990 7f* 7g 7f⁵ 10f⁵ 7m⁶ 7m⁶ 6s⁵ 7d] compact, workmanlike filly: modest handicapper: won maiden at Newcastle in May: uncertain to stay much beyond 7f: acts on firm going (ran fairly well on soft): visored (never placed to challenge or knocked about) sixth start: sold 1,650 gns Doncaster November Sales. *M. J. Camacho.*

CRIBELLA (USA)   3 b.f. Robellino (USA) 127–Crinoline 72 (Blakeney 126)   — [1989 7.3v⁵ 1990 11.5g⁶ 10.1m⁵ 8f 17.6m] strong, workmanlike filly: modest form when well-beaten fifth in listed race at Newbury and minor event at Windsor: tailed off in maiden final start: should prove best over middle distances. *K. M. Brassey.*

CRICKET FAN   3 br.c. Gorytus (USA) 132–Nollet (High Top 131) [1989 6m* 7m **63 §** 7g 7g 1990 8g 7g⁴ 7f⁶ 7m 7d³ 6m 8m] leggy, sparely-made, angular colt: has a quick action: modest at best: visored, ran in snatches and looked ungenuine in handicap final start, in June: suited by 7f: acts on firm and dead going: has pulled hard: usually on toes: inconsistent. *S. Dow.*

CRIMINAL LAW   3 b.c. Law Society (USA) 130–Indian Maid 117 (Astec 128) **103** [1989 8.2d 6g⁶ 1990 12.5f* 14m* 16.2f⁵ 14.8m²] big, lengthy, unfurnished colt: has plenty of scope: has a long, rather round action: made virtually all to win maiden (on toes) at Wolverhampton in April and minor event at York in May: easily better effort in listed races won by River God after when very good length second of 4 at Newmarket in July, leading until inside final 1f: stays 1¾m well: acts on firm going: game. *R. Hollinshead.*

CRIMSON CLOUD (IRE)   2 ch.c. (May 7) Red Sunset 120–Shangara (Credo **77** 123) [1990 5f 5g 5g⁶ 6g⁴ 6g⁴ 7g⁴ 7g² 7g 8m³ 8.2s² 8m³ 7v² 7d⁴ 8.2s³ 7s⁴] 13,000Y: rather sparely-made colt: moderate mover: brother to 1¼m seller winner Chic Carolyn and half-brother to several other winners here and abroad, including useful middle-distance stayer Pal's Bambino (by Pal's Passage): dam won twice over 5f at 2 yrs in Ireland: modest maiden: best efforts when given good test of stamina: acts on good to firm ground and heavy: has sweated. *N. Tinkler.*

CRIMSON CONQUEST (USA)   2 ch.f. (Feb 10) Diesis 133–Sweet Ramblin **83** Rose (USA) (Turn-To) [1990 6f* 7g² 7m⁶] $300,000Y: lengthy, sparely-made filly: fluent mover: sister to modest maiden Two Words and half-sister to several winners, including Sword Blade (by Damascus), stakes winner at around 1m: dam, stakes-placed winner at up to 6f, is half-sister to very smart Fleet Velvet: odds on, comfortable winner of maiden at Yarmouth in August: fair form in minor event at Kempton and £7,500 contest won by Dartrey at Newmarket: stays 7f. *H. R. A. Cecil.*

CROCKADORE (USA)   3 ch.f. Nijinsky (CAN) 138–Flo Russell (USA) (Round **102** Table) [1989 NR 1990 8g* 11g² 12m² 12g² 10d⁴] IR 420,000Y: fifth foal: half-sister to useful 8.2f winner Double Encore (by Nodouble) and winners in USA by Affirmed and Damascus: dam placed in USA: 11/8 on, won maiden at Phoenix Park by 8 lengths in April: useful form behind Knight's Baroness in Kildangan Stud Irish Oaks (staying on never able to challenge) and Khalafiya in Meld Stakes at the Curragh third and fourth starts: blinkered, below-form favourite in listed race final one: suited by 1½m. *D. K. Weld, Ireland.*

CROESO   2 b.g. (Jan 25) Sayf El Arab (USA) 127–Coral Princess (Imperial Fling **64** (USA) 116) [1990 6m 6g⁵ 7d 6d 8d] 8,000Y, 16,000Y: lengthy, good-quartered gelding: first foal: dam won in Norway: quite modest maiden: stays 1m. *C. A. Horgan.*

CROFTER'S CLINE   6 b. or br.g. Crofter (USA) 124–Modena (Sassafras (FR) **61 d** 135) [1989 6m² 6m* 6f 6f* 6f⁶ 6g* 6m² 6m⁶ 7.5m⁵ 7f 6g 1990 6m⁴ 6f² 5g 6g 10g 6g

6f 6f] strong gelding: quite modest handicapper: below form after second outing: best at 6f: acts on any going: usually blinkered or visored: apprentice ridden. *M O'Neill.*

CROFT IMPERIAL 3 ch.c. Crofthall 110–Farinara (Dragonara Palace (USA) 115) [1989 5d* 5d² 5d² 5g² 5f* 5g³ 5f³ 5m³ 5g* 5s⁵ 1990 5f 5f⁵ 5m³ 6m 5g 6s 5s] workmanlike, good-quartered colt: keen walker: has a quick action: fairly useful performer at his best: ran well in Group 3 event at Newmarket and Kempton minor event in the spring: well below form on all 4 outings afterwards: should prove best at 5f: seems to act on any going: twice blinkered, including at Kempton: tends to idle: trained until after third start by J. Berry. *J. Balding.* — **94 d**

CROFT VALLEY 3 ch.c. Crofthall 110–Sannavally (Sagaro 133) [1989 6f⁶ 6f⁴ 5g 1990 6m³ 6g² 6d³ 6m 6m⁶ 6f² 6m* 6f⁶ 7m 6g⁴ 6f a7g⁵ a6g⁴ a6g a8g³ a10g] workmanlike colt: modest performer: on toes, won handicap at Ripon in August, soon pushed along then leading inside final 1f: best efforts at 6f: acts on firm and dead going: visored 5 times, including at Ripon. *R. M. Whitaker.* — **71**

CRONK'S COURAGE 4 ch.g. Krayyan 117–Iresine (GER) (Frontal 122) [1989 6s⁴ 6d⁵ 6m 6m 5f 1990 6m 6m 5m 6d 6m² 6g³ 6d* 6f⁴ 5m 6m² 6g² 6m 5d 6g 6m 6d* 5.8d] big, strong, lengthy gelding: has a quick action: modest handicapper: successful at Haydock (making all) in July and Nottingham in October: best at 6f: has won on firm going, but goes particularly well on dead nowadays: visored or blinkered. *G. Lewis.* — **69**

CRONK'S DOMINION 2 ch.f. (Apr 23) Dominion 123–Zanubia 81 (Nonoalco (USA) 131) [1990 6m 7m 7m 7s] angular filly: fifth foal: half-sister to 1986 2-y-o 5f winner Bothy Ballad (by Final Straw) and a winner in Italy: dam, 7f winner, is half-sister to dam of Knockando out of half-sister to Connaught: always behind in minor event and maidens (not at all knocked about on final start): bandaged behind final 2 starts. *G. Lewis.* — **53**

CRONK'S QUALITY 7 b.g. Main Reef 126–Ozone (Auction Ring (USA) 123) [1989 5g 1990 6m 6m 6m 6d³ 6s a6g a8g] small, good-quartered gelding: moderate mover: fair winner early as 5-y-o: lightly raced nowadays, and below form in 1990: effective at 5f and 6f: unsuited by firm going, acts on any other: ran poorly when blinkered: bandaged at 7 yrs: sometimes taken down early. *G. Lewis.* — **57**

CROSBY 4 b.c. Music Boy 124–Yelney 65 (Blakeney 126) [1989 6s 7s 5f 6m 6f⁵ 7m* 7m a6g⁶ a8g 1990 6f³ 7.6m a5g⁴ a7g²] good-bodied, quite useful-looking colt: modest handicapper: better suited by 6f and 7f than 5f: seems to act on any going: sometimes on toes, and often sweats: trained until after second outing by J. Payne. *P. A. Kelleway.* — **66**

CROSBY PLACE 4 gr.f. Crooner 119–Royal Bat 69 (Crowned Prince (USA) 128) [1989 10v 7s⁶ 6f³ 7f⁶ 8f⁴ 7f 7g² 8.2f 7.6m 1990 a7g⁵ a10g⁴ a10g* a10g⁶ a10g² a10g² 10.2f* 10.8m a10g² 10m a12g 10g a10g] workmanlike, close-coupled filly: quite modest handicapper: won at Lingfield in February and Doncaster (ladies) in March: off course 4 months after tenth outing and tailed off last 3: suited by 1¼m: easily best efforts on a sound surface: blinkered: has worn bandages. *M. J. Haynes.* — **60 d**

CROSSILLION 2 b.c. (May 29) Rousillon (USA) 133–Croda Rossa (ITY) (Grey Sovereign 128§) [1990 6m⁴ 7m²] lengthy, angular colt: good walker: easy mover: half-brother to 3-y-o Rockridge (by Chief Singer) and 3 winners, including smart 5f to 1¼m winner Dancing Rocks (by Green Dancer) and useful 1984 2-y-o 6f winner Red Rocks (by Grundy): dam won 3 of 4 races in Italy, and is half-sister to Italian Derby winner Cerreto: ¾-length second of 12, shaken up 2f out then staying on really well final furlong, to Knock To Enter in maiden at Warwick in October: will be suited by 1m: sure to improve again, and win a race. *G. Wragg.* — **78 p**

CROSS MAGS 3 ch.f. Hasty Word 84–Red Squaw 61 (Tribal Chief 125) [1989 5f³ 6m⁵ 1990 8m 7f 12.5g] small, stocky, plain filly: poor maiden. *G. Price.* — **—**

CROUPIER 3 b.c. Night Shift (USA)–Countess Walewski 85 (Brigadier Gerard 144) [1989 6m² 6m⁴ 7g* 1990 8g 8f⁶ 8f* 8m⁴] rather leggy, attractive colt: useful performer: returned to form when winning handicap at Newmarket in August: 200/1, very good 14 lengths fourth of 10, staying on from rear, to Markofdistinction in Queen Elizabeth II Stakes at Ascot: stays 1m: acts on firm going. *C. E. Brittain.* — **105**

CROWN ANGEL (USA) 2 ch.f. (Mar 6) The Minstrel (CAN) 135–State Treasure (USA) (Secretariat (USA)) [1990 5m⁵ 6g 8m⁵] IR 105,000Y: leggy, angular filly: fifth foal: closely related to a winner in USA by Dixieland Band and half-sister to a winner there by Linkage: dam, U.S. 2-y-o 6f winner from only 3 starts, is half-sister to Media Starguest and from excellent family: over 12 lengths fifth of 11, — **51 p**

never near to challenge, to Glowing Ardour at Chepstow in August, best effort in maidens: worth keeping an eye on. *R. Hannon.*

CROWN BALADEE (USA) 3 b. or br.c. Chief's Crown (USA)–Naseem — Baladee 82 (Kris 135) [1989 7.3g⁴ 7m⁴ 8f² 1990 10g 8m] strong, close-coupled, chunky colt: quite modest maiden at 2 yrs: faced very stiff task in handicap final start in 1990: slowly away in similar event 6½ months earlier: stays 1m. *A. A. Scott.*

CROWNING AMBITION (USA) 3 b.f. Chief's Crown (USA)–Fabulous 65 Notion (USA) (Somethingfabulous (USA)) [1989 6g 8.2s³ 6g⁶ 1990 7m² 7g* 7g] leggy, workmanlike filly: modest form: favourite, held on by a head in maiden at Salisbury in August: wandered and no extra having again led 2f out in similar event previous start, raced too freely in handicap (blinkered) on final one: stays 7f: acts on good to firm ground: wore net muzzle final start at 2 yrs. *R. Charlton.*

CROWN RESERVE 2 br.c. (Feb 29) Another Realm 118–Stardyn (Star Appeal 64 133) [1990 6f² 6m² 7g³ a6g] sturdy colt: first reported foal: dam maiden suited by 1½m: quite modest form when second in maidens at Brighton and Folkestone: well beaten facing stiff task in Southwell nursery on final outing, first for 4 months: should be better suited by 7f than 6f *M. J. Ryan.*

CROWPOST 2 gr.c. (Mar 31) Lucky Wednesday 124–Alpha Centauri 56 (Grey — Mirage 128) [1990 5m 5m 8m] smallish, leggy colt: fourth living foal: dam won 6f seller at 3 yrs: of no account. *S. R. Bowring.*

CRUACHAN (USA) 2 b.c. (Apr 23) Lear Fan (USA) 130–Sugar Hollow (USA) 96 p (Val de L'Orne (FR) 133) [1990 7g²] $12,000Y: second foal: dam never ran: bit burly and green, ½-length second of 11, disputing lead racing keenly then staying on well, to Golden Birch in mixed-aged event at Newmarket in November: moved short to post: sure to improve, and win a race. *G. Harwood.*

CRU EXCEPTIONNEL 2 b.c. (Apr 8) Scottish Reel 123–Elton Abbess 86 59 P (Tamerlane 128) [1990 6m⁶] 7,000Y: strong, good-bodied colt: half-brother to 1989 Irish 2-y-o 5f winner Murur (by Never So Bold) and 2 other winners, including useful 1985 2-y-o Roaring Riva (by Music Boy): dam won 3 sprint races and stayed 1m: in need of race and green, 11 lengths sixth of 14, very slowly away when catching eye not at all knocked about, to Volksraad in maiden at Newmarket in November: sure to improve considerably, and win a race or two. *P. J. Makin.*

CRUISE PARTY (IRE) 2 b.c. (May 4) Slip Anchor 136–Cider Princess (Alcide 78 p 136) [1990 7m⁵ 8g⁴] 64,000F, 52,000Y: big, lengthy colt: has plenty of scope: half-brother to Irish 3-y-o 1½m winner Blackdown (by Rainbow Quest), good-class miler Tender King (by Prince Tenderfoot) and a winner in Italy: dam Irish 9f winner, is from successful family: modest form in maidens at Newmarket (staying on well) and Pontefract (carried head high) in the autumn: will do better at 3 yrs. *W. Jarvis.*

CRUISING HEIGHT 3 b.f. Shirley Heights 130–Nomadic Pleasure 91 (Habitat 112 134) [1989 NR 1990 10.6s* 12.2g* 12s² 12g⁴ 10g³ 14.6g] big, rangy filly: has a short, scratchy action: fourth foal: sister to 4-y-o 11f to 14.6f winner Highflying and half-sister to Park Hill Stakes winner Trampship (by High Line): dam, 9f winner, is half-sister to Prix Vermeille winner Paulista: favourite, impressive winner of maiden at Haydock and minor event at Warwick in June: contested pattern events afterwards, setting pace when about 7½ lengths behind Hellenic in Yorkshire Oaks at York fourth start: ran poorly (held up) in Park Hill Stakes at Doncaster: stayed 1½m: probably not at her best on very soft going: stud. *B. W. Hills.*

CRY FOR THE CLOWN 6 b.h. Cawston's Clown 113–Bayberry 77 (Henry The — § Seventh 125) [1989 9g 8f 1990 8.2m] leggy, sparely-made horse: moderate mover: useful at his best: pulled up lame near-hind only outing (May) at 6 yrs: best at around 1m: acts on dead going and unsuited by firm: usually blinkered or visored: often bandaged: thoroughly inconsistent. *C. Spares.*

CRYPTIC GIRL 3 b.f. Tower Walk 130–Lucky Saran 72 (Lucky Wednesday 124) — [1989 5f 6m⁶ 6g 1990 9m 12m] sparely-made filly: poor plater: sold 1,000 gns Doncaster September Sales. *W. J. Pearce.*

CRYSTAL BEAM 3 b.g. Crystal Glitters (USA) 127–Jem Jen 85 (Great Nephew 79 126) [1989 6f⁴ 7.3g* 7m⁵ 8.5g⁴ 7g 1990 9g⁵ 8.5g⁶ 10.4d⁴ 12d 8m⁵ 8m⁴ 10.8m⁴ 8m⁵ 8d⁶] leggy gelding: fair performer: stays 10.8f: acts on good to firm ground: twice blinkered: has run well for 7-lb claimer: retained by trainer 52,000 gns Ascot February Sales: winning hurdler. *P. A. Kelleway.*

CRYSTAL GAZING (USA) 2 b.f. (Feb 17) El Gran Senor (USA) 136–Crystal 104 p Bright 75 (Bold Lad (IRE) 133) [1990 6m² 6m* 7d*] sturdy, compact filly: half-sister to fair but untrustworthy 3-y-o 1m and 1¼m winner Staunch Rival (by Sir Ivor): dam, placed at 5f at 2 yrs, later winner at about 1m in USA: well-backed

Bottisham Heath Stud Rockfel Stakes, Newmarket—
Crystal Gazing (left) just holds on from Lee Artiste

favourite, won Blue Seal Stakes at Ascot in September easily by 4 lengths, leading on bridle around 2f out: odds on and again looking really well, followed up in Bottisham Heath Stud Rockfel Stakes at Newmarket following month, quickening 2f out then holding on by a short head from Lee Artiste: will stay at least 1m. *L. M. Cumani.*

CRYSTAL HEIGHTS (FR) 2 ch.c. (Feb 23) Crystal Glitters (USA) 127–Fahrenheit 69 (Mount Hagen (FR) 127) [1990 7m 6g3] big, strong, lengthy colt: half-brother to 1987 2-y-o 6f winner Full Blast (by Sayyaf), later stayed 1½m but unreliable, and 6f and 1m winner Start-Rite (by Comedy Star): dam placed at 7f and 1m: over 2 lengths third of 17, headway 2f out then unable to quicken final 50 yds, to Rocton North in maiden at Yarmouth: green and showed clear signs of ability on debut: will stay 1m: sort to do better at 3 yrs. *W. A. O'Gorman.*   **72 p**

CRYSTAL JACK (FR) 2 b.g. (Apr 19) Crystal Glitters (USA) 127–Cackle (USA) (Crow (FR) 134) [1990 5f4 5f4 5d* 5f4 5g3 6f* 7s 6g 6g3 7d] 220,000 francs (approx £21,200) Y: leggy, quite good-topped gelding: has a quick action: second foal: dam French minor 1½m winner, is out of half-sister to good American miler Well Mannered: fair performer: successful at Chester in maiden in May and minor event in July: better at 6f than 5f, and is bred to stay 7f: acts on firm and dead ground: tends to get on edge, and often sweats: races keenly: inconsistent. *F. H. Lee.*   **88**

CRYSTAL PARK 4 b.f. Head For Heights 125–So Precise (FR) (Balidar 133) [1989 9f 10.2m 11g a14g2 a14g 1990 a11g* a11g5 a12g5 a14g3] workmanlike filly: won claimer at Southwell in January: stays 1¾m: inconsistent. *J. Wharton.*   **47**

CRYSTAL PATH (FR) 2 ch.f. (Apr 7) Crystal Glitters (USA) 127–Flower Parade (Mill Reef (USA) 141) [1990 7m2 6m* 7d3] workmanlike filly: has scope: third reported foal: half-sister to quite modest hurdler Wind of Flower (by Pharly): dam, placed over 1m at 2 yrs and 10.5f at 3 yrs in France, is half-sister to very smart French colt Bilal: won maiden at Newmarket by a neck from Lapland Lights: over 3 lengths third of 6, one pace final 2f, to Crystal Gazing in Bottisham Heath Stud Rockfel Stakes later in October: will stay 1m: can improve again. *M. Moubarak.*   **95 p**

CRYSTAL RING (IRE) 2 b.f. (Feb 28) Kris 135–Crown Treasure (USA) (Graustark) [1990 7m2 7g2] lengthy, rather sparely-made filly: has scope: sister to 3-y-o stayer Crystal Spirit and half-sister to several winners, notably Diamond Shoal and Glint of Gold (both by Mill Reef): dam very useful at 2 yrs in USA when winner at 5f: fair form, staying on, in minor event won by Shadayid at Ascot in September and Janbiya at York month later: seems one paced, and will be much better suited by middle distances. *I. A. Balding.*   **83**

208

CRYSTAL SPIRIT 3 b.g Kris 135–Crown Treasure (USA) (Graustark) [1989   95
7m⁶ 1990 11d⁴ 11.7f² 11.7f⁶ 16g* 16m⁵ 16.2m³ 14g 17.6g* 16.2m⁴ 18d] rangy,
workmanlike gelding with plenty of scope: has rather round action: fairly useful
performer: won maiden at Nottingham in June and £7,400 handicap at Haydock in
September: ran poorly at York and Newmarket (Cesarewitch, close up 1¾m)
seventh and final starts: suited by forcing tactics and thorough test of stamina: acts
on good to firm ground, possibly not on dead: winning hurdler. *I. A. Balding.*

CRYSTAL SPRAY 4 b.f. Beldale Flutter (USA) 130–Crystal Fountain (Great   62
Nephew 126) [1989 10g 12g 10m⁶ 10.4m² 10g⁵ a 12g² a 13g³ a 12g 1990 a 12g⁵ 13f³ 14g*
12.8m³] medium-sized filly: modest form when placed in handicaps here, trained
until after first outing in 1990 by H. Candy: sent to Ireland and won maiden at Down
Royal: stays 1¾m: blinkered last 2 starts. *M. Grassick, Ireland.*

C SHARP 3 ch.g. Song 132–Simply Jane (Sharpen Up 127) [1989 5g³ 5g⁶ 5g³ 1990   50
7f 5g⁵ 5.3h 5m⁴ 5g 6f⁶] sparely-made gelding: shows a quick action: plating-class
sprint maiden: possibly best with give in the ground: blinkered last 5 outings, twice
edgy: usually sweating. *K. M. Brassey.*

CUILLIN RIDGE 3 ch.g. Dalsaan 125–Cailin Oir (Sallust 134) [1989 NR 1990 7g   —
10.1g 10.1m 10g 12d a10g] IR 14,000Y: big, good-topped gelding: third foal:
half-brother to Irish 1¾m and 2m winner Adapt (by Smoggy): dam never ran: no
worthwhile form, including in claimers: blinkered last 2 starts. *M. D. I. Usher.*

CULLINAN (USA) 3 b.c. Diamond Prospect (USA)–Meshuggenah (Sharpen Up   92
127) [1989 7m³ 6d* 7g² 7g 1990 7m 5d* 5s⁶] well-made, attractive colt: useful
performer at 2 yrs: off course 4 months after landing odds in minor event at
Beverley in June: well below form in Free Handicap at Newmarket and Haydock
minor event otherwise as 3-y-o: should prove best beyond 5f: best efforts on an easy
surface, though below form on very soft going. *L. M. Cumani.*

CUMBRIAN CEILIDH 3 ch.g. Simply Great (FR) 122–Elm 88 (Realm 129)   70
[1989 NR 1990 9.1m³ 8g² 8g⁶ 8.2m⁵ a8g 10m* 10g⁵] 6,000Y, 10,500Y: angular,
workmanlike gelding: good walker and mover: sixth foal: half-brother to quite
useful sprinter Bold Realm (by Bold Lad (IRE)), also successful in Italy: dam won
over 5f on her first 2 starts: modest performer: below best last 4 starts, hanging
right and leading inside final 1f to win moderately-run seller (no bid) at Ripon in
August: claimed to join L. Lungo £6,250 final start: stays 1¼m. *M. H. Easterby.*

CUMBRIAN EXPRESS 5 b.g. Bay Express 132–Astral Suite 82 (On Your   76
Mark 125) [1989 6d 5f 5f 1990 6f 6f 5m 6m* 5f³ 6m* 6g 6m⁴ 6f 5m⁵ 6f⁵ 6g] strong,
quite attractive gelding: poor mover: made all or virtually all to win handicap at
Thirsk in May and claimer (claimed out of M. H. Easterby's stable £11,258) at
Newcastle in June: below form after, finishing lame final outing (heavily bandaged in
front): stayed 6f: seemed unsuited by very firm going: effective with or without
blinkers: dead. *C. R. Beever.*

CUMBRIAN SINGER 3 b.g. Chief Singer 131–Bloomsday 69 (Sparkler 130)   61
[1989 6f⁴ 6g⁴ 5g³ 7m 7v 6g 1990 7g 7m⁶ 6m⁴ 7d³ 7g 6m³ 6g³ 6d 6f 7d] rather leggy,
good-topped gelding: moderate mover: quite modest maiden: effective at 6f and 7f:
acts on good to firm ground, possibly unsuited by heavy: races keenly: visored final
start: sold 5,200 gns Newmarket Autumn Sales, probably to race in Italy. *M. H.
Easterby.*

CUMBRIAN WALTZER 5 ch.g. Stanford 121§–Mephisto Waltz 98 (Dancer's   96
Image (USA)) [1989 5g⁵ 5m⁵ 6m⁵ 6f³ 5m⁵ 6f 5g⁵ 6m³ 6m⁵ 5m* 5g* 5m² 1990
5m² 5g³ 5m² 6m 5m³ 6m² 6m⁵ 5.6g⁵ 6d⁴ 5m 0s⁴] leggy gelding: often dull in coat:
good mover: fairly useful handicapper: ran well most starts as 5-y-o, on eighth and
ninth staying on strongly in Tote-Portland at Doncaster (badly hampered 1f out) and
Ladbrokes (Ayr) Gold Cup: ideally suited by 6f or stiff 5f: acts on any going:
blinkered once: has sweated: tough, genuine and tremendously consistent. *M. H.
Easterby.*

CUM LAUDE 3 b.f. Shareef Dancer (USA) 135–With Distinction (USA) 102
(Distinctive (USA)) [1989 8g 1990 11f² 12m⁴ 11.5g* 12m⁴ 10f* 10g² 10m* 10g²
10.5v] rangy filly: has plenty of scope: moderate mover: fairly useful performer:
twice odds on when winning maiden at Yarmouth in July, handicap at Redcar
(sweating, wandered) in August and 3-runner £7,500 contest at Yarmouth in
September: 7 lengths second to Ruby Tiger in Premio Lydia Tesio at Rome and in
mid-division for Group 3 contest at Saint-Cloud last 2 starts: effective at 1¼m and
1½m: acts on firm going. *H. R. A. Cecil.*

CUNNING PLAN 2 gr.g. (Mar 21) Belfort (FR) 89–Chinese Princess (Sunny   57
Way 120) [1990 6f² 5f⁶ a7g⁴ 7g⁵ 8.5m⁶ 6g⁴ a6g a6g³ a7g⁵] 4,800Y: leggy, rather

unfurnished gelding: good walker: half-brother to several winners on flat and over jumps, including 1978 2-y-o 1m seller winner Magic Kit (by Namnan): dam unraced half-sister to very smart Streetfighter: fair plater: ran creditably in claimers at Southwell on final 2 starts: stays 1m: swerved badly left stalls second outing: dosen't look an easy ride. *T. D. Barron.*

CUPIDS BOWER   7 b.m. Owen Dudley 121–Cupid's Delight 84 (St Paddy 133)   — [1989 NR 1990 a14g] leggy, lightly-made mare: of little account: has worn blinkers: has been to stud. *Mrs S. Oliver.*

CUP OF TRICKS (USA)   3 br.f. Clever Trick (USA)–Cup of Honey (USA)   — (Raise A Cup (USA)) [1989 5m3 6g* 7h2 7m 8g3 1990 8.5g5 8g 7d6 7g6] close-coupled filly: fair winner at 2 yrs: showed signs of return to form in £7,200 handicap at Epsom in June on third start in 1990, ran poorly in similar event at Lingfield later in month: stays 1m: acts on hard ground. *B. Hanbury.*

CURIA REGIS (USA)   3 b.c. Deputy Minister (CAN)–Katie Cochran (USA)   **104** (Roberto (USA) 131) [1989 6m* 6f2 7m* 7g3 1990 8m2 12s* 10g3 10.1g4] attractive colt: has a rather round action: useful efforts in July when winning 4-runner listed race at Haydock and about 2 lengths third of 7 to Husyan in Scottish Classic (held up in rear than staying on well) at Ayr: stays 1½m: acts on good to firm ground and soft: sent to race in USA. *Major W. R. Hern.*

CURLILOCKS   2 ch.f. (Apr 17) Glenstal (USA) 118–Merry Sharp (Sharpen Up   — 127) [1989 5d] second foal: half-sister to a winner in Italy: dam from family of very smart stayer May Hill: always in rear in maiden at Catterick in October. *Mrs Barbara Waring.*

CURRACALL   5 br.g. Indian King (USA) 128–Callixena (Kalamoun 129) [1989 8s   — 9m2 9.5m3 12d 1990 12m6 10m 10.6d a6g a8g a7g] lengthy ex-Irish gelding: third foal: half-brother to useful Irish 1986 2-y-o 6f and 1m winner Inanna (by Persian Bold): dam won over 7.9f at 2 yrs in Ireland: won handicap at Naas as 3-y-o: no worthwhile form in 1990: needs further than 6f and stays 1¼m: acts on firm and dead going: has been tried in blinkers. *J. Parkes.*

CURTAIN CALL   4 ch.c. Final Straw 127–Hathaway (Connaught 130) [1989 10g4   **100** 8f 7g3 8f2 8m2 7m2 7h* 7f3 8f* 8g* 9g 1990 8g 8f 8.2m2 8f2 8m3 8m* 8f 7.6m5 8m2] strong colt: useful handicapper: had fine season: won apprentice event at Ascot in July: neck second of 32 to Pontenuovo in Royal Hunt Cup at Royal Ascot fourth outing: suited by 1m: goes extremely well on top-of-the-ground: blinkered once: often sweats, and has got on edge: has turn of foot: tough and consistent: sold to race abroad. *P. J. Makin.*

CURTAIN UP (FR)   3 ch.g. Sicyos (USA) 126–Angelina d'Or (Sun Prince 128)   — [1989 NR 1990 7g 8g 7m] 340,000 francs (approx £31,100) Y: angular gelding: moderate mover: third foal: closely related to a winner in Italy by Bellypha: dam, French provincial 1½m winner, is half-sister to The Parson and daughter of Ribblesdale and Park Hill Stakes winner Bracey Bridge: no show in maidens. *R. Guest.*

CURVED BLADE (FR)   3 ch.c. Kris 135–Kaliopa (FR) (Zeddaan 130) [1989   **86** 5m2 6g2 6g* 7m2 1990 7.6m3 6m] rather leggy, attractive colt: fair performer: creditable third at Lingfield, leading 5f and better effort in handicaps in first half of 1990: stays 7.6f: races keenly: edgy and sweating final start. *J. Gosden.*

CURVET (USA)   5 b.m. Ack Ack (USA)–Jingle Jan (USA) (In Reality) [1989 NR   — 1990 8g 10m6 6g 8d 10.2s4 a6g a8g] small, angular ex-French mare: third foal: half-sister to French 9f winner Minnesinger (by Sassafras): dam won 7 times in USA, including in minor stakes company, at up to 9f: won maiden as 2-y-o: retains only a modicum of ability: stays 1¼m: acts on heavy going. *M. C. Chapman.*

CUT A CAPER   8 b.g. Gay Fandango (USA) 132–Brilliant Gem 83 (Charlottown   — 127) [1989 10s2 12s6 10f2 10h5 10.2h2 10m* 1990 a10g6] small gelding: poor mover: poor handicapper: stays 1¼m well: probably acts on any going: ran freely in blinkers: has won for apprentice. *R. J. O'Sullivan.*

C U TECHNIMECH   4 b.f. Chukaroo 103–Karyobinga 66 (So Blessed 130) [1989   — 6f 1990 6g 5f 5g] lengthy, good-topped filly: retains little ability. *M. W. Eckley.*

CUTE ENCHANTRESS   3 b.f. Enchantment 115–Chalk Your Cue (Pals   — Passage 115) [1989 5d 1990 11.7m 17.6m3] leggy filly: no worthwhile form in maidens, sweating as 3-y-o. *T. B. Hallett.*

CUT FOR KINGS   2 b.f. (Feb 17) King of Spain 121–Razor Blade 65 (Sharp Edge   **36** 123) [1990 5f 6m 8m] 4,200F: small, good-quartered filly: sixth foal: half-sister to 3 winners here and abroad, including sprinter Keen Edge (by Good Times): dam 2-y-o 5f and 7f winner: poor form in maidens and an apprentice seller. *C. C. Elsey.*

CUT IN STONE (USA) 3 b.f. Assert 134–Bally Knockan (USA) (Exclusive 72 Native (USA)) [1989 NR 1990 10.1g⁶ 10.2g² 12g⁵] $32,000Y: leggy, angular filly: second foal: half-sister to Irish 6f and 1m winner To Die For (by Diesis): dam out of smart winner at up to 9f Ferly, won 6f stakes at 5 yrs and also placed in stakes at up to 8.5f: 15 lengths second of 5 to Narwala in minor event at Doncaster in September: below that form in Pontefract maiden 6 weeks later: should stay 1½m: gave trouble at stalls first 2 starts. *J. R. Fanshawe.*

CUTLASS PRINCESS (USA) 3 b.f. Cutlass (USA)–T N T Gal (USA) (Baldski — (USA)) [1989 5g⁵ 6f⁴ 7m 8.5f 1990 7.6d 12h] smallish, sparely-made filly: poor maiden: has joined J. J. O'Neill. *R. Guest.*

CUT OUT 3 ch.c. Claude Monet (USA) 121–Luscinia 73 (Sing Sing 134) [1989 NR — 1990 a6g a7g 6m 6g] 6,000Y: leggy, angular colt: poor mover: half-brother to several winners on flat and over hurdles, including 5f and 6f winner Nariz (by Brigadier Gerard): dam won over 1m: no sign of ability in claimers: with M. Brittain later, when stable-companion Sayyaf's Lad mistakenly ran in his place in Wolverhampton handicap in July. *C. Spares.*

CUT THE MUSIC (IRE) 2 b.g. (Feb 22) Sure Blade (USA) 128–Monaco 67 Melody 103 (Tudor Melody 129) [1990 6f⁵ 7g² 8f 7g 7.6v⁵] IR 24,000Y: big, lengthy gelding: moderate mover: eighth foal: half-brother to 5 winners, including useful 1983 2-y-o 5f winner Jeema (by Thatch) and Irish 1m (at 2 yrs) and 1½m winner Northern Ace (by Shareef Dancer): dam 6f winner: quite modest maiden: easily best effort at Chester in August: should stay 1m: possibly unsuited by extremes of going. *M. Bell.*

CUT THE MUSTARD (IRE) 2 b.c. (Apr 15) Niniski (USA) 125–Cutlers Cor- 54 p ner 111 (Sharpen Up 127) [1990 8m 8s] 30,000Y: big, rangy colt: has plenty of scope: third foal: half-brother to 1988 2-y-o 5f winner Sawaik (by Dominion) and Irish 3-y-o 7f winner Clean Cut (by Formidable): dam 5f winner: green and backward, always behind in maiden at Newmarket and minor race at Newbury in October. *J. L. Dunlop.*

CUTTING NOTE (USA) 3 ch.c. Diesis 133–Hasty Key (USA) (Key To The 93 Mint (USA)) [1989 6g² 7m* 8g⁵ 1990 9f3] quite attractive colt: useful form as 2-y-o, winning maiden at Newmarket and about 8 lengths last of 5 in Racing Post Trophy (on toes) at Newcastle: third in minor event at Ripon in April on only start in 1990, taking keen hold, pushed along 3f out and staying on at one pace: stays 1m. *G. A. Huffer.*

CUT UP ROUGH 6 b.g. Mummy's Pet 125–Albany 120 (Pall Mall 132) [1989 6v — 8d 6f⁴ 5.8h⁴ 6f3 6f⁵ 6m⁴ 6g 6f* 5m 7m 1990 5g 6f 8m 6f 7g 5m 6f 10f] leggy, quite attractive gelding: little show since winning maiden claimer (edgy and sweating) as 5-y-o: suited by 6f: acts on firm going: blinkered and visored once: trained until after seventh outing by G. Cottrell. *J. H. Baker.*

CUVEE ROSE 3 b.f. Lafontaine (USA) 117–Champers Club (Run The Gantlet 60 (USA)) [1989 6m 6f² 6g3 7m 7m* 8g* 8f 1990 10.6f 8m3 10g² 10f* 12m⁶ 10.6v a10g] small, leggy filly: moderate walker: poor mover: quite modest performer: below form after struggling to land odds in 4-runner claimer at Yarmouth in August: should stay 1½m: probably acts on firm going: sweating and edgy fifth start. *C. E. Brittain.*

CYDALIA (USA) 3 b. or br.f. Cresta Rider (USA) 124–Slam Bid (USA) (Forli 109 (ARG)) [1989 7s* 1990 7m⁴ 8g⁴ 8g² 7d⁴ 8d 6d3 7g] first foal: dam lightly-raced French 1m winner out of half-sister to dam of L'Emigrant and Salpinx: successful at Maisons-Laffitte in newcomers race in November at 2 yrs and Prix Imprudence in April: strong-finishing fourth in Poule d'Essai des Pouliches (held up in rear) at Longchamp and narrowly-beaten third in Prix de Seine-et-Oise at Maisons-Laffitte second and sixth outings: seems effective at 6f to 1m: yet to race on firm going, acts on any other. *F. Boutin, France.*

D

DAARIK 3 b.c. Diesis 133–Bay Street 114 (Grundy 137) [1989 6f* 7m* 6f* 6g* 103 6g² 1990 7m⁴ 8g⁶ 7f* 7f 7.6f² 6m 7g*] leggy, rather shallow-girthed colt: has a fluent, round action: useful performer: won minor event at Chepstow in May and listed event at the Curragh (favourite) in September: seems best at around 7f: acts on firm ground: to race in USA. *H. Thomson Jones.*

DAAZAM (IRE) 2 b.f. (Apr 23) Mazaad 106–Jamie's Girl (Captain James 123) **57**
[1990 5g 5d⁴ 6m⁴ 7g⁴ 5d² 6g* 6f⁴ 8.5m 6d] 1,000 2-y-o: lengthy filly: has a round
action: third foal: half-sister to 1m and 1¼m winner By Choice (by Sallust): dam
unraced: improved plater: sweating and edgy, won at Nottingham (no bid) in July:
looked in need of race penultimate outing, first for 2 months: ran badly final start:
probably ideally suited by 6f: best form on an easy surface: blinkered fifth to eighth
starts: trained by Ronald Thompson except for final start. *W. W. Haigh.*

DADDY'S DARLING 5 b.m. Mummy's Pet 125–Annie Get Your Gun 69 **52**
(Blakeney 126) [1989 12m 10f⁶ 10f 10m³ 10h² 12f⁴ 12m³ 12m³ 12g⁶ 12g⁴ 1990 a12g*
a10g a12g⁵ a16g³ 12f* 12f* 12g⁶ 12m² 12g² 12m] small, rather sparely-made mare:
plating-class handicapper: improved as 5-y-o, winning at Lingfield in January,
Brighton in April and Folkestone in May: best short of 2m: acts on hard and dead
going: effective with or without blinkers or visor. *J. T. Gifford.*

DAHLAWISE (IRE) 2 b.f. (Apr 18) Caerleon (USA) 132–Cornish Heroine **76**
(USA) 101 (Cornish Prince) [1990 a6g* 6m² 7m⁶] IR 30,000Y: leggy, sparely-made
filly: fourth foal: closely related to 3-y-o 11f winner Pinecone Peter (by Kings Lake),
later winning hurdler, and fairly useful 7f winner Lomax (by Lomond): dam 1m (at 2
yrs) and 12.2f winner: green, comfortable winner of maiden at Southwell in
September: ridden by 5-lb claimer, very good staying-on second in nursery at
Newmarket following month: will stay 1m +. *W. J. Haggas.*

DAILY SPORT BOY 2 b.c. (May 20) Jalmood (USA) 126–Knavesmire 82 **57 §**
(Runnymede 123) [1990 5m 5g 5f³ 5d* 7m 5g⁴ 8.2s] 6,000F, 6,000Y, resold 1,000Y:
unfurnished colt: seventh foal: half-brother to 5f performer Bluemede (by Blue
Cashmere) and a winner in Italy: dam best at 2 yrs: fair plater on his day: stayed on
strongly when winning (no bid) at Catterick in July: should be suited by further than
5f: has run creditably for 7-lb claimer: has hung right: bolted to start third
appearance: one to treat with caution: trained by J. Berry first 3 outings: sold 2,000
gns Newmarket Autumn Sales. *M. W. Easterby.*

DAILY SPORT SOON 5 b.h. Star Appeal 133–Pritillor 93 (Privy Councillor **66 §**
125) [1989 14f² 16g 12.3g⁴ 16.1m 14.8m⁶ 14.6g⁶ 13.3m 1990 12f⁴ 14.8m* 16d 14f⁵
12m⁶ 12m²] small, rather sparely-made horse: led final strides when winning
handicap at Warwick in April: stays 2m: acts on firm and dead going: winning hurdler
in 1989/90: not one to rely on. *J. R. Jenkins.*

DAISY DANCE (FR) 3 b.f. Alzao (USA) 117–Polly Duckins (Dike (USA)) [1989 **111**
6.5d 7g⁶ 7d 8m 1990 10.7g³ 12g⁴ 9g² 10m⁵ 8g* 9g² 8d² 10g⁴ 8d⁵ 9f] eighth foal:
half-sister to Irish 1½m winner Miss Duckins and fairly useful maiden Nokuru (both
by Simbir) and to a winner in Belgium: dam poor half-sister to smart animals Crozier
and Monatrea: won maiden at Saint-Cloud in June: ¾-length second of 15 to Lady
Winner in Prix d'Astarte at Deauville seventh start: probably stays 1¼m: acts on
dead ground. *Y. Porzier, France.*

DAISY GIRL 4 b.f. Main Reef 126–Mellow Girl 88 (Mountain Call 125) [1989 **64**
10.2g 10.4m⁵ 8m² 10.6d 1990 12.3d 9s 12m 10g* 10m* 10.4d⁶ 11s] sturdy, workmanlike filly: successful in handicaps at Chepstow in June (showing improved form)
and August: suited by 1¼m and a sound surface (yet to race on very firm). *J. Mackie.*

DAISY GREY 2 ro.f. (May 7) Nordance (USA)–Great Grey Niece 74 (Great —
Nephew 126) [1990 9g] 3,200F, 10,500Y: half-sister to 3-y-o Calahonda Dave (by
Song) and 4 winners here and abroad, including sprinters Absolution (by Absalom)
and Peckitt's Well (by Lochnager): dam placed over 5f at 2 yrs: always behind in
claimer at York in October. *A. Hide.*

DAISY MY LOVE 3 b. or br.f. Sharpo 132–Carmen Maria (Bold Lad (IRE) 133) —
[1989 NR 1990 5f] fourth foal: sister to Irish 5f and 6f winner My Precious Daisy:
dam once raced from family of Honorius and Suni: 50/1 and blinkered, very slowly
away when tailed off in seller at Bath in May. *B. R. Millman.*

DAKIN BROOK 3 b.f. Prince Ragusa 96–Minster Melody 73 (Highland Melody —
112) [1989 8f 1990 11g] no worthwhile form in maiden auction events: has joined Mrs
G. Plowright. *S. G. Norton.*

DAKI (USA) 2 ch.f. (Mar 27) Miswaki (USA) 124–Devon Diva (USA) (The **86 p**
Minstrel (CAN) 135) [1990 6g³ 6d* 6g²] workmanlike filly: second foal: dam 9f
winner at 4 yrs in USA, is daughter of Devon Ditty: odds on, won maiden at
Goodwood in September: good running-on second of 6 to Punch N'Run in listed
event at York following month: will stay 7f. *J. H. M. Gosden.*

DALBY DANCER 6 b.m. Bustiki–Wensum Girl (Ballymoss 136) [1989 14.8d* **71**
16.2g* 15.8m² 14m* 10.6g⁶ 12g² 16.2g⁵ 14.8f* 14g⁵ 16f⁴ 14f⁴ 14g 14f³ 1990 13.3m
14g² 14s 16m 15.3m² 14m² 14.8f* 14f⁴ 17.6f³ 16m⁵ 17.6f⁴ 13.3g 15.3g⁴ 18d] rather

leggy, workmanlike mare: moderate mover: modest handicapper: favourite, won at Warwick in July: stays well: acts on any going: bandaged penultimate outing: has won for apprentice: tough. *B. A. McMahon.*

DALE HILL DAISY 2 b.f. (Apr 22) Mummy's Game 120–Just Irene 50 (Sagaro 133) [1990 5m² 5m* 5m 5f* 5g⁶ 5m⁶ 5d³] small, sturdy filly: poor mover: third foal: half-sister to 3-y-o Sacoshe (by Swing Easy): dam plater won at 1¼m: fairly useful filly: successful in maiden, making all, at Nottingham in June and nursery at Wolverhampton in August: very good third, racing keenly and rallying well, to Snowy Owl in listed race at Doncaster: speedy: possibly suited by a soft surface. *B. A. McMahon.* — 93

DALE PARK 4 b.c. Kampala 120–Coshlea 63 (Red Alert 127) [1989 10v³ 10.6s² 8.2g² 11m³ 10.2f 9m 11s 10s⁵ 12g 13v* a12g 1990 12d 12g 12d 15v 14.6d³ 15d⁵ 16.5d] leggy, sparely-made colt: has round action: won claimer as 3-y-o: no worthwhile form in 1990: should stay 1¾m: acts on any going, with possible exception of firm: best efforts when ridden up with pace: unbeaten over hurdles in 1989/90. *N. Tinkler.* —

DALESIDE 2 gr.c. (Apr 22) Full Out (USA)–All Regal (Run The Gantlet (USA)) [1990 5m⁵ 6g⁴ 6d² 7.5f] 19,000F, 23,000Y: good-topped, rather leggy colt: has scope: half-brother to useful Italian stayer Damascus Regal (by Damascus) and a listed winner in USA: dam French 1½m winner also successful in USA: plating-class maiden: ridden by 7-lb claimer, best efforts final 2 starts: looks a stayer. *T. Fairhurst.* — 52

DALESIDE LADYBIRD 4 b.f. Tolomeo 127–Dawn Redwood 63 (Mummy's Pet 125) [1989 7f⁶ 7.5f⁶ 6f 6f² 5m⁴ 8.5g 6g⁴ 6f3 5f 7g 6f² 7d 7g 1990 6m 6f² 7g 6g² 6f² 6m 6d⁴ 5f³ 6f⁶ 6f³ 7m⁶ 6f⁴ 6m⁵ 6g 5f 6g 6g 10m 8g] rather leggy, good-topped filly: carries condition: usually looks really well: has a round action: poor handicapper: best at 6f: acts well on firm ground (not discredited on dead seventh outing): visored fourteenth to sixteenth starts: has sweated: sometimes slowly away: has won only one of her 41 races. *T. Fairhurst.* — 55 d

DALEY BRIOCHE 2 b.c. (May 29) Pharly (FR) 130–Flaretown 63 (Town Crier 119) [1990 5m⁶ 7d* 7.5f² 8d 7g⁴ a7g⁴] 4,800Y: sparely-made colt: moderate mover: half-brother to 3-y-o Swiftwind (by Dalsaan) and 2 winners, including 8.2f winner St Louis Blues (by Cure The Blues): dam third over 5f and 6f at 2 yrs: ridden by 7-lb claimer, won 11-runner maiden auction at Edinburgh by a length: ran well in nurseries after, particularly on all-weather: should stay 1m. *M. H. Tompkins.* — 79

DAL MISS 3 b.f. Dalsaan 125–Loyal And Regal 51 (Royal And Regal (USA)) [1989 5m 1990 6s 8g 5m 6g 7d] workmanlike filly: has round action: no worthwhile form: blinkered final outing. *R. E. Peacock.* —

DALMORE 4 b.g. Runnett 125–Fade To Grey (Gay Fandango (USA) 132) [1989 NR 1990 12m 12g] leggy, sparely-made gelding: plater: has looked ungenuine: twice winner over hurdles in October. *F. Watson.* — §

DAL PASCATORE 2 br.g. (Feb 20) Noalto 120–Priors Dean 61 (Monsanto (FR) 121) [1990 7m 7f 7f 8m 8.2g] 1,300Y: lengthy, dipped-backed gelding: third foal: dam ran only at 2 yrs: when ridden at 6f: of little account. *F. J. Yardley.* —

D'ALTAGNAN 4 ch.g. Dalsaan 125–Fresh As A Daisy (Stanford 121§) [1989 8h³ 6m³ 7m* 7f³ 8.3m⁴ 7g² 7.6f³ a8g a7g 1990 8m⁶ 8g⁴ 8f* 8m² 8.3m³ 8f 8m³ 8g 10g] workmanlike gelding: modest handicapper: won at Bath in July: stays 1m: acts on firm going: has looked unsuited by track at Brighton: sold 6,000 gns Newmarket Autumn Sales. *R. Hannon.* — 68

DAMAAZ (IRE) 2 ch.g. (May 1) Mazaad 106–Sharpwinds (Tumble Wind (USA)) [1990 5g 7m 6f⁶ 7f a7g² a6g⁴ a6g⁶ 7g 7d 6s a6g³ a6g⁶] IR 7,200Y: medium-sized, quite good-topped gelding: has a round action: second foal: half-brother to poor Irish 4-y-o Sharp Flyer (by Exhibitioner): dam Irish 6f winner: ridden by 7-lb claimer, very good third of 12 in claimer at Southwell late in year: a modest plater on other form: stays 7f: best form on turf on an easy surface: blinkered or visored last 8 outings: races keenly. *J. S. Wainwright.* — 64

DAMART (USA) 6 b.g. Verbatim (USA)–Ice Wave (USA) (Icecapade (USA)) [1989 10v 12m 12m³ 12.3m 12g⁴ 12f4 12m 11s a11g⁴ 1990 a11g⁵ a7g³ a8g³ a8g⁶ a7g a7g⁴ 10.2f 9f² 8m* 10d² 8d⁵ 7g⁵ 10.6s] neat gelding: moderate mover: won selling handicap (no bid) at Edinburgh in May: stays 1½m, but at least as effective at 7f and 1m: acts on any going: blinkered once, often visored: trained until after penultimate start by M. Naughton: winning selling hurdler. *Miss L. C. Siddall.* — 42

DAMASKEEN (USA) 4 b.g. Caveat (USA)–Double Damask (USA) (Damascus (USA)) [1989 6f 6m⁶ 6g⁴ 6m² 5m⁵ 6g 5m* 5f³ 6m 1990 5m 6m 5m a5g² 5m⁴ 5m⁴ 5m⁴ 5m⁴ 6m 5m⁶ 5.3f* 5m² 5m⁵] compact gelding: has a quick, fluent action: quite — 60

modest handicapper: blinkered only time, led final strides when winning at Brighton in September: pulled up after breaking blood vessel third outing: best at 5f: acts on firm going: has won for apprentice: sometimes sweats. *Mrs S. Armytage.*

DAME D'AMOUR 3 ch.f. Ballad Rock 122–Behroz (Relko 136) [1989 NR 1990 **60** 7m 7g³ 7m 7.2d] IR 60,000Y: lengthy, unfurnished filly: fourth foal: dam winning Irish stayer: quite modest maiden: easily best effort second start: will be suited by further: edgy final outing. *C. F. Wall.*

DAM INQUISITIVE 6 br.g. Don 128–Inquisitive Girl 97 (Crepello 136) [1989 **—** 8g⁴ 10f 8.2d⁶ 6s 1990 7m 7g a7g] big gelding: plater: well-backed favourite, hung left and found little second start: trained until after then by J. Payne, and off course 7 months after: needs further than 6f: blinkered final outing: wears bandages. *C. A. Dwyer.*

DANCE AHEAD 2 b.f. (Jan 17) Shareef Dancer (USA) 135–Shoot Clear 111 (Bay **81** Express 132) [1990 7f* 7f⁴ 7m⁵] sturdy, good-quartered filly: good walker: has quick action: third foal: half-sister to 3-y-o 1¼m winner Elmaftun (by Rainbow Quest) and useful 1½m winner Shoot Ahead (by Shirley Heights): dam 5f to 7f winner at 2 yrs and fourth in 1000 Guineas, is half-sister to Sally Brown and Untold: won 4-runner maiden at Newmarket in July by 5 lengths, showing turn of foot: ran creditably in smallish fields for listed race there and Group 3 event at Goodwood after: will stay 1¼m. *M. R. Stoute.*

DANCE BUSTER 3 b.c. Bustino 136–Dance In Rome 79 (Dance In Time **—** (CAN)) [1989 7g 1990 7.6g⁴ 8g a8g] rather unfurnished colt: plating-class form: easily best effort in claimer on reappearance: should stay 1¼m: hung right penultimate start: blinkered final one: sold out of Sir Mark Prescott's stable 7,800 gns Newmarket July Sales in between. *G. P. Enright.*

DANCE MOVE 3 b.f. Shareef Dancer (USA) 135–Rapide Pied (USA) 117 (Raise **—** A Native) [1989 NR 1990 7m] first foal: dam, French 7f and 1m winner, half-sister to smart French middle-distance filly Joli Vert: last of 10 in maiden at Lingfield in August: sold 13,500 gns Newmarket December Sales. *A. A. Scott.*

DANCE OF A GUNNER 3 ch.f. Gunner B 126–Kilttaley 74 (Tower Walk 130) **—** [1989 6g 1990 7d 10.1m 10.6v 10d] leggy gelding: well beaten, including in sellers. *R. J. Holder.*

DANCE OF GOLD 3 b.c. Jalmood (USA) 126–Prima Ballerina (FR) (Nonoalco **—** (USA) 131) [1989 7g 7m⁵ 1990 8v 7.5d 12g³] strong, angular colt: showed signs of ability at 2 yrs, little (including in seller) in 1990: should stay 1m: sold 1,250 gns Doncaster June Sales. *M. H. Easterby.*

DANCE ON SIXPENCE 2 b.c. (Mar 1) Lidhame 109–Burning Ambition (Troy **82** 137) [1990 7f⁴ 6m² 5m* 5m² 6d⁵] 6,000Y: rangy colt: has scope: first foal: dam well-beaten half-sister to One In A Million out of half-sister to Deep Run: fair performer: won median auction at Windsor in August: ran well in nurseries after: should stay 7f. *H. J. Collingridge.*

DANCE PARTOUT (IRE) 2 ch.c. (Mar 5) Glow (USA)–Coven (Sassafras (FR) **77** 135) [1990 7d³ a7g² 7m⁶ 8g 8f² 8m⁶ 10s²] 45,000F, IR 90,000Y: good-topped colt: has plenty of scope: fifth live foal: half-brother to 4 winners, all at least fairly useful, including smart 1989 2-y-o 6f and 7f winner Balla Cove (by Ballad Rock), since successful in USA: dam won at 6f to 1¼m in Ireland: modest maiden: stays well: acts on any going: sold 25,000 gns Newmarket Autumn Sales. *N. A. Callaghan.*

DANCER'S FIRST (USA) 3 b.f. Green Dancer (USA) 132–Beauvoir (Artaius **—** (USA) 129) [1989 NR 1990 7m 11.7m⁴ 12h⁴ 10f⁴ 8f 7f] second reported foal: half-sister to 1989 3-y-o maiden Beau's Delight (by Lypheor): dam, French 1m winner, is half-sister to smart French 1¼m winner Sangue, later top class in USA: well beaten in maidens and selling handicaps: probably doesn't stay 1½m: sold out of G. Lewis' stable 2,500 gns Newmarket July Sales after second start. *P. Howling.*

DANCERS WAGER 3 br.g. Mashhor Dancer (USA)–Betyle (FR) (Hardicanute **—** 130) [1989 NR 1990 8f 12.2m] sparely-made gelding: sixth reported foal: closely related to a winner in Norway by Fabulous Dancer and half-brother to a pattern-placed animal in Italy: dam, who has been in Italy, never ran: poor form in claimers: sold 1,700 gns Doncaster June Sales. *J. M. P. Eustace.*

DANCE SPECTRUM (USA) 4 b.c. Lyphard (USA) 132–Rainbow Connection **114** (CAN) (Halo (USA)) [1989 10g* 12d* 10.6s⁶ 12m²ᵈⁱˢ 12s⁶ 1990 14m* 16m² 16m² 18g 16.2m* 16m²] strong, well-made colt: has a short, sharp action: developed into smart stayer, successful in handicaps under 10-0 at Sandown in April and Ascot (£10,000 event) in September: best effort ¾-length second of 7, well clear, to Great Marquess in Jockey Club Cup at Newmarket final outing: stays 2m: acts on good to firm going and is unsuited by soft: looked tremendously well last 2 starts: genuine: sold to race abroad. *G. Harwood.*

DANCING BERRY 3 b.f. Sadler's Wells (USA) 132–Red Berry 115 (Great — Nephew 126) [1989 NR 1990 10m 8s6] compact filly: closely related to useful 7f winner Lidhame (by Nureyev) and half-sister to several winners, including very useful 1m to 10.5f winner New Berry (by Sir Gaylord): dam second in Cheveley Park Stakes: well beaten in maidens at Yarmouth and Newcastle. *L. Cumani.*

DANCING BREEZE 3 ch.f. Horage 124–Lady's Guest (Be My Guest (USA) 53 126) [1989 5.3g 5g4 5g 5f4 5m2 5m2 5m4 5f5 5m 1990 5f 5s5 6g a8g3 8m2 8.5g 8d 8g6 8f3 8.3m6 10f 10m a8g2 7.6d 10g a8g6] lengthy, workmanlike filly: plating-class maiden: worth a try over 7f: acts on firm going, probably unsuited by dead. *Pat Mitchell.*

DANCING BRIDE 3 ch.f. Caerleon (USA) 132–Bahrain Vee (CAN) (Blushing 65 Groom (FR) 131) [1989 NR 1990 8f2 8m 10.2f5 13.1h5 12m] tall, leggy filly: first foal: dam twice-raced daughter of close relation to top Canadian colt Giboulee: quite modest maiden: blinkered and facing stiff task, raced freely disputing lead 1m then eased in handicap final start: stays 13f: gave trouble at stalls third start. *J. P. Hudson.*

DANCING CHIEF 2 br.g. (Mar 31) Lidhame 109–Darlinga 98 (Derring-Do 131) — [1990 6m 6m] 7,000F, 12,500Y: leggy, unfurnished gelding: third living foal: dam 3 times successful over 5f at 2 yrs, lightly raced at 3 yrs: better for race, weakened 2f out in maidens at Ripon and Pontefract. *Denys Smith.*

DANCING COVE 3 b.c. Shareef Dancer (USA) 135–Fanny's Cove 89 (Mill Reef 60 (USA) 141) [1989 NR 1990 10f a12g 11g* a14g 12m] 14,000Y: leggy, quite attractive colt: fourth foal: closely related to useful 1988 2-y-o 7f and 1m winner Prince Ibrahim (by Be My Guest) and a winner in Italy by Dance In Time: dam won over 1¼m on only start: 10/1, first form in maidens when making all in auction event at Edinburgh in June: ran badly in handicaps after: should stay 1½m: on toes first 2 outings: trained until after fourth by Sir Mark Prescott. *G. G. Gracey.*

DANCING DAYS 4 ch.c. Glenstal (USA) 118–Royal Agnes 71 (Royal Palace 131) 62 [1989 10v5 8g* 8m3 10f4 10m3 10g* 10m4 12.3g3 11s 1990 12.4f6 11f3 a12g2 12m 12d 11d3 a12g a12g2 10d a12g4 a12g6] smallish, attractive colt: moderate mover: quite modest performer: best at up to 1½m: probably unsuited by heavy going: effective with or without blinkers or visor: sometimes wanders under pressure: sold out of J. W. Watts's stable 11,000 gns Doncaster September Sales after eighth outing. *J. Parkes.*

DANCING DELIGHT 3 ch.g. Music Boy 124–Open Country (Town And — Country 124) [1989 NR 1990 7d 8m6] big, strong gelding: third foal: dam unraced: well beaten in maiden at Lingfield and competitive minor event at Chepstow in October. *R. Hannon.*

DANCING EARL 3 gr.g. Lomond (USA) 128–Baccalaureate 109 (Crowned 57 Prince (USA) 128) [1989 8g3 7g 1990 7f3 10g4 12.3d 10m a8g2 a11g 7.6m] small, sturdy gelding: plating-class maiden, not seen out after July: easily best effort from last 5 starts when second in handicap at Southwell, having been virtually tailed off at halfway: stays 1m. *C. E. Brittain.*

DANCING LEGEND (IRE) 2 b.c. (Apr 15) Lyphard's Special (USA) 122– 57 Princess Nabila (USA) (King Pellinore (USA) 127) [1990 8m 7m 6g 8.2s5] 8,000Y, 11,500 2-y-o: big, lengthy colt: has scope: second foal: half-brother to a winner in Belgium: dam lightly-raced daughter of smart French 5f to 10.5f winner Guile Princess: easily best effort fifth of 18, staying on well, in nursery at Hamilton in November: will be well suited by 1¼m +: acts well on soft ground. *M. O'Neill.*

DANCING MAY 3 b.f. Tina's Pet 121–Breckland Lady 62 (Royalty 130) [1989 5g — 6f6 6h3 7f 7m6 6m 10.6d 1990 8g 9f 10m] sparely-made filly: has a round action: poor plater: bandaged second start. *P. Howling.*

DANCING MONARCH 5 ch.h. Dara Monarch 128–Maiden's Dance 65 89 (Hotfoot 126) [1989 8m* 8f 8.2g2 8f 8m 10.6g3 8f2 8f2 8g3 8d 8g 1990 8f3 8h3 8g 8.2m 9f* 9m 8f] strong, lengthy, quite attractive horse: moderate walker and mover: fairly useful handicapper: won at Redcar in June, leading close home having travelled smoothly long way then edged left final 1f: not seen out after running poorly in Royal Hunt Cup at Royal Ascot: needs further than 7f and stays 9f: best on a sound surface: visored fifth and sixth (slowly away) starts: held up and ideally suited by strong gallop: has hung. *R. Hollinshead.*

DANCING MUSIC 3 ch.c. Music Boy 124–Miss Rossi (Artaius (USA) 129) 107 [1989 5s* 5d2 6g 6f 5g* 5f* 5m4 5m2 5s* 5m3 6g 1990 5m2 5m4 5d6 5g* 5f2 5g5 5g 6g3 5d2] rather leggy, workmanlike colt: usually dull in coat: good walker and mover: useful sprinter: won listed race at Tipperary in July: clearly best subsequent efforts when second, running on well, to Argentum in King George Stakes at Goodwood and Ra'a in listed race at Newmarket: suited by 5f: acts on any going: sometimes drifts left. *J. Berry.*

DANCING NORTH   5 b. or br.g. Shareef Dancer (USA) 135–Icena 117 (Jimmy Reppin 131) [1989 NR 1990 6m⁵ 10.1m 8m⁶] big, heavy-topped gelding: carries plenty of condition: bad mover: fifth foal: half-brother to 2¼m winner Teevano (by Blakeney): dam won Lowther Stakes: showed signs of a little ability on debut, none afterwards: has started slowly. *C. J. Benstead.*   —

DANCING PADDY   2 b.c. (Apr 26) Nordance (USA)–Ninotchka 72 (Niniski (USA) 125) [1990 6g] 11,500Y: leggy, quite attractive colt: first foal: dam maiden stayed 1¼m, is half-sister to useful sprinter Novello out of sister to high-class Pyjama Hunt: slowly away, green and soon well behind in maiden at Nottingham in July. *J. D. Czerpak.*   —

DANCING RIVER   4 b.g. Niniski (USA) 125–River Chimes 43 (Forlorn River 124) [1989 NR 1990 11m³] fifth foal: half-brother to very speedy 1984 2-y-o Absent Chimes (by Absalom): dam sister to high-class Rapid River: favourite, 10¾ lengths third of 5 in maiden at Edinburgh in April: won 5 times over hurdles as a juvenile. *W. A. Stephenson.*   —

DANCING SENSATION (USA)   3 b.f. Faliraki 125–Sweet Satina (USA) (Crimson Satan) [1989 5m³ 6d³ 6g 1990 6m⁴ 6g⁵ 7f³ 7f⁶ 8m⁵ 7m² 7f* 7m⁴ 7m 7.6m³ a8g⁵ a11g] big, good-topped filly: fluent mover: quite modest handicapper: won moderately-run race at Yarmouth in July: should stay 1m: acts on firm going: has run creditably sweating and on toes: retained by trainer 6,400 gns Newmarket Autumn Sales. *J. W. Hills.*   68

DANCING STREET   2 ch.f. (Apr 27) Scottish Reel 123–Florence Street (Final Straw 127) [1990 6m 6f 7g] leggy, workmanlike filly: first foal: dam once-raced half-sister to useful 1985 2-y-o 6f winner Bambolona: poor form in maidens and a median auction event: very slowly away on debut: will stay 1m: may do better. *R. M. Whitaker.*   42

DANCING TUDOR   2 b.c. (Mar 8) Absalom 128–String of Beads 63 (Ile de Bourbon (USA) 133) [1990 6f⁵ 7f² 7.5f² 7g 7g 8d a7g⁶] lengthy colt: good walker: first foal: dam (of doubtful temperament) stayed 2m, is half-sister to very smart 1983 2-y-o Creag-An-Sgor: modest maiden: off course around 2 months after fourth start, and showed little on return: should stay 1m: possibly unsuited by a soft surface. *J. Etherington.*   71

DANCING WAY   3 b.c. Sadler's Wells (USA) 132–Waterway (FR) 112 (Riverman (USA) 131) [1989 8d 1990 12m] big, workmanlike colt: has a rather round action: bit backward and green, slowly away and well beaten in maidens at Thirsk and Newbury. *Major W. R. Hern.*   —

DANDOON   3 b.c. Rainbow Quest (USA) 134–Good Lass (FR) (Reform 132) [1989 NR 1990 10m⁶ 12m²] seventh living foal: half-brother to 4 middle-distance winners, notably 4-y-o Ile de Nisky, useful Bonne Ile (both by Ile de Bourbon) and useful 1989 French 1½m and 2½m winner Hi Lass (by Shirley Heights): dam French 2-y-o 1m winner out of half-sister to Blakeney and Morston: about 4 lengths sixth of 15 in maiden at Leicester having been ridden along virtually throughout: made running when easily beaten 10 lengths by River God in similar event at Doncaster in May. *G. A. Huffer.*   65

DANDY KIM (IRE)   2 b.c. (Apr 21) Mazaad 106–Papoosette (Raise You Ten 125) [1990 5g⁶ 5m*] IR 8,500F, 8,200Y: strong, good-topped colt: half-brother to several winners, including 1982 2-y-o 5f winner Final Set (by Tumble Wind): dam ran twice: made all in maiden at Lingfield in May: sent to Italy and has won there. *K. M. Brassey.*   67

DANDY'S GIRL   5 ch.m. Record Token 128–Miss Rockefeller (Richboy 117) [1989 8.5g⁶ 12f³ 14m⁵ 1990 a8g] big, plain mare: of little account: has worn crossed noseband. *R. F. Marvin.*   —

DANE ROSE   4 b.f. Full of Hope 125–Roella (Gold Rod 129) [1989 9g³ 10.2f⁶ 1990 12.5f] no worthwhile form in varied company, including selling: wore crossed noseband only outing at 4 yrs: sold 825 gns Ascot May Sales. *M. B. James.*   —

DANESH   3 gr.g. Kalaglow 132–Demia (FR) (Abdos 134) [1989 NR 1990 10m 12.2m³] leggy, workmanlike gelding: fourth living foal: half-brother to fairly useful 1¼m winner Danishgar (by Shergar), French 1¼m winner Diya (by Top Ville) and very useful stayer Demawend (by Mill Reef): dam French 1m and 10.5f winner: 16/1,   —

Mr K. Abdulla's "Dangora"

13 lengths third of 6 to Tour Eiffel in maiden at Catterick in June: moved moderately down: sold 8,000 gns Newmarket Autumn Sales and gelded. *M. R. Stoute.*

DANGORA (USA) 2 b.f. (Apr 23) Sovereign Dancer (USA)–Mofida 115 (Right Tack 131) [1990 6m* 6f* 6m²] strong-quartered filly: has scope: has a quick action: eighth foal: closely related to smart miler Zaizafon (by The Minstrel): dam very tough winner of 6 races at up to 7f, is grandam of Elmaamul: green, comfortable winner of maiden at Ascot in July and minor event at Haydock in August: heavily-backed favourite but bit edgy, good second to Only Yours in 'Pacemaker Update' Lowther Stakes at York: will stay 7f: improving. *B. W. Hills.* — 98

DANNEMAN 2 b.c. (May 3) Daring March 116–Lillemor (Connaught 130) [1990 5f 5m² a6g* 6f² 5m 6d* 5m⁵ 6d²] tall, leggy colt: first foal: dam twice-raced half-sister to smart Italian winner Alpherat out of half-sister to Steel Heart: modest performer: won maiden at Southwell in July and claimer at Haydock in September: will stay 7f: acts on firm and dead ground: blinkered final 3 starts: sold 12,000 gns Doncaster October Sales. *R. Boss.* — 77

DANNY BLANCHFLOWER 3 ch.g. Rabdan 129–Caffre Lily (Hittite Glory 125) [1989 6f 5f⁴ 5f 7g 6v 6g 1990 10f 8g 12m⁵ 12f a12g³ a11g⁴ 10d 10d⁶] workmanlike gelding: moderate walker: has a round action: poor plater: acts on top-of-the-ground: found little sixth start. *P. S. Felgate.* — —

DANRAB 4 b.g. Rabdan 129–Friendly Pet (Be Friendly 130) [1989 7d³ 7m⁴ 8.2f² 8m³ 10m 10.6g 9s 1990 7.5d a7g² a7g³] compact, good-bodied gelding: moderate mover: plating-class maiden: stays 1m: visored twice: ridden by claimer. *M. J. O'Neill.* — 47

DANSE D'ESPRIT 2 b.f. (Mar 2) Lidhame 109–Bel Esprit (Sagaro 133) [1990 6g 6d⁴ 7g* 7m 8d 8d] rather sparely-made filly: fourth foal: half-sister to 6f and 7.3f — 54

217

winner Fille d'Esprit (by Cragador): dam no form on flat or over jumps: plating-class performer: won maiden at Edinburgh in June: ran poorly for 7-lb claimer final outing: stays 1m: carried head high second start. *G. H. Eden.*

DANSEUSE DU SOIR (IRE)   2 b.f. (Feb 7) Thatching 131–Dance By Night 84 **108** (Northfields (USA)) [1990 5g* 5.5g² 5.5g*] 40,000Y: second foal: half-sister to 3-y-o Sarah Georgina (by Persian Bold), fair 6f winner at 2 yrs: dam won twice at 7f at 2 yrs: very useful filly: successful in maiden at Longchamp in May and 9-runner Prix Robert Papin at Maisons-Laffitte (by head from Divine Danse) in July: will stay 6f. *E. Lellouche, France.*

DANSON BOATHOUSE   4 b.g. Niniski (USA) 125–Boathouse 116 (Habitat —
134) [1989 10m 1990 10h] lengthy gelding: no promise in claimer or maiden (well tailed off) over 10 months later. *F. J. O'Mahony.*

DANZA HEIGHTS   4 br.c. Head For Heights 125–Dankal:a (Le Levanstell 122) —
[1989 7g 8f 1990 12d⁶ 8f⁶ 8.2m 10m 18d 16s] tall, quite good-topped colt: has a round action: well beaten in varied events. *P. S. Felgate.*

DANZANTE (USA)   2 b.f. (Apr 4) Danzig (USA)–Bold Captive (USA) **107**
(Boldnesian) [1990 6.5g² 7g³ 6.5d*] half-sister to several winners, including 1¼m Breeders' Cup Classic winner Skywalker (by Relaunch) and 6f to 9f winner Pac Mania (by Ramsinga): dam sprinter: useful filly: won listed Criterium d'Evry in September by a head from Crack Regiment: 3¾ lengths third to Green Pola in Prix du Calvados at Deauville previous month: will stay 1m. *A. Fabre, France.*

DANZARIN (IRE)   2 b.c. (Apr 20) Kings Lake (USA) 133–Sodium's Niece **77**
(Northfields (USA)) [1990 6m³ 6m 6g⁶ 6m*] 15,500Y: leggy, quite good-topped colt: third foal: half-brother to 3-y-o Francis Furness (by Burslem): dam lightly raced, was placed at 8.5f as 2-y-o in Ireland: showed much improved form to win £18,100 nursery at Newmarket in August by neck from Princess Tara: will stay further. *R. Hannon.*

DANZIG LAD (USA)   2 b.c. (May 13) Ziggy's Boy (USA)–Sexy Ways (USA) **65**
(Our Native (USA)) [1990 5m³ 6g⁵ a6g³ 7g 8d a7g³] $32,000Y: smallish, quite good-bodied colt: has a long stride: half-brother to several minor winners in USA: dam minor winner at 3 yrs in USA: sire best at 6f or 7f: quite modest maiden: visored

*Philip Cornes Nickel Alloys Nursery Handicap, Newmarket—
Danzarin (No. 10) just holds off Princess Tara*

in selling nursery sixth start: probably stays 1m: sold out of J. Gosden's stable 5,000 gns Newmarket Autumn Sales before final outing. *M. P. Naughton.*

DARA DEE   3 b.f. Dara Monarch 128–Not Mistaken (USA) (Mill Reef (USA) 141) 85 [1989 6m⁵ 7m⁵ 7m⁵ 7m² 7v⁶ 1990 8g³ 8g* 8d³ 7m* 7m 7m² 8m] leggy, close-coupled filly: has a markedly round action: fair performer: made virtually all to win minor event at Goodwood in June and £11,300 handicap at Newmarket in July: ran very well penultimate outing: at least as effective over 7f as 1m: acts on good to firm ground, possibly unsuited by heavy: has tended to hang under pressure. *C. E. Brittain.*

DARAGENCY   2 b.f. (Feb 7) Dara Monarch 128–Rashah 67 (Blakeney 126) [1990 — 5g 7g 8.2s 10.6s] 4,000F: leggy filly: first foal: dam would have been suited by 1¼m: poor form in maidens and sellers: off course nearly 4 months after debut: took good hold for 7-lb claimer penultimate outing. *J. S. Wilson.*

DARAKAH   3 ch.f. Doulab (USA) 115–Ladytown (English Prince 129) [1989 5m² 78 6g⁵ 5m⁵ 5m* 1990 6m 5m⁵ 6m⁶ 6m³ 7f* 7g 7g³ 7g⁵ 7.6d 7g² a7g] leggy filly: modest handicapper: well drawn, made all at Lingfield in July: ran well seventh to tenth starts, badly in Southwell claimer on final one: stays 1m: acts on firm and dead going: sold out of J. Benstead's stable 13,500 gns Newmarket Autumn Sales after penultimate outing. *C. J. Hill.*

DARA LOCH (IRE)   2 b.c. (May 10) Dara Monarch 128–Kumari (FR) 78 53 (Luthier 126) [1990 7d⁶ 8d 8.2s⁶ 8v 8d] IR 3,600Y: leggy, close-coupled colt: has a very round action: half-brother to very useful stayer Angel City (by Carwhite): dam 1¼m winner: poor maiden: sweating final start. *C. Tinkler.*

DARANIYDA   3 b.f. Mouktar 129–Dramatic Lady (Lyphard (USA) 132) [1989 41 a7g⁴ 1990 a8g³] odds-on third of 6 at Southwell in January, better effort in maidens. *M. R. Stoute.*

DARA PRINCE   3 ch.c. Dara Monarch 128–Dowcester 63 (Habitat 134) [1989 — 5g⁵ 5m⁴ 5g⁴ 5m 5f 1990 7m 5m 6g 8m 12m 9m⁶ 10m 8f⁶ 8f 6g 6g] small, sturdy colt: poor handicapper: probably stays 9f: blinkered 6 times, 5 of them in 1990: sold 1,100 gns Doncaster September Sales. *D. W. Chapman.*

DARAROYAL   3 ch.c. Dara Monarch 128–Palace Guest (Be My Guest (USA) 48 126) [1989 a8g 1990 12f 9m⁶ 7m 5g 7d 5m⁵ 6m⁴ 7m 10.8m 8f 7m* 8f² 7f²] leggy, workmanlike colt: has round action: fair plater: 33/1, won handicap (no bid) at Yarmouth in September: twice good second at Brighton: stays 1m: acts on firm ground: often blinkered, though not last 3 starts: once visored: bandaged eighth start: bolted and unseated rider (withdrawn) intended sixth. *Mrs N. Macauley.*

DARBY SKY (USA)   3 b.c. Darby Creek Road (USA)–Wimborne Sky (USA) (Sir 72 Wimborne (USA) 118) [1989 6g⁴ 6g⁶ 1990 8.2s⁶ 10g 11.7g 12m 12.3g⁶ 10m* 10.6d⁵ 10.6d² 10d⁴ a10g] close-coupled, rather sparely-made colt: has a round action: modest handicapper: made all at Ripon in August: below form at Lingfield final start: possibly worth another try at 1½m: acts on good to firm ground and dead: has run creditably for amateur: sweating (faced very stiff task) fourth outing. *M. E. D. Francis.*

DARIKA LAD   2 gr.g. (Jan 25) Belfort (FR) 89–Lindrake's Pride (Mandrake 69 Major 122) [1990 7m⁵ 6g⁵ 7.5m* 7g] workmanlike gelding: has scope: second foal: half-brother to modest maiden Touchlin Pride (by Touch Boy): dam never ran: won maiden auction at Beverley in September in good style: found little in nursery at York following month: stays 7.5f. *Miss L. C. Siddall.*

DARING JOY   3 b.f. Daring March 116–African Berry 84 (African Sky 124) [1989 57 7g 1990 9g 12f6 14g² 18d⁶ 14.6d⁵] workmanlike filly: plating-class handicapper on most form: should prove best short of 2¼m: acts on dead going. *B. A. McMahon.*

DARING LADY   2 br.f. (Mar 23) Daring March 116–Ash Gayle 49 (Lord Gayle — (USA) 124) [1990 6m 7m 8.2v] 1,050Y: sturdy filly: fifth foal: closely related to 1m and 1½m winner Taylormade Boy (by Dominion) and half-sister to a winner in Italy: dam (plater) won at up to 11f: backward, well beaten, including in seller. *M. D. I. Usher.*

DARING MAID   2 br.f. (Apr 25) Daring March 116–Pirate Maid (Auction Ring 40 (USA) 123) [1990 5f 6d a5g⁶] leggy filly: third foal: dam ran once: poor form in maidens: sold 700 gns Ascot December Sales. *P. T. Walwyn.*

DARING TIMES   5 gr.g. Good Times (ITY)–She Who Dares (Bellypha 130) 84 [1989 8d 10m⁶ 10f⁴ 10f³ 10g 8m² 9f 9f 9g 8m 8g 10g 1990 8f* 10m* 12.3f⁴ 8f⁶ 10.2g 8m² 7m* 7g*] strong, rangy gelding: formerly inconsistent, but in excellent form in handicaps as 5-y-o: successful at Doncaster (landing big gamble) and Beverley in

March and in quite valuable events at Newmarket in October: effective at 7f and stays 1¼m: acts on firm going: suitable mount for inexperienced rider: sold 20,000 gns Newmarket Autumn Sales. *Mrs J. R. Ramsden.*

DARI SOUND (IRE) 2 b.c. (Mar 26) Shardari 134–Bugle Sound 96 (Bustino 136) [1990 8.5m² 8g] 8,000F, 14,500Y: compact, rather sparely-made colt: half-brother to 1984 Irish 2-y-o 1¼m winner Over The Waves (by Main Reef), Irish 6f winner Sound of Victory (by Thatch) and a disqualified 1¾m winner by Beldale Flutter: dam stayed 1¾m, is out of Melodina, dam also of Dubian and See You Then: bit backward and green, second of 7, staying on strongly, in maiden at Beverley in September: bandaged near-hind and blinkered, ran poorly in similar event at Newcastle following month: will stay at least 1¼m. *J. G. FitzGerald.* **67**

DARK CITY 3 b.f. Sweet Monday 122–City's Sister 72 (Maystreak 118) [1989 5h 6h 1990 6v] slightly dipped-backed, sparely-made filly: soundly beaten in maidens then seller. *G. Richards.* **—**

DARK GISELLE 5 b.m. King of Spain 121–Giselle 104 (Pall Mall 132) [1989 8s a6g 1990 5m⁵ 6g 8f] lengthy mare: poor mover: plater: stays 7f: acts on good to firm and dead going: sold 1,500 gns Ascot November Sales. *R. J. Hodges.* **—**

DARK HERITAGE 7 b.g. Scorpio (FR) 127–Mother of The Wind 82 (Tumble Wind (USA)) [1989 10f 1990 a12g] big, strong, good-bodied gelding: quite modest winner as 5-y-o: bandaged behind, never placed to challenge in Lingfield handicap in November, only second subsequent outing on flat: best form at 1¼m: acts on firm going: ran moderately in blinkers: has sweated: has won for apprentice. *D. J. G. Murray-Smith.* **—**

DARK ISLE 2 b.g. (Mar 21) Mashhor Dancer (USA)–Dark Amber 68 (Formidable (USA) 125) [1990 7g 7d⁵] 3,700F, 4,200Y: tall gelding: second foal: dam 1m winner at 4 yrs, is half-sister to Rakaposhi King: ridden by 7-lb claimer, around 3 lengths fifth of 18 in maiden auction at Goodwood in October: backward on debut: will stay 1m. *M. McCourt.* **61**

DARK KRISTAL (IRE) 2 b.f. (May 11) Gorytus (USA) 132–Kristallina 84 (Homeric 133) [1990 5m⁵ 5f⁶ 5m⁵ 6d³] small filly: fourth reported foal: half-sister to fairly useful 2-y-o sprint winners Dona Krista (by King of Spain) and Krisfield (by Anfield): dam won over 13.8f: quite modest maiden: ran well in nursery final start: will stay 7f: acts on good to firm ground and dead. *R. Hannon.* **66**

DARLING DIANNE (IRE) 2 ch.f. (Apr 29) Burslem 123–Escalado (Homing 130) [1990 5f 6m* 6m 6d a7g] IR 4,000Y: compact filly: has a quick action: fourth foal: half-sister to 3-y-o Northern Blues (by Tender King) and Irish 1¼m winner Excavate (by Nishapour): dam placed 3 times at up to 7.5f in Ireland: won 11-runner seller (bought in 8,400 gns) at Windsor by 2½ lengths: twice blinkered, including when successful, visored final start: trained first 4 starts by R. Holder. *M. P. Naughton.* **55**

DARTING MOTH 3 br.f. Mansingh (USA) 120–Crescent Dart 103 (Sing Sing 134) [1989 6g⁶ 5g⁴ 1990 7.6d 6d⁶ a6g² a6g⁶] lengthy, slightly dipped-backed filly: plating-class maiden: clearly best efforts as 3-y-o in claimers at Southwell last 2 starts: should stay 7f. *G. A. Pritchard-Gordon.* **56**

DARTINGTON HALL 3 ch.g. Free State 125–Westonbirt 93 (Queen's Hussar 124) [1989 NR 1990 9m 10g 12g 11.5g] 10,500Y: strong, workmanlike gelding: third living foal: dam 2-y-o 6f winner is sister to useful miler Boscage: well beaten in maidens and handicap. *A. Hide.* **—**

DARTREY (IRE) 2 b.f. (Feb 27) Darshaan 133–Secala (USA) (Secretariat (USA)) [1990 7m*] **107 P**

Since it was initiated in 1987 Newmarket's Oh So Sharp Stakes, a seven-furlong minor event for two-year-old fillies that opens the card on Cambridgeshire day, has not been won by an animal anywhere nearly so good as the fillies' triple crown winner it commemorates; but its latest winner Dartrey is already prominent in the betting for both the One Thousand Guineas and the Oaks, and looks to be a filly with a bright future. At this early stage, we'd imagine that as she's a daughter of the Prix du Jockey-Club winner Darshaan, who is already proving a marked influence for stamina, out of a Secretariat mare who won at up to nine furlongs, a mile and a half is more likely than a mile to bring the best out of her; but we wouldn't entirely discount her chances of proving effective at a mile early on, for she revealed a fine turn of foot at Newmarket in what was a moderately-run race. Dartrey, a leggy, sparely-made filly, was one of three runners in the eight-strong field

Oh So Sharp Stakes, Newmarket—newcomer Dartrey lives up to her reputation; Diamond City is a promising second

owned by Sheikh Mohammed (who, of course, also owned Oh So Sharp) and the most fancied in the betting, too, although one of his other participants, Diamond City, not seen on the racecourse since winning a maiden at Leicester over two months earlier, attracted late support. Easily the most interesting of the five remaining runners, three with winning form, was Cumani's debutante Kadizadeh, a half-sister by Darshaan to the dual Derby winner Kahyasi; she'd reportedly been working well at home, and eventually shared favouritism with Dartrey at 11/4. Of the two market leaders Dartrey looked more in need of the run, but she always held the call over Kadizadeh in the race and ran out a most impressive winner. Soon close up in a race in which the pace didn't increase until three furlongs out, at which point Sheikh Mohammed's runners were first, second and third, Dartrey was sent to the front shortly afterwards, quickened two or three lengths clear virtually straight away, and then kept on strongly to win by three lengths as Diamond City came clear in second with an even larger gap back to Kafiyah in third. Although Dartrey wasn't extending her advantage in the closing stages she was back on the bridle at the line, and won with her ears pricked. The performances of Kafiyah, an unlucky second in a listed event at Newbury two outings earlier, and sixth-placed Crimson Quest tend to suggest the form is well up to standard. Dartrey, more than any of her opponents, seems set to improve a good deal at three, and we've a strong feeling that she's going to be concerned in the finish of more important races than the Oh So Sharp Stakes in 1991.

		Darshaan (br 1981)	Shirley Heights (b 1975)	Mill Reef
Dartrey (IRE) (b.f. Feb 27, 1988)				Hardiemma
			Delsy (b or br 1972)	Abdos
				Kelty
		Secala (USA) (ch 1975)	Secretariat (ch 1970)	Bold Ruler
				Somethingroyal
			Aladancer (b 1968)	Northern Dancer
				Mock Orange

Darshaan's five individual winners of six pattern races in Europe in 1990 all won at either a mile and a quarter or a mile and a half; Zayyani, in 1989, is the only pattern winner of his at less than a mile and a quarter. Dartrey's dam Secala has already produced a middle-distance winner in the quite useful Irish colt Sir Simon (by Sir Ivor), who won two races in 1983 including the eleven-and-a-half-furlong Ulster Harp Derby; both her other winners, though, by Artaius and Habitat, seemed best at seven furlongs. Another of her foals, Aljood (by Kris), ran the best race of her ultimately disappointing career when fourth over a mile in the 1988 Prix Marcel Boussac. Secala is from a first-rate family. Her dam Aladancer, who won nine races including the California Oaks, is related to the high-class Italian middle-distance stayer Duke of Marmalade; and, further removed, numbers the good-class French one-mile to mile-and-a-quarter performer Gabina, the very smart French middle-distance colt Galetto and the high-class American colt Cryptoclearance, earner of over 3,000,000 dollars, among her better relatives. *M. R. Stoute.*

Prix Eugene Adam, Saint-Cloud—a long-looking three-length victory for Dashing Blade; the other British challenger Starstreak comes fourth

DARUSSALAM 3 ch.f. Tina's Pet 121–Chinese Falcon 81 (Skymaster 126) [1989 6f³ 5m³ 8f⁶ 7f 7g 1990 8f⁶ 7m⁶ 7h 8g 6g⁵ 6f² 6m* 6m⁴ 6g 6f⁴ 5m 6m⁴ 5m 5f 5g 5d] **49** §
sparely-made filly: has a round action: best effort when winning seller (bought in 7,600 gns) at Hamilton in June, slowly away and leading 2f out: stays 6f: acts on firm going: usually visored: blinkered eighth start: sold 2,500 gns Doncaster October Sales: inconsistent and not one to trust. *Denys Smith.*

DASCH (SWE) 3 b.g. Diligo (FR) 115–Baczyna (POL) (Mehari 123) [1989 NR —
1990 10f a12g] Swedish-bred gelding: ran 4 times unplaced in Scandinavia in 1989: well beaten in maidens at Brighton and Southwell in summer: returned to Sweden. *E. Eldin.*

DASHING BLADE 3 b.c. Elegant Air 119–Sharp Castan 101 (Sharpen Up **115**
127) [1989 6m* 6m* 7f³ 7g* 7g* 1990 8f 8m⁴ 10m* 10g² 10.5g 12g*]
Believe it or not, Dashing Blade was well on his way towards half a million pounds in prize-money by the time he was retired in September. His progress along that road as a three-year-old owed a lot to a realistic appraisal of his ability and some shrewd placing by connections. The 1989 Three Chimneys Dewhurst Stakes winner found it tough going in top company in Britain in the latest season, his six-and-a-half-length fourth to Shavian in the St James's Palace Stakes at Royal Ascot being the only reward from three outings; he was well beaten in the Guineas, following an injury-interrupted preparation, and in the Juddmonte International. But Dashing Blade didn't always chase shadows. He missed the Eclipse in favour of the Group 2 Prix Eugene Adam at Saint-Cloud, missed Goodwood in favour of the Group 1 Grosser Mercedes Benz Preis-Bayerisches Zuchtrennen at Munich, and after York was sent on for the Group 1 Gran Premio d'Italia-Trofeo Saima at Milan rather than for any of the alternatives on home soil. Those trips netted a sum of over £200,000 through wins at Saint-Cloud and Milan and second place at Munich.
There was nothing of the calibre of Shavian against Dashing Blade in the Eugene Adam. None of the seven runners had won a pattern race during 1990 in fact, so, by the conditions of the race, all escaped penalty. Starstreak started favourite but faded into fourth as Dashing Blade kept up a good gallop in front from four furlongs out and won by a long-looking three lengths from the French colt Verre Bleu. Dashing Blade met older horses for the first time in the Bayerisches-Zuchtrennen, and one of them, the German four-year-old Turfkonig, squeezed through to pip him and Treble Eight by a length and a neck. By Group 1 standards the race wasn't particularly well contested. The same could be said of the Gran Premio d'Italia, whose handsome purse is seldom enough to entice horses away from the Prix de l'Arc de Triomphe. On form the twelve-runner race seemed to lie between Dashing Blade and the

Gran Premio d'Italia-Trofeo Saima, Milan—Dashing Blade gets the trip and storms home

Derby Italiano winner Houmayoun, though Dashing Blade had never been tried at a mile and a half before. Dashing Blade ran away from Houmayoun over the last three furlongs, and was virtually unchallenged over the last two, coming home six lengths in front of a couple of imports, the ex-English Bold Passion and the ex-Irish Teach Da Mhile.

Dashing Blade (b.c. 1987)	Elegant Air (br 1981)	Shirley Heights (b 1975)	Mill Reef / Hardiemma
		Elegant Tern (b 1971)	Sea Bird II / Prides Profile
	Sharp Castan (ch 1977)	Sharpen Up (ch 1969)	Atan / Rocchetta
		Sultry One (ch 1961)	Tropique / Sweet Heart V

As outlined in *Racehorses of 1989* Dashing Blade was the fifth winner, from as many foals, out of the 1979 Hoover Fillies' Mile third Sharp Castan; among the others was the useful Navarzato (by Dominion) and the Ayr Gold Cup second Fairways Girl (by Young Generation). Her two-year-old of 1990 Sharp Chief (by Chief Singer) has shown signs of ability. Dashing Blade's sire, Elegant Air, had to be put down in April following the rapid onset of an illness that turned out to be caused by a cyst compressing the spinal chord. Some consolation for the loss of the leading first-season sire of 1989 lies in that he'd already covered thirty-four mares in the spring and looks set to have a fair-sized last crop to represent him. Elegant Air showed his best form at a mile and a quarter (he finished twelfth to Secreto in the Derby on his only outing at a mile and a half) but his best two runners to date, Dashing Blade and the Prix Saint-Alary winner Air de Rien, have stayed a mile and a half. Elegant Air also showed improved form in his third season. Because of leg trouble Dashing Blade will not have the opportunity of doing the same. He has been retired to the Littleton Stud in Hampshire at a fee of £5,000 (October 1st). Quite an attractive colt, a good mover, he acted on good to firm going and never raced on soft. *I. A. Balding.*

DASHING FELLOW (IRE) 2 b.c. (Apr 19) Sure Blade (USA) 128–Belle Viking (FR) (Riverman (USA) 131) [1990 7g 7g 7m 6d] IR 70,000Y: rather angular colt: has a round action: closely related to smart middle-distance performer Sirk (by Kris) and half-brother to 4 other winners, including 1986 2-y-o 7f winner D'Azy (by Persian Bold): dam French 1m and 1¼m winner from family of Vitiges: well beaten in maidens and nursery (faced very stiff task). *P. F. I. Cole.* —

DASHING PRINCE 2 ch.c. (Apr 25) Prince Sabo 123–Daisy Star (Star Appeal 133) [1990 6m 5g4 6m4 5g 5f2 5f2 5f5 5f4 5f4] angular colt: poor mover: first foal: dam poor half-sister to 1½m and 2¼m winner Baron Blakeney out of 5f winning half-sister to high-class stayer Grey Baron: plating-class performer: suited by 5f: blinkered final outing: usually bandaged: has run creditably for 7-lb claimer: trained first 3 starts by D. Browne: sold 4,000 gns Newmarket Autumn Sales: consistent. *R. W. Stubbs.* 56

DASHING SENOR 3 b.c. El Gran Senor (USA) 136–Zillionaire (USA) (Vaguely Noble 140) [1989 6m2 7g3 7g6 1990 7g* 7m5 10d3 10.2m* 10m 10.2g3 9m6 8d2 8m] strong, good-bodied colt: carries condition: fairly useful performer: won maiden at Epsom in April and slowly-run handicap (wore tongue strap) at Doncaster in June: ran well in competitive handicaps sixth to eighth starts: stays 1¼m: acts on good to firm ground and dead: sweating third and fourth starts. *A. C. Stewart.* 94

DASHING STYLE (IRE) 2 b.c. (Mar 10) Red Sunset 120–Rare Sound 69 (Rarity 129) [1990 6d 7m6 7d6 6d a7g* a7g] 14,000Y: small, sturdy colt: poor mover: first foal: dam 2-y-o 5.1f winner: won 14-runner maiden, showing greatly improved form, at Lingfield late in year by ¾ length: ran moderately in nursery at Southwell afterwards: suited by 7f: found little off bridle third start: unseated rider leaving stalls fourth. *R. Guest.* 60

DASHING TYKE 2 gr.g. (Mar 23) Flying Tyke 90–Habatashie 62 (Habat 127) [1990 5m] 4,000Y: third foal: brother to 6f seller winners Mischievous Tyke and Master Tyke, latter also successful in 7f claimer: dam plating-class maiden: last of 11 in maiden auction at Redcar in September. *A. Smith.* —

DASHWOOD (USA) 3 ch.g. The Minstrel (CAN) 135–Jane Austen (USA) 76 (Arts And Letters) [1989 NR 1990 10f 10.1g 11.5g 12.5g6] 66,000Y: strong gelding: —

has a round action: fifth foal: half-brother to 3 winners in USA: dam, stayed 1¼m, is half-sister to Elegant Air: no show in maidens and minor events, sweating final start: virtually pulled up time before: wears crossed noseband. *D. C. Jermy.*

DASWAKI (CAN) 2 b.c. (Feb 17) Miswaki (USA) 124–Nice Manners (CAN) 86 (Barachois (CAN)) [1990 7m⁶ 7m⁴ 7m³ 6m³ 5m⁵ 6d* 6m*] IR 45,000Y: rather angular colt: moderate walker: second foal: dam minor winner in USA: improved colt: readily won claimers at Goodwood and Leicester in October: seems suited by 6f: acts on good to firm ground and dead. *R. Hannon.*

DATURA 4 b.f. Simply Great (FR) 122–Marie Louise 86 (King Emperor (USA)) — [1989 9v 10v 11m⁴ 8m³ 9m⁵ 10m⁵ 9f* 10f³ 9m 12g 8d 10v 1990 7m 8m 12d 17.1f 13.1h⁶ 8f] neat ex-Irish filly: fifth living foal: half-sister to 1m to 1½m winner Spurn The Odds (by Run The Gantlet): dam won twice at around 7f: won maiden at Tramore as 3-y-o: tailed off in varied events, including seller, in 1990: stays 1¼m: acts on firm going: bandaged and blinkered (pulled hard) final outing. *A. J. Chamberlain.*

DAUNTESS 3 ch.f. Formidable (USA) 125–Cantico 58 (Green Dancer (USA) 132) 81 [1989 6g 6g² 1990 7g* 8g 6g³ 8m⁵ 8m] lengthy, sparely-made, angular filly: fair performer: won maiden at Kempton in June: bandaged behind, ran creditably in £11,700 handicap and listed race (sweating and on toes, headstrong) at Ascot last 2 outings: stays 1m: tends to be a handful at the start, and has once refused to enter stalls. *D. R. C. Elsworth.*

DAUNTLESS KNIGHT (USA) 2 ch.c. (Feb 15) Sir Ivor 135–Colinear (USA) 70 p (Cohoes) [1990 7g 8.2d⁴] $170,000Y: good-topped, lengthy colt: half-brother to several winners, including very smart 6f to 1¼m winner Hardgreen and Richmond Stakes winner Castle Green (both by Irish Castle): dam won 6f claiming race: around 6 lengths fourth of 15, staying on, to Hip To Time in minor event at Nottingham in October: will be well suited by 1¼m: will improve again. *G. Harwood.*

DAVID'S FLIGHT 2 ch.c. (Apr 26) Absalom 128–Djimbaran Bay (Le Levanstell 66 122) [1990 5f² 5m² 5f 6g³ 7g³ 7g⁴] 11,000Y: lengthy colt: fluent mover: half-brother to numerous winners here and abroad, including useful 1¼m winner Bettyknowes (by Satingo) and fair 6f winner Portvasco (by Sharpo): dam won at up to 1¼m in France: quite modest maiden: stays 7f: pulled too hard fifth start: ran well when sweating. *R. Hollinshead.*

DAVINA'S DOUBLE 2 b.f. (Feb 17) Absalom 128–Double Stitch 74 (Wolver — Hollow 126) [1990 6m] 3,000Y: smallish, sturdy filly: third foal: half-sister to 3-y-o Short Encounter (by Blakeney): dam 8.2f winner: backward, soon struggling in maiden at Nottingham in September: dead. *W. Jarvis.*

DAWADAR (USA) 3 b.c. Exceller (USA) 129–Damana (FR) (Crystal Palace 93 (FR) 132) [1989 NR 1990 10m² 12.3m* 12d* 12v] lengthy, rather sparely-made colt: second foal: half-brother to winning jumper Damanour (by Lypheor): dam won from 1m to 1¾m in France: favourite, won maiden at Ripon (hung under pressure) in August and handicap at Haydock (always prominent) in September: will be suited by further: seems unsuited by heavy going: sold to join N. Tinkler 31,000 gns Newmarket Autumn Sales. *L. M. Cumani.*

DAWES OF NELSON 5 b. or br.g. Krayyan 117–Killyhevlin (Green God 128) 47 [1989 7.6f 6m 7m⁴ 6g 6m 7d 1990 6f 6f 6m⁴ 6g⁵ 6g² 5g* 6m⁵ 6m³ 6d⁴ 5.8d⁴] workmanlike gelding: has long stride: won for first time in handicap at Hamilton in July: ran well afterwards: probably stays 7f: acts on good to firm and dead going: hung badly left fifth start. *M. J. Bolton.*

DAWN BELL 5 b.m. Belfort (FR) 89–Dobrina (FR) (Our Mirage 123) [1989 10d 44 7d 5g 5f 1990 a6g a5g 5f² 5m 6m* 6m 5m] good-bodied mare: carries plenty of condition: moderate mover: appeared to show improved form when winning claimer at Chepstow in July: well beaten otherwise last 4 outings, sweating and edgy first of them: best at 6f: acts on firm going: has worn blinkers. *J. M. Bradley.*

DAWN DECISION 3 br.c. Dawn Johnny (USA) 90–Asicion 89 (Above Suspicion — 127) [1989 NR 1990 a12g] rangy, workmanlike colt: half-brother to 2 sprint winners by Laxton and 1977 2-y-o 5f winner Maysus (by Maystreak): dam won over 5f and 6f at 2 yrs: tailed off in maiden at Southwell in August: joined J. Czerpak. *M. R. Leach.*

DAWN GREY 2 gr.c. (Apr 22) Nishapour (FR) 125–Geoffrey's Sister 102 69 (Sparkler 130) [1990 6g² 8d 8d³] 16,000F: small, angular colt: half-brother to 3-y-o Go Buy Bailey's (by Rousillon), 1m winner at 2 yrs, very useful 6f and 7f performer Mac's Fighter (by Hard Fought) and poor 12.2f winner Keep Hoping (by Busted): dam miler: modest maiden: will stay 1¼m. *C. W. Thornton.*

DAWNING STREET (IRE) 2 ch.c. (Mar 3) Thatching 131–Dawn Star 94 80 p (High Line 125) [1990 7m 7g*] well-made colt: third foal: half-brother to fair 6f winner Dawn Storm (by Runnett): dam 1¼m and 1lt winner, is half-sister to useful 1982 2-y-o 5f and 6f winner Domynsky, later stakes winner in USA: won maiden at Salisbury in October by a neck from Young Buster: carried condition on debut: will probably improve again. *J. L. Dunlop.*

DAWN'S DELIGHT 12 b.g. Dawn Review 105–Bird of Passage (Falcon 131) **72 ?** [1989 6d⁴ 6v³ 6v⁴ 6s* 6m 6m 5.6g 6s 6m 6d* 6s⁶ 6v 1990 6f 6m 6s 6m 6d⁵ 6m a7g 6m] leggy, workmanlike gelding: moderate mover: successful in Haydock handicaps in 1989, gaining his nineteenth victory (apprentice ridden) on second occasion: sign of retaining his ability only on fifth outing: best at 6f: suited by plenty of give in the ground: has worn blinkers, visor and bandages: often on toes: usually gets behind and is suited by strong gallop. *K. T. Ivory.*

DAWN SUCCESS 4 br.c. Caerleon (USA) 132–Dawn Echo (Don (ITY) 123) **93** [1989 8s² 7d 8.5s² 10f 8f 10g 8m² 8m⁵ 9g² 8m 6d* 1990 7.5v⁶ 8g 7g⁶ 8f 8f⁶ 9g⁵ 7.6g 7m 9m 6s] leggy, close-coupled colt: quite useful on his day: best efforts as 4-y-o in valuable handicaps fifth, sixth and ninth (ridden by 7-lb claimer, seventh of 40 to Risen Moon in Cambridgeshire at Newmarket) outings: effective at 6f, and stays 9f: acts on any going: inconsistent. *C. E. Brittain.*

DAWSON CITY 3 ch.g. Glint of Gold 128–Lola Sharp (Sharpen Up 127) [1989 6f² **97** 6f* 7f² 1990 9f² 10v* 10.6s² 11.5f⁴ 8m 11d* 10.4v⁵] sturdy gelding: fairly useful handicapper: won at Ayr in April and September, always close up and showing improved form to win £6,200 contest in latter: stays 11.5f: best effort on a soft surface: winning hurdler. *M. H. Easterby.*

DAYDAYSI 2 b.f. (Mar 6) Dawn Johnny (USA) 90–Mayab 100 (Maystreak 118) **—** [1990 6m 8.2g] small, sparely-made filly: fifth live foal: half-sister to 7f seller winner Laxay and fair sprinter Mayor (both by Laxton): dam 5f winner: bit backward, well beaten in maiden and a seller at Nottingham. *M. R. Leach.*

DAYJUR (USA) 3 br.c. Danzig (USA)–Gold Beauty (USA) (Mr Prospector **137** (USA)) [1989 6m* 6m² 1990 7m 6f* 6m² 5m* 5d* 5m* 6g* 5g* a6f²]
'No chance', they said. Despite his starting favourite for the Breeders' Cup Sprint on the dirt track at Belmont Park late in October, there were knowledgeable racing men on both sides of the Atlantic convinced that Europe's top sprinter Dayjur faced insuperable problems in his bid to succeed where Green Desert, Committed, Double Schwartz and eight others from Europe had failed against the home-based specialists since the series began. Princess Tracy's fifth in the inaugural running in 1984 had been Europe's highest placing. Good as he might be on turf, Dayjur had never raced on dirt; he'd never raced round a bend; nor had he experience of the cut-throat dash from the stalls for a good position on the bend and the protracted hurly-burly usual in American sprints; on top of that there was the travel, at the end of a long season. In the end Dayjur found nothing insuperable except the previous year's second, Safely Kept, and he would have beaten her except for one eventuality no-one foresaw—his hurdling a shadow about fifty yards out. The Breeders' Cup Sprint must have been one of the most dramatic races seen on the course since Secretariat won the last leg of his triple crown by thirty-one lengths seventeen years earlier. Two horses went onto the deck early on,

King's Stand Stakes, Ascot a tremendous performance from Dayjur in this famous race; and a highly commendable one from runner-up Ron's Victory as well

Keeneland Nunthorpe Stakes, York—
nothing can live with Dayjur as he lowers the course record

7/1-chance Mr Nickerson bringing down the long-shot Shaker Knit with fatal consequences to both. From his outside draw Dayjur missed the trouble but was immediately off the bridle, pushed along vigorously to make up for a slowish break. After a furlong or so, entering the turn, he'd gone up to be a close second to best-away Safely Kept, and as the two sped round the bend only Glitterman could live with them. Into the straight they soon began to drop Glitterman, drawing away together, hammer and tongs. Dayjur seemed the stronger, though he received a couple of cracks of the whip, and he held a neck lead when he came to the stand's shadow and tried to jump it. Breaking stride cost him the advantage and there was no time to recover; he was even shying at another shadow as he passed the post a neck down, well clear of those behind. A sheepskin noseband—shadow roll in America—might have prevented the distraction. But Dayjur had done enough to vindicate his reputation; enhance it even. The locals were unstinting in their praise, and demand for his services is certain to be very great at Shadwell Farm in Kentucky where he has now been retired at a fee of 50,000 dollars. Reportedly one of the mares visiting him will be Safely Kept.

At home Dayjur's reputation stood sky-high when he left for New York. A run of victories in top races had established him as the season's leading sprinter; their authority and style pointed firmly to his being among the best seen over a much longer period. His trainer nominated him as the best sprinter he'd ever handled, his jockey regarded him as unbeatable over five furlongs and only slightly vulnerable over six, the best sprinter he'd ever ridden. Compliments indeed! While Hern is recognised first and foremost for sending out classic winners, he has, in his long career, trained fast horses of the calibre of Boldboy and Galivanter; and Carson definitely hadn't forgotten the brilliant filly Habibti, for one, when he made his assessment. It all began with Dayjur's win in the King's Stand Stakes at Royal Ascot on his fifth outing of the season, a win followed by others in the Keeneland Nunthorpe Stakes at York, the Ladbroke Sprint Cup at Haydock and the Ciga Prix de l'Abbaye de Longchamp which made him the first to achieve the feat in one season (he lost his chance of a clean sweep in the sprint championship when pulled out of the July Cup because of a mild bout of coughing). Dayjur dominated his fourteen King's Stand opponents almost from the stalls, went clear at halfway and kept up so blistering a gallop that nothing could get near him, not even Ron's Victory who came six lengths clear of third-placed Lugana Beach in finishing second.

A large part of Dayjur's career before Royal Ascot had been taken up with finding out what kind of horse he was. After finishing seventh in the Free Handicap (he'd received 8-1 originally as a result of promising two-year-old form), he'd been dropped back to six furlongs, then to five. He'd progressed nicely, winning a small race at Nottingham, just losing to Tod in the

Ladbroke Sprint Cup, Haydock —
Dayjur beats the July Cup winner and clinches the sprint championship

Hue-Williams Stakes at Newbury, then comfortably accounting for Tigani, Statoblest and other older sprinters in the Sears Temple Stakes at Sandown where, significantly, previous attempts to hold him up had been abandoned. Naturally, when Dayjur next turned out in the Nunthorpe in August riding tactics were unchanged from Sandown and Ascot: he would attempt to take the opposition, who included the very welcome Mr Nickerson, off its feet. The objective was breathtakingly achieved. Soon in full flow, he quickly had all his eight opponents except Statoblest in trouble, and by halfway he held a lead of two lengths whilst cruising comfortably on the bridle. Statoblest had closed to not much more than a length approaching the furlong-pole, but Dayjur quickened when shaken up, and with great zest extended his advantage to four lengths by the line. It was a performance worthy to mark the return of the name of Nunthorpe to the race title after fifteen years. Not in the history of this famous race had the winner covered the distance so quickly. Dayjur lowered Committed's 1984 course record by more than a second, in so doing achieving the exceptional timefigure of 1.69 fast, equivalent to a timerating of 142, and on a par with Habibti's at Haydock in 1983 when she won the Vernons Sprint Cup by seven lengths from Soba.

The latest version of the Vernons, the Ladbroke Sprint Cup, came next on Dayjur's agenda two weeks later. Although the race is run over six furlongs he started at 2/1 on, against the July Cup winner Royal Academy, the Prix Maurice de Gheest winner Dead Certain, the July Cup second Great Commotion, Ron's Victory, Statoblest, Pharaoh's Delight, Tod and Duck And Dive. He'd shown no signs of stopping in any of his races during his spell at five furlongs; furthermore the ground, which can be testing at Haydock at that time of year, was good. Dayjur, very much on his toes beforehand, gave another scintillating front-running display which lost little of its force by the fact of Royal Academy's difficulties in finding a way through or Dead Certain's poor showing. Carson quickly had him across to the stand rail in front of Tod and Dead Certain, and got an instant response when he asked him to go. While

227

Ciga Prix de l'Abbaye de Longchamp—jumping shadows . . . . .

Royal Academy looked for a gap, Dayjur was surging into an unassailable lead of at least five lengths; Royal Academy came late, but Dayjur was scarcely challenged in winning by a length and a half. Once more the field finished spread out, Pharaoh's Delight, third as at York, was beaten six and a half lengths. After this the five-furlong Ciga Prix de l'Abbaye de Longchamp looked a formality in the absence of Royal Academy and Ron's Victory. Only Statoblest, Pharaoh's Delight, Lugana Beach, Boozy and Touch of White took Dayjur on again, and he started at 10/1 on, the minimum odds on the Pari-Mutuel. The home-trained Whippet was due to run but unshipped his rider and had to be withdrawn. The outcome of the race was something less than the complete rout generally anticipated, under three lengths covering

Breeders' Cup Sprint, Belmont Park— . . . . . and again!

the first four home. Nevertheless in the middle of the race Dayjur, who sweated up beforehand, again showed himself in a different league from the opposition. Having seemed not to be moving particularly strongly through the first two furlongs the colt changed his legs and accelerated, electrifyingly, when Carson pushed him along, so that in another furlong he'd gone from a length up to at least five. He was still well clear when he shied at something, lost concentration and was eased off, still having two lengths to spare over Lugana Beach at the finish. His shying, probably at a shadow, passed almost without comment at the time.

So where does Dayjur, who'd won four of Europe's top races by an aggregate of ten lengths, value more, stand among sprinters? We have had his trainer's and jockey's opinion already, and at the end of the season we got others from the Horse of the Year poll of racing journalists and from the International Classification. The Horse of the Year voting went as follows: Dayjur fourteen, Salsabil thirteen, In The Groove two, Saumarez one, Timeless Times one, Bean Boy one. A narrow squeak for Dayjur, but the real significance in the vote lies in that his performances were sufficiently impressive to overcome the prejudice in Britain against pure speed, in favour of milers and middle-distance horses, that has clearly existed down the years. These polls have been taken in one form or other since 1959 yet only twice before, in 1980 (Moorestyle) and 1983 (Habibti) have sprinters come out on top. The International Classification rated Dayjur at 133. Timeform ratings have been going longer than the Horse of the Year award or International Classifications: they cover a period of more than forty years now. The highest-rated sprinter of the many thousands assessed in that period is Abernant (142), twice winner of the July Cup, King George Stakes and Nunthorpe Stakes, winner of the King's Stand Stakes, described by Sir Gordon Richards as the best sprinter he had ever ridden. Pappa Fourway (139) who as a three-year-old in 1955 never looked like being beaten in his eight races, including the King's Stand Stakes, July Cup and Diadem Stakes, is the only other sprinter ahead of Dayjur in the Timeform Annual ratings. On the same mark as Dayjur are Moorestyle and two colts who put up tremendous weight-carrying feats in the Portland in the days before top horses were excluded from handicaps, Princely Gift and Right Boy. A pound behind them on 136 come Habibti, the Nunthorpe winner Floribunda and the July Cup winner Thatch.

		Danzig (USA)	Northern Dancer	Nearctic	
		(b 1977)	(b 1961)	Natalma	
Dayjur (USA)			Pas de Nom	Admiral's Voyage	
(b.c. 1987)			(b or br 1968)	Petitioner	
		Gold Beauty (USA)	Mr Prospector	Raise A Native	
		(b 1979)	(b 1970)	Gold Digger	
			Stick To Beauty	Illustrious	
			(b 1973)	Hail To Beauty	

A feature common to most in this distinguished group is their versatility as far as distance is concerned: most, while brilliantly speedy, got six furlongs well, some even further. Dayjur's record, taken literally, bears out Carson's summing up—unbeatable over five, slightly vulnerable over six—but it is hair-splitting to conclude he was more effective at one distance than the other. He was a formidable opponent at either. As to ground, in proving his ability on dirt Dayjur seized an opportunity not afforded any of the others; Abernant at Belmont is something that fires the imagination but, alas, he was foaled well before inter-continental racing took off. On turf Dayjur proved himself on firm and dead; he never raced on softer, and ran on dead at Royal Ascot at the insistence of his owner. In appearance Dayjur has a lot of the sprinter about him: he's a robust, good-quartered colt who carries condition; his action is a free, yet rather round one. When it came to assessing Dayjur's chances at Belmont Park his pedigree was held to be in his favour. And rightly so, since he is bred for the job, by Danzig out of a champion sprinter by Mr Prospector. The dam Gold Beauty was selected best North American sprinter of 1982 after winning the first six of her seven races as a three-year-old, including one over the Belmont Park six furlongs, the Grade 2 Fall Highweight Handicap. The following year the gelding Chinook Pass took over

Hamdan Al-Maktoum's "Dayjur" (W. Carson)

as best sprinter, but Gold Beauty topped the *Daily Racing Form* Free Handicap for female sprinters, 3 lb clear, and won another handicap at Belmont Park, this time a Grade 3 event. She won at distances up to seven furlongs, racing mainly over six. The next dam Stick To Beauty was a minor stakes winner at seven furlongs, out of the unraced Hail To Beauty, a sister or half-sister to numerous winners, among them the dam of the Grade 1 Mother Goose Stakes winner Caesar's Wish. Dayjur is Gold Beauty's second foal. The first, Maplejinsky (by Nijinsky), was a good-class filly endowed with more stamina than Dayjur; she won two Grade 1 events, the Alabama Stakes over a mile and a quarter and the Monmouth Oaks over a furlong less. Gold Beauty subsequently produced a sister to Maplejinsky and a sister to Dayjur, both of whom followed Dayjur's route to Britain, via the Keeneland July Selected Yearling Sale. Sheikh Hamdan Al-Maktoum's Shadwell Estate Company, who bought Dayjur for 1,650,000 dollars there in 1988, paid 1,600,000 dollars for the Nijinsky (called Gracious Beauty, now in training with Hern) in 1989 and 1,850,000 dollars for the Danzig in 1990. It is regrettable that Dayjur won't be in training alongside these two in the next season. Yet the decision to retire him was entirely predictable when his value at stud was weighed against another year's potential earnings on the track, when no fresh fields were there for him to conquer, and when account was taken of the injury scare towards the end of his two-year-old days (he suffered a bad cut under a hind joint that a fraction deeper might have severed a tendon). Dayjur, incidentally, is a notable advertisement for the success of the wind operation pioneered by Sir Frederick Hobday. A hobdayed horse is one which has undergone an operation on the larynx and vocal chords aimed at remedying a wind infirmity which manifests itself as 'whistling' or 'roaring' after the horse has been asked to exert itself. Partial paralysis of the vocal chords can cause the amount of air able to enter the windpipe to be restricted; and obviously if the horse can't get sufficent air he can't give of his best on the racecourse. The operation can be extremely beneficial, as it was in the two instances that played a big part in bringing it to wider notice in the early-'sixties—those of the good sprinters Bleep-Bleep and Shamrock Star, whose form improved almost out of recognition afterwards. Another recent high-class sprinter who has had this operation is Perion. Dayjur was operated on at the end of 1989. Dayjur has gone to stud abroad, but will not be forgotten. Every so often comes an occasion on a racecourse when those present count themselves fortunate to have been there. Nunthorpe day at York was one, when Dayjur clinched our vote, at least, for Racehorse of the Year. *Major W. R. Hern.*

DAYMER BAY 3 b.f. Lomond (USA) 128–Clarista (USA) 67 (Riva Ridge (USA)) — [1989 NR 1990 7m 8f³ a12g] 64,000Y: lengthy, angular filly: third foal: half-sister to French provincial 11f winner Visions of Eden (by Persepolis): dam, maiden, stayed 1¼m and looked ungenuine, is half-sister to Topsy and Teenoso: plating-class maiden: stays 1m: blinkered final start. *W. Haggas.*

DAYS OF THUNDER 2 ch.c. (Mar 6) Vaigly Great 127–Silent Prayer 58 **68** p (Queen's Hussar 124) [1990 7m⁴] 11,000Y: sixth foal: brother to 1988 2-y-o 6f winner Vaigrant Wind and half-brother to 3-y-o Arabian Silence (by Sayf El Arab): dam won maiden auction at Goodwood in June. *C. A. Cyzer.*

DAZZLE THE CROWD (IRE) 2 b.g. (Apr 15) Simply Great (FR) 122–Katie — Roche (Sallust 134) [1990 6g] 9,000Y: strong, angular gelding: fourth foal: brother to a winner in Italy and half-brother to 6f winner Teresa Deevey (by Runnett): dam Irish 1m winner: green and backward, prominent 4f in maiden at Goodwood in June. *C. A. Cyzer.*

DAZZLINGLY RADIANT 3 gr.f. Try My Best (USA) 130–Elvina (FR) **80** (Dancer's Image (USA)) [1989 5m³ 5m³ 8m 8g 8f² 7f⁶ 7f² 7g³ 6g* 5.8m² 6m* 6g³ 6m⁴ 6m⁵ 6d] leggy, quite good-topped filly: moderate walker and mover: fair handicapper: successful in summer events at Chepstow and Kempton: ran very well in quite valuable event at Newmarket penultimate start, moderately final one: suited by 6f: acts on firm going: hung left and ran wide on turn at Folkestone. *R. Hannon.*

DEAD CERTAIN 3 b.f. Absalom 128–Sirnelta (FR) (Sir Tor) [1989 5m² **123** § 5f* 5f* 6g² 6m* 6m* 1990 7.3d 6g² 6m⁶ 6.5g* 6g 6m]
  It's inevitable, but some racehorses turn out to be most inappropriately named. Wasn't it, for instance, rather tempting fate to come up with the likes of Rapid Mover, Simply First Class, Stroke of Luck, Theprincessofspeed and, even, Pride of Shipley? The very smart filly Dead Certain had little in common with her name as a three-year-old. How she would perform became one of the great imponderables, though by the end of the year it seemed that she was set on running more bad races than good. Her good runs were an improvement on what she'd shown as a game and progressive two-year-old when from six starts she was second twice and won the rest, including the Queen Mary, Lowther and Cheveley Park Stakes. In her second season Dead Certain added the Prix Maurice de Gheest at Deauville when up against a small field that included Machiavellian who started odds on but ran appallingly, and Rock City who had to concede her 9 lb. Perhaps this wasn't the stiffest of tasks but Dead Certain accomplished it well, held up then coming through smoothly to lead one furlong out and beat Rock City a length. At Royal Ascot she'd come within a head of a fifth pattern victory in the Cork And Orrery Stakes, dominating the centre of the track and keeping on strongly under the whip only to lose out to Great Commotion close home. That was an excellent performance given the

Prix Maurice de Gheest, Deauville—the good side of Dead Certain;
she wins from Rock City (No. 1) and Pole Position

11-lb penalty for her two-year-old Group 1 success, a truly remarkable one given her dire showing on her only previous start of the year in the Fred Darling Stakes at Newbury back in April. With her running only at sprint distances as a two-year-old, connections and public alike were eager to learn more about her prospects of staying a mile for the Guineas, but it wasn't the extra distance which beat her. At the time, it looked more like some grave physical disorder as, having set off in front, Dead Certain was back-pedalling before the two-furlong marker then stopped rapidly, throwing her head about in alarming fashion. We'd thought beforehand that Dead Certain would stay a mile but after a rest, the Guineas having gone, and then her fine run at Royal Ascot, connections clearly felt the option wasn't worth pursuing. It seemed, however, to be a case of either very good or very bad for Dead Certain in 1990 and those runs at Royal Ascot and Deauville were her only good ones. She was beaten about fifteen lengths in the Carroll Foundation July Cup at Newmarket, twenty-five lengths in the Krug Diadem Stakes at Ascot and almost too far to calculate in the Ladbroke Sprint Cup at Haydock. She'd been edgy and swished her tail repeatedly in the paddock before being asked to contest the break-neck early pace at Newmarket but we wouldn't like to make any excuses for Dead Certain otherwise. She dramatically failed to play her part in what had been billed as the 'sprint showdown' at Haydock, giving a thoroughly temperamental display and a nightmarish ride for her new jockey Munro, this time dropping herself right out after only a couple of furlongs as Dayjur kicked up the turf in front of her.

		Abwah	Abernant
	Absalom	(gr 1969)	The Creditor
	(gr 1975)	Shadow Queen	Darius
Dead Certain		(ch 1965)	Shadow
(b.f. 1987)		Sir Tor	Round Table
	Sirnelta (FR)	(b 1963)	Never Too Late
	(b or br 1971)	Finelta	Fine Top
		(b or br 1959)	Sanelta

Dead Certain's pedigree was discussed at some length in *Racehorses of 1989*. She cost just 5,800 guineas as a foal despite being a half-sister to six winners, including the useful mile-and-a-quarter handicapper Fire Top (by Hotfoot). Their dam, the French one-mile to mile-and-a-quarter winner Sirnelta, is out of a sister to the 1963 Prix du Jockey-Club and Grand Prix de Paris (then run over fifteen furlongs) winner Sanctus II. Dead Certain never gave herself the chance to prove whether or not she'd stay beyond six furlongs. She acted on firm going, and Newbury was the only occasion on which she encountered a soft surface. Before if not during a race, those who

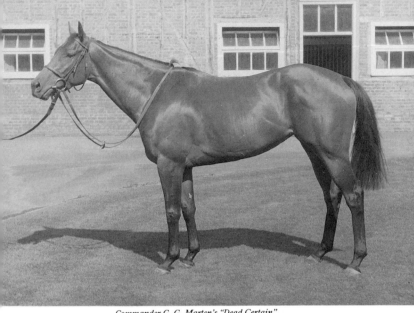

Commander G. G. Marten's "Dead Certain"

saw her must have found Dead Certain a most attractive individual; a robust, round-barrelled filly who carried condition, she is a grand walker and displayed a powerful, fluent action to post. She's to visit Thatching in 1991. *D. R. C. Elsworth.*

DEADLOCK 3 ch.c. The Minstrel (CAN) 135–Roses To Rachel (Artaius (USA) 129) [1989 8v 1990 11d 12f 10m⁴ 10m⁶ 10g⁶ 12m 12g⁶ 12m³ 11.7m⁴] well-made colt: moderate walker and mover: modest maiden: stays 1½m: acts on good to firm ground: has run well for 7-lb claimer: often makes the running. *D. R. C. Elsworth.* — 69

DEADLY TOUCH 2 b.c. (Mar 20) Touching Wood (USA) 127–Katharina 105 (Frankincense 120) [1990 6g a7g 7f 8g] 3,700F, 4,200Y: neat, good-bodied colt: half-brother to smart 5f (at 2 yrs) to 7.3f winner Derring Miss (by Derrylin) and 2 winners abroad: dam useful at up to 1m: behind in maidens, including auctions. *P. Howling* —

DEAREST 3 b.f. Alzao (USA) 117 Lover's Rose (King Emperor (USA)) [1989 NR 1990 7m⁹ 7g⁵ a12g⁶] 54,000Y: rangy, rather unfurnished filly: sister to smart 5f (at 2 yrs) to 7.3f winner Pass The Peace and half-sister to 2 winners by Auction Ring, including quite useful 6f winner Lover's Bid: dam, half-sister to very smart stayer Swell Fellow, won at around 9f in Ireland: quite modest maiden: off course 6 months before final start when gave impression did not stay 1½m: retained by trainer 24,000 gns Newmarket December Sales. *P. F. I. Cole.* — 63

DEAR MIFF 5 ch.m. Alias Smith (USA)–Dear Jem 78 (Dragonara Palace (USA) 115) [1989 12.3s⁵ 11.7d⁴ 14g 10f 12m 8.5g 10m² 9m a12g⁵ 1990 10.2f⁴ 9f 8m] plain mare: poor handicapper: best short of 1½m: acts on any going: blinkered last 3 outings at 4 yrs: sometimes sweats: twice winner over hurdles in autumn. *M. R. Channon.* — 29

DEAR MIMI (USA) 3 b.f. Roberto (USA) 131–Carnival Princess (USA) (Prince John) [1989 NR 1990 10.6s 12.2f³] $120,000Y: leggy filly: half-sister to high-class 7f and 1m performer Salse (by Topsider) and a modest winner by Key To The Mint: dam, minor 6f winner in USA at 3 yrs, is half-sister to Italian Oaks winner Carnauba: —

233

blinkered, 7½ lengths third of 8 to Muse in maiden at Warwick in July, readily outpaced and wandering under pressure: moved moderately down and showed nothing on soft ground on debut. *M. R. Stoute.*

DEAR OLD GIRL 3 gr.f. Carwhite 127–Curfew 76 (Midsummer Night II 117) — [1989 5.3g 5d 6m 8m 1990 a11g 10g5 10m5 a11g 8m a11g 10d] smallish filly: poor maiden: stays 1¼m: visored final start: sold 1,100 gns Newmarket Autumn Sales. *D. T. Thom.*

DEAUVILLE DUCHESS 3 gr.f. Ballad Rock 122–Miss Deauville (Sovereign — Path 125) [1989 NR 1990 8m5 10.2m] 12,500F: neat filly: half-sister to a listed winner in Italy by Mummy's Pet: dam twice-raced sister to very useful 6f to 1m winner Miss Paris: bandaged behind, no worthwhile form in seller (blinkered) and claimer: sold to join P. Hobbs 4,000 gns Newmarket July Sales. *Mrs L. Piggott.*

DEBACH DAISY 3 b.f. Ahonoora 122–Princess Seal 108 (Prince Tenderfoot 61 (USA) 126) [1989 6m2 1990 8f4 7g3 7m2 7g 8g 7d 8g5] workmanlike filly: quite modest form when narrowly beaten in maidens second and third starts: well behind subsequently, including in handicap: best form over 7f: blinkered final start. *C. E. Brittain.*

DEBBIE HARRY (USA) 4 b.f. Alleged (USA) 138–Tie A Bow (USA) (Dance 70 Spell (USA)) [1989 NR 1990 10f 8v6 14.8f2 15.8g2 14.8f3 16m6] heavy-bodied filly: carries lot of condition: has rather round action: modest handicapper: will be suited by good test of stamina: acts on firm going: has run well for 7-lb claimer. *P. F. I. Cole.*

DEBBIE'S CHOICE 4 b. or br.f. Record Run 127–Anna's Pet (Mummy's Pet — 125) [1989 NR 1990 11.5m 6f] lengthy filly: little promise in maidens and handicap: sweating and on toes on reappearance: sold 1,150 gns Ascot November Sales. *R. Curtis.*

DEBJANJO 2 b.g. (Apr 17) Critique (USA) 126–Miss White (FR) (Carwhite 127) 68 [1990 6m4 5m2 6g4 6f3 6m 6g] 8,200Y: leggy gelding: moderate mover: second foal: half-brother to French 3-y-o 9f and 1¼m winner Montez (by Lyphard's Wish), successful at 4.5f and 1m at 2 yrs: dam closely related to dam of Mendez: quite modest form in varied events: took keen hold and ran poorly when blinkered final outing: will probably be better suited by 7f: has run well for apprentice: sometimes sweating and edgy. *J. R. Jenkins.*

DEB'S BALL 4 b.f. Glenstal (USA) 118–De'b Old Fruit (Levmoss 133) [1989 7m6 43 8.2m5 7g3 1990 7f 7f 8g 9.1m3 8m 12f] quite good-topped filly: quite modest maiden at best: stays 9f: visored fourth and fifth starts: winner over hurdles twice early in 1990/1. *D. Moffatt.*

DECEIT 3 b.c. On Your Mark 125–Second Movement (Music Boy 124) [1989 5s 62 5s4 5.3m2 5f 5f5 5g4 1990 5d 5g 5g* 5m* 5g 5m* 5g4 5g5 5g4 5f 6g 5m 5m 5d 5d] small, good-quartered colt: has a quick action: quite modest performer: made all in claimers at Wolverhampton in May and Lingfield in May and Chepstow (claimed out of G. Lewis' stable £10,760) in June: showed little facing stiff tasks in the autumn: best at 5f: acts on firm going: often blinkered, including when successful: sold 2,800 gns Newmarket Autumn Sales. *N. Tinkler.*

DECIDED (CAN) 7 b.g. Affirmed (USA)–Expediency (USA) (Vaguely Noble — 140) [1989 NR 1990 16.2s] big, strong, good-topped gelding: moderate walker and mover: fair winner as 4-y-o when trained by H. Cecil: needed race only outing in 1990: stays 1½m well: useful hurdler/chaser. *Miss H. C. Knight.*

DEDICATED 2 b.c. (Apr 18) Valiyar 129–Mischiefmaker 73 (Calpurnius 122) 87 [1990 6g3 6m2 8.5m* 8m2 8s2] 16,000Y: workmanlike colt: has scope: good mover: fifth living foal: half-brother to ungenuine 3-y-o Chloe's Pet (by Local Suitor) and a winner in Norway: dam 1m seller winner at 2 yrs stayed 1¼m: fair performer: quickened well to win maiden at Beverley in September: second in minor event at Bath and listed race at Turin later: better suited by 1m + than 6f. *W. Jarvis.*

DEE AND EM 5 ch.g. Crofter (USA) 124–Cousin Clare (Pontifex (USA)) [1989 43 5m 5m 6f 6f3 6m 6f* 6m 5m 5.3f4 6g 6m 6g 1990 5f 6g 8f5 7h 5m3 5m* 5m6 5m 5m 7m 7m 5m] compact, workmanlike gelding: poor handicapper: won at Lingfield in June: ideally suited by sprint distances: acts on firm and dead going: effective with or without blinkers: bandaged behind ninth outing: has seemed unsuited by course at Catterick: has carried head high: sold to join M. Chapman's stable 1,000 gns Newmarket Autumn Sales. *B. R. Millman.*

DEEGEE 2 ch.f. (Apr 18) Bay Express 132–Join The Club 67 (Dance In Time 49 § (CAN)) [1990 5m 5g4 5m] rather unfurnished filly: fourth foal: half-sister to 11f winner Brigadiers Glory (by Castle Keep): dam 5f winner from 4 starts at 2 yrs: hung left when fourth of 6 in maiden (fractious when mounted) at Wolverhampton in

June· reared in stalls and unseated rider third start then withdrawn after repeatedly unseating rider in preliminaries next intended outing: one to leave alone. *B. A. McMahon.*

DEE JAY PEE   4 ch.g. Electric 126–Lady Gaston 76 (Pall Mall 132) [1989 8g 7g —8.5f 9m 1990 a14g] angular gelding: has a round action: no worthwhile form in varied company on flat. *B. Preece.*

DEEP REEF   4 ch.g. Main Reef 126–Kareela (FR) (Deep Diver 134) [1989 6f³ 8d —6v 7g 1990 6f 7g 7m 6m 8m 11.7m] lengthy, rather angular gelding: fair handicapper at one time: no worthwhile form since first outing at 3 yrs: stays 6f: acts on firm and dead going: bandaged near-hind fourth: has joined J. Baker. *B. R. Millman.*

DEEP SELECTION (IRE)   2 b.f. (Jan 25) Deep Run 119–Random Select —(Random Shot 116) [1990 5m 5m⁵] IR 5,800F: compact filly: first reported racing: dam winning Irish jumper: visored and carrying condition, over 6 lengths fifth of 7 in maiden at Newbury in June: very green, slowly away and hung right on debut: will stay much further. *Mrs Barbara Waring.*

DEEP TAW   6 br.m. Kala Shikari 125–Florence Mary 51 (Mandamus 120) [1989 5f —5m⁴ 5h 5f⁴ 5f⁴ 5f⁶ 8m 1990 5m⁶ 5f] small non-thoroughbred mare: carries plenty of condition: poor mover: poor handicapper: doesn't stay 1m: acts on firm going. *C. J. Hill.*

DEEP WATER BAY   6 b.g. Lochnager 132–Cateryne (Ballymoss 136) [1989 NR —1990 8m a13g] small gelding: modest at best, but has deteriorated: stays 1¼m: acts on good to firm and heavy going: well beaten when blinkered: winning selling hurdler. *B. J. McMath.*

DEERCAL DANCER   4 ch.g. Ballacashtal (CAN)–Lookslike Reindeer (Bonne —Noel 115) [1989 7d⁶ 7.5d² 7g³ 6f⁴ 7m³ 7m 7m⁶ a6g 1990 7m] small gelding: quite modest form at best as 3-y-o: tailed off in seller in March: stays 7.5f: acts on firm and dead going: blinkered twice: sold 875 gns Ascot April Sales. *R. Simpson.*

DEERNESS LAD   3 b.g. Kala Shikari 125–Il Regalo (Meadow Mint (USA) 120) —[1989 5g 6f⁵ 7.5f 7f 8.5f 1990 12.2m³ 12.2m 15g] leggy, angular gelding: poor plater: visored, pulled hard and looked ungenuine final start: stays 7.5f. *D. H. Topley.*

DEFENSIVE PLAY (USA)   3 b.c. Fappiano (USA)–Safe Play (USA) **118**(Sham (USA)) [1989 7m³ 8m* 1990 10m* 11.5m⁴ 12m⁴ 10.6m* 11s* a8f³]

Like those of an increasing number of European-trained horses, Defensive Play's earnings were transformed by a visit to North America in the autumn. Baylis, Fire The Groom and Defensive Play were winners there who comfortably doubled their career earnings at one blow, Aldbourne very nearly did so with her three North American runs while the victories of Ruby Tiger and Cacoethes boosted theirs by over seventy per cent. It wasn't as if Defensive Play had done badly over here; some way off the best, yes, but he'd won two Group 3 contests to add to his success in a Newmarket maiden as a two-year-old. The first of those came in the Guardian Classic Trial at Sandown on his reappearance when he was made 7/4 favourite to account for, in betting order, Missionary Ridge, Rock Hopper, Marienski, Victory Piper and Karinga Bay. The Guardian Classic Trial had looked like establishing a pre-eminent reputation among the Derby trials at one stage but neither Gulf King, Galitzin or, believe it or not, Old Vic had done much to excite the Derby betting with its victory in the previous three editions. It was the same with Defensive Play who was available at 40/1 after beating Rock Hopper a length. This subdued reaction must have been partly due to the awkward way in which Defensive Play, with his long stride, negotiated the turn but there was plenty to like about him as an individual (he's a big, strong, lengthy colt) and his enthusiasm (he kept increasing the pace, and made every yard). Both winner and second were quickly given another chance to impress, with contrasting results, in the Lingfield Derby Trial. Despite a 3-lb penalty, Defensive Play was again made favourite but this time his problems with the downhill turn seemed even more pronounced and once in line for home he was soon headed, eventually being beaten ten lengths. Defensive Play did not appear in the Derby field nor indeed, in that for any of the top races in Europe. It was over two and a half months before we saw him again, when he probably needed the race in the Gordon Stakes at Goodwood; next Defensive Play bounced back with as good a performance as any he produced here to emerge best from a three-way

Man o'War Stakes, Belmont Park—a Grade 1 win for Defensive Play

photo with Maximilian and Alphabel for the Burtonwood Brewery Rose of Lancaster Stakes at Haydock.

In six runs in Britain, then, Defensive Play won £67,170. The Grade 1 Man o'War Stakes at Belmont Park in late-September had a first prize of 284,160 dollars—or about £150,000 at prevailing exchange rates. Now an eleven-furlong turf contest, the Man o'War Stakes was won by Secretariat, Dahlia and Snow Knight in consecutive years in the 'seventies but Defensive Play didn't look to have a top-class opponent in the latest running. He was scheduled to but the 1989 Canadian triple crown winner With Approval was withdrawn after heavy rain turned the ground soft. Second-favourite Defensive Play, whom had hitherto raced only on good to firm ground, was again allowed to stride on and again was never headed. Shy Town, winner of two Grade 3 handicaps earlier in the season, got closest at half a length with the French-trained favourite Ode three and a quarter lengths behind him.

		Mr Prospector (b 1970)	Raise A Native
Defensive Play (USA) (b.c. 1987)	Fappiano (USA) (b 1977)		Gold Digger
		Killaloe (b 1970)	Dr Fager
			Grand Splendor
	Safe Play (USA) (b 1978)	Sham (b 1970)	Pretense
			Sequoia
		Bori (b 1972)	Quadrangle
			Lucretia Bori

Defensive Play's dam Safe Play was rated just 3 lb off the best of her sex as a three-year-old in the USA but registered her biggest success in the Grade 1 La Canada Stakes over nine furlongs the following year. She's had a troubled time at stud, however, having one barren year and twice not being covered. Defensive Play is her second foal following the French provincial eleven-furlong winner Livry (by Lyphard) and she had a Mr Prospector colt in 1988. It's hard to know where to start when listing the good winners in this family. The second dam Bori wasn't one of them, in fact she didn't win a race of any

Mr K. Abdulla's "Defensive Play"

description, but she's produced the One Thousand Guineas winner Musical Bliss and is a half-sister to the very useful staying two-year-olds Draw The Line and Bob's Majesty. The third dam Lucretia Bori was a close relation to the Ebor winner Sostenuto and half-sister to the high-class miler Romulus. Defensive Play is from the fourth crop of Fappiano who died in September following an injury to his off-hind. Successful in ten of his seventeen races, including the Grade 1 Metropolitan Handicap, and best at up to a mile, Fappiano was rated 119 and 7 lb off the best of his age by the Experimental Free Handicap or Daily Racing Form Free Handicaps in all of his three seasons on the racetrack. He far surpassed those achievements as a stallion. Having initiated an excellent record as a circ of two-year-olds with his first crop, Fappiano entered the top six in the General Sire list as soon as he had three crops of racing age, and never left it. In 1990, chiefly through the Kentucky Derby and Breeders' Cup Classic winner Unbridled, he vied for top position in the General Sire List with another stallion who died in the autumn, Alydar. Fappiano had very little impact in Europe—Defensive Play was his first European pattern-race winner—prompting many to conclude that his stock are far more effective on the dirt tracks in North America. Defensive Play was second reserve for the Breeders' Cup Classic on dirt and it's no surprise that he stayed on that side of the Atlantic, finishing third in the Grade 3 Affirmed Handicap at Hollywood Park in December for S. McGaughey's stable. *G. Harwood.*

DEFICIT (USA) 3 ch.c. Deputy Minister (CAN)–Go Leasing 121 (Star Appeal **71**
133) [1989 6m 8m^3 1990 11.7f4 12.2m* 13.3m^4 13.1m4] robust colt: good mover, with quick action: modest form: favourite, won claimer at Catterick in May: stays 13.3f: on toes third start: sold 20,000 gns Newmarket July Sales. *B. W. Hills.*

DEGANNWY 3 br.f. Caerleon (USA) 132–Delagoa (FR) (Targowice (USA) 130)   **52**
[1989 7f⁴ 1990 10m 10m 10m 12g* 12f³ 10f 12m³ 10.6s 15d²] small filly: plating-class
handicapper: rallied to win 3-runner race at Edinburgh in June: ran well when placed
after, in slowly-run race final start: probably stays 15f: acts on firm and dead
(possibly not soft) ground: has pulled hard. *Dr J. D. Scargill.*

DEGREE OF FORCE 2 b.g. (Mar 21) Stanford 121§–Scotch Rocket 60 (Roan   **57**
Rocket 128) [1990 5g 6g 6g² 6m² 7m 7m 8d] 8,000Y: well-grown, workmanlike
gelding: has plenty of scope: second foal: half-brother to 3-y-o 6f winner Northern
Rocket (by Northern Tempest): dam 7f winner: runner-up in sellers at Nottingham
and Doncaster: off course at least 7 weeks before each of last 2 starts, backward on
final one: should stay beyond 6f: sold 2,000 gns Newmarket Autumn Sales. *Mrs J. R.
Ramsden.*

DEHAR BOY 4 b.g. Buzzards Bay 128§–Nahawand 51 (High Top 131) [1989 10s   **44**
9f³ 10.2f⁵ 11m 10m⁶ 10g⁴ 8f⁵ 9f⁵ 1990 8m 8m² 8.3g 10g⁵ a8g⁶ a8g] strong, lengthy
gelding: moderate mover: plating-class form at best: effective at 1m to 1¼m: acts on
firm going: mostly blinkered at 4 yrs. *D. Morris.*

DELIGHTFUL DIANE 3 b.f. Kalaglow 132–Whip Finish 77 (Be Friendly 130)   **—**
[1989 5.8m⁵ 6g 1990 8g 10.2f⁴ 11.7m] tall, unfurnished filly: plating-class maiden:
always behind and tended to hang left in June handicap final start: appears suited by
1¼m: pulled hard on reappearance: sold 950 gns Ascot October Sales. *R. J. Holder.*

DEMESNE FLYER 3 ch.g. Tower Walk 130–Covenant 75 (Good Bond 122)   **54**
[1989 6g 1990 a5g 8.5m 5f 5g 5m 6m 6d] strong, workmanlike gelding: plating-class
maiden: stays 6f: acts on firm going. *R. Hollinshead.*

DEMOCRATIC (USA) 2 ch.c. (Apr 23) Miswaki (USA) 124–Allegra (USA) **101**
(Alleged (USA) 138) [1990 5g² 5m³ 6.5g⁴ 7m* 8g² 7m³ 8v³] $42,000F, $80,000Y:
sturdy colt: carries condition: fourth reported foal: dam unraced, from family of
Secretariat and Sir Gaylord: useful performer: won slowly-run maiden at Leicester
in September: placed after in minor event at Newbury, moderately-run Somerville
Tattersall Stakes at Newmarket and Prix des Chenes at Saint-Cloud: stays 1m. *M.
Bell.*

DEMONSTRABLE (USA) 3 b.c. Alleged (USA) 138–Lovin' Lass (USA)   **82**
(Cutlass (USA)) [1989 NR 1990 10.1m 10.1m² 12m² 12m⁴ 14f* 16d⁴] big, lengthy
colt: has a rather round action: fifth foal: half-brother to fairly useful but temperamental maiden Danbury (by Danzig) and multiple winners in USA by Graustark and
To The Quick: dam stakes-placed winner at 6f and 7f in USA: fair performer:
favourite, always close up when winning maiden at Redcar in October: soundly-
beaten co-favourite in Chester handicap 2 weeks later: stays 1¾m: acts on firm
going: sold A. Falourd 29,000 gns Newmarket Autumn Sales. *B. W. Hills.*

DENBY HOUSE LAD (CAN) 3 br.g. Assert 134–Queens Club (USA) (Cyane)   **—**
[1989 NR 1990 12m⁶ 16.2d⁴ 14m⁵] $7,700Y: big, lengthy gelding: ninth foal:
half-brother to 4 winners in North America, including a 2-y-o stakes-placed filly by
Al Hattab: dam unraced sister to Beldame Stakes runner-up Fourdrinier: quite
modest maiden: ridden along over 1m out when gambled-on fourth of 7 at Beverley,
best effort: faced stiff task 9 days later in June: subsequently gelded. *S. G. Norton.*

DENCAST 3 b.c. Battle Hymn 103–Ishiyama 62 (Owen Anthony 102) [1989 7d   **—**
a6g a6g 1990 8g a7g] rather sparely-made colt: seems of little account. *C. R. Beever.*

DENHAM GREEN 4 b.g. Dominion 123–Ariadne 79 (Bustino 136) [1989 7g³   **56**
6v⁶ 6d 9f 5m³ 5g² 5g 6m 5s 5m 1990 5f 6s 5f 5g* 5m a5g³ a7g 5g a6g⁵ 5s² 6g⁶]
lengthy, good-quartered gelding: has a roundish action: fairly useful as 2-y-o, but
has deteriorated: won seller (bought in 7,600 gns) at Hamilton in May: stays 6f:
probably unsuited by firm going, acts on any other: blinkered and taken down early
last 2 starts: sold 1,600 gns Doncaster October Sales: inconsistent. *M. H. Easterby.*

DENHAM HOUSE 3 ch.g. Jalmood (USA) 126–Ariadne 79 (Bustino 136) [1989   **—**
5v³ 5s⁵ 5g 7g 10.6d 1990 10m 12m⁶ 12g a7g 8g a11g] workmanlike, good-quartered
gelding: carries condition: no longer appears of any account. *T. Kersey.*

DENITZ (FR) 8 ch.g. Sharpman 124–Djerba (My Swallow 134) [1989 8f 8f 7d⁵   **44**
1990 a10g² a10g a12g² a10g a12g³ a12g² 10.8m 10m⁶ 11.5m a7g⁵ 10g a10g]
good-bodied gelding: has been hobdayed: poor handicapper: stays 1½m: best with
give in the ground and acts on heavy: bandaged eighth outing: visored tenth. *C.
Holmes.*

DENSBEN 6 b.g. Silly Prices 110–Eliza de Rich 57 (Spanish Gold 101) [1989 5g⁴   **74**
5g* 6v* 6.1f³ 6f 6m 6m³ 5m 6m 6m² 6f 6m 5s⁴ 6s 6m 6d⁵ 6g² 5s 5d⁶ 1990 5f 6m*
6v⁵ 6f* 6m 6d⁴ 6m 6g⁴ 7m 6d 6g 6s 7d 7d] smallish, sparely-made gelding: modest
handicapper: tends to run particularly well in spring: successful at Newcastle in

March and Haydock in May: below form after eighth outing: suited by 6f: acts on any going: visored last 2 outings: good mount for inexperienced rider: has started slowly: inconsistent. *Denys Smith.*

DEN'S SONG 4 ch.g. Sallust 134–Princess Ru (Princely Gift 137) [1989 7s 8m 7f5 7m4 7m5 7m3 8.2f 7m* 7d6 7d 1990 a7g3 a8g 8g 7f] compact gelding: has a long stride: easily best effort when winning handicap (apprentice ridden) at Redcar as 3-y-o: suited by 7f: acts on good to firm going: sold 1,300 gns Ascot July Sales: resold 1,200 gns Ascot September Sales. *W. Carter.*

DENTICULATA 2 ch.c. (Apr 17) Domynsky 110–Melody Song 74 (Saintly Song 128) [1990 a8g] 15,500Y: sixth reported foal: half-brother to 1m winner Moon Melody (by Silly Season), 4-y-o sprinter Ayodessa (by Lochnager) and another winner abroad: dam 2-y-o 5f and 6f winner: tailed-off last of 11 in claimer at Southwell in December. *Ronald Thompson.*

DEPLOY 3 b.c. Shirley Heights 130–Slightly Dangerous (USA) 122 **131** (Roberto (USA) 131) [1989 8v3 1990 10.6f* 12f2 12d* 12g2]

Deploy's season was as regrettably short as Quest For Fame's and Sanglamore's, and unlike them he won't be in training at four; but at least he got the opportunity to show why he'd been regarded as the pick of the stable's Derby entrants in the early-spring. The opportunity came in the last of his five races, in the Budweiser Irish Derby at the Curragh in July. He'd been supplemented at a cost of IR £60,000 in a serious attempt to win; not merely, as some thought, to act as pacemaker for Quest For Fame. Having set off in front, he managed to stay there until Salsabil produced the better turn of foot going into the final furlong, and he continued to battle on so well under pressure that he finished within a length of the winner, well clear of the rest led by Belmez. This performance made Deploy a leading contender for the St Leger. He was due to have a preparatory run for Doncaster in the Great Voltigeur Stakes at York in August (having been withdrawn from the Geoffrey Freer Stakes at Newbury a few days earlier on account of anticipated firm ground) when he strained a near-fore tendon on the gallops, bringing about his retirement.

In 1991 Deploy will stand at his owner-breeder's Eagle Lane Farm, near Newmarket, at £5,000 with the October 1st concession. The fee reflects Mr Abdulla's policy of pricing nominations low in order to help his stallions to

Mr K. Abdulla's "Deploy" (P. Eddery)

a good start at stud. It could justifiably have been higher for a colt of Deploy's record and breeding, though admittedly there is a strong element of 'what might have been' about his career and some disagreement about the value of the Irish Derby form. For our part we have given him full credit for running Salsabil to three quarters of a length, making the assumption that the modest early gallop contributed to the proximity of those relatively ordinary animals down the field. Whatever view is taken of the form, Deploy clearly improved substantially on his previous efforts as a three-year-old—wins in a maiden race at Haydock in April and a minor race at Leicester in June, and a close second to Private Tender in another minor race at Newmarket in between. He finished lame on the firm going at Newmarket so wasn't risked on it again, as a result missing the King Edward VII Stakes at Royal Ascot. The ground was good to soft at Leicester, where he gave weight and a decisive beating to Down The Flag and Beauchamp Express, in the style of a developing stayer.

		Mill Reef	Never Bend
Deploy	Shirley Heights	(b 1968)	Milan Mill
(b.c. 1987)	(b 1975)	Hardiemma	Hardicanute
		(b 1969)	Grand Cross
	Slightly Dangerous (USA)	Roberto	Hail To Reason
	(b 1979)	(b 1969)	Bramalea
		Where You Lead	Raise A Native
		(ch 1970)	Noblesse

The smallish, well-made Deploy possesses an excellent pedigree. The distaff side has been kept to the fore in recent years through Rainbow Quest and Warning, both grandsons of Where You Lead; it had already earned a place in the history of the Oaks through the efforts of Noblesse (the ten-length winner in 1963), and Where You Lead and Slightly Dangerous (each of them second in their day). The top-class miler Warning (by Known Fact) is a half-brother to Deploy; he was the dam's second foal, after the very useful middle-distance colt Timefighter (by Star Appeal); the third foal, Deploy's brother Highly Dangerous, was in training at Beckhampton but a catalogue of set-backs kept him off the course and he was sold for 21,000 guineas at Newmarket in October. *R. Charlton.*

DEPOSKI 2 ch.c. (Jan 23) Niniski (USA) 125–Deposit 73 (Thatch (USA) 136) **66**
[1990 8g⁵ 8g] sparely-made, unfurnished colt: second foal: dam second at 6f at 2 yrs won in West Indies: around 4 lengths fifth of 16, staying on well, in maiden at Kempton in September: never able to challenge in similar event at Newmarket following month: will stay 1¼m. *M. R. Stoute.*

DEPUTY TIM 7 ch.g. Crofter (USA) 124–Kindle (Firestreak 125) [1989 8.2v* **69**
9f* 8m² 8.2g 7.6h 7m* 8m 7.5m 7f 8s⁵ 9f 7m 1990 a7g 8f 8m² 8.2f 9g 10f⁵ 10m⁴ 11m⁴ 8.2g* 8.2g* 8f a7g² a8g 10.4g⁵ 8.2m 8m* 8.2d* a8g⁵ a7g⁶] neat gelding: carries plenty of condition: moderate mover: modest handicapper: won at Nottingham and Hamilton (making virtually all) in July and Pontefract and Nottingham in October: ridden by 7-lb claimer, never placed to challenge nor knocked about final outing: best form at around 1m: acts on any going: best without blinkers: best ridden up with pace: has hung left: tough. *R. Bastiman.*

DERAILED 3 ch.g. Siberian Express (USA) 125–Lasani (FR) (Appiani II 128) **—**
[1989 NR 1990 a8g 10m 12.5f 8f 8.3g 7m 17.6m² a12g⁵ 12.5m 12d] lengthy, angular gelding: fourth foal: half-brother to poor and headstrong maiden Proposal (by Sharpo): dam 1m to 10.5f winner in France: poor form, including in sellers: mulish at stalls on third start: blinkered sixth: trained first 3 by M. Johnston: has joined R. Holder. *C. A. Austin.*

DERBY CUP (USA) 2 ch.c. (Feb 2) Raise A Cup (USA)–Pretty Derby (USA) **68**
(Master Derby (USA)) [1990 5m 5g 5f² 6m⁶ a6g³ a8g* 8d 10.6s 8d a8g² a7g⁵] $22,000Y: compact, good-quartered colt: moderate mover: first foal: dam never ran: ridden by 7-lb claimer, won 18-runner seller (bought out of W. O'Gorman's stable 7,500 gns) at Southwell by ½ length: better suited by 1m than shorter: easily best form on all-weather, and unsuited by soft ground on turf: blinkered eighth outing. *M. W. Easterby.*

DERECHEF 3 ch.f. Derrylin 115–Songe d'Inde (Sheshoon 132) [1989 7.3v 1990 **—**
7m⁴ 8g 7g 7.6d 8m 11.5g] rangy, unfurnished filly: little worthwhile form after about 10 lengths fourth to Hasbah in minor event at Leicester in May: should stay at least 1m. *T. Thomson Jones.*

DERISBAY (IRE) 2 b.c. (Apr 22) Gorytus (USA) 132–Current Bay (Tyrant — (USA)) [1990 6m 7m 7d 10s] 4,100Y: big colt: has plenty of scope: sixth foal: brother to useful 3-y-o winning sprinter Katzakeena, closely related to 1985 French 2-y-o 7f winner Lac Aux Dames (by Kings Lake) and half-brother to another winner in France: dam won from 6.5f to 1m in Italy and France: bit backward, poor form in varied events. *P. J. Arthur.*

DEROUET (IRE) 2 b.g. (Apr 22) Tate Gallery (USA) 117–Gay Surrender 70 (Sir 55 Gaylord) [1990 6f⁴ 7g 5f² 6m² 6m⁶ 6m] IR 7,800F, 26,000Y: smallish, lengthy gelding: half-brother to a winner in Canada: dam 10.2f winner, is half-sister to good-class middle-distance stayer Riverside (dam of Riverqueen) and good 6f to 1¼m winner Double-U-Jay: plating-class performer: hung left and looked difficult ride fourth and final starts, running poorly final one: should stay 7f: blinkered final 2 starts: sold 2,700 gns Newmarket Autumn Sales. *D. Morley.*

DERRING PET (IRE) 2 b.rg. (Mar 30) Daring March 116–Mummy's Whistler — (Mummy's Pet 125) [1990 5m] leggy, quite good-topped gelding: fourth reported live foal: half-brother to 7f seller winner Pokey's Pet (by Uncle Pokey): dam poor plater: bit backward, slowly away and always behind in maiden at Beverley in September: sold 1,100 gns Doncaster September Sales. *W. W. Haigh.*

DERRY LOVE 3 gr.f. Derrylin 115–Rough Love 105 (Abwah 118) [1989 NR 1990 — 8f 7.2d 7m] fourth reported foal: half-sister to 1m winner See No Evil (by Bold Lad): dam sprinter: well beaten in minor events and maiden, twice slowly away. *L. J. Barratt.*

DERRY REEF 3 b.f. Derrylin 115–Ballyreef (Ballymore 123) [1989 7d 6s 1990 46 8m 8.2f 10.6f⁶ 12m² 12m³ 16m 14g³] good-topped filly: moderate mover: plating-class performer: effective at 1½m to 1¾m (stumbled and unseated rider over 2m): acts on good to firm ground. *Mrs J. R. Ramsden.*

DERRY RHYTHM 5 b. or br.g. Derrylin 115–French Music (French Beige 127) — [1989 7m 8h 10m 10.1m 10f³ 12.2f a14g 1990 a12g] workmanlike gelding: carries plenty of condition: poor performer: faced very stiff task in Southwell claimer in November: stays 1¼m: acts on firm and dead going: tends to get on toes. *P. Burgoyne.*

DERWENT WATERS 3 b.g. Lomond (USA) 128–Jemarjo Pet (USA) (Peter — Peter) [1989 NR 1990 8g 10f⁵ 12f 10g] 86,000F, IR 100,000Y: lengthy, good-topped gelding: half-brother to several winners, notably good-class sprinter Orojoya (by Gold Stage) and very smart American colt Bywayofchicago (by Well Mannered), successful at up to 9f: dam won at up to 1m: plating-class maiden: carried head high and tailed off as if something amiss in June handicap final outing: should prove best at up to 1¼m. *T. Thomson Jones.*

DESERT DIRHAM (USA) 2 ch.c. (Mar 11) Blushing Groom (FR) 131– 79 p Capricorn Belle 115 (Nonoalco (USA) 131) [1990 7m*] tall colt, rather unfurnished: has scope: good mover: first foal: dam won from 6f (at 2 yrs) to 9f (in USA): coltish, green and easy to back, won maiden at Newmarket in August by a length from Paris of Troy, leading 2f out and pushed along firmly: will stay 1m: sure to improve. *M. R. Stoute.*

DESERT FOREST 2 ch.c. (Feb 21) Hotfoot 126–Sequoia 87 (Sassafras (FR) 49 p 135) [1990 7g] 8,000F, 8,600Y: smallish, lengthy, rather dipped-backed colt: half-brother to several winners, including useful 7f and 1m handicapper Travelguard (by Nishapour): dam 2-y-o 6f winner: bit backward, slowly away, green and moderate headway 2f out when in mid division in 23-runner median auction at York in October: will improve. *J. M. P. Eustace.*

DESERT GEM 2 b.f. (Apr 3) Green Desert (USA) 127–Jem Jen 85 (Great 87 Nephew 126) [1990 6m³ 6.5g 8m] 44,000Y: big, good-bodied filly: has lots of scope: half-sister to several winners, including 11.5f winner Northern Moon (by Ile de Bourbon): dam 1¼m winner: progressive filly: never-dangerous ninth of 12 in Brent Walker Fillies' Mile at Ascot, best effort: better suited by 1m than 6f. *P. A. Kelleway.*

DESERT OF STARS (USA) 3 b.c. Desert Wine (USA)–Vesuvius (USA) 77 (Exclusive Native (USA)) [1989 NR 1990 10g⁴ 14g³] lengthy, good-bodied colt with plenty of scope: third foal: dam unraced: sire high-class performer at 1m to 1¼m: modest form in minor event (slowly away) at Nottingham and maiden (favourite but still green and wandered under pressure) at Redcar in June: lacks turn of foot, and will be suited by test of stamina. *M. R. Stoute.*

DESERT PALM 5 b.m. Palm Track 122–Diascia (Dike (USA)) [1989 NR 1990 — 15.5f] leggy, lengthy mare: winning plater (visored) as 3-y-o: 50/1, tailed off in amateurs handicap at Folkestone in September: stays 1¾m: acts on good to firm going: winning claiming hurdler in October. *R. J. Hodges.*

DESERT SPLENDOUR 2 b.c. (Jan 30) Green Desert (USA) 127–Lost 95 Splendour (USA) (Vaguely Noble 140) [1990 5g³ 5m⁴ 7g³ 7m 7g² 7m* 7m* 6d 8v] robust, useful-looking colt: fifth foal: half-brother to 1989 2-y-o 5f and 6f winner Tadeus (by Final Straw) and 2 other winners, including 1m and 1¼m winner Count Nulin (by Pas de Seul): dam unraced daughter of Roussalka, a sister to Our Home and half-sister to Oh So Sharp: fairly useful performer: looked tremendously well when winning nurseries by wide margin at Ascot and Newmarket in October: creditable seventh of 19 to Chipaya in Racecall Gold Trophy at Redcar: soundly beaten in Gran Criterium at Milan in November: should be suited by 1m: acts on good to firm and dead going: strong-running type. *C. E. Brittain.*

DESERT SUN 2 b.c. (Mar 21) Green Desert (USA) 127–Solar 120 (Hotfoot 93 P 126) [1990 7s*]
    Although he finished champion trainer for the sixth time in nine years Henry Cecil had a fairly quiet season on the two-year-old front, winning just twenty-two races despite having over a hundred juveniles under his care. The prolonged spell of dry weather undoubtedly played a significant part in keeping the total low, as Cecil rarely risks promising horses when the ground is very firm; and it was also noticeable that quite a few of those who did make the racecourse weren't so forward as one normally expects with two-year-old runners from Warren Place. However, as the ground began to ease towards the end of the season the stable introduced several horses who could pay to keep a close eye on in 1991—Hip To Time, an impressive winner at Nottingham, Sharp Imposter, who stormed home in a back-end maiden at Leicester, Volksraad and Perpendicular, and the strong, lengthy Green Desert colt Desert Sun who looked considerably above the average in winning his only start with plenty in hand. Desert Sun made his debut in a big field of maidens at Doncaster in October on the same day that his stable-companion Peter Davies gave Warren Place their sole two-year-old pattern race win of the season in the Racing Post Trophy. The opposition to Desert Sun amounted to nothing special, and most of them looked short of peak fitness. Still, there was a lot to like about the way Desert Sun saw them off. After displaying a long, round action to post he was soon travelling smoothly in front. He was shaken up and responded immediately once asked to quicken over two out, gradually forging clear under hands and heels to beat Saint Ciel by six lengths easing down with the favourite Straw Beret close up in third.

		Danzig	Northern Dancer
	Green Desert (USA)	(b 1977)	Pas de Nom
	(b 1983)	Foreign Courier	Sir Ivor
Desert Sun		(b 1979)	Courtly Dee
(b.c. Mar 21, 1988)		Hotfoot	Firestreak
	Solar	(br 1966)	Pitter Patter
	(ch 1973)	L'Anguissola	Soderini
		(b 1967)	Posh

    Desert Sun cost his connections 135,000 guineas at the Highflyer Sale. His sire Green Desert was a smashing racehorse—good looking, well bred, capable of high-class form at up to a mile and splendidly consistent. He looked an excellent stallion prospect on his retirement to the Shadwell Stud in 1987, and although it's early days there's no denying he's made a promising start. All told Green Desert had twenty-four runners from his first crop. Fifteen of them were successful at least once—a very high proportion, which also included a couple of other Cecil-trained horses in Sedair and Volksraad as well as the useful Irish filly Inishdalla—and although Bering ran him close Green Desert ended the year as the leading first-season sire judged on prize-money won in Britain and Ireland. Surprisingly, Green Desert achieved this without having a pattern winner. It'll be most surprising if he doesn't put that right in 1991. Desert Sun's dam Solar was one of the leading two-year-old fillies of 1975, when she won twice and finished a close third in the Cheveley Park Stakes. She wasn't such a force at three but showed very useful form at up to ten furlongs, and she's produced winners over a variety of distances, including the useful sprinter Cutler's Corner (by Sharpen Up) and the winning stayer Solamente (by High Line). Solar's dam L'Anguissola, a useful two-year-old who had a rather disappointing second season, has proved very successful as a broodmare. Besides Solar her offspring include the Portland Handicap winner Walk By and Smarten Up, a very smart sprinter on her day who recently returned to the fore as the dam of the top sprinter Cadeaux Genereux. Desert Sun is quite an imposing colt—just the type to go on—and the chances are he'll stay a mile. We'll get a better idea of how high he can go once he's taken on some stronger opposition, but for the moment suffice to say that he's a most interesting prospect, almost certainly capable of a good deal better than his one appearance at two permits us to rate him. *H. R. A. Cecil.*

DESERT VICTRESS (USA) 2 ch.f. (Mar 19) Desert Wine (USA)–Elegant Victress (CAN) (Sir Ivor 135) [1990 5m 6g⁴ 8g] lengthy filly: has plenty of scope: seventh foal: half-sister to several winners, including 1986 2-y-o 7f winner Sharp Victor (by Sharpen Up) and 1987 Breeders' Cup Juvenile fourth Flying Victor (by Flying Paster): dam sprinting half-sister to leading 1983 Canadian 3-y-o Northern Blossom: sire high-class 1m to 1¼m performer: easily best effort when 9 lengths seventh of 16, travelling strongly over 5f, to Clare Heights in maiden at Yarmouth in October: carrying condition in 4-runner minor event at York time before, first run for over 2 months: sort to do better at 3 yrs. *C. F. Wall.* — 70 p

DESERT WARBLER (USA) 3 ch.c. The Minstrel (CAN) 135–Thats The Reason (USA) (Bold Reason) [1989 NR 1990 7m a8g 9m] IR 22,000Y: unfurnished colt: fourth foal: dam, showed some ability in USA, is half-sister to Turf Classic winner Noble Fighter and Grand Prix d'Evry winner Vagaries: soundly beaten in maidens and claimer: sold to join N. Waggott 1,450 gns Newmarket September Sales. *D. J. G. Murray-Smith.* — —

DESIGNER STUBBLE 2 ch.g. (May 11) Final Straw 127–Miami Melody (Miami Springs 121) [1990 7f⁶ 6g² 6f² 7m⁵ 7g⁶] 3,400Y: fourth foal: dam placed over 6f and 1½m in Ireland: quite modest maiden: stays 7f. *G. B. Balding.* — 67

DESIRED LACE 2 b.f. (Mar 10) Grey Desire 115–Dragon Lace (Dragonara Palace (USA) 115) [1990 6f2 6g3 6g3 5f6 5g 5m6 5m 5v] leggy, lightly-made filly: has a quick action: second foal: half-sister to 3-y-o Northern Lace (by Northern Tempest): dam never ran: plater: easily best efforts first 2 starts: better suited by 6f than 5f: sold 540 gns Doncaster October Sales. *M. Brittain.* — 51 d

DESIRE'S DOUBLE 2 gr.c. (May 10) Grey Desire 115–Strip Fast 71 (Virginia Boy 106) [1990 5f4 6g4 6g3 6g4 5m4 5g4 7f 6g 6g 8f] 3,300Y: leggy colt: has round action: fifth foal: half-brother to winners abroad by Noalto and Ahonoora: dam won 4 races from 1m to 10.2f, one at 9 yrs: plating-class maiden: stays 7f: consistent. *M. Brittain.* — 50

DETOUR (IRE) 2 br.f. (Feb 1) Soughaan (USA) 111–Lost Path (Sovereign Path 125) [1990 a7g5 6f4 a6g* 7m* 7g a6g] IR 4,700F, IR 3,700Y: smallish, angular filly: half-sister to many winners here and abroad, including 1988 2-y-o 5f and 6f seller winner Ryan's Girl (by Tanfirion) and 13f and 1¾m winner Ivelostmyway (by Relko): dam of little account: quite modest performer: won 16-runner maiden at Southwell and 6-runner nursery at Goodwood: ran moderately last 2 starts: probably better suited by 7f than 6f. *W. J. Haggas.* — 68

DE VALERA 2 b.f. (Feb 20) Faustus (USA) 118–Dame du Moulin 81 (Shiny Tenth 120) [1990 6s3 6m6 6g 6g 8d 7s] 3,600F, 5,000Y: workmanlike filly: has a round action: second foal: dam, 2-y-o 7f winner, is half-sister to useful middle-distance fillies Rollrights and Rollfast: third of 5 in maiden at Hamilton in May, only form: sweating final start. *W. Bentley.* — 41

DEVA'S GEM 2 b.f. (Apr 15) Green Ruby (USA) 104–Deva Rose 80 (Chestergate 111) [1990 5f 5g] workmanlike filly: has scope: half-sister to several winners, including 3-y-o 5f winner Eager Deva (by Lochnager) and fair sprinter Rosie Dickens (by Blue Cashmere): dam won 4 times at 5f: poor form in maidens at Catterick and Wolverhampton (swerved start) in autumn. *R. Hollinshead.* — 39

DEVILS DIRGE 4 b.f. Song 132–Devils Alternative 67 (Hotfoot 126) [1989 6s 5m4 5f3 5g2 5f2 5.3h2 5m5 6m2 5.3f3 1990 7f4 6m 6f 7f4 a11g 6h5] lengthy, sparely-made, angular filly: has a round action: plating-class maiden: probably stays 7f: acts on hard ground: blinkered final start. *G. A. Pritchard-Gordon.* — 53

DEVIL'S SOUL 2 b.g. (Jan 28) Faustus (USA) 118–Ragged Moon 72 (Raga Navarro (ITY) 119) [1990 6m] 20,000Y: neat gelding: second foal: dam won 1m — 57 p sellers: better for run, around 10 lengths eleventh of 15 in maiden at Salisbury in June: should improve. *R. Akehurst.*

DEVIOSITY (USA) 3 b.c. Spectacular Bid (USA)–Reinvestment (USA) (Key **64** To The Mint (USA)) [1989 NR 1990 10m 7m 9g3] $125,000Y: lengthy, good sort: fourth foal: half-brother to useful Italian 1m to 1¼m performer Lonely Bird (by Storm Bird): dam unraced half-sister to Posse: edgy, third of 7 at Ripon in July, first form in maidens: should stay 1¼m: very fractious in preliminaries on debut. *B. W. Hills.*

DIABLE AU CORPS (FR) 3 gr.c. Akarad (FR) 130–Dictia (FR) (Caro 133) **111** [1989 NR 1990 10g2 10g* 10g* 10.5g3 9d6] 120,000 francs (approx £11,000) Y: fifth foal: half-brother to a 9f winner in France by Iron Duke: dam French 1m to 1¼m winner: won maiden at Evry and Group 3 event at Frankfurt in April: 4 lengths third to Epervier Bleu in Prix Lupin at Longchamp then well beaten in Prix Daphnis at Evry in July. *J. E. Hammond, France.*

DIACO 5 b.g. Indian King (USA) 128–Coral Cave 79 (Ashmore (FR) 125) [1989 8f **67** 7.6m 8h6 8h4 7m3 7m2 7.6f2 8h4 7m2 7.6m6 1990 6g 7f 7m5 7g 7.6g5 7m3 6f6 8f* 8f* 7m 8.2d2] leggy, quite attractive gelding: usually looks very well: formerly disappointing, but in good heart in second half of year: dropped to selling company, won handicaps at Brighton in August (bought in 7,000 gns) and September (retained 6,200 gns): best at 1m nowadays: acts on hard and dead going: blinkered once at 3 yrs and fifth to seventh outings: has looked ungenuine: goes well with waiting tactics, particularly on switchback track, and for A. Munro. *M. A. Jarvis.*

DIADAD 3 ch.g. Doulab (USA) 115–Numidia (Sallust 134) [1989 5f4 5m6 5m4 5m4 **46** 5g5 5m 1990 5s 5f a5g6 a6g6 6g 5m6] sturdy gelding: carries condition: plating-class performer: faced stiff tasks in handicaps: likely to prove best at 5f: visored on reappearance: blinkered last 2 starts: has given trouble at stalls: sold 950 gns Doncaster August Sales. *F. H. Lee.*

DIAMOND BAY 3 b.f. Buzzards Bay 128§–Czar's Diamond 66 (Queen's Hussar — 124) [1989 5m 8m 8f 1990 11.7f] soundly beaten in maidens and minor event. *J. R. Bosley.*

DIAMOND BLUE 3 b.g. Dunphy 124–Tumble And Toss (USA) (Rough'n — Tumble) [1989 NR 1990 9f6 10.6s 8m6] IR 1,250F, 2,500Y: leggy gelding: half-brother to Irish 1½m winner Sinead's Princess (by Sun Prince), fairly useful 6f winner Sailor's Frolic (by Deck Hand) and numerous winners abroad: dam minor winner at up to 9f in USA: well beaten in maidens then auction event in the summer, though has shown signs of ability. *C. W. C. Elsey.*

DIAMOND CITY (USA) 2 b.f. (Mar 24) Mr Prospector (USA)–Honey's Flag **100** p (USA) (Hoist The Flag (USA)) [1990 7f* 7m2] $450,000Y: leggy, rather angular filly: has a roundish action: third foal: dam once-raced half-sister to dam of Preakness winner Aloma's Ruler: favourite, comfortable winner of maiden at Leicester in July: much better effort when 3 lengths second to Dartrey in £7,500 event at Newmarket over 2 months later, staying on really well without being knocked about: will be much better suited by 1m + : sure to win more races. *H. R. A. Cecil.*

DIAMOND CUT (FR) 2 b.c. (Apr 19) Fast Topaze (USA) 128–Sasetto (FR) (St **75** Paddy 133) [1990 7f3 7m6 8m5] 700,000 francs (approx £64,800) Y: half-brother to winners at up to 11f in France by Nice Havrais and Bikala: dam half-sister to Perfect Match and Kirchner: modest maiden: will stay 1¼m. *M. Moubarak.*

DIAMONDING (USA) 4 b.c. Diamond Shoal 130–Gwynn (USA) (Native **46** Dancer) [1989 10.5v 7d 1990 12h 12g 8g5 11.5d4 7g5 8m5 7f6 6g 8m] smallish ex-French colt: poor mover: half-brother to several winners in USA, including Creamette City (by In Reality), stakes winner at up to 1m: dam ran only twice: plating-class form at best at 4 yrs: stays 1m: has worn blinkers: changed hands 3,000 gns Doncaster June Sales: resold 1,150 gns Doncaster October Sales. *N. Tinkler.*

DIAMOND INTHE DARK (USA) 2 b.c. (Apr 14) Diamond Prospect **67** (USA)–Implicit (Grundy 137) [1990 a6g6 a6g6 5m3 6g a6g2 a5g5] angular, rather dipped-backed colt: brother to 3-y-o Diamond Sprite, fair miler Magic At Dawn and 2 winners in USA, and half-brother to 2 other winners: dam showed little ability: quite modest maiden: ran poorly when blinkered and sweating fourth outing: bred to stay beyond 6f. *S. G. Norton.*

DIAMOND PATH 4 ch.g. Morston (FR) 125–Glide Path 91 (Sovereign Path — 125) [1989 10g2 12f4 12m2 12m3 12g 10g3 1990 16.2f5 14f5 9m] strong gelding: has a quick action: fairly useful on his day as 3-y-o: well beaten in varied events in first half of 1990: stays 1½m: ran badly in visor: sweated freely final outing: doesn't find much: sold out of R. Boss's stable 25,000 gns Doncaster March Sales before reappearance. *N. Tinkler.*

DIAMOND SHOES (USA) 3 b.f. Diamond Shoal 130–Raise A Baby (USA) 91 (Raise A Native) [1989 7g² 1990 7m³ 10f* 8m⁴ 10m⁶ 10.2m³ 8g] strong, good-bodied filly: good walker: 6/4 on, won maiden at Salisbury in June: appeared to run very well when third of 4 to Cameo Performance in Newcastle listed race, moderately starts either side: needs further than 1m, and may well stay beyond 1¼m: acts on firm going: wore net muzzle last 4 starts. *G. Harwood.*

DIAMOND SINGH 3 b.c. Mansingh (USA) 120–Prime Thought 69 (Primera — 131) [1989 5d 5d⁴ 5g 6g 8.2g 1990 8v 11g 10g 14g 15.3g] rather unfurnished colt: poor mover: poor maiden. *J. S. Wainwright.*

DIAMOND SPRITE (USA) 3 b.g. Diamond Prospect (USA) 126–Implicit — (Grundy 137) [1989 7m² 7m³ 8m⁶ 8.2f 1990 8g⁶ 7.5g⁵ 8f⁴] dipped-backed, good-quartered gelding: moderate walker: good mover: quite modest maiden at best: last of 4 in July handicap final start: stays 1m: has twice sweated: sold 1,000 gns Doncaster October Sales. *J. Etherington.*

DIAMOND WIND (USA) 2 b.f. (Feb 2) Wind And Wuthering (USA) 132– 49 Diamond Oyster 72 (Formidable (USA) 125) [1990 5.3h⁵ 5d 6m³ 6h⁵ a7g⁵ 7f 7g⁶ 8m 8m³ 10m] leggy, sparely-made filly: has a round action: first known foal: dam maiden here at 2 yrs won at around 6f in North America: moderate plater: seems not to stay 1¼m: has run well for apprentice: inconsistent: sold 600 gns Newmarket Autumn Sales. *C. A. Cyzer.*

DIBLOOM 2 b.g. (May 5) Nomination 125–Tosara 84 (Main Reef 126) [1990 7m] — first foal: dam 1¼m and 10.2f winner, is half-sister to smart French stayer Chawn: always towards rear in maiden at Goodwood in September. *H. Candy.*

DIDDLEY (IRE) 2 ch.c. (Mar 18) Sandhurst Prince 128–Regal Rhapsody (Owen — Dudley 121) [1990 5f⁵] 5,000Y: leggy, angular colt: first foal: dam ran once at 3 yrs in Ireland: backward, well-beaten fifth of 7, moderate late headway after slow start, in maiden at Newmarket in May: sold 500 gns Newmarket September Sales. *N. A. Callaghan.*

DIET 4 b.g. Starch Reduced 112–Highland Rossie 67 (Pablond 93) [1989 8.2v 8g 76 8.2g 11m 8.2f³ 7m* 6f* 6f⁶ 7m² 6f 7g⁶ 7m 6g* 6m 6s 6s³ 6s 1990 6m⁶ 6v² 5m⁴ 6f⁵ 6m² 6m⁶ 5g 6m⁴ 6m⁴ 6g 5m* 6d 7d 6s³] angular gelding: carries condition: modest handicapper on his day: won at Pontefract in September: best over 6f or stiff 5f: acts on any going: usually visored: has hung under pressure: suited by forcing tactics: inconsistent. *J. S. Wilson.*

DIGRESSION (USA) 3 b.c. Seattle Slew (USA)–Double Axle (USA) (The Axe 110 II 115) [1989 7m² 7g* 8m* 1990 10m⁵ 12g] big, powerful, good-bodied colt: good walker and mover: put up smart performance to win 1m Royal Lodge Stakes at Ascot at 2 yrs: in need of race, took keen hold and hung right when about 5 lengths fifth of 6 to Razeen in moderately-run Predominate Stakes at Goodwood: ran badly in Ever Ready Derby at Epsom 2 weeks later, always behind: stays 1¼m: flashed tail at Ascot and Epsom: to race in USA. *G. Harwood.*

DIGS 2 b.c. (Apr 13) Doulab (USA) 115–Helcia 86 (Habitat 134) [1990 7m³ 6m* 6g² 84 6g³ 7.3g 8d] 17,500F, 18,500Y: sturdy colt: has a quick action: half-brother to several winners, including useful 1980 2-y-o 6f winner Chirk Castle (by Welsh Pageant) and 1¾m winner Talus (by Kalaglow): dam runner-up from 6f to 11.5f: fair performer: won maiden at York in July: ran well in nurseries next 2 starts: best form at 6f: possibly unsuited by dead ground: blinkered final start. *R. F. Johnson Houghton.*

DI MODA 3 ch.c. Buzzards Bay 128§–Diamond Talk (Counsel 118) [1989 NR 1990 — 10.1g 10.1g 12m] lengthy colt: brother to 1987 2-y-o 7f winner Buzzards Crest and half-brother to several winners, including fairly useful miler Corn Street (by Decoy Boy) and sprinter Pusey Street (by Native Bazaar): dam unraced: bit backward, always behind in minor events and maiden. *J. R. Bosley.*

DIMPLE STAR 3 b.g. The Brianstan 128–Hanovia Gold 72 (Yellow River 114) — [1989 5h⁶ 7m 1990 8g] leggy gelding: soundly beaten in seller and maidens: may well improve when returned to sprint distances: has joined Miss P. O'Connor. *S. Dow.*

DINNINGTON BUMBLE 3 ch.f. Miramar Reef 100§–Sandra's Secret 88 41 (Most Secret 119) [1989 7f 1990 7.5f 8m 10.2m 8g⁶ 12.2d⁶ 10m⁵ 8.2g] leggy, lengthy filly: plater: stays 1¼m: visored (led 1m) third start, blinkered final one: has carried head high and been awkward in preliminaries: sold to join D. Morrill 1,500 gns Doncaster October Sales. *R. M. Whitaker.*

DIRECTORS' CHOICE 5 b.g. Skyliner 117–Hazel Gig (Captain's Gig (USA)) **60** §
[1989 10f⁵ 10f 10g 1990 10d³] tall, leggy gelding: has a long stride: quite useful at 2
yrs: has deteriorated, but showed he retains some ability in apprentice handicap at
Goodwood in October: winner over hurdles week later: stays 1¼m: acts on any
going: blinkered 4 times, including at Goodwood, visored once: ungenuine. *W.
Carter.*

DIRECT SOURCE 2 b.f. (Feb 19) Noalto 120–Love Unspoken 54 (No Mercy **40**
126) [1990 6f 5m 5.3h 5f 7m 6g a6g⁶ a5g] plain filly: has a round action: sister to 3-y-o
Granitobi and half-sister to winners in Italy and Scandinavia by Absalom: dam
showed form only at 5f: poor maiden: ran well in blinkers penultimate outing. *A.
Moore.*

DISCORD 4 b.g. Niniski (USA) 125–Apple Peel 109 (Pall Mall 132) [1989 8s⁵ 6d —
11m* 11m 13.3g* 1990 8.3m⁶ 14g] tall gelding: modest winner at 3 yrs: shaped well
over inadequate trip on reappearance, then never a threat in Tote Ebor at York
(reportedly injured near-fore) 3 weeks later: stays 13.3f well: best efforts on a sound
surface. *W. Hastings-Bass.*

DISCOVER GOLD 9 br.g. Junius (USA) 124–More The Perrier (Rarity 129) **35**
[1989 NR 1990 8f³ 7d] poor handicapper: best at 7f or 1m: acted on any going:
blinkered once: dead. *K. S. Bridgwater.*

DISK MAKER 5 b.g. Crooner 119–Sirette 42 (Great Nephew 126) [1989 NR 1990 **58**
10m⁴ 11.7f⁶ 10m³ 12f* 12m⁴ 12m* 10f³ 12f² 12m] neat gelding: improved
handicapper: favourite, won at Folkestone in June and July: ran well in amateurs
race next outing: stays 1½m: acts on firm going: sweated on reappearance: usually
apprentice ridden. *R. Curtis.*

DISMISS 5 b.m. Daring March 116–Sweet Jane 59 (Furry Glen 121) [1989 9v³ **85**
10s* 8s⁵ 12m 10m² 10f 10g² 1990 10g³ 10m⁴] tall, leggy mare: fair handicapper:
creditable third to Starlet in valuable event at Epsom in April: not seen out after
following month: suited by 1¼m: acts on good to firm and soft going: has won for
apprentice: well below form when sweating and edgy. *R. V. Smyth.*

DISSONANT (USA) 4 ch.g. Diesis 133–Nashualee (USA) (Nashua) [1989 8d² **94**
10.6s² 10f⁴ 10m² 10g⁶ 1990 10m 10m² 10f³ 10m⁶] good mover: fairly useful
handicapper: apprentice ridden, ran creditably second to fourth outings, edging left
and demoted last of them: stays 1¼m: acts on any going: has sweated. *H. R. A. Cecil.*

DISTANT RELATION 5 b.m. Great Nephew 126–Perchance 77 (Connaught —
130) [1989 12g 19g 16g a13g 1990 17.1f⁶ 16m 16.5f] lengthy mare: bad mover: won in
French Provinces and Jersey: well beaten in varied events on flat in Britain: stays
11f: unsuited by firm going: often blinkered: bandaged at 5 yrs: successful 4 times
over hurdles in 1989/90. *K. O. Cunningham-Brown.*

DISTANT RELATIVE 4 b.c. Habitat 134–Royal Sister II (Claude) [1989 **128**
7g* 8m³ 7f³ 8g* 7.3g* 8m* 8m³ 7m* 1990 8m² 8m³ 8d² 8f* 8g³ 8g* 8m²]
'Riding Distant Relative is like opening a bottle of champagne: you have
to shake him up to make him fizz, but once you do he explodes'. Jockey
Michael Hills's words seemed more apt than ever in the latest season as
Distant Relative came with a late surge to win both the Sussex Stakes and the
Emirates Prix du Moulin, two of Europe's most prestigious prizes over a mile.
Unfortunately for Hills, he wasn't the one who got to pop the cork. By
Goodwood in August, he'd lost his stable retainer, and the mount on Distant
Relative went to Carson in the Sussex Stakes; to Pat Eddery after that. The
ride had belonged to Hills throughout Distant Relative's three-year-old
career, and in the colt's first three races at four, in each of which he'd reached
a place, finishing second to Safawan in the Lockinge Stakes at Newbury in
May, third behind Markofdistinction in the Queen Anne Stakes at Royal
Ascot, and second to Zoman in the Phoenix International at Phoenix Park.
Distant Relative's three-quarter-length defeat by Zoman, conceding the
three-year-old 11 lb from weight-for-age, was a particularly good effort,
but he started only third favourite in a field of seven for the Sussex Stakes.
The St James's Palace Stakes winner Shavian was made favourite at 100/30
after his stable-companion Chimes of Freedom had been withdrawn earlier in
the day due to the prevailing ground. Green Line Express, who'd been beaten
three lengths into second by Zilzal in the same race twelve months earlier,
was second best at 7/2, with Zoman at 5/1, the once-raced Lord Charmer 7/1,
Great Commotion at 15/2 and Call To Arms at 50/1. Distant Relative looked

Sussex Stakes, Goodwood—
Green Line Express is runner-up for the second successive year
as Distant Relative keeps on well; Shavian (centre) takes third

particularly well in the paddock at Goodwood, as he tended to throughout his career, and moved poorly to post, which was also a trait of his. He gave a typical performance in the race, too, starting slowly and soon getting behind even though his jockey scrubbed him along from the stalls. He was still last turning for home, where Shavian continued to set a strong pace tracked most closely by Green Line Express, but so well did he quicken on the inside that from being a good six lengths down three furlongs out he was almost two lengths clear inside the final hundred yards. Green Line Express rallied near

Emirates Prix du Moulin de Longchamp—
Distant Relative gets up in the final strides from Linamix,
with Priolo in close attendance

the finish but Distant Relative held on by three quarters of a length with Shavian a length further away, and the remainder another seven lengths or more adrift.

The Sussex Stakes, Goodwood's only Group 1 race, went unsponsored in the latest season, much of the added prize money, which for the previous six years had been put up by the Swettenham Stud, having to come instead out of racecourse coffers, though the Levy Board did grant £40,000 towards a total of £150,000. By contrast, Longchamp's Emirates Prix du Moulin, one of France's two most important mile races, enjoyed Arab sponsorship for the first time. As a horserace, it was a virtual rematch of the other, the Prix du Haras de Fresnay le Buffard Jacques Le Marois, run at Deauville three weeks earlier, the first three from Deauville, Priolo, Linamix and Distant Relative, all renewing rivalry. Priolo had run on most strongly over the straight mile at Deauville, winning by half a length from his stable-companion Linamix, the winner of the French Guineas. Distant Relative, who again got behind early on, eventually quickened so well that he led briefly in the centre of the track at the distance, but he couldn't sustain his run, and was beaten a neck for second. There was again little between the trio at Longchamp, but on the different type of track Distant Relative was able to turn the tables. With Reinstate doing a good job as pacemaker for the Boutin-trained pair, the six runners were soon strung out in single file. Linamix raced in second followed immediately by the outsider Pole Position, while Distant Relative, once again, had to be niggled along to stay in touch. He was under much stronger pressure early in the straight, and for long enough didn't look as though he'd get on terms, as Linamix went into a two-length lead, but he responded with tremendous courage to what's come to be known as the full Eddery treatment, and headed Linamix on the post as Priolo finished well to be under a length behind in third. Eddery again took the mount on Distant Relative in the Queen Elizabeth II Stakes at Ascot's Festival of Racing later in the month. The colt again found himself well behind early on, but in a very strongly-run race both he and Markofdistinction came surging through in the closing stages. In a ding-dong battle, Markofdistinction proved the stronger by a length, but Distant Relative finished eight lengths clear of Green Line Express in third and lost no caste in defeat.

Distant Relative (b.c. 1986)	Habitat (b 1966)	Sir Gaylord (b 1959)	Turn-To
			Somethingroyal
		Little Hut (b 1952)	Occupy
			Savage Beauty
	Royal Sister II (b 1977)	Claude (b 1964)	Hornbeam
			Aigue-Vive
		Ribasha (b 1967)	Ribot
			Natasha

Distant Relative was set to renew rivalry with Markofdistinction, and Priolo, in the Breeders' Cup Mile but a recurrence of an old injury while exercising on the course on the morning of the race forced his withdrawal, and it was announced shortly afterwards that he'd been retired to the Whitsbury Manor Stud in Hampshire at a fee of £6,000. Sons of his sire Habitat, who died in 1987, haven't always made the expected impact at stud, and none has yet come close to emulating his sire, who has claims to being one of the most successful European-based stallions of the modern era. In the latest season he overtook Mill Reef as the leading sire in terms of cumulative money won in Great Britain and Ireland. Habitat's influence was generally for speed, and among his regular flow of pattern race winners were Marwell, Habibti, Double Form and Sigy, all of whom were successful in the Prix de l'Abbaye. There's stamina on the maternal side of Distant Relative's pedigree. His dam, whose only other winner so far is Lightning Thunder (winner of a ten-furlong seller in the latest season), was successful in eight races, seven in Italy and a mile-and-a-quarter apprentice handicap in Ireland. Her half-sister Ribarbaro was second in the Chester Cup and won races from a mile and a half to two miles. Another of Natasha's granddaughters Arkadina (by Ribot and hence closely related to Ribasha) is the dam of Irish St Leger winner Dark Lomond, whilst Arkadina's brother Blood Royal won the Jockey Club Cup and has proved a strong influence for stamina as a stallion. This is also the family of

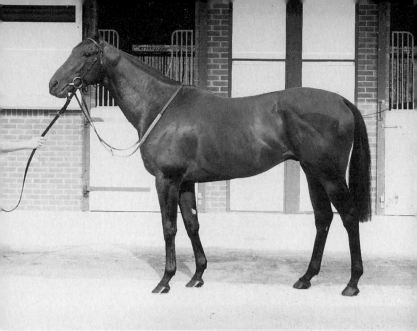

Mr Wafic Said's "Distant Relative"

the good two-year-old Mukaddamah, whose dam Tash shares the same grandam as Distant Relative's dam Royal Sister II. A yearling colt by Last Tycoon out of Royal Sister made 360,000 guineas at the Newmarket Highflyer Yearling Sales in October, and will be a two-year-old in training with Stoute in 1991. Distant Relative won a maiden over six furlongs as a two-year-old but raced exclusively over seven furlongs and a mile at three and four. He won a handicap at Newmarket on his reappearance at three, but raced only in pattern races afterwards and was never out of a place in fourteen further starts, a remarkable record. He won eight of his eighteen races in all, including the Phoenix International, the Beefeater Gin Celebration Mile at Goodwood, the Gardner Merchant Hungerford Stakes at Newbury and the Bisquit Cognac Challenge Stakes at Newmarket at three, when he also finished third behind Shaadi in the Irish Two Thousand Guineas. As his record suggests, the strong, lengthy, useful-looking Distant Relative was a most genuine and consistent colt and, though he often needed to be ridden along early on, he could produce a fine turn of foot. He did most of his racing on a sound surface but his performance against Zoman in Ireland suggests he acted equally well on dead going. He was a great credit to his trainer. *B. W. Hills.*

DISTANT RULER 6 b.h. Indian King (USA) 128–Faraway Places (Flair Path 122) [1989 5s 5f 5f5 5g3 5g* 5f4 5g 5m 5f 5g6 1990 5g 5m 5m4 5m* a5g* 5m3 5m5] lengthy, good-topped horse: has a quick action: successful at Sandown (for fourth time) in claimer, making all, in May and Southwell in handicap over week later: suited by forcing tactics at 5f: acts on firm and dead going: occasionally blinkered, visored last 5 outings: needs plenty of driving: sold 3,100 gns Newmarket Autumn Sales. *C. R. Nelson.* **73**

DISTINCTLY NORTH (USA)   2 b.c. (Feb 2) Minshaanshu Amad (USA) **115**
91–Distinctiveness (USA) (Distinctive (USA)) [1990 5m* 5g⁴ 5m* 6f² 6m²
5g* 6m² 6d²]

Game and genuine, an honest tryer capable of taking on the best if not
quite up to beating them regularly, are remarks which might apply equally to
the smart sprinting two-year-old Distinctly North and his trainer Jack Berry.
Both were seldom out of the limelight in the latest season. Distinctly North
was easily the best horse in Berry's Moss Side Racing Stable in Lancashire,
and like most of his stable-companions was sent far and wide in search of
winning opportunities. He was a splendid advertisement for his trainer and
his methods, showing much better form at the end of a long campaign, during
which his physical condition often took the eye, than he had at its outset; and
at Doncaster in September he picked up a pattern-race success in the Flying
Childers Stakes. Berry himself had a marvellous season. He became the first
northern-based trainer since Dobson Peacock in 1932 to train one hundred
winners in a flat season, when Heaven-Liegh-Grey went in at Brighton in
August; he broke William Elsey's record, set in 1905, of a hundred and
twenty-four winners in a flat season by a northern-based trainer when
Sizzling Saga won at Catterick in October, and by the close of the turf year,
when his tally had increased to a hundred and twenty-seven, stood second
only to Cecil in the total number of winners trained in any flat season this
century. Moss Side's total was achieved with a collection of two-year-olds,
modest handicappers and selling platers. The two-year-olds have since been
largely dispersed to make way for the next crop, for racing youngsters is the
backbone of the operation. Distinctly North himself, who may have proved
difficult to place in Britain, was sold in the autumn and will continue his career
in the States.

By the time the Flying Childers came to be run Distinctly North had
already had five races, winning two of them, a maiden (in excellent style) at
Goodwood and a minor event at Sandown, finishing less than a length second
to Mac's Imp in two others, the Scottish Equitable Richmond Stakes at
Goodwood and the Heinz '57' Phoenix Stakes, but managing only fourth in the
Norfolk Stakes at Royal Ascot. Though his form at six furlongs read better
than that at five, his performance at Phoenix Park on his fifth outing, where he
and Mac's Imp showed terrific speed and had the Royal Ascot five-furlong
winners On Tiptoes and Gipsy Fiddler beaten soon after halfway, suggested a
return to five wouldn't greatly inconvenience him, and Distinctly North was
backed down to 6/4-favourite at Doncaster to give Berry only his second

Flying Childers Stakes, Doncaster—
the game and speedy Distinctly North holds off Mujadil (noseband),
Vintage Only and Line Engaged (rails)

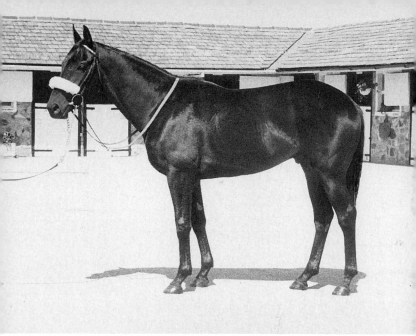

Mr R. E. Sangster's "Distinctly North"

pattern-race win in Britain, following that of Almost Blue in the Molecomb
Stakes two years earlier. Opposed by five others, including Mujadil, who'd run
him to a short head at Sandown, the Norfolk winner Line Engaged conceding 5
lb, the Gimcrack runner-up Vintage Only, and the St Hugh's Stakes winner
Dominio, Distinctly North, looking a little dull in condition, was soon disputing the lead then responded in typically generous fashion when brought
under pressure to hold off Mujadil by a length and a half with Vintage Only
three quarters of a length back in third. Three weeks later Distinctly North
proved once again that five and six furlongs come alike to him with a fine
second in the Newgate Stud Middle Park Stakes at Newmarket. Looking
much better in himself than he had at Doncaster, really taking the eye in
appearance, Distinctly North ran his usual type of race, setting out to make
all. Two furlongs from home it seemed as though he might hold on, but though
he battled on splendidly he was cut down virtually on the line and beaten half a
length by the French challenger Lycius. By now Distinctly North was booked
for the States, but with only 8-5 in the Racecall Gold Trophy at Redcar his
departure was delayed in order to take what seemed a first-rate chance of
ending his racing days in Britain on a lucrative winning note. In the end the
weather turned against him, and he wasn't able to produce his best form on
the dead ground that prevailed; having led Chipaya and the few others racing
on the far side, he was eased when the filly went beyond recall, ending five
lengths down in second place.

Distinctly North, a tall, strong, close-coupled colt, a good walker and
particularly fluent mover, was bought for 62,000 dollars at one of the
numerous 'breeze up' sales for two-year-olds in the States eight months after
being led out from the Ocala Breeders Yearling Sale unsold at just 12,000

		Northern Dancer (b 1961)	Nearctic
	Minshaanshu		Natalma
	Amad (USA)	Tappahannock	Chieftain II
Distinctly North (USA)	(b or br 1979)	(b 1971)	Princess Ribot
(b.c. Feb 2, 1988)		Distinctive	Epigram
	Distinctiveness (USA)	(b 1943)	Curtsey
	(b or br 1972)	New Love	Pardal
		(b or br 1963)	Stavroula

dollars. His sire Minshaanshu Amad, who'd been standing in Florida, has had an eventful career. A 700,000-dollar yearling, he was thrown in at the deep end as a two-year-old, finishing well beaten in the Royal Lodge Stakes and the Horris Hill on his only starts, turned temperamental as a three-year-old, deteriorated even further during the following season and ignominiously ended his career, still a maiden, by trying to savage an opponent's jockey. Being a son of Northern Dancer, however, he got an opportunity at stud, and though he hasn't proved popular at the sales—in 1989 the average price for one of his yearlings was less than 2,500 dollars—he's had plenty of winners, minor ones mostly. Distinctly North is to the best of our knowledge the fifth winner from his dam Distinctiveness, a half-sister to the American Derby winner Determined King and dam also of the useful 1980 two-year-old sprinter Steelinctive (by Steel Heart) and the useful 1989 American youngster Break The Mold (by Nodouble). Minshaanshu Amad seemed to find a mile and a quarter too sharp, and probably stayed two miles. Distinctly North looked first and foremost a sprinter in Britain. He may stay seven furlongs, or even a mile, on the sharp American tracks, though, and he seems just the type to adapt well. *J. Berry.*

DISTINCT NATIVE 3 ch.c. Be My Native (USA) 122–Miami Life (Miami 89 Springs 121) [1989 8g 1990 8g 12d 12g³ a12g* 12m²] strong, lengthy colt: won maiden (moved moderately down) at Southwell in August: placed in valuable handicaps at Royal Ascot and York, always front rank and rallying when second of 7 to Arzanni at York: will stay further: acts on good to firm ground: progressive. *R. W. Armstrong.*

DIVIDIA 3 b.f. Pas de Seul 133–Divina (GER) (Alpenkonig (GER)) [1989 5m⁶ 40 6m³ 5f² 6m 6m 8.2s⁵ 1990 7.5m⁵ 7g a7g 10m⁶ 10m⁵ 11m⁶] smallish, sparely-made filly: moderate mover: quite moderate plater: stays 1¼m: probably acts on any going. *M. Brittain.*

DIVINE BREEZE (IRE) 2 b.f. (Apr 25) Godswalk (USA) 130–Mother of The 39 Wind 82 (Tumble Wind (USA)) [1990 5.8f⁴ 5f 5m] leggy filly: moderate walker: sixth foal: half-sister to 9f and 1¼m winner Dark Heritage (by Scorpio) and a winner in Italy by Runnett: dam 2-y-o 7f winner: poor maiden: swished tail and looked reluctant under pressure final start. *D. J. G. Murray-Smith.*

DIVINE DANSE (FR) 2 ch.f. (Mar 20) Kris 135–Dance Quest (FR) 117 114 (Green Dancer (USA) 132) [1990 6g* 5g² 5.5g² 6d² 5g* 6m³ 7s³]
'Freddy's Revenge' is the title of Jack Sholter's follow-up to the cult horror movie 'A Nightmare On Elm Street'. There may be a similar sequel to a nightmare of an altogether different kind if Divine Danse and Freddie Head return for the One Thousand Guineas to Newmarket's Rowley Mile, scene of their hapless third in the Tattersalls Cheveley Park Stakes in October, after which the beleaguered Head was widely condemned for a badly-judged ride. Divine Danse was an unlucky enough loser of the Cheveley Park, traditionally a good pointer to the classic, for us to take the unusual step of rating her as if she'd won. Divine Danse, who looked in magnificent condition, was steadied leaving the stalls and soon travelling easily at the rear of the eleven-runner field but began to run into trouble at halfway where she was unable to switch to the outside as her rider intended. As Capricciosa and Imperfect Circle, the eventual first and second, went for home under two furlongs out Divine Danse was still back in eighth place and probably six lengths down at least; when finally switched back inside and given a tap with the whip she fairly flew through the final hundred and fifty yards, running on strongly into third just three lengths down. Given the ease with which she'd travelled through the race, the style in which she'd quickened when clear and the fact that the first

252

*Prix d'Arenberg, Longchamp—Divine Danse resumes winning ways,
at the chief expense of Polemic*

two were ridden out fully, we think it probable that had she been able to begin
her run sooner Divine Danse would have been the narrow winner.

Divine Danse started favourite for the Cheveley Park on the evidence of
her trainer's fine record in the race—she'd been successful previously with
Ma Biche in 1982 and Ravinella in 1987, both of whom went on to win the
Guineas—and her good form in France, where she'd won twice, including in
the Prix d'Arenberg at Longchamp on her most recent outing, and finished
second on her three other starts, all in pattern events. Divine Danse's run of
second places began in the Prix du Bois at Longchamp in July, less than a
month after winning a newcomers race at Chantilly, continued in the Prix
Robert Papin at Maisons-Laffitte, where she lost by a neck to Danseuse du
Soir, then ended in the Prix Morny Agence Francaise at Deauville where,
despite carrying her head a little high and tending to hang, she finished only a
length and a half behind Hector Protector. Unlike Capricciosa and Imperfect
Circle, who were retired for the year after the Cheveley Park, Divine Danse
was kept on the go, and she reappeared in the Criterium de Maisons-Laffitte
later in October. One of three second favourites behind the Grand Criterium
runner-up Masterclass, Divine Danse ran a creditable race on her first
attempt at seven furlongs, finishing third, three lengths and two behind the
colts Ganges and Prix Eclipse winner Crack Regiment, without ever
threatening to win the race. We wouldn't lay blame for her defeat at the door
of ground or distance: she was most probably beaten by better animals in what
was one of the most strongly-contested two-year-old races in France all year.

		Sharpen Up	Atan
	Kris	(ch 1969)	Rocchetta
	(ch 1976)	Doubly Sure	Reliance II
Divine Danse (FR)		(b 1971)	Soft Angels
(ch.f. Mar 20, 1988)		Green Dancer	Nijinsky
	Dance Quest (FR)	(b 1972)	Green Valley
	(b 1981)	Polyponder	Barbizon
		(ch 1974)	Second Thought

Divine Danse, a tall, angular filly who's a good walker but less fluent a
mover in her faster paces, having a rather round action, is by Kris, sire of four
other pattern-race winners in Europe in 1990, out of the Green Dancer mare
Dance Quest, a smart sprinter as a two-year-old in France who was kept to
sprinting, with some success, as a three-year-old. Dance Quest is a half-sister
to the 1984 Prix de la Salamandre winner Noblequest out of the smart filly
Polyponder, who won over seven furlongs and a mile as a three-year-old but
was at her best at four years over five furlongs when she won three pattern
events and came fourth in the Prix de l'Abbaye. Divine Danse will probably
stay a mile, but, knowing her stable, she may well be seen sprinting again in
the coming season. She has yet to race on very firm ground but acts on any
other. *Mme C. Head, France.*

253

DIVINE HEROINE 3 b.f. Valiyar 129–Pellinora (USA) (King Pellinore (USA) — 127) [1989 NR 1990 7f] fourth foal: half-sister to 1½m winner Peleus (by Irish River): dam 6 times unplaced in France, is half-sister to Park Hill winner I Want To Be: chased leaders 5f in maiden at Folkestone in April: sold 1,350 gns Newmarket July Sales barren to Music Boy. *A. A. Scott.*

DIVINE PET 5 br.g. Tina's Pet 121–Davinia 92 (Gold Form 108) [1989 6v 5s 6f* 74 5.8h⁴ 6m⁵ 6g 6f² 6h* 6m 5.8f⁶ 1990 6f 6f 5m⁴ 6d 6f² 6h⁶ 5g³ 5m³ 5d 6s⁴ 5.8d³] strong, good-topped gelding: carries plenty of condition: has been hobdayed: has a quick action: modest handicapper: finds easy 5f on sharp side and stays 6f: acts on any going except possibly heavy: sweating and on toes ninth start: usually gets behind. *W. G. R. Wightman.*

DIVING (USA) 2 b.c. (Mar 2) Silver Hawk (USA) 127–Challenging Stage (USA) 69 (Gold Stage (USA)) [1990 8g 7g⁵ 7m] $100,000Y: lengthy colt: has scope: poor walker: first foal: dam ran twice: quite modest maiden: should stay 1m: possibly needs an easy surface. *R. Charlton.*

DIXTON (USA) 2 b.c. (Apr 15) Dixieland Band (USA)–Cosmic Tiger (USA) (Tim 77 The Tiger (USA)) [1990 5g* 5d⁶ 6f⁶ 6f] $190,000Y: workmanlike, deep-girthed colt: has scope: moderate walker: first foal: dam good class at 2 yrs, won at up to 9f: modest performer: won maiden at Wolverhampton in May and nursery at Chepstow in June: ran poorly final outing: better suited by 6f than 5f: sold 7,400 gns Newmarket Autumn Sales. *R. Charlton.*

DIZZY (USA) 2 gr.f. (Mar 31) Golden Act (USA)–Bergluft (GER) (Literat) [1990 81 6g 6m 7m3] 12,500Y: rangy, workmanlike filly: has scope: moderate mover: half-sister to several winners abroad: dam successful in Germany: 3 lengths third of 18, keeping on well, to Noble Destiny in maiden at Leicester in October: will stay 1¼m. *B. W. Hills.*

DJANILA 3 ch.f. Fabulous Dancer (USA) 124–Happy River (Riverman (USA) 131) — [1989 7m⁵ 7f* a7g 1990 a10g] small, strong filly: won minor event at Ostend at 2 yrs: well beaten 3 starts here, sweating and on toes final one at 2 yrs. *G. G. Gracey.*

DOC LODGE 4 b.f. Doc Marten 104–Cooling 89 (Tycoon II) [1989 8.2g 9s² 8.2d³ — 7g⁴ a8g³ 1990 a7g a8g a8g] big, lengthy filly: quite modest maiden at best: soundly beaten in handicaps at Southwell at 4 yrs: best run at 7f. *R. D. E. Woodhouse.*

DOCTOR ROY 2 ch.c. (Mar 21) Electric 126–Pushkar (Northfields (USA)) [1990 70 p 6d 8f 8m 8d⁴] 1,650Y: strong, angular colt: has scope: fifth foal: half-brother to 3 winners, including one in USA and smart 5-y-o Eradicate (by Tender King), 6f to 10.5f winner later runner-up in Grade 1 company in USA: dam never ran: progressive form in maidens: fourth of 9, soon close up and unable to quicken, to Fair Average at Leicester in October: will be suited by 1¼m: likely to improve again. *N. Bycroft.*

DOCTOR'S REMEDY 4 br.g. Doc Marten 104–Champagne Party (Amber — Rama (USA) 133) [1989 7d 5f 8m⁶ 10f⁵ 10g⁴ 12f a8g 1990 8m a12g] sturdy, rather dipped-backed gelding: carries condition: has a round action: little worthwhile form in varied events on flat for long time: winning selling hurdler in April: has joined G. Moore. *M. Tate.*

DODGER DICKINS 3 gr.g. Godswalk (USA) 130–Sronica (Midsummer Night 53 § II 117) [1989 6m⁵ 5d 5d a6g⁶ a7g 1990 10.6f 8.2g 6m⁶ 8g* 8m⁴ 8.2m* 8m⁴ 8f⁶ 8f³ 10m 8.2m 12m 9f] workmanlike gelding: plating-class handicapper: won at Doncaster in June and Nottingham (on toes, coming from rear to win by 5 lengths) in July: below form subsequently: best at around 1m: acts on good to firm ground: ridden by apprentice in 1990: has carried head high: unreliable. *R. Hollinshead.*

DODGY 3 b.c. Homing 130–Beryl's Jewel 86 (Silicone 121) [1989 6f 7m 1990 8m⁶ 72 7.6g* 8m⁵ 8f* 7f² 8g 7.6d 7g] workmanlike colt: poor mover: modest performer: won claimers at Lingfield in June and Newmarket (gamely) in August: stays 1m: acts on firm ground: usually bandaged: tail swisher. *W. J. Haggas.*

DO-I-KNOW-YOU 4 b.f. Kafu 120–Galaxy Scorpio (Saritamer (USA) 130) [1989 40 5f5 5.1m⁶ 5f⁵ 6h³ 5g⁴ 5m 5g 6g 6g a6g a6g⁵ 1990 a6g 5.1f² a6g 5m 6m⁵ 5f⁵ 5.1m⁴ 5m] lengthy, good-quartered filly: moderate mover: plating class at best since 2 yrs: stays 6f: seems to act on any going: has won blinkers, hood and severe bridle: inconsistent, and seems temperamental: sold 1,500 gns Newmarket Autumn Sales. *C. N. Williams.*

DOIRE 2 gr.g. (Apr 9) Belfort (FR) 89–Derrygold §§ (Derrylin 115) [1990 7m³ 7g⁴ 57 § a6g⁵ 8.2g 8m 6g 7d a8g³] 5,500F, 16,500Y, resold 15,000Y: leggy gelding: third foal: half-brother to 3-y-o Vals Jewel (by Van Der Linden) and 1m winner Emsleys Choice (by Windjammer): dam fairly useful 6f and 7f winner at 2 yrs refused to race last 3 outings on flat, but won over hurdles: fair plater: best effort final start: virtually refused to race previous 2 outings: stays 1m: blinkered sixth outing: trained first 2 by D. Morley: carries head high: one to be very wary of. *T. Fairhurst.*

DOKKHA OYSTON (IRE) 2 b.c. (Mar 26) Prince Sabo 123–I Don't Mind 97 **91** (Swing Easy (USA) 126) [1990 5m⁴ 6g* 6d² 6m³ 6m³ 6g 6d] lengthy colt: shade unfurnished: has scope: eighth foal: half-brother to fair middle-distance stayer/good hurdler Swingit Gunner (by Gunner B) and 2-y-o sprint winners by Dublin Taxi, Decoy Boy and Music Boy: dam won 10 races at 5f and 6f: fairly useful performer: progressed after winning Hamilton maiden in June, best efforts in nurseries on fifth and sixth starts: stays 6f: acts on good to firm ground and dead: retained 10,000 gns Doncaster October Sales. *J. Berry.*

DOLLAR SEEKER (USA) 6 b.h. Buckfinder (USA)–Syrian Song (USA) **74 d** (Damascus (USA)) [1989 NR 1990 a12g³ a12g a11g³ a12g² a12g⁵ 12f 12m 13m³ 12.3g 11g⁵ a11g a11g 11d⁵ a12g⁶] compact horse: moderate mover: modest handicapper: tailed off in apprentice race seventh outing, mostly ran moderately afterwards: stays 13f: possibly best on an easy surface nowadays: usually blinkered or visored: wears bandages. *A. Bailey.*

DOLLY BOD 2 b.f. (Mar 22) Kabour 80–Argostone (Rockavon 120) [1990 5f⁵ 5s **—** 7g] 750Y: deep-girthed, close-coupled filly: good walker: half-sister to 3-y-o Just Go (by All Systems Go), 6f seller winner at 2 yrs, and 1m winner/successful hurdler Little Miss Horner (by Sit in The Corner): dam poor: well beaten, including in seller. *M. H. Easterby.*

DOLPOUR 4 b.c. Sadler's Wells (USA) 132–Dumka (FR) 117 (Kashmir II 125) **116** [1989 10m² 10m* 10.5m² 10.1d* 10g² 1990 10m* 10m⁵ 10.5g⁵ 12s 12d⁴] leggy, attractive colt: has quick action: high-class form at best late on as 3-y-o: won Gordon Richards EBF Stakes at Sandown in April by 2 necks from penalized Ile de Chypre and Batshoof: fair fifth, edging left, to In The Groove in 10.5f Juddmonte International Stakes at York: ran poorly after in Group 1 event at Baden-Baden and EBF Blandford Stakes at the Curragh: should stay 1½m: acts on good to firm and dead going: sent to D. Elsworth. *M. R. Stoute.*

DOMAIN 2 b.c. (Feb 20) Dominion 123–Prelude 85 (Troy 137) [1990 7g] first foal: **61 p** dam stayer: 7 lengths seventh of 17 to Dawning Street in maiden at Salisbury in October: will stay middle distances: should improve. *I. A. Balding.*

DOME LAWEL (USA) 2 b.f. (Mar 30) Blushing Groom (FR) 131–Par Excel- **79 p** lance (CAN) (L'Enjoleur (CAN)) [1990 6m² 5m*] sturdy, quite attractive filly: good walker: sixth foal: half-sister to Royal Lodge runner-up Khozaam (by Seattle Slew) and very useful 1986 2-y-o 6f winner Canadian Mill (by Mill Reef): dam won 9f

Gordon Richards EBF Stakes, Sandown—
Dolpour holds on from Ile de Chypre (left) and Batshoof (right),
with Observation Post fourth

Canadian Oaks: odds on, won maiden at Sandown in September easily by 3 lengths from Hidden Bay, quickening clear over 1f out and eased towards line: sure to do better, and is a useful sprinting prospect. *M. R. Stoute.*

DOMIANA 2 br.f. (Apr 13) Primo Dominie 121–Tatiana 59 (Habitat 134) [1990 6g 6d4] 18,000Y: first foal: dam maiden stayed 1m, is out of half-sister to Derby second Cavo Doro: 6 lengths fourth of 17 in maiden at Folkestone in November: will probably stay 7f. *M. Blanshard.* **55**

DOMICKSKY 2 b.c. (Mar 6) Dominion 123–Mumruffin 101 (Mummy's Pet 125) [1990 6d5 7f*] 13,500Y: fourth foal: half-brother to winning sprinter Grand Prix (by Formidable) and a winner in Malaysia: dam very speedy half-sister to very useful 1972 2-y-o Claudius: won maiden at Brighton in September by ½ length from Fast Run, leading 2f out looking likely to win in good style but needing to be hard ridden inside last: likely to prove at least as effective returned to 6f: sure to improve further. *M. J. Ryan.* **67 p**

DOMINICUS 4 b.g. Dominion 123–Pulcinella 95 (Shantung 132) [1989 12g 12s5 12.3m6 12f 10.5g 8s a11g a16g 1990 a13g 10.2f 11s 12.5f 12.5f 8.5g 12.5g5 12g4 9f4] smallish, lengthy gelding: fair at best, but has deteriorated considerably: stays 1½m: blinkered once, visored 3 times: sold out of M. Naughton's stable 5,000 gns Doncaster May Sales after seventh outing. *A. Mullins, Ireland.* **36**

DOMINIE STAR 2 b.f. (Mar 7) Primo Dominie 121–Starlust 79 (Sallust 134) [1990 6g 6g4] smallish, sturdy filly: fifth foal: half-sister to 1¼m winner Travel Storm (by Lord Gayle) and useful 6f and 1m winner Bronzewing (by Beldale Flutter): dam 2-y-o 5f winner, is half-sister to Welsh Pearl, very useful at up to 1m: created very favourable impression in autumn maidens at Thirsk and Newcastle, particularly when over 4 lengths fourth of 13 to Emilia Romagna, set plenty to do then running on strongly under considerate ride and giving impression might have won had run started sooner: sure to do lot better, and win a race. *R. M. Whitaker.* **60 p**

DOMINIO (IRE) 2 b.f. (Mar 27) Dominion 123–La Tuerta 96 (Hot Spark 126) [1990 5m4 5f2 5m* 6m3 5g* 5g5] rather leggy, workmanlike filly: has a quick action: second foal: half-sister to 3-y-o La Cabrilla (by Carwhite), fairly useful 5f and 6f winner at 2 yrs: dam sprinting half-sister to Cadeaux Genereux and quite useful stayer Brightner: much improved performer: won maiden at Salisbury in June and **92**

Strathclyde Stakes, Ayr—Dominion Gold looks a good prospect

Mr P. D. Savill's "Dominion Gold"

listed event (by 3 lengths from Almasa) at Newbury in August: respectable fifth of 6 to Distinctly North in Flying Childers Stakes at Doncaster: suited by 5f. *P. T. Walwyn.*

DOMINION GOLD   2 b.c. (Mar 20) Domynsky 110–Lush Gold 91 (Goldhill 125) **103** [1990 6g* 6d² 6s* 6m* 6d⁶ 6m³ 6g⁴ 6d⁶] unfurnished colt: has a round action: eighth foal: half-brother to 6f winner Eastbrook and 1988 2-y-o winner Grimston Again (both by Lochnager): dam 5f and 1m winner, is sister to very useful sprinter Lush Park: useful colt, successful in maiden at York in May, and £9,200 event at Haydock and Strathclyde Stakes (by 8 lengths) at Ayr in July: ran creditably in Prix Morny Agence Francaise at Deauville next start but moderately after: will stay 7f: acts on good to firm and soft ground. *M. H. Easterby.*

DOMINO DANCING   2 br.c. (Mar 16) Lidhame 109–Atlantic Air (Air Trooper **55** 115) [1990 5m⁴ 5f⁴ 5f* 5.3f] 20,000Y: strong colt: second foal: half-brother to a winner in Belgium; dam won in Italy: made all in maiden at Folkestone, showing much improved form, in August: ran poorly at Brighton after. *K. M. Brassey.*

DOMINO TEMPEST   2 b.f. (Apr 13) Northern Tempest (USA) 120–Penna **56** Bianca (My Swallow 134) [1990 7m 7g³ 7m⁶ 7m² 8m 7d⁶] 8,000Y: sturdy filly: fifth foal: half-sister to 3-y-o 1m winner Appelania (by Star Appeal) and 1988 2-y-o 6f winner Musianica (by Music Boy): dam won in Italy: plating-class maiden: probably stays 1m: visored final outing: has run well for claimer: sold 8,600 gns Newmarket Autumn Sales. *M. H. Tompkins.*

DOMINOE TURBO   2 gr.c. (Apr 15) Primo Dominie 121–Katysue 98 (King's **—** Leap 111) [1990 5g⁴] 7,000Y: sixth foal: half-brother to unreliable 3-y-o 1¼m and 11.5f winner Golden Daffodil (by Jalmood), 4-y-o 6f winner Pattie's Grey (by Valiyar) and Sinclair Lady (by Absalom), fairly useful 1986 2-y-o 5f winner, later temperamental: dam won 5 times over 5f at 2 yrs: around 7 lengths fourth of 9 in maiden auction at Carlisle in May: dead. *C. Tinkler.*

DOMINORA 2 b.f. (Mar 19) Dominion 123–True Nora 99 (Ahonoora 122) [1990 6g⁵ 6d³] lengthy, rather angular filly: first foal: dam 5f performer best at 2 yrs, is half-sister to Mac's Reef, very useful at up to 1½m, and daughter of half-sister to Goodwood Cup winner Tug of War: bit backward and green, shaped fairly well in autumn maidens at Folkestone and Leicester: will improve again. *C. R. Nelson.* **62 p**

DOMINO TRICK 2 b.f. (Apr 9) Primo Dominie 121–Tricky Tracey (Formidable (USA) 125) [1990 5m² 5m² 5g* 5g* 5g³ 5d⁴ 5f⁶ 5f 5m] small, sturdy filly: third foal: half-sister to French 1m winner Trickiest (by Try My Best): dam unraced: trained by J. Berry when successful in maiden auction (despite hanging left) at Epsom and seller (unimpressively at 7/4 on, then sold 13,000 gns) at Nottingham: ran well when in frame in nurseries afterwards: speedy: easily best form on an easy surface. *S. Dow.* **63**

DOMINUET 5 b.m. Dominion 123–Stepping Gaily 79 (Gay Fandango (USA) 132) [1989 5m 6h⁶ 6f 5m³ 6m 5m⁴ 1990 5m⁵ 5g⁴ 5m⁴ 5f⁵ 6g⁴ 5d* 5g² 5g* 5g² 6m⁴ 5m³ 5f 5m 5g⁶ 6s 5d] lengthy, quite attractive mare: formerly temperamentally unsatisfactory, but vastly improved in summer: won handicaps at Beverley and Ripon (apprentice ridden) in June: better effort when second to Bella Seville at Ayr, but didn't reproduce that form: best form at 5f on an easy surface: has often given trouble in preliminaries and is now taken down early. *J. L. Spearing.* **65**

DOMRUN 3 b.f. Runnett 125–Dominion Blue 66 (Dominion 123) [1989 5g⁵ 5m³ 5f⁶ 5m⁴ 6f² 6g 5g⁶ 5m² 6f⁶ 5v² 5m⁵ a8g 1990 6v 7m] leggy, close-coupled filly: has a roundish action: plater: below form in spring as 3-y-o: stays 6f: appears suited to plenty of give in the ground. *N. Tinkler.* **—**

DOM WAC 2 b.c. (Mar 28) Dominion 123–Noble Wac (USA) (Vaguely Noble 140) [1990 8.2d a7g⁴] robust colt: has scope: third foal: half-brother to 9f winner Fact Or Fiction (by Known Fact): dam unraced half-sister to Lear Fan: 20/1 and burly, around 9 lengths eighth of 15, one pace, to Hip To Time in minor event at Nottingham: below that form in maiden at Southwell later in autumn: looks sort to do better. *M. Bell.* **65 p**

DONATIST 4 b.c. Dominion 123–Kaftan 68 (Kashmir II 125) [1989 8v³ 8d⁴ 8g⁴ 9.2m* 1990 10f 10d] rather angular, quite attractive colt: has a quick action: won claimer as 3-y-o: tailed off in seller and apprentice handicap (blinkered) in autumn: should stay 1¼m: acts on good to firm and dead going. *Miss L. Bower.*

DONNA BOLD 3 b.f. Never So Bold 135–Domynga 85 (Dominion 123) [1989 6f 6m 1990 7m 7m 7m] sturdy, good-quartered filly: has a quick action: plating-class maiden: little worthwhile form as 3-y-o, blinkered in July handicap final start. *J. D. Bethell.* **—**

DONNA ELVIRA 4 b.f. Chief Singer 131–Countess Olivia (Prince Tenderfoot (USA) 126) [1989 8m³ 8.5m⁴ 7g² 1990 7f 6s 7.6m⁴ 7m⁶ 8d 7d⁶ 8v] quite attractive filly: has a quick action: fair maiden at best: best efforts at 7f: acts on good to firm going: bandaged near-hind fourth outing. *C. F. Wall.* **71**

DONNA KATRINA 3 gr.f. Kings Lake (USA) 133–Rocketina 57 (Roan Rocket 128) [1989 NR 1990 7g 6f] 41,000Y: smallish, good-quartered filly: half-sister to very useful 1983 5f and 6f winner Rocket Alert (by Red Alert), later successful over 7f in USA: dam won 1m seller: speed 4f when down in maiden at Newbury and minor event at Kempton in the spring: sold 1,300 gns Newmarket Autumn Sales. *R. Hannon.* **—**

DONNA LORENZA 3 br.f. Ahonoora 122–Lockwood Girl 81 (Prince Tenderfoot (USA) 126) [1989 5d 5f² 6f³ 6h³ 6h 8m⁵ 7g a7g⁵ a8g⁶ 1990 7f⁴ 9s 10f 8h] small, lengthy filly: quite modest form at best at 2 yrs: lost her form, blinkered and sweating on final 3-y-o start in May: stays 1m: acts on hard ground: has run respectably for 7-lb claimer: has joined C. Weedon. *R. Hannon.* **—**

DONNA MARTINI 3 b.f. Martinmas 128–Racine City 71 (Dom Racine (FR) 121) [1989 NR 1990 7g 7m 7m⁶ 8m 10f 8f⁵ 10f⁶ 12g] leggy filly: first foal: dam, best at 2 yrs over 5f, is out of half-sister to Irish Oaks second Tuscarora: plater: stays 1¼m. *M. P. Muggeridge.* **—**

DONNA VENEZIANA 3 b. or br.f. Ela-Mana-Mou 132–Camogie (Celtic Ash) [1989 NR 1990 10f⁴ a12g⁵ 11.7h²] IR 24,000F, IR 20,000Y: angular filly: moderate walker: half-sister to several winners, including very useful 5f and 1m winner Never A Lady (by Pontifex) and 1m winner Maestrette (by Manado): dam unraced daughter of leading 1963 2-y-o Mesopotamia: plating-class maiden: stayed 1½m: blinkered final start: sold 3,300 gns Ascot September Sales: dead. *J. L. Dunlop.* **47**

DONOSA 5 ch.m. Posse (USA) 130–Love Supreme 84 (Sallust 134) [1989 10f 6f 5f 1990 a8g a13g] probably of little account: visored once. *B. Richmond.*

DONOVAN ROSE 5 b.h. Song 132–Piccadilly Rose 63 (Reform 132) [1989 6v² 73
6v³ 6m 6g⁴ 6m* 6f⁶ 6h* 7m 6g⁴ 6m³ 7g² 7s⁴ 6s 6s 1990 6m² 6s⁴ 7f⁴ 6g* 6g⁵ a7g
6g⁴ 6g² 7g⁴ 7m⁴ 6h² 6m² 6m⁴ 7g] good-quartered, quite attractive horse: modest
handicapper: led final strides when winning at Hamilton in May: suited by 6f or 7f:
acts on any going: has won for apprentice: usually blinkered or visored: tough,
genuine and consistent: sold 8,600 gns Newmarket Autumn Sales. *J. Berry.*

DONT BEAT THE BABY 2 br.f. (Apr 23) Sulaafah (USA) 119–Molucella 52
(Connaught 130) [1990 6m⁵ 6g 6m 7g 8d⁶] small, good-bodied filly: first foal: dam
poor half-sister to smart miler Fair Season: poor form in varied races: probably
stays 1m: bolted going down for 7-lb claimer second start: very edgy final outing. *C.
R. Barwell.*

DON'T GIVE UP 2 b.c. (Apr 28) Nomination 125–Tug Along (Posse (USA) 130) 82
[1990 5f⁴ 5.3f* 5m⁶ 6m⁶ 6g 5.8f² 6m 7m 7m² 6m 6m] 5,000Y: workmanlike colt: has
a quick action: second foal: dam ran 3 times as 3-y-o: fair performer: won Brighton
maiden auction in April: best efforts ninth and tenth starts: had very stiff task final
outing: stays 7f: visored final 3 starts, sometimes blinkered before. *R. A. Bennett.*

DON'T PRESUME 2 b.f. (Mar 23) Pharly (FR) 130–Roxy Hart (High Top 131) 84
[1990 7f³ 6m* 7d 7d⁶] IR 22,000Y: strong, quite attractive filly: has scope:
half-sister to 3-y-o 7f winner Sawaki and fair 6f and 7.6f winner Farras (both by
Song) and 7f and 1m winner Super Lunar (by Kalaglow): dam unraced half-sister to
good sprinter Music Maestro and smart 1985 2-y-o Outer Circle: fair performer:
won maiden at Pontefract in August: very good eleventh of 20, never dangerous, in
Cartier Million at Phoenix Park: will probably stay 1m: edgy and bit reluctant to go
down on final start. *M. H. Tompkins.*

DONTWORRYABOUTIT 3 ch.g. Aragon 118–Spanish Chestnut (Philip of 43 §
Spain 126) [1989 5m⁵ 6m³ 7m⁶ 5f⁴ 5.3h⁶ 6g 7f a8g a8g a6g 1990 a7g⁴ a5g⁴ a8g 8m
5m² 6f] shallow-girthed, angular gelding: modest plater: 25/1 and visored, hung
badly left when good head second in non-selling handicap at Wolverhampton in
April: blinkered, swished tail and didn't run on later in month: stays 7f: acts on firm
going: twice blinkered: has twice bolted to post: best left alone. *Mrs N. Macauley.*

DOODLIN 6 ch.g. Matsadoon (USA)–Grankie (USA) (Nashua) [1989 8m 1990 —
10f] workmanlike, plain gelding: modest maiden at best: barely stayed 9f: acted on
good to firm going: bandaged only start at 6 yrs: dead. *M. D. Hammond.*

DOOLAR (USA) 3 b.c. Spend A Buck (USA)–Surera (ARG) (Sheet Anchor) 84
[1989 7g² 7m³ 1990 10m⁴ 10m⁴ 12.2m⁴ 10f² 10f^wo 10. 1m² 11.7m 12m] rather angular,
deep-girthed colt: has a powerful, round action: fair performer: walked over in
maiden at Folkestone in July: good second in minor event (made most) at Windsor,
easily best subsequent effort: seems best at 1¼m: sold to join P. Dalton 30,000 gns
Newmarket Autumn Sales. *P. F. I. Cole.*

DOREEN'S DELIGHT 4 ch.c. Bay Express 132–Elizabeth Howard 74 38
(Sharpen Up 127) [1989 NR 1990 8.5g 10h⁶ 9m 11d⁴ 9s⁵] strong colt: second foal:
dam middle-distance winner: showed a little ability in handicaps last 2 outings:
better suited by 11f than 9f: acts on soft going. *S. T. Harris.*

DORIMAR 3 b.g. Wolverlife 115–Ahoy Dolly (Windjammer (USA)) [1989 7.5f 9g 54
1990 9m 8g⁴ 7m⁵] leggy, rather unfurnished gelding: plater: from only when
33/1-tourth of 17 at Leicester in June: stays 1m: has joined K. Wingrove. *M. H.
Tompkins.*

DORIS GIRL 3 gr.f. Absalom 128–Targos Delight (Targowice (USA) 130) [1989 41
5g 5d 5f 5m² 5m 6g³ 6m 1990 7.5m 8m 6m 7.5d 0m 7f 9f² 9f⁵ 11m³ 10g] good-bodied,
workmanlike filly: fair plater at her best: stays 11f: acts on firm ground: sold 2,500
gns Newmarket September Sales. *W. J. Pearce.*

DORKING LAD 8 b.g. Cawston's Clown 113–High Voltage 82 (Electrify) [1989 65
6g 6f 6f⁵ 7g 6f 6m² 6m⁵ 6s⁵ 6m 6g³ 6g 6v 1990 6f 6f⁶ 6m 6m 6m⁶ 6d⁵ 6s⁶ 6s⁴ 6d 6s³
a7g] lengthy, dipped-backed gelding: has a round action: quite modest handicapper,
on the decline: suited by 6f: not at his best on firm going, acts on any other:
blinkered twice, sweating and edgy second time: sometimes apprentice ridden:
usually gets behind and is suited by strongly-run race. *M. H. Tompkins.*

DORMERS DELIGHT (IRE) 2 ch.c. (Mar 9) Hatim (USA) 121–Tuna 63 68
(Silver Shark 129) [1990 7g⁴ 7g⁵] IR 70,000Y: half-brother to numerous winners,
notably Carroll House (by Lord Gayle): dam poor maiden: shaped fairly well in
autumn maidens at Salisbury and Folkestone (stayed on from rear): may do better.
D. R. C. Elsworth.

DORSET DELIGHT 3 gr.f. Red Sunset 120–Tippity Top 56 (High Top 131)   —
[1989 7f a7g a6g 1990 8f 7h 8.5d 10.2f] smallish, workmanlike filly: no sign of ability;
blinkered and tailed off in selling handicap final start. *T. Thomson Jones.*

DORSET DUKE 3 b.g. Beldale Flutter (USA) 130–Youthful (FR) (Green Dancer   92 d
(USA) 132) [1989 6m* 6m* 1990 10m2 10.5g6 12m 10.5g6 9m 10m4 10.5g5] rather
leggy, attractive gelding: good mover: useful winner in July at 2 yrs and second of 3
to Theatrical Charmer in listed Newmarket Stakes: disappointed in 2 pattern events
then handicaps, taking keen hold and disputing lead 1m on final one: should prove
suited by further than 9f, and stay 1½m: particularly headstrong when blinkered
third start, wore severe noseband afterwards: sweating fifth start. *G. Wragg.*

DORSEY 3 ch.g. Music Boy 124–Miss Trilli 89 (Ardoon 124) [1989 NR 1990 6f 6m   54
6m3 6d6 6d a5g6] 8,000F, 2,200 2-y-o: small gelding: fourth foal: half-brother to 7f
winner Twiller (by Noalcoholic) and 12.2f claimer winner Princegate (by Absalom):
dam 5f handicapper: worthwhile form only when staying on in seller and claimer
third and fourth outings: should be better suited by 7f: blinkered and wore eyeshield
final start, visored previous three. *P. J. Feilden.*

DOSTOYEVSKY (USA) 3 b.c. Nureyev (USA) 131–Mairzy Doates (USA)   89
(Nodouble (USA)) [1989 7g 1990 8g3 9g* 12g3 10m4 8m] rather leggy colt: good
mover: fairly useful performer: won maiden at Ripon in June: ran well in minor
event at Leicester next start, making most at good pace: suited by middle distances:
best efforts on an easy surface: bandaged near-hind first 4 starts: sold 17,000 gns
Newmarket Autumn Sales. *M. R. Stoute.*

DOTTEREL (IRE) 2 b.g. (Apr 23) Rhoman Rule (USA)–Miysam 60 (Supreme   39
Sovereign 119) [1990 5m5 5f 6g] 7,200Y: leggy, sparely-made gelding: second foal:
half-brother to 1987 2-y-o 5f winner Tapestry Prints (by On Your Mark): dam 2-y-o
5f winner: sire 7f to 9f winner: poor form, including in sellers. *M. H. Easterby.*

DOUBLE DUTCH 6 b.m. Nicholas Bill 125–Dutch Princess 70 (Royalty 130)   100
[1989 16s* 16s2 14s* 14f6 16f4 16g3 16m* 18g* 16g4 1990 18f4 16g2 16m4 14m2 18g6]
lengthy, sparely-made mare: usually fails to impress in paddock: turns fore feet out:
much improved as 5-y-o, winning Tote Cesarewitch at Newmarket penultimate
outing: best effort in 1990 second to Barrish in handicap at Sandown in July: never
near to challenge when sixth to Al Maheb in Doncaster Cup 2 months later: suited
by testing conditions at 1¾m and stays 2¼m: acts on any going: often sweats: has a
turn of foot and best in strongly-run race: splendidly tough, genuine and consistent:
a credit to her trainer. *Miss B. Sanders.*

DOUBLE ECHO (IRE) 2 br.c. (May 2) Glow (USA)–Piculet 69 (Morston (FR)   66
125) [1990 6g 7g4 7m5] IR 53,000Y: compact colt: fifth living foal: half-brother to
3-y-o True George (by King of Clubs), 6f winner at 2 yrs, and a winner in Italy by
Rusticaro: dam half-sister to Dominion and Prominent: quite modest maiden: will
be better suited by 1m. *J. D. Bethell.*

DOUBLE ENCORE (USA) 4 ch.c. Nodouble (USA)–Flo Russell (USA)   65
(Round Table) [1989 8.2m* 8m4 1990 10d5 9.5g4 8d 8f2 8h2 8g 8f 8m 8h4 8h* 10.1g
10g6 8f4] rather leggy, good-topped colt: has a quick action: useful at one time:
favourite, not at his best when winning minor event at Brighton in August: best
form at 1m on top-of-the-ground: visored eighth start: takes keen hold: sold 37,000
gns Newmarket Autumn Sales. *C. R. Nelson.*

DOUBLE ENTENDRE 4 br.f. Dominion 123–Triumphant 90 (Track Spare   67
125) [1989 7d 7g 7f6 7g 6m 8s* 8m 8g 1990 10g 8g* 9m3 8m6 8g* 8g a10g] leggy filly:
quite modest handicapper: won apprentice race (on toes) at Sandown in May and
22-runner event at Kempton in September: ran poorly last 2 outings, off course 3
months in between: effective at 1m and 9f: goes particularly well with give in the
ground. *M. J. Haynes.*

DOUBLE HANDFULL 4 gr.f. Pas de Seul 133–Love Tangle 77 (Wollow 132)   26
[1989 8s3 8s6 8g 7g 1990 10f 8.2s 8f 8m 8.3g 8f6 8.3m6 8f] compact, workmanlike
filly: moderate mover: poor plater: best run at 1m on soft going: blinkered sixth
outing: has joined J. Roberts. *R. J. Hodges.*

DOUBLE STRAND 3 ch.f. Crofthall 110–Excavator Lady 65 (Most Secret 119)   —
[1989 NR 1990 8f 8f 6s 6f 8f] angular filly: poor mover: first foal: dam stayed 1¾m on
flat and won selling hurdles: no show, in sellers last 2 starts. *R. M. Whitaker.*

DOUBLOVA (IRE) 2 ch.f. (Apr 26) M Double M (USA)–Danova (FR) (Dan   83
Cupid 132) [1990 5f* 5f* 6m2 5f3 5m* 6d*] 3,800Y: smallish, rather dipped-
backed filly: half-sister to 1987 2-y-o 7f seller winner Saddique (by Skyliner) and
several winners abroad, including good 1985 Norwegian 2-y-o Big Band Beat (by
Orchestra): dam French 10.5f winner: fair performer: successful in maiden at

Warwick and claimers at Beverley in July, Pontefract in September and Catterick (didn't have to run to best form) in October: seems suited by 5f: bandaged near-hind penultimate outing: retained 14,000 gns Doncaster October Sales. *J. Berry.*

DOULAB'S IMAGE   3 ch.c. Doulab (USA) 115–Haneena 118 (Habitat 134) [1989   **67**
6m⁴ 7v² 6g⁴ 6g⁵ 1990 6g 6m⁵ 6m 5g² a7g⁴ a5g a7g a7g*] smallish, good-bodied colt: good mover: 25/1 and apprentice ridden, returned to near his best when winning handicap at Southwell in December: stays 7f: acts on good to firm ground and heavy: usually blinkered: trained until after fourth start by H. Thomson Jones. *J. A. Glover.*

DOULALLY   3 ch.f. Doulab (USA) 115–June Maid 56 (Junius (USA) 124) [1989 5f⁵   **47**
5m⁵ 6m³ 5f³ 5f⁵ 6g⁵ 6g⁴ 6f 6f* 6g 1990 6g 6d 5f³ 5m⁶ 6m⁶ 6g⁵ 5m 5g] small, lengthy filly: plating-class handicapper: suited by 6f: acts on firm going: blinkered last 3 starts and last 4 at 2 yrs: none too consistent. *R. Allan.*

DOUNHURST   3 b.f. Saher 115–Wernlas (Prince Tenderfoot (USA) 126) [1989   **—**
6g⁵ 5f² 5f⁶ 6g a7g⁴ 1990 6f 7f 6f] small, lengthy, well-made filly: moderate mover with a quick action: quite modest maiden: below form in first half of 1990, easily best effort on second start: stays 7f. *R. Hannon.*

DOVALE   2 ch.f. (Mar 3) Superlative 118–Astonishing (Jolly Good 122) [1990 5g³   **66**
5m* 6g 7m⁴ 6m] sturdy, lengthy filly: third foal: half-sister to 3-y-o 1¼m winner Wake Up (by Night Shift), 5f winner at 2 yrs: dam poor half-sister to very smart stayer Mr Bigmore: quite modest filly: won maiden at Wolverhampton in August: ran moderately in nursery final outing: stays 7f. *W. Jarvis.*

DOVEHOUSE   2 b.f. (Apr 10) Petoski 135–Karietta (Wollow 132) [1990 6g 5f]   **—**
1,700Y: second foal: half-sister to 3-y-o 6f and 7f winner Anna Karietta (by Precocious): dam poor half-sister to Karelia, very useful at up to 1½m: always behind in maidens, slowly away second occasion. *R. Earnshaw.*

DOVEKIE   3 b.c. Ela-Mana-Mou 132–Sacred Ibis (Red God 128§) [1989 7m* 1990   **105**
10m² 12g³ 16.2f] tall, good sort: put up very useful performances when beaten 3 lengths by Anvari in Derrinstown Stud EBF Derby Trial at Leopardstown and 6 lengths behind Houmayoun in 22-runner Derby Italiano at Rome: broke leg in Queen's Vase at Royal Ascot following month: stayed 1½m. *G. Harwood.*

DOVESGATE   2 b.c. (May 3) Superlative 118–Venetian Sky 85 (Touch Paper   **62** ?
113) [1990 5m 6f 7m 8.2s 8m 5s* 6d 6d a5g] 20,000F, 16,000Y: second foal: dam 7f winner is out of half-sister to high-class miler Hilal: won 11-runner claimer at Edinburgh by ½ length from South Crofty, soon ridden along in rear in very strongly-run race and possibly flattered: little worthwhile form otherwise, including in apprentice seller: evidently best at sprint distances: acts well on soft ground: blinkered last 4 starts: sold out of N. Callaghan's stable 2,500 gns Doncaster November Sales. *D. W. Chapman.*

DOWLAND (USA)   2 b.c. (Feb 5) Sovereign Dancer (USA)–Grace Note (FR) 99   **94**
(Top Ville 129) [1990 7g* 8d³] second foal: closely related to top-class middle-distance 3-y-o Belmez (by El Gran Senor): dam 1¼m winner stayed 1½m from good family: won 21-runner maiden at the Curragh in September: 3 lengths third of 6 to Approach The Bench in Juddmonte EBF Beresford Stakes there following month: will stay at least 1¼m. *M. Kauntze, Ireland.*

DOWN THE FLAG (USA)   3 ch.c. Stalwart (USA)–Hunt's Lark (CAN) **116**
(Knightly Dawn (USA)) [1989 NR 1990 12m* 12d² 12s 12f⁴ 10m³ 12m* 12s*]
Since its inception in 1969 the St Simon Stakes has, more often than not, been won by a late-developing horse and the trend continued in the latest season. Unraced as a two-year-old, Down The Flag began with a promising victory in a Doncaster maiden in May then, after a near seven-week absence through late-summer, ran well to reach the frame in two competitive handicaps at Ascot and won another at Newmarket in the autumn. At Newmarket he put up a useful performance under 9-6 in beating Berillon by three lengths in a field of thirteen, staying on strongly to win going away. That performance alone gave him a fair chance at Newbury and further improvement was on the cards, but his ability to act on the prevailing ground had to be taken on trust. As usual the ground for the St Simon was very much on the easy side. Down The Flag had only raced on ground as soft once before, running poorly when favourite for the Old Newton Cup at Haydock in July. The stable had been very much out of sorts at the time, though, and on dead he'd run an excellent race in a Leicester minor event in June, beaten only half a length by Deploy with Beauchamp Express a further four lengths back. Sent

261

St Simon Stakes, Newbury—Down The Flag and Hajade draw clear of the rest

off 5/1 third favourite in a field of eight at Newbury, behind the Cecil-trained pair Spritsail and Sardegna, Down The Flag was always prominent travelling well. Sent to the front over half a mile from home and pushed clear, he never looked like being caught, beating another improving colt Hajade staying on by a length and a half. The pair pulled seven lengths clear of a below-par Spritsail who seemed unsuited by the ground, whilst Sardegna ran badly.

		Stalwart (USA) (b 1979)	Hoist The Flag (b 1968)	Tom Rolfe Wavy Navy
Down The Flag (USA) (ch.c. 1987)			Yes Dear Maggy (b 1972)	Iron Ruler Yes Dear
		Hunt's Lark (CAN) (ch 1976)	Knightly Dawn (b 1970)	Sir Gaylord Breath O'Morn
			Lark O'War (b 1965)	Cohoes War Tide

Down The Flag was bought at the Irish National Yearling Sales for IR 24,000 guineas. His pedigree probably won't be familiar to many readers. The seventh foal of Hunt's Lark, he's a half-brother to four winners in the States, most notably the Washington DC International winner Lieutenant's Lark (by Lt Stevens), successful eight times at up to eleven furlongs. Hunt's Lark herself was placed once from five starts as a two-year-old. She's a half-sister to four winners, including the extremely tough Woodbine Dancer, a winner twenty-one times at up to a mile and a quarter in minor company through nine consecutive seasons. Down The Flag's grandam Lark O'War won three times at up to a mile in minor company. She is related to numerous winners and is also half-sister to the dam of Guilty Conscience, champion older sprinter in the States in 1981. Down The Flag's sire Stalwart raced only as a two-year-old, winning a Grade 1 event over eight and a half furlongs. He's had few runners in Europe, his best besides Down The Flag being the smart French colt Bad Conduct, third in the Prix Lupin. He's sired over a hundred winners, notably the Belmont Stakes runner-up Kingpost. Down The Flag, a rangy colt with plenty of scope, stays a mile and a half and acts on good to firm ground and soft. He seems sure to do well as a four-year-old and follow in the path of similar horses from the stable, Per Quod and Beau Sher two notable examples. *B. Hanbury.*

262

DOWN THE MIDDLE   2 b.g. (Mar 30) Swing Easy (USA) 126–Into The Fire 74   **70**
(Dominion 123) [1990 5m 5g* 5g⁴ a6g* 6m² 7m⁴ 6m* a6g⁶ a6g³ 6m] 4,100F,
7,000Y: leggy, workmanlike gelding: first foal: dam stayed 1¼m here, won in
Guernsey: smart plater, successful at Carlisle (bought in 3,200 gns) in May and
Southwell (retained 4,000 gns after winning by 12 lengths) in June and in claimer
(hung left) at Nottingham in July: gave impression needed race final outing: suited
by 6f: slowly away all starts. *J. Berry.*

DOWN THE VALLEY   4 b.f. Kampala 120–Abertywi 87 (Bounteous 125) [1989   **54**
8f 8m³ a8g³ a8g a8g⁵ a11g a11g² 1990 a11g²] strong, heavy-topped filly: carries
condition: plating-class handicapper: stays 11f: acts on any going: blinkered 3 times,
including last 2 starts. *R. Hannon.*

DOWNTOWN BELLE   3 ch.f. Belfort (FR) 89–Chance Match 73 (Royal Match   —
117) [1989 a8g4] fifth foal: sister to a winner abroad: dam Irish 1½m winner:
ridden by 7-lb claimer, well-beaten fourth of 5 in maiden at Lingfield in January:
twice unruly and withdrawn afterwards, trained by I. Campbell on second occasion,
in July: sold 960 gns Newmarket September Sales. *R. Simpson.*

DRAG ARTIST   5 br.g. Artaius (USA) 129–Drag Line (Track Spare 125) [1989   **51**
12d 12d 12g⁵ 12g⁵ 12m⁵ 12g a11g² a11g² a14g² a14g5 1990 a13g³ a11g³ a12g a12g4]
small, plain, dipped-backed gelding: moderate mover: plating-class performer: stays
1¾m: particularly well suited by give in the ground: seems effective with or without
blinkers: has run well for 7-lb claimer: tends to wander: sold 1,300 gns Doncaster
October Sales. *M. Brittain.*

DRAGONS NEST   3 b.g. Welsh Term 126–Laxmi 108 (Palestine 133) [1989 7f   —
1990 10m 12f⁶] well beaten in maidens: ridden by lad in paddock and awkward at
stalls on reappearance: uncertain to stay middle distances. *Miss A. J. Whitfield.*

DR BILL   2 ch.g. (Feb 18) Domynsky 110–Miss Barnaby 75 (Sun Prince 128) [1990   **66**
6f³ 7m⁵ 6g 6m³ 6g⁵ 6g] sturdy, close-coupled gelding: carries condition: has a round
action: half-brother to 3 winners by Lochnager, including 1¼m and 11f winner
Barnaby Benz, and modest 1987 2-y-o Cat-Arrowed (by Sonnen Gold): dam won at
1½m and stayed 13f: quite modest maiden: ran too freely when visored penultimate
start: likely to prove better suited by 7f than 6f. *M. H. Easterby.*

DREAMAWHILE   3 b.f. Known Fact (USA) 135–Forgotten Dreams (FR) 82   **85**
(Shoemaker 121) [1989 6g⁶ 5f² 1990 7m* 7d 7.6d³ 8m⁶ a7g² a7g⁴] leggy, useful-
looking filly: fair performer: won maiden at Goodwood in May: ran creditably in
listed races and handicaps last 4 starts: effective at 7f and 1m: acts on good to firm
ground and dead: somewhat headstrong. *P. T. Walwyn.*

DREAM CARRIER (IRE)   2 b.c. (Apr 21) Doulab (USA) 115–Dream Trader   **65**
(Auction Ring (USA) 123) [1990 6g 5m⁵ 6f6 6m 6g 6m⁴ 6g⁴ 7s 6d] 13,000Y: strong,
close-coupled colt: has scope: moderate walker: second foal: half-brother to 3-y-o
Prince of Clubs (King of Clubs): dam sister to useful 1983 Irish 2-y-o Grey
Dream: quite modest maiden: suited by 6f: best form on top-of-the-ground: has run
well for 7-lb claimer. *R. Hannon.*

DREAM FOR TWO   2 ch.f. (Mar 16) Reach 122–Dream Chaser 92 (Record   **65** p
Token 128) [1990 6g 7m⁴] unfurnished filly: first foal: dam suited by 6f: 6 lengths
fourth of 22, soon prominent and keeping on despite hanging left, in maiden at
Chepstow in October: likely to improve again. *R. Hannon.*

DREAMING SPIRES   3 b.f. Sadler's Wells (USA) 132–Impossibility (Posse   —
(USA) 130) [1989 6m⁴ 8f 1990 11.5g] lengthy filly: soundly beaten in maidens since
debut: bred to stay 1m. *C. E. Brittain.*

DREAM OF TOMORROW   2 b.c. (Apr 17) Today And Tomorrow 78–Targow   **75**
Girl (Targowice (USA) 130) [1990 5f² a5g² 6h4 a6g* 6f* 6m² 6m 6m² 6g a6g*]
3,500Y: leggy colt: third foal: dam well beaten: modest performer: successful in
maiden auction (sweating) at Southwell, claimer at Lingfield and nursery at
Southwell again: better suited by 6f than 5f: races keenly: game and genuine. *J.
Berry.*

DREAM ON   2 ch.f. (Mar 3) Absalom 128–Great Exception 84 (Grundy 137) [1990   **54**
5f⁶ 5g 5d 5d⁵ a6g³ a7g] 4,800F, 6,000Y, 7,000 2-y-o: small filly: first foal: dam won
over 12.2f and 14.7f: plating-class maiden: ran poorly in nursery at Southwell on final
start: should be suited by 7f. *M. Johnston.*

DREAMS EYES   2 b.c. (Apr 21) Dreams To Reality (USA) 113–Hairbrush (USA)   **64**
(Sir Gaylord) [1990 5f 7m³ 8.2m 7m 6m² 8f⁶ 8d 6s a7g] 6,000Y: lengthy colt: has a
moderate action: closely related to a winner in France by Pharly and half-brother to
several other winners, including 5f and 7.6f winner Ashraf Dancer (by Fabulous
Dancer), as well as dam of high-class French colt Highest Honor: dam won at up to

263

7f in USA: quite modest maiden: claimer-ridden second of 24 to Second Star in seller (claimed out of) G. Huffer's stable £6,001) at Redcar: ran poorly on all-weather final outing: should stay 1m: acts on top-of-the-ground and seems unsuited by a soft surface: has worn bandages. *R. Bastiman.*

DREAMS TO RICHES 4 b.f. Busted 134–Divine Thought 102 (Javelot 124) — [1989 10d 14g 1990 12.3g 11m6 14m] tall, lengthy filly: behind in varied events, including handicaps: should stay well. *L. M. Cumani.*

DREAM TALK 3 b.c. Dreams To Reality (USA) 113–Lala 91 (Welsh Saint 126) 86 [1989 6m5 5m* 5m* 5m2 1990 5m4 5d 5f3 5m* 5d2 5m6] leggy colt: fair handicapper: won at York in June, racing alone far side: good second in £16,400 event at Ascot, easily better subsequent effort: should stay 6f: yet to race on soft going, acts on any other: blinkered last 3 starts: not seen out after July. *J. Berry.*

DRESS PARADE 3 b.c. Sadler's Wells (USA) 132–Steel Habit (Habitat 134) 101 + [1989 NR 1990 11d2 10m3 10g*] IR 250,000Y: rather leggy, useful-looking colt: has scope: moderate mover: third foal: brother to very smart 4-y-o Batshoof, successful from 7f to 10.5f: dam, winner twice in Italy, is sister to very useful 1983 Irish 2-y-o Ancestral, daughter of Cherry Hinton winner Ampulla and closely related to high-class sprinter Steel Heart: odds on, placed behind Quest For Fame in maiden at Newbury and Anvari in £7,400 event at Newmarket: off course 4 months then easily landed odds of 1/10 in maiden at Ripon in September: should stay 1½m: tends to carry head bit high: probably capable of better. *H. R. A. Cecil.*

DRESS PERFORMANCE (USA) 3 b.f. Nureyev (USA) 131–Hortensia (FR) 62 + 119 (Luthier 126) [1989 6g 1990 6g3] leggy, workmanlike filly: half-sister to Glacial Storm (by Arctic Tern): weak second favourite on first run for 10½ months, 7 lengths third of 5 to My Ballerina in maiden at Brighton in May, weakening final 2f. *B. W. Hills.*

DRINKS PARTY (IRE) 2 b.f. (Jan 17) Camden Town 125–Holy Water 53 (Monseigneur (USA) 127) [1990 a6g 6g4 6g a8g 6m6 8m* 10m3 7d5 a7g4] 1,000Y: compact filly: poor mover: second foal: half-sister to 3-y-o Caswell (by Saher): dam unraced daughter of sister to Deep Diver and half-sister to Irish 2000 Guineas winner King's Company: won 17-runner apprentice seller (bought in 3,200 gns) at Warwick by a short head: ran creditably in nurseries after: stays 1¼m: acts on top-of-the-ground and soft going. *J. Wharton.*

DRINNY'S DOUBLE 3 ch.g. Connaught 130–Caramel 93 (Crepello 136) [1989 — 6g 8s 8.2s 1990 12.3f 11v] small, sturdy gelding: no worthwhile form on flat: bred to stay 1¼m: sold 2,300 gns Ascot May Sales: winning selling hurdler for R. Frost. *J. S. Wilson.*

DR MACCARTER (USA) 3 gr.c. Dr Carter (USA)–Now Voyager (USA) 83 (Naskra (USA)) [1989 a7g2 a8g4 a7g2 1990 a7g4 a8g2 a10g3 a10g* a12g6 a10g2] sturdy colt: carries condition: fair handicapper: won at Lingfield (made most to win easily) in November: off course 8½ months after second start: should stay 1½m: blinkered or visored. *W. A. O'Gorman.*

DRMANUM 2 b.c. (Apr 27) Dreams To Reality (USA) 113–Village Idol 74 53 (Blakeney 126) [1990 7m4 8f 8m5] 7,200F, 9,000Y: neat colt: half-brother to 7f seller winner Sporting Idol (by Mummy's Game) and 2 winners abroad: dam stayed 1½m: plating-class form in maidens: stays 1m: has run creditably for 7-lb claimer. *G. A. Huffer.*

DR ROBERT 3 ch.c. Commanche Run 133–Fresh (High Top 131) [1989 NR 1990 77 8g3 11g* 11m* 11m6 12g5 10.6d6 10.6d] rangy, good-bodied colt: has plenty of scope: moderate mover: third foal: half-brother to useful 6f winner Be Fresh (by Be My Guest): dam, good middle-distance performer in Italy, is half-sister to high-class middle-distance filly Free Guest, dam of Shamshir: fair performer: won maiden at Edinburgh and handicap at Hamilton in June: ran moderately in amateurs handicap final start: stays 1½m: yet to race on extremes of going. *L. Cumani.*

DR SOMERVILLE (USA) 3 b.c. Chief's Crown (USA)–Icing 112 (Prince 117 Tenderfoot (USA) 126) [1989 7d5 7g2 9g* 9m* 10v 1990 11d5 9g2 10d 10g* 10g*] $450,000Y: half-brother to several winners, notably very smart 1988 2-y-o Al Hareb (by El Gran Senor), successful at 7f and 1m, and Ulster Harp Derby winner Rising (by Relkino): dam won from 5f to 1m at 2 yrs: won minor event at Evry and Prix de Conde at Longchamp as 2-y-o and listed race at Deauville and La Coupe de Maisons-Laffitte (by neck and 1½ lengths from Goofalik and Agent Bleu) as 3-y-o: stayed 1¼m: probably needed a sound surface: died following routine vitamin injection in October. *Mme C. Head, France.*

DRUMHEAD 4 ch.g. High Line 125–Wig And Gown (Mandamus 120) [1989 12g² 95
12m 12f⁶ 14d² 15s* 19g⁴ 14m⁴ 1990 16g* 18.4d⁵ 16m 16m⁴ 15g² 17.4d⁴ 18d]
workmanlike gelding: moderate walker: fairly useful handicapper: 25/1, won £7,700
event at Kempton in April: ran well when in frame in Northumberland Plate at
Newcastle and in both Tennent Trophy and 15-runner race at Ayr: suited by test of
stamina: probably unsuited by firm going, acts on any other: visored last 4 outings:
sometimes sweats (did so badly on final outing) and gets on toes: has won for
amateur: winning hurdler in December. *P. T. Walwyn.*

DRUMMER'S DREAM (IRE) 2 b.f. (Mar 17) Drumalis 125–Peaches And 48
Cream (FR) (Rusticaro (FR) 124) [1990 6g⁴ 5f² 5f] IR 1,000F: small filly: first foal:
dam placed at 9f and 9.5f in Ireland: second of 16, racing alone, in seller at
Wolverhampton in July: always behind in maiden there around 6 weeks later: should
be well suited by further than 5f. *J. Mackie.*

DRUM SERGEANT 3 b.g. Elegant Air 119–Cala-Vadella 110 (Mummy's Pet 73
125) [1989 6d⁴ 1990 6m² 6m² 6s a6g³ a6g] strong, sturdy gelding: good walker:
modest maiden: narrowly beaten at Newmarket (subsequently gelded) and Redcar
(moved moderately down) 6 months later: faced stiff task third start and below
form in Southwell claimers: will stay 7f: sold out of W. Jarvis's stable 6,400 gns
Newmarket Autumn Sales after third start. *J. Parkes.*

DRU RI'S BRU RI 4 b.g. Kafu 120–Bru Ri (FR) (Sir Gaylord) [1989 12.2d 10d —
12.2d 7.5d 12.2m 8m⁶ 12m 1990 a13g⁵] rather leggy gelding: moderate walker: poor
mover: little worthwhile form in varied events, including sellers: blinkered twice at
3 yrs. *W. Bentley.*

DRY POINT 4 ch.g. Sharpo 132–X-Data 93 (On Your Mark 125) [1989 6g* 5m³ 83
6g⁶ 6m⁴ 1990 6s 6g* 6f* 6m² 6m 5m⁵ 6m³ 6d 6d 6s] strong, angular, workmanlike
gelding: has a round action: fair handicapper: won at Lingfield in June and Thirsk in
July: better suited by 6f than 5f: seems to need a sound surface: occasionally
bandaged: wears crossed noseband: gave trouble stalls on reappearance. *J. A. R.
Toller.*

DR ZEVA 4 b.c. Busted 134–Dance In Rome 79 (Dance In Time (CAN)) [1989 51
10v⁶ 12s 8.5g 10m⁶ 9g⁴ 10g⁶ 11.7f⁶ 8.2g⁴ a8g⁶ a10g² a11g 1990 10f* 10m² 10m 8m
10g* 10m 10m 10f5 10f 8.2v 10s⁶] big, deep-girthed colt: poor handicapper: won at
Brighton (selling event, bought in 7,200 gns) in April and Lingfield (pulling hard for
apprentice) in June: below form last 6 outings, including for amateur: suited by
1¼m: acts on firm going: blinkered tenth start. *J. R. Jenkins.*

DUAL CAPACITY (USA) 6 b.g. Coastal (USA)–Fenney Mill 99 (Levmoss 133) 36
[1989 14s 14s 12m⁵ 11.5f⁶ 12g* 12f² 10m* 12g 12g 1990 a13g³ 10.2f5] tall gelding:
poor mover: poor handicapper: not seen out after March: suited by good gallop at
1¼m and stays 1½m: appears to act on any going: usually has tongue tied down: has
won for lady and when bandaged. *W. J. Musson.*

DUBAI VIEW 3 b.c. Doulab (USA) 115–Anglo Irish (Busted 134) [1989 6d 1990 —
6f] leggy, rather angular colt: soon outpaced in maidens: sold 2,400 gns Newmarket
July Sales. *D. Morley.*

DUBLIN BREEZE 3 b.g. Dublin Taxi–Dusty Foot (Simbir 130) [1989 5m 7m 6g 50
10.6d* 8g² 1990 12.5g 12m⁴ 12m 12f⁶ 12m 10d³] leggy, rather sparely-made gelding:
plating-class handicapper: favourite, very good third of 22 in selling event at
Nottingham in October, slowly away and stumbling 3f out then staying on strongly:
will be suited by return to 1½m: acts on firm ground and dead: took keen hold
penultimate start. *M. H. Tompkins.*

DUC DE BERRY (USA) 2 ch.c. (Apr 9) Chief's Crown (USA)–L'Extravagante 93 p
(USA) (Le Fabuleux 133) [1990 7d²] $260,000Y: tall, good-topped colt: not a good
walker: half-brother to several winners, notably smart Irish 1¼m winner Montelimar (by Alleged): dam, winner 3 times at up to 1m, is daughter of outstanding filly
Franfreluche, dam also of L'Enjoleur and Medaille d'Or: 20/1, ¾-length second of
11, quickening to lead under 2f out and staying on well, to Junk Bond in valuable
minor event at Newmarket in October: will stay 1¼m: sure to improve, and win a
race. *G. Harwood.*

DUCK AND DIVE 3 ch.c. Lomond (USA) 128–Avec L'Amour 75 (Realm 129) 111
[1989 5g³ 5m* 6f 5g* 6d² 6m⁵ 6m⁵ 1990 6f* 5m² 6m* 5d⁵ 5m⁴ 5m⁴ 6m² 6g⁴ 6g⁶]
lengthy, well-made colt: has a quick, short action: won minor event at Folkestone in
April and Group 3 EBF Greenlands Stakes (bumped and awarded race) at the
Curragh in May: very good short-head second to La Grange Music in Newbury
listed race seventh start: well beaten in Ladbroke Sprint Cup at Haydock on final
one: stays 6f: yet to race on soft going, acts on any other: consistent. *R. Hannon.*

DUCK HANDS (IRE) 2 b.f. (Apr 17) Prince Tenderfoot (USA) 126–Mock **45**
Auction 55 (Auction Ring (USA) 123) [1990 5g⁵ 6g* 6g 6f² 6g⁶ 7f⁴ 7f⁵ a6g] leggy,
lengthy filly: has a quick action: sixth foal: half-sister to 2-y-o sprint winners
Fairfield Lad (by Krayyan) and Dutch Auction (by Taufan): dam out of half-sister to
good stayer New Brig, ran only at 2 yrs: modest plater: won seller (bought in 6,800
gns) at Yarmouth in June: ran badly at Southwell on final start: will stay 1m: suitable
mount for a claimer: inconsistent. *M. H. Tompkins.*

DUCKINGTON 6 b.h. Bustino 136–Cribyn 96 (Brigadier Gerard 144) [1989 **85**
6.1f* 6f² 6m 7m* 6f² 1990 6f 6m⁴ 6m 6g 6f⁴ a7g³ 6g⁴ 7m 7g] leggy, close-coupled
horse: has had soft palate operation: fair handicapper: ideally suited by strong gallop
at 6f and has won over 1m: particularly well suited by firm going: probably unsuited
by track at Epsom: best covered up: consistent. *M. H. Easterby.*

DUFFER'S DANCER 8 ch.g. Miami Springs 121–Evening Chorus (Mountain —
Call 125) [1989 6h⁵ 5f⁴ 6g⁵ 6h⁶ 6m 7g 6g 1990 a7g 8.5g 8f 5m 7g] small, dipped-
backed gelding: poor handicapper: well beaten at 8 yrs: best at 6f: used to act well on
top-of-the-ground: ran poorly in visor, sometimes blinkered: bandaged fourth start.
T. Kersey.

DUGGAN 3 b.c. Dunbeath (USA) 127–Silka (ITY) (Lypheor 118) [1989 7m 7g 7d **76**
1990 10g⁶ 10f* 10.6f* 10m² 12.2g* 12m³ 12m³ 12.3g* 14m⁶ 12m 12m⁶ 13.3g 12s]
lengthy, rather sparely-made colt: modest handicapper: successful at Salisbury and
Haydock (apprentices) in May, Catterick in June and Ripon in July: below form last 5
starts: suited by 1½m: best form with give in the ground, though has won on firm:
quite often apprentice ridden: usually looks very well. *R. J. R. Williams.*

DUKE OF IMPNEY 3 b.g. Roscoe Blake 120–Top Secret 90 (Manacle 123) —
[1989 a8g 1990 a8g 10g 7g] lengthy, workmanlike gelding: soundly beaten in
maidens: unlikely to stay 1¼m (pulled hard second start): wore severe noseband
final start: trained until after reappearance by F. Jordan: joined C. Vernon Miller and
gelded. *Miss H. C. Knight.*

DUKE OF PADUCAH (USA) 3 gr.c. Green Dancer (USA) 132–Flordelisada **110**
(USA) (Drone) [1989 7g* 1990 9g² 11.5m* 12g⁶ 12m⁴] rangy, attractive colt: has
scope: good walker: 7/2 on, won 2-runner minor event at Lingfield in May: 9 lengths
sixth of 18 to Quest For Fame in Ever Ready Derby at Epsom and about 2¾ lengths
fourth of 8 to Private Tender in King Edward VII Stakes at Royal Ascot: stays 1½m
well: very useful. *G. Harwood.*

DUKE'S DUET (USA) 3 b.c. Seattle Song (USA) 130–Haute Sanga (Guillaume **67**
Tell (USA) 121) [1989 8v⁵ 1990 8f³ 12f⁶] angular, leggy, lengthy colt: modest form
in maidens, easily best effort at Kempton on reappearance: prominent 9f then
wandered under pressure at Salisbury later in May: bred to stay middle distances.
G. Lewis.

DULCIMAL (IRE) 2 b.f. (Apr 16) Heraldiste (USA) 121–Ultimate 77 —
(Galivanter 131) [1990 5g 6m⁶ a6g 5m] IR 7,500Y: small, angular filly: half-sister to
Irish 5f and 6f winner Picante (by Stanford) and a winner abroad: dam 2-y-o 5f
winner: little worthwhile form in varied races: looked headstrong second outing. *M.
Bell.*

DULVERTON 3 ch.c. Ela-Mana-Mou 132–Parsimony 121 (Parthia 132) [1989 NR —
1990 8m 10s] 26,000Y: half-brother to several winners, including smart sprinter
Scarcely Blessed (by So Blessed) and very useful 5f to 7f winner Petty Purse (by
Petingo): dam won July Cup and is half-sister to good sprinters Mummy's Pet and
Arch Sculptor: showed signs of a little ability in maiden at Goodwood and minor
event at Nottingham: sold to join J. Parkes 3,200 gns Newmarket Autumn Sales. *G.
Harwood.*

DULZURA 2 b.f. (Apr 30) Daring March 116–Comedy Lady 46 (Comedy Star —
(USA) 121) [1990 6g 6g 5m] 1,500Y: leggy filly: half-sister to 1987 2-y-o 5f winner
Only In Gest (by Aragon): dam won 8.3f seller: well beaten in maiden auctions. *B.
Richmond.*

DUMAYLA 3 b.f. Shernazar 131–Dumka (FR) 117 (Kashmir II 125) [1989 NR 1990 **78** +
10.2g³ 8m³] rangy, rather unfurnished filly: eighth foal: closely related to useful 6f
and 1m winner Dolka (by Shergar) and half-sister to 6 winners, all at least useful,
including 2000 Guineas winner and Derby third Doyoun (by Mill Reef), very smart
6f performer Dafayna (by Habitat) and high-class 1¼m winner Dolpour (by Sadler's
Wells): dam won French 1000 Guineas: fair form in minor events won by Narwala at
Doncaster and Remthat Naser at Leicester (swished tail) in the autumn: will be well
suited by return to 1¼m. *M. R. Stoute.*

DUMBRECK 3 b.f. Another Realm 118–Eagle's Quest 62 (Legal Eagle 126) [1989 **66**
6f⁴ 6m⁴ 7m⁵ 6f⁴ 6m 6s* 6v⁴ 7g⁴ 1990 6m 6g⁵ 7g⁴ 7.6g 7m 8d⁵ 6s 6s] workmanlike,
good-quartered filly: quite modest handicapper: best 3-y-o efforts on third, fourth
and sixth (£19,000 event at Ayr) starts: will be suited by return to further: acts well
on soft ground. *A. P. Stringer.*

DUMDUMSKI 3 b.c. Niniski (USA) 125–Live Ammo 94 (Home Guard (USA) **64**
129) [1989 6m³ 7m⁴ 1990 8.5m² 9m] sparely-made colt: modest maiden: pulled up
lame in handicap at York in May: stayed 8.5f: dead. *Lord John FitzGerald.*

DUNMAGLASS 3 b.c. Sayf El Arab (USA) 127–Stubble 93 (Balidar 133) [1989 —
5f⁵ 6f 6d 1990 7d] leggy colt: plating-class maiden: well-backed favourite, not
entirely discredited in seller (claimed £6,550) at Leicester in June, weakening over
1f out: stays 6f: best efforts on dead ground. *Sir Mark Prescott.*

DUNMOUNIN 3 ro.f. Alias Smith (USA)–Poly Negative (Polyfoto 124) [1989 6g⁶ **42**
7g 6m 6m 7f 6g⁴ 6s a8g 1990 7m 12.3f 12.2m 7g 9m 7d² 7g⁴ 7m⁴ 7m 6g 7f 7d] lengthy
filly: moderate mover: poor performer: well below form last 3 starts: suited by 7f:
acts on good to firm ground and dead: has run creditably for 7-lb claimer. *W. Bentley.*

DUN SHINING 3 b.g. Lochnager 132–Miss Barnaby 75 (Sun Prince 128) [1989 —
5g 5d² 5m³ 6m 6m² 6g 1990 5s 8f 8g 6m] medium-sized gelding: easy mover:
plating-class maiden: below form in handicaps, seller on final outing: stays 6f:
looked unsuited by soft ground: sold 680 gns Doncaster August Sales. *M. H.
Easterby.*

DUNSTAR 3 b.g. Dunphy 124–Starlit Way 92 (Pall Mall 132) [1989 5v⁴ 5d² 5g⁶ —
6m 6m 6v 6s⁴ a8g 1990 8.2s 8.2g] sparely-made gelding: poor mover: plater: stays
6f: best form on soft ground: sold 880 gns Doncaster June Sales. *M. Brittain.*

DUPLICITY (IRE) 2 b.c. (May 7) Double Schwartz 128–Goirtin (Levmoss 133) **61** p
[1990 6g] 9,200 2-y-o: leggy colt: has scope: fifth living foal: half-brother to 9.4f
winner Lyapkin-Tyapkin and winning hurdler Winged Foot (both by Tap On Wood)
and another winning hurdler: dam Irish 1¼m winner: backward, around 9 lengths
ninth of 17, soon going rather slow after slow start then running green 2f out and not
knocked about, in maiden at Newbury in October: sure to improve. *L. J. Holt.*

DURHAM ROAD 2 b.f. (May 12) Carriage Way 107–Central Carpets 70 (Garda's **46**
Revenge (USA) 119) [1990 6d 5m⁴] sparely-made filly: third foal: sister to poor 1988
2-y-o plater Valentine Lady, later successful abroad: dam sprinter: over 4 lengths
fourth of 7 in maiden at Redcar in July: very slowly away on debut. *Denys Smith.*

DURKHAN (USA) 3 ch.c. Irish River (FR) 131–Dukayna 103 (Northfields **89** +
(USA)) [1989 NR 1990 8.2d 8f*] leggy, good-bodied colt with plenty of scope: has a
quick action: fourth living foal: dam, 1m winner, is closely related to 4-y-o Dolpour
and half-sister to Dalsaan, Dafayna and Doyoun: bit green, won 9-runner maiden at
Newmarket in July by 3 lengths from Waki Gold, quickening well: soon pushed along
towards rear in similar event at Haydock: looked likely to improve again, but wasn't
seen out again. *L. M. Cumani.*

DURLEY SONG 4 gr.g. Cree Song 99–Donrae 106 (Don (ITY) 123) [1989 7f⁶ —
7.5m 6m³ 1990 7f⁶ 8f] leggy, angular gelding: best effort third of 4 in minor event at
Thirsk as 3-y-o: reluctant at stalls on reappearance. *M. H. Easterby.*

DURNELTOR 2 br.c. (Mar 20) Hard Fought 125–Pounelta 91 (Tachypous 128) **82**
[1990 6m³ 6m⁵ 6g 6m* 6s] workmanlike colt: has scope: first foal: dam 2-y-o 7f
winner, probably stayed 1½m, is half-sister to Dead Certain: fair colt: won maiden at
Folkestone in October: will stay at least 7f: seems unsuited by soft ground. *R.
Hannon.*

DUST DEVIL 5 b.h. Horage 124–Witch of Endor 80 (Matador 131) [1989 8d 10m —
10g⁵ 10m² 10g² 12g⁴ 11s⁴ 12d 1990 10g 10m 10.6g⁵] strong, lengthy horse: very
useful as 3-y-o: lightly raced and never able to challenge in valuable handicaps in
1990: probably stays 1½m: yet to race on firm going, acts on any other: usually
blinkered: sold 3,100 gns Newmarket Autumn Sales. *J. L. Dunlop.*

DUST D'THRONE (USA) 2 b.c. (May 3) Bob's Dusty (USA)–Dethroned —
(USA) (Grenfall (USA)) [1990 7v 8d a7g 10.2s] quite attractive colt: has a round
action: fourth foal: half-brother to a winner in North America by Pass The Tab: dam
minor winner at up to 9f: sire very useful at 9f: bit backward, little sign of ability in
maidens or a minor event: didn't handle bend well at Edinburgh. *S. G. Norton.*

DUTCH BLUES 3 b.g. Dutch Treat 112–My Polyanna 81 (Polyfoto 124) [1989 **53**
NR 1990 10g⁵ 13m⁵] leggy, plain gelding: fifth foal: half-brother to a winning
hurdler: dam, thoroughly genuine and consistent, stayed 1½m: plating-class form in

claimers at Nottingham and Ayr (maiden) in the summer: may prove best short of 13f: has joined Mrs S. Austin. *R. M. Whitaker.*

DUTCH CZARINA 2 b.f. (Feb 21) Prince Sabo 123–Dutch Princess 70 (Royalty 130) [1990 7m⁵ 8g⁵] sturdy, useful-looking filly: fifth foal: half-sister to Cesarewitch winner Double Dutch (by Nicholas Bill): dam staying maiden: 10 lengths fifth of 8, soon ridden along and staying on steadily, in 1m minor event at Sandown in September: will stay well, and do better in time. *Miss B. Sanders.*   **53 p**

DUTCH DESIRE 2 gr.f. (Apr 26) Grey Desire 115–Dutch May 109 (Maystreak 118) [1990 5m 5g 5m] sparely-made, dipped-backed filly: fifth reported foal: half-sister to useful 5f to 7f winner Lucky Dutch (by Lucky Wednesday): dam won 7 sprint races at 2 yrs and 3 yrs: well beaten in sellers: dead. *M. W. Easterby.*   **—**

DUTCH SCHULTZ 4 b.g. Uncle Pokey 116–Double Duchess 55 (Connaught 130) [1990 NR 1990 11g] compact gelding: second foal: dam poor maiden at 2 yrs: 33/1, never dangerous in claimer at Hamilton in July. *I. Semple.*   **—**

DUTEST 3 b.c. Aragon 118–Indian Call 72 (Warpath 113) [1989 6g⁵ 6g 8m⁵ 1990 9m* 12m 8m] leggy, quite attractive colt: good walker: modest handicapper: favourite, improved when winning at Wolverhampton in April, leading 3f out: below form later in the spring: stays 9f well: sold 3,000 gns Newmarket Autumn Sales. *A. C. Stewart.*   **70**

DUTYFUL 4 b.f. Bold Owl 101–My Duty 70 (Sea Hawk II 131) [1989 7s⁶ 9f 12f⁵ 16m 12m² 12f* 10m⁵ 13.3d 1990 12f 11.7g 11.5m⁴ 12g² 12m⁵ 14m⁶ 14g⁵ 16f³ 16.2d⁴ 16s² a16g⁴] sturdy, workmanlike filly: quite modest handicapper: stays 2m: acts on any going: visored once at 2 yrs: wore small bandages behind final outing. *M. J. Haynes.*   **64**

DUXFORD LODGE 3 b.f. Dara Monarch 128–Simmay (Simbir 130) [1989 6m 7g⁴ 6m 8.5f 1990 8f 7m 11m 12m⁴ 12f⁶ a14g 11s 10d 12s] close-coupled, sparely-made filly: poor plater: should stay 1¾m: acts on firm and dead going: blinkered second start. *J. F. Bottomley.*   **27**

DWADME 5 b.g. High Top 131–Durun 89 (Run The Gantlet (USA)) [1989 14g* 14m 14f⁴ 15f³ 14f 16m² 1990 18.4d] tall, rather sparely-made gelding: won handicap at Salisbury as 4-y-o: well beaten in Chester Cup (Handicap) in May: stays 2m: acts on firm going: has got on toes: useful staying novice hurdler in 1989/90 (damaged tendon on reappearance). *O. Sherwood.*   **—**

DYNAMIC QUEST 3 ch.g. Posse (USA) 130–Do Your Best 89 (Try My Best (USA) 130) [1989 NR 1990 a7g⁶ a10g] 2,000Y: second foal: half-brother to 4-y-o Ardross Best (by Ardross): dam 1m winner: tailed off in claimers in January: gelded and sold 525 gns Ascot November Sales. *J. A. Bennett.*   **—**

DYNAMIC STAR 6 b.g. Lord Gayle (USA) 124–Stellarevagh (Le Levanstell 122) [1989 NR 1990 11s] rather leggy gelding: plating-class handicapper at best: tailed off in Hamilton maiden in April: stays 1½m: best form on soft going: a difficult ride: sold 1,700 gns Doncaster September Sales. *C. C. Trietline.*   **—**

DZET (USA) 3 b.g. Caerleon (USA) 132–Tendresse (USA) (Secretariat (USA)) [1989 8.2d 8m 1990 10f 12.5g 10g 14m⁵] lengthy gelding: has round action: no form, including in selling and ladies handicap: blinkered first 2 starts, looking unsatisfactory on first: trained until after third by Mrs L. Piggott. *K. G. Wingrove.*   **—**

E

EAGER DEVA 3 b.c. Lochnager 132–Deva Rose 80 (Chestergate 111) [1989 5f* 5m 6v 1990 a6g⁶ 5f* 6f⁴ 6m 5.8f² 5g 5m³ 6m 5f⁵ 5g 6g⁴ 5d 5.6g 5d 5m⁶ 5m³ 5g⁴ 5g³] robust, good-quartered colt: has plenty of scope: usually looks well: good walker and easy mover: fair handicapper: won at Doncaster in March: stays 6f: seems best on top-of-the-ground. *R. Hollinshead.*   **83**

EAGLE BID (IRE) 2 b.c. (Apr 28) Auction Ring (USA) 123–Gay Folly (Wolver Hollow 126) [1990 7m] IR 11,500F, 14,000 2-y-o: fourth living foal: dam never ran: very backward in maiden at Leicester in September. *S. Dow.*   **—**

EAGLE EDDY 3 b.c. Longleat (USA) 109–Princess Tam (Prince Regent (FR) 129) [1989 NR 1990 8.2g] 2,500F: half-brother to 3 winners in Scandinavia, notably Dalby Mustang (by Welsh Saint), also very useful performer at up to 1m here: dam placed once from 8 starts in Ireland: tailed off in apprentice maiden at Hamilton in May. *J. S. Wilson.*   **—**

EARLY BREEZE 4 b.g. Tumble Wind (USA)–Dawn Hail 74 (Derring-Do 131) 55
[1989 6s⁶ 6s* 6m² 6m⁶ 7g⁴ 7m 7g 6m 7d 1990 a7g 6m 8m⁶ 10.8g³ 10g⁶ 6d⁵ 7g]
compact gelding: modest winner early as 3-y-o: well below his best in 1990: stays
1¼m: suited by give in the ground: visored last 3 starts: winning hurdler in August.
M. McCourt.

EARTHLY PLEASURE 4 b.f. Music Boy 124–May Fox 67 (Healaugh Fox) 29
[1989 10.1g 12m 12m³ 12g⁴ 15.3g⁵ 10g 10.6s 1990 12g a8g 8f⁵] good-topped filly:
plating class at best: stays 1½m: acts on firm going: blinkered 3 times as 3-y-o: sold
out of P. Makin's stable 3,700 gns Doncaster March Sales before reappearance. *K.
White.*

EAST BARNS (IRE) 2 gr.c. (May 13) Godswalk (USA) 130–Rocket Lass 56
(Touch Paper 113) [1990 5f⁶ 5m⁴ 5g⁶ 5f³ 6g³ 6g 7m* 7g 7m 6d 7d] IR 5,600Y:
close-coupled colt: has a quick action: second foal: brother to 3-y-o Codys Boy: dam
placed over 5f at 2 yrs in Ireland: plating-class performer: won maiden auction at
Catterick in July: behind in nurseries and a claimer after: best form at 6f and 7f on a
sound surface: blinkered or visored 5 of final 6 starts. *J. S. Wainwright.*

EASTDENE MAGIC 3 ch.f. Nicholas Bill 125–Step Softly 81 (St Chad 120) —
[1989 6f⁶ 7f² 7f³ 7.5m⁵ 7f* 7m 7m² 1990 10.6s 8.5g] leggy, sparely-made filly: good
mover: quite modest winner at 2 yrs: soundly beaten in amateur handicaps in summer of 1990: should be suited by further than 7f: acts on firm going: gave trouble at
stalls as 3-y-o, refusing to enter them in August: changed hands 6,500 gns
Doncaster October Sales. *Mrs G. R. Reveley.*

EASTER BABY 4 ch.f. Derrylin 115–Saintly Miss 63 (St Paddy 133) [1989 a6g —
1990 a6g⁴ a12g⁴ a16g⁴ 10.1g 12.5g] lengthy filly: little sign of ability in varied events:
blinkered last 2 outings. *P. D. Cundell.*

EASTERN AURA (IRE) 2 ch.f. (Feb 21) Ahonoora 122–Sybaris 91 (Crowned 49
Prince (USA) 128) [1990 5m 6m 7d⁶] IR 140,000Y: second foal: half-sister to 1988
Irish 2-y-o 7f winner Millennium Queen (by Mendez): dam 2-y-o 5f winner later
successful in USA: poor form in maidens. *B. W. Hills.*

EASTERN EMBER 4 br.f. Indian King (USA) 128–Pithead 70 (High Top 131) 85
[1989 8.2s 8s 6s* 5m* 5m 6m⁶ 5g⁵ 5g* 5f³ 6f³ 6f 5m³ 6m 6m 5f 6s 5m 1990 7.6d
7.5d* 7m* 8.2m⁵ 8.2s⁶ 8g⁵ 7m⁴ 6m² 6f 8m³] leggy, lengthy filly: poor mover: fair
handicapper: led final strides when winning at Beverley and Thirsk in May: stays
1m: acts on any going: usually blinkered or visored: apprentice ridden at 4 yrs
except seventh outing: inconsistent: covered by Hubbly Bubbly. *S. G. Norton.*

EASTERN MAGIC 2 b.c. (May 3) Faustus (USA) 118–Hithermoor Lass 75 (Red 83 p
Alert 127) [1990 7g³ 7g*] IR 60,000Y: rather leggy colt: good mover: fourth
reported foal: half-brother to very useful sprinter Poyle George (by Sharpo): dam
placed from 5f to 7f, is out of poor sister to smart handicapper Idiot's Delight:
favourite, won maiden at Salisbury in October by 2 lengths from Lodestar: will stay
1m: can improve further. *J. W. Hills.*

EASTERN MUSIC 2 b.c. (Apr 20) Music Maestro 119–Eastern Romance 73 76
(Sahib 114) [1990 5f³ 5f³ 5m⁴ 6g* 6f³ 6g³ 6g 6d⁴ 7s⁶] IR 15,000Y, resold IR 12,000Y:
lengthy, rather sparely-made colt: half-brother to 3-y-o Age of Romance (by
Chukaroo) and 3 winners, including fair miler Miss Cuddles (by Mummy's Pet): dam
won 6f seller at 2 yrs: modest performer: made all in maiden at Chepstow in June:
suited by 6f: probably acts on any going. *R. Hollinshead.*

EASTERN PARTNER (USA) 3 b.c. Damascus (USA)–Tennis Partner (USA) —
(Northern Dancer) [1080 NR 1990 7d] 3295,000Y: compact, attractive colt: first foal:
dam unraced sister to Ajdal and half-sister to Formidable and Fabuleux Jane:
well-beaten eighth of 19 in maiden at Lingfield in October: showed quick action: sold
6,000 gns Newmarket Autumn Sales, probably to race in Singapore. *P. F. I. Cole.*

EASTERN PLAYER 7 ch.g. Royal Match 117–Cigarette 61 (Miralgo 130) [1989 —
NR 1990 21.6m⁶ 15.8d⁵] of little account: blinkered 3 times: bandaged at 7 yrs: dead.
Miss G. M. Rees.

EASTERN PLEASURE 3 gr.g. Absalom 128–First Pleasure 73 (Dominion 54
123) [1989 NR 1990 8g a7g⁶ a8g 10.5g⁴] sturdy gelding: moderate walker: first foal:
dam, suited by 1m, is half-sister to useful 9f to 1½m winner Celtic Pleasure: better
for race and bandaged, first form when fourth of 8 in selling handicap at York in
October: will be well suited by 1½m +: sold 5,000 gns Doncaster October Sales and
gelded. *J. Wharton.*

EASTERN SUNSET 3 b.c. Scott Joplyn 108–Victory Corner 68 (Sit In The —
Corner (USA)) [1989 NR 1990 7m 7.6g 10d] workmanlike colt, with scope: has round
action: third reported foal: half-brother to 18.8f winner Silver Thorn (by Record

269

Run) and 8.3f and 10.1f seller winner Easter Rambler (by Tower Walk): dam stayed 6f: behind in maiden, claimer and seller: trained first 2 starts by P. Butler. *H. J. Collingridge.*

EASTERN WHISPER (USA)   3 gr.c. Arctic Tern (USA) 126–Mazyoun (USA)   **69** 57 (Blushing Groom (FR) 131) [1989 NR 1990 10g 12f* 12d⁵ 12m 10d 10.6v 9.1s³] compact, rather angular colt: second foal: half-brother to 4-y-o Handsome Leader (by Green Forest): dam, placed at 6f and 7f, is from family of Mysterious and J O Tobin: won claimer (claimed out of B. Hanbury's stable £25,000) at Kempton in May, running on strongly to lead inside final 1f: easily best subsequent effort on final start: stays 1½m: acts on any going: looked unco-operative in ladies event (visored) fourth start: winning hurdler: somewhat temperamental. *Denys Smith.*

EASTERN WIND (IRE)   2 b.c. (Mar 14) Tumble Wind (USA)–Western Wendy   **41** 50 (Young Emperor 133) [1990 6m 7f⁶ 6m] IR 9,500F, 36,000Y: strong, useful-looking colt: has scope: has a round action: second living foal: dam 2-y-o 6f winner: behind in maidens, tailed off final start: blinkered first 2: wore a tongue strap second outing: changed hands 1,400 gns Newmarket Autumn Sales. *N. A. Callaghan.*

EASTER TERM   2 b.f. (Feb 25) Welsh Term 126–Silly Woman (Silly Season 127)   **—** [1990 5f] 8,000Y: fourth live foal: half-sister to useful 6f to 1m winner Serious Trouble (by Good Times) and smart 1985 2-y-o 5f and 7f winner Moorgate Man (by Remainder Man): dam unraced: very slowly away and always well behind in maiden at Doncaster in March. *R. J. Holder.*

EAST SUNRISE   2 ch.c. (Mar 11) Gabitat 119–Rueful Lady (Streetfighter 120)   **38** [1990 6m 6m⁵] rather angular colt: first reported foal: dam (very closely in-bred to Streetfighter) won over hurdles: visored over 5 lengths fifth of 17, staying on, in seller at Goodwood in August. *B. Gubby.*

EASY BUCK   3 b.g. Swing Easy (USA) 126–Northern Empress 80 (Northfields   **64** p (USA)) [1989 NR 1990 8d²] leggy gelding: fifth living foal: half-brother to 3 winners, including 6f and 7f winner Nevada Mix (by Alias Smith) and 8.2f and 11f (in French Provinces) winner Bold Mac (by Comedy Star): dam ran 3 times: 25/1 and bit backward, held up when 2 lengths second of 11 to eased Forty Or More in claimer at Leicester in October: should improve: winning hurdler. *N. A. Gaselee.*

EASY KIN   8 ch.g. Great Nephew 126–Ardneasken 84 (Right Royal V 135) [1989   **—** NR 1990 15.3g 16m 10m] lightly raced and soundly beaten in handicaps on flat since 1986: stays 2m: acts on firm and dead going: has worn blinkers and a visor: wears bandages: has been tried in crossed noseband. *R. E. Peacock.*

EASY LINE   7 ch.g. Swing Easy (USA) 126–Impromptu 88 (My Swanee 122)   **91** [1989 6f 6f² 6f² 6f 6m* 6f³ 6f³ 6m⁴ 6f⁴ 1990 6m 6m⁴ 6m⁴ 6g³ 6m* 6f³ 6m* 6m 6m 5m⁴ 5m² 6m 5m* 6d⁶ 7d] tall, lengthy gelding: moderate mover: fairly useful handicapper: won at Kempton (same race for second year running) in June, Newmarket in July and Pontefract (quickening really well from rear to lead close home) in October: ideally suited by 6f or stiff 5f: probably not at his best on soft going, acts on any other: visored once: often hangs, and is best covered up. *P. J. Feilden.*

EASY OVER (USA)   4 ch.g. Transworld (USA) 121–Love Bunny (USA) (Exclu-   **—** sive Native (USA)) [1989 8g* 10v² 10.2g 10.5m a10g 1990 10f6] big, workmanlike gelding: won slowly-run apprentice maiden at Newcastle early as 3-y-o: below form in handicaps after next outing: suited by 1¼m: acts on heavy going: has sweated: winning hurdler in autumn. *G. M. Moore.*

EASY PREP   3 b.g. Reasonable (FR) 119–Professor's Choice 86 (Mount Hagen   **89** (FR) 127) [1989 6m⁶ 6m* 5g⁴ 6s³ 1990 7m³ 8m³ 7g* 7d] angular gelding: fair handicapper: 20/1, slowly into stride and came from last of sixteen 3f out to win £20,000 Norwest Holst Trophy at York in May: broke leg at Leicester following month: may have proved ideally suited by 7f: acted on good to firm ground and soft: best with strong handling. *G. A. Pritchard-Gordon.*

EASY PURCHASE   3 br.c. Swing Easy (USA) 126–Dauphiness 76 (Supreme   **67** Sovereign 119) [1989 7f 1990 10m a8g 9m⁵ 10.2f² 12.5g² a12g⁵ 10g² 12m a11g³ a12g*] big, angular colt: has a quick action: quite modest performer: second favourite, won 16-runner handicap at Lingfield in December, leading inside final 1f: stays 1½m: possibly needs an easy surface. *D. Haydn Jones.*

EASY TIME (GER)   5 b.g. High Line 125–Easily (Swing Easy (USA) 126) [1989   **—** 15.5s 11.7d 10.1m 12m 12h* 12f* 16m⁵ 12f² 1990 a12g³ 12f 12f5 12g4 17.1m⁶] rangy, workmanlike gelding: poor handicapper: seems best at 1½m: acts on hard going: blinkered twice at 4 yrs and on fourth outing (slowly away): sold to join W. Clay 1,000 gns Newmarket Autumn Sales. *P. F. I. Cole.*

EASY TOOMEY 2 br.g. (Apr 29) Swing Easy (USA) 126–Miss Twomey (Will 42 Somers 114§) [1990 6m⁶ 5m⁶ a7g⁶ 6m] 4,800Y: lengthy gelding: brother to a winner in Italy and half-brother to several other winners, including 5f performer Miss Poinciana (by Averof): dam poor Irish maiden: poor maiden: carried head high third outing: ran as if something badly amiss final start. *J. R. Jenkins.*

EBONY CHARM 4 ch.f. Mr Fluorocarbon 126–Ma Pierrette 77 (Cawston's — Clown 113) [1989 NR 1990 10m 6m 8h] no show in poor company. *O. O'Neill.*

EBONY ENTERTAINER (IRE) 2 br.c. (Apr 9) Kafu 120–Naval Artiste 64 (Captain's Gig (USA)) [1990 6m⁵ 5m⁶ 6g] 9,400Y: good-topped colt: poor mover: ninth foal: half-brother to several winners, including sprinters Naval Fan (by Taufan) and Karla's Star (by Kampala): dam Irish 2-y-o 5f winner: very green, around 8 lengths fifth of 7 in maiden at Ascot in July, best effort: off course for around 2 months after second start. *S. Dow.*

EBRO 4 ch.g. Aragon 118–Caribbean Blue (Blue Cashmere 129) [1989 8g³ 10f² — 10m 8.2f 10f⁶ 10f³ 12f 10g 1990 12m 10f³ a12g 10f] big, workmanlike gelding: turns fore-feet out: quite modest form at best: little show as 4-y-o: stays 1¼m: acts on firm going. *Mrs L. Piggott.*

ECCOLINA 4 ch.f. Formidable (USA) 125–Chili Girl 112 (Skymaster 126) [1989 — 6s⁶ 8g⁵ 8.5f 8m a7g³ 1990 a10g⁶ 10s 9m⁵ 10m 7m] rather angular filly: poor walker: moderate mover: quite modest maiden: ran poorly in handicaps last 2 outings: seems to stay 1¼m: blinkered last 3 starts: has given trouble in preliminaries: not one to trust implicitly. *J. L. Dunlop.*

ECHO LADY (IRE) 2 b.f. (Jan 29) Vaigly Great 127–Final Act 64 (Decoy Boy 58 129) [1990 5m 5f⁴ 6g 6m 6d 6d] IR 13,000F, 12,000Y: good-topped filly: sister to 3-y-o Elwadi and very useful 1984 2-y-o sprinter Vaigly Oh, and half-sister to a winner in Belgium: dam won three 1m sellers: plating-class maiden: ran moderately in nurseries on final 3 outings. *G. B. Balding.*

ECHO ONE 4 b.g. Ercolano (USA) 118–Miss Monte Carlo 75 (Reform 132) [1989 — 9g⁸ 11g* 12g* 1990 7m 12.5f 8g 13m 9g 15.8d 13.8d] leggy gelding: first foal: dam placed over 6f at 2 yrs: successful 4 times at up to 1½m in Belgium: bought 2,600 gns Ascot February Sales: well beaten in modest company in Britain. *K. B. McCauley.*

ECHO PRINCESS 3 b.f. Crofter (USA) 124–What A Breeze (Whistling Wind 55 123) [1989 5m 5m³ 5g² 5g² 5f² 6d 5m³ 5m² 5g² 5f² 5f* 5s³ 1990 6m⁶ 5d⁵ 5m⁴ 6s⁴ 6g⁴ 6m⁵ 5.3h⁴ 6m 6g] lengthy, good-quartered filly: quite modest performer at her best: best form at 5f: acts on any going: has given trouble inside stalls: blinkered sixth and eighth starts: hung right for apprentice final one: changed hands 5,200 gns Doncaster February Sales: sold 1,600 gns Doncaster October Sales. *J. Berry.*

ECKIY (IRE) 2 b.c. (Apr 20) Drumalis 125–Tabriya 61 (Nishapour (FR) 125) 36 [1990 5m 6s 5m 6g 5m 8m 5g] IR 5,600Y: compact colt: second foal: half-brother to winner in Italy: dam lightly raced: bad maiden: slowly away when blinkered or visored final 2 starts. *P. Burgoyne.*

ECKS'AMPLE (USA) 2 b.g. (May 13) Lines of Power (USA)–Honey Wama 48 (USA) (Wajima (USA)) [1990 6d 7m] medium-sized, rather leggy gelding: closely related to a minor winner by Marshua's Dancer and half-brother to 2 others: dam never ran: never dangerous in autumn maidens at Lingfield (backward and green) and Chepstow. *M. A. Jarvis.*

ECONOMY EXPRESS 2 b.f. (May 22) Bay Express 132–Massawa (FR) 34 (Tennyson (FR) 124) [1990 6g 6g 7g 6d a7g⁴] 1,750Y: sparely-made filly: third foal: dam French maiden: poor maiden: ran in a seller third start: ran creditably for 7-lb claimer when considerably handled on all-weather final start: stays 7f. *W. J. Musson.*

ECOSSAIS DANSEUR (USA) 4 ch.c. Arctic Tern (USA) 126–Northern 67 Blossom (CAN) (Snow Knight 125) [1989 10.2d² 12f⁶ 10m⁴ 9.1f* 10.5m⁵ 9g² 1990 a12g⁴ 12g⁵ 12f³ 10m] lengthy, rather angular colt: moderate mover: fair winner at 3 yrs: not discredited second outing in 1990: best at around 1¼m: has won on firm going, and goes well on a soft surface: trained until after third start by B. Hills: sold IR 1,200 gns Goffs November Sales. *T. Stack, Ireland.*

ECRAN 4 b.f. Kings Lake (USA) 133–High Finale 100 (High Line 125) [1989 99 13.3m⁶ 16m³ 17.6f* 17.6m* 16m 18g³ 19g³ 1990 16d 16m 16m⁶ 22d³ 20f² 18g 20g⁴] rangy, workmanlike filly: carries condition: has quick, round action: 66/1, sweating and wearing tongue strap, appeared to run excellent race when second of 7 to Lucky Moon in Goodwood Cup: no comparable form as 4-y-o, and always behind in

271

Doncaster Cup 6 weeks later: suited by thorough test of stamina: acts on firm and dead ground: can't be relied upon. *J. L. Dunlop.*

EDGE OF THE GLEN 2 b.g. (May 31) Alleging (USA) 120–Scotch Bonnet — (Supreme Sovereign 119) [1990 5.8h 5m] 900F, 4,600Y: half-brother to a minor winner abroad: dam twice-raced daughter of half-sister to 1000 Guineas second Glen: tailed off in maiden auction at Bath (slowly away, seemed reluctant to race) and seller at Lingfield. *C. J. Hill.*

EDGEWISE 7 b. or br.g. Tanfirion 110–Regency Girl 89 (Right Boy 137) [1989 — 8.2g 1990 a6g a8g a7g 7f 7.6m 7h] compact gelding: poor handicapper: best at up to 7f: acts on any going: occasionally visored: has sweated, and been taken early to post. *D. Morris.*

EDUCATED RITA 3 b.f. The Brianstan 128–Sobriquet (Roan Rocket 128) [1989 **41** 6g 6m 7d 1990 10m 8f5 10m3 10g 12.5g5] angular filly: plater: probably stays 1½m. *Miss L. C. Siddall.*

EDWARD LEAR (USA) 4 b.c. Lear Fan (USA) 128–Coed (USA) (Ribot 142) **65 d** [1989 9m4 11g2 1990 10.6s 10g a8g3 8.2m2 a12g 10m5 11m4 10.4d 8d6] workmanlike colt: moderate mover: quite modest handicapper: easily best effort in 1990 on fourth start: stays 11f: acts on good to firm going: bandaged third start, sweating fourth: winning selling hurdler in November. *J. G. FitzGerald.*

EDWARD'S CORNER 12 b. or br.m. Sit In The Corner (USA)–Guid Tassie 66 — (French Beige 127) [1989 NR 1990 16.5m] plain mare: modest winning hurdler/ chaser: 50/1, tailed off throughout in ladies maiden at Doncaster in June. *J. Dooler.*

EDWARD SEYMOUR (USA) 3 b.c. Northern Baby (CAN) 127–Regal Leader **86 p** (USA) (Mr Leader (USA)) [1989 NR 1990 8g 9g2] $135,000Y: lengthy, useful-looking colt: fourth foal: half-brother to 2 winners by Private Account, including Crown The Leader, useful winner at up to 1m: dam showed only little ability: stayed on strongly when second of 7 to Scottish Jester in maiden (moved moderately down) at Ripon in July: has joined S. Mellor: may well be capable of better. *L. M. Cumani.*

EECEE TREE 8 ch.g. Young Generation 129–Golden Treasure 106 (Crepello 136) [1989 5f6 5f 5m5 5m 1990 5f6 5m 5m 5g 7.6g 5m5 5g 5m6 5m 5.3f] good-topped gelding: moderate mover: poor handicapper: best at 5f: acts on any going: often sweats and gets on edge: has worn blinkers and a crossed noseband: has been taken down early: trained until after seventh outing by C. Holmes. *P. J. Arthur.*

EFFERVESCENT 5 ch.h. Sharpo 132–Never So Lovely 87 (Realm 129) [1989 **53** 7g 7f 6f6 7.5m 7f6 7.6h4 7f5 8f* 8m3 9f3 8.3m2 8f* 8.5g 1990 8f 8.5f3 9g2 8f 9g 7f5 8m] rather leggy, useful-looking horse: poor walker and mover: quite modest handicapper: pulled up badly lame final outing: suited by around 1m: acted on firm and dead going: wore blinkers: dead. *G. Lewis.*

EIDOLON 3 b.f. Rousillon (USA) 133–Eider 80 (Niniski (USA) 125) [1989 NR — 1990 14d] smallish, angular filly: first foal: dam 2-y-o 9f winner well beaten both starts at 3 yrs: 50/1, moved poorly down and tailed off in maiden at Haydock in September. *B. Palling.*

EIGHTEENTHIRTYFOUR (IRE) 2 b.c. (May 6) Ballad Rock 122–Weavers' — Tack (Weavers' Hall 122) [1990 7g 7s] IR 3,200F: leggy, good-topped colt: half-brother to Irish 1m winners De Payur (by Touch Paper) and Handsome Devil (by Wolverlife): dam Irish 4-y-o 17.8f winner: bit backward, always behind in autumn maidens at Folkestone and Lingfield. *A. Moore.*

EIGHTSOME (USA) 3 ch.c. Sharpen Up 127–Clever Dancer (Mr Prospector **112** (USA)) [1989 NR 1990 8g* 9g4 9d2 10d3 10g4 9.7g 10v3] $400,000Y: first foal: dam twice-raced 2-y-o 5f winner in Ireland, out of California Oaks winner Aladancer: won newcomers race at Saint-Cloud in May: beaten 6 lengths by Candy Glen then 1½ lengths behind Antisaar in Prix Daphnis at Evry and Prix Guillaume d'Ornano at Deauville, third and fourth starts: stays 1¼m: acts on dead ground. *A. Fabre, France.*

EIRE LEATH-SCEAL 3 b.c. Legend of France (USA) 124–Killarney Belle **83** (USA) (Irish Castle (USA)) [1989 5d3 6m5 6f2 6m2 7m* 7.5m* 7m2 7m* 8m2 8g3 7g 7m5 7g3 8g5 1990 9.1m4 8.2f* 8f3 8m 9m4 10.6s5 9g 8m2 9m 10.2g 8d6 8g4 9g 10.2s5 7d] small, attractive colt: usually looks well: poor mover: fair handicapper: won £6,300 event at Haydock in April: goes well with forcing tactics at 1m, and should stay 1¼m: acts on firm and dead going, unsuited by soft: bandaged off-fore eighth start: tough and genuine. *M. Brittain.*

EJAY HAITCH 5 b.h. Be My Native (USA) 122–Miss Spencer (Imperial Fling **38** (USA) 116) [1989 21.6d 18s4 1990 18m 18m 16.5g3 16.2g3] good-topped horse: poor handicapper: suited by a good test of stamina and give in the ground: has sweated and got on toes: bandaged last 2 outings. *T. Kersey.*

ELA-AYABI-MOU 4 ch.f. Absalom 128–Fairfields 73 (Sharpen Up 127) [1989 7g⁶ 8f 8m 7g 7m 7f⁶ 6f 7d⁵ 1990 a8g] quite modest handicapper on her day as 3-y-o: suited by 7f: acts on firm and dead going: often apprentice ridden. *Dr J. D. Scargill.* —

ELADHAM 4 b. or br.c. Lyphard's Special (USA) 122–Derrede (Derring-Do 131) [1989 8m⁶ 10f 12g 12.5f⁵ 10.5g* 1990 8.5g² 8m⁴ 10g⁴ 10d 8.2m³ 10.2m* 11f³] angular, sparely-made colt: claimed out of D. Morley's stable £6,666 fourth outing: confirmed promise of next run when winning handicap at Newcastle in July in good style, making all and well clear 2f out: suited by 1¼m: acts on good to firm going: apprentice ridden last 3 starts. *M. D. Hammond.* 62

ELA-GORRIE 2 gr.f. (Mar 18) Valiyar 129–Bishah (USA) 86 (Balzac (USA)) [1990 5m² 6g 6g⁴ 7f⁶ 7m 5m] 2,800Y: leggy filly: moderate mover: first foal: dam 11f winner, is daughter of half-sister to dam of Pawneese: poor maiden: sometimes blinkered: gave plenty of trouble to post penultimate outing: seems unsatisfactory temperamentally. *C. N. Allen.* 32 §

ELAPSE (USA) 3 gr.g. Sharpen Up 127–Bygones (USA) (Lyphard (USA) 132) [1989 5s³ 6f² 5m* 5f³ 1990 6m² 6f⁶ 6m² 5d 5m] big, strong, close-coupled gelding: fair performer: made most when second in Abernant Stakes at Newmarket and minor event at Goodwood: ran poorly in handicaps in the summer, carrying head high first occasion: stays 6f: acts on good to firm going: bandaged near-hind fourth start. *B. W. Hills.* 83

EL ARAB 3 ch.g. Sayf El Arab (USA) 127–Sally Conkers (Roi Lear (FR) 126) [1989 5s 5s 6f 6f³ 6f² 6f* 6m⁴ 7m 6v² 7g⁵ 1990 6m³ 6g 6m* 6g⁵ 6m⁶ 6g⁴ 7g³ 6m⁶ 6d 6m² 6f⁵ 7.2g³ 7d⁵ 6s a7g² a6g*] leggy, good-topped gelding: often dull in coat: moderate mover: fair handicapper: won at Pontefract in April and Southwell (by 3 lengths, running on strongly from rear) in November: stays 7f: acts on any going: often visored, including at Pontefract: below form for 7-lb claimer. *E. J. Alston.* 84

ELA-YEMOU 3 ch.g. Dara Monarch 128–Micro Mover (Artaius (USA) 129) [1989 5g 6m⁵ 6m* 6m² 6m³ 5d⁴ 1990 7f³ 6g³ 6g³ 6m² 6g⁵ 6f 6d 6m⁵ 8h⁴ 6g 7m 7g a8g⁴ a10g⁴] tall gelding: fair handicapper on most form: easily best efforts last 6 starts when fourth (moved poorly down) in claimer and handicap at Lingfield: evidently stays 1¼m: acts on firm going, ran moderately (when edgy) on dead: blinkered fifth and seventh starts: moody and probably ungenerous. *C. N. Allen.* 81 §

EL BABY (IRE) 2 ch.c. (May 15) Burslem 123–Granville Lady (High Hat 131) [1990 5m] close-coupled colt: half-brother to useful 1984 2-y-o 6f winner Downing Street (by Martinmas) and very useful Irish 7f and 9f winner Red Russell (by Tap On Wood): dam, Irish middle-distance winner, is sister to Dewhurst winner Hametus: bit backward and very green, eased when beaten 2f out in maiden at Pontefract in June. *C. E. Brittain.* —

ELBIO 3 b.c. Precocious 126–Maganyos (HUN) 112 (Pioneer (USA)) [1989 NR 1990 6m⁴ 6s* 5m* 5m* 6m] 29,000Y: rather leggy, attractive colt: first foal: dam, much-travelled filly, won from 6f to 1½m and also over hurdles: won maiden at Hamilton (hung right) in May and handicaps (impressively) at Sandown (on toes, heavily backed) and Newmarket (made all) in June: again favourite, prominent long way then eased in £7,500 handicap at Newmarket in July: best form at 5f. *P. J. Makin.* 97

EL DINERO (IRE) 2 b.c. (Mar 19) Last Tycoon 131 Eltisley (USA) 82 (Grey Sovereign 128§) [1990 5.1g* 6f³ 7d⁶ 7.3g⁶] IR 12,000Y, 26,000 2-y-o: leggy, attractive colt: half-brother to several winners here and abroad, including useful 7f winner Applemint (by Sir Ivor) and useful sprinter Dare Me (by Derring-Do): dam 2-y-o 5f winner: fairly useful colt: comfortable winner of maiden at Yarmouth in June: ran well when sixth of 20, going on having been quite badly impeded over 2f out, in Cartier Million at Phoenix Park, then moderately when sixth of 9 in Vodafone Horris Hill Stakes at Newbury: stays 7f. *W. Jarvis.* 95

EL DOMINIO 2 b.c. (May 2) King of Spain 121–Domicile (Dominion 123) [1990 6g⁵ 5g² 6m 6m² 6f³ 7m⁴ 7g⁵ 8m 8d*] 5,400F, 6,800Y, 8,000 2-y-o: close-coupled colt: keen walker: fourth foal: brother to 6f (at 2 yrs) and 7f winner Premier Prince: dam lightly raced: won maiden at Bath in October, showing much improved form, by 5 lengths from Rustiman: clearly well suited by 1m and a soft surface. *K. O. Cunningham-Brown.* 83 ?

EL DOUBLE (IRE) 2 b.c. (Mar 11) Doulab (USA) 115–Eulalie 85 (Queen's Hussar 124) [1990 6m³ 5f* 6f 6m⁵ 6s] 20,000F, 26,000Y: leggy, good-topped colt: has scope: eighth foal: half-brother to useful 7f and 1m winner Electric Lady (by 82

273

Electric), 9f and 1¼m winner Rattle Along (by Tap On Wood) and a winner in Norway: dam winner at up to 10.8f, is half-sister to very useful Suni and Honorius: fair performer: comfortable winner of maiden at Salisbury in July: ran well in nursery fourth start, carried head high and raced on probably unfavoured part of track final outing: stays 6f: usually on toes: sold 15,000 gns Newmarket Autumn Sales. *G. Harwood.*

ELEANOR CROSS 5 br.m. Kala Shikari 125–Ribofleur 74 (Ribero 126) [1989 — NR 1990 9f 7f] tall mare: poor maiden: probably stays 1m. *B. Richmond.*

ELECTRIC DANCER 4 br.g. Electric 126–Chicory (Vaigly Great 127) [1989 **48** 10g 12f⁶ 10.1m 11.7m 12g² 12s⁴ 16f 1990 a12g 16g 17.6g² 17m* 17.1d] rather leggy gelding: won poor handicap at Pontefract in October: dyed-in-the-wool stayer: acts on good to firm going: bandaged first start. *C. A. Horgan.*

ELECTRIC MONEY 4 b.c. Kafu 120–Silver Bullion (Silver Shark 129) [1989 — 6m⁵ 6m 6f 1990 6m 7f] rather leggy, workmanlike colt: quite modest winner at 2 yrs: always behind both outings in spring: best form at 6f. *W. G. Turner.*

ELECTRIC ROSE 5 ch.m. Electric 126–Rose And The Ring (Welsh Pageant **48** 132) [1989 6g 7f 8m² 7m 12.3m 12m 10f 1990 6f 8m 8.5g³ 8f* 8g* 8m 7.6g⁴ 7.6g 8m⁴ 9.1m⁵ 8f 7m] leggy, good-topped mare: bad mover: attracted no bid after winning selling handicaps at Carlisle and Yarmouth early in summer: suited by around 1m: acts on firm going: usually visored: bandaged near-hind eleventh outing: wears severe bridle or crossed noseband. *C. N. Allen.*

ELECTROJET 2 b.f. (Apr 9) Electric 126–Shy Talk 93 (Sharpen Up 127) [1990 5s **52** 5g⁶ 6m⁴ 6f* 6m 6d] 1,900Y: smallish, angular filly: moderate mover: fourth foal: half-sister to 6f winner Shy Mistress (by Cawston's Clown): dam sprinter: lowered in class, won seller (no bid) at Leicester in July, making most and rallying gamely: ran poorly in selling nursery at Ripon (swerved right and bumped start) and claimer at Haydock (possibly something amiss) after: should prove better suited by 7f. *B. A. McMahon.*

ELEGANT APPROACH 2 b.f. (Jan 28) Prince Ragusa 96–Honest Opinion 68 **46** (Free State 125) [1990 7g 8.2g³ 8g] 2,500Y: sparely-made filly: fifth foal: half-sister to 1¼m seller winner Fast Approach and 1985 2-y-o 5f seller winner Positive Approach (both by Daring March): dam 5f winner at 2 yrs: poor form, including in seller: will stay 1¼m. *W. W. Haigh.*

ELEGANT MONARCH 4 ch.c. Ardross 134–Supremely Royal (Crowned **62** Prince (USA) 128) [1989 12.5f³ 14f 11f 12f⁴ 10.6d 12.3m 16m* 17.4s 16.2d 1990 16.5m 16.2g⁵ 16.5m³ 16.2g* 18.4f³ 16f³ 17.4d 15.3g] big, rangy colt: has a markedly round action: quite modest handicapper: won 6-runner event at Beverley in July: stays well: acts on firm going, probably unsuited by soft: has run well when edgy. *F. H. Lee.*

ELEGANT PEARL 3 b.f. Ardross 134–Sombreuil 95 (Bold Lad (IRE) 133) [1989 — NR 1990 a12g 10m] rather leggy filly: fifth foal: half-sister to French 10.5f and 1½m winner Pearl Drift (by Busted) and French provincial 9.5f to 11.2f winner Keep The Rhythm (by Dance In Time): dam best at 1m: well beaten in maidens at Southwell (wore eyeshield) and Yarmouth (never able to challenge) in August. *Sir Mark Prescott.*

ELEGANT ROSE 4 ch.f. Noalto 120–Shapina 105 (Sharp Edge 123) [1989 10.2g **72** 7m³ 8m⁵ 7.6m³ a10g⁵ a8g² a8g² 1990 a8g² a6g* a7g a7g² a7g³ a6g³ 6m² 6f 7g³ 6m* 6m a7g a5g⁵ a6g] sturdy filly: won maiden at Lingfield in January and handicap at Windsor in June: best form at 6f or 7f: possibly needs sound surface: goes well blinkered: good mount for apprentice. *O. O'Neill.*

ELEGANT SPIRIT 2 b.f. (Feb 26) Elegant Air 119–On To Glory 78 (Welsh **31** Pageant 132) [1990 6f 7f 8m] 1,100Y: first foal: dam 1¼m winner: poor maiden. *Mrs N. Macauley.*

ELEGANT STRANGER 5 b.g. Krayyan 117–Tumvella (Tumble Wind (USA)) — [1989 7g 8f² 8g 1990 8m] good-quartered, attractive gelding: form on flat for long time only when second in handicap at Leicester as 4-y-o: hampered only start in 1990: suited by 1m: acts on any going: won 3 times over hurdles in 1989/90. *M. H. Tompkins.*

ELEMENTARY 7 b.g. Busted 134–Santa Vittoria 100 (Ragusa 137) [1989 10s³ **110** 12g² 12g* 10m³ 9f* 12m³ 9g² 9g 1990 8g² 10g* 8g⁴ 9m³ 12.3d*] strong, quite attractive gelding: useful performer: won listed race at Phoenix Park in May and minor event (easily in face of simple task) at Down Royal in November: ran well under 10-7 when third in handicap at Leopardstown: effective from 1m to 1½m: acts on any going: blinkered last 4 outings as 4-y-o: good hurdler: tough, genuine and consistent. *J. S. Bolger, Ireland.*

ELEMIS (USA) 3 ch.f. Sir Ivor 135–'tis A Kitten (USA) (Tisab (USA)) [1989 7g **70** 8g 1990 8f 7f² 8g³ 7g*] sparely-made filly: has a quick action: favourite but edgy, improved form when making all in handicap at Wolverhampton in July: suited by 7f: sweating second start. *J. R. Fanshawe.*

ELEVEN LIGHTS (USA) 6 ch.g. Lyphard (USA) 132–Eleven Pelicans (USA) **44** (Grey Dawn II 132) [1989 12d 12g 12f² 12g⁶ 12h² 13.6f⁴ 12g 12h³ 12m⁴ 12g⁴ 15g⁶ 1990 12h* a12g⁴ 15m* 15.8d⁴ 15d] small gelding: moderate walker and mover: poor handicapper: successful at Carlisle in July and Edinburgh (apprentice ridden) in September: stays 15f: acts well on top-of-the-ground: has sweated: often finds little off bridle: winning hurdler in August. *Mrs G. R. Reveley.*

ELFASLAH (IRE) 2 b.f. (Mar 1) Green Desert (USA) 127–Fair of The Furze 112 **71** (Ela-Mana-Mou 132) [1990 6g⁶ 7f³ 7m] 145,000Y: workmanlike filly: has plenty of scope: first foal: dam Irish 1m and 1¼m winner stayed 1½m: over 2 lengths third of 15, keeping on well, in maiden at Redcar in October: below that form in similar event final start: will stay 1m: may do better. *H. Thomson Jones.*

ELFING 3 b.f. Fairy King (USA)–Near The End (Shirley Heights 130) [1989 5m — 1990 6m 6f 5h³ 5.3h 5m] neat, well-made filly: poor maiden: third at Bath, only form: should be suited by return to further, and is bred to stay 1m. *R. Hannon.*

ELHUDHUD 3 ch.c. Habitat 134–Green Lucia 116 (Green Dancer (USA) 132) **70** [1989 NR 1990 6s² 8g⁴ 7g² 6f² 9m 7d⁶ 8g 7d a6g a8g³ a10g²] IR 120,000Y: leggy, quite good-topped colt: moderate walker and mover: third foal: half-brother to 1988 2-y-o 7f winner Muthaiga (by Kalaglow) and Irish 1¾m winner Euromild (by Shirley Heights): dam placed in Irish Oaks and Yorkshire Oaks: modest maiden: blinkered, best efforts for some time when placed in Lingfield claimers: stays 1¼m: also blinkered third (ran well) and fourth (also hooded) starts: sold out of R. Charlton's stable 13,000 gns Newmarket September Sales after fourth. *R. W. Stubbs.*

ELITE ETOILE 5 b.m. Gorytus (USA) 132–Antipol (Polyfoto 124) [1989 NR — 1990 16.2m 12g] workmanlike mare: half-sister to several winners, including useful 1983 Irish 2-y-o 5f and 1m winner Shindella and Irish 1m and 9f winner Borraderra (both by Furry Glen): dam never ran: always behind in maiden at Beverley (sweating and edgy) and minor event at Carlisle in spring. *B. Preece.*

ELIZA WOODING 2 b.f. (Mar 2) Faustus (USA) 118–Red Gloves 83 (Red God **70** 128§) [1990 6g⁴ 7f* 7m⁴ 7m 8g 8m⁶ 8m 8m⁵ 8d⁴] 6,600Y: tall, leggy filly: fourth reported live foal: half-sister to fairly useful 6f and 1m winner Takdeer (by Sharpo) and quite useful 6f and 7f winner Master Palehouse (by Moorestyle): dam placed at 6f and 7f at 2 yrs later winner in Norway, is out of half-sister to leading French 1969 2-y-o filly Vela: quite modest performer: won seller (bought in 8,500 gns) at Newmarket in July: ran well in nurseries at Leicester (for 7-lb claimer) and Doncaster on final 2 starts: will be suited by 1¼m: yet to race on very soft going, acts on any other: not particularly consistent: sold to join C. J. Hill 5,000 gns Newmarket Autumn Sales. *P. A. Kelleway.*

ELLA STREET 3 b.f. King of Spain 121–More Fun (Malicious) [1989 7m⁶ 1990 — 8v 8g 10.2m 8.2g] workmanlike filly: well beaten, including in handicaps. *N. Tinkler.*

ELLEBANNA 2 b.f. (Feb 19) Tina's Pet 121–Mainly Dry (The Brianstan 128) **68** d [1990 5g* 5g³ 5[5m⁴ 5s⁴ 5a⁵] 35,000Y: leggy, quite attractive filly: has rather round action: fourth foal: closely related to useful sprinter Iod (by Petoriuo) and half-sister to one-time fair sprinter Great Chaddington (by Crofter): dam never ran: made all in maiden at Kempton in April: didn't reproduce that form: off course 3 months after fourth start, sweating and edgy final one: speedy: unsuited by soft ground. *J. Berry.*

ELMAAMUL (USA) 3 ch.c. Diesis 133–Modena (USA) (Roberto (USA) **125** 131) [1989 7m* 8g* 1990 8g* 8f 10m² 12g³ 10m* 10.5g² 10g* 10d4]

While no Nashwan, this tough colt made a more than adequate replacement for connections with some excellent big-race displays in 1990, notably the one which won them the Coral-Eclipse at Sandown in July for the second year running. As usual the Eclipse afforded an early opportunity for the classic crop to be tested against its predecessors. The field for the race, slightly substandard, had the three-year-olds Elmaamul, Razeen and Call To Arms facing the four-year-olds Creator, Relief Pitcher and Terimon and the five-year-old Ile de Chypre. The French-trained Creator, who went into the race on a long winning run, started at 6/5 on. Razeen started second favourite

Coral-Eclipse Stakes, Sandown—
the Derby third Elmaamul beats his elders Terimon and Ile de Chypre

although Elmaamul had finished well ahead of him in the Derby on their most recent appearance. Elmaamul had been enjoying a good season. His seventh in the Guineas, hampered by Machiavellian, was perhaps his worst effort. He'd won a classic trial on his reappearance, caught the eye in another, then gone on to finish third behind Quest For Fame at Epsom, beaten four and a half lengths, always prominent and battling on under pressure in the straight. Elmaamul's Derby form was clearly an improvement on his previous best— his defeat of Raj Waki in the BonusPrint Easter Stakes at Kempton and his second to Razeen (received 3 lb), following a valiant effort to recover from a hefty bump in the straight, in the NM Financial Predominate Stakes at Goodwood—and it appeared to put him in the Eclipse with a fair chance, though Creator's superior claims were hard to deny. In the event Creator took little interest in proceedings. Up front Ile de Chypre, Elmaamul and Relief Pitcher between them ensured a strong gallop, Relief Pitcher being prevented from dominating affairs. Ile de Chypre kicked on round the home turn and for a moment looked like breaking away, but the other two held fast, and as the runners made their way up the straight Terimon began to creep into the picture as well. Elmaamul got to Ile de Chypre a furlong and a half out, passed him quickly with a fine burst of acceleration, then had to fend off a challenge

Phoenix Champion Stakes, Phoenix Park—another brave display;
Elmaamul is driven out to beat Sikeston

from Terimon through the last furlong. In a driving finish Elmaamul always had the edge; as the pair drew right away from the others he held on very gamely by half a length. Razeen, thought to have had a recurrence of wind trouble, finished fifth; 100/1-chance Call To Arms finished last.

So a three-year-old had come out on top in the meeting of the generations. The same thing happened in Elmaamul's three subsequent races, though in only one, the Phoenix Champion Stakes, did his number go up in the winner's frame. Elmaamul continued to pursue a mile-and-a-quarter programme, running next in the Juddmonte International at York in August. Carson had been adamant that the colt had failed to stay in the Derby, despite what seemed evident to the contrary at the time. At York Elmaamul turned in another splendid effort, only to find In The Groove too good at the weights. Once again impeded—he was involved in the incident which saw Dashing Blade squeezed out passing the two-furlong marker—he obtained a run just as the winner had gone on and battled away under the whip for second place, a length and a half down. That the Phoenix Champion Stakes followed just twelve days on from York made no difference to Elmaamul. He was a worthy winner of the final running of the race at the now-closed Phoenix Park venue. Very relaxed in the preliminaries as usual, in contrast to some of the opposition, he settled nicely in second or third place behind the outsider Tanwi but looked briefly in trouble as Sikeston quickened up to the leader two and a half furlongs from home. Switched outside, Elmaamul caught up with the leaders in half a furlong or so, took a while to wear down the stronger of the pair Sikeston, then stayed on under pressure to beat him a length and a half. Batshoof, third at York, lost third place to Kostroma here; the well-fancied French challenger Saumarez ran as badly as Creator had done at Sandown. A long, hard campaign might have been telling on even Elmaamul by now, for his performance lacked a bit of its customary sparkle in the Dubai Champion Stakes at Newmarket in October, his swan-song. However, as he showed no sign of it in the paddock beforehand perhaps the change in the going was responsible instead: he'd never run on softer than good before. Elmaamul, having shown prominently from the start, challenged Linamix under driving as soon as the latter went on three furlongs out but simply couldn't get the better of him, and had shot his bolt on the rising ground, where he was relegated to fourth by In The Groove and Legal Case; the winner In The Groove beat him almost six lengths.

Elmaamul has been retired along with Dayjur to Shadwell Farm in Kentucky; his fee is to be 10,000 dollars. The two stable-companions' pedigrees have one obvious common element in speed in the bottom line. Elmaamul's fourth dam is Cheb, winner eight times over five furlongs. Her daughter Wold Lass was a sprinting half-sister to the Molecomb and Lowther Stakes winner Reet Lass and to Cheb's Lad, a smart and speedy two-year-old who later stayed a mile. Wold Lass's daughter Mofida also won eight races; she was smart, too, at up to seven furlongs. Her foals include the 1985 Queen Elizabeth II Stakes third Zaizafon and the latest Lowther Stakes runner-up Dangora. Their half-sister Modena never ran, and was sold carrying Elmaamul for 85,000 dollars at Keeneland in 1986. Elmaamul himself was sold there as a foal for 185,000 dollars, and resold at the Cartier Million Yearling Sale for IR 320,000 guineas. Incidentally, looking back now it seems a stroke of good fortune for those who took part that coughing forced him to miss the Million race. Modena's second foal Modesto (by Al Nasr) showed promise in a seven-furlong maiden at Leicester in September.

Elmaamul (USA) (ch.c. 1987)	Diesis (ch 1980)	Sharpen Up (ch 1969)	Atan
			Rocchetta
		Doubly Sure (b 1971)	Reliance II
			Soft Angels
	Modena (USA) (b 1983)	Roberto (b 1969)	Hail To Reason
			Bramalea
		Mofida (ch 1974)	Right Tack
			Wold Lass

Elmaamul developed into a medium-sized, quite attractive colt at three. His best form was at a mile and a quarter, it would be fair to say, without necessarily agreeing with his jockey about his performance in the Derby.

Hamdan Al-Maktoum's "Elmaamul" (W. Carson)

Elmaamul ran his best races on good to firm or good going. He had the ideal temperament, and in his toughness, honesty and consistency showed other qualities which went towards making him a thoroughly admirable performer. *Major W. R. Hern.*

ELMAFTUN 3 b.c. Rainbow Quest (USA) 134–Shoot Clear 111 (Bay Express 132) [1989 NR 1990 10m* 10.2m³ 14g 10m⁵ 9g] 160,000Y: compact colt: carries condition: has rather round action: second foal: half-brother to fairly useful 12.3f winner Shoot Ahead (by Shirley Heights): dam, 2-y-o 5f to 7f winner and 1000 Guineas fourth, is half-sister to Sally Brown and Untold: won maiden at Sandown in June: faced stiffish tasks in quite valuable handicaps, well beaten except in slowly-run 5-runner race at Yarmouth fourth start: will be suited by 1½m: to join D. Hayes in Australia. *H. Thomson Jones.* **87**

ELMAJARRAH (CAN) 3 ch.f. Caro 133–Play Around Honey (USA) (Exclusive Native (USA)) [1989 NR 1990 7m² 8g² 11.5g³ 8d 8m 8g] lengthy filly with scope: good mover: first foal: dam half-sister to Siberian Express: modest maiden: ran fairly well third outing but out of form subsequently: may prove best short of 11.5f: sold 23,000 gns Newmarket December Sales. *H. Thomson Jones.* **77**

ELMAYER (USA) 4 ch.c. Sharpen Up 127–Dancing Lesson (USA) (Nijinsky (CAN) 138) [1989 10.5m² 12g 8m 10m 12d³ 1990 10.2f* 10f⁴ 12d 10m 10m 10f 11.5m⁶] tall colt: not a good walker: useful at his best: justified favouritism in maiden at Doncaster in March: ran poorly in handicaps last 3 outings, setting too strong a gallop in amateurs event final one: suited by 1¼m: acts on firm and dead going: ran poorly when sweating and edgy, including when blinkered fifth start. *P. A. Kelleway.* **94 d**

ELMDON PRINCE 3 b.g. Ela-Mana-Mou 132–Be My Queen 84 (Be My Guest 61
(USA) 126) [1989 8s 8.2g 1990 8f 12m² 12g⁶ 12m³ 12m a14g⁴ 10m] leggy gelding:
quite modest form: ran moderately in handicaps after good third at Edinburgh in
June: suited by 1½m: acts on good to firm ground: visored final start: subsequently
gelded. *M. Bell.*

ELMURAQASH 3 gr.c. Ela-Mana-Mou 132–Queen's Counsellor 92 (Kalamoun —
129) [1989 8m⁵ 8.2g* 1990 9g] strong, workmanlike colt: won minor event at
Nottingham as 2-y-o: broke pelvis in listed race at Newmarket in April: should have
been suited by 1¼m +: dead. *P. T. Walwyn.*

EL NIDO 2 ch.c. (Apr 26) Adonijah 126–Seleter (Hotfoot 126) [1990 5g 5d⁵ 6g 6m 49
7f 7d] leggy, workmanlike colt: has scope: second foal: half-brother to 3-y-o 7.5f to
12.4f winner Calachuchi (by Martinmas): dam in rear, including in sellers: poor form
in varied company: will stay 1m: sweating, edgy and taken very quietly down on
penultimate start. *M. J. Camacho.*

ELOFAHABIT 4 b.g. Headin' Up–Eleonora 70 (Falcon 131) [1989 7s⁶ 6m 6g 8g 33
1990 a6g⁶ 7m 6f a7g 5g 5g⁶ 6f⁵ 7f⁶ 9f 10.4g 6g 6m] sturdy gelding: carries condition:
poor handicapper: should stay 6f: blinkered 3 times at 4 yrs: wore crossed noseband
third to fifth outings: taken down early fourth. *L. J. Barratt.*

EL PASO 3 b.c. Alzao (USA) 117–Invery Lady 65 (Sharpen Up 127) [1989 6g³ 7f* 104
1990 8g⁵ 8m* 8.2f⁴ 10.6s³ 9m⁵ 9f³ 12m⁶] big, leggy colt: fluent mover: useful
handicapper: led post in £7,400 event at Newmarket in May: ran well next 3 outings
(off course 3 months before slow-starting fifth in listed race at York) but well below
form subsequently in apprentice race at Lingfield (ill at ease on track and none too
keen) and listed race at Newmarket: should stay 1½m: acts on any going: very edgy
fifth (also sweating) and sixth starts. *L. M. Cumani.*

EL REY 6 b.h. King of Spain 121–Powderhall 81 (Murrayfield 119) [1989 8g⁴ 6g 90
1990 8g⁶ 8g 8m⁵ 8g³ 8m⁴ 8d 8m³ 7.6v⁶] tall horse: moderate mover: fairly useful
handicapper: equal-third to Grey Owl in £11,000 event at Ascot in October: best
form at up to 1m, but needs testing conditions at 6f: acts on good to firm and soft
going: good mount for apprentice: sold 16,000 gns Newmarket Autumn Sales. *W.
Hastings-Bass.*

EL SHADDAI 2 br.c. (Feb 7) Green Ruby (USA) 104–Miss Serlby 65 (Runnett 35
125) [1990 5g 6m⁶ 5f 5m] 7,200Y: neat colt: has a quick action: second foal: dam
maiden best at 5f: poor maiden: looked difficult ride when visored final start. *M.
O'Neill.*

ELUSIVE LADY 3 b.f. Blakeney 126–Bewitched 63 (African Sky 124) [1989 6f —
1990 12m 10g] lengthy filly: well beaten in maidens: sweating and edgy final start:
sold 750 gns Ascot December Sales. *W. G. R. Wightman.*

ELUSIVE SPIRIT 2 ch.f. (Feb 29) Absalom 128–Sister Jinks 88 (Irish Love 117) 48
[1990 5s³ 6g 7.5d 8m⁴ 8.2d] 6,400Y: leggy, rather angular filly: has a roundish
action: seventh foal: half-sister to 3-y-o Barankya, 7f winner at 2 yrs, and fairly
useful 1988 2-y-o 5f and 7f winner James Payne (both by Horage): dam Irish 2-y-o 9f
winner: plating-class filly: tailed off final start: will be suited by 1¼m: hampered
start second outing, slowly away fourth one. *Dr J. D. Scargill.*

ELVOL 3 ch.f. Whistling Deer 117–Haleys Mark (On Your Mark 125) [1989 5f —
6m⁵ 6m a6g 1990 5f 7m] leggy, unfurnished filly: well beaten, including in selling
handicap: usually slowly away. *P. J. Arthur.*

EL VOLADOR 3 br.c. Beldale Flutter (USA) 130–Pharjoy (FR) 85 (Pharly (FR) 68
130) [1989 5s 5d 5.8h³ 7.5f³ 1990 10g 8f* 8f³ 10d⁴ 8m⁵ 10g 10f] medium-sized colt:
poor mover: quite modest handicapper: won at Bath in May: well below form at Ayr
in July final outing: stays 1¼m: acts on firm and dead going: has run well when
sweating and edgy. *M. R. Channon.*

ELWADI 3 b.c. Vaigly Great 127–Final Act 64 (Decoy Boy 129) [1989 6m 6d 7g —
1990 8g 7m] lengthy colt: carries condition: has a round action: well beaten in
maidens and handicaps: sweating and very edgy on reappearance: sold to join M.
Usher 5,000 gns Newmarket July Sales. *C. J. Benstead.*

EL YASAF (IRE) 2 b.c. (Mar 27) Sayf El Arab (USA) 127–Winsong Melody 72
(Music Maestro 119) [1990 5g⁵ 5g* 5m] 4,200Y: first foal: dam poor maiden never
ran beyond 7f: won maiden at Carlisle in June: bandaged near-hind, ran moderately
in minor event at Beverley following month. *R. W. Stubbs.*

ELZAEEM (USA) 4 b.c. Secreto (USA) 128–Billy Sue's Rib (USA) (Al Hattab —
(USA)) [1989 8.5s⁵ 10g 1990 8g 8h 8.2s] smallish, robust colt: tends to take the eye:
has a quick, rather round action: fairly useful winner as 2-y-o: lightly raced after, but

gave indications of retaining ability final outing (June): bred to stay 1¼m. *J. L. Dunlop.*

EMALLEN (IRE) 2 b.g. (Feb 12) Prince Regent (FR) 129–Peperonia (Prince Taj 123) [1990 7m⁶ 7m 6g 8.2g 8m] robust gelding: has scope: good walker: brother to 3 winners, including useful middle-distance winner Prince Pepe, and half-brother to other winners here and abroad: dam minor French 1¼m winner: soundly beaten in varied races: faced very stiff tasks in nurseries final 2 starts: will stay 1¼m. *D. A. Wilson.* **33**

EMDEO 2 b.c. (Jan 16) Starch Reduced 112–Lana's Secret 79 (Most Secret 119) [1990 6m 6d] big, rangy colt: fourth reported foal: dam 5f winner: bit backward, always behind in maidens at Newmarket (slowly away) and Doncaster (steadied stalls) in November. *R. Hollinshead.* **—**

EMERALD GULF (IRE) 2 br.f. (Mar 30) Wassl 125–Gaelic Jewel 89 (Scottish Rifle 127) [1990 6g] 10,000Y: lightly-made filly: third foal: half-sister to 3-y-o Irish Emerald (by Taufan), successful at 5f (at 2 yrs) and 10.6f: dam 1¼m winner, is daughter of very useful miler Red Ruby, a half-sister to Laser Light: slowly away, green and always behind in maiden at York in May: joined R. Whitaker after. *M. Brittain.* **—**

EMERALD MOON 3 b.g. Auction Ring (USA) 123–Skyway 76 (Skymaster 126) [1989 6f 6f 6g⁴ 6g 1990 7f 7d 7m 8m⁵ 12m] angular gelding: quite modest maiden: stays 1m: acts on good to firm ground and dead: hung right third start, ran creditably for lady on fourth: trained until after third start by R. Hollinshead: sold to join W. G. Turner 1,200 gns Ascot November Sales. *R. Simpson.* **73**

EMERALD SEA (USA) 3 ch.g. Coastal (USA)–Emerald Reef 104 (Mill Reef (USA) 141) [1990 12.3g 12.3g⁴ 10g³] tall, leggy gelding: third foal (previous 2 by Key To The Mint): dam, most disappointing sister to Diamond Shoal and Glint of Gold, stayed 1¾m: third of 9 in claimer at Salisbury in October, first worthwhile form: should be suited by return to 1½m: sold 18,000 gns Newmarket Autumn Sales. *I. A. Balding.* **56**

EMERALD SUNSET 5 b.g. Red Sunset 120–Kelly's Curl (Pitskelly 122) [1989 10g 8m 1990 8f] ex-Irish gelding: modest maiden as 3-y-o: no form on 3 runs at Brighton: pulled up in uncompetitive minor event in April: blinkered once: changed hands 750 gns Ascot October Sales: winning selling hurdler in November. *A. R. Davison.* **—**

EMERITUS 3 b.g. Niniski (USA) 125–Her Grace 101 (Great Nephew 126) [1989 NR 1990 15.3m² 16.2d*] workmanlike gelding: fourth foal: half-brother to 3 winners, including Goodnight Moon (by Ela-Mana-Mou), a fairly useful winner here and successful in USA in 1990: dam, 6f winner at 2 yrs, is half-sister to smart miler Long Row: favourite, won maiden at Beverley in June, soon struggling in rear then staying on strongly from over 2f out: looks out-and-out stayer: sold 8,600 gns Newmarket Autumn Sales and gelded. *P. F. I. Cole.* **68**

EMILIA ROMAGNA (USA) 2 b.f. (Apr 19) Forli (ARG)–Pailleron (USA) (Majestic Light (USA)) [1990 7m² 6g*] $180,000Y: rather leggy, close-coupled filly: moderate mover: sister to a minor winner in North America and half-sister to another: dam unraced sister to Grade 1 winners Prince True and Hidden Light: odds on, won maiden at Newcastle in October by a neck from Russian Mink, leading travelling well 2f out but not finding so much as expected: quickened really well in moderately-run race on debut: stays 7f: likely to improve further. *B. W. Hills.* **72 p**

EMMA MAY 3 b.f. Nicholas Bill 125–Nonsensical 99 (Silly Season 127) [1989 8.2g 8g 1990 12.3m⁶ 11s] smallish, workmanlike filly: moderate mover: no sign of ability in modest company. *N. Bycroft.* **—**

EMMA'S SPIRIT 4 b.f. Thatching 131–Emma Royale 69 (Royal And Regal (USA)) [1989 7f 10.6m 1990 11g 8g a7g⁴ 5g a7g] workmanlike filly: of little account. *B. Preece.* **—**

EMMA TOM BAY 5 b.g. Bay Express 132–Counsel's Verdict (Firestreak 125) [1989 7g 9f 7g 8.3d 1990 a8g⁴ a6g a7g⁵] good-bodied gelding: poor mover: poor maiden: visored twice at 5 yrs: dead. *Mrs Barbara Waring.* **—**

EMPEROR CHANG (USA) 3 b.g. Wavering Monarch (USA)–Movin Mitzi (USA) (L'Heureux (USA)) [1989 7g 7g 8s 1990 10g 10m⁵ 8d 9f³ 12g* 12m² 12g 12.3g⁴ 12f 12g 12m] $9,000F, IR 35,000Y: compact gelding: first foal: dam, from family of Sayf El Arab, won at around 6f in USA: made most to win maiden at Fairyhouse in June: 300/1, flattered when seventh of 9 to Salsabil in Irish Derby at the Curragh seventh start: well below that form in Ulster Harp Derby at Down Royal and 3 quite valuable handicaps here afterwards: suited by 1½m: acts on good **96 d**

Daniel Prenn Royal Yorkshire Stakes, York—
Emperor Fountain (rails) makes all again; Akaroa (left) comes second,
ahead of the grey Tarikhana and Irish challenger Victorious Deed

to firm ground: trained until after eighth start by L. Browne: gelded after final one. *J. Sutcliffe.*

EMPEROR FOUNTAIN 3 b.c. Chief Singer 131–Set Sail 64 (Alpenkonig   **99**
(GER)) [1989 NR 1990 10m³ 10m⁴ 10m* 10.5m* 10m 11d⁴ 12m] 100,000Y: workmanlike colt: moderate mover: third foal: half-brother to very smart 7f (at 2 yrs) to
1½m winner Spritsail (by Kalaglow) and quite modest 1½m to 17f winner Comedy
Sail (by Comedy Star): dam half-sister to Slip Anchor, Lancashire Oaks winner
Sandy Island and German 2000 Guineas winner Swazi: set good pace and made all in
maiden at Newbury in May and listed event at York in June: good, never-dangerous
fourth of 6 to Pirate Army at Ayr, easily better effort in listed races last 2 starts:
should stay 1½m: yet to race on extremes of going. *J. A. R. Toller.*

EMPERORS WARRIOR 4 ch.g. High Line 125–Cocoban (Targowice (USA)   **54**
130) [1989 10g⁵ 12f 11.3f² 13.1f⁵ 18g 1990 18f 11.5m 12f⁶ 15d² 16.5f²] lengthy gelding:
moderate mover: plating-class maiden: stays 2m: acts on firm and dead going: twice
bandaged behind: has joined C. Broad. *P. F. I. Cole.*

EMPIRE BLUE 7 b.g. Dominion 123–Bold Blue 82 (Targowice (USA) 130) [1989   **98**
12s* 12m 11v* 12d⁴ 1990 12g*] workmanlike gelding: fairly useful handicapper:
looking tremendously well, showed himself as good as ever when winning Great
Metropolitan Stakes at Epsom in April first time out for third year running, keeping
on well to beat Silver Owl 2 lengths: best form at 1½m on an easy surface: has worn
blinkers, but not for long time: has gone freely to post: goes very well fresh: has
joined N. Henderson. *P. F. I. Cole.*

EMPIRE JOY 5 ch.g. Sallust 134–Vivchar 80 (Huntercombe 133) [1989 9d 7g 7f   **61**
10f 8m³ 7m⁶ 8m 1990 6m² 7g* 7m² 7m³ 8m³ 7m 6g 7g] good-bodied gelding: carries
condition: poor mover: quite modest handicapper: well-backed favourite, won at
Goodwood in June: stays 1m: acts on good to firm going: visored final start: tended
to hang left and carry head awkwardly on third. *C. A. Horgan.*

EMPIRICIST 3 ch.c. Lomond (USA) 128–Spartan Helen (Troy 137) [1989 NR   **62** §
1990 9g⁵ 10m⁶ 12f5 12f³ 12g⁵ 10.2g 11s 11v] IR 65,000Y: compact colt: moderate
mover: first foal: dam unraced daughter of staying half-sister to Blakeney and
Morston: quite modest maiden: should stay beyond 1½m: blinkered first (edgy) and
last 4 starts, visored third: sold out of J. Gosden's stable 8,200 gns Newmarket
September Sales after fifth outing and no form afterwards, reluctant to race last 2
starts: one to avoid. *N. Tinkler.*

EMPRESS OF CANADA 3 b.f. Dominion 123–Canadian Charisma (Supreme —
Sovereign 119) [1989 NR 1990 7g] fourth foal: dam ran twice: 33/1, tailed off after
slow start in maiden at Newbury in April. *S. Dow.*

EMPRESS WU 3 b.f. High Line 125–Elm Park (Aberdeen 109) [1989 8f⁴ 1990 8g] —
leggy, quite good-topped filly: keen walker: fourth in maiden at Wolverhampton in
October at 2 yrs: prominent 5f in claimer over 8 months later: sold out of H. Cecil's
stable 4,600 gns Ascot April Sales. *A. Hide.*

EMPSHOTT (USA) 3 b.c. Graustark–Call The Queen (USA) (Hail To Reason) — §
[1989 6h³ 6m² 7f² 7f² 7f⁴ 8f³ 7g² 7g 1990 8g 10.2f³ 12m 10h⁴ 9g 9m⁶ 10d] good-
bodied colt: good walker: disappointing and ungenuine maiden: stays 1¼m: acts on
firm going: blinkered last 2 starts at 2 yrs: sold 3,600 gns Newmarket Autumn Sales.
G. Harwood.

EMRYS 7 ch.g. Welsh Pageant 132–Sun Approach 84 (Sun Prince 128) [1989 NR —
1990 a7g] workmanlike gelding: modest winner as 4-y-o: 16/1 from 8/1 on only race
on flat since, never dangerous in claimer (wore severe noseband) at Southwell in
November: stays 1½m: acts on any going: has been taken down early: made all in
handicap hurdle in September. *D. Burchell.*

EMSBOY 2 b.g. (Apr 15) Lidhame 109–Fille de Phaeton (Sun Prince 128) [1990 6g 34
6d 5v⁵ 6d a7g] small, sparely-made gelding: eighth foal: half-brother to 2 winners in
Belgium: dam never ran: poor maiden: blinkered, second-last in 21-runner nursery
at Newmarket on penultimate outing. *P. D. Cundell.*

EMSLEYS CHOICE 4 ch.g. Windjammer (USA)–Derrygold §§ (Derrylin 115) 37
[1989 10f⁵ 8.5g 9f 8.2f² 8h* 9f 8m⁴ 12g⁶ 9f⁵ 8f 8.5f⁶ 10m 9f 1990 a8g⁴ a7g⁶] leggy,
good-topped gelding: modest handicapper at best: stayed 1¼m: acted on hard going:
dead. *T. Fairhurst.*

EMTYAAZ (USA) 4 b.c. Danzig (USA)–The Wheel Turns (USA) (Big Burn 77
(USA)) [1989 6m³ 1990 6f* 7m* 6f⁴] robust, good sort: easy winner of 3-runner
affairs for minor event (unruly at stalls and pulling hard) and apprentice race at
Lingfield in July: again odds on, found nothing there following month: clearly
difficult to train: sent to join G. Jones in USA. *L. M. Cumani.*

EMVEN 3 b.f. Dara Monarch 128–La Vosgienne (Ashmore (FR) 125) [1989 7m 8f⁴ 60
10g 1990 12m* 12f⁴ 14g] leggy, lengthy filly: quite modest performer: won maiden at
Beverley in April: stayed 1½m: acted on firm going: sweating final start at 2 yrs,
edgy at 3 yrs: dead. *C. E. Brittain.*

ENCHANTED TALE (USA) 5 b.m. Told (USA)–Fairest Forest (USA) (Big —
Spruce (USA)) [1989 7.5m 6f 7g⁶ 8g 1990 13.8m] leggy, quite attractive mare: quite
modest maiden at best: tailed off in handicaps last 2 outings: stays 7f: has worn
crossed noseband. *W. Bentley.*

ENCHANTING HABIT 3 b.g. Enchantment 115–Miss Worth 73 (Streak 119) 60
[1989 6m⁵ 6f⁴ 7m² 6f² 6f 6s⁵ 6v⁶ 1990 8f 8g⁴ 8.2g 8g³ 7g² a8g 7m⁵ 7g 8g]
medium-sized gelding: quite modest maiden: best efforts in handicaps when placed:
suited by 7f: acts on any going: blinkered fifth to seventh starts: trained until after
seventh by W. Pearce. *C. A. Horgan.*

ENCORE AU BON 2 gr.c. (Apr 18) Petong 126–White's Pet (Mummy's Pet 125) 74
[1990 5g 6g 8f 8f* 7g] 12,000Y: good-bodied colt: first foal: dam never ran: won
nursery at Brighton in tremendous style by 6 lengths from Dance Partout: below
that form in similar event at York (slowly away) later in October: suited by 1m: acts
well on firm ground: sold 26,000 gns Newmarket Autumn Sales. *L. M. Cumani.*

ENDLESS JOY 3 b.f. Law Society (USA) 130–La Joyeuse (USA) 95 (Northern —
Dancer) [1989 5f³ 6m* 6f³ 6g⁵ 7m³ 7g³ 8g* 7g 1990 8.5g 10m] small, lengthy,
robust filly: carries condition: has a quick action: fairly useful winner as 2-y-o but
well beaten in listed races since: on toes and went down well when facing very stiff
task at Newbury in June, final start in 1990: suited by 1m. *R. J. R. Williams.*

ENERGETIC SPARK 5 b.g. Energy Plus 69–Grimsby Lady (Hot Spark 126) —
[1989 NR 1990 11m a8g] of little account. *C. Dwyer.*

ENERGIA 4 gr.f. Alias Smith (USA)–Ermione (Surumu (GER)) [1989 12.3d² 12d —
16.2m² 16f⁵ 12g⁶ 1990 18m⁵ 17.6g⁶] smallish, angular filly: modest form at best:
tailed off in minor event and claimer (blinkered) as 4-y-o: should prove suited by
further than 1½m. *P. A. Blockley.*

ENGLISH RAJ (USA) 2 ch.g. (Mar 21) Raja Baba (USA)–Salem Ho (USA) —
(Salem (USA)) [1990 7g 7g] $50,000Y: deep-girthed gelding: seventh foal: half-
brother to fair 1987 9f winner Green's Old Master (by Forli) and a minor 2-y-o 5f
winner in USA by Avatar: dam, minor stakes winner at 2 yrs, won 6 times at up to 7f:

always behind in minor event at Kempton (green) and maiden at Salisbury in autumn. *D. R. C. Elsworth.*

ENHANCEMENT   2 ch.g. (Mar 5) Noalto 120–Crimson Queen 49 (Crimson   46
Beau 124) [1990 6g³ 5f⁶ 7f 7m 6m⁵ 6d] 5,000Y, 3,800 2-y-o: leggy, lengthy gelding: third foal: dam, plater, ran only at 2 yrs: poor maiden: bandaged, visored and better for run, ran well in Leicester claimer fifth start: seems best at 5f or 6f. *P. D. Evans.*

ENHARMONIC (USA)   3 ch.c. Diesis 133–Contralto 100 (Busted 134) [1989 111
6f* 1990 7m* 7.6f⁵ 7m* 7d³] angular, good-topped colt: very useful performer: stayed on strongly from rear to win minor event at Leicester in March and listed race (edgy, beat Sheer Precocity 1½ lengths) at York in August: set plenty to do when creditable third of 6 to Anshan in Group 3 event at Goodwood: stays 7f: yet to race on soft going, acts on any other: headstrong, refused to settle second start. *W. Hastings-Bass.*

ENJOY (IRE)   2 b.f. (Apr 10) Mazaad 106–Faddle (St Paddy 133) [1990 5g 5g⁴ 6m]   —
IR 4,400Y: workmanlike filly: fourth foal: dam third over 1½m at 3 yrs in Ireland: little worthwhile form in maidens, one an auction event: sold 800 gns Newmarket December Sales. *M. J. Haynes.*

ENQELAAB (USA)   2 b.c. (Feb 13) Chief's Crown (USA)–Affirmatively (USA)   74
(Affirmed (USA)) [1990 7m⁴ 7m³ 8g³] $425,000Y: strong, close-coupled, attractive colt: has scope: second foal: half-brother to useful French 3-y-o Mais Oui (by Lyphard), successful at 1m: dam, won at up to 1¼m, is from good family: modest maiden: best effort third of 17 to Nasab at Newcastle final start: will be very well suited by 1¼m +: sure to win a race. *M. R. Stoute.*

ENSHARP (USA)   4 b.c. Sharpen Up 127–Lulworth Cove 114 (Averof 123) [1989   73
7s³ 7s³ 7f² 7m² 9m 1990 7f⁶ 7f³ 8h 6f³ 6f⁶ 6f² a7g* 6g a8g⁵] sturdy, good-bodied, attractive colt: carries plenty of condition: evens, won (for only time) claimer at Southwell in August: stays 7f: acts on any going: blinkered eighth start: apprentice ridden at 4 yrs: sold 3,500 gns Doncaster September Sales. *T. D. Barron.*

ENTERPRISE LADY (FR)   3 ch.f. Gorytus (USA) 132–Calder Hall (Grundy   56
137) [1989 6f² 6f³ 7g 6f² 6g 1990 8g⁴ 10m⁶ 8.3m* 8.3g* 8m² 8g 8.2s² 10d²] leggy, unfurnished filly: useful plater: no bid then sold out of P. Makin's stable 4,800 gns when winning twice at Windsor in August: good second afterwards: stays 1m: acts on any going: has run creditably for apprentice: sometimes sweating and edgy. *R. J. Hodges.*

ENTERPRISE PRINCE   4 b.g. Lucky Wednesday 124–Avona (My Swallow   —
134) [1989 7g⁶ 10.6m 10g 1990 a7g a8g⁶ a11g⁶] leggy, angular gelding: turns fore feet out: poor mover: won seller at 2 yrs: showed he retains a little ability in Southwell claimer second outing: should stay 1m: sold 1,700 gns Ascot May Sales. *Ronald Thompson.*

ENVIRONMENT FRIEND   2 gr.c. (Mar 19) Cozzene (USA)–Water Woo   89 p
(USA) (Tom Rolfe) [1990 7g⁶ 7m*] 23,000Y: close-coupled, useful-looking colt: has scope: sixth reported foal: half-brother to a winner in Italy: dam French 6f winner at 2 yrs, is daughter of Waterloo: co-favourite following most promising debut, won 18-runner maiden at Newmarket in October by ½ length from Fly To The Moon, pushed along 3f out and staying on really well final furlong to lead virtually on line: will stay 1m: looks a useful prospect. *J. R. Fanshawe.*

ENZO (USA)   2 ch.c. (Mar 16) Solford (USA) 127–Sacred Squaw (USA) (Olden 100
Times) [1990 7m² 7m* 7d³ 9d*] fourth foal: closely related to 1987 Irish 2-y-o 1m winner Bedford Ranger (by Bedford) and half-brother to a winner in USA: successful in maiden at Limerick in September and listed event (by 3 lengths, clear, from Favoured Nations) at the Curragh in November: around 5½ lengths third to Kooyonga in Group 3 event at Leopardstown in between: will stay 1¼m: acts on good to firm ground and dead. *J. S. Bolger, Ireland.*

EPERVIER BLEU   3 b.c. Saint Cyrien (FR) 129–Equadif (FR) (Abdos 134) 131
[1989 NR 1990 10s* 10f* 10.5s* 10.5g* 12m² 12m* 12g²]
Epervier Bleu came within an ace of winning the two biggest races in France, caught close home by Sanglamore in the Prix du Jockey-Club Lancia then just failing to catch Saumarez in the Ciga Prix de l'Arc de Triomphe. These can hardly be classified as blemishes on his record but, then again, they are the only races he's lost. Four smooth wins gained in little over two months in the spring elevated Epervier Bleu to the status of France's 'great white hope'. Not having been raced at two, he was brought out at virtually the first

opportunity in 1990 for the Prix Verso II, the second newcomers race of the Parisian season, at Saint-Cloud on March 10th. Starting at approximately 6/1 third favourite in a field of sixteen, Epervier Bleu won by ten lengths. The margin of victory shrunk as he was steadily upped in class in three outings at Longchamp, though not nearly so much as his starting price—11/10 in the listed Prix de Courcelles; 6/10 in the Group 2 Prix Greffulhe; and 1/10 in the Group 1 Prix Lupin. The impression left by Epervier Bleu in each of these was the same—that of having plenty in hand. In the Courcelles it was a case of 's'imposant dans un veritable canter' by six lengths from seven opponents headed by the subsequent Derby Italiano winner Houmayoun. Among his opponents in the Greffulhe was Bleu de France who was very much the talking horse of the spring and co-favourite for the Derby at the time of this, his reappearance. That distinction, however, didn't prevent Epervier Bleu from from beating him comprehensively. Epervier Bleu didn't have to be shown the whip and his jockey was looking round over a furlong out as Bleu de France faded badly, leaving Theatre Critic to finish second, beaten two and a half lengths, and Priolo another length and a half back in third. In a weaker field for the Lupin three weeks later, Boeuf set Epervier Bleu more to do and again got a fine response as his mount was shaken up then needed just one tap down the neck before striding out to catch Tarvisio in the last half furlong and win by one and a half lengths, going away.

One and a half miles looked well within Epervier Bleu's compass and so, therefore, did victory in the Prix du Jockey-Club at Chantilly. He'd reportedly shown his form at home too late to be entered for Epsom. At Chantilly, Epervier Bleu faced eleven opponents and was made an even-money favourite. Carrying plenty of condition and looking very well, he took the preliminaries in his stride and for much of the race he was the most likely winner. He was held up travelling smoothly towards the outside while Sanglamore, the only one going anything like so well as they turned into the straight, lost a couple of lengths on him as the two of them looked for a challenging position. About a furlong out, Epervier Bleu took the lead only to be cut down by Sanglamore's late run and be beaten half a length. Owner Daniel Wildenstein has never won the Prix du Jockey-Club but has had three victories (with Allez France, All Along and Sagace) in the Prix de l'Arc de Triomphe and it was quickly announced that Epervier Bleu would bid to give him a fourth. It was over three months before we saw him again, in the Prix Niel on Longchamp's day of Arc trials, and at odds of 2/5 he was unimpressive. Epervier Bleu looked well and didn't blow unduly afterwards but having taken the lead just inside the last two furlongs, he couldn't extend it and tended to hang, having nothing in hand to hold Antisaar by a head with Passing Sale (sixth in the Prix du Jockey-Club) closing, a length back, in third. The reported confidence of Epervier Bleu's connections for the Arc never wavered, however, and he rewarded it with a performance of the top class. There is very little between Epervier Bleu and Saumarez, the top-rated middle-distance performer of 1990, the difference between them in the Arc being Saumarez's turn of foot which took him about

Prix Lupin, Longchamp—Epervier Bleu at 10/1 on

Prix Niel, Longchamp—
Epervier Bleu scrapes home from Antisaar with Passing Sale third

four lengths clear early in the straight. Epervier Bleu had been travelling strongly in eleventh place, tracking Snurge, on the final turn then summoned a tremendous effort to emerge best of Saumarez's pursuers. The post, however, always looked like coming just too soon. Five days earlier Boeuf, who rode Epervier Bleu in all his races, had reacted to Epervier Bleu's latest piece of work with an ebullient summary of his Arc prospects. 'He slaughtered galloping companions he was only just beating a fortnight ago', he said. 'In fact he worked so well that it will stop me sleeping at nights—I just cannot wait for the race to come.' In this case, the partnership will probably get a second chance; Wildenstein is going to let Epervier Bleu have one more crack at the Arc, at least.

		Saint Cyrien (FR) (b 1980)	Luthier (b or br 1965)	Klairon Flute Enchantee
Epervier Bleu (b.c. 1987)			Sevres (b 1974)	Riverman Saratoga
		Equadif (FR) (b 1976)	Abdos (b or br 1959)	Arbar Pretty Lady
			Gracilla (b 1963)	Prince Bio Altagracia

Perhaps he'd have had second thoughts had Epervier Bleu possessed a stronger pedigree. Epervier Bleu's achievements came as a late fillip to the reputation of his dam Equadif who made an untrumpeted exit from the mainstream of European racing at Tattersalls in 1988 when she was sold for 6,200 guineas and exported to Spain. Her stay in the Wildenstein Stud had been a short one—he bought her carrying Epervier Bleu—and prior to her 1988 sale (in foal to Legend of France) Equadif had produced two unraced fillies and been barren twice, the Spanish interest in her presumably chiefly due to her one runner, La Potita (by Dom Pasquini), who won four races in Spain and was third in the Premio Banesto or Spanish Oaks. Equadif ran twenty-two times in France, winning minor events over nine furlongs and a mile and a half at Le Croise-Laroche but mostly bringing up the rear in provincial handicaps. She was, however, the only winner out of the Prix Cleopatre runner-up Gracilla. Gracilla raced and produced for Marcel Boussac and was mated to Abdos on each of her last three seasons, the resultant offspring being inbred to the excellent broodmare Pretty Lady who was dam of Equadif's unraced grandam Altagracia as well as Abdos, dual Champion Stakes winner Dynamiter and the Vermeille third Dalama. Epervier Bleu's sire Saint Cyrien, like Abdos, was a winner of the Grand Criterium. Unlike him, Saint Cyrien was able to race as a three-year-old but he couldn't recapture his form and only had three more races, never tried beyond nine furlongs. Saint Cyrien's stud record had been fairly unremarkable until Epervier Bleu came along but he headed the sires' table for money won in France in 1990, Epervier Bleu providing him with over half of it. The strong, deep-bodied, angular Epervier Bleu will have to wait at least another year before he gets his chance at stud. He seems ideally suited by an easy surface and, if he gets the chance, should stay beyond a mile and a half. A row of form figures can provide a misleading record of horse performance but in the case of Epervier Bleu it seems to present a fair assessment: he's genuine, consistent and a credit to his trainer. *E. Lellouche, France.*

EPHEMERAL   3 b.f. Shernazar 131–Swanilda (FR) (Habitat 134) [1989 NR 1990   **90**
10g* 12.5m³] 58,000Y: sparely-made filly: half-sister to several winners, including 1988 2-y-o 6f winner Plumbe Tempest (by Lyphard) and useful stayer Arizelos (by Shirley Heights): dam won over 1m in France and is half-sister to Super Dan, a very useful winner at up to 9f: led close home to beat Escrime in maiden at Sandown: 5/1 on, found nothing off bridle when 4¾ lengths third of 5 to Applecross in slowly-run Wolverhampton minor event later in May. *L. Cumani.*

EQUATOR   7 ch.g. Nijinsky (CAN) 138–Sound of Success (USA) (Successor)   —
[1989 14.6g 1990 9s] leggy, lengthy, plain gelding: lightly-raced maiden: suited by further than 1¼m: bandaged only start at 7 yrs: has run creditably for amateur and apprentice: winning hurdler in December. *J. S. Haldane.*

John Smith's Magnet Cup, York—the remarkable Eradicate goes on winning; Halkopous is a clear second

EQUINOR 3 b.c. Norwick (USA) 120–Cithern 91 (Canisbay 120) [1989 5s 5f 5.8h **57** 6m⁶ 7m⁶ 7f 8f⁶ 10g a8g⁶ 1990 a10g⁴ a10g² a10g³ a10g⁵ 12f² 12f³ 14g 10m 13.8m* 16.2f] workmanlike colt: moderate walker: plating-class handicapper: won at Catterick by a short head: well out of depth at Royal Ascot 12 days later: stays 1¾m: acts on firm going: winning hurdler. *R. A. Bennett.*

ERADICATE 5 b.h. Tender King 123–Pushkar (Northfields (USA)) [1989 8g³ 8s **115** 8f 9g² 8g⁶ 8m⁵ 8s 10.5m 10g² 10g 1990 10m* 10f* 10f* 10.5m* 10.6m⁶ 12f² 10f³ 12g] lengthy, well-made horse: usually looks very well: has a long, round stride: had a tremendous season, winning handicaps at Newmarket (2), Redcar and York: quickened into lead over 1f out when beating Parador ¾ length in £24,300 Zetland Gold Cup at Redcar and Halkopous 2½ lengths in £41,800 John Smith's Magnet Cup at York: sold to join J. Canani in California after next outing and runner-up in Grade 1 Oak Tree Invitational at Santa Anita: stays 1½m: acts very well on top-of-the-ground: blinkered sixth outing at 4 yrs, visored last 2: suited by strong handling: smart. *P. Calver.*

ERDELISTAN (FR) 3 br.c. Lashkari 128–Eunomia (FR) (Abdos (FR) **124** 134) [1989 NR 1990 10.5d* 12g³ 12m³ 11s* 12g 12v*]

Erdelistan's Gran Premio del Jockey Club provided Luciano d'Auria with clearly his biggest success of the year but he's unlikely to claim this as one of his greatest training feats. Up until two days before the race Erdelistan had been trained by Alain de Royer-Dupre. In his hands the colt was produced to go close in the Prix du Jockey-Club, in only the third race of his life and then to put up another very smart effort in the Prix de l'Arc de Triomphe. Although still very inexperienced in comparison to the majority of Arc runners, with improvement by no means out of the question, Erdelistan did look exposed after that race as one lacking the turn of foot necessary to join the top rank at a mile and a half. A longer trip would have suited him very well but whether he'll get the chance to prove it now is questionable—he'll still be a big fish over a mile and a half in Italy.

The Aga Khan's runners in the Prix du Jockey-Club always command the utmost respect—in the previous eleven editions he had a placed horse (and four winners) on each occasion that he had a runner—but Erdelistan's participation looked rather optimistic. Although his debut as short-priced favourite for a maiden at Saint-Cloud less than two months earlier had been a winning one, two heads were all that prevented him from coming third; then, like the Aga Khan's most recent French Derby winner Natroun, Erdelistan had contested the Prix de l'Avre at Longchamp, a listed race, as his warm-up for the Jockey-Club but whereas Natroun had won it by five lengths, Erdelistan finished third. Erdelistan started at 13/1 in a twelve-runner field at Chantilly. Stablemate Mahshari helped cut out a strong pace but Erdelistan couldn't hold a close position at halfway nor quicken with Epervier Bleu and Sanglamore in the straight. In the last few strides however he was running on strongest of all, beaten a length. A similar lack of acceleration when the race began in earnest told heavily rounding the final turn in the Arc when Erdelistan was tracking Saumarez one moment then floundering some four lengths adrift of him the next; he eventually finished seventh of twenty-one, five and three quarter lengths behind the winner. To win his two pattern races Erdelistan had to go outside France, to Germany for the Group 3 Furstenberg-Rennen at Baden-Baden, and, as we've said, to Italy for the Group 1 Gran Premio del Jockey Club at Milan. In both he looked a cut above his rivals beforehand and started odds on. He was probably a bit backward in Germany on his first run for nearly three months, because he had to work hard to beat the German Oaks first and third Highness Lady and Surikhana. In Italy he was much more convincing in accounting for Teach Dha Mhile by three and a half lengths and Heart of Groom another two in the colours of the Lady M Stable which had made the similarly successful (and late) purchase of another Aga Khan colt, Houmayoun, for the Derby Italiano back in May.

Erdelistan comes from the family of Marcel Boussac's closely in-bred 1949 Arc de Triomphe winner Coronation V, a sister to Erdelistan's third dam Ormara. Coronation failed to throw a single foal from fourteen consecutive coverings but Ormara, who never raced, was the dam of several winners including Locris who in five seasons reached the places in the Champion Stakes, Jacques le Marois, d'Ispahan, Moulin and Ganay. His half-sister Iroma

Erdelistan (FR) (br.c. 1987)	Lashkari (b or br 1981)	Mill Reef (b 1968)	Never Bend
			Milan Mill
		Larannda (ch 1971)	Right Royal V
			Morning Calm
	Eunomia (FR) (br 1975)	Abdos (b or br 1959)	Arbar
			Pretty Lady
		Iroma (b 1965)	Iron Liege
			Ormara

was a much more minor winner at around a mile and a quarter as indeed was her daughter, Erdelistan's dam, Eunomia. Probably the best of Iroma's offspring, from the days when Fabre still trained jumpers, was the very useful hurdler/mile-and-a-quarter winner Imyar. Erdelistan is the sixth middle-distance winner from as many foals out of Eunomia and the others, only one of which made its racecourse debut earlier than Erdelistan, include the smart filly Euliya (by Top Ville), and Erdel (by Crystal Palace) who was also placed in the Prix de l'Avre as, for that matter, was Erdelistan's sire Lashkari. Lashkari gained his greatest European success in the Prix du Conseil de Paris but garnered far greater rewards in two visits to the United States for the Breeders' Cup Turf, winning it in 1984 and coming fourth twelve months later. The useful filly Yalanoura is another from Lashkari's first crop. It is certain that, like her, Erdelistan will stay beyond a mile and a half; connections thought it necessary to provide him with a pacemaker on all but his debut. Erdelistan has yet to race on firm going but acts on any other. *L. d'Auria, Italy.*

EREVNON 3 b.c. Rainbow Quest (USA) 134–Embryo (Busted 134) [1989 8g⁶ 1990 10m 12.3v³ 14.6d a12g³ a14g*] rather unfurnished colt: ridden by 7-lb claimer, improved form when winning handicap at Southwell in December easing up by 8 lengths: clearly much better suited by 1¾m than shorter, and will stay 2m: trained until after reappearance by R. Hern. *C. E. Brittain.* **73**

ERIC'S PET 3 gr.c. Petong 126–When I Dream (Sparkler 130) [1989 6m 6f 7.6m 6g 1990 6g 8.2f 7f 8h 6f⁵ 7d 7m 10m³ 8m³ 12h⁶ 10m 8f* 8f⁵] rangy colt: plater: won handicap (bought in 4,100 gns) at Bath in September: stays 1m: best efforts on firm going: blinkered third and fourth starts. *M. D. I. Usher.* **41**

ERIK ODIN 3 b.g. Nordico (USA)–Assurance (FR) (Timmy Lad 130) [1989 7g 6g 6g³ a7g* a7g⁴ 1990 a7g² 5f 6f 6g a8g 6d a6g³ a7g a6g²] sturdy gelding: poor walker and mover: quite modest performer: stays 7f and needs further than 5f: inconsistent. *Mrs L. Piggott.* **64**

ERIN'S TOWN 4 b.g. Town And Country 124–Erin's Hospitality (Go-Tobann) [1989 10g⁴ 10f³ 1990 8.5g 12g 11.5g a12g²] smallish, workmanlike gelding: ran best race for a long time when second in handicap at Lingfield in September: will stay further than 1½m: bandaged off-hind second outing. *W. Carter.* **50**

ERIVAN 4 ch.g. Shakapour 125–Eurissia (FR) (Sir Gaylord) [1989 7m* 8.5m 10.1m⁴ 1990 8.2g 6m 9g⁵ 8d 8g 9f 11d] sparely-made gelding: has a round action: form in handicaps in 1990 only on third start: stays 1¼m: acts on good to firm going: bandaged off-hind sixth outing, blinkered seventh: trained on reappearance by I. Semple. *R. Allan.* **—**

ERNANI 3 b.c. Sadler's Wells (USA) 132–Godzilla 106 (Gyr (USA) 131) [1989 5g² 6g* 7g² 7g³ 8g² 1990 8v³ 9g³ 7f 7g² 6g* 6.2g* 7d² 7g⁴] strong, close-coupled colt: useful performer: successful in minor events at Evry as 2-y-o and at Bordeaux and Lyon in September, 1990: very good fourth to Septieme Ciel in Prix de la Foret at Longchamp final start, not entirely discredited in Jersey Stakes at Royal Ascot on third: seems best short of 1m, though bred to stay further: acts on heavy going. *R. Collet, France.* **108**

ERNIE 2 b.c. (May 17) Miller's Mate 116–Bempton 57 (Blakeney 126) [1990 8g] leggy colt: has scope: eighth foal: closely related to very smart middle-distance stayer Banket (by Glint of Gold), 2 middle-distance performers by Mill Reef, and half-brother to 1½m and 13.4f winner Mr Pintips (by Kris) and 3-y-o 10.2f winner Chirrup (by Chief Singer): dam second over 1m and 9f, is half-sister to Shirley Heights (by Mill Reef): better for race, soundly beaten in maiden at York in October. *D. Morley.* **— p**

ERRIS EXPRESS 5 b.g. Bay Express 132–Royal Home 69 (Royal Palace 131) [1989 7d⁶ 7d 8m 8.3g⁶ 6f* 6m 5m* 6f² 6m* 6s⁶ 6s 5m 1990 5f 5g 6f 5m 5g 5m³ 5m³ 6g* 5m* 5m* 6m 5m 6g³ 5m 5d⁶ 6d] attractive gelding: poor mover: in very good **77**

288

form in June, winning handicaps at Pontefract and Newbury and 3-runner claimer at Sandown in between: effective at 5f to 6f: not at best on soft going, acts on any other: wears bandages: best racing up with pace. *F. Durr.*

ESCAPE HATCH 4 b.g. Thatching 131–La Troublerie (Will Somers 114§) [1989 **46** 7g³ 7m⁴ a8g* a7g⁴ 1990 8.2s 8m 8f 7f 8f² 7.6g 8m] workmanlike gelding: moderate mover: dropped in class, form as 4-y-o only when second, not finding much, in seller (wore tongue strap) at Brighton: stays 1m: acts on firm going: blinkered second to sixth starts: very slowly away final one: sold to join B. McMath's stable 2,100 gns Newmarket Autumn Sales: one to treat with caution. *R. Hannon.*

ESCAPE TALK 3 gr.f. Gabitat 119–Getaway Girl 63 (Capistrano 120) [1989 5g 5s **47** 5m* 5f³ 6m³ 5f* 5f* 6f³ 7f* 8.2g 7g 1990 7m 7.5f⁴ 9f 8.5d⁴ 8m⁴ 8f⁶ 10.2m⁵ 9m⁶ 9g 7m 9f⁶ 10f³ 12m⁴ 13.8m³ 12g 12f 10m⁴ 10m 10d] smallish, close-coupled filly: moderate mover: plating-class handicapper: stays 13.8f: goes well on firm ground, but acts on dead: often edgy: blinkered penultimate start: claimed out of Mrs J. Ramsden's stable £6,000 second outing: sold to rejoin her 3,300 gns Doncaster October Sales. *M. Brittain.*

ESCRIBANA 5 b.m. Main Reef 126–Amorak 85 (Wolver Hollow 126) [1989 12.5g **40** 10.1m 14f 14m 11.5m 1990 16.2m⁵] good-topped mare: first sign of ability on flat in maiden at Beverley in March, losing her position soon after halfway: will be suited by extreme test of stamina: winning hurdler in 1989/90. *J. R. Jenkins.*

ESCRIME (USA) 3 b.f. Sharpen Up 127–Doubly Sure 59 (Reliance II 137) [1989 **92** 7g⁵ 1990 10m² 10g² 8m* 10g* 9g] big, angular, raw-boned filly: shows plenty of knee action: fairly useful performer: made virtually all when game winner of maiden at York in June and minor event at Sandown in September: facing stiff task, front rank over 7f when well behind in Newmarket listed race: should prove best at up to 1¼m: acts on good to firm going. *H. R. A. Cecil.*

ESPRIT D'ETOILE (USA) 5 b.g. Spectacular Bid (USA)–Star Pastures 124 **104** (Northfields (USA)) [1989 10m* 8m 1990 8g* 10f] Irish gelding: capable of useful form, but is very lightly raced: won Group 3 Kilfrush EBF Concorde Stakes at Phoenix Park in June by short head from Lotus Pool: never a threat in valuable handicap at the Curragh following month: effective at 1m and stays 13f: yet to show his form on firm going, acts on any other. *M. V. O'Brien, Ireland.*

ESTEFAN 3 b.f. Taufan (USA) 119–Benita 94 (Roan Rocket 128) [1989 5g³ 5s⁴ **48** 1990 5f³ 6g 5f⁶ 6m⁵ 7g⁵ 5g⁵ 6f⁴ a7g a6g 5m⁶ a5g] tall, good-topped filly: poor walker: plating-class maiden: easily best efforts after reappearance in handicaps sixth and seventh starts: stays 6f: probably acts on any going: blinkered sixth to ninth starts: trained until after fourth by P. Felgate. *M. W. Easterby.*

ESTONIA 4 b.f. Kings Lake (USA) 133–Paddy's Joy (Run The Gantlet (USA)) **—** [1989 10s² 12m 10d⁶ 11f* 11m 10d 1990 a11g] fourth foal: half-sister to useful Irish hurdler Bikaloy (by Bikala): dam unraced half-sister to Ballymore: won maiden at Killarney as 3-y-o: no subsequent form: stays 11f: acts on any going: blinkered fourth and fifth starts in 1989: seems inconsistent. *N. Tinkler.*

ETERNAL FLAME 2 br.f. (Mar 19) Primo Dominie 121–Cameroun 106 (African **73** Sky 124) [1990 5m⁴ 6d³ 6m³] lengthy filly: quite good mover: first foal: dam 2-y-o 5f winner stayed 6f: modest maiden: off course 3½ months after debut: will probably stay 7f: best run on dead ground. *J. W. Hills.*

ETERNAL TRIANGLE (USA) 4 b.f. Barachois (USA)–Clover Lady (USA) **—** (Iron Constitution (USA)) [1989 8g⁵ 8h 8g⁴ 7m⁶ 10g 1990 a7g a6g] close-coupled, workmanlike filly: quite modest handicapper at best; slowly away and always behind both outings early in year: stays 1m: best efforts on good ground: occasionally sweats and gets on toes. *J. D. Czerpak.*

ETERNITY STAR (USA) 2 br.c. (Feb 26) Majestic Light (USA)–Northern **107** Eternity (USA) 108 (Northern Dancer) [1990 6d* 7d⁴ 8m² 7.5d⁴ a8.5f] first foal: dam 2-y-o 6f winner also second in Lowther Stakes, is half-sister to good 1980 French 2-y-o 5f and 7f winner Miswaki: sire top-class middle-distance performer: won newcomers race at Saint-Cloud in June by 6 lengths: in frame in listed race at Deauville, Prix La Rochette (length second of 7 to Beau Sultan, leading halfway up straight to near line) at Longchamp and Prix Eclipse (over a length fourth to Crack Regiment) at Saint-Cloud: last of 11 in Breeders' Cup Juvenile at Belmont Park: will stay 1¼m: acts on good to firm ground and dead: wore a tongue strap at Longchamp. *F. Boutin, France.*

ETHAN FROME (FR) 3 ch.c. Pharly 130–Festive Lady (Margouillat 133) **111** [1989 NR 1990 9g³ 12g* 12g⁵ 15m² 15g⁵ 15g² 15g² 15g] first reported foal: dam French provincial 12.5f winner: won maiden at Saint-Cloud in April: second in Prix

Berteux at Chantilly, Prix Kergorlay (beaten 1½ lengths by Al Maheb) at Deauville and listed race at Longchamp: never travelling smoothly in Group 3 contest at Longchamp final start, giving impression worth a try in blinkers or a visor: stays 15f: very useful. *D. Smaga, France.*

ETON LAD   3 b.c. Never So Bold 135–Carolside 108 (Music Maestro 119) [1989 **107** 8m² 1990 7m³ 8.2g² 8.5g* 8g⁴ 8.5g* 8m 8g⁵ 9g] sparely-made colt: fluent mover, with a long stride: useful performer: gamely made virtually all when successful at Epsom in £10,700 event in April and Diomed Stakes (by ½ length from Landyap) in June: ran poorly fourth and last 3 starts, racing freely in blinkers on final one: will be suited by 1¼m: needs to be able to set pace. *N. A. Callaghan.*

EUCHAN GLEN   3 b.c. Wolverlife 115–Down The Line 74 (Brigadier Gerard **83** 144) [1989 6f* 6m 6s⁴ 6m 6g⁴ 7g* 1990 7f⁶ 6v⁶ 7g* 7h 7g⁵ 8.2f⁶ 8g² 8m⁴ 11g* 12m* 11f* 12m] leggy colt: fair form: successful in claimers at Carlisle (making all) in April and generally uncompetitive events at Hamilton (twice) and Ayr in July: pulled hard in lead when well behind in £8,100 handicap final start: best form at 1m: acts on firm ground: has run well for 7-lb claimer and lady: consistent. *J. S. Wilson.*

EUROBLAKE   3 b.g. Roscoe Blake 120–Pie Eye 88 (Exbury 138) [1989 5f⁴ 6m **79** 5f⁵ 7f⁴ 7.5m* 7f⁶ 7f⁶ 7.5m³ 8m⁴ 7g 8f⁶ 7d⁶ 8g 1990 8f 8.5m⁴ 8.2f² 8g² 10.6f⁵ 8f⁵ 8g 8g⁶ a8g² 8f² 8f* 8h⁶ 7.5g* 8m 7.5m 8m⁶ 7d² a7g* a7g] compact, good-quartered gelding: turns off-fore in: modest performer: won handicap at Newcastle in July, seller (no bid) at Beverley in August and handicap (making most and showing improved form) at Southwell in November: stays 1m: acts on firm and dead ground: sometimes takes keen hold: tends to be on toes: has sweated: has sometimes hung markedly. *T. D. Barron.*

EUROCON   6 b.g. Ile de Bourbon (USA) 133–Consistent 90 (Connaught 130) **52** [1989 13.8d* 13.8d² 17f⁵ 15.8m 15.8m² 16f⁶ 16g³ 15.8f³ 15.8g⁵ 16.2f⁴ 17f 15.8g* 15g 1990 a16g² 18d² 17.1d⁴ a16g] small gelding: good mover: plating-class handicapper on his day: stays well: acts on firm and dead going: best ridden up with pace: has won for apprentice: slowly away when tried in visor: has run moderately when sweating: goes very well at Catterick: inconsistent. *T. D. Barron.*

EURODOLLAR   6 gr. or ro.r. Sparkler 130–Silver Berry (Lorenzaccio 130) [1989   — NR 1990 8f] leggy, lengthy rig: has a rather round action: modest handicapper: 50/1 and carrying condition, much better than position suggests in Lincoln Handicap at Doncaster in March, running on well far side after being hampered 2f out: not seen out again: stays 9f: probably acts on any going: sold 900 gns Newmarket Autumn Sales. *W. Carter.*

EURO GALAXY   3 ch.g. Crofthall 110–Patent Pending (Goldhill 125) [1989 6f⁴ **75** 1990 7h³ 7g* 7f² 7m³] leggy, lengthy, sparely-made gelding: turns fore-feet out: won maiden at Thirsk in August: good second in Thirsk minor event, better effort following month: should prove best at 6f or 7f: acts on hard ground: refused to enter stalls on intended reappearance. *R. M. Whitaker.*

EUROLINK THE LAD   3 b.g. Burslem 123–Shoshoni Princess (Prince **93** Tenderfoot (USA) 126) [1989 6f⁶ 6m⁴ 7g 6f² 7m³ 6d⁴ 6f² 6f* 6v⁴ 7d 1990 6m 7f² 7f³ 7g* 7.6m⁴ 7.3g* 7m⁵ 8g] rather unfurnished gelding: fairly useful performer: quickened well to lead close home and win handicaps at Newbury in August and September: below form last 2 starts, particularly so on final one (on toes): stays 7f: has won on firm going, but best effort with some give. *J. L. Dunlop.*

EURO MARK (IRE)   2 ch.g. (Mar 28) On Your Mark 125–Old Acquaintance **53** (Virginia Boy 106) [1990 5.8m 5m 6m⁶ 5.3h² 5m⁵ 7m 5f⁴] IR 3,200F, 2,200Y, 1,500 2-y-o: sturdy gelding: eighth living foal: dam unraced, from family of Knockroe: fair plater: hung left when running well fourth and fifth (median auction) outings: best form at 5f: visored final start. *M. Madgwick.*

EVADING   2 br.f. (Apr 23) Petoski 135–Hiding 84 (So Blessed 130) [1990 7f 8m⁵ **61** 9g a7g*] 8,000Y: rather sparely-made filly: half-sister to 3-y-o 6f winner Lurking (by Formidable) and 1986 2-y-o 5f winner Aid And Abet (by Pas de Seul): dam lightly-raced 2-y-o 5f winner from same family as Bassenthwaite: quite modest performer: visored first time, won 14-runner maiden at Southwell in November by a neck: fifth of 30 in Newmarket seller on second outing: should stay 9f. *W. Hastings-Bass.*

EVASIVE PRINCE (USA)   2 b.c. (Apr 4) Secreto (USA) 128–Overstate (USA) **87** P (Speak John) [1990 7m² 7s*] $80,000Y: unfurnished colt: good mover: half-brother to many winners, notably champion Canadian colt Overskate (by Nodouble), successful at up to 1½m: dam winner at up to 6f at 2 yrs: odds on, won maiden at Lingfield in October very easily by 1½ lengths from Oka Flow, soon travelling strongly on unfavoured part of track and never off bridle: will stay at least 1m: sure to do good deal better, and appeals as one to follow. *M. R. Stoute.*

EVENING AFFAIR 4 b.f. Red Sunset 120–Miss Flirt (Welsh Pageant 132)   74
[1989 11.3m⁶ 12f⁴ 11.5m⁶ 16m 12.5m⁶ 11.7f² 8f* 9f² 8g² 7g 1990 10f² 10.2m⁶ 9g⁴ 10g⁵ 10h* 10h⁶ 9f²] lengthy, sparely-made filly: moderate worker: modest handicapper: won at Brighton in July: stays 1¼m: acts well on very firm going: usually blinkered: suited by strong handling: not one to trust implicitly: sold 6,800 gns Newmarket December Sales. *R. Boss.*

EVENING HOUR 5 ch.m. Glenstal (USA) 118–Field Lady 71 (Habitat 134)   —
[1989 6d 7m 7h⁵ 7g* 7f 1990 a11g⁵ 7m⁶ 8m] good-quartered mare: won handicap at Yarmouth as 4-y-o: well beaten early in 1990, in selling event (blinkered) final outing: form only at 7f: sometimes sweats: bought 2,700 gns Doncaster January Sales: inconsistent. *P. A. Blockley.*

EVENING RAIN 4 b.c. Hays 120–Fine Form (USA) (Fachendon) [1989 8s 8g*   —
8.2g* 10m⁵ 9m 1990 8f 8f 8f 7m] big, workmanlike colt: little show since quite modest winner of spring handicaps as 3-y-o: sweating and mulish at stalls final start (June): stays 1m. *R. J. Hodges.*

EVENING STAR 4 b.f. Red Sunset 120–Avereen (Averof 123) [1989 8m⁵ 8m⁵   71
10f 7.6f 8g a8g³ a8g³ a8g³ 1990 a8g* a8g⁴ a8g² a8g³ a8g⁵ a8g² 8f 9f 8m 8m 8.2m a8g⁴ 8g* 8g a8g* a8g* a8g a8g⁴] leggy filly: ran well most starts on all-weather, winning at Southwell in maiden in January and handicaps (apprentice ridden) in November: form on turf at 4 yrs only when winning handicap at Salisbury in October: stays 1m: seems to need give in the ground: used to wear visor (didn't last 7 outings). *A. Hide.*

EVENING SUNSET 4 b.g. Red Sunset 120–Princess Elinor (Captain James   —
123) [1989 8m 10.1g 10.1d⁴ 10.2f 1990 12f 10m 16.5m⁶ a12g⁴ a18g] sturdy gelding: well beaten in varied events. *Miss G. M. Rees.*

EVENTIDE 4 ch.f. Red Sunset 120–Tagik (Targowice (USA) 130) [1989 7m³ 8g   —
8m⁴ 8m 7m⁵ 7g 1990 a10g⁴ a11g] sparely-made filly: shows traces of stringhalt: poor form, including in sellers: suited by 1m: blinkered twice, visored once at 3 yrs: has looked unenthusiastic. *D. Burchell.*

EVERGLADES (IRE) 2 b.c. (Feb 18) Green Desert (USA) 127–Glowing With   76
Pride 114 (Ile de Bourbon (USA) 133) [1990 7m⁴ 7m] sturdy colt: carries condition: third foal: dam 7f and 10.5f winner: over 5 lengths fourth of 12, progress from halfway until no extra final furlong, in maiden at Yarmouth in September: well-backed second favourite, found little off bridle in similar event at Leicester following month. *G. Wragg.*

EVER RECKLESS 4 ch.f. Crever 94–Gold Spangle 97 (Klondyke Bill 125)   62 §
[1989 5s⁴ 5s 5g 5f⁴ 5f⁶ 5m 5m 5.8h* 5g 5f 5m⁴ 5m⁶ 5m* 5g 5f 5.1g 5m 1990 5m 8m 5d⁶ a5g² a7g 6f⁶ 5f⁴ 5m⁴ 7m² 7d a5g⁴ 6m⁵ 5m* 5f⁵ a5g* 5m 5m³ 5m a6g a5g³ a5g² a6g] leggy, lengthy, unfurnished filly: poor walker: won handicaps at Catterick (apprentices) and Southwell in August: best at 5f: acts well on top-of-the-ground: usually wears blinkers or visor: wore bandages behind on all-weather late in year: often sweats: has been taken down early: has looked unenthusiastic and goes well for tender handling: retained 4,200 gns Newmarket Autumn Sales: inconsistent. *D. T. Thom.*

EVER SHARP 6 b.g. Sharpo 132–Blue Jane 81 (Blue Cashmere 129) [1989 5g⁵ 5f   —
5g 5m 5m 1990 5m 5g 6d] big, lengthy, workmanlike gelding: poor mover: smart at one time in 1988, but below his best towards end of that season and disappointing since: suited by 5f: acts on any going: blinkered and visored once: has found little off bridle, swished tail under pressure and is suited by waiting tactics: sold to join C. Holmes's stable 1,200 gns Newmarket Autumn Sales. *P. J. Makin.*

EVER SO ARTISTIC 3 ch.c. Claude Monet (USA) 121–Ever So 78 (Mummy's   58
Pet 125) [1989 NR 1990 7f 7f a7g 6m⁵ 6m⁶ 5m 5m 6f⁵ 5.1m 5.3f 6g a5g*] sparely-made colt: first foal: dam 2-y-o 6f winner: plating-class sprinter: 33/1, improved form to win 8-runner claimer at Lingfield in December: mostly visored, including at Lingfield: badged behind seventh (sweating and edgy) start, near-hind on fourth: changed hands 700 gns Ascot November Sales before final one. *P. Howling.*

EVER SO SHARP 7 br.h. Caruso 112–Sealed Contract 76 (Runnymede 123)   34
[1989 6f 5f 7m 5f 5m a7g a6g 1990 a11g a11g a8g a5g a6g 5m⁴ 5m 5g⁶ 5.8h³ 5.8f 5f 5f 6m 5m 5m 8.2v] small, workmanlike horse: bad mover: poor handicapper: suited by 5f: acts on hard going: usually blinkered: has carried head high: inconsistent. *J. P. Smith.*

William Hill Lincoln Handicap, Doncaster—a high draw proves essential in the early-season lottery; Evichstar wins from Vilanika (striped sleeves), with the 1989 winner Fact Finder (striped cap) taking fifth behind Inishpour and Vanroy (rails)

EVERWELL WIN (IRE) 2 ch.g. (Mar 6) Hard Fought 125–Flat Refusal (USA) — (Ribero 126) [1990 6m 6g 5v] IR 2,900F, 9,400 2-y-o: compact gelding: half-brother to numerous winners, including modest sprinter Tread Lika Prince (by Prince Tenderfoot): dam won twice over 6f in North America: soundly beaten in maidens and a seller in autumn: sold 880 gns Doncaster November Sales. *J. Parkes.*

EVERY ONE A GEM 3 ch.g. Nicholas Bill 125–Lady Bequick 81 (Sharpen Up 57 127) [1989 7m 8.2g 8g5 1990 10f 10m 8m5 9f3 11.5g2] big, good-bodied gelding: plating-class maiden: seems suited by 1½m: blinkered (only form in 1990) last 3 starts. *M. J. Ryan.*

EVICHSTAR 6 ch.g. Jasmine Star 113–Chive (St Chad 120) [1989 6m 6f 8.2m 89 7m4 8m5 8g3 10g4 10.2g 10.6m6 10f3 8.2d2 8g2 8g* a7g* a7g3 1990 a8g* a8g2 a7g 8f* 8f* 8f6 10g6] close-coupled, good-quartered gelding: returned to his best in first half of year: successful in handicaps at Southwell in January, Doncaster (33/1, making all in £48,000 William Hill Lincoln Handicap) in March and Newcastle in April: best racing up with pace over 1m: acts on any going: wears blinkers: has worn bandages: used to sweat, get on edge and prove difficult to settle, but became more tractable: taken down early: sold to race in Holland 8,000 gns Ascot October Sales. *J. G. FitzGerald.*

EXCELSIS 4 b.c. Shirley Heights 130–Sacred Ibis (Red God 128§) [1989 8f5 10m2 52 12m 11.7m4 10h3 10m a10g a10g6 1990 a12g 10m 10.1m5 11.5f2 11.7f2 12f5 12m6] neat colt: plating-class maiden: stays 11.7f: acts on firm going: visored first outing: trained until after then by J. Dunlop. *J. R. Jenkins.*

EXCEPTIONAL BID (USA) 5 b.h. Spectacular Bid (USA)–Gulls Cry (USA) 83 (Sea-Bird II 145) [1989 10f2 13.3f5 10m2 11.5m* 12m5 12g 1990 7g4 10.6d] angular, useful-looking horse: poor mover: fair performer: first outing for 11 months, good fourth, outpaced early, to If Memory Serves in ladies race at Doncaster in September: stays 1½m: acts on good to firm going, possibly unsuited by dead: sold 7,600 gns Newmarket Autumn Sales. *H. R. A. Cecil.*

EXCHANGE FAYRE 3 ch.c. Burslem 123–Sanibel (Ahonoora 122) [1989 6m — a6g 1990 a6g3 a6g a7g 6m 8f6 10f] close-coupled, sparely-made colt: poor plater: moved badly and pulled up third start: doesn't stay 1¼m: blinkered debut: sold 525 gns Ascot November Sales. *R. O'Leary.*

EXCLUSIVE VIRTUE (USA) 2 b.f. (Mar 20) Shadeed (USA) 135–Exclusive 80 p Order (USA) (Exclusive Native (USA)) [1990 7g2 7m*] lengthy filly: has a powerful, round action: fourth foal: half-sister to 2 winners in France, including useful 1988 2-y-o 5.5f and 7f winner Irish Order (by Irish River): dam French 6f to 7f winner stayed 1m: ¾-length second of 15, staying on strongly, to Fragrant Hill in valuable minor event at Newbury in September: didn't need to run to that form when landing odds in workmanlike style in maiden at Leicester following month: will stay 1m: strong-running sort: likely to improve. *M. R. Stoute.*

EXECUTION ONLY (IRE) 2 b.c. (Mar 10) Sure Blade (USA) 128–Headin' 41 Home 105 (Habitat 134) [1990 6m4 a6g a6g] 23,000Y: heavy-topped colt: half-brother to several winners, including Day Is Done (by Artaius), very useful at up to 9f, and 7f and 1m winner Instinctive (by Known Fact): dam won at 7f and 1m: 10 lengths last of 4, slowly away and fading from over 1f out, in maiden (coltish, unruly beforehand) at York in July: always towards rear in similar events at Southwell. *J. W. Watts.*

EXECUTIVE LADY   3 ch.f. Night Shift (USA)–Rosier 99 (Hotfoot 126) [1989 NR 1990 8m 6g4 7.5f3 a8g 7g2 7m 7m3 7g 7d] sturdy filly: poor walker: third foal: dam, 2-y-o 6f winner who promised to stay 1¼m, is half-sister to 1½m winner Night Sky and winner at up to 1m Town Sky, both useful: quite modest form at best, including in seller: stays 7f: acts on good to firm ground: has had tongue tied down, including for best effort seventh outing. *I. Campbell.*   **59**

EXHAUST MAN   6 b.g. Crooner 119–Silk Fashion 61 (Breeders Dream 116) [1989 12g 12s5 16m5 1990 15.5f* 14.8m3 8m] small, compact gelding: plating-class handicapper: first race for over 10 months, won at Folkestone in April, hanging right over 1f out: stays 2m: particularly well suited by top-of-the-ground: ran moderately in blinkers: suitable mount for inexperienced rider. *Miss B. Sanders.*   **55**

EXHELLA (IRE)   2 ch.f. (May 22) Exhibitioner 111–Junella 95 (Midsummer Night II 117) [1990 5m 7.5d3 7d 6f4 7.5f 7f 7d 8.2s] IR 2,200Y: close-coupled, workmanlike filly: half-sister to plating-class stayer Joist (by Malinowski): dam won from 1¼m to 2m: plating-class maiden at best: ran moderately when visored or blinkered fourth and fifth (trained until after then by M. H. Easterby) starts. *K. B. McCauley.*   **51 d**

EXHIBITION ROAD   3 ch.c. Exhibitioner 111–The Way She Moves (North Stoke 130) [1989 5d 5g 6d 7m5 1990 17.6m] strong, compact, sprint type: poor form at 2 yrs: tailed off in August maiden, only start in 1990. *D. H. Barons.*   **—**

EXIT TO NOWHERE (USA)   2 b.c. (Mar 11) Irish River (FR) 131–Coup de Folie (USA) 112 (Halo (USA)) [1990 8g2 8m2 7.5d*]   **121 p**

Machiavellian's half-brother Exit To Nowhere, and not his stable-companion Hector Protector, seems likely to be Boutin's representative in the Two Thousand Guineas at Newmarket if the trainer's remarks after Exit To Nowhere's runaway victory in the Prix Thomas Bryon at Saint-Cloud in October were reported correctly. For much of the season the unbeaten Hector Protector had appeared the obvious choice, but Exit To Nowhere is apparently considered likely to be the better suited by Newmarket's straight mile, and in any case he's a very smart colt in his own right. Indeed, Exit To Nowhere's form is almost as good as Guineas second Machiavellian's at the same stage of his career, and if he is brought over to Newmarket he'll be a very interesting contender.

Exit To Nowhere took his place at Saint-Cloud as one of only two maidens in a nine-runner field. He'd finished second in both his previous races, going down by a nose to Tel Quel in a newcomers event at Longchamp at the beginning of September then coming out best at the weights, but still

Prix Thomas Bryon, Saint-Cloud—
Machiavellian's half-brother Exit To Nowhere comes into the classic picture;
he gives a substantial beating to Reason To Trick
and other useful French two-year-olds

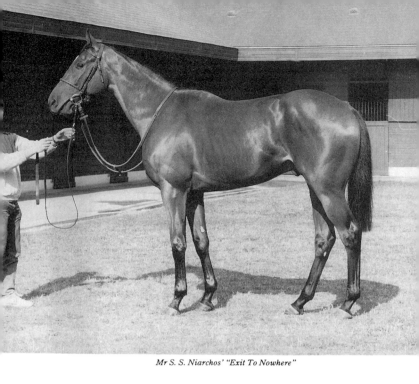

Mr S. S. Niarchos' "Exit To Nowhere"

finding the subsequent Grand Criterium runner-up Masterclass half a length
too good, in a maiden over the same course and distance later in the month.
His most formidable opponents at Saint-Cloud seemed to be the multiple
winner Booming, whose only defeat in seven races had been when third to
Hector Protector and Lycius in the Prix de la Salamandre, the Prix Eclipse
runner-up As Que To, and the unbeaten Zanadiyka. Exit To Nowhere
improved dramatically on his previous form, which had come on a sounder
surface, and ran out a thoroughly convincing five-length winner. Turning for
home in fifth position Exit To Nowhere made his move halfway up the home
straight and impressed so much with his finishing effort that the chief writer
for the French racing daily *Paris-Turf* reported excitedly that he was 'going
practically twice as quickly as his opponents', adding that he 'took five lengths
out of the runner-up Reason To Trick in less than a hundred and fifty metres'.
While much of Exit To Nowhere's improvement can probably be attributed to
the good to soft ground, which one might have anticipated since he has a
round action, he'd quite likely come on in the four weeks since his previous
run (when he still looked on the weak side); and possibly, too, from being held
up even longer. Whatever the reasons for his upturn in form Exit To Nowhere
is clearly a very smart colt. While too much notice shouldn't be taken of a
collateral form-line linking him to Hector Protector through fifth-placed
Booming, who ran below form and may have been feeling the effects of a long
season, third-placed As Que To, while perhaps better at a shorter trip, ran
near enough to her best to suggest Exit To Nowhere's form is almost as good
as any two-year-old's in France or Britain.

```
                              ┌Riverman          ┌Never Bend
                ┌Irish River (FR) ┤  (b 1969)     ┤River Lady
   Exit To      │  (ch 1976)   └Irish Star        └Klairon
Nowhere (USA)  ┤                 (b 1960)          ┌Botany Bay
 (b.c. Mar 11, 1988)              ┌Halo            ┤Hail To Reason
                └Coup de Folie (USA)┤  (b or br 1969)└Cosmah
                   (b 1982)        └Raise The Standard┌Hoist The Flag
                                     (b 1978)        └Natalma
```

Exit To Nowhere, as previously mentioned, is a half-brother to Machiavellian (by Mr Prospector), whose pedigree was dealt with extensively in *Racehorses of 1989* and is summarised in his entry this year. Exit To Nowhere, a tall, well-made colt, altogether a handsome individual and with plenty of scope, as his portrait shows, is by the top-class French miler Irish River, who is much more of an influence for stamina than Mr Prospector, and numbers such as the stayer Orban and the middle-distance performers Grand Pavois, Ballinderry and Mashkour among his better winners. Machiavellian stayed a mile, but was a rather headstrong individual, particularly in his early days, and was brought back in distance at the end of his career. Exit To Nowhere seems of calmer disposition, and quite possibly he'll stay at least a mile and a quarter. He seems set for a good season as a three-year-old. *F. Boutin, France.*

EXPLOSIVE SPEED (USA) 2 b.c. (Feb 23) Exceller (USA) 129–Strait Lane (USA) (Chieftain II) [1990 7n₁⁵] half-brother to 5 winners, notably smart French 1½m performer Silver Lane and Hawkster, Grade 1 winner at 8.5f (at 2 yrs) and 1½m in USA (both by Silver Hawk): dam unraced: backward, never better than mid-division in 12-runner maiden at Leicester in September: showed a fluent, round action: sure to improve, particularly over further. *M. Moubarak.*   **52 p**

EXPRESS ACCOUNT 3 b.f. Carr de Naskra (USA)–Miss Audimar (USA) (Mr Leader (USA)) [1989 7m³ 6f³ 1990 8g 8m* 8m 8d 10f⁵ 8h⁴ a8g 9m⁶ 8g* 8g⁴ 10m* 9m³ 10d a10g⁵ a12g⁴ a11g] leggy, rather dipped-backed filly: modest handicapper: won at Thirsk (maiden, made all) in May then at Kempton (came from rear) and Redcar (apprentices) in September: well below form final start: stay 1½m: acts on hard going, ran badly on dead: blinkered sixth to eighth (sweating, edgy and raced too freely) outings: bandaged near-hind penultimate one: goes well for 7-lb claimer. *R. J. R. Williams.*   **77**

EXPRESS EDITION 3 b.f. Comedy Star (USA) 121–June Fayre (Sagaro 133) [1989 5s 6f 7m⁶ 7m³ 7m⁶ 7g⁵ 6g 6g* 6g 1990 8g 8.2g* a8g 9g* 9g 10g 9g 9f³ 9f³ 9f 8.2s] small, angular filly: poor walker and mover: plating-class performer: successful in claimers (claimed out of M. Tompkins' stable £10,252 on second occasion) at Hamilton in May and June: inconsistent afterwards: stays 9f: acts on firm ground: blinkered in 1990 (except fifth start) and when successful at 2 yrs: bandaged near-hind penultimate start: sold 1,850 gns Doncaster October Sales. *C. R. Beever.*   **54 d**

EYE BEE AITCH 5 b.m. Move Off 112–River Petterill 89 (Another River 89) [1989 7f 8f 11g 11s 1990 8v 8g⁶ 8m³ 12g] bad plater. *W. Storey.*   **17**

EYES ON THE PRIZE 3 ch.f. Lomond (USA) 128–Girl Friday (USA) 106 (Secretariat (USA)) [1989 8m 10g 1990 7.2d⁶ 10.6s⁴ 16s⁵] strong, good-bodied filly: no worthwhile form but showed signs of ability in handicaps at Haydock and Newcastle (visored) last 2 outings: should stay at least 1¾m. *W. Hastings Bass.*   **— p**

F

FABLED ORATOR 5 b.g. Lafontaine (USA) 117–Brompton Rose 98 (Sun Prince 128) [1989 6s⁵ 6v 7d 7.6f 6f² 7f* 6f a10g 1990 8m] tall, angular gelding: moderate mover: modest handicapper on his day: stays 7f: acts well on firm going: has worn blinkers, including when successful at 4 yrs: suited by forcing tactics and seems best racing apart from others. *G. G. Gracey.*   **—**

FABRICIOUS (IRE) 2 ch.g. (Mar 31) Precocious 126–Pale Silk (FR) (Shantung 132) [1990 5f 5f⁵ 6g 7g⁴ 7g⁵ 7m* 7.5f* 7m* 7f 6m⁴ 7g³ 7d* 7s] close-coupled gelding: half-brother to winners in France at 1m+ by Margouillat and Fabulous Dancer: dam lightly-raced French maiden: much improved: made all in claimer at Redcar, nursery at Beverley and sellers at Newcastle (retained 4,100 gns) in July and Catterick (no bid) in October: will stay 1m: acts on firm and dead ground, but   **76**

may be unsuited by soft: best in blinkers: sold 13,000 gns Newmarket Autumn Sales. *M. W. Easterby.*

FABULOUS DEED (USA) 3 ch.f. Shadeed (USA) 135–Fabulous Salt (USA) 88 **77** (Le Fabuleux 133) [1989 7g 1990 10g³ 10f²] leggy, rather unfurnished filly: moderate mover: modest form when placed in summer maidens at Beverley and Brighton: sold 5,200 gns Newmarket December Sales. *M. R. Stoute.*

FABULOUS QUEEN (FR) 7 b.m. Fabulous Dancer (USA) 124–Moquerie — (FR) 120 (Beaugency (FR) 126) [1989 10f 1990 11.5m4] lengthy ex-French mare: sister to French 1m winner Mouette and half-sister to several other winners, including very useful 1½m and 1¾m winner Quemora (by Riverman): dam dead-heated in Prix de Pomone and was suited by 1½m +: successful over 1m at 2 yrs, 3 yrs and 4 yrs, including in listed event at Evry: showed she retains a little ability in claimer at Lingfield in May, no extra final 2f: may be suited by return to shorter. *J. A. Glover.*

FABULOUS SHAUN 4 b.g. Petong 126–High State 72 (Free State 125) [1989 **39** 7d 8m⁶ 6f 9m 8m 6m 6g 6s 1990 8m 10m 8f² 8m 7d 7m] workmanlike gelding: plating-class maiden at best: form at 4 yrs only on third outing: stays 1m: acts on firm going: often blinkered or visored. *P. S. Felgate.*

FACE NORTH (IRE) 2 b.g. (Apr 22) Fayruz 116–Pink Fondant (Northfields **67** (USA)) [1990 5f* 5f* 5g² 6m4] IR 4,500F, IR 7,200Y: small, sturdy gelding: moderate mover: first foal: dam ran twice at 2 yrs: quite modest performer: successful in sellers (retained 11,000 gns on first occasion, 5,600 gns on second) at Wolverhampton in April and Bath in May: neck second to Timeless Times in minor event at Edinburgh: stays 6f. *K. M. Brassey.*

FACE THE ODDS 2 ch.g. (Mar 27) Faustus (USA) 118–Character Builder 92 **74** (African Sky 124) [1990 6m³ 7d* 7s] IR 11,000Y: fifth foal: half-brother to 3-y-o Tyrian (by Elegant Air) and a winner in Italy by Milford: dam best at 2 yrs when successful from 5f to 7f: modest form: won maiden auction at Goodwood by a short head: hung right from halfway when running creditably in nursery at Doncaster later in October. *R. W. Armstrong.*

FACE UP 3 br.c. Top Ville 129–Pomade 79 (Luthier 126) [1989 NR 1990 8m⁵ 7g² **81** 8g* 8m] smallish, angular colt: moderate walker and mover: third foal: half-brother to modest staying maiden/winning hurdler Pomatum (by General Assembly): dam disqualified 9f winner on sole outing: favourite, won claimer (claimed out of H. Cecil's stable in £9,500 gns) at Newmarket in June, running on strongly: never able to challenge in £15,400 handicap there following month: bred to stay further. *J. Wharton.*

FACILITY LETTER 3 gr.g. Superlative 118–Facetious 88 (Malicious) [1989 5f4 **66** 6g² 6m³ 6g* 7f 6m4 6g² 5m6 7g² 6v² 7d 1990 a6g³ 7m⁵ 7d⁵ 7m 8.5g² 7d] sturdy gelding: good walker: quite modest handicapper, not seen out after June: stays 8.5f: has form on top-of-the-ground but best efforts with some give: has been tried in blinkers, better form without: sold to join G. Moore 5,200 gns Newmarket Autumn Sales. *W. J. Haggas.*

FACT FINDER 6 br.h. Known Fact (USA) 135–Idealist (Busted 134) [1989 8g* **88** 8d 1990 8f⁵ 7m 8f4 8g 8m 8m² 8f 8m* 8f² 8m² 8g⁵ 8m 8g4 8g⁵] good-topped horse: bad mover: fairly useful handicapper: ridden some way out when winning at Salisbury in June: best at 1m: acts on any going. *R. Akehurst.*

FACT OR FICTION 4 br.g. Known Fact (USA) 135–Noble Wac (USA) (Vaguely **65** Noble 140) [1989 8.2m 11.7m 16m 10.2f³ 8s 10g a11g³ a10g4 1990 9f² 10.6f 10.1g⁶ 9g² 8.2m 8m⁵ 9f* 8f² 10f³ 10f 8m⁵ a10g* a10g² a10g⁵] strong, angular gelding: quite modest performer: won apprentice claimer at Wolverhampton in July and apprentice handicap at Lingfield (making all) in November: probably best short of 11f: acts on firm going: mostly blinkered or visored nowadays: sold out of H. Candy's stable 7,000 gns Newmarket Autumn Sales after eleventh start. *Miss B. Sanders.*

FACTOTUM 7 b.g. Known Fact (USA) 135–Blue Shark (Silver Shark 129) [1989 — 10h4 10f 10f 1990 11.5g 10m 16f4 16f³] small, good-bodied gelding: carries plenty of condition: good mover: quite modest handicapper at best: below form as 7-y-o: should stay beyond 1¼m: acts on hard going: wore small bandages on reappearance: inconsistent: winner 4 times over hurdles in 1989/90 before turn of year. *R. Akehurst.*

FACTUELLE 3 ch.f. Known Fact (USA) 135–Cayla (Tumble Wind (USA)) [1989 **60** 5s* 6f² 6g³ 5f 1990 5d 5m 5g 5m² 5g³ 5f4 5m 5m 5m 5g] small, stocky filly: quite modest sprinter: good fourth in handicap at Sandown in July: faced stiff tasks afterwards: stays 6f: acts on any going. *M. J. Fetherston-Godley.*

FAILAND   3 b.f. Kala Shikari 125–What A Mint (Meadow Mint (USA) 120) [1989   55
5m³ 6h⁵ 6f 5m⁴ 6g 7f⁴ 6g⁶ 7f² 8.2g 1990 8m 8f 7f⁴ 7f² 7m* 7.6g³ 8f⁵ 7m 7m 8g 7g]
poor walker: has a quick action: plating-class performer: won amateurs handicap at
Chepstow in June: below form last 5 starts: best at around 7f: acts on firm going. *R. J.
Holder.*

FAIR AVERAGE   2 ch.c. (Apr 8) Ahonoora 122–Fair Head 87 (High Line 125)   89 p
[1990 6g 7g⁴ 8d*] workmanlike colt: has scope: fifth foal: half-brother to 2 winning
hurdlers by Kalaglow: dam won over 7.6f at 2 yrs later poor plater: won maiden at
Leicester in October, showing much improved form, by 7 lengths from Single File,
quickening under 2f out and soon clear: will be suited by 1¼m: acts on dead ground:
can improve again. *H. Candy.*

FAIR DARE   2 b. or br.f. (Mar 11) Daring March 116–Fair Madame 88 (Mon-   65
seigneur (USA) 127) [1990 6m⁴ 6d4] leggy filly: second living foal: dam 5f and 6f
winner: quite modest form in maidens at York (backward) in August and Doncaster
in November: will stay 7f. *C. B. B. Booth.*

FAIRE FAILLITE   3 b.f. Bustino 136–Coverham Lass (Whitstead 125) [1989   —
NR 1990 12g] small, workmanlike filly: first foal: dam never ran: soon tailed off in
maiden at Pontefract in October: sold 1,150 gns Doncaster November Sales. *A. W.
Jones.*

FAIR ENCHANTRESS   2 b.f. (Feb 29) Enchantment 115–Pts Fairway (Runny-   47
mede 123) [1990 6g 6m² 7f 6m] 2,200Y: workmanlike, good-quartered filly: has
scope: keen walker: sixth foal: sister to 1988 2-y-o 5.8f winner Roheryn and half-
sister to 2 winning platers, including 1m winner On Impulse (by Jellaby): dam well
beaten both starts at 2 yrs: 50/1, second of 6, keeping on under very hard riding, in
maiden at Nottingham in July: ran moderately after in maiden auction and nursery.
J. A. Bennett.

FAIRFIELD LAD   5 b.g. Krayyan 117–Mock Auction 55 (Auction Ring (USA)   42
123) [1989 6.1f 6f 6g⁵ 6m 6m 5s 6g⁵ 6m 1990 5m⁶ 6g 6g 6m 5g 5s 7d 6s⁴ a6g a6g]
quite attractive gelding: moderate mover: fourth in seller at Hamilton: suited by 6f
or stiff 5f: acts on any going: has worn blinkers, but best form without. *J. Dooler.*

FAIRFIELDS CONE   7 ch.m. Celtic Cone 116–Bond's Best 56 (Good Bond 122)   —
[1989 NR 1990 13.3m] lengthy mare: second foal: half-sister to winning hurdler
Buckskin's Best (by Buckskin): dam 15f winner, successful over hurdles: modest
hurdler, winner 4 times in 1988/9: 66/1, always behind in listed race at Newbury in
May. *R. Dickin.*

FAIR REASON (IRE)   2 ch.f. (Feb 29) Reasonable (FR) 119–Fair Colleen (King   41
Emperor (USA)) [1990 5m⁶ a6g⁶ 5.1m³ 5m] IR 2,000Y: smallish, sturdy filly: poor
mover: half-sister to 1984 French 2-y-o 7.2f winner Flying Liner (by Skyliner): dam
unraced half-sister to Double Jump and Royalty: ridden by 5-lb claimer, third in
seller at Yarmouth in August, easily best effort: unfavourably drawn final start:
suited by 5f. *Pat Mitchell.*

FAIR TITANIA   3 b.f. Fairy King (USA)–Miss Robust (Busted 134) [1989 6m⁵   96
5.8h² 5f* 5m⁶ 5f5 6m* 7h* 7m⁴ 8g³ 7g⁵ 1990 6f4 8m 8m⁴ 8g³ 9s⁴ 8m 8g⁵ 8g* 8m]
lengthy, workmanlike filly: moderate walker and mover: fairly useful performer:
favourite, narrow winner of listed race at Milan in September: last of 10 facing stiff
task in similar event at Ascot following month: stays 9f: acts on any going: suitable
mount for 7-lb claimer: has run well when on toes and sweating. *M. Bell.*

FAIR WICKET   3 ch.g. Norwick (USA) 120–Fairford Lass (Sandford Lad 133)   62 d
[1989 8.2g 8.2d 1990 9s² 8f 8.2s 12.5g] big, rangy gelding: no form other than when
second in maiden at Hamilton in April, wandering under pressure: will stay beyond
9f: acts on soft going: trained until after third start by J. Berry. *B. Preece.*

FAIRY FLAX (IRE)   2 b.f. (Apr 18) Dancing Brave (USA) 140–Fairy Tern 109   83 p
(Mill Reef (USA) 141) [1990 6g⁶ 6m²] sturdy, angular filly: fluent mover: fifth foal:
half-sister to 3-y-o 7.6f winner Fairy Fortune (by Rainbow Quest), very useful 6f (at
2 yrs) and 1m winner Hoy (by Habitat) and 1986 2-y-o 6f winner Greencastle Hill (by
High Top): dam 5f and 7f winner, is closely related to smart 1¼m colt Elegant Air:
well-backed second favourite, 4 lengths second of 4, leading over 4f, to easy winner
Crystal Gazing in £9,800 event at Ascot in September: will stay 1m: should win a
race. *I. A. Balding.*

FAIRY FOLK (IRE)   2 b.f. (May 23) Fairy King (USA)–Tripoli (Great Heron   81 p
(USA)) [1990 6d³ 6s*] IR 37,000Y: half-sister to several winners abroad: dam lightly
raced, showed a little ability: favourite, won 18-runner maiden at the Curragh in
October by a head: will stay 1m: likely to do better. *M. V. O'Brien, Ireland.*

FAIRY FORTUNE 3 ch.f. Rainbow Quest (USA) 134–Fairy Tern 109 (Mill Reef 78 (USA) 141) [1989 6d 1990 7g⁴ 8g³ 7m² 7f⁴ 7g² 8m³ 7.6m* 8m⁵ 8m² 8m⁶] leggy, angular filly: fair performer: made most on favoured stand side to win maiden at Lingfield in September: ran creditably afterwards, including in amateur riders handicap: stays 1m: acts on good to firm ground: visored sixth start: has carried head high. *I. A. Balding.*

FALCON BLUE 3 ch.g. Blue Cashmere 129–Tralee Falcon 82 (Falcon 131) 52 [1989 5f 5f² 5m⁵ 6m³ 5g 1990 a8g⁶ 7m³ 6f³ 8m 10.4g³] lengthy, rather sparely-made gelding: plating-class handicapper: stays 7f: acts on firm going: has run well for 7-lb claimer, moderately in visor: sold 6,400 gns Newmarket July Sales to race in Scandinavia. *J. G. FitzGerald.*

FALCON FLIGHT 4 ch.g. Tampero (FR) 115–Kemoening 78 (Falcon 131) [1989 — 8g⁴ 7f² 8.5g² 8h⁴ 6m² 7f⁵ 6g² 7m 1990 a7g⁶] smallish, rather sparely-made gelding: modest at 3 yrs: favourite and bandaged, well beaten in claimer at Southwell in January: possibly best at up to 7f: acts on firm going. *J. Mackie.*

FALCONS DAWN 3 b.c. Exhibitioner 111–African Bloom (African Sky 124) 69 [1989 5s* 5d⁵ 5f² 5f 5d 6d 1990 7f 5g⁴ 6m⁵ 6m⁵ 8.2m² 8g³ 8d³ 8g⁶ 8m⁴] leggy, quite good-topped colt: has a round action: modest handicapper: suited by 1m: acts on any going: usually visored at 3 yrs: retained 2,800 gns Doncaster May Sales after third start. *M. O'Neill.*

FALCON'S DOMAIN (IRE) 2 b. or br.c. (Mar 21) Hegemony 112–Cova 80 Kestrel (Ovac (ITY) 120) [1990 5m² 5f* 5d⁵ 6f⁴ 6g³ 6m 7s] IR 12,500Y: compact colt: first foal: dam Irish 7f winner: fair performer: won maiden auction at Chepstow in May: good third in valuable listed-restricted race at the Curragh: better suited by 6f than 5f: seems unsuited by soft ground. *J. M. P. Eustace.*

FALDO (USA) 2 gr.g. (Mar 12) Caro 133–Binky (FR) 113 (Faraway Son (USA) — 130) [1990 7s 7m 7f] 500,000 francs (approx £48,000) Y: seventh foal: half-brother to 4 minor winners in USA: dam 5.5f and 6.5f winner at 2 yrs in France out of half-sister to smart French middle-distance stayer Budapest: well beaten in varied events, including a valuable restricted race at Deauville: blinkered final outing. *P. A. Kelleway.*

FALLOW DEER 3 ch.f. Jalmood (USA) 126–Regent's Fawn (CAN) 72 (Vice 59 Regent (CAN)) [1989 6f⁵ 5f⁵ᵈⁱˢ 1990 a8g³ a8g² 8m⁵ 7g⁵ 9f³ 8m² 7g⁶ 10m⁴ 10m² 10m³ 10m* a12g] small, lengthy filly: moderate mover: quite modest performer: downgraded to sellers, led close home to justify favouritism at Lingfield (sold out of B. Hills's stable 6,600 gns) in September: showed nothing in non-selling handicap 2 months later: stays 1¼m: has given impression ill at ease on firm ground: not an easy ride but has run well for an apprentice, including when successful. *D. J. Wintle.*

FALSE ALLEGATION (USA) 3 b.c. Alleged (USA) 138–Reckoning (USA) 64 (Olden Times) [1989 NR 1990 10g 10m⁴ 11g² 14g a12g⁶] close-coupled, quite attractive colt: fifth foal: brother to maiden 1989 3-y-o Alleged Account and half-brother to a stakes-placed winner in USA by Inverness Drive: dam lightly-raced sister to champion American 1982 2-y-o Roving Boy: form in first half of 1990 only when second of 6 in maiden at Edinburgh: should stay 1½m: blinkered last 3 starts. *B. Hanbury.*

FALSE PASSPORT 3 ch.g. Alias Smith (USA)–Hussy 82 (Queen's Hussar 124) — [1989 NR 1990 a10g 12d] 4,000Y: robust gelding: third living foal: half-brother to a prolific winner in Norway by Rhodomantade: dam stayed 1½m: tailed off in maidens at Lingfield (ran wide turns) and Folkestone in November. *M. J. Bolton.*

FAME AND GLORY 5 b.h. Shareef Dancer (USA) 135–Oh So Fair (USA) — (Graustark) [1989 14.8s 16s 12s 12g 12s 1990 17.1f] lengthy, quite attractive horse: tubed: made all in 1¾m handicap at Sandown as 3-y-o: no subsequent form: sold 850 gns Ascot November Sales: to stand at Starlyte Stud, Warwickshire. *J. D. Bethell.*

FAMILY AT WAR (USA) 2 b.f. (Mar 27) Explodent (USA)–Sometimes 71 Perfect (USA) (Bold Bidder) [1990 5f² 5m* 5g⁵ 5s²] $32,000Y: quite good-topped, attractive filly: has scope: half-sister to 3 minor winners in North America: dam minor winner at around 6f at 2 yrs, is half-sister to very useful 1986 French 2-y-o 1m winner Tiger Run: sire won at up to 8.5f: quite modest form: faced simple task in 2-runner maiden event at Pontefract in August: never a threat from halfway in minor events at Ripon and Ayr after. *J. Etherington.*

FAMILY LINE 2 b.c. (Mar 9) High Line 125–Princess Dina 87 (Huntercombe 65 p 133) [1990 8g] fourth living foal: half-brother to 1988 2-y-o 7f winner Labelon Lady (by Touching Wood): dam, in frame at up to 9f, is half-sister to good French middle-distance stayer Paddy's Princess and daughter of half-sister to Connaught:

burly, around 8 lengths seventh of 21, keeping on not knocked about, in maiden at Pontefract in October: will stay well: sure to improve. *M. J. Camacho.*

FAMOUS BEAUTY 3 br.f. Vision (USA)–Relfo 124 (Relko 136) [1989 6g² 6g*   **68** 6f² 6m 8g 1990 10.6f² 10.2m 10g⁵ 12h² 12.3g 12m⁵ 12d⁶ 12m⁵ 12m* 13.6d⁶ 16s] sparely-made filly: keen walker: modest handicapper: led close home in apprentice contest at Chepstow in October: never placed to challenge afterwards: should stay 1¾m: acts on hard ground, possibly unsuited by a soft surface: has run creditably when sweating: claimer ridden: inconsistent. *R. Hollinshead.*

FAMOUS DANCER 2 b.c. (Mar 29) Top Ville 129–Dancing Place (FR) (Green   **— P** Dancer (USA) 132) [1990 8g] 30,000Y: tall, lengthy, attractive colt: rather unfurnished: second foal: half-brother to a winner in Italy by Alleged: dam French 1m winner, is half-sister to smart French sprinter Gem Diamond: 33/1, eye-catching seventh of 15, beaten around 18 lengths, in maiden at Newmarket in October won by Sharifabad, held up, switched over 3f out, good headway not at all knocked about: sure to improve considerably. *D. R. C. Elsworth.*

FAMOUS FELLOW (IRE) 2 b.g. (Apr 18) Valiyar 129–Naturally Fresh 91   **55** (Thatching 131) [1990 6g 5m³ 5m³ 8m 6g⁶ a6g] 15,500Y: smallish, workmanlike gelding: first foal: dam 2-y-o 5f winner out of half-sister to smart Romper: plating-class maiden: stays 1m: blinkered last 3 starts. *J. A. Glover.*

FANATICAL (USA) 4 b.c. Lear Fan (USA) 130–Gal A Tic (USA) (Assagai)   **78** [1989 8.5f 12.4m* 14.8m³ 12m³ 12g 12.4g⁵ 1990 12.8g* 12.3g] rather good-topped colt: carries plenty of condition: moderate mover: fair handicapper: won at Ripon in May by neck having looked likely to win more easily over 1f out: bandaged, ran moderately 3 weeks later: suited by 1½m: acts on good to firm going: ran creditably in blinkers: sold to join J. Baker's stable 9,200 gns Ascot July Sales. *J. W. Watts.*

FANCY ME 2 b.f. (Apr 28) Dunbeath (USA) 127–Friendly Thoughts (USA) (Al   **71** Hattab (USA)) [1990 7g 6m 6g* 7m] angular filly: fourth live foal: half-sister to 1¼m seller winner Thanks A Million (by Simply Great): dam never ran: carrying condition, won maiden at Newcastle in good style by 1½ lengths from Knifebox: creditable seventh in nursery at Newmarket later in October: stays 7f: may do better. *W. Jarvis.*

FANELLAN 3 b.f. Try My Best (USA) 130–Scotia Rose (Tap On Wood 130) [1989   **69 +** 6g* 6g⁵ 1990 8g⁶ 7m] quite attractive, rather unfurnished filly: modest form, winning maiden at Yarmouth at 2 yrs and sixth in handicap (held up and short of room over 1f out) at Leicester: forced wide entering straight then never dangerous in Sandown handicap in June: worth a try over further than 1m. *M. R. Stoute.*

FANILLE 4 b.c. Top Ville 129–Flying Fantasy (Habitat 134) [1989 9g 10s 1990   **—** 10.6d] smallish, lengthy colt: little promise in maidens and claimer: winning hurdler in December. *H. A. T. Whiting.*

FANLIGHT 2 b.c. (Jan 28) Beldale Flutter (USA) 130–Carib Flash (Mill Reef   **—** (USA) 141) [1990 6s 6m⁴] quite attractive colt: first foal: dam unraced daughter of very useful sprinter Oscilight: poor form in maidens at Haydock (unfavourably drawn) and Nottingham (ridden along before halfway). *C. F. Wall.*

FANMAN 5 b.h. Taufan (USA) 119–Courreges 75 (Manado 130) [1989 12g 11g 8m   **40** 1990 9f 5m³ 5g⁴ 5g⁴ 6g 6g 5g⁴] leggy, rather angular horse: poor walker: poor handicapper: stays 7f: blinkered once at 4 yrs. *C. Parker.*

FARA 3 gr.f. Castle Keep 121–Faridetta 107 (Good Bond 122) [1989 6m³ 6f³ 6m⁶   **56** 8s⁴ 7g⁵ 8g 1990 12.2g⁴ 10g³ 9.1m⁶ 8.5g³ 10m* 10.6v] leggy, angular filly: plater. 7/1, won 18-runner handicap (no bid) at Redcar in September: appeared to stumble on turn final start: should stay 1½m: acts on good to firm ground and soft. *Miss S. E. Hall.*

FARAT (USA) 2 ch.c. (May 19) Woodman (USA) 126–Solac (FR) (Gay Lussac   **74 p** (ITY) 116) [1990 6g4] $40,000Y: good-bodied, medium-sized colt: half-brother to fairly useful 1988 Irish 2-y-o 1m winner Solar Myth (by Lypheor) and 2 winners in Italy: dam half-sister to Italian Derby winner Sirlad: backward and very green, around 3 lengths fourth of 11, headway over 2f out then keeping on, to Chimayo in maiden at Newmarket in October: should improve. *J. L. Dunlop.*

FAR DARA 4 ch.f. Pharly (FR) 130–Sardara 106 (Alcide 136) [1989 8g³ 8d 12.5f   **—** 10.6m 16.2g 10m 16.2m 10.2g 8f 15s 13s 1990 10.2f 12f 10s] small, close-coupled filly: has a round action: no longer of much account. *N. Bycroft.*

FARFELU 3 b.c. Lyphard's Special (USA) 122–Spring Azure 98 (Mountain Call   **86 ?** 125) [1989 5d⁴ 5d² 5g³ 5f* 6m² 6f* 5g⁴ 7m⁵ 1990 6m⁵ 5g² 6m³ 5.8h* 6m 5g⁴ 7.6d 6m³ 6s] robust, good-quartered, sprint type: fair performer: below form after winning handicap at Bath in July: stays 6f: acts on hard going, showed nothing on soft: blinkered fourth to sixth starts. *K. M. Brassey.*

FAR FROM HOME   3 b.f. Habitat 134–Miss By Miles 91 (Milesian 125) [1989   **73**
NR 1990 7g 7.6d 7m³ 7g³ 7.3m³ 9m⁵ 8m⁴ 7f² 6g* 6s 6s] lengthy, workmanlike filly: good walker: has a quick action: half-sister to 4 winners, including smart 6f and 1m winner Missed Blessing (by So Blessed) and useful and game 1¼m and 1½m winner Buzzbomb (by Bustino): dam game miler: modest performer: won maiden at Nottingham in September, leading near finish: effective at 6f, and should stay 1m: acts on firm ground: has given impression worth a try in blinkers: likely to prove best with exaggerated waiting tactics: possibly irresolute: sold 20,000 gns Newmarket December Sales. *R. F. Johnson Houghton.*

FARISI (USA)   2 ch.c. (Jan 12) Shahrastani (USA) 135–Fashada (USA) 83   **74**
(Riverman (USA) 131) [1990 7m⁴ 8.2g] medium-sized colt: first foal: dam 2-y-o 6f winner later stayed 1m, is daughter of Felix Culpa, very useful at around 1¼m in France: over 3 lengths fourth of 16, keeping on well, to Shamshir in maiden at Newmarket in August: soon beaten in minor event at Haydock following month: should be better suited by 1m than 7f. *M. R. Stoute.*

FARMER JOCK   8 ch.h. Crofter (USA) 124–Some Dame 72 (Will Somers 114§)   **65**
[1989 6s 5f³ 5.1m 6f³ 5f³ 5m* 6m⁶ 5g² 5m* 5f² 5f 5.1f* 5f³ 5g³ 6f 5m 5g 5m 5.6g² 5.1g⁶ 5m 5f⁵ 5m 1990 a5g² a5g³ a7g⁴ a5g² a6g³ a6g⁵ a6g⁵ 5f 5m 5.8h² 5g⁵ 6d 5m 5g⁴ 6g 5f⁴ 5.8h³ 6h* 6m⁴ 6h⁴] strong, good-bodied horse: carries condition: quite modest handicapper: won at Brighton in July: best at 5f or 6f: not at his best on soft going, acts on any other: effective with or without blinkers or visor: has worn bandages: tends to hang: needs strong handling and to be held up. *Mrs N. Macauley.*

FARMIN   3 b. or br.c. Rousillon (USA) 133–Jendeal (Troy 137) [1989 8g⁴ 1990   **90**
10m² 12g³ 14d* 14d 14d* 14.6d²] rather sparely-made colt: moderate walker: fairly useful performer: won maiden at Haydock in September and handicap (easily) at Newmarket in October: ran moderately fourth start: should stay 2m: yet to race on extremes of going: sold 62,000 gns Newmarket Autumn Sales to race in Italy. *A. C. Stewart.*

FAR MORE   4 ch.g. Gorytus (USA) 132–Demare (Pardao 120) [1989 7d 8f⁴ 10m⁴   —
13.3m 16m⁵ 12h³ 12m 10m⁵ 8.5m⁵ 8m 8s 8f⁴ 8f a10g⁵ 1990 14g 18f 10.6s 11.5m 12m⁴] workmanlike gelding: moderate mover: quite modest maiden at best: sweating, showed signs of retaining a little ability last 2 outings: winner over hurdles later in summer: stays 1½m: acts on hard going, probably unsuited by a soft surface: below form in blinkers: often bandaged: has had tongue tied down and worn crossed noseband: not the easiest of rides: changed hands 11,000 gns Doncaster March Sales. *F. Durr.*

FARM STREET   3 b.g. Henbit (USA) 130–Mill Hill (USA) (Riva Ridge (USA))   **88**
[1989 NR 1990 8m³ 10m⁴ 12f⁴ 8.5d* 8d 8.5m 8m 10m 8d] workmanlike, good-quartered gelding: moderate mover: fourth living foal: brother to poor hurdler Going Up and half-brother to French 1¼m and 11f winner Optimise (by Relkino): dam, placed at up to 9f in France, is half-sister to smart sprinter Peterhof out of half-sister to Mill Reef: fairly useful handicapper at his best: ran poorly after making all in £13,900 event at Epsom in June: best at around 1m: acts on dead going: edged left final start. *P. T. Walwyn.*

FARNDALE   3 gr.c. Vaigly Great 127–Beloved Mistress 84 (Rarity 129) [1989   —
5d³ 5g² 5g⁶ 5m⁵ 6g⁵ 6m 1990 a8g 10f⁵ 12.5f a12g] angular colt: moderate mover: plating-class form at best: pulls hard, and is most unlikely to stay middle distances: bandaged on reappearance. *Miss S. J. Wilton.*

FAR PAVILION (IRE)   2 b.f. (May 7) Pennine Walk 120–Fair Abode (Habitat   **74**
134) [1990 6g* 6g⁴] 10,000Y: lengthy, workmanlike filly: has scope: fifth foal: half-sister to a winner in Austria: dam unraced half-sister to Fair Salinia: bit backward and green, made all in minor event at Windsor in August: around 2½ lengths fourth of 16 to Jimlil in similar event at Doncaster following month: started favourite both times: will be better suited by 1m +. *R. Charlton.*

FARRANFORE EXPRESS (IRE)   2 b.g. (Mar 28) Mazaad 106–Golden Arum   —
67 (Home Guard (USA) 129) [1990 5m⁶ 5g 6g a7g] IR 3,600F, IR 7,800Y: quite good-topped gelding: has a round action: third reported foal: dam placed over 5f on debut at 2 yrs lost form after: little sign of promise: looked temperamentally unsatisfactory on second start, when trained by M. McCormack: blinkered final start. *C. N. Allen.*

FAR TOO LOUD   3 b.g. Taufan (USA) 119–Octet (Octavo (USA) 115) [1989 8v   **72**
1990 12d³ 11g² 15.8d 15.8m² 13.8m*] workmanlike colt: has a round action: modest

performer: wearing tongue strap, won 4-runner handicap at Catterick in August: stays 2m: seems to need a sound surface: will prove best with forcing tactics: sold to join N. Gaselee 30,000 gns Doncaster August Sales. *J. G. FitzGerald.*

FASCINATING LADY 2 ch.f. (Apr 9) Enchantment 115–Formula 72 (Reform 132) [1990 7g 6m 8m] leggy filly: half-sister to a winning plater: dam 1m winner: seems of little account: wears bandages behind. *M. D. I. Usher.* —

FASCINATION WALTZ 3 b.f. Shy Groom (USA)–Cuckoo Weir (Double Jump 131) [1989 6g³ 5m 6m² 1990 7m 6m* 6m* 6m] angular, sparely-made filly: fair handicapper: won at Newmarket and Ripon (£14,500 event) in August, in latter leading 1f out and hanging markedly right: creditable eighth of 13 in £15,800 contest at York afterwards: sweating, pulled hard and saddle slipped on reappearance: suited by strongly-run 6f. *J. Mackie.* 83

FASHION SCENE (USA) 4 ch.f. London Bells (CAN) 109–Yes Please 108 (Mount Hagen (FR) 127) [1989 8d 8m⁴ 10g a10g 1990 8v 8m⁵ 11g⁶] rangy, sparely-made filly: poor maiden: stays 1m: acts on good to firm going. *W. Storey.* 34

FAST AND FREE 4 b.g. Kafu 120–Santa Maria (GER) (Literat) [1989 7s* 7d 8m 8m 1990 8.3g 12g] leggy, lightly-made gelding: poor walker: has a round action: easily best effort when winning seller early as 3-y-o: stays 7f: evidently needs soft going. *P. J. Feilden.* —

FAST APPROACH 4 br.f. Daring March 116–Honest Opinion 68 (Free State 125) [1989 10f* 9f 10f 8f 10f⁴ 10f⁵ 10g 1990 10f 10g 10.6d] big, lengthy filly: turns fore feet in: moderate mover: winning plater in 1989: well beaten as 4-y-o, but showed signs of retaining ability in claimer final outing: suited by 1¼m: acts on firm going: sweating, very edgy and wore tongue strap second start: sold after out of J. Dooler's stable 5,000 gns Doncaster August Sales: not an easy ride. *M. D. Hammond.* —

FASTAUFAN 3 b.g. Taufan (USA) 119–Maggie Mine 85 (Native Prince) [1989 6g 7.5f 1990 8m 10f 12m⁵ 12g] good-topped gelding: no worthwhile form, including in handicaps, but showed signs of ability last 2 starts. *R. M. Whitaker.* —

FAST OPERATIVE 3 ch.c. Absalom 128–Thorganby Victory 82 (Burglar 128) [1989 6f³ 7m³ 6f 7d 6s⁴ 1990 7d⁶ 7.6m³ 7m³ 8m³ 7h³ 7h 8h 7f⁵ 5m⁶ 7f⁵ 7v] smallish, angular colt: has a roundish action: plater: may well prove suited by 6f or 7f: acts on any going: visored final outing at 2 yrs: usually apprentice ridden. *W. G. M. Turner.* 48

FAST RUN (IRE) 2 ch.g. (May 16) Commanche Run 133–Starlite Night (USA) 105 (Star de Naskra (USA)) [1990 6m 7f4 7f2 7f 9g a8g] leggy gelding: second foal: dam 7f winner: ½-length second of 6, running on well, to Domicksky at Brighton, best effort in maidens: ran moderately last 3 outings: should be suited by a test of stamina: blinkered final start: sold 1,750 gns Ascot November Sales. *P. F. I. Cole.* 66 d

FAST-TALKIN TINKER (IRE) 2 b.g. (Apr 8) Bold Owl 101–Our Ena (Tower Walk 130) [1990 7f² 8.2g⁶ 8.2s⁵] IR 8,600F, 21,000Y: workmanlike gelding: has scope: fourth foal: half-brother to 2 winners, including 1987 2-y-o 6f seller winner Right Path (by Ya Zaman): dam second over 5f at 3 yrs in Ireland: modest form, staying on, in maiden at Ayr and minor event at Haydock first 2 starts: stays 1m: unsuited by soft ground. *G. Richards.* 75

FATAL FRIENDSHIP (USA) 2 ch.c. (Jan 21) Blushing Groom (USA) 131–Leap Lively (USA) 116 (Nijinsky (CAN) 138) [1990 7m⁵] big, good-topped colt: has plenty of scope: half-brother to Forest Flower (by Green Forest) and to poor maiden Shot And Shell (by Damascus): dam won Hoover Fillies' Mile and third in Oaks: favourite but carrying condition, over 5 lengths fifth of 7, challenging briefly 2f out then not knocked about when beaten, to Big Blow in minor event at Ascot in September: will stay 1m: should improve, and win a race. *I. A. Balding.* 73 p

FATEFUL (USA) 2 b.f. (Feb 12) Topsider (USA)–Fate's Reward (USA) (Key To The Mint (USA)) [1990 6d*] $200,000Y: first foal: dam won at up to 9f: well-backed favourite but green, won 21-runner maiden at Doncaster in November by a length, clear, from Sariah, leading over 1f out and running on strongly: will stay 7f: sure to improve. *J. H. M. Gosden.* 90 p

FATHER FIGURE 2 ch.c. (Mar 23) Crofthall 110–Farinara (Dragonara Palace (USA) 115) [1990 6m⁶ 7f³ 8m⁶ 7m 8m⁵ 10s] 4,000F, 33,000Y: sturdy, useful-looking colt: second foal: brother to 3-y-o Croft Imperial, fairly useful 5f winner at 2 yrs: dam unraced daughter of useful 5f mare Faridina: modest maiden: seems to stay 1m: ran poorly when blinkered fourth start. *R. Hannon.* 69

FATHER TIME 6 ch.g. Longleat (USA) 109–Noddy Time 97 (Gratitude 130) [1989 8f 7.6f 8.3m* 8m 8.3m 7s 8s 1990 12d 16d²] strong, workmanlike gelding: carries plenty of condition: quite modest performer: clear second in celebrity race at 62 +

Sedgefield in November: effective at 1m and appears to stay 2m: unsuited by firm going, acts on any other: effective with or without blinkers: goes well with forcing tactics: inconsistent. *M. H. Tompkins.*

FAULTLESS SPEECH   3 ch.c. Good Times (ITY)–Fine Asset (Hot Spark 126)   **71**
[1989 6m 6d6 1990 6m5 6d 5m 5g 7m6 5m 6m* 7g6] strong, stocky colt: moderate walker and mover: modest performer: won 22-runner handicap at Leicester in September: tailed off in apprentice event previous start, below form (found little) in handicap on final one: probably best at 6f: blinkered last 2 outings. *G. Lewis.*

FAUSTINGER   2 b.c. (Mar 11) Faustus (USA) 118–Solo Singer 66 (Song 132)   **43**
[1990 6m 6g 7.5f] 7,600F, 16,000Y: angular colt: good walker: moderate mover: first foal: dam maiden suited by 6f, is half-sister to smart French jumper Khorassan: caught eye staying on well under very considerate handling in seller at Doncaster in June on second start: never placed to challenge, again tending to hang left, in auction event at Beverley following month. *Ronald Thompson.*

FAUSTUS LAD   2 gr.c. (May 12) Faustus (USA) 118–Rich Lass (Broxted 120)   **44**
[1990 7m 7.5m a7g 8m 8.2s] 7,000Y: close-coupled colt: third foal: half-brother to 3-y-o San Greco (by Mandrake Major) and fairly useful 1987 2-y-o 6f winner Fortinbras (by Junius): dam poor daughter of half-sister to smart miler Richboy: poor maiden at best: should stay 1m. *M. Brittain.*

FAVOSKI   4 b.c. Niniski (USA) 125–Favoletta 115 (Baldric II 131) [1989 8s 10m4   **57**
11.7m 1990 14.6f4] small, quite attractive colt: quite modest maiden: stayed 1¾m: acted on firm ground: won over hurdles in February: dead. *I. P. Wardle.*

FAVOURED NATIONS (IRE)   2 b. or br.c. (Jan 31) Law Society (USA)   **94**
130–Lady Lavery (USA) (Northern Dancer) [1990 7d* 9d2] first foal: dam thrice-raced half-sister to Irish St Leger winner Leading Counsel, Princess Royal winner Sylph and very useful American winner (at up to 11f) Present The Colors: odds on, won 10-runner maiden at Leopardstown in October by 1½ lengths: 3 lengths second of 11, clear, to Enzo in listed race at the Curragh in November: will stay 1½m. *M. V. O'Brien, Ireland.*

FAX ME   4 b.g. Red Sunset 120–Hill of Howth (Sassafras (FR) 135) [1989 NR 1990   —
9m 11.7f] second foal: half-brother to a minor stakes winner in USA by Welsh Saint: dam won over 11f in Ireland: tailed off in ladies race on debut: pulled up lame in claimer 7 weeks later: wore bandages: dead. *R. Simpson.*

FAYAFI   3 b. or br.f. Top Ville 129–Muznah 92 (Royal And Regal (USA)) [1989   **69**
8m3 10g4 1990 10m4 14d2 14m2 15v6] smallish, workmanlike filly: modest maiden: faced very stiff task in handicap final start: will stay 2m: acts on good to firm ground and dead: sold 6,500 gns Newmarket December Sales. *H. Thomson Jones.*

FAY EDEN (IRE)   2 ch.f. (Apr 5) Fayruz 116–Dainty Eden 53 (Orbit 106) [1990   **43**
6m 6m 5m 5g 5.8d] IR 2,600F: small, workmanlike filly: closely related to a poor maiden by Jester and half-sister to useful sprinter Bri-Eden (by The Brianstan) and a bumpers winner: dam won 1m seller and stayed 2m: poor plater: ran well for 7-lb claimer in non-selling nursery final start: may well stay 7f. *R. J. Hodges.*

FAYGATE   4 ch.f. Vaigly Great 127–Fayette 80 (Dom Racine (FR) 121) [1989   —
8.5m2 8m6 7g 1990 7f] sparely-made filly: modest maiden at best: may prove best at 1m: isn't the easiest of rides. *R. J. Holder.*

FAYNAZ   4 ch.c. Tumble Wind (USA)–Ceduna (FR) (Right Tack 131) [1989 7f   **73**
8.3m3 7g 1990 7g 7.6m6 6m4 6f* 6m 8.2m4 7m* 8g4 8g] well-made colt: modest handicapper: won at Folkestone in August and Warwick in October: possibly ideally suited by 7f: yet to race on soft surface: blinkered third to fifth starts: has worn bandages behind and been taken down early. *K. M. Brassey.*

FAY'S DANCER (IRE)   2 b.f. (Feb 12) Fayruz 116–Granny Stock (Imperial   **47** d
Fling (USA) 116) [1990 5f4 5.8h 5f 6m6 a6g 6m 6d 7d] 2,600Y: smallish, rather angular filly: moderate walker: first foal: dam ran once in Ireland: quite modest plater: failed to progress. *M. D. I. Usher.*

FAY'S SONG (IRE)   2 ch.f. (Mar 27) Fayruz 116–Harp (Ennis 128) [1990 5.8m5   **84**
5f* 5g5 5m2] IR 3,000F, 3,000Y: compact, angular filly: half-sister to 3 winners, including 1980 Irish 2-y-o 5f winner Harp Auction (by Auction Ring): dam never ran: fair performer: won minor event at Folkestone in September: should stay 6f: trained on debut by W. Brooks. *R. Akehurst.*

FEARLESS FIGHTER   5 b.g. Formidable (USA) 125–Wild Asset (Welsh   — §
Pageant 132) [1989 9m 10f4 8m 1990 11.7g 10m5 11.5m 10m 8m] workmanlike, angular gelding: poor maiden judged on most form: appeared to stay 11.5f: visored once at 3 yrs: ungenuine: dead. *G. P. Enright.*

FEARLESS NATIVE 4 br.g. Final Straw 127–Nativity (USA) 91 (Native — Royalty (USA)) [1989 8g⁶ 8.2f⁴ 10f* 11m⁴ 10g 9.2m⁵ 10f 10g⁵ 10s² 1990 10g] leggy, close-coupled gelding: won maiden claimer at Ayr as 3-y-o: ran poorly since next outing: suited by 1¼m: acts on firm ground: blinkered seventh (reluctant to race) and eighth starts at 3 yrs: retained 3,700 gns Ascot April Sales. *R. J. Manning.*

FEARLESS PHIL (USA) 2 b.c. (Mar 13) Ziggy's Boy (USA)–Ancient Glory — (USA) (Sir Ivor 135) [1990 7m] $22,000Y: workmanlike colt: half-brother to 2 winners in North America by Full Partner: dam placed at 3 yrs: sire best at 6f or 7f: better for race, weakened 2f out in maiden at Chepstow in October: sold 4,000 gns Newmarket Autumn Sales. *D. J. G. Murray-Smith.*

FEARLESS REVIVAL 3 ch.f. Cozzene (USA)–Stufida (Bustino 136) [1989 6g³ 101 6g* 7m* 7g² 1990 7.3d 10m³] sparely-made, rather angular filly: good mover, with a quick action: progressive performer at 2 yrs: front rank long way and eased in Fred Darling Stakes at Newbury in April: 6 lengths third to Native Twine in listed race at same course 3 months later: stays 1¼m: acts on good to firm ground. *M. R. Stoute.*

FEARSOME 4 gr.g. Formidable (USA) 125–Seriema 72 (Petingo 135) [1989 7g 8s — 7d 7m 8.5d⁶ 7.5f 8m⁶ 7m 8g² 10g⁴ 10g² 10f 1990 8g 11.5m 12g 10.1m⁶ 10m⁶ 8.3m a 12g a8g a11g] compact gelding: poor mover: quite modest at best as 3-y-o: best form at 1¼m: acts on good to firm going: often blinkered. *K. O. Cunningham-Brown.*

FEDORIA 4 b.c. Formidable (USA) 125–Zepha 88 (Great Nephew 126) [1989 7s* 108 1990 8g⁵ 7.6d 7m* 8f 7m* 7f* 7.3g² 7g 7d⁵] strong, attractive colt: progressed extremely well in summer, finishing excellent second to Norwich in Gardner Merchant Hungerford Stakes at Newbury: successful in handicaps at Doncaster in June and Newmarket (twice, first time beating Nayiand short head in £20,700 Ladbroke Bunbury Cup) in July: acts on any going: awkward at stalls second and third outings, and has started slowly: has good turn of foot. *M. A. Jarvis.*

FELENA FLYER (IRE) 2 ch.f. (May 21) Gorytus (USA) 132–Foxoale Flyer — (USA) (Foolish Pleasure (USA)) [1990 6g] 1,700F: smallish, close-coupled filly: half-sister to 1½m winner Sly Vixen (by Akarad): dam unraced daughter of half-sister to Eclipse Stakes winner Solford: slowly away and always behind in maiden at Newcastle in October: reluctant to go down. *W. J. Pearce.*

FELLOWS DREAM 3 b.f. Milk of The Barley 115–Stonebow Lady 52 (Wind- — jammer (USA)) [1989 5f 6f 1990 10.8f] leggy, compact filly: no sign of ability in maiden and sellers: edgy, sweating then took keen hold only start in 1990. *L. J. Codd.*

FENAMICA 3 b.f. Trojan Fen 118–My Tootsie 88 (Tap On Wood 130) [1989 7m — 7g 1990 11.5g a12g⁴ 16m 12.5g 16m] close-coupled filly: poor maiden: should stay beyond 1½m: blinkered last 2 starts, setting too strong a pace first occasion. *M. J. Ryan.*

FENNEL 2 b.f. (Feb 18) Slew O' Gold (USA)–Fenney Mill 99 (Levmoss 133) [1990 97 p 6m* 6.5g³] 155,000Y: rather sparely-made filly: half-sister to useful 7f and 14.7f winner Red Guitars (by Nijinsky) and modest 1¼m and 1½m winner Dual Capacity (by Coastal): dam Irish 1¼m winner stayed 1½m, is out of Irish 1000 Guineas and St Leger winner Pidget: odds on, won maiden at Newmarket in August in very good style by 5 lengths from Road To The Isle: close third of 17, keeping on strongly, to Nazoo in Tattersalls Tiffany Yorkshire Stakes at Doncaster following month: will be well suited by 7f or 1m: likely to improve again, and win more races. *M. R. Stoute.*

FENOUILLE 3 b.g. Ile de Bourbon (USA) 133–Foreseen (Reform 132) [1989 NR 77 1990 10g³ 11.5g² a10g²] rather unfurnished gelding: first foal. dam unraced half-sister to Derby Italiano winner My Top: modest maiden: ran wide home turn at Sandown on debut: should prove better at 1½m than 1¼m. *D. R. C. Elsworth.*

FENTON LAKE 2 b.g. (May 5) Tina's Pet 121–Kakisa 81 (Forlorn River 124) 76 [1990 6f³ 5d² 5m³ 5g² 6m²] 10,000Y: good-topped gelding: has scope: second foal: brother to winning 3-y-o sprinter Lake Mistassiu: dam 5f and 6f winner: modest maiden: may stay 7f: races keenly: took very strong hold to post third and fourth starts, taken down quietly final one: consistent. *G. A. Pritchard-Gordon.*

FERMENTATION (IRE) 2 b.c. (Mar 14) Pitskelly 122–Santa Chiara 79 (Aztec 38 128) [1990 a6g a6g 6g 7m³ 7f⁵ a8g 8.5m 10m] IR 4,000Y, 2,500 2-y-o: neat colt: half-brother to 5f winner Native Hero (by African Sky), a winner in Jersey and a winner over hurdles: dam stayer: poor plater: no form on all-weather: should be well suited by 1m +: blinkered final 2 starts: sold 1,300 gns Doncaster October Sales. *J. Wharton.*

FEROX 4 b.g. Formidable (USA) 125–La Grange 79 (Habitat 134) [1989 6g⁴ 6m⁴ 79 6f³ 1990 6f⁴ 5g 5m⁶ 8.3m 6d 5g* a6g a5g²] strong, good-bodied gelding: has a quick action: apprentice ridden, won for first time when beating Glencroft by length in handicap at Salisbury in October: stays 6f: may prove suited by give in the ground: usually bandaged: has joined Mrs J. Cecil. *D. R. C. Elsworth.*

FESTIVAL OF MAGIC (USA) 3 b.f. Clever Trick (USA)–Santa Linda (USA) **73** (Sir Ivor 135) [1989 NR 1990 7m⁴ 7g⁶ 8m² a8g* a8g] $70,000Y: workmanlike filly: second foal: half-sister to fairly useful 1¼m and 12.5f winner Gold Pavilion (by Lemhi Gold): dam unraced half-sister to smart middle-distance colt Noble Saint out of half-sister to Tom Rolfe and Chieftain: modest form: easily landed odds in maiden at Southwell in August: clearly best other effort when racing alone and beaten short head at Yarmouth: stays 1m: sold 2,000 gns Newmarket December Sales. *R. W. Armstrong.*

FESTIVE FALCON 4 ch.g. Sandhurst Prince 128–Caelidh 98 (Silly Season 127) **60 ?** [1989 8d 8s 10m⁶ 8s 10g a12g² 1990 11g* 10m* a12g² a12g a8g a12g] tall, close-coupled gelding: won claimers at Hamilton (maiden, apprentice ridden) in May and Newmarket (claimed out of P. Makin's stable £9,551, making all to land gamble) in June: ran poorly in similar event final outing: stays 1½m: acts on firm going. *O. O'Neill.*

FESTIVE SEASON (USA) 3 b.f. Lypheor 118–Marie Noelle (FR) **114 —** (Brigadier Gerard 144) [1989 NR 1990 7g 10.2f] 160,000Y: rather leggy filly: has rather round action: fourth foal: half-sister to 2 winners, notably Prix Marcel Boussac winner Mary Linoa (by L'Emigrant): dam French 2-y-o 7.5f winner later successful at up to 1¼m in USA: never able to challenge in maidens at Wolverhampton and Bath (pulled hard, eased last 1f) in the summer: sold 16,000 gns Newmarket December Sales, probably to Italy. *J. Gosden.*

FETTLE UP 2 ch.g. (Jun 4) Lyphard's Special (USA) 122–Fire Risk (Thatch **—** (USA) 136) [1990 8f 10s a8g] 6,200Y: neat gelding: fourth foal: dam unraced half-sister to high-class milers Final Straw and Achieved: little worthwhile form in maidens, one an auction event. *J. Wharton.*

FIABA 2 b.f. (Mar 13) Precocious 126–Historia 71 (Northfields (USA)) [1990 5m³ **66** 5.3f² 5g* 5d³ 6g⁶ 5m 6d³ 7f⁵] 7,000Y: close-coupled, sparely-made filly: second foal: half-sister to 3-y-o Gilded Past (by Glint of Gold): dam, ran once at 2 yrs, is out of half-sister to high-class Moulton and Derby third Freefoot: quite modest performer: won maiden auction at Hamilton in June: stays 7f: best efforts on an easy surface: sold 6,000 gns Newmarket Autumn Sales. *C. F. Wall.*

FIDDLING 3 ch.f. Music Boy 124–Penny Pincher 95 (Constable 119) [1989 NR **74** 1990 5m* 5d² 5g] workmanlike, good-quartered filly: good walker: moderate mover: sister to useful sprinter Clantime and a winner in Jersey and half-sister to 2 sprint winners, including Tobermory Boy (by Mummy's Pet): dam 5f sprinter: comfortably won maiden at Edinburgh in April: favourite for quite valuable handicaps in May, checked on turn then staying on well and beaten neck at Chester: jockey reported he thought she had broken down (after stumbling stalls) at York 8 days later. *Mrs J. R. Ramsden.*

FIELD GLASS (USA) 3 b.c. Mr Prospector (USA)–Stellarette (CAN) (Tentam **100** (USA)) [1989 7g* 1990 8m* 8m⁴ 7.2s⁴ 7g⁵ 8m² 7g⁵] rather leggy, quite attractive colt: has a quick action: useful performer: tended to idle when winning Esher Cup Handicap at Sandown in April: ran creditably in competitive events next 4 starts, particularly so when second in £19,100 handicap at Newmarket: below-form favourite for Leopardstown listed race in August: stays 1m: has form on soft going, but may be ideally suited by top-of-the-ground: found little third start: to join F. Schulhofer in USA. *M. R. Stoute.*

FIELD RUNNER 3 ch.g. Precocious 126–Orange Squash 78 (Red God 128§) **—** [1989 NR 1990 10.1m⁴] IR 14,000Y: tall, rather unfurnished gelding: fifth foal: half-brother to 3 winners, including French 9.2f and 9.7f winner Voussac (by Great Nephew) and very useful 1½m and 1¾m winner Prime Assett (by Welsh Pageant): dam won 3 times at around 1m: green, late headway when about 15 lengths fourth of 14 to Sunderland in minor event (moved poorly down) at Windsor in July: gelded and sold to join G. Pritchard-Gordon 5,800 gns Newmarket Autumn Sales. *A. C. Stewart.*

FIELDS OF FORTUNE 3 ch.f. Anfield 117–Suffolk Broads (Moulton 128) **—** [1989 7m 7m 10g 1990 12m] leggy, lightly-made filly: well beaten in maidens. *J. L. Spearing.*

FIERCE 2 ch.g. (Apr 3) Carwhite 127–Nosey 96 (Nebbiolo 125) [1990 7m 7m⁵ 7f⁴ **68** 8m⁴ 8m] 7,800F, 11,000Y: tall, close-coupled gelding: looks weak: first foal: dam Irish 2-y-o 5f and 6f winner, half-sister to 2 Irish middle-distance winners: modest maiden: ran poorly final outing: stays 1m. *J. R. Jenkins.*

FIERY SUN   5 b.g. Sexton Blake 126–Melanie Jane (Lord Gayle (USA) 124) [1989   —
11d³ 12.3g 1990 a14g⁵ 13.8m⁵ 18g⁴ 17.6g] sturdy gelding: poor handicapper: stays
2¼m, at least in slowly-run race: acts on firm and dead going: sometimes visored:
bandaged off-hind second start: winning hurdler. *G. R. Oldroyd.*

FIESOLE   4 ch.f. Sharpo 132–Flaming Peace 104 (Queen's Hussar 124) [1989 8s   31
8g 8m 10g⁶ 8m⁴ 8m 8f 9m 8f 10f⁶ 1990 8m 8.2s 8f³ 8m 8f 8m* 8f³ 8.2m⁵ 8f] leggy
filly: won seller (no bid) at Ayr in July: failed to confirm that improvement, pulling
hard eighth outing: stays 1m: acts on firm going: best with strong handling: sold to
join G. Moore's stable 4,000 gns Newmarket Autumn Sales and won over hurdles
afterwards. *Don Enrico Incisa.*

FIFE (IRE)   2 b.f. (Apr 26) Lomond (USA) 128–Fiddle-Faddle 85 (Silly Season   75 p
127) [1990 8m³] 64,000F: eighth foal: half-sister to 3 winners, including useful
stayer El Conquistador (by Shirley Heights) and 7f and 1m winner Talk of Glory (by
Hittite Glory): dam 1½m and 2m winner, is half-sister to Irish St Leger winner
Mountain Lodge: promising third of 10, staying on really well and coming clear, to
Brockette in maiden at Leicester in September: sure to improve, and win a staying
maiden. *B. W. Hills.*

FIGHTER COMMAND   4 ch.g. Milford 119–Olga Wagner (ITY) (Sharpen Up   47
127) [1989 NR 1990 16.2m⁴] workmanlike gelding: second foal: half-brother to
useful winner in Italy by Dance In Time: dam won 5 races in Italy: won NH Flat
races at Southwell and Lingfield in February: favourite, travelled strongly long way
when 6 lengths fourth of 13 in maiden at Beverley following month: dead. *J. A.
Glover.*

FIGHTING BRAVE   3 b.g. Gorytus (USA) 132–Lady Habitat (Habitat 134)   77 §
[1989 NR 1990 8f⁵ 8f⁶ 8g⁶ 10g 10f² 10g² 10m² 11.5g² 11.7m* 12m³ 12s] lengthy
gelding: modest performer: favourite, won handicap at Bath in October, keeping on
steadily to lead close home: suited by 1½m: acts on firm going, probably not on soft:
blinkered last 7 starts, swerving left on first occasion: has carried head awkwardly
and looked reluctant: not one to rely on. *N. A. Graham.*

FIGHTING BREEZE   3 b.f. Hard Fought 125–Be Gustful (Ballymore 123)   53
[1989 NR 1990 a8g² 8g⁴ 10g 12m 10f] 1,650Y: angular filly: fourth foal: sister to 4-y-o
Gushy, successful from 7f (at 2 yrs) to 8.2f, and half-sister to 1985 2-y-o 6f winner
Strive (by Try My Best): dam Irish 7f winner: plating-class form first 3 starts: tailed
off in handicap final one: would have proved best short of 1½m: dead. *S. Dow.*

FIGHTING CHRISTINE (USA)   3 ch.f. Fighting Fit (USA)–Born Anew   65
(USA) (Avatar (USA)) [1989 NR 1990 a8g⁴ a8g⁴ a7g* 8g⁵ a8g 8m 7m² 8.2v² 7g]
rangy filly: has a quick action: first foal: dam lightly-raced maiden out of half-sister
to very smart middle-distance stayer Boucher: won maiden at Southwell in June:
clearly best effort after when second in claimers: should stay further than 1m: acts
on good to firm ground and heavy: sold 8,200 gns Newmarket Autumn Sales. *J. H. M.
Gosden.*

FIGHTING GORYTUS   5 b.h. Gorytus (USA) 132–Stella Urbis (GER) (Upper   71
Case (USA)) [1989 NR 1990 12m³ 12m 14s 12m³ 10g² 12.4m⁴ 11g⁶] good-topped
horse: moderate mover: modest handicapper: stays 1½m: acts on good to firm and
heavy going: sold 3,600 gns Doncaster November Sales. *C. C. B. Booth.*

FIGHTING SON (USA)   2 ch.c. (Mar 7) Fighting Fit (USA)–Sonseri 95 (Prince   —
Tenderfoot (USA) 126) [1990 5g⁵ 6m] 20,000Y: sturdy, good-bodied colt: moderate
mover: fifth foal: dam 5f and 6f winner stayed 1m, is half-sister to very useful 6f to
1m winner Apres Demain: sire won from 6f to 9f: bit backward, poor form in maidens
at Newmarket in April and Carlisle (weakened quickly if out) over 2 months later.
M. A. Jarvis.

FIGHTING SUN   3 ch.g. Hard Fought 125–Sunny Waters (High Top 131) [1989   —
a7g a8g 1990 a8g⁴ 10g 8m 11.7m 14m] rather leggy, heavy-topped gelding: has a
round action: well beaten, including in handicaps: blinkered third start. *H. J.
Collingridge.*

FIGHT TO WIN (USA)   2 b.g. (Apr 29) Fit To Fight (USA)–Spark of Life (USA)   — p
(Key To The Mint (USA)) [1990 8m] sturdy gelding: has scope: fifth reported foal:
half-brother to several winners, including very useful middle-distance colt Fire of
Life (by Nijinsky): dam best at 4 yrs when very smart winner at up to 1¼m: sire won
from 6f to 1½m: around 16 lengths eleventh of 14, not knocked about, in maiden at
Newmarket in October: sure to improve. *I. A. Balding.*

FIGMENT   3 b.f. Posse (USA) 130–Honey Thief 77 (Burglar 128) [1989 5v 6s⁵   75
a6g⁴ 1990 5m⁵ 5g⁶ 5m³ 5f² 5m* 6f³ a5g 5m² 5g* 6m* 5m 5m 7m 5g] strong,
good-topped filly: modest handicapper: successful at Wolverhampton in July and in

Dr K. E. Rohde's "Filia Ardross"

very good style at Beverley and Newmarket in August: well below form afterwards: stays 6f: probably acts on any going: blinkered after fifth start, except on thirteenth: also wore eyeshield on seventh (subsequently sold out of Sir Mark Prescott's stable 4,000 gns Ascot July Sales): trained next 4 by J. Mackie: has failed to respond to pressure, is somewhat temperamental, and seems to go well with tender handling. *D. W. Chapman.*

FIGURE OUT (USA) 4 b.c. Alleged (USA) 138–Preceptress (USA) (Grey **84** Dawn II 132) [1989 10.2g⁴ 10.1m* 12m⁴ 12f² 12m⁴ 1990 12d⁴ 12m⁴ 12g 13g] lengthy, useful-looking colt: useful form as 3-y-o: shaped quite well first 2 starts in 1990, ran as though something amiss next 2: should stay further than 1½m: acts on firm going: has won when sweating. *B. Hanbury.*

FILAGO (USA) 3 b.c. Foolish Pleasure (USA)–Derly (USA) 113 (Lyphard (USA) **115** 132) [1989 7d* 7d* 7g* 8m⁵ 1990 10g³ 8.5m² 10d⁵ 9g² 9.7g³ 8g³ 10v² 8v⁴] smart French colt out of half-sister to Detroit: successful as 2-y-o in newcomers event at Evry and listed race and valuable restricted event at Deauville: placed in listed races in 1990 and very good 1½ lengths third to Agent Bleu in Ciga Prix Dollar at Longchamp fifth start: stays 9.7f: yet to race on very firm ground, probably acts on any other. *Mme C. Head, France.*

FILIA ARDROSS 4 b.f. Ardross 134–Sari Habit (Saritamer (USA) 130) [1989 **108** 8g* 8g* 11d* 11g* 12g² 8s² 11g⁵ 9.2g³ 1990 10m⁶ 8.5g³ 7m² 7.3g⁵ 10m² 10m³ 10d⁵] strong, good-topped filly: winner of German 1000 Guineas and Oaks in 1989: useful form here at 4 yrs: second at Goodwood in listed event and Abtrust Select Stakes and also ran creditably in Sun Chariot Stakes (ridden along halfway) and Dubai Champion Stakes at Newmarket last 2 outings: stays 1½m, and effective at much shorter: acts on good to firm and soft going: consistent. *A. C. Stewart.*

FILICAIA 4 ro.f. Sallust 134–Fine Flame (Le Prince 98) [1989 5d 5m 5m 6f 6f⁴ 6f⁵ **56** 6g 1990 6f 7f 7m 7f³ a7g 7m⁴ 6g 7m³ 6f³ 6m 6m³ 6m* 5f⁴ 6g 6s] compact filly:

plating-class handicapper: 25/1-winner of 16-runner event at Ripon in August: stays 7f: acts on firm and dead going: visored 4 times, including at Ripon: often slowly away: has got on edge: inconsistent. *Don Enrico Incisa.*

FILL THE SAIL (IRE)   2 b.f. (Mar 18) Tumble Wind (USA)–Lady Mary (Sallust 134) [1990 5g⁶ a6g a5g 5g⁴ 6m 5.3h⁶ 6f] IR 1,400F, 400Y: rather unfortunate filly: has a round action: half-sister to winning sprinter Tanfen (by Tanfirion): dam third over 5f and 9f in Ireland: poor plater: stays 6f: sweating fifth start: has run moderately for girl apprentice: sold 540 gns Newmarket September Sales. *K. M. Brassey.*   39

FILM LIGHTING GIRL   4 ch.f. Persian Bold 123–Mey 78 (Canisbay 120) [1989 12f⁶ 12.8f² 11g 1990 a11g a11g] leggy, light-framed ex-Irish filly: half-sister to several winners, including smart 7f to 1½m winner Perchance (by Connaught): dam best at 1¼m, is half-sister to smart animals Albany and Magna Carta: 8 lengths second in maiden at Wexford as 3-y-o: blinkered, unseated rider at start final outing that year: well beaten in claimers at Southwell in January: stays 12.8f: best form on top-of-the-ground. *J. L. Harris.*   —

FINAL ACE   3 ch.c. Sharpo 132–Palmella (USA) 89 (Grundy 137) [1989 7m² 1990 5f* 6g 6m 5m³ 6s 8d] robust, sprint type: injured shortly after winning minor event (edgy, flashed tail) at Pontefract in April: best subsequent effort when fair staying-on third in claimer at Sandown: stays 7f (never placed to challenge over 1m): acts on firm going, seems unsuited by soft. *J. Etherington.*   76

FINAL ALI   3 ch.g. Final Straw 127–Bargouzine 67 (Hotfoot 126) [1989 NR 1990 8.2d 10.4m⁶ 10.2f⁵ 7m³ 8m⁴ 7f 11d a8g] 2,600Y: big, plain gelding: shows traces of stringhalt: second foal: half-brother to ungenuine D'Yquem (by Formidable): dam, half-sister to very useful sprinter As Friendly, stayed 1m: poor maiden: stays 1m: form only on good to firm ground. *Capt. J. Wilson.*   45

FINAL DEED   2 gr.g. (Apr 27) Final Straw 127–Birch Creek (Carwhite 127) [1990 6g³ 7g* 7m² 6m⁴ 7g 8m 8v 7s] 10,500Y: good-bodied, workmanlike gelding: has a roundish action: second foal: half-brother to 3-y-o Arethusa Leisure (by Homing): dam French maiden placed in pattern company in Italy: fair performer: won minor event at Ayr in June: best effort second of 4 in similar event at Chester: below best final 4 outings, on first 2 occasions on toes: seems best at 7f. *F. H. Lee.*   83

FINAL ENIGMA   3 ch.c. Final Straw 127–Mystery Ship 105 (Decoy Boy 129) [1989 5d 6m 5v 1990 6f 10f⁵ 8h* 7f* 7m* 7m² 7f⁶] neat, good-quartered colt: quite modest handicapper: favourite, successful at Brighton in May (seller, bought in 4,600 gns) and June and Folkestone (most impressively) in July: stays 1m: acts on hard ground: blinkered final start at 2 yrs: sold 3,000 gns Newmarket Autumn Sales. *P. J. Makin.*   60

FINAL HARVEST   3 ch.f. Final Straw 127–Gas Only 63 (Northfields (USA)) [1989 6f³ 6m² 6f⁵ a5g 1990 a6g³ a7g⁵ a5g³ a7g⁵ a8g⁶ a5g³ 5f 5g 7m 6g] small filly: has a sharp action: poor maiden on most form: best 3-y-o effort on all-weather: probably needs further than 5f: sometimes blinkered: sold 920 gns Doncaster September Sales. *D. W. Chapman.*   42

FINAL OFFER (USA)   2 gr.f. (Apr 25) Spectacular Bid (USA)–Geiger Countess (USA) (Mr Prospector (USA)) [1990 6m⁴ 6g a6g] $80,000Y: half-sister to several winners, including Oakworth (by Vice Regent), useful 6f winner at 2 yrs in 1987: dam won twice at up to 7f at 2 yrs: 6½ lengths fourth of 9 to Fennel at Newmarket, best effort in maidens: gave plenty of trouble at stalls at Doncaster in September and was withdrawn: blinkered final start: has worn bandages: sold 5,200 gns Newmarket December Sales. *A. A. Scott.*   57

FINAL SHOT   3 br.f. Dalsaan 125–Isadora Duncan (Primera 131) [1989 5d 5m* 5f² 7f² 5d³ 6m³ 1990 5f⁵ 5d 6m 7m² 7g² 6m* 7f³ 6m⁶ 6m³ 6d* 6g 7.6v] small,   91

Ladbrokes (Ayr) Gold Cup—
Final Shot bursts through to land a gamble decisively from the customary big field

workmanlike filly: fairly useful handicapper: successful at York in July and in £53,300 Ladbrokes (Ayr) Gold Cup in September, in latter held up then leading over 1f out to beat Bertie Wooster 2½ lengths: tenderly handled last 2 starts, facing stiff task first occasion: stays 7f: acts on firm and dead ground: game and consistent. *M. H. Easterby.*

FINDON 3 ch.f. Kris 135–Fine Honey (USA) (Drone) [1989 NR 1990 10.2g5] — strong, lengthy, angular filly: fifth foal: half-sister to fairly useful 1986 2-y-o 7f winner Pollenate (by High Line), subsequently successful in USA, and a winner in Belgium: dam lightly-raced 2-y-o 5f winner from family of Bates Motel, Super Asset and Hatim: weak favourite and very green, well-beaten last of 5 to impressive Narwala in minor event at Doncaster in September: gave a lot of trouble at stalls. *R. Charlton.*

FINEST 5 bl.m. Final Straw 127–Finest View 66 (Bold Lad (IRE) 133) [1989 9f3 10f 10m4 11f3 10m a8g6 1990 a8g a8g5 10g] leggy, quite good-topped mare: moderate mover: plating-class maiden: possibly best at up to 1¼m: acts on firm going: has worn crossed noseband. *P. Calver.*

FINE WARRIOR 3 b.c. Anita's Prince 126–Thistle Grove (Sagaro 133) [1989 — 5f3 5f3 6f4 1990 8m] bad plater: best effort over 6f: sold out of J. Berry's stable 3,500 gns Doncaster May Sales. *W. Clay.*

FINGEST 7 b.g. Imperial Fling (USA) 116–Derry Daughter (Derring-Do 131) **41** [1989 14.8s4 17.1m5 16m 1990 18f 13s 10.4g4] close-coupled, lightly-made gelding: poor maiden: stays 2m: acts on any going: usually blinkered: often bandaged: won 3 times over fences in 1989/90. *P. D. Evans.*

FINJAN 3 b.c. Thatching 131–Capriconia (Try My Best (USA) 130) [1989 7f3 6d5 **87** 1990 7m* 7m 6m2 6g* 6m2 6d2] strong, sturdy colt: keen walker: fair performer: made all in maiden at Newcastle in June and apprentice handicap at Newbury in August: very good second in handicap at Ayr final start: effective at 6f and 7f: best efforts on an easy surface: remains in training. *P. T. Walwyn.*

FINLUX SKY DESIGN 3 b.c. Ballad Rock 122–Slip The Ferret 109 (Klairon **41** 131) [1989 8g5 8s 6f 1990 8f5 10f 8.2m5 8m 8.2g 8.2v 12.2d6] leggy, workmanlike colt: poor mover: poor maiden: should stay beyond 1m: acts on good to firm ground: sold 3,800 gns Newmarket Autumn Sales. *E. Weymes.*

FINNAIR FINESSE 4 b.f. Camden Town 125–Shady Glade (Sun Prince 128) — [1989 6m 7g 1990 a10g a7g a6g] leggy, close-coupled filly: modest winner as 2-y-o: behind in subsequent handicaps: visored at 3 yrs: tends to sweat. *J. D. Czerpak.*

FIORENTIA 2 br.f. (Feb 4) Final Straw 127–Chellaston Park 117 (Record Token **92** 128) [1990 5m4 5m4 5m* 5f6 6m5 5m4 6g 5m 5m4 5d4] 5,600Y: small, sturdy filly: second foal: half-sister to 3-y-o Babicos (by Free State): dam sprinter: fairly useful performer: won maiden at Warwick in May: much better form after, excellent fourth, running on well having been outpaced, to Mujadil in Cornwallis Stakes at Ascot and Snowy Owl in listed event at Doncaster on final 2 starts: seems ideally suited by strongly-run 5f on stiff track: acts on good to firm ground and dead: sold 15,500 gns Newmarket Autumn Sales. *M. D. I. Usher.*

FIORINI 2 br.f. (Mar 9) Formidable (USA) 125–Egnoussa 76 (Swing Easy (USA) **43** 126) [1990 5g4 6d] 8,200Y: neat filly: fifth foal: sister to middle-distance maiden Enoussian Breeze: dam, half-sister to very smart Devon Ditty, won over 7f: bit backward, always mid-division in 19-runner maiden at Ayr in September: very slowly away on debut. *C. B. B. Booth.*

FIRAGA (IRE) 2 ro.f. (Mar 8) Horage 124–Fire-Screen 92 (Roan Rocket 128) — [1990 5f5 5g6 6f5 7m3 a7g6] 8,000Y, 10,000Y: lengthy filly: half-sister to 4 winners, including 13f and 1¾m winner Fire Rocket (by Busted) and fairly useful 1981 2-y-o 7f winner Marquessa d'Howfen (by Pitcairn): dam won at 1¼m: bad plater: blinkered and ridden by 7-lb claimer final start. *K. M. Brassey.*

FIREGLOW 2 b.f. (Mar 19) Mummy's Game 120–Burnt Amber (Balidar 133) **46** [1990 7m 8m 6m5 6d] angular, plain filly: first foal: dam unraced half-sister to Lockton: poor form, including in sellers: possibly suited by 6f: bandaged final 2 starts. *J. A. R. Toller.*

FIRE GOLD 3 b.f. Never So Bold 135–Seein Is Believin (USA) (Native Charger) — [1989 6g 7g5 6f 1990 7f 8f 10.6v] angular, dipped-backed, sparely-made filly: moderate walker and mover: poor maiden: well beaten in claimers and selling handicaps in 1990. *W. M. Perrin.*

FIREHALMS 3 b.g. Reesh 117–Halmsgiving (Free State 125) [1989 NR 1990 9g 50 8.5g 8.5g⁴ 7g] rather unfurnished gelding: first foal: dam placed in 9f seller: plating-class maiden: best effort fourth in claimer at Beverley. *M. H. Easterby.*

FIRE LADY 4 ch.f. Hotfoot 126–Hindu Flame 83 (Shiny Tenth 120) [1989 6s 6f³ 41 5m 6f 1990 8.3g 8f 10.1m² 11.7m] big, lengthy filly, rather dipped-backed: modest plater on her day: stays 1¼m: acts on firm going. *J. R. Jenkins.*

FIRE OF TROY 2 br.f. (May 6) Ilium 121–Rekindle 70 (Relkino 131) [1990 6m 45 6g² 7g 7m 8m 10m a8g] smallish, sparely-made filly: third foal: half-sister to 4-y-o Spark of Wit (by Comedy Star): dam poor half-sister to useful 1½m to 2m winner No Bombs: ½-length second of 8 to Angel Train in seller at Warwick in June: no comparable form, and has looked temperamental: should stay 1m: blinkered fifth and sixth starts, running much too freely on sixth. *R. J. Holder.*

FIRESTREAM 4 br.f. Blazing Saddles (AUS)–Dovey (Welsh Pageant 132) [1989 45 7m⁴ 8g³ 7f² 8f⁴ 7s 7g 1990 7m 7g 8d 7m³ 7m] angular filly: poor maiden: unseated rider final outing: better suited by 1m than 7f: acts on firm going, possibly unsuited by soft surface: sold 720 gns Doncaster October Sales. *G. M. Moore.*

FIRE THE GROOM (USA) 3 b.f. Blushing Groom (FR) 131–Prospector's Fire 115 (USA) (Mr Prospector (USA)) [1989 7g 1990 8.5d* 8.2m* 8d 7m 8m* 8m* 8f*] leggy, workmanlike filly: has a rather round action: smart performer: progressed extremely well: successful in maiden at Epsom, minor event at Nottingham, £11,700 handicap and listed race (heavily-backed favourite, by ¾ length from Samsova) at Ascot, then Aqueduct Budweiser Breeders' Cup Handicap (by ¾ length from Sally Rous at level weights) at Aqueduct: suited by strong pace at 1m, and may be worth a try over further: yet to race on very soft going, acts on any other: reportedly to join Bill Shoemaker in USA. *L. M. Cumani.*

FIRE TOP 5 br.h. Hotfoot 126–Sirnelta (FR) (Sir Tor) [1989 9d² 8s⁴ 8f 10g² 10f* 94 10f⁶ 10g* 10f⁵ 10g* 10g* 1990 10g 10g⁴ 10.4d 10g* 10m³ 10.5m 10m 10f² 10m² 10.6g³ 10g 10.2s² 10g] sparely-made horse: usually looks really well: fairly useful performer: successful in strongly-run £19,000 handicap at Epsom in June by 1½ lengths from Gran Alba: ran well when placed in listed event and handicaps afterwards: stays 1¼m well: acts on any going: visored once: races up with pace: tremendously tough, game and genuine. *R. Akehurst.*

FIRMAMENT (USA) 3 gr.c. Spectacular Bid (USA)–Star In The North (USA) — 94 (Northern Dancer) [1989 NR 1990 8m 10m 8m a10g⁵] workmanlike colt with scope: has a free, rather round action: sixth foal: closely related to good U.S. 1m to 1¼m performer Cool (by Bold Bidder) and half-brother to 3 winners, notably very smart 11f to 1¾m winner Mountain Kingdom (by Exceller): dam 1¼m and 1½m winner from good family: little promise in maidens, visored final start: sold 3,700 gns Newmarket December Sales. *J. H. M. Gosden.*

FIRST ADMIRAL 4 b.c. Lord Gayle (USA) 124–Grecian Blue 68 (Majority Blue — 126) [1989 8.2m 10m 10.8m 8.2g⁶ 10m 1990 13s] rather finely-made, workmanlike colt: has a short, quick action: plating-class form at best: should stay 1¼m: blinkered twice. *D. J. Wintle.*

FIRST AVENUE 6 b.g. Tina's Pet 121–Olympus Girl 65 (Zeus Boy 121) [1989 50 8m 11.7m⁵ 10f* 10f* 10.2f⁴ 10f* 1990 11.5m⁵ 10g⁵ 11.7m⁶ 10h⁶ 10f² 10f* 10f⁵ 12m⁴] compact gelding: plating-class handicapper: won race at Folkestone for fourth time in apprentice race in September: stays 1½m: acts very well on firm going: has worn blinkers and visor: good mount for apprentice: bolted to post seventh outing: consistent. *Andrew Turnell.*

FIRST BID 3 ch.g. Crofthall 110–Redgrave Design 77 (Nebbiolo 125) [1989 6v 62 1990 10g 10d 12.2d⁴ 10d³ 9s 10.2s] workmanlike gelding: form only when in frame, keeping on well, in claimer (blinkered) at Catterick and handicap (visored, made most) at Redcar: stays 1½m: yet to race on top-of-the-ground: also blinkered fifth start. *R. M. Whitaker.*

FIRST BILL 7 ch.g. Nicholas Bill 125–Angelica (SWE) (Hornbeam 130) [1989 — 12d 11.7g³ 12g* 11.7m³ 12g 1990 12f4 12.3d 12g⁵ 11.7m] smallish, well-made gelding: moderate mover: quite modest handicapper: not discredited first and third outings: suited by 1½m: goes particularly well on an easy surface: sometimes sweats: suitable mount for apprentice. *H. Candy.*

FIRST BLESSED 3 b.f. Music Boy 124–Blessit 79 (So Blessed 130) [1989 5g 6g — 1990 6m⁵ 5m 9s 7d] neat filly: poor maiden: better at 6f than 5f: sold 1,200 gns Doncaster November Sales. *W. J. Pearce.*

FIRST BORN 3 br.f. Be My Native (USA) 122–Feat of Arms (Jaazeiro (USA) 127) 43 [1989 5d⁶ 5f⁵ 7g 6m 7g 1990 8m⁴ 8f⁵ 10d⁵ 12m² 12g] leggy, light-framed filly: has a round action: quite moderate plater: suited by 1½m: acts on good to firm ground and dead: ridden by 7-lb claimer first 3 starts. *D. Dutton.*

FIRST DREAM 3 b.f. Dreams To Reality (USA) 113–Khloud 76 (Pitskelly 122) —
[1989 5g² 5f³ 5v⁴ 6s* 1990 8.2g 6g 8.2g⁶ 10g a8g] leggy, sparely-made filly: quite modest winner at 2 yrs: below form in 1990: better at 6f than 5f, unlikely to stay 1¼m: acts on soft going: sweating and edgy fourth start: sold 2,600 gns Newmarket July Sales. *M. Johnston.*

FIRST EMERALD 2 b.f. (Apr 9) Sulaafah (USA) 119–Mavela (USA) (Empery 47
(USA) 128) [1990 7.5g⁵ 7m 8m² a8g] 500Y: first foal: dam once-raced daughter of half-sister to very smart 1979 2-y-o Many Moons: 3½ lengths second of 17 to Sharp Glow in apprentice seller at Warwick: ran moderately for 7-lb claimer on final start: will probably stay 1¼m. *N. A. Graham.*

FIRST ERROR 6 ch.g. Creetown 123–Greeana 65 (Green God 128) [1989 NR —
1990 8g 8.2g⁶ 8f] big, good-topped gelding: poor mover: poor maiden: stays 1m. *K. S. Bridgwater.*

FIRST EXHIBITION 3 b.f. Claude Monet (USA) 121–All Hail 112 (Alcide 136) —
[1989 7m³ 1990 10g 10m⁵ 7.5g 8g] leggy, sparely-made filly: plating-class maiden, form only on debut: should stay 1m: sold 2,200 gns Newmarket July Sales. *J. R. Fanshawe.*

FIRST FASTNET 5 b.m. Ahonoora 122–Jolie Brise (Tumble Wind (USA)) [1989 —
5d* 6g 5m 5f³ 5m⁴ 5m* 5g 5g 6f 5m⁴ 5.3f 5m a5g 1990 a5g] workmanlike mare: below her best since winning handicaps at Catterick (apprentices) and Windsor as 4-y-o: suited by 5f: used to race on soft going, acts on any other: blinkered twice at 4 yrs: sold 3,400 gns Doncaster January Sales: inconsistent. *F. Durr.*

FIRST FLUSH 4 b.g. Precocious 126–Rosananti 107 (Blushing Groom (FR) 131) 42
[1989 7d 6f 6f⁴ 6f 6m 5m 6g 8.2d a8g 6g 1990 6f a5g 7g* 7f a7g⁵ a6g* 5m a6g 5m] sturdy gelding: carries condition: poor walker: successful in handicaps at Yarmouth in June and Southwell in August: stays 7f: acts on firm ground: visored twice at 3 yrs: wears bandages: sometimes on toes: inconsistent. *K. T. Ivory.*

FIRST FOR APRIL 2 b.f. (May 8) Welsh Captain 113–Glorious Spring 41 —
(Hittite Glory 125) [1990 6m 5f] useful-looking filly: first foal: dam poor plater at 2 yrs: soundly beaten in sellers. *M. P. Muggeridge.*

FIRST HOME 3 b.g. Homing 130–Mill Wind 68 (Blakeney 126) [1989 5d⁶ 5f 6m —
5.1m⁶ 5f² 6m⁴ 6f² 6f³ 6f⁵ 6m 7g 6g a7g a8g 1990 a8g⁴ a11g⁶ 11.5g⁴ 10f 11.5f⁶ 8f a10g⁶] rather leggy gelding: has a quick action: inconsistent plater: stays 7f. *Pat Mitchell.*

FIRST MISTAKE 3 b.f. Posse (USA) 130–Gentle Star 77 (Comedy Star (USA) —
121) [1989 5f 6g⁴ 6g⁶ 6m⁴ 1990 7.5g] big, rangy filly: plating-class maiden: 20/1, bandaged near-hind and bit backward on first run for nearly 10 months, pulled hard in May handicap on only start in 1990: worth another try at 5f. *M. W. Easterby.*

FIRST SUCCESS (IRE) 2 gr.c. (Apr 10) Wassl 125–Ardmay 57 (Roan Rocket 78
128) [1990 6m 8.2d⁵ 7m⁶ 7.3g 6m³ 5d] 27,000Y: good-quartered, useful-looking colt: has plenty of scope: fifth foal: half-brother to 3-y-o Northern Heights (by Pharly), 7f winner at 2 yrs, and 3 other winners, including Irgaim (by Valiyar), fair 6f and 1m winner here, later better in Italy: dam sister to Gairloch and Whistlefield: best efforts fourth and fifth starts, never-dangerous eighth of 9 in Horris Hill Stakes at Newbury and third of 14 to Volksraad in maiden at Newmarket: ran poorly final outing: stays 7f: blinkered final 2 outings, racing freely on first occasion. *R. Boss.*

FIRST TRADITION 5 ch.m. Sayyaf 121–Traditional Miss 90 (Traditionalist —
(USA)) [1989 5f 7m 8m 6m⁵ 7f³ 7m 6m³ 6f⁵ 1990 8f a6g] lengthy, good-bodied mare: poor performer: best form at 6f to 7f: acts on firm going: blinkered and sweating third outing at 4-y-o: has won for apprentice. *C. J. Hill.*

FIRST VICTORY 4 gr.c. Concorde Hero (USA) 101–Cestrefeld 94 (Capistrano 101
120) [1989 7s 7fʷᵒ 9m⁵ 10.2g 10g* 12g* 1990 11m² 14m* 13.3m⁴ 12f² 16m⁵ 14g⁴ 13.3g* 12m⁴ 12s] tall, angular colt: useful handicapper: progressed well as 4-y-o, winning at Sandown in May and Newbury (£20,400 'Coral' Autumn Cup, coming back on bridle in straight and running on strongly to beat Clare Court 3 lengths) in September: mostly ran well in between, including in Tote Ebor at York: gives impression will prove best at up to 1¾m: acts on firm going, seemingly unsuited by soft: hung left fifth start: usually comes from behind, and is suited by strong gallop. *R. Hannon.*

FIRST VINTAGE (USA) 3 b.c. Ruthie's Native (USA)–Champagneandlace 51
(USA) (Champagne Charlie (USA)) [1989 6f 6d³ 1990 8f 8f 10.4g 9g a6g⁴ 6g 6d]

good-quartered colt: edgy, form as 3-y-o only when fourth of 16 in handicap at Southwell: blinkered facing stiff task, edged left in claimer next start: seems best at 6f: often sweating: sold 1,000 gns Newmarket Autumn Sales. *S. G. Norton.*

FISHERMAN'S CROFT   4 b.c. Dunbeath (USA) 127–Russeting 76 (Mummy's — Pet 125) [1989 7f 8.2m 6g 8f4 8g* 8g5 8g5 1990 10.6d 10m] sparely-made, medium-sized colt: has a markedly round action: quite modest winner of claimer as 3-y-o: needed race both starts in 1990: stays 1m: seems suited by a sound surface: prolific winning hurdler in 1989/90. *N. Tinkler.*

FISHIN' TACKLE (USA)   2 b.c. (Apr 13) Sportin' Life (USA)–Perilune (USA) — p (Soy Numero Uno (USA)) [1990 7m] $38,000Y: well-made colt: good walker: fourth foal: half-brother to a winner in USA by Clev Er Tell: dam minor winner at 3 yrs: sire stayed 9f: carrying condition, not knocked about final 3f when behind in maiden at Newmarket in July: should improve. *A. A. Scott.*

FISHKI   4 b.f. Niniski (USA) 125–Ladyfish 79 (Pampapaul 121) [1989 10.5f6 a8g4   63 1990 a8g a12g6 11.5f* 12f3 9g 12s* 15v*] workmanlike, angular filly: made all in claimer (claimed out of B. Hanbury's stable £4,110) at Yarmouth in July and handicaps at Hamilton (unchallenged by 5 lengths, eased considerably) in September and Ayr in October: claimed out of R. Stubbs's stable £8,704 fourth outing: stays 15f: has won on firm going, but clearly goes particularly well in the mud: occasionally bandaged behind: winning novice hurdler in November. *M. D. Hammond.*

FITAHL (USA)   2 br.c. (Jan 28) Chief's Crown (USA)–Love's Dream (FR) (Rhein-   79 gold 137) [1990 5m* 6m 5m3] 560,000Y: rather leggy, close-coupled, attractive colt: has a keen, round action: third foal: half-brother to modest 1m winner In The Rigging (by Topsider): dam half-sister to Light Cavalry and Fairy Footsteps: impressive winner of May maiden at Leicester: very edgy, staying-on third to Bit of A Lark in minor event at Pontefract in October, first run since finishing last in Coventry Stakes at Royal Ascot: should be suited by further than 5f. *H. Thomson Jones.*

FITNESS FANATIC   2 b.g. (Mar 25) Nishapour (FR) 125–Bustling Nelly 94 — (Bustino 136) [1990 7g 8g 6d] 3,600Y: third foal: half-brother to 1½m winner Passion And Mirth (by Known Fact) and 2m winner Silk Degrees (by Dunbeath): dam middle-distance winner, is daughter of Cambridgeshire winner Flying Nelly: well beaten in autumn maidens. *D. A. Wilson.*

FIT THE BILL   2 b.c. (Apr 11) Nicholas Bill 125–Golden Windlass 79 (Princely   74 Gift 137) [1990 6m3 6m 5d 8d4 8.2g2] 4,500F, 12,000Y: lengthy colt with plenty of scope: half-brother to 2 winners, including miler Haddfan (by Lorenzaccio): dam won over 1m: much improved in nurseries (well-backed favourite both times) final 2 starts, second at Nottingham in September: will stay 1¼m. *Mrs G. R. Reveley.*

FITZROY BELL   3 ch.g. Red Sunset 120–Gaychimes (Steel Heart 128) [1989 8g — a8g6 a7g 1990 a12g] workmanlike gelding: well beaten in maidens and claimers: most unlikely to stay 1½m: visored only start in 1990: blinkered previous two. *M. Bell.*

FIVE CASTLES   2 b.c. (May 8) Castle Keep 121–Teftu 85 (Double Jump 131) — [1990 8g 7s 6d] compact colt: second reported foal: dam 2-y-o 6f winner: always behind in autumn maidens. *G. P. Enright.*

FIVESEVENFIVEO   2 ch.f. (Feb 10) Enchantment 115–Miss Times 78 (Major   77 Portion 129) [1990 5g 5g* 6f2 5m2 6m4 5m3 6m] 2,000F, 3,000Y: close-coupled, good quartered filly: has quick action: sister to 2-y-o 5f winners Mr Charmer and Enchanted Times: dam 6f seller winner at 2 yrs, is out of half-sister to very smart sprinter Runnymede: modest performer: won maiden auction at Redcar in June: ran well most starts after, but badly in seller final outing: stays 6f: has hung left. *J. Berry.*

FIZZ TIME   2 b.c. (Feb 24) Good Times (ITY)–More Fizz (Morston (FR) 125) — p [1990 5d 5d 6d] 32,000Y: leggy, rather angular colt: first foal: dam French 9.2f winner from family of Zeddaan: poor form in maidens: slowly away first 2 starts: not given hard race final one: will be better suited by 7f+: may be worth keeping an eye on. *Mrs J. R. Ramsden.*

FLAMBOYANCE   3 b.f. Exhibitioner 111–Mock Auction 55 (Auction Ring (USA) — 123) [1989 a6g 1990 a6g6] small filly: well beaten in maidens at Lingfield: blinkered second of them: sold 1,050 gns Ascot April Sales. *J. Ringer.*

FLAME FLOWER   8 gr.m. Runnymede 123–Headliner (Pampered King 121) — [1989 NR 1990 a12g] sparely-made mare: poor maiden: tailed off in handicap at Southwell in May, only outing since 1986: used to be suited by middle distances: blinkered once: has been to stud. *N. Kernick.*

311

FLAMENCO PARK 3 b.f. Mummy's Pet 125–Appleby Park 98 (Bay Express —
132) [1989 NR 1990 8m a7g⁵ 7m⁶ 6s] tall, lengthy filly: fourth living foal: half-sister
to useful 7f and 1m winner Cromwell Park (by Moorestyle): dam lightly-raced 2-y-o
7f winner: fifth in maiden at Southwell: off course 4 months and stiff tasks
afterwards, no chance final start: pulls hard. *J. Wharton.*

FLAMING GLORY 3 b.c. Alzao (USA) 117–Engage (Whistling Wind 123) [1989   72
6m⁵ 6m³ 7g* 8m² 9g 1990 12.3d⁶ 12d³ 12g 16.2f⁴ 16f⁶ 16.2g² 18g] stocky colt:
modest handicapper: stays 2m: acts on firm ground and dead: blinkered last 5 starts:
ran wide on turn at Epsom: inconsistent: sold 7,200 gns Newmarket Autumn Sales.
M. Bell.

FLAMINGO POND 4 b.f. Sadler's Wells (USA) 132–Anegada 79 (Welsh   101
Pageant 132) [1989 10.5f⁴ 10.1m* 10m⁵ 10m* 10.2m³ 11s⁵ 1990 10f 10m* 10m⁵ 10m⁵
10d] angular, sparely-made filly: useful performer: made all in 3-runner minor event
at Lingfield in June: below form afterwards: should stay 1½m: best efforts on
top-of-the-ground: has won when sweating. *R. Charlton.*

FLANAGAN 3 br.c. Comedy Star (USA) 121–Bold Blue 82 (Targowice (USA) —
130) [1989 7m 1990 10.8m] neat colt: half-brother to useful 1¾m winner Cadmium
(by Niniski) and 5.8f to 1½m winner Empire Blue (by Dominion): dam won over
1¼m: well beaten in maidens, moving badly to post only start in 1990: sold 675 gns
Ascot July Sales. *P. F. I. Cole.*

FLASH DANCER (IRE) 2 b.c. (Feb 23) Tate Gallery (USA) 117–Vaguely —
Deesse (USA) (Vaguely Noble 140) [1990 7f⁵ 6f⁵ 6g] 64,000Y: workmanlike colt:
second foal: dam ran once: soundly beaten in maidens and minor event (blinkered
and edgy, particularly at stalls): sold 3,700 gns Newmarket Autumn Sales. *Mrs L.
Piggott.*

FLASHFOOT 2 ch.c. (Apr 20) Rousillon (USA) 133–Miellita 98 (King Emperor   67
(USA)) [1990 8g⁵ 8m] big, lengthy colt: has plenty of scope: seventh foal:
half-brother to 3-y-o Lomond Lady (by Lomond), 8.5f winner Sonbere (by Electric)
and middle-distance winner In The Shade (by Bustino): dam 2-y-o 6f winner, stayed
at least 1¼m: bit backward, quite modest form in minor event at Newbury (slowly
away) and maiden at Newmarket in autumn. *I. A. Balding.*

FLASH OF REALM (FR) 4 b.c. Super Moment (USA)–Light of Realm 116   ?
(Realm 129) [1989 10v* 11d 10.5m⁴ 12d⁶ 1990 12g* 12g⁴ 10.6m 11d⁶] good-bodied
colt: useful at his best, winner of listed event at Saint-Cloud and fourth in Prix Lupin
at Longchamp as 3-y-o: successful in spring when trained by H. Pantall in minor
race at Nantes: claimed out of N. Tinkler's stable £22,222 third outing: 200/1, last of
6 in Ayr listed event won by Pirate Army: stays 1½m: probably acts on any going. *P.
Monteith.*

FLASS VALE 2 b.g. (Mar 21) Final Straw 127–Emblazon 91 (Wolver Hollow 126)   61
[1990 5f 5m 6g³ 7m⁴ 7d³ 7.5f⁴ 7f⁴ 7f⁶] 4,200Y: good-topped gelding: carries
condition: has a round action: sixth foal: half-brother to 3-y-o Walkern Witch (by
Dunbeath), 6f winner at 2 yrs, and 3 other winners here and abroad, including
modest 6f and 1m winner Taranga (by Music Boy): dam winner at up to 1½m, is
daughter of good staying 2-y-o Slip Stitch: quite modest maiden: will stay further:
acts on firm and dead ground: suitable mount for 7-lb claimer. *T. Fairhurst.*

FLEET FOOTED 7 b.g. Tachypous 128–More Or Less 64 (Morston (FR) 125) —
[1989 12f 8m 10m 10m* 8.5f³ 10g⁴ 10f³ 10g 1990 11m⁵ 9.1m] close-coupled, quite
attractive gelding: moderate mover: poor handicapper: ideally suited by around
1¼m: suited by a sound surface: blinkered 3 times: seems to need plenty of driving:
retained 3,200 gns Doncaster May Sales: winning hurdler. *Mrs G. R. Reveley.*

FLEET SPECIAL 8 gr.g. High Top 131–Rockney 84 (Roan Rocket 128) [1989   44
10f 10h² 12h⁵ 8h² 10f³ 1990 10.2m⁶ 8.2s 8m 9f⁶ 12g* 12.8g⁵ 12d⁵ 11m²
11m³ a12g³ 12m⁴ a12g⁵ 10m⁴] lengthy,
sparely-made gelding: plating-class handicapper: seems to stay 1½m: suited by a
sound surface: visored sixth outing: often wears a tongue strap. *P. Monteith.*

FLEURCONE 8 ch.g. Celtic Cone 116–Little Fleur (Tudor Wood 96) [1989 NR —
1990 a12g a16g] little worthwhile form on flat since debut as 3-y-o: bandaged near-
hind in 1990. *K. White.*

FLIGHT FANTASY (USA) 5 b.m. Air Forbes Won (USA)–Prisoner's Song   45
(USA) (Stop The Music (USA)) [1989 NR 1990 10m 8m 9f⁶ 12g* 12.8g⁵ 12d⁵ 11m²
11m³ a12g³ 12m⁴ a12g⁵ 10m⁴] leggy, quite good-topped mare: moderate mover:
20/1-winner of handicap at Beverley in May: stays 1½m: acts on good to firm going:
blinkered twice at 3 yrs: suitable mount for apprentice: sometimes edgy, and has
sweated. *J. Parkes.*

312

FLIGHT OF FREEDOM (USA) 2 b.c. (Apr 14) Lear Fan (USA) 130– 92 p
Runaway Lady (USA) (Caucasus (USA)) [1990 7g³ 7d⁴] $60,000Y: well-made colt:
has a quick action: second foal: dam minor winner at up to 9f in North America:
burly, around a length fourth of 11, losing position over 2f out then staying on well, to
Junk Bond in valuable minor event at Newmarket in October: will be better suited
by 1m: likely to improve further. *J. W. Hills.*

FLIGHT OF PLEASURE (USA) 2 b.f. (Mar 11) Roberto (USA) 131–Journey 74
(USA) (What A Pleasure (USA)) [1990 a5g 6g* 7g* 7m⁶ 7h³ 8m] $100,000F,
$120,000Y: leggy, unfurnished filly: good mover: sister to a graded stakes-placed
winner in North America and half-sister to several other winners, including 1m
winner Lambourn Citizen (by L'Emigrant): dam unraced: successful in maiden at
Yarmouth and minor event (flashed tail under strong pressure) at Warwick in June:
best form at 7f: acts on hard ground. *B. Hanbury.*

FLIGHTY ANGEL 3 b.f. Precocious 126–Angel Beam (SWE) 115 (Hornbeam —
130) [1989 NR 1990 7f] good-bodied filly: half-sister to 6 winners, including Royal
Hunt Cup winner Governorship (by Dominion) and fairly useful 5f and 6f winner
Young Oak (by Young Generation): dam, smart over 5f and 6f at 2 yrs, needed 1¼m
at 3 yrs: backward, weakened quickly last 2½f in claimer at Salisbury in August:
sold 950 gns Newmarket September Sales. *I. A. Balding.*

FLIGHTY GUEST 2 gr.f. (Feb 21) Be My Guest (USA) 126–Julia Flyte 91 44
(Drone) [1990 7m 7g⁶ 8m] 21,000F, 20,000Y: lengthy filly: fourth foal: half-sister to
a winner in Italy: dam 2-y-o 6f winner, is half-sister to very useful Miss Petard (dam
of Rejuvenate): never able to challenge in quite valuable events at Sandown and
Salisbury and maiden (visored) at Chepstow: may do better. *I. A. Balding.*

FLIRTING A LITTLE (USA) 3 gr.f. Little Current (USA)–On My Knee 80
(USA) (Secretariat (USA)) [1989 NR 1990 8g⁶ 10g³] $52,000Y: sturdy filly: has
scope: second foal: half-sister to a winner in USA by Summing: dam unraced
half-sister to 3 winners by Little Current, including Hollywood Oaks winner Prize
Spot: fair form, staying on, in maidens at Newmarket and Goodwood in the summer:
will be suited by 1½m. *J. H. M. Gosden.*

FLITCHAM 3 b.f. Elegant Air 119–Seldom (Rarity 129) [1989 6m 1990 8.2g³ 8m 57 d
10g 10g 10g a13g a13g a16g⁵] small, close-coupled, angular filly: quite modest
maiden: should stay 1¼m: retained by trainer 1,600 gns Newmarket Autumn Sales.
W. J. Musson.

FLOATING LINE 2 ch.c. (Mar 12) Bairn (USA) 126–County Line 75 (High Line 74
125) [1990 6m* 7m] 3,200Y: sparely-made colt: second foal: half-brother to 3-y-o 7f
winner Moscow Dynamo (by Siberian Express): dam middle-distance maiden: won
maiden auction at Pontefract by 2½ lengths from Dance On Sixpence: ridden by 7-lb
claimer, well beaten in nursery later in August: withdrawn intended debut (refused
to enter stalls) in May. *P. Wigham.*

FLOATING NOTE 5 ch.m. Music Boy 124–Red Crest 64 (Red God 128§) [1989 — §
6d 6m 5f 6f 7f 6m 8.5m 6m 1990 a5g a7g 6g 7m 7f 8m a8g 7m] leggy, close-coupled
mare: no longer of much account: has worn blinkers and visor: has sweated, and
often got on edge. *J. S. Wainwright.*

FLORADO 2 b.f. (Mar 4) Faustus (USA) 118–Fuchsia 66 (Hot Spark 126) [1990 5f 48
6m⁵ 7m³ 8.2g 8m] small, close-coupled filly: first foal: dam maiden suited by 6f:
plating-class maiden: edged right third start, reluctant to race next outing: should
stay 1m. *M. Blanshard.*

FLORET (USA) 3 b.c. Roberto (USA) 131 Floreia (USA) (Bold Bidder) [1989 47
NR 1990 6f⁵ a8g 9m 11v⁶ 12d⁴ a12g⁴] $105,000Y: leggy, good-topped colt: third foal:
half-brother to successful U.S. 4-y-o 7f winner Flower Ridge (by Cox's Ridge): dam unraced
daughter of top-class U.S. filly Gallant Bloom: form only when fourth in seller
(blinkered and bandaged, carried head high) at Edinburgh and claimer at Lingfield:
worth a try at 1¼m. *R. W. Stubbs.*

FLORIDA GOLD 3 b.c. Hard Fought 125–Klairelle (Klairon 131) [1989 6m⁵ 7f⁵ 38
7m⁴ 7m² 7f³ 8g 8g 6m 8.2s 1990 7g 8.3g 10f 7m⁵ 8f⁶ 8.3m 10f* 8h 12m⁶ 10m]
compact colt: moderate mover: plater: virtually only form as 3-y-o when 8-length
winner of handicap (no bid) at Lingfield in August, making all: stays 1¼m: acts on
firm ground: blinkered seventh, eighth and final outings: has run creditably for 7-lb
claimer. *D. A. Wilson.*

FLORIDA SECRET 3 b.g. Miami Springs 121–Close Secret 80 (Reliance II 137) 58
[1989 6m 6m² 7g* 1990 12m 12f 10m³ 8.5g⁴ 9m⁵ 8g 9m] sparely-made gelding: has a
round action: plating-class performer: found little in handicaps, including ladies,
fifth and sixth starts: gelded afterwards, and burly on return over 3 months later:

best at up to 1¼m: acts on good to firm ground: has worn bandages: has been slowly away and swished tail under pressure. *J. Pearce.*

FLOWER DANCER 2 b.c. (Apr 3) Mashhor Dancer (USA)–Raina Perera 71   **44**
(Tyrnavos 129) [1990 7f 7m] first foal: dam maiden (stayed 7f) here at 2 yrs later won in Italy: around 13 lengths thirteenth of 22, keeping on, in maiden at Chepstow in October, second and better effort: will be better suited to 1m. *Miss A. J. Whitfield.*

FLOWER GIRL 3 ch.f. Pharly (FR) 130–Dancing Meg (USA) 113 (Marshua's **108**
Dancer (USA)) [1989 6f* 7g³ 6g 1990 7m⁴ 6f² 6g* 6f* 6g 6g* 6m] good-topped, robust filly: has a free, rather round action: useful performer: won £7,200 event (sweating) at Newmarket and listed race at Haydock in August and Group 3 contest at Baden-Baden in August: always behind in Cork And Orrery Stakes and Diadem Stakes at Ascot: should prove as effective at 7f: acts on firm going. *H. Thomson Jones.*

FLOWER MELODY 2 b.f. (Mar 3) Liboi (USA) 76–Milford Moss (Record **48** p
Token 128) [1990 a8g⁶] first live foal: dam unraced: weak in market, sixth of 7 behind 8-length winner Statajack after slow start in maiden at Lingfield: may improve. *H. Candy.*

FLOWER OF SCOTLAND 2 b.f. (Mar 29) Hotfoot 126–La Piccolina 85 **53**
(Tudor Rhythm 112) [1990 6g 6m⁵ 7m 7f 10s⁴] leggy, angular filly: fourth reported foal: dam won from 1m to 12.2f: 50/1-fourth of 21, staying on steadily, to Matahif in maiden at Nottingham in October: clearly suited by a test of stamina: acts on soft ground. *P. Calver.*

FLOWN 3 b.c. Hotfoot 126–My Own II 96 (El Relicario 124) [1989 NR 1990 10.1m⁴ **86**
10f* 12m³ 12g 12g] lengthy, attractive colt: has plenty of scope: brother to fairly useful middle-distance stayer Fleeting Affair and half-brother to several winners, including good middle-distance performer Haul Knight (by Firestreak): dam won from 1m to 11f: won maiden at Newmarket in August: easily best effort in handicaps next time, held up then staying on well only final 1f: suited by 1½m, possibly by top-of-the-ground: taken down early and moved moderately final start: retained by trainer 27,000 gns Newmarket Autumn Sales. *R. Hannon.*

FLUENT IN SPANISH 2 b. or br.f. (Feb 29) King of Spain 121–Linguistic 95   —
(Porto Bello 118) [1990 6g a6g 7g] 14,500Y: rather leggy filly: half-sister to 4 winners, including stayers Castle Douglas (by Amboise) and Relatively Easy (by Relkino): dam 2-y-o 5f winner: carrying condition, well beaten in large-field maidens and a minor event. *M. W. Easterby.*

FLUIDITY (USA) 2 b.c. (Apr 6) Robellino (USA) 127–Maple River (USA) **80** p
(Clandestine) [1990 7m⁴ 7m⁵ 7m a7g* a7g*] $100,000Y: good-bodied colt: has scope: moderate mover: brother to useful 10.5f winner Hello Ernani and half-brother to 2 winners in North America: dam won twice at sprint distances at 3 yrs: progressive stayer, winner of 12-runner maiden and 13-runner nursery (by 3½ lengths from Castcareaway at Lingfield) in December: likely to improve again at 1m + . *J. H. M. Gosden.*

FLUORESCENT FLO 3 ch.f. Ballad Rock 122–Ridans Girl 89 (Ridan (USA)) **68**
[1989 NR 1990 8m 8g 5g³ 6g 6m 7f 7f] IR 10,500Y: sixth foal: half-sister to Belgian 6f to 1m winner Schuygulla (by Dara Monarch): dam, 2-y-o 5f and 6f winner, is sister to good 1977 2-y-o Aythorpe and half-sister to smart performer at up to 7f Royal Boy: third in maiden at Mallow in April, virtually only show: well beaten in minor event (sweating) and maiden here: trained until after fifth start by T. Stack. *D. Moffatt.*

FLYAWAY (FR) 5 ch.h. Touching Wood (USA) 127–Flying Sauce 107 (Sauce   —
Boat (USA)) [1989 12g⁵ 12s³ 12f⁴ 18f⁵ 12.3m⁶ 16.5m⁶ 12s 14g⁵ 12.4g⁵ a12g³ 1990 a14g 16m 15.3g 16.2s] lengthy horse: carries condition: poor walker and mover: modest handicapper on his day as 4-y-o: well beaten in autumn of 1990: should stay 1¾m: ideally suited by an easy surface: blinkered 4 times as 3-y-o: bandaged final start: a difficult ride. *J. L. Harris.*

FLY AWAY SOON (USA) 2 b.c. (Apr 21) Lear Fan (USA) 130–Awenita (Rarity **72** p
129) [1990 7f²] 30,000Y: workmanlike colt: third foal: closely related to a minor winner in North America by Darby Creek Road: dam never ran: bit backward and green, 2½ lengths second of 7, wandering but keeping on well, to Alnaab in maiden at Goodwood in August: will improve. *P. F. I. Cole.*

FLY BY NORTH (USA) 2 b.c. (Apr 24) Northern Horizon (USA)–Lazy E **41**
(CAN) (Meadow Court 129) [1990 7g a8g a8g] smallish, close-coupled colt: has a quick action: second known foal: dam never ran: behind in maidens. *R. Hannon.*

FLY FURTHER 2 b.f. (Apr 22) Move Off 112–Foreign Bird 92 (Lauso) [1990 7d   —
7d] leggy filly: half-sister to 5f winner Debris (by Coded Scrap) and 2m winner

Foreign Embassy (by Mandamus), both winners over jumps: dam won at up to 1¼m: backward in seller at Catterick and maiden at Edinburgh in autumn. *W. A. Stephenson.*

FLYING BRAVE 2 b.c. (Mar 14) Persian Bold 123–Flying Sauce 107 **101** (Sauce Boat (USA)) [1990 6g* 6d3 7f2 7m* 8g4]

The inaugural running of the Tattersalls Tiffany Highflyer Stakes, a £25,000 added open race for two-year-old colts and geldings at Newmarket in August, offering bonuses totalling £850,000 to owners of the first six horses to finish which were sold at the previous year's Highflyer Yearling Sales, attracted plenty of disparaging comment from all sides of the industry throughout the year, and it came as no surprise to learn in November that the race will be dropped in 1992. The compromise reached between Tattersalls, Britain's largest bloodstock sales company, and the Jockey Club, whose opposition to a completely restricted event run on the same lines as Ireland's Cartier Million left open the farcical possibility that Highflyer-sold horses need not even finish in the frame to scoop the huge bonuses; the bonuses themselves, as John Dunlop, trainer of the winning horse Flying Brave and third-placed Time Gentleman, complained, were funded entirely by the breeders and vendors and not by Tattersalls or Tiffanys; the publicity afforded the race (as for its sister event, the Tattersalls Tiffany Yorkshire Fillies Stakes at Doncaster, later in the year) was inadequate to say the least; and the idea of tying a two-year-old bonus race to a sale like the Highflyer, with its heavy emphasis on classic second-year pedigrees, lacked foresight. In the end a shortage of suitably precocious animals contributed at least as much to the paucity of runners (seventeen, from an initial entry of just fifty-nine) at Newmarket, as the general indifference and prevailing firm ground which were blamed officially. Things aren't likely to look up much in 1991, either, although the re-siting of the race later in the Calendar and extension of the bonuses down to tenth place, while incorporating the fillies race at the same time, should offset the effect of the smaller 1990 Highflyer catalogue. Bonus races have proved to be popular in other countries where flair in race planning is encouraged, but the Jockey Club's stilted approach to the whole concept ensured the Highflyer Stakes was always going to be an ungainly compromise that sat uncomfortably and unwanted amongst the general pattern.

Flying Brave was bought for 54,000 guineas as a yearling by a syndicate specially formed to try and win the £500,000 first-bonus. He ran three times before the Highflyer Stakes, winning a maiden at Goodwood in July by a short head then showing progressive form in a minor event at Ascot and the Lanson Champagne Vintage Stakes at Goodwood. The quick-actioned Flying Brave was never travelling with any fluency on the dead ground at Ascot, and made hard work of reaching a place, but he looked a different horse on much firmer ground at Goodwood six weeks afterwards, staying on well to finish a clear second to the length-and-a-half winner Mukkaddamah. Flying Brave's form, although only fairly useful, looked to be clearly the best of the Highflyer contestants; yet he didn't win as well as might have been anticipated. On his toes and edgy beforehand, as is usual with him, Flying Brave came through from the rear when chased along three furlongs out, tended to hang and swish his tail when brought to challenge, but then ran on well to lead near the finish

Tattersalls Tiffany Highflyer Stakes, Newmarket—
bought as a yearling specifically to win this race, Flying Brave lands the £500,000 bonus,
responding to strong pressure to catch Shalford (rails) late on

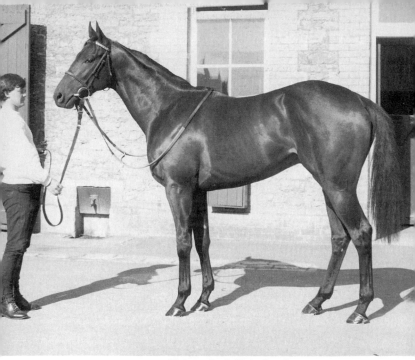

Mr Aubrey Ison's "Flying Brave"

and win by a length from the nursery winner Shalford. On his only subsequent outing Flying Brave contested the Panasonic Beresford EBF Futurity over a mile at the Curragh. Back on easy ground—we weren't sure it was so soft as was returned officially—Flying Brave was unable to produce his best form and finished a modest fourth of six behind Misty Valley.

Flying Brave (b.c. Mar 14, 1988)	Persian Bold (br 1975)	Bold Lad (b 1964)	Bold Ruler Barn Pride
		Relkarunner (b or br 1968)	Relko Running Blue
	Flying Sauce (b 1980)	Sauce Boat (ch 1975)	Key To The Mint Missy Baba
		Fly To Post (b or br 1972)	Assagai Flying Fable

Flying Brave, a compact, attractive colt, is easily the best of the four winners from his dam Flying Sauce, a useful two-year-old in France in the early 'eighties when her two victories included the listed Prix Herod over a mile. Two of her other winners, the dual-purpose performer Flyaway (by Touching Wood) and the French colt Flying Falcon (by In Fijar) have won over middle distances, and it's very likely that Flying Brave will stay at least a mile and a quarter as a three-year-old. He acts well on firm going and is possibly unsuited by a soft surface. *J. L. Dunlop.*

FLYING CROOKED 2 b.c. (Apr 14) Town And Country 124–Glittering Gem 77 — (Silly Season 127) [1990 5f a6g 6g] leggy, sparely-made colt: has a round action:

second foal: dam placed from 7f to 1½m: no worthwhile form in maidens and a seller: hung left final outing. *D. J. G. Murray-Smith.*

FLYING DEER (IRE)   2 ch.f. (Apr 13) Mazaad 106–Green Idol (Green God 128)   —
[1990 6g 7f 5f] IR 9,800Y: lengthy filly: has a long stride: seventh foal: dam Irish 2-y-o 5f winner: well beaten in maidens and a seller (blinkered). *K. M. Brassey.*

FLYING DIVA   3 b.f. Chief Singer 131–Flying Fantasy (Habitat 134) [1989 6g*   100
7g* 1990 8.5g5dis 8d2 8g 10m3] good-quartered filly: fairly useful performer: staying-on second in £9,600 handicap at Ascot, best effort: well beaten in listed races starts either side (got poor run at Epsom on reappearance) and when last of 3 in £7,500 contest (found to have been doped) at Yarmouth: better at 1m than shorter: acts on dead ground. *B. W. Hills.*

FLYING DOWN TO RIO (IRE)   2 b.c. (May 21) Try My Best (USA) 130–Gay   85
France (FR) 91 (Sir Gaylord) [1990 7g6 7m4 7g4] 22,000Y: workmanlike colt: has scope: half-brother to 3-y-o 1½m winner Tour Eiffel and very useful 1985 2-y-o 7f winner Lucayan Princess (both by High Line), fair 8.5f winner French Sonnet (by Ballad Rock) and winners abroad: dam 2-y-o 6f winner: best effort 4 lengths equal-fourth of 17, running on strongly, to Flying Brave in Tattersalls Tiffany Highflyer Stakes at Newmarket in August: well backed, one pace in maiden at Sandown following month: will stay at least 1m. *R. Hannon.*

FLYING FLO JO (USA)   3 b.f. Aloma's Ruler (USA)–Madam Cherry (USA)   56
(Master Derby (USA)) [1989 NR 1990 8m6 7g 6f 7f4 6f* 7h5] $18,000Y, $57,000Y: leggy, lengthy filly: third reported foal: half-sister to a winner in USA by Full Out: dam won at up to 1m: sire won Preakness Stakes: won handicap at Brighton in June, always travelling comfortably: poor last of 5 in similar event there nearly 2 months later: stays 7f: acts on firm ground. *P. F. I. Cole.*

FLYING HORSESHOES   2 ch.f. (Mar 13) Stanford 121§–Cast Party 68 (Hello   —
Gorgeous (USA) 128) [1990 6g 7.5d 7g 7.5g 7f 8g 8v] 800Y: angular filly: first foal: dam 5f winner at 2 yrs later in Italy: poor form in varied events: blinkered or visored (including in sellers) third to fifth starts. *N. Bycroft.*

FLYING PETAL   2 gr.f. (Apr 24) Petong 126–Careless Flyer 66 (Malicious)   —
[1990 5f 6m] 2,800F, 6,200Y: good-bodied filly: half-sister to 3-y-o Say A Prayer (by Sayf El Arab), 1983 2-y-o 7f seller winner Miss A Beat (by Song) and a winning hurdler: dam 6f winner: backward, tailed off in auction races at Chepstow (maiden) in May and Salisbury (visored, swerved stalls) in June. *C. J. Hill.*

FLYING PROMISE   2 ch.c. (Mar 30) Stanford 121§–Impailand (Imperial Fling   66
(USA) 116) [1990 5f 5g4 5m4 5g6 5d a5g2 a5g2] 5,200Y: strong, lengthy, plain colt: first foal: dam never ran: quite modest maiden: runner-up in nurseries at Southwell, running well behind Friendly Claim on final outing: off course over 6 months after fourth start: speedy. *R. A. Bennett.*

FLYING ROOFER   4 b.f. Jester 119–Forest Glen (Tarqogan 125) [1989 8m4 6g   — §
6m 7m 10f 1990 a7g a13g6 10f] smallish, quite well-made filly: little sign of ability: temperamental. *J. D. Roberts.*

FLY THE STREAM   3 b.f. Paddy's Stream 80–Fly Blackie (Dear Gazelle 113)   —
[1989 NR 1990 12f] fourth foal: dam unraced on flat, placed in novice hurdle: 33/1 and ridden by 7-lb claimer, tailed-off last in maiden at Chepstow in May. *J. H. Baker.*

FLY TO THE MOON (USA)   2 ch.f. (Apr 24) Blushing Groom (FR) 131– Dis-   83 p
coniz (USA) (Northern Dancer) [1990 6m2 7m2] $700,000Y: neat, quite attractive filly: fifth reported foal: sister to very useful 1987 2-y-o 5f and 6f winner Digamist: dam very small stakes winner at up to 1½m: ½-length second of 18, soon prominent, to Environment Friend in maiden at Newmarket in October, second and much better effort: will be suited by 1m: sure to improve again, and win a race. *H. R. A. Cecil.*

FOLK DANCE   8 b.g. Alias Smith (USA)–Enchanting Dancer (FR) (Nijinsky   78
(CAN) 138) [1989 16s3 16s* 14s3 14g4 14g 12f3 18g6 1990 14m4 16m3 16m 14m5 14.8m* 16m3 14m3 14g] big, strong, quite attractive gelding: modest handicapper: won at Warwick in June: ran moderately (sweating) in Tote Ebor at York final outing: stays well: acts on any going: usually visored: has won for apprentice: none too enthusiastic and best covered up: winning jumper: consistent. *G. B. Balding.*

FOLLOW THE SEA   4 b.c. Tumble Wind (USA)–Seapoint (Major Point) [1989   61
6v3 5v 10f 8g 8m6 8m 9m 8.2g 1990 8.3m 9m2 9g 10g5] sturdy, lengthy colt: quite modest maiden: stays 9f: acts on good to firm and heavy going. *R. Akehurst.*

FOND KISS   5 b.m. Young Generation 129–Firente 85 (Firestreak 125) [1989 9d   —
10s 10s6 9f 10m 8m 8.2d 9.2d5 7.6m 1990 a10g3 12d 10g] workmanlike, rather

angular mare: modest winner (including for apprentice) as 3-y-o: little show in subsequent handicaps and claimer: stays 1¼m: best with a bit of give in the ground (possibly unsuited by soft going): sold 2,000 gns Newmarket Autumn Sales. *C. A. Cyzer.*

FONTAINE LADY 3 b.f. Millfontaine 114–Lady Begorra (Roi Soleil 125) [1989 41 5f⁶ 5.8f⁶ 1990 10.1g 8g 10.1m 10m 6m* 7g 6m 6f 8f 5m³ 5m 6d] leggy filly: good walker: poor performer: won apprentice selling handicap (bought in 3,100 gns) at Windsor in July: very good third in handicap at Warwick: stays 6f: acts on firm going: blinkered last 8 starts: usually ridden by 7-lb claimer B. Thomas. *E. A. Wheeler.*

FOOD OF LOVE 2 ch.f. (Apr 25) Music Boy 124–Shortbread 104 (Crisp And 91 Even 116) [1990 5g³ 5m* 5m² 5f 5f² 5g⁴ 5m* 5m² 5d³] 7,800F, 16,000Y: close-coupled filly: moderate mover: half-sister to 1982 2-y-o 5f winner Puff Pastry (by Realm) and a winner in Italy by Vitiges: dam won over 7f here and 1½m in Norway: fairly useful performer: made all in maiden at Newbury in May and seller at Newcastle (odds on, bought in 12,000 gns) in August: ran very well in minor event at York and listed race at Ayr final 2 starts: speedy: tends to hang left. *J. Berry.*

FOO FOO (IRE) 2 ch.f. (Mar 23) The Noble Player (USA)–Unmistakable 83 44 (Hello Gorgeous (USA) 128) [1990 6g 5m 7m⁴ 7g 5m⁴ 6d³ a7g] IR 1,700Y, resold 8,200Y: workmanlike filly: has markedly round action: first foal: dam 7f winner also successful in Italy: poor maiden: ran badly only outing on all-weather: probably stays 7f. *D. Marks.*

FOOLISH TOUCH 8 b.g. Hot Spark 126–Nushka (Tom Fool) [1989 6v 7d⁶ 6g⁵ 74 7m* 6m 7m⁵ 7m³ 6m³ 6m 7m 6v⁴ 7g 1990 6s 6v* 6m 6m 6d⁶ 6g 7g 6m² 6f* 6m 7m³ 7g 7g 7m 7g² 8d 7d⁵ a8g⁵ a8g⁶] lengthy gelding: poor walker and moderate mover: modest handicapper: last at halfway when winning at Ayr (£7,800 event) in April and Pontefract in July: suited by 7f or stiff 6f: acts on any going: has worn blinkers, often visored: usually bandaged: sometimes sweats: usually starts slowly, gets behind and is a difficult ride: has won 5 times at Newmarket. *W. J. Musson.*

FOOT SOLDIER 3 b.g. Hotfoot 126–Gunnard 62 (Gunner B 126) [1989 5m⁴ 6m 62 6m 7g⁵ 8f 8g⁶ 1990 7f 10.6f 11g* 14g² 13g³ 12.4f⁴ 16m³] workmanlike, sparely-made gelding: moderate walker: quite modest handicapper: led close home to win at Hamilton in May: ran creditably all subsequent outings: stays 2m: acts on firm going. *Mrs J. R. Ramsden.*

FORBEARANCE 2 ch.f. (Apr 26) Bairn (USA) 126–For Instance (Busted 134) 77 p [1990 8g*] sturdy filly: second foal: dam ran 3 times at 4 yrs: 33/1 and burly, won 21-runner maiden at Pontefract in October by a head from High Savannah, challenging approaching final furlong and running on well: will stay 1¼m: sure to improve. *M. Johnston.*

FORBIDDEN CITY (NZ) 3 b.c. Babaroom (USA)–The Empress (NZ) — (Imperialist (USA)) [1989 7g a7g 1990 10.1g 7m 8g 12f] leggy colt: plating-class maiden: form only on Lingfield Equitrack: headstrong: sold to join F. Jestin 1,700 gns Doncaster August Sales. *J. R. Jenkins.*

FORCELLO (USA) 7 b.g. Forli (ARG)–Heavenly Bow (USA) (Gun Bow) [1989 — 10s³ 8d 1990 a10g a12g] strong, good-bodied gelding: has a quick action: lightly-raced handicapper: best at 1m to 1¼m: probably not at his best on firm going, acts on any other: visored once: well served by forcing tactics: occasionally sweats. *D. Burchell.*

FORD KING 3 b.f. Sandhurst Prince 128–Douala (GER) (Pentathlon) [1989 5g 57 7m 6g 7d⁴ 7g³ 1990 7f 7f* 7m 7d] sparely-made, leggy filly: quite modest handicapper: 20/1 on first run for over 5 months, easily best effort to win 16-runner race at Catterick in September: will stay 1m: acts on firm going, possibly unsuited by dead. *M. O'Neill.*

FOREIGN ALLIANCE 2 br.c. (Mar 21) Lidhame 109–Pour Moi 73 (Bay 44 Express 132) [1990 5f 5d 6g 6f⁴ 6g⁶ 6f⁴ 7f 7m⁴ 7g 8m⁵] 8,200F, 8,800Y: small, sparely-made colt: has a quick action: second live foal: half-brother to plating-class maiden Always Take Profit (by Noalto): dam placed over 5f and 6f: poor form in varied company: probably stays 1m: blinkered fourth to eighth outings: inconsistent: sold 575 gns Ascot October Sales. *G. Lewis.*

FOREIGN ASSIGNMENT (IRE) 2 b.c. (May 10) Reasonable (FR) 119–Lady 48 Pitt (Pitskelly 122) [1990 6g 6m 6g] rangy colt: has scope: moderate walker: fourth foal: half-brother to Irish 6f winner Deep In The Valley (by Wolver Hollow): dam never ran: poor form for 7-lb claimer in maidens and a minor event: showed signs may be capable of better final start. *G. Lewis.*

FOREST FAWN (FR)   5 b. or br.m. Top Ville 129–Red Deer (FR) (Kirkland   —
Lake) [1989 10.1m² 12f² 12h⁵ 11.5f 13.4m⁶ 10.2f⁵ 10g⁶ a10g⁶ 1990 a11g⁶] rather
sparely-made mare: plating-class maiden: stays 1¼m. *E. A. Wheeler.*

FOREST NYMPH (NZ)   5 b.m. Oak Ridge (FR)–Lively Lass (NZ) (Lionhearted   66
117) [1989 NR 1990 8m⁴ 7m 11.5m² 12d 10g] sturdy mare: winner over 1m in New
Zealand as 3-y-o: in frame in minor event at Pontefract and ladies race at Lingfield in
first half of 1990: stays 11.5f. *Mrs S. Oliver.*

FOREVER DIAMONDS   3 ch.g. Good Times (ITY)–Mel Mira 68 (Roi Soleil   65
125) [1989 5v 5d* 5f⁶ 1990 6s 5v³ 8.2g² 6g⁵ 6m 6d³ 6d⁶ 6s] leggy, rather sparely-
made gelding: quite modest handicapper: stays 1m: possibly best on an easy surface:
ran moderately in blinkers last 2 starts. *J. S. Wilson.*

FORGE   2 ch.g. (Feb 12) Formidable (USA) 125–Red Shoes 74 (Dance In Time   —
(CAN)) [1990 5d 7g] close-coupled, deep-girthed gelding: moderate walker: first
foal: dam stayed 1½m, is daughter of Oaks and St Leger winner Dunfermline: bit
backward in maidens at Newbury, off course 4 months in between: sold 3,800 gns
Ascot October Sales. *I. A. Balding.*

FORGE BAY   3 b.c. Buzzards Bay 128§–Korresia (Derring-Do 131) [1989 NR   —
1990 7.2d⁵ 9m⁵ 7d a10g] leggy, good-topped colt: has a round action: fifth foal: dam
ran once: no worthwhile form, though showed signs of some ability (prominent 7f)
in handicap final start. *H. J. Collingridge.*

FORGE BEAU   5 b.g. Swing Easy (USA) 126–Korresia (Derring-Do 131) [1989   —
8m 5f 7m⁵ 8f 7g 7g³ 8f 1990 8f 7f a7g⁵ 7d] lengthy, angular gelding: poor plater. *G.
Blum.*

FORMAL PROFILE   2 ch.f. (Feb 14) Miramar Reef 100§–Classic Profile (Hello   —
Gorgeous (USA) 128) [1990 5m 5f⁵ 7m⁶ 10m 7d] 520F: leggy, angular filly: second
foal: dam twice-raced daughter of Oaks third Aureoletta: soundly beaten in sellers
and claimers: looked ungenuine third start: bandaged behind final 2 outings: sold
650 gns Doncaster October Sales. *J. G. FitzGerald.*

FORMATION   4 b.g. Tanfirion 110–Imagination (FR) (Dancer's Image (USA))   49
[1989 8s 12.2m³ 13.8m* 11f³ 16.2g 13.8g² 18m³ 16m⁵ 13.8g⁵ 13.8d 1990 13.8m 12g
13.8m⁵ 14g 15.8g 12.2d4] workmanlike gelding: carries condition: usually doesn't
take the eye: moderate walker and mover: plating-class handicapper: ran poorly last
3 outings, visored 2 of them: stays 2¼m: suited by a sound surface: sweating and
mulish at stalls on reappearance: sold to join Mrs A. Knight's stable 4,600 gns
Doncaster August Sales. *E. Weymes.*

FORMIDABLE TASK   3 ch.f. Formidable (USA) 125–Light O'Battle 97   —
(Queen's Hussar 124) [1989 5f 6f⁵ 1990 9.1f³ 8m³ 9m] sturdy filly: has round action:
plating-class maiden: faced stiff tasks in 1990: should stay further than 6f: retained
by trainer 17,000 gns Doncaster August Sales after second start. *Miss S. E. Hall.*

FORM KEY   3 b.f. Lochnager 132–Good Form 54 (Deep Diver 134) [1989 NR 1990   35
8.5m 6f⁵ 7m 6g 8d] leggy, workmanlike filly: sister to winning sprinter Loch Form:
dam stayed 1¼m: poor form in the summer, best effort fifth in claimer at Redcar. *M.
H. Easterby.*

FOR NOTHING   5 gr.h. Bay Express 132–Flitterdale 81 (Abwah 118) [1989 10d4   58 d
10d 9g 8.2g 8.5f 1990 a7g* a7g² a7g* a8g a7g a7g 8.2m a7g⁶ a8g] good-bodied horse:
winner twice in handicaps at Southwell early in year: below form after, but showed
signs of retaining ability eighth outing: best form at up to 1m: blinkered once at 3
yrs. *J. A. Glover.*

FOR PETE'S SAKE   2 b.f. (Apr 17) Kirchner 110–Bunnycraft (The Go-Between   42
129) [1990 5d³ 5f 5g⁶ 6m 6m] leggy, angular filly: good walker: fourth reported living
foal: half-sister to ungenuine sprint plater Bunnyloch and poor maiden A Bit of
Alright (both by Lochnager): dam poor maiden: poor plater: stays 6f: sold 720 gns
Doncaster September Sales. *J. Etherington.*

FOR REAL   3 ch.f. Tina's Pet 121–Golden Decoy 73 (Decoy Boy 129) [1989 5g³   62
5f⁴ 5f* 5m* 5m* 5m2dis 5m 5f³ 6g² 6f⁴ 6m* 6f⁵ 5m 1990 5f 6f³ 5f⁶ a5g 6m* 6f* 6g³
6g² 6g⁴ 6m³ 6f* 6m⁵ 6g⁵ 5f⁵ 6m⁴ 6g a6g² a7g³] small, good-quartered filly: useful
plater: successful at Leicester (bought in 5,000 gns) in May, Folkestone (no bid) in
June and Thirsk (bought out of J. Berry's stable 9,200 gns in August: ran creditably in non-sellers at Southwell last 2 starts: stays 7f: acts on firm going: usually
wanders: has sweated. *J. Etherington.*

FORTAN PRINCE   3 b.g. Burslem 123–Hark Hark 75 (Sing Sing 134) [1989 5f⁴   53
5f⁴ 5h⁴ 5f³ 5f⁶ 5g a5g 1990 5f 5g 6s³ 7g⁵ 6d 6g³ 6m³ 6f² 6g 6g⁵ 10s] lengthy gelding:

Britannia Handicap, Ascot—Fox Chapel causes a major upset;
Gulmarg (rails) is second and Colourist (left) third

plating-class maiden: suited by 6f: acts on firm going: bandaged off-fore final outing:
blinkered penultimate (ran fairly well) start and once at 2 yrs. *S. T. Harris.*

FORT SORENO (DEN) 2 gr.c. (Jan 14) Belfort (FR) 89–Gavea (African Sky 60
124) [1990 6m⁴ 7g] first reported foal: dam twice-raced half-sister to very smart 1m
to 1¼m performer Cataldi: plating-class form in maidens at Redcar (slowly away)
and Newmarket in June. *R. Guest.*

FORTUNE'S WHEEL (IRE) 2 b.c. (May 27) Law Society (USA) 130–North 106
Forland (FR) 99 (Northfields (USA)) [1990 5g³ 6d⁴ 7.5g⁵ 7.5g⁶ 8g* 9g³ 10s³ 10v*
8v⁶] sixth foal: half-brother to very useful French 7.5f and 1m winner Harmless
Albatross (by Pas de Seul) and useful winner at up to 1m in France, Libertine (by
Hello Gorgeous): dam, 1¼m winner and second in Ribblesdale Stakes, is half-sister
to very smart French middle-distance mare Infra Green: useful French colt: won
seller at Longchamp in October and Premio Guido Berardelli at Rome in November:
6½ lengths third to Pistolet Bleu in Criterium de Saint-Cloud on seventh outing:
suited by a good test of stamina: acts well on heavy going: blinkered first 2 starts. *R.
Collet, France.*

FORTY OR MORE 3 ch.g. Yashgan 126–Infanta (USA) (Intrepid Hero (USA)) 73
[1989 NR 1990 8m 8m² 8d* 10d] IR 9,000F, 7,000Y: lengthy gelding: fourth foal:
half-brother to modest 1986 2-y-o 5f winner Take A Hint (by Pitskelly), a Swedish
1m winner in 1990: dam twice-raced half-sister to dam of Robellino: on toes, easy
winner of claimer at Leicester in October: behind in handicap following month:
stays 1m: best effort on dead going (moved poorly down second start on good to
firm). *C. F. Wall.*

FOUNTAIN LOCH 3 b.f. Lochnager 132–Fountain 90 (Reform 132) [1989 6m 67
5g 1990 6f* 6s⁵ 6m 7m 6s² 6g⁶ 6f⁴ 6m² 7g* 6d⁵ 6m 6g 7d 5s] small, good-quartered
filly: has quick action: modest performer: won claimer at Redcar in May and
handicap (gamely) at Kempton in September: probably better at 7f than 6f: acts on
any going: ran poorly when sweating and edgy fourth outing: pulled too hard on
sixth: retained 6,200 gns Doncaster October Sales. *R. M. Whitaker.*

FOUR AWAY 3 br.c. Valiyar 129–Edwins' Princess 75 (Owen Dudley 121) [1989 —
7g 7f 8m 1990 10m] leggy, rather close-coupled colt: good walker: no worthwhile
form in maidens and claimer. *N. A. Callaghan.*

FOURHEARTSDOUBLED 2 b.c. (May 23) Mashhor Dancer (USA)–Sunset 42
Ray 74 (Hotfoot 126) [1990 a8g a8g a8g⁶] 2,500F, 3,000Y: small colt: fifth foal:
half-brother to 3-y-o 1½m winner Miss Adventure (by Adonijah): dam won from 1m
to 2m: poor form in maidens at Southwell and Lingfield. *Dr J. D. Scargill.*

FOURSINGH 2 br.g. (Feb 20) Mansingh (USA) 120–Maycrest (Imperial Fling 75
(USA) 116) [1990 5f* 6g² 6g 6m 6m³ 6f³ 7f 8.2g] 12,500Y: smallish, lengthy,
attractive gelding: moderate walker: has a quick action: first foal: dam ran once:

320

modest performer: won maiden at Bath in May: best form at 6f: carries heads high, and seems rather irresolute. *J. Berry.*

FOURWALK   6 br.h. Godswalk (USA) 130–Vaunt (USA) (Hill Rise 127) [1989 5g   **62**
6f⁵ 6m⁴ᵈⁱˢ 6m 7f⁵ 6m* 6f² 6g² 6f 6m⁵ 6m³ 5.6g 1990 a5g a7g⁵ a6g 6f³ 6m] strong, close-coupled, plain horse: poor walker and bad mover: quite modest handicapper: tailed off final outing (May): stays 6f: acts on any going: visored twice, blinkered final outing at 5 yrs: has worn tongue strap: has won only once since early 1987. *Mrs N. Macauley.*

FOX CHAPEL   3 b.g. Formidable (USA) 125–Hollow Heart 89 (Wolver Hollow   **86 ?**
126) [1989 6m 6m* 7g 1990 7m 10.1m⁵ 8d* 8m 8f 7d 8g 8m] good-bodied gelding: 100/1, easily best effort when winning 26-runner Britannia Handicap at Royal Ascot: evidently suited by 1m: best form on dead going, though has won on good to firm: unreliable. *R. Hannon.*

FOXES DIAMOND   2 b.f. (Mar 1) Sallust 134–Rahesh 111 (Raffingora 130) [1990   **55**
6g³ 5m² 6f⁶ 6g 5d 5m 8f 7d] 2,200Y: workmanlike filly: half-sister to minor 2-y-o winners Monsarah (by Monsanto) and Homing In (by Homing): dam speedy 2-y-o: plating-class maiden: easily best efforts when placed: should be suited by further than 6f: seems unsuited by dead ground: blinkered sixth outing: has been bandaged off-hind. *D. Dutton.*

FOXTROT OSCAR   3 b.c. Mummy's Game 120–Glint of Silver 69 (Sallust 134)   **65**
[1989 5f* 5g 1990 5f⁴ 5m 7f 8f 5.1m] robust colt: modest performer: below form after reappearance: may prove suited by 6f: yet to race on soft ground, acts on any other: blinkered and wore crossed noseband final (slowly away) start: hung left second start at 2 yrs, wore brush pricker and ran badly on third: sold 2,900 gns Newmarket Autumn Sales. *J. A. R. Toller.*

FOXTROT PIE   2 ch.f. (Mar 24) Shernazar 131–Round Dance 73 (Auction Ring   **77**
(USA) 123) [1990 7m 7m 10s²] sturdy, angular filly: fifth foal: half-sister to 3-y-o Plaything (by High Top) and a winner in Italy by Shirley Heights: dam 7f winner: 50/1 and bit backward, 5 lengths second of 21 to Matahif in maiden at Nottingham in October, easily best effort: will stay 1½m: acts on soft ground. *G. A. Pritchard-Gordon.*

FOXY (IRE)   2 ch.f. (Apr 30) Coquelin (USA) 121–Djory (USA) (Prince John)   **—**
[1990 6m] IR 1,500F, 1,100Y: small filly: seventh foal: half-sister to 2 winners at up to 9f in USA by Bold Lad (IRE) and Super Concorde (also successful at 9f in France): dam unraced: on toes, not knocked about when beaten last 2f in seller at Lingfield in September: sold 400 gns Ascot December Sales. *C. James.*

FOXY SUE   3 ch.f. Cree Song 99–Persian Breakfast 50 (Deep Diver 134) [1989   **—**
NR 1990 6m 6m 6g] good-quartered filly: sixth foal: half-sister to fair 1985 2-y-o 5f and 6f winner Calixtus (by Sonnen Gold): dam plater: no sign of ability in claimers and seller: may need further: sold 950 gns Doncaster September Sales. *D. W. Chapman.*

FRAAR (USA)   2 b.c. (Mar 21) Topsider (USA)–Alchaasibiyeh (USA) 85 (Seattle   **97 p**
Slew (USA)) [1990 6d* 7m³ 8m*] rather leggy, good-topped colt: first foal: dam placed from 6f to 1m, is out of a smart sprinter: won valuable event at Ascot in June and minor event at Bath (by 4 lengths, running on strongly, from Dedicated) in October: better suited by 1m than shorter: should progress further. *H. Thomson Jones.*

FRAGRANT HILL   2 b.f. (Apr 18) Shirley Heights 130 English Spring (USA)   **82**
116 (Grey Dawn II 132) [1990 8m³ 7g* 7d⁶] lengthy, workmanlike filly: has scope: moderate walker: second foal: half-sister to modest 3-y-o 1½m winner Spring To Glory (by Teenoso): dam stayed 1¼m: still carrying condition, won minor event at Newbury in September by ¾ length from Exclusive Virtue, making all and keeping on well despite swishing tail: well beaten in Bottisham Heath Stud Rockfel Stakes at Newmarket following month: will stay 1¼m. *I. A. Balding.*

FRAGRANT PARK   3 ch.f. Gorytus (USA) 132–Park Lady 82 (Tap On Wood   **—**
130) [1989 7m 8m³ 1990 10f 10m⁶ 12f 16f⁶ 16f³ 12f] small, sparely-made, angular filly: modest maiden at best: well beaten after slowly-run handicap second start: seems best at up to 1¼m: blinkered last 2 starts, very edgy on first of them: sold 1,000 gns Newmarket Autumn Sales. *J. W. Hills.*

FRANCISCAN   3 b.g. Godswalk (USA) 130–Athenian Primrose (Tower Walk   **65**
130) [1989 NR 1990 8.2s 8f 10.6f⁴ 10s⁵ 10f 8.2g* 8m² 11m³ 10g a8g⁶ 8.2d a8g] 13,000Y: well-made gelding: first foal: dam lightly-raced half-sister to useful 1982 2-y-o sprinter Carolside: modest handicapper: won at Hamilton in June: stays 11f:

acts on good to firm ground: wandered under pressure eighth outing: trained until after then by W. Pearce: winning hurdler. *B. Preece.*

FRANCIS FURNESS 3 b.f. Burslem 123–Sodium's Niece (Northfields (USA)) **46**
[1989 6f4 6m 7.5f 7m a7g4 a8g5 1990 6v3 8.2g6 7g 6m 7g 8.2m2 10f2 11m3 11m 11s5] leggy, rather sparely-made filly: has a round action: plating-class maiden: ran moderately in handicap and claimer last 2 starts: stays 11f: acts on any going: has run creditably for 7-lb claimer: has joined C. Brooks. *Denys Smith.*

FRANCIS ROSE 4 ch.f. Salmon Leap (USA) 131–Brief Agenda (Levmoss 133) —
[1989 12.5s 7f3 7f6 7m 8g 7g2 8d 6d 8s 1990 a7g 9f 8f5 7h 8g] ex-Irish filly: half-sister to Irish 1¼m winner Bold And Brief and 6f winner Ladenda (both by Bold Lad (IRE)): dam, placed over 9.5f in France, daughter of 1000 Guineas winner Pourparler: poor maiden: stayed 7f: dead. *B. Stevens.*

FRANSYLCO 2 b.c. (Feb 22) Bold Owl 101–Sodina 75 (Saulingo 122) [1990 7.5d6 **61**
7g5 7f5 a7g5 8d 8d5] 4,600F, 8,800Y: neat colt: fifth live foal: dam ran only at 2 yrs, winning at 5f: quite modest maiden: ran well in nursery at Ayr final start: stays 1m: consistent. *A. Bailey.*

FREAK TOSS (ARG) 3 ch.c. Egg Toss (USA)–Frau Lamanche (ARG) (Frari **80**
(ARG)) [1989 NR 1990 6g4 10g3 10m5 7g6 a6g5 a8g2 a8g] lengthy colt: dam half-sister to dam of very smart 1m to 1½m winner Free Guest and good Italian middle-distance filly Fresh: successful over 6f in Argentina in March: fair form here when in frame in minor events in August then handicap (beaten short head) at Lingfield in November: best effort at 1m: visored last 4 starts, hanging right first occasion. *J. M. P. Eustace.*

FREAKY DEAKY 3 b.g. Prince Tenderfoot (USA) 126–Maylands (Windjammer **73**
(USA)) [1989 NR 1990 8g 9s 8g6 8d3 9.5m2 10m6 9.5m6 8m 8m5 8m 8d] 10,500F: good-bodied gelding: good walker: third foal: brother and half-brother to undistinguished animals: dam, who promised to stay 1¼m, is sister to French and Italian miler El-Muleta: placed in maiden at Gowran Park and minor event at Dundalk in May: no form in Leicester claimers last 2 starts: probably stays 1¼m: acts on good to firm ground and dead: blinkered fourth to ninth starts: trained until after ninth by M. Kauntze. *B. J. Curley.*

FREDDIE LLOYD 2 b.c. (May 23) Tate Gallery (USA) 117–Jemarjo Pet (USA) **58**
(Peter Peter) [1990 6m 6d6 7m] 6,200F, 7,500Y: compact colt: half-brother to several winners, notably good-class sprinter Orojoya (by Gold Stage) and very smart American colt Bywayofchicago (by Well Mannered), successful at up to 9f: dam won at up to 1m: over 8 lengths sixth of 7 in maiden at Yarmouth in July: held up and never near to challenge in similar event at Newmarket following month: may do better. *N. A. Callaghan.*

FREDDIE'S STAR 3 b.c. Tina's Pet 121–Wellington Bear (Dragonara Palace **37**
(USA) 115) [1989 5s3 5g4 6f 6m 6f3 7m2 7m6 7m* 6g a8g 1990 a8g a7g 7f 6g 6g 8f 10m 8d 10g 10f5 7m 8.3m4 8.3m 8h] leggy colt: quite modest winner (ridden by 7-lb claimer) as 2 yrs: well below that form in handicaps: probably ideally suited to 7f: acts on firm going: takes a keen hold: often edgy: bandaged final start: didn't handle bends at Catterick. *R. A. Bennett.*

FREE AT LAST 3 b.f. Shirley Heights 130–Brocade 121 (Habitat 134) [1989 5m2 **115**
6f2 7f* 7m* 7g* 1990 8m4 8d4 8g4 10g2 8.5f*] neat, good-quartered filly: has a quick action: very useful performer: off course 3 months after 8½ lengths fourth to Salsabil in General Accident 1000 Guineas at Newmarket on reappearance: in frame in pattern events at Deauville and the Curragh then £50,000 contest at Belmont Park, running very well to be beaten only ¾ length by Relief Pitcher at Belmont: remained in USA, winning 8.5f $100,000 Carmel Handicap at Bay Meadows in November: stays 1¼m: trained until after penultimate start by G. Harwood. *N. Drysdale, USA.*

FREEDOM 3 b.f. Free State 125–Pied A Terre (Ribocco 129) [1989 5g 6m 1990 8g —
10g 12m 12d] smallish, sparely-made filly: good mover: poor performer: blinkered final start. *J. Pearce.*

FREEDOM WEEKEND (USA) 2 ch.f. (May 18) Shahrastani (USA) 135– — p
Glorious Quest (USA) (Hawaii) [1990 6m] 15,000Y: quite good-topped, attractive filly: half-sister to useful 1987 American 2-y-o Crown Quest (by Chief's Crown) and a winner by Vigors: dam winner at around 1m in USA: very burly and green, slowly away and always behind, not knocked about, in maiden at Kempton in July: sort to do better. *J. R. Fanshawe.*

FREE FOR ALL 2 ch.c. (Apr 21) Mummy's Game 120–Free On Board 73 (Free **51**
State 125) [1990 6m 6m 6m 5g5 6g] lengthy colt: good walker: first foal: dam stayed 1¼m: plating-class maiden: stays 6f. *L. J. Holt.*

FREE MINX   4 b.g. Free State 125 Musical Minx 75 (Jukebox 120) [1989 8g³ 8s   51
7m 11m 8g 1990 10.2f 11s² 10v⁴ 12g] sturdy gelding: plating-class maiden: stays 11f:
best form on an easy surface and acts on heavy going: blinkered once, visored final
outing: very slowly away on reappearance: has been taken down early and been
reluctant at stalls. *M. J. Camacho.*

FREESIA   3 b.f. Shirley Heights 130–Free Dance (FR) (Green Dancer (USA) 132)   78
[1989 NR 1990 12g* 12d 11.7m⁶] workmanlike filly: fifth foal: sister to fair 1¾m
winner Fresco and half-sister to 1¾m winner Freestone (by Great Nephew) and
1¼m and 1½m winner Free Fact (by Known Fact): dam French 8.5f and 9f winner:
won maiden at Newbury in August, always in touch, running on well to lead close
home despite edging left: disappointing in handicaps: should stay 1¾m. *Major W. R.
Hern.*

FREE THINKER (USA)   3 b.f. Shadeed (USA) 135–Top Hope 115 (High Top   100
131) [1989 6m² 1990 8m* 8m² 8m* 10m⁵ 8m⁴ 8.5f] leggy, lengthy filly: useful
performer: won minor event at Warwick in April and listed race at Milan in June:
behind in Grade 3 event at the Meadowlands final start: ran creditably in listed races
otherwise: may prove ideally suited by 1m: to remain in USA. *I. A. Balding.*

FREEZING (IRE)   2 gr.f. (Feb 29) Siberian Express (USA) 125–Field Day 87   49 p
(Northfields (USA)) [1990 7m⁶] fifth foal: half-sister to 3-y-o 2m winner Besito (by
Wassl) and 3 other winners, including 15.3f winner Amigo Feo (by Tap On Wood)
and 6f to 1¼m winner, including in pattern company in Italy, Darweesh (by Cure
The Blues): dam 1¼m and 1½m winner, is daughter of sister to Irish 2000 Guineas
third Sovereign Edition: 11½ lengths sixth of 13, prominent 5f, in minor event at
Lingfield in August: should improve. *K. M. Brassey.*

FRENCH BAY   3 ch.c. Pharly (FR) 130–Finbay (ITY) 82 (Canisbay 120) [1989 8g   —
a7g³ a8g* 1990 10v⁶ 12.3d⁵ 12f a8g] compact, workmanlike colt: modest winner in
December at 2 yrs: carried condition and well below form last 2 outings in 1990, off
course nearly 3 months in between: should stay 1½m: bandaged final start. *D.
Haydn Jones.*

FRENCH GLORY   4 b.c. Sadler's Wells (USA) 132–Dunette (FR) 127 (Hard To   118
Beat 132) [1989 10m⁶ 10m* 12d⁴ 12.5g* 12d² 12g 1990 12d⁵ 12g³ 12d* 12.5g*
12.5g³ 10d⁴ 12s* 12g 12f] good-class colt: favourite, won 10-runner Grade 1
Rothmans International at Woodbine in October by 1¼ lengths from Sky Classic:
ran exclusively in French pattern races earlier in season, beating Tycana a head in
La Coupe at Longchamp and Lights Out a nose in Prix Maurice de Nieuil at

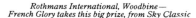

*Rothmans International, Woodbine—
French Glory takes this big prize, from Sky Classic*

Mr K. Abdulla's "French Glory"

Maisons-Laffitte: well beaten in Breeders' Cup Turf at Belmont Park and never reached leaders in Japan Cup at Tokyo last 2 starts: suited by 1½m: best form with give in the ground and acted on soft: sold to stud in Japan. *A. Fabre, France.*

FRENCH HOUSE 3 ch.c. Coquelin (USA) 121–Ottina (GER) (Luciano) [1989 NR 1990 a8g a7g 7f 10m 12.5g⁴ 12d] IR 1,400Y: compact, angular colt: third foal: half-brother to 2 winners abroad: dam won 3 times in Germany: plater: form only when 50/1-fourth of 16 at Wolverhampton. *J. Wharton.*   **54** ?

FRENCH IVY (USA) 3 ch.c. Nodouble (USA)–Lierre (USA) (Gummo (USA) 117) [1989 NR 1990 10.6d⁵ 13.6m² 12g² 12d⁶] $35,000F: leggy colt: first foal: dam successful 3 times at up to 1m in USA: fair maiden: shapes like a stayer: possibly needs a sound surface: visored except for third start: sold out of J. Gosden's stable 22,000 gns Newmarket Autumn Sales after third. *Mrs A. L. M. King.*   **87**

FRENCH SENOR (USA) 3 b.c. El Gran Senor (USA) 136–French Poem (USA) (Sharpen Up 127) [1989 NR 1990 8m² 8f⁴ 7h* 8m 8m² 7.6d²] $85,000Y: smallish, sturdy colt: moderate mover: first foal: dam French 5f winner: fairly useful performer: won maiden at Thirsk in August: best effort when neck second of 16 in handicap at Lingfield final start, quickening really well from rear to lead inside final 1f then unable to sustain effort close home: suited by 1m: yet to race on soft ground, acts on any other: often has tongue tied down. *H. R. A. Cecil.*   **89** +

FRESCOBALDO (USA) 4 b.c. Run The Gantlet (USA)–Voice of The River (USA) (Speak John) [1989 10g³ 12m² 14g⁴ 1990 11s 12.3f² 12g² 16f 12m 12m* 12.4m² 13f⁶ 12.3m⁵] leggy, rather sparely-made colt: has a rather round action: modest   **72**

324

handicapper: sweating, won for first time in apprentice race at York in June: stays 1½m: acts on firm going, unsuited by soft: pulled hard in visor fourth outing: lacks turn of foot: game. *M. P. Naughton.*

FRESH FROM VICTORY 6 b.g. Hotfoot 126–Triumphant 90 (Track Spare 125) [1989 10s 10s* 10.1m 10f5 12h 10f 12m 1990 a12g] workmanlike, angular gelding: won selling handicap in spring as 5-y-o: stays 1¼m: possibly needs a soft surface nowadays: probably best with strong handling (pulled hard only outing at 6 yrs). *A. Moore.*

FRESH LINE 4 b.f. High Line 125–Snow Tribe 94 (Great Nephew 126) [1989 12.2d2 12.3d4 12f 12g 1990 a14g] leggy, sparely-made filly: quite modest maiden at best: tailed off in Southwell handicap in May: should have been suited by good test of stamina: possibly needed a soft surface: ran badly in blinkers: usually edgy and gave trouble at stalls: in foal to Dunbeath. *J. Hetherton.*

FRIARS HILL 3 b.g. Doc Marten 104–Dancing Amber (Broxted 120) [1989 5f 5g 6g 1990 5f4 6g2 6f3 8g a6g] angular gelding: rather unfurnished: poor mover: plating-class performer: virtually pulled up penultimate start: hampered in rear over 3f out at Southwell in August: stays 6f: acts on firm going: bandaged near-hind: hung right first 2 starts. *M. W. Ellerby.* 51

FRIDAYATPISSARRO'S 2 b.f. (May 17) Prince Sabo 123–Contadina (Memling) [1990 5m 6g2 6m3 7m 8.2v] 6,800Y: leggy filly: half-sister to several winners, including very useful colts Manor Farm Boy (by Mansingh) and Conbrian (by The Brianstan): dam never ran: quite modest maiden: off course 3 months after third start: best form at 6f: possibly unsuited by heavy ground. *M. R. Channon.* 65

FRIDAY FOURBALL 2 ch.g. (Apr 6) Monsanto (FR) 121–Sparkling Ears 61 (Sparkler 130) [1990 6g 6g 7m4 7m 7g2 a8g4 7f5 10.6s 7d 7d2 a8g] workmanlike gelding: poor mover: fourth foal: dam maiden stayed 1¼m: fairly useful plater: ran moderately both starts on all-weather: best form at 7f: acts on dead ground: inconsistent. *E. Weymes.* 55

FRIEDLAND (USA) 2 b.c. (Mar 25) Nijinsky (CAN) 138–Fenella 92 (Thatch (USA) 136) [1990 7d] quite good-topped colt: seventh foal: closely related to 3-y-o Leonella (by Caerleon) and 2 winners, including useful middle-distance stayer Kashi Lagoon (by Ile de Bourbon), and half-brother to 2 winners, including Queen Anne winner Trojan Fen (by Troy): dam, from good family, won over 7.6f: backward and green, swerved left stalls, held up and always behind in valuable minor event at Newmarket in October: moved moderately down: seems sure to do better. *H. R. A. Cecil.* 65 p

FRIEND IN DEED (FR) 2 b.c. (Mar 20) Comrade In Arms 123–Ergo 82 (Song 132) [1990 5g4 a5g* 5f4] 5,200Y, 10,000 2-y-o: plain, rather sparely-made colt: half-brother to several winners here and abroad, including 1982 2-y-o 5f winner Henceforth (by Full of Hope): dam 5f winner at 2 yrs: made all in 7-runner maiden at Southwell, beating Jet Pet by 4 lengths: dead. *Denys Smith.* 62

FRIENDLY CLAIM (IRE) 2 b.c. (Mar 17) Petorius 117–Pitaka (Pitskelly 122) [1990 5m6 5f 5g* 5g* 6f a6g* a5g*] 7,000Y: compact colt: fifth foal: closely related to poor and inconsistent maiden Puno (by Aragon) and half-brother to 4-y-o Wanda (by Taufan), 5f winner at 2 yrs: dam never ran: successful in seller (retained 5,000 gns) at Pontefract, nursery at Hamilton and claimer and nursery (by 2 lengths from Flying Promise) at Southwell: effective at 5f and 6f: best form on all-weather: seems unsuited by firm ground: mulish stalls second outing: suitable mount for a claimer. *T. D. Barron.* 84

FRIENDLY COAST 4 b.g. Blakeney 126–Noreena (Nonoalco (USA) 131) [1989 7d 8g5 8m 7f 11.7m 10m4 12m5 15.3g3 14g6 14m 12g5 8f2 10d5 9m 10f 1990 a16g* a13g* 12f3 14g] leggy gelding: plating-class handicapper: twice won at Lingfield (also successful over hurdles there) early in year: stays 2m: acts on firm going: visored twice: seemed unreliable at 3 yrs. *D. T. Thom.* 53

FRIEND OF A FRIEND 2 b.f. (May 18) Nishapour (FR) 125–Marista (Mansingh (USA) 120) [1990 7m] 15,000Y: sixth foal: half-sister to useful 1988 2-y-o 5f winner Four-Legged Friend (by Aragon), 2 winners by Free State, including 6f and 1m winner Hanseatic, and a winner here and in Holland: dam lightly-raced half-sister to useful sprinter Cedar Grange, looked temperamental: burly, never near leaders in maiden auction at Leicester in September. *Dr J. D. Scargill.*

FRIMLEY DANCER 2 b.f. (Apr 17) Northern Tempest (USA) 120–Taylors Renovation 58 (Frimley Park 109) [1990 5f6 6m 6g 5f4 5g4 6m4] 2,200Y: plain filly: 52

poor mover: first foal: dam 2-y-o 6f and 7f winner appeared to stay 1¼m: fair plater: improved on final 2 starts: will stay 7f. *C. J. Hill.*

FRIMLEY PARKSON 6 br.g. Frimley Park 109–Frimley Grove (Tower Walk 130) [1989 5s² 5.8h 5f⁶ 6f 5g² 5m⁵ 5f³ 5f⁴ 5g³ 5m 5d³ 5m² 6m⁵ 5d² a6g a6g 1990 5m² 5g* 6m 6m⁵ 5m² 5f⁶ 5m⁶ 5m 5m⁵ 5d⁶ 5d³] sturdy, compact gelding: carries plenty of condition: bad mover: quite modest handicapper: won at Epsom in April despite drifting left: unseated rider and bolted thirteenth intended outing: effective at 5f and 6f: acts on any going: usually wears blinkers or visor: sweated first 3 starts: has carried head bit high, and is not the easiest of rides. *P. J. Arthur.* **63**

FROGS FIRST 4 b.f. Beldale Flutter 130–Lareyna 98 (Welsh Pageant 132) [1989 8d 8.2g 10m⁶ 7m 7m 5m 7.6m⁴ 8m⁴ 8g 1990 8m³ 8f 10f 8.3m 8.3g 6m 8.2m] workmanlike filly: no form as 4-y-o after reappearance (tended to carry head awkwardly): stays 1m: acts on good to firm going: bandaged second and third outings: sometimes sweats and gets on edge: often taken down early. *Mrs Barbara Waring.* **43** d

FROMOZ 2 br.c. (Feb 2) Full On Aces (AUS)–Hard To Forget (AUS) (Mount Hagen (FR) 127) [1990 5f 5m 5g 6g a6g 7g 8.2g] 2,300F: angular, plain colt: has a round action: half-brother to several winners in Australia: dam and sire won in Australia: bad maiden. *A. W. Potts.* **35**

FRONT LINE ROMANCE 3 ch.f. Caerleon (USA) 132–Bottom Line 90 (Double Jump 131) [1989 6g⁶ 7f* 7m³ 8g² 1990 10m³ 10f 12m⁶] rather sparely-made, workmanlike filly: fair winner at 2 yrs: good third of 7 to Moon Cactus in moderately-run Lupe Stakes at Goodwood on reappearance, pulling hard: bolted in Lingfield handicap and Newmarket minor event later in summer: stays 1¼m: acts on firm going. *M. A. Jarvis.* **89**

FRONT PAGE 3 ch.c. Adonijah 126–Recent Events (Stanford 121§) [1989 7g 6m⁴ 6f⁵ 7s⁴ 6g 7g³ 1990 8g 6m³ 7d 6g² 6m⁶ 6m* 7g 6f⁴ 6m a8g] workmanlike colt: carries condition: returned to near 2-y-o form when winning apprentice seller (bought in 4,500 gns) at Nottingham in July by 6 lengths: stays 7f: acts on any going: blinkered final start: has run creditably when sweating: sometimes edgy: found little fifth start: trained until after sixth by Mrs L. Piggott: isn't one to trust implicitly. *J. Akehurst.* **54**

FROZEN FOREST 2 ch.c. (Apr 5) Touching Wood (USA) 127–Ever So Cool (FR) (Never Say Die 137) [1990 8m 8d 7s 10.2s a8g] strong, compact colt: carries condition: half-brother to several winners here and abroad, including 3-y-o 10.2f winner Allez-Oops (by Moulin) and ex-French 15f winner Laxdaela (by Sagaro): dam French 11f winner: plating-class maiden: ran poorly in Southwell nursery final start: stays 1¼m: acts on soft going. *M. Johnston.* **50**

F S WILLIAMS 2 br.f. (Mar 30) Gold Claim 90–Lack-A-Penny (Bivouac 114) [1990 6s⁵ 6g] sparely-made filly: second reported foal: dam of little account over jumps: soundly beaten in maidens at Hamilton. *I. Semple.* —

F-TROOP (IRE) 2 b.f. (May 8) Nordico (USA)–Adorable Princess 91 (Royal Palace 131) [1990 7m 6d] 10,500Y: leggy filly: moderate mover: sister to Irish 3-y-o 6f (at 2 yrs) to 1½m winner Nordic Surprise, and a winner in Hong Kong: dam Irish 1½m winner at 4 yrs, from family of Double Schwartz: little sign of ability in claimer (slowly away) at Yarmouth and seller at Lingfield. *Mrs L. Piggott.* **41**

FUGLER'S FOLLY 3 b.g. King of Spain 121–Djellaba 74 (Decoy Boy 129) [1989 7m 7g 1990 a10g² 12f⁴ 10g² 12f² 14f³ 13.8m⁵ 12m* 12f* 12f* 14f²] angular gelding: had a quick action: modest performer: won claimer at Goodwood in June then handicaps at Salisbury and Beverley in July: stayed 1¾m: acted on firm going: dead. *W. J. Haggas.* **75**

FUJAIYRAH 3 b.f. In Fijar (USA) 121–Ananiyya (FR) (Faristan 123) [1989 6f* 7m² 8m³ 7g 1990 11.3d⁶ 10m⁴ 12d] big, strong, close-coupled filly: fairly useful performer: creditable fourth to Moon Cactus in moderately-run Lupe Stakes at Goodwood, making most: edgy, well beaten in Cheshire Oaks (bit backward) at Chester and Ribblesdale Stakes (sweating, pulled hard) at Royal Ascot: stays 1¼m: possibly best on top-of-the-ground. *A. A. Scott.* **89**

FULL BELT (USA) 3 b.f. Full Extent (USA) 113–Snow Ridge (USA) (King Pellinore (USA) 127) [1989 5s 5s 5g 1990 9f] lengthy filly: last in sellers and claimer: blinkered final start at 2 yrs. *R. J. Holder.* —

FULL HEARTED (USA) 6 b.g. Full Out (USA)–Heladi (Traffic Judge) [1989 NR 1990 8.2s⁶ 8v 12g] rather leggy, good-topped gelding: modest winner as 3-y-o: —

bandaged, never able to challenge in Scottish handicaps (first 2 selling) in spring: should stay 1½m: acts on any going: has worn blinkers and visor: has run moderately when sweating: has worn crossed noseband. *W. J. Musson.*

FULL MONTY 4 ch.g. Raga Navarro (ITY) 119–Miss Quay (Quayside 124) [1989 8d 7f 12m⁴ 12h⁵ 1990 16m⁵] leggy, plain gelding: good walker: plating-class form at best: ran fairly well in slowly-run race over 1½m, doesn't stay 2m: winning hurdler. *Denys Smith.* —

FULL OF PLUCK (IRE) 2 b.c. (Apr 21) Try My Best (USA) 130–Tomona (Linacre 133) [1990 8m² 8g⁴ 7g* 8v⁵] IR 8,000F: tall colt, rather unfurnished: has scope: good mover: third foal: half-brother to Irish 3-y-o 1¼m winner Hegemonic (by Godswalk): dam successful over 11f and 1½m from 4 yrs to 6 yrs and over hurdles in Ireland: won 23-runner median auction at York in October: 5 lengths fifth of 16 to Steamer Duck in Gran Criterium at Milan in November: will stay 1¼m: acts on heavy going. *B. Hanbury.* **103**

FULL ORCHESTRA 3 b.f. Shirley Heights 130–Harp Strings (FR) 109 (Luthier 126) [1989 6f² 7g³ 1990 10.1m² 12m 13.3g⁴] rather angular filly: has a quick action: fair performer: sweating, won maiden at Windsor in August: behind in York listed race (edgy, led 1m) and below form in Newbury handicap afterwards: should stay 1½m. *Major W. R. Hern.* **83**

FULL QUIVER 5 br.g. Gorytus (USA) 132–Much Pleasure (Morston (FR) 125) [1989 7g 7f² 7f6 8f⁵ 8m⁵ 8m² 8m² 8m² 8m6 8m³ 11v 1990 11.7g* 10m 11.7m* 10m⁴ 12g³ 12s 10.2s⁵] leggy gelding: gained his only 2 wins in handicaps at Windsor in May and July: ran very well when in frame at Newbury (quite valuable event won by Madame Dubois) and Salisbury: stays 1½m: acts on firm going, not discredited on soft final outing: blinkered once, effective with visor or without: sometimes sweats: has worn tongue strap: often finds little and best waited with. *Mrs Barbara Waring.* **85**

FUNAMBULE (USA) 3 b.c. Lyphard (USA) 132–Sonoma (USA) 121 (Habitat 134) [1989 8g* 8g* 1990 8d⁵ 8m³ 7g* 7d* 6d⁶ 7g] smart French colt out of sprinting sister to Sigy: 4½ lengths third to Linamix in Poule d'Essai des Poulains at Longchamp: won Prix du Palais Royal (by ½ length from Rock City) and Prix de la Porte Maillot there in the summer: off course 3 months then below form after, in Prix de la Foret final outing: possibly best at 7f: yet to race on extremes of going. *Mme C. Head, France.* **118**

FUNATTHEFARMER'S 2 b.f. (Apr 26) Moor House 84–Peggy Jet 69 (Willipeg 112) [1990 5f 5f⁵] rather sparely-made filly: fifth reported foal: dam won at up to 7f: tailed off in sellers in spring. *D. R. Tucker.* —

FUNUN (USA) 3 b.f. Fappiano (USA)–Toutski (USA) (Baldski (USA)) [1989 6f⁴ 7m 1990 5f* 6g 6g³ 7.3m⁴ 7g* 7m 6d⁵ 6s] lengthy, unfurnished filly: has a quick action: fair performer: won maiden at Folkestone in April and handicaps at Lingfield in June and Haydock (£7,300 event, best effort) in September: ran poorly in quite valuable handicaps sixth and final starts: stayed 7f: acted on firm and dead going: visits Shaadi. *P. T. Walwyn.* **84**

FURAJET (USA) 2 ch.f. (Mar 25) The Minstrel (CAN) 135–Zummerudd (Habitat 134) [1990 5m* 5d* 5f³ 6m⁵] sturdy, attractive, sprint type: has a quick action: third foal: dam twice-raced daughter of Cherry Hinton winner Ampulla, a half-sister to Steel Heart: modest performer: comfortable winner of maiden at Sandown in May and £7,400 event at Beverley in June: third in Queen Mary Stakes at Royal Ascot and fifth in Cherry Hinton Stakes at Newmarket: seems to stay 6f: keen sort. *A. A. Scott.* **77**

FURIELLA 2 ch.f. (Mar 30) Formidable (USA) 125–Palmella (USA) 89 (Grundy 137) [1990 5f 6g⁶ 6g 5f⁴ 5.1m² 5m⁶ 6d] stocky filly: poor mover: sixth foal: half-sister to 3-y-o 5f winner Final Ace (by Sharpo), 1¼m winner Tino-Ella (by Bustino) and fairly useful middle-distance winner Norpella (by Northfields): dam 1¼m winner stayed 1½m, is half-sister to Teenoso and Topsy: modest plater: should be suited by further than 5f: blinkered third and fourth outings. *P. J. Feilden.* **50**

FURNACE MILL 5 b. or br.g. Tumble Wind (USA)–Jane Bond 59 (Good Bond 122) [1989 10.2g 12s 1990 11s] compact gelding: winning plater as 3-y-o: stayed 1¼m: acted on good to firm and dead going: bandaged once at 4 yrs: dead. *A. P. Stringer.* —

FURTHER FLIGHT 4 gr.g. Pharly (FR) 130–Flying Nelly 107 (Nelcius 133) [1989 8d 7s 10m* 11.7m 1990 11.7f* 12.3d* 12f 12d² 15g* 14g* 18d²] leggy, angular gelding: has a rather round action: vastly improved handicapper, winning £69,900 Tote Ebor at York (co-favourite) in August by 1½ lengths, idling, from Bean King: **102**

Tote Ebor Handicap, York—greys galore as the vastly improved Further Flight wins idling from Bean King (left), Holy Zeal and First Victory (rails)

earlier successful at Bath and Chester in May and Ayr (most impressively in £15,400 contest) in July: favourite, better still when clear second to Trainglot in Tote Cesarewitch at Newmarket, driven clear 4f out: suited by test of stamina: best runs with a bit of give in the ground: bandaged behind last 2 outings, off-hind only on fourth: game, genuine and consistent. *B. W. Hills.*

FUSILIER   8 b.g. Habitat 134–Formentera (FR) (Ribot 142) [1989 7m² a7g 1990   **54** §
a8g⁶ a10g³ a10g a10g* a10g⁵] big, strong, good-topped gelding: carries plenty of condition: not a good walker or mover in slower paces: plating-class handicapper on his day: led final strides when winning apprentice event at Lingfield in January: stays 1¼m: suited by a sound surface: has worn blinkers, but not since 1988: wears bandages: unreliable. *T. Thomson Jones.*

FUTUH (USA)   2 gr.f. (Feb 18) Diesis 133–Hardship (USA) (Drone) [1990 6d²   **95**
6f* 6m² 6d⁵ 5d²] $200,000Y: small, quite good-topped filly: has a long, roundish stride: sister to 3-y-o Patchwork and half-sister to winners in USA by Plugged Nickle (very useful filly Rose Park) and Elocutionist: dam very useful 2-y-o in North America: fairly useful performer: made all in maiden at Redcar in August: good second after in Salisbury minor event won by Lee Artiste and Doncaster listed race won by Snowy Owl: speedy: yet to race on very soft going, acts on any other. *H. Thomson Jones.*

FUTURE GAMBLE   5 b.g. Auction Ring (USA) 123–Silja (FR) (Masetto) [1989   **42**
8s³ 10m 8.2f² 8h 8m² 8f² 8f* 1990 9f 10m 8m² 7.6g⁶ 8f³ 8m⁵ 8f 8f 8m] sturdy gelding: bad mover: poor handicapper: stays 1m well: acts on any going: effective with or without visor: has worn bandages: has wandered under pressure: sold 850 gns Doncaster November Sales. *P. J. Feilden.*

FUTURE GLORY   4 b.g. Ile de Bourbon (USA) 133–Bombshell 76 (Le   **62**
Levanstell 122) [1989 12.3m⁵ 10.2m 1990 12m 9f⁶ 11g⁴ 12.2m² 12.3g 10m a12g] lengthy, dipped-backed gelding: moderate mover: won maiden as 2-y-o but has deteriorated: well beaten in seller and claimer last 2 outings: stays 1½m: best effort on soft going: sweating and edgy fifth start: sold out of Miss S. Hall's stable 1,800 gns Doncaster October Sales after sixth. *A. W. Potts.*

FYAS   2 b.f. (Mar 18) Sayf El Arab (USA) 127–Joking 81 (Ribero 126) [1990 6g³ 6f⁶   **52**
7g⁴ 6f⁴ 7f² 7f³ 6m 6m⁶] 1,500F, 1,900Y: small, leggy filly: eighth foal: half-sister to a minor winner in USA by Dalsaan: dam, half-sister to Queen's Hussar, won over 1½m: plating-class performer: will stay 1m. *M. H. Easterby.*

328

Mr S. Wingfield Digby's "Further Flight"

G

GAASID 5 ch.h. Kings Lake (USA) 133–Le Melody 102 (Levmoss 133) [1989 14s² 88
18.4m⁵ 12m* 12f 16g 13.3m⁸ 12m 12m² 11v 12d 1990 12f* 12g³ 12d² 12f 11s⁵ 12s]
lengthy, quite attractive horse: carries plenty of condition: poor mover: fair handicapper: favourite, won at Kempton in April: shaped as though retaining most of his
ability at Newbury (first run for 4 months) and Doncaster (seventh to Azzaam in
November Handicap) in autumn: probably best at up to 1¾m: acts on any going, but
seems unable to take repeated racing on firm: occasionally sweats, and got on edge
at Doncaster: suited by waiting tactics: very useful novice hurdler. *R. Akehurst.*

GABARDOON 3 b.g. Gabitat 119–Its For Sure 63 (Ardoon 124) [1989 6m 1990 —
6m 5g 6m 6m 8m] lengthy, angular gelding: poor maiden: usually sweating, edgy
when visored third start: changed hands 900 gns Ascot February Sales: trained until
after fourth start by B. Gubby. *J. D. J. Davies.*

GABBIADINI 3 b.g. Taufan (USA) 119–Galerida (Silver Shark 129) [1989 5f 6m⁵ 80
6f* 6m 6f* 6m⁵ 7m* 7m 7s 7g⁵ 6m² 1990 6g 7g⁶ 7h* 8.5d² 7m² 7m 8d 7.5f 8f² a8g*
8g⁶ 7.6m³ 7m] close-coupled, angular gelding: fair handicapper: successful at
Thirsk in May and Southwell (£8,100 event) in August: ran well when placed, poorly
for 7-lb claimer at Newmarket final start: stays 8.5f: acts on hard and dead ground.
M. H. Tompkins.

GABBY HAYES 2 ch.g. (Apr 10) Gabitat 119–Night Cap (SWE) (Hornbeam 130) 44
[1990 6g 7m a8g] 2,000Y, 3,800 2-y-o: lengthy, angular gelding: has round action:
sixth reported foal: half-brother to 7f seller winner Asian King and a winning jumper
(both by Roman Warrior): dam, bred in Sweden, reportedly won twice at 2 yrs: poor
maiden: ridden by 7-lb claimer when soundly beaten on all-weather. *P. Mitchell.*

329

GABIBTI (IRE) 2 ch.f. (Jan 30) Dara Monarch 128–Torriglia (USA) (Nijinsky 82
(CAN) 138) [1990 5f 5g* 5d* 6m³ 6f⁴ 6f³ 6d 6m* 7.3g] IR 5,600Y, resold IR 6,000Y:
small, good-quartered filly: has a quick action: half-sister to 2 winners in Italy and a
winner over jumps in France: dam French maiden: fair performer: successful in
maiden at Newbury in April, minor event at Beverley in May and nursery at
Leicester in September: should stay 7f: yet to race on very soft going, acts on any
other: keen sort: tends to sweat. *B. Gubby.*

GABISH 5 b.g. Try My Best (USA) 130–Crannog (Habitat 134) [1989 7g 10m 8m —
10f 12h 12m 8f 1990 a12g4] compact gelding: modest winner early as 3-y-o, but has
deteriorated considerably: stays 1m: acts on firm and dead going: blinkered 3 times:
winning selling hurdler in August. *J. Ffitch-Heyes.*

GABRIELLA MIA 5 b.m. Ranksborough 117–Gin And Lime 75 (Warpath 113) —
[1989 13.3f 9m 1990 10m³] strong, deep-girthed mare: tailed off in varied events on 3
outings. *P. J. Arthur.*

GABRIELLE'S ANGEL 3 br.f. Another Realm 118–Leaplet (Alcide 136) [1989 —
5f 1990 11.7f] seems of little account. *P. Butler.*

GADABOUT (USA) 3 ch.c. Mr Prospector (USA)–Playmate (USA) (Buck- 90
passer) [1989 NR 1990 8g 10m* 12g 10f³ 12f⁵ 14g] $350,000F: leggy, rather sparely-
made colt: seventh foal: brother to two 2-y-o winners, notably high-class Irish 6.3f
and 1m winner Woodman, closely related to a North American winner by Conquistador Cielo and half-brother to 3 winners, including very useful but unreliable
miler Accompanist (by The Minstrel): dam, placed once from 5 starts, is sister to
Numbered Account: won maiden at Sandown in May: easily best efforts in handicaps
on fourth (took good hold, set strong pace) and fifth starts: may prove best at 1¼m:
acts on firm going. *R. Charlton.*

GAELIC BIRD (FR) 3 b.f. Gay Mecene (USA) 128–Orange Bird (USA) (Sea 111
Bird II 145) [1989 7m⁵ 7d 8d 9g* 1990 8d² 8g⁴ 9d³ 10.5d⁴ 8m* 9d* 8d 9.2g 10g]
40,000Y: half-sister to very useful French 1¼m winner Gold Bird (by Rheingold),
the dam of Gabina and Galleto: dam, French 1m winner, is half-sister to very smart
performer Duke of Marmalade and Aladancer: won maiden at Compiegne in
November at 2 yrs then Prix Sandringham (by neck from Mais Oui) at Chantilly and
Prix Chloe at Évry in summer of 1990: good seventh in Yellow Ribbon Stakes at
Santa Anita final start: stays 1¼m: acts on good to firm and dead ground. *F. Doumen,
France.*

GAELIC CHIEF 2 b.c. (Apr 1) Lidhame 109–Celtic Sonata (Music Boy 124) 70
[1990 6f* 6g 7f⁶] compact colt: second foal: dam once-raced granddaughter of Irish
Oaks winner Celina: won maiden at Thirsk in August: ran creditably in nursery at
Haydock, next and easily best subsequent effort: stays 6f. *C. Tinkler.*

GAELIC DANCER 3 ch.c. Town And Country 124–Verily Jane 53 (Royben 125) 69
[1989 NR 1990 10m a8g³ 10g⁶ a8g⁴ 16m] 3,500Y: rather sparely-made colt: poor
mover: first foal: dam 7d plater here at 2 yrs later won in Belgium: in frame in maiden
and handicap at Southwell: showed little otherwise, hanging badly right on debut:
should stay 1¼m: bandaged first 4 starts. *L. J. Codd.*

GAELIC HOPE 3 ch.g. Horage 124–Amiga Mia 71 (Be Friendly 130) [1989 NR —
1990 8s 8m 5g a8g] IR 11,000Y: lengthy, rather unfurnished gelding: poor mover:
fifth foal: half-brother to 3 winners, including fairly useful sprinter Gallant Hope (by
Ahonoora) and 1986 2-y-o 5f winner Arapiti (by Runnett), later winner in Italy: dam
won over 6f: behind in maiden (trained by P. Prendergast) at Tralee and claimers
here. *B. R. Millman.*

GAIETY 3 b.f. Sadler's Wells (USA) 132–Wish You Were Here (USA) 81 70 p
(Secretariat (USA)) [1989 NR 1990 9s⁵ 7d³ a8g²] IR 275,000Y: second foal: dam 7f
and 1¼m winner out of top-class middle-distance performer Summer Guest: placed
in maidens at the Curragh and Southwell in November, 2/1 on when staying-on
½-length second of 16 to Stack Rock: should stay beyond 1m: may well improve. *T.
Stack, Ireland.*

GALACTIC SCHEME (USA) 3 b.g. Exclusive Era (USA)–Cosmic Time 61
(USA) (Jig Time (USA)) [1989 6f* 6g 6m² 1990 7.6m 10m 8m 6f⁴ 8f⁶] close-coupled
gelding: modest winner as 2-y-o: easily best effort in 1990 when fourth of 7 in
claimer at Goodwood: should stay beyond 6f: has worn tongue strap, including third
(sweating and edgy) outing: gelded after final one. *R. Hannon.*

GALAGAMES (USA) 3 ch.c. Lyphard (USA) 132–Morning Games (USA) (Grey 76 ?
Dawn II 132) [1989 8v 1990 10f² 12h² 11.5m³ 14m³ 14f⁴ 14d a13g] round-barrelled
colt: carries condition: modest maiden: placed in small fields: below best last 4

starts, racing freely in blinkers on penultimate one: should stay 1¾m: acts on hard ground: lacks turn of foot: sold 10,600 gns Ascot December Sales. *G. Harwood.*

GALALAW 2 br.f. (Feb 20) Persian Bold 123–Rubista 116 (Crowned Prince (USA) — 128) [1990 7s] leggy filly: fifth foal: half-sister to middle-distance winner Rushluan (by Kalaglow) and 1m winner Ponjan (by Kris): dam speedy 2-y-o, appeared not to train on: slowly away, never better than mid-division in 22-runner maiden at Doncaster in October. *A. A. Stewart.*

GALATEA PEARL 3 b.f. Rabdan 129–Bridal Wave (Julio Mariner 127) [1989 45 5g6 1990 5 7.6v4 7f 12.5m5 10.2m3 8g6 10g4 10f 10f 8.2v5 10d4 a12g a14g] quite good tupped filly: has a markedly round action: poor maiden: faced stiff task in Southwell claimers: stays 1¼m: acts on heavy going, probably unsuited by firm: wandered under pressure when blinkered seventh start: often set plenty to do. *B. A. McMahon.*

GALAXY EXPRESS 2 ch.g. (Mar 23) Bay Express 132–Heaven And Earth — (Midsummer Night II 117) [1990 5f 5f] 2,500F, 5,000Y: brother to winning hurdler After The Gloom (disappointing on flat) and half-brother to fairly useful 1979 2-y-o 5f winner Our Mother (by Bold Lad, IRE): dam ran twice: no show in maiden auctions at Bath and Warwick. *G. H. Eden.*

GALAXY GLOW 2 b.f. (Mar 9) Kalaglow 132–Lone Galaxie (USA) 69 (Nodouble — (USA)) [1990 7.5f6 7m 7f] 6,000F: first foal: dam maiden stayed 6f: poor maiden. *C. Tinkler.*

GALAXY RANGER 2 b.g. (Feb 21) Caerleon (USA) 132–Fallen Rose (Busted — 134) [1990 7m 8.2s] strong, quite attractive gelding: seventh foal: half-brother to smart sprinter Sharp Reminder (by Sharpo) and 1m winner Floating Pearl (by Wollow): dam, half-sister to high-class filly First Bloom, won small 7.5f race in France: bit backward, weakened last 2f in autumn maidens at Newmarket and Haydock. *W. Jarvis.*

GALLANT HOPE 8 ch.g. Ahonoora 122–Amiga Mia 71 (Be Friendly 130) [1989 76 5s 6f 5f4 5g** 6m* 6f4 6f 6m5 5g 6m 5.6g3 6s 7m 5m 1990 5g 6d 5m3 5m 6m 6m 5m6 6m 5.8f 6g3 5m6 6s a6g] small, stocky gelding: carries plenty of condition: has been hobdayed: fairly useful handicapper at one time: ran creditably on eleventh start (10 lb out of handicap) behind Sloe Berry in £16,800 event at Ascot in October: effective at 5f to 6f: unsuited by soft going, acts on any other: best blinkered: used to be best with strong handling: sometimes gets behind. *B. R. Millman.*

GALLERY ARTIST (IRE) 2 ch.c. (May 7) Tate Gallery (USA) 117–Avec 61 L'Amour 75 (Realm 129) [1990 5g 6g2 6f 6d2 6v3 6g3 6d5 a7g6] 4,200Y: small, compact colt: poor mover: sixth foal: closely related to useful sprinting 3-y-o Duck And Dive (by Lomond): dam disappointing granddaughter of very speedy 2-y-o Pharsalia: runner-up in seller at Yarmouth and selling nursery at Lingfield: ran creditably in non-selling nurseries on last 4 starts: will be suited by 1m: possibly suited by easy ground: blinkered second and third starts. *R. Guest.*

GALLERY LADY (IRE) 2 b.f. (Apr 10) Tender King 123–London Spin 86 — (Derring-Do 131) [1990 6m a6g 6g 7m] 1,500Y: smallish, sturdy filly: poor mover: half-sister to several winners on flat and over hurdles, including 7f and 1m performer Bu-Sofyan (by Runnett): dam stayed 1m: little worthwhile form in sellers: blinkered, bandaged and sweating final outing: sold 820 gns Doncaster September Sales. *J. Wharton.*

GALLEY BAY 4 b.f. Welsh Saint 126–Locust Grove 80 (Sassafras (FR) 135) 55 [1989 8s5 7f2 10d 7d6 7g6 10d4 1990 8m 14m6 12g a14g* 10f6] ex-Irish filly: half-sister to two 2-y-o 6f winners by Camden Town and a winner in Spain: dam, 1¾m winner, is sister to high-class middle-distance stayer Ashmore: won for first time on flat in amateurs handicap at Laytown in August: never dangerous in apprentice race at Chepstow month later: stays 1¾m: sometimes blinkered: trained until after fourth outing by P. Prendergast: winning hurdler. *B. R. Millman.*

GALLOWAY RAIDER 6 br.g. Skyliner 117–Whispering Breeze (Caliban 123) 43 [1989 NR 1990 a13g 13v 12g2 14g5 13g5 18m2 16.2d4 16m* 16.5g2 16.2g5 16m 15m5 16m6 16f4 18g6] tall, leggy gelding: has a round action: poor handicapper: won slowly-run event at Redcar in June: stays 2¼m: acts on hard going: raced freely in visor: nails turn of foot, and suited by galloping track. *Denys Smith.*

GALWEX LADY 4 gr.f. Mendez (FR) 128–Shadiliya 90 (Red Alert 127) [1989 — 8d6 9m5 10m4 10.2h3 12m 11.7m 1990 8.5g] lengthy filly: plater: should stay 1½m: acts on hard ground: blinkered twice, visored (virtually bolted to post) final start at 2 yrs: winning hurdler in 1989/90 with M. Pipe. *C. R. Beever.*

331

GAMEFISHER 3 br.c. Claude Monet (USA) 121–Resurgence (Runnymede 123) —
[1989 7g 1990 10g] leggy colt: tailed off in maidens. *F. A. Wheeler.*

GAMEOVERBALLBURST 4 ch.f. My Top–Second Service (Red Regent 123) —
[1989 9v 9s 7m 10m 12f 1990 9s] smallish, workmanlike ex-Irish filly: first reported
foal: dam behind in varied company: no sign of ability: sold 1,300 gns Doncaster May
Sales. *M. Johnston.*

GAME PLAN 3 b.f. Darshaan 133–Formulate 119 (Reform 132) [1989 NR **118**
1990 10g³ 10m² 12d² 10g* 12g⁶ 12m]

Only Salsabil beat the 50/1-outsider of eight Game Plan in the Gold Seal
Oaks. No horse has won the race at such long odds since 1833 and Game Plan
never really threatened to do so though she caused some minor inconvenience to the winner, getting her boxed in, when the South African jockey
Marcus produced Game Plan on the outside three furlongs out. The final
margin between the two, however, was five lengths. A month earlier Game
Plan hadn't contested a race of any description. A third in a Sandown maiden
revealed plenty of promise, a second to Moon Cactus in the Lupe Stakes more
than useful ability and three weeks after the Oaks Game Plan showed her
performance at Epsom was no flash in the pan by winning the Group 2 Sea
World EBF Pretty Polly Stakes at the Curragh. Given the impression gained
in the Oaks that Game Plan would prove as effective over a mile and three
quarters as a mile and a half, the step down to one and a quarter miles in the
Pretty Polly certainly didn't represent an easy opportunity to lose her maiden
status despite an obvious chance on form. So it proved, with Game Plan
chasing the leaders into the straight but taking time to wear them down and
hanging right, into the whip, as she did so. The outsider Caerless Writing and
heavily-penalized Braiswick were both tightened up in the last furlong but
Game Plan won on merit by one and a half lengths; the Ballymacoll Stakes
winner Native Twine (who started favourite) and Kostroma followed close
behind. A stewards inquiry and appeal followed before Game Plan was allowed
to keep the race. It would have been a great pity for connections if she hadn't
been, because Game Plan never looked like winning another one, finishing
last in both the Yorkshire Oaks and Princess Royal Stakes.

Game Plan's dam Formulate also finished second in the Lupe Stakes but,
in marked contrast to that of her daughter, Formulate's performance was a
disappointment as she'd been the top staying filly as a two-year-old when her
victories included the Waterford Candelabra Stakes, the May Hill and the
Hoover Fillies Mile. She started odds on in the Lupe and had just one other

Sea World EBF Pretty Polly Stakes, the Curragh—
Game Plan (second left) follows up her good Oaks run;
Caerless Writing (third left) finishes second, Braiswick (star on cap) third

race at three years, never able to challenge in the Coronation Stakes. Formulate's five previous living foals didn't have anything like Game Plan's ability although they included four winners, namely the two-year-old one-mile winner Senane (by Vitiges), the mile-and-a-quarter winner Far Top (by High Top), a stayer in Almarreekh (by Glint of Gold) and Tasjil (by Posse) who wasn't around for long in Britain but proved very successful, renamed Handsome, as a three-year-old in Malaysia. Formulate threw the Rainbow Quest filly Colour Quest before being sold by Someries Stud for 75,000 guineas in foal to Rousillon in 1990. The second dam Tabulator, a French one-mile and mile-and-a-quarter winner, also produced the useful seven-furlong and mile-and-a-half winner High Season and Double Zero, a poor staying maiden here who went on to confound a lowly sale price by producing two American classic runners-up in Twice A Prince, who was beaten virtually out of sight (thirty-one lengths) by Secretariat in the Belmont Stakes,and Play The Red who lost out to Elocutionist in the Preakness three years later.

			Shirley Heights	Mill Reef
	Darshaan	(b 1975)		Hardiemma
	(br 1981)	Delsy		Abdos
Game Plan			(b or br 1972)	Kelty
(b.f. 1987)		Reform		Pall Mall
	Formulate	(b 1964)		Country House
	(ch 1976)	Tabulator		Never Say Die
		(ch 1963)		Two Fold

Game Plan, a close-coupled filly and a good walker, showed her best form over a mile and a half in the Oaks and hasn't encountered extremes of going. She was sweating prior to both those disappointing last two starts. *C. E. Brittain.*

GANGER CAMP 4 bl.f. Derrylin 115–Way of Life 61 (Homeric 133) [1989 7f 7f 7f — 7m⁴ 8s² 8.2m⁴ 7d 8g⁴ a8g⁴ a10g 1990 11.7m 10m] sturdy, good-bodied filly: poor mover: quite modest maiden as 3-y-o: still needed race second outing in 1990, refused to enter stalls next intended one: should stay further than 1m: acts on soft going, possibly unsuited by firm: visored twice at 3 yrs. *M. P. Muggeridge.*

GANGES (USA) 2 b.c. (Apr 29) Riverman (USA) 131–Paloma Blanca 119 (USA) (Blushing Groom (FR) 131) [1990 7.5g⁶ 7.5g³ 8s* 9g⁴ 7s*]
Francois Boutin's Lamorlaye Stables housed three of France's leading two-year-old colts in the latest season. Less well known than the unbeaten Hector Protector and Machiavellian's half-brother, Exit To Nowhere, is the progressive Ganges who left his best until last when winning the Criterium de Maisons-Laffitte in October from as good a field as any that was assembled for a two-year-old race in France during 1990. Ganges had made his debut over two months earlier at Deauville's August Festival but evidently needed a couple of runs to put him straight, for after a break of a month he ran right away with a maiden at Maisons-Laffitte in September then put up a useful performance, his best up to that point, when finishing over three lengths fourth of twelve to Pistolet Bleu in the nine-furlong Prix de Condé at Longchamp. Ganges, whose finishing effort at Longchamp suggested that a drop back in distance would bring about further improvement, started at 14/1 at Maisons-Laffitte, eighth choice behind the odds-on Masterclass, a two-and-a-half-length second to Hector Protector in the Grand Criterium at Longchamp earlier in the month; also in the nine-runner field were Divine Danse, winner of the Prix d'Arenberg at Longchamp (after finishing second to Hector Protector in the Prix Morny) and an unlucky third in the Cheveley Park at Newmarket; the Prix Eclipse winner Crack Regiment; the Challenge d'Or Piaget winner Hello Pink, who'd seemingly had his limitations exposed when fifth to Hector Protector in the Prix de la Salamandre; and Masterclass' highly-regarded stable-companion Ski Chief, who'd made his debut in the Eclipse and acquitted himself well in that race after a shaky start to finish seventh. The soft ground and seven furlongs combined to elicit a much improved performance from Ganges. Soon in touch, Ganges really stamped his authority on the race in the final quarter mile as Masterclass began to struggle in the testing conditions, and he settled matters decisively, coming

*Criterium de Maisons-Laffitte—Ganges copes well with the testing conditions;
Crack Regiment comes second*

away from Crack Regiment and Divine Danse in the final furlong to win by three lengths and two. There can be little doubt that the form is up to its usual standard. Second-placed Crack Regiment, himself an improving colt, had mastered conditions nearly as soft in the Prix Eclipse, while third-placed Divine Danse had shown she could handle soft ground in the Prix Morny, and both were fairly beaten. It usually takes a good horse to win the Criterium—Septieme Ciel, Lead On Time, Procida, L'Emigrant and Zino are among its recent winners—and Ganges' clear-cut victory suggests he, too, is a smart colt, little, if anything, behind his more renowned stable-companions.

		Riverman (USA) (b 1969)	Never Bend (b 1960)	Nasrullah Lalun
Ganges (USA) (b.c. Apr 29, 1988)			River Lady (b 1963)	Prince John Nile Lily
		Paloma Blanca (USA) (b 1980)	Blushing Groom (ch 1974)	Red God Runaway Bride
			Satania (b 1975)	Ruritania Slapton Sands

Ganges was acquired by owner Allen Paulson at the Nelson Bunker Hunt Dispersal at Keeneland in January, 1988, when he purchased the dam Paloma Blanca, in foal to Riverman, for 510,000 dollars. At the time of the sale the unraced Paloma Blanca had already produced the eight-and-a-half-furlong California Oaks winner Abrojo (by Big Spruce) and the minor American winner Super Pal (by Super Concorde); Ganges is her fourth foal and third winner. Paloma Blanca is a daughter of the Ruritania mare Satania, a half-sister to the good middle-distance performer Riboboy and the smart French filly Sea Level as well as several other winners, but an infrequent producer herself since retiring from the racecourse where she won four races at up to nine furlongs. On his pedigree, and the evidence of his performances on the racecourse, Ganges is likely to prove best at up to a mile and a quarter, though it's interesting to see that he's already been entered for the Irish Derby, as well as for the Irish Two Thousand Guineas. Ganges has yet to race on top-of-the-ground, and seems particularly well suited by very soft. *F. Boutin, France.*

GANT BLEU (FR) 3 ch.g. Crystal Glitters (USA) 127–Gold Honey (Artaius 63 (USA) 129) [1989 6g3 5d5 5g6 1990 7f 6f3 6m 8f6 7d 9f6 7.5g 8m3 7m2 8d a8g] leggy, rather sparely-made gelding: moderate mover: quite modest maiden: stays 1m: acts on firm going: well below form in visor fifth outing: inconsistent. *R. M. Whitaker.*

GANTON GORSE (USA) 2 b.f. (May 24) Marfa (USA)–Volatile Gal (USA) — (Explodent (USA)) [1990 6m 7f] $37,000Y: workmanlike filly: half-sister to 2 winners in USA by Stalwart: dam won at up to 9f: sire very smart at 3 yrs, best at 9f: blinkered, well beaten in autumn maidens at Nottingham and Brighton (reminders leaving stalls): sold 1,300 gns Newmarket Autumn Sales. *W. Jarvis.*

GARDA'S GOLD 7 b.g. Garda's Revenge (USA) 119–Mielee (Le Levanstell 122) 44 [1989 12s6 1990 11s6 12m 11.5m* 10g 10m4 10m] leggy, narrow gelding: moderate mover: poor handicapper: 25/1, won slowly-run event at Sandown in June: ran very well when slow-starting fourth in apprentice race at same course: stays 1½m: acts on good to firm and soft going: blinkered or visored first 5 starts: has worn crossed noseband: has run well when sweating. *R. Dickin.*

GARDENERS BOY 2 ch.g. (Feb 10) Ballacashtal (CAN)–Rockery 91 (Track 60 Spare 125) [1990 6m5 6m4 6m 10.2s6] tall, rather angular colt: seventh living foal: half-brother to fair 1½m and 2m winner Rough Stones (by Blakeney): dam 2-y-o 6f winner: plating-class maiden: held up and not knocked about in minor event at Doncaster in November, first run for almost 3 months: should stay 1¼m. *P. F. I. Cole.*

GARGOOR 4 ch.c. Kris 135–Icena 117 (Jimmy Reppin 131) [1989 13v5 12d 1990 — a8g6] big, strong colt: poor maiden. *N. A. Callaghan.*

GARTH 2 gr.c. (Feb 22) Petong 126–Doppio 62 (Dublin Taxi) [1990 5d 5g* 5m] 77 sturdy, rather dipped-backed colt: has scope: first foal: dam 2-y-o 5f winner out of sister to Runnett: won maiden at Warwick by 5 lengths from Rainbow Fleet: well-backed favourite, slowly away and ran poorly in nursery at Leicester later in July. *P. J. Makin.*

GARTH LADY 4 ch.f. Jalmood (USA) 126–Lady Capilano 87 (Nebbiolo 125) — [1989 7m3 1990 12g a12g6 12d 12v] rather unfurnished filly: modest maiden at best: probably stays 1½m: bandaged only start at 3 yrs. *Miss A. J. Whitfield.*

GAVIN ALLEN 2 ch.g. (May 6) Heraldiste (USA) 121–Vernair (USA) 73 (Super 68 Concorde (USA) 128) [1990 a6g6 6f3 a6g3 7m5 7g3 7d3 7m4] 6,200Y: small, sparely-made gelding: first living foal: dam 6f winner also successful in Italy: quite modest maiden: will be suited by 1m: acts on firm and dead ground: suitable mount for a claimer: consistent. *C. N. Allen.*

GAY GLINT 3 b.g. Glint of Gold 128–Gay Hellene 111 (Ela-Mana-Mou 132) [1989 92 NR 1990 10m* 12g6 11.5m4 11.7m3 14m* 14g5 16m2 16.2m2] 11,000 2-y-o: unfurnished gelding: good walker: first foal: dam 1¼m and 10.5f winner, is daughter of Irish 1000 Guineas winner Gaily: progressed into fairly useful performer and won maiden (made all) at Leicester in March and handicap at Sandown in July: very good second in quite valuable handicaps at Newmarket and Ascot: suited by test of stamina. *N. A. Graham.*

GAY REVENGE 2 b.g. (Apr 16) Sweet Monday 122–Mummys Colleen 75 — (Mummy's Pet 125) [1990 6g a6g] 580Y: half-brother to winning sprinter Jesters Pet (by Cawston's Clown) and a winner abroad: dam won twice over 5f: well beaten in maidens at Chepstow and Southwell. *D. Burchell.*

GAY RUFFIAN 4 b.g. Welsh Term 126–Alcinea (FR) 93 (Sweet Revenge 129) 58 [1989 10.2h 12m2 12g 1990 13s* a12g] lengthy, sparely-made gelding: has a round action: justified favouritism in handicap at Hamilton in April: carrying condition, tailed off in similar event on all-weather over 4 months later: stays 13f well: goes very well on soft going: has run well when sweating: fairly useful hurdler, easy winner in November. *D. Burchell.*

GAZZYMAZ 4 ch.g. Longleat (USA) 109–Vaguely Hopeful 65 (Fortino II 120) 46 [1989 12h5 14f4 15s6 15g 1990 13g4 16.2d2 18m3 a14g2] workmanlike gelding: poor maiden: will stay extreme distances: probably suited by an easy surface: bandaged last 2 starts. *S. G. Norton.*

GDANSK VICTORY (USA) 2 b.f. (Mar 20) Danzig Connection (USA)–Lulu **83** p
Mon Amour (USA) (Tom Rolfe) [1990 7m*] fourth foal: closely related to useful
sprinter Nicholas, Irish 1m winner Danlu and a winner in USA (all by Danzig): dam,
winner at around 1m, is half-sister to Nordance (also by Danzig), smart stakes
winner at up to 1m: sire top class at 2 yrs and 3 yrs: dead-heated with other co-
favourite Duharra in maiden at Tipperary in September: well related, and likely to
do much better. *J. S. Bolger, Ireland.*

GEBLITZT 6 b.h. Tumble Wind (USA)–Tatty Kay (Tarqogan 125) [1989 10.1m3 —
1990 7.6m 9m 10m] sparely-made horse: poor maiden: stays 1¼m: acts on firm and
dead going: bandaged at 6 yrs. *J. E. Long.*

GEMDOUBLEYOU 2 b.f. (Apr 17) Magnolia Lad 102–Amber Windsor 52 **56**
(Windjammer (USA)) [1990 5g3 5m6 6g3 5g3 6m5 a6g4 5d3 6f* 6f2 6m* 5.8h5 7g6
7f5 6m4 7g6 6g5] 500 (privately) F: close-coupled filly: has a quick action: second
foal: dam 7f winner: won nursery at Warwick in July and seller (no bid) at
Nottingham in August: stays 7f: acts well on firm ground: often slowly away: below
form on all-weather: has run well for 7-lb claimer: inconsistent. *R. Hollinshead.*

GEMINI FIRE 6 br.g. Mansingh (USA) 120–Sealady (Seaepic (USA) 100) [1989 **82**
5g 6v 5g 5f 5m4 5m2 5f5 6f4 5m3 6m 5g 5d3 5d* 1990 5g 5g 5d 5s* 5m3 5m 5g6 5d 5d
6g 6s] sparely-made gelding: fair handicapper on his day: won at Haydock in July:
ran as though something amiss last 2 outings: stays 6f: acts on any going except
probably heavy: has worn visor: often edgy: inconsistent. *M. P. Naughton.*

GENAIR (FR) 5 ch.h. General Assembly (USA)–Metair 118 (Laser Light 118) **74**
[1989 7.6m6 8.5d3 8f2 9f2 8f3 8m* 8g3 8f5 9f3 8.2g 8.2d 8g* 8m6 8m 8g 1990 8.2s5
8g4 8m6 8.2s6 8m* 8m3 8.5f* 10.2m4 10f6 8f* 8.2d 8m 8g6 8m4 8g 9m 8d] big,
rather dipped-backed horse: has had soft palate operation: modest handicapper: won
at Redcar in July and August and Beverley in between: suited by strongly-run race
at 1m: best efforts on top-of-the-ground: visored twice as 3-y-o: has run moderately
for claimer: often gets behind, but didn't when successful. *G. M. Moore.*

GENERAL IDEA 5 ch.g. General Assembly (USA)–Idealist (Busted 134) [1989 —
12f4 14v4 1990 22d6] third foal: half-brother to Lincoln Handicap winner Fact Finder
(by Known Fact): dam winner twice over 1½m in Ireland: winner of 3 NH Flat races
in first half of year, including IR £7,400 event (odds on) at Phoenix Park: well-
beaten sixth of 8 in Queen Alexandra Stakes at Royal Ascot. *D. K. Weld, Ireland.*

GENERAL MEETING 3 ch.g. General Assembly (USA)–La Marne (USA) **40**
(Nashua) [1989 NR 1990 8f 7f 8.5m4 7f 8g5] small gelding: turns fore feet out: poor
mover: brother to plating-class 1¼m winner Town Meeting and half-brother to
several winners, including fair 5f to 1m winner Akram (by Sandford Lad): dam
lightly-raced half-sister to leading 2-y-o fillies Crimea II and Bravery: poor maiden,
not seen out after May: bandaged behind: sold 580 gns Doncaster October Sales. *M.
Brittain.*

GENERALS DAUGHTER (USA) 3 ch.f. General Holme (USA) 128–Evelle —
(USA) (Gentlemans Game) [1989 6g2 6m3 7m5 8m 1990 8g] leggy, narrow, light-
framed filly: poor walker: quite useful third in Ripon listed race at 2 yrs, easily best
effort: bandaged behind, virtually bolted to post and soon tailed off in June claimer
only start in 1990: should stay further than 6f. *N. A. Callaghan.*

GENEROUS (IRE) 2 ch.c. (Feb 8) Caerleon (USA) 132–Doff The Derby **115**
(USA) (Master Derby (USA)) [1990 5m* 6m2 7f3 6d 8g* 7d*]
The second half of the 1990 season was an extremely rewarding one for
the trainer-jockey combination of Paul Cole and Richard Quinn. Knight's
Baroness started the ball rolling at the Curragh in mid-July with her hard-
fought win in the Kildangan Stud Irish Oaks; that fine servant Ibn Bey kept it
in motion with a Group 1 win at Dusseldorf the following week, while at
Doncaster in September Snurge gave the partnership their biggest success to
date in the St Leger. More was to follow. During the autumn Snurge ran a
cracking race to finish third behind Saumarez and Epervier Bleu in the Arc,
while Ibn Bey took his career prize money to nigh-on a million pounds by
winning the Irish St Leger and chasing home Unbridled in the Breeders' Cup
Classic at Belmont Park. Elsewhere Zoman and the much-improved filly Ruby
Tiger each chipped in with pattern-race successes abroad, and for good
measure there was also a big two-year-old success at Newmarket in October
when Generous became the longest-priced winner so far of the Dewhurst
Stakes.

Three Chimneys Dewhurst Stakes, Newmarket—
Generous (dark colours) finishes strongest;
Bog Trotter is a good second ahead of Surrealist (right), Mujtahid and Stark South

But let's begin at the beginning. Generous was up against four winners when he made his debut in the Garter Stakes at Ascot in May. Despite looking just in need of the race he won a shade cleverly, and connections immediately announced him an intended starter for Royal Ascot's Coventry Stakes seven weeks later. Generous started fourth favourite at 8/1 in the Coventry. He never really looked like heading the more experienced Mac's Imp, but he kept on strongly to finish a clear second, and his jockey Carson—deputising for the suspended Quinn— voiced the opinion that Generous was likely to be Group 1 material in time. Generous had another couple of defeats against his name before Carson was vindicated. The first came behind Mukaddamah in the Lanson Champagne Vintage Stakes at Goodwood where Generous got himself in a stew during the preliminaries. He didn't perform too badly in finishing third of six, but in the Prix Morny at Deauville a couple of weeks later he was never at ease, eventually trailing home a soundly-beaten tenth of twelve behind Hector Protector after reportedly becoming upset in his stable near the sales pavilion on the night before the race. By this stage Generous seemed fairly well exposed. A smooth defeat of the newcomer Radhari and two moderate animals in the Reference Pointer Stakes over a mile at Sandown in September told us little new about his merit, but it did show that he was over whatever had ailed him in France, and on lining up for the Dewhurst, sponsored for the third time by Three Chimneys Farm, he started at 50/1 in a field of eight.

During the 'seventies the Dewhurst became widely accepted as Europe's premier test for two-year-olds, with winners like Mill Reef, Grundy and The Minstrel going on to prove themselves champions at three. The early 'eighties threw up El Gran Senor, but some top owners and trainers nowadays avoid the race, preferring easier options. The latest renewal eventually posed almost as many questions as it answered, though beforehand it seemed to have attracted three colts of particular promise in the unbeaten Mujtahid, Anjiz and Sedair. Mujtahid started favourite at 5/4 on and fully deserved to do so on form after highly impressive wins at Newmarket and York. However, he didn't impress greatly in the paddock, and once racing he gave the impression the rain-softened ground was against him, at no stage looking likely to produce the eye-catching finishing speed which characterised his previous efforts. Anjiz and Sedair gave nothing like their true running in the Dewhurst either, the former finishing distressed and the latter reportedly breaking a blood vessel. But enough of the Dewhurst disappointments—what of those who did produce their best? The Laurent-Perrier Champagne Stakes winner Bog Trotter, an 8/1 chance, certainly did. Apparently, connections had been disappointed when he'd been unable to beat Peter Davies, giving him 6 lb, in the Somerville Tattersall Stakes on fast ground over course and distance two weeks previously. That wasn't a particularly strongly-run race, though, and the combination of a more forceful ride and easier ground for the Dewhurst saw Bog Trotter in a much more favourable light. Indeed, with a little under two furlongs to run he looked an assured winner after quickening from the front to open up a three- to four-length advantage. However, Generous, who'd been held up for the first time in his career, began to stay on really strongly at that point. He'd reduced the deficit to two lengths passing the furlong pole, and with Quinn putting his whip down inside the last furlong Generous sustained his challenge in admirable fashion, forging ahead with about thirty yards to run and passing the post three quarters of a length to the good, with the progressive Sandown maiden-race winner Surrealist staying on strongly up the hill to finish another two and a half lengths away in third; Mujtahid was two lengths further back in fourth, the same distance in front of Stark South with Anjiz, the rank outsider Kohinoor and Sedair all beaten out of sight. That Generous improved considerably in the Dewhurst is indisputable, but by how much and why? Not least among the possible explanations is that the Dewhurst was the first time he'd been granted a really good test of stamina on ground with plenty of give in it. Assessing the form is rather more difficult, but we reckon the Irish colt Stark South is as good a yardstick as any. Stark South had run three times prior to the Dewhurst, winning the first two then finishing a very good fifth of twenty behind Rinka Das under similar conditions in the Cartier Million at Phoenix Park just six days earlier. Assuming Stark South ran close to form in the Dewhurst, then that shown by both Generous and Bog Trotter looks at least 10 lb short of what's required to win an average Two Thousand Guineas.

Caerleon's record from four crops as a stallion is highly respectable, though he's not yet had a top-class three-year-old, and a feature of his stud career so far has been his ability to produce plenty of good winners over a variety of distances ranging from fast horses like Caerwent and Corwyn Bay through to staying types like the Park Hill winner Casey and the St Leger Italiano winner Welsh Guide. Generous' dam Doff The Derby, a daughter of the Preakness Stakes winner Master Derby, never made the racecourse. Indeed, she was covered by the smart American miler Jaklin Klugman while still a two-year-old, a union which produced a minor stakes winner over seven furlongs called Windy Triple K. Doff The Derby was then sold to join the Barronstown Stud in Ireland. She has produced three foals there all by Northern Dancer line stallions; the first was Wedding Bouquet (by Kings Lake), a very useful performer at up to a mile; the second was Generous and the third a colt by Lomond. Further back, ability and resilience feature in full measure. Doff The Derby's dam Margarethen showed smart form over a long period during the 'sixties, winning sixteen of her sixty-four starts at up to nine furlongs; she's also made quite a name for herself at stud as the dam of the tremendously tough and genuine Trillion, herself the dam of Triptych.

Generous, an angular colt with scope, and a fluent mover with a round action, was sold for IR 80,000 guineas as a foal; the IR 200,000 guineas he fetched a year on made him the top-priced Caerleon yearling to be sold at auction in 1989. Judged on his pedigree and style of running there's every chance he'll stay at least a mile and a quarter at three. However, enterprising placement might be necessary if he's to win more good races, for as a consequence of his Dewhurst win he'll now have to carry a penalty in all bar the best. His trainer is well versed in the art of locating opportunities abroad for horses who aren't quite top class at home, and if Generous does fall short he could still emulate the Balding-trained 1989 Dewhurst winner Dashing Blade, who in his second season managed to pick up prestigious prizes in France and Italy. *P. F. I. Cole.*

GENOBRA 6 b.g. Young Generation 129–Dobra Star (FR) 61 (Right Royal V 135) — §
[1989 NR 1990 10.6d] has a round action: fairly useful on his day as 4-y-o: bit backward and bandaged on only run on flat since, tailed off in amateurs handicap at Haydock: best form at up to 1½m: used to go very well in the mud: has run in snatches, including when blinkered: sold 1,150 gns Doncaster November Sales: not to be trusted. *D. McCain.*

GENOTIN 7 b.g. Pitskelly 122–Bazaar Goddess (USA) (Bazaar) [1989 10.2g 8m[5] —
9.2f[2] 8f[4] 10m[2] 10.6d 8m* 8m* 1990 8m 10m 9m 8m 7m 8m[4] 10f 12d 10m 10.2s]
leggy, good-topped gelding: quite modest winner of 2 handicaps (first for apprentices) as 6-y-o: very little show in similar events and seller in 1990: stays 1½m, but at least as effective at 1m: acts on any going: has worn bandages: has often hung (badly so fifth outing). *S. Mellor.*

GENTLE ARIA 2 b.f. (Mar 8) Elegant Air 119–Lady Capilano 87 (Nebbiolo 125) 101 p
[1990 7m* 8.2v*] tall, unfurnished filly: third foal: half-sister to 3-y-o Dominiana (by Dominion) and modest maiden Garth Lady (by Jalmood): dam 1½m winner: won maiden at Lingfield in September and minor event at Haydock (by 8 lengths from Lassoo, making all and staying on strongly) following month: will stay 1¼m: acts very well on heavy ground. *Miss A. J. Whitfield.*

GENTLE GAIN 3 ch.f. Final Straw 127–Regain 86 (Relko 136) [1989 5f[6] 6g 1990 58
7g[6] 7g 7m[3] 8g 10.2m 10g] deep-girthed filly: quite modest maiden: should be suited by further than 7f: bandaged behind final outing: sweating first two. *H. Candy.*

GENTLE HERO (USA) 4 ch.g. Hero's Honor (USA)–Tender Camilla 115 83
(Prince Tenderfoot (USA) 126) [1989 5s[3] 5m* 6g* 6m* 6s* 1990 6v 6m[5] 6m 7m[5]
6m 6m[5] 6m[3] 7m 6d] sturdy gelding: blind in right eye: moderate mover: modest handicapper: stays 7f: acts on good to firm and soft going: visored 3 of last 4 starts: has hung under pressure. *M. P. Naughton.*

GENTLE MELODY (USA) 2 b. or br.f. (Apr 20) Chief's Crown (USA)– — p
Courting Days (USA) (Bold Lad (USA)) [1990 7m] $155,000Y, resold 60,000Y: neat filly: half-sister to 4 winners in Ireland and USA, including smart 7f (at 2 yrs) to 1½m winner Magesterial (by Northern Dancer): dam Irish 1¼m winner, is half-sister to very smart 9f and 1¼m stakes winner Glowing Tribute and from family of Allez France: 25/1, pushed along 3f out and little impression in maiden at Yarmouth in August: should do better. *M. R. Stoute.*

GENTLE SATIN 3 b.c. Anita's Prince 126–Drora (Busted 134) [1989 5m a7g 56 d
a8g[3] 1990 a10g2 a10g a8g 7f[6] 6f[4] 6f a8g 7m 7d 7m 6m 6d] rangy colt: has been tubed: moderate mover: quite modest maiden: little form after first run: finds 6f on short side and stays 1¼m: tailed off in blinkers ninth start. *P. Mitchell.*

GENTLY GENTLY 3 b.c. Prince Tenderfoot (USA) 126–Domani 106 (Mourne —
126) [1989 NR 1990 6m[6] 6m 6m 8m] IR 9,400F, 15,500Y. lengthy colt: has quick action: brother to plating-class middle-distance maiden Best Foot Forward and fairly useful sprinter Bonseri and half-brother to 3 winners, notably very useful 6f to 1m winner Apres Demain (by King Emperor): dam won over 6f and 7f: little sign of ability, blinkered in selling handicap final start. *R. Hannon.*

GENUINE GIFT (CAN) 5 ch.h. Blushing Groom (FR) 131–Barb's Bold (USA) —
112 (Bold Forbes (USA)) [1989 11.5m[2] 12m[3] 12g[6] 1990 9f 12f a13g] strong, workmanlike horse: poor mover: lightly-raced maiden: soundly beaten last 4 outings: stays 1½m. *J. J. Bridger.*

GEORGE JET 3 gr.g. Relaunch (USA)–Eleven Pelicans (USA) (Grey Dawn II 42
132) [1989 NR 1990 8g 7m[4]] strong, workmanlike gelding: fourth foal: half-brother to 6-y-o 1½m and 15f winner Eleven Lights (by Lyphard): dam winning half-sister to very useful 1982 staying 2-y-o Alligatrix and daughter of sister to very smart animals Cabildo and Canal: sire smart from 7f to 1½m: bit backward, led over 5f when fourth of 6 in seller at Warwick: sold 8,000 gns Newmarket July Sales. *Mrs L. Piggott.*

Hamdan Al-Maktoum's "Gharam"

GEORGE WILLIAM 9 b.h. Import 127–Bloomsbury Girl 63 (Weepers Boy — 124) [1989 6m 5m 1990 6g] strong, good-bodied horse: carries plenty of condition: moderate mover: modest handicapper on his day, but is very lightly raced nowadays: ideally suited by 6f or stiff 5f: probably needs give in the ground: has been tried in blinkers and visor: has often worn bandages. *J. S. Wilson.*

GEORGIAN DANCER (USA) 3 b.c. Nijinsky (CAN) 138–Strike A Pose 86 (USA) (Iron Ruler (USA)) [1989 NR 1990 10f² 10g* 12.5f³] good-topped colt: seventh foal: closely related to a minor North American winner at around 1m by Green Dancer and half-brother to 4 winners there, including useful 1979 2-y-o Tonka Wakhan (by Big Spruce) and 6f stakes winner Wedding Picture (by Blushing Groom): dam won 4 times at up to 7f: fair form, justifying favouritism in maiden at Sandown in September: probably stayed 1½m: dead. *J. H. M. Gosden.*

GERAGHTYFIRSTPASS 3 b.g. Kafu 120–Swan River 70 (Roan Rocket 128) — [1989 NR 1990 6g] IR 12,000Y: deep-girthed, rather angular gelding: third foal: half-brother to Irish 9f winner Krismas River (by Kris) and fairly useful 6f and 1m winner Alsabiha (by Lord Gayle): dam, suited by 1¼m, is daughter of Park Hill winner Parmelia, herself a half-sister to St Paddy: reared at stalls when tenth of 16 in maiden at Nottingham in April: dead. *G. A. Huffer.*

GERALIA 2 b.f. (Mar 30) Last Tycoon 131–Gerania (FR) (Arctic Tern (USA) 126) 53 [1990 7m 7g 6d] compact filly: first foal: dam once-raced half-sister to smart French middle-distance performer Glaros: plating-class form in maidens: ran poorly final start: will be suited by 1m + . *C. C. Elsey.*

GERSHWIN 7 b.g. Gold Song 112–Firey Kim (CAN) (Cannonade (USA)) [1989 48 6v 5s 6f 7h³ 6h* 6m⁶ 6m⁵ 6h 7.6f 5m 6f 7m 1990 5.8h⁶ 6m⁵ 6g³ 6m² 5m] tall gelding: plating-class handicapper: effective at 6f and 7f: probably unsuited by soft going, acts on any other: effective with or without visor: has won for apprentice: has been taken very quietly to post. *J. Berry.*

GESNERA 2 br.f. (Mar 14) Rusticaro (FR) 124–Joie d'Or (FR) (Kashmir II 125) **51**
[1990 6g 7g³ 7f 7f] lengthy filly: has a roundish action: sixth foal: half-sister to 7f/1m
performers Joie de Rose and Gurteen Boy (both by Tickled Pink): dam of little
account: form only when third in maiden at Wolverhampton in July: possibly
requires an easy surface. *M. Blanshard.*

GET GOING 3 b.f. Petorius 117–Regal Promise (Pitskelly 122) [1989 6m⁴ 6m* **68**
6v² 7d 1990 8.2f⁵ 7d⁶ 8m 7m 8g⁵ 7g⁶ 7f⁴ 8g⁶ 7g 10.4d] smallish, close-coupled filly:
has a round action: quite modest handicapper: stays 1m: acts on any going: blinkered
third start: visored next 2: sold 5,400 gns Newmarket Autumn Sales. *C. W. C. Elsey.*

GHADBBAAN 6 b.h. Kalaglow 132–Firework Party (USA) 115 (Roan Rocket **69**
128) [1989 12d a7g² 1990 9f 9f* 8g* 8f³ 10.6s³ 10g⁵ 8d² 7g³ 8m² 11.5f* 10m*
10.4g² 8f* 10.6d³ 8.2v⁶ 10.2s³] lengthy, leggy horse: scratchy mover: prolific
winner in modest company: justified favouritism in sellers at Redcar (women riders,
no bid) in May, Lingfield (bought in 10,000 gns) in July and Chepstow (retained
12,000 gns) in September and in claimers at Carlisle in May and Windsor and Redcar
in August: effective at 1m and stays 1½m: acts on any going except possibly heavy:
genuine and consistent: sold 11,000 gns Newmarket Autumn Sales. *N. Tinkler.*

GHARAH (USA) 3 b.f. Shadeed (USA) 135–Bolt From The Blue (USA) (Blue **79**
Times (USA)) [1989 7g⁵ 7s⁴ 1990 8g² 10.2h² 12.2g² 10f³ 10f² 9m³ 10.4g⁶ 10m⁵]
rangy, quite attractive filly: fair maiden: sweating, wandered under pressure when
running fairly well in amateurs handicap sixth start: didn't get best of runs both
subsequent outings: should stay 1½m: acts on hard ground: edgy second start: sold
17,000 gns Newmarket December Sales. *P. T. Walwyn.*

GHARAM (USA) 3 ch.f. Green Dancer (USA) 132–Water Lily (FR) 116 **108**
(Riverman (USA) 131) [1989 6m* 7m² 1990 8g³ 12d 12d³ 9m] leggy, sparely-made,
quite attractive filly: capable of useful form but disappointing: third in Dubai Poule
d'Essai des Pouliches at Longchamp: 13 lengths third to Hellenic in Ribblesdale
Stakes (outpaced on turn then staying on steadily) at Royal Ascot, only sign of
retaining her ability: sweating and bit edgy before leading 6f in listed race final start:
evidently stayed 1½m: suffered knee injury second outing at 2 yrs: visits Kris. *A. C.
Stewart.*

GHAYAAT (USA) 3 ch.f. Lyphard (USA) 132–Goodbye Shelley (FR) 116 (Home —
Guard (USA) 129) [1989 6f 1990 7g 7m⁴ 10g] small, angular filly: plating-class form
at best: will be suited by return to shorter: sold 6,400 gns Newmarket December
Sales. *P. T. Walwyn.*

GHILAN (USA) 4 b.g. Linkage–Chuckle (Shecky Greene (USA)) [1989 8g³ 7g⁴ **70**
7g⁶ 1990 a6g⁵ a8g* a8g³ 8h 7h² 8f 7f² 7.6f³ 7.6m² 8g⁶ 8f³] angular gelding: won
claimer at Lingfield in January: better efforts when placed in handicaps on turf
afterwards: below form in seller (claimed to join B. Llewellyn's stable £6,100) final
outing: stays 1m: acts on hard and dead going: has started slowly. *R. Akehurst.*

GHYLLDALE 2 b.f. (Mar 15) Sweet Monday 122–Dreamy Desire 50 (Palm —
Track 122) [1990 a6g a7g 7f] leggy filly: first live foal: dam free-racing plater,
seemed not to stay 1½m: well beaten in sellers: bandaged final start. *R. Bastiman.*

GHZAALH (USA) 3 ch.f. Northern Dancer–Give Thanks 123 (Relko 136) [1989 **87**
NR 1990 7g 10.4d²] sturdy, useful-looking filly: second foal: closely related to fair
12.2f winner (awarded race) Saffaanh (by Shareef Dancer): dam very tough winner
from 9f to 1½m, including of Irish Oaks, and second in Park Hill Stakes, is from
excellent family: still carrying condition, made most when second in maiden at
Chester in May: visits Machiavellian. *Major W. R. Hern.*

GIBBOT 5 b.g. Taufan (USA) 119–Gaychimes (Steel Heart 128) [1989 10.2g⁵ 10g **54**
10.8d 10f 10f 10m 10m⁶ 1²g 10.0d² 11v 10m 10g² 10g⁵ a10g³ a10g² a10g² 10.2f⁶ 9f*
a10g⁸ 8m² 10m³ 9m⁶ 8m⁶ 10m⁶ 9g⁵ 10d 10s a10g a13g] close-coupled, workmanlike
gelding: carries plenty of condition: has a round action: plating-class handicapper:
won girl apprentices event at Kempton in April: below form last 4 outings: effective
at 1m to 1¼m: acts on any going: slowly away when blinkered: bandaged ninth
outing: has worn tongue strap. *P. Howling.*

GIBRALTAR WALK 2 b.c. (Feb 24) Dreams To Reality (USA) 113–Jolliffe's —
Treble (Lochnager 132) [1990 5m a6g] 3,850Y, 2,000 2-y-o: third foal: half-brother
to 1987 2-y-o Barnby Moor (by Raga Navarro), disqualified 6f winner at 2 yrs: dam
never ran: no show in sellers. *J. R. Jenkins.*

GIJON 2 b.g. (Feb 29) Coquelin (USA) 121–Elan's Valley (Welsh Pageant 132) —
[1990 6m] 16,000F, 7,400Y: leggy, rather unfurnished gelding: first foal: dam French
8.5f winner: blinkered and green, soon struggling in seller at Windsor in June: sent
to Norway. *Sir Mark Prescott.*

GILBERT'S GIRL   3 b.f. Castle Keep 121–Traditional Miss 90 (Traditionalist   **40**
(USA)) [1989 7m 1990 10m 10.1m 8f 10m² 12d³] leggy, sparely-made filly: poor
plater: form only on last 2 starts: may prove ideally suited by 1¼m: acts on good to
firm ground and dead: tends to wander under pressure. *C. J. Hill.*

GILDED OMEN   2 b.f. (Feb 24) Faustus (USA) 118–Fine Asset (Hot Spark 126)   **37**
[1990 a5g⁵ 6g⁴ a6g⁵ a7g a7g] close-coupled, deep-girthed filly: third living foal:
half-sister to 3-y-o 6f winner Faultless Speech (by Good Times): dam bred
half-sister to smart 7f performer Tudor Mill: poor plater: slowly away first 3 starts:
wore eyeshield final 2 outings: sold 640 gns Newmarket September Sales. *Sir Mark
Prescott.*

GILDED PAST   3 ch.g. Glint of Gold 128–Historia 71 (Northfields (USA)) [1989   **62** d
7m 6m⁶ 8f⁴ 7.5f⁵ 1990 8f 10f⁴ 12g 10m⁴ 10g⁵ 10f 10m 10m] close-coupled gelding:
has a quick action: quite modest maiden: ran poorly in handicap and sellers last 3
starts: should stay 1½m: acts on firm ground: twice reluctant at stalls: gelded after
final outing. *A. N. Lee.*

GILDERDALE   8 ch.g. Gunner B 126–Mertola (Tribal Chief 125) [1989 7g⁶ 7f*   **87**
7g⁴ 8f⁴ 8m² 7f⁵ 8f³ 8.5g 7m 8m² 8g⁵ 1990 8f 7m 9m* 8f⁴ 8m² 8f 9m* 10g* 9m⁵
9m 8m⁵] close-coupled gelding: has quick action: fair performer: successful in
handicaps at Goodwood in June and August (amateurs) and in amateurs race at
Sandown in September, quickening well for last 2 successes: stays 1¼m: goes
particularly well on top-of-the-ground: usually held up: tough. *J. W. Hills.*

GILT PREFERENCE   3 b.g. Pitskelly 122–Mandolin 74 (Manado 130) [1989   **80**
NR 1990 a8g 10.1g 10.6d 12m* 12g²] IR 18,000Y: tall, unfurnished gelding: has
scope: first foal: dam 10.2f winner out of half-sister to high-class French filly Pitasia:
first worthwhile form when winning 18-runner handicap at Leicester in October:
favourite, good second in similar event at Newmarket: stays 1½m: sold out of M.
Jarvis' stable 31,000 gns Newmarket Autumn Sales after penultimate start. *M. C.
Pipe.*

GILT PREMIUM   3 b.c. Precocious 126–Nonabella 82 (Nonoalco (USA) 131)   **60**
[1989 NR 1990 6g 8.2g 8g⁵ 7d* 8g 8.2s 7f³ 14,000F, IR 14,000Y: lengthy colt:
moderate mover: first foal: dam 7f and 1m winner out of game and useful staying
2-y-o Fiordiligi: tended to wander when winning seller (sold out of M. Jarvis' stable
4,500 gns) at Leicester in June: easily best other effort when third of 20, staying on
never able to challenge, in claimer at Newmarket: suited by 7f: acts on firm and dead
ground: blinkered last 6 starts: sold 4,600 gns Doncaster October Sales. *M. H. B.
Robinson.*

GIN AND ORANGE   4 b.g. Mummy's Pet 125–Amberetta 72 (Supreme   **64**
Sovereign 119) [1989 7d* 8m³ 7f 8m⁵ 8m 8s a7g 1990 10.6f⁵ 8f⁶ 9g³ 10m² 11.7m]
rangy, quite attractive gelding: moderate mover: quite modest handicapper: hung
left final outing: stays 1¼m: acts on firm and dead going: probably best with waiting
tactics: sold to join J. Jenkins' stable 8,000 gns Newmarket Autumn Sales. *C. R.
Nelson.*

GINA'S CHOICE   4 b.f. Ile de Bourbon (USA) 133–Modern Romance (Dance In   **22**
Time (CAN)) [1989 10g 8.5f 7m 6m 7m 1990 10g 8f4] big, rather plain filly: has a
round action: first form when fourth in Yarmouth selling handicap in July: doesn't
stay 1¼m: sometimes bandaged. *J. Wharton.*

GINA'S DELIGHT   2 ch.f. (May 26) Valiyar 129–City Swinger (Derrylin 115)   **41**
[1990 5g 6d a6g] leggy, good-topped filly: has a quick action: third foal: half-sister to
3-y-o Ilewin (by Ile de Bourbon): dam, of little account, is half-sister to smart 5f
sprinter Bold And Free and good sprinter Watergate: poor form in maidens and a
claimer. *J. Wharton.*

GINETTA   2 ch.f. (Apr 14) Giacometti 130–Thorganby Tina 72 (Averof 123) [1990   —
5d 6m⁵ 7f 7f] 500Y: leggy filly: turns fore-feet in: sixth foal: half-sister to 3-y-o 5f
winner Maison des Fruits (by Balidar): dam stayed 1m: well beaten in sellers and a
maiden auction: blinkered first 2 starts. *A. Smith.*

GINGERNUT (USA)   3 ch.c. Timeless Moment (USA)–United Appeal (USA)   **45** §
(Valid Appeal (USA)) [1989 5m⁴ 6f⁵ 5f⁴ 5.8h² 5h² 5.8f³ 6m³ 6g³ 7g⁶ a7g a6g 1990
6m 8m 6g⁴ 6f* 5g 6g 7d 6f 7f 5m⁶ 6m 8m] smallish, good-quartered colt: good
mover: poor performer: showed little after winning apprentice handicap at Salisbury
in May: stays 6f: acts on firm going: visored seventh start: has sweated and been on
toes: sometimes hangs left: temperamental and not one to trust. *M. D. I. Usher.*

GINGER'S GONE   3 b.f. Ginger Brink (FR) 117–Away And Gone (Comedy Star   —
(USA) 121) [1989 5m 6f 6g 1990 8.2d⁶ 10.4g] angular, plain filly: poor form in maidens
and claimers: stays 1m. *E. H. Owen jun.*

GIPPESWYCK LADY 3 b.f. Pas de Seul 133–Estivalia (Persian Bold 123) [1989 **83**
6m 6g⁵ 8.2g³ 8d⁶ 1990 10t 10g² 12m² 14m³ 14m* 16m² 15.3g² 14d⁴ 16s*] leggy,
workmanlike filly: fair handicapper: ridden by 7-lb claimer, won at Yarmouth in July
and Lingfield in October: stays 2m well: acts on good to firm ground and soft. *M. H.
Tompkins.*

GIPSY FIDDLER 2 b.c. (Apr 8) Bairn (USA) 126–Miss Cindy 95 (Mansingh **107**
(USA) 120) [1990 5g* 5f* 5d* 5m⁵ 6m³] 10,000Y: well-grown, close-coupled colt:
moderate mover: half-brother to several winners here and abroad, including 1986
2-y-o 5f and 6f seller winner Miss Drummond (by The Brianstan): dam 5f to 7f
performer, is sister to Petong: useful colt, successful in maiden at Hamilton, minor
event at Pontefract and Windsor Castle Stakes at Royal Ascot: good third, never
able to challenge, to Mac's Imp in Heinz '57' Phoenix Stakes at Phoenix Park: better
suited by 6f than 5f: sure to win another race or two. *J. J. O'Neill.*

GIPSY KING 2 gr.g. (Feb 22) Magic Mirror 105–Sarah Gillian (USA) (Zen **59**
(USA)) [1990 6g⁵ 6g² 7m⁶ 7m 7.5g⁴ 8m⁶ 7g a7g⁵] 2,800Y: leggy, rather sparely-
made gelding: has rather round action: second foal: dam well beaten: plating-class
maiden: stays 7.5f: has been bandaged off-hind: carries head awkwardly, and gives
impression ungenuine. *P. A. Kelleway.*

GIPSY RAMBLER 5 gr.g. Move Off 112–Gipsy Silver (Pongee 106) [1989 7d **—**
6v⁵ 1990 10v] rather sparely-made gelding: form on flat only when winning nursery
in 1987: blinkered once: often races freely: winning novice hurdler in November. *N.
Chamberlain.*

GIRL GEORGIE 4 ch.f. Music Boy 124–Rely On Guy 73 (Reliance II 137) [1989 **—**
NR 1990 a6g a8g] first foal: dam 7f winner: behind in maidens: sold 1,200 gns
Doncaster June Sales. *A. Bailey.*

GIUTURNA (IRE) 2 b. or br.f. (May 28) Alzao (USA) 117–Saranita 70 (Thatch **51**
(USA) 136) [1990 6m 6g³ 6m] IR 9,000Y: small filly: fifth foal: dam 1m winner in
France: plating-class maiden: will stay 7f. *Lord John FitzGerald.*

GIVE IN 3 gr.c. Harlow (USA) 111–Moment of Weakness 76 (Pieces of Eight 128) **56**
[1989 5s* 5s⁶ 6m³ 6f⁴ 7m² 6m⁴ 7f⁴ 7m⁵ 6f² 6g 6g 6g 6m⁴ 6f a6g a8g* 1990 a7g²
a8g* a8g⁵ a8g⁵ 9m 8.2f 6m 8g 7.5f⁶ a7g a7g] leggy, narrow colt: plating-class
performer: 5/2 on and ridden by 7-lb claimer, won 3-runner handicap at Southwell in
January: needs further than 6f, and stays 1m: possibly unsuited by top-of-the-ground
nowadays: sometimes visored at 2 yrs: inconsistent. *Mrs N. Macauley.*

GIVEMEACALL 2 b.c. (Mar 26) Kind of Hush 118–Darymoss 79 (Ballymoss **48**
136) [1990 5m⁵ 6s 6g 6g 7.5g⁶ 7.5m 8.2s 10.6s³ a8g 10.2s] 4,800Y: workmanlike colt:

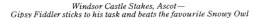

*Windsor Castle Stakes, Ascot—
Gipsy Fiddler sticks to his task and beats the favourite Snowy Owl*

poor mover: fourth foal: half-brother to 3-y-o Myverygoodfriend (by Swing Easy) and a winner over hurdles: dam, maiden, best at up to 1m: modest plater: ran well final 3 starts: will stay well: suited by soft ground: blinkered fourth start: has given impression unsatisfactory temperamentally. *N. Tinkler.*

GIVE ME HOPE (IRE) 2 b.f. (Apr 29) Be My Native (USA) 122–Diamond Gig (Pitskelly 122) [1990 6g 7s 4] leggy, quite attractive filly: second living foal: sister to 1989 2-y-o 6f selling winner Native Gem: dam placed over hurdles in Ireland, is half-sister to smart 10.5f and 1½m winner Amyndas: around 7 lengths fourth of 22 to Desert Sun in maiden at Doncaster in October: will be suited by at least 1m: likely to improve again. *R. W. Armstrong.* **70 p**

GIVENTIME 2 ch.g. (Mar 23) Bustino 136–Duck Soup 55 (Decoy Boy 129) [1990 a7g a8g3] 6,000Y: sturdy gelding: has a round action: sixth foal: half-brother to 5 winners, including fairly useful 1985 2-y-o Crete Cargo (by King of Spain) and 1½m winner Joseph (by Rolfe): dam won over 7f from 3 starts: bit backward, over 5 lengths third of 10, staying on well, to Moving Out in maiden at Southwell: will be suited by 1¼m: will improve again. *Andrew Turnell.* **54 p**

GIVUS ABID 2 ch.c. (Feb 12) Primo Dominie 121–Formidable Dancer 70 (Formidable (USA) 125) [1990 5f 7.5m] 2,200F, 5,400Y: first foal: dam maiden, stayed 1½m: well backed, prominent to halfway then not knocked about in seller at Windsor in August: reared stalls and withdrawn at Beverley month later: may improve. *R. O'Leary.* **40 p**

GLACIAL STORM (USA) 5 b.h. Arctic Tern (USA) 126–Hortensia (FR) 119 (Luthier 126) [1989 12m2 12g4 12f4 12m5 13.3g4 1990 15.5f* 16m6 16m3 12d2 12d] lengthy, heavy-topped, most attractive horse: has rather a round action: generally disappointing after reaching place in Ever Ready Derby and Budweiser Irish Derby in 1988: ran one of his better races when winning Prix de Barbeville at Longchamp in April by nose from Turgeon: continued on the decline after, tailed off in La Coupe at Longchamp in June final outing: stayed 2m: had form on all types of going, but seemed unable to take much racing on top-of-the-ground: often blinkered, but wasn't at 5 yrs: to stand at Ballysheehan Stud, Co. Tipperary. *J. E. Hammond, France.* **105 §**

GLAD TO BE GREY 2 ch.c. (May 21) Song 132–Faraway Grey 99 (Absalom 128) [1990 5f 6d a5g6] small, rather sparely-made colt: first reported foal: dam 2-y-o 5f winner stayed 1m: well beaten in maidens: off course 6 months after debut. *R. J. R. Williams.* **42**

GLADYS PUGH 4 b.f. Comedy Star (USA) 121–Nylon Pirate 80 (Derring-Do 131) [1989 8g 7.3m 8g 6m 7m 1990 10f] strong, workmanlike filly: little worthwhile form, including in selling company. *M. R. Channon.* **—**

GLANCE OF GOLD (USA) 2 ch.c. (Apr 2) Mr Prospector (USA)–Over Your Shoulder (USA) 77 (Graustark) [1990 6m3] $320,000Y: lengthy, workmanlike colt: third foal: half-brother to modest maiden Rakan (by Danzig), stayed 10.8f: dam, sister to very smart American 6f to 1¼m winner Proctor, was middle-distance stayer: favourite but bit backward, over 2 lengths third of 8, headed under 2f out, no extra and not knocked about, to Go Executive in maiden at Goodwood in June: moved moderately down: not seen out after. *G. Harwood.* **70 p**

GLASS CASTLE (FR) 6 b.h. Crystal Palace (FR) 132–Halliana (USA) (Bold Reason) [1989 10g3 10.6m4 12g3 12g 1990 10.2f 10.1g 10m 10.6s5] workmanlike horse: poor maiden: barely stays 1½m: acts on good to firm and soft going: raced too freely in blinkers third start: often bandaged: has hung and raced with head high: sold 1,650 gns Ascot July Sales. *A. Hide.* **—**

GLASTONDALE 4 b.g. Beldale Flutter (USA) 130–Glastonbury 73 (Grundy 137) [1989 12m3 12.2m6 12m* 12m6 12.3g* 12.2m2 10f* 10m6 10.2g2 10.4m6 12f3 12.2m 1990 a12g4 a11g a14g4 10.2f3 10m2 12f5 12.4f2 12f 12m2 12g6 10m 11m6 11d2 12g* 12f2 12f2 12.3g3] compact gelding: carries condition: plating-class handicapper: apprentice ridden, made all at Edinburgh in July: stays 1½m: acts on firm and dead going: visored twice at 2 yrs: has run well when sweating: lacks turn of foot, and suited by forcing tactics: consistent. *T. D. Barron.* **52**

GLAZERITE 3 b.c. Dunphy 124–Rust Free 58 (Free State 125) [1989 7g6 7m* 8m 8g* 8m 1990 8m 12f6 10d3 12g4 13.1m3 a18g5 16m6 13v3 16d2 16s6 a14g5] strong colt: modest handicapper: stays 13f: below form on firm going, probably acts on any other: visored last 5 starts: has needed plenty of driving and may prove best with strong handling. *R. Guest.* **75 d**

GLEAMING WATER 2 gr.f. (Mar 13) Kalaglow 132–Idle Waters 116 (Mill Reef (USA) 141) [1990 6m* 6m3 6m] 16,000Y: sparely-made filly: sister to very useful **81 p**

stayer Shining Water and half-sister to winning stayer Ancient Mariner (by Wollow) and 3-y-o 12.5f to 1¾m winner Secret Waters (by Pharly): dam smart 1½m to 14.6f winner: won minor event at Windsor in July, hanging left 2f out: third of 5 to Jimmy Barnie in minor event then always outpaced in 'Pacemaker Update' Lowther Stakes at York: will be very well suited by middle distances. *R. F. Johnson Houghton.*

GLEBELANDS GIRL 3 b.f. Burslem 123–Genzyme Gene 38 (Riboboy (USA) — 124) [1989 5g 5s⁶ 5m⁴ 6f 5f⁶ 7m³ 7f⁵ 7m⁶ 7f 8g 8m 1990 a10g⁶ a10g³ a10g 10f 12.2m 10m⁵ 12.2g⁵ 11.7m 13.8m⁴] small, sparely-made filly: has a round action: plater: suited by 1¼m: has run well for 7-lb claimer: winning selling hurdler. *R. A. Bennett.*

GLENAIRLIE (IRE) 2 b.f. (Mar 6) Glow (USA)–Celtic Symphony (Orchestra 52 118) [1990 6m 6m⁴ 8m⁴ 8m] IR 28,000Y: smallish, good-topped filly: second foal: dam 1½m winner in Ireland: plating-class performer: probably better suited by 1m than 6f: has run well for 7-lb claimer. *J. S. Wilson.*

GLENASLENA (IRE) 2 b.f. (Apr 11) Gorytus (USA) 132–Scalded (Hotfoot 126) — § [1990 6m a6g⁴ 6m 7m] IR 9,000Y: sparely-made filly: has a quick action: second foal: dam unraced half-sister to good Italian sprinter Swing Fire: poor form in sellers: carries head high: best left alone: retained 1,900 gns Newmarket September Sales. *Sir Mark Prescott.*

GLENBURY 5 ch.g. Morston (FR) 125–Glenside Lady 79 (So Blessed 130) [1989 — NR 1990 10.8m] probably of little account. *J. D. Roberts.*

GLENCOE LADY 3 b.f. Thatching 131–Borgia (GER) (Orsini 124) [1989 7m 7f 37 1990 9m³ 12.5g 10.6s 10f⁵ 10.4g 15.3f⁶] angular filly: has a round action: poor on most form: probably best short of 1½m: acts on good to firm going. *D. Haydn Jones.*

GLENCROFT 6 b.g. Crofter (USA) 124–Native Fleet (FR) (Fleet Nasrullah) 82 [1989 5f 6f⁶ 6m 5m⁵ 5g 5m 5g 6m 6m 5d 1990 a5g⁶ a5g³ 5f* 5f* 5m* 5m a5g 5m 5g 5m⁵ 5m⁶ 5g 5d* 5g² a6g* 6s 5s² a5g* a6g⁴ a5g⁴ a6g³] big, strong gelding: prolific winner in 1988 after being hobdayed: in excellent heart again in autumn, winning handicaps at Edinburgh and Southwell (twice): also successful in claimers at Redcar (twice) and Chepstow in first half of season: better suited by 5f than 6f (looked unsuited by 6f track at Lingfield final outing): seems to act on any going nowadays: blinkered first time in some while at Edinburgh and all subsequent starts: has been tubed and reportedly broke blood vessel second outing. *D. W. Chapman.*

GLENELIANE (IRE) 2 b.f. (Apr 14) Glenstal (USA) 118–Sweet Eliane (Bird- 58 brook 110) [1990 6g 5f³ 5d⁶ 5f² 5m³ 6f⁴ 5f² a6g² 5m⁶ 6d⁶ 5m⁵ 7g⁴ 8m] IR 6,200Y, 5,000 2-y-o: lengthy, good-quartered filly: half-sister to 3-y-o 1m winner Tartar's Bow (by Gorytus) and 2 winners, including 1983 2-y-o 6f winner Sir Humpherson (by Music Boy): dam poor maiden: plating-class maiden: best form at up to 7f: has run creditably for 7-lb claimer: tail flasher: sold 3,200 gns Doncaster October Sales: consistent. *Pat Mitchell.*

GLENFIELD GRETA 2 ch.f. (Apr 6) Gabitat 119–Glenfield Portion 86 58 (Mummy's Pet 125) [1990 5g² 5f⁵ 6g 5f³ 5f* 5m⁴ 6m 6d⁵] 5,000Y: small, sturdy filly: third live foal: half-sister to winning sprinter Bernstein Bette (by Petong): dam 2-y-o 5f winner well beaten at 3 yrs: plating-class performer: ridden by claimer, made all in maiden auction at Haydock in August: unseated rider leaving stalls third outing, awkward at them sixth one: stays 6f: acts on firm and dead ground: carries head high: races keenly. *P. S. Felgate.*

GLEN FINNAN 2 ch.f. (Mar 5) Ballacashtal (CAN)–Glen Kella Manx 97 — (Tickled Pink 114) [1990 5.8f⁶ 6m 6m 5.8f⁶ 5m] compact filly: has a round action: first foal: dam 5f and 6f winner stayed 7f: soundly beaten in minor events and maidens. *J. C. Fox.*

GLEN KATE 3 b.f. Glenstal (USA) 118–Miss Kate (FR) (Nonoalco (USA) 131) 102 [1989 7m* 1990 6m* 7f* 9g⁶ 8d] rangy filly: successful in minor event (edgy and swishing tail beforehand, swerved over 1f out) at Warwick and £11,600 handicap (coming from well off pace) at Newmarket in the spring: off course nearly 3 months then below form in Evry listed race and behind in Group 2 event at Deauville: should stay 1m: sold out of H. Cecil's stable after second start, eventually to race in USA. *N. Clement, France.*

GLEN MADDIE 3 b.f. Reasonable (FR) 119–Iresine (GER) (Frontal 122) [1989 55 5d 5d⁴ 1990 8.2g 6g 8.2v 5s a6g*] strong, dipped-backed filly: carries condition: poor mover: won handicap at Southwell in December: better suited by 6f than 5f: trained until after fifth start by J. S. Wilson. *J. Mackie.*

GLENMERE PRINCE 4 b.g. Prince Tenderfoot (USA) 126–Ashbourne Lass (Ashmore (FR) 125) [1989 11v 12.2d 6f⁴ 7f⁴ 7m³ 8.2f 8m 8f 1990 8.2f] leggy gelding:

poor form, including in sellers: may prove suited by 1m: acts on firm going: blinkered twice. *P. J. Feilden.*

GLEN OAK 5 b.g. Glenstal (USA) 118–Neeran (Wollow 132) [1989 NR 1990 14g] —
tall, lengthy gelding: poor maiden: tailed off in handicap only start at 5 yrs: stays 1½m: acts on firm going (has won on soft over hurdles): visored and blinkered once: has swished tail: difficult ride. *J. D. Roberts.*

GLENORTHERN (IRE) 2 ch.c. (Feb 6) Glenstal (USA) 118–Lady Tyrrel (Pall   79
Mall 132) [1990 6m⁴ 6m⁶ 6g 7m⁵ 8d*] IR 28,000Y: smallish colt: easy mover: half-brother to 4 winners here and abroad, including useful 9f to 2m winner Bold Connection (by Persian Bold): dam Irish 11f winner: won 17-runner nursery, showing much improved form, at Goodwood in October by 5 lengths from Princess Moodyshoe: will stay 1¼m: acts well on dead ground: sold 23,000 gns Newmarket Autumn Sales. *J. L. Dunlop.*

GLENSAY 4 gr.f. Sayf El Arab (USA) 127–Blanche Neige 75 (Forlorn River 124)   —
[1989 NR 1990 6g 10.1g 7m 7f 5f 5g] small, close-coupled filly: second foal: dam, half-sister to sprinters Kind Music and Boy Trumpeter: well beaten in varied events, often slowly away: sold 1,100 gns Ascot July Sales. *M. McCourt.*

GLENSCAR 4 gr.g. Glenstal (USA) 118–Caranina (USA) (Caro 133) [1989 6m 5m   49
7m⁶ 6m* 6g² 6f⁵ 6g 1990 5m 5f 6m 7m 6g⁵ a8g 6m² 6g 7m 5d⁶ 6d 6m⁶ 8g²] angular, sparely-made gelding: poor walker and mover: poor handicapper: needs further than 5f and stays 1m: acts on good to firm and dead going: often slowly away: sold out of M. Charles's stable 3,200 gns Doncaster August Sales after seventh outing: inconsistent. *J. L. Spearing.*

GLENSTAL ABBEY (USA) 4 ch.g. Gregorian (USA) 115–Full Delivery (USA)   —
(Irish Ruler (USA)) [1989 12m 12f⁴ 10f³ 12g 12g 12g⁵ 1990 a12g³ 12.5f a12g] lengthy, workmanlike ex-Irish gelding: moderate mover: seventh foal: half-brother to 4 winners in USA: dam won at around 1m in USA: poor maiden: blinkered 4 times (including last 2 starts): winning selling hurdler in May. *R. Akehurst.*

GLENSTAL PRINCESS 3 ch.f. Glenstal (USA) 118–Jessamy Hall 77 (Crown-   69
ed Prince (USA) 128) [1989 5f⁵ 6f* 1990 7d 6m 5.8m⁶ 7.6f³ 7f 7.6g 6m⁴ 6m 6s] lengthy filly: modest performer: mostly faced very stiff tasks in handicaps, running well at Chester and Goodwood (£11,400 event) sixth and seventh starts: may be suited by return to further, and is bred to stay 1m: acts on firm going: visored and sweating penultimate start. *R. Guest.*

GLENSTAL PRIORY 3 b.f. Glenstal (USA) 118–Jumbola (Wolver Hollow 126)   52
[1989 6m⁵ 7m 8g 1990 7m 8g³ 10m² 10.2f⁶ 12m⁵ 9m⁵] small filly: has a quick action: plating-class performer: claimed out of G. Balding's stable £9,000 when second in claimer at Sandown: suited by 1¼m: acts on good to firm ground. *P. F. I. Cole.*

GLINTING CURRENCY (USA) 2 b.f. (Mar 21) Glint of Gold 128–Current   — p
Pattie (USA) 102 (Little Current (USA)) [1990 6m⁵] fourth foal: half-sister to fairly useful 1¼m and 1½m winner Timothy's Toy (by High Top): dam fourth in Cheveley Park Stakes on second of 2 starts at 2 yrs, is out of half-sister to dam of Nonoalco: 12½ lengths fifth of 9, front rank over 4f, to Fennel in maiden at Newmarket in August: sure to improve over further. *C. E. Brittain.*

GLINT IN THE EYE (IRE) 2 b.f. (Mar 17) Glint of Gold 128–Babilla (USA)   42
(Raja Baba (USA)) [1990 5m 6m 7d⁵] 28,000F: leggy filly: third foal: dam unraced daughter of very useful 1974 Irish 2-y-o 5f and 6f winner Tender Camilla, later placed in Coronation Stakes: poor maiden: stays 7f: sweating and edgy second start: sold 2,300 gns Newmarket Autumn Sales. *C. F. Wall.*

GLITTERBIRD 3 br.f. Glint of Gold 128–Dovetail 80 (Brigadier Gerard 144)   55
[1989 7g⁶ 7m 1990 10g 14m⁴ a12g⁶ 10g 10f²] big, workmanlike filly: plating-class maiden: blinkered, good second in claimer at Newmarket in July: may well be suited by return to further: lacks turn of foot: sold 2,500 gns Doncaster September Sales. *G. A. Pritchard-Gordon.*

GLITTERING EYES (FR) 2 ch.c. (Apr 2) Crystal Glitters (USA) 127–   —
Seventeen Roses (USA) (Lyphard (USA) 132) [1990 6m 9g] 190,000 francs (approx £17,600) Y: compact colt: fifth foal: half-brother to 2 French middle-distance winners in Fijar: dam unraced: soundly beaten in maiden at Ripon and claimer (backward) at York 2½ months later: sold 800 gns Newmarket Autumn Sales. *M. H. Tompkins.*

GLOWING ARDOUR 2 b.f. (Feb 18) Dancing Brave (USA) 140–Cocotte 111   94
(Troy 137) [1990 7m² 7m² 8m* 8m* 8m] strong, lengthy filly: has plenty of scope: first foal: dam 1¼m winner, is granddaughter of Irish 1000 Guineas winner Gaily: fairly useful filly: won maiden at Chepstow in August and Silken Glider EBF Stakes

(by ½ length, with Shimmering Sea 2 lengths back in third) at Leopardstown in September: weakened quickly final furlong when modest seventh in Brent Walker Fillies' Mile at Ascot: will be suited by 1¼m. *M. R. Stoute.*

GLOWING PRAISE 3 b.c. Wassl 125–Rossitor 78 (Pall Mall 132) [1989 NR 1990 8g] well-made, good sort: half-brother to several winners, notably top-class middle-distance colt Kalaglow (by Kalamoun) and useful Irish 7f and 1¼m winner Glowing Embers (by Nebbiolo): dam, winning stayer, raced and produced in error as Aglow: showed nothing in maiden at Yarmouth in June: moved moderately down: sold to join T. Kersey 1,650 gns Doncaster August Sales. *C. E. Brittain.* —

GLOWING STAR 4 gr.c. Kalaglow 132–Freddy My Love (Thatch (USA) 136) [1989 8s³ 9s⁴ 10m³ 10m* 12g⁵ 9m⁴ 10d⁵ 9g⁴ 11g³ 12s 10d⁴ 1990 12g* 10m³ 14m* 12m³ 14f⁴ 14g⁶] third foal: dam, won 3 times in Italy, is half-sister to very smart 1m to 1½m winner Free Guest and good Italian middle-distance filly Fresh: successful in minor events at Tipperary in May and Leopardstown (odds on) in June: very good third to Batshoof in Tattersalls EBF Rogers Gold Cup at the Curragh in between: stayed on, never a threat, when sixth in Irish St Leger at last-named: stays 1¾m. *Joseph M. Canty, Ireland.* **107**

GLOWLAMP (IRE) 2 b.f. (Mar 8) Glow (USA)–Astania (GER) (Arratos (FR)) [1990 7f⁴ 7m² 7f² 9m* 7.3s³ 8v] IR 54,000Y: big filly: quite good mover: closely related to temperamental 10.2f and 1½m winner Northants and winning hurdler Eskimo Mite (both by Northern Baby) and half-sister to 2 winners by Naskra: dam, Irish 13f winner, is half-sister to dam of Alpenkonig, leading German middle-distance colt: sire 7f to 9f winner: fairly useful filly: made all in 4-runner maiden at Wolverhampton in October: around 4 lengths third of 6 to Shaima in listed event at Newbury: well beaten in Premio Dormello at Milan in November: will be suited by 1¼m. *B. Hanbury.* **93**

GLOW OF SUMMER 2 b.f. (Mar 25) Glow (USA)–Summer Madness 88 (Silly Season 127) [1990 7f 7d] 8,200F, 14,500Y: half-sister to several winners, including 1987 2-y-o 5f winner Favourite Girl (by Mummy's Pet): dam won at up to 1m: one-paced seventh of 18 in maiden auction at Goodwood in October, second outing: will stay 1m: may improve again. *M. Bell.* **50 p**

GO AND GO 3 ch.c. Be My Guest (USA) 126–Irish Edition (USA) (Alleged (USA) 138) [1989 6g⁶ 7g* 7m* 7g a8.5g* a8.5f 1990 8m* 10m⁴ a12f* a10f a10f a9f³] **?**

The Belmont Stakes, final leg of the American triple crown, has produced some of the most memorable moments in post-war racing history, including the thrilling battle between Affirmed and Alydar in 1978 and Secretariat's thirty-one-length victory in 1973, the most impressive classic win of modern times. Go And Go's victory in the one hundred and twenty-second running earned him a place in Belmont Stakes history as the first European-trained winner of the race, indeed of any of the races that comprise the American triple crown. European challengers for the classic races in North America, all of which are run on dirt, are a rarity. British-trained Bold Arrangement finished second to Ferdinand in the Kentucky Derby in 1986, and French-trained Le Voyageur finished third to Easy Goer and Sunday Silence in the 1989 Belmont—but Go And Go's presence in the Belmont line-up was still considered a curiosity. He wasn't unknown to the Americans, however. He had been sent across the Atlantic twice as a two-year-old, gaining a hard-fought victory in the Laurel Futurity in October and finishing eighth of twelve in the Breeders' Cup Juvenile at Gulfstream Park the following month. Both races were on dirt, the Laurel Futurity having been transferred after heavy rain had made Laurel's turf course unraceable. Go And Go's form as a two-year-old in Ireland, where he won two of his four races, earned him fifth place in the Irish Classification. He was the only two-year-old to appear in the International Classification in Europe (assessed at 110, joint fiftieth) and in North America's Experimental Free Handicap (assessed at 115, joint twenty-third in the division for colts and geldings, joint thirty-seventh overall). The final decision to send Go And Go for the Belmont was taken after he managed only fourth, following a successful reappearance in a listed event at Phoenix Park, in the Derrinstown Stud EBF Derby Trial at Leopards- town. According to his trainer, Go And Go would almost certainly have been aimed at the Ever Ready Derby if he'd won at Leopardstown.

Most of the top European trainers favour transporting their trans-atlantic challengers as late as possible nowadays and Go And Go arrived in New York from Ireland only three days before the Belmont. He started fourth favourite in a field of nine and, wearing a visor for the first time, trounced the home-trained opposition, quickening clear in tremendous style in the final furlong to win by eight and a quarter lengths, a staggering margin in a top race. Thirty Six Red and Baron de Vaux came second and third after disputing the lead for a long way; the short-priced favourite Unbridled was a disappointing fourth. Unbridled's performance contrasted sharply with those he'd recorded in the Kentucky Derby and the Preakness Stakes, the first two legs of the triple crown; Unbridled won at Churchill Downs and finished second at Pimlico where the Derby runner-up Summer Squall (who didn't contest the Belmont) turned the tables on him. Unbridled raced on the drug lasix in the Kentucky Derby and the Preakness but wasn't allowed to do so in New York where the racing authorities operate a ban on medication at the time of racing. Unbridled was unfairly dismissed in some quarters after the Belmont as a horse dependent on medication to produce his best form. Unbridled and Go And Go—unplaced in the Travers Stakes at Saratoga on a further visit to the States in the interim—met again at Belmont Park almost five months later in the world's most valuable race the Breeders' Cup Classic. Unbridled, beaten in two of his three races since the Belmont, restored his early-season reputation with a victory in the Breeders' Cup Classic from British-trained Ibn Bey and Thirty Six Red. Go And Go trailed home last of fourteen after being struck into in the first part of the race which turned out to be his last for his Irish stable. Go And Go was afterwards transferred permanently to the United States to be trained by D. Wayne Lukas for whom he finished a very

Belmont Stakes, Belmont Park—Irish-trained Go And Go gains an historic victory in the last leg of the American triple crown

Moyglare Stud's "Go And Go"

close third in the nine-furlong Native Diver Handicap at Hollywood Park in early-December on his first appearance.

	Be My Guest (USA) (ch 1974)	Northern Dancer (b 1961)	Nearctic
			Natalma
		What A Treat (b 1962)	Tudor Minstrel
Go And Go (ch.c. 1987)			Rare Treat
	Irish Edition (USA) (b 1980)	Alleged (b 1974)	Hoist The Flag
			Princess Pout
		Grenzen (ch 1975)	Grenfall
			My Poly

Go And Go's sire and dam were both bred in North America and raced in Europe where they remained for stud. The Northern Dancer stallion Be My Guest was a high-class miler but some of his best progeny have been suited by longer distances, including the Irish and French Derby winner Assert and, in the most recent season, the Geoffrey Freer Stakes winner Charmer; Go And Go stays a mile and a half well. Go And Go's dam Irish Edition gained her only victory over nine and a half furlongs in a fillies' maiden at Dundalk. She is a daughter of the Kentucky Oaks runner-up Grenzen who won stakes races on turf and dirt from six to nine furlongs. Go and Go is Irish Edition's second foal, following the Kris colt Latest Release who is also a winner in the States; her third foal Complex Situation (by King's Lake) was also in training there in the latest season. *D. K. Weld, Ireland.*

GO BOY GO 3 b.g. All Systems Go 119–Chubby Ears (Burglar 128) [1989 5s⁵ 5s² 5m 1990 a10g⁵ 7m 5f 6m] leggy, quite good-topped gelding: plating-class maiden: below form in handicaps and sellers as 3-y-o: should stay beyond 5f: blinkered last 3 outings: sold 1,650 gns Ascot June Sales. *K. M. Brassey.* —

GO BUY BAILEY'S 3 b.g. Rousillon (USA) 133–Geoffrey's Sister 102 (Sparkler 130) [1989 8.2g² 8m 8g* 7d⁴ 1990 8.2f 8m 9m 9m³ 12m] small gelding: modest **70**

handicapper: form as 3-y-o only when fair third at Hamilton, pushed along some way out then staying on well: should be suited by further than 9f: best form on an easy surface. *M. Johnston.*

GOD BLESS YOU 3 b.c. Vision (USA)–Maestrette 77 (Manado 130) [1989 7g 1990 8.2s* 10v³ 9m⁵ 10.6s 10d* 10.6g 10.2g 10m 10.6v³ 10d] lengthy, sparely-made colt: modest handicapper: won at Hamilton (maiden, edged right) in April and Beverley in June: stays 1¼m: yet to race on firm going, acts on any other: refused to race eighth (blinkered) and final starts, and isn't one to trust. *S. G. Norton.* **76 §**

GODLY LIGHT (FR) 4 b.f. Vayrann 133–Western Goddess 95 (Red God 128§) [1989 NR 1990 a8g a6g⁶ 8.3g³] half-sister to useful 5f to 1m winner Hollywood Party (by Be My Guest) and French 1m winner Western Flag (by Bustino): dam, winning Irish sprinter, is half-sister to high-class miler Mr Fluorocarbon: staying-on third of 17 in seller at Windsor in August: slowly away in maidens early in year. *P. F. I. Cole.* **47**

GODMAIDFLOWERS (IRE) 2 gr.f. (Apr 28) Godswalk (USA) 130–Fresh As A Daisy (Stanford 121§) [1990 6m 6f⁶ 7f⁵] 7,000Y, 2,400 2-y-o: lengthy filly: third foal: half-sister to 7f winner D'Altagnan (by Dalsaan): dam lightly raced: plating-class maiden: stayed 7f: dead. *S. Dow.* **52**

GODOUNOV 7 b.g. Godswalk (USA) 130–Grilse Run 94 (Stupendous) [1989 NR 1990 12m⁶] close-coupled gelding: poor maiden: barely stays 1½m: acts on hard going: blinkered and visored twice: highly strung. *T. Fairhurst.*

GODSALL 3 gr.f. Godswalk (USA) 130–Sallail (Sallust 134) [1989 5f 5m² 5m⁴ 6m 5f³ 7m⁶ 7m 5.1m³ 6f 1990 6g 7v] leggy, sparely-made filly: poor form in varied races at 2 yrs, none at 3 yrs: effective at 5f and seems to stay 7f: bandaged on re-appearance: has ducked markedly under pressure, and seems bit temperamental. *Mrs N. Macauley.*

GODSCHARM (IRE) 2 b.f. (Mar 8) Godswalk (USA) 130–Polynesian Charm (USA) (What A Pleasure (USA)) [1990 5f³ 5m² 5f* 5f 5d² 6m⁴ 5d⁵ 5m³ 6f² 7h 6m³ 6m 6m] 5,400Y: leggy filly: poor walker: moderate mover: half-sister to 1¼m winner August (by Sensitive Prince), 6f winner Tiger Trap (by Al Hattab) and several winners in USA: dam half-sister to smart 1969 American 2-y-o Clover Lane: quite modest performer: made all in early-season minor event at Beverley: inconsistent afterwards: stays 6f: tends to wander, but is a suitable mount for a claimer. *M. Brittain.* **66**

GODS GIFT 2 b.f. (Feb 21) Godswalk (USA) 130–Asturiana (Julio Mariner 127) [1990 a5g⁶ 5s a5g] 2,000Y: light-framed filly: first foal: dam, half-sister to Musidora winner Escorial, ran 4 times at 2 yrs: soundly beaten in varied events: apparently finished lame when bandaged behind final outing. *K. T. Ivory.* **—**

GODS LAW 9 gr.g. Godswalk (USA) 130–Fluently (Ragusa 137) [1989 12f⁵ 12m 12m⁴ 12.3m⁶ 12m* 15m³ 12g² 12m² 12m⁶ 12m² 12.3m 1990 12m² 12g⁴ 13.6d a12g⁵] leggy, good-topped gelding: plating-class handicapper: suited by 1½m and a sound surface: blinkered twice: often pulls hard: takes keen hold to post (bolted on re-appearance), and has been taken down early: winner over hurdles twice in September, but isn't one to trust implicitly. *Mrs G. R. Reveley.* **53**

GODSMINT 2 b.c. (Apr 10) Godswalk (USA) 130–What A Mint (Meadow Mint (USA)) [1990 7m 7g] workmanlike colt: fourth reported foal: half-brother to 3-y-o 7f winner Failand (by Kala Shikari): dam won at up to 1½m in Ireland and several times at up to 2½m over hurdles here: always behind in October maidens at Chepstow (slowly away) and Salisbury. *R. J. Holder.* **—**

GODS SOLUTION 9 g.rh. Godswalk (USA) 130–Campitello (Hornbeam 130) [1989 6d** 7d 7m⁴ 6f⁴ 7m⁴ 6f* 6f² 6f³ 6g 7m⁵ 6g 6f 1990 6m³ a6g 6m* 7m 6m² 6m 6g⁴ 6f 6d⁶] rangy horse: poor mover: quite modest handicapper: showed himself as good as ever when winning at Pontefract in April: stays 7f: not at his best on soft going, acts on any other: has worn blinkers, but not for long time: goes very well with forcing tactics on a turning track, and has won 7 times at Catterick. *T. D. Barron.* **63**

GO DUTCH (USA) 3 ch.c. Lyphard's Wish (FR) 124–Parema (USA) (Explodent (USA)) [1989 6m 6g 7g² 6g³ 6m⁵ 1990 a7g* a7g 8g² 7g² 7f³ 8f³ 7m*] leggy, sparely-made colt: fairly useful handicapper here: won at Southwell (maiden, made all) in March and Sandown in June: sent to D. Combs in USA and much improved, about 7¾ lengths behind Royal Academy in Breeders' Cup Mile at Belmont Park: stays at least 9f: acts on firm going: has run creditably when sweating and edgy. *C. R. Nelson.* **113 ?**

GO ELECTRIC 3 ch.g. Electric 126–Anadyomene 101 (Sea Hawk II 131) [1989 NR 1990 10m 12.2d⁵] 5,800F, 8,000Y: lengthy, good-topped gelding: closely related **—**

GOL

to quite modest 11.3f winner Watershed (by Blakeney) and half-brother to 2 other flat winners, including ungenuine 11f and 1½m winner Hello Benz (by Hello Gorgeous): dam 11f and 13f winner out of Cheveley Park winner Lalibela: soundly beaten in minor event and claimer in the summer. *M. H. Easterby.*

GO EXECUTIVE 2 b.g. (Apr 18) Sharpo 132–Staritsa (USA) (Alleged (USA) **75** 138) [1990 5d 6g2 6m*] IR 20,000Y: leggy, close-coupled gelding: keen walker: moderate mover: fourth foal: half-brother to temperamental 1987 2-y-o 5f winner Miss Caro Star (by Rusticaro): dam unraced daughter of very smart Roussalka, sister to Our Home and half-sister to Oh So Sharp: won maiden at Goodwood in August by a neck from Alqwani: swished tail under pressure second outing: looked to be progressing well, but not seen out again. *C. E. Brittain.*

GO FOR GLORY 3 b. or br.g. My Dad Tom (USA) 109–Ardtully Lass 64 (Cavo **—** Doro 124) [1989 6g6 6m 7g a6g a7g5 1990 8g 7.5g 8f] leggy, quite attractive gelding: good walker: poor maiden: should stay 7f: hung left on reappearance: sold 580 gns Doncaster November Sales. *J. J. O'Neill.*

GO FORUM 5 ch.g. Tumble Wind (USA)–Devine Lady (The Parson 119) [1989 **—** 12s 12m 12f 12m 11.5g3 14m3 12f3 12h5 14f5 14g2 14m2 13.3m a12g2 a12g 1990 11.1m 14m 11.7m 14g 14g 14g5] sturdy, good-bodied gelding: fair handicapper as 4-y-o: well below form in 1990: stays 1¾m: acts on firm going: blinkered once. *J. Sutcliffe.*

GO GO BOY 3 b.g. All Systems Go 119–Sandra's Sovereign (Workboy 123) [1989 **—** 5g 5f a6g 1990 a8g 10d a12g] probably of little account. *S. R. Bowring.*

GO GOTT 2 b.g. (Apr 23) All Systems Go 119–La Bird 61 (Le Johnstan 123) [1990 **—** 6g] third foal: dam won at 1m and 1¼m: backward in maiden at Ripon in June. *J. Balding.*

GO HOLIMARINE 3 gr.f. Taufan (USA) 119–Standing Ovation (Godswalk **58** (USA) 130) [1989 6g5 6g 5.1f5 7m* 7m5 8g4 7.3m 7g4 7g 1990 8f3 7m 7m6 6f] leggy filly: moderate walker and mover: plating-class performer: stayed 1m: acted on firm going: blinkered last 2 starts at 2 yrs: dead. *C. N. Williams.*

GOLAN HEIGHTS 3 b.g. Shirley Heights 130–Grimpola (GER) (Windwurf **100** (GER)) [1989 7g2 8.2g* 8m 1990 9g3 10.1g* 12s2 12m 14g3 12g5] good-bodied gelding: carries condition: has a rather round action: capable of useful form: won minor event at Windsor in April: easily best subsequent efforts when placed in listed race at Haydock and minor event (made most) at York: shapes like a stayer: acts on soft going: genuine. *H. R. A. Cecil.*

GOLD AISLING 2 gr.f. (May 10) Sonnen Gold 121–My Aisling 72 (John de **38** Coombe 122) [1990 8m 5f6 5m] second foal: dam disqualified 7f and 1¼m winner at 2 yrs: poor maiden: may well be suited by 6f. *R. J. Holder.*

GOLDBUSTER 5 b.h. Busted 134–Coryana 104 (Sassafras (FR) 135) [1989 NR **94** 1990 10.2f 10f 10.8m3 14f* 12d] good-topped, attractive horse: poor mover: half-brother to 3 winners, notably very smart miler Waajib (by Try My Best): dam Irish middle-distance performer: favourite, showed much improved form on first run in handicap when winning at Salisbury in May: tailed-off last of 7 in £22,400 Epsom handicap month later: will stay 2m: reared over in preliminaries on debut: hung left third and fourth starts. *G. Harwood.*

GOLD CITY (IRE) 2 b.g. (May 4) Red Sunset 120–God's Kiss (Godswalk (USA) **—** 130) [1990 5.3f4 7f 6m 7m] IR 3,200F, 5,600Y: neat gelding: third foal: dam Irish maiden: no show, including in sellers: 3 times visored: sold 950 gns Newmarket Autumn Sales. *R. Hannon.*

GOLD DIVER 3 ch.g. Main Reef 126–Ice Baby (Grundy 137) [1989 7g 7m 8f5 **54** 8.5f6 8.2s 1990 12d4 8g4 11f2 11m5 13.8d4] lengthy, dipped-backed gelding: plating-class maiden: stays 11f: acts on firm going, seems unsuited by a soft surface: blinkered last 4 starts and final one at 2 yrs. *M. W. Easterby.*

GOLD EMBLEM 2 b.f. (May 26) Tina's Pet 121–Bar Gold 80 (Lucky Brief 128) **46** [1990 6m3 6m3 7m3 8m 6m a7g] 2,100F, 5,000Y: angular filly: half-sister to several winners here and abroad, including fair 1985 2-y-o Lily Fogg (by Swing Easy) and stayer Gold Rifle (by Scottish Rifle): dam won twice at around 1¼m: modest plater: below best last 3 starts: should stay 1m. *Miss S. E. Hall.*

GOLDEN 3 ch.f. Don 128–Roll Up (Roll of Honour 130) [1989 NR 1990 10.6f4 **69** 12m3 12m 12.4f* 16f3 16m6 15d5 16g2] IR 3,000Y: angular, workmanlike filly: good walker: seventh foal: sister to Irish maiden Carriglegan Rose and half-sister to 3 winners, including 6f and 7f winner Reveille (by Ahonoora) and 6f (at 2 yrs) to 11.7f winner Up To Uncle (by Saher): dam won at 1½m and 2m in Ireland: modest

351

handicapper: won at Newcastle in July: stays 2m: seems to act on firm and dead going: consistent. *C. W. C. Elsey.*

GOLDEN ANCONA   7 ch.g. London Bells (CAN) 109–Golden Darling 86   **71**
(Darling Boy 124) [1989 6v2 7d 6g 6m3 6m4 6m 6m5 5.6g4 6s 6g5 6v6 6d4 1990 7f5
6v4 8g 8.2s 8f 7m5 7m a7g 8m 8m5 8d 7m 7m 8g4 7.6v5 a8g5] close-coupled,
lightly-made gelding: poor mover: modest handicapper: stays 1m: particularly well
suited by give in the ground: has worn blinkers and a visor, but better without:
usually gets behind. *M. Brittain.*

GOLDEN AWARD   2 b.f. (Mar 12) Last Tycoon 131–Golden Glint (Vitiges (FR)   **65**
132) [1990 6m 6g] 32,000Y: leggy filly: second foal: half-sister to 3-y-o Shining Spear
(by Commanche Run): dam lightly-raced half-sister to Main Reef and smart
middle-distance filly Moonlight Night: prominent to 2f out in minor event at
Goodwood in September, first and better effort: will be suited by 1m + . *M. R. Stoute.*

GOLDEN BEAU   8 b.g. Crimson Beau 124–Kantado 93 (Saulingo 122) [1989 8g   **64**
8d4 8m 9f6 8f 9f 8m2 8m6 8.2m 8f* 8m 7m3 8g2 8m 8s 8m5 8.2d 1990 a8g 8f6 8.2s
8m4 8f4 9f5 9g6 8m2 8g2 8m 8.2s4 8m* 8m2 8.2d 8g3 8d 8m 8v3 8d5 8m] sparely-
made, rather hollow-backed gelding: good mover: quite modest handicapper: won at
Ayr (same race for second successive year) in July: suited by about 1m: acts on any
going, except possibly hard: blinkered once: effective with or without visor:
excellent mount for inexperienced rider: has often sweated and got on edge. *M. P.
Naughton.*

GOLDEN BIRCH   2 gr.c. (Apr 20) Heights of Gold–Silver Birch 122 (Silver   **95 p**
Shark 129) [1990 5f3 7g 6m3 6m2 6g* 7g*] big, lengthy colt: has plenty of scope:
half-brother to 2 winners at up to 1m by High Top: dam stayed 1m: successful in
maiden (made all to win by 5 lengths) at Folkestone in October and mixed-aged
event (led 2f out and held on gamely from Cruachan) at Newmarket following
month: will stay 1m: progressing extremely well. *W. G. R. Wightman.*

GOLDEN CAP (USA)   2 ch.f. (Mar 31) Hagley (USA)–Mrs Hat (Sharpen Up   **70 p**
127) [1990 5f*] $37,000Y: sister to 1988 Irish 2-y-o 6f winner Plume Poppy and a
winner in Italy: dam winner at around 6f in North America, is granddaughter of Glad
Rags II: sire won over 1m: co-favourite but very green, won maiden at Wolverhampton in September by a neck from Negeen, disputing lead and running on well
under considerate ride: sure to improve. *P. F. I. Cole.*

GOLDEN DAFFODIL   3 gr.f. Jalmood (USA) 126–Katysue 98 (King's Leap 111)   **66 §**
[1989 NR 1990 10f* 11m 11.5g* 10f6 12.4f 10f2 12m 10m 10m4] 11,000Y: leggy,
workmanlike filly: poor mover: fifth foal: half-sister to fairly useful 1986 2-y-o 5f
winner Sinclair Lady (by Absalom), later temperamental, and 4-y-o 6f winner
Pattie's Grey (by Valiyar): dam won 5 times over 5f at 2 yrs: favourite, won seller at
Nottingham in May (bought in 10,000 gns) and claimer (odds on) at Yarmouth in
July: stays 11.5f: acts on firm going: set strong pace in blinkers eighth start: sold
7,000 gns Newmarket Autumn Sales: inconsistent and not one to rely on. *Mrs L.
Piggott.*

GOLDEN DARLING (USA)   3 ch.f. Slew O' Gold (USA)–Close Control (USA)   **55**
(Dunce) [1989 NR 1990 11.5g 10f3] rangy filly: half-sister to several winners in North
America, notably very smart 1982 2-y-o filly Sophisticated Girl (by Stop The Music):
dam minor 6f winner at 2 yrs: weak 7/1 and still green, close up over 1m when third
of 10 to Prince Hannibal in maiden at Brighton in June. *L. M. Cumani.*

GOLDEN DELLA   3 b.f. Glint of Gold 128–Shindella 104 (Furry Glen 121) [1989   **59**
7g 1990 12m6 12f6 12m3 14m 10m 9m4 8.2g* 9s 8.2v5 8v] leggy, workmanlike filly:
quite modest form: co-favourite, won claimer (claimed out of I. Balding's stable
£10,000) at Hamilton in September: stays 1½m: acts on good to firm ground, not
very soft: has joined D. Moffatt. *J. S. Wilson.*

GOLDEN DIVOT   3 b.g. Chief Singer 131–Action Belle (Auction Ring (USA)   **54**
123) [1989 NR 1990 10m 10m 10.2m2 12.4f 16f2] sturdy, attractive gelding: has
scope: moderate mover: second foal: half-brother to Holster (by Gorytus), plating-
class 5f and 6f winner at 2 yrs: dam sister to good 7f and 1m performer
Meis-El-Reem: form only when second in claimers at Doncaster (wandered under
pressure, claimed out of A. Stewart's stable £10,205) and Redcar (3-runner event,
behind wide-margin winner) in the summer: seems to stay 2m: worth a try in
blinkers or visor: sold 2,600 gns Doncaster October Sales. *Mrs G. R. Reveley.*

GOLDEN FLIGHT   3 ch.f. Remainder Man 126§–Wigeon 80 (Divine Gift 127)   **—**
[1989 5d6 5f6 5m2 7m3 6g 8.2d 7.5f6 8.2g 1990 6g 12g 12m5 6m6 10f 6g 9s] leggy,
plain filly: has a round action: poor maiden: stays 1½m: acts on good to firm going:

visored penultimate outing: sweating and bandaged off-hind on fourth: often edgy: sometimes hangs. *E. J. Alston.*

GOLDEN GENERAL 2 ch.c. (Apr 28) Blushing Scribe (USA) 107–Broken 55 Paws (Busted 134) [1990 5f⁵ 6m⁴ 7f³ 7f 7f 7f⁵ 8f] 5,000F: big, strong colt: has scope: second foal: dam never ran: plating-class maiden at best: should be suited by 1m: twice slowly away: sold 2,800 gns Ascot December Sales. *W. G. R. Wightman.*

GOLDEN GENERATION 4 b.g. Young Generation 129–Song of Gold 85 — (Song 132) [1989 10g 8m⁶ 7h² 6f 7.6f 1990 6f 8h 8g 11.7m 11.7m 10g 7m 8f] big, strong, good-topped gelding: very little form as 4-y-o, in seller final outing: retained by trainer 2,500 gns Newmarket Autumn Sales: headstrong, and has worn severe noseband. *B. R. Millman.*

GOLDEN GUNNER (IRE) 2 ch.g. (Feb 8) Mazaad 106–Sun Gift (Guillaume — Tell (USA) 121) [1990 7d⁵ a6g] IR 8,600F, 17,500Y: third foal: half-brother to 1989 2-y-o 6f winner Times Gift (by Burslem): dam unraced: well beaten in maidens at Yarmouth (showed a little promise when green) and Southwell. *M. H. Tompkins*

GOLDEN IMAGE 4 ch.f. Bustino 136–Kingston Rose (Tudor Music 131) [1989 — 8s⁴ 10g 8.2g⁴ 10m 12g 1990 18g⁶ 16f] sturdy filly: plating-class form at best: may prove best short of 2¼m: possibly needs give in the ground: ridden by 7-lb claimer and visored at 4 yrs: winning selling hurdler in February. *M. Dods.*

GOLDEN ISLE 6 b.h. Golden Fleece (USA) 133–Dunette (FR) 127 (Hard To 48 Beat 132) [1989 10f 1990 12f³ 14d a12g a11g 14g⁴ a16g a12g³] strong horse: carries plenty of condition: poor mover, with a round action: useful winner in 1987: showed he retains a little ability when in frame in handicap and claimer in second half of year: possibly better suited by 1¾m than 1½m: suited by an easy surface (probably not at best on very soft going): headstrong (ran too freely in blinkers second outing). *B. J. Curley.*

GOLDEN LOFT 3 b.f. Thatching 131–Often (Ballymore 123) [1989 7g⁴ 1990 69 a8g² a8g⁶ 7m 8d² 10v 8g² a8g] unfurnished filly: quite modest performer: should stay further than 1m: acts on dead going: has run well for 5-lb claimer: bandaged behind final start. *D. J. G. Murray-Smith.*

GOLDEN MADJAMBO 4 ch.c. Northern Tempest (USA) 120–Shercol 74 38 (Monseigneur (USA) 127) [1989 10.2g 12s 8.2m 12g 1990 12.5m⁶ 10.8m 12.5f² 10.8f⁴ 10s 14g³ 16.5m⁵] leggy, angular colt: poor maiden: stays 1¾m: acts on any going: sweating and on toes fourth and final outings: has pulled hard, and worn crossed noseband. *B. A. McMahon.*

GOLDEN MILL (USA) 3 b.f. Mr Prospector (USA)–Mill Queen 86 (Mill Reef 73 (USA) 141) [1989 NR 1990 8g 10f³ 12f*] good-topped filly: fourth foal: dam won over 7f and 9f: won 6-runner maiden at Folkestone in September: very reluctant at stalls and quickly pulled up (lame) on debut: will prove better at 1½m than 1¼m. *G. Harwood.*

GOLDEN MINTAGE (USA) 2 b.c. (Apr 27) The Minstrel (CAN) 135–Golden 102 Bowl (USA) 100 (Vaguely Noble 140) [1990 6g 7f³ 7m* 7g² 7d³ 10s] IR 25,000Y: closely related to a winner in USA by Be My Guest: dam 7f and 1½m winner, is daughter of outstanding filly Rose Bowl, a half-sister to Ile de Bourbon: won 10-runner maiden at Galway in July by 2½ lengths: placed afterwards in Reference Point EBF Tyros Stakes at the Curragh and Cartier Million (under 2 lengths third of 20 to Rinka Das) at Phoenix Park: well-beaten eighth of 9 in Criterium de Saint-Cloud final start: should stay beyond 7f: acts on good to firm and dead: blinkered last 2 starts: useful. *D. K. Weld, Ireland.*

GOLDEN ORCHY 2 b.g. (Mar 24) Uncle Pokey 116–Strath of Orchy 96 (Loch 55 nager 132) [1990 7.5d 6d⁴ 6g 7f] 6,000Y: workmanlike gelding: second reported foal: dam 2-y-o 6f winner: best effort fourth in claimer at Haydock in July: not knocked about after, in need of run final start: will stay 7f. *C. Tinkler.*

GOLDEN REVERIE (USA) 2 b.c. (Feb 28) Golden Act (USA)–Our Reverie 39 (USA) (J O Tobin (USA) 130) [1990 5m 6g 8.2s] sparely-made colt: first reported foal: dam stakes winner at up to 11f is half-sister to Sharrood, smart 1985 2-y-o 6f and 7.3f winner and later graded-stakes winner at up to 1¼m in USA, and daughter of very smart Angel Island: poor form in maidens and a claimer: should prove suited by 1m +: coltish first 2 starts, when trained by G. Harwood: hung left second outing. *M. D. Hammond.*

GOLDEN SABRE 4 b.c. Sayf El Arab (USA) 127–Bohemian Rhapsody 86 (On 42 Your Mark 125) [1989 6s 6g⁴ 5.8m³ 6m⁶ 7f 7f 7f⁶ 7m 6f³ 7m³ 6g 1990 5g 7f 6g⁴ 7m 6d⁵ 6m⁴ 6m] small colt: has a quick action: poor maiden: suited by 6f: acts on firm and dead going: blinkered final outing, visored last 3 at 3 yrs: sold 1,450 gns Ascot September Sales. *J. L. Spearing.*

GOLDEN SCISSORS   4 gr.f. Kalaglow 132–Hide Out (Habitat 134) [1989   52
12.2m⁵ 12h⁵ 11.7m² 1990 14.6f⁴ 16.2m* 14.8m 14.8f 17.6m 16f] lengthy, angular filly: won maiden at Beverley in March despite hanging right under pressure: well beaten in handicaps after: stays 2m: acts on firm going: wore small bandages behind fifth outing: active type, takes keen hold: won 3 novice hurdles in autumn. *M. R. Channon.*

GOLDEN SUNRISE   2 ch.c. (Apr 3) On Your Mark 125–Seraphino (Formidable   39
(USA) 125) [1990 5f 5g 6g] IR 3,400F, IR 3,000Y, 3,000 2-y-o: angular, workman-like colt: poor walker: first foal: dam ran once: poor form in sellers and a maiden: blinkered, sweating profusely and very edgy when running badly final outing. *P. A. Blockley.*

GOLDEN SWALLOW   4 ch.f. Creetown 123–Polysee (Polyfoto 124) [1989 NR   —
1990 10.2f 9f 8.5d 8f] leggy, workmanlike filly: moderate mover: seventh living foal: half-sister to 1m to 10.6f winner Seven Swallows (by Radetzky): dam ran once: well beaten, including in selling company: has sweated. *M. J. Camacho.*

GOLDEN TOPAZ   6 br.h. African Sky 124–Lochboisdale 76 (Saritamer (USA)   —
130) [1989 NR 1990 9s] leggy horse: of little account: has worn blinkers and visor: gave trouble at stalls only start at 6 yrs. *J. Parkes.*

GOLDEN TORQUE   3 br.g. Taufan (USA) 119–Brightelmstone 105 (Prince   74
Regent (FR) 129) [1989 5m³ 6m⁵ 6g* 6d⁴ 6s 8s* 7g⁶ 7d⁶ 1990 9.1m* 9m 8f 9m² 9m 11m 10m] strong, close-coupled gelding: good walker: modest performer: won claimer (claimed out of Mrs J. Ramsden's stable £24,000) at Newcastle in March: well-backed favourite, easily best effort in handicaps when good second at Hamilton: stays 9f: acts on good to firm ground and soft: effective with or without a visor: has looked an awkward ride. *R. Bastiman.*

GOLDEN TREASURY (USA)   3 b.f. Lyphard (USA) 132–Belle Pensee (USA)   75
(Ribot 142) [1989 7g 1990 8m² 10g⁴ 10f³ 12.2d³ 12.2m* 12h³ 11.5m⁶ 12m] strong, sturdy filly: has a rather round action: modest performer: won maiden at Catterick in July: ran moderately in handicaps afterwards, slowly away and edging left closing stages for 7-lb claimer penultimate start: should stay beyond 1½m: acts on firm going. *H. R. A. Cecil.*

GOLDEN TUNE   2 b.g. (Apr 2) Song 132–Mrs Webb (Sonnen Gold 121) [1990   42
7.5f 7f 7f] 9,000Y: lengthy, good-quartered gelding: third foal: half-brother to 3-y-o Whitewebb (by Carwhite): dam lightly raced and well beaten at 2 yrs: poor form in varied auction events. *C. Tinkler.*

GOLDEN VINTAGE   4 ch.g. Glint of Gold 128–Boissiere (High Top 131) [1989   —
8d 10g⁵ 10g 11.7m³ 12g 1990 a11g] quite modest maiden at best: tailed-off last in Southwell handicap in September: winner of 2 selling hurdles later in month: stays 11.7f. *S. Dow.*

GOLD FLAIR   4 ch.f. Tap On Wood 130–Suemette (Danseur 134) [1989 10s⁵   68
16.5g⁴ 1990 a12g³] big, leggy filly: fairly useful maiden at best, but is very lightly raced: stays 1½m: best form on good going: sweating and edgy final start at 3 yrs: has looked less than an ideal mount for amateur. *P. F. I. Cole.*

GOLD FUTURES (IRE)   2 b.c. (Feb 18) Fayruz 116–Fair Chance (Young   88
Emperor 133) [1990 5f* 5m² 5g² 5g³ 5m⁶] IR 14,000Y: close-coupled colt: scratchy mover: sixth foal: half-brother to Irish 3-y-o 1m winner Burella (by Burslem) and a winner in Belgium: dam Irish 2-y-o 5f and 7f winner: fair performer: won maiden auction at Wolverhampton in April: third of 7 to Line Engaged in Norfolk Stakes at Royal Ascot: blinkered, never dangerous in listed event at Newmarket final start: best form on good ground. *W. A. O'Gorman.*

GOLD LAW (IRE)   2 b.c. (Apr 27) Law Society (USA) 130–Golden Oriole (USA)   73 p
(Northern Dancer) [1990 8m² 8f*] IR 300,000Y: second foal: brother to Irish 3-y-o Sunny Morning: dam Irish 6f winner, is sister to El Gran Senor and Try My Best: favourite, won maiden at Wolverhampton in September by a neck from Someone Brave, leading 3f out: will be suited by 1¼m: will improve. *P. F. I. Cole.*

GOLDLINE SEEKER   2 b.c. (Feb 12) Damister (USA) 123–Bottom Line 90   72
(Double Jump 131) [1990 8.2d 10.2s³] quite attractive colt: seventh foal: half-brother to several winners here and abroad, including useful 1988 1½m winner Knight Line Dancer (by Caerleon), later better in Italy, and fairly useful 1983 2-y-o 5f winner Red Line Fever (by Bay Express): dam won from 1m to 1½m: third of 14, keeping on despite drifting left, to Knifebox in minor event at Doncaster in November: slowly away on debut: stays 1¼m. *M. A. Jarvis.*

GOLDMINE (DEN) 2 b.c. (Mar 21) Indian King (USA) 128–Pithead 70 (High — Top 131) [1990 6m 6g] tall colt: brother to fair 5f to 7.5f winner Eastern Ember and half-brother to 2 winners, including French 1½m winner What A Paper (by What A Guest): dam Irish 1½m winner also successful over hurdles, is sister to smart Miner's Lamp: bit backward, behind in maiden at Salisbury (bandaged) and minor event at Windsor in August. *C. C. Elsey.*

GOLD MINORIES 6 b.h. Baptism 119–Viva La Weavers (Weavers' Hall 122) 90 d [1989 7f 6f 6f 7f* 7.6f* 7m⁵ 1990 10m 9.2g 7.6f² 7.6g 6s a7g a7g] rather lightly-made, close-coupled horse: moderate mover: fairly useful handicapper at best: well beaten last 4 outings, including in seller: best at around 7f: suited by top-of-the-ground: has run well for apprentice and when sweating: well served by forcing tactics: has won 5 times at Lingfield: sold out of G. Harwood's stable 4,400 gns Newmarket Autumn Sales after fourth start. *J. Parkes.*

GOLD MINSTREL (IRE) 2 ch.c. (Mar 14) Fayruz 116–Pass No Problem (Pas — de Seul 133) [1990 5.8m a6g 6m 8.2g] 1,700Y, 2,000 2-y-o: small colt: poor mover: first foal: dam unraced: of little account. *Miss A. L. M. King.*

GOLD NOSTALGIA 3 ch.f. Glint of Gold 128–Crepellora (Crepello 136) [1989 — 7g³ 7m* 8g⁵ 8m⁶ 1990 8m 10m 12m 11.5g 8g] good-bodied filly: fair form at 2 yrs, none in minor events, listed race and handicap in autumn of 1990: should stay 1½m: sweating third outing: blinkered fourth: retained by trainer 62,000 gns Ascot February Sales: sold 9,800 gns Newmarket December Sales. *P. A. Kelleway.*

GOLD PROSPECT 8 b.g. Wolverlife 115–Golden Darling 86 (Darling Boy 124) 93 d [1989 7d 8s 8.2g³ 1990 8.2s 8g³ 8.2s² 7.6f⁵ 8.3m⁴ 8m⁶ 7.2g⁵ 8m 8d] lengthy gelding: often impresses in appearance: moderate mover: fair handicapper: best at 7f to 1m: suited by an easy surface: ran moderately when edgy: best with extreme waiting tactics. *G. B. Balding.*

GOLD STRATA 4 b.g. Gold Song 112–French Strata (USA) 76 (Permian (USA)) — [1989 12d⁵ 1990 a6g⁵] strong, sturdy gelding: little sign of ability in maidens and handicap: pulled hard when visored at 3 yrs: sold 1,000 gns Ascot April Sales. *J. White.*

GOLDSTREAM (USA) 3 b.c. Slew O' Gold (USA)–Someway Somehow (USA) — (What Luck (USA)) [1989 NR 1990 10.1m 10.1m⁵ 10m 11.7g 10.6d] $190,000Y: rangy colt: moderate mover: fifth foal: half-brother to a winner at around 6f in USA by Quiet Fling and to modest maiden Cape Pigeon (by Storm Bird): dam, sister to 1983 champion older mare Ambassador of Luck, won 3 times in USA, including minor 6f stakes event: well-beaten fifth of 23 in minor event at Windsor in June: faced stiffish tasks in handicaps: sweating fourth start: tends to hang: sold 3,200 gns Newmarket Autumn Sales. *J. R. Fanshawe.*

GOLD TOUCH 7 b.g. Strong Gale 116–Nordic Maid 84 (Vent du Nord) [1989 NR — 1990 10h³] rangy, rather angular gelding: extremely lightly raced: sold out of P. Makin's stable 3,100 gns Ascot May Sales before only outing at 7 yrs. *S. Dow.*

GOLD TRUST 3 b.c. Bellypha 130–Abbey (FR) (Jim French (USA)) [1989 NR — 1990 10.2s] 20,000F, 52,000Y: rangy colt with scope: half-brother to several winners in France, all at 1m or more: dam French 10.5f winner, is half-sister to Ashmore: 50/1 and burly, last of 17 in competitive minor event at Doncaster in November. *P. J. Makin.*

GOLDVEIN (SWE) 2 b.g. (Mar 5) Superlative 118–Follow Me Follow 92 — (Wollow 132) [1990 6g] 18,500F, 25,000Y: neat, good-quartered gelding: fourth foal: half-brother to 3-y-o Blow A Kiss (by Auction Ring): dam 5f winner at 2 yrs from family of Honeyblest: blinkered, prominent to halfway, giving impression needed race, in maiden at Newcastle in October. *W. A. O'Gorman.*

GOLFER'S SUNRISE 5 b.g. Red Sunset 120–Miss Stradavinsky (Auction — Ring (USA) 123) [1989 12.5g² 9f⁴ 14m⁶ 8f 12.5f 1990 a11g a14g 12.3d] workmanlike gelding: poor maiden: stays 12.5f: acts on firm going: sometimes blinkered: has carried head high: winning selling hurdler in March. *K. White.*

GOMARLOW 3 gr.c. Belfort (FR) 89–Tringa (GER) (Kaiseradler) [1989 6g 7g² 68 1990 7m 6m⁴ 7m⁴ 8g⁴ 10s 10g 7d] lengthy, rather angular colt: quite modest on most form: second in maiden at Newmarket at 2 yrs, easily best effort: stays 1m: visored (carried head high) third start: not one to trust implicitly. *D. Morley.*

GONDO 3 br.g. Mansingh (USA) 120–Secret Valentine 71 (Wollow 132) [1989 5m 63 7g 5.1f 8g 6s² a6g⁴ 1990 7d a7g⁴ 7m 6d 7v³ 6d 6d³ a6g a6g* a7g a6g⁵] compact gelding: has a quick action: quite modest performer: sweating, always prominent when winning claimer (claimed out of M. Ryan's stable £4,100) at Southwell in

November: best efforts at 6f: acts on soft going: visored sixth to eighth starts. *E. J. Alston.*

GONE SAVAGE 2 b.c. (Mar 9) Nomination 125–Trwyn Cilan 89 (Import 127) **85**
[1990 5g² 5d² 5m* 5g] 23,000Y: strong, good-bodied colt: carries condition: has scope: good walker: second foal: closely related to useful 3-y-o 5f winner Rivers Rhapsody (by Dominion): dam best at 5f: favourite, won maiden at Lingfield very easily by 2½ lengths: ran poorly in Norfolk Stakes at Royal Ascot later in June, and not seen out again: speedy: acts on good to firm ground and dead. *P. F. I. Cole.*

GO NOBLEY 4 b.g. Gorytus (USA) 132–Noblanna (USA) 85 (Vaguely Noble 140) —
[1989 10f 12m 10.1g 1990 a16g] medium-sized, lengthy gelding: well beaten on flat: easy winner of 4 novice hurdles on all-weather in 1989/90. *T. Thomson Jones.*

GOODBYE MR MARKS (IRE) 2 b.c. (Apr 30) On Your Mark 125–Ciao **59**
(Mandamus 120) [1990 6m⁵ 7g a6g²] IR 4,500F, 2,800Y, 3,000 2-y-o: workmanlike colt: half-brother to 2 winners, including 1983 Irish 2-y-o 6f winner Flingamus (by Imperial Fling): dam Irish 5f winner: easily best effort second of 9, quickening turn and keeping on well, in seller at Southwell in August. *N. Bycroft.*

GOODFELLOWS LOT 3 br.g. Blazing Saddles (AUS)–Just Kidding (USA) **60**
(Jester) [1989 6g⁴ 5d³ 1990 5g³ a5g³ 5m 5g 5f 5d] good-quartered gelding: quite modest maiden: below form in handicaps last 4 starts: should stay 6f: acts on dead going: sold 1,200 gns Doncaster November Sales. *W. W. Haigh.*

GOOD FOR A LOAN 3 b.c. Daring March 116–Game For A Laugh 72 **75**
(Martinmas 128) [1989 NR 1990 10.1g 8g⁵ 9g 8.2g⁵ 7f 11.5m² 12g⁵ 10d] well-made, good sort: moderate walker and mover: first foal: dam 7f and 7.6f winner out of half-sister to very smart sprinter Great Bear: modest maiden: ran poorly in apprentice handicap final start: gives impression may prove best with waiting tactics in strongly-run race at 1¼m: acts on good to firm ground, possibly not on dead: sold to join R. Lee 16,000 gns Newmarket Autumn Sales. *A. C. Stewart.*

GOOD FOR THE ROSES 4 b.g. Kampala 120–Alleyn (Alcide 136) [1989 10g **46**
8.2f 7m 7m² 7m 8.2f³ a8g² 1990 8g 8m⁶ 10g⁴ a8g⁵ a8g³] leggy gelding: has a round action: poor maiden: stays 1¼m: acts on firm ground: tended to carry head high second start: trained until after fourth one by G. Pritchard-Gordon. *M. McCormack.*

GOOD GRACE 3 b.f. Longleat (USA) 109–Shaky Puddin (Ragstone 128) [1989 —
NR 1990 12f 10f 16.2d⁶ 10f] leggy, workmanlike filly: sixth foal: sister to modest 1987 2-y-o plater Hidden Flame: dam poor maiden: little promise, including in seller and amateurs handicap: trained first 3 starts by C. Cyzer. *P. J. Hobbs.*

GOOD HAND (USA) 4 ch.g. Northjet 136–Ribonette (USA) (Ribot 142) [1989 **84**
10.2f 12f³ 13.6f² 16.2g* 16f² 17.6d² 16m⁵ 1990 16f* 18.4d⁴ 18m* 20m⁴ 20.4m* 17.4d⁶ 16.2s 18d] close-coupled, sparely-made gelding: fair handicapper: won at Ripon in April, Doncaster in May and Ayr (odds on, slowly-run 3-runner event) in July: a thorough stayer: acts on firm and dead going (probably unsuited by soft): blinkered on final outing and 3 times at 3 yrs: probably best on a galloping track: usually soon off bridle, and isn't the easiest of rides. *J. W. Watts.*

GOOD HOLIDAYS 4 b.f. Good Times (ITY)–Mistress Bowen (Owen Anthony —
102) [1989 7.6m 5m 5m 5m 5m 7.6m 6g 1990 a8g] rather sparely-made filly: has a long stride: no longer of much account: visored last 2 outings at 3 yrs: reluctant to go down final one. *D. Burchell.*

GOOD IMPRESSION 2 b.c. (Mar 31) Blushing Scribe (USA) 107–Derring —
Venture (Camden Town 125) [1990 7m 6m 8.2g a7g] 7,800Y: neat colt: third foal (all by Blushing Scribe): dam last on only start, at 2 yrs: soundly beaten, including in sellers. *R. Champion.*

GOOD MEDICINE 5 b.g. Star Appeal 133–Jacoletta 74 (Artaius (USA) 129) —
[1989 12m 14m 11g 12g³ a14g³ a12g³ a16g 1990 a11g a12g] workmanlike gelding: poor performer: best at up to 1½m: possibly unsuited by soft going, acts on any other: blinkered once, often visored: sold out of P. Feilden's stable 5,700 gns Ascot April Sales after first outing: inconsistent. *D. Burchell.*

GOOD POLICY (IRE) 2 b.f. (Mar 22) Thatching 131–Good To Follow 82 **76**
(Wollow 132) [1990 6m⁵ 6g⁶ 8m² 7m² 8.2m*] leggy, good-quartered filly: fifth foal: half-sister to very smart 1989 French 10.5f and 13.5f winner Borromini (by Henbit) and middle-distance handicapper Vintage (by Noalcoholic): dam 7f winner, is half-sister to good sprinter Sayyaf: made all in minor event at Nottingham in September, beating Mac's Princess 2 lengths: better suited by 1m than shorter. *P. T. Walwyn.*

GOOD PROFILE (USA) 2 b.c. (Mar 10) Liloy (FR) 124–I Sparkle (USA) **74 p**
(Gleaming (USA)) [1990 6d⁵ 7d²] angular colt: half-brother to several minor

winners in USA: dam never ran: ½-length second of 11, keeping on strongly, to Sunny Davis in maiden at Edinburgh in October: green and swerved left start on debut: will be suited by 1m: likely to improve again. *S. G. Norton.*

GOODREDA 3 b.f. Good Times (ITY)–Gundreda 93 (Gunner B 126) [1989 6m⁶ — 8g 5d⁴ 7d⁴ a7g 1990 8.2g] rather unfurnished filly: plating-class maiden: facing stiff task, pulled too hard in handicap in June: should stay 1m: needs to settle. *C. E. Brittain.*

GOOD SESSION 3 ch.g. Milk of The Barley 115–Rapid Rhythm 63 (Free State — 125) [1989 NR 1990 8g 10m⁵ 9g 12m 12d] 6,000 2-y-o: rather leggy, close-coupled gelding: has round action: first foal: dam placed over 5f at 2 yrs, her only season to race: no show, in selling handicaps last 2 starts: gets on toes. *A. W. Potts.*

GOOD SKILLS 3 b.f. Bustino 136–Gunner's Belle 67 (Gunner B 126) [1989 7m — 7m⁶ 1990 10m a8g] leggy filly: plating-class maiden: backward at 3 yrs, weakening rapidly 2f out in 1m handicap in June: bred to stay 1½m, but pulls hard: sold 2,500 gns Newmarket Autumn Sales. *G. A. Pritchard-Gordon.*

GOOD SPARK 4 b. or br.g. Good Times (ITY)–Bright Spark 65 (White Fire III) — [1989 6v 7v? 7g³ 7s⁵ 12t⁶ 12f* 12f³ 9.5f² 8.5g 11g⁵ 12g² 1990 9m 12m] ex-Irish gelding: half-brother to winners in Belgium and Norway: dam poor half-sister to smart animals Ovaltine and Guillotina: made all in maiden at Tramore as 3-y-o: well beaten in amateur events in 1990: stays 1½m: acts on any going: often blinkered, but wasn't when successful: good mount for apprentice: quite useful hurdler as juvenile. *J. Akehurst.*

GOOD TIME BOY 2 b.c. (Mar 5) Good Times (ITY)–Galetzky 86 (Radetzky 69 123) [1990 5m³ 5s* 5m 5m⁴ 6g⁵] 2,200Y: lengthy, rather angular colt: second foal: half-brother to poor 1989 3-y-o Kelly's Bid (by Pitskelly): dam won twice at 1m and stayed 1¼m: quite modest performer: apprentice ridden, won maiden at Hamilton in April: ran well last 2 starts, in summer: will stay 7f: sold 1,400 gns Doncaster November Sales. *M. Brittain.*

GOODY FOUR SHOES 2 gr.f. (May 23) Blazing Saddles (AUS)–Bronzamer 86 67 (Saritamer (USA) 132) [1990 5m⁵ 5m* 5m 6d⁶ 5s⁶] 1,050F: compact filly: third reported foal: dam 6f and 1m winner: made all in claimer at Edinburgh in September, beating Caerulia by 5 lengths: ran well in nursery at Newmarket next start: should stay 6f: easily best efforts on a sound surface: withdrawn lame intended debut. *W. W. Haigh.*

GOOFALIK (USA) 3 b.c. Lyphard (USA) 132–Alik 113 (Targowice (USA) 130) 114 [1989 9g² 7s² 8d² 1990 8g* 10g² 10d⁵ 10g² 10g* 8v⁶] fifth foal: closely related to French 4-y-o maiden Alypheor (by Lypheor) and half-brother to French 1m winner Auberge Rouge and 9f winner Alyka (both by Riverman): dam French 1m winner out of sister to dam of Irish River: won minor event at Maisons-Laffitte in March and listed race at Longchamp in October: second in La Coupe de Maisons-Laffitte: stays 1¼m: very useful and consistent. *Mme C. Head, France.*

GO ON SMILE (USA) 4 ch.c. Diesis 133–Key Tothe Minstrel (USA) 108 (The 80 Minstrel (CAN) 135) [1989 8m⁴ 8f 10f⁴ 8f* 8f⁶ 8g 1990 8f3 8f 8m* 9f3 9g4 8f] small, strong, good-topped colt: poor mover: looking really well, won amateurs race at Warwick in May: swishing tail in paddock, tailed off in Royal Hunt Cup (Handicap) at Royal Ascot final outing: best at around 1m: acts on firm going: mulish at stalls fifth start. *A. A. Scott.*

GO ON THE GRAIN 3 ch.g. Remainder Man 126§–Femme Fatale 67 (King's — Leap 111) [1989 7m 8.2d 8s 8.2g 1990 12g 11g⁵ 16.5m⁶] lengthy, workmanlike gelding: poor form at 2 yrs: none in amateurs events in 1990, carrying 34 lb overweight on first occasion: dead. *J. S. Wilson.*

GO PATHFINDER 3 b.g. Swing Easy (USA) 126–Pollinella 108 (Charlottown 44 127) [1989 6g a8g 1990 a6g 8f⁶ 10m 9g² 8m] leggy, workmanlike gelding: poor maiden: sweating, wandered and seemed none too keen when second in handicap at Wolverhampton in June: faced stiff task following month: stays 9f: acts on firm ground: blinkered last 2 outings: usually slowly away. *J. Sutcliffe.*

GO RABALL GO 4 br.g. All Systems Go 119–Rabeeb 64 (Home Guard (USA) ? 129) [1989 10g 7g a7g 1990 a10g a8g 8f] small, leggy gelding: modest winner at 2 yrs: no subsequent form in Britain: suited by 7f: acts on firm and dead going: visored second outing: tends to flash tail: sold 2,300 gns Doncaster March Sales: since winner in Sweden. *C. N. Allen.*

GORDANO 3 ch.g. Muscatite 122–Coral Star (Tarboosh (USA)) [1989 7m 6m 8m 34 7f⁵ 7g a6g 1990 7m⁴ 5f 10.2f⁶ 10.1m 12f⁶] neat gelding: poor plater: appeared to run well in slowly-run apprentice race final start: winning selling hurdler. *R. J. Holder.*

GORDONS DREAM 3 b.g. Kafu 120–Dane Valley (Simbir 130) [1989 NR 1990   81 d
8.2g* 8g 9m² 9m⁴ 9m 9g a8g] 5,000Y: leggy, rather sparely-made gelding: good
walker: half-brother to 3 winners, including 1987 2-y-o 1m winner Valley of Danuata
(by Taufan): dam ran once: capable of fair form: easily best efforts winning apprentice maiden at Hamilton in May and second in claimer at Goodwood in August: broke
blood vessel and pulled up final start: stays 9f. *C. N. Allen.*

GORINSKY (IRE) 2 ch.c. (Apr 21) Gorytus (USA) 132–Grapette (Nebbiolo 125)   89
[1990 5f⁵ 6m* 5d² 6m* 5m² 5f³ 5g² 5d² 6v* 5g] 3,800F, 3,400Y: sturdy colt: has a
quick action: third foal: dam Irish 1¼m and hurdles winner: fair performer: made all
in sellers at Lingfield (no bid) in May and Goodwood (retained 8,800 gns) in June and
claimer (didn't have to run to best form) at Ayr in October: ran well in nurseries
seventh, eighth and final starts: suited by 5f: acts on any going. *J. Berry.*

GORYTUS STAR 4 ch.g. Gorytus (USA) 132–Bean Siamsa (Solinus 130) [1989   —
6m² 1990 a6g] close-coupled gelding: good second in handicap in June, 1989: always
struggling in Lingfield claimer, only other outing since 2 yrs: stays 6f well: acts on
good to firm and soft going: sold out of J. Hudson's stable 2,200 gns Ascot July Sales.
D. Haydn Jones.

GO SOUTH 6 b.g. Thatching 131–Run To The Sun (Run The Gantlet (USA))   79 §
[1989 12.2s² 12g* 12m 16m* 14m² 19f⁶ 14f⁶ 14g³ 18g a13g* a14g a16g* a16g² 1990
a13g⁴ 18f 15.5f⁴ 14m² 14g⁶ 14.8m⁵ 14.8m³ 16m 16.5f³ 16.2s* 18d⁵ 16s⁶ a14g⁴ a16g*
a16g³] sturdy gelding: moderate mover: fair handicapper on his day: won at
Haydock in October and Lingfield in December: stays 2m: probably acts on any
going: blinkered: often drops himself out, takes little interest and is not one to rely
on. *J. R. Jenkins.*

GO TALLY-HO 2 b.f. (Mar 15) Gorytus (USA) 132–Brush Away (Ahonoora 122)   66
[1990 5m* 5m*] 5,000F: workmanlike filly: has scope: second foal: half-sister to
useful Irish 3-y-o Takwim (by Taufan), successful at up to 7f: dam unraced half-
sister to useful stayer Princess Genista: comfortable winner of maiden in June and
3-runner minor event (by 4 lengths made all) at Hamilton following month: will stay
6f: tends to hang right. *J. Berry.*

GOTCHER 3 b.f. Jalmood (USA) 126–Sipapu 90 (Targowice (USA) 130) [1989 6f*   62 §
7m⁵ 6m³ 6g⁵ 5g⁴ 6d³ 1990 6f⁴ 7d⁴ 7m 7m⁴ 6g 7f 6m 6m 7f⁴] strong, lengthy filly:
quite modest handicapper: stays 7f: acts on firm and dead ground: blinkered fifth and
eighth starts: irresolute. *W. Carter.*

GOTHIC FORD 6 b.g. Stanford 121§–Gothic Lady (Godswalk (USA) 130) [1989   69
7d³ 7d³ 7d² 6m⁵ 8m* 7m 7m² 7f* 7m 7m 7g 7f⁵ 7g⁵ 7m a7g⁵ a6g² a8g² a7g² 1990
a8g* a7g⁴ a7g² a7g³ a7g* a7g³ a8g² a8g³ a7g² a7g³ a8g 8f 7.5m a8g a8g⁶ a8g a8g⁶
a11g] short-legged, rather dipped-backed gelding: moderate mover: generally in
good form on all-weather early in 1990 and justified favouritism in handicaps at
Southwell in January: off course 6 months after eleventh outing and below his best
subsequently: ideally suited by 7f or 1m: acts on any going: has been tried in visor
and severe bridle: wore eyeshield last 2 outings, as well as blinkers on final one:
goes well on turning track. *C. Tinkler.*

GOTT'S DESIRE 4 ch.g. Sweet Monday 122–Steel Lady 60 (Continuation 120)   68
[1989 7.5d³ 8.2f 8m² 7m* 7m⁶ 7f 8.2d³ 7m* 7.6m 7g² 7d³ a7g³ 1990 a8g⁴ a7g 7.6m
7m⁵ 7f* 7f⁴ 7g² 7m⁴ 7m* 7m 7.6m* 7m 8m 8.2d 7d] angular gelding: quite modest
handicapper: won at Redcar (selling event, no bid) in July and Lingfield (twice, on
second occasion ridden by 7-lb claimer) in September: soundly beaten last 4 starts,
very slowly away second of them: keen sort, suited by about 7f: probably acts on any
going. *R. Bastiman.*

GOULD'S DELIGHT 4 b.f. Deep Roots 124–Brun's Toy (FR) (Bruni 132)   —
[1989 NR 1990 10m a7g] sparely-made filly: lightly raced and little sign of ability:
bandaged and edgy final outing: sold 1,500 gns Doncaster September Sales. *R. F.
Marvin.*

GOVERNORSHIP 6 ch.g. Dominion 123–Angel Beam (SWE) 115 (Hornbeam   61 §
130) [1989 7d 8f⁵ 8f 8f³ 8m⁶ 8f 1990 7m 9f 7.6m* 6f 8.3m 8.5f 8f 6g 7d 11d] lengthy,
good-topped gelding: poor walker: has a quick action: one-time fairly useful
handicapper: favourably drawn, fair way below his best when making all in claimer at
Lingfield in June: no other form as 6-y-o, including in sellers: suited by 1m: acts on
firm and dead going: best in blinkers: sold out of J. Hills's stable 4,800 gns Ascot
October Sales after seventh outing: thoroughly unreliable. *D. W. Chapman.*

GO WITH THE FLO 4 br.f. Indian King (USA) 128–Doon Belle (Ardoon 124)   51
[1989 11.7d 8m 8m 6g 6g² 6f* 1990 6g 5f⁴ 6f 5m] workmanlike filly: quite moderate
winner at 3 yrs: form in spring handicaps only on second outing, tending to hang and

swish tail: best at sprint distances: blinkered final start: apprentice ridden: wears crossed noseband: has had tongue tied down. *J. Mackie.*

GOZONE   3 ro.g. Carwhite 127–Perlesse 88 (Bold Lad (USA)) [1989 7d⁵ a7g⁵ a8g   **54** 1990 10.1m 7m 6d³ 6s⁵ 5g a6g⁶ a7g a8g²] leggy gelding: plating-class maiden: stays 1m: acts on dead going. *E. Eldin.*

GRABEL   7 b.m. Bold Owl 101–Gay Dawn (Gay Fandango 132) [1989 14g* 16g³   **—** 13m⁶ 22.2f⁴ 14m 14v* 1990 22d 14m⁴ 14d] Irish mare: fairly useful winner as 6-y-o: well beaten in Queen Alexandra Stakes (well-backed favourite) at Royal Ascot, then in listed event and handicap: stays extremely well: acts on any going: good mount for inexperienced rider: high-class hurdler. *P. Mullins, Ireland.*

GRACEBRIDGE (USA)   2 ch.f. (Jan 30) Miswaki (USA) 124–Ball Star (ARG)   **83** (Snow Ball) [1990 6s² 6m* 6m 6.5g 7g 7s] 52,000Y: rather leggy, angular filly: half-sister to fairly useful 1¼m winner Sabatina (by Verbatim) and winners in North America and France: dam graded winner in Argentina later successful in USA: fair performer: won maiden at Nottingham in August by 5 lengths: ran well in Tattersalls Tiffany Yorkshire Stakes at Doncaster fourth start: should stay 7f: acts on good to firm ground: sold 20,000 gns Newmarket Autumn Sales. *L. M. Cumani.*

GRACE CARD   4 b.g. Ela-Mana-Mou 132–Val de Grace (FR) (Val de Loir 133)   **55** [1989 NR 1990 16.2m² 16.2f⁶ 17.6m⁶ 16m 17m² 18g a16g a14g] lengthy, workmanlike gelding: half-brother to several winners, including Gracefully (by Lyphard), dam of Prix de Diane winner Lypharita, and fairly useful middle-distance performer Grace Note (by Top Ville), dam of Belmez: dam, French 10.5f winner, out of half-sister to Prix de Diane winner Fine Pearl: won NH Flat race at Southwell in February: plating-class form in maidens and handicap on flat: ran poorly last 3 outings: suited by test of stamina. *R. Hollinshead.*

GRACELAND LADY (IRE)   2 b.f. (Feb 20) Kafu 120–Theda 61 (Mummy's Pet   **55** 125) [1990 5f 5m³ 5g* 5m 5g⁶ 5g⁴ 6d] 5,800Y: leggy, quite attractive filly: poor mover: second foal: dam stayed 7f: plating class performer: won maiden auction at Ripon in June: below that form after: carried head high fourth start, seemed unsuited by track at Chester next outing. *M. H. Easterby.*

GRACE O'MALLEY   3 ch.f. Yashgan 126–Perestrella (Relkino 131) [1989 NR   **67** 1990 12g a12g 12f³ 12m a12g² a12g⁵ a11g⁴] 11,000Y: leggy filly: third foal: dam unraced half-sister to high-class middle-distance performer Calaba: quite modest maiden: worthwhile form only when placed: worth a try over further: blinkered last 3 starts: sold 1,300 gns Newmarket December Sales, probably to Italy. *J. A. R. Toller.*

GRACEWING   3 br.f. Gorytus (USA) 132–Bellinote (FR) 71 (Noir Et Or 125)   **43** [1989 NR 1990 8.5d 8d 8g 8m⁵ 8.2f 8.2m 6m⁶ 7f⁵ 7m³ 7.2d⁵ 7v⁵ 12d⁶ 7d 6s⁵] compact filly: first foal: dam maiden half-sister to smart 1981 French 2-y-o stayer Beau Pretender: poor form: should stay beyond 7f: acts on firm going: often on toes: trained by J. W. Watts first 2 outings. *P. Monteith.*

GRAIN LADY (USA)   2 ch.f. (Mar 8) Greinton 119–Countess Belvane (Ribot   **—** 142) [1990 7d] $160,000Y: leggy, unfurnished filly: half-sister to numerous winners, including useful Irish 6f winner Merta (by Jaipur): dam minor winner: whipped around leaving stalls and refused to race in minor event at Leicester in October. *D. Nicholson.*

GRAMINIE (USA)   4 gr.g. Graustark–Etoile d'Orient (Targowice (USA) 130)   **—** [1989 8m⁴ 14g⁵ 10m⁵ 8g 1990 11 7g⁵] lengthy, angular gelding: modest maiden at best: probably stays 1½m: blinkered final outing at 3 yrs. *P. J. Hobbs.*

GRAMMOS (USA)   2 b.c. (Jan 31) Bailjumper (USA)–Rheine Falls (USA)   **89 p** (Rheingold 137) [1990 7m* 10g⁶] 34,000Y: big, workmanlike colt: has plenty of scope: half-brother to 2 winners in USA: dam minor winner in USA, is half-sister to Cambridgeshire winner Baronet: sire smart over 1m and 9f: won maiden at Yarmouth in September by ¾ length from Evasive Prince: favourite, sixth of 9, pulling very hard and eased when beaten under 2f out, in listed race at Newmarket in November: likely to do better. *H. R. A. Cecil.*

GRAMY AWARD (USA)   2 b. or br.c. (Mar 23) Mr Prospector (USA)–Gramy   **?** (FR) (Tapioca II (FR) 123) [1990 8d² 8d*] $500,000Y: half-brother to several winners, including good-class 1985 French staying 2-y-o Fieldy (by Northfields), later stakes winner in USA, and to French middle-distance winner Grisant (by Margouillat): dam smart French middle-distance performer: second to Pistolet Bleu in newcomers race at Saint-Cloud in September before winning 8-runner maiden there following month, apparently most impressively, by 2½ lengths: will probably stay 1¼m: likely to do better as 3-y-o. *A. Fabre, France.*

GRAN ALBA (USA)   4 gr.c. El Gran Senor (USA) 136–Morning Games (USA)   **104** d
(Grey Dawn II 132) [1989 10f* 10f4 12g6 12f2 10d* 11s4 12m 9g4 10g5 1990 8f6 10f5 10g2 10m 9g 10.6g4 9m 10.4v2] heavy-topped colt: carries condition: moderate walker: has a roundish action: useful on his day: by far his best effort as 4-y-o when clear second in strongly-run £19,000 handicap at Epsom in June: needs further than 1m and stays 1½m: needs an easy surface: sometimes blinkered or visored: bandaged off-fore fifth outing: changed hands 21,000 gns Newmarket Autumn Sales. *R. Hannon.*

GRANBERA (USA)   2 b.f. (Apr 26) El Gran Senor (USA) 136–Satin Ribera   **70** p
(USA) (Mickey McGuire (USA)) [1990 7s2] 42,000Y: light-framed filly: third foal: dam won 17 races in USA and was third in 8.5f Grade 1 event: weak 10/1-shot, 3 lengths second of 17, travelling well, challenging 2f out then no extra, to Knifebox in maiden at Lingfield in October: will stay at least 1m: should improve. *B. W. Hills.*

GRAND BLUSH (USA)   4 gr.f. Blushing Groom (FR) 131–Versatile (FR)   **100**
(Versailles II) [1989 7s 7g3 7g 1990 6f2 6m6 7g 6m 8m* 8.3m* 9m6 8g3 8m 8f] rather leggy, close-coupled filly: useful performer: successful in handicaps at Pontefract (in good style) and Windsor in August: 28/1, improved again when third of 9, pulling hard then not having clear run 2f out, to Tabdea in listed event at Doncaster: behind in £60,000 handicap at Aqueduct, USA, last outing: suited by 1m: acts on firm going, possibly unsuited by soft: used to wear tongue strap: has got on edge: mounted on track and went freely down seventh start. *M. Moubarak.*

GRAND HARBOUR   10 br.g. Dragonara Palace (USA) 115–Top of The Tree 66   —
(Lorenzaccio 130) [1989 NR 1990 a7g] tall, good-topped gelding: fairly useful handicapper in 1985: acted as pacemaker next 2 seasons: prominent 4f in Southwell claimer in February: effective at 7f and 1m: acts on soft going but has done all his winning on a sound surface. *R. Champion.*

GRAND ISLAND   5 ch.g. Thatching 131–Okavamba 82 (Wollow 132) [1989 NR   —
1990 13.8m4 12h 13.8m4] workmanlike gelding: has a scratchy action: quite modest maiden at best, but has deteriorated: appeared ungenuine when visored. *E. Weymes.*

GRAND MORNING (IRE)   2 b.f. (Apr 25) King of Clubs 124–Northern   **77**
Chance 78 (Northfields (USA)) [1990 5m* 5m* 5f4 6g2] IR 25,000Y: rather leggy, good-quartered filly: sixth foal: half-sister to fair 1987 2-y-o 5f winner Toshair Flyer (by Ballad Rock), Irish 1¼m and 11f winner Northern Pet (by Petorius) and a winner in Italy: dam 1m winner: successful in maiden at Phoenix Park and listed race at the Curragh in May: over 4 lengths fourth of 12 to On Tiptoes in Queen Mary Stakes at Royal Ascot: not seen out after short-head second of 16 in valuable resticted race at the Curragh in August: stays 6f. *Patrick Prendergast, Ireland.*

GRAND PARTY   5 ch.m. Revlow 108–Grand Melody (Song 132) [1989 5f a10g   **39**
1990 a5g6 a6g3 a6g6 10f6 a7g] lengthy, workmanlike mare: poor maiden: raced freely fourth outing, and not certain to stay 1¼m: bandaged behind last 4 outings: sold 1,750 gns Doncaster September Sales. *J. M. Bradley.*

GRAND PRIX   5 b.h. Formidable (USA) 125–Mumruffin 101 (Mummy's Pet 125)   **81**
[1989 5.8h 5g5 5.8h* 6m2 6f2 6f 6h 6m 5g 1990 5g 5.8h 5m4 5m* 5m5 5m 6m* 5m 5m5 5g6] neat, good-bodied horse: moderate mover: fair handicapper: successful at Salisbury in August and Goodwood (making all in £11,400 contest) following month: best at 6f or stiff 5f: seems to need top-of-the-ground: often sweating and on edge: sometimes starts slowly: has gone freely to post: withdrawn lame at start tenth intended outing. *D. R. C. Elsworth.*

GRANITTON BAY   3 b.g. Prince Tenderfoot (USA) 126–Miss Redmarshall 80   **78**
(Most Secret 119) [1989 5m3 5g* 5f 5f4 5m* 5m2 5g 5g6 1990 5f 5v 7h2 5d5 7m3 8m* 7m* 7g* 7m5 7.6g5 8.5m4 9m 8m 8g 8m* 9m 8d] lengthy, rather dipped-backed gelding: moderate walker and mover: fair performer: successful in seller (no bid) and handicap at Doncaster in May then handicap at Epsom in June and claimer (returned to form) at Leicester in September: needs further than 5f, and stays 8.5f: acts on hard and dead going: mostly visored after third start: gelded after final one. *R. M. Whitaker.*

GRANITTON PRINCESS   2 b.f. (Mar 21) Creetown 123–Ackabarrow 97   **36**
(Laser Light 118) [1990 5f 5m 5d 6f4 5v 7d 5s a7g] 2,300F, 2,400Y: lengthy, angular filly: half-sister to three 2-y-o winners and to 5f seller winner Acka's Boy (by Town And Country): dam won 6 times over 5f: poor form in varied races, including sellers: visored final outing. *R. M. Whitaker.*

GRANNY'S BIRTHDAY 5 b.m. Young Generation 129–Gallant Believer —
(USA) (Gallant Romeo (USA)) [1989 NR 1990 a7g] lengthy mare: little worthwhile
form: has tended to carry head high. *J. D. Czerpak.*

GRANNY'S GIRL 2 b.f. (May 7) Mummy's Game 120–Michaelmas 72 (Silly 45
Season 127) [1990 5m 6g a8g5] close-coupled filly: sixth foal: half-sister to 7f seller
winner Coldwater Canyon (by Dominion) and modest 1984 2-y-o 1m winner
Rowanberry (by Great Nephew): dam thrice-raced half-sister to high-class miler
Martinmas: still better for race, around 10 lengths fifth of 12, eased 2 lengths or so
when beaten, to Access Flyer in maiden at Lingfield, final and best effort: worth a
try at 7f. *I. A. Balding.*

GRATCLO 4 gr.f. Belfort (FR) 89–Shagra (Sallust 134) [1989 5s 6m 6g 6f 6m 7m 65
8f 8f 8f 7f* 6f4 6g* 1990 6f 7f* 7f* 8h2 7m 8f3 7.6m 8m6 8.3f 7m] strong, workmanlike filly: has a quick action: successful in spring handicaps at Wolverhampton
and Salisbury: possibly ideally suited by 7f: acts well on firm ground: has started
slowly: reluctant to race for 7-lb claimer seventh outing at 3 yrs: has often hung left.
C. J. Hill.

GRAVETTE 2 ch.f. (Apr 26) Kris 135–Highland Light 105 (Home Guard (USA) 79
129) [1990 7m 6m 7g2] angular, workmanlike filly: has scope: has a roundish action:
sixth foal: half-sister to fairly useful 6f (at 2 yrs) and 1m winner Church Light and to
1½m winner and Italian St Leger winner Welsh Guide (both by Caerleon), and to a
winner in Scandinavia: dam sprinter: 20/1, 1½ lengths second of 20, soon prominent
then staying on well, to Campestral in maiden at Newmarket in November, easily
best effort: will stay 1m: keen sort: likely to win a race. *H. R. A. Cecil.*

GRAVITATE 2 b.c. (Apr 16) Song 132–Sheer Bliss 76 (St Paddy 133) [1990 7g 8g 51
7s] 17,000Y: leggy, angular colt: half-brother to several winners, including useful
Irish middle-distance winner Sheringham (by Blakeney): dam maiden, best at 2 yrs:
caught eye in median auction at York (very slowly away) and maiden at Pontefract:
tailed off final outing. *P. Calver.*

GREAT AFFAIR 2 ch.c. (Apr 22) Mummy's Game 120–Pretty Great 63 (Great 45
Nephew 126) [1990 5f4 6g5] leggy colt: first foal: dam maiden stayed 1m, is half-
sister to very smart sprinter Crew's Hill: poor form in minor event (slowly away)
and seller. *J. M. P. Eustace.*

GREAT CHADDINGTON 5 b.g. Crofter (USA) 124–Mainly Dry (The 71
Brianstan 128) [1989 5g3 5s 5m 5f2 5f4 5m2 5m6 5d 1990 5f2 5f2 5d4 5s4 5m* 5f5 5g
5d4 a5g 5m4 5g2 6m 5d3 5g] tall, leggy, close-coupled gelding: moderate mover:
modest handicapper: won for only time since early as 2-y-o in apprentice race at
Edinburgh in May: withdrawn lame at start eleventh intended outing: suited by 5f:
acts on any going: effective with or without blinkers or visor. *J. Berry.*

GREAT COMMOTION (USA) 4 b.c. Nureyev (USA) 131–Alathea 123
(Lorenzaccio 130) [1989 7d* 8m5 8m2 8f4 7f* 7.3g2 8m2 1990 6g2 6g* 6m2 8f4
6g4 8h3]
    The decision to try Great Commotion over six furlongs was fully vin-
dicated: he bettered his three-year-old seven-furlong and one-mile form and
established himself just about the best of a substandard collection of older
sprinters by winning the Cork And Orrery Stakes and finishing second in the
Carroll Foundation July Cup. Great Commotion had been persevered with
over further for much longer than most of the season's leading sprinters:
three-year-olds Dayjur, Royal Academy, Ron's Victory and Dead Certain all
started off in Guineas trials but none of them attempted beyond six furlongs
more than twice in the spring. After winning impressively on his debut in a
Newmarket maiden, Great Commotion spent the rest of his three-year-old
season in pattern company, never running a poor race and winning the
Beeswing Stakes at Newcastle and finishing second in the Irish Two
Thousand Guineas at the Curragh. It had become customary to ride him up
with the pace, so it was unexpected to see Eddery electing to tuck him in
behind the leaders when the horse was brought back to six furlongs for the
first time on his reappearance in the Duke of York Stakes at York. He finished
strongly but couldn't quite get the better of Lugana Beach, leaving the
impression that six furlongs was a minimum. In that respect he was helped by
the uphill finish and easing ground conditions which made for a stiffer test of
stamina in the Cork And Orrery at Royal Ascot. The race was contested by the
meeting's biggest field outside a handicap; of the seventeen that lined up
the Poule d'Essai des Pouliches second Pont Aven, Greenham runner-up

Cork And Orrery Stakes, Ascot—Great Commotion (right) gets it on the nod after a magnificent duel with the filly Dead Certain

Montendre, Dead Certain and Great Commotion attracted most of the interest. One couldn't help but be impressed with Great Commotion's appearance in the paddock or by his battling qualities in the race. Having come under strong pressure over a furlong out, he steadily wore down Dead Certain after a terrific duel and got the verdict on the nod.

Trainer and owner, endeavouring to repeat their previous year's success with Cadeaux Genereux, supplied a third of the runners for the July Cup with the Prix du Gros Chene winner Nabeel Dancer and Magic Gleam joining Great Commotion in a field lacking Dayjur. Rock City, like Royal Academy attempting six furlongs for the first time since two years, shaded favouritism over Dead Certain, better in with Great Commotion than at Royal Ascot. Great Commotion, a 16/1 chance, ran the race of his life despite having sweated and got on his toes and a bit coltish in the preliminaries on what was a muggy, oppressive afternoon. He profited to an extent from the leaders' going off too fast for their own good, picking up ground from the back of the field as they began to tire and coming to challenge for the lead with Keen Hunter around two furlongs out. Great Commotion then held a narrow advantage until Royal Academy took it up inside the final furlong, and afterwards kept on well to hold off Rock City for second by a neck, three parts of a length adrift of Royal Academy. Great Commotion ran poorly back at a mile in the Sussex Stakes at Goodwood, soon off the bridle at the rear of the field and never in the race. The stable was under a cloud at the time and didn't send out a winner for six weeks from mid-July. Great Commotion was again below his best in the Ladbroke Sprint Cup at Haydock, readily left behind when Dayjur quickened two furlongs out, after which he was sent to continue his career in California with Neil Drysdale. According to reports he was unlucky not to win on his American debut in the Grade 3 Kelso Handicap at Belmont Park, finishing strongly and going down by only a neck after weaving his way through the field up the straight. It was claimed that the winner Expensive Decision set a new world record for a mile on turf in the race, but his time was well outside Chase The Door's at Brighton in July.

Great Commotion is a brother to Lead On Time, a good-class sprinter and the winner of the Prix Maurice de Gheest at Deauville on the last of his five outings. Lead On Time now stands at the Haras du Quesnay, his first

		Northern Dancer	Nearctic
	Nureyev (USA)	(b 1961)	Natalma
	(b 1977)	Special	Forli
Great Commotion (USA)		(b 1969)	Thong
(b.c. 1986)		Lorenzaccio	Klairon
	Alathea	(ch 1965)	Phoenissa
	(b 1975)	Vive La Reine	Vienna
		(b 1969)	Noble Lassie

runners due on the track in 1991. Another mating between Nureyev and Alathea, the latter a lightly-raced maiden acquired by Gainsborough Stud after Lead On Time's success, produced a French provincial winner at around a mile. Alathea's three other winning foals include the very useful French miler Keyala (by Key To The Mint), later successful nine times in North America. Alathea, a half-sister to the Champagne Stakes winner R B Chesne, is a daughter of Vive La Reine, a winning sister to Vaguely Noble out of the Lancashire Oaks winner Noble Lassie. Great Commotion possesses most of the attributes sought after in a racehorse: looks, speed, versatility, good temperament, durability. He's an attractive colt, a medium-sized, quite good-topped one; he is effective at six furlongs and stays a mile; he has yet to race on soft going, but acts on any other. *A. A. Scott.*

GREAT DESIGN 2 b.c. (Feb 14) Primo Dominie 121–Great Optimist 55 (Great 75 Nephew 126) [1990 7g* 7m 8d6] 15,500F, 18,500Y: robust colt: half-brother to several winners, including 6f winner Matou (by Mummy's Pet): dam in frame over middle distances: won maiden at Salisbury by ¾ length from Blues Club: ran well in face of stiff tasks in nurseries later in October: stays 1m. *J. H. M. Gosden.*

GREATEST OF ALL (IRE) 2 ch.f. (Apr 2) Ela-Mana-Mou 132–Red Jade 82 62 (Red God 128§) [1990 6m6 6.5g 7m] 29,000F, 23,000Y: tall, leggy, plain filly: half-sister to 5 winners here and abroad, including fairly useful 4-y-o sprinter Hinari Televideo (by Caerleon) and useful 7f and 7.3f winner Mahogany (by Tap On Wood): dam 2-y-o 5f winner: best effort fifteenth of 17, slowly away and always behind, in Tattersalls Tiffany Yorkshire Stakes at Doncaster second start. *R. Hannon.*

GREAT FRIENDSHIP 3 b.g. Bairn (USA) 126–Badwell Ash (Morston (FR) 54 125) [1989 NR 1990 8.2g6 10g5 10g 10d 8m3 8m] leggy, angular, rather sparely-made gelding: sixth foal: half-brother to very useful 8.5f and 1¼m winner Validate (by Valiyar), fairly useful 1m winner New Tick (by Young Generation) and a winner in Scandinavia: dam unraced close relative of Cheshire Oaks winner Hunston: 33/1, set fair bit to do when strong-finishing third of 21 in handicap at Pontefract, only worthwhile form: should stay 1¼m. *C. W. Thornton.*

GREAT GUSTO 4 b.g. Windjammer (USA)–My Music 68 (Sole Mio (USA)) — [1989 10.1m 10m 10.6m 12.3m* 14m 10f3 10g 10m 8m* 8m 8.2f3 8g* 8.5f 1990 16.5g 10.4g a11g 8m a12g a7g] leggy, good-topped gelding: quite modest winner (including for lady and apprentice) as 3-y-o: little show in 1990: probably best at around 1m: acts on firm going: often on toes, and has sweated: trained on reappearance by Ronald Thompson. *C. Dwyer.*

GREAT HAND 4 b.c. Tumble Wind (USA)–Great Aunt 74 (Great Nephew 126) 57 [1989 6d5 8.5d 7.5f 8h 8f3 9m3dis 9f 1990 a10g a8g 9f6 8f6 8m3 10f* 8.2f2 8g2 10m 10.6d 10m 10s] leggy colt: quite modest handicapper: won (for only time) slowly-run race at Nottingham in May: off course 4½ months after ninth outing then well beaten: stays 1¼m: acts on firm going: sweating and on toes tenth and eleventh starts: often tends to edge. *D. A. Wilson.*

GREAT HEIGHTS 3 b.g. Shirley Heights 130–As You Desire Me 112 94 p (Kalamoun 129) [1989 7g4 1990 10m* 11.5m3] big, good-topped, attractive gelding: has a quick, shortish action: 7/4 on, made all in maiden at Newmarket in April: still inexperienced when 6 lengths third of 5 to Rock Hopper in Group 3 event at Lingfield following month, running very wide on home turn, and staying on well inside final 1f: subsequently gelded: will stay 1½m: has joined Mrs J. Cecil: may well be capable of better. *H. R. A. Cecil.*

GREAT LAKES 4 b.c. Lomond (USA) 128–Costly Wave (FR) 117 (Caro 133) 107 [1989 8v2 8d* 8m* 1990 7g* 10g] Irish colt: half-brother to several winners, including very useful French 9f and 1¼m winner Swept Away (by Kris): dam, smart French miler, is out of Oaks third Arctic Wave: very lightly raced, but capable of useful form: won listed race at Phoenix Park in May at 3 yrs and Group 3 EBF Gladness

Stakes (by head from Mr Brooks) at the Curragh almost year later: never reached leaders in listed race later in April: stays 1m. *M. V. O'Brien, Ireland.*

GREAT MARQUESS 3 b.c. Touching Wood (USA) 127–Fruition 89 **115** p (Rheingold 137) [1989 NR 1990 10m* 14g² 14.6g⁵ 16m*]
This colt is true to his breeding: a late-maturing stayer as was his half-brother Kneller (by Lomond). Although Great Marquess' achievements amount to less than his half-brother's at the same stage, and he seems to have lesser powers of acceleration, he's better than many who've done well in the Cup races in recent seasons and has a future in good long-distance events. The unbeaten Kneller, also trained by Cecil, ran once as a two-year-old. Thereafter the two horses' careers have followed a very similar pattern; in Great Marquess' case beginning with a run over a barely-adequate distance in a maiden race at Pontefract in the spring, then a spell off the track followed by a short, late summer-early autumn campaign over further at York, Doncaster and Newmarket. Great Marquess improved greatly on the form of his Pontefract win when a rallying head second to Shambo in the strongly-contested Racecall Melrose Handicap at York, for which his stable-companion Millionaire's Row started a hot favourite. It was hard to envisage his beating another stable-companion River God in the St Leger next time out, let alone some of the other runners, and in coming fifth of eight to Snurge, beaten around eight lengths, never able to challenge but again staying on, he showed further improvement. Kneller had gone on from the Ebor and the Doncaster Cup to the Jockey Club Cup, a Group 3 race over two miles at Newmarket. Great Marquess went on from York and Doncaster to the same event, the only three-year-old in a field that also included Ashal, Al Maheb and Teamster. Despite the assistance of a pacemaker and a strong gallop which made for a good test of stamina, Ashal, penalized for his Gold Cup win, found Great Marquess and Dance Spectrum too sharp for him as the race evolved to rest between the three of them from half a mile out. Ashal pushed on five furlongs out, Dance Spectrum soon challenged, and then Great Marquess, steadily responding to pressure, also joined issue. Dance Spectrum and Great Marquess then began to pull away, both flat out; Great Marquess got his head in front just inside the last and stayed on well to win the sustained duel by three parts of a length, the pair eight lengths clear of Ashal.
Great Marquess, a close-coupled colt, was bought for only 30,000 guineas as a yearling; admittedly Touching Wood wasn't the height of fashion

Jockey Club Cup, Newmarket—Great Marquess (right) follows in Kneller's footsteps; Dance Spectrum easily beats Ashal for second

Mr C. A. B. St George's "Great Marquess"

Great Marquess (b.c. 1987)	Touching Wood (USA) (b 1979)	Roberto (b 1969)	Hail To Reason
			Bramalea
		Mandera (b 1970)	Vaguely Noble
			Foolish One
	Fruition (b 1978)	Rheingold (b 1969)	Faberge II
			Athene
		Welsh Flame (b 1973)	Welsh Pageant
			Electric Flash

as a sire, and none of the dam's three other foals besides Kneller had won, but Kneller had taken the Jockey Club Cup only two weeks earlier. The family has remained in the limelight since, for the dam, the quite useful middle-distance mare Fruition, is a half-sister to Salsabil's dam Flame of Tara. Great Marquess moves moderately in his slower paces. He proved effective on good to firm going at Newmarket and has yet to race on ground easier than good. *H. R. A. Cecil.*

GREAT MILL 3 b.c. Simply Great (FR) 122–Milly Lass (FR) 85 (Bold Lad (USA)) [1989 6m⁶ 7f² 7g 9g² 8m⁴ 10g⁴ 8g³ 1990 8f 10m⁶ 12.3g⁶ 14g 12m⁴ 14g] rather **61** leggy, close-coupled colt: has a quick action: quite modest maiden: should stay 1¾m: acts on good to firm ground: blinkered final outing at 2 yrs: has looked a hard ride: sold 10,500 gns Ascot October Sales: winning hurdler for K. Bailey. *M. E. D. Francis.*

GREAT MUSIC   2 ch.c. (Apr 6) Music Boy 124–Amadina 96 (Great Nephew 126)   **62**
[1990 5f 5g² 5g⁶ 5m] 8,000Y: robust, rather angular colt: has scope: has a round
action: half-brother to several winners, including fairly useful 1983 2-y-o 7f winner
Court And Spark (by Relkino), later winner at 1¼m: dam, half-sister to very useful
1972 2-y-o Claudius, won at 6f to 8.5f: quite modest maiden. *J. S. Wainwright.*

GREAT SERVICE   3 ch.c. Vaigly Great 127–Janlarmar 69 (Habat 127) [1989 5g⁵   **63**
5v* 6f⁵ 7f 7g a8g 1990 a8g⁴ a7g³ a8g⁴ a8g* a8g⁵ 9s⁴ 11v² 12d 12d 12.3g 16.2d a11g
a14g 9f 8v⁵ 8g* 8d³] angular colt: has a rather round action: quite modest
handicapper: won at Southwell in January: form after April only in October when
winning at Pontefract then good third at Doncaster (bandaged near-hind, soon off
bridle) day later: stays 11f: acts on heavy ground, and seems unsuited by firm:
blinkered and sweating on reappearance: sometimes edgy: changed hands 13,500
gns Newmarket Autumn Sales. *Ronald Thompson.*

GREAT SONG   3 ch.f. Vaigly Great 127–Suzannah's Song (Song 132) [1989 5g 7f   **— §**
7m 5g³ 5f 5.1m 6g 5g 6m⁴ 6g a7g a6g⁴ a5g⁵ 190m a6g a5g] small, lengthy filly: plater:
moved poorly to post, ran wide into straight then tended to hang and look reluctant
on reappearance: stays 6f: blinkered nowadays: sold 1,150 gns Doncaster May Sales:
unreliable. *T. Fairhurst.*

GREAT STAR   2 ch.f. (Apr 27) Vaigly Great 127–Cracked Up (Busted 134) [1990   **70**
6f³ 8f⁵ 7d⁴ 9m³] 4,000Y: leggy, lengthy filly: moderate mover: fourth foal: half-
sister to a winner in Austria by Relkino: dam never ran: quite modest maiden: ran
well last 2 starts: stays 9f: drifted left third start: very troublesome at stalls once
and was withdrawn. *E. Weymes.*

GRECIAN REBEL   2 b.g. (May 5) Absalom 128–Navarino Bay 102 (Averof 123)   **47 p**
[1990 a7g⁵ 5m 7m⁵] 14,500Y: leggy, unfurnished gelding: has a round action: fourth
foal: half-brother to a disqualified winner over hurdles: dam won over 5f at 2 yrs and
stayed 1½m: poor form in maidens and a claimer: seems much better suited by 7f
than 5f. *M. Bell.*

GREEK FLUTTER   5 b.g. Beldale Flutter (USA) 130–Greek Blessing 83 (So   **75**
Blessed 130) [1989 12g 1990 12f³ 12f² 13.8m² 12.3d 12m*] rather leggy, good-topped
gelding: carries condition: has a scratchy action: quite modest handicapper: won strongly-
run event at Edinburgh in May: suited by 1½m +: best on a sound surface: bandaged
second and third starts: goes well for K. Fallon: best ridden up with pace. *J. G.
FitzGerald.*

GREEK LAD   3 ch.c. Decoy Boy 129–Corinth Canal 77 (Troy 137) [1989 NR 1990   **—**
8m 8m 7m 7g⁵ 8.3f] 11,000 2-y-o: compact colt: first foal: dam once-raced sister to
Helen Street: poor maiden: best effort over 7f on good ground: dead. *Mrs Barbara
Waring.*

GREEN ARCHER   7 b.g. Hardgreen (USA) 122–Mittens (Run The Gantlet   **—**
(USA)) [1989 14s 21.6d⁵ 18s 16.5g⁶ 20.4g* 17f⁵ 1990 18f 16d⁴] close-coupled
gelding: poor handicapper: had very stiff task both outings at 7 yrs: suited by
extreme test of stamina: appears to act on any going. *Mrs J. R. Ramsden.*

GREEN BUCK   2 b.c. (Feb 25) Green Ruby (USA) 104–Habitab (Sovereign Path   **51**
125) [1990 5m⁴ 5m 5m³ 6g 5f 6g⁵ 5m⁵ 8d a5g] 4,400Y: small colt: fourth foal: half-
brother to 5.1f winner Lime Brook (by Rapid River): dam never ran: fair plater: stays
6f: acts on top-of-the-ground and dead: visored fifth start: races keenly. *B. Palling.*

GREENDALE (FR)   2 b.c. (Apr 7) Green Desert (USA) 127–Lastcomer (USA)   **74 p**
100 (Kris 135) [1990 6d⁴] rather leggy colt: first foal: dam 6f (at 2 yrs) and 1¼m winner from family of Gorytus: backward and green, under 4 lengths fourth of 10, slowly
away then staying on well not knocked about, to Fraar in valuable minor event at
Ascot in June: seemed sure to improve, but not seen out again. *C. E. Brittain.*

GREEN DANUBE (USA)   2 ch.f. (Jan 29) Irish River (FR) 131–Chere Amie   **52 p**
(FR) (Gay Mecene (USA) 128) [1990 7m] neat filly: first foal: dam French 1m winner
seemed to stay 1¼m: around 11 lengths ninth of 22, slowly away and green then
running on well final 2f, in maiden at Chepstow in October: will stay 1m: sure to
improve. *W. Hastings-Bass.*

GREEN DOLLAR   7 b.g. Tickled Pink 114–Burglars Girl 63 (Burglar 128) [1989   **80**
5s 5f³ 7m 5.8h 6f⁴ 5f⁵ 6m² 6m* 6f² 5g³ 6m 6m² 7f 6g 6f* 6m⁵ 6s³ 6m³ 5m⁶ 6g 1990
6g 5m⁵ 6f⁵ 6m⁵ 6m* 6f⁵ 7g 6d 6m* 6f* 5m 6f⁴ 6m 6m 6m⁶ 6f² 6h* 6m 5m⁵ 6m 6m⁶
6d] smallish gelding: fair handicapper: successful at Lingfield in May, Goodwood in
June and Brighton later in June and in August: best at 6f: goes particularly well on
top-of-the-ground: has worn blinkers and visor, but not for some time: has run well
when sweating: tough. *E. A. Wheeler.*

GREEN EMPEROR   4 b. or br.c. Head For Heights 125–La Padma (Sassafras   **71** d
(FR) 135) [1989 8m⁶ 10f⁴ 13.3m² 16f 13.3m 14m⁶ 10g* 10g² 1990 10f⁵ 12m² 10f 9m
a12g 11.5m 18.1m⁵] leggy, close-coupled colt: has a round action: fair handicapper at
3 yrs: well beaten last 3 outings in 1990, racing much too freely last 2: effective at
1¼m and 1½m: acts on good to firm going: has sweated and got on toes: suited by
forcing tactics: sold 9,000 gns Ascot October Sales. *R. W. Armstrong.*

GREEN ENTERPRISE   2 b.f. (Apr 10) Glenstal (USA) 118–Branch Out (Star   **59**
Appeal 133) [1990 5g 6g* 5.1m⁴ 7f² 7m² 7m 7g² 8.2g⁵ 8m] 3,600F, 3,400Y: workmanlike filly: keen walker: first foal: dam lightly-raced free runner: plating-class
performer: won maiden auction at Yarmouth in June: ran well fifth and seventh
starts: should stay 1m: tail swisher: sold 3,000 gns Newmarket December Sales. *B.
Hanbury.*

GREEN GLOW   2 b.g. (Feb 28) Green Ruby (USA) 104–Jonesee 64 (Dublin   **66**
Taxi) [1990 6m⁴ 5d³ 5m* 5m³ 6d 8.2s⁴] sturdy gelding: poor mover: second foal:
half-brother to 5f and 6f winner Respectable Jones (by Tina's Pet): dam won 7f seller
at 3 yrs: won 3-runner maiden at Hamilton in July: well-backed favourite, very good
fourth, keeping on never dangerous, in nursery at Hamilton: stays 1m: acts on good
to firm ground and soft: hung left for 7-lb claimer second start. *M. H. Tompkins.*

GREENHAM (USA)   3 b.c. Green Dancer (USA) 132–Cameo Shore (Mill Reef   **103**
(USA) 141) [1989 NR 1990 10g* 10f* 14.6g³ 12m 14g*] robust, attractive colt:
moderate walker and mover: fifth foal: half-brother to fairly useful 1¼m winner
Cambo (by Roberto) and 11f winner Bronte (by Bold Forbes): dam useful winner
over 7f and 10.5f in France: won maiden at Leicester in May and minor events at
Folkestone in June and York (by neck from Crack) in October: should stay 2m:
probably best on an easy surface: sold 105,000 gns Newmarket Autumn Sales to
race abroad. *G. Harwood.*

GREENHILLS LAD (IRE)   2 b.c. (May 14) Mazaad 106–Kimstar 61 (Aureole   **66**
132) [1990 5m 6m⁴ 7f³ 7f⁶ 7g⁶ 8g 7g 7d] IR 11,500Y, 10,500Y, 6,600 2-y-o: small,
useful-looking colt: keen walker: half-brother to 3-y-o Suspect Device (by Dublin
Taxi), 1m winner Pale Star (by Kampala) and winning Irish middle-distance stayer
Tawkin (by Taufan): dam maiden stayed 13f: quite modest maiden: ran poorly final 2
outings: stays 1m: looks a hard ride, and may do better in blinkers. *R. Akehurst.*

GREENHILLS PRIDE   6 b.g. Sparkling Boy 110–Soheir 74 (Track Spare 125)   **50**
[1989 10.2g³ 10s³ 8f 10v* 12.4g 12s 1990 11s 9s⁶ 12m⁴ 11.5m³ 11g² 11g³ 13f³] tall,
close-coupled gelding: plating-class handicapper: stays 1½m: possibly unsuited by
firm going, acts on any other: tried in blinkers and visor at 4 yrs: has joined J.
Jenkins. *H. J. Collingridge.*

GREENHILLS STAR   5 ch.m. Mansingh (USA) 120–Soheir 74 (Track Spare   **—**
125) [1989 NR 1990 a11g] seems of little account and of suspect temperament:
blinkered twice, visored once. *J. R. Jenkins.*

GREEN LANE (USA)   2 ch.c. (Feb 28) Greinton 119–Memory Lane (USA) 100   **77**
(Never Bend) [1990 6m 8m* 8.2g 7g 8m⁶] leggy, close-coupled colt: good mover:
half-brother to several winners, notably useful middle-distance performer Fields of
Spring (by The Minstrel): dam, sister to Mill Reef, won Princess Elizabeth Stakes:
bandaged near-hind, made all in maiden at Chepstow in August: eye-catching sixth
of 22 in nursery at Warwick on final start, finishing fast from poor position over 1f
out and giving impression might well have won comfortably had run begun sooner:
will stay 1¼m: acts well on good to firm ground. *I. A. Balding.*

GREEN LIGHTNING (IRE)   2 b.c. (Apr 16) Green Desert (USA) 127–Etoile   **87**
de Paris 116 (Crowned Prince (USA) 128) [1990 6m² 6g* 6m* 6g³] IR 175,000Y:
sixth foal: half-brother to 3-y-o Summing Up (by Law Society) and 11f winner The
Soviet (by Nureyev): dam Irish 6f and 7f winner, is half-sister to high-class 1m to
1½m performer Northern Treasure: successful in maiden (by 4 lengths) at Phoenix
Park and minor event (by ½ length) at Tipperary: 2 lengths third of 6 to Time
Gentlemen in Group 3 event at the Curragh: quite useful. *J. S. Bolger, Ireland.*

GREEN LINE EXPRESS (USA)   4 ch.c. Green Forest (USA) 134–Lay-   **126**
litna (USA) (Key To The Mint (USA)) [1989 8.2g* 8f² 8g⁴ 8m⁴ 8f 1990 8m⁶
7.6f* 8f² 8g 7g* 8m³ 9f³]
   The Queen Elizabeth II Stakes at Ascot has attracted outstanding fields
since it became the centre piece of the Festival of British Racing in 1987, so
much so that it seems well on the way to becoming established as the European mile championship. The honours in the latest race went to the older

division, and the first three home went on to fill the same three places in the International Classification for older milers. Third-placed Green Line Express is a rather better animal than his one length and eight lengths defeat behind Markofdistinction and Distant Relative suggests. He did easily best of the five that forced the cut-throat pace, but when the two principals came at him, just as he'd worn down Shavian around two furlongs out, he had little left to offer except resolution. Green Line Express had met Distant Relative on four previous occasions, three of them as a four-year-old, and not once had he finished in front of him. In the Lockinge Stakes on his reappearance, when he refused to settle, and in the Jacques Le Marois at Deauville Green Line Express ran well below his best, but his half-length second, rallying strongly, when 7/2 second favourite in the Sussex Stakes at Goodwood was as well as he'd run in his career, the equal of his three-length second to Zilzal when a 100/1-chance in the same race twelve months earlier. Those places at Goodwood and Ascot earned connections over £86,000. Green Line Express has now won around £225,000, less than a fifth of which is attributable to his three wins. Two of those came in the latest season, in a five-runner listed race at Lingfield and the Kiveton Park Stakes, his first in pattern company, at Doncaster. Green Line Express took full advantage of Lord Florey's lacklustre display at Lingfield and having made the running quickened clear for a comfortable six-length success. At Doncaster matters were a lot tighter, a short head to be precise, and it took the judge some time to announce him rather than Sally Rous the winner. Switched to the stand rail leaving the stalls, Green Line Express led virtually throughout and rallied after being headed briefly inside the final furlong. He failed to secure a place in the line-up for the Breeders' Cup Mile and ended his season which had started almost six months earlier with a third in the Grade 3 Knickerbocker Handicap at Aqueduct.

Green Line Express's family was discussed at length in *Racehorses of 1989*. His sire Green Forest was the top European miler of 1982, having taken three of the four Group 1 races open to colts in France as a two-year-old. Green Forest's three other winners in Britain and Ireland in 1990 all came from the same stable, the best of them the useful sprinter Centerland. Laylitna's three previous living foals included two winners, one in North America by Silver Hawk. Laylitna, thrice-raced as a two-year-old, is a

Kiveton Park Stakes, Doncaster—
a well-deserved pattern-race win for Green Line Express,
who beats Sally Rous (noseband)

Ecurie Fustok's "Green Line Express"

	Green Forest (USA) (ch 1979)	Shecky Greene (b 1970)	Noholme II
Green Line			Lester's Pride
Express (USA)		Tell Meno Lies (gr 1971)	The Axe II
(ch.c. 1986)			Filatonga
	Laylitna (USA) (b 1978)	Key To The Mint (b 1969)	Graustark
			Key Bridge
		Furl Sail (b 1964)	Revoked
			Windsail

daughter of Furl Sail, the champion American three-year-old filly of 1967, and a half-sister to the two-year-old seven-furlong winner Wedgewood Blue, dam of Spode's Blue who won a maiden at Redcar and a minor event at Chester over a mile and a half in October. Green Line Express is a good-quartered, quite attractive colt who stays nine furlongs. He lacks the turn of foot of some of his contemporaries and needs riding up with the pace to be seen to best advantage; on more than one occasion he's looked well worth a chance over a mile and a quarter. He acts on firm going and has yet to race on a soft surface. He sweated up at Goodwood and Deauville and, like most of the stable's runners, had the tongue strap dispensed with in the latest season. Green Line Express is due to stay in training as a five-year-old. *M. Moubarak.*

GREEN POLA (USA) 2 b.f. (Apr 25) Nijinsky (CAN) 138–Irish Valley (USA) **109** p
(Irish River (FR) 131) [1990 7g* 7g*] $112,000Y: second foal: sister to Irish 3-y-o 11f winner Gaelic Myth: dam half-sister to Green Dancer (by Nijinsky): successful in maiden at Saint-Cloud and Prix du Calvados (by ¾ length from Magic Night, pair

clear) at Deauville: injured herself just before Prix Marcel Boussac at Longchamp in October: will stay 1¼m: highly regarded. *G. Mikhalides, France.*

GREEN'S CANALETTO (USA) 4 b.c. Hagley (USA)–Gaucherie (USA) **102** (Sharpen Up 127) [1989 6f2 6m3 6f 6m* 6m3 5g2 6m5 5g 1990 6f5 7.2f5 6m4 6g 5m] tall, leggy, lengthy colt: really good mover with a long stride: useful winner as 3-y-o: form in 1990 only when fourth to Sharp N' Early in listed event at Lingfield: effective at 5f and 6f: yet to race on soft going, appears to act on any other: trained until after second outing by W. Jarvis. *R. Akehurst.*

GREEN'S CASSATT (USA) 2 ch.f. (Mar 6) Apalachee (USA) 137–Royally **74** Rewarded (USA) (Bold Forbes (USA)) [1990 5f2 5m2 6f* 7g2] $50,000Y: leggy, rather angular filly: moderate walker: half-sister to 2 winners in North America: dam minor winner at 3 yrs: modest performer: won 4-runner minor event at Folkestone: short-head second of 4 finishers in similar event at Warwick later in June: better suited by 7f than shorter. *P. F. I. Cole.*

GREEN'S COROT 3 b.g. Prince Tenderfoot (USA) 126–Song Beam 84 (Song **74** 132) [1989 a6g* 1990 8f3 7m 7.6g2 7.6f5 a8g3 7g] big, lengthy gelding: modest performer: stays 1m: acts on firm going: has wandered under pressure, and didn't find much on final start: sold 7,600 gns Newmarket Autumn Sales, probably to race in Italy. *P. F. I. Cole.*

GREEN'S FERNELEY (IRE) 2 gr.c. (Apr 12) Taufan (USA) 119–Rossaldene **97** 79 (Mummy's Pet 125) [1990 7m3 7m* 8.2d3 8m3 9v] IR 32,000Y: neat colt: half-brother to several winners, including fairly useful 1985 2-y-o 5f winner Lammastide (by Martinmas): dam 5f winner at 2 yrs: improving colt: won maiden at Yarmouth in August by 4 lengths: third after in 4-runner minor event at Haydock and listed race at Ascot, and around 8 lengths seventh of 16 to Steamer Duck in Gran Criterium at Milan: better suited by 1m than 7f: yet to race on very firm ground, acts on any other: blinkered last 2 starts. *W. J. Haggas.*

GREEN'S GUARDI (USA) 3 b.c. Hagley (USA)–Carobreuse (FR) (Caro 133) **53** [1989 NR 1990 12.5f 12m4 12m6 10m2 10g3] $65,000Y: rangy, workmanlike colt: moderate walker: has rather round action: fifth foal: brother to Italian 1989 9.8f winner Soft Caresse and Schnell, winner of 8 minor races in North America, and half-brother to 2 minor winners in North America: dam twice-raced in USA: plating-class maiden: best efforts when blinkered and making most last 3 starts, in seller final one: suited by 1¼m: sold 11,000 gns Newmarket July Sales. *W. Jarvis.*

GREENSIDE 2 b.f. (May 3) Hotfoot 126–Akola (Hard Tack 111§) [1990 a5g4 a6g2 **47** a7g2 7.5f 7f3 7h a6g a7g a8g] 5,000Y: angular, sparely-made filly: has a roundish action: seventh foal: dam unraced: poor maiden: stays 7f. *R. Thompson.*

GREEN'S MAUD EARL 2 b.f. (Apr 18) Night Shift (USA)–Brittle Grove 79 **—** (Bustino 136) [1990 6d4 5v6] 9,000F, 14,000Y: compact, attractive filly: first foal: dam twice-raced daughter of half-sister to top-class Italian stayer Weimar: backward, well beaten in maidens at Chester on consecutive days in October: sold 1,800 gns Newmarket Autumn Sales. *W. Jarvis.*

GREEN'S MOILLON (USA) 2 b.f. (May 3) Hagley (USA)–My Mademoiselle **41** (USA) (Buckaroo (USA)) [1990 5g6 5f5 6m a6g 5.1m5 8m6 8.2g 7f] $25,000Y: close-coupled filly: moderate walker: has a round action: third reported foal: dam ran once: poor plater: best form at 5f: bought out of W. Haggas's stable 1,800 gns Newmarket July Sales after first outing. *J. L. Harris.*

GREEN'S PORTRAIT (IRE) 2 b. or br.c. (Mar 5) Gianchi–Tin Mary 96 (Tin **82** King 126) [1990 6m 6g 5.8m4 7f2 7m 7m* 7.3g* 8d 7m] IR 9,400Y, 16,500 2-y-o: tall, rather unfurnished colt: has scope: half-brother to several winners, including useful 1m to 1¾m winner Gallant Welsh (by Welsh Pageant): dam stayed 1m: sire, fourth in Italian Derby, is son of Niniski: fair colt: successful in claimer at Salisbury and nursery at Newbury (idled) in September: not at all knocked about in Newmarket nursery final outing: should stay 1m: possibly unsuited by dead ground: trained first 5 outings by R. Hannon: sold 14,000 gns Newmarket Autumn Sales. *R. Akehurst.*

GREEN'S SEAGO (USA) 2 ch.g. (Apr 17) Fighting Fit (USA)–Ornamental **70** (USA) (Triple Crown (USA)) [1990 a5g5 5m4 6m6 6m3 5m4 8m4 7m4 8.2d a8g a8g* a7g2 a8g] $55,000Y: rather sparely-made gelding: easy mover: half-brother to 2 minor winners in North America: dam unraced: sire won from 6f to 9f: won 12-runner claimer at Lingfield in November, showing improved form, by 2½ lengths: good second in nursery at Southwell later in year: stays 1m: acts well on all-weather, best form on turf on top-of-the-ground: has tended to hang: trained first 5 starts by R. Hannon, next 3 by R. Akehurst then sold 3,200 gns Newmarket Autumn Sales. *J. L. Harris.*

GREEN'S STUBBS 3 b.g. Ballad Rock 122–Aventina 83 (Averof 123) [1989 5g⁴ —
5m² 5m³ 6m* 6m⁴ 1990 6m 6m 6m] close-coupled, strong gelding: has a sharp
action: modest winner at 2 yrs: faced stiff tasks in claimers and handicap (sweating)
in summer of 1990: should stay 7f: blinkered final start: sold 1,950 gns Newmarket
September Sales and subsequently gelded. *P. F. I. Cole.*

GREEN'S TRILOGY (USA) 2 b.g. (Mar 22) Lyphard's Wish (FR) 124–Capitol 80
Caper (USA) (Senate Whip (USA)) [1990 6m⁵ 5m* 7g 8m* 9g²] tall, leggy,
sparely-made gelding: looks weak: moderate mover, with rather round action:
second foal: dam twice-raced half-sister to Play Fellow, Grade 1 winner at up to 11f
in USA: modest performer: won maiden at Windsor in August and nursery at
Pontefract in September: good second to Strike Fire in nursery at Sandown: ran
poorly third start: will stay 1¼m. *W. Jarvis.*

GREEN'S VAN GOYEN (IRE) 2 b.g. (Apr 3) Lyphard's Special (USA) 61
122–Maiden Concert (Condorcet (FR)) [1990 6m 7g 7g] IR 17,000F, IR 40,000Y:
lengthy gelding: has scope: third foal: half-brother to 3-y-o Candy Glen (by
Glenstal), successful from 5f (at 2 yrs) to 9f, including in Italian 2000 Guineas: dam
once-raced half-sister to dam of Irish 1000 Guineas winner More So: quite modest
form in southern maidens: will be better suited by 1m +: trained first 2 starts (bit
backward) by R. Hannon. *R. Akehurst.*

GREEN TIN HUT (USA) 3 b.g. Strike Gold (USA)–Cazeez (USA) (Cannonade —
(USA)) [1989 8d 1990 8m 10.1m 8.2m] angular, rather unfurnished gelding: no form,
including in handicap: pulled hard on reappearance: moved badly to post next start.
M. H. Tompkins.

GREEN TURBAN 2 b.c. (Apr 6) Shareef Dancer (USA) 135–Miss Petard 113 82 p
(Petingo 135) [1990 7g⁵ 8m] small, sturdy colt: ninth living foal: brother to 3-y-o
10.4f winner Jubilee Trail and half-brother to Musidora and Park Hill winner
Rejuvenate (by Ile de Bourbon) and useful miler Cracking Form (by Habitat): dam
won at up to 1½m: around 2 lengths fifth of 14, always prominent and not knocked
about when beaten, to Jahafil in minor event at Doncaster: co-second favourite,
remote seventh of 8, slowly away, in Royal Lodge William Hill Stakes at Ascot later
in September: evidently thought capable of better. *B. W. Hills.*

GREENWICH BAMBI 2 b.f. (May 23) Music Boy 124–Coca (Levmoss 133) 63
[1990 5m⁴ 5f⁴ 6d⁵ 7d⁴] 8,400Y: rather unfurnished filly: seventh foal: half-sister to

Timeform Nursery Handicap, Pontefract—
note Munro's distinctive riding style on Green's Trilogy,
who gets the better of Bolt near the finish

3-y-o Rexy Boy (by Dunbeath), smart 7f (at 2 yrs) and 9f winner Greenwich Papillon (by Glenstal), Irish 11.5f winner Antiguan Reef (by Mill Reef) and winners abroad: dam, placed over 11f at 3 yrs in French Provinces, is granddaughter of 1000 Guineas winner Hypericum: quite modest maiden: stays 7f. *W. Carter.*

GREEN WITH ENVY   2 b.c. (Mar 22) Green Ruby (USA) 104–Pearl Pet 56   — (Mummy's Pet 125) [1990 6m 6f] 6,400Y, 5,200 2-y-o: rather leggy, useful-looking colt: first foal: dam maiden stayed 10.8f: behind in maiden at Goodwood and seller (claimed £6,500) at Leicester. *A. R. Davison.*

GREETLAND GRIT   3 ch.f. Ballacashtal (CAN)–Tempered Wind (Fleece 114)   30 [1989 5g⁵ 7m 6v 6s 1990 6s⁵ 8m⁶ 8m⁶ 8g⁵ a11g] sparely-made filly: poor mover: plater: best effort fourth start: trained until after then by J. Berry. *B. Preece.*

GREETLAND ROCK   2 ch.g. (Apr 2) Ballacashtal (CAN)–Zamindara (Crofter   65 (USA) 124) [1990 a5g a6g⁴ 5m² 5m⁴ 5m² 5f* 5m³ 5v⁶ a5g⁴] 4,000Y: neat gelding: first foal: dam poor maiden stayed 1m: fairly useful plater: made all at Folkestone (bought in 3,800 gns) in September: ran creditably when in frame in non-selling nurseries at Redcar and Southwell (sweating profusely) afterwards, moderately in seller at Ayr in between: better suited by 5f than 6f: not ideally suited by heavy ground. *J. Berry.*

GREGORAVICH   3 ch.c. Nijinsky (CAN) 138–Pagan Queen 83 (Vaguely Noble   — 140) [1989 NR 1990 12.5f] leggy, angular colt: fifth reported foal: brother to 1989 1½m winner La Gracile and closely related to 1½m winner Green Steps (by Green Dancer): dam won at 1½m and 1¾m: tailed off in maiden at Wolverhampton in April: sold 9,400 gns Newmarket July Sales. *G. Wragg.*

GREY ADMIRAL   5 gr.g. Alias Smith (USA)–Beech Tree 67 (Fighting Ship 121)   47 [1989 NR 1990 12f⁴ 12f] leggy, rather sparely-made gelding: good mover: poor maiden: best form at up to 1½m on soft going: winning selling hurdler in May: sold 6,000 gns Ascot July Sales. *K. A. Morgan.*

GREY AREA   3 gr.c. Petong 126–Little Mercy 90 (No Mercy 126) [1989 6d 1990   63 7m² 7f⁶] good-topped colt: has plenty of scope: second to Anna Karietta in maiden at Lingfield in August, making most: edgy, took good hold to post and in race for minor event 9 days later: should prove best at sprint distances. *Mrs N. Macauley.*

GREY CHIMES   2 ch.f. (Apr 22) Grey Desire 115–Cowbells (Mountain Call 125)   — [1990 5f] half-sister to 1¼m winner Magic Mink (by Record Token) and 2 winners by Dublin Taxi: dam unraced: behind in seller at Redcar in June: sold 650 gns Doncaster September Sales. *M. Brittain.*

GREY COMMANDER   2 gr.c. (Feb 28) Grey Desire 115–Melowen 75 (Owen   50 Dudley 121) [1990 5m⁶ 5g a5g³ 6g 8d] leggy, sparely-made colt: moderate mover: second foal: half-brother to temperamental animal Sunny Jorvick (by Mansingh): dam 6f and 7f winner stayed 1m, is out of close relation to outstanding sprinter Floribunda: poor maiden: off course 3 months after running well on all-weather: probably stays 1m. *M. Brittain.*

GREY DANCER   2 gr.c. (Feb 27) Petong 126–Infelice (Nishapour (FR) 125)   59 [1990 8g 7g 10.2s] 9,800Y: compact colt: third foal: dam from family of smart Catherine Wheel: bit backward, plating-class form in maidens and a median auction: probably best short of 1¼m. *C. N. Allen.*

GREY EARL   2 gr.c. (Feb 16) Today And Tomorrow 78–Runager 74 (Lochnager   — 132) [1990 5g 5m 7f 7d] big, lengthy, good-topped colt: first foal: dam 2-y-o 5f winner: well beaten in sellers: raced very freely when blinkered final 2 starts. *W. J. Pearce.*

GREY GYPSY   4 gr.f. Absalom 128–Nyeri 104 (Saint Crespin III 132) [1989 6s² 6v   50 6m 6f⁵ a6g 1990 a10g a11g³ a14g* 12m a14g 16s⁴ a13g] angular, good-bodied filly: moderate mover: plating-class handicapper: won at Southwell in February: probably stays 2m: acts on soft going: blinkered once at 3 yrs: doesn't find much off bridle: sold 4,600 gns Newmarket December Sales. *P. T. Walwyn.*

GREY ILLUSIONS   2 gr.c. (Apr 14) Nishapour (FR) 125–Morica 88   66 (Moorestyle 137) [1990 6g 6d⁶ 6g²] 5,800Y: strong colt: moderate walker: first foal: dam 2-y-o 6f winner, stayed 1¼m, is half-sister to Aragon out of half-sister to Song: progressive maiden: second to Ageetee at Folkestone in October: will be better suited by 7f. *L. J. Holt.*

GREY MERLIN   3 gr.g. Derrylin 115–Sea Kestrel 82 (Sea Hawk II 131) [1989 6g⁵   56 6m⁵ 6m 7m³ 7m 8.2g 8d⁴ 1990 8g 8m⁶ 8.2d² 10.4g⁵ 9g 8.2v⁶] sturdy gelding: has a markedly round action: plating-class maiden: best efforts in claimers third and fourth (blinkered) starts: stays 1¼m: acts on dead going: has run well for 7-lb claimer. *Miss L. C. Siddall.*

GREY NORTH 2 b.f. (May 3) Grey Desire 115–Northgate Lady 54 (Fordham (USA) 117) [1990 a8g] third foal: half-sister to modest plater Crofter's Court (by Crofthall) and 4-y-o Telegraph Callgirl (by Northern Tempest), successful at 7f and 1m: dam little worthwhile form, including in sellers: tailed-off last of 12 in claimer (unruly start) at Southwell late in year. *M. Brittain.* —

GREY OWL (USA) 3 gr.c. Caro 133–Demure (USA) (Dr Fager) [1989 7g⁵ 1990 8g⁶ 8m³ 10m³ 10f² 8m⁵ 9g³ 8.2g* 8g² 8m³ 8m* 8d⁴ 9g⁶] big, good-topped colt: carries condition: fairly useful performer: won maiden (simple task) at Hamilton in September then in good form in handicaps, leading close home to win £11,000 event at Ascot in October: below form in £19,600 event at Newmarket final start: should prove as effective at 1¼m as 1m: acts on firm ground: visored last 9 outings: flashed tail fifth start: has taken keen hold: to join S. McGaughey in USA. *J. Gosden.* 94

GREY POWER 3 gr.f. Wolf Power (SAF)–Periquito (USA) (Olden Times) [1989 6g 7d⁶ 1990 8f² 10.2m² 11m 12m⁶ 12m³ 13.3g³] good-topped filly: modest maiden: third in October handicaps at Ascot and Newbury, tending to wander first occasion: stays 13f: acts on good to firm ground. *W. Hastings-Bass.* 74

GREY REALM 2 ch.f. (Jan 30) Grey Desire 115–Miss Realm 86 (Realm 129) [1990 5d⁶ 5d a5g⁴ 6g³ 7d 6g a8g 8m 6m] 10,000Y: close-coupled, deep-girthed filly: moderate mover: third foal: half-sister to 3-y-o Spanish Realm (by King of Spain), quite modest 5f winner at 2 yrs: dam 2-y-o 5f winner: moderate plater at best: stays 7f: sold 560 gns Doncaster October Sales. *M. Brittain.* 45

GREY RECORD 2 gr.c. (Feb 28) Grey Desire 115–Record Lady (Record Token 128) [1990 6g 6d³ 5v³ a7g⁶] 10,000Y: rather angular colt: second foal: half-brother to 3-y-o Sireesh (by Reesh): dam unraced daughter of half-sister to Chellaston Park: plating-class form in maidens: ran moderately on all-weather: should prove suited by further than 5f: acts on heavy going. *M. Brittain.* 57

GREY ROOSTER (USA) 2 gr.c. (Apr 10) Diesis 133–Chickery Chick (USA) (Hatchet Man (USA)) [1990 5g* 5m³ 5g 5.8h² 5g⁶ 5f⁵] $65,000Y: shallow-girthed, smallish, lengthy colt: fluent mover: third reported foal: half-brother to a minor winner in North America by Slewpy: dam winner at around 1m as 4-y-o: fair performer: won maiden at Newmarket in April: excellent second in nursery at Bath: ran badly final start: much better suited by 6f than 5f. *W. Jarvis.* 89

GREY RUM 5 gr.g. Absalom 128–Cuba Libre (Rum (USA)) [1989 6g 8m 8h⁵ 7.5m 8.2g⁵ 8g² 7f² 8f⁵ 8.3d² 7s² 7g* 7m* 7m⁶ a8g⁶ 1990 a7g a6g⁵ a7g³ 7m⁵ 7.5m³ 8f 7g 8.2m 6f⁵ 8f³ 7.6m² 7f³ 7m⁵ 7f* 7f² 6m² 7m 7m] workmanlike gelding: plating-class handicapper: won apprentice race at Folkestone in August: effective over stiff 6f to 1m: acts on any going: effective with or without blinkers: good mount for inexperienced rider: sold to join R. Lee's stable 17,000 gns Newmarket Autumn Sales: tough. *W. J. Pearce.* 52

GREY SHIMMER (USA) 3 gr.c. Caro 133–Beauty's Image (USA) (Wajima (USA)) [1989 7g 8g 1990 8f² 8g* 8m 7m] big, lengthy colt: has a quick action: modest form: odds on, won apprentice maiden at Warwick in July, making most: below form in handicaps at Newmarket: may prove best at up to 1m: very edgy and withdrawn on intended debut. *L. Cumani.* 72

GREY SONATA 3 gr.f. Horage 124–The Grey (GER) (Pentathlon) [1989 6f³ 5m 5f 7g⁴ 7.3m a7g 7g 1990 11.7f 8f⁶ 6m 7m] leggy filly: poor walker and mover: quite modest maiden at best: soundly beaten in seller and amateurs handicap (blinkered) last 2 starts: stays 1m: acts on firm going: has looked unsatisfactory: winning hurdler. *C. L. Popham.* 53

GREY STARLING 2 b.f. (Mar 12) Pharly (FR) 130–Jolly Bay 108 (Mill Reef (USA) 141) [1990 8g 7m⁶] rather leggy, quite attractive filly: third reported foal: half-sister to a winner in Austria by Comedy Star: dam, winner of Pretty Polly Stakes, is daughter of Juliette Marny, a sister to Julio Mariner and half-sister to Scintillate: disputed lead over 5f when around 6 lengths sixth of 22 in maiden at Chepstow in October: green and slowly away on debut: will stay 1¼m: sure to do better. *R. Charlton.* 64 p

GREY TUDOR 3 gr.g. Import 127–Grey Morley 78 (Pongee 106) [1989 6f⁴ 6s a6g* a6g 1990 a6g⁶ 5f 5s² 7g 5g a7g 7m 10f³ 10f 10m 6m⁶ 6g 6d* 5s⁴ a6g a6g⁴ a7g] leggy, workmanlike gelding: plating-class performer: soon pushed along in rear when winning 21-runner apprentice selling handicap (no bid) at Leicester in October: should prove suited by at least 6f: probably acts on any going: blinkered, edgy and unruly to post eleventh start: has been slowly away. *C. N. Allen.* 59

GREY WOLF   3 gr.g. Bellypha 130–Matinee 119 (Zeddaan 130) [1989 7g² 6d 1990   **66 d**
6f⁴ 6m² a7g 5.8h³ 6m 8f a8g⁶ a8g a6g⁵] tall gelding: poor mover: quite modest
maiden: narrowly beaten, running on well, at Newmarket and Haydock (claimer) in
May: claimed out of R. J. R. Williams' stable £3,133 fifth start, trained by M. Channon
on sixth: should s.ay beyond 6f. *K. O. Cunningham-Brown.*

GRIFFITH (IRE)   2 ch.c. (May 25) Glow (USA)–Ashton Amber (On Your Mark   **52**
125) [1990 7m 8.2d 8m 10s] IR 34,000Y: deep-girthed colt: has a long stride: eighth
foal: half-brother to Irish 2000 Guineas second Mr John (by Northfields) and to
several other winners here and abroad: dam once-raced sister to Red Alert: bit
backward, behind in maidens, easily best effort penultimate outing: should stay
1¼m. *B. Hanbury.*

GRIS ET VIOLET (FR)   3 ch.g. Iron Duke (FR) 122–Darkeuse (FR) (Dark   **—**
Tiger) [1989 NR 1990 12m] 90,000 francs (approx £8,200) Y: workmanlike gelding:
seventh foal: brother to French 9.2f to 10.5f winner Waterloo Revenge and half-
brother to several middle-distance winners: dam successful 8 times (5 at 2 yrs) in
France at up to 10.2f: bit backward, green and well beaten in claimer at Beverley in
September: winning hurdler. *J. G. FitzGerald.*

GRONDOLA   3 b.f. Indian King (USA) 128–Trysting Place (He Loves Me 120)   **54 d**
[1989 7.5f 8f³ 7g a8g 1990 a8g* a10g⁶ a10g³ 8.5m⁵ 10f³ 8g⁶ 8m] leggy, close-coupled
filly: plating-class performer: below form after making all in 5-runner maiden (odds
on) at Lingfield in January: keen sort, seems best at 1m: trained until after sixth
start by P. Kelleway: winning hurdler. *D. Burchell.*

GROOMBRIDGE (USA)   2 ch.c. (Feb 5) Blushing Groom (FR) 131–Double   **76 +**
Axle (USA) (The Axe II 115) [1990 5m⁴ 6m* 6m] sturdy, strong colt: half-brother to
several winners, including 3-y-o Digression (by Seattle Slew), smart 7f and 1m
winner at 2 yrs: dam won 4 races at up to 1m: favourite, won maiden at Goodwood in
May comfortably by 2½ lengths: never travelling well in Coventry Stakes at Royal
Ascot following month, and not seen out again. *G. Harwood.*

GROVE ARIES (IRE)   2 b.c. (May 12) Doulab (USA) 115–Habanna 107 (Habitat   **97**
134) [1990 6d³ 6m* 6f 6g⁶ 7m⁴ 7.3g⁴] 8,000Y: compact colt: has scope: moderate
mover: half-brother to several winners, including Manhatten Miss (by Artaius),
fairly useful at up to 7f in Ireland: dam Irish 2-y-o 5f and 6f winner: fairly useful
performer: won 3-runner maiden at Yarmouth by 6 lengths in July: much better
efforts final 3 outings in listed race at Kempton, moderately-run Somerville
Tattersall Stakes at Newmarket and Vodafone Horris Hill Stakes (travelled strongly
over 5f when fourth of 9 to Sapieha) at Newbury: gives impression may prove better
suited by 6f than 7f. *M. H. Tompkins.*

GROVE SERENDIPITY (IRE)   2 b.c. (Mar 18) Glenstal (USA) 118–Huppel   **77**
83 (Huntercombe 133) [1990 6m 7g⁶ 7f² 7m 7.6v⁶] 19,000F: close-coupled, workmanlike colt: half-brother to a winner in Italy by Mill Reef: dam 7f and 1m winner:
modest maiden: well beaten in nurseries final 2 starts, at Chester (first run for 2
months) second occasion: sold 14,500 gns Newmarket Autumn Sales. *M. H.
Tompkins.*

GROWN AT ROWAN   3 b.f. Gabitat 119–Hallo Rosie 67 (Swing Easy (USA)   **75**
126) [1989 6f 6f 6m 6f³ 1990 6h⁶ 5.3h³ 5g² 6f³ 5m² 5m² 7m* 8g 6m⁶] rather leggy
filly: modest performer: won £7,200 handicap at Sandown in August, leading close
home: unseated rider to post and weakened final 1f next start: probably best at 6f or
7f: acts on hard ground: consistent. *M. Madgwick.*

GUAPA   2 b.f. (May 4) Shareef Dancer (USA) 135–Sauceboat 120 (Connaught 130)   **— p**
[1990 8g] medium-sized, lengthy, useful-looking filly: seventh foal: closely related
to a winner in France by Dance In Time and half-sister to 4 winners here and in
France, including smart 1m to 11f winner Kind of Hush (by Welsh Pageant) and
smart 8.5f and 10f winner Dusty Dollar (by Kris): dam won at 6f (at 2 yrs) and stayed
1¼m: favourite but edgy and green, considerably handled and never better than
mid-division in 13-runner maiden at Wolverhampton in October: will stay middle
distances: sure to improve. *M. R. Stoute.*

GUARANTEE   3 b.c. Persian Bold 123–Kendie Blue (FR) (Kenmare (FR) 125)   **—**
[1989 6m⁶ 6f 7g 6m³ 5f² 5d 8f 8s⁶ 5g a5g² a6g⁵ a5g 1990 a8g 5m 6f 5.3f] neat colt:
moderate walker: quite modest maiden: well beaten as 3-y-o, including in handicaps: bred to stay at least 7f: blinkered sixth start: has run well for 7-lb claimer: has
hung left, and worn tongue strap: inconsistent: sold to join C. Popham 5,200 gns
Ascot November Sales. *C. A. Austin.*

GUAYAMINA PRINCESS   2 b.f. (Apr 27) Nishapour (FR) 125–Petingalyn   **—**
(Petingo 135) [1990 8.2d] tall, leggy, angular filly: half-sister to several winners,

including 1¼m winner Bronze Runner (by Gunner B): dam of no account: tailed off in autumn minor event at Nottingham. *J. Parkes.*

GUECA SOLO 2 ch.f. (Mar 24) Pharly (FR) 130–Atitlan (Relko 136) [1990 6m⁶] 10,000Y: second foal: half-sister to a winner in Italy: dam French 1m and 1¼m winner: favourite but better for race, around 5 lengths sixth of 11, soon in touch after slow start then no extra final furlong and not knocked about, in maiden at Yarmouth in September: went freely down: sure to improve, particularly at 7f+. *H. R. A. Cecil.*   **68** p

GUEST RIGHT 3 b.c. Be My Guest (USA) 126–Miss Allowed (USA) (Alleged (USA) 138) [1989 NR 1990 8.2s 8.2g² 11g 12d⁶ 10g 9m 10.5g⁶ 10d] IR 5,400F: lengthy, angular colt: fourth foal: brother to Irish 7.9f winner Norquest and Italian 1990 1¼m winner Okay Brazil and closely related to 1986 Irish 2-y-o 6f and 7f winner Best Try (by Try My Best), later successful in USA: dam unraced daughter of very useful middle-distance filly Miss Toshiba: quite modest maiden: second in apprentice event at Hamilton in May, best effort: should stay 1¼m. *M. Brittain.*   **59** d

GUIDOBALDO (USA) 4 b.c. Sir Ivor 135–Hankow Willow (USA) (No Robbery) [1989 7s² 8s 8f 8g 1990 8f 9g a8g a11g⁶ a12g⁶] leggy colt: poor mover: second in maiden as 3-y-o, only worthwhile form: should stay 1m: possibly needs soft going: bandaged, trained on reappearance by S. Dow. *C. N. Allen.*   —

GUILTY CONSCIENCE 3 b.g. Pitskelly 122–Sweet Shop 62 (Sweet Revenge 129) [1989 NR 1990 12g 12m 16g] IR 4,000Y: sturdy, lengthy gelding: half-brother to 4 winners in Ireland, including fairly useful 1¼m performer Madam Slaney (by Prince Tenderfoot): dam won over 13f: no show in claimers and maiden: very much on toes on debut, blinkered final start: dead. *P. Burgoyne.*   —

GULFLAND 9 ch.g. Gulf Pearl 117–Sunland Park (Baragoi 115) [1989 12.2s⁵ 12s 12f² 12.4m 11s 12.2f⁴ 12g⁶ a12g⁵ 1990 a12g³ 12g² 12m² 12.4m⁵ 12g* a12g⁵ 12d⁶ 12m* 12.2m 12g] workmanlike, good-bodied gelding: carries condition: moderate mover: quite modest handicapper: won 4-runner race at Hamilton in July and slowly-run amateurs event at Pontefract in September: suited by 1½m: acts on any going, but particularly well on an easy surface: usually ridden by 5-lb claimer A. Peate: held up: tough. *G. A. Pritchard-Gordon.*   **59**

GULF PALACE (USA) 5 ch.h. Green Dancer (USA) 132–Sanctum Sanctorum (USA) (Secretariat (USA)) [1989 12s⁴ 12d² 11.7m⁴ 10f* 12f⁵ 12m³ 12m* 10g² 12f² 12m² 10m 12m 1990 12m² 12d⁵ 10m² 10m 12f² 12f³ 12s³] rangy, well-made horse: moderate mover, with a quick action: fair handicapper: stays 1½m well: acts on any going, but particularly well on top-of-the-ground: usually held up: consistent. *R. Akehurst.*   **88**

GULF REESH 3 b.c. Reesh 117–Ro (Absalom 128) [1989 NR 1990 7m 6m 7d] 24,000Y: leggy colt: has a round action: second foal: brother to 1988 2-y-o 5f seller winner No More Mas: dam unraced from family of Dominion: in mid-division for sellers in the summer: should prove best beyond 6f. *G. A. Huffer.*   —

GULLANE 4 b.g. Valiyar 129–Olivian 79 (Hotfoot 126) [1989 12s² 11v⁴ 12.2d 12f 10m⁵ 12m 15g³ a16g³ 1990 a16g a12g⁶] sturdy, heavy-bodied gelding: moderate mover: poor maiden: stays 2m: acts on soft going: blinkered second and fourth starts in 1989: visored fifth: often pulls hard: trained on reappearance by Allan Smith: ungenuine and one to leave alone. *M. J. Ryan.*   — §

GULMARG 3 b.c. Gorytus (USA) 132–Kashmili 3now 03 (Shirley Heights 130) [1989 6m³ 8m 6d⁴ 6g⁴ 1990 7g⁵ 7f⁴ 8d² 8m⁴ 8f* 9m* 9m] rangy, attractive colt: moderate mover: fairly useful performer: successful in August in 4-runner maiden (8/1 on) at Thirsk and handicap (best effort, comfortably) at Wolverhampton: ran poorly in Cambridgeshire Handicap at Newmarket final start: suited by 9f: acts on firm and dead going. *H. Candy.*   **90**

GULSHA 4 b.f. Glint of Gold 128–Mai Pussy 91 (Realm 129) [1989 7g⁵ 1990 a7g² 10.2f⁴] workmanlike filly: quite modest form in maidens: stays 1¼m: sold to join N. Twiston-Davies' stable 16,000 gns Doncaster March Sales. *B. Hanbury.*   **62**

GUNBOAT 4 ch.g. Relaunch (USA)–Ferjima's Gem (USA) (Wajima (USA)) [1989 6m² 6f² 6m 6f³ 7g 1990 6f 6m 5m 5m6 9f⁶ 8g 7m² 6s] good-topped gelding: fair at best: showed he retains some ability when short-head second of 20 in selling handicap at Yarmouth in September: stays 7f: acts on firm going: has got an edge. *K. M. Brassey.*   **61**

GUNRUNNER GIRL 3 ch.f. Longleat (USA) 109–Witchingham Lass 83 (Sweet Revenge 129) [1989 6g 7g 1990 7m 7f 5m] rangy, rather unfurnished filly: no sign of ability, in handicaps last 2 outings. *R. Voorspuy.*   —

GUNS AND ROSES 3 ch.c. Ballad Rock 122–Sweet Reprieve (Shirley Heights 85
130) [1989 NR 1990 a7g² a6g* 6m³ 7m⁶ 7f⁶ 5m³ 6m⁵ 5m* 6m⁴ 5m² 6d 6d 6s³ 5s
a6g² a7g³] 10,000Y: leggy, close-coupled colt: second foal: dam, placed over middle
distances in Ireland, is half-sister to William Hill Futurity winner Sandy Creek: won
maiden at Lingfield in February and handicap at Newmarket in July: in frame in
handicaps after, finishing well when narrowly beaten at Doncaster and Lingfield
(twice) last 3 occasions: stays 7f: probably acts on any going: often gets behind, and
is worth a try in blinkers or a visor. *W. A. O'Gorman.*

GURTEEN BOY 8 ch.g. Tickled Pink 114–Joie d'Or (FR) (Kashmir II 125) [1989 44
11v² 1990 13s³ 12s] strong, sturdy, plain gelding: has a round action: shows signs of
stringhalt: poor handicapper: stays 13f: goes particularly well with plenty of give in
the ground: has been tried in blinkers, visor and hood: suitable mount for
apprentice: winning hurdler in 1989/90. *J. J. O'Neill.*

GUSHY 4 ch.c. Hard Fought 125–Be Gustful (Ballymore 123) [1989 8.2m* 9f⁴ 8g 59
8.2g² 10s³ 9s³ 1990 8.2s 8v 8m³ 8m* 8.2s³ 8f⁵ 8m* 8m⁵ 8g⁵ 8d³ 8m⁶ 8f³] smallish,
workmanlike colt: moderate walker and mover: fairly useful plater: won handicaps
at Pontefract in April (no bid) and June (sold out of M. W. Easterby's stable 7,000
gns): suited by 1m: acts on any going: usually blinkered or visored: has worn
bandages: sold 1,250 gns Ascot October Sales. *C. R. Beever.*

GUTHRIE COURT 3 b.f. Daring March 116–Gangawayhame 91 (Lochnager 45
132) [1989 5m* 6f² 5f* 1990 7g 7.5d 5m 5g 5d 6g] stocky filly: good walker: modest
plater: easily best effort as 3-y-o in non-selling handicap at Carlisle fourth start:
suited by 5f: acts on firm ground: visored fifth start: sold 1,950 gns Ascot July Sales.
M. H. Easterby.

GYMCRAK FORTUNE (IRE) 2 b.g. (Mar 2) Kafu 120–Forlorn Chance 51
(Fighting Don) [1990 5m⁶ 5g⁵ a6g⁵ 7g³ a7g³ 8m] 6,000Y: lengthy, angular gelding:
moderate mover: half-brother to several winners, including 1½m winner Shanipour
(by Nishapour) and very useful French middle-distance winner Dieter (by Lord
Gayle): dam once-raced sister to very smart sprinter Forlorn River: modest plater:
stays 7f: blinkered first and penultimate starts: has flashed tail: sold 575 gns Ascot
October Sales. *M. H. Easterby.*

GYMCRAK GAMBLE 2 b.g. (Apr 4) Beldale Flutter (USA) 130–Baridi 82 52
(Ribero 126) [1990 a6g⁶ 7g⁴ a6g a7g⁵ 8.2g 10.6s] 5,200F, 7,600Y: leggy gelding:
fourth foal: half-brother to 4-y-o Island Jetsetter (by Tolomeo): dam placed at 6f and
1½m: plating-class maiden: should stay 1¼m: has been slowly away: sold 850 gns
Doncaster October Sales. *M. H. Easterby.*

GYMCRAK LOVEBIRD 3 b.f. Taufan (USA) 119–Waadi Hatta (USA) 47 84
(Upper Nile (USA)) [1989 5g 5h* 6m* 7f* 7f² 7m 1990 7g⁴ 8m² 7.5g² 9m* 10.2m⁵
9m² a8g⁵ 10g* 10.2g 10m⁴] leggy, lengthy filly: moderate mover with a markedly
round action: fair handicapper: won at Hamilton in June and Sandown (£6,400 event,
by short head) in August: gives impression should stay beyond 1¼m: acts on hard
ground: retained 2,100 gns Doncaster October Sales. *M. H. Easterby.*

GYMCRAK PREMIERE 2 ch.g. (Feb 26) Primo Dominie 121–Oraston 115 68
(Morston (FR) 125) [1990 5f²] 6,600F, 12,000Y: workmanlike gelding: half-brother
to 14.6f winner Rum Cay (by Our Native) and a winner in Italy by To The Quick: dam
won 1¼m Premio Lydia Tesio and is half-sister to smart French 1m and 1¼m
performer The Abbot: green, short-head second of 5 in maiden at Haydock in May.
M. H. Easterby.

GYMCRAK SOVEREIGN 2 b.g. (Jan 20) Ballacashtal (CAN)–Get Involved 79 48
(Shiny Tenth 120) [1990 6g 7.5g² 5f 7f 8d 8v] 7,000Y: leggy, quite good-topped
gelding: has a round action: sixth foal: brother to a winner over hurdles and
half-brother to 1m seller winner Comedy Prince (by Comedy Star): dam sprinter:
modest plater: stays 1m: possibly unsuited by extremes of ground. *M. H. Easterby.*

GYMYNSKY 2 b.g. (Feb 19) Domynsky 110–Swinging Baby 73 (Swing Easy 38
(USA) 126) [1990 5g⁴ 5f] 8,800Y: strong, robust gelding: fourth foal: dam 5f winner,
is half-sister to good Italian horse Hoche: little show in maidens at Edinburgh
(5-runner) and Beverley (auction): sold 1,200 gns Doncaster September Sales. *M.
H. Easterby.*

GYPSY QUEEN (FR) 2 gr.f. (Feb 26) Kenmare (FR) 125–Venise Pleasure — p
(USA) (Honest Pleasure (USA)) [1990 8g] useful-looking filly: first live foal: dam ran
once, is half-sister to smart French 1m and 9f winner Verria and very useful 1980
French 2-y-o 6f to 1m winner Vorias: backward, prominent 5f in 18-runner maiden at
Newmarket in October: sure to do better. *B. Hanbury.*

GYPSY RIVER (USA) 3 ch.c. Alydar (USA)–Seven Springs (USA) 114 (Irish 77
River (FR) 131) [1989 NR 1990 8m^2 7.6d^2 7m^2 8.2m* 8.3m^6 8g 10m^3] tall, rather
leggy colt: first foal: dam, half-sister to very smart Regal State, won 3 times at
around 6f at 2 yrs in France and later stayed 1m: modest form: won maiden at
Nottingham in August, running on strongly despite edging left: below form in
handicaps: suited by 1m: sold 42,000 gns Newmarket Autumn Sales. *R. Charlton.*

H

HABAAYIB 2 ch.c. (Feb 27) Blushing Groom (FR) 131–Awaasif (CAN) 130 86 P
(Snow Knight 125) [1990 7g^2] leggy colt: has scope: fourth foal: brother to promoted
Oaks winner Snow Bride, successful from 7f (at 2 yrs) to 1½m, and half-brother to
3-y-o 8.2f winner Jarraar (by Mr Prospector) and 1987 2-y-o 7f winner Salaadim (by
Seattle Slew): dam middle-distance half-sister to 1000 Guineas second Konafa and
very smart American colt Akureyei: easy to back, most promising second to Balaat
in 21-runner maiden at Newbury in August, progress 3f out then running on really
well towards finish: will stay 1¼m: sure to improve a good deal, and win races. *M. R.
Stoute.*

HABETA (USA) 4 ch.c. Habitat 134–Prise (Busted 134) [1989 8d 8f 10m^6 8g 7s 68
8.2d^2 8.2g* a8g^3 a10g* a11g 1990 10.2m 8m* 8.2s^4 8g^6 8m^6 8.2m^6 8g* 8g^5 8g^4 a8g^5
a10g^4] quite good-topped colt: carries plenty of condition: quite modest handicapper: won at Doncaster in May and Newcastle in October: ran creditably after,
including for apprentice and amateur: effective at 1m and 1¼m: yet to show form on
very firm going, acts on any other: suited by good gallop. *J. W. Watts.*

HABIBTI DANA 3 ch.f. Bairn (USA) 126–Southern Swanee 86 (My Swanee —
122) [1989 NR 1990 8m 8g] 3,200Y: lengthy, sparely-made filly: fourth foal: dam
genuine 2-y-o sprinter: slowly away, behind in maiden and claimer in the summer.
G. A. Huffer.

HABITANCY 4 b.f. Habitat 134–Bright Landing 78 (Sun Prince 128) [1989 7g —
5m^2 5s^2 5g^3 6d 1990 6m] lengthy, good-quartered filly: moderate walker and mover,
with a quick action: placed in useful company as 3-y-o: bit backward, prominent 4f in
valuable York handicap in May: should stay 6f: acts on good to firm and soft going. *R.
F. Johnson Houghton.*

HACIENDA 3 b.c. Habitat 134–Bare Minimum (Bustino 136) [1989 NR 1990 7f^6 68
10f^6 8g a8g* a8g* 9m 8d a8g] 8,000F: well-made colt: third foal: dam unraced
half-sister to 1000 Guineas third Joking Apart, dam of Galtres winners Sans Blague
and Deadly Serious: won handicaps at Southwell in May and June, best effort making
all in latter: behind in similar events after: suited by 1m: sweating badly penultimate
start: sold D. Burchell 9,400 gns Doncaster November Sales. *J. W. Watts.*

HACKFORTH 4 ch.c. Hard Fought 125–Sweet And Sour 96 (Sharpen Up 127) 75
[1989 6s 6m 10f^6 7m* 8m^2 7g 7g 6f^6 8f^6 a8g* a10g a8g 1990 a8g^3 a8g^3 a7g^3 a7g a7g^5
7m* 7f* 7.6d* a7g^2 7.6g* 7.2g 7m 7g^5 7.6v] neat colt: improved and had fine
season, winning handicaps at Catterick, Thirsk and Chester (apprentice ridden,
£14,600 event) in spring and Chester again in September: best at 7f to 1m: acts on
firm and dead going (unsuited by heavy): has turn of foot: consistent. *J. D. Bethell.*

HADLEIGHS CHOICE 3 b.g. Fairy King (USA)–Jillette (Fine Blade (USA) —
121) [1989 6g 7.6m^4 7.5f 8f 7g 1990 12f^5 12f 10m 10g 10m^6 10g] close-coupled
gelding: plating-class maiden at best: probably stays 1½m: acts on firm going: blinkered final start at 2 yrs: sold 800 gns Doncaster November Sales. *H. J. Collingridge.*

HAFHAFAH 3 b.f. Shirley Heights 130–Shurooq (USA) 94 (Affirmed (USA)) 66
[1989 8f* 8.2g 1990 8g 10.2f^2 10g 10m^5 10f^3 10m 10m^3 9m^3 10m] leggy, shallow-
girthed filly: quite modest handicapper: stays 1¼m: probably needs top-of-the-
ground: below form sweating final start: sold 6,400 gns Newmarket December
Sales. *H. Thomson Jones.*

HAIL CAESAR (USA) 3 ch.c. Roberto (USA) 131–Princess Roycraft (USA) 88
(Royal Note) [1989 NR 1990 12f^3 12f* 16.2m^4 19f^4] $350,000Y: big, angular colt:
brother to 2 winners, notably good stakes winner from 9f to 1m Royal Roberto,
and half-brother to 6 winners: dam very useful winner at up to 1m: odds on, won
4-runner maiden at Brighton in June: ran well in moderately-run £10,400 handicap
at Ascot next start, as though something amiss on final one: stays 2m. *G. Harwood.*

HAILSHAM (CAN) 2 b.c. (Feb 14) Riverman (USA) 131–Halo's Princess (CAN) 89
(Halo (USA)) [1990 6g* 6m 7g 8m^4] $125,970Y: lengthy, quite attractive colt: has a
powerful, round action: first foal: dam winner at up to 9f, was one of leading 2-y-o

fillies in Canada in 1983: fair performer: best effort 11 lengths fourth of 8, keeping on well, to Mujaazif in Royal Lodge William Hill Stakes at Ascot: earlier won maiden at Newmarket in May: will stay beyond 1m. *C. E. Brittain.*

HAITHAM 3 b.c. Wassl 125–Balqis (USA) 93 (Advocator) [1989 8g² 8d⁵ 1990 **73** 10m⁴ 11f⁴ 14g* 16.2d⁶ 12m³] rather leggy colt: moderate mover: modest performer: awkward at stalls, made all in maiden at Yarmouth in June: below form in handicap and amateurs contest (made most) following month: stays 1¾m: acts on firm going: sold 12,000 gns Newmarket Autumn Sales: winning hurdler for R. Akehurst. *H. Thomson Jones.*

HAJADE 3 b.c. Ile de Bourbon (USA) 133–Timbale d'Argent (Petingo 135) [1989 **113** NR 1990 9f³ 10g* 12f* 12f* 14.6g 12s²] IR 65,000Y: angular, good-topped colt: good walker: closely related to French 9f to 13f winner Tambour du Roi (by Green Dancer) and half-brother to 3 other winners, including 1m to 1¼m winner Tireuse de Carte (by In Fijar): dam, showed a little ability in France, is granddaughter of Never Too Late: won maiden at Goodwood in June and 4-runner races for minor event at Newmarket in July and listed race at Goodwood in August: well beaten in St Leger at Doncaster then very good second of 8, clear, to Down The Flag in St Simon Stakes at Newbury: should have stayed beyond 1½m: acted on any going: died during operation on off-hind in November. *L. Cumani.*

HAJAIM (IRE) 2 ch.c. (Feb 28) Doulab (USA) 115–Sharrara (CAN) 61 (Blushing **69** Groom (FR) 131) [1990 7m⁴ 7f* 7m] rather leggy, attractive colt: has a quick action: third foal: half-brother to 6f to 8.3f winner Juvenara (by Young Generation): dam lightly-raced maiden stayed 1¼m: won maiden at Brighton in September by a short head from Lease Back: ran moderately in minor event at Ascot following month: will stay 1m. *C. E. Brittain.*

HAKY (FR) 2 ch.c. (Jan 27) Miswaki (USA) 124–Honey Stage (USA) (Stage Door **80** Johnny) [1990 6f⁴ 7m 7g² a8g*] 38,000Y: rangy colt: has scope: half-brother to a winner in France by Stop The Music: dam French 2-y-o 1m winner: 5/2 on, won 17-runner maiden at Southwell when ridden by 5-lb claimer comfortably by ½ length from Just John: stays 1m: blinkered second start: pulled hard and tended to hang third outing. *W. A. O'Gorman.*

HALA 3 b.f. Persian Bold 123–True Respect (USA) (Baldski (USA)) [1989 5d⁴ 5f — 5g⁴ 6g³ 7f 7m³ 7g 8g 1990 a8g a8g⁵ 8m 10.2f⁴ 10.1m] leggy, sparely-made filly: moderate walker: has a fluent, round action: plating-class maiden at best: should be suited by further than 7f: has pulled hard: sweating final start: sold out of C. W. C. Elsey's stable 975 gns Ascot April Sales after second: resold 1,000 gns Newmarket July Sales. *G. G. Gracey.*

HALEIM 3 ch.c. Formidable (USA) 125–Miss Reasoning (USA) (Bold Reasoning **79** (USA)) [1989 5f³ 6g* 6m 1990 6m² 6f² 7f] sturdy colt: fair performer: good second in minor events in the spring: sweating, behind facing stiff task in handicap (moved moderately down) 3½ months later: should stay 7f. *Dr J. D. Scargill.*

HALF A PINK JO 3 ch.c. Absalom 128–Habitual Beauty (Habat 127) [1989 5g⁵ — 1990 7m 6f⁴ 7f] compact, good-quartered colt: third foal: half-brother to bad sprint maiden Vagara (by Vaigly Great): dam never ran: well beaten in varied company: sold to join S. Turton 1,300 gns Ascot October Sales. *M. McCormack.*

HALF A TICK (USA) 2 b.c. (Apr 1) Timeless Moment (USA)–Moon Star Miss **104** ? (USA) (Star Envoy (USA)) [1990 5f* 6m² 6g⁴ 7g* 7f² 7f⁶ 7f³ 8.5f⁵] $25,000Y: neat, quite attractive colt: moderate walker: has a roundish action: fifth foal: half-brother to a minor stakes winner in USA: dam stakes winner at up to 1m: useful performer: successful in maiden at Salisbury in May and minor event (comfortably) at Chester in June: very good fifth of 13 to River Traffic in Laurel Futurity at Laurel: suited by 1m: sweating and virtually pulled up seventh outing. *P. F. I. Cole.*

HALKOPOUS 4 b.g. Beldale Flutter (USA) 130–Salamina 106 (Welsh Pageant **81** 132) [1989 10.6s* 9f⁴ 12f⁵ 12g⁶ 12m* 12g⁴ 10.5m* 10g 1990 10g 12g³ 10m⁴ 10m⁴ 10.5m² 12f 12.3g² 12g⁵ 13d 12m⁴ 9m 12m 11s* 12s] compact gelding: carries plenty of condition: moderate mover: fair handicapper: visored first time, won £7,600 event at Newbury in October, idling final 1f: always behind when blinkered in November Handicap at Doncaster 2 weeks later: stays 13f: acts on any going: tough. *M. H. Tompkins.*

HALLOWED GROUND (IRE) 2 b.f. (Mar 23) Godswalk (USA) 130–Stony **60** Ground (Relko 136) [1990 5f⁵ 5m 5m³] IR 10,000Y: leggy filly: moderate walker: half-sister to several winners here and abroad, including 1983 2-y-o 7f winner Green Mist (by Derrylin) and modest miler/smart hurdler Bank View (by

Crofter): dam Irish 1½m winner: quite modest maiden: gave impression something amiss second and third starts: will stay 6f. *C. F. Wall.*

HALOX (USA) 4 b.g. Little Current (USA)–Noble Legion (CAN) (Vaguely Noble 140) [1989 10g 8m 1990 a6g³ a7g a7g⁶] strong, angular gelding: showed signs of ability in maidens: harshly treated in handicaps, blinkered final outing: bred to be suited by middle distances: very lightly raced. *J. Sutcliffe.* —

HALSTON PRINCE 3 b.c. Petorius 117–Repicado Rose (USA) (Repicado 108 (CHI)) [1989 6f² 7g² 1990 8g* 7f* 8m² 8f³ 8d² 10m* 10g⁵] compact, robust colt: moderate walker and mover: won maiden at Yarmouth and 2-runner minor event at Warwick in July then £11,650 handicap (best effort, setting modest pace) at Ascot in October: favourite, well below form in listed event at Newmarket final start: stays 1¼m: best efforts on top-of-the-ground. *H. R. A. Cecil.*

HALVOYA 5 gr.m. Bay Express 132–Porsanger (USA) (Zeddaan 130) [1989 5d 5f 58 6f² 6m 5f3 6f* 5f² 6f 5g⁵ 5g³ 5m 5f 1990 5g² 5m³ 5m⁴ 5m 5g* 5g⁴ 5m* 5m 5m⁶ 5m 6g 5m 5d 5m³ 5.8d a6g⁵ a6g a5g² a5g* a5g⁶ a5g³] leggy, rather angular mare: quite modest handicapper: successful at Warwick and Catterick in summer and Lingfield in December: suited by 5f: possibly needs sound surface nowadays: blinkered 5 times: best with forcing tactics and tender handling. *J. L. Spearing.*

HAMADRYAD (IRE) 2 b.c. (May 2) Fairy King (USA)–Clifden Bottoms 86 (Wolver Hollow 126) [1990 7m⁵ 7g³ 7m² 7d] IR 62,000Y: leggy, quite attractive colt: brother to 3-y-o Jackie's Wish and half-brother to a winner in Holland and a winner over hurdles: dam Irish 8.5f winner from family of Waajib: fair maiden: second of 7, looking likely winner when challenging 1f out but unable to quicken, to Big Blow in minor event at Ascot: creditable thirteenth of 20 in Cartier Million at Phoenix Park later in October: will be better suited by 1m. *W. Carter.*

HAMILTON LADY (IRE) 2 b.f. (Jan 11) Zino 127–Villasanta (Corvaro (USA) 43 122) [1990 6m 5d 8.2d 8.2v] IR 5,200Y: lengthy, rather angular filly: first foal: dam French maiden from family of Romildo and Pevero: never able to challenge in maidens and minor event: should stay 1m. *C. W. C. Elsey.*

HAMLET CROFT 2 b.f. (Feb 3) Manor Farm Boy 114–Haverhill Lass 67 (Music 53 Boy 124) [1990 6m a6g² a8g⁴] lengthy filly, rather unfurnished: second reported live foal: dam sprinter: plating-class form for girl apprentice in claimer at Southwell and maiden at Lingfield: showed promise in Newmarket seller on debut: stays 1m. *A. Bailey.*

HAMOUDI 2 b.g. (Mar 29) Miller's Mate 116–Wanton 106 (Kris 135) [1990 6m 41 8.2d 6d] 5,200Y: compact gelding: moderate walker: first foal: dam sprinter, best at 2 yrs: poor maiden. *D. Morley.*

HANA MARIE 3 b. or br.f. Formidable (USA) 125–Milk And Honey 102 (So 101 § Blessed 130) [1989 6m² 5f* 5g 6f* 1990 6f³ 5m⁴ 6m² 6d³ 6m² 6m 5f⁴ 5m 7g] workmanlike filly: good walker: useful sprinter: 33/1, ran particularly well when about 1¾ lengths fourth of 14 to Argentum in King George Stakes at Goodwood seventh start, outpaced then staying on: no show in listed race (well behind early on) and handicap after: acts on firm going: visored last 7 outings: mainly consistent, but has looked ungenerous and is probably not one to trust: sold 52,000 gns Newmarket Autumn Sales, reportedly to join J. Hammond in France. *G. A. Huffer.*

HAND IN GLOVE 4 b.g. Star Appeal 133–Cash Limit 62 (High Top 131) [1989 51 10.1m 12g² 14g⁶ 14m⁶ 1990 13g a14g⁵ 10d³ 10.2f²] angular, deep-girthed gelding: plating-class maiden: stays 1¼m: acts on firm and dead going: apprentice ridden at 4 yrs: takes keen hold: has joined R. Brotherton. *W. J. Haggas.*

HAND PAINTED 6 br.g. Rabdan 129–Morkulla (SWE) 49 (Royal Park 114) 51 ? [1989 NR 1990 10m⁶ 10f 11.5f⁴ 12m⁶ 10.8m² 10m⁴ 10g⁵] leggy gelding: has a round action: poor maiden: easily best effort penultimate outing: stays 1½m: acts on firm ground and is unsuited by a soft surface: often wears bandages: has got on edge: sold 800 gns Doncaster January Sales. *J. Pearce.*

HANDSOME LEADER (USA) 4 b.g. Green Forest (USA) 134–Mazyoun — (USA) 57 (Blushing Groom (FR) 131) [1989 9f 10f 1990 7f 8m 10.1g 12.5g 8.3m 7m 8m] lengthy gelding: of little account: blinkered twice. *G. H. Eden.*

HANNAH AUTOSOUND 2 b.c. (Feb 23) Nordance (USA)–Sense of Pride — (Welsh Pageant 132) [1990 5f] 10,500F, 8,400Y: first foal: dam Irish middle-distance winner: backward in maiden auction at Haydock in August. *P. Monteith.*

HANNAH BROWN (IRE) 2 ch.f. (Apr 19) Carlingford Castle 126–Liebeslied — 91 (Dike (USA)) [1990 a6g] fifth living foal: half-sister to a winner in Italy by Thatch: dam 5.9f and 1m winner at 2 yrs later successful over hurdles, is half-sister to

Cheshire Oaks winner Hardiesse: tailed off in maiden at Southwell in August. *H. A. T. Whiting.*

HANNAH'S BOY 4 ch.g. Smackover 107–Saint Motunde 84 (Tyrant (USA)) 58 [1989 NR 1990 6m 5d³ 6m 6d 6g⁶ 6m 5f a5g⁴ a6g⁶ 6m⁴ a6g⁴ 5g³ 6m⁴ 5f⁵ 5d⁵ 6d³] big, lengthy, sparely-made gelding: poor mover: plating-class handicapper: stays 6f: best on an easy surface: sometimes blinkered: has started slowly: sold 2,500 gns Doncaster November Sales. *B. A. McMahon.*

HANNAH'S CHOICE 3 b. or br.f. Kampala 120–Cape of Storms (Fordham — (USA) 117) [1989 a6g 1990 a6g⁴ a7g⁶ a8g] poor form in maiden and claimers at Southwell: sold 1,300 gns Doncaster May Sales. *P. A. Blockley.*

HANNAH'S SECRET 4 ch.f. Starch Reduced 112–Lana's Secret 79 (Most 36 Secret 119) [1989 5f⁴ 5h 5f 5f⁵ 5f⁴ 5g 6m 5m 5f⁵ 5m 5g⁶ 1990 5m a5g 5f⁶ 5m⁶ 5g⁶ 5g 5m 6g⁶ 5m 5m 5g] medium-sized filly: poor maiden: suited by 5f: acts on firm going: blinkered 3 times at 3 yrs, hooded last 2 outings at 4 yrs: has been slowly away: retained by trainer 2,000 gns Ascot October Sales. *B. Palling.*

HANSOM LAD 7 b.g. Dublin Taxi–Trackalady 96 (Track Spare 125) [1989 6s 5m 76 5g 5m 5g 6m 6g a6g* a6g⁴ 1990 a6g⁴ a6g² a6g 5m 5g a5g a7g 6s a6g a6g² a5g* a6g³] big, good-topped gelding: carries plenty of condition: won handicap at Southwell in December: no form on turf since spring, 1988: suited by sprint distances: wore blinkers and crossed noseband third outing at 6 yrs: none too genuine. *W. W. Haigh.*

HAPPY RESULT (USA) 2 b.f. (Apr 17) Diesis 133–Sainera (USA) 89 (Stop — p The Music (USA)) [1990 7f] 23,000Y: quite attractive filly: half-sister to several winners here and abroad, including useful 1985 2-y-o 6f winner Miscrown (by Miswaki): dam 2-y-o 7f winner: disputed lead almost 5f then eased significantly when beaten in maiden at Redcar in October: moved well down: will do better. *J. H. M. Gosden.*

HARBOUR BAR (USA) 3 b.c. Cure The Blues (USA)–Little Deep Water 98 88 (General Assembly (USA)) [1989 6f² 6m* 5f⁵ 7m³ 8m² 10v³ 1990 8.2g⁵ 10.6f³ 10g² 8m⁴ 8g⁶ 7g⁴ 6g 8v⁵] tall, quite attractive colt: useful winner at 2 yrs: below form in minor events first 2 outings in 1990: ran in Italy afterwards, in frame in listed race and Group 2 event third and fourth outings: probably stays 1¼m: acts on good to firm ground: trained until after third start by M. Jarvis. *A. Renzoni, Italy.*

HARBOUR KNIGHT (IRE) 2 b.c. (Jan 11) Caerleon (USA) 132–So Directed 58 98 (Homing 130) [1990 5g³ 6g 6m 8.2d] IR 35,000Y: lengthy, unfurnished colt: poor walker: first foal: dam Irish 2-y-o 5f winner: plating-class maiden: caught eye when seventh of 16 at Folkestone on third outing: should stay beyond 6f: possibly unsuited by dead ground. *J. M. P. Eustace.*

HARDALE 3 b.f. Beldale Lark 105–Jachar (Lighter 111) [1989 8m 1990 a10g a10g] — angular filly: well beaten, in seller on debut. *C. Holmes.*

HARD AS IRON 7 b.g. Ardoon 124–Prancer 70 (Santa Claus 133) [1989 10f* 8f* 97 8f 9f* 8m* 9f* 9m* 9g 1990 8g⁵ 10f 8m⁴ 9g 8g] tall gelding: carries plenty of condition: poor walker: fairly useful handicapper: best effort as 7-y-o fourth to Curtain Call in apprentice event at Ascot in July: best at 1m to 1¼m: best form on top-of-the-ground: blinkered twice: tends to idle, and best suited by waiting tactics: winner over hurdles twice in autumn: genuine. *M. H. Tompkins.*

HARDIHERO 4 b.g. Henbit (USA) 130–Hardirondo 93 (Hardicanute 130) [1989 — 12s² 16d⁴ 12.5f 1990 11g 14f⁴] leggy, quite attractive gelding: plating-class maiden as 3-y-o: well beaten in handicaps in July: will prove suited by thorough test of stamina: probably acts on any going: can creditably in blinkers: winning hurdler. *Denys Smith.*

HARDIHEROINE 3 b.f. Sandhurst Prince 128–Hardirondo 93 (Hardicanute 69 130) [1989 7m⁴ 7h* 7m 8.2f² 8f² 8.2f⁵ 1990 10f⁴ 12d⁶ 12.3g 17.1f⁵ 8.2m⁴ 7f] smallish, sparely-made filly: good walker: has a quick, moderate action: modest winner at 2 yrs: virtually only form in 1990 in handicap penultimate start: should stay beyond 1m: acts on hard ground. *M. C. Pipe.*

HARD SELL 3 ch.g. Hard Fought 125–Misoptimist 111 (Blakeney 126) [1989 6f⁵ 71 6m 8g 1990 7f* 8f² 8m⁶ 7f³ 6f⁴ 7m 6g 8m a7g* a7g²] leggy gelding: modest handicapper: won apprentice event at Salisbury in May and Southwell in November: stays 1m: acts on firm going: wore eyeshield last 2 starts: sold out of R. Hannon's stable 6,400 gns Newmarket Autumn Sales after eighth: often hangs, and may well be ungenuine. *J. G. FitzGerald.*

HARD TO FIGURE 4 gr.c. Telsmoss 91–Count On Me 77 (No Mercy 126) 85 [1989 8d 6g 5.8m 6m 6f³ 6m* 5.8m* 5f* 8h³ 1990 5f⁶ 6f³ 7g* 7m 7.6d 7g⁴ 6d 5f² 5m* 6g³ 6m⁶ 5m 6d 10.6v] rather leggy, workmanlike colt: fair handicapper on his day: successful at Epsom (showing improved form) in April and Sandown (suffering interference and awarded race) in July: effective at 5f and stays 7f: acts on firm going, unsuited by soft surface. *R. J. Hodges.*

HARD TO GET 3 b.c. Rousillon (USA) 133–Elusive 94 (Little Current (USA)) [1989 6m5 7m6 6m2 6g3 7f5 7g3 9g3 10g5 1090 10f5 12g 10m 10m 12.5g] close-coupled, angular colt: quite modest form at 2 yrs, none at 3 yrs: stays 9f: best efforts on an easy surface: blinkered twice: tends to carry head high and looks a difficult ride: sold to join A. Jones 3,100 gns Doncaster October Sales. *J. Wharton.*

HARD TO NAME 3 b.c. Connaught 130–Printafoil (Habat 127) [1989 7m 7m 76 8.5f* 1990 12f3 11.7g6 12f2 11f* 12g3 10.2m 10f4 12g4 12d4 12v 12s 5s 7d6] strong, workmanlike colt: moderate mover: modest handicapper: won at Redcar in June: fourth in Norsk Derby at Ovrevoll eighth start: should prove ideally suited by 1½m: acts on firm going, probably not on soft: sold out of E. Eldin's stable 21,000 gns Newmarket Autumn Sales after tenth start. *M. McCourt.*

HARD TO SNUB 2 b.c. (Apr 7) Shardari 134–Snub (Steel Heart 128) [1990 8s] 8,800Y: rangy colt: fourth foal: half-brother to 3-y-o 9f winner Highly Desireable (by High Top) and modest 7f and 11.7f winner Heart of Fire (by Kalaglow): dam won over 7f and 9f in Ireland and later in USA: backward, slowly away and soon tailed off in minor event at Newbury in October. *P. J. Arthur.*

HARDY HAWK (FR) 5 b.g. Zino 127–My Hawk (FR) (Sea Hawk II 131) [1989 8s 9s3 9g 9d6 9g* 8g 10d5 9g6 12g* 9.2g 1990 8f 10f 8f 12f 14g 7.6g 15.3m6 a12g] rangy gelding: sixth reported living foal: half-brother to 5 winners in France, including middle-distance winners Hawkish (by King of Macedon) and Hawkeye (by Riverman): dam unplaced half-sister to French St Leger winner Agent Double and very smart middle-distance stayer Air de Cour: successful in quite valuable events at Evry and Maisons-Laffitte at 4 yrs: lost his form completely in 1990: stayed 1½m: acted on good going: blinkered and edgy fourth (virtually bolted with 7-lb claimer) and sixth outings: dead. *C. A. Austin.*

HAREDEN (USA) 2 b.c. (Feb 26) Cougar (CHI)–Chippewa (USA) (Jacinto) 85 [1990 6g3 6d6 7f2 7f* 8g5] $45,000Y: good-topped colt: first foal: dam winner at up to 9f: sire top-class performer at up to 1¾m in USA: fair performer: won nursery at Salisbury going away by a length from Blue Aeroplane: favourite, ran creditably in similar event at Sandown later in August: will stay 1¼m. *G. Harwood.*

HAREFOOT 3 b.f. Rainbow Quest (USA) 134–Swiftfoot 119 (Run The Gantlet 92 ? (USA)) [1989 NR 1990 11d5 11.3d 12f5 11.7m5 11.5m* 11.5g4 12g2 14.6d6] tall, leggy, lengthy filly: third foal: half-sister to quite useful 1987 2-y-o 1m winner Bannister (by Known Fact): dam Irish Oaks and Park Hill winner from good family: won 4-runner maiden at Lingfield in September: blinkered first time, easily best effort when neck second to Rudjig in minor event at Salisbury: should stay beyond 1½m: acts on good to firm ground: also blinkered last start: should prove best on galloping track. *Major W. R. Hern.*

HARKEN PREMIER 5 gr.g. Hard Fought 125–Maraquiba (FR) (Kenmare (FR) 46 § 125) [1989 7.5g 7m 7m 8f4 10f6 10m 11f* 8.2g5 8.2d 9g6 8.5f 12f* 1990 12f4 11.7g 10h2 12h3 10m6 a12g 10g] strong, lengthy gelding: poor handicapper: stays 1½m: acts on hard going: often blinkered, but not when successful at 4 yrs: ungenerous, and is inconsistent. *J. R. Jenkins.*

HARLEQUIN GIRL 2 ch.f. (Mar 24) Primo Dominie 121–Song of Gold 86 (Song — 132) [1990 5m 7f] 6,000Y: seventh foal: half-sister to 3-y-o 1¼m winner Modern British (by Elegant Air) and 3 other winners here and abroad, including 6f and 7f winner Postorage (by Pyjama Hunt): dam sprinter: no show in maidens at Windsor (slowly away) and Brighton. *J. White.*

HARLEQUIN LAD (USA) 3 ch.c. Erins Isle 121–Doha (FR) (New Chapter — 106) [1989 NR 1990 10.1m 11.7m 12m 16m] 65,000 francs (approx £6,000) Y: lengthy colt: moderate mover: half-brother to winners in France and North America: dam quite useful French maiden: no sign of ability, including in handicap. *K. O. Cunningham-Brown.*

HARMER (IRE) 2 b.f. (Apr 30) Alzao (USA) 117–Native Flower (Tumble Wind 72 (USA)) [1990 6f2 6g] IR 6,000F, 30,000Y: half-sister to a winner in Italy: dam behind all 3 starts at 3 yrs in Ireland: 2 lengths second of 6 to Crimson Conquest in maiden at Yarmouth in August: dull in coat, good speed over 4f in similar race at Kempton month later. *Lord John FitzGerald.*

HAROON 3 ch.c. Ahonoora 122–Gold Paper (FR) (Rheingold 137) [1989 NR 1990 83 6m 6f 8m2 10.5m* 11.5m3] leggy, quite attractive colt: third living foal: half-brother

Hamdan Al-Maktoum's "Hasbah"

to Irish 8.5f winner Suir Surprise (by Rusticaro): dam daughter of half-sister to Grand Prix de Paris winner White Label: fair form: won maiden at York and third of 5 in handicap at Yarmouth in September: should prove suited by 1½m. *L. M. Cumani.*

HARPIST 2 ch.f. (Mar 23) Music Boy 124–Haywain 58 (Thatching 131) [1990 5m5 6m5 5v 5s 6s] 4,200 2-y-o: small filly: bad mover: first foal: dam 7f winner: poor maiden at best: sweating final 2 outings: sold 400 gns Ascot December Sales. *J. S. Wilson.* — **48**

HARPLEY 3 gr.c. Beldale Flutter (USA) 130–Jellygold 95 (Jellaby 124) [1989 NR 1990 8m 8g] sturdy colt: first foal: dam 6f winner at 2 yrs: slowly away and well beaten in summer maidens: joined Mrs G. Reveley. *H. J. Collingridge.* — —

HARRY HEARTS 4 b.g. Seven Hearts 98–Our Melody 78§ (Song 132) [1989 NR 1990 7.6g] smallish gelding: half-brother to modest 2-y-o 5f winners Powder Puff and Ole Flo (both by Frimley Park): dam placed numerous times over sprint distances: always behind in claimer at Lingfield: dead. *P. Burgoyne.* — —

HARRY PEA (IRE) 2 b.c. (Jan 28) Runnett 125–Chiarella (Relkino 131) [1990 5g5 6m] 10,000Y: leggy colt: first reported foal: dam won in Italy: poor maiden: dead. *J. Berry.* — **32**

HARRY'S COMING 6 b.g. Marching On 101–Elegant Star 86 (Star Moss 122) [1989 5f* 7f2 6f* 6f* 5f6 6f6 1990 5f* 5m* 5g4 6f 5g3 5g5 5m* 6d5 5.8f5 5m2 5m 5m5 5f4 6f5 5g] leggy, good-topped gelding: quite modest handicapper: improved in first half of season, winning at Folkestone, Wolverhampton and Lingfield: best form at 5f on a sound surface: tried in blinkers and visor at 3 yrs: often apprentice ridden. *R. J. Hodges.* — **60**

HARRY'S GEM (IRE) 2 br.g. (Apr 4) Green Ruby (USA) 104–Miami Blues 54 (Palm Track 122) [1990 7g] first foal: dam 1m and 1¼m sellers winner: never placed to challenge or knocked about, beaten under 11 lengths, in maiden at Salisbury in October: will do better. *M. E. D. Francis.* — **58 p**

HARRY'S JOY 2 b.f. (Jan 25) Aragon 118–Happy Donna 106 (Huntercombe 133) [1990 a7g] eighth known foal: half-sister to 6f to 1m winner Imperial Friend (by Imperial Fling): dam 2-y-o 5f winner: slowly away and always behind in 11-runner claimer at Southwell in December. *C. J. Hill.* — —

382

HARRY'S LADY (IRE) 2 b.f. (Mar 8) Alleging (USA) 120–Lucky Engagement 56 p
(USA) 75 (What Luck (USA)) [1990 6m³] IR 7,000Y: leggy filly: third foal: dam
maiden stayed 7f: bit backward, edgy and bandaged, 2 lengths third of 17, ridden
along at halfway and staying on strongly, to Green's Trilogy in maiden at Windsor in
August: will improve, particularly at 7f+. *T. Thomson Jones.*

HARTLEY 3 gr.g. Final Straw 127–She Who Dares (Bellypha 130) [1989 6f 6m⁵ 59
5g* 5f 5g⁶ 1990 6s 6m 8f 8f⁴ 8.2d³ 8m 6d⁴ 6g² 6s 7d a7g] angular, rather leggy
gelding: poor mover: quite modest performer on his day: should stay 7f: probably
unsuited by top-of-the-ground, acts on soft: none too consistent. *T. Fairhurst.*

HARVEST MINSTREL 3 ch.g. Final Straw 127–Smagiada (Young Generation 43
129) [1989 5m² 8m 6d 1990 6m⁴ 6f a7g³ a8g a12g] strong, angular gelding: plating
class at best since debut: bred to stay 1m: blinkered third and fourth starts: sold out
of M. H. Easterby's stable 2,500 gns Doncaster June Sales after fourth. *D. Burchell.*

HARVEST SPLENDOUR (USA) 3 b.f. Solford (USA) 127–Autumn Splen- 54
dour (USA) (Luskin Star (AUS)) [1989 7m 1990 8f 6m 7m 8g³ a8g⁶ 7v 7d a11g]
leggy filly: clearly best effort when third in handicap at Doncaster in June, leading 3f
out then hanging left and weakening close home: may prove best at 7f: sold out of J.
W. Watts's stable 3,400 gns Newmarket Autumn Sales after sixth start. *M. H.
Tompkins.*

HASBAH 3 ch.f. Kris 135–Al Bahathri (USA) 123 (Blushing Groom (FR) 131) 111
[1989 6g² 7f* 1990 7m³ 8m 7g³ 7m* 8f² 8f³ 7m⁵ 8g* 8f] lengthy, good-topped filly:
very useful performer: won minor event at Leicester in June and listed race (very
edgy in stalls) at Phoenix Park in September: narrowly beaten in Nell Gwyn Stakes
at Newmarket on reappearance and 5 lengths second to Chimes of Freedom in
Coronation Stakes at Royal Ascot: ran in USA final start: stayed 1m: acted on firm
going: tended to be on toes, very edgy then didn't settle in 1000 Guineas on second
start: hung right on seventh: best with forcing tactics: inconsistent: visits Mr
Prospector. *H. Thomson Jones.*

HASTY THRILL (USA) 3 b.c. Lines of Power (USA)–Ashbud (Ashmore (FR) 56
125) [1989 6f a8g 1990 a10g⁶ a10g² a10g² 12f a12g⁶ 10m 11.5f] quite modest form first
3 starts: ran poorly after, including in seller: should stay further than 1¼m: joined A.
Chamberlain. *R. Hannon.*

HATAY 5 ro.m. Alias Smith (USA)–Panay 77 (Arch Sculptor 123) [1989 6f 5g² 5g —
5g 5g 6m 6f 5m 1990 8f 10.8m 5m] strong, good-bodied mare: worthwhile form for
long time only on second start at 5f: suited by 5f and give in the ground:
occasionally blinkered: probably needs strong handling. *P. A. Blockley.*

HATEEL 4 b.c. Kalaglow 132–Oatfield 69 (Great Nephew 126) [1989 8g 10s⁵ 106
15.3f² 12f² 14m* 13.3g⁵ 13.3m⁶ 14m* 14.6g 10m³ 12g* 1990 12f* 10g² 11m* 12d³

*Bessborough Stakes (Handicap), Ascot—Hateel and First Victory (grey) meet again;
The Prussian is third*

12f* 12s* 12f³ 13.4g 12m] strong, well-made colt: useful handicapper: much improved at 4 yrs, winning at Haydock (twice, on sixth outing by length from Cambo in £22,700 Old Newton Cup), Newbury and Royal Ascot (£14,900 Bessborough Handicap): ran poorly in listed races seventh and eighth starts: suited by 1½m: acts on any going. *P. T. Walwyn.*

HATTA FORT 3 bl.c. Formidable (USA) 125–Hatta 114 (Realm 129) [1989 NR 1990 5f 5f² 6f⁴ 5m⁵ 5g⁶] strong colt: eighth foal: half-brother to 6f and 7f winner Al Amead (by Brigadier Gerard) and a winner in USA: dam won Molecomb Stakes: quite modest maiden: first past post at Thirsk in May, hanging left and demoted for interference: stays 6f: blinkered (ran in snatches) third start: visored last 2, sweating and edgy on first occasion, running poorly second: sold 8,200 gns Newmarket July Sales to race in Denmark. *J. W. Watts.*   **67**

HAUNTING BEAUTY (USA) 3 ch.f. Barachois (CAN)–Vitale (Vitiges (FR) 132) [1989 5f* 5f* 5f* 6m⁵ 5m 1990 7.3d² 6f² 6g4] close-coupled filly: useful performer: ran well in Fred Darling Stakes at Newbury, listed race (beaten short head) at Haydock and Cork And Orrery Stakes (very edgy) at Royal Ascot: effective at 6f and 7f: set to race on soft going, acts on any other: reportedly sold to race in USA. *M. R. Stoute.*   **110**

HAUNTING OBSESSION (USA) 2 ch.f. (Jan 20) Barachois (CAN)–Vitale (Vitiges (FR) 132) [1990 5f² 5m*] well-grown, rather angular filly: has scope: sister to useful 3-y-o sprinter Haunting Beauty and 2 minor winners in USA: dam ran once: still better for run, won minor event at Warwick in August by ½ length from Princess Who, running on well to lead close home: will improve again. *J. Etherington.*   **59 p**

HAVE A BARNEY 9 ch.g. Laurence O 111–Barney's Girl (My Smokey 125) [1989 NR 1990 14m⁵ 22d] Irish gelding: smart chaser, third to Desert Orchid in Jameson Irish Grand National at Fairyhouse in April: 25/1, 9½ lengths fifth of 9 to Flustered in amateurs event at Leopardstown: soundly beaten in Queen Alexandra Stakes at Royal Ascot over week later. *A. L. T. Moore, Ireland.*   **—**

HAVERTON 3 b.g. Carwhite 127–Rosie Pug (Mummy's Pet 125) [1989 6f⁵ 6m 7m⁶ 6v 1990 6g 8f 7m 7d 6m 6m⁵ 7h4] strong gelding: moderate mover: poor performer: may be ideally suited by 6f: acts on hard ground, seems unsuited by heavy: has run well for 7-lb claimer: blinkered fourth to sixth starts. *T. Casey.*   **45**

HAVEYOUALLDONE (IRE) 2 b.c. (May 12) Auction Ring (USA) 123–Elated 80 (Sparkler 130) [1990 7g 7m] 16,000F, 4,800Y: angular, unfurnished colt: poor mover: sixth living foal: brother to modest 8.2f winner Auchinate and half-brother to fairly useful 7f and 1m winner Monetarist (by Monseigneur): dam won over 1m at 2 yrs: well beaten in minor event and maiden in autumn. *S. Dow.*   **48**

HAWAIIAN REEF 3 b.c. Henbit (USA) 130–Raffmarie 78 (Raffingora 130) [1989 7m 1990 10.1m 10g 8m] rather leggy, attractive colt: showed some ability on first 2 of only 4 starts. *J. P. Hudson.*   **—**

HAWAIIAN ROMANCE (USA) 4 ch.f. Hawaii–Chateau Princess (USA) (Majestic Prince) [1989 7g 8m 10f 12f 10f 1990 10s* 12g⁶ 12g 10d] big, lengthy filly: has a rather round action: first race for over 10 months, won strongly-run handicap at Nottingham (sweating and edgy) in May: no form after: stays 1¼m: seems to need soft going. *R. Curtis.*   **64**

HAWAII STORM (FR) 2 b.c. (Mar 7) Plugged Nickle (USA)–Slewvindaloo (USA) (Seattle Slew (USA)) [1990 6m 8.2d⁶ 7g⁶ 8d] 8,000F, 24,000Y: leggy colt: first reported foal: dam little sign of ability in 6 starts in North America: sire won from 7f to 9f: plating-class maiden: best effort third start: well beaten in nursery final start. *Miss A. J. Whitfield.*   **60**

HAWAIT AL BARR 2 b.f. (Mar 18) Green Desert (USA) 127–Allegedly Blue (USA) 106 (Alleged (USA) 138) [1990 7m³ 7f⁵] 250,000Y: well-grown, useful-looking filly: has plenty of scope: good mover: second foal: half-sister to fair stayer Owen Falls (by Mill Reef): dam 1½m winner suited by 1¾m, is daughter of sister to Crowned Prince and Kentucky Derby winner Majestic Prince: bit backward, quite modest form, one paced, in autumn maidens at Salisbury (moderately run) and Redcar: will be much better suited by 1m +: sort to do lot better. *M. R. Stoute.*   **71 p**

HAWWAM 4 b.c. Glenstal (USA) 118–Hone 79 (Sharpen Up 127) [1989 8s* 8m² 10m 8f 8m² 8m³ 8g⁴ 9g 1990 8g 8g 8f 9m 8g⁶ 10m⁶ 8d 10m⁴ 9m 8d³ 10.2s³] good-topped, quite attractive colt: usually takes the eye: one-time useful handicapper: best efforts as 4-y-o in veterans race (carrying 18 lb overweight) at Ascot and 29-runner event at Newmarket eighth and tenth outings: stays 1¼m: acts on any going, except perhaps firm: has sweated and got on edge: has worn severe bridle: **68**

has wandered and idled, and is best with waiting tactics and strong handling: sold to join S. Mellor's stable 24,000 gns Newmarket Autumn Sales. *C. J. Benstead.*

HAWWAR (USA) 3 b. or br.c. Lypheor 118–Berkeley Court 102 (Mummy's Pet 125) [1989 NR 1990 16g3 15.8m4 17.6m4 16.2s] $150,000Y: rather leggy, quite attractive colt: has a fluent, round action: good walker: first foal: dam French 2-y-o 1m winner later won at up to 9f in USA: showed signs of ability in maidens: soon off bridle, tailed off in handicap final start: should stay extreme distances: best effort on good going: sold to join Mrs A. King 5,000 gns Newmarket Autumn Sales. *A. C. Stewart.* —

HAXBY LAD 2 gr.g. (Jan 17) Faustus (USA) 118–Vignargenta (Absalom 128) [1990 5m3 5d4 5g2 5f6 5f5 5f] 7,000F, 4,800Y: sturdy gelding: second foal: half-brother to thoroughly ungenuine animal Timber's Girl (by Southern Arrow): dam won in Italy: plating-class form in varied company: will stay 6f: seems suited by an easy surface: bolted before start final outing. *C. Tinkler.* 56

HAYLEY CLAIRE 3 b.f. Free State 125–Lucky Love 65 (Mummy's Pet 125) [1989 NR 1990 10g6 10.2m] 6,600Y: compact filly: first foal: half-sister to a winner in the West Indies: dam won 6f seller at 3 yrs: burly, scant promise in maiden and claimer. *J. Ringer.* —

HAZEL MILL 3 br.f. Elegant Air 119–Teye (Mummy's Pet 125) [1989 NR 1990 9g6 12.3m3 12m2 12m6 10g] 2,400Y: leggy filly: moderate mover: fourth foal: half-sister to modest 6f winner Hazel Bee (by Starch Reduced) and winning hurdler Aber Cothi (by Dominion): dam showed little ability: poor maiden: seems to stay 1½m: blinkered final outing: hasn't ideal attitude. *P. Calver.* 47

HAZY HEATH 3 b.f. Wolver Heights 99–Bumfuzzle (USA) (Fleet Nasrullah) [1989 7g 6f 1990 10g a8g] workmanlike filly: has a rather round action: no form, including in amateur riders handicap. *E. J. Alston.* —

HEADBEE 4 b.f. Head For Heights 93–Plaits 93 (Thatching 131) [1989 10f6 10g 11.7m 8.3d3 10f4 9m 12g2 12g5 1990 10.8m 14m] leggy filly: poor maiden: stays 1½m: acts on firm going: winner of novice selling hurdle in September. *K. White.* —

HEAD GROOM 3 ch.c. Shy Groom (USA)–Solarina (Solinus 130) [1989 6m5 7g6 5f 6g 1990 a7g a10g3 a10g 12f] compact colt: poor form: stays 1¼m: blinkered last 3 starts: edgy final one: sold 2,000 gns Ascot April Sales. *J. D. Bethell.* 39

HEAD OF AFFAIRS (USA) 3 ch.f. Full Pocket (USA)–Affair 78 (Bold Lad (IRE) 133) [1989 NR 1990 10.4d] angular, sparely-made filly: second foal: half-sister to fair 1989 1½m winner Scandal (by Blood Royal): dam, 2-y-o 6f winner who showed little subsequently, is daughter of useful 7f and 9f winner Guest Night: 33/1, tailed off in maiden at Chester in May. *C. W. C. Elsey.* —

HEADREST 3 b.f. Habitat 134–Guillotina 118 (Busted 134) [1989 NR 1990 8m 12.2g6 14d 18d] workmanlike filly: sister to fairly useful 1988 2-y-o 7f winner Head-quarters, useful 2-y-o 7f winner Shorthouse and Princess Royal winner One Way Street, and half-sister to 2 winners: dam middle-distance stayer: no worthwhile form, but showed signs of ability in handicap final start. *A. C. Stewart.* —

HEAD TURNER 2 b.f. (May 1) My Dad Tom (USA) 109–Top Tina (High Top 131) [1990 6g4 6d] second foal: dam unraced: plating-class form in autumn maidens at Folkestone. *J. P. Hudson.* 54

HE AINT MUCH GOOD (IRE) 2 ch.g. (Mar 26) Thatching 131–La Troublerie (Will Somers 114§) [1990 6f6g 7v] 12,000F, IR 12,000Y: smallish, lengthy gelding: brother to 1m winner Escape Hatch and half-brother to 1m winner Nobody's Perfect (by Vitiges) and 2 minor middle-distance winners in France: dam won 7 times at up to 1¼m, including in Prix d'Ispahan: poor maiden: seems to stay 7f: races keenly: sold 3,400 gns Doncaster October Sales. *J. Berry.* 41

HEAR A NIGHTINGALE 3 br.g. Pitskelly 122–Calarette 85 (Caliban 123) [1989 5m4 6f4 5f4 7s6 8.2s* 1990 10g 12m6 11g3 14.8m2 16.2s6 17.1f* 15.3g4 16.1m3 a18g6 16g3 18.1m4 16.2s3 18d] small gelding: has a rather round action: modest handicapper: won at Bath in June: stays 17f: acts on any going: visored third to fifth outings: blinkered third at 2 yrs. *T. Thomson Jones.* 74

HEARD A WHISPER 2 b.c. (Feb 3) Bellypha 130–Breadcrumb 111 (Final Straw 127) [1990 5m5 6d* 6m* 6m2 6f 5d*] 33,000Y: lengthy, angular, useful-looking colt: has scope: has a quick action: first foal: dam 6f and 7f winner from sprinting family: won strongly-run Harry Rosebery Challenge Trophy at Ayr in September by a length from Sir Harry Hardman, staying on well having been slowly away and soundly outpaced to halfway: earlier successful in maiden at Epsom and 105

Harry Rosebery Challenge Trophy, Ayr—Heard A Whisper (rails) comes back strongly to beat Sir Harry Hardman after being outpaced

minor event at Doncaster in June: should stay beyond 6f: acts very well on dead ground. *G. Lewis.*

HEARD IT BEFORE (FR) 5 b.h. Pharly (FR) 130–Lilac Charm 87 (Bustino 136) [1989 10.2g 12d 10f4 9f* 8h3 10m5 10m5 8g4 9g3 8m* 10f 8f 8f3 1990 a8g] smallish, attractive horse: poor mover: plating-class winner as 4-y-o: faced stiff task only outing (February) in 1990: stays 1¼m: acts on any going: good mount for apprentice: genuine. *R. P. C. Hoad.* —

HEARTBURN 2 ch.f. (Feb 26) Hard Fought 125–Sweet And Sour 96 (Sharpen Up 127) [1990 5m 5f 5m] 3,000Y: leggy, sparely-made filly: fourth foal: sister to 7f to 1m winner Hackforth and half-sister to quite modest 12.2f winner Buy G's (by Blakeney): dam 2-y-o 5f winner: poor form in varied events: hampered at start final outing: will be better suited by 6f. *J. D. Bethell.* 46

HEARTHRUG 3 br.f. Persian Bold 123–Chauffeuse 76 (Gay Fandango (USA) 132) [1989 6f 1990 7m6 8.5d 7m4 5.1f 7m6 9f 8.2s] smallish, rather leggy filly: little worthwhile form: sold 3,000 gns Newmarket Autumn Sales. *P. T. Walwyn.* —

HEART OF DARKNESS 2 br.c. (Feb 11) Glint of Gold 128–Land of Ivory (USA) 109 (The Minstrel (CAN) 135) [1990 6f4 7g* 7m*] strong, good-bodied colt: first foal: dam 5f (at 2 yrs) and 1m winner, is half-sister to high-class Gold And Ivory: useful colt: showed good turn of foot when winning 4-runner Washington Singer Stakes at Newbury in August by 1½ lengths from Caerdydd: continued the upgrade in GPA National Stakes at the Curragh following month, held up, hard ridden from over 2f out then staying on well despite drifting right to win by a head from Malvernico: will stay middle distances: likely to improve again. *I. A. Balding.* 106 p

GPA National Stakes, the Curragh—these two-year-olds come under strong pressure before Heart of Darkness (right) prevails over Malvernico (rails) and Prodigal Blues

Mr Paul Mellon's "Heart of Darkness"

HEART OF JOY (USA)   3 b.f. Lypheor 118–Mythographer (USA) (Secre- **120** ?
tariat (USA)) [1989 6d* 1990 7m* 8m² 8g² 8f³ 7.3g³ 10.2m² 9.2g⁵]

Ante-post backers and layers were left in something of a quandary when
one of the most important One Thousand Guineas trials, the Nell Gwyn
Stakes at Newmarket, resulted in three fillies separated by just short heads.
After setting a fair early pace, Hasbah was joined on the line by Heart of Joy
and In The Groove with the judge eventually calling Heart of Joy the winner.
This was a most inconclusive trial. The bookmakers' conclusion as advertised
the next day was, generally speaking, Heart of Joy 4/1 for the Guineas and the
other two at eights with, to complicate matters further, the fourth horse Sally
Rous having her odds cut in half to 12/1. The backers' conclusion was to turn
to Salsabil for whom no photo-finish print was needed in the Fred Darling
Stakes three days later. Heart of Joy probably owed her market position to
earlier weight of money following glowing gallop reports — despite the popular
mythology of a Stoute 'hoodoo' in the One Thousand Guineas, backers have
never been disinterested in Stoute's favoured candidate. She hadn't been a
leading two-year-old, indeed she'd raced only once at two years, but that run
was a winning one against a large field of maidens at Newbury, gained in good
style. One mile for the Guineas looked sure to suit her well. The Guineas
provided a graphic illustration of the uncertainties of racing with the first
three in the Nell Gwyn this time spread over more than twenty-five lengths.
Heart of Joy did easily the best of them and ran Salsabil to three quarters of a
length; she moved comfortably into the lead over two furlongs out and battled
on most determinedly, drawing five lengths clear of third home Negligent. It
was a very smart performance which Heart of Joy could not repeat. She
started a clear favourite for three of her remaining five starts but didn't win

Nell Gwyn Stakes, Newmarket—left to right, Hasbah (third), Heart of Joy (winner), Sally Rous (fourth) and In The Groove (second)

again. Salsabil's absence from the Goffs Irish One Thousand Guineas made Heart of Joy an obvious choice only for In The Groove to confound her Newmarket Guineas form in spectacular fashion, beating Heart of Joy three lengths. That represented a turnaround of twenty-four lengths on their efforts of just over three weeks earlier and it was Hasbah's turn to do the same when she met Heart of Joy next in the Coronation Stakes at Royal Ascot, the two of them filling the minor places behind Chimes of Freedom. A step down in trip saw Heart of Joy comprehensively outpointed in the Hungerford Stakes, then a step up to a mile and a quarter for the listed Virginia Stakes at Newcastle had her leading everywhere except where it mattered, short-headed by her only opponent of note Cameo Performance. Any chance Heart of Joy might have had in the moderately-run Prix de l'Opera over an extended nine furlongs at Longchamp was lost when she got stuck on the rails until the final furlong; she didn't have much more to give at the finish having run on well initially.

Heart of Joy (USA) (b.f. 1987)	Lypheor (b 1975)	Lyphard (b 1969)	Northern Dancer
			Goofed
		Klaizia (b 1965)	Sing Sing
			Klainia
	Mythographer (USA) (b 1977)	Secretariat (ch 1970)	Bold Ruler
			Somethingroyal
		Arachne (ch 1967)	Intentionally
			Molecomb Peak

Heart of Joy was purchased for 63,000 dollars as a foal in the Tartan Farms Dispersal Sale in November 1987. Her dam Mythographer fetched 290,000 dollars. Mythographer had failed to win (running eight times for three second placings) but was an immediate success at stud with her first three foals (Heart of Joy was the fourth) all winners and the first two of them, the Hold Your Peace pair Uene and Ataentsic, both stakes winners of over 150,000 dollars. The grandam Arachne had herself won a similar amount nearly twenty years before, when her ten victories included one in the six-furlong Correction Handicap, and two of her offspring won over twice as much; Acaroid won three graded events, notably the Grade 1 nine-and-a-half-furlong United Nations Handicap. The third dam Molecomb Peak, who was bred on very similar lines to Nearctic, won a one-mile maiden race at Leicester as a three-year-old. The leggy, rather sparely-made Heart of Joy is to try her luck in the United States. She has a fluent, markedly round action and acts on good to firm ground and dead. Her best form is at a mile. *M. R. Stoute.*

Jimmy Heal Memorial Trophy Nursery, Brighton—
Heaven-Liegh-Grey gives Jack Berry his one-hundredth winner of the season,
a total rarely achieved by a northern trainer

HEAVEN-LIEGH-GREY 2 gr.f. (Mar 18) Grey Desire 115–North Pine **92**
(Import 127) [1990 5m* 5g⁴ 5m² 5f² 5.3h* 5m* 5f³ 5g⁵] 5,600Y: workmanlike filly:
second foal: half-sister to 1988 2-y-o 5f seller winner Springlake's Lady (by Music
Boy): dam poor half-sister to top-class sprinter Lochnager: fairly useful performer:
wide-margin winner of maiden auction at Doncaster in May and nurseries at
Brighton and Windsor (despite veering left) in August: below form final start:
speedy. *J. Berry.*

HEAVENLY HOOFER 7 b.g. Dance In Time (CAN)–Heavenly Chord 89 **32**
(Hittite Glory 125) [1989 7d⁵ 8m³ 8.2f⁶ 8f 1990 8g 12g⁵ 12g⁴ 11m³ 12h³] lengthy
gelding: poor handicapper: very slowly away final outing: stays 1½m: acts well on
top-of-the-ground: well beaten when blinkered: suitable mount for inexperienced
rider: winner 3 times over hurdles in 1989/90: inconsistent. *W. Storey.*

HEAVENLY QUEEN 2 b.f. (Mar 5) Scottish Reel 123–Celeste 83 (Sing Sing **—**
134) [1990 5f 5m 6g] 1,700Y: workmanlike filly: half-sister to several winners,
including 5f and 7f winner Sharp Celeste (by Sharpen
Up): dam stayed at least 6f: little worthwhile form in maiden auctions and a seller:
continually hung right second outing. *G. Blum.*

HEAVY LAND (FR) 4 b.f. Recitation (USA) 126–Vitelline (FR) (Pharly (FR) **—**
130) [1989 NR 1990 8f] third foal: half-sister to 2 winners in French Provinces: dam
never ran: virtually pulled up in claimer at Pontefract in May. *R. Boss.*

HEBBA (USA) 3 b.f. Nureyev (USA) 131–Likely Exchange (USA) (Terrible **80**
Tiger (USA)) [1989 6m* 5g⁴ 8m² 8.5g⁴ 8m² 8g] sparely-made filly: fair performer:
second in minor event at Newmarket: well beaten in listed races otherwise at 3 yrs,
racing keenly and weakening last 2f final start: stayed 1m: usually on toes, very
much so final outing: stud. *M. R. Stoute.*

HECTOR PROTECTOR (USA) 2 b.c. (Mar 4) Woodman (USA) 126– **122 p**
Korveya (USA) 116 (Riverman (USA) 131) [1990 5g* 6d* 6g* 6d* 7g* 8g*]
  'Plus ca change, plus c'est la meme chose'. The long, hot summer of 1989
was followed by another in 1990 and Deauville's August meeting drew to a
close as it had the previous year with an unbeaten colt representing the
Boutin-Head-Niarchos triumvirate, and descending from Mr Prospector on
his sire's side and out of a mare formerly trained by Boutin, heading the
French two-year-old rankings by reason of a recent success in the Prix Morny
Agence Francaise. By the end of the season that colt, Hector Protector, had
followed his predecessor Machiavellian to the top of the International
Classification, adding the Prix de la Salamandre to his tally, as had Machiavel-
lian, before taking a step beyond and crowning his first season with a hard-

389

*Prix Morny Agence Francaise, Deauville—right to left,
Divine Danse, Hector Protector, Polemic and Acteur Francais*

earned victory in the Grand Criterium, in doing so becoming only the sixth, following Grey Dawn II in 1964, My Swallow in 1970, Blushing Groom in 1976, Irish River in 1978 and Green Forest in 1981, to complete this particular Group 1 treble in the post-war period. But the relevance of Alphonse Karr's aphorism that 'the more things change, the more they stay the same' stops here: the importance and kudos attached to two-year-old racing has diminished significantly in Europe in the last decade or so, even in France where the pace of change has been slower, and Hector Protector's achievements can't be regarded as highly as they might have been in the past. The overall level of his form seems significantly lower than that of Green Forest and the others. If that's correct he has some improvement to make to stay on top at three, yet it could be that Hector Protector, unbeaten in six races from five furlongs to a mile and on the racecourse from May to October, was so near the finished article at two that further Group 1 successes will elude him once his second season gets into full swing and the slower developers come along; and his most realistic chance of classic victory will be in either the Two Thousand Guineas or the Poule d'Essai des Poulains.

Hector Protector was certainly ready early as a two-year-old, and he made his debut in a newcomers race over five furlongs at Chantilly in May, the Prix d'Orgemont, which played host to both Grey Dawn II and Blushing Groom in their day; Hector Protector succeeded where they failed with a narrow, if apparently unexpected, victory over his stable-companion Blackbeard, chosen by stable-jockey Head, in the four-runner event. Thirteen days later Hector Protector made it two from two with a two-length success in the listed Prix La Fleche over six furlongs at Evry; then, at Deauville at the beginning of August, he warmed up for the Prix Morny by conceding weight all round in the Group 3 Prix de Cabourg and winning by a neck and two and a half lengths from Belle Bleue and Polski Boy. Despite the narrowness of his win in the Cabourg, which his connections attributed to travelling and racing on a sweltering day, Hector Protector started a hot favourite for the strongly-contested Morny. He was one of three pattern winners—the others being the Norfolk Stakes winner Line Engaged and the Prix du Bois winner The Perfect Life—in a twelve-runner field which also contained the Chesham Stakes second Dominion Gold, the Lanson Champagne Vintage third Generous, the Prix Yacowlef second Crack Regiment and the Prix Robert-Papin and du Bois second Divine Danse, as well as the highly-regarded once-raced winners Acteur Francais and Polemic. Hector Protector justified his position in the market and improved Boutin's fine record in the race—he'd previously won it on four occasions, including in the two preceding years—with a workmanlike display. In a race run on heavily-watered dead ground, at a relentless gallop

Prix de la Salamandre, Longchamp—
Lycius and Booming become two more of Hector Protector's victims

and in the teeth of a headwind, Hector Protector gave the strong impression that a move up to seven furlongs would bring about further improvement: once he took up the running at the four-hundred-metre pole, having held a prominent position from the start, he did little more than maintain a slender advantage under strong riding until coming clear approaching the finish. At the line he had a length and a half and the same to spare over Divine Danse and Acteur Francais.

The Morny and the Salamandre are different types of races, and to win both requires adaptability and flexibility. Whereas the Morny is a sprint over a straight, flat six furlongs the Salamandre is run over an extra furlong (nominally anyway, though research suggests the course falls significantly short of its advertised distance), involves negotiating a descent and the long, sweeping turn into Longchamp's home straight; and, being run in September, it is usually contested by later-maturing, stouter-bred horses. Judged by his record over the years no trainer understands what it takes to win the Salamandre better than Boutin: Hector Protector's victory, at the expense of the subsequent Newgate Stud Middle Park Stakes winner Lycius, was Boutin's tenth in the event since Nonoalco set the ball rolling in 1972. Hector Protector was provided for the first time with a pacemaker, Mousequetaire, who's shown fair form in three races without winning. Rather unsatisfactorily, Mousequetaire didn't set a particularly stringent gallop and was able to hold the lead until a furlong and a half out where Hector Protector started to break free from the bunch and went over half a length up on Lycius and the fourth-favourite Booming. Not for the first time, Hector Protector had to dig into his reserves of courage and determination, and in the face of a persistent challenge he responded in his accustomed style to keep Lycius at bay by a length with Booming, who was suffering his first defeat in six races, half that distance back in third and River Traffic, winner of the Grade 3 Laurel Futurity on his next appearance, two lengths further back as fourth of the seven runners.

Neither Lycius nor Booming was anywhere to be seen when Hector Protector reappeared in the one-mile Grand Criterium at Longchamp in October; only five runners went to post, the smallest for France's premier two-year-old event since Abdos won in 1961, leaving Hector Protector, assisted again by Mousequetaire, to defend his unbeaten record against the Prix La Rochette winner Beau Sultan and two promising young stayers, Masterclass,

Ciga Grand Criterium, Longchamp —
a notable treble for the unbeaten Hector Protector
who is well on top of Masterclass at the end

an impressive winner from Hector Protector's good stable-companion Exit To Nowhere in a maiden over the course and distance the previous month, and, from Britain, the once-raced Country Lady Stardom Stakes winner Selkirk. Hector Protector, who looked tremendously well in the paddock, rippling with muscle and on excellent terms with himself, put his challengers in their place with his best and most impressive performance of the season which owed much to better work from Mousequetaire. As Mousequetaire, who'd set a blistering gallop, weakened quickly entering the final straight Hector Protector went into a two-length lead; and though he was pressed briefly by Masterclass with over a furlong to run he never relaxed his grip and passed the post two and a half lengths in front with Beau Sultan and Selkirk, neither of whom had an answer when Hector Protector put the question, another two and a half lengths behind.

An outbreak of 'Woodmania' at the autumn sales followed the performances of Hector Protector and his Newmarket-based contemporary Mujtahid (in whose essay details of Woodman can be found) in the middle of the summer. Their earnings helped Woodman finish the year leading juvenile sire (ahead of his sire Mr Prospector) as well as leading first-season sire if prize monies in France and North America are taken into account: the upper echelons of the latter list, incidentally, were dominated in the second half of the year by the family of Mr Prospector who, at its end, had four other sons in the top eleven as well as a grandson in the top few. Hector Protector was bought back by his owner for the comparatively modest sum of 35,000 dollars, less than the average paid for a yearling by Woodman in 1989, apparently after failing to make his reserve at Keeneland's September Sale. He's the second foal of Korveya after the quite modest maiden Yemanja (by Alleged) who ran unplaced three times for Charlton in the latest season. Korveya was a smart filly in France as a three-year-old (having been unraced at two), winning her first three races, including the nine-furlong Prix de Chloe, demonstrating a degree of versatility too with fourth place in the six-furlong Prix de Seine-et-Oise then ending her racing career with third place in the one-mile Premio Bagutta at Milan. Korveya's half-sister Proskona (by Mr Prospector) was a high-class sprinter when conditions were testing and ran clean away with the Prix de Seine-et-Oise and the Premio Umbria as a three-year-old. Boutin knows this family well: besides training Proskona and Korveya he also had care of another half-sister Carnet Solaire, who showed useful form at around a

Mr S. S. Niarchos' "Hector Protector"

mile as a two-year-old in 1986. Their dam Konafa, whose second place at 66/1 in the 1976 One Thousand Guineas bore no resemblance to any of her other form, is illustriously related too: she's a half-sister to the good American colt Akureyei, whose five-from-twelve record included wins in the (now graded) Pilgrim Stakes over nine furlongs as a two-year-old and the Grade 3 Fountain of Youth Stakes over an extended mile, and the top-class middle-distance filly Awaasif, successful in the Yorkshire Oaks, a close third in the Arc and more recently the dam of the 1989 Oaks 'winner' Snow Bride. Konafa is also out of a full sister to the dual Canadian champion handicap horse Dance Act.

Hector Protector (USA) (b.c. Mar 4, 1988)	Woodman (USA) (ch 1983)	Mr Prospector (b 1970)	Raise A Native
			Gold Digger
		Playmate (ch 1975)	Buckpasser
			Intriguing
	Korveya (USA) (ch 1982)	Riverman (b 1969)	Never Bend
			River Lady
		Konafa (b 1973)	Damascus
			Royal Statute

Machiavellian kept his form long enough to run second in the Two Thousand Guineas: Hector Protector, if reports from France late in the year prove correct, is sixty-forty to stay in France and contest the Poule d'Essai des Poulains over the Criterium distance. Boutin, when asked in an interview on December's *Racing World* video to draw parallels between the pair, was translated as saying 'It is very difficult to compare . . . Machiavellian really exerts himself in the morning, he is outstanding . . . Hector Protector, on the other hand, is very relaxed in the mornings, he doesn't tire himself. He is superior to Machiavellian in that he can pace himself, he gains from every race. But in terms of pure class I don't believe he is superior to Machiavellian'. Boutin gave no opinion at the time on the matter of how far Hector Protector may stay. We believe that although Hector Protector won four races over sprint distances as a two-year-old, stamina was his first suit: he was at his best in the Criterium where the scorching pace and forceful ride he was given combined to grind his opponents into defeat. Certainly, Hector Protector was as strong at the end as he had been when striking for home, and there's not much doubt that he'll stay a mile and a quarter. The good-bodied Hector Protector, who has so far raced only on easy ground, should train on: he's a handsome individual whose succession of tough races at two didn't prevent his progressing steadily, and he's got the scope to grow a bit yet. At the end of the day, though, game and genuine racehorse that he is, Hector Protector probably needs, as we said, to improve a good deal further to maintain his standing at three; that proved beyond Machiavellian, whose form as a two-year-old was virtually on a par with Hector Protector's, and it may prove beyond Hector Protector too. *F. Boutin, France.*

HEEMEE 4 br.f. On Your Mark 125–Beyond The Rainbow (Royal Palace 131) 39
[1989 5f3 5m 5f3 5f 6g 6f 5m6 1990 5f 5m 5m 5f3 5d 7m 7f] sparely-made filly: moderate walker and poor mover: fair winner as 2-y-o, but has deteriorated: best at 5f: unsuited by a soft surface: blinkered twice: sometimes sweating and on toes: trained until after third start by P. Blockley. *M. J. Camacho.*

HEIR OF EXCITEMENT 5 b.g. Krayyan 117–Merry Choice (Yankee Gold 43
115) [1989 10.2g6 7d 8f 8m2 9f 8g5 12f3 11f2 10f3 10.6d 10m 10.2g 1990 a12g4 10.2m* 11f6 10s 11m3 10.2m6] lengthy gelding: carries plenty of condition: usually looks well: has looked irresolute but battled on well under strong pressure when winning (for only time) handicap at Newcastle in March: stays 11f: acts on any going: visored second to fifth outings in 1989, blinkered ninth: has worn a tongue strap: winning hurdler in August. *A. P. Stringer.*

HELAWE 7 ch.g. Last Fandango 125–Pigmy (Assagai) [1989 6m6 6f 6g2 6f2 6m4 76
5.3f5 6g 1990 6g4 7m* 7h* 7h3 8m 7h2 7f3 7f* 7f* 7f2 7m4 7g a7g8* a7g4] big, lengthy, angular gelding: good walker: modest handicapper: had good season, successful at Edinburgh (making all) in April, Brighton (has now won there 5 times) in May, August and September and Lingfield in November: stays 7f: best on sound surface: lazy sort, who needs blinkers: goes very well on switchback track: tough and consistent. *Sir Mark Prescott.*

HELD IN SUSPENSE (USA) 2 gr.g. (Mar 12) Tri Jet (USA)–Knickers (USA) 76
(Paraje (ARG)) [1990 6f* 6f2 7g 7g2 8g] $11,000Y: well-grown, close-coupled gelding: half-brother to 2 minor winners in USA: dam minor winner at around 6f at 4 yrs: sire best at up to 1¼m: modest performer: won maiden at Doncaster by a short head in July: ran creditably after: promises to stay 1m. *J. Etherington.*

HELEN'S BOWER (IRE) 2 gr.f. (Apr 15) Bellypha 130–Queen Helen 112 62 p
(Troy 137) [1990 7g5] first foal: third foal (at 2 yrs) and 14.6f winner: backward, 8½ lengths fifth of 13, keeping on one pace, in maiden at Kempton in September: will stay middle distances: sure to improve. *N. A. Graham.*

HELEN'S GUEST 3 ch.f. Be My Guest (USA) 126–Helenetta 97 (Troy 137) 82
[1989 7g4 7g5 1990 10g2 11.3d5 10m6 10.5d 10m* 10g5 10.2g] leggy, unfurnished filly: fair performer: dropped from pattern company (had set pace), won maiden at Nottingham in July: creditable fifth at Sandown, better effort in quite valuable handicaps after: suited by 1¼m: stud. *G. Wragg.*

HELENSVILLE (IRE) 2 ch.f. (Apr 27) Horage 124–Calaloo Sioux (USA) 100 71
(Our Native (USA)) [1990 6m6 6g5 7g2 a7g 7m5 8f2 8m] leggy, sparely-made filly: first living foal: dam 7.6f winner, is out of half-sister to very speedy fillies Hecla, Mange Tout and Rose Dubarry: quite modest maiden: ran poorly final start: suited by 1m: sold 3,600 gns Doncaster November Sales. *M. A. Jarvis.*

HELIOS 2 br.c. (Apr 5) Blazing Saddles (AUS)–Mary Sunley 62 (Known Fact 66
(USA) 135) [1990 5g5 6d6 7v3] 4,300F, 6,200Y: leggy colt: moderate walker: first foal: dam maiden suited by 1¼m, is half-sister to Roseate Tern and Ibn Bey out of half-sister to Teleprompter: best effort around 6 lengths sixth of 10 to Fraar in valuable minor event at Ascot in June: ridden by 7-lb claimer, soundly-beaten third of 5 when facing stiff task in minor event at Chester nearly 4 months later. *R. Simpson.*

HELLENIC   3 b.f. Darshaan 133–Grecian Sea (FR) 107 (Homeric 133) [1989 125
8g⁴ 1990 10.5g* 12d* 12g* 11.0g² 12g]

'Look at the stars! Look, look up at the skies!'—Gerard Manley Hop-
kins. Those connected with Hellenic must have done plenty of that, her plans
being so contingent on give in the ground in a season when rainfall was a
commodity in very short supply. Hellenic raced only six times all told and her
participation in those events she did contest was usually the subject of a
late decision; she was withdrawn on the day of the race when short-priced
favourite for the Irish Oaks. That excepted, however, Hellenic managed to
run in all the big races she was intended to and made an immediate impact.
The going had been firm on the Wednesday of Royal Ascot but persistent rain
on the Thursday turned it good to soft by the time of the penultimate race on
the card, the Ribblesdale Stakes. Having justified heavy support in the quite
valuable BBA Middleton Graduation Stakes at York in May, Hellenic was
made co-third favourite on just her third start. It was the only time that she
encountered a soft surface and the field was spreadeagled. The Musidora third
Ivrea was beaten six lengths by Hellenic, the Pouliches third Gharam thirteen
lengths, Spode's Blue eighteen lengths and then came seven other stragglers,
including the Oaks fifth Ahead and Cheshire Oaks winner Pharian. Hellenic
had moved up comfortably from the back of the field on the home turn, taken
the measure of stable-companion Ivrea just inside the two-furlong marker
then responded to a couple of smacks to stride clear.

Victory was much harder to gain on her next appearance, after the
abortive trip to Ireland, in the Aston Upthorpe Yorkshire Oaks at York.
Compared to Ascot, Hellenic had half the number of opponents but they were
of a different quality: Swinburn's preferred mount, the Nassau Stakes winner,
Kartajana; the Oaks runner-up Game Plan; Dahlia's daughter Wajd; the clear
paddock pick Cruising Height; and Ruby Tiger who wouldn't have started 33/1
after her campaign in the autumn. Although Hellenic clearly had to excel
herself to emerge best from this field, we believe strongly that the faster
ground also contributed to the very different manner of her victory. She was
again held up in last place but this time had to struggle from the turn (over
four furlongs out) to make progress and was hanging left as she did so. Three
furlongs out Hellenic was still last some six lengths adrift of Kartajana who'd
moved smoothly to the front. Swinburn must have been very confident of
having made the right choice of rides (he'd passed over the 1986 winner
Untold) but Kartajana couldn't extend her advantage and Hellenic gradually

Ribblesdale Stakes, Ascot—Hellenic pulls well clear

*Aston Upthorpe Yorkshire Oaks, York—stiffer opposition this time,
provided by Kartajana (centre) and Wajd*

worked her way through the field to lead close home, still edging left. The
stable's conviction that their sturdy, moderate-actioned filly would not handle
top-of-the-ground conditions was by now well enough known but that was the
only proviso in Hellenic's future engagements. She'd looked in excellent
shape at Royal Ascot and York, had proved herself to be high-class and was
progressing well. It was decided to let her stamina come into full play in the St
Leger and she started favourite. But for the first time in the season Hellenic
had to give second best. The Leger developed into a two-horse race from
three out as she and Snurge drew clear of River God but, both horses giving
their utmost, Hellenic lost out by three quarters of a length. We've no doubt
that she stayed—she just lost to a better horse. Hellenic's final race came in
the Prix de l'Arc de Triomphe. Longchamp's daily going forecasts began at
soft but steadily retreated from that point and that was probably the end of
Hellenic's chance. Her prospects of turning the form around with Snurge at
the shorter trip weren't bright and without a flat-out gallop it wasn't surprising to see others outpace Hellenic in the straight as well; she wasn't at all
discredited to be beaten seven lengths, eighth of the twenty-one runners.

			Shirley Heights	Mill Reef
	Darshaan		(b 1975)	Hardiemma
	(br 1981)		Delsy	Abdos
Hellenic			(b or br 1972)	Kelty
(b.f. 1987)			Homeric	Ragusa
	Grecian Sea (FR)		(ch 1968)	Darlene
	(ch 1978)		Sea Venture	Diatome
			(b or br 1973)	Knighton House

Pattern-class performers are not a rarity in Hellenic's family. She is a
half-sister to the King Edward VII Stakes runner-up New Trojan (by Troy)
and to Golden Wave (by Glint of Gold) who filled the same position in the
Lanson Champagne Vintage Stakes and Solario Stakes. Their dam Grecian
Sea won a maiden at Saint-Cloud and was fourth in the Prix du Calvados as a
two-year-old when trained in France and showed useful form, though not
managing to win, for Major Hern at three; she was beaten just over five
lengths when tenth of fourteen in Fairy Footsteps' One Thousand Guineas.
The second dam Sea Venture made the frame in a Guineas trial, at Ascot, and
the third, Knighton House, was another to contest the Guineas itself but
finished well beaten after early scrimmaging. Knighton House did much
better, reaching the places, in the Fred Darling Stakes, the Coronation Stakes
and the Sun Chariot but would have been a highly-prized broodmare even if
she hadn't as she's a sister to Reform. More recent winners in the family are
Grecian Sea's half-brother, the 1989 Gran Criterium second Naval Party, and

Lord Weinstock's "Hellenic"

half-sister, the 1988 Meld Stakes winner Sailor's Mate who's by Shirley Heights and therefore bred along very similar lines to Hellenic. Grecian Sea had two other foals before Hellenic, the lightly-raced White Caps (also by Shirley Heights) and the modest mile-and-a-half winner Troyes (by Troy), and her three since are Gulf Sailor (by Darshaan), Celtic River (by Caerleon) and another colt by Darshaan. She visited Reference Point in 1990. *M. R. Stoute.*

HELLENIC PRINCE 4 b.c. Ela-Mana-Mou 132–Pipina (USA) 81 (Sir Gaylord) — [1989 10s⁵ 10d⁴ 10.4m 12f 1990 9f³ 12.5f⁵ 10h⁴] close-coupled, workmanlike colt: modest maiden at best: below form in spring, running poorly last 2 outings: should stay 1½m: acts on soft going, possibly unsuited by top-of-the-ground: blinkered final outing: has worn crossed noseband: winning hurdler in January. *J. Pearce.*

HELLESPONT (IRE) 2 b.c. (Mar 12) Beldale Flutter (USA) 130–Thalassa 79 (IRE) 94 (Appiani II 128) [1990 6d⁴ 7m⁵ 6f³ 8m 7m 10s³] leggy colt: brother to French 11f winner Turret Water and half-brother to several other winners, including useful but unreliable middle-distance performer Miramar Reef (by Mill Reef): dam middle-distance winner here and in France: fair maiden: will stay 1½m: acts on any going: carried head awkwardly final start: tends to hang. *C. E. Brittain.*

HELLO MY DARLING (IRE) 2 b.c. (Apr 18) Law Society (USA) 130–Hela- 80 p plane (USA) 68 (Super Concorde (USA) 128) [1990 7.6s⁵] IR 68,000Y: good-bodied colt: third live foal: half-brother to useful miler Strike Force (by Gorytus): dam maiden, should have stayed 1m: carrying condition, 12 lengths fifth of 6, pushed along 3f out, to Time Line in listed race at Lingfield in October: should improve. *K. M. Brassey.*

HELLO VANOS 2 b.g. (Feb 28) King of Spain 121–Flaming Peace 104 (Queen's — Hussar 124) [1990 6g 7m 5m 10m] 11,000F, 4,800Y: rather unfurnished gelding: has a round action: half-brother to several winners, including 1980 2-y-o 6f winner Sovereign Flame (by Supreme Sovereign), middle-distance stayer Fair And Wise and 3-y-o 1m and 1¼m winner High Beacon (both by High Line): dam 2-y-o 7f winner: poor form in varied events, final one a selling nursery. *J. A. Glover.*

HENLEY REGATTA 2 br.c. (Jan 27) Gorytus (USA) 132–Straw Boater 89 **61** (Thatch (USA) 136) [1990 6m 7m 7m³ 7g 7f⁶ 7s] 10,000Y: tall, leggy colt: first foal: dam 9.4f winner: quite modest form in maidens and nurseries: shaped well penultimate start, faced stiff task final one: may be better suited by 1m. *G. B. Balding.*

HENRIETTA PLACE 6 b.m. Sayyaf 121–Gilana (Averof 123) [1989 10m 9m 8f³ — 1990 7f 8m 8g 7m] smallish mare: poor handicapper: no form at 6 yrs: probably best at 1m: acts on any going: usually claimer ridden. *G. A. Pritchard-Gordon.*

HENRI LE COMTE 3 gr.g. Sunley Builds 102–Countess Mariga (Amboise 113) — [1989 NR 1990 8f 8g 12m 11.5f 10f a8g] leggy gelding: has a round action: second foal to thoroughbred stallion: dam never ran: no form, mostly in claimers: worth a try in blinkers: sometimes sweating: trained until after fifth start by S. Woodman. *M. McCormack.*

HENRYK 6 ch.g. Gay Fandango (USA) 132–Clouds 70 (Relko 136) [1989 12m⁶ 12f **58** 11.7m 11.7m 12f 1990 14d³ 14f⁴ 14m*] angular gelding: well-backed co-favourite, won handicap at Nottingham in September: stays 1¾m: best form on top-of-the-ground: bandaged near-hind at 6 yrs: has sweated and got on toes: excellent mount for apprentice. *B. J. Curley.*

HENRY LODGE (USA) 2 b.c. (Feb 1) Dixieland Band (USA)–Lodging (USA) — (King Pellinore (USA) 127) [1990 6m] $100,000Y, resold 40,000Y: long-backed colt: first foal: dam won at up to 9f in USA: prominent long way in minor event at Newmarket in August: sold 1,400 gns Newmarket Autumn Sales, resold 700 gns Ascot December Sales. *L. M. Cumani.*

HENRY'S WOLFE 5 b.g. Coquelin (USA) 121–Grangemore (Prominer 125) — [1989 5f 5f 5f 6f⁵ a6g a6g 1990 6f 5m] lengthy, good-quartered gelding: has a round action: quite modest winner as 3-y-o: well below his best since, including in selling contests: suited by sprint distances: possibly unsuited by soft going, acts on any other: blinkered or visored. *P. J. Feilden.*

HENRY WILL 6 b.g. Nicholas Bill 125–Silver Cygnet 71 (My Swanee 122) [1989 **66** 6d⁴ 6d 6f 7m 6f⁵ 7m⁵ 7f⁵ 6f² 6g* 7.6m 6f⁶ 6f⁴ 6g 6m⁶ 6f⁶ 6g³ 7g 7g³ 6d 6f 6g 7m 1990 6f³ 6g* 6f⁴ 7.6d 7m³ 6g 6g* 6g² 6g* 6m 6g² 6m² 6f⁶ 7m 7f 7m 6g] workmanlike, angular gelding: moderate mover: quite modest handicapper: won at Nottingham in April and Yarmouth (apprentices) and Ripon in June: off course 7 weeks after fourteenth outing then below form last 3: best at 6f to 7f: acts on any going: blinkered final start, and usually late on in 1989. *T. Fairhurst.*

HENRY WILLIAM 5 b.g. Known Fact (USA) 135–Kesarini (USA) 87 (Singh **40** (USA)) [1989 5d 5f 5g³ 5m 5f² 5.1f⁴ 1990 5m 5g 5m² 5.1f³ 5m a5g⁵ 6f⁴ 5f 5m 5g a5g⁴] small, short-backed gelding: poor maiden: best efforts at sprint distances: acts on firm going. *Pat Mitchell.*

HENSHAW 6 ch.g. Crofter (USA) 124–Jabula 99 (Sheshoon 132) [1989 NR 1990 — 10m 10f 12m⁶] ex-Irish gelding: half-brother to several winners, including fairly useful 1976 2-y-o 5f and 7f winner The Bowler (by Bold Lad (IRE)): dam won at up to 1½m: well beaten in varied events, including seller. *T. B. Hallett.*

HERBERTO (USA) 3 b.c. Roberto (USA) 131–Her Silver (USA) (Herbager 136) **80** [1989 NR 1990 12g⁴ 12m² 12h* 11.7m 14g⁶ 12g⁵] $385,000F, $875,000Y: close-coupled colt: fifth foal: half-brother to 1986 French 2-y-o 7.5f winner Hot Silver (by Nureyev): dam unraced half-sister to high-class 2-y-o Banquet Table and good 1m to 1¼m performer State Dinner: fair form: 10/1 on, won poor apprentice maiden at Brighton in July: clearly best effort in handicaps in apprentice event final start: will be well suited by return to further: sold to join N. Tinkler 13,500 gns Newmarket Autumn Sales. *L. M. Cumani.*

HERCLE (FR) 4 b.c. Fabulous Dancer (USA) 124–L'Exception (FR) (Margouil- **62** lat (FR) 124) [1989 8v* 9.6s 8g* 8s 8m³ 8g² 10g* 11m 8.2d⁴ 8.2d 8g⁵ 8.2d⁴ 8v 1990 a8g⁶ a7g 7m³ 8v² 8m* 8m 8g 8m 8.2v 8.2d 7d² 6s 8d] compact, rather sparely-made colt: moderate mover: quite modest form at best in Britain: co-favourite, won selling handicap (no bid) at Edinburgh in April: effective at 7f and stays 1¼m: acts on good to firm and heavy going. *N. Tinkler.*

HERCULES 3 gr.g. Bay Express 132–Firdale Rosie 78 (Town Crier 119) [1989 5f — 6m 6s 1990 6m 7m 6f 6m] close-coupled gelding: plater: blinkered third start, visored final one: sold 1,050 gns Ascot July Sales. *P. Burgoyne.*

HERE COMES A STAR 2 b.c. (Mar 24) Night Shift (USA)–Rapidus (Sharpen — Up 127) [1990 6d a7g] 13,000F, 16,500Y: sturdy, lengthy colt: half-brother to 3 winners, including 1984 2-y-o 5f winner Rapid Glory (by Hittite Glory) and 1¼m seller winner Beau Echarpe (by Relkino): dam ran only 3 times: burly, soundly beaten in maidens at Doncaster and Southwell. *J. Etherington.*

HERE HE COMES 4 b.g. Alzao (USA) 117–Nanette 100 (Worden II 129) [1989 59 6v⁶ 7s⁵ 7f² 7f⁴ 8m 8.3g 19m 10.2f 8f a10g 6f 7g 7m⁶ 7m 9g 10m⁵ 10f 10d* 10g⁴ 10d] angular gelding: showed improvement on previous 4-y-o form when winning apprentice handicap at Goodwood in October: stays 1¼m: acts on firm and dead going: blinkered once at 2 yrs and 3 yrs: trained until after second start by R. Akehurst. *W. Carter.*

HERESHEIS 4 b.f. Free State 125–Gambela (USA) 88 (Diplomat Way) [1989 69 10m 1990 10f 10m 12m⁴ 10.6s² 12.3g* 12g² 16m* 16.2g² 14m* 12f⁶] angular, workmanlike filly: carries condition: poor walker: generally ran well in amateur handicaps in summer, winning at Ripon, Chepstow and Yarmouth: stays 2m: acts on good to firm and soft going: consistent. *J. Pearce.*

HERIZ 2 ch.c. (May 13) Persian Bold 123–Home Address 83 (Habitat 134) [1990 77 5g² 6m³ 6m² 8m³ 7m 8m] 14,000Y: close-coupled, sparely-made colt: third foal: half-brother to 3-y-o Post Code (by Teenoso) and disappointing maiden Homely Touch (by Touching Wood): dam 10.8f winner, is out of 1969 1000 Guineas winner Full Dress II: modest maiden: suited by 1m: found little off bridle when blinkered fifth outing: a hard ride: sold 8,800 gns Newmarket Autumn Sales. *G. Wragg.*

HERMITAGE LANE 3 ch.c. Habitat 134–Ramiana (USA) 68 (Blushing Groom — (FR) 131) [1989 NR 1990 8m 9f] IR 17,500Y, resold IR 20,000Y: workmanlike colt: poor walker and mover: brother to useful 1980s 2-y-o 6f winner Heart of Arabia and half-brother to Irish 1½m and 1¾m winner Helenikos (by Ela-Mana-Mou) and a winner in Italy: dam 11f winner: no sign of ability in newcomers event at Newmarket and seller (blinkered) at Ripon: sold 2,200 gns Doncaster May Sales. *N. A. Callaghan.*

HERMITAGE ROCK 3 ch.c. Ballad Rock 122–Verde Dimora (Sir Ivor 135) 70 [1989 6m⁵ 6h* 6m⁵ 6h 7f⁵ 7m⁵ 7m* 7s³ 8g³ 1990 7m 6m 7g³ 7m 6m 7g³ 8m 7d⁴ 8d] good-bodied colt: modest handicapper: stays 1m: best with give in the ground nowadays: ran well in blinkers: sold 7,500 gns Newmarket Autumn Sales. *G. Lewis.*

HERN BAY 2 ch.f. (Apr 19) Lyphard's Special (USA) 122–Best Bidder 78 40 (Auction Ring (USA) 123) [1990 5m 6m 5m] small filly: fourth foal: half-sister to 3-y-o 5f winner Tender Charm (by Tumble Wind): dam sprinter: poor form in maidens and a claimer: sold 580 gns Doncaster October Sales. *M. A. Jarvis.*

HERNE 4 ch.c. Miami Springs 121–Tarvie 101 (Swing Easy (USA) 126) [1989 6v² 93 5v² 6g³ 5m* 5g* 5m* 5g⁵ 5d* 5g⁵ 1990 7g 5m 5g 5g³ 5g² 5g⁴ 6g 5m 5d³] half-brother to very speedy 1985 2-y-o Stalker (by Kala Shikari) and Young Ghillie (by Young Generation), a modest maiden here successful from 1¼m to 13f on the Continent: dam game sprinter: quite useful performer: second in handicaps at Phoenix Park and the Curragh prior to running very well when fourth to Boozy in Group 3 event at former in September: bandaged off-hock, behind in £9,900 handicap at Ascot eighth outing: best at 5f: yet to race on firm going, probably acts on any other: sold 14,500 gns Newmarket December Sales *J. C. Hayden, Ireland.*

HEROES SASH (USA) 5 b.h. Lyphoor 118–Salish (USA) (Olden Times) [1989 93 6d? 6g 8m bt 8h⁶ 9m² 8g 8f⁶ 7.6f⁵ 7m⁴ 1990 7m⁵ 8f⁵ 7m 8f 7g³ 8g] useful-looking horse: poor mover: fairly useful on his day, but has not won since only start at 2 yrs: stays 9f: acts on firm and dead going: blinkered once at 4 yrs: often sweats, and has got on toes. *R. Guest.*

HERO'S CRY (NZ) 3 b. or br.c. Babaroom (USA)–Erivari (NZ) (Sharivari — (USA)) [1989 NR 1990 a12g 16m⁴ 10f⁵ 10f] New Zealand-bred colt: well behind, in seller final outing: blinkered last 2 starts. *J. R. Jenkins.*

HE'S A KING (IRE) 2 b.g. (Apr 21) Fayruz 116–Bally 74 (Balidar 133) [1990 6d — a7g a6g] 1,500Y: third foal: half-brother to 3-y-o Balishy (by Shy Groom), 5f and 6f winner at 2 yrs: dam best effort at 1m: soundly beaten in varied events: blinkered final start. *N. Bycroft.*

HICKLAM MILLIE 3 ch.f. Absalom 128–Embarrased 81 (Busted 134) [1989 5d 34 6m⁶ 8f 1990 7.5g 6f⁶ a7g a8g³ 7f⁶ 8f⁶ 10m⁴ 8.2g⁴ 10m] angular filly: poor mover: moderate plater: stays 1¼m: acts on firm going. *P. Calver.*

HICKORY WIND   3 ch.g. Dalsaan 125–Derrain (Prince Tenderfoot (USA) 126)   **70**
[1989 5v⁵ 6m³ 7f* 7f² 8.2d 1990 10v 9m 7m² 7m 7g 8f³ 7m 7d] big, angular gelding:
turns off-fore in: modest performer: suited by 1m: acts on firm going: visored last 7
outings: has run well for apprentice: inconsistent. *Denys Smith.*

HIDDEN BAY (IRE)   2 b.c. (Apr 14) Lyphard's Special (USA) 122–Fast Bay   **70**
(Bay Express 132) [1990 5g² 5g⁴ 5m³ 5m² 5g 7f 6m³] IR 9,200Y, 11,000 2-y-o:
smallish, angular colt: has a roundish action: third foal: half-brother to a winner in
Macao: dam lightly raced: modest maiden: ran poorly fifth start: should be suited by
further than 5f: sold 9,400 gns Newmarket Autumn Sales. *W. J. Haggas.*

HIDDEN BEAUTY   4 ch.f. Vaigly Great 127–Phoebe Ann 76 (Absalom 128)   **—**
[1989 7g 9g 7d⁵ 7f 7f 10f⁶ 8f² 7m⁴ 7.6m 8s 1990 a7g a10g] workmanlike, sparely-
made filly: poor maiden: stays 1m: acts on firm going: often bandaged. *D. Burchell.*

HIDDEN COVE (IRE)   2 b.g. (Feb 13) Slip Anchor 136–Glancing 113 (Grundy   **75 p**
137) [1990 8s⁵] 56,000F, IR 135,000Y: angular gelding: fourth foal: half-brother to
fair 6f and 7f winner Inshad and 1988 2-y-o 6f winner Sweeping (both by Indian
King): dam 2-y-o 5f and 6f winner, is half-sister to high-class 1984 2-y-o Bassenthwaite and daughter of very smart filly Splashing: around 8 lengths fifth of 14 to
Another Bob in minor event at Newbury in October: should improve. *I. A. Balding.*

HIDDEN QUIVER (USA)   4 b.g. Secreto (USA) 128–Feather Bow (USA) (Gun   **—**
Bow) [1989 12.3d 1990 12d 12.3g 11.7m 14m] heavy-topped gelding: bandaged, well
beaten as 4-y-o, including in handicaps. *K. A. Morgan.*

HIDDEN (USA)   3 ch.f. Secreto (USA) 128–Shark Song 103 (Song 132) [1989   **74**
10g⁵ 8g² 1990 10g 11.7g⁴ 14f* 14g⁵ 14m 13.6d a14g* a14g*] deep-girthed filly: has a
quick action: modest handicapper: won at Redcar in May and Southwell in
November and December: will prove best at up to 1¾m: acts on firm going:
blinkered last 4 starts: difficult to settle: bandaged at 2 yrs. *H. Thomson Jones.*

HIDEAWAY (USA)   2 ch.f. (Mar 25) Secreto (USA) 128–Out Distance (USA)   **62**
(Forli (ARG)) [1990 7m⁶ 7g 7m³ 8m⁶ 9g] $67,000Y: rather angular filly: half-sister
to 2 winners by Spectacular Bid, one stakes placed: dam ran several times in France
and USA: quite modest maiden: reared stalls final outing: gives impression will stay
well: has been bandaged: sold 900 gns Ascot December Sales. *A. A. Scott.*

HIGH ALOFT   6 b.h. Cut Above 130–Think Ahead 104 (Sharpen Up 127) [1989   **—**
12s 16s 16.2g⁴ 18h⁴ 1990 a13g a14g⁵ 14m⁵] leggy, workmanlike horse: has a quick
action: poor handicapper: suited by a test of stamina: acts on any going: usually
blinkered: inconsistent: winning hurdler in March. *T. Casey.*

HIGH BARON   3 br.g. Baron Blakeney 83–High Finesse (High Line 125) [1989   **—**
NR 1990 10m 13.3m] tall, workmanlike gelding: first foal: dam NH Flat race winner
out of good hunter chaser Black Baize: well beaten in maidens, pulling hard and
close up 1m second occasion. *P. T. Walwyn.*

HIGH BEACON   3 ch.g. High Line 125–Flaming Peace 104 (Queen's Hussar   **100**
124) [1989 7g 7g³ 8m 8g* 1990 10g* 12g³ 12m⁵ 16.2f⁶ 16m⁴ 16m³] sturdy, workmanlike gelding: keen walker: easy mover: useful performer: 25/1, won handicap at
Kempton in April: ran well at Newmarket in £7,700 handicap (bandaged off-hind)
and listed race (won by Arzanni) last 2 starts: stays 2m: acts on good to firm ground:
gelded after final start. *H. Candy.*

HIGH BOURNE   2 b.c. (May 4) High Top 131–Crimbourne 83 (Mummy's Pet   **64**
125) [1990 7m 6m³ 5d⁶] strong, compact colt: second foal: dam maiden best at 7f, is
daughter of smart 1m to 1½m winner Lucent, herself daughter of very good sprinter
Lucasland: quite modest maiden: should stay beyond 6f. *M. McCormack.*

HIGHBROOK (USA)   2 b.f. (Apr 10) Alphabatim (USA) 126–Tellspot (USA)   **76 p**
(Tell (USA)) [1990 8g⁶] half-sister to several winners in North America: dam placed
once in 16 starts: 7½ lengths sixth of 16, prominent over 5f, to Clare Heights in
maiden at Yarmouth in October: sure to do better. *J. H. M. Gosden.*

HIGH CASTE   3 ch.g. Carwhite 127–Brazen 83 (Cash And Courage 116) [1989   **55**
8.2g 8g 1990 12.5f 12.3d 12m⁴ 16g 16f* 15.3f³ 17.6f⁶] angular gelding: plating-class
handicapper: won 3-runner race at Chepstow in July: best other effort next time:
stays 2m: acts on firm going: sweating and edgy second start: sold to join B. Morgan
10,000 gns Newmarket Autumn Sales then gelded. *R. J. Holder.*

HIGH ELEGANCE   3 b.f. Elegant Air 119–Tula Singh 66 (Mansingh (USA) 120)   **63**
[1989 6g 1990 8.2g⁵ 6f² 6f] workmanlike filly: poor walker: well-backed second of 4
in maiden at Hamilton, only form in the summer: faced stiff task in handicap: pulls
hard, and probably best short of 1m: hung badly left on debut. *M. Johnston.*

HIGHER HAMILL   3 b.c. Taufan (USA) 119–Judy's Pin (Ballymore 123) [1989 5g⁵ 5v² 5d* 5m⁴ 6s 6m 6g* 7g* 1990 10v 9m] leggy, close-coupled colt: moderate walker: fair winner at 2 yrs: well beaten in long handicaps in 1990: best form at 7f on good ground: sweating final start: early best efforts when ridden by M. Birch: sold 550 gns Ascot October Sales. *N. Tinkler.* —

HIGHEST DEGREE   2 b.c. (Feb 11) Superlative 118–Hot Momma 81 (Free State 125) [1990 6f³ 6m³ 6g 7f³ 7d] 10,000F: smallish, well-made colt: good walker and mover: first foal: dam 1¼m winner but better at 2 yrs: quite modest maiden: ran poorly in sellers final 2 (visored latter one) starts: better suited by 7f than 6f: possibly unsettled by dead ground: sold 2,200 gns Doncaster November Sales. *J. Etherington.*   59

HIGHEST PRAISE (USA)   7 ch.g. Topsider (USA)–Prides Promise (USA) (Crozier (USA)) [1989 7v⁶ 7d 7g 7g⁶ 7g 7f⁴ 7m³ 7s⁶ 7d 1990 7f* 7m 7m 7g 7m⁶ 7.6g² 7v⁴.6m⁶ a7g] strong, good-bodied gelding: moderate mover: modest handicapper: below his best after winning slowly-run event at Newcastle in April: stays 7f: acts on any going: good mount for apprentice. *D. Morris.*   74 d

HIGHFIELD PRINCE   4 b.g. Prince Tenderfoot (USA) 126–Parler Mink (Party Mink) [1989 7d⁴ 8m⁵ 12m³ 8g 9f* 12f⁵ 1990 12g] rather lengthy, sparely-made gelding: moderate mover: winning plater as 3-y-o: faced stiff task only outing in 1990: effective at 9f and 1½m: easily best efforts on top-of-the-ground. *R. O'Leary.*   —

HIGHFIRE   8 b.g. High Top 131–Home Fire 99 (Firestreak 125) [1989 NR 1990 a11g 12g 12m⁶] big, lengthy gelding: well beaten in maiden and handicaps in spring: successful in novice chase in March: stays 1½m: acts on dead going: visored and blinkered once: has joined K. Bailey. *O. O'Neill.*   —

HIGHFLYING   4 br.g. Shirley Heights 130–Nomadic Pleasure 91 (Habitat 134) [1989 9f 1990 8.5g³ 8.5g 11m* 12.4m* 12g⁴ 12m* 10.6m² 12.3g* 14m* 14.6g² 12m³ 14.6d* 12s] strong, good-bodied gelding: carries plenty of condition: usually impresses in appearance: poor mover: progressed very well in handicaps, winning at Redcar and Newcastle in June, Pontefract and Ripon in August, York in September and Doncaster (easily by 8 lengths) in October: effective at 1½m and 1¾m: acts on good to firm and dead going (unsuited by very soft): genuine and consistent: a credit to his trainer. *R. A. Harrison.*   95

HIGH FOUNTAIN   3 ch.f. High Line 125–Crystal Fountain (Great Nephew 126) [1989 NR 1990 10g* 12.5f² 15d⁶ 16.2m 16.5d* 16m] leggy filly: fifth foal: sister to quite useful 1¼m winner Flood Mark and half-sister to Irish 4-y-o 1¾m winner Crystal Spray (by Beldale Flutter): dam once-raced half-sister to Royal Palace: useful form: won maiden at Beverley in May and minor event (set strong pace, beat 9/4-on shot Crack 25 lengths) at Doncaster in October: well beaten in listed race at Newmarket final start, leading 1½m: reared stalls third start then stumbled leaving them and unseated rider on fourth: stays well: goes well on a soft surface. *H. R. A. Cecil.*   102

HIGH GRADE   2 b.c. (Feb 20) High Top 131–Bright Sun (Mill Reef (USA) 141) [1990 10.2s³ a8g] 90,000Y: sturdy, lengthy colt: good walker: second foal: half-brother to 3-y-o Sunflower Seed (by Mummy's Pet): dam unraced sister to Milford and half-sister to Height of Fashion, dam of Unfuwain and Nashwan: bit backward and green, 8 lengths third of 15, staying on well despite flashing tail and hanging left, to Persian Halo in minor event at Doncaster: slowly away and always behind in maiden at Southwell following month: will stay 1½m. *P. F. I. Cole.*   71

HIGH HAGBERG   4 b.g. Cree Song 99–Persian Breakfast 50 (Deep Diver 134) [1989 NR 1990 10h⁵ 10f] fifth foal: half-brother to fair 1985 2-y-o 5f and 6f winner Calixtus (by Sonnen Gold): dam plater: well beaten in apprentice race and maiden at Brighton. *J. E. Long.*   —

HIGH I KEW   4 b.c. High Top 131–Klewraye (Lord Gayle (USA) 124) [1989 8s⁶ 11.7m² 10m* 10g³ 11.7m* 11.7d² 11s² 1990 11.7g 12.3d² 11.1m⁵ 12g* 12.3m⁴ 12g² 16g² 12m* 12m⁵] useful-looking colt: good mover: fair handicapper: won at Carlisle (making all) in June and Beverley (ridden by 7-lb claimer) in September: stays 2m: acts on good to firm and soft going: sold to join M. Pipe 15,000 gns Newmarket Autumn Sales. *C. F. Wall.*   83

HIGH KICKING   2 b.f. (Mar 31) Kalaglow 132–Can Can Girl 69 (Gay Fandango (USA) 132) [1990 7m 8g] 14,000Y: lengthy filly: third reported foal: half-sister to 3-y-o Languedoc (by Rousillon): dam lightly-raced half-sister to speedy Noiritza, dam of Al Sylah: poor form in large-field autumn maidens at Newmarket and Pontefract. *J. W. Watts.*   45

HIGHLAND BIDDER 3 b.f. Ring Bidder 88–Highland Rossie 67 (Pablond 93) **39**
[1989 7m 7g³ 7.5f 8m 8g 1990 10m 12h⁴ 12½n³ 8g a12g⁵ a12g³ 15.3m⁵ 8f⁶ 10m 10m⁵
11m⁴] smallish, rather leggy filly: has round action: poor performer: stays 15f: acts
on hard ground: blinkered last 2 starts and last 3 at 2 yrs. *G. H. Eden.*

HIGHLAND CEILIDH (IRE) 2 b.f. (Mar 5) Scottish Reel 123–Savage Love **78**
78 (Wolver Hollow 126) [1990 7g 7m² 8f*] IR 10,000Y: workmanlike filly: good
walker: has a round action: first foal: dam lightly-raced granddaughter of leading
1963 2-y-o Mesopotamia: well-backed favourite, won 21-runner maiden auction race
at Redcar in October by a neck from Kind Style, holding on well after making most:
may well stay beyond 1m. *J. L. Dunlop.*

HIGHLAND CHIEFTAIN 7 b.h. Kampala 120–La Primavera (Northfields **–**
(USA)) [1989 10d 10.5f⁶ 10g 10f² 11g³ 11f* 11s* 10s* 1990 12v] finely-made, quite
attractive horse: keen walker: has a quick action: good-class performer at his best:
winner of numerous pattern events, all but one of them abroad, exception being
Brigadier Gerard Stakes at Sandown at 5 yrs: out of frame in Grade 1 event at
Rosehill, Australia, in April: stayed 1½m: acted on any going: reportedly suffered
back trouble: tough and genuine: retired to Gestut Pliesmuhle, near Cologne, fee
DM 10,000 (approx £3,500). *J. L. Dunlop.*

HIGHLAND HERO 3 b.g. Doc Marten 104–Lush Secret 50 (Most Secret 119) **82**
[1989 NR 1990 8.2g 6s* 6s] 9,400Y: lengthy gelding: fourth live foal: half-brother to
modest miler Knights Secret and very useful 6f and 7f performer Bollin Knight
(both by Immortal Knight): dam plater: 25/1, won minor event at Hamilton in
September in good style by 1½ lengths from Minstrel Dancer, quickening well to
lead last ½f: chased leaders 4f then eased in handicap at Haydock: reared stalls on
debut: may be capable of better. *M. H. Easterby.*

HIGHLAND LAKE (FR) 2 b.c. (Feb 14) Kings Lake (USA) 133–Pokhara (FR) **–**
(Kashmir) [1990 8g 9g a8g⁵] seventh foal: half-brother to 3 winners (by Moulin,
Trepan and Ginger Brink) at 1m+: dam French 11.5f winner: out of first 6 in
maidens at Compiegne and Le Croise-Laroche when trained by A. Fabre: well-
beaten fifth of 8 to Wicked Things in maiden at Lingfield. *C. A. Austin.*

HIGHLAND MADNESS 3 b.c. Monsanto (FR) 121–Contessa (HUN) (Peleid **–**
125) [1989 6m 6m 6g 1990 10m 6m 8m] sparely-made colt: of little account. *A. J.
Chamberlain.*

HIGHLAND MAGIC (IRE) 2 b.c. (Apr 29) Stalker 121–Magic Picture (Deep **75**
Diver 134) [1990 5g6 5g6 5g4 6m² 6d a6g⁴ a7g*] 7,600Y: compact colt: fourth
foal: dam Irish sprint maiden: modest performer: won 12-runner maiden at Lingfield in December by ½ length: probably better suited by 7f than shorter. *M. J.
Fetherston-Godley.*

HIGHLAND MEETING 2 ch.c. (Mar 23) Scottish Reel 123–Neenah 107 (Bold **75**
Lad (IRE) 133) [1990 5g 6m 6g6 7f³ 7g⁵ 8m² 8f³] close-coupled, rather unfurnished
colt: fifth reported foal: half-brother to 1987 2-y-o 5f winner Amenaide (by Known
Fact) and very useful 1¼m and 11.5f winner N C Owen (by Bustino): dam 2-y-o 6f
winner stayed 1½m, is half-sister to Irish Oaks winner Swiftfoot: modest
performer: will stay further than 1m: ran too freely in blinkers fourth outing: sold
10,000 gns Newmarket Autumn Sales. *H. Candy.*

HIGHLAND PARK 4 ch.g. Simply Great (FR) 122–Perchance 77 (Connaught **–**
130) [1989 11m 12m³ 11f⁵ 12m⁵ 12.2f* 12.4f² 12.3m⁶ 12m 12m⁵ 1990 12f 12.5f⁴ 14g⁶
13.8m 15m 15d⁴] deep-girthed, workmanlike gelding: quite modest winner as 3-y-o:
little worthwhile form in 1990, running poorly (blinkered) final outing: stays 1½m:
acts on firm going, possibly unsuited by dead: visored 3 occasions: has looked a
difficult ride. *F. Watson.*

HIGHLAND ROWENA 5 ch.m. Royben 125–Highland Lassie 62 (Highland **53**
Melody 112) [1989 5f* 6m³ 5f* 5m⁴ 5g* 5m 5g⁴ 5m 5d* 5f⁵ 1990 5m a5g 5g 5g³
5m³ 5g* 5f 5g] good-quartered mare: poor mover: plating-class handicapper: won
at Wolverhampton in very close finish in July: sweating, ran poorly final outing:
speedy: goes well on a sound surface: tailed off only start on all-weather. *B. A.
McMahon.*

HIGHLAND RUBY 2 b.f. (Apr 6) Green Ruby (USA) 104–Highland Rossie 67 **46**
(Pablond 93) [1990 5f⁴ 6m⁶] 2,000Y: workmanlike filly: fourth foal: half-sister to
3-y-o Highland Bidder (by Ring Bidder), 6f and 7f winner Diet (by Starch Reduced)
and ungenuine plater The Overnight Man (by Smackover): dam won sellers at 7f and
1m: poor form in maidens at Warwick and Ripon. *B. A. McMahon.*

HIGHLAND SPIRIT 2 ch.f. (Mar 23) Scottish Reel 123–Salacious (Sallust 134) **78**
[1990 5g 5g⁵ 6g⁴ 5g 6f* 6f⁴ 7g³ 7m* 7f² 7g⁵ 6d] 7,000Y: small, angular filly: has a

round action: third living foal: half-sister to a minor winner in USA: dam Irish 7f and 9f winner: modest performer: won maiden auction at Redcar in July and nursery at Newcastle in August: looked past best final outing: better suited by 7f than shorter and will stay at least 1m: sometimes slowly away. *R. M. Whitaker.*

HIGH LIVING 3 b.g. Good Times (ITY)–Visible Asset (Vitiges (FR) 132) [1989 **49** 6m 6g 5m 6g 1990 9s* 10.2f 8g 8.2d] sturdy gelding: clearly best effort when winning handicap at Hamilton in April: off course 4 months before final start: stays 9f (stumbled badly over 10.2f): best effort on soft ground. *Mrs J. R. Ramsden.*

HIGHLY DESIRABLE 3 b.f. High Top 131–Snub (Steel Heart 128) [1989 NR **76** 1990 9m* 9f³] good-bodied filly: third foal: half-sister to 7f and 11.7f winner Heart of Fire (by Kalaglow) and poor plater Jolly Vic (by Mr Fluorocarbon): dam Irish 7f and 9f winner and later in USA: won claimer at Wolverhampton by 6 lengths: modest 9 lengths last of 3 to Madame Dubois in minor event at Wolverhampton later in April: sold 4,200 gns Newmarket December Sales in foal to Primo Dominie. *W. J. Haggas.*

HIGHLY NOTED 3 ch.f. Music Boy 124–Hysterical 68 (High Top 131) [1989 NR — 1990 5g 6f⁵ 7h] 5,200Y: strong, lengthy filly: third foal: half-sister to 1m winner Courageous Bidder (by Known Fact) and useful 7f to 9f winner Comic Talent (by Pharly): dam won at 1½m at 4 yrs, her only season to race: no worthwhile form: broke leg in Thirsk maiden: dead. *F. H. Lee.*

HIGHLY SECURE 3 b.c. Shirley Heights 130–Caring (Crowned Prince (USA) **76** + 128) [1989 7g 1990 8.5m² 10m⁴ 8g² 8d 8d 8m] compact, quite attractive colt: good walker: modest maiden: faced stiff tasks in handicaps last 3 starts, staying on under tender handling and running well at Newmarket on final one: should be suited by return to 1¼m: possibly needs a sound surface. *J. L. Dunlop.*

HIGH MARINER 4 ch.f. Julio Mariner 127–High Lee 71 (Will Hays (USA)) — [1989 9m 1990 10m 12f] leggy, angular filly: has a round action: no sign of ability, including in seller. *J. D. Roberts.*

HIGH ON HIGH (FR) 4 ch.f. Ginger Brink (FR) 117–Highdinoa (FR) (Card **38** King (USA) 127) [1989 10d⁶ 10g⁶ 10g 8s 1990 a7g 12.5f 10.1g 10g⁶ 15.3g⁶ 10.1m 10.1m 12g³ 16s⁵ a12g 10d⁵] leggy, workmanlike ex-French filly: moderate mover: half-sister to 2 winners in France, including 1m and 9f (listed event) winner Wingtip (by Moulin): dam French 1m and 9.2f winner: showed signs of ability in autumn, twice in sellers: seems to stay 2m: acts on heavy going: sometimes blinkered: has been mulish at stalls. *C. A. Austin.*

HIGH PLATEAU (USA) 3 ch.c. Raise A Native–Soft Horizon (USA) (Cyane) **77** [1989 NR 1990 12f² 14f² 16.2f 15.8m³ 16m⁴] $160,000Y: big, strong colt: fourth reported foal: half-brother to 2 winners in USA: dam lightly-raced sister to 3 stakes winners: fair maiden: well beaten last 3 starts, in listed race at Royal Ascot on first occasion: stays 1¾m: sold 16,500 gns Newmarket Autumn Sales. *P. F. I. Cole.*

HIGH PREMIUM 2 b.c. (Mar 9) Forzando 122–High Halo 64 (High Top 131) **54 p** [1990 6g 5d 5d] 16,000Y: sturdy, good-topped colt: has scope: first foal: dam thrice-raced 1m winner, would have stayed further: never dangerous in minor event and maidens, catching eye going on well under considerate ride having been well behind final 2 starts: will do better, particularly over further, and is one to bear in mind in better company. *Mrs J. R. Ramsden.*

HIGH PURSE 3 ch.c. High Line 125–Petty Purse 115 (Petingo 135) [1989 7g **77** 8.2g⁴ 8g² 1990 10f² 8g* 10f] workmanlike colt: modest form: won maiden at Carlisle in May: ridden by 7-lb claimer in facing stiff task, ran well in mid-division for Zetland Gold Cup Handicap at Redcar later in month: should stay 1½m: carries head high: doesn't look easiest of rides and may prove best with strong handling. *G. A. Huffer.*

HIGH QUINTA 4 ch.f. High Line 125–Jacquinta 95 (Habitat 134) [1989 10g 12m — a8g² a8g 10m a8g a8g] deep-girthed, workmanlike filly: second in maiden at Southwell as 3-y-o, only form: visored final outing: takes keen hold: sold 2,900 gns Ascot February Sales. *N. A. Graham.*

HIGH RODING 3 b.c. High Top 131–Ryoanji 100 (Lyphard (USA) 132) [1989 7g **66** 10g 1990 12f⁴ 10g 14f³ 10g⁶] heavy-bodied colt: carries condition: quite modest maiden: looked headstrong prior to best effort in finishing third of 6 at Yarmouth, no extra final 1f: sold 3,800 gns Newmarket Autumn Sales: resold 2,000 gns Doncaster November Sales. *C. E. Brittain.*

HIGH SAVANNAH 2 ch.f. (May 5) Rousillon (USA) 133–Stinging Nettle 90 **77 p** (Sharpen Up 127) [1990 7m⁴ 8g²] rangy filly: has scope: second foal: dam, winner at 6f at 2 yrs on debut lightly raced and no form after, is half-sister to very smart 7f to 1¼m winner Gairloch and smart miler Whistlefield: close second of 21, leading 2f out and keeping on well, to Forbearance in maiden at Pontefract in October: likely to improve again: should win a race. *M. A. Jarvis.*

HIGH SPIRITED   3 b.f. Shirley Heights 130–Sunbittern 112 (Sea Hawk II 131)   80 p
[1989 7g³ 1990 10m⁶ 12f⁴ 13.3m³ 14m* 14m² 16f*] strong, close-coupled filly: moderate mover: fair performer: won handicaps at Yarmouth in July and Thirsk (favourite, comfortably made most) in August: stays 2m: progressive. *J. L. Dunlop.*

HIGH STOY   4 br.g. My Top–Dorcetta (Condorcet (FR)) [1989 12.8m³ 12f² 12g   48
12m 9.5m 1990 8v 11g⁵ 12g] leggy gelding: first foal: dam won 1½m claimer in France: plating-class maiden: pulled up lame and destroyed at Hamilton in June: stayed 1½m: acted on firm going: winning claiming hurdler in February. *P. Monteith.*

HIGH TIME GIRL (IRE)   2 b.f. (Feb 7) Nicholas Bill 125–Carnival Fugue 58   —
(High Top 131) [1990 6g 7m] 7,200Y: lengthy filly: seventh foal: closely related to fairly useful 1¼m winner Honey Line and 3 winners abroad (all by High Line) and half-sister to 6f winner Party Game (by Red Alert): dam poor maiden: well beaten in large-field maidens at Salisbury and Chepstow. *C. J. Hill.*

HIGHTOWN EXECUTIVE (IRE)   2 b.f. (May 26) Reasonable (FR) 119–
Tintale (Tin Whistle 128) [1990 5f⁶ 7f³ a5g a8g] IR 2,000Y: half-sister to several winners here and abroad, including 1983 2-y-o 5f winner Buckminster Boy (by Sweet Revenge), later successful in 10.8f seller: dam ran 4 times: bad maiden: beaten in a seller second start when trained by R. Hannon: soundly beaten in Lingfield maidens over 5 months later: stays 7f. *J. S. Moore.*

HIGHTOWN-PRINCESS (IRE)   2 gr.f. (May 26) King Persian 107–Ambient   — p
68 (Amber Rama (USA) 133) [1990 6d] 2,500Y: half-sister to several winners, including useful sprinter Westacombe (by Huntercombe) and fair 1984 2-y-o 6f winner Ambit (by Kampala): dam lightly raced: ridden by 7-lb claimer, over 13 lengths seventh of 17, prominent 4f, in maiden at Folkestone in November: should improve. *R. J. Hodges.*

HIGH WATER   3 ch.g. High Line 125–Sextant 98 (Star Appeal 133) [1989 8m 8s⁴   59
8f⁴ 1990 9s 10.2f² 12g 11m⁵ 10g 11m² 10f 8h 10.2m 10m² 12d 10d⁶ 10m] strong, round-barrelled gelding: has a round action: quite modest handicapper: should be suited by 1½m: acts on any going: ran poorly when tongue tied down eleventh start: reportedly broke blood vessel on eighth: inconsistent. *T. Fairhurst.*

HILLDYKE MAC   4 b.g. Lochnager 132–Companion 76 (Compensation 127)   —
[1989 6s 5d 6g⁵ 5m 5s 5s 6g 1990 5f 5f 5m 6f a5g 5d] compact gelding: poor walker and mover: of little account: visored fifth outing. *N. Bycroft.*

HILLMOOR BELLA   3 ch.f. Creetown 123–Confleur 81 (Compensation 127)   —
[1989 7m 6g 5v 1990 12.2m] workmanlike, plain filly: soundly beaten, including in seller. *J. Norton.*

HILL'S HALO   4 b.g. Kampala 120–Clanjingle (Tumble Wind (USA)) [1989 10s   51 §
12f³ 12f³ 16m⁵ 1990 a13g a12g³ a10g⁴ a12g] good-topped, quite attractive gelding: has a round action: plating-class maiden: looked ungenuine final outing: suited by 1½m: blinkered last 3 starts. *J. A. C. Edwards.*

HILLS OF HOY   4 b.g. Teenoso (USA) 135–Fairy Tern 109 (Mill Reef (USA) 141)   66
[1989 NR 1990 8.5g 7m 8.5d 7.6g 8.5g² 7g³ 8f 9g 12m⁵] compact, quite attractive gelding: has been hobdayed: moderate mover: third foal: half-brother to very use-ful Hoy (by Habitat), winner at 6f (at 2 yrs) and 1m, and 1986 2-y-o 6f winner Greencastle Hill (by High Top): dam, winner at 5f and 7f, is closely related to smart 1¼m performer Elegant Air: quite modest maiden: may well prove ideally suited by 1¼m: sold to join K. Bailey's stable 3,200 gns Newmarket Autumn Sales. *I. A. Balding.*

HILLZAH (USA)   2 ch.c. (Feb 29) Blushing Groom (FR) 131–Glamour Girl   92
(ARG) (Mysolo 120) [1990 7m* 7g³ 7g 8m] $125,000Y: workmanlike colt: moderate walker: half-brother to 1987 2-y-o 7f winner True Gent (by Lord Gaylord) and a minor winner in USA: dam good Argentinian winner: won maiden at Sandown in July: on toes, ran well in £6,000 event at Salisbury next start, moderately in Group 3 event (sweating) at Sandown and listed race at Ascot: should stay 1m. *P. T. Walwyn.*

HILTI'S HUT (USA)   2 b.c. (Feb 19) Blushing Groom (FR) 131–Northernette   92
(CAN) (Northern Dancer) [1990 6m⁶ 8m* 8m⁶] rather leggy, attractive colt: moderate mover: half-brother to several winners, notably very smart 1984 Irish 2-y-o 7f and 1m winner Gold Crest (by Mr Prospector): dam, sister to Storm Bird, was top Canadian filly at 2 yrs and 3 yrs, successful in 9f Canadian Oaks: made most in maiden at Newmarket, rallying gamely to win by ½ length from Another Bob: on toes, creditable sixth of 11, swishing tail under pressure and fading from over 1f out, in listed race at Ascot later in October: has twice given trouble at stalls. *R. Charlton.*

HIMIKO (IRE)   2 b.f. (Mar 10) Green Desert (USA) 127–Fear Naught 99   **91**
(Connaught 130) [1990 6in² 6m* 6m⁴ 6.5g⁴ 6d² 6m] 70,000Y: sturdy filly: has a
quick action: half-sister to 1½m winner Malipiero (by Persian Bold) and Without
Reserve (by Auction Ring), useful at up to 1m in Ireland: dam won Royal Hunt Cup:
fairly useful performer: won maiden at Ripon (swerved left over 1f out) in August:
staying-on second to Imperfect Circle in listed race at Ayr, best effort after: will be
suited by 7f: possibly suited by an easy surface: reared over at stalls on debut. *B. W.
Hills.*

HIMMAH (USA)   3 b.f. Habitat 134–Charmie Carmie (USA) (Lyphard (USA)   **85**
132) [1989 6g* 7d* 1990 7v* 8d⁶ 7m⁴ 7d⁶ 7g⁶ 7d] smallish, workmanlike filly: has a
quick action: fair handicapper: won £7,000 contest at Ayr in April by 8 lengths: ran
very well at York penultimate start: should have stayed 1m: acted on heavy going:
visits Doyoun. *H. Thomson Jones.*

HINARI HI FI   5 b.m. Song 132–Sarah Siddons (Reform 132) [1989 5m 6m 6f³ 5g   **52**
5m⁶ 6h 6m⁴ 5d 6f 6g⁵ 6m³ 6g 1990 a6g a6g 6f² 5f⁵ 7f 6f³ 6m⁶ 6g* 6d² 6m³ 6m 6g
6m³ 6g³] sparely-made mare: showed much improved form when winning claimer
at Carlisle in June: suited by 6f: acts on firm and dead going: good mount for
apprentice: has worn crossed noseband. *W. W. Haigh.*

HINARI SUNRISE   4 ch.g. Tap On Wood 130–Miss Markey 98 (Gay Fandango   —
(USA) 132) [1989 8g⁴ 10f⁵ 12f* 13.8m² 12m* 12m⁵ 13.3d 12g 1990 12f 12f 12g] leggy,
sparely-made gelding: modest winner as 3-y-o: ran moderately last 5 outings: suited
by 1½m: acts on firm going: bandaged off-hind and edgy on reappearance: has joined
J. Mackie and won over hurdles in December. *M. Johnston.*

HINARI TELEVIDEO   4 b.f. Caerleon (USA) 132–Red Jade 82 (Red God 128§)   **91**
[1989 6s⁵ 5f³ 5m³ 5f* 5f 5m 5g 1990 5m 5d 5g⁵ 5m 5m 5m² 5m a5g 6m* 6m 5.6g 6d
5m 5g³ 5m 6s 5s a7g] lengthy, good-quartered filly: has a quick action: quite useful
handicapper on her day: won £7,200 event at Newcastle in August: effective at 5f to
6f: best form on a sound surface: often gives trouble at stalls (withdrawn fourth
intended start): best waited with and has turn of foot: inconsistent. *M. Johnston.*

HINARI VIDEO   5 b.g. Sallust 134–Little Cynthia 76 (Wolver Hollow 126) [1989   **69**
5g 5d 5g* 5f 5m 5f⁶ 5g² 5m 5f 5f⁴ 5d⁶ 5s⁶ a5g³ 1990 a5g* a5g a5g* a5g a5g⁵ a5g²
5g⁶ 5g 5d² 5g⁴ 5g⁴ a5g² 5g 5m³ a5g a5g 6m* 6m 6m 5d* 6d 6s a6g⁵] smallish,
workmanlike gelding: moderate mover: modest handicapper: won at Southwell
(making all) and Lingfield in January, Hamilton in August and Ayr (getting up close
home) in September: effective at 5f to 6f: possibly not at best on extremes of going:
has worn blinkers, including in amateurs event (ran moderately) thirteenth outing:
changed hands 6,400 gns Doncaster May Sales: inconsistent. *M. S. Johnston.*

HINARI VISION   3 b.f. Kings Lake (USA) 133–Get Ahead 58 (Silly Season 127)   **44**
[1989 NR 1990 8f⁵ 9m 8.2g⁶ 12s] IR 8,000Y: rather unfurnished filly: sixth foal:
sister to useful 4-y-o 1¼m to 1½m winner Sultan's Son and half-sister to several
winners, including fairly useful middle-distance handicapper Main Reason (by Main
Reef) and stayer Sugar Palm (by Gay Fandango): dam daughter of smart middle-
distance stayer Guillotina: poor form in the spring: bred to stay further than 1m (led
9f over 1½m). *M. Johnston.*

HINTLESHAM HARRY   3 b.g. Pas de Seul 133–Silver Glimpse 108 (Petingo   **60**
135) [1989 7m 7.5f³ 8m⁵ 8g 1990 8m a11g⁵ 8g 8g⁵ 10m* 10f* 11.5f* 12m⁶] lengthy
gelding: quite modest handicapper: won at Sandown (claimer) and twice at Yarmouth in space of 9 days in July: creditable sixth of 8 in slowly-run race at Pontefract: probably stays 1½m: acts on firm going: blinkered last 5 starts: sometimes
edgy: carries head high, wanders under pressure and is a difficult ride. *G. A.
Pritchard-Gordon.*

HIP TO TIME (USA)   2 b.c. (Mar 17) Roberto (USA) 131–Luv Luvin' (USA)   **83 P**
(Raise A Native) [1990 8.2d*] rangy, good sort: has plenty of scope: half-brother to
useful French 5.5f and 7f winner Or Vision (by Irish River) and a winner in North
America: dam stakes-placed winner at up to 7f: 8/1, won 15-runner minor event at
Nottingham in October in good style by 4 lengths from Arak, travelling strongly in
second, leading 1f out and drawing clear comfortably: sure to improve considerably.
H. R. A. Cecil.

HITCHENSTOWN   7 b.g. Town And Country 124–Veinarde (Derring-Do 131)   **33**
[1989 8d³ 8.5d 8f⁶ 8.2g⁶ 7.6m 8f² 8m² 1990 10.6f 8f 5s 12f* 13g a12g 7.6m⁵ 8f⁴ 8h⁵
12m 10.4g⁶] strong, lengthy gelding: carries plenty of condition: poor handicapper:
won 5-runner event at Pontefract in May: effective at 1m and stays 1½m: acts on any
going: occasionally blinkered: has sweated: usually apprentice ridden. *M. J. O'Neill.*

HIT THE HIGH SPOTS   4 b.f. High Top 131–Criminelle (Crepello 136) [1989   80
10f 11m a12g* a14g* 1990 a13g3 a12g5 12m6 14.8m2 14.6g6 14d] rangy filly: fair
handicapper on her day: should stay 2m: acts on good to firm going, possibly
unsuited by dead: bandaged off-fore when winning at 3 yrs: hung right and carried
head awkwardly fourth outing: sold 11,500 gns Doncaster November Sales. *J. L.
Dunlop.*

HIZEEM   4 b.g. Alzao (USA) 117–Good Member (Mansingh (USA) 120) [1989 7d   45 §
7.5d 8d 8.2g3 10f 8.2f3 10f2 10f5 12f6 8m6 7.5f6 7m2 8m 7g* 7m 8.2g6 8.2g 1990 8f5 8f
7f 10m 8f 7g* 8m5 8m 7f5 8m3 8.2m 9g] small gelding: poor handicapper: won
selling event (no bid) at Edinburgh in June: effective at 7f to 1¼m: acts on firm
going: often wears blinkers, but didn't last 7 outings: inconsistent and probably
ungenuine. *K. B. McCauley.*

H M GEAR   2 b.c. (May 9) Mansingh (USA) 120–Huntergirl (Huntercombe 133)   —
[1990 5g6 5m 5m 6m] 4,000Y: strong, lengthy colt: has scope: sixth reported foal:
half-brother to 1988 2-y-o 5f winner Jump Dyke (by Longleat): dam bad plater: well
beaten, including in a seller: headstrong: sold 580 gns Doncaster November Sales.
W. J. Pearce.

HOKUSAI (USA)   2 b.c. (May 22) Fighting Fit (USA)–Angling (USA) (Angle   99 p
Light (USA)) [1990 6g* 7m*] $45,000Y: quite attractive colt: second known foal:
dam ran twice: sire won from 6f to 9f: favourite, won minor event at Nottingham
(comfortably by 3 lengths) in June and slowly-run listed Bernard Van Cutsem
Stakes at Newmarket following month by 1½ lengths from Jameelaty, staying on
strongly under pressure to lead inside final 1f: will stay 1m: looked sure to improve
further and win again, but not seen out after. *H. R. A. Cecil.*

HOLD COURT (IRE)   2 ch.c. (May 28) The Noble Player (USA) 126–Sindos 89   65
(Busted 134) [1990 7g 8.2s 6d*] 23,000Y: rather leggy colt: first foal: dam 7.2f and
1¼m winner: made all in maiden at Catterick in October, keeping on well, having
flashed tail when hit, to win by a neck from Benno: should stay 1m: races keenly:
sold 14,000 gns Newmarket Autumn Sales. *N. A. Callaghan.*

HOLD FAST (IRE)   2 b.g. (May 20) Dara Monarch 128–No Flight (Nonoalco   46
(USA) 131) [1990 a7g a8g4] 12,000F, 9,800Y: third foal: dam unraced daughter of
very useful Child Stakes winner Rose Above: poor form in Lingfield maidens in
December: should stay 1m. *H. Candy.*

HOLDFORTH   3 b.g. Sayyaf 121–Chief Dilke 82 (Saulingo 122) [1989 7g 8g 1990   —
12s 11f4 12m 11g 10m 9g] plating-class maiden at best: carried head high second
start: visored (3 times) and blinkered when running poorly after: stays 11f. *Denys
Smith.*

HOLLOW WONDER   8 b.m. Revlow 108–Honey Beam 71 (Heswall Honey 120)   —
[1989 NR 1990 a11g] sparely-made mare: fourth foal: half-sister to a winning jumper
by Gambling Debt: dam, raced at 2 yrs on flat, winning hurdler: in need of race, slowly
away and soon tailed off in claimer at Southwell in January. *Mrs N. Macauley.*

HOLME HALE (USA)   4 b.c. General Holme (USA) 128–Fleet Moment (USA)   —
(Turn And Count (USA)) [1989 8.5d2 10g 1990 11.5g] rather leggy, lengthy colt: has a
short, quick action: lightly-raced maiden: well beaten in handicaps last 2 outings:
should stay beyond 1m. *J. H. Baker.*

HOLY ZEAL   4 b.g. Alzao (USA) 117–Crystal Halo 78 (St Chad 120) [1989 11.7d6   92
11.7m 14f5 13f* 14f* 14g2 14.8m 14m* 13.3m 16.2d4 1990 14m3 14g3 16m* 14m6
16m3 12.3m2 14g3 14.6g4] useful-looking gelding: fairly useful handicapper: had fine
season, winning moderately-run £12,900 event at Kempton in May: given plenty to
do when very good third of 22, hanging left, to Further Flight in Tote Ebor at York
on seventh outing: effective at 1½m and stays 2m: acts on firm going: has had
tongue tied down, but not at 4 yrs: genuine and consistent. *D. W. P. Arbuthnot.*

HOME JANE   2 b.f. (May 25) Homeboy 114–Rhythm 64 (Bleep-Bleep 134) [1990   47
6m 7g 5m] compact filly: sister to 3-y-o Compos Mentis, 6f winner at 2 yrs, and
half-sister to several other winners, including useful 1979 2-y-o sprinter Pink Blues
(by Tickled Pink) and Vocalist (by Crooner), very useful at up to 9f in USA: dam,
non-thoroughbred, seemed to stay 1½m: poor form in minor events and a maiden. *R.
J. Holder.*

HOME JOHN   3 b.c. Homeboy 114–Fantasy Royale 84 (Breeders Dream 116)   —
[1989 5m 5m 6f6 6g 1990 8f 10.6v] sturdy colt: poor mover: bad plater. *R. J. Hodges.*

HOME LOAN   3 b.f. Homing 130–Rambert (Mandamus 120) [1989 NR 1990 8.2m   43
8d6 12d] leggy filly: half-sister to a winner in Denmark by Fine Blue: dam ran once:
bit backward, made most when sixth in Leicester claimer: well beaten in maidens,
swishing tail on debut. *J. L. Spearing.*

HOMESTEAD LAD 2 b.g. (Apr 28) Homing 130–Greenstead Lady 67 (Great — Nephew 126) [1990 7.5m 7f a8g] 6,000Y: leggy gelding: first foal: dam 1½m and 1¾m winner: well beaten, including in a Redcar seller. *D. W. Chapman.*

HOME STRAIGHT 4 b.g. Homing 130–Fast Asleep (Hotfoot 126) [1989 5g⁴ **32** 6g⁶ 6g 8s⁵ 10g 9s 1990 10.2f 5g⁵ 6h⁵ 7f] leggy, rather dipped-backed gelding: moderate mover: plating-class form at best: stayed 1m: dead. *W. Storey.*

HOMESTYLE 2 b.c. (Feb 14) Homing 130–Kinz (Great Nephew 126) [1990 7.5f 8d 7f] leggy, sparely-made colt: first foal: dam poor daughter of half-sister to Music Maestro: poor form, including in seller: sweating final start: sold 600 gns Doncaster October Sales. *M. Brittain.*

HOME TRUTH 3 ch.f. Known Fact (USA) 135–Dance Card 69 (Be My Guest **98** (USA) 126) [1989 NR 1990 7m⁴ 7g* 7h* 7.3m⁶ 8f³ᵈⁱˢ 7g² 8g⁶ 8m³ 8m* 8g] rather angular filly: has a quick action: third foal: half-sister to fairly useful 1988 2-y-o 6f winner Chief's Image (by Chief Singer), successful in USA in 1990: dam second over 1m on second start became disappointing: useful performer: won maiden (dead-heated) at York and minor events at Brighton and Chepstow: ran well most other starts, including in Schweppes Golden Mile at Goodwood and Leopardstown listed race: stays 1m well: acts on hard ground. *B. W. Hills.*

HOMILE 2 b.c. (Mar 17) Homing 130–Rocas 48 (Ile de Bourbon (USA) 133) [1990 **61** 7m⁵ 7m 7g⁶ a6g⁵ a7g³] leggy, lengthy colt: first reported foal: dam stayer: quite modest form: 4½ lengths third of 13 to Fluidity in Lingfield nursery, having run poorly on course previous outing: will be suited by at least 1m. *R. Hannon.*

HOMING RUN 3 b.g. Homing 130–Emma Royale 69 (Royal And Regal (USA)) **59** p [1989 NR 1990 a12g³] sparely-made gelding: third foal: half-brother to bad 4-y-o Emma's Spirit (by Thatching): dam 1½m winner: 33/1, 5 lengths third of 17 to Cosimo in claimer at Southwell in November, slowly away then headway 5f out, green then staying on well: joined B. Preece: sure to improve and should win a modest race. *R. Hollinshead.*

HOMME D'AFFAIRE 7 br.g. Lord Gayle (USA) 124–French Cracker (Klairon — 131) [1989 10d 12g² 12g 1990 16d] well-made, quite attractive gelding: modest handicapper, but is very lightly raced on flat nowadays: stays 1½m: not at his best on firm going, acts on any other: good mount for apprentice: winning hurdler in October. *R. J. O'Sullivan.*

HONEY BOY SIMBA 4 ch.g. Mansingh (USA) 120–Continental Divide 50 **53** (Sharp Edge 123) [1989 7s 7m³ 7m³ 7h² 8f² 8f² 8.2m 9m 10.2f⁶ 8m 8f 6g 7g 8.2g 7d⁴ 7d⁶ 1990 7m⁴ 8m³ 8m 8.5g* 9s 10f a8g² 8g 8f* 8m³ 8m⁵ 8.5m⁵ 8.2d 8g³] smallish, lengthy gelding: carries condition: poor mover: plating-class handicapper: won apprentice events at Beverley in May and Thirsk in July: best form at 7f to 1m: below form on hard ground, probably acts on any other: usually visored. *M. J. O'Neill.*

HONEY MILL 4 b.f. Milford 119–Sharp Venita 84 (Sharp Edge 123) [1989 10f 8g — 7f 6f³ 7m² 6g a7g 1990 a6g a8g⁴ a8g 7g a5g a6g] rangy filly: quite modest maiden at one time: well below her best in 1990: should stay at least 1m: acts on good to firm going: often blinkered. *O. O'Neill.*

HONEY'S FORTUNE 3 gr.c. Magic Mirror 105–Close To You 44 (Nebbiolo — 125) [1989 8.2s 1990 8g 8.2m 7g 10f] angular colt: no worthwhile form: sold 750 gns Doncaster September Sales. *I. Semple.*

HONG KONG GIRL 4 br.f. Petong 126–Ballad Island 83 (Ballad Rock 122) **71** [1989 5m 5h⁵ 5f* 5g 5g⁴ 5s* 5g² 5g 5m⁵ 5d 1990 5m 5m⁵ 5g⁶ 6s] rather leggy filly: fairly useful handicapper at her best: showed she retains some ability last 3 outings: best at 5f: acts on any going: sweating second start: trained until after reappearance by J. Berry. *P. J. Makin.*

HONING STONE (IRE) 2 b.c. (May 22) Flash of Steel 120–Prestigious (Cure **75** The Blues (USA)) [1990 7g⁴ 7m³ 7m² 7g⁶ 8m⁵ 8d 8g³ 8m a7g⁵ a7g² a8g*] IR 10,000Y: good-quartered colt: moderate mover: second foal: half-brother to 4-y-o Preservationist (by Sadler's Wells): dam Irish maiden daughter of Nanticious: modest performer: won 16-runner nursery at Southwell comfortably by 1½ lengths: will stay 1¼m: seems unsuited by a soft surface: has had tongue tied down. *C. N. Allen.*

HONORARY CONSUL 9 b.g. Bruni 132–Isadora Duncan (Primera 131) [1989 — NR 1990 13m⁶ 15m] strong gelding: bad mover: seems no longer of much account. *T. Craig.*

HONOR RAJANA (USA) 3 b.c. Hero's Honor (USA)–Rajana (USA) (Rajab 113 (USA)) [1989 7d* 7g² 8d³ 8m³ 1990 8d⁴ 8m⁶ 8g⁵ 8g² 10g⁴] good-looking colt: won maiden at Longchamp at 2 yrs: ran well last 2 starts as 3-y-o, length second to Zoman in Ciga Prix du Rond-Point at Longchamp and 3¼ lengths fourth to Relief Pitcher in £50,000 event at Belmont Park: stays 1¼m: yet to race on extremes of going: blinkered once at 2 yrs. *P. Bary, France.*

HONOR YER PARTNER 2 b.c. (Apr 21) Ahonoora 122–Lady Gaylass (USA) 58 (Sir Gaylord) [1990 5m 6s 7h⁵ 8m] neat colt: moderate mover: half-brother to 4 winners, all over middle distances: dam winner at up to 1m in France, is out of half-sister to Blakeney and Morston: plating-class maiden: stays 1m: sold 3,600 gns Newmarket Autumn Sales. *Major W. R. Hern.*

HONOURS GRADUATE 4 br.g. Petorius 117–Princess Virginia (Connaught — 130) [1989 NR 1990 a8g 6f] rather sparely-made gelding: soundly beaten in maidens and minor event: blinkered and bandaged at 4 yrs: sold 1,250 gns Ascot October Sales. *L. J. Codd.*

HOORAY LADY 6 ch.m. Ahonoora 122–Song Beam 84 (Song 132) [1989 8g 8f 84 8.2m⁴ 8h* 8.5m⁵ 10f⁴ 8h* 10g 8m³ 8f 12h³ 8m² 10m³ 8m 1990 8m⁴ 8m² 9m 8g 8m⁴ 8g] strong, lengthy mare: good mover: fair handicapper: effective at 1m and has seemed to stay 1½m: unsuited by soft going and goes well on firm: blinkered once: fell third start: suited by strong pace and waiting tactics: a course specialist at Brighton. *G. B. Balding.*

HOOTING DON 2 gr.g. (Mar 10) Bold Owl 101–Donna Pavlova (Don (ITY) 123) 79 [1990 6g³ 6f³ 6g³ 7g² a7g³ a7g⁴ 7.5g* 8g⁶ 8d³ 9g] 16,500Y: close-coupled gelding: brother to 1985 2-y-o 5f seller winner Dancing Owl and 3 winners abroad, and half-brother to 1981 2-y-o 5f winner Little Ballerina (by Brittany): dam poor maiden: modest performer: won nursery at Beverley in August: better suited by around 1m than shorter: acts well on easy ground. *J. Berry.*

HOPEA (USA) 4 ro.f. Drone–Hope So (USA) (Tudor Grey 119) [1989 10.1g 1990 60 a11g* a11g² a10g⁵ a10g 12g] rather leggy, good-topped filly: carries condition: moderate mover: 33/1, won maiden at Southwell in February: raced left in handicaps at Lingfield (bandaged behind) and Goodwood (sweating) last 2 outings: stays 11f: sold 2,300 gns Doncaster August Sales. *D. T. Thom.*

HOPPING AROUND 6 b.g. Prince Tenderfoot (USA) 126–Wurli 70 (Wolver — Hollow 126) [1989 12.4g³ 13v⁵ 12d² 12f⁴ 12g⁵ 12m⁴ 12d 15g* 16m⁴ 15s² 15g³ a13g⁶ 1990 12m⁵ 13g⁶] neat gelding: poor mover: quite modest handicapper: faced stiffish tasks both outings early in summer: stays 2m: ideally suited by an easy surface: has won for apprentice: tends to carry head high: often doesn't find great deal under pressure: winning hurdler in January. *C. W. Thornton.*

HOPSCOTCH 3 b.f. Dominion 123–Tartan Pimpernel 109 (Blakeney 126) [1989 — 7f³ 8m² 9g² a8g⁶ 1990 a10g⁶] lightly-made filly: moderate mover: quite modest maiden on flat: should stay 1¼m: sold 11,400 gns Ascot April Sales: prolific winning hurdler for M. Pipe. *W. Hastings-Bass.*

HORALDO 3 ch.g. Horage 124–Nebanna 74 (Nebbiolo 125) [1989 7f 8g 10g 1990 — 8.2g 10m] leggy, sparely-made gelding: poor form: faced very stiff tasks in summer handicaps, well tailed off final start. *Mrs J. R. Ramsden.*

HORN DANCE (USA) 4 b.c. Green Dancer (USA) 132–Fair Salinia 125 93 ? (Petingo 135) [1989 14f³ 17.6d⁶ 16m 1990 12m 12f⁶ 14g 14.6g] close-coupled, finely-made colt: capable of useful form, but probably of unsatisfactory temperament: pulled hard then dropped away tamely final outing: stays 1¾m: blinkered second and last starts: often sweating and on edge: sent to join D. Hayes in Australia. *G. Harwood.*

HORN PLAYER (USA) 3 ch.c. The Minstrel (CAN) 135–Qualique (USA) 72 (Hawaii) [1989 8g 1990 8m⁵ 8m 8.5d² 12.3g³ 12g] big, lengthy colt: has scope: poor mover: modest maiden: stays 12.3f: acts on good to firm ground and goes well: gave trouble at stalls third start: sold to join F. Jordan 17,000 gns Newmarket Autumn Sales. *B. W. Hills.*

HORRIBLE HORACE 2 b.g. (Mar 8) Homing 130–Holdall 80 (Manacle 123) — [1990 5m 6m 6f 5m] leggy gelding: turns near-fore out: first reported foal: dam 6f (at 2 yrs) and 7f (seller) winner: seems of little account. *R. P. C. Hoad.*

HORSEFLY 2 b.f. (May 26) Balliol 125–Erstung 83 (Shantung 132) [1990 5m] — third living foal: half-sister to 1½m winner Dellwood Renown (by Connaught): dam placed over 1m at 2 yrs, won over hurdles: behind in median auction at Windsor in August. *W. Holden.*

HORSTAY (IRE) 2 b.g. (Apr 9) Horage 124–Short Stay (Be My Guest (USA) **61**
126) [1990 5m³ 5g⁶ 6g⁴ 6f² 7.5f⁴ 7f⁵ 7.5g⁴ 6g³ 8m] IR 2,000Y, 6,600 2-y-o: small,
sturdy gelding: turns fore-feet in: moderate mover: first foal: dam Irish maiden,
stayed middle distances: quite modest performer: ran well at York in strongly-run
seller and nursery (slowly away) final 2 starts: stays 1m: may do better in blinkers:
sold 1,700 gns Doncaster October Sales. *C. Tinkler.*

HOSPITABLE 6 ch.g. Be My Guest (USA) 126–Harmonise 113 (Reliance II 137) **65**
[1989 10g* 9g* 11g* 11g* 12g* 1990 a12g² a12g4] winner of 5 races in Belgium in
1989, 3 of them at Ostend in July: quite modest form in Britain: in frame at Lingfield
(bandaged behind) in January in claimer and apprentice handicap: stays 1½m. *John
Mark Capitte, Belgium.*

HOSTESS QUICKLY 3 b.f. Hotfoot 126–Linda Dudley 81 (Owen Dudley 121) **59**
[1989 7f 8.2f5 1990 12f5 a12g² 12m* a11g² 12m a11g4 12m 13v2] leggy filly: poor on
most form, winning handicap at Edinburgh in June: 20/1, improved form in Ayr
claimer final start: will stay 1¾m: has won on good to firm ground, clearly goes well
on heavy: sold to join P. Hedger 7,000 gns Newmarket Autumn Sales. *Dr J. D.
Scargill.*

HOSTILE ACT 5 b.g. Glenstal (USA) 118–Fandetta (Gay Fandango (USA) 132) **57**
[1989 NR 1990 11.5m⁶ 12d 12.3g5 11.5g² 10m3 10.2m 10m² 12m] rather leggy
gelding: half-brother to sprint winner Alnashme (by Godswalk): dam unraced half-
sister to Molecomb Stakes winner Hatta: plating-class maiden: stays 11.5f: acts on
good to firm going: has hung left: wears bandages. *Miss P. Hall.*

HOT COMPANY 5 ch.g. Hotfoot 126–Campagna (Romulus 129) [1989 12g 14m3 **64** §
13.6f⁶ 12m⁴ a14g4 1990 a12g*] angular, sparely-made gelding: won claimer at
Lingfield (claimed to join P. Bevan's stable £8,401) in January: suited by 1¼m: yet to
race on soft going, acts on any other: usually blinkered: ungenuine. *D. Burchell.*

HOT DESERT 2 b.g. (May 9) Green Desert (USA) 127–Hayya (FR) (Shergar **92**
140) [1990 5m* 5m3] leggy, lengthy gelding: second foal: half-brother to a winner in
Scandinavia by Shareef Dancer: dam unraced half-sister to Luderic, smart in France
at up to 9f: impressive winner of maiden at Newcastle in June: well-backed favourite, around a length third of 7, making most and tending to edge left last 1f, to
Seductress in listed race at Newmarket following month: speedy: seemed likely to
improve further, and win another race or 2 but not seen out again. *Major W. R. Hern.*

HOTFOOT HENRY 3 ch.g. Hotfoot 126–Courting Day 90 (Right Boy 137) **—**
[1989 5d⁶ 5d 6m 5f 6g a6g a7g 1990 9g 10m] leggy, angular gelding: poor form,
including in seller: bred to stay at least 1m: has given trouble at stalls, getting loose
from them and withdrawn when blinkered at 2 yrs: edgy in 1990. *A. Smith.*

HOT GIRL 8 b.m. Hot Grove 128–Gloria Maremmana (King Emperor (USA)) **—**
[1989 10m⁴ 1990 8f] lengthy mare: poor mover: poor handicapper: bandaged and
backward only outing at 8 yrs: stays 1½m: probably acts on any going: has worn
blinkers: usually slowly away. *B. R. Millman.*

HOT HOPE 3 b.f. Blazing Saddles (AUS)–Return Home (Nonoalco (USA) 131) **42**
[1989 5v 5g⁶ 5f 6g a6g a6g 1990 a6g4 a6g5 a5g* 5f4 5m4 6f 5m5 5g 5g 5m a5g a7g]
plain filly: poor handicapper: made all at Lingfield in March: no form after seventh
start: best at 5f: acts on firm going: has run creditably when sweating and edgy. *J. J.
Bridger.*

HOT PERFORMER 3 ch.f. Hotfoot 126–Show Business 72 (Auction Ring **48**
(USA) 123) [1989 6h 5f4 6g6 7.5g² 7m* 7f³ 7g* 7m 7g* 7g 1990 8f6 7m 8.2f5 7h6
8.2g 7g 8d 10g5 12f* 10g 13.8f 10m? 11v] tall, lengthy filly: moderate walker:
plating-class handicapper. ridden by 7-lb claimer, won selling event (no bid) at
Beverley in July: only show after when second at Redcar: should prove suited by
further than 1¼m: acts on firm going, tailed off on heavy: somewhat temperamental,
and looked most unsuitable mount for 7-lb claimer at 2 yrs. *T. Fairhurst.*

HOT RUMOUR 3 ch.g. Hotfoot 126–Clear As Crystal 80 (Whitstead 125) [1989 **83**
6h 8.2s5 8m 10g² 1990 10.2f 12d4 12g* 12f3 14g 17.6g] lengthy, angular gelding: poor
mover: fair performer: won maiden auction at Beverley in May and amateurs event
at Hamilton in June: unlucky next start then faced stiff tasks in Ebor Handicap at
York and £7,400 handicap (ran poorly) at Haydock: should stay at least 1¾m: acts on
firm and dead ground: blinkered last 2 starts at 2 yrs: gives trouble at stalls,
withdrawn on intended reappearance: sold 12,000 gns Doncaster November Sales.
S. G. Norton.

HOT STAR 4 b.g. Hotfoot 126–La Camargue (Wollow 132) [1989 8s 8.2m 10f 9.1f5 **62**
12.3f 13s² 15s* 12.4g4 1990 18f 13v* 14s 16m 15g6] leggy gelding: has a markedly
round action: quite modest handicapper: won at Ayr in April, only form at 4 yrs:

stays 15f well: goes very well in the mud: usually sweats and gets on toes. *J. F. Bottomley.*

HOT SUNDAY SPORT   2 b.f. (Mar 27) Star Appeal 133–Alpine Alice 94 (Abwah 118) [1990 6g 7f³ 8m] 8,200Y: neat filly: poor mover: half-sister to 3 winners, including middle-distance performer Steppey Lane (by Tachypous): dam 2-y-o 7f winner, is daughter of 1000 Guineas third Alpine Bloom: little worthwhile form, slowly away, in maidens and a seller. *P. A. Kelleway.* —

HOT TAN   4 ch.f. Hotfoot 126–Tanara 93 (Romulus 129) [1989 7g 10f 8f 7g⁵ 1990 a7g] small, quite good-topped filly: moderate mover: sign of ability only on final start at 3 yrs: sold 4,000 gns Doncaster January Sales. *Ronald Thompson.* —

HOT TOOTSIE   3 b.f. Hotfoot 126–Lady of The Isle 72 (Pitskelly 122) [1989 5f⁴ 5f 5m 5f⁵ 5g* 5f⁴ 6m* 6m 6f² 5s 6v⁵ 6g 1990 6g 6m] small, good-bodied filly: useful plater at 2 yrs: below form both outings in July, 1990: suited by 6f: seems to act on any going: sometimes hangs, and is a difficult ride: inconsistent. *J. Balding.*

HOUMAYOUN (FR)   3 b.c. Shernazar 131–Halwah (FR) (The Minstrel (CAN) 135) [1989 8g³ 8m* 10v⁴ 1990 10f² 10.5d⁶ 12g* 12g 11g* 12g⁶] fourth foal: half-brother to twice-raced French 1988 2-y-o 1m winner Haratiyna (by Top Ville) and useful French 1¼m to 12.5f winner Hanzala (by Akarad): dam French 12.5f winner: won 2-y-o maiden at Longchamp, 22-runner Derby Italiano (by 4½ lengths) at Rome in May and minor event at Milan in September: ran poorly in Group 1 events at Milan fourth and final starts: suited by 1½m: acts on firm going: changed hands after second start, left A. de Royer-Dupre's stable after third: seems unreliable. *L. d'Auria, Italy.* **114**

HOUSATONIC (USA)   3 b.f. Riverman (USA) 131–Hippodamia (USA) 130 (Hail To Reason) [1989 NR 1990 7g 8g⁶ a7g* a12g⁴] sparely-made filly: tenth foal: half-sister to 2 winners in USA, notably Globe (by Secretariat), graded-stakes winner at up to 11f: dam high-class French 2-y-o 5.5f and 1m winner also successful in USA at up to 9f: favourite, won maiden at Southwell in July: appeared to run creditably when well-beaten fourth of 13 in handicap there following month, ridden long way out: stays 1½m: sold 56,000 gns Newmarket December Sales. *J. H. M. Gosden.* **59**

HOUSE OF FRUIT   3 b.g. Mansingh 120–Rheinbloom 66 (Rheingold 137) [1989 7g⁵ 7m³ 7m 8.2g 8.2g 1990 a10g] tall, rather unfurnished gelding: quite modest form at best as 2-y-o: soundly beaten in maiden at Lingfield in January: stays 7f. *C. N. Allen.* —

HOUSEPROUD (USA)   3 br.f. Riverman (USA) 131–Proud Lou (USA) (Proud Clarion (USA)) [1989 5g³ 5.5g* 8g² 1990 8s* 8g* 10.5d 8g⁶ 9f⁴] **115**

The latest Dubai Poule d'Essai des Pouliches was a modest edition. Only two of the fourteen runners (none of the first eight finishers) went on to win a race of any description later in the season and we rate the winner Houseproud as having shown the worst form of any French classic winner since the 1965 Pouliches winner La Sarre. And whereas La Sarre's victory was only confirmed in a three-way photo, Houseproud's superiority was clear before the race and at the finish. Her two-length second to Salsabil in the Marcel Boussac the previous October wasn't looking any worse with the passage of time and she'd made a winning return in the Prix de la Grotte over course and distance three weeks earlier. Houseproud was made 9/10 favourite in the Pouliches to see off a foreign challenge comprising Pharaoh's Delight,

Dubai Poule d'Essai des Pouliches, Longchamp—
odds-on Houseproud wins from Pont Aven and Gharam (near side)

Mr K. Abdulla's "Houseproud"

Princess Taufan, Gharam, Tatwij and Wedding Bouquet and a home contingent that included the first four in one of France's most important trials, the Prix Imprudence. She did so by showing easily the best turn of foot. Pont Aven emerged best of the Imprudence runners, moving to the front fairly comfortably entering the straight, but she'd hardly done so before Houseproud was galvanised by Eddery into an irresistible run from mid-division, leading approaching the final furlong and ridden out to win by two lengths, Pont Aven coming in half a length in front of Gharam. It didn't take long, however, for Houseproud's colours to be lowered as, four weeks later, she finished in the ruck behind Rafha in the Prix de Diane Hermes. Trying to come from the back in a moderately-run race, it was probably a creditable effort, but Houseproud had hung badly right when asked to go about her business and it was four months before she was seen out again, in the Group 3 Prix du Rond-Point at Longchamp on Arc day. Despite her stiff task, effectively giving weight all round when allowances for age and sex are taken into account, Houseproud was made an even-money favourite but, as with the 1988 Pouliches winner Ravinella, she failed to recapture the glory of her efforts in the spring. On her final start Houseproud attempted to emulate Ravinella's victory in the All Along Stakes at Laurel Park in the United States; again she ran virtually up to her best form and again that wasn't enough to win.

Houseproud is the fourth foal out of Proud Lou following unraced animals by J. O. Tobin and Irish River and the once-raced 1984 three-year-old

		Never Bend	Nasrullah
	Riverman (USA)	(b 1960)	Lalun
	(b 1969)	River Lady	Prince John
Houseproud (USA)		(b 1963)	Nile Lily
(b.f. 1987)		Proud Clarion	Hail To Reason
	Proud Lou (USA)	(b 1964)	Breath O'Morn
	(b 1979)	Baby Louise	Exclusive Native
		(b 1972)	Careful Turn

Brosna (also by Irish River). Houseproud is closely related to all of those descendants of Never Bend, therefore, and sister to the two-year-old Stornoway who has finished fourth twice from as many starts, also trained by Fabre. Proud Lou raced at two, three and four years, only managed to win at two but showed very useful form in doing so, the most important of her four successes coming with a comfortable pillar-to-post triumph in the Grade 1 Frizette Stakes over a mile. A 550,000-dollar addition to the Juddmonte Farms assets in 1985, Proud Lou is a half-sister to five winners, none of them of her class, including another of Fabre's current charges Boston Two Step who showed useful form as a two-year-old but didn't progress in his second season. The Kentucky Derby winner Proud Clarion and lightly-raced two-year-old stakes winner Baby Louise are Houseproud's maternal grandparents. Houseproud has been retired to stud in the United States. Her run in the Prix de Diane was inconclusive as regards stamina but we can say that she probably stayed nine furlongs and acted on any going. *A. Fabre, France.*

HOUSE WARMING   3 ch.c. Habitat 134–Be Sweet 117 (Reform 132) [1989 NR 1990 10.1g 9m 10.2h 7f 6m] sturdy colt: moderate mover: sixth foal: half-brother to 3 winners, including useful 1984 2-y-o 7f and 1m winner Top Bee (by Shirley Heights) and 13.3f winner King Menelaos (by Ile de Bourbon): dam, half-sister to Royal Hive and Attica Meli, smart at up to 1½m: no sign of ability, in apprentice selling handicap (blinkered) final start: sold 1,700 gns Ascot July Sales. *D. A. Wilson.*   —

HOW   4 b.c. Horage 124–Rathcoffey Dodo 108 (Jukebox 120) [1989 8m 10.2f⁴ 10m 11.7f* 13.8d⁶ 1990 10.8m a12g⁵ a14g] sturdy, useful-looking colt: moderate mover: won maiden claimer as 3-y-o: no worthwhile form in handicaps in spring: suited by 1½m: acts on firm going: sold 4,200 gns Newmarket July Sales. *Mrs L. Piggott.*   —

HOWJAL (USA)   5 b.g. Conquistador Cielo (USA)–Taylor Park (USA) (Sir Gaylord) [1989 NR 1990 12g] angular, well-made gelding: won maiden at Beverley at 3 yrs: backward on first intended run on flat since, bolted to post and unseated rider: never dangerous in amateurs handicap later in October: stays 1½m: possibly needs give in the ground. *J. R. Bostock.*   —

HOW'S YER FATHER   4 b.g. Daring March 116–Dawn Ditty 100 (Song 132) [1989 6s 6s 7m⁶ 6m⁴ 6f² 5m⁵ 5m³ 6m⁵ 1990 a6g² a6g 6g⁶ 6f 6d 5m⁴ 5f⁴ 5.3f⁶ 5g³ 5m⁶] leggy, sparely-made gelding: plating-class maiden: effective at 5f and 6f: acts on any going with possible exception of soft: sometimes blinkered: has run creditably when sweating and edgy: trained until after fifth outing by J. McConnochie. *R. J. Hodges.*   53

HOZAY (USA)   3 b.c. Cresta Rider (USA) 124–Chellita (Habitat 134) [1989 NR 1990 8m 8f 8.2s⁵ 8.2g 10g] 39,000Y: big, heavy-topped colt: moderate walker: half-brother to smart 1988 2-y-o 7f and 1m winner Tessla (by Glint of Gold) who ran creditably over 1¼m in 1989, and to 2 other winners, including 1984 Irish 2-y-o 5f winner Zenetta (by Bellypha): dam ran once: behind in varied events: bandaged third start: sweating when blinkered on fourth: has worn tongue strap. *Mrs L. Piggott.*   —

HTHAAL (USA)   2 b. or br.c. (Jan 7) Caro 133–Endurable Heights (USA) (Graustark) [1990 6d⁵] $240,000Y: rather leggy colt: has scope: moderate walker: fourth foal: brother to fairly useful 1986 2-y-o 5f and 7f winner Inshirah and half-brother to 2 other winners: dam thrice-raced half-sister to very smart stakes winner Batonnier and daughter of leading 1964 2-y-o Mira Femme: bit backward and green, lost place by halfway in 6-runner maiden at Chester in October: showed a roundish action. *H. Thomson Jones.*   —

HUCKLEBERRY WIN (USA)   3 ch.c. Riverman (USA) 131–Waterloo 120 (Bold Lad (IRE) 133) [1989 NR 1990 7f³ 10g 8d⁴ 7.2d³ 8v* 7.6v] $120,000Y: compact colt: brother to Irish maiden White Water Lady, best at up to 7f, closely related to good 1985 2-y-o 6f and 7f winner Water Cay (by J O Tobin), later successful at 1m, and half-brother to several other winners: dam won Cheveley Park Stakes and 1000   78

Guineas: favourite, won handicap at Ayr in October: wearing tongue strap, soon pushed along in £9,700 Chester handicap 8 days later: worth another try over 1¼m: best efforts with plenty of give in the ground: sold to join M. Hammond 40,000 gns Newmarket Autumn Sales. *J. W. Watts.*

HUD HUD (USA)   2 b.f. (Feb 20) Alydar (USA)–Tax Dodge (USA) (Seattle Slew — p
(USA)) [1990 7g] $650,000Y: unfurnished filly: first foal: dam won at up to 9f, including in stakes: showed signs of ability in maiden at Kempton in September. *A. A. Scott.*

HUDSON BAY TRADER (USA)   3 b.g. Sir Ivor 135–Yukon Baby (USA)   76
(Northern Dancer) [1989 7g 1990 8f 10g3 10.6f* 11.7g5 11m 12g 10g4] strong, attractive gelding: modest handicapper: on toes, won at Haydock in May: ran moderately fifth and sixth outings: should be suited by 1½m + : acts on firm ground: has joined N. Henderson. *C. F. Wall.*

HUMALONG   5 b.m. Bay Express 132–Hum 69 (Crooner 119) [1989 10f 7f6 7g2 7f   36
7m2 7.6m5 6m2 6g 1990 6m 7f 7g5 6m3 7m4 7f2 7g 7m 6g 6m] rangy, workmanlike mare: poor maiden stays 7f: acts on firm going: sold 1,800 gns Ascot November Sales. *L. J. Holt.*

HUNDRA (USA)   2 ch.c. (Mar 23) Arctic Tern (USA) 126–Nur Jahan (USA) (Raja   85 p
Baba (USA)) [1990 8s4] $65,000Y, resold 26,000Y: close-coupled, workmanlike colt: second known foal: dam won at around 1m in USA: around 3 lengths fourth of 22, staying on well final 2f, to Another Bob in minor event at Newbury in October: sure to improve, particularly over further. *P. A. Kelleway.*

HUNDRED ISLANDS   3 br.f. Hotfoot 126–Bally Tudor 75 (Henry The Seventh   37
125) [1989 NR 1990 7.5d 8m 15g5 10m3 13.8m3] lengthy, good-topped filly: has a long stride: eighth foal: dam won over 1¼m: plater: best effort in 4-runner non-selling handicap at Catterick final start, no chance with leaders then staying on steadily: stays 13.8f: usually on toes: should be suited by more enterprising tactics. *M. J. Camacho.*

HUNG OVER   4 b.f. Smackover 107–Passionate 57 (Dragonara Palace (USA) 115)   46
[1989 6f 5m 6f4 5f 6g4 a8g a6g3 1990 a7g2 6f6 a5g] leggy, lengthy filly: poor maiden: stays 7f: best on an easy surface: blinkered last 2 starts: sold 1,700 gns Ascot July Sales: resold 2,500 gns Ascot September Sales. *B. A. McMahon.*

HUNKY DORIUS   3 b.f. Petorius 117–Always Smiling (Prominer 125) [1989 5f   37 §
5m 5m3 5h3 5f2 5f3 6g 5d4 6g 5f5 1990 5f6 5m6 5m4 6m6 5.8f 7g 8m5 8.3g 10m6 10m 12.5m 10d6] leggy, sparely-made filly: poor maiden: stays 1¼m: acts on firm and dead going: blinkered 6 times, once at 3 yrs: wears bitless bridle: tends to carry head high, often edgy and hasn't ideal attitude: changed hands 4,000 gns Doncaster February Sales: sold 980 gns Doncaster November Sales. *Capt. J. Wilson.*

HUNTED   3 ch.g. Busted 134–Madam Cody (Hot Spark 126) [1989 NR 1990   84
10.5m4 14m5 12m3] 13,500Y: sturdy gelding: has a quick action: second foal: half-brother to a winner in USA by Night Shift: dam second over 7f at 2 yrs in Ireland: easily best effort in maidens at Folkestone on final start: will prove suited by 1½m + : sold to join M. Pipe 15,500 gns Newmarket Autumn Sales. *A. C. Stewart.*

HUNTING HORN (USA)   3 b.c. Northern Dancer–Buzz My Bell (USA)   71
(Drone) [1989 6g 1990 8.2m2 8m6 10f4] lengthy, rather angular colt: modest maiden: ran moderately after reappearance: may be worth another try short of 1m. *M. R. Stoute.*

HUNZA'S CHOICE   3 b.c. Exhibitioner 111–Romantic Air 62 (He Loves Me   38
120) [1989 5m4 5m 6m 6m5 6f5 6m 6g6 7f 8f a6g3 a7g 1990 a7g6 a10g3 a8g4 12f a12g3 /m 12m5 11g6 13m 8.2m 9f6 10f] small, rather sparely-made colt: poor maiden: stays 1½m: possibly best with give in the ground nowadays: blinkered sixth outing. *P. Mitchell.*

HURRICANE POWER   3 br.c. Wolverlife 115–Libby Jayne 67 (Tumble Wind   77
(USA)) [1989 6f5 1990 6m2 6m* 5d 6m4 6s a7g3] rangy, quite attractive colt: modest handicapper: favourably drawn, won maiden at Lingfield in June: easily best efforts after when in frame at York and Lingfield (first run for 2 months): stays 7f: acts on good to firm ground: sweating third start: trained until after penultimate one by J. Hudson. *J. D. Bethell.*

HUSO   2 ch.g. (May 18) Sharpo 132–Husnah (USA) 85 (Caro 133) [1990 6m6 6m 6m   64
6m5 6g4] leggy gelding: first foal: dam 1½m and 1¾m winner: quite modest maiden: will be better suited by 7f: has run creditably for 7-lb claimer: sold 12,000 gns Newmarket Autumn Sales. *C. E. Brittain.*

HUSYAN (USA) 4 b.c. Alleged (USA) 138–Close Comfort (USA) (Far North 115 (CAN)) [1989 12g* 10.1g* 12m² 1990 12g 10m* 12d⁵ 10g* 12m 11.1g⁵] strong, lengthy colt: smart on his day: won Brigadier Gerard Stakes at Sandown in May (setting steady pace), by 2½ lengths from Scenic and Scottish Classic at Ayr in July by 2 lengths from Alcando: well beaten otherwise at 4 yrs: best at 1¼m: acts well on good to firm ground: sent to race in USA. *P. T. Walwyn.*

HYDE AND PEAK 3 b.f. King of Spain 121–Vivchar 80 (Huntercombe 133) — [1989 NR 1990 10m 7m⁵ a8g 10.6d] 3,100Y: strong, workmanlike filly: fifth foal: half-sister to 5-y-o 7f winner Empire Joy (by Sallust): dam 2-y-o 5f winner: well beaten in maidens and claimers: not bred to stay 1¼m: sold 1,700 gns Ascot November Sales. *J. A. Glover.*

HYDEONIAN 3 ch.g. Viking (USA)–Precious Lady (Home Guard (USA) 129) — [1989 6f⁵ 7.5f 6m 1990 8g 8m 8g] sparely-made gelding: no sign of ability, in selling handicap (visored, sweating and on toes) final start: sold 1,350 gns Doncaster August Sales. *C. Tinkler.*

HYDEONIUS 5 b.g. Crystal Palace (FR) 132–Razannda (FR) (Labus (FR)) [1989 60 10f 8f 10m⁶ 9m⁴ 10m 1990 12.3g 10m² 11m* 14m* 12f⁴ 12g* 12f* 15d⁴ 12.2f² 15.5f 12m⁶ 13.8d 13.6d 16d* a14g⁶ a16g] workmanlike gelding: keen walker: moderate mover, with quick action: in excellent form in handicaps in summer, winning at Hamilton, Nottingham (slowly-run race) and Hamilton again (2 ran) in July then Thirsk in August and September: justified favouritism in celebrity race at Sedgefield in November: below his best on all-weather last 2 outings: stays 2m: acts on firm and dead going: has sweated: trained until after reappearance by J. Glover. *C. Tinkler.*

HYDROPIC 3 b.g. Kabour 80–Hydrangea 73 (Warpath 113) [1989 7f 8m a8g a7g 43 1990 a6g² a10g⁵ 6m 6m a8g] leggy gelding: poor maiden: well beaten except when second in handicap at Lingfield: seems suited by 6f. *D. W. Chapman.*

HYMN OF HARLECH 7 b.g. Welsh Chanter 124–Church Bay 76 (Reliance II 82 137) [1989 7.6m 8m* 9m 8g² 8m⁵ 8g³ 8m⁵ 1990 7.6m² 8m* 9m⁴ 8.3m 7m a8g] smallish gelding: has a quick action: rallied to win apprentice handicap at Newbury in June for second year running: below form on all-weather final outing: stays 9f:

Scottish Classic, Ayr—Scotland's only pattern race on the flat is won comfortably by Husyan

Hamdan Al-Maktoum's "Husyan"

ideally suited by top-of-the-ground: wears blinkers: races up with pace: has looked none too enthusiastic and best handled tenderly: winning novice hurdler in November. *D. R. C. Elsworth.*

HYPNOTIST 3 b.g. High Top 131–Tamilian 89 (Tamerlane 128) [1989 NR 1990 10f³ 10f⁴ 10f² 10m 8m*] 3,200Y: workmanlike gelding: has a round action: half-brother to 1984 2-y-o 1m winner Grundy Lane (by Grundy) and 2 winners in Hong Kong: dam won at up to 1¼m: quite modest performer: always front rank when winning apprentice handicap at Sandown in July, wandering for inexperienced rider: possibly suited by 1m. *C. A. Cyzer.*   **69**

HYSSOP 2 ch.g. (Mar 8) Absalom 128–Willow Herb 68 (Habat 127) [1990 5g⁶ 6d 7f* 7f³ 7g 7g⁶ 8.5m] 8,000Y: rangy gelding: sixth foal: half-brother to a winner in Italy: dam 6f winner, is daughter of half-sister to Queen's Hussar: lowered in class, easily made all in seller (retained 8,000 gns) at Yarmouth in July: best effort after on next start: seems suited by 7f: acts on firm ground, possibly unsuited by dead. *J. Derry.*   **63**

HYTHE 4 b.g. Teenoso (USA) 135–Full Dress II 115 (Shantung 132) [1989 NR 1990 10.8m] small, stocky gelding: no sign of ability: blinkered and taken down early only outing at 4 yrs: sold 1,150 gns Doncaster November Sales. *P. A. Blockley.*   **—**

I

IBN BEY 6 ch.h. Mill Reef (USA) 141–Rosia Bay 102 (High Top 131) [1989 13.3f² 16f⁵ 14f* 12.5m* 13.3g* 12s* 12f⁶ 1990 10.5d³ 12g³ 12g⁴ 12g* 12s² 14g* a10f²]   **126**

For the second time Paul Cole won the International Racing Bureau's Derby award for the leading British trainer overseas: his haul of £1,341,456 put him more than £650,000 ahead of the next man Guy Harwood: third-placed

Grosser Preis der Berliner Bank, Dusseldorf—
Ibn Bey finishes clear of Mondrian and the rest

John Dunlop also topped the £600,000-mark on foreign soil, while four others, Brittain, Cecil, Hills and Balding earned over £400,000. That splendidly tough, genuine and consistent old war-horse Ibn Bey was the Cole stable's star traveller, during the course of the year taking in eight Grade 1 or Group 1 races in seven different countries for approximately £675,000 in overseas prize-money. Nearly two-thirds of that total came as the result of one astonishing run—his second to the Kentucky Derby winner Unbridled in the world's richest race, the Breeders' Cup Classic at Belmont Park in October. Racing on dirt for the first time and over the shortest trip he'd encountered since his two-year-old days, Ibn Bey was refitted with blinkers; he'd first worn them when beating Mondrian in the Europa-Preis at Cologne in 1989 but had twice raced too freely in them since. Ibn Bey was always close up in a maximum-sized field of fourteen lacking Sunday Silence, Easy Goer and Criminal Type through injury or retirement, and turned for home in second behind Thirty Six Red. He drew alongside the leader with a hundred yards to go, just as Unbridled squeezed between the pair, then kept on to go down by a length, the same distance by which he held off Thirty Six Red.

Other than when blinkered in the Gran Premio di Milano, Ibn Bey had given a good account of himself in each of his races earlier in the season. In his

Jefferson Smurfit Memorial Irish St Leger, the Curragh—
the six-year-olds Ibn Bey and Mr Pintips put on a grandstand finish

Breeders' Cup Classic, Belmont Park—
Ibn Bey (No. 3, new colours) makes astonishingly light of the unfamiliar
and runs Kentucky Derby winner Unbridled to a length

only one in Britain, in the Hanson Coronation Cup at Epsom, he was outpaced over two furlongs out having tried to steal a march rounding the home turn, then stayed on again late, gaining on In The Wings and Observation Post at the line. His second trip to Germany, for the Grosser Preis der Berliner Bank at Dusseldorf, finished much the same way as his first—a resounding victory over Mondrian who was having his first outing since being virtually pulled up in the Coronation Cup. Ibn Bey quickly had things sewn up after being sent for home three furlongs out and had four lengths to spare at the post. Cauthen was criticised by Mondrian's trainer for his handling of his horse and was replaced by Hofer in the Grosser Preis von Baden. Ibn Bey was denied the hat-trick by the Hofer/Mondrian combination, who swept past in the final furlong to score by a length, with Per Quod a length and three quarters away in third. Per Quod was one of eleven opponents that Ibn Bey found himself up against in an older-horse dominated Jefferson Smurfit Memorial Irish St Leger at the Curragh, a race in which he finished well beaten as a three-year-old. Ibn Bey went off joint-second choice in the betting with Braashee behind the short-priced Michelozzo, who was by now arguably living on his reputation. Michelozzo was one of the first beaten whereas Ibn Bey and Braashee turned for home second and third behind Thetford Forest. Quinn was pushing Ibn Bey along by that stage, but having been passed by Mr Pintips and looking held two furlongs out, the horse showed tremendous courage and kept responding to wear down Mr Pintips close home and beat him a length, the two six-year-olds three lengths clear of Braashee. Ibn Bey ran his best races when ridden up with the pace, and he was totally unsuited by the ride he was given by a Japanese jockey in the Japan Cup on his final outing. He never threatened to play a prominent part and was beaten about five lengths after passing a few stragglers in the final quarter of a mile.

			Never Bend		Nasrullah
		Mill Reef (USA)	(b 1960)		Lalun
		(b 1968)	Milan Mill		Princequillo
Ibn Bey			(b 1962)		Virginia Water
(ch.h. 1984)			High Top		Derring-Do
		Rosia Bay	(b 1969)		Camenae
		(b 1977)	Ouija		Silly Season
			(b or br 1971)		Samanda

Ibn Bey was one of three winners for his dam, the mile-winner Rosia Bay, in the latest season. Roseate Tern (by Blakeney) won the General Accident Jockey Club Stakes at Newmarket on her reappearance, while the three-year-old filly Barakat (by Bustino) took four runs to get off the mark, then won a poor maiden at Yarmouth and the £18,400 Cognac Courvoisier Handicap at Doncaster, both over a mile and three quarters. Rosia Bay's matings to Diesis in 1988 and El Gran Senor in 1989 both resulted in colts and she's now in foal to Nashwan. A granddaughter of hers by Reference Point out of Cerise Bouquet was knocked down to the BBA for 170,000 guineas at the Newmarket Highflyer Sales in October on behalf of a Japanese client. More details of the family, whose other members include Teleprompter, can be found in the essays on Ibn Bey and Roseate Tern in *Racehorses of 1989*. It's

Y. Sohma's "Ibn Bey"

impossible not to be impressed by Ibn Bey's record. He won ten of his twenty-nine races, at least one in each of his five seasons, in pattern company in the last four. A big, strong, powerful-galloping horse, he proved effective at a mile and a quarter to a mile and three quarters and on ground ranging from firm through to soft on turf, as well as on dirt. His eighth placing in the Japan Cup—the three British runners Cacoethes (third), Belmez (seventh) and Ibn Bey earned over £200,000 between them at Tokyo—took his total career earnings past the £1,000,000-mark. Ibn Bey has now been retired to stud in Japan. *P. F. I. Cole.*

IBN NAAS (USA) 4 ch.g. Diesis 133–La Vie (USA) (Le Fabuleux 133) [1989 12s⁴ 9f 1990 a8g] rather sparely-made, attractive gelding: quite modest form at best: tailed off in handicap at Southwell in January: should be suited by middle distances: of doubtful temperament. *B. Richmond.*

IBN SINA (USA) 3 b.c. Dr Blum (USA)–Two On One (CAN) (Lord Durham (CAN)) [1989 6f 7m² 8g³ 1990 7h³ 10m 11.5m³ 12.3f² 12m⁶] lengthy, well-made colt: has a round action: fair form at 2 yrs: below best in minor event then claimers in 1990: should stay well: pulled hard and ran poorly final start: sold to join M. Robinson 6,200 gns Newmarket Autumn Sales. *P. F. I. Cole.* 68

IBN ZAMAN (USA) 4 b.c. Graustark–Wake Robin (Summer Tan) [1989 10.1m 12m⁵ 14m⁶ 1990 15.5f 12m] sturdy colt: slow maiden: tailed off in handicaps in spring, running too freely in visor second: sold 900 gns Ascot May Sales. *C. C. Elsey.*

ICANSEEFORMILES (IRE) 2 gr.c. (May 31) Godswalk (USA) 130–Saintly Tune (Welsh Saint 126) [1990 6g] IR 8,400Y: well-grown, close-coupled colt: rather unfurnished: brother to 3-y-o Walking Saint, successful at 7f (at 2 yrs) and 8.5f, and half-brother to a bumpers winner by Don: dam won at up to 1¾m on flat and up to 2½m over hurdles in Ireland: slowly away and always behind in maiden at Newmarket in October. *R. Hannon.*

ICARNAFORDIT 3 b.f. The Dissident 85–Italian Summer 83 (Silly Season 127) — [1989 7f 8.2f 1990 9f4] poor form in claimers and seller. *W. G. M. Turner.*

ICE BREAKER (FR) 7 b.h. Arctic Tern (USA) 126–Figure de Proue (FR) — (Petingo 135) [1989 8g 12d 1990 10f 12g5] rather leggy, good-topped horse: moderate mover: poor handicapper: stays 11f: seems to need a soft surface: bandaged final outing: wore net muzzle at 7 yrs. *I. Semple.*

ICE MAGIC 3 ch.c. Red Sunset 120–Free Rein (Sagaro 133) [1989 6m3 6m4 6f6 72 1990 6g 8f3 10g* 11m3 13.8m2 12g6 12f3 13.8f2] sparely-made colt: modest handicapper: won at Nottingham in June despite edging left: stays 1¾m: acts on firm going: lacks turn of foot: consistent. *P. Calver.*

ICY VIEW (IRE) 2 b.c. (Apr 15) Vision (USA)–Icefield (Northfields (USA)) — [1990 a6g 7g] IR 4,200F, 7,000Y: leggy, rather close-coupled colt: sixth foal: half-brother to 1984 2-y-o 6f winner Harvester King (by Pitskelly): dam unraced daughter of Portland Handicap winner Gold Pollen: no show in claimer at Southwell (slowly away and green) and maiden at Chester (seemed unsuited by track) in August. *B. A. McMahon.*

IDLE CHAT (USA) 3 ch.f. Assert 134–Gossiping (USA) (Chati (USA)) [1989 93 8.2f* 7g 1990 10m2 11.5m3] workmanlike filly: fairly useful performer: beaten short head by sole opponent Petite Mou in minor event (on toes, led over 9f) at Nottingham and about 5 lengths behind Rafha in listed race at Lingfield in the spring: will stay 1½m: acts on firm going: genuine. *B. W. Hills.*

IF MEMORY SERVES (USA) 4 b.c. Youth (USA) 135–Royal Recall (USA) 102 (Native Royalty (USA)) [1989 7m* 10.1g2 10m 10g* 1990 10m2 10.2m4 8m*dis 10g6 7g* 8g* 8m* 10g6] lengthy, rather leggy colt: has a quick action: useful performer: first past the post in ladies races at Ascot (£6,600 event, neck in front of Akdam but swerving right stalls and disqualified) in July and Doncaster in September, minor event at Newbury later in September and apprentice contest at Ascot in October: stays 1¼m: acts on good to firm going: occasionally bandaged off-hind: pulled too hard second start: wears severe noseband: taken quietly to post. *J. H. M. Gosden.*

IJTIHAAD (USA) 3 b.c. Arctic Tern (USA) 126–Corita (Satingo 129) [1989 8m3 103 1990 10f* 10m3 13.3g5 10.2g5 12m 10m*] well-made, attractive colt: has a fluent, round action: useful form: won maiden at Newmarket in July and 5-runner minor event (made all) at Leicester in October: ran as if something amiss in Group 2 event third outing and weakened quickly on turn in £71,300 Ascot handicap (stiff task) on fifth: stays 1¼m well: acts on firm going: remains in training. *Major W. R. Hern.*

IKDAM 5 b.h. Glint of Gold 128–Run To The Sun (Run The Gantlet (USA)) [1989 — 18g4 16s3 17.6d 17.4s5 16m 18g 1990 16d5] quite attractive, good-bodied horse:

Breitling 'Spitfire' Stakes For Lady Amateur Riders, Doncaster— Lydia Pearce gains some compensation for If Memory Serves's controversial disqualification at Ascot

usually looks really well: fluent mover: modest handicapper early as 4-y-o: well beaten last 5 outings on flat: needs extreme test of stamina: acts on any going: blinkered last 2 outings at 4 yrs: useful hurdler. *R. J. Holder.*

IKSAB 3 b.g. Lyphard's Special (USA) 122–Some Dame 72 (Will Somers 114§) **75** [1989 NR 1990 7f* 8.2g⁶ 7m³ 6m* 7d 6m 6s* 6m 6f³ a7g] 34,000F: rangy gelding: moderate mover: half-brother to sprint winners Reggae (by Gay Fandango) and Farmer Jock (by Crofter) and winners in France and Belgium: dam, half-sister to high-class Record Run, won over 1¼m: modest performer: won maiden at Doncaster in March and claimers at Haydock in May and July: below form last 3 starts, moving badly to post before handicap at Southwell: may prove best at 6f: acts on any going: keen sort, wears crossed noseband: wore tongue strap second and third starts. *R. Boss.*

IKTESHAF 2 b.c. (Mar 1) Green Desert (USA) 127–Colourful (FR) 97 (Gay **76** Mecene (USA) 128) [1990 6g³ 5f² 6g³ 6m*] 105,000Y: workmanlike, good-bodied colt: has scope: second foal: half-brother to 3-y-o 9f and hurdles winner Bookcase (by Siberian Express): dam French 2-y-o 5f winner, is half-sister to middle-distance performer First Prayer out of high-class French staying 2-y-o First Bloom: modest form: won maiden at Kempton in July, making most: sweating and coltish time before: will be suited by 7f. *B. Hanbury.*

IL BAMBINO 2 ch.g. (May 22) Bairn (USA) 126–Trapani (Ragusa 137) [1990 6m **58** 7m² 7f³ 7s a7g] 1,150 2-y-o: leggy, lightly-made gelding: eighth foal: half-brother to several winners here and abroad, including fairly useful 5f and 1m winner Prince Ragusa (by English Prince): dam ran 3 times: plating-class maiden: soundly beaten in nursery on all-weather final start: will stay 1m: possibly unsuited by soft ground. *P. F. I. Cole.*

IL CORSAIR (IRE) 2 b.c. (Mar 19) Horage 124–Corozal (Corvaro (USA) 122) **95** [1990 6g 7d⁴ 6d⁵ 7m* 8s* 9v*] IR 1,600Y, resold IR 15,000Y: leggy, useful-looking colt: first foal: dam 9.5f winner in Ireland: progressive colt: won maiden at Chepstow (bandaged near-hind) in October and listed races at Turin and Milan (latter by a neck from All The King's Men) in November: will stay 1¼m: well suited by very soft ground. *A. A. Scott.*

ILDERTON ROAD 3 br.f. Noalto 120–Mac's Melody (Wollow 132) [1989 8v **74** 1990 10m⁴ 10m³ 7g⁵ 7f³ 8.2m⁵ 8m⁵ 10g³ 8m² 8g⁴] big, rangy filly: modest form: stays 1¼m: acts on firm going: has run creditably when sweating and on toes: consistent. *Mrs Barbara Waring.*

ILE DE CHYPRE 5 b.h. Ile de Bourbon (USA) 133–Salamina 106 (Welsh **120** Pageant 132) [1989 8g 10m² 10m* 12g² 10m² 10.5f* 10g³ 12f 1990 10m² 9.2g⁶ 10m³ 10.8m*] strong, rangy, attractive horse: carries deal of condition: high class as 4-y-o, winner of Juddmonte International at York: best effort in 1990 second to Dolpour in Gordon Richards EBF Stakes at Sandown: third to Elmaamul in Coral-Eclipse on latter course later: well below best when struggling to land the odds

Hoover Cumberland Lodge Stakes, Ascot—
Ile de Nisky (right) makes good use of the 5 lb concession from Cacoethes

H. H. Prince Yazid Saud's "Ile de Nisky"

(reportedly lost a special protective shoe) in minor event at Warwick in October: stays 1½m, but better allowed to stride on over 1¼m: unsuited by soft going and acts very well on top-of-the-ground: mulish at stalls third start: races with head high: taken steadily to post: showed plenty of temperament as 3-y-o, but has since proved himself to be thoroughly tough and genuine: a credit to his trainer. *G. Harwood.*

ILE DE NISKY 4 b.c Ile de Bourbon (USA) 133–Good Lass (FR) (Reform 132) **117** [1989 10.3n1* 12g4 12g3 10g2 10g6 1990 12g4 12m2 11g3 12d2 12m4 12g2 11.1g4 12m* 12g] big, rather sparely-made colt: good walker: has a very powerful, round action: smart performer: won Hoover Cumberland Lodge Stakes at Ascot in September by ½ length from Cacoethes, pair clear: ran well when second (hanging right under pressure) to Assatis in Hardwicke Stakes at Royal Ascot fourth outing: 74/1, well beaten in Ciga Prix de l'Arc de Triomphe at Longchamp final one: better at 1½m than 1¼m, and should stay further: acts on good to firm and dead going: set strong pace sixth (unseated rider to post) and seventh (mounted on track) starts: consistent: to race in Saudi Arabia. *G. A. Huffer.*

ILE DE REINE 4 b.f. Ile de Bourbon (USA) 133–Fair Fight 84 (Fine Blade (USA) **64** 121) [1989 11.7d 12f4 14f 1990 14.8m* 16f2 14g 16m4 17m3 18d] big, rangy filly: good mover with a long stride: first race for almost a year, made all in 5-runner handicap at Warwick in May: ran poorly when blinkered final outing: suited by good test of stamina: acts on firm going, possibly unsuited by dead: edgy last 2 outings, sweating second time. *H. Candy.*

ILE DE ROMA   3 b.c. Ile de Bourbon (USA) 133–Romara 105 (Bold Lad (IRE)   **96**
133) [1989 7g² 7m³ 8s* 1990 11g³ 10.6f* 9f] workmanlike, deep-girthed colt: fairly
useful form when third to Belmez in £6,000 event at Newbury and winning 4-runner
minor event at Haydock in the spring: last of 7 in Grade 3 event at Arlington, USA, in
September: may prove best at around 1¼m: acts on any going: tends to carry head
high: to be trained by F. Brothers in USA. *G. Wragg.*

ILLOGICAL   3 br.f. Ile de Bourbon (USA) 133–Modern Romance (Dance In Time   —
(CAN)) [1989 NR 1990 a11g 12.5g 10m⁶ 12.4s⁴] sturdy, plain filly: bad mover: fourth
foal: sister to poor 4-y-o Gina's Choice: dam never ran: signs of ability on flat only in
claimer final start, taking keen hold, disputing lead over 1m and carrying head high:
winning selling hurdler. *J. Wharton.*

I'LL SOON KNOW   3 ch.f. Known Fact (USA) 135–Soolyn (Dominion 123)   **57**
[1989 5m⁴ 6g 6d 1990 6m 6m⁴ 6g² 6f* 7f 7m⁶] smallish, angular filly: plating
handicapper: on toes, won at Chepstow in July: didn't get best of runs afterwards,
staying on well when good sixth of 22 at Chepstow: flashed tail when hit and edged
left second start: should stay 1m: acts on firm going: has joined B. Palling. *R. J.
Holder.*

ILLUME   2 b.f. (Mar 10) Ilium 121–Raffinrula 75 (Raffingora 130) [1990 a6g a7g   —
6g⁶] small filly: half-sister to 3-y-o 7f to 1m winner Cee-Jay-Ay (by Free State) and a
winner in Belgium: dam won twice over 5f at 2 yrs: no form in sellers: sold 800 gns
Newmarket Autumn Sales. *W. J. Musson.*

ILLUSORY   3 b.f. Kings Lake (USA) 133–Bold Fantasy 115 (Bold Lad (IRE) 133)   **68**
[1989 5m³ 6d² 1990 6m* 6s] small, good-bodied filly: first run for a year, won
maiden at Redcar in October by a head: third favourite but facing stiff task, virtually
pulled up in Doncaster listed race following month: bred to stay 1m: stud. *R.
Charlton.*

IMAGE BOY (IRE)   2 br.c. (May 24) Flash of Steel 120–Gay Pariso 82 (Sir   —
Gaylord) [1990 7g 7m 7d] 1,000 Y-o: sturdy colt: half-brother to 4 winners, including smart 1984 2-y-o 6f winner Northern Chimes (by London Bells): dam,
daughter of Musidora Stakes winner Jakomima, won over 1m: no show in claimers
and a maiden auction: bandaged first 2 starts. *J. A. Bennett.*

IMAGINARY PLANE   2 b.g. (Feb 4) Petoski 135–Dalmally 89 (Sharpen Up   —
127) [1990 8m 8f 8.2g] 9,400Y: rather angular gelding: fourth foal: dam 6f and 8.5f
winner: never able to challenge in maidens and a seller: will be better suited by
1¼m +. *M. H. Easterby.*

IMAGINING   3 b.c. Fairy King (USA)–Shancarnan (AUS) (Galway Bay (FR))   **70**
[1989 NR 1990 7g⁵ 8m* 8m 8.2m³ 9m 8d] IR 1,000F: sturdy colt: second foal: dam
well beaten on 4 starts in Ireland: modest form: won claimer at Newmarket in July:
third in similar event at Nottingham, easily best subsequent effort: stays 1m: acts on
good to firm ground. *J. W. Hills.*

IMCO AFFIRMATION (IRE)   2 b.c. (Mar 18) Glow (USA)–Affirmation (FR)   **62**
(Affirmed (USA)) [1990 7m 8.2m 8.5m⁴ 7g] IR 36,000Y: strong, attractive colt:
moderate walker: second foal: half-brother to 3-y-o Chandanne (by Ballad Rock):
dam minor French 11f winner at 4 yrs, is from good family: quite modest form: ran
poorly final outing: stays 8.5f: sold 4,100 gns Newmarket Autumn Sales. *M. A.
Jarvis.*

IMHOTEP   3 gr.c. Claude Monet (USA) 121–Miss Melmore (Nishapour (FR) 125)   **56**
[1989 5s⁴ 6m 6m⁵ 6g² 8g 6f³ 6m 7g 1990 5g⁶ 7m⁶ 6f² 5m³ 7m³ 7g⁴ 6f 6m] tall, rather
angular colt: has a rather round action: plating-class maiden nowadays: stays 7f: acts
on good to firm ground: joined S. Kettlewell. *A. M. Robson.*

IMITATE (IRE)   2 b.f. (Feb 17) Tate Gallery (USA) 117–Exemplary 106 (Sove-   **72**
reign Lord 120) [1990 5f⁴ 5g² 6s* 5d⁴ 6m⁵] 14,000Y: compact filly: has a moderate
action: closely related to a winner abroad by Northfields and half-sister to numerous
other winners, including 6f and 1¼m winner Run For Ever (by Runnett): dam best at
5f: quite modest performer: landed odds in maiden at Hamilton in May: better
efforts starts either side: best efforts at 5f on an easy surface: sweating final outing:
tends to hang: sold 2,100 gns Doncaster November Sales, and has joined D. Chapman. *J. Etherington.*

IMPERFECT CIRCLE (USA)   2 b.f. (Feb 1) Riverman (USA) 131–Avi-   **111 p**
ance 112 (Northfields (USA)) [1990 6f² 6d* 6m2]
   Unlike her half-sister Chimes of Freedom, who was forward enough to
make her debut in the May of her first season, Imperfect Circle, an unfurnished filly, tall but attractive, did not see a racecourse until the middle of

Shadwell Estates Firth of Clyde Stakes, Ayr—
Chimes of Freedom's half-sister Imperfect Circle looks very promising
in winning this listed race easily

July, when she ran second, beaten a neck by Only Yours, in a field of six maidens at Newmarket. By her return to the racecourse, at Ayr in September for the listed Shadwick Estates Firth of Clyde Stakes, Only Yours had finished second in the Princess Margaret Stakes at Ascot and won the 'Pacemaker Update' Lowther Stakes at York, and if one were to judge Imperfect Circle's run at Newmarket on the evidence of what Only Yours achieved in these races the conclusion would be that she put up a useful performance. This line of reasoning is false. Only Yours's performances no more provided a boost for the form of her Newmarket race than Imperfect Circle's subsequent displays did. Linking maiden form to that of a listed or pattern event may be an easy way out for thought-lazy commentators, and it doubtless makes strong appeal to those with a penchant for believing what it suits them to believe, but in practice it doesn't work, not where inexperienced two-year-olds are concerned, at any rate. This may be axiomatic, but we never cease to be amazed how frequently form students, and others, would have us believe otherwise. Experience has long since taught us to look upon a clash such as the initial one between Only Yours and Imperfect Circle as nothing more than a brief encounter in infancy, from which the protagonists go their separate ways.

As we have said, Imperfect Circle's path took her next to Ayr for the Firth of Clyde Stakes, and in a field of eleven which included some pretty useful fillies—Ivory Bride, Futuh and It's All Academic, for example—she was an impressive winner, stamping her authority on the race in no uncertain manner in the last furlong and pulling almost five lengths clear. Only Yours would not have beaten Imperfect Circle in this race. Coincidentally, the paths of the two fillies reconverged two weeks after the Firth of Clyde Stakes, in the Tattersalls Cheveley Park Stakes at Newmarket, though one could have been excused for not noticing. As Imperfect Circle drew out with Capricciosa in the last furlong to engage in a brief struggle from which she was to emerge three quarters of a length down, so Only Yours dropped away to ninth of the eleven runners.

In the brouhaha which followed Divine Danse's unfortunate run, the promise inherent in Imperfect Circle's second place tended to pass by without

423

Imperfect Circle (USA) (b.f. Feb 1, 1988)	Riverman (USA) (b 1969)	Never Bend (b 1960)	Nasrullah
			Lalun
		River Lady (b 1963)	Prince John
			Nile Lily
	Aviance (ch 1982)	Northfields (ch 1968)	Northern Dancer
			Little Hut
		Minnie Hauk (b 1975)	Sir Ivor
			Best In Show

comment. Which was a pity. She had attained, in just three starts, a level of form in our opinion surpassed only marginally by Chimes of Freedom in five appearances in 1989. More importantly, for a filly bred to be suited by further, she had shown the speed more than to hold her own in a Group 1 race over a sprint distance. Whether Divine Danse would have won the Cheveley Park with a clear run is one of those indeterminate things which will always remain a matter of opinion, but we fancy it will take a filly better than the one Divine Danse showed herself to be in her races in France to beat Imperfect Circle, when it comes to racing over a mile in the One Thousand Guineas. Of the other two-year-old fillies whose form may reasonably be regarded as better than Imperfect Circle's, Shadayid and Shamshir have already had a chance to show what they can do over a mile, against fillies not renowned for pace at a time when a mile was more a test of stamina and less one of speed than it is likely to be in the One Thousand Guineas. Their superiority over Imperfect Circle could be more apparent than real. The rub is that the One Thousand Guineas may come a little early for a filly who did not blossom until the autumn, though this is something over which we may leave Roger Charlton to do the worrying. Imperfect Circle's family details may be referred to in the comment on Chimes of Freedom in *Racehorses of 1989*. Riverman, her sire, has produced a host of good horses, most notably that tough mare Triptych, the Arc winners Detroit and Gold River, and the top-class milers Irish River and Rousillon. *R. Charlton.*

IMPERIAL BRUSH 6 b.g. Sallust 134–Queen of The Brush (Averof 123) [1989 NR 1990 14m] leggy, sparely-made gelding: fairly useful winner as 3-y-o: blinkered on only second race on flat since, prominent until 2f out in strongly-run handicap at Sandown in April: stays 1¾m well: acts on good to firm and soft going: has run well when sweating: fairly useful hurdler. *D. R. C. Elsworth.* —

IMPERIAL FRIEND 6 b.m. Imperial Fling (USA) 116–Happy Donna 106 (Huntercombe 133) [1989 6v 8d 6f 7.6f 7g4 8.3m 8m3 8f 7d 1990 9f3 8f4 7h3] deep-bodied mare: poor handicapper: stays 9f: best form on a sound surface: has won for apprentice. *C. J. Hill.* 35

IMPERIAL GLORY 5 b.g. Ahonoora 122–Sovereign Bloom (Florescence 120) [1989 6d 1990 a6g] rather leggy gelding: extremely lightly raced but has shown a little ability. *S. Mellor.* —

IMPORTANT GUEST 3 b.f. Be My Guest (USA) 126–Riboule 69 (Ribero 126) [1989 8f 7f6 1990 8.2v a8g] unfurnished filly: moderate walker and mover: plating-class maiden: no form in autumn at 3 yrs, in claimer on reappearance: bred to stay middle distances: changed hands 2,200 gns Newmarket July Sales. *Miss S. E. Hall.* —

IMPUNITY 5 b.g. Blakeney 126–Lantern Light 86 (Le Levanstell 122) [1989 12d4 12g 12f4 12h3 18h2 15f4 12f5 15.8m2 16f5 14f 1990 15.8d] neat gelding: moderate mover: poor maiden: stays 2¼m: acts on hard and dead going: visored seventh outing (didn't look keen) in 1989 and final 2 at 3 yrs: often apprentice ridden. *R. M. Whitaker.* —

INAAD 6 b.h. Mill Reef (USA) 141–Rambling Rose 118 (Silly Season 127) [1989 9f3 10f* 10g5 12f 10m3 10.5m2 1990 9g2 10f4 10m3 10.5m3 10m3 10g] rather leggy, quite attractive horse: usually looks very well: good mover: fairly useful handicapper: ran particularly well on fourth outing when third to Eradicate in £41,800 event at York, staying on strongly having had poor run for most of straight: should stay 1½m: best form on a sound surface: has run well for inexperienced rider: suited by strong gallop: tough and consistent: sold 25,000 gns Newmarket December Sales. *H. Thomson Jones.* 91

IN A WHIRL (USA) 2 br.f. (Feb 7) Island Whirl (USA)–Hurry Marie (USA) (Hurry To Market) [1990 6m* 5d5 6d] tall, close-coupled filly: has scope: sister to a minor winner in North America and half-sister to several others, one in minor 60 +

stakes: dam won 9 races at up to 1¼m: sire very smart stakes winner at up to 1¼m: won maiden at Lingfield in May by ½ length after slow start: never able to challenge in £8,000 event (reared stalls) at Epsom and Chesham Stakes at Royal Ascot. *N. A. Callaghan.*

INBIHAR 3 br.f. Doulab (USA) 115–Silojoka 95 (Home Guard (USA) 129) [1989 — 6g 1990 5f 6f 6g 7g⁵ 7m 9f⁵ 10.2m] sparely-made filly: little worthwhile form: stays 7f: has been mulish at stalls and sweated. *C. J. Benstead.*

INCARESS 2 ch.f. (Apr 6) Royal Vulcan 83–Solatia 75 (Kalydon 122) [1990 8m 8d] close-coupled, angular filly: has a round action: ninth foal: half-sister to a winner in Hong Kong: dam 1½m winner: behind in autumn maidens at Leicester: slowly away on debut. *N. A. Callaghan.*

INCOLA 4 b.g. Liboi (USA) 76–Sdenka (FR) 79 (Habitat 134) [1989 7f⁵ a10g 1990 51 a11g a10g a12g⁴ 12f 10s⁴ 12f⁴ 11.5g* 12f² 12f* 12f⁴] small, angular gelding: plating-class handicapper: made all at Lingfield in June and Folkestone in August: suited by 1½m: best form on sound surface: blinkered fifth outing. *H. Candy.*

IN CONCERT 2 ch.f. (Feb 17) Absalom 128–Hum 69 (Crooner 119) [1990 6g⁵ 6g⁴ 47 6m⁶ a7g⁶] 5,000Y: lengthy, rather angular filly: has a round action: sister to 2-y-o sprint winners Absolutely Humming (stays 1m) and Skybolt and half-sister to a 6f winner by Averof: dam stayed 1½m: poor maiden: probably stays 7f: sold 720 gns Doncaster October Sales. *M. Brittain.*

IN COUNCIL 3 b. or br.c. Blakeney 126–Regal Lady (FR) 93 (Relko 136) [1989 67 NR 1990 10.6d³] heavy-topped colt: brother to Oaks third Britannia's Rule and 1981 2-y-o 1m winner Born Hero, and half-brother to winning stayer Ile de Roi (by Ile de Bourbon): dam won at up to 13f and is half-sister to Vaguely Noble: 12/1, blinkered and burly, 7½ lengths third of 5 to Scribbling in maiden at Haydock in August, weakening over 1f out: sold to join D. N. Carey 1,700 gns Newmarket Autumn Sales. *J. H. M. Gosden.*

INDELIBLE MARK 4 b.c. Bustino 136–Current Pattie (USA) 102 (Little — Current (USA)) [1989 10g⁵ 10g 1990 8m 10h⁵ a14g⁴ 10.4g 8g] lengthy, attractive colt: no rateable form: sold to join H. Whiting's stable 2,900 gns Newmarket Autumn Sales. *C. E. Brittain.*

INDEPENDENT AIR 2 gr.g. (Jun 25) Elegant Air 119–Tranquility Base 112 47 (Roan Rocket 128) [1990 6g 6f 7m 7f 7f 5f 6h² 5f⁶ 6g 7f⁵ 6m 8f4] 6,600Y: smallish, good- quartered gelding: half-brother to numerous winners here and abroad, including fair sprinter Padre Pio (by Mummy's Pet) and fairly useful 6f winner Spanish Calm (by King of Spain): dam at her best at 2 yrs, when 5f and 6f winner: poor maiden: stays 7f: visored final outing: ran poorly when bandaged near-fore penultimate start. *D. T. Thom.*

INDIANA SCARLETT 3 ch.f. Blazing Saddles (AUS)–Littleton Song 73 (Song — p 132) [1989 1990 7m 10.1m⁵ 10m] compact filly: moderate walker and mover: third foal: dam, 6f winner at 2 yrs, is closely related to quite useful sprinter Chin-Chin: well beaten in maidens and 10.1f minor event: bit backward, never placed to challenge or knocked about final start: may do better. *C. A. Horgan.*

INDIAN BABA 5 b.g. Indian King (USA) 128–Norfolk Bonnet (Morston (FR) 70 125) [1989 NR 1990 14g 16.2d³] tall, angular gelding: fair winner as 3-y-o: showed he retains some ability when third to Morley Street in minor event at Goodwood: suited by test of stamina: yet to race on soft going, acts on any other: on edge when blinkered: somewhat unsatisfactory. *G. P. Enright.*

INDIAN CHIEF 3 b.c. Indian King (USA) 128–Gay Broad 78 (Gay Fandango 55 (USA) 132) [1989 5d⁵ 6g 6m⁴ 6h* 6v 1990 6g 6m 7m 7m⁶ 6m 6s²] strong, lengthy colt: good walker: moderate mover: modest winner as 2-y-o: second favourite and blinkered on first run for over 3 months, form at 3 yrs only when neck second of 13 in seller at Hamilton: stays 6f: possibly unsuited by heavy going: has joined L. Bowman. *R. Hannon.*

INDIAN FLUTE 3 b.f. Indian King (USA) 128–Corista (Tudor Music 131) [1989 54 NR 1990 11g⁴ 8.2g⁴ 11s³ 12m 11.5g⁵] IR 3,800F, IR 7,000Y: rangy filly: half-sister to winning Irish stayers Golden Oak (by Tap On Wood) and Gayla Orchestra (by Lord Gayle): dam, won over 7f at 2 yrs and 1½m at 4 yrs, is sister to Orchestra: plating-class form: should stay at least 1½m: possibly needs an easy surface: bandaged fourth start. *W. J. Musson.*

INDIAN MAESTRO 4 b.g. Music Maestro 119–Indian Wells (Reliance II 137) 58 [1989 6m* 7m 6h² 8h⁵ 6m* 7g 6g⁴ 7m⁴ 7g⁵ 1990 8m 7f⁵ 6m 10g³ 10g⁵ 9m² 10f⁴ 8h⁵] leggy, angular gelding: quite modest handicapper: effective at 6f and seems to stay

1¼m: acts on hard going: often apprentice ridden: has pulled hard, and goes well with forcing tactics: sold 1,600 gns Doncaster October Sales. *Pat Mitchell.*

INDIAN PLUME 3 b.g. Commanche Run 133–Fettle (Relkino 131) [1989 7m³ 1990 8.5g⁴ 8g² a8g* 12.3g 12d 9g a14g a11g*] compact gelding: moderate mover: successful in maiden in August, leading 1f out and hanging left, and claimer (claimed £6,500) in November, blinkered and making all: well beaten in between, moving down badly on first occasion: stays 11f: to join D. Burchell. *M. H. Easterby.* **75**

INDIAN QUEEN 5 ch.m. Electric 126–Taj Princess 88 (Taj Dewan 128) [1989 8g 12s 10f⁴ 10g* 10d⁴ 10d³ 9.2g 12s* 1990 12g 13.5d³ 11.1g⁶ 15.5v*] leggy, quite good-topped mare: very useful performer: 24/1, dead-heated with Braashee, pair 6 lengths clear, in Prix Royal-Oak at Longchamp in October having made running: stays 2m: best with plenty of give in the ground: usually blinkered or visored: has run creditably when sweating and on toes: tough and genuine. *W. Hastings-Bass.* **115**

INDIAN SLAVE (IRE) 2 ch.c. (Feb 1) Commanche Run 133–Commanche Belle 74 (Shirley Heights 130) [1990 7m 7m⁴ 7s⁵] leggy colt: first foal: dam middle-distance maiden half-sister to Band and Zimbalon: best effort fourth in maiden at Chepstow in October: raced on unfavoured part of track final outing: will be suited by 1m +: bandaged first 2 starts. *R. Guest.* **69**

INDIAN SNAKE 3 br.f. Mansingh (USA) 120–Boa (Mandrake Major 122) [1989 5m⁵ 5m* 5g 6d 1990 6m 6g] sturdy filly: carries condition: keen walker: steadily dropped in class but well beaten since quite modest winner at 2 yrs: best form at 5f: edgy final start: refused to enter stalls once at 2 yrs: sold 1,000 gns Ascot November Sales. *C. F. Wall.* **—**

INDIAN SPIRIT 4 ch.g. Mansingh (USA) 120–Funny-Do (Derring-Do 131) [1989 5d 5m 1990 a5g] good-topped gelding: of little account: blinkered once. *M. W. Ellerby.* **—**

INDIAN STAR 3 b.f. Indian King (USA) 128–Salique (Sallust 134) [1989 5g³ 5g* 5d⁵ 6f⁵ 5m⁶ 5m³ 6m⁴ 6f⁵ 5f 6m 6d⁶ 6g 1990 5f 6m³ 6g* 6m³ 7m 7g 6g³ 6m³ 7f⁴ 6g 7g 7d] leggy, light-framed filly: moderate walker: has round action: quite modest handicapper: game winner at Ripon in May: suited by 6f: yet to race on very soft ground, acts on any other: ran fairly well in visor ninth start, moderately for apprentice next one. *M. Brittain.* **58**

INDIA'S TWIST 3 ch.c. Exhibitioner 111–West Bank (Martinmas 128) [1989 5s 5f² 6f⁴ 5m² 5m* 5g⁶ 1990 6m 7m] rather leggy, workmanlike colt: modest winner at 2 yrs: ran moderately in May handicaps at 3 yrs: best form at 5f. *J. D. Bethell.* **—**

INDIGO 2 ch.f. (Feb 9) Primo Dominie 121–Blueit (FR) 101 (Bold Lad (IRE) 133) [1990 5m* 5d 5f³ 5f⁴ 5f* 5f⁴ 5m] 8,400Y: close-coupled, rather angular filly: moderate walker: fifth foal: half-sister to fairly useful sprinter Blues Indigo (by Music Boy) and fair sprinter King of Spades (by King of Spain): dam 2-y-o 5f winner: modest performer: successful in maiden at Catterick in March and nursery (quickening really well from rear to lead line) at Thirsk in August: unlucky at **78**

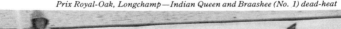

Prix Royal-Oak, Longchamp—Indian Queen and Braashee (No. 1) dead-heat

Redcar sixth start: speedy: acts well on firm ground: tends to get on toes. *R. M. Whitaker.*

INDIGO LADY (IRE)   2 b.f. (Mar 18) Salmon Leap (USA) 131–Late Spring 101   —
(Silly Season 127) [1990 6m 7m 7d] IR 15,000Y: half-sister to numerous winners, including Spindrifter (by Sandford Lad), winner of 13 races at 2 yrs and successful at up to 9f, and modest miler Sand-Dollar (by Persian Bold): dam 2-y-o 5f winner: poor form in maidens and claimer: sold 2,800 gns Newmarket Autumn Sales. *Sir Mark Prescott.*

INDIVISIBLE   4 ch.f. Remainder Man 126§–Red Ragusa 62 (Homeric 133) [1989   39
8g³ 12f 12f 12.2g 8f 8f 1990 a11g² a12g a11g³ 10.2f 10.6f 8f⁶ 8f² 8m⁴ a8g⁶ 8g 8f 8.2m 10.4g] leggy filly: poor maiden: fell eleventh start, hit rail and sustained bad gash on last: suited by 1m: acts on firm going: inconsistent. *R. Hollinshead.*

IN DREAMS   7 b.g. High Line 125–Blissful Evening (Blakeney 126) [1989 14m   —
16f⁴ 14g 1990 16.5m 12g a12g 18m 14m 14g⁶] narrow, rather leggy gelding: fair winning stayer as 5-y-o: little sign of retaining ability: bandaged and trained first 4 starts by T. Kersey. *R. F. Johnson Houghton.*

INDUBITABLE   5 ch.m. Sharpo 132–Veracious 86 (Astec 128) [1989 11.7m⁵   80
13.3m⁴ 1990 12d 12.3g2] workmanlike mare: fair winner as 3-y-o: lightly raced since, but has shaped well most starts: stays 13.3f: acts on good to firm and dead going. *G. B. Balding.*

IN EXCESS   3 b.c. Siberian Express (USA) 125–Kantado 93 (Saulingo 122) [1989 116 ?
6f* 6g⁴ 1990 6m* 6g⁴ 7g* 7f] big, leggy, useful-looking colt: useful form, successful in minor event at Leicester in March and £11,100 contest at Newmarket in May: sent to join P. Jackson in USA after disappointing as second favourite for Jersey Stakes at Royal Ascot, winning 3 races including 2 Grade 3 handicaps: stays 9f: yet to race on a soft surface: tended to sweat and get on toes. *W. A. O'Gorman.*

INFEB   3 gr.f. Another Realm 118–Sweet Rosina 61 (Sweet Revenge 129) [1989   43
NR 1990 8.2g 10g⁶ 12.5g 8g 10m 9f³ 12m² 10f³ 12m 10g] 5,000F: stocky filly: sister to modest 7f to 11.5f winner Taylor's Realm and half-sister to several other winners here and abroad: dam in frame over 5f and 6f: poor form: stays 1½m: acts on firm ground: has run well for 7-lb claimer. *J. L. Spearing.*

INFERRING   2 b.c. (Mar 5) Alleging (USA) 120–Be My Darling 82 (Windjammer   54 p
(USA))   [1990 10s 10.2s4] 44,000Y: good-topped, angular colt: fourth foal: half-brother to 3-y-o Okaku and French 9f and 9.5f winner Tony's Guest (both by Be My Guest): dam 6f winner suited by 1¼m, is out of half-sister to high-class 1969 2-y-o Divine Gift: blinkered, around 25 lengths fourth of 14, weakening final 2f, in minor event at Doncaster in November: backward and green on debut: will stay 1½m: likely to improve again. *Mrs L. Piggott.*

INFINITY ZOOM (IRE)   2 b.g. (Feb 22) Alzao (USA) 117–Carthagian (Thatch   54
(USA) 136) [1990 7g⁴ 5m³ 6f³ 7m 8d] IR 19,000F, 25,000Y: strong, lengthy gelding: fourth foal: dam lightly raced in Ireland, is half-sister to Princess Royal winner Alia: plating-class maiden: should be suited by at least 7f: blinkered final outing: has carried head high: sold 2,000 gns Newmarket Autumn Sales. *M. H. Easterby.*

INGLEBERG   2 ch.c. (Apr 20) Ballacashtal (CAN)–Flying Sister (St Paddy 133)   —
[1990 7s] strong, workmanlike colt: third foal: dam maiden granddaughter of Oaks winner Steady Aim: soundly beaten in late-season maiden at Doncaster. *M. Johnston.*

INHERITANCE (IRE)   2 b.c. (Mar 25) Last Tycoon 131–Unknown Lady (USA)   68
(Hoist The Flag (USA)) [1990 7m 7m] 86,000Y: leggy, good-topped colt: fourth foal: half-brother to French 9.2f winner Lady Is A Tramp (by Mr Prospector): dam French 1¼m winner: blinkered, over 10 lengths tenth of 17, slowly away then one pace last 2f, in Tattersalls Tiffany Highflyer Stakes at Newmarket in August, second and better effort: will stay 1m: sold 8,600 gns Newmarket Autumn Sales. *G. Harwood.*

INISHDALLA (IRE)   2 b.f. (Mar 18) Green Desert (USA) 127–Costly Wave   96
(FR) 117 (Caro 133) [1990 6m² 5g² 6m* 6m⁵ 6g² 6m² 5g²] half-sister to several winners, including useful 7f and 1m winner Great Lakes (by Lomond) and very useful French 9f and 1¼m winner Swept Away (by Kris): dam, smart French miler, out of Oaks third Arctic Wave: fairly useful Irish filly: won maiden at Phoenix Park in July: around 6 lengths fifth to Mac's Imp in Heinz '57' Phoenix Stakes there following month: then runner-up on 3 occasions, twice behind Capricciosa, including in Moyglare Stud Stakes at the Curragh in September on penultimate outing: stays 6f. *D. K. Weld, Ireland.*

427

INISHPOUR   8 b.h. Nishapour (FR) 125–Miss Britain (Tudor Melody 129) [1989   **74** d
8s* 8m 10f6 8.2g4 9m2 8m5 10.2m6 8m3 8f 8.2d 1990 8f3 10g 8h 7m 9m6 8m 12g2
11g2 13d] tall, leggy, lengthy horse: usually looks very well: moderate mover:
creditable third to Evichstar in Lincoln Handicap at Doncaster in March: below form
after, though not discredited seventh and eighth outings: seems to stay 1½m: acts
on any going: ran moderately when blinkered: good mount for apprentice. *A. M.
Robson.*

INNERGLOW   3 gr.f. Kalaglow 132–Intoxication 73 (Great Nephew 126) [1989   **69**
NR 1990 12.2g4 11.5m6 10m4 15.3m3 15.5f4 13.8d2] 25,000Y: leggy, angular filly:
first foal: dam stayed 1½m, daughter of Princess Royal winner Shebeen: modest
form: 7/1 from 12/1, good second of 18 in handicap at Catterick: stays 15.3f: acts on
good to firm ground and dead. *A. C. Stewart.*

IN ORBIT   5 b.g. Habitat 134–Aryenne (FR) 125 (Green Dancer (USA) 132) [1989   **54**
NR 1990 9g 10g6 10m*] good-bodied gelding: has a rather round action: won (for
first time) handicap at Beverley in July: not sure to stay much beyond 1¼m: ran
poorly on soft going. *A. P. Stringer.*

INOVATE   3 b.g. King of Spain 121–Octavia (Sallust 134) [1989 NR 1990 8m]   —
21,000Y: workmanlike gelding: sixth foal: half-brother to several winning platers,
including 6f to 10.8f winner Neat Style (by Sweet Monday): dam showed a little
ability: burly, well beaten in claimer at Leicester in September: sold 1,650 gns
Doncaster August Sales. *J. Parkes.*

IN PLACE (USA)   2 b.c. (Mar 16) Roberto (USA) 131–Placer Queen (Habitat   **58** p
134) [1990 8g 8.2d] big, strong colt: has plenty of scope: has a markedly round
action: second known foal: half-brother to 3-y-o Invisible Halo (by Halo), 6f winner
at 2 yrs: dam ran 3 times here before winning at up to 1¼m in Canada: led or
disputed lead until 2f out in maiden at Kempton in September: held up and never
dangerous in minor event at Nottingham following month: should do better. *P. W.
Harris.*

IN PURSUIT   3 ch.g. Rainbow Quest (USA) 134–Silk Stocking 109 (Pardao 120)   **83**
[1989 8v 1990 10.8m5 10.1g5 13.3m3 12.3g2 14m2 14m* 12m* 12s] leggy, rather
unfurnished gelding: has long, rather round stride: fair performer: favourite, made
most to win maiden at Yarmouth in September and claimer at Newmarket in
October: 20/1, prominent 9f when in mid-division for November Handicap at
Doncaster: suited by forcing tactics at 1½m, and stays 1¾m: acts on good to firm
going. *W. Hastings-Bass.*

INSEYAB   2 b.f. (Mar 27) Persian Bold 123–Strike Home 82 (Be My Guest (USA)   **53**
126) [1990 5d 6d5 7d] close-coupled filly: moderate walker: first foal: dam 11.7f
winner, is half-sister to Ballad Rock: fifth of 11, ridden before halfway and fading
over 1f out, in maiden at Lingfield in October, only form: pushed along from start
final outing: should be suited by 7f + : bandaged off-hind: sold 3,000 gns Newmarket
Autumn Sales. *A. A. Scott.*

IN SHARP FOCUS   3 ch.f. Final Straw 127–Little Change 70 (Grundy 137)   —
[1989 5m3 5m3 7g 5f2 7f3 6m4 5g 7g 1990 6m] small, lengthy filly: keen walker:
moderate mover: quite modest performer: in need of race only start at 3 yrs: suited
by 6f: sold 3,400 gns Ascot May Sales. *M. Johnston.*

INSPIRED LOVE   5 gr.m. Dalsaan 125–Inspiring (Home Guard (USA) 129)   **44** d
[1989 7g 8.5g 8.5f2 10.2m2 10.6d 8.2g 13.6g 1990 9g 10f2 10g 12d 12m 12f6 10f3 10m3
12f* 12g 10.6d 12.2m 10.2s] strong, lengthy mare: carries plenty of condition:
moderate mover: won for only time in 5-runner handicap at Folkestone in August:
no form afterwards: stays 1½m: acts on firm going: blinkered 3 times at 3 yrs: has
run well for inexperienced rider. *F. J. Yardley.*

INSTANT DESIRE (USA)   3 ch.f. Northern Dancer–Pink Topaze (FR) (Dja-   **73**
kao (FR) 124) [1989 6g3 7m3 1990 8.5d5 10m3 10m3 10m6 8m2 7.6m4 7m] strong,
lengthy, good-quartered filly: modest maiden: stays 1¼m: acts on good to firm
ground: wore tongue strap first 3 outings: often edgy: inconsistent. *M. Moubarak.*

INSWINGER   4 br.g. Swing Easy (USA) 126–Cheri Berry 87 (Air Trooper 115)   **37**
[1989 6g5 5h 6f 6m 5.3h a6g5 1990 a8g6 a6g5 a5g4 a6g2 5f 7f 5m 6m a6g4] small,
lengthy, slightly dipped-backed gelding: carries condition: poor maiden: no form on
turf at 4 yrs: suited by 6f: acts on firm going: blinkered twice, visored third outing.
W. G. R. Wightman.

INTEGRITY BOY   3 b.g. Touching Wood (USA) 127–Powderhall 81 (Murray-   **43**
field 119) [1989 6f 6g 6m 8.5f2 10.6d3 8g* 10g 1990 10.2f 8g 12g6 12g3 11m6 10.1m4
11s6] medium-sized gelding: modest winner as 2-y-o: well below that form in 1990,

favourite for selling handicap penultimate start: should be suited by middle distances: blinkered last 3 starts, also last 4 at 2 yrs: hung on fifth outing: winning selling hurdler. *R. O'Leary.*

INTERLOPER 2 b.c. (Mar 29) Robellino (USA) 127–Blushing Cousin (Great   **68** Nephew 126) [1990 6f 7m³ 7d⁶] 14,000F, 10,000Y: first foal: dam (showed a little ability in USA) is out of half-sister to Blushing Groom: around ½-length third of 17 to Regent's Folly in maiden auction at Leicester in September: should stay 1m: possibly unsuited by dead ground. *J. H. M. Gosden.*

INTERNAL AFFAIR 2 gr.f. (May 12) Aragon 118–Alicia Markova 64 (Habat   **48** 127) [1990 5m⁶ 5m⁵] 2,600F, 3,000Y: ninth foal: half-sister to 3 winners, including 1987 2-y-o 6f winner Markstyle (by Moorestyle): dam, half-sister to Music Maestro, Saulingo and Outer Circle, ran 3 times at 2 yrs: poor form in maidens at Lingfield and Redcar in September: will be better suited by 6f. *A. C. Stewart.*

INTERROGATE 2 b.f. (Mar 5) In Fijar (USA) 121–Artipiar 106 (Tyrant (USA))   **—** [1990 6d⁵] 9,400Y: well-grown, rather leggy filly: fourth foal: half-sister to 1985 2-y-o 6f winner Faye (by Monsanto) and a winner in Norway: dam sprinter: backed at long odds, 18 lengths fifth of 8, prominent around 4f then eased when beaten, to impressive Shadayid in maiden at Ascot in June: looked sure to improve, but not seen out again. *R. Boss.*

IN THE CLUB (IRE) 2 b.c. (Apr 26) King of Clubs 124–Drora (Busted 134)   **57** [1990 5m² 6g 6g⁵ 7g] 5,600 2-y-o: leggy colt: poor walker and mover: sixth foal: half-brother to Dunenny (by Dunphy) and Beechwood Cottage (by Malinowski), winners at up to 1m: dam ran once: plating-class maiden: virtually pulled up final outing: should be suited by 7f. *Denys Smith.*

IN THE FRAME 2 br.g. (Mar 14) Claude Monet (USA) 121–Venetian Joy 80§   **58** (Windjammer (USA)) [1990 7f 7g 8m 8m] 2,000F, 3,200Y: rangy gelding: moderate mover: fourth foal: dam maiden suited by 1m: plating-class maiden: ran moderately in visor final outing: seems to stay 1m: wears bandages. *G. H. Eden.*

IN THE GROOVE 3 b.f. Night Shift (USA)–Pine Ridge 80 (High Top 131) **127** [1989 5m² 6g² 6m* 7g³ 1990 7m² 8m 10.5m* 8g* 12d⁴ 10.5g* 12m³ 12g 10d*]

None produced a telling and eye-catching turn of foot more often in British and Irish pattern races in the latest season than In The Groove. She won three Group 1 races, the Goffs Irish One Thousand Guineas at the Curragh, the Juddmonte International at York and the Dubai Champion Stakes at Newmarket. Two of those successes were gained in open-aged competition, something even her close rival Salsabil didn't achieve, yet in the voting for Horse of the Year just two members of the panel cast their vote for In The Groove, while thirteen went for Salsabil, one fewer than for the winner Dayjur. The result was no doubt influenced by In The Groove's disappointing runs in the two English fillies' classics, both of which Salsabil won, but it exaggerates the difference between them in terms of merit. Indeed, the International Classification assessed In The Groove 1 lb ahead of Salsabil (we rate Salsabil slightly the better).

Tattersalls Musidora Stakes, York—In The Groove leaves her Guineas form behind; Sardegna (rails) just beats Ivrea for second

Goffs Irish One Thousand Guineas, the Curragh—from last to first,
In The Groove storms past Heart of Joy and Performing Arts (rails)

In The Groove first showed the finishing speed that was to become her hallmark in the Tattersalls Musidora Stakes at York in May. She came to the race under something of a cloud, having trailed in eighth of ten in the General Accident One Thousand Guineas earlier in the month, beaten more than twenty lengths behind Salsabil after pulling hard early on. At York she was allowed to go off at 15/2 in a field of five. Sardegna, who'd won the Pretty Polly Stakes at Newmarket on her previous start, was confidently expected to strengthen her position in the Oaks betting, and started at 6/5 on. Berry's Dream and Ivrea were also preferred in the market, but In The Groove put up an improved performance, quickening well to beat Sardegna easing up by a length and a half, having been held up last into the straight. Waiting tactics seemed to explain much of her improvement and Cauthen, who'd had to relinquish his ride to Cochrane that day, continued with them in the Goffs Irish One Thousand Guineas at the Curragh later in the month. In The Groove started second favourite in a field of twelve, just in front of the home-trained pair The Caretaker and Wedding Bouquet. Heart of Joy, who'd finished a good second to Salsabil in the Guineas, and had beaten In The Groove a short head in the Nell Gwyn Stakes at Newmarket in April, was heavily backed at 6/4 on, but In The Groove turned the tables unequivocally. Held up, as the outsider Performing Arts set a steady pace, In The Groove was still last early in the straight, just behind the favourite, but stormed through on the outside to win going away by a long-looking three lengths from Heart of Joy. Performing Arts completed a clean sweep of the places for English-trained runners, half a length further back, with The Caretaker another length behind in fourth, Lady of Vision fifth and Aminata sixth.

In The Groove's margin of victory at the Curragh was over two lengths greater than Salsabil's in the Guineas, but the Newmarket form looked stronger overall, and it was Salsabil who started favourite at 2/1 when the pair renewed rivalry in the Gold Seal Oaks. In The Groove, who was ridden by Asmussen, was heavily backed at 85/40, but her finishing burst wasn't forthcoming and she kept on at one pace under hard riding (Asmussen was suspended for two days for misuse of the whip) in the final two furlongs, beaten a length and a head by Game Plan and Knight's Baroness for the places behind the five-length winner Salsabil. The Oaks was In The Groove's fourth race in five weeks and two months passed before her next, the Juddmonte International Stakes at York. The field of nine wasn't a vintage one, but included the Derby third Elmaamul, fresh from his win in the Coral-Eclipse at Sandown, and the Eclipse runner-up, the four-year-old Terimon. Another four-year-old Batshoof, who'd beaten Terimon into third in the Prince of Wales's Stakes at Royal Ascot, started favourite at 5/2, with Elmaamul at 7/2, but In The Groove, who started at 4/1, again showed much the best finishing speed. Cauthen was at pains to settle her in the early stages and still had her two lengths last turning for home, as Relief Pitcher and Dashing Blade set a good gallop. In The Groove had to be eased towards the outside to make her challenge halfway up the straight, but quickened smartly and was always getting the better of Elmaamul as the pair drew clear from the distance. At the line, In The Groove was a length and a half in front, with Batshoof, who got involved in scrimmaging chiefly with fourth-placed Terimon, a further two and a half lengths back in third, and Dolpour fifth.

In The Groove's win at York revived a theory, which gained wide currency after her Oaks defeat, that she's at her best fresh, but her subsequent record showed she can take her races. She had three more after York, culminating in the Dubai Champion Stakes at Newmarket in October. Before that, she made two trips to France, on the first of them finishing third behind Salsabil at Longchamp in September in the Prix Vermeille, a Group 1 event for three-year-old fillies over the same course and distance as the Arc de Triomphe. Salsabil, the winner by a neck from Miss Alleged, was having her first race since the Irish Derby in July, and was expected to come on for the run, but In The Groove, only half a length further behind, looked an unlucky loser, finishing strongly having been out of her ground in a race that developed into a sprint up the straight. In the Arc she reversed placings with

Juddmonte International Stakes, York—the colts,
three-year-old Elmaamul the best of them, are put in their place

Dubai Champion Stakes, Newmarket—In The Groove rounds off a marvellous season with a battling victory over the grey Linamix and the 1989 winner Legal Case

Salsabil by a short head, but came only ninth of twenty-one, beaten around nine lengths, having travelled strongly in the rear for a long way. In The Groove was ridden in the Arc by Fox, a last-minute replacement for Reid, injured when his mount Whippet threw him approaching the stalls in the previous race the Prix de l'Abbaye. Cauthen, claimed for Belmez at Longchamp, was back in the saddle for the Champion Stakes. The race is normally run less than two weeks after the Arc, but in recent years defeat at Longchamp has been no bar to success at Newmarket and In The Groove became the fourth winner in the last five runnings to have been beaten in the Arc, following on from Legal Case in 1989 and Triptych in 1986 and 1987. Legal Case, sixth in the latest Arc, was among a field of ten at Newmarket, but three-year-olds dominated the betting. The filly Kartajana started a hot favourite at 13/8, having been an impressive winner of the Sun Chariot Stakes over course and distance earlier in the month. In The Groove was at 9/2, with Elmaamul, who'd won the Phoenix Champion Stakes since York, at 5/1, Legal Case a point longer, Terimon 12/1 and the French Two Thousand Guineas winner Linamix next best at 14/1. In The Groove had already been beginning to look wintry at Longchamp and she looked woolly at Newmarket, but it didn't affect her performance in the slightest. Held up as Albadr set a strong pace for Elmaamul, she was still on the bit when Linamix went on three furlongs out and, as the field fanned across the track, she swept through to lead inside the distance. Cauthen had to ride her out firmly to make sure, but she held on well to win by a length and a half from Linamix, with Legal Case over three lengths clear of the remainder in third, Elmaamul fourth, Filia Ardross fifth and Kartajana a well-beaten sixth.

In The Groove (b.f. 1987)	Night Shift (USA) (b 1980)	Northern Dancer (b 1961)	Nearctic
			Natalma
		Ciboulette (b 1961)	Chop Chop
			Windy Answer
	Pine Ridge (b 1980)	High Top (b 1969)	Derring-Do
			Camenae
		Wounded Knee (ch 1973)	Busted
			La Lidia

In The Groove's success at Newmarket took her first-prize money earnings for the season to well over half a million pounds and helped give her trainer his highest finishing position in the trainers' table, behind only Cecil,

Cumani and Stoute. Elsworth made his name as a trainer of jumpers, notably through his handling of Desert Orchid, and he was champion National Hunt trainer in 1987/8, the same season Rhyme'N' Reason won him the Grand National. In The Groove was his first classic winner, but he had Mighty Flutter placed in the Derby in 1984, and Naheez placed in the French and Irish equivalents in 1987. Naheez was bought for just 16,000 guineas as a yearling and In The Groove cost little more, being picked up for 20,000 guineas at Newmarket. Her pedigree would probably have caught a jump trainer's eye as the third dam La Lidia, a half-sister to the Irish Derby winner Your Highness, is the dam of Sinzinbra, dam of such as Young Snugfit, Cashew King and Grand National runner-up Mr Snugfit. In The Groove's dam Pine Ridge produced two previous foals, the fairly useful miler Spanish Pine (by King of Spain) and the minor American winner Stripped Pine (by Sharpo). The two-year-old filly Pineapple (by Superlative) shaped promisingly in a Newbury maiden for Stoute on her only start in 1990, and Pine Ridge's 1989 foal, a colt by Sharpo since named Stylus, fetched 38,000 guineas at the Newmarket Highflyer Yearling Sales in October. She has since produced a colt by Formidable. Pine Ridge herself won a couple of races over a mile and a half, and her dam Wounded Knee was successful twice at up to a mile and three quarters. In The Groove has shown her best form to date over ten furlongs, but she almost certainly has it in her to win more top races over a mile, and she clearly stays a mile and a half, at least when conditions aren't testing. Her trainer was careful not to risk her on very firm ground as a two-year-old, when she won just one of her four races, and she's yet to race on very soft going, but appears to act on anything in between. A very robust filly, who carries plenty of condition and usually impresses in appearance, she's a good mover with a powerful action. There's no reason to think she won't train on, every reason to think she will,

Mr Brian Cooper's "In The Groove"

and with her versatility and turn of foot In The Groove could become to the 'nineties what Triptych was to the 'eighties. *D. R. C. Elsworth.*

IN THE HOG 2 ch.f. (May 16) Music Boy 124–Emlyn Princess (Julio Mariner 127) [1990 6d4 7f] 4,400Y: sturdy, angular filly: second foal: dam useful hurdler and winning chaser: fourth in maiden auction at Catterick in July: backed at long odds, weakened from 2f out in seller 3 months later: sold 2,100 gns Newmarket Autumn Sales. *M. H. Tompkins.* **40**

IN THE MOOD 2 b.f. (Apr 17) Lidhame 109–Siliferous (Sandy Creek 123) [1990 6m5 7m3 6m3] small, sparely-made filly: has free, rather round action: third foal: half-sister to 3-y-o The Goofer (by Be My Native), successful twice at around 1¼m: dam unplaced 4 times at 2 yrs, is closely related to useful 1m to 1¼m performer Kahaila: lowered in class, keeping-on third in seller at Lingfield in September: likely to prove at least as effective at 7f as 6f. *M. J. Fetherston-Godley.* **54**

IN THE PAPERS 3 b.f. Aragon 118–Mistress Gay 76 (Lord Gayle (USA) 124) [1989 5f2 5m* 5m* 6m 1990 5d 5g6 6d3] strong, compact filly: fair form: set stiff tasks at 3 yrs, appearing to run well when third of 5 in minor event at Goodwood in October: stays 6f: acts on good to firm ground and dead. *J. Sutcliffe.* **78**

IN THE PRINT 2 b.c. (Apr 14) Night Shift (USA)–Filwah (High Top 131) [1990 7d] 9,600 2-y-o: second foal: dam never ran: last in maiden auction at Goodwood in October. *J. White.* **—**

IN THE WINGS 4 b.c. Sadler's Wells (USA) 132–High Hawk 124 (Shirley Heights 130) [1989 10d* 12g 1990 10.5d2 12g* 12g* 12m5 12m* 12g4 12g*] **128**

So much else happened at the Breeders' Cup meeting at Belmont Park in October that In The Wings's victory in the Breeders' Cup Turf tended to be pushed into the background. Compared to some of the other races, the Breeders' Cup Turf was fairly uneventful, In The Wings steadily weaving his way through from near the back of the fourteen-strong field to pick off the opposition one by one, finally wearing down the 1989 Canadian triple crown winner With Approval to score by half a length. And the result lost some of its significance through the below-par performances of the Arc winner Saumarez and Cacoethes, the latter the recent course and distance winner—from Breeder's Cup Turf runners Alwuhush and El Senor, as well as With Approval—in the Turf Classic Invitational. Nevertheless, the winner's performance was a high-class one which brought France's total of victories in the Breeders' Cup series to five, following those of Lashkari, Last Tycoon, and the two from Miesque; Britain has still just one, through Pebbles. Furthermore In The Wings had gone one better than Fabre's most prominent

Hanson Coronation Cup, Epsom—In The Wings produces an impressive turn of foot to account for Observation Post and Ibn Bey

Grand Prix de Saint-Cloud—In The Wings and the fillies Ode and Zartota

previous runners in the race, the Arc winner Trempolino and the filly Sierra
Roberta.

In The Wings was ridden at short notice at Belmont by the American
jockey Stevens after Eddery had been claimed for the Rothmans International
winner French Glory. The stable-companions started favourite, coupled at
9/5, though on their European form neither was entitled to be regarded the
equal of Saumarez who'd had In The Wings over three lengths back in fourth
place in the Arc. In The Wings had shown substantially better form than
French Glory in Europe. His career had finally got going in the latest season,
following two severely limited by a knee injury sustained as a two-year-old,
and he'd justified favouritism in the Hanson Coronation Cup, the Grand Prix
de Saint-Cloud and the Prix Foy. The Coronation Cup at Epsom in June was
only the sixth race of In The Wings's career. His fourth had been Carroll
House's Arc, in which he'd come eleventh, beaten around six lengths, starting
favourite; his fifth had been France's first big race of the season for older
horses, the Prix Ganay at Longchamp in April, in which he'd come a promising
second to Creator. For one of such inexperience In The Wings was ridden
with remarkable confidence at Epsom, being dropped out and set a lot to do
from Tattenham Corner, giving Ibn Bey eight lengths start and Observation
Post six. Early in the straight he was involved in a collision with Mondrian
which affected the German challenger more; In The Wings made up ground
very smoothly, collaring first Ibn Bey then Observation Post in the second-
last furlong and going on to beat them three lengths and a length and a half
respectively.

Breeders' Cup Turf, Belmont Park—In The Wings is the third European-trained winner,
following Lashkari and Pebbles

By the time In The Wings was returned to Britain for the King George VI and Queen Elizabeth Diamond Stakes at Ascot in July he'd added the Grand Prix de Saint-Cloud to his Coronation Cup. The story at Saint-Cloud was much as it had been at Epsom—he was held up, quickened through to lead a furlong out, then comfortably held off the Grand Prix d'Evry winner Ode by one and a half lengths. In The Wings headed the market for the King George on Salsabil's defection, despite doubts about his effectiveness on firmish ground. On the way down he showed a pronounced knee action, as on several occasions on easier going in the past. In the race he was unable to mount a serious challenge and was beaten on merit, though a bump from Cacoethes over three furlongs out could not have helped matters; he crossed the line in fifth, the best part of eight lengths behind Belmez. On similar going next time out In The Wings landed the odds in the Prix Foy at Longchamp, but for a leading Arc candidate made pretty hard work of seeing off Zartota by half a length. He improved on that on easier ground in the Arc, showing good acceleration when switched outside in the straight to improve his position considerably; and he kept running on until held in the final hundred yards.

In The Wings (b.c. 1986)	Sadler's Wells (USA) (b 1981)	Northern Dancer (b 1961)	Nearctic
			Natalma
		Fairy Bridge (b 1975)	Bold Reason
			Special
	High Hawk (b 1980)	Shirley Heights (b 1975)	Mill Reef
			Hardiemma
		Sunbittern (gr 1970)	Sea Hawk II
			Pantoufle

The game and genuine In The Wings is one of a record six Grade 1 or Group 1 winners from Sadler's Wells's first crop—the others being Braashee, French Glory, Old Vic, Prince of Dance and Scenic. His dam High Hawk

Sheikh Mohammed's "In The Wings"

436

improved at a rapid rate of knots as a three-year-old after finishing second in a modest race at Folkestone; she went on to prove herself one of the toughest, most genuine fillies of her generation, as well as one of the best. Only light framed, she thrived on a busy season and won five races, including the Ribblesdale Stakes at Ascot and the Park Hill Stakes at Doncaster where she turned the tables on the Irish Guinness Oaks winner Give Thanks. Stamina was another strong point of High Hawk's and there seemed no reason why she shouldn't have been as good or even better over two miles or more, given the chance. High Hawk was bought by Sheikh Mohammed as a yearling for 31,000 guineas at the Newmarket Highflyer Sales. Her first foal Swooping (by Kings Lake) proved slow, while the two that succeeded In The Wings, the Kris filly Shajan and Sure Blade colt Falconry, have yet to race. She has since produced colts by Dancing Brave and Sadler's Wells. Another good member of the family is High Hawk's three-parts sister Infamy who won the Sun Chariot Stakes at three and the Rothmans International at four. Their dam Sunbittern won her first three races as a two-year-old and was a good fourth to stablemate Jacinth in the Cheveley Park Stakes, but temperament got the better of her the following year and she refused to race at all on her last appearance, at Epsom on the day of Morston's Derby. Further back in In The Wings's pedigree can be found Etoile de France, grandam of the Irish Two Thousand Guineas winner Northern Treasure and sister to Irish Derby winner Fidalgo. In The Wings is a small, sturdy colt. He was particularly well suited by some give in the ground, although he never encountered very testing conditions. He did most of his racing over a mile and a half, held up to make the most of his outstanding turn of foot. His last race his best, he has been retired to the Kildangan Stud, Co Kildare, at a fee of IR £20,000 (October 1st terms), alongside Shaadi and Sure Blade. Fifteen nominations are to be made available to French breeders, with Sheikh Mohammed retaining sole ownership. *A. Fabre, France.*

INTIMISTE (USA) 3 ch.c. Arctic Tern (USA) 126–Bubble Company (Lyphard 108 (USA) 132) [1989 6d* 10g² 10v* 1990 11d* 12m⁶ 12m] close-coupled, rather sparely-made colt: has a round action: half-brother to French 2000 Guineas second Candy Stripes (by Blushing Groom): dam sister to Sangue: successful in 3 of his 6 races, notably Criterium de Saint-Cloud (on demotion of Snurge) in November at 2 yrs and Group 2 Prix Noailles in April: well beaten in Prix Hocquart at Longchamp and Prix du Jockey-Club at Chantilly: should stay 1½m: evidently needs an easy surface. *F. Boutin, France.*

INTO THE FUTURE 3 b.g. Mummy's Game 120–Valley Farm 88 (Red God 41 128§) [1989 NR 1990 6m 7g 8m 10m 8g 8f³ 9.1m⁴ 10m⁵ 10m⁴ 10.8m⁴ 11m a12g⁶ a14g] 6,200F, 8,600Y: smallish, good-quartered gelding: half-brother to several winners, including 1¼m to 15.8f winner Valls d'Andorra (by Free State) and 1986 2-y-o 6f winner Margam (by African Sky): dam won over 6f: plater: keen sort, may be suited by return to 1m or 1¼m: bandaged behind final start: sold out of J. Toller's stable 4,200 gns Newmarket July Sales after fifth. *A. P. Stringer.*

INTREPID LASS 3 b.f. Wassl 125–Risk All 90 (Run The Gantlet (USA)) [1989 57 7g 7m 8g⁵ 1990 12m 11.7g 14g⁴ 14g⁴ a12g⁴ a14g²] tall, leggy filly: moderate mover: plating-class maiden: favourite, made most when second in handicap at Southwell in August: suited by 1¾m. *H. Candy.*

INTRICACY 2 b.f. (May 16) Formidable (USA) 125–Baffle 87 (Petingo 135) [1990 — 6g 7m] sturdy, quite attractive filly: has a quick action: half-sister to 3-y-o Wonderment and very useful 6f and 7f winner Mister Wonderful (both by Mummy's Pet) and to several other winners, including 4-y-o Castle Secret (by Castle Keep) successful from 1½m to 16.2f: dam, from good staying family, won over 13.3f: soon struggling in autumn maidens at Kempton and Leicester. *Lady Herries.*

INTRIGUE 3 b.g. Mummy's Pet 125–Subtlety (Grundy 137) [1989 5f 1990 a8g⁴ 52 d a10g a8g a6g 7m 10.2h 8g 8.2g 6m] lengthy, rather finely-made gelding: little worthwhile form: blinkered seventh start: often ridden by 7-lb claimer: rather headstrong: has carried head high and looked ungenerous. *M. P. F. Murphy.*

INTROVERT 6 b.g. Niniski (USA) 125–Consister 89 (Burglar 128) [1989 14s — 1990 2 1.6m] leggy gelding: of little account: blinkered twice: bandaged only start at 6 yrs. *A. Smith.*

IN TRUTH 2 ch.c. (Feb 13) Dreams To Reality (USA) 113–Persian Express 66 (Persian Bold 123) [1990 8d 8g 10s 8.2s*] rangy colt: second live foal: dam poor daughter of half-sister to very smart Tacitus: won nursery at Hamilton in November, showing greatly improved form, by 1½ lengths from Richmond: well worth another try over 1¼m: acts well on soft ground. *R. Earnshaw.*

INTUITIVE JOE   3 b.g. Petorius 117–Super Girl (Super Sam 124) [1989 5s 5g⁵ 57
5.1f⁴ 5m⁴ 6g⁴ 5f² 5f⁴ 6g⁴ 6f* 6g 1990 8f³ 8g 8m⁵ 8g³ 8.2m⁶ 7.6g 8m* 8.3m 7f a8g
a7g² 10f² 10f] smallish, attractive gelding: plating-class handicapper: made most to
win seller (bought in 6,000 gns) at Leicester in July: second in claimer and
apprentice race (set strong pace, kept on well), easily best efforts after: stays 1¼m:
acts on firm going: taken down early: has looked a hard ride. *G. Lewis.*

IN UNISON   3 b.f. Bellypha 130–Celtic Assembly (USA) 95 (Secretariat (USA))   ?
[1989 NR 1990 8m* 9v⁴ 8g⁵ 10.5v² 10.5s⁴ 11v] quite attractive filly: second foal:
half-sister to modest 1989 maiden Prefabricate (by Kings Lake): dam 10.6f winner
out of top Irish 2-y-o filly of 1975 Welsh Garden: co-favourite and wearing tongue
strap, won maiden at Warwick in March: ran solely in Italy afterwards, including in
listed races: off course nearly 6 months after third start: probably stays 10.5f: sold
17,500 gns Newmarket December Sales. *J. Gosden.*

INVERTIEL   6 b.g. Sparkling Boy 110–Phyl's Pet (Aberdeen 109) [1989 9f² 7h*   70
8f⁶ 1990 7.5d³ 8f 8g 8m⁴ 7m 7g⁴ 8d] quite good-topped gelding: easy mover: modest
handicapper: probably better suited by 7f than 1m: acts on hard going: sweating and
on toes on reappearance: has won for apprentice. *Mrs G. R. Reveley.*

INVISIBLE HALO (USA)   3 b.f. Halo (USA)–Placer Queen (Habitat 134)   —
[1989 5f 6g* 7m⁴ 8m⁶ 7g 1990 8m] leggy filly: modest winner at 2 yrs: well beaten in
handicaps last 3 starts: suited by 7f. *P. W. Harris.*

INVITATION WALTZ   3 b. or br.f. Be My Guest (USA) 126–Sabre Dancer   92
(AUS) (Twig Moss (FR)) [1989 NR 1990 7g* 7m* 7m² 7f* 8f⁶] 60,000Y: leggy,
rather narrow, angular filly: second foal: dam successful in 5 races at up to 7f in
Australia: fairly useful performer: successful in maiden at Wolverhampton and in
smallish fields for minor events at Catterick and Chepstow: good sixth in handicap
at Newmarket in August: stays 1m: sent to race in California. *L. M. Cumani.*

INVOCATION   3 ch.c. Kris 135–Royal Saint (USA) (Crimson Satan) [1989 NR   —
1990 10m 10f⁵ 12g⁵ 12d⁶] good-bodied colt: has scope: moderate walker: bad
mover: fourth foal: dam, winner at 1m to 1¼m in USA, is half-sister to dam of Mount
Livermore and Magical Wonder: signs of ability second and third starts but looked of
little account afterwards: blinkered final outing: wore bandages first 2 starts: sold
out of Mrs L. Piggott's stable 3,800 gns Newmarket July Sales and off course 5
months after third. *A. Moore.*

I PERCEIVE   3 b.g. Vision (USA)–Wavetree (Realm 129) [1989 6f 6g⁵ 7d² 1990   87 d
10.6f² 8.2m⁵ 8.2d⁶ 10.6d 10.6v] tall, good-bodied gelding: fairly useful effort, leading
until close home, when second in minor event at Haydock in May: no comparable
form as 3-y-o: stays 10.6f: best effort on firm going: broke loose and bolted before
second start: gelded after final one. *F. H. Lee.*

IRENE LOCK   2 b.c. (May 11) Lock And Load (USA) 72–Porto Irene 73 (Porto   —
Bello 118) [1990 8d a7g a8g] sturdy colt: first reported foal: dam, stayed 1¼m, is out
of half-sister to high-class sprinter Import: soundly beaten in maidens at Leicester
(backward) and Lingfield. *D. C. Tucker.*

IRENE'S CHARTER   5 b. or br.m. Persian Bold 123–Crestia (Prince Ten-   71
derfoot (USA) 126) [1989 9f⁴ 9f⁵ 10f² 10f⁴ 8m³ a12g³ a10g* a10g 1990 a8g* a8g³
a8g* 10f⁶] leggy, workmanlike mare: moderate mover: successful at Lingfield in
claimer (claimed out of D. Murray-Smith's stable £9,101) in February and handicap
following month: withdrawn lame at start at Doncaster later in March, and ran
moderately 5 days later: probably best short of 1½m: acts on firm going: bandaged
last 2 appearances: consistent. *K. O. Cunningham-Brown.*

IRENE'S FANCY (IRE)   2 ch.f. (Mar 13) On Your Mark 125–Bermuda Princess   42
(Lord Gayle (USA) 124) [1990 6h⁴ 5f] IR 1,500Y: third foal: dam Irish maiden: 100/1,
fourth of 5 in maiden at Carlisle: never able to challenge in maiden auction at
Beverley later in July: better suited by 6f than 5f. *P. A. Blockley.*

IRISCAR   4 b.f. Valiyar 129–Dellwood Iris 71 (Firestreak 125) [1989 6g 1990 a7g   —
a7g] sturdy filly: of little account. *W. Holden.*

IRISH DITTY (USA)   3 ch.c. Irish River (FR) 131–Devon Ditty 122 (Song 132)   55
[1989 NR 1990 8.5d 7d⁵ 7m] rather angular colt: fifth foal: half-brother to useful 1985
2-y-o 1m winner Ivybridge (by Sir Ivor) and 2 winners in North America, including
1988 2-y-o Tom Cobbley (by Seattle Slew): dam, best 2-y-o filly in Britain in 1978,
subsequently won 9f stakes race in USA: form in maidens only when fifth of 11 at

Catterick in July, no extra final 1f: swerved leaving stall on debut: sold to join K. Morgan 3,700 gns Newmarket September Sales. *J. H. M. Gosden.*

IRISH EMERALD 3 b.c. Taufan (USA) 119–Gaelic Jewel 89 (Scottish Rifle 127) 83 [1989 5s* 5d³ 6g 6g⁶ 6v 5g 1990 7m 8m³ 10.6s* 12g 10g⁴ 10d2] close-coupled, workmanlike colt: moderate mover: fair handicapper: won £7,900 event at Haydock in June: suited by 1¼m: acts on good to firm ground and goes well on soft: has rejoined trainer at 2 yrs C. Bravery. *M. H. Tompkins.*

IRISH FLASHER 3 b.g. Exhibitioner 111–Miss Portal (St Paddy 133) [1989 8.2g — 6v⁴ 6s 1990 6f 5m 9f] tall, rather plain gelding: well beaten since second start at 2 yrs, including in sellers: should stay beyond 6f: acts on heavy going: carries head high: sold 750 gns Doncaster May Sales. *M. O'Neill.*

IRISH GROOM 3 b.g. Shy Groom (USA)–Romany Pageant (Welsh Pageant 132) 47 [1989 8.2g 7g 1990 6m 10.2f 8g² 8.2m 8.2m⁵ a8g⁶ 8m³ 8d⁶] angular gelding: moderate mover: poor performer: worth another try over 1¼m: acts on good to firm ground and dead: blinkered 6 times (ran creditably last 3 outings), twice sweating: has looked none too keen. *J. P. Smith.*

IRISH IMPULSE (USA) 2 b.f. (Apr 14) Irish River (FR) 131–Exclusively 50 Raised (USA) 116 (Exclusive Native (USA)) [1990 6m⁶ 6.5g] 29,000Y: half-sister to useful 7f (at 2 yrs) and 8.5f winner Shuja (by Kalaglow) and French 11f winner Lady Goldsboro (by Kris): dam smart staying 2-y-o: poor form in maiden at Windsor and Tattersalls Tiffany Yorkshire Stakes at Doncaster: will be better suited by 7f + . *R. J. Williams.*

IRISH NATIVE (IRE) 2 b.g. (Feb 16) Be My Native (USA) 122–Irish Bride — (Track Spare 125) [1990 7s] IR 8,200f, 26,000Y: angular gelding: half-brother to 5 winners, including fairly useful 1981 2-y-o 5f and 7f winner Major Irish (by Malinowski) and fairly useful miler Red Paddy (by Red Sunset): dam never ran: bandaged behind, soon off bridle in maiden at Doncaster in November. *H. Candy.*

IRISH PASSAGE 7 gr.g. Welsh Captain 113–Honey's Queen (Pals Passage 115) 75 [1989 8d 8f² 7.5g² 8f 8f⁵ 8f 7.5m 8g 8m³ 8g³ 1990 a8g³ a8g* a8g* a8g* a8g* a8g* a8g³ a8g 8.5f* 8f⁴ 8.5f² 8m² a8g⁴ 8g⁵ 8f* 8.5m³ 8g a8g] workmanlike gelding: carries plenty of condition: good mover: had excellent season, winning 4 handicaps and a claimer at Southwell early in year then handicaps at Beverley (apprentices, first run for 4½ months) in July and Carlisle in September: stays 9f: possibly unsuited by soft going, acts on any other: blinkered once: has hung left under pressure: held up: goes very well for apprentice A. Greaves: consistent. *T. D. Barron.*

IRISH SUNSET 3 b.f. Red Sunset 120–Meisha (On Your Mark 125) [1989 6m — 8.5f 7m 1990 8v 12.2m 12h] workmanlike, good-quartered filly: moderate mover: no worthwhile form in maidens and sellers. *Denys Smith.*

IRISH VALUE (DEN) 2 gr.c. (Mar 10) Valiyar 129–Killarney Belle (USA) 52 (Irish Castle (USA)) [1990 8.2m 7m 7f⁴ 10s a8g] rather angular colt: half-brother to tough and fairly useful 7f and 7.5f (at 2 yrs) and 8.2f winner Eire Leath-Sceal (by Legend of France) and quite modest 1989 3-y-o 1m and 10f winner Booby Prize (by Bustino): dam unraced: plating-class maiden: seems to stay 1¼m: acts on any going: blinkered second outing. *R. Guest.*

IRON KING 4 gr.c. Tender King 123–Zanskar (Godswalk (USA) 130) [1989 6s 5s 59 6f³ 7h³ 7m⁵ 6f² 6m⁴ 6m 5f* 6f a6g⁵ a6g⁴ a7g⁴ 1990 5f⁷ 6f 6f⁴ 5.0h 5m² 5f³ 6m 6m 5f⁴ 5m 6t³ 6m 5m 6f⁶ 6m] sturdy, useful-looking colt: poor mover: plating-class handicapper on his day: effective at 5f and stays 7f: best form on a sound surface: ran creditably when visored, moderately when blinkered penultimate outing: sold 5,500 gns Newmarket Autumn Sales: not one to rely on. *R. Hannon.*

IRON MIKE 3 b.g. Glenstal (USA) 118–Salabella 64 (Sallust 134) [1989 NR 1990 — 6f⁴ 8v 7h⁵ 5.8f 7h 7g 8.3g] 12,500Y: sparely-made gelding: third foal: half-brother to 1986 2-y-o 6f winner Rockfella (by Ballad Rock) and 7f and 1m winner Silk Petal (by Petorius), both useful: dam, half-sister to Irish St Leger winner M-Lolshan, stayed 11f: poor plater: should stay 1m: blinkered last 4 outings, ran very slowly away on first occasion: sold 1,600 gns Newmarket September Sales. *W. Carter.*

IRON RED 2 b.f. (Mar 19) Never So Bold 135–Rosie Pug (Mummy's Pet 125) 62 [1990 6m 5d 6g a5g⁴ a6g³] 21,000Y: lengthy, useful-looking filly: second foal: half-sister to 4-y-o Haverton (by Carwhite): dam lightly-raced sister to smart sprinter The Pug and closely related to Music Boy: quite modest maiden: best efforts on all-weather: better suited by 6f than 5f. *M. A. Jarvis.*

ISABEAU 3 b.f. Law Society (USA) 130–Elodie (USA) (Shecky Greene (USA)) — [1989 NR 1990 9g 10.6s 10.1m⁴ a12g 10m⁶] 43,000Y: rather sparely-made filly: first foal: dam 11f and 1½m winner in France: best effort in Haydock maiden second start: on toes, ran badly in Southwell handicap on fourth: should stay 1½m: sold 3,600 gns Newmarket September Sales: winning claiming hurdler for K. Morgan. *J. R. Fanshawe.*

ISAMBARD   3 b.c. Star Appeal 133–Mertola (Tribal Chief 125) [1989 NR 1990 **82** d 10m3 11.5m4 9m3 12d a12g] close-coupled colt: half-brother to 4-y-o 5f winner Mertola's Pet (by Tickled Pink) and 3 other winners, including 7f to 1¼m winner Gilderdale (by Gunner B): dam ran once: easily best effort when staying-on third in maiden at Lingfield on debut: off course nearly 4 months before third start: stays 1¼m: joined P. Cole. *G. Harwood.*

ISAYSO   3 b. or br.g. Oh Say (USA)–Needs Supporting 79 (Home Guard (USA) **64** 129) [1989 NR 1990 11m 8g4 8m5] 2,400F: sturdy gelding: moderate mover: brother to useful 9f and 1½m winner Random Rover and half-brother to poor plater Needs A Shot (by Brave Shot): dam suited by 1½m: fourth in maiden at Edinburgh in June: bred to stay beyond 1m: dead. *J. S. Wilson.*

I SEE ICE   3 b.f. High Top 131–Climb The Heights (USA) (Majestic Light (USA)) **73** [1989 7m 7f5 1990 a8g2 a8g3 10f a11g2 12f* 13.8m2 12g3 10.2f] medium-sized filly: modest handicapper: won at Folkestone in July: ran fairly well next 2 starts, sweating and pulled too hard in lead on first occasion: suited by 1½m: acts on firm going. *B. W. Hills.*

ISIPINGO   3 b.c. Pitskelly 122–Nemoralis (Great White Way (USA)) [1989 7f6 **—** 1990 11d 7g] leggy, rather angular colt: tailed off in maidens. *D. A. Wilson.*

ISLAND JETSETTER   4 ch.g. Tolomeo 127–Baridi 82 (Ribero 126) [1989 **62** 10.2g3 12.3d 8f6 8.2g3 8.2g 10m 8s6 1990 10.6s3 12.3g 8g4 8.5g3 10f3 12f5 8.5g2 10m 9s] workmanlike, angular gelding: has a rather round action: fair maiden at best: stays 1¼m: acts on any going: wore small bandages behind final outing: winning hurdler in March: trained until after sixth start by M. H. Easterby. *N. Tinkler.*

ISLAND JEWEL   2 ch.c. (Apr 10) Jupiter Island 126–Diamond Talk (Counsel **—** 118) [1990 6g 6g 7m] tall colt: half-brother to several winners, including fairly useful miler Corn Street (by Decoy Boy) and sprinter Pusey Street (by Native Bazaar): dam never ran: bit backward in maidens and a minor event: had tongue tied down final start. *J. R. Bosley.*

ISLAND LOCKSMITH   6 b.g. Brigadier Gerard 144–Lake Naivasha 101 **—** (Blakeney 126) [1989 11g* 1990 a12g a16g] dipped-backed gelding: no worthwhile form in Britain: winner at Ostend in August, 1989. *M. J. Ryan.*

ISLAND RULER   3 b. or br.f. Ile de Bourbon (USA) 133–Dominant 86 **79** (Behistoun 131) [1989 7m4 1990 10.6s2 12f3 11.5g] leggy, rather sparely-made filly: fair maiden: ran poorly in minor event on final start: should prove better at 1½m than 1¼m: seems to act on any going: bandaged in front on reappearance, near-fore only last 2 starts. *A. C. Stewart.*

ISLAND SPIRIT   3 b.g. Ile de Bourbon (USA) 133–Zeyneb 65 (Habitat 134) **75** [1989 8v 8g 1990 10m4 14f2 16.5m* 17.1f3] rather angular gelding: modest form: landed odds in ladies race at Doncaster in June: ran creditably when placed in handicaps, final start in July: stays 17f: acts on firm ground: has edged left. *B. W. Hills.*

ISLAND UNIVERSE (USA)   2 b.c. (Mar 25) Lyphard (USA) 132–Care- **112** p fully Hidden (USA) (Caro 133) [1990 6m*]

As usual Luca Cumani introduced some promising two-year-olds in the autumn, none more so this time than Island Universe who romped home by nearly ten lengths—officially seven—in the valuable Duke Of Edinburgh Stakes over six furlongs at Ascot in October on his only start. None of the seven other newcomers in opposition had any sort of answer as Island Universe set sail for home two furlongs out, and even the best of them, Arylh, who ran clean away with a maiden at Leicester later in the month, was made to look flat-footed as Island Universe, without being particularly hard ridden, kept increasing his advantage to win in most impressive fashion. As with most races contested solely by newcomers it's difficult to know exactly what the form's worth. But though the subsequent performances of fourth-placed Aellopous, sixth-placed Swell Time, and last-placed Jesters Farewell contrast with those of Arylh and another later winner Takaddum and cast doubt over the form, Island Universe, a rangy colt, short of peak fitness and noticeably green in the preliminaries, probably achieved more at the first time of asking

Sheikh Mohammed's "Island Universe"

than most of his contemporaries and seems sure to develop into a cracking good three-year-old, probably at around a mile. Indeed, with another run under his belt he could well become a live candidate for the Two Thousand Guineas.

Island Universe (USA) (b.c. Mar 25, 1988)	Lyphard (USA) (b 1969)	Northern Dancer (b 1961)	Nearctic
			Natalma
		Goofed (ch 1960)	Court Martial
			Barra II
	Carefully Hidden (USA) (b 1979)	Caro (gr 1967)	Fortino II
			Chambord
		Treasure Chest (b 1962)	Rough'n Tumble
			Iltis

Island Universe is a full brother to the smart if somewhat temperamental Ensconse, who gave Cumani his first classic success for Sheikh Mohammed when winning the Irish One Thousand Guineas in 1989. Cumani now receives approaching twenty yearlings per season from Sheikh Mohammed, and he explained in an interview with the *Thoroughbred Times* in July how their association came about. 'My relationship with him started after I was sitting next to his manager on a plane on the way back from an Irish sale. There was a bomb scare as we landed in London, and we were all taken to some outpost at Heathrow Airport. We were all ready to jump out onto the wing and onto the tarmac. But instead we were all kept sitting all night in the airport waiting for luggage to be identified, so we spent all night talking horses. The next day he rang me and asked if I would be interested in taking a few of Sheikh Mohammed's horses.' Perhaps the best Cumani has trained for Sheikh Mohammed is Pirate Army. Ensconse wouldn't be far behind though, and there's every chance that Island Universe, also a close relative of the minor two-year-old winners Jathibiyah (by Nureyev) and Rimsh (by Storm Bird) out of a seven-furlong-winning half-sister to the smart filly Kanz and the dams of Glint of Gold, Diamond Shoal, Media Starguest and I Want To Be, will top the lot. He's already been entered for the Irish Two Thousand Guineas, but, interestingly, not, as yet, the Irish Derby. Island Universe showed a round, moderate action at Ascot, one usually associated with a soft-ground performer, but he clearly isn't inconvenienced by good to firm. *L. M. Cumani.*

ISLAND WEDDING (USA) 3 b.f. Blushing Groom (FR) 131–South Sea Dancer (USA) (Northern Dancer) [1989 7f³ 7m³ 1990 8m² 7d³ 8.5g* 7g* 7.6v] sparely-made, rather shallow-girthed filly: good mover with a quick action: progressive form when justifying favouritism in minor event at Beverley in July and handicap at York in October: seems suited by 7f: probably doesn't act on heavy going. *M. R. Stoute.*   **89**

ISLE OF ARRAN 3 b.c. Ile de Bourbon (USA) 133–Marzooga 84 (Bold Lad (IRE) 133) [1989 8m 9g* 8g 10g 1990 12m 12.3g⁵ 16.2d² 15g 16f* 12.3m⁴ 19f² 13.8f³] strong, close-coupled colt: carries condition: fair performer: very easy winner of handicap at Lingfield in July: suited by test of stamina and firm ground: visored last 4 starts: sweating and edgy (ran well) penultimate one: has looked none too keen, and is not one to trust implicitly. *R. Hollinshead.*   **85 §**

ISLE OF GLASS (USA) 2 b.f. (Feb 2) Affirmed (USA)–Liffey Lass (USA) 95 (Irish River (FR) 131) [1990 6g* 6m⁵ 7g*] second foal: dam 2-y-o 7f winner, is out of half-sister to high-class colts Home Guard and Boone's Cabin: fairly useful Irish filly: successful in maiden event and CL Weld EBF Park Stakes (by ½ length from Spring To Light) at Phoenix Park in September: will stay 1m. *J. Oxx, Ireland.*   **94**

ISOLA FARNESE 3 b.f. Hotfoot 126–Immaculate Girl 67 (Habat 127) [1989 NR 1990 8g 8.2m 9m⁶] 6,200Y: stocky filly: second foal: half-sister to Italian 7f to 9f   **—**

Sheikh Mohammed's "Isle of Glass"

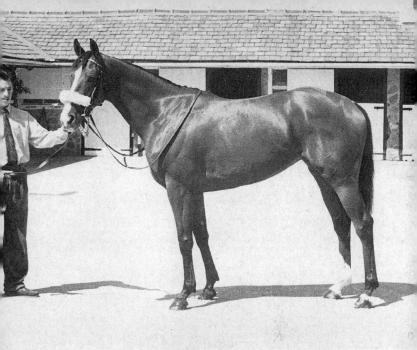

Academy Leasing Ltd's "It's All Academic"

winner Barbara Alberti (by Windjammer): dam, lightly raced, should have stayed 1¼m: no promise in maiden and auction races. *Don Enrico Incisa.*

ITDOESNTMATTER   3 b.f. Saher 115–Debnic 86 (Counsel 118) [1989 NR 1990 16f³ 12f⁵ 17.6m⁵ 15.3f 16m] IR 2,000Y: angular filly: has little scope: half-sister to several winners, including fair 1¼m winner Miss Polyanna (by Polyfoto) and 1987 2-y-o 7f seller winner Royal Course (by On Your Mark): dam, who stayed 1m, is half-sister to French 1000 Guineas third Bagheera: little form in maidens, sellers and handicap: sold 1,000 gns Doncaster October Sales. *M. O'Neill.*   —

ITQAN (IRE)   2 b.f. (Mar 11) Sadler's Wells (USA) 132–Photo 83 (Blakeney 126) [1990 7g 7f] 74,000Y: sturdy, good-bodied filly: has scope: very good walker: fifth foal: closely related to useful sprinter Quick Snap (by Try My Best) and half-sister to 3-y-o Photo Call (by Chief Singer), successful at 9f (at 2 yrs) and 11f: dam 1m and 9f winner, is daughter of 1000 Guineas second Photo Flash, a half-sister to Welsh Pageant: favourite, plating-class form in maidens at Kempton (hampered 4f out then kept on under tender handling) and Redcar (found little off bridle): very headstrong: looks sort to do better. *B. W. Hills.*   60 p

ITSAGAME   2 br.c. (Mar 22) Mummy's Game 120–Immodest Miss 73 (Daring Display (USA) 129) [1990 5f* 5f* 5f² 5m] 12,500Y: close-coupled, sturdy colt: seventh foal: half-brother to useful 1985 2-y-o 5f and 6f winner Prince Peccadillo (by Dragonara Palace) and a winner abroad: dam won 1¼m seller: modest performer: successful in minor events at Doncaster in March and Pontefract in April: faced stiff task in listed race final start: will be better suited by 6f. *S. Dow.*   73

IT'S ALL ACADEMIC (IRE)   2 b.f. (Feb 27) Mazaad 106–Princess of Nashua (Crowned Prince (USA) 128) [1990 5m* 5d* 5m³ 5d* 5f² 5m² 5f² 5g⁵ 6d] 21,000Y: compact, workmanlike filly: has scope: has a quick action: fourth living foal: half-   91

443

sister to fairly useful 1988 2-y-o 5f winner Sky Royale (by Skyliner) and a prolific winner in Italy by Kampala: dam unraced granddaughter of high-class filly Victoria Cross: fairly useful filly: successful in minor events at Pontefract in April and Chester in May and £8,000 contest at Epsom in June: consistent until running moderately final 2 starts: best at 5f: sold 40,000 gns Doncaster September Sales. *J. Berry.*

IT'S ME   4 gr.f. Good Times (ITY)–Rykneld (Warpath 113) [1989 8g* 8h* 8m 8m⁵   **52**
10m³ 8s 10.6d 1990 10f³ 10m 8g³ 8.5f² 9f 8m⁴ 8.2m] lengthy, workmanlike filly: good walker: plating-class handicapper: stays 1¼m: acts on firm going: sold out of Miss S. Hall's stable 8,200 gns Doncaster August Sales after sixth outing, resold 925 gns Ascot December Sales. *N. Tinkler.*

IT'S NOT MY FAULT (IRE)   2 b.c. (Feb 8) Red Sunset 120–Glas Y Dorlan 80   **42**
(Sexton Blake 126) [1990 6f a7g 8m 10s] 9,000F, 8,000Y, 2-y-o: first foal: dam 11f and 1½m winner: well beaten in varied events. *Dr J. D. Scargill.*

IT'S THE PITS   3 b.c. Tender King 123–Pithead 70 (High Top 131) [1989 NR   **64**
1990 6f3 7g 7m³ 8.2s* 9g⁴ 9g⁴ 8.2g⁴ 10f 12g 12m 12m* 11v² 15.8d⁵] 9,200Y, big, strong colt: has plenty of scope: moderate mover: half-brother to 4-y-o 5f to 7.5f winner Eastern Ember (by Indian King) and French 1½m winner What A Paper (by What A Guest): dam, sister to smart Miner's Lamp, won over 1½m in Ireland and over hurdles: quite modest handicapper: won at Haydock in June, in rear over 2f out, and Folkestone in October, always prominent: stays 1½m: acts on good to firm ground and heavy: looked reluctant sixth and seventh (blinkered) starts: hard ride: has joined L. Lungo. *G. Lewis.*

ITTISAAL   3 b. or br.f. Caerleon (USA) 132–House Tie (Be Friendly 130) [1989   **64**
5f4 1990 6m² 5g² 6f² 6m⁶] leggy, rather close-coupled filly: quite modest maiden: may be suited by further: acts on firm going: sold 35,000 gns Newmarket December Sales. *H. Thomson Jones.*

IVAN THE TERRIBLE (IRE)   2 ch.g. (Apr 27) Siberian Express (USA)   **75**
125–Chrisanthy 81 (So Blessed 130) [1990 6m⁶ 6d⁶ a6g⁴ 7d 8.2d a8g⁶ a7g*] 13,500F, 12,500Y: lengthy, workmanlike gelding: has scope: fourth reported foal: half-brother to 3-y-o Satis Dancer (by Mashor Dancer), successful at 7f (at 2 yrs) and 1m, and a winner in Hong Kong by Sayyaf: dam 2-y-o 5f winner failed to train on: much-improved winner of nursery at Southwell in December: suited by 7f: seems unsuited by a soft surface: blinkered penultimate start. *P. F. I. Cole.*

I'VE GOTTA TELL YA   4 b.g. Petong 126–Super Jennie 80 (Stephen George   **46**
102) [1989 8g 12.5f 10.6m 16.2g 13f⁴ 11f⁴ 11m⁵ 14d 1990 10.6f 12m* 14g² 12m⁴ 16.2d⁵ 15m* 12g³ 13m⁶ 16f 15.8d a14g] big, rather leggy gelding: moderate mover: poor handicapper: won at Edinburgh in April and June (apprentice ridden in slowly-run race): off course over 2½ months after eighth outing and not at his best last 3: possibly ideally suited by slightly shorter than 2m: acts on firm and dead going. *Capt. J. Wilson.*

IVOROSKI   8 b.g. Malinowski (USA) 123–Fado (Ribero 126) [1989 12.4g⁵ 10v   **36**
12g³ 12g⁵ 12h⁵ 12.3m⁴ 12m³ 15m 12g⁴ 12h² 11f³ 10f² 10.6d⁴ 10m³ 10.2g* 12.3m⁴ 10.6m a12g⁵ a14g⁵ 1990 10.2f 10.2m⁴ 12.3f⁵ 12.4f⁵ 12m⁵ 9f³ 10d 12.8g 11m 12f² 10f⁴ 10.2m 16d] workmanlike gelding: poor handicapper: has won only once in over 3 years: stays 1½m: probably not at his best on soft going, acts on any other: blinkered once: occasionally sweats: suitable mount for claimer. *Denys Smith.*

IVORS GUEST   4 b.g. Be My Guest (USA) 126–Ivor's Date (USA) (Sir Ivor 135)   **—**
[1989 8m 10g 1990 9g 10.1m⁵] leggy, quite good-topped gelding: moderate mover: lightly-raced maiden: should stay 1¼m: fairly useful hurdler as a juvenile. *Mrs J. Pitman.*

IVORS MELODY   3 b.f. Music Maestro 119–Double Birthday (Cavo Doro 124)   **47**
[1989 NR 1990 6f6 7g 6s 5g 7d⁶ 9f² 8f³ 8f⁴ 10.6d 10g] sturdy filly: third reported foal: half-sister to 5f (at 2 yrs) and 1m winner Major Ivor (by Mandrake Major): dam ran once: plating class at best: stays 9f: probably needs top-of-the-ground. *Mrs G. R. Reveley.*

IVORY BRIDE   2 b.f. (Apr 23) Domynsky 110–Ivoronica 89 (Targowice (USA)   **93**
130) [1990 5m³ 6g² 5d³ 6s* 6m* 6m 6d⁴ 6m] 18,000Y: leggy, unfurnished filly: half-sister to 3-y-o Muarij (by Star Appeal) and 4 winners, including one-time useful 5f and 6f winner Lochonica (by Lochnager) and sprinter Diamond Appeal (by Star Appeal): dam 2-y-o 5f winner: quite useful performer: made all in maiden at Haydock and Manton Rose Bowl Stakes at Newbury in July: good fourth to Imperfect Circle in listed race at Ayr, easily better of last 2 starts: much better

suited by 6f than 5f: yet to race on very firm ground, acts on any other: visored final 2 starts. *M. H. Tompkins.*

IVORY'S OF RADLETT 3 b.g. Alzao (USA) 117–La Croisette (Nishapour (FR) 125) [1989 6m 6m 5f5 5f* 5f5 5.3h² 5.8f6 5.1m² a6g a5g a6g5 a7g6 a8g 1990 7.5f6 8f4 7m³ 10f4 10f 8m 8g 8m a8g 7g4] small, sparely-made gelding: modest plater: stays 7.5f: acts on firm going: sometimes visored: has run well when on toes and for 7-lb claimer: sometimes bandaged: has joined M. Castell: probably ungenuine. *K. T. Ivory.*   **46** §

IVORY WAY (USA) 4 b.c. Sir Ivor 135–Frederick Street (Traffic Judge) [1989 9f 10f³ 10.4m* 12g 1990 10.4d 12g4 12f5 12m² 14f² 12f² 16.1m5 14.6g 12m² 12m* 12s4 12s³] strong, attractive colt: carries plenty of condition: fairly useful handicapper: won amateurs event at Ascot in October: ran well when placed behind Secret Society in £71,300 race (awkward at stalls) at same course previous outing and Azzaam in William Hill November Handicap (ran in snatches) at Doncaster: stays 1¾m: acts on any going: visored last 7 outings: none too resolute: sent to join D. Hayes in Australia. *J. H. M. Gosden.*   **93** §

IVREA 3 b.f. Sadler's Wells (USA) 132–Ivy (USA) (Sir Ivor 135) [1989 7f* 1990 10.5m³ 12d² 12s³] big, angular filly: won maiden at Leicester in October at 2 yrs: set pace or ridden close to it in 1990, showing useful form in Tattersalls Musidora Stakes (edging right) at York and Ribblesdale Stakes (beaten 6 lengths by Hellenic) at Royal Ascot: below form in Lancashire Oaks at Haydock final start, in July: will stay 1¾m: to join Frank Brothers in USA. *M. R. Stoute.*   **109**

IVY COTTAGE 2 br.f. (May 24) Damister (USA) 123–Debutina Park 87 (Averof 123) [1990 5f² 5m³ 5d4 6d] lengthy, good-quartered filly: fourth foal: half-sister to winning sprinters Super Deb (by Superlative) and Avidal Park (by Horage): dam 2-y-o 6f winner ran only once afterwards: quite modest maiden: off course over 5 months after second start: favourite, ran poorly final outing: should stay 6f. *J. Etherington.*   **66**

I WONDER WHEN 9 ch.g. Levanter 121–Gretna Wonder 46 (Elopement 125) [1989 NR 1990 12m] poor form in modest company on flat: needs further than 1m. *G. Price.*   —

IZADYAR 6 b.h. Akarad (FR) 130–Ilyaara (Huntercombe 133) [1989 NR 1990 13s] has been hobdayed: modest winner over 1m from 2 starts as 3-y-o: bandaged, always behind in Hamilton handicap in April. *I. Semple.*   —

IZIOFF 4 ch.g. Sayyaf 121–Maroua (FR) (The Marshal 118) [1989 8s6 1990 a6g³ a6g² a10g6 a8g 10s] smallish ex-Irish gelding: seventh reported foal: dam 2-y-o 5f winner in France on only start: plating-class maiden: probably stays 1m. *R. Akehurst.*   **48**

J

JABARABA (USA) 9 b.g. Raja Baba (USA)–Time To Step (USA) (Time Tested (USA)) [1989 14s 12s 12f 1990 10m 10m] tall gelding: plating-class winner as 7-y-o: lightly raced and no subsequent form: stays 1½m: used to be suited by top-of-the-ground: showed nothing in blinkers or visor: handicapped at 0 yrs: sold out of J. Bennett's stable 2,100 gns Ascot May Sales before reappearance: resold 500 gns Newmarket September Sales. *D. A. Wilson.*   —

JACAMAR 4 b.c. Jalmood (USA) 126–Streamertail 81 (Shirley Heights 130) [1989 12s5 8m 8f4 7m 7m 7.6g 8f* 8g 8.3g 8g 9g a7g4 a10g5 a8g* a10g² 1990 a8g² a10g* a10g²] lengthy, good-topped colt: keen walker: has a quick action: fair on his day, but has often looked ungenuine: won handicap at Lingfield in January: stays 1¼m: goes well on firm going and unsuited by a soft surface: has won for 5-lb claimer: wearing tongue strap, virtually pulled up sixth start in 1989: can't be relied upon. *B. Hanbury.*   **82** §

JACK BOY 5 b.g. Sparkling Boy 110–Miss Deed 83 (David Jack 125) [1989 5g 6f 5m 5f 5d 5m 5g 1990 5f4 5g6 5g* 5m6 5d² 5d4 5g³ 5f 5d 5g5 5d] small, sturdy gelding: carries condition: has a round action: plating-class handicapper: won apprentice race at Edinburgh (on toes) in June: suited by sprint distances: goes particularly well with give in the ground (yet to race on very soft): blinkered once. *J. Balding.*   **52**

JACK TULLY 3 b.c. Mouktar 129–Fabulous Luba (Luthier 126) [1989 7g 1990 12.5f6 10m] leggy, rather angular colt: moderate walker: bit backward, no worth-   —

445

Mrs P. J. Sheen's "Jaffa Line"

while form in maidens in July but gave impression capable of better: bred to stay 1¼m. *G. A. Huffer.*

JACQUELINE'S GLEN 4 b.f. Furry Glen 121–June's Slipper (No Argument 107) [1989 NR 1990 16d] half-sister to 2 winning jumpers: dam unraced half-sister to very useful stayer Tamerslip: won NH Flat race at Sedgefield in October: well tailed off in celebrity race there following month. *J. Parkes.* —

JADAAL 2 b.c. (May 11) Runnett 125–Tarte Tatin (FR) (Busted 134) [1990 6m] 1,600Y: big, lengthy, dipped-backed colt: third foal: half-brother to 3-y-o Return To Sender (by Auction Ring) and Irish 7f winner Sallustar (by Sallust): dam French maiden half-sister to Noir Et Or: very green and bandaged, swerved stalls and soon tailed off in Lingfield seller in May. *J. D. Czerpak.*

JADEBELLE 4 b.f. Beldale Flutter (USA) 130–Precious Jade 72 (Northfields (USA)) [1989 7s 8f 8m² 8f⁴ 8g³ 10m⁵ 12f² 1990 a10g⁶] small, strong, lengthy filly: carries condition: quite modest at 3 yrs: well beaten only outing (January) in 1990: stays 1½m: acts on firm going. *W. G. M. Turner.*

JADEITE (FR) 4 b.c. Crystal Glitters (USA) 127–Jawhara 93 (Upper Case (USA)) [1989 8g⁴ 10m* 10.6m* 10.6g⁴ 12f 10m³ 8.2g* 8f 10f⁴ 10g⁶ 1990 a8g 10.4d 8.2m* 8.2s* 8g 8.2s 10.5m 8.2f⁶ 8.2d* 9m] tall, lengthy, good-topped colt: carries condition: usually looks really well: has a rather round action: successful in handicaps at Haydock in May (£6,600 contest), June and August, recording fifth course win when racing alone far side in straight last occasion: unable to dominate and below form otherwise at 4 yrs: best at 1m: acts on good to firm and soft going: wears crossed noseband: goes very well with forcing tactics: sold 4,000 gns Doncaster November Sales. *R. Boss.* **86**

JADE 'N AMBER 5 b.m. Sonnen Gold 121–Madame Quickly 80 (Saint Crespin III 132) [1989 10f 10.1m 1990 8f] leggy, rather angular mare: well beaten in sellers. *T. B. Hallett.* —

JADE ROBBERY (USA) 3 br.c. Mr Prospector (USA)–Number (USA) (Nij- 113
insky (USA) 138) [1989 6d² 7g* 8d² 8m* 1990 8d³ 8m⁵ 9.2g⁵] a leading French
2-y-o of 1989, successful in listed race and Ciga Grand Criterium (by ¾ length from
Linamix, quickening really well but veering right) at Longchamp: disappointed in
Prix de Fontainebleau, Poule d'Essai des Poulains (carrying head high) and Prix
Jean Prat at Longchamp early on in 1990: free-running sort, uncertain to stay much
beyond 1m: may have proved suited by waiting tactics: reportedly suffered virus and
serious lung infection: likely to stand in Japan. *A. Fabre, France.*

JAFFA LINE 2 b.f. (Feb 17) High Line 125–Jacquinta 95 (Habitat 134) [1990 6d⁴ 96
7m³ 7m* 7m* 8m⁴ 7d⁴] 9,000F, 19,500Y: sturdy, angular filly: keen walker: has
powerful, round action: fifth foal: sister to 4-y-o High Quinta and closely related to
7f winners Toohami and 3-y-o Nicquita (both by Nicholas Bill): dam, 2-y-o 6f winner,
is daughter of Jacinth: fairly useful filly: successful at Goodwood in maiden in July
and Teacher's Whisky Prestige Stakes (by a neck from Ausherra) in August: ran
well after in Brent Walker Fillies' Mile at Ascot and Bottisham Heath Stud Rockfel
Stakes at Newmarket: will be suited by middle distances. *D. R. C. Elsworth.*

JAGGED EDGE 3 ch.c. Sharpo 132–Tura (Northfields (USA)) [1989 6m 6f² 5d* –
6v 1990 6g 6m 6m 7m 7d 6s 8g] neat colt: modest winner at 2 yrs: little form, mostly
facing stiff tasks, in handicaps in 1990: should stay 7f: probably acts on heavy going:
blinkered last 2 outings: changed hands 1,500 gns Ascot November Sales. *R. J.
Holder.*

JAGJET 3 ch.c. Vayrann 133–Ritsurin 79 (Mount Hagen (FR) 127) [1989 5v 5.3g* 51
5m 7m² 7m⁶ 9g⁵ 7g⁵ 8g 7d 1990 10v 8f⁶ 6m 7m 10g 10m⁴ 10m⁵ 9f* 10f* 12f⁴]
smallish, good-topped colt: poor mover: fair plater: led inside final 1f to win (no bid)
at Redcar and Folkestone in August: stays 1¼m: acts on firm ground: visored third
start: hung right for 7-lb claimer on fourth: sold to join Miss S. Wilton 5,000 gns
Newmarket September Sales. *W. Carter.*

JAHAFIL 2 b.c. (Feb 22) Rainbow Quest (USA) 134–River Spey 96 (Mill Reef 108 p
(USA) 141) [1990 7g⁴ 8g* 7g* 8m²] 200,000Y: big, rangy, attractive colt: has plenty
of scope: fluent mover: second foal: half-brother to 3-y-o Loch Spey (by For-

Hamdan Al-Maktoum's "Jahafil"

midable): dam 2-y-o 7.3f winner later stayed middle distances, is out of sister to very smart Joking Apart: progressive colt: 3½ lengths second of 8, staying on well, to Mujaazif in Royal Lodge William Hill Stakes at Ascot in September: successful earlier in month in minor events (making all and keeping on really well, despite wandering near finish on second occasion) at Sandown and Doncaster: will be well suited by middle distances: strong-galloping sort: sure to win more races. *Major W. R. Hern.*

JAHZEELAN   2 b.c. (Mar 23) Never So Bold 135–Misty Halo 93 (High Top 131)   66
[1990 a7g⁴ 7.5f⁴ 7h² 8d] 52,000Y: tall, lengthy colt: has plenty of scope: second foal: half-brother to 3-y-o 1¼m winner Rock Face (by Ballad Rock): dam prolific winner at 1m to 2¼m: quite modest maiden: will stay 1¼m: acts on hard ground. *Sir Mark Prescott.*

JAHZEEN   4 b.g. Shareef Dancer (USA) 135–Dancing Meg (USA) 113 (Marshua's   —
Dancer (USA)) [1989 10.8s² 10g 1990 14f] moderate mover: form only on first of 3 outings: should be suited by further than 11f. *J. Mackie.*

JAILBREAKER   3 ch.g. Prince of Peace 109–Last Farewell (Palm Track 122)   —
[1989 7f 1990 12d] well beaten in maidens. *B. R. Millman.*

JAKI'S ROULETTE   2 ch.f. (Mar 17) Rolfe (USA) 77–Stephouette 47 (Stephen   —
George 102) [1990 7g a8g] good-bodied filly: third reported foal: sister to quite modest maiden Handy Mo and half-sister to a bumpers winner: dam plater best at 1m, later won over hurdles: carrying condition, well beaten in maidens at Salisbury and Lingfield. *J. S. King.*

JALDI (IRE)   2 b.f. (May 21) Nordico (USA)–Havara 82 (African Sky 124) [1990   — p
6g] fourth foal: half-sister to 3-y-o 7f winner Brother Ray (by Chief Singer): dam 6f winner: shaped quite well in maiden at Folkestone in October, staying on having got behind: should improve. *J. Sutcliffe.*

JALEES   4 b.g. Precocious 126–Walladah (USA) 71 (Northern Dancer) [1989 6v⁵   —
7s 7s 7f 6m 1990 8m 12m 12f] compact, good-bodied gelding: little show in varied events: blinkered twice: dead. *G. G. Gracey.*

JALINGO   3 ch.g. Jalmood (USA) 126–Linguistic 95 (Porto Bello 118) [1989 NR   —
1990 10m] 16,000Y: leggy, workmanlike gelding: half-brother to several winners, including stayers Castle Douglas (by Amboise) and Relatively Easy (by Relkino): dam won twice over 5f at 2 yrs: bit backward, disputed lead over 7f then eased right down in maiden at Leicester in April: showed a quick action. *P. J. Makin.*

JALJULI   4 b.f. Jalmood (USA) 126–Anjuli (Northfields (USA)) [1989 7m⁵ 7m 1990   —
8m⁴ 7g 5m 6m] compact, attractive filly: has a fluent, rather round action: useful as 2-y-o: gave indication of retaining some ability in £7,400 race at Newbury and listed event at Sandown on first and third outings in 1990: on toes, raced with head high final start: needs further than 5f and should stay 1m: best efforts on an easy surface: sold 78,000 gns Newmarket December Sales. *C. E. Brittain.*

JALLAD (USA)   2 b.c. (Mar 30) Blushing Groom (FR) 131–Petrava (NZ) (Im-   89
posing (AUS)) [1990 6m* 7g] heavy-topped colt: carries condition: second foal: dam won from 6.5f to 9f in South Africa, where champion filly at 3 yrs: won maiden at York in August comfortably by ½ length, clear, from Wolf Hall, quickening well inside final furlong then edging right and left: well-backed favourite, found little under pressure last 1½f and eased in minor event at Kempton following month: should stay 7f. *P. T. Walwyn.*

JALMUSIQUE   4 ch.g. Jalmood (USA) 126–Rose Music 86 (Luthier 126) [1989   85
10v 9f* 8.2m 10.6g³ 8f² 8g 1990 8f² 8f* 8g 10f 8g 8m⁶ 10m² 9f³ 8.2d 8m⁵] strong, good-bodied gelding: carries condition: has a long stride: fair handicapper: won at Thirsk (bandaged near-hind) in April: needs riding with enterprise over 1m, but uncertain to stay beyond 1¼m: suited by top-of-the-ground: visored fifth start. *M. H. Easterby.*

JAMAICA GEORGE   5 br.g. Sexton Blake 126–Summer Serenade (FR) 96   60
(Petingo 135) [1989 NR 1990 a16g³ 16g⁴] sparely-made gelding: moderate mover: quite modest winner (apprentice ridden) as 3-y-o: showed he retains ability in handicaps at Lingfield in December: stays well: visored final start. *T. Thomson Jones.*

JAMAICA JOE   2 b.c. (Mar 8) Music Boy 124–Pasha's Dream (Tarboosh (USA))   57
[1990 5m 5f⁴ 6m 6f 6g⁵ 7g 6m⁶ 6d a6g] 15,000F, 24,000Y: leggy, good-quartered colt: poor mover: has scope: sixth living foal: half-brother to 1m and 1¼m seller winner Obeliski (by Aragon) and 5f winner Davill (by Record Token): dam half-sister to smart middle-distance performer Jimsun: fair plater: better suited by 6f

than 5f: possibly ideally suited by an easy surface: blinkered last 3 outings: has sweated: sometimes races too freely. *R. Hannon.*

JAMEELATY (USA) 2 ch.f. (Mar 18) Nureyev (USA) 131–Bright Omen (USA) 90 (Grey Dawn II 132) [1990 5g⁵ 6g* 6m* 7m² 7f² 6m] $250,000Y: tall, leggy, sparely-made filly: has a smooth, quick action: first foal: dam modest sister to Grade 1 winner Bounding Basque: fairly useful filly: successful in maiden at Leicester in May and minor event at York in July: better efforts when runner-up in listed races won by Hokusai and Trojan Crown at Newmarket: ran moderately in Moyglare Stud Stakes at the Curragh: will probably stay 1m: sweating and edgy third and fourth outings, more settled fifth. *A. A. Scott.*

JAMESIE 3 ch.g. Noalto 120–Ann Wilson (Tumble Wind (USA)) [1989 7f 7m 6g — 1990 a6g⁶] seems of little account. *D. C. Jermy.*

JAMES IS SPECIAL (IRE) 2 b.c. (Apr 14) Lyphard's Special (USA) 122–High — Explosive (Mount Hagen (FR) 127) [1990 7f 7s] 10,000Y: tall colt: half-brother to several winners, including 6f and 9f winner Ultra Light (by Superlative) and quite useful sprinter Myra's Special (by Pitskelly): dam poor staying maiden: never dangerous in large-field autumn maidens at Chepstow and Doncaster. *H. J. Collingridge.*

JAMES RIVER 4 ch.c. Star Appeal 133–Yorktown (Charlottown 127) [1989 10m⁴ — 11.5f 16f⁶ 12f a12g a16g⁵ a12g⁴ 1990 a11g⁶] leggy, light-framed colt: worthwhile form only on final start at 3 yrs: should stay beyond 1½m: blinkered last 2 starts (very fractious in preliminaries second of them): sold to join Mrs A. Knight's stable 900 gns Ascot February Sales. *J. L. Dunlop.*

JAMESTOWN BOY 2 b.g. (Mar 8) King of Clubs 124–Jhansi Ki Rani (USA) 94 — (Far North (CAN) 120) [1990 7f 7f⁶ 7f] IR 13,000Y: third foal: half-brother to fair 7f and 1m winner Kikala (by Kalaglow) and 11f winner Kings Rank (by Tender King): dam 7f and 1m winner: no show in maidens and a claimer. *Sir Mark Prescott.*

JAMIN 3 b.c. Teenoso (USA) 135–Miss Longchamp 94 (Northfields (USA)) [1989 85 6m 1990 8.2g³ 10.4d 10g² 10m 10f⁵ 12f* 12m³ 12m² 13d³ 16m³ 14d] strong, lengthy colt: has a quick, fluent action: fair handicapper: won handily-run race at Goodwood in August, leading inside final 1f: largely consistent afterwards but looked a hard ride: probably stays 2m: acts on firm and dead going: takes keen hold: sold 38,000 gns Newmarket Autumn Sales: somewhat ungenuine. *G. Wragg.*

JANBIYA (IRE) 2 ch.f. (Mar 31) Kris 135–Spark of Fire (Run The Gantlet 89 (USA)) [1990 6d⁶ 7g* 7.6s⁶] IR 370,000Y: quite attractive filly, rather unfurnished: fluent mover: sister to Irish 2000 Guineas winner Flash of Steel and half-sister to 3 other winners: dam, from very successful family, showed little ability in Ireland: sweating profusely, won 5-runner minor event at York by 2½ lengths from Crystal Ring, running on well: last of 6 in listed race at Lingfield later in October: will stay 1m: seems unsuited by soft ground. *H. Thomson Jones.*

JANE'S BRAVE BOY 8 b.g. Brave Shot–Jane Merryn (Above Suspicion 127) — [1989 8g 7m⁶ 7m 7f 7.5f³ 7g* 7.5m 7s 7g 7m⁶ 1990 a6g 7m 8g⁶ 8.5g 6g a7g 8m⁴ 8m 7f] workmanlike gelding: carries plenty of condition: poor handicapper: little form at 8 yrs: suited by 7f and a turning track: possibly unsuited by soft going, acts on any other: often apprentice ridden: has joined T. Craig. *D. W. Chapman.*

JANE'S FANTASY 2 ro.f. (Feb 19) Enchantment 115–Sea Farer Lake 74 — (Gairloch 122) [1990 7g 6h⁶] quite good-topped filly: has scope: second foal: sister to 3-y-o Sirse, 6f sellers winner at 2 yrs: dam 1m and 1¼m winner: behind in maiden (slowly away) and claimer in July. *Ronald Thompson.*

JANIE-O 7 ch.m. Hittite Glory 125–Tweezer (Songedor 116) [1989 7m 10m 8.2d — 1990 8f a11g] compact, good-bodied mare: lightly raced and below form since first half of 1988: bandaged, pulled up lame final outing: best at 7f to 1m with forcing tactics: ideally suited by an easy surface: blinkered twice, usually visored: often wears crossed noseband: has sweated and got on toes. *J. Dooler.*

JANISKI 7 b.g. Niniski (USA) 125–Seasurf 106 (Seaepic (USA) 100) [1989 16f⁶ 77 d 16m⁴ 16.1m⁴ 1990 14.8m² 16m² 16.2m 14g 17.1m⁴ 16.2d 14.6d⁵] strong gelding: has a quick action: modest handicapper: below his best after second outing: suited by around 2m and top-of-the-ground: has run well in blinkers, usually visored: has looked a difficult ride. *Mrs Barbara Waring.*

JARRAAR (USA) 3 b.c. Mr Prospector (USA)–Awaasif (CAN) 130 (Snow 78 Knight 125) [1989 NR 1990 8m⁶ 8.2f* 8m] tall colt with scope: third foal: half-brother to very smart 7f (at 2 yrs) to 1½m winner Snow Bride (by Blushing Groom) and 1987 2-y-o 7f and 1989 U.S. winner Salaadim (by Seattle Slew): dam top-class middle-distance filly from good family: easily landed odds in 3-runner maiden at

Haydock: second favourite, some late headway then eased in 13-runner handicap at Newbury later in May: may well stay further: joined F. Brothers in USA in June. *J. Gosden.*

JARRWAH 2 ch.f. (Mar 3) Niniski (USA) 125–Valiancy 87 (Grundy 137) [1990 7s] 60,000Y: sister to a listed winner in Germany and closely related to 13. If winner Valfleury (by Ile de Bourbon): dam, 1¼m winner, is daughter of Oaks second Val's Girl: well beaten in maiden at Doncaster in October: will stay well. *B. Hanbury.* —

JARZON DANCER 2 br.c. (Mar 19) Lidhame 109–Long Valley 71 (Ribero 126) [1990 6g4 7f5 6m5] 5,200F, 8,000Y: leggy, rather sparely-made colt: has a roundish action: half-brother to 3 winners, including tough 1983 2-y-o 5f winner Who Knows The Game (by John de Coombe): dam showed a little ability at 2 yrs: plating-class form in maiden auctions and a claimer: gave impression second outing possibly ill at ease on firm ground (hung badly): stays 6f. *C. F. Wall.* 55

JASCHA 4 b.f. Music Boy 124–Ardmay 57 (Roan Rocket 128) [1989 7f 7.6m3 5g 6f 6d a8g4 1990 a7g4 a8g* a7g* a8g5 a7g 7g 6f 8.3m] strong, sturdy filly: won claimers at Lingfield in January and February: no form afterwards: stays 1m: has sweated: sometimes taken down early: sold out of F. J. Houghton's stable 9,000 gns Ascot February Sales after fourth outing: resold 2,100 gns Ascot September Sales. *M. Bell.* 46 d

JATHIBIYAH (USA) 3 b.f. Nureyev (USA) 131–Carefully Hidden (USA) (Caro 133) [1989 7m* 8.2s2 1990 9g3 10f3 10m3 8f3 7m2] leggy, quite attractive filly: good walker: fairly useful performer: best effort in handicap at Lingfield second start: stayed 1¼m: acted on any going: blinkered last 3 starts, taking keen hold: mulish when mounted and taken down early final outing: carried head high: visits Kris. *H. Thomson Jones.* 89

JAVERT 5 ch.g. Kings Lake (USA) 133–Red Berry 115 (Great Nephew 126) [1989 10d 8.5g4 1990 11s 9s4 8g2 7.5d 8.2g 8.2g a8g3 8.2m4 9s] smallish, lengthy gelding: plating-class maiden: acts on good to firm going, possibly unsuited by soft: bandaged first 2 starts: changed hands 3,200 gns Doncaster August Sales: resold 4,100 gns Doncaster October Sales. *M. Brittain.* 54

JAWAB (CAN) 3 ch.c. Vice Regent (CAN)–Rare Secretary (USA) (Secretariat (USA)) [1989 NR 1990 7m* 7h2 8.2m2 7f*] $220,000Y: well-made colt: fifth foal: half-brother to 2 winners in USA: dam won twice at up to 1m in USA: comfortable winner of maiden (showed a round action) at Lingfield in May and 5-runner minor event at Brighton in July: stays 1m: remains in training. *A. C. Stewart.* 95

JAWANI (IRE) 2 b.c. (Apr 7) Last Tycoon 131–Fabled Lady (Bold Lad (IRE) 133) [1990 6m 7m6 8m] 27,000F, 48,000Y: big, rather leggy colt: has scope: half-brother to a winner in Germany: dam poor Irish maiden: progressive maiden: but backward on first run for over 3 months, around 9 lengths seventh of 13, never placed to challenge or knocked about, at Leicester in October: may well improve further. *Dr J. D. Scargill.* 60 p

JAYDEEGLEN 3 b.f. Bay Express 132–Friendly Glen (Furry Glen 121) [1989 5f2 5g4 1990 5g 6f 5g 5g 8f 10m5] leggy, sparely-made filly: poor on most form since debut. *R. A. Harrison.* —

JAY MARCHING 2 gr.f. (Mar 4) Marching On 101–Tootsie Jay 48 (Alias Smith (USA)) [1990 5d 6m6] sparely-made, plain filly: first foal: dam temperamental plater: green, soundly beaten in sellers. *M. P. Naughton.* —

JAZAF (USA) 3 b.g. Hero's Honor (USA)–Fleeing Partner (USA) (Fleet Nasrullah) [1989 8g3 1990 7f* 7m* 7d2 8m3 a7g 7g3 7m] workmanlike, good-quartered gelding: moderate mover: fairly useful performer: won maiden at Folkestone in March and handicap at Lingfield in May: easily best efforts after when placed in competitive handicaps and a ladies event: stays 1m: yet to race on soft going, acts on any other: ridden by 7-lb claimer third to fifth outings: sold 17,000 gns Newmarket Autumn Sales. *P. F. I. Cole.* 91

J BRAND 3 b.c. Persian Bold 123–Napa Valley 89 (Wolver Hollow 126) [1989 7m 7g 6f5 a7g 1990 12f* 12m* 12.3d 11f6 11.7m* a12g] workmanlike colt: has a short, sharp action: quite modest handicapper: made all at Folkestone and Leicester in April then led inside final 1f to win at Windsor in June: favourite, ran as if something amiss at Southwell in July: stays 1½m: acts on firm going. *P. F. I. Cole.* 64

J CHEEVER LOOPHOLE 5 gr.g. King of Spain 121–Sally's Silver 62 (No Mercy 126) [1989 5g5 5f 5f2 5.8f5 5d 5d a6g2 a6g* a5g5 a6g2 1990 a5g3 a6g2 a6g* 5f2 5g 6m6 5m 5m5 5g5 5m a6g2 a5g4 a6g] lengthy gelding: fair handicapper: goes well on all-weather, and won at Southwell in March: suited by 6f: probably acts on any going: blinkered twice, visored once: has appeared unsuited by track at Epsom: goes well with forcing tactics. *C. Tinkler.* 81

JEALOUS LOVER 6 gr.m. Alias Smith (USA)–Drawing Room Car (Chingac- 39
gook 128) [1989 10s² 10f 15.3m 12h² 10f⁵ 12f* 12.2f³ a11g 1990 a12g⁵ 11.5f⁴ 10.8m
15.5f⁵ 12f] small mare: good mover: poor plater: better at 1½m than 1¼m: acts on
any going: usually blinkered: has also worn a hood. *P. J. Makin.*

JEAN DOUGAL 3 ch.f. Star Appeal 133–Brandy (Busted 134) [1989 NR 1990 38
10m 12m 15g³] sparely-made filly: has a quick action: half-sister to fair 1981 2-y-o 1m
winer Gin and 1½m seller winner Carouser (both by Warpath): dam poor daughter of
half-sister to top sprinters Lucasland and So Blessed: poor plater: will be suited by
further: may benefit from a visor or blinkers: awkward at stalls last 2 starts. *J. W.
Watts.*

JEANNE DE LORRAINE 3 ch.f. Shadeed (USA) 135–Poquito Queen (CAN) —
113 (Explodent (USA)) [1989 6.3m³ 6m⁶ 6g⁶ 6g⁶ 1990 8m 8.5d⁵ 7d] sturdy filly: good
walker: second foal: half-sister to minor stakes winner in USA: dam maiden, placed
in Oaks, is daughter of very useful stayer Senorita Poquito: quite modest form at
best in maidens when trained at 2 yrs by J. Oxx in Ireland: no form at 3 yrs: should be
suited by further than 1m: twice blinkered, tailed off on final start: sold 2,800 gns
Newmarket September Sales. *J. R. Fanshawe.*

JEANS VALENTINE 2 gr.f. (Feb 14) Green Ruby (USA) 104–Roanette (Roan 55
Rocket 128) [1990 5f³ 6g* 6g² 6m⁴ 6g⁴ 6m* 6f³ 6f* 6m⁶] 2,200Y: leggy, workmanlike filly: moderate mover: half-sister to a winning plater, a winner abroad and a
winning hurdler: dam daughter of sister to Gimcrack winner Sovereign Lord:
plating-class filly: made all in maiden auction at Hamilton in May and sellers (no bid)
at Ripon in July and Redcar in August: stays 6f: hung right and flashed tail seventh
start: consistent. *J. Berry.*

JEBALI 3 ch.c. Good Times (ITY)–Penitent 85 (Sing Sing 134) [1989 6m⁴ 7m² 64
7g² 7f 1990 8f⁵ 7f² 7g] big, lengthy colt: quite modest maiden: raced too freely in
lead at Epsom final start, in April: probably best short of 1m: joined V. Young. *R.
Hannon.*

JEETHGAYA (USA) 2 ch.f. (Apr 15) Critique (USA) 126–Born Anew (USA) 56 p
(Avatar (USA)) [1990 7m 8f³] 6,600Y: workmanlike filly with scope: second foal:
half-sister to 3-y-o 7f winner Fighting Christine (by Fighting Fit): dam lightly-raced
maiden out of half-sister to very smart stayer Boucher: well backed both starts,
game third, beaten under length by Highland Ceilidh after disputing lead all way, in
maiden auction event at Redcar in October: may well improve again. *A. Hide.*

JEHOL 4 b.g. Teenoso (USA) 135–Buz Kashi 123 (Bold Lad (IRE) 133) [1989 10m³ 98
12m* 12m⁶ 1990 10f³ 12g 11g 10m 10m 10m* 10f⁵ 12.3g* 11d⁴ 12m] lengthy, attractive gelding: useful handicapper: won slowly-run races at Ripon in July (£9,000
event) and September: taken down early, ran poorly final outing: stays 1½m: acts
on firm going (stiff task on dead): takes keen hold, and usually held up. *G.
Wragg.*

JENDALI (USA) 2 b.c. (Feb 12) Nijinsky (CAN) 138–Jellatina (Fortino II 120) 86 p
[1990 8g⁴] $375,000Y: strong, good-topped colt: brother to very useful 7f (at 2
yrs) and 1½m winner Maksud, closely related to top-class miler Northjet (by
Northfields) and half-brother to several winners, notably Italian sprinter Madang
(by Habitat): dam Irish 9f winner: burly and very green, around 5 lengths fourth of
15, unable to quicken from under 2f out and not knocked about, to Sharifabad in
maiden at Newmarket in October: showed a quick action: sure to improve. *H. R. A.
Cecil.*

JENNIES' GEM 2 b.f. (Mar 21) Sayf El Arab (USA) 127–Melindra 83 (Gold Form 95
108) [1990 6f⁵ 5f* 5g* 6m 5m* 5d⁴ 5m] 7,400Y: rather angular filly: moderate
walker: third living foal: sister to fair 2-y-o 5f winner The Irish Sheikh and
half-sister to 5f seller winner Mia Scintilla (by Blazing Saddles): dam sprinter:
comfortable winner of maiden auction at Hamilton in July, auction event at Haydock
in August and minor event (easily best effort, making all to beat Food of Love 1½
lengths) at York in September: ran moderately final 2 outings, went too fast early
first occasion: suited by 5f. *R. Boss.*

JENNY B QUICK 3 ch.f. Mandrake Major 122–Clairwood (Final Straw 127) —
[1989 5s 5f 1990 7m 9s] lengthy, workmanlike filly: no form, including in seller. *T.
Craig.*

JENNY'S CALL 2 gr.f. (Mar 9) Petong 126–Jenny Splendid 101 (John Splendid — p
116) [1990 6d] 31,000Y: angular filly: fifth foal: half-sister to 1984 2-y-o 5f winner
Shelley Marie (by Gunner B) and winning sprinter Shari Louise (by Radetzky): dam
won from 5f to 7f: bit backward, behind in maiden at Goodwood in October: should
improve. *B. W. Hills.*

Summerhill Stud Ltd's "Jimmy Barnie"

JENPAT 2 b.f. (Apr 25) Mashhor Dancer (USA)–Russeting 76 (Mummy's Pet 125) —
[1990 6f] 18,500Y: fifth foal: closely related to modest 7f and 1m winner Sanawi (by
Glenstal) and half-sister to 1m winner and prolific winning hurdler Fisherman's
Croft (by Dunbeath): dam 2-y-o 5f winner, is sister to high-class sprinter Runnett
and very useful 1977 2-y-o 5f performer Cala-Vadella: slowly away and always
behind in maiden auction at Yarmouth in August: sold 640 gns Newmarket
September Sales. *W. Jarvis.*

JENUFA (IRE) 2 br.f. (Jan 24) Last Tycoon 131–Love Lost (Home Guard (USA) **87**
129) [1990 6g* 6g*dis 7m] 15,500Y: lengthy, unfurnished filly: first foal: dam little
form: first past post in maiden auction at Salisbury in August and nursery (disqualified for slightly hampering beaten horse over 1f out) at Doncaster in September: respectable seventh of 8 to Dartrey in £7,500 event at Newmarket: will stay
1m. *J. W. Hills.*

JEROZA (USA) 4 b.f. Shareef Dancer (USA) 135–Tarpoon (USA) (Vaguely —
Noble 140) [1989 8g 8.2m 1990 a11g 17.6g⁵ 12g] good-bodied, attractive filly: poor
mover: well beaten, including in sellers. *M. R. Channon.*

JESS REBEC 2 br.f. (Mar 29) Kala Shikari 125–Laleston 73 (Junius (USA) 124) **63**
[1990 5f⁶ 6d⁴ 6d⁵ a5g⁴ a5g² a5g⁴] smallish, workmanlike filly: has a quick action:
first foal: dam 5f winner: quite modest maiden: probably better at 5f than 6f: ridden
by 7-lb claimer first 2 outings. *G. A. Huffer.*

JESTERS FAREWELL (USA) 2 ch.f. (Apr 14) The Minstrel (CAN) —
135–Forever Waving (USA) (Hoist The Flag (USA)) [1990 6m 6d] rather leggy filly:
has scope: moderate walker: third reported foal: half-sister to 3-y-o Prayer Flag
(by Forli): dam, winner at up to 9f, is half-sister to top 1976 American 3-y-o filly

452

Revidere: bit backward and green, slowly away and behind from halfway in maidens at Ascot and Leicester in October: free to post. *P. W. Harris.*

JET PET 2 b.g. (Mar 31) Tina's Pet 121–Spinnaker Lady 70 (Windjammer (USA)) 64 [1990 5m4 a5g2 6m 6m a6g5 a7g6 6m3 8.2s3 6m5 8d 6s* a8g3] 1,800F, 4,200Y: small, angular gelding: moderate mover: first foal: dam won 1¼m seller: made all in claimer at Hamilton in November, winning by 10 lengths: visored, third of 16, leading to 1f out, in nursery at Southwell in December: stays 1m: acts well on soft ground: has been bandaged: retained by trainer 2,600 gns Newmarket Autumn Sales. *D. T. Thom.*

JET SKI LADY (USA) 2 ch.f. (Feb 20) Vaguely Noble 140–Bemissed (USA) 106 (Nijinsky (CAN) 138) [1990 6m* 6m3 7g* 8g] $335,000F: third foal: half-sister to a winner at around 1m in North America by Sir Ivor: dam good-class filly at 2 yrs in USA later third in Kentucky Oaks: successful in maiden and a nursery (under 9-7, by ¾ length) at Leopardstown: around 5 lengths seventh of 9, leading 6f, to Shadayid in Prix Marcel Boussac at Longchamp in October: will stay 1¼m. *J. S. Bolger, Ireland.*

JIGGING 2 ch.g. (Mar 15) Scottish Reel 123–Kesarini (USA) 87 (Singh (USA)) 73 p [1990 8d5] 25,000F: fourth foal: half-brother to useful 1988 2-y-o 5f winner That's The One (by Known Fact) and 3-y-o Amazake (by Rousillon): dam 2-y-o 5f winner, is out of Coronation Stakes winner Kesar Queen: green, over 6 lengths fifth of 22, held up then staying on well final 2f, to Character in maiden at Ayr in September: gave trouble stalls: will improve. *Miss S. E. Hall.*

JIMLIL 2 b.f. (Apr 7) Nicholas Bill 125–Ozra 63 (Red Alert 127) [1990 5f4 5f2 6d3 88 6m2 7f6g* 7m 6d* 7s] workmanlike filly: has a round action: second foal: half-sister to a poor maiden: dam 6f and 7f winner: successful in minor events at Doncaster in September and October, latter by 10 lengths from Sinclair Lad: best form at 6f: suited by an easy surface: sometimes gives trouble at stalls. *B. Palling.*

JIMMY BARNIE 2 ch.c. (Feb 9) Local Suitor (USA) 128–Sharper Still (Sharpen 102 Up 127) [1990 6m2 6m* 6m* 5f*dis 6d* 5m] lengthy colt: fifth foal: half-brother to 1986 2-y-o 6f winner Summerhill Streak (by Imperial Fling) and 6f seller winner Summerhill Spruce (by Windjammer): dam never ran: useful colt, first past post in maiden at Lingfield in June, minor event at York in July, 4-runner Molecomb Stakes (disqualified after beating Poets Cove ½ length, having hung left final furlong and caused interference) at Goodwood in August and Group 2 event at Baden-Baden in September: ran poorly in Cornwallis Stakes at Ascot final start: likely to prove equally effective at 5f and 6f. *J. L. Dunlop.*

JIMMY GRIFFIN (IRE) 2 b.g. (May 23) Burslem 123–Quantas 91 (Roan — Rocket 128) [1990 5m 5d5 6g 7.5g 7m a7g] IR 3,800Y: leggy, angular gelding: moderate mover: half-brother to several winners, including sprinter Stepping Gaily and hurdler Clover Hill Lad (both by Gay Fandango): dam 2-y-o 6f winner: little worthwhile form, including in sellers. *M. W. Easterby.*

JIM'S WISH (IRE) 2 b.c. (Jan 26) Heraldiste (USA) 121–Fete Champetre 80 82 (Welsh Pageant 132) [1990 6m* 6m3 6m6 6m3 7m4 7f5 8g4 8m 7v4 8d] 23,000Y: workmanlike colt: first foal: dam twice-raced half-sister to very smart sprinter Le Johnstan: fair performer: won Newbury maiden in May: very good fourth in Sandown nursery seventh start: suited by 1m: best form on a sound surface. *M. D. I. Usher.*

JINGA 5 b.h. Castle Keep 121–Eldoret 100 (High Top 131) [1989 12v2 12d* 14s4 73 14m6 16m 16.2m* 16.5m3 13.1f4 14.8m2 1990 14m6 12m 12g6 13.1h4] lengthy, quite attractive horse: modest handicapper on his day: stays well: acts on any going: moody. *Lady Herries.*

JIVE MUSIC 4 b.f. Music Boy 124–Swift To Conquer 87 (Solinus 130) [1989 5s5 33 5d 6m4 5m4 6g4 5f 5m 5g 5m5 1990 6m4 6f 5f 5m3 5f5 5d 5m 5m5 5m 5f 5g a5g 8.5f 5m2 5m5 5m4 5f3 5.3f 5d] smallish, good-quartered filly: bad mover: poor maiden: effective at 5f and 6f: acts on firm and dead going: sometimes blinkered or visored: has sweated and got on edge. *N. Bycroft.*

JOE BLOW 2 b.c. (Feb 15) Today And Tomorrow 78–Baby Bunting (Pyjama 47 Hunt 126) [1990 5g2 6m3 5d5 7g 7.5g a6g 6m 5v5] rather sparely-made colt: first foal: dam never ran: modest plater: best effort when blinkered final start. *W. J. Pearce.*

JOE BUMPAS 4 b.g. Noalto 120–Montana Moss (Levmoss 133) [1989 12.2d5 48 10v6 11f 13m 10g 12.2g 17f 10v 13.8d5 9s3 12g2 1990 a14g^ 13.8m* 13s6 12.4f4 13.8m 15.8g 14m 13g2 12g4 15.8d4 15.8m5] sturdy gelding: shows plenty of knee action: poor handicapper: won at Catterick in March: stays 1¾m: probably acts on any going: usually apprentice ridden: fair hurdler as a juvenile: inconsistent: has joined Miss G. Rees. *T. D. Barron.*

JOE SUGDEN 6 b.g. Music Boy 124–Sum Star 67 (Comedy Star (USA) 121) 89
[1989 5f2 5f* 5m3 5f2 5g5 5m 5m4 5f4 5g3 g2 5m3 5g2 5d5 5s 6s 5m* 5d 5d3 1990 5f3 5g3 5m3 5d2 5g2 6d* 6d 5f6 a5g4 5m3 g3 5.6g3 6m2 5m 6d4 6d2 5s5] tall gelding: moderate mover: fairly useful handicapper; nearly always runs well, and in June won £8,800 event at Epsom: effective at 5f to 6f: acts on any going: has been tried in visor: has won for apprentice: splendidly tough and consistent. *P. Howling.*

JOHANNA THYME 3 b.f. Reesh 117–Sea Thyme (Persian Bold 123) [1989 6g —
6g 1990 5s6 6g a7g] lengthy filly: poor mover: no worthwhile form in maidens (2 auction events) and handicaps. *R. Bastiman.*

JOHNNY COME LATELY (IRE) 2 b.c. (Feb 18) Le Johnstan 123–Invisible —
(King Emperor (USA)) [1990 6g 7g] IR 2,700F, IR 13,500Y: leggy, lengthy colt: has scope: half-brother to fairly useful 1982 2-y-o sprinter Hunter's Grove (by Our Mark) and quite modest 11.7f winner Ela-Re-Koumpare (by Hardgreen): dam ran 3 times: backward, well beaten in maiden (green) at Newcastle and median auction at York in October. *J. S. Wainwright.*

JOHN O'DREAMS 5 b.g. Indian King (USA) 128–Mississipi Shuffle 78 (Steel 58
Heart 128) [1989 8v 1990 10m 5m5 7m 5m6 6d2 5.8d2 5s5] sturdy ex-Irish gelding: poor walker and moderate mover: fourth foal: half-brother to French 1m and 8.5f winner Dunshufflin (by Dunbeath): dam sprinting daughter of July Cup winner Merry Madcap: close second in handicaps at Nottingham (vast improvement on form shown earlier in season) and Bath in October: needs further than 5f and had form over 1½m in Ireland: acts on soft going: blinkered twice at 3 yrs: effective with or without visor. *Miss J. Thorne.*

JOHNS GAMBLE 2 b.c. (Feb 10) Alleging (USA) 120–Fair Filly (Silver Shark 56
129) [1990 5f5 6d3 7m a6g 5d6 6d5] 5,400F: good-quartered colt: has scope: moderate mover: half-brother to 2-y-o winners by Northern Baby (at 1m) and Hard Fought (at 6f): dam Irish 11f winner, is half-sister to top 1974 Irish 2-y-o Sea Break: plating-class maiden: ran poorly final 3 starts, first occasion sweating and edgy: should be suited by further than 6f: visored or blinkered 4 times: usually claimer ridden. *T. Fairhurst.*

JOHNS JOY 5 b.g. Martin John–Saybya (Sallust 134) [1989 8f 8f 8g5 1990 8m 9m 80 §
10m3 8f4 9m2] angular gelding: has a round action: fairly useful winner as 3-y-o: lightly raced since, hanging right under pressure when second in handicap at Sandown in July: stays 9f: acts on firm going: has found little, and is one to treat with caution. *D. R. C. Elsworth.*

JOHN'S REEF 5 ch.g. Main Reef 126–Embustera 73 (Sparkler 130) [1989 NR —
1990 8g 12g] of no account: bandaged at 5 yrs. *T. Kersey.*

JOIE DE ROSE 5 b.m. Tickled Pink 114–Joie d'Or (FR) (Kashmir II 125) [1989 64
6d 7g 7.6f 7f3 7f* 7m2 6f 7m 7f 7f3 7f 7m4 8m 7.6m4 8f6 7g 1990 7.5m4 7.5m6 7f 7m* 7g 7m 7.6m5 7f3 8.2m* 8.3f* 8.3m2 8m3 8g 8m4 8m 8m3] plain mare: usually unimpressive in coat: has a round action: quite modest handicapper: formerly thoroughly inconsistent, but in fine form in summer, winning at Doncaster (apprentice race for second successive year), Nottingham (making most) and Windsor: best at 7f or 1m: acts on any going: blinkered once: usually races up with pace. *M. Blanshard.*

JOIE DE SOIR 2 b.f. (Apr 20) Caerleon (USA) 132–Late Evening (USA) 73 p
(Riverman (USA) 131) [1990 a7g2 a7g*] 19,000F: unfurnished filly: second foal: half-sister to a winner in Italy: dam French maiden: favourite, won 16-runner maiden at Southwell by ¾ length, clear, from Pacific Rim, leading after 1f and keeping on well near finish: will be better suited by 1m: may improve. *R. F. Johnson Houghton.*

JOKERS PATCH 3 ch.g. Hotfoot 126–Rhythmical 69 (Swing Easy (USA) 126) 76
[1989 7f2 7.5f2 8f2 a8g5 1990 8f2 8m3 10m* 10d] workmanlike gelding: has a quick action: modest performer: favourite, won claimer at Goodwood in September, staying on steadily to lead close home: stays 1¼m: acts on firm going, seems unsuited by dead: ran creditably when sweating second outing: takes keen hold: trained until after third start by P. Makin. *P. Leach.*

JOKIST 7 ro.g. Orchestra 118–What A Picture 80 (My Swanee 122) [1989 6s 6v6 65 §
6s6 6f 6g 6m2 6m* 6d 6g 1990 5f 6f* 6m 6m 6m 5m 6f* 7f6 7m5 6m 7g3 7d] workmanlike gelding: quite modest handicapper on his day: won at Kempton in April and Redcar in July: effective at 6f and 7f: acts on any going: blinkered twice,

including sixth outing: unruly at stalls on reappearance; thoroughly inconsistent. *P. S. Felgate.*

JOLEJESTER 5 b.m. Relkino 131–Mirthful 73 (Will Somers 114§) [1989 14g 1990 — 16.2f³ 12m 16.2g⁴ 15g] sturdy mare: no worthwhile form: not seen out after July: will be suited by thorough test of stamina. *C. W. C. Elsey.*

JOLI'S GREAT 2 ch.f. (Feb 6) Vaigly Great 127–Jolimo 92 (Fortissimo 111) **64** [1990 7d² 7m 7f] small filly: fifth foal: half-sister to several winners, including 1½m winner and very smart hurdler Osric (by Radetzky) and 11f winner Joli's Girl (by Mansingh): dam won from 1½m to 2¼m: form only when second in Yarmouth maiden in July: never placed to challenge in similar event final start: will stay 1m: may well do better. *M. J. Ryan.*

JOLI'S PRINCESS 2 br.f. (Mar 20) Prince Sabo 123–Joli's Girl 79 (Mansingh **93** 120) [1990 6f* 6m* 6f 7g² 7m⁴ 7m 6g²] close-coupled filly: first foal: dam 9f winner stayed 1½m: successful in maiden at Brighton in June and minor event at Windsor in July: best effort in York nursery final start: probably better suited by 6f than 7f: not particularly consistent. *M. J. Ryan.*

JOLIZAL 2 ch.f. (Mar 30) Good Times (ITY)–New Central 74 (Remainder Man **52** 126§) [1990 7f 7g³ 8.2g⁵ a8g⁵ a8g³] 1,700F: lengthy filly: first foal: dam 6f to 1m winner: a modest plater on turf: showed improved form in Lingfield maidens on all-weather last 2 starts: stays 1m. *D. Morris.*

JOLLY FISHERMAN (IRE) 2 ch.c. (Apr 30) Montekin 125–Ruby Relic **62** (Monseigneur (USA) 127) [1990 a7g 5f a7g² a7g 6g 8.5m a6g a5g² a6g⁶ 7s a7g* a5g a7g a6g⁶ a7g a8g⁴] IR 3,600F, 6,200Y, 3,000 2-y-o: neat colt: good mover: third living foal: dam never ran: quite modest performer: won nursery at Southwell in November: will stay 1¼m: best form on all-weather: inconsistent. *M. C. Chapman.*

JOLLY FLIER 2 br.g. (Apr 26) Prince of Peace 109–Ceile (Galivanter 131) [1990 — 7m] plain, close-coupled gelding: third foal: dam of little account on flat and over hurdles: tailed off in maiden at Chepstow in October: moved badly down. *N. Kernick.*

JOMANA 4 ch.f. Roman Warrior 132–Tina's Magic (Carnival Night) [1989 5f³ 6f⁶ **47** 6g⁵ 5m 5m 6f 8g⁶ 6g a6g 1990 7f 7f⁶ 5.8f 8m⁶ 10f⁶ 8.3m² 9f² 10m⁵ 8f] tall filly: poor performer nowadays: seems to stay 1¼m: best form on top-of-the-ground: blinkered final start at 3 yrs. *J. C. Fox.*

JONBEL 2 b.c. (Mar 2) Norwick (USA) 120–Two Shots (Dom Racine (FR) 121) **44** [1990 7d⁶ 7m 7g 7f 8.2s⁴ 8v 7d⁴ a8g] 5,200Y: rather dipped-backed colt: fourth foal: half-brother to 3-y-o Two Toffs (by Another Realm), speedy plater at 2 yrs: dam ran twice at 2 yrs: modest plater: best effort (in Hamilton maiden) fifth start: suited by 1m: acts well on soft ground: blinkered fourth outing, hooded next 2: very slowly away on all-weather: changed hands 6,200 gns Newmarket Autumn Sales. *R. W. Stubbs.*

JONDEBE BOY 6 b.g. John de Coombe 122–Simply Jane (Sharpen Up 127) [1989 **87** NR 1990 6v 5g² 6g² 5m* 5g⁴ 6g⁵ 5g³ 5g 5f* 5f 5m] lengthy, rather shallow-girthed gelding: fair handicapper: made all, well clear by halfway, at Goodwood (£12,800 event) in May and Hamilton in July: faced stiff task next outing, unable to dominate and well beaten on final one: very speedy, and best at 5f: has won on heavy going but goes very well on top-of-the-ground: has run well for 7-lb claimer. *G. M. Moore.*

JONJAS CHUDLEIGH 3 ch.g. Aragon 118–Lizabeth Chudleigh (Imperial **107** Fling 116) [1989 6g⁵ 6d² 6m⁶ 8g 8.5g²* 8d 7g³ 8d⁵ 1990 8g² 11g² 12f² 9m⁵ 8.5m²8m* 10g* 8m* 8g*] IR 2,800Y: second foal: half-brother to quite modest 1988 2-y-o 6f winner Syrus P Turntable (by King of Spain): dam never ran: won maiden at Galway at 2 yrs: progressed into a useful handicapper in 1990, completing 4-timer at Phoenix Park, Leopardstown, then in Davy Stockbrokers Irish Cambridgeshire and Old Vic Series Final at the Curragh (both under 9-10, leading close home): best form at 1m to 1¼m: probably acts on firm going, yet to race on soft: game and consistent. *C. P. Harty, Ireland.*

JORURI 5 ch.g. High Line 125–Dancing Sally 100 (Sallust 134) [1989 NR 1990 12f⁵ — 12.3g 10m⁶ 10.6d a12g] rather leggy, close-coupled gelding: carries plenty of condition: useful winner as 3-y-o: little worthwhile form in 1990: stays 1½m: best form on a sound surface: has run in snatches, and is not an easy ride. *F. J. Yardley.*

JOSHYKIN 4 b.g. Montekin 125–Miss Annie 73 (Scottish Rifle 127) [1989 7s⁵ — 8d³ 6m 7m⁶ 1990 a10g a10g a11g] leggy gelding: has a round action: moderate plater at best: soundly beaten in non-selling handicaps and claimer in January: suited by 1m: acts on dead going: wears bandages. *K. T. Ivory.*

JOUD 2 b.f. (Apr 26) Dancing Brave (USA) 140–Rapide Pied (USA) 117 (Raise A 93 Native) [1990 6m* 8g⁵ 7d⁵] leggy filly: second foal: half-sister to 3-y-o Dance Move (by Shareef Dancer): dam French 7f and 1m winner: highly impressive wide-margin winner of minor event at Newmarket in August, making all and clear 2f out still on bridle: heavily-backed favourite, pulled very hard and beaten 3f out in May Hill Stakes at Doncaster then found little off bridle in 6-runner Bottisham Heath Stud Rockfel Stakes at Newmarket: bred to stay 1m: headstrong. *M. R. Stoute.*

JOURNEYMAN (IRE) 2 ch.g. (May 19) Montekin 125–Maiden's Dance 65 — (Hotfoot 126) [1990 7.5d 7.5m 8f 10s] 7,000Y: good-topped, workmanlike gelding: has scope: fourth foal: half-brother to 3-y-o 7f winner Taylors Prince (by Sandhurst Prince) and 1m and 9f winner Dancing Monarch (by Dara Monarch): dam stayed 1m but possibly temperamental, is half-sister to 2 very useful 1m to 1½m performers: poor form in maidens, first 3 auction races: backward first 2 starts: sold 1,500 gns Doncaster November Sales. *C. Tinkler.*

JOVIAL KATE (USA) 3 gr.f. Northern Jove (CAN)–Flashy Feet (USA) (Pre- 63 d tense) [1989 6g 7f 5f⁵ 6g⁵ 6f a6g² a6g² a6g² 1990 a6g² a6g² a5g³ a6g³ a6g² a6g⁴ 5m 5f 5.8f⁵ 6f 6m 6m 5.3h³ 7f⁶ 5m⁵ 6g] lengthy, workmanlike filly: maiden: showed modest form on the all-weather but didn't reproduce that on turf: stays 6f: blinkered tenth start: usually wears bandages behind: has carried head awkwardly: sometimes sweating: not one to trust implicitly. *M. D. I. Usher.*

JOYCE'S CARE (USA) 4 gr.f. Green Dancer (USA) 132–Imminent (USA) 75 (Secretariat (USA)) [1989 12d² 16d² 14f² 16.2g⁵ 15s³ 18g 1990 16f² 18.4d 12m 15.8g³ 16.2g⁶ 13m² 16.5f⁶ 16f⁵] leggy, sparely-made filly: modest maiden: below form last 4 outings, looking none too keen in visor final one: needs further than 13f and stays 2¼m: best on a sound surface: lacks a turn of foot: sold to join J. Allen's stable 6,300 gns Doncaster August Sales. *Miss S. E. Hall.*

JOYEUSE MARQUISE (IRE) 2 ch.f. (Mar 6) Fabulous Dancer (USA) 108 124–Gay Secretary (USA) (Secretariat (USA)) [1990 7g⁵ 8g* 8g⁴ 8g⁵] first foal: dam French maiden: narrow winner of maiden at Clairefontaine in August: much better form in Prix d'Aumale and Prix Marcel Boussac (4 lengths fifth of 9 to Shadayid) at Longchamp in autumn: will stay 1¼m: useful. *B. Secly, France.*

J P MORGAN 2 b. or br.c. (May 8) Law Society (USA) 130–Queen of The Brush 69 (Averof 123) [1990 8m⁴] 105,000Y: leggy, shallow-girthed, angular colt: seventh foal: half-brother to several winners, including useful stayer Princess Genista (by Ile de Bourbon) and 8.3f winner Mashobra (by Vision): dam Irish 1½m winner, is half-sister to Old Country: blinkered, 5 lengths fourth of 13, soon in touch after slow start but finding little under pressure, in maiden at Leicester in October: will stay well: sold 9,500 gns Newmarket Autumn Sales. *J. H. M. Gosden.*

J R JONES 3 b.g. Blakeney 126–Bonne Baiser 88 (Most Secret 119) [1989 6g 6h* 57 6g⁴ 8m 7g* 7g 7.3d 1990 7f 11.7m³ 8f 7m 12m⁵ 17.1d³] small, good-quartered gelding: has round action: quite modest winner as 2-y-o: first form in 1990 (fell on reappearance) when third in handicap at Bath final outing: stays well: best efforts on an easy surface: sweating second start: trained until after reappearance by J. Berry: winning hurdler. *D. Burchell.*

JR'S PET 3 b.f. Auction Ring (USA) 123–What A Pet (Mummy's Pet 125) [1989 7g — 1990 7g 8f⁵] unfurnished filly: moderate mover: no form in large-field maidens then apprentice claimer: very slowly away in last-named. *R. J. R. Williams.*

J-TEC BOY 4 gr.g. Orange Reef 90–Fotostar (Polyfoto 124) [1989 8.2s 12f 1990 — a7g⁵] leggy, sparely-made gelding: little worthwhile form in varied company, in- cluding selling. *I. Semple.*

JUBILATA (USA) 2 ch.f. (Feb 16) The Minstrel (CAN) 135–All Gladness (USA) 65 (Alydar (USA)) [1990 7f⁵ 7f³] $350,000Y: first foal: dam unplaced from 6 starts: quite modest form in maidens at Yarmouth and Brighton: sold 6,000 gns Newmarket December Sales. *M. R. Stoute.*

JUBILEE TRAIL 3 b.f. Shareef Dancer (USA) 135–Miss Petard 113 (Petingo 82 135) [1989 7g⁴ 1990 10g⁵ 10.2f² 12f² 10.4g* 10m] rather leggy, workmanlike filly: has round action: fair form: well-backed favourite, made virtually all to win maiden at Chester in September: ran well in £8,300 Newmarket handicap final start: stayed 1½m: acted on firm going: stud. *B. W. Hills.*

JUBILYNSKY 2 b.f. (Jun 8) Domynsky 110–Most Jubilent 64 (Most Secret 119) — [1990 6g 7f] strong, workmanlike filly: fourth reported foal: dam 1m winner: bit backward, always behind in maidens at Thirsk and Redcar (not knocked about). *M. H. Easterby.*

JUBRAN (USA) 4 b.g. Vaguely Noble 140–La Vue (USA) (Reviewer (USA)) 54
[1989 11.7m⁶ 12g³ 1990 12f 13s 12m⁴ 12g⁶ a11g] quite attractive, close-coupled
gelding: lightly-raced maiden: helped out strong gallop when visored fourth outing,
off course 6 months after⸱ stays 1½m: trained first 4 starts by J. S. Willson. *M. P.
Naughton.*

JUDGEMENT CALL 3 b.c. Alzao (USA) 117–Syllabub (Silly Season 127) [1989 86
5g² 5m² 6f* 5m² 5f⁵ 5m² 5f* 5f* 5f* 5m³ 6g* 5g² 1990 6f³ 6f⁴ 7d 7m 6m⁴ 5d
6m* 6f* 7m⁴ 5m³ 7.6m⁶ 6g³] close-coupled, good-quartered colt: has a quick
action: fair performer: well-backed favourite, won claimers at Catterick and Ayr (5
days later) in July: goes well on top-of-the-ground, possibly unsuited by
dead: visored once at 2 yrs: bandaged seventh to ninth outings, near-fore only on
final one: sold to join P. Howling 21,000 gns Newmarket Autumn Sales. *M. H.
Easterby.*

JUDICIAL HERO 3 b.c. Law Society (USA) 130–Prattle On 112 (Ballymore 123) 102 p
[1989 NR 1990 10m 12g⁴ 12m* 14m²] 25,000Y: leggy colt: second foal: half-brother
to Irish 7.5f winner Summit Talk (by Head For Heights): dam 9f to 1¼m winner in
France, is half-sister to smart sprinter Petipa: 33/1, won 7-runner minor event at
Newmarket by short head from Advie Bridge: 15/2, 1½ lengths second of 4 to River
God in listed race (went down well) at Goodwood later in August, not finding as
much as seemed likely over 1f out: should prove at least as effective back at 1½m:
should continue to improve. *J. P. Hudson.*

JUDICIAL (USA) 3 b.f. Law Society (USA) 130–Northern Valley (USA) 76
(Northern Dancer) [1989 NR 1990 10.6s⁵ 14d³ 15d³ 16m] $108,000Y: sturdy filly:
moderate mover: first reported foal: dam unraced close relation to several winners,
notably Green Dancer, and half-sister to several others, including smart French
1¼m and 1½m winner Ercolano: modest maiden: stays well: almost certainly needs
an easy surface: visored final start: sold 5,600 gns Newmarket December Sales. *D.
J. G. Murray-Smith.*

JUDICIAL WIT (USA) 2 br.c. (Mar 9) Alleged (USA) 138–Bold Bikini (USA) 85 p
(Boldnesian) [1990 8d*] brother to Irish Derby winner Law Society, closely related
to high-class 1978 American 2-y-o Strike The Colors (by Hoist The Flag) and
half-brother to several other winners, including high-class middle-distance stayer
Legal Bid (by Spectacular Bid): dam 8.5f stakes winner at 4 yrs: odds on, won 13-
runner maiden at Leopardstown in October by ¾ length: will stay 1½m: sure to go
on to better things. *M. V. O'Brien, Ireland.*

JULFAAR (USA) 3 b.c. Arctic Tern (USA) 126–Nijit (USA) (Nijinsky (CAN) 91
138) [1989 NR 1990 10m⁶ 12m* 14g⁴] 74,000Y: rather leggy colt: moderate walker:
has a rather round action: second reported foal: half-brother to North American
winner Diadancer (by Diamond Shoal): dam stakes-placed sprint winner in USA out
of Bitty Girl: odds on but still green on first run for over 5 months, won maiden at
Pontefract in September: took keen hold and quickly eased once held 2f out in 1¾m
minor event at York: stays 1½m well. *A. C. Stewart.*

JULIE HUFF (IRE) 2 b.f. (Feb 2) Petorius 117–Brilleaux 73 (Manado 130) —
[1990 a6g 6m 8m] 3,000F: close-coupled, angular filly: second foal: half-sister
to useful miler Welsh Flame, should have stayed 1¼m: poor plater. *W. G. M. Turner.*

JULIE'S STAR (IRE) 2 ch.f. (May 29) Thatching 131–Red Roman 87 (Solinus —
130) [1990 6g 7m] IR 7,000Y: strong, lengthy filly with scope: fourth foal: half-sister
to 2 winners abroad: dam 2-y-o 5f winner mainly disappointing afterwards, is out of
speedy half-sister to dam of Roland Gardens: never better than mid-division in
autumn maidens at Kempton and Chepstow. *C. James.*

JULIETSKI 2 gr.f. (Feb 28) Niniski (USA) 125 Plum Blossom (USA) (Gallant — p
Romeo (USA)) [1990 10s] angular, rather sparely-made filly: seventh foal:
half-sister to fairly useful 1986 2-y-o 5f winner Plum Drop (by Take By Storm) and
winners in USA and Italy: dam never ran: well-beaten seventh of 21 in maiden at
Nottingham in October: should improve. *Mrs L. Piggott.*

JUMBY BAY 4 b.g. Thatching 131–Ridge The Times (USA) 78 (Riva Ridge 70 §
(USA)) [1989 7f⁴ 10m⁵ 8f 8f* 8m² 1990 8g 8m 8f 6g⁴ 8d a7g³ a6g³ a6g²] big, rangy
gelding: easily best efforts for some time when placed in claimers at Southwell late
in year: effective at 6f and stays 1m: acts on firm going: sweating and edgy when
blinkered fourth and fifth outings: takes strong hold: has hung markedly left: trained
first 2 starts by M. Pipe: not one to trust. *M. Johnston.*

JUNE'S FANCY 4 ch.f. Mr Fluorocarbon 126–Havaneza 65 (Simbir 130) [1989 —
8m 7m 11.7f⁴ 15.5f 11.7f 1990 10m 16m] sparely-made filly: poor mover: poor maiden:
suited by 1½m. *D. R. Tucker.*

JUNGLE DANCER (IRE) 2 b.c. (May 23) Sadler's Wells (USA) 132–Forlene 72 p
108 (Forli (ARG)) [1990 8g5 8.2d3] IR 725,000Y: angular, unfurnished colt: sixth
foal: closely related to 1984 Irish 2-y-o 7f winner Palais Glide and French 1¼m and
10.5f winner Gloria's Dancer (both by Northern Dancer): dam Irish 2-y-o 7f and 1m
winner out of very smart Arkadina: over 5 lengths third of 15, driven along over 3f
out and keeping on well, to Hip To Time in minor event at Nottingham in October:
will be well suited by 1¼m: sure to improve again, and win a race. *M. R. Stoute.*

JUNGLE KNIFE 4 b.g. Kris 135–Jungle Queen (Twilight Alley 133) [1989 8g6 79
8g2 7.5m5 10d 10m 9f 1990 8v4 9s* 10d*] tall, workmanlike gelding: moderate
walker and mover: successful in handicaps at Hamilton (hacking up) and Folkestone
(well-backed favourite) within a week in November: stays 1¼m: probably needs an
easy surface, and acts on heavy: winning hurdler in December. *M. H. Tompkins.*

JUNK BOND 2 b.c. (Apr 13) Last Tycoon 131–What A Pity 97 (Blakeney 102 p
126) [1990 6g* 7d*]
  The top-class sprinter/miler Last Tycoon has made a good start as a
stallion. At present the pick of his first crop, which includes numerous
winners throughout Europe, is the French-trained Selima Stakes winner
Tycoon's Drama. Two colts likely to do a great deal better at three, however,
are the current Two Thousand Guineas favourite Marju, a half-brother to
Salsabil, and the unbeaten Junk Bond, who followed his highly impressive
debut in an eighteen-runner six-furlong maiden at Newbury in September,
where he was ridden by the stable's chief work rider Raymont and started
at 25/1, with victory in the Philip Cornes Houghton Stakes at Newmarket.
At Newbury, Junk Bond belied his starting price and slightly backward
appearance with a sparkling performance in a faster time than that for the
preceding Group 2 Rokeby Farms Mill Reef Stakes, quickening smoothly
from a moderate position at halfway to be just behind the leaders two furlongs
out then switching outside the runner-up Kalashandi and running on well
(after a corrective slap with the whip) to win by two lengths and four. Junk
Bond apparently returned with cuts to his legs, which were probably sustained when Soleil Dancer in the next stall reared over and lashed out; that
would account for his very slow start, but he wasn't kept off the course for
long and he reappeared a month later at Newmarket on Champion Stakes day.
Conceding upwards of 7 lb to ten rivals, including several well-bred newcomers from the top Newmarket stables, Junk Bond won less easily than at
Newbury, coming off the bridle when the modest gallop increased three
furlongs out, getting to the leaders quickly but then having to buckle down to

*Philip Cornes Houghton Stakes, Newmarket—a win for a 'good little un';
Junk Bond (second right) beats newcomers Duc de Berry (right) and
Tetradonna (behind winner), with Flight of Freedom fourth*

account for Duc de Berry a shade comfortably in the end by three quarters of a length with three others close up and a five-length gap back to the rest. The Houghton Stakes is usually a stepping stone to a higher grade—Shadeed is its best recent winner—and Junk Bond seems likely to develop into a very useful performer in the coming season; he is a very genuine sort.

			Northern Dancer
		Try My Best	Sex Appeal
	Last Tycoon	(b 1975)	Mill Reef
	(b 1983)	Mill Princess	Irish Lass II
Junk Bond		(b 1977)	Hethersett
(b.c. Apr 13, 1988)		Blakeney	Windmill Girl
	What A Pity	(b 1966)	So Blessed
	(b 1980)	Scarcely Blessed	Parsimony
		(b 1974)	

Junk Bond, who is on the small side, was purchased for 33,000 guineas as a yearling at Newmarket's October Sales. He's the third foal of the lightly-raced seven-furlong winner What A Pity following a winner in Italy by Tap On Wood and a filly by Pharly. What A Pity is from a family that has thrown up many good sprinters over the years. Scarcely Blessed, whose several other winning foals include the useful six- and seven-furlong winner Breadcrumb and the useful 1983 two-year-old Pagan of Troy, showed smart form as a three-year-old and won the five-furlong King George Stakes at Goodwood in the same season as her half-sister Petty Purse passed the post in the frame in the Queen Mary Stakes, Molecomb Stakes and Cheveley Park Stakes. Their dam Parsimony, who won the Cork And Orrery Stakes and the July Cup in 1972, is a half-sister to Mummy's Pet and Arch Sculptor. Few members of the family have stayed much beyond a mile. So far he's raced only on an easy surface. *R. Charlton.*

JUNKET DISH 2 b.c. (Apr 21) Tremblant 112–Whey 85 (Sallust 134) [1990 7m] — smallish colt: second foal: dam 2-y-o 5f winner, bred to stay at least 1m: tailed off in maiden at Salisbury in June. *J. D. Czerpak.*

JUNUH 4 br.f. Jalmood (USA) 126–Adeebah (USA) 94 (Damascus (USA)) [1989 8g 8f 1990 8g 8m] smallish, lightly-made filly: easy mover: fair winner as 2-y-o: lightly raced and no subsequent form, including in seller: has been slowly away. *G. Richards.*

JUPITER SOUND 2 b.f. (May 7) Jupiter Island 126–Carribean Sound 76 (Good   47 Times (ITY)) [1990 6m 7f² 7f 8m⁴ 10.6s] medium-sized filly: first foal: dam 7f winner: plating-class maiden: should stay further than 1m. *C. E. Brittain.*

JURA 2 ch.c. (Apr 11) Rousillon (USA) 133–Reuval 102 (Sharpen Up 127) [1990   90 p 7g²] angular colt: third foal: dam suited by 1m: favourite, ¾-length second of 16, caught near line having led 1f out, to Surrealist in maiden at Sandown in September: sure to improve, and win a race. *H. R. A. Cecil.*

JURO VISA (IRE) 2 b.f. (May 23) Petorius 117–Travel (Saritamer (USA) 130)   45 [1990 5g⁴ 5g³ 5m 5d 7f⁵ 6m⁶ 6m² a6g⁶ 5f⁵ 6g⁵ 6m⁵] IR 2,500Y: leggy, good-topped filly: half-sister to 1985 2-y-o 7f winner Nervous Ride and a winner in USA (both by Beldale Flutter): dam lightly raced: modest plater: below form at Southwell: seems suited by 6f: races keenly: has twice hung badly left, and wore martingale final outing: has run creditably for an apprentice. *Pat Mitchell.*

JURRAN 5 ro.h. Formidable 125–Queen's Counsellor 92 (Kalamoun 129)   — § [1989 8h⁴ 8.5m⁶ 1990 10m 10m] strong, lengthy horse: has a free action: fairly useful at his best: very lightly raced and well below form since 3 yrs: acted as pacemaker final outing: stays 1m: acts on firm and dead going: ran moderately in blinkers: ungenuine. *H. Thomson Jones.*

JURZ (IRE) 2 b.c. (Jun 1) Pennine Walk 120–Kawkeb (USA) 72 (Vaguely Noble   70 p 140) [1990 8.2s 7m²] strong, workmanlike colt: has plenty of scope: third foal: half-brother to fairly useful 7.5f and 10.8f winner Annaf (by Topsider): dam 1¾m winner: 2 lengths second of 22, hanging left over 1f out and soon headed, to Il Corsair in maiden at Chepstow in October: backward and green on debut: will stay 1¼m: sure to improve again. *H. Thomson Jones.*

JUSTAGLOW 4 b.f. Kalaglow 132–Justicia 87 (Nonoalco (USA) 131) [1989 8f*   — 1990 12m⁶] useful-looking, shallow-girthed filly: made all in 3-runner maiden at Ayr (swishing tail and idling) at 3 yrs: pulled hard only outing (May) in 1990: should stay 1¼m: acts on any going. *B. W. Hills.*

JUST A LOOK   2 ch.c. (Mar 8) Doulab (USA) 115–Gentle Look (Tower Walk 130)   57
[1990 5f a6g a6g³ a8g⁶] 8,400Y, 9,500 2-y-o: sparely-made colt: second foal: brother
to 3-y-o Do Look: dam lightly raced, from family of Bay Express: plating-class form
when blinkered in all-weather maidens won by Dahlawise and Toshiba Comet Too:
stays 1m: raced very keenly and tended to hang third start. *D. J. G. Murray-Smith.*

JUST A STEP   4 br.c. Lochnager 132–My Louise 54 (Manado 100) [1989 6v⁶ 7s³   70
6g² 7f* 7m⁵ 7g 1990 a7g 7g 7m⁴ 7m² 7m⁵ 7m² 7.6m⁴ a6g⁴ a6g 7m 7g⁵ a7g 7d] small,
sturdy colt: moderate mover: modest handicapper: suited by 6f to 7f: acts on firm
going: has sweated, and got on edge: goes well with forcing tactics. *M. McCormack.*

JUSTASUNDAYSPORT   2 ch.f. (Jan 29) Star Appeal 133–Justine (GER) (Lu-   53 p
ciano) [1990 7g] 26,000Y: sister to useful 1¼m winner Always On A Sunday and 3
other winners here and abroad, and half-sister to 3 winners here and in Germany:
dam won in Germany: slowly away and never able to challenge in maiden at
Kempton in September: should do better. *P. A. Kelleway.*

JUST A TREAT (IRE)   2 b.f. (May 17) Glenstal (USA) 118–Another Treat   47
(USA) 82 (Cornish Prince) [1990 5g 5g* 5m 8.2d] 20,000F: lengthy, good-topped
filly: half-sister to 3 winners, including Irish 1m winner Wurud (by Green Dancer):
dam lighty-raced half-sister to dams of Golden Fleece and Be My Guest: won
maiden at Ayr in June: bit backward when last in nurseries at Leicester in July and
Nottingham in October. *J. Berry.*

JUST GILL   2 ch.f. (Mar 26) Tina's Pet 121–City Link Lass 92 (Double Jump 131)   52 p
[1990 7g⁵] 11,500Y: leggy filly: has scope: fifth foal: half-sister to 6.5f winner Vague
Lass and 6f and 7f winner Sporting Simon (both by Vaigly Great): dam 2-y-o 5f and 6f
winner: bit backward and very green, slowly away when last of 5 to Janbiya in minor
event at York in October: should improve. *Sir Mark Prescott.*

JUST GO   3 ch.f. All Systems Go 119–Argostone (Rockavon 120) [1989 5s² 5g⁶   —
6m⁶ 5g³ 6m² 6g* 6m 1990 6f 6g 5g⁶] small filly: poor mover: has run moderately
since winning seller at 2 yrs: will stay 7f: blinkered final outing. *M. H. Easterby.*

JUST GREAT   4 br.g. Simply Great (FR) 122–Bourton Downs 74 (Philip of Spain   43
126) [1989 8s⁵ 10m² 8.2s⁵ 8m⁶ 12f 12m 10g⁴ 11s 10g 10g 12g 1990 a11g* a12g² a12g²
a12g⁶ 10.2f³ 9f 10.8m⁶ 12f] leggy, sparely-made gelding: poor handicapper: won at
Southwell in January: stays 1½m: acts on any going: blinkered twice, visored final
outing in 1989: below form when sweating: inconsistent: has joined R. Juckes. *D. T.
Thom.*

JUST IMAGINE   3 b.f. Head For Heights 125–Lochboisdale 76 (Saritamer   —
(USA) 130) [1989 5f⁶ 5m⁵ 6g 6f 8.5f 8.2f 6m² 7f⁶ 7d 1990 6m⁶ 8.2g 8.5m 12m 8m]
compact filly: poor mover: plater: best form at 6f though bred to stay further: seems
suited by a sound surface: sometimes slowly away: on toes last 2 starts, visored final
one: sold 880 gns Doncaster June Sales: has looked a difficult ride and unsatisfactory. *T. Fairhurst.*

JUST JEAN   3 b.f. Kala Shikari 125–Curzon House 73 (Green God 128) [1989 5d   —
7s³ 8g⁴ 1990 a8g 12m] workmanlike, good-quartered filly: plating-class maiden:
well beaten facing stiff tasks in handicaps: appears to stay 1m. *R. J. O'Sullivan.*

JUST JENNINGS   5 ch.g. Horage 124–Sally St Clair (Sallust 134) [1989 6f⁶ 5.8h   73
5f⁵ a6g³ 1990 a7g⁶ a7g 8f a7g* 7m³ 6m⁴ 6s⁶ 6m⁵ a7g* a6g²] close-coupled gelding:
successful at Lingfield in handicap in April and claimer (claimed out of D. Haydn
Jones's stable £10,000) in August: ridden by 7-lb claimer, ran well final outing:
effective at 6f and stays 1m: acts on firm going, and not discredited on soft seventh
outing: usually blinkered: has often sweated and got on toes. *W. A. O'Gorman.*

JUST JOHN   2 ch.c. (Mar 15) Smackover 107–Saint Motunde 84 (Tyrant (USA))   74
[1990 5m⁴ 5m 6g 5m⁵ 5m⁵ 5m² 5f 7g 6m 6m⁶ a8g³ a7g a7g³ a8g²] leggy,
unfurnished colt: fourth reported foal: brother to sprinter Hannah's Boy and
half-brother to sprinter Saint Navarro (by Raga Navarro): dam best at 2 yrs, later
won at 6f to 1m: modest maiden: much improved towards end of year: suited by 1m:
best form on all-weather, acts on top-of-the-ground on turf: blinkered tenth start:
has run well for 7-lb claimer: often gives trouble stalls or starts slowly, and was
reluctant to race twelfth outing. *B. A. McMahon.*

JUST MY BILL   4 ch.g. Nicholas Bill 125–Misnomer 85 (Milesian 125) [1989 8v*   78
10g⁶ 10.5f³ 12m⁴ 12g 10.5f 10s³ 10.6s 1990 13v² 12.3d³ 12m⁵ 14s 12g² 12m⁵] leggy,
rather sparely-made gelding: fair form in varied events: not seen out after July:
probably suited by about 1½m and give in the ground: worth a try in blinkers or
visor. *C. W. C. Elsey.*

JUST ONE (IRE)   2 b.c. (Mar 10) Stalker 121–Angelica (SWE) (Hornbeam 130)   59
[1990 6g 7d 7m a6g⁵ a7g a8g² a8g⁴] 7,000Y: good-quartered colt: moderate mover:

half-brother to 1½m winner First Bill (by Nicholas Bill) and 5f winner Young Angel (by Young Generation): dam unraced sister to smart 1971 2-y-o Angel Beam: ¾-length second of 10 to Rare Detail in maiden at Lingfield in December, easily best effort: suited by 1m: blinkered or visored last 4 starts. *M. McCormack.*

JUST PULHAM 5 b.g. Electric 126–Lady Acquiesce 67 (Galivanter 131) [1989 12m 11.5m⁶ 11g 8fa 12g⁶ 1990 a16g⁶ a14g] smallish gelding: showed he retains a little ability in first of 2 Southwell handicaps in December: winning selling hurdler. *G. A. Huffer.* — 35

JUST READY (IRE) 2 b.g. (Apr 2) Petorius 117–Lacey Brief (USA) (Roi Dagobert 128) [1990 7m 7m 7g 8v] IR 25,000Y: workmanlike gelding: half-brother to fairly useful 1983 Irish 2-y-o 7f winner Rustic Lace (by Rusticaro) and a winner in Italy: dam Irish 9f winner: always behind in maidens and a nursery (slowly away, faced stiff task). *Sir Mark Prescott.* —

JUST RUN (IRE) 2 b.f. (Jan 13) Runnett 125–Wild Justice 76 (Sweet Revenge 129) [1990 5m] IR 1,800F, 5,100Y: leggy, lengthy filly: half-sister to Irish 7f winner Boa Restrictor (by Balbao) and winning Irish sprinter Gentle Rain (by Tower Walk): dam placed over 7f and 1m at 2 yrs, from same family as Kris: behind in maiden auction at Doncaster in May. *W. G. M. Turner.* —

JUST SEYMOUR 4 ch.g. Seymour Hicks (FR) 125–Pennycress 99 (Florescence 120) [1989 7d 7g a8g 1990 6m a6g] leggy gelding: behind in varied events since 2 yrs: sweated when visored: sold 700 gns Ascot September Sales: resold 550 gns Ascot October Sales. *B. Gubby.* —

JUST SUPER 5 b.m. Star Appeal 133–Striped Shirt (USA) (Dunce) [1989 NR 1990 11.5f³] leggy mare: first form when third in seller at Lingfield in July. *J. Ffitch-Heyes.* 33

JUST THREE 4 b.c. Tina's Pet 121–Mio Mementa 61 (Streak 119) [1989 8g 7s² 7s* 7g* 7.6f 7f* 7f 7g³ 7.6f* 7g* 7g⁶ 7m⁴ 8g² 7d³ 1990 8f 8f³ 7.2f² 8g* 8m 7.2s⁵ 8g* 7m³ 8g⁵ 8g⁴ 8m 8g] lengthy, useful-looking colt: usually impresses in appearance: very useful performer: successful in listed events at Phoenix Park in May and the Curragh (making all and beating Vague Shot easily by 5 lengths) in July: ran creditably in Group 3 race at latter ninth outing: suited by 7f or 1m: acts on any going: suited by forcing tactics: genuine. *M. McCormack.* 111

JUST TOO BRAVE 7 b.g. Beldale Flutter (USA) 130–Georgina Park 88 (Silly Season 127) [1989 a10g 1990 a11g 12m] big, strong gelding: poor mover: plating-class maiden at best: stays 1½m: suited by a bit of give in the ground (unsuited by heavy): blinkered 3 times, including first start at 7 yrs: trained until after then by M. McCourt: bandaged next time. *M. J. Ryan.* —

JUST VIRGINIA 2 b.f. (Feb 29) Petong 126–First Experience 58 (Le Johnstan 123) [1990 5f⁵ 5d 5g 6g 5f 6m] leggy, unfurnished filly: first foal: dam 5f winner, is sister to smart 1982 2-y-o 5f winner Cat O'Nine Tails: poor form, including in sellers: sometimes unruly stalls: blinkered final outing: trained first 4 by P. Felgate: very headstrong. *R. M. Whitaker.* 39

JUVENARA 4 b.g. Young Generation 129–Sharrara (CAN) 61 (Blushing Groom (FR) 131) [1989 8m 7m 5m⁵ 6f⁶ 6f³ 8f⁴ 7m⁴ 8f⁴ 7s 9f³ 8m* a8g² a10g 1990 6s³ 5m 6f* 8g⁴ 6f⁶ 6f² 6d 8f⁶ 6f⁶ 8f⁴ 8.3m* 6m 6h 8h 8.3g 8f³ 8f² 10f³] small, workmanlike gelding: poor walker: won handicap at Brighton in April and claimer at Windsor in July: needs further than 5f and stays 1¼m: acts on any going: has run well when edgy: often claimer ridden: inconsistent. *R. J. Hodges.* 64

K

KABCAST 5 b.g. Kabour 80–Final Cast 50 (Saulingo 122) [1989 5d 5m⁵ 5.1m² 5m² 5f* 5g* 5f* 5m* 5m* 5m² 5g² 5g 5g² 5.6g 5f 5g⁵ 5g³ 5m⁵ 5d a5g⁴ 1990 a6g⁵ a5g³ 5f 5m 5m 5m 5f 5d 5g³ 5f⁴ 5f 5m² 5m 5f 5m* 5.3f] good-bodied gelding: quite modest handicapper nowadays: apprentice ridden, was at Edinburgh in September: very slowly away previous outing: best at 5f on a sound surface: well in blinkers: often sweats. *D. W. Chapman.* 59

KABELLA 4 ch.f. Kabour 80–Right Abella 74 (Right Boy 137) [1989 6g 6g 1990 a8g a6g a7g 6f 6g] tall, leggy filly: well beaten in varied events. *D. W. Chapman.* —

KABERA 2 b.g. (Feb 12) Kabour 80–Boldera 69 (Persian Bold 123) [1990 6d] 2,000Y: strong, compact gelding: first foal: dam won from 8.2f to 13.8f at 3 yrs and 4 yrs: backward in maiden at Ayr in September. *D. W. Chapman.* —

KACHINA MAID   5 b.m. Anfield 117–Grey Twig 68 (Godswalk (USA) 130) [1989   **37**
8d 7f 8f 7m² 7f² 6f³ 7h³ 7f⁶ 7f⁴ 7m³ 1990 6f 7h⁵ 7m 8m 7f⁴ 7m⁵ 8m 8h⁵ 8f² 8f 8f]
sturdy, workmanlike mare: poor plater: ideally suited by 7f or easy 1m: yet to race
on soft going, acts on any other: blinkered once: occasionally slowly away: sometimes taken down early. *L. G. Cottrell.*

KADAN (GER)   6 b.g. Horst-Herbert–Ling Lady (GER) (Marduk (GER)) [1989   **56**
8f* 8g³ 1990 7f³] rather sparely-made gelding: moderate mover: quite modest
handicapper: probably best around 1m: possibly unsuited by soft going, acts on any
other: improved hurdler in 1989/90, winner of 4 of his 6 races. *M. H. Tompkins.*

KADIM (USA)   3 ch.c. Diesis 133–Alghuzaylah 90 (Habitat 134) [1989 6g² 7m*   **97**
8m⁶ 7.3d⁶ 1990 6m² 6m² 6m* 6m³ 6m⁴ 6m] sturdy, quite attractive colt: shows
some knee action: fairly useful performer: won listed Scherping-Rennen at Baden-
Baden: ran creditably in valuable handicaps at York, Newcastle and Goodwood later
in summer: seems suited by 6f: acts on good to firm ground: game: to join D. Hayes
in Australia. *H. Thomson Jones.*

KADIZADEH (IRE)   2 b.f. (May 23) Darshaan 133–Kadissya (USA) (Blushing   **86**
Groom (FR) 131) [1990 7m⁴ 8g] rather leggy filly: fourth foal: closely related to fair
1¼m winner Kassiyda (by Mill Reef) and half-sister to dual Derby winner Kahyasi
(by Ile de Bourbon): dam French 1¼m winner: 8 lengths fourth of 8 to Dartrey in
£7,500 event at Newmarket: again favourite, ridden along 3f out and steadily
outpaced last 2f in maiden at Yarmouth later in October: will prove suited by middle
distances. *L. M. Cumani.*

KADWAH (USA)   3 b.f. Mr Prospector (USA)–Castilla (USA) (Bold Reason   **80**
(USA)) [1989 NR 1990 7m³ 8m* 10d* 8m] $800,000Y: workmanlike filly: second
foal: dam, half-sister to Cougar II, was high-class American turf performer with wins
including 1¼m Yellow Ribbon Stakes: won maiden (not handling turn well) at
Kempton in May and slowly-run minor event (9/4 on, easily) at Leicester in June:
sweating and keen to post, hampered 2f out then soon beaten in listed race at Ascot
final start, first for 4 months: stayed 1¼m: visits Polish Precedent. *J. Gosden.*

KAFFIE (IRE)   2 b.f. (Mar 9) Kafu 120–Santa Maria (GER) (Literat) [1990 5m   **41**
5g⁵ 5g⁵ 7d 7d 6s] leggy filly: moderate mover: third foal: sister to 7f seller winner
Fast And Free: dam daughter of half-sister to very useful Irish middle-distance filly
Santa Roseanna and good German middle-distance performer San Vincente: poor
maiden: stays 7f: acts on soft ground: raced much too freely penultimate start. *R.
Earnshaw.*

KAFIYAH (USA)   2 ch.f. (Apr 2) Shadeed (USA) 135–Bolt From The Blue (USA)   **90**
(Blue Times (USA)) [1990 6m* 6m² 6m 7m³] lengthy filly: third foal: sister to 3-y-o
Gharah and half-sister to poor maiden Bin Daahir (by Blushing Groom): dam winner
from 9f to 1½m in USA, is half-sister to Alydar's Best: quite useful filly: won maiden
at Newbury in June: 1½ lengths second of 6 to Ivory Bride in Manton Rose Bowl
Stakes at Newbury following month, giving impression would have just about won
with clear passage: good third to Dartrey in £7,500 event at Newmarket: likely to
prove better suited by 7f than 6f: sold 40,000 gns Newmarket December Sales. *P. T.
Walwyn.*

KAGRAM QUEEN   2 b.f. (May 12) Prince Ragusa 96–Arodstown Alice (Sahib   **61**
114) [1990 5g 7g⁵ 6g⁵ 7f* 7f² 7m⁵ 7f 7f²] lengthy, dipped-backed filly: half-sister
to several winners, including 1985 2-y-o 6f and 7f winner Improvise (by Record
Token): dam ran 3 times: plating-class performer: backed at long odds, won seller
(no bid) at Redcar in July: will be suited by 1m: consistent. *Mrs G. R. Reveley.*

KAHALA BAY   2 b.c. (Mar 10) Belfort (FR) 89–Firey Kim (CAN) (Cannonade   **—**
(USA)) [1990 6f⁵] 8,000F, 8,000Y: leggy colt: sixth foal: half-brother to quite useful
sprinter P J Kelly and 6f and 1¼m seller winner Gershwin (both by Gold Song) and a
winner abroad: dam unraced: tailed off in 5-runner maiden at Brighton in June: sold
2,000 gns Doncaster October Sales. *J. White.*

KAHEEL (USA)   3 ch.c. Caro 133–Escaline (FR) 123 (Arctic Tern (USA) 126)   **113**
[1989 7m² 1990 8m³ 12g⁴ 12g 10d⁶ 9.7g] small, lengthy colt: capable of very useful
form: 7 lengths fourth of 18 behind Quest For Fame in Ever Ready Derby at Epsom,
having had fair bit to do on inside entering straight, then 10 lengths eighth of 9 to
Salsabil in Budweiser Irish Derby at the Curragh, held up taking keen hold and
never able to challenge: disappointed in listed race at Deauville and Group 2 contest
(bandaged, last of 11) at Longchamp afterwards: suited by 1½m: trained until after
fourth start by A. Stewart: clearly one to have reservations about. *G. Mikhalides,
France.*

462

KAHER (USA)   3 b.c. Our Native (USA)–June Bride (USA) (Riverman (USA)   96
131) [1989 7g³ 1990 10g² 11.5g* 12g² 12m⁴ 12.5f* 12m] compact colt: fairly useful
performer: won maiden at Lingfield in June and 3-runner minor event at Wolverhampton in September: led 1¼m in £71,300 handicap at Ascot final start: should stay
1¾m: acts on firm going: takes keen hold. *A. C. Stewart.*

KAHHAL (IRE)   2 gr.f. (Apr 27) Doulab (USA) 115–Queen's Counsellor 92   — p
(Kalamoun 129) [1990 6d] compact filly: sixth foal: half-sister to 1989 2-y-o 8.2f
winner Elmuraqash (by Ela-Mana-Mou) and 3 other winners, including winning
stayer Assaglawi (by Troy): dam won over 6f at 2 yrs and later stayed 1m: backward,
beginning to fade when bumped 2f out in maiden at Doncaster in November: should
do better. *H. Thomson Jones.*

KAHSHED   3 ch.g. Wolverlife 115–Lady Margaret (Yellow God 129) [1989 6f 6m⁵   —
7m 7g 1990 12.5g 10g⁴ 12m] lengthy, angular gelding: plater: staying-on fourth at
Ripon, best effort in summer as 3-y-o: should stay beyond 7f. *M. H. Tompkins.*

KAIKOURA   2 b.r.f. (Feb 1) Full On Aces (AUS)–Jandell (NZ) (Shifnal) [1990 7s⁶]   — p
ninth foal (first in Northern Hemisphere): dam New Zealand bred: around 30
lengths sixth of 19 in maiden at Doncaster in November: should do better. *W. Jarvis.*

KAILUA   3 b.f. Kafu 120–Gilana (Averof 123) [1989 NR 1990 5m 8m⁴ 8.2g 6m] IR   —
1,500Y, 14,000 2-y-o: tall filly: fourth foal: sister to thrice-raced Irish 1988 2-y-o
Progressive Girl and half-sister to winning 1m plater Henrietta Place (by Sayyaf):
dam disqualified winner over 7f in Ireland at 4 yrs: no form in varied events: unruly
at stalls second start: trained first by M. H. Easterby. *P. Monteith.*

KAIPHAS   3 b.c. Pharly (FR) 130–Kaiserslaut (GER) (Dschingis Khan) [1989 NR   73
1990 7m⁴ 8m] sturdy, attractive colt: first foal: dam, winner of 3 races in Germany
and second in German Oaks, is from good German family: fourth in maiden at
Sandown in June: again favourite, chased leader until ridden along 3½f out then
badly hampered in similar event at York in September: will stay further. *I. A.
Balding.*

KALABRIDGE   2 gr.f. (May 24) Kalaglow 132–Tickton Bridge (Grundy 137)   57 +
[1990 6m 6g 8f 6d 6d² 6d²] 2,100Y: leggy, unfurnished filly: second foal: half-sister
to 3-y-o 1¼m winner Tara's Delight (by Dunbeath): dam unraced half-sister to
Connaught Bridge and Rhein Bridge: improved on final 2 starts, staying on well in
nurseries at Newmarket and Folkestone in November: will be suited by 7f + : seems
suited by a soft surface. *M. J. Ryan.*

KALA EAGLE   4 gr.g. Kalaglow 132–Mamzelle 85 (King's Troop 118) [1989 10d⁴   —
12g³ 10m 8s⁴ 10.6s⁴ a10g² 1990 10.8g 14.8m] leggy, quite good-topped gelding: poor
walker: has a fluent, slightly round action: fair maiden as 3-y-o: soundly beaten in
Warwick handicaps in June: stays 1¼m: acts on soft going and possibly unsuited
by top-of-the-ground: blinkered twice: sometimes unruly at stalls: one to have
reservations about. *J. C. McConnochie.*

KALAHARI PRINCE (IRE)   2 b.c. (Mar 1) Green Desert (USA) 127–Lauretta   88 p
111 (Relko 136) [1990 7g*] 84,000F, IR 280,000Y: half-brother to 4 winners,
including fairly useful 12.3f winner Helenetta (by Troy) and quite useful 1¼m
winner Brinkley (by Moulton): dam middle-distance winner: landed odds by a short
head in 12-runner maiden at the Curragh in August: should do better over 1m + . *M.
V. O'Brien, Ireland.*

KALALEE   3 ch.g. Doulab (USA) 115–Silk Empress (Young Emperor 133) [1989   —
7g 8m 1990 12m⁵ 15.3m 16f4] leggy, workmanlike gelding: well beaten in maiden:
twice bandaged: not bred to stay 1½m: winning claiming hurdler: sold to join Mrs E.
Heath 9,000 gns Doncaster October Sales. *F. Durr.*

KALAN (IRE)   2 ch.c. (Apr 28) Sharpo 132–Zumurrudah (USA) 82 (Spectacular   —
Bid (USA)) [1990 6m] IR 44,000Y: strong, good-quartered colt: first foal: dam 1m
winner, half-sister to top-class middle-distance filly Awaasif, top-class American
colt Akureyri and 1000 Guineas runner-up Konafa: carrying condition, lost touch 2f
out in maiden at Yarmouth in September: may do better. *C. E. Brittain.*

KALAPARTY   4 gr.f. Kalaglow 132–Firework Party (USA) 115 (Roan Rocket 128)   53 §
[1989 7g 10g 8f6 11m 10g⁵ 11.7m 10m 8m⁴ 10d a12g 1990 11.7g² 11.1m³ 12m 11.5m 8g²
11.7m² 10f* 10f² 10f² 10g⁵ 10m² 9m⁶ 12g⁵ 10s] workmanlike filly: moderate mover: won
handicap at Newmarket in July despite wandering right: stays 1½m: acts on firm and
dead going: often blinkered: reluctant to go down sixth outing: usually finds little,
and is not one to trust implicitly. *C. J. Benstead.*

KALA'S PRINCESS   3 b.f. Kampala 120–Dasa Girl (Prince de Galles 125) [1989   —
5f 6m 6m⁶ 1990 10f 7m 7m 8f 7f 11m] medium-sized filly: shows a round action: poor
plater. *D. A. Wilson.*

KALEIDOS 3 b.c. Rainbow Quest (USA) 134–Sagar 74 (Habitat 134) [1989 NR 78
1990 10f³ 12h* 11.5m 10.1m²] 48,000Y: well-made colt: third foal: half-brother to
French 1¼m winner Suruba (by Top Ville) and Gold Ducat (by Young Generation),
modest winner over 5f at 2 yrs: dam won small 10.5f race in France: long odds on,
won 3-runner maiden at Brighton in May: better effort in handicaps on final start,
making most: probably stays 1½m: sold 18,000 gns Newmarket July Sales, changed
hands 11,000 gns Ascot October Sales: winning hurdler for N. Tinkler. *J. H. M.
Gosden.*

KALI KOPELLA 4 ch.f. Ahonoora 122–Restless Lady (Sandford Lad 133) [1989 —
6s 5d³ 5m 5m² 5m* 5f 5.3h⁴ 5m 5g 5d 1990 5m 6g 8m a5g 5m 5m 5.1m 5m] big,
lengthy filly: poor walker and mover: quite modest handicapper at best: little show
since winning at Edinburgh as 3-y-o: form only at 5f: acts on hard and dead going:
blinkered or visored fourth to sixth outings. *J. W. Payne.*

KALININ 2 ch.c. (Feb 24) Niniski (USA) 125–Kalaya (Tanerko 134) [1990 7f 8m 50
7m] IR 30,000Y, resold 14,000Y: rather leggy, quite attractive colt: closely related
to French 11f winner Darroze (by Gorytus) and half-brother to 3-y-o African Guest
(by What A Guest) and 3 more winners in France: dam, French provincial 9.5f and
10.5f winner, is half-sister to Kalamoun: plating-class form in maidens: will be much
better suited by middle distances: sold 6,400 gns Newmarket Autumn Sales. *J. L.
Dunlop.*

KALMADENE 3 gr.c. Kalaglow 132–Almadena 73 (Dairialatan 111) [1989 NR 100 p
1990 12.5f³ 12f* 12g 11.5f² 12m* 12g*] leggy, quite attractive colt: half-brother to
very useful 6f and 7f winner Scarrowmanwick (by Tickled Pink) and 1¼m winner
Cumrew (by Gunner B): dam placed on debut at 2 yrs: won maiden (odds on, didn't
handle bends well) at Folkestone in May and handicaps at Salisbury in August and
Kempton (£11,500 event, leading inside final 1f) in September: stays 1½m well: acts
on firm going: progressive. *G. Harwood.*

KALOGY 3 gr.f. Kalaglow 132–Coyote 94 (Welsh Pageant 132) [1989 NR 1990 62
12.4m² 15d 12g] lengthy, workmanlike filly: fourth foal: half-sister to 3 winners,
including 1¼m winner Cynomis (by Shergar) and useful 10.4f and 1¾m winner
Range Rover (by High Top): dam genuine middle-distance stayer: beaten ½ length
by sole rival Shilinski in maiden at Newcastle in August, travelling strongly in lead
long way but green and headed close home: well beaten in Ayr minor event and
Pontefract maiden: should stay beyond 1½m though headstrong: sold to join M.
McCourt 3,000 gns Doncaster November Sales. *G. A. Pritchard-Gordon.*

KALOOKI QUEEN 2 ch.f. (Jan 28) Joshua 129–Hill of Fare (Brigadier Gerard 38
144) [1990 6g⁶ 5m 6m 6d 6g⁶] leggy, angular filly: third foal: half-sister to a winner in
Belgium: dam lightly raced and little form at 2 yrs: poor form, including in sellers. *B.
Stevens.*

KALSHANDI (IRE) 2 ch.c. (Apr 9) Ballad Rock 122–Kaliala (FR) (Pharly (FR) 88
130) [1990 5d³ 6g² 6g³ 5d] sturdy colt, shade unfurnished: has a quick action: third
foal: dam French 1m winner: fair form behind Junk Bond in maiden at Newbury in
September and Punch N'Run in listed race at York following month: needs further
than 5f, and will stay 7f: races keenly. *L. M. Cumani.*

KALVEE DANCER 3 b.f. Kalaglow 132–Clonavee (USA) (Northern Dancer) —
[1989 5g 1990 12m 12.2g] lengthy, rather unfurnished filly: no worthwhile form. *E.
Weymes.*

KAMAKAZE GIRL 4 b.f. Kampala 120–Glencara 104 (Sallust 134) [1989 6s⁵ 64
8g⁶ 7f 7m³ a8g 1990 8.2s* 8f 8m 7d⁴ a8g 8.2v*] big filly: moderate walker and
mover: won handicap at Hamilton in April and claimer at Haydock in October:
effective at 7f and 1m: seems to need soft surface nowadays: blinkered fourth and
fifth outings: sold to join J. Mackie's stable 8,000 gns Newmarket Autumn Sales. *M.
J. Ryan.*

KAMAROCK 8 b.h. Kampala 120–Hey Dolly (Saint Crespin III 132) [1989 NR —
1990 a12g] small horse: visored and bandaged on only run on flat since 1985, pulled
up after 3f in handicap at Southwell in March: often used to wear blinkers. *C. Spares.*

KAMART 2 gr.f. (Feb 17) Belfort (FR) 89–Practicality (Weavers' Hall 122) [1990 66
5m³ 6m* 6g 6m⁶] rather unfurnished filly: seventh live foal: half-sister to minor
winners in Belgium and France: dam once-raced half-sister to very smart miler
Poacher's Moon: won maiden at Carlisle in June: ran moderately after, running very
wide on home bend at Catterick final start. *Denys Smith.*

KANAFA (IRE) 2 ch.g. (Jan 28) Dara Monarch 128–Miss Victoria (Auction Ring —
(USA) 123) [1990 7m 7m] IR 29,000Y: compact gelding: first foal: dam Irish maiden,

placed at 7f: well beaten in maiden and claimer at Yarmouth: sold 850 gns Doncaster October Sales. *G. A. Pritchard-Gordon.*

KANDARA (FR)   2 b.f. (Apr 24) Dalsaan 125–Kantado 93 (Saulingo 122) [1990   **88 ?**
5g4 5g* 5d2 5f 6m a6g3 6m* 6g 6d4] 13,500 2-y-o: lengthy, dipped-backed, strong-quartered filly: has scope: seventh living foal: half-sister to 4 winners, including 3-y-o In Excess (by Siberian Express), useful winner at 6f to 9f here and in USA, and 1¼m winner Beau Fils (by Crimson Beau): dam raced mainly at 5f: fair performer: won maiden auction at Carlisle in May and nursery at Newcastle in August: much better suited by 6f than 5f: inconsistent. *M. Johnston.*

KANOOZ (IRE)   2 br.g. (Apr 12) Wassl 125–Countess Candy 106 (Great Nephew   **62**
126) [1990 8d a8g4] IR 88,000Y: leggy gelding: has scope: second foal: dam, Irish 2-y-o 7f and 8.5f winner, is half-sister to very useful Irish middle-distance filly Countess Tully: quite modest form when fourth in maiden at Lingfield in December: will stay 1¼m. *Sir Mark Prescott.*

KARANNJA (USA)   2 ch.f. (Feb 25) Shahrastani (USA) 135–Kareena 110   **55 p**
(Riverman (USA) 131) [1990 7g6] third living foal: closely related to useful 1¼m winner Karaferya (by Green Dancer): dam won 4 times at around 1m: co-favourite, over 14 lengths sixth of 17, eased once held last 1f, in maiden at Salisbury in October: sure to do better. *M. R. Stoute.*

KARAZAN   3 gr.c. Nishapour (FR) 125–Celestial Path 101 (Godswalk (USA) 130)   **90**
[1989 8.5f4 8f* 8g* 1990 9f5 8g 10.2m3 10.5m4 9g 7d3 9m] big, strong colt: has scope: fairly useful handicapper: ran well when in frame, in John Smith's Magnet Cup at York and £6,000 event (stayed on strongly) at Ayr last 2 occasions: blinkered, well beaten in Cambridgeshire at Newmarket final start: clearly effective at 7f with plenty of give in the ground, but should stay 1½m: acts on firm and dead ground: ran moderately when on toes fifth start. *J. G. FitzGerald.*

KARBAJ   6 ch.g. Arctic Tern (USA) 126–Jadhringa (Petingo 135) [1989 12g4 16g5   **—**
12m3 16f* 18h* 20f 1990 12m5 12m] close-coupled gelding: quite modest winner as 5-y-o: faced stiffish task both outings in 1990: suited by test of stamina: acts well on very firm going: occasionally bandaged. *C. A. Horgan.*

KARENA'S LAD   3 ch.g. Chabrias (FR) 103–Karena Park (Hot Spark 126) [1989   **—**
NR 1990 a7g 10m 10m6] close-coupled gelding: second reported foal: dam close relation of very useful 6f and 1m winner Dun Habit, showed little worthwhile form: burly, no show in maiden and sellers. *J. L. Harris.*

KARENS PRINCE   3 b.g. Ampney Prince 96–Karen's Girl (Joshua 129) [1989   **—**
5g5 6s a7g a5g 1990 a6g] leggy gelding: has a round action: well beaten in varied races. *Mrs R. Wharton.*

KARENS STARLET   4 b.f. Ampney Prince 96–Karen's Girl (Joshua 129) [1989   **52**
5m 6f 5m5 9f5 10g4 1990 8g 8f 11m*] lengthy, dipped-backed filly: has a rather round action: showed improved form to win seller (sold to join P. Monteith's stable 3,000 gns) at Hamilton in August: appears better suited by 11f than shorter: acts on good to firm going: blinkered once: has looked none too easy a ride: trained first 2 outings by Mrs P. Barker. *M. D. Hammond.*

KARIBA DAM   2 b.c. (Feb 16) Damister (USA) 123–Flooding (USA) (Irish River   **60**
(FR) 131) [1990 8f4] 33,000Y: neat colt: first foal: dam unraced, from good American family: better for race and green, over 6 lengths fourth of 18, hard ridden 3f out then staying on well final ½f, to Mujaazif in maiden at Thirsk in September: will stay well: sold 5,200 gns Newmarket Autumn Sales. *J. H. M. Gosden.*

KARIM'S KID (IRE)   2 b.c. (Mar 16) Petorius 117–Light of Eire (USA)   **65**
(Majestic Light (USA)) [1990 5m4 6m2 6g 5g* 5m 5f2 5f4 bm2] IR 10,000F, 15,000Y: strong, workmanlike colt: fifth foal: half brother to fair 7f and 1m winner Aquaglow (by Caerleon) and useful Italian middle-distance winners by Glint of Gold and Arctic Tern: dam ran twice: quite modest performer: easy winner of maiden at Lingfield in June: mostly ran creditably after: speedy: pulled hard when running poorly in visor third outing: has hung right: not an easy ride. *R. Boss.*

KARINGA BAY   3 ch.c. Ardross 134–Handy Dancer 87 (Green God 128)   **114**
[1989 5f6 6m* 7g* 7.3d 1990 10m3 10.5g2 12g5 12m* 12g3 14.6g6]

Karinga Bay, the winner of two of his four races as a two-year-old, including the Washington Singer Stakes at Newbury, appeared to be the North's main classic hope for 1990. In fact he turned out to be its only serious contender, training on into a smart colt but some way behind the best of his generation. Karinga Bay made a good impression in his preparation for the Ever Ready Derby. On his last outing before Epsom he finished one and a half

Gordon Stakes, Goodwood–
Karinga Bay (third left) gradually wears down Starstreak and Blue Stag (rails);
Defensive Play takes fourth

lengths second to Sanglamore in the William Hill Dante Stakes at York, improving on his third to Defensive Play and Rock Hopper in the Guardian Classic Trial at Sandown on his seasonal reappearance, even though his bit had slipped. At York he gave the impression that he'd get the Derby distance and would be capable of further improvement, though he left a doubt as to whether he'd handle the unorthodox Epsom track. Confidence in his chance increased in the run-up to the race, particularly after Sanglamore won the Prix du Jockey-Club, and Karinga Bay started at 14/1 at Epsom. He did well to finish fifth, looking ill at ease on the track; he stayed on strongly to recover much of the ground he lost down Tattenham Hill and was beaten eight lengths by Quest For Fame.

Karinga Bay missed the Irish Derby, appearing next in the Gordon Stakes at Goodwood which had been won in each of the previous four seasons by a horse unplaced in the Derby—Allez Milord, Love The Groom, Minster Son and Warrshan. Karinga Bay turned Epsom tables on Blue Stag, but not before he'd again shown himself a difficult ride, especially on a sharp track. Rouse had to work hard to get him into contention, then to keep him there as the colt hung right. Karinga Bay is thoroughly genuine though, and he kept on to force his head in front of Starstreak and Blue Stag well inside the final furlong. Karinga Bay's main objective was now the St Leger. His preparation for it went much less encouragingly than for the Derby, for he was beaten very decisively into third place behind Belmez and Snurge in the Great Voltigeur Stakes at York; both beat him eight lengths, and the winner gave him 5 lb into the bargain. The Leger went much the same as the Voltigeur for Karinga Bay. Trained to the minute, looking in tremendous shape, he led early but was gradually left behind as the principals pressed for home. He finished just over nine lengths down on Snurge in sixth place.

Karinga Bay (ch.c. 1987)	Ardross (b 1976)	Run The Gantlet (b 1968)	Tom Rolfe / First Feather
		Le Melody (ch 1971)	Levmoss / Arctic Melody
	Handy Dancer (ch 1977)	Green God (ch 1968)	Red God / Thetis II
		Miss Golightly (ch 1972)	Jimmy Reppin / Gracious Gal

Karinga Bay will probably be returned to middle distances. There was no evidence at Doncaster that he stays so well as his sire or his brother, the modest Gydaros who won over a mile and three quarters. Karinga Bay was

Ardross' best winner in 1990. The dam stayed well for a daughter of two sprinters and won three races over a mile and a quarter; she is also the dam of the useful middle-distance stayer Roll A Dollar (by Spin of A Coin), a winner by The Brianstan and Karinga Bay's stable-companion Slender (by Aragon), a modest maiden. The third dam, Gracious Gal, was best at six or seven furlongs. The big, strong Karinga Bay, a fluent mover, seems suited by a sound surface. He should train on from three to four but unless he makes more than normal improvement he won't be easy to place in Britain. *Denys Smith.*

KARTAJANA 3 b.f. Shernazar 131–Karamita 119 (Shantung 132) [1989 NR **123** 1990 10m* 10m* 12d 10f* 12g² 10m* 10d⁶]

Karamita was the present Aga Khan's second pattern-race winner trained in Britain and it now looks as if her daughter Kartajana might be his second last. On November 20th the Aga Khan's 1989 Oaks winner Aliysa was disqualified as a result of a routine test showing up hydroxycamphor, a metabolite of the prohibited substance camphor, after which—on December 4th—the Aga Khan announced that his ninety or so horses trained in Britain would be removed and that he would not have a runner in Britain until the scientific management of racing here had reached a standard he considered acceptable. The central scientific issues of the case—whether that hydroxy-camphor had been produced by camphor at all and, as a corollary, whether camphor should be on the prohibited list anyway—cannot be entered into here. Suffice to say that they are complicated and controversial. The many implications of the case are largely contentious as well, except that the Aga Khan's withdrawal is a loss to horseracing in Britain, most directly, of course, to the stables of his trainers Stoute and Cumani. Every year the Aga Khan's massive breeding operation can be relied upon to produce horses worth their place in some of the best races in Europe. Now, unless the Aga Khan has a change of heart, none of them will be seen in Britain.

In 1990, the best here was Kartajana. Salt must have been rubbed in the wounds when she trailed in last of eight then had to have a routine dope test in her Gold Seal Oaks, a race for which she'd disputed favouritism over the preceding fortnight, but Kartajana went on to show that her Epsom run was an aberration. Before the Oaks she'd run twice and won twice. She's a far from imposing individual physique-wise, a moderate mover, and looked a bit back-ward as well before her debut, but word had clearly got out about her ability before that first run, in a Leicester maiden in April, as she was backed down to 11/4 on in a field of fifteen. A length victory gained a shade comfortably over Ambrose, the first two having drawn well clear, set Kartajana up for the William Hill Trial at Newbury and an even more clear-cut win, by three lengths from Katsina which left no doubts that her next race would be the

Vodafone Nassau Stakes, Goodwood—Kartajana wins from Starlet

Cheveley Park Stud Sun Chariot Stakes, Newmarket—same order, and Kartajana beats her rival more decisively this time

Oaks. Notwithstanding the fact that she had something to find against proven fillies Salsabil and In The Groove, Kartajana's performance at Epsom was lamentable. She showed a very short action to post, then if she was ever going well in the race it was only for the first half mile; she was ridden along vigorously at the top of the hill and that was the end of her challenge. Connections had no explanation at the time though it later emerged that Kartajana was slightly lame behind.

In the circumstances it wasn't surprising that the promise of her first two starts was largely forgotten and that she started third favourite of six in the Vodafone Nassau Stakes at Goodwood in early-August, backers preferring the Prix de Diane runner-up Moon Cactus and the much improved handicapper Starlet. The race was run at a good pace set, surprisingly, by Moon Cactus with the rest of the field needing to be niggled along to stay with her; but when Kartajana moved to the front over two furlongs out Moon Cactus quickly gave way and it was Starlet who did best of the pursuers, Kartajana beating her two lengths. As Kartajana was running on so strongly at the finish in the Nassau and it clearly hadn't been the trip that beat her in the Oaks, another try at a mile and a half seemed a risk well worth taking. It came in the Aston Upthorpe Yorkshire Oaks for which Swinburn had to make another enviable but difficult choice of rides; he sided with Kartajana, only to be beaten by stable-companion Hellenic. Three furlongs out Kartajana looked the winner, so easily had she taken the lead, but Hellenic got to her inside the last half furlong. The margin between them would have been about a length had Swinburn not snatched up Kartajana as Hellenic edged left in front of her close home. Back to a mile and a quarter and lesser company in the Cheveley Park Stud Sun Chariot Stakes at Newmarket, Kartajana won as easily as it had fleetingly appeared she might at York. She was clearly the best filly in the field and started 11/10 favourite but the way she trounced her six opponents couldn't be anticipated. Having chased the leaders on the outside, Kartajana took over nearing the Bushes and was out on her own by the furlong marker from which point Swinburn spent most of his time looking round at the rest, headed again by Starlet; then came Filia Ardross, Line of Thunder, Mamaluna, Arpero and Bex. Kartajana's eventual winning margin, misleadingly, was a length and a half. On the strength of that Kartajana also started favourite— she did so in five of her seven races—to beat In The Groove and the colts in the Champion Stakes but couldn't make it third time lucky for the Group 1 success. The dead ground, which she'd also encountered at Epsom, very probably contributed to her modest showing; she weakened up the hill and was eased.

Like so many of the Aga Khan's, Kartajana's family can read like an exhausting list of good winners. The fourth dam Baghicheh won the Prix de la Grotte and was placed in the Pouliches and Diane, the third dam Cherry was second in the Irish Oaks and produced the very useful French one-mile and thirteen-furlong winner Shahinaaz who, in her turn, produced that exception-

H. H. Aga Khan's "Kartajana"

			Busted (b 1963)	Crepello Sans Le Sou
	Shernazar (b 1981)			
		Sharmeen (b 1972)	Val de Loir Nasreen
Kartajana (b.f. 1987)				
		Shantung (b 1956)	Sicambre Barley Corn
	Karamita (b 1977)			
		Shahinaaz (b 1965)	Venture VII Cherry

ally game stayer Karadar and the dam of the smart globetrotting mile-and-a-quarter filly Khariyda. That's not to mention Kartajana's dam Karamita. She was a game and consistent filly with a good turn of foot, progressive too as she moved through the ranks to win a maiden and a handicap before the Extel Stakes at Goodwood then, on her final start, the Group 3 Princess Royal Stakes at Ascot. Karamita produced three living foals before Kartajana but only one of them raced—that, however, was Kazaviyna (by Blakeney) who, like her dam, won the Extel. Karamita didn't run at two years and neither did Kartajana or her year-younger brother Karazani, both of whom were late foals. Kartajana wasn't three years old when she ran in the Oaks. Her sire Shernazar was a late developer too, of course. He won the Alycidon Stakes, Geoffrey Freer and September Stakes (beating Slip Anchor) on the trot as a four-year-old before being knocked out of contention on the home turn when second favourite (coupled) for the Arc. On the debit side at stud, he's the first of seven not to have produced a winner from a mating with Dumka, Dumayla being their three-year-old of 1990, but his first crop also includes useful performers in Houmayoun and the Irish pair Outside Pressure and Cheering News as well as a high-class one in Kartajana. Kartajana has now been retired. A close-coupled, angular filly, she's a moderate mover who sometimes sweated in the preliminaries. She seemed ideally suited by a mile and a quarter, probably by a sound surface. *M. R. Stoute.*

KASAYID 3 br.c. Niniski (USA) 125–Raabihah 98 (Shirley Heights 130) [1989 NR **98** 1990 8m* 10.5g³ 12f* 16.2f³ 14.8m³ 20f³ 16g³] lengthy, lightly-made colt: moderate mover: first foal: dam 6f and 7f winner: fairly useful performer: won Newmarket Challenge Whip and maiden at Chepstow in May: best efforts in listed race at Newmarket and Goodwood Cup fifth and sixth starts: odds on, ran poorly in 3-runner minor event at Thirsk final one: stays 2½m: remains in training. *H. Thomson Jones.*

KASHMIR GOLD 2 ch.c. (Feb 8) Glint of Gold 128–Eastern House 83 (Habitat **51** 134) [1990 5f⁶ 6g 6g 7f a7g* a7g⁶ a8g 8.2g⁶ 10.6s] 2,300Y, 13,000 2-y-o: lengthy colt: poor mover: first foal: dam won over 7f and 1m: won seller (retained 4,400 gns) at Southwell in August: took keen hold and looked difficult ride penultimate start: stays 7f: blinkered final 2 starts: inconsistent: sold 600 gns Doncaster October Sales. *Pat Mitchell.*

KASHTALA 3 b.f. Lord Gayle (USA) 124–Khatima (Relko 136) [1989 NR 1990 8g **102** 8g* 10f³ 10m* 10g³ 10g³ 10.6v* 11s² 10.2s³] rangy, workmanlike filly: has a rather round action: third living foal: half-sister to 4-y-o Khaydara (by Indian King), useful 6f winner: dam French 12.5f winner: useful performer: won maiden at Carlisle in June and handicaps at Ripon in August and Haydock in October: creditable second in £7,600 handicap at Newbury, rallying well under very hard ride: will stay 1½m: goes well on heavy going: mulish in preliminaries fifth start, mounted outside paddock on next. *L. M. Cumani.*

KASHTEH (IRE) 2 b.f. (May 12) Green Desert (USA) 127–Klarifi 91 (Habitat **79** 134) [1990 6g 7m* 8g⁶ 8m⁴] 65,000Y: tall, leggy filly: has scope: half-sister to Irish middle-distance winner Ezy Koter (by Lomond): dam Irish 7f winner, is out of disqualified Irish Oaks winner Sorbus: won maiden at Newcastle in August: very good fourth in nursery at Yarmouth: had stiff task in between: stays 1m. *B. Hanbury.*

KATAHDIN 3 b.c. Sandhurst Prince 128–Grand Teton 64 (Bustino 136) [1989 6g **51** 7g⁶ 6f⁵ 6f⁴ 6g 1990 8m⁶ 7g³ 6f² 6s 6g⁶ 7m 8g*] neat colt: plating-class performer: ridden by 7-lb claimer, won 20-runner claimer at Leicester in July, leading inside final 1f: stays 1m: acts on firm going, and possibly unsuited by soft: sold 10,500 gns Newmarket July Sales. *G. Wragg.*

KATANGO BEAT 3 b.f. Dunbeath (USA) 127–Kittycatoo Katango (USA) **—** (Verbatim (USA)) [1989 7m 8.2f a8g 1990 a10g⁶ 10f³ 8h a11g 12m⁶ 10f⁶] angular filly: moderate walker: poor plater: twice blinkered: joined P. Blockley. *P. A. Blockley.*

KATES CABIN 3 ch.f. Habitat 134–Old Kate 110 (Busted 134) [1989 NR 1990 **96** 8m⁴ 8g* 8m⁴ 10s⁴ 9m² 10.2s⁶] good-bodied filly: carried condition: fourth foal: half-sister to 4-y-o 1¾m winner Take One (by Teenoso), very useful 11f and 1½m winner Kalakate (by Kalaglow) and Irish 1¼m winner Keepcalm (by Auction Ring), later listed winner in Italy: dam, 9f and 10.2f winner, is sister to very smart soft-ground stayer Old Bill: favourite, soon off bridle when winning maiden at Kempton in September: best efforts in listed race at Ascot and Newmarket minor event third and fifth starts: should have stayed 1¼m: probably unsuited by soft going: stud. *G. Wragg.*

KATHS CHOICE 2 b.f. (May 1) Dunbeath (USA) 127–Beaufort Star 95 (Great **45** Nephew 126) [1990 7m 6g 6d] 10,000Y: fourth living foal: half-sister to modest 1m and 10.6f winner Touching Star (by Touching Wood) and a winner in Italy by Julio Mariner: dam sprinting sister to Uncle Pokey: poor form in minor event and maidens. *H. J. Collingridge.*

KATHTEEN 4 b.f. Teenoso (USA) 135–Kath (Thatch (USA) 136) [1989 10g 8d **—** 8m³ 7m 7h 8m 1990 a8g 7m 6v 7m] lengthy filly: third in seller (sweating) as 3-y-o, only form: visored on reappearance. *D. H. Topley.*

KATHY COOK 5 b.m. Glenstal (USA) 118–Belmont Blue 75 (Kashmir II 125) **— §** [1989 16f 12m 16.2m³ 17f⁶ a16g 1990 18f] good-topped mare: moderate mover: unreliable maiden: stays 17f: acts on firm going: tail swisher: not genuine. *R. Hollinshead.*

KATHY FLYNN 2 b.f. (Feb 1) Import 127–Runasca 49 (Runnymede 123) [1990 **—** 5m 6d] 2,100Y: smallish, workmanlike filly: third foal: half-sister to plating-class 1986 2-y-o Run To Work (by Workboy): dam plater, ran only at 2 yrs: well beaten in seller and claimer: off course 5 months in between. *W. G. M. Turner.*

KATIE JO 4 b.f. Taufan (USA) 130–Wyn Mipet (Welsh Saint 126) [1989 8m 8m⁶ **73** 8g³ 7.6m² 9m² 1990 10.2f⁶ 10f² 9g* 10f 10g⁵ 10m 10g⁴ 10m³ 12m² 12m² 10.6d⁵ 12m³ 12g 10g² 10d* a12g* a12g⁴] stocky, quite attractive filly: showed improved form when winning well-contested handicap at Kempton in April: not as good later in season, including when justifying favouritism in seller (bought in 6,200 gns, then left M. Ryan's stable) at Folkestone and claimer at Lingfield in November: best efforts at around 1¼m on good ground (yet to race on very soft): good mount for apprentice. *J. Akehurst.*

KATIE SCARLETT 4 b.f. Lochnager 132–Final Request 63 (Sharp Edge 123) 49 d
[1989 7d⁴ 7g 6s⁶ 7f 5f 6f⁶ 6f 6m a8g a12g 1990 a10g* a16g⁴ 10f 12g 10g a10g] big, short-backed, workmanlike filly: good mover with a long stride: 25/1, form on flat for long time only when winning 7-runner Lingfield maiden in February: stays 1¼m: has run well when sweating and on edge, and when ridden by claimer: won novice hurdle in December. *J. J. Bridger.*

KATIES FIRST (USA) 3 b.f. Kris 135–Katies 125 (Nonoalco (USA) 131) [1989 98
NR 1990 7f⁵ 6f² 5h* 6d⁴ 5m 5m* 6m 5g 5g⁴ 5.6g² 5m 6m² 6s*] IR 105,000Y: sparely-made filly: first foal: dam won Coronation Stakes and Irish 1000 Guineas: fairly useful sprinter: made virtually all to win maiden at Bath in May, handicap at Chester in July and listed race (beat Nicholas 1½ lengths) at Doncaster in November: neck second in Tote-Portland Handicap at Doncaster and £8,400 handicap at Newmarket: looked most ill at ease on track at Epsom: acts on any going. *G. Lewis.*

KATIE VALENTINE 2 gr.f. (Feb 14) Belfort (FR) 89–Call Me Kate 72 46
(Firestreak 125) [1990 5m 5m⁴ 5g² 5g⁴ 6d 6m 6m³ 7g⁶ 7m 6d² 6v⁶ 6d 6s⁶] 4,400Y: rather sparely-made filly: seventh foal: sister to 3-y-o 6f winner Belfort Ruler and quite modest 1987 2-y-o 5f and 6f winner Defence Call, and half-sister to a winner in Denmark: dam 4-y-o 1¼m winner: poor maiden: suited by 6f: best form in visor: has worn bandages: changed hands 3,500 gns Newmarket Autumn Sales. *Dr J. D. Scargill.*

KATILIUM 2 br.f. (Apr 19) Ilium 121–Hunt's Katie (Daring March 116) [1990 a7g] —
first foal: dam, maiden probably stayed 1m: slowly away and always well behind in 12-runner maiden at Lingfield in December. *J. White.*

KATSINA (USA) 3 b.f. Cox's Ridge (USA)–Katsura (USA) (Northern Dancer) 98
[1989 7f² 7g* 1990 10m³ 10m² 10g 9g⁶ 9m³] compact, good-quartered filly: fairly useful performer: ran well in listed races at Newbury and Newmarket second and fourth outings: ran as if something amiss in Group 2 event at the Curragh in between: would have stayed 1½m: stud. *B. W. Hills.*

KATSUE 3 ch.g. Noalto 120–Gamma (GER) (Zank) [1989 7f 10g 1990 10g 12m 11d] —
close-coupled, plain gelding: poor plater: blinkered final start. *Miss L. C. Siddall.*

KATWIL 2 b.c. (Feb 18) Gabitat 119–Pas de Chat (Relko 136) [1990 5m³ 5m* 5m⁵ 88
6m* 6m⁶ 6s⁴] compact colt: moderate mover: brother to 3-y-o Wilvick, 5.8f (at 2 yrs) and 7f winner, and half-brother to thoroughly unreliable 5f and 7f winner Jovick (by Swing Easy): dam ran twice: progressive colt, successful at Windsor in maiden in June and nursery in July: first run for nearly 3 months and bandaged near-fore, excellent staying-on fourth in nursery at Newbury final start: better suited by 6f than 5f: acts on good to firm ground and soft: sold only 2,100 gns Newmarket Autumn Sales. *R. Akehurst.*

KATY LOU 4 gr.f. Nishapour (FR) 125–Emmylou (Arctic Tern (USA) 126) [1989 —
10f 8h⁴ 12f⁵ 10.1m 10.1m⁶ 10f⁴ 12h⁶ 1990 a12g] small, lengthy filly: poor form: probably stays 1¼m: blinkered or visored last 5 outings: races freely: winning hurdler. *Miss B. Sanders.*

KATY'S LAD 3 b.c. Camden Town 125–Cathryn's Song (Prince Tenderfoot 66
(USA) 126) [1989 5s* 5s³ 5m⁶ 7.5f⁴ 7g⁴ 7m⁴ 8.2g² 1990 7m⁵ 9m² 8m* 10.6f³ 8.5d³ 8f 7.6g⁶ 8.5m 8f⁶ a8g 9m⁵ 8m 10.8m⁴ 10.4d⁵] leggy colt: has a quick action: quite modest handicapper: made most to win at Warwick in April: stays 1¼m: seems to act on any going: has worn blinkers, but best form without: inconsistent. *B. A. McMahon.*

KATY'S PET 2 b.f. (Mar 3) Tina's Pet 121–Our Katy 68 (Dragonara Palace (USA) 68
115) [1990 6g³ 6m⁵ 6g³ 6g⁵ 6d²] 420F, 8,000Y: smallish, sparely-made filly: second foal: dam won two 6f sellers: quite modest maiden: will be better suited by 7f. *D. Morley.*

KATZAKEENA 3 b.f. Gorytus (USA) 132–Current Bay (Tyrant (USA)) [1989 94
5g² 5g² 6g² 1990 6g* 6f³ 5m* 6m* 5m³ 6m⁵ 6m⁴ 6g⁶] close-coupled, good-quartered filly: fairly useful performer: justified favouritism in maiden at Nottingham in April then £7,600 handicap at Newcastle and £23,500 William Hill Trophy Handicap at York in June, making virtually all first occasion then held up afterwards:

William Hill Trophy (Handicap), York—Katzakeena withstands the late rally
of the grey Norton Challenger on Timeform Charity Day.
The twentieth annual Charity Day had record-breaking receipts topping £120,000,
which raised the overall total to £1,350,000

ran well in listed races sixth and seventh starts, moderately (blinkered and edgy) on final one: stays 6f: acts on firm going. *P. J. Makin.*

KAWARAU QUEEN 3 b.f. Taufan (USA) 119–Hasty Goddess 72 (Nebbiolo 125) **67**
[1989 5g 5m³ 5m² 5g² 1990 8.2g³ 8g³ 7.5g³ 8.2m* 8g³ 9m 8m 6g⁴ 6d 8m 6d] workmanlike, deep-girthed filly: modest performer: mostly below form after winning maiden auction race at Hamilton in June: stays 1m: acts on good to firm ground: ran wide into straight and swished tail at Ripon seventh start: has sweated. *S. G. Norton.*

Leslie And Godwin Spitfire Handicap, Goodwood—
blinkered Kawtuban is produced late to catch Aromatic (No. 2) and Baylis

KAWTUBAN 3 b.c. Law Society (USA) 130–Thünderflash (FR) (Northfields **100**
(USA)) [1989 6m 1990 7f⁵ 6m⁴ 7d 8f* 8g 9m² 10m² 10f* 12g⁴ 12m³ 10m] leggy colt:
useful handicapper: won at Salisbury in May and £31,600 Leslie And Godwin Spitfire
Handicap (sweating and edgy, led post) at Goodwood in August: stays 1½m: best on
top-of-the-ground: ran poorly for 5-lb claimer: blinkered 3 times, including when
virtually running away with his jockey on final outing: formerly coltish and somewhat temperamental in preliminaries: to join D. Hayes in Australia. *R. Charlton.*

KAWWAS 5 b.h. Persian Bold 123–Tifrums 77 (Thatch (USA) 136) [1989 8g 8d **61**
6f³ 7m⁵ 6f* 7f 7f⁵ 6g³ 7m⁶ 7g 6m 1990 7g 7g² 7g² 7f* 8h⁶ 7m 7f² 8m 7m 8d 8m]
smallish, attractive horse: poor mover: quite modest handicapper: well-backed
favourite, won at Yarmouth in July: stays 7f: seems to need a sound surface:
blinkered once: sometimes gets on toes, and has sweated: has given trouble at stalls
and tended to hang: inconsistent. *W. Holden.*

KAYEMBEE 2 b.g. (Apr 16) Trojan Fen 118–By Surprise 68 (Young Generation **47**
129) [1990 5m 6m 7m 6g 7f⁵ 6m 6f⁵] 7,600Y: compact, rather dipped-backed gelding:
carries condition: good mover: second foal: brother to 3-y-o 7f and 1m winner
Sapphirine: dam 1m winner from family of Little Wolf: poor maiden: needs further
than 6f: visored fourth outing: bandaged near-hind penultimate start: had tongue
tied down final one. *C. Tinkler.*

KAYMONT 2 b.f. (Mar 26) Germont–Kaymay 76 (Maystreak 118) [1990 6d⁶ 5s] **—**
workmanlike filly: fifth reported living foal: half-sister to 1988 2-y-o 5f winner Brave
Melody (by Heroic Air): dam won at up to 1m: well beaten in autumn claimers at
Catterick and Edinburgh. *Capt. J. Wilson.*

K-BRIDGE DOMINION 4 b.g. Dominion 123–Mariko (Dancer's Image **—**
(USA)) [1989 10g 12f⁵ 10.1m 10g 12m 1990 10.1m 8.3m] leggy, good-topped gelding:
moderate mover: form only on second outing as 3-y-o: bandaged on reappearance,
blinkered next start. *G. G. Gracey.*

K-BRIGADE 3 b.h. Brigadier Gerard 144–Kajetana (FR) (Caro 133) [1989 8g² **54**
10g⁴ 12d⁶ 10f 12.4g 10g⁶ a16g³ 1990 13v⁴] big horse: modest handicapper at best:
stays 2m: possibly not at his best on firm going, acts on any other: visored once at 4
yrs: lacks a turn of foot and is normally ridden up with pace: game. *C. W. C. Elsey.*

K C RAPIDE 3 b.c. Rapid River 127–Duty Watch 40 (Import 127) [1989 NR 1990 **55**
6m² 5d 5m⁵ 6d a7g] smallish, sturdy colt: second foal: half-brother to 4-y-o
Hakedma (by Van Der Linden): dam sprint plater: plating-class form: moved poorly
down and withdrawn under veterinary advice intended fourth start: off course 4
months and showed little after: stays 6f. *R. Hollinshead.*

KEEN EDGE 6 b.h. Good Times (ITY)–Razor Blade 65 (Sharp Edge 123) [1989 **67**
5s 5s⁴ 6f* 6m⁵ 6f³ 6m 6f 6f 6f⁵ 6f⁴ 6m⁵ 5m 1990 5m⁴ 5m⁴ 6m] small, compact horse:
quite modest handicapper: speedy, and best at sprint distances: probably acts on any
going: has worn blinkers, but not since 1987: sold 2,100 gns Newmarket Autumn
Sales: genuine. *P. Mitchell.*

KEEN HUNTER (USA) 3 ch.c. Diesis 133–Love's Reward (Nonoalco (USA) **110 p**
131) [1989 6g⁵ 1990 6m* 6m* 6m⁵] tall, quite attractive colt: odds on, most
impressive in winning small-field minor events at Nottingham and Newmarket in
June: 4/1, 4¾ lengths fifth of 9 to Royal Academy in strongly-run Carroll Foundation
July Cup at Newmarket, leading over 1f out then no extra: looked very smart
performer in the making. *J. Gosden.*

KEEN MELODY (USA) 3 b.f. Sharpen Up 127–Sweet Abandon (USA) **60 d**
(Lyphard (USA) 132) [1989 6g 6f⁶ 8f⁶ 1990 8m⁶ 8g⁶ 7m² 8g 7m 7g a10g a7g⁶] small,
sparely-made filly: quite modest maiden: below form after second in handicap at
Warwick in August: stays 1m: acts on good to firm ground: blinkered (slowly away)
final outing: hung left second: changed hands 2,800 gns Newmarket December
Sales. *R. Hannon.*

KEEN VISION (IRE) 2 b.c. (May 4) Vision (USA)–Calvino (Relkino 131) [1990 **43**
7m 7g 7g] 6,000F: workmanlike colt: fourth foal: half-brother to 1987 2-y-o 7f
winner Y V Tucker (by Valiyar) and temperamental maiden Regal Vine (Prince
Tenderfoot): dam second over 7f at 2 yrs in Ireland: poor form in autumn maidens,
backward first 2 starts. *D. W. P. Arbuthnot.*

KEEP BIDDING 4 br.g. Hays 120–Keep Chanting (Auction Ring (USA) 123) **46**
[1989 8g 8m 8m³ 6m 10s 1990 7.5m 7f 7f² 8m² 8g³ 12f* 9f 12g 10.2g] big, lengthy
gelding: has a round action: poor handicapper: beat sole rival Glastondale by head at
Thirsk in July: ran moderately last 3 outings: seems to stay 1½m: acts on firm going:
sometimes blinkered: winner twice over hurdles in autumn. *M. W. Easterby.*

KEEP IN TRIM 2 ch.f. (Mar 3) Pharly (FR) 130–Silverhall (Sparkler 130) [1990 — 6g] workmanlike filly: third foal: half-sister to 3-y-o Silver Lodge (by Homing): dam unraced half-sister to Swiss Maid: backward, behind from halfway in maiden at Newbury in August: moved poorly down. *D. Marks.*

KEEP LOOKING (USA) 3 b.f. Mr Prospector (USA)–Kind Hope (USA) — (Chieftain II) [1989 NR 1990 7g 8m 10.2f4] sturdy filly: third foal: half-sister to Kindled (by Mummy's Pet), modest 6f winner here successful over middle distances in Belgium in 1990: dam unraced half-sister to Known Fact: showed signs of ability in 3 summer maidens: favourite, stumbled early on final start. *J. H. M. Gosden.*

KEEP YOUR WORD 4 ch.f. Castle Keep 121–So True 116 (So Blessed 130) 72 [1989 10f 9m3 10m 1990 10g 8m 8g* 8f 9g* 9s2 10.6v5 10d5] tall, sparely-made filly: poor walker: moderate mover: successful in handicaps at Chepstow in June and Kempton (apprentices) in September: ran very well next outing: should stay 1¼m: acts well on soft going, probably not at best on firm. *G. B. Balding.*

KELLYEM 3 gr.f. Absalom 128–Pitroyal 74 (Pitskelly 122) [1989 NR 1990 8m — 8.5m] 3,700Y: leggy, sparely-made filly: third foal: half-sister to modest 16.2f winner Par Avion (by Beldale Flutter): dam won over 1½m: well beaten in minor event and claimer (12/1 from 25/1) in April. *W. G. M. Turner.*

KELLYS KINGDOM (IRE) 2 b.c. (Mar 17) King Persian 107–Kellys Risc 65 (Pitskelly 122) [1990 5m 5f4 5m2 5m* 6m4 6m2 6f4 6m 6m4 a8g] 4,800Y: small, compact colt: moderate walker and mover: second reported living foal: dam unraced: modest performer: last-stride winner of maiden auction at Catterick in April: mostly ran creditably in nuseries afterwards though well beaten final start: suited by 6f: has run creditably for 7-lb claimer. *R. A. Bennett.*

KELLY'S KITE 2 br.f. (Feb 29) Buzzards Bay 128§–Bold Kelly 83 (Pitskelly — 122) [1990 5g 6g] leggy filly: second foal: dam 2-y-o 6f winner: little worthwhile form in autumn maidens at Wolverhampton and Folkestone. *H. J. Collingridge.*

KELTIE (USA) 2 ch.c. (Feb 29) Storm Bird (CAN) 134–Classy Twist (USA) 78 (Twist The Axe (USA)) [1990 8m3 8d3 10.2s2] sturdy, long-backed colt: half-brother to 2 winners in USA by Fappiano, including 9f graded-stakes winner With A Twist: dam stakes-placed winner at up to 1m in USA from 3 yrs to 5 yrs: placed in maidens at Leicester and a minor event (staying-on second to Persian Halo) at Doncaster in autumn: acts on good to firm ground and soft going: capable of winning a race over middle distances. *G. Harwood.*

KEMBLA 2 br.f. (Jan 27) Known Fact (USA) 135–Oscura (USA) 82 (Caro 133) 59 [1990 5.8h*] second foal: dam 1m winner, is half-sister to champion grass horse Johnny D: won 5-runner minor event at Bath in August by ½ length from Marynetta, leading over 1f out then green and hanging badly: sold 7,400 gns Newmarket Autumn Sales. *R. Charlton.*

KENILWORTH CASTLE 4 b.c. Dunbeath (USA) 127–Ravenshead (Charlot- 61 town 127) [1989 14f6 14f3 15.3f 18g6 1990 a14g2 a13g* a12g5] leggy colt: made all in handicap at Southwell in January: stays 1¾m: blinkered at 4 yrs: winning hurdler in 1989/90. *R. Hollinshead.*

KENTFIELD 3 b.f. Busted 134–Girton 68 (Balidar 133) [1989 NR 1990 11.7m6] — angular, sparely-made filly: sixth foal: half-sister to useful Irish 4-y-o sprinter Puissance (by Thatching), 5f winner Moorestyle Girl (by Moorestyle) and a winner in Denmark: dam won over 5f and 6f: bit backward, well beaten in maiden at Bath in July. *M. R. Stoute.*

KENTON LADY 2 br.f. (Apr 2) Carriage Way 107–Parade Girl 57 (Swing Easy — (USA) 126) [1990 5m] first foal: dam suited by 5f: never dangerous in seller at Thirsk in May. *Denys Smith.*

KENTRA 4 ch.f. Grey Ghost 98–La Raine 93 (Majority Blue 126) [1989 5s2 5f 5m6 49 5m 1990 6m 5m3 5d3 a5g3 a5g3 a5g6 a5g6] lengthy, angular filly: keen walker: has a quick action: plating-class maiden: best at 5f: acts on good to firm and soft going: blinkered final start at 3 yrs: sweating on reappearance: apprentice ridden first 6 outings: sold 1,150 gns Doncaster September Sales. *T. D. Barron.*

KERFUFFLE (USA) 5 ch.g. Irish River (FR) 131–Women's Wear (USA) — (Groton) [1989 NR 1990 14.6f 12m6 11.7f5 15.5f a16g] rather leggy gelding: fifth foal: half-brother to 3 graded-stakes winners: dam 2-y-o winner in North America: won NH Flat race at Lingfield in February: little sign of ability otherwise: sold out of G. Harwood's stable 3,200 gns Newmarket Autumn Sales after fourth outing. *Dr J. D. Scargill.*

KERRY BOY 3 ch.g. Sallust 134–Silk Imp 72 (Imperial Fling (USA) 116) [1989 — NR 1990 a7g⁶ a7g³ a6g⁶ 6m 7g⁵ 12.5g 7d] 5,600Y: small, sturdy gelding: first foal: dam 1m winner stayed 1¼m: poor maiden: tailed off in July seller final start: should be suited by 1m +: trained first 6 starts by M. Tompkins. *P. J. Feilden.*

KESTREL FORBOXES (IRE) 2 b.g. (May 9) Seymour Hicks (FR) 90 125–Dance Mistress (Javelot 124) [1990 5m⁶ 5f² 5g³ 5.8m* 6m* 6f⁶ 6f* 6m³ 6g⁵] IR 3,800F, IR 5,000Y: close-coupled, fair sort: moderate mover: half-brother to 3 winners, including fairly useful stayer Sunley Builds (by Patch) and 1m seller winner Hunky (by Nonoalco): dam from same family as Nonoalco: fair performer: made all in maiden auction at Bath, seller (bought in 8,200 gns) at York and nursery at Windsor in summer: will be suited by 7f: game, genuine and consistent. *J. Berry.*

KESTREL KAYSIS (IRE) 2 b.f. (Apr 27) Soughaan (USA) 111–Faradiya — § (Rusticaro (FR) 124) [1990 5f⁴] IR 900Y, resold 700Y: compact filly: first foal: dam French maiden: bit backward, last of 4 in maiden auction at Wolverhampton in April: unseated rider to post then, and again before being withdrawn from seller there in May: clearly temperamental. *J. Berry.*

KEVINSBELLE 2 b.f. (Mar 25) Belfort (FR) 89–Manna Green (Bustino 136) 64 [1990 5m⁶ 5m² 5f⁵ 7f² 7f* 7m 7f 6m 7d] 5,400Y: close-coupled filly: fifth foal: half-sister to 3 winners, including 9f claimer winner Taxi Man (by Dublin Taxi): dam ran twice: quite modest performer: ridden by 7-lb claimer and on toes, readily made all in maiden auction at Redcar in August: ran moderately after, pulling hard first 3 occasions: better suited by 7f than 5f. *E. Eldin.*

KEVINSLINE (IRE) 2 b.c. (May 17) Montelimar (USA) 122–Priceless Pin 33 (Saint Crespin III 132) [1990 5f 5m 5g 7f 7g] 3,200Y: leggy colt: half-brother to several winners, including fairly useful 7f to 2m winner Weavers' Pin (by Weavers' Hall) and modest 6f and 7f performer Nawwar (by Thatching): dam ran twice at 2 yrs in Ireland: poor form in maiden auctions and a claimer. *E. Eldin.*

KHALAFIYA 3 b.f. Darshaan 133–Khalisyin 96 (Shakapour 125) [1989 8d² 1990 104 8g* 8g² 10m⁵ 12g* 12d] first foal: dam 3-y-o 1m and 7f winner: won maiden at Leopardstown in March and EBF Meld Stakes (by length from Crockadore) at the Curragh in August: well beaten in Blandford Stakes at the Curragh final start: stays 1½m. *J. Oxx, Ireland.*

KHARIF 6 b.g. Formidable (USA) 125–Pass The Rulla (USA) (Buckpasser) [1989 42 12d 12g² 13m⁵ 15s 1990 16m*] well-made gelding: poor handicapper: has looked none too keen, but did nothing wrong (given excellent ride) when winning slowly-run handicap at Newcastle in March: effective from 1½m to 2m: acts on good to firm and dead going: best form without blinkers or visor: well suited by waiting tactics and tender handling: much improved hurdler. *R. Allan.*

KHAYAMOUR 4 gr.c. Habitat 134–Khayra (FR) (Zeddaan 130) [1989 8m³ 1990 71 6g⁴ 8g 8g] smallish, angular colt: moderate mover: modest form at best: harshly treated in handicap final outing: better suited by 1m than 6f. *R. F. Johnson Houghton.*

KHAYDARA 4 b.f. Indian King (USA) 128–Khatima (Relko 136) [1989 7g⁵ 7g³ 86 6m* 6m³ 6m² 6g* 5g 1990 6f⁴ 6d 6m 7.2g 6m] big, strong, good-bodied filly: has a quick action: progressed into useful performer as 3-y-o, winner of quite valuable contests at Newmarket and York: shaped well on reappearance, but below form afterwards: suited by 6f: acts on firm going, possibly unsuited by dead. *L. M. Cumani.*

KHIOS (USA) 3 b.g. Lord Gaylord (USA)–Monelia (USA) (Mongo) [1989 8m⁵ 6d — 1990 8f 12 5g 16.2d 10f 10m] compact gelding: no worthwhile form: heavily bandaged on reappearance: changed hands 7,000 gns Newmarket July Sales after third start: winning hurdler. *F. Durr.*

KHOJOHN 2 ch.g. (Feb 29) Chief Singer 131–Pirate Lass (USA) 90 (Cutlass 43 (USA)) [1990 5g 6s 6g⁶ 6g 8d] 10,500Y: plain gelding: second foal: half-brother to 1989 2-y-o 1¼m seller winner Fyfield House (by Gorytus): dam 6f and 7f winner at 2 yrs, is out of half-sister to smart Father Hogan: poor maiden: stays 1m. *C. W. C. Elsey.*

KHOREVO 5 b.g. Tyrnavos 129–Amina 80 (Brigadier Gerard 144) [1989 8s 10s 39 § 8d 5f a11g 1990 10f* 10.8m 10.1g 8g 10f 12f³ 12f²] sturdy gelding: moderate mover: made all in selling handicap (no bid) at Folkestone in April: suited by middle distances: acts on firm going, possibly unsuited by soft: visored first 2 and last 2 starts: apprentice ridden in 1990: reluctant to race fourth outing at 4 yrs: not one to rely on. *I. Campbell.*

KHULM 3 b.c. Kafu 120–Little Wild Duck 78 (Great Heron (USA) 127) [1989 6m 66 6g 1990 6m⁶ 5m 6f* 6m⁴ 6m 5m 7m³ 8m⁵ 7g 8m] leggy, close-coupled colt: quite modest performer: sweating and on toes, won maiden at Newmarket in May, leading close home: well worth a try over further: acts on firm going: hung right for 7-lb claimer: joined M. Madgwick. *L. J. Holt.*

KIBBLE 4 ch.f. Kabour 80–Hilly's Daughter (Hillandale 125) [1989 NR 1990 a6g a8g a8g 6m] strong filly: first foal: dam no form in modest company: no worthwhile form: broke out of stalls fourth intended outing: dead. *D. W. Chapman.* —

KIBREET 3 ch.g. Try My Best (USA) 130–Princess Pageant 95 (Welsh Pageant 132) [1989 NR 1990 11d 8f 7g⁵ 8m 10.1m⁴ 8g² 8g 8m⁴ 10d²] 17,500F, IR 50,000Y: lengthy, workmanlike gelding: has scope: fourth foal: brother to useful Italian 1987 2-y-o Pink Jam and closely related to Vaga Pierina (by Northfields), prolifically successful in Italy at 1¼m: dam 7f to 1½m winner later placed in USA: capable of fair form: best effort strong-finishing second in Goodwood claimer final start: will prove better at 1¼m than 1m: acts on good to firm ground and dead: has run creditably for 7-lb claimer: inconsistent: winning hurdler. *D. R. C. Elsworth.* 80

KICKED OUT 2 br.c. (Apr 7) Undulate (USA)–Midsummer Girl (Midsummer Night II 117) [1990 6m 6f 7m] angular colt: fourth live foal: dam won over hurdles: no show, including in seller: hung left soon after start and pulled up at halfway (got loose to start) on debut. *B. Stevens.* —

KID LEWIS 3 b.g. Thatching 131–Mirkan Honey 83 (Ballymore 123) [1989 7m 7m 1990 8.2s⁶ 7g 7d² 8m 8d] quite attractive gelding: good walker: quite modest maiden: ran poorly in claimers last 2 starts: should stay 1m: easily best effort on dead going: found nothing under pressure final start, and is probably ungenuine: sold to join Mrs A. Knight 2,250 gns Ascot November Sales. *J. L. Dunlop.* 64 §

KIEGY 2 b.f. (Feb 6) Mansingh (USA) 120–Blickling 64 (Blakeney 126) [1990 5g 6g] 7,000Y: smallish filly: seventh foal: sister to 7f winner S D Demo and a winner over hurdles, and half-sister to 1½m to 2m winner Saxon Court (by Mummy's Game) and a winner in Spain: dam needed long distances: well beaten in maidens (backward and slowly away on debut) at Carlisle in spring. *G. Richards.* —

KILDONAN 3 b.g. Welsh Captain 113–Madam Import 63 (Import 127) [1989 6h² 7f 7m 8.2f⁴ 8.5f* 8.2f⁴ 8f⁵ 1990 a8g⁵ a7g² a8g⁴ a10g² a10g 12f] big, good-topped gelding: carries condition: quite modest handicapper: well beaten last 2 outings, off course 4½ months in between: stays 1¼m: acts on firm ground: sold out of T. Barron's stable 7,000 gns Doncaster March Sales after fifth start. *P. A. Blockley.* 60

KILGETTY 4 b.c. Welsh Saint 126–Duchess 91 (Electrify) [1989 NR 1990 8.5g⁶] second reported foal: dam 2-y-o 7f and 1m winner, later successful in Belgium: 33/1, well beaten in maiden at Beverley in May. *M. J. Camacho.* —

KILLIMOR LAD 3 b.c. Tina's Pet 121–Jeldi 58 (Tribal Chief 125) [1989 7s 7m 1990 8m 8.2s] sparely-made colt: has a quick action: poor maiden. *M. McCormack.* —

KILLINGHALL (IRE) 2 b.c. (May 11) Glow (USA)–Joma Kaanem (Double Form 130) [1990 5d 5f³ 6g] IR 22,000Y: lengthy, good-quartered colt with scope: third foal: half-brother to fair miler Fenjaan (by Trojan Fen): dam ran once at 3 yrs in Ireland, is out of sister to smart Selhurst and half-sister to Royal Palace: third of 13 in maiden at Catterick in September: raced keenly on unfavoured part of track following month: should stay 6f. *J. W. Watts.* 55

KIMBERLEY PARK 2 b.f. (Jun 4) Try My Best (USA) 130–Georgina Park 88 (Silly Season 127) [1990 a6g⁶ 5m⁴ 5d] compact filly: fifth foal: half-sister to 3 winners, including fairly useful miler Sandicliffe Star (by High Top) and useful sprinter Melody Park (by Music Boy): dam 2-y-o 7f winner: fourth in minor event at Pontefract in October: worth another try over 6f: possibly unsuited by a soft surface. *J. Wharton.* 62

KIMBERS (IRE) 2 b.c. (Apr 24) Lomond (USA) 128–Take Your Mark (USA) (Round Table) [1990 8g 7m* 7.6s⁴] IR 36,000F, IR 47,000Y: lengthy, useful-looking colt: good mover: closely related to Irish 1¼m winner Dame Kiri (by Sadler's Wells) and 2000 Guineas runner-up Charmer (by Be My Guest), later winner at up to 13.3f, and half-brother to 2 other winners: dam lightly-raced half-sister to dam of Leading Counsel: won minor event at Ascot by 1½ lengths from Balaat, leading over 1f out and staying on strongly: 6 lengths fourth of 6 to Time Line in listed event at Lingfield later in October: will probably stay 1¼m. *C. R. Nelson.* 93

KINDLY LADY 2 b.f. (Mar 2) Kind of Hush 118–Welcome Honey 70 (Be Friendly 130) [1990 5.3f⁶ 5m 5f⁴ 5g a6g a8g] 2,000F, 800Y: leggy, rather sparely-made filly: half-sister to a poor animal: dam won 1m claimer: of little account. *C. J. Hill.* —

KIND OF SHY 4 ch.f. Kind of Hush 118–Peta 93 (Petingo 135) [1989 8.5f 9f 8g 38 8m² 8.2f² 8.2g 7.5m² a8g a11g 1990 a7g a8g 8.2m⁶ 9f 8f⁶ 8f⁴ 8f⁴ 8m 10.2s] leggy, sparely-made filly: poor plater: stays 1m: suited by top-of-the-ground: blinkered once: takes keen hold. *R. Hollinshead.*

KIND STYLE (IRE) 2 ch.c. (Apr 5) Doulab (USA) 115–Dankalia (Le Levanstell 60 122) [1990 5f³ 5m 5g 5g 6g 6g³ 6g 8f² 8m 8d a8g a8g⁵ a8g³] IR 12,000F, 5,600Y: compact colt: moderate walker and mover: half-brother to several winners here and abroad, including fairly useful 1984 2-y-o 6f winner Dan Thatch (by Thatch): dam winner at 3 yrs in Italy: quite modest maiden: seems suited by 1m: acts on firm going: tends to hang, and looks difficult ride. *R. Hollinshead.*

KING AL 3 b.c. Indian King (USA) 128–Impudent Miss 105 (Persian Bold 123) 97 [1989 6g³ 6m* 6f² 6g 1990 8f² 7f² 7g 8m³ 7.6f* 8m⁶ 7m* 7m] leggy colt: quite useful performer: won handicaps at Lingfield in July and Newmarket in August: possibly in need of race when well beaten in £71,900 handicap at Ascot final start: best at around 7f: acts on firm going: usually ridden up with pace: tends to wander under pressure. *Dr J. D. Scargill.*

KING ARBRO 3 b.c. Tumble Wind (USA)–Double Habit (Double Form 130) 78 [1989 NR 1990 7f² 7f² 8.2g² 6f* 6f* 6m] 16,500F, IR 42,000Y: strong, lengthy colt: second foal: half-brother to 4-y-o 6f and 7f winner Too Eager (by Nishapour): dam never ran: won apprentice maiden at Pontefract and minor event (on toes, made all) at Folkestone in July: looked extremely well but ran moderately in handicap final start: best at 6f: acts on firm going: sold 6,400 gns Newmarket Autumn Sales. *B. W. Hills.*

KING CRACKER 3 ch.c. King of Clubs 124–Brenda (Sovereign Path 125) [1989 54 6m⁴ 1990 9m⁴ 8m⁶ 10f⁵ 10f 15m³] leggy, close-coupled colt: has light, quick action: plating-class maiden: sweating and edgy, didn't handle turn or look keen in Edinburgh handicap final start: probably stays 15f: claimed out of L. Cumani's stable £12,555 second start. *M. D. Hammond.*

KING DANCER 3 b.c. Kafu 120–Gay Parthia 84 (Gay Fandango (USA) 132) — [1989 NR 1990 8m] IR 4,600Y: sturdy colt: fourth foal: half-brother to winning sprinter Laleston (by Junius): dam won twice over 5f at 2 yrs, her only starts: 25/1, moved badly down and tailed off in seller at Carlisle in June. *M. Brittain.*

KING FERDINAND 3 b.c. King of Spain 121–Gundi 57 (Mummy's Pet 125) — [1989 NR 1990 7g] 29,000Y: workmanlike colt: fourth reported foal: brother to plating-class maiden King Trevisio and half-brother to useful sprinter Orient (by Bay Express): dam poor maiden: 20/1, burly and green, last of 11 in mixed-aged contest at Newmarket in November: moved moderately to post. *P. J. Makin.*

KING HIGH 3 b.c. Shirley Heights 130–Regal Twin (USA) 77 (Majestic Prince) 91 § [1989 8m⁶ 1990 10m⁶ 14g² 16g² 17.6m* 17.6g] rather leggy, lengthy colt: carries condition: moderate mover: fair form in maidens, facing simple task to land odds at Wolverhampton in July: ducked badly left at stalls and found little final 2f when putting up best effort previous start: tailed off in handicap (very edgy) on final one: stays well: blinkered last 2 starts: lacks turn of foot: sold to join Dr J. Scargill 5,200 gns Newmarket Autumn Sales: one to be wary of. *J. L. Dunlop.*

KING MARCOS (USA) 3 b.c. His Majesty (USA)–Spanish Fake (USA) (Sham 67 (USA)) [1989 NR 1990 11.5m²] $12,000Y: small, workmanlike colt: half-brother to a winner in North America by Silent Screen: dam very useful stakes winner at up to 1m: sire very smart winner at up to 9f. 10/1, ridden by 7-lb claimer and wearing tongue strap, short-head second of 10 in maiden at Lingfield in June: will be suited by further. *B. Hanbury.*

KING NODDY 2 b.c. (Apr 8) Starch Reduced 112–Kathy King (Space King 115) 48 [1990 5m 5m⁶ 5m 5g 6g⁵ 7f 7m 8m² 8.2g 8d a8g a7g] leggy colt: moderate mover: brother to useful sprinter Kathred, 3-y-o Atlantic Clear, 2 poor animals and a winner in Sweden, and half-brother to poor 6f to 1m winner Little Newington (by Most Secret): dam well beaten: good second to Runham in selling nursery at Leicester: little other form: suited by 1m: raced too freely in visor seventh start: not one to rely on. *B. Palling.*

KING OF MILEEN 4 b.g. Castle Keep 121–Port Meadow 83 (Runnymede 123) 67 [1989 10.1m 8f³ 10.1m 10.6s 10g⁴ 10g 1990 10m⁶ a8g 8.3m³ 10f³ 8.2m⁴ 10g⁶] lengthy, quite attractive gelding: quite modest handicapper: stays 1¼m: acts on firm ground (shaped well on soft). *W. Carter.*

KING OF SAILORS 6 br.g. King of Spain 121–Found At Sea (USA) (Pieces of — Eight 128) [1989 5g 10s 8f a8g a14g a16g⁵ 1990 a14g⁵ a8g] rangy, angular gelding: has shown only a modicum of ability: blinkered first 3 starts at 5 yrs: sold 2,000 gns Doncaster October Sales. *R. Thompson.*

KING OF SHADOWS 3 b. or br.c. Connaught 130–Rhiannon 65 (Welsh   —
Pageant 132) [1989 NR 1990 10.4m[5] 14d 16.5d[6] a12g[5] a12g] sturdy colt: fourth foal: brother to a middle-distance winner in Italy and half-brother to modest 7f winner Prince of The Lake (by Lochnager): dam stayed 1m as 2-y-o: well beaten, in claimer final start. *R. Hollinshead.*

KING OF TALES 4 b.c. Sadler's Wells (USA) 132–Tales To Tell (USA) (Donut King) [1989 NR 1990 12m 11s a16g[6]] tall, quite attractive colt: has a powerful, round action: won minor event at Doncaster on second of 2 outings as 2-y-o: no worthwhile form in handicaps in autumn, but showed signs of retaining ability: will prove suited by 1½m + . *C. E. Brittain.*

KING OF THE CLOUDS 5 b.g. Sonnen Gold 121–Misfired 101 (Blast 125)   **43**
[1989 NR 1990 10g 7.5d[5] 10.8g[5] 8g[3] 8.2g 7m 8.2m] smallish, lengthy gelding: poor maiden: possibly doesn't stay 11f: acts on good to firm and heavy going: visored twice, blinkered last 5 starts: trained until after fifth outing by K. Bridgwater. *J. L. Spearing.*

KING PHILIP 3 b.c. King of Spain 121–Midnight Music (Midsummer Night II   **44**
117) [1989 5g 5d 6m 6s[6] 6g 1990 6g 5g[5] 5g a6g a8g 6g 6g 5m] small, stocky, attractive colt: good walker: moderate mover: poor maiden: faced stiff tasks and no worthwhile form in handicaps last 6 starts: stays 6f: acts on soft going: blinkered third and last 3 starts. *J. S. Wainwright.*

KINGS ALDERMAN 3 b.g. Kings Lake (USA) 133–Keep The Thought (USA)   —
84 (Valdez (USA)) [1989 8.2f[6] 8.5f[3] 10g[3] 10g 1990 a8g[5] a8g 9.1m 8m 8g[5] 10m 10s 11.5g] rather leggy gelding: modest maiden at 2 yrs: ran moderately in 1990, including in seller: probably better at 1¼m than 1m: retained 750 gns Ascot November Sales: winning selling hurdler. *W. J. Musson.*

KINGS CLUB 3 b.c. Local Suitor (USA) 128–Clymene 86 (Vitiges (FR) 132)   —
[1989 NR 1990 10g 10.2g[5] 12f 10g] IR 21,000Y: strong, lengthy colt: second foal: dam, 7f winner at 2 yrs on only start, is half-sister to useful 6f and 7f winner Saluzzo and daughter of staying half-sister to smart Harmony Hall: appears of little account: sold 2,000 gns Newmarket Autumn Sales. *C. E. Brittain.*

KINGS CRESCENT 3 b.g. Fairy King (USA)–Pennycress 99 (Florescence 120)   —
[1989 NR 1990 7m 8m] IR 11,500F, IR 21,000Y: robust, good-quartered gelding: moderate mover: half-brother to several winners, including useful sprinter Ponchielli (by Pitskelly) and fair middle-distance performer Video Man (by Guillaume Tell): dam won twice over 5f at 2 yrs: always behind in summer maidens, bandaged near-hind second start: joined G. Balding then sold 1,000 gns Newmarket Autumn Sales. *M. H. Easterby.*

KING'S CRUSADE 7 ch.g. Reform 132–Crusader's Dream 88 (St Paddy 133)   —
[1989 NR 1990 a8g] small, lightly-made gelding: moderate mover: well beaten in amateur races as 4-y-o and Southwell handicap (bit backward, bandaged) in November. *D. J. Wintle.*

KING'S LADY (FR) 4 ch.f. Ti King (FR) 121–Harold's Girl (FR) (Northfields   **36**
(USA)) [1989 8v[6] 10s 11m[3] 10.5g[4] 10d 11.5d 10g 10g* 9.5g[6] 10d[6] 1990 a8g[4] a8g[4] a12g[6]] ex-French filly: third foal: half-sister to 2 winners in France, including useful French 6f to 1¼m winner Tout Est Permis (by Pyjama Hunt): dam 6f winner at 2 yrs in France: won minor event at Vichy as 3-y-o: poor form at best in Lingfield claimers early in year: stays 11f. *W. J. Musson.*

KINGSLEY 3 b.f. Kings Lake (USA) 133–Bushti Music 63 (Bustino 136) [1989   **63**
NR 1990 8f 12s[2] 12f[2] 12g[2] 13g[2] 12.4f[6] a14g[5] 12g 10d[5] 12.5g[2] 12m*] IR 9,000Y: leggy, sparely-made filly: third foal: dam, who stayed 9f, is half-sister to very useful spinters Hanu and Sanu: quite modest performer: won seller (bought in 6,500 gns) at Pontefract in October: one paced, and should stay well: probably acts on any going: goes well with forcing tactics: ran creditably for amateur, moderately for 7-lb claimer at Southwell. *M. Johnston.*

KINGS MEETING 3 b.c. Kings Lake (USA) 133–Meeting Adjourned 94   **42** d
(General Assembly (USA)) [1989 7.5f 7f 7m[5] 8f 1990 11g[4] 12g[4] 12m[6] 14f 13m 12m[6] a14g[6] 15.3m 8.2g 11m] leggy, lightly-made colt: moderate mover: poor maiden: ran poorly last 6 starts: stays 1½m: blinkered ninth start: bandaged fourth: sold to join W. Clay 820 gns Doncaster October Sales. *M. Brittain.*

KINGSMERE 3 ch.g. Kings Lake (USA) 133–Mrs Hippy (Tudor Music 131)   —
[1989 5f[5] 6m 6m 6g a6g a7g 1990 10f 12m 12m 10.1m 10f 10.8m 10d] smallish,

good-quartered gelding: moderate mover: poor plater: bred to stay 1¼m: trained until after sixth start by R. Hannon. *M. R. Channon.*

KING'S REALM   2 b.c. (Apr 17) Another Realm 118–My Cervantes (Hill Clown   35
(USA)) [1990 7g 7m 7m 8m 10m] 6,000F: small, compact colt: good walker: has a round action: brother to quite modest maiden Levitt Lady and half-brother to 3 minor winners here and abroad: dam poor half-sister to smart miler Maystreak: poor plater: best effort in blinkers final start: stays 1¼m: sold 4,000 gns Newmarket Autumn Sales. *Mrs L. Piggott.*

KING'S SHILLING (USA)   3 b.g. Fit To Fight (USA)–Pride's Crossing (USA)   68
(Riva Ridge (USA)) [1989 6m⁵ 7g³ 8.2d⁴ 8s² 1990 8.5m* 10g 10.2f² 10d 9g⁵ 9m 8h⁵
8m 7m 7.6d⁵ 8m] leggy, sparely-made gelding: modest handicapper: bit edgy and sweating, won maiden at Beverley in March: stays 1¼m: inconsistent: sold to join P. Mitchell 11,000 gns Newmarket Autumn Sales and gelded. *I. A. Balding.*

KING TREVISIO   4 b.g. King of Spain 121–Gundi 57 (Mummy's Pet 125) [1989   47
7s 1990 6g 6g⁶ 8.2g⁴ 6m³ a8g² 8.2m 6d] workmanlike gelding: poor mover: poor maiden: stays 1m. *Mrs J. R. Ramsden.*

KING VICTOR (IRE)   2 b r c (May 1) Tender King 123–Wyn Mipet (Welsh   —
Saint 126) [1990 5d 6m 8.2g 6m] neat colt: has a round action: fourth foal: half-brother to 3-y-o 7f winner Little Kraker (by Godswalk), 9f to 1½m winner Katie Jo (by Taufan) and 1986 2-y-o 5f and 6f winner Victory Ballard (by Ballad Rock): dam placed over 5f at 2 yrs in Ireland: little worthwhile form in sellers: blinkered final start. *R. O'Leary.*

KING WILLIAM   5 b.g. Dara Monarch 128–Norman Delight (USA) (Val de   59 d
L'Orne (FR) 130) [1989 10m 8f⁵ 8f⁶ 10g⁶ 10f² 12m² 10.2g 12g* 10.6m 13.6f a11g⁶
1990 12m⁴ 12f* 12f³ 12.2m 12g 12m³ 12g⁴ 12m 12f³ 12g⁵ a12g] robust gelding: carries condition: moderate mover: plating-class handicapper: apprentice ridden, won at Beverley in March: best at 1½m: acts on firm going and ran badly on soft: blinkered twice: has won when sweating: sold out of D. Smith's stable 7,400 gns Doncaster January Sales: retained 17,000 gns Doncaster August Sales: twice winner over hurdles after: inconsistent. *J. L. Spearing.*

KINKAJOO   3 b.f. Precocious 126–Skyey 70 (Skymaster 126) [1989 6g 1990 8g   —
8m a8g] leggy, angular filly: no worthwhile form in maidens and handicap: may prove best short of 1m. *M. A. Jarvis.*

KINLACEY   3 b.f. Aragon 118–Mimika 85 (Lorenzaccio 130) [1989 5m⁶ 6m⁴ 8m⁶   69
8m 8.2s⁴ 1990 7g 6f² 7m* 8f⁵ 8f⁴ 7d³] workmanlike filly: good walker: has a long stride: modest performer: won maiden at Leicester in July: needs further than 6f: acts on firm going (faced stiff task on dead). *B. A. McMahon.*

KINLET VISION (IRE)   2 b.f. (Mar 31) Vision (USA)–Verandah (Jaazeiro   56
(USA) 127) [1990 5m³ 5m² 5.3h* 6m⁶ 6g⁴ 6m* 6g⁵ 6d] leggy filly: second foal: half-sister to 3-y-o Rainton Leap (by Salmon Leap): dam Irish 1m winner, is from family of Knockroe: useful plater: bought in 3,700 gns to 5,500 gns after winning at Brighton in May and Yarmouth in September: will stay 7f: acts well on top-of-the-ground. *J. Berry.*

KINO   3 b.g. Niniski (USA) 125–Relkina (FR) 85 (Relkino 131) [1989 7m 8m³ 7g⁵   69
1990 10g 12d 12m⁴ 14m³ 16.2f 16.1m⁶] leggy, unfurnished gelding: modest maiden: stayed on when in frame in handicaps: seems suited by 1¾m: best efforts on good to firm ground: has run well when sweating: sold to join S. Sherwood 10,000 gns Doncaster August Sales then gelded: winning hurdler. *C. E. Brittain.*

KINOKO   2 ch.g. (Mar 4) Bairn (USA) 126–Octavia (Sallust 134) [1990 5m² 6g²   65 §
6m² 6s⁴ 7m 6d⁴ a7g⁴] 10,500Y: rangy gelding, rather unfurnished: half-brother to several minor winners here and abroad, including 6f to 10.8f winner Neat Style (by Sweet Monday): dam showed a little ability: quite modest maiden: should stay 7f: acts on top-of-the-ground and a soft surface: usually troublesome in preliminaries and was withdrawn after twice unseating rider at stalls once: inconsistent, and one to treat with caution. *R. Hollinshead.*

KINTARO   2 b.c. (Feb 15) Glint of Gold 128–Tzarina (USA) (Gallant Romeo   —
(USA)) [1990 7d] 13,500Y: fifth reported foal: half-brother to 3-y-o All Night Deli (by Night Shift) and fairly useful sprinter Mandub (by Topsider): dam placed 3 times in USA: slowly away and always behind in maiden auction at Goodwood in October. *D. J. G. Murray-Smith.*

KIRALYI (FR)   3 b.f. Kings Lake (USA) 133–Vivante 87 (Bold Lad (IRE) 133)   —
[1989 NR 1990 12g a12g] 80,000Y: sister to plating-class maiden Lady of Shalott and half-sister to several winners, including high-class 1½m winner Head For Heights

(by Shirley Heights): dam, 6f winner, is half-sister to dam of Le Johnstan: well beaten in maidens at Newmarket (apprentices) and Southwell. *M. H. Tompkins.*

KIRAM (USA) 5 b.h. Gold Stage (USA)–Alight (FR) (Habitat 134) [1989 6d 6d 10v 8d 7.6f6 7m 7.6f 7.6h 8.2g 10.2f 7g 10f 10f 1990 10f 10f] small, quite attractive horse: poor mover: won maiden at Dundalk as 2-y-o: has lost his form completely: often blinkered. *J. E. Long.*

KIRBY OPPORTUNITY 2 ch.f. (Apr 14) Mummy's Game 120–Empress   37
Catherine 73 (Welsh Pageant 132) [1990 5m 5g4 6g4 6g3 6g 7f 6m 5m 6m] 2,000Y: leggy filly: third foal: closely related to fair 7f and 1m winner Green's Seascape (by Mummy's Pet): dam 1½m winner out of sister to Connaught: poor plater: stays 6f: blinkered sixth outing: sometimes sweating, and on toes. *G. Blum.*

KIRBY'S BEST 3 ch.f. Sayf El Arab (USA) 127–Betty's Bid (Auction Ring (USA)   32
123) [1989 5d 5f5 5g 5.1m 6g 6f 1990 6m 6g 5g 6g3 7f 7m 7m 7f 6d a7g] small, close-coupled filly: has a markedly round action: plater: ran moderately last 4 starts: probably stays 7f: blinkered twice at 2 yrs. *G. Blum.*

KIR (IRE) 2 ch.g. (Apr 10) M Double M (USA)–Wolver Rose (Wolver Hollow 126)   —
[1990 7m 8m] 25,000Y: second foal: half-brother to 1989 Irish 2-y-o 5f winner Never Wrong (by Kafu): dam ran twice: soundly beaten in maiden at Goodwood and minor event at Bath in autumn. *M. McCormack.*

KIRRIEMUIR 2 b.f. (Mar 4) Lochnager 132–Maxine's Here 52 (Copte (FR))   56
[1990 5m* 5f3 6m3 6f4 6m a8g] strong, close-coupled, workmanlike filly: fifth foal: sister to a poor plater and half-sister to 3-y-o 11f winner Big Surprise (by Comedy Star) and a winning 1½m plater by Cawston's Clown: dam, winner of 2-runner 5f seller at 2 yrs, stayed 1m: won 10-runner maiden at Leicester: soundly beaten in small-field minor events and nurseries afterwards: should stay beyond 5f: trained first 4 outings by W. G. M. Turner. *R. Akehurst.*

KIRSHEDA 5 b.m. Busted 134–Mellow Girl 88 (Mountain Call 125) [1989 12.3s   51
16g 15m2 12m 18m 1990 16g6 16.8f2 16f6] angular, sparely-made mare: plating-class maiden: appears to stay 2¼m and to act on any going: winning hurdler in August. *J. Mackie.*

KIRSTENBOSCH 3 b.g. Caerleon (USA) 132–Flower Petals (Busted 134)   61
[1989 6g5 7f4 8g3 1990 8f 7.5m5 8m 8m 8.5d3 10d4 10g3 a12g3 a11g5 10m5 10g2 12d5] leggy, quite attractive gelding: has a fluent, slightly round action: quite modest maiden: claimed out of T. Barron's stable £6,550 in seller penultimate start: well below form in similar event over 7 weeks later: best at up to 1¼m: acts on dead ground: often edgy: one paced: keen sort: gelded after final start. *L. Lungo.*

KISKA (USA) 2 ch.f. (Feb 7) Bering 136–Hortensia (FR) 119 (Luthier 126) [1990   69 p
8g2] big, leggy, sparely-made filly: sixth foal: closely related to Derby second Glacial Storm, later 15.5f winner in France, and modest maiden Helen's Song (both by Arctic Tern) and half-sister to 2 middle-distance winners: dam smart at around 1¼m in France: 5 lengths second of 13, headed over 1f out and keeping on well, to Melpomene in maiden at Wolverhampton in October: will be suited by 1¼m +: sure to improve, and win a race. *B. W. Hills.*

KISSAVOS 4 ch.c. Cure The Blues (USA)–Hairbrush (USA) (Sir Gaylord) [1989   53
5v2 6s 6m5 6m5 6g5 6g* a6g 1990 6g 5m 5m 6f a6g2 a7g3 a8g4 6m5 6m2 a6g a7g4 a6g6] small, angular colt: plating-class handicapper: effective at 6f to 1m: acts on good to firm and heavy going: blinkered last 5 outings. *N. A. Callaghan.*

KISU KALI 3 ch.g. Kris 135–Evita 111 (Reform 132) [1989 NR 1990 10.2f2 10f3   75
10d4 9m2 12m4] big, good-bodied gelding: has a markedly round action: sixth foal: brother to once-raced 1987 2-y-o Kriformi and half-brother to fair 1½m winner Southern Comfort (by Ile de Bourbon), later prolifically successful in Italy: dam won Nell Gwyn Stakes: modest maiden: should stay 1½m: seems unsuited by a soft surface: joined C. Brooks then gelded. *H. R. A. Cecil.*

KIT 2 b.f. (May 16) Green Ruby (USA) 104–Crowebrass (Crowned Prince (USA)   34
128) [1990 5f3 5f4 5s 5g6 5g 6f] 1,900Y: leggy filly: has a round action: half-sister to 1985 2-y-o 5f seller winner Crowemetals (by Starch Reduced): dam poor maiden: poor plater: tailed off final start: trained by R. Hollinshead on debut. *B. Preece.*

KITSBEL 2 ro.g. (Mar 30) Belfort (FR) 89–Fair Kitty 73 (Saucy Kit 76) [1990 8m   60
7m 6m6] half-brother to 1¾m winner and successful hurdler Kitty Come Home (by Monsanto): dam useful jumper, stayed well: quite modest form when backward in maidens first 2 starts: needs further than 6f. *W. Carter.*

480

KITTY RUSSE 3 b.f. Nureyev (USA) 131–Kittyhawk 113 (Bustino 136) [1989 8f² 65
1990 12f² 10m] quite attractive filly, rather unfurnished: modest maiden: off course
over 3½ months before last of 7 (bandaged off-hind) at Beverley. *B. W. Hills.*

KIYA (USA) 4 b.f. Dominion 123–Melodrama 102 (Busted 134) [1989 8g* 10m⁴ 72
8g* 8m* 8m* 8m 9g⁴ 1990 8f 8g 8m 8g² 7.6m 8m 9m 8d⁵ 8g² 8m⁵ a10g] leggy,
lengthy filly: often unimpressive in appearance: modest handicapper: suited by 1m:
acts on good to firm and dead going. *W. Hastings-Bass.*

KLAIROVER 3 b.f. Smackover 107–Klairove 74 (Averof 123) [1989 6m 5g 1990 —
8m 5.8f 5.8m⁵] big, workmanlike filly: poor mover: bit backward, no worthwhile
form, in seller and handicap last 2 starts: bred to stay 1m. *C. J. Hill.*

KLUTE 11 b.h. Bigivor–Carminway (Nearest 88) [1989 NR 1990 5m²] non- —
thoroughbred horse: has been at stud: totally outclassed in 2 matches over 5f. *Miss
Lesley Bruce.*

KNAVE OF CLUBS 3 ch.g. King of Clubs 124–La Calera (GER) (Caracol (FR)) 71
[1989 6m⁶ 6f 8g³ 1990 10m 10m³ 10g³ 12g* 12m² 12.2f³] angular gelding: has a
rather round action: modest performer: won handicap at Hamilton in September:
ran well in lady riders handicap at Catterick final start: should stay further: acts on
firm going: sweating first 2 starts, very edgy on third: claimed out of M. Camacho's
stable £6,270 after seller on third: winning hurdler. *P. A. Blockley.*

KNIFEBOX (USA) 2 b.c. (Mar 12) Diesis 133–Matoki (USA) (Hail To Reason) 96
[1990 6g² 7m⁴ 7s* 10.2s* 8v] $190,000Y: small, sparely-made colt: has a markedly
round action: half-brother to several winners abroad, including 9f graded-stakes
winner Parochial (by Mehmet): dam minor winner at 3 yrs: favourite, made all or
most in maiden at Lingfield in October and minor event (won by 10 lengths from
Wings of Freedom) at Doncaster following month: around 10 lengths tenth of 16 in
Gran Criterium at Milan: suited by 1¼m: acts very well on soft ground. *J. H. M.
Gosden.*

KNIGHT OF KIRKTON 3 b.g. State Trooper 96–Musical Piece 91 (Song 132) 43
[1989 6d 7f 1990 8f 8m 10.2f⁵ 10m 10f] good-topped gelding: form only where fifth in
maiden claimer at Bath in June: sold 1,000 gns Doncaster October Sales. *R. Hannon.*

KNIGHT OF MERCY 4 b.g. Aragon 118–Little Mercy 90 (No Mercy 126) 106
[1989 6d⁵ 6d² 6f* 6f⁴ 6m³ 6m⁴ 7g³ 6f 6m⁴ 7.3m 6g⁶ 6v 6d 1990 8g 6m⁴ 6m³ 7g⁴
7m* 6d* 6m* 6d 7m⁶ 6d⁵ 6s³]
'He's going to be a decent handicapper this year; there's probably a little
listed race in him, too' commented Richard Hannon on the recently-gelded
Knight of Mercy in a *Timeform Interview* in April. Knight of Mercy took a
while to come to hand and was dropped to claiming company at Goodwood in
June to gain his first victory for over a year. Fortunately for connections he
failed to attract a claim, for on his next two starts Knight of Mercy fully
justified his trainer's earlier optimism by winning the Wokingham Stakes at
Royal Ascot and William Hill Stewards' Cup at Goodwood. Emulating Calibina
in 1977 and Petong in 1984 by winning the summer's two biggest sprint

*Wokingham Stakes (Handicap), Ascot—Knight of Mercy,
Amigo Menor (rails) and Hana Marie dominate the finish of this competitive sprint*

William Hill Stewards' Cup (Handicap), Goodwood—Knight of Mercy does the double;
Amigo Menor and Masnun are with him on the far side,
stand-side runner Bocas Rose gets up for second

handicaps, Knight of Mercy earned over four times more in first prize money than the £20,000 for which he was eligible to be claimed at Goodwood. The money wasn't easily won. It took a strong ride from Pat Eddery to get Knight of Mercy home under a 7-lb penalty at Royal Ascot. Driven along from halfway he made steady headway through the field, came with a strong burst up the centre of the course to head long-time leader Amigo Menor in the last fifty yards and won going away by three quarters of a length. Racing off the same mark in the Stewards' Cup—the weights were published on the eve of the Wokingham—Knight of Mercy was again outpaced and left with plenty to do at halfway. Running on strongly under a powerful ride, this time from Raymond (Eddery was claimed to ride Ajanac), he got the best of a close finish with stable-companion Bocas Rose, Amigo Menor and Masnun, the quartet separated by two necks and a head. Knight of Mercy will have to improve to win one of the lesser listed races. However, he's still by no means weighted out of contention in handicaps. He ran creditably on each of his last four starts, finishing third to Amigo Menor in a competitive event at Newbury on his final outing. He ended the season on a mark only 6 lb higher than when successful at Royal Ascot and Goodwood.

		Mummy's Pet	Sing Sing
	Aragon	(b 1968)	Money For Nothing
	(b 1980)	Ica	Great Nephew
Knight of Mercy		(gr 1974)	Intent
(b.g. 1986)		No Mercy	Fortino II
	Little Mercy	(gr 1968)	Crowning Mercy
	(gr 1978)	Petite Rock	Goldhill
		(b 1968)	Channel Rock

Knight of Mercy is effective at six and seven furlongs; he looked in need of the race on his only attempt at a mile. Though Aragon is known chiefly as a sire of sprinters, he stayed a mile and there is more stamina on the distaff side of Knight of Mercy's pedigree. The first three dams on the bottom line, all winners, each stayed at least a mile. Little Mercy was a game and consistent handicapper at seven furlongs to a mile, successful eight times in the early-'eighties. Her only foal prior to Knight of Mercy, Silent Sister (by Kind of Hush), won over six furlongs as a two-year-old; her latest foal to race is the modest maiden Grey Area (by Petong). Knight of Mercy has the look of both his parents, in that he's a strong, good-bodied type who carries condition, and he also takes after them in his gameness. He acts on any going with the possible exception of heavy. He started slowly when tried in blinkers once as a three-year-old. *R. Hannon.*

482

Mr M. W. Grant's "Knight of Mercy"

KNIGHT'S BARONESS 3 b.f. Rainbow Quest (USA) 134–Knights **116**
Beauty (USA) (True Knight (USA)) [1989 7m² 7m* 8g² 1990 11.5m² 12d³
12m* 14.6g⁴]

Where Bint Pasha, Ibn Bey, Insan and Zoman had all failed, the rather
less talented Knight's Baroness succeeded in adding a major classic victory to
Zaizoom's 1987 Derby Italiano for owner Fahd Salman, trainer Paul Cole and
jockey Richard Quinn. Following her Irish Oaks triumph, the three of them
did it again with Ibn Bey in the Irish St Leger just one week after Snurge had
done what was asked of him for another of the stable's patrons in the St Leger
at Doncaster. Knight's Baroness lined up for the Kildangan Stud Irish Oaks at
the Curragh having been comprehensively outpointed by Salsabil in the Gold
Seal Oaks at Epsom five weeks earlier when she'd been given a hard ride
(Quinn hit her eighteen times and received a three-day suspension) into the
bargain. She certainly didn't have an easy time of it to justify favouritism at
the Curragh either but turned in another thoroughly game performance. The
non-participation of Hellenic on account of the firmish ground, and the poor
showing by Pharian removed what had looked to be Knight's Baroness'
biggest threats but the modest early pace wouldn't have suited and although
Quinn had her racing close up in third, Knight's Baroness couldn't initially
match the dual Italian classic winner Atoll on whom Gary Moore kicked clear
just inside the two-furlong marker. Three hundred yards later, however, and
Knight's Baroness had come into her element. Atoll was tiring and with
long-time leader Assertion finding only the one pace, Knight's Baroness
stayed on strongly between horses to get up by a neck and the same. Atoll's
connections were reportedly angry that Moore had disobeyed instructions
and gone on so soon on what was the beginning of a bad week for the jockey,

who four days later received a five-and-a-half-year world ban and near-£100,000 fine following betting-related charges brought by the Royal Hong Kong Jockey Club. The proximity of some pretty modest Irish challengers—Assertion had only recently lost her maiden certificate at the eighth attempt and started 50/1—makes the overall form of the Irish Oaks hard to gauge but there aren't any doubts as to the merit of Knight's Baroness. She was as consistent as she was game, never out of the frame in seven starts. After winning a maiden at Yarmouth as a two-year-old, Knight's Baroness lost out to subsequent Prix de Diane winner Rafha in both the May Hill Stakes at Doncaster and the Marley Roof Tile Oaks Trial at Lingfield, in the latter race beaten a neck in receipt of 6 lb on her reappearance. Knight's Baroness' fourth to Madame Dubois in the Park Hill at Doncaster, conceding weight, was perhaps a little below her best but she did enough to satisfy us that she stayed the trip and was later found to be lame.

Knight's Baroness (b.f. 1987)	Rainbow Quest (USA) (b 1981)	Blushing Groom (ch 1974)	Red God Runaway Bride
		I Will Follow (b 1975)	Herbager Where You Lead
	Knights Beauty (USA) (b 1977)	True Knight (b or br 1969)	Chateaugay Stealaway
		Broadway Beauty (b 1973)	Chompion Grass Roots

Knight's Baroness is by the 1985 Arc winner Rainbow Quest who has made such an excellent start at stud; Knight's Baroness is probably the least talented—though not the least important—of the four pattern winners from his first crop, the others being Saumarez, Quest For Fame and Splash of Colour. Fahd Salman was the purchaser of Rainbow Quest's ten-year-old sister Red Comes Up (in foal to Danehill) for 200,000 guineas at the latest Newmarket December Sales. Knight's Baroness' dam Knights Beauty went through the sale-ring at 13,000 dollars as a yearling in 1978, 400,000 dollars in 1985 and her value was probably on the wane again following the unsuccessful efforts of her first two foals Stormy Beauty (by Storm Bird) and Captive Heart (by Conquistador Cielo). The price paid for Knight's Beauty was a fairly typical price for one of the Grade 1 mile-and-a-quarter winner True Knight's second crop of yearlings but Knight's Beauty was most untypical of his runners, a very useful and tough individual who raced for five seasons and gained twelve victories, including three stakes races from six and a half to eight and a half furlongs as a four-year-old. True Knight's covering fee was just 2,000 dollars in 1990. Knights Beauty stands out similarly on her dam's side of the pedigree although a protracted search reveals that this is also the family of Exclusive Native, Deputy Minister and Gala Performance. Knights Beauty produced the Dancing Brave colt Royal Decree in 1988 but died in

Kildangan Stud Irish Oaks, the Curragh—
Knight's Baroness stays on strongly between Atoll and Assertion (rails)

1989. Knight's Baroness is to visit Polish Precedent in 1991. She is a leggy, lightly-made filly, a moderate walker who has a quick action in her faster paces. *P. F. I. Cole.*

KNIGHT'S GLANCE   3 b.g. Castle Keep 121–Coming Out (Fair Season 120)   —
[1989 NR 1990 8m 12f 10f⁵ 10.2f 10f] leggy gelding: second foal: dam unraced daughter of Parthian Glance, also dam of Prix Gladiateur winner Knight Templar: maiden, form only when fifth at Brighton: sold 725 gns Ascot November Sales. *M. McCormack.*

KNIPHOFIA   3 ch.c. Norwick (USA) 120–Miss Hippolyta 82 (High Line 125)   50
[1989 NR 1990 8g 10f 10f 8m 11.5f* 12h 16m 16s a12g] compact colt: moderate walker: fourth living foal: dam 10.8f winner: 20/1, won strongly-run handicap at Lingfield in July, running on well to lead post: only occasional form otherwise: probably stays 2m: acts on firm going. *C. P. Wildman.*

KNOCKAVON   2 b.c. (Mar 17) Belfort (FR) 89–Miss Merlin 79 (Manacle 123)   75
[1990 a5g 5m* 5g* 5m* 5f⁶ 5g] 10,000Y: leggy, rather sparely-made colt: half-brother to fairly useful sprinting 3-y-o Lyndseylee (by Swing Easy), two 2-y-o 5f seller winners and a winning hurdler: dam won twice at 6f: modest performer: successful in maiden at Edinburgh in May, claimer (had simple task) at Ayr in July and nursery (making all and quickening well) at Windsor in August: ran poorly, dropping out quickly, in nurseries after: speedy: on toes fourth and fifth starts. *J. Berry.*

KNOCK KNOCK   5 ch g. Tap On Wood 130–Ruby River (Red God 128§) [1989   80
10s⁶ 10.8d⁶ 10f³ 10f³ 10f 9m* 10g² 9f² 8m* 10m* 9.2d³ 10g⁴ 10g⁵ 1990 10.2f 9g 10.8f² 8h⁶ 9g³ 8g* 10f* 8m³ 10h⁴ 10g³ 9m⁴ 10.6d 10m³] good-quartered gelding: goes extremely well for lady rider and justified favouritism at Redcar in June and Salisbury (easily) in July: stays 1¼m: best efforts on a sound surface: best without blinkers or visor: finds little in front, and is suited by good gallop, waiting tactics and tender handling. *I. A. Balding.*

KNOCK TO ENTER (USA)   2 b.c. (Mar 11) Diesis 133–Privy (USA) (Tisab   80 p
(USA)) [1990 7m*] $130,000Y: leggy, angular colt: moderate walker: second foal: dam minor winner at around 7f: well-backed favourite, won maiden at Warwick in October by ¾ length from Crossillion, quickening to challenge over 1f out, looking likely to win well, but needing to be pushed out vigorously: moved poorly down: will stay 1m: sure to improve, and win again. *M. R. Stoute.*

KNOSSINGTON BOY   2 ch.g. (Mar 27) Norwick (USA) 120–Lizzie Lightfoot   —
(Hotfoot 126) [1990 6g 7g 7f] 8,200F: lengthy, workmanlike gelding: half-brother to 7f and 1m winner Neds Expressa and modest 1984 2-y-o 5f winner Bay Bazaar (both by Bay Express): dam unraced close relative of very useful 1¼m colt Light Fire: no form, including in sellers: slowly away first 2 starts. *G. M. Moore.*

KOHINOOR (IRE)   2 b.c. (Feb 17) Shareef Dancer (USA) 135–Freddy My Love   76
(Thatch (USA) 136) [1990 6d 7m* 8.2g 7d] IR 28,000Y: close-coupled, good-topped colt: half-brother to Irish 1m (at 2 yrs) to 1¾m winner Glowing Star (by Kalaglow): dam, winner in Italy, is half-sister to Free Guest and Fresh: made all in maiden at Newmarket in August, to win by 3 lengths from Honing Stone: well beaten after in minor event at Haydock and Three Chimneys Dewhurst Stakes (looked well, on toes) at Newmarket: should stay 1m: seems unsuited by easy ground. *C. E. Brittain.*

KOKOSCHKA   8 gr. or ro.g. Alias Smith (USA)–Opinion 71 (Great Nephew 126)   —
[1989 14.8s 1990 14.8m⁶ 17.1f 17.1f] strong gelding: carries plenty of condition: no longer of much account: blinkered twice, including final outing: sometimes bandaged: sold 1,300 gns Ascot July Sales: resold 1,050 gns Ascot October Sales. *G. Roe.*

KOLINSKY   4 ch.g. Dunbeath (USA) 127–Kolomelskoy Palace 77 (Royal Palace   51
131) [1989 12g 11m 16.2g 12f² 11m* 12g² 11g² 11f* 12.3f 12m⁴ 12.2g⁶ 10.6m 10v 1990 10m 12g³ 12g⁵ 12f² 12m 12g 11f² a12g² a11g⁶ a12g³ 10.2m 10.6s a11g a12g⁴ a14g³ a14g⁴] tall, leggy, good-topped gelding: carries condition: moderate mover: plating-class handicapper: stays 1½m: acts on firm going: blinkered or visored tenth to thirteenth starts: has run well when sweating, and has got on edge: goes well with forcing tactics: sold out of F. Lee's stable 6,600 gns Newmarket Autumn Sales after thirteenth outing: none too keen. *M. C. Chapman.*

KOLONAKI   3 b.c. Busted 134–Nuppence 79 (Reform 132) [1989 6m 7g⁵ 6g⁴   55 d
1990 6g 9f 7d 7.6m 11.5g³ 12m 12.2m⁶ 10g] big, good-bodied colt: has a quick action: quite modest maiden: form as 3-y-o only on fifth start: should stay 1½m: wore severe noseband final start: sold out of G. Lewis' stable 9,200 gns Newmarket July Sales after fifth: has joined J. P. Leigh. *A. W. Potts.*

M. C. Throsby's "Kooyonga"

KOMOMBO (IRE)   2 b.c. (Apr 4) Sadler's Wells (USA) 132–Gertrude Lawrence **56 p** (Ballymore 123) [1990 6m] IR 260,000Y: close-coupled, rather unfurnished colt: half-brother to quite useful Irish 6f and 1m winner Lady Ambassador (by General Assembly) and Irish 1¾m winner Gertrudes Daughter (by Niniski): dam unraced daughter of Sarah Siddons, also dam of Seymour Hicks and Princess Pati: weak 14/1-shot and green, never dangerous or knocked about in maiden at Newmarket in November: sure to improve good deal. *G. Harwood.*

KOOYONGA (IRE)   2 ch.f. (May 12) Persian Bold 123–Angjuli (Northfields **101** (USA)) [1990 7m* 7g* 7d² 7d*] IR 62,000Y: sixth foal: half-sister to 3-y-o Proof of Purchase (by Wassl), useful 1988 2-y-o 5f and 6f winner Jaljuli (by Jalmood) and fairly useful Irish 6f and 7f winner Hatton Gardens (by Auction Ring): dam unraced half-sister to Roland Gardens: useful filly, successful in maiden at Gowran Park, EBF Silver Flash Stakes (by a head from African Dance) at Phoenix Park and EBF Leopardstown Stakes (by 4 lengths from Smooth Performance) at Leopardstown: 1½ lengths second of 20 to Rinka Das in Cartier Million at Phoenix Park: will stay 1¼m. *M. Kauntze, Ireland.*

KORACLE BAY   3 b.f. Kind of Hush 118–Sea Aura 89 (Roi Soleil 125) [1989 6m* **75** 7g³ 1990 6g 6m 7.3m⁵ 7.6g 7f⁵ a8g⁶ a8g 10.6d⁶] big, lengthy filly: moderate mover: modest handicapper: creditable staying-on sixth in amateurs event at Haydock final start: visored, found little and ran moderately in claimer time before: stays 10.6f: acts on good to firm ground and dead: ran poorly at Chester. *C. F. Wall.*

KOSTROMA   4 b.f. Caerleon (USA) 132–Katie May 103 (Busted 134) [1989 10m* **116** 11m² 10d⁶ 10d⁴ 8m⁵ 1990 10g* 10m 10g⁴ 10g⁵ 10f³ 9m* 8m* 8g* 10g³ 10g] leggy, sparely-made filly: half-sister to 3 winners in France, notably high-class 1m to 1¼m winner Grise Mine (by Crystal Palace): dam, out of best 2-y-o filly of 1970 Cawston's Pride, won over 7f and 1m and stayed 1¼m, and is half-sister to Solinus: progressed extremely well, winning listed events at the Curragh in April and Leopardstown in July and August and Group 3 EBF Desmond Stakes at the Curragh later in August by neck from Bold Russian: creditable third, never able to reach leaders, to Elmaamul in Phoenix Champion Stakes: effective at 1m to 1¼m: best form on a sound surface: blinkered once at 3 yrs: smart. *T. Stack, Ireland.*

KOTASHAAN (FR) 2 b.c. (May 4) Darshaan 133–Haute Autorite (USA) 111 **?** (Elocutionist (USA)) [1990 8v² 9v*] first foal: dam French 7f (at 2 yrs) and 1m winner: narrow second in newcomers race at Saint-Cloud in November before winning maiden at Maisons-Laffitte later in month by 1½ lengths: will stay 1½m: potentially very useful. *Mme C. Head, France.*

KOVALEVSKIA 5 ch.m. Ardross 134–Fiordiligi 109 (Tudor Melody 129) [1989 **55** 10s³ 12d 12m* 14g⁵ 15.5f 13s 12g* a12g 12g a10g* 1990 a10g⁴ 12f⁵ 12.5m 11.5m 15.5f⁶ 12g 12m 12g* 12d a12g⁴ a10g a10g] small, sparely-made mare: won same amateurs handicap (20 ran) at Folkestone in October for second successive season: little other form at 5 yrs: stays 1½m well: possibly unsuited by firm going, acts on any other: best ridden up with pace: inconsistent. *D. A. Wilson.*

KREISCHIM (IRE) 2 b.g. (Apr 10) Kreisler–Chimela (Ela-Mana-Mou 132) **61** [1990 5g⁴ 6g 6m 6d 6m⁵ 7m⁴ 7g a6g⁴ 7m⁴ 6g⁴ 6d⁵ 6d a7g a5g³] IR 2,600Y: angular, workmanlike gelding: has a roundish action: first foal: dam showed some ability at 2 yrs in Ireland: sire unraced half-brother to Habibti: quite modest maiden: best effort (in Southwell nursery) final start: should stay 1m: blinkered fifth outing: carries head high: has sweated: reportedly sold 2,000 gns Doncaster October Sales: resold 3,000 gns Ascot November Sales. *Pat Mitchell.*

KREMLIN GUARD 5 ch.m. Home Guard (USA) 129–Laurel Wreath (Sassafras **60** (FR) 135) [1989 7g³ 7f⁵ 7m² 7g³ 8g⁵ 8g a10g⁵ 1990 10.1g 10m⁵ 10m² a8g] leggy mare: has a rather round action: best effort in 1990 neck second in seller at Lingfield in September: stays 1¼m: acts on firm and dead going: visored and sweating on reappearance: has got on toes: winning hurdler in January: sold 3,100 gns Newmarket Autumn Sales. *M. H. Tompkins.*

KRISFIELD 5 b. or br.g. Anfield 117–Kristallina 84 (Homeric 133) [1989 7g⁶ 7s³ **58** 6m 6g 10g⁵ 1990 6g⁵ 7m 6m 6m⁶ 6s 6s 6d 7d] lengthy gelding: poor mover: quite modest handicapper on his day: ran poorly last 3 outings: stays 7f: best form with

Mr R. E. Sangster's "Kostroma"

give in the ground: ridden by inexperienced 7-lb claimer second to fourth starts: sold out of M. Brittain's stable 5,400 gns Ascot February Sales: inconsistent. *O. Brennan.*

KRISSOS 3 b.c. Good Times (ITY)–Chrysicabana 88 (Home Guard (USA) 129) — [1989 NR 1990 16m⁶ 10m 12m] lengthy, heavy-topped colt: shows knee action: second foal: half-brother to 1987 2-y-o 6f winner Dominion Treasure (by Dominion): dam 1¼m winner: soundly beaten in maidens then claimer: sold to join M. Murphy 2,400 gns Newmarket Autumn Sales. *C. E. Brittain.*

KRISTIN'S LIGHT 3 b.f. Noalto 120–Parez 67 (Pardao 120) [1989 5.3h⁴ 6m² — 6f² 6h³ 7m* 7g 6f⁶ 7m 7g 1990 a7g] leggy, sparely-made filly: poor mover: modest plater: has shown nothing since successful at 2 yrs: suited by 6f: visored once at 2 yrs: sold 920 gns Newmarket July Sales. *R. W. Stubbs.*

KRISTIS GIRL 3 ch.f. Ballacashtal (CAN)–Fleur d'Amour 85 (Murrayfield 119) **76** [1989 5d* 5m³ 5.8h³ 6m⁵ 6m² 1990 a7g 6m² 5v* 7d² 6m² 7.2s⁶ 5d 5m⁴ 6f⁶ 7.6g 7m 6d] plain, angular filly: moderate mover: modest handicapper: made all at Ayr in April: shaped as if retaining her ability, prominent 5f, in competitive events last 3 starts: needs testing conditions at 5f, and stays 7f: probably best with give in the ground. *D. Haydn Jones.*

KRIUS 2 b.c. (Apr 14) Shirley Heights 130–Meliora 73 (Crowned Prince (USA) — p 128) [1990 7s] good-topped colt: sixth live foal: half-brother to good-class stayer Weld (by Kalaglow) and 3 other winners, including 1984 2-y-o 5f winner Upper (by Cure The Blues): dam 7f winner: burly, switched right leaving stalls then ran on steadily from halfway to finish in mid-division in 19-runner maiden at Doncaster in November: sure to do better over further. *W. Jarvis.*

KRONPRINZ (IRE) 2 b.c. (Apr 23) Local Suitor (USA) 128–Kaiserchronik **69** (GER) (Cortez (GER)) [1990 7g³ 8.2s⁵ a8g] leggy colt: half-brother to 4 winners in Germany: dam 6f and 10.5f winner in Germany from good family: quite modest form in maidens on first 2 starts: poor seventh of 12 from slow start in Southwell claimer final outing: will stay 1¼m: bought out of I. Balding's stable 5,000 gns Doncaster November Sales after second appearance. *A. P. Stringer.*

KTOLO 4 b.f. Tolomeo 127–Miss Kate (FR) (Nonoalco (USA) 131) [1989 7g 8m³ **68** 11.5f⁴ 10g⁴ 12f³ 12m 14m 12f* 12f³ 12s* 1990 10m 11.5m 11.7m² 11.7m⁴ 12m⁵ 12d] leggy filly: has a round action: modest handicapper nowadays: best effort as 4-y-o on third outing (edged left): stays 1½m: acts on any going: bandaged last 5 starts: takes keen hold. *R. Akehurst.*

KUMADA 3 b.g. Vision (USA)–Fan The Flame 69 (Grundy 137) [1989 5s⁵ 5m² **52 §** 6m⁴ 5f² 5f² 5f² 7m⁵ 6f³ 6g⁶ 1990 9s 9m⁴ 8m 6g² 6s 6m 7v] slightly dipped-backed gelding: easy mover: plating-class maiden: off course nearly 5 months before final start: should prove best short of 9f: acts on firm going: often blinkered or visored: often hangs left: sold 1,550 gns Doncaster October Sales: ungenuine. *F. H. Lee.*

KUMMEL KING 2 b.g. (Mar 19) Absalom 128–Louise 71 (Royal Palace 131) **61** [1990 5f 5g² 5g* 5m⁵ 5f⁴ 5f⁵ 5m⁴ 5m⁶ 7s] 7,000Y: strong, compact gelding: half-brother to 3 winners, including 7f winner Acapulco (by Music Boy): dam 1½m winner: quite modest performer: wide-margin winner of maiden at Catterick in June: should stay beyond 5f: best form on easy ground: blinkered seventh start: sold out of J. Berry's stable 4,600 gns Doncaster September Sales before final outing. *Capt. J. Wilson.*

KUMZAR 6 br.m. Hotfoot 126–Welsh Jane 71 (Bold Lad (IRE) 133) [1989 NR 1990 — 7m 10.2f 7f 9f] good-bodied mare: bad maiden. *J. M. Bradley.*

KURDISH PRINCE 6 b.g. Dunphy 124–Lea Landing 81 (Meadow Court 129) — [1989 16m 18.1g⁵ 1990 8m 12g 12g 10.2f] small gelding: moderate mover: of little account: brought down second outing: blinkered twice. *M. J. Charles.*

KURRAJONG 2 br.c. (Feb 11) Known Fact (USA) 135–Metair 118 (Laser Light **55** 118) [1990 5d⁵] workmanlike colt: eighth foal: brother to 1m winner Connue and half-brother to several other winners, including useful sprinters Meteoric (by High Line) and Fine Edge (by Sharpen Up): dam game sprinter: second favourite but bit backward, around 5 lengths fifth of 11, prominent 4f, in maiden at Newbury in April: went very freely to post. *R. Charlton.*

KUWAIT MUTAR 8 b.g. Martinmas 128–Willowy (Mourne 126) [1989 NR 1990 — a14g⁴] strong gelding: winning stayer in Belgium in 1986: lightly raced and no form in Britain: bandaged last 2 outings. *R. Guest.*

KUWAIT SUNSET (IRE) 2 ch.f. (May 14) Exhibitioner 111–Kuwait Night 67 — (Morston (FR) 125) [1990 6g] leggy filly: second foal: dam, 1½m winner, is sister to useful middle-distance stayer Mubarak of Kuwait: slowly away and always tailed off in seller at Nottingham in July. *J. D. Czerpak.*

KWACHA 4 b.c. Reesh 117–Madame Quickly 80 (Saint Crespin III 132) [1989 12g 11f 8m 7m 10.2h 15.3g 1990 a14g 13g] rather leggy, workmanlike colt: little sign of ability, including in seller: blinkered once at 3 yrs. *T. Craig.* —

L

LAAHIJ (USA) 2 b. or br.c. (Mar 14) Roberto (USA) 131–My Royal Guest (Be My Guest (USA) 126) [1990 7m] $37,000F, 60,000Y: workmanlike colt: first foal: dam unraced half-sister to Bog Road and Royal Hobbit: in mid-division in maiden at Salisbury in June: sold 2,200 gns Newmarket Autumn Sales. *Major W. R. Hern.* —

LA BALLERINE 4 b.f. Lafontaine (USA) 117–Kirsova (Absalom 128) [1989 8m³ 8m⁵ 10g³ 9g* 11s 10.5g³ a11g⁶ 1990 8m⁴ 10f 14.8f* 12m³ 10g³ 11.5g⁵ 13g 12m 14f² 14m 13.8d a12g⁴] medium-sized filly: moderate walker: plating-class handicapper: won at Warwick in May by neck, putting head in air: finds 1¾m on short side and stays 15f: acts on firm going: occasionally sweats: best with strong handling and exaggerated waiting tactics. *C. E. Brittain.* 53

LA BAMBA 4 br.g. Laxton 105–Ribamba 82 (Ribocco 129) [1989 NR 1990 7m³ 7m⁴ 8g⁶ 7f² 7m⁶ 7m 7m* 7m⁵ 7g* 7d*] leggy gelding: sixth live foal: half-brother to very smart 1m to 1¼m winner Commodore Blake (by Blakeney): dam, half-sister to Bruni, placed at 1m and 9f: developed into a fair handicapper, winning at Redcar, Yarmouth (very impressively by 5 lengths after starting slowly) and Doncaster in autumn: should stay 1m: acts on firm and dead going: has wandered. *G. A. Pritchard-Gordon.* 84

LABEEBA (IRE) 2 ch.f. (Apr 16) Thatching 131–Badiya (USA) (Sir Ivor 135) [1990 6m 6m³ 8m] sparely-made filly: first foal: dam unraced granddaughter of Juliette Marny, sister to Julio Mariner and half-sister to Scintillate: best effort third in seller at Yarmouth in September: should stay beyond 6f: sold 2,600 gns Newmarket Autumn Sales. *B. Hanbury.* 42

LABEKA LAO (USA) 3 ch.f. Laomedonte (USA) 116–Pitty Pal (USA) (Caracolero (USA) 131) [1989 7f 7m* 7g 7m 8.5f 10.6d 1990 8m 11v] lengthy, angular filly: form only when winning poor seller at 2 yrs. *J. Berry.* —

LA BELLE VIE 4 b.f. Indian King (USA) 128–Engage (Whistling Wind 123) [1989 7s 10.1m 9.2f 7f 6f* 7m⁴ 6g 6g* 7g 6g* 7g⁵ 6f* 6g⁶ 1990 7m⁵ 7f² 6g³ 6m² 7m* 6g 7f⁶ 6m⁴ 6m 6m² 7m³ 6m² 6m⁵ 6m 7g⁵ 8g 7g² 7d] workmanlike, good-quartered filly: moderate mover: modest handicapper: won at Yarmouth (for fourth time) in June: stays 7f: acts well on top-of-the-ground: suitable mount for apprentice: tough. *D. A. Wilson.* 73

LA BUCA 2 b.f. (Mar 3) Giacometti 130–Sarah Louise 66 (Double-U-Jay 120) [1990 a7g] 480Y: sparely-made filly: second reported foal: dam poor novice hurdler/chaser won 5f seller at 2 yrs: tailed-off last of 16 in maiden at Southwell. *D. Yeoman.* —

LA CABRILLA 3 gr.f. Carwhite 127–La Tuerta 96 (Hot Spark 126) [1989 5m⁴ 5m* 6m* 6m³ 7s⁶ 1990 8g³ 8.5g³ 7g 7f³ 7m 7d⁴ 7g⁴] good-bodied, quite attractive filly: good walker: fair performer: good third in £8,800 event at Kempton, listed race at Epsom and minor event at Chepstow: mostly faced stiff tasks otherwise in 1990: stays 1m: acts on firm going, possibly unsuited by soft. *P. T. Walwyn.* 82

LA CASSONADE 2 b.f. (Mar 21) Sulaafah (USA) 119–My Sweet Melody 62 (Music Boy 124) [1990 6g 6m a6g] smallish, good-quartered filly: first foal: dam poor maiden best at 5f: plating-class form in maidens and a minor event. *M. D. I. Usher.* 55

LA CASTANA 4 ch.f. Dunbeath (USA) 127–Din Brown (USA) (Tom Rolfe) [1989 7g 12f⁵ 10f 8.2f³ 8.2m³ 8m⁶ 8.2f² 10f³ 12f 12g* 1990 13.6g⁶ 15.8d 18.8f³] angular filly: winning plater: form in handicaps in summer only when third in poor 5-runner event at Warwick: appears to stay 2¼m: acts on firm going: below form in blinkers: won 4 times over hurdles in 1989/90: sold 6,000 gns Doncaster August Sales. *C. R. Beever.* 53

LACE PAROSOL 4 ro.f. Neltino 97–Anglophil 61 (Philemon 119) [1989 NR 1990 8m 9g 7f⁴ a6g] close-coupled filly: fifth living foal: dam 2-y-o 6f winner: well beaten in varied events: sweated on debut. *C. Holmes.* —

LA CHIQUITA 6 b.m. African Sky 124–La Cita (Le Levanstell 122) [1989 5m* 5f³ 5f* 5m* 6f⁴ 5f 1990 5f² 5g 5g⁵ 5m³ 5m⁴ 6g 6m 5m³ 5d⁵ 5g⁵] lengthy, good- 82 d topped mare: modest handicapper: suited by 5f: acts well on top-of-the-ground: has swished tail. *T. Craig.*

LACONIC 2 ch.g. (Feb 12) Nicholas Bill 125–Hi-Conkers 86 (Sica Boy 132) [1990   — 6g 6d 8d] 4,000Y: rather sparely-made gelding: brother to 1m winner Joint Services and half-brother to several other winners, including very useful sprinter Swinging Sam (by Swing Easy): dam 2-y-o 5f winner: poor maiden: should be suited by further than 6f. *J. M. Jefferson.*

LADDERMAN 4 ch.g. Salmon Leap (USA) 131–Joanne's Joy (Ballymore 123)   **48** [1989 8.2s² 8f³ 10g 7m 8f 1990 7g 10.1g⁴ 11.5m 10m 8f5] lengthy gelding: disappointing maiden: stayed 1¼m: probably acted on any going: sweating and edgy second start: difficult ride: dead. *R. V. Smyth.*

LA DOMAINE 3 b.f. Dominion 123–La Galette 76 (Double Form 130) [1989 5f⁵   **75** 5f⁵ 6g⁵ 6g* 6g³ 6s² 6g 1990 6.5g³ 8d* 7m 7m 8g 8g⁵ 8f³ 8.3m a8g a8d* 8g] lengthy, good-quartered filly: good walker: has a fluent, roundish action: modest performer: successful at Cagnes-sur-Mer in March and in 24-runner £19,000 handicap at Ayr (by short head having been soon outpaced) in September: stays 1m: acts on any going: inconsistent. *C. R. Nelson.*

LADY ALONE 3 ch.f. Mr Fluorocarbon 126–Empress Corina 74 (Free State 125)   **52** [1989 5d² 5m² 5f³ 6m⁶ 5.1f² 6g a5g 1990 6f 5m 5m⁶ 5m* 6m⁵ 5m⁵ a5g] leggy, sparely-made filly: moderate mover: plating-class handicapper: favourite, won at Catterick in June, soon pushed along then staying on strongly to lead close home: below form after, withdrawn lame intended seventh start and not seen for 5 months afterwards: stays 6f: acts on any going. *J. D. Czerpak.*

LADY BARAKA (IRE) 2 b.f. (May 13) Shernazar 131–Lady Wise (Lord Gayle   **52** (USA) 124) [1990 6f⁴ 7m² 5m 7d] IR 2,000F: small filly: moderate mover: half-sister to 1985 Irish 2-y-o 5f winner Before The Storm (by Thatching): dam placed over 8.6f at 2 yrs in Ireland, is half-sister to Middle Park winner Spanish Express: in frame in maiden at Brighton and claimer at Yarmouth: never able to challenge after: will be suited by at least 1m: trained first 2 outings by R. Guest. *J. Pearce.*

LADY BLUES SINGER 4 ch.f. Chief Singer 131–Moaning Low 85 (Burglar   **33** 128) [1989 6s⁴ 5f 5.8h³ 8.2f 6g³ a8g a6g⁴ a6g 1990 a7g4] close-coupled filly: poor maiden: seems to stay 7f: acts on any going: blinkered twice at 2 yrs. *A. J. Chamberlain.*

LADY BRAVE (IRE) 2 ch.f. (Feb 14) Commanche Run 133–Gerona (GER)   — (Herero) [1990 a7g 7f 8.2g] IR 2,000Y: neat filly: half-sister to several winners, notably Cataldi (by Wolver Hollow), very smart on his day at up to 1¼m: dam versatile winner of 7 races, including 1¼m German Oaks and 6f Goldene Peitsche: well beaten in maiden auctions and a seller. *R. Curtis.*

LADY BUNTING 3 b.f. Well Decorated (USA)–Lady's Flag (USA) (Fifth Marine   **56** (USA)) [1989 7m 8v 8g⁴ 1990 8f³ 8m 7m 7m³ 8m 8m 7m 8m³] leggy filly: quite modest form: best efforts (mostly in handicaps) on days when placed, making most last 2 occasions: stays 1m: acts on firm going: blinkered seventh start. *L. G. Cottrell.*

LADY CHALONER 4 bl.f. Sparkling Boy 110–Dras Lass 86 (Don Carlos) [1989   **49** NR 1990 6m a7g 5m 5m⁵ 5m] small, workmanlike filly: keen walker: first form when fifth, soon pushed along, in maiden at Warwick in August: should be better suited by 6f: has joined P. Bevan. *B. A. McMahon.*

LADY DICTATOR 2 gr.f. (May 11) Blushing Scribe (USA) 107–Milnsbridge   **42** (Dragonara Palace (USA) 115) [1990 5m 5m 6m⁴] 1,600Y: sturdy filly: second foal: half-sister to 1988 2-y-o 5f to 7f winner Crowthers (by Mandrake Major): dam poor maiden: keeping-on fourth at Lingfield in May, only form in sellers: unseated rider leaving paddock and was withdrawn at Nottingham following month. *D. Haydn Jones.*

LADY DOOLITTLE 2 b.f. (Mar 21) King of Spain 121–Mondoodle 63 (Mon-   **52** santo (FR) 121) [1990 6g 8m⁶ 6d⁵ a7g] 2,000F, 4,300Y: tall, lengthy filly: has scope: second foal: dam 2-y-o 6f winner: plating-class maiden: sixth of 17 in apprentice seller at Warwick: ran poorly on all-weather: seems suited by 6f: active sort. *J. A. Glover.*

LADY ELECTRIC 4 b.f. Electric 126–Romping (Sir Gaylord) [1989 9f 7m 8f   **46** 11.7f 12g* 18g⁴ 1990 12f⁵ 12.2m 12m⁴ 14m⁵ 14m² 16g³ 12.2m 17.1d5] workmanlike filly: plating-class handicapper: should prove best at up to 2m: probably unsuited by firm going: good mount for apprentice. *R. J. Hodges.*

LADY EMMA 3 b.f. Kafu 120–Nadja 77 (Dancer's Image (USA)) [1989 5m 5f 5m   — 5m⁵ 5f⁵ 1990 10.2m] tall, leggy filly: moderate mover: poor form at 2 yrs: first run for 14 months, badly tailed off in apprentice handicap only start in 1990. *B. R. Millman.*

LADY GHISLAINE (FR)   3 b.f. Lydian (FR) 120–Planeze (FR) (Faraway Son   —
(USA) 130) [1989 6g 1990 7m 6g⁶ 8m⁶ 6d] workmanlike, plain filly: has a round
action: no worthwhile form, in selling handicap final start. *T. Casey.*

LADY GRENVILLE   3 b.f. Aragon 118–Tri'as (Tyrant (USA)) [1989 6f 6g 7m   40
6g⁴ a7g⁴ 1990 a8g⁶ a7g³ a8g⁶ 6f⁴ 7f] medium-sized filly: quite modest maiden
at best: below form at 3 yrs, staying on after slow start in apprentice handicap
(sweating) fourth outing: seems best at 6f: acts on firm going. *M. D. I. Usher.*

LADY GWENMORE   2 b.f. (Apr 11) Town And Country 124–Ment More 62   —
(Sahib 114) [1990 8m 8.2m 7m] workmanlike filly: fourth reported foal: half-sister
to winning plater Jetmore (by Mljet): dam poor maiden on flat, won over hurdles:
always behind in maidens and minor event. *R. Hannon.*

LADY HOMILY   6 b.m. Homing 130–Taryn 76 (Crooner 119) [1989 NR 1990 8f]   —
rather leggy, workmanlike mare: winning plater as 4-y-o: tailed off in apprentice
handicap at Warwick in May: used to be well suited by 7f and top-of-the-ground:
blinkered once. *E. A. Wheeler.*

LADY IN ACTION (FR)   2 b.f. (Mar 12) Fast Topaze (USA) 128–Gracious Girl   —
(USA) (Forli (ARG)) [1990 a6g] second foal: half-sister to 3-y-o Shannon Flood (by
In Fijar): dam French 2-y-o 6.5f winner, is half-sister to Prix de Diane winner Lady
In Silver: slowly away and soon well behind in 11-runner claimer at Southwell in
December. *M. H. Tompkins.*

LADY IN RED (FR)   2 b.f. (May 1) Shareef Dancer (USA) 135–Dressed In Red   74 p
(Red Alert 127) [1990 6g 6m⁵ 6.5g] 31,000F, 31,000Y: leggy, attractive filly: sixth
foal: half-sister to leading Italian sprinter Tinterosse (by Kenmare): dam won in
Italy: progressive maiden: still carrying condition when thirteenth of 17 in Tatter-
salls Tiffany Yorkshire Stakes at Doncaster in September: likely to improve again.
R. Charlton.

LADY IN THE LAKE   3 b.f. Kings Lake (USA) 133–Trouble Me Not (USA)   —
(Nodouble (USA)) [1989 6f 7g 10g 1990 12.2m 12m] angular, plain filly: of little
account: blinkered final outing. *R. O'Leary.*

LADY JEMMA (IRE)   2 b.f. (Apr 12) Prince Tenderfoot (USA) 126–Flame Up   55
(Bustino 136) [1990 6g 7m 6g 8m³ 10m⁶] IR 1,900F: small filly: moderate walker:
second foal: dam Irish 2-y-o 5f winner: ridden by apprentice, sixth of 18, keeping on
never dangerous, to Long Furlong in selling nursery at Leicester in October: suited
by 1¼m: has been bandaged: sold 800 gns Newmarket Autumn Sales, resold 500 gns
Ascot December Sales. *M. H. Tompkins.*

LADY KALLISTE   2 gr.f. (Feb 23) Another Realm 118–Lady Killane 62 (Reform   —
132) [1990 5m 7s] 3,500F, 3,200Y, 4,000 2-y-o: workmanlike filly: poor mover: first
foal: dam maiden suited by 1½m out of very useful 6f sprinter Cease Fire: bit
backward in maidens at Folkestone and Lingfield (showed up to 2f out) in October:
may well do better. *P. Mitchell.*

LADY KEYSER   4 b.f. Le Johnstan 123–Fanny Keyser (Majority Blue 126) [1989   —
6d 5.8m 5m 5.3h 5f⁶ 5m 5f* 5.1f⁶ 5f 5m⁴ 1990 a5g] angular, workmanlike filly:
plating-class winner of handicap as 3-y-o: well beaten at Lingfield in January: suited
by 5f: yet to race on soft going, acts on any other: blinkered once at 3 yrs. *D. W.
Chapman.*

LADY LACEY   3 b.f. Kampala 120–Cecily (Prince Regent (FR) 129) [1989 NR   75
1990 8.3f2 7f* 8g⁴ 8m³ 8.2v² 8m² 8g³] IR 1,300Y: rather lightly-made, quite
attractive filly: fourth living foal: half-sister to 1m and 9f winner Xylophone (by Tap
On Wood): dam Irish 11.2f winner: progressive form: won claimer at Salisbury in
August: will stay further: acts on any going. *G. B. Balding.*

LADYLIKE (USA)   3 b.f. Sir Ivor 135–Ethics (USA) (Nijinsky (CAN) 138) [1989   71
NR 1990 10.4g 10.6d⁶ 12d2] workmanlike filly: second foal: half-sister to smart
French 4-y-o middle-distance stayer Robertet (by Roberto): dam unraced sister to
high-class middle-distance colt Solford: first worthwhile form when second of 12 to
Mingus in maiden at Folkestone in November: better at 1½m than 1¼m. *J. H. M.
Gosden.*

LADY LONGLEAT   3 ch.f. Longleat (USA) 109–Kip's Sister (Cawston's Clown   —
113) [1989 6g⁵ 5f² 6g 5g 5s 1990 a8g 11m a11g 8.3m 10m 8f 10m 8.2m] small, angular
filly: moderate mover: poor maiden: possibly best at up to 1m: visored last 2 starts:
blinkered once at 2 yrs. *M. Brittain.*

LADY MADINA   3 b.f. Legend of France (USA) 124–Double Touch (FR)   52
(Nonoalco (USA) 131) [1989 7g 6m 1990 12f4 10g 14g³ a14g³ 15.3m*] work-

manlike filly: plating-class perfomer: held up when winning handicap at Wolverhampton in August, edging left: suited by test of stamina. *M. J. Ryan.*

LADY MAGENTA 3 ch.f. Rolfe (USA) 77–Heliotrope (King Emperor (USA)) 35
[1989 NR 1990 9f 10.2f 7m 8f⁴ 10f 10.8f³ 12m 10h³ 12m] lengthy filly: fourth reported foal: dam of little account: plater: form only at around 1¼m: blinkered fifth and seventh starts: sold out of R. Simpson's stable 3,000 gns Ascot September Sales after eighth. *Miss L. Bower.*

LADY MIAMI 3 ch.f. Mansingh (USA) 120–Miami Star 80 (Miami Springs 121) 36
[1989 6m 6g 1990 5f 8.3g 6f 6m⁴] sparely-made filly: plater: doesn't stay 1m: sweating second start. *T. Casey.*

LADY OF LIGHT (IRE) 2 b.f. (May 5) Glow (USA)–Silent Sun 90 (Blakeney —
126) [1990 6g 7s a7g] 2,000F: second foal: half-sister to 3-y-o Closed Shop (by Auction Ring), 6f to 1m winner at 2 yrs: dam won at 1¼m here and 1m in France: shaped quite well in maidens on first 2 starts: soundly beaten in similar event on all-weather. *D. J. G. Murray-Smith.*

LADY OF THE FEN 2 b.f. (Jan 9) Myjinski (USA)–Flying Glory (Flying 56
Mercury) [1990 5g⁵ 5g 6f⁵ 5m⁵ 5f⁵ 5f³ 5f* 6m⁵ 5f⁶ 5m⁴ 5m² 5f⁶ 5f⁵ 6m⁵ 7g 7f⁴ 6m 8d] lengthy, sparely-made filly: has a quick action: sixth foal: half-sister to 7f and 1m seller winner Clipsall (by Petitioner) and a winner abroad: dam unraced: fairly useful plater: ready winner at Wolverhampton (retained 6,000 gns) in July: mostly consistent after: stays 7f: acts well on firm ground: visored third and fourth outings, bandaged first 3: carries head high, and has looked ungenuine. *Mrs N. Macauley.*

LADY PHILIPPA (IRE) 2 b.f. (Feb 7) Taufan (USA) 119–Katie Koo 82 77
(Persian Bold 123) [1990 a6g³ a8g²] third foal: half-sister to 1987 Irish 2-y-o 6f and 7f winner Hakari (by Glenstal): dam won at 11.7f and 13.1f: placed in Lingfield maidens, caught inside final furlong when length second of 8, well clear, to Wicked Things in December: sure to win a race. *B. W. Hills.*

LADY POLY 2 b.f. (Feb 25) Dunbeath (USA) 127–First Temptation (USA) (Mr —
Leader (USA)) [1990 6m 6m 7f] medium-sized filly: second foal: half-sister to 3-y-o Sam The Man (by Aragon): dam maiden on flat suited by test of stamina, won a hurdle race: poor form in quite modest company: may do better over further. *Miss B. Sanders.*

LADY PRIMROSE 4 b.f. Reesh 117–Caerinion 76 (Royal Palace 131) [1989 NR — §
1990 7m 7g a6g] close-coupled, angular filly: has a round action: fourth in seller as 2-y-o, only form: looked temperamentally unsatisfactory final outing: sold to join B. Forsey 2,600 gns Ascot December Sales. *G. Blum.*

LADY REMAINDER 3 ch.f. Remainder Man 126§–My Aisling 72 (John de —
Coombe 122) [1989 NR 1990 7g 10.2m⁶ 8m 10.6d 14m] sturdy filly: first foal: dam, first past post twice as 2-y-o but disqualified both times, stayed 1¼m: no worthwhile form but showed signs of ability second and fourth starts: probably better at 1¼m than 1m: tends to sweat and be on edge: winning selling hurdler. *Mrs J. R. Ramsden.*

LADY ROSANNA 5 b.m. Kind of Hush 118–Rosaceae 99 (Sagaro 133) [1989 12v 72
14.8d⁵ 12f² 14f* 14g⁶ 14f³ 14m* 13.1f² 12g³ 1990 14.8m⁵ 12m³ 14.8f⁶ 12g 16.2m⁶] robust, quite attractive mare: moderate mover: won 2 handicaps at Sandown as 4-y-o: below her best in 1990, running moody race third outing then off course 5 months: suited by about 1¾m: acts on any going, except possibly heavy: good mount for claimer: winning hurdler in 1989/90. *I. A. Balding.*

LADY ROSEMARY 3 b.f. Burslem 123–Sweet Foot (Prince Tenderfoot (USA) —
126) [1989 5f⁵ a6g a6g 1990 a8g⁴ a8g] small filly: no worthwhile form since debut: blinkered twice: sold 560 gns Doncaster February Sales. *I. Campbell.*

LADY SCOTFIELD (IRE) 2 b.f. (May 6) Tate Gallery (USA) 117–Costalunga —
(Baldric II 131) [1990 a6g 8.2m a7g a5g a6g a7g] IR 4,600F: sparely-made filly: fifth foal: half-sister to a winner in Italy by Hoche: dam unraced daughter of half-sister to smart middle-distance performer Dancing Rocks: soundly beaten in varied events at Southwell and Nottingham: blinkered penultimate start. *R. J. Muddle.*

LADY SHALOTT (IRE) 2 b.f. (Mar 18) Caveat (USA)–Carillon Miss (USA) —
(The Minstrel (CAN) 135) [1990 7d 7m] 4,800Y: good-topped filly: moderate mover: half-sister to a minor winner in USA: dam unraced daughter of Sex Appeal, dam also of Try My Best and El Gran Senor (both by Northern Dancer): sire won 1½m Belmont Stakes: backward and slowly away in maiden auction at Goodwood and minor event (on toes) at Ascot in October. *J. O'Donoghue.*

LADY'S MANTLE (USA) 6 ch.m. Sunny Clime (USA)–Alchemilla (USA) 41
(Quadrangle) [1989 6d 5f 5m⁵ 5m² 5.1m* 5f* 5m⁵ 5h⁴ 5f² 5f⁴ 5m² 5.1f³ 5g 5m⁵ 5.1g

1990 5m 5f 6m 5m 5m³ 5f² 5g⁴ a5g⁵ 5m⁴ 5m⁶ 5f⁴ 5m² 5m³ 5m 5f* 5.1m³ 5.3f⁴ 5d⁵ 5d⁶] compact, good-bodied mare: carries plenty of condition: moderate mover: poor handicapper: made all at Folkestone in September: below her best only outing on all-weather: suited by 5f: acts on hard and dead going: has been tried in blinkers and visor: often wears crossed noseband: often claimer ridden, but wasn't at Folkestone. *R. Bastiman.*

LADY SNOOBLE 3 b.f. King of Clubs 124–Ides of March 87 (Mummy's Pet 125) **50** [1989 8.2f5 1990 5s² 6f 7f² 7g 7m⁶ 6m 7g 8g a8g] small, sturdy filly: plating-class maiden who lost her form: best effort over 7f: probably acts on any going: blinkered sixth and eighth starts: trained until after sixth by R. Boss: has run poorly for apprentice and looked none too keen: one to be wary of. *R. J. Hodges.*

LADY SPEED STICK 4 b.f. Tender King 123–Tetrazzini 70 (Sovereign Path **40** 125) [1989 8.5f 7g5 7m 6g⁶ 6f 7f 6f⁴ 7m 1990 7f 7m⁵ 7g³ 8g³ 8m 8.2g² 10g 12g 8g⁵ 8m⁴ 10f a8g] smallish, lengthy filly: moderate walker and mover: poor and inconsistent maiden: stays 1m: best on a sound surface: blinkered 3 times as 3-y-o: has sweated and got on edge: sold 2,000 gns Doncaster October Sales. *W. Bentley.*

LADY STOCK 4 ch.f. Crofter (USA) 124–Millingdale 65 (Tumble Wind (USA)) **52** [1989 6g 5h 6f 7m 7f* 7h 7g 8d 6f 1990 8.3m⁴ 10.1m⁴ 8f 8.3g] smallish, close-coupled filly: carries condition: best effort at 4 yrs in seller on second outing: stays 1¼m: acts on firm going: twice bandaged near-hind: inconsistent. *J. White.*

LADY TALECA (IRE) 2 ch.f. (Apr 9) Exhibitioner 111–Morelia 76 (Murrayfield **49** 119) [1990 5s 6g⁶ 5m³ 6m³ 7f 6d] IR 2,800F, 2,000Y: chunky filly: carries condition: poor mover: half-sister to 3 winners, including 11f winner Porter (by Mummy's Pet) and 1987 2-y-o 5f winner Warring States (by Kafu): dam 2-y-o 7f winner: plating-class maiden: should stay further than 6f: possibly unsuited by dead ground: sold 1,200 gns Doncaster October Sales. *F. H. Lee.*

LADY TAP 4 ch.f. Red Sunset 120–Park Lady 82 (Tap On Wood 130) [1989 5m **78** 6m² 5m 5d 1990 5m 5g⁵ 5m⁶ 6m* 5m² 6m⁴] compact filly: good walker: modest handicapper: won at Yarmouth in September: effective at 5f and 6f: never raced on soft going, acted on any other: visored once at 3 yrs: in foal to Sharrood. *W. Hastings-Bass.*

LADY TOPAZ 3 b.f. Jalmood (USA) 126–Town Lady 93 (Town Crier 119) [1989 **52** 6g 5m³ 6g⁴ 7m 7g 1990 7m 8g³ 8m 8g 7m⁴ 7f 7g⁶ 8.2s a8g] small, sturdy filly: plating-class maiden: easily best efforts as 3-y-o when in frame in handicaps at Leicester: stays 1m: acts on good to firm ground: gave a lot of trouble at stalls seventh start: visored final one: sold 800 gns Newmarket December Sales. *T. Thomson Jones.*

LADY TOPPING (USA) 3 b.f. Lyphard (USA) 132–Miss Derby (USA) (Master **51** Derby (USA)) [1989 6.3m 7g⁴ 7g⁴ 8g⁶ 1990 a7g 8m 8.5g⁶ 10m⁵ 9f] $120,000Y: small filly: fifth foal: closely related to French 2-y-o 8.5f winner Madame Nureyev (by Nureyev): dam, winner at up to 9f, is granddaughter of notable broodmare Treasure Chest: plating-class maiden: best efforts fourth in Irish maidens as 2-y-o: sweating, form in 1990 only in handicap fourth outing: stays 1¼m: sold out of J. Oxx's stable 10,000 gns Newmarket Autumn (1989) Sales: sold 8,000 gns Newmarket December Sales. *Lord John FitzGerald.*

LADY VIOLET 3 gr.f. Superlative 118–Declamation 93 (Town Crier 119) [1989 **—** NR 1990 8m 8s⁴] leggy filly: eighth foal: half-sister to 3 winners, including useful middle-distance stayer Aim To Please (by Gunner B): dam second over 6f on only start: 66/1, 14 lengths fourth of 6 to impressive Susurration in maiden at Newcastle in November, never placed to challenge: may improve again. *Don Enrico Incisa.*

LADY VIXEN (USA) 3 b.f. Sir Ivor 135–T V Vixen (USA) (T V Lark) [1989 NR **—** 1990 12f⁵ 10.6s 10.2f⁵ 9f 8g] rather leggy, good-quartered filly: half-sister to 2 minor winners in USA by Raise A Native: dam won 9 stakes races at 3 yrs in USA, notably 8.5f Fantasy Stakes: well beaten in maidens and handicaps: blinkered final start. *P. F. I. Cole.*

LADY WESTGATE 6 b.m. Welsh Chanter 124–Church Bay 76 (Reliance II 137) **46** [1989 NR 1990 12f 12m 16g* 16m² 16.5f* 16f⁵ 14m⁶] leggy, rather plain mare: successful in handicaps at Chepstow (carrying head high) in June and Folkestone (odds on) in July: ran moderately last 2 outings: suited by 2m: acts on firm going: visored once: placed in point-to-points. *G. B. Balding.*

LADY WESTOWN 6 b.m. Town And Country 124–Hay-Hay (Hook Money 124) **53** [1989 12g 16m³ 16.2m* 16m³ 16.5m⁵ 1990 16m⁶ 16.5f* 16.2g* 16m³] small mare: favourite, won handicaps at Doncaster in July and Beverley (odds on for 4-runner event, sent clear 4f out) in August: reportedly broke down final outing: suited by test of stamina: acts on firm ground: has sweated. *R. J. Holder.*

LADY WINIFRED (IRE) 2 ch.f. (May 28) The Noble Player (USA) 126– 51 Pollymere (Scorpio (FR) 127) [1990 7m 7g 6g] IR 1,500F, IR 5,400Y: rather leggy filly: has scope: first foal: dam never ran: plating-class form in maidens and minor event in autumn. *R. Hannon.*

LADY WINNER (FR) 4 ch.f. Fabulous Dancer (USA) 124–Ameridienne (FR) 121 79 (Targowice (USA) 130) [1989 8s6 8g* 8g5 8g2 8g* 9.2g6 9s* 8.5s* 8.5g* 1990 8g2 9.2g5 8d4 8d* 8g4 9f2 9.2g2 8g] good-class French filly: successful in Prix d'Astarte at Deauville by ¾ length from Daisy Dance: in frame after in Prix Jacques le Marois (over length fourth to Priolo) at same course, Beverly D Stakes at Arlington and Ciga Prix de l'Opera (not having best of runs behind Colour Chart) at Longchamp: beaten around 3 lengths when eighth to Royal Academy in Breeders' Cup Mile at Belmont Park: effective at 1m to 9f: acts on any going: tough and consistent. *M. Zilber, France.*

LAFKADIO 3 b.g. Gay Mecene (USA) 128–Lakonia (Kris 135) [1989 5f 1990 8g4 41 8g a8g a11g a12g a14g4] good-bodied gelding: form on flat only when fourth in maiden at Edinburgh and handicap at Southwell: stays 1¾m: blinkered third start: sold out of J. Gosden's stable 1,800 gns Newmarket July Sales after that: winning selling hurdler. *M. C. Chapman.*

LA FOUDRE 2 ro.c. (Mar 22) Show-A-Leg 107–Land of Ginger (Young Man (FR) – 73) [1990 5m 6g 7m 7m] workmanlike colt: second foal: dam never ran: well beaten in maidens and minor event: blinkered final 2 (raced very freely first occasion) starts. *Miss A. J. Whitfield.*

LA FUMATA 3 br.f. Valiyar 129–Manela Lady (Ela-Mana-Mou 132) [1989 NR – 1990 7.6m] small, lengthy filly: first foal: dam, ran twice in Ireland, is daughter of useful Irish 1979 2-y-o 5f winner Smokey Lady, sister to Steel Heart and half-sister to dam of Chilibang: bit backward, well beaten in maiden at Lingfield in September: sold 800 gns Newmarket December Sales. *T. Thomson Jones.*

LA GALERIE 3 b.c. Glenstal (USA) 118–Tizzy 79 (Formidable (USA) 125) [1989 87 5s 5d2 5g* 5g* 5f6 5f3 6m5 5m2 6g2 6f3 5s3 6g4 1990 8f5 8v4 7.6m 6d] lengthy colt: had a quick action: fairly useful performer at 2 yrs: off course 5 months after creditable fourth of 5 in minor event at Ayr in April: broke leg in Ayr Gold Cup: probably stayed 1m: dead. *W. Carter.*

LA GRANGE MUSIC 3 ch.c. Music Boy 124–Great Care 66 (Home Guard 111 (USA) 129) [1989 NR 1990 6m* 6m* 6g3 6m* 6m2 7g5 6g*] 5,600Y: leggy, good-topped colt: has plenty of scope: sixth foal: half-brother to modest 9f winner Hamper (by Final Straw): dam sprinter from family of top-class middle-distance filly Grease: won minor event at Thirsk in May, £7,000 handicap (on toes) at Newbury in June and listed races at Newbury in July and the Curragh (by head from Milieu) in September: close third in Cork And Orrery Stakes at Royal Ascot: best at 6f: sometimes sweating: occasionally slowly away: very useful. *G. A. Huffer.*

LAIRD OF BALMORAL 3 b.c. Lochnager 132–Baggin Time 91 (Pinsun 108) 88 [1989 6m4 6m6 6m 6g* 8.2d* 8g 6v3 1990 8d5 9m 8m2] compact, good-quartered colt: good walker: fair performer: shaped well before good second in auction race at Redcar in June: should stay beyond 1m: acts on good to firm ground and heavy. *M. H. Easterby.*

LAKELAND BEAUTY 3 b.f. Mummy's Pet 125–Skiddaw (USA) (Grey Dawn II 96 132) [1989 6g4 6f* 6g6 1990 7.3d6 8m 6m* 7d] leggy, lengthy, rather angular filly: has a round action: fairly useful performer: won minor event at Leicester in May: sweating and edgy, behind in 1000 Guineas (swished tail) at Newmarket and June handicap (mulish in preliminaries) at Epsom starts either side: headstrong, and may prove best at sprint distances: yet to race on soft going: acts on any other: trained until after second start by W. Brooks. *J. H. M. Gosden.*

LAKE MISTASSIU 3 b.f. Tina's Pet 121–Kakisa 81 (Forlorn River 124) [1989 85 6m5 6f4 5f* 5.3f2 5s* 5g 1990 5f2 5g5 5g3 5m6 5d 5g4 5s3 5g] smallish, strong filly: fair handicapper: will prove best at 5f: acts on any going: on toes, hung badly right second start. *G. A. Pritchard-Gordon.*

LALLAPALOOSA 2 b.f. (Apr 29) Superlative 118–Tsar's Bride (Song 132) 84 [1990 6m5 6m4 6f5 6g* 6m6 6m5] 11,500Y: workmanlike filly: has a quick action: sixth foal: half-sister to 1986 2-y-o 6f winner Tender Tiff (by Prince Tenderfoot) and 1¼m winner Winter Palace (by Persian Bold): dam lightly raced: fair performer: blinkered first time, won nursery at Windsor in August by 7 lengths: respectable fifth to Punch N'Run in similar event at Ascot after, only comparable form and only other time blinkered. *J. L. Dunlop.*

LALLUMETTE 3 br.f. Royal Match 117–La Piccolina 85 (Tudor Rhythm 112) —
[1989 NR 1990 6m 8.3f 7m³] lengthy filly: third reported foal: half-sister to 2 poor maidens by Riboboy: dam 1m to 12.2f winner: behind in claimer (moved poorly down) and minor events. *B. R. Millman.*

LA MARIQUITA 2 b.f. (Mar 2) Ballacashtal (CAN)–La Perricholi (FR) 80   50
(Targowice (USA) 130) [1990 6m³ 7g* 7m³ 7h⁵ 8m 8.2s] sparely-made filly: moderate mover: second foal: dam 6f winner: fair plater: sold out of J. Hetherton's stable 15,000 gns after winning very comfortably at Redcar in June: below that form after, blinkered final outing: should stay 1m: seems unsuited by soft going: sold 1,050 gns Doncaster October Sales. *M. H. Easterby.*

LAMARSH (IRE) 2 ch.c. (Feb 5) Be My Guest (USA) 126–Annabella 88   69
(Habitat 134) [1990 7m 7g 7s³] stocky colt: fifth living foal: half-brother to fair middle-distance maiden Lexden (by Blakeney): dam 5f winner at 2 yrs winner is out of high-class 5f and 1m winner Sovereign and half-sister to Irish Derby second Lucky Sovereign: 50/1, third of 14, leading on favoured stand rail 4f, in maiden at Lingfield in October, only form: should stay 1m: possibly suited by soft ground. *J. H. M. Gosden.*

LA MASAAS (USA) 2 b.c. (Jan 7) Miswaki (USA) 124–Skeeb (USA) 94   80
(Topsider (USA)) [1990 5g 5m* 5f³ 5d² 6d 5g⁵ 5d] neat colt: poor mover: first foal: dam, 2-y-o 6f winner, is sister to million-dollar earner North Sider: modest performer: hung left when winning maiden at Thirsk in May: best effort neck second to Vintage Only in minor event at Beverley following month: better form at 5f than 6f: blinkered final outing, getting very upset in preliminaries: has worn tongue strap: sold 12,500 gns Doncaster October Sales. *A. A. Scott.*

LAMBADA GIRL (IRE) 2 b.f. (Apr 28) Petorius 117–Spear Dance (Gay   62
Fandango (USA) 132) [1990 5.8m 5.8h³ 6m 6g 6m 5.8d] IR 6,000Y: small, workmanlike filly: poor mover: second foal: sister to Irish 3-y-o 11f and 1½m winner Masai Warrior: dam Irish 7f and 1m winner, is sister to Jersey Stakes winner Rasa Penang: around 6 lengths tenth of 16 in very valuable listed-restricted race at the Curragh in August, fourth and apparently best effort: only poor form otherwise: will stay 7f: blinkered final 3 starts. *D. W. P. Arbuthnot.*

LAMBOURN RAJA 4 b.g. Indian King (USA) 128–Take A Chance (FR) (Baldric   85
II 131) [1989 8.2g 1990 8f³ 8m² 8.2v* 8.2d⁴ 7g* 7g* a7g*] lengthy, rather angular gelding: in excellent heart in autumn, winning claimers at Haydock and Southwell and handicaps, making all, at Newbury (apprentices) and Salisbury in between: better at 7f than 1m: has form on firm going, but clearly goes very well with some give: visored once: sold out of J. Hudson's stable 6,800 gns Ascot April Sales. *M. C. Pipe.*

LAMBSON 3 b.g. Petorius 117–Julie Be Quick (USA) (Selari) [1989 NR 1990 8m   57
9f⁵ 8g⁶ 9g⁴ 10m 8.2m 10m 11d] 17,000Y: leggy gelding: moderate walker and mover: half-brother to 3 winners here and abroad, including fairly useful 6f and 7f winner Blue Emmanuelle (by Lochnager), later successful at around 1m in USA: quite modest form at best: showed little last 4 starts: should stay 1¼m: acts on firm ground. *R. M. Whitaker.*

LAMBTON LAD 3 b.g. Sahar 115–Illaqua (USA) (Empery (USA) 128) [1989 a8g   —
1990 8f 8f 10.6f 8.5g 8g 11.5g³ 8m a7g⁶ 7m 12.5g] lengthy, sparely-made gelding: poor plater: should be suited by further than 7f: blinkered sixth to ninth starts. *E. Eldin.*

LA MEZERAY 2 b.f. (May 18) Nishapour (FR) 125–La Pythie (FR) 89 (Filiberto   —
(USA) 123) [1990 5f] 1,000Y: angular, plain filly: seventh foal: half-sister to 3-y-o Barcham (by Blakeney), 7f winner at 2 yrs, and 7f winner Mark Birley (by Night Shift): dam 2-y-o 7f winner, is granddaughter of top-class La Sega: slowly away and soon behind in seller at Warwick in May. *B. Palling.*

LAND AFAR 3 b.c. Dominion 123–Jouvencelle 68 (Rusticaro (FR) 124) [1989   82
6m* 6g⁵ 1990 8.2f⁶ 8m⁵ 10m³ 10.6s² 10.6m⁴ 9m*] good-quartered colt: fair handicapper: won claimer (claimed out of W. Jarvis' stable £21,587 to join J. O'Shea) at Goodwood in August, staying on strongly to lead inside final 1f: may well stay further than 10.6f: acts on good to firm ground and soft: blinkered fourth start: consistent. *W. Jarvis.*

LAND OF HOPE 3 b.f. Dominion 123–Vielle 123 (Ribero 126) [1989 6m⁵ 1990   61
7m 7.6d⁶ 10g 8.3m 8f² 8g a8g a10g] lengthy, quite good-topped filly: quite modest maiden: below form last 3 outings, including for amateur: stays 1m: best efforts on

top-of-the-ground: visored last 4 starts: sold 2,400 gns Newmarket December Sales. *P. T. Walwyn.*

LAND OF WONDER (USA) 3 b.g. Wind And Wuthering (USA) 132–Heat — Haze (USA) 66 (Jungle Savage (USA)) [1989 5d⁵ 5s⁴ 7m 1990 10m 8.3m 14f⁶ 7h] leggy gelding: has a round action: poor maiden: better at 7f than 5f: blinkered and edgy second start: sold 1,700 gns Ascot July Sales: seems of dubious temperament. *C. A. Cyzer.*

LAND O' THE LEAL (IRE) 2 b.f. (Apr 4) Tate Gallery (USA) 117–Land Ho — (Primera 131) [1990 6g 7m⁴] IR 14,000F, IR 24,000Y: close-coupled, angular filly: half-sister to several winners, including very useful 1976 2-y-o 5f winner Easy Landing (by Swing Easy) and dam of Upper Strata: dam daughter of very smart sprinter Lucasland: fourth of 8, prominent nearly 5f, in maiden at Leicester in October: dead. *M. Bell.*

LAND SUN (IRE) 2 b.c. (Feb 13) Red Sunset 120–Great Land (USA) (Friend's 63 § Choice (USA)) [1990 5g 5g 5f⁵ 5g⁴ 5g* 6m⁴ 6g⁶ 6m⁴ 5m* 6f 5m⁶ 5.8h 6m 5m* 6g 5f² 5m 5m 5m 5v* 5m 6s 5g] 9,400Y: small, sturdy colt: moderate mover: third foal: dam won 9 races at up to 9f in North America: modest performer: successful in seller (retained 7,000 gns) at Wolverhampton in May, claimer at Bath in July and nurseries at Redcar (tended to hang left) in August and Haydock in October: well beaten, quite often tailed off, in his other races: suited by 5f: acts on any going: effective with or without blinkers or visor: thoroughly unreliable. *M. R. Channon.*

LANDYAP (USA) 6 b.h. Fappiano (USA)–My Candidate (USA) (Prince John) 112 [1989 NR 1990 13.3m³ 10m⁶ 8.5g² 10g³ 10.1g² 10m³ 12s⁵ 9g⁴] rangy horse: half-brother to 2 winners in USA, including stakes-placed County Seat (by Dewan): dam won once at around 7f as 3-y-o: winner of 5 of his 36 races in USA, including in stakes company: placed as 6-y-o in listed events at Newbury and Windsor on first and fifth outings and in Group 3 races at Epsom, Deauville and Goodwood: probably best at 1m to 1¼m: possibly unsuited by soft going: very useful. *D. R. C. Elsworth.*

LANGHAM LADY 4 b.f. Dunbeath (USA) 127–Rosinante (FR) 65 (Busted 134) — [1989 5.8m 7m³ 7m 6g a7g a6g⁵ 1990 a7g] leggy, close-coupled filly: modest winner as 2-y-o: generally well below form since, tailed off in blinkers at Southwell in January: should be suited by further than 6f: suited by an easy surface. *D. Haydn Jones.*

LANGTON (IRE) 2 gr.f. (Mar 21) Fayruz 116–Regency Girl 89 (Right Boy 137) — [1990 5d] 5,200Y: neat filly: half-sister to several winners, including useful 1986 2-y-o sprinter Fille and fair 6f and 7f winner Edgewise (both by Tanfirion): dam stayed 6f: bit backward and green, always behind in seller at Beverley in June. *N. Tinkler.*

LANGTRY LADY 4 b.f. Pas de Seul 133–Arianna Aldini (Habitat 134) [1989 6s* 91 7g² 7s⁴ 7m⁶ 8g 7g⁴ 1990 a8g* a8g² a7g⁴ 8f* 8g 8m 8m 7f a7g⁶ 8m² 8g² 8s³ 8g³] leggy, sparely-made filly: improved handicapper: successful at Southwell in March and Kempton (£21,000 Jubilee Handicap Stakes) in May: ran well last 4 starts, behind Silk Petal in Cologne listed race and Petipa in £8,200 event at York last 2: suited by 1m: acts on any going: often ridden by claimer: has carried head high. *M. J. Ryan.*

LANGTRY LASS 3 b.f. Tina's Pet 121–Nimble Star (Space King 115) [1989 6m⁴ 78 6g⁴ 1990 7f³ 8m⁴ 7m 6f* 7d 6m 8d⁵ 6m⁵ 6f 6f* 6m 6m² 6g² 6f* 6d 6s] lengthy, good-topped filly: has a round action: fair handicapper: won at Redcar in June, Brighton (led on post) in September and Redcar in October: suited by 6f and a sound surface: sweating and on toes sixth outing: has hung left, including when blinkered ninth outing: seems best with waiting tactics: sold 11,000 gns Newmarket Autumn Sales. *M. J. Ryan.*

LANGUEDOC 3 b.c. Rousillon (USA) 133–Can Can Girl 69 (Gay Fandango 71 (USA) 132) [1989 6m² 6m⁴ 1990 7m³ 6m 5m⁴ 5m] attractive, good-quartered colt: modest form: easily best efforts as 3-y-o when in frame in minor event and handicap: somewhat headstrong, and likely to prove best at sprint distances: sold to join K. McCauley 16,000 gns Newmarket Autumn Sales. *K. B. McCauley.*

LANYARD 2 b. or br.c. (Mar 6) Sure Blade (USA) 128–Prudence 68 (Grundy 137) 48 [1990 6m⁴ 6m⁴] good-quartered, attractive colt: second foal: half-brother to a winner in Germany: dam seemed to stay middle distances, is half-sister to Ribblesdale winner Strigida and daughter of Ribblesdale winner Catalpa: poor form in maidens: will be suited by further: sold 3,100 gns Newmarket Autumn Sales. *J. L. Dunlop.*

LANZAROTE 3 b.f. Longleat (USA) 109–Bel Esprit (Sagaro 133) [1989 5s² 5g⁵ — 5m⁵ 7g⁴ 8s 6g⁵ 7g 7g 1990 a7g⁵ 8m 7f] workmanlike filly: quite modest maiden: below form as 3-y-o: stayed 7f: ran well for 7-lb claimer: dead. *A. Bailey.*

LA PEREET (IRE) 2 b.f. (Mar 21) Vision (USA)–Great Alexandra (Runnett 61 125) [1990 5m⁶ 6g 5f⁵ 7m⁴ 7f⁴ 7g 7.5g³] 2,000Y: leggy, rather angular filly: has a round action: first foal: dam Irish 1½m winner: plating-class maiden: ran creditably in visor final start: much better suited by 7f than shorter. *C. N. Allen.*

LAPIERRE 5 b.h. Lafontaine (USA) 117–Lucky Omen 99 (Queen's Hussar 124) — [1989 10.5f 7.5s 10f⁵ 10f⁵ 10.2m² 10.5f 10d⁵ 10.2g³ 1990 10g 10g⁶ 10g 10m 10m⁶ 12f 10g⁶] rangy, quite attractive horse: bad mover: smart at his best in first half of 1988, winning Prix Jean Prat Ecurie Fustok at Longchamp: has deteriorated considerably: probably stays 1¼m: suited by give in the ground. *C. E. Brittain.*

LA PLACE 3 ch.f. Mansingh (USA) 120–Pegs Promise (Tumble Wind (USA)) — [1989 5g 5m 6g 1990 5m 6m 5m] angular, sparely-made filly: poor form at best: ran badly in handicaps. *D. W. Chapman.*

LAPLAND LIGHTS (USA) 2 b.f. (Mar 17) Northern Prospect (USA)– 85 Blushing Emy (USA) (Blushing Groom (FR) 131) [1990 6m² 5d] $27,000Y: lengthy filly: has scope: fourth foal: half-sister to 6f to 8.3f winner Royal Dartmouth (by Czaravich): dam minor sprint winner in North America: promising neck second of 11 to Crystal Path in maiden at Newmarket, travelling strongly when poorish run over 1f out then running on really well: weak in market and gone in coat, soon outpaced in listed event at Doncaster later in October: will be better suited by 7f. *A. C. Stewart.*

LA RAPTOTTE 3 b.f. Alzao (USA) 117–Maypole Hie (Bold Lad (IRE) 133) [1989 51 5f⁶ 6m 5m⁵ 5.1f⁶ 7m³ 7m⁵ 1990 7m* 8m² 7f 7g⁶ 7g 8.2m 10m 8g 8m⁴ 8.2s⁶] angular, narrow filly: inconsistent handicapper: won selling event (bought in 5,200 gns) at Wolverhampton in April: stays 1m: acts on good to firm ground: blinkered last 2 starts: ran moderately in visor at 2 yrs: good mount for claimer: retained by trainer 1,250 gns Ascot November Sales. *M. J. Charles.*

LARA'S BABY (IRE) 2 ch.f. (Feb 4) Valiyar 129–Tapiola 71 (Tap On Wood 130) 78 [1990 6m 7m 7g 7m² 7s³] 8,800Y: sturdy filly: second foal: dam 7f winner at 2 yrs: modest maiden: will stay 1¼m: trained on debut by W. Brooks. *R. Akehurst.*

LARA'S ELEGANT 3 b.c. Elegant Air 119–Lara's Song (USA) 69 (Russian — Bank (USA) 110) [1989 7m 1990 9g² 17.6m] smallish, lengthy, robust colt: 66/1, no chance with Thakib in 3-runner minor event at Wolverhampton: tailed off in maidens, bandaged and finishing lame final start. *K. White.*

LARCH IMAGE LADY 5 ch.m. Music Maestro 119–Unexpected 75 (Laser — Light 118) [1989 NR 1990 a5g] leggy mare: of little account. *R. P. C. Hoad.*

LARS PORSENA 3 b. or br.g. Trojan Fen 118–Apocalypse (Auction Ring (USA) 84 § 123) [1989 5s 6m³ 5g² 5f² 5m* 5m 5m 5s 1990 6f² 6g⁵ 6m³ 5m 7m² 7g 7m⁶ 6m⁶ 8m⁴ 8m² 8f² 8h² 8f⁴ 7.6m² 7g³ 8.2m* 8d⁵] close-coupled, good-quartered gelding: carries condition: fair handicapper: mostly ran creditably, winning at Nottingham in September by a head: effective over 7f and 1m: acts on hard going: trained until after eighth start by P. Felgate: irresolute and best covered up. *R. M. Whitaker.*

LASSOO 2 ch.f. (Apr 18) Caerleon (USA) 132–Siouan 78 (So Blessed 130) [1990 87 7d² 8.2v²] 16,500F: tall, unfurnished filly: half-sister to 3-y-o 12.3f winner Tomahawk (by De My Guest) and 3 other winners, including very smart middle-distance colt Apache (by Great Nephew): dam 1½m winner, is half-sister to high class middle-distance stayer Dakota and very useful Warpath: stayed on well when runner-up in maiden at Ayr in September and minor event won by Gentle Aria at Haydock following month: will be well suited by middle distances: sure to win a race. *C. W. Thornton.*

LAST BLESSING 3 b.f. Final Straw 127–Bless The Match 101 (So Blessed 130) 73 [1989 NR 1990 7m* 7m³ 7m³ 8f* 7m⁵] big, well-made filly: has plenty of scope: third foal: half-sister to fair 1988 2-y-o 6f winner Bryant (by Touching Wood): dam winning sprinter: modest form in visor: won maiden (33/1) at Goodwood, wandering under pressure, and 5-runner apprentice claimer (favourite) at Warwick, making all: stays 1m. *P. W. Harris.*

LA ST CLAIR 2 ch.f. (Jun 4) Music Boy 124–Soosjoy 89 (Sexton Blake 126) [1990 — 5m a6g] neat filly: second foal: dam won from 7f (at 2 yrs) to 10.2f: slowly away and always behind in maidens at Folkestone and Lingfield. *J. White.*

LAST CRUSADE (IRE) 2 b.g. (Apr 27) Last Tycoon 131–Berengaria (ITY) 48 (Teodoro Trivulzio) [1990 6g 6d 8d a7g a7g] 22,000F, IR 20,000Y: lengthy gelding: half-brother to several winners abroad: dam (unraced) from good Italian family: poor maiden: pulled hard to post second and third starts and also very free in race third: sold 1,500 gns Ascot November Sales. *R. F. Johnson Houghton.*

LA STRAVAGANZA　2 b.f. (May 5) Slip Anchor 136–St Isadora (Lyphard (USA) 132) [1990 7m⁵] third living foal: half-sister to quite modest 1988 2-y-o Sicaire (by Bustino), since successful over 1m in France, and to 1½m winner Akaroa (by Kalaglow): dam winner twice over extended 9f in France at 4 yrs: 4 lengths fifth of 10, slowly away then unable to quicken final 2f, in maiden at Redcar in September: should improve further. *W. Jarvis.*　**64 p**

LAST SHOWER　5 ch.m. Town And Country 124–Rainbow's End 83 (My Swallow 134) [1989 NR 1990 17.1d] workmanlike mare: quite modest maiden at best: weakened final 3f in handicap at Bath in October: blinkered once at 3 yrs. *J. S. King.*　—

LAST STRAW　2 b.c. (Mar 31) Blushing Scribe (USA) 107–Straw Reef 64 (Final Straw 127) [1990 5f 6d 6s] sturdy colt: first foal: dam lightly raced, best at 2 yrs: showed a little ability in Doncaster maiden in March: twice burly and well beaten in autumn. *A. W. Jones.*　**45**

LAST TAKE　2 b.c. (Apr 27) Ballacashtal (CAN)–Take To Heart 72 (Steel Heart 128) [1990 6m 7g 8g 7m] lengthy, workmanlike colt: fifth foal: dam in frame at 5f and 6f, ran only at 2 yrs: poor maiden: sold 1,150 gns Newmarket Autumn Sales. *M. D. I. Usher.*　**36**

LA STUPENDA　3 ch.f. Chief Singer 131–Lap of Honour 100 (Final Straw 127) [1989 NR 1990 7g⁵ 7.6d 6m* 6m 5m⁶ 6g* 6d² 6s] compact, workmanlike filly: has a quick action: first foal: dam 6f and 7f winner out of half-sister to Oaks second Vielle: favourite, won maiden at Carlisle in June and minor event at Kempton in September: very good second to Ra'a in minor event at Goodwood: moderately drawn in Doncaster listed race final start: evidently best at 6f: goes well on dead going. *W. Jarvis.*　**92**

LATHOM LAD　2 b.c. (Apr 17) Creetown 123–Belle Year (Quorum 126) [1990 6g] 2,000F: lengthy, good-quartered colt: half-brother to several winners here and abroad: dam apparently of no account: edgy and green, tailed off in maiden at Thirsk in August. *M. O'Neill.*　—

LATIN LEEP　3 b.c. Castle Keep 121–Balatina 85 (Balidar 133) [1989 a6g⁶ a6g⁵ a7g⁶ 1990 a7g² a8g* a8g⁶ a10g* a8g⁶ 8h³ 11.5m⁴ 12m⁵ 10g³ 10.1m³ 10f* 10.2f⁴ 10f⁴] sturdy colt: quite modest performer: successful in claimers at Southwell and Lingfield in February then Newmarket in July: may prove best at 1¼m: acts on firm going: has run creditably for lady rider: blinkered fourth to sixth outings. *J. Pearce.*　**69**

LATIN MASS　2 ch.f. (Apr 25) Music Boy 124–Omnia 80 (Hill Clown (USA)) [1990 5f² 5m³ 5m² 5m³ 5g³ 5m⁴ a6g⁵ 5m] 15,500Y: workmanlike filly: has quick action: sister to modest 7f winner Stanhope and half-sister to 4 winners, including smart 1982 2-y-o 6f and 7f winner All Systems Go (by Bay Express): dam won at 1½m: plating-class maiden: below form on all-weather: withdrawn after getting loose and bolting intended eighth start: better form at 5f than 6f: sometimes bandaged behind: retained 4,000 gns Doncaster October Sales. *J. Berry.*　**53**

LATIN QUARTET　2 b.g. (Feb 16) Chief Singer 131–Pampas Miss (USA) (Pronto) [1990 7m 7m 8.2d] strong, attractive gelding: poor mover: seventh foal: half-brother to 3-y-o 1¾m and 2m winner Rainbow Stripes (by Rainbow Quest) and 3 other winners in Ireland and abroad, including very useful French 9f and 11f winner Samalex (by Ela-Mana-Mou): dam lightly-raced daughter of top-class American filly Bayou: well beaten in maidens. *W. J. Haggas.*　—

LATOSKY　2 br.c. (May 1) Teenoso (USA) 135–Patosky 94 (Skymaster 126) [1990 7s] half-brother to several winners, including one-time very smart sprinter Crews Hill (by High Top) and 1¾m winner and hurdler Blake's Progress (by Blakeney): dam suited by 7f and 1m: better for race, around 17 lengths ninth of 22, soon mid-division after slow start then hands and heels last 2f, in maiden at Doncaster in October: will improve, particularly over further. *M. J. Camacho.*　— p

LATOUR　2 b.c. (Mar 4) Lafontaine (USA) 117–Lucky Omen 99 (Queen's Hussar 124) [1990 7g⁵ 7m 7m] 25,000Y: well-grown colt: brother to one-time smart 6f and 9.2f winner Lapierre and half-brother to several other winners here and abroad, including very useful sprinter Lucky Hunter (by Huntercombe): dam 5f and 6f winner at 2 yrs: over 3 lengths fifth of 11, staying on well, to Corrupt in maiden at Newmarket in July: never able to challenge in better company there after: will stay 1m. *C. E. Brittain.*　**75**

LAUNDE ABBEY　2 ch.f. (Mar 20) Absalom 128–More Fun (Malicious) [1990 6g² 5m* 6f] lengthy, good-topped filly: fourth foal: half-sister to 3-y-o Ella Street (by King of Spain), 1988 2-y-o 5f winner Like Amber (by Aragon) and 1½m winner　**75**

Magic Tower (by Tower Walk): dam never ran: modest form: won maiden at Chester in July by 2½ lengths from Lucy Dancer: likely to prove suited by further than 5f. *C. E. Brittain.*

LAURAVALE 2 b.f. (Apr 5) Kind of Hush 118–Fuddled 74 (Malacate (USA) 131) 36 [1990 8m 7f] 1,700F, 2,600Y: medium-sized, angular filly: has a round action: third foal: dam 1½m winner: poor form in maiden at Edinburgh (slowly away, ran very wide home turn) and seller at Redcar. *D. H. Topley.*

LAUREL QUEEN (IRE) 2 ch.f. (Apr 18) Viking (USA)–Prima Bella 76 (High 56 Hat 131) [1990 5m⁴ 6f³ 7f* 7f 7g* 7f⁴ 7m* 7g⁵ a8g] 5,600Y: neat filly: keen walker: half-sister to several winners here and abroad, including 5f (at 2 yrs) to 1½m winner No More The Fool (by Jester) and 1m to 9f winner Monteros Boy (by Crofter): dam stayed well: successful in sellers at Yarmouth (bought in 6,500 gns) and Thirsk (bought in 3,200 gns) in summer and in claimer at Yarmouth in September: ran moderately on all-weather final start: should stay 1m: hung left persistently fourth outing. *J. Berry.*

LAVAN VEMUZAR (IRE) 2 ch.c. (Apr 17) Heraldiste (USA) 121–Blink (Dike — (USA)) [1990 a7g] IR 4,200F, IR 4,600Y, 9,600 2-y-o. plain colt. half-brother to several winners, including 1986 2-y-o 6f winner Annie Noonan and 1985 Irish 2-y-o 5f winner Isabella Cannes (both by Ahonoora): dam of little account: slow-starting last of 9 in maiden at Southwell in July. *C. N. Allen.*

LA VISIR (USA) 4 b.f. Sir Ivor 135–Vireo (USA) (True Knight (USA)) [1989 10g 78 12g³ 12m⁴ 10s 18g* 14s⁴ 1990 11.7m⁶ 16.1m 17.6f* 16m* 17.6g⁵] big, leggy filly: has a round action: fair handicapper: won at Wolverhampton (returned to form) and Newcastle (moderately-run event) in August, squeezing through to lead close home both times: suited by test of stamina: acted on any going: in foal to Mashhor Dancer. *B. Hanbury.*

LAVROSKY (USA) 6 b.g. Nijinsky (CAN) 138–Just A Game 108 (Tarboosh — (USA)) [1989 8.3m 8.3m 10g 12g⁴ 1990 14.8m 12f 16.2m] lengthy, rather finely-made gelding: has been pin-fired: moderate mover: fair maiden at best, but has deteriorated: should stay further than 1½m: acts on good to firm and heavy going: blinkered last 2 outings: usually bandaged: resold 2,700 gns Doncaster May Sales: resold 5,500 gns Doncaster October Sales. *B. Stevens.*

LAWFUL 3 b.f. Law Society (USA) 130–Dunette (FR) 127 (Hard To Beat 132) 76 [1989 NR 1990 10m² 10.6f²] 26,000Y: workmanlike filly: fourth foal: half-sister to smart French middle-distance 4-y-o French Glory (by Sadler's Wells) and one-time useful Irish winner at up to 1½m Golden Isle (by Golden Fleece): dam won French Oaks: second in very small fields for maidens at Ascot (£10,000 event) and Haydock in the summer: will be suited by 1½m. *C. R. Nelson.*

LAWHILL 4 b.c. Lomond (USA) 128–Fair Abode (Habitat 134) [1989 10.6g 1990 — 8.2d] strong, lengthy, good-topped colt: modest form in maidens as 2-y-o: always behind in handicap at Nottingham in October, only second subsequent outing. *K. A. Morgan.*

LAWNSWOOD JUNIOR 3 gr.c. Bairn (USA) 126–Easymede 85 (Runnymede 74 d 123) [1989 5f 5.8m² 5m³ 7m* 7m 8g 7g⁴ 1990 8.2f⁴ 12.3d⁴ 9m 10g⁴ 9m⁵ 8g 8d 9g⁵ 8m⁵ 11d² 12.4s³] workmanlike colt: moderate mover: modest handicapper: should prove ideally suited by 1¼m: possibly best on a sound surface: has run fairly well when sweating: visored last 4 outings: sold privately 5,000 gns Doncaster November Sales. *R. Hollinshead.*

LAW STUDENT 3 ch.f. Precocious 126–Star Court 102 (Aureole 132) [1989 7g — 1990 8g 8f⁴ 10m 10d] second filly: form in maidens only on second start at 3 yrs: tailed off in handicaps, off course 6 months in between: stays 1m: worth a try in blinkers. *P. T. Walwyn.*

LAXEY BAY 3 b.c. Caerleon (USA) 132–Franconia (AUS) (Rheingold 137) [1989 99 7.3g⁶ 7g³ 7m² 8f* 10g³ 1990 8.2f² 8m² 10.5g⁴ 8.5g 8m² 10g*] compact, workmanlike colt: carries condition: moderate walker and mover: useful performer: won minor event at Ripon in August: ran well in Dante Stakes at York and £6,600 ladies race at Ascot third and fifth starts, poorly in Diomed Stakes at Epsom in between: stays 1¼m: acts on firm going: tends to sweat and to get on edge: sent to race in USA. *B. W. Hills.*

LAXMI (USA) 2 b.c. (Feb 26) Lyphard's Wish (FR) 124–Camarina (USA) 79 (Vaguely Noble 140) [1990 7g⁵ 8d⁵] $92,000Y: rather leggy colt: second foal: dam twice raced here later successful in USA, is daughter of smart sprinter Lullaby Song: fifth of 16, keeping on despite looking green, to Surrealist in maiden at

Sandown in September: favourite, ran moderately in similar event at Leicester following month: should stay 1m. *M. R. Stoute.*

LEABRANNAGH LASS   2 ch.f. (Mar 4) Ballad Rock 122–Kenton's Girl 86   —
(Record Token 128) [1990 5g 5f⁶ 6d] sturdy filly: second foal: dam 2-y-o 5f winner: poor form in quite modest company: off course for 3 months after second outing. *R. E. Peacock.*

LEACROFT   6 b.g. Domitor (USA) 98–Whitmarsh 56 (Hessonite 88) [1989 7.5g⁶   —
7m 7h³ 8g⁴ 10f* 10.2f⁴ 10f³ 9m⁶ 9f 1990 9f 11f] good-bodied gelding: carries plenty of condition: moderate mover: plating-class winner (apprentice ridden) of handicap as 5-y-o: ran poorly (slowly away) final outing in 1990: stays 1¼m: acts on firm going: probably best with tender handling: winning selling hurdler in March. *W. W. Haigh.*

LEADING GUEST   5 b.g. What A Guest 119–Light House (Primera 131) [1989   43
10.8s 11.7d 10.8d 9f 8f 10f² 1990 12m 8m⁶ 8f⁵ 8g² 10.2f* 10.8g 12f⁵ 9f 7h⁶] big, lengthy gelding: has a round action: plater: favourite, won for only time when making all in selling handicap (no bid) at Bath in June: suited by 1m to 1¼m and forcing tactics: acts on hard going: slowly away when blinkered final outing: often pulls hard: sold 3,000 gns Ascot November Sales: inconsistent. *R. J. Hodges.*

LEAH JAY   3 ch.g. Sayyaf 121–Patriots Day (Red Regent 123) [1989 6g 1990 10g   —
10.1m 10.1m⁶ 11.7m 10d] compact, workmanlike gelding: has a moderate, quick action: well beaten, including in handicaps. *E. A. Wheeler.*

LEAN'N MEAN (IRE)   2 b.c. (Mar 8) Heraldiste (USA) 121–Pyjama Game 56   55
(Cavo Doro 124) [1990 8m⁴ 7d³ a8g a8g⁴] IR 4,600F, IR 4,500Y: sparely-made colt: half-brother to winners in Germany and Belgium: dam, half-sister to Grey Desire, placed at up to 2m: fair plater: will be suited by 1¼m: ridden by claimer. *M. Bell.*

LEAR LEADER (USA)   2 br.c. (Mar 30) Lear Fan (USA) 130–Tolstoya (North-   66
fields (USA)) [1990 5m* 5f² 7m⁶ 6f*] neat, good-quartered colt: shows knee action: first known foal: dam Irish 2-y-o 5f winner: quite modest performer: won maiden at Sandown in April and 3-runner minor event (odds on, none too impressively) at Lingfield in July: probably stays 7f. *C. R. Nelson.*

LEASE BACK (USA)   2 ch.c. (Apr 26) Secretariat (USA)–Go Leasing 121 (Star   69
Appeal 133) [1990 8f⁴ 7f² 7m⁶] close-coupled, sturdy colt: third foal: half-brother to 3-y-o 12.2f winner Deficit (by Deputy Minister): dam 6f to 1¼m winner and third in 1000 Guineas, later won at 9f in USA: quite modest form in autumn maidens: will be suited by 1¼m: sold 19,000 gns Newmarket Autumn Sales. *G. Harwood.*

LEAVE IT TO LIB   3 b.f. Tender King 123–Nuit de Vin (Nebbiolo 125) [1989 6g²   47
6f² 5m³ 6f⁵ 6g⁶ 1990 6f 6g 7m* 7d] small, sparely-made filly: plating-class performer: worthwhile form at 3 yrs only when justifying favouritism in claimer at Edinburgh in September: may well stay 1m: acts on firm ground. *P. Calver.*

LE CHIC   4 b.g. Kabour 80–Boom Shanty 66 (Dragonara Palace (USA) 115) [1989   64 §
5m 5m 5.1g⁵ 5g 5f 1990 5m² 5m* 5f⁴ 5g⁵ 5d³ 5g 5g² 5m² 6f² 5m³ 5m 5d 5g 5m³ 5m²
5d 6d a6g a5g³] strong, workmanlike gelding: quite modest handicapper: successful at Catterick in May: stays 6f: acts on firm and dead going: blinkered final start in 1989: usually apprentice ridden: doesn't find much, and best covered up: not one to trust implicitly. *D. W. Chapman.*

LE CORSAIRE (USA)   2 br.c. (Apr 2) Nureyev (USA) 131–Little Bonny 126   80 p
(Bonne Noel 115) [1990 7m⁶ 7m⁴] $500,000Y: strong, deep-girthed colt: fifth foal: closely related to 11f winner Hanoof (by Northern Dancer) and Irish 1½m winner Bonny Irish Lass (by The Minstrel): dam 1m and 1¼m winner second in Irish Oaks, is sister to good colt Noelino: bit backward, fair form in autumn minor events at Ascot: bandaged near-hind on debut: will stay 1¼m: looks sort to do much better. *L. M. Cumani.*

LEE ARTISTE   2 b.f. (Apr 14) Tate Gallery (USA) 117–Mirkan Honey 83   104
(Ballymore 123) [1990 5m³ 6m² 5m* 6m* 7d² 8v⁶] 17,000Y: smallish, workmanlike filly: moderate walker: half-sister to 3-y-o Kid Lewis (by Thatching) and useful Scandinavian colt Tiger Bill (by General Assembly): dam Irish 4-y-o 2m winner: won maiden at Newbury in July and minor event at Salisbury in September: excellent second, running on really well, to Crystal Gazing in Bottisham Heath Stud Rockfel Stakes at Newmarket: soundly beaten in Premio Dormello at Milan in November: should be suited by 1m: possibly unsuited by heavy ground. *P. F. I. Cole.*

LEFT RIGHT   7 b.m. Marching On 101–Beryl's Gift 80 (Sayfar 116) [1989 6s 6d   39 §
5f⁶ 6m⁵ 6f 5g⁴ 5m 7.5f² 7.5m 6f 5g 5m 5s³ a6g 1990 a6g² a5g 6g⁶ 6g 5f a6g 6d
a6g] leggy, good-topped mare: poor handicapper: stays 7.5f: acts on any going: has

worn blinkers, probably best without: often sweats and gets on toes: sometimes bandaged: often starts slowly: sold 875 gns Ascot November Sales: inconsistent and not genuine. *P. S. Felgate.*

LEGAL BEAGLE 3 b.g. Law Society (USA) 130–Calandra (USA) 114 (Sir Ivor **84 p** 135) [1989 NR 1990 12m²] 34,000Y: well-made gelding: fifth foal: half-brother to 1¾m winner Reef Lark (by Mill Reef) and useful Irish 1m winner Golden Temple (by Golden Fleece): dam Irish 1m and 1¼m winner and fourth in Irish Oaks: 16/1 and bit backward, 2½ lengths second of 15 to Ballet Classique in maiden at Folkestone in October: will stay 1¾m. *G. Harwood.*

LEGAL CASE 4 b.c. Alleged (USA) 138–Maryinsky (USA) (Northern **126** Dancer) [1989 8.5f* 10.1m* 10.1d² 10d* 12g 10g* 1990 10m⁴ 12m⁵ 12m 12g⁶ 10d³ 10s*]

A season that had promised so much at the outset for Legal Case threatened for most of its duration to be a major disappointment, and it wasn't until its final weeks that he restored his reputation as a colt to be reckoned with in the highest class. The prolonged dry spell was all against him. Legal Case's return to form coincided with his return to racing on easy ground which he'd not encountered since his most important win, in the Champion Stakes the previous autumn. Legal Case's form got progressively worse on his three runs on top-of-the-ground in the summer and he was absent from the track for more than two months after finishing tailed off in the King George VI and Queen Elizabeth Diamond Stakes. His sixth place in the Ciga Prix de l'Arc de Triomphe at Longchamp on his return was a splendid effort in the circumstances: he was the second-highest placed older horse in the race behind In The Wings and finished almost as close as he'd done as a three-year-old when, admittedly, he was stopped several times in his run. At Newmarket two weeks later he looked in excellent shape and ran as well in defeat as he'd done in victory the year before, staying on well in third behind the three-year-olds In The Groove and Linamix having been held up and pushed along half a mile from home. Time was running out for Legal Case to get off the mark for the year and he was supplemented for the Premio Roma, the last scheduled Group 1 race in Europe in 1990. An odds-on chance, he won comfortably by two lengths from Candy Glen and Sikeston, who were to finish second and first, respectively, in the rearranged Premio Vittorio di Capua at Milan later in the month.

Legal Case, the seventh British-trained winner of the Premio Roma in the last twelve years and the second trained by Cumani, following Old Country in 1985, provided his rider Dettori with a first Group 1 win in his native Italy. Dettori enjoyed a tremendous first season as stable-jockey to Cumani and looks destined to become champion one day barring mishap. When riding Line of Thunder to victory in the Ferry Stakes at Chepstow at the end of August he became the first teenager to ride a hundred winners in a season since Piggott in 1955. The highlight of his career so far came at the Festival of British Racing at Ascot when in the space of three quarters of an hour he rode Markofdistinction and Shamshir to victory in the Queen Elizabeth II Stakes and the Brent Walker Mile Stakes. Dettori ended the season fourth in the championship behind Eddery, Carson and Cauthen with one hundred and forty winners on the turf (he had another four on the all-weather) and had other notable successes in North America. He and Munro, denied the chance of reaching his century through injury, are two of the most talented riders to emerge since Eddery himself.

The unraced 1990 two-year-old La Sky, in training with Cecil, is the product of the second of three matings (she was barren to the first) between Law Society, a son of Alleged, and Legal Case's dam Maryinsky, a winner twice in America at up to nine furlongs as a three-year-old. La Sky was sold for 260,000 guineas as a yearling at the Newmarket Highflyer Sales; her brother was knocked down to Brittain for 42,000 guineas at the same sale a year later. Maryinsky, who has since produced a filly by Persian Bold, visited To The Quick in her first two years at stud; their second daughter To The Dancer won four races at up to nine furlongs. Maryinsky is one of eleven winners foaled by Extra Place, two of which, Bold Place, dam of the Prix du Gros Chene winner Gem Diamond, and Card Table were graded stakes winners in the States.

Sir Gordon White's "Legal Case"

Extra Place, successful twice at up to a mile, is also the grandam of Belle Chanson, winner of the Schweppes Australasian Oaks.

Legal Case (b.c. 1986)	Alleged (USA) (b 1974)	Hoist The Flag (b 1968)	Tom Rolfe / Wavy Navy
		Princess Pout (b 1966)	Prince John / Determined Lady
	Maryinsky (USA) (b 1977)	Northern Dancer (b 1961)	Nearctic / Natalma
		Extra Place (b 1963)	Round Table / Rich Relation

Legal Case has often given the impression that he should be at least as effective at a mile and a half as a mile and a quarter, but on the four occasions he has run over a mile and a half he has yet to produce his very best. What is for sure is that he needs give in the ground to show it. Legal Case, a lengthy, attractive colt, sweated up on his first two starts in the latest season, on the second of which, in the slowly-run Princess of Wales's Stakes, he pulled hard and tended to hang left. Given the right conditions, he could still make up into the top-class horse he promised to become in the autumn as a three-year-old. *L. M. Cumani.*

LEGAL FANTASY 3 br.c. Law Society (USA) 130–Never Never Land (Habitat 134) [1989 NR 1990 8g 8f 8.5d 10.1m⁴ 8m] IR 95,000Y: rather leggy, good-topped colt: seventh foal: half-brother to 2 winners by Bold Lad, notably top-class sprinter Never So Bold: dam unraced half-sister to dam of Bruni: signs of ability in minor

— §

502

event and handicap (soon off bridle) last 2 starts: slowly away first 2 starts and reluctant to race on first of them: one to avoid. *C. R. Nelson.*

LEGAL PROFESSION (IRE) 2 b.c. (Feb 1) Law Society (USA) 130–Palais Rose (USA) (Northern Dancer) [1990 6s*] first foal: dam, Irish 1m winner, is granddaughter of Coronation Stakes winner Lisadell: odds-on winner of 9-runner maiden at the Curragh in October by 4 lengths: promising. *M. V. O'Brien, Ireland.* **87 p**

LEGAL STREAK 3 b.c. Mr Fluorocarbon 126–Streakella 79 (Firestreak 125) [1989 5m⁵ a8g 1990 a8g⁵ 12.3f 10.6v 8.2s⁴] leggy, sparely-made colt: poor maiden on flat: off course 6 months after second start: should stay beyond 1m: acts on soft going: sold to join Miss S. Wilton 7,500 gns after winning selling hurdle in November. *B. A. McMahon.* **43**

LEGAL TINA 5 ch.m. Ballacashtal (CAN)–Pitapat (Shantung 132) [1989 12.5g⁶ 10.1m 1990 8.3m³ 9f⁶] leggy mare: poor mover: poor form in modest company: seems to stay 9f: bandaged twice: sweating and on toes on reappearance: winning claiming hurdler in September. *S. Dow.* **45**

LEGAL VIEW (USA) 2 b.c. (Apr 10) Riverman (USA) 131–Dictina (FR) (Dictus (FR) 126) [1990 7d] $725,000Y: close-coupled, rather leggy colt: second reported foal: dam winner of 4 races, including Grade 3 9f event, is from family of Caro: around 7 lengths eighth of 11, losing position gradually last 2f, to Junk Bond in valuable minor event at Newmarket in October: sure to improve. *L. M. Cumani.* **74 p**

LEGAL WIN (USA) 2 ch.c. (May 10) Arctic Tern (USA) 126–Banker's Favorite (USA) (Lyphard (USA) 132) [1990 7s⁶] $180,000Y: fourth foal: half-brother to 3 minor winners in USA, one placed in graded stakes: dam winner at up to 9f, is half-sister to champion sprinter Plugged Nickle: around 19 lengths sixth of 15, racing on unfavoured side, to Suomi in maiden at Newcastle in November: sure to do better. *M. Bell.* **53 p**

LEGATAIRE (USA) 2 b.f. (Jan 10) Arctic Tern (USA) 126–Belleval (FR) (Val de L'Orne (FR) 130) [1990 9v*] sixth foal: half-sister to several winners in France, including 3-y-o 1¼m winner Baracelli (by Hero's Honor): dam French 1m and 8.5f winner, is half-sister to high-class French stayer Bourbon: claimer-ridden 6-length winner of 19-runner maiden (with rest well strung out) at Maisons-Laffitte in November: likely to make very useful middle-distance stayer. *Mme C. Head, France.* **93 p**

LEGEND OF SCOTLAND 2 b.c. (Mar 15) Scottish Reel 123–Visitation 84 (Tarqogan 125) [1990 5m 6g a7g] 8,000Y: leggy colt: half-brother to several winners, including 3-y-o Scatter (by Sharpo), 6f winner at 2 yrs, and fairly useful 1985 2-y-o 5f winner Little Pipers (by Music Boy): dam stayed 1½m: always behind in varied events, including a Southwell seller. *J. D. Czerpak.* **—**

LEGION OF HONOUR 2 b.c. (Feb 22) Ahonoora 122–Shehana (USA) 86 (The Minstrel (CAN) 135) [1990 6m³] lengthy colt: first foal: dam 2-y-o 9f winner apparently stayed 1½m: bit green, 10 lengths third of 8, travelling comfortably, edging right 2f out then not knocked about, to Island Universe in maiden at Ascot in October: moved moderately down: sure to improve. *W. Jarvis.* **79 p**

LEIGH BOY (USA) 4 b.g. Bates Motel (USA)–Afasheen (Sheshoon 132) [1989 11.7d 10g 12d* 12m⁶ 15.3m² 14.8m⁶ 16.2d 14m 1990 16m² 17m⁶] workmanlike gelding: modest handicapper: stays 2m: acts on good to firm and dead going: goes well with forcing tactics: fair hurdler, winner twice in autumn. *G. M. Moore.* **71**

LEITRIM PRIDE 2 b.g. (Feb 10) Law Society (USA) 130–Sweet Soprano 80 (High Line 125) [1990 7m⁵ 7g* 7f] 30,000Y: useful-looking gelding: third foal: dam 7f and 11f winner, is out of half-sister to Royal Hive and Attica Meli: favourite, won maiden at Ayr in July by length from Crimson Cloud: disputed lead 5f and eased when beaten in nursery at Goodwood following month: will stay 1m. *G. Lewis.* **69**

LE JOUEUR (USA) 3 ch.g. Riverman (USA) 131–Happy Bride 116 (Royal Match 117) [1989 NR 1990 10m⁵ 14f] $100,000Y: medium-sized gelding with scope: second foal: dam successful from 6f to 1¼m in Ireland later good winner in USA: 25/1 and ridden by 7-lb claimer, easily better effort in maidens when fifth of 8 at Redcar, never able to challenge: gelded after refusing to enter stalls (wore crossed noseband) intended debut: sold to join Mrs P. Barker 8,000 gns Newmarket Autumn Sales. *J. H. M. Gosden.* **—**

LE LINGOT (USA) 2 gr.c. (Apr 7) Northern Jove (CAN)–Winthataway (USA) (Blushing Groom (FR) 131) [1990 6m⁵ 6f* 7f³] $27,000Y: smallish, close-coupled colt: good walker and mover: first foal: dam minor winner at around 6f in USA: odds on, won maiden at Pontefract in July when trained by C. Wall: good staying-on third of 5 to Plan of Action in minor event at Newmarket: sent to Italy, and won over 7.5f at Florence in September. *A. Pecoraro, Italy.* **86**

LEONELLA (USA) 3 b.f. Caerleon (USA) 132–Fenella 92 (Thatch (USA) 136) — [1989 NR 1990 7m5] closely related to useful middle-distance stayer Kashi Lagoon (by Ile de Bourbon) and 1½m winner Fenlands (by Kings Lake) and half-sister to 3 other winners, including Queen Anne winner Trojan Fen (by Troy): dam, from good family, won over 7.6f: 12/1, ridden halfway when well-beaten fifth of 9 in maiden at Newmarket in November: will be suited by further: may do better. *J. H. M. Gosden.*

LEOTARD 3 b.c. Lyphard's Special (USA) 122–Tondbad (Furry Glen 121) [1989 97 NR 1990 12.2m2 14.8m2] IR 29,000Y: workmanlike colt: good walker and mover: first foal: dam Irish 1¾m winner also successful 2m hurdler: fairly useful form in maidens won by Tour Eiffel at Catterick and Rubicund at Newmarket in June: shapes like a thorough stayer. *A. C. Stewart.*

LE PASSE TEMPS 3 ch.c. King Persian 107–Darius Royal (Royal Match 117) — [1989 NR 1990 a12g6 10m6 12m] IR 2,600F, 1,900Y, 14,000 2-y-o: third foal: half-brother to a winner in Hong Kong: dam never ran: plating-class form when sixth in September maidens: tailed off facing very stiff task in claimer. *R. J. R. Williams.*

LE PELLEY'S ISLE 3 b.g. Pitskelly 122–Belitis 109 (Tudor Melody 129) [1989 — NR 1990 8m 7g 10.2s] IR 5,400F, IR 24,000Y: half-brother to 4 winners in Ireland, including fairly useful 1980 2-y-o 6f winner Passion Wagon (by Bay Express), and 2 in France, including prolific 9f to 11f winner Bizantus (by Sassafras): dam 5f to 1m winner out of top 1963 2-y-o filly Mesopotamia: no worthwhile form in late-season, 13 lengths seventh of 11 in mixed-aged event at Newmarket second start: out of depth week later. *G. B. Balding.*

LEPOUSHKA 4 b.f. Salmon Leap (USA) 131–Polifontaine (FR) (Bold Lad (USA)) 97 [1989 8m3 8g4 7g* 6g5 8s2 8d 1990 8g 8g* 7m5 9g 7g 8m3 8g* 7s2] Irish filly: third foal: closely related to winner in USA by Try My Best: dam quite useful winner as 2-y-o in France, half-sister to Millfontaine and Katies: won maiden at Down Royal as 3-y-o and handicap in April and listed race (making virtually all) in September, both at the Curragh: 2 lengths second to The Caretaker in Leopardstown listed contest: effective at 7f and 1m: acts on good to firm and soft going. *P. Hill, Ireland.*

LE RUBIS VERT 2 b.f. (Apr 15) Green Ruby (USA) 104–Dourne (Dom Racine — (FR) 121) [1990 5g 6m 7.5g] 1,100Y: dipped-backed filly: first reported foal: dam never ran: well beaten in sellers: subsequently sold 920 gns Doncaster August Sales. *J. Balding.*

LES AMIS 3 b.f. Alzao (USA) 117–Les Sylphides (FR) (Kashmir II 125) [1989 6h5 59 5f4 6g* a6g 1990 6m4 6g 9m 8g 8m 6d4 7g5 a7g4 7d a10g2 a10g6 a8g3dis a8g] sturdy, workmanlike filly: quite modest performer: second in handicap at Lingfield in November, short-headed having quickened clear over 1f out: below form after, twice for apprentice: stays 1¼m: possibly needs an easy surface: blinkered eighth (ran creditably) and ninth outings. *M. J. Ryan.*

LES ANIMAUX NUAGES (FR) 2 b.c. (May 4) Primo Dominie 121–Elmira 96 (FR) (Sir Gaylord) [1990 5d* 5m2 6m2 6m4 7m3 7g* 7.6s3] 160,000 francs (approx £15,400) Y: quite attractive, leggy colt: has scope: has a quick action: fifth foal: dam French 1¼m winner: fairly useful performer: successful in maiden at Newbury in April and £6,000 event (by ¾ length from Joli's Princess, showing much improved form) at Salisbury in August: good third of 6 to Time Line in listed event at Lingfield after: much better suited by 7f than shorter: acts very well on an easy surface: trained first 4 outings by R. Hannon: sweating fifth start: tends to get on toes. *R. Akehurst.*

LE SAULE D'OR 3 br.f. Sonnen Gold 121–Richesse (FR) (Faraway Son (USA) 67 130) [1989 6f6 8m* 7g6 7d 1990 8.2f 8m4 10.2m4 8f 10m6 8g4 8.5m 9m5 8.2d] leggy, sparely-made filly: quite modest handicapper: stays 1¼m: acts on good to firm ground and dead: wandered badly when successful at 2 yrs: often slowly away: blinkered last 5 outings: bandaged near-hind penultimate one: rather inconsistent: joined B. McMath. *J. W. Watts.*

LESBET 5 b.m. Hotfoot 126–Remeta 67 (Reform 132) [1989 15.5s 19f6 19f5 1990 — a16g5] plating-class winner as 3-y-o: soundly beaten in subsequent handicaps: suited by test of stamina: form on flat only with plenty of give in the ground, though has won on firm over hurdles. *C. P. Wildman.*

LES SYLPHIDES 3 b.c. Top Ville 129–Nadia Nerina (CAN) 82 (Northern 87 Dancer) [1989 7g 1990 8g 7m2 7g3 10m2 10m2 10m* 10.2g] good-topped, attractive colt: carries plenty of condition: moderate walker and mover: fair performer: sweating and edgy, won maiden at Yarmouth in August: lacks turn of foot, and may prove better suited by 1½m: sold 48,000 gns Newmarket Autumn Sales. *H. R. A. Cecil.*

LES YEUX D'AMOUR   4 br.f. Vision (USA)–Adorit 76 (Habat 127) [1989 6m 6f   —
5g 5f 5.3h 6f 7f 1990 a7g a7g] small, sparely-made filly: quite modest winner as
2-y-o: well beaten in varied events since, including seller: stays 6f: acts on soft
going, possibly unsuited by top-of-the-ground. *W. Holden.*

L'ETE (IRE)   2 b.f. (Mar 18) Kafu 120–Miss Merryweather (Sexton Blake 126)   85
[1990 5g² 5m⁶ 5m² 5m² 5m 5g*] 3,200Y: good-quartered, workmanlike filly: second
foal: half-sister to 3-y-o Kabaka (by Krayyan): dam lightly raced in Ireland: made all,
showing much improved form, in maiden at Wolverhampton in October, beating
Fenton Lake 5 lengths: suited by sharp 5f. *P. Mitchell.*

LE TEMERAIRE   4 b.c. Top Ville 129–La Mirande (FR) (Le Fabuleux 133) [1989   ?
10s 12v³ 12m³ 12g* 11g 1990 12g³ 10.5g³ 11d 12g⁶ 10.5g⁵ 10g⁴ 10d 12.4s] leggy ex-
French colt: fifth foal: half-brother to 4 winners, notably Washington International
and Japan Cup winner Le Glorieux (by Cure The Blues): dam very useful middle-
distance filly, sister to Oaks third La Manille: won maiden at Chantilly as 3-y-o:
never a threat in claimers at Ayr (running on steadily from rear) and Newcastle last
2 outings: stays 1½m: trained until after sixth outing by P. Bary: winning hurdler. *N.
Tinkler.*

LET FLY   3 ch.c. Kris 135–Cut Loose 118 (High Top 131) [1989 7g 1990 10m 10m   68
16m² 18.1m] rather sparely-made colt: form only when second in handicap at
Warwick in August, held up and ridden along in rear 7f out: broke leg and destroyed
at Yarmouth: suited by test of stamina. *G. Wragg.*

LET'S BE ON   2 b.f. (May 14) State Diplomacy (USA)–Wings At Night (Decoy   —
Boy 129) [1990 6f] second reported foal: dam poor sister to useful 5f performer
Urray Harry: slowly away and always behind in maiden at Carlisle in September. *P.
Beaumont.*

LETSBEONESTABOUTIT   4 b.g. Petong 126–My Bushbaby 100 (Hul A Hul   83
124) [1989 8.2s 6s 5.8m* 6m 6m² 7g 6f* 6f 7g⁵ 5f⁵ 7h⁵ 6g 6g³ 6f² 6f³ 6f³ 6g⁴ 5d a6g
1990 6f⁴ 6f⁵ 6f* 7f³ 6m 6f² 6m* 6d³ 6m² 6d 6g 6f³ 6m⁴ 6m 7f⁴ 6g⁶ 6m* 5.6g 6d] tall,
strong gelding: poor mover: fair handicapper: once ungenerous, but a reformed
character as 4-y-o and won at Salisbury in May, Goodwood in June and Redcar in
August: best at 6f: ideally suited by top-of-the-ground: has been tried in visor,
usually blinkered: consistent, and a credit to his trainer. *Mrs N. Macauley.*

LET'S GO LOCHY   4 b.f. Lochnager 132–Happy Donna 106 (Huntercombe 133)   —
[1989 NR 1990 5m 10m] good-bodied filly: poor walker: seventh foal: half-sister to 6f
to 1m winner Imperial Friend (by Imperial Fling) and several poor animals: dam won
3 times over 5f at 2 yrs: slowly away, tailed off in claimer and seller. *C. J. Hill.*

LETTYFANA (USA)   2 b.f. (Mar 12) Fappiano (USA)–Letty's Pennant (USA)   ?
(Bold Forbes (USA)) [1990 8s*] $150,000F: first foal: dam, winner at up to 9f, is
half-sister to 1987 champion 3-y-o filly Sacahuista: won 17-runner newcomers race
at Saint-Cloud in November by 2 lengths: sure to go on to better things. *F. Boutin,
France.*

LEVADE   2 b.c. (Mar 17) Elegant Air 119–Silent Pool 68 (Relkino 131) [1990 6g 6g   66
8m⁴ 8g⁶ 9g⁶] 13,000Y: good-bodied colt: sort to carry condition: fourth foal:
half-brother to 3-y-o 9f and 1¼m winner Water God (by Dominion): dam slow
daughter of Park Hill Stakes winner Idle Waters: quite modest maiden: ran
creditably in blinkers final start: will be suited by further: sold 4,000 gns Newmarket Autumn Sales. *I. R. Fanshawe.*

LEVEL XING   2 ro.c. (Apr 2) Stanford 121§–Lucky Song 91 (Lucky Wednesday   88
124) [1990 5f² 5g* 5m 6m* 6g² 6m² 6m⁴ 6m² 6m⁵ 6g⁵ 6m 7m] 7,800Y: strong,
useful-looking colt: good walker: moderate mover: first foal: dam 5f and 7f winner:
fair performer: successful at Kempton in maiden (after slow start) in April and minor
event in May: ran well in nursery at Ascot penultimate outing: best form at 6f. *R.
Hannon.*

LEVEN BABY   3 br.f. Blazing Saddles (AUS)–Farababy (FR) (Faraway Son   46
(USA) 130) [1989 5m⁴ 6m 7g⁴ 1990 8f 7g 8g⁶ 9m 10m 9f*] leggy filly: fair plater: form
as 3-y-o only when winning at Redcar (no bid) in August: stays 9f: acts on firm
ground: twice slowly away: winning hurdler: seems somewhat temperamental. *Mrs
G. R. Reveley.*

LEVISHAM   5 ch.r. Valiyar 129–Bridestones 92 (Jan Ekels 122) [1989 13.8d 1990   —
16.2m 12f] sturdy rig: moderate mover: poor maiden: stayed 1¾m: suited by give in
the ground: dead. *R. D. E. Woodhouse.*

LEVITT LADY   4 gr.f. Another Realm 118–My Cervantes (Hill Clown (USA))   41
[1989 7d⁵ 1990 7f 5g⁶ a6g a7g³ 8h] lengthy, angular filly: good mover: poor form at

best at 4 yrs: tailed off in selling handicap final outing: best form at 6f as 2-y-o: possibly unsuited by hard going. *D. Haydn Jones.*

LEXDEN 4 b.g. Blakeney 126–Annabella 88 (Habitat 134) [1989 10s² 12g 12g⁵ 11.7m² 1990 16.2s] well-made gelding: modest maiden at best: stays 1½m: acts on good to firm and soft going: has joined M. Pipe. *W. M. Perrin.*

LEZAYRE 3 b.f. Dalsaan 125–Tallantire (USA) (Icecapade (USA)) [1989 NR 1990 8m] 1,050 2-y-o: first foal: dam unplaced at 1m on only start: 33/1 and backward, last of 9 finishers in maiden at York in September. *A. W. Potts.*

LIANE BEAUTY 4 b.f. Castle Keep 121–Princess Fair (Crowned Prince (USA) 128) [1989 7f 7f 10h 10.1m 8.3m⁵ 8f⁶ 8.3d 1990 a8g a12g⁶ 8.3m 11.7f⁶] leggy filly: little form, including in sellers: visored once at 3 yrs. *Mrs S. Armytage.*

LIAR'S POKER (IRE) 2 br.g. (Apr 11) Alzao (USA) 117–Goldwyn Princess 72 (Native Prince) [1990 6m 6g 6m] 10,000Y: good-bodied gelding: moderate mover: half-brother to 3 winners, including King's Stand winner African Song (by African Sky) and modest 1984 2-y-o 5f and 6f winner Cornwall (by Sexton Blake): dam ran twice: little worthwhile form, slowly away, in maidens and a seller: blinkered final outing. *J. W. Hills.*

LIBERTO 3 b.g. Seymour Hicks 87–Countess Decima (USA) (Sir Gaylord) [1989 6f 8.2g 6g 1990 11g 8.5g 12.2m] dipped-backed gelding: little sign of ability, blinkered, raced too freely penultimate start. *T. Fairhurst.*

LIBK 2 b.c. (Feb 16) Kalaglow 132–Balqis (USA) 93 (Advocator) [1990 7m 8m* 91 8g* 8m] strong, well-made colt: has scope: second foal: half-brother to 3-y-o 1¾m winner Haitham (by Wassl): dam 2-y-o 5f and 6f winner, is half-sister to dam of Hollywood Derby winner Slew The Dragon: fair performer: successful in maiden at Yarmouth in September and minor event (by 1½ lengths from Quaglino, running on well after meeting trouble) at Wolverhampton following month: modest eighth of 11 in listed race at Ascot after: will stay 1¼m. *H. Thomson Jones.*

LIB'S PET 2 b.f. (Apr 22) Tina's Pet 121–Miss Maud 57 (Tennyson (FR) 124) [1990 a5g 5m] close-coupled filly: first live foal: dam maiden stayed 1¼m: behind in maiden and seller in spring. *K. M. Brassey.*

LIDANZIA 2 br.f. (Apr 15) Lidhame 109–Lady Antonia 66 (Owen Anthony 102) 49 [1990 5f⁵ 6d] 2,500F: leggy, sparely-made filly: moderate mover: half-sister to winning hurdler Man In The Moon (by Mansingh): dam lightly-raced half-sister to dam of good English and German colt Whip It Quick: stayed on well when fifth of 8 in maiden at Bath in September: dropped out halfway in similar event (unruly stalls) at Leicester following month. *R. J. Holder.*

LIFESONG 4 b.f. Song 132–Blakesware Saint 74 (Welsh Saint 126) [1989 7g 6s⁶ 5g 5m 6m 5m⁵ 1990 a8g] rangy filly: of little account. *S. E. Kettlewell.*

LIFETIMES AMBITION 2 br.c. (Apr 15) Hotfoot 126–Consistent Queen 55 60 (Queen's Hussar 124) [1990 5m 5g 6f 5m³ 5d 8m 8g 10.2s] 4,400Y: compact colt: half-brother to winning platers Royal Rabble (by Rabdan) and Dencott Lady (by Swing Easy): dam won 1m seller: quite modest performer: suited by a test of stamina: acts well on soft ground: looked temperamental when blinkered third start: usually very edgy. *E. J. Alston.*

LIFEWATCH CHECK 3 b.g. Tumble Wind (USA)–Habilite 94 (Habitat 134) [1989 5h⁴ 5f⁴ 7.5f⁵ 6m 7f⁴ 7d a7g⁴ a8g⁵ 1990 a10g⁶] leggy, rather sparely-made gelding: plating-class maiden: sole outing as 3-y-o in January: suited by 7f+: possibly unsuited by a soft surface. *M. Johnston.*

LIFEWATCH VISION 3 b.c. Vision (USA)–Maellen (River Beauty 105) [1989 107 6f³ 6m* 6m* 6g* 7f⁵ 6.3g⁵ 7.3d⁵ 6g 1990 8f* 8.5g² 8g² 10f⁵ 8m 10.1g 8m² 9g] workmanlike colt: has a rather round action: useful performer: won 3-runner minor event at Thirsk in April: second in £10,700 event at Epsom, IR £137,500 handicap at the Curragh and £11,600 contest at Newmarket: stays 1¼m: yet to race on very soft ground, acts on any other: pulled too hard in blinkers fifth start. *M. Johnston.*

LIFFEY LACE (USA) 3 b.f. Sagace (FR) 135–Liffey (FR) (Irish River (FR) 131) 83 [1989 7m* 8.2f² 8.2s* 9s* 1990 12.2g⁴ 10m⁵ 10m 8m² 8d] leggy filly: fair performer: blinkered for first time, form as 3-y-o only when running-on 40/1-second of 11 in quite valuable handicap at Ascot in September: should stay further than 9f: acts on any going: also blinkered final start: sold 25,000 gns Newmarket December Sales. *J. L. Dunlop.*

LIFT AND LOAD (USA) 3 b.c. Lyphard's Wish (FR) 124–Dorit (USA) 106 (Damascus (USA)) [1989 7m³ 7g² 7m² 7f² 7m⁵ 8d* 1990 8d 8m⁴ 10d* 12g* 12s⁵ 12g* 12m⁶ 12s⁴] lengthy, good-quartered colt: shows knee action: useful per-

Troy Stakes, Doncaster—
Lift And Load shows more resolution than Spinning or Bawbee

former: successful in £7,500 handicap at Epsom and King George V Stakes Handicap at Royal Ascot in June then listed race at Doncaster in September: ran in Festival Handicap (creditably) at Ascot and November Handicap at Doncaster last 2 starts: suited by 1½m: acts on good to firm ground, but goes very well with some give: occasionally on toes: sometimes wanders: lazy but game. *R. Hannon.*

LIGHT DANCER 4 ch.g. Niniski (USA) 125–Foudre 76 (Petingo 135) [1989 12m4 10.8f4 10f6 12g 12.4g 1990 15m] compact, sparely-made gelding: no worthwhile form on flat, including in handicaps: winning hurdler in September. *L. J. Codd.* —

LIGHT GREEN (USA) 3 b.g. Green Dancer (USA) 132–Linklighter 89 (Busted 134) [1989 NR 1990 12d5 a8g a5g] third foal: dam, 1¼m winner also successful at 6f at 2 yrs, is out of half-sister to Great Voltigeur winner Patch: well beaten in maiden and claimers, bolting to post before final start. *R. V. Smyth.* —

LIGHT HAND 4 br.f. Star Appeal 133–No Cards 109 (No Mercy 126) [1989 10m 12g5 8m2 8m4 10f* 10s 10f* 11g 1990 10g* 10m3 10f2 9m3 10d* 10.6d*] leggy, workmanlike filly: moderate mover: won handicap at Leicester in June and claimers at Ayr and Haydock (apprentice ridden) in September: suited by 1¼m (blinkered and raced freely over 11f): acts on firm and dead going. *M. H. Tompkins.* 75

LIGHTNING THUNDER 3 b.g. Dara Monarch 128–Royal Sister II (Claude) [1989 7g 7d a8g4 1990 12m 12h2 12.2m5 10f* 12.3g 8g] lengthy, workmanlike gelding: good walker: moderate mover: fair plater: favourite, won at Redcar (sold out of D. Morley's stable 7,000 gns) in May, hanging repeatedly left, looking none too keen but leading final strides: behind in lady riders non-selling handicaps after: stays 1½m: acts on hard ground: blinkered final outing, visored previous 4: has joined D. Yeoman. *Denys Smith.* 50

LIGHT OF MORN (USA) 4 b.c. Alleged (USA) 138–Flaming Leaves (USA) 108 (Olden Times) [1989 10.6g* 12f 10g* 10m* 10m* 9f2 9.7m 9g3 8g* 1990 7.2f3 8d 8m4 10g6] strong, good-topped colt: usually impresses in appearance: progressed extremely well as 3 y o, winning listed contest at Newmarket: below his best in varied events in 1990, on final outing well beaten in Scottish Classic at Ayr in July: stays 1¼m, but at least as effective at 1m: acts on firm going: takes keen hold, and has worn hackamore bridle: has often worn tongue strap. *B. Hanbury.* 103

LIGHT-OF-THE-LOCH 2 b.f. (Jan 25) Lightning Dealer 103–Balmenoch (Queen's Hussar 124) [1990 5m4 5d6 5d 5v4 6s2] 800Y: leggy filly: has a round action: third foal: dam poor plater: poor maiden: will be suited by 7f: acts well on soft ground: sweated up final outing: retained 4,800 gns Ascot December Sales. *A. W. Potts.* 45

LIGHT ON HER TOES 3 b.f. Cragador 110–Oscilight 112 (Swing Easy (USA) 126) [1989 5g 6g 7m 1990 7m 8.2s] lengthy, angular filly: seems of little account. *M. J. Bolton.* —

LIGHTS OUT (FR) 4 b.c. Crystal Glitters (USA) 127–Light A Star (Wollow 132) [1989 10s* 12m6 11g* 12g* 12d6 13.5g* 12g* 12g5 1990 12s 12g* 12d 12.5g2 12g2] second foal: dam placed at up to 12.5f, half-sister to very smart Light The Lights: won minor event at Evry and 4 times (twice in listed races) in Provinces as 3-y-o: showed improved form to beat Robertet 2½ lengths in Prix Jean de Chaudenay at 119

Saint-Cloud in May: ran poorly in Grand Prix d'Evry, then caught final strides by French Glory in 4-runner Prix Maurice de Nieuil at Maisons-Laffitte in July on fourth outing: suited by 1½m. *A. de Royer-Dupre, France.*

LIHBAB 7 ch.g. Ballad Rock 122–Sovereign Bloom (Florescence 120) [1989 8f3 — 1990 8f] rangy gelding: lightly-raced plater: swerved left start and tailed off at Chepstow in September: stays 9f: acts on any going with possible exception of soft: wears bandages: winning novice hurdler in November. *J. M. Bradley.*

LIKE AMBER 4 ch.f. Aragon 118–More Fun (Malicious) [1989 5s 5s4 5m 5m4 5g 60 1990 6m 6m 7g2 7m 7f 5g 5g* 5m 7g] quite modest handicapper: won at Wolverhampton in October by 3 necks, pushed along virtually throughout: stays 7f: acts on any going: inconsistent. *C. E. Brittain.*

LILAC TIME 4 b.f. Town And Country 124–Harp Strings (FR) 109 (Luthier 126) — [1989 10m 12f 10.6d 12g 1990 a12g a12g4 12m6 a12g] workmanlike filly: plating-class form at best: should stay at least 1¼m: visored once at 3 yrs. *R. Hollinshead.*

LILIAN BAYLISS (IRE) 2 b.f. (Apr 4) Sadler's Wells (USA) 132–Godzilla 106 96 p (Gyr (USA) 132) [1990 6g2 7d*] lengthy, rather sparely-made filly: has a roundish action: sister to very useful French 3-y-o Ernani, 6f winner at 2 yrs, closely related to high-class French miler Phydilla (by Lyphard) and half-sister to several winners, including Observation Post (by Shirley Heights), 7f and 8.2f winner at 2 yrs later suited by 1¼m/1½m: dam won at up to 7.5f at 2 yrs in Italy and showed form at 6f here: odds on but still bit green, won minor event at Chester in October by 5 lengths from So Romantic, quickening over 1f out and soon clear: will stay at least 1m: sure to improve further, and win again. *M. R. Stoute.*

LILLY CAMILLY 3 ch.f. Electric 126–Be Sharp 85 (Sharpen Up 127) [1989 5g 5f 43 1990 8m 8f* 8m] lengthy, sturdy filly: won seller (no bid) at Thirsk in August: hampered early when behind in handicap 3 weeks later: may well stay further. *Miss L. C. Siddall.*

LILY'S LOVER (USA) 4 b.g. Sensitive Prince (USA)–Rushing Stream (USA) — (Delta Judge) [1989 8g 7g 9f5 11f2 12f4 12m 10f4 12g 12d 1990 10.4d 12m 12f 10m] tall, sparely-made gelding: moderate walker and mover: fair handicapper at one time: completely out of form in first half of 1990: blinkered, bolted going down and soon tailed off in Newmarket claimer final outing: suited by 1½m: best form on sound surface. *G. A. Pritchard-Gordon.*

LILY'S SUN 3 gr.g. Kala Shikari 125–Lily of France 81 (Monsanto (FR) 121) 69 d [1989 5f6 6d 1990 6f2 6g 5g3 5h6 5g6 6h 7g 5.3f5 7g a5g] leggy, lengthy gelding: moderate mover: quite modest maiden: generally well below form after third start: will prove best over sprint distances: acts on firm going: bandaged behind at 2 yrs and sixth start: on toes and hung left on fifth. *W. G. R. Wightman.*

LILY SUGARS 2 ch.f. (Feb 15) Ardross 134–Bobo Ema 81 (Auction Ring (USA) — 123) [1990 a7g a8g] IR 1,500Y: second foal: sister to 3-y-o Bellezza: dam 2-y-o 6f winner out of French middle-distance maiden: ridden by 7-lb claimer, well beaten in maidens at Lingfield: bandaged near-fore final start. *J. S. Moore.*

LIMEBURN 4 b.c. Young Generation 129–Brickfield Queen (High Top 131) 94 [1989 11f3 10.1m 12d2 10m2 12g2 10g 1990 10m 10m5 11.5m* 12m 10f5 12m4 12m2 10d4] robust colt: blind in right eye: quite useful handicapper: made all at Sandown in July: ran well when second in amateurs race at Ascot: intended pacemaker in pattern events fourth and sixth (appearing to show improved form) outings: stays 1½m: acts on good to firm and dead going: usually blinkered, but wasn't at Sandown: sometimes slowly away: sold 23,000 gns Newmarket Autumn Sales. *G. Harwood.*

LIME ST NIGHTMAIR 2 b.g. (May 25) Elegant Air 119–Bernice Clare 68 — (Skymaster 126) [1990 8g] 9,800Y: medium-sized gelding: half-brother to several winners here and abroad, including quite modest 8.2f winner Question of Degree (by Known Fact): dam won over 1m at 4 yrs: burly in maiden at Newmarket in October. *A. C. Stewart.*

LINAMIX (FR) 3 gr.c. Mendez (FR) 128–Lunadix (FR) (Breton 130) [1989 127 8g* 8d* 8m2 1990 8d* 8m* 12g 8g2 8g2 8m6 10d2]

Boutin's stable supplied the favourite for the first colts' classic in both Britain and France. The day after Machiavellian was beaten in the Guineas, Linamix won the Dubai Poule d'Essai des Poulains at Longchamp. Linamix had only six opponents and started at evens. He'd accounted for four of them—Jade Robbery, Funambule, Honor Rajana and pacemaker Reinstate— with some authority in the Prix de Fontainebleu over the same course on his

508

Dubai Poule d'Essai des Poulains, Longchamp—
Linamix wins in course-record time from Zoman and Funambule

seasonal reappearance three weeks earlier. Of the others Book the Band seemed fairly well exposed going into the race while fellow British challenger Zoman was taking a huge step up in class. Zoman, however, came out a clear second best without ever getting on terms with Linamix who, having raced second to Reinstate, took over early in the straight and ran on strongly under pressure to hold on by a length and a half. The gallop had been a good one on the firmish ground, and for the third year in the last four, following Soviet Star and Kendor, the Poulains winner lowered the track record.

Most years the Poulains field is inferior to that at Newmarket. It's debatable whether the latest was, and Linamix turned out to be an above-average Poulains winner, even though he failed to win again. He had five more races, the first of them the Derby for which he started second favourite but ran below form in finishing ninth of eighteen behind Quest For Fame. In the end he seemed not to stay the trip. Before that, he'd had an uncomfortable time on Tattenham Hill, losing a good place and becoming short of room when his jockey steadied him. Linamix was let down after Epsom, and his forward showing on his return in the one-mile Prix du Haras de Fresnay-le-Buffard Jacques le Marois at Deauville in August apparently took connections by surprise. Yet another high-class stable-companion, Priolo, won the race. Linamix, one of the first to be ridden, stuck to his task so well on the rails that he remained in contention right to the line, Priolo coming late to beat him and Distant Relative by half a length and a neck. Three weeks later the same horses fought out the finish of another Group 1 mile race, the Emirates Prix du Moulin de Longchamp. Linamix was ridden in a very similar manner to when he won the Poulains but on this occasion, having taken over from Reinstate some way out, was just caught; Distant Relative beat him a short head, Priolo finishing best in third, three quarters of a length down. Judged on these last two performances Linamix held as good a chance as any in the Queen Elizabeth II Stakes at Ascot later in September, and we are rather at a loss to explain his modest showing, unless it was that the leaders (good horses on this occasion) went too fast to allow him to take up his customary forward position. He was never travelling comfortably in mid-division, dropped back to last on the turn just when he might have been expected to have improved, and made only a little late headway into a remote sixth place. We saw a very different Linamix in the Dubai Champion Stakes. Allowed to stride on behind the pacemaker Albadr as if no doubts existed about his staying the stiff ten furlongs, he took it up fully three furlongs out, soon saw off Elmaamul, and though unable to match In The Groove for finishing speed, he kept on gamely and strongly under pressure up the hill to make sure of second, only a length and a half behind. Afterwards Linamix's jockey Head received a two-day suspension for using the whip with excessive frequency; the decision seemed harsh in view of the way the colt had responded.

The now-retired Linamix got a mile and a quarter better than did his sire, the 1984 Moulin winner Mendez, also a free-running sort but one who pulled harder. The dam Lunadix, a minor winner over six furlongs at two and a mile

509

J-L. Lagardere's "Linamix"

Linamix (FR) (gr.c. 1987)	Mendez (FR) (gr 1981)	Bellypha (gr 1976)	Lyphard
			Belga
		Miss Carina (gr 1975)	Caro
			Miss Pia
	Lunadix (FR) (gr 1972)	Breton (b or br 1967)	Relko
			La Melba
		Lutine (gr 1966)	Alcide
			Mona

at four in France, had previously produced a very smart middle-distance colt in Long Mick (by Gay Mecene). Long Mick was somewhat controversially rated fourth behind El Gran Senor, Rainbow Quest and Lear Fan in the 1983 International Classification for two-year-olds on a win in the ten-furlong Prix de Conde at Longchamp; he won the Grand Prix d'Evry later on and was placed in some better races in the States as well as in France during a long career. He is now at stud in Japan, as is Mendez. Lunadix's winners don't end at Long Mick and Linamix; she has produced three others in France, including Moonbeam (by Bolkonski), useful at up to a mile and a quarter. The grandam Lutine also got a mile and a quarter—she won over the distance at Windsor—but her dam, the fairly useful Mona, had no pretensions to staying beyond six furlongs. Linamix, a big, lengthy, angular colt with a powerful, round action, tended to go freely to post and did, as we've said, run freely in his races. He seemed best served by being allowed to bowl along up near the front, tactics that both Head and Mosse, the latter of whom came in for criticism from sections of the British Press at Epsom, used to advantage on him. Linamix acted on good to firm and dead going; he was never raced on extremes. He has been retired to the Haras du Val-Henry. *F. Boutin, France.*

LINAVOS   7 b.h. Tyrnavos 129–Linmill 74 (Amber Rama (USA) 133) [1989 5f⁴ 5f   —
1990 a6g] compact horse: poor performer: first run for 20 months, faced very stiff task in Lingfield claimer in December: stays 6f: acts on firm and dead going: suitable mount for apprentice: occasionally sweats. *P. Howling.*

LINCHMERE LAD (IRE)   2 b.c. (May 6) Petorius 117–Adamantos 92 (Yellow   69 p
God 129) [1990 7g⁵ 7g⁴] 7,000F, 16,000Y: compact, quite attractive colt: half-brother to several winners here and abroad, including fair 1m and 1¼m winner Sergeant Smoke (by Known Fact) and 1¼m and 12.2f winner Arkan (by Prince Tenderfoot): dam 2-y-o 7f winner, is half-sister to top 1960 2-y-o colt Typhoon: 4 lengths fourth of 16 to Mulciber in maiden at Folkestone in October: took keen hold when green on debut: may well improve again. *Lady Herries.*

LINCSTONE BOY (IRE)   2 b.g. (Mar 28) Kafu 120–Babylon (Hello Gor-   59
geous (USA) 128) [1990 6g 6g 5m* 5m] IR 1,700Y, resold 3,600Y: tall, plain gelding: first foal: dam unraced: won maiden auction at Redcar in September, showing much improved form, by a neck from Oliroan, making all: looked awkward ride when last in Warwick nursery after: blinkered final 2 starts: one to be wary of. *J. Balding.*

LINDFIELD BELLE (IRE)   2 b.f. (Feb 21) Fairy King (USA)–Tecmessa   78
(Home Guard (USA) 129) [1990 6m⁵ 5m⁴ 5f* 5g⁴ 6m⁵ 6d 5m⁶ 6s 7s] stocky, lengthy filly: carries condition: has a quick action: modest performer: made all in maiden at Lingfield in August: ran well in listed races at Newbury and Ayr fourth and sixth starts: stays 6f: acts on firm and dead ground, but seems unsuited by soft: sweating final start. *D. A. Wilson.*

LINE ENGAGED (USA)   2 b.c. (Apr 10) Phone Trick (USA)–Quick Nurse   108
(USA) (Dr Fager) [1990 5m³ 5g* 6m* 6d 5g⁴ 6g⁵] $47,000Y: lengthy, angular colt: has a quick action: half-brother to several winners in USA, one placed in 6f Grade 3 event: dam never ran: sire smart sprinter: useful colt, successful in Norfolk Stakes at Royal Ascot in June by a length from Sylva Honda and minor event at Windsor in July by 5 lengths from Timeless Times: good fourth of 6 to Distinctly North in Flying Childers Stakes at Doncaster: raced freely when running moderately in

Norfolk Stakes, Ascot—Line Engaged improves to beat Sylva Honda,
Gold Futures and Distinctly North (No. 1)

Mr I. Karageorgis' "Line Engaged"

Rokeby Farms Mill Reef Stakes at Newbury on final start: seems equally effective at 5f and 6f: acts on good to firm ground and dead. *D. R. C. Elsworth.*

LINE OF THUNDER (USA) 3 b.f. Storm Bird (CAN) 134–Shoot A Line 127 **103** (High Line 125) [1989 6g³ 6m* 6d* 6m² 1990 12d⁶ 7m* 8g² 10m⁴] lengthy, good-quartered filly: has a quick action: useful performer: 6/5 on, won 3-runner minor event at Chepstow in August: ran creditably in listed race at Doncaster and Sun Chariot Stakes at Newmarket afterwards: stays 1¼m: yet to race on extremes of going: reportedly to race in USA. *L. M. Cumani.*

LINE OF VISION (USA) 3 gr.c. Liloy (FR) 124–Invision (USA) (Grey Dawn II **85** 132) [1989 6g⁶ 5f⁴ 6f² 7g 1990 8f³ 8g*dis 9m 10.6s 9g³ 10f 10f* 12m⁴ 9g⁶ 8m⁶ 9m³] rangy, rather unfurnished colt: fair handicapper: first past post in maiden (disqualified as jockey weighed in 2 lb light) at Carlisle in April and when ridden by 7-lb claimer at Pontefract in July: very good third of 40 to Risen Moon in £61,600 William Hill Cambridgeshire at Newmarket final start, always prominent: suited by further than 1m: acts on firm ground: races freely (pulled too hard for amateur fourth start): carries head high: sold 54,000 gns Newmarket Autumn Sales, reportedly to race in Saudi Arabia. *Mrs J. R. Ramsden.*

LINGFIELD LASS (USA) 3 b.f. Advocator–Royal Caprice (USA) (Swaps) **60** [1989 6g 6f⁶ 8g⁶ 7m 1990 a8g³ a10g* a10g³ 12f⁵ 12g⁵ 10.6f⁴] sparely-made filly: quite modest handicapper: won at Lingfield in February: stays 10.6f: acts on firm going: sold to join I. Campbell 14,000 gns Newmarket July Sales. *W. J. Musson.*

LINK MARKET (USA) 4 b.f. Linkage (USA)–Motor Mouse (USA) (Outing **71** Class) [1989 8s³ 10g 8.2m 9m 1990 14g² 14g* 14m³ 14d⁴ a14g² a12g* a12g* 14m⁵ a16g* a13g* a13g² a14g a16g²] rangy filly: poor mover: successful in handicaps on all-weather at Southwell (twice) in July and Lingfield (twice) in November: also winner of similar event at Nottingham in June: stays 2m: best runs on all-weather: genuine and consistent. *M. J. Ryan.*

LINKRIS 2 ch.f. (May 4) Norwick (USA) 120–Powderhall 81 (Murrayfield 119)   — §
[1990 5f 5f 6g 5m⁵ 7g] 2,100F, 2,000Y: leggy filly: half-sister to several winners, including quite useful 6f and 1m winner El Rey (by King of Spain) and fair 1m winner Clarandal (by Young Generation): dam won 4 times at up to 6f: seems of little account: looked ungenuine when blinkered third outing: bandaged behind final 4 outings. *R. W. Stubbs.*

LINPAC LIGHT 3 gr.f. Kalaglow 132–North Page (FR) 81 (Northfields (USA))   67
[1989 5m⁴ 8d² 1990 10m 12m⁶ 12d³ 12v a12g⁴] unfurnished filly: quite modest maiden: in frame, staying on well, in handicaps at Beverley and Southwell: should be suited by 1¾m: acts on dead ground. *C. W. C. Elsey.*

LINPAC WEST 4 b.c. Posse (USA) 130–North Page (FR) 81 (Northfields (USA))   97
[1989 8.2v* 9s² 10.6s* 9f 10g³ 1990 10g 12m² 12s⁴ 10g⁴ 14g 13.4g⁴ 13d⁴ 12m⁶ 12s] lengthy, angular colt: poor mover: had 2 good performances to his credit at Ayr in 1990, fourth to Husyan in Scottish Classic on fourth start (100/1) and to Aahsaylad, beaten 3 necks, in Bogside Cup (Handicap) on seventh: ran poorly in Tote Ebor at York and November Handicap at Doncaster fifth and final starts: should stay 1¾m: best on an easy surface, and acts well in the mud: has edged under pressure. *C. W. C. Elsey.*

LIOSEAN 4 gr.g. Silly Prices 110–Manche 82 (Palestine 133) [1989 NR 1990 11g   —
12m] brother to fair sprinter Not So Silly: dam second in three 5f races at 2 yrs: very mulish going down and at stalls when withdrawn on intended debut in March: well beaten in maiden claimer and seller later in spring. *N. Chamberlain.*

LISALEE (IRE) 2 b.f. (Apr 19) Montekin 125–Ivy Holme (Silly Season 127)   34
[1990 6s⁴ 6d⁵ 6f] IR 950Y: workmanlike filly: moderate mover: third foal: half-sister to 3-y-o Singh Holme and a winner in Italy (both by Mansingh): dam ran once: poor form in sellers: slowly away second start: should prove suited by further than 5f. *J. Parkes.*

LISA ROSA 3 b.f. Ardross 134–Macaw 85 (Narrator 127) [1989 NR 1990 10m 10f]   —
big, lengthy filly: half-sister to several winners, including useful 6f to 1m winner Northleach (by Northfields) and 5-y-o 12.3f winner Red Jam Jar (by Windjammer): dam won over 1m: backward, no form in summer claimers at Newmarket: bandaged final start. *W. J. Musson.*

LITMORE DANCER 2 br.f. (Feb 27) Mashhor Dancer (USA)–Daring Charm   —
(Daring March 116) [1990 7g] lengthy, angular filly: first foal: dam unraced daughter of half-sister to Huntercombe: prominent almost 4f in large-field maiden at Newmarket in November: showed a round action. *J. D. Bethell.*

LITTLE BIG 3 b.c. Indian King (USA) 128–Route Royale (Roi Soleil 125) [1989   84
6g⁴ 7g 1990 a8g* 7f² 8.2f³ 8.5d* 10.6s 8d 7.6f⁴ a8g 10d³ 10d 8d 8m a10g⁶] useful-looking colt: fair performer: led well inside final 1f when winning maiden at Lingfield in March and handicap (on toes, sweating and went freely down) at Beverley in May: suited by 1¼m: acts on any going: blinkered ninth (ran well) and tenth starts: trained until after tenth by R. Boss. *B. J. Curley.*

LITTLE CARIAD 3 ch.f. Fine Blue 103–Crisp Venture (Crisp And Even 116)   —
[1989 NR 1990 7g 5g a8g] leggy, close-coupled filly: fifth reported foal: dam tailed off in novice hurdle: tailed-off last in claimer and maidens' blinkered and on toes final start. *M. B. James.*

LITTLE CONKER 2 ch.c. (Feb 23) All Systems Go 119–L'Irondelle (On Your   34
Mark 125) [1990 6m 7g 5d 6f⁶ 8.5m 6m a7g] 600F: workmanlike colt: has a round action: second foal: dam never ran: bad plater: best form at 5f and 6f. *A. Smith.*

LITTLEDALE (USA) 4 b.c. Lypheor 118–Smeralda 105 (Grey Sovereign 128§)   63
[1989 8g³ 1990 11s⁵ 10.8m⁶ a10g 9g³ 10m⁶] lengthy colt: best efforts in spring in handicaps at York (ladies) and Sandown last 2 outings: seems to stay 1¼m. *D. J. G. Murray-Smith.*

LITTLE FLASHER (IRE) 2 ch.g. (Jan 15) Exhibitioner 111–Eskaroon   70
(Artaius (USA) 129) [1990 5f 5m* 5m* 5d² 5g⁴ 5g³ 5f³ 5f 5m² 5m⁵ a5g a6g⁵ a5g*] IR 5,000F, 8,000Y: sturdy, good-quartered gelding: has a quick action: third foal: half-brother to 3-y-o Puffy (by Wolverlife), successful from 5f (at 2 yrs) to 7f: dam unraced half-sister to Oaks and Irish Oaks runner-up Bourbon Girl: no bid when successful in early-season sellers at Beverley and Nottingham: won 15-runner nursery at Southwell in November by ½ length from Flying Promise: better at 5f than 6f: effective with or without blinkers. *M. W. Easterby.*

LITTLEGO 5 b.g. Croghan Hill 106–Iamstopped (Furry Glen 121) [1989 12d² 16m — 12.3d 1990 11.5m³] sparely-made ex-Irish gelding: second foal: half-brother to 7f (at 2 yrs) and 1m winner Murphy (by Touch Paper): dam placed at up to 1m in Ireland: on toes, 10 lengths third of 16, slowly away and never nearer, in claimer at Lingfield in May: should be suited by further than 1½m: acts on good to firm and dead going: winning hurdler in April. *J. R. Jenkins.*

LITTLE GOOSE GIRL 4 ch.f. Alias Smith (USA)–Mother Goose (Absalom — 128) [1989 10f⁶ 8.3m 1990 11.7f 8f 1990 a13g⁴] lengthy filly: no sign of ability in poor company. *C. P. Wildman.*

LITTLE KRAKER 3 b.f. Godswalk (USA) 130–Wyn Mipet (Welsh Saint 126) 69 [1989 6g⁵ 6m⁶ 6g 1990 7m⁴ 8h⁴ 7d* 8m 8f⁶ 8.3f² 7m⁶ 10.6d 10m⁴ 10g⁵] smallish, shallow-girthed filly: moderate mover: modest performer: won claimer at Epsom in June: may stay beyond 1¼m: acts on firm and dead going, seems unsuited by hard: rather inconsistent. *R. Hannon.*

LITTLE MONK (IRE) 2 b.g. (Jan 22) Mazaad 106–Smurfette (Baptism 119) 42 [1990 5s 5f 5m 5m⁴ 6f] IR 4,200F, IR 11,000Y: robust gelding: first foal: dam never ran: poor form, including in sellers: blinkered final 2 starts: sold 1,000 gns Doncaster August Sales. *M. W. Easterby.*

LITTLE PRESTON (IRE) 2 b.f. (May 13) Pennine Walk 120–Blessingtonia 79 53 (So Blessed 130) [1990 5f 6m a7g² a7g⁵] 6,000Y, 5,000 2-y-o: leggy, lengthy, unfurnished filly: half-sister to 2-y-o 5f winners Dunloring (by Dunphy) and Tennis Penny (by Auction Ring): dam raced only at 5f, winning once at 2 yrs: former plater: ½-length second of 14 in maiden at Lingfield late in year, best effort: suited by 7f: trained on debut by G. Lewis. *N. A. Callaghan.*

LITTLE RIPPER 3 br.f. Belfort (FR) 89–Harem Queen 66 (Prince Regent (FR) 35 129) [1989 6m* 7m⁴ 6f⁴ 7.5f 6f⁵ 7m* 6g 7m 7m a7g a8g 1990 a5g³ a6g a7g a5g² 7m 5f 7m 8h⁵ 5g⁴ 5f] small, sparely-made filly: fairly useful plater in summer at 2 yrs: poor form in first half of 1990, often in non-selling events: better at 7f than shorter: effective with or without blinkers: visored last 3 outings: tends to flash tail: has joined K. White. *M. D. I. Usher.*

LITTLE SAFFRONS 3 b.g. Hard Fought 125–Miss Pinkerton (Above — Suspicion 127) [1989 5v⁶ 5m 5m³ 5f⁶ 7m⁵ 7f⁵ 6m 7f 1990 7f 9f 10m 10m] lengthy, workmanlike colt: poor mover: plating-class form at 2 yrs, none in sellers in 1990: stays 7f: ran poorly in blinkers then visor last 2 starts at 2 yrs: carries head bit high. *T. W. Cunningham.*

LITTLETON (USA) 2 b.f. (Apr 23) El Gran Senor (USA) 136–Daeltown (FR) 75 117 (Dictus (FR) 126) [1990 5m² 7f* 8.2m⁵] small, sturdy filly: good walker: closely related to a minor stakes-placed winner by Storm Bird: dam French filly stayed 1¼m, much improved at 4 yrs: won maiden at Brighton by ½ length from Glowlamp: favourite, eased when beaten in minor event at Nottingham later in September: should be much better suited by 1m + than 7f. *R. Charlton.*

LIU LIU SAN (IRE) 2 ch.f. (May 7) Bairn (USA) 126–The Saltings (FR) 44 (Morston (FR) 125) [1990 6m 7m] 2,600Y: unfurnished filly: third foal: half-sister to 1988 2-y-o 7f winner Accessofhornchurch (by Coquelin): dam twice-raced half-sister to useful sprinter Dare Me, herself dam of good sprinter Fortysecondstreet: never better than mid-division in autumn maidens at Goodwood (slowly away) and Chepstow. *P. Mitchell.*

LIVE ACTION 3 b.c. Alzao (USA) 117–Brig O'Doon (Shantung 132) [1989 NR 97 p 1990 8.5d³ 8.5g² 8m* 12m 10.2s* 9.1s*] 82,000Y: good-bodied colt: half-brother to several winners, including high-class miler Young Generation (by Balidar) and useful 1977 2-y-o 6f winner Beldale Record (by Jukebox): dam poor maiden: successful in maiden at Sandown in July, soon pushed along and leading post, then impressively in handicap at Doncaster and minor event at Newcastle in the autumn: stays 1¼m well: goes very well on soft ground: useful performer in the making. *L. M. Cumani.*

LIVING IMAGE 2 b.c. (Feb 19) Taufan (USA) 119–Visible Form 99 (Formidable 86 p (USA) 125) [1990 7g² 8.2d*] 36,000F, 48,000Y: quite attractive colt: good walker: third foal: half-brother to 1988 2-y-o 6f winner Azeb (by Young Generation): dam, 6f and 1¼m winner, is out of half-sister to very smart stayer Raise You Ten: won 4-runner minor event at Haydock in September gamely in close finish from Ocean Air and Green's Ferneley: better suited by 1m than 7f: likely to improve again. *W. Jarvis.*

LIVING PROOF 6 ch.g. Known Fact (USA) 135–Lady Esmeralda 79 (Karabas 41 132) [1989 5f² 5m⁶ 5m 1990 5m 5g 5f³ 5f⁴ 5m⁴ 5g⁶ 6g 5g⁵ a5g⁶ a5g] strong, angular gelding: carries condition: poor handicapper: best at 5f: acts on firm going: usually taken down alone and very quietly. *J. P. Smith.*

LIYOUN (IRE) 2 b.c. (Apr 21) Shernazar 131–Lisana 97 (Alleged (USA) 138) 85 P [1990 8m4] first foal: dam 1½m winner, is out of half-sister to top-class French 1½m performers Acamas, Akarad and Akiyda: very green, 3 lengths fourth of 14, staying on really well having been flat-footed when pace increased, to Hilti's Hut in maiden at Newmarket in October: will be suited by middle distances: sure to improve considerably and win races. *M. R. Stoute.*

LIZZY CANTLE 3 b.f. Homing 130–Muninga 108 (St Alphage 119) [1989 5f 5f5 52 ? 6m a6g3 1990 a5g4 a5g4 a7g* a7g3 a7g5 a6g 8f] small, good-bodied filly: poor handicapper: won at Lingfield in January: beat only 2 home afterwards, and not seen out after May: withdrawn lame intended fourth start: stays 7f: blinkered sixth outing. *C. P. Wildman.*

LIZZY LONGSTOCKING 8 br.m. Jimsun 121–Darling Emma (Dairialatan 111) — [1989 NR 1990 10.1m] second foal: dam never ran: backward, slowly away and always behind in minor event at Windsor in July: winning hurdler twice early in 1990/1 season. *T. B. Hallett.*

LLANDOVERY 3 br.c. Caerleon (USA) 132–Copy Conforme (FR) (Top Ville 75 129) [1989 7m 1990 10.1g6 10m 10.1m4 10.4g* 12.2d* 10m 12m* 12m4 10m3 12m* 12m* 12m4 12.2d3] smallish, lengthy colt: moderate mover: modest performer: won claimers at Chester, Catterick, Pontefract, Goodwood and Beverley: better at 1½m than shorter, and will stay further: acts on good to firm ground and dead: blinkered nowadays: sold 22,000 gns Newmarket Autumn Sales, probably to Italy. *B. W. Hills.*

LLANELLY (FR) 3 gr.f. Kenmare (FR) 125–Grey Valley (USA) (Vigors (USA)) 51 ? [1989 8g 7s 7s 1990 10.5d 10.5g 9s 8g 9d6 8d* 9f5 8.3g4 10g 10d] angular, sparely-made filly: second foal: half-sister to French provincial 1¼m and 1½m winner Galana Sagan (by Bellman): dam French 12.5f winner out of half-sister to Vitiges: won claimer (claimed out of B. Secly's stable approx £9,400) at Evry in June: staying-on fourth in seller (claimed out of M. Pipe's stable £6,050) at Windsor in August, clearly best effort here: should stay beyond 1m: blinkered third to eighth and final starts. *Graeme Roe.*

LLANTRISANT (USA) 3 b.g. Private Account (USA)–Ambry (USA) (Gallant 72 Man) [1989 6m 1990 8.2m3 8.2s] good-topped gelding: third in moderately-run Nottingham minor event, easily better effort in the spring: can do better over middle distances: probably unsuited by soft ground. *J. Gosden.*

LLENNODO 3 ch.f. Castle Keep 121–Incarnadine 67 (Hot Spark 126) [1989 5m5 43 6f5 5g3 6g3 8.2f 6f 1990 9f 7.5d2 a7g] small, sparely-made filly: quite modest plater: stayed 9f: acted on firm and dead going: blinkered (ran poorly) final outing: usually sweating and edgy at 2 yrs: dead. *J. G. FitzGerald.*

LOADPLAN LASS 4 b.f. Nicholas Bill 125–Strathclair (Klairon 131) [1989 8g — 6m 8.2d 10g 12g 1990 a7g] leggy, narrow filly: well beaten since 2 yrs, including in sellers: bred to stay middle distances: blinkered and edgy final start at 3 yrs: twice reluctant at stalls: sold out of C. Booth's stable 3,700 gns Doncaster January Sales before only run in 1990. *A. P. James.*

LOCAL DERBY 2 ch.g. (Apr 12) Scottish Reel 123–Green Pool 39 65 (Whistlefield 118) [1990 7.5g2 8f] 8,600F, 5,000 (privately) Y: smallish, workmanlike gelding: first foal: dam plating half-sister to Rich Charlie: neck second in maiden auction at Beverley in August, soon close up travelling well, leading 2f out but caught close home: below that form in maiden at Thirsk following month. *A. P. Stringer.*

LOCAL DERBY 3 ch.c. Local Suitor (USA) 128–Honey Match 98 (Match III 135) 97 [1989 NR 1990 10.2f* 12.3d 12f* 12g 12m 12m* 14g 14m2 12m] big, strong colt: has plenty of scope: carries condition: half-brother to several winners, including useful 1¼m winners Hatched and Brown Thatch (both by Thatch): dam, 1¼m winner, is half-sister to numerous good winners: fairly useful performer: won maiden at Newcastle in April and handicaps at Haydock in May and August: stays 1¾m: acts on firm going. *J. W. Watts.*

LOCALITY 5 b.m. Lochnager 132–Declamation 93 (Town Crier 119) [1989 10f6 38 12f5 12.8m6 12.4m5 11f3 10m5 12.3m 12d 12g 11s3 10v 12d 1990 9s4 11f 9s5 8f] close-coupled, heavy-topped mare: poor maiden: probably stays 1½m: acts on any going: trained first 2 starts by N. Tinkler: sold 850 gns Doncaster October Sales. *Don Enrico Incisa.*

LOCAL LASS 3 b.f. Local Suitor (USA) 128–Sorebelle 95 (Prince Tenderfoot 90 (USA) 126) [1989 NR 1990 7g 7m 6g2 7g* 7f 8m4 7g 6d3 6m] lengthy, good-quartered filly: has plenty of scope: fifth foal: half-sister to useful 5f and 7f winner

Abuzz (by Absalom): dam best at up to 1m: won 5-runner maiden at Leicester in June: ran very well when staying-on third of 28 to Final Shot in £53,300 Ladbrokes (Ayr) Gold Cup, poorly when favourite in £8,400 Newmarket handicap 2 weeks later: at least as effective at 6f as 1m, where there's plenty of give in the ground: faced very stiff task on firm going: edgy (ran well) third start. *C. E. Brittain.*

LOCH DUICH 4 ch.c. Kris 135–Sleat 112 (Santa Claus 133) [1989 10.6g 10g3 14g 1990 10m5 12.5f* 10m* 10m6 8d] leggy colt: won claimer at Wolverhampton (didn't have to be at his best) in April and handicap at Sandown (leading final strides) month later: below form when final outing, first for 4 months: needs at least 1¼m and stays 1½m: has run well when sweating: takes keen hold: sold to join J. Baker's stable 7,200 gns Newmarket Autumn Sales. *W. Jarvis.* — 77

LOCHERRE 6 gr.g. Lochnager 132–Chemin de Guerre 78 (Warpath 113) [1989 NR 1990 12m] workmanlike gelding: moderate mover: showed signs of ability as 3-y-o: wearing brush pricker on off-side, never dangerous in handicap at Leicester in March: tailed off when blinkered: winning novice hurdler in January. *O. Brennan.* — —

LOCH FRUIN 3 b.c. Lomond (USA) 128–Miralove 91 (Mount Hagen (FR) 127) [1989 7m2 7g 8g4 1990 12m3 14f* 16g4 10.2f*] lengthy, attractive colt: carries condition: fair form: favourite, won maiden at Redcar in June, swishing tail and leading post, and amateurs race at Doncaster in July, leading 7f out: stays 2m: has won on firm but best efforts with give in the ground: blinkered last 2 starts: lacks turn of foot: sold 5,000 gns Newmarket Autumn Sales. *B. W. Hills.* — 89

LOCH SPEY 3 ch.f. Formidable (USA) 125–River Spey 96 (Mill Reef (USA) 141) [1989 6g 8g 1990 8g 10m 11d5 8m] strong, sturdy filly: plating-class form at best: blinkered, sweating profusely and very edgy when tailed off in claimer final start: seems to stay 1¼m. *G. A. Pritchard-Gordon.* — —

LOCK KEEPER (USA) 4 b.g. Riverman (USA) 131–Jamila (Sir Gaylord) [1989 8d 8.2d2 1990 11g3 12g 12d5] stocky, attractive gelding: moderate walker: lightly-raced maiden: stays 11f. *J. Mackie.* — 55

LOCO TYCOON 3 ch.g. Nicholas Bill 125–Sabala 93 (Tribal Chief 125) [1989 NR 1990 8v 10m 11g 10g 8g 12f 15m] 19,000Y: leggy, quite good-topped gelding: poor mover: fourth living foal: half-brother to 3 winners, including 7f and 1m winner Timber Tycoon (by Dragonara Palace) and 1986 2-y-o 5f winner Jaisalmer (by Castle Keep), both fairly useful: dam won at 6f and 7f: no form, including in sellers and handicaps: races freely, and doesn't stay middle distances: visored final start: mulish at stalls second: sold out of Sir Mark Prescott's stable 5,200 gns Newmarket July Sales and gelded after fifth. *A. P. Stringer.* — —

LODESTAR (IRE) 2 b.c. (Jan 26) Rainbow Quest (USA) 134–Air Distingue (USA) 120 (Sir Ivor 135) [1990 7g2] second foal: half-brother to 3-y-o Vaudeville Lady (by Top Ville): dam (from good family) won from 6f to 8.5f, including in USA, and was third in French Oaks: second favourite, kept on well when 2 lengths second of 13 to Eastern Magic in maiden at Salisbury in October: will be suited by further: sure to do better. *G. Harwood.* — 78 p

LODGING 3 ch.c. Longleat (USA) 109–Mollified 67 (Lombard (GER) 126) [1989 NR 1990 8g 8f5 10g 8m4 8h6 a8g4 8m3 7g 8m4 9g3 8m] rather angular colt: fifth foal: half-brother to 4-y-o 1¼m winner Carpet Slippers (by Daring March) and a winning hurdler: dam stayed 1¼m: quite modest maiden: should stay 1¼m: below form on hard ground: visored last 5 starts. *J. D. Bethell.* — 66

LOFT BOY 7 b.g. Cawston's Clown 113–Burglar Tip 73 (Burglar 128) [1989 5m2 6f3 6f3 6f 5f3 5m3 5.6g6 5m4 5g4 5d5 5d a6g6 1990 5.8h* 5m5 5.8f2 5f6 5m3 5f* 5.8h2 5m2 5.8f4 5m 6g3 6s] sturdy gelding: fair handicapper: won at Bath in May and Sandown (making most) in July: effective at 5f to 6f: acts on any going: usually blinkered or visored: occasionally bandaged off-hind: tough and consistent. *J. D. Bethell.* — 82

LOFTY LADY (IRE) 2 b.f. (May 6) Head For Heights 125–Octavia Girl 104 (Octavo (USA) 115) [1990 8m* 8m] sturdy, attractive filly: fourth foal: half-sister to fairly useful 7f and 1m winner Festival Mood (by Jalmood): dam 2-y-o 6f winner later stayed 1m: second favourite but bit backward, won maiden at Salisbury by short head from Subtle Change, leading over 1f out and running on under hand riding: ran creditably in face of stiff task in Brent Walker Fillies' Mile at Ascot later in September: will stay 1¼m. *B. W. Hills.* — 81

LOGAMIMO 4 br.c. Lord Gayle (USA) 124–Miss Morgan (Native Prince) [1989 8d 10v 10.6s 11f2 8g 11f6 10.2g 12g6 11m* 11f* 12.2m* 11g* 12.2g* 10.2f3 10f4 12g 1990 a12g6] rather leggy, quite good-bodied colt: good mover: successful 5 times, mostly in handicaps, as 3-y-o: favourite, never able to challenge at Southwell in — —

February: better at 1½m than 1¼m: acts on firm going: usually blinkered: changed hands 10,000 gns Doncaster January Sales: winner over hurdles (has worn tongue strap, claimed to join J. Hellens' stable in May). *N. Tinkler.*

LOGICAL LADY 3 b.f. Tina's Pet 121–Lady Andrea (Andrea Mantegna) [1989 **71** 5d 5d 5d³ 6f* 7f 7m² 8f⁶ 7.3v⁶ 1990 7m 10m⁵ 8m⁶ 10f⁶ 8g⁵ 10.2f* 11.7m³ 10.6v] close-coupled filly: modest handicapper: won at Bath in September, held up travelling well, leading inside final 1f despite hanging left: stays 1½m: acts on firm ground, seems unsuited by heavy: blinkered last 4 starts: has sweated and got on edge: winning hurdler: not an easy ride. *R. J. Holder.*

LOGWOOD BLACK 2 b.c. (Jan 20) Aragon 118–Little Egret 74 (Carwhite 127) — [1990 6m a7g] 6,600F: first foal: dam winner in Italy stayed 1½m, is half-sister to very useful French middle-distance winner Natchitoches: slowly away and always behind in claimers at Leicester and Southwell. *R. Hollinshead.*

LOKI (IRE) 2 ch.c. (Apr 16) Thatching 131–Sigym (Lord Gayle (USA) 124) [1990 **77 p** 6m 6d 7m*] IR 72,000Y: strong colt: has a fluent action: first foal: dam suited by 1¼m: 12/1 from 25/1, made all, quickening 2f out and staying on well, in maiden at Warwick in October, beating Top Shereek 1½ lengths: well backed time before: better suited by 7f than 6f. *G. Lewis.*

LOLITA 3 b.f. Wassl 125–Lady Bennington (Hot Grove 128) [1989 NR 1990 a7g³ **37** a7g 8g 6m⁶] leggy filly: has a round action: second foal: dam well behind in 3 races on flat and didn't complete over hurdles: form only in sellers first and final (apprentice handicap) starts: worth another try over further: sold 2,700 gns Newmarket July Sales. *Lord John FitzGerald.*

LOMAX 4 b.g. Lomond (USA) 128–Cornish Heroine (USA) 101 (Cornish Prince) **96** [1989 8f⁶ 7f 7g 1990 7m*] lengthy, attractive gelding, rather dipped-backed: recaptured form shown as 2-y-o when making all in £16,600 Insulpak Victoria Cup (Handicap) at Ascot in May: should stay 1m: acts well on top-of-the-ground: wears blinkers: sold 12,000 gns Newmarket Autumn Sales. *G. Harwood.*

LOMBARD FLYER 3 b.g. Exhibitioner 111–Quirina (GER) (Marduk (GER)) — [1989 7g 8.2g 8m⁴ 8.2s 1990 10.6f 8.5d a7g] tall, leggy gelding: plating-class form at 2 yrs, little at 3 yrs: stays 1m: best effort on top-of-the-ground: visored last 2 starts: sold 1,700 gns Doncaster August Sales. *M. O'Neill.*

LOMBARD SHIPS 3 ch.f. Orchestra 118–Tina's Star (Simbir 130) [1989 NR **73** 1990 8f⁵ 8.2f² 8.2m⁴ 8g⁵ 8.2g³ 7f 7g² 7f² 7.2d² 8.2v* 8m⁴ 7d] IR 540Y, 5,600 2-y-o: sparely-made filly: has a quick action: first reported foal: dam lightly-raced half-sister to Park Hill runner-up Lady Pavlova: modest performer: favourite, won claimer at Haydock in October by 10 lengths: bred to stay beyond 1m: acts on any going: on toes fifth and sixth starts: wandered under pressure on penultimate one: ran poorly final start, consistent otherwise. *M. O'Neill.*

LOMBARD THATCH 3 ch.f. Thatching 131–Molly Malone (Bold Lad (IRE) — 133) [1989 5m⁶ 5d 7g 1990 5m⁶ 7g⁶ 8.2s] small, dipped-backed filly: poor maiden: worth a try over 6f: acts on good to firm ground: visored final start. *M. O'Neill.*

LOMBOK 3 ch.c. Lomond (USA) 128–Enthralment (USA) 78 (Sir Ivor 135) [1989 — 7g 1990 10g 10g 8g⁶ 8g] small, angular colt: moderate mover: no worthwhile form, including in handicap: worth another try over further. *Miss G. M. Rees.*

LOMINDA (IRE) 2 b.f. (Feb 6) Lomond (USA) 128–Olinda 101 (Sassafras (FR) **80** 135) [1990 6g 6m* 6d³] 25,000Y: lengthy filly: sister to a winner in Italy, closely related to 2 winners abroad by Try My Best and half-sister to a winner abroad: dam Irish 7.5f winner at 2 yrs: won maiden at Yarmouth in September by a short head from Wish of Luck: on toes, disputed lead 4f in minor event at Doncaster following month: will be suited by 7f: possibly unsuited by a soft surface. *J. W. Hills.*

LOMOND LADY 3 b.f. Lomond (USA) 128–Miellita 98 (King Emperor (USA)) — [1989 6g 1990 12g 12f] leggy filly: no worthwhile form in maidens: pulled up lame final start: dead. *I. A. Balding.*

LONDINIUM 3 b.c. Top Ville 129–Nophe (USA) 95 (Super Concorde (USA) 128) — [1989 NR 1990 10g] leggy, attractive colt: second foal: dam 5f winner at 2 yrs who didn't train on: showed nothing in maiden at Kempton in April: sold to join O. Brennan 1,400 gns Newmarket Autumn Sales. *J. H. M. Gosden.*

LONDON LOUISE 4 b.f. Ile de Bourbon (USA) 133–Miss St James's 92 — (Sovereign Path 125) [1989 10f³ 12m a12g² a10g 1990 a14g a8g] leggy, lightly-made filly: poor maiden: probably stays 1½m: blinkered final outing: has worn bandages behind. *R. J. R. Williams.*

LONDON PRIDE (USA) 3 b.f. Lear Fan (USA) 130–Dance Empress (USA) **106** (Empery (USA) 128) [1989 NR 1990 8f* 7.3d³] strong, angular filly with scope: third foal: half-sister to 1988 2-y-o 7f winner Intebah (by The Bart), once-raced at 3 yrs: dam, 3-y-o 6f winner in USA, is half-sister to dam of very useful 1985 2-y-o Truely Nureyev: won moderately-run minor event at Leicester in March, making virtually all: 20/1, about 6 lengths third of 8 to Salsabil in Fred Darling Stakes at Newbury following month, always close up: should have been suited by return to 1m: sent to N. Drysdale in USA. *P. F. I. Cole.*

LONDON STANDARD 5 b.g. Shack (USA) 118–Red Realm (Realm 129) [1989 **64** 6d⁶ 6f 7f 1990 a6g³ a8g* a7g² 8m a10g⁴ a7g³ a8g³ 11.7m a7g⁵ a8g³ a6g³ a6g a7g a10g a8g] workmanlike gelding: previously irresolute, but did nothing wrong when winning handicap at Lingfield in March: below form last 4 outings: ideally suited by further most 6f, and stays 1m: often used to wear blinkers, but didn't in 1990: has worn bandages behind. *P. Mitchell.*

LONDON WINDOWS 8 b.g. Balliol 125–Chebs Lass 84 (Chebs Lad 120) [1989 **37** 8m 10.1m 10f 10h⁶ 10m⁶ 10f8f11f² 12g* 12f³ 10m 12f⁴ 11.7m 1990 18.8f⁴] tall gelding: poor handicapper: seems to stay 2¼m: acts on firm going: blinkered or visored 4 times: winning chaser in 1989/90. *B. C. Morgan.*

LONELY LASS 4 b.f. Headin' Up–Lonely Dawn (USA) 63 (Plenty Old (USA)) **35** [1989 6m 5m² 6g 1990 a6g 5g a7g⁵] lengthy, rather sparely-made filly: poor maiden: stays 6f. *L. J. Barratt.*

LONELY STREET 9 b.m. Frimley Park 109–Abalone (Abwah 118) [1989 6v² **—** 6g⁵ 5s³ 6f⁴ 6f 6f⁶ 6f 5g⁵ 6s 6d 6v 1990 6m⁶ 6d] plain, close-coupled mare: usually dull in coat: fair performer in spring of 1989, but generally below form subsequently: better suited by 6f than 5f: well suited by plenty of give in the ground: has worn blinkers and a visor, but not for some time: excellent mount for apprentice: has sweated. *P. J. Arthur.*

LONG ARM OF TH'LAW 4 ch.g. Longleat (USA) 109–Burglar Tip 73 **—** (Burglar 128) [1989 5m² 5m 6m 6g³ 6s² 6s 5s a7g 1990 6f⁴ 5g 6g 8.2s 6f 6d] rather leggy, close-coupled gelding: quite modest on his day: form as 4-y-o only on reappearance (not finding great deal): stays 6f: acts on any going: best in blinkers: inconsistent: sold 2,800 gns Newmarket July Sales. *W. J. Pearce.*

LONG BAY 8 b.h. Song 132–Sundream (Petingo 135) [1989 10.2g 8.2f⁵ 8m 7.6h⁵ **26** 10m³ 10g⁶ 10h⁵ 7g* 7g 8f⁵ 1990 a10g⁴ a8g⁵ a10g⁴ 10f 8.2f 10m 8m 8m 7f] sturdy, workmanlike horse: carries condition: moderate mover: bad performer: stays 1¼m: acts on firm going: has worn blinkers and won for apprentice. *H. J. Collingridge.*

LONGDRUM 3 ch.g. Sayf El Arab (USA) 127–Geppina Umbra (Sheshoon 132) **49** [1989 6m³ 6f⁶ 1990 8g 12.5g² 12m⁴ 10d⁴ 12d] tall, strong, rangy gelding: plating-class maiden: stays 1½m well: best efforts on an easy surface: has run creditably for apprentice: awkward to post and at stalls third outing. *M. J. Fetherston-Godley.*

LONG FURLONG 2 b.g. (May 18) Castle Keep 121–Myrtlegrove (Scottish Rifle **71** 127) [1990 6m⁵ 6m 8.2g² 10m*] leggy gelding: has scope: third foal: dam unraced daughter of half-sister to High Line: blinkered, won selling nursery (sold 4,250 gns) at Leicester in October, showing much improved form, by 5 lengths from Wotamona: will stay 1½m: carries head high, and doesn't look easiest of rides. *J. L. Dunlop.*

LONGIRL SISTER 4 ch.f. Longleat (USA) 109–Refectory (Reform 132) [1989 **—** NR 1990 10f 7h² 5g 8f 7.6g 8f] small, angular filly: sister to Long Girl, 1987 2-y-o listed winner in Belgium, and half-sister to 13.8f seller winner Uno's Pet (by Tina's Pet): dam never ran: successful 4 times in Belgium at 2 yrs: no worthwhile form in Britain, including in selling company: sold 1,000 gns Doncaster November Sales. *J. Ffitch-Heyes.*

LONG ISLAND 3 b.f. Law Society (USA) 130–Palm Dove (USA) (Storm Bird **—** (CAN) 134) [1989 5v⁵ 6m* 6g⁴ 6f⁴ 7m* 7m² 7m³ 7g 8g⁶ 1990 8g⁵ 8.5g] leggy, unfurnished filly: fair performer: creditable fifth in £8,800 event at Kempton: broke shoulder when hampered and fell in listed race at Epsom later in April: may well have been better suited by 1¼m: bandaged near-hind: dead. *N. A. Callaghan.*

LONG KNIVES 2 b.c. (Feb 21) Known Fact (USA) 135–Ides of March 87 **77** p (Mummy's Pet) [1990 5f² 6g⁴] IR 52,000/: good-bodied colt: has scope: second foal: half-brother to 3-y-o Lady Snooble (by King of Clubs): dam sprinting half-sister to very useful 1981 2-y-o 6f winner Foam Bath and jumper/middle-distance stayer Cima: favourite, modest form in maidens won by Tiber Flow at Sandown in July and Junk Bond at Newbury over 2 months later: will improve. *G. Harwood.*

LONG LANE LADY 4 ch.f. Longleat (USA) 109–Teresa Way 66 (Great White 42 Way (USA)) [1989 NR 1990 6m a7g³ a7g⁵ 6d a7g] lengthy, good-quartered filly: fifth reported foal: half-sister to quite useful sprinter Master Cawston and 7f winner Brizlincote (both by Cawston's Clown): dam placed over 5f at 2 yrs: poor form in maiden (ran very wide home turn) and claimer at Southwell second and third outings: gambled on, withdrawn lame from Nottingham handicap in September: has got on toes. *J. Mackie.*

LONG LEAVE 2 b.c. (Feb 3) Night Shift (USA)–Stuff And Nonsense 86 — (Crooner 119) [1990 7g a6g a8g] strong, round-barrelled colt: seventh foal: half-brother to 3-y-o Clock Golf (by Mummy's Game), smart 7f and 1m performer Folly Foot (by Hotfoot), 1m and 9f winner Sillitoe (by Tachypous) and a winner in Belgium: dam 1¼m winner: poor form in minor event and maidens. *R. F. Johnson Houghton.*

LONGLYN 3 b.f. Longleat (USA) 109–Quenlyn (Welsh Pageant 132) [1989 5m 5m — 1990 8m 7m 5f] small filly: no form, including in sellers: blinkered final start: sold 700 gns Ascot May Sales. *W. Carter.*

LONGSHOREMAN 3 gr.g. Longleat (USA) 109–Cabotage 54 (Sea Hawk II 131) 74 [1989 6m 7m³ 8.5f² 7g 7d 1990 a11g² a12g² 13.3m 11.7m* 14m⁵ 12d³ a12g³] sturdy gelding: modest performer: made all in maiden at Bath in July: stays 1½m (got poor run over 13f): acts on good to firm and dead going: blinkered final start at 2 yrs: lacks turn of foot, and is suited by forcing tactics: sold 23,000 gns Newmarket Autumn Sales: winning hurdler for N. Tinkler. *R. F. Johnson Houghton.*

LONGWOOD LEGEND 2 b.c. (Apr 23) Legend of France (USA) 124–Phlox 40 101 (Floriana 106) [1990 a6g 8m a8g a6g a6g] 4,200F, 4,500Y: leggy, rather sparely-made colt: poor mover: eighth foal: half-brother to 3 winners, including Indian Flower (by Mansingh), fairly useful 5f winner here and later successful at up to 7f in USA, and a winner in Italy by Dragonara Palace: dam won 4 times over 5f: soundly beaten in varied races, including a seller. *Pat Mitchell.*

LOOKINGFORARAINBOW (IRE) 2 ch.c. (Mar 8) Godswalk (USA) 57 130–Bridget Folly (Crofter (USA) 124) [1990 5m 5m⁵ 5m² 5g³ 6m⁵ 5g] IR 8,200F, 3,600Y: compact colt: first foal: dam Irish maiden: plating-class maiden: hung left over 1f out final outing, clipping heels of winner and falling: out of depth when tried at 6f. *A. M. Robson.*

LOOK KEW 2 b.f. (May 18) Precocious 126–Klewraye (Lord Gayle (USA) 124) 48 p [1990 6g] 3,400Y: sixth foal: closely related to 3-y-o 6f winner Caffarelli (by Mummy's Pet) and half-sister to 3 winners here and abroad, including 1¼m and 11.7f winner High I Kew (by High Top) and quite useful 1986 2-y-o 6f winner Pas d'Enchere (by Pas de Seul): dam Irish 2-y-o 7f winner: around 10 lengths ninth of 17, never a threat, in maiden at Yarmouth in October: should improve. *C. F. Wall.*

LOOTING (USA) 4 b. or br.g. Pirate's Bounty (USA)–Bank Examiner (USA) 72 (Buckfinder (USA)) [1989 7m 6m 7.6f a8g⁶ a6g* 1990 a6g³ a6g³ a6g² a7g² a6g⁴ a7g* a6g⁶ 7f 7m 6d* 6m* 6m³ 6g 6f 6h] strong, good-bodied gelding: modest handicapper: successful at Lingfield in March and Leicester and Kempton in June: suited by 6f: acts on good to firm and dead going: sweated eleventh outing, and has got on edge. *R. J. O'Sullivan.*

LORD ADVOCATE 2 br.c. (Feb 28) Law Society (USA) 130–Kereolle 48 (Riverman (USA) 131) [1990 5g 5m 6m 8m] 54,000Y: medium-sized colt: moderate mover: seventh foal: half-brother to very useful stayer Arden (by Ardross) and fair 1m winner Knyf (by Kris): dam second over 6f at 2 yrs in France but mainly disappointing, is half-sister to very good broodmare Miss Manon: plating-class maiden: should stay at least 1m: sold 6,800 gns Newmarket Autumn Sales. *R. Charlton.*

LORD BERTIE (USA) 3 b.c. Roberto (USA)–Honorine (USA) (Blushing 86 Groom (FR) 131) [1989 6f 6m⁴ 8.2d² 1990 10m⁵ 8f⁵ 8d 10g³ 9m* 10f*] close-coupled colt: moderate walker: shows plenty of knee action: won handicaps at Sandown in July and Newmarket in August: stays 1¼m: acts on firm and dead going: taken last and very quietly to post third outing: blinkered last 3 starts. *J. Sutcliffe.*

LORD CHARMER (USA) 3 b.c. Seattle Slew (USA)–Embellished (USA) 105 (Seattle Slew (USA)) [1989 NR 1990 8m* 8f⁶ 7m] $550,000Y: strong, round-barrelled colt: has a powerful, round action: third foal: half-brother to Seattle Dawn (by Grey Dawn), a graded-stakes winner at 9f and 1¼m in 1990: dam 6f maiden winner at 3 yrs in USA, is half-sister to numerous winners including champion U.S. 2-y-o filly Althea and smart middle-distance gelding Native Courier: most impressive in winning £6,700 maiden at Newmarket in May: well beaten in Sussex

Sheikh Mohammed's "Lord Florey"

Stakes (held up, never able to challenge) at Goodwood and disappointing favourite for listed race (still carrying condition) at York in August: will prove suited by further than 7f. *J. Gosden.*

LORD DANUM 2 b.c. (Feb 22) Miramar Reef 100§–Pink Ebony (Indianira **31** (USA)) [1990 6g⁵ 6g 6f 7d a8g] 3,100Y: sparely-made colt: first foal: dam never ran: little worthwhile form, including in seller: should be suited by further than 7f: acts on dead ground: sold 920 gns Doncaster November Sales. *Ronald Thompson.*

LORD DAVID S (USA) 4 b.c. Nijinsky (CAN) 138–Mirthful Flirt (USA) 107 **92** (Raise A Native) [1989 8g 8m² 10m* 10m* 10.2g⁶ 1990 10m² 11m 10m³ 10m⁵ 10.6g⁶ 12m] big, strong, rangy colt: carries condition: has a rather round action: fairly useful handicapper: best efforts at 4 yrs when placed behind Eradicate at Newmarket and Jehol at Ripon: sweating and easy to back fourth outing, ran moderately next time: suited by 1¼m: acts well on good to firm going. *B. W. Hills.*

LORD FLOREY (USA) 3 b.c. Blushing Groom (FR) 131–Remedia (USA) (Dr **119** **?** Fager) [1989 7m³ 7g² 1990 7g* 8m* 8m³ 7.6f³ 8m³ 10m⁵] strong, good sort: smart performer: impressive in winning maiden at Newmarket in April and listed race at Kempton in May: clearly best effort, giving strong impression would have won ridden closer to the pace, when 1½ lengths third to Shavian in St James's Palace Stakes at Royal Ascot: not entirely discredited in Group 2 contest at Goodwood penultimate start, best effort after: suited by 1m: possibly unsuited by very firm ground: to race in USA. *L. M. Cumani.*

LORD FUTURE (IRE) 2 ch.g. (Apr 2) The Noble Player (USA) 126–Little **46** Spinner 57 (Tachypous 128) [1990 a8g⁶ a7g] IR 6,800F, 5,600Y: leggy gelding: second foal: dam 1¼m winner: slowly away then staying on in maidens at Southwell: will be better suited by 1¼m+. *G. A. Pritchard-Gordon.*

LORD IT OVER (USA) 7 b.g. Best Turn (USA)–Idle Hour Princess (USA) **—** (Ribot 142) [1989 10s 12h⁵ 13.8m⁴ 1990 a8g a12g] compact, attractive gelding: no longer of much account: blinkered once, visored last 2 outings in 1989: sold 900 gns Doncaster January Sales before reappearance: resold 700 gns Doncaster September Sales. *M. C. Chapman.*

Duke of Devonshire's "Lord of The Field"

LORD LAMMAS 5 gr.g. Tap On Wood 130–Seriema 72 (Petingo 135) [1989 NR 1990 15.3m] compact, well-made gelding: plating-class maiden at 3 yrs: tailed off when pulled up lame only subsequent outing on flat: probably stays 1½m: blinkered twice in 1988: difficult ride. *A. W. Jones.* —

LORD MAGESTER (FR) 3 ch.c. Magesterial (USA) 116–Lady Zia (FR) (Sir Tor (FR)) [1989 7m 7g5 1990 7g 7f4 7m 6s 6f3 5.3f2 6m5] lengthy, good-quartered colt: may prove best at 6f, though bred to stay at least 1m: acts on firm going, seems unsuited by soft: sold 9,400 gns Newmarket Autumn Sales. *L. Cumani.* 64

LORD OBERON (IRE) 2 b.g. (May 10) Fairy King (USA)–Vaguely Jade (Corvaro (USA) 122) [1990 7f4 6m4 8d4 7m] 11,000F, 16,000Y: angular, lengthy gelding: third foal: half-brother to 3-y-o 1m winner Shining Jewel (by Exhibitioner) and modest 1m and 10.2f winner Aardvark (by On Your Mark): dam unraced: modest maiden: best effort over 1m: acts on good to firm and dead going: blinkered final start. *B. Hanbury.* 76

LORD OF THE FIELD 3 b.c. Jalmood (USA) 126–Star Face (African Sky 124) [1989 7g* 1990 8f2 9g* 8f 10d4 11.1g* 12m5] good-topped, attractive colt: has scope: easy mover: won listed Feilden Stakes at Newmarket in April and strongly-run BonusPrint September Stakes (unseated rider to post, came from rear to beat Roseate Tern 2 lengths) at Kempton in September: took keen hold early when running poorly in Hoover Cumberland Lodge Stakes at Ascot final start: swerved away from whip when good fourth in Prix Guillaume d'Ornano at Deauville: should stay 1½m: yet to race on soft going, probably acts on any other: smart. *J. A. R. Toller.* 115

LORD OF TUSMORE 3 b.c. Al Nasr (FR) 126–Princess Toy (Prince Tenderfoot (USA) 126) [1989 6g6 1990 8f* 8.2m2 9m2 10f 9g2 10g* 9m] good-topped, attractive colt with plenty of scope: impresses in appearance: has a quick, rather round action: developed into useful performer, winning maiden at Doncaster in March and £24,400 handicap at Newbury (quickening well to lead inside final 1f) in September: third favourite, raced centre of track when well beaten in Cambridgeshire Handicap at Newmarket final start: stays 1¼m: best efforts on good ground. *B. W. Hills.* 103

LORD RANDOLPH 2 b.c. (Apr 17) Norwick (USA) 120–Inca Girl (Tribal Chief   39
125) [1990 7m 7d a8g] 5,400Y, 2,100 2-y-o: half-brother to 1986 2-y-o 5f and 6f seller
winner Good Time Girl (by Good Times) and a winner in Scandinavia: dam placed
over 5f and 7f in Ireland: poor form in maidens, one an auction, and a claimer. *J. E.
Long.*

LORD'S FINAL 3 ch.c. Royal Match 117–White Cone (Celtic Cone 116) [1989   —
NR 1990 8m] first foal: dam, no sign of ability in novice hurdles and point-to-points,
is out of sister to fairly useful out-and-out stayer Amberwood: 100/1, behind in
competitive minor event at Chepstow in October. *C. R. Barwell.*

LORD WINDERMERE 5 b.g. Taufan (USA) 119–Repercussion 90 (Roan   —
Rocket 128) [1989 10.1m 1990 12f 9g] leggy, lengthy gelding: of little account: dead.
J. M. Bradley.

LOREN'S COURAGE (USA) 5 ch.g. Solford (USA) 127–Roman Luster (USA)   93
(Proudest Roman (USA)) [1989 12m⁵ 12f⁶ 12m* 12g* 12.3g² 14f 12d 1990 14g 14g²
13.3g⁵ 12g² 16.2m³] strong, good-topped gelding: carries plenty of condition: fairly
useful handicapper: ran well last 4 starts, third in £10,600 event won by Nafzawa at
Ascot: stays 2m: best on a sound surface: has won for amateur: goes well with
enterprising tactics: winning novice hurdler in January. *G. Harwood.*

LORETTO (USA) 3 b.c. Danzatore (CAN) 127–Desirable (AUS) (Without Fear   —
(FR) 128) [1989 NR 1990 a12g] 26,000Y: half-brother to 4 winners in Australia,
notably Grade 2 1m Champion Fillies Stakes winner Entrancing (by Bright Finish):
dam won 10 races at up to 7f from 22 starts at 2 yrs to 4 yrs in Australia, and was
outstanding 2-y-o: showed nothing in maiden at Lingfield in December. *R. F.
Johnson Houghton.*

LOSING PATIENCE 2 ch.f. (May 19) Adonijah 126–Ptarmigan 75 (Hill Clown   —
(USA)) [1990 5g 6m 7f⁴] 2,300Y: sparely-made filly: sister to a winner in Austria,
half-sister to moderate 7f and 1m winner Danish Express (by Music Boy) and 1985
2-y-o 5f winner Haverhill Girl (by Cawston's Clown): dam stayed 1½m: soundly
beaten in sellers and a maiden auction: blinkered final start. *M. J. Haynes.*

LOSMANAR 2 b.c. (Apr 1) Los Santos (FR)–Mana (GER) (Windwurf (GER))   61
[1990 6m³ 6m⁴ a7g*] neat colt: first known foal: dam won at 2 yrs in Germany: sire
won 6 races in Germany, seeming best at around 1m: quite modest form in maidens,
making all and winning readily by 4 lengths at Southwell in June: will stay 1m. *J.
Etherington.*

LOST CITY (USA) 2 ch.c. (Feb 8) Golden Act (USA)–Avie's Gold (USA) (Lord   57
Avie (USA)) [1990 7g 7m 7m] $31,000Y: strong colt: first foal: dam unraced: sire
top-class middle-distance performer: never better than mid-division in autumn
maidens: carried condition and green first 2 starts, not knocked about final one: sold
6,000 gns Newmarket Autumn Sales. *R. Hannon.*

LOST EMPIRE 3 b.c. Lomond (USA) 128–Fantasy Land (Nonoalco (USA) 131)   71
[1989 6g 1990 6m³ a8g* 7m] useful-looking colt: moderate mover: favourite, made
most when dead-heating for maiden at Southwell in May: faced very stiff task in
Newmarket handicap over 4 months later: stays 1m: sold 6,400 gns Newmarket
Autumn Sales. *B. W. Hills.*

LOST INNOCENCE (USA) 3 ch.c. Blushing Groom (FR) 131–Olamic (USA)   90
(Nijinsky (CAN) 138) [1989 7g 1990 8g* 8m* 9m⁴ 9g 8m 9m] lengthy, attractive
colt: favourite, successful in maiden (awarded race) at Carlisle in April and handicap
(leading inside final 1f) at Newbury in May: faced stiffish tasks in quite valuable
handicaps and Cambridgeshire Handicap (visored, well beaten) at Newmarket
subsequently: stays 9f: moved poorly down fourth outing. *M. R. Stoute.*

LOTHIAN 3 b.g. Top Ville 129–Cojean (USA) 86 (Prince John) [1989 7g 1990   86
10.1g⁴ 10.1g 11.7h* 11.5m* 12.3g 16f⁶ 17.1m²] leggy, quite attractive gelding: fair
performer: won maiden claimer at Bath in July and handicaps at Lingfield in August
and September: stays well: possibly best on top-of-the-ground. *B. W. Hills.*

LOTS OF LUCK 7 gr.m. Neltino 97–Safe Passage (Charlottown 127) [1989 8s   72
10.8d² 9f6 12m⁶ 8.2f 12g⁴ 8.2g* 8m 9f⁵ 8.2d⁴ 8m⁶ 9.2d² 9g a10g 1990 8m 8m³ 8m⁴
10g* 10m 10.5m 10f² 10f 10g⁶ 10m³ 10g 10.6d* 10.6v 10.4d] smallish, workmanlike
mare: moderate mover: modest handicapper: won at Yarmouth in June and Haydock
(amateurs) in September: effective at 1m and stays 11f: acts on any going: tried in
blinkers at 5 yrs: none too consistent: winning hurdler in December. *J. Pearce.*

LOTTIE ROSE 3 b.f. Blakeney 126–Voir Tout En Beau (USA) (Cloudy Dawn   —
(USA)) [1989 NR 1990 10m⁶ 14f 12.2d 9s] 820F: fifth foal: half-sister to a winner in
Italy and a winning hurdler: dam unraced half-sister to outstanding broodmare
Peace: no form in maidens, claimer and handicap. *Miss S. E. Hall.*

LOTUS POOL (USA) 3 b. or br.c. Spectacular Bid (USA)–Golden Petal (USA) **114** (Mr Prospector (USA)) [1989 NR 1990 7g* 8g* 8m³ 8g² 10f² 12g⁴ 8g²] tall, leggy colt: second foal: half-brother to U.S. winner Golden Gorse (by His Majesty): dam maiden out of half-sister to very smart 1m to 1¼m filly Reine Mathilde: favourite, won maiden at the Curragh in March and listed Harp Lager EBF 2000 Guineas Trial at Phoenix Park in April: beaten length or under in Airlie/Coolmore Irish 2000 Guineas at the Curragh, Kilfrush Concorde Stakes at Phoenix Park and Windfields Farm Gallinule Stakes at the Curragh next 3 starts: stays 1¼m: acts on firm going: below form in blinkers final start: very useful. *D. K. Weld, Ireland.*

LOUDEST WHISPER 2 b.c. (May 9) Reach 122–Dancela 74 (Ela-Mana-Mou **61** p 132) [1990 6g a8g³] close-coupled, angular colt: second foal: dam disappointing half-sister to useful Irish middle-distance winner Sir Simon and granddaughter of Aladancer: ridden by 7-lb claimer, over 5 lengths third to Access Flyer in maiden at Lingfield, easily better effort: slowly away on debut: may improve again. *C. E. Brittain.*

LOUIS CYPHRE 4 b.c. Niniski (USA) 125–Princesse Timide (USA) (Blushing **117** Groom (FR) 131) [1989 12m³ 12g⁵ 11g* 10m 10d⁴ 12m² 10g² 1990 12d⁶ 9.2g⁴ 12d* 9.5f] medium-sized, attractive colt: smart performer: won minor event at Evry in July by neck: easily best other effort at 4 yrs when around 1½ lengths fourth to Creator in Prix d'Ispahan at Longchamp: behind in Grade 2 event in USA, also in July: stays 1½m: acts on good to firm and soft going. *F. Boutin, France.*

LOUKARA GOLD 3 b.g. Taufan (USA) 119–Blue Parrot (FR) (Lyphard (USA) **62** 132) [1989 NR 1990 10f 7m 10m 7g 15.5f² 16m⁴ 13.8d] IR 9,400Y: neat gelding: sixth foal: half-brother to useful 1983 2-y-o 6f winner Catching and a winner in Belgium (both by Thatching): dam minor 11f winner at 4 yrs in France: quite modest form in handicaps last 3 starts: may prove ideally suited by around 1¾m. *R. Akehurst.*

LOUVE BLEUE (USA) 3 b.f. Irish River (FR) 131–Lupe 123 (Primera 131) **113** [1989 10s⁵ 10g² 10.5g⁵ 10g⁶ 10s⁶] seventh reported foal: sister to French 10.5f and 1½m winner Lascaux and half-sister to several winners, including 1m and 9f winner Legend of France (by Lyphard) and French 1m and 9.2f winner Louveterie

D. Wildenstein's "Louve Bleue"

(by Nureyev), both very smart: dam won Oaks and Coronation Cup: won newcomers event at Longchamp in April: second in Prix Saint-Alary and listed race (caused interference and demoted to fifth) at Longchamp: below form after in Group 3 race at Deauville and E P Taylor Stakes at Woodbine, Canada: should stay 1½m. *A. Fabre, France.*

LOVEALOCH (IRE) 2 b.f. (May 4) Lomond (USA) 128–Civility 108 (Shirley Heights 130) [1990 6m 7m*] 52,000Y: rather leggy, good-topped filly: third living foal: half-sister to 9f winner Paper Craft (by Formidable) and to a winner in Italy: dam first past post twice at around 1½m but suited by 1¾m, is half-sister to smart 1976 2-y-o 5f performer Piney Ridge and very useful 1¼m winner Hill's Yankee: won maiden at Redcar in September by ½ length from Lucky Noire: will be better suited by 1m: likely to improve again. *M. Bell.* **73 p**

LOVE AND LEGEND (USA) 2 ch.f. (Mar 18) Lyphard's Wish (FR) 124–Lore 'n Legend (USA) (Bold Forbes (USA)) [1990 8g4] $85,000Y: third foal: half-sister to a graded stakes-placed winner by Danzig: dam minor winner at around 6f: weak 10/1-shot, shaped promisingly when 3½ lengths fourth of 16 to Clare Heights in maiden at Yarmouth in October, slowly away then keeping on well under considerate ride: certain to do better. *H. R. A. Cecil.* **84 p**

LOVE FORTY 3 b.f. Superlative 118–Spin Dry (High Top 131) [1989 NR 1990 11s] 23,000Y: fifth foal: half-sister to 3 winners, including quite modest 1½m winner In A Spin (by Windjammer): dam showed little worthwhile form in France: 20/1 and on toes, always behind in claimer at Hamilton in September: sold 1,600 gns Newmarket Autumn Sales. *D. T. Thom.* **—**

LOVE LEGEND 5 ch.h. Glint of Gold 128–Sweet Emma 108 (Welsh Saint 126) [1989 5m* 5f3 6m2 6f 5g 5.6g 5g 6d3 1990 a5g* a6g4 a6g* 5g* 5m 5m2 5g 5m 5m* 6m 5m 6m 5g* 5.6g* 5m] smallish, sparely-made horse: poor walker: has a quick action: quite useful handicapper: much improved as 5-y-o, winning at Lingfield (twice), Kempton, York (£9,200 contest), Chester and Doncaster: battled on gamely to lead close home and beat Katies First a neck in £20,500 Tote-Portland Handicap at last-named: effective at 5f to 6f: acts well on sound surface: effective with blinkers or without: sometimes bandaged behind: has won for apprentice: genuine. *D. W. P. Arbuthnot.* **95**

LOVELY FLOWER 4 ch.f. Hello Gorgeous (USA) 128–Apricot Rose (Mill Reef (USA) 141) [1989 7g3 7.6m 7m 1990 10.8m 8g3 8m 10.6s] lengthy, angular filly: quite modest maiden: broke leg and destroyed at Haydock in June: should have stayed 1¼m: possibly best with give in the ground. *W. Jarvis.* **57**

LOVELY LAGOON 4 b.f. Mill Reef (USA) 141–Tweedling (USA) (Sir Ivor 135) [1989 NR 1990 11s*] twice-raced filly: won maiden at Hamilton in April: will stay at least 1½m. *C. E. Brittain.* **68**

LOVELY MONEY 2 br.c. (May 7) Primo Dominie 121–Linda's Design (Persian Bold 123) [1990 5g 6m 6m 6s] 7,000F, 15,500Y: compact colt: third foal: half-brother to plating-class maiden Madonijah (by Adonijah): dam soundly-beaten daughter of half-sister to very smart animals Prominent and Dominion: plating-class maiden: **54**

Tote-Portland Handicap, Doncaster—
Love Legend (far side) and Katies First battle it out ahead of Joe Sugden

possibly unsuited by soft ground: sold 3,300 gns Newmarket Autumn Sales. *P. T. Walwyn.*

LOVELY WONGA   4 b.g. Tanfirion 110–Teala (Troy 137) [1989 7s 7f 7m 10.1m — 12m6 12g 1990 8.3g] plain gelding: plater: little show on flat since 2 yrs: probably stays 1½m: best form on top-of-the-ground: blinkered 3 times. *D. A. Wilson.*

LOVE OF THE ARTS (IRE)   2 b.f. (Mar 15) Tate Gallery (USA) 117–Royal   80 Daughter (High Top 131) [1990 5m 6m* 6s2 6m4] 16,000F: workmanlike filly: keen walker: has a round action: third foal: dam placed over 1½m, is half-sister to Goodwood Cup winner Tug of War: fair performer: won maiden at Yarmouth in June: 2½ lengths second of 5 to Dominion Gold in £9,200 event at Haydock following month: gave impression something possibly amiss in 4-runner Princess Margaret Stakes at Ascot: will stay 7f: best form on soft ground. *M. H. Tompkins.*

LOVE PRINCE   4 b.g. Indian King (USA) 128–Chanrossa (High Top 131) [1989   56 6v 6g6 5f* 6f 5f6 5g 5d 1990 5m 6m 8f 7f5 8f6 8m 7m 7f2] leggy, quite good-topped gelding: plating-class handicapper on his day: stays 7f: acts on firm going: blinkered once at 3 yrs: often starts slowly: inconsistent. *W. Carter.*

LOVE RETURNED   3 b.f. Taufan (USA) 119–Miss Loving 89 (Northfields   94 (USA)) [1989 5f2 5m2 5m6 6g2 1990 5s* 5v5 5m2 5.8h6 6g2 5g* 5g 6g3 5.6g 5m4 5d] lengthy, unfurnished filly: moderate mover: fairly useful performer: won maiden auction race at Hamilton in April and handicap at Lingfield in June: good fourth to Blyton Lad in listed race at Newmarket penultimate start: likely to prove best over sharp 5f: acts on any going, with possible exception of heavy: has sometimes found little off bridle: consistent. *W. Jarvis.*

LOVER'S MOON   3 b.c. Ela-Mana-Mou 132–Ce Soir (Northern Baby (CAN)   99 127) [1989 7m5 8g* 1990 12g3 16m4 16.2f6 17.6f*] strong, lengthy colt: fairly useful performer: blinkered, won handicap at Wolverhampton in September: suited by thorough test of stamina: acts on firm going: sold 7,000 gns Newmarket Autumn Sales. *G. Harwood.*

LOVERS' PARLOUR   4 b.f. Beldale Flutter (USA) 130–Ready And Willing 82 — (Reliance II 137) [1989 7g4 1990 10f4 8g] lengthy, quite good-topped filly: 6/4 favourite, 4½ lengths fourth of 15 in maiden at Newmarket early as 3-y-o: beaten 10 lengths or more in minor event at Pontefract (moved down poorly) and maiden at Ripon (pulled hard) in spring: should be suited by at least 1m. *G. Wragg.*

LOVE STREET   3 b.f. Mummy's Pet 125–Crime of Passion 115 (Dragonara   59 Palace (USA) 115) [1989 5f4 5m 5m4 5m5 1990 6f2 6h3 5m 6f3 5.3f6] leggy, sparely-made filly: quite modest maiden: below form last 3 starts: unlikely to stay much beyond 6f: acts on hard ground: has run well for 7-lb claimer: blinkered penultimate start. *P. F. I. Cole.*

LOVE TALK   2 br.f. (Mar 29) Hotfoot 126–Sirnelta (FR) (Sir Tor) [1990 8s6]   69 p 4,100F, 58,000Y: lengthy, sparely-made filly: sister to useful 1m and 1¼m winner Fire Top and half-sister to smart 3-y-o sprinter Dead Certain (by Absalom) and several other winners: dam won from 1m to 1¼m in France: around 8 lengths sixth of 14, green at halfway then staying on well, to Another Bob in minor event at Newbury in October: will stay 1¼m: likely to improve, and win a race. *D. R. C. Elsworth.*

LOVEYA LYNSEY   3 b.f. Relkino 131–Guiletta 63 (Runnymede 123) [1989 NR — 1990 10g 10g 10g 12d] 2,200Y: lengthy, angular filly: moderate walker and mover: half-sister to several winners, including fairly useful 1988 2-y-o 5f and 6f winner Paddy Chalk (by Tina's Pet) and middle-distance stayer Fiorenzo (by Filiberto): dam ran 3 times: no form in sellers, showing signs of ability on second start. *Miss L. C. Siddall.*

LOW DALBY   4 ch.f. Longleat (USA) 109–Bridestones 92 (Jan Ekels 122) [1989   60 8d3 8f5 11m5 11.7m3 11.5m 10.6d5 10v4 12s3 1990 10f* 12f2 10f 10g3 10m] strong filly: quite modest handicapper: won uncompetitive event at Leicester in March: effective at 1¼m and 1½m: best efforts on sound surface: good mount for apprentice. *J. A. R. Toller.*

LOXLEY RANGE (IRE)   2 ch.c. (Apr 7) Hatim (USA) 121–Chantal 74 (Charlot- — tesville 135) [1990 5g 7m] 7,000Y: leggy colt: half-brother to Derby third Scintillating Air (by Sparkler), winning stayer Chance of Stardom (by Star Appeal) and a winner in Belgium: dam placed at 1¼m: well beaten in maidens at Nottingham (slowly away) and Doncaster (seemed very headstrong in auction event) in June. *O. Brennan.*

LOYALTY (IRE)   2 b.c. (Apr 19) Stalker 121–Opening Flight (Falcon 131) [1990 — 7g 8.2g] IR 5,000Y, resold 2,500Y: neat colt: fifth live foal: half-brother to 2 winners, notably fairly useful 1983 Irish 2-y-o 5f winner Deasy's Delight (by Tanfirion): dam Irish 9f winner: well beaten in sellers at Thirsk and Nottingham: subsequently sold 720 gns Doncaster October Sales. *N. Tinkler.*

LUAGA 4 b.f. Tyrnavos 129–Lady Rushen (Dancer's Image (USA)) [1989 8m 6m **41** 7m 9g 8f³ 10.8m⁵ 1990 10f² 11.7f 8g⁵ 10f³ 10g⁶ 12m³ 10g⁴ 14m 12g 10g] tall, leggy filly: moderate walker and mover: poor maiden: stays 1½m: acts on firm going: has often sweated and got on edge. *M. Blanshard.*

LUCAYA 2 br.c. (Feb 20) Gabitat 119–Queen's Bidder 84 (Auction Ring (USA)) — 123) [1990 5m 6m 6g 5m] lengthy colt: has a long stride: fifth live foal: dam 2-y-o 5f winner: poor maiden: visored, sweating and edgy final start. *B. Gubby.*

LUCEDEO 6 ro.g. Godswalk (USA) 130–Lucy Limelight 98 (Hot Spark 126) [1989 **97** 6m⁶ 5f⁴ 5m⁴ 5f⁴ 6f² 5m² 5m⁶ 5h⁶ 5g* 5m² 5m² 5f⁵ 5m⁵ 5m⁶ 5f 5f³ 5m⁶ 6f* 6m³ 5g* 6g 1990 5m⁴ 5f* 5m* 5m* 6f* 6f⁴ 5m³ 5g* 5g³ 5m³ 6d⁶ 6m⁵ 5m³ 5m 5m* 5m 5d 5.6g 5m⁶ 5m 5g⁶ 5m] sturdy, compact gelding: carries condition: vastly improved handicapper, winning at Thirsk, Catterick (apprentices), Beverley and Ripon within 8 days in April, York (£10,800 event) in May and Newbury (dead-heating with Our Freddie) in July: ideally suited by stiff 5f: best on a sound surface: went down freely in blinkers final outing: often slowly into stride and best held up: excellent mount for inexperienced rider: splendidly tough and consistent: a credit to his trainer. *J. L. Spearing.*

LUCKNAM DREAMER 2 b.g. (Apr 10) Macmillion 110–River Damsel (Forlorn **79** ? River 124) [1990 6m³ 6m 6m² 6m²] big, rangy gelding: has plenty of scope: half-brother to middle-distance winner Joja Roly (by Souvran) and out-and-out staying hurdler Rivertino (by Ivotino): dam won in Holland: modest maiden: will be better suited by 7f: usually on toes. *Mrs Barbara Waring.*

LUCKNAM STYLE 2 b.g. (Mar 17) Macmillion 110–Mrs Currie 74 (He Loves **78** Me 120) [1990 6g⁶ 7m* 6g³] 1,400Y: leggy, sparely-made gelding: second reported living foal: half-brother to a winner in Belgium: dam ran only at 2 yrs, winning at 1m: made all in maiden auction at Leicester in September: better at 7f than 6f: wears a tongue strap: tends to get on toes. *Mrs Barbara Waring.*

LUCK O' THE IRISH 3 ch.g. Sallust 134–Sweet Hostess (Candy Cane 125) **46** [1989 7g 8.2d 8g 1990 11v⁶ 8.2g³ 8g⁴ 12.2m⁶ 9g⁴ a8g 8g] leggy, workmanlike gelding: poor maiden: stays 9f: hung left on reappearance, wore severe noseband fourth outing: blinkered fifth and final starts: sold to join G. Gracey 500 gns Ascot October Sales. *N. Tinkler.*

LUCK'S CHANGED 2 ch.f. (May 8) Sweet Monday 122–Dutch Girl 78 **34** § (Workboy 123) [1990 5f⁵ 5f⁶ 5d 5g 6m⁴ 6m⁶ 6m 5f] small, lengthy, unfurnished filly: has round action: fifth foal: half-sister to modest 5f and 6f winner Golden Flats (by Sonnen Gold): dam, daughter of smart sprinter Dutch Gold, won 5 times over 5f: poor plater: persistently hung right fifth outing: blinkered final one: twice unruly at stalls: one to treat with caution. *M. W. Easterby.*

LUCKY AGAIN 3 br.c. Ile de Bourbon (USA) 133–Soft Pedal 92 (Hotfoot 126) **80** [1989 NR 1990 8m⁴ 7m 10. 1m³] stocky colt: sixth foal: half-brother to very useful 7f to 10.2f winner Lucky Scott (by Crimson Beau), subsequently stakes placed in USA, and modest 1986 2-y-o 5f winner Joyful Gemma (by Dunphy): dam won 5 times at around 6f: fair maiden: best effort third of 14, hanging left, in minor event at Windsor in July: stays 1¼m: sold 11,000 gns Newmarket Autumn Sales. *P. F. I. Cole.*

Homeowners Sprint (Handicap), York—
the admirable grey Lucedeo and apprentice Gavin Husband
gain the fifth of their six wins together, beating Almost Blue a neck

LUCKY ASSET 2 b.f. (Apr 14) Nomination 125–Wild Asset (Welsh Pageant 132) 40 [1990 6d a8g a7g⁵] 7,400F, 10,500Y: half-sister to 3-y-o Frivolous (by Bairn), smart 7f and 1m winner Attempt (by Try My Best) and Irish middle-distance winner Gentle Stream (by Sandy Creek): dam poor maiden: poor form in maidens and claimers. *G. A. Pritchard-Gordon.*

LUCKY BARNES 3 b.g. Lucky Wednesday 124–Hutton Barns 92 (Saintly Song 58 128) [1989 5f* 6m² 6g 6g⁶ 6g⁴ 6g⁴ 5m² a6g 1990 8.2g 8m² 7g⁵ 7g² 8f* 12f³ 8.2g²] workmanlike gelding: moderate mover: useful plater: looked awkward ride when winning 5-runner event (no bid) at Thirsk in July, leading inside final 1f: stays 1m: acts on firm ground: effective with or without blinkers: trained until after sixth start by W. Pearce. *P. A. Blockley.*

LUCKY BLUE 3 b.g. Blue Cashmere 129–Cooling 89 (Tycoon II) [1989 5f 5m² 69 1990 6m 6g* 6f* 6m* 6g⁵ 6m³ 6m⁶ 6f² 6m 5m⁵ 6m] workmanlike gelding: quite modest performer: inconsistent after winning apprentice claimer (claimed out of M. H. Easterby's stable £6,500) at Nottingham and handicaps at Thirsk and Lingfield in June: better at 6f than 5f: acts on firm going: ran poorly when visored final start and blinkered ninth: drifted right but ran creditably for 7-lb claimer. *R. W. Stubbs.*

LUCKY BOTHA 2 b.c. (May 8) Germont–Lucky Rub (Rubor 88) [1990 5m⁴ 5g⁴ 41 6g] workmanlike colt. turns fore feet out: third foal: dam lightly raced over hurdles: sire unraced brother to Ancestral: poor form in minor events and a maiden in summer. *C. Parker.*

LUCKY CRYSTAL 4 ch.f. Main Reef 126–Please Oblige (Le Levanstell 122) — [1989 6d³ 7f 8f 8f⁴ 1990 7.6m 9m] lengthy filly: fair winner at her best at 2 yrs: wearing crossed noseband, ran poorly in 1990: best efforts over 6f: acts on good to firm and dead going: sold 940 gns Ascot December Sales. *C. A. Horgan.*

LUCKY FROSTY (USA) 3 br.g. What Luck (USA)–Frosty Stare (Targowice 45 (USA) 130) [1989 5f² 6m⁵ 6m⁴ 6m⁵ 5m³ 5f 6m 1990 a8g⁵ 6f⁶ 6m 8m⁵ 10f 6m 5f 7.5g⁴] compact, rather angular gelding: has a quick, moderate action: quite modest maiden at 2 yrs: below form in 1990, in seller final start: stays 6f: retained by trainer 11,000 gns Ascot February Sales: sold 4,200 gns Newmarket Autumn Sales: one to treat with caution. *P. A. Kelleway.*

LUCKY GUEST 3 bl.c. Be My Guest (USA) 126–Gay Fantasy (Troy 137) [1989 108 NR 1990 10g² 12m² 10g* 12d³ 10f 10d* 9g* 9g²] rather leggy, attractive colt: has quick action: third foal: half-brother to fair 7f and 9f winner Trust Troy (by Gorytus) and 1987 2-y-o 8.2f seller winner Promise Kept (by Castle Keep): dam unraced half-sister to very useful middle-distance filly Miss Petard: won maiden at Epsom in June, listed race at Baden-Baden in August and £6,400 handicap at York in October: very good second in £19,600 handicap at Newmarket: seems best on an easy surface at distances short of 1½m: edged badly left second start: looked really well last 3 outings: progressive. *J. L. Dunlop.*

LUCKY MANLEY 2 b.c. (Apr 8) Ballacashtal (CAN)–Herminda 80 (King of 61 Spain 121) [1990 5g⁴ 6g² 5.8h* 5g⁴ 6f⁴ 5m⁵ 6m] leggy colt: moderate mover: first foal: dam disappointing maiden, form only at 5f at 2 yrs: plating-class performer: won maiden auction event at Bath in May: gives impression will prove as effective at 5f as 6f: sold 2,700 gns Doncaster October Sales. *J. Berry.*

LUCKY MOON 3 b.c. Touching Wood (USA) 127–Castle Moon 79 (Kalamoun 104 129) [1989 8.2d 1990 10f⁶ 10.2h⁵ 14g* 12f* 12.3g* 16.1f* 20f* 18g] lengthy, quite

Goodwood Cup—Lucky Moon graduates from handicaps

attractive colt: moderate mover: useful performer: favourite, clear-cut winner of handicaps (made all) at Nottingham, Thirsk and Ripon in space of 9 days in June and Newmarket (£7,700 event) in July then beat Ecran 2½ lengths in Goodwood Cup in August: again favourite, ran moderately in Doncaster Cup final start: stays well: acts on firm going. *J. L. Dunlop.*

LUCKY NATIVE   4 br.c. Be My Native (USA) 122–Change of Luck (Track Spare   51
125) [1989 8.2s⁴ 6f 12g* 1990 10.1g 10.6s⁴ 14m 12.3g² 12m² 16m 14g⁴ 15.3m⁴]
good-topped colt: has a round action: plating-class handicapper: stays 2m: acts on
good to firm and soft going: has pulled hard. *D. Marks.*

LUCKY NOIRE   2 b.f. (Apr 30) Aragon 118–Noire Small (USA) (Elocutionist   72
(USA)) [1990 6g 7m⁶ 7m³ 7m² 8m] strong, compact filly: second foal: half-sister to
3-y-o Badgers Dash (by Jalmood): dam won 3 races in Italy and has run over hurdles
here: modest maiden: hampered several times then eased in nursery final start: may
prove suited by 1m. *G. Harwood.*

LUCKY OAK   4 ch.g. Tap On Wood 130–Zalinndia (FR) (Brigadier Gerard 144)   —
[1989 10f⁵ 8.2m 10h³ 12h⁴ 9m 12g 12g 1990 10f⁴ 8m a10g 11.5m 8f 10m 12f⁴ 10.1m 10f⁴
11.5f⁶ 12f 10g 12m] medium-sized, close-coupled gelding: poor mover: poor maiden:
suited by 1¼m: form only on top-of-the-ground: blinkered fourth outing: winning
selling hurdler. *R. P. C. Hoad.*

LUCKY VERDICT   4 b.g. Touching Wood (USA) 127–Noor 76 (Mill Reef (USA)   88
141) [1989 8d 8.5d 10.8m³ 12.2m⁴ 16g⁵ 16f⁴ 14m³ 16m* 17.6g² 16m* 16g³ 1990 18f*
16g³ 18.4d 20m²] smallish, sturdy gelding: has rather round action: favourite: put up
impressive performance when winning £9,600 handicap at Doncaster in March: in
splendid shape, very good second to Retouch in £14,800 Ascot Stakes (Handicap) at
Royal Ascot, looking sure to win when leading over 2f out: suited by good test of
stamina and top-of-the-ground: best in blinkers: best held up on a galloping track:
very useful hurdler as a juvenile. *M. C. Pipe.*

LUCY DANCER (IRE)   2 ch.f. (Mar 16) No Pass No Sale 120–Daoulas   68
(Thatching 131) [1990 5m⁵ 6m 5m² 5f 5g* 5m] IR 2,000Y: compact filly: moderate
mover: first foal: dam French 9f and 1¼m winner: quite modest performer: won
maiden at Chester in August: should stay 6f: best effort on good ground. *M.
McCormack.*

LUCY JOHNSTON'S (IRE)   2 ch.f. (Apr 23) Burslem 123–Trekking 34   —
(Homing 130) [1990 6s 6m 5f⁵ 7f a8g] IR 1,000Y: leggy filly: third foal: dam, plater,
stayed 1¼m: no worthwhile form in maidens and claimers. *E. J. Alston.*

LUCY MANETTE   3 ch.f. Final Straw 127–Lady Tippins (USA) 83 (Star de   53
Naskra (USA)) [1989 NR 1990 5h⁵ 6m 6m³] neat filly: second foal: half-sister to
ungenuine 4-y-o Access Travel (by Auction Ring), useful 6f winner at 2 yrs: dam 6f
and 7f winner: 33/1, third of 16 in maiden at Lingfield in June, slowly away, plenty to
do at halfway then running on well not knocked about: should stay beyond 6f. *P. W.
Harris.*

*Duke of York Stakes, York—front-running Lugana Beach (blinkers)
holds on by the skin of his teeth from Great Commotion*

Mr Ray Richards' "Lugana Beach"

LUFAH LADY 2 b.f. (May 2) Sulaafah (USA) 119–Remainder Lady (Connaught — 130) [1990 a8g] smallish, sparely-made filly: first foal: dam poor daughter of half-sister to 2000 Guineas and Derby-placed Remainder Man: very green, soon well behind in 17-runner claimer at Southwell in November. *B. Preece.*

LUGANA BEACH 4 br.c. Tumble Wind (USA)–Safe Haven (Blakeney 126) 116 [1989 5m 6f5 5m* 5m* 5g* 5g* 1990 6g* 5m6 5d3 6m 5m6 5g 5g2 5v4 6s3] compact, useful-looking colt: moderate mover: smart sprinter: held off Great Commotion by short head, making all, in Duke of York Stakes in May: best efforts after behind Dayjur in King's Stand Stakes at Royal Ascot, Keeneland Nunthorpe Stakes at York and Ciga Prix de l'Abbaye de Longchamp on third, fifth and seventh outings: effective at 5f and 6f: never showed his best form on extremes of going: wore blinkers: sometimes started slowly: retired to Spa Stud, Worcestershire, fee £1,000 n.f.n.f. *D. R. C. Elsworth.*

LUKE'S BRAVE BOY 2 ch.c. (May 18) Prince Ragusa 96–Golden Baby 52 52 p (Sharpen Up 127) [1990 7m 9g] 1,200F: workmanlike colt: has a fluent, rounded action: second foal: dam plater: staying-on eighth of 19 in claimer at York in October: backward on debut: will stay 1¼m at least: likely to improve. *A. Hide.*

LUKS AKURA 2 b.c. (Mar 11) Dominion 123–Pacificus (USA) 65 (Northern 48 Dancer) [1990 6d4 5s4 a7g5 a7g6] 8,000Y, 25,000 2-y-o: small, sturdy colt: second foal: closely related to leading juvenile hurdler Philosophos (by High Top): dam 13f winner: plating-class maiden: respectable sixth of 14 to Ivan The Terrible in nursery at Southwell late in year: stays 7f. *M. Johnston.*

LUNA BID 7 b.g. Auction Ring (USA) 123–Moonscape 87 (Ribero 126) [1989 6v* 83 6d5 6g 6f5 6m2 6f3 6m 6m3 6m2 6m* 6m5 6m6 6s5 6m* 6g6 6g 6v 6d 1990 6f 6m 6m6 6m6 6s 6m4 6m3 6g 6m2 6m3 6m 6g 7m 6d 6s 6s] good-topped gelding: carries plenty of condition: turns fore-feet in markedly: poor mover: fair handicapper:

below form last 6 outings: best at 6f: acts on any going: usually gets behind: has reportedly broken blood vessels. *M. Blanshard.*

LUNA PROBE   3 b.f. Pas de Seul 133–Dancing Song 87 (Ridan (USA)) [1989 5d⁵ — 5s 5d 5f 6f⁶ 5g 5g² 5m 7m 6f 5g 1990 7m 6g 8m 8m 5d⁵ 6g] sparely-made filly: keen walker: has a round action: plating-class maiden: no worthwhile form in 1990: best form at 5f on easy surface, and for 7-lb claimer: once appeared reluctant to race. *J. H. Johnson.*

LUNAR MAGIC   2 b.g. (Feb 1) Henbit (USA) 130–Lunaria (USA) (Twist The Axe   **42** (USA)) [1990 5m⁶ 6d⁶ a8g a7g a8g] workmanlike gelding: good walker and mover: fourth live foal: half-brother to 5-y-o 1½m winner Super Gunner (by Homing) and quite modest maiden Best Effort (by Try My Best): dam thrice-raced half-sister to smart sprinter Abeer: poor maiden: slowly away first 2 starts: off course over 5 months after debut. *R. Hollinshead.*

LUNAR MOVER (USA)   4 b.c. Sharpen Up 127–Intentional Move (USA) **111** ? (Tentam (USA)) [1989 8s* 7d² 8m⁶ 1990 8f* 8m 8m] useful-looking colt: good mover: fractured cannon bone when sixth in 2000 Guineas at Newmarket in 1989: justified favouritism in listed Doncaster Mile in March on first subsequent outing: 50/1, well beaten in Queen Anne Stakes at Royal Ascot, and wasn't seen out again: will prove best at up to 1m: acts on any going: reportedly pulled muscles in quarters second start: carries head high. *C. R. Nelson.*

LUNCH BOX   5 ch.m. Great Nephew 126–Supper Time 71 (Shantung 132) [1989 **40** 10.2g 10m 12.3m² 11.7g² 10.6d 12g³ 13.6g a14g* 1990 12f⁵ 10.1g³] workmanlike, rather angular mare: moderate mover: quite modest at her best: stays 1¾m: acts on good to firm and heavy going: effective with or without visor: suitable mount for inexperienced rider: has joined N. Graham. *W. Hastings-Bass.*

L'UOMO CLASSICS   3 b.g. Indian King (USA) 128–Sperrin Mist 83 (Camden **82** Town 125) [1989 5m* 5g⁴ 6g 6g³ 6m 1990 7m⁵ 7m* 8d⁵ 8m⁴ 7g 9m² 9m 8m] good-quartered gelding: keen walker: moderate mover: fair handicapper: won at York in June: very good second to Gulmarg at Wolverhampton, easily best effort last 4 starts: stays 9f: acts on good to firm ground and dead: will prove best with strong handling, and worth a try in blinkers or a visor. *Mrs J. Pitman.*

LUPESCU   2 ch.f. (Apr 28) Dixieland Band (USA)–Keep Me Posted (USA) (Stage **92** p Door Johnny) [1990 7m² 7m² 7.3s⁴] 29,000Y: lengthy, good-topped filly: has plenty of scope: good walker: half-sister to 2 winners in USA: dam never ran: looked green when beaten short head by Sumonda in maiden at Leicester: co-favourite, and 4 lengths fourth of 6, beaten when checked inside final furlong, to Shaima in listed event at Newbury later in October: will stay 1½m: sure to do better, and win races. *H. R. A. Cecil.*

LUREX GIRL   6 ch.m. Camden Town 125–Klairelle (Klairon 131) [1989 NR 1990 — 17.1f] sturdy mare: poor handicapper: tailed-off last of 8 at Bath in May: suited by 2m and plenty of give in the ground. *D. R. Tucker.*

LURKING   3 b.f. Formidable (USA) 125–Hiding 84 (So Blessed 130) [1989 6m 5f⁴ **58** 7g² 6v a7g³ 1990 a7g² a6g² a7g² a6g* 7d 7m⁵ 7g 6g 7d³ 7g a8g⁶] workmanlike filly: moderate mover: quite modest performer: won apprentice maiden at Southwell in March, leading close home: stays 7f well: acts on dead (seems unsuited by heavy) ground: visored fourth and final starts: wore crossed noseband fifth to eighth, sweating on first of them. *W. Hastings-Bass.*

LUST OF LOVE   4 b.f. Sallust 134–Aridje 79 (Mummy's Pet 125) [1989 6s 5g⁵ **63** 7m² 7m* 6g 6m⁵ 5m 1990 7f 7f² 7m⁵ 7m² 7g 7f⁵ 6m 7m] leggy, rather sparely-made filly: poor walker and mover: quite modest handicapper on her day: stays 7f: acts well on top-of-the-ground: blinkered (ran moderately) final outing: carried head awkwardly under pressure second start: inconsistent. *Miss L. C. Siddall.*

LUSTREMAN   3 ch.g. Sallust 134–Miss Speak Easy (USA) (Sea Bird II 145) **55** [1989 7m 8v 8g 1990 10.1g 10m 10g 10f² 11m* 10f⁶ 12h⁴] workmanlike, close-coupled gelding: plating-class handicapper: sweating, led post at Ayr in July: should stay 1½m: acts on firm going: trained until after second start by B. Stevens. *M. R. Channon.*

LUSTY LAD   5 b.g. Decoy Boy 129–Gluhwein (Ballymoss 136) [1989 7f 6f⁴ 6m 9m — 8h⁵ 1990 a7g a10g] rather sparely-made gelding: modest handicapper as 3-y-o: lightly raced since and long way below his best: stays 7f: acts on firm going: hooded once at 4 yrs: winning hurdler early in 1989/90 (reportedly broke blood vessel next time). *M. J. Haynes.*

LUSTY RON   3 ch.g. Sallust 134–Roya (Roan Rocket 128) [1989 NR 1990 12.2d] — IR 3,500Y: workmanlike gelding: seventh reported foal: half-brother to 1987 2-y-o

8.2f winner Donroya (by Don) and Irish 12.4f winner Rodagglo (by Pitskelly). dam, granddaughter of champion 2-y-o filly Opaline II, won over 5f in France on debut: 33/1 and visored, well tailed off in claimer at Catterick in July. *C. Tinkler.*

LUTHIOR (FR) 4 gr.c. Carwhite 127–Luthiana (FR) (Luthier 126) [1989 10m³ 86 11d³ 12.5d 12m* 12.5g⁵ 10.5d⁶ 1990 12m⁴ 12f⁵ 8h³] leggy ex-French colt: moderate walker: has a rather round action: first reported foal: dam 1¼m winner in France: won maiden at Saint-Cloud as 3-y-o: 20/1 and apprentice ridden, staying-on 5½ lengths third of 8 in minor event at Brighton in August: stays 1½m. *R. Simpson.*

LUZUM 6 ch.h. Touching Wood (USA) 127–Velvet Habit 89 (Habitat 134) [1989 103 8m* 1990 8.5g 7g⁴ 7m 7.3g³ 7m³ 7.6v] small, sturdy horse: moderate performer: easily best efforts as 6-y-o when in frame in Group 3 contest at Newmarket, handicap at Newbury and minor event won by Rami at Warwick: suited by 7f to 1m: acts on any going except seemingly heavy: wears blinkers: bit coltish on reappearance: sold to join J. Glover 9,200 gns Newmarket December Sales. *H. Thomson Jones.*

LYCIUS (USA) 2 ch.c. (Feb 29) Mr Prospector (USA)–Lypatia (FR) (Lyp- 116 p hard (USA) 132) [1990 6d⁴ 7d⁴ 7g² 6m*]

The Middle Park Stakes, sponsored for the first time by Newgate Stud in 1990, has been won twice by a subsequent Two Thousand Guineas winner in the last twenty years: in 1970, by Brigadier Gerard, and in 1979 by Known Fact, who was awarded the Guineas on the disqualification of Nureyev. Lycius, its latest winner, hasn't the level of form that Brigadier Gerard or Known Fact showed at two, nor is it certain that he'll return to Britain rather than stay in France for the Poule d'Essai des Poulains, but if he does line up at Newmarket he'll possess better credentials for the classic than most recent Middle Park winners and shouldn't be taken lightly. Considering that Lycius was reverting to six furlongs in the Middle Park having shown his best form over seven, and was encountering top-of-the-ground for the first time; and that he has plenty of scope, and is sure to be suited by the step up to a mile as a three-year-old, he's certainly not the long shot that the betting suggests. While he may not be a top-class colt on form he wasn't far short of the best of his contemporaries at two, and he'll make a good-class miler in the coming season we're sure.

The tall, good-topped, angular Lycius was brought over for the Middle Park in October, for which he was supplemented at a cost of £10,000, fresh from a second place in the seven-furlong Prix de la Salamandre at Longchamp;

Newgate Stud Middle Park Stakes, Newmarket—French raider Lycius (right) is a narrow but convincing winner from Distinctly North

in a race truly run by French standards, he had gone down by a length to Hector Protector after coming from fifth place of seven entering the short straight then quickly holding every chance. That defeat was his second in three outings—he'd finished fourth on his debut in the Prix Yacowlef, a traditionally-important race for newcomers at Deauville in August—but his form was improving rapidly, not deteriorating, and he lined up at Newmarket with a first-rate chance of adding to his half-length defeat of the useful River Traffic in a seven-furlong listed event at Deauville and becoming the first French-trained runner to win the Middle Park since Venture VII in 1959. In those days, much more than of late, the Middle Park was a highly prestigious event—between 1944 and 1966, for example, nine of its winners topped the Free Handicap, and Venture VII himself was rated second only to Sing Sing—but the latest running was typical of the modern trend and attracted a relatively undistinguished field, with only the consistent Distinctly North, successful in the Flying Childers Stakes on his previous start, and the unbeaten and highly-regarded Majlood among the eight other runners seeming to provide serious opposition to Lycius. The race, worth over £78,000 to the winner, swiftly took its expected shape as Distinctly North, with a strong wind at his back, set out to make all the running; and passing halfway he led by a couple of lengths with Lycius back in seventh, last of the main bunch. Two furlongs out Lycius still had plenty of ground to make up, but once he met the rising ground he began to run on with great purpose, collared Distinctly North thirty yards out, and went away to win easing up by three quarters of a length with Majlood, who'd got to Distinctly North over a furlong out but was unable to make any further impression a length and a half back in third. It was a very smart performance by Lycius, albeit about a stone

Sheikh Mohammed's "Lycius"

below what would have been required to win the race in its heyday, and one which if it had been repeated in the Three Chimneys Dewhurst Stakes later in the month, for which he had been supplemented shortly before meeting with injury, would have taken him very close to winning. His set-back was said to be a minor one and Lycius apparently remains on course for the classics. His trainer has expressed doubts about his staying a mile, but his rider, Asmussen, who seems set to lose the ride to Cauthen, is reportedly much more positive about his prospects. We believe Lycius will have no trouble with Newmarket's mile, and if he does make the journey he'll go there, as did the eventual second Venture VII in 1960, with fair each-way prospects.

		Raise A Native	Native Dancer
Lycius (USA) (ch.c. Feb 29, 1988)	Mr Prospector (USA) (b 1970)	(ch 1961)	Raise You
		Gold Digger (b 1962)	Nashua
			Sequence
	Lypatia (FR) (b 1975)	Lyphard (b 1969)	Northern Dancer
			Goofed
		Hypatia (ro 1968)	High Hat
			Purple Queen

Lycius' sire Mr Prospector, who'll be twenty-one in 1991, is now well and truly established as the leading stallion in North America. Clear at the top of the leading active sire list, around 6,000,000 dollars ahead of his closest pursuer Nijinsky and nearly three times that ahead of his youngest active rival Seattle Slew, Mr Prospector has over a hundred stakes winners to his name from thirteen crops for earnings of over 40,000,000 dollars, including nearly 4,000,000 dollars in 1990 when his stakes winners besides Lycius included the Grade 1 winners Rhythm and Fantastic Law. Surprisingly perhaps, he's not the most sought-after stallion at the yearling sales—that position, based on yearling averages, has been held for the past three years by Danzig—but, nonetheless, his fifty or so yearlings sold at public auction in the last two years have averaged almost 600,000 dollars. Lycius was bought for 500,000 dollars at the Keeneland July Selected Sale. He's the sixth winner from seven foals from his dam Lypatia, a minor winner at six and a half furlongs in France and a mile in North America, whose previous best progeny was the widely-travelled Abakir (by Riverman), successful from a mile to an extended nine furlongs in France then at up to a mile and a half in North America, where he improved to win twice in graded stakes. Neither Lypatia's dam Hypatia, who raced in Britain for Timeform's founder Phil Bull, nor grandam Purple Queen, a daughter of the very speedy Crimson, won beyond a mile. But Hypatia has produced the Park Hill third Lynwood Sovereign and Lypatia the winning jumper (at up to three miles) Chico Valdez (by Valdez), and on the whole Lycius' pedigree isn't one noticeably lacking in the stamina to stay a mile. He acts on good to firm and dead going. *A. Fabre, France.*

LYDIA MARIA   2 b.f. (Feb 9) Dancing Brave (USA) 140–Connaught Bridge 124   **70 p**
(Connaught 130) [1990 8g⁶ 8g⁶] strong, deep-girthed filly: sixth living foal: half-sister to 3-y-o Class Adorns (by Sadler's Wells) and 4 winners, including 1½m to 1¾m winner Wassl Reef (by Mill Reef): dam high-class middle-distance performer: bit backward, beaten at least 10 lengths in maidens at Wolverhampton and Newmarket in October: will improve at 1¼m: will improve later. *P. W. Harris.*

LYNAM PRINCE (IRE)   2 br.c. (May 7) Fairy King (USA)–Come True (FR)   **— p**
(Nasram II 125) [1990 7m] 52,000Y: brother to 3-y-o 7f winner Cosmic Princess and half-brother to several winners, including useful 1m to 1¼m winner Spanish Prince (by Gay Fandango): dam Irish 1½m winner: held up and never placed to challenge or knocked about in maiden at Yarmouth in September: will do better. *A. C. Stewart.*

LYNCARA   2 b.f. (May 4) Lyphard's Special (USA) 122–Nicara (Rusticaro (FR)   **38**
124) [1990 5m⁴ 5d 7s] 650Y: small, angular, light-framed filly: first foal: dam Irish 2-y-o 6f winner: poor form in minor and maiden events: best effort first start: off course around 7 months after. *C. W. C. Elsey.*

LYNDSEYLEE   3 b.f. Swing Easy (USA) 126–Miss Merlin 79 (Manacle 123)   **96**
[1989 5d* 5m* 5m* 5f 5f* 5f³ 5m² 5m³ 5m 5m² 6g 1990 5d⁶ 5d 5f⁴ 5g* 5g 5m² 5f* 5f² 5m⁶ 5g 5g] workmanlike, good-quartered filly: has a quick action: fairly useful performer: won handicap (dead-heated) at Epsom in June and claimer at Sandown in July: best form at 5f on top-of-the-ground: occasionally sweating and edgy: tends to

be bit slow into stride: sometimes taken down quietly: has won for 7-lb claimer. *J. Berry.*

LYPHAR DANCER 2 b.g. (Apr 27) Bellypha 130–Western Gem 86 (Sheshoon 62
132) [1990 6m 7g6 8m] 110,000Y: attractive gelding: seventh foal: half-brother to 4
winners, including 3-y-o 1m and 8.5f winner Akimbo (by Bold Lad) and 1989 3-y-o
1m winner Steffi (by Precocious): dam, half-sister to very smart performers
Western Jewel and Mr Fluorocarbon, placed over 7f and 1½m: quite modest maiden:
should be better suited by 1m than shorter: sold 10,500 gns Newmarket Autumn
Sales. *G. Harwood.*

LYPHAROS 3 b.g. Lyphard's Special (USA) 122–Cocarde (Red God 128§) [1989 44 §
6g 6d6 6d 1990 8m 10m4 11g6 11m6] leggy, sparely-made gelding: poor maiden:
seems to stay 1¼m: takes good hold: sometimes sweating: has hung badly left (ran
out on debut) and looks ungenuine. *P. Mitchell.*

M

MABTHUL (USA) 2 b.c. (Apr 11) Northern Baby (CAN) 127–Persuadable 72
(USA) (What A Pleasure (USA)) [1990 8g6 8.2s3 10s] $42,000Y: big, rangy colt: has
plenty of scope: keen walker: second reported foal: dam won at up to 9f: third of 13,
keeping on steadily, to Red Rainbow in maiden at Haydock: looking well and
carrying condition, weakened from over 2f out in similar event won by Matahif at
Nottingham later in October: possibly doesn't stay 1¼m. *D. Morley.*

MACCONACHIE 3 b.c. Good Times (ITY)–High Point Lady (CAN) (Knightly 50
Dawn (USA)) [1989 NR 1990 8.2s 8f 8f5 11g6 12d5 12m5 10m3 10f3 10m 11d6 a7g4]
3,000Y: leggy, angular colt: poor maiden: seventh foal (fourth in Britain): half-
brother to fair middle-distance performer Stated Case (by Beldale Flutter) and a
winner in USA: dam won 7f claimer at 2 yrs: plating-class maiden: probably stays
1½m: acts on firm going: will prove useful bound by strong handling: gives strong
impression worth a try in blinkers or a visor. *T. D. Barron.*

MACE-BEARER 6 b.g. Martinmas 128–Annatown 68 (Charlottown 127) [1989 —
NR 1990 a6g] leggy, workmanlike gelding: poor maiden: stays 6f: acts on good to
firm going: visored last 2 outings at 4 yrs: sold 620 gns Doncaster March Sales. *M.
C. Chapman.*

MACEDONAS 2 b.c. (May 12) Niniski (USA) 125–Miss Saint-Cloud 102 67
(Nonoalco (USA) 131) [1990 7g5 7m] 12,500Y: tall, leggy colt: looks weak: second
foal: half-brother to 3-y-o Chez Jarrasse (by Pharly): dam 7f to 1¼m winner:
never-dangerous fifth of 17 to Stark South in minor event at Kempton in September:
favourite, well beaten in maiden auction at Leicester later in month. *Miss A. J.
Whitfield.*

MACFARLANE 2 br.c. (Mar 14) Kala Shikari 125–Tarvie 101 (Swing Easy (USA) 79
126) [1990 5m5 5m2 5f3 6s3 5d*] 38,000Y: stocky, lengthy colt: poor mover: brother
to very speedy 1985 2-y-o Stalker and half-brother to 3 other winners, including
1989 Irish 2-y-o 5f winner Regal Peace (by Known Fact): dam game sprinter:
modest performer: ran on well after troubled run when winning nursery at
Doncaster in November by length from Party Treat: easily best form at 5f: well
suited by some give in the ground. *M. J. Fetherston-Godley.*

MACHIAVELLIAN (USA) 3 b.c. Mr Prospector (USA)–Coup de Folie 123
(USA) 112 (Halo (USA)) [1989 6d* 6g* 7g* 1990 7m* 8f2 8m4 6.5g5]

Machiavellian's second season turned out less successful than the first,
and those who'd thought him a budding champion were to be disappointed,
their disappointment no doubt compounded by his meeting trouble when Tirol
ended his winning run in the General Accident Two Thousand Guineas then
yet again when the same horse beat him in the Airlie/Coolmore Irish Two
Thousand Guineas. Hopes of an autumn come-back were dashed when he
finished last of five behind Dead Certain in the Prix Maurice de Gheest at
Deauville; news of the completion of negotiations for his sale to Sheikh
Mohammed and his retirement to Dalham Hall Stud, on offer at £100,000 per
share, soon followed. His first season fee has now been fixed at £20,000
(October 1st).

Machiavellian headed the International Classification for two-year-olds
in 1989, 5 lb clear, following wins in the Prix Yacowlef and two Group 1 races,

Prix Djebel, Maisons-Laffitte—Machiavellian wins his trial;
Ron's Victory (blaze) takes second, then is returned to sprinting

the Prix Morny and the Prix de la Salamandre. He'd become favourite for the Two Thousand Guineas after beating the filly Qirmazi for a second time, with the previously-undefeated British colt Rock City in fourth, in the Salamandre. Whether he deserved such a high rating caused some argument during the winter but he remained favourite for the big race up to the 'off'. Machiavellian's Guineas warm-up victory in the Prix Djebel at Maisons-Laffitte in April fuelled the debate. His trainer expressed himself well pleased with the performance, adding that he regarded Machiavellian as good as Nonoalco, but behind Nureyev, at the same stage. We were none too impressed with the time the horse took to assert his superiority in the course of landing the odds by two and a half lengths from Ron's Victory, and though there was clearly plenty of physical improvement in him, his odds of 6/4 seemed to represent very poor Guineas value, particularly as he wasn't certain to stay a mile. However, still 6/4 on the day, he finished a good second to Tirol and would have been closer than the two lengths with a better ride. Having taken the preliminaries well, he was held up towards the stand rail, tracking Tirol who turned out the right horse to track. But the chance to improve position two furlongs out was missed, and in the moments that passed before the next one came Tirol had made his move. In order finally to deliver a challenge Machiavellian was switched to his right, cutting across the weakening Elmaamul and causing Welney to check slightly. Machiavellian's turn of speed at this point of the race was impressive; it took him into second place going into the Dip, but he made little inroad into Tirol's lead up the hill and was well held over the last hundred yards. The decision to reoppose Tirol in Ireland backfired on connections, inasmuch as while he finished more than a length closer than at Newmarket he came only fourth, and probably neither himself nor the winner was seen at his best in a muddling race. As at Newmarket, Machiavellian looked in superb shape (he had his tongue tied down on this occasion). The tactics were unchanged—he was settled towards the rear, taking a good hold behind a modest early pace, and was in a handy seventh-of-nine position at halfway, racing towards the outside. He kept handy until Royal Academy improved on the wide outside going into the second-last furlong and boxed him in behind the eventual third Lotus Pool. To get out of this fix Machiavellian had to be checked back and switched round Royal Academy, losing ground away, obviously. Once in the clear he failed to accelerate as well as anticipated, just keeping on steadily, to be nearest at the finish.

Given the contrast between the way Machiavellian was finishing at a mile and the way he finished his sprint races as a two-year-old, his return to six and a half furlongs in the Prix Maurice de Gheest promised to be both interesting and illuminating. In fact he ran no sort of race, failing to quicken under pressure when the pace hotted up two furlongs out and trailing in six and a half lengths behind the winner Dead Certain. That fact that he'd been off the course for twelve weeks may have counted against him.

			Raise A Native	Native Dancer
	Mr Prospector (USA)		(ch 1961)	Raise You
	(b 1970)		Gold Digger	Nashua
Machiavellian (USA)			(b 1962)	Sequence
(b.c. 1987)			Halo	Hail To Reason
	Coup de Folie (USA)		(b or br 1969)	Cosmah
	(b 1982)		Raise The Standard	Hoist The Flag
			(b 1978)	Natalma

As Machiavellian left the stage so his two-year-old half-brother Exit To Nowhere (by Irish River) was about to make his bow. That colt took three runs to get off the mark, but when doing so in the Prix Thomas Bryon at Saint-Cloud in October he showed himself potentially top class, and there would seem every chance that he'll be attempting to go one better than Machiavellian in the Guineas in 1991. The pair are the first two foals of the mare Coup de Folie, a very useful winner in France at up to a mile as a two-year-old and up to a mile and a quarter at three. She was bought as a yearling in the United States, the same year that her sire Halo finished leading sire with the Kentucky Derby winner Sunny's Halo and the champion two-year-old Devil's Bag among his representatives. The late E. P. Taylor bred her, out of an unraced half-sister to Northern Dancer. The close-coupled, good-topped Machiavellian showed a quick, powerful action; he acted on firm going. A keen sort, he stayed a mile but that distance was probably his limit. *F. Boutin, France.*

MACHININGDUN 2 b.f. (Apr 5) Dunbeath (USA) 127–Ryoanji 100 (Lyphard (USA) 132) [1990 5m 5f5 5m6 5m 5f 6m6] 4,800Y: close-coupled filly: has a quick action: eighth foal: half-sister to 3-y-o High Roding (by High Top), unreliable 7f and 1¾m winner Miss Annie (by Scottish Rifle) and 1983 2-y-o 6f winner Ritsurin (by Mount Hagen): dam ran only at 2 yrs when 7f winner: poor form, including in seller: sweating and on toes final 2 outings. *N. Bycroft.*

MACHO MAN 5 br.g. Mummy's Game 120–Shoshoni 72 (Ballymoss 136) [1989 11s 8.2g 10v 1990 12s5 5] smallish gelding: winning plater: shaped as though retaining plenty of ability in non-selling handicap at Hamilton in November: twice winner over hurdles afterwards: should stay 1½m: acts on good to firm ground and soft: has worn blinkers, but not since 3 yrs: goes well with forcing tactics: inconsistent. *J. J. O'Neill.*

MAC KELTY 3 b.c. Wattlefield 117–Thevetia 65 (Mummy's Pet 125) [1989 5g 6m 6g 6m 6g* 6v3 5m4 7g5 7d a5g 1990 5s6 7f 6g 8.2g2 11m 9g6 7g 8g4 6m4 6g 9s6 10.5g 8d4 8d a5g a6g a11g] stocky colt: plating-class handicapper: seems best at 1m/9f: acts on good to firm ground and heavy: blinkered seventh to tenth starts: lacks pace. *N. Bycroft.* — 51

MACKENZIES 5 ch.m. Homing 130–Miss Henry 78 (Blue Cashmere 129) [1989 7g 10m 8g 8m 7.6h 7m 7f6 8m 8g3 12g a11g a10g2 1990 a12g a11g] lengthy, workman-like mare: poor mover: poor maiden: stays 1¼m: visored fourth to eighth outings at 4 yrs. *M. J. Ryan.* —

MAC RAMBLER 3 b.c. Hotfoot 126–Arkengarthdale (Sweet Story 122) [1989 7m 1990 8v5 8.2g 10g 12g] no worthwhile form, including in handicap. *N. Bycroft.* —

MACREE 3 b.f. Another Realm 118–Mrs Willie (St Paddy 133) [1989 6f 7f5 7h5 1990 10f 10m 10.1m 12f] workmanlike filly: well beaten, in selling handicaps last 2 starts. *A. Moore.* —

MACROBIAN 6 b.g. Bay Express 132–White Domino 67 (Sharpen Up 127) [1989 6m* 6m5 6m* 6m* 6g 6m3 6g 6g2 6g* 1990 6m 6m5 6m4 6m6 5m 6m* 6m 6m5 6m 6d 5g] good-bodied gelding: fairly useful handicapper: successful at Ripon in July: suited by 6f: best on a sound surface: suited by forcing tactics: visored twice, blinkered twice: has had operation for soft palate. *M. H. Easterby.* — 92

MAC'S BEST (USA) 3 ch.g. Borzoi (USA) 117–Happy Satan (USA) (Crimson Satan) [1989 NR 1990 a6g5 a6g6] $7,500Y: half-brother to 2 minor winners in USA: dam ran twice: well beaten in maiden and claimer: sold 825 gns Ascot February Sales. *M. McCormack.* —

MAC'S FIGHTER   5 ch.h. Hard Fought 125–Geoffrey's Sister 102 (Sparkler 105 130) [1989 6g² 6g 6m⁴ 7.2g³ 6f* 8f 1990 6f* 6m⁴ 5f⁶ 7g⁶ 6s] compact horse: moderate mover: favourite on first run for 8 months: beat Savahra Sound very cleverly by ½ length in listed Cammidge Trophy at Doncaster in March: below form after in similar events and Group 3 contests: burly final outing, first for over 4 months: suited by stiff 6f: possibly unsuited by soft going, acts on any other: wears blinkers or visor: usually taken very quietly to post: waited with and is suited by strong gallop. *W. A. O'Gorman.*

MAC'S IMP (USA)   2 b.c. (Feb 12) Imp Society (USA)–Flaming Reason 116 (USA) (Limit To Reason (USA)) [1990 5f² 5f* 6m* 6m* 6m* 6f² 6f* 6m*]

Racegoers who enjoy watching good sprinters seemed in for a fairly thin time at the start of the 1990 season, as most of the established stars—notably Cadeaux Genereux, Silver Fling, Golden Opinion and Danehill—had been retired with no obvious candidates to take their place. A similar scenario looks set to prevail in the early part of 1991. Dayjur and Royal Academy, who between them won all four British and French Group 1 sprints in the latest season, will both be at stud, as will Statoblest and several of the others who played supporting roles. The French colt Ron's Victory is one who will be around, and if he can reproduce the form which enabled him to run away with the Diadem Stakes at Ascot in September he'll take all the beating. Overall, though, the scene looks set for some of the three-year-olds to come to the fore in the sprinting division. Mac's Imp should be one of them. He's no Dayjur, not at the moment that's for sure, and the curtain came down on his first season before most of the prestige events for two-year-olds of his type took place. However, by that time he'd already built up a record of six wins from eight races, three of which were in pattern company, and his physique and the improvement he made as the season progressed suggest he'll be at least as good if not better as a three-year-old.

Mac's Imp was backed as if victory was a formality for his debut in a maiden race at Nottingham on the first day of May. In the event he couldn't cope with the more experienced Poet's Cove, but he made no mistake in similar company at Newmarket on Two Thousand Guineas day, beating Madagans Grey by nearer seven lengths than the official verdict of five, and further emphatic wins in minor events at Goodwood and Newbury stamped him as an ideal type for the Coventry Stakes. And so it proved. The twelve colts who took him on at Royal Ascot were all winners. None had form within hailing distance of Mac's Imp's, though, and he rewarded those who made him 2/1-favourite in style, quickening clear with ease over two out and never looking likely to be pegged back, passing the post two lengths clear of the well-regarded Generous with Bold Nephew keeping on well after a sluggish start to finish clear of the remainder in third. At this stage Mac's Imp had the best form of any two-year-old in Britain, and initially connections seemed inclined towards a tilt at the Prix Robert Papin, a race in which O'Gorman had gone close twice during the 'eighties with Superlative and Superpower. In the event Mac's Imp was turned out rather earlier for the Anglia Television July Stakes at Newmarket. Even with a 5-lb penalty for his Ascot win he still

Coventry Stakes, Ascot—Mac's Imp comes out on top in an all-winner field;
Generous (centre) beats Bold Nephew for second

Scottish Equitable Richmond Stakes, Goodwood—Mac's Imp beats Distinctly North

seemed to have a fair amount in hand of his three rivals, but after racing clear for almost four furlongs he was left standing by the once-raced Mujtahid, being pushed out once clearly held to pass the post a long-looking seven lengths adrift. Our first reaction to that race was that Mac's Imp had been beaten fairly and squarely by a colt of immense promise, and that view was lent weight by the winner's timefigure which was equivalent to a timerating of 121. However, Mac's Imp was reportedly less than a hundred per cent on his return home, and it's also arguable he was put at a disadvantage by being allowed to force a really searching gallop from the start. Mac's Imp didn't take too long to bounce back from that defeat—before another five weeks had elapsed he'd put up a couple of very smart performances to win the Scottish Equitable Richmond Stakes at Goodwood and the Heinz '57' Phoenix Stakes at Phoenix Park. Mac's Imp was faced with strong opposition in both races, his Goodwood rivals including Distinctly North, Mujadil and the progressive Time Gentlemen, who'd won the Group 3 John Roarty EBF Railway Stakes at the Curragh with plenty in hand on his most recent start. Mac's Imp looked in cracking shape, and under a slightly more restrained ride than at Newmarket he won with authority, quickening from the front soon after halfway and responding well once driven along to beat Distinctly North, who'd been set plenty to do, by a length, the pair drawing clear in a fast time. Distinctly North was in the line-up again in Ireland for what was almost certainly the final running of the Phoenix Stakes; the Queen Mary winner On Tiptoes and the Windsor Castle winner Gipsy Fiddler were also in the field of thirteen, while judged on the market the leading home-trained challenger was the O'Brien filly Capricciosa, who'd made all in a maiden race at the Curragh on her only previous start. Mac's Imp was sent off a strong favourite for the seventh time in eight outings and continued the British domination of the race with his best effort. Predictably, with several very speedy horses in opposition, the field was soon well strung out, and it seemed On Tiptoes held a slender advantage for the first couple of furlongs. Mac's Imp and Distinctly North (given his head

538

much earlier this time) soon came through to do battle, though, and with the rail to help him Mac's Imp kept on bravely to fend off the sustained challenge of the runner-up by a neck. Gipsy Fiddler, three lengths away, ran a fine race in keeping on for third, while On Tiptoes (sixth) and Capricciosa (tenth) ran better than their final positions, the former shaping like a five-furlong performer and the latter finding the combination of a high draw and inexperience too much of a burden. Several autumn targets were pencilled in for Mac's Imp after his Phoenix Park win, among them the Racecall Gold Trophy and the Laurel Futurity at the end of October, but he was found to be suffering from a high temperature in the lead up to the Newgate Stud Middle Park Stakes which led to his being put away for the season.

Unlike some trainers, O'Gorman doesn't attend the sales with vast fortunes at his disposal, and the policy over the years has been to excuse shortcomings in pedigree in order to concentrate on the way a prospective purchase looks and moves. Naturally, such tactics call for a highly skilled eye, and to say that the stable's methods have stood the test of time would be an understatement. The list of moderately-priced horses who fly the O'Gorman flag in good company lengthens by the year, and even in the unlikely event of their never winning another race both Mac's Imp and Timeless Times have already done more than enough to earn favourable comparison with predecessors such as Abdu, Sayf El Arab, Superlative, Superpower, Sayyaf and the brilliantly speedy Brondesbury. Mac's Imp was bought for only 25,000 dollars at the Keeneland September Sale. His sire Imp Society didn't race at two. At three and four he became known as a tough and very smart performer at up to a mile and a quarter, winning thirteen of twenty-five races including the Grade 2 Oaklawn and Razorback Handicaps and also breaking the track record under top weight in the John B. Campbell Stakes at Pimlico. Imp Society will be represented by his third crop in 1991. Mac's Imp was by far the biggest earner among his second, and the most notable performer among his first was Retiring Imp, who won the Group 3 Premio Certosa over five

Heinz '57' Phoenix Stakes, Phoenix Park — a repeat of Goodwood,
and a fine finish between these two likeable and speedy two-year-olds

furlongs at Milan on the same day Mac's Imp made his debut. Mac's Imp is the second foal produced by Flaming Reason. The first, also by Imp Society, is a minor winner in the States, while the third, a colt by Silver Hawk, went to the Shadwell Estate Company for 290,000 dollars at the latest Keeneland July Sale. Flaming Reason won four times at up to seven furlongs without scaling any great heights, but there are some notable performers close up in her pedigree. French Wind, who won the Display Stakes over nine furlongs as a two-year-old in 1963, has bred numerous winners, including the good French staying juvenile La Girouette, while her dam Flaming Wind is a half-sister to none other than Nijinsky's dam, the champion Canadian filly Flaming Page.

Mac's Imp (USA) (b.c. Feb 12, 1988)	Imp Society (USA) (ch 1981)	Barrera (b 1973)	Raise A Native Minnetonka
		Trotta Sue (b 1966)	Promised Land Blue Norka
	Flaming Reason (USA) (b 1980)	Limit To Reason (b or br 1968)	Hail To Reason Sailors Hunch
		French Wind (b 1961)	Menetrier Flaming Wind

There's some stamina in Mac's Imp's pedigree, and the fact that the Laurel Futurity over an extended mile was under consideration as one of his late-season options suggests there's a good chance he'll be allowed to tackle one of the Guineas trials during the spring. However, the likelihood is that he'll prove best employed over five and six furlongs. He's certainly a sprinter in appearance—robust and good-quartered with the scope to go on—and he also has a sprinter's demeanour in that it's thought necessary to take him very quietly and early to post. Moreover, once racing, Mac's Imp tends to be very keen to get on with the job; and he's always likely to prove suited by forcing tactics and possibly by a firm surface if the opinion of his trainer proves accurate. It was noticeable in his wins at Newbury and Royal Ascot that he tends to drift left once under pressure to quicken, but there's no suggestion he's of dubious temperament. On the contrary, Mac's Imp is a really game colt, and we'll be most surprised if he doesn't win another good prize or two. *W. A. O'Gorman.*

MACS MAHARANEE 3 b.f. Indian King (USA) 128–High State 72 (Free State 125) [1989 5m⁴ 5f⁴ 5g³ 6g² 6f⁶ 6g² 1990 6f 6m⁶ 5m⁴ 5g* 6m² 5m² 5f⁴ 5g 6m* 6f⁵] leggy filly: moderate mover: fair handicapper: won at Doncaster (made all) in June and Yarmouth (best effort) in September: seems ideally suited by 6f: acts on good to firm ground. *P. S. Felgate.* **81**

MAC'S MUSIC 4 ch.g. Music Boy 124–Annathena 83 (Homeric 133) [1989 NR 1990 6g 5g] sturdy gelding: fifth foal: half-brother to 1¼m seller winner Marsoom (by Full of Hope): dam suited by 1m: 50/1, over 6 lengths seventh of 16 in 5f Hamilton seller in May. *L. J. Barratt.* **—**

MAC'S PRINCESS (USA) 2 b.f. (Apr 26) Sovereign Dancer (USA)–Jungle Princess (USA) (Jungle Road) [1990 8.2m² a7g⁵ 7s] $37,000Y: half-sister to numerous winners aboard, including American Derby winner Pocket Zipper (by Full Pocket): dam third in Hollywood Oaks: hung left when 2 lengths second of 14 to Good Policy in minor event at Nottingham in September: well beaten after in maidens at Southwell and Doncaster: seems unsuited by soft ground. *W. A. O'Gorman.* **67**

MADAGANS GREY 2 gr.g. (Mar 19) Carwhite 127–Cheri Berry 87 (Air Trooper 115) [1990 5f² 6g* 6g 6d⁵ 6m⁴ 5m 7g 8g* 8g 8m 10g⁴] 4,000F, 6,000Y: leggy gelding: moderate mover: half-brother to 3-y-o Allsorts (by Noalto): dam sprinter: fair performer: successful in maiden auction at Newmarket in May and nursery at Sandown in August: good fourth of 9 to Matahif in listed race at Newmarket: suited by 1¼m: acts on good to firm and dead ground: blinkered fifth and sixth starts: wears crossed noseband: inconsistent. *R. Boss.* **88**

MADAME DUBOIS 3 ch.f. Legend of France (USA) 124–Shadywood 96 (Habitat 134) [1989 7g 1990 9m* 9f* 10m² 10m* 12m² 14.6g* 12.5g*] **121**

Eighteen years after winning the Prix de Royallieu at Longchamp on 65/1-shot Guillotina, Pat Eddery, standing in for Cauthen, won the race again on another filly bred and owned by the Cliveden Stud. There were no fancy prices this time—Madame Dubois, carrying a 7-lb penalty for a previous

540

A. F. Budge Park Hill Stakes, Doncaster—
stable-companions Madame Dubois and Applecross dominate the finish

Group 2 victory, started at 10/9 on in a field of eight in the Ciga-sponsored event in October. Soon prominent, but niggled along as early as halfway in a race two furlongs shorter than her previous one, Madame Dubois was sent to the front with under a quarter of a mile to run and, rousted along, soon opened up a two-length lead. A furlong or so later she looked in danger of defeat as the French-trained pair Spendomania and Echoes began to close, but she responded magnificently to very firm driving to hold on by what was described officially as a short neck and a neck. There was talk of returning to Longchamp for the Prix Royal-Oak but apparently connections were unsure of her staying the two miles and decided to retire her. For our part we think there was a good chance she would have stayed; what was certain was that victory in the Royallieu brought a fitting end to a splendid career which saw her improve tremendously as a three-year-old.

Madame Dubois had picked up her penalty when gaining a clear-cut win in the A. F. Budge Park Hill Stakes at Doncaster the previous month. The field for the Park Hill was quite a strong one—much stronger than the four-runner affair in 1989. Madame Dubois, who had been narrowly and unluckily beaten into second place behind Madiriya in the Galtres Stakes at York last time, started 2/1 favourite in an open-looking contest, receiving weight from a couple of her seven opponents, the Irish Oaks winner Knight's Baroness and the French filly Whitehaven. Madame Dubois and her stable-companion Applecross dominated the finish, the former coming through to take the lead off the latter two furlongs out then staying on strongly under firm riding to draw two and a half lengths clear, with Whitehaven and Knight's Baroness filling the frame. Madame Dubois had come to prominence with time and distance. She'd begun, like others from her stable in recent seasons, in minor races at Wolverhampton in the spring. Twice a winner on that course, she'd first looked useful when coming second to stable-companion Native Twine in the Ballymacoll Stud Stakes, a listed race over a mile and a quarter at Newbury in June. She'd impressed even more in winning the Steventon Stakes over the same distance there in July from the colts Stapleford Manor and Ijtihaad. Then followed York, Doncaster and Longchamp.

Ciga Prix de Royallieu, Longchamp—
Madame Dubois defies a penalty over the shorter distance,
holding on from Spendomania and Echoes

Madame Dubois (ch.f. 1987)	Legend of France (USA) (b 1980)	Lyphard (b 1969)	Northern Dancer / Goofed
		Lupe (b 1967)	Primera / Alcoa
	Shadywood (ch 1982)	Habitat (b 1966)	Sir Gaylord / Little Hut
		Milly Moss (ch 1970)	Crepello / Bally's Mil

Madame Dubois is the first foal of Shadywood, not the third as was stated in *Racehorses of 1989*. The dam's family has been trained at Warren Place for many years, and even the sire Legend of France and his dam, the Oaks winner Lupe, were once housed there. Shadywood showed fairly useful form over middle distances. She's a sister to the quite moderate mile-and-a-quarter winner Touchez Le Bois and a half-sister to three other winners, including the smart six-furlong to one-mile winner Kashmir Lass. Madame Dubois' grandam Milly Moss won the Cheshire Oaks and is a sister to Mil's Bomb who was good enough and versatile enough to win both the Nassau Stakes and Park Hill Stakes. Madame Dubois is easily the best to date of the relatively small number of runners Legend of France has had. Legend of France was exported to France in 1989 having previously stood at Derisley Wood Stud at Newmarket. His best other progeny are Girl of France, a winner in listed company in France, and the fairly useful handicapper Eire Leath-Sceal, another notably genuine animal. Madame Dubois, a lengthy, rather angular filly, a moderate mover in her slower paces, raced only on a sound surface. She has a superb temperament and was a very genuine sort. She's to visit Kris. *H. R. A. Cecil.*

MADAM JAC 4 b.f. Anfield 117–Lucky Petina 88 (Mummy's Pet 125) [1989 NR 1990 a7g 6f3 7f3 7f 7f 7.6m4 7.6g a10g3] medium-sized filly: fourth reported foal: half-sister to 5f winner Hi-Tech Leader (by Swing Easy): dam sprinting half-sister to Manor Farm Boy: plating-class maiden: stays 7.6f: acts on firm going: sweating and on toes fourth outing: bandaged behind on seventh. *R. Akehurst.*   53

MADAM TAYLOR 5 b.m. Free State 125–Hourglass (Mansingh (USA) 120) [1989 10.2g4 12d 10m 9f 10m3 10m 10.6d* 9m2 10g6 11s3 10.6m 8g 1990 a12g 10.6d 10.4g 10m 10.2s2 12s] dipped-backed mare: moderate mover: plating-class winner for apprentice as 4-y-o: form in 1990 only in seller on fifth outing: stays 11f: has won on firm going, but suited by an easier surface nowadays: not discredited in blinkers: has worn bandages behind: trained until after reappearance by H. Collingridge: reluctant to race third outing. *R. E. Peacock.*   36

MADELEY'S PET 3 ch.f. Tina's Pet 121–Thorganby 75 (Decoy Boy 129) [1989 5d3 5f3 5g2 5d2 5d2 1990 5v6] sturdy, good-quartered filly, slightly dipped backed: moderate mover: quite modest maiden: not entirely discredited facing very stiff   —

542

*Galtres Stakes, York—Madiriya is pressed late on by Madame Dubois,
having shown a fine turn of foot to go clear*

task in April handicap on sole outing in 1990: may stay 6f: has run creditably for 7-lb
claimer: sometimes on toes. *Denys Smith.*

MADEMOISELLE CHLOE 3 b.f. Night Shift (USA)–Emerald Rocket 69 **105**
(Green God 128) [1989 5m* 5m* 5s* 6m⁶ 1990 7.3d⁵ 6g³ 5d⁵ 6g] lengthy, good-
quartered filly: moderate mover: useful performer: best effort as 3-y-o staying-on 9
lengths fifth to Dayjur in King's Stand Stakes at Royal Ascot third start: not
discredited in Duke of York Stakes (held up taking keen hold) at York and Prix de
Ris-Orangis at Evry starts either side: probably stays 6f: yet to race on very firm
going, probably acts on any other: has joined W. O'Gorman. *C. B. B. Booth.*

MADIRIYA 3 ch.f. Diesis 133–Majanada (Tap On Wood 130) [1989 6g⁴ 8f* 1990 **119**
9m⁴ 10g³ 10.1m* 10m* 12m* 12m⁶] lengthy, rather sparely-made filly: moderate

H. H. Aga Khan's "Madiriya"

walker: has a free, rather round action: successful in handicaps at Windsor and Newbury then listed Galtres Stakes (quickening to lead 2f out and holding on by ½ length from Madame Dubois) at York: improved markedly again when about 2 lengths sixth of 9 to Salsabil in Prix Vermeille at Longchamp, keeping on never dangerous: stays 1½m: smart. *L. M. Cumani.*

MADIYLA 3 gr.f. Darshaan 133–Manntika 77 (Kalamoun 129) [1989 NR 1990 10g⁵ 12d*] leggy, rather sparely-made filly: second foal: half-sister to poor winning stayer Premier Princess (by Hard Fought): dam 1¼m winner: favourite, easily won maiden at Folkestone in November: moved poorly down on debut previous month: sold to join J. Redmond 7,400 gns Newmarket December Sales: looked capable of better. *L. M. Cumani.* — 73 p

MADONETTA 2 ch.f. (Mar 23) Sharpo 132–Woodwind (FR) 103 (Whistling Wind 123) [1990 6g 7d4] leggy, rather close-coupled filly: moderate mover: half-sister to several winners, including useful 6f and 7f winner Mummy's Favourite (by Mummy's Pet) and very useful miler Tahilla (by Moorestyle): dam 6f winner: first run for 2 months, fourth of 7, one pace last 2f, to Lilian Bayliss in minor event at Chester in October: will probably improve again. *R. Charlton.* — 70 p

MAERD ROO 4 b.f. Beldale Lark 105–Briana 64 (The Brianstan 128) [1989 NR 1990 11g⁶ 12g] angular filly: sixth foal: dam placed over 5f at 2 yrs: tailed-off last of 6 in maiden at Edinburgh: hampered and fell after 1½f in Hamilton amateurs race later in June. *I. Semple.* — —

MAGDALENE HEIGHTS 2 ch.c. (Mar 28) All Systems Go 119–Carreg-Wennol (Dublin Taxi) [1990 7m 8g] lightly-made colt: first foal: dam of little account: soundly beaten in maidens at Newcastle. *D. H. Topley.* — —

MAGDALENE (IRE) 2 b.f. (Apr 26) Runnett 125–Grattan Princess (Tumble Wind (USA)) [1990 6f 6d⁴ 5s] 3,600Y: well-grown, workmanlike filly: has scope: sixth foal: closely related to 3-y-o Perspicacity (by Petorius) and half-sister to 6f seller winner Twilight Falls (by Day Is Done) and a winner in Belgium: dam lightly-raced Irish maiden: well beaten in maiden auctions and a 4-runner Catterick minor event. *T. Fairhurst.* — —

MAGGIE SIDDONS 2 b.f. (Mar 17) Night Shift (USA)–Sarah Siddons (Reform 132) [1990 6m 5.8m 5m 7g³ 6m 7g* 7m² 5.8d* 7s³] 6,600F, 5,400Y: good-topped filly: carries condition: has a round action: ninth foal: closely related to 1986 2-y-o 6f seller winner Sands of Time (by Dance In Time) and half-sister to 2 winners, including 5f and 6f winner Hinari Hi Fi (by Song): dam French 8.5f winner, is half-sister to top Italian 2-y-o Anguillo: former plater: much improved final 4 starts, winning nurseries at Wolverhampton and Bath in October: stays 7f: acts on good to firm and soft going. *C. J. Hill.* — 81

MAGGIES LAD 2 b.g. (Apr 24) Red Johnnie 100–Busted Love (Busted 134) [1990 5f 5m 5m³ 5f³ 6g³ 5g⁴ 5g³ 7.5d⁵ 7f⁴ 5f⁴ 8f⁵ 8v⁶ 7d a7g³] 5,000Y: workmanlike gelding: has scope: second living foal: brother to 1¾m winner Johnsted: dam never ran: plating-class maiden: ran creditably on all-weather: stays 1m: effective with or without blinkers or visor: good mount for a claimer. *T. Fairhurst.* — 56

MAGIA (USA) 3 b.f. Vaguely Noble 140–My Sister 101 (Nonoalco (USA) 131) [1989 7g 1990 8f⁶ 10m⁴ 10g 12m] leggy, close-coupled filly: first run for 4 months, form in maidens only when fourth of 6 at Sandown: soundly beaten in handicaps: should stay 1½m: trained until after reappearance by C. Wall. *J. R. Fanshawe.* — 61

MAGICAL DEED (USA) 3 b.c. Shadeed (USA) 135–Cornish Genie (USA) (Cornish Prince) [1989 NR 1990 8g 12g 8m⁵ 10d 10m] sturdy colt: seventh foal: half-brother to 3 winners in USA, including stakes winners at up to 11f by Vigors and up to 1¼m by Grey Dawn II: dam 6.5f and 1m winner in France: 25/1, first show in maidens when staying-on fifth at York: blinkered when well beaten in handicaps: should prove better at 1¼m than 1m: sold 5,600 gns Newmarket Autumn Sales. *A. A. Scott.* — 68

MAGICAL DREAM (USA) 2 ch.f. (Mar 22) Lyphard's Wish (FR) 124–Green Lass 98 (Green God 128) [1990 5f 5g³ 5g³ 6g* 6g² 6g² 7.5g* 7m³ 7.5f³ 8.2g* 8m³ 8v⁵] $17,000F, $25,000Y: neat filly: sister to quite useful American 1987 2-y-o 5.8f winner Green Lyph and half-sister to a minor winner: dam 2-y-o 1m winner later won in Italy: modest performer: successful in sellers (no bid) at Nottingham in June and Beverley in July and nursery at Nottingham in September: suited by 1m: best on a sound surface: sweating and edgy fifth and sixth starts: genuine. *J. Etherington.* — 71

MAGICAL SPIRIT 3 b.f. Top Ville 129–Anegada 79 (Welsh Pageant 132) [1989 NR 1990 8m⁶ 10.4g² 11.5g³ 12g] lengthy, attractive filly: has scope: half-sister to 5 winners, including useful 4-y-o 1¼m winner Flamingo Pond (by Sadler's Wells) and — 70 +

good 7f to 1½m winner John French (by Relko): dam sister to dam of Saumarez and half-sister to Derrylin: placed in minor event at Chester and maiden at Lingfield: had stiff task final outing: may well prove best at 1¼m: sold 23,000 gns Newmarket December Sales. *M. R. Stoute.*

MAGICAL VEIL 2 ch.f. (Mar 25) Majestic Light (USA)–Jameelapi (USA) 94 **64 p** (Blushing Groom (FR) 131) [1990 8m4] smallish, rather sparely-made filly: third foal: half-sister to winning Irish middle-distance stayer Jameel Ridge (by Cox's Ridge): dam 2-y-o 6f winner: over 6 lengths fourth of 11, keeping on after slow start, to Lofty Lady in maiden at Salisbury in September: sure to improve. *M. R. Stoute.*

MAGIC ANA 3 b.f. Magic Mirror 105–Ana Gabriella (USA) (Master Derby (USA)) **57** [1989 6d 7g* 7g2 8g3 7g 7g3 8.9s 7.5d4 a8g4 1990 a7g2 a6g2 a6g* 7f] shallow-girthed ex-French filly: plating-class performer: landed odds in claimer at Southwell: ran poorly in Doncaster handicap later in March: stays 7f: usually bandaged. *M. C. Pipe.*

MAGIC AT DAWN (USA) 5 ch.g. Diamond Prospect (USA) 126–Implicit **57** (Grundy 137) [1989 8h5 9f5 8f5 1990 9f5 8m 11m 12.2m5 9f] sturdy, deep-girthed gelding: has been operated on for a soft palate: quite modest handicapper: suited by 1m, front-running tactics and firm going: blinkered final start: winning hurdler in August: inconsistent. *G. M. Moore.*

MAGIC BULLET (USA) 3 b.f. Northern Baby (CAN) 127–Probation (USA) **—** (Bold Ruler) [1989 5g 5d 6m 1990 5m 7g] leggy, rather unfurnished filly: poor form at 2 yrs: didn't get best of runs in handicap on reappearance then showed nothing in similar event 2 weeks later: bred to stay 1m: twice slowly away: wore severe bridle at 2 yrs: sold 2,300 gns Newmarket July Sales. *J. Etherington.*

MAGIC CRYSTAL 3 b.f. Ahonoora 122–Carntino (Bustino 136) [1989 7g 1990 **—** 10m4 10.1g 12d4 a12g4 12m4] rather unfurnished filly: little worthwhile form: sold 800 gns Newmarket December Sales. *Lord John FitzGerald.*

MAGIC EXPRESS (USA) 3 ch.c. Green Forest (USA) 134–Secretariat Flag **98** (USA) (Secretariat (USA)) [1989 7g 1990 8f4 8.5g4 8.2g*dis 8m5 10f2 10f2 9m2 9m* 9m 9f* 10d] stocky colt: moderate walker: has quick action: fairly useful performer: first past post in handicap (disqualified after steroid test) at Nottingham in June and apprentice races (made all) at Ripon in August and Lingfield in September: out of depth final start: best efforts at 9f: acts on firm going: has worn tongue strap, not last 5 starts: ran in snatches when held up fourth start, and best with forcing tactics. *M. Moubarak.*

MAGIC FLAME 3 b.f. Sayf El Arab (USA) 127–Sterlonia 96 (Sterling Bay **70** (SWE)) [1989 NR 1990 6m* 6f5 7g2 8m4 7d6 6s3] leggy, quite good-topped filly: poor mover: sixth foal: half-sister to 3 winners, including useful 1986 2-y-o 5f winner Nutwood Lil (by Vaigly Great): dam won at 7f and 1m: 20/1 and ridden by 7-lb claimer, led post in claimer (slowly away) at Nottingham in April: easily best other efforts in similar events here on next 2 outings: sent to Scandinavia, successful over 6.7f at Taby in September: stays 7f. *E. Eldin.*

MAGIC GLEAM (USA) 4 b.f. Danzig (USA)–All Agleam (USA) (Gleaming **112** (USA)) [1989 8d 7f* 8f2 8g* 8g3 10.5f4 1990 8m3 8m5 8.5g6 8m4 6m4 8d5 9f] big, strong, lengthy filly: carries condition: good walker: fluent mover: very smart as 3-y-o, winner of Child Stakes at Newmarket: not so good in 1990, on fifth outing fourth to Royal Academy in strongly-run Carroll Foundation July Cup at Newmarket, staying on well from halfway: ideally needs further than 6f, and stays 1m: acts on firm going, probably unsuited by a soft surface: sent to continue career with N. Drysdale in USA. *A. A. Scott.*

MAGIC MILLY 4 b.f. Simply Great (FR) 122–Supreme Fjord 92 (Targowice **—** (USA) 130) [1989 10s 9f 6g a8g 1990 10.8m 14g 11.7f] small, sparely-made filly: quite modest winner as 2-y-o: no form since, including in sellers: best form at 1m with give in the ground. *B. R. Millman.*

MAGIC NIGHT (FR) 2 b.f. (Mar 9) Le Nain Jaune (FR) 121–Pin Up Babe **107** (Prominer 125) [1990 6g* 7g2 7g2 8g* 8g6] fourth known foal: half-sister to a modest maiden in France: dam French 10.5f and 11f winner: sire stayer: useful filly: successful in newcomers race at Saint-Cloud in June and Prix d'Aumale (by ½ length and the same from Sha Tha and Caerlina) at Longchamp in September: ¾-length second to Green Pola in Prix du Calvados at Deauville on third start: never-dangerous sixth of 9, staying on, to Shadayid in Prix Marcel Boussac at Longchamp on final one: will stay 1½m. *P. Demercastel, France.*

MAGIC POTION 2 gr.c. (Mar 11) Sayf El Arab (USA) 127–Mercy Cure 81 (No **65 p** Mercy 126) [1990 7g 6g6] 4,600Y: lengthy, unfurnished colt: half-brother to 3 winners, including 3-y-o Sister Sal (by Bairn), 6f winner at 2 yrs, and 5f to 7f winner Last Recovery (by Final Straw): dam firm-ground sprinter: 7 lengths sixth of 10, never able to challenge, to Roger de Berksted in maiden at York in October: may well improve again. *M. E. D. Francis.*

MAGIC SECRET 2 b.c. (Mar 30) Local Suitor (USA) 128–Meissarah (USA) 78 (Silver Hawk (USA) 127) [1990 6m⁴ 7g³ 7f² 7.5f³ 7.5g² 8f² 8.2s*] rather leggy colt: has a round action: first foal: dam never ran: modest performer: won maiden at Hamilton in September by 7 lengths from Crimson Cloud: will be suited by 1¼m: acts on firm ground, but goes very well on soft. *B. Hanbury.*

MAGIC TOP 2 b.c. (Feb 8) Doulab (USA) 115–Enchanted 116 (Song 132) [1990 48 5m⁶ 5g⁵ 5g⁵ 5m] IR 24,000Y: strong, neat colt: half-brother to several winners, including useful 11f and 11.7f winner Woodpecker (by Touching Wood): dam sprinter, best at 2 yrs: poor maiden: visored, bit backward and swerved stalls final outing, first for 3½ months: looked unco-operative when also visored time before: sold 1,000 gns Doncaster October Sales. *M. Bell.*

MAGNATE'S CROWN (IRE) 2 b.c. (Feb 15) Last Tycoon 131–Chapelet 71 73 (Habitat 134) [1990 6g⁴ 6m² 6m² 7m] 46,000Y: strong, compact colt: second foal: dam lightly-raced maiden from family of Beldale Flutter: modest maiden: probably stays 7f. *P. W. Harris.*

MAGNETIZE 3 b.f. Electric 126–Silver Birch 122 (Silver Shark 129) [1989 5m 58 6m² 6f³ 6m⁴ 5m⁵ 6g 1990 6f 7m 10f 8.3m 6f⁵ 7.6m³ 7.6d 8m 7g] sturdy, lengthy filly: carries condition: plating-class maiden: apparently best efforts at Lingfield sixth and seventh starts: should stay 1m: acts on firm ground and dead: has run creditably when sweating: ran badly for apprentice final start: sold 980 gns Newmarket December Sales. *W. G. R. Wightman.*

MAHAT 3 b.f. Rainbow Quest (USA) 134–Rivers Maid 83 (Rarity 129) [1989 NR —
1990 10m 10m] 33,000Y: tall, angular filly: half-sister to 1985 2-y-o Nomination (by Dominion), a high-class performer at up to 7f: dam won over 7f at 2 yrs and is sister to very useful middle-distance performer and good hurdler Decent Fellow: 33/1, towards rear in maidens at Sandown and Newbury in the spring. *R. F. Johnson Houghton.*

MAHFIL 2 b.c. (Apr 19) Head For Heights 125–Polavera (FR) (Versailles II) 72 p [1990 7m⁴ 8.2s⁴] useful-looking, good-topped colt: has scope: sixth foal: half-brother to minor French 9f winner Riviere Polaire (by Irish River): dam minor French 6.5f and 1m winner: 4 lengths fourth of 13, fading last 1f, to Port Sunlight in maiden at Haydock in October: well-backed favourite on debut in July: will probably improve again. *A. C. Stewart.*

MAHIR (USA) 2 ch.c. (Mar 1) Sharpen Up 127–Vie En Rose (USA) (Blushing 74 p Groom (FR) 131) [1990 7m³ 8d⁴] $220,000Y: workmanlike colt: has a long stride: brother to 1m and 1¼m winner Marksmanship, later successful in USA, and half-brother to a winner in Italy: dam, half-sister to smart French 6f to 1m winner Vorias and good French miler Verria, showed some ability in USA: 3 lengths fourth of 13, travelling smoothly, unable to quicken then not knocked about, to Straldi in maiden at Leicester: shaped well on debut earlier in October: sure to do better. *J. H. M. Gosden.*

MAHONG 2 gr.g. (Apr 12) Petong 126–Balearica 90 (Bustino 136) [1990 6g⁵ 7s²] 74 18,000Y: quite good-topped gelding: third foal: brother to fair 1989 2-y-o 6f winner Jacomino and half-brother to 4-y-o Where's The Money (by Lochnager), fair 5f winner at 2 yrs: dam, placed from 6f to 1m, is daughter of sister to Runnett: modest form in maidens at Newmarket (slowly away) and Newcastle (eased) in autumn. *J. W. Hills.*

MAHRAH (USA) 3 b.f. Vaguely Noble 140–Montage (USA) (Alydar (USA)) 89 [1989 7m² 7g⁶ 1990 11f³ 8g* 9g² 10m] rather unfurnished filly: shows knee action: fair form: won maiden at Ripon in May, off bridle virtually throughout: much better effort when second in minor event at Wolverhampton following month: should have stayed 1¼m: best efforts on an easy surface: visits Dancing Brave. *A. C. Stewart.*

MAHRAJAN 6 b.h. Dominion 123–Dame Julian 84 (Blakeney 126) [1989 9d* 71 10g³ 8m 10m 9g 8d 1990 9g 10m⁵ 11.5m⁵ 11.7m* 11.7g* 12g 12g] rangy horse: moderate mover: successful in August handicaps at Windsor: stays 1½m: acts on any going: inconsistent. *C. J. Benstead.*

MAIDEN BIDDER 8 b.m. Shack (USA) 118–Wolveriana 78 (Wolver Hollow 40 126) [1989 6f5. 1m³ 6m³ 7f* 6f* 6m 6f⁵ 6f⁵ 5g 7f 7.6f 5m 6g² 6f 6m 5m 7g 6m 6g 1990 5m 6g⁴ 6d 7m³ 7.6g 6f 6h⁶ 7m 7f 7m 5m 6g] lengthy mare: generally well below her best since winning handicaps (first for amateurs) on successive days as 7-y-o: stays

7f: probably unsuited by soft going, acts on any other· blinkered 3 times: has found little in front and best with waiting tactics: inconsistent. *D. A. Wilson.*

MAID MARINER   8 br.m. Julio Mariner 127–Molly Polly (Molvedo 137) [1989 — NR 1990 14g] lengthy mare: first race on flat since 3 yrs, soundly beaten in handicap at Nottingham in April: inconsistent handicap hurdler, winner at Market Rasen in June. *Miss G. M. Rees.*

MAID OF ESSEX   4 b.f. Bustino 136–Magelka 77 (Relkino 131) [1989 7d 9g 1990   **66** d 10.2f3 10.2f3 14m 12m4 8m5 10m5 10.2g 7g6 8g3 8.2d] attractive filly: quite modest handicapper: best at 1m to 1¼m: acts on firm going: often sweats and gets on edge: races keenly. *C. E. Brittain.*

MAID OF HONOR (USA)   3 ch.f. Blushing Groom (FR) 131–Summer Legend   — (USA) (Raise A Native) [1989 NR 1990 7g 7m] $225,000Y: leggy, angular filly: half-sister to several winners in North America, including top 1988 Canadian 2-y-o filly Legarto (by Roberto): dam winner at up to 7f from good family: no worthwhile form in maidens at Newbury and Goodwood (very edgy in stalls, tailed off) in spring. *I. A. Balding.*

MAID OF MOONSHINE (IRE)   2 b.f. (May 3) Green Ruby (USA) 104–Mount   **38** of Light 61 (Sparkler 130) [1990 5m 6g 6m 6m] leggy filly: fifth living foal: half-sister to 1907 2-y o 5f and 6f seller winner Rustic Dawn (by Rusticaro): dam, half-sister to smart miler Richboy, stayed 1½m: poor form, including in a seller. *G. B. Balding.*

MAID WELCOME   3 br.f. Mummy's Pet 125–Carolynchristensen 58 (Sweet   **77** Revenge 129) [1989 5d 5s 5.8f 6f 1990 a6g4 6f4 5g 5f4 6m 5g 5m6 5.8h2 5f 5.1f5 5.3h* 6f2 6m4 6m 6f4 5f 5.3f 6d 5g* a5g2 a6g6 a5g5] sturdy filly: has a round action: modest performer: won handicap at Brighton in August and claimer at Pontefract in October: stays 6f: acts on hard going: blinkered nowadays: suitable mount for apprentice: trained until after sixth start by M. Haynes: inconsistent. *Mrs N. Macauley.*

MAILMAN   11 ch.g. Malacate (USA) 131–Sallail (Sallust 134) [1989 10s5 10v2 11.7d   **46** 9f 10m 11.7m 12f4 12m* 15.5f* 12m3 1990 11.7f 11.7g 12f 12m6 15.5f3] tall gelding: well below form in 1990: stays 15.5f: acts on any going: excellent mount for inexperienced rider. *I. A. Balding.*

MAIN FLEET   3 br.c. Lord Gayle (USA) 124–Fleetsin (FR) (Jim French (USA))   **74** [1989 NR 1990 11d 10m a12g3 a12g*] easy mover: fifth foal: half-brother to useful 5.8f and 7f winner Fleet Form (by Double Form), successful in USA in 1990, and a winner in USA by Hello Gorgeous: dam French middle-distance winner: won claimer at Southwell in December, leading close home: well beaten in Newbury maidens: better at 1½m than shorter. *C. R. Nelson.*

MAIORO (CAN)   4 b.f. Bates Motel (USA)–Toys Are Fun (USA) (Go Marching   — (USA)) [1989 NR 1990 9g 12g] fourth foal: half-sister to minor winner in USA: dam winner 6 times at up to 9f: well beaten in ladies race at Kempton (bandaged near-hind) and apprentice maiden at Newmarket: sold 1,050 gns Doncaster October Sales. *M. H. B. Robinson.*

MAI PEN RAI   2 ch.g. (Jan 19) All Systems Go 119–Jersey Maid 82 (On Your   **70** Mark 125) [1990 6g 6g 6m2 6m2 6m3 6m3 7f 7f3 8m* 8.2d] 2,100Y: sparely-made, angular gelding: first foal: dam 2-y-o 5f winner stayed 7f: modest performer: won nursery at Pontefract in October, showing much improved form, by 1½ lengths from Carnbrea Cuddy: will stay 1¼m: best form on a firm surface. *P. Calver.*

MAISON DES FRUITS   3 b.f. Balidar 133–Thorganby Tina 72 (Averof 123)   **57** [1989 5f5 5m3 5g6 a6g² a5g 1990 a5g7 a6g4 6g5 5g 5g* 5g] workmanlike filly: shade unfurnished: quite modest form: best effort when dead-heating in handicap at Epsom in June: probably stayed 6f: sometimes bandaged: sweating third start: dead. *C. N. Allen.*

MAIS OUI (USA)   3 b.f. Lyphard (USA) 132–Affirmatively (USA) (Affirmed **108** (USA)) [1989 8g* 6.5s4 1990 8g 8m* 8m2 8f4 10g5 8d 9.2g] $275,000Y: deep-girthed filly: first foal: dam minor winner at up to 1¼m in USA out of outstanding American racemare Straight Deal: successful in newcomers race at Maisons-Laffitte in October at 2 yrs and in listed race at Longchamp in May, 1990: useful form in pattern events third to fifth starts (never able to challenge when 8 lengths fourth in Coronation Stakes at Royal Ascot) but below form afterwards: stays 1¼m: possibly unsuited by a soft surface. *F. Boutin, France.*

MAJED (IRE)   2 b.c. (Mar 25) Wolverlife 115–Martin Place (Martinmas 128)   **78** p [1990 7m 8d2 7g3] IR 5,000F: useful-looking colt: good walker: second foal: half-brother to 3-y-o Martinstar (by Norwick): dam little worthwhile form in 3 outings: modest form when placed in maiden at Leicester and minor event at Newmarket

(ridden by 7-lb claimer, edged right last 2f) in autumn: will stay 1m: should improve, and win a modest race. *N. A. Callaghan.*

MAJESTIC GAMBLER 2 b.c. (Apr 6) Enchantment 115–Wessex Kingdom 68 **61** d (Vaigly Great 127) [1990 6g* 6g⁶ 6f⁶ 7g 5g²] 4,000F, 6,600Y: useful-looking colt: first foal: dam 5f winner: won maiden auction race at Pontefract in June: below that form after, including in sellers: blinkered final 2 starts: dead. *W. J. Pearce.*

MAJESTIC JEM 4 b.f. Majestic Maharaj 105–Mia Samira (Allangrange 126) — [1989 8d 8.2m 1990 5m 6m] workmanlike filly: well beaten in modest company. *R. J. Hodges.*

MAJLOOD (USA) 2 b.c. (Mar 13) Danzig (USA)–Qui Royalty (USA) (Native **110** p Royalty (USA)) [1990 6f* 6g* 6m³] $2,100,000Y: leggy, unfurnished colt: sixth foal: brother to very useful 3-y-o Qui Danzig, 6f winner at 2 yrs, closely related to Bakharoff (by The Minstrel) and half-brother to 2 other winners, notably Sum (by Spectacular Bid), successful at up to 1¼m, including in graded stakes: dam very useful stakes-placed winner at up to 1m: heavily-backed favourite but green, won

Hamdan Al-Maktoum's "Majmu"

maiden at Goodwood in August and BonusPrint Sirenia Stakes (by ½ length,
rallying well having become unbalanced 1f out, from Shalford) at Kempton in
September: 2 lengths third of 9 to Lycius in Newgate Stud Middle Park Stakes at
Newmarket: will stay 7f: likely to improve again, and win another race or two. *M. R.
Stoute.*

MAJMU (USA) 2 b.f. (Feb 26) Al Nasr (FR) 126–Affirmative Fable (USA) **105**
(Affirmed (USA)) [1990 7f³ 7m² 8g* 8m⁶] $140,000Y: good-topped, attractive filly:
first foal: dam minor winner at around 1m: useful filly: won 7-runner May Hill Stakes
at Doncaster in September, showing much improved form, by a short head, clear,
from Shamshir, leading 3f out, joined almost immediately then staying on very
gamely: looked past best and ran moderately in Brent Walker Fillies' Mile at Ascot:
will be suited by 1¼m. *J. H. M. Gosden.*

MAJOR INQUIRY (USA) 4 b.g. The Minstrel (CAN) 135–Hire A Brain (USA) **91**
92 (Seattle Slew (USA)) [1989 14m² 14f* 14m² 10g² 1990 14f³ 18.4d 20m³] sturdy
gelding: first foal: dam Irish 7f winner, is daughter of Grenzen, a high-class winner
at up to 9f: fairly useful performer: looking very well, good third to Retouch in
£14,800 2½m Ascot Stakes (Handicap) at Royal Ascot: subsequently gelded: stays
extreme distances: acts well on top-of-the-ground: fairly useful hurdler (has broken
blood vessel) as a juvenile. *D. R. C. Elsworth.*

MAJORITY HOLDING 5 b.h. Mandrake Major 122–Kirkby 85 (Midsummer **—**
Night II 117) [1989 9d 7v 8.3m 8g 10.1m 10.1m 8m* 8.3m 9m⁴ 8s 10.6d* a10g² a12g⁵
a12g⁵ 1990 10.1g] lengthy, rather dipped-backed horse: plating-class winner of 2
handicaps (second for apprentices) as 4-y-o: never placed to challenge in Windsor
claimer in April: stays 10.6f: acts on good to firm and heavy going: usually bandaged:
inconsistent. *K. T. Ivory.*

549

MAJOR IVOR 5 ch.h. Mandrake Major 122–Double Birthday (Cavo Doro 124) — [1989 7f³ 8.2g 7f³ 8f* 8f² 8f* 9f³ 8.2d³ 1990 8g 7m 8m] big, workmanlike horse: carries condition: modest handicapper: not seen out after July: suited by around 1m: acts on firm and dead going: well suited by strong handling. *Mrs G. R. Reveley.*

MAJOR JACKO 7 b.h. Mandrake Major 122–Toreadora 103 (Matador 131) [1989 **46** 5d⁵ 6d² 6f 6m 6g 6m a7g* 1990 a7g 6f 8m 6f³ 7h⁴ 6m⁶ 7f⁵ 7m 7f³ 6m⁶ 6f* 6g 6m 6m a6g⁴ a6g³ a7g] big, lengthy horse: moderate mover: plating class at best judged on most recent form: led final strides when winning handicap at Folkestone in September: effective at 6f to 7f: acts on any going: blinkered twice: often apprentice ridden. *R. Hannon.*

MAJOR ROGERS (USA) 2 ch.c. (Apr 19) Sauce Boat (USA)–European Passer **61** (USA) (Caucasus (USA)) [1990 7g 7g³ 6g a7g³ a7g* a8g⁵] 17,500Y: stocky colt: second foal: dam minor winner at up to 1¼m at 4 yrs in North America: won 13-runner maiden at Lingfield in November: gambled on time before: best form at 7f: visored last 2 starts. *D. J. G. Murray-Smith.*

MAKBUL 3 b.c. Fairy King (USA)–Royaltess (Royal And Regal (USA)) [1989 6f* **80** + 6f* 1990 9.1s²] compact, good-quartered colt: successful in June as 2-y-o in minor event at Pontefract and £7,700 race at Ascot: second favourite, 6 lengths second of 7 to eased Live Action in minor event at Newcastle in November, 1990, no chance with winner from over 2½f out: will prove suited by further than 6f: remains in training. *D. Morley.*

MAKE CONTACT (USA) 4 b.c. Fappiano (USA)–Touch (USA) **94** [1989 11.7m 12m⁶ 12h² 15.3m* 16m² 14g 1990 16m⁶ 16m* 16.2m² 16.2f*] rangy, quite attractive colt: progressive handicapper as 4-y-o: favourite, won at Newbury in July and Goodwood (£7,570 event) in August: well suited by test of stamina: acted on hard ground: blinkered once at 3 yrs: dead. *R. Akehurst.*

MAKEMEASTAR (IRE) 2 ch.f. (Feb 29) Horage 124–Sally St Clair (Sallust **61** p 134) [1990 6m⁵ a7g*] 12,000Y: third foal: sister to 3-y-o Potter's Dream and 6f and 7f winner Just Jennings: dam winner in Canada, is half-sister to Superlative, smart at up to 7f: won maiden at Southwell in July: looked likely to improve further, but not seen out again. *W. A. O'Gorman.*

MAKESHIFT 3 b.f. Night Shift (USA)–Fall To Pieces (USA) 101 (Forli (ARG)) **81** [1989 NR 1990 5f 7g a7g⁴ 7f² 7f* 8m* 8f* 7g] 25,000Y: smallish filly: eighth living foal: half-sister to useful 1989 sprinter Splintering (by Sharpo) and 3 minor 2-y-o winners, including Tchoupitoulas (by Grundy) who later won in USA: dam won over 7f and 1m: progressed well, winning handicaps at Doncaster, Edinburgh and Wolverhampton (coming from towards rear and edging markedly left) in the summer: off course 2 months before behind in £8,400 handicap final start: stays 1m: acts on firm going: trained debut by R. Smyth: wore tongue strap afterwards. *A. N. Lee.*

MALACANANG 6 b.m. Riboboy (USA) 124–Gold Spangle 97 (Klondyke Bill — 125) [1989 NR 1990 12m] workmanlike mare: tailed off in handicap in March, only outing on flat since 3 yrs. *J. P. Smith.*

MALENOIR (USA) 2 b.c. (Jan 28) Solford (USA) 127–Viewed (USA) (Alydar — (USA)) [1990 10s 10.2s] $8,000Y, resold 9,500 (privately) Y: first foal: dam never ran: soundly beaten in maiden (showed a very round action) at Nottingham and minor event (slowly away) at Doncaster in autumn. *M. Bell.*

MALIBASTA 4 b.f. Auction Ring (USA) 123–Basta 72 (Busted 134) [1989 8f² 8f² **83** 1990 9m 8m 8m² 8m⁵ 10g⁵ 8d⁶ 8g*] quite attractive filly: fair handicapper: favourite, won at Bath in October: best at 1m: acts on firm and dead going. *D. R. C. Elsworth.*

MALIBU MAGIC (IRE) 2 b.g. (Mar 5) Be My Native (USA) 122–Nishapours **82** Baby (Nishapour (FR) 125) [1990 6m⁵ 8.2d² 8d⁵] IR 7,000Y, 18,500 2-y-o: lengthy, unfurnished gelding: first foal: dam ran twice: easily best effort head second of 17, clear, to Paris of Troy in maiden at Haydock in September: will probably stay 1¼m. *J. M. P. Eustace.*

MALINDI BAY 3 gr.c. (Mar 6) Grey Desire 115–Malindi (Mansingh (USA) 120) **46** [1990 5m⁶ 6g 6g a6g 7g 6m⁵ 8.2g 6d] 4,000Y: compact colt: carries condition: third living foal: half-brother to 10.5f seller winner Lindi's Gold (by Sonnen Gold): dam never ran: modest plater: best effort on all-weather: probably doesn't stay 1m: blinkered final start. *B. J. McMath.*

MALLAU 4 b.c. Runnett 125–Brierley Lodge 67 (Lorenzaccio 130) [1989 6s 6s **48** 8d⁵ 6f 5.8h 6m² 6m 6f* 7f² 5.3h⁶ 7f* 7m⁵ 7m 1990 6f 8f 6m 6m 6g 7m 6g 7g a6g* a7g a6g a7g] good-topped colt: 25/1 and apprentice ridden, returned to form on first outing on all-weather when winning handicap at Lingfield in November: effective at 6f and easy 7f: acts on firm ground: blinkered once at 3 yrs: inconsistent. *L. J. Holt.*

MALLYAN 3 b.f. Miramar Reef 100§–Charlie's Sunshine 77 (Jimsun 121) [1989 8d 1990 a12g 10m 13.8f4] behind in varied events: sweating and on toes, hampered on turn in Catterick claimer second start. *D. T. Garraton.* —

MALMESBURY 3 ch.g. Burslem 123–Malmsey (Jukebox 120) [1989 6m 7g 7g4 8g 1990 7g 9f4 10g] workmanlike gelding: has a long stride: quite modest form at 2 yrs: well beaten facing stiff tasks in 1990 but shaped as if retaining ability in claimer final start, not at all knocked about: will stay 1¼m. *G. B. Balding.* —

MALSMAN 2 br.c. (Apr 24) Mansingh (USA) 120–Montana (Mossborough 126) [1990 5m 5.3f 7s] 3,700Y: leggy colt: seventh foal: half-brother to several winners, including 1½m winner Wisconsin (by Mummy's Game) and 1m winner Iowa (by So Blessed), both subsequently successful over hurdles: dam poor maiden on flat and over hurdles: soundly beaten in autumn maidens and minor event. *P. Butler.* —

MALTBY HYUNDAI (IRE) 2 b.c. (May 11) Tumble Wind (USA)–Beltich-bourne 73 (Targowice (USA) 130) [1990 7f] IR 5,000F, 2,000Y: strong, compact colt: brother to 1987 2-y-o 5f winner Michellor and half-brother to 2 other winners, one over hurdles: dam placed at up to 1¼m: carrying condition, took keen hold and weakened quickly over 1f out in maiden auction at Thirsk in August. *R. V. King.* —

MALTHOUSE MAESTRO (IRE) 2 b.c. (Apr 27) Kafu 120–Taotl (Yellow God 129) [1990 5m6 5m6] IR 6,400Y: good-topped colt: has scope: moderate mover: half-brother to useful Irish 1982 2-y-o 6f winner Certain Something (by Solinus): dam unraced: carrying condition, speed 3f in minor event at Windsor and maiden (carried head high) at Catterick: sold 1,500 gns Doncaster November Sales. *K. M. Brassey.* 43

MALUNAR 5 gr.g. Mummy's Pet 125–Tranquility Base 112 (Roan Rocket 128) [1989 6s 6d* 7s 6g4 5.8h 6m 1990 5g6 6g2 6m4 6g4 6m5 6g 6m4 6m6 7m4 6d4 6s4 6g2 6d 5s2 a6g3 a7g2] close-coupled gelding: modest handicapper: ran creditably (without winning) most starts as 5-y-o: stays 7f: acts on good to firm and soft going: blinkered 3 times: effective with or without visor: has sweated: best with strong handling: sold out of R. Shaw's stable 8,500 gns Newmarket Autumn Sales after thirteenth outing. *M. H. Tompkins.* 75

MALVERNICO (IRE) 2 b.c. (Mar 9) Nordico (USA)–Malvern Beauty 100 (Shirley Heights 130) [1990 5m* 5g* 6g2 5m* 6.3g* 7m2] IR 7,000F: second living 105

Shernazar EBF Curragh Stakes, the Curragh—
Malvernico gets up in the last stride from Downeaster Alexa (rails)

Mrs D. Mahony's "Malvernico"

foal: dam 10.5f winner, is granddaughter of 1000 Guineas second Photo Flash: useful Irish colt: successful in maiden at Leopardstown, minor event at Phoenix Park and Shernazar EBF Curragh Stakes and Dunmurry Stud EBF Anglesey Stakes at the Curragh: had very hard race when beaten a head, caught near line, by Heart of Darkness in GPA National Stakes at the Curragh on final start (September): will stay 1m. *J. S. Bolger, Ireland.*

MAMALAMA 2 ch.f. (Feb 24) Nishapour (FR) 125–Gauloise 93 (Welsh Pageant **50** 132) [1990 5f 6m³ 6m 6f³ 7f 7g 8m] 6,000F: leggy, angular filly: seventh foal: half-sister to middle-distance winner Persillant (by Persian Bold) and 2m winner Green's Collection (by High Top): dam winner twice at around 1m, is half-sister to smart 6f to 1m performer Gwent: plating-class maiden: ran moderately in apprentice seller final outing: should stay 1m. *L. J. Holt.*

MAMALUNA (USA) 4 ch.f. Roberto (USA) 131–Kadesh (USA) (Lucky Mel) **108** [1989 10f² 12m³ 10d² 10f* 10g⁴ 10g 1990 10s 10f⁴ 10m⁵] rangy filly: has a rather round action: smart as 3-y-o, making all in Vodafone Nassau Stakes at Goodwood: lightly raced and not quite so good in 1990, on last 2 outings fourth in Nassau Stakes and fifth in Sun Chariot Stakes at Newmarket, both won by Kartajana: stays 1½m: probably acts on any going: suited by forcing tactics. *G. Harwood.*

MANALAPAN 3 b.f. Superlative 118–Hsian (Shantung 132) [1989 NR 1990 7g* **71** d 7m 8m⁵ 8m⁶ 8g 8g 8.2v³] 2,800F, 17,500Y: workmanlike filly: third foal: half-sister to 4-y-o Princess Wu (by Sandhurst Prince): dam lightly-raced half-sister to smart 6f to 1m winner Bas Bleu and very useful middle-distance performer Primerello: 20/1, won maiden at Carlisle in May: clearly best subsequent effort when fifth in handicap at Ripon: stays 1m: acts on good to firm ground: looked difficult ride, and was blinkered then visored last 2 starts. *J. Etherington.*

MANAOLANA 2 b.f. (Feb 17) Castle Keep 121–Ladysave (Stanford 121§) [1990 **— p** 7d] big, heavy-bodied filly: second foal: half-sister to 3-y-o 2m winner Powersurge (by Electric): dam ran twice: backward and very green, weakened fi om 2f out in maiden at Ayr in September: will improve. *Denys Smith.*

MANCHESTERSKYTRAIN 11 b.g. Home Guard (USA) 129–Aswellas 93 (Le Levanstell 122) [1989 8h 6f 7f 1990 7.6m⁶ 9g 10.2f] workmanlike gelding: retains only a modicum of ability: stays 1m: acts on any going: blinkered once: sometimes sweats: often gives bit of trouble at stalls. *B. R. Millman.* —

MANDERLEY BOY 4 b.g. Absalom 128–Phlox 101 (Floriana 106) [1989 7s⁴ 7.5d 8d 6m 6m⁶ 7g⁶ 1990 a6g 10f] small, sparely-made gelding: no longer of much account. *W. T. Kemp.* —

MANDY'S LOVE 5 b.m. Tower Walk 130–Our Mandy (Mansingh (USA) 120) [1989 5f 1990 7f 5m⁶] lengthy, rather dipped-backed mare: winning plater as 3-y-o: little other form, running in better company: gambled on on reappearance: suited by 5f and a soft surface. *C. J. Hill.* —

MAN FROM ELDORADO (USA) 2 b.c. (Feb 21) Mr Prospector (USA)– Promising Girl (USA) (Youth (USA) 135) [1990 7g⁴ 7s²] IR 360,000Y: big, lengthy colt: has plenty of scope: second foal: half-brother to 3-y-o 7f (at 2 yrs) and 8.2f winner Star of The Future (by El Gran Senor): dam stakes-placed winner at up to around 1m in USA, is half-sister to very smart 6f to 1¼m performer Beau's Eagle: co-favourite, 2½ lengths second of 19, travelling strongly, drifting left then running on well, to Perpendicular in maiden at Doncaster in November: will stay 1m: sure to win a race. *G. Harwood.* **90**

MANGO MANILA 5 b.h. Martinmas 128–Trigamy 112 (Tribal Chief 125) [1989 8g 8m⁵ 7m* 8.2g 7m 8g 1990 7g* 6m 6m² 7m 8m] robust horse: bad mover: modest handicapper on his day: 33/1, won for third time at Newmarket in moderately-run event in May: effective at 6f and 7f: acts on good to firm and dead going: sometimes wears crossed noseband: inconsistent. *C. A. Horgan.* **75**

MANGROVE MIST (IRE) 2 b.f. (Apr 10) Nishapour (FR) 125–Antiguan Cove (Mill Reef (USA) 141) [1990 8g a8g a7g⁶] IR 3,200F, 8,500Y: first foal: dam never ran: poor form in maidens at Yarmouth and Lingfield. *Sir Mark Prescott.* **38**

MANHATTAN RIVER 4 ch.g. Gorytus (USA) 132–East River (FR) (Arctic Tern (USA) 126) [1989 8.2m² 8f³ a7g 1990 a7g³ a8g 7m* 6f 7f] compact gelding: 20/1, sweating and edgy, won 19-runner seller (no bid) at Catterick in March: ran poorly final outing: possibly best at 7f: acts on good to firm going: sold out of E. Weymes's stable 4,500 gns Doncaster January Sales after second start. *S. E. Kettlewell.* **60**

MANHUNT 4 b.f. Posse (USA) 130–Macarte (FR) (Gift Card (FR) 124) [1989 7s 7.6m⁶ 6f 6f³ a6g a7g 1990 a8g] sparely-made filly: poor maiden: probably stays 7f: form only on top-of-the-ground: inconsistent: sold 950 gns Ascot February Sales. *J. L. Dunlop.* —

MANJANIQ 6 b.g. Kings Lake (USA) 133–Ivory Home (FR) (Home Guard (USA) 129) [1989 12d⁵ 17.6f 12f 1990 a12g] attractive gelding: moderate mover: fair winner as 3-y-o: very lightly raced and little subsequent worthwhile form on flat: stays 13.3f: acts on heavy going: sold 1,050 gns Doncaster March Sales. *D. Chapman.* —

MANNICK (NZ) 3 b.c. Babaroom (USA)–Keesh (NZ) (Heir Presumptive (USA) 87) [1989 NR 1990 a11g 10m 10m] neat New Zealand-bred colt: no worthwhile form in autumn sellers: mulish leaving paddock and refused to race second start. *J. R. Jenkins.* — §

MANSE KEY GOLD 3 ch.f. Vaigly Great 127–Carafran (Stanford 121§) [1989 5d⁵ 5g² 6m³ 6f 7f⁴ 6m 6g⁵ 5g⁶ 6s* 1990 6f³ 6g³ 7g* 7.5g⁴ 7f 7g² 8g⁴ 7m 7g² 7m 7m 7d⁴ a8g] compact filly: quite modest handicapper: won at Carlisle in May: ran very well at Doncaster ninth outing: tailed off at Southwell on final one: ideally suited by 7f: best with give in the ground. *R. Earnshaw.* **65 ?**

MANSONNIEN (FR) 6 ch.h. Tip Moss (FR)–Association (FR) (Margouillat (FR) 133) [1989 10v³ 10.5s³ 9.2g⁴ 11d* 11f² 10d² 12g 1990 10g* 10f⁴ 10.5d 9.2g 10g 10g⁵ 10d⁵ 10g⁵] French horse: smart at his best: won Prix Exbury at Saint-Cloud in March: fair fourth to Creator in Prix d'Harcourt at Longchamp 2 weeks later: ran moderately after in pattern and listed company: stays 1½m: probably acts on any going. *N. Pelat, France.* **110**

MANTON MEMORIES 2 b.g. (Apr 2) Uncle Pokey 116–Carnation 64 (Runny-mede 123) [1990 6m⁶ 6g 7f³ 7f³ 8m] 7,800Y: compact gelding: moderate walker: fourth reported live foal: brother to 1988 2-y-o 6f winner Virginia's Bay: dam best at 5f: quite modest maiden: stays 7f. *C. Tinkler.* **66**

MANTRAKI 3 ch.c. Good Times (ITY)–Tota Tora (Home Guard (USA) 129) 76 [1989 7m³ 8.2g³ 1990 8f4 12m 9f² 10g 8f 8m* 9g] leggy, workmanlike colt: has a quick action: modest performer: made most and battled on well to win handicap at Goodwood in September: easily best other effort third start: should stay 1¼m: acts on firm going: on toes, took keen hold and hung right second outing: sold to join N. Tinkler 15,500 gns Newmarket Autumn Sales. *N. Tinkler.*

MANX PRINCESS 3 b.f. Roscoe Blake 120–Princess Scarlett (Prince Regent — (FR) 129) [1989 6g⁶ 6m 7g⁵ 1990 7g⁶ 6m 7m 10g 15.8d] leggy, sparely-made filly: poor maiden: should be suited by further than 7f: has got on edge. *Mrs J. R. Ramsden.*

MA PETITE CHOU 3 gr.f. Known Fact (USA) 135–Boule de Suif 88 (Major 52 Portion 129) [1989 6f 1990 8m⁴ 8g 8g 8f⁶ 10m] smallish, sturdy filly: plating-class maiden: staying-on fourth at Warwick, best effort: hung right and found little in claimer fourth start, showed nothing on final one: sold to join P. Hayward 1,550 gns Newmarket December Sales. *G. Wragg.*

MAPLE WALK 3 b.f. Tumble Wind (USA)–Littoral (Crash Course 128) [1989 — NR 1990 7m 6m 8f] 5,000Y: compact filly: fourth foal (previous 3 by Don): dam won over 1½m in Ireland and is half-sister to useful 5f to 7f winner Cooliney Prince, later successful in USA: showed little in minor events and maiden. *M. E. D. Francis.*

MARAAKIZ (USA) 2 ch.c. (Feb 13) Roberto (USA) 131–River of Stars (USA) 91 (Riverman (USA) 131) [1990 7m* 7f² 8.2g³ 7m³ 7v²] 64,000Y: strong colt: first foal: dam minor winner in USA from family of Beldale Flutter: fairly useful performer: won maiden at Sandown in July: ran well in minor events at Ascot and Chester final 2 starts: will stay 1¼m: seems to act on any going: sweating and edgy fourth start. *J. L. Dunlop.*

MARA ASKARI 2 b.c. (Feb 24) Night Shift (USA)–Madam Cody (Hot Spark 126) 80 [1990 7m² 8g⁴] good-bodied colt: third foal: brother to a winner in USA: dam second over 7f at 2 yrs in Ireland: shaped well when ½-length second of 5 to Alnaab in minor event at Goodwood in August: odds on, ran moderately in similar event at Wolverhampton nearly 6 weeks later. *G. Harwood.*

MARAATIB (IRE) 2 b.f. (May 15) Green Desert (USA) 127–Shurooq (USA) 94 92 (Affirmed (USA)) [1990 5f² 5m* 5f⁵ 6m³ 5m* 6d²] small, good-topped filly: has a quick action: second foal: half-sister to 3-y-o Hafhafah (by Shirley Heights), 1m winner at 2 yrs: dam 6f and 7f winner at 2 yrs stayed 1½m: quite useful performer: easy winner of maiden at Haydock in May and minor event at Bath in October: stays 6f: acts on good to firm ground and dead. *H. Thomson Jones.*

MARASOL 3 gr.f. Siberian Express (USA) 125–Macarte (FR) (Gift Card (FR) 65 § 124) [1989 5.8f² 6f² 5f² 8m* 7s² 8f a8g 1990 a8g⁴ a8g 8g⁶ 8f⁴ 7m⁶ 8m 8g⁴ 10g² 9m*] angular, sparely-made filly: moderate walker and mover: quite modest handicapper: evens, won claimer (claimed to join M. Pipe £12,001) at Wolverhampton in July: stays 1¼m: acts on any going: difficult ride and probably ungenuine. *J. L. Dunlop.*

MARBLE HILL (IRE) 2 b.c. (Apr 6) Mummy's Treasure 84–Thai Sabai — (Double Form 130) [1990 6m 6g 6g] 2,000 (privately) Y: close-coupled, good-quartered colt: has scope: second foal: brother to a winner in Hong Kong: dam Irish maiden: behind in minors at Warwick and Nottingham. *P. Burgoyne.*

MARCELLINA 8 ch.m. Welsh Pageant 132–Connarca (Connaught 130) [1989 — 12g⁶ 1990 16.5d⁴] strong, stocky mare: carries plenty of condition: poor maiden on flat: won twice over hurdles in 1989/90. *E. J. Alston.*

MARCH ABOVE 4 ch.g. Cut Above 130–Marchesana 77 (March Past 124) [1989 — 9m* 1990 9f 9f 10.1g 12f 17.1f⁶] angular ex-Irish gelding: fourth foal: dam won at up to 13.8f: won maiden at Tipperary in July, 1989: soundly beaten in varied events, including handicaps, as 4-y-o: has worn bandages: winning selling hurdler in November. *B. Stevens.*

MARCHAM (IRE) 2 b.c. (Mar 30) Sadler's Wells (USA) 132–Dazzling Light 116 110 p (Silly Season 127) [1990 7m* 8s³] 260,000F: half-brother to several winners, including fair 1988 2-y-o 5f winner Arc Lamp (by Caerleon) and useful 6f and 1¼m winner Lady Sophie (by Brigadier Gerard): dam, smart over 7f and 1m, is half-sister to Welsh Pageant: heavily-backed favourite, won maiden at Goodwood in September in good style by 3½ lengths from Amigos, travelling smoothly from start and running on strongly final furlong: much better form when 4 lengths third of 4 to Peter Davies in Racing Post Trophy at Doncaster following month, shaken up under 3f out, one pace from over 1f out: will stay at least 1¼m: sure to win more races. *B. W. Hills.*

Schweppes Golden Mile, Goodwood—
a fine piece of training as lightly-raced March Bird (nearest camera, bandaged)
is produced to win this valuable handicap; Milligan (rails) finishes second

MARCH BIRD 5 ch.g. Dalsaan 125–Late Swallow (My Swallow 134) [1989 NR 1990 9m 8m* 8m⁴ᵈⁱˢ 8f*] strong, lengthy gelding: moderate mover: fair handicapper: won £64,400 Schweppes Golden Mile at Goodwood by 1½ lengths from Milligan, hanging right after leading over 1f out: successful at Sandown earlier in summer: stays 1m well: acts on firm and dead going: bandaged off-hind second outing, in front last 2: sweating first and third (also on toes) starts. *J. Sutcliffe.* — **81**

MARCH GENERATION 4 b.c. Young Generation 129–Walk By 113 (Tower Walk 130) [1989 NR 1990 8g] half-brother to fair sprinter Scintillio (by Hot Spark) and a winner in Belgium: dam sprinting half-sister to smart fillies Smarten Up (dam of Cadeaux Genereux who's by Young Generation) and Solar: 33/1, never near to challenge in Edinburgh maiden in June. *J. P. Hudson.* — —

MARCHING PAST 2 br.c. (Mar 9) Daring March 116–Storm Crest 80 (Lord Gayle (USA) 124) [1990 6g³ 7f² 5m² 6g² 6d²] well-made colt: sixth foal: brother to very useful sprinter Ongoing Situation and a winner in Norway: dam won over 5f at 2 yrs and stayed 1½m: fair maiden: very good second in nursery at Haydock final start: may improve bit further back at 7f. *A. C. Stewart.* — **78**

MARCHING STAR 4 ch.f. Marching On 101–Elegant Star 86 (Star Moss 122) [1989 6v⁶ 7.5d 6m 7m 8f⁶ 8g 6f 7m 7g a6g⁶ a6g 1990 a8g 8m 8f⁵ 5m 7g⁵ 8g 12g 5g 7f² 7f 9g 7f 7d⁵ 6s] neat filly: unreliable plater: unruly in stalls and very slowly away in amateurs race tenth outing: probably stays 1m: acts on any going: used to wear blinkers or visor: bandaged behind last 4 starts: trained until after fifth outing by T. Fairhurst. *J. S. Haldane.* — **37 §**

MARCH PAST (USA) 2 b.c. (May 11) Far North (CAN) 120–Slow March 105 (Queen's Hussar 124) [1990 6h⁵ 6f² 5m 5m] $26,000F, 13,000Y: good-topped colt: moderate mover: seventh foal: half-brother to 3 winners, including 1986 2-y-o 6f winner Misk (by Miswaki) and 1½m winner Silent Journey (by Gregorian): dam won from 6f to 1¼m in Ireland and stakes placed in USA: form only when second of 5 in maiden at Thirsk in August. *J. Berry.* — **62**

MARCROFT 4 ch.f. Crofthall 110–Squires Girl (Spanish Gold 101) [1989 6g 7g³ 7m⁵ 6m 7s² 6m 6f⁶ 1990 8f 7f 7.6d⁴ 7g 7g 6m⁶ 7.6m³ 7m² 7f⁵ 7m* 8m⁴ 8m 7.6g⁵ 7m 7d 7f 7m 6s 7d³ 7d⁵ 7d] sparely-made, close-coupled filly: modest handicapper: won at Catterick in August: best at 7f to 1m: acts on any going: ran poorly when visored fifth outing: tends to carry head high: none too reliable. *R. M. Whitaker.* — **76**

MARCUS THORPE (USA) 2 ch.c. (Mar 24) Palace Music (USA) 129–Guilty Miss (USA) (Mr Redoy (USA)) [1990 8g² 10g³] 26,000Y: quite good-topped colt: has scope: has a quick action: first foal: dam minor winner in USA at around 5f: fairly useful form behind Commendable in maiden at York (green) in October and Matahif in listed race at Newmarket following month: will stay 1½m: likely to improve again, and is sure to win a race. *H. R. A. Cecil.* — **94 p**

MARDESSA 2 b.f. (Apr 28) Ardross 134–Marquessa d'Howfen 93 (Pitcairn 126) [1990 6s⁶ 7f² 7.5f⁵ 8g 7g 8d⁵] workmanlike filly: fourth foal: sister to 2 maidens, including poor stayer Quessard, and half-sister to 3-y-o Another Marquessa (by — **62**

555

Beldale Flutter): dam 2-y-o 7f winner: quite modest maiden: pulled hard final start: stays 1m: acts on firm and dead ground. *F. H. Lee.*

MARDIOR 2 b.f. (Mar 7) Martinmas 128–Diorina 91 (Manacle 123) [1990 5m 6g 7m 6g a6g] leggy filly: half-sister to 3-y-o 6f winner Bodamist (by Swing Easy), fair sprinter Cheri Berry (by Air Trooper) and a winning hurdler: dam best at 2 yrs, when 5.3f winner: bad maiden: tailed off at 7f. *W. G. R. Wightman.* **39**

MARDONIUS 4 b.c. Persian Bold 123–Dominica (GER) (Zank) [1989 10m* 10.5d³ 12.5m² 12g² 15m* 15.5g5 1990 15.5d² 15g*] French colt: successful at Longchamp in newcomers race and Ciga Prix de Lutece as 3-y-o and in September in listed event by 3 lengths at odds on in 1990: off course 4 months after running well there in Prix Vicomtesse Vigier (beaten ¾ length by Turgeon) on reappearance: suited by test of stamina: acts on good to firm and dead going: usually blinkered. *A. Fabre, France.* **112**

MARGS GIRL 3 b.f. Claude Monet (USA) 121–Aquarian Star (Cavo Doro 124) [1989 5f 5f² 6m 7m* 6m⁴ 7m³ 7m³ 7m³ 7m² 8.2s³ 8m⁶ 6g5 6g² 1990 6m5 6f 7g* 7g5 6g6 7g⁴ 7d³ 7g² 7.5f* 8h* 7.5g5 8g a8g* 7d 8v² 8d⁴ a8g4] leggy filly: poor mover: modest performer: won claimers at Carlisle in April and Beverley and Carlisle in July then handicap at Southwell in September: very good second in Ayr handicap fifteenth start: stays 1m well: acts on any going: has run creditably when on toes: suitable mount for 7-lb claimer: genuine and largely consistent. *T. Fairhurst.* **71**

MARGUB (USA) 5 b. or br.h. Topsider (USA)–Kissapotamus (USA) (Illustrious) [1989 6.5s5 8g5 8f 7f 1990 8f⁴ 10f³ 10.6s* 10.6s³ 10.6m*] big, strong, good sort: fair performer: won claimers at Haydock in June and August: stays 1¼m: acts on any going: sold 9,000 gns Newmarket Autumn Sales. *J. H. Baker.* **80**

MARIA CAPPUCCINI 2 ch.f. (Mar 19) Siberian Express (USA) 125–Mary Martin (Be My Guest (USA) 126) [1990 5m* 5g² 5f 5m] 15,500Y: smallish filly: good mover: second foal: half-sister to 3-y-o Pacific Gem (by Valiyar), 6f winner at 2 yrs: dam unraced half-sister to very smart sprinter Greenland Park (dam of Fitnah) and Red Sunset: won maiden at Newmarket in April: better effort staying-on 2 lengths second of 5 to On Tiptoes in minor event there: well beaten in pattern company after, bit backward final start, first for over 3 months: will stay 6f: trained first 3 outings by R. Boss. *I. A. Balding.* **70**

MARIA DONIA 2 ch.f. (May 13) Siberian Express (USA) 125–Nafla (FR) (Arctic Tern (USA) 126) [1990 5g5] small filly: second foal: half-sister to 3-y-o Urfan (by Valiyar): dam French 7f to 1¼m winner, is granddaughter of Park Hill winner Cursorial: around 8 lengths fifth of 12 in maiden at Kempton in April: joined I. Balding afterwards. *R. Boss.*

MARIA GRAZIA 2 ch.f. (Apr 23) Night Shift (USA)–Grace Note 104 (Parthia 132) [1990 5m* 5f³ 5m⁶ 5m5 5g 7.5v] 4,100Y: small, sturdy filly: good walker: half-sister to several winners here and abroad, including fairly useful 7f winner Coda (by Reform): dam seemed to stay 7f: won maiden auction at Beverley in March: joined A. Renzoni in Italy after third outing. *R. Boss.* **58**

MARIAN EVANS 3 b.f. Dominion 123–Kindjal 84 (Kris 135) [1989 6g 1990 7m⁴ 7f³ 6g a6g] sturdy filly: quite modest maiden: will be suited by return to further: sold 1,150 gns Ascot November Sales. *P. W. Harris.* **—**

MARIANO 5 b.g. Aragon 118–Macarte (FR) (Gift Card (FR) 124) [1989 6m 6f 6f 1990 a7g a7g] leggy, close-coupled gelding: modest winner as 3-y-o: well beaten since in handicaps and claimer: suited by 6f to 7f: acts on firm and dead going: never going well in blinkers (including final start when also wearing crossed noseband): bandaged at 5 yrs: difficult ride, who finds little in front. *T. Thomson Jones.* **—**

MARIENSKI (USA) 3 b.c. Nureyev (USA) 131–Highclere 129 (Queen's Hussar 124) [1989 6m³ 7m* 8m⁶ 1990 10m5 7m³ 8.2f³ 7.2s³ 7f6] rangy, good sort: has a fluent action: useful performer: got poor run when good third in listed race at Haydock fourth start: looked very well but ran moderately in Jersey Stakes at Royal Ascot 11 days later: best form here at up to 1m: acts on any going: blinkered first and last 2 outings: edgy, took keen hold and tended to hang on reappearance: won 9f allowance race at Saratoga in August on second start for N. Howard in USA. *Major W. R. Hern.* **103**

MARIE SWIFT 5 b.m. Main Reef 126–Sarus 76 (Amber Rama (USA) 133) [1989 NR 1990 10.2f 11s 8f 8f 10g] lengthy, angular mare: carries plenty of condition: fourth foal: half-sister to 2 poor animals: little sign of ability. *R. Dickin.* **—**

MARIE ZEPHYR 6 b.m. Treboro (USA) 112–Thimothea (FR) 43 (Timmy My Boy 125) [1989 NR 1990 16d6] good-bodied mare: carries plenty of condition: **—**

moderate mover: modest maiden at best: has deteriorated; stays 13f: acts on any going. *C. W. C. Elsey.*

MARINE DIVER 4 b.g. Pas de Seul 133–Marine Life (Deep Diver 134) [1989 97 d 10d³ 10.4f² 12m 10f² 10g 1990 10f² 10g 11m⁶ 10h² 9g² 10g² 10m] quite attractive gelding: carries condition: good walker: has a slightly round action: fairly useful on his day: probably stays 1½m: acts on firm and dead going: doesn't often go through with his effort: not one to rely on. *P. F. I. Cole.*

MARINERS LAW 7 b.g. Julio Mariner 127–Gallic Law 91 (Galivanter 131) [1989 — NR 1990 12h] good-topped, close-coupled gelding: well beaten in modest company: blinkered once at 5 yrs. *Miss G. M. Rees.*

MARINERS MIRROR 3 b.f. Julio Mariner 127–Sujono 58 (Grey Mirage 128) — [1989 NR 1990 9g⁴ 12.5m] leggy, workmanlike filly: first reported living foal: dam, second over 9f on flat, won 2 juvenile hurdles: no form in minor event and maiden (sweating, on toes, mounted on track and took good hold) at Wolverhampton: winning hurdler. *M. Scudamore.*

MARINE SOCIETY 2 b.c. (Feb 2) Petoski 135–Miranda Julia 73 (Julio Mariner 81 p 127) [1990 7g⁶ 8g 8m⁵ 7m] 18,000F, 14,500Y: well-made colt: grand walker: first foal: dam 7f winner: best effort fifth of 14, keeping on well from mid-division, in maiden at Newmarket: held up and never able to challenge in nursery there later in October: likely to do better over 1¼m or more. *D. R. C. Elsworth.*

MARIOLINO 3 b.c. Buzzards Bay 128§–Banking Coyne 76 (Deep Diver 134) — [1989 5v⁴ 5s⁴ 5s⁵ 7m⁶ a7g 1990 8m 7m 5m 6m 8d 10d] workmanlike colt: plating-class maiden at best: blinkered third to fifth starts: has sweated. *P. J. Arthur.*

MARISTOW MAIDEN 3 b.f. Night Shift (USA)–Rapidus (Sharpen Up 127) — [1989 NR 1990 9m 9f 9m 7m] robust filly: sixth foal: half-sister to 1984 2-y-o 5f winner Rapid Glory (by Hittite Glory), 1¼m seller winner Beau Echarpe (by Relkino) and a winner in Belgium: dam ran 3 times: little sign of ability, including in seller: trained first 2 starts by W. Jarvis. *P. J. Feilden.*

MARJONS BOY 3 ch.c. Enchantment 115–Nevilles Cross (USA) 67 (Nodouble 66 (USA)) [1989 7m⁶ 7m 8.2f³ 8f² 8g⁴ 1990 a10g* a10g² 12f⁴ 13.1h 12m 11.5g⁶ 10g 10m⁶ 10m² 10d 8m⁴ 8g*] big, angular colt: moderate mover: quite modest performer: won maiden at Lingfield (odds on) in February and handicap (ridden by 7-lb claimer, return to form) at Salisbury in October: stays 1¼m: acts on firm going: blinkered last 5 starts. *M. Bell.*

MARJORIE PETONG 2 gr.f. (Feb 13) Petong 126–Speed The Plough (Grundy — § 137) [1990 5g 6m 6g 5m] 4,000F: close-coupled, workmanlike filly: fifth foal: half-sister to 1m and 9f winner Mottram's Gold (by Good Times): dam lightly raced and no sign of ability: soundly beaten in maidens and minor events: visored, sweating and looked reluctant to race final outing: usually gives trouble stalls: one to avoid. *J. J. Bridger.*

MARJORIE WOOD (IRE) 2 ch.f. (Apr 18) Dreams To Reality (USA) 113– 33 Beechwood (USA) (Blushing Groom (FR) 131) [1990 5m⁴ 5g 6d 8m 7d] 7,200Y: neat filly: has round action: first foal: dam French 10.8f winner: poor form, including in seller: seems to stay 1m. *S. G. Norton.*

MARJU (IRE) 2 br.c. (Mar 12) Last Tycoon 131–Flame of Tara 124 (Artaius 99 P (USA) 129) [1990 7m*]
Impressive performances, whether on the gallops or on the racecourse, invariably excite the imagination, but it takes an unusually fertile mind to endorse the impressive York winner Marju's position at the head of the betting for the Two Thousand Guineas. Marju, who was side-lined by a viral infection after winning his only race, the Avondale New Zealand Graduation Stakes over seven furlongs in September, and then wasn't risked in any of the established top two-year-old races in the autumn, is a very well-bred colt— he's a half-brother to Salsabil—of immense potential and almost certainly a great deal better than we are able to rate him. All the same, to have him sharing Guineas favouritism with the top French colt Hector Protector, for example, who's already shown he's not far short of the required standard with victories in three Group 1 events, is premature, to say the least.
We should probably have been in a better position to judge Marju had he made his debut at York in June, as was the original intention, instead of in September; he developed a slight swelling on his leg shortly before his intended debut and had to be put on the easy list for a month. His trainer

Avondale New Zealand Stakes, York —
Salsabil's half-brother Marju makes a big impression

wanted to introduce Marju over six furlongs on his return from injury if the opportunity allowed, but eventually he was re-routed to York where he started odds on in an eleven-runner field, with only Road To The Isle, a five-length second in a Newmarket maiden on his previous start, seriously backed to beat him. Marju, a sturdy, lengthy colt, just in need of the race, won with the minimum of fuss, pulling double over his rivals from early in the straight, joining Road To The Isle on the bridle approaching the final furlong and then, having been chased along for a stride or two with hands and heels, drawing right away to win by eight (it was officially six) lengths and three. One couldn't help but be impressed with the acceleration Marju showed in pulling clear quickly, his superiority unmistakably evident throughout the race, and there's little doubt that he's an exciting prospect who's likely to win races at a much higher level. But without dampening enthusiasm too much it should be said that nothing Marju achieved at York couldn't have been accomplished by any of the top fifty two-year-olds—fifth-placed Tartan Tinker, for example, is a thoroughly modest northern maiden, on the verge of selling class—and with plenty still to find Marju is not, on what's been seen of him so far, a worthy favourite for the Guineas.

		Try My Best	Northern Dancer
	Last Tycoon	(b 1975)	Sex Appeal
	(b 1983)	Mill Princess	Mill Reef
Marju (IRE)		(b 1977)	Irish Lass II
(br.c. Mar 12, 1988)		Artaius	Round Table
	Flame of Tara	(b 1974)	Stylish Pattern
	(b 1980)	Welsh Flame	Welsh Pageant
		(b 1973)	Electric Flash

Marju, a 440,000-guinea buy at the Irish National Yearling Sale, is from the initial crop of the versatile Last Tycoon, in 1986 the best horse over five furlongs in Europe and winner by a neck from Palace Music of the Breeders' Cup Mile. The latter tested Last Tycoon's stamina fully but it's on the cards that he'll get plenty of horses who stay further than he did—his dam Mill Princess won over a mile and a quarter in France, and is related to the Irish Derby winner Irish Ball as well as the better-known middle-distance trio of

Assert, Bikala and Eurobird—and Marju, for one, seems likely to stay at least a mile and a quarter. Salsabil, and her full sister Nearctic Flame (by Sadler's Wells), were at their best over middle distances and their dam, Flame of Tara, won at a mile and a half and wasn't beaten far over a mile and three quarters. If Marju should win the Two Thousand Guineas his dam Flame of Tara will become the fourth mare this century to foal a winner of both Newmarket classics following Doris (dam of Sunstar and Princess Dorrie), Donnetta (Diadem and Diophon) and Crepuscule (Honeylight and Crepello). *J. L. Dunlop.*

MARK AIZLEWOOD 5 b.h. Nicholas Bill 125–Lunar Queen 96 (Queen's 56 Hussar 124) [1989 12f 12g 12m⁵ 11f⁴ 11m⁵ 10m⁴ 12.3m 11s⁶ 11s² 1990 12f² 13s⁵ 12.4f 11f] good-topped horse: turns fore feet in: poor mover: plating-class handicapper: stays 1½m: has form on firm going, but ideally suited by an easy surface nowadays: sometimes visored: a difficult ride, and is none too genuine. *R. M. Whitaker.*

MARK-EDEN 7 b.g. On Your Mark 125–Dainty Eden 53 (Orbit 106) [1989 NR 31 1990 8.2s³ 8v] leggy, angular gelding: poor form: stayed 1m: acted on soft going: wore bandages: dead. *G. M. Moore.*

MARKOFDISTINCTION 4 b. or br.c. Known Fact (USA) 135–Ghislaine 130 (USA) 71 (Icecapade (USA)) [1989 8m⁴ 7.6h* 8f³ 7g² 7g³ 1990 8m* 8m⁴ 8m* 9.5f⁴ 8m* 8g]
Markofdistinction had looked a rattling good miler in the making as early as his second outing when he finished within two lengths of Nashwan in the Two Thousand Guineas without the benefit of a previous run that season. A number of set-backs restricted him to just four more races and prevented him from confirming that impression as a three-year-old, but he more than made up for lost time in the latest season. He proved unbeatable in Britain granted the right set of conditions and in the Queen Elizabeth II Stakes at Ascot in September, more than sixteen months after the Guineas, gave a performance no other horse was able to match all year over a mile in Europe. As time went by, it became evident that to show to best advantage Markofdistinction needed a strongly-run race, waiting with and the ground to be on the firm side. He had the first and last prerequisites in the Queen Elizabeth, and his jockey Dettori saw to it that the tactics were right. Yet Markofdistinction still faced a formidable task, up against just about as strong a field as the miling brigade could muster: the first three in the Sussex Stakes—Distant Relative, Green Line Express and Shavian—were all in the line-up, as were Guineas winners Linamix, Tirol and Candy Glen, plus Citidancer and Croupier. Brought back in distance after a below-par effort behind Steinlen in the Grade 2 Caesars

Queen Anne Stakes, Ascot—
the meeting opens with a neck win for Markofdistinction from Mirror Black

Queen Elizabeth II Stakes, Ascot—Markofdistinction at his best,
as he and Distant Relative come clear of a good field

International Handicap at Monmouth Park over nine and a half furlongs (the furthest he attempted), Markofdistinction was dropped out in the rear as Shavian set as furious a pace as he had in the Sussex Stakes. Rounding the home turn Shavian led by a couple of lengths from Green Line Express with Markofdistinction still travelling comfortably in seventh, ahead of Linamix, Distant Relative and Croupier. When most of those who'd been close up from the start found it impossible to sustain the pace any longer and capitulated early in the home straight, Markofdistinction, between horses, and Distant Relative, on the outside, were produced to challenge, and throughout the final furlong and a half were engaged in a tremendous duel with riders and horses giving their all. Markofdistinction, who'd accelerated impressively, drifted to his right onto the rail when in front but marginally held the upper hand inside the last furlong and eventually got the better of Distant Relative by a length. The two drew eight lengths clear of Green Line Express, who comfortably beat off the other early pace-setters, and a further five in front of rank-outsider Croupier, who stayed on late through tired horses. Markofdistinction's timefigure of 1.30 fast, the equivalent of a timerating of 133, was the best recorded over the distance in 1990 and confirmed his run as one right out of the top drawer.

When Distant Relative was pulled out because of injury, Markofdistinction was left as the sole British representative in the Breeders' Cup Mile at Belmont Park. Although unable to reproduce his Ascot form he was far from disgraced, beaten only around two and a half lengths in seventh behind Royal Academy after flattering briefly in the home straight. The ground wasn't so fast as connections hoped for—they'd attributed his one defeat on this side of the Atlantic in the year, in the Juddmonte Lockinge Stakes at Newbury in May, to heavily-watered ground. In a somewhat muddling affair at Newbury, he'd found little after looking the certain winner at the distance. Markofdistinction turned the Lockinge Stakes form on its head in the Queen Anne Stakes at Royal Ascot. He'd already met six of his eight opponents at least once in the spring, four of them in the Trusthouse Forte Mile at Sandown on his reappearance, when he'd accounted for Citidancer impressively by two

Mr Gerald Leigh's "Markofdistinction"

lengths, and four of them in the Lockinge. Last after three furlongs in a strongly-run Queen Anne, Markofdistinction moved up smoothly to track the leaders two furlongs out and having waited for a gap to appear he burst into the lead on the rail just inside the final furlong, and kept on strongly, despite carrying his head awkwardly to one side, to thwart the persistent challenge of Mirror Black by a neck. The pace resulted in the field finishing well strung out, with the best part of a furlong covering the nine runners. The Lockinge winner Safawan and third Monsagem were among those down the field, while the Lockinge runner-up Distant Relative was beaten over five lengths in third.

Markofdistinction (b. or br.c. 1986)	Known Fact (USA) (b 1977)	In Reality (b 1964)	Intentionally
			My Dear Girl
		Tamerett (b or br 1962)	Tim Tam
			Mixed Marriage
	Ghislaine (USA) (b 1981)	Icecapade (gr 1969)	Nearctic
			Shenanigans
		Cambretta (b or br 1975)	Roberto
			Cambrienne

Markofdistinction's victory in the Queen Elizabeth II Stakes came ten years after that of his sire in the same race and two after that of another of Known Fact's sons, Warning. Markofdistinction's dam Ghislaine ran twice for Harwood late as a three-year-old in 1984, winning a mile-and-a-quarter maiden at Sandown by seven lengths before disappointing when second favourite for the Princess Royal Stakes at Ascot. Ghislaine's second foal, the three-year-old Shirley Heights filly Ahead, did rather better in the Princess Royal, finishing third to Narwala, having previously romped home in a minor event at Salisbury and made much of the running when fifth to Salsabil in the

Oaks. Ghislaine, who has since produced two more fillies by Shirley Heights, is a half-sister to four winners, all at least useful, including the Prix du Chemin de Fer du Nord winner Pluralisme and the middle-distance filly Singletta. The last-named was being carried by Cambretta, an Irish nine-furlong winner and a half-sister to Critique, when Cambretta was sold by Markofdistinction's owner to Sheikh Mohammed for 1,000,000 dollars at the Keeneland November Sale in 1982. The rangy, short-actioned Markofdistinction confounded the theory that moderate movers are best with some give in the ground—he showed his best form on top-of-the-ground. He never had any difficulty going the pace in his races and possessed a top-class turn of foot. He has joined the ever-increasing band of horses sold to stand at stud in Japan. *L. M. Cumani.*

MARLEE LOCH   2 b.f. (Apr 20) Rolfe (USA) 77–Cadenette 76 (Brigadier Gerard   —
144) [1990 5m⁶] first foal: dam suited by 1¼m: over 10 lengths sixth of 8 in maiden at
Ayr in July. *Denys Smith.*

MARLIN DANCER   5 b.g. Niniski (USA) 125–Mullet 75 (Star Appeal 133) [1989   43
NR 1990 11.7g 10.8f⁶ 16m⁴] workmanlike, angular gelding: has a round action: poor
maiden: stays 2m. *J. D. J. Davies.*

MARLINGFORD   3 ch.g. Be My Guest (USA) 126–Inchmarlo (USA) (Nashua)   —
[1989 7f⁶ 1990 13.6m] good-topped gelding: well beaten in maidens at Leicester and
Redcar: sold 4,500 gns Newmarket Autumn Sales: winning hurdler for Mrs J.
Jordan. *G. Harwood.*

MARQUETRY (USA)   3 ch.c. Conquistador Cielo (USA)–Regent's Walk (USA)   110
(Vice Regent (CAN)) [1989 7m* 7g² 1990 10m² 10.1g⁵ 12f⁵ 9f⁶] big, strong colt:
carries condition: has an easy, fluent action: useful performer: made the running
when beaten short head by Starstreak in £9,100 event at Ascot in May: off course 4
months then below form in Windsor minor event but ran well when in mid-division
for Grade 1 events at Santa Anita and Hollywood Park: probably stays 1½m. *G.
Harwood.*

MARSDALE   5 b.m. Royal Palace 131–Jamuna (Canisbay 120) [1989 NR 1990   —
8h 11.7f] rather angular mare: half-sister to 1978 2-y-o 5f and 6f winner Royal
Connection (by Royalty): dam placed over 1m in France: soon tailed off in minor
event and claimer. *M. P. Muggeridge.*

MARSH HARRIER (USA)   9 b.g. Raise A Cup (USA)–Belle de Jour (USA) 74   —
(Speak John) [1989 11.7m 11.7g 10g² 10f⁴ 12m⁴ 10f 1990 a10g a13g] big, strong, rangy
gelding: below form in handicaps since finishing second in claimer in August, 1989:
stays 1¼m: suited by a sound surface: ran creditably when blinkered and sweating:
best with strong handling: has worn a tongue strap. *A. Moore.*

MARSH'S LAW   3 br.g. Kala Shikari 125–My Music 68 (Sole Mio (USA)) [1989   55
5m 7m 7m⁵ 6m 6s⁵ 1990 6m a8g⁵ a7g a11g⁶ 7m 10.2s⁵ 10g³ 8d²] sturdy gelding: fair
plater at best: easily best effort when third in claimer at Newmarket in November:
gambled-on favourite in handicap at Doncaster week later: better at 1¼m than
shorter: best effort on good ground: often bandaged. *J. Wharton.*

MARSH WARBLER   2 b.g. (Jun 1) Wattlefield 117–Be Lyrical 95 (Song 132)   —
[1990 7m 7m] lengthy, good-bodied gelding: good walker: first foal: dam sprinter,
best at 2 yrs: behind in maidens at Newmarket (bandaged behind) and Yarmouth. *G.
A. Pritchard-Gordon.*

MARTINA   2 b.f. (May 22) Tina's Pet 121–Tin Tessa 87 (Martinmas 128) [1990   —
a7g a7g⁶] sixth foal: half-sister to 7f winner Actress (by Known Fact) and 1986 2-y-o
5f winner Tiszta Sharok (by Song): dam best at 2 yrs, successful over 5.8f: beaten at
least 13 lengths in late-year maidens at Southwell. *J. Wharton.*

MARTINI EXECUTIVE   2 b.c. (May 13) King of Spain 121–Wigeon 80 (Divine   76
Gift 127) [1990 a6g* 6f³ 7f⁵ 6m* 6m² 7.3g⁶] 8,200Y: lengthy, workmanlike colt:
eighth foal: half-brother to 6f winner Premier Lad (by Tower Walk) and 5f to 1¼m
winner Ma Pierrette (by Cawston's Clown): dam won at up to 1¼m: modest
performer: won seller (bought in 8,000 gns) at Southwell in July and nursery at
Ripon in August: stays 7f: possibly unsuited by very firm ground: pulled hard and
didn't handle bend at Thirsk third outing. *W. J. Pearce.*

MARTINI'S COURIER   3 br.g. Lucky Wednesday 124–Be My Sweet 78   52
(Galivanter 131) [1989 5d 6m⁶ 5m 7m³ 6g⁵ 6s³ a6g² 1990 7.5f⁵ 6v a7g 10.2m 8m⁴
7.5f 8f⁴ 10m] leggy gelding: turns off-fore in: fair plater: stays 1m: acts on firm
ground: hung right and carried head awkwardly when blinkered: takes keen hold:
has sweated and got on edge: sometimes wears crossed noseband: trained until

after fifth start by W. Pearce: sold 1,250 gns Doncaster September Sales: somewhat unsatisfactory. *Ronald Thompson.*

MARTIN-LAVELL POST 3 b.f. Tina's Pet 121–Stradey Park 103 (Murrayfield 119) [1989 5m⁵ 5m* 1990 5s a5g⁴ a5g³ a6g 6h⁴ 6f³ 6m⁴ 6f 6g] workmanlike filly: plating-class handicapper: stays 6f: acts on firm going: wore eyeshield sixth (reared stalls) to eighth starts, running well first 2 of them. *Sir Mark Prescott.*   **52**

MARTINOSKY 4 b.g. Martinmas 128–Bewitched 63 (African Sky 124) [1989 6s⁵ 8s 5s³ 6f² 6m* 6m 6h² 8m 8f 7m⁶ 6f 6m 1990 6m 6f⁴ 6f* 5f² 6m 8h⁶ 6m³ 6g⁶ 6m] big gelding: good walker: quite modest handicapper: led close home when winning at Brighton in July: best at 6f or stiff 5f: acts on any going: usually blinkered: has run poorly for apprentice. *W. G. R. Wightman.*   **62**

MARTINSTAR 3 b.f. Norwick (USA) 120–Martin Place (Martinmas 128) [1989 6g 6g a6g 1990 7m³ 8f⁵ 8f⁵ 8h 7g] leggy, sparely-made filly: poor handicapper: should be better suited by 1¼m: acts on firm going: sweating second start, edgy (ran poorly) final one: sold to join Mrs A. Knight 2,100 gns Ascot September Sales. *M. J. Fetherston-Godley.*   **35**

MARWAD (IRE) 2 b.c. (Apr 14) Runnett 125–Splendid Chance (Random Shot 116) [1990 6m] 76,000Y: quite attractive, unfurnished colt: brother to good 1985 2-y-o 5f and 6f Luqman, closely related to a winner in Sweden and half-brother to French 1¼m winner Splendid Day (by Day Is Done): dam stoutly-bred Irish 1¼m winner stayed 1¾m: green, 14 lengths eighth of 14, soon pushed along and never dangerous, in maiden at Newmarket in November: moved fluently down: sold 2,000 gns Doncaster November Sales. *A. A. Scott.*   —

MARWELL BIANCA 2 b.f. (Mar 30) Carwhite 127–Lily of France 81 (Monsanto (FR) 121) [1990 5g 5f⁶ 5.3h⁴ 5.8h² 5m⁶ 6d a5g³ a7g² a7g] neat filly: second foal: dam sprinter: plating-class maiden: stays 7f. *W. G. R. Wightman.*   **58**

MARY FROM DUNLOW 2 ch.f. (Apr 24) Nicholas Bill 125–Abrasive 53 (Absalom 128) [1990 a5g² 5.1m* 5d² 5f 5.3h* 5f 5m] 5,800Y: plain filly: second foal: dam stayed 6f, ran only at 2 yrs: poor performer: bought in 4,400 gns then 3,500 gns when winning sellers at Yarmouth in June and Brighton in August: will be better suited by 6f: acts on hard and dead ground: inconsistent. *J. Berry.*   **49**

MARYLAND WILLIE 3 b.c. Master Willie 129–Maryland Cookie (USA) 101 (Bold Hour) [1989 7g⁶ 1990 10f³ 12f* 12d² 12g⁶ 14.8m⁴] angular, workmanlike colt: fairly useful performer: won maiden at Salisbury in May: good second at Epsom, better effort in handicaps: sweating, always behind in July listed race at Newmarket final outing: stays 1½m: acts on firm and dead going: bandaged at 3 yrs. *D. R. C. Elsworth.*   **89**

MARYNETTA (IRE) 2 b.f. (Mar 24) Runnett 125–Mary Mullen 88 (Lorenzaccio 130) [1990 5m³ 5m² 5f² 5.3h* 5.8h⁴] 7,200F, 7,400Y: leggy, quite good-topped filly: half-sister to 4 winners here and abroad, including 1981 2-y-o 6f winner Lucayan Lady (by Swing Easy): dam 2-y-o 5f winner: quite modest performer: won maiden at Brighton in August, making all: stays 6f: consistent: sold 7,800 gns Newmarket Autumn Sales. *K. M. Brassey.*   **60**

MASAI MARA (USA) 2 ch.c. (Feb 19) Mogambo (USA)–Forever Command (USA) (Top Command (USA)) [1990 8m] well-grown colt: first reported foal: dam won at up to 11f, including in stakes: sire best at around 1m: green, around 16 lengths eighth of 11, never able to challenge, in minor event at Newmarket in November: sure to do better. *L. M. Cumani.*   — p

MASAKEN 3 ch.f. (Mar 8) Doulab (USA) 115–Amalee 57 (Troy 137) [1990 0m 7m 6g³] workmanlike filly: third foal: half-sister to 3-y-o Shahriza (by Persian Bold) and 1988 2-y-o 6f winner Musil (by Mummy's Pet): dam maiden stayed 14.6f, may have been temperamental: quite modest form in maidens: better suited by 7f than 6f, and will stay 1m. *B. Hanbury.*   **70**

MASCALLS LADY 5 b.m. Nicholas Bill 125–Whisper Gently 91 (Pitskelly 122) [1989 NR 1990 a10g] rather plain, leggy mare: plater: form only when winning at Brighton in May, 1988: stays 1m: sometimes pulls hard. *W. G. Turner.*   —

MASELLA 3 ch.f. Aragon 118–Winter Resort (Miami Springs 121) [1989 5m⁴ 5f⁶ 6g³ 7f a8g⁵ 1990 a7g 6m³ 6g* 6m 7g 7d a6g] leggy, close-coupled filly: fair plater: clearly best effort when gamely making all in apprentice non-selling handicap at Yarmouth in July: stays 6f. *J. W. Hills.*   **50**

MASHHOR JOHN 2 b. or br.c. (May 6) Mashhor Dancer (USA)–Dastina 80 (Derring-Do 131) [1990 7m⁶ 7f⁶ 8.5m³ 7f² 8m⁵ 7d⁴ 8.2s] 7,000F, 32,000Y: sturdy colt: good walker: half-brother to 4 winners here and abroad: dam second over 7f at   **69**

2 yrs, is sister to smart 7f performer Tudor Mill: quite modest maiden: stays 8.5f: best form on firm ground: blinkered last 3 starts: carried head high third start. *D. Morley.*

MASILIC 2 ro.f. (Feb 22) Grey Desire 115–Pendle's Secret 73 (Le Johnstan 123) [1990 5f 6m 7d] leggy, narrow filly: fifth reported foal: half-sister to 1986 2-y-o 8.2f winner Rivers Secret (by Young Man): dam 1¼m winner: well beaten, including in a seller: blinkered final start: trained on debut by D. Smith. *D. Yeoman.* —

MASKED BALL 10 b.h. Thatch (USA) 136–Miss Mahal (Taj Dewan 128) [1989 12.3s⁶ 12d² 12m³ 12m⁴ 12g⁴ 12m³ 12m³ 11s 12ga 12g⁴ 1990 a11g³ a11g* a11g² a12g³ 10.2f* 10.2m³ 10.6f² 12f* 12m² 10.6s² 10.6s* 12f* 10m⁶ 10.6g] lengthy, good-topped horse: fair performer: successful in claimers at Southwell in January and Haydock in July and handicaps at Doncaster in March and July (both apprentices) and Haydock in May: ran poorly final outing: best at 1¼m to 1½m: acts on any going: wears bandages: excellent mount for apprentice: held up: splendidly tough and consistent: a grand old servant. *P. Calver.* **79**

MASKOONA 5 b.m. Electric 126–Hound Song 84 (Jukebox 120) [1989 NR 1990 a12g a14g] of little account: blinkered final outing. *D. W. Chapman.* —

MASNUN (USA) 5 gr.g. Nureyev (USA) 131–Careless Kitten (USA) (Caro 133) [1989 6d⁴ 6s 5s 6f⁶ 6f* 6f² 6f⁶ 6m 6f 6h² 6m* 6v⁵ 1990 5g 6f⁶ 6m 6d 6m⁵ 7m 6m⁴ 6m³ 6m* 6m 6g⁶ 6s⁶] strong, sturdy gelding: quite useful handicapper: won £15,800 event at York in September, quickening well to lead close home: suited by 6f: seems to act on any going, but goes particularly well on top-of-the-ground: often on toes: has hung right. *R. J. O'Sullivan.* **95**

MASROUG 3 b.g. Dunbeath (USA) 127–Fleur Rouge 71 (Pharly (FR) 130) [1989 NR 1990 a8g² a10g a8g] 2,700 2-y-o: lanky gelding: first foal: dam 2-y-o 6f winner out of William Hill Gold Cup winner Boswellia: easily best effort in maidens on debut: gelded after second start then looked thoroughly temperamental on return (wearing tongue strap, sweating) 4½ months later. *Mrs L. Piggott.* **52** §

MASSLAMA (FR) 2 ch.f. (Feb 2) No Pass No Sale 120–Marmana (USA) (Blushing Groom (FR) 131) [1990 8g* 8g*] third foal: half-sister to winners in France at 9f to 1½m by The Wonder and Vayrann: dam French middle-distance maiden: successful in 15-runner newcomers race at Saint-Cloud in September and 8-runner Prix des Reservoirs (by a neck from After The Sun) at Longchamp in October: will stay 1¼m: useful. *A. de Royer-Dupre, France.* **111**

MASTERCLASS (USA) 2 ch.c. (Apr 16) The Minstrel (CAN) 135–Monroe (USA) 102 (Sir Ivor (USA) 135) [1990 8m* 8g² 7s⁴] strong, compact, attractive French colt: good walker: seventh foal: closely related to 3 winners, including French 3-y-o 5f winner Victoriana (by Storm Bird) and quite useful 1988 2-y-o 6f winner Didicoy (by Danzig), and half-brother to 2 winners, including 1m to 10.4f winner Esquire (by High Line): dam Irish sprinting sister to Malinowski and good 2-y-o Gielgud and half-sister to dam of Try My Best and El Gran Senor: won maiden at Longchamp in September in good style by ½ length from Exit To Nowhere: 2½ **116**

Prix des Aigles, Longchamp—
newcomer Masterclass impresses in appearance and performance;
he buckles down to beat Exit To Nowhere and Balleroy

lengths second of 5, tending to wander, to Hector Protector In Ciga Grand Criterium at same course following month: odds on, possibly unsuited by ground when modest fourth of 9 to Ganges in Criterium de Maisons-Laffitte later in October: will stay 1¼m: smart. *A. Fabre, France.*

MASTER DANCER 3 b.g. Mashhor Dancer (USA)–Silent Dancer 76 (Quiet Fling (USA) 124) [1989 8f³ 9g⁶ 1990 12d 14f 15.8d] leggy gelding: has a round action: quite modest form at 2 yrs, none in maiden auction race and handicaps in 1990: gives impression should stay well: sold 5,000 gns Doncaster October Sales: winning hurdler for Miss L. Siddall. *R. M. Whitaker.* —

MASTER GLEN 2 ch.c. (Feb 27) Rabdan 129–Rage Glen 67 (Grey Mirage 128) [1990 6m 8g 8d] smallish, quite sparely-made colt: moderate mover: second foal: brother to useful 1989 2-y-o 5f and 6f winner Lord Glen: dam headstrong 8.2f and 1¼m winner also successful over jumps: best effort seventh of 12, pulling hard then one pace, in minor event at Wolverhampton, second start: slowly away in maiden later in October. *R. Champion.* 59

MASTER LINE 9 ch.h. High Line 125–Fair Winter 111 (Set Fair 129) [1989 11.7m³ 11f⁴ 12m² 12.2m* 11.7m⁴ 12m⁴ 11.7d³ 12f 12m 12.2m⁵ 1990 12.2m⁶ 11.7g* 11.7m⁵ 12g⁶ 12g a12g⁴ 12g⁶] small, sparely-made horse: has a sharp action: quite modest handicapper: won at Windsor in April: below form after: stays 13f: probably not at best on extremes of going: bandaged near-hind final outing: excellent mount for apprentice: occasionally sweats: genuine. *H. Candy.* 70 d

MASTER OFTHE HOUSE 4 b.g. Kind of Hush 118–Miss Racine (Dom Racine (FR) 121) [1989 6s 6v² 6d⁴ 5m⁴ 5m⁵ 6g⁴ 6s² 5.3f² 6f⁶ 6g a6g 1990 6m⁶ 8f 5g 6m 7g³ 8m⁴ 7g³ 7m² 7f² 7m³ 6m⁶ a7g³ 7m³ 7d 7d⁴] sturdy gelding: poor mover: quite modest maiden: possibly best at 7f nowadays: acts on any going: has been tried in blinkers and visor: has got on toes, and sweated tenth start: sold to join M. Hammond's stable 4,600 gns Newmarket Autumn Sales. *D. W. Chapman.* 60

MASTER OF TROY 2 b.g. (May 2) Trojan Fen 118–Gohar (USA) (Barachois (CAN)) [1990 8.2d] 24,000Y: half-brother to 2 minor winners in USA: dam 5f claimer winner at 2 yrs, is half-sister to good American and Canadian performer Par Excellance, dam of very smart 1984 2-y-o stayer Khozaam: green, around 9 lengths seventh of 15, outpaced 3f out then staying on well final 2f, to Hip To Time in minor event at Nottingham in October: sure to improve, particularly at 1¼m. *B. Hanbury.* 66 p

MASTER PIERRE 3 b. or br.g. Gabitat 119–Emerglen (Furry Glen 121) [1989 5m⁵ 5m 6m 6m² 6g 5g³ 1990 6m 7g⁶ 7m⁵ 8.3m 8m⁵ 8f⁴ 8m⁵ 10g 8m³ 8g a10g⁶ a12g³ a12g³] lengthy, good-topped gelding: has a round action: plating-class maiden: stays 1½m: acts on firm ground: sometimes sweating and on toes. *L. J. Holt.* 54

MASTER PLAN (FR) 4 b.g. Carwhite 127–Manene (FR) (Tapioca (FR) 123) [1989 10s⁴ 11.7m⁶ 10f 8f⁴ 9m* 19m9 a8g⁵ a12g 10.2f⁶ 10.6f 10m 8h⁴ 9g 9s 8g⁴ 10.6s 12g⁴ 12.3g⁵ 8.5g⁵ 9g* 8m⁵ 10f⁶ 8m* 8.2m 10.6g 8m⁶ 8g² 8m] compact gelding: moderate mover: quite modest on his day: won apprentice handicaps at Hamilton in July and Pontefract in August: probably best at 1m to 1¼m: acts on hard going, possibly unsuited by soft nowadays. *J. S. Wilson.* 63

MASTER POKEY 6 br.g. Uncle Pokey 116–September Fire (Firestreak 125) [1989 6m 5f⁶ 5.6g⁵ 6s 1990 6m 6m* 6m 6g* 6m* 5.6g 6d⁵ 6g] sturdy, good-quartered gelding: carries plenty of condition: fairly useful handicapper: successful at Doncaster in May and Nottingham and Ayr (£14,900 event) in July: favourite, good fifth of 29 to Final Shot in Ladbrokes (Ayr) Gold Cup: ideally suited by 6f: probably not at his best on soft going, acts on any other: often heavily handaged in front. *M. W. Easterby.* 89

MASTER SANDY (USA) 3 b.c. Master Willie 129–Whose Broad (USA) (Hoist The Flag (USA)) [1989 NR 1990 10m 13.3m 14g] $3,000Y, resold 12,000Y: big, lengthy, attractive colt: has plenty of scope: brother to useful 1987 2-y-o 5f and 7f winner William's Bird and modest 1989 maiden Just Susanna, and half-brother to a minor winner in USA: dam never ran: well beaten in maidens, blinkered and sour in preliminaries final start: sold 3,600 gns Doncaster August Sales. *J. L. Dunlop.* —

MASTER TYKE 5 gr.g. Flying Tyke 90–Habatashie 62 (Habat 127) [1989 8m 8.3m a8g⁵ a6g³ 1990 a6g⁴ a8g⁵ a8g⁵ a7g* a7g² 10f a6g 7.6m 7.6m a8g a10g a8g] sturdy gelding: moderate mover: won claimer at Lingfield in March: below form after next outing: stays 1m: effective with or without blinkers: has won for apprentice: inconsistent. *R. P. C. Hoad.* 45

MATA CARA 2 b. or br.f. (Mar 9) Storm Bird (CAN) 134–Fatah Flare (USA) 121 (Alydar (USA)) [1990 6m⁴ 6m⁴] compact, deep-girthed filly: second foal: half-sister to fairly useful 1989 2-y-o 6f winner Fire And Shade (by Shadeed): dam 6f (at 2 yrs) 73 p and 10.5f winner, is from excellent family: better for runs, quite modest form in maidens won by Crystal Path at Newmarket and Sixofus at Redcar in October: will be better suited by 7f: likely to improve. *L. M. Cumani.*

MATADOR (USA) 3 ch.c. Nureyev (USA) 131–Allicance (USA) 113 (Alleged **93** (USA) 138) [1989 NR 1990 11.7f³ 12m* 14f 11.7m² 12g³ 13.3g*] leggy colt: has a long stride: third foal: brother to French provincial 11.5f and 1½m winner Beaute Dangereuse: dam, French 10.5f winner who stayed 1½m, is half-sister to numerous winners including Blushing Groom: won maiden at Kempton in July and handicap at Newbury in October: will be suited by return to further: best efforts with give in the ground. *R. Charlton.*

MATAHIF (IRE) 2 b. or br.c. (Mar 30) Wassl 125–Reves Celestes (USA) 82 **97** (Lyphard (USA) 132) [1990 6d² 7m² 8.2m² 8d² 7m³ 10s* 10g*] IR 30,000Y: leggy, sparely-made colt: easy mover: second live foal: half-brother to fair 1m (at 2 yrs) and 1½m winner Keswa (by Kings Lake): dam 1m winner stayed 1¼m, is half-sister to Celestial Storm and to dam of very smart French middle-distance filly River Memories: improving colt: made all in maiden at Nottingham in October, beating Foxtrot Pie impressively by 5 lengths, and Jennings The Bookmakers Zetland Stakes at Newmarket following month, given excellent ride to beat Walim by ¾ length: will stay 1½m +: acts on good to firm ground and soft: likely to prove best with forcing tactics. *R. W. Armstrong.*

MATAMATA 2 br.g. (Apr 30) Jalmood (USA) 126–Macarte (FR) (Gift Card (FR) **67** 124) [1990 6m 6m 6g 8f³] round-barrelled gelding: has scope: fifth foal: half-brother to 3-y-o Marasol (by Siberian Express), successful at 1m (at 2 yrs) and 9f, and to 6f winner Mariano (by Aragon): dam minor French 1m and 9f winner: easily best effort around 3 lengths third of 11 to Gold Law in maiden at Wolverhampton in September: will stay 1¼m. *J. L. Dunlop.*

MATASIETE (USA) 3 b.g. Diamond Shoal 130–Babalowa (USA) (Raja Baba — (USA)) [1989 6f8.2g⁶ 6m 1990 8f 5g⁶ a8g 6g 8.2g] lengthy, quite attractive gelding: plating-class maiden: soundly beaten since second start at 2 yrs: better at 1m than 6f. *J. G. FitzGerald.*

MATCHING LINES 3 ch.f. Thatching 131–Irish Limerick 89 (Try My Best **58** (USA) 130) [1989 5g⁵ 5g* 5m 1990 6m⁴ 8g 6m 7g⁴ 5f 7f 7g 5d³ 5s*] leggy, work-manlike filly: has had soft palate operation: moderate mover: quite modest handi-capper: clearly best effort since reappearance when winning at Hamilton in November: effective at 5f with plenty of give in the ground, and stays 6f: retained by trainer 1,200 gns Doncaster November Sales. *Mrs J. R. Ramsden.*

MATERIAL GOLD 3 b.g. Sonnen Gold 121–Miss Whitley (Hot Spark 126) [1989 **49** 5d 5f⁴ 7m⁶ 7.5g 7f³ 6g 7d 1990 8g 6s⁶ 6f⁴ 6m 8g⁴] leggy, good-quartered gelding: moderate walker: has a round action: modest plater: stays 1m: acts on firm going: blinkered last 3 starts at 2 yrs: pulls hard. *C. Parker.*

MATE'S MIRAGE 2 ch.g. (May 3) Music Boy 124–Gay Shadow 99 (Northfields — (USA)) [1990 a5g⁶ 5f] 12,500Y: half-brother to 5 winners, including quite modest 11f winner Schweppes Tonic (by Persian Bold) and plating-class 7f and 1m winner Sahara Shadow (by Formidable): dam 2-y-o 5f and 6f winner, is half-sister to very smart sprinter Honeyblest: poor form in maiden and claimer in spring. *T. D. Barron.*

MATHEMA 3 ch.f. Rousillon (USA) 133–Blue Doc (Majority Blue 126) [1989 NR **68** 1990 a8g⁴ a8g* a10g⁶ a8g² a8g⁴ 8.2d 10d] workmanlike filly: has a quick action: sixth reported foal: half-sister to 2 winners, including Irish 1m winner Dock Leaf (by Wolver Hollow): dam, successful twice at up to 7f in Ireland, is half-sister to Lingfield Oaks Trial winner Gift Wrapped, dam of Reach: modest form at Southwell, winning maiden in March and best efforts, wearing eyeshield and staying on well, in frame in claimer and £8,100 handicap on consecutive days in August: should stay 1¼m: sold 7,500 gns Newmarket Autumn Sales. *Sir Mark Prescott.*

MATHKURH (USA) 2 b.f. (Mar 24) Riverman (USA) 131–Manal (FR) 74 **78** p (Luthier 126) [1990 5d*] neat, quite attractive filly: fifth foal: half-sister to Princess Margaret winner Muhbubh (by Blushing Groom) and a winning plater: dam thrice-raced sister to French Derby second Twig Moss and very smart middle-distance winner Tip Moss, and half-sister to Brush Aside: green, won maiden at Chester in May by 3 lengths from Simmie's Special: looked sure to improve and win more races, but not seen out again. *H. Thomson Jones.*

MATOMANI 3 b.f. Beldale Flutter (USA) 130–Bundu (FR) 88 (Habitat 134) [1989 **68** NR 1990 8g 8g⁴ 8m⁵ 10.6s 9m] leggy filly: second foal: half-sister to fair 1m winner Mbulwa (by Be My Guest): dam 1¼m and 10.6f winner: quite modest maiden: ran poorly last 2 outings: should be suited by 1¼m: seems unsuited by soft ground: sold to join D. Murray-Smith 1,200 gns Newmarket December Sales. *G. Wragg.*

MATTER OF FACT 2 br.f. (Feb 13) Known Fact (USA) 135–Matoa (USA) (Tom 58 Rolfe) [1990 5m⁵ 5f³ a6g⁴ 6m] neat filly: sister to French 9f winner De Facto and half-sister to several winners here and abroad, including fairly useful 1m to 15f winner Prince Spruce (by Big Spruce) and 6f and 1m winner Rear Action (by Home Guard): dam won twice at up to 1m in USA: plating-class maiden: seemed reluctant to race at Southwell penultimate start, then stayed on well final 2f under tender handling: ran poorly final outing: should be much better suited by 6f than 5f: sold 2,200 gns Newmarket Autumn Sales. *B. W. Hills.*

MATTER OF LAW 3 ch.g. Blakeney 126–Opera Star (FR) 70 (Appiani II 128) 51 [1989 NR 1990 a12g⁵ 12f 15.3m 16.2d 15.3g 10g 12f³ 14f² 13.8m² 14m³ 15.3f⁴] 6,000Y: stocky gelding: has a rather round action: turns fore-feet in: sixth foal: brother to 1¼m seller winner Baydon Queen and half-brother to 2 middle-distance winners in France, notably 1¼m winner Lyn's Star (by Derrylin): dam won at 1¼m here and 1½m in France: fair plater: should prove suited by test of stamina: acts on firm going: blinkered and on toes sixth start: one paced: sold 3,700 gns Newmarket Autumn Sales. *C. A. Cyzer.*

MATTS BOY 2 b.c. (Mar 30) Runnett 125–Thatchville 65 (Thatch (USA) 136) p [1990 6m] good-topped, attractive colt: first foal: dam sprinter: carrying condition and green, never-dangerous seventh of 13, moderate late progress, in maiden at Ripon in July: should improve. *Miss S. E. Hall.*

MATUSADONA 3 b.f. Tumble Wind (USA)–Ceiling (Thatch (USA) 136) [1989 — NR 1990 6g 7d a8g⁶ a8g⁵] 16,000F, 9,400Y: workmanlike filly: third foal: sister to plating-class maiden Nessfield: dam, second over 1¾m at 4 yrs in Ireland, is half-sister to Knockroe: 7½ lengths fifth of 16 at Southwell, first sign of ability in maidens. *P. A. Kelleway.*

MAURSKI 3 br.f. Undulate (USA)–Bay Girl (Persian Bold 123) [1989 NR 1990 8m — 10f] small, workmanlike filly: has a round action: first foal: dam ran once at 2 yrs: no promise in minor event and seller: sold 900 gns Ascot May Sales. *B. Stevens.*

MAXIGROOM (USA) 2 b.c. (Apr 22) Blushing Groom (FR) 131–Maximova 99 p (FR) 121 (Green Dancer (USA) 132) [1990 8s² 7v*] fourth foal: brother to fairly useful French 1¼m winner Balchaia and half-brother to 2 animals by Seattle Slew, notably Prix de la Foret winner Septieme Ciel: dam good class at up to 1m: beaten narrowly in newcomers race at Saint-Cloud in November before winning maiden at Maisons-Laffitte in December by a short head: will stay 1¼m: sure to go on to better things. *Mme C. Head, France.*

MAXIMILIAN (USA) 3 b.c. Mr Prospector (USA)–Mystery Mood (USA) (Night 114 Invader (USA)) [1989 NR 1990 8g* 8m* 8g⁴ 8g* 10.6m⁴ 9m⁶ 10d] $975,000Y: leggy colt: half-brother to several winners, including smart 1981 American 2-y-o filly Mystical Mood (by Roberto) and quite useful Darting Groom (by Blushing Groom), a winner at up to 1¼m in Britain: dam best at 2 yrs when smart stakes winner at up to 1m: won maiden at Newmarket in May, £7,400 event at Newbury in June and Group 3 Ostermann-Pokal at Cologne in July: ran well when demoted neck second to Defensive Play in 10.6f Group 3 event at Haydock on fifth outing, edging left: needs more forcing tactics at 9f, and should prove suited by further: acts on good to firm ground, seems unsuited by dead: takes keen hold: has joined F. Schulhofer in USA. *J. Gosden.*

MAX THE LID 2 br.g. (Mar 27) Sayf El Arab (USA) 127–Home In Pasadena — (Home Guard (USA) 129) [1990 6g] 7,600F, 8,400Y: well-made gelding: half-brother to 2 winners in Italy: dam never ran: backward in minor event at Doncaster in September: moved poorly down. *G. A. Pritchard-Gordon.*

MAYAASA (FR) 2 b.f. (Mar 24) Green Desert (USA) 127–Fitnah 125 (Kris 135) 65 [1990 5m* 6g] strong-quartered, compact filly: first foal: dam French 9.5f and 1¼m winner and second in French Oaks, is out of good sprinter Greenland Park, a sister to Red Sunset: won 5-runner maiden at Newmarket in May by ¾ length from Milly Black: slowly away, never able to challenge and eased in nursery at York over 5 months later. *A. A. Scott.*

MAY BE BOLD 3 b.f. Never So Bold 135–Plum Run (USA) 87 (Run The Gantlet 53 (USA)) [1989 NR 1990 8m⁶ 8m 7d⁴ 8m 10g] 7,000Y: leggy, good-topped filly: fifth foal: half-sister to 1986 2-y-o 7f winner Assultan (by Troy), later fair but unguenine hurdler: dam winner at up to 8.2f from family of Arts And Letters: plating-class maiden: clearly best effort third start: blinkered and edgy, tailed off in claimer final one: should stay 1¼m: probably needs easy surface: ridden by 7-lb claimer, except for second start. *J. A. R. Toller.*

MAYBE LUCKY 3 b. or br.f. Monsanto (FR) 121–Eddie Brooks (Palm Track 122) [1989 NR 1990 10f 10f 10.1m] 320Y: smallish, leggy filly: first foal: dam unraced: well beaten in maidens and minor event: edgy and pulled hard final start. *A. Moore.* —

MAYFLY GIRL 3 b.f. Mr Fluorocarbon 126–Illiney Girl 66 (Lochnager 132) [1989 NR 1990 6m⁶ a7g] sparely-made filly: first foal: dam 5f and 6f seller winner: bandaged behind, last in minor event and maiden. *T. P. McGovern.* —

MAY HINTON 3 ch.f. Main Reef 126–Jeanne Avril 99 (Music Boy 124) [1989 6g² 6g* 6m⁴ 6f* 6s³ 1990 7f 6m⁶ 5d] small, angular filly: made all or most when fair winner twice as 2-y-o: faced stiff tasks in 1990, last of 18 in £16,400 handicap on final start, in June: acts on any going. *J. L. Dunlop.*

MAY QUEEN 3 b.f. Dara Monarch 128–Markon (On Your Mark 125) [1989 8g 1990 12.2m² 7g] leggy, angular filly: moderate mover: soundly beaten in maidens and claimer. *S. E. Kettlewell.* —

MAY REEF (IRE) 2 b.f. (Mar 2) Simply Great (FR) 122–Mey 78 (Canisbay 120) [1990 6f* 5m* 6m 6s] sparely-made filly: good mover: half-sister to several winners, including smart 7f to 1½m winner Perchance (by Connaught): dam, best at 1¼m, is half-sister to smart animals Albany and Magna Carta: successful in seller (retained 6,200 gns) at Folkestone in August and nursery (led post) at Nottingham in September: ran poorly in nurseries at Ascot and Newbury (raced on possibly unfavoured part of track) after: will stay at least 1¼m. *A. N. Lee.* 71

MAY SQUARE (IRE) 2 ch.g. (Feb 6) Nicholas Bill 125–Casa Rosada (Known Fact (USA) 135) [1990 8g 8g] 18,000Y: angular gelding: first foal: dam poor daughter of Nell Gwyn winner Evita: backward, never better than mid-division in 16-runner maiden at Kempton in September: weakened quickly last 2f in similar event at Pontefract following month. *D. Morley.* 53

MAZAG (USA) 3 b.c. Mr Prospector (USA)–Rose O'Riley (USA) (Nijinsky (CAN) 138) [1989 7g³ 7m³ 1990 7g 7m⁴ 8d 8.3m⁶] attractive, rather leggy colt: has a sharp action: fairly useful at 2 yrs: well below form in first half of 1990, getting poor run second and third starts in Lingfield maiden and Britannia Handicap at Royal Ascot: should stay at least 1m: found little final start: to join Brad McDonald in USA. *M. R. Stoute.* ?

MAZARINE BLUE 2 b.f. (Feb 4) Bellypha 130–Maiden Pool 85 (Sharpen Up 127) [1990 5m⁶] light-framed filly: half-sister to several winners, including very useful sprinter Rich Charlie (by Young Generation) and 5f and 1m winner Consulate (by Absalom): dam 5f winner: around 7 lengths sixth of 8, veering left stalls then prominent over 3f, in maiden at Newcastle in June. *M. A. Jarvis.* —

MAZATLAN 2 b.g. (Jan 29) Mazaad 106–Ashbocking 55 (Dragonara Palace (USA) 115) [1990 7g⁶ 6d 7g] 14,000Y: workmanlike, good-quartered gelding: easy mover: second foal: half-brother to a winner in Italy: dam 1¼m seller winner: plating-class form in varied events. *J. G. FitzGerald.* 60

MAZIN 2 b.c. (May 11) Faustus (USA) 118–Polly Oligant (Prince Tenderfoot (USA) 126) [1990 5d 5f⁵ 5f⁶ 7g 6m⁶ a7g⁵] 17,500F, 31,000Y: sturdy colt: fifth foal: half-brother to 3-y-o Friendship Renewed (by Vaigly Great), 6f winner at 2 yrs, and fair 5f to 1m winner Swift's Pal (by Record Token): dam fair 5f winner at 2 yrs in Ireland: poor maiden: ran creditably in nurseries last 3 starts, including on all-weather at Lingfield: likely to prove better suited by 7f than 6f: retained by trainer 3,400 gns Newmarket Autumn Sales. *C. J. Benstead.* 42

MAZWOOD (IRE) 2 b.c. (May 7) Mazaad 106–Putt Wood 62 (Record Token 128) [1990 5g 7m] IR 6,600Y: close-coupled colt: first reported foal: dam maiden suited by 1¼m, is out of half-sister to Tudor Music: ridden by 7-lb claimer, never dangerous in maiden at Windsor and minor event (blinkered) at Lingfield 4 months later. *M. McCourt.* —

MCA BELOW THE LINE 2 ch.c. (Jan 28) Lucky Wednesday 124–Delayed Action 113 (Jolly Jet 111) [1990 5g⁶ 5m² 5f* 5d⁴ 7f* 7.5f⁵ 7g² 7m³ 7f⁶] dipped-backed colt: moderate mover: seventh living foal: brother to 3-y-o What Happens Next and half-brother to fairly useful sprinter Force of Action (by Galivanter) and Manx 1m winner Rapid Action (by Gunner B): dam won seven 5f races: fairly useful plater: no bid after winning at Redcar and Brighton in June: stays 7.5f: acts on firm going, possibly unsuited by a soft surface: blinkered final 5 starts. *W. J. Pearce.* 58

MCA LUCKY STAR 4 gr.f. Lucky Wednesday 124–Starkist 81 (So Blessed 130) [1989 5v⁴ 7g⁴ 6f 8.3g 7.5m⁵ 6g 1990 10.8m] compact, good-bodied filly: has a rather — §

568

round action: modest winner at 2 yrs: little show since first outing in 1989, including in seller: stays 6f: acts on heavy going, probably unsuited by firm: temperamental and one to avoid. *G. H. Jones.*

MEADS BROW 4 b.c. Petong 126–Pams Gleam 89 (Sovereign Gleam 117) [1989 6f4 7f 6h 6f6 6g 7d 1990 6f 7.6m 7f 9m 7.6m 10.1m 8.3m3 8f3 7f a6g] compact colt: carries plenty of condition: has a quick action: poor form at best in handicaps at 4 yrs: probably doesn't stay 1¼m: best form on top-of-the-ground: blinkered 6 times, including last 5 starts. *R. Voorspuy.*   33

MEALLWASHA (IRE) 2 b.f. (Apr 24) Wassl 125–Nathacha (Thatch (USA) 136) [1990 6g 7d] IR 8,500F, IR 13,000Y: unfurnished filly: sixth foal: half-sister to useful 1988 2-y-o 7f winner Double Prosperity (by Kings Lake): dam thrice-raced half-sister to Boldboy: showed signs of ability in maidens at Nottingham (auction) and Catterick in autumn. *J. R. Fanshawe.*   —

MEANIE MINNA 4 b.f. Derrylin 115–Pirate Maid (Auction Ring (USA) 123) [1989 7d 7f4 6f3 5.8h5 1990 8.2s] workmanlike, angular filly: quite modest maiden at best: stays 7f: acts on firm going. *J. Norton.*   —

MEAN TO ME 4 b.f. Homing 130–Mac's Melody (Wollow 132) [1989 10.6m 1990 a10g3 a12g] tall, leggy, sparely-made filly: form only when third in Lingfield maiden in February: sweated profusely only outing at 3 yrs. *Mrs Barbara Waring.*   47

MECADO 3 b.g. Ballacashtal (CAN)–Parma Nova 58 (Dominion 123) [1989 6g a6g 1990 7m 8g 10.2m 10m 9f 12.5g 12.5m] compact gelding: no worthwhile form, including in sellers: blinkered fifth start: visored 3 times. *F. J. Yardley.*   —

MEDAILLE D'OR 2 ch.c. (Apr 4) Primo Dominie 121–Alezan Dore 82 (Mountain Call 125) [1990 5m3 5m6 5f* 5m5] 23,000F, 21,000Y: rather leggy, useful-looking colt: good walker: closely related to a winner in Italy by Dominion and half-brother to 4 winners, including 5f winners Nazela (by Another Realm) and Deux Etoiles (by Bay Express): dam half-sister to smart middle-distance filly Aloft, stayed 7f: made all, showing improved form, in maiden at Wolverhampton: favourite but edgy, fair fifth in nursery (moved moderately down) at same course later in August: will stay 6f: hung left on debut. *J. W. Payne.*   72

MEDIA STAR 5 ch.m. Star Appeal 133–Linduna (Derring-Do 131) [1989 12g 12f3 12f 8f 16.5g 12g 12f* 10m 14f3 12f 14g 1990 a11g a16g6 10.2f 14m4 18f 15.3g4 15.8d3 15.8m6 13.8d] leggy, angular mare: has a round action: inconsistent plater: stays 2m: acts on firm and dead going: usually wears bandages. *T. Kersey.*   —

MEESON CODE 3 b.c. Coded Scrap 90–Meeson Secret (Most Secret 119) [1989 NR 1990 8g 8.2m a12g 12f 15m] leggy, close-coupled colt: second foal: brother to 4-y-o plater Meeson Scrap: dam ran 4 times at 2 yrs: no sign of ability on flat, in seller on debut: winning selling hurdler for B. McMath. *M. P. F. Murphy.*   —

MEESON GOLD 2 b.c. (May 30) Sonnen Gold 121–Meeson Secret (Most Secret 119) [1990 5m 5m4 5g2 5m6 5f4 5f 6s] close-coupled colt: moderate mover: third foal: half-brother to poor plater Meeson Scrap (by Coded Scrap): dam ran 4 times at 2 yrs: fair plater: ran poorly when blinkered sixth start: best form at 5f on a sound surface. *M. P. F. Murphy.*   53

MEESON KAMP 4 b.g. Kampala 120–Turin Rose (Martinmas 128) [1989 5v* 5d2 5m6 5m* 5m6 5f2 5g2 5m6 5d5 a6g3 a5g 1990 5g2 5g2 5m4 5g 5g5 5f* a5g 5g 5m] leggy, lengthy gelding: has a roundish action: modest handicapper: won at Wolverhampton in July: best at 5f: acts on any going: has got on edge: has hung right when ridden by 7-lb claimer: below form at Chester and Southwell. *J. Berry.*   73

MEESON KING 9 br.g. Space King 115–Meeson Girl (Tyrant (USA)) [1989 6s a6g a6g5 a6g 1990 a5g] small, lengthy, workmanlike gelding: plating-class handicapper on his day, very lightly raced nowadays: stays 6f: acts on any going: blinkered once: has run well for inexperienced rider: often goes freely to post. *B. A. McMahon.*   —

MEESON SCRAP 4 b.g. Coded Scrap 90–Meeson Secret (Most Secret 119) [1989 5f 6m 5.8h6 5f6 5m 6g 6g3 a6g 1990 a6g] tall, leggy gelding: plater: stays 7f: best form with give in the ground. *B. Preece.*   —

MEESON TIMES 2 b.f. (May 2) Enchantment 115–National Time (USA) (Lord Avie (USA)) [1990 6m 6m* 6m 6d 6d 8d a5g] sturdy, compact filly: second foal: dam ran twice at 2 yrs: fair plater: won at Windsor (bought in 3,700 gns) in July: well beaten after, twice unfavourably drawn in nurseries: stays 6f: visored and bandaged final 2 outings: trained first 4 by M. Usher. *B. Ellison.*   52

MEGAN'S FLIGHT 5 ch.m. Welsh Pageant 132–Escape Me Never 75 (Run The Gantlet (USA)) [1989 12s4 12s2 14.8d4 12m2 12d3 14g a14g* a16g* a14g4 1990 17.6m 14s 16g a18g3 14g* 14g2 14d 12m] leggy, workmanlike mare: won for first time   68 on turf in handicap at Sandown in September: ran well on all-weather previous outing: stays 2¼m: yet to race on firm going, acts on any other: ran moderately when blinkered and apprentice ridden third outing: best racing up with pace: has been reluctant at stalls: sold 7,000 gns Newmarket December Sales. *Lady Herries.*

MEINE VONNE LADY   5 br.m. Jalmood (USA) 126–Gold Rupee 86 (Native   —
Prince (USA)) [1989 8.2v 8d 8.2m 8g⁴ 8f 8.2d 8f⁴ 8f² 8f 8v 1990 8.2f] leggy mare:
carries plenty of condition: moderate mover: winning plater as 3-y-o: suited by
about 1m: acts on any going: sold 2,000 gns Doncaster May Sales. *D. McCain.*

MELANCOLIA   4 b.f. Legend of France (USA) 124–Fardella (ITY) (Molvedo   —
137) [1989 8f³ 10g* 1990 8m 9m⁴ 9g] has a quick action: won Newmarket claimer
late on as 3-y-o: faced stiff tasks in handicaps and apprentice race in summer: will be
suited by 1½m: acts on firm ground. *R. M. Whitaker.*

MELARINOS (USA)   2 b.c. (May 3) Greinton 119–Gay Current (USA) (Little   65 p
Current (USA)) [1990 7g] $90,000Y: close-coupled, rather plain colt: third reported
foal: half-brother to a minor winner in USA by L'Emigrant: dam minor winner at
around 1m in USA, is sister to smart French 1m to 1¼m performer Look Fast:
beaten around 5 lengths, never able to challenge, in mid-division for 17-runner
minor event at Kempton in September: should improve. *G. Harwood.*

MELBURY (USA)   3 ch.f. Forli (ARG)–Her World (USA) (Transworld (USA)   76 ?
121) [1989 5m* 5m⁵ 6m² 5g² 5f⁶ 5g 1990 5f⁶ 6m 5.8f⁶] medium-sized filly: shows a
short, quick action: fair performer at best: deteriorated as 3-y-o, running in June
seller final start: stays 6f: sweating and on toes fifth outing at 2 yrs, swerved right
leaving stalls penultimate one in 1990. *C. R. Nelson.*

MELDON SONG   2 b.f. (Mar 5) Pitskelly 122–Daughter of Song 73 (Song 132)   45
[1990 6m³ 7f⁵] 6,400Y: leggy filly: poor mover: sister to a winner in Italy and
half-sister to 2 winners, including modest sprinter Gorgeous Girl (by Dragonara
Palace): dam won 5f seller: backed at long odds, 8 lengths third of 10 in maiden at
Ayr in July: tailed off (eased when headed 2f out) in similar event there 3 days later.
W. Bentley.

MELFA   5 b.m. Auction Ring (USA) 123–Nejwah (Morston (FR) 125) [1989 10m 6f   36
a8g a14g a12g a8g 1990 a10g a8g² a8g⁵ 7.6g 10m 10g] sparely-made ex-Irish mare:
second in claimer at Lingfield in January, only worthwhile form in Britain: stays 9f:
acts on firm going: has worn blinkers: occasionally sweats: trained until after fifth
start by J. Davies. *A. W. Denson.*

MELICUS (USA)   5 b.h. Providential 118–Melodina 118 (Tudor Melody 129)   —
[1989 NR 1990 14.8m] well-made horse: has a round action: won maiden at Redcar as
3-y-o: well beaten in March handicap at Warwick, only subsequent outing on flat:
suited by test of stamina: acts on good to firm going: sold 5,200 gns Newmarket
Autumn Sales. *P. F. I. Cole.*

MELISSA MINSTER   3 br.f. Head For Heights 125–Hymettus 103 (Blakeney   —
126) [1989 NR 1990 8.3f 10.1g] 2,500Y: lightly-made filly: third foal: dam won 1½m
Galtres Stakes: no form in minor events at Windsor: bandaged off-hind second start:
sold 1,100 gns Doncaster September Sales: resold 725 gns Ascot November Sales.
R. Hannon.

MELLOTTIE   5 b. or br.g. Meldrum 112–Lottie Lehmann 69 (Goldhill 125) [1989   85 p
NR 1990 10.2f 9f⁶ 12g⁵ 10m³ 9f* 9f⁴ 8g 10m³ 9f* 11f² 9g³ 9m* 10m* 9m²]
good-topped gelding: carries plenty of condition: first foal: dam, winner over 7f and
8.2f, stayed middle distances: progressed extremely well in handicaps, winning at
Redcar in May and July and York and Leicester in September: well supported and
ran better still when second of 40, leading 1f out and keeping on well, to Risen Moon
in William Hill Cambridgeshire at Newmarket: best at around 1¼m with strong
handling: acts well on top-of-the-ground: has turn of foot: genuine and consistent: a
credit to his trainer. *Mrs G. R. Reveley.*

MELPOMENE (USA)   2 b.f. (Mar 23) Lear Fan (USA) 130–Melodrama 102   80 p
(Busted 134) [1990 8g* 7d²] good-topped filly: half-sister to several winners,
including fair miler Kiya (by Dominion) and useful 2-y-o 6f and 7f winner Quiet
Weekend (by Town And Country): dam 6f and 1m winner, is daughter of smart
sprinter Matinee: won maiden at Wolverhampton by 5 lengths from Kiska: looked
past best when creditable 5 lengths second of 5, finding little having quickened
clear, to Sharp Imposter in minor event at Leicester later in October: worth another
chance to confirm debut promise. *W. Hastings-Bass.*

MEL'S ROSE   5 ch.g. Anfield 117–Ragtime Rose (Ragstone 128) [1989 8d² 9f⁵   82
7m* 7f³ 7m* 7g 8m 7m 7g 7m 8g a8g² 1990 7f³ 7m* 7f³ a7g 8m³ 7m 8m² 7d a10g³
a8g] tall gelding: has a quick action: fair handicapper: won at Yarmouth (third win

there) in July: appeared to show improved form when second at Newmarket in November: below that form last 3 outings: suited by 7f to 1m: acts on firm and dead going: blinkered once: good mount for apprentice. *G. A. Huffer.*

MELTING TEARS 2 b.f. (Feb 13) Noalto 120–Davemma 81 (Tachypous 128) 47 [1990 6g6 5d6 7g* 7.5f 7m2 7m5 7m 8.2s] 2,000Y: leggy filly: first foal: dam disappointing maiden, stayed 1½m: poor performer: won maiden auction at Edinburgh in July: should be well suited by 1m: seems unsuited by a soft surface. *J. S. Wilson.*

MEMORIVE (USA) 2 b.f. (Apr 21) Riverman (USA) 131–Le Vague A L'Ame 75 p (USA) (Vaguely Noble 140) [1990 7f2] good-topped filly: has plenty of scope: sister to good-class French and American middle-distance filly River Memories and half-sister to 2 other winners, including French 7f (at 2 yrs) to 1m winner Raise A Memory (by Raise A Native): dam placed from 1m to 1½m in France, is half-sister to Celestial Storm: very green, promising length second of 15 to Nunivak in maiden at Redcar in October, soon close up after slow start and keeping on well final 2f despite hanging left: will stay 1¼m: sure to improve, and win races. *G. Harwood.*

MENDIP MIST 2 ch.f. (Apr 30) Known Fact (USA) 135–Silver Surprise 78 (Son 48 of Silver 123) [1990 6m 7g3 5m5 6m5 5.8h6 7m 6m] small filly: fourth foal: dam 1¼m winner and successful hurdler: poor maiden at best: stays 7f. *R. J. Holder.*

MERANDI SPECIAL 3 b.g. Coquelin (USA) 121–Mountain Chase (Mount — Hagen (FR) 127) [1989 8g 1990 13.3m 16g 13m] workmanlike gelding: no sign of ability in maiden events: sold to join J. Thomas 2,000 gns Ascot September Sales. *M. E. D. Francis.*

MERCALLE (FR) 4 gr.f. Kaldoun (FR)–Eole Des Mers (FR) (Carvin 127) [1989 108 11g8* 8g* 9.5g* 12g3 11g* 12g3 12.5d5 11g2 12s2 12.5m6 11g* 12g2 1990 10g 15.5f4 12g4 20g* 20f6] leggy, workmanlike filly: moderate walker: shows plenty of knee action: winner 1½m and 13f winner Lonesome Devil: dam won over 6.5f (at 2 yrs) and 1¼m: winner 5 times in French Provinces as 3-y-o, including in listed events: appeared to show much improved form when beating Cossack Guard 5 lengths in Prix du Cadran at Longchamp in May, allowed to establish clear advantage and never challenged: tailed-off last of 6 in Goodwood Cup nearly 2½ months later: stays extreme distances. *M. Bouland, France.*

MERCEDES GIRL (IRE) 2 b.f. (Apr 7) Alzao (USA) 117–Daring Mistress — (Crash Course 128) [1990 5g 6g 5d5] 6,000 2-y-o: small, sparely-made filly: first foal: dam Irish maiden: little worthwhile form, including in seller: sold 900 gns Doncaster September Sales. *N. Tinkler.*

MERCERS MAGIC (IRE) 2 ch.c. (Apr 25) Dalsaan 125–Rixensart 77 (Credo — 123) [1990 7f6 8m 8.2d] IR 4,200Y: half-brother to several winners here and abroad, including 1981 Irish 2-y-o 7.5f winner Pixie (by Pitcairn) and 1986 2-y-o 5f winner Strike Rate (by Wolver Hollow): dam 6f winner at 2 yrs, is half-sister to Irish 2000 Guineas winner Furry Glen: well beaten in maidens. *D. Haydn Jones.*

MERCHANT HOUSE (IRE) 2 ch.c. (May 7) Salmon Leap (USA) 131–Persian — p Polly 99 (Persian Bold 123) [1990 5m] 10,000F, 11,000Y: fifth foal: brother to 1¼m and 1½m winner Salmonid and half-brother to 3 winners, including 3-y-o Treble Eight (by Kings Lake) successful at 1m (at 2 yrs) and 10.1f: dam Irish 2-y-o 7f winner: favourite, ridden halfway after slow start and never able to challenge in maiden at Lingfield in September: clearly thought capable of better. *R. W. Stubbs.*

MERCHANT OF VENICE 2 b.c. (Mar 7) Precocious 126–Silka (ITY) (Lyp- 54 heor 118) [1990 7g 10.2s a8g6] 16,500Y: good-topped colt: third reported foal: half-brother to fair 4-y-o 1¼m and 1½m winner Duggan (by Dunbeath) and 6f and 7.5f winner Cluzo (by Sharpo): dam won in Italy: plating-class form in varied races: stays 1¼m. *W. J. Pearce.*

Prix du Cadran, Longchamp—Mercalle, the filly from the Provinces, slips the field for a surprise victory

MERDON DANCER 2 b.c. (Apr 12) Mashhor Dancer (USA)–Crystal's Solo 55
(USA) (Crystal Water (USA)) [1990 7f2 8f6] second foal: half-brother to ungenuine
1988 2-y-o 7f winner Crystal Heights (by Wolver Heights): dam second once from 12
starts in USA: plating-class form, keeping on never a threat, in autumn maidens at
Brighton and Wolverhampton: sold 4,200 gns Newmarket Autumn Sales. *I. A.
Balding.*

MERITSU (IRE) 2 ch.f. (May 4) Lyphard's Special (USA) 122–Ferry Lane (Dom 51
Racine (FR) 121) [1990 5m4 5f5 6g 6m 7g a7g4] IR 8,400Y: small, angular filly: good
walker: fourth foal: half-sister to winners in France and Belgium: dam poor half-
sister to Royal Boy, a smart performer at up to 7f: modest plater: ran best race (for
7-lb claimer) in maiden on all-weather: suited by 7f: blinkered fourth outing. *D. R. C.
Elsworth.*

MERMAID'S PURSE (CAN) 3 ch.f. Devil's Bag (USA)–Oceana (USA) —
(Northern Dancer) [1989 7m* 7.3v 1990 9m] sparely-made, plain filly: poor walker:
moderate mover: dead-heated in maiden at Redcar at 2 yrs, rallying strongly: well
beaten in listed race at Newbury and minor event (wore crossed noseband, chased
leaders 7f) at Wolverhampton: stays 7f well: probably unsuited by heavy ground:
joined D. Bell (Canada) in May. *J. Gosden.*

MERPET 2 b.f. (Apr 19) Petong 126–Spanish Mermaid (Julio Mariner 127) [1990 —
7g 8.5m3 8m a8g] smallish, angular filly: has a quick action: second foal: dam never
ran: poor maiden: ran in seller on debut: sold 1,100 gns Doncaster November Sales.
M. J. Camacho.

MERRYHILL MAID (IRE) 2 ch.f. (May 21) M Double M (USA)–Piazza 71
Navona (Upper Case (USA)) [1990 a6g 6f4 6g3 5m* 6g 5g 6m 6d* 6d3] IR 1,000Y,
resold IR 2,000Y: leggy, angular filly: half-sister to 2 winners, including 1m winner
Bank Parade (by Dom Racine): dam won over 7f and 1¼m in Italy: modest performer: successful in seller (no bid) at Lingfield in August and claiming nursery (by
5 lengths, showing much improved form) at Newmarket in November: will stay 7f:
none too consistent. *J. L. Harris.*

MERRY NUTKIN 4 ch.g. Jalmood (USA) 126–Merry Cindy 63 (Sea Hawk II 131) 84
[1989 10.4m6 13f* 16.2g* 1990 16m*] strong, workmanlike gelding: moderate
walker: has a long stride: unbeaten in handicaps on last 3 outings, but is very lightly
raced: idled in front when beating All Is Revealed 2 lengths at Newmarket in May:
stays 2m: acts on firm going: looked unsuited by track at Chester (sweating) on
reappearance at 3 yrs. *W. J. Haggas.*

MERRY ROUS 2 br.f. (May 10) Rousillon (USA) 133–Merry Weather 69 (Will 66
Somers 114§) [1990 6d* a7g] small, narrow filly: half-sister to several winners,
including smart sprinter Tina's Pet and 7f to 1¼m winner Bickerman (both by
Mummy's Pet): dam 9f winner: bit backward and very green, won 12-runner maiden
at Leicester by a head from Caroles Express: co-favourite, well beaten in nursery at
Southwell in November. *Sir Mark Prescott.*

MERSEYSIDE MAN 4 b.g. My Dad Tom (USA) 109–Chanita (Averof 123) 79 d
[1989 7f 7f4 8m3 8f3 8f3 7g 8f 1990 a8g* a8g* a7g* a8g* a8g3 a7g 8f 8f 8h4 9m4
a8g3] lengthy, workmanlike gelding: poor mover: successful in 4 handicaps at
Lingfield early in year: long way below form on turf and when returned to all-
weather (didn't look keen) in November: stays 1m: acts on firm going: usually wears
visor and ridden by 7-lb claimer: often slowly away: retained by trainer 4,100 gns
Newmarket July Sales, then 1,000 gns Ascot October Sales. *Dr J. D. Scargill.*

MERTOLA'S PET 4 b.f. Tickled Pink 114–Mertola (Tribal Chief 125) [1989 5h4 68
5.8h4 5.3f4 a6g5 1990 5.8h4 5m* 5g 5f5 5m2 5.8h 5m 5m 5f6 5.3f5 5d] small, quite
good-quartered filly: made all in handicaps at Lingfield and Bath in June: speedy,
best at 5f: acts well on top-of-the-ground. *L. G. Cottrell.*

MERTON MILL 3 b.f. Dominion 123–Brookfield Miss 73 (Welsh Pageant 132) 65
[1989 7g 1990 10.1g5 10g 11.7m6 10m* 10.6s3 10.4d2 11.5g3 12s6] workmanlike filly:
moderate mover: quite modest handicapper: won selling event (bought in 8,000 gns)
at Nottingham in September: ran well next 3 starts: stays 11.5f: acts on good to firm
ground and soft: has run well for apprentice. *D. Morley.*

MESLEH 3 b.c. Alleged (USA) 138–Forlene 108 (Forli (ARG)) [1989 NR 1990 82
8m5 10f2] 190,000F, 460,000Y: strong, lengthy colt with scope: moderate mover:
fifth foal: half-brother to Irish 2-y-o 7f winner Palais Glide and French 1¼m and
10.5f winner Gloria's Dancer (both by Northern Dancer): dam Irish 2-y-o 7f and 1m
winner out of very smart Arkadina: fair form in the spring in newcomers event at
Newmarket, soon having plenty to do then running on strongly, and maiden (odds

on) at Nottingham, never going well and tending to hang: gives strong impression will prove best with give in the ground. *J. Gosden.*

MESSAGE PAD   3 ch.c. Rousillon (USA) 133–Ouija 104 (Silly Season 127) [1989   **105**
7g* 7g 1990 7m⁶ 7g⁴ 8d 8m⁵ 8.2f* 8m* 9m² 7m] rangy colt: good walker: has a long stride: useful performer: successful in smallish fields for handicaps at Haydock and Newcastle in August: ran well in listed race won by Va Toujours at York next start, moderately in £71,900 handicap at Ascot over 3 weeks later: stays 9f: acts on firm ground, seems unsuited by dead: headstrong, and often taken down early: has been equipped with special noseband and severe bridle, not last 4 starts. *J. W. Watts.*

METAL BOYS   3 b.g. Krayyan 117–Idle Gossip (Runnett 125) [1989 5m⁵ 5f⁵ 5h*   **84**
5m 6m² 5f³ 6f³ 6f⁴ 6v 5g* 1990 5f* 5f⁵ 5d³ 6g] medium-sized gelding: poor mover: fair performer: made most to win handicap at Beverley in March: ran well in listed race at Haydock and handicap at Newbury next 2 starts: best over 5f: acts on hard ground and dead: gelded after final start, in May. *R. Hollinshead.*

METRO LINER   4 br.g. Zino 127–Bellinzona (Northfields (USA)) [1989 7m³ 8m   **—**
10d⁶ 8s⁵ 1990 8f] first foal: dam French provincial 9.5f winner out of sister to leading 1975 2-y-o Pasty: showed ability when trained in Ireland, on first outing as 3-y-o third in maiden at Tipperary: well beaten in similar event at Brighton in April: stays 1m. *R. Akehurst.*

MEVLEVI   3 b.f. Shareef Dancer (USA) 135–Meliora 73 (Crowned Prince (USA)   **—**
128) [1989 NR 1990 10g] fifth live foal: half-sister to 4 winners, including very smart stayer Weld (by Kalaglow): dam 7f winner: well behind in maiden at Sandown in September: sold 5,000 gns Newmarket December Sales. *H. R. A. Cecil.*

MEXICAN VISION   3 b.g. Vision (USA)–Mexican Two Step (Gay Fandango   **54**
(USA) 132) [1989 7g 10g 7g 1990 8m 8f⁴ 6g 7m 7f⁵ 7g* 7m 8.2m 9m 8.2v4] strong, lengthy gelding: has a round action: plating class as 3-y-o, best effort when winning seller (sold out of Mrs L. Piggott's stable 9,000 gns) at Leicester in August: faced stiff tasks last 3 starts: stays 7f: probably best with give in the ground: mostly blinkered after second start: sometimes sweated: bandaged on reappearance. *I. Campbell.*

MEZAAJ (USA)   2 br.g. (Mar 24) Shadeed (USA) 135–Honor To Her (USA) (Sir   **— p**
Ivor 135) [1990 6g] $300,000Y: sturdy, compact gelding: fourth foal: half-brother to useful 1985 French 6.5f and 7f winner Savannah's Honor (by Storm Bird), later stakes-placed winner at up to 1½m in USA, and French 3-y-o 9f and 1½m winner Anna's Honor (by Alleged): dam unraced: backward, prominent over 3f in maiden at Newmarket in October: should improve. *M. A. Jarvis.*

MEZHIROV (USA)   3 b.c. Lemhi Gold (USA) 123–Santa Moira (USA) (Ex-   **52**
clusive Native (USA)) [1989 7g 1990 7f⁴ 8m] quite good-bodied colt: showed a markedly round action: staying-on fourth in maiden at Leicester in March: broke leg and destroyed at Warwick following month: should have been well suited by 1¼m. *J. H. M. Gosden.*

MIAD   3 b. or br.f. Wassl 125–Al Khazaama (USA) 78 (Alydar (USA)) [1989 NR   **64**
1990 7g 7.6m 7.2d² 8.2d] leggy filly: first foal: dam, probably stayed 9f, is daughter of high-class winner at up to 9f Drama Critic: quite modest maiden: set modest pace when second at Haydock: well beaten in handicap over 3 weeks later: should stay 1m: possibly needs an easy surface: sold 2,400 gns Newmarket December Sales. *R. W. Armstrong.*

MIA FILLIA   3 b.f. Formidable (USA) 125–As Blessed 101 (So Blessed 130) [1989   **56**
7m 5m 0.5f⁴ 7g a6g a7g⁴ 1990 0m 7f 8g⁵ 8.2m 7m 8g⁴ 10f⁶ 10g⁷ 11.5m⁴ 8m] strong, compact filly: has a quick action: plating-class maiden: suited by 1¼m: possibly best with give in the ground, though seems unsuited by soft: sold to join N. Tinkler 6,000 gns Newmarket Autumn Sales. *R. W. Armstrong.*

MIAMI BANKER   4 ch.c. Miami Springs 121–Banking Coyne 76 (Deep Diver   **96**
134) [1989 5s* 6v 5s* 5s* 5m 5f⁵ 5m² 5g* 5f² 5g 5m 1990 6m⁶ 5m⁶ 6m⁶ 5g* 6d 5d² 5.6g 5m 5d 5s6] strong, lengthy colt: moderate mover: fairly useful handicapper: won £13,900 event at Epsom in June by head from Joe Sugden, leading post: best at 5f: acts on any going: blinkered last 7 starts: has got on toes: tends to idle and is suited by strong handling and waiting tactics. *P. J. Arthur.*

MIAMI BEAR   4 b.g. Miami Springs 121–Belinda Bear (Ragstone 128) [1989   **—**
8.2v⁵ 11m 9m 10.4g⁴ 12.2f⁴ 11s 12m³ 1990 12m⁵] strong, good-bodied gelding: has a round action: plating-class maiden: probably stays 1½m: best effort on soft ground: keen sort: winning hurdler. *J. Berry.*

MIAMI PRIDE   4 b.f. Miami Springs 121–Gwynpride (Val de L'Orne (FR) 130)   **—**
[1989 5d 5m 6g 5f 1990 a7g a7g 10m] sparely-made filly: moderate mover: plater:

well behind last 6 outings: has worn blinkers, visor and bandages: trained on reappearance by T. Kersey. *Ronald Thompson.*

MIA SCINTILLA 4 ch.f. Blazing Saddles (AUS)–Melindra 83 (Gold Form 108) **43** [1989 NR 1990 a8g a7g a6g a5g6 a6g a5g4 5m 6g a7g a6g 6g4 a5g 5g6 a5g* a5g4 6g a5g3 a6g] lengthy filly: poor mover: poor handicapper: 20/1 and ridden by 7-lb claimer, won 16-runner event at Southwell in July, making most and holding on gamely: soon clear and ran very well in similar event penultimate outing: best at 5f: blinkered third and ninth starts: wears bandages. *S. R. Bowring.*

MICDAN 3 gr.g. Exhibitioner 111–Galaxy Scorpio (Saritamer (USA) 130) [1989 5d **48** 5d* 7g 6m 6g a7g5 1990 a7g2 a7g a8g2 a7g2 a7g3 7d 7m 6d5] close-coupled, rather unfurnished gelding: moderate mover: fair plater: ran creditably on all-weather, and in apprentice handicap final start: probably stays 1m: acts on dead going: often blinkered. *C. N. Williams.*

MICHELOZZO (USA) 4 b.c. Northern Baby (CAN) 127–Tres Agreable (FR) **117 d** (Luthier 126) [1989 8.2s* 12g3 14m* 14.6s* 1990 13.4d2 12d6 14g 16.2d2 15.5v4] finely-made, attractive colt: poor mover, with a rather scratchy action: impressive winner of St Leger Stakes at Ayr final outing as 3-y-o, but was disappointing in 1990: odds-on second to Braashee in slowly-run Ormonde EBF Stakes at Chester and Morley Street in minor event at Goodwood: reportedly spread plate and returned lame second outing, then well beaten in Irish St Leger 3 months later: suited by test of stamina: seems to need soft going: to join J. Hammond in France. *H. R. A. Cecil.*

MICHIKA (IRE) 2 b.f. (Jan 27) Runnett 125–Soudchika (GER) (Dschingis **41** Khan) [1990 5m 6d6 6d] medium-sized filly: has a roundish action: first reported foal: dam from family of Dubian and See You Then: poor form in maidens. *E. A. Wheeler.*

MICK'S CHOICE 2 b.c. (Mar 30) Petoski 135–Holy Day 82 (Sallust 134) [1990 **65** 6g5 6m2 7.5d4 7.5f 7m4 a7g 8m 8g a8g6 a7g2 a7g3 a7g a6g4 a7g3 a8g5] 7,600Y: compact, good-quartered colt: easy mover: first living foal: dam best at 2 yrs, when 5f winner: quite modest maiden: best form at 7f: blinkered last 7 outings: has been bandaged off-fore: has had tongue tied down: has run poorly for claimer: inconsistent. *M. W. Easterby.*

MICRO LOVE 6 ch.h. Vaigly Great 127–Minne Love 67 (Homeric 133) [1989 **83** 5m4 5f6 5g6 5h* 5m* 5m2 5.8h2 5g 5m* 5g4 5m 1990 5g6 5m* 5g6 5m3 6m 5m 6m 6m6 5m 5.8f] small, strong, workmanlike horse: good mover: modest handicapper: won £7,300 contest at Sandown in April: ran poorly last 2 outings, blinkered first time: finds easy 5f on sharp side nowadays: best on top-of-the-ground: has won when sweating: tends to be a little on edge. *L. G. Cottrell.*

MIDAS BLUE (IRE) 2 ch.f. (Apr 28) Burslem 123–Lady's Guest (Be My Guest **52** (USA) 126) [1990 6f 7f3 7d a7g a7g2 a7g] IR 2,000Y, resold 3,600Y: second foal: half-sister to 4-y-o Dancing Breeze (by Horage): dam placed from 1m to 1¼m in Ireland: plating-class maiden: will be better suited by 1m: ran respectably after starting slowly when visored final outing. *A. Bailey.*

MIDDLE HALF 5 b.g. Formidable (USA) 125–Moiety Bird (Falcon 131) [1989 **46** NR 1990 10.1g2 11.7g 12g3 10.8g4 10m5 12f5] medium-sized gelding: carries plenty of condition: moderate mover: poor maiden: stays 1½m: acts on good to firm going: blinkered third and fifth starts. *P. F. I. Cole.*

MIDDLE KINGDOM (USA) 3 b.c. Northern Dancer–Puget Sound 95 (High **100** Top 131) [1989 6g 1990 8f4 8.5g4 12m* 12d* 11.5f3 12m6] strong, good-topped colt: moderate walker and mover: won maiden at Haydock in May, running on strongly to lead close home despite edging left, and 3-runner £10,200 event at Ascot in June, making most: sweating and swishing tail beforehand, well-beaten last of 6 in Gordon Stakes at Goodwood in July: should stay further: acts on firm and dead going: useful. *B. W. Hills.*

MIDFIELDER 4 ch.g. Formidable (USA) 125–Pampas Flower 80 (Pampered — King 121) [1989 7g2 8f* 8f 8m 1990 8f 10.6d] deep-girthed, workmanlike gelding: quite useful winner at 3 yrs: never dangerous in handicaps (second one for amateurs) in 1990, off course 6 months in between: stays 9f: acts on any going: very much on toes when running moderately final start at 3 yrs: useful hurdler. *P. J. Hobbs.*

MIDNIGHT FLAME 4 gr.g. Kalaglow 132–Midnight Flit 89 (Bold Lad (IRE) — 133) [1989 10.1m a8g6 a12g 1990 11.5f a8g] rangy gelding: lightly raced and little sign of ability: sold 750 gns Ascot December Sales. *M. J. Fetherston-Godley.*

MIDNIGHT JESTOR (IRE) 2 b.f. (May 16) Jester 119–Midnight Patrol — (Ashmore (FR) 125) [1990 6m 7f 7m 8m 6d] leggy filly: third foal: sister to 6f winner Viceroy Jester and half-sister to 1988 2-y-o 7.5f winner Punta Baluarte (by Viking): dam placed over 1¼m in Ireland: of little account: visored penultimate start, blinkered final one: has been bandaged. *B. Stevens.*

MIDNIGHT LASS 2 b.f. (Feb 28) Today And Tomorrow 78–Capel Lass (The 59 ?
Brianstan 128) [1990 5m² 5f⁴ 5m² a6g⁶ 5f* 5.1m*] 2,500Y: leggy filly: moderate mover: first foal: dam never ran: useful plater: no bid after making all at Windsor and Yarmouth (hung left most of way) in August: will prove best at 5f. *J. Berry.*

MIDNIGHT OWL (FR) 3 b.f. Ardross 134–Midnight Lady (FR) 89 (Mill Reef —
(USA) 141) [1989 NR 1990 14f] sparely-made filly: seventh foal: half-sister to several winners, including useful French pair Party Doll (by Be My Guest), successful at up to 1m, and 1986 2-y-o 6.5f winner Microcosme (by Golden Fleece): dam, 6f winner from 2 starts at 2 yrs, is daughter of very smart Mia Pola: made most when well beaten in maiden at Redcar in October. *H. R. A. Cecil.*

MIDNIGHT SAGA 2 b.c. (May 10) Mashhor Dancer (USA)–Honey Pot 111 —
(Hotfoot 126) [1990 a7g] 26,000Y: half-brother to 5 winners, including useful 1987 2-y-o 5f winner Ship of Fools (by Windjammer) and quite useful 6f to 1m winner Great Northern (by Dom Racine): dam sprinting 2-y-o: weak 14/1-shot, well beaten in 16 runner maiden at Southwell in December. *Sir Mark Prescott.*

MIDNIGHT STRIKE (USA) 6 b.g. Topsider (USA)–Revels End 79 (Welsh —
Pageant 132) [1989 NR 1990 10.6m⁶] close-coupled gelding: 33/1 and blinkered, always mid-division in claimer at Haydock in August, only second race on flat: winner over hurdles, but isn't one to trust. *J. H. Baker.*

MIDSUMMER BREEZE 3 b.f. Tumble Wind (USA)–Pam Story (Sallust 134) —
[1989 5f* 5f 1990 5m 5m⁶] sparely-made filly: odds on, won maiden at Wolver-hampton at 2 yrs: behind in Molecomb Stakes at Goodwood later in 1989: ran and handicaps in summer 1990: sold 1,600 gns Ascot September Sales. *J. P. Hudson.*

MIDSUMMER COMMON 2 b.f. (Feb 24) Hotfoot 126–Summer Fayre 64 42
(Reform 132) [1990 5m 5g³ 6m⁶ 6g⁵ 7g 7m³ 7.5g⁵ 8m] small, rather sparely-made filly: has a round action: second foal: dam appeared to stay 1¼m: quite moderate plater: had stiff task final start: should be suited by 1m: sold 850 gns Newmarket Autumn Sales, resold 740 gns Ascot December Sales to join A. Moore. *D. Morley.*

MIDWEST 3 ch.g. Kabour 80–Boom Shanty 66 (Dragonara Palace (USA) 115) —
[1989 5g 1990 6m 6m 5m 5d 6d 9s] sturdy gelding: appears of no account: blinkered fifth start: once refused to enter stalls. *D. W. Chapman.*

MIEKA 3 ch.g. Longleat (USA) 109–Secret Pearl (Gulf Pearl 117) [1989 8g⁶ 7g 64
5g* 1990 5d 6m⁴ 5g⁵ 10m 7m 8m² 14g 8m 10s a8g] leggy, quite good-topped gelding: poor mover: quite modest handicapper: should stay at least 1½m: acts on good to firm ground: swished tail in preliminaries and taken down last and quietly sixth outing: trained until after seventh by R. Boss. *B. J. Curley.*

MIGHTY DRAGON (IRE) 2 b.c. (Mar 19) Taufan (USA) 119–Honagh Lee 73
(Main Reef 126) [1990 6m⁴ 6d² 6g⁴ 5.8f² 6m*] 16,500F, 17,000Y: leggy colt: moderate mover: first foal: dam never ran: modest performer: odds on, comfortably made all in maiden at Nottingham in July: hung first 2 starts and looked unco-operative when blinkered third: should stay 7f: carries head awkwardly: sold 10,000 gns Newmarket Autumn Sales. *J. L. Dunlop.*

MIGHTY GLOW 6 gr.g. Kalaglow 132–Faridetta 107 (Good Bond 122) [1989 10s 73 d
10.2g 12m 13m² 12f 13f⁴ 12t⁶ 12g³ 16f⁴ 12m 15.3g⁵ 10m 15.5f⁶ 15s 1090 a13g 16m⁶
14m* 12.5m 12f4 14g* 12h 12m 10.6s 12g 14d 16m 16.2f³ 16m 10g 12m] leggy, workmanlike gelding: moderate mover: has looked ungenuine and is thoroughly unreliable, but did nothing wrong when winning handicaps at Nottingham in April under strong handling: stays 2m: acts on firm going: often visored: winning hurdler in October. *C. Tinkler.*

MILADY-SAL 3 ch.f. Milford 119–Bralanta 71 (Green God 128) [1989 5m 5m⁶ 6g —
a7g a8g 1990 a7g 7m 10f] small, good-quartered filly: poor mover: poor plater: visored, swished tail under pressure final start. *R. T. Juckes.*

MILAN FAIR 6 b.g. Mill Reef (USA) 141–Fairweather Friend (USA) 69 (Forli —
(ARG)) [1989 6d 8m 10.1m* 10m 11.7m² 12f⁶ 12m⁵ 1990 8.3m] lengthy gelding: poor winner of claimer (apprentice ridden) as 5-y-o: bandaged, last of 18 in similar event in July: stays 11.7f: acts on good to firm and good going: blinkered or visored on 4 of last 5 appearances in 1988: inconsistent. *P. D. Cundell.*

MILBURN LEISURE 3 br.g. Kala Shikari 125–Paperwork (Brigadier Gerard —
144) [1989 7m 1990 7.5d] no show in maiden auction race and seller. *A. Smith.*

MILCLERE 4 ch.f. Milford 119–Great Lass (Vaigly Great 127) [1989 7f 10f 8f 37
a12g⁵ 1990 a10g 12m 16.5m⁵ a14g⁴ 10m⁵ a11g² a12g⁶] leggy filly: poor maiden: stays
1¾m: blinkered first start, visored fifth: trained until after first outing by W.
Wightman: keen sort. *J. A. Glover.*

MILFORD MAGIC 2 ch.f. (Mar 25) Mummy's Game 120–Toccata (USA) 64 (Mr —
Leader (USA)) [1990 5f 6m a7g⁶ a6g 6g 6g] 1,500Y: lengthy filly: has a round action:
closely related to fair 1m winner Stage Villain (by Mummy's Pet), later temperamental, and half-sister to quite modest 5f to 7f winner Orchard's Pet (by Petong):
dam sprint maiden: seems of little account. *P. Howling.*

MILHOLM 3 ch.c. Milford 119–Hagen's Bargain 62§ (Mount Hagen (FR) 127) —
[1989 7f 6f 1990 7f 11.7f] small colt: no form in maidens and claimers. *G. B. Balding.*

MILIEU 5 b.h. Habitat 134–Lady Graustark (USA) (Graustark) [1989 8d⁶ 9g 8f⁶ 111
7f* 8m⁴ 8g* 7m⁴ 7d* 1990 6m* 7g⁵ 8g³ 6m³ 8g 6g² 9g] big, strong horse: won 3
listed events in 1989 and landed the odds by neck in another at Leopardstown in
March: placed after in similar contests at Phoenix Park and the Curragh (beaten
head by La Grange Music) and behind demoted A Prayer For Wings in EBF
Greenlands Stakes at the Curragh in between: effective at 6f and stays 9f: acts on
any going: very useful. *D. K. Weld, Ireland.*

MILITARY FASHION 4 ch.c. Mill Reef (USA) 141–Smarten Up 119 (Sharpen 101
Up 127) [1989 8g* 10mʷᵒ 10g³ 1990 10m² 9m* 12s] tall, good-topped colt: moderate
walker: has a quick action: suffered hairline fracture of cannon bone in spring:
returned in good form late in season, making all in £7,100 event (odds on) at
Newmarket: raced too freely in November Handicap at Doncaster:
stays 1¼m: acts on good to firm going. *L. M. Cumani.*

MILITARY SHOT (USA) 3 b.g. Lyphard's Wish (FR) 124–Pavahra 93 85
(Mummy's Pet 125) [1989 6m³ 6m⁶ 6f* 7m⁵ 1990 7f⁵ 8m 7m² 7.6g⁴ 7m⁶ 7f 7g 7d²]
leggy, workmanlike gelding: fair handicapper: well worth another try over 1m: acts
on firm and dead going: sometimes slowly away: sweating second start: sold 21,000
gns Newmarket Autumn Sales. *G. A. Pritchard-Gordon.*

MILL DE LEASE 5 b.h. Milford 119–Melting Snows 88 (High Top 131) [1989 —
8.5f4 12.3f⁵ 10f⁵ 17f a11g 1990 a14g] leggy, workmanlike, angular horse: winning
plater as 3-y-o: bandaged, tailed off in non-selling handicap at Southwell in December, first run for year: stays 1½m: probably acts on any going: moved down
poorly second start at 4 yrs. *J. Dooler.*

MILLFIELDS LADY 3 b.f. Sayf El Arab (USA) 127–Ma Pierrette 77 75
(Cawston's Clown 113) [1989 6h* 7f⁴ 7h³ 6g³ 6g 8m² 10f⁴ 8.2g³ 1990 8d³ 8m 8m*
8m* 10f⁴ 10m 10f 10g⁵ 8d] leggy filly: moderate mover: modest handicapper: won at
Goodwood in May and June: inconsistent afterwards: best form over 1m, though
should stay further: yet to race on soft going, acts on any other: visored, slowly into
stride and tailed off most of way final start: bandaged seventh. *R. Simpson.*

MILL FLIGHT (IRE) 2 b.f. (May 18) Millfontaine 114–Diyala (FR) (Direct 46
Flight) [1990 5m 5g⁶ 6d³ 6g a7g 7d] IR 800F: leggy filly: second foal: dam French
11.5f winner: third in maiden at Catterick in July, only worthwhile form: tailed off in
seller final outing: should be suited by 7f. *Mrs P. A. Barker.*

MILLFORD HAVEN 5 b.g. Welsh Saint 126–Flute (FR) (Luthier 126) [1989 —
NR 1990 11g⁵ 11.5f] rather sparely-made ex-Irish gelding: third foal: half-brother to
Any Song (by Bold Lad, IRE), fairly useful winner who stayed 9f: dam poor maiden:
first past the post in maiden at Limerick and handicap (demoted) at Mallow as 3-y-o:
pulled up lame in seller in July, and not seen out again: stays 1¼m. *Dr J. D. Scargill.*

MILLIE (USA) 2 ch.f. (Feb 29) Master Willie 129–La Zonga (USA) (Run The 65 p
Gantlet (USA)) [1990 7g] $9,700F, $36,000Y: smallish filly: second foal: dam ran 7
times: around 9 lengths eighth of 16, keeping on under considerate ride, in maiden
at Sandown in September: moved moderately down: should improve. *H. Candy.*

MILLIGAN 5 ch.h. Tap On Wood 130–Rose Music 86 (Luthier 126) [1989 8g* 8g 86
9.2f* 8f⁵ 8.2g⁴ 8m⁶ 8g 1990 8f 8g⁴ 8.2m 8f² 8m² 9m* 10.4g] strong, compact horse:
has a markedly round action: fair on his day: odds-on neck winner, hard ridden, of
5-runner claimer at Lingfield in August: ran well previous 2 outings, including in
Schweppes Golden Mile at Goodwood: effective at 1m to 9f: acts on firm going:
occasionally sweats: has worn a tongue strap: usually equipped with martingale
nowadays: none too consistent: sold to race abroad. *Sir Mark Prescott.*

MILLIONAIRE'S ROW 3 b.c. Niniski (USA) 125–One In A Million 125 (Rarity 86 +
129) [1989 NR 1990 12m² 12m* 12h² 14g] 115,000Y: rangy, angular colt: has a rather
round action: sixth foal: half-brother to top-class miler Milligram (by Mill Reef) and
useful 1986 3-y-o 7f winner Someone Special (by Habitat): dam won 1000 Guineas:

odds on, won maiden at Newbury in July and minor event at Thirsk in August: heavily-backed favourite, didn't settle and weakened final 2f in £15,900 handicap at York in August: should be suited by return to 1½m: carries head high: may well be capable of better. *H. R. A. Cecil.*

MILLION HEIRESS 3 b.f. Auction Ring (USA) 123–Irish Isle 67 (Realm 129) — [1989 6m 7g 6g 1990 6m 7g⁴ 7f⁶ 8f] workmanlike, good-quartered filly: poor maiden: should stay 1m: sold 1,100 gns Ascot October Sales. *G. B. Balding.*

MILLION MILES (USA) 2 b.c. (Feb 14) Dixieland Band (USA)–Highly Noble 70 p (USA) (Vaguely Noble 140) [1990 6m⁵ 8d⁶ 7m³] $85,000F, IR 88,000Y: attractive colt, rather dipped backed: has a round action: half-brother to 3 winners in North America: dam minor winner at 3 yrs: quite modest form in maidens: will improve, particularly back at 1m + : bandaged near-hind on debut. *B. W. Hills.*

MILLPOND BOY 6 ch.g. Connaught 130–Nonsensical 99 (Silly Season 127) 49 [1989 10.2g 1990 11.7g² 10m 14g] workmanlike gelding: has quick action: plating-class winner (apprentice ridden) as 4-y-o: form since only when second in Windsor handicap (hanging left) in August: stays 13f: acts on any going: sweated only start at 5 yrs. *R. J. Hodges.*

MILL POND (FR) 4 ro.c. Mill Reef (USA) 141–Royal Way (FR) (Sicambre 135) 105 [1989 11m² 12m* 12g⁵ 12g⁵ 12d 15m 1990 12f³ 15v³ 15.5d⁴ 12m⁶ 22d² 14g* 15g⁴] plain, close-coupled, good-topped colt: carries condition: moderate walker: capable of useful form: in frame in first half of year when trained by J. FitzGerald, including in Prix Vicomtesse Vigier at Longchamp and Queen Alexandra Stakes at Royal Ascot: then returned to France and winner of quite valuable race at Vichy in August: stays extreme distances: probably acts on any going: bandaged last 2 outings in Britain: ran moderately in ladies race (wore tongue strap, sweated and got very much on edge) fourth start: somewhat unreliable. *A. de Royer-Dupre, France.*

MILL RUN 3 b.f. Commanche Run 133–Gay Milly (FR) 74 (Mill Reef (USA) 141) 96 [1989 7m⁴ 7m⁴ 1990 10f* 10m*] tall, leggy filly: won slowly-run races for 2-runner maiden at Yarmouth in July and minor event (beat Ruby Setting 2½ lengths) at Salisbury in August: sold 12,500 gns Newmarket December Sales. *L. M. Cumani.*

MILLSOLIN (IRE) 2 b.c. (Apr 8) Millfontaine 114–Isolin (Saulingo 122) [1990 44 6m 7m 6d] 2,100 2-y-o: leggy, workmanlike colt: third foal: dam Irish maiden: well beaten, including in a seller (swerved stalls). *A. R. Davison.*

MILLY BLACK (IRE) 2 b.f. (Apr 8) Double Schwartz 128–Milly Lass (FR) 85 63 (Bold Lad (USA)) [1990 5m² 6m] 8,400Y: quite good-topped filly: half-sister to out-and-out stayer Otabari (by Welsh Pageant), 7.6f winner Azyaa (by Kris) and a winner in Hong Kong: dam 2-y-o 7f winner, is half-sister to smart Kashmir Lass: burly, staying-on ¾-length second of 5 to Mayaasa in maiden at Newmarket in May: prominent to halfway in similar event at Goodwood over 4 months later. *W. Jarvis.*

MILLY-MANDY 2 b.f. (Apr 16) Dominion 123–Ulla Laing 107 (Mummy's Pet — p 125) [1990 6d] leggy, light-framed filly: second foal: dam 2-y-o 5f and 6f winner is out of staying mare Goosie-Gantlet: green, good speed over 4f in unfavoured centre of track in maiden at Lingfield in October: should improve. *R. Akehurst.*

MILLY SHARP 3 ch.f. (Feb 25) Nishapour (FR) 125–Becky Sharp 66 (Sharpen 44 Up 127) [1990 5g³ 5m 6g 5g 7m⁴ 7f⁴ 7f³ 7g⁶ 6m⁵ 6m] 6,000Y: angular, leggy filly: has a very round action: second living foal: dam 1m winner: moderate plater: should stay 1m: sold 920 gns Doncaster November Sales. *H. J. Collingridge.*

MILNE'S WAY 3 ch.f. The Noble Player (USA) 126–Daring Way (USA) 78 68 (Alydar (USA)) [1989 6f⁵ 6f³ 6g 6m 6m* 5.8f* 6g² 7g³ 1990 6g 6g⁶ 6m 8.5d⁵ 8m 8h* 8f³ 8.3m 7m⁵ 10d 8g⁴ 8m] workmanlike filly: has a round action: modest handicapper: gambled on, returned to form when winning at Bath in July: easily best subsequent efforts when in frame: better at 1m than shorter: acts on hard going: usually edgy. *G. Lewis.*

MILTON BURN 9 b.h. Sexton Blake 126–Neasden Belle 66 (Sovereign Path — 125) [1989 16s² 12v³ 12s² 14f 12m 12f 14g⁴ 13.3m 18g 1990 16.2m 16s] narrow, leggy horse: poor walker: has rather a round action: modest handicapper: usually at his best in spring: effective at 1½m and stays very well: ideally suited by an easy surface: has worn blinkers and a visor: often on toes: none too consistent. *C. A. Austin.*

MIMINING 4 ch.f. Tower Walk 130–Louisianalightning (Music Boy 124) [1989 55 7g 7.3s 6d 6s² 5m 6m 5d 5s 6s 7d 1990 6m 5m⁵ 5g³ 6g a7g⁵ a5g 6g* 5d³ a6g* 6g] lengthy, good-quartered filly: turns near-fore in: moderate mover: plating-class handicapper: won at Nottingham and Southwell in June: ideally suited by 6f: acts on heavy going: blinkered once at 3 yrs, visored fifth and sixth starts: often used to sweat and get on toes. *P. S. Felgate.*

MIMI'S MACHINE   2 ch.f. (May 25) Bairn (USA) 126–Camarilla (Posse (USA)   **36**
130) [1990 6m³ 5.1m⁵ 5f⁶ 6m⁵ 6f] 1,500Y: neat filly: first foal: dam unraced daughter
of Park Hill second Wolverene: poor plater: will probably be better suited by 7f. *J. R.
Jenkins.*

MIND THE STEP   3 b.c. Shareef Dancer (USA) 135–Mytinia 94 (Bustino 136)   **74 +**
[1989 NR 1990 10.6s⁶ 10d* 10.2s] lengthy, quite attractive colt: has a quick action:
third foal: half-brother to 4-y-o Mytaski (by Niniski): dam, 11.7f winner, is sister to
very smart 1½m winner Bustomi: favourite on first run for over 4½ months,
comfortably won 3-runner minor contest at Leicester in October: well beaten in
competitive minor event following month: should stay 1½m: green all starts, coltish
first 2 occasions. *G. Harwood.*

MINDY (IRE)   2 b.c. (May 27) Salmon Leap (USA) 131–Malija (FR) (Malicious)   **—**
[1990 6f 7m 8d 7g 8m 6d] IR 4,200F: workmanlike colt: has scope: closely related to
2 winners in Italy and half-brother to another: dam French middle-distance winner
also successful in Italy: well beaten in varied events. *N. A. Callaghan.*

MINERS LAW (IRE)   2 b.c. (Mar 23) Law Society (USA) 130–Lighted Lamp   **—**
(USA) (Sir Gaylord) [1990 7m 7g 7m] 17,000Y: rather leggy colt: has a round action:
half-brother to numerous winners, including smart French 7f to 1½m performer
Lighted Glory (by Nijinsky) and smart middle-distance stayer Torus (by Ribero):
dam half-sister to Crocket: bit backward, soundly beaten in maidens at Newmarket,
Salisbury and Chepstow: likely to do better over further. *G. Lewis.*

MINE'S A DOUBLE   5 b.g. Crofter (USA) 124–Modena (Sassafras (FR) 135)   **—**
[1989 7d 6s 5f 5m 6f 6m* 6f 5m 5f⁵ 7g 7m³ 8f* 7g⁴ a7g 1990 7m 8m 7.5m a7g 7m 7m
6m a7g 8f 7m 7m] strong, compact gelding: winning plater as 4-y-o: no form in 1990:
stays 1m: acts on firm going: visored final start: sold 6,200 gns Doncaster January
Sales: resold 1,500 gns Doncaster September Sales. *R. Hollinshead.*

MING COURT   2 br.f. (Feb 12) Daring March 116–Slick Chick 89 (Shiny Tenth   **55**
120) [1990 5m⁵ 6g 6m 6d 8m a7g] 8,200Y: good-topped filly: eighth living foal:
half-sister to several winners here and abroad, including quite useful 5f to 1¼m
winner Basil Boy (by Jimsun): dam stayed 13f: plating-class maiden: caught eye
given considerate ride in Warwick nursery penultimate outing: ran badly final start:
should stay 1m: seems unsuited by a soft surface. *S. Dow.*

MINGUS (USA)   3 b.c. The Minstrel (CAN) 135–Sylph (USA) 110 (Alleged (USA)   **89 p**
138) [1989 8m² 1990 10g² 12g³ 12d*] compact, heavy-topped colt: landed odds in
maiden at Folkestone in November: fairly useful effort when third to Rudjig in
Salisbury minor event on first run for 1½m months: better at 1½m than shorter: may
be capable of better. *G. Harwood.*

MINIMIZE   3 b.c. Alzao (USA) 117–Timinala 58 (Mansingh (USA) 120) [1989 7m   **90**
7f² 7g² 1990 8f² 8.5g² 10d⁶ 10f* 10f⁴ 10m² 9m 10s² 12s] strong, close-coupled colt:
fairly useful performer: won maiden at Brighton in June: ran well after when in
frame for quite valuable handicaps and minor event, poorly in Cambridgeshire
Handicap at Newmarket and November Handicap at Doncaster: stays 1¼m well:
acts on any going. *L. M. Cumani.*

MINIZEN DANCER   2 b.c. (Mar 22) Fulmar (USA)–Reperage (USA) (Key To   **58**
Content (USA)) [1990 5m³ 5f⁵ 5f⁵ 6g 6m² 6f 6g 8.2g 6g] 12,000Y: rather angular
colt: moderate mover: first foal: dam French 2-y-o 1m winner: sire French 1m to
1¼m winner: plating-class maiden: ran moderately in nurseries final (visored last) 4
outings: stays 6f: sometimes sweats: sold 1,500 gns Doncaster November Sales. *M.
Brittain.*

MINIZEN MINSTREL (IRE)   2 ch.c. (Apr 26) Fayruz 116–Sassess (Sassafras   **41**
(FR) 135) [1990 5s⁴ 5m 6g 7g 7m 6d 8m] IR 8,000F, 5,000Y: leggy, sparely-made
colt: third foal: half-brother to a winner abroad by Horage: dam placed at 1m at 3 yrs
in Ireland: poor maiden: best form at 7f: bandaged behind final 2 outings: sold 720
gns Doncaster October Sales. *M. Brittain.*

MINIZEN MUSIC (IRE)   2 b.g. (Apr 6) Anita's Prince 126–Northern Amber   **64**
(Shack (USA) 118) [1990 5g* 5m 6g 6g 5m⁶ 5m 5v² 5m a5g 5d] 5,200Y:
sparely-made gelding: moderate mover: second foal: half-brother to 3-y-o Persian
Spring (by King Persian): dam ran several times: 3-length winner of large-field
sellers at Beverley (no bid) and Thirsk (bought in 10,000 gns) in May: ran
moderately on all-weather late in year: better suited by 5f than 6f: acts on top-
of-the-ground and heavy: blinkered (running creditably) sixth start: inconsistent.
M. Brittain.

MINIZEN STAR (IRE)   2 ch.c. (Feb 8) Thatching 131–Rose Linnet (USA) (Mr   **52**
Prospector (USA)) [1990 a5g³ 5v⁶ 5g a6g a8g] 2,400F, 12,500Y: small colt: first foal:

dam unraced from family of Critique: plating-class maiden: easily best effort on first outing: off course for over 5 months after third. *M. Brittain.*

MINKES BOY (IRE) 2 ch.g. (Mar 31) Krayyan 117–Willow Bird 74 (Weepers Boy 124) [1990 7f4 a7g 8m] IR 18,000Y: strong, lengthy gelding: has scope: good walker: half-brother to several winners, including fair 6f to 1m winner Willow Red (by Red Alert) and 5f winner Flying Dolphin (by Deep Diver): dam stayed 1m: poor form in minor event and maiden auction: slowly away final start. *J. S. Wainwright.* **32**

MINSK 4 ch.f. Kabour 80–Wedded Bliss 76 (Relko 136) [1989 8m6 8.2m4 8m5 8f 1990 a7g a5g 8m5 7m 7g 6g 7f 8f6 12m 8f 10m] workmanlike filly: bad plater: doesn't stay 1½m. *D. W. Chapman.* **—**

MINSKIP MISS 3 ch.f. Lucky Wednesday 124–Sofica 56 (Martinmas 128) [1989 5f4 5m6 6m 5g 1990 6g 6f4 6m a7g 7m3 7f 6m4 6g] small, leggy filly: poor walker: poor maiden: should be suited by return to 7f: easily best efforts on good to firm ground. *Don Enrico Incisa.* **41**

MINSKIP (USA) 2 ch.f. (May 6) The Minstrel (CAN) 135–Fabulous Native (USA) (Le Fabuleux 133) [1990 5m4 5m* 5m6 6m] neat filly: moderate walker: closely related to useful 1983 Irish 2-y-o Ballet de France (by Northern Dancer) and half-sister to very smart middle-distance performer St Hilarion (by Sir Ivor): dam half-sister to useful Irish 6f to 1¼m performer Muscovite out of close relation to Exclusive Native: odds on, made all in maiden at Wolverhampton in July: best form at 5f, but should stay further. *B. W. Hills.* **62**

MINSTER LADY 2 b.f. (Mar 28) Damister (USA) 123–Stately Girl (Free State 125) [1990 7m 7f 7f] leggy, sparely-made filly: moderate walker: fourth foal: dam won 6 races in Italy: prominent to 2f out in sellers and a claimer. *M. Bell.* **34**

MINSTER TIMES 2 ch.c. (Apr 4) Good Times (ITY)–Gunnera (Royal Gunner (USA)) [1990 7.5d 7m2 8m 8.2g 8f] 5,000Y: leggy, rather shallow-girthed colt: has quick action: seventh foal: half-brother to a winner in Belgium: dam unraced: plating-class maiden: visored, speed 6f then weakened quickly in auction event final start: sold 1,400 gns Doncaster November Sales. *C. Tinkler.* **60**

MINSTREL DANCER (USA) 3 b.c. The Minstrel (CAN) 135–Belle Gallante (USA) (Gallant Man) [1989 6g 1990 6m3 5g* 6f* 8f4 8m6 6s2] quite attractive colt: moderate mover: fairly useful performer: landed odds in maiden at Beverley and minor event at Thirsk in July: ran well when in frame in minor events afterwards: moved badly down fifth start: stays 1m: acts on any going. *L. M. Cumani.* **96**

MIRACLES HAPPEN 2 ch.f. (Feb 24) Superlative 118–Pilfer 81 (Vaigly Great 127) [1990 5g2 a6g3 5g 5m 5f5 6h2 6f3 6m 5g 6m] 5,400Y: small, sturdy filly: second foal: half-sister to a winner in Belgium: dam placed over 7f at 2 yrs: modest plater: claimed out of K. Brassey's stable on debut: stays 6f: ran poorly in blinkers fifth outing: suitable mount for 7-lb claimer: trained second to eighth outings by M. Tompkins. *Mrs S. Oliver.* **46**

MIRANDA JAY 2 b. or br.f. (Feb 3) Night Shift (USA)–Assisi (Habitat 134) [1990 7g3 7m*] compact filly: quite good mover: first foal: dam twice-raced half-sister **80 p**

Offa's Dyke Maiden Fillies Stakes, Chepstow —
Miranda Jay (centre) is Pat Eddery's two-hundredth winner of the season

to smart 7f to 2m winner Harly: favourite, won 22-runner maiden at Chepstow in October shade comfortably by a length from Lara's Baby, leading over 1f out: will stay 1m: likely to do better. *M. A. Jarvis.*

MIRROR BLACK 4 b.c. Alzao (USA) 117–Flaxen Hair (Thatch (USA) 136) [1989 **119** 8.2g* 8f* 8f* 8f3dis 8m3 8f3 7g2 8v3 1990 8g* 8.5g4 8m2 8m4 8s* 7m4] close-coupled, good-bodied colt: smart performer: won Badener Meile in May and Elite Preis at Cologne in September: ran best races when clear neck second of 9, hanging left 1f out, to Markofdistinction in Queen Anne Stakes (reportedly returned lame) at Royal Ascot and fourth to Sally Rous in Jameson Irish Whiskey Challenge Stakes at Newmarket in October: stays 8.5f: acts on any going: has a good turn of foot: usually looks extremely well: tough and consistent: a credit to his trainer: sold to race in Saudi Arabia. *P. J. Makin.*

MIRROR'S IMAGE 2 ch.f. (Feb 19) Never So Bold 135–Mirabiliary (USA) 74 — (Crow (FR) 134) [1990 6f6] 22,000Y: first foal: dam 1¼m winner: chased leaders to halfway, hung left and soon dropped out in 6-runner maiden at Yarmouth in July. *G. A. Pritchard-Gordon.*

MISALLAH (IRE) 2 b. or br.f. (Apr 22) Shirley Heights 130–Turkish Treasure — (USA) 111 (Sir Ivor 135) [1990 7m 8m 8.2v] rangy filly: poor walker: closely related to smart Irish 7f to 13f winner The Miller (by Mill Reef) and half-sister to several other winners, including useful Irish 2-y-o's Magic Mirror (by Nureyev) and Treasure Trove (by Try My Best): dam won over 6f and 7f at 2 yrs: well beaten in autumn in maidens at Sandown (slowly away) and Leicester (pulled hard) and minor event at Haydock: should stay middle distances: sold 13,000 gns Newmarket December Sales. *J. L. Dunlop.*

MISCHAK (USA) 3 b.g. Miswaki (USA) 124–Chuckles (USA) (Riverman (USA) **58** 131) [1989 NR 1990 8m 8g5 8g 10m4 8g a8g4 a12g2 a14g a10g3 a11g] $210,000Y: workmanlike gelding: moderate walker: first foal: dam once-raced daughter of Kentucky Oaks third Funny Cat: easily best efforts when placed in claiming events at Southwell and Lingfield: suited by 1½m: tends to sweat: ridden by claimer last 4 starts: very slowly away and looked to take little interest in claimer (claimed out of A. Scott's stable £6,000 and subsequently gelded) on fifth. *W. A. O'Gorman.*

MISCHIEVOUS TYKE 4 ch.f. Flying Tyke 90–Habatashia 62 (Habat 127) **36** [1989 7d6 8.2s 7.5f 6m* 6f3 7m 7m5 6g 6g 8f5 8m 1990 8.2f a7g3] leggy, good-topped filly: carries condition: winning plater as 3-y-o: stays 7f: acts on firm and dead going. *A. Smith.*

MISDEMEANOURS GIRL (IRE) 2 b.f. (May 2) Fairy King (USA)–Dar-A- **49** Meter (Dara Monarch 128) [1990 5m 5.3h6 5f3 6m] 5,600Y: small filly: first foal: dam Irish maiden: plating-class form: should prove suited by 6f + . *M. R. Channon.*

MISHAB 3 ch.c. Local Suitor (USA) 128–Jeema 102 (Thatch (USA) 136) [1989 NR — 1990 6f 8m 8.2m] IR 23,000Y: good-topped colt: moderate mover: first foal: dam, best at 2 yrs, won 3 times at 5f: ridden by 7-lb claimer, behind in maidens and minor event in the summer. *G. A. Huffer.*

MISS ABBI 3 b.f. Jalmood (USA) 126–The Shrew 92 (Relko 136) [1989 6m 1990 — 8.2v 12.2d 12d a14g] rather unfurnished filly: bad plater. *C. Tinkler.*

MISS ABOYNE 5 b.m. Lochnager 132–Mia Cosa (USA) 78 (Ragusa 137) [1989 **57** 7d 8.2v4 8f 6f 12f4 8f* 8.5g2 10g3 7f6 1990 5s2 10.6s 12g 12g4 5g* 10f 7m 8m] lengthy, workmanlike mare: won amateurs handicap at Edinburgh in July: best other efforts in similar races as 5-y-o at Hamilton and Ayr (carried 11 lb overweight) on first and sixth starts: effective at 5f and seems to stay 1¼m: acts on any going: blinkered once: has hung right: trained until after sixth outing by J. S. Wilson. *J. A. Glover.*

MISS ACKLAM 2 b.f. (Feb 25) Lochnager 132–Lady of Leisure 75 (Record Run — 127) [1990 7f] 2,000Y: first foal: dam won twice over 5f, including at 2 yrs: slowly away and always behind in claimer at Carlisle in September. *B. W. Murray.*

MISS ADVENTURE 3 b.f. Adonijah 126–Sunset Ray 74 (Hotfoot 126) [1989 6m **69** 7m2 7m4 8m5 8g3 8m3 10f2 1990 9m6 12g* 13g3 16.2s2 15.3g 14d 18d] angular filly: moderate mover: quite modest performer: won claimer at Newmarket in May: stiff tasks in handicaps last 2 starts: should prove suited by further than 1½m: acts on any going: winning hurdler. *M. H. Tompkins.*

MISS ALCAZAR 3 b.f. Aragon 118–Permutation 79 (Pinza 137) [1989 5d5 5m **28** 7g5 8g 1990 9.1m 8f 8m 7.5d 8.2s 7g 7d5 6m4 8m 7f 5m 7f 6m] leggy, lengthy filly: plater: seems suited by 6f: blinkered once at 2 yrs. *Denys Smith.*

Prix de Malleret, Longchamp—
Ruby Tiger comes third behind the French fillies Miss Alleged and Whitehaven

MISS ALLEGED (USA)   3 b.f. Alleged (USA) 138–Miss Tusculum (USA) **123** p
(Boldnesian (USA)) [1989 NR 1990 11g* 10.5g* 12d* 12m²]
   The Prix Vermeille at Longchamp in September unearthed one of the standard French Prix de l'Arc de Triomphe candidates in the runner-up Miss Alleged, an improving, lightly-raced three-year-old filly. But unfortunately she finished sore and couldn't take her place in the Arc; a cracked pedal bone was diagnosed and she subsequently underwent a successful operation for its repair which may enable her to return to the track as a four-year-old. Miss Alleged put up a very smart performance to divide Salsabil and In The Groove, beaten a neck: well handled, she challenged for the lead at about the same time as the winner, and though she never got in front she battled on so well that she was steadily pegging her back over the last furlong. That was Miss Alleged's first defeat. She didn't run as a two-year-old and the sum of her experience before the Vermeille amounted to three outings in small fields of fillies at Longchamp between May 15th and June 24th, beginning with a newcomers event. She progressed from there to the Group 3 Prix de Royaumont in which she comfortably accounted for weak opposition, then to the Group 2 Prix de Malleret. Miss Alleged seemed to have a stiff task in the Malleret, conceding 3 lb to her three opponents who included Whitehaven and Ruby Tiger, the former a very useful recent winner at Chantilly. Whitehaven led from Miss Alleged until giving way approaching the final furlong, Miss Alleged quickening on to score easily by two lengths; Ruby Tiger finished third, beaten a further length, having had every chance.

		Hoist The Flag	Tom Rolfe
	Alleged (USA)	(b 1968)	Wavy Navy
	(b 1974)	Princess Pout	Prince John
Miss Alleged (USA)		(b 1966)	Determined Lady
(b.f. 1987)		Boldnesian	Bold Ruler
	Miss Tusculum (USA)	(b 1963)	Alanesian
	(b 1970)	Sailor Town	Sailor
		(b 1965)	Dashing

   Miss Alleged's sire was a late-developer himself: a contemporary and stable-companion of the Derby winner The Minstrel, he finished second in the St Leger and progressed to win two Arcs. He has been standing in the United States since his retirement from racing, and Miss Alleged was bought over there, for 250,000 dollars as a yearling at Keeneland. The dam Miss Tusculum is an unraced mare from an American family whose standing she has helped to improve since she went to stud; the second dam has placed three times in twenty starts, the third dam never ran. All three have minor stakes winners among a collective total of twenty-plus winners. Miss Tusculum has two from five previously successful in the United States—Bold Josh (by Tentam) and Nancy's Champion (by Northern Jove), both of whom stayed at least a mile. Miss Alleged stays a mile and a half well. Before her injury she had shown form on ground both on the firm side of good and on the easy side. Where her future lies remains to be seen: hopefully, she'll be able to have a shot at the Arc another year. *P. Bary, France.*

MISS APPROPRIATE   2 br.f. (Feb 20) Touching Wood (USA) 127–Plaits 93   —
(Thatching 131) [1990 7f a7g] 1,500F, 7,800Y: smallish, workmanlike filly: second

581

foal: half-sister to middle-distance plater Headbee (by Head For Heights): dam unreliable maiden, stayed 7f: always behind in maiden auction at Doncaster and seller at Southwell. *M. W. Easterby.*

MISS ARAGON   2 b.f. (Mar 20) Aragon 118–Lavenham Blue (Streetfighter 120)   **48**
[1990 6d 5v³ 5s] rangy, good sort: has plenty of scope: good mover: third foal: dam poor maiden: poor form, including in seller: gambled-on favourite in Edinburgh seller final start: should stay beyond 5f. *M. P. Naughton.*

MISS ARK ROYAL   5 b.m. Broadsword (USA) 104–Starboard Belle 85 (Right   —
Tack 131) [1989 NR 1990 18m] medium-sized mare: quite modest maiden at best as 3-y-o: tailed off in handicap in June: stays 1½m: ran poorly in blinkers: sometimes sweats: winning selling hurdler in May. *A. R. Davison.*

MISS BATCHWORTH   4 ch.f. Ballacashtal (CAN)–Soft Secret (Most Secret   —
119) [1989 6m 6m 5.1m 6g 5m 5m 7m 1990 5f 6m 5m⁶] small, workmanlike filly: moderate mover: little form since 2 yrs: barely stays 5f when conditions are testing: bandaged behind last 2 outings: trained until after reappearance by C. Holmes: sold 775 gns Ascot November Sales. *R. Akehurst.*

MISS BEA   3 b.f. Petorius 117–Stop The Cavalry (Relko 136) [1989 NR 1990 a7g⁴
a8g⁶ a10g 8g 7d 6m 7g 7m 7f a6g] 7,400F, 9,000Y: lengthy filly: third foal: half-sister to modest 1988 2-y-o maiden Kiwi Magic (by Try My Best), later successful in USA, and to a winner in Italy by Auction Ring: dam never ran: poor plater: probably best at up to 7f: mostly blinkered or visored: often slowly away: seems rather highly strung. *A. Bailey.*

MISS BELL RINGER   2 b.f. (Mar 28) Belfort (FR) 89–Immatation (FR) 67   **42**
(Polyfoto 124) [1990 5.8f⁵ 5f⁶ 6d⁵ a6g⁶ a7g] 3,000 (privately) Y: workmanlike, good-quartered filly: half-sister to a winner in Belgium and a winner in Hong Kong: dam winning sprinter: poor maiden: stays 6f: acts on a soft surface. *C. J. Hill.*

MISS BOBBY BENNETT   3 b.f. Kings Lake (USA) 133–Karen Lee M (USA)   **78**
(Roman Line) [1989 NR 1990 8g 8m⁴ 10g⁵ 12.4m⁵ 13.1m² 11.7m* 11.7m* 12g⁶ 11.7g 11.5m⁵] quite good-topped filly: fifth reported living foal: half-sister to 2 winners in USA: dam ran twice: modest handicapper: below form after winning twice at Windsor in July: stays 13f: visored final start: has twice hung badly left, including on second victory: has joined M. Pipe. *C. R. Nelson.*

MISS BRIGHTSIDE   2 ch.f. (May 14) Crofthall 110–Fidget (Workboy 123)   —
[1990 5d] fifth foal: dam unraced: behind in maiden at Catterick in October. *A. Smith.*

MISS BURFIELD   2 ch.f. (Feb 6) Faustus (USA) 118–Lady Acquiesce 67   **47**
(Galivanter 131) [1990 5m 7g 6d a6g a7g4] 2,600F, 1,700Y: fifth foal: dam, 2-y-o 5f winner, is half-sister to smart sprinter Chellaston Park: poor maiden: stays 7f. *R. Hannon.*

MISS CALCULATE   2 ch.f. (Apr 4) Mummy's Game 120–Antique Bloom 101   **59**
(Sterling Bay (SWE)) [1990 5m 5f 5m³ 5f6 6g 6g 5g² a6g* 6f² a7g* a6g* 7g 7d⁵ a8g4] 1,050F, 2,200Y: lengthy, angular filly: has a moderate action: sixth living foal: sister to 3-y-o Weekender and half-sister to a winner abroad: dam 2-y-o 5f winner didn't train on: successful in sellers (retained 4,400 gns first occasion, 5,500 gns second, winning easily both times) and a claimer at Southwell: best form at 6f and 7f: best efforts when blinkered: trained first 12 outings by M. W. Easterby. *Capt. J. Wilson.*

MISS CARANGE (IRE)   2 ch.f. (Jan 18) Henbit (USA) 130–Carange (Known   —
Fact (USA) 135) [1990 5m 7m] 2,100Y: first foal: dam no sign of ability: backward, no show in seller at Lingfield and claimer at Salisbury. *C. J. Hill.*

MISS CHALK   4 ch.f. Dominion 123–Stoney 73 (Balidar 133) [1989 7d 8m 7m⁵   **42**
7h² 5.8h⁴ 6m 7m 7m 6m 6f 7f4 10f4 1990 8.3g² 10g* 8g 10.2f3 10.1m] sparely-made filly: plater: co-favourite, won handicap at Leicester (no bid) in May: suited by 1¼m: acts on hard ground: bandaged at 4 yrs: winner over hurdles, but has reportedly broken blood vessel. *M. C. Pipe.*

MISS CHRISSY   5 b.m. Ballacashtal (CAN)–Miss Meg 68 (John Splendid 116)   —
[1989 5g⁵ 6f 5g 1990 6m] strong, workmanlike mare: has a quick action: modest form at best since 2 yrs: best form at 5f with give in the ground: wears blinkers or visor: sometimes sweats. *K. B. McCauley.*

MISS COOKIE   2 ch.f. (Apr 25) Nicholas Bill 125–Maryland Cookie (USA) 101   **59** p
(Bold Hour) [1990 6g4] medium-sized, quite attractive filly: fifth foal: closely related to 3-y-o 1½m winner Maryland Willie and fairly useful 1986 2-y-o 7f winner Amber Cookie (both by Master Willie): dam sprinter: around 8 lengths fourth of 24 to

Sharpthorne in maiden at Kempton in September: will stay 1¼m· wore small bandage on off-hind: should improve. *H. Candy.*

MISS CRUSTY 2 gr.f. (Feb 24) Belfort (FR) 89–Blue Empress (Blue Cashmere 45 129) [1990 5f3 6g5 7m a6g] small filly: has a round action: fifth foal: half-sister to 3-y-o Cove Cottage (by Swing Easy) and 3 winners here and abroad, including 1m and 1¼m seller Miami Blues (by Palm Track): dam showed no ability: poor maiden: ran in sellers first 2 starts: well beaten in Southwell nursery final outing. *R. J. Holder.*

MISS DAMISTER 2 b.f. (Apr 25) Damister (USA) 123–Portrait (USA) (Lyphard 39 (USA) 132) [1990 6f5 6m 6f5] 440Y: leggy, close-coupled filly: first foal: dam ran 3 times: poor maiden: sweating and edgy final 2 starts. *M. Brittain.*

MISS DELILAH 4 b.f. Humdoleila 103–Pem Pem (Blakeney 126) [1989 9g 8m 29 1990 11s 8v3 8.2s] poor maiden: form only on second outing: stays 1m: acts on heavy going: changed hands 2,000 gns Ascot July Sales. *P. D. Evans.*

MISS DEMONSTRATIVE (IRE) 2 ch.f. (Feb 10) Montekin 125–North Lady — (Northfields (USA)) [1990 5m 8m] IR 8,000F, 5,000 2-y-o: leggy filly: dam poor half-sister to Lowther winner Miss Demure: well beaten in maiden at Wolverhampton and apprentice seller (looked irresolute) at Warwick: dead. *P. D. Evans.*

MISS ECHO 2 ch.f. (Apr 19) Chief Singer 131–Uranus (Manacle 123) [1990 6f3 85 7d3 7m4 8d4] rather leggy, close-coupled filly: half-sister to several winners, including smart 7f and 1m winner Tellurano (by Guillaume Tell) and very useful colt at up to 9f here and in USA, Bruiser (by Persian Bold): dam won twice over 5f at 2 yrs in Ireland: progressive maiden: fourth of 16 in nursery at Redcar final start: will stay 1¼m: likely to win a race. *M. H. Tompkins.*

MISSED AGAIN 2 b.f. (Mar 15) High Top 131–Out of Shot 116§ (Shirley Heights 71 130) [1990 7m2 7m3] rangy filly: second foal: dam winner disqualified from third in Oaks, was temperamental: stayed on steadily in maidens won by Neroli at Sandown and Jaffa Line at Goodwood in July: will be much better suited by stiffer test of stamina. *J. L. Dunlop.*

MISS EL ARAB (IRE) 2 ch.f. (Mar 17) Sayf El Arab (USA) 127–Shining Bright 75 (USA) (Bold Bidder) [1990 5m* 5f4 5d6 5d3 5g* 6s4 5m 5g6 5d5 5m] IR 4,600Y, resold 2,000Y: workmanlike filly: has a quick action: third foal: half-sister to 4-y-o 5f and 8.2f winner Shawiniga (by Lyphard's Wish), also successful in France at 2 yrs: dam never ran: modest performer: successful in early-season maiden auction at Leicester and minor event at Ayr in June: suited by 5f: acts on good to firm and dead ground: has sweated up: races keenly: inconsistent. *E. J. Alston.*

MISS EMMAJANE 3 b.f. Dublin Taxi–Linanbless (So Blessed 130) [1989 NR — 1990 8m 7.5d 8g 8d] IR 3,400Y: big, lengthy, rather sparely-made filly: fourth foal: sister to 1985 2-y-o 5f winner Lady Chantry: dam never ran: poor plater. *J. G. M. O'Shea.*

MISS EUROLINK 3 br.f. Touching Wood (USA) 127–Sule Skerry 78 (Scottish — Rifle 127) [1989 5v* 5d4 8g 1990 10f6 12m3 9m 12f] leggy, sparely-made filly: poor performer: bred to stay well: probably acts on any going: ran creditably when sweating second start: trained reappearance by J. Dunlop: winning hurdler for M. Pipe. *R. Hollinshead.*

MISS FEE FEE 3 b.f. Red Johnnie 100–Miss Macfee (Forlorn River 124) [1989 — 5m4 6f2 6m4 5f3 5m5 6t4 5g6 5s0 7g·0 1990 6f5 7f 7m6 6m a8g 7.6m5 8d 6g] leggy, sparely-made filly: shows a round action: quite modest form at best at 2 yrs, little in 1990: easily best effort at 7f with give in the ground: visored fifth start: has run respectably for a 7-lb claimer: sometimes bandaged: sold to join N. Callaghan 1,700 gns Newmarket Autumn Sales. *P. Howling.*

MISS FORMIDARE 2 b.f. (Mar 10) Formidable (USA) 125–Relatively Sharp 86 52 (Sharpen Up 127) [1990 6g2 5m2 6f3 6f4 5m 7m 6d] 6,200Y: leggy filly: third foal: half-sister to poor maiden You're The Tops and a winner in Italy from by Head For Heights): dam winning sprinter, much improved at 4 yrs, is half-sister to Tirol: plating-class maiden: stays 6f: possibly unsuited by dead ground: hung left when blinkered fifth outing: started head awkwardly third one. *G. A. Huffer.*

MISS FOXTROT 2 b.f. (Apr 19) Bustino 136–Java Jive 63 (Hotfoot 126) [1990 61 p 7m 7g5] compact, quite attractive filly: second foal: half-sister to 3-y-o Nikkris (by Song): dam best at sprint distances: over 5 lengths fifth of 23, staying on, in median auction at York in October: will be better suited by 1m +: will improve again. *J. L. Dunlop.*

Sir Gordon White's "Missionary Ridge"

MISS GOLDIE LOCKS 3 ch.f. Dara Monarch 128–Really Sharp (Sharpen Up —
127) [1989 5g 1990 6g⁴ 7m 5.1f 7m] lengthy filly: no worthwhile form, in selling
handicap final start: sold 900 gns Ascot November Sales. *Dr J. D. Scargill.*

MISS GREEN GABLES 2 br.f. (Mar 7) Green Ruby (USA) 104–Redcross Miss —
64 (Tower Walk 130) [1990 5f] 1,300Y: lengthy, plain filly: first living foal: dam
middle-distance maiden: backward and on toes, tailed off in maiden at Thirsk in
April. *J. Balding.*

MISS HIRON 2 b.f. (Mar 29) Smackover 107–Passionate 57 (Dragonara Palace **43**
(USA) 115) [1990 7f⁶ a7g⁴ a6g⁵ 6m² 6d 8.2g a7g] 740Y: compact filly: fourth foal:
dam placed at 5f and 5.8f: poor maiden: best effort claimer-ridden second of 18 in
selling nursery at Ripon: suited by 6f: possibly unsuited by a soft surface. *R. Guest.*

MISS HOSTESS 3 gr.f. Petong 126–Rosalina 71 (Porto Bello 118) [1989 5m 5f⁵ —
5m⁵ 7m⁵ 7m³ 7m 7m 8g 1990 11g 11m 8g⁶ 7m⁶ 8g⁵ 8d 7g 8m⁶ 8.2m 12g] leggy, quite
good-topped filly: poor maiden: no form last 5 starts: stays 1m: acts on good to firm
ground: twice blinkered at 2 yrs: sometimes takes keen hold. *T. Craig.*

MISSIONARY RIDGE 3 ch.c. Caerleon (USA) 132–Shellshock 110 (Salvo 129) **114**
[1989 7g 7m³ 7g⁶ 8f* 7.3d³ 1990 10m⁴ 12.3d³ 12g 10.2m* 10f* 10.5g⁶ 10m* 12f]
sturdy colt: keen walker: has a fluent, round action: very useful performer: won
minor event (11/10 on) at Newcastle in June, Windfields Farm EBF Gallinule Stakes
at the Curragh in July and Abtrust Select Stakes (well ridden, made all and held on
by ½ length from Filia Ardross) at Goodwood in September: seems best at 1¼m:
possibly best on top-of-the-ground: sold to join R. Frankel in USA, and finished in
mid-division in Hollywood Turf Cup in December. *B. W. Hills.*

MISSISSAUGA 2 b.f. (Feb 14) Superlative 118–Marton Maid 74 (Silly Season —
127) [1990 6m 6f⁶ 6m 7d] 1,300Y: smallish, plain filly: poor mover: third foal:
half-sister to quite modest 1989 2-y-o 5f winner Megan Blaze (by Sayf El Arab):
dam, inconsistent maiden, is half-sister to good-class sprinter Haveroid: little
worthwhile form, including in sellers: visored final outing: sold 520 gns Doncaster
October Sales. *J. Hetherton.*

584

MISSISSIPPI BEAT (USA) 3 b.g. Dixieland Band (USA)–Jungle Dance 46
(USA) (Graustark) [1989 6g⁵ 6g 1990 8.2s 9f⁴ 12h⁵ 12g² 13.8m⁴ 12m⁴ 15g⁴ 13m⁶
11m⁴ a12g² 12g⁵ a11g⁵ 16m 12d³ a14g a16g⁴ a14g²] lengthy, dipped-backed gelding:
moderate mover: plater: should prove suited by a test of stamina: acts on firm and
dead going: often visored: appeared not to respond to pressure early on third start:
has sweated up. *M. P. Naughton.*

MISS JAVA 3 ch.f. Persian Bold 123–Miss Bali 95 (Crepello 136) [1989 6d² 6g² 78
7g⁵ 1990 8g 8g⁴ 8m* 7g³ 9m 9m³ 10m³ 11.5m⁴ 10m] deep-girthed filly: modest
handicapper: won at Doncaster in June, always in touch: made running (soundly
beaten) final start but held up otherwise in 1990, putting up best efforts seventh and
eighth outings: stays 11.5f: acts on good to firm ground: mostly blinkered after third
outing: edgy on sixth. *G. Wragg.*

MISS JON PIERRE 3 b.f. Full of Hope 125–Cala Galera 45 (Mummy's Pet 125) —
[1989 NR 1990 8h] second foal: half-sister to a bad animal: dam plater: got loose and
was withdrawn once at 2 yrs: tailed off in seller in May. *R. P. C. Hoad.*

MISS KATANGA 2 b.f. (Feb 12) Lochnager 132–Moment To Remember (USA) —
(Assagai) [1990 5f³ 7g] 2,100F: sturdy filly: seventh foal: half-sister to several
winners, including quite modest 7f to 8.3f winner Hogan's Run (by Tender King)
and stayer Moody Girl (by Relko): dam second over 5f and 1½m in Ireland: 8 lengths
third of 4 to Pod's Daughter in seller at Doncaster when trained by W. G. M. Turner:
tailed off when backward in maiden at Sandown over 6 months later. *J. A. B. Old.*

MISS KELLYBELL 3 ch.f. Kirchner 110–California Split (Sweet Revenge 129) 48
[1989 6f 5f 6g⁴ 1990 a8g⁵ a8g³ 7.5f 7f 6f 7m⁴ 6g* 5f⁶ a6g 6g 6g 6d² a6g] small,
angular filly: poor walker and bad mover: poor plater on most form but much better
efforts when winning handicap (made all far side) at Thirsk in August and second in
apprentice handicap at Leicester: appears best at 6f, probably with give in the
ground: sometimes edgy and sweating: has joined H. Whiting. *R. Thompson.*

MISS KERRY 3 ch.f. Royal Blend 117–Miss Plumes 62 (Prince de Galles 125) —
[1989 NR 1990 8.2s 9m 10f⁶ 12.5g⁶ 12.5m⁶ 12d] sparely-made filly: sixth living foal:
dam plater, won from 1m to 1¼m: no worthwhile form in sellers though showed
signs of ability third to fifth outings, giving impression would prove suited by test of
stamina: winning claiming hurdler. *P. D. Evans.*

MISS KILPATRICK 4 ch.f. Noalto 120–Ann Wilson (Tumble Wind (USA)) 37 d
[1989 10g 8f 1990 a7g⁵ a8g² a10g a7g 10f 10f 8.3g 10f 10m 8f a10g] sturdy filly: has a
round action: easily best effort second in claimer at Lingfield in February: stays 1m:
blinkered sixth, seventh and final starts: has sweated. *D. C. Jermy.*

MISS KIVE 4 b.f. Kabour 80–Final Cast 50 (Saulingo 122) [1989 5d 5m 5f⁶ 6m⁵ 6f —
5m⁶ 5g⁶ 6s 5m 1990 a5g 5m 5.1m⁵ a5g] compact filly: plating-class maiden as 3-y-o:
below form in 1990, though showed a little on third outing: form only at 5f: visored
debut: blinkered otherwise: has sweated: retained 880 gns Doncaster September
Sales: has looked irresolute. *D. W. Chapman.*

MISS KNIGHT 3 ch.f. Longleat (USA) 109–Ethel Knight (Thatch (USA) 136) 57
[1989 5d 5g⁴ 6g 5s⁵ 5m 5v³ 5m 1990 a6g² a7g* a5g* a6g⁴ a5g³ 5f⁵ 5s³ 6f 6g 7m 7m
6g³ 6m* 7m 5m a6g a5g 6g a6g] smallish, compact filly: moderate walker: quite
modest handicapper at best: won twice at Southwell in January: easily best subsequent effort when leading post at Nottingham in June: effective at 5f and stays 7f
well: acts on firm going: sometimes sweating and unruly in preliminaries: has been
taken down early: occasionally slowly away. *R. Bastiman.*

MISS MAC 3 ch.f. Smackover 107–Stewart's Rise 52 (Good Bond 122) [1989 5s⁵ —
5g 6m 6g⁴ 7f 1990 9f 10m] small, lightly-made filly: good walker: bad plater. *B. A.
McMahon.*

MISS MARJORIE HILL 4 ro.f. Royal Match 117–Overseas 48 (Sea Hawk II —
131) [1989 NR 1990 a12g] smallish, lengthy filly: fifth reported foal: half-sister to 3
winners, including 9f seller winner Turtle Bay (by Anax): dam poor maiden: tongue
tied down, tailed off final 5f in maiden at Southwell in November: sold 1,000 gns
Doncaster November Sales. *M. C. Chapman.*

MISS MARTINA 2 b.f. (May 8) Martinmas 128–Rosaceae 101 (Sagaro 133) [1990 66
6g 5m³ 7m 7g³] neat filly: good mover: half-sister to winners by Kind of Hush,
including middle-distance stayer Lady Rosanna: dam 10.2f and 1½m winner, is
half-sister to very useful 1¼m to 2m winner Capricorn Line: easily best effort in
maidens 10 lengths third of 17 to Aghaadir at Salisbury final start: will stay at least
1m. *I. A. Balding.*

MISS MATTERS 3 b.f. Strong Gale 116–Miss Filbert 95 (Compensation 127) —
[1989 5.3m 6f⁵ 6d 1990 10m 8m] leggy, plain filly: poor maiden: bred to stay 1m. *M. McCourt.*

MISS MEASURE 2 b.f. (May 14) Electric 126–Gentle Gypsy 94 (Junius (USA) —
124) [1990 5d 5d 6f 7.5g a6g] small filly: second foal: half-sister to 3-y-o Vinegar Bob
(by Blushing Scribe): dam 2-y-o 5f winner, seemed not to train on: little worthwhile
form in sellers: blinkered final 2 starts, unseating rider to post first time: sold 780
gns Doncaster August Sales. *M. W. Easterby.*

MISS MICROCHIP 3 b.f. Dreams To Reality (USA) 113–Strawberry Ice (Arctic 30
Storm 134) [1989 8g 1990 a7g a8g a12g⁶ 12m⁴ 15.3f 12d⁵] small, rather leggy filly:
poor plater: may prove ideally suited by 1¼m: acts on good to firm ground and dead:
ridden by 7-lb claimer last 2 starts. *J. Wharton.*

MISS MIRROR 2 gr.f. (Apr 23) Magic Mirror 105–Rhein Symphony 74 (Rhein- 77 p
gold 137) [1990 7m⁵] leggy, unfurnished filly: sixth living foal: half-sister to 3-y-o
Tesekkurederim and a listed winner in Scandinavia (both by Blazing Saddles): dam
1½m winner: over 4 lengths fifth of 18, going on well having missed break, to Noble
Destiny in maiden at Leicester in October: sure to improve. *W. J. Haggas.*

MISS MITCHELL 5 gr.m. Sexton Blake 126–Knapping (Busted 134) [1989 87
10m³ 12.8f* 12m² 16g* 14g* 12g 16d* 1990 14g² 16m⁴20m5 14m 16g] workmanlike,
rather unfurnished mare: second reported foal: half-sister to bumpers and hurdles
winner Derrynap (by Derrylin): dam ran twice: much improved as 4-y-o, winning IR
£27,000 NCB Leopardstown November Handicap on final outing: 33/1, fair fifth of 18
to Retouch in Ascot Stakes (Handicap) at Royal Ascot, travelling strongly long way:
then off course nearly 3 months and behind in handicaps at the Curragh in autumn:
stays extremely well: acts on firm and dead going: good mount for apprentice. *R. Lister, Ireland.*

MISS MOODY 4 ch.f. Jalmood (USA) 126–Ice Galaxie (USA) (Icecapade (USA)) —
[1989 5f 6f 5.8h 6f 6s⁴ 1990 5f 7m 5f] workmanlike, good-quartered filly: maiden
plater: stays 6f: acts on soft going: has sweated, and on toes. *J. M. Bradley.*

MISS PATDONNA 4 b.f. Starch Reduced 112–Karousa Girl (Rouser 118) [1989 —
8d 8.2s 8m 6m 9f 10g 10f⁴ 12.5f 12g 1990 a13g⁶] lightly-made filly: winning plater as
2-y-o: well beaten since in varied events: stays 1m: best efforts on an easy surface.
B. Palling.

MISS PINOCCHIO 3 b.f. Noalto 120–Floral 82 (Floribunda 136) [1989 5d⁴ 5d 51
5h² 5f* 6m 5g5 5f6 5s 5f³ 1990 7m⁴ 6f 5m5 5g 6m³ 6m 5f⁴ 6m* 6m³ a5g 5m 7m5]
angular filly: fair plater: below form after winning at Ayr (bought in 5,200 gns) in
July: needs further than 5f, and stays 7f: best form on top-of-the-ground: ran well
when on toes: sold 1,800 gns Doncaster September Sales. *J. Berry.*

MISS PISTACHIO 3 b.f. Swing Easy (USA) 126–Unexpected 84 (Laser Light —
118) [1989 NR 1990 6m5 5s 6d] 380F, 300Y: workmanlike filly: fifth living foal:
half-sister to 3 maidens, one very temperamental: dam 4-y-o 7.6f winner: well
beaten in apprentice race, minor event (first run for 4 months) and claimer. *B. A. McMahon.*

MISS POKEY 4 b.f. Uncle Pokey 116–Silken Swift 83 (Saulingo 122) [1989 8d 65
10.2m 10f 12f² 12g* 16f⁴ 1990 12m 17.1d* 16.5d6] leggy filly: poor mover: quite
modest handicapper: confirmed promise of reappearance and showed improved
form when winning at Bath in October: stays well: best effort on dead going: has
worn blinkers: winning hurdler in December. *R. J. Holder.*

MISS PORTIA 3 ch.f. Import 127–Mistress Meryll 61 (Tower Walk 130) [1989 44
NR 1990 7g 8g 7g 6m6 a6g 6g² 5s a5g5] good-topped filly: has quick action: sixth
foal: half-sister to 7f to 8.3f winner Sergeant Meryll (by Marching On) and a winner
in Austria and Germany: dam sprinter: poor form: wandered under pressure when
second in handicap at Thirsk: best effort at 6f: possibly unsuited by soft going: sold
675 gns Ascot December Sales. *J. W. Watts.*

MISS PRASLIN 2 ch.f. (May 3) Nordance (USA)–Carrivos (Tyrnavos 129) [1990 40
6m 6f5 6f 7.5m 7f] 720F, 2,500 2-y-o: sparely-made filly: second foal: dam, promised
to stay 2m, is out of half-sister to very smart 1973 2-y-o Welsh Harmony: poor
maiden: stays 7.5f. *D. Morris.*

MISS PRECOCIOUS 2 b.f. (Mar 26) Precocious 126–Hissy Missy 70 (Bold Lad 50
(IRE) 133) [1990 6d5 a7g a7g] 4,800F: fifth foal: half-sister to some poor animals:
dam in frame over 7f at 2 yrs: over 7 lengths fifth of 17 to Takaddum in maiden at
Folkestone: well below that form on all-weather. *M. J. Haynes.*

MISS PRO VISION 2 b.f. (May 9) Daring March 116–The Silver Darling 75 **32**
(John Splendid 116) [1990 5g 5d 5m 7.5g 5f 5m 7f] 5,000Y· neat, strong filly:
half-sister to several winners, including very useful sprinter Sylvan Barbarosa (by
Native Bazaar): dam second in Britain before winning in Belgium: poor plater:
sweating badly and very unimpressive in appearance final start. *W. Bentley.*

MISS RELSUN 6 ch.m. Le Soleil 96–Relax 73 (Seminole II) [1989 11f² 10f* 9.1f* **61**
9f⁴ 10m* 10.2g³ 1990 10d³ 10f 10.2m³ 10d⁴ 11m 10f⁶ 10.2m² 10f³ 10g³ 10.2m² 10m⁵
9m² 12g² 10m⁶] leggy, workmanlike mare: carries condition: quite modest handicapper: stays 1½m: acts on firm and dead going: suitable mount for apprentice. *Mrs
G. R. Reveley.*

MISS SARAHSUE 4 br.f. Van Der Linden (FR)–Blakesware Dancer 68 (Dance **36**
In Time (CAN)) [1989 9f 7m⁵ 7f 7m 7m⁵ 7h⁵ 1990 10.1g 6f⁵ 7.6m 12f⁶ 11.5f⁵ 10h²
10m⁵ 10f a12g] leggy, sparely-made filly: poor maiden: stays 1¼m: acts on hard
going: blinkered once at 3 yrs: occasionally sweats: broke blood vessel seventh
intended outing in 1989. *J. E. Long.*

MISS SARAJANE 6 b.m. Skyliner 117–Taffeta 72 (Shantung 132) [1989 10.4m **65**
9f² 8.2m 9f³ 10f² 8g 8.2m³ 8m⁶ 8.2g 9m² 10.4m 10.2g 8g* 10g a8g 1990 a8g 8f 8m* 8f
8m 9g 8m 8g⁴ 8.2s 8f² 8m 9s 8.2v 8g 8m⁶] leggy, workmanlike mare: good mover:
quite modest handicapper: won apprentice event at Wolverhampton in April: mainly
well below her best in second half of year: stays 1¼m: probably unsuited by soft
going nowadays, acts on any other: good mount for claimer: usually races up with
pace, though often slowly away. *R. Hollinshead.*

MISS SHARPO 2 b.f. (Feb 3) Sharpo 132–Taiga 69 (Northfields (USA)) [1990 **69**
6m 6m⁵ 6f⁴ 7m² 7d³] 15,500Y: small, sparely-made filly: second foal: half-sister to
9f winner Polonez Prima (by Thatching): dam 1¼m winner stayed 1½m, is out of
sister to Park Hill winner Quay Line: progressive maiden: ran well at Leicester in
auction event and nursery final 2 starts: broke loose from stalls and withdrawn in
between: will stay 1m: acts on good to firm ground and dead. *R. Hannon.*

MISS SIMONE 4 b.f. Ile de Bourbon (USA) 133–Nanga Parbat (Mill Reef (USA) **—**
141) [1989 9f 9f⁶ 8.2g 10f 1990 a12g] small, leggy filly: moderate mover: modest
maiden at 2 yrs: lightly raced since and has shown nothing: should be well suited by
middle distances: blinkered twice in 1989: sold 950 gns Ascot December Sales. *P.
Liddle.*

MISS SIMPLICITY (IRE) 2 b.f. (Feb 21) Simply Great (FR) 122–Mexican **75**
Two Step (Gay Fandango (USA) 132) [1990 7m 8g* 7.3s⁶] 7,400Y: close-coupled
filly: has scope: sixth foal: sister to Irish 7f and 9f winner Hear Me and half-sister to
useful 1¼m to 1½m winner Busted Rock (by Busted), 3-y-o 7f winner Mexican
Vision (by Vision) and a winner in USA: dam fairly useful Irish 2-y-o 6f winner: ran
on strongly to win 16-runner maiden at Kempton in September: looked past best and
dropped away quickly 2f out, having raced keenly, in listed race at Newbury
following month: will stay 1¼m. *D. R. C. Elsworth.*

MISS SUNPUSS (USA) 2 gr.f. (Jan 14) Gato Del Sol (USA)–Redecorate (USA) **50**
(Hatchet Man (USA)) [1990 7m⁶ 7g³ 6m 7f⁴ 6m] 15,000Y: leggy, angular filly:
second reported foal: sister to 3-y-o Casa d'Isabel: dam winner at up to 7f: plating-
class maiden at best: will probably stay 1m. *R. Akehurst.*

MISS TATTING (USA) 3 ch.f. Miswaki (USA) 124–Petit Rond Point (USA) **89**
(Round Table) [1989 NR 1990 7f⁴ 8f⁴ 8f³ 7m³ 7f* 7f² 7h* 8m* 8g⁶] IR 140,000Y:
lengthy filly: half-sister to several winners in USA, including a minor stakes-placed
winner at up to 9f by Nijinsky: dam, unplaced from 6 starts, is half-sister to dam of
Lyphard's Wish: in fine form in the summer, making all in handicaps at Folkestone,
Brighton (odds on) and Goodwood (bandaged near-hind): well beaten in listed race
final start: stays 1m: acts on hard ground: has run creditably when sweating. *C. F.
Wall.*

MISS TENAVILLE 3 b.f. Kala Shikari 125–La Bambola 95 (Be Friendly 130) **—**
[1989 5s² 5m² 5f 1990 8m 7f] sturdy, workmanlike filly: turns fore-feet out: plating-
class maiden at best: no show in apprentice handicap (sweating and edgy on first run
for 14 months) and claimer as 3-y-o. *S. Dow.*

MISS THE POINT (FR) 2 gr.c. (Mar 3) Sharpo 132–Miss Suntan (Bruni 132) **101**
[1990 7g* 7.5m⁵ 7.5g² 7.5g 8g⁴ 10v⁴] 19,000Y: quite good-topped colt: third foal:
half-brother to 3-y-o Mothers Son (by Mummy's Pet): dam French 1½m winner
from family of Wolver Hollow: showed improved form when fourth, beaten under 3
lengths, in Group 2 Premio Guido Berardelli at Rome in November: very impressive
winner of maiden at Wolverhampton in June on only start outside Italy: suited by
1¼m: acts well on heavy ground. *J. H. M. Gosden.*

MISS TINO 2 b.f. (Apr 21) Relkino 131–Miss Horatio (Spartan General 109) [1990 —
7m 8d a8g] rather leggy filly: shows knee action: third reported living foal: dam won
3m novice hurdle: no form in maidens. *A. J. Wilson.*

MISS U LIKE CRAZY (USA) 2 ch.f. (Apr 19) Miswaki (USA) 124–Summer- 75 p
sault (USA) (Vaguely Noble 140) [1990 6m6 6g*] $34,000Y: sturdy filly: half-sister
to 1988 2-y-o 1m winner Swing Shift (by Night Shift) and a winner in USA: dam won
at around 6f in USA: won 18-runner maiden at Folkestone in October by 3 lengths
from Noble Flutter, drifting left soon after halfway and running on well: bit
backward and green on debut: will improve again. *J. W. Hills.*

MISS UPSHIRE 3 b.f. Norwick (USA) 120–Longgoe 70 (Lorenzaccio 130) [1989 —
NR 1990 10.6s 16g] sparely-made filly: fourth foal: dam showed some ability at 2 yrs
but little at 3 yrs: showed little in maidens (sweating, took keen hold second start)
in the summer. *D. W. Browne.*

MISS WAGER 3 ch.f. Crested Lark 78–Mrs Love It 70 (Rapid River 127) [1989 —
NR 1990 7d] second reported foal: dam sprinter: 100/1, behind in maiden at Catterick
in October. *Miss G. M. Rees.*

MISS WASSL 3 b.f. Wassl 125–Arena 86 (Sallust 134) [1989 7m4 1990 8m* 8.5g 64
11.5m5] leggy, sparely-made filly: shows plenty of knee action: quite modest form
when justifying favouritism in claimer at Warwick in March: ran poorly in Epsom
handicap next start, well out of depth on final (May) one: should stay beyond 1m:
changed hands 2,400 gns Ascot February Sales. *P. A. Kelleway.*

MISS WESLEY 5 b.m. Raga Navarro (ITY) 119–Balcanoona 87 (Cawston's 35
Clown 113) [1989 5f5 5m 5m 6f 5f 5f3 6f 1990 5g4 a5g 5m 5m3 7g6] small, lengthy
mare: poor mover: poor handicapper: yet to race on soft going, acts on any
other: visored once (slowly away) at 4 yrs, blinkered fourth start: sold afterwards
out of A. Turnell's stable 2,000 gns Ascot September Sales: inconsistent. *D. W.
Browne.*

MISS WILLOW 4 b.f. Horage 124–Nebanna 74 (Nebbiolo 125) [1989 8m 8m 10g2 —
10m6 12m 10m5 14g 10.6g 1990 10s 11m 10g 14m6] leggy filly: has a round action:
quite modest at best: no form in 1990: stays 1¼m: acts on good to firm going: twice
blinkered, once visored: inconsistent. *H. J. Collingridge.*

MISTER GOFF 2 b.c. (May 21) Taufan (USA) 119–Spring Bride 57 (Auction —
Ring (USA) 123) [1990 6m 8g 6d] lengthy colt: looks weak: half-brother to 3-y-o
Stanway (by Sandhurst Prince), useful sprinter Hafir (by Tender King) and 1986
2-y-o 7f winner Lightening Laser (by Monseigneur): dam, raced only at 2 yrs, is
sister to very useful 1979 2-y-o Highest Bidder and half-sister to good American
horse Peregrinator and smart sprinter Royal Ride: well beaten in maidens: very
green and on toes on debut. *S. G. Norton.*

MISTER LAWSON 4 ch.g. Blushing Scribe (USA) 107–Nonpareil (FR) 92 —
(Pharly (FR) 130) [1989 6s 7m 6v 1990 7f] close-coupled gelding: fairly useful as
2-y-o: behind in subsequent handicaps: best form at 5f on top-of-the-ground:
sometimes sweats: winning hurdler in spring: sold to join B. Forsey's stable 4,400
gns Ascot June Sales. *Mrs J. Pitman.*

MISTER MAJOR 2 ch.g. (Mar 19) Absalom 128–Gay Tamarind (Tamerlane 128) 46
[1990 5m 6m 6m4 7f5 6m 8.2d] 14,000F, 17,000Y, 14,500 2-y-o: strong, workmanlike
gelding: has a round action: fifth reported living foal: half-brother to 7.5f winner La
Jambalaya (by Reform) and 7f and 8.5f winner Tamertown Lad (by Creetown): dam
tailed off only start: poor maiden. *L. J. Holt.*

MISTER MARCH 7 b.g. Marching On 101–Jetwitch 56 (Lear Jet 123) [1989 6m —
5m3 5m2 5m6 5f 5m 5m 5m6 7f 6m 7m3 7f6 5.1g 7m 8f 5g 5m 1990 a7g a7g6 6m 5f]
leggy, sparely-made gelding: has a quick action: poor handicapper: effective at 5f
and stays 7f: suited by a sound surface: tailed off in blinkers: inconsistent. *D. W.
Chapman.*

MISTER ODDY 4 b.g. Dubassoff (USA)–Somerford Glory 44 (Hittite Glory 125) —
[1989 7s4 7s 8f 6m 1990 12m 10s] leggy, workmanlike gelding: modest maiden at one
time: well below his best since first outing at 3 yrs: stays 7f: acts on heavy going:
winning hurdler in December. *J. S. King.*

MISTER PETARD 8 b.g. Sandy Creek 123–Miss Upward 77 (Alcide 136) [1989 —
NR 1990 16.2m] compact, sturdy gelding: poor mover: of little account: often wears
blinkers. *B. Ellison.*

MISTER RIV (FR) 5 b.h. River River (FR) 117–Mrs Annie (Bolkonski 134) 115
[1989 14d3 12m2 12m 11d6 15g6 14.5d* 12m2 12g2 12g3 11v 1990 12g2 11d3 10.5g*
10.5g6 8.5g 8.5g3 10g* 10d2 12g 8s 9g] first foal: dam won over 7f in France at 2 yrs:

showed much improved form when winning Prix Gontaut-Biron at Deauville by 2 lengths from Relief Pitcher: reproduced that running when second to Saumarez in Prix du Prince d'Orange at Longchamp: never better than mid-division in Ciga Prix de l'Arc de Triomphe next outing: also successful in handicap at Longchamp in May: best form at 1¼m with a bit of give in the ground. *A. Spanu, France.*

MISTER SAYERS   2 b.c. (Apr 14) Balliol 125–Deer Forest (Huntercombe 133)   **49**
[1990 6m a7g² 7m] 4,100Y: leggy, light-framed colt: brother to an animal of little account and half-brother to 3 winners, including 7f and 1m winner Ballnacarn (by Firestreak): dam showed no form in 3 outings: easily best effort in seller at Southwell in August. *W. Carter.*

MISTER SICY (FR)   4 ch.c. Sicyos (USA) 126–Mrs Annie (Bolkonski 134) [1989   **113**
10.5s⁴ 8m⁴ 8g* 8m* 9g 7d⁴ 8v² 1990 8g* 8g² 8g⁴ 8d*] smart colt: successful in first half of year in valuable event at Saint-Cloud by 2 lengths from Ocean Falls and Prix du Chemin de Fer du Nord at Chantilly by neck and nose from Monsagem and Val des Bois: divided Val des Bois and Ocean Falls when beaten 2 lengths in Prix Edmond Blanc at Saint-Cloud: suited by 1m: yet to race on firm going, acts on any other: trained until after third outing by F. Boutin. *N. Clement, France.*

MISTER'S SISTER   3 ch.f. Tumble Wind (USA)–Joanelle (Brigadier Gerard   **—**
144) [1989 6m 5m⁶ 5d 1990 7.5d 6m a8g] leggy, rather sparely-made filly: poor form, second favourite in 17-runner seller (unruly at stalls) on reappearance: wore crossed noseband final start: sold 2,100 gns Doncaster September Sales. *M. Johnston.*

MISTITLED (USA)   2 b.f. (Apr 14) Miswaki (USA) 124–Untitled 98 (Vaguely   **54**
Noble 140) [1990 5g* 6m 5m 5m] $22,000Y: well-grown, leggy filly: closely related to very useful French 1m winner Private Views (by Mr Prospector) and half-sister to 3 other winners, including useful 7f and 1¼m winner Jungle Pioneer (by Conquistador Cielo) and a middle-distance winner by Nureyev: dam 1m winner, is half-sister to Dactylographer: won maiden at Chester (trained by S. Norton) in June: blinkered, creditable seventh in nursery at Wolverhampton final start: should be suited by further than 5f. *E. Eldin.*

MISTRAL GIRL (IRE)   2 b.f. (Apr 23) Tumble Wind (USA)–Arthashat   **—**
(Petingo 135) [1990 5m 7f a7g] IR 9,000Y: half-sister to several winners in Italy: dam, placed in Italy, from family of Bassenthwaite: poor form in auction events and a maiden. *R. Hannon.*

MISTRAL'S DANCER   3 br.f. Shareef Dancer (USA)–Mythical Assembly   **—**
(General Assembly (USA)) [1989 6g 7m⁴ 10s 8d 1990 8g 8.2g⁵ 8f 10m 12m 10g 12.2m⁵ a8g⁵ a8g] IR 26,000Y: smallish, workmanlike ex-Irish filly: moderate walker: first foal: dam unraced half-sister to top-class miler Northjet: plating-class maiden: soundly beaten last 4 starts, including in handicap: best effort over 7f on good to firm ground: bought out of K. Prendergast's stable 12,000 gns Newmarket December (1989) Sales. *R. Hollinshead.*

MISTRESS CARROLL   3 ch.f. Simply Great (FR) 122–Cariole 84 (Pardao 120)   **57**
[1989 6g 1990 7g⁵ 8m³ 7d⁵ 7d* a8g 6g] leggy, quite good-topped filly: quite modest form: favourite, won seller (sold out of G. Pritchard-Gordon's stable 6,500 gns) at Yarmouth in July: ran poorly afterwards, in ladies event penultimate start: should stay 1¼m: acts on good to firm ground and dead: edgy first 2 outings, sweating first occasion, bandaged second: lacks turn of foot. *J. G. M. O'Shea.*

MISTRESS MONET   3 b.f. Claude Monet (USA) 121–Skysted (Busted 134)   **56**
[1989 6f⁶ 6m 6f⁵ 7g 1990 8m 7.5d 8.2v⁴ 7v² 7d*] strong, good-bodied filly: plater: favourite, won at Edinburgh (no bid) in October, edging right: seems suited by 7f: acts on heavy going: sold to join Mrs A. Knight 4,600 gns Doncaster November Sales. *M. J. Camacho.*

MISTY EYES   3 b.f. High Top 131–Ringed Aureole 77 (Aureole 132) [1989 7m 8m   **59** §
7m 8.2s² 8.2s⁶ 1990 12f² 12g² 11g² 12h⁴ 11f6] tall, lengthy, leggy filly: plating-class maiden: edgy, sweating and looked ungenerous final start: should stay beyond 1½m: possibly best with some give in the ground: has run well for 7-lb claimer: tail swisher: sold 5,500 gns Newmarket Autumn Sales. *Sir Mark Prescott.*

MISTY GLOW   3 gr.f. Kalaglow 132–Six Ashes (Bruni 132) [1989 NR 1990 10f⁴   **55**
12m 10g² 12.2g²] tall, leggy filly: first foal: dam unraced half-sister to several winners, including useful miler Greenwood Star: worthwhile form only when second in apprentice claimer at Nottingham and handicap at Catterick in June: ridden by 7-lb claimer first 3 starts. *J. Etherington.*

MISTY GODDESS (IRE)   2 gr.f. (Feb 29) Godswalk (USA) 130–Silent Sail   **63**
(Aglojo 119) [1990 6g 7f³ 8m⁵ 7m 7f* 8d²] sturdy filly: half-sister to 3 winners here

and abroad, including fair 1m winner Russell Creek (by Sandy Creek) and 5.3f winner Jellabia (by Pal's Passage): dam Irish 1¼m winner, is half-sister to Jellaby: quite modest performer: lowered in class, won seller (no bid) at Redcar in October: very good second of 20, staying on, in selling nursery at Doncaster: gives impression will be suited by 1¼m. *M. A. Jarvis.*

MISTY NIGHT   2 gr.f. (May 1) Grey Desire 115–Maha (Northfields (USA)) [1990   52
5g⁵ 6g 5m³ 6m 8f 8.2s⁶ 10.6s 8d] small, workmanlike filly: second foal: dam well
beaten in NH Flat race: sixth of 17, staying on well, in selling nursery at Hamilton in
September, easily best effort: stays 1m: acts well on soft ground. *P. Monteith.*

MISTY VALLEY (USA)   2 ch.c. (Apr 24) Majestic Light (USA)–Orchid Vale 104 p
(USA) (Gallant Man) [1990 7g² 7g* 8g*] half-brother to several winners in Australia, including graded-stakes winner Lady's Slipper (by Dancer's Image): dam unraced sister to champion American filly Gallant Bloom: improving colt: successful in
maiden at Fairyhouse and Panasonic Smurfit EBF Futurity Stakes (by 2½ lengths
from Star of Gdansk) at the Curragh in September: will stay 1¼m. *M. Kauntze,
Ireland.*

MITILINI   10 ch.g. Julio Mariner 127–Charming Thought (USA) (Stage Door   —
Johnny) [1989 NR 1990 11.7m] strong, short-coupled gelding: fairly useful as 3-y-o:
very little subsequent form on flat and extremely lightly raced nowadays: stays
1½m: used to act well on heavy going: blinkered once: sold 2,000 gns Doncaster
October Sales. *J. White.*

MIZAJ   6 ch.g. Thatching 131–Stickpin 74 (Gulf Pearl 117) [1989 10.2g* 10g 10d³ 9f   —
10m² 10.8f² 10f 10.2m² 10v 1990 10v 8.2d] rangy, deep-girthed gelding: has a rather
round action: quite modest winner as 5-y-o: shaped well on second outing in 1990,
but then ran as though something amiss over hurdles: stays 11f: acts on any going:
not the easiest of rides, and best with waiting tactics: trained on reappearance by G.
Richards. *M. D. Hammond.*

MIZUWARI   4 ch.f. Blazing Saddles (AUS)–River Aire 82 (Klairon 131) [1989   68
7.3m⁶ 6m⁶ 6g* 6f* 7g³ 7.3m⁶ 1990 6m 7g⁶ 7m⁶ 7f⁵ 7f⁴ 7g 8g⁴ 7g] lengthy filly:
quite modest handicapper: stays 1m: acts on firm going: slowly away and always
behind when visored last outing: occasionally sweats. *G. B. Balding.*

MIZYAN (IRE)   2 b.c. (Mar 23) Melyno 130–Maid of Erin (USA) (Irish River (FR)   —
131) [1990 6m] 3,800Y: rather leggy, angular colt: second foal: half-brother to 3-y-o
My Mavournin (by L'Emigrant): dam, ran once in France, is sister to good-class
River Dancer and from family of Sun Princess: never able to challenge in maiden at
Newmarket in November. *J. D. Czerpak.*

MOAT GARDEN (USA)   2 b.c. (Apr 14) Sportin' Life (USA)–Round Tower 93   82
(High Top 131) [1990 8g⁴ 8g⁶] rather leggy, good-topped colt: has plenty of scope:
easy mover: fifth foal: closely related to 3-y-o Royal Archive (by Shadeed) and
half-brother to 3 winners, including useful 1986 2-y-o 7f winner Roundlet (by
Roberto) and 1½m winner Windsor Park (by Bold Forbes): dam 10.1f and 10.6f
winner, is out of half-sister to Highclere: on toes, around a length fourth of 15,
travelling smoothly then going on best of all, to Prince Russanor in minor event at
Newbury in September: odds on, little impression from 3f out and not knocked
about in 7-runner maiden at York following month: will stay 1¼m. *I. A. Balding.*

MODEL CHILD   2 ch.f. (May 1) Bairn (USA) 126–Reform Princess 80 (Reform   —
132) [1990 a6g] 15,000Y: first foal: dam stayer: always towards rear in maiden at
Southwell in August: sold 1,000 gns Newmarket Autumn Sales. *C. F. Wall.*

MODEL NURSE   3 b.f. Exhibitioner 111–Majestic Nurse 80 (On Your Mark 125)   55
[1989 7f⁵ 1990 7d 8m 7h² 7h 8.3g² a8g³ a8g* 8g⁵ a8g] close-coupled filly: has a
quick action: fifth foal: half-sister to 4-y-o 7f winner Awesome Power (by Vision)
and 1987 2-y-o 8.5f winner Musical Nurse (by Ballad Rock): dam successful here and
in Ireland at 1m to 1¼m: plating-class performer: 5/4 on, won 16-runner claimer at
Southwell in September: should stay 1¼m: trained debut by P. Finn in Ireland. *C. R.
Nelson.*

MODEL VILLAGE   3 ch.f. Habitat 134–It's Terrific (Vaguely Noble 140) [1989 101
NR 1990 7g² 7m* 7m² 8f 8g* 8g⁵ 7m] 165,000Y: smallish, angular filly: has a quick
action: sister to French provincial 8.2f winner Ile Mude and half-sister to several
winners in Italy: dam won from 1¼m to 13f in Ireland: useful performer: quickened
well to win maiden at Newmarket in May and £8,200 handicap at Newbury in
August: set plenty to do last 3 starts, creditable fifth in listed race at Doncaster then
well beaten in £71,900 handicap at Ascot: stayed 1m: keen sort: stud. *B. W. Hills.*

MODERN BRITISH   3 b.g. Elegant Air 119–Song of Gold 85 (Song 132) [1989   69
NR 1990 7f⁶ 7f⁶ 10m 8f⁶ 7d 5m⁵ 6g³ 6m 6m² 7f² a7g⁶ 7m 7m⁵ 6d 6d⁴ a8g² a10g*]

19,000F, 6,600Y: lengthy, workmanlike gelding: moderate mover: sixth foal: half-brother to 3 winners here and abroad, including 6f and 7f winner Postorage (by Pyjama Hunt): dam sprinter: modest performer: won maiden claimer at Lingfield in December: stays 1¼m: acts on firm and dead going: has run creditably sweating, and for inexperienced rider: retained 3,600 gns Newmarket Autumn Sales. *C. A. Cyzer.*

MODERN JAZZ 3 b.g. Swing Easy (USA) 126–Abstract 73 (French Beige 127) —
[1989 NR 1990 11.5g 10m⁴] 4,500F: rather leggy gelding: scratchy mover: half-brother to 3 winners, including ungenuine 5-y-o Take Issue (by Absalom) and useful 1979 2-y-o 7f performer Summary (by Mandamus): dam won over 10.8f: well beaten in October minor events, pulling hard second start. *C. C. Elsey.*

MODEST HOPE (USA) 3 b.c. Blushing Groom (FR) 131–Key Dancer (USA) 73
(Nijinsky (CAN) 138) [1989 7g 1990 10m 10m³ 11.7g² 12f³] big, rather angular colt: poor walker and mover: modest maiden: placed last 2 starts in handicaps at Windsor and Haydock in May: suited by 1½m: acts on firm going: sold to join G. Eden 5,200 gns Newmarket Autumn Sales. *A. A. Scott.*

MODESTO (USA) 2 b.c. (Feb 11) Al Nasr (FR) 126–Modena (USA) (Roberto 72 p
(USA) 131) [1990 7m⁴] IR 220,000Y: useful-looking colt, rather unfurnished: second foal: half-brother to high-class 3-y-o Elmaamul (by Diesis): dam unraced half-sister to smart miler Zaizafon and daughter of Mofida, very tough winner of 8 races at up to 7f: around 5 lengths fourth of 11, taking keen hold then staying on despite poor run, to Democratic in maiden at Leicester in September: sure to improve. *B. W. Hills.*

MOD SQUAD 4 ch.f. Montekin 125–Fauchee (Busted 134) [1989 NR 1990 8v] —
ex-Irish filly: fifth foal: dam lightly-raced 1½m winner in Ireland: showed ability on 3 runs at up to 1m as 2-y-o when trained by J. Bolger: 50/1, never a threat in Ayr maiden in April: blinkered twice. *W. Storey.*

MOFADOR (GER) 6 br.h. Esclavo (FR)–Mantilla (GER) (Frontal 122) [1989 78
7.2s 8m⁴ 9g⁵ 8m 7.6m 8v 7m 1990 7m 8.2f 8f a7g* a7g* a8g² 7g² a7g* a8g⁴ 8.2m*
9s 8.2d³ 8v a8g² 7d] lengthy, round-barrelled horse: took very well to all-weather, winning handicaps at Southwell in June (twice) and July: also successful on turf at Hamilton in August: stays 1m: unsuited by soft going: blinkered second outing: good mount for apprentice: has won when sweating. *F. H. Lee.*

MOGUL PRINCE 3 b.g. Mansingh (USA) 120–Valadon 72 (High Line 125) [1989 — §
5s 6f³ 6m 6m² 5.8m³ 7m* 7f 7m 7.3m 7g 1990 8g 9f 7m 8.2g 8m 8m] leggy gelding: good walker: modest performer (awarded nursery) at 2 yrs: behind in handicaps in 1990: suited by 7f: blinkered 5 times: visored once at 2 yrs: has worn tongue strap: sold 1,450 gns Newmarket Autumn Sales: one to treat with caution. *M. D. I. Usher.*

MOHARABUIEE 4 b.f. Pas de Seul 133–Clonavee (USA) (Northern Dancer) —
[1989 7.6m 8.5f 10.2h⁵ 10m 10f² 10f⁶ 7.6m 9f 9g a8g³ a8g a8g⁵ a7g 1990 a7g⁶ a7g
10.2f 7m⁶ 8m] workmanlike filly: poor plater: stays 1¼m: probably acts on any going: inconsistent, and has found little off bridle: sold to join R. Frost's stable 1,400 gns Ascot May Sales. *R. Hollinshead.*

MOHAWK CHIEF (IRE) 2 b.c. (Feb 10) Ahonoora 122–Ringtail 102 (Auction 90
Ring (USA) 123) [1990 6d* 6m² 6g⁵ 6g⁶] IR 30,000Y: small, quite attractive colt: moderate mover: first foal: dam 2-y-o 5f winner: fairly useful performer: won maiden at Yarmouth in July: ran well when never-nearer fifth of 8 to Majlood in listed race at Kempton, moderately in 7-runner Rokeby Farms Mill Reef Stakes at Newbury. *G. Wragg.*

MOHINI 3 ch.f. Sharpo 132–Girl's Brigade (Brigadier Gerard 144) [1989 5m 5g —
7f⁵ 7f 8.2f 7f⁵ 7d 1990 8g 8g 6m 7g 7m 8f] leggy fIlly: moderate walker: plater: edgy, soundly beaten in 1990: stays 1m: best form on firm ground: blinkered then visored last 2 outings: didn't handle Chester track: bandaged second start. *M. D. I. Usher.*

MOHSSEN (FR) 9 ch.g. Sharpen Up 127–Showery Summer (FR) (Tanerko 134) —
[1989 10.6g 1990 12f⁴ 10m 15.3m 12f³ 10f⁶ 10.6d] workmanlike gelding: plating-class winner of ladies event as 7-y-o: lightly raced and very little subsequent form: better suited by 1¼m than 1½m: suited by a sound surface: wears bandages: sweating on reappearance. *L. J. Barratt.*

MO ICHI DO 4 b.g. Lomond (USA) 128–Engageante (FR) (Beaugency (FR) 126) —
[1989 8.5g³ 10f⁵ 10.2g 10g² 10m³ 1990 12.3f] has a rather round action: modest maiden at best: stays 1¼m: possibly unsuited by top-of-the-ground: successful twice over hurdles in autumn. *Miss S. J. Wilton.*

MOLLERS 2 ch.f. (Mar 25) Foolish Pleasure (USA)–Musical Sally (USA) (The 52
Minstrel (CAN) 135) [1990 6g⁶ 6m⁶ 6m⁵ 6d⁶ 6f³ 7m] dipped-backed, good-quartered filly: fourth foal: dam never ran: poor maiden: gives impression may do

better at 5f: blinkered final 2 starts: sold 980 gns Doncaster September Sales. *J. W. Watts.*

MOLLY'S MOVE 3 ch.f. Kabour 80–Sallyanda 65 (Marcus Superbus 100) [1989 **40** 6m 7d 6s 1990 6v 8m3 12m5 8m2 10f4 8g4 8f 9m2 8h 9f4 9f3 10m4 8f 11m6 10m 11m] sparely-made, plain filly: plater: consistent until last 3 starts: ridden by 7-lb claimer, bolted to post then stumbled and unseated rider early in race on penultimate one: probably stays 1½m and acts on any going. *W. Storey.*

MOLLY SPLASH 3 b.f. Dunbeath (USA) 127–Nelly Do Da 78 (Derring-Do 131) **63** [1989 8g 1990 a8g6 8m 10f4 8m2 8g 9f4 8g2 9m 8m] small, compact filly: quite modest maiden: ran moderately last 2 starts: stays 9f: acts on firm ground: bandaged behind on reappearance. *C. A. Cyzer.*

MOLO 3 b.g. Castle Keep 121–Eldoret 100 (High Top 131) [1989 6f 7f6 8g 1990 7f] — leggy gelding: poor form in maidens: tailed off in handicap in May: bred to stay middle distances. *Lady Herries.*

MOMENT OF TRUTH 6 b.g. Known Fact (USA) 135–Chieftain Girl (USA) **45** (Chieftain II) [1989 NR 1990 16m2 12m] close-coupled, good-topped gelding: good mover: very lightly raced on flat: may prove best slightly short of 2m: wore crossed noseband on reappearance: useful novice chaser. *P. Monteith.*

MOMENTSOFMUSIC 2 ch.c. (Apr 22) Music Boy 124–Sweet Relief 90 (Sweet **73** Revenge 129) [1990 5m3 5m* 7g] 3,700F, 20,000Y: good-topped colt: half-brother to 3-y-o 7f winner Star Leader (by Kafu), 1983 2-y-o 7f winner Forge Close (by Swing Easy) and a winner in Italy: dam won three 6f races: won maiden at Ayr in July by 1½ lengths from L'Ete: not discredited, soon ridden along, in Chester nursery over 6 weeks later: probably stays 7f: trained by J. Berry on debut. *C. Tinkler.*

MOMSER 4 ch.g. Mr Fluorocarbon 126–Jolimo 92 (Fortissimo 111) [1989 10.6m **63** 10m3 10.6d6 10m2 12f 13.6g2 a12g 1990 a13g 12f6 11f 12f2 12g5] leggy gelding: quite modest handicapper: sweating, saddle slipped and rider lost irons final outing: stays 13.6f: acts on firm and dead going: often claimer ridden: found little second outing. *M. J. Ryan.*

MONARCH EXPRESS (USA) 2 b.g. (May 8) Key To The Kingdom (USA)– **68** Pleasingly Quick (USA) (To The Quick (USA)) [1990 8.2d 8d3] $13,000Y: brother to a winner at up to 7f and half-brother to another winner: dam never ran: 7 lengths third of 18 to El Dominio in maiden at Bath in October: slowly away on debut: may improve again. *N. A. Graham.*

MONARDA 3 ch.g. Pharly (FR) 130–Emaline (FR) 105 (Empery (USA) 128) [1989 **65** 7m 8g6 1990 a7g5 6f 12.5g* 13.1h2 12d* 13.3m5 12m4] leggy, close-coupled gelding: has a round action: quite modest handicapper: won at Wolverhampton (wandering under pressure) in May and Beverley (making most and rallying well) in June: should be well suited by 1¾m + : yet to race on soft going, acts on any other: has run well for 7-lb claimer. *P. F. I. Cole.*

MONA'S PRINCE 3 b. or br.g. Class Distinction–Princess Mona 56 (Prince — Regent (FR) 129) [1989 a7g 1990 a6g 10m 11.5m 10f6 7m] workmanlike gelding: no sign of ability, in selling handicaps last 2 starts. *C. J. Benstead.*

MONASTERY 4 b.g. General Assembly (USA)–Sweet Habit (Habitat 134) [1989 — 8f* 9m 10m* 10f4 10m2 9m2 10m* 10g* 10g 1990 10m 12d4 10m6 10.5m 10f 10g 9m 10.6v] leggy gelding: progressed well as 3-y-o, winning £24,200 handicap at Newbury and listed event at Goodwood: failed to reproduce that form in 1990: suited by 1¼m: acts on firm going: bandaged on reappearance: moved down poorly next outing: has run creditably when sweating. *Mrs L. Piggott.*

MONDRIAN (GER) 4 ch.c. Surumu (GER)–Mole (GER) (Espresso 122) [1989 **120** 9g* 10.5g3 11g* 11g* 12s* 12g* 12g* 12g* 12s2 1990 12g* 12g 12g6 12g2 12g* 12s* 12s* 12s] angular, good-topped colt: carries plenty of condition: good-class performer: winner of 11 of his 14 races in Germany since 2 yrs, notably 7 Group 1 contests: easily landed the odds in Aral-Pokal at Gelsenkirchen-Horst and Geno Europa-Preis at Cologne, and in between accounted for Ibn Bey by length in Grosser Preis von Baden in 1990: successful also in Group 2 Gerling-Preis at Cologne in April: behind on all his 3 starts outside Germany as 4-y-o: moved down moderately, reportedly pulled muscle when virtually pulled up in Coronation Cup at Epsom: stays 1½m: acts on soft going: to join P. Cole. *U. Stoltefuss, Germany.*

MONESTA 2 ch.f. (Apr 1) Claude Monet (USA) 121–Esta Bonita (USA) 69 — (To-Agori-Mou 133) [1990 8g] angular filly: first foal: dam ran twice at 2 yrs: bit backward and blinkered, slowly away and always behind in maiden at Newcastle in October: sold 980 gns Doncaster October Sales. *R. F. Marvin.*

MONETARY FUND 6 b.g. Red Sunset 120 Maida (Majority Blue 126) [1989 — 14.8s* 15.5s⁵ 14g³ 16f³ 1990 13v⁶ 14m] tall, close-coupled gelding: quite modest winner of handicap early as 5-y-o: stays 2m: acts on any going: ran poorly in blinkers: sometimes sweats: held up and suited by strong gallop: has run in snatches. *R. Akehurst.*

MONIGA 4 b.f. Blazing Saddles (AUS)–Misuumi (Artaius (USA) 129) [1989 7d 94 7m² 7f² 7m* 6m* 6m 6g³ 6m³ 6m 6v 1990 6f 6m 6m* 6m* 6s³ 6g 6.5g³ 6g⁴ 6d] fairly useful filly on her day: successful in early-summer handicaps at Newbury and York (£11,900 contest): below form in listed event at Phoenix Park (sweating) and Ladbrokes (Ayr) Gold Cup, last of 28 finishers, last 2 outings: suited by 6f: best efforts in Britain on top-of-the-ground: has run creditably for 5-lb claimer: not particularly consistent: sold 14,500 gns Newmarket December Sales. *I. A. Balding.*

MONKEY LOVE 3 gr.c. Carwhite 127–Minne Love 67 (Homeric 133) [1989 5f 50 6f⁶ 6d 5g² 1990 7g 7f³ 7f 8m] good-topped, workmanlike colt: plating-class maiden: easily best efforts when placed in handicaps: stays 7f: acts on firm going. *L. G. Cottrell.*

MONOLULUS SURPRISE (IRE) 2 b.f. (Apr 2) Primo Dominie 121–Atilla 42 The Hen 64 (Hot Spark 126) [1990 16m 6g 6m³ 6f 5.1m] 3,300Y: compact filly: fifth foal: dam 2-y-o 5f winner, is half-sister to smart 1973 2-y-o 5f performer Eveneca: poor maiden: ran badly in sellers final 2 (blinkered second) starts. *G. A. Huffer.*

MON REGRET 5 ch.g. Record Token 128–Charlotte's Image (Towern 96) [1989 — NR 1990 a12g] ex-French gelding: second foal: dam never ran: no sign of ability. *J. A. B. Old.*

MONSAGEM (USA) 4 b.c. Nureyev (USA) 131–Meringue Pie (USA) (Silent 112 Screen (USA)) [1989 8d* 8m⁵ 10.5f* 9.2g³ 8g* 8g⁶ 1990 7m* 8m³ 8d² 8m 8g] lengthy, round-barrelled colt: moderate walker: poor mover: smart performer at 3 yrs: favourite on first run for almost 10 months, made all in 5-runner listed Leicestershire Stakes in April: ran well when placed in Juddmonte Lockinge Stakes (edging left) at Newbury and Prix du Chemin de Fer du Nord at Chantilly: ran as though something amiss in Queen Anne Stakes at Royal Ascot and Prix Quincey at Deauville (off course 2 months in between): ideally suited by 1m or 9f: acts on firm and dead going, though possibly unable to take much racing on firm. *H. R. A. Cecil.*

MONSCOMA (USA) 2 b.c. (May 5) Montelimar (USA) 122–Scoma (Lord Gayle 49 (USA) 124) [1990 7d 6g⁶ 6d] IR 3,600F, 2,800 2-y-o: first foal: dam poor maiden in Ireland, second once over 1½m: best effort sixth of 11 in maiden at Folkestone in October: slowly away on debut: likely to prove suited by further than 6f. *A. R. Davison.*

MONSIEUR MORUE 3 b.g. Pas de Seul 133–Footway 97 (Sovereign Path 125) — p [1989 NR 1990 11.7f 10d] close-coupled, quite attractive gelding: fifth foal: half-brother to fair stayer Harreek (by Tap On Wood) and 1¼m seller winner Footstool (by Artaius): dam, sister to 1000 Guineas winner Humble Duty, won 4 of 7 starts in Ireland, from 6f to 1m: showed signs of ability, never placed to challenge, in maiden at Bath (slowly away) and claimer at Ayr (not knocked about) nearly 5 months later. *R. J. Holder.*

MONTAUK (IRE) 2 br.g. (Mar 9) Gorytus (USA) 132–East River (FR) (Arctic 55 Tern (USA) 126) [1990 5m⁴ 5f⁴ 5g 5m 5m⁶] 21,000F, 10,000Y: smallish, round-barrelled gelding: second living foal: brother to 7f seller winner Manhattan River:

Grosser Preis von Baden, Baden-Baden—Mondrian repulses a strong overseas challenge led by Ibn Bey and Per Quod

dam minor French 11f winner: plating-class maiden: ran poorly final 2 starts, looking temperamental on second one: blinkered 3 times. *M. H. Easterby.*

MONTENDRE 3 b.c. Longleat (USA) 109–La Lutine 95 (My Swallow 134) [1989 **108** ? 6g² 6f* 6g* 1990 7g² 6g 6m⁴ 7f⁵ 7g 6s] leggy, rather angular colt: fluent mover: useful performer: in frame in Greenham Stakes at Newbury and £7,500 handicap at Newmarket: well below form in Group 3 events and listed race last 3 outings: should prove as effective over 7f as 6f: trained until after fourth start by L. Cumani. *M. Johnston.*

MONTEROS BOY 5 ch.g. Crofter (USA) 124–Prima Bella 76 (High Hat 131) **66** [1989 8h 10f 8.5m 8m⁴ 8h⁴ 10f³ 9m* 8.3m⁵ 9f⁵ 12g 10f³ 10g 1990 9f 9g 8m* 10f⁶ 8m³ 8f* 8f² 8m² 7f² 10.2g⁶ 8m⁴] good-topped gelding: quite modest handicapper: won at Kempton (apprentices) in May and Pontefract in July: finds fast 7f on sharp side and stays 1¼m: probably acts on any going: effective with blinkers or without: good mount for apprentice: consistent. *B. W. Hills.*

MONTPELIER LAD 3 br.g. Elegant Air 119–Leg Glance 87 (Home Guard **74** (USA) 129) [1989 NR 1990 a7g* 10d 9.5g 10g³ 8m⁵ 8m⁵ 7g⁵ 8g 8g² 8m 7g²] tall gelding: carries condition: third foal: dam 2-y-o 7f winner: modest performer: won maiden at Lingfield in January: second in handicaps at Sandown and Newbury: stays 1m: seems best on an easy surface: visored fourth and ninth starts: has worn crossed noseband: may well prove best with waiting tactics: sold to join G. Richards 30,000 gns Newmarket Autumn Sales. *W. Hastings-Bass.*

MONTYKOSKY 3 b.g. Montekin 125–Reliable Rosie (Relko 136) [1989 7m 6g **54** 8m 7d 1990 a8g 12m a12g² 15.3f³ 16m 15.3g] sturdy gelding: form only when placed in sellers, claimed £6,811 out of E. Eldin's stable on second occasion: moved poorly down and tailed off in handicap final start: should prove suited by good test of stamina. *B. Preece.*

MONYA 3 b.f. Explodent (USA)–Fandangerina (USA) (Grey Dawn II 132) [1989 **—** NR 1990 7m⁴ 10d⁶ a8g 10g 8d] sturdy filly: poor mover: half-sister to very useful 6f to 1m performer Western Gun (by Lypheor): dam won at up to 1m: no worthwhile form, in claimers last 2 starts: wore crossed noseband: sold 850 gns Doncaster November Sales. *R. Boss.*

MOONA (USA) 2 b.f. (May 8) Lear Fan (USA) 130–Dance Empress (USA) **52** (Empery (USA) 128) [1990 a5g⁶ 7f 6d4] leggy, close-coupled filly: fourth foal: sister to 3-y-o 1m winner London Pride and half-sister to 1988 2-y-o 7f winner Intebah (by The Bart): dam 6f winner, is half-sister to dam of very useful 1985 2-y-o Truely Nureyev: first race for 3½ months, around 10 lengths fourth of 17 in maiden at Folkestone in November, easily best effort: should stay 7f. *P. F. I. Cole.*

MOON CACTUS 3 b.f. Kris 135–Lady Moon 101 (Mill Reef (USA) 141) **118** [1989 6g² 7m* 7m* 8m² 1990 10m* 10.5d² 10f³]
    The useful staying two-year-old Moon Cactus had her share of problems at three and and her racecourse appearances were few, but she still managed to emerge from the season with a good deal of credit. An abscess under a tooth made training her difficult early on, and she didn't reappear until late-May in the Sheraton Park Tower Lupe Stakes at Goodwood, only just over a fortnight before her major objective of the Gold Seal Oaks or its French equivalent, the Prix de Diane Hermes. Looking very fit though not at all well in her coat, she quickened clear off a slow pace in a matter of strides when shaken up over a furlong out but, as in the past, began to idle and needed to be driven out to hold subsequent Oaks runner-up Game Plan by a length and a half. The pair pulled five lengths clear of the remaining five runners. Cecil expressed himself very pleased with Moon Cactus over the next few days; the main problem now was deciding whether to go to Epsom or Chantilly. After much deliberation the latter was chosen, one of the chief reasons cited being that Chantilly's right-handed track would be more suitable in view of the filly's restricted vision in her left eye. Sent off at 3/1 coupled with pacemaker Helen's Guest and Fabre's Colour Chart in a field of fourteen, she passed the post a very good third, in a race not run to suit her. Helen's Guest failed to set a good gallop and the contest developed into a sprint from about two furlongs out. As in the Lupe, Moon Cactus was held up and pulled extremely hard; turning into the straight she had plenty to do but buckled down really well under hard riding and was going on well at the finish, in the end beaten half a length and two by stable-companion Rafha and Colour Chart, with the favourite Air de Rien alongside Moon Cactus; Colour Chart was subsequently demoted to fourth for

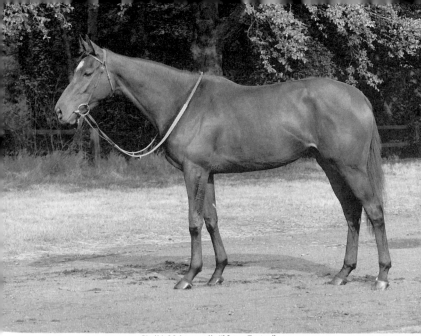

Sheikh Mohammed's "Moon Cactus"

interfering with the favourite. Moon Cactus seemed sure to win another good prize and looked to hold sound claims for her next start, the Vodafone Nassau Stakes at Goodwood, for which she started a very well-backed 5/4 favourite. Cauthen allowed her to stride on on this occasion and she was soon leading at a strong pace; the writing was on the wall though when Kartajana ranged upsides her over two furlongs out and Moon Cactus could offer only token resistence. She wasn't knocked about when clearly held inside the last furlong.

Moon Cactus (b.f. 1987)	Kris (ch 1976)	Sharpen Up (ch 1969)	Atan
			Rocchetta
		Doubly Sure (b 1971)	Reliance II
			Soft Angels
	Lady Moon (b 1980)	Mill Reef (b 1968)	Never Bend
			Milan Mill
		Moonlight Night (ch 1972)	Levmoss
			Lovely Light

Moon Cactus' pedigree was detailed in *Racehorses of 1989*. Her two-year-old half-brother Wakashan (by Dancing Brave), also in training with Cecil, raced just once, shaping promisingly when third in a Newbury maiden. Sire Kris goes from strength to strength, and an update on his winners can be found in the essay on Shamshir. Moon Cactus, a leggy, workmanlike filly, showed a free, rather round action, and was an active sort who pulled hard. She stayed a mile and a quarter, and acted on good to firm ground and dead. Following a series of minor injuries she was retired in October. *H. R. A. Cecil.*

MOON FESTIVAL   2 gr.f. (May 8) Be My Guest (USA) 126–Castle Moon 79   **68** p (Kalamoun 129) [1990 7m⁵ 7g⁶] leggy, sparely-made filly: has a round action: half-sister to several winners, including Sheriff's Star (by Posse), Moon Madness (by

Vitiges) and 3-y-o Lucky Moon (by Touching Wood): dam, winner at 1m to 13f, is sister to good middle-distance stayer Castle Keep and half-sister to Gold Cup winner Ragstone: 6 lengths sixth of 20, staying on, in maiden at Newmarket in November: very green and slowly away on debut: will be well suited by middle distances: likely to do better. *Lady Herries.*

MOONFLUTE (USA) 2 ch.f. (Apr 17) The Minstrel (CAN) 135–Top Hope 115 82 (High Top 131) [1990 6m* 7f³ 6.5g] 70,000Y: sparely-made, angular filly: fourth foal: half-sister to 3-y-o 1m winner Free Thinker (by Shadeed): dam 7f winner at 2 yrs, stayed 1m: fair performer: raced freely when winning maiden at Kempton in July and when third of 6 to Trojan Crown in listed race at Newmarket: creditable tenth of 17 in Tattersalls Tiffany Yorkshire Stakes at Doncaster: stays 7f. *I. A. Balding.*

MOONJID 2 b.c. (Jan 23) Shirley Heights 130–Psylla 96 (Beldale Flutter (USA) 60 130) [1990 8g 7m 8d] compact colt: moderate walker and mover: first foal: dam 9f and 1¼m winner, is out of half-sister to Kris and Diesis: quite modest form, never better than mid-division, in minor event at Newbury and maiden at Newmarket first 2 starts. *P. T. Walwyn.*

MOONLIGHT SAIL 3 ch.f. Main Reef 126–Moonlight Sonata 78 (So Blessed 50 130) [1989 5s⁵ 6m² 7g² 8d 8g 7s 8d 6d 6s 1990 7m 6m 7s 7.9m 10f a8g* 8g² 10m⁶ a8g a8g a8g⁵ a12g⁵ a11g] IR 5,000Y: sparely-made filly: fourth foal: dam 6f winner at 2 yrs who didn't train on: won handicap at Laytown and second in claimer (claimed out of K. Prendergast's stable £3,050) at Tralee in August: poor form here, mostly in claimers: stays 1m: visored penultimate start often blinkered, including when successful: winning selling hurdler. *R. W. Stubbs.*

MOON REEF 4 ch.f. Main Reef 126–Malmsey (Jukebox 120) [1989 9g⁶ 10.5f 12.3g⁶ 12.3f² 12.3g⁵ 17.4s 1990 11.7g 12m⁵ 14g⁵ 14m 12m a11g] big, rangy filly: modest handicapper as 3-y-o: below her best in 1990: best form at up to 1½m: acts on any going: ran poorly in visor final outing: has joined C. Broad. *J. M. P. Eustace.*

MOONTALK 4 br.f. Dubassoff (USA)–Gay Picture 62 (Linacre 133) [1989 7f 8f 44 1990 12g² a13g] lightly-raced maiden: form only when short-head second in seller at Folkestone in October: stays 1½m. *R. Akehurst.*

MOOR FROLICKING 4 ch.f. Morston (FR) 125–Woodland Frolic (Hittite 45 Glory 125) [1989 6s 6v² 6s² 6m 6f 6f 7g 10m 10m 1990 a8g* a7g a7g 8m* 8m⁶ 8m 8m] small filly: keen walker: has a round action: successful in claimer at Lingfield in February and selling handicap at Leicester (no bid, making virtually all) in March: stays 1m: acts on good to firm and heavy going: bandaged final start: inconsistent. *T. M. Jones.*

MOORS COUNTRY 2 b.g. (Apr 19) Aragon 118–Open Country (Town And 63 Country 124) [1990 7g 7f³ 7m⁴ 8f⁶ 8.2d a7g⁴ a8g] leggy, close-coupled gelding: has a round action: fourth foal: dam never ran: quite modest maiden: should stay 1m: possibly unsuited by a soft surface. *R. Hannon.*

MOOSANCE 2 b. or br.f. (May 12) Mummy's Game 120–Tabasheer (USA) 40 (Indian Chief II) [1990 5g 5m² 5.8h⁴ 6g⁵] 1,600Y: leggy, sparely-made filly: closely related to 2 winners by Mummy's Pet, including fairly useful sprinter Tremellick, and half-sister to 2 winners abroad: dam never ran: poor maiden: best effort at 5f: sold 1,200 gns Newmarket Autumn Sales. *R. Guest.*

MORAL TALES (IRE) 2 b.g. (Mar 22) The Noble Player (USA) 126–Bellinote — (FR) 71 (Noir Et Or 125) [1990 7v] 9,000Y: second foal: half-brother to 3-y-o Grace-wing (by Gorytus): dam maiden half-sister to smart 1981 French staying 2-y-o Beau Pretender: slowly away and always behind in maiden at Ayr in October. *D. Moffatt.*

MORCINDA 4 ch.g. Ballacashtal (CAN)–Montelimar 108 (Wolver Hollow 126) 66 [1989 10f⁵ 1990 5g³ 7m⁵ 5g² 6g 6g 5m⁵ 8.2m⁶ 7d⁵ 8g 6s⁶] strong, lengthy gelding: quite modest maiden: should stay 1m: acts on good to firm and dead going: bandaged first 2 starts: tends to get on edge: has started slowly. *P. Monteith.*

MORE ICE 4 b.f. Runnett 125–Spoons (Orchestra 118) [1989 10g 16m⁶ 10s 1990 — a11g] ex-Irish filly: second foal: dam unraced: little sign of ability in modest company. *C. Tinkler.*

MOREIRWEN 3 b. or br.f. Bold Owl 101–Neophyte II (Never Say Die 137) [1989 — a7g a7g 1990 a8g³ a8g] little sign of ability in maidens. *J. O'Donoghue.*

MORE LARKS (IRE) 2 b. or br.c. (Feb 20) Godswalk (USA) 130–Charmeuse — (Cut Above 130) [1990 5v] 19,000F, 14,000Y: first foal: dam unraced, from family of Brocade: carrying condition, well beaten after slow start in maiden auction at Chester in October: sold 500 gns Ascot December Sales. *M. McCormack.*

MORGANNWG (IRE) 2 br.f. (Jan 24) Simply Great (FR) 122–Kitty's Sister 54 p
(Bustino 136) [1990 7g] 23,000Y: sparely-made filly: third foal: sister to fairly useful
1989 Irish 2-y-o 6f winner Mistral's Collette, since successful in 9f listed event in
Italy: dam, sister to Lowther winner Kittyhawk (dam of Nomadic Way), very useful
at up to 1m: slowly away and behind from 2f out in minor event at Doncaster in
September: should improve. *M. Bell.*

MORLEY STREET 6 ch.g. Deep Run 119–High Board (High Line 125) [1989 83 p
NR 1990 16.2d*] second foal: dam unraced daughter of top-notch hunter
chaser/point-to-pointer Matchboard: won minor event at Goodwood in October by
head, well clear, from below-form Michelozzo: high-class jumper. *G. B. Balding.*

MORNING JOY 3 b.f. Mummy's Pet 125–Satellite (Busted 134) [1989 5d 5f4 —
5m3 5f4 5g 1990 6m 7f] workmanlike filly: moderate mover: poor maiden: faced stiff
tasks in selling handicaps as 3-y-o: should prove better at 6f than 5f: edgy on reappearance: sold 1,200 gns Newmarket Autumn Sales. *W. J. Pearce.*

MORPICK 3 ro.g. Morston (FR) 125–Pickwood Sue 74 (Right Boy 137) [1989 5d4 58
1990 6m 5d 5g5 5m5 5m6 a6g6 5d a6g4 a6g4 a5g2 a6g2] close-coupled, plain gelding:
poor walker: plating-class maiden: stays 6f: yet to race on extremes of going: has
run creditably when sweating and on toes, and for apprentice. *J. P. Leigh.*

MOSCOW DYNAMO 3 br.c. Siberian Express (USA) 125–County Line 75 83
(High Line 125) [1989 6g3 1990 7.6d4 7m* 8.5d4] lengthy, attractive colt: fair form:
6/5 on, won maiden at Catterick in May: green and wandering under pressure:
fourth in £13,900 handicap at Epsom following month: stays 8.5f: acts on good to
firm ground and dead: taken down very early and steadily at Catterick, wore severe
noseband on reappearance. *M. R. Stoute.*

MOSSWOOD PRINCE 2 ch.c. (Apr 25) Country Classic–Morse Princess 69 —
(Communication 119) [1990 6f a6g 6m] leggy, workmanlike colt: first reported foal:
dam plater stayed 1m: little worthwhile form, including in sellers: unseated rider
before halfway on debut: pulled hard in blinkers final start. *R. O'Leary.*

MOSSY ROSE 4 b.f. King of Spain 121–Mosso 81 (Ercolano (USA) 118) [1989 6d3 65
6d 6m 7.3m 7f3 6m4 7g 7g 1990 a6g3 6s 7.6m 6m 6d 7m a6g* a6g2 6m 7g4 a7g a7g
a7g] strong, good-bodied filly: poor mover: 25/1, led close home having started
slowly when winning (for only time) handicap at Southwell in September: easily
best other effort at 4 yrs on next outing: stays 7f. *Pat Mitchell.*

MOSTIMUS 2 ch.f. (Mar 5) Doulab (USA) 115–Jennyjo 64 (Martinmas 128) [1990 63
5m* 6m5 6g a6g a7g a7g] 15,000Y: good-quartered, sprint type: half-sister to fairly
useful 1986 2-y-o 5f winner Ultra Nova (by Tina's Pet) and modest 1987 2-y-o 6f
winner Mill Bridge (by Tender King): dam 7f winner: won maiden at Pontefract in
July by 2½ lengths from Kevinsbelle: should stay 6f: bandaged behind third outing:
usually ridden by 7-lb claimer. *G. R. Oldroyd.*

MOST OF ALL 4 gr.f. Absalom 128–Beech Tree 67 (Fighting Ship 121) [1989 —
7m5 7m 1990 8f 10f] workmanlike filly: lightly-raced maiden: well beaten in May
handicaps: withdrawn lame at start next intended outing (trained by T. Kersey) 5½
months later: blinkered on reappearance. *Dr J. D. Scargill.*

MOTCOMBS 3 gr.f. Glenstal (USA) 118–Roof (Thatch (USA) 136) [1989 6g5 6d 64
1990 6f* 6f 6m5 8.2s 8m 7f 8m4] workmanlike, good-quartered filly: quite modest
performer: won maiden at Brighton in April: apparently easily beat subsequent
effort when in face of very stiff task in Warwick minor event final start: probably
stays 1m: acts on firm going: visored and slowly away third start: blinkered fifth:
retained 4,700 gns Ascot July Sales. *M. McCormack.*

MOTHER HEN 5 b.m. Ardross 134–Lucayan Lady 81 (Swing Easy (USA) 126) —
[1989 NR 1990 12m 12.3g 9s] strong, lengthy mare: winning plater as 3-y-o: well
beaten in handicaps in 1990: withdrawn lame on intended reappearance: stays 1¼m:
tends to get warm in preliminaries, and has got on edge. *K. B. McCauley.*

MOTHERS SON 3 b.g. Mummy's Pet 125–Miss Suntan (Bruni 132) [1989 NR —
1990 8g 7m 10g] leggy, lengthy gelding: second foal: dam French 1½m winner from
family of Wolver Hollow: well beaten in maidens and minor event: sold to join R.
Simpson 6,000 gns Newmarket September Sales. *R. Simpson.*

MOUFAJAH (IRE) 2 b.c. (Feb 7) Touching Wood (USA) 127–Nuit d'Ete (USA) 72 p
90 (Super Concorde (USA) 128) [1990 6m 7g5] first living foal: dam 2-y-o 5f and 6f
winner: still bit backward, around 6 lengths fifth of 21, progress at halfway then no
extra final furlong, to Balaat in maiden at Newbury in August: pulled hard and edged
left on debut: will improve again. *B. Hanbury.*

MOUKTARPOUR (IRE) 2 br.c. (Feb 14) Mouktar 129–Jam Treacle (USA) — p
(Jaipur) [1990 8d] IR 20,000Y: lengthy colt: half-brother to several winners here and
abroad, including smart 1977 French staying 2-y-o Orange Marmalade (by Aureole)
and 14.7f winner Golden Curd (by Nice Havrais): dam French 1¼m winner:
backward and green, seventh of 13, outpaced soon after halfway and not knocked
about, in maiden at Leicester in October: should improve. *C. F. Wall.*

MOUNTAIN GLOW 3 gr.g. Siberian Express (USA) 125–Bombshell 76 (Le 71
Levanstell 122) [1989 NR 1990 9g⁵ 10.2g 11m² 10f⁴ 10g³ 10m 10g³] compact, rather
angular gelding: half-brother to several winners, including 4-y-o Future Glory (by
Ile de Bourbon), 1m winner at 2 yrs, and 1¾m winner Orlandoland (by Reliance II):
dam 8.5f winner: modest maiden: may prove ideally suited by 1¼m: probably
unsuited by firm going: sold to join J. L. Harris 3,000 gns Doncaster October Sales.
Miss S. E. Hall.

MOUNTAIN KINGDOM (USA) 6 b.h. Exceller (USA) 129–Star In The 113
North (USA) 94 (Northern Dancer) [1989 9g⁴ 12g* 12d⁴ 13.4f* 14f* 12g⁶ 14f² 1990
9.5v³ 12v⁴ 16m² 20d 13.3g³ 12.5g 12m] lengthy, quite attractive horse: very useful
performer: ran creditably when placed behind Teamster in Henry II EBF Stakes at
Sandown and Charmer in 5-runner Geoffrey Freer Stakes at Newbury: below his
best in Grand Prix de Deauville Lancel and Cumberland Lodge Stakes (keen hold in
blinkers and tailed off) at Ascot last 2 outings: ran twice in Australia early in year:
stays 2m: has won on heavy going, but best form in Britain on top-of-the-ground:
has joined D. Elsworth. *C. E. Brittain.*

MOUNTAINOUS 4 br.g. Lochnager 132–September Fire (Firestreak 125) —
[1989 NR 1990 a6g a11g] very big gelding: half-brother to 3 winners, including 6f and
7f winner Master Pokey (by Uncle Pokey): dam never ran: no show in claimers at
Southwell in November: bandaged off-fore and very slowly away first time, fitted
with tongue strap second. *M. W. Easterby.*

MOUNTAIN VISION (IRE) 2 b.f. (Feb 16) Vision (USA)–Mountain Heather 37
(Daring Display (USA)) [1990 5m⁶ 5g⁶ 5m 5g] IR 850F: small, close-coupled
filly: moderate walker: dam unraced close relation of very useful 1971 2-y-o Pert
Lassie: poor form, including in sellers. *E. J. Alston.*

MOUNTAIN WIND 3 b.g. Tumble Wind (USA)–Bustina (FR) (Busted 134) —
[1989 6g 7g 1990 8f 10.1g 7m⁵ 10.8g 10h] IR 26,000F, IR 56,000Y: sturdy ex-Irish
gelding: brother to 2 winners in Ireland, one a sprinter the other a stayer, and half-
brother to quite useful Irish 6f to 1m winner Miss Lillian (by Sandford Lad): dam
fourth of 16 on only start at 2 yrs in France: poor form at best: trained at 2 yrs by L.
Browne: gelded after final start. *J. Sutcliffe.*

MOUNT IDA (USA) 3 b.f. Conquistador Cielo (USA)–Suspicious (USA) 79
(Damascus (USA)) [1989 NR 1990 10.6f² 8m² 8.5d⁴ 8m² 10.2f* 12f 10g] $95,000Y:
good-topped, attractive filly: has scope: half-sister to a minor winner by Alydar: dam
won at up to 1¼m: sire champion colt in USA stayed 1½m: fair performer: favourite,
won maiden at Bath in June: behind after in £27,900 handicap (very stiff task) at
Goodwood and £5,100 handicap (bit burly, visored) at Newbury: stays 1¼m: acts on
firm ground: takes keen hold. *C. R. Nelson.*

MOVEABLE FEAST 2 b. or br.f. (Jan 18) Primo Dominie 121–Cottage Pie 106 —
(Kalamoun 129) [1990 5m] 12,000Y: good-bodied filly: has scope: half-sister to 1986
2-y-o 5f winner Sauce Diable (by Moorestyle): dam useful staying 2-y-o, is half-
sister to Yorkshire Cup winner Riboson: bit backward, slowly away, green and
always behind in maiden auction at Sandown in June. *J. R. Williams.*

MOVING FORCE 3 b.g. Muscatite 122–Saint Simbir 82 (Simbir 130) [1989 6m 74
6m 1990 7h⁶ 5.8f* 5f⁵ 5f5 7f⁴ 7f⁴ 5m⁶ 7.6d* 8g] rather leggy, unfurnished gelding:
modest performer: won seller (edgy, no bid) at Bath in June and handicap at
Lingfield in October: best at around 7f: acts on firm and dead ground: consistent. *R.
Akehurst.*

MOVING OUT 2 b.c. (Feb 20) Slip Anchor 136–New Generation 91 (Young 65 p
Generation 129) [1990 8d a8g*] close-coupled colt: has knee action: second foal:
half-brother to 1988 2-y-o 5f winner Noble Habitat (by Formidable): dam won at up
to 1m: odds on but still green, won 10-runner maiden at Southwell in November by
1½ lengths from Western Ace: will stay 1¼m: will improve again. *Sir Mark Prescott.*

MOWTHORPE 5 ch.g. Ballad Rock 122–Simeonova (Northfields (USA)) [1989 —
NR 1990 10.2m⁵] strong, dipped-backed gelding: quite modest winner at 2 yrs:
bandaged, never able to challenge in slowly-run handicap at Newcastle in March:
should stay 1¼m: acts on firm and dead going: winning hurdler. *M. W. Easterby.*

MOY RIVER (IRE) 2 b.c. (Apr 22) Dominion 123–Allaigah (Be My Guest 91 ?
(USA) 126) [1990 6m⁶ 6g* 6m² 6f³] 13,000Y: lengthy, quite attractive colt: poor
mover: third foal: half-brother to modest 1989 2-y-o 8.5f winner Toast The Host (by
Elegant Air) and a winner in Italy: dam poor daughter of half-sister to high-class
middle-distance colt Pelerin: won auction race at Epsom in June by 6 lengths: odds
on, better effort in minor events after when second of 5 to Heard A Whisper at
Doncaster: seemed unsuited by firm ground at Chester: will stay 7f. *J. L. Dunlop.*

MR BROOKS 3 b.c. Blazing Saddles (AUS)–Double Finesse 97 (Double Jump 106
131) [1989 7d* 1990 7g² 8m⁵ 12g 5g² 6m³] strong, close-coupled colt: won maiden at
Leopardstown in October at 2 yrs: placed in Gladness Stakes at the Curragh and
listed races (blinkered) at Tipperary and Phoenix Park: good fifth in moderately-run
Irish 2000 Guineas: visored and edgy, raced freely when last in the Derby: not bred
to stay beyond 1m: useful. *K. Connolly, Ireland.*

MR BURFIELD 2 br.c. (Mar 23) Faustus (USA) 118–Grey Twig 68 (Godswalk 66
(USA) 130) [1990 5g 5m* 6m⁵ 6m 6m 7f 8g] 11,000Y: smallish, lengthy colt:
moderate walker: fourth living foal: half-brother to 1986 2-y-o 5.8f and 6f winner
Grey Wolf Tiger (by Rolfe) and 7f winner Kachina Maid (by Anfield): dam ran only at
2 yrs: quite modest performer: won maiden auction at Sandown in May: best form at
up to 6f: sold 4,200 gns Newmarket Autumn Sales. *R. Hannon.*

MR BUSH (USA) 3 gr.c. Fappiano (USA)–Future Fun (USA) (What A Pleasure 59
(USA)) [1989 NR 1990 a8g⁵ a8g*] $165,000F: sturdy colt: second foal: half-brother
to successful North American 4-y-o Fun Fun Fun (by Sovereign Dancer): dam
stakes-placed sprinter: second favourite, won maiden at Southwell in August in
good style, making most: will stay further: sold 5,800 gns Newmarket Autumn
Sales. *J. H. M. Gosden.*

MR C FOX (USA) 3 ch.c. Devil's Bag (USA)–Sugar Plum Time (USA) (Bold 88
Ruler) [1989 NR 1990 9.1f² 12.5g² 12m⁴] big, leggy, angular colt: half-brother to
3 winners in North America: dam best at 4 yrs when good-class winner at up to 11f:
fair maiden: best efforts at Newmarket and Newcastle first 2 starts: will be suited by
return to 1¼m: sold 20,000 gns Newmarket Autumn Sales. *B. W. Hills.*

MR CHEEKYCHOPS 3 ch.g. Blue Cashmere 129–Tzu-Hsi 66 (Songedor 116) 53
[1989 5s 5m⁶ 7f 1990 a10g 7.5f² 8.2s⁴ 9f² 7m⁵ 7.5d* 11m 8m 8g] leggy, angular
gelding: fair plater: favourite, won at Beverley (no bid) in May: then ran moderately
and not seen out after June: stays 9f: acts on firm and dead going: often sets pace:
has been bandaged. *M. Brittain.*

MR CHRIS CAKEMAKER 6 ch.m. Hotfoot 126–Polonaise (Takawalk II 125) 57
[1989 10d 10.2g 10.6g 11m² 11s 11s² 1990 8.2s² 8v* 12g 9s³ 10d 8g 8.2s² 10.6d 10d 9s]
lengthy mare: poor mover: plating-class handicapper: favourite, won selling event
(no bid) at Ayr in April: effective at 1m to 11f: acted very well in the mud: visored
once: won for apprentice, but wasn't the easiest of rides: often sweated and got on
edge: in foal to Roaring Riva. *M. P. Naughton.*

MR CHRIS GATEAUX 8 gr.g. Gay Fandango (USA) 132 Snap Cobwebs 31
(Silver Shark 129) [1989 NR 1990 6g 7m 8.3m 8h⁴ 9f 6m] workmanlike gelding: poor
maiden: form only at around 1m: acts on firm going: effective with or without
blinkers: visored final outing. *B. C. Morgan.*

MR DORMOUSE 4 b.g. Comedy Star (USA) 121–Tea-Pot 77 (Ragstone 128) —
[1989 12m³ 12f5 16.2g 14d 16.2d 18g 1990 16g⁶] close-coupled gelding: moderate
mover: poor handicapper: shapes like out-and-out stayer: best run on top-of-the-
ground: blinkered or visored last 3 outings: winning hurdler in April: has joined I.
Balding. *C. W. C. Elsey.*

MR KEWMILL 7 b.g. Homing 130–Muninga 108 (St Alphage 119) [1989 5f 6f⁵ 6f — §
6f⁵ 10g 8.3m 7f 10m 10.8m³ 10f 8m a8g 1990 8.2f 12m] close-coupled gelding: has
a round action: bad handicapper: probably best short of 1¼m: blinkered 3 times,
usually visored: sometimes bandaged: not one to rely on. *J. A. Bennett.*

MR MAD 2 b.g. (Feb 19) Good Times (ITY)–Mistress Bowen (Owen Anthony —
102) [1990 5m 5f⁴ 5g 7f] 2,400F, 3,800Y: close-coupled gelding: seventh foal:
brother to plating-class maiden Good Holidays: dam ran 3 times: well beaten,
including in a seller: ran very wide home bend at Carlisle final start, first for 4
months. *C. Tinkler.*

MR MOCCASIN 3 b.g. Doc Marten 104–Some Cherry 41 (Some Hand 119) [1989 58
NR 1990 8.2s⁵ 8v³ 8.2g⁴ a8g a8g a11g] close-coupled gelding: second foal: dam
effective from 5f to 1m: deteriorated after showing quite modest form in maidens
first 2 starts: possibly needs the mud. *J. A. Glover.*

MR NICKERSON (USA)   4 b.c. Slewpy (USA)–Municipal Bond (USA) (Nas-   ?
hua) [1989 NR 1990 a6f* a6f* a6f* a7s⁵ a6f* a6f* a6f³ 5m a6f² a6f² a6f] very strong,
powerful colt: sixth foal: closely related to 2 winners by Seattle Slew, notably stakes
winner Tax Dodge, and half-brother to another winner in USA: dam graded-placed
winner at up to 1¼m: a leading American sprinter, winner of 10 of his 25 races and of
over $500,000 in prize money: successful on dirt in stakes races in January and
February and Grade 3 Bold Ruler Stakes in April, all at Aqueduct, and in Grade 3
Roseben Handicap (3 ran) and Grade 2 True North Handicap (4 ran) at Belmont Park
in June: 18/1, chased leaders over 3f when around 8 lengths seventh of 9 to Dayjur in
Keeneland Nunthorpe Stakes at York (showed quick action) in August, only race on
turf: suffered heart attack and died in Breeders' Cup Sprint at Belmont Park in
October. *Mark Reid, USA.*

MR OPTIMISTIC   3 ch.g. King Persian 107–Saybya (Sallust 134) [1989 8s⁵ 8.2d   —
7v 8.2s² 10g⁶ 1990 10v 8.2g⁵ 12s 15v⁵ 16s] leggy gelding: modest maiden at 2 yrs:
below form in 1990: should be suited by return to shorter than 2m: acts on soft
going, yet to race on top-of-the-ground: changed hands 9,600 gns Doncaster November Sales. *J. J. O'Neill.*

MR PINTIPS   6 b.h. Kris 135–Bempton 57 (Blakeney 126) [1989 16d⁵ 16m 1990   115
13.4d⁵ 16m⁴ 12s 12.5g* 14g² 12d³ 12v* 12v³] rather leggy, quite attractive horse:
poor mover: won amateurs race at Deauville in August and listed race at Maisons-
Laffitte in November: smart form in between behind Ibn Bey in Jefferson Smurfit
Memorial Irish St Leger and Sesame in EBF Blandford Stakes, both at the Curragh:
suited by test of stamina: best with give in the ground and acts on heavy: tough: sold
96,000 gns Newmarket December Sales. *W. Hastings-Bass.*

MR REINER (IRE)   2 br.g. (Apr 17) Vision (USA)–Yvonne's Choice (Octavo   56
(USA) 115) [1990 5f 6m³ 8f 7m] IR 7,000F, 9,400Y: leggy gelding: poor walker: first
reported foal: dam Irish 4-y-o 9.5f winner: plating-class maiden: should be suited by
further than 6f: visored final start. *Denys Smith.*

MRS BARTON (IRE)   2 gr.f. (Feb 29) Faustus (USA) 118–Phar Lapa 59   41
(Grundy 137) [1990 5g 6g 6m² 7g] small filly: good mover: second foal: half-sister to
3-y-o Prince Carnegie (by Taufan): dam staying maiden: poor form, including in
sellers: will be suited by 1m +. *B. W. Hills.*

MRS CLAYPOOL   2 br.f. (Mar 22) Petong 126–Rare Legend 69 (Rarity 129)   59
[1990 7m 6m⁶ 7d⁴ a8g³] smallish, sparely-made filly: first foal: dam 14.6f winner:
plating-class maiden: ran well for claimer final start: suited by 1m: trained first 2
starts by M. Tompkins: bandaged near-hind on debut. *M. A. Jarvis.*

MRS GRAY   3 gr.f. Red Sunset 120–Haunting 79 (Lord Gayle (USA) 124) [1989   —
5d³ 5f⁵ 5m* 5f⁶ 5f⁴ 5f⁴ 5s 5m⁵ 1990 6f 5f⁶ 6m⁵] smallish, sparely-made filly: quite
modest winner at 2 yrs: faced stiff tasks in handicaps and claimer in summer of 1990,
slowly away and wandering under pressure second outing: best form at 5f: blinkered
once at 2 yrs: sometimes sweats: inconsistent. *Mrs G. R. Reveley.*

MRS HENNY PENNY   3 ch.f. Absalom 128–Flopsy (Welsh Pageant 132) [1989   60
6f⁵ 6f⁴ 6f⁶ 7.3m⁴ 7g 1990 8m² 8.2g⁵ 8m] small, sturdy filly: quite modest maiden:
fell and broke leg at Warwick in June: stayed 1m: acted on good to firm ground:
usually bandaged behind at 2 yrs: dead. *D. W. P. Arbuthnot.*

MRS KEPPEL   2 b.f. (Mar 13) Castle Keep 121–Coming Out (Fair Season 120)   67
[1990 6m⁵ 7f²] unfurnished filly: third foal: sister to 3-y-o Knight's Glance and
modest maiden Castle Dance: dam unraced half-sister to Prix Gladiateur winner
Knight Templar: bit backward, quite modest form in maidens at Newbury and
Chester in summer: will be suited by 1m: sold 7,000 gns Doncaster November Sales.
J. L. Dunlop.

MRS MEYRICK   9 b.m. Owen Dudley 121–Social Bee 108 (Galivanter 131) [1989   —
12m 8.2f 8h⁶ 10f 13f* 13.8m* 15m* 15.8g⁶ 12.3f 1990 a14g a12g] leggy, lengthy
mare: winner 3 times in poor company as 8-y-o: bandaged, tailed off in handicaps at
Lingfield and Southwell early in year: better suited by 13f than shorter and seems to
stay 2m: acts on firm going. *R. M. Whitaker.*

MR SMILEY   3 b.g. Pharly (FR) 130–Yelming 76 (Thatch (USA) 136) [1989 NR   —
1990 7m 7m 7m⁵ 7m 8m 7m 10f a10g] 31,000Y: small gelding: half-brother to several
winners here and abroad, including 1¼m winner Follow The Band (by Dance In
Time) and quite useful 1983 2-y-o 1m winner Feasibility Study (by Welsh Pageant),
later winner in USA: dam, placed at up to 7f, is half-sister to Bassenthwaite: quite
modest form at best: showed nothing in handicaps last 2 starts: should stay beyond
7f: trained until after seventh outing by Mrs J. Pitman. *G. Lewis.*

MRS PEEDODY 3 ch.f. Trampler 79–Midsummer Sparkle (Agapornis) [1989 —
NR 1990 9m 12.2m 10m 11.5g⁶] sparely-made filly: first reported living foal: dam
never ran: no show, including in seller. *J. Pearce.*

MRS SKINNER 3 ch.f. Electric 126–Equal Chance 95 (Hitting Away) [1989 7m —
6m 1990 8g⁵ 8g⁶ 8g 10f⁶ 10m 10m] leggy filly: plater: stays 1m: below form when
sweating and edgy: sold to join Mrs P. Barker 750 gns Ascot November Sales. *C.
James.*

MR TAYLOR 5 b.g. Martinmas 128–Miss Reliant 65 (Reliance II 137) [1989 12d⁴ 37
12g³ 12f 12g* 12h² 12.4m 12m⁶ 15.3g⁴ 14m⁶ 12g 15g 14g⁵ 1990 12m⁶ 12.5m 18f³ 16.2g
18m³ 16m 10.6s 16.5d a16g] leggy, angular gelding: poor mover: poor handicapper:
stays 2¼m: yet to race on soft going, acts on any other: none too reliable. *H. J.
Collingridge.*

MR WADDILOVE 4 b.c. Bold Lad (IRE) 133–Friendly Sound 82 (Be Friendly 62 d
130) [1989 7g 6d 5g 5f³ 6f 5m* 5f⁶ 6m 5f⁵ 5d* 5g 1990 5f⁴ 6f⁴ 5g 8g⁶ 7g 6g] strong
colt: quite modest handicapper: out of form after second outing: effective at 5f and
6f: acts on firm and dead going: often wears blinkers: sold 1,000 gns Newmarket
Autumn Sales: inconsistent. *W. J. Pearce.*

MR WISHING WELL 4 ch.g. Dunbeath (USA) 127–Little Change 70 (Grundy 72
137) [1989 8.2d* 10m² 10m6 1990 8.2s 10.5m⁵ 10m] good-quartered gelding: fairly
useful winner at 3 yrs: 50/1 and apprentice ridden, never-nearer fifth to Eradicate in
£41,800 handicap at York in July: tailed off in Ripon handicap month later: stays
1¼m: acts on good to firm and dead going: sweating final start (July) at 3 yrs:
retained by trainer 10,500 gns Newmarket Autumn Sales. *R. J. R. Williams.*

MUARIJ 3 ch.f. Star Appeal 133–Ivoronica 89 (Targowice (USA) 130) [1989 6m —
1990 7m 6m 8.3m 8m 10f] lengthy filly: good mover: no show, including in handicaps,
and may be temperamentally unsatisfactory: sold 2,100 gns Ascot October Sales. *C.
J. Benstead.*

MU-ARRIK 2 b. or br.c. (Mar 13) Aragon 118–Maravilla 73 (Mandrake Major 122) 51
[1990 5f⁴ 6d⁶] 36,000Y: first foal: dam maiden stayed 1m, is half-sister to useful
miler Deadly Nightshade: plating-class form in maidens at Redcar and Doncaster:
off course 6 months in between: may do better. *H. Thomson Jones.*

MUDAFFAR (IRE) 2 b.c. (Feb 10) Simply Great (FR) 122–Baleen (Lochnager 68
132) [1990 7s⁴ 7s] 12,000F, 33,000Y: neat colt: second foal: dam Irish maiden, is
half-sister to Horris Hill winner Gouriev: 6 lengths fourth of 17 at Lingfield, better
effort in autumn maidens. *R. W. Armstrong.*

MUDAHIM 4 b.g. Shareef Dancer (USA) 135–Mariska (FR) (Tanerko 134) [1989 — p
NR 1990 10.8m] good-topped, useful-looking gelding: seventh living foal: brother to
useful Irish 1m winner Triple Kiss, who stayed 1¾m, and half-brother to several
winners, notably 1980 2-y-o 1m winner Wolver Heights (by Wolver Hollow), later
good winner in USA: dam twice-raced sister to Relko: 33/1, over 15 lengths seventh
of 16 in maiden at Warwick in April: winning hurdler in November: should improve.
D. J. Wintle.

MUDDY LANE 2 b.c. (Apr 9) Ilium 121–Monstrosa 70 (Monsanto (FR) 121) 52
[1990 5m² 6g³ 5f⁵ 8f⁶] plain colt: first foal: dam 2-y-o 5f winner, stayed 1m: plating-
class maiden: should stay 1m: twice very troublesome at stalls. *B. R. Millman.*

MUESTA 3 b.f. Bustino 136–Misguided 106 (Homing 130) [1989 5f³ 6f 1990 10f⁵ 46
10g 14.8f a11g⁴ a8g⁴ a8g] medium-sized filly: poor maiden: form only when fourth in
handicaps at Southwell: stays 11f: wore net muzzle on reappearance. *K. M. Brassey.*

MUIRFIELD VILLAGE 4 b.g. Lomond (USA) 128–Ukelele (USA) (Riva Ridge 68 §
(USA)) [1989 8g⁵ 1990 10.1g 6f² 10m* 10m 10g 10m 10s⁵] big, lengthy, good-bodied
gelding: split a pastern at 2 yrs: landed gamble on first run in handicap at Lingfield in
May: stays 1¼m: not genuine. *S. Dow.*

MUIZENBERG 3 b.c. Mashhor Dancer (USA)–Allotria 86 (Red God 128§) [1989 70
NR 1990 8g a7g* 7m 7.6m⁴] 24,000Y: useful-looking colt: reportedly cracked a
sesamoid as 2-y-o: sixth foal: half-brother to middle-distance winner and good
hurdler Aldino (by Artaius): dam won at 6f and 1m from 4 starts, and is half-sister to
Wollow: modest form to win maiden at Southwell in June, edging left: fair fourth in
handicap (swished tail) at Lingfield: sold to join J. Edwards 7,500 gns Newmarket
Autumn Sales. *R. W. Armstrong.*

MUJAAZIF (USA) 2 b.c. (Mar 9) Alydar (USA)–Miss Snowflake (USA) 116
(Snow Sporting (ARG)) [1990 6m² 6f³ 8f* 8m* 8s⁴]
   It's around forty years since Stan last showed his paces on the
racecourse, twenty or so since the latest incarnations of Sid and Eric made

their debuts, and every Tom, Dick and Harry has come and gone since racehorses names were first registered in the *General Stud Book*. The name given to a racehorse is, of course, primarily at the discretion of the owner; names, like most other things, fall in and out of fashion as times change. A consequence of the vastly increased number of Arab-owned horses in training over the past decade is the plethora of Arabic names on the racecourse, some of them, it would seem, contravening Appendix E of the *Rules of Racing* advising that names unacceptable for registration include those which are 'similar to those already registered' and '. . . which would cause confusion in the administration of racing and breeding'. Students of phonetics, if not of Arabic, might delight in the subtle differences between Mujaazif, Mujadil, Mujtahid, Mukaddamah, Mukddaam, Mudaffar and the as-yet unraced Muka-afah—the first five of which, at least, could be deemed preferable to their English equivalents 'risk taker', 'argumentative', 'studious', 'prelude', and 'courageous'—but there's no disputing that their outward similarity, plus the fact that those so named carry near-identical colours and hold much the same engagements, invite misunderstanding. Our advice? Watch your bets!

The risk-taking Mujaazif was very well suited by a distance of ground and a sound surface as a two-year-old; on the only occasion he encountered soft, in the one-mile Racing Post Trophy at Doncaster in October, for which he was co-favourite at 2/1, he finished tailed-off last of the four runners. Mujaazif wasn't given the opportunity to exploit his stamina until his third outing, having been placed in a six-furlong maidens at Newbury, where he started a hot favourite, and Goodwood; then, in a fairly weakly-contested maiden at Thirsk over a mile, he won in good style by two and a half lengths from Magic Secret, leading on the bridle two furlongs out and passing the post with an inestimable amount in hand. The task that faced Mujaazif in the eccentrically-renamed Royal Lodge William Hill Stakes at Ascot later in the

Royal Lodge William Hill Stakes, Ascot—
Mujaazif is a stylish winner of this usually-informative two-year-old race,
from the favourite Jahafil

Maktoum Al-Maktoum's "Mujaazif"

month, for which he started co-second favourite in a field of eight behind the twice-successful Jahafil, was a stiff one, but the searching gallop set by the National Stakes third Prodigal Blues then maintained by Jahafil brought forth a greatly improved performance. Mujaazif, in excellent condition, looked certain to play a prominent role in the finish turning for home; quickening through a gap between Jahafil and the weakening Prodigal Blues under two furlongs out, he put his head in the air briefly then applied himself to the task in hand, shaking off the persistent Jahafil inside the final furlong and going away to win by three and a half lengths with the Laurent-Perrier Champagne third Stone Mill filling the minor place again another four lengths behind. We can't believe the level of the form was so moderate as the Racing Press mostly made it out to be—after all, the field was very well strung out and the time for the race compared favourably with the Brent Walker Fillies' Mile (which was widely acknowledged as being a strongly-contested event)—and though the form isn't top class, and perhaps lower than the standard we'd normally expect, it's still pretty good. In that sort of form Mujaazif should have gone very close to winning the Racing Post Trophy. He shouldn't be written off after one poor run, and given firmer ground he'll be a prominent contender for one of the classic trials over a mile and a quarter or more in the spring.

In twenty-four hours in November the North American breeding industry, which has suffered the loss of more than its share of leading stallions in the past two and a half years, lost another two of its best-known sires, Alydar and Northern Dancer. Northern Dancer, the most influential thoroughbred stallion in the world over the past twenty years, had been retired since 1987, but Alydar was only fifteen at the time of his death, caused by fractures to his right hind leg. Alydar was a top-class racehorse whose position in racing

603

		Raise A Native	Native Dancer
	Alydar (USA)	(ch 1961)	Raise You
	(ch 1975)	Sweet Tooth	On-And-On
Mujaazif (USA)		(b 1965)	Plum Cake
(b.c. Mar 9, 1988)		Snow Sporting	Snow Cat
	Miss Snowflake (USA)	(b 1966)	Extatica
	(b 1978)	Bold Jewel	Any Time Now
		(b 1973)	Bold Contessa

folklore was founded more on the part he played in the thrilling triple crown of 1978, when he was second to Affirmed in all three legs, than for any of his fourteen victories, six of which were in Grade 1 events, from twenty-three other starts. Retired to Calumet Farm, who bred and owned him, Alydar proved an enormous success at stud (overshadowing Affirmed) and is currently third on the leading sire list behind Mr Prospector and Nijinsky with progeny earnings of around 35,000,000 dollars, having topped the general sire list in 1990 when for the first time earnings from the Japan Cup were included. Alydar has sired eighteen Group 1 or Grade 1 winners including 'America's horse' Alysheba, winner of the Kentucky Derby and Breeders' Cup Classic and still the world record money-earner with 6,679,242 dollars; the 1988 champion two-year-old and 1989 Belmont Stakes winner Easy Goer; and the top-class older horse Criminal Type, who was strongly in the running for the Horse of the Year award in 1990 and who would have been standing beside Alydar at Calumet in 1991; and, in Europe, Cacoethes, Alydar's Best and Alydaress. Mujaazif may well fall short of those in terms of ability, but he was the best two-year-old Alydar had running for him in 1990 on either continent. A 1,000,000-dollar yearling, costing just over twice the average for two hundred and forty or so Alydar yearlings sold at public auction since 1981, Mujaazif is the fifth foal of his dam Miss Snowflake. Her first foal, Snow Chief, by the modest stallion Reflected Glory, won over 3,000,000 dollars in prize money and a leg of the triple crown, the Preakness Stakes; but none of her next three, by the equally-unfashionable stallions The Irish Lord and Irish Stronghold, made the racecourse. Snow Chief aside, Mujaazif's pedigree on his dam's side is a moderate one. Miss Snowflake was a minor winner at around six furlongs in the States, and although all his next three dams were winners they have produced only a couple of unimportant stakes winners between them. Mujaazif is already a smart colt, and he seems likely to get a little better in the coming season, when he'll be suited by middle distances. Given top-of-the-ground, he seems sure to pay his way. *M. R. Stoute.*

MUJADIL (USA) 2 b.c. (Mar 16) Storm Bird (CAN) 134–Vallee Secrete **119** (USA) (Secretariat (USA)) [1990 6g⁵ 5m* 5m² 6f⁵ 5g* 5g² 5m*]

In 1988 Hadif, a colt owned by Sheikh Hamdan Al-Maktoum and trained by Armstrong, put up an improved performance to win Ascot's Cornwallis Stakes in a style which persuaded us to nominate him as one who might make his presence felt against the best sprinters the following year. Unfortunately for connections and those who followed him, it wasn't to be—Hadif ran respectably in pattern company on a couple of occasions in 1989 yet ended the season with no wins from seven attempts, eventually being sent to continue his career in the States. In the latest season another American-bred colt representing the same connections, Mujadil, produced improvement to win the Cornwallis. He doesn't impress as a top-notcher, but we'll be surprised if his second season doesn't yield a good deal more success than Hadif's. Mujadil didn't make the most auspicious of starts to his career, swerving markedly left as the stalls opened and eventually finishing over a dozen lengths behind the impressive Dominion Gold in a maiden race at York in May. Nevertheless, his work during the middle part of the race suggested he'd do quite a bit better in due course, and except for one hiccup his subsequent record was one of constant improvement. Mujadil's first win came at Doncaster later in May, when he made all to beat Latin Mass very easily by eight lengths. He was then forced to miss an intended engagement in the Norfolk Stakes because of a pricked foot, but was back in action in a minor event at Sandown in July and put up a fine performance to be beaten a whisker by Distinctly North, the pair well clear. The remainder of Mujadil's season

Cornwallis Stakes, Ascot—five furlongs suits Mujadil ideally at this stage of his career; he is a clear-cut winner from Clifton Charlie and Vintage Only (No. 7)

was spent in pattern or listed company, beginning with the Scottish Equitable Richmond Stakes at Goodwood in which he ran a lack-lustre race. We shouldn't necessarily put it down to the fact that he was returning to six furlongs. Indeed, Mujadil began to find the principals Mac's Imp and Distinctly North too strong well over a furlong from home and it's likely there was another reason for his moderate performance. Mujadil's next outing came at York in the Roses Stakes, where he justified strong support with authority, making all and needing only to be nudged along from two out to beat Sir Harry Hardman by two and a half lengths. He then went down fighting when runner-up behind Distinctly North in the Flying Childers Stakes at Doncaster, and on lining up for the Cornwallis he started 9/4 favourite in a field of eleven. The Cornwallis field included the winners of twenty-five races between them; notably Jimmy Barnie, winner of a Group 2 race at Baden-Baden on his latest start, Vintage Only, three quarters of a length behind Mujadil in the Flying Childers, and Clifton Charlie, a progressive colt seeking a hat-trick after winning a couple of competitive nurseries at the Cambridgeshire meeting. Mujadil, ridden for the first time by Cauthen instead of the suspended Carson, beat them all handsomely. The pace was taxing from the start, with Mujadil, Clifton Charlie, Vintage Only and Never In The Red all vying for the lead to halfway. However, Mujadil began to get on top soon after, and despite edging slightly right he was firmly in command in the final furlong, passing the post three and a half lengths clear of Clifton Charlie with Vintage Only close up in third and the rest well strung out. There's no reason to suppose that Vintage Only didn't run right up to his best form at Ascot and, assuming he did, Mujadil improved by the best part of a stone. Moreover, in breaking Sizzling Melody's two-year-old track record by more than a quarter of a second Mujadil recorded a timefigure of 0.84 fast, equivalent to a time-rating of 121. The fact he could do so without being at all hard ridden suggests he'll have a say in some good races in 1991.

Mujadil cost IR 300,000 guineas as a yearling. His sire Storm Bird made an early impact at stud with the likes of Indian Skimmer and Bluebird, and in

Hamdan Al-Maktoum's "Mujadil"

Mujadil (USA) (b.c. Mar 16, 1988)	Storm Bird (CAN) (b 1978)	Northern Dancer (b 1961)	Nearctic
			Natalma
		South Ocean (b 1967)	New Providence
			Shining Sun
	Vallee Secrete (USA) (b 1977)	Secretariat (ch 1970)	Bold Ruler
			Somethingroyal
		Midou (br 1970)	Saint Crespin III
			Midget II

the latest season he was also responsible for the good-class staying two-year-old Mukaddamah and the Preakness Stakes winner Summer Squall. Mujadil's dam Vallee Secrete, who won over a mile in France, produced four live foals prior to him. The first by Double Form didn't amount to much; the second, Kombus (by Known Fact), showed fair form for Stoute as a two-year-old and went on to win in stakes company over six furlongs in the States; the third was the very useful Irish miler Sagamore (by Simply Great); while the fourth is a brother to Mujadil called Lyrebird who was trained at Ballydoyle in the latest season but didn't make the racecourse. Vallee Secrete has some illustrious relatives, particularly fillies. Her dam Midou, very useful at around a mile, is a sister to the Cheveley Park winner Mige out of Midget II, another Cheveley Park winner and one who trained on to win the Coronation Stakes and Prix de la Foret at three and the Queen Elizabeth II Stakes the following year. Midget II also made a name for herself as a broodmare. Mige was probably the best of her nine winners, but she also produced Madge, dam of the Cheveley Park and One Thousand Guineas winner Ma Biche.

Mujadil is quite an attractive colt. It's unlikely he'll stay a mile, but his trainer expects him to show his form over six furlongs in due course and we share that view. Mujadil is clearly fully effective on a sound surface—his Ascot performance proves that beyond question. However, he's by no means an impressive mover, and it could be significant that his one disappointing effort in the Richmond Stakes was the only time he came across very firm. *R. W. Armstrong.*

MUJTAHID (USA) 2 ch.c. (Mar 13) Woodman (USA) 126–Mesmerize **118** (Mill Reef (USA) 141) [1990 6m* 6f* 6g* 7d⁴]

They were a particularly interesting bunch of first-season sires represented in Britain during the latest season. Dancing Brave, the best of them on the racecourse, produced a couple of useful animals in Bravefoot and Glowing Ardour from a small number of runners; Bering, runner-up in Dancing Brave's Arc, got the Racing Post Trophy winner Peter Davies; while that good horse Green Desert and the ill-fated Tate Gallery also met with plenty of success, though mainly at a lower level. But arguably the most significant impact made by a first-season sire in 1990 was that of the Mr Prospector stallion Woodman. As a yearling Woodman cost Robert Sangster 3,000,000 dollars and went into training with Vincent O'Brien. He wasn't far behind the best juveniles in 1985—winning his first three starts and finishing fifth in Huntingdale's Dewhurst—yet the following season he managed only one very disappointing effort before being retired to stand at a fee of 15,000 dollars at the Ashford Stud in Kentucky. Woodman didn't have the owners of the most fashionably-bred mares beating a path to his door. Plenty of breeders were keen to use him, though, and the success of his first crop in Europe and America was such that, for the moment at least, he's become one of the most sought-after young stallions around. In America Woodman's best representative was Hansel, who gained his most notable success at Arlington in September by overcoming trouble in running to win the Grade 2 Arlington-Washington Futurity. Woodman hit the headlines in France with the unbeaten Hector Protector, the winner of four pattern races from six starts; and from only a handful of British representatives he produced Mujtahid, who looked a potential champion during the summer only to perform well below expectations when odds-on for the Three Chimneys Dewhurst Stakes.

Mujtahid's position at the head of the Dewhurst market seemed fully deserved. Like his sire he'd had three outings prior to the race. The first was in a maiden at Newmarket in late-June. In a field of eleven he started 7/4 favourite after reportedly working in good style with the well-regarded Mujadil, and he justified the confidence with plenty in hand, making all and quickening clear from the distance to beat Pigalle Wonder by four lengths. Mujtahid was then stepped up in class over the same course and distance twelve days later for the Anglia Television July Stakes, a race which for the third year in succession attracted a mere four runners. Mac's Imp, the clear form choice following his all-the-way win in the Coventry Stakes, was sent off

Anglia Television July Stakes, Newmarket—Mujtahid runs clean away from Mac's Imp

Scottish Equitable Gimcrack Stakes, York—another clear-cut win

favourite at 5/4; Mujtahid was far from friendless on 2/1, with the Coventry third Bold Nephew on 11/4 and The Old Firm, who'd finished a close fourth in a listed race the previous day, more or less ignored at 16/1. Thanks to Mac's Imp the pace was searching from the outset with the field soon strung out at intervals of two lengths. Mujtahid had to be niggled along just to hold third after a couple of furlongs, but soon after halfway the picture changed very swiftly. Mac's Imp, in hindsight, might have set off too fast for his own good, and couldn't quicken; Mujtahid, on the other hand, was now in full flight. He swooped to challenge the leader with just under two furlongs to run, and inside the last it was a one-horse race, Mujtahid storming clear under hand riding to beat Mac's Imp by a long-looking seven lengths in a new two-year-old track record time with The Old Firm a length and a half away in third and Bold Nephew, who'd hindered his chance by hanging, a neck away in fourth. As we've said on numerous occasions in the past, the fact that a horse lowers a track record doesn't necessarily mean that he or she has put up an exceptional performance, and there's no doubt that conditions for the July meeting were very fast indeed. Even so, Mujtahid's timefigure worked out at 0.84 fast—equivalent to a timerating of 121—as good as anything recorded by a two-year-old in Britain all season, and he posted another fast time at York six weeks later in the Scottish Equitable Gimcrack Stakes.

Truth to tell, the opposition to Mujtahid at York was nothing special. Only four took him on: the useful northern colt Vintage Only, the Newmarket maiden race winners Mystiko and Regal Sabre and the Bath winner Asterix. At 2/1-on Mujtahid retained his unbeaten record in the manner his form entitled him to, gradually taking the measure of the front-running Vintage Only from the two-furlong pole and forging clear to beat him four lengths. The performance received rather mixed reviews in the Press, and most of the major ante-post bookmakers kept his Two Thousand Guineas odds at eight or ten to one. Mujtahid was supplemented for the Dewhurst at a cost of £10,000, but heavy rain which fell in the hour or so leading up to the race seemed to turn the ground against him. He didn't look at his peak either, and after travelling fairly strongly under restraint for almost four furlongs he found little once asked to quicken, carrying his head a bit high in the closing stages and passing the post fourth of eight, a little over five lengths behind the 50/1-winner Generous.

Woodman's success with Mujtahid, Hansel and Hector Protector has seen demand for his stock increase considerably. 'Woodmania' was how one reporter in the *Thoroughbred Times* summed it up, and although that phrase was clearly tongue in cheek there's no doubt buyers at the latest Keeneland September Sale were impressed with the stallion's record. The twenty-three Woodman yearlings on offer there sold at an average of almost 120,000 dollars, more than double the stallion's average for 1989 despite the fact that the general market trend is downward. Mujtahid himself cost 165,000 dollars, which made him the third-highest priced yearling from Woodman's first crop. His dam Mesmerize was sold for 105,000 guineas at the Highflyer Sales in

608

Hamdan Al-Maktoum's "Mujtahid"

1983 and sent to the States. Mujtahid is her second foal. The first (by State Dinner) is unraced, while the third is a colt by In The Groove's sire Night Shift. Mesmerize never made it to the racecourse, but had she done so it's a fair bet she'd have stayed reasonably well. Her dam Jeanie Duff won twice at up to a mile and a half. Jeanie Duff has since bred several winners, including the useful Italian filly Marina Duff, and is from a very successful family. Mujtahid's third dam Turf showed smart form over a mile and a half and more during the early-'sixties, winning the Galtres Stakes and finishing second in the Newbury Autumn Cup. Moreover, Turf is also a close relation to the dam of the good stayer Celtic Cone and a half-sister to Beaver Street, whose descendants include such good horses as Dowsing, Royal And Regal, Glory Forever and the Kentucky Oaks winner Native Street.

Mujtahid (USA) (ch.c. Mar 13, 1988)	Woodman (USA) (ch 1983)	Mr Prospector (b 1970)	Raise A Native Gold Digger	
		Playmate (ch 1975)	Buckpasser Intriguing	
	Mesmerize (b 1982)	Mill Reef (b 1968)	Never Bend Milan Mill	
		Jeanie Duff (b or br 1972)	Majestic Prince Turf	

Mujtahid, a lengthy colt, is a fine walker and in his faster paces moves with a fluency which suggests fast conditions will always be to his advantage. His best form so far is at six furlongs, but he'll have no problem staying seven or a mile, and on breeding the possibility of his getting even further in due course can't be ruled out. As regards the coming season, Mujtahid seems most unlikely to contest the Two Thousand Guineas now—he suffered a stress fracture to the off-fore cannon bone in December. The latest news on the injury is that the colt is making satisfactory progress and connections are guardedly optimistic that he'll eventually make a full recovery. *R. W. Armstrong.*

MUKADDAMAH (USA) 2 b.c. (Mar 21) Storm Bird (CAN) 134–Tash **120 p** (USA) (Never Bend) [1990 6g* 7f* 8s2]

For all but the final stride of the last three furlongs Mukaddamah looked certain to add the Racing Post Trophy at Doncaster in October to his earlier pattern success in the Lanson Champagne Vintage Stakes at Goodwood. Never much more than two lengths ahead, but comfortably so for the most part from his closest pursuers Peter Davies and Marcham, Mukaddamah started to waver from a true line as the post approached; then, in the last gasp, he had the lead snatched from him as Peter Davies, who'd been under strong pressure from the moment Mukaddamah took up the running, got up to win by a whisker. One journalist to draw the positive conclusion that Mukaddamah would have won had he been waited with was Michael Tanner who timed the Racing Post Trophy furlong by furlong for his sectional timing column in the *Sporting Life Weekender*. Electrically-recorded sectional times are part and parcel of racing in North America where the tracks are laid out to the same pattern, and they are frequently returned from the major courses in France, too. In Britain though, they almost invariably have to be taken by hand, usually from a video recording; many courses in Britain still lack basic electrical timing. Taking a sectional time at the racecourse or from television pictures is by and large an impracticable task. Just try timing the third-last furlong of the Racing Post Trophy, the start of which is roughly from where Mukaddamah took over, and which was hand-timed by Tanner at 10.96 seconds. As the camera follows the runners, who kept to the centre of the track, it's not even possible to see the three-furlong pole until the runners have gone, at a guess, ten yards past; and neither does the angle of the television camera to the track make it possible to judge exactly when the field had reached the two-furlong line. In these unsatisfactory circumstances, remembering too that the ground was soft and the wind negligible, to state as Tanner did, that the time for the third-last furlong was 'an outstanding fraction', and then to draw the conclusion that this increase in pace ultimately told on Mukaddamah, is unsound. Forming solid opinions from inexact methods, without precise regard for other essential information, such as whether the furlong-markers are indeed a furlong apart, which our research at Doncaster suggests they are not, is dangerous practice. Until such time as all racecourses are equipped with full electric timing, are measured and marked exactly, and accurate sectional standards are established, sectional timing will remain an irrelevance. Whatever fraction Mukaddamah recorded for the third-last furlong, he lost no caste in defeat. It was a smart performance,

Lanson Champagne Vintage Stakes, Goodwood—
Mukaddamah lengthens his stride in pleasing fashion; Flying Brave follows him through,
but Generous (rails) can do no more

Hamdan Al-Maktoum's "Mukaddamah"

among the best of the season by a two-year-old, and one which entitles him to realistic consideration at this juncture for the Two Thousand Guineas.

Mukaddamah (USA) (b.c. Mar 21, 1988)	Storm Bird (CAN) (b 1978)	Northern Dancer (b 1961)	Nearctic
			Natalma
		South Ocean (b 1967)	New Providence
			Shining Sun
	Tash (USA) (b or br 1977)	Never Bend (b 1960)	Nasrullah
			Lalun
		Natashka (b 1963)	Dedicate
			Natasha

All things considered, Mukaddamah probably has a brighter future than some of the season's other leading youngsters. A rangy, attractive colt, just the sort to thrive as a three-year-old, he's been lightly campaigned, having had just three races, and has a particularly effective turn of foot which enabled him to settle his first two races swiftly and took him from last to first in a matter of strides at Doncaster. Mukaddamah was impressive when pulling two and a half lengths and six clear in a maiden at Nottingham in July, and made short work too of the stiffer task that confronted him in the six-runner Champagne at Goodwood the following month. Looking very well, Mukaddamah took a keen hold in a race run at a good gallop, moved through strongly two furlongs out then quickly went clear in the final furlong to win by a length and a half from Flying Brave with Generous (who wasn't in the same form that later won him the Dewhurst) three lengths away in third. Mukaddamah's performances tend to suggest a mile may be his ideal distance, but it's well

611

worth noting that he settled better than at Goodwood in the less strongly-run Racing Post Trophy, and on pedigree he'd stay a mile and a quarter. Interestingly, he has already been entered for the Irish Derby.

Mukaddamah, who was bought for 375,000 dollars at the Keeneland July Selected Sale, is the fifth winner from the six-furlong winner Tash. None of the first three, who include Mukaddamah's full brother Contempt, successful twice as a two-year-old in the States in 1987, has won beyond seven furlongs, but his three-year-old half-sister Queen of Women (by Sharpen Up) won over an extended mile and a quarter in the French Provinces late in the year. Generally, there's no shortage of stamina in Mukaddamah's pedigree. Tash's half-sisters, for example, include the Oaks and Irish Oaks placed Arkadina, herself the dam of the Irish St Leger winner Dark Lomond, and the smart Ivory Wand, dam of the high-class middle-distance stayer Gold And Ivory; while Tash's half-brothers include the smart colt Gregorian, third in the Eclipse and King George, and Arkadina's brother Blood Royal, a good winner over two miles. Their dam Natashka, a leading performer in the States in her day, is out of a half-sister to the St Leger winner Black Tarquin. *P. T. Walwyn.*

MUKDDAAM (USA) 3 b.c. Danzig (USA)–Height of Fashion (FR) 124 (Bustino **111** 136) [1989 7m* 1990 8f* 8g⁴ 12m²] big, strong, rangy colt: has a lot of scope: has a powerful, round action: made all in minor event at Kempton in April: didn't quite come up to expectations afterwards but put up very useful efforts behind Tirol in Craven Stakes at Newmarket, leading 6f then outpaced and badly hampered, and Private Tender in King Edward VII Stakes at Royal Ascot, staying on steadily from mid-division: will prove better suited by forcing tactics over 1½m: acts on firm going, yet to race on a soft surface: ducked right stalls first 2 outings: stays in training. *Major W. R. Hern.*

MUKIR 4 ch.g. Kris 135–Velvet Habit 89 (Habitat 134) [1989 8m 8.2g³ 8m⁴ a8g —
1990 7.6g 10.6d] big, strong, workmanlike gelding: modest maiden at 3 yrs: shaped as though retaining ability in amateurs handicap (pulling hard) final outing: suited by 1m: best effort with give in the ground. *P. T. Walwyn.*

MULCIBER 2 b.c. (Apr 11) Head For Heights 125–Quisissanno 76 (Be My Guest **83** (USA) 126) [1990 7m² 7f² 7m² 7g*] IR 18,000Y: unfurnished colt: third foal: half-brother to Irish 3-y-o 1½m to 1¾m winner Montezuma (by Commanche Run) and a winner in Austria: dam won at 1½m: fair performer: won maiden at Folkestone in October by 2 lengths from Rival Bid: will be better suited by 1m+: acts on firm ground: has carried head bit awkwardly. *G. Harwood.*

MULL HOUSE 3 b.g. Local Suitor (USA) 128–Foudre 76 (Petingo 135) [1989 **85** 6m⁶ 7m* 1990 8m 11.7g 11m* 13.3m* 13.3m⁵ 16.1m* 12m 18d] strong, rangy gelding: has a markedly round action: progressive form when winning handicaps at Newbury (on both occasions pushed along some way out) in June and Newmarket in August: out of depth penultimate start, behind in Cesarewitch (14/1) at Newmarket on final one: suited by 2m: acts on good to firm ground: sometimes sweating and edgy.*J. Sutcliffe.*

MULOOF 2 ch.c. (May 21) Rousillon (USA) 133–Troyenne 81 (Troy 137) [1990 **59** 7f⁴ 7h⁴ 6g] lengthy colt: has scope: second foal: half-brother to 3-y-o Footpath (by Final Straw): dam 1¾m winner, is half-sister to Knockando: plating-class form in maidens at Brighton: will stay 1m. *P. F. I. Cole.*

MUMMY'S BAIRN 2 b.f. (Feb 1) Bairn (USA) 126–Mummy's Glory 82 **55** (Mummy's Pet 125) [1990 6m³ 6m⁶ 7m⁶ 7m⁴ a7g²] leggy filly: fourth foal: half-sister to untrustworthy maiden Tambuli (by Mr Fluorocarbon): dam best at 2 yrs, raced only at 5f: fair plater: better form at 6f than 7f: got loose at stalls first 2 outings: sold 3,000 gns Doncaster August Sales. *M. J. Camacho.*

MUMMY'S EMERALD 2 ch.f. (Apr 5) Mummy's Game 120–Emerald Eagle 78 **72** (Sandy Creek 123) [1990 5m⁶ 6m⁴ 6m* 6m 6g] leggy filly: has free, rather round action: first foal: dam 6f to 1m winner: dead-heated with Swingawan Lady in maiden at Ayr in July: ran moderately after in minor event and nursery: should stay 7f. *C. B. B. Booth.*

MUMMY'S FOX 3 b.c. Mummy's Game 120–May Fox 67 (Healaugh Fox) [1989 —
5s⁵ 5d⁵ 7m⁵ 7g 7f² 7m 7g² 7m 8f 6g a7g 1990 10f 10g 7m 8f 8g] small, close-coupled colt: fair plater: showed little in non-selling events in 1990: should stay 1m (stiff task and pulled hard over 1¼m): sometimes sweating and edgy: inconsistent. *J. C. Fox.*

MUNDAY DEAN 2 ch.g. (Apr 13) Kind of Hush 118–Nancy Brig 63 (Brigadier **67** p
Gerard 144) [1990 6g*] 6,400Y, 13,000 2-y-o: good-quartered gelding: half-brother

to 5f winner Bridge of Gold (by Balidar) and fairly useful French miler Filiatra (by Music Boy): dam placed at 9f: 12/1, carrying condition and very green, won 22-runner maiden auction at Nottingham in September by 3 lengths from Saafend, leading at halfway and running on strongly: will stay at least 7f: sure to improve. *Sir Mark Prescott.*

MUPHRID 2 br.c. (May 30) Sharpo 132–Favorable Exchange (USA) (Exceller (USA) 129) [1990 6s 8m] 4,200F, 11,000Y: first living foal: dam French 10.7f to 1½m winner: poor form in maiden and seller: dead. *Lord John FitzGerald.* —

MURANGO 4 b.c. Shirley Heights 130–Eldoret 100 (High Top 131) [1989 10g* 97 12.3m* 12m⁵ 13.3m 12m⁶ 1990 10m³ 10m³ 12.3m² 12f⁵ 12m* 12m⁶ 11s³] strong, compact colt: fairly useful handicapper: well ridden when making all at Salisbury in September: stays 1½m: acts on any going: bandaged off-hind: occasionally sweating and on toes: takes keen hold: hung under pressure third start: sold 40,000 gns Newmarket Autumn Sales: consistent. *J. L. Dunlop.*

MURDERER'S ROW (USA) 3 ch.c. Nodouble (USA)–Mazda's Miracle (USA) — (New Policy) [1989 NR 1990 10g] 60,000Y: strong, angular colt: seventh foal (fifth by Nodouble): brother to 2 winners in USA, including stakes winner at about 1m M Double M, and half-brother to another winner by Pia Star: dam, winner at about 6f at 3 yrs, is half-sister to very useful winner at up to 1¼m Double Discount and Chain Store (both by Nodouble), latter dam of Al Bahathri: very green, about 14 lengths twelfth of 22 in maiden at Kempton in June, tenderly handled: refused to enter stalls at Lingfield later in month. *J. H. M. Gosden.*

MURMURING 4 b.f. Kind of Hush 118–Beryl's Jewel 86 (Siliconn 121) [1989 6f 62 6m³ 6f² 6f² 6f² 6m a6g² 1990 a6g⁴dis a6g⁵ a6g* a6g 5g 6m 5m⁶ 5m 6h² 6f 6h 5m 7f a5g³ a6g⁴] workmanlike, angular filly: good walker: has a quick action: made all in maiden at Lingfield in February: best effort after second in handicap: stays 6f: acts on hard ground: usually apprentice ridden at 4 yrs: has got on edge: inconsistent. *S. Dow.*

MUSABIQ 2 gr.c. (Mar 7) Superlative 118–Lammastide 93 (Martinmas 128) [1990 72 6g⁶ 6m* 6m 6m] 26,000Y: well-made colt: first foal: dam 2-y-o 5f winner: won maiden at Nottingham in August narrowly, rallying well: easily best other effort in Ascot nursery final start: strong-running sort: sold 15,500 gns Newmarket Autumn Sales. *P. T. Walwyn.*

MUSAFIRIE 4 b.c. What A Guest 119–Perbury 88 (Grisaille 115) [1989 8v⁴ 10g — 11f⁵ 14.8m⁵ 12m⁵ 16.2d⁵ 14m⁶ 1990 14.8m⁴ 14g 11.7f] lengthy, fair sort: has a long, round action: modest handicapper as 3-y-o: below form in spring: best at around 1½m: acts on firm and dead going: bandaged on reappearance. *Mrs Gill E. Jones.*

MUSCADINE 3 b.f. Muscatite 122–Bee Hawk 87 (Sea Hawk II 131) [1989 NR — 1990 10g 8g] IR 1,100F, 6,000Y: leggy, lengthy filly: half-sister to several winners, including fairly useful 1978 2-y-o 6f winner Persian Sapphire (by Wolver Hollow) and Irish 9f winner Run Again (by Runnett): dam needed long distances: bandaged, no show in maidens at Kempton. *J. Ringer.*

MUSE 3 ch.g. High Line 125–Thoughtful 86 (Northfields (USA)) [1989 NR 1990 78 10g³ 10g⁶ 10.1m 13.1m⁵ 12.2f* 12m* 13.1h² 14g⁵ 14g⁴] leggy gelding: has a rather round action: third foal: dam, 1¼m winner, is half-sister to Princess Royal Stakes winner Heavenly Thought, dam of Homing and Water Mill: modest performer: made virtually all to win maiden at Warwick in July and apprentice handicap at Kempton in August: will be suited by test of stamina: acts on hard ground: lacks turn of foot, and suited by forcing tactics: sold to join D. Elsworth 22,000 gns Newmarket Autumn Sales. *Major W. R. Hern.*

MUSHROOM MAN 2 b.c. (Mar 17) Undulate (USA)–Smokey's Sister (Forlorn — River 124) [1990 6g 5g] leggy, angular colt: brother to 1985 2-y-o 7f seller winner Solent Express and half-brother to winners over hurdles: dam won 6 races in Scandinavia: tailed off in claimer (unruly at start) and seller (got rid of rider at stalls beforehand) in summer. *K. M. Brassey.*

MUSHY BOFF 2 ch.f. (May 28) Tina's Pet 121–Rely On Guy 73 (Reliance II 137) 65 [1990 5m⁴ 5m³ 5s* 5g⁶ 5d³ 5v³ 5.8d⁵ 5d] 3,000Y: sturdy filly: has scope: second foal: dam 7f winner: quite modest performer: won maiden auction at Haydock in June by 4 lengths: ran moderately final outing: stays 6f: acts well on soft ground: sold 2,600 gns Doncaster November Sales to join C. Hill's stable. *J. Berry.*

MUSICAL FLASH 3 ch.c. Music Boy 124–Martin-Lavell News 90 (Song 132) 64 [1989 5m³ 5m 5f⁵ 5f³ 5m² a6g 1990 a5g² 5f³ 5s* 5d 5m² 5f³ 6m⁶ 5f⁵ 5f² 5m 5d 5d 5m] neat, strong colt: quite modest handicapper: won at Hamilton in April: ran poorly last 2 starts: should stay 6f: acts on any going: has run creditably for 7-lb claimer: sometimes slowly away: sold 5,000 gns Newmarket Autumn Sales. *R. Hannon.*

MUSICAL IVY   3 b.f. Aragon 118–Park Parade 94 (Monsanto (FR) 121) [1989 5v⁵ — §
5g 5f 5f 1990 a6g 7m 5f] narrow, leggy, sparely-made filly: has a round action: poor plater: bred to stay at least 7f: probably ungenuine. *J. R. Bosley.*

MUSICAL LYRICS   2 b.f. (Apr 27) Song 132–Spanish Ribbon (Pieces of Eight   36
128) [1990 5f² 5f² 5f 5d⁴ 5m] 2,700F, 2,700Y: small, sparely-made filly: moderate mover: seventh living foal: sister to a winner abroad and half-sister to 7f and 8.3f winner Hachimitsu (by Vaigly Great): dam never ran: poor plater: hung left on debut: inconsistent: sold 4,000 gns Doncaster September Sales. *J. Berry.*

MUSICAL MOMENTS   4 b.f. Vision (USA)–Miami Melody (Miami Springs   37
121) [1989 8g 6f 7m⁴ 1990 12f 10.8f² 8h⁵] rather angular filly: moderate mover: poor maiden: stays 10.8f: acts on hard going: raced freely in blinkers final start at 3 yrs. *J. D. Roberts.*

MUSICAL NOTE   3 ch.f. Sharpo 132–Fair And Wise 75 (High Line 125) [1989   37
6m 7g 8m 6m 1990 12m 14g 10f 10m 10.6v²] leggy filly: moderate mover: poor maiden: second in selling handicap at Haydock in October: stays 10.5f: seems suited by plenty of give in the ground. *M. Blanshard.*

MUSIC MY SON   9 b.g. Tumble Wind (USA)–Negante 68 (Negotiation) [1989   —
NR 1990 11.7g 17.6m] plain gelding: no longer of any account: has worn blinkers, bandages and a crossed noseband. *Mrs N. S. Sharpe.*

MUST BE MAGICAL (USA)   2 ch.g. (Mar 1) Temperence Hill (USA)–   43
Honorine (USA) (Blushing Groom (FR) 131) [1990 8d 7s 7s] $20,000Y: third foal: half-brother to fairly useful 3-y-o 9f and 1¼m winner Lord Bertie (by Roberto): dam placed at 1m in France: poor form in maidens: bit backward first 2 starts: visored, led 5f on unfavoured side final outing. *F. H. Lee.*

MUTAFANI   3 b.c. Top Ville 129–Nepula 105 (Nebbiolo 125) [1989 NR 1990 12m   75
10d³ 10m⁶ 8g² 12m² 10m 9g² 12m² 10m³ 8d] 41,000Y: rather sparely-made colt: second foal: closely related to once-raced French 1989 3-y-o Circo (by High Top): dam 7f and 1m winner at 2 yrs lost form as 3-y-o: modest form when placed in maidens in Ireland and veteran jockeys race (penultimate start) at Ascot: stays 1½m: acts on good to firm ground and dead: equipped with severe bridle and took keen hold at Ascot: sold 17,500 gns Newmarket Autumn Sales, probably to race in Italy. *K. Prendergast, Ireland.*

MUTAH (USA)   3 ch.c. Topsider (USA)–Bank On Love (USA) (Gallant Romeo   103
(USA)) [1989 6m* 6g* 1990 8.5g³ 7g³ 8d] strong, good-quartered colt: moderate mover, with a quick action: useful performer: unlucky and rated as having won when third of 16 in £20,000 handicap at York second start, switched and quickening in tremendous style from rear over 1f out: looking really well, never got clear run in Britannia Handicap at Royal Ascot 5 weeks later: may prove best at up to 7f: joined S. Penrod in USA. *H. R. A. Cecil.*

MUTAMARRID   2 br.c. (Feb 11) Sure Blade (USA) 128–Raabihah 98 (Shirley   85 p
Heights 130) [1990 7m*] leggy, attractive colt: has scope: second foal: half-brother to 3-y-o 1m and 1½m winner Kasayid (by Niniski), effective also at 2½m: dam 6f (at 2 yrs) and 7f winner: well backed, won 19-runner maiden at Chepstow in October by ½ length from Mulciber, leading 1f out and running on well: will stay 1m: sure to improve. *H. Thomson Jones.*

MUTE SWAN (USA)   3 ch.f. The Minstrel (CAN) 135–Pantomime (USA) (The   61
Axe II 115) [1989 NR 1990 8m 11m³ 7f² 10f*] leggy, sparely-made filly: sixth foal: half-sister to 4 winners, including Stark Drama (by Graustark), a stakes-placed winner at up to 9f, and smart American 1986 2-y-o 7f winner Damascus Drama (by Damascus): dam, very useful 8.5f stakes winner, is half-sister to good filly Grafitti: quite modest form: made all in maiden at Brighton in August: stays 11f. *J. H. M. Gosden.*

MUTHAIGA   4 gr.c. Kalaglow 132–Green Lucia 116 (Green Dancer (USA) 132)   60
[1989 NR 1990 13.3m⁵ 12f 8m 8g 8g⁶ a11g³ a12g a11g] big, leggy, lengthy colt: useful winner at 2 yrs: reportedly suffered leg injury in 1989: apparently easily best effort in 1990 on fourth start: ran in Southwell claimers last 3, well beaten last 2 occasions: should prove effective at middle distances: often bandaged: sold out of J. Toller's stable 4,700 gns Newmarket Autumn Sales after fifth outing. *N. Tinkler.*

MUWFIQ   3 b.c. Formidable (USA) 125–Triple First 117 (High Top 131) [1989 6m⁶   82
6m* 1990 7m² 7f 7m⁴ 7m] robust, good sort: carries plenty of condition: has a round action: fair performer: in frame in minor event and handicap: eased right down as if something amiss otherwise in first half of 1990: stays 7f well: didn't handle turn at

Catterick: sold 7,800 gns Newmarket Autumn Sales, probably to race in Italy. *P. T. Walwyn.*

MUZO (USA) 3 b.c. Irish River (FR) 131–Dance Flower (CAN) (Northern Dancer) [1989 NR 1990 10m⁵ 12.3m³ 12m³ 10.6d*] strong, well-made colt: first foal: dam 6f to 1m winner in USA out of half-sister to The Minstrel (by Northern Dancer): fairly useful form: best effort when winning maiden at Haydock in September, leading 4f out and staying on strongly: will prove as effective returned to 1½m: has joined Mrs J. Cecil. *H. R. A. Cecil.* **96**

MY ADMIRAL 3 b.c. Montelimar (USA) 122–Sherbourne (FR) (Sharpman 124) [1989 NR 1990 8.2m⁴ 11g⁵ 10.1g⁴ 12g² 12f* 14f] 800F, IR 11,000Y: leggy, close-coupled colt: first living foal: dam French 3-y-o 6.5f to 1¼m winner: fair performer: won auction at Beverley in July, leading 6f out and keeping on well: second in Austrian Derby at Freudenau previous start, well beaten facing stiff task in £7,500 handicap (moved poorly down) in August: stays 1½m well: acts on firm ground: blinkered last 2 starts. *C. F. Wall.* **84**

MY ALIBI (IRE) 2 ch.c. (Apr 3) Hatim (USA) 121–Serriyya 53 (Tap On Wood 130) [1990 6f⁴ 6f* 6f² 6m⁴ 7g⁵ 7.3g] IR 3,200Y, 6,400Y: compact colt: first foal: dam 2-y-o 6f seller winner: lowered in class, won seller (retained 3,000 gns) at Brighton in June: ran well in nurseries next 3 starts: stays 7f: blinkered final 5 outings. *W. Carter.* **59**

MY ALMA (IRE) 2 b.f. (Jan 23) Reasonable (FR) 119–Lady Bidder (Auction Ring (USA) 123) [1990 5f³ 5d³ 5m* 5f² 6g 5f³ 6g² 5m] IR 9,200Y: small, rather sparely-made filly: has a quick action: fifth foal: half-sister to fair miler Classic Suite (by Ya Zaman) and 1984 2-y-o 6f winner High Bidder (by Skyliner): dam unraced daughter of sister to good sprinter Holborn: modest performer: won maiden at Thirsk in May: best form at 5f: acts well on firm ground: none too consistent. *R. M. Whitaker.* **72 ?**

MY BALLERINA (USA) 3 b.f. Sir Ivor 135–Emmaline (USA) (Affirmed (USA)) [1989 NR 1990 12g⁶ 12g⁶ 10f* 10m⁴ 12g⁵] $200,000Y: leggy filly: first foal: dam, winner at up to 9f in USA, is closely related to very smart middle-distance winner Hatim, later Grade 1 winner in USA, and half-sister to 1979 Horris Hill winner Super Asset and high-class 8.5f to 1¼m winner Bates Motel: successful in small fields for maiden at Brighton in May and minor contest (made all) at Lingfield in July: creditable fifth in listed race at Evry: stays 1½m: sent to N. Drysdale in USA. *P. F. I. Cole.* **94**

MY BED TIME 2 b.f. (Jun 5) Blakeney 126–Noddy Time 97 (Gratitude 130) [1990 6g⁴] smallish, workmanlike filly: half-sister to several winners, including smart 5f to 7f winner Grey Desire (by Habat) and smart 1¼m performer The Dunce (by High Hat): dam stayed 1m: bit backward and green, over 5 lengths fourth of 10, staying on well, to Roger de Berksted in maiden at York in October: sure to improve, particularly over 1m or more. *M. H. Tompkins.* **65 p**

MY CHIARA 4 b.f. Ardross 134–My Tootsie 98 (Tap On Wood 130) [1989 11.3m 8f⁴ 9m⁵ 10g⁶ 14m⁶ 12g⁵ 14.8m⁴ 10m⁶ 12g³ 12g² 12g a10g* 12d³ a10g² a10g 1990 10g⁵ 10m 12g 12f 11.7m⁴ 11.7m⁵ 11.7m 12m* 16.2m 11s] leggy, quite good-topped filly: usually looks very well: keen walker: has a fluent action: modest handicapper: 25/1, returned to form when winning apprentice race at Ascot (hanging right) in September: pulled up (saddle slipped) next outing: has appeared to find 1¼m on sharp side, and stays 1¾m: seems unsuited by extremes of going: goes well with forcing tactics: tough. *M. D. I. Usher.* **71**

MY COQUETTE 3 ch.f. Coquelin (USA) 121–River Lane (Riverman (USA) 131) [1989 6g 1990 8m 10.6s⁴ 8f² 10.4g 8m 8.2v 7d⁶] tall, leggy filly: quite modest form when in frame in maiden and minor event, making most: may prove best over 1m: acts on any going, except possibly heavy. *C. E. Brittain.* **68 d**

MY DESIRE 2 ch.f. (May 14) Grey Desire 115–Another Move 69 (Farm Walk 111) [1990 7g 8g a7g] leggy, unfurnished filly: fourth foal: half-sister to 1½m and 14.6f winner/successful hurdler Tancred Sand (by Nicholas Bill) and 5f and 7f winner Ela-Yianni-Mou (by Anfield): dam 1½m winner, is sister to very useful middle-distance stayer Move Off: poor form in maidens and a median auction. *Mrs G. R. Reveley.* **—**

MY DIAMOND RING 5 b.m. Sparkling Boy 110–Bells of St Martin 89 (Martinmas 128) [1989 6v 6d 8m⁴ 9f⁵ 8g* 8h⁵ 8.2f⁵ 10.8m 8.3g* 8.5m 8.3m⁴ 8.3m² 1990 a8g⁶ a8g a8g³ a8g⁵ 8m⁵ 7m 7f⁶ 8f 8m 8.3m⁵ 8d³ 10f⁵ 8.2m 8g 8m 8d 8g] light-framed mare: moderate mover: appeared to run easily her best race since 2 yrs when second in handicap at Bath in August: suited by 1m: probably acts on any **50 ?**

going: sometimes sweats: sometimes slowly away: not one to rely on. *M. D. I. Usher.*

MYFONTAINE 3 b.c. Persepolis (FR) 127–Mortefontaine (FR) (Polic 126) [1989 55 NR 1990 8f a11g⁶ 14g 11.7m* 11.5m⁵ 11.7m⁶ a14g 10m 11.5g a12g⁴ a11g⁵] 9,200Y: leggy colt: half-brother to several winners, including high-class miler Katies (by Nonoalco) and very useful middle-distance performer Millfontaine (by Mill Reef): dam, French 1m winner, is sister to very smart Polyfoto: plating-class handicapper: won at Windsor (first form) in June: stays 1½m: acts on good to firm going: has gone down keenly. *K. T. Ivory.*

MYFOR 4 ch.g. Be My Guest (USA) 126–Forliana 75 (Forli (ARG)) [1989 8g³ 8m² — § 8m⁴ 10.2f² 8g 1990 14.6f] close-coupled gelding: poor walker: fair maiden at best: dropped out quickly final 2f at Doncaster in March: stays 1¼m: acts on firm ground: irresolute: winning hurdler in December. *M. C. Pipe.*

MYHAMET 3 b.c. Gorytus (USA) 132–Honey Bridge 99 (Crepello 136) [1989 79 7m⁴ 8m² 8.2f² 8f* 1990 13.3m 12m⁵ 14g 13.3g] rangy colt: good mover: progressed into fair performer at 2 yrs: clearly best effort in handicaps when fifth at Salisbury in August: should stay 1¾m + : trained until after third start by R. Hern: sold 8,400 gns Ascot November Sales. *C. E. Brittain.*

MY HARRY BOY 3 b.g. Castle Keep 121–Escape Me Never 75 (Run The — Gantlet (USA)) [1989 NR 1990 10g 10m] 1,300F: compact gelding: brother to poor maiden Maid Maleen and half-brother to several winners, including 1½m winner Galesa and 5-y-o 1¾m and 2m winner Megans Flight (both by Welsh Pageant): dam, half-sister to smart miler Trusted, won over 1m: no sign of ability in summer maidens. *W. G. M. Turner.*

MY HELENE 2 b.f. (Jun 9) Mummy's Game 120–Il Regalo (Meadow Mint (USA) — 120) [1990 7m] leggy filly: seventh foal: half-sister to a winner in Italy by Frimley Park: dam placed over 1m and 1¼m: slowly away then stayed on into mid-division in 14-runner seller at Newmarket in August: sold 800 gns Newmarket Autumn Sales, resold 520 gns Ascot December Sales. *M. H. Tompkins.*

MY HOSTESS 2 b.f. (Mar 24) Gabitat 119–Its For Sure 63 (Ardoon 124) [1990 6g — 7m] leggy, lengthy filly: third foal: sister to 3-y-o Gabardoon: dam lightly-raced 5f performer: always behind in maidens at Leicester (backward, mulish stalls) and Lingfield over 3½ months later: sweating and very edgy, refused to enter stalls next intended appearance. *B. Gubby.*

MY IMPRESSION 4 b.g. Lomond (USA) 128–Wish You Were Here (USA) — (Secretariat (USA)) [1989 NR 1990 13.3m] lengthy gelding: first foal: dam 7f and 1¼m winner, is out of top-class middle-distance mare Summer Guest: 50/1 and carrying condition, always behind in listed race at Newbury in May: moved down moderately. *H. Candy.*

MY KIA 3 ch.f. Good Times (ITY)–Troy Moon (Troy 137) [1989 NR 1990 7g⁵] — good- topped filly: first foal: dam maiden who stayed 1½m, out of half-sister to Sharpen Up: 33/1, backward, green and edgy, showed signs of ability when running-on fifth of 10 in maiden at Epsom in April: refused to enter stalls before Sandown claimer in July. *R. P. C. Hoad.*

MY LADY MINSTREL 4 ch.f. Brotherly (USA) 80–Lady Peggy (Young Nelson 27 106) [1989 5m 6f 5.8h⁵ 6m 5f² 5f 5.8h² 6f 5.3h⁵ 6g 5g 6m 7g 1990 6f 6f³ 7m 7g⁶ 5m 5.8f 6m a7g 5.8h 5m⁴ 5f⁶ 6m] small filly: moderate walker and mover: poor maiden: stays 6f: acts on hard ground: occasionally blinkered: below form when sweating: inconsistent. *J. L. Spearing.*

MY LADYS TEARS 3 gr.f. Godswalk (USA) 130–Vital Spirit 65 (Tachypous — 128) [1989 5f² 6g 6f 5g 1990 6m 8.2s] leggy filly: little worthwhile form since debut: pulls hard and has hung: sold 800 gns Newmarket Autumn Sales. *F. J. Yardley.*

MY LAMB 5 b.h. Relkino 131–Lambay 88 (Lorenzaccio 130) [1989 8d 10.2g* 11f* 104 12m² 12f 1990 10m 12g²] big, useful-looking horse: usually looks very well: has very long stride: useful handicapper: creditable second of 4, setting slow pace, to Alphabel in listed event at Newmarket in June: stays 1½m: acts on any going: suited by forcing tactics: splendidly genuine and consistent. *D. R. C. Elsworth.*

MY LIFE'S AMBITION (IRE) 2 b or br.g. (Apr 30) Wolverlife 115–Car- — p nation For Me (Kala Shikari 125) [1990 3m] IR 4,200F, 3,00CY: workmanlike gelding: fourth foal: dam showed ability on flat and over jumps in Ireland: ridden by 7-lb claimer, shaped with promise when in mid-division in 30-runner seller at Newmarket in October: should improve. *M. H. Tompkins.*

MYLORDMAYOR 3 ch.g. Move Off 112–Sharenka (Sharpen Up 127) [1989 5d 5f **52**
5f 7f 7m² 7m² 7g 8.5f a6g a6g³ a7g⁵ 1990 a7g⁵ a7g⁶ a⁷g⁴ ⁷m 8†] sparely-made
gelding: plating-class maiden: best efforts on all-weather: stays 7f: inconsistent:
sold to join W. Price 1,900 gns Ascot May Sales. *Ronald Thompson.*

MY LORD (USA) 3 b.c. Nijinsky (CAN) 138–Euphrosyne (USA) (Judger (USA)) **98**
[1989 7g⁶ 8m⁶ 8g* 1990 10.6g* 12s] lengthy, good-topped colt: carries condition:
has plenty of scope: won £15,500 handicap at Haydock in September, rallying
strongly to beat Baylis ¾ length: favourite but never going well in November
Handicap at Doncaster: should stay 1½m: game: clearly difficult to train. *J. H. M.
Gosden.*

MY LUCKY LADY 2 br.f. (Feb 24) Lucky Wednesday 124–Saran (Le Levanstell —
122) [1990 5m 5m 5g⁶ 6m] leggy, plain filly: has a round action: eighth foal: sister to
8.5f seller winner Lucky Grove and half-sister to useful sprinter Cyril's Choice (by
Malicious): dam ran twice: seems of little account: sold 780 gns Doncaster
September Sales. *Ronald Thompson.*

MY LUCKY STAR 4 gr.f. Ballacashtal (CAN)–La Comedienne (Comedy Star —
(USA) 121) [1989 6g 6f 8h⁶ 7m 7h* 7f⁶ 7f³ 7h 8f⁵ 7.6m 1990 8.3g 10.2f]
sparely-made, dipped-backed filly: winning plater as 3-y-o: suited by 7f: acts on hard
going: inconsistent. *Andrew Turnell.*

MY OPINION 4 b.f. Beldale Flutter (USA) 130–Opinion 71 (Great Nephew 126) **45**
[1989 NR 1990 11f⁵ 8.5g 8g 11.5m 12f a14g 10v³ a16g⁵] compact filly: fifth foal:
half-sister to 3 winners, including fairly useful 1½m winner Stratford Ponds (by
High Top): dam, 1½m winner, is half-sister to very useful stayer Kambalda: form in
handicaps only at Ayr (better effort) and Lingfield last 2 starts: should stay 2m:
possibly needs plenty of give in the ground. *E. Eldin.*

MY PAL POPEYE 5 br.g. Runnett 125–Staderas (Windjammer (USA)) [1989 **74**
5.8h² 6f⁵ 5f 5g* 5m⁵ 5f³ 5f³ 5.8f 5.3f a6g6 a6g* a7g⁵ 1990 a6g* a5g⁴ a6g⁴ a6g*
a7g⁶ a6g* a7g² a6g 5.8h a5g a6f³] tall, leggy, lengthy gelding: modest handicapper:
winner 4 times on all-weather at Lingfield, on last occasion in March: never-nearer
third of 7 in Teleprompter Stakes at Arlington final outing: stays 7f: unsuited by soft
going and acts well on firm: sometimes sweats and gets on toes: has given trouble at
stalls: often taken down early: has often hung and not looked genuine: goes well for
tender handling. *P. Mitchell.*

MY PRAYER 6 ch.m. Buckskin (FR) 133–Yellow Idol (Yellow God 129) [1989 NR —
1990 13.8m] leggy, angular mare: no form. *G. M. Moore.*

MY PRETTY NIECE 4 b.f. Great Nephew 126–Melbourne Miss (Chaparral —
(FR) 128) [1989 12m 10.6g 10g 1990 10.1m 8.3m 8f 8f⁵] workmanlike filly: no form in
varied events. *C. Holmes.*

MY REEF 5 ch.h. Main Reef 126–Lassalia (Sallust 134) [1989 NR 1990 8f 10f 10m —
8g⁶ a8g 7f 12f] rather sparely-made horse: no longer of much account: blinkered
final outing. *J. R. Bostock.*

MY RUBY RING 3 b.f. Blushing Scribe (USA) 107–Bells of St Martin 89 **46**
(Martinmas 128) [1989 6d 6g 1990 8m 8m 8.2f 6g⁴ 6m⁵ 6d 6m 6m 8.3m 7f] leggy,
angular filly: poor maiden, not seen out after July: bred to stay beyond 6f: very
slowly away between starts: hung left fourth. *M. D. I. Usher.*

MY SCENE (FR) 4 b.f. Gay Mecene (USA) 128–My Hawk (FR) (Sea Hawk II **78** ?
131) [1989 NR 1990 11.2g* 10g² 10g 8g⁵ 7m⁵ 8g 8g 7d⁵ a8g a6g⁶] leggy ex-French
filly: seventh reported living foal: half-sister to 6 winners in France, including 5-y-o
Hardy Hawk (by Zino): dam unraced half-sister to French St Leger winner Agent
Double and very smart middle-distance stayer Air de Cour: winner and runner-up in
minor races in Provinces in May: ran poorly last 2 starts: has been taken down early:
trained until after seventh outing by J. Hammond. *C. A. Austin.*

MY SERENADE (USA) 6 b.m. Sensitive Prince (USA)–Mau Mae (USA) —
(Hawaii) [1989 5f⁶ 8m 6m 6f 5f 7f 8.5f⁵ 7f 9g 12f⁵ 1990 7f⁶ 5f a5g 6f 6g a7g 9f] small,
lengthy, light-framed mare: poor mover: no longer of much account: blinkered once:
taken early to post fourth outing. *P. J. Bevan.*

MY SHAFY 3 ch.f. Rousillon (USA) 133–Lys River (FR) 119 (Lyphard (USA) 132) **92** +
[1989 NR 1990 7m² 8g* 7.3m² 8d*] sparely-made filly: half-sister to 3
winners, including quite moderate 2m winner Tirwadda (by Troy) and fairly useful
1982 2-y-o 7f winner Blushing River (by Blushing Groom): dam smart middle-
distance performer in France: won maiden at Edinburgh and £9,700 handicap
(impressively) at Ascot in June: unlucky in Newbury handicap in between: will stay
1¼m: progressed very well. *B. Hanbury.*

MY SHOUSHOU 2 b.f. (Mar 23) Shirley Heights 130–Crystal Fountain (Great Nephew 126) [1990 7g⁶] 220,000Y: leggy, workmanlike filly: has scope: sixth foal: half-sister to one-time useful 1¼m winner Flood Mark (by High Line) and winning Irish stayer Crystal Spray (by Beldale Flutter): dam once-raced half-sister to Royal Palace: around 6 lengths sixth of 15, headway 3f out and keeping on under hand riding, to Fragrant Hill in minor event at Newbury in September: will improve, particularly over further. *B. W. Hills.* **68** p

MY SISTER ELLEN 3 ch.f. Lyphard (USA) 132–Cat Girl (USA) (Grey Dawn II 132) [1989 7g³ 1990 8.2g⁴ 7f* 7m* 8m⁵ 8m² 6s] good-bodied filly: has scope: fairly useful form: pushed out to win maiden (made all) at Folkestone and 3-runner minor event (led final ½f) at Yarmouth in September: good second in minor contest at Chepstow: stays 1m: acts on firm going: swishes tail: has looked temperamentally unsatisfactory, particularly so on debut and reappearance. *H. R. A. Cecil.* **97**

MY SPARKLING RING 4 b.g. Sparkling Boy 110–Bells of St Martin 89 (Martinmas 128) [1989 10s 11.7m 10.1m 8.3m 8.3m³ 8.3d 8f 9f 10f 1990 8m] good-bodied gelding: little show except when third in seller at 3 yrs: should prove best at up to 1m: visored last 5 starts in 1989: has looked none too keen. *M. D. I. Usher.* **—**

MY SPORTING LADY 4 b.f. My Dad Tom (USA) 109–Ardtully Lass 64 (Cavo Doro 124) [1989 5s³ 6m 5h 8f 7h 1990 a6g] small, leggy filly: plating-class maiden at best: should stay beyond 5f: possibly needs a soft surface. *P. J. Arthur.* **—**

MYSTERIOUS GLEN (FR) 2 b.c. (Mar 2) Glenstal (USA) 118–Hotbee 101 (Hotfoot 126) [1990 6f⁴ 6m² 6m* 7.5m² 7f⁴] 8,400F, 26,000Y: quite attractive colt, rather unfurnished: first foal: dam won Molecomb Stakes: quite modest performer: won maiden at Redcar in June: stays 7.5f: acts on good to firm ground. *C. Tinkler.* **70**

MYSTERIOUS MAID (USA) 3 ch.f. L'Emigrant (USA) 129–Body Heat (USA) (Sir Ivor 135) [1989 NR 1990 10f⁴ 8m³ 8g³ 10.2f* 10m] $33,000F, IR 30,000Y: lengthy, rather angular filly: second foal: dam never ran: quite modest form: won handicap at Bath in May: ran moderately in similar event following month: may well stay further: acts on firm going. *P. F. I. Cole.* **68**

MYSTERY BAND (USA) 4 b.c. Dixieland Band (USA)–Lindaria (USA) (Sea Bird II 145) [1989 8g³ 12g 8g² 10f⁵ 10m 8g 1990 10m⁶ 8f⁶ 8g³ 12.3g 9m⁴ 8m⁶ 10.8f* 12f⁴ 10m³ 11m² 10.8m⁵ 10m 10m⁵ 12m⁴ a11g² 10m⁴ 12m⁶] big, angular colt: poor mover: fairly useful plater: bought out of G. Huffer's stable £7,158 third outing: won at Warwick (bought in 4,800 gns) in July: showed better form most starts afterwards: stays 1½m: acts on firm ground: lost near-eye after third start as 3-y-o, has worn eyecover since. *C. R. Beever.* **55**

MYSTERY CARGO (USA) 2 b.c. (Apr 16) Storm Bird (CAN) 134–Verset Holiday (USA) (Ribots Holiday (USA)) [1990 6m⁴ 6m] $80,000F, IR 110,000Y: quite good-topped colt: half-brother to 2 winners in USA, including smart Canadian turf filly Baldski's Holiday (by Baldski), successful at up to 9f: dam winner in Puerto Rico: over 7 lengths last of 4 in maiden at Ascot in September: well below that form in similar event at Folkestone following month. *N. A. Callaghan.* **63**

MYSTICAL FLOWER 2 b.f. (Jun 12) Scorpio (FR) 127–Hagen Queen 65 (Mount Hagen (FR) 127) [1990 6g 5f⁶ 6g] 800Y, 1,100 2-y-o: leggy, workmanlike filly: poor mover: second foal: dam won over hurdles: soundly beaten, including when blinkered in a seller at York. *R. D. E. Woodhouse.* **—**

MYSTICAL LADY 3 ch.f. Sagaro 133–L'Angelo di Carlo 46 (Record Token 128) [1989 5g 5.3g⁴ 5g⁴ 5m⁶ 6f 1990 10.1m] small, leggy filly: little worthwhile form, including in sellers: bandaged, saddle broke and ran very wide only start in 1990, in July. *Miss L. Bower.* **—**

MYSTICAL MELI 2 ch.f. (Mar 1) Faustus (USA) 118–La Millie (Nonoalco (USA) 131) [1990 5f⁴ a7g⁴ a6g a6g 8m 7d a8g] 2,200F: lengthy filly: first living foal: dam French maiden: 5 lengths fourth of 13 to Makemeaster in maiden at Southwell: ran moderately after, including in sellers: best form at 7f: sold 800 gns Doncaster November Sales. *J. Wharton.* **49** d

MYSTIC BID 3 br.c. Auction Ring (USA) 123–Relic Spirit (Relic) [1989 6f 5f⁴ 6g 1990 8g a8g a7g 9f⁶] leggy colt: poor mover: poor form at 2 yrs, none in 1990: bred to be best at up to 1m: sold to join W. Clay 1,600 gns Doncaster September Sales. *J. Etherington.* **—**

MYSTIC CRYSTAL (IRE) 2 b.f. (May 13) Caerleon (USA) 132–Bolivia (GER) (Windwurf (GER)) [1990 8m⁵ 7m⁶ 6m 6d⁴ 8d a8g² a7g* a7g*] 45,000Y: leggy, rather sparely-made filly: second foal: dam useful filly in Germany at 2 yrs: ridden by apprentice when comfortable winner of claimer and nursery (by ½ length from **85**

Green's Seago) at Southwell in November; best form at 7f: best form on all-weather, acts on dead ground on turf. *W. A. O'Gorman.*

MYSTIC MONKEY 5 ch.g. Royal Match 117–Thorganby Melody (Highland — §
Melody 112) [1989 12h 10.1m a10g 1990 11.7f] workmanlike gelding: of little account
and seems temperamental. *T. B. Hallett.*

MYSTIKO (USA) 2 gr.c. (Feb 22) Secreto (USA) 128–Caracciola (FR) (Zeddaan 97 p
130) [1990 6m² 6f* 6g³] \$150,000Y: sturdy, angular colt: has a quick action: half-
brother to French 8.5f winner Mer Belle and a winner in North America (both by Far
North): dam French maiden, is half-sister to good filly Calderina, third in French
Oaks: progressive colt: won maiden at Newmarket by 2 lengths, clear, from Wolf
Hall, making all: ridden with much less enterprise when over 6 lengths third of 5 to
Mujtahid in Scottish Equitable Gimcrack Stakes at York later in August, and made
headway only near finish: will be much better suited by 7f or 1m: sweating final 2
starts: sure to win another race or two. *C. E. Brittain.*

MY SWAN SONG 5 b.g. Soul Singer 97–Palmaria (Be Friendly 130) [1989 10d²
12.5g* 12g 10f 12f⁵ 12.5f 12m a11g⁶ 1990 a11g a12g⁴ a14g a11g⁴ a14g a12g]
close-coupled gelding: poor in all his paces: stays 12.5f: seems to act on any going:
blinkered second to fourth starts: inconsistent. *J. P. Smith.*

MY TAI-PAN 3 b.g. King of Clubs 124–Orchestration 116 (Welsh Pageant 132) 45
[1989 6g² 7m⁶ 8m 7g 1990 a8g 10m 9m⁴ 8d 10.1m a7g³ 6m 7m] leggy gelding: poor
maiden: easily best efforts as 3-y-o when in frame, making most, in claimers: should
stay 1¼m: blinkered third and fifth starts, visored after: trained until after third by
R. Hollinshead. *K. T. Ivory.*

MYTASKI 4 b.c. Niniski (USA) 125–Mytinia 94 (Bustino 136) [1989 10m³ 12f² 12g 81
14m³ 1990 16g 11.7f³ 12m] lengthy colt: fair maiden: stays 1¾m: acts on firm going:
lacks turn of foot: a difficult ride: sold 4,200 gns Ascot November Sales. *Major W. R.
Hern.*

MY TURN NEXT 2 b.f. (Apr 19) King of Spain 121–Its My Turn 80 (Palm Track 53
122) [1990 6s 6m 6f⁵ 8.2v 6d] big, lengthy filly: second foal: half-sister to 3-y-o
Silverdale Fox (by Sweet Monday), fair 6f winner at 2 yrs: dam miler: plating-class
maiden: doesn't stay 1m: best efforts on top-of-the-ground: slowly away first 3
starts. *R. Hollinshead.*

MY-UGLY-DUCKLING 3 ch.g. Longleat (USA) 109–Snow Goose (Santa Claus —
133) [1989 7m 8m 9g 8g 1990 12f⁶ 12.5g 14g 15.3g 10.1m] leggy, rather sparely-made
gelding: plating-class form at 2 yrs: keen sort, appears not to stay 1½m: has worn
severe noseband and been taken down steadily: sold to join K. Wingrove 920 gns
Doncaster September Sales. *C. N. Allen.*

MY VALENTINE CARD (USA) 4 ch.f. Forli (ARG)–Super Valentine (USA) — §
(Super Concorde (USA) 128) [1989 8g 10f⁶ 8h 8f⁶ 8m 1990 a8g] leggy, rather angular
filly: moderate mover: plating-class maiden at best: probably stays 1¼m: acts on
firm going: reluctant to race in blinkers final start at 3 yrs: visored only once in 1990:
has sweated badly: winning selling hurdler in January: pulls hard: one to treat with
caution. *S. G. Norton.*

MYVERYGOODFRIEND 3 b.g. Swing Easy (USA) 126–Darymoss 79 67
(Ballymoss 136) [1989 5f³ 5m⁴ 6m 7m⁴ 6m² 1990 6f 8m⁴ 8m 7m 10f⁵ 8.2m³ 7g²
7.6m⁵ 7d] angular, close-coupled gelding: carries condition: quite modest maiden:
best efforts when placed, making most and rallying gamely on second occasion:
stays 1m: acts on good to firm ground: blinkered last 4 starts. *Andrew Turnell.*

N

NAAR CHAMALI 3 ch.f. Salmon Leap (USA) 131–Reliant Nell (Reliance II 137) —
[1989 NR 1990 10g] 2,600F: lengthy, workmanlike filly: closely related to 2 winners
in France by Northfields, including 10.2f and 1½m winner Reliquais: dam 1½m and
15.5f winner in France also successful over jumps: 33/1 and a bit backward, moved
moderately down when tailed off in claimer at Nottingham in June. *J. D. Czerpak.*

NABEEL DANCER (USA) 5 b.h. Northern Dancer–Prayers'n Promises 120
(USA) (Foolish Pleasure (USA)) [1989 6s* 7.2s 6f³ 5g⁴ 6f² 5f⁶ 6g² 6g³ 6m⁴ 5g³ 6s
1990 5f 5g² 5m 5m* 5d 6m] lengthy, good sort: shows plenty of knee action: ran
consistently well in good company as 4-y-o: disappointed on 4 of his 6 outings in
1990, but most impressive in Prix du Gros Chene at Chantilly in June: made all and
soon well clear when beating Ron's Victory by 5 lengths: blinkered then and again

*Prix du Gros Chene, Chantilly—blinkers do the trick,
and Nabeel Dancer dominates the race*

when setting very strong pace, dropping away quickly, in July Cup on final start:
suited by 5f: easily best form on a sound surface: sometimes sweated, became
coltish and gave trouble at stalls, particularly in his early races: retired to
Derrinstown Stud, Co Kildare, fee IR £5,000 (live foal). *A. A. Scott.*

NAD ELSHIBA (USA) 4 b.c. Nijinsky's Secret (USA) 113–Terska (USA) **81**
(Vaguely Noble 140) [1989 12g² 12d 14g⁴ 1990 14m⁶ 10f⁴ 11.1m² 10.8g] big, rangy
colt: has a rather round action: fair maiden: probably suited by around 1½m: acts on
good to firm going: active type, who wore severe bridle at 4 yrs: reluctant at stalls
final outing (June): sold 18,000 gns Newmarket Autumn Sales. *Major W. R. Hern.*

NADI AL QADISIYA 3 b.c. Reesh 117–Swinging Baby 73 (Swing Easy (USA) **—**
126) [1989 NR 1990 6f 7m] IR 1,400Y, resold 9,200Y: sturdy colt: third foal: brother
to Irish maiden Golden Share and closely related to a maiden by Lochnager, both
quite modest: dam, 5f winner, is half-sister to good Italian winners Travolta and
Hoche: burly, behind in maiden (ridden by 7-lb claimer) at Newmarket and
apprentice race at Lingfield in May. *G. A. Huffer.*

NADMA (USA) 3 b.f. Northern Dancer–Beaconaire (USA) (Vaguely Noble 140) **82 +**
[1989 NR 1990 10m* 10m²] close-coupled, rather angular filly: sixth foal: closely
related to top-class American filly Sabin (by Lyphard) and half-sister to Fatah Flare
(by Alydar) and useful 1985 2-y-o 6f winner Soughaan (by Riverman): dam, winner at
up to 1¼m in France, is half-sister to high-class filly Kittiwake, dam of very good
American filly Miss Oceana: won maiden at Pontefract in April: beaten 12 lengths by
Spinning in minor event there in June: will be well suited by 1½m. *H. R. A. Cecil.*

NAFHAAT (USA) 3 ch.f. Roberto (USA) 131–Distant Horizon (USA) (Exclusive **91**
Native (USA)) [1989 7s² 1990 8m⁴ 10f² 12f* 12m⁵ 15d² 16d² 14.6d⁴] rather
sparely-made filly: good mover: fairly useful performer: won maiden at Haydock in
August: ran well next 3 starts in listed races at York and the Curragh and (in
between) minor event at Ayr: stayed well: acted on any going: has had tongue tied
down: visits Polish Precedent. *H. Thomson Jones.*

NAFPLION 5 b.m. Young Generation 129–Time For Thought 75 (Crooner 119) **—**
[1989 8d 8m 10.6g 8.5g 12.2m⁶ a11g 1990 8g a8g a8g 10.6f 5s⁶ 6f 7m] rather leggy,
workmanlike mare: no longer of much account: blinkered fifth outing in 1989,
visored first 2 at 5 yrs. *R. E. Peacock.*

NAFUAT 6 b.g. Taufan (USA) 119–Jerusalem (Palestine 133) [1989 7d 6m⁴ 7g a7g **47 §**
a7g a6g⁶ 1990 6s 7f 8g³ 7m⁶ 8g⁴ 8m 6g 6d] rather leggy, sparely-made gelding:
moderate mover: fairly useful handicapper at his best, but has deteriorated: best
run as 6-y-o on fourth outing: stays 7f: used to be best on an easy surface: often
blinkered, visored fourth outing: sold out of J. W. Watts's stable 4,000 gns
Doncaster January Sales: unenthusiastic. *Mrs P. A. Barker.*

NAFZAWA (USA) 3 ch.f. Green Dancer (USA) 132–Nawazish (Run The Gantlet **101**
(USA)) [1989 7f² 7.3v³ 1990 12m² 14m³ 16m² 16m* 14g 17.6g⁶ 16.2m* 16m⁴] leggy,
rather angular filly: good mover: useful performer: had simple task (9/1 on) in
3-runner Newcastle maiden in July then led 4f out and stayed on strongly to win
£10,600 handicap at Ascot in October: below best in listed event at Newmarket final
start: should stay beyond 2m: probably acts on any going. *M. R. Stoute.*

NAGEM 7 b.m. Headin' Up–Eleonora 70 (Falcon 131) [1989 6s 5f 6f⁶ 6m⁴ 5d 6m³   53
7g 1990 a6g a6g 6m 6g a5g⁵ 5g³ 5g² 6d⁴ 6f⁵] strong, lengthy mare: has run tubed:
poor mover: one-time modest front-running sprint handicapper: ran her best races
for long while (fair way out of handicap) on seventh and eighth outings: acts on any
going: blinkered last 2 outings in 1989, unruly first of them: usually on edge:
retained 1,200 gns Doncaster November Sales. *L. J. Barratt.*

NAI HARN 2 b.c. (Mar 29) Petong 126–Pacific Polly (Mount Hagen (FR) 127)   71
[1990 6g 6f* 6f⁵ 6g³ 7f 7m] 10,000Y: leggy colt: second foal: half-brother to quite
modest maiden Aquatic (by Mummy's Game): dam never ran: modest performer:
won maiden auction at Pontefract in July: should stay 7f. *C. F. Wall.*

NAILEM 3 b.c. Absalom 128–La Reine de France (Queen's Hussar 124) [1989 5s⁵   —
5m⁵ 5m⁴ 5f* 5m⁴ 5f⁵ 6m³ 1990 a8g] sturdy colt: has a roundish action: carries
condition: modest winner at 2 yrs: soundly beaten in handicap in February: best
form at 5f: acts on firm going. *R. P. C. Hoad.*

NAIYSARI (IRE) 2 gr.c. (Feb 12) Mouktar 129–Naiymat (Troy 137) [1990 8m³]   67 P
workmanlike colt: second foal: dam French 1½m winner from family of Shergar and
Shernazar: green, 6 lengths third of 11, slowly away then staying on well final 2f
under tender handling, to impressive Polish King in minor event at Newmarket in
November: sure to improve considerably, particularly at 1¼m +, and win races. *L.
M. Cumani.*

NAJAAH 2 b.f. (Feb 14) Green Desert (USA) 127–Sarajill (High Line 125) [1990   — p
7s] 74,000Y: neat filly: fourth foal: dam poor sister to Nicholas Bill, Centroline and
Centrocon (dam of Time Charter): green and burly, slowly away and never able to
challenge in maiden at Lingfield in October: should improve. *R. W. Armstrong.*

NAJAT 3 b.f. Tender King 123–Brave Ivy 68 (Decoy Boy 129) [1989 5f⁴ 5f* 5f⁶ 5g   — §
5m 1990 6f⁶ 8m a6g] tall, sparely-made filly: good walker: plating-class winner at
2 yrs: very slowly away and always behind in handicaps first 2 starts in 1990:
blinkered and edgy final one, first for 4 months: sold 600 gns Ascot October Sales:
one to avoid. *Dr J. D. Scargill.*

NAJEEBA (USA) 3 ch.f. Blushing Groom (FR) 131–La Noblesse (USA) 85 (Key   —
To The Mint (USA)) [1989 NR 1990 5g⁴] $280,000Y: light-framed filly: second foal:
dam lightly-raced 9f winner out of sister to Crowned Prince and Majestic Prince:
second favourite, staying-on fourth of 8 in maiden at Beverley in July: will be well
suited by further. *A. C. Stewart.*

NAJMAH (USA) 3 ch.f. Nijinsky (CAN) 138–Double's Nell (USA) (Nodouble   73 d
(USA)) [1989 NR 1990 7g 11.5m⁴ 10h² 8m 10f⁴ 8g⁶] $400,000Y: angular, unfurnished
filly: sixth foal: half-sister to several winners, notably good-class winner at up to 1m
Nell's Briquette (by Lanyon), the dam of Sanquirico and Love The Groom: dam
unraced: modest form in frame in listed race at Lingfield and maiden at Brighton:
ran poorly in maidens last 3 starts, twice pulling hard in lead: may prove best short
of 11.5f: blinkered final start: sold 30,000 gns Newmarket December Sales: best left
alone. *J. L. Dunlop.*

NAKORA BISTRAYA (USA) 3 b.f. Robellino (USA) 127–Calypsa (USA) 83   79
(The Minstrel (CAN) 135) [1989 6m 8g⁵ 1990 8m³ 8.2s* 10m⁵ 8.2s* 8m⁴ 9m]
close-coupled filly: has a markedly round action: won minor event (on toes) at
Nottingham in May and apprentice handicap (best effort, staying on from rear) at
Haydock in July: soundly beaten from apparently modest draw in Cambridgeshire
Handicap at Newmarket on first run for 3 months: stays 1¼m: goes well on soft
ground. *G. A. Pritchard-Gordon.*

NA LA GIRI 4 b.g. Nishapour (FR) 125–Les Sylphides (FR) (Kashmir II 125)   —
[1989 10d³ 10s 10m 8f* 8m 8h² 7m 9f² 10g 8f⁵ 10h 11.7g 8g 1990 10f] leggy gelding:
moderate mover: winning plater as 3-y-o: bandaged and blinkered, ran poorly only
outing (March) on flat in 1990: stays 1¼m: acts on firm and dead going: tends to pull,
and has worn severe bridle: rather inconsistent. *R. Simpson.*

NAME THE BRAVE (IRE) 2 b.g. (Mar 23) Nomination 125–Bold Loren (Bold   60
Lad (IRE) 133) [1990 5m³ 5v² 5g³ 6m 6g⁶ 6d 7f³ 7d⁵] 16,000F, 22,000Y: rangy
gelding: has plenty of scope: good walker: first foal: dam twice-raced half-sister to
dam of Gallic League: quite modest maiden: ran in sellers last 2 starts: stays 7f:
probably acts on any going: blinkered third and final 4 starts. *M. H. Easterby.*

NAMTY 3 b.f. Thatching 131–Riverine (FR) (Riverman (USA) 131) [1989 NR 1990   —
8m] 27,000Y: sturdy, close-coupled filly: fourth foal: half-sister to 3 winners,
including fairly useful 1986 2-y-o 6f winner Lucayan Knight (by Dominion): dam
1¼m winner in France: burly, no promise in maiden at Kempton in July: sold 2,400
gns Newmarket Autumn Sales. *J. H. M. Gosden.*

Queen Mother's Cup (Lady Amateur Riders), York—
a useful performance by Nangarar (right) to beat Bold Fox

NANCY ARDROSS   4 b.f. Ardross 134–Classy Nancy (USA) (Cutlass (USA))   —
[1989 12g 16.2m⁶ 15g 1990 12.5m] lengthy, sparely-made filly: has a free, rather
round action: little worthwhile form in maidens and handicaps: should prove best
short of 2m: winning selling hurdler in March: sold 4,000 gns Doncaster November
Sales. *Dr J. D. Scargill.*

NANGARAR (USA)   4 b.c. Topsider (USA)–Nawazish (Run The Gantlet (USA))   96
[1989 8m² 10f* 10f* 1990 12m* 10.5m 10.6g] rangy, angular colt: put up improved
performance when beating Bold Fox 1½ lengths in valuable ladies event at York in
June: returned lame when tailed off in £41,800 handicap there next outing: suited by
1½m: has raced only on sound surface: sold 17,500 gns Newmarket Autumn Sales.
M. R. Stoute.

NAN'S BOY   2 b.c. (May 1) Blakeney 126–Classy Nancy (USA) (Cutlass (USA))   —
[1990 5.8m 7m 7d 7g] 4,400Y: workmanlike colt: fifth foal: half-brother to 3-y-o 5f
winner Bold Lez (by Never So Bold) and 4-y-o Nancy Ardross (by Ardross): dam
won at up to 6f in USA: well beaten in maidens, including auctions. *J. Ffitch-Heyes.*

NAOCHAR (IRE)   2 b.f. (Mar 11) Sallust 134–Her Name Was Lola (Pitskelly   45
122) [1990 5g 6g⁴ 7.5d 6m⁶ 6f 7g⁴ 6m⁶ 8m] IR 4,600F, IR 3,100Y: leggy, sparely-
made filly: has a round action: third foal: dam ran 3 times at 2 yrs in Ireland: modest
plater: blinkered, raced keenly in apprentice seller final start: stays 7f: sold 1,750
gns Ascot November Sales. *R. Simpson.*

NAO FAZ MAL   2 b. or br.f. (Mar 26) Chief Singer 131–Pine Away 74 (Shirley   66
Heights 130) [1990 6m 7m⁵ 7m 7m] 11,000F, 26,000Y: leggy, sparely-made filly:
first foal: dam 2-y-o 6f winner out of smart 5f performer Piney Ridge: easily best
effort fifth in maiden at Yarmouth in August. *Lord John FitzGerald.*

NAOMI'S KEEPSAKE   2 b.f. (May 12) Nomination 125–Rebecca (Quorum 126)   38
[1990 7d 7d a6g] half-sister to several winners here and abroad, including 7f and 1m
winner Swinging Rebel (by Swing Easy): dam poor half-sister to Steel Pulse: never
dangerous in varied races, including a 20-runner seller at Catterick. *C. W. Thornton.*

NARWALA   3 b.f. Darshaan 133–Noufiyla 68 (Top Ville 129) [1989 7g² 1990   120
10.2g* 10fʷᵒ 12m* 12g²]
    Blink, and you might have missed Narwala. Some could have forgotten
her in the more than ten months which separated her second in a Newmarket
maiden as a two-year-old and her reappearance, after which Narwala appeared
just three times in Britain in the space of a month, once in a walk-over when
most of the racegoers would have been on their way home. What we did see of
Narwala, however, put her comfortably into the top ten middle-distance fillies
trained in Britain. The others had established their reputations long before

Princess Royal Stakes, Ascot—Narwala makes up for lost time,
leading throughout to beat Applecross and Ahead

Narwala reappeared with a runaway win over four opponents in a minor event
at Doncaster in September. It seemed that she was relatively unfancied that
day, starting co-third favourite, but so impressive was she, asked to quicken
three furlongs out and winning by fifteen lengths easing down, that nothing
stood its ground for Narwala's second intended run of the year, in a similar
contest at Brighton. As it was then, Narwala had to go straight into pattern
company for the Princess Royal Stakes at Ascot. Turned out in excellent
condition, she was keen in the paddock and the race, setting up a six-length
lead after about half a mile. At that stage it looked as if Narwala was going too
fast for her own good but Pat Eddery was able to give her a breather, allowing
the others to catch up, before kicking on again coming off the turn from which
point she never looked like being caught. Narwala didn't have to be hard
ridden in beating the other co-favourite Applecross two lengths, with the
same distance back to Ahead narrowly in front of Sesame. That was her third
and last outing in Britain but Narwala did have one more run, under top weight
in the Grade 2 Long Island Handicap at Belmont Park the day after the
Breeders' Cup. This time she gave an even bigger beating to Ahead (four and a
half lengths, giving 4 lb) but found one too good for her at the weights in the
American four-year-old Rigamajig.

Narwala (b.f. 1987)	Darshaan (br 1981)	Shirley Heights (b 1975)	Mill Reef
			Hardiemma
		Delsy (b or br 1972)	Abdos
			Kelty
	Noufiyla (b 1982)	Top Ville (b 1976)	High Top
			Sega Ville
		Noureen (b 1973)	Astec
			Nubena

Narwala is by the excellent Darshaan out of a formerly undistinguished
daughter of another of the Aga Khan's Prix du Jockey-Club winners Top Ville.
Darshaan comes from one of the Boussac families purchased by the Aga Khan
and Top Ville from his Dupre acquisitions, whereas Narwala's dam Noufiyla
can be traced back to Teresina, one of the first mares to race and produce in
Europe for the Aga Khan's grandfather. Narwala is Noufiyla's first foal, the
second being a colt by Lashkari. Noufiyla was barren to Kalaglow in 1989.
Trained by Johnson Houghton, she reached the frame in maiden races on each
of her four runs but failed to win. She's a half-sister to the Cherry Hinton
winner and Coronation Stakes third Nasseem, the present Aga Khan's first
pattern winner trained in Britain, out of the unraced Noureen. The third dam
Nubena was third in the 1960 Irish Oaks. Narwala is a sparely-made filly who,
like most of Darshaan's progeny, stays one and a half miles well. She flashes
her tail under pressure. *L. M. Cumani.*

NASAB 2 ch.c. (Apr 14) Nordance (USA)–Piccadilly Etta 76 (Floribunda 136) **77**
[1990 7m 8.2m³ 8g*] IR 12,500F, 27,000Y: lengthy, rather angular colt: good mover:

half-brother to several winners, including 1986 2-y-o 6f winner Einstein (by Mummy's Pet), fairly useful sprinter Jose Collins (by Singing Bede) and fair 1m winner Vitigeson (by Vitiges): dam won from 1½m to 2m: progressive colt: won 17-runner maiden at Newcastle in October by a length from Thibaain, quickening 2f out and staying on well: will stay 1¼m. *D. Morley.*

NASEBY (IRE)   2 b.f. (Mar 23) Kafu 120–First Contact 79 (Simbir 130) [1990 5m   **49**
5v³ 5d 6g⁶ 5m] IR 6,200Y: leggy filly: half-sister to winning 2-y-o platers by Crofter and London Bells: dam stayed 1m: plating-class maiden: stays 6f: acts on heavy ground. *D. Haydn Jones.*

NASEEM ELBARR (USA)   2 ch.c. (Feb 10) The Minstrel (CAN) 135–   **— p**
Doubling Time (USA) 117 (Timeless Moment (USA)) [1990 7f⁴] $600,000Y: third reported foal: half-brother to useful miler Timely (by Kings Lake), later successful in North America: dam suited by 1¼m, is out of unraced half-sister to Faraway Son and Liloy: favourite but green, over 10 lengths fourth of 5, soon niggled along then not knocked about final 2f, in maiden at Yarmouth in July: should improve. *A. C. Stewart.*

NASHAAT (USA)   2 b.c. (Mar 14) El Gran Senor (USA) 136–Absentia (USA) 108   **— p**
(Raise A Cup (USA)) [1990 6m] IR 420,000Y: medium-sized, quite good-topped colt: closely related to very useful sprinter Dancing Dissident (by Nureyev) and half-brother to a winner in Japan: dam useful miler in France later smart in USA: very green, around 8 lengths eighth of 18, chasing leaders 4f then not knocked about unduly, in maiden at Newbury in June: looked sure to improve, but not seen out again. *Major W. R. Hern.*

NASHID   5 b.g. Be My Guest (USA) 126–Whispering Sands (Kalamoun 129) [1989   **96 d**
11.7m* 13.3m* 14m* 12m 16g⁵ 1990 12g² 16.2d⁵ 14g 13d 12g] good-topped, quite attractive gelding: fairly useful handicapper at his best: good second to Bold Fox at Leicester in June, but failed to reproduce that form: effective at 1½m to 1¾m: probably acts on any going: has given trouble in preliminaries: takes keen hold: sold 11,000 gns Newmarket Autumn Sales. *A. C. Stewart.*

NASWARA (USA)   2 br.f. (Jan 27) Al Nasr (FR) 126–Sound Of Summer (USA)   **— p**
(Drone) [1990 7m] $47,000F, $200,000Y: strong, rangy filly: has scope: half-sister to several winners, one placed in minor stakes: dam winner at up to 9f, including in graded company: around 9 lengths eleventh of 18, slowly away then fading from 2f out, in maiden at Leicester in October: reared over in paddock: should improve, particularly over further. *H. R. A. Cecil.*

NATARAYA (USA)   3 b.f. Nijinsky (CAN) 138–Beautiful Morning (USA)   **74**
(Graustark) [1989 NR 1990 10.2f² 12f³ 12f⁴ 15.3g⁵ 12g a12g⁶ a12g] $90,000Y: big, leggy filly: ninth foal: closely related to graded-placed winner Scarlet 'N Gray (by Secreto) and half-sister to 2 winners by Roberto, including useful 6f (at 2 yrs) and 1½m winner Fool's Prayer, later graded winner in USA: dam unraced: modest maiden: stays 1½m: acts on firm going: on toes second start: refused to enter stalls intended fourth: below form with forcing tactics and for amateur: sold 12,000 gns Newmarket December Sales. *G. Harwood.*

NATIVE FLAIR   5 b.m. Be My Native (USA) 122–Tuyenu 77 (Welsh Pageant   **81**
132) [1989 12d 10m⁶ 1990 a10g² a10g² 12.3f* 12.2m⁴ 12f³ 10g⁴ 12g² 12m³ 11.5m⁶] tall, rather sparely-made mare: moderate mover: fair handicapper: won at Ripon in April: ran well after until final outing: stays 1½m: acts on any going: game and consistent: sold 4,200 gns Newmarket December Sales in foal to Superlative. *R. W. Armstrong.*

NATIVE GUILE   3 b.f. Lomond (USA) 128–Merlins Charm (USA) 113 (Bold   **—**
Bidder) [1989 6m 7m* 7m³ 8g 1990 10m] lengthy filly: fair winner at 2 yrs: has contested pattern and listed events since, tailed off in Lupe Stakes (bandaged off-hind) at Goodwood in May: should stay 1m: sold 30,000 gns Newmarket December Sales. *B. W. Hills.*

NATIVE KNIGHT   5 b.g. Be My Native (USA) 122–Lady Pitt (Pitskelly 122)   **48**
[1989 12m² 12m⁴ 12f² 1990 12m 12m⁵ 10h⁴ 12m³] leggy, lengthy gelding: poor maiden: effective at 1¼m and 1½m: acts well on top-of-the-ground: ran moderately when blinkered: sometimes sweats: lacks a turn of foot. *R. Akehurst.*

NATIVE MAGIC   4 ch.f. Be My Native (USA) 122–Tuyenu 77 (Welsh Pageant   **91**
132) [1989 10.1m⁴ 8m³ 10.2f* 10f³ 13.3d* 1990 13.3m² 12f⁶ 12s 14d³ 12g³ 12s a14g] sparely-made, angular filly: fairly useful handicapper: ran well at Haydock on fourth outing (first for 3 months), moderately on all-weather final one: stays 1¾m: unsuited by soft going, acts on any other. *R. W. Armstrong.*

NATIVE MISSION 3 ch.g. Be My Native (USA) 122–Sister Ida (Bustino 136) **76** [1989 NR 1990 14f³ 13.6m⁵] IR 6,200F, IR 19,000Y: unfurnished gelding: first foal: dam never ran: modest form, never able to challenge, in maidens at Redcar in October: should be suited by 2m: winning hurdler. *J. G. FitzGerald.*

NATIVE SCOT 4 ch.f. Be My Native (USA) 122–Bunduq 67 (Scottish Rifle 127) **34** [1989 10g 9f⁵ 10.6m 12f 9f 10m 9g 10.6d 9s² 1990 10.6f³ 10m 11d] tall filly: poor maiden: stays 1¼m: acts on any going: visored once at 3 yrs: sweating, hit rail second outing: has shown signs of temperament. *F. H. Lee.*

NATIVE STREAM 2 ch.f. (Apr 10) Deep River 103–Native Love 77 (Native **—** Prince) [1990 5m⁶ 6d] angular, sparely-made filly: sister to poor maiden Native River and half-sister to 1976 2-y-o 6f seller winner Market Fresh (by Tamerlane), a winner in Denmark and a winning hurdler: dam placed over 6f: always behind in minor event (very green, slowly away) and maiden at Doncaster in autumn. *E. H. Owen jun.*

NATIVE SUITOR 3 b.g. Local Suitor (USA) 128–Bronte (USA) 88 (Bold Forbes **—** (USA)) [1989 5s 5m⁴ 6m 1990 8f 8.5g a7g 8m⁴] lengthy, good-quartered gelding: plating-class maiden: suited by 1m: sold to join P. Blockley 2,100 gns Ascot September Sales. *R. Hollinshead.*

NATIVE TRIBE 3 b.g. Be My Native (USA) 122–More Fuss (Ballymore 123) **96** [1989 6m⁴ 6m⁴ 7f* 7f* 8g² 1990 7d 10d² 12g 10.2m⁶ 10.6g 13d 12v²] rather leggy, close-coupled gelding: usually looks well: fairly useful handicapper at his best: second at Epsom and Haydock, losing lot of ground on turn in latter: stays 13f: has form on any going, though best in 1990 with plenty of give: has joined G. Balding. *B. Hanbury.*

NATIVE TWINE 3 b.f. Be My Native (USA) 122–Twine (Thatching 131) [1989 **114** 6m² 6f* 6d² 6f* 1990 8m² 10m* 10g4] leggy, rather sparely-made filly: shows a round action: very useful performer: justified favouritism in listed race at Newbury: again favourite, below form in Pretty Polly Stakes at the Curragh later in June, travelling strongly long way: unlikely to stay beyond 1¼m: sold to USA, winning 8.5f stakes race at Louisiana Downs in September: behind in Yellow Ribbon Stakes at Santa Anita in November. *H. R. A. Cecil.*

NAUGHTY NORA 2 b.f. (May 2) Lir 82–Amberush 41 (No Rush) [1990 a7g] **—** third reported foal: sister to winning hurdler Lirchur: dam plater on flat stayed 1½m, won over hurdles: slowly away and always behind in late-year maiden at Lingfield. *A. Moore.*

NAUGHTY REBEL 3 b.c. Swinging Rebel 105–Halma (Hallez (FR) 131) [1989 **—** NR 1990 12d] fifth reported living foal: dam no worthwhile form: 33/1 and ridden by 7-lb claimer, tailed off in maiden at Folkestone in November. *R. J. Hodges.*

NAVAL FAN 4 b.g. Taufan (USA) 119–Naval Artiste (Captain's Gig (USA)) [1989 **81** 5v* 5.8m⁶ 5m² 5m² 5g⁵ 5m* 5g 5s² 1990 6v 5g⁴ 5g⁴ 5m* 5m⁵ 5m* 5g⁵ 5m* 5g* 6g*] leggy, rather angular gelding: has a round action: successful in second half of year in handicap at Hamilton, claimer at Pontefract, seller at Beverley (odds on, no bid), handicap at Newcastle and seller (bought in 7,000 gns) at York, easily best 2 of his wins in the handicaps: suited by 5f: acts on good to firm and heavy going: sold 14,500 gns Newmarket Autumn Sales. *M. H. Easterby.*

NAVARESQUE 5 b.m. Raga Navarro (ITY) 119–Esquinade 84 (Silly Season 127) **52** [1989 10.2f 8f 1990 7h 8h 7m³ 7f* 8g⁵ 8f² 8m* 10h 8f⁵ 8.2m³ 6g* 6g 6d⁶ 7d³] leggy, angular mare: has a round action: successful in handicaps (making most in first 2) at Brighton (apprentices) in June, Sandown in July and Nottingham (appearing to show much improved form racing on favoured stand rail) in September: effective at 6f and stays 9f: acts on firm and dead going. *R. J. Hodges.*

NAWASSI (USA) 3 b.f. Shadeed (USA) 135–Scintillate 119 (Sparkler 130) [1989 **69** 5m² 1990 6g³ 6g² 7m⁴ 7m² 7.5d 6s] strong-quartered, attractive filly: sixth foal: half-sister to useful 1985 2-y-o 6f winner Alshinfarah (by Great Nephew) and Danish winner Salib (by Be My Guest): dam, Oaks winner, is half-sister to Juliette Marny and Julio Mariner: quite modest maiden: trained reappearance by R. Charlton: bred to stay further: acts on good to firm ground: sold to join K. Cunningham-Brown 11,000 gns Newmarket Autumn Sales. *K. Prendergast, Ireland.*

NAWWAR 6 ch.h. Thatching 131–Priceless Pin (Saint Crespin III 132) [1989 6f⁶ **73** 6g* 6m⁴ 6m³ 1990 7g 6m 7m⁵ 6m 7m² 7m² 7m 7m³ 7g 7m a7g] strong, close-coupled horse: modest handicapper: best at 6f or 7f: acts on good to firm and dead (probably unsuited by very soft) going: has sweated and been slowly away. *C. J. Benstead.*

NAYLAND 4 ch.c. Be My Guest (USA) 126–Troytops 66 (Troy 137) [1989 8m⁶   **98**
10.6g⁵ 8f² 1990 8g² 7.6d⁵ 8g² 8f 8m* 7m² 8f⁵ 8g³ 7m²] lengthy, angular colt:
moderate mover: generally gave good account of himself in valuable handicaps,
winning £7,200 event at Newmarket in June: better efforts second to Fedoria in
£20,700 race at same course and to Pontenuovo in £71,900 contest at Ascot
(gambled-on favourite) next and final outings: stays 1m: possibly not at best on firm
going, yet to race on soft: has wandered under pressure, and best with waiting
tactics: consistent. G. Wragg.

NAZAKAT 3 ch.f. Known Fact (USA) 135–Royal Home 69 (Royal Palace 131)   **41**
[1989 5m⁶ 5f³ 5f* 6g 1990 5g 5.8f 5f 5m 5f 7f 6f 6m 5m a6g] strong, sturdy filly: has a
quick action: quite modest winner at 2 yrs: generally well below form in handicaps
since: should stay at least 6f: visored penultimate start. L. J. Holt.

NAZARE BLUE 3 b.g. Absalom 128–Top Stream 87 (Highland Melody 112)   **52**
[1989 5v² 5g 5m3 5f² 6f⁵ 6f⁴ 6m⁵ 1990 7f 6f 6m² 5g 6m³ 6f 6g 7m 6g 6d] big, rather
angular gelding: quite good mover: plating-class maiden: below form last 5 starts,
slowly away first 2 occasions and in amateurs event on third: stays 6f: acts on any
going. Mrs Barbara Waring.

NAZELA 3 gr.f. Another Realm 118–Alezan Dore 82 (Mountain Call 125) [1989   **91**
5m⁴ 5m2 5m* 6f² 6g 1990 5f² 6g 5f* 5m³ 6m 5f* 5g⁶] lengthy, sturdy filly: carries
condition: good walker: poor mover: fairly useful handicapper: won at Kempton in
May and Redcar in August: suited by strongly-run 5f and top-of-the-ground. J. W.
Payne.

NAZMIAH 4 b.f. Free State 125–Irish Ballad 65 (Irish Ball (FR) 127) [1989 11.5m⁴   **57**
12m 12m⁴ 11f⁶ 10d* 10m⁶ 1990 10f 11m 10m 10m 10g² 10f³ 10g* 10m 10.2g 12m]
leggy filly: quite modest handicapper: won at Leicester in August having had lots to
do: best efforts at 1¼m: seems ideally suited by an easy surface: occasionally
sweats, and has got on toes: usually led or taken early to post: wore crossed
noseband final outing: inconsistent. A. Hide.

NAZOO (IRE) 2 b.f. (Mar 31) Nijinsky (CAN) 138–La Dame du Lac (USA)   **99 p**
(Round Table) [1990 6g* 7d* 7m* 6.5g*] 580,000Y: sister to 2 winners including
useful 1987 Irish 2-y-o 6f winner Lake Como (also 1m winner in France), closely
related to a winner in USA and half-sister to a stakes-placed winner by Exceller:
dam unraced, from very good family: Irish filly: made all and ran on gamely in
Tattersalls Tiffany Yorkshire Stakes at Doncaster in September, beating Atlantic

Tattersalls Tiffany Yorkshire Fillies Stakes, Doncaster—
Nazoo (No. 14) touches off Atlantic Flyer in the first and last running
of this very valuable event

Maktoum Al-Maktoum's "Nazoo"

Flyer by a neck: earlier successful twice at Phoenix Park (dead-heating in a minor event on second start) and in a listed race at Leopardstown: will stay 1m: acts on good to firm ground and dead. *J. S. Bolger, Ireland.*

NDITA 4 b.f. Be My Native (USA) 122–Orangery (Realm 129) [1989 8s* 8g* 7.6f **63** 8m 8m 8m 1990 9g 10m⁴ 10.6s⁴ 11m 11v³ a8g] tall, leggy filly: moderate walker: has a quick action: modest winner in spring as 3-y-o: easily best efforts since when fourth in claimers at Newmarket and Haydock: stays 10.6f: acts on good to firm and soft going: sold 1,550 gns Ascot December Sales. *M. H. Tompkins.*

NEARCTIC BAY (USA) 4 b.g. Explodent (USA)–Golforette (USA) (Mr Randy) **58** [1989 10f 10g 1990 14.6f³ 13s 12f⁶] robust gelding: easily best effort third in maiden at Doncaster in March: stays 1¾m: acts on firm ground, unsuited by soft: tongue tied down last 2 outings: sold privately to join T. Bill's stable 11,500 gns Doncaster August Sales. *Mrs P. A. Barker.*

NEARROE 4 ch.g. Noalto 120–Incarnadine 67 (Hot Spark 126) [1989 10.1g⁶ **37** 11.7m⁶ 12g 1990 10v 11g⁶ 12g 7.5d⁶ 8g 8f² 7.5g⁶ 8m³ 9g] compact, good-bodied gelding: poor walker: poor maiden: ideally suited by further than 1m, and stays 1½m: acts on firm going: slowly away when visored last 2 outings: has given trouble at stalls. *M. P. Naughton.*

NED'S AURA 5 br.g. Dalsaan 125–My Natalie 64 (Rheingold 137) [1989 7.5d 6d⁶ **93** 7f 6m 7f² 7f² 8f² 7f 6g 6m³ 6f² 7m² 7s³ 7g* 7m² 1990 8f* 7g³ 9m* 8f 8m⁴ 9g* 9m³ 7d* 9m] good-topped gelding: moderate mover: fairly useful handicapper: successful at Redcar in May, York in June and August (£12,700 Andy Capp Handicap by ¾ length from Lord of Tusmore) and Ayr in September: ran poorly in Cambridgeshire

627

Michael Sobell Handicap, York—
Ned's Aura gets the nine furlongs all too well for Pandy and St Ninian (rails)
on his first attempt at the trip since his three-year-old days

final start: effective at 7f and stays 9f: acts on any going: has worn blinkers and visor, but didn't at 5 yrs: sold 60,000 gns Newmarket Autumn Sales. *R. M. Whitaker.*

NEEDHAM LAD (IRE) 2 b.g. (Mar 3) Wassl 125–Blue Shark (Silver Shark   54
129) [1990 7m⁶ 8.2m 10s] IR 18,000Y: close-coupled gelding: half-brother to several winners, notably high-class miler Sandhurst Prince (by Pampapaul): dam little form: plating-class maiden: best effort at Nottingham second outing. *P. A. Kelleway.*

NEEDS MUST 3 gr.g. Another Realm 118–Miss Monte Carlo 75 (Reform 132)   —
[1989 6m 6f³ 6g* 6g 8s⁴ 6v 1990 9s 6v] workmanlike, angular gelding: shows a rather round action: useful plater at 2 yrs: well below form in April, 1990: suited by 1m: acts on soft going: sold 1,750 gns Ascot June Sales. *C. Tinkler.*

NEEDWOOD IMP 4 ch.g. Joshua 129–The Doe 82 (Alcide 136) [1989 8g 8.2g   —
8f⁵ 7m² 7m⁵ 7m 6s 7d 1990 6v 7m 7g⁵ 8m 8f 11m⁶ 10m] lengthy, angular gelding: has a long, rather round stride: poor maiden: little form in 1990: suited by 7f: acts on good to firm going: visored third to sixth starts. *B. C. Morgan.*

NEEDWOOD MUPPET 3 b.g. Rolfe (USA) 77–Sea Dart 55 (Air Trooper 115)   64
[1989 5g 5.1m 5g 5f 1990 5g 5m 5m⁴ 5g 5d 5m³ 5m⁵] angular gelding: has a round action: second foal: half-brother to 4-y-o 7f winner Needwood Sprite (by Joshua): dam 10.8f seller winner out of half-sister to Cesarewitch winner Centurion: modest maiden: well beaten in handicaps last 3 outings, initially facing stiff tasks: should be suited by 1¼m: yet to race on top-of-the-ground: apprentice ridden except third start. *B. C. Morgan.*

NEEDWOOD NIGHTLIFE 3 b.f. Decoy Boy 129–Johnny's Pride (Frimley   40
Park 109) [1989 5g 5.1m 5g 5f 1990 5g 5m 5m⁴ 5g 5d 5m³ 5m⁵] small, lengthy filly: shows a quick action: poor sprint maiden. *B. C. Morgan.*

NEEDWOOD POPPY 2 b.f. (May 17) Rolfe (USA) 77–Needwood Nap (Some   —
Hand 119) [1990 6f 7g 6d] angular filly: has a quick action: fourth live foal: half-sister

to 6f winner Needwood Nut (by Royben): dam poor plater: poor form in sellers and a claimer: ridden by 7-lb claimer first 2 starts. *B. C. Morgan.*

NEEDWOOD SPRITE 4 ch.f. Joshua 129–Sea Dart 55 (Air Trooper 115) [1989 **53**
7.5d5 8.2g5 7m* 8g2 10m3 8m2 9g 1990 9g 9s4 10g 8.2s3 11g4 10.4g3 10.6g 12s2 13.8d4 13.6d 12s4] plain filly: plating-class performer: stays 13.8f: acts on good to firm and soft going. *B. C. Morgan.*

NEEHA 4 b.g. Nishapour (FR) 125–Acantha 77 (Prince Tenderfoot (USA) 126) **—**
[1989 10m 8f 6f6 5m4 5f 5f4 6h3 6m 7m4 7f a8g3 1990 a8g] workmanlike gelding: modest form at best: seemed to stay 1m: acted on any going: blinkered 5 times, including only start (well beaten) in 1990: dead. *R. Simpson.*

NEENAWN 3 gr.f. Bairn (USA) 126–Rustling 68 (Rusticaro (FR) 124) [1989 NR **74**
1990 10m3 10m3 10m* 10.2f2] leggy filly: first foal: dam maiden best at 9f or 1¼m: modest form when winning claimer at Sandown in August and second in handicap at Bath in September: claimed out of C. Nelson's stable £6,500 second start. *J. Akehurst.*

NEGEEN (USA) 2 b.f. (Mar 31) Danzig (USA)–Sunny Smile (USA) (Boldnesian) **78 p**
[1990 5g6 5f2 5.5g* 6d2] $700,000Y: rather unfurnished filly: half-sister to several winners, notably Smile (by In Reality), 1986 Breeders' Cup Sprint winner and top class at up to 9f: dam multiple winner: odds on, won maiden at Wolverhampton by a head, clear, from Serious Hurry: good second of 21, eased, to Chipaya in nursery at Nottingham later in October: improving. *A. C. Stewart.*

NEGLIGENT 3 gr.f. Ahonoora 122–Negligence 66 (Roan Rocket 128) [1989 6g3 **109**
7g* 1990 8m3 10.5g 9m3] angular, rather unfurnished filly: moderate mover: very useful performer: won Bottisham Heath Stud Rockfel Stakes at Newmarket at 2 yrs: 5¾ lengths third to Salsabil in General Accident 1000 Guineas at Newmarket: off course 3½ months then well beaten in Juddmonte International and 1¼ lengths third of 8 to Va Toujours in listed race, both at York: should stay 1¼m: purchased privately by Sheikh Mohammed. *B. W. Hills.*

NELSON'S LASS (IRE) 2 b. or br.f. (Mar 20) Carwhite 127–Praise The Lord **38**
(Lord Gayle (USA) 124) [1990 5f 5m5 6f4 7f 6m5 6g] IR 700F, IR 1,800Y: small,

Mrs J. M. Corbett's "Negligent"

narrow filly: has a round action: first foal: dam Irish maiden: poor maiden: should be suited by further than 6f. *Mrs S. M. Austin.*

NEPTUNE'S LAW (USA)   2 br.c. (Apr 27) Proud Appeal (USA)–Bold Mermaid   66
(USA) (Sea Bird II 145) [1990 6g⁶ 6h* 7f⁵ 7m³ 8m] leggy, close-coupled colt: half-brother to several minor winners in USA: dam placed once from 12 starts: sire high class from 5.5f to 9f: quite modest performer: won maiden at Carlisle in July: ran well next 2 starts, moderately for 5-lb claimer final one: should stay 1m. *J. Etherington.*

NEPTUNE'S PET   2 b.c. (Apr 9) Tina's Pet 121–Abalone (Abwah 118) [1990 5m³   65
6g⁶ 5f 5f⁵ 6m] 10,000Y: tall, workmanlike colt: has scope: half-brother to 3 winners over sprint distances, including useful Lonely Street (by Frimley Park): dam unraced: quite modest maiden: good fifth in nursery at Wolverhampton: stays 6f: slowly away and ran wide on bend at Warwick third start. *W. Carter.*

NEROLI   2 b.f. (Apr 18) Nishapour (FR) 125–Norska 67 (Northfields (USA)) [1990   72 ?
6d 7m* 7m 6f] lengthy, angular filly: third foal: half-sister to 2 winners in Italy: dam staying maiden at 2 yrs not so good as 3-y-o: form only when making all in maiden at Sandown in July, quickening home turn and keeping on gamely despite carrying head high: needs further than 6f, and will stay 1¼m. *R. Hannon.*

NETTINA (IRE)   2 b.f. (Mar 6) Runnett 125–Inner Pearl (Gulf Pearl 117) [1990   57
6m⁶ 6g² 6m 6f 5m⁴ 8.2g] 8,000F, 14,000Y: good-bodied filly: half-sister to 2-y-o 5f winners Inner Ring (in France) and Market Gem (both by Auction Ring): dam won from 4f to 9f in France: plating-class maiden: doesn't stay 1m: blinkered penultimate outing: active sort. *K. M. Brassey.*

NEVADA MIX   6 gr.h. Alias Smith (USA)–Northern Empress 80 (Northfields   58
(USA)) [1989 7m 7f 7f 6f³ 6f⁴ 6f⁵ 6g* 7g a6g a7g⁵ 1990 6f 6f 7f²] strong, stocky horse: modest handicapper at best judged on most form: not seen out after July: effective at 6f and 7f: acts on any going: sweated when tried in blinkers: good mount for apprentice: inconsistent. *N. A. Gaselee.*

NEVERDOWN   3 ch.f. Never So Bold 135–Bourton Downs 74 (Philip of Spain   50
126) [1989 7g 1990 8g 8m 9m 8m³ 8.2m* 8m⁶ 8g 8g] leggy, lengthy filly: plating-class form at best: won maiden claimer at Hamilton in July, ridden along in rear 4f out: well worth another try beyond 1m. *M. Bell.*

NEVER GIVE UP   3 b.g. Law Society (USA) 130–Hardiemma 81 (Hardicanute   —
130) [1989 NR 1990 11.5g] 8,000Y: lengthy gelding: half-brother to several winners, notably Derby and Irish Derby winner Shirley Heights (by Mill Reef): dam made up to 11f: 33/1 and bit backward, well behind in minor event at Lingfield in October. *Mrs Barbara Waring.*

NEVER IN   4 b.g. Aragon 118–Recent Events (Stanford 121§) [1989 6m 6m² 7m²   40
7m 6f² 6f⁴ 6f 7g 1990 6m 7m⁶ 8f⁶ 8d] big, angular gelding: plater: keen sort, possibly best at up to 7f: acts on firm going: visored once at 3 yrs, blinkered last 2 outings in 1990: bought 2,300 gns Doncaster May Sales. *K. R. Burke.*

NEVER IN THE RED   2 b.c. (May 15) Wattlefield 117–Swing Gently 78 (Swing   98
Easy (USA) 126) [1990 5f² 5s⁵ 5m* 5f* 5m³ 5g² 5m⁵] 3,300Y, 6,800 2-y-o: leggy, lengthy, rather shallow-girthed colt: fifth living foal: half-brother to 2 winners, including 1986 2-y-o 5f winner Jonleat (by Gunleat), later successful in USA: dam poor maiden: useful colt, successful (made all) in maiden at Edinburgh and nurseries at Warwick and Redcar in summer: excellent second to Rivers Rhapsody in all-aged listed race at Doncaster: creditable fifth, wandering in front, in Cornwallis Stakes at Ascot: very speedy: possibly unsuited by very soft ground: consistent. *J. Berry.*

NEVER SO FAIR   3 b.f. Never So Bold 135–Favoletta 115 (Baldric II 131) [1989   65
NR 1990 8m 8m 8m⁵] well-made filly: closely related to smart 5f performer Amaranda (by Bold Lad) and half-sister to numerous winners, notably Favoridge (by Riva Ridge), very smart at up to 1m: dam won Irish 1000 Guineas and is half-sister to Furioso, dam of Teenoso: first form when about 5¾ lengths fifth of 8 to Sajjaya in minor event at Newmarket in August, never placed to challenge: may be capable of better. *G. Wragg.*

NEVER SO HIGH   3 b.c. Never So Bold 135–High Gait 90 (High Top 131) [1989   84
7g 1990 7g a8g² 8d⁶ a10g²] leggy, quite attractive colt: fair form when second in handicap at Lingfield in November: much better at 1¼m than shorter. *R. W. Armstrong.*

NEVER SO SURE   2 br.g. (May 27) Never So Bold 135–Amerella (Welsh   68
Pageant 132) [1990 5g⁵ 6g² 6s* 7g 8d] 15,500Y: workmanlike gelding: moderate mover: eighth foal: half-brother to several winners, including smart sprinter

Cragside (by Hot Spark) and fair 6f and 1m winner Mudrik (by Sparkler); dam Irish 1¼m winner, is out of Molecomb winner Lowna: quite modest performer: won maiden at Haydock in July by ¾ length, wandering under 2f out then staying on strongly: should stay 1m: acts on soft ground: changed hands 6,800 gns Newmarket Autumn Sales. *Mrs J. R. Ramsden.*

NEWARK ANTIQUEFAIR 2 b.c. (May 25) Rolfe (USA) 77–Sea Dart 55 (Air —
Trooper 115) [1990 8d 10.2s] small, angular colt: third foal: half-brother to 7f seller winner Needwood Sprite (by Joshua): dam 10.8f seller winner, is out of half-sister to Cesarewitch winner Centurion: soundly beaten in maiden at Leicester and minor event at Doncaster. *B. C. Morgan.*

NEW ARRANGEMENT 4 b.g. Trojan Fen 118–Cariole 84 (Pardao 120) [1989
12g⁵ 12.3m² a10g* 1990 12f 14.8m⁵ 16g] workmanlike gelding: fair winner at 3 yrs: never dangerous in handicaps in spring: stays 1½m: winning juvenile hurdler in January. *J. R. Jenkins.*

NEW CHANDELIER 4 b.g. Alzao (USA) 117–New Light 78 (Reform 132) [1989 —
7f⁵ 7m 7f² 1990 10f 7f 8f] angular gelding: has a quick action: form only in slowly-run maiden on final outing at 3 yrs: blinkered last start. *P. W. Harris.*

NEW MEXICO 6 br.g. Free State 125–Trigamy 112 (Tribal Chief 125) [1989 10d   86
10f 10m 10.6d 10g³ 10.6m³ 8v* 8g* 7g³ 1990 a7g 8.2s 8m 10d* 10f* 10g* 10f³ 8m⁴
10f*] strong, sturdy gelding: carries plenty of condition: moderate mover: fair handicapper: successful at Beverley (gambled-on favourite) and Pontefract in May, Ayr in June then Beverley again (struck into after post and severed tendon) in July: effective at 7f to 1¼m: acts on any going: takes keen hold: tough. *M. F. D. Morley.*

NICE AND SHARP 3 b.c. Sharpo 132–Lune de Miel 80 (Kalamoun 129) [1989 7f   62 d
8g⁶ 1990 8.2m6 8g³ 8.2g* 8m 8g³ 9g³ 8g 8f³ 9m⁵ 8m 8.2g 11s 9m] rather sparely-made colt: moderate mover: quite modest handicapper: won at Hamilton in May: stays 9f: best efforts on good ground: sold 3,100 gns Newmarket Autumn Sales. *R. Hollinshead.*

NICE DAY 3 br.f. Shirley Heights 130–Keyboard 88 (High Top 131) [1989 6f² 6g*   73
7d⁵ 1990 6m⁴ 6m⁶ 7.6g 9m⁴ 10f³] leggy, sparely-made filly: modest form: ran well, staying on, in July handicaps at York and Ayr last 2 starts, beaten by 7-lb claimer and set a lot to do in latter: stays 1¼m: acts on firm going. *J. Etherington.*

NICE DICE 2 b.c. (Apr 29) Double Schwartz 128–Danaka (FR) (Val de Loir 133) — p
[1990 7s] eighth reported foal: half-brother to several winners, including 1986 2-y-o 7f winner Bills Henry (by In Fijar): dam, minor French 11f winner, is closely related to good middle-distance performer Val d'Aoste: eighth of 15 in Newcastle maiden in November, soon in touch after slowish start, joining leaders halfway then green and not knocked about: should improve. *M. J. Camacho.*

NICE MANA (FR) 5 ch.m. Nice Havrais (USA) 124–Salmana (FR) 111 (Manado   53
130) [1989 NR 1990 8m 8f* 12m 10m⁶ 8f 12m 8g] lengthy, robust mare: carries plenty of condition: moderate mover: first foal: dam very useful 2-y-o: ran 13 times in Scandinavia as 4-y-o, winning on 3 occasions at up to 11f at Jagersro: won apprentice race at Carlisle in May, setting slow pace: little form after, in seller on sixth outing: sold to join P. Blockley's stable 1,400 gns Newmarket Autumn Sales: winning selling hurdler in November. *W. J. Pearce.*

NICE PICTURE (IRE) 2 b.c. (Apr 21) Kings Lake (USA) 133–Nana Mana Mou   49
(Ela-Mana-Mou 132) [1990 7m 8g 7g 8d a8g] IR 22,000F, 9,400 2-y-o: sturdy, dipped-backed colt: third foal: half-brother to Irish 3-y-o Navy Admiral (by Be My Guest), successful at 7f and 1m, and a winner abroad by Salmon Leap: dam unraced half-sister to 2000 Guineas winner Nebbiolo and daughter of best German 2-y-o of 1967, Hovara: plating-class maiden: will stay 1¼m. *R. Champion.*

NICHOLAS MARK 6 ch.g. Gunner B 126–Bargain Line 68 (Porto Bello 118)   75
[1989 12f 12m 15.8m⁴ 12m³ 13f² 12g 13m² 13g² 11f⁴ 12f 12m* 12m² 12.2g* 12m
12.2m² 14g⁴ 13.8d a12g 1990 12m 12m⁶ 15.8g* 13.6g² 12m² 13g 15.8m* 14.8f² 12h*
13.8m* 12m 17.6f] close-coupled, useful-looking gelding: poor walker: has a quick action: modest handicapper: made all at Catterick (has now won there 7 times) in June, July and August and Thirsk (3-runner event) earlier in August: effective at 1½m and unlikely to stay stiff 2m: best on a sound surface: has run creditably for lady rider: tough and genuine. *R. M. Whitaker.*

NICHOLAS PAYNE 3 ch.g. Salmon Leap (USA) 131–Erin Lassie (USA) (Bold   52 §
Lad (IRE) 133) [1989 NR 1990 8m 10.1g⁶ 10f⁶ 10m 11.7m 10m⁵ 10f 8m 7f] 28,000F,
16,000Y: lengthy gelding: moderate mover: half-brother to several winners here and in USA, including modest sprinter Ma Petite Lassie (by Pas de Seul): dam, French 1m winner, is sister to 1000 Guineas winner Waterloo: plating-class form at

*Biddlestone All-Aged Stakes, Chepstow—a minor race makes headlines,
as Lester rides his first winner since his comeback; Nicholas (right) beats Amigo Menor*

best: reported by rider to have hung badly on turn at Windsor fifth start: stays 1¼m:
sweating and coltish third start: has taken good hold, virtually bolting penultimate
start: blinkered last 2: sold 1,600 gns Doncaster November Sales: one to treat with
caution. *J. W. Payne.*

NICHOLAS (USA)   4 b.c. Danzig (USA)–Lulu Mon Amour (USA) (Tom Rolfe) **104**
[1989 NR 1990 10.2m² 10m⁶ 7f² 7m⁶ 7g⁶ 7m³ 6m* 5d⁵ 6s²] big, good-topped colt:
second foal: brother to Irish 1m winner Danlu: dam winning half-sister to Nordance
(by Danzig): successful 3 times in USA, including once in 1990: useful form in
Britain: landed the odds in all-aged event at Chepstow in October: ran well in
£71,900 handicap at Ascot and in Doncaster listed race previous and final starts:
best at 6f and 7f: probably acts on any going: often gets on edge: has worn tongue
strap. *Mrs L. Piggott.*

NICHOLESS   2 ch.f. (May 23) Nicholas Bill 125–Lunar Queen 96 (Queen's   —
Hussar 124) [1990 a7g] 6,400F: sister to 9f and 1¼m winner Mark Aizlewood and
French 1¼m winner Triera, and half-sister to several other winners here and
abroad, including sprinter Parabems (by Swing Easy): dam won three 5f races at 2
yrs: eighth of 16 in maiden at Southwell in December. *H. Candy.*

NICKEL SILVER (FR)   6 ch.g. Son of Silver 123–Dana's Return (USA) 87   —
(Turn-to) [1989 NR 1990 12d 12s] chunky, strong gelding: winner in France early as
3-y-o: shaped as though retaining a little ability in handicaps in September: stays
10.7f: blinkered at 2 yrs and on first outing at 3 yrs. *G. Richards.*

NICKI RA RA   2 ch.f. (Mar 24) Nicholas Bill 125–Ra Ra Girl 77 (Shack (USA) 118)   —
[1990 5m⁶ 5f] first foal: dam 6f winner: no worthwhile form in maiden and seller at
Wolverhampton in summer. *B. A. McMahon.*

NICKLE JOE   4 ro.g. Plugged Nickle (USA)–Travois (USA) (Navajo (USA))   —
[1989 NR 1990 8m 10m 12m] tall, leggy, quite good-topped gelding: poor maiden: no
form at 4 yrs. *M. Tate.*

NICOLAKI   5 gr.g. Busted 134–Nicholas Grey 100 (Track Spare 125) [1989 12d   —
12g 1990 17m 11.7g 12f] good-topped gelding: modest winner in September, 1988:

finished lame next outing and well beaten in subsequent handicaps: best form at 1½m: blinkered first 2 starts: sold to join W. Clay's stable 1,700 gns Doncaster May Sales. *T. M. Jones.*

NICQUITA 3 ch.f. Nicholas Bill 125–Jacquinta 95 (Habitat 134) [1989 5m² 6m⁴ 5g⁴ 5f³ 6v 1990 7m 6m 7m 6f⁶ 6f³ 7m⁵ 7m* 7f 7g² 7g 8g 7m² a7g a10g] leggy, quite good-topped filly: has round action: quite modest handicapper: ridden by 7-lb claimer, won at Warwick in August: good second at Kempton and Warwick, best subsequent efforts: suited by 7f: acts on any going: visored nowadays. *C. C. Elsey.* 65

NIDOMI 3 ch.c. Dominion 123–Nicholas Grey 100 (Track Spare 125) [1989 6f⁵ 1990 7f 7f⁵ 7g⁴ 7.5g 9g 7m] leggy, good-topped colt: moderate mover: plating-class maiden: below form in handicaps last 3 starts, facing very stiff task in amateurs event on final one: may prove suited by middle distances: hung left fifth outing: subsequently sold out of Sir Mark Prescott's stable 12,500 gns Newmarket July Sales. *G. P. Enright.* 53

NIGEANDBOB (IRE) 2 ch.f. (Apr 23) Millfontaine 114–Atedaun (Ahonoora 122) [1990 6s 7.5f 7m] third foal: half-sister to 3-y-o Al Badeto (by Hays): dam placed at 1m at 3 yrs in Ireland: of no account: retained by trainer 900 gns Doncaster September Sales. *J. Norton.* —

NIGEL'S LUCKY GIRL 2 gr.f. (Feb 19) Belfort (FR) 89–Haiti Mill 68 (Free State 125) [1990 7f⁵ 6f² 6g* 6m² 6m⁶ 7d] 2,700F, 7,000Y: leggy, quite good-topped filly: has plenty of scope: has fluent action: first foal: dam maiden suited by 1m, is out of sister to high-class Petong: modest performer: won maiden auction at Ripon in August: seems better suited by 6f than 7f: possibly needs a sound surface. *R. Guest.* 77

NIGHT AT SEA 3 gr.f. Night Shift (USA)–Into Harbour (Right Tack 131) [1989 6g⁵ 5f* 6m* 1990 6f² 6m⁶ 6g 5g⁴ 5d³ 5m* 5f 6m] workmanlike, good-quartered filly: capable of useful form: 12/1, easily best effort winning listed Trafalgar House Sprint at Sandown in July by 3 lengths from Boozy: behind afterwards in King George Stakes at Goodwood and listed race (on toes and sweating, last of 11) at Newmarket: suited by 5f: goes particularly well on top-of-the-ground: flashes tail under pressure. *L. M. Cumani.* 107 ?

NIGHTBOURNE 4 ch.g. Night Shift (USA)–Catulle (Roan Rocket 128) [1989 8g 7g 8m⁴ 8.2d⁶ 11s⁶ 10m⁶ 1990 10.2f] smallish, workmanlike gelding: plating-class maiden at best: should stay beyond 1m: acts on good to firm and dead going. *S. Dow.* —

NIGHT CLUB (GER) 6 ch.g. Esclavo (FR)–Nightlife (GER) (Priamos GER) 123) [1989 12.2g5 10f a8g 1990 a11g6 a11g a8g a7g³ a8g⁵ a7g² a7g a8g 8f⁵] tall, lengthy, sparely-made gelding: showed much improved form when second in maiden at Southwell in July: stays 7f: blinkered eighth and final (not discredited) outings: has sweated and got on edge. *J. P. Smith.* 53

NIGHT JAR 3 b.f. Night Shift (USA)–Fodens Eve 80 (Dike (USA)) [1989 6m 7d 1990 6f⁵ 5g* 6g² 7m³ 6m] lengthy filly: fair form: won minor event at Chepstow in June: placed in apprentice handicap at Newbury and £7,000 handicap at Sandown: stays 7f. *W. Hastings-Bass.* 82

NIGHTMARE KNAVE 3 ch.c. King of Clubs 124–Mary's Dream (Midsummer Night II 117) [1989 6g a6g* 1990 6m 7m a6g 6m 5.3f a7g] small, lengthy colt: modest form when winning maiden at Lingfield late on at 2 yrs: below form in handicaps: should have been suited by 7f+: blinkered fifth start: dead. *W. Carter.* —

NIGHT OF STARS 4 b.f. Sadler's Wells (USA) 132–Glinting 105 (Crepello 136) [1989 8m² 8d³ 1990 8.5m* 8m³ 8g² 8g* 8g⁵ 8m⁶] angular ex-French filly: fourth foal: half-sister to smart ⁷/t and 1m performer Hadeer (by General Assembly) and fair 1¼m winner Flaunting (by Kings Lake): dam, from very successful family, was best at up to 1m: won maiden (wandered left under pressure) at Beverley in April and listed event narrowly at Munich in July: stayed 8.5f: covered by Warning. *N. A. Graham.* 89

NIGHT PROWLER 2 b.f. (Feb 16) Night Shift (USA)–Aphrosina (Known Fact (USA) 135) [1990 7d a8g a8g⁵] 15,500Y: good-quartered filly: first foal: dam poor half-sister to smart sprinter Enchantment: quite modest form: third to Akeem in late-year maiden at Lingfield: sold 1,800 gns Ascot November Sales. *P. F. I. Cole.* 62

NIGHT-SHIRT 3 b.g. Night Shift (USA)–Vestina 85 (Run The Gantlet (USA)) [1989 7m 8f 8f² a7g² 1990 12.2m 11m* 11.7g³ 11.5m* 11.5m³ 11g* 11.5g* 11.5f* 12.2m* 12h*] workmanlike, deep-girthed gelding: good mover: progressed into fairly useful performer: won maiden (blinkered) at Edinburgh then handicaps at Ayr (amateurs, on sixth start), Lingfield (3 times), Catterick (on toes, idled inside final 1f) and Brighton: pulled hard in ladies event fifth start: stays 1½m well: acts on hard 99

Mr Garth Insoll's "Night-Shirt"

ground: tough and consistent: reportedly sold to race in Saudi Arabia. *Sir Mark Prescott.*

NIGHT TRADER (USA)   4 br.f. Melyno 130–Disco Girl (FR) (Green Dancer (USA) 132) [1989 8.5m⁶ 8.2g⁶ 1990 a8g a12g] big, workmanlike filly: well beaten in maidens and handicap. *R. F. Marvin.* —

NIGHT TRANSACTION   3 ch.f. Tina's Pet 121–Beech Tree 67 (Fighting Ship 121) [1989 8m 8g 1990 8m 10m 8g 10g 8m⁵ 9f² 9m² 9m 8d] stocky filly: poor maiden: probably stays 1¼m: acts on firm ground (stiff task on dead): blinkered fourth and fifth starts. *A. Hide.* **45**

NIJMEGEN   2 b.c. (Feb 6) Niniski (USA) 125–Petty Purse 115 (Petingo 135) [1990 6d] 84,000Y: good-bodied colt: sixth foal: closely related to a winner abroad by Ile de Bourbon and half-brother to 3-y-o 1m winner High Purse (by High Line) and a winner abroad by Final Straw: dam 5f to 7f winner, is out of very smart sprinter Parsimony: backward and green, around 18 lengths eighth of 21, running on steadily from halfway under hand riding, in maiden at Doncaster in November: sure to do better. *W. Jarvis.* — p

NIK-A-DORE   2 b.f. (Apr 30) Cragador 110–Rodi (Le Dieu d'Or 119) [1990 5m 8.2g] 500F: lengthy filly: half-sister to 4 winners in Italy: dam never ran: backward, tailed off in maiden at Beverley and seller (looked reluctant) at Nottingham in September. *G. P. Kelly.* —

NIKATINO   4 b.f. Bustino 136–Latakia 80 (Morston (FR) 125) [1989 8.5s 12h⁶ 11.7m* 12m² 11.7m* 12f³ 12f⁵ 1990 11.7g⁶ 11.7g⁴ 11.5m³ 11.5g² 13.1h* 14g] leggy, rather sparely-made filly: has a round action: plating-class handicapper: won at Bath in July: should stay 1¾m: acts on hard ground. *R. Akehurst.* **54**

NIKITAS   5 b.g. Touching Wood (USA) 127–Hi There 89 (High Top 131) [1989 11f 12f³ 12f 10f⁵ 11.7m 1990 14f² 14m⁴ 14s² 14m⁴ 12m 14f³ 14f* 16g² 14g⁴ 16f⁶ 14d] **75**

634

good topped gelding: modest handicapper: won for only second time when making all, soon clear, in 4-runner event at Haydock in August: stays 2m: acts on any going: has looked a difficult ride, and seemed not to come down hill well at Lingfield final outing. *Miss A. J. Whitfield.*

NIKKI DOW 4 b.g. Tanfirion 110–Amboselli 73 (Raga Navarro (ITY) 119) [1989 —
6m* 5m2 5m2 5m2 5g3 5g a6g 1990 5f 6f 5m6 5m a6g 6g 5g6 a6g] small, angular gelding: moderate mover: won claimer as 3-y-o: very little form in 1990, twice slowly away: suited by 6f or stiff 5f: acts on hard and dead going. *P. Howling.*

NIKKRIS 3 ch.f. Song 132–Java Jive 63 (Hotfoot 126) [1989 5m6 5m6 5.1m6 5m5 32
5g4 1990 a5g5 a6g5 a5g5 a6g 5f6 5f5 5m6 5f a7g6] small, angular filly: turns fore-feet in: moderate mover: plating-class maiden at 2 yrs: below form in 1990, in sellers last 2 starts: should stay 6f: sold 720 gns Newmarket July Sales. *R. W. Stubbs.*

NIKLAS ANGEL 4 b.g. Petorius 117–The Woodbird (Tudor Melody 129) [1989 43
8.2s5 10v 8.3m* 7f 8h* 8.5g 8f 10f6 7.5m4 7g 8f2 a8g* a8g2 a7g2 a8g3 1990 8m 9g 6d
7f 8f 10.2m 8m* 8g6 a8g4 8d a7g] leggy, lightly-made gelding: poor mover: first worthwhile form as 4-y-o when winning selling handicap (bought in 4,400 gns) at Warwick in October: didn't look keen ninth outing: effective at 7f and 1m: suited by a sound surface: often blinkered, including at Warwick: has sweated. *C. N. Allen.*

NIKOLAYEVICH 3 b.c. Niniski (USA) 125–Rexana (Relko 136) [1989 NR 1990 —
11d 12f3 15.3m] strong, workmanlike colt: has scope: sixth reported foal: brother to very useful stayers Princess Sobieska and Sergeyevich and half-brother to 2 winners at 1½m + : dam French 1m and 1½m winner: soundly beaten in maidens in the spring, running in snatches last 2 starts: should be suited by test of stamina: sold to join D. Jermy 5,000 gns Newmarket Autumn Sales. *J. L. Dunlop.*

NIKOZETTE (IRE) 2 b.f. (Apr 11) Auction Ring (USA) 123–Tondbad (Furry —
Glen 121) [1990 5m6 7g] 6,800Y: big, good-topped filly: second foal: half-sister to 3-y-o Leotard (by Lyphard's Special): dam Irish 1¾m winner also successful over hurdles: bandaged, edgy and green, swerved stalls and always behind in maiden at Goodwood: unseated rider soon after start in minor event at Newbury 4 months later. *R. W. Armstrong.*

NIL BLEU 3 ch.c. Valiyar 129–Neomenie (Rheffic 129) [1989 9g 10d2 1990 12d2 108
10.5m2 15m* 12g* 15g 15.5v6] fourth foal: half-brother to French provincial 11f winner Nile Palace (by Crystal Palace) and 2 winning jumpers: dam 15f winner on flat and good jumper in France: won Prix Berteux at Chantilly and listed race at Toulouse in June: creditable 13 lengths sixth of 11 to Braashee and Indian Queen in Prix Royal-Oak at Longchamp: stays 15f: yet to race on firm ground, probably acts on any other. *J-P. Gallorini, France.*

NILU (IRE) 2 b.f. (Apr 7) Ballad Rock 122–El Pina (Be My Guest (USA) 126) 58
[1990 6g6 6g3 6g* 5f3 6f5 7m5 5f 6v5] IR 15,000Y: angular filly: third foal: half-sister to useful Irish 6f and 7f winner Mansion House and Irish 1¼m winner Beau Beauchamp (both by Thatching): dam unraced daughter of Princess Royal winner Aloft: plating-class performer: won maiden at Doncaster in June: probably better suited by 7f than shorter: seems unsuited by heavy ground: blinkered or visored final 3 starts: suitable mount for 7-lb claimer. *G. A. Huffer.*

NINEOFUS 4 b.g. Lochnager 132–Mountain Child 70 (Mountain Call 125) [1989 —
NR 1990 16m6] good-topped gelding: good walker and mover: first race on flat since 2 yrs, raced keenly in handicap at Newcastle in June: likely to prove best short of 2m: much improved and winner 5 times over hurdles in autumn. *M. H. Easterby.*

NINETY NINE (IRE) 2 b.c. (Mar 11) Pitskelly 122–Nighty Night (Sassafras 47 p
(FR) 135) [1990 7m 8g a7g5] IR 5,200Y, resold IR 7,500Y: sturdy colt: has a round action: half-brother to several winners, including middle-distance performer Celtic Bhoy (by Red Sunset): dam unraced half-sister to 1969 Criterium des Pouliches winner Vela: plating-class form, particularly catching eye on first 2 starts, in maidens: may well be one to keep an eye on in modest company. *R. W. Armstrong.*

NIPOTINA 4 b.f. Simply Great (FR) 122–Mothers Girl (Huntercombe 133) [1989 51
7d4 8f 8g 8.2m5 8f 7m6 10.4m4 11g6 a11g 1990 a11g2 a11g4 a14g4 a11g4 a8g6 12.5f2
12.5g3 12m6 a12g5 10.2f4 12.2m3 13.1h2 12f4 13.1h3 11m* a12g6 12.2m6] small filly:
moderate mover: favourite, got off mark in apprentice handicap at Redcar in August:
stays 13f: acts on hard and dead going: has run well when sweating and edgy: claimer ridden. *R. Hollinshead.*

NISHA 2 gr.f. (Feb 8) Nishapour (FR) 125–Eary Glas (Reform 132) [1990 7g 7g] 64
leggy, workmanlike filly: fourth reported foal: half-sister to 1986 2-y-o 6f winner Greensward (by Tower Walk): dam, a twin, unraced sister to high-class sprinter New Model and very useful sprinter Latest Model: quite modest form, not knocked

about, in minor event (awkward stalls) at Newbury and median auction at York in autumn. *W. J. Haggas.*

NISHAPOUR KID   2 b.c. (Apr 18) Nishapour (FR) 125–Crane Beach (High Top **35** 131) [1990 6m 7g] 6,200F, IR 2,000Y: leggy colt: third foal: half-brother to 1988 2-y-o 7f winner Cassibella (by Red Sunset): dam unraced: bit backward and slowly away in seller at Goodwood and claimer at Leicester. *B. Gubby.*

NISHCOR   2 gr.c. (Apr 26) Nishapour (FR) 125–Corsage (FR) (Nureyev (USA) **64** 131) [1990 6g4 7m 6f4 6v4 7d6 8.2s6] small, angular colt: second foal: dam French 1m winner: quite modest maiden: stays 1m: acts on any going. *Miss S. E. Hall.*

NISHKINA   2 b.g. (Mar 25) Nishapour (FR) 125–Varishkina 103 (Derring-Do 131) **53** [1990 6f3 6f2 7g 7f] leggy, lengthy gelding: third living foal: dam useful from 7f to 10.5f: shaped well in sellers first 2 starts: raced very keenly after: should prove better suited by 7f than 6f: blinkered final outing. *M. H. Easterby.*

NO BEATING HARTS   7 b.g. London Bells (CAN) 109–Movement 79 (Daring — Display (USA) 129) [1989 5g 5s2dis 5g* 5m 6f2 5f3 6f 5g5 5g5 6g3 5.6g 5g6 5d 1990 5f 5g 6f 6g 5m4 5f a5g] rangy, good-bodied gelding: carries plenty of condition: moderate mover: modest handicapper as 6-y-o, well below his best in 1990: ideally suited by 5f and an easy surface: best form without blinkers or visor: has got on toes and often sweats: none too keen and best with waiting tactics. *W. G. Turner.*

NOBLE BRAVE   3 b.g. Indian King (USA) 128–Windy Lady (Whistling Wind — 123) [1989 6f 1990 9m 10m] rather leggy, long-backed gelding: no form, in seller final start. *R. Hannon.*

NOBLE DESTINY   2 b.f. (Mar 1) Dancing Brave (USA) 140–Tender Loving **89** p Care 105 (Final Straw 127) [1990 7m*] lengthy, angular filly: has a long stride: first foal: dam 2-y-o 7f winner, is half-sister to useful 2-y-o's Satinette and Silk Pyjamas: well-backed favourite but green, won 18-runner maiden at Leicester in October by 1½ lengths from Super Staff, leading 2f out and running on strongly: will stay 1m: sure to improve, and win more races. *M. R. Stoute.*

NOBLE ENDEAVOUR   3 b.c. Try My Best (USA) 130–Lady Probus 70§ **86** (Shantung 132) [1989 NR 1990 8m4 8m5 8.2m6 10m* 10.2g5 12d* 13.3g2] IR 19,000Y: rangy colt: fifth foal: half-brother to Irish 1m and 8.5f winner Ronald Ivor (by Bold Lad (IRE)): dam showed ability at 2 yrs but became most disappointing: in good form in handicaps, winning at Yarmouth (edgy) in August and Goodwood in October: should stay 1¾m: acts on good to firm ground and dead: sweating and went freely down when running poorly third start: sold 35,000 gns Newmarket Autumn Sales. *A. C. Stewart.*

NOBLE FELLOW   3 b.c. The Noble Player (USA) 126–Fravelot (Javelot 124) **54** [1989 NR 1990 8.2m 8f2 7g4 8g 8m 10g2 12f* 16m 12s5 13.8d] IR 4,100F, IR 6,200Y: close-coupled, useful-looking colt: has a round action: half-brother to The Very Thing (by Jupiter Pluvius), a fair middle-distance winner and very useful hurdler, and 2 other winners: dam won over 1½m: plating-class handicapper: 6/5 on and ridden by 7-lb claimer, won 4-runner event at Pontefract in July: should stay further than 1½m: acts on any going: blinkered on fifth start: claimed out of B. Hanbury's stable £6,850 on sixth: sold 750 gns Ascot December Sales. *Mrs J. R. Ramsden.*

NOBLE FLUTTER (IRE)   2 ch.f. (Mar 29) The Noble Player (USA) 126–Night **67** of Wind 101 (Tumble Wind (USA)) [1990 5m2 6m2 6m3 6m4 6g2 5d2] rather unfurnished filly: has a quick action: second foal: half-sister to 1988 2-y-o 5f winner Howling Gael (by Peterhof): dam won Queen Mary: quite modest maiden: stays 6f: acts on good to firm ground and dead: consistent. *B. W. Hills.*

NOBLE LUSTRE (USA)   4 b.f. Lyphard's Wish (FR) 122–Crowned (Royal And **61** Regal (USA)) [1989 8f 7m3 8g2 7m3 10m 1990 10.6f 8g6 6m* 6m3 6m 6m6 6m 6m 6m] sturdy filly: quite modest handicapper on her day: won at Kempton in May despite wandering: effective at 6f and stays 1m: acts on good to firm going: sweated badly sixth start: usually taken last and quietly to post: inconsistent. *C. F. Wall.*

NOBLE MATCH   3 ch.f. The Noble Player (USA) 126–Marylove (Kalydon 122) **93** [1989 5d* 5m* 5f3 5m5 1990 5d* 5m6 5m6 5m5 5s5 5g5 5s] leggy filly: fairly useful sprinter: won handicap at Newbury in April: off course 5 months after third start, easily best subsequent effort when 2¼ lengths fifth of 13 to Blyton Lad in listed race at Newmarket on return: seems unsuited by very soft ground: visored final start. *I. A. Balding.*

NOBLE PARTNER   3 b.c. Blushing Scribe (USA) 107–Super Fortune (USA) **61** (Super Concorde (USA) 128) [1989 7g 8g 1990 a12g3 a12g 12m] angular, useful-looking colt: form in maidens only when third of 11 at Southwell: tailed off in handicaps: probably stays 1½m. *D. J. G. Murray-Smith.*

NOBLE PATRIARCH 3 b.c. Alzao (USA) 117–Pampala (Bold Lad (IRE) 133) **113**
[1989 7g 7m⁴ 8g* 8g* 8m* 1990 8g⁶ 8g⁴ 8m 8.5g 10m⁴ 10d⁴ 9g 10s⁰] stocky, quite
attractive colt: very useful performer: made all to beat Relief Pitcher ½ length in
listed race at Goodwood in October: easily better effort subsequently when good
sixth to Legal Case in Premio Roma: suited by 1¼m: goes well on a soft surface: has
been bandaged near-fore: goes well with forcing tactics. *J. L. Dunlop.*

NOBLE SAVAGE 4 ch.c. Caerleon (USA) 132–Indian Maid 117 (Aztec 128) **109** d
[1989 10f³ 16f⁶ 15g³ 14f³ 14m³ 16m* 19g² 15.5g 1990 14m* 14g⁵ 16m⁵ 20d 14m⁵]
strong, lengthy colt: easy mover: appeared to put up much improved performance
when winning strongly-run £7,400 handicap under 9-10 at Newmarket in April,
making all and soon clear: failed by long way to reproduce that effort, easy to back
and found little once headed final outing: probably best with forcing tactics at around
1¾m: acts well on top-of-the-ground: sweated second start: acted as pacemaker on
fourth. *G. Harwood.*

NOBLE SOCIETY 2 b.c. (Apr 10) Law Society (USA) 130–Be Noble (Vaguely **74** p
Noble 140) [1990 8g⁵ 8d²] 5,000Y: lengthy, angular colt: half-brother to several
winners here and abroad: dam pulled up only start, is out of high-class 1958 2-y-o Be
Careful: bit backward, 3 lengths second of 12, staying on well, to Baatish in maiden
at Edinburgh in October: will be suited by 1¼m: likely to improve again. *E. Weymes.*

NOBLE SON 4 b.g. Thatching 131–Eden Quay (King's Bench 132) [1989 10m⁴ **39**
8.2f 8f 1990 a11g a7g⁴ a8g 7m 9s 12.5f⁴ 12.5f 11m³ 15g⁴ 15m⁴ 12g 15m⁴ 11m 11m*
12.2f⁵ 11v⁵ a12g a12g] workmanlike gelding: inconsistent plater: ridden by 7-lb
claimer, won poor non-selling handicap at Edinburgh in September: faced stiff tasks
last 3 outings: stays 15f, at least in slowly-run race: acts on firm going: visored first 5
starts. *M. P. Naughton.*

NOBLE SOUL 3 ch.f. Sayf El Arab (USA) 127–Fleet Noble (USA) (Vaguely **67**
Noble 140) [1989 a7g⁵ 1990 a8g* a7g²] quite modest form: 15/8 on, easy winner of
3-runner maiden at Lingfield: good second of 4 in handicap there later in January:
stays 1m. *D. R. Laing.*

NO CANDLES TONIGHT 2 b.f. (Apr 5) Star Appeal 133–Kochia 54 (Fire- **74** p
streak 125) [1990 8d³] small, workmanlike filly: fourth foal: half-sister to very useful
3-y-o Starstreak (by Comedy Star), successful from 6f (at 2 yrs) to 1¼m: dam 1m
seller winner: length third of 13, leading 3f out then green and no extra final furlong,
to Straldi in maiden at Leicester in October: will stay 1¼m: will improve, and win a
race. *M. Johnston.*

NO COMEBACKS 2 b.f. (Feb 28) Last Tycoon 131–Dead End (Bold Lad (IRE) **70** p
133) [1990 6m²] fifth reported foal: dam unraced half-sister to Irish 1000 Guineas
winner Katies and Extel Handicap winner Millfontaine: second of 6, leading 2f out
and headed near line, to Possessive Dancer in maiden at Newmarket in November:
should improve. *R. J. R. Williams.*

NOCTURNAL REVERIE (USA) 3 b.f. Assert 134–Grey Dream 101 (Auction **46**
Ring (USA) 123) [1989 NR 1990 12g 14m⁴ 9m 12.5m⁴ 12d a14g²] leggy filly: moderate
mover: first foal: dam useful 5f and 6f winner in Ireland at 2 yrs later stakes placed in
USA: plater: blinkered, second in claimer at Southwell in November: better at 1¾m
than shorter. *J. Pearce.*

NO DECISION 3 br.g. King of Spain 121–Really Fine VII (pedigree unknown) **67**
[1989 NR 1990 7g 6s⁴ 6m 6g 6m⁶ a6g³ a7g a8g* a8g²] heavy-topped gelding with
scope: has rather round action: first foal: dam never ran: quite modest performer:
won claimer at Southwell in August: better at 1m than shorter: often slowly away.
M. W. Easterby.

NODOLYA 3 b.f. Niniski (USA) 125–Press Corps 93 (Realm 129) [1989 6f⁵ 1990 **70**
7g 6g a8g 10m³ 10g* 10.5g² 10g] leggy, lengthy filly: modest performer: favourite,
comfortable winner of claimer at Salisbury in October: creditable second in selling
handicap at York, tending to hang but easily better effort after: will be suited by
further: acts on good to firm ground: joined J. Ffitch-Heyes. *B. Hanbury.*

NODS GAME 2 b. or br.g. (Mar 31) Mummy's Game 120–Nadron 59 (Thatching **46**
131) [1990 6m 6m⁵ 7g] workmanlike gelding: second foal: dam, seemed to stay 7f, is
out of sister to high-class miler Hilal: poor form: sweating, on toes and mulish stalls,
pulled hard and looked none too keen under pressure in seller final start: seems to
stay 7f: bandaged near-hind on debut: temperament under suspicion. *M. J. Camacho.*

NOELREAC JULIAN 2 b.c. (Apr 11) Caerleon (USA) 132–Interviewme **78** p
(USA) (Olden Times) [1990 6g²] 14,000Y: lengthy, quite good-quartered colt:
moderate walker: brother to fairly useful Irish 7f and 1m winner Caerforme, closely
related to modest winner in France by Gorytus and half-brother to 4 other winners:

dam 2-y-o 6f winner in USA, is half-sister to dam of high-class miler Jaazeiro: 1½ lengths second of 5f, disputing lead over 5f, to Chimayo in maiden at Newmarket in October: moved short to post: gave trouble at stalls and withdrawn at Doncaster following month: should improve, and win a race: retained by trainer 30,000 gns Newmarket Autumn Sales. *C. E. Brittain.*

NO FINESSE 2 b.f. (Mar 12) Daring March 116–Hound Song 84 (Jukebox 120) [1990 5g 6m 5f 6d] 5,200Y: stocky filly: moderate mover: fifth foal: dam sprinter: little worthwhile form, including in seller: sold 1,100 gns Newmarket Autumn Sales. *R. Hannon.* —

NO GUTS NO GLORY 3 b.g. Mansingh (USA) 120–Lyn Affair 62 (Royal Palace 131) [1989 NR 1990 10s] big, lengthy gelding: third reported foal: dam stayed 1½m: 50/1 and bandaged off-hind, tailed off in minor event at Nottingham in October: gave trouble at stalls: has joined R. Holder. *P. Leach.* —

NO HARD FEELINGS (IRE) 2 b. or br.f. (Feb 26) Alzao (USA) 117–Coshlea 63 (Red Alert 127) [1990 5m* 5m² 6m² 6m³ 6g* 6m³ 6d⁵ 7f* 7g⁴ 8v* 8d³] 16,500Y: strong, sturdy filly: carries condition: has a roundish action: third foal: half-sister to fair 5f (at 2 yrs) to 13f winner Dale Park (by Kampala) and fair 1987 2-y-o 6f winner Glamgram's Best (by Taufan): dam placed from 11f to 15f: fair performer: successful in minor events at Newcastle in March and Carlisle in June, a claimer at Carlisle in September and nursery at Ayr in October: suited by 1m: best form on an easy surface: game, genuine and consistent. *N. Tinkler.* **86**

NO MISTRESS 2 ch.f. (Mar 29) Master Willie 129–Regent Miss (CAN) (Vice Regent (CAN)) [1990 6g⁴ 6m⁴ 7m⁶] leggy filly, rather unfurnished: fourth foal (all by Master Willie): sister to very smart Deputy Governor, best at up to 1¼m here later successful in USA: dam and great-grandam won Canadian Oaks: modest form when fourth in maidens at Newbury and Nottingham: broke a leg final start: dead. *H. Candy.* **74**

NO MORE THE FOOL 4 ch.g. Jester 119–Prima Bella 76 (High Hat 131) [1989 10.6s⁵ 10.4f 12g 12f* 12m* 11m* 12d 12.2g 12.2d 1990 12f⁶ 12.5m⁵ 10.4d⁶ a12g* a12g* 11m* a11g* a12g⁵ a14g] tall, leggy, lengthy gelding: has a long stride: modest handicapper: made all or most when winning 3 times at Southwell and once at Redcar (odds on in apprentice race) in summer: ran as though something amiss eighth outing, off course over 5 months after: stays 1½m: acts on firm going: blinkered or visored last 7 outings: good mount for claimer. *J. Berry.* **77**

NON CONSTAT (USA) 6 b.g. Vaguely Noble 140–Jamila (Sir Gaylord) [1989 a16g 1990 a12g⁴ a14g 12g a12g³ 13.6g⁴ 14.8m⁴ a12g³ a8g⁵] tall, attractive gelding: easily best efforts in handicaps at 6 yrs on all-weather at Southwell on first and fourth outings: stays 2m: acts on hard and dead going: has worn blinkers, visor and crossed noseband: has won for amateur: trained until after sixth outing by R. Thompson: has found nothing off bridle: not one to rely on. *R. J. Muddle.* **71 §**

NONE GO BY 2 br.f. (Mar 2) Daring March 116–River Aire 82 (Klairon 131) [1990 7g] sturdy filly: half-sister to 3 winners, including 6f winner Mizuwari (by Blazing Saddles) and Irish middle-distance stayer Boggy Peak (by Shirley Heights): dam placed over 7f and 1m: backward, always behind in minor event at Newbury in September: moved moderately down. *G. B. Balding.* —

NOORA PARK (IRE) 2 ch.f. (May 6) Ahonoora 122–Miss Audimar (USA) (Mr Leader (USA)) [1990 5g³ 6g* 5m* 6m⁴] third reported foal: half-sister to 3-y-o 1m and 1¼m winner Express Account (by Carr de Naskra): dam graded stakes-placed winner at up to 11f in USA: successful in 6-runner maiden at Tipperary and 5-runner minor event at Phoenix Park: very good fourth of 13 to Mac's Imp in Heinz '57' Phoenix Stakes: better suited by 6f than 5f: dead. *J. S. Bolger, Ireland.* **101**

NO QUARTER GIVEN 5 b.g. Don 128–Maggie Mine 85 (Native Prince) [1989 6s⁶ 6d* 6g⁴ 6m* 5d 6g³ 5g³ 6g² 6s⁴ 5d 5s* 1990 6s⁶ 5g⁵ 7f³ 7.6m 6m³ 6g³ 6d³ 5g³ 6g³ 5g* 6f² 5m* 5m 5d⁴ 5d⁴ 5g² 5s] rangy, well-made gelding: carries plenty of condition: fair handicapper: successful at Leicester (making all) in July and Nottingham (on toes) following month: probably best at sprint distances: acts on any going: good mount for apprentice: has been taken down early: consistent: credit to his trainer. *P. S. Felgate.* **79**

NO QUESTIONS 2 gr.f. (Mar 20) Another Realm 118–Our Mother 95 (Bold Lad (IRE) 133) [1990 5f 6m 6f⁴ a6g³ 6g* 6m 7f] 3,100Y: rather sparely-made filly: good walker: has a quick action: half-sister to 3 winners here and abroad, including 6f and 7f winner Bold Habit (by Homing): dam ran only at 2 yrs, winning at 5f: made most in seller (bought in 4,500 gns) at Yarmouth in July, easily best effort: stays 6f: trained by J. Berry first 4 outings: tends to hang. *J. L. Harris.* **52**

NORABLASSIE 3 b.f. Norwick (USA) 120–Aberdeen Lassie 102 (Aberdeen — 109) [1989 7m 5f 8g 1990 8m 8m 7f⁶ 8f 10.8m 10m⁶ 12.5m] leggy filly: moderate mover: poor maiden: probably stays 1m: sweating final start: retained by trainer 900 gns Ascot February Sales: sold 800 gns Doncaster October Sales. *H. J. Collingridge.*

NORDIC BRAVE 4 b.c. Indian King (USA) 128–Belle Viking (FR) (Riverman **69** (USA) 131) [1989 9v⁴ 6d* 7s⁵ 7g⁶ 6g⁵ 1990 6s 6m* 6f³ 6m 5m 6g 6m⁴ 7m² 7g 7d 6d 7g] leggy, lightly-made, angular colt: moderate mover: 50/1 and sweating, showed improved form when winning £11,700 handicap at York in May: best efforts after when in frame in handicaps at same course on consecutive days: effective at 6f to 7f: best efforts on top-of-the-ground: has won for apprentice: goes well with forcing tactics: inconsistent. *M. Brittain.*

NORFOLK GEM 3 b.f. Blakeney 126–Pencuik Jewel (Petingo 135) [1989 NR **53** 1990 a12g⁴ 12m⁴] fifth living foal: half-sister to 4 winners, including fairly useful 7.6f and 1¼m winner Risk All (by Run The Gantlet) and 1¼m winner Celtic Ring (by Welsh Pageant): dam lightly-raced half-sister to Ragstone, Castle Keep and dam of Moon Madness and Sheriff's Star: staying-on fourth of 11 in maiden at Southwell in July: well beaten in Goodwood claimer 2 months later: dead. *Lady Herries.*

NORFOLKIEV (FR) 4 b.c. In Fijar (USA) 121–Touraille (FR) (Jim French **79** (USA)) [1989 6g a6g 1990 6m⁶ 6h² 7g* 6g 7m⁶ 6m 6m² 6m² 6g* 6s] good-bodied colt: moderate mover: fair handicapper: won at Catterick in June and Salisbury (comfortably better effort) in October: probably better suited by 6f than 7f: acts on hard going: used to have tongue tied down. *M. Moubarak.*

NORFOLK LADY 2 br.f. (Apr 29) Norwick (USA) 120–Belle (DEN) (Comedy — Star (USA) 121) [1990 8g 6d] 3,000Y: sixth foal: sister to 1989 Irish 2-y-o 1m winner Relaxing Lady and half-sister to fairly useful 6f and 1m winner Touch of Grey (by Blakeney) and a winner in Italy: dam won 3 times in Scandinavia: soundly beaten in autumn maidens at Yarmouth and Doncaster. *D. T. Thom.*

NORFOLK LASS 3 b.f. (May 7) Blakeney 126–Balgreggan (Hallez (FR) 131) — [1990 7g] angular, plain filly: half-sister to several winners, including useful 6f to 1m winner Sailor's Song (by Song) and sprinters Manton Dan (by Tower Walk) and Street Market (by Porto Bello): dam twice-raced half-sister to smart stayer Golden Love: green, tailed off in maiden at Newmarket in November: showed a round action. *M. A. Jarvis.*

NORMAN INVADER 6 b.g. Nicholas Bill 125–Floricelle 92 (Derring-Do 131) — [1989 NR 1990 11.7m 11.7g] leggy, angular gelding: has a round action: fair winner as 4-y-o: backward, well beaten in Windsor handicaps in summer: withdrawn lame intended reappearance: stays 1½m: acts on firm going. *J. S. King.*

NORMEAD LASS 2 b.f. (May 5) Norwick (USA) 120–Meads Lass (Saritamer — (USA) 130) [1990 6g] second reported foal: dam never ran: prominent halfway in maiden at Folkestone in October: showed a moderate action. *R. Akehurst.*

NORMHURST 4 ch.g. Lucky Wednesday 124–Bronze Princess 72 (Hul A Hul — 124) [1989 10d 10.6s 10.6m 12.3m 9g⁵ 11s* 12s 1990 16.2d] lengthy gelding: poor mover: quite modest winner of handicap as 3-y-o: ran as though something amiss in June: stays 11f: acts on soft going: visored once at 3 yrs: occasionally sweats: sold 1,250 gns Doncaster November Sales. *C. Tinkler.*

NORQUAY (USA) 5 ch.g. Arctic Tern (USA) 126–Godetia (USA) 119 (Sir Ivor **70** 135) [1989 10.2g⁶ 8g⁵ 9f 9.2f⁶ 8m 8 5g* 8m⁵ 7f⁵ 10.6m⁴ 8.2d* 1990 a8g⁴ 8.2s² 8f 8f* 8.2g³ 8g² 8.2s³ 8.2g⁵ 8.5f² 8f 8v⁶ 8d a8g a11g] close-coupled, workmanlike gelding: moderate mover: modest handicapper: won at Carlisle in May: ran moderately on all-weather last 2 outings: stays 1¼m: acts on any going: visored once at 4 yrs: has won for amateur: sometimes wears bandages behind: usually held up: retained 2,000 gns Newmarket Autumn Sales. *N. Tinkler.*

NORSTOCK 3 b.f. Norwick (USA) 120–Millingdale 65 (Tumble Wind (USA)) — [1989 6g 7f 8f 1990 7m a8g³ 8m⁵ 8.2m 10g 8g a10g⁴] workmanlike filly: has a round action: poor maiden: probably stays 1¼m. *J. White.*

NORTHANTS 4 b.g. Northern Baby (CAN) 127–Astania (GER) (Arratos (FR)) **80 d** [1989 12d* 14f⁵ 10.2f* 12m* 12f 12.5f³ 11d² 10f 10g² 12g* 13.3d³ 12d 1990 10.4d⁵ 12.3d⁵ 16.2m 10.6s⁵ 12.2g³ 10f 11f 12.3g 10.6g 12s⁴ 16s³] sturdy, medium-sized gelding: capable of fair form, winner 4 times as 3-y-o, but is temperamentally unsatisfactory: stays 2m: acts on any going: often blinkered, but not last 6 outings: trained until then by Mrs L. Piggott: has been reluctant to race and usually gets well behind: winning hurdler in October. *W. Storey.*

EBF Trusthouse Forte Sapphire Stakes, Phoenix Park—
Northern Goddess (No. 5) wins a useful sprint with a fine burst of speed;
Takwim (left) rallies gamely to deprive Mr Brooks of second spot

NORTH BASE 3 b.c. Hard Fought 125–Bases Loaded (USA) (Northern Dancer) **52**
[1989 NR 1990 8.2g 6m 8f² 6g 9f² 8f⁵ 7.5g³ 7d 8m 8v] 2,600F: sturdy colt: half-brother to smart middle-distance 4-y-o Relief Pitcher (by Welsh Term) and 2 other winners, including 1¼m winner The Dice Man (by Key To The Mint): dam won over 7f in USA: twice successful in sprint races in Belgium in 1989: plating-class form here: stays 9f: acts on firm going: visored fourth and final starts: inconsistent: sold 1,600 gns Doncaster October Sales. *J. S. Wilson.*

NORTH COL 3 b.c. Head For Heights 125–Night Encounter (Right Tack 131) **116**
[1989 9g* 1990 10d² 12g³ 12d4 12g* 12.5g 15g*] fifth foal: half-brother to modest 1½m winner Tyro Prince (by Prince Tenderfoot) and a winner in Austria: dam, sister to Take A Reef, won at up to 12.5f in France: won newcomers event at Evry in October at 2 yrs, Grand Prix de Vichy (by 3 lengths from Per Quod) in August and Ciga Prix de Lutece (23/1, by ½ length from Amour Royal) at Longchamp in October: stays 15f well: blinkered last 3 starts. *J. E. Pease, France.*

NORTH COUNTRY 3 b.c. Nordico (USA)–Loren (Crocket 130) [1989 6g⁵ 6g² **82**
1990 5f² 6f* 7m⁶ 6m³ 7.6g* 6m] neat, good-quartered colt: has a rather round action: fair performer: made all in maiden (4/1 on) at Folkestone and handicap at Chester: ran badly after slow start for 7-lb claimer in July handicap final outing: stays 7.6f: acts on firm going. *H. R. A. Cecil.*

NORTHENER 3 ch.g. Reasonable (FR) 119–Northampton (Northfields (USA)) **—**
[1989 7.5f 6m 7f 1990 11s] small, angular, plain gelding: poor plater: visored at 2 yrs. *C. R. Beever.*

NORTHERN CONQUEROR (IRE) 2 ch.c. (Apr 17) Mazaad 106–Gaylom **80**
(Lord Gayle (USA) 124) [1990 5m³ 5m² 5m³ a5g* 6g² 5m4 6m⁵ 6f⁵ 7g² 7g² 8m⁵ 9g4 7m] 6,600F, 8,800Y: lightly-made colt: easy mover: half-brother to 7f and 1m winner Cumute (by Main Reef), also successful in Norsk 2000 Guineas: dam won over 5f at 4 yrs in Ireland: bought out of J. Berry's stable 8,000 gns after making all in seller at Southwell in June: best form on good ground: visored final start: sometimes edgy: suitable mount for 7-lb claimer: sold 9,500 gns Newmarket Autumn Sales. *C. N. Allen.*

NORTHERN CREST 4 ch.g. Anfield 117–Contadina (Memling) [1989 8d 11.7m **53**
14g⁵ 16f³ 16m³ 14d 1990 a10g² 12m a12g⁶] tall, angular gelding: easy mover: quite modest maiden: off course over 8 months after reappearance: stays 2m: blinkered once at 3 yrs: has sweated: difficult ride. *C. L. Popham.*

NORTHERN FLYER 2 ch.c. (Mar 21) Bairn (USA) 126–Fly The World (USA) **65**
74 (Empery (USA) 128) [1990 6m 6g 7m] 8,600Y: lengthy, rather sparely-made colt: second foal: dam 1m winner: best effort in maidens seventh of 13 at Warwick final start: will stay 1m. *P. T. Walwyn.*

NORTHERN GALLERY (IRE) 2 ch.c. (Feb 12) Tate Gallery (USA) **—**
117–Cliona (FR) (Ballymore 123) [1990 6m a8g] IR 2,700Y: leggy, good-topped individual: sixth foal: half-brother to a middle-distance winner in France by Bold

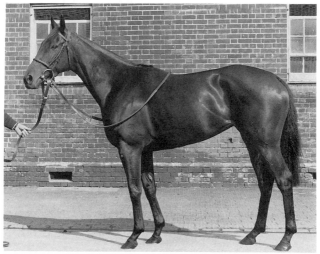

Nigel Harris' "Northern Goddess"

Lad (IRE): dam useful French 1¼m winner, is out of very useful sister to Floribunda: soundly beaten in maidens at Folkestone (blinkered) and Southwell (eyeshield). *Mrs L. Piggott.*

NORTHERN GODDESS 3 b.f. Night Shift (USA)–Hearten (Hittite Glory 125) **111**
[1989 5d⁵ 5f* 5m² 5.8f³ 1990 6g 5.8f* 6g⁶ 6m² 5d 5g* 6m* 6g* 6m²] compact, attractive filly: very useful performer: won handicaps at Bath in May and Beverley (sweating) in July, rallying well, then held up and quickened in good style to win listed race (very keen in preliminaries) and Group 3 contest at Phoenix Park in August: swished tail when 10 lengths second to Ron's Victory in Krug Diadem Stakes at Ascot final start: stays 6f: acts on firm going, possibly unsuited by dead: tends to get on toes: swerved left fourth start: progressive. *I. A. Balding.*

NORTHERN HABIT 4 ch.g. Salmon Leap (USA) 131–Manx Millenium 66 **84**
(Habitat 134) [1989 7m² 8f² 1990 6f 8m³ 7f³ 7.5f³ 8m² 7.6g⁴ 8g 8m 8g²] leggy, quite good-topped gelding: fair maiden: stays 1m: has raced only on sound surface: wore net muzzle last 5 outings. *I. A. Balding.*

NORTHERN HAL 3 b.c. Sadler's Wells (USA) 132–Northern Script (USA) 95 **101**
(Arts And Letters) [1989 6g³ 1990 8.2m* 11g⁴ 10.1m² 12m⁵ 10m* 8g² 8m] good-topped, lengthy colt: has a quick action: useful performer: won Nottingham minor events in April and September, rallying very well first occasion then idling having led over 2f out on second: effective at 1m to 1¼m: acts on good to firm ground: may well prove best held up. *P. T. Walwyn.*

NORTHERN HOST (IRE) 2 br.c. (Feb 12) Petorius 117–Special Guest 67 (Be **62**
My Guest (USA) 126) [1990 5f 5m* 5m⁵ 5m⁴ 5f⁴ 6m² 5m 5.3h² 5f⁴ 5m 5g⁵] 7,400Y: sturdy colt: moderate walker: first foal: dam 2-y-o 7f winner stayed 9f: quite modest performer: won early-season minor event at Catterick: creditable fifth in selling nursery final start: stays 6f: has worn blinkers, visor (ran moderately) and a hood: sold 4,000 gns Newmarket Autumn Sales. *R. W. Stubbs.*

NORTHERN LACE 3 gr.c. Northern Tempest (USA) 120–Dragon Lace (Drag- **38**
onara Palace (USA) 115) [1989 5f 6m 6g a6g 1990 a6g³ 6m⁶ 5s³ 6v 6g³] small, lightly-

made colt: poor mover: poor maiden: should stay beyond 6f: acts on soft ground: sold 600 gns Doncaster June Sales. *M. Brittain.*

NORTHERN NATION 2 b.c. (Mar 2) Nomination 125–Ballagarrow Girl 66 **67** (North Stoke 130) [1990 5f 5m⁵ 5f⁵ 5m⁵ 5m* 5g² 5m⁵ 5g⁶ 5v] 7,200Y: workmanlike, good-quartered colt: has scope: fourth foal: half-brother to temperamental 1988 2-y-o Sky Hill (by Windjammer): dam suited by 1¼m, is half-sister to smart 6f and 7f winner The Quiet Bidder: quite modest performer: won maiden at Redcar in July: ran well in nurseries at Haydock (despite veering badly left) and Redcar (sweating and edgy) next 2 starts: likely to prove best at 5f: acts on good to firm going, and seems unsuited by heavy: visored fourth outing: carries head high: looks a difficult ride: sold 6,600 gns Doncaster November Sales. *E. J. Alston.*

NORTHERN OPTIMIST 2 b.f. (Apr 22) Northern Tempest (USA) 120–On A **70** Bit 66 (Mummy's Pet 125) [1990 5g³ 6g⁵ 6f* 7m 7g] close-coupled, angular filly: has rather round action: half-sister to several winners, including 3-y-o Wallingfen Lane (by Lochnager), successful at 1m and 8.5f, and fair 9f and 1¼m winner White Sapphire (by Sparkler): dam placed at up to 9f: modest performer: won maiden at Carlisle in September: better subsequent effort in nurseries at Redcar (slowly away, never able to challenge) next start: should stay 1m. *J. G. FitzGerald.*

NORTHERN PARK (USA) 2 b.c. (Feb 11) Northern Dancer (CAN)–Mrs **92 p** Penny (USA) 127 (Great Nephew 126) [1990 8g*] $2,800,000Y: fourth foal: closely related to fair 1988 2-y-o 6f winner Mrs Jenney (by The Minstrel), later successful in USA, modest maiden Pennysylvania (by Northjet) and half-brother to a poor maiden: dam won Cheveley Park, Prix de Diane and Prix Vermeille: won new-comers race at Longchamp in September by a short head: will stay 1¼m. *A. Fabre, France.*

NORTHERN PET 3 b.f. Petorius 117–Northern Chance 78 (Northfields (USA)) **103** [1989 6m² 8g² 7d³ 7g 8s* 1990 9g⁵ 8g³ 10m³ 10d* 8m³ 11g* 10g 10f⁶ 19m³ 10m³ 12g⁶ 14g 10d⁶ 12d⁵] IR 15,500Y: fifth foal: half-sister to 2 winners, notably fair 1987 2-y-o 5f winner Toshair Flyer (by Ballad Rock): dam 1m winner: useful performer, successful in £5,700 contest at Gowran Park in May and listed race at Phoenix Park in June: well beaten in Irish St Leger and Blandford Stakes at the Curragh twelfth and final starts: stays 11f: acts on any going. *Kevin Prendergast, Ireland.*

NORTHERN PRINTER 5 ch.g. Baptism 119–Stradey Lynn 57 (Derrylin 115) **84** [1989 8g 7s 8m³ 7f⁵ 8.2m³ 8.2g 7m³ 8f²ᵈⁱˢ 7f⁶ 8.2d 7.6m⁵ 7g 8g² 9g 10.6s⁶ 7m 8d 1990 a8g⁴ 8f 7f² 8h 8g 6f² 6m⁵ 7.5f* 8.2f⁵ a7g 7.6g] strong, sturdy gelding: poor mover: fair handicapper: generally runs with credit, but seldom wins and was gaining only success since final start in 1988 at Beverley in July: stays 1m: possibly not at his best on soft going, acts on any other: usually claimer ridden: has carried head high, and probably needs holding up as long as possible. *M. J. O'Neill.*

NORTHERN RAIN 4 ch.g. Ballacashtal (CAN)–Summer Rain (Palestine 133) **—** [1989 5s 7g a8g a8g³ 1990 a7g a8g a8g⁶] compact gelding: successful early on as 2-y-o: easily best effort in last 2 seasons when third in Lingfield claimer: appears to stay 1m: visored on reappearance: sold 1,600 gns Ascot May Sales. *C. N. Allen.*

NORTHERN RAINBOW 2 b.c. (Feb 25) Rainbow Quest (USA) 134–Safe **78 p** House 81§ (Lyphard (USA) 132) [1990 6m² 8d³] 38,000Y: lengthy colt: fifth foal: half-brother to 3-y-o Shelter (by Teenoso) and 2 winners, including 1986 2-y-o 6f winner Safety Pin (by Grundy): dam temperamental, won at 10.8f: modest form in maidens won by Bold Nephew at Newbury in May and Peking Opera at Leicester (not knocked about) over 5 months later: will be suited by 1¼m +: likely to do better. *P. F. I. Cole.*

NORTHERN RISING 2 ch.c. (Mar 23) Bairn (USA) 126–Lucky Petina 88 **—** (Mummy's Pet 125) [1990 6m⁶ 6s⁴] 21,000Y: leggy, close-coupled colt: fifth reported foal: half-brother to 5f winner Hi-Tech Leader (by Swing Easy): dam sprinting half-sister to Manor Farm Boy: beaten around 10 lengths in maidens at Hamilton. *A. N. Lee.*

NORTHERN ROCKET 3 b.g. Northern Tempest (USA) 120–Scotch Rocket **56** 60 (Roan Rocket 128) [1989 5d 5s 6m 6g 8.5f 6g⁵ a5g⁵ a6g* a7g⁴ 1990 a7g 7.5d 6m² 6g 5g⁶ 6m⁵ 7m⁶ a6g⁶ a6g⁵ a6g 6d a6g] leggy gelding: quite modest performer: best efforts at Southwell: suited by 6f: visored fourth and fifth outings: effective with or without blinkers: has run creditably for 7-lb claimer and when sweating: races freely. *J. P. Leigh.*

NORTHERN RULER 8 br.g. Rolfe (USA) 77–Sanandrea (Upper Case (USA)) **—** [1989 12s 1990 a14g⁶] neat gelding: retains little ability: possibly doesn't stay extreme distances: acts on any going: blinkered twice. *R. Thompson.*

NORTHERN SPARK 2 b.c. (May 26) Trojan Fen 118–Heavenly Spark (Habitat 65 134) [1990 5g* 6m⁴ 6g 6d 8v] 8,000Y: leggy colt: brother to modest maiden Trojan Heart and half-brother to 4 minor winners in France and USA: dam ran once: won maiden at Edinburgh in June: hampered final outing: should be suited by further than 6f. *C. W. Thornton.*

NORTHERN STREET 3 ch.g. Glenstal (USA) 118–Moaning Low 85 (Burglar 44 128) [1989 5m 6g⁴ 6d 1990 6m⁴ 8g] smallish, quite attractive gelding: plating-class maiden: should stay further than 6f. *J. P. Hudson.*

NORTHERN VILLAGE 3 ch.g. Norwick (USA) 120–Merokette 83 (Blast 125) — [1989 8.2g 1990 7g 8m 9m⁶ 10f 8.5g 10g] workmanlike gelding: moderate mover: no worthwhile form, including in handicaps: should stay 1¼m. *S. Dow.*

NORTHGATE GIRL (IRE) 2 ch.f. (Feb 5) Gorytus (USA) 132–Red Line 57 Fever 94 (Bay Express 132) [1990 5f 5m⁴ 5f³ 5m³ 5m² 5d⁴ 5g 5d⁶ a5g] IR 7,800Y: neat, good-quartered, sprint type: third foal: half-sister to 3-y-o Minizen Leader (by Salmon Leap): dam 2-y-o 5f winner: plating-class maiden: below best in selling nursery at Wolverhampton on seventh outing: acts on top-of-the-ground. *M. Brittain.*

NORTHGATE KING 3 b.c. Fairy King (USA)–Dollyful (Track Spare 125) 60 [1989 5v 5d⁵ 5g 5m² 1990 7.5g 7.5d* 8g⁶ a8g 9g² 8.2g² 8.2m⁴ 11m² 10g⁴ 10m 10.2m⁶ 9g] neat colt: bad mover: quite modest handicapper: 25/1-winner at Beverley in June: mostly ran well afterwards, but well below form in apprentice event at Kempton final start: stays 11f: acts on good to firm ground and dead. *M. Brittain.*

NORTH OF WATFORD 5 ch.h. Jasmine Star 113–Wallie Girl (Right Track 131) 64 [1989 5g⁶ 5f 5f 5m⁶ 5m 5m⁵ 5g 5m³ 5g⁶ 6f 5.8f³ 5f⁶ 5g⁴ 8f³ 8f 7d 1990 5m³ 5g³ 5g* 5g 6g* 5d* 6g* 6m 5g⁴ 5f 5m⁵ 5g⁴ 6g 6s 5s a5g² a6g⁵] lengthy, good-quartered horse: poor walker: moderate mover: quite modest handicapper: far more reliable in summer than in past, making all or most at Hamilton, Carlisle, Edinburgh and Ripon: best form at 5f or 6f: yet to show his form on extremes of going: has won when sweating: probably unsuited by track at Chester. *K. B. McCauley.*

NORTHUMBRIAN KING 4 b.g. Indian King (USA) 128–Tuna 63 (Silver 60 § Shark 129) [1989 10.2g⁴ 11f* 12f* 12.4m⁶ 12h⁴ 12.3g 12f⁴ 14f⁶ 13.6g⁶ 1990 a14g² 14g⁴ a14g³ 14g 15m³ 15.8d] tall, close-coupled gelding: moderate walker and mover: quite modest handicapper: stays 15f: acts on firm going: blinkered twice: carries head high and is ungenuine: winner 5 times over hurdles early in 1990/1. *C. W. Thornton.*

NORTH WIND (IRE) 2 b.f. (Feb 10) Lomond (USA) 128–Spirit of The Wind 82 p (USA) (Little Current (USA)) [1990 7g 8g³] strong, lengthy filly: first foal: dam unraced half-sister to Grade 1 1¼m winner Dawn's Curtsey: over 4 lengths third of 15 to Sharifabad in maiden at Newmarket in October: will stay 1¼m: likely to improve again. *B. W. Hills.*

NORTHWOLD STAR (USA) 4 br.f. Monteverdi 129–Its A Romp (Hotfoot 71 126) [1989 10.5f 12f 10m 12h 16.2g² 16f⁵ 14m³ 17.6m² 16m³ 18.1g* 1990 16g 14m 18.4d a14g² 14g³ 15.3g² 16m 18.8f* 16.5f⁵ a14g⁴ 18d 18g* a16g² a16g² a16g⁴ a16g⁶] smallish, close-coupled filly: turns off-fore in: modest handicapper: won at Warwick in July and Pontefract in October: suited by good test of stamina: probably not ideally suited by firm going, acts on any other: blinkered once, often visored: usually makes running. *D. T. Thom.*

NORTON CHALLENGER 3 gr.c. Absalom 128–Klaire 85 (Klairon 131) [1989 98 5s* 5d* 1990 5v⁴ 7g² 6m⁷ 6m⁷ 8m⁵] rangy, good-topped colt: has plenty of scope: good walker and mover: useful handicapper: beaten head (running on well) in valuable events at York and Newcastle (best effort) third and fourth starts: not seen out after late-July: should prove ideally suited by 7f: acts on good to firm ground and heavy. *M. H. Easterby.*

NORWAY'S LIGHT (ITY) 3 b.c. Alzao (USA) 117–Corniola (Red God 128§) — [1989 NR 1990 10g⁵ 10.1m⁶ 8g] workmanlike colt: half-brother to winners in Italy, including 1¼m and 1½m winner Cicciobomber (by Cut Above): dam unraced: showed signs of ability in June, best effort when sixth (close up long way) in minor event at Windsor. *B. Hanbury.*

NORWICH 3 b.c. Top Ville 129–Dame Julian 84 (Blakeney 126) [1989 7m² 118 7m⁴ 1990 7m* 7m* 7g² 7f⁴ 7m* 7m* 7.3g* 7g⁴ 7g²]

The revelation by the Jockey Club in late-September that two big-race favourites at the St Leger meeting had been 'nobbled' had an effect akin to releasing a fox into a hen house. The Press and media had a field day on skulduggery in racing and, for a while, the impact was chastening. There were arguments within the sport about the effectiveness of arrangements for stable and racecourse security, and widespread speculation about a conspiracy involving bookmakers. Wider afield, horseracing's integrity was thrown into serious question as the story received sensationalised treatment. The flames were fanned further a few weeks later when a third case was confirmed, involving Flying Diva in a three-horse race at Yarmouth a week after Doncaster. Norwich, fourth when 11/4 joint-favourite in the Kiveton Park Stakes on the second day at Doncaster, and Bravefoot, last of five when 11/8 favourite for the Laurent-Perrier Champagne Stakes on the next day, were the first proven cases of horses being doped to lose since that of Alloway Lad, who started favourite for the Egmont Handicap at Epsom on Derby Day 1969. 'Nobbling' of racehorses hadn't received publicity on such a scale since the convictions of dopers in October 1963 and February 1966 which led to precautions at trainers' yards—where horses were most usually 'got at'—and at racecourses being strengthened. Access to racecourse stables nowadays is confined to stable-hands in charge of horses, senior stable staff and trainers—all of whom carry passport identification—and owners and their spouses who can be admitted by the trainer or someone acting on his or her behalf. Both Norwich and Bravefoot were found positive to the standard test for a tranquiliser: the fast-acting but short-lived acetylpromazine (ACP) was the substance used and it seems certain that it was administered at the racecourse stables, possibly by injection as close as half an hour before the races in which Norwich and Bravefoot took part. Norwich's rider said of his mount: 'When he cantered down to the start he was as dead as a doornail'. Norwich ran below his best, soon being headed by the eventual winner Green Line Express and hanging left when vigorously shaken up about two furlongs out; he was beaten about five lengths. The file relating to investigations into the doping cases, conducted by South Yorkshire police assisted by the Jockey Club's security services, is in the hands of the Crown Prosecution Service at the time of writing. Norwich suffered no lasting ill-effects from his experience at Doncaster and came a good second to Septieme Ciel in the Prix de la Foret at Longchamp the following month on his only subsequent outing.

Norwich had arrived at the Kiveton Park Stakes in cracking form, the winner of five of his seven races in the current season. Starting with an

Gardner Merchant Hungerford Stakes, Newbury—progressive Norwich makes all; the upgraded Fedoria (left) is a good second

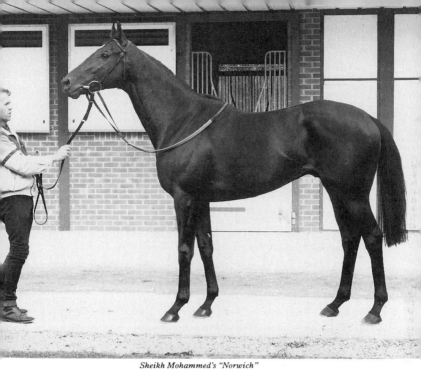

Sheikh Mohammed's "Norwich"

impressive victory in a graduation event at Catterick in April, Norwich rose through the ranks, winning another graduation race at Lingfield and then events of listed status at Leopardstown in July and Phoenix Park in August. Both visits to Ireland resulted in comfortable victories, though he reportedly broke a blood vessel in the EBF Platinum Hardwicke Cup at Phoenix Park. Norwich gained the most important victory of his career to date in the Gardner Merchant Hungerford Stakes at Newbury, nine days after Phoenix Park, making all and looking in no danger after quickening clear two furlongs out to beat Fedoria by four lengths. Norwich was sweating and on his toes before the Hungerford, indicative, like his free-running style of racing, of a natural inclination to get on with things. No longer so headstrong as in his two-year-old days, he nonetheless usually races up with the pace and often makes the running. Norwich has raced only at seven furlongs; he acts on firm going and has yet to race on a soft surface.

Norwich (b.c. 1987)	Top Ville (b 1976)	High Top (b 1969)	Derring-Do
			Camenae
		Sega Ville (b 1968)	Charlottesville
			La Sega
	Dame Julian (br 1976)	Blakeney (b 1966)	Hethersett
			Windmill Girl
		March Spray (bl 1958)	March Past
			Cup Tie

The big, useful-looking Norwich is the second foal by the Prix du Jockey Club winner Top Ville out of Dame Julian following St Ville, a winner on the all-weather over a mile and a half and two miles. All four previous foals out of the fair one-mile winner Dame Julian were also winners, the best of them being Fair Dominion (by Dominion), useful at up to a mile and a quarter and later successful in the States, and her sister Domynga, a listed-race winner over seven furlongs. After Norwich, Dame Julian visted Top Ville twice without issue: she now has another foal by Dominion. Although Norwich's pedigree suggests at first glance that he has sound prospects of staying beyond a mile, there is plenty of speed in the earlier generations. The grandam March Spray was a useful sprinter and produced two better ones in Daring Boy and Daring March. March Spray's dam Cup Tie was raced only at two years old and was apparently a short runner. *B. W. Hills.*

NORWICK STAR 2 b.f. (May 25) Norwick (USA) 120–Gentle Star 77 (Comedy — Star (USA) 121) [1990 a7g] 2,500Y: rather angular filly: third foal: half-sister to 3-y-o First Mistake (by Posse) and 1988 2-y-o 5f seller winner Tell Me This (by Goldhills Pride): dam 6f winner: green, soon struggling in maiden auction at Southwell in August. *K. T. Ivory.*

NO SHARPS OR FLATS (USA) 3 ch.f. Sharpen Up 127–Orientate (Hotfoot — 126) [1989 6f2 7m 1990 7g 8.5d 8m] workmanlike, dipped-backed filly: quite modest form on debut: edgy in 1990, sweating and carrying little condition final start (June). *J. R. Fanshawe.*

NO SID NO STARS (USA) 2 ch.g. (Mar 25) Diamond Shoal 130–Side Saddle 60 p (USA) (Codex (USA)) [1990 8.2m] rather sparely-made gelding: second foal: half-brother to a winner in North America by Fappiano: dam minor winner at around 1m, is half-sister to Breeders' Cup Mile winner Cozzene: under 15 lengths seventh of 17 to Circus Light in maiden at Nottingham in September, stumbling and soon in rear then staying on well last 3f until no extra inside final 1f: will stay 1¼m: certain to improve. *D. Morley.*

NO SUBMISSION (USA) 4 b.c. Melyno 130–Creeping Kate (USA) (Stop The 81 Music (USA)) [1989 8.5d* 8f4 8.2m 8f5 1990 8g 8f 8.2s3 8f 8.3m2 8m5 8d 10m4] tall, leggy, quite attractive colt: poor mover: fair handicapper: easily best efforts as 4-y-o on third and fifth (would have won but for hanging left) outings: stays 1¼m: acts on any going: sometimes on edge. *C. R. Nelson.*

NOTANOTHERONE (IRE) 2 b.g. (Apr 23) Mazaad 106–Maltese Pet 74 61 (Dragonara Palace (USA) 115) [1990 5m4 5.3h3 6m 7g 6d a6g5 a7g5] IR 5,200Y, 1,500 2-y-o: leggy, close-coupled gelding: third live foal: dam 7f winner: quite modest maiden: ran poorly third to fifth starts, including in a selling nursery: stays 6f. *J. E. Long.*

NOTHING'S FREE 3 b.f. Free State 125–Wayward Polly 63 (Lochnager 132) 58 [1989 5d2 5f2 6g 7m 8s6 6s 1990 7.5f3 8f2 7f4 6f2 6m 8m] rather leggy, useful-looking filly: moderate mover: useful plater: sweating, ran poorly final start, in June: probably stays 1m: seems to act on any going: on toes at 3 yrs: blinkered second (taken down early) and last 3 starts, visored third. *M. W. Easterby.*

NOTLEY 3 b.g. Formidable (USA) 125–Riviere Bleue (Riverman (USA) 131) — [1989 6g2 6d* 1990 6m5] strong, sturdy gelding: favourite, fairly useful form when making virtually all to win maiden at Newbury in October at 2 yrs: carrying condition, outpaced from halfway when over 10 lengths fifth of 7 in £8,000 event won by Tod at same course in May: subsequently gelded: should stay further. *R. Hannon.*

NOT QUITE FREE 3 b.f. Gabitat 119–Free Range 78 (Birdbrook 110) [1989 NR — 1990 7g 6f 7m 6m 6f 6m 6m] workmanlike, rather plain filly: has a round action: first foal: dam 5f to 7f winner: no form, including in selling handicap: sold 900 gns Ascot July Sales. *L. J. Holt.*

NOT YET 6 b.g. Connaught 130–Ritratto (Pinturischio 116) [1989 8d 8.5d5 9f* 9f5 61 10f 10f5 10.6d2 8g* 9f 8.2g4 1990 8f 8.5g5 9f5 10d* 10g2 10m5 8.5f5 10.6d3 8m* 8.5m 8.2d 8m] small, compact gelding: carries plenty of condition: bad mover: quite modest handicapper: successful at Beverley in June and Newcastle (same apprentice race for second successive year) in August: stays 1¼m: appears to act on any going: excellent mount for apprentice: sometimes sweats, and has got on toes: usually held up. *E. Weymes.*

NOUSHY 2 ch.f. (Mar 2) Ahonoora 122–Bolkonskina (Balidar 133) [1990 5m 6m4 75 5m5 6.5g 7m6 8g] 12,000Y: small, workmanlike filly: seventh foal: sister to 3-y-o 1m winner Zizania: dam sister to Bolkonski, won in Italy: modest filly: stays 7f. *C. E. Brittain.*

NOW BOARDING   3 b.f. Blazing Saddles (AUS)–Strictly 3wing 89 (3wing Easy   5G
(USA) 126) [1989 NR 1990 6m⁶ 7d² 6m² 8h⁴] lengthy filly: fourth foal: half-sister to
a winner in South Africa by Ardross: dam, who won 4 times at 5f, is half-sister to
good-class middle-distance performer Bold Arrangement: ridden by 7-lb claimer,
second in seller and maiden claimer (claimed out of W. Hastings-Bass's stable
£7,100) in July: stays 1m: acts on hard and dead going. *R. J. Hodges.*

NOW DANCE   2 gr.f. (Jan 31) Belfort (FR) 89–Tresanna (Treboro (USA) 112)   —
[1990 5m⁵ 5f] first foal: dam unraced: well beaten in maiden and seller at Wolverhampton in July: sold 810 gns Doncaster September Sales. *J. L. Harris.*

NOWHISKI   2 b.c. (Apr 27) Petoski 135–Be Faithful 93 (Val de Loir 133) [1990   —
7m 6d] 17,500Y: rangy colt: has scope: half-brother to 3-y-o 11f and 11.5f winner
Cleonte (by Dominion) and several other winners, including fair 9f winner Top Wing
(by High Top): dam 2-y-o 7f winner, is half-sister to high-class sprinter Apollo Nine
and to dam of Enstone Spark: well behind in autumn maidens at Leicester and
Doncaster: will stay middle distances. *H. J. Collingridge.*

NOW LISTEN (USA)   3 b.c. Miswaki (USA) 124–Nowanna (USA) (Envoy) 111
[1989 NR 1990 7f* 8.2g* 8f] $170,000Y: sturdy, attractive colt: carries condition:
seventh foal: half-brother to 5 winners, notably stakes winner at up to 1m Chick Or
Two (by Topsider): dam ran 6 times: bit green, easily landed odds in maiden (made
most) at Folkestone in March and minor event (quickening in impressive style to
beat Eton Lad 2½ lengths) at Nottingham in April: third favourite, never dangerous
and eased once beaten in 2000 Guineas at Newmarket: stays 8.2f: to be trained by R.
Frankel in USA. *G. Harwood.*

NOW THEN MINIZEN   2 ch.c. (Apr 10) Forzando 122–Grand Opera 92 (Great   55
Nephew 126) [1990 6g 7f⁶ a8g] 6,600F, 10,500Y: neat colt: sixth foal: half-brother to
several winners, including late 1¼m performer and winning hurdler Operatic Score
(by Kind of Hush): dam 7f winner at 2 yrs: plating-class maiden: form only on second
outing: should stay 1m. *M. Brittain.*

NUCLEAR EXPRESS   3 b.g. Martinmas 128–Halka (Daring March 116) [1989   79
5g* 5d* 5d² 6g 5f⁴ 5d³ 5g 1990 6s⁵ 5m* 5m² 5g² 5.8f³ 5m⁶ 5g⁵ 5f* 5m⁶ 5g 5d]
leggy, workmanlike gelding: turns fore-feet in: fair handicapper: won at Wolverhampton in April and Warwick in July: ran moderately at Chester (soon pushed
along in rear) and Haydock (blinkered) last 2 starts: stays 5.8f: acts on firm and dead
going: has run creditably for 7-lb claimer: tends to hang and carry head high. *J. Berry.*

NUCLEON (USA)   4 ch.c. Mr Prospector (USA)–Nonoalca (FR) 120 (Nonoalco   94
(FR) 131) [1989 8m 7g³ 9g⁴ 11g⁵ 1990 a6g* a6g* a6g* 6f⁴ 6f³ 7m 5d⁴ 8.3m] big, lengthy,
angular ex-French colt: fourth foal: half-brother to French 10.5f winner Narmada (by
Blushing Groom) and French 7.5f (at 2 yrs) to 1½m winner Narghile (by Foolish
Pleasure), later successful in USA: dam second in Poule d'Essai des Pouliches: won
maiden at Lingfield and handicap at Southwell early in year: fairly useful form at
best in varied events after, well beaten final outing (July): should be suited by
further than 6f: below form when blinkered, sweating freely and edgy fifth outing:
flashed tail time before: has worn crossed noseband. *W. A. O'Gorman.*

NUJOOM (USA)   3 b.f. Halo (USA)–Bird of Dawning (USA) (Sea Bird II 145)   —
[1989 7m⁵ 1990 8g 8f] lengthy, unfurnished filly: form only in maiden at Newmarket
as 2-y-o: behind in similar event and minor contest in 1990: sold 800 gns Newmarket
December Sales. *J. M. P. Eustace.*

NUMBER ELEVEN   3 b.f. Local Suitor (USA) 128–Babycham Sparkle 80 (So   57
Blessed 130) [1989 5m² 5g⁴ 6g³ 1990 7m³ 6g⁵ 6m*] rather sparely-made filly:
plating-class performer: sweating and on toes, made all in maiden claimer at
Chepstow in July: stays 7f: acts on good to firm ground: has given trouble at stalls.
Sir Mark Prescott.

NUNIVAK (USA)   3 ch.f. (Apr 2) Bering 136–Snow The Judge (USA) (Court   77 p
Recess (USA)) [1990 7f³ 7f*] $130,000Y: workmanlike filly: half-sister to several
winners in North America, one in minor stakes: dam, maiden, showed a little ability
from 6 starts: made most in maiden at Redcar in October, beating Memorive by a
length: favourite on debut over 2 months earlier: will stay at least 1¼m: sure to
improve again. *A. C. Stewart.*

NUNKI (ITY)   3 br.c. Clever Trick (USA)–Lacey (CAN) (His Majesty (USA))   —
[1989 NR 1990 8m 10f⁴ 12g 11.5m⁴ 12g 12v] leggy, workmanlike colt: moderate
mover: second reported foal: dam stakes winner from 2 yrs to 5 yrs over 6f to 7½f:
little worthwhile form in maidens here and Group 1 events in Italy. *C. E. Brittain.*

NUSAKAN (ITY)   3 ch.c. Spring Heights–Present Arms (Artaius (USA) 129)   87
[1989 8.2d⁶ 1990 10m² 10m⁵ 10.6s³ 12g 14g⁶ 8m² 8v] workmanlike colt: fair maiden:

head second to Philharmonia at Goodwood in September: well beaten in Group 2 event at Rome 7 weeks later: probably stays 1½m: acts on soft ground. *C. E. Brittain.*

NYONYA BESAR 3 b.f. Ballad Rock 122–Nekhbet 74 (Artaius (USA) 129) [1989 6g 1990 6m⁵ 6m⁶ 5s⁵] useful-looking filly: moderate walker: quite modest maiden at best: tailed off in minor event and well beaten in July handicap (stiff task) last 2 starts: should be suited by further than 6f: bandaged on reappearance. *C. F. Wall.* —

O

OAKBOURNE 2 b.c. (Feb 9) Daring March 116–Jacoletta 74 (Artaius (USA) 129) [1990 6d 6g 8d⁶] 9,200Y: leggy, workmanlike colt: fourth foal: half-brother to 2-y-o 6f winners by Star Appeal and Kind of Hush: dam placed over 7f at 2 yrs: progressive maiden: staying-on sixth of 18 to El Dominio at Bath in October: stays 1m. *T. Thomson Jones.* 68

OAKES DAY 5 ch.m. Derrylin 115–Persian Breakfast 50 (Deep Diver 134) [1989 7.5d 6m 6f⁵ 7h⁵ 6f 6g 5g 5m³ 5g 5m 5f 5f 6f 5m 1990 6g 5g⁴ 7g a5g 5m⁶ 6g 5f 5m] good-bodied mare: poor mover: bad maiden: stays 6f: acts on firm going: sold 1,050 gns Ascot October Sales. *Don Enrico Incisa.* —

OAKHURST 2 b.f. (Mar 19) Mandrake Major 122–Rock Psalm (Saintly Song 128) [1990 6m⁵ 6f³ 6m] 5,200Y: leggy, useful-looking filly: moderate walker: sister to fairly useful 1987 2-y-o 5f and 6f winner Belle Canticle and temperamental but successful sprinter Major's Review: dam of no account: plating-class maiden at best: gave thoroughly temperamental display second start: awkward on other occasions too (withdrawn once) and should be treated with caution: has joined Ronald Thompson. *N. Tinkler.* 53 §

OAK PARK (IRE) 2 br.g. (Jun 3) Prince Tenderfoot (USA) 126–Louisa Stuart (FR) (Ruysdael II 122) [1990 7d 5.8m 6f⁵ 6g⁶ 6d a6g² a5g² a6g⁵] 7,200Y: half-brother to 3 winners here and abroad, including 6f to 1½m winner Brave Louise (by Brave Shot): dam French 2-y-o 7f winner, is half-sister to Irish Oaks winner Aurabella: quite modest maiden: should stay 7f: acts well on all-weather, and seems suited by an easy surface on turf. *R. W. Stubbs.* 63

OBELISKI 4 b.g. Aragon 118–Pasha's Dream (Tarboosh (USA)) [1989 8d³ 8m 8f 10g² 10s* 12s² 1990 12v 12s*] leggy, angular gelding: has a round action: successful in handicap at Hamilton in November by short head, rallying gamely: suited by 1½m: goes very well on soft going: won twice over hurdles early in year. *M. H. Tompkins.* 61

O'BERON'S DAUGHTER 3 b.f. Fairy King (USA)–Precocious Angel (Persian Bold 123) [1989 NR 1990 6m a8g⁵ a7g³ a7g⁵ 9g a8g⁵ 9f⁴ 8d a7g a8g] 1,200 2-y-o: tall, leggy, narrow filly: first foal: dam once-raced daughter of half-sister to Irish 2000 Guineas winner Pampapaul: plating-class form: off course 3 months then showed little last 3 starts: stays 9f: acts on firm going: has been mulish in preliminaries: temperamental. *R. Thompson.* 51 §

OBLIGATION (USA) 2 ch.c. (Feb 2) Nepal (USA)–Line of Duty (USA) (Buffalo Lark (USA) [1990 7m² 7m* 8m³ 7f²] $45,000Y: leggy colt: has a round action: half-brother to winners in North America by Fluorescent Light and Rise Jim: dam lightly-raced half-sister to Lear Fan and Pirate Army: sire, best at 5 yrs, won at up to 9f: fairly useful performer: won minor event at Lingfield in August very comfortably by 3 lengths: one pace last 2f in listed race won by Selkirk at Goodwood and minor event won by Woodman's Mount at Folkestone after: stays 1m. *G. Harwood.* 92

OBOLOV 3 ch.g. Vaigly Great 127–Dortia (Martinmas 128) [1989 5m² 6g 5d 5g³ 1990 5f 6d a6g] small, shallow-girthed gelding: turns off-fore in: plating-class maiden: little show in handicap and claimers in 1990: form only at 5f: possibly unsuited by dead ground: sold 900 gns Doncaster November Sales. *P. Calver.* —

OBSERVATION POST 4 b.c. Shirley Heights 130–Godzilla 106 (Gyr (USA) 131) [1989 10m² 10.5f² 12g² 1990 10m⁴ 10m² 12g² 12.5g³ 11d⁵ 12m⁵] tall, rather leggy, attractive colt: has a quick action: very smart at his best, but has not won since 2 yrs: second in 1990 in Festival Stakes at Goodwood and Hanson Coronation Cup at Epsom, finding little on both occasions: off course 2 months after fourth outing, and ran poorly in autumn: stays 1½m: possibly not at his best on firm going: best treated with caution. *B. W. Hills.* 121 d

OCCAMIST (USA) 5 ch.g. Diesis 133–Solo Naskra (USA) (Naskra (USA)) [1989 —
a 10g 1990 11.5m] leggy, sparely-made, angular gelding: plating-class maiden at best:
winning selling hurdler in October. *B. Preece.*

OCEAN AIR 2 b.f. (May 24) Elegant Air 119–Fandangerina (USA) (Grey Dawn II 89
132) [1990 7m* 8.2g* 8.2d²] 58,000Y: big-topped filly: half-sister to 3-y-o Monya
(by Explodent) and very useful 1987 2-y-o 6f and 7f winner Western Gun (by
Lypheor): dam won at up to 1m: fair performer: successful in maiden at Yarmouth in
August and minor event at Haydock in September: second to Living Image in minor
event at Haydock: will stay 1¼m: acts on good to firm ground and dead. *H. R. A.
Cecil.*

OCEAN FALLS 4 b.c. Wassl 125–Homing Pigeon (FR) (Habitat 134) [1989 7v* 111
8d² 8m³ 7m 1990 8g² 8g³ 8g5 7g* 8g³ 8g² 8g* 7g 8s³ 8v] very useful colt: won
listed race at Longchamp in July and Prix Quincey (by 1½ lengths from River of
Light) at Deauville following month: placed in good company, behind Taffeta And
Tulle in Prix Perth at Saint-Cloud in November: well beaten in Prix de la Foret at
Longchamp previous outing: effective at 7f and 1m: never raced on firm going, acted
on any other: trained until after third start by A. Fabre: retired to Haras de Meautry,
20,000 francs (Oct 1st). *Mme M. Bollack-Badel, France.*

OCKY'S FLIER 6 bl.g. Aban 80–Ceile (Galivanter 131) [1989 16.2m 12m 1990 —
10.8m5 12m] leggy, close-coupled gelding: form only in 1m seller (hung left) on first
outing in 1988: often used to wear blinkers or visor. *N. Kernick.*

ODE (USA) 4 ch.f. Lord Avie (USA)–Ouro Verde (USA) (Cool Moon) [1989 121
10d5 9g² 8g6 11g* 10.5g* 9.2g5 12m³ 1990 10f6 10.5d* 12d* 12g² 11s³ 10f² 12f2]
    Asked to name the best four-year-old middle-distance filly trained in
Europe, followers of British racing would most likely go for Starlet or Roseate
Tern. But on her seconds in the Grand Prix de Saint-Cloud and in the
Budweiser International and Japan Cup later in the year, the French filly Ode
takes the palm. Stabled at Chantilly with Lellouche, who took over the
training of most of Wildenstein's horses in 1989 on the death of Douieb, Ode
had her last race in France when chasing In The Wings home at a length and a
half in the Grand Prix de Saint-Cloud on the first day of July. She'd gone into
that race a winner at Evry on her last two starts, recording her first pattern
success when prevailing by a length in the Prix Corrida and then coming more
to the attention of those on this side of the Channel when beating Per Quod
and Pirate Army by half a length and one and a half in the Grand Prix d'Evry,
giving her owner his second successive victory in the race following that of
Star Lift. Ode had also won at Evry in listed company as a three-year-old, a
season which she began with Fabre, ended by reaching a place in the Group 2
Prix du Conseil de Paris at Longchamp, and in the middle of which she was
beaten on two of her three outings in the Provinces. Put away after Saint-
Cloud specifically for an autumn campaign in the States and a tilt at the Japan
Cup, Ode reappeared in the Man o' War Stakes at Belmont Park in September
and was beaten four and three quarter lengths into third by Defensive Play.
She stepped up on that effort a month later when one and a quarter lengths
second at Laurel Park in the Budweiser International won by Fly Till Dawn,
whose trainer Darrell Vienna has a further claim to fame, apparently, as a
co-writer of the popular American television series Hill Street Blues. One of
two French challengers for the Japan Cup in Tokyo, the other, French Glory,
having likewise spent much of the autumn in North America, Ode ran a very
game race and nearly got up in a three-way photograph. She produced a
tremendous finishing effort, having been seventh and forced slightly wide on
the home turn, and caught Cacoethes in the dying strides, only to be outdone
by Better Loosen Up by a head. According to her owner the suspensory
tendon went on her off-fore during the race and as a result she was to be
retired to the paddocks.

		Lord Gaylord	Sir Gaylord
	Lord Avie (USA)	(b 1970)	Miss Glamour Gal
	(b 1978)	Avie	Gallant Man
Ode (USA)		(b 1963)	Evilone
(ch.f. 1986)		Cool Moon	Nearctic
	Ouro Verde (USA)	(b 1968)	Mamounia
	(b 1976)	Sanelta	Tourment
		(b 1954)	Satanella

Wildenstein and Lellouche enjoyed considerable success in 1990 and both finished in the top three of their respective owners' and trainers' prizemoney lists in France. Agent Bleu, Boxing Day, Epervier Bleu and Pistolet Bleu, as well as Ode, were all major contributors. Another of Wildenstein's good horses, by the way, the Prix de Meautry winner Pole Position is to join Julie Cecil and will be the first horse Wildenstein has had in training in Britain since his split with Henry Cecil in 1985. Ode's sire Lord Avie was the champion two-year-old of 1980 in North America, and showed high-class form the following year when he won the nine-furlong Florida Derby. Her dam Ouro Verde won over seven and a half furlongs in France as a two-year-old and later over a mile in stakes company in the States. Ode is Ouro Verde's fourth reported foal; the third, Orangerie (by Arctic Tern), won over eleven furlongs in the French Provinces in 1989, while the fifth, Onde Bleu Marine (by Sagace), won twice in the latest season, including in a listed contest at Evry over an extended mile and a quarter. Ouro Verde is a half-sister to the Prix du Jockey-Club and Grand Prix de Paris winner Sanctus II and to Finelta, the grandam of Dead Certain. Ode, a genuine and consistent filly, was effective at a mile and a quarter and a mile and a half and acted on any going. *E. Lellouche, France.*

ODILEX 3 b.g. Mummy's Pet 125–Odile (Green Dancer (USA) 132) [1989 6m⁵ 70
8.2s⁴ 6g 1990 7m⁵ 6f⁵ 8h* 8.5g* 8f²] sturdy gelding: modest performer: won seller (bought in 5,200 gns) at Brighton and claimer (claimed out of M. Jarvis' stable £10,500) at Epsom: very good second in handicap at Brighton later in summer: stays 8.5f well: yet to race on heavy going, acts on any other: joined N. Gaselee. *S. Dow.*

ODIN'S FLAME (IRE) 2 b.g. (Feb 13) Viking (USA)–Sunley Saint 79 (Artaius —
(USA) 129) [1990 5g 7d 6g⁵] IR 3,300F, IR 9,000Y: sturdy gelding: has round action: first foal: dam maiden suited by 1½m: no worthwhile form in poor company: slowly away first 2 starts, swerved left final one: visored final 2 outings: sold 1,000 gns Doncaster August Sales. *J. S. Wilson.*

OFFICER CADET 3 b.g. Shernazar 131–Selection Board 75 (Welsh Pageant 63
132) [1989 7m⁶ 6f⁵ 6f 1990 10.6f 11f⁵ 8g* 10g* 11m⁵ 10.6d⁴ 9s 11d* a12g³] closecoupled gelding: moderate mover: quite modest handicapper: won at Carlisle (made all) in June, Nottingham in July and Edinburgh in October: will prove best at up to 1½m: best with give in the ground: wandered markedly when blinkered second start. *J. W. Watts.*

OFFSHORE TRYST (IRE) 2 b.f. (Mar 14) Try My Best (USA) 130–Crestia 55
(Prince Tenderfoot (USA) 126) [1990 7m 7g] IR 77,000Y: fair sort: fourth foal: half-sister to modest 7f and 1¼m winner Irene's Charter (by Persian Bold): dam Irish 6f winner, is half-sister to very smart stayer El Badr: well beaten in maidens at Sandown and Newmarket over 2 months later. *R. Hannon.*

OFF THE RECORD (FR) 5 ch.g. Don Roberto (USA)–Farce (FR) (Bon Mot 89
III 132) [1989 8d 10.2g 12f² 12m 1990 12f² 11f⁴ 12m 12m³ a14g* 16m* 16.2m*
14g 16.2m* 16.2m² 18d] good-topped gelding: carries plenty of condition: formerly thoroughly unreliable, but in excellent form for most of summer: won maiden at Southwell, quite valuable handicaps at Sandown and Ascot (given excellent ride by M. Roberts both times) and handicap (very confidently ridden) at Beverley: ran badly in Ebor and Cesarewitch ninth and final outings: best at 1¾m to 2m: suited by a sound surface: blinkered once: suited by waiting tactics. *C. W. Thornton.*

OFF THE WALL 3 b.g. Auction Ring (USA) 123–Fraudulent (Sexton Blake 126) 41
[1989 7m 1990 a7g³ a8g 7m⁶ 7f] strong gelding: has scope: poor maiden: well worth another try over 1m: visored (stiffish tasks) last 2 outings: sometimes slowly away: sold 6,800 gns Ascot May Sales: winning selling hurdler for M. Pipe. *W. Hastings-Bass.*

OH DANNY BOY 6 br.g. Rabdan 129–Musical Princess 66 (Cavo Doro 124) 49
[1989 12d 12f 12.8m⁴ 10f 12m² 10m² 10.2g 12.3g² 10f* 10.6d 1990 10f 10m 10d 12m
12.8g² 10m 12g² 10m² 12.3m³ 12.3m 12.3g 10m³] lengthy gelding: moderate mover: poor handicapper: effective at 1¼m and 1½m: probably needs a sound surface nowadays: goes well with forcing tactics and at Beverley. *E. Weymes.*

OH MERCY (FR) 2 ch.f. (Feb 8) Be My Guest (USA) 126–Grammene (Grey 71 p
Dawn II 132) [1990 6m⁵] second foal: closely related to French 3-y-o 8.2f winner Paradise City (by Sadler's Wells): dam French 1m and 9.5f winner: around 7 lengths fifth of 9, slowly into stride then staying on final 2f, to Shihama in maiden at Newmarket in November: sure to improve, particularly over 7f + . *H. R. A. Cecil.*

OH SO FINE 3 b.g. Welsh Term 126–Miss Ultra Sound (USA) (Groshawk (USA)) —
[1989 NR 1990 11.5m 10.1m 11.5g] IR 2,200Y, resold IR 2,600Y: leggy, plain gelding:
third foal: dam unraced: no sign of ability in maiden and minor events. *R. Akehurst.*

OH SO RISKY 3 b.c. Kris 135–Expediency (USA) (Vaguely Noble 140) [1989 6g3 **94**
7g* 1990 8m3 11.5m* 12g 10f] tall, useful-looking colt: fairly useful performer:
favourite and edgy, won handicap at Sandown in May: below form in King George V
Stakes at Royal Ascot and £8,000 handicap at Newmarket: well suited by middle
distances: acts on good to firm ground: winning hurdler. *D. R. C. Elsworth.*

OHSO SCARLET 2 ch.f. (Feb 1) Blushing Scribe (USA) 107–Soho 63 (Camden —
Town 125) [1990 5g6 6m a6g] workmanlike filly: third foal: dam lightly-raced
daughter of Prix Morny and French 1000 Guineas winner Solitude: broke a leg at
halfway in claimer at Lingfield in November. *Pat Mitchell.*

O I OYSTON 14 b.g. Martinmas 128–Last Lap 75 (Immortality) [1989 8v* 8d5 —
7.6m 8.2d 8.2d 1990 8m] big gelding: carries plenty of condition: a grand old servant,
now retired, who won 22 times on flat: best at up to 9f: very well suited by plenty of
give in the ground: excellent mount for claimer: best without blinkers: suited by
forcing tactics: went particularly well on a turning track: tough and genuine: a credit
to his trainer. *J. Berry.*

OKA FLOW 2 b.c. (Feb 20) Vaigly Great 127–Atoka 97 (March Past 124) [1990 **80 p**
7m 7s2] 21,000Y: leggy, angular colt: has a quick action: sixth foal: half-brother to
3 winners, including fairly useful 1985 2-y-o 5f winner Oh Boyar (by Young
Generation) and 1m and 1¼m seller winner Love To Dance (by Dominion): dam won
from 6f to 15f: 1½ lengths second of 14 to very easy winner Evasive Prince in maiden
at Lingfield in October, leading on favoured stand rail 2f out and keeping on: will
stay 1m: likely to improve again. *J. R. Fanshawe.*

OKAKU 3 b.g. Be My Guest (USA) 126–Be My Darling 82 (Windjammer (USA)) —
[1989 7m 1990 8m a8g a7g 8m] strong, good-topped gelding: seems of little account:
blinkered last 2 starts: trained until after reappearance by Mrs L. Piggott. *K. G.
Wingrove.*

OK CORRAL (USA) 3 gr.g. Malinowski (USA) 123–Tiger Trap (USA) 80 (Al **52**
Hattab (USA)) [1989 7g4 1990 8f4 a8g 10m6] big, rather leggy gelding: quite modest
form: stays 1¼m: sold 12,500 gns Ascot July Sales: winning hurdler for J. White. *W.
Hastings-Bass.*

O K NURSE 6 gr.m. Mandrake Major 122–Grisma (Grisaille 115) [1989 10m5 12f —
1990 9m4 8.5m] lengthy mare: well beaten in varied events. *J. Mulhall.*

OK RECORDS 3 b.g. Cure The Blues (USA)–Last Clear Chance (USA) (Alleged —
(USA) 138) [1989 a8g5 1990 8f 8.2m] angular, lightly-made gelding: well beaten,
including in seller: sold out of W. Hastings-Bass's stable before reappearance 2,100
gns Ascot May Sales. *O. O'Neill.*

OKYPOUS 6 b.g. High Top 131–Grazia 90 (Aureole 132) [1989 NR 1990 8g 8g6 —
11m5 10m] sturdy gelding: poor mover: half-brother to several winners, including 6f
and 7f winner Faiz (by Prince Tenderfoot), subsequently successful at up to 1m in
USA: dam 2-y-o 6f winner: plating-class form in maidens second and third outings:
apprentice ridden first 3 starts. *Mrs S. M. Austin.*

O-LA-LE 6 ch.h. Virginia Boy 106–Winning Wave (USA) (Victory Morn) [1989 —
7d4 7.5d* 8d 7.5g* 7.5m 6g 8f 1990 8m 7f5 7m] rather sparely-made horse: poor
mover: won handicaps at Beverley early as 5-y-o: no worthwhile form last 5 outings:
stays 7.5f: needs give in the ground: sold 800 gns Ascot October Sales. *W. G A.
Brooks.*

OLD COMRADES 3 ch.g. Music Boy 124–Miss Candine 66 (King Emperor —
(USA)) [1989 5s5 5m 5d3 5f3 1990 5g 5m 5g5] workmanlike, good-quartered gelding:
quite modest sprint maiden: faced very stiff tasks in handicaps. *L. G. Cottrell.*

OLD DEFENSIBLE 2 b.g. (Apr 12) Sulaafah (USA) 119–Impregnable 66 **50**
(Never Say Die 137) [1990 a7g a7g a7g6 a8g] IR 5,200Y, 5,200 2-y-o: narrow, very
leggy gelding: half-brother to several winners, including 7f performer Mystery Ship
(by Decoy Boy): dam 1½m winner: plating-class maiden: ran well for apprentice
final start: will be suited by 1¼m: gave trouble stalls second appearance. *R. J.
Muddle.*

OLDE CYDER 5 b.g. Royal Boxer 112–Cider Drinker (Space King 115) [1989 NR —
1990 12.2m6] lengthy gelding: fourth foal: dam poor maiden on flat and over hurdles:
300/1, tailed-off last of 6 in maiden at Catterick in June: sweating, on toes and gave
bit of trouble at stalls. *J. M. Bradley.*

OLD HUBERT 9 ch.g. Gulf Pearl 117–Wise Counsel (Counsel 118) [1989 NR   **64**
1990 15.3g 18g³ 16.5d a16g* a16g⁶] workmanlike gelding: made all and impressive
winner of handicap at Southwell in December: set strong gallop when well beaten in
similar event 10 days later: well suited by good test of stamina: acts on any going:
blinkered once: usually wears bandages. *A. Bailey.*

OLD MOTHER GOOSE 4 b.f. Jalmood (USA) 126–Snow Goose (Santa Claus   **—**
133) [1989 9s 9f 12d 1990 13.8m 15.8g 12g 16.2m⁶] lengthy, angular filly: poor walker
and mover: appears of little account. *N. Bycroft.*

OLD PEG 2 b.f. (Mar 26) Reach 122–Lizarra 74 (High Top 131) [1990 7g 7s a7g   **56**
a6g⁴] rather angular filly: first foal: dam placed over 6f at 2 yrs, only season to race:
around 2 lengths fourth of 12, finishing well, to Balsmo in claimer at Southwell,
easily best effort: should be suited by further than 6f. *M. H. Easterby.*

OLD VIC 4 b.c. Sadler's Wells (USA) 132–Cockade 104 (Derring-Do 131) **130**
[1989 11d* 10s* 12.3m* 12g* 12g* 1990 12d³ 12m²]
       Just as the connections of Sunday Silence and Easy Goer were denied
much reward for keeping North America's top three-year-olds of 1989 in
training, so those of Europe's best middle-distance colt of that year Old Vic
suffered similar disappointment. Injury forced Sunday Silence and Easy Goer
into early retirement after just two and three races respectively, whilst Old
Vic proved difficult to train because of the prolonged dry spells and was
restricted to just two outings at Ascot in the summer. The dual Derby winner
had been absent for just short of a year when he made his come-back in the
Hardwicke Stakes at the Royal meeting, a race which also saw the reappearance of the Arc winner Carroll House. Old Vic, who started odds on,
and Carroll House both ran as though needing the race, and it was the
50/1-shots Assatis and Ile de Nisky who came from off a strong pace to battle it
out at the finish. The intention was to give Old Vic another race before the
King George VI and Queen Elizabeth Diamond Stakes, but in the event he was
returned to Ascot after a racecourse gallop with Monsagem at Newbury. The
decision to allow Old Vic to run on ground considered faster than ideal in the
King George was apparently an agonising one and was finally made only five
minutes before declaration time on the afternoon of the race after the trainer
had walked the track. Cecil explained, 'The last time I walked a course was
before The Minstrel's King George in 1977. I opted to let Lucky Wednesday
take his chance—and he broke down'. Old Vic didn't win the King George, but
he very nearly did and put up a terrific performance, all things considered, in
going down by only a neck to his year-younger stable-mate Belmez. Sweating

Sheikh Mohammed's "Old Vic" (S. Cauthen) goes to post for the King George

and edgy in the preliminaries, Old Vic went off second favourite behind the Coronation Cup winner In The Wings. He gradually quickened the pace from the front, held a two-length lead entering the straight and rallied most courageously despite tending to wander and change his legs. For the first time a trainer had saddled the first two home in the King George, the fact that both colts suffered an interrupted preparation making the feat all the more praiseworthy. While Cecil went on his way to becoming champion trainer for the ninth time, Old Vic remained on course for the Arc until shortly before his intended warm-up race—the Prix Foy—when he rapped a tendon while galloping after racing at Nottingham in company with Shellac. The results of Old Vic's third season are more likely to discourage than encourage the owners of classic winners to keep them in training. Similar ventures have met with mixed results recently. While Miesque, Moon Madness and Triptych went on to do well, the other eight classic winners kept in training in Britain and Ireland in the last five years were very lightly raced and brought little financial reward for their owners. It might be argued that Old Vic would have been able to command a higher fee at stud had his retirement come in the autumn of 1989 when his Derby victories were still relatively fresh in the mind. As it is, he is to stand at Dalham Hall in 1991 at a fee of £25,000 with the October 1st concession, with Sheikh Mohammed retaining sole ownership.

		Northern Dancer	Nearctic
	Sadler's Wells (USA)	(b 1961)	Natalma
	(b 1981)	Fairy Bridge	Bold Reason
Old Vic		(b 1975)	Special
(b.c. 1986)		Derring-Do	Darius
	Cockade	(b 1961)	Sipsey Bridge
	(b 1973)	Camenae	Vimy
		(b 1961)	Madrilene

Salsabil may have been Sadler's Wells's only three-year-old pattern winner of 1990 in Europe, but the strength in depth of his first crop was emphasised again in the latest season with Batshoof, Braashee, Dolpour, French Glory, In The Wings, as well as Old Vic, continuing to play a prominent part in proceedings. The four sold at public auction as yearlings (Dolpour and In The Wings were home bred) were all knocked down to Arab owners, Old Vic the most expensive at 230,000 guineas. Old Vic is the fifth living foal of his dam Cockade, a sister to the Two Thousand Guineas winner High Top and the Jersey Stakes winner Camden Town. Her four other winners on the flat include Green Lucia (by Green Dancer), placed in both the Irish Guinness Oaks and the Yorkshire Oaks, and the lightly-raced three-year-old Splash of Colour (by Rainbow Quest), who got up to beat Ile de Nisky in the Royal Whip Stakes at the Curragh in August on only his second outing. All her winners have shown form at a mile and a half or more. How her Green Desert 1990 two-year-old Muthhil, a 500,000-guinea yearling in training with Michael Jarvis, turns out will be interesting. Cockade won over a mile, but her dam Camenae was a stayer and won a maiden (albeit a poor race) over an extended mile and three quarters in the mud. Old Vic, a rangy, good-bodied colt, was suited by forcing tactics and a mile and a half. A tremendous mover with a very powerful action, he won on soft going and ran an excellent race on good to firm in the King George. The ground was good when he won the French Derby with a performance which ranks amongst the best of the decade. *H. R. A. Cecil.*

OLGA'S PET 3 br.g. Tina's Pet 121–Aunt Winnie (Wolver Hollow 126) [1989 6g 6g 1990 6g 7m] leggy gelding: seems of little account: sold 1,550 gns Doncaster May Sales. *J. Balding.*

OLIFANTSFONTEIN 2 b.c. (Apr 11) Thatching 131–Taplow (Tap On Wood 130) [1990 7g] 15,000Y: lengthy colt: first foal: dam never ran, from family of Bassenthwaite and Hadeer: very green, prominent over 4f in minor event at Doncaster in September: should improve. *R. Simpson.*

OLIROAN 2 gr.g. (Apr 11) Vin St Benet 109–Olibanum 61 (Frankincense 120) [1990 5m3 5m 6f a6g2 6d2 a6g6 5m2 5m3] 1,150Y: plain, angular gelding: half-brother to winning sprinters Capeability Pound (by Balboa), Blochairn Skolar (by Most Secret) and a winner in Belgium: dam plater: plating-class maiden: seems suited by 5f. *M. W. Ellerby.*

OLIVERS MOUNT (USA) 2 b.c. (Mar 24) Lyphard's Wish (FR) 124–Olivera **67** (GER) (Kaiseradler) [1990 8m* 8g] 9,000Y: rangy colt, with plenty of scope: half-brother to a winner in Germany: dam unraced daughter of leading 1970 German 2-y-o Orpheline: green, edgy and very much in need of race, won maiden auction at Redcar in August by short head from Crimson Cloud: bit slipped through mouth (running best ignored) in Doncaster nursery following month: sold 23,000 gns Newmarket Autumn Sales. *T. D. Barron.*

OLYMPIAN 3 ch.g. High Line 125–Elysian 94 (Northfields (USA)) [1989 8f6 8g **63** 1990 11.7f3 15.3m5 14g 13.1m6] stocky gelding: quite modest maiden: should stay beyond 11.7f: looks hard ride, and is worth another try in visor (wore one pen-ultimate start) or blinkers: winning hurdler for T. McGovern. *P. T. Walwyn.*

OLYMPIC CHALLENGER 6 b.g. Anfield 117–Calibina 101 (Caliban 123) **52** [1989 12g 8m 6s 6g a6g5 1990 a7g5 a6g 5g 6g3 6g6 6d5 6g3 6d 11g3] lengthy gelding: has a rather round action: poor handicapper: needs further than 5f and seems to stay 11f: best with give in the ground: usually wears blinkers or visor: tends to get long way behind: trained until after seventh start by J. Mackie: winning hurdler in August. *J. H. Johnson.*

OMORSI 3 b.f. Prince Tenderfoot (USA) 126–Her Name Was Lola (Pitskelly 122) — [1989 7g 1990 a8g4 10.2f 10m 16m 12m2 12f3 16.2g3] leggy filly: plating-class maiden: ran in amateur events last 5 outings: stays 1½m: acts on firm ground. *M. J. Fetherston-Godley.*

O MY DARLING (USA) 2 b.f. (Apr 13) Mr Prospector (USA)–Midnight **76 p** Pumpkin (USA) (Pretense) [1990 7g4 7g] $650,000Y: lengthy, good-quartered filly: sister to Preakness winner Tank's Prospect and half-sister to a minor winner by Northjet: dam won at up to 9f: 5½ lengths fourth of 5, travelling comfortably around 5f after slow start, to Janbiya in minor event at York in October: never placed to challenge or knocked about unduly in maiden at Newmarket following month: may well do better and one to keep an eye on. *C. F. Wall.*

ONAWAY 3 ch.f. Commanche Run 133–Lulubo (USA) (Native Charger) [1989 NR **84** 1990 12.5m2 12.2g* 12f8 12m 14.6g 14d6] IR 19,000Y: strong, lengthy, workmanlike filly: half-sister to 2 winners in USA: dam graded-stakes winner at up to 9f: favourite, won maiden at Catterick in June and minor event (7/1 on, struggled to beat sole opponent) at Pontefract in July: towards rear in listed race at York and handicaps at Doncaster (£18,400 event) and Newmarket (blinkered): should be well suited by further than 1½m. *H. R. A. Cecil.*

ONCE UPON A TIME 3 b.f. Teenoso (USA) 135–Pas de Deux 80 (Nijinsky **77** (CAN) 138) [1989 6g 7f5 8.5f* 1990 8.5g4 10.2f3 11m5 10m2 11.7m* 12g5 10g 10g] small filly: modest handicapper: odds on, won 3-runner race at Windsor in August by 15 lengths: wearing pricker near-side, below form in quite valuable events afterwards: stays 1½m: acts on firm going: takes keen hold: possibly unsatisfactory. *I. A. Balding.*

ON DISPLAY (IRE) 2 ch.c. (Apr 2) Exhibitioner 111–That's Easy (Swing Easy **86** (USA) 126) [1990 5m2 5d* 5g2 5g5 5g2 6m2 7m 6d] fourth foal: dam Irish 9f winner: Irish colt: made all in maiden at Naas in March: runner-up afterwards in minor events at Phoenix Park, Bellewstown and Gowran Park: never able to challenge in Norfolk Stakes at Royal Ascot on fourth start: stays 6f: acts on good to firm ground and dead: blinkered fourth and last 3 starts. *M. A. O'Toole, Ireland.*

ONE DEVONSHIRE 4 b.g. Sandhurst Prince 128–Raregirl (Rarity 129) [1989 **47 §** 10s 8f 12.3f2 12m4 12g3 1990 9g a12g 10m4 12m] angular gelding: poor walker: poor maiden: virtually refused to race second outing: stays 1½m: acts on firm going: visored last 2 starts: one to treat with caution. *M. H. Tompkins.*

ONE FOR IRENE 3 gr.f. Hotfoot 126–Vila Real 76 (Town Crier 119) [1989 6g **45** 5m6 1990 7.5d4 8m 7.5d 10m2 10.8f4 9f2 9f 10g 10d] workmanlike filly: has a free, roundish action: plater: may prove ideally suited by return to 1m: acts on firm ground and dead: likely to prove best with waiting tactics: sold 2,700 gns Doncaster October Sales, and later won claiming hurdle for G. H. Jones. *R. M. Whitaker.*

ONE FOR THE BOYS 3 ch.g. Superlative 118–Contenance (GER) (Luciano) **50** [1989 5m 6m 6f6m 6g 1990 10f 10.4d 9m 10.1m 12m* 14f3 13.8m3 17.4d a14g] sturdy gelding: plating-class performer: made all in selling handicap (bought in 7,000 gns) at Pontefract in July, hanging right: probably stays 1¾m (no chance over 17.4f): acts on good to firm ground: twice ridden by lad in paddock: bandaged on reappearance: may be best setting pace: winning hurdler, sold out of F. Durr's stable 10,800 gns following November seller after eighth start on flat. *M. C. Chapman.*

ONE FOR THE CHIEF 2 b.g. (Mar 9) Chief Singer 131–Action Belle (Auction 53
Ring (USA) 123) [1990 7m⁵ 7g⁶ 8.2m 8.2g] 30,000Y: rather angular gelding:
moderate mover: third foal: brother to 3-y-o Golden Divot and half-brother to 1988
2-y-o 5f and 6f winner Holster (by Gorytus): dam sister to good-class 7f and 1m
performer Meis-El-Reem: well beaten in varied races, including a nursery. *R. M.
Whitaker.*

ONE FOR THE POT 5 ch.g. Nicholas Bill 125–Tea-Pot 77 (Ragstone 128) 70
[1989 21.6d 15.8m 16.2m³ 15f⁶ 16.2g² 20.4g⁴ 17f⁴ 1990 11s* 12f* 12.4f* 10v³ 12d⁴
12g* 13d² 12v*] 16.5d⁴] strong, short-backed gelding: since changing stables in 1989
has shown much improved form: successful in handicaps at Hamilton (apprentices),
Pontefract and Newcastle in spring and Doncaster and Haydock in autumn: stays
2m: acts on any going, but particularly well on easy surface: used to sweat and get on
edge: suited by waiting tactics: winning hurdler in November. *Mrs J. R. Ramsden.*

ONE MAGIC MOMENT (IRE) 2 b.f. (Apr 14) Thatching 131–Debutante 78 67
(Silly Season 127) [1990 a6g⁵ a7g² 6g⁴ 6d* 6m] 7,000Y: leggy, workmanlike filly:
half-sister to several winners here and in Italy, including Italian Derby winner Don
Ozario (by Homing) and 7f winner Ghassanah (by Pas de Seul): dam 7f winner: quite
modest performer: made all in maiden at Ayr in September, beating Arabian King by
1½ lengths: stays 7f: possibly unsuited by top-of-the-ground. *C. A. Cyzer.*

ONENINEFIVE 4 ch.f. Sayyaf 121–Pink Ribbon (Riboboy (USA) 124) [1989 NR —
1990 10f⁵ 12f 10f] second foal: dam French provincial 9f winner: well beaten in
maiden and apprentice races. *G. A. Ham.*

ONE TO NOTE 6 br.h. Star Appeal 133–Town Lady 93 (Town Crier 119) [1989 —
NR 1990 12.2m 8m] smallish, lengthy horse: moderate mover: quite modest winner
of handicap at 3 yrs: bandaged, soundly beaten in similar company in spring: stays
1½m: acts on heavy going: blinkered once. *M. P. Muggeridge.*

ONLY JOKING 6 b.m. Balinger 116–Comical (Comedy Star (USA) 121) [1989 NR —
1990 17.1f] workmanlike mare: has a round action: seems no longer of much account.
Mrs A. Knight.

ONLY MALONEY 2 b.c. (May 16) Cadoudal (FR) 124–Sprimonte (USA) (Big —
Spruce (USA)) [1990 a7g] 560F, 900Y: first foal: dam never ran: tailed off in 14-
runner maiden at Lingfield in November. *J. S. Moore.*

ONLY THE LONELY 3 b.g. Mummy's Game 120–Izobia (Mansingh (USA) —
120) [1989 5d 7g 7f 7g 1990 7g 10f] workmanlike gelding: good walker: poor maiden
on flat: won 2-runner hurdle for G. Balding. *R. Hannon.*

ONLY YOURS 2 b.f. (Mar 21) Aragon 118–Welsh Jane 71 (Bold Lad (IRE) 133) 98
[1990 6m³ 6f* 6m² 6m* 6m 6d⁵] rangy, workmanlike filly: has scope: quite good
mover: sixth reported foal: half-sister to 3 winners, including 3-y-o Osario, smart 5f
and 6f winner at 2 yrs, and 6f to 1m winner Dramatic Event (both by Kind of Hush):
dam seemed to stay 1m, is out of speedy Abbot's Isle: fairly useful filly: won

*'Pacemaker Update' Lowther Stakes, York—
Only Yours (No. 8) wins a closely-contested event from Dangora*

Mrs M. Butcher's "Only Yours"

9-runner 'Pacemaker Update' Lowther Stakes at York in August by a head from Dangora with several others close up, disputing lead at halfway and staying on gamely: earlier made all in Newmarket maiden: creditable fifth of 19, hanging left, to Chipaya in Racecall Gold Trophy at Redcar: will stay 7f: acts on firm and dead ground: apparently in season when hanging badly third start. *R. Hannon.*

ON MY MERIT   4 ch.g. Bold Lad (IRE) 133–Borehard (Bonne Noel 115) [1989 8.5d 6m⁶ 7g⁴ 8m* 8g* 8f* 8f³ 8m* 8g 1990 8f 8f⁶ 6f 7m 9f² 7.5f⁵ 8.2d 9m] big, lengthy gelding: fair winner of 4 handicaps as 3-y-o: easily best effort in 1990 second at Redcar in July: stays 9f: acts on firm going: visored fourth start: sweating and on toes on last: has often hung. *F. H. Lee.*   **72 ?**

ON STRIKE (IRE)   2 gr.g. (Apr 2) Caerleon (USA) 132–Kaysanniya (Nishapour (FR) 125) [1990 5g 6g 7f² 7m* 7m* 7g³ 8m² 8g 8f³] 11,500Y: small, leggy gelding: has a quick action: second reported foal: dam never ran: quite modest performer: successful in sellers at Edinburgh (no bid) and Catterick (retained 8,400 gns) in August: ran well after when placed: better suited by 1m than shorter and will stay 1¼m: visored fourth, fifth and final 3 starts: sold 6,000 gns Newmarket Autumn Sales. *M. H. Tompkins.*   **67**

ON THE EDGE   2 b.c. (Apr 16) Vaigly Great 127–Final Request 63 (Sharp Edge 123) [1990 6g⁵ 6g 7s 6s] 8,000 (privately) Y: quite attractive colt: has scope: sixth foal: brother to Italian 3-y-o 1m to 10.5f winner If One Day and half-brother to 3 winners, including 5f winner Lakedge and 1¼m winner Katie Scarlett (both by Lochnager): dam 1¼m and 1½m sellers winner: fifth of 16 in minor event at Doncaster in September: well below that form after: should stay 7f. *T. D. Barron.*   **66**

ON THE LINE   2 b.c. (May 7) Belfort (FR) 89–Queen's Parade (Sovereign Path 125) [1990 5m⁵ 5s*] 6,800Y: close-coupled colt: looks weak: seventh foal: half-   **66**

656

*Queen Mary Stakes, Ascot—bargain-buy On Tiptoes dominates,
with It's All Academic a clear second*

brother to 7f winner Life Guard (by Absalom) and winning hurdler Rowlandsons
Trophy (by Vaigly Great): dam poor maiden: odds on, won claimer at Hamilton in
April by 7 lengths: not seen out again. *M. H. Easterby.*

ON THE REBOUND 2 br.f. (Apr 23) Lidhame 109–Janlarmar 69 (Habat 127) —
[1990 6g 6m] 3,100Y: leggy, angular filly: poor mover: half-sister to 3-y-o 5f (at 2 yrs)
and 1m winner Great Service and 6f seller winner Crimpsall (both by Vaigly Great):
dam won 6f seller: well beaten in large fields of platers at York (slowly away and
hung left) and Redcar: sold 1,000 gns Doncaster October Sales. *W. W. Haigh.*

ON THE SAUCE 3 b.g. Kala Shikari 125–Kingsfold Flash 50 (Warpath 113) —
[1989 NR 1990 10.1g 8m] lengthy gelding with scope: fifth foal: half-brother to useful
1m and 9f winner Kingsfold Flame (by No Loiterer): dam plater: well behind in
Windsor minor event: pulled up in Goodwood maiden. *M. J. Haynes.*

ON TIPTOES 2 b.f. (Mar 3) Shareef Dancer (USA) 135–Pennyweight (Troy 137) **98**
[1990 5f* 5g* 5f* 6m⁴ 6m⁶] 7,000Y: big, good-bodied filly: has plenty of scope: easy
mover: third foal: closely related to useful 6f and 7f winner Penny Candle (by Be My
Guest) and half-sister to 3-y-o Sunset Dreams (by Habitat): dam poor half-sister to
Wassl: fairly useful filly, successful in maiden at Ripon in April, minor event at
Newmarket in May and Queen Mary Stakes (readily by 2½ lengths from It's All
Academic, making all) at Royal Ascot in June: ran creditably when fourth to
Chicarica in Hillsdown Cherry Hinton Stakes at Newmarket and sixth to Mac's Imp
in Heinz '57' Phoenix Stakes at Phoenix Park: stays 6f. *J. P. Leigh.*

ON WITH THE DANCE 3 ch.f. Formidable (USA) 125–Plie (USA) (Raja Baba —
(USA) [1989 NR 1990 8m 10.2f] angular, workmanlike filly: third foal: dam
twice-raced half-sister to very smart French 1m to 1¼m perfomer Majuscule: well
beaten in June maidens, hanging badly right second start: sold 800 gns Ascot November Sales. *P. W. Harris.*

ON Y VA (USA) 3 ch.f. Victorious (USA)–Golden Moony (Northfields (USA)) —
[1989 6m² 7f⁴ 7m⁴ 6f³ 6g 1990 10g⁶ 10m 11.5m 10f³] sparely-made, angular filly:
quite modest maiden at best: well below form in claimers and handicap in 1990:
stays 7f: sold 1,450 gns Ascot October Sales. *R. J. R. Williams.*

OOGIE POOGIE (USA) 3 b.f. Storm Bird (CAN) 134–Cascapedia (USA) —
(Chieftain II) [1989 7f² 1990 8f 10m⁴ 12.3m⁶] rangy, angular filly: turns fore feet in:
quite modest maiden at best: probably stays 1¼m. *M. R. Stoute.*

OPALKINO 5 ch.m. Relkino 131–Opalescent 71 (Gulf Pearl 117) [1989 8d 9f 7m **36**
5g 1990 a8g 10.2f 7g 8m³] angular, sparely-made mare: poor maiden: stays 1m:
below form in blinkers: trained until after third start by A. Jones: very awkward at
stalls and withdrawn fifth intended start: has worn crossed noseband. *A. Bailey.*

OPEN CHAMPION (USA) 3 b.c. To-Agori-Mou 133–Lightning Record 96 —
(Le Johnstan 123) [1989 6s⁶ 1990 10m 10.6s 9g 8m] workmanlike colt: has round
action: little worthwhile form in varied company: may prove best short of 1¼m.
M. McCormack.

OPERA GHOST 4 b.c. Caerleon (USA) 132–Premier Rose 117 (Sharp Edge 123) **87**
[1989 10.1m⁶ 10m³ 8f* 10.1m³ 8.3m⁵ 9m⁴ 10.6s 1990 12f² 12f* 12m* 12m* 12f
14g 13.3g] close-coupled, quite good-topped colt: carries plenty of condition: fair
handicapper: in excellent form in first half of season, winning at Thirsk, Doncaster,
Kempton and York: below form in valuable events last 3 outings: better suited by

1½m than shorter: acts really well on top-of-the-ground: sweated and reared stalls sixth start: most genuine. *P. W. Harris.*

OPERA HOUSE 2 b.c. (Feb 24) Sadler's Wells (USA) 132–Colorspin (FR) **100** P 118 (High Top 131) [1990 7m*]
The colours of Helena Springfield Ltd haven't been much in evidence on the racecourse since Colorspin won the Irish Oaks and Milligram and Bella Colora both went close to winning the One Thousand Guineas in a purple patch for the domestic textile company in the mid-'eighties. Those three fillies reside at the company's Meon Valley Stud now, and some of their foals have already come up for sale at Newmarket's Highflyer Yearling Sales, where the stud is one of the leading vendors. Sheikh Mohammed has been one of Meon Valley's best customers, and both parties have good reason to be satisfied with his purchases so far. In 1988 he spent 520,000 guineas on Stagecraft (by Sadler's Wells out of Bella Colora), who seemed misplaced in the betting for the Derby on the evidence of an inauspicious debut, but who really found his form in the second half of 1990 and could well be one to follow in the top events at a mile and a quarter or thereabouts in 1991; and in 1989 he paid 340,000 guineas for another colt by Sadler's Wells, out of Bella Colora's half-sister Colorspin. Named Opera House, that colt made his debut in a maiden at Leicester in October, started odds on and spreadeagled the opposition in tremendous style. A leggy, close-coupled sort, rather green in the preliminaries, Opera House showed great promise, leading on the bridle under three furlongs out, going clear soon afterwards without being extended and reaching the post ten lengths ahead of another debutant, Rivertino, with another four lengths back to the rest. It would be imprudent to make much of the fact that only third-placed Mahir of the five behind who ran subsequently did anything to advertise the race: collateral form between two-year-olds, particularly ones so lightly raced, is notorious for being misleading. Opera House certainly looked a cut above the average Leicester maiden-race winner and with plenty of improvement assured he seems certain to go on and hold his own in better company.

		┌Northern Dancer	┌Nearctic
	┌Sadler's Wells (USA)	│ (b 1961)	│Natalma
	│ (b 1981)	└Fairy Bridge	└Bold Reason
Opera House	│	│ (b 1975)	│Special
(b.c. Feb 24, 1988)	│	┌High Top	┌Derring-Do
	└Colorspin (FR)	│ (b 1969)	│Camenae
	(b 1983)	└Reprocolor	┌Jimmy Reppin
		(ch 1976)	└Blue Queen

Sadler's Wells needs no introduction; almost the same could be said of Colorspin, whose first foal Opera House is. Colorspin won three races in all, two of them as a two-year-old, including the listed Rochford Thompson Fillies Stakes, but was at her best on Irish Oaks day when, encountering soft ground for the only time in her career, she was one of the easiest winners of the classic in living memory. Colorspin has the pedigree to match her racing record; not only is she a half-sister to Bella Colora and the very useful Rappa Tap Tap, both of whom were best at up to a mile and a quarter, she's also a daughter of the Lancashire Oaks winner and Oaks fourth Reprocolor. Reprocolor is still active at the Meon Valley Stud: she had a colt by Ajdal in 1989 but was barren to Slip Anchor in 1990. Colorspin's second foal, by Lomond and so a close relation of Opera House, was sold for 44,000 guineas at the latest Highflyer Sales. Opera House will stay a mile and a half. He's emphatically one to follow. *M. R. Stoute.*

OPERATION WOLF 4 ch.g. Adonijah 126–Sesta (Artaius (USA) 129) [1989 **100** 10.2g² 10m⁴ 10m* 10g² 11s³ 8f* 10g 1990 8m⁵ 9m⁴ 9g 10.2s] lengthy, good-topped gelding: useful performer: very good fourth of 40 to Risen Moon in William Hill Cambridgeshire (Handicap) at Newmarket in October: ran poorly in Doncaster minor event final outing: probably best at 1m to 1¼m: acts on any going. *C. E. Brittain.*

ORATEL FLYER 3 gr.c. Kirchner 110–Hyperion Princess (Dragonara Palace **44** (USA) 115) [1989 6m 6g 6g a5g a5g⁶ 1990 a5g² 5f⁴ 5m 5m a5g 7f 7m 6g² 5f 7m 6f³ 5m 5.8d a6g⁴ a6g⁴ a5g] close-coupled, rather angular colt: poor maiden: probably suited by 6f: acts on firm going: sometimes wears severe noseband: took keen hold and edged left in amateurs handicap sixth start: visored last 10: inconsistent. *R. Thompson.*

ORBA GOLD (USA) 2 br.f. (Jan 23) Gold Crest (USA) 120–Miss Derby (USA) 64 (Master Derby (USA)) [1990 5f3 5g4] IR 17,000Y: lengthy, rather angular filly: keen walker: moderate mover: sixth foal: half-sister to 1985 French 2-y-o 6f winner Madame Nureyev (by Nureyev) and 3-y-o Lady Topping (by Lyphard): dam, minor winner in USA, from family of Glint of Gold and Diamond Shoal: quite modest form in maiden at Lingfield and minor event at Ripon (soon ridden along and tended to carry head bit high): slowly away: will be suited by further. *P. A. Kelleway.*

ORBITAL BOY 2 gr.g. (Mar 17) Swing Easy (USA) 126–Mummy's Chick 77 — (Mummy's Pet 125) [1990 6d a5g a8g] 3,000F, 8,200Y: first foal: dam 2-y-o 5f winner: last in maidens at Folkestone and Lingfield (2). *J. Akehurst.*

ORBIT (USA) 3 ch.f. Sunny's Halo (CAN)–Female Star (USA) (Johnny Apple- 68 seed (USA)) [1989 6g4 1990 a8g2 8f* 10g4 10m] rather unfurnished filly: favourite, won maiden at Bath in May: creditable fourth (finding little) at Lingfield, easily better effort in handicaps: stays 1¼m: acts on firm ground. *B. W. Hills.*

ORCHANDA 2 b.f. (Feb 24) Pennine Walk 120–My Fair Orchid 71 (Roan Rocket 49 128) [1990 6m 6g a7g5 6m 8.2s5 7d3 a8g6] neat filly: bad mover: third reported foal: half-sister to 3-y-o Lipperosa (by Music Boy) and fair 7f winner Oriental Splendour (by Runnett): dam plater, showed form only at 5f: fair plater: stays 1m: acts well on a soft surface: sold 1,700 gns Doncaster November Sales. *M. J. Camacho.*

ORCHARD COURT (USA) 3 ch.c. Believe It (USA)–Quilting Bee (USA) 80 (Tom Rolfe) [1989 7m4 6m6 7m* 7g3 7f* 7g 7g2 7g2 a7g* a7g* 1990 a7g* a8g* a7g* a8g* 7f 8m3] sturdy, quite attractive colt: moderate mover: fair performer: evens, completed 6-timer at Southwell when winning £5,000 claimer in March: stays 1m: acts on good to firm ground: suitable mount for claimer: sold to race in USA. *T. D. Barron.*

ORCHARD'S PET 4 gr.c. Petong 126–Toccata (USA) 64 (Mr Leader (USA)) 56 [1989 8s 6d5 7.5d 6m 7g 5f* 5m 6m2 6m6 6f4 7f5 7f 6f5 6m* 1990 a6g a6g4 a6g a6g2 a6g2 a6g 8f 8f 7h 6h5 6d2 6f 7m3 6f5 a7g2 a7g2 8f] leggy, good-topped colt: has a roundish action: plating-class handicapper: stays 7f: has won on firm going, but possibly needs an easier surface nowadays: effective with or without blinkers or a visor: suitable mount for apprentice. *W. G. M. Turner.*

ORDER OF MERIT 5 b.g. Cut Above 130–Lady Habitat (Habitat 134) [1989 9f 12f 14f3 12m 10.1m* 12f 10m 10f 11.7d 8.5f 1990 9g 10f5 10.8m] small, sturdy gelding: dropped in class, won seller at Windsor in July, 1989: no subsequent form, including in amateur events: suited by 1¼m: bolted to post on reappearance, and is a difficult ride: sold 1,900 gns Ascot September Sales. *J. White.*

ORDER PAPER 5 b.g. Taufan (USA) 119–Lady of Surana (Shirley Heights 130) 57 [1989 8g 12g 12d 13s2 10v2 13.6g 1990 a14g 11s 13v 12g 12s 12m3] narrow, leggy, close-coupled gelding: form as 5-y-o only in seller on final outing: best at 1¼m to 1½m: acted on good to firm going and went well with plenty of give: visored once: won for apprentice: dead. *J. S. Wilson.*

ORIENT AIR 2 b.f. (Mar 9) Prince Sabo 123–Chinese Falcon 81 (Skymaster 126) 60 p [1990 5f* 5m] half-sister to unreliable 3-y-o 6f seller winner Darussalam (by Tina's Pet) and useful 5f performer Miss Import (by Import): dam 2-y-o 6f winner: won maiden at Catterick in September comfortably by 1½ lengths from Serious Hurry: not discredited after slow start in nursery at Warwick following month. *T. D. Barron.*

ORIENTAL CHARM 5 ch.g. Krayyan 117–Little Angle (Gulf Pearl 117) [1989 37 10.2g 8v 1990 a8g 10f 10v 8.2s5 12g 10.6s 9m5] strong gelding: moderate mover: poor maiden: stays 9f: acts on good to firm and soft going: blinkered and visored twice: sold 2,500 gns Doncaster August Sales. *D. Moffatt.*

ORIENTAL EXPRESS 7 b.g. Whitstead 125–Miss Argyle 92 (Mountain Call — 125) [1989 NR 1990 10.2s6] leggy, sparely-made gelding: has a round action: plater: stays 1½m: probably best with give in the ground nowadays: reluctant at stalls only outing at 7 yrs: sometimes sweats. *Ronald Thompson.*

ORIENTAL MUSIC 2 b.f. (Mar 2) Music Boy 124–Orien (Goldhill 125) [1990 58 5m4 5g3 5g4 6d] strong, good-bodied filly: fifth foal: dam never ran: plating-class maiden: off course over 2 months after second start: should stay 6f. *J. Etherington.*

ORIENTAL MYSTIQUE 3 ch.f. Kris 135–Miss Toshiba (USA) 113 (Sir Ivor 97 135) [1989 6d6 1990 8m2 10.5m5 8g* 7g* 7m2 8m] rangy, quite attractive filly: fairly useful performer: won maiden at Edinburgh in June and 4-runner minor event at Yarmouth in July: behind in Group 3 event at the Curragh in September: somewhat headstrong, and seems best short of 1¼m: acts on good to firm ground: on toes first 2 outings. *B. W. Hills.*

ORIENTAL NATIVE (USA) 3 ch.g. Raise A Native–Etoile d'Orient (Targowice (USA) 130) [1989 5g 1990 8g 8g 6s 8.2g] strong, workmanlike gelding: no form in maidens or handicap (tongue tied down, ran as though something amiss): unlikely to stay 1m: blinkered last 3 outings. *W. J. Pearce.* —

ORIENTAL SPLENDOUR 4 b.f. Runnett 125–My Fair Orchid 71 (Roan Rocket 128) [1989 8.5s 7f4 7g 8f 7f* 7.6m5 7s5 7.6f5 1990 7.5m* 7m6 7m3 7g 7.5g* 7m 7.5m6] compact, workmanlike filly: fair handicapper: travelled strongly much of way when winning at Beverley in April and August: suited by 7f: acts well on top-of-the-ground: blinkered twice at 2 yrs: inconsistent. *Miss S. E. Hall.* 80

ORIENTAL TREASURE (USA) 5 ch.g. Irish River (FR) 131–Etoile d'Orient (Targowice (USA) 130) [1989 8s4 7d 8m 10f 8.3m a11g5 a10g 1990 a12g a8g] strong, medium-sized gelding: little worthwhile form since 3 yrs: stays 1m: blinkered 5 times: sold 1,400 gns Ascot February Sales. *J. W. Hills.* —

ORLEANS GIRL 3 b.f. Dixieland Band (USA)–Philassa (USA) (Forli (ARG)) [1989 6m5 6m5 5f2 7g 1990 5f2 6f2 6f6 6g2 7m5 10.1m 8g 5m4 5.3f3 6m 6g* 7g 7d] rather sparely-made filly: moderate mover: quite modest performer: led post in handicap at Folkestone in October: below form after, moving poorly to post on first occasion: should prove best at 6f or 7f: acts on firm going: has run creditably for 7-lb claimer: sweating sixth start: sold to join R. Hodges 4,000 gns Newmarket December Sales. *R. V. Smyth.* 62

ORLEANS SOUND 6 b.g. Duc d'Orleans 76–What A Performance (Gala Performance (USA)) [1989 11.7g 1990 12g a14g] smallish gelding: seems of little account: sold 3,600 gns Doncaster August Sales. *S. Mellor.* —

OR NOR 3 b.f. Cure The Blues (USA)–Barely Hot (Bold Lad (IRE) 133) [1989 5v 5s 5g 5f5 5m 5m 5f* 5f2 5g5 5g 5.3f4 1990 a5g5 a5g 5m 5m 6m 6s] lengthy filly: has a roundish action: ungenerous plater: mostly faced stiff tasks in non-selling handicaps: will stay 6f: blinkered twice, visored once: sold out of W. Carter's stable 2,000 gns Newmarket September Sales after sixth start. *J. S. Wilson.* — §

ORSETT (USA) 4 ch.g. Our Native (USA)–Ornamental (USA) (Triple Crown (USA)) [1989 7m4 10g6 1990 a10g6 a8g 8m] lengthy, rather angular gelding: lightly-raced maiden: tailed off when blinkered second outing: winning selling hurdler: sold to join M. Pipe's stable 7,500 gns Ascot May Sales. *Dr J. D. Scargill.* —

ORUJO (IRE) 2 b.c. (Mar 14) Try My Best (USA) 130–Oyace (ITY) (Hogarth (ITY)) [1990 8m*] IR 17,000Y: strong, close-coupled colt: half-brother to a winner in Italy and a winner over hurdles: dam winner in Italy, is half-sister to Italian 2000 Guineas winner Ovac: green, won 13-runner maiden at Leicester in October by 1½ lengths from Tyrian Purple, always prominent and staying on strongly despite drifting right: will stay 1¼m: sure to improve. *Sir Mark Prescott.* 80 p

ORVIETTO 3 ch.c. Try My Best (USA) 130–Ventimiglia (Bruni 132) [1989 7v 10g6 10g5 1990 8m 7.6m* 9m* 8.2f5 10g3 10m] tall, leggy colt: moderate mover: fair handicapper: impressive winner at Lingfield and York within 4 days in May: ran poorly in £35,800 event at Sandown in July final outing: stays 1¼m: acts on good to firm ground. *N. A. Callaghan.* 81

OSARIO 3 b.c. Kind of Hush 118–Welsh Jane 71 (Bold Lad (IRE) 133) [1989 5g* 6m2 6f2 6m3 6g* 1990 7m2 7d6 8m4 6s] big, robust, angular colt: capable of smart form, but clearly difficult to train: won Racecall Gold Trophy at Redcar at 2 yrs: easily best effort (off course 5½ months after) in 1990 when second in European Free Handicap at Newmarket: showed signs of retaining ability penultimate start but soon struggling when favourite for Doncaster listed race (moderately drawn) on final one: should prove as effective at 6f as 7f: acts on good to firm going. *R. Hannon.* 107 ?

OSGATHORPE 3 ch.g. Dunbeath (USA) 127–Darlingka 77 (Darling Boy 124) [1989 6m 6d4 1990 6m3 7f3 6m2 7m* 6m5 6m 8m 6m 6g 7m4 9f 8m5 7d] big, good-bodied gelding: quite modest performer: mostly below form after winning maiden at Edinburgh in June: stays 1m: acts on firm going: blinkered ninth outing, headstrong time before: gelded after final start. *E. Weymes.* 68 d

OSHAWA 3 br.f. Alzao (USA) 117–O'Shaunessy (Charlottesville 135) [1989 NR 1990 8g5 10m2 10.2f* 12f2 12v 12g* 16.5d*] 28,000Y: rangy filly: half-sister to a winner in Norway: dam placed in Irish bumper at 4 yrs: won maiden at Bath (odds on) in July and November handicaps (improved form) at Newmarket and Doncaster: 97 stays 2m: acts on firm and dead going (stiff task on heavy): has run creditably for amateur. *B. W. Hills.*

OTTERBURN (USA)   4 b.c. Raise A Man (USA)–Summertime Lady (USA) (No   — §
Robbery) [1989 10m⁴ 7.5m² 10f² 8f 1990 a10g⁶ 10h 10m⁶ 10f a13g] angular colt: modest maiden as 3-y-o: blinkered 3 times in 1990: trained first 2 starts by R. O'Sullivan: reluctant to race next time, and is one to leave alone. *F. J. O'Mahony.*

OTTERGAYLE   5 br.h. Lord Gayle (USA) 124–Otterhill 67 (Brigadier Gerard   **86**
144) [1989 8g² 8d* 7d 8s 8f 10m⁴ 9g 8d 1990 8g 7.6d³ 8m⁶ 8f 8m² 8m 10g 8g] small, finely-made horse: good mover: fair handicapper on his day: ran best races as 5-y-o when placed at Chester in May and Newmarket (4-runner £7,200 event) in June: very slowly away penultimate outing: suited by 1m: goes particularly well with give in the ground: has run creditably when sweating: has won for lady. *P. T. Walwyn.*

OUR AISLING   2 b.f. (Mar 15) Blakeney 126–Mrs Cullumbine 60 (Silly Season   **47 p**
127) [1990 6m 7d⁵] workmanlike filly with scope: third foal: half-sister to 3-y-o Caught Unawares (by Longleat) and fairly useful 7f and 1½m winner Rakes Lane (by Pitskelly): dam, stayed 1½m, half-sister to useful 6f winner Chantry Bridge: over 8 lengths fifth of 13, pushed along in rear 3f out then staying on well, in maiden at Ayr in September: bit backward on debut: will stay 1¼m: will improve again. *S. G. Norton.*

OUR FAN   4 b.c. Taufan (USA) 119–Crufty Wood (Sweet Revenge 129) [1989 5f*   **65**
5f⁵ 6g³ 6h* 6f³ 5m³ 6f² 6f* 5m⁴ 6m 5s 1990 5.8h 5d 5f⁵ 6g³ 6f² 6f² 5m⁶ 6m⁵ 5f² a6g] neat, good-quartered colt: quite modest form in handicaps as 4-y-o: stays 6f: acts on any going with possible exception of soft: suitable mount for claimer. *J. Berry.*

OUR FREDDIE   6 br.g. Cajun 120–So Valiant 80 (So Blessed 130) [1989 **104**
5s² 5m 5f* 5f⁴ 5g 5m³ 5g* 5g 5m² 5f3dis 6m 1990 5m³ 5g³ 5f* 5f* 5m² 5m* 5m² 5g³ 5m⁴]
    The very speedy Our Freddie had a tremendous 1990: he improved by leaps and bounds and was never out of the frame in nine races, successful in three of them. Not bad for a horse branded with a 'squiggle' and noted as thoroughly inconsistent in *Racehorses of 1987.* He'd shown little in the following two seasons to suggest what was in store but, as seems to happen more regularly with sprinters than their counterparts over longer distances, he took on a new lease of life. He got off the mark in a handicap at Redcar in May, making all and scoring unchallenged by three lengths, and followed up at the same course later in the month. Again he showed blistering speed, equalling the course record, and taking his tally at Redcar to four wins from as many starts there. By September he'd earned the right to tackle better company and went to post for the listed Doncaster Bloodstock Sales Scarbrough Stakes at the St Leger meeting. Quickly taking up his customary position, he led the field a merry dance for much of the way only to tie up close home, but nonetheless finished an excellent third to Rivers Rhapsody. Our Freddie had earlier dead-heated with another much-improved performer, Lucedeo, in a Newbury handicap in July, and in a very competitive handicap at Haydock in August he was able to show a clean pair of heels to two other noted front-running handicappers, Sigama and Jondebe Boy, before finally going down by half a length to Absolution.

		Red Regent	Prince Regent
	Cajun	(b 1972)	Redowa
	(ch 1979)	Ermyn Lass	Ennis
Our Freddie		(ch 1963)	Rye Girl
(br.g. 1984)		So Blessed	Princely Gift
	So Valiant	(br 1965)	Lavant
	(br 1971)	Moghari	Djebe
		(ch 1960)	Roman Triumph

    Our Freddie is the eighth foal of So Valiant, and the fifth winner; he's a half-brother, by the Middle Park Stakes winner Cajun, to the useful 1985 two-year-old five-furlong winner West Carrack (by Tachypous) and the fairly useful but temperamental 1979 two-year-old five-furlong winner Heroic Air (by Song). So Valiant also won over five furlongs at two years; she's a half-sister to the fair miler Sandring and moderate sprinter Our Audrey. Our Freddie's grandam Moghari won over eleven furlongs. Our Freddie, a well-made gelding, is a poor mover in his slower paces but acts on any going. He wears a hood and blinkers and is suited by tender handling. He once refused to go to post as a five-year-old but showed no such tendencies at six and proved a great credit to connections. *W. Carter.*

OUR MARTHA 2 br.f. (Mar 19) Sulaafah (USA) 119–Before Long (Longleat (USA) 109) [1990 8g 7d 7m] 1,200Y: workmanlike filly: first foal: dam never ran: little worthwhile form in maidens, one an auction: virtually pulled up on debut. *C. R. Barwell.*   **41**

OUR NITORIOUS 2 b.c. (May 8) Petorius 117–Night Encounter (Right Tack 131) [1990 6s 6g 8d 8f] 3,300F, 8,000Y: leggy, sparely-made colt: half-brother to 1½m winner Tyro Prince (by Prince Tenderfoot), French 3-y-o Group 3 1½m and 15f winner North Col (by Head For Heights) and a winner in Austria: dam, sister to Take A Reef, won at up to 12.5f in France: always behind in maidens. *G. R. Oldroyd.*   —

OUR PATRICK 2 b.g. (Apr 5) Morston (FR) 125–Sambell 71 (Sammy Davis 129) [1990 7f] half-brother to several winners, including quite useful middle-distance performer House Hunter (by Dubassoff) and 1981 2-y-o 5f winner Sammy Waters (by Rapid River): dam won 1m seller: slowly away and tailed off in maiden at Wolverhampton in July. *B. Preece.*   —

OUR RON 3 b.g. Daring March 116–Sweet Jane 59 (Furry Glen 121) [1989 6f³ 6m² 5m 5m 8.5g⁵ 7.3m⁶ 1990 7f 10g⁵ 11.7g 12h* 11.7m 11.5m² 10g⁵ 12m⁶ 7g⁵ a12g⁴ a13g⁴ a13g⁶ a10g³] leggy, quite attractive gelding: turns off-fore in: quite modest handicapper: won at Brighton in May: ran creditably 3 of last 4 starts at Lingfield: should be suited by return to further: best turf efforts on top-of-the-ground: edgy second start, sweating on third: has taken good hold, and wore net muzzle in apprentice race ninth start: sometimes taken down early. *R. V. Smyth.*   **66**

OUR SLIMBRIDGE 2 b. or br.g. (Apr 26) Top Ville 129–Bird Point (USA) 87 (Alleged (USA) 138) [1990 7m 7d 7g] 10,500Y: rather leggy gelding: second foal: half-brother to 3-y-o Trull (by Lomond): dam 9f to 10.1f winner: quite modest form, never dangerous or knocked about, in maiden and a minor event at Newmarket first 2 starts: showed little final one: may do better. *C. N. Williams.*   **66**

OUR TOPSIE 3 b.f. My Dad Tom (USA) 109–Tops 73 (Club House 110) [1989 NR 1990 7.2d⁶] 900 2-y-o: leggy filly: has scope: fourth reported foal: sister to a poor maiden: dam won 7f seller at 2 yrs and stayed 1½m: 25/1, behind in moderately-run maiden at Haydock in September. *H. J. Collingridge.*   —

OUR VISION 3 b.c. Vision (USA)–Faiblesse (Welsh Saint 126) [1989 7g⁴ 7m 7m⁵ 10g 1990 7f* 7m 8m⁴ 9g] rangy colt: moderate walker and mover: quite modest performer: off course over 6 months after winning handicap at Doncaster in March: raced very freely when blinkered and ridden by 7-lb claimer in £19,600 handicap at Newmarket final start: worth another try at 1¼m: acts on firm going: joined R. Holder. *C. E. Brittain.*   **67**

OUT OF FUNDS 4 b.g. Ela-Mana-Mou 132–Overspent 85 (Busted 134) [1989 12g⁶ 12.3m² 14f² 16m 1990 18.4d] useful-looking gelding: moderate walker: lightly-raced maiden, but has shown himself capable of fair form: 33/1 and sweating, close up until over 2f out when well beaten in Chester Cup in May: should stay 2m: acts on firm going. *R. Hollinshead.*   —

OUTSTANDING BILL 4 ch.g. Nicholas Bill 125–Hardwick Amber 58 (Tanfirion 110) [1989 8f 7h 7.5m 5m 6s⁴ 12g⁶ 1990 10.2f⁵ 10v] leggy, close-coupled gelding: quite modest maiden: should stay 1½m: seems to act on any going. *J. M. Jefferson.*   **64**

OVER MY HEAD 4 b.f. Bay Express 132–Mystic Halo (Aureole 132) [1989 NR 1990 a7g] smallish filly: well beaten in maidens as 2-y-o and claimer in August. *N. A. Callaghan.*   —

OVERPOWER 6 b.g. Try My Best (USA) 130–Just A Shadow (Laser Light 118) [1989 8d⁴ 8f 8m⁶ 8g* 8g³ 8.2g 8f⁴ 8g⁴ a8g⁴ a8g⁵ 1990 8f⁵ 7.6d 10m² 10g³ 10h³ 10m 9g³ 8f⁶] sparely-made gelding: quite modest handicapper: effective at 1m to 1¼m: probably not at his best on soft going, acts on any other: blinkered twice: has sweated and got on edge: not the easiest of rides: trained until after second outing by J. W. Watts. *M. H. Tompkins.*   **63**

OWER (IRE) 2 b.f. (Feb 18) Lomond (USA) 128–Argon Laser 107 (Kris 135) [1990 7f² 7g] 52,000Y: smallish, sparely-made filly: first foal: dam 7f winner, is half-sister to smart middle-distance stayer Torus: quite modest form, not knocked about, in maidens at Newmarket won by Dance Ahead in July (very green) and Campestral in November: likely to do better. *J. L. Dunlop.*   **68 p**

OWLANDISH 2 b.c. (Apr 19) Bold Owl 101–Whipalash 73 (Stephen George 102) —
[1990 8.2s 8g 10.2s] 2,500F, 4,000Y: rather leggy, unfurnished colt: seventh foal:
brother to a winner in Holland and modest sprint maiden James Owl: dam placed at
7f: well beaten in maidens and a minor event. *M. O'Neill.*

OWT ON 3 ch.g. Sweet Monday 122–Young April 46 (Young Man (FR) 73) [1989   **69**
6m 5f 6g 6g 1990 7f* 8g² 8.2s³ 7m] big, angular gelding: modest handicapper: won at
Newcastle in April: ran moderately final start (June), hanging right and not looking
keen: suited by 1m: acts on any going: flashed tail second outing: sold privately to
join J. Fort 10,000 gns Doncaster August Sales. *Mrs J. R. Ramsden.*

OXBOW 3 b.c. Trojan Fen 118–Shannon Princess (Connaught 130) [1989 8g⁵ 1990   **75**
8f 10m³ 12g 12.3m⁵ 12v⁶ 12g² 10d²] compact colt: good mover: modest maiden:
stays 1½m: acts on good to firm ground and dead: visored fifth start: sold out of P.
Walwyn's stable 24,000 gns Newmarket Autumn Sales after sixth. *R. Akehurst.*

OXFORD PADDY 3 b.g. Taufan (USA) 119–Spyglass (Double Form 130) [1989 —
7m 1990 7m⁶ 8g 8m 8g⁶ a11g⁴ a14g] leggy, close-coupled gelding: moderate walker:
poor form: blinkered last 3 outings. *R. O'Leary.*

OZONE FRIENDLY (USA) 3 ch.f. Green Forest (USA) 134–Kristana 96 —
(Kris 135) [1989 5f² 5f⁴ 6g* 5.5g* 6g⁴ 6m 1990 6m 6s] leggy, unfurnished filly:
useful performer as 2-y-o when made all in maiden at Newmarket and Prix Robert
Papin at Maisons-Laffitte: ran poorly in listed races in 1990, off course 5 months in
between: should stay 1m: best form on good ground. *B. W. Hills.*

P

PACIFIC GEM 3 br.g. Valiyar 129–Mary Martin (Be My Guest (USA) 126) [1989   **72**
5g⁶ 6f* 6m 7g 7d 1990 7d 8.2f 7m³ 8.2s 10f⁴ 9m⁴ 10d⁵ 9m 8v] medium-sized gelding:
modest handicapper: stays 1¼m: acts on firm and dead going: has worn severe
noseband and been taken last and quietly to post: sold 9,200 gns Doncaster November Sales. *P. Calver.*

PACIFIC RIM 2 ch.g. (Apr 10) Absalom 128–Spare Wheel 67 (Track Spare 125)   **76 p**
[1990 a7g² a8g*] 3,700F, 7,400Y: second foal: dam 1½m seller winner also successful over hurdles: 6/4 on, won 11-runner late-year claimer at Southwell comfortably
by 1½ lengths: stays 1m: suitable ride for apprentice. *W. A. O'Gorman.*

PACKET LINE 3 ch.f. High Line 125–Another Packet (Main Reef 126) [1989 NR —
1990 14m⁶] first foal: dam lightly-raced maiden out of half-sister to smart middle-
distance stayer Capstan: weak 14/1 and bit backward, tailed off in 6-runner maiden at
Yarmouth in September. *L. M. Cumani.*

PACTOLUS (USA) 7 b.g. Lydian (FR) 120–Honey Sand (USA) (Windy Sands) —
[1989 NR 1990 16g] leggy, rather finely-made gelding: keen walker: has a round
action: one-time quite useful handicapper: never able to challenge in £7,700 event
at Kempton in April, only race on flat since 1987: out-and-out stayer: possibly
unsuited by a soft surface: edgy when blinkered, on first occasion pulling hard and
hanging left. *S. Christian.*

PADDY CASH 3 b.g. Pas de Seul 133–Kachela (Kalamoun 129) [1989 5m 1990   **46 ?**
6m⁶ 8.2s 6g 6g⁴ 7g⁵ 6m 6g 7f 10m] leggy, rather sparely-made gelding: poor form at
best: should stay 7f: acts on good to firm ground: blinkered (led 6f) final start:
trained until after sixth by J. S. Wilson. *M. W. Easterby.*

PADDY'S LINE 3 ch.g. Crimson Line–Paddys Belle 47 (St Paddy 133) [1989 NR —
1990 11.7f 8d] strong, plain gelding: second foal: dam, plater, possibly stayed 1¼m:
backward, tailed off in maiden and claimer (sweating and edgy) 5½ months later. *D.
C. Tucker.*

PADDY TEE 2 b.c. (Jun 7) Nicholas Bill 125–Sabala 93 (Tribal Chief 125) [1990   **54**
6g 6g 7f⁴ 7m] 4,700Y: leggy colt: fifth living foal: brother to 3-y-o Loco Tycoon and
half-brother to 3 winners, including 7f and 1m winner Timber Tycoon (by Dragonara
Palace) and 1986 2-y-o 5f winner Jaisalmer (by Castle Keep): dam 6f and 7f winner:
plating-class maiden: will probably stay 1m. *M. R. Channon.*

PAGO 3 ch.c. Sallust 134–Fire Dance (FR) (Habitat 134) [1989 5g⁵ 6m 5d* 6v 6g —
1990 6d 5g⁶] close-coupled, workmanlike colt: turns fore-feet in: moderate walker
and mover: quite modest winner at 2 yrs: well below form in handicap and claimer
(in mid-division, tailed off at halfway) in October, 1990: needs further than 5f
nowadays, and should stay 1m: acts on dead ground: blinkered at 3 yrs. *J. J. O'Neill.*

PAINT THE LILY 2 ch.f. (Feb 4) Claude Monet (USA) 121–Screen Goddess 65 **62** (Caliban 123) [1990 6d⁴ 6s a8g³ a8g³] leggy filly: half-sister to 3-y-o Cocked Hat Girl (by Ballacashtal), 1¾m winner/successful hurdler Walcisin (by Balboa) and a winner in Malaysia: dam placed at up to 1½m, is half-sister to Cambridgeshire winner Negus: quite modest maiden: good third in Southwell claimer final outing: suited by 1m. *P. J. Makin.*

PALABORA (USA) 3 gr.g. Wolf Power (SAF)–Peeping (USA) (Buckfinder — (USA)) [1989 5g* 5f⁴ 6g 5.8h⁴ 6m⁴ 7m 7g³ 6f⁵ 6v a7g⁶ 7g 1990 6m 7m 8.2g 6f 6m 8m] plain, angular colt: quite modest but inconsistent winner at 2 yrs: no worthwhile form in 1990: stays 7f: appears unsuited by heavy ground: blinkered last 2 starts: edgy on reappearance: has joined D. C. O'Brien. *P. Burgoyne.*

PALACE COURT 3 b.g. Anita's Prince 126–Court Hussar (Queen's Hussar 124) — [1989 6m 8.2g 8g 1990 12f 12g 12.5g 15.3m 12m] smallish, good-quartered gelding: well beaten, including in seller: visored final start: blinkered previously at 3 yrs. *P. Burgoyne.*

PALACE LADY 4 b.f. Ballacashtal (CAN)–Belle (DEN) (Comedy Star (USA) — 121) [1989 8g 5f 10f 1990 11g 6g 7g 6m 7m 5d⁶ 6m] tall, workmanlike filly: showed signs of a little ability at Edinburgh fifth and sixth outings: sweating and blinkered fourth start. *T. Craig.*

PALACE MILL 4 b.g. Simply Great (FR) 122–Ballet Violet (Stradavinsky 121) **45** [1989 10v 11.7d 12.5f⁶ 1990 16g 17.6m⁶ 14g⁴ 17.1f⁶ 10g⁵] big, workmanlike gelding: moderate walker and mover, with a round action: poor maiden: needed further than 1¼m, but possibly best short of 2¼m: acted on good to firm going: dead. *R. J. Hodges.*

PALACE STREET (USA) 3 ch.f. Secreto (USA) 128–Majestic Street (USA) **103** (Majestic Prince) [1989 6g³ 6m⁵ 6g* 8g 1990 8g² 8m⁵ 8m² 7.2s* 8d⁴ 7m⁴ 7.3g⁶ 8g⁴ 7d² 8m³ 6s] close-coupled, wiry filly: keen walker: shows plenty of knee action: useful performer: won listed race at Haydock in June: placed afterwards behind Anshan in Group 3 contest at Goodwood and Fire The Groom in listed race (weakening final 1f) at Ascot: seems ideally suited by 7f: to race on firm going, possibly suited by some give: game and consistent. *G. B. Balding.*

PALAIS DE DANSE 6 ch.h. Dance In Time (CAN)–Dunfermline 133 (Royal — Palace 131) [1989 8.5d⁶ 10m 10.4m 9s 1990 a8g a13g 8g 10m⁶ 8g 10.6s⁵ 9s] tall, deep-girthed, rather short-backed horse: poor maiden: stays 1¼m: acts on good to firm and soft going. *A. W. Potts.*

PALATIAL STYLE 3 b.g. Kampala 120–Stylish Princess (Prince Tenderfoot **92** (USA) 126) [1989 5m⁴ 5f⁶ 5d 5g⁴ 1990 7f² 8g* 9m 8m² 8g* 8m² 8f³ 10m 9g⁴ 9m² 10.2g* 12s] leggy, angular gelding: fairly useful handicapper: won at Carlisle in April, Ripon (£7,800 event) in June and Doncaster (£8,600 event in fine style after not getting clear run) in September: set a lot to do and weakened final 1f when well-beaten eighth of 24 in November Handicap at Doncaster: suited by 1¼m, possibly by a sound surface: consistent. *M. Avison.*

PALE WINE 3 b.c. Rousillon (USA) 133–Opale 117 (Busted 134) [1989 7m 1990 **83** 13.3m*] rangy, rather unfurnished colt: favourite, won maiden at Newbury impressively by 6 lengths from Rhodes: destroyed after breaking off-fore on gallops in July: looked capable of a good deal better. *A. C. Stewart.*

PALEY PRINCE (USA) 4 b.c. Tilt Up (USA)–Apalachee Princess (USA) **106** (Apalachee (USA) 137) [1989 5m 5m 5f 5g⁴ 5f* 5m⁵ 5m³ 5m* 1990 5f⁴ 5m³ 5f 5m⁵ 5m³ 5d 5m 5m 6m 6f³ 5m* 5g⁴ 5m⁵ 5m 5m 5g a5g⁵] strong-quartered, good-topped, slightly dipped-backed colt: good mover: favourably drawn, returned to form when winning £8,700 handicap at Sandown in August: ran creditably in all-aged listed event at Doncaster and £9,900 handicap at Ascot next 2 outings: best at 5f: suited by a sound surface: useful. *M. D. I. Usher.*

PALLIUM (IRE) 2 b.c. (Apr 16) Try My Best (USA) 130–Jungle Gardenia **68 §** (Nonoalco (USA) 131) [1990 5g⁵ 6g 5f² 5m² 5m⁶] 4,800Y, 19,000 2-y-o: good-bodied colt: third foal: half-brother to a winner in Italy by Dominion: dam, from family of Pampapaul, He Loves Me and Common Land, ran several times at 2 yrs in Ireland: quite modest performer: ran poorly final outing: should stay 6f: blinkered or visored final 2 starts: hangs right, and looked thoroughly unco-operative penultimate appearance: one to be wary of. *M. P. Naughton.*

PALMAS PRIDE 3 b.g. Dalsaan 125–Sabirone (FR) (Iron Duke (FR) 122) [1989 **65** 6g⁵ 7m 6m³ 6g² 6m² 7d² 1990 8.2f⁴ 8.2g* 7d³ 7m² 7f* 8h³] sturdy gelding: moderate walker: quite modest performer: won handicaps at Nottingham in June (awarded race much later) and Ayr (made all) in July: stays 1m: yet to race on soft ground, acts on any other: has run creditably for apprentice: blinkered or visored fourth start and last 3 at 2 yrs: claimed out of D. Morley's stable £7,655 fourth outing: winning hurdler. *M. D. Hammond.*

PALMION 8 b.g. Dominion 123–Blessed Palm 76 (St Paddy 133) [1989 NR 1990 a7g] lengthy, attractive gelding: quite modest handicapper in 1987: never able to challenge at Lingfield in December, only subsequent outing: best over 7f or easy 1m: yet to show his form on soft going, acts on any other: has won for apprentice: ideally suited by sharp track. *R. Curtis.* —

PALM REEF 6 b.g. Main Reef 126–Fingers (Lord Gayle (USA) 124) [1989 12s 7.9m 6f 8m 8g 7s 12f a12g 1990 a8g6] well-made gelding: modest maiden as 3-y-o: no subsequent form: occasionally blinkered: sold 1,600 gns Ascot February Sales. *M. Madgwick.* —

PALM SWIFT 4 b.f. Rabdan 129–Swiftsand 65 (Sharpen Up 127) [1989 7m 7f a8g 1990 12m a7g] leggy filly: no worthwhile form in varied events. *A. J. Chamberlain.* —

PALMY (USA) 3 b.f. Buckfinder (USA)–Pampas 99 (Pampapaul 121) [1989 NR 1990 8g 8g6 12f 10g] workmanlike filly: second foal: half-sister to Strover (by Sir Ivor), 7f (at 2 yrs) and 9.5f winner in Ireland: dam 5f winner here and in Ireland, later raced in USA: no worthwhile form in maidens and handicap: joined S. Leadbetter. *C. W. C. Elsey.* —

PALVIC GREY 6 gr.m. Kampala 120–Ambient 68 (Amber Rama (USA) 133) [1989 NR 1990 12h] leggy, angular mare: well beaten in modest company. *Miss G. M. Rees.* —

PAMIANBE 2 ch.f. (Mar 25) Music Boy 124–City Link Rose (Lochnager 132) [1990 6m] second foal: half-sister to 5f winner City Link Pet (by Tina's Pet): dam showed signs of a little ability: very slowly away and soon struggling in maiden at Newmarket in November. *D. A. Wilson.* —

PANALO 3 gr.g. Magic Mirror 105–Radinka (Connaught 130) [1989 6m 7f 7m4 6f 5g4 5m6 6m 6g 5g 6f6 5f2 5m3 5g5 6s3 a6g* 1990 7f 6g 7h4 7g a7g 7g2 7g* 8m 7f] smallish, sparely-made gelding: won seller (no bid) at Catterick in July: below form later in summer: suited by 7f: acts on any going: best form in blinkers or a visor: has worn bandages. *J. Hetherton.* 56

PANAMA PATTI (IRE) 2 b.f. (Apr 29) Alzao (USA) 117–Stamina 78 (Star Appeal 133) [1990 5m 5m5 5f 5f6 7f 7m] 8,000Y, 4,000 2-y-o: sturdy, close-coupled filly: moderate walker: second foal: dam 10.1f winner, is daughter of useful middle-distance performer Swift Harmony: little worthwhile form: should be suited by further than 5f: sold 1,050 gns Newmarket Autumn Sales. *R. Hollinshead.* 32

PANAMA PETE (IRE) 2 b.c. (May 22) Horage 124–Cheerleader 90 (Floribunda 136) [1990 5m 5g 5d* 6g* 7f* 7m5 7f* 7g 7f6 7m2 7m 7m5] IR 6,500Y: small, stocky colt: carries plenty of condition: brother to 1¼m winner Another Wish and a winner in Switzerland and half-brother to several winners in Italy: dam 2-y-o 5.1f winner later successful in Italy, is daughter of half-sister to On Your Mark: successful in sellers (no bid) at Beverley and Ripon and in non-selling nurseries at Lingfield in July and Redcar in the summer: will be better suited by 1m: yet to race on very soft going, acts on any other: game and genuine: sold 17,000 gns Newmarket Autumn Sales. *M. H. Easterby.* 77

PANCHOS PEARL (USA) 2 b.f. (Apr 13) Pancho Villa (USA)–Jackie Pearl (USA) (Ruffled Feathers) [1990 6d3 6m2 6f* 6m 6m* 6d2 6m] $90,000Y: angular, unfurnished filly: has a fluent, round action: half-sister to Italian St Leger winner Rough Pearl (by Tom Rolfe) and a winner in North America: dam very useful winner at up 1m: sire seemed best from 6f to 1m: quite useful performer: successful at Goodwood in maiden in August and a minor event in September: ran well after when third to Imperfect Circle in listed race at Ayr and seventh of 11 to Capricciosa in Tattersalls Cheveley Park Stakes at Newmarket: will be better suited by 7f: acts on firm and dead ground. *C. R. Nelson.* 95

PANDESSA 3 b.f. Blue Cashmere 129–Jeanne du Barry 74 (Dubassoff (USA)) [1989 6f5 5m5 1990 6m6 8m] lengthy, unfurnished, plain filly: poor form in varied events. *J. H. Johnson.* —

PANDY 4 b.g. Thatching 131–Hot Stone (Hotfoot 126) [1989 8.2g5 8m* 8g 10g 1990 10m3 10.4d 10f5 9m2 10m2 11f* 10.6m3 10.5g4] lengthy, useful-looking gelding: has a quick action: modest handicapper: comfortably landed odds in 4-runner event at Redcar in July: hung left final start: stays 11f: seems well suited by top-of-the-ground: sold to join G. Thorner's stable 12,000 gns Newmarket Autumn Sales. *J. W. Hills.* 77

665

PAN E SALAM 3 gr.g. Ile de Bourbon (USA) 133–Norton Princess 76 (Wolver 72 +
Hollow 126) [1989 NR 1990 10m 12s* 12d³ 12g] 9,000Y: smallish, angular gelding:
second foal: dam 6f winner at 2 yrs seemed not to train on: won maiden auction race
at Hamilton in May: 33/1, easily better effort in minor events in summer, appearing
to show improved form, when third of 6 to Tyrone Bridge in moderately-run race at
Beverley: stays 1½m well. *Dr J. D. Scargill.*

PANICO 3 b.c. Superlative 118–Ex Dancer (USA) (Executioner (USA)) [1989 6f 56
7g 1990 7g⁶ 6g 8f³ 10m 8f² 8m 7.2d⁴] strong colt: plating-class maiden: ran well,
making most, at Thirsk (edgy) and Haydock (moderately-run race, tended to put
head in air last 2f) fifth and final starts: stays 1m (very slowly away over 1¼m): acts
on firm and dead going: visored last 3 starts: retained by trainer 17,000 gns
Doncaster August Sales after fifth. *Miss S. E. Hall.*

PANIC RISING (USA) 2 b.c. (Feb 6) Master Willie 129–Sticky Habit 79 — p
(Habitat 134) [1990 6d] fifth foal: half-brother to several winners, including very
useful 6f to 8.5f winner Aim For The Top (by Irish River) and 7f winner Surmise (by
Alleged): dam, from good family, won at 1m and 1¼m: around 15 lengths ninth of 17
in maiden at Folkestone in November. *C. A. Cyzer.*

PANIENKA (POL) 6 b.m. Dom Racine (FR) 121–Pointe Rousse (FR) —
(Margouillat (FR) 133) [1989 NR 1990 16g] good-topped mare: quite modest handicapper as 4-y-o, successful on 3 occasions: soundly beaten only subsequent outing:
suited by test of stamina: possibly unsuited by firm going and used to act well on
soft. *J. Mackie.*

PANIKIN 2 gr.g. (Apr 9) Red Sunset 120–Haunting 79 (Lord Gayle (USA) 124) 85
[1990 a7g* a6g⁴ 7s³ 7s] 8,000Y: unfurnished gelding: brother to 3-y-o Mrs Gray, 5f
winner at 2 yrs, closely related to useful 1986 2-y-o 5f and 6f winner Amigo Sucio (by
Stanford) and one-time fairly useful 6f and 7f winner Valley Mills (by Red Alert), and
half-brother to several other winners: dam stayed 1m: won maiden at Southwell in
July: better efforts in nurseries at Doncaster on last 2 starts: stays 7f: acts well on
soft ground. *J. Wharton.*

PANORAMIC 3 b.c. Rainbow Quest (USA) 134–Immense (USA) (Roberto (USA) 118
131) [1989 8g² 9g⁴ 1990 11s* 12g* 12m⁵ 12g² 12v] IR 130,000Y: second foal:
half-brother to successful U.S. filly On The Avenue (by Caro): dam, 3-y-o Grade 3
8.5f winner, is half-sister to joint top U.S. 2-y-o filly of 1975 Dearly Precious: won
handicap in April and listed race in May, both at Longchamp: about 3½ lengths fifth
to Sanglamore in Prix du Jockey-Club at Chantilly and good second in Prix du
Conseil de Paris at Longchamp 4½ months later: stays 1½m: seems unsuited by
heavy going, yet to race on firm. *A. Fabre, France.*

PANSONG 4 b.c. Absalom 128–Sea Chant (Julio Mariner 127) [1989 10.2g 9v²
8.2s 8.2m 12.2m 8h⁵ 9f⁵ 7m 9f⁵ 8f 8.5m 10s⁴ 9s 1990 8m 5g 8f a7g 10m 7.6m 10.8f
a11g] leggy colt: poor walker and mover: fair plater at his best in 1989: has lost his
form: stays 1¼m: probably acts on any going: sometimes blinkered or visored:
sweating third and fourth outings: sold out of T. Fairhurst's stable 1,800 gns
Doncaster March Sales. *M. B. James.*

PAPER CRAFT 3 b.g. Formidable (USA) 125–Civility 108 (Shirley Heights 130) 64
[1989 NR 1990 a7g 7d⁶ 8m³ 10.2g 9s*] IR 10,000Y: lengthy gelding: second living
foal: dam, first past post twice at around 1½m but suited by 1¾m, is half-sister to
smart 1976 2-y-o 5f performer Piney Ridge and very useful 1¼m winner Hill's
Yankee: quite modest performer: 16/1, improved form to win 17-runner handicap at
Hamilton in September: stays 9f: goes well on soft ground: coltish first 3 outings
and susequently gelded: tends to hang, and is not an easy ride. *M. Johnston.*

PAPER DANCE 2 b.c. (May 13) Mashhor Dancer (USA)–April Days 75 (Silly 73
Season 127) [1990 8m³ 8g 7m] rangy, shallow-girthed colt: half-brother to 3-y-o
Trying Days (by Teenoso) and several winners here and abroad, including a 1¼m
plater by Bay Express: dam 10.4f winner, is out of Oaks second Maina: modest form,
shaping promisingly, in maiden at Chepstow and minor event at Newbury first 2
starts: ran poorly in maiden after: will be suited by 1¼m + . *R. J. Holder.*

PAPER DART (USA) 2 b.c. (Feb 5) Lear Fan (USA) 130–Forelie 88 (For- 66
midable (USA) 125) [1990 7m⁶ 6d² 7g] 16,000Y: rather unfurnished colt: second foal:
half-brother to 4-y-o Cavalcanti (by Sir Ivor): dam, 6f winner who only raced at 2 yrs,
is half-sister to Derby Italiano winner My Top: 5 lengths second of 11 to Reed Bed in
maiden at Lingfield in October: stays 7f. *P. T. Walwyn.*

PAPER SHOES 4 b.f. Workboy 123–Two Friendly 54 (Be Friendly 130) [1989 61
5d⁶ 5f 5m 5f4 5f 5g* 5f 5g 5s⁴ 1990 a5g⁴ a6g 5g⁴ a5g 5f² 5g 5d⁵ 5s³ a5g* a5g⁶]
leggy filly, rather unfurnished: quite modest handicapper: made all at Southwell in

December: best at 5f: seems to act on any going: effective with or without blinkers: inconsistent. *R. Earnshaw.*

PAPPAGALLO 3 ch.c. Lomond (USA) 128–Glasshouse (AUS) (Boone's Cabin 73 (USA)) [1989 NR 1990 8m 7g⁴ 7m⁵ 8d 8.2d³ 10m² 10f⁶ 10f* 10m²] sturdy, attractive colt: has plenty of scope: moderate mover: third foal: dam 6f winner at 3 yrs in Australia from good family: modest performer: won 5-runner claimer at Yarmouth in August, leading close home: stays 1¼m: acts on firm and dead going: lacks turn of foot. *W. Jarvis.*

PAQUERETTE 2 b.f. (May 14) Crofthall 110–Bouchette 76 (Current Coin 118) — [1990 6m] plain filly: seventh foal: dam 7f seller winner: backward, green and bandaged, slowly away and always tailed off in maiden at Pontefract in September. *A. Smith.*

PARADIGM'S VISION (IRE) 2 b.f. (May 22) Vision (USA)–Echo Repeating 45 (Ballymore 123) [1990 7.5g⁶ 7f⁶ 8m 10.6s] IR 1,400Y: leggy filly: poor mover: half-sister to a winner over hurdles in Ireland: dam unraced close relation of Cumberland Lodge winner Fingal's Cave: poor maiden: should stay beyond 1m: seems unsuited by soft ground. *J. Parkes.*

PARADOR 4 ch.c. Be My Guest (USA) 126–Keep Shining (USA) 77 (Stage Door 98 Johnny) [1989 5h 7h⁴ 6f⁴ 10.2f* 10m* 10f³ 9m* 9g 10g 1990 10.2m* 10f² 10f⁴ 10g⁴ 9m] angular, unfurnished colt: fairly useful handicapper: won slowly-run race at Doncaster in May: ran well after when in frame in valuable events at Redcar (unlucky), Goodwood and Newbury: suited by 1¼m and a sound surface: has won for apprentice: carries head bit high and best held up. *G. Harwood.*

PARBOLD HILL 2 ch.c. (May 25) Carwhite 127–Coppice (Pardao 120) [1990 40 8.2m 8.5m⁶ 8g] 5,000Y: leggy, close-coupled colt: seventh foal: half-brother to fair 1m to 10.2f winner Madame Bovary (by Ile de Bourbon), 1986 2-y-o 5.1f winner Nightdress (by Pyjama Hunt) and winners in Italy and Belgium: dam second in small 9f race in France: well beaten in maidens and a minor event. *K. R. Burke.*

PAR DE LUXE 3 b.f. Superlative 118–Parbold 54 (Sassafras (FR) 135) [1989 7g⁵ 63 1990 7g³ 8.5g⁵] strong, workmanlike filly: quite modest form in maidens in May: probably stays 8.5f. *C. W. C. Elsey.*

PAREVA (USA) 3 b.c. Pas Seul (USA)–Bare Eva (USA) (Barrera (USA)) [1989 — NR 1990 11v a12g] medium-sized colt: first reported living foal: dam minor sprint winner in USA: sire unraced son of Northern Dancer: tailed-off last in claimer then maiden (blinkered, pulled hard) nearly 4 months later. *J. S. Wainwright.*

PARIOS (FR) 2 ch.c. (Mar 2) Sicyos (USA) 126–Parga (FR) (Gay Mecene (USA) 75 128) [1990 5g⁴ 5m⁴ 5m 5m³ 5d² 5g] 34,000Y: rather unfurnished colt: first foal: dam unraced: modest performer: ran as if something amiss final start: will probably be better suited by 6f: acts on good to firm and dead going. *J. W. Payne.*

PARISH CHIMES (IRE) 2 b. or br.f. (May 2) Dalsaan 125–Parish Bell 59 (Monseigneur (USA) 127) [1990 6m a6g⁴ a7g⁶] IR 700F: small, good-bodied filly: third foal: half-sister to 1988 French 2-y-o 6f winner Convocation (by General Assembly): dam unraced half-sister to Coronation Cup winner Sea Chimes: plating-class maiden: well beaten on all-weather. *R. Guest.*

PARISIAN EXPRESS (FR) 2 gr.f. (Feb 18) Siberian Express (USA) 125– 41 Parisana (FR) (Gift Card (FR) 124) [1990 7d 9m⁵] 8,200Y: lengthy, angular filly: first foal: dam unraced daughter of Oaks winner Pia, grandam of Chief Singer: soundly beaten in maiden auction at Goodwood and 5-runner maiden at Wolverhampton in October: sold 3,000 gns Ascot December Sales, and has joined K. Cunningham-Brown. *M. A. Jarvis.*

PARISIAN GIRL 7 br.m. Blue Cashmere 129–Confleur 81 (Compensation 127) — [1989 7f 6m⁵ 6s 1990 5s 6s a6g] lengthy mare: poor maiden: ideally suited by 6f and give in the ground: well beaten when visored: often apprentice ridden. *E. J. Alston.*

PARIS MATCH 8 b. or br.g. Bold Lad (IRE) 133–Miss Paris 111 (Sovereign Path — 125) [1989 15.8m 1990 11f⁵] big, lengthy gelding: poor maiden: fair handicapper at his best at 3 yrs: best form at 1m: acted on firm going: blinkered twice: winning selling hurdler twice in August: dead. *G. M. Moore.*

PARIS OF TROY 2 b.c. (Feb 13) Trojan Fen 118–Little Loch Broom 60 (Reform 82 132) [1990 7m³ 7m² 7m 8.2d*] 21,000Y: leggy, quite attractive colt: fifth foal: half-brother to 4 winners, including fairly useful 11f and 13.3f winner Musaahim (by Pharly) and very useful 1983 2-y-o 6f winner Fawzi (by Young Generation): dam placed over 1m and 1¼m, is daughter of very useful Sleat, grandam of Reprimand: won 17-runner maiden at Haydock in September by a head, clear, from Malibu

Magic: better suited by 1m than 7f: acts on good to firm ground and dead. *M. A. Jarvis.*

PARKBORO LAD   3 b.c. Kala Shikari 125–Great Lass (Vaigly Great 127) [1989 — 5s 5f6 1990 a6g] sturdy, lengthy, workmanlike colt: well beaten in maidens and claimer: dead. *J. Wharton.*

PARK FORUM   3 ch.c. Dunbeath (USA) 127–Heavenly Gaze (FR) (Gay Mecene — (USA) 128) [1989 5m 1990 a8g a10g6] well beaten in minor event and maidens. *J. Sutcliffe.*

PARKING BAY   3 b.g. Bay Express 132–Sophie Avenue (Guillaume Tell (USA)   67 121) [1989 6f6 8m 8g3 1990 8.2f* 9m6 9g5 10g5 10.2g] tall, good-topped gelding: has scope: quite modest performer: won handicap at Nottingham in May: stays 9f: acts on firm going: not entirely discredited for lady rider. *G. A. Pritchard-Gordon.*

PARKLANDS BELLE   6 b.m. Stanford 121§–Kelly's Curl (Pitskelly 122) [1989   34 8s 6v 7g5 8d 8m 7f 8.2g3 a8g2 a7g 1990 7f3 5m 8f4 8f 5g a8g6] smallish mare: poor plater judged on most form: stays 1m: acts on any going: has won when sweating and for amateur: inconsistent. *C. J. Hill.*

PARK STREET   5 b.g. Runnett 125–Chieftain Girl (USA) (Chieftain II) [1989 NR — 1990 a10g5] rangy gelding: fair handicapper as 3-y-o: weakened and eased final 1f when fifth of 7 at Lingfield in February: suited by strongly-run 1m: probably acts on any going: winning but unreliable hurdler. *O. Sherwood.*

PARKWAY EXPRESS   4 ch.f. Sagaro 133–Parrot Fashion 86 (Pieces of Eight — § 128) [1989 NR 1990 11.5m 12h5 a14g] sparely-made filly: fifth foal: dam best at 1¼m: of no account and is also ungenuine: bandaged final outing. *B. Stevens.*

PARLIAMENTARY   2 ch.c. (Apr 11) Parliament 117–Barefoot Contessa   49 (Homeric 133) [1990 7m 7m 7f5 6s] 3,200Y: leggy, sparely-made colt: half-brother to 4 winners, including sprinter Shay (by Hays) and 1986 2-y-o 7f winner Imperial Way (by Runnett): dam never ran: best effort fifth in seller at Redcar in October: reared stalls continually and withdrawn intended third outing: appears to need further than 6f, and will stay 1m. *M. Brittain.*

PARLIAMENT PIECE   4 ch.g. Burslem 123–Sallywell (Manado 130) [1989 8f4   84 7f* 10g 7m2 7.6g6 6g 7f2 7g4 7g2 7g4 7g6 1990 7f3 8g4 7m 7m6 8m4 7m4 7f2 8f4 8f5 7m] big, lengthy gelding: poor mover: fair handicapper: ran creditably most starts as 4-y-o, on eighth behind March Bird in £64,400 Schweppes Golden Mile at Goodwood: ridden by 7-lb claimer, didn't lead and found little next time: stays 1m: acts on firm ground: visored seventh to ninth starts: unsuited by Chester track: goes well with forcing tactics. *R. M. Whitaker.*

PARR (IRE)   3 b.c. (Apr 10) Salmon Leap (USA) 131–Mums 88 (Mummy's Pet   66 p 125) [1990 7g 8g6] lengthy, workmanlike colt: has scope: good walker: second foal: dam ran only at 2 yrs, winning at 5f: quite modest form in minor events at Kempton and Newbury in September: will probably improve bit further. *M. R. Stoute.*

PARSONSANNCO   2 b.f. (Mar 6) Blushing Scribe (USA) 107–Pink Robber   42 (USA) 85 (No Robbery) [1990 5f 6m5 6g 7.5d 7f2 a7g3 7f6 a7g6] 800F, 3,000Y: leggy filly: second foal: dam 6f winner at 2 yrs: modest plater: ran poorly final 2 outings, last one for 7-lb claimer: looked reluctant sixth start: seems suited by 7f: acts on firm ground: sometimes bandaged. *K. T. Ivory.*

PARTING MOMENT (USA)   3 ch.c. The Minstrel (CAN) 135–Farewell 103 Letter (USA) (Arts And Letters) [1989 7m 7g* 7f 8.5g2 8g2 10g4 1990 10g3 12m2 12d* 16.2f2 14.5g* 15g 15g6 16m5] rather leggy, attractive colt: good walker: useful performer: successful in smallish fields for listed race at Lyon in June and St Leger Italiano (by 8 lengths) at Turin in July: ran well in Prix de Lutece at Longchamp (held up) and listed race won by Arzanni at Newmarket last 2 starts: suited by test of stamina: yet to race on soft going, acts on any other: usually makes the running: genuine and consistent. *I. A. Balding.*

PARTY TREAT (IRE)   2 ch.f. (Mar 12) Millfontaine 114–Party Dancer (Be My   69 Guest (USA) 126) [1990 5m4 5f3 5f2 5g3 5m2 5m3 6d 5d2 6d5] IR 1,500Y: workmanlike filly: carries condition: half-sister to 1986 2-y-o 5f seller winner Broon's Answer (by Junius): dam ran twice: very useful plater: good second in non-selling nursery at Doncaster penultimate start: should stay 6f: acts on good to firm ground and dead: blinkered final 4 starts: usually bandaged: tends to wander: trained first 3 outings by B. Stevens. *T. Casey.*

PAS DE REEF   3 ch.f. Pas de Seul 133–La Paille 113 (Thatch (USA) 136) [1989   49 7.5g 7f5 1990 9s2 11v 8.2g 9m2 12m2 10m* 11g* 12g2 a12g3 a12g6 12m 12s] workmanlike filly: plating-class handicapper: 5-length winner at Beverley (seller, no bid) and Hamilton in July: slipped and unseated rider final start: stays 1½m: acts on good to firm ground and soft. *M. Brittain.*

PASHM   4 ch.c. Morston (FR) 125–Poshteen 86 (Royal Smoke 113) [1989 NR 1990 7.6f a8g a11g] tall colt: poor form in modest company. *O. O'Neill.*   —

PASHTO   3 b.g. Persian Bold 123–Epure (Bellypha 130) [1989 NR 1990 8m 10m² 13.3m⁴ 14g* 13.3m 14g³ 15d* 16m* 18d] 42,000Y: rather leggy, workmanlike gelding: shows knee action: first foal: dam, 11.5f winner in France, is closely related to high-class French 1m and 11f winner Al Nasr and half-sister to 3 other at least useful animals: won maiden at Nottingham in July, amateurs event at Ayr in September and £7,700 handicap at Newmarket in October: 9/1 and looking very well, soundly beaten in Cesarewitch at Newmarket: should stay beyond 2m: acts on good to firm ground and dead: genuine: joined N. Henderson. *B. W. Hills.*   101

PASSAGE HOME   3 b.f. Blakeney 126–Maze (Silly Season 127) [1989 NR 1990 10f⁵ 11g³ 12m a12g] leggy filly: half-sister to fair 1986 1m and 1¼m winner Sweet Domain (by Dominion): dam twice-raced half-sister to very useful middle-distance handicapper Polish Warrior: form in maidens then handicap in the summer only when close third of 8 in auction race at Edinburgh. *C. W. C. Elsey.*   55

PASSED PAWN   3 b.g. Blakeney 126–Miss Millicent (Milesian 125) [1989 8m 7d⁴ 8.2s 1990 12m² 14g 12m⁴ 12m² 12m⁵ a12g* a11g* a11g³ a14g* 16.2s⁵ 15d* 16.5d] small gelding: modest performer: successful in seller (bought in 8,200 gns) and apprentice handicap at Southwell on consecutive days in August then in handicaps at same course in September and Edinburgh (comfortably) in October: suited by around 1¾m: acts on good to firm ground and dead. *M. H. Tompkins.*   68

PASSING SALE (FR)   3 b.c. No Pass No Sale 120–Reachout And Touch (USA) (Youth (USA) 135) [1989 8g⁶ 7g 7s⁴ 1990 8f 11s² 9.7g* 12g* 12m⁶ 10g² 10g* 12m³ 12g*] 65,000 francs (approx £5,950) Y: strong, angular colt: second foal: dam unraced daughter of Musidora winner Everything Nice: won handicap at Longchamp, listed races at Maisons-Laffitte and Deauville (Piaget d'Or) and Prix du Conseil de Paris (by short neck from Panoramic) at Longchamp: good third in Prix Niel at Longchamp: stays 1½m well: acts on good to firm ground and dead: smart. *B. Secly, France.*   119

PASSION AND MIRTH   3 b.f. Known Fact (USA) 135–Bustling Nelly 94 (Bustino 136) [1989 8g 1990 8f 10.1m 16m² 12h³ a11g³ 12m 12f* 10m⁴ a11g³ 12g⁶ 12d] small filly: fair plater: won apprentice handicap (no bid) at Brighton in September: 51

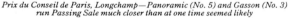

Prix du Conseil de Paris, Longchamp—Panoramic (No. 5) and Gasson (No. 3) run Passing Sale much closer than at one time seemed likely

stays 1½m: acts on firm going: sold 3,200 gns Newmarket Autumn Sales. *C. A. Cyzer.*

PASSION KING 5 ch.g. Dara Monarch 128–Ardent Runner 94 (Runnymede — 123) [1989 NR 1990 7m 10.2f] leggy gelding: quite modest handicapper as 3-y-o: never placed to challenge both outings in July: should stay beyond 7f: acts on firm going: has carried head awkwardly and edged right: apparently needs to be covered up. *G. B. Balding.*

PATAUDI (USA) 10 b.h. Apalachee (USA) 137–Bonavista (Dead Ahead) [1989 — NR 1990 12d 11.5g6] bandaged and backward on only runs on flat since 2 yrs, tailed off in minor event and handicap in June. *P. Howling.*

PATCHWORK (USA) 3 gr.f. Diesis 133–Hardship (USA) (Drone) [1989 NR — 1990 10g5 10.2f6 12h3] $250,000Y: leggy, rather angular filly: has rather round action: fourth foal: half-sister to 2 winners in USA, notably very useful filly Rose Park (by Plugged Nickle): dam very useful at 2 yrs in USA, placed in 1m Grade 1 event: quite modest maiden: soon ridden along when well-beaten third of 5 at Brighton: sold 7,000 gns Newmarket December Sales. *J. H. M. Gosden.*

PATHERO 6 ch.g. Godswalk (USA) 130–Canoodle 66 (Warpath 113) [1989 14s — 13v 13v 12d 16g 1990 13g6] smallish, sturdy gelding: carries plenty of condition: moderate mover: quite modest winner as 4-y-o: lightly raced and well below form subsequently: stays 2m: probably not suited by firm going and used to go extremely well with plenty of give: blinkered once: occasionally sweats: has won for apprentice. *N. Bycroft.*

PATHFINDER FORCE (IRE) 2 b.g. (May 4) Tate Gallery (USA) 117–Sister — Eucharia (Oats 126) [1990 6g 6m] 10,000Y: medium-sized gelding: has scope: first reported living foal: dam Irish 1¼m winner: backward, showed signs of a little ability in maiden and auction race. *J. Sutcliffe.*

PATH OF CONDIE 3 b.c. Vaigly Great 127–Goosie-Gantlet 63 (Run The 66 Gantlet (USA)) [1989 7g 7f5 1990 7g 10.2m3 10m3 12g3 15.5f 13.8d4] rather leggy, angular colt: has a quick action: quite modest maiden: best form at 1½m to 1¾m with give in ground: sold to join M. Pipe 12,500 gns Newmarket Autumn Sales. *B. W. Hills.*

PATIENCE CAMP 4 b.f. Bustino 136–Short Rations (Lorenzaccio 130) [1989 — 12g2 14m2 16g2 16m5 14g* 16f* 16g2 1990 16.2f4 20m 18m3] tall, lengthy, plain filly: useful winner as 3-y-o: ran badly on fourth outing (visored) that season and all 3 in 1990: stays well: best run on good ground: has had tongue tied down: one to leave alone: sold 26,000 gns Newmarket December Sales. *M. R. Stoute.*

PATIENCE CREEK 4 ch.f. Mummy's Game 120–Brandon Creek 79 (Be My 58 Guest (USA) 126) [1989 7g5 8f 8f5 8m 8f2 8d* 8g 1990 a8g6 8g 8d a8g5 a10g5] workmanlike filly: has a round action: quite modest winner of handicap at Goodwood as 3-y-o: shaped as though retaining most of her ability in autumn: should stay 1¼m: acts on firm and dead going. *C. P. Wildman.*

PATRICIA (USA) 2 ch.f. (Feb 3) Assert 134–Passionist (USA) (Buckpasser) — p [1990 7m] $20,000Y: useful-looking filly: half-sister to several minor winners: dam minor winner at up to 9f: well backed, twice impeded before halfway then not knocked about when beaten in maiden at Leicester in October: moved poorly down: should improve. *H. R. A. Cecil.*

PATRICK JOHN LYONS 9 b.h. Cavo Doro 124–Latin Spice (Frankincense — 120) [1989 12.2s 10s 15.5s 10.1m 12.2m 11.7m 11.7m 11.7m 1990 10m 10m] robust, compact horse: no longer of much account. *P. J. Arthur.*

PATROCLUS 5 b.g. Tyrnavos 129–Athenia Princess 80 (Athens Wood 126) 34 § [1989 16m6 19f 12f 19g5 1990 15.5f6 17m3] workmanlike gelding: has a round action: quite modest winner early as 3-y-o, but has deteriorated: suited by test of stamina: probably acts on any going: blinkered once at 3 yrs: takes a lot of driving, and is ungenuine. *R. Voorspuy.*

PATSBERIC 3 b.g. Blushing Scribe (USA) 107–Manageress 74 (Mandamus 120) — [1989 7f 7m 1990 9m6 12m5 11.7h6] sturdy gelding: little form, in handicap and maiden claimer (blinkered) last 2 outings: swished tail repeatedly in preliminaries on reappearance. *R. J. Holder.*

PATSY'S PET 2 b.f. (Apr 1) Tina's Pet 121–Emperor Star (King Emperor (USA)) 59 [1990 5f 6h2 a6g4 7g6 6v5 6d 8d a6g a7g] 2,500F, 8,000Y: leggy, rather shallow-girthed filly: closely related to 3 winners, including very useful 6f and 7f winner Not For Show (by Mummy's Pet) and half-sister to another winner: dam of little account: quite modest maiden: stays 7f: probably not ideally suited by soft ground: blinkered (pulled hard) seventh start: has run well for 7-lb claimer. *T. Fairhurst.*

PATTIE'S GREY   4 gr.f. Valiyar 129–Katysue 98 (King's Leap 111) [1989 7.5m⁴   61
1990 5g⁵ 7m² 7.5d⁶ 5f⁵ a6g* a6g 6m⁶ a6g 6d] workmanlike, good-quartered filly: moderate walker and mover: favourite, made all in 16-runner handicap at Southwell in August: found little next outing: stays 7f: blinkered last 6 starts: sold 2,200 gns Doncaster November Sales. *J. Etherington.*

PAULINES VALENTINE   2 b.f. (May 16) Aragon 118–My Haven 77   43
(Godswalk (USA) 130) [1990 5m 7f⁴ 7d 7f 8v] 3,000Y: third foal: dam 2-y-o 7f winner: poor maiden: well beaten last 3 starts, including in a seller: stays 7f: twice slowly away. *J. S. Wilson.*

PAVERS GOOD SHOES   2 b.f. (Mar 18) Good Times (ITY)–Windy Sea 105   —
(Sea Hawk II 131) [1990 6g] 1,400Y: medium-sized, angular filly: half-sister to fairly useful 6f and 8.2f winner Sharp Sea (by Sharpen Up) and a winner in Holland: dam won over 7f and 1¼m: better for race, behind in maiden auction at Kempton in September. *M. Brittain.*

PAY HOMAGE   2 ch.g. (May 1) Primo Dominie 121–Embraceable Slew (USA)   94
(Seattle Slew (USA)) [1990 5d² 5f² 6d⁵ 5.8f³ 7f* 7g⁴ 7g⁶ 8m⁴] 13,000Y: rather leggy, angular gelding: moderate walker: second foal: half-brother to 3-y-o Smile of Fortune (by Nodouble): dam 4-y-o 7f winner in USA: fairly useful performer: won nursery at Goodwood in August: hung right when good fourth in similar event at York (unruly stalls), next and best subsequent effort: should be suited by 1m: blinkered fourth outing. *I. A. Balding.*

PAY THE BANK   3 b.f. High Top 131–Zebra Grass 85 (Run The Gantlet (USA))   81
[1989 7g⁵ 7m³ 8f* 1990 8.5g⁵ 10m³ 10.6m⁴ 10m a10g] rather leggy, close-coupled filly: modest performer: first run for 3 months when third at Newbury, no extra final 1f but best effort in handicaps: stays 1m: acts on firm ground. *B. W. Hills.*

PAY TO DREAM (IRE)   2 b.g. (Mar 16) Runnett 125–Pursue 78 (Auction Ring   55
(USA) 123) [1990 6g 7s a6g⁵] 9,200Y: compact colt: first foal: dam 2-y-o 5f winner, is half-sister to smart miler Alert: plating-class maiden: hung left second start. *J. Sutcliffe.*

PAYVASHOOZ   5 b.m. Ballacashtal (CAN)–Abercourt 89 (Abernant 142) [1989   64
6v 6d 6.1f 7m 7m 6d 6s* 7m³ a8g⁵ a7g* 1990 a8g³ a7g a8g³ a8g² a8g² a8g⁶ a8g⁶ 8f 6v 7m³] good-topped mare: quite modest handicapper on her day: not seen out after April: stays 1m: possibly not at best on firm nowadays: blinkered once: suitable mount for apprentice: inconsistent. *M. Brittain.*

PEACE KING   4 ch.g. Adonijah 126–Flaming Peace (USA) 64 (Lyphard (USA)   79
132) [1989 NR 1990 8f* 12h* 11.5m⁵ 13.3m³] strong, chunky gelding: good walker: fluent mover: ½-length winner of maiden at Brighton in April and amateurs race (odds on) at Thirsk 2 weeks later: ran creditably in 5 runner Newbury handicap final outing: stays 13.3f: changed hands 35,000 gns Newmarket July Sales: won 2 novice hurdles in autumn. *G. Harwood.*

PEACE TALK   3 br.f. Warpath 113–War Talk (USA) 90 (Assagai) [1989 7f⁶ 8g   —
1990 10g a11g 12g 10f] smallish, sparely-made filly: well beaten, in selling handicap final start: has hung left for apprentice. *I. Campbell.*

PEAK DISTRICT   4 b.g. Beldale Flutter (USA) 130–Grand Teton 64 (Bustino   —
136) [1989 8m² 10m² 11.7d⁶ 10.5m⁴ 8g 1990 10.8m 10.8m 12g 10g 8g 11d] small, lengthy gelding: bad mover: modest maiden at best: well beaten in handicaps in 1990: stays 10.5f: bandaged on reappearance. *K. S. Bridgwater.*

PEANDAY   9 b.g. Swing Easy (USA) 126–Parradell 104 (Pandofell 132) [1989 12f   —
10f 10g 1990 8m 8m] tall, good-topped gelding: carries plenty of condition: poor mover: 100/1, showed he retains a little ability in first of 2 amateur events in summer: stays 1¼m: used to go well with plenty of give in the ground: has worn blinkers, but not for long time: bandaged at 9 yrs. *Lady Herries.*

PEARL DOVE   3 b.f. Oats 126–Nimble Dove 62 (Starch Reduced 112) [1989 5s⁶   —
5g 1990 7f 12m] small, light-framed non-thoroughbred filly: well beaten in maidens and handicap: bred to need middle distances, but pulls hard. *G. Price.*

PEARL ESSENCE (USA)   2 b.f. (Jan 26) Conquistador Cielo (USA)–Frau   —
Daruma (ARG) (Frari (ARG)) [1990 6g 7g] $160,000Y: workmanlike filly: has scope: fourth foal: sister to very useful 7f and 1m winner Zelphi, later successful in North America, and half-sister to a winner by Spectacular Bid: dam won Argentinian Oaks: well behind in large fields of maidens at Newbury and Newmarket. *C. F. Wall.*

PEARL RUN   9 ch.g. Gulf Pearl 117–Deep Down (Deep Run 119) [1989 14.8s⁶   **61**
16d⁴ 17.1m⁴ 1990 14.8m 14.8m⁴ 18f* 16g 14s 20m 16g 14.8m⁶] good-bodied gelding:
moderate mover: quite modest handicapper: successful at Nottingham in May:
below form afterwards: suited by a test of stamina: unsuited by soft going nowadays,
acts on any other: wears bandages: good mount for apprentice: has won Heart of
England Handicap (now re-named after him) at Warwick 4 times. *G. Price.*

PECHE D'OR   6 ch.g. Glint of Gold 128–Fishermans Bridge 113 (Crepello 136)   —
[1989 NR 1990 8m 10.6s 12.3g 12m 16m] compact, workmanlike gelding: modest
maiden as 3-y-o: no form in amateur events in 1990: stays 1¾m: acts on any going:
has worn blinkers and visor: sweating final start. *B. W. Hills.*

PECKING ORDER   6 b.m. Henbit (USA) 130–Daring Lass 87 (Bold Lad (IRE)   —
133) [1989 6d 5f⁵ 1990 5m 5f 7m⁵ a7g 8f 7f 8.5g⁶ 8f⁶] lengthy mare: retains only a
modicum of ability: probably best at 7f nowadays: has sweated, got on edge and been
taken down early. *F. J. Yardley.*

PEDANTRY (IRE)   2 gr.g. (Apr 23) Rusticaro (FR) 124–Sweet Hostess (Candy   **46**
Cane 125) [1990 5g⁶ 6g 7g 5f 7m 7g 8.5m³ 8m 10.6s⁶ 8.2s a7g] IR 5,600Y, 5,500
2-y-o: leggy gelding: half-brother to several winners, including 1m and 1½m winner
Mrs Pistol (by Camden Town) and fairly useful 1980 2-y-o 5f winner Katysue (by
King's Leap): dam never ran: modest plater: ran respectably on all-weather: best
form at around 1m: blinkered third start: sometimes hangs left, and is difficult ride.
D. W. Chapman.

PEE A DOUBLE YOU   2 b.c. (Mar 8) Balliol 125–Token of Truth (Record   —
Token 128) [1990 6g 5f] lengthy colt: first live foal: dam granddaughter of Cry of
Truth, best 2-y-o filly of 1974: soundly beaten in claimer (backward) at Leicester
and seller at Wolverhampton in summer. *B. Preece.*

PEERGLOW   6 br.m. Raga Navarro (ITY) 119–Go Perrys 66 (High Hat 131) [1989   — §
10.8m 1990 10f] leggy, shallow-girthed mare: moderate mover: ungenuine plater:
sometimes wears blinkers. *C. N. Williams.*

PEGASUS HEIGHTS   4 ch.g. Air Trooper 115–Confetti Copse 71 (Town And   —
Country 124) [1989 9f 1990 10.8m] lengthy, plain gelding: tailed off in minor event
and maiden in the Midlands. *R. J. Hodges.*

PEGGOTTY   2 gr.f. (May 12) Capricorn Line 111–Silver Empress 63 (Octavo   **50**
(USA) 115) [1990 6g 6d⁴] leggy filly: first foal: dam maiden suited by 7f, is out of
sister to smart Catherine Wheel: 7 lengths fourth of 8 to Triviality in maiden at
Goodwood in October: will be better suited by 7f + . *P. Hayward.*

PEGGY SUE   2 ch.f. (Apr 14) Hotfoot 126–Presentable 60 (Sharpen Up 127) [1990   —
5.1m⁶] half-sister to 3 winners, including 1985 2-y-o 1m winner Centrepoint (by
Reform): dam placed over 1½m: is half-sister to Gimcrack winner Wishing Star:
slow-starting sixth of 7 in seller at Yarmouth in June: gave trouble at stalls and
withdrawn from similar event there following month. *M. H. Tompkins.*

PEKING OPERA (IRE)   2 b.c. (Mar 14) Sadler's Wells (USA) 132–Braneakins   **91** p
(Sallust 134) [1990 7m² 8g² 8d*] small, close-coupled colt: has a quick action:
second living foal: half-brother to modest maiden Akin To Fame (by Ahonoora): dam
Irish 1½m winner, is half-sister to Park Appeal, Desireable and Alydaress: long
odds on, won maiden at Leicester in October in good style by 5 lengths from Majed:
second previously in Newmarket maidens won by Sapieha and Sharifabad: very
much a staying type: sure to do better. *M. R. Stoute.*

PELAGIAN ZEST   5 b.g. Magnolia Lad 102–Enthusiasm (Abwah 118) [1989 NR   —
1990 12f 10m] of no account. *J. Dooler.*

PELAW   2 b.c. (Mar 20) Persian Bold 123–No Restraint 84 (Habitat 134) [1990 5m   **37**
5g 6g⁶ 7f a7g³ a7g] 4,000Y: close-coupled colt: poor walker: first foal: dam 1m and
1¼m winner, is half-sister to very smart staying filly Sorbus: poor plater: will stay
1m: blinkered final start. *T. Fairhurst.*

PELENG (IRE)   2 ch.c. (May 8) Mille Balles (FR) 124–Prosodie (FR) (Relko   **80**
136) [1990 7g² 7g⁴ 8m] 110,000 francs (approx £10,200) Y: angular, workmanlike
colt: fifth foal: half-brother to French 7f to 9f winner Preston and French 10.5f
winner Prologue (both by Fabulous Dancer): dam French 10.5f winner, is out of
half-sister to dam of Prix Morny winners Regal State and Seven Springs: fair
maiden: 8 lengths fourth of 5 in Laurent-Perrier Champagne Stakes at Doncaster:
tailed off in Royal Lodge William Hill Stakes at Ascot: should stay 1m. *P. A. Kelleway.*

PELIGROSO   4 ch.g. Star Appeal 133–Sarah Gillian (USA) (Zen (USA)) [1989 8m   —
14g⁶ 10m⁶ a10g⁵ 1990 a12g] neat gelding: little sign of ability: not bred to stay much
beyond 1¼m. *P. A. Kelleway.*

PELLS CLOSE   7 gr.g. He Loves Me 120–Seriema 72 (Petingo 135) [1989 NR — §
1990 16f⁴] plain gelding: has shown signs of ability, but isn't genuine: visored twice,
often blinkered: winning novice chaser in 1989/90. *S. Dow.*

PELORUS   5 b.h. High Top 131–St Isabel (Saint Crespin III 132) [1989 10d 10v³ 107 ?
10f* 10.6g² 1990 8m³ 10m 8g 10.2s] leggy horse: usually looks well: smart winner as
4-y-o: shaped as though retaining ability in £7,400 race at Newbury in June: well
beaten in Prince of Wales's Stakes at Royal Ascot (taken last to post) 6 days later
and in listed event and minor contest (blinkered) in November: suited by about
1¼m: probably acts on any going: has started slowly. *W. Jarvis.*

PENANDO   2 b.g. (Apr 30) Dreams To Reality (USA) 113–Pendona 72 (Blue   70 ?
Cashmere 129) [1990 5f³ a5g⁴ 5m⁵ 5m⁵ 6m² 6m⁶ 7g 6m³ 6d 5f⁶ 5g a5g⁵ a6g²]
smallish, workmanlike gelding: has a round action: first reported foal: dam maiden
best at 5f, is daughter of useful sprinter Calibina: short-head second of 8, showing
much improved form, to Clear Comedy in late-year maiden at Lingfield: only a fair
plater on other form: really needs further than 5f and stays 7f: effective with or
without blinkers. *E. A. Wheeler.*

PENDOR DANCER   7 b.g. Piaffer (USA) 113–Bounding (Forlorn River 124)   79
[1989 5d 5s⁴ 6m 6m 5m* 5m* 5m* 5g* 5g 5g³ 5.6g 5m⁴ 5d 1990 5g 5.8h 5m² 5g 5m⁵
5m* 5f 5m⁶ 5g 5.8f 5d⁴ 5m] lengthy gelding: fair handicapper: winner at Kempton in
July: best efforts after on last 2 starts: best over 5f: acts on any going: effective with
or without blinkers or visor: has worn bandages behind: usually sweating and on
toes. *W. Carter.*

PENHILL FLAME   4 ch.f. Main Reef 126–Debian 71 (Relko 136) [1989 5m⁴ 7f   35
a7g 1990 6m⁶ 8.3m⁶ 9f 8f] close-coupled filly: plater: may prove best at 7f. *D. Haydn
Jones.*

PENNIES WOOD   3 b.g. Star Appeal 133–Deep River (FR) (Val de Loir 133)   —
[1989 NR 1990 10f 7f⁵] 1,000Y: leggy, narrow gelding: second foal: half-brother to
modest maiden Diana Dee (by Blakeney): dam won 3 times in Italy: 50/1, well
beaten in maiden (chased leaders 1m) at Salisbury and minor event (had no chance)
at Chepstow in May. *B. R. Millman.*

PENNINE STAR (IRE)   2 b.f. (Feb 29) Pennine Walk 120–Sterna Regina 102   53 p
(Royal And Regal (USA)) [1990 6g⁴ 6g] 16,500Y: sturdy filly: has scope: half-sister
to several winners here and abroad: dam Irish 7.5f (at 2 yrs) and 1½m winner, is
half-sister to Star Appeal: slowly away, switched over 2f out and kept on well when
in mid-division in 16-runner minor event at Doncaster in September: backward and
green on debut: will improve again, particularly at 7f + . *C. W. C. Elsey.*

PENNY FORUM   6 b.g. Pas de Seul 133–Kind Thoughts 71 (Kashmir II 125)   76
[1989 14g³ 16g³ 14m² 14f 1990 a12g⁶ 18f⁵ 14.8m* 14m 16.2d² 16g* 18.4f* 16.2m⁵
14g] compact gelding: modest handicapper: favourite, won at Warwick in March and
Chester in June and July: ran creditably in Tote Ebor at York, but wasn't seen out
again: suited by test of stamina: acts on any going, except possibly heavy: usually
blinkered: suitable mount for apprentice: bandaged near-fore: suited by waiting
tactics. *J. Sutcliffe.*

PENNY MINT   2 ch.f. (Jan 27) Mummy's Game 120–School Road 88 (Great   82
Nephew 126) [1990 5s 5g² 6g* 6f* 6d] 2,600F, 2,000Y: plain filly: moderate mover:
sixth living foal: half-sister to 3 winners, including 1988 2-y-o 5f winner Gleeful (by
Sayf El Arab) and 6f winner Dorney (by Tachypous): dam sister to smart miler
Saher, ran only at 4 yrs when 6f and 7f winner: fair performer: won maiden auction at
Leicester in July comfortably by 4 lengths and nursery at Newmarket (by 1½
lengths from Allinson's Mate) in August: off course for nearly 2 months after: much
better suited by 6f than 5f: possibly unsuited by softish ground. *J. M. P. Eustace.*

PENNY PIPEDREAM   2 ch.f. (May 3) Night Shift (USA)–Elevena (AUS) (Just   —
Great 127) [1990 7f⁶ 7m 6g] half-sister to good Australian middle-distance stayer
Chiamare (by Claude): dam winner 4 times in Australia, is sister to leading 1972/3
Australian 2-y-o filly Just Topic: well beaten in maidens: carried condition first 2
starts: sold 2,400 gns Newmarket Autumn Sales. *R. V. Smyth.*

PENSERAPH   2 br.c. (Apr 29) Precocious 126–Rosalka (ITY) (Relko 136) [1990   38
5g⁶ 5m⁵ 5.8h⁶ 5f 6g 5m a7g] 5,000Y: leggy, close-coupled colt: closely related to fair
5f performer Bella Rossi (by Mummy's Pet) and half-brother to 2 other winners,
including French 7f and 1m winner John Hawkwood (by Irish River): dam won 4
times in Italy: poor maiden: not discredited in Lingfield seller penultimate start:
blinkered or visored last 5: sold out of D. Elsworth's stable 1,350 gns Newmarket
Autumn Sales. *P. Howling.*

673

PENTAGON ROSE   4 b.f. Kafu 120–All Gold Rose (Rheingold 137) [1989 6d 5s⁴   **43** §
6m 5m 5.3h⁴ 5m* 5g 5f⁵ 5m 5m 5f 5.1g 5m* 5.3f 5f⁶ 6f² 5g 1990 5f⁴ 5m 5m⁴ 5g 5m³
5g² 5g 5m a5g 5m] leggy, sparely-made filly: has a quick action: poor handicapper:
stays 6f: probably acts on any going: blinkered twice: wore tongue strap third
outing: sold to join M. O'Neill's stable 2,100 gns Newmarket September Sales:
inconsistent, and none too genuine. W. Carter.

PENTHOUSE C (USA)   9 b.g. Cannonade (USA)–Poundcake (USA) (Hail To   —
Reason) [1989 NR 1990 a16g6] big, tall gelding: lightly-raced maiden. A. R. Davison.

PENTRIDGE   2 ch.f. (May 20) Pennine Walk 120–Pennycuick 101 (Celtic Ash)   —
[1990 6m] 20,000Y: lengthy, plain filly: half-sister to several winners, including very
useful 1978 2-y-o 5f winner Penny Blessing (by So Blessed) and speedy 1988 2-y-o
Wasimah (by Caerleon): dam sprinting half-sister to Mummy's Pet, Arch Sculptor
and Parsimony: backward, slowly away and soon tailed off in maiden (reluctant
stalls) at Newmarket in October: moved poorly down. G. Lewis.

PENULTIMATION   5 b.h. Young Generation 129–Maiden Pool 85 (Sharpen Up   —
127) [1989 6d² 7d 6f 6m 1990 6s] strong, good-bodied horse: moderate mover: fairly
useful winner as 3-y-o: lightly raced and little subsequent worthwhile form: best
form at 6f or 7f: probably unsuited by firm going: blinkered final outing at 4 yrs: sold
1,500 gns Newmarket Autumn Sales. G. Harwood.

PERANG PERCY   4 b.g. Bay Express 132–Carcosa 103 (Sovereign Lord 120)   —
[1989 NR 1990 a7g⁴] half-brother to French 5f winner Flash Connection (by Hot
Spark) and to useful 6f to 1m winner Perang Tejam (by Sharpen Up): dam won over
6f and 7f at 2 yrs: didn't get clear run 2f out when 9 lengths fourth of 15 in claimer at
Southwell in February. T. Casey.

PERCY'S PET   4 b.f. Blakeney 126–Oula-Ka Fu-Fu 67 (Run The Gantlet (USA))   —
[1989 12.4g 12f 10.5g⁴ 12g⁴ a8g⁴ 1990 a11g a11g 9f 11m⁵ 12.5g 8f 8m] rather angular
filly: poor maiden: no form as 4-y-o, including in selling company: looked unenthusiastic third outing: usually blinkered: awkward in stalls final start: sold to join K.
Bailey's stable 5,600 gns Newmarket July Sales: winning hurdler following month.
C. B. B. Booth.

PERDIKKAS (USA)   3 b. or br.c. Chief's Crown (USA)–Oeuf Ivoire (USA) 91   —
(Sir Ivor 135) [1989 NR 1990 10m 10.6s 12.3g⁴ 13.1m] $525,000Y: sturdy, attractive
colt: first foal: dam, winner twice at about 1¼m, sister to Oaks d'Italia winner Ivor's
Image: well beaten in maidens and handicap in the summer: should stay 1½m:
visored final start: sold 2,800 gns Newmarket Autumn Sales. M. R. Stoute.

PERESKIA   2 b.f. (Apr 19) Petoski 135–Mytinia 94 (Bustino 136) [1990 6m 7m²]   **66** p
medium-sized, leggy filly: fourth foal: half-sister to 3-y-o 1¼m winner Mind The
Step (by Shareef Dancer): dam 11.7f winner, is sister to very smart 1½m winner
Bustomi: 2½ lengths second of 8, keeping on well, to Exclusive Virtue in maiden at
Leicester in October: sure to do better, particularly over 1m + . C. E. Brittain.

PERFECT CHANCE   4 b. or br.f. Petorius 117–Perfect Line 102 (Rarity 129)   **75**
[1989 7m* 8f⁴ 6g 6g² 7g* 7m 1990 6m⁴ 6m⁵ 7m³ 7g⁶] lengthy, good-quartered filly:
modest handicapper: stays 7f: acts on good to firm going: tailed off in tongue strap
final start at 3 yrs: sold 8,200 gns Newmarket December Sales. B. Hanbury.

PERFECT PRINCE (IRE)   2 gr.c. (Feb 1) Anita's Prince 126–Perfect Run   —
(Godswalk (USA) 130) [1990 7m 7m 8.2g 6m] IR 3,000F, 2,400Y: angular colt:
moderate mover: first foal: dam ran once at 2 yrs in Ireland: little worthwhile form,
including in a seller: took keen hold when blinkered final outing, and didn't look
completely genuine: sold 1,025 gns Ascot November Sales. P. F. I. Cole.

PERFOLIA (USA)   3 ch.f. Nodouble (USA)–Perfect Example (USA) (Far North   **87** +
(CAN) 120) [1989 NR 1990 10g³ 7m* 8v] lengthy, angular filly: has round action:
second foal: half-sister to a minor winner in USA: dam unraced half-sister to Grade 1
winner at up to 1¼m French Charmer (dam of Zilzal) and to the dam of Polish
Precedent: not seen out until late-October, easily landing odds in maiden at
Newmarket following month by 3½ lengths from Bold Habitat, winning maiden:
in Group 3 contest at Milan: stays 1¼m: should be capable of better. J. H. M. Gosden.

PERFORMER   2 gr.f. (May 17) Green Ruby (USA) 104–Susie Hall (Gold Rod   —
129) [1990 5m 5m] 6,000Y: angular filly: seventh foal: half-sister to 4 winners,
including milers Golden Game (by Mummy's Game) and Foolish Ways (by Comedy
Star): dam unraced half-sister to top 1970 2-y-o filly Cawston's Pride: bit backward,
well beaten in seller and maiden auction in spring. J. Balding.

PERFORMING ARTS   3 ch.f. The Minstrel (CAN) 135–Noble Mark 120 (On   **104**
Your Mark 125) [1989 5m* 6f* 5f³ 6g⁴ 6s² 7g⁴ 1990 8g⁴ 8g³ 7f⁵ 8f² 8m⁴] small,
good-topped filly: 25/1, best effort when third to In The Groove in moderately-run

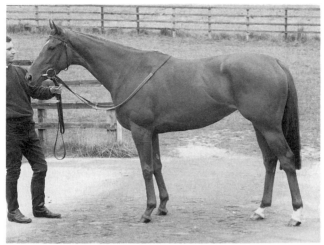

Mr R. E. Sangster's "Performing Arts"

Goffs Irish 1000 Guineas at the Curragh, leading 7f: useful performances in Jersey Stakes at Royal Ascot and Group 3 event at the Curragh third and final starts: suited by 1m: best form on a sound surface. *B. W. Hills.*

PERION 8 ch.g. Northfields (USA)–Relanca (Relic) [1989 6s³ 5m⁵ 5g 5f 5g³ 5m 5g 5g⁵ 5g⁶ 5m 1990 5f 5m 5g⁵ 5d] lengthy, angular gelding: twice hobdayed: poor mover: smart at his best in 1988: deteriorated considerably, and showed virtually nothing as 8-y-o: suited by 5f: used to be particularly well suited by an easy surface: blinkered once: needed strong handling: retired. *M. Bell.* —

PERISTYLE 4 br.f. Tolomeo 127–Persevering 95 (Blakeney 126) [1989 12h⁶ 11f 12.2f⁵ 16f³ 13.8g³ 13.8g 12.5f⁶ 12.2d⁴ 12m² 1990 10m⁵] leggy, sparely-made filly: poor maiden: out of her depth only outing at 4 yrs: apparently suited by 1½m: acts on good to firm going: won 4 times over hurdles in 1989/90. *R. Lee.* —

PERJURY (IRE) 2 b.g. (Mar 5) Try My Best (USA) 130–Riverine (FR) (Riverman (USA) 131) [1990 6g⁵ 6m⁶ 6g] 16,500Y: leggy gelding: fifth foal: half-brother to 1988 French 7.2f 2-y-o winner Kennebec (by Kenmare), quite useful 1986 2-y-o winner Lucayan Knight (by Dominion) and a winner in Belgium: dam French provincial 1¼m winner: caught eye keeping on strongly from rear, not knocked about, in maiden at Ripon on debut: first run for nearly 4 months, since leaving J. Payne's stable, never dangerous in Folkestone maiden final outing: may do better. *D. R. C. Elsworth.* 55

PERMANENTLY PINK 4 b.g. Auction Ring (USA) 123–Hawaiian Joss (USA) (Hawaii) [1989 6s⁶ 6f 8h 10.2f 1990 8m³ 12.5f 8.3g] lengthy, angular gelding: moderate mover: winning plater at 2 yrs: form in varied events since only on re-appearances at 3 yrs and 4 yrs: changed hands 800 gns Ascot February Sales: inconsistent. *R. J. Hodges.* 34

PERPENDICULAR 2 b.c. (Apr 14) Shirley Heights 130–Pris (Priamos (GER) 123) [1990 7s*] good-topped colt: has scope: sixth foal: brother to 3-y-o Precipice and half-brother to Lockinge winner Prismatic (by Manado) and 9f and 1¼m winner Psylla (by Beldale Flutter): dam unraced half-sister to Kris, Diesis and Presidium: co-favourite, made all in 19-runner maiden at Doncaster in November, keeping on 95 P strongly despite flashing tail to win by 2½ lengths from Man From Eldorado: will stay at least 1¼m: a very useful performer in the making. *H. R. A. Cecil.*

PERPIGNAN   3 br.f. Rousillon (USA) 133–Heart 'n' Soul 101 (Bold Lad (IRE)   **76** 133) [1989 NR 1990 7g³ 6g* 6g] IR 18,000Y: sturdy, workmanlike filly: half-sister to a winner in Belgium by Final Straw: dam useful sprinting 2-y-o in Ireland: co-favourite, comfortably made all despite hanging left last 3f in maiden at Lingfield in June: facing stiff task, soon outpaced in handicap there in August: well worth another try over 7f: keen sort, wears net muzzle. *G. Harwood.*

PER QUOD (USA)   5 b.g. Lyllos (FR)–Allegedly (USA) (Sir Ivor 135) [1989 10v*   **115** 12d² 10s² 10m⁴ 12d³ 12m³ 10.1d³ 12g² 12s⁴ 12d* 1990 12g⁵ 10m⁴ 12d² 16m 12g² 12s³ 14g⁵ 12m³ 12g³ 12v² 14s* 12v] leggy, workmanlike gelding: usually looks very well: has a quick, round action: smart performer: rarely runs a poor race, and won Group 3 Premio Roma Vecchia in November by 4½ lengths from Pier Damiani: did particularly well in Grand Prix d'Evry won by Ode and Grosser Preis von Baden won by Mondrian on third and sixth outings: suited by testing conditions at 1¼m and stays 1¾m: not at his best on firm going, goes very well on a soft surface: splendidly tough, genuine and consistent: a credit to his trainer. *B. Hanbury.*

PERSIANALLI (IRE)   2 b.c. (Apr 2) Persian Bold 123–Alligatrix (USA) 111   **85** (Alleged (USA) 138) [1990 6m* 6m] IR 40,000Y: tall, close-coupled colt: fourth foal: half-brother to 3-y-o Alidiva (by Chief Singer), successful from 6f (at 2 yrs) to 1m: dam 2-y-o 7f winner third in Hoover Fillies' Mile, is out of sister to very smart animals Cabildo and Canal: won maiden at Yarmouth in September, running on well under hand riding: uneasy favourite but looking really well, never able to challenge in nursery at Newmarket following month. *J. H. M. Gosden.*

PERSIAN DYNASTY   6 br.h. Persian Bold 123–Parez 67 (Pardao 120) [1989 7f   **50** 7m⁶ 8m⁵ 7f 10.2f⁶ 8f⁵ 10.2f* 12.2f⁵ 1990 8f 10f 8f* 9g 8h⁵ 10.8m⁴ 7f* 10m³ 8.2m* 10g⁶ 8f⁵ 9f⁶ 8h 7m 10.2f³ 10.2m 8m] small horse: poor handicapper: successful at Warwick (apprentices) and Chepstow (reared leaving stalls) in May and Nottingham in June: needs at least 7f and stays 1¼m: acts well on top-of-the-ground: good mount for claimer. *J. M. Bradley.*

PERSIAN EMPEROR   5 ro.h. Persepolis (FR) 127–Rosananti 107 (Blushing   **54** § Groom (FR) 131) [1989 7f⁶ 9m 10m 8g 8g⁴ 9f 8g⁶ a10g⁴ 1990 a8g⁵ 8f⁴ 12.5m³ 14g⁶ 13.8m³ 10f⁶ 10.4d 12f⁶ 12f⁴] compact horse: has a quick action: capable of plating-class form, but has won only once (maiden as 3-y-o) and isn't one to rely on: stays 1¾m: best form on a sound surface: ran poorly in visor and blinkers: trained until after seventh outing by R. Hollinshead: a difficult ride. *R. Simpson.*

PERSIAN HALO (IRE)   2 b. or br.c. (May 4) Sunny's Halo (CAN)–Persian   **83** p Susan (USA) (Herbager 136) [1990 8d³ 10.2s*] IR 23,000Y: tall, leggy, lengthy colt: half-brother to several winners in USA: dam won at up to 9f in USA: well-backed favourite, won 15-runner minor event at Doncaster in November by 3 lengths from Keltie, soon travelling well, quickening 2f out and clear final furlong under hand riding: will stay 1½m: clearly acts well on soft ground. *M. Kauntze, Ireland.*

PERSIAN HAT (IRE)   2 ch.g. (Mar 16) Hatim (USA) 121–Persian Myth   — (Persian Bold 123) [1990 6d] IR 13,500F, 14,500Y: third foal: half-brother to 3-y-o Musca Myth (by Muscatite), successful in Holland: dam ran once at 2 yrs in Ireland: no show in claimer at Goodwood in October: sold 4,200 gns Newmarket Autumn Sales. *W. J. Haggas.*

PERSIAN HOUSE   3 ch.g. Persian Bold 123–Sarissa 105 (Reform 132) [1989 NR   **73** 1990 12s⁴ 13g³ 12.3m⁴ 10.2g 13d 13.6d²] IR 7,400Y: big, good-topped gelding: eighth foal: closely related to fair 1983 2-y-o 5f winner Valkyrie (by Bold Lad) and half-brother to 1988 2-y-o 7f winner Wassling (by Wassl), Irish 1½m to 17f winner Inquest (by Caerleon) and smart middle-distance performer Sabre Dance (by Dance In Time): dam won over 5f and 6f at 2 yrs: modest form, staying on steadily never dangerous, in maidens and handicaps: should stay further: acts on good to firm ground and good: lacks turn of foot, and should prove suited by more forcing tactics: winning hurdler. *J. M. Jefferson.*

PERSIAN LORD   3 b.c. Persian Bold 123–Tres Bien (Pitskelly 122) [1989 NR   **62** 1990 8f 10.1g 10m 9m 10m* 10m* 10g 9g 10f² 10.2m 10d 12m 8.2d] IR 24,000Y: good-bodied colt: second foal: half-brother to poor Irish maiden Kelly Bien (by Octavo): dam showed only a little ability in USA: quite modest handicapper: won apprentice handicaps at Kempton (ran wide home turn) and Sandown (made most) in July: ran badly last 4 starts, wearing tongue strap last 2: stays 1¼m: acts on good to firm ground: blinkered eleventh and final outings: sold 13,000 gns Newmarket Autumn Sales. *H. Candy.*

PERSIAN SATAN (IRE) 2 b.f. (May 5) King Persian 107–Irish Myth (St 38 Paddy 133) [1990 5g 5f⁵ 5f 7m 7f 8.2g 8m] 680Y: angular filly: poor mover: fourth foal: dam lightly raced: poor plater: probably stays 1m: unruly start fourth outing. C. J. Hill.

PERSIAN SOLDIER 3 b.c. Sandhurst Prince 128–Persian Case (Upper Case 73 (USA)) [1989 a7g* 1990 9m 8g⁴ 8m 8d] workmanlike colt: good walker: won maiden at Lingfield in December at 2 yrs: easily best effort in handicaps when fourth at Kempton in June: stays 1m: visored final start: sold to join G. Moore 11,000 gns Newmarket Autumn Sales. P. T. Walwyn.

PERSIAN SPRING 3 ch.f. King Persian 107–Northern Amber (Shack (USA)) — 118) [1989 6m⁶ 6m 5m 5g 5g 1990 7f 7m 6f a6g] compact filly: moderate mover: of little account: blinkered last 2 outings: sold 1,050 gns Ascot July Sales. B. Stevens.

PERSIAN SULTAN 3 br.c. Persian Bold 123–Florita 86 (Lord Gayle (USA) 35 124) [1989 5v 5d 6m 6m³ 6h² 7m² 7g⁴ 7m⁴ 1990 a7g 7.6g 6m 10h 10h⁴] small, quite attractive colt: plater: best effort in summer as 3-y-o on final start: seems to stay 1¼m: visored third to sixth starts: often taken down very early: races freely: sweating on reappearance: sold to join Miss L. Bower 800 gns Ascot November Sales. A. Moore.

PERSILLANT 6 b.h. Persian Bold 123–Gauloise 93 (Welsh Pageant 132) [1989 82 14g* 12m* 12f4 13s 1990 12f 16g³ 12m 13f⁴] good-topped horse: moderate mover: fairly useful winner of handicaps at 5-y-o: not discredited at Royal Ascot (Bessborough Stakes) and Chester first 2 starts in summer: likely to prove best at up to 1¾m: probably acts on any going: ran moderately in blinkers third start: often gets on edge: useful hurdler in 1989/90. N. Tinkler.

PERSONALITY CLASH 2 b.f. (Mar 8) High Top 131–Five Farthings 90 48 (Busted 134) [1990 6m 6m 5m] 40,000Y: smallish, sparely-made filly: first foal: dam 1½m and 1¾m winner, is out of half-sister to top 1981 2-y-o filly Circus Ring: around 4 lengths seventh of 16 in maiden at Newbury in July: gave impression something amiss next time, and off course 3 months before running moderately again: bred to be better suited by 1m+. T. Thomson Jones.

PERSPECTIVE 2 b.f. (Feb 21) Never So Bold 135–Geopelia 109 (Raffingora 130) — [1990 a7g] 17,000Y, 1,550 2-y-o: sister to 3-y-o Brown Carpet and half-sister to ungenuine 1m winner Flitteriss Park (by Beldale Flutter) and 2 winners in South Africa: dam sprinter: slowly away, raced wide and always behind in 12-runner claimer at Southwell in December. M. H. Tompkins.

PERSPICACITY 3 b.f. Petorius 117–Grattan Princess (Tumble Wind (USA)) — [1989 NR 1990 7m 7m 11.5g 8g 6d] 5,000Y: sturdy filly: fifth foal: half-sister to 6f seller winner Twilight Falls (by Day Is Done), useful 1985 2-y-o sprint maiden Pop The Cork and a winner in Belgium (both by Kampala): dam lightly-raced Irish maiden: plating-class maiden: probably stays 1m: takes keen hold: sold 3,000 gns Newmarket Autumn Sales. M. E. D. Francis.

PERSUASIUS (IRE) 2 b.c. (Mar 13) Petorius 117–Be A Dancer (Be Friendly 64 130) [1990 6f 6g⁵ 6g³] IR 15,000F, IR 11,000Y: leggy colt: fifth foal: half-brother to a winner in Norway: dam Irish 7f and 9f winner: burly, best effort when third of 22 to Nigel's Lucky Girl in maiden auction at Ripon in August. W. J. Pearce.

PERSUASIVE 3 b.f. Sharpo 132–Queen's Eyot 79 (Grundy 137) [1989 NR 1990 72 9s* 11v* 12h² 12g3dis 12m⁵ 10.6g 10d² 10.6d⁶ 10v⁶] 1,800 2-y-o: lengthy, rather sparely-made filly: has a round action: first foal: dam suited by 1¼m: modest performer: clear-cut winner of April claimers at Hamilton and Ayr: ran creditably most starts (including in amateur events) but soundly beaten having taken strong hold on final one: stays 1½m: acts on any going. J. S. Wilson.

PERU 2 b.c. (Mar 23) Conquistador Cielo (USA)–Dance Flower (CAN) (Northern — Dancer) [1990 7s] compact colt: second foal: half-brother to 3-y-o 10.6f winner Muzo (by Irish River): dam 6f to 1m winner in USA, is out of half-sister to The Minstrel (by Northern Dancer): better for race and on toes, always behind in maiden at Doncaster in October. J. W. Watts.

PERUZZI 4 ch.g. Simply Great (FR) 122–Okavamba 82 (Wollow 132) [1989 12d — 10.6g 14m⁵ a12g³ a16g 19m0 8m 10.2m 8.3g⁵ 10g] workmanlike gelding: disappointing maiden: needs further than 1m and stays 1½m: sometimes bandaged. M. D. I. Usher.

PESIDANAMICH (IRE) 2 b.c. (Apr 28) Mummy's Treasure 84–Bay Supreme 67 (Martinmas 128) [1990 6m⁵ 6f⁵ 6m⁶ 7f² 6v* 7d a7g⁶] IR 2,200F, IR 4,000Y, 5,000 2-y-o: sturdy colt: third foal: brother and half-brother (by Jester) to winners in Scandinavia: dam unraced: quite modest performer: won 7-runner nursery at Ayr by a head from Super Spacemate: ran moderately afterwards: stays 7f: acts on any going: suitable mount for a claimer. *T. D. Barron.*

PETALOUDA   6 ch.m. Avgerinos 121–Normandy Velvet (Normandy) [1989 NR   —
1990 a13g⁶] seemingly of no account. *P. Howling.*

PETAMO   4 b.g. Coquelin (USA) 121–Kissing 98 (Sing Sing 134) [1989 8g 10f 10.6g   —
12m 12h³ 12f 14m 15.5f² 15.3f⁵ 12g 1990 14.8f] close-coupled, quite attractive
gelding: plating class on most form: stays 15f: acts on firm ground: carried head high
and flashed tail under pressure when blinkered fifth outing at 3 yrs: winning novice
hurdler in August. *J. L. Harris.*

PETAVIOUS   5 b.g. Mummy's Pet 125–Pencuik Jewel (Petingo 135) [1989 10g³   **67** d
8g 10m⁶ 8.3m⁴ 8f a10g⁴ a12g a11g* 1990 a12g² a12g³ 12g⁶ 12m² 12m³ 10m⁵ 12m 12g]
leggy gelding: moderate mover: ran creditably on all-weather in January: easily best
effort in summer handicaps on fourth outing: ran badly last 2: suited by 1½m: acts on
good to firm going: suitable mount for apprentice. *Lady Herries.*

PETER DAVIES (USA)   2 ch.c. (Mar 3) Bering 136–French Flick (USA)   **120** p
(Silent Screen (USA)) [1990 7m* 7m* 8s*]
    Having sold the subsequent Arc winner Saumarez to American interests
mid-way through the season without so much as a pattern-race win from him,
then having had St Leger winner Michelozzo beaten by the jumper Morley
Street in a minor event at Goodwood, owner Charles St George might have
wished being spared the suspense of the photo finish of the last Group 1 race
of the season in Britain, the one-mile Racing Post Trophy at Doncaster in
October, involving his colt Peter Davies. St George, who was also narrowly
denied a piece of history when his Lupescu failed by a short head to give
Lester Piggott a winner on his come-back ride in Britain, had the verdict in his
favour at Doncaster, but for much of the straight must have been resigned
to second (at best) again as Peter Davies was flat out and making little
impression. The Racing Post Trophy had been building into an exciting
contest from the five-day declaration stage, and by race-day looked set to
influence considerably the order of merit among the leading staying two-
year-olds; after all, it pitched the top staying colt Mujaazif, fresh from his
comfortable victory in the Royal Lodge William Hill Stakes, against the top
staying filly Shamshir, successful in the Brent Walker Fillies' Mile, as well as
the unbeaten trio Peter Davies, conqueror of the subsequent Dewhurst
second Bog Trotter in the Somerville Tattersall Stakes on his most recent
outing, the smart Lanson Champagne Vintage Stakes winner Mukaddamah,
and the highly-regarded Sadler's Wells colt Marcham, an impressively easy
winner of a Goodwood maiden on his only start. The race indeed lacked
nothing in excitement, but the finish concerned neither Mujaazif, the 2/1
favourite, who failed to act on the soft ground and finished tailed off, nor
Shamshir, who was withdrawn as her trainer considered the ground to be too
testing; nor did the result clarify the already confused two-year-old picture.
Conditions were very testing, certainly—in our opinion the ground was much
softer than was returned officially—and stamina and courage, attributes
possessed in abundance by Peter Davies, won the day. Peter Davies, who'd
been found wanting for pace after setting a modest gallop for five furlongs,
galloped on relentlessly to snatch victory from the faltering Mukaddamah on
the line with Marcham, who'd had a good battle for second place until the
furlong pole, four lengths away in third. This very close finish to the final
two-year-old pattern race in Britain was in keeping with the trend of the
season. Much like the year before, the best two-year-olds seen in public
weren't an outstanding collection by any means, and it's questionable how
much relevance the result of the Racing Post Trophy, or any of the other
two-year-old pattern races for that matter, will have to the top races by the
middle of 1991. In his favour Peter Davies will be very well suited by middle
distances, and has been more lightly campaigned than any of Be My Chief,
High Estate or Sanquirico (who was also owned by St George), the best
staying two-year-olds of the three previous seasons, all of whom failed to train
on; against Peter Davies, though, is that he lacks a turn of foot, had a gruelling
race in severe conditions at Doncaster, and that his form, smart though it may
be, is not in the same bracket as Reference Point's, for example, Cecil's best
previous winner of the race, or even Lanfranco's, St George's other previous

Racing Post Trophy, Doncaster—stamina wins the day;
Peter Davies (right) wears down Mukaddamah under strong driving

winner, both of whom kept their form really well the following season. We find it difficult to envisage Peter Davies, at the time of writing Derby favourite, progressing to the top, but he lacks nothing in spirit and he should, at the least, add to his winning tally.

If one thing above all else will hold Peter Davies back at the top level as a three-year-old it's this lack of an instant change of pace. In the Somerville Tattersall Stakes at Newmarket earlier in October, Peter Davies had been left flat-footed when the pace had quickened very much in the same manner as at Doncaster; then, pushed along vigorously from halfway, he'd struggled for the best part of two furlongs before running on strongly to account for Bog Trotter going away by two lengths. Things had been much easier for Peter Davies when he had made his debut in a maiden race at Leicester in September. Looking fitter than most of the newcomers in the field, Peter Davies made all the running and stayed on strongly from two furlongs out to win easing down by four lengths. In all his races, but particularly at Doncaster, where he might have done better had more use been made of him from the start, Peter Davies struck us very much as an enthusiastic, strong-galloping type, long on stamina. As a two-year-old he was the more effective the further he went, and he'll require at least a mile and a quarter, more probably a mile and a half, and a true gallop to be seen to best advantage at three.

		Arctic Tern	Sea Bird II
	Bering	(ch 1973)	Bubbling Beauty
	(ch 1983)	Beaune	Lyphard
Peter Davies (USA)		(ch 1974)	Barbra
(ch.c. Mar 3, 1988)		Silent Screen	Prince John
	French Flick (USA)	(ch 1967)	Prayer Bell
	(b 1978)	Tres Jolie	Herbager
		(b 1967)	Leallah

The Prix du Jockey-Club winner Bering has made a fine start to his time at stud; besides Peter Davies he's sired the good French staying two-year-old Beau Sultan, the Gran Criterium winner Steamer Duck and several other lesser winners, including the Redcar seven-furlong winner Nunivak. Bering was a one of the best in France in recent years, who came into his own over middle distances but had the misfortune to run up against Dancing Brave in the best Arc for some time. Bering wasn't a widespread commercial success when his first crop reached the sales—his six yearlings sold at public auction in North America in 1989, of which Peter Davies was one, averaged 69,500 dollars, 5,500 dollars less than his initial covering fee, and those sold in Europe varied between 5,000 guineas in Ireland and 4,100,000 francs (around £380,000) at Deauville—but his early results on the racecourse, particularly considering how stoutly bred he is, should see his improving his position in the market place. At 20,000 dollars at Keeneland's September Yearling Sale, the leggy Peter Davies, who has his sire's four white stockings and white blaze, was the second-cheapest of Bering's progeny sold in the States. The dam French Flick, a winner of five races at up to nine furlongs, including in minor stakes as a five-year-old, produced only a poor winner in the States by Northjet from four foals before Peter Davies. French Flick's dam Tres Jolie, successful twice including at six and a half furlongs, didn't have a great deal of success at stud, French Flick being her only winner; but the same couldn't be said of her grandam Leallah, the best two-year-old filly in the States in 1956, who bred numerous winners, including several who won minor stakes and others who have gone on to produce minor stakes winners. Interestingly, the 1956 volume of the *Bloodstock Breeders Review* reported that Leallah's only defeat during her two-year-old campaign could be attributed to the mud, 'which none of her family can handle'. Peter Davies, however, is very much at home on soft ground, and proved on his first two starts that he can act on good to firm as well. In January it was announced that Japanese stud owner Tomohiro Wada had purchased a substantial share in the colt. *H. R. A. Cecil.*

PETERHOUSE 3 b.c. Habitat 134–Kanz (USA) 115 (The Minstrel (CAN) 135) **77**
[1989 6g 6g* 1990 8m 8.2s 8m³ 7m] small, close-coupled colt: modest performer: easily best effort in handicaps in the summer when fair third at Salisbury, quickening clear 3f out but weakening inside last: unlikely to stay beyond 1m: acts on good to firm ground: coltish second and third outings: joined C. Brooks. *G. Harwood.*

PETER MARTIN 9 ch.g. Monsanto (FR) 121–Bouboulina (Hornbeam 130) [1989 **— §**
14s⁴ 17f² 16m⁶ 15.8m⁶ 16.2m⁴ 16f³ 15m² 16.2m⁴ 14.8f² 14g⁴ 16.2m² 18m⁴ 1990 16.5f] workmanlike gelding: moderate mover: ungenuine handicapper: stayed well: acted on any going: often blinkered or visored: usually held up and suited by strong gallop: sold out of F. Lee's stable 3,400 gns Doncaster May Sales: dead. *Miss G. M. Rees.*

PETER PUMPKIN 2 b.g. (May 12) Tickled Pink 114–Wild Pumpkin (Auction **36**
Ring (USA) 123) [1990 5m 5.3h⁴ 6m 5m⁶ 7f 7f⁴ 7m 6m a7g] workmanlike gelding: poor mover: third foal: brother to 5f winner Pink Pumkin and a poor maiden: dam poor maiden: stays 7f: often blinkered: races freely: difficult at stalls third outing: rather temperamental. *R. Voorspuy.*

PETIPA (USA) 3 gr.c. Encino (USA)–Connie O (USA) (Oxford Flight (USA)) **88**
[1989 5.3m* 5g² 5m⁴ 7m* 7g 1990 8.2f 8m⁶ 8m 8.5d³ 8d⁴ 10f 8m 10f⁶ 8m⁶ 8g⁴ 8m 8g* 8g] useful-looking colt: good walker: fair handicapper: won £8,200 contest at York in October: co-favourite, ran badly at Newbury 2 weeks later: should stay beyond 1m: acts on good to firm ground and dead: genuine: sold 37,000 gns Newmarket Autumn Sales. *R. Hannon.*

PETITE AMIE 2 gr.f. (Mar 21) Petoski 135–Amourette (Crowned Prince (USA) **46**
128) [1990 6s⁵ 6g 7d⁶ 8v] 5,000Y: sixth reported foal: closely related to 3-y-o Pomme d'Amour and a winner in Italy (both by Niniski) and half-sister to a winner in Italy: dam never ran: one-paced sixth of 13 in maiden at Ayr in September, best effort: faced stiff task after: should stay at least 1m. *C. W. Thornton.*

PETITE ANGEL 5 ro.m. Burslem 123–Lavinia (Habitat 134) [1989 8.5f 7f 8h 5f **—**
6f⁶ 8h⁴ 8f 8m 8f 5f⁴ 8f a8g 1990 a5g] small, sturdy mare: bad plater: sold 1,700 gns Ascot February Sales. *R. Hollinshead.*

PETITE BUTTERFLY 3 b.f. Absalom 128–Girl of Shiraz 84 (Hotfoot 126) **66**
[1989 5m 6m a7g* 1990 a6g* a6g³ 6m 6g a8g³ a6g 6m* 7g⁵ 7g 7.6d] smallish, lengthy filly: keen walker: has quick action: quite modest performer: won handicap at Southwell in January and seller (bought in 4,600 gns) at Windsor in August: stays 7f: acts on good to firm ground, possibly unsuited by dead. *W. Carter.*

PETITE ELITE 3 b.f. Anfield 117–Gimima 54 (Narrator 127) [1989 NR 1990 12d **—**
a8g⁶ a6g] small, sturdy filly: sister to 5-y-o Final Pass, poor maiden here successful over 7f and 1m in Belgium, and half-sister to several winners here and abroad, including 1988 2-y-o 5f winner Gallery Pot Girl (by Philip of Spain): dam won 1m

seller: no worthwhile form, 8/1 from 20/1 but slowly away in claimer (wore eye-shield) at Southwell final outing: ridden by 7-lb claimer last 2 starts. *J. G. FitzGerald.*

PETITE MELUSINE (IRE) 2 b.f. (Jan 14) Fairy King (USA)–Grace de Bois 50 (Tap On Wood 130) [1990 5f³ 5m² 5g 6m⁶ 7s a7g a5g] 17,000Y: small, angular filly: first foal: dam minor winner in France at around 9f: plating-class maiden: ran moderately after second start: should stay 6f. *R. Thompson.*

PETITE MOU 3 b.f. Ela-Mana-Mou 132–Petite Bourguoise (Crowned Prince 93 (USA) 128) [1989 6m* 7g 8v 1990 10m* 8v 12d³ 10g 10m⁶ 12m⁶ 10f* 10g⁵] compact filly: won 2-runner minor event at Nottingham in April and handicap at Lingfield in August: ran in Italian pattern events otherwise as 3-y-o except for fifth start: third in Oaks d'Italia at Milan: probably stays 1½m: acts on any going: ran moderately when sweating fifth start. *B. Hanbury.*

PETITE ROSANNA 4 b.f. Ile de Bourbon (USA) 133–Let Slip 77 (Busted 134) 89 [1989 9f⁵ 10g* 10f* 12g 10m⁴ 10f 10f⁵ 9.2d⁴ 10m 12m⁵ 1990 10g 10h* 10g 10g⁶ 10h* 10m⁵ 10m² 10m* 10.2g⁴ 12m³ 12m³ 12g] smallish, good-quartered filly: fairly useful handicapper: successful at Brighton in May and August and Salisbury in September: ran very well at Newmarket penultimate outing: effective at 1¼m and 1½m: suited by a sound surface: blinkered (raced keenly) final start at 3 yrs: usually wears tongue strap. *W. Carter.*

PETITESSE 2 gr.f. (Mar 14) Petong 126–Foudroyer (Artaius (USA) 129) [1990 55 5m 6g 5g⁵ 5.1m² 6g⁴ 5f* 5f² 5f⁵ 6m² 6f⁵ 5f 6m* 6m⁶ 5m] 3,300Y: small, dipped-backed filly: fourth foal: dam twice-raced half-sister to smart animals Lighted Glory and Torus: fair plater: no bid after winning at Lingfield in July and September: probably better suited by 6f than 5f: acts on firm going: blinkered ninth to eleventh starts: has been mounted on track, and usually mulish to post: inconsistent. *G. Blum.*

PETIVARA 3 b.f. Petong 126–Avahra 108 (Sahib 114) [1989 6g⁶ 6g⁶ 1990 6f 7m 48 6f² 6m⁴ 6f⁵ 6m 6f⁶ 7g 6g⁴ a10g] leggy, workmanlike filly: plating-class maiden: should stay 7f, not 1¼m: acts on firm ground: visored (ran well) penultimate start. *S. Dow.*

PETLOVA 3 b.f. Petorius 117–Vlassova (FR) 69 (Green Dancer (USA) 132) [1989 63 6g 1990 7m* 8.2s a8g 11m⁶ 10m 16m] lengthy filly: first foal: dam French 11.5f to 15f winner: won 4-runner maiden at Edinburgh in May: sixth of 7 at Redcar, virtually only shown in handicaps: yet to show she stays beyond 7f, doesn't stay 2m: visored (on toes, took keen hold) fifth start. *S. G. Norton.*

PETMER 3 b.g. Tina's Pet 121–Merency 75 (Meldrum 112) [1989 6g 1990 10f⁴ 57 p 10.1m⁵] tall, leggy gelding: quite modest form: ran on never placed to challenge in maiden at Brighton and minor event at Windsor in the summer, giving impression capable of better: stays 1¼m. *R. Akehurst.*

PETONY (IRE) 2 b.f. (May 16) Petorius 117–Norme (FR) (Dark Tiger) [1990 5f² 51 5m⁴] IR 1,800Y: half-sister to 3 winners here and abroad, including 1m seller winner Pride of Kirby (by Pas de Seul): dam French 1m winner: plating-class form in maiden auctions at Beverley (slowly away) and Redcar: off course over 2 months in between: will be better suited by 6f. *C. W. C. Elsey.*

PETRACO (IRE) 2 b.c. (Mar 31) Petorius 117–Merrie Moira (Bold Lad (IRE) 64 133) [1990 6f³ 7d 5d⁵] IR 40,000Y: workmanlike colt: has a quick action: half-brother to several winners, including Irish 1m to 1½m winner Party Prince (by Lord Gayle) and Steward's Cup winner Autumn Sunset (by African Sky): dam raced 5f and 6f winner in Ireland: quite modest form in maidens at Goodwood and Redcar first and final starts: seventeenth of 20 in Cartier Million at Phoenix Park: stays 6f. *L. J. Codd.*

PETROL BLUE 3 b.g. Tumble Wind (USA)–Petrina 87 (Petingo 135) [1989 6g 58 1990 6f 5f⁶ 5f⁴ 6g* 8f⁵ 7f⁴ 6m² 6g 6f 6m 6g³ 7m] angular gelding: quite modest handicapper: won at Carlisle in May: stays 1m: acts on firm ground: blinkered last 2 outings, running creditably first of them: edged left much of way second start. *M. H. Easterby.*

PETROPOWER (IRE) 2 b.c. (Apr 26) Petorius 117–Gay Honey (Busted 134) 57 [1990 5g³ 5g* 6g³ 5g* 5m⁴] IR 6,400F, 12,500YS: lengthy, rather angular colt: moderate mover: fifth reported foal: half-brother to a winning Irish hurdler: dam never ran: plating-class performer: wandered when winning claimers at Leicester in May and Edinburgh in June: went left leaving stalls and raced virtually alone when respectable fourth in Edinburgh claimer: stays 6f: blinkered final 2 starts: sold 3,400 gns Newmarket Autumn Sales. *J. Berry.*

PETRULLO 5 b.h. Electric 126–My Therape 112 (Jimmy Reppin 131) [1989 9g² **114** 10s⁴ 11g 10f⁶ 12m⁶ 10g³ 10d* 12g 10g 1990 9m⁵ 10.5d⁴ 10m⁶ 10m⁴] strong, rangy horse: usually looks well: has a quick action: much improved as 4-y-o, winning La Coupe de Maisons-Laffitte: ran creditably in first half of 1990, in Earl of Sefton EBF Stakes at Newmarket and Prix Ganay (fourth to Creator) at Longchamp on first 2 outings: suited by 1¼m: unsuited by firm going, acts on any other: tends to hang, and is suited by strong handling and waiting tactics. *J. R. Fanshawe.*

PET SHOP BOY 2 gr.c. (Apr 21) Petong 126–Moben 73 (Counsel 118) [1990 5m **59** 5m³ 6h 5g² 5m* 6m] 16,000Y: useful-looking colt, shade unfurnished: has scope: half-brother to 4 winners (all by Mummy's Pet), including very useful 5f to 1m winner Teacher's Pet: dam 7f winner, is half-sister to high-class stayer Grey Baron: won maiden at Nottingham in June: last in nursery following month: virtually pulled up third outing, hung right from halfway on fourth: should stay 6f: blinkered final 2 starts. *K. M. Brassey.*

PETTICOAT POWER 4 b.f. Petorius 117–Red Realm (Realm 129) [1989 7g 6g **68** 6m 7g 6g 6m 6d 6m⁴ 6g* 1990 a7g⁴ a7g² 6f⁵ 6m³ 6d⁴ 6m⁵ 7m* 6f⁶ 7.6m⁴ 7m⁴ 7m 7m³ 7g⁵ 7m³ 7g³ 7d*] workmanlike, sparely-made filly: modest handicapper: won at Kempton (well backed) in June and Folkestone (favourite, making all) in November: effective at 6f to 7f: acts on firm and dead going: suitable mount for inexperienced rider: consistent. *G. B. Balding.*

PFALZ 2 b.f. (Feb 4) Pharly (FR) 130–Leipzig 107 (Relkino 131) [1990 7g²] third **81 p** foal: sister to 1988 2-y-o 6f winner Zaitech: dam 6f and 1m winner, from family of Braashee, Hadeer and Bassenthwaite: ½-length second of 14 to Jahafil in minor event at Doncaster in September, with winner most of way and keeping on well near line: will stay at least 1¼m: sure to improve, and win a race. *M. R. Stoute.*

PHALAROPE (IRE) 2 b.g. (May 17) Petorius 117–Magee (Weavers' Hall 122) **52** [1990 6f 6g 7.5m⁵ 7g⁶ 8m⁶] IR 37,000Y: rather leggy, close-coupled gelding: has scope: third living foal: closely related to 6f and 7f winner Choritzo (by Runnett) and half-brother to 6f and 7f winner Eastern Song (by Ballad Rock): dam disappointing Irish maiden: plating-class maiden: good sixth in York nursery final start: stays 1m: tends to carry head high. *M. H. Easterby.*

PHANAN 4 ch.g. Pharly (FR) 130–L'Ecossaise (Dancer's Image (USA)) [1989 8f **68** 8f⁵ 14m³ 16.5g³ 17.6f² 10.1m² 12.2g* 11.7m* 14m⁴ 12g a10g 1990 12f 10.4d² 12.3d⁴ 10m 10m* 11.7m³ 11.7m⁴ 12f³ 12.3m³ 10.4g⁴] leggy, workmanlike gelding: modest handicapper: given excellent ride when winning at Lingfield in June: best efforts over middle distances: acts on firm and dead going: usually wears small bandage off-hind: lacks turn of foot, and is suited by forcing tactics. *F. Durr.*

PHARAMINEUX 4 ch.g. Pharly (FR) 130–Miss Longchamp 94 (Northfields **65** (USA)) [1989 7s 7g 8m 10f 8m⁴ 8m 10m³ 10m 8f a10g 1990 11.7m² 11.7m³ 11.7m³ 14m* 14g* 14g* 16.2m⁶ 16.2s] strong, workmanlike gelding: has a quick action: progressed very well in handicaps, winning at Sandown in July and September and Salisbury (well-backed favourite) in August: stays 1¾m: possibly unsuited by extremes of going: blinkered final start at 3 yrs. *R. Akehurst.*

PHARAOH'S DELIGHT 3 b.f. Fairy King (USA)–Ridge The Times (USA) 78 **112** (Riva Ridge (USA)) [1989 6m⁶ 5f* 6m* 6d* 6g² 1990 8g⁶ 8f⁵ 6m 6d² 5m³ 6g³ 5g²

Shadwell Stud Cheshire Oaks, Chester—outsider-of-eight Pharian makes a winning debut, staying on strongly from Ruby Tiger and Wajna

*Lancashire Oaks, Haydock—Pharian causes another upset,
and has six lengths in hand of Cruising Height*

6m⁵ 5g³] quite attractive filly: very useful performances in Prix de Meautry
(hanging right) at Deauville, Keeneland Nunthorpe Stakes at York and Ladbroke
Sprint Cup at Haydock fourth to sixth starts, and in Prix de l'Abbaye de Longchamp
on final one: blinkered, set strong pace when below form penultimate outing: best at
sprint distances: yet to race on very soft going, acts on any other: has been bandaged. *J. P. Hudson.*

PHARIAN (USA)   3 ch.f. Diesis 133–Pharlette (FR) (Pharly (FR) 130) [1989 NR   **114**
1990 11.3d* 12d 12s* 12m 13.5d 4] $95,000Y: small, angular, sparely-made filly: third
reported foal: sister to American winner Aletta Maria and half-sister to a winner in
USA by Full Pocket: dam unraced: led 1f out and stayed on strongly to win Shadwell
Stud Cheshire Oaks at Chester in May and 4-runner Lancashire Oaks (on toes, beat
Cruising Height 6 lengths) at Haydock in July: soundly beaten in Ribblesdale Stakes
at Royal Ascot and below form in Irish Oaks at the Curragh and Prix de Pomone at
Deauville: stayed 1½m: acted on soft going, seemed unsuited by good to firm: stud.
C. E. Brittain.

PHARLY FIZZ   3 ch.g. Pharly (FR) 130–Amber Fizz (USA) (Effervescing (USA))   **36**
[1989 NR 1990 8f a12g³ 10g a11g] 3,800Y: sturdy gelding: poor mover: second foal:
dam once-raced half-sister to very smart 1978 American 2-y-o Groton High, from
family of Bold Ruler: well beaten in sellers after third (no extra final 1f) at Southwell.
J. S. Wainwright.

PHARMOPI   3 b.f. Pharly (FR) 130–Motion Picture 73 (Irish River (FR) 131)   **—**
[1989 NR 1990 7g 8.5d 7m 8.3m] 32,000Y: sturdy filly: first foal: dam twice-raced
daughter of Odeon, very useful at up to 1¾m: no form, including in handicap: bred to
stay further: sold 3,100 gns Newmarket Autumn Sales. *C. J. Benstead.*

PHAROAH'S GUEST   3 ch.g. Pharly (FR) 130–Exuberine (FR) 82 (Be My   **—**
Guest (USA) 126) [1989 NR 1990 8m 10.1g 8g 9g 11.7m 13.1m 10f 10d] 4,500Y: strong,
compact gelding: moderate mover: second foal: half-brother to Irish 1½m and 1¾m
winner Classy Trick (by Head For Heights): dam 1m winner: poor maiden: should
stay 1¼m in blinkers or a visor. *P. T. Walwyn.*

PHARYNX   3 b.g. Pharly (FR) 130–Pamina 110 (Brigadier Gerard 144) [1989 NR   **—**
1990 7m 8.2d 10m] strong, rangy gelding: moderate walker: fourth foal: half-brother
to fairly useful 1m to 11.7f winner Tamino (by Tap On Wood): dam, very useful at up
to 1¼m, is daughter of very smart Magic Flute: no sign of ability in maidens: sold
2,000 gns Ascot July Sales and gelded. *P. T. Walwyn.*

PHIL-BLAKE   3 br.g. Blakeney 126–Philogyny 94 (Philip of Spain 126) [1989   **62**
6m⁴ 6g 6d 1990 10g 8m² 8m⁵ 11m 8d] leggy, workmanlike gelding: quite modest
form: ran moderately in handicaps last 3 outings: should prove better over 1¼m
than shorter: gelded after fourth start: winning hurdler. *C. A. Horgan.*

PHILHARMONIA 3 ch.f. Caerleon (USA) 132–Melody (USA) (Lord Gayle 98
(USA) 124) [1989 NR 1990 8m* 7m⁵ 10s* 10g²] sturdy, angular filly: moderate
mover: seventh foal: sister to 1987 2-y-o 7f winner St Cadoc and half-sister to
several winners, including 1988 2-y-o 6f winner Creole (by Sadler's Wells) and
smart 7f filly Guest Performer (by Be My Guest): dam Irish 7f to 1½m winner:
progressive form: won maiden at Goodwood in September and minor event at
Nottingham in October: staying-on ¾-length second of 7 to eased Stagecraft in
listed race at Newmarket: should stay 1½m. *J. W. Hills.*

PHILIPPA'S HEIR 3 b.f. Elegant Air 119–Ebb And Flo 82 (Forlorn River 124) 51
[1989 6m 7m³ 7g 8.2s 1990 9s⁶ 8.5m³ 10f⁴ 8g⁴ 12.2m⁴ 12m⁴ 15.8m⁶ 10f⁴] leggy,
shallow-girthed filly: plating-class maiden: showed little last 2 outings, bandaged on
first of them: stays 1½m: acts on firm going, seems unsuited by soft: visored last 3
starts, blinkered final one at 2 yrs: sold to join R. Lee 5,000 gns Newmarket Autumn
Sales. *R. W. Stubbs.*

PHILIPPI (FR) 4 b.c. Zino 127–Parforce (FR) (Mill Reef (USA) 141) [1989 8d⁵ 112
5g 9g⁶ 9g² 8s* 8d* 1990 8g⁴ 8g⁶ 7s* 7g⁴ 7d² 8g⁶ 8g 7d* 7g³] French colt: won
listed races at Longchamp in April and September: in frame in between in Group 3
events won by Funambule at same course, and ran very well there on final start
when 4½ lengths third to Septieme Ciel in Prix de la Foret: suited by 7f: goes very
well with give in the ground. *N. Clement, France.*

PHILJOY 4 b.f. Bustino 136–Formana (Reform 132) [1989 12d⁴ 12.3m⁴ 12m⁶ 16f² 64
1990 13s² 16f⁴ 18.4d⁶ 14.8m³] workmanlike filly: poor mover: quite modest maiden:
stays 2m: acts on any going: hung on reappearance. *C. W. C. Elsey.*

PHILOSOPHOS 4 b.g. High Top 131–Pacificus (USA) 65 (Northern Dancer) —
[1989 10g⁶ 11.7m² 12g 13.3d² 1990 17.6g] smallish, angular gelding: poor walker:
modest maiden at best: shaped as though retaining ability only outing at 4 yrs: likely
to prove best at up to 2m: acts on good to firm and dead going: useful hurdler. *J. H.
Baker.*

PHIL'S FOLLY 3 b.f. Glasgow Central 91–Katebird 89 (Birdbrook 110) [1989 —
5.8f⁴ 5m 1990 6v 6m] smallish, deep-girthed filly: poor maiden. *W. Carter.*

PHILS FRIEND 4 ch.g. Sunley Builds 102–Our Denise 63 (Bend A Bow (USA)) —
[1989 NR 1990 12g] fourth reported foal: dam probably stayed 1m: 33/1, tailed off
from halfway in seller at Folkestone in October. *J. J. Bridger.*

PHILSTAY 3 b.f. Bustino 136–Magelka 77 (Relkino 131) [1989 6f 6m 8g⁶ 10.6d —
1990 8f 12.2m 12h 8h² 9f] smallish, workmanlike filly: apparently of little account. *T.
Fairhurst.*

PHISUS 3 b.f. Henbit (USA) 130–Daring Lass 87 (Bold Lad (IRE) 133) [1989 5d³ —
5s⁴ 5s⁵ 5f 6m 6g 8g 1990 10m a5g 5.8h⁶ 6f⁴] workmanlike filly: poor maiden: stays
1m: acts on any going: sometimes on toes. *J. White.*

PHOENIX JULE 3 b.g. Coquelin (USA) 121–Ariel Sands (USA) (Super —
Concorde (USA) 128) [1989 6f⁶ 6m 6g² 6s² a8g³ a7g⁶ a8g 1990 a8g] quite attractive
gelding: quite modest form when placed in claimers: stays 1m: blinkered last 3
outings: sold to join B. Crawford 2,600 gns Doncaster May Sales. *J. G. FitzGerald.*

PHOTO CALL 3 b.f. Chief Singer 131–Photo 83 (Blakeney 126) [1989 7s⁶ 8.2g⁵ 65
9f* 1990 10.6f⁶ 8.2s 8g 11f* 11.5m 12f³ 15.5f³ 12f⁵ 16m] sturdy, angular filly:
moderate walker and mover: quite modest handicapper: bit edgy, won at Redcar
(edged left and swished tail when hit with whip) in August: stays 1½m: goes well on
firm going: blinkered third start: rather inconsistent and may be unsatisfactory. *M.
A. Jarvis.*

PHOUNTZI (USA) 4 ch.c. Raise A Cup (USA)–Pushy 112 (Sharpen Up 127) 104
[1989 7d³ 8g* 1990 8m⁴ 7f4 10.1g⁵ 8g⁴ 8m⁴ 8s] leggy, quite attractive colt: good
mover: won maiden at Newmarket (reportedly split a pastern) in spring as 3-y-o:
best efforts in 1990 in Trusthouse Forte Mile at Sandown, minor event at Newbury
and £11,500 race at Newmarket (staying on strongly behind Raj Waki) on first,
fourth and fifth outings: suited by 1m: acts on good to firm going: trained until after
fifth start by M. Stoute. *A. Fabre, France.*

PHUSSANDBUSSLE 2 b.f. (Mar 11) Pharly (FR) 130–Sophonisbe (Wollow —
132) [1990 7m 6g] 5,000Y: leggy, dipped-backed filly: second living foal: half-sister
to a winner in Germany: dam French 11f winner, is half-sister to Steinlen: little
worthwhile form in autumn maidens at Lingfield (slowly away and moderate late
progress) and Folkestone: will probably be much better suited by 1m + . *J. L. Dunlop.*

PICK AND CHOOSE 2 b.f. (Apr 30) Nomination 125–Plum Bold 83 (Be My 48
Guest (USA) 126) [1990 a6g 6d⁵ 6d] close-coupled filly: moderate walker: fifth foal:

half-sister to 3-y-o Roman Walk (by Petorius), 6f winner at 2 yrs, 1987 2-y-o Irish 5f winner Very Welcome (by Main Reef) and 1m winner Kaleidophone (by Kalaglow): dam 6f winner: poor form in maidens: will stay 7f. *J. P. Leigh.*

PICKLES   2 b.c. (Mar 3) Petoski 135–Kashmiri Snow 83 (Shirley Heights 130)   78 p
[1990 7m⁴ 8g³] rangy, quite attractive colt: has plenty of scope: second foal: half-brother to 3-y-o 1m and 9f winner Gulmarg (by Gorytus): dam 1m winner: over a length third of 16 to Road To The Isle in maiden at Kempton in September: will stay 1½m: likely to improve again, and win a race. *H. Candy.*

PIC NEGRE   3 b.g. Lochnager 132–Sallusteno 80 (Sallust 134) [1989 6m 6g⁶ 6g   54
5g a5g 1990 a6g⁴ 6g⁶ a7g⁶ 7.5d 8m 10g 6m a8g³ a8g a8g 10.6v⁵ 10d] workmanlike gelding: plating-class maiden: easily best efforts when in frame at Southwell: stays 1m: visored ninth start: twice blinkered. *S. G. Norton.*

PIER DAMIANI (USA)   3 b.c. Shareef Dancer (USA) 135–All A Lark (General 106 ?
Assembly (USA)) [1989 7s⁵ 7g 1990 10m³ 8.5g⁵ 12f⁵ 12g² 12g 12s³ 10g* 14.6g 14s²] deep-girthed colt: has scope: easily best efforts when 4½ lengths second to Houm-ayoun in Derby Italiano and Per Quod in Premio Roma Vecchia at Rome: only fair form otherwise, awarded race when bumped and beaten short head in maiden at Beverley in August and tailed off in St Leger at Doncaster: stays 1¾m: acts on soft ground: hung right and looked ungenuine sixth start. *C. E. Brittain.*

PIGALLE WONDER   2 br.c. (Jan 22) Chief Singer 131–Hi-Tech Girl 93   75
(Homeboy 114) [1990 5m² 6g⁶ 5d⁶ 6m² 5m⁴ 7m 6g 5g⁶ 6s] 34,000Y: robust, close-coupled colt: good walker: fluent mover: first foal: dam 2-y-o 5f winner suited by 6f: modest form in varied events: ran well when in mid-division in 18-runner nursery at Haydock on third-last outing: moved poorly down final one: probably better suited by 6f than 5f (had stiff task over 7f): possibly unsuited by softish ground: sold 12,000 gns Newmarket Autumn Sales. *C. E. Brittain.*

PIGEON LOFT (IRE)   2 gr.f. (May 10) Bellypha 130–Dovetail 80 (Brigadier   47
Gerard 144) [1990 6m 8m⁶ 8f] medium-sized filly: has scope: sister to French 1m and 1¼m winner Diamond Dove and half-sister to 2 winners abroad: dam, 1¼m winner, is daughter of Sun Chariot and Child Stakes winner Duboff: poor form in maiden at Edinburgh (gave trouble at stalls) and maiden auction at Redcar: very green on debut. *P. Calver.*

PIGEON VOYAGEUR (IRE)   2 b.c. (Mar 10) Saint Estephe 123–Homing 111
Pigeon (FR) (Habitat 134) [1990 7g 7.5g² 9d* 10s²] 15,000Y: half-brother to several winners, including very useful French 7f and 1m winner Ocean Falls (by Wassl) and Irish Derby fourth Vanvitelli (by Ela-Mana-Mou): dam Irish 1m winner, is granddaughter of Oaks winner Long Look: progressive colt: well beaten in minor event at Vichy on debut but 2 outings later won Prix Saint-Roman at Longchamp by ¾ length from Clark Store: 4 lengths second of 9 to Pistolet Bleu in Criterium de Saint-Cloud in November: will stay 1½m: acts very well on soft ground. *A. Fabre, France.*

PILAR   2 gr.f. (Mar 6) Godswalk (USA) 130–Old Silver (Bold Lad (IRE) 133) [1990   67 d
5f 6g 5g 6m 5f⁴ 7f³ 7m* 7g³ 7m⁵ 8.2g 7f* 6m 6d⁶ a8g a7g a6g] 6,600Y: neat filly: poor mover: fourth foal: dam (modest) placed over 7.9f at 2 yrs in Ireland: quite useful plater: successful in nursery (retained 5,000 gns) at Wolverhampton in August and at Redcar (no bid after winning comfortably) in October: below form on all-weather: suited by 7f: acts well on firm ground: blinkered fifth start: has worn bandages: inconsistent. *Mrs N. Macauley.*

PILGRIM'S PATH   3 gr.g. Godswalk (USA) 130–Lassalia (Sallust 134) [1989   75
5m⁶ 6m⁴ 6d 1990 6g² 6m* 6m⁴ 6m⁴ 7m 7m² 7f³ 6g⁵] good-topped, workmanlike gelding: modest handicapper: won at Haydock in May: stays 7f: acts on firm going: visored (ran fairly well) in apprentice race final start: hung left and swished tail on reappearance: has edged right: sold 13,500 gns Newmarket Autumn Sales. *G. B. Balding.*

PILOT   4 ch.f. Kris 135–Sextant 98 (Star Appeal 133) [1989 7g⁴ 10.5f² 1990 9m]   —
angular, medium-sized filly: keen, active type, takes a good hold: won slowly-run maiden at Newmarket in April, 1989: evens, ½-length second to Snow Bride in Tattersalls Musidora Stakes at York following month: afterwards found to have cracked a pastern: well backed, well-beaten ninth of 10 in Earl of Sefton EBF Stakes at Newmarket in April, only subsequent outing: stayed 10.5f. *Major W. R. Hern.*

PIMSBOY   3 b.g. Tender King 123–Hitopah (Bustino 136) [1989 5m 7m* 1990   58
8.2g³ 8.5d 8.2g 8f⁵ 8.2m³ 10m 8m 7.5m² 8.2d⁶ 7m 7d⁴ 7d⁶] rather angular gelding: quite modest handicapper: claimed out of W. Haggas' stable £14,000 after claimer on reappearance: best efforts after when placed: should stay 1¼m (hampered at trip):

acts on good to firm ground and dead: blinkered (ran fairly well) ninth and tenth starts. *J. Parkes.*

PIMS CLASSIC 2 gr.c. (Feb 24) Absalom 128–Musical Maiden 76 (Record **75** Token 128) [1990 6m 6g⁴ a7g² a7g²] 5,200 2-y-o: well-made colt with scope: good mover: second foal: dam 2-y-o 7f winner is out of half-sister to top 1975 2-y-o filly Pasty: modest maiden: runner-up to Catundra and Mystic Crystal at Southwell: seems better suited by 7f than 6f: bandaged off-fore third start. *W. J. Haggas.*

PIMS GUNNER (IRE) 2 b.g. (Feb 11) Montelimar (USA) 122–My Sweetie **78** p (Bleep-Bleep 134) [1990 5m⁶ 6f* 7g 6m⁴ 8m²] IR 7,800F, IR 13,500Y: rangy gelding: has scope: has a round action: seventh reported foal: half-brother to 7f and 1¼m winner Wizzard Art (by Wolver Hollow), Irish 8.5f winner Colonel Gay (by Scorpio) and a winner over hurdles: dam lightly-raced half-sister to smart Air Trooper: won maiden auction at Yarmouth in August by 2½ lengths: ran well in nursery final start: will stay 1¼m: likely to improve further. *W. J. Haggas.*

PINCTADA 8 b.g. Mummy's Pet 125–Pinaka 69 (Pitcairn 126) [1989 7g* 8g 7d 7s **72** + 7g 7m⁴ 7g² 8.3m 7g⁶ 7.3m³ 7g 7g* 7m 7g 1990 7g⁵] strong, compact gelding: carries plenty of condition: poor mover: fair winner of handicaps as 7-y-o: not discredited only outing (April) in 1990: better suited by 7f than 1m: ideally suited by an easy surface: usually held up: excellent mount for inexperienced rider. *R. Simpson.*

PINEAPPLE 2 ch.f. (Feb 26) Superlative 118–Pine Ridge 80 (High Top 131) **68** p [1990 6g⁵] angular, unfurnished filly: fourth foal: half-sister to high-class 3-y-o In The Groove (by Night Shift), successful from 6f (at 2 yrs) to 10.5f, including in Irish 1000 Guineas, and to fairly useful miler Spanish Pine (by King of Spain): dam 1½m winner: around 8 lengths fifth of 18, ridden along 2f out and staying on strongly, to Junk Bond in maiden at Newbury in September: will stay 7f: sure to improve, and win a race. *M. R. Stoute.*

PINECONE PETER 3 ch.g. Kings Lake (USA) 133–Cornish Heroine (USA) 101 **59** (Cornish Prince) [1989 8.2g 1990 8.2g⁴ 11m* 9g³ 9m 9g] leggy, angular gelding: moderate mover: quite modest performer: won claimer at Edinburgh in May, hanging right: needs further than 9f, and stays 11f well: sold 5,600 gns Ascot September Sales: winning hurdler for O. Brennan. *J. Berry.*

PINE GLEN PEPPER 2 ch.c. (Mar 7) Aragon 118–The Ranee (Royal Palace **58** 131) [1990 5f³ 5g³ 5m²] leggy colt: third foal: half-brother to 7f and 1m winner Alipura (by Anfield): dam behind in modest company: quite modest form in maidens and a minor event in spring: will be better suited by 6f. *S. Dow.*

PINE RIDGE LADY 3 gr.f. Castle Keep 121–Red Lady 78 (Warpath 113) [1989 **—** NR 1990 7m⁵ 10.1g] workmanlike filly: third foal: half-sister to Mazurkanova (by Song), plating-class 2-y-o 6f winner: dam 13f winner: well beaten in minor events at Kempton (slowly away and soon tailed off) and Windsor. *S. Dow.*

PING PONG 2 br.f. (Mar 16) Petong 126–Conway Bay 74 (Saritamer (USA) 130) **65** [1990 5m⁵ 5f³ 5m 6m 5g⁵ 5m³ 5m⁶ 5m 6m⁴ 7f⁶ 5d⁶ a7g² a6g*] compact filly: moderate mover: sister to 4-y-o James's Pet, 6f seller winner at 2 yrs, and half-sister to 8.2f seller winner Light The Way (by Nicholas Bill) and 6f winner Conway King (by King of Spain): dam placed over 5f at 2 yrs, appeared not to train on: won 10-runner claimer at Southwell late in year by 5 lengths: best at 6f: best form on all-weather: blinkered sixth and seventh starts: has run creditably for 7-lb claimer: sometimes slowly away: changed hands 1,650 gns Doncaster October Sales. *T. Fairhurst.*

PINISI 5 ch.g. Final Straw 127–Bireme 127 (Grundy 137) [1989 12m⁵ 12m⁵ 1990 **—** 11s 21.6m] strong, lengthy gelding: good walker: showed signs of ability as 4-y-o: well beaten subsequently over hurdles and in maiden (blinkered) and handicap (visored, raced too keenly) in spring. *G. M. Moore.*

PINK BELLS (USA) 3 ro.f. Pass The Tab (USA)–Zenica (FR) (Faraway Son **54** § (USA) 130) [1989 NR 1990 10f 8f 8m 11.7m 10f⁶ 11.7h⁵ 11.7h⁴] IR 40,000Y: angular filly: fifth foal: sister to 2 winners in USA, including 1988 2-y-o stakes winner Just A Tab, and half-sister to a winner by Sweet Candy: dam won 3 times from 9f to 11f in French Provinces: ungenuine maiden: stays 1m: ran poorly in blinkers final start: sold 2,000 gns Newmarket December Sales. *P. F. I. Cole.*

PINK BUBBLES 3 ch.f. Blushing Scribe (USA) 107–Swing The Cat (Swing **39** Easy (USA) 126) [1989 NR 1990 7m 6m 7f 7m⁶] 500F, 2,400Y: sparely-made filly: half-sister to 4 winners, including fair 6f and 7f winner Tamdown Flyer (by Hotfoot): dam never ran: plater: form only when sixth in handicap (edgy) at Newmarket: swerved left at stalls in apprentice event second start: sold 800 gns Doncaster October Sales. *R. Guest.*

PINK GIN 3 ch.g. Tickled Pink 114–Carrapateira (Gunner B 126) [1989 6s³ 7v **55**
1990 8v 8.2g⁴ 10d⁶ 10.2m³ 10d⁴] good-topped gelding: plating-class maiden: easily
best efforts as 3-y-o when in frame, staying on well, in handicaps: well worth a try
over 1½m: acts on good to firm ground and soft. *Miss S. E. Hall.*

PINK SUNSET (IRE) 2 ch.c. (Mar 9) Red Sunset 120–Pink Rose 75 (Ragusa **36**
137) [1990 7m 6s⁵ 6m⁴ a7g 7.5g] 12,500F, IR 6,000Y, 5,000 2-y-o: leggy, rather
sparely-made colt: brother to a winner in Belgium and half-brother to several
winners, including 9f and 1¼m winner Good Ruler (by Bold Lad): dam 1¾m winner:
poor maiden: soundly beaten in sellers third and fourth starts: unruly stalls, carried
head high and hung badly left second outing: sold 920 gns Doncaster September
Sales. *N. Tinkler.*

PINNACLE POINT 3 b.c. Lochnager 132–Wollow Maid 73 (Wollow 132) [1989 **87**
5g 5m³ 6m⁴ 6m* 6h⁶ 7m⁶ 6m² 5f 1990 5m³ 6g* 6f* 6g² 6d² 6g* 6m 5g³ 6m⁵ 6f² 6m
6m* 6g 6m⁶ 6m⁵ 7m² 7g 7g 8m] strong, robust colt: has a rather round action: fair
handicapper: won at Carlisle in April, Thirsk in May, Hamilton in June and Nottingham (£7,500 event) in August: excellent second at Redcar in September: stays 7f:
best efforts on top-of-the-ground: hung left for 7-lb claimer: blinkered twice at 2
yrs: has sweated. *J. Pearce.*

PINTAIL BAY 4 b.g. Buzzards Bay 128§–Pin Hole 83 (Parthia 132) [1989 9f³ **58**
1990 12g 10g⁶ 10m 12g³ 10.6d⁴ 12g² 10.6v 11.5g] big, strong gelding: carries plenty of
condition: has a round action: quite modest maiden: better suited to 1½m than
1¼m: acts on dead going. *H. J. Collingridge.*

PIPERS HILL 3 ch.g. Creative Plan (USA)–Kindle (Firestreak 125) [1989 6m **63**
8m⁶ 8m⁴ 10f³ 1990 9m 7m* 5f 6f⁵ 6h² 6m 7d⁴ 7f³ 7.6g 7f⁴ a10g] smallish, shallow-
girthed gelding: quite modest performer: won selling handicap (no bid) at Warwick
in April: may prove suited by 7f: yet to race on soft going, acts on any other: has run
well for apprentice. *M. R. Channon.*

PIPING HOT 2 br.g. (Mar 31) Daring March 116–Rosette 91 (Red Alert 127) **67 p**
[1990 6f* 7g] big, lengthy gelding: has plenty of scope: sixth living foal (all by Daring
March): brother to quite useful 6f and 7f winner Pick of The Pack, 7f winner Highly
Recommended and a winner in Belgium: dam won over 5f and 6f at 2 yrs: won
5-runner maiden at Brighton in June by a length, running on strongly after getting
outpaced: in need of race in Kempton nursery 3 months later, never placed to
challenge or knocked about. *R. V. Smyth.*

PIPISTRELLE 3 b.f. Shareef Dancer (USA) 135–Latin Melody 109 (Tudor **62**
Melody 129) [1989 8g 1990 12m 12f⁴ 13.8m² 13m* 13.8d* 16f² 14f 15m⁴ 13.8f⁴ 16m]
sturdy, angular filly: quite modest handicapper: short-priced favourite and
apprentice ridden, won at Hamilton in June and Catterick in July: stays 2m: acts on
firm ground and dead. *Dr J. D. Scargill.*

PIPITINA 3 b.f. Bustino 136–Pipina (USA) 81 (Sir Gaylord) [1989 7g⁶ 1990 10g⁴ **91**
11.5g² 12f² 14g⁴ 16g* 15d* 18d 16m⁶] lengthy, good-quartered filly: fluent mover:
fairly useful performer: successful in autumn minor events at Thirsk and Ayr: well
beaten after in Cesarewitch Handicap and listed event at Newmarket: stays 2m: acts
on dead going: stud. *G. Wragg.*

PIPPA'S DREAM 3 b.f. Doulab (USA) 115–Chaldea (Tamerlane 128) [1989 5f* **65**
7h⁴ 6g² 6f 6g⁴ 6g⁴ 1990 8f⁴ 8.5g 7f⁴ 8m] workmanlike filly: moderate mover: quite
modest handicapper: ridden by 7-lb claimer, good fourth at Brighton on reappearance: in mid-division for IR £138,000 event at Leopardstown final start, in June:
stays 1m: acts on firm ground: sold 4,200 gns Newmarket Autumn Sales. *P. F. I.
Cole.*

PIPSQUEAK 2 g.r.f. (Mar 12) Alleging (USA) 120–Silver Berry (Lorenzaccio 130) **— p**
[1990 7m] 52,000Y: big, good sort: half-sister to several winners, including good
3-y-o sprinter Argentum (by Aragon) and fair miler Eurodollar (by Sparkler): dam
poor half-sister to very smart 1¼m filly Cranberry Sauce: backward and very green,
steadied stalls and never placed to challenge under considerate ride in maiden at
Newmarket in October: sure to do better. *R. Charlton.*

PIQUANT 3 b. or br.g. Sharpo 132–Asnoura (MOR) (Asandre (FR)) [1989 5s³ **80 §**
5m* 5m⁵ 6m* 6m 6v³ 7d 1990 6f⁵ 6m 6m 6g 7g 6d* 6s 6s⁴ a7g³] stocky gelding:
capable of fair form: led close home in handicap at Ayr in September: stays 7f: acts
on any going: twice visored: swished tail vigorously fourth outing and looked none
too genuine: inconsistent and not one to trust implicitly. *W. Hastings-Bass.*

PIRATE ARMY (USA) 4 br.c. Roberto (USA) 131–Wac (USA) (Lt Stevens **114**
(USA)) [1989 8s* 12f² 1990 9m³ 10m² 12d³ 12m* 11d* 9.7g² 12g⁵] big, rather leggy

Doonside Cup, Ayr—
Pirate Army is extended by Berry's Dream and Spritsail

colt: good walker: has a powerful, slightly round action: smart performer: favourite, won £12,500 event at Chepstow (odds on, making all) in July and listed race at Ayr (in workmanlike style by 1½ lengths from Berry's Dream) in September: mostly placed in pattern contests otherwise, on last occasion making most and running very well in Ciga Prix Dollar won by Agent Bleu at Longchamp: takes strong hold, and probably best short of 1½m: looked ill at ease on firm going final outing (May) as 3-y-o, acts on any other: consistent. *L. M. Cumani.*

Sheikh Mohammed's "Pirate Army"

PISTOLET BLEU (IRE)   2 b.c. (Apr 19) Top Ville 129–Pampa Bella (FR) **118** p
115 (Armos) [1990 8g* 9d* 10s*]

    There's no better horse with which to begin a list of contenders for the Prix du Jockey-Club, the French Derby, than the unbeaten Pistolet Bleu, who at this early stage looks like being a worthy successor to his stable-companion, his owner's Epervier Bleu, second to Sanglamore in the event in 1990. Pistolet Bleu couldn't have made a more promising start to his racing career, winning all three of his races, two of them pattern events, and leaving the clear impression in the last of them, the Group 1 Criterium de Saint-Cloud in November, that he's potentially a high-class middle-distance colt.

    Pistolet Bleu made his debut less than two months earlier in a new-comers race at the same course. Races for newcomers are much more common in France than they are in Britain, and those on the Parisian tracks in particular are used regularly by the top trainers to introduce their better horses: Pistolet Bleu won his, which was over a mile, by a neck from Andre Fabre's Gramy Award, who, if reports from France are correct, seems set also to become another good horse for Khalid Abdulla. Two weeks into October Pistolet Bleu lined up for the Group 3 Prix de Conde over nine furlongs at Longchamp. He might have been second favourite in the betting behind the maiden Kashan, who'd gone into many note-books when an eye-catching second in another newcomers race on his only start, but he came out comfortably on top in the race, making virtually all the running and coming home two and a half lengths ahead of Balleroy, third to Masterclass and Exit To Nowhere in a good maiden on his most recent appearance. The proximity in third place of the selling-race winner Fortune's Wheel initially seemed to call the form into question, but his later performances were of similar merit, and by the time Pistolet Bleu reappeared in the Criterium de Saint-Cloud at the start of November fourth-placed Ganges had paid the form a compliment by handsomely defeating a strong field in the Criterium de Maisons-Laffitte. Few looked beyond Pistolet Bleu to win the Criterium—he was chosen by nineteen of the twenty-two journalists listed in *Paris-Turf*—and he ran out an untroubled winner, making headway from fifth position on the home turn to lead with more than a furlong left, then coming four lengths clear of the Prix Saint-Roman winner Pigeon Voyageur with Fortune's Wheel two and a half lengths further back in third and Widyan, best of the three Anglo-Irish challengers, fourth. There was some interference in the straight, which prompted Widyan's rider Quinn to object to Fortune's Wheel, but the incident didn't concern Pistolet Bleu, who showed a tendency to hang left himself when clear in the final furlong. The Criterium, usually the final Group 1 race for two-year-olds in Europe, was belatedly elevated in status in 1988 after being won by subsequent classic winners Escaline, Darshaan, Mouktar and Fast Topaze; it was 'won' again by a subsequent classic winner in 1989, when Snurge passed the post well clear only to be disqualified. Pistolet Bleu, described by his trainer at the end of the year as 'a top-class horse who stays and loves the soft ground' could well be the next to make the grade.

Criterium de Saint-Cloud—
Widyan is fourth behind Pistolet Bleu, Pigeon Voyageur and Fortune's Wheel;
his stable-companion Snurge was first past the post in this Group 1 event in 1989

		High Top	Derring-Do
	Top Ville	(b 1969)	Camenae
	(b 1976)	Sega Ville	Charlottesville
Pistolet Bleu (IRE)		(b 1968)	La Sega
(b.c. Apr 19, 1988)		Armos	Mossborough
	Pampa Bella (FR)	(ch 1967)	Ardelle
	(ch 1981)	Kendie	Klairon
		(b 1963)	Amagalla

There's no doubt that Pistolet Bleu will stay a mile and a half. He's a son of the Prix du Jockey-Club winner Top Ville, who despite being represented by the specialist seven-furlong performer Norwich in the latest season is an overwhelming influence for stamina, numbering the high-class middle-distance winners Princess Pati, Shardari, Darara and Saint Estephe among his progeny. And Pistolet Bleu has as his dam the very useful French ten-and-a-half-furlong winner Pampa Bella, who also finished third in the Prix de Diane. Pampa Bella is a sister or half-sister to the useful French middle-distance winner Armos to numerous winners in France, most of whom stayed at least a mile and a quarter. So far Pistolet Bleu has raced only on an easy surface, showing his best form when the ground was softest. Reportedly Pistolet Bleu will follow a similar programme to that taken in 1990 by Epervier Bleu; if so we can look forward to his trying to enhance his Jockey-Club claims in the Prix Greffulhe and the Prix Lupin at Longchamp in the spring. *E. Lellouche, France.*

PITCAIRN PRINCESS 2 b.f. (Mar 21) Capricorn Line 111–Queendom 109 — (Quorum 126) [1990 5m⁵ 6g 7s] fifth reported living foal: half-sister to 4 winners, including Chester Cup winner Charlotte's Choice (by Blakeney) and Queen's Niece (by Great Nephew), fair winner at up to 1m: dam genuine and consistent at up to 9f: tailed off in maidens. *D. A. Wilson.*

PIT PONY 6 b.g. Hittite Glory 125–Watch Lady (Home Guard (USA) 129) [1989 — 13v⁴ 1990 11s] neat gelding: moderate mover: poor maiden: should stay beyond 1m: acts on good to firm and dead going: untrustworthy hurdler: has been tried in blinkers and visor. *J. S. Wilson.*

PITSEA 4 b.c. Tina's Pet 121–Here's Sue 76 (Three Legs 128) [1989 5s⁵ 6m² 6f⁴ 60 6f* 7g 7g 6v a6g 1990 a7g a7g³ 7g 6m 7.6m] tall, rather leggy colt: has a round action: modest winner of handicap as 3-y-o: below form since, well tailed off in claimer final outing: best form at 6f on top-of-the-ground: sold 1,200 gns Ascot July Sales. *R. Hannon.*

PLAGUE O' RATS 6 b.g. Pitskelly 122–Hillbrow 100 (Swing Easy (USA) 126) — [1989 NR 1990 16g] workmanlike gelding: carries plenty of condition: fairly useful winner as 2-y-o: has deteriorated considerably, and soon tailed off in handicap in June: best form at around 7f: probably acts on any going: sometimes blinkered: won 3-runner novice hurdle in May. *R. G. Frost.*

PLAIN FACT 5 b.g. Known Fact (USA) 135–Plain Tree 71 (Wolver Hollow 126) 96 d [1989 5s 6f⁴ 5m⁴ 5f* 6f² 6f² 6m 6m 6m⁵ 5s³ 1990 6v 6m 6m² 6d 7m³ 6g² 5m² 6s⁵ 6s] compact, workmanlike gelding: useful handicapper at his best: below form after finishing second at Lingfield in May: needs a stiff 5f and probably stays 7f: acts on any going: apparently suffers from brittle feet. *Sir Mark Prescott.*

PLAN OF ACTION (IRE) 2 b.c. (May 9) Krayyan 117–Lady Anna Livia 92 (Ahonoora 122) [1990 6m² 7f* 7f* 7g² 7g³] IR 6,000F, 7,000Y: leggy, lengthy colt: good walker: second foal: dam won in Holland: fairly useful colt, successful in maiden at Yarmouth in July and minor event at Newmarket in August: ran well after behind Sedair in £14,900 event at York and Radwell in Group 3 event at Sandown: will stay 1m: sold 72,000 gns Newmarket Autumn Sales. *G. Lewis.*

PLATINUM DISC 3 b.g. Song 132–Pennies To Pounds 80 (Ile de Bourbon 76 (USA) 133) [1989 5d 5g 1990 7f* 6g² 5m 6g⁵ 7m 7g² 7g³] strong, good-bodied gelding: modest performer: made all in maiden at Leicester in March: ran well in handicaps at Kempton (leading until post) and York last 2 starts: effective over 6f and 7f: acts on firm going: sold 12,500 gns Newmarket Autumn Sales. *W. Hastings-Bass.*

PLATINUM ROYALE 3 b.c. Dominion 123–Zerbinetta 96 (Henry The Seventh 76 125) [1989 NR 1990 10.1m⁴ 12m³ 12.2m*] strong, good-topped colt: half-brother to 4-y-o Amadora (by Beldale Flutter) and several winners, including very useful Italian filly Stufida (by Bustino) and sprinter General Wade (by Bold Lad): dam sprinter: modest form: 4/1 on, ridden along 3f out and led close home to win 6-runner maiden at Catterick in August: should stay 1¾m: sold 10,000 gns Newmarket Autumn Sales. *A. C. Stewart.*

PLATONIQUE 3 b.f. Dunbeath (USA) 127–Plato's Retreat 73 (Brigadier Gerard 83 144) [1989 6m* 6m⁶ 6d* 8g* 7g⁴ 8m⁴ 1990 8f⁴ 12f⁵ 10.2m⁴ 10.2g⁴ 8m 12v 10d 7d⁴ a8g⁵] leggy, workmanlike filly: fair performer: mostly ran creditably in varied company as 3-y-o, although disappointing favourite in apprentice handicap on seventh outing: stays 1¼m: acts on good to firm ground and dead: retained 22,000 gns Newmarket Autumn Sales. *Mrs J. R. Ramsden.*

PLATOON 3 gr.c. Petong 126–Shelton Girl 64 (Mummy's Pet 125) [1989 6m 7g⁵ 66 6f² 6v⁶ 1990 7f 6f 7d* 7g a7g] workmanlike colt: easy mover: modest performer: not seen out until September as 3-y-o, easily best effort when making all in maiden at Catterick in October: stays 6f: acts on any going. *T. D. Barron.*

PLAUSIBLE 5 b.h. Neltino 97–False Evidence 53 (Counsel 118) [1989 12d 58 d 12.3m² 11.7g⁴ 14m 12m² 12m 12g⁶ 12g* a12g 1990 21.6m³ 16g⁴ 16.2m⁶ 14g⁶ 16g 16m] leggy horse: moderate mover: plating class on his day: doesn't stay extreme distances: yet to race on firm going, acts on any other: sometimes blinkered or visored: has looked reluctant, and is suited by exaggerated waiting tactics: not one to trust implicitly. *K. O. Cunningham-Brown.*

PLAX 3 ch.c. The Noble Player (USA) 126–Seapoint (Major Point) [1989 6m⁶ 7f⁶ — 6d 1990 7m 7m 9m⁶ 10m] big, workmanlike colt: good walker: has run moderately since second start at 2 yrs, in handicaps (co-favourite final start) in 1990: should stay 1m: bandaged behind penultimate outing. *R. Akehurst.*

PLAYFUL POET 3 ch.g. The Noble Player (USA) 126–Phamond 61 (Pharly 84 (FR) 130) [1989 5s 5d* 5s² 5d 1990 6m 5d 5g² 5m 6s² 5s*] deep-girthed, strong-quartered gelding: moderate mover: fair handicapper: favourite, made virtually all to win 22-runner contest at Doncaster in November: stays 6f: goes well with plenty of give in the ground: trained until after reappearance by K. Brassey. *M. H. Easterby.*

PLAYING TALENT (IRE) 2 ch.g. (Mar 3) The Noble Player (USA) 126– 54 Tallantire (USA) (Icecapade (USA)) [1990 5m² 5g 6g⁴] 6,200Y: strong, good-bodied gelding: carries condition: has scope: second foal: dam ran once: best effort second in maiden auction at Doncaster in May: fourth in seller there: will stay 7f. *Mrs J. R. Ramsden.*

PLAYING WITH FIRE 4 ch.f. Mr Fluorocarbon 126–Cinderwench 95 — (Crooner 119) [1989 8d 7m 7f 1990 a10g] smallish, workmanlike filly: no worthwhile form: well backed last 2 outings: bred to stay 1m: sold 1,100 gns Ascot September Sales. *M. Bell.*

PLAYSAYYAF (IRE) 2 b.c. (Mar 1) Sayyaf 121–Playtime (Primera 131) [1990 — 5m 7g] IR 4,400F, 3,000Y: angular, sparely-made colt: half-brother to several winners here and abroad: dam poor half-sister to good 1½m horse Auroy: always behind in maidens at Windsor (slowly away) and Salisbury. *B. Gubby.*

PLAY THE ACE 2 b.c. (Mar 26) Mansingh (USA) 120–Boa (Mandrake Major 64 122) [1990 5g 5f* 5d* 6f⁶ 5g²] 4,800Y: big, lengthy, rather angular colt: third foal: brother to 3-y-o Indian Snake, 5f winner at 2 yrs, and winning sprinter Snake Song: dam lightly-raced half-sister to useful stayers Frog and Ophite: progressive colt, successful in maiden auction at Carlisle in May and seller (by 5 lengths, no bid) at Beverley in June: good second in claimer at Beverley: stays 6f. *J. Berry.*

PLAY THE BLUES 3 gr.f. Cure The Blues (USA)–Casual Pleasure (USA) 59 (What A Pleasure (USA)) [1989 6g 5d 1990 a8g² 8m 6m 8g] leggy, sparely-made fllly. has a round action: quite modest form when second in maiden at Southwell: well beaten in claimers after, racing very freely penultimate start: may well prove best at up to 1m: sold to join J. Joseph 4,000 gns Newmarket July Sales. *B. Hanbury.*

PLAY THE GAME 3 br.f. Mummy's Game 120–Christine 102 (Crocket 130) 64 ? [1989 5f² 5f³ 5g³ 6g² 5f* 6m⁶ 6f 1990 6m 5g 6f⁴ 5m 5.8d a6g] small filly: quite modest performer: faced stiff tasks in handicaps first 3 outings, best effort on fourth: probably stays 6f: acts on firm going: unruly stalls, slowly away and looked temperamentally unsatisfactory penultimate outing at 2 yrs: twice blinkered: has run well for 7-lb claimer. *J. Berry.*

PLAYTHING 3 b.f. High Top 131–Round Dance 73 (Auction Ring (USA) 123) 69 [1989 7g⁵ 1990 8f*] second of 10 in maiden at Kempton in May, staying on after slow start: awarded race much later. *A. C. Stewart.*

PLAYUP 2 ch.f. (Apr 11) High Line 125–Putupon 89 (Mummy's Pet 125) [1990 6d 56 7m 6d⁶] leggy filly: good walker: second foal: half-sister to French 3-y-o Group 3 6f winner Pole Position (by Sharpo): dam 2-y-o 5f winner, is sister to high-class 1983 2-y-o sprinter Precocious and half-sister to middle-distance stayer Jupiter Island: bandaged behind, travelled strongly 5f when under 9 lengths seventh of 16 to Shamshir at Newmarket, second and best effort in maidens. *Mrs L. Piggott.*

PLEASANT COMPANY 3 b.f. Alzao (USA) 117–Keeping Company (King's Company 124) [1989 NR 1990 7g⁴ 8.2g⁶ 8m 8g 7g a12g 8f a6g] 3,000 2-y-o: small filly: fifth foal: half-sister to a winner in Austria: dam Irish middle-distance winner from family of L'Attrayante: poor plater: showed ability first 2 starts but little after: blinkered twice, visored once: sold out of M. Johnston's stable 1,750 gns Newmarket July Sales after fifth start: trained next 2 by Mrs A. Knight. *M. B. James.* —

PLEASANT EXHIBIT 3 ch.c. Exhibitioner 111–Miss Fandango 56 (Gay Fandango (USA) 132) [1989 NR 1990 5g³ 5.3f* 6s⁴ a6g⁵] IR 9,000F, IR 16,000Y: good-quartered colt: third foal: dam, raced 7f, is half-sister to smart performer at up to 7f Royal Boy and good 1977 2-y-o Aythorpe: favourite, won maiden at Brighton in October: creditable fourth in handicap, better subsequent effort at Lingfield: stays 6f: trained until after third start by J. Hudson. *J. D. Bethell.* 71

PLEASANT TIMES 2 ch.c. (Mar 12) Absalom 128–Lady Warninglid (Ela-Mana-Mou 132) [1990 7m 7f] 7,600F, 16,500Y: sparely-made colt: poor mover: first foal: dam, unraced, from family of Rock City and Kerrera: well beaten in slowly-run minor event at York and maiden at Ayr in July. *M. Brittain.* —

PLEASE BELIEVE ME 3 b.f. Try My Best (USA) 130–Believer 112 (Blakeney 126) [1989 5f* 5f* 5f² 6g⁶ 6m⁴ 1990 7v² 6m 6m 6m 5g⁴ 5.6g⁶ 8m⁶] well-grown filly: good walker: fairly useful performer: ran in valuable handicaps at York, Doncaster (Portland Handicap, staying on) and Ascot (visored, not disgraced after being bumped 2f out) last 3 outings: worth another try at 7f or 1m: acts on firm going: tends to get on toes. *M. H. Easterby.* 90

PLEASE PLEASE ME (IRE) 2 b.f. (Apr 21) Tender King 123–Tacama 64 (Daring Display (USA) 129) [1990 8m 6m] IR 7,800F, IR 11,500Y: leggy, sparely-made filly: half-sister to fair 1988 2-y-o 6f winner Eeezepeeze (by Alzao) and winners in Hong Kong and Italy: dam, plater, half-sister to useful stayer Drishaune: edgy, slowly away and always behind in sellers (wandered badly on second occasion) at Newmarket in October: sold 1,100 gns Newmarket Autumn Sales. *A. N. Lee.* —

PLEASURE AHEAD 3 b.c. Taufan (USA) 119–Nan's Mill (Milford 119) [1989 5s 5d⁵ 5.3m² 5m² 6m⁶ 5m³ 6f 6g 1990 8g 8f 8m 8m³ 7f⁴ 8.3m⁴ 7h² 7g 8.3g 8f⁵ 6f³ 7m 7f⁶] leggy, close-coupled colt: poor mover: plating-class maiden: stays 1m: acts on hard ground: sweating and edgy (below form) ninth start. *M. R. Channon.* 52

PLEASURE FLIGHT 3 b.f. Jalmood (USA) 126–Third Movement 75 (Music Boy 124) [1989 5m³ 1990 8g a8g⁶ a11g*] lengthy, rather angular filly: quite modest performer: won handicap at Southwell in June, outpaced 5f out then staying on well to lead inside last: will stay further. *W. J. Haggas.* 71

PLECTRUM 2 b.f. (Mar 15) Adonijah 126–Cymbal 80 (Ribero 126) [1990 7m⁶] half-sister to 1¼m winner Beau Mirage (by Homing) and a winner abroad by Moulton: dam middle-distance winner, is half-sister to smart performers Band and Zimbalon: under 9 lengths sixth of 10, unable to quicken last 2f and not knocked about, in maiden at Sandown in August: can improve. *B. W. Hills.* 58 p

PLIE 3 ch.f. Superlative 118–La Pirouette (USA) 73 (Kennedy Road (CAN)) [1989 5f² 5.8f* 6g⁴ 5m⁶ 6m 1990 5m 5f 7f⁶ 8h⁶ 7m⁵ 7g⁶ 8f⁵ 7m 8g³] good-quartered filly: plating-class performer: stays 1m: acts on firm ground. *D. W. P. Arbuthnot.* 57

PLYNLIMON 2 b.c. (Apr 11) Starch Reduced 112–Joie de Galles 72 (Welsh Pageant 132) [1990 5f² 6g⁶ 5f⁶ 5g⁶ 6g] 6,000Y: compact colt: fifth foal: half-brother to 1½m winner Welshman (by Final Straw), and 1987 2-y-o 7f winner Rave Review (by Jalmood): dam 1½m winner: poor maiden: blinkered and on toes, ran very freely in seller final start: hung left from halfway second outing: should stay 6f. *B. Palling.* 54 d

POACHERS THEME 2 b.f. (Feb 12) Song 132–Tickled Trout 70 (Red Alert 127) [1990 5m 5m² 5g² 6s 6m 6m] 7,200F: unfurnished filly: first foal: dam, plater, won at 5f and 6f at 2 yrs: plating-class maiden: suited by 5f: blinkered final start, sweating and on toes time before. *J. Berry.* 53 ?

PODRIDA 4 gr.f. Persepolis (FR) 127–Pot Pourri 97 (Busted 134) [1989 12g⁵ 14m⁵ 13.8f* 14.8m* 14g³ 1990 14.8f³ 14g²20m a18g 13.8d] good-bodied filly: carries condition: moderate mover: fair handicapper at best: ran poorly last 2 outings, off course 2 months before each of them: should prove best around 2m: acts on firm going: has won when sweating badly: lacks turn of foot: sold to join B. Stevens' stable 9,000 gns Newmarket Autumn Sales: winning selling hurdler in December. *W. Jarvis.* 75

POD'S DAUGHTER (IRE) 2 b.f. (Mar 5) Tender King 123–Make Your Bid 79 **43**
(Auction Ring (USA) 123) [1990 5f* 5m⁴ 5g⁶ 5d³ 6g 5f² 6f] IR 4,600F, IR 3,400Y:
neat filly: turns off-fore in: second foal: half-sister to a winner abroad: dam 1m and 9f
winner: quite modest plater: won 4-runner event (no bid) at Doncaster in March:
better form at 5f: acts on firm ground. *C. Tinkler.*

POETS COVE 2 b.c. (Apr 26) Bay Express 132–Miss Milton (Young Christopher **100**
119) [1990 5m² 5m 5f* 5f* 5f* 5g³ 5g⁶ 5m] strong, compact non-thoroughbred colt:
progressed physically: good walker: has active action: first reported foal: dam lightly
raced on flat: fairly useful colt, successful in maiden at Nottingham in May, minor
event at Thirsk in July and 4-runner Molecomb Stakes (awarded race on
disqualification of ½-length winner Jimmy Barnie) at Goodwood in August: very
good third to Mujadil in listed race at York, easily best subsequent effort: speedy. *W.
Carter.*

POET'S DREAM (IRE) 2 b. or br.c. (Apr 25) Storm Bird (CAN) 134–Lisadell **95**
(USA) 122 (Forli (ARG)) [1990 8.3g² 7m⁵] eighth foal: brother to Irish 3-y-o Karri
Valley, closely related to very useful Irish 6f performer Yeats (by Nijinsky) and
fairly useful Irish 7f and 1m winner Lisaleen (by Northern Dancer) and half-brother
to another winner in Ireland at 7f by Secretariat: dam, Coronation Stakes winner, is
sister to top-class Thatch and half-sister to King Pellinore and Marinsky: odds on,
short-head second of 14 in maiden at the Curragh: showed plenty of improvement
when over 4 lengths fifth of 8, unable to quicken from over 2f out, to Heart of
Darkness in GPA National Stakes there: sure to win a maiden at 7f or 1m. *M. V.
O'Brien, Ireland.*

POINTE OF LAW (FR) 3 b.f. Law Society (USA) 130–Ninoushka (USA) **55**
(Nijinsky (CAN) 138) [1989 6m⁵ 6m³ 8f³ 9g 1990 a10g³ 12f² 12m² 14.8f⁴ 12g³]
sparely-made, plain filly: poor walker and mover: plating-class maiden, not seen out
after May: will be suited by 2m: acts on firm going: retained by trainer 7,500 gns
Ascot February Sales: consistent. *P. A. Kelleway.*

POINT TAKEN (USA) 3 b.c. Sharpen Up 127–Furry Friend (USA) (Bold **—**
Bidder) [1989 7m 6g 6g² 1990 7m 7f 8m 7g] well-made, attractive colt: modest form
when second in maiden at Redcar: well below form in early-season handicaps:
unlikely to stay beyond 1m. *L. M. Cumani.*

POIRE DU NORD 2 b.c. (Feb 22) Legend of France (USA) 124–Polly's Pear **—**
(USA) (Sassafras (FR) 135) [1990 7m⁴ 7f 7s] 5,500F, 10,000Y: stocky, angular colt:
first foal: dam never ran: soundly beaten in minor event (4 ran) and maidens. *R.
Hollinshead.*

POKEREE 7 gr.g. Uncle Pokey 116–Border Squaw 84 (Warpath 113) [1989 2 1.6d **35**
12m³ 15s⁴ 13s 16g⁶ 1990 9s² 13g* 13g⁴ 12g⁶ 12m⁴ 15d 12s 18d] big, lengthy gelding:
moderate mover: poor handicapper: won for only time on flat at Hamilton in June:
ran moderately last 2 outings: has appeared to stay 15f: acts on good to firm and soft
going: visored 3 times in 1989: mostly apprentice ridden: has looked none too keen:
sold out of D. Moffatt's stable 17,000 gns Ascot October Sales after seventh outing.
R. Dickin.

*Molecomb Stakes, Goodwood—Poets Cove, who enjoys a trouble-free run up the rails,
is awarded the race on the disqualification of Jimmy Barnie (left);
in between are It's All Academic (noseband) and Seductress*

POKE THE FIRE 3 ch.c. Never So Bold 135–Home Fire 99 (Firestreak 125) **79**
[1989 6f3 6f6 5f* 6f4 6d 6g4 5m 1990 5g* 6g 5m5 6m 6g2] smallish, robust colt: good
walker: has a quick action: fair on his day: won at Cagnes-sur-Mer in March: creditable second in apprentice claimer at Nottingham in June, hanging right: should stay
7f: acts on firm ground: tends to sweat: ran poorly in blinkers. *C. R. Nelson.*

POKEY'S PRIDE 7 b.g. Uncle Pokey 116–Strawberry Ice (Arctic Storm 134) **70**
[1989 12d2 18.4m 14m5 12h* 12f3 12m3 12f* 12m6 14f 14m3 13s3 12m6 14g* 12g4 12d
1990 11.7g 12m2 12m2 12.8g3 16m 12m2 14f3] leggy, quite attractive gelding:
moderate mover: modest handicapper: effective at 1½m and stays 2m: acts on any
going: ideally suited by strong handling: held up: consistent. *M. H. Tompkins.*

POLAR BIRD 3 b.f. Thatching 131–Arctic Winter (CAN) (Briartic (CAN)) [1989 **111**
5m* 5f* 5g* 6g* 7.3v 1990 6g6 6g 6m* 7m6 6g2 6m4] strong, attractive filly: has a
quick action: very useful performer: won £7,500 handicap at Newmarket in July:
looked really well last 2 starts, excellent second in £12,500 handicap at York then
beaten about 11 lengths behind 10-length winner Ron's Victory in Diadem Stakes at
Ascot: suited by 6f: goes very well on a sound surface, and probably unsuited by
heavy ground. *B. W. Hills.*

POLAR VISION 4 b.g. Lyphard's Special (USA) 122–Arctic Drama (Northern **58**
Baby (CAN) 127) [1989 9g 10f 11m3 10m3 12g 12d2 10m4 12m 1990 10.8m6 10g6 12m
11m 14m6 a12g 14g3 12g3 14d] leggy, useful-looking gelding: poor mover: quite
modest maiden: appeared to run very well second outing, but well below that form
afterwards: probably stays 1¾m: possibly best with give in the ground nowadays:
blinkered and visored twice: changed hands 7,000 gns Ascot May Sales: winning
novice hurdler in November. *C. C. Elsey.*

POLEMIC (USA) 2 ch.f. (Apr 22) Roberto (USA) 131–Solartic (CAN) (Briartic **104**
(USA)) [1990 6.5g* 6d4 5g2 8g] seventh foal: sister to smart 6f (at 2 yrs) to 1½m
winner Tralos and half-sister to 2 winners, including fairly useful 1984 2-y-o 5f
winner Solo Native (by Exclusive Native), later successful at up to 1¼m in USA:
dam won at up to 1m and second in 9f Canadian Oaks: successful in newcomers race
at Deauville: in frame in Prix Morny Agence Francaise (around 3 lengths fourth to

Mr R. E. Sangster's "Polar Bird"

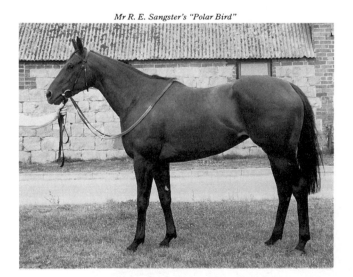

Hector Protector) at Deauville again and Prix d'Arenberg (2 lengths second to Divine Danse) at Longchamp: under 6 lengths last of 9 to Shadayid in Prix Marcel Boussac at Longchamp: will stay 1¼m. *A. Fabre, France.*

POLEMOS   6 ch.h. Formidable (USA) 125–Polemia (USA) (Roi Dagobert 128)   — [1989 12s 14f⁶ 12m⁶ 10m² 1990 14f⁶] angular horse: good mover: fair performer: stays 1½m: acts on any going: blinkered once: bandaged second outing at 5 yrs and only one in 1990: usually acts as pacemaker. *H. Thomson Jones.*

POLE POSITION   3 b.c. Sharpo 132–Putupon 89 (Mummy's Pet 125) [1989 5g*   **116** 7.5g³ 6.5s* 1990 5g⁵ 6.5g³ 6d* 8g⁵ 6d 7g⁵] smart French colt: dam sister to Precocious and half-sister to Jupiter Island: won 11-runner Prix de Meautry at Deauville by length from Pharaoh's Delight: ran creditably in Prix Maurice de Gheest at Deauville and Prix du Moulin de Longchamp (about 5 lengths fifth of 6 to Distant Relative) starts either side: seems effective at 6f and 1m: acts on soft going, yet to race on top-of-the-ground: to join Mrs J. Cecil. *A. Fabre, France.*

POLICIANE (FR)   2 ch.f. (Apr 8) Policeman (FR) 124–Pharlane (FR) (Pharly   **53** (FR) 130) [1990 5m⁶ 6g⁶] workmanlike filly: second reported foal: half-sister to French 2-y-o 1m winner King Ken (by Kenmare): dam French 9f winner: around 10 lengths sixth of 24 in maiden at Kempton in September: green and slowly away 5 months earlier: should be much better suited by further. *P. Mitchell.*

POLISH HONOUR (USA)   2 b.f. (Apr 22) Danzig Connection (USA)–Royal   **61** p Honoree (USA) (Round Table) [1990 7m] sturdy filly: closely related to useful 1988 Irish 2-y-o 5f and 6f winner Honoria (by Danzig) and half-sister to several winners, including Irish St Leger runner-up Father Rooney (by Val de L'Orne) and smart French 1982 2-y-o 1m winner Allverton (by Alleged): dam, winner 3 times at up to 6f, is sister to top 1972 French 2-y-o Targowice and half-sister to dam of Manila and Stately Don: burly and green, shaped better than mid-division position suggests in 18-runner maiden at Leicester in October, chased along under hand riding until fading final furlong: sure to improve. *Mrs L. Piggott.*

POLISH KING (USA)   2 gr.c. (Mar 16) Danzig (USA)–Sintra (USA)   **85** P (Drone) [1990 8m*]

The Soham House Stakes, a minor event for two-year-olds over a mile at Newmarket in November, fell to Dancing Brave, Kayhasi and Belmez in the second half of the 'eighties and was won we should guess by another budding star, more probably at around a mile than over middle distances, in Polish King in 1990. From a leading stable and by one of the world's top stallions, Polish King already had plenty going for him before his tremendously impressive appearance at Newmarket, where, even though he won by only two lengths, he was one of the easiest winners there we've seen for a long time. A weak 13/2-shot in the face of support for Hern's newcomer Alrayed, Polish King was soon travelling supremely well, went to the front three furlongs out and, with his rider doing little more than adjusting his reins and taking several looks behind, won with an incalculable amount in hand. The bare form of the race isn't worth a great deal: second-placed Caithness Cloud had looked very much a stayer when ninth of fifteen in a similar event at Nottingham on his previous outing, and Bosambo, seven and a half lengths back in fourth, had finished among the stragglers in the maiden won by Sharifabad over the course and distance the previous month. But there's much more to enthuse about in the considerable superiority Polish King had over his rivals from halfway, if not in the unsatisfactory manner in which his rider Swinburn failed to use the opportunity to educate him more thoroughly, and though it's unwise to get too excited about him—post-race quotes of

Soham House Stakes, Newmarket—exciting prospect Polish King has plenty in hand;
he is pursued by Caithness Cloud, Bosambo (rails) and eventual third Naiysari

between 14/1 and 25/1 for the Two Thousand Guineas and Derby seem on the mean side, particularly for the Derby—it was difficult not to be impressed by his performance, and he seems sure to graduate successfully in much stronger company.

Polish King (USA)
(gr.c. Mar 16, 1988)

	Danzig (USA) (b 1977)	Northern Dancer (b 1961)	Nearctic
			Natalma
		Pas de Nom (b or br 1968)	Admiral's Voyage
			Petitioner
	Sintra (USA) (ro 1981)	Drone (gr 1966)	Sir Gaylord
			Cap And Bells
		Misty Plum (b 1969)	Misty Day
			Plumage

Polish King, a 450,000-dollar purchase at Keeneland's July Selected Sale, is by Danzig, sire of a whole array of top-class performers from five furlongs (Dayjur) to a mile and a half (Danzig Connection) out of the seven- and eight-and-a-half-furlong graded stakes winner Sintra. Sintra, whose second foal Polish King is, is the only noteworthy winner from the minor stakes winner (at up to seven furlongs) Misty Plum; the third dam Plumage never ran. Curiously, Polish King is bred on vaguely similar lines to Dancing Brave, being by a son of Northern Dancer out of a mare by Drone, but whether he'll stay so far as a mile and a half is open to question: both sides of his pedigree, and his performance at Newmarket to a lesser extent, spell speed rather than stamina. Whatever his ideal distance, Polish King is very much one to keep on the right side. *M. R. Stoute.*

POLISH PATRIOT (USA) 2 b.c. (Mar 24) Danzig (USA)–Maria Waleska 95 (Filiberto (USA) 123) [1990 6m² 6f* 5f² 5f² 6f* 6m⁵] $375,000Y: strong, good-quartered colt: brother to modest 1989 3-y-o Polish Princess and half-brother to 2 winners: dam won Italian Oaks and Gran Premio d'Italia: fairly useful performer: made all in maiden at Goodwood in August and all-aged minor event (by wide margin) at Folkestone in September: good fifth of 9, outpaced from 2f out, to Lycius in Newgate Stud Middle Park Stakes (very free to post) at Newmarket: held up when below best fourth outing: better suited by 6f than 5f, and is bred to stay at least 7f: rather headstrong, and has worn a net muzzle. *G. Harwood.*

POLISTATIC 3 br.f. Free State 125–Polyandrist 92 (Polic 126) [1989 6m 6f⁴ 53 1990 8f⁶ 9m⁵ 9g⁶ 11.7m 7m 10.1g 8m⁶] smallish filly: plating-class maiden: stays 9f: acts on firm going. *C. A. Horgan.*

POLL TAX PARTY 2 b.f. (Mar 15) Mansingh (USA) 120–Anita's Choice 45 52 (Shantung 132) [1990 6g a6g² a6g⁵ 6g⁴ 5f⁶ 5g³ 5m] 1,200Y: workmanlike filly: moderate mover: sister to a winner in Hong Kong and half-sister to a winner in Switzerland: dam untrustworthy 1½m winner also won over hurdles: fair plater: very good third in nursery at Wolverhampton: spread plate before running poorly final start: seems best at 5f: sold 920 gns Doncaster October Sales. *J. Berry.*

POLLY MULDOWNEY 3 ch.f. Precocious 126–Follow The Stars 86 (Sparkler 58 130) [1989 6g 1990 7m⁶ 7g 7f⁶ 8g⁶ 8g³ 8m a7g] workmanlike filly: moderate mover: plating-class maiden: good staying-on third in handicap at Wolverhampton in October: stays 1m: acts on firm ground: sold out of D. Elsworth's stable 5,600 gns Newmarket Autumn Sales after sixth start. *R. W. Stubbs.*

POLLY'S KAROS (FR) 2 b.f. (Apr 7) Kenmare (FR) 125–Polly's Harde (FR) ? (Lyphard (USA) 132) [1990 8s*] half-sister to several winners in France, including very useful 1983 staying 2-y-o Polly's Ark (by Arctic Tern): dam French 1m winner out of sister to 2000 Guineas winner Right Tack: won 17-runner newcomers race at Saint-Cloud in November by a short neck from Maxigroom: will stay 1¼m. *F. Boutin, France.*

POLONEZ PRIMA 3 ch.c. Thatching 131–Taiga 69 (Northfields (USA)) [1989 81 6g 1990 7f⁴ 8m³ 8m³ 8m³ 9m* 9g² 10d² 10.2s a10g⁶] good-bodied colt: fair performer: won auction event at Redcar in September: second in quite valuable handicaps at York and Newmarket (apprentices): suited by 1¼m: seems unsuited by very soft ground. *G. A. Huffer.*

POLYKRATIS 8 b.h. He Loves Me 120–Blue Persian 112 (Majority Blue 126) 68 § [1989 6v 5s 6f 6f³ 6m³ 6m⁵ 6f 6m* 6m³ 6h⁴ 6g 6g a6g⁶ 1990 8g 6f 6m 6g 7.6m 7f⁵ 6m 6m] rather leggy horse: good mover with a slightly round action: smart sprinter at his best in 1986: has won only Pontefract handicap since, and proved disappointing: acts on any going: usually finds little and tends to get behind: best left alone. *M. E. D. Francis.*

696

Royal Hunt Cup, Ascot—Pontenuovo (rails) rallies to get the verdict from Curtain Call;
the four just behind are, right to left, Pride of Araby (third), Gilderdale (fourth),
Superoo (sixth) and Heroes Sash (fifth)

POLYPLATE 2 b.f. (Mar 31) Song 132–Countless Countess 65 (Morston (FR) **49**
125) [1990 6g 7f 7m⁶ 8.2g 8m] 5,000Y: leggy, quite attractive filly: has scope: first
foal: dam 2m winner: plating-class maiden: best effort third start: set plenty to do in
nurseries after: hung right second outing. *M. J. Ryan.*

POLYROLL 4 b.c. Kampala 120–Hail To Feathers (USA) (Hail To All) [1989 8d* **—**
8s³ 7s² 8.5m³ 9m 7.3m 7g⁵ 8m 1990 9g 10g] big, lengthy colt: moderate mover:
fairly useful winner in spring as 3-y-o: generally well below his best subsequently,
and not seen out after April: best up to 8.5f: acts on good to firm and soft going:
ridden up with pace: apprentice ridden as 3-y-o, except for fourth start. *Miss B.
Sanders.*

POMERANIA (USA) 3 b.f. Danzig (USA)–Smuggly (USA) 121 (Caro 133) [1989 **56**
6g 1990 7g³ 7m³] strong, sturdy filly: has a round action: plating-class form in
maidens at Epsom and Goodwood (giving impression would prove suited by easy
surface) in the spring: will be better suited by 1m. *J. Gosden.*

POMME D'AMOUR 3 gr.f. Niniski (USA) 125–Amourette (Crowned Prince **44** §
(USA) 128) [1989 7f⁴ 7f⁴ 7m 6g 1990 8f 10f 10f³ 12h⁴ 10.8m] sparely-made, lengthy
filly: poor maiden: suited by 1¼m: acts on firm going: visored 3 times: has given
trouble in preliminaries, and been ridden by lad in paddock: sold 2,000 gns
Newmarket Autumn Sales: temperamentally unsatisfactory. *N. A. Graham.*

POMPUSE LORD 4 ch.g. Posse (USA) 130–Laxay 69 (Laxton 105) [1989 7m **—**
a8g 1990 a8g] compact gelding: lightly raced and little sign of ability. *M. R. Leach.*

PONT AVEN 3 b.f. Try My Best (USA) 130–Basilea (FR) (Frere Basile (FR) 129) **109**
[1989 6d³ 5d* 5g³ 5g² 1990 7m³ 6.5s* 8g² 6g 6d³ 6d⁵ 7g⁶] very useful performer:
won listed race at Evry and second in Dubai Poule d'Essai des Pouliches at Longchamp in the spring: ran poorly in Cork And Orrery Stakes (well-backed favourite,
wore tongue strap and looked tremendously well) at Royal Ascot fourth start, not
discredited in Prix de la Foret at Longchamp on final one: may prove best short of
1m: acts on soft going: keen sort. *R. Collet, France.*

PONTENUOVO 5 b.g. Kafu 120–Black Gnat (Typhoon 125) [1989 a8g a7g 1990 **99**
9f* 8m 8f* 8m 8m* 8m² 7m* 9m] rangy gelding: has a rather round action: useful

Stud Lite L.A. Lager Stakes (Handicap), Ascot—
another big handicap goes Pontenuovo's way;
Nayland (noseband) and Nicholas can't get to grips

performer: had a tremendous season, winning claimer at Ripon in April and handicaps at Ascot in June, July and September: beat Curtain Call a neck in £33,200 Royal Hunt Cup and Nayland 2½ lengths in £71,900 Stud Lite L A Lager Stakes on third and seventh outings: on toes, led apparently unfavoured far-side group 1m in Cambridgeshire final one: suited by 7f or 1m: acts very well on top-of-the-ground, yet to race on a soft surface: bandaged second start: hung left and swished tail on sixth: goes very well with forcing tactics: genuine. *D. R. C. Elsworth.*

PONTYNYSWEN 2 b.g. (Apr 25) Ballacashtal (CAN)–Tropingay (Cawston's — Clown 113) [1990 6g 7m5 a6g a7g] neat gelding: second foal: brother to poor maiden Rose's Pride: dam well beaten: little worthwhile form in sellers and a maiden: will be suited by 1m. *D. Burchell.*

POOH WEE 2 b.f. (Apr 28) Music Boy 124–Nicoletta 81 (Busted 134) [1990 6m5 **71** 6d* 7s] 20,000Y: strong, compact filly: has scope: poor mover: fifth foal: half-sister to fairly useful 7f (at 2 yrs) to 1½m winner Nickle Plated (by Auction Ring), fair 1m to 1¾m performer Sir Percy (by Blakeney) and disappointing Nicoridge (by Riva Ridge): dam 9f winner, is half-sister to Irish 1000 Guineas winner Favoletta and dam of Teenoso: won 5-runner maiden at Chester in October in good style by 5 lengths from Run Milady, hanging right when taken to front then staying on strongly: good tenth of 21 when facing stiff task in Doncaster nursery: stays 7f: bandaged behind. *M. J. Camacho.*

POPPY CHARM 3 b.f. Star Appeal 133–Pop Music (FR) (Val de Loir 133) [1989 **54** 6g* 7m2 7m6 8s2 8m 8g 1990 9f3 12h3 10g3 8f 8m 9m] sparely-made filly: fair plater: ran moderately last 3 starts, badly hampered first of them: should stay 1½m: acts on any going. *M. H. Tompkins.*

POPSI'S LEGACY 3 ch.f. Little Wolf 127–Popsi's Poppet 89 (Hill Clown (USA)) — [1989 NR 1990 10g] third reported living foal: dam 2m winner: 50/1, backward and green, slowly away when tailed-off last in maiden at Epsom in June. *M. J. Haynes.*

PORICK 2 b.c. (Mar 9) Marching On 101–Natina-May 59 (Mandrake Major 122) — [1990 5m 6m 7f] leggy, close-coupled colt: first reported foal: dam 2-y-o 6f and 7f winner later stayed 1¼m: seems of little account: blinkered final start. *D. Yeoman.*

PORTER RHODES (USA) 4 b.c. Hawaii–Stella Matutina (FR) 103 (Bolkonski **113** + 134) [1989 8g2 8m* 10m* 1990 9m6 10.5d] strong, good-bodied colt: has a quick action: has a lot of ability, but difficult to train: odds-on winner of Newmarket maiden and Group 2 Windfields Farm EBF Gallinule Stakes at the Curragh (hanging left) in May, 1989: shaped well when under 4 lengths sixth of 10, not much room over 1f out, to Terimon in Earl of Sefton EBF Stakes at Newmarket in April: reportedly lame in Prix Ganay later in month: stays 1¼m: acts on good to firm going. *H. R. A. Cecil.*

PORT ISAAC (USA) 2 br.f. (Jan 22) Seattle Song (USA) 130–Key Link (USA) **64** p (Bold Ruler) [1990 6m 7m4] $35,000Y: lengthy filly: half-sister to several minor winners: dam twice-raced sister to Key To The Kingdom and half-sister to Fort Marcy and Key To The Mint: uneasy favourite, around 4 lengths fourth of 10 in maiden at Redcar in September: will be better suited by 1m. *M. R. Stoute.*

PORTLY STAN 2 b.c. (Feb 4) Stanford 121§–Portland Dancer 63 (Wolverlife **66** 115) [1990 5g 5f2 6g* 5m a6g4] 6,200Y, 11,500 2-y-o: leggy, useful-looking colt: first foal: dam poor maiden, probably best at 5f: quite modest performer: won maiden auction at Pontefract in June, making all: respectable fourth in claimer at Southwell: better suited by 6f than 5f and will probably stay 7f: ridden by girl apprentice. *T. D. Barron.*

PORTOFINO 4 ch.g. Coquelin (USA) 121–Decoy Duck 67 (Decoy Boy 129) [1989 **62** 8m 8m 9m 8v 12g 1990 10g 8f5 8f a11g* a12g*] rangy gelding: apprentice ridden, won handicaps comfortably at Southwell in September: needs further than 1m and stays 1½m: on toes when running poorly on heavy going. *P. J. Makin.*

PORT OF SPAIN (USA) 3 b.c. El Gran Senor (USA) 136–Four Runs (USA) — (Reviewer (USA)) [1989 NR 1990 10g 10m 12.5g5 13.6m] leggy, angular colt: poor walker and mover: closely related to a minor winner at up to 9f by Storm Bird and half-brother to a winner by Fluorescent Light, both in USA: dam lightly-raced winner at about 6f: well beaten in maidens and minor events: sold to join R. Curtis 3,200 gns Newmarket Autumn Sales. *J. L. Dunlop.*

PORTO HELI 3 b.g. Precocious 126–Coral Heights 86 (Shirley Heights 130) **73** [1989 7m3 1990 11d 10.4d5 9f2 14g 8g] strong, quite attractive gelding: poor mover: modest maiden on flat: best effort over 9f on firm ground: winning hurdler for M. Pipe. *C. E. Brittain.*

PORT SHARER   3 b.f. Runnett 125–Amorak 85 (Wolver Hollow 126) [1989 NR   **39**
1990 a8g² a10g⁵ a10g² a10g 8m a10g⁴] 4,600F: third foal: half-sister to 4-y-o winning
selling hurdler Tap Dancing (by Sallust): dam won at 1m and stayed 1½m: poor
maiden: no show last 3 starts, including in seller: stays 1¼m: visored third to fifth
starts. *D. W. P. Arbuthnot.*

PORT SODERICK (USA)   3 b.c. Affirmed (USA)–Queen of Cornwall (USA)   **70**
109 (Cornish Prince) [1989 6m 1990 10.5g⁴ 10g 10d³ 8m² 11d⁶] lengthy, attractive
colt: modest form: in frame in minor event and claimers: showed a scratchy action
to post and ran poorly final start: seems effective at 1m and 1¼m: yet to race on
extremes of going: bandaged off-fore last 3 starts: sold 5,200 gns Newmarket
Autumn Sales. *B. W. Hills.*

PORT SUNLIGHT (IRE)   2 ch.c. (Feb 2) Tate Gallery (USA) 117–Nana's Girl   **80**
109 (Tin Whistle 128) [1990 6m³ 6m⁶ 5m⁵ 8g⁴ 8.2s*] strong, workmanlike colt: has
a quick action: half-brother to numerous winners, including good 1977 2-y-o
Aythorpe (by Ridan) and Royal Boy (by Realm), smart at up to 7f: dam, useful at up
to 1m, is sister to very smart Tin King: stayed on well to win maiden at Haydock in
October, showing much improved form: much better suited by 1m than shorter: acts
very well on soft ground. *R. Hannon.*

PORT VAUBAN   2 b.c. (Apr 9) Tumble Wind (USA)–Cruise Port 73 (Homeric   **85**
133) [1990 6m 6f* 7.3m⁵ 7f⁴ 7f² 7g* 8m³ 8g 8d 7m] 12,500F, 30,000Y: lengthy colt:
has scope: modest mover: second foal: half-brother to poor 1½m winner Almetingo
(by Touching Wood): dam placed here at 2 yrs, won over 1m at 4 yrs in France: fair
performer: won maiden at Brighton in June and nursery at Leicester in August:
easily best effort after on next start: stays 1m: best form on a sound surface: sold
19,000 gns Newmarket Autumn Sales. *R. Hannon.*

POSITIVE ACCLAIM   2 b.f. (Feb 2) Vaigly Great 127–Acclimatise 116 (Shirley   **73 p**
Heights 130) [1990 7m 6g³] leggy, unfurnished filly: first live foal: dam 7f (at 2 yrs)
to 1¼m winner stayed 1½m: favourite, under 2 lengths third of 11, keeping on well
when headed, to Chimayo in maiden at Newmarket in October: will stay 1m: likely to
improve further. *R. Hannon.*

POSITIVE ATTITUDE   5 br.m. Red Sunset 120–Wilderness 88 (Martinmas   **73**
128) [1989 7f 7f⁴ 6f 8.3m² 8m* 9f⁴ 8g* 8f⁵ 8.2d* 8s 9g 1990 8m⁵ 8m⁶ 8m³ 9m]
workmanlike mare: fair handicapper at her best as 4-y-o, winner on 3 occasions:
suited by 1m: possibly unsuited by soft going, acted on any other: wore blinkers:
suited by waiting tactics: in foal to Bairn. *M. Bell.*

POSITIVELY GREAT (USA)   4 ch.g. Achieved 125–Sable Linda (USA)   **—**
(Graustark) [1989 6v³ 6h³ 8m 8f³ 9m 9g³ 10m 11g 1990 9s⁶ 9f⁶ 12f 8m] big, lengthy
gelding: quite modest maiden at best: below form last 6 outings: stays 9f: acts on
firm going: tended to hang right and looked difficult ride final start: usually edgy and
taken down early: sold 1,350 gns Doncaster June Sales. *M. P. Naughton.*

POSSEBELLE   3 ch.f. Posse (USA) 130–Belle Origine (USA) (Exclusive Native   **—**
(USA)) [1989 7m 1990 7g⁵ 6f 7m⁶ 6f⁴ 7.6m a8g] leggy, rather angular filly: plating-
class maiden: stays 7f: possibly needs an easy surface: visored (tailed off) final start:
sold 800 gns Ascot December Sales. *M. J. Haynes.*

POSSESSIVE DANCER   2 b.f. (May 14) Shareef Dancer (USA) 135–   **71 p**
Possessive (Posse (USA) 130) [1990 6m*] 20,000Y: second foal: half-sister to 3-y-o
1m winner Possessive Lady (by Dara Monarch): dam unraced half-sister to smart
miler Long Row and daughter of Irish 1000 Guineas winner and good broodmare
Front Row: weak in market, won 6-runner maiden at Newmarket in November by a
neck from No Comebacks, ridden 2f out and leading line: will stay 1m: sure to
improve. *A. A. Scott.*

POSSESSIVE LADY   3 ch.f. Dara Monarch 128–Possessive (Posse (USA) 130)   **62**
[1989 6g 1990 8.2g⁶ 8f* 8g* 10g² 8m⁴ 8g² 8.2m 9m 8.2d] leggy, lightly-made filly:
quite modest performer: favourite, won claimers at Salisbury and Newmarket
(claimed £11,020 out of A. Scott's stable) in May: worth another try at 1¼m: acts on
firm going, possibly not on dead: edgy and sweating fourth start when trained by N.
Tinkler: sold 5,200 gns Newmarket Autumn Sales: inconsistent. *A. A. Scott.*

POSTAGE STAMP   3 ch.g. The Noble Player (USA) 126–Takealetter (Wolver   **76**
Hollow 126) [1989 7g 1990 11d 10.4d⁴ a11g* 10m 8m³ 9m³ 10f² 10.6d a12g⁵ 10m⁶
10d³] rangy, good-topped gelding: good walker: has rather round action: modest
performer: landed odds in maiden at Southwell in May: ran creditably in handicaps
most starts afterwards, in £8,200 apprentice event final start: will be suited by
return to 1½m: acts on firm and dead ground: gelded after final start. *J. W. Hills.*

POTATO KING 5 b.g. Hard Fought 125–Fenland Queen (King's Troop 118) [1989 NR 1990 15d] leggy gelding: poor maiden: suited by 7f: acts on any going: hung right in blinkers: bought 4,000 gns Doncaster June Sales: sold 2,100 gns Ascot November Sales. *J. J. O'Neill.* —

POTERIUM 2 b.c. (Apr 10) Persian Bold 123–Cryptomeria 86 (Crepello 136) [1990 7g⁴] 10,000F, IR 82,000Y: brother to a winner in Japan and half-brother to 1985 2-y-o 6f winner Stedham (by Jaazeiro) and a winner in Italy: dam middle-distance filly: 4¼ lengths fourth of 13 to Eastern Magic in maiden at Salisbury in October: will be suited by further: sure to do better. *J. H. M. Gosden.* **73 p**

POTTER'S DREAM 3 ch.g. Horage 124–Sally St Clair (Sallust 134) [1989 5g⁵ 6m² 6g² 6g 7g 1990 8m⁴ 7d 8g 8m 7m² 7m⁵ 10d³ 10d 9g⁴] leggy, workmanlike gelding: modest maiden: good 33/1-fourth of 13 in £19,600 handicap at Newmarket final start: blinkered, hung left and tailed off in claimer time before: stays 1¼m: acts on good to firm ground and dead: tends to wander: visored fifth start: trained until after then by G. Balding: inconsistent. *R. J. R. Williams.* **77**

POWER BOAT 4 ch.g. Jalmood (USA) 126–Bedeni 100 (Parthia 132) [1989 10s 10.1m 12.2d 15g a14g⁶ 1990 a16g⁴] sturdy gelding: well beaten in varied events. *M. Avison.* —

POWERFUL PIERRE 2 br.g. (Mar 5) Mummy's Game 120–Harmonious Sound (Auction Ring (USA) 123) [1990 5f 5m 5m⁴ 5f³ 5m 5m] 6,600F, 5,800Y: big gelding: has scope: third foal: half-brother to 1½m winner Puff Puff (by All Systems Go): dam unraced: plating-class maiden: ran poorly final start: will be better suited by 6f: sweating penultimate start. *L. J. Holt.* **56**

POWER OF PRAYER 3 ch.f. The Noble Player (USA) 126–Sandra's Choice (Sandy Creek 123) [1989 7m 8g 7f 1990 6h 8.3f] angular filly: behind in maidens and handicaps: bred to stay beyond 1m. *R. Akehurst.* —

POWERSURGE 3 b.c. Electric 126–Ladysave (Stanford 121§) [1989 NR 1990 12m⁴ 16f* 15d] workmanlike colt: first foal: dam ran twice: 13/8 on, won 4-runner maiden at Thirsk in July: burly and soon struggling in handicap at Edinburgh nearly 3½ months later. *Denys Smith.* **64**

POWER TAKE OFF 4 b.f. Aragon 118–Law And Impulse 104 (Roan Rocket 128) [1989 7m³ 8m² 8m* 10m³ 1990 8g* 8g³ 7g 9g³ 8g⁵] big, angular, rather sparely-made filly: good mover: first race for over 9 months, won £16,300 handicap at York in May: stayed on from rear when third in listed events at Sandown and Newmarket: stays 1¼m: acts on good to firm going: swerved left stalls third outing. *D. R. C. Elsworth.* **102**

POYLE GEORGE 5 br.h. Sharpo 132–Hithermoor Lass 75 (Red Alert 127) [1989 5g⁴ 6m 5m* 1990 5f 5d⁴ 5m 5f 5m] smallish, robust horse: has a quick action: very useful performer: won listed event at Newmarket in October, 1989: 20/1, never-nearer fourth of 15 to Dayjur in King's Stand Stakes at Royal Ascot, easily best effort at 5 yrs: best at 5f: has won on good to firm going, but possibly needs an easier surface nowadays: sweated freely on reappearance. *D. R. C. Elsworth.* **113**

PRAIRIE AGENT 5 b.m. Main Reef 126–Regal Guard 60 (Realm 129) [1989 10s 10f 10m 15.3m⁶ 16.2g 12f 15.3g² 17.6f⁵ 12g 1990 16m⁴] rather sparely-made mare: moderate mover: bad plater: seems to stay 15f: acts on firm going: has given trouble in preliminaries and started slowly. *R. J. Muddle.* —

PRAYER FLAG (USA) 3 ch.f. Forli (ARG)–Forever Waving (USA) (Hoist The Flag (USA)) [1989 5m⁶ 6f 5f 1990 6m⁶ 6g 10m⁴ 10m⁶ 12f] small, sparely-made filly: plater: stays 1¼m: sometimes sweating and edgy: sold to join J. D. J. Davies 850 gns Ascot November Sales. *P. W. Harris.* **43**

PRAYER WHEEL 3 b.f. High Line 125–Heaven Knows 113 (Yellow God 129) [1989 7g 1990 12m⁶ 12f4 16m³ 16.5m⁴ 13m⁴ 12m³] lengthy, good-quartered filly: turns fore-feet in: has a rather round action: plating-class maiden: suited by test of stamina: mulish beforehand then took strong hold when below form in ladies event. *G. A. Pritchard-Gordon.* **52**

PRECELLA THE HUN 3 b.f. Precocious 126–Amerella (Welsh Pageant 132) [1989 5d 5s⁴ 5f⁵ 6g 6f³ 7m⁵ 6g 6g 1990 7m 7g 7.5d] smallish, angular filly: moderate walker: poor mover: poor maiden: best run at 7f: probably acts on any going: blinkered twice: sometimes on toes: sold 2,800 gns Doncaster May Sales: resold 575 gns Ascot October Sales. *N. Tinkler.* —

PRECENTOR 4 ro.c. Music Boy 124–La Magna 104 (Runnymede 123) [1989 6s³ 5m* 5f 5f² 5g 5g 6d 6g a6g 1990 6m 5m 5m⁴ 5g² 5m³ 6m² 6f⁴ 6m* 6m⁴ 5m⁴ 6g⁵ 5.8d⁵] strong, close-coupled colt: moderate mover: plating-class handicapper: **53**

Cecil Wiggins' "Poyle George"

well-backed favourite, won at Pontefract in September: effective at 5f and 6f: acts on firm and dead going: blinkered. *J. D. Bethell.*

PRECIOUS AIR (IRE)   2 ch.f. (Jan 25) Precocious 126–Astra Adastra (Mount Hagen (FR) 127) [1990 5m³ 5f* 6d³ a6g⁶ a7g³] IR 32,000Y: sixth foal: half-sister to fairly useful 1½m winner Baraz (by Busted) and a winner abroad: dam Irish 2-y-o 5f winner, is half-sister to sprinter Ballad Rock: claimer-ridden winner of 8-runner maiden at Bath by 2 lengths: good third of 12, staying on well, to Teanarco in nursery at Haydock: ran poorly both starts on all-weather: better suited by 6f than 5f. *B. W. Hills.*   **82**

PRECIOUS BALLERINA   5 ch.m. Ballacashtal (CAN)–Jenny's Rocket 90 (Roan Rocket 128) [1989 9m 9f 1990 a7g² 9f⁴ a8g³ a7g] tall mare: quite modest maiden at best: easily best effort for long time when third in amateurs handicap at Southwell in December, first run for over 8 months: best form at 1m to 1¼m: has sweated and got on edge: often finds little. *J. Hetherton.*   **54**

PRECIOUS BOY   4 b.g. Taufan (USA) 119–Carrigeen Moss (Red God 128§) [1989 8.2s* 8s 9f³ 10m⁴ 12f 12g 1990 11d] compact, workmanlike gelding: fair winner early as 3-y-o: needed race only outing on flat in 1990: stays 1¼m: acts on any going: winning hurdler in November. *M. O'Neill.*   **—**

PRECIOUS CAROLINE (IRE)   2 b.f. (May 10) The Noble Player (USA) 126–What A Breeze (Whistling Wind 123) [1990 a6g⁵ 5f a6g² 6m] 4,000 (privately) Y: workmanlike, good-quartered filly: good walker: has a roundish action: half-sister to several winners, including useful Irish 6f and 7f winner Mistral Man (by Sweet Revenge) and 1987 2-y-o 6f winner Lauries Treasure (by Don): dam ran 3 times: best effort runner-up in claimer at Southwell: possibly unsuited by top-of-the-ground: sold 3,200 gns Doncaster October Sales. *J. Berry.*   **60**

PRECIOUS DAMSEL   3 b.f. Precocious 126–Blessed Damsel 99 (So Blessed 130) [1989 NR 1990 6m] fifth live foal: half-sister to 1¼m winner Al-Walled (by Young Generation) and winning stayer Bustamante (by Busted): dam won from 5f to 7f at 2 yrs: always behind in seller at Leicester in May: sold 720 gns Newmarket September Sales. *D. Morley.*   **—**

PRECIOUS MEMORIES 5 br.g. Kabour 80–Kings Fillet (King's Bench 132) — §
[1989 12.4g 12f 10f 10.2g 8m 1990 a14g⁶ a14g⁵] leggy, sparely-made gelding: poor
mover: winning plater as 3-y-o: well beaten in subsequent non-selling handicaps:
best form at 1¼m to 1½m: acts on firm and dead going: blinkered 5 times, including
when successful: often wanders and races with head up: sold 3,100 gns Doncaster
October Sales. *J. P. Leigh.*

PRECIOUS SPIRIT 3 b.f. Simply Great (FR) 122–Arctic Drama (Northern —
Baby (CAN) 127) [1989 5g³ 5m⁶ 5m 5g² 5m* 7f⁴ 6m 1990 6f 8.5m 7m] narrow,
sparely-made filly: quite modest winner at 2 yrs: well beaten in 1990, including in
seller and handicap: should stay at least 1m: acts on firm going: sold 600 gns Doncaster October Sales. *M. Brittain.*

PRECOCIOUSLY 4 ch.f. Precocious 126–Grankie (USA) (Nashua) [1989 7s 31
10s² 10f⁶ 9f 10f* 8m 12g 1990 10f⁵ 10f⁵ 8m] close-coupled filly: moderate mover:
winning plater: should stay 1½m: acts on any going: visored last 6 starts: winning
claiming hurdler: sold to join B. Forsey's stable 2,400 gns Ascot May Sales. *S. Dow.*

PREDESTINE 5 b.g. Bold Owl 101–Combe Grove Lady (Simbir 130) [1989 NR 61
1990 8m 11.7g 16.2m 12g* 12m 8.3f] small, leggy gelding: confirmed promise of
previous 2 outings when winning handicap at Kempton in June, kicked clear under
2f out: best at 1½m: suited by give in the ground. *M. Madgwick.*

PREDICTABLE 4 ch.g. Music Boy 124–Piccadilly Etta 76 (Floribunda 136) 51
[1989 6s⁴ 6d⁶ 5m² 5g³ 5m³ 5m⁴ 6g 6s⁵ 6g⁴ 6f⁶ 5g 7g 1990 a7g* a7g a6g⁵ 6v 5m⁴ 5g
5m 7m⁵ 6m⁴ 8m* 8d⁴ 8g 8.5f⁵ 8g⁶] lengthy, angular gelding: moderate walker and
mover: won claimer at Southwell in January and handicap at Edinburgh in June:
stays 1m: acts on good to firm and soft going: effective with or without visor: sold
3,700 gns Doncaster October Sales. *Mrs A. Knight.*

PREENING 3 b.f. Persian Bold 123–Glinting 105 (Crepello 136) [1989 NR 1990 62
7m⁵ 8.5d⁶ 8m a8g⁵ 12g³ 12m* 12m⁴ 12d] leggy, workmanlike filly: has a round
action: fifth foal: half-sister to 4-y-o 1m and 8.5f winner Night of Stars (by Sadler's
Wells), smart 7f and 1m performer Hadeer (by General Assembly) and fair 1¼m
winner Flaunting (by Kings Lake): dam, from very successful family, was best at up
to 1m: quite modest handicapper: won at Goodwood in August: suited by 1½m,
probably by a sound surface: ran poorly in blinkers fourth start: sweating and found
little on final one: sold 61,000 gns Newmarket December Sales. *W. Hastings-Bass.*

PRELECTOR 2 bl.g. (Apr 12) Primo Dominie 121–Pearl Wedding 86 (Gulf Pearl 46
117) [1990 5m⁵ 6g 5m³ 7m] 6,200Y: sparely-made gelding: half-brother to 3 winners,
including William Hill Cambridgeshire winner Century City (by High Top) and a
winner in Italy: dam 1¼m and 1½m winner: poor form in claimers and maiden
auctions: stays 7f. *C. Tinkler.*

PREMIER CHOICE (IRE) 2 b.c. (Mar 17) Petorius 117–Numidia (Sallust 134) 45
[1990 5g 6m 6g 5g] 6,600F, 14,000Y: smallish, angular colt: good walker: second
foal: half-brother to 3-y-o Diadad (by Doulab): dam stayed 9f, is half-sister to very
useful French middle-distance winner Dieter: poor form in northern maidens. *W. J.
Pearce.*

PREMIER DANCE 3 ch.g. Bairn (USA) 126–Gigiolina (King Emperor (USA)) 63
[1989 5m³ 7f³ 1990 a7g² a8g³ 10m⁵ 12m 7.6m⁵ 8.2s⁴ 7m a8g⁴ 8.2m² 8.2d² 8m]
compact gelding: moderate mover: quite modest maiden: stays 1m: acts on any
going: blinkered sixth and seventh outings: inconsistent. *D. Haydn Jones.*

PREMIER DEVELOPER 3 b.c. Precocious 126–Arderelle (FR) 80 (Pharly 79
(FR) 130) [1989 5g⁵ 5s⁵ 5m* 1990 6g 5g² 5f³ 6f* 5f⁵ 7g 6d 6g² 5m⁴ 6f³] leggy colt:
has a rather round action: fair handicapper: led post at Ayr in July: stays 6f: acts on
firm going: wears crossed noseband: looked none too keen when blinkered second
and third starts, very edgy and pulling hard first occasion: hangs under pressure:
sold 11,000 gns Newmarket Autumn Sales. *W. J. Pearce.*

PREMIERE MOON 3 ch.f. Bold Owl 101–Silvery Moon (Lorenzaccio 130) 70
[1989 5g 5f⁵ 6g⁴ 5f³ 7m³ 7m* 7g³ 7g 1990 7g 8g 7m⁴ 8m* 7m 8f 10.6d 8.2v³]
sparely-made filly: poor mover: modest handicapper: other 3 starters involved in
accident when winning at Warwick in June: probably best subsequent effort when
well-beaten third of 16 in claimer at Haydock, slowly away, plenty to do then staying
on very well: stays 1m: best form on good to firm ground: sometimes bandaged
behind: retained by trainer 5,000 gns Ascot February Sales. *H. J. Collingridge.*

PREMIER LADY 3 b.f. Red Sunset 120–Be A Dancer (Be Friendly 130) [1989 5f 32
6m 7g 1990 12m 16g⁵ 13.8d⁵ 14f⁴] close-coupled, sturdy filly: poor maiden: stays
1¾m: acts on firm going: visored (best effort) final start: edgy at 3 yrs, sweating first
2 starts: joined N. Gaselee. *D. T. Thom.*

PREMIER PRINCE 4 b.c. King of Spain 121–Domicile (Dominion 123) [1989 6d 61
7f⁶ 7f 9m 8f⁵ 8.2g⁵ 6g² 8m³ 6g⁵ 6s⁶ 6m 1990 6m 7g 7m⁴ 7.6m⁶ 7f* 7m⁵ 8d 7m⁶ 7g⁶
7g] strong, workmanlike colt: quite modest handicapper: won at Leicester in July:
stays 7f: acts on firm and dead going: suited by waiting tactics. *L. G. Cottrell.*

PREMIER PRINCESS 4 b.f. Hard Fought 125–Manntika 77 (Kalamoun 129) 43
[1989 15g⁵ 15.8m² 16f⁴ 13.8g⁴ 16m⁴ 12g 18g 1990 21.6m⁵ 13.8f 17m⁴ 15.8d*]
workmanlike filly: won for first time on flat and showed improved form in handicap
at Catterick in October: also successful over hurdles 3 times in autumn: stays well:
best effort on dead going. *W. Bentley.*

PREMIER ROYALE (IRE) 2 b.c. (Feb 29) Indian King (USA) 128–Rince Si 58
(Malinowski (USA) 123) [1990 5f⁶ 5f² 5g² 5m² 5m³ 7f⁶] IR 13,500Y: lengthy, workmanlike colt: third foal: dam never ran: plating-class maiden: looked ungenuine final
outing: should be suited by further than 5f: acts on firm ground: blinkered (ran
moderately) penultimate start. *W. J. Pearce.*

PREMIER TOUCH 3 b.c. Petorius 117–Fingers (Lord Gayle (USA) 124) [1989 93
5m³ 5f* 5f³ 1990 7g 6s² 8m* 7m³ 8m 6g³ 6g⁶ 7.2g⁶ 7d 6s³ 6g] leggy colt: moderate
walker and mover: fairly useful performer: won auction event at Redcar in June:
seems best at 6f or 7f: probably acts on any going: blinkered last 2 starts, pulling
hard and weakening quickly on final one: often sweating: has wandered under
pressure: sold 27,000 gns Newmarket Autumn Sales. *W. J. Pearce.*

PREMIER VENUES 2 b.c. (Feb 23) Gorytus (USA) 132–Tarnished Image 88 —
(Targowice (USA) 130) [1990 5f] 15,000Y: compact colt: half-brother to winners in
Italy and France: dam 2-y-o 5f winner: prominent 4f when last of 10 in maiden at
Ripon in April. *W. J. Pearce.*

PRENONAMOSS 2 b.g. (Mar 10) Precocious 126–Nonabella 82 (Nonoalco 91
(USA) 131) [1990 6g 5m² 5g² 5g⁴ 5m* 6d³ 5g²] 4,600F, 7,000Y: lengthy, rather
angular gelding: has scope: second foal: brother to 3-y-o 7f winner Gilt Premium:
dam 7f and 1m winner: progressive colt: quickened well to win maiden auction at
Warwick in October: ran very well after in nurseries at Newmarket, on final start
blinkered first time: possibly best at 5f: acts on good to firm ground and dead. *D. W.
P. Arbuthnot.*

PREOBLAKENSKY 3 b.c. Blakeney 126–Preobrajenska 93 (Double Form 130) 79
[1989 NR 1990 12f⁴ 10g 12m³ 14f] tall, rather leggy colt: first foal: dam won at 5f and
6f as 2-y-o but seemed to go wrong way temperamentally as 3-y-o: fair form in frame
in moderately-run races for minor event at Newmarket and 4-runner maiden at
Kempton: tailed off otherwise: stays 1½m: trained until after third start by D.
Elsworth: sold to join G. Richards 16,000 gns Newmarket Autumn Sales: one to
treat with caution. *B. W. Hills.*

PREPARE (IRE) 2 b.f. (Mar 10) Millfontaine 114–Get Ready 91 (On Your Mark 58
125) [1990 7f 5m⁵ 6d 7g] IR 11,000Y: half-sister to several winners, including
high-class sprinter Anita's Prince (by Stradavinsky) and fair 1982 2-y-o 6f winner
Picaroon (by Taufan): dam best at 5f: best effort second outing: tailed off in
Salisbury maiden final one. *R. J. Holder.*

PREPOLLO 4 gr.c. Precocious 126–Rosie Black 80 (Roan Rocket 128) [1989 8g —
6m⁵ 6f 6g 6g 6m 7g 1990 7m 5f⁶ 6v 7g 10m 8.5g 10m] strong, heavy-topped colt: has
rather a round action: modest maiden at best, but has shown very little since 2 yrs:
tailed off in blinkers and visor: heavily bandaged and wore severe noseband final
outing: trained until after third by E. Weymes. *R. A. Harrison.*

PRESAGE 4 b.c. Petong 126–Discreet 104 (Jukebox 120) [1989 7s 7.5d 9d⁴ 9m⁶ 45
5g 7.5m 1990 a7g⁴ a8g a7g³ a5g a7g a7g a6g 7m 6f⁵] leggy, close-coupled colt:
moderate mover: poor maiden: stays 7f: visored twice, blinkered last 3 outings: sold
1,150 gns Doncaster May Sales after. *J. P. Leigh.*

PRESENT TIMES 4 b.g. Sayf El Arab (USA) 127–Coins And Art (USA) —
(Mississipian (USA) 131) [1989 a11g 1990 a7g⁶ a7g 10d] close-coupled, deep-girthed
gelding: lightly-raced maiden: backed at long odds in seller final start, first for 8
months: stays 7f: sold out of K. Wingrove's stable 2,100 gns Ascot February Sales
after second outing. *A. Moore.*

PRESET 3 ch.c. Homing 130–Constanza 94 (Sun Prince 128) [1989 6g 1990 8m³ 72
8.2m³ 12.4f³ 12m⁵ 12.3g 14g] workmanlike colt: modest performer: wore crossed
noseband when below form last 2 starts, edgy and pulling hard first occasion then
sweating and on toes on second: stays 1½m: sold to join J. Spearing 11,500 gns
Doncaster October Sales. *P. Calver.*

PRESIDENT GEORGE 3 b.g. Be My Native (USA) 122–Mother White 36
(Jukebox 120) [1989 5f⁵ 6m 8m 1990 10.2f⁵ 8f⁶ 8g 8m 8g 7.5g 7m 8m 10m] leggy

gelding: moderate mover: poor plater: stays 1m: blinkered 3 times: sold 780 gns Doncaster October Sales. *M. Brittain.*

PRESIDENTIAL STAR (USA) 4 b.f. President (FR)–Out of This World 76 —
(High Top 131) [1989 8g 9s 8.2s⁵ 8m 8.2m 8h⁴ 10.4g⁵ 8g 10f 8f 1990 a10g] angular filly: carries condition: moderate mover: poor on most form: well beaten last 5 starts: best form at 1m: probably suited by soft going: blinkered 3 times at 3 yrs: visored only outing in 1990: takes good hold. *P. Butler.*

PRESIDIO 4 ro.g. Beldale Flutter (USA) 130–Danielle Delight (Song 132) [1989 —
8d 11.7m 10f⁴ 10m 10m 1990 a8g a10g] lengthy, shallow-girthed gelding: poor maiden: should stay beyond 1m: best form on an easy surface: won twice over hurdles in 1989/90: sold 980 gns Doncaster June Sales. *J. White.*

PRESQUE NOIR 2 br.c. (Mar 23) Latest Model 115–Orlaith 68 (Final Straw 71 p
127) [1990 6m⁵] well-grown colt: has scope: first foal: dam third over 6f at 2 yrs on only start, is out of half-sister to Irish Oaks winner Swiftfoot: 7 lengths fifth of 14, soon chasing leaders and keeping on, to Volksraad in maiden at Newmarket in November: will improve. *H. Candy.*

PRESSED FOR TIME 3 b.f. Buzzards Bay 128§–Sweet Paper (Jellaby 124) —
[1989 8g 1990 12f⁶ 8m⁴ 8m 10m] big, angular filly: no worthwhile form, including in seller. *M. O'Neill.*

PRESSURE 3 b.f. Pharly (FR) 130–Hay Reef 72 (Mill Reef (USA) 141) [1989 NR 94
1990 7g*· 10m⁴ 10m] close-coupled, rather angular filly: has a round, scratchy action: fifth foal: half-sister to 3 winners here, including 1½m winner Legendary Dancer (by Shareef Dancer) and 1983 2-y-o 5f winner Fluctuate (by Sharpen Up): dam 1¼m winner closely related to Wassl: led close home to win Newbury maiden in April: about 3 lengths fourth of 6 to Sardegna at Newmarket, setting slow early pace then staying on well again inside final 1f, easily better effort in summer listed races: will be suited by further. *H. R. A. Cecil.*

PRESTANCIA (FR) 5 b. or br.m. Ile de Bourbon (USA) 133–Princesse Kay —
(FR) (Roi Lear (FR) 126) [1989 12g 12g⁶ 12g⁵ 12d* 10s 12g 1990 10f⁵ 8f⁵ 8m 14g 12g⁶
10.6d] leggy ex-French mare: has a round action half-sister to 2 winners in France and another in Italy: dam French 1¼m and 1½m winner: successful 3 times in French Provinces, including handicap in July, 1989: no form in minor events or handicaps in Britain: stays 1½m. *M. Bell.*

PRETONIC 2 b.f. (Jan 26) Precocious 126–Northern Ballerina 52 (Dance In Time 58
(CAN)) [1990 6d 6g⁴ a6g³] 6,400Y: workmanlike filly: second foal: half-sister to 3-y-o Simple Truth (by Known Fact): dam won sellers at 7f and 8.2f: improving filly: one-paced third of 16 in maiden at Southwell in August: will be better suited by 7f. *C. F. Wall.*

PRETTY DUET 3 b.f. Song 132–Liberation 63 (Native Prince) [1989 5g 5f 1990 —
7g 5g 5m⁶ 5m] leggy filly: no worthwhile form, including in handicaps: sold 1,150 gns Ascot October Sales. *C. Holmes.*

PRETTY IN PINK 4 b.f. Formidable (USA) 125–Londonderry Air 84 (Bally- —
moss 136) [1989 NR 1990 a7g⁶ 9f] half-sister to several winners here and abroad, including useful 1m winner Persian Market (by Taj Dewan) and Irish 1¼m winner Vitalise (by Vitiges): dam 5f winner from only 3 starts at 2 yrs: little promise in maiden (visored) and claimer in spring. *D. Moffatt.*

PRETTY MUCH 2 gr.f. (Apr 23) Absalom 128–Pakpao 77 (Mansingh (USA) 120) 33
[1990 5m 5m⁵ 5f⁵] lengthy filly: sixth foal: half-sister to 2-y-o winners by Sparkling Boy and Blue Cashmere: dam 2-y-o 5f winner: poor form in sellers: bolted at Nottingham in May, injured herself and was put down. *T. Fairhurst.*

PRETTY POPPY 2 b.f. (May 2) Song 132–Moonlight Serenade 66 (Crooner 119) 67
[1990 5m² 5f* 5d] 4,200Y: good-quartered filly: good walker and mover: sixth foal: half-sister to 3-y-o 10.5f winner Applianceofscience (by Bairn), 5f winner Stocious (by Petong) and useful 7f and 1m winner King Balladeer (by Dominion): dam, to smart sprinter Blackbird, stayed 1m: odds on, won maiden auction at Redcar in May by 3 lengths: last of 7 in £7,400 event at Beverley following month. *J. Hetherton.*

PRETTY PRECOCIOUS 4 b.f. Precocious 126–Siouxsie 90 (Warpath 113) 41 §
[1989 6m 7m 6m 5m 6m⁶ 9s* 9f 10.6s 10f 8g⁶ 1990 a8g a5g 8m² 8m⁴ 8.2s⁶ 8m⁴ 8f 7g
8.3m 9f 8m³ 8.2v 8d⁵ 10d⁵] tall filly: has a rather round action: poor plater: stays 9f: acts on good to firm and soft going: headstrong, and is a difficult ride: sold 1,500 gns Doncaster November Sales. *J. L. Spearing.*

PRETTY SUPER 2 b.f. (Mar 10) Superlative 118–Strapless 84 (Bustino 136) 39
[1990 5f 5f 5m⁵ 5m⁶ 5d⁵ 5g 7g] IR 8,200Y: small, close-coupled filly: third foal:

half-sister to ungenuine maiden Elenos (by Trojan Fen): dam 6f winner, is out of Cheveley Park second Dame Foolish: poor maiden: very unruly in preliminaries fourth (visored) and fifth starts, and is temperamental: sold to join J. Bridger 500 gns Newmarket September Sales. *J. Hetherton.*

PRICELESS BOND (USA) 2 ch.f. (Jan 28) Blushing Groom (FR) 131–Pied **75** Princess (USA) (Tom Fool) [1990 6g³ 7m² 8.5m² 9m*] $350,000Y: smallish, angular filly: half-sister to numerous winners, notably high-class middle-distance colt Majesty's Prince (by His Majesty): dam unraced: modest performer: odds on, won 5-runner maiden at Wolverhampton in October, making all: stays 9f. *M. R. Stoute.*

PRICELESS FANTASY 3 ch.f. Dunbeath (USA) 127–Linda's Fantasy 108 **76** (Raga Navarro (ITY) 119) [1989 6g⁵ 5m³ 7m⁶ 1990 7.5d 8d³ 9m* 10m² 9g⁴ 10m⁴ 10d² 10.2s a10g] smallish, lengthy filly: has a round action: good walker: modest handicapper: won at Ripon in August: very good second at Redcar seventh start, well beaten in Doncaster minor event and Lingfield handicap after: stays 1¼m well: acts on good to firm and dead ground: sold out of J. Fanshawe's stable 5,200 gns Newmarket December Sales before final start. *I. P. Wardle.*

PRICELESS HOLLY 2 b.c. (May 6) Silly Prices 110–Holly Doon (Doon 124) — [1990 7s a7g] half-brother to several winners, including middle-distance stayers Yorkshire Holly (by Bivouac) and Holly Buoy (by Blind Harbour): dam poor plater: tailed off in maidens at Newcastle and Southwell. *Mrs G. R. Reveley.*

PRICELESS LOOT 2 b.f. (Apr 21) Ardross 134–Pulcinella 95 (Shantung 132) **48** [1990 6m⁶ 7.5d] 5,600Y: lengthy, angular filly: seventh foal: half-sister to fairly useful 1983 2-y-o sprinter Preobrajenska (by Double Form) and a winner in Switzerland: dam 1m winner: green, never dangerous in maiden at Goodwood: ridden along by halfway when well below that form in auction event later in June. *C. A. Cyzer.*

PRIDE OF ARABY (USA) 4 b.c. Sovereign Dancer (USA)–Miss Manon (FR) **109** (Bon Mot III 132) [1989 10s³ 10.6g² 10m* 1990 8g 8f² 8m² 8f³ 7.6f4] tall, rather finely-made colt: good mover: very useful performer: improved each time when placed in valuable handicaps in first half of year, third of 32, favourite and sweating, to Pontenuovo in £33,200 Royal Hunt Cup at Royal Ascot: ran moderately in listed event following month: best at 1m: acts well on top-of-the-ground: keen sort, who pulled too hard on reappearance. *R. Charlton.*

PRIDE OF SHIPLEY 2 b.c. (May 11) Scorpio (FR) 127–L'Angelo di Carlo 46 — (Record Token 128) [1990 a6g 6m] 3,400Y: workmanlike colt: third foal: half-brother to 2 poor animals: dam stayed 7f: slowly away and always behind in seller at Southwell and maiden auction at Pontefract. *D. W. Chapman.*

PRIESTGATE 5 ch.g. Stanford 121§–Change of Luck (Track Spare 125) [1989 — 5g⁴ 5f³ 6m 6m 5g² 6m 6m* 6g⁴ 7g 1990 7f 6m 5d 6g 6d a8g a6g a8g] lengthy, workmanlike gelding: won same seller at York for second successive season in October, 1989: no form at 5 yrs: best at sprint distances on a sound surface: blinkered last 3 outings as 4-y-o and on fourth start: often bandaged: good mount for apprentice: has sweated. *J. Wharton.*

PRIMA CAVALLA 2 b.f. (Mar 27) Primo Dominie 121–Highest Tender 56 — (Prince Tenderfoot (USA) 126) [1990 a6g] third foal: half-sister to a winner in Norway: dam plater: bit backward, green and bandaged, soon behind in claimer at Southwell in August. *P. S. Felgate.*

PRIME DISPLAY (USA) 4 ch.g. Golden Act (USA)–Great Display (FR) **98 d** (Great Nephew 126) [1989 12s⁴ 12f⁴ 14g² 1990 16m⁵ 16m* 20m 18.4f⁵ a18g] big, strong, rangy gelding: carries plenty of condition: has a round action: favourite, made all in listed Saval Beg EBF Stakes at Leopardstown in May: lost his form afterwards: stays 2m: acts on any going: sold to join O. Sherwood's stable 15,500 gns Newmarket Autumn Sales. *P. F. I. Cole.*

PRIME MOVER 2 b.g. (Apr 12) Mummy's Game 120–Feast-Rite (Reform 132) **65 p** [1990 6g⁶ 6d a6g*] 20,000Y: quite good-topped gelding: fourth living foal: brother to fair 1988 2-y-o 5f winner Fire Sprite, closely related to 1987 6f winner Daddy's Dilemma (by Mummy's Pet) and half-brother to a winning sprinter by Dragonara Palace: dam twice-raced half-sister to smart 1984 2-y-o Brave Bambino: won 7-runner maiden at Lingfield by ¾ length from Oak Park, soon pushed along vigorously, hanging left on turn then running on strongly: likely to improve again. *Sir Mark Prescott.*

PRIMETTA PRINCE 6 ch.g. Morston (FR) 125–Russian Princess 99 (Henry — The Seventh 125) [1989 NR 1990 a12g a12g⁵] lengthy gelding: modest maiden at 2 yrs: very lightly raced and little subsequent form: blinkered once. *W. J. Pearce.*

PRIME WARDEN 4 b.c. Blakeney 126–Misguided 106 (Homing 130) [1989 10.1m 10g 8g⁴ 7g a12g 1990 12g 10g] strong, compact colt: has a free, rather round action: modest maiden at best: ran poorly in handicaps in June: should be suited by further than 1m. *J. Ffitch-Heyes.*　—

PRIMITIVE SINGER 2 b.g. (Feb 22) Chief Singer 131–Periquito (USA) (Olden Times) [1990 8s 10.2s⁵] workmanlike, deep-girthed gelding: has scope: moderate mover: seventh foal: half-brother to several winners, notably very useful 7f (at 2 yrs) to 2m winner Primitive Rising (by Raise A Man): dam ran 4 times: beaten around 10 lengths in minor events at Newbury (took keen hold) and Doncaster late in season. *W. Hastings-Bass.*　70

PRIMO SUNDAY SPORT 2 b.g. (Feb 28) Primo Dominie 121–Miss Import 101 (Import 127) [1990 6g⁵] 2,200Y: rather unfurnished gelding: second foal: dam 5f performer: tailed off in 5-runner minor event at Chester in September, running very wide home turn then weakening rapidly. *J. Berry.*　—

PRIMULA AGAIN 5 ch.g. Free State 125–Silent Prayer 58 (Queen's Hussar 124) [1989 NR 1990 10.2s] small, lengthy gelding: plating-class maiden at best: bandaged and burly only outing at 5 yrs: best at up to 13f: best form on a sound surface: blinkered once: inconsistent. *W. Bentley.*　—

PRINCE BOLLINGER 3 b.c. Head For Heights 125–Almuadiyeh 69 (Thatching 131) [1989 NR 1990 11d 8g a8g⁵ 12h³] 18,000F, 60,000Y: strong, lengthy colt: has scope: good walker: first foal: dam, out of half-sister to smart stayers Frascati and The Admiral, raced only at 2 yrs when placed over 7f: plating-class maiden in the spring: takes keen hold, and may prove best at around 1¼m: tends to carry head high: hung right second start: joined D. Arbuthnot. *P. F. I. Cole.*　—

PRINCE CARNEGIE 3 b.g. Taufan (USA) 119–Phar Lapa 59 (Grundy 137) [1989 NR 1990 10m 12d⁵ 11.5m 8m 10h⁵] 10,000Y: leggy, workmanlike gelding: first foal: dam staying maiden: poor maiden: probably stays 1¼m: visored twice, blinkered once: sold 1,900 gns Doncaster November Sales. *D. Morley.*　33

PRINCE ENGELBERT 5 br.g. Persian Bold 123–Polyester Girl (Ridan (USA)) [1989 6v 9g 9.5f 9.5f⁵ 7g 9g⁵ 8g 1990 a8g 6m] leggy ex-Irish gelding: brother to fairly useful 1982 2-y-o Irish 7f winner Persian Polly and half-brother to Hazy Vision (by Vision), successful over 6f in Ireland in 1988: dam Irish 6f winner: bad maiden: sold 3,000 gns Ascot July Sales. *J. Ffitch-Heyes.*　—

PRINCE HANNIBAL 3 b.c. High Top 131–Fluctuate 87 (Sharpen Up 127) [1989 7g 1990 8f4 8.5g³ 10f² 10f* 10m* 12f⁶ 12m* 12m 12g] rangy colt: fairly useful handicapper: won at Brighton (maiden) in June, Kempton (rather idling) in July and Goodwood (hanging left) in September: pulled hard and ran poorly final start: stays 1½m: best efforts on top-of-the-ground: best with waiting tactics. *J. L. Dunlop.*　88

PRINCE HURRICANE (IRE) 2 b. or br.c. (Feb 24) Tender King 123–Storm Lass 65 (Typhoon 125) [1990 6g a7g⁶ a7g 6m] IR 4,000Y: leggy, sparely-made colt: half-brother to several winners abroad and a winning hurdler: dam placed at up to 9f in Ireland: little worthwhile form: blinkered in seller final start: sold 650 gns Doncaster October Sales. *Pat Mitchell.*　—

PRINCE IBRAHIM 4 b.c. Be My Guest (USA) 126–Fanny's Cove 89 (Mill Reef (USA) 141) [1989 10.2d³ 10m³ 11s⁶ 8m 1990 8m³ 8g 10f 10m 8h² 9m² 8g⁴ 8m] lengthy, angular colt: has a long stride: quite useful handicapper on his day: stays 1¼m: probably acts on any going: blinkered last 4 starts, taken down early first time: often sweats and gets on edge: probably best on a galloping track: lacks turn of foot and requires enterprising tactics: sold 25,000 gns Newmarket Autumn Sales. *J. L. Dunlop.*　87

PRINCE LIVERMORE (USA) 3 ch.c. Mt Livermore (USA)–Abbey Leix (USA) (Banquet Circuit (USA)) [1989 6g 6g 1990 6m² 7m 10f* 12g] tall, angular colt: moderate mover: quite modest form: won claimer at Folkestone: pulled hard and never able to challenge in similar event later in May: stays 1¼m: joined Mrs M. Kendall. *N. A. Callaghan.*　60

PRINCE OF DREAMS 3 ch.c. Gabitat 119–Icacos Bay 58 (Martinmas 128) [1989 6g 1990 8.5g 10.2f⁶ 10m⁵ 10m] big, strong, close-coupled colt: plating-class form: should have been suited by return to shorter: blinkered and edgy final start: dead. *J. G. M. O'Shea.*　—

PRINCE OF HUTTON 2 b.g. (Mar 7) Prince Sabo 123–Wayward Polly 63 (Lochnager 132) [1990 5f 5g] 13,500Y: robust gelding: has scope: third foal: dam won 5f seller at 2 yrs: backward, never on terms in maidens at Haydock (slowly away) and Ripon in spring. *M. W. Easterby.*　—

PRINCE OF IRELAND (IRE) 2 b.c. (May 14) Anita's Prince 126–Mooned 64 **47**
(Fair Season 120) [1990 5v⁴ 5d⁵ 5g 5g⁴ 6m⁵ 5g⁴ 5d a5g] IR 3,000Y, resold 1,950Y:
workmanlike, dipped-backed colt: has a quick action: second foal: half-brother to
4-y-o Xhube (by Reasonable): dam daughter of half-sister to Irish Oaks winner Celina, family of See You Then and Sure Blade: poor form in varied events: blinkered
and found little off bridle in seller penultimate start, and off course 6 months after:
best efforts over 5f on good ground. *N. Bycroft.*

PRINCE OF ROCK (IRE) 2 b.c. (Apr 22) Ballad Rock 122–Prasia (Prince **50**
Regent (FR) 129) [1990 7g 7m 7m 6d a7g] IR 9,600Y: well-made colt: has scope:
moderate mover: half-brother to 2 winners, including 1¼m winner Mandolin (by
Manado): dam, placed over middle distances in France, is half-sister to high-class
French filly Pitasia: plating-class maiden: best effort third start (reluctant stalls):
faced stiff task in nursery penultimate outing: will be suited by 1m: may do better in
blinkers. *R. F. Johnson Houghton.*

PRINCE OF THE SEA (IRE) 2 gr.c. (Feb 12) Double Schwartz 128–Baracuda **69 p**
(FR) (Zeddaan 130) [1990 6d²] 14,000F, 9,200Y: half-brother to French middle-
distance winner Baloa (by Card King): dam French maiden: 5 lengths second of 17,
keeping on, to Samurai Gold in maiden at Folkestone in November: should improve.
D. W. P. Arbuthnot.

PRINCE PEDRO 2 b.c. (Feb 22) King of Spain 121–La Bambola 95 (Be Friendly **32**
130) [1990 5s⁵ 5m⁵ 5m a6g⁵ 6m] 4,600Y: neat colt: half-brother to 3-y-o Miss
Tenaville (by Kala Shikari): dam won from 7f to 14.7f: poor form in sellers and a
claimer. *N. Tinkler.*

PRINCE RUSSANOR 2 b.c. (Apr 13) Rousillon (USA) 133–Pellinora (USA) **84**
(King Pellinore (USA) 127) [1990 8g* 8.2d⁵] 25,000Y: lengthy, rather angular colt:
fifth foal: closely related to fairly useful 1½m winner Peleus (by Irish River): dam,
once-raced half-sister to Park Hill winner I Want To Be, from an excellent family:
bit backward, won minor event at Newbury in September by ½ length from Democratic, idling and edging right: odds on, modest fifth of 15, pulling hard and running in
snatches, in similar event at Nottingham following month: created a favourable
impression at Newbury. *J. L. Dunlop.*

PRINCE SOBUR 4 b.g. Jalmood (USA) 126–Ultra Vires 87 (High Line 125) **63**
[1989 10v² 11m 13.3g 14m² 16.1m 1990 16d² 16.2m 14s* 16.2d 17.6g³ 17.4d³ 14d⁵
18d] rangy gelding: moderate mover: quite modest handicapper: won at Haydock in
June: better efforts when third at Haydock again and Ayr: virtually pulled up,
seemingly lame, in Cesarewitch final outing: suited by good test of stamina: best
with give in the ground and acts on heavy. *M. Blanshard.*

PRINCESS ACCORD (USA) 4 b.f. D'Accord (USA)–Cohutta Princess (USA) **106**
(Groton) [1989 7d* 8.2m* 7g* 8g* 9g* 10g⁴ 1990 8m³ 7.2s² 8g³ 8m⁶ 9f⁵ 9f³ 9f]
sparely-made filly: moderate walker and mover: progressed very well as 3-y-o and
won listed races at Ascot (idled) and Newmarket: ran with credit for most of 1990, in
similar company at Sandown and Kempton on first and third starts: would have won
comfortably with clear run fourth one: stays 9f: acts on any going: usually bandaged
off-hind: tough and consistent. *L. M. Cumani.*

PRINCESS CAERLEON 4 ch.f. Caerleon (USA) 132–Tigeen (Habitat 134) **63**
[1989 5s 5m 5m⁶ 5f⁴ 5f 5g 5f 5d 1990 5g⁴ 5g 5g⁶ 5m³ 5m³ 5f² 5m³ 5g⁶ 5m²] lengthy,
rather dipped-backed filly: moderate walker and mover: quite modest handicapper:
best at 5f: acts on firm and dead going: very slowly away third start: sweating and
edgy seventh and last. *C. H. Eden.*

PRINCESS JENNY 8 b.m. Home Guard (USA) 129–Princess of Verona 95 **—**
(King's Leap 111) [1989 NR 1990 12m] big, plain mare: appears no longer of much
account: blinkered once: has given trouble at stalls. *M. Tate.*

PRINCESS JESSICA 3 ch.f. Anfield 117–Maid of Warwick 96 (Warwick 110) **—**
[1989 5d 5.3g 5d² 6f⁵ 5m⁵ 5g 6f⁶ 1990 a6g⁵ a7g 5f 5f a5g] small, sturdy filly:
moderate plater: should stay 6f: acts on good to firm ground and dead: visored
(always behind) penultimate start: trained until after second by B. Smart. *P. Butler.*

PRINCESS JESTINA (IRE) 2 b.f. (Apr 4) Jester 119–Royal Aunt (Martinmas **57**
128) [1990 5f² 5f* 5g 5f5 6f³] IR 5,000Y: leggy, sparely-made filly: half-sister to 1986
2-y-o 5f seller winner Flag Bearer (by Runnett): dam modest Irish 2-y-o 6f winner:
plating-class performer: won maiden auction at Kempton in April: ran moderately
in 3-runner minor event (wandered badly) at Lingfield final start: sold 800 gns
Newmarket December Sales. *M. J. Haynes.*

PRINCESS KATIE 2 b.f. (Feb 7) Forzando 122–Jianna 60 (Godswalk (USA) **52**
130) [1990 5f 6m⁴ 7h 6f⁴ 6m⁴ 7f⁴ 6m 7g a8g] 540F: sturdy filly: moderate mover:

first foal: dam, maiden, stayed 6f: modest plater: stays 7f: best form on firm ground. *A. Moore.*

PRINCESS LUCY 3 b.f. Local Suitor (USA) 128–Jalapa (FR) 117 (Luthier 126) —
[1989 7g 6m 1990 12h⁴ 16m] big, plain filly: poor form: faced very stiff task in handicap. *P. F. I. Cole.*

PRINCESS MODENA 2 gr.f. (May 7) Prince Sabo 123–Mary of Modena 90   **43**
(Crowned Prince (USA) 128) [1990 6m 8.2m] rather angular filly: sixth living foal: half-sister to modest 1¼m winner Modena Reef (by Mill Reef): dam 6f winner: poor form in maiden and minor event (faded from 2f out) at Nottingham in September: sold 1,900 gns Newmarket Autumn Sales. *B. Hanbury.*

PRINCESS MONOLULU (IRE) 2 b.f. (Apr 20) Salmon Leap (USA) 131–San —
Salu (Sallust 134) [1990 5s⁶ 6g 6g] IR 1,700Y: small filly: third foal: dam fair Irish 2-y-o, placed in 5f listed event: well beaten, including in a seller: sold 850 gns Doncaster October Sales. *J. Hetherton.*

PRINCESS MOODYSHOE 2 ch.f. (Mar 24) Jalmood (USA) 126–Royal Shoe   **63**
(Hotfoot 126) [1990 5f³ 6m 6m 6m⁴ 6g 7g⁵ 8d²] plain filly: has a round action: first foal: dam winning jumper: quite modest maiden: ran well in nursery at Goodwood final start: suited by 1m: best form on dead ground. *L. J. Holt.*

PRINCESS NELL 2 b.f. (Apr 21) Damister (USA) 123–Nell of The North (USA)   **53**
(Canadian Gil (CAN)) [1990 6m⁶ 7m] leggy, unfurnished filly: looks weak: fourth reported foal: half-sister to 3-y-o Regal North (by Regalberto) and a winner in North America: dam won at up to 9f in USA: around 13 lengths sixth of 12 in maiden at Nottingham in August: should prove suited by 7f+: sold 1,250 gns Doncaster October Sales. *J. Etherington.*

PRINCESS OF BASRA 3 ch.f. Bairn (USA) 126–Miss Nelski 84 (Most Secret —
119) [1989 5g 1990 6f 6f⁶ a7g⁴ 8m 7d a8g] lengthy filly: poor plater: probably stays 7f: visored last 2 starts: sold out of W. Haigh's stable 800 gns Doncaster June Sales after fourth: resold 1,000 gns Ascot July Sales: has shown signs of temperament. *J. L. Harris.*

PRINCESS ROXANNE 3 b.f. Prince Tenderfoot (USA) 126–Godwyn (Yellow   **61**
God 129) [1989 NR 1990 8f⁶ 10f⁴ 10m⁵ 10.4g⁵ a8g⁶ 15d⁵ 9m 12m a12g⁵] IR 5,000F, IR 5,000Y: lengthy filly: moderate walker: eighth foal: half-sister to fairly useful Irish 1982 2-y-o 5f winner Kimbernic (by Lord Gayle), Irish 1m winner Flamante (by Steel Heart) and 2 winning jumpers: dam, half-sister to very useful Pianissimo, won over 6f in Ireland: quite modest maiden: below form in varied events last 4 outings, including amateurs contest: stays 1¼m: acts on firm going: blinkered seventh and eighth starts. *A. Bailey.*

PRINCESS SONATA 3 b.f. Music Boy 124–Jovenita (High Top 131) [1989 5d —
5f⁶ 5m 5g 1990 5g 7g] leggy, angular filly: poor form at best in varied company: bandaged off-hind on reappearance. *D. W. P. Arbuthnot.*

PRINCESS TANIMARA 3 b. or br.f. Vision (USA)–Tanimara (Sassafras (FR) —
135) [1989 7.5f 7f 7f 6g 1990 10m 12.5g 10m 14f⁵] small, leggy filly: has a round action: poor maiden: seems not to stay middle distances: visored then blinkered last 2 starts: sold 680 gns Newmarket September Sales. *G. H. Eden.*

PRINCESS TARA 2 br.f. (Feb 14) Prince Sabo 123–La Magna 104 (Runnymede   **76**
123) [1990 5g 5d² 6m* 6s³ 6f 6m² 6m² 6m⁴ 7m] 6,600Y: rather leggy, good-quartered filly: half-sister to numerous sprint winners, notably class French colt Kind Music and very useful Boy Trumpeter (both by Music Boy): dam 2-y-o 5f winner: modest filly: won auction event at Salisbury in June: ran well when in frame in nurseries after at Newmarket, Chepstow and Ascot: should be as effective at 7f as 6f: seems unsuited by soft ground: has run well when edgy and sweating. *G. Lewis.*

PRINCESS TAUFAN 3 b.f. Taufan (USA) 119–Guindilla (Artaius (USA) 129)   **98**
[1989 5d* 5d* 5f* 5f⁵ 6d⁵ 6m³ 6m⁴ 1990 8v⁴ 8g 10m 10g 8d] close-coupled filly, rather unfurnished: fairly useful performer: 7 lengths fourth of 13 to Atoll in Premio Regina Elena at Rome in April: behind in Poule d'Essai des Pouliches at Longchamp and listed races at Newbury (showed quick action), Fairyhouse and the Curragh: stays 1m: acts on any going: trained until after third start by Dr J. Scargill. *J. C. Hayden, Ireland.*

PRINCESS WHO 2 gr.f. (Mar 4) Lidhame 109–Norton Princess 76 (Wolver   **67**
Hollow 126) [1990 5m⁴ 5g² 5f³ 5m 5g* 5f² 5m 5m² 5.3f³] 11,000Y: leggy filly: third foal: half-sister to 3-y-o 1½m winner Pan E Salam (by Ile de Bourbon) and plating-class 1988 2-y-o Blazing Away (by Blazing Saddles): dam 6f winner at 2 yrs seemed not to train on: quite modest performer: comfortably made all in maiden at Wolver-

hampton in June: speedy: blinkered fourth and final outings: sometimes on toes: consistent: sold 5,000 gns Ascot October Sales. *M. McCormack.*

PRINCESS WU 4 b.f. Sandhurst Prince 128–Hsian (Shantung 132) [1989 8d 10m 10m⁶ 11.3f³ 10g a13g 1990 a12g] sparely-made filly: plating-class maiden: no form last 3 outings: should be suited by 1½m: acts on firm going: sold 850 gns Ascot May Sales: resold 1,200 gns Ascot September Sales. *R. W. Stubbs.* —

PRINCE VALIYAR 3 b.g. Valiyar 129–Lusitanica 89 (Pieces of Eight 128) [1989 8m 10g 1990 10.1g 13.1h 12h⁶ 10m] leggy gelding: no worthwhile form, in seller final start: should stay 1¼m: pulled hard in lead when blinkered second start: trained until after third by M. Jarvis: winning selling hurdler. *A. Moore.* —

PRINGIPOULA 4 b.f. Dominion 123–Another Princess 83 (King Emperor (USA)) [1989 6s² 5s² 6s 6g* 6m⁴ 5f³ 6g⁴ 7m 6m 1990 8.5f⁴ 7g] sturdy, good-bodied filly: carries plenty of condition: has a quick action: fair winner as 3-y-o: ran moderately at Epsom in April, and wasn't seen out again: should stay 1m: probably suited by a sound surface. *C. E. Brittain.* —

PRIOLO (USA) 3 b.c. Sovereign Dancer (USA)–Primevere (USA) 91 (Irish River (FR) 131) [1989 7d* 1990 8g* 10.5s³ 9g* 9.2g* 10d² 8g* 8g³ 8g³] **127**

Like the cavalier party guest, Priolo made an eye-catching late arrival at the business end of three of the top mile races. He turned heads, coming from off the pace and finishing strongest of all, in the Prix du Haras de Fresnay-le-Buffard Jacques le Marois at Deauville, the Emirates Prix du Moulin de Longchamp and the Breeders' Cup Mile at Belmont Park, leaving no doubt that he was a colt all the best milers of 1990 had to reckon with. Priolo didn't always come out on top, however. In fact, of those three big races in the second half of the season he won only the Marois. He was one of three Boutin-trained colts in the field, the most fancied in the betting being the Poulains winner Linamix whose owners ran Reinstate as a pacemaker. The two other home-trained runners Lady Winner and Septieme Ciel were also preferred as were the Coronation Stakes winner Chimes of Freedom, who started favourite, and the recent Sussex Stakes one-two Distant Relative and Green Line Express. The field was completed by Candy Glen and Sikeston. A very strong collection then, and Priolo was best of them on the day despite encountering trouble in running. Two furlongs out Priolo was behind a line of horses spread across the track, only the pacemaker was out of it; then, taken back towards the rails by his jockey Lequexo, Priolo found a gap approaching the final furlong. Distant Relative and Linamix had just about come out best of the others when Priolo emerged from between Candy Glen and Lady Winner to lead close home and win by half a length. The first three took each other on again in the Moulin three weeks later. This time, however, although Priolo got a perfectly clear run in the smaller field, he had too much to do after the pacemaker had carried out his job assiduously. The writing was on the wall early in the straight when he was at least five lengths down on Linamix for although he ran on really strongly, without being given a hard race, he couldn't quite catch his stable-companion, nor Distant Relative who got up on the line. In the Breeders' Cup Mile, Priolo was very much up against it before he'd gone even a furlong. He found himself a detached last after being badly baulked on the inside then, after passing a few stragglers on the turn, he

Prix Jean Prat, Longchamp—Satin Wood divides the French pair Priolo and Septieme Ciel

*Prix du Haras de Fresnay-le-Buffard Jacques le Marois, Deauville—
home runners continue to dominate this event,
as Priolo beats stable-companion Linamix and Distant Relative*

couldn't keep pace with Royal Academy initially before coming with another powerful run at the death, once more finishing a never-nearer third beaten under a length. A third prize of 108,000 dollars isn't to be scoffed at but Priolo's connections must have counted themselves unlucky not to take home rather more.

These three were high-class performances, clearly Priolo's best. He'd earlier been tried over further—and with some success. Over nine furlongs in May he'd beaten Boxing Day one and a half lengths in the listed Prix Matchem at Evry, and Satin Wood the same distance, with Septieme Ciel third, in the Prix Jean Prat at Longchamp to add to earlier wins in a two-year-old maiden at Deauville and an Evry minor event. Priolo had been well held, however, by both Epervier Bleu in the Prix Greffulhe (hanging left into the centre of the track when asked for his effort) and Saumarez in the Grand Prix de Paris, appearing to run creditably at the time but in hindsight below his best.

			Northern Dancer	Nearctic
	Sovereign Dancer (USA)		(b 1961)	Natalma
	(b 1975)		Bold Princess	Bold Ruler
Priolo (USA)			(gr 1960)	Grey Flight
(b.c. 1987)			Irish River	Riverman
	Primevere (USA)		(ch 1976)	Irish Star
	(br 1982)		Spring Is Sprung	Herbager
			(b 1973)	Pleasant Flight

Priolo has done a lot better in France than either his sire or dam. After four runs (for one second placing) in North America as a three-year-old, Sovereign Dancer was fitted with blinkers and won two minor events at around a mile and a quarter and was second in the one-and-a-half-mile Grand Prix de Vichy for Mme Head as a four-year-old. Priolo is his best representative in Europe by a long chalk, though he had Thakib, Pride of Araby and Dangora in Britain in 1990, but his reputation on the other side of the Atlantic (he stands at Lane's End Farm) had already undergone a dramatic improvement through his having the 1984 Preakness winner Gate Dancer in his first crop. Breeders' Cup Mile runner-up Itsallgreektome is also by Sovereign Dancer. Priolo's dam Primevere was a fairly useful winner over seven furlongs at two years and a mile and a quarter at three years for Boutin, and Priolo is her first foal. Her dam Spring Is Sprung's standing as a broodmare, by contrast, has never been very high. Starting with the best opportunities, she produced a winner by Mr Prospector but only two others have followed—she was represented with no distinction by the three-year-old Bric Lane here in the latest season— and she was sold for 7,500 dollars in November 1989 believed to be in foal to

Ecurie Skymarc Farm's "Priolo"

the Blushing Groom stallion Westheimer. Spring Is Sprung raced only once but she deserved every chance at stud as a granddaughter of the outstanding Grey Flight, dam of What A Pleasure (brother to Priolo's third dam), the champion filly Misty Morn and, interestingly, Sovereign Dancer's dam Bold Princess amongst a host of stakes winners: another daughter of Grey Flight by Bold Ruler was Clear Ceiling, dam of One Thousand Guineas winner Quick As Lightning.

Priolo, who has yet to race on top-of-the-ground, stays nine furlongs but has achieved his best performances running on strongly over a mile. Expect to see him arrive late on the scene—and to some effect—in more of the top races in 1991. *F. Boutin, France.*

PRIOR CHARGE 3 ch.f. Tender King 123–Priors Mistress 71 (Sallust 134) **70** d
[1989 NR 1990 a8g⁴ a10g⁴ 10m 10m a8g⁴ a8g⁶ a10g a8g] angular, sparely-made filly: has quick action: third foal: half-sister to 1¼m seller winner Super Idea (by Red Sunset): dam disappointing: won maiden at Lingfield in February: should stay 1¼m. *Pat Mitchell.*

PRIORITY PAID 3 ch.f. Try My Best (USA) 130–Anna Carla (GER) (Windwurf **69** (GER)) [1989 5m* 1990 7f⁵ 6g⁵] lengthy, useful-looking, angular filly: won maiden at Windsor in June at 2 yrs: good fifth in August minor event at Leicester final start, slowly away, not getting best of runs 3f out then running on well: may prove best at 6f: gave trouble at stalls at Leicester. *W. Hastings-Bass.*

PRIORY BAY 4 b.f. Petong 126–Salt of The Earth 85 (Sterling Bay (SWE)) [1989 **32** 8g 10m⁴ 7m⁴ 10f 8f 8m⁵ 10g 1990 8f 8m 8f² 12m 8h⁴] leggy filly: poor maiden: should prove best at up to 1m: acts on any going: visored twice as 3-y-o, visored fourth (didn't handle descent at Lingfield) and fifth starts. *J. C. Fox.*

PRIORY CLOUD 3 b.f. Castle Keep 121–Misfired 101 (Blast 125) [1989 8m 1990 **—** 7f⁴ 7m⁶ 8.2m 8m] workmanlike filly: plating-class maiden: should have stayed 1m: dead. *A. P. Stringer.*

PRIVATE ACCESS (USA) 2 b.c. (Mar 12) Private Account (USA)–Empress of 82 Canada (CAN) (Accomplish) [1990 7g⁴ 8g²] $107,000Y: well-made, good sort: good walker: half-brother to several winners here and in North America, including fair 1983 2-y-o 1m winner Maricourt (by One For All): dam won 6 times at up to 7f: fair form behind Jahafil in minor event at Doncaster and Miss Simplicity in maiden at Kempton (caught near line having quickened clear) later in September: will stay 1¼m: should win a race. *I. A. Balding.*

PRIVATE TENDER 3 b.c. Shirley Heights 130–Select Sale (Auction Ring 116 ? (USA) 123) [1989 NR 1990 12f* 12m 10.2m* 12m* 12m 12m⁵ 15.5v] strong, round-barrelled colt: carries condition: first foal: dam unraced daughter of half-sister to Abwah and Owen Dudley: won minor events at Newmarket and Doncaster and King Edward VII Stakes (favourite, by 2½ lengths from Mukddaam) at Royal Ascot: behind in handicap at Newbury, Princess of Wales's Stakes at Newmarket, Gordon Stakes (moved moderately down) at Goodwood and Prix Royal-Oak at Longchamp: stayed 1½m: acted on firm going: edged right under pressure: sold to Turkish Jockey Club for stud. *H. R. A. Cecil.*

PRIVATE THOUGHTS 2 b.c. (Apr 12) Jupiter Island 126–Placid Pet 65 — (Mummy's Pet 125) [1990 7m 8.2s] 11,500Y: medium-sized, leggy colt: seventh live foal: half-brother to 3 sprint winners and a winner abroad: dam 1m winner, is sister to Runnett: never dangerous in maidens at Leicester (auction event) and Haydock. *M. O'Neill.*

PRIVY GIRL 2 b.f. (Apr 15) Librate 91–Privy Court 73 (Adropejo 114) [1990 8m — 8m] seventh foal: dam showed a little ability at 2 yrs: tailed off in minor event at Bath and seller at Warwick. *J. M. Bradley.*

PRIX DU NORD (USA) 4 b.g. Northern Prospect (USA)–Bisouloun (FR) — § (Sharpman 124) [1989 8.2m 12h 10.2f 10f 8.5m 1990 a11g⁶] well-made gelding: little worthwhile form in varied company: blinkered last 5 starts: winning selling hurdler: hasn't impressed with attitude, and is one to be wary of. *K. G. Wingrove.*

PRODIGAL BLUES (USA) 2 b.c. (Feb 26) The Minstrel (CAN) 135–Street 103 Savy (USA) (Foolish Pleasure (USA)) [1990 5m⁶ 6m² 6d³ 7f* 7g³ 7m³ 8m⁶] $25,000Y: rangy colt: has scope: good walker: has a roundish action: first foal: dam minor winner at up to 9f: useful colt: very good third, staying on well, to Heart of

King Edward VII Stakes, Ascot—
Private Tender wins going away from Mukddaam (striped cap),
Air Music (rails) and Duke of Paducah

Cliveden Stud's "Private Tender"

Darkness in GPA National Stakes at the Curragh penultimate start: earlier won minor event at Redcar in July very easily: pulled quite hard when well beaten in Royal Lodge William Hill Stakes at Ascot: should be suited by 1m: yet to race on very soft going, acts on any other. *J. W. Hills.*

PROFILIC 5 b.h. Ballacashtal (CAN)–Sea Charm 70 (Julio Mariner 127) [1989 6m 6m 6m4 6f 6g4 6f* 6f 8.2g 6m 6f 6m6 6m5 7g5 6s 6m2 6g2 6f2 6g5 6d5 1990 6f* 6m 6m 6m 6m3 6f* 7g5 6d 7m 6f3 6f* 6m3 6m 6g 6m 6d 6d 6g 6s6] big, strong, lengthy horse: usually looks very well: has a long, round stride: fair handicapper: won at Ripon in April, Chepstow in May and Doncaster in July: never near to challenge last 7 outings: suited by strongly-run race at 6f and stays 7f: acts on any going: blinkered 3 times at 4 yrs: usually gets behind and ideally needs strong handling. *Capt. J. Wilson.* **88**

PROFIT A PRENDRE 6 b.g. Tina's Pet 121–Brave Ballard (Derring-Do 131) [1989 6v 7.6f 7f6 7.6f 6f 7.6h 5f 7m 7f* 8g5 7s* 8s4 8g3 8m 7m 1990 7g 7m2 9g5 6f* 7m 7m 7f 8m 8g 7m6 8d 8m 7m 6m 6s] big, lengthy gelding: quite modest handicapper: won for amateur for fifth time and at Redcar for third when justifying favouritism in good style in May: little worthwhile form after: effective at 6f to 1m: acts on any going: carries head high: has hung left and is suited by waiting tactics. *D. A. Wilson.* **69**

PROHIBITION 3 b.g. Music Boy 124–Green Chartreuse 91 (French Beige 127) [1989 5g2 5g3 5m 6m2 6m* 6m* 6m3 7m 6d 6s 6m 6g3 a6g3 1990 6m* 6f2 6g* 6g3 6d* 6d 6m 6m2 6m 6f5 6m2 6g* 6d4 5g5] workmanlike gelding: fair handicapper: won at Warwick in March and Epsom in April and June: didn't recapture that form, although won claimer (blinkered) at Ripon in August: best form at 6f on an easy **88 ?**

713

surface: also blinkered and visored once at 2 yrs: tends to hang left: genuine. *J. Berry.*

PROMEGG 4 ch.c. Music Boy 124–Rosy Lee (FR) (Le Haar 126) [1989 8m 10s² — 10g⁵ 1990 11g] rather sparely-made colt: quite modest maiden at best: stays 1¼m: acts on good to firm and soft going: sold 1,600 gns Ascot September Sales. *G. A. Pritchard-Gordon.*

PROPAGANDA 2 b.c. (Apr 16) Nishapour (FR) 125–Mrs Moss 81 (Reform 132) — [1990 8m] workmanlike colt: half-brother to numerous winners, including very smart middle-distance stayer Jupiter Island (by St Paddy) and high-class 1983 2-y-o sprinter Precocious (by Mummy's Pet): dam 2-y-o 5f winner: bit backward, dropped away 3f out when last of 11 in minor event at Newmarket in November. *C. E. Brittain.*

PROPERS 4 ch.f. Noalto 120–Budget Queen 101 (Good Bond 122) [1989 7s 7f² **53** 8.5m 8m⁴ 7g 7g 1990 7.6m⁵ 6m⁴ 7g 8m³ 8.2g⁶ 7m⁶ 8f³ 10f⁵ 6m] leggy filly: plating-class maiden: probably best over 7f or 1m: acts on any going: has sweated and got on toes: sold 4,200 gns Newmarket Autumn Sales. *P. Mitchell.*

PROSPECTIVE RULER (USA) 2 b.c. (Apr 25) Northern Prospect (USA)– **95** Swan Song (USA) (Ribot 142) [1990 6g² 6m⁵ 7m* 7m⁴ 8g⁵ 7g* 8v] $55,000Y: leggy colt: half-brother to several winners, one placed in graded stakes over 7f: dam unraced: successful in 3-runner maiden at Warwick in June and nursery (in really good style) at Kempton in September: around 9 lengths eighth of 16 in Gran Criterium at Milan in November: stays 1m: probably acts on any going: blinkered or visored last 2 starts. *M. R. Stoute.*

PROSPECTORS MOON (USA) 3 ch.f. Miswaki (USA) 124–Moon Min (USA) — (First Landing) [1989 6g³ 7m⁴ 6f⁴ 1990 7m 8f 8g 6s] leggy, lengthy filly: has scope: moderate walker: plating-class maiden: faced stiff tasks in handicaps and claimer after reappearance, blinkered and looking ungenuine (swerving at stalls, not responding to pressure) final start: bred to stay beyond 1m. *C. F. Wall.*

PROSPORT 2 b.c. (Feb 20) King of Spain 121–Greensward Blaze 50 (Sagaro 133) **45** [1990 6m⁴ 6g 6g 8d 6v] workmanlike colt: has a round action: fourth foal: dam won 1m seller: poor maiden: best effort on debut: last in nurseries when facing stiff tasks final 2 outings: slowly away and hung left in seller second run. *N. Bycroft.*

PROST (USA) 3 b.g. Raise A Cup (USA)–Wrap It Up (Mount Hagen (FR) 127) **69** [1989 8m 1990 a8g⁶ a10g³ a10g⁴ 12g³ 11.7g 14g⁴ 17.1f² 14m⁶ 11.5g⁶ 16f⁵] quite attractive gelding: moderate walker: good mover: modest maiden: stayed 17f: acted on firm going: sold out of W. O'Gorman's stable 16,000 gns Newmarket July Sales after eighth start: winning hurdler: dead. *I. Campbell.*

PROUD BRIGADIER (IRE) 2 b.g. (Apr 29) Auction Ring (USA) 123– **35** Naughty One Gerard (Brigadier Gerard 144) [1990 6f⁶ 5m 5.3f⁶] 4,600Y: sixth foal: half-brother to 1985 Irish 2-y-o 1m winner General Symons (by Dominion): dam never ran: poor form, including in a seller. *W. Carter.*

PROUD PATRIOT 5 ch.g. Kalaglow 132–Sandforinia 86 (Sandford Lad 133) — [1989 12f 12.2f a12g* 1990 12m 12f⁶ 11.5m] workmanlike gelding: moderate mover in slower paces: made all in claimer at Lingfield as 4-y-o, only form on flat for long time: suited by 1½m: has broken blood vessels over hurdles: sold 1,100 gns Ascot July Sales. *R. Akehurst.*

PROVENCE 3 ch.c. Rousillon (USA) 133–Premier Rose 117 (Sharp Edge 123) **83** p [1989 NR 1990 12m⁶ 12g³] rangy colt with scope: fourth foal: half-brother to 4-y-o 1m and 1½m winner Opera Ghost (by Caerleon) and 1987 2-y-o 6f winner Rose Bouquet (by General Assembly): dam, sister to useful 7f and 1m filly Shapina, stayed 1m: 16/1 and very green, promoted fourth of 11 in maiden at Pontefract in October, badly bumped 2f out then staying on despite hanging left: can improve again. *P. W. Harris.*

PRUDENT MANNER 3 ch.c. Cure The Blues (USA)–Prudent Girl 92 **114** (Primera 131) [1989 NR 1990 9m² 7f* 9m* 9g* 9m² 10g³] IR 140,000Y: tenth foal: half-brother to several winners, including top-class American middle-distance performer Providential (by Run The Gantlet) and top 1981 French staying 2-y-o filly Play It Safe (by Red Alert): dam, half-sister to Hethersett, won over middle distances: successful in maiden at the Curragh in July and in smallish fields for minor event and listed race at Phoenix Park in August: subsequently beaten ½ length by Citidancer in Group 3 contest (not getting best of runs) at Leopardstown and 2¾ lengths behind Relief Pitcher in State of New York Stakes at Belmont Park: stays 1¼m: yet to race on a soft surface: very useful. *D. K. Weld, Ireland.*

PSYCHO SONNY 3 b.g. Aragon 118–Sunny Reproach (High Top 131) [1989 a6g⁶ **53 d**
1990 a7g* a7g⁴ a7g⁴ a6g⁵ 7m 7m⁵ 8.2g 8m⁵ 7.6m a7g⁴ 7g a7g 10m 8g 7f] small,
sparely-made gelding: poor walker and mover: plating-class performer: won claimer
at Southwell in January: well beaten last 3 starts: probably stays 1m: ran creditably
for 7-lb claimer: visored twice, blinkered once: wore hood twelfth outing: sold to
join Mrs A. Knight 1,400 gns Ascot September Sales. *Mrs A. Knight.*

PUESTO DEL SOL (IRE) 2 b.c. (Mar 21) Red Sunset 120–Mount Isa (Miami **74 p**
Springs 121) [1990 6d⁶ 6g 6g⁶] IR 20,000Y: well-made, quite attractive colt: has
scope: good mover: first foal: dam placed over 5f in Ireland, is out of sister to
Floribunda: modest form in maidens: bit backward, around 4 lengths sixth of 17,
switched 2f out and running on well not knocked about, at Newbury final start:
withdrawn having been awkward at stalls at Newmarket next intended outing: will
stay 7f: appeals as one to keep an eye on in handicap company. *D. R. C. Elsworth.*

PUFF PUFF 4 b.f. All Systems Go 119–Harmonious Sound (Auction Ring (USA) **56**
123) [1989 6g 6m⁶ 7f³ 8.5m 8.3m⁵ 7g 6m 1990 7m 6d a10g a12g* a12g² a10g⁴ a12g²]
rather leggy filly: backed at long odds, returned to form when winning handicap at
Lingfield in November: good second in similar events there after: unseated rider
leaving stalls third outing, first for 4 months: stays 1½m: acts on firm going: trained
first 2 starts by J. Czerpak. *Miss B. Sanders.*

PUFFY 3 ch.g. Wolverlife 115–Eskaroon (Artaius (USA) 129) [1989 5d⁴ 5m* 5f³ **71 §**
7f⁵ 6g⁶ 8f 6g* 7g⁴ 5v* 7g² 1990 7f 8.5f⁵ 6v² 7g² 7.5d 7m 8m 8h⁵ 7m 8m 5g 7d* 7d³]
leggy, rather sparely-made gelding: shows a quick action: modest performer:
visored in handicaps last 2 starts, winning at Edinburgh in October: otherwise
mostly never placed to challenge or knocked about facing stiff tasks after being
claimed £7,050 out of M. W. Easterby's stable fourth start: stays 7.5f: acts on heavy
going: sometimes blinkered: temperamental and one to treat with caution. *Ronald
Thompson.*

PULIGNY 3 b.g. Glenstal (USA) 118–No Distractions 78 (Tap On Wood 130) **64**
[1989 5m⁶ 5f⁶ 6g² 7m² 8s* 1990 7f 8.5d⁶ 8f 8m⁴ 12.4m³ 10.6v*] lengthy, well-made
gelding: quite modest handicapper: favourite and dropped in class, won seller
(bought in 7,700 gns) at Haydock in October: stays 1½m: acts on good to firm
ground and heavy: sold 9,000 gns Newmarket Autumn Sales. *Mrs J. R. Ramsden.*

PULLOVER 5 ch.m. Windjammer (USA)–Woolcana 71 (Some Hand 119) [1989 5g **37**
6d 6.1f 6f 7f⁶ 7.5m 7f 1990 8m 8f 7f⁴ 7m⁴ 8g] strong, workmanlike mare: carries
plenty of condition: moderate mover: poor handicapper: stays 7f: possibly needs a
sound surface: inconsistent: sold 1,200 gns Doncaster August Sales: resold 2,200
gns Ascot November Sales. *J. C. McConnochie.*

PULPIT ROCK 3 ch.f. Lomond (USA) 128–Piney Ridge 116 (Native Prince) **56**
[1989 5m⁶ 1990 7g⁴ 6g⁶] lengthy, workmanlike filly: easily best effort in the summer, showing plating-class form, when fourth in maiden at Wolverhampton: best
effort over 7f: sold 1,900 gns Newmarket December Sales. *R. F. Johnson Houghton.*

PULSINGH 8 br.h. Mansingh (USA) 120–Pulcini 61 (Quartette 106) [1989 12m⁶ **38**
12f* 12f⁶ 11.7d 12m⁴ 12.2m 12fa12g 1990 11.7g 11.5m⁵ 12f 11.5m² 11.5g⁴ 12f⁴] strong,
good-topped horse: carries plenty of condition: poor handicapper: suited by around
1½m: acts on firm going and probably unsuited by soft: always behind in blinkers. *C.
J. Benstead.*

PUMPKIN 3 b.f. Top Ville 129–Bumpkin 108 (Free State 125) [1989 7g 1990 8m **64**
8.5d 8f⁴ 10g⁴ 10.2f* 10h³ 10g 10.2f 10m⁶ 8m a10g⁴ a10g] leggy, angular filly: quite
modest handicapper: won moderately-run race at Doncaster in July: easily best subsequent efforts when in frame: worth a try over 1½m: acts on hard going: visored
final start. *T. Thomson Jones.*

PUNCH N'RUN 2 b.c. (Apr 15) Forzando 122–Wrangbrook (Shirley Heights **101**
130) [1990 6m³ 6m³ 6f² 7f* 7g⁵ 6d² 6m* 6g* 6d³] 19,500Y: smallish colt: moderate
mover: first foal: useful performer: won maiden at Salisbury in July,
nursery at Ascot in September and 6-runner Dewhirst Rockingham Stakes (by 3½
lengths from Daki, running on strongly) at York in September: ran well after when
third of 19, keeping on, to Chipaya in Racecall Gold Trophy at Redcar: seems ideally
suited by 6f: acts on firm and dead ground: suited by forcing tactics: has tended to
hang: often on toes. *R. Hannon.*

PUNCH THE AIR 2 ch.f. (Mar 13) Northjet 136–Joyfully (FR) (Dilettante II 121) **—**
[1990 7m 8d] rather leggy, unfurnished filly: half-sister to several winners in
France, all over 1m +: dam French 9f winner: well beaten in maidens at Leicester in
October. *W. J. Haggas.*

PUNDLES PET 3 b.c. Petong 126–Goody Goody 84 (Mummy's Pet 125) [1989 —
5d 5f 5m* 5f² 5f⁵ 6g⁵ 5g 5v⁶ 1990 6f] good-quartered colt: moderate walker: won
seller at 2 yrs: behind in May claimer only start at 3 yrs: likely to prove best at 5f:
acts on any going: often blinkered: sometimes edgy and slowly away: doubtful
temperamentally: sold 600 gns Newmarket July Sales. *W. J. Pearce.*

PUPPET SHOW 6 b.g. Mummy's Pet 125–Contralto 100 (Busted 134) [1989 8g —
8f 1990 10.1g 8g 9g 8.3m] rather leggy, good-topped gelding: modest winner as
4-y-o: lightly raced and no subsequent worthwhile form, including in selling company: stays 1m: acts on hard going: has won when sweating. *S. T. Harris.*

PURE BLISS 3 b.f. Idiot's Delight 115–Julie Emma (Farm Walk 111) [1989 NR —
1990 7d 10s 12d] lengthy filly: fifth foal: dam, no worthwhile form on flat, later
winning selling hurdler: ridden by 7-lb claimer and backward, well beaten in late-
season maidens and minor event. *R. J. Hodges.*

PURE CLASS 3 ch.g. Habitat 134–On The Fringe (USA) 87 (Vaguely Noble 140) 68
[1989 NR 1990 8m 7g 7m4] 52,000Y: sturdy gelding: carries condition: fifth foal:
brother to useful 7.2f and 1m winner Edge of Town, a minor winner in USA and 1986
2-y-o 5f- and 6f-placed Nabras: dam placed from 7f to 1¼m on all 3 starts at 3 yrs, is
half-sister to high-class Ribofilio: progressive form in maidens in the spring: subsequently gelded. *B. W. Hills.*

PURE GREEN (USA) 3 ch.f. Green Forest (USA) 134–Malakya (Artaius (USA) 75
129) [1989 NR 1990 6f3dis 6f² 7m3dis 6m4dis 5m2dis 5f⁶ 5.1m* 5d⁶ 5m] strong,
lengthy filly: fourth foal: dam French 2-y-o 1¼m winner: modest performer:
apprentice ridden, won handicap at Yarmouth in September: pulls hard, and best at
sprint distances: acts on good to firm ground and dead: blinkered (ran creditably)
final start: didn't wear tongue strap on last 5: difficult ride who has swerved right
and hangs: disqualified third to fifth starts after positive tests for steroids. *M.
Moubarak.*

PURE PRIMULA 2 b.g. (Feb 22) Say Primula 107–Miss Primula 81 (Dominion —
123) [1990 6g 6m 6g 7m 7f 8.2s 7f] compact gelding: first foal: dam sprinter: seems of
little account: blinkered fourth outing: sold 800 gns Doncaster October Sales. *W.
Bentley.*

PURSUIT 3 ch.f. Posse (USA) 130–St Louis Sue (FR) 79 (Nonoalco (USA) 131) —
[1989 NR 1990 8m 7f⁶ 10g⁵] leggy, angular filly: fifth foal: half-sister to very useful
sprinter Whippet (by Sparkler): dam stayed 1¼m: no sign of ability in maidens then
minor event. *C. A. Austin.*

PUSEY STREET BOY 3 ch.c. Vaigly Great 127–Pusey Street 96 (Native 74
Bazaar 122) [1989 7f⁴ 7m² 7g 1990 8d 8m⁴ 7m* 8.2s⁵ 7f⁶ 8f 7f a7g a7g] leggy,
lengthy, dipped-backed colt: modest handicapper: won at Sandown in May: easily
best subsequent effort when fifth at Haydock: needs strong pace over 7f, and stays
1m: acts on any going. *R. Hannon.*

PUSSY FOOT 4 b.f. Red Sunset 120–Cats 85 (Dance In Time (CAN)) [1989 6v² 72
6s⁴ 6f² 5m* 5.3h² 5g* 6m⁴ 5.3f* 5d 1990 5m 5g³ 5m⁴ 5m⁵ 5m⁴ 5f² 5f³ 5f 5.3f² 5d]
strong, workmanlike filly: modest handicapper: suited by 5f and a sound surface:
blinkered sixth and last 2 starts: sometimes edgy. *Sir Mark Prescott.*

PYTCHLEY NIGHT 3 b.c. Red Sunset 120–Lili Bengam (Welsh Saint 126) 81
[1989 6m² 6m³ 1990 8f⁶ 8f² 7.6d⁶ 7g 8f² 7d 8f 8m 9g a8g*] lengthy, quite
good-topped colt: 20/1, won 18-runner handicap at Southwell in December: should
prove as effective over 7f as 1m: acts on firm going, probably unsuited by dead: keen
sort. *D. Morris.*

Q

QANNAAS 6 br.g. Kris 135–Red Berry 115 (Great Nephew 126) [1989 12g⁴ 1990 —
12m⁵] strong, sturdy horse: fair handicapper at best: stays 1¾m: acts on any going:
blinkered only start at 6 yrs: has sweated and got on toes: races up with pace:
consistent: had fine season over hurdles in 1989/90, and won novice chase in November. *Mrs D. Haine.*

QASWARAH 3 b.f. Commanche Run 133–Donna Sabina (Nonoalco (USA) 131) —
[1989 7m⁶ 7f³ 1990 10g 10f⁶] close-coupled, angular filly: modest maiden: ran poorly
in summer as 3-y-o, in handicap final start: bred to stay 1m + : sold 1,400 gns
Newmarket December Sales. *A. C. Stewart.*

QATHIF (USA) 3 b.c. Riverman (USA) 131–Al Bayan (USA) 82 (Northern 93
Dancer) [1989 6g* 8g³ 1990 7m 6m 6f² 6m] robust, deep-girthed, attractive colt:
good mover: useful as 2-y-o, winning minor event at Ascot and third in Racing Post
Trophy (found little) at Newcastle: easily best effort in 1990 when second of 4 in
minor event at Thirsk in July, making most: best form at 1m: sold A. Falourd 28,000
gns Newmarket Autumn Sales. *H. Thomson Jones.*

Q-EIGHT (IRE) 2 b.c. (Apr 13) Vision (USA)–Warning Sound (Red Alert 127) — p
[1990 6d] IR 55,000Y: third foal: half-brother to Irish 1¼m winner Second Guess (by
Ela-Mana-Mou) and 3-y-o Remthat Naser (by Sharpo), winner at 5f (at 2 yrs) and
1m: dam Irish 5f to 1¼m winner: backward, around 17 lengths seventh of 21, running
on steadily from halfway, in maiden at Doncaster in November: should improve. *G.
A. Huffer.*

QIRMAZI (USA) 3 ch.f. Riverman (USA) 131–Cream'N Crimson (USA) 113
(Vaguely Noble 140) [1989 6g* 6d* 6g² 7g² 8g⁵ 1990 7m⁵ 9.2d* 10g³ 8d 8g] close-
coupled, attractive filly: has a round action: very useful 2-y-o: comfortably won
Group 3 Prix Vanteaux at Longchamp in April: creditable third of 9 to Air de Rien in
Prix Saint-Alary there 3 weeks later, best subsequent effort: stayed 1¼m: acted on
dead ground: very useful: stud. *A. Fabre, France.*

QISMAT 3 b.g. Doulab (USA) 115–Borshch (Bonne Noel 115) [1989 5d 1990 7m —
7m⁶] leggy gelding: sixth of 14 at Sandown in June, only sign of ability in maidens:
dead. *R. Guest.*

QUAGLINO (USA) 2 b.c. (Mar 30) Robellino (USA) 127–Affair 78 (Bold Lad 85
(IRE) 133) [1990 5f³ 7f* 7g 8.2g⁴ 8g² 6g⁵] workmanlike, good-topped colt: quite
good mover: third foal: half-brother to fair 1989 1½m winner Scandal (by Blood
Royal): dam, 2-y-o 6f winner who showed little subsequently, is daughter of useful
7f and 9f winner Guest Night: fair performer: won maiden at Wolverhampton in July
by 8 lengths from Marching Past: ran well in listed event (never able to challenge)
won by Punch N'Run at York final start: stays 1m: consistent. *P. T. Walwyn.*

QUALITAIR AVIATOR 4 b.g. Valiyar 129–Comtec Princess 73 (Gulf Pearl 79
117) [1989 12g⁶ 11f 12m* 16.2g⁴ 12.4m 12g⁴ 12.3m³ 12f⁵ 14m 14m 12s⁶ a14g* a11g*
a14g 1990 a13g* a12g² a16g³ a14g* 12f 12.3d 14g⁵ a14g a16g² a14g⁶] close-coupled,
workmanlike gelding: moderate mover: made all or virtually all to win 4 handicaps
on all-weather, last of them at Southwell in March: returned to form penultimate
outing: stays 2m: probably unsuited by firm going: often takes keen hold: suited by
forcing tactics. *J. F. Bottomley.*

QUALITAIR BLAZER 3 ch.f. Blazing Saddles (AUS)–Midfirna (Midsummer 39
Night II 117) [1989 5s 5g² 6m⁶ 6g 8g 1990 7g 7g 10g 10f⁵] compact filly: poor
maiden: may well stay beyond 1¼m: looked unenthusiastic second start. *J. F.
Bottomley.*

QUALITAIR CHOICE (IRE) 2 b.f. (Apr 23) Stalker 121–Ardrums (Native —
Prince) [1990 7f a7g⁴] 3,000F, 4,000Y: neat filly: half-sister to many winners,
including 5f to 7f winner Embroideress (by Stanford) and 7f and 1¼m winner Mugh-
tanim (by Red Sunset): dam 2-y-o 5f winner in Ireland: one-paced fourth of 15 in
seller at Southwell in August. *J. F. Bottomley.*

QUALITAIR DREAM 3 b.f. Dreams To Reality (USA) 113–Maputo Princess 73
(Raga Navarro (ITY) 119) [1989 5g⁴ 5f⁶ 7g⁴ 7m² 6g* 6d² 6g* 6m 7d 1990 6g⁵ 6m 6m
7m² 8₁₁ 8m 7.2g 7d 6d 6m 6d 7d³ 9g] small, workmanlike, good-quartered filly: has a
round action: modest handicapper, but somewhat inconsistent: ran well when third
in £9,600 contest (battling on under very strong pressure) at Redcar, moderately in
£19,600 contest at Newmarket 4 days later: needs testing conditions at 6f, and stays
1m: acts on good to firm ground and dead. *J. F. Bottomley.*

QUALITAIR DUTCHESS 5 br.m. Enchantment 115–Conte Bleu (Jan Ekels —
122) [1989 NR 1990 a12g 10m 13.8m a12g 13.8m 15.3g] small, strong mare: carries
plenty of condition: no longer of much account: often blinkered. *J. F. Bottomley.*

QUALITAIR FIGHTER 3 ch.g. Hard Fought 125–Venus of Stretham 107 —
(Tower Walk 130) [1989 NR 1990 8.2g 10.6s 9g a12g a12g] IR 3,000F, 6,400Y:
half-brother to a winner abroad by Busted: dam won 10 races at up to 1¼m, 7 of them
at 2 yrs: of no account on flat: winning selling hurdler. *J. F. Bottomley.*

QUALITAIR MELODY 2 b.g. (Mar 21) Bairn (USA) 126–Melody Park 104 —
(Music Boy 124) [1990 5f 5f 7f a6g⁵ a7g⁵ a7g 8.5m] 9,200Y: sturdy gelding: first foal:
dam sprinter: poor maiden: blinkered penultimate outing: sold 720 gns Doncaster
October Sales. *J. F. Bottomley.*

QUALITAIR PROMISE 2 ch.f. (Mar 29) Reach 122–Maputo Princess (Raga —
Navarro (ITY) 119) [1990 6g a7g 6g 8m] 5,000Y: angular filly: has a round action:

fourth foal: half-sister to 3-y-o Qualitair Dream (by Dreams To Reality), fair 6f winner at 2 yrs, and platers by Wattlefield and Rabdan: dam behind in varied company: little worthwhile form, including in sellers. *J. F. Bottomley.*

QUALITAIR REALITY   2 b.f. (Apr 7) Dreams To Reality (USA) 113–Blushing Nurse (Saritamer (USA) 130) [1990 6g⁵] 6,200Y: second foal: dam of little account: around 10 lengths fifth of 11 in maiden auction at Hamilton in May. *J. F. Bottomley.*   —

QUALITAIR SONG   2 b.f. (Feb 16) Song 132–Hellene (Dominion 123) [1990 6m 6m 6m 5v] 9,000Y: quite good-topped filly: good walker: second live foal: sister to 6f winner Sideloader Special: dam never ran: little worthwhile form in sellers and a maiden: has twice led to 2f out on unfavoured part of track. *J. F. Bottomley.*   —

QUALITAIR SOUND (IRE)   2 b.c. (Apr 6) Mazaad 106–A Nice Alert (Red Alert 127) [1990 8.2m⁴ 8m 6v² 8d 7s] IR 3,000F, IR 7,000Y, resold 3,400Y: workmanlike colt: has plenty of scope: has a round action: third living foal: dam never ran: modest performer: best short of 1m: best efforts on a soft surface. *J. F. Bottomley.*   73

QUALITAIR SUPREME   3 ch.f. Exhibitioner 111–Glendalough (USA) (High Finance) [1989 NR 1990 7m⁵ 8.2g 10.6s] IR 3,000Y: workmanlike filly: eighth foal: half-sister to 1988 2-y-o 1m seller winner Dewdrop (by Viking) and 1987 2-y-o 5.8f winner What A Challenge (by Sallust): dam won over 9f and 9.5f at 3 yrs in Ireland: no worthwhile form in minor event, claimer and maiden in first half of season. *J. F. Bottomley.*   —

QUALITAIR SWEETIE   3 ch.g. Sweet Monday 122–Right Abella 74 (Right Boy 137) [1989 6m 7m⁶ 8m 1990 11g 12m* 12.4m 13g² 12m 12d 13d 13.6d a12g] workmanlike gelding: quite modest handicapper: sweating, led post at Pontefract in June: creditable second at Ayr, clearly best subsequent effort: should stay 1¾m: acts on good to firm going: blinkered seventh and eighth starts. *J. F. Bottomley.*   59 d

QUATRE FEMME   3 b.f. Petorius 117–Irish Kick (Windjammer (USA)) [1989 NR 1990 5m² 6g² 6f* 6s 6m] IR 10,000Y: leggy, angular filly: fifth foal: closely related to smart 4-y-o 6f winner Sharp N' Early (by Runnett) and half-sister to fair 1985 2-y-o 5f winner St Croins Castle (by Godswalk) and 6f and 7f winner Irish Cookie (by Try My Best): dam never ran: modest performer: won maiden at Chepstow in September: soon struggling in minor event then always behind in £8,400 handicap: will stay 7f: acts on firm going. *M. Johnston.*   76

QUAVERING   3 b.c. The Minstrel (CAN) 135–Flicker Toa Flame (USA) 85 (Empery (USA) 128) [1989 7m 7g³ 1990 8g*] good-bodied colt: second favourite, won 19-runner maiden at Yarmouth in June: rather headstrong, and wears a crossed noseband: should have improved again. *J. Gosden.*   98

QUEEN ANGEL   4 b.f. Anfield 117–More Or Less 64 (Morston (FR) 125) [1989 10.2m⁶ 11.7m* 11.1f* 12m³ 1990 11m] lengthy, good-bodied filly: moderate mover: fair winner in spring as 3-y-o: 33/1, tailed off in £7,900 handicap at Newbury in May: stays 1½m: acts on firm going. *Miss B. Sanders.*   —

QUEEN OF DREAMS   2 ch.f. (Feb 26) Ti King (FR) 124–Humeur de Reve (USA) (Lord Avie (USA)) [1990 a8g⁶ a8g² a8g⁴] 1,000 2-y-o: first foal: dam ran once: ½-length second of 11, keeping on, to Toshiba Comet Too in late-year maiden at Lingfield, easily best effort: will be suited by 1¼m. *Dr J. D. Scargill.*   58

QUEEN OF INDIA (USA)   2 gr.f. (Mar 20) Chief's Crown (USA)–Queen of Luck (USA) (Drone) [1990 7m 8d⁴] $200,000Y: angular, rather plain filly: second reported foal: dam minor winner at 2 yrs, is half-sister to 6f to 1½m winner Fit To Fight: quite modest form in maiden at Goodwood and similar event at Edinburgh: will stay 1¼m: sure to improve. *J. H. M. Gosden.*   63 p

QUEEN OF SHANNON (IRE)   2 b.f. (May 10) Nordico (USA)–Raj Kumari (Vitiges (FR) 132) [1990 6m 6g²] leggy, angular filly: first foal: dam poor form in 3 races: 1½ lengths second of 17, pulling hard early then keeping on well, to West Riding in maiden at Newbury in October. *C. A. Horgan.*   74

QUEEN OF THE CLUB   3 ch.f. King of Clubs 124–Goosalley (Run The Gantlet (USA)) [1989 5v⁵ 5s² 5f* 5g 1990 a7g 8m] IR 26,000Y: small filly: third foal: half-sister to an Italian 1m winner by Home Guard: dam, French 1¼m winner, is half-sister to very smart stayer El Badr: won maiden at Mallow in May at 2 yrs: well beaten in claimers here in March, 1990: bred to stay much further than 5f: blinkered last 2 starts at 2 yrs when trained by D. K. Weld. *R. Akehurst.*   —

QUEENS COURIER   4 ch.f. Sayf El Arab (USA) 127–Veneziana 91 (Tiger 125) [1989 NR 1990 a7g] rather leggy, good-quartered filly: little show in maidens. *J. Balding.*   —

QUEENS TOUR 5 b.h. Sweet Monday 122–On Tour 60 (Queen's Hussar 124) **58**
[1989 10d* 12v 10g⁵ 12s 12f 10.6d a10g⁵ 10g 1990 10g 12g⁴ 12m 12g⁶ 12g⁵ 12d⁶]
small, lightly-made horse: poor walker and mover: fair handicapper at one time: well
below his best in first half of 1990: should stay 1¾m: best with give in the ground:
bandaged first 2 starts: suitable mount for apprentice. *M. Brittain.*

QUELUZ (USA) 2 b.f. (Feb 13) Saratoga Six (USA)–Mariella (USA) 106 (Roberto **59**
(USA) 131) [1990 6d 7f² 7m] workmanlike filly: second foal: half-sister to 3-y-o
Ballet Russe (by Nijinsky): dam middle-distance winner, is daughter of Monade:
quite modest maiden: will probably be better suited by 1m. *M. R. Stoute.*

QUESSARD 6 ch.g. Ardross 134–Marquessa d'Howfen 93 (Pitcairn 126) [1989 **—**
12d⁵ 16g 17.6f⁴ 15g 17f 15g² 1990 a16g a14g] strong, lengthy gelding: has shown
traces of stringhalt: powerful galloper with a round action: fair maiden at best, but
has deteriorated considerably: stays 15f: best with give in the ground: visored once
at 4 yrs. *F. H. Lee.*

QUEST FOR FAME 3 b.c. Rainbow Quest (USA) 134–Aryenne (FR) 125 **127**
(Green Dancer (USA) 132) [1989 8v² 1990 11d* 12.3d² 12g* 12g5]
The Derby clings to its title of the 'world's premier flat race'. It is
probably still the race most owners want to win and provides entertainment —
around twenty million pounds is wagered annually on the result — on a scale
that no other flat race in Britain approaches. But the race owes its world-wide
status nowadays to its glorious tradition. Although the Ever Ready Derby is
by some way the richest undistorted prize in British racing — the winner
earned a record £355,000 in 1990 — it barely scrapes into the world's most
valuable twenty races. The first prize for the Ciga Prix de l'Arc de
Triomphe — £496,525 in 1990 — exceeds that for the Derby among European
races but monetary rewards are even greater in North America, Japan and
Australia, whose races dominate the world's top twenty. The Breeders' Cup
Classic was worth the equivalent of £692,308 in 1990, making it the world's
richest race, while the Japan Cup carried a first prize equivalent to £572,000
and the Melbourne Cup £539,352.
In guaranteeing total minimum prize money for the latest Derby of
£600,000, the owners of Epsom made an expensive misjudgement. Added
money for the Derby was originally £250,000, made up of contributions from
the race-sponsors Ever Ready, United Racecourses and the Levy Board, but
the £262,560 contribution from owners in entry and declaration fees fell short
of that expected, leaving a deficit of £87,444 to be made up by United
Racecourses. The reason for the short-fall was that only one hundred and
twenty-six horses were entered by the time the Derby closed on February
28th. The initial entry fee for the Derby has remained unchanged at £1,320 for
the past four years but the total cost to run — there's a forfeit stage in late-May
(a further £2,500) and a confirmation of entry five days before the race
(£1,180) — has more than doubled in the period and the number of entries has
fallen each year (there were two hundred and eight in 1987). The initial entry
stage for the Derby has been closer to the race — little more than three
months before — than for nearly all other big races in Europe and has worked
well enough without the supplementary entry stage used for races such as the
Irish Derby and the Prix de l'Arc. The three-month deadline has been late
enough to ensure that virtually all the best available talent has been entered
for the Derby (the British-trained winners of the two latest editions of the
Prix du Jockey-Club, Old Vic and Sanglamore, were also entered for Epsom
and ran at Chantilly for preference). Starting with the 1993 edition, however,
the Derby will revert to having a yearling entry stage which is expected to
help to boost the total value of the race to £750,000. Nominations will be
made, at a cost of £200, in December 1991. The first forfeit, costing £800, will
not be until early-March in the year of running, and will be followed by a final
forfeit, costing £2,500, in May 1993 and a confirmation to run, of £1,500, on the
Friday before the race. There will be an option of a second entry, costing
£10,000, in early-March 1993. The total cost of running a horse entered as a
yearling will therefore be £5,000 (the same as in 1990); it will cost £14,000 for
a horse put in as a three-year-old. The system differs significantly from the
much more ambitious proposal put forward to the Jockey Club, with the
support of the Horseracing Advisory Council, by United Racecourses who

wanted to introduce a yearling entry stage in April 1991 (£250), followed by two further confirmation stages in April 1992 (£250) and April 1993 (£1,000) before the forfeit stage in May (£2,500) and the five-day confirmation of entry (£1,000)—still making a total of £5,000 to run, as at present. There would have been an option of a £100,000 supplementary entry five days before the Derby's traditional running on the first Wednesday in June (though there's talk of switching the race to a Saturday from 1993 or 1994). The April deadline favoured by Epsom was timed to allow yearlings to be advertised in sales catalogues as being entered for the Ever Ready Derby, providing publicity for the race and its sponsors as well as theoretically making the yearlings themselves more commercially attractive (though no yearling purchased in Britain or Ireland has gone on to win the Derby since Grundy in 1975, and only four sold as yearlings at public auction—all of them purchased in Kentucky—have been successful since). A breeders' prize of £50,000 was to have been provided for the 1993 Derby, for yearling entrants only. Based on estimates of around 1,600 yearling entrants, Epsom would have been able to guarantee total minimum prize money of £1,000,000, with the winner receiving at least £600,000, putting the Derby once again in the forefront of the world's richest races. Supplementary entries, which weren't taken into account in Epsom's calculations, could have made a sizeable contribution to the prize-money pool—there were three supplementary entries at IR £60,000 each for the 1990 Budweiser Irish Derby—as well as providing a way in for good horses that for one reason or another were not originally entered. The effects of late supplementary entries on the ante-post market on the Derby—which starts the previous autumn, continues to take shape over the winter and gathers pace once the new season opens—has always been a contentious issue and is said to have figured in the Jockey Club's deliberations (though they were

Ever Ready Derby, Epsom—
rounding Tattenham Corner Quest For Fame (second left) is ideally placed,
up with Treble Eight (rails), Elmaamul (striped cap), River God and Missionary Ridge (left);
Blue Stag has only four behind him, tucked in towards the inside
behind Kaheel (epaulets, blaze)

Ever Ready Derby, Epsom—the finish.
Quest For Fame has three lengths to spare over Blue Stag;
Elmaamul comes third, Kaheel fourth and Karinga Bay (centre track) fifth

almost certainly more strongly influenced by views about Epsom's proposal received on behalf of breeders and trainers). The Irish Derby and the Prix de l'Arc were both won in the latest season by supplementary entries—Salsabil and Saumarez.

It's difficult to envisage that a provision for eleventh-hour supplementary entries could have added much, if anything, to the confusion in the latest Derby ante-post market. The phrase 'survival of the fittest' took on a literal meaning as prominent fancy after prominent fancy fell by the wayside in the weeks leading up to the race, resulting in the most volatile Derby ante-post market in memory. William Hill's Derby betting a month before the race had the Royal Lodge winner Digression (who had still to reappear as a three-year-old) as favourite at 7/1, followed by the Chester Vase winner Belmez at 8/1, the Guineas third Anshan at 14/1, then—all on 16/1—the one-time ante-post favourite Be My Chief, the Guardian Classic Trial winner Defensive Play, the Poule d'Essai des Poulains winner Linamix, Nashwan's half-brother Mukddaam, the Chester Vase runner-up Quest For Fame, Belmez's stable-companion Shavian, and the Poulains runner-up Zoman. Rock Hopper (20/1) and Duke of Paducah and Elmaamul (both 25/1) completed the list of those quoted. A number of horses had already dropped out of the Derby picture after being prominent in the betting, chiefly among them the one-time first or second favourites Bleu de France (who began the season as the principal French-trained hope for the race) and Sasaki. Betting on the Derby was unusually light in the period leading up to the event—'the market is weaker than canteen coffee' said a Hill's spokesman—and by the time Digression reappeared, in the last of the recognised trials, the listed NM Financial Predominate Stakes, he had shortened to 7/2. No other Derby hope had captured the imagination sufficiently to displace him as favourite. Shavian and another possible Derby hope for Warren Place stables, Razeen, opposed Digression at Goodwood, as did the Two Thousand Guineas fifth Elmaamul. Digression's Derby odds were back out to 16/1 after his fifth-of-six placing in the Predominate which the improving Razeen won by four lengths from Elmaamul to promote himself to joint favouritism with William Hill for the Derby at 4/1, to which odds Rock Hopper (winner of the Calor Derby Trial at Lingfield) was also shortened. Already out of the reckoning by this stage were Belmez (tendon injury), Anshan, Be My Chief, Defensive Play (ringworm) and Mukddaam (bruised foot). These were joined soon afterwards by Rock Hopper who was withdrawn after lameness interrupted the final stages of his Derby preparation.

Of the top ten in the ante-post betting a month before the Derby, only Digression (out to 14/1 on the day), Linamix (11/2 second favourite), Zoman (third favourite at 6/1) and Quest For Fame (7/1) were in the eventual line-up. Razeen was favourite at 9/2 in a field which contained some moderate horses by Derby standards, seven of the eighteen runners starting at 50/1 or longer. The first eleven in the betting had collectively won twenty-one of their

721

thirty-eight starts but, Linamix and Digression apart, none had been successful in a pattern race. Most had been very lightly raced at two; Razeen wasn't
raced at that age at all because of a respiratory problem and didn't see a
racecourse until a little over six weeks before the Derby. Digression, Linamix
and Karinga Bay (runner-up in the William Hill Dante and a 14/1-shot for the
Derby) were the only prominent Derby hopes that had even contested a
pattern race in their first season. Zoman had won a Chepstow maiden event on
his only start; Blue Stag (8/1 for the Derby on the strength of a defeat of
Saumarez in the Dee Stakes at Chester) had won a maiden at Nottingham over
a mile and a quarter on the second of only two starts; Elmaamul (10/1) had won
on both his starts, looking a good horse in the making; and Duke of Paducah
(14/1) had won his only race, the Philip Cornes Houghton Stakes at Newmarket. Quest For Fame had ended his first season a maiden after finishing
second in a big field at Newbury in October. He won a maiden at the same
course on his return in April, prior to coming a length second in the three-
runner Dalham Chester Vase, and was one of five of his owner's horses among
the thirty left in the Derby at the May forfeit stage, along with Digression,
Defensive Play, Aromatic (who was started at Epsom as a pacemaker for
Quest For Fame and Digression) and the William Hill Dante winner Sanglamore. Quest For Fame was announced as Mr Abdulla's 'main hope' for the
Derby by the owner's racing manager soon afterwards, though Sanglamore—
considered by connections of roughly equal merit to Quest For Fame—
remained a possible runner until the week before the race when he was
switched to the Prix du Jockey-Club, run on the Sunday before Epsom.
Sanglamore's victory set up the prospect of a notable Chantilly-Epsom Derby
double for his owner, trainer and jockey, last achieved thirty-seven years
earlier when Scratch II and Galcador were successful in the Boussac colours
for trainer Semblat and jockey Johnstone.

The rangy, good-looking Quest For Fame was one of several to take the
eye in the paddock and the parade before the Derby—Razeen, Zoman and
Elmaamul were others who looked tremendously well—and he went on to
gain a decisive victory. Aromatic missed the break and the headstrong Treble
Eight, who had come fourth in the Derby Italiano, made most of the running.
Quest For Fame was close up throughout and quickened in good style when
given the office about two furlongs out, depriving the fading Treble Eight of
the lead well over a furlong out and never looking likely to be caught. Eddery
kept Quest For Fame up to his work as he drew away for a three-length win
from the late-challenging Blue Stag (the fourth Derby runner-up saddled by
trainer Hills), with Elmaamul a length and a half away in third after being
prominent all the way; the maiden Kaheel came fourth, followed by Karinga
Bay, Duke of Paducah, Zoman (who found the trip too far) and Treble Eight.
Linamix and Digression failed to run anywhere near their best though both
finished in front of Razeen who beat only four home after seeming to be
travelling comfortably coming down the hill.

Pat Eddery described Quest For Fame as 'the easiest of my Derby
winners' (he also won on Grundy and Golden Fleece). Eddery's understandable enthusiasm for Quest For Fame—'he quickened up the hill like only a
good horse can'—had to be tempered by the near-certainty that the Derby
field he had beaten was substandard, an impression confirmed when only six
of the runners managed to win a race of any kind on the flat during the rest of
the season. Only Karinga Bay, successful in the Gordon Stakes at Goodwood,
went on to pattern-race success over the Derby trip; Linamix and Elmaamul,
the best horses in the Derby field along with the winner, were both put back to
shorter distances and confirmed themselves high-class performers, as did
Zoman, put back to a mile. But Blue Stag and Kaheel were among those beaten
in their subsequent races. Blue Stag and Kaheel ran next in the Budweiser
Irish Derby at the Curragh in July when Quest For Fame started 5/4 favourite
in a line-up which also included the One Thousand Guineas and Oaks winner
Salsabil and the now-recovered Belmez. Quest For Fame's owner invested IR
£120,000 in an attempt to win the Irish Derby, supplementing both Quest For
Fame and his stable-companion Deploy. Deploy did the better of the pair,
going down by three quarters of a length to Salsabil, with Quest For Fame
only fifth, separated from his stable-companion by Belmez and Blue Stag, and

beaten over five lengths by the winner. Quest For Fame was lame on his return from Ireland and spent the rest of the season on the side-lines recovering from an injury to his near-fore. The injury took longer than expected to respond to treatment but it was confirmed in November that Quest For Fame stays in training as a four-year-old. He had looked just the lightly-raced, progressive type to train on after winning the Derby, having shown improved form on each of his four outings, and it is good news that he is to have the chance to realize his potential. For the present, however, judged strictly on what he achieved at Epsom, he has been rated well below par for a Derby winner. In five races, incidentally, he has not yet encountered top-of-the-ground conditions.

The triumphs of Quest For Fame and Sanglamore—who also sadly missed the second half of the season—were among the highlights of a brilliant season for Pat Eddery who won the jockeys' championship in Britain for the eighth time. Eddery became only the fourth jockey in British flat-racing history to ride two hundred winners or more in a season, ending with a score of two hundred and nine. Fred Archer, Tommy Loates and Gordon Richards are the only others to have achieved the feat, Richards achieving it for a record twelfth time in 1952, the year Eddery was born. The British record of two hundred and sixty-nine winners, set in 1947, also stands to Richards. Eddery is a naturally gifted horseman and a fine jockey, particularly strong and determined in a finish. Driving ambition and an appetite for hard work are other attributes of Eddery's make-up: he usually rides at two meetings a day when evening fixtures supplement the racing programme during the summer and seldom turns down a ride, adopting the philosophy that 'I can't ride winners sitting in the weighing room'. Eddery's schedule also includes numerous overseas assignments, mainly for his retainer Mr Abdulla. Prince Khalid Abdulla does not use his royal title—he is a member of the ruling family of Saudi Arabia—and shuns publicity. He has spent millions building up a racing empire on the scale of those controlled by members of the Al-Maktoum family and by the Aga Khan. He has been runner-up three times in the list of leading owners in Britain and has never slipped below fourth in the past seven seasons. The classic victories of Quest For Fame and Sanglamore helped to give their trainer Roger Charlton a magnificent start in his first season in charge at Beckhampton stables after serving twelve years as assistant to Jeremy Tree. Tree, who retired at the end of 1989, and Guy Harwood provided Mr Abdulla with most of his major victories in the 'eighties, including those of Quest For Fame's sire Rainbow Quest (saddled by Tree) and of the best horse to carry the green, pink and white Abdulla colours Dancing Brave (Harwood).

Quest For Fame (b.c. 1987)	Rainbow Quest (USA) (b 1981)	Blushing Groom (ch 1974)	Red God
			Runaway Bride
		I Will Follow (b 1975)	Herbager
			Where You Lead
	Aryenne (FR) (br 1977)	Green Dancer (b 1972)	Nijinsky
			Green Valley
		Americaine (ch 1968)	Cambremont
			Alora II

Quest For Fame, the Grand Prix de Paris and Prix de l'Arc winner Saumarez and the Irish Oaks winner Knight's Baroness were all members of Rainbow Quest's first crop. Rainbow Quest showed top-class form at two, three and four, finishing second in the Dewhurst, in the frame in three classics and then crowning a fine career with victories in the Coronation Cup and the Prix de l'Arc de Triomphe (on a disqualification) in his third season. Rainbow Quest also had good looks and an excellent pedigree to recommend him to breeders. His owner didn't syndicate him and priced nominations at a very reasonable £25,000. Rainbow Quest attracted a wide range of high-class mares and proved excellent value; only three of the thirty-three yearlings sold at auction in his first two years made less than the covering fee. Rainbow Quest stands at the Banstead Manor Stud at Newmarket where he is advertised at a fee of £20,000 plus £20,000 (Oct 1st) for 1991. Quest For Fame's dam Aryenne was acquired by Mr Abdulla after her racing days were over. She won Group 1 races at two and three, the Criterium des Pouliches

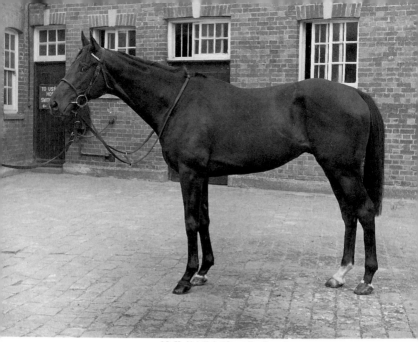

Mr K. Abdulla's "Quest For Fame"

(now the Prix Marcel Boussac) and the Poule d'Essai des Pouliches (French Guineas); she was a genuine and consistent racehorse—she just came off worst in a memorable battle with Mrs Penny for the Prix de Diane—and had an excellent turn of foot. Aryenne produced two colts to Habitat before being sent to Rainbow Quest: Vestris, a lightly-raced maiden on the flat who has subsequently shown no sign of ability over hurdles after changing hands for only 880 guineas at the end of his three-year-old days; and In Orbit who won for the first time in July, in a handicap over a mile and a quarter at Beverley (like Vestris, In Orbit began his racing career with Harwood and was sold cheaply—fetching 4,100 guineas—at the Newmarket Autumn Sales as a three-year-old). Aryenne's fourth foal Silver Rainbow, a brother to Quest For Fame, was in training with Harwood in the latest season but wasn't seen out; her fifth foal, a filly by Kris, unnamed at the time of writing, will be in training with Charlton in 1991. Aryenne is a half-sister to the very useful racemare Apachee (by Sir Gaylord), the dam of the Gran Premio del Jockey Club winner Antheus and the very useful Alexandrie who started favourite for the Oaks in Sun Princess' year (Alexandrie's first foal Animatrice came third in the 1988 Oaks). Americaine, the dam of Aryenne and Apachee as well as of the unraced Ameridienne (dam of Lady Winner), was a winning half-sister to the Poule d'Essai des Poulains winner Adamastor. More distantly, this is also the family of the outstanding racemare Roseliere, winner of the Prix de Diane and Prix Vermeille and the dam of the Champion Stakes and dual Queen Elizabeth II Stakes winner Rose Bowl and the King George VI Stakes winner Ile de Bourbon, sire of the 1988 Derby winner Kahyasi. *R. Charlton.*

QUESTIONING (USA) 3 b.f. Miswaki (USA) 124–Ask Me How (USA) ?
(Secretariat (USA)) [1989 NR 1990 7m] $100,000Y: robust, quite attractive filly:
third foal: half-sister to a winner in North America by Sovereign Dancer: dam
successful at up to 7f at 3 yrs and 4 yrs: weak favourite, seventh of 11 in maiden at
Goodwood in May: sent to G. Jones in California, successful at Del Mar in August. *J.
Gosden.*

QUESTION OF HONOR 2 b.c. (Apr 7) Legend of France (USA) 124–Snow 55
Goose (Santa Claus 133) [1990 7m5 7f3 7g 8m a8g] 1,250F: close-coupled, quite
attractive colt: half-brother to several winners, including quite useful 1983 2-y-o 7f
winner Scaldante (by Hotfoot) and quite modest middle-distance winner Obergurgl
(by Warpath): dam unraced: plating-class maiden: off course 2 months after finishing tailed off third start. *R. Hollinshead.*

QUICK PROFIT 3 b.f. Formidable (USA) 125–Penny Blessing 112 (So Blessed 78
130) [1989 5m 1990 6f4 6f2 7d 7.6g 7m* 8h2 8m4 7g 8f2 8g5 8m6] leggy filly: modest
performer: won maiden at Chepstow in July: stays 1m: acts on hard going, seems
unsuited by a soft surface: never going well in blinkers eighth start: sold 13,000 gns
Newmarket December Sales. *R. F. Johnson Houghton.*

QUICK RANSOM 2 ch.c. (May 4) Hostage (USA)–Run Amber Run (Run The 77
Gantlet (USA)) [1990 6g 6g a6g5 6g 8.2s 7s2 a8g4 a8g4 a8g2] 6,000Y: leggy colt:
half-brother to a winner in USA by Somethingfabulous: dam minor winner in USA, is
half-sister to Irish 2000 Guineas second Mr John: modest maiden: excellent second,
staying on well, in nurseries at Doncaster and Southwell: will be suited by a test of
stamina: acts well on soft ground. *M. Johnston.*

QUICK STEEL 2 b.c. (Apr 28) Alleging (USA) 120–Illiney Girl 66 (Lochnager 41
132) [1990 a6g 8d 6d] sparely-made colt: first foal: dam winning sprinter: poor form
in maidens: bandaged behind on debut. *T. P. McGovern.*

QUICK TEMPO 3 b.c. Shareef Dancer (USA) 135–Mineown 85 (Roan Rocket —
128) [1989 6m 5.8f4 6h3 1990 12m 11.5f 10d a8g] smallish, stocky colt: quite modest
maiden: well beaten in handicaps and claimers in 1990: should stay 1m: sold out of C.
Brittain's stable 8,000 gns Doncaster August Sales after second start. *C. Weedon.*

QUI DANZIG (USA) 3 b.c. Danzig (USA)–Qui Royalty (USA) (Native Royalty 108
(USA)) [1989 6m* 6f2 7g2 1990 7g4 7f3 8g5] rather leggy, quite attractive colt: has a
rather round action: useful performer: 11/1, best effort when about 2½ lengths third
of 15 to Sally Rous in Jersey Stakes at Royal Ascot: about 11 lengths behind
Septieme Ciel in Prix Messidor at Maisons-Laffitte over 3 weeks later, weakening
final 1f: seems suited by 7f: acts on firm going: keen sort. *M. R. Stoute.*

QUIET ACHIEVER (CAN) 5 ch.g. Overskate (CAN)–From Nine To Five —
(USA) (Secretariat (USA)) [1989 10.2g 8.5f6 10f6 10m 10m5 5f 8f* 1990 10g] rangy
gelding: has a round action: wearing tongue strap, showed improved form when
winning apprentice handicap at Pontefract in October, 1989: faced stiff task in
claimer year later: best at 1m: acts on firm going. *C. E. Brittain.*

QUIET PLEASE 2 b.f. (Jan 31) Kind of Hush 118–Woodfold 80 (Saritamer (USA) —
130) [1990 6g 6m] small filly: first reported living foal: dam sprinter: never able to
challenge in maiden (backward) at Kempton and claimer at Leicester in autumn. *W.
A. O'Gorman.*

QUIET RIOT 8 b.g. Hotfoot 126–Tuyenu 77 (Welsh Pageant 132) [1989 10.8s 49
10.2g 14m4 14f* 12m4 14.8m2 18.8f5 a13g 1990 10.1g6 11.7g 12m 12f* 8m 11.7f4]
strong, good-topped gelding: has a round action: bandaged and dropped in class, won
selling handicap (no bid) at Brighton in July: ran moderately final outing: stays 1¾m:
acts on any going: blinkered and visored once: good mount for apprentice. *J. White.*

QUINTA (IRE) 2 b.g. (Mar 28) Truculent (USA) 121–Feliscoa (FR) (Royal 45
Ascot) [1990 a7g 7g 8.2s a7g a8g a7g] 8,000Y: lengthy gelding: moderate walker:
fifth foal: half-brother to a winner in Spain: dam won in Spain: poor form, including in
sellers: blinkered final start. *M. W. Easterby.*

QUINTA ROYALE 3 b.g. Sayyaf 121–Royal Holly (Royal Buck) [1989 5f2 6g2 75 d
5g3 1990 7f* 8m6 8m 8.2m6 8m4 8d] strong, lengthy gelding: moderate mover:
modest performer: won handicap at Salisbury in May: below form after, including in
claimers last 3 starts: stays 1m: acts on firm going. *R. Akehurst.*

QUINTESSENTIAL 2 b.c. (Mar 25) Music Boy 124–Questa Notte 104 (Mid- 66
summer Night II 117) [1990 6d a6g2 a6g3] 8,800Y: workmanlike colt: has scope: has
a quick action: half-brother to several winners here and in Italy, including fair sprinter Quaver (by Song) and 5f winner Quilting (by Mummy's Pet): dam 6f performer: 2
lengths second of 9 to very easy winner Relentless Pursuit in maiden at Lingfield,
best effort: gives impression will be better suited by 7f + . *Sir Mark Prescott.*

QUINTO 4 b.g. Tumble Wind (USA)–Con Carni (Blakeney 126) [1989 8g 8f 10.1m —
10f² 12f³ 10f³ 9f⁶ 10f³ 10f³ 1990 10f 10m] close-coupled gelding: moderate walker
and mover: plater: bandaged, ran poorly in spring: probably stays 1½m: acts on firm
going: often blinkered or visored: takes good hold: has tended to hang. *Miss P. Hall.*

QUINZII MARTIN 2 b.c. (Apr 10) Song 132–Quaranta 83 (Hotfoot 126) [1990 **63**
6m 5m² 5m² 5.3h² 5m³] strong, good-bodied colt: has plenty of scope: has a quick
action: closely related to 3-y-o 5f and 5.8f winner Tinkerbird (by Music Boy) and
half-brother to 3 winners, including Cambridgeshire winner Quinlan Terry (by
Welsh Pageant), also successful at 1½m: dam 2-y-o 5f winner, is half-sister to smart
5f to 7f performer Quy: improving colt: one-paced third in maiden at Wolverhampton in August: well worth another try over 6f: yet to race on easy surface. *Sir
Mark Prescott.*

QUIP 5 ch.g. High Line 125–Sans Blague (USA) 108 (The Minstrel (CAN) 135) **53**
[1989 13.8d 10f 12g⁴ 16f 12.3f⁶ 12m 10g 10m 11g⁴ 12g⁵ 13s⁴ 12.2f* 12s⁵ 1990 12g 12g
12g* 12d 12g* 11d⁴ 12.3g 12g 12f² 15m² 12.2m4] leggy gelding: has a long stride:
plating-class handicapper: has gained all his 3 wins when ridden by 7-lb claimer Jaki
Houston: rallied very gamely when successful twice at Edinburgh in June: effective
at 1½m and stays easy 15f: suited by sound surface: best without visor: sometimes
sweats: headstrong and best allowed to stride on: usually taken down early or very
steadily: game. *M. P. Naughton.*

QUITE A FIGHTER 3 b.f. Hard Fought 125–Snow Tribe 94 (Great Nephew —
126) [1989 6m² 7f³ 6g⁵ 8m 8.2s 1990 12d] rangy, angular filly: moderate mover:
quite modest form in minor events on first 3 starts at 2 yrs: edgy, pulled up lame in
June handicap only start in 1990: should be suited by 1m +. *J. Hetherton.*

R

RAAHIN (USA) 5 ch.h. Super Concorde (USA) 128–Bonnie Hope (USA) **69**
(Nijinsky (CAN) 138) [1989 14f³ 14f³ 14f* 16f³ 14m⁵ 16f² 14m 1990 16.2m⁴ 18m⁴ 12g]
lengthy horse: moderate mover: quite modest handicapper: may prove best at up to
2m: acts on any going: visored once: goes well with forcing tactics. *R. Akehurst.*

RA'A (USA) 3 ch.f. Diesis 133–Shicklah (USA) 106 (The Minstrel (CAN) 135) **106**
[1989 6g* 5g* 1990 8m 6m³ 6m³ 6m³ 5g³ 5g* 6d* 5d*] compact filly: moderate
mover: useful sprinter: made all in £7,000 event at Newbury in September then
minor contest at Goodwood and listed race (favourite, by 1½ lengths from Dancing
Music) at Newmarket in October: seemed ideally suited by an easy surface:
sweating when pacemaker on reappearance: game and consistent: visits Woodman.
H. Thomson Jones.

RABBIT'S FOOT 2 b.f. (May 9) Touching Wood (USA) 127–Royal Custody — p
(Reform 132) [1990 7m] small filly: third foal: dam unraced half-sister to several
winners, including Ragstone and Castle Moon (dam of Moon Madness, Lucky Moon
and Sheriff's Star): green and ridden by 7-lb claimer, moderate late headway having
been tailed off in maiden at Chepstow in October: will stay well: should improve.
Lady Herries.

RACECALL GOLD CARD 3 ch.g. Camden Town 125–Polly Royal 75 (Music **42 §**
Boy 124) [1989 7g 1990 10.8m 8f⁶ 7f 7f³ 7f 7m 7m 8f⁴ 7h³ 7m] good-topped gelding:
poor performer: best effort in handicap at Folkestone fourth start, making most and
flashing tail: stays 7f: visored fifth start: sweating final one: probably unsatisfactory:
sold 7,500 gns Ascot December Sales, reportedly to join A. Potts. *M. McCormack.*

RACE TO TIME (IRE) 2 b.g. (May 20) Runnett 125–Plunket's Choice (Home **63**
Guard (USA) 129) [1990 6g⁶ 5g⁴ 7g⁶ a6g⁴ a7g⁴ a8g³] IR 5,200Y: leggy, quite
attractive ex-Irish gelding: third foal: half-brother to 1989 Irish 2-y-o 6f winner Maid
of Mourne (by Fairy King): dam never ran: quite modest performer: stays 1m:
trained by K. Connolly first 3 outings. *R. Akehurst.*

RACEY NASKRA (USA) 4 b.f. Star de Naskra (USA)–Langness (USA) 97 —
(Roberto (USA) 131) [1989 7f⁵ 7.5m* 7g⁵ 7.6f⁴ 1990 a7g a12g] rather angular filly:
modest winner as 3-y-o: behind in claimer (blinkered) and handicap at Southwell
early in 1990: doesn't stay 1½m: acts on firm going: sold 3,300 gns Doncaster March
Sales. *N. Tinkler.*

RACHEL'S DANCER (IRE) 2 b.f. (Mar 30) Lomond (USA) 128–Passing **75**
Fancy (USA) (Buckpasser) [1990 6m⁶ 7d* 8.2v⁴ 7d⁵] 30,000Y: leggy filly: closely
related to Triumph Hurdle winner Solar Cloud (by Northfields): dam Irish 1¼m
winner from very good family: modest performer: stayed on well to win maiden at

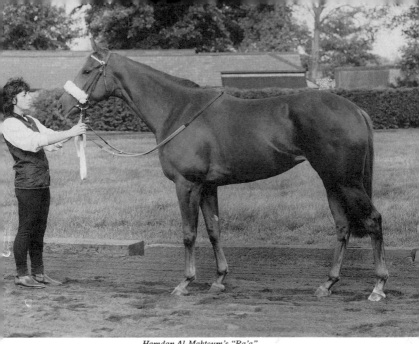

Hamdan Al-Maktoum's "Ra'a"

Ayr in September in very close finish: well beaten but not discredited, keeping on
steadily, in minor events at Haydock and Chester after: will stay 1¼m. *B. W. Hills.*

RACING RASKAL 3 b.c. Dunphy 124–Raskaska (Aureole 132) [1989 NR 1990   **46**
10g 10.2m 12.3g 12m 15g² 13.8m⁶ a12g⁶ 15.3m² 16m 18d] IR 1,400 2-y-o: smallish,
quite attractive colt: moderate mover: half-brother to disqualified Irish 2m winner
Dance For Gold (by Stradavinsky) and a winning Irish point-to-pointer: dam
once-raced half-sister to very smart French miler Hadrianus: signs of ability only
when second in maiden claimer and handicap (ridden by 7-lb claimer): suited by test
of stamina: acts on good to firm going. *Capt. J. Wilson.*

RACKETEER (IRE) 2 b.f. (Apr 8) Stalker 121–Splendid Yankee (Yankee Gold   **89**
115) [1990 6g 5f² 5f* 5g² 5m⁴ 5f 5g⁴ 5m⁵ 5m] IR 4,800Y: leggy, rather sparely-made
ex-Irish filly: moderate walker: first reported foal: dam Irish maiden on flat and over
hurdles: fair performer: claimer-ridden winner of maiden at Warwick in July and
nursery (made all) at Newbury in September: very good third of 14, making most, in
nursery at Newmarket: ran moderately in Cornwallis Stakes at Ascot final start:
speedy: yet to race on soft going, acts on any other: races keenly, and best making
running. *B. R. Millman.*

RADAR KNIGHT 2 b.c. (Feb 23) Beldale Flutter (USA) 130–Eurynome (Be My   **50**
Guest (USA) 126) [1990 5g 7m 7m³ 7f² 7f⁶ 8m] 1,900F, 4,000Y: leggy, workmanlike
colt: has a roundish action: first foal: dam 1¼m winner in France: plating-class
maiden at best: should be suited by 1m+. *R. A. Bennett.*

RADICAL CHIC 2 b.f. (Jan 26) Sadler's Wells (USA) 132–Santa Roseanna 111   **83** p
(Caracol (FR)) [1990 7m⁵] 150,000F: smallish, workmanlike filly: sister to Irish
3-y-o Stadler, successful at 1m (at 2 yrs) and 1½m, and half-sister to 2 winners,
including very useful Irish 6f and 7f performer King's College (by Golden Fleece):
dam, from good family, won from 7f to 9f in Ireland and stayed 1½m: bit backward
and green, around 9 lengths fifth of 8, staying on well after slow start, to Dartrey in

£7,500 event at Newmarket in October: will be better suited by 1m + : certain to improve, and win a race. *L. M. Cumani.*

RADIO CAROLINE   2 b.g. (Mar 21) All Systems Go 119–Caroline Lamb 74   **63**
(Hotfoot 126) [1990 6g 7m² 6m⁴ 8m⁶ 7f 8d² 8f4] 4,400Y: close-coupled, rather sparely-made gelding: fifth foal: half-brother to winning hurdler/chaser Master Lamb (by Absalom): dam won over 1m and over hurdles: quite modest maiden: claimed out of Miss S. Hall's stable after second start: suited by 1m: acts on firm going and dead. *A. Harrison.*

RADISH 'N' LEMON   4 b.c. Young Generation 129–Lady of Chalon (USA)   —
(Young Emperor 133) [1989 8h*dis 8g 8f 1990 12.3f] leggy, lengthy, rather sparely-made colt: disqualified winning plater as 3-y-o: no form in subsequent handicaps: stays 1m: acts on hard ground: visored once at 3 yrs: bandaged only start in 1990. *B. Stevens.*

RADWELL   2 b.c. (Mar 17) Dunbeath (USA) 127–Integrity 108 (Reform **112 p**
132) [1990 6g* 6f* 7g*]
'Unbeaten, very useful and likely to improve again over further' is a succinct summation of Radwell, whose hard-earned half-length victory in the seven-furlong Imry Solario Stakes at Sandown in August, after which he was retired for the season, places him within striking distance of the best of his contemporaries. Successful in both of his previous races, a twelve-runner maiden at Ripon and a minor event at Windsor, the workmanlike, good-bodied Radwell was sent off as one of the outsiders at Sandown in a nine-runner field headed by dual Goodwood winner Alnaab, and Sea Level, second to Bravefoot in a maiden at Newmarket before winning a similar event at Kempton. Radwell's form was nowhere near as far behind theirs as the betting suggested, and there seemed good reason to expect him to improve on it: not only was he racing over seven furlongs (and on a stiff course too) for the first time, having been educated over six, but he had looked far from the finished article at Ripon, where he had just prevailed in a tight finish; and then had left the impression he had had more in hand than the head by which he beat Buster in a strongly-run race at Windsor. There's no doubt that at Sandown the round-actioned Radwell was suited by the extra distance, and possibly the easier ground too, for he recorded easily his best performance. Three furlongs out he was still plumb last as Act of Diplomacy, having set a scorching gallop, began to tire; but the complexion of the race soon changed as Radwell came through to dispute the lead with Alnaab who stayed on the stronger, despite edging right, as the pair drew six lengths clear of the Acomb Stakes third Plan of Action. Unfortunately neither second nor third ran again, and although fourth-placed Sea Level (who may well have run better than his position suggests anyway, as he was the only one to chase Act of Diplomacy in the early stages) subsequently won the listed Bovis Autumn Stakes at Ascot several of the other contestants' later performances suggest the level of the form wasn't quite so good as we perceived it to be at the time. Nevertheless, Radwell seems a lazy type whose narrow winning margins could be deceptive. He's certainly one we're expecting to train on and do well in the coming season, even if he finds winning the better races beyond his capabilities.

		Grey Dawn II	Herbager
	Dunbeath (USA)	(gr 1962)	Polamia
	(b 1980)	Priceless Fame	Irish Castle
Radwell		(b or br 1975)	Comely Nell
(b.c. Mar 17, 1988)		Reform	Pall Mall
	Integrity	(b 1964)	Country House
	(gr 1978)	Cry of Truth	Town Crier
		(gr 1972)	False Evidence

Radwell, a 6,800-guinea foal, was sold again nearly a year later at New-market for 14,000 guineas. He's the fifth foal of his dam Integrity, a useful sprinter ideally suited by six furlongs, who has also produced the French eight-and-a-half-furlong winner Elan's Valley (by Welsh Pageant) and minor six-furlong winners by Petong and Tyrnavos. Integrity is easily the best foal in the disappointing stud career of the top-class 1974 two-year-old filly Cry of Truth. There's plenty of speed on this side of Radwell's pedigree, but several members of his family have stayed quite well—Cry of Truth's dam False

Lord Vestey's "Radwell"

Evidence and only winning colt On Oath both stayed a mile and a half—and it's quite probable that Radwell, by the Royal Lodge and William Hill Futurity winner Dunbeath, already emerging as something of an influence for stamina, will be another who'll stay a mile and a quarter. Radwell has yet to race on soft ground, but his action suggests it shouldn't inconvenience him. *J. R. Fanshawe.*

R A EXPRESS   5 b.g. Bay Express 132–Pinaka 69 (Pitcairn 126) [1989 7.6m 5m   **63**
6g⁴ 5s⁵ 5s 1990 5m² 5m⁰ 5m² 6f 6d* 5m⁶ 6s³ 5g 6f a5g⁶ 5g 5d² 5d³ 5m⁵ 6d] rather leggy, good-topped gelding: has shown signs of stringhalt: poor mover: carrying 16 lb more than proper mark, won (for only time) handicap at Chester in May: probably suited by 5f: best form on a soft surface: sometimes bandaged: usually makes running. *B. A. McMahon.*

RAFHA   3 b.f. Kris 135–Eljazzi 92 (Artaius (USA) 129) [1989 6f* 6g² 7g² 8g*   **123**
1990 8.5g* 11.5m* 10.5d*]
Rafha might never have reached the racecourse at three. Twice first, twice second from four outings as a juvenile, and assessed at 8-7 in the Free Handicap, she apparently didn't enter her trainer's calculations as a serious contender for major honours in 1990. He believed she would be difficult to place with a penalty for a Group 3 win in Doncaster's May Hill Stakes and, moreover, described her as 'knee high to a bumble bee'. Maybe Cecil also had in the back of his mind the dam Eljazzi, who failed to progress as anticipated over middle distances having won her only start at two, when he suggested an early departure to the paddocks for Rafha. However, owner/breeder Prince

729

Marley Roof Tile Oaks Trial, Lingfield—Rafha (left) and Knight's Baroness
run encouraging trials for Chantilly and Epsom respectively; Idle Chat is well held in third

Faisal wasn't dissuaded from persevering, and the filly overcame all the perceived obstacles to reward him handsomely. Even so, Rafha's season spanned less than seven weeks. It started on a high note, if a rather subdued one at the time, when she romped to a ten-length success in the listed Princess Elizabeth Stakes at Epsom in April, a race marred by an incident in which Long Island broke her shoulder when brought down over a furlong out. Paddock inspection beforehand had brought no surprises, Rafha was still small and sturdy after the winter. Her lack of inches seemed no bar to her

Prix de Diane Hermes, Chantilly—Rafha shows speed and courage;
subsequently-demoted Colour Chart is a clear second
ahead of Moon Cactus (No. 4), Air de Rien (No. 5),
almost-hidden Vue Cavaliere, Guiza and Atoll (No. 10)

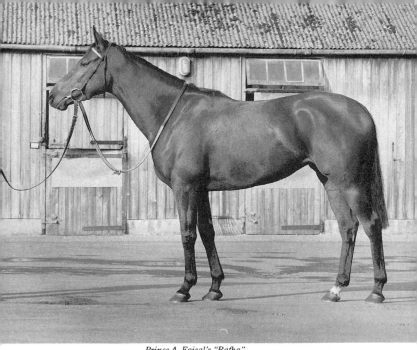

Prince A. Faisal's "Rafha"

progress, though. Next came the transition to middle distances in the Marley Roof Tile Oaks Trial at Lingfield, a fairly smooth transition once Rafha had been man-handled into the stalls after proving troublesome. Conceding 6 lb to each of her four rivals, she took the tight turns like a polo pony and gradually asserted herself for a narrow victory, gained without recourse to the whip, over subsequent Irish Oaks winner Knight's Baroness, whom she'd also beaten in the May Hill eight months previously. Little doubt now that Rafha had trained on into a very useful filly, yet connections declined to fulfil an engagement in the Oaks, fearing rather timidly perhaps that the pre-race hullaballoo at Epsom could be her undoing. Her stable wasn't represented in the Oaks, but fielded two in the Prix de Diane Hermes a day later at Chantilly, Rafha passed over by Cauthen in favour of Moon Cactus, a clear-cut winner of the Lupe Stakes on her reappearance. The Prix Saint-Alary winner Air de Rien, the 24/10 favourite, the Sheikh Mohammed-owned grouping of Moon Cactus, Colour Chart and Helen's Guest, and the classic winners Houseproud (Poule d'Essai des Pouliches) and Atoll (Premio Regina Elena and Oaks d'Italia) all figured in the betting ahead of Rafha, a 9/1-shot in a field of fourteen. Stable jockey and punters alike had underestimated Rafha to their cost. Her temperament was equal to the occasion, though she had become noticeably warm by the off and went rather keenly through the opening furlong or so, partly at least due to her jockey Carson having to recover a stirrup; but Rafha soon relaxed better than most as the pacemaker Helen's Guest set an unexceptional gallop. Having tracked the leaders, Rafha took a little time to find top gear once the race began in earnest but still stole a march on the somewhat unenterprisingly-ridden trio who were to emerge as her closest pursuers. Bursting to the front approaching the final furlong, she then responded gamely to pressure to repel the challenge of Colour Chart by half a length, if anything going away again at the line. Moon Cactus came through strongly from the rear to snatch third, two lengths further adrift, from a clutch of three, Air de Rien, Vue Cavaliere and Guiza, separated by short heads; Atoll seemed unable to quicken in seventh, while Houseproud hung badly right when ridden and wasn't persevered with. Despite the modest pace, some slightly questionable tactics, and a bunched finish Rafha was indubitably a worthy winner. Similarly, the much improved Colour Chart was second best on merit. However, the stewards found that Asmussen on Colour Chart had interfered with Air de Rien when switched abruptly to challenge and, considering the margins involved, they had little option but to place her behind that rival.

A proposed late-summer campaign for Rafha never materialised, various explanations being proffered for her missing engagements such as the Nassau Stakes (jarred up), the Yorkshire Oaks (slightly below-par) and the Sun Chariot (missed important gallop after pulling out a bit stiff). The form of the Diane was upheld in her absence, but Rafha can't be rated as highly as Highclere, Mrs Penny, Madam Gay and Indian Skimmer, the other British-trained winners of the race.

Rafha (b.f. 1987)	Kris (ch 1976)	Sharpen Up (ch 1969)	Atan Rocchetta
		Doubly Sure (b 1971)	Reliance II Soft Angels
	Eljazzi (b 1981)	Artaius (b 1974)	Round Table Stylish Pattern
		Border Bounty (b 1965)	Bounteous B Flat

Rafha joins an impressive band of middle-distance fillies sired by Kris in his first six crops, notably Oh So Sharp, Unite, Kozana, Fitnah and Sudden Love, with Shamshir waiting in the wings from his seventh. As was outlined in *Racehorses of 1989*, there's enough stamina in Rafha's pedigree to suggest she would have stayed the full mile and a half well if tried. Her grandam, the very useful middle-distance stayer Border Bounty, foaled the high-class miler Pitcairn (sire of Ela-Mana-Mou) as well as the Irish St Leger third Valley Gorge before Eljazzi. Rafha is Eljazzi's second foal. The third, a Slip Anchor colt named Sarawat, is also at Warren Place and was the subject of promising reports at two. Rafha is a fluent mover with a round action; she encountered neither very firm nor very soft ground but acted on any other. *H. R. A. Cecil.*

RAGE 3 ch.g. Final Straw 127–Nasty Niece (CAN) (Great Nephew 126) [1989 NR 1990 6f5 6m 5g 7m4 8.5d2 8f* 8g3 11m] rangy gelding: good mover: eighth foal: half-brother to several winners, including fairly useful 1m to 1¼m winner Penelope Strawbery (by Anfield) and 1988 2-y-o 6f winner Specialised Boy (by Mummy's Game), useful 7f to 9f winner in Italy in 1990: dam won over 7f at 2 yrs in Canada: quite modest performer: bandaged off-hind, won handicap at Thirsk in June, always close up: not seen out after July: suited by 1m: acts on firm and dead going. *M. H. Easterby.*   65

RAGTIME 3 b.c. Pas de Seul 133–Boldella (Bold Lad (IRE) 133) [1989 6m4 7m 1990 8m 10m 10m 12f 10d] neat, strong colt: good walker: plating-class form at best: should stay at least 1m: sold 2,700 gns Ascot October Sales. *C. W. C. Elsey.*   —

RAGTIME COWBOY 3 b.g. Indian King (USA) 128–F Sharp 83 (Formidable (USA) 125) [1989 6m 1990 7g a8g 9m 10g5 12m] workmanlike gelding: has a round action: little worthwhile form (including in selling handicap) but has shown signs of ability: should stay 1¼m. *C. W. Thornton.*   —

RAHAAM (USA) 3 gr.f. Secreto (USA) 128–Fager's Glory (USA) (Mr Prospector (USA)) [1989 6g2 1990 7m* 10m 10m2] useful-looking filly: good mover with a quick action: 9/4 on, won maiden at Newmarket in April: off course nearly 6 months then well beaten in £8,300 handicap (pulled hard) at Newmarket and good 4 lengths second of 5 to Ijtihaad in minor event at Leicester: stays 1¼m. *H. R. A. Cecil.*   91

RAHDARI (IRE) 2 br.c. (Apr 18) Darshaan 133–Ramanouche (FR) 112 (Riverman (USA) 131) [1990 8g2] big, rangy colt: has plenty of scope: sixth living foal: half-brother to several winners, including fairly useful 1½m winner Rashtoun (by   84 p

Shareef Dancer) and Roubayd (by Exceller), fairly useful at up to 2m: dam very useful winner at up to 7f in France, is out of very smart 9f to 13f filly Bubunia: better for race and green, 1½ lengths second of 4, leading over 1f out and not knocked about when headed, to Generous in minor event at Sandown in September: will stay 1½m: sure to improve, and win a race. *M. R. Stoute.*

RAHIF   2 b.c. (Apr 2) Shirley Heights 130–Vaguely 92 (Bold Lad (IRE) 133) [1990   — p
7g⁴] 380,000Y: well-made colt: brother to Shady Heights, top-class winner at up to 10.5f, and half-brother to useful 1m and 1¼m winner Dimmer (by Kalaglow) and useful 1985 2-y-o 6f winner Top River (by High Top): dam 1m and 1¼m winner: easy-to-back favourite, tailed-off last of 4 in Washington Singer Stakes at Newbury in August, taking keen hold, shaken up 2f out then weakening quickly: clearly thought capable of good deal better. *R. W. Armstrong.*

RAH WAN (USA)   4 ch.c. Riverman (USA) 131–Thorough 115 (Thatch (USA)   68
136) [1989 8m⁴ 8.2g² 7g* 1990 10f 10m 9m⁵ 7.5f 8.3f⁵] leggy, quite attractive colt: moderate walker: fairly useful winner at 3 yrs: best effort in 1990 on final start: stays 1m: blinkered and bandaged off-fore second start: sold 2,800 gns Newmarket Autumn Sales. *N. A. Callaghan.*

RAINBOW BRIDGE   3 br.g. Godswalk (USA) 130–Regal Entrance (Be My   63 d
Guest (USA) 126) [1989 5d⁴ 5f⁵ 5m⁶ 7f 6f 7m 6g* 6m* 6m 6g² 6v 1990 6m⁵ 7f 6f³ 6s² 6m 7g 8g 7d⁴ 8f⁶ 7f 8h³ 11d] strong, close-coupled gelding: carries condition: quite modest winner at 2 yrs: best form at 6f: acts on any going: often edgy: blinkered 3 times: trained until after seventh start by P. Felgate, then until after penultimate one by M. W. Easterby: winning selling hurdler: ungenuine and one to avoid. *J. J. O'Neill.*

RAINBOW CHASER (IRE)   2 b.f. (Feb 9) Rainbow Quest (USA) 134–Scotia   54
Rose (Tap On Wood 130) [1990 6f³ 8m a8g³] IR 26,000Y: close-coupled, rather angular filly: second foal: half-sister to 3-y-o Fanellan (by Try My Best), 6f winner at 2 yrs: dam Irish middle-distance winner, is half-sister to dam of Greenland Park (dam of Fitnah) and Red Sunset: third in small fields in maidens at Brighton and Lingfield (beaten 8 lengths by Statajack): stumbled and unseated rider in between. *P. F. I. Cole.*

RAINBOW FLEET   2 b.f. (May 1) Nomination 125–Olderfleet 59 (Steel Heart   66
128) [1990 5m 5m² 5m³ 5g² 5f* 6f⁶ 5m] 94,000Y: strong, workmanlike filly: has scope: closely related to 2 winners by Dominion, including useful 1987 2-y-o 5f and 6f winner Peace Girl, and half-sister to winning sprinter Runaway (by Godswalk): dam second 3 times over 1m: quite modest performer: quickened well to win nursery at Folkestone in July: ran creditably final start, first for over 2 months: stays 6f: reportedly in season when running moderately fourth outing. *L. J. Holt.*

RAINBOW RING   3 b.f. Rainbow Quest (USA) 134–Circus Ring 122 (High Top   —
131) [1989 NR 1990 10f⁶] 46,000Y: fourth foal: half-sister to very useful 7f (at 2 yrs) and 1¼m winner Lady Shipley (by Shirley Heights) and French 1½m winner Douglas Fir (by Busted): dam unbeaten at 2 yrs, including in Lowther Stakes, ran once afterwards: 12/1, slow-starting 16 lengths sixth of 8 in maiden at Lingfield in July. *C. E. Brittain.*

RAINBOW STRIPES   3 ch.c. Rainbow Quest (USA) 134–Pampas Miss (USA)   60
(Pronto) [1989 7g 10m 10m 10m⁵ 10s 10g⁴ 11.7m 15g³ 12.2m⁴ 14m* 12f⁴ 15.5f 16m* 16d] big, rather unfurnished colt: quite modest performer: won maiden claimer at Yarmouth in August and 18-runner handicap at Warwick in October: soundly beaten at Chester final start: suited by test of stamina and a sound surface: below form (made most) in blinkers seventh start: not an easy ride, best with strong handling: trained until after tenth start by R. Guest. *P. A. Blockley.*

RAINBOW TRUST   2 b.c. (Mar 22) Rainbow Quest (USA) 134–Bandit Queen   — p
(FR) (Jim French (USA)) [1990 7s⁵] 74,000Y: tall, leggy, close-coupled colt: looks weak: half-brother to 3 winners, including 1¼m winner Matrah (by Northfields): dam unraced half-sister to dam of Kings Lake and Salmon Leap: backward, around 20 lengths third of 19, outpaced and green then going on well, to Perpendicular in maiden at Doncaster in November: sure to improve. *A. A. Scott.*

RAIN GOD   2 b.c. (Feb 24) Lidhame 109–Rainbow Star (Star Appeal 133) [1990   60
7f³ 8m 7s] close-coupled, quite attractive colt: second foal: dam well-beaten half-sister to useful 1976 2-y-o sprinter Namara: plating-class form in maidens at Brighton and Leicester first 2 starts: probably stays 1m. *Miss A. J. Whitfield.*

RAINIBIK (FR)   4 b.c. Bikala 134–Rains Came (ITY) (Bold Forbes (USA)) [1989   114
10v* 12s⁵ 10.5m* 12g 10d⁴ 10g³ 10s³ 10d 9.7m 10m³ 10s⁴ 1990 10g* 10f² 11g⁶ 11s

733

10g 10g 11d² 11d⁶ 10v³] French colt: third foal: dam ran twice at 3 yrs in France: won valuable event at Maisons-Laffitte in March: ran well when 3 lengths second to Creator in Prix d'Harcourt at Longchamp following month: placed only twice in Group 2 and 3 races in Germany and Italy after, on final outing demoted a place in Premio Carlo Porta at Milan: suited by 1¼m: probably acts on any going. *F. Boutin, France.*

RAIN-N-SUN   4 gr.g. Warpath 113–Sun Noddy (Tom Noddy 104) [1989 8m 1990 a11g] lengthy, angular, plain gelding: well beaten: visored only start at 4 yrs. *J. L. Harris.*   —

RAINSTONE   2 ch.f. (Mar 7) Rainbow Quest (USA) 134–Emaline (FR) (Empery (USA) 128) [1990 a8g² a8g³] rather sparely-made filly: third foal: half-sister to 3-y-o Monarda (by Pharly): dam French 2-y-o 7f winner: plating-class form, staying on well, in maidens at Lingfield: will be suited by 1¼m + . *P. F. I. Cole.*   57

RAINTON LEAP   3 b.g. Salmon Leap (USA) 131–Verandah (Jaazeiro (USA) 127) [1989 NR 1990 8f 7m 7.5d 11m 10m 11m³ 12d⁶] IR 15,500F, IR 4,100Y: tall gelding: first foal: dam, winner at around 1m in Ireland, is from family of Knockroe: poor plater: should prove best at up to 11f: joined P. Davis. *T. D. Barron.*   34

RAISE A RUBY   2 b.f. (Apr 19) Green Ruby (USA) 104–Fashion Lover 70 (Shiny Tenth 120) [1990 6g⁵ 6g⁶ 6g⁴ 5g⁶] leggy filly: third foal: half-sister to 3-y-o Star of Fashion (by Comedy Star): dam won 1m seller: poor maiden: flashed tail third start. *J. Berry.*   45 d

RAJAYA (USA)   2 b.c. (Apr 5) Nureyev (USA) 131–Don't Sulk (USA) 115 (Graustark) [1990 6m] unfurnished colt: fourth foal: brother to 2 winners, including useful 1½m winner Professional Girl, and half-brother to a winner in France: dam, winner of 1½m Prix de Royallieu, is sister to Kentucky Derby and Belmont Stakes second Jim French: well beaten, never a factor, in maiden at Newmarket in November: should improve. *A. A. Scott.*   — p

RAJPUT RAJAH   3 b.g. Indian King (USA) 128–Take A Chance (FR) (Baldric II 131) [1989 NR 1990 7g 7m⁵ 6f 7g 7g] 25,000Y: neat gelding: brother to 4-y-o 7f and 8.2f winner Lambourn Raja and half-brother to several winners, including useful 7f and 1m winner That's My Son (by Busted): dam won Prix Yacowlef and is sister to high-class French 2-y-o Without Fear: no worthwhile form in maidens and handicaps. *E. A. Wheeler.*   —

RAJ WAKI (USA)   3 b.c. Miswaki (USA) 124–Script Approval (USA) (Silent Screen (USA)) [1989 7f* 1990 8g² 8f 10.5g 8f² 7m³ 8f* 8g³ 8m* 9g*] well-made colt: moderate mover: very useful performer: won minor event at Brighton in September then led about 1f out when successful at Newmarket following month in £11,600 contest by 1½ lengths from Lifewatch Vision and listed race by neck from Theatrical Charmer: stays 9f: acts on firm ground. *G. Harwood.*   111

RAKEEN (USA)   3 b.c. Northern Dancer–Glorious Song (CAN) (Halo (USA)) [1989 NR 1990 9m* 8g² 10.2s*] compact, attractive colt: fifth foal: half-brother to 2 winners, notably Rahy (by Blushing Groom), useful 6f and 1m winner here later high-class miler in USA: dam champion older mare in USA successful in 4 Grade 1 9f events: won minor events at Wolverhampton (drifting right) in October and Doncaster (17-runner race by 5 lengths from Balish) in November: stays 1¼m well: useful and progressive: sold to go to South Africa. *J. H. M. Gosden.*   99 +

RAKES LANE   5 b.g. Pitskelly 122–Mrs Cullumbine 60 (Silly Season 127) [1989 NR 1990 14m] big, workmanlike gelding: fairly useful winner in 1988: well beaten in April handicap at Newmarket: stays 1½m well: acts on any going: blinkered 3 times at 3 yrs: very useful novice hurdler in 1989/90. *J. R. Jenkins.*   —

RAMASIS   2 br.g. (Apr 14) Dawn Johnny (USA) 90–Laxay 69 (Laxton 105) [1990 6m] second foal: dam 7f seller winner: slowly away and tailed off halfway in minor event at Nottingham in September. *M. R. Leach.*   —

RAMBADALE   3 ch.f. Vaigly Great 127–Corinthia (USA) (Empery (USA) 128) [1989 6m² 6f² 6m* 7m⁶ 6g 1990 6m 8m⁵ 8g³ 8.2g⁴ 8g] small, workmanlike filly: good walker: plating-class handicapper: stays 8.2f: acts on firm ground: blinkered (took keen hold) final start, in June. *M. H. Tompkins.*   56

RAMBO CASTLE   4 b.g. Castle Keep 121–Rampage 93 (Busted 134) [1989 10s 10m² 12h* 12g 12g² a12g³ 1990 12f⁵ 18.4d² 16m⁶ 20m 14d] angular, sparely-made gelding: 25/1, ran well when second to impressive Travelling Light in Ladbroke Chester Cup (Handicap) in May: lightly raced and below form after: suited by good test of stamina and an easy surface: winning hurdler as a juvenile: sold out of S. Norton's stable 16,500 gns Doncaster March Sales. *N. Tinkler.*   81

Sheikh Mohammed's "Rakeen"

RAMBO EXPRESS 3 b. or br.c. New Express 95–Saul Flower (Saulingo 122) **90**
[1989 6g 6g 1990 6m⁶ 6s 6m 6g⁵ 5m⁴ 5.1f⁶ a5g 5.1m 5.3f³ 5d² a6g* a6g⁵ a6g*] smallish, workmanlike colt: favourite, much improved form to win claimers at Southwell
in November and December, both in good style having made all unchallenged: stays
6f: acts on dead going: blinkered fourth start: visored last 4: needs to be able to
dominate. *G. A. Huffer.*

RAMI (USA) 3 br.c. Riverman (USA) 131–Ancient Regime (USA) 123 (Olden **115**
Times) [1989 6g³ 7g* 1990 7g³ 8f 6m* 7m* 7m³] leggy, quite attractive colt: has a
quick action: smart performer: favourite, won minor events at Lingfield (10/1 on) in
May and Warwick in October: good staying-on third of 8 to Sally Rous in Challenge
Stakes at Newmarket final start: well beaten in 2000 Guineas there second outing:
worth another try at 1m: acts on good to firm ground: has been taken quietly to post:
stays in training. *P. T. Walwyn.*

RAMSEY STREET 3 b.f. Mummy's Game 120–Green Jinks (Hardgreen (USA) —
122) [1989 5f³ 1990 7d⁵ 8g 10f] rather leggy filly: 20/1 and ridden by 7-lb claimer on
first run for 11 months, keeping-on fifth of 20 in seller at Yarmouth, edging left: ran
poorly in claimers later in July, claimed out of M. Tompkins' stable £4,411 on first
occasion: should stay 1m: best effort on dead going. *K. S. Bridgwater.*

RANCHO MIRAGE 3 ch.g. Superlative 118–Que Sera 91 (Music Boy 124) [1989 **73**
NR 1990 6m³ 5g* 5g⁶ 5d⁴ 6m] 21,000Y: robust, sprint type: first foal: dam 2-y-o 5f
winner out of half-sister to Chapel Cottage: 7/4 on, won maiden at Beverley in May:
ran well in handicaps at Epsom and Ascot (£16,400 event) next 2 starts, moderately
at York in July: may prove best at 5f: has been taken early and quietly to post. *J. W.
Watts.*

RANDAMA 3 b.f. Akarad (FR) 130–Ramanouche (FR) 122 (Riverman (USA) 131) **77**
[1989 NR 1990 10m³ 12.2g a12g² a12g³ 14m³ 16m² 16d⁵] unfurnished filly: fifth

735

living foal: half-sister to 4 winners, including 1½m winner Rashtoun (by Shareef Dancer) and Roubayd (by Exceller), successful at up to 2m: dam, daughter of very smart 9f to 13f filly Bubunia, winner at up to 7f in France: modest maiden: will stay well: acts on good to firm ground: sold to join K. McCauley 4,000 gns Newmarket December Sales. *M. R. Stoute.*

R AND B UPDATE 4 b.g. Longleat (USA) 109–Neringulla (African Sky 124) [1989 6g3 6d 6m 7m 8m 6g6 1990 7m9 a7g] leggy, good-topped gelding: disappointing maiden: wearing tongue strap, virtually pulled up in handicap at Southwell in January: may stay beyond 6f: possibly unsuited by top-of-the-ground. *J. D. Czerpak.* —

RANGERS LAD 5 b.g. Sallust 134–Flaxen Hair (Thatch (USA) 136) [1989 10.8s 10m* 9f 10m 8f5 10.1m3 10f6 10.6d4 a14g5 1990 a10g* 10f] compact gelding: carries condition: poor mover: won handicap at Lingfield in January: well beaten 8 months later: should stay beyond 1¼m: possibly unsuited by soft going, acts on any other: blinkered once at 3 yrs: none too genuine: sold 1,150 gns Ascot November Sales. *P. Mitchell.* 41

RANWELI REEF 4 b.g. Superlative 118–Grace Poole (Sallust 134) [1989 8m 7m 6m 7m 6g 1990 10.2f 8m 8m 11.7g 10.6s 7m 10f 6m] good-topped gelding: modest winner as 2-y-o: no longer of much account: blinkered once at 3 yrs, visored final outing in 1990: sold 700 gns Ascot November Sales. *D. R. Tucker.* —

RAPIDARIS 4 b.g. Rapid River 127–Stellaris (Star Appeal 133) [1989 9f 9f 11g 10f 1990 8m] smallish, lengthy gelding: appears of little account: bandaged only start at 4 yrs. *B. R. Cambidge.* —

RAPID CORACLE (IRE) 2 b.c. (Mar 29) Welsh Term 126–Canoeing (Tap On Wood 130) [1990 6m5 6f2 8g6 7m4 7d2 6d*] 7,400F, 6,000Y: tall, leggy colt: second foal: half-brother to 3-y-o Sail On (by No Pass No Sale): dam twice-raced daughter of very useful 1½m winner Rapids, a half-sister to Hawaiian Sound: won nursery at Newmarket in October, showing greatly improved form, by a length from Teanarco, staying on really strongly from over 1f out: may well improve further back at 7f: acts well on dead ground. *R. Hannon.* 97

RAPID LAD 12 b.g. Rapid River 127–Seacona (Espresso 122) [1989 10d 10.8d 10d6 10f4 10f2 10m* 10.8m5 10m 10f2 10m3 10f* 10m 10m3 10f4 10f 1990 10.8m 10m2 10d5 10f4] compact gelding: good mover: quite modest handicapper: successful 12 times at Beverley, and has not won elsewhere since 1982: not seen out as 12-y-o after May: best at 1¼m: needs top-of-the-ground: has worn blinkers, but not for long time: held up and is suited by strong gallop: particularly well handled by D. Nicholls: tough. *J. L. Spearing.* 55

RAPID MOVER 3 ch.g. Final Straw 127–Larive 80 (Blakeney 126) [1989 6m 6f 7g 7.5g5 8g 1990 11m4 8.2g6] leggy gelding: poor maiden: visored once at 2 yrs. *T. Craig.* —

RAPPORTEUR (USA) 4 b.g. His Majesty (USA)–Sweet Rapport (USA) (Round Table) [1989 10g5 12f 10m5 a10g5 a10g* 1990 a10g6 a10g* a12g3 a10g3 a8g2 a10g* a8g4 9g 11.7f2 10.4d 10m2 12m6 10g* 10.5m 9m4 9m2 10g3 a10g* a10g* a10g3 a10g*] leggy, angular gelding: fairly useful handicapper: successful 6 times at Lingfield in 1990, on turf in June otherwise on all-weather: effective at 1¼m and 1½m: acts on good going, seems unsuited by dead: wore bandages late in season: has won for apprentice: goes very well with forcing tactics, particularly on switchback track: consistent. *C. C. Elsey.* 92

RARE DETAIL (IRE) 2 ch.f. (Jan 31) Commanche Run 133–Sharp Dresser (USA) (Sharpen Up 127) [1990 a8g*] first foal: dam unraced half-sister to Alleging and Nomrood: 13/2 and wearing eyeshield, slow-starting ¾-length winner from Just One of late-year maiden at Lingfield: will stay 1¼m: should improve. *Mrs L. Piggott.* 56 p

RASAN 3 ch.c. Dominion 123–Raffle 82 (Balidar 133) [1989 6g6 6f4 6f4 1990 7m 5m6 7m* 7.6m* 7m 7.6m* 7.6f*] good-bodied colt: progressed extremely well in the summer, successful in maiden at Sandown and 3 handicaps (making virtually all) at Lingfield, by 7 lengths in 5-runner race on final start: stays 7.6f: acts on firm going. *R. W. Armstrong.* 106

RASHEED 3 b.c. Chief Singer 131–Enchanting Dancer (FR) (Nijinsky (CAN) 138) [1989 6m 7g 1990 11d 8m 10.6s 7m 8.2g 10m4 11.7g4 14d5 12m2 12s 10g4 10g] close-coupled colt: moderate mover: plating-class maiden: needs strong pace at 1¼m, and will probably be best at 1½m: best effort on good to firm ground, unsuited by soft: often races freely: bandaged off-hind fifth and sixth outings, behind last 4: visored sixth: trained until after eighth by M. Blanshard. *N. A. Callaghan.* 56

RASHITA 3 b.f. Alzao (USA) 117–Apapa Port 80 (My Swanee 122) [1989 NR 1990 8.5g 10g4 10.6d 13v4 12.4s6] IR 6,000F, 70,000Y: lengthy filly: keen walker: fifth 58

foal: half-sister to 1988 Irish 2-y-o 6f winner Port Arms (by Sandhurst Prince) and Irish 9f winner Papa Port (by Kampala): dam 5f mudlark: plating-class maiden: easily best effort at Nottingham (showed quick action, led 7f) second start, off course nearly 4 months after: ran in claimers last 2 outings: may be suited by return to shorter: blinkered final start. *D. Morley.*

RASMOOR SONG 2 b.f. (May 20) Cree Song 99–Malmo (Free State 125) [1990 — 7f a7g a6g] sparely-made filly: first foal: dam poor daughter of a hurdling half-sister to smart sprinter Bream: always behind in maidens and a claimer. *D. Lee.*

RATHAGE 4 b.f. Horage 124–Rathcoffey Duchy (Faberge II 121) [1989 8g⁵ 12v² — 12g* 12g 10.6m⁵ 12g 13v⁶ 12.6g⁶ 1990 a14g 10d a12g a12g] lengthy, shallow-girthed filly: won handicap at Leicester early as 3-y-o: little subsequent worthwhile form: suited by 1½m: acts on good to firm and heavy going: blinkered final outing: trained until after reappearance by R. Guest: sold 1,500 gns Ascot December Sales. *M. Madgwick.*

RATHBRIDES JOY 3 gr.g. Kafu 120–Great Meadow (Northfields (USA)) [1989 **68** d 5d⁶ 6m 7f* 7m 8.2f² 8g 1990 8.5m 10f² 12m² 10.2m a11g 12f⁶ 10m³ 10.6v] tall, leggy gelding: moderate mover, with a round action: useful plater: clearly best effort at Thirsk on third start: suited by 1½m: best efforts on top-of-the-ground: visored fourth start: tends to carry head high: not particularly consistent. *J. S. Wainwright.*

RATHER GORGEOUS 5 br.m. Billion (USA) 120–Fair Sara 65 (McIndoe 97) **37** § [1989 NR 1990 12h 12.3g 11m⁶ 16f 18g 13.8f* 13.8d] tall, lengthy, angular mare: first foal: dam winning hurdler: 33/1, first worthwhile form when winning 9-runner handicap at Catterick (pulled hard) in September: stays 1¾m: acts on firm going: unsatisfactory temperamentally. *Capt. J. Wilson.*

RATHVINDEN HOUSE (USA) 3 b.g. Hostage (USA)–Great Verdict (USA) **67** 110 (Le Fabuleux 133) [1989 10g⁶ 1990 8f⁴ 10.1m 10f² 10m 11.5g⁴] tall, sparely-made gelding: clearly best efforts in frame for handicaps at Brighton and Yarmouth (gambled on in latter): acts on firm going: sweating first 2 starts: joined T. Thomson Jones. *R. Boss.*

RATION OF PASSION 5 b.m. Camden Town 125–Bellagold (Rheingold 137) **39** [1989 5d² 6d³ 5s 5m 5m 5s a6g⁶ 1990 a6g a6g³ a6g⁶ a6g⁶ a6g⁴ a5g² a6g⁴ a5g⁵] big, angular mare: poor maiden: best at sprint distances: probably acts on any going: visored first outing: has sweated: inconsistent. *J. J. Bridger.*

RAVENHURST 2 br.g. (May 12) Bustino 136–Ravens Peak (High Top 131) **55** [1990 6m 8m 6d 7f⁶ 8m] 2,600 2-y-o: smallish, sturdy gelding: first foal: dam lightly-raced half-sister to very useful 1981 staying 2-y-o Ashenden: plating-class maiden: stays 7f: tends to edge left. *T. Fairhurst.*

RAVEN'S AFFAIR 4 b.g. Tower Walk 130–Femme Fatale 67 (King's Leap 111) — [1989 9f 6m⁵ 8.2d 1990 8f⁶ 10m 8.2m 8.2v] medium-sized gelding: has shown only a little ability. *M. Tate.*

RAVENSWICK (IRE) 2 ch.f. (Mar 3) Raise A Native–Pitty Pal (USA) — (Caracolero (USA) 131) [1990 5f 5m⁴] lengthy filly: first known foal: dam lightly raced, was minor stakes-winning sprinter at 2 yrs: not knocked about in maidens at Haydock and Doncaster in spring. *M. W. Easterby.*

RAWAABE (USA) 2 ch.f. (Mar 30) Nureyev (USA) 131–Passerine (USA) (Dr **87** Fager) [1990 5m⁴ 5m⁴ 5d* 5g⁴] $625,000Y: sturdy, useful-looking filly: good walker: closely related to 2 winners, notably very useful sprinter Doulab (by Topsider) and half-sister to another winner: dam 6f winner, is half-sister to high-class performer at up to 1¾m Properantes: made all in maiden at Catterick in October, winning easily by 7 lengths from Parios: respectable fourth, not finding so much as anticipated off bridle having led over 3f, in nursery at Newmarket after: speedy. *H. Thomson Jones.*

RAWAAN (FR) 3 b.g. Labus (FR)–Rose Ness (Charlottesville 135) [1989 NR ? 1990 10.7g³ 11g² 12g* 12g⁵ 14g² 12g⁶ 13v⁶ 12.2d 11d] tall gelding: brother to 2 French middle-distance winners and half-brother to several winners, notably very smart 7f and 1m winner Raykour (by Dalsaan): dam, half-sister to Prix de Diane winner Crepellana, ran 4 times at 3 yrs in France, placed once over 7.5f: won maiden at Bordeaux in May: bit backward, well beaten in claimers here: probably stays 1¾m: trained until after sixth start by A. de Royer-Dupre: winning selling hurdler. *N. Tinkler.*

RAW TALENT 3 br.g. Gorytus (USA) 132–Welcome Break (Wollow 132) [1989 **51** + NR 1990 8g⁶ a11g³ 12.2m⁵ 11.5m³ 14g⁶] 45,000Y: workmanlike gelding: moderate mover: fourth foal: half-brother to smart 6f to 1¼m winner Invited Guest (by Be My Guest), later good winner in USA: dam unraced half-sister to Interval and daughter of Cambridgeshire winner Intermission: plating-class maiden: sixth in handicap at Nottingham, travelling well then hampered and no extra: may be suited by return to 1½m: sold 6,200 gns Newmarket Autumn Sales. *W. J. Haggas.*

RAY'S BOY 3 b.c. Rabdan 129–Ticky Tachs Girl (Tachypous 128) [1989 NR 1990 10.8m⁶] second foal: dam lightly-raced maiden out of sister to smart sprinter Lazenby: 100/1, well beaten in Warwick minor event: dead. *Mrs N. Macauley.* —

RAYS MEAD 2 gr.f. (Apr 30) Tremblant 112–Free Range 78 (Birdbrook 110) [1990 5g] leggy filly: second foal: half-sister to 3-y-o Not Quite Free (by Gabitat): dam 5f to 7f winner: soon struggling in minor event at Windsor in April. *L. J. Holt.* —

RAZEEN 5 ch.g. Be My Guest (USA) 126–Fast Motion 86 (Midsummer Night II 117) [1989 10.2g⁵ 9v⁶ 8m 1990 a8g⁴ a11g⁶ a11g2] lengthy, rather sparely-made gelding: moderate mover: fair maiden at best in Britain: sent to race in Scandinavia and is a winner there: stays 11f: probably unsuited by heavy going: sometimes blinkered. *J. G. FitzGerald.* 52

RAZEEN (USA) 3 b.c. Northern Dancer–Secret Asset (USA) (Graustark) [1989 NR 1990 8g* 8g* 10m* 12g 10m⁵] $1,175,000F: rangy, good sort: has been operated on for wind problem: has a rather short action: sixth foal: brother to smart 7f to 1½m winner Warrshan, closely related to high-class middle-distance performer Assatis (by Topsider) and half-brother to 2 winners: dam unraced daughter of champion 2-y-o filly Numbered Account: won maiden at Newbury, minor event at Sandown and moderately-run N M Financial Predominate Stakes (by 4 lengths from Elmaamul) at Goodwood: favourite, ran poorly in Ever Ready Derby at Epsom: creditable fifth to Elmaamul in Coral-Eclipse Stakes at Sandown: should stay 1½m: to race in USA. *H. R. A. Cecil.* 113

RAZZBERRY (FR) 3 br.f. Be My Guest (USA) 126–Wool Princess (FR) (Direct Flight) [1989 6g⁴ 7g2 6g2 7f⁴ 1990 8m³ 10g⁶ 11g⁴ 14f 14d] lengthy, sturdy filly: modest maiden at 2 yrs: not so good in 1990, best effort fourth in handicap at Hamilton: doesn't stay 1¾m: acts on firm going: sold 3,000 gns Newmarket December Sales. *M. A. Jarvis.* 56

READING LIGHT (IRE) 2 b.f. (Apr 5) Thatching 131–Lundylux 88 (Grundy 137) [1990 6g 7g] compact, rather sparely-made filly: first foal: dam, half-sister to Derby Italiano winner Welnor, needed at least 1½m: behind in large-field autumn maidens at Newbury (slowly away and green) and Newmarket. *R. Hannon.* —

READY WIT 9 br.g. Bay Express 132–Brevity 76 (Pindari 124) [1989 7g a8g⁶ a7g⁴ 1990 a12g⁵ 8m⁵ 10.1g* 10s³ 10f 10.6s 10.6s] lengthy, workmanlike gelding: won claimer at Windsor in April: below form in handicaps after next outing: stays 1¼m: unsuited by firm going and goes very well in the mud: sometimes visored as 6-y-o: trained until after reappearance by R. Hannon: apprentice ridden afterwards. *M. P. Muggeridge.* 46

REALISM 5 b.g. Known Fact (USA) 135–Miss Reasoning (USA) 108 (Bold Reasoning (USA)) [1989 8g 8d 7s 9.2f a10g⁶ a8g 1990 a10g⁵ a12g⁴ a12g* 12f] lengthy, angular gelding: has a quick action: led final strides when winning handicap at Lingfield in February: ran moderately month later: stays 1½m: acts on soft going, possibly unsuited by firm. *K. O. Cunningham-Brown.* 56

REALM (USA) 3 b.f. Mr Prospector (USA)–State (USA) (Nijinsky (CAN) 138) [1989 8g⁶ 1990 9m² 10f² 10.2h³ 9g2] angular, sparely-made filly: modest form: favourite, short-head second of 11, staying on well, in handicap at Redcar in June: stays 1¼m: acts on hard going. *A. C. Stewart.* 72

N.M. Financial Predominate Stakes, Goodwood—
Razeen (USA) wins a muddling race from Elmaamul (extreme right)
and goes on to start favourite for the Derby

Sheikh Mohammed's "Razeen (USA)"

REAL STUNNER 3 ch f Chief Singer 131–Real Party 68 (Realm 129) [1989 NR **78**
1990 5f* 6m 5g5 5g 5m4 5m6 6d 6m4 6s 5s] 13,000Y, 4,000 2-y-o: big, strong,
close-coupled filly: seventh foal: half-sister to French provincial 11.7f and 12.7f
winner Express Party (by Bay Express), a prolific winner in Italy and to the dam of
smart sprinter Carol's Treasure: dam, half-sister to Madam Gay, won over 5f at 2
yrs: modest performer: 25/1, won minor event at Thirsk in April: stays 6f: seems
ideally suited by top-of-the-ground. *M. P. Naughton.*

REAMUR 3 b. or br.f. Top Ville 120 Brilliant Reay 74 (Ribero 126) [1989 NR 1990 **68**
10.4g3 12f2 10g4] rather leggy, sparely-made filly: half-sister to several winners,
including fairly useful 7f (at 2 yrs) and 1m winner Test of Time (by Bay Express):
dam won over 10.4f: quite modest maiden: stays 1½m. *L. M. Cumani.*

REAPERS REWARD 2 b.f. (Mar 7) Oats 126–Red Ragusa 62 (Homeric 133) **—**
[1990 5g 8d] leggy, rather angular filly: fourth foal: half-sister to 6f winner Via Vitae
(by Palm Track): dam plater: well beaten in maidens at Chester (on toes, slowly
away) and Leicester: off course 4 months in between. *R. Hollinshead.*

REASONABLE KID 3 ch.c. Reasonable (FR) 119–Trust Sally 65 (Sallust 134) **79**
[1989 5m5 6g5 6d* 5g5 1990 5f3 6f* 7g] angular colt: moderate mover: fair
performer: won strongly-run claimer at Haydock, leading close home having been
outpaced: never near to challenge in Epsom handicap later in April: needs further
than 5f and should stay 7f: yet to race on soft ground, acts on any other. *R. Boss.*

REASON TO TRICK (USA) 2 b.c. (Feb 27) Clever Trick (USA)–Hail Hail **110**
(USA) (Hail To Reason (USA)) [1990 7.5g3 7.5g* 7.5d2 8v*] $77,000Y: closely re-
lated to a winner in North America by Icecapade and half-brother to 2 other winners,
including 5f-winning dam of smart French 6.5f to 1m winner Northern Premier: dam

minor winner in USA, is half-sister to dam of high-class middle-distance mare Hush Dear: won maiden at Deauville in August and 5-runner Prix des Chenes at Saint-Cloud (by 4 lengths) in November: 5 lengths second of 9 to Exit To Nowhere in Prix Thomas Bryon at Saint-Cloud in between: very useful. *J. E. Hammond, France.*

REBEL RAISER (USA)   6 ch.g. Raise A Native–Lady Oakley 94 (Gulf Pearl   **38** 117) [1989 7g³ 7m* 6h² 7m 7h⁶ 7m 7.6m 7m 6f a7g 1990 a11g⁴ a8g⁶ 7f² 7h⁶ 6h³ 7g 7f 7f⁵ 6f³ 7f⁴ 7m⁵ 7h⁴ 7g] compact, good-quartered gelding: moderate mover: useful as 2-y-o, only poor nowadays: needs further than 5f and stays 7f: acts on hard going: visored once: has sweated and got on edge: has won for apprentice: winning selling hurdler in August: not one to rely on: sold 1,500 gns Ascot December Sales. *M. J. Ryan.*

RECALDE   2 b.c. (Apr 26) King of Spain 121–Kissimmee (FR) (Petingo 135) [1990   **81** 5.1g² 6m⁴ 7g* 7m⁶ 7g⁴] 7,400F, 14,500Y: leggy, close-coupled colt: eighth foal: brother to quite modest 1988 2-y-o 7f winner Viva Suenos and half-brother to a winner in Mexico: dam placed at 1½m in French Provinces: fair performer: won minor event at Leicester in July: ran creditably in nursery final outing: much better suited by 7f than shorter: best efforts on good ground: pulled hard fourth outing. *G. Wragg.*

RECHANIT (IRE)   2 b.f. (Apr 25) Local Suitor (USA) 128–Claretta (USA) 82   **— p** (Roberto (USA) 131) [1990 7m⁶] 5,000Y, 6,600 2-y-o: half-sister to 3-y-o Saville Way (by Gorytus), smart middle-distance stayer Sapience (by Niniski) and winners in Belgium and Jersey: dam 2-y-o 7f winner, is half-sister to Italian 1000 Guineas winner Rosananti and good English and German performer Claddagh: very green, soon struggling when over 12 lengths sixth of 11 in minor event at York in September: should improve. *C. N. Allen.*

RECHARGEABLE   4 b.g. Music Boy 124–Ciliata (So Blessed 130) [1989 8m   **—** 8.2f⁵ 1990 8.3m] rangy gelding: quite modest maiden at best: led early to post only start in 1990: stays 7f: bandaged first outing at 3 yrs: sold 6,200 gns Newmarket July Sales. *R. Akehurst.*

RECIDIVIST   4 b.f. Royben 125–On Remand 83 (Reform 132) [1989 7s 6s 8d² 8f   **37** 8m 10f⁵ 8m 1990 7m⁶ 8g⁶ 8f⁵] leggy filly: poor walker: moderate mover: poor maiden: should stay 1¼m: possibly requires an easy surface. *R. J. Hodges.*

RECIPE   3 ch.f. Bustino 136–Rosetta Stone 89 (Guillaume Tell (USA) 121) [1989   **—** 9f³ 1990 10.2h⁴ 14g 14m] angular filly: easily best efforts when in frame in maidens: soundly beaten in June handicap final start: bred to stay well. *M. R. Stoute.*

RECITAL (USA)   3 b.f. Danzig (USA)–Dancealot (USA) (Round Table) [1989 NR   **70** 1990 7m² 7g 6f⁴] strong, lengthy filly: moderate mover: closely related to 3 winners by Nijinsky, notably Tights, a smart winner at 3 yrs up to 1¼m, and half-sister to 4 winners: dam one of leading 2-y-o fillies in USA in 1973: favourite, quite modest form in maidens: easily best effort at Goodwood on debut: may stay 1m. *A. C. Stewart.*

RECORD EDGE   3 ch.g. Roman Warrior 132–Record Red 61 (Record Run 127)   **—** [1989 NR 1990 10m] first reported foal: dam showed ability once at 2 yrs: burly, slowly away and well beaten in maiden at Nottingham in July. *K. S. Bridgwater.*

RECORD PRICE   4 b.g. Simply Great (FR) 122–Silk Trade (Auction Ring (USA)   **—** 123) [1989 10s 10d³ 8.5g² 10f² 8.2g 1990 a8g a12g] sparely-made, angular gelding: moderate walker and mover: modest maiden at best: ran poorly last 3 outings: stays 1¼m: acts on firm and dead going. *J. P. Leigh.*

RECTILLON   3 b.c. Rousillon (USA) 133–Rectitude 99 (Runnymede 123) [1989   **78** 6m⁶ 1990 a10g* 10g³ 10.2f* 10.6s 10.2m⁴ 10f⁵ 10f⁴] lengthy colt: good mover: modest handicapper: landed odds in maiden at Lingfield in March and 5-runner contest at Bath in May: facing stiff task, hung left when well beaten final start: should prove as effective over bit shorter: acts on firm going: carries head rather awkwardly: ran moderately in blinkers sixth start: trained until after then by B. Hills: sold only 1,100 gns Newmarket Autumn Sales. *J. P. Hudson.*

RED BISHOP (USA)   2 b. or br.c. (Mar 31) Silver Hawk (USA) 127–La   **77 p** Rouquine (Silly Season 127) [1990 7m³] $100,000Y: fifth foal: half-brother to 2 minor winners in North America by Bold Forbes: dam French 1m winner later stakes-placed winner in USA: co-favourite, under 5 lengths third of 12, pushed along 3f out and keeping on, to Grammos in maiden at Yarmouth in September: should improve. *J. H. M. Gosden.*

RED BLISTER   3 ch.g. Hotfoot 126–Hindu Flame 83 (Shiny Tenth 120) [1989   **—** NR 1990 a8g 5d] seventh foal: brother to 4-y-o sprint plater Fire Lady and closely related to 1983 2-y-o 5f winner Dellwood Iris (by Firestreak): dam 5f winner at 2 yrs: burly and ridden by 7-lb claimer, slowly away when tailed off in maiden and minor event. *W. Holden.*

RED CRESCENT   2 b.c. (Feb 4) Red Sunset 120–Temple Heights 72 (Shirley   65
Heights 130) [1990 7g 7g 7s] 19,000Y: compact colt: first foal: dam 2m winner out of game stayer Hardirondo: around 13 lengths ninth of 16 in maiden at Salisbury on debut: soundly beaten on soft ground. *J. R. Jenkins.*

REDDEN BURN (IRE)   2 b.c. (Feb 7) Green Desert (USA) 127–Red Letter   88
Day 100 (Crepello 136) [1990 6g² 6g* 7m* 7m*] IR 120,000Y: neat, attractive colt: has quick action: half-brother to 1982 2-y-o 5f winner Holy Day (by Sallust): dam won over 6f and 1m: fair performer: odds on, won maiden at Ripon and small-field minor events at Newcastle (easily by 5 lengths) and Chester (by short head from Final Deed, making all) in summer: stays 7f. *H. R. A. Cecil.*

RED DOLLAR   5 ch.g. Tachypous 128–Burglars Girl 63 (Burglar 128) [1989 8s 7f   —
1990 a7g⁶] rangy, workmanlike gelding: good mover: modest winner early as 3-y-o, very lightly raced nowadays: suited by 7f and forcing tactics: acts on good to firm and soft going: possibly best in visor: sometimes sweats and gets on edge. *B. Gubby.*

RED FORMATION   3 b.f. Formidable (USA) 125–Red Velvet 114 (Red God   —
128§) [1989 NR 1990 7m⁵ 7.6m 5.3f⁴] neat filly: half-sister to 4-y-o Scarlet Veil (by Tyrnavos) and several winners, including useful 7f to 9f winner Scarlet Blade (by Kris) and very useful 1974 2-y-o sprinter Red Cross (by Crepello): dam at her best at 2 yrs when winner over 5f and 6f: no worthwhile form in maidens: blinkered final start. *W. Jarvis.*

RED GALE   3 b.g. Blushing Scribe (USA) 107–Moraine (Morston (FR) 125) [1989   54
6g⁵ 6f³ 6g² 7f 8g 1990 8.2g 8m 8g⁶ 9m* 10g] leggy, angular gelding: returned to selling company when winning at Redcar (no bid) in June: favourite, ran moderately 17 days later: stays 9f: acts on firm going. *C. W. C. Elsey.*

RED HENRY (USA)   3 ch.c. Red Ryder (USA)–Bay Line Girl (USA) (Sailing   78
Along (USA)) [1989 5g* 5d² 5m² 5f* 5f² 6d 1990 5f⁶ 5f] leggy, good-topped colt: fairly useful winner at 2 yrs, second in Molecomb Stakes at Goodwood: ran fairly well in listed race at Haydock on reappearance, moderately in Group 3 contest (gave trouble at stalls) at Newmarket later in spring: best at 5f: acted on firm going: effective with or without blinkers: dead. *W. A. O'Gorman.*

RED HOT ROSIE   2 gr.f. (May 25) Absalom 128–Cloister Rose 70 (Track Spare   —
125) [1990 5f 6g 6m] 1,100Y: leggy, close-coupled filly: eighth foal: dam stayed 1½m: always behind, including in seller: subsequently sold 800 gns Newmarket Autumn Sales. *B. R. Millman.*

RED INDIAN   4 ch.g. Be My Native (USA) 122–Martialette (Welsh Saint 126)   58
[1989 6s 7g³ 8m⁴ 8.2m³ 7m² 6f 7m 7m² 7m⁶ 6g 8.2f 7m 10f² 10g² 10g 1990 8.5f⁴ 10.2f⁴ 10.4g 9g* 8.5m² 9f 8.2d] tall, leggy, lengthy gelding: moderate mover: won (for first time) handicap at Hamilton in September: pulled hard when running well next outing: stays 1¼m: acts on firm ground: visored once at 3 yrs: has worn crossed noseband and tongue strap: winning novice hurdler in November. *W. W. Haigh.*

RED JAM JAR   5 ch.g. Windjammer (USA)–Macaw 85 (Narrator 127) [1989   48
10.8m² 10m² 10f² 12.3m* 12.3g 12.2g 1990 a11g³ a12g⁵ 10f³ 10s] good-bodied gelding: moderate mover: poor handicapper: stays 1½m: acts on firm and dead going: has worn tongue strap, crossed noseband and been taken down early: tends to carry head high: changed hands 8,000 gns Doncaster May Sales after final start: resolution under suspicion. *J. Mackie.*

RED MAYDAY   2 b.f. (Mar 24) Domynsky 110–May Kells (Artaius (USA) 129)   43
[1990 5m⁴ 5d⁴ 6g⁶ 5g 6g] 2,000Y: leggy, workmanlike filly: moderate mover: first foal: dam unraced: poor maiden: should be better suited by 6f than 5f. *E. H. Owen jun.*

REDNET   3 b.f. Tender King 123–Red For Go (Tanfirion 110) [1989 5m⁴ 5g 5d 5m   62
1990 a5g* a5g 5g⁶ 5g³ 5g* 5f⁶ a5g³ a5g a5g a5g a6g] tall, good-topped filly: moderate mover: quite modest handicapper: won at Southwell in May and Warwick (rallying well) in July: ran well at Southwell seventh start, poorly after: will prove best at 5f: ran moderately when sweating and on toes: has worn tongue strap. *D. W. Chapman.*

RED PADDY   5 ch.g. Red Sunset 120–Irish Bride (Track Spare 125) [1989 7m 8f³   —
8m* 9g⁶ 10m 7m⁶ 7.6m⁵ 8f a10g] sparely-made gelding: fairly useful winner as 4-y-o: no rateable form in 1990, but ran tremendous race in circumstances when second home on unfavoured far side in Royal Hunt Cup (Handicap) at Royal Ascot

(sweating) on third outing: off course 5 months after: stays 9f: acts on firm going: slowly away first 2 starts: has tended to hang, and probably best with waiting tactics. *P. J. Makin.*

RED PENCIL 5 ch.g. Krayyan 117–Blue Gulf 68 (Gay Fandango (USA) 132) 70 [1989 NR 1990 10.2f 11s² 10f 10m³] angular gelding: has a quick action: modest maiden: not seen out after April: stays 11f: acts on any going: apprentice ridden last 3 starts. *R. Hollinshead.*

RED PIPPIN 3 b.g. Blushing Scribe (USA) 107–Orchard Road 74 (Camden Town 63 125) [1989 6f³ 5m⁴ 1990 6m³ 6f⁶ 5m⁵ 6m⁴ 5.8f³ 5f² 5f 6f 5m 7f 5m⁵] leggy, close-coupled gelding: quite modest maiden: good second in handicap at Sandown in July: no form in varied events after: stays 6f: acts on firm ground: sometimes sweating: usually blinkered: wanders under pressure. *Mrs N. Macauley.*

RED PLANET 5 b.g. Sir Ivor 135–Miss Mars 95 (Red God 128§) [1989 10.2g⁶ — § 12m⁶ 1990 a12g⁶ a12g] sturdy gelding: bad mover: poor maiden: blinkered twice: sold 1,700 gns Doncaster March Sales. *Denys Smith.*

RED POPPY (IRE) 2 b.f. (Feb 25) Coquelin (USA) 121–Special Thanks 58 (Kampala 120) [1990 6g⁴ a6g⁵] IR 8,700Y: leggy, rather sparely-made filly: first foal: dam Irish 7f winner: plating-class form in maidens: hung right and carried head high on debut: found little off bridle second outing. *G. A. Pritchard-Gordon.*

RED PROCESSION 6 ch.g. Red Sunset 120–Procession 118 (Sovereign Path 125) [1989 NR 1990 15g 12g⁶] leggy, rather angular ex-Irish gelding: half-brother to several winners, including useful sprinter Marching On (by Tudor Melody): dam 5f winner: poor maiden: sometimes blinkered. *P. Liddle.*

RED RAINBOW 2 b.c. (Mar 17) Rainbow Quest (USA) 134–Red Berry 115 105 (Great Nephew 126) [1990 6s² 7g⁴ 7m⁴ 8g³ 8.2s* 7.3g² 10v²] 80,000Y: leggy colt: half-brother to several winners, including very useful 1m to 10.5f winner New Berry (by Sir Gaylord) and useful 7f winner Lidhame (by Nureyev): dam second in Cheveley Park Stakes: useful colt: well-backed favourite, won maiden at Haydock in October by 8 lengths from Baatish, quickening clear 2f out: better efforts in Vodafone Horris Hill Stakes at Newbury (beaten 4 lengths by Sapieha) and Group 2 Premio Guido Berardelli at Rome (beaten neck) after: will stay 1½m: yet to race on firm ground, acts on any other: strong-galloping sort. *B. Hanbury.*

RED RIVER BOY 7 b.g. Latest Model 115–Count On Me 77 (No Mercy 126) 56 [1989 8.5d 7g 8h³ 8.5m 7f6 8f² 5.8h* 6h⁵ 7f 7f⁶ 5m³ 6g⁴ 5.8f* 6m 5g⁵ 6g 1990 5.8h 8.3m 7g⁴ 6m² 7m² 5.8f⁶ 8f 6m⁵ 7d⁵ a6g⁶ a7g⁵] lengthy gelding: carries plenty of condition: has a round action: plating-class handicapper: finds easy 5f on sharp side and stays 1m: acts on any going: has been tried in blinkers: has run well for inexperienced rider. *R. J. Hodges.*

RED ROGER 2 ch.g. (May 9) Nishapour (FR) 125–Tasimah (FR) (Petingo 135) — [1990 5f⁶ 6m] 850F, 3,300Y: leggy, sparely-made gelding: half-brother to 3 winners abroad: dam French maiden: soundly beaten in auctions, first a maiden: dead. *C. P. Wildman.*

RED ROSEIN 4 b.f. Red Sunset 120–Vain Deb 66 (Gay Fandango (USA) 132) 61 [1989 6s 5d 6d 5m 5m 6f³ 6f⁶ 6f³ 6g⁵ 6m³ 6m² 6g⁵ 7s 6g² 6f 6g³ 1990 6f⁶ 6f⁶ 6m 6d 6f⁴ 6f 5g² 5d 5m 6s 6d] leggy, sparely-made filly: has a quick action: quite modest handicapper: below form last 4 outings: stays 6f: best form on a sound surface: blinkered tenth outing: usually bandaged behind: often slowly away: has not won since debut at 2 yrs. *N. Tinkler.*

RED SECRET (IRE) 2 br.f. (Apr 14) Valiyar 129–Freeze The Secret (USA) 118 45 p (Nearctic) [1990 a7g⁵ a8g⁵] half-sister to several winners, including useful Irish 7f to 8.5f performer Certain Secret (by Known Fact) and Irish middle-distance stayer Security Clearance (by General Assembly): dam second in 1000 Guineas and Oaks: beaten some way when fifth in maidens at Lingfield: wore eyeshield both starts. *Mrs L. Piggott.*

RED SPARKY 2 b.f. (Feb 24) Green Ruby (USA) 104–Electrified 67 (Gunner B 43 126) [1990 5f 5f⁵ 6g² 6g 6g⁶ 7f 7.5g] 2,500Y: medium-sized filly: has a round action: first foal: dam won over hurdles: moderate plater: stiff task final start: should stay 7f: has been bandaged. *J. Balding.*

RED TIGER 2 ch.g. (May 7) Blushing Scribe (USA) 107–Nonpareil (FR) 92 57 (Pharly (FR) 130) [1990 6m 5g³ 5m⁵ 5m² 5g³ 5m] 29,000Y: leggy, sparely-made gelding: third foal: brother to 1989 2-y-o 5.8f winner Access Leisure and fair 1988 2-y-o 5f winner Mister Lawson: dam best at 2 yrs: plating-class maiden: blinkered fourth start: tends to hang right and doesn't look particularly genuine: sold 3,400 gns Doncaster September Sales. *J. Berry.*

RED TOTO 3 ch.c. Habitat 134–Soumana (FR) (Pharly (FR) 130) [1989 6g⁴ 7v **108** 1990 8m* 9m³ 8.5d 10m* 10f* 10f⁴ 10m* 9m] medium-sized colt: comfortable winner of maiden at Warwick in April and handicaps at Yarmouth in June and Newmarket (£8,000 event) in July: led inside final 1f to win slowly-run 5-runner £9,100 handicap at Yarmouth in September: never dangerous facing stiff task in Cambridgeshire at Newmarket: suited by 1¼m: acts on firm ground, seems unsuited by heavy. *A. C. Stewart.*

RED VICTOR 3 b.c. Bellman (FR) 123–Red Sharp (FR) (Sharpman 124) [1989 6d **48** 7g 1990 a10g⁵ 8f 8f 10m⁵ 8.5g³ 9g⁶ 10m 10f⁵ 10m⁵ 12.5m 12d] close-coupled colt: good walker: moderate mover: plater: stays 1¼m: acts on good to firm ground: usually blinkered. *R. F. Johnson Houghton.*

REED BED (IRE) 2 b.c. (Mar 13) Thatching 131–Kye-Hye 61 (Habitat 134) **78 p** [1990 6f⁵ 6g⁶ 6d*] IR 9,600F, 60,000 francs (approx £5,800) Y: tall, leggy colt: has scope: half-brother to several winners, including very good French miler Justicara (by Rusticaro) and useful 6f and 1m winner Naar (by North Stoke): dam placed at up to 1¾m: won maiden at Lingfield in October, showing much improved form, by 5 lengths from Paper Dart: may well improve further at 7f. *R. Hannon.*

REEDLING (USA) 5 b.g. Riverman (USA) 131–Mary Biz (USA) (T V Lark) — [1989 10.1m 11.7m 16f⁴ a10g 1990 10m] big, rangy gelding: showed promise on debut, but very little on other 6 outings on flat: tailed off in seller in September: blinkered once in 1989. *P. Butler.*

REEF WIND 3 b.c. Tumble Wind (USA)–Hollow Reef (Wollow 132) [1989 5g 5s **50** 5m⁶ 6m 7f 7m 5f a6g⁴ a7g 1990 10.6s⁶ 9g 10.6s 13m³ 13.8m² 11.5f⁵ 13.8m⁴ 10f² 6f 8.2g⁵ 11.7f³ 7m a11g] small, light-framed colt: plating-class maiden: shaped as if stayed 13.8f: acted on any going: ran poorly in visor: blinkered once at 2 yrs: took keen hold: sometimes bandaged: trained first 5 outings by S. Norton: winning selling hurdler: dead. *R. W. Stubbs.*

REEL FOYLE (USA) 3 ch.f. Irish River (FR) 131–Abergwaun 128 (Bounteous **71** 125) [1989 6m³ 5g* 5m⁴ 5m⁶ 1990 5f³ 5g⁵ 5d 5m⁵ 7f] strong, muscular filly: modest performer: should prove suited by 5f: acts on firm ground: blinkered (ridden along leaving stalls, below form) penultimate start. *Mrs L. Piggott.*

REEM ALBARAARI 2 b.f. (Mar 5) Sadler's Wells (USA) 132–Habibti 136 **81 p** (Habitat 134) [1990 6g³ 6m³] 510,000Y: small, stocky filly: fluent mover, with a sharp action: first living foal: dam outstanding sprinter, also third in 1000 Guineas: backward and green, demoted second of 16 to Jimlil in minor event at Doncaster, keeping on well despite wandering: better effort over 4 lengths third of 4 to Crystal Gazing in £9,800 event at Ascot later in September: will stay 7f. *M. R. Stoute.*

REFERENCE LIGHT (USA) 3 b.c. Diesis 133–Lulworth Cove (Averof **107** 123) [1989 6g³ 6g* 1990 8m³ 8f⁵ 7.6g² 7g² 6d*] workmanlike colt: capable of useful form: won £8,400 handicap at Newmarket in October by a short head, always prominent and rallying well: taken quietly to post, ran moderately in amateurs race at Doncaster time before, hanging left: ideally suited by 6f: acts on dead going, possibly unsuited by firm. *M. R. Stoute.*

REFLECTIVE 3 br.g. Magic Mirror 105–Thanks Edith (Gratitude 130) [1989 6g **34** 7.5f 8f 8f³ 8.2s 1990 8f 8g 7m 12m 10f³ 12.2d a12g] leggy, sparely-made gelding: plater: worthwhile form as 3-y-o only on fifth (first for over 4½ months) start: best form over 1m: seems suited by firm going: blinkered fourth and fifth outings: trained until after latter by Mrs R. Wharton. *W J Pearce.*

REGAL CREST (USA) 2 br.c. (Feb 27) Gold Crest (USA) 120–Ambrellita (FR) **92** (Misti IV 132) [1990 5f⁵ 5g* 5d 5g⁴ 5m⁴ 7m⁵] $65,000Y: leggy, double-coupled colt: moderate mover: half-brother to fair 1¼m performer Amber Loch (by Lomond) and 2 winners in France: dam won from 7.5f to 13f in France: fairly useful colt: won maiden at Nottingham in June by 7 lengths: better efforts in varied events final 3 starts, making running over 5f when 5 lengths last of 5 behind Bog Trotter in Somerville Tattersall Stakes at Newmarket: worth a try at 6f. *J. Berry.*

REGAL LOOK (IRE) 2 b.f. (Apr 25) Vision (USA)–Latin Guest (Be My Guest **46** (USA) 126) [1990 5m 6g⁶ 6d 7m 5.8d] 13,000Y: small filly: fourth foal: half-sister to winner in Belgium by Pas de Seul: dam lightly-raced half-sister to champion 1978 Irish 2-y-o Sandy Creek: poor form in varied events, including a seller: will stay 1m: sold out of W. Jarvis' stable 1,100 gns Doncaster August Sales after second start. *B. R. Millman.*

REGAL NORTH 3 b.g. Regalberto (USA)–Nell of The North (USA) (Canadian — Gil (CAN)) [1989 6m⁶ 6f⁵ 6m² 7g 8f⁵ 1990 8g 10.2m] leggy, rather shallow-girthed gelding: quite modest maiden at 2 yrs: faced very stiff task in handicap final start in

1990, in May: should stay further than 6f: ran wide on turn at Catterick: retained 480 gns Doncaster October Sales. *J. Etherington.*

REGAL PEACE   3 br.f. Known Fact (USA) 135–Tarvie 101 (Swing Easy (USA)   **94** 126) [1989 5d⁴ 5m* 6d 5g³ 1990 5m⁵ 7f 5g⁶ 6m⁵ 7m⁵ 6m⁶ 5g⁶ 6g⁴ 9s⁶ 7d⁴] 26,000Y: small, sparely-made filly: half-sister to several winners, notably very speedy 1985 2-y-o Stalker (by Kala Shikari): dam game sprinter: fairly useful performer: won listed race at the Curragh in May at 2 yrs: ran creditably in Group 3 event at Phoenix Park and listed race at the Curragh seventh and eighth starts: chiefly below form otherwise at 3 yrs, tailed off in Jersey Stakes at Royal Ascot: best at sprint distances: acts good to firm ground. *J. McLoughlin, Ireland.*

REGAL REFORM   7 b.g. Prince Tenderfoot (USA) 126–Polly Packer 81   **107** (Reform 132) [1989 12d 12g* 14g² 12m³ 12g⁶ 14f* 16.1m* 14.8m³ 18f* 1990 12m 16.2f* 22d* 16.1f⁴ 18m² 18g³ 16m⁵ 18d⁴] workmanlike, good-bodied gelding: useful performer: successful in minor event at Haydock and Queen Alexandra Stakes (by 8 lengths from Mill Pond) at Royal Ascot: ran very well when third of 10 to Al Maheb in Doncaster Cup, creditably when fourth to Trainglot in Tote Cesarewitch (Handicap) at Newmarket final outing: out-and-out stayer: acts on firm and dead going: tough, genuine and consistent: a credit to his trainer. *G. M. Moore.*

REGAL ROMPER (IRE)   2 b.c. (Mar 4) Tender King 123–Fruit of Passion   **49 p** (High Top 131) [1990 6d 6g] IR 14,500F, 11,000Y: rather leggy, good-topped colt: has scope: has a round action: second foal: half-brother to a winner in Hong Kong: dam unraced: backward, prominent to around 2f out in maidens at Ayr and York in autumn: sure to do better. *F. H. Lee.*

REGAL SABRE (USA)   2 b.c. (Feb 15) Sharpen Up 127–Royal Heroine 121   **104 p** (Lypheor 118) [1990 6m³ 6m* 6g⁴ 7.3g³] IR 250,000Y: strong, good-topped colt with scope: thrived physically: has a powerful action: second reported foal: dam 6f to 9.2f winner later won Breeders' Cup Mile: useful colt: won maiden at Newmarket in July: better subsequent effort in pattern events when over 4 lengths third of 9,

Queen Alexandra Stakes, Ascot—a severe test of stamina, and a clear-cut winner in Regal Reform who beats the roan Mill Pond; the horse next to Mill Pond is fourth-placed Ceciliano

carrying condition but staying on well having been outpaced 3f out, to Sapieha in Vodafone Horris Hill Stakes at Newbury: will be suited by 1m: looks sort to do better at 3 yrs. *R. Hannon.*

REGAL STING (USA) 3 b.c. Drone–Momma Taj (USA) (Bupers) [1989 7g — 1990 8g] heavy-topped colt: never placed to challenge in maidens at Newmarket and Newbury: sold 2,100 gns Newmarket Autumn Sales. *G. Harwood.*

REGAL THATCH 3 ch.c. Thatching 131–Kolomelskoy Palace 77 (Royal Palace   63 131) [1989 6f² 6f² 6f 7g³ 7m⁴ 8m⁴ 8g 7m* 6v 7d³ 1990 8g 8m 8d 7m⁵ 7f 6f⁴ 8g 9m] workmanlike, angular colt: fair winner at 2 yrs, generally well below form in 1990: stays 1m: acts on any going: blinkered 5 times as 3-y-o: sold to join G. Richards 10,500 gns Newmarket Autumn Sales. *C. E. Brittain.*

REGAL VALUE 2 b.c. (Apr 18) Nomination 125–Be Royal 97 (Royal Palm 131)   47 [1990 6m 6g] 17,500Y: good-bodied colt: fifth reported foal: half-brother to useful 6f and 7f winner Native Oak (by Tower Walk): dam 2-y-o 5f winner, is half-sister to dam of Pas de Seul: behind in sellers at Goodwood and Nottingham (tended to wander, and looked ungenuine) in summer: sold to join A. Harrison 3,500 gns Doncaster August Sales. *W. Jarvis.*

REGAN (USA) 3 b.f. Lear Fan (USA) 130–Twice A Fool (USA) (Foolish   60 Pleasure (USA)) [1989 NR 1990 10m 12m³] rather angular filly: fifth foal: half-sister to 3 winners in USA, including stakes winner at up to 1m by Full Intent: dam unraced daughter of sister to top-class miler Habitat: strong-finishing third of 12 in claimer at Leicester in September, pushed along with a lot to do over 4f out: very green and moved poorly down 8 days earlier: sold 8,500 gns Newmarket Autumn Sales. *B. Hanbury.*

REGENT LAD 6 b.g. Prince Regent (FR) 129–Red Laser 95 (Red God 128§)   80 [1989 8g* 8.5d² 8f* 8m* 8f³ 8f 8f⁴ 8f² 7.5m* 8f³ 7f* 7m 8f⁵ 8g⁶ 1990 8f 8h 7.5f⁴ 8f⁶ 7.5g² 8m 9m⁴ 8g⁴ 8.5m⁴ 8g 9f² 10m⁵ 8d² 8m³ 7d] leggy gelding: good walker: fair handicapper: probably best short of 1¼m: acts on any going except possibly heavy: best without blinkers: consistent but none too resolute, and is ideally suited by waiting tactics. *Miss L. C. Siddall.*

REGENT'S FOLLY (IRE) 2 ch.f. (Mar 5) Touching Wood (USA) 127–   83 p Regent's Fawn (CAN) 72 (Vice Regent (CAN)) [1990 7m 7m* 7g*] IR 9,000Y, resold 10,500Y: good-bodied filly: second foal: half-sister to 3-y-o 1¼m winner Fallow Deer (by Jalmood): dam maiden suited by 1½m, is sister a top-class Canadian middle-distance filly Bounding Away and close relation to high-class 1¼m winner Ascot Knight: progressive filly, game neck winner of maiden auction at Leicester in September and nursery at York following month: will be well suited by 1¼m +: quite useful middle-distance handicapper in the making. *W. Jarvis.*

REGENT'S INLET (USA) 3 b.g. It's Freezing (USA)–Lawyer's Wave (USA)   60 (Advocator) [1989 NR 1990 9g³ 12m 10.1m 8m 8f 6m 8m* 8.2m] workmanlike gelding: has scope: moderate walker and mover: second reported foal: dam, minor 3-y-o 8.5f stakes winner, is sister to smart American colt Kirrary: form only when winning handicap at Yarmouth in August by 4 lengths, soon ridden along in rear: evidently suited by 1m: blinkered last 3 starts: edgy and pulled hard final one: joined T. Caldwell. *C. E. Brittain.*

REGGAE BEAT 5 b.g. Be My Native (USA) 122–Invery Lady 65 (Sharpen Up   59 127) [1989 10g 8f* 9m² 10m³ 12m 1000 n10g⁴ a12g* a13g⁶ 10f 10.8d⁰ 11.5g⁴] leggy, lightly-made, angular gelding: has a light action: plating-class handicapper: won at Lingfield in March and Sandown (wearing tongue strap) in September: stays 1½m: acts on any going: suitable mount for 7-lb claimer: winning hurdler in October. *I. Campbell.*

REGIMENTAL ARMS (USA) 3 b.c. Sir Ivor 135–Durtal 121 (Lyphard (USA)   96 § 132) [1989 NR 1990 10m⁴ 10.4d* 10m⁶ 12m 12g⁶ 10m² 14g⁵] small, sturdy colt: has a round action: seventh foal: half-brother to useful miler True Panache (by Mr Prospector) and Gold Cup winner Gildoran (by Rheingold): dam, winner of Cheveley Park and Fred Darling Stakes, is half-sister to Arc winner Detroit: capable of quite useful form, winning maiden at Chester in May and just over 5 lengths last of 6 in Predominate Stakes at Goodwood: ran poorly in King Edward VII Stakes at Royal Ascot and listed race (moved poorly down) next 2 starts and found nothing in minor events last 2: should be well suited by 1½m +: sold 21,000 gns Newmarket Autumn Sales: clearly one to be wary of. *B. W. Hills.*

REGINA ROYALE (USA) 3 b.f. Eternal Prince (USA)–Lizzie's Light (USA)   41 (Icecapade (USA)) [1989 6m 6g 1990 8g 10.1m⁶ 8.3g 8f 7m⁴ 8m² 8.2s⁵ a6g] leggy filly: has a round action: plater: stays 1m: acts on good to firm ground and soft: trained first 3 starts by W. Jarvis: visored last three. *C. R. Nelson.*

REGORDES 3 b.f. Commanche Run 133–Smageta (High Top 131) [1989 NR 1990   **91 +**
10.6s* 11.5g² 14.6g] lengthy filly: fourth foal: closely related to 1987 Italian 2-y-o winner Rusoli (by Ardross) and half-sister to 1990 Italian 7f and 1m winner Ruchetee (by Ahonoora): dam won 3 times in Italy at 2 yrs: 20/1-winner of maiden at Haydock in June: improved considerably when second in minor event at Sandown, rallying strongly: 16/1, led over 9f when tailed off in Park Hill Stakes at Doncaster: should be suited by 1¾m. *L. M. Cumani.*

REINDEER WALK 8 gr.g. Godswalk (USA) 130–Carcajou (High Top 131)   **47 d**
[1989 NR 1990 a6g a8g³ 8f 8.2s⁵ 6f 7f a7g⁶ 10d 8f 8f] robust gelding: poor handicapper: best at 7f or 1m: acts on any going: visored twice: trained until after ninth start by D. Chapman: ungenuine. *M. P. Muggeridge.*

REINE D'BEAUTE 4 gr.f. Caerleon (USA) 132–As You Desire Me 112 (Kala-   **97 p**
moun 129) [1989 NR 1990 9f* 8m*] rangy filly: fluent mover: fourth foal: half-sister to 3 winners, all at least quite useful, including untrustworthy filly Intimate Guest (by Be My Guest), successful from 6f to 1m: dam, from very good family, won 3 times at around 1m in France: made all to justify favouritism in minor events at Ripon and Pontefract (long odds on) in April: will stay further than 9f. *H. R. A. Cecil.*

REINE DE DANSE (USA) 3 gr.f. Nureyev (USA) 131–Bernica (FR) 114 (Caro   **78 ?**
133) [1989 NR 1990 7g² 7m⁵ 8g³ 7d⁵ 7m] $400,000Y: angular filly: fifth foal: sister to smart 1985 French 2-y-o 6f winner Excalibur's Lake and half-sister to 3 winners in France: dam very useful at up to 1¼m in France: modest maiden: deteriorated, edging right and finding little third start. *B. W. Hills.*

REJOICE (IRE) 2 b.f. (Apr 14) Damister (USA) 123–Rocket Alert 110 (Red Alert   **80 p**
127) [1990 a7g*] angular, rather unfurnished filly: third foal: half-sister to useful 1¼m and 10.6f winner Ardlui (by Lomond): dam 5f to 7f winner: ridden by 5-lb claimer, won 16-runner maiden at Southwell comfortably by 3 lengths, clear, from Joie de Soir: will stay 1m: sure to improve. *W. A. O'Gorman.*

REJONEO (USA) 3 b.c. El Gran Senor (USA) 136–Chateau Dancer (USA) 104   **85**
(Giacometti 130) [1989 7m³ 6g⁶ 1990 7g³ 8g² 8.2m⁴ 10f* 10m⁴] tall, close-coupled colt: has rather round action: fair form: won 4-runner maiden at Folkestone in August: stayed 1¼m: ran as if something amiss third start: dead. *J. Gosden.*

REKLAW 3 b.g. Hard Fought 125–Rubina Park 64 (Ashmore (FR) 125) [1989 8s   **—**
1990 8m 7m⁴ 8f 8g 10g] angular, sparely-made gelding: shows plenty of knee action: poor form at best: behind in handicaps, well-backed favourite penultimate outing: should stay middle distances. *Mrs J. R. Ramsden.*

RELAX AGAIN 3 gr.f. Durandal 114–Relax 73 (Seminole II) [1989 NR 1990 7g 8g   **—**
6f 8h⁵] smallish, angular filly: sixth reported living foal: half-sister to plating-class 1989 9.1f and 1¼m winner Miss Relsun (by Le Soleil): dam stayed well: no form in claimers (very slowly away on debut) and apprentice maiden. *Mrs G. R. Reveley.*

RELENTLESS PURSUIT (IRE) 2 b.c. (Feb 6) Thatching 131–Daring Way   **71 p**
(USA) 78 (Alydar (USA)) [1990 6m⁶ 6g a6g*] well-made colt: has scope: second foal: half-brother to 3-y-o Milne's Way (by The Noble Player), 5.8f and 6f winner at 2 yrs:

State of New York Stakes, Belmont Park —
Relief Pitcher and Free At Last give the visitors a good start to Breeders' Cup day

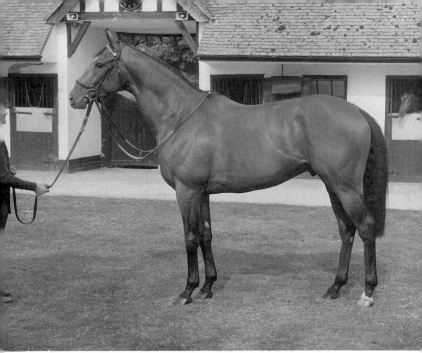

Mrs John Wallinger's "Relief Pitcher"

dam won over 7f at 3 yrs: favourite, won 9-runner maiden at Lingfield late in year very easily by 2 lengths from Quintessential: will stay 7f: sure to improve further. *B. W. Hills.*

RELIANT   3 b.c. Shirley Heights 130–Swift And Sure (USA) 98 (Valdez (USA))   **78**
[1989 8.2d³ 8v 1990 10.8m 12m⁴ 12g⁴ 14m² 12m⁶ 12m⁶ 11.7m⁵] short-legged, strong, lengthy colt: moderate walker and mover: modest maiden: stays 1¾m: lacks turn of foot: sold 10,000 gns Newmarket Autumn Sales, probably to race in Italy. *I. A. Balding.*

RELIEF PITCHER   4 b.c. Welsh Term 126–Bases Loaded (USA) (Northern   **120** Dancer) [1989 9g⁵ 10g² 11.7m³ 10f² 10f* 12f³ 12m² 12f² 10g* 11.1m² 10d⁴ 1990 9m 10m⁵ 10m* 10m² 10m⁴ 10g² 10.5g 10d² 10g*] big, deep-girthed colt: carries plenty of condition: good-class performer: won State of New York Stakes at Belmont Park in October by ¾ length from Free At Last: best efforts earlier in season in listed race (beat Observation Post ½ length) at Goodwood, Prince of Wales's Stakes (caught final strides by Batshoof) at Royal Ascot and in another Goodwood listed contest on eighth start: effective at 1¼m and 1½m: acts on good to firm and dead going: too free in visor seventh outing: has sweated and got on toes: splendidly tough and consistent. *P. T. Walwyn.*

RELPOUR   2 gr.c. (May 3) Nishapour (FR) 125–Reflected Glory (SWE) (Relko   **73** 136) [1990 6g² 5f* 6f³ 5m* 5m 6g³] 3,200Y: rather leggy colt: half-brother to several winners in Sweden: dam poor staying maiden: modest performer: won maiden auction at Beverley in July and nursery at Goodwood in August: stays 6f: has been bandaged: often on toes: ran well when sweating penultimate start: consistent. *Mrs N. Macauley.*

REMEMBER THE ALAMO 4 b.g. Scorpio (FR) 127–Chelsea Charmer —
(Ballymore 123) [1989 8s 9s 6g 12f² 12m³ 12g 1990 15d 10.6d] leggy ex-Irish gelding:
half-brother to a winner in USA by Cut Above: dam Irish 1m winner: placed in
handicaps at Mallow as 3-y-o: no show in amateurs race and claimer in September:
stays 1½m: acts on firm going. *J. J. O'Neill.*

REMTHAT NASER 3 b.f. Sharpo 132–Warning Sound (Red Alert 127) [1989 **91**
5d* 6g² 7g² 7g⁵ 6g 1990 6m⁵ 7g² 8m* 8m* 7g⁵] neat filly: fairly useful performer:
successful in smallish fields for minor events at Warwick and Leicester (dead-
heated) in October: soon recovered from very slow start but well below form in
mixed-aged contest at Newmarket final start: stays 1m: acts on good to firm ground
and dead. *G. A. Huffer.*

REMWOOD GIRL 4 b.f. Remainder Man 126§–Aliwood Girl 64§ (Broxted 120) —
[1989 6s² 7.5d* 7f 8.2g 8v 8m 1990 a7g a7g⁶ 10m⁴ 8m 7d] small, plain filly: keen
walker: moderate mover: winning plater as 3-y-o: easily best effort in 1990 on third
outing: stays 1¼m: acts on good to firm and soft going: tried in blinkers (hung left) at
2 yrs. *K. S. Bridgwater.*

RENDEZVOUS BAY 4 b.f. Mill Reef (USA) 141–Figure de Proue (FR) (Petingo —
135) [1989 10m 10.6g 12.2m a13g a14g 1990 a11g] sparely-made filly: modest maiden
at 2 yrs: no subsequent form. *J. L. Dunlop.*

RENO'S JEM 4 b.f. Starch Reduced 112–Miss Purchase 62 (Sterling Bay (SWE)) — §
[1989 NR 1990 a11g] leggy, plain filly: no sign of ability and appears ungenuine:
blinkered, pulled up in Southwell maiden in February: sold 1,550 gns Ascot June
Sales: resold 1,050 gns Ascot July Sales. *R. T. Jukes.*

RENTINA 3 b.f. Adonijah 126–Gay Charlotte 95 (Charlottown 127) [1989 7m⁶ **67**
1990 10.2g³ 14f² 12f³ 10m⁵] sparely-made filly: quite modest maiden: should stay
1½m: carried head high last 2 outings. *H. R. A. Cecil.*

REPACKER 4 ch.f. Aragon 118–Golden October 62 (Young Generation 129) —
[1989 7m a10g 1990 a7g⁵ a10g] leggy filly: sign of ability only when fifth in maiden
claimer at Southwell in January: stays 7f: usually bandaged: has worn tongue strap.
C. N. Allen.

REPECHAGE 3 b.f. Tina's Pet 121–Lady's Walk (Pall Mall 132) [1989 NR 1990 **70**
9m 12.5g* 12.2d⁵ a12g] sparely-made, angular filly: half-sister to several winners,
including prolific 1979 2-y-o 5f winner Davidgalaxy Affair (by Tower Walk) and fairly
useful 5f winner Deportment (by So Blessed): dam lightly raced: modest form:
easily won seller (sold out of J. Fanshawe's stable 7,000 gns) at Wolverhampton in
October: easily best other effort (moved badly down on debut) in apprentice race
next time: stays 1½m: acts on dead going. *B. A. McMahon.*

REPIQUE (USA) 2 ch.f. (Apr 1) Sharpen Up 127–Repetitious 103 (Northfields **88** p
(USA)) [1990 6m²] 210,000Y: sister to 1988 2-y-o 1m winner Sharp 'N Shine, later
one to treat with caution, and half-sister to 3 other winners, including good French
1¼m and 10.5f winner Sarhoob (by Alydar): dam 6f to 1m winner, is sister to smart
filly Nanticious: green, short-head second of 9, soon prominent and running on
strongly, to Shihama in maiden at Newmarket in November: showed a round action:
sure to improve, particularly at 7f+. *L. M. Cumani.*

REPLICATE 2 ch.f. (Apr 24) Vaigly Great 127–Remould 83 (Reform 132) [1990 **56**
6m 6d³ 6g] smallish, sparely-made filly: half-sister to middle-distance winner Deal
On (by Quiet Fling) and 2 winners abroad: dam 2-y-o 5f winner: best effort staying-
on third of 25 in claimer at Goodwood in October: will probably stay 7f. *J. W. Hills.*

REPROTOPPER 2 b.f. (Apr 16) High Top 131–Reprocolor 114 (Jimmy Reppin **74** p
131) [1990 7g⁶ 7m⁵] rangy filly: really good walker: powerful galloper, with a round
action: eighth foal: sister to Irish Oaks winner Colorspin and half-sister to very
smart 6f to 1¼m winner Bella Colora (by Bellypha) and useful 6f and 1m winner
Rappa Tap Tap (by Tap On Wood): dam won Lingfield Oaks Trial and Lancashire
Oaks: 7 lengths fifth of 9, staying on steadily, to Shadayid in minor event at Ascot in
September: will be suited by 1m+: sure to win a race. *M. R. Stoute.*

RE-RELEASE 5 ch.m. Baptism 119–Release Record (Jukebox 120) [1989 7g⁴ **90**
8s⁶ 8.5d⁵ 8f² 8.2m²ᵈⁱˢ 8.2g³ 9g³ 12d² 1990 13.3g³ 9m 12s] rangy, angular mare:
fairly useful handicapper: shaped well when third in £20,400 event at Newbury in
September and not discredited when ninth of 40 to Risen Moon in 9f Cambridgeshire at Newmarket (soon outpaced) 2 weeks later: will stay 1¾m: acts on any
going: wears blinkers or visor: winning but moody hurdler. *M. C. Pipe.*

RESEARCHING (USA) 3 b.c. Mr Prospector (USA)–Solartic (CAN) (Briartic —
(CAN)) [1989 NR 1990 10m 10m⁴ 10s] lengthy, workmanlike colt with scope: good
mover: sixth foal: brother to In Toto and closely related to Solo Native (by Exclusive

Native), both fairly useful 2-y-o 5f winners and latter also successful at up to 1¼m in USA, and half-brother to smart 6f (at 2 yrs) to 1½m winner Tralos (by Roberto): dam successful at up to 1m and second in 9f Canadian Oaks: form only when fourth of 8 in moderately-run maiden at Redcar: hung left first 2 starts, headstrong on final one: sold 10,500 gns Newmarket Autumn Sales. *G. Harwood.*

RESHIFT   2 b.f. (Apr 9) Night Shift (USA)–Repoussee (Jimmy Reppin 131) [1990   **77 p**
6g 6g² 6d* 8v] angular, good-topped filly: fourth foal: dam ran once: progressive filly: ridden by 7-lb claimer, won 18-runner maiden at Doncaster in November by 2 lengths from Collins Avenue: seventh of 10 in Premio Dormello at Milan later in month: keen sort: probably stays 1m. *M. Bell.*

RESIDENCY   6 b.g. Dominion 123–Restive 96 (Relic) [1989 NR 1990 a8g] strong,   —
good-topped gelding: moderate mover: modest maiden as 3-y-o: very lightly raced nowadays: best effort at 7f: possibly unsuited by extremes of going. *J. Webber.*

RES IPSA LOQUITUR   3 b.g. Law Society (USA) 130–Bubbling (USA) (Stage   **69**
Door Johnny) [1989 6m⁴ 7g⁴ 7g⁴ 10g 1990 9g⁶ 10.4d⁶ 8m 12m⁵ 10f⁴ 12.2f² 12g⁵] well-made gelding: modest maiden: amateur ridden, moved poorly down and ran poorly in handicap final start: will be suited by stiffer test of stamina: trained until after fourth start by R. Hollinshead. *R. Simpson.*

RESISTING (USA)   2 b.c. (May 25) Desert Wine (USA)–Fool's Miss (USA)   —
(Saltville) [1990 8f 8g 9g] $100,000Y: lengthy colt: has scope: half-brother to 5 winners in USA, notably Delicate Vine (by Knights Choice), high-class 1986 2-y-o winner at up to 1m: dam ran 3 times: sire high class at 1m to 1¼m in USA: very green, poor form in maidens and a claimer (travelled well to 3f out then carried head bit high and found little) in autumn. *J. H. M. Gosden.*

RESOLUTE BAY   4 b.g. Crofthall 110–Spinner 59 (Blue Cashmere 129) [1989 5g   **89**
6m⁵ 6m 5f⁴ 6m⁴ 6f* 6m* 6f 6m 6f 1990 6g 5m 5m² 6f* 6m 6g⁵ 6m² 6m 5.6g 6g 7g⁴ 6d 7d] lengthy gelding: has a rather round action: quite useful handicapper: edged right when first past the post at Sandown (demoted) and Chester in July: very good second in £7,200 event at Newcastle in August: effective over stiff 5f and should prove as good at 7f as 6f: appears ideally suited by top-of-the-ground: best visored (blinkered final start): has started slowly. *R. M. Whitaker.*

RESPECTABLE JONES   4 ch.g. Tina's Pet 121–Jonesee 64 (Dublin Taxi)   **89**
[1989 6m⁶ 5g³ 5f⁴ 6g 6g 7.6m 5d* 5d⁴ 1990 6m⁵ 6g² 6d² 5m* 6m² 5d⁶ 6g⁴ 6m⁵ 6m* 5g³ 6s⁶ a6g*] leggy, lengthy gelding: fair handicapper: successful in 1990 at Windsor (apprentices), Chepstow (ladies) and Lingfield (showing improved form, easily by 5 lengths): hung badly right fifth start: stays 6f: acts on any going: often visored, but not last 6 starts: consistent. *G. B. Balding.*

RESTLESS DON   5 b.h. Mandrake Major 122–La Fille 58 (Crooner 119) [1989 5g   **65**
5f⁴ 5f 5m* 5g³ 6m 5g⁴ 5m 5m⁵ 5m 5m 1990 5f 5d 5g 5f⁵ 5d 6m 5g 5m⁶ 5m] lengthy, dipped-backed horse: fair winner as 4-y-o: below his best in 1990: suited by 5f and a sound surface: has shown tendency to hang: inconsistent. *G. M. Moore.*

RESTLESS RHAPSODY   7 ch.g. Young Generation 129–Bohemian Rhapsody   —
86 (On Your Mark 125) [1989 5m 5f 6m 7m 7g² 1990 a8g a6g a6g a7g] robust gelding: form for long time only final start at 6 yrs: stays 7f: possibly suited by an easy surface nowadays: effective with or without blinkers: usually bandaged off-fore: sold 975 gns Ascot April Sales. *J. G. M. O'Shea.*

RESTORE   7 ch.g. Habitat 134–Never So Lovely 87 (Realm 129) [1989 6v⁴ 5s 6f*   **86 d**
6f* 6f 6m 6m 6m 6g³ 6g 1000 6f⁶ 6m 0f⁰ 0d 6d 6m⁴ 6f* 6d 6g 6m⁵ a7g⁶] useful-looking gelding: hobdayed twice: one-time useful sprinter: had excellent chance on best form when winning claimer at Goodwood in August: little show afterwards: suited by 6f and a sound surface: has worn visor, blinkered nowadays: not suited by track at Epsom: often on edge: usually taken early to post: best with strong handling. *G. Lewis.*

RESUCADA   4 b.g. Red Sunset 120–Camden Dancer (Camden Town 125) [1989   **37**
6s 5s 6d 6m³ 6f 6f⁴ 6m* 5f⁵ 6h⁴ 5m 1990 6m 6f 5f 5f 5m 5g 10m⁴ 8.2g 8m⁵ 8f³ 8h 7.5f] strong, lengthy gelding: carries condition: moderate walker: modest winner as 3-y-o, not so good in 1990: best form at 6f: needs a sound surface, and acts on hard ground: usually blinkered or visored, but wasn't last 2 starts. *T. Fairhurst.*

RETIRING IMP (USA)   3 ch.c. Imp Society (USA)–Merry And Gay (USA)   **102**
(Majestic Prince) [1989 NR 1990 5g* 6v² 5g* 5g 5f 5v 6s] $25,000Y, 2,000 2-y-o: seventh foal: half-brother to 3 winners in North America: dam never ran: sire best at 4 yrs when successful in graded events from 8.5f to 1¼m: useful sprinter: successful in minor event at Rome in March and Group 3 Premio Certosa (by short neck from Barn Five South) at Milan in May: below form after, trained by W.

O'Gorman for King George Stakes at Goodwood (soon behind) on fifth start. *B. Agriformi, Italy.*

RETOUCH 4 b.c. Touching Wood (USA) 127–Nelly Do Da 78 (Derring-Do 131)   **94**
[1989 10g 12f 10f* 13.8g² 11.7f³ 14m⁵ 1990 14g⁴ 16m² 20m* 17.6g² 16.2m⁴ 14.6d³]
workmanlike, rather sparely-made colt: quite useful performer: swished tail when
winning £14,800 Ascot Stakes (Handicap) at Royal Ascot by 2 lengths from Lucky
Verdict: ran well after when placed in £7,400 handicap at Haydock and minor event
won by Yalanoura at Doncaster: suited by good test of stamina: acts on good to firm
and dead going. *P. F. I. Cole.*

RETURN TO SENDER 3 b.c. Auction Ring (USA) 123–Tarte Tatin (FR)   —
(Busted 134) [1989 7g 1990 7f 11d 7f 7g] lengthy, workmanlike colt: well beaten in
maidens and handicaps: bred to stay 1m+: has flashed tail. *R. J. R. Williams.*

REVEL 2 ch.c. (Mar 8) Sharpo 132–Waltz 75 (Jimmy Reppin 131) [1990 5s³] fifth   —
foal: dam, 1m winner, is sister to Joking Apart: 12 lengths third of 5, slowly away and
never able to challenge, to Able Jet in minor event at Ayr in October: sold 3,000 gns
Doncaster November Sales. *W. Hastings-Bass.*

REVEREND MOTHER 4 b.f. Class Distinction–Black Veil 53 (Blakeney 126)   —
[1989 NR 1990 12f a12g 10.8g] lengthy, plain filly: poor mover: of little account:
blinkered final outing. *N. Kernick.*

REVIF (FR) 2 gr.c. (Mar 18) Kenmare (FR) 125–Reverente (FR) (Riverman   **65** p
(USA) 131) [1990 6m] quite good-topped colt: half-brother to several winners
abroad, including useful miler (in France and USA) Revolutionary (by Formidable):
dam French 1m winner at 2 yrs, is half-sister to French St Leger winner Agent
Double and good middle-distance colt Air de Cour: backward and green, over 7
lengths seventh of 10 to Act of Diplomacy in maiden at Newmarket in July, fading
last 2f not knocked about: looked sure to do better, but not seen out again. *A. C. Stewart.*

REVOKE (USA) 3 ro.f. Riverman (USA) 131–Queens Only (USA) (Marshua's   **70** d
Dancer (USA)) [1989 6f³ 5g³ 5m² 5m⁶ 6g⁴ 1990 8m⁵ 8m² 8f⁶ 9m 8m³ 8d³ a8g]
small, sparely-made filly: maiden: below form after second start, sweating
when third in claimers: suited by 1m: acts on good to firm going: sold out of B. Hills's
stable 4,300 gns Newmarket September Sales after third start. *A. N. Lee.*

REXY BOY 3 b.c. Dunbeath (USA) 127–Coca (Levmoss 133) [1989 NR 1990 8f 8v   —
8m a12g 12m a12g] 6,800Y: good-bodied colt: sixth foal: half-brother to useful 7f and
9f winner Greenwich Papillon (by Glenstal), Irish 11.5f winner Antiguan Reef (by
Mill Reef) and winners in Norway and Hong Kong: dam, placed over 11f at 3 yrs in
French Provinces, is granddaughter of 1000 Guineas winner Hypericum: well
beaten, in claimer final start: has worn crossed noseband and sweated. *W. J. Pearce.*

REZA 2 gr.g. (Feb 20) Superlative 118–Moon Charter 45 (Runnymede 123) [1990   **52**
6g 6m⁶ 5m 7m] 11,000Y: sturdy gelding: second foal: dam plater best run at 7f as
2-y-o: plating-class form, including for 7-lb claimer, in maidens, first an auction
event: stays 7f. *G. A. Huffer.*

RHEIN LEGEND (IRE) 2 b.c. (Apr 7) Trojan Fen 118–Rhein Honey (Rhein-   **63**
gold 137) [1990 6f a6g³ 7d 7.5f⁶ 7f² 8m*] IR 5,000Y: leggy, close-coupled colt:
half-brother to a winner in Belgium: dam quite useful Irish sprinter: quite modest
performer: won nursery at Warwick in August, making all and staying on well to
beat Highland Meeting ½ length: sweating and pulled hard time before: was suited
by 1m: dead. *J. W. Watts.*

RHODES 3 ch.g. Pharly (FR) 130–Beacon Hill 81 (Bustino 136) [1989 NR 1990   **75**
10g 13.3m² 14.8m³ 16m²] lengthy gelding: has a round action: second living foal:
dam, placed over 1¼m from 3 starts, is sister to Height of Fashion, the dam of
Unfuwain and Nashwan: modest maiden: favourite, led until post at Nottingham
final outing: stays 2m: lacks turn of foot: sold to join J. Akehurst 16,000 gns
Newmarket Autumn Sales. *Major W. R. Hern.*

RHYMING KATE 5 b.m. Rymer 121–Gokatiego (Huntercombe 133) [1989 NR   —
1990 a8g a11g a7g 10.2f 10m⁶ 12.4f 10d a8g 7f 10m] lengthy, rather sparely-made
mare: second foal: dam unraced: of little account: sold 1,800 gns Doncaster August
Sales. *D. W. Chapman.*

RHYTHMIC DANCER 2 b.c. (Apr 28) Music Boy 124–Stepping Gaily 79 (Gay   **91**
Fandango (USA) 132) [1990 5f³ 5f² 5d² 5f* 5g⁴ 5f* 5m² 5d] leggy, close-coupled
colt: fifth foal: brother to a winner in Belgium and half-brother to 5f winner
Dominuet (by Dominion) and 3-y-o 5f winner The Auction Bidder (by Auction Ring):
dam winning sprinter: improved colt: successful in maiden (made all) at Haydock in
May and nursery at Wolverhampton in September: excellent second in nursery at

Ascot Stakes (Handicap), Ascot—Retouch wears down the blinkered Lucky Verdict

Newmarket after: speedy: best form on top-of-the-ground: keen sort: taken down very early final 2 starts. *J. Berry.*

RIACE 2 ch.c. (Mar 7) Town And Country 124–Cygne 44 (Piaffer (USA) 113) [1990 5f³ 6m 7m 7m 7g] first foal: dam plater, stayed 1m: plating-class maiden: slowly away and very green on debut: off course nearly 4 months before penultimate start: should stay 7f. *C. P. Wildman.* **52**

RIBOKEYES BOY 8 b.g. Riboboy (USA) 124–Molvitesse 75 (Molvedo 137) [1989 10s³ 10s⁵ 10f 1990 a12g² 12f] close-coupled gelding: plater: probably stays 1½m: acts on good to firm and soft going: usually bandaged: occasionally slowly away. *A. R. Davison.* **44**

RICARDO BOOTS 4 ro.g. Remainder Man 126§–Mountainette (Peter Wrekin 108) [1989 NR 1990 a11g] strong, good-bodied gelding: seemingly of little account. *B. Preece.* **—**

RICHARD'S HILL 7 br.g. Fidel 106–Baroness Vimy (Barrons Court) [1989 NR 1990 12m⁵] brother to winning hurdler Richard's Kate: dam very lightly-raced Irish hurdler: progressive hurdler in 1989/90, winner 4 times late in season: 100/1 and apprentice ridden, well beaten in maiden at Pontefract in September. *T. B. Hallett.* **—**

RICHMOND (IRE) 2 ch.g. (Mar 25) Hatim (USA) 121–On The Road (On Your Mark 125) [1990 6f 6g 7m⁴ 7m a7g⁶ 8v² 8d³ 8.2s² a8g² a8g⁵] IR 9,200Y: sturdy gelding: moderate mover: fourth live foal: half-brother to 1m and 8.5f winner Xafu Xafu (by Kafu): dam modest Irish 5f winner at 2 yrs: modest performer: much improved since blinkered first time on sixth start, though ran moderately final start: will be suited by 1¼m: acts well on soft ground. *J. S. Wainwright.* **73**

RICHMOND PARK 3 b.c. Aragon 118–The Ranee (Royal Palace 131) [1989 6m⁶ 6f⁵ 8m 7d⁵ 8g⁵ 1990 9m 8.2g 7.6d⁵ 7m] sparely-made colt: plater: sweating, never dangerous in amateurs handicap final start, in June: should stay 1¼m: best form on an easy surface: blinkered once at 2 yrs. *L. J. Barratt.* **—**

RICKETTY (IRE) 2 b.g. (Mar 19) Reasonable (FR) 119–Kilteelagh Lady (King's Leap 111) [1990 5g 7m 5d* 5m³ 6d] 8,700Y: useful-looking gelding: half-brother to 2 winners over hurdles: dam Irish 2-y-o 6f winner: well-backed favourite following promising runs in better company, won seller (no bid) at Haydock in July: bit backward and not knocked about in nursery final start: should be suited by further than 5f. *M. W. Easterby.* **71**

751

RICKSHAW QUEEN 3 b.f. Alzao (USA) 117–Sorrow (Wolver Hollow 126) **39**
[1989 NR 1990 8g 10g⁶ 10.6s 8g⁶ 9m⁵ 11.7h 8.2d⁵ 10m a8g] IR 10,000F, IR 18,000Y:
angular filly: poor mover: second living foal: half-sister to 1986 2-y-o plating-class
maiden Ingliston (by Cajun): dam lightly-raced daughter of close relation to Song:
poor maiden: possibly best at up to 1m (tailed off lame over 11.7f): sold 1,500 gns
Newmarket Autumn Sales. *R. Hollinshead.*

RIDGE END (USA) 2 br.f. (Mar 9) Cox's Ridge (USA)–Lipika (USA) (Nijinsky —
(CAN) 138) [1990 7m] sturdy filly: first reported foal: dam, 1m winner (at 2 yrs) in
Ireland, is closely related to useful sprinter Flawless Image: bit backward, hampered early then always behind in moderately-run maiden at Salisbury in September:
moved moderately down. *Mrs L. Piggott.*

RIDGEPOINT 3 ch.c. Gorytus (USA) 132–Cooliney Princess 98 (Bruni 132) **102**
[1989 8m⁴ 8.2d* 1990 11.5m² 10.5g⁵ 12g 11s* 12g⁴ 10v] lengthy, rather
dipped-backed colt: beaten 3 lengths by sole rival Duke of Paducah in Lingfield
minor event and about 15 lengths in Dante Stakes at York: behind in Derby Italiano
at Rome: trained until after then by C. Brittain, subsequent runs in Italy including
win in listed race at Rome and fourth to Dashing Blade in Group 1 event at Milan in
September: seems to stay 1½m. *S. Saggiomo, Italy.*

RIDWAN 3 b.c. Rousillon (USA) 133–Ring Rose 86 (Relko 136) [1989 NR 1990 —
12m⁴] useful-looking colt: sixth foal: half-brother to very useful 11f winner Balladier
(by Busted) and French 1m and 6.5f (at 4 yrs) winner Tangle Thorn (by Thatching):
dam middle-distance winner out of very smart Heath Rose: soundly-beaten last of 4
in maiden at Kempton in July: sold to join K. Morgan 5,400 gns Newmarket
September Sales. *M. R. Stoute.*

RIESENER 4 ch.g. Touching Wood (USA) 127–Sharp Run (Sharpen Up 127) —
[1989 9g 10.6m 16.2g 12.4m 8g⁵ 10g 1990 a7g 14.8f⁵] leggy gelding: little worthwhile
form: visored first outing. *Mrs P. A. Barker.*

RIEVAULX 4 b.g. Petorius 117–Sister Sala (Double-U-Jay 120) [1989 8f⁴ 10.6g —
8g⁶ 8m 1990 8f 10m 6g] lengthy, plain gelding: quite modest form at best: always
behind in claimers and handicap at 4 yrs: stays 1m: blinkered final outing: has joined
J. FitzGerald. *W. J. Pearce.*

RIFFA PARK 2 b.f. (Apr 8) Domynsky 110–Hunslet 72 (Comedy Star (USA) 121) —
[1990 5f 6g 6m 8.5m] workmanlike filly: second foal: half-sister to 3-y-o Shalaglen
(by Lochnager): dam 7.2f winner, is sister to useful 1m and 1¼m winner and smart
jumper Starfen: well beaten, including in sellers. *M. H. Easterby.*

RIGHT STEP (FR) 5 ch.g. Noalcoholic (FR) 128–Right Dancer 97 (Dance In —
Time (CAN)) [1989 10f³ 12f* 12h 1990 12f] lengthy, good-topped gelding: moderate
mover: won seller at Thirsk at 4 yrs: 33/1 and ridden by 7-lb claimer, well beaten in
handicap at same course in September: suited by 1½m: acted on firm going: winning
hurdler: dead. *M. D. Hammond.*

RINCE DEAS (IRE) 2 b.f. (Apr 29) Alzao (USA) 117–Flaxen Hair (Thatch **53**
(USA) 136) [1990 5g² 5d⁵ 5m³ 6d 5m 5m 5f⁶ 5.8h⁵ 5f⁴ a5g³ a5g] small, workmanlike
filly: has a roundish action: fifth foal: sister to smart miler Mirror Black and
half-sister to 1¼m seller winner Rangers Lad (by Sallust), 3-y-o 7.5f and 1m winner
Colourist (by Petorius) and a winning hurdler: dam unraced: inconsistent maiden:
perhaps worth another try at 6f: has run creditably for apprentice: sold 4,200 gns
Newmarket December Sales. *M. McCormack.*

RING APPEAL 3 ch.g. Star Appeal 133–Sally Gal 101 (Lord Gayle (USA) 124) —
[1989 5.8m 8g a7g 1990 8.2f 12.5g] small, sparely-made gelding: well beaten in
maidens and handicap: sold 1,200 gns Newmarket July Sales. *C. E. Brittain.*

RING O'ROSES (IRE) 2 b. or br.f. (Mar 16) Auction Ring (USA) 123–Coupe —
d'Hebe 87 (Ile de Bourbon (USA) 133) [1990 7m 7f] medium-sized, unfurnished filly:
good walker: first foal: dam won only start, over 1m at 2 yrs: green, unfavourably
drawn in maiden at Lingfield in September: well-backed favourite, never able to
challenge in seller at Redcar following month: will be better suited by 1m +. *W.
Hastings-Bass.*

RING RACECALL 3 b.g. Montekin 125–Right Minx (Right Tack 131) [1989 6m —
7m 6f² 6f³ 6f⁶ 7g 1990 a10g a10g⁴] compact, rather sparely-made gelding: has a
quick action: plating-class maiden: ran poorly last 4 starts, blinkered on last 3 and
not seen out after February: should stay 7f. *J. W. Hills.*

RINJA (USA) 3 b.c. Robellino (USA) 127–Dijla 82 (Hittite Glory 125) [1989 6m⁵ **75**
6f 7.6m* 8g⁶ 7g⁶ 1990 10g⁴ 8m 8m² 8d 8m⁶ 8.2m⁴ 9g 9m²] lengthy colt: modest
handicapper: stays 9f: acts on good to firm ground: took keen hold in lead when
below form penultimate start: usually bandaged behind. *D. W. P. Arbuthnot.*

Cartier Million, Phoenix Park—Rinka Das (centre) quickens to win the third running of this extremely valuable race decisively from Kooyonga (rails) and Golden Mintage (blinkers), with Too Conspicuous fourth and Stark South (rails) fifth

RINKA DAS (USA) 2 b.c. (Feb 9) Nureyev (USA) 131–Tremulous (USA) 102 **107** (Gregorian (USA) 124) [1990 6m⁴ 7g* 7d*] IR 260,000Y: first reported foal: dam 1¼m and 1½m winner stayed 1¾m, later successful in USA, is half-sister to Seismic Wave: successful in 8-runner maiden and 20-runner Cartier Million (by 1½ lengths from Kooyonga, always travelling well and showing improved form) at Phoenix Park in September: will be suited by 1m +: useful. *D. K. Weld, Ireland.*

RIO PIEDRAS 6 b.m. Kala Shikari 125–Glory Isle 60 (Hittite Glory 125) [1989 **62** 10s² 9v* 8.5d 8g 8f 9m³ 10m 10m² 8m⁴ 10g⁶ a10g 10g* 1990 a12g⁶ 10.2f 9f 9g 10g 10g⁵ 10.6s 10f⁴ 10.2f² 9f4 10g³ 10.4g* 10.6g³ 10d⁶ 9m⁵ 10m² 10d* 10.4d 10d] smallish, lightly-made mare: usually runs with credit, and won claimer at Chester in September and apprentice handicap at Newmarket in October: well below her best last 2 outings: ideally suited by around 1¼m: acts on any going: ran poorly when visored or blinkered: often wears severe noseband: has sweated and got on edge: has looked none too keen: sold 6,400 gns Doncaster November Sales. *A. Bailey.*

RIO TEJO (USA) 2 b. or br.f. (Feb 18) Tsunami Slew (USA)–Celebration Song **89** (USA) (J O Tobin (USA) 130) [1990 5g³ 6m³ 5f* 5m⁵ 5.3f* 5m⁶] $110,000Y: good-topped, quite attractive filly, with scope: good walker: first foal: dam in frame at 6f and 1m in Ireland and later placed in USA, is half-sister to Seattle Song (by Seattle Slew): sire good class, best at 9f or 1¼m: won minor event at Brighton in September, showing much improved form: earlier made all in maiden at Redcar: mulish stalls in between, never able to challenge in Cornwallis Stakes at Ascot final start: should be at least as effective at 6f as 5f: best form on firm ground. *J. H. M. Gosden.*

RIPYANA 3 ch.f. Bairn (USA) 126–Correct Number (Exdirectory 129) [1989 NR **—** 1990 7f a6g⁵ 6f 7g] 3,200Y: leggy filly: second foal: dam Irish 1¼m winner: no show here, including in seller: successful over 1m in Yugoslavia in August. *J. D. Czerpak.*

RISATINA 4 ch.f. Sallust 134–Saga's Humour 61 (Bustino 136) [1989 7s 10s 12f **—** 10.2f³ 10f³ 11.7f⁵ a12g a10g 1990 a16g] small filly: moderate mover: form only when third in claimer and apprentice race as 3-y-o: badly tailed off last 3 starts: blinkered last 6 outings. *D. Burchell.*

RISBOROUGH GIRL 2 b.f. (Feb 14) Glow (USA)–River Maiden (FR) 86 **—** (Riverman (USA)) [1990 6f⁶ 5.3h⁶ 5f] 4,000Y: lengthy, sparely-made filly: third foal: half-sister to 3-y-o The Swamp Fox (by Mummy's Pet): dam 7f winner: little worthwhile form in sellers: blinkered final start. *P. D. Cundell.*

RISEN MOON (USA) 3 b.c. Hawaiian Sound (USA) 129–Uvula (USA) (His **107 +** Majesty (USA)) [1989 7g 1990 7g* 7f² 8m 7g* 9m*] tall, leggy colt: progressed well

physically: won maiden at Warwick in July, 22-runner handicap (in tremendous
style) at Doncaster in September and £61,600 William Hill Cambridgeshire Handicap at Newmarket: 7/1 favourite, put up another most impressive performance to
beat Mellottie 1½ lengths at Newmarket, coming from back of a 40-runner field to
lead inside final ½f and win going away: effective at 7f to 9f: acts on good to firm
ground: wore special bit last 2 starts: has excellent turn of foot: sold to race in Saudi
Arabia. *B. W. Hills.*

RISE OVER   4 ch.f. Smackover 107–Stewart's Rise 52 (Good Bond 122) [1989   —
8.5d 8d⁴ 10.6g 8m⁵ 1990 10v⁶ 8f 9g] big, unfurnished filly: has a round action: easily
best effort on second outing at 3 yrs: stays 1m: has worn bandages: often sweats. *K.
White.*

RISE UP SINGING   2 ch.c. (Mar 4) Noalto 120–Incarnadine 67 (Hot Spark 126)   84
[1990 7m 7m 7m⁶ 7.3g 8m* 7.6v 7s*] 5,000F, 14,000Y: strong colt: has scope:
moderate mover: fourth foal: half-brother to 3-y-o Llennodo (by Castle Keep) and
modest 1987 2-y-o 5f and 6f winner Roedean Honey (by Good Times): dam won over
7f and 1m: successful, making most, in 30-runner seller (retained 13,500 gns) at
Newmarket in October and 21-runner nursery (by ½ length from Quick Ransom) at
Doncaster following month: stays 1m: acts on good to firm ground and soft but
apparently not heavy: slowly into stride final 3 starts. *R. Hannon.*

RISK FACTOR   4 b.g. Auction Ring (USA) 123–Flying Anna (Roan Rocket 128)   57
[1989 10s 12m 9m⁶ 8.2d 1990 8v⁴ 8f³] sturdy, workmanlike gelding: moderate
mover: first sign of ability and better effort in spring when fourth in maiden at Ayr.
D. Moffatt.

RIVAL BID (USA)   2 b.g. (Mar 1) Cannonade (USA)–Love Triangle (USA) (No-   74
double (USA)) [1990 7g⁴ 8m 7g²] $30,000Y: workmanlike, close-coupled gelding:
first foal: dam winner at up to 9f: sire won Kentucky Derby: modest maiden: should
stay 1m: possibly unsuited by top-of-the-ground. *M. A. Jarvis.*

RIVA (USA)   3 b.f. Riverman (USA) 131–Valderna (FR) (Val de Loir 133) [1989 5f³   66
1990 10h³ 10m⁵] smallish, close-coupled filly: keen walker: quite modest form in
maidens in the summer: may well stay further: sold 27,000 gns Newmarket September Sales. *B. W. Hills.*

RIVE-JUMELLE (IRE)   2 b.f. (Feb 23) M Double M (USA)–Riverwave (USA)   58
(Riverman (USA) 131) [1990 7m 7m² 7.5m²] IR 7,000Y: lengthy, unfurnished filly:
moderate mover: third foal: dam placed at up to 13f in Ireland: sire won from 6f to 9f:

second in claimer at Salisbury and maiden auction (ran on strongly having taken keen hold) at Beverley in September: will stay further. *C. N. Allen.*

RIVERAIN   2 b.f. (Apr 29) Bustino 136–Gold Rupee 86 (Native Prince) [1990 6g⁶   **65** 7.5d² 7m* 7f³ 7.5g⁶ 9g⁶ a8g²] 8,000Y: workmanlike filly: moderate mover: half-sister to several winners, including fairly useful sprinter Alakh (by Sharpen Up): dam 6f winner: quite modest performer: won 19-runner maiden auction at Doncaster: should stay at least 1¼m: bought out of M. Jarvis' stable 4,700 gns Doncaster November Sales before final start. *T. D. Barron.*

RIVER CHASE (IRE)   2 ch.f. (Jan 18) Salmon Leap (USA) 131–Amboselli 73   **—** (Raga Navarro (ITY) 119) [1990 a7g] third reported foal: half-sister to 3-y-o 7f winner Yankee Trader (by Stanford) and modest sprinter Nikki Dow (by Tanfirion): dam placed over 5f at 2 yrs: slowly away and moderate headway around halfway in late-year maiden at Lingfield. *Sir Mark Prescott.*

RIVER CONSORT (USA)   2 bl.c. (Apr 21) Riverman (USA) 131–Queens Only   **80 p** (USA) (Marshua's Dancer (USA)) [1990 7m³ 7g*] sturdy colt: eighth foal: brother to fair 3-y-o Revoke and half-brother to several winners, including quite useful 1988 2-y-o 6f winner Roback (by Roberto) and smart 1982 American 2-y-o 1m and 9f winner Only Queens (by Transworld): dam, 6f to 1m winner in USA, is closely related to Native Royalty, smart at around 9f: favourite, won maiden at Salisbury in October by a neck from Haky, held up travelling strongly, quickening ahead over 1f out and keeping on well despite swishing tail and running green: will be better suited by 1m: likely to improve further. *G. Harwood.*

RIVER DRAGON   5 b.g. Rarity 129–Wet Powder (Above Suspicion 127) [1989   **53** 12s 12s⁵ 16g* 16f² 16.5g³ 16g⁵ 16.5m² 16m³ 1990 15.3g 15.3f² 16m] sturdy gelding: carries plenty of condition: moderate mover: quite modest winner as 4-y-o: ran moderately final outing (August) in 1990: should stay further than 2m: acts on firm and dead going: blinkered or visored last 2 starts: bandaged at 5 yrs: not the easiest of rides, and probably needs strong handling: has joined P. Kelleway. *J. W. Payne.*

RIVER GOD (USA)   3 b.c. Val de L'Orne (FR) 130–Princess Morvi (USA)   **121 p** (Graustark) [1989 7g³ 1990 12m* 12g 16.2f* 14.8m* 14m* 14.6g³]

Hot on the heels of firm ground for the two major jumps festivals of 1990 at Cheltenham and Liverpool, the climate continued to prove a hindrance during the latest flat season. The effects of the dry spell were felt on a wide scale behind the scenes, where the availability of all-weather gallops and equine swimming pools often dictated the state of fitness in which runners reached the track. The tracks themselves did their best to alleviate the

Tia Maria March Stakes, Goodwood—River God books his place in the St Leger

Sheikh Mohammed's "River God"

situation through watering, but, unfortunately, at a number of venues the system in operation seems nowhere near so efficient as it ideally ought to be. Some horses coped with the extreme ground and weather conditions better than others. The rigours of a summer campaign looked like catching up with River God, who returned home dehydrated and distressed after struggling to land odds of 4/1 on in a listed race at Newmarket's July meeting. It seemed obvious at the time that River God was below par; Criminal Law, a length second, and Kasayid, five lengths third at Newmarket, had been beaten out of sight by him on terms only 5 lb worse in the Queen's Vase at Royal Ascot three weeks earlier. Thankfully this proved merely a hiccup in River God's impressive progress. Following two contrasting and relatively uninformative displays to open his campaign—he'd hacked up from weak opposition in a maiden at Doncaster before managing only sixteenth of eighteen when allowed to take his chance in an open-looking Derby—the Queen's Vase had gone a lot further towards establishing his merit, River God, market leader at 6/4, giving short shrift to the nine who remained after second-favourite Dovekie broke a leg passing the stands. River God won going away by six lengths, Parting Moment staying on resolutely for second, fully ten lengths clear of Kasayid. Incidentally, the Jockey Club announced in December that the Queen's Vase is to be restored to Group 3 status in the next season as part of the revision of the staying pattern, bringing it level in status with the Goodwood Cup which is reduced in distance to two miles.

River God went on to become the first Queen's Vase winner since Baynoun in 1984 to contest the St Leger. An authoritative front-running performance in the Tia Maria March Stakes at Goodwood on his appearance after Newmarket served to illustrate his well-being, but a length-and-a-half and a neck beating of Judicial Hero and Crack, both receiving 4 lb, didn't read like classic-winning form. Though unable to match Baynoun's neck second to Commanche Run in the Leger, River God ran well to finish four and three quarter lengths third, prominent from the outset and rallying having been tapped for speed by Snurge and Hellenic. River God doesn't possess the finishing pace to trouble the best middle-distance stayers. What he does have is the ability to sustain a powerful gallop over long distances, which will make him a formidable contender in the Cup races. His lightly-raced stable-companion Great Marquess, three and a half lengths further adrift at Doncaster, took care of the older brigade in the Jockey Club Cup at Newmarket the following month, and competition in the staying division for 1991 doesn't look strong at this stage.

		Val de Loir	Vieux Manoir
	Val de L'Orne (FR)	(b 1959)	Vali II
	(b 1972)	Aglae	Armistice III
River God (USA)		(b 1965)	Aglae Grace
(b.c. 1987)		Graustark	Ribot
	Princess Morvi (USA)	(ch 1963)	Flower Bowl
	(ch 1975)	Silana	Silnet
		(b 1965)	Anabara

A well-made individual with plenty of scope, River God is a fine-looking racehorse, as was his sire the 1975 French Derby winner Val de l'Orne, and is the type to go on from three to four. Val de l'Orne has already been responsible for one smart stayer, Valuable Witness, as well as the Grade 1 Hollywood Derby winner Victory Zone and River God's full brother Pay The Butler. Picked up for 74,000 guineas at Newmarket's Highflyer Yearling Sales less than two months prior to Pay The Butler's finest hour in the Japan Cup, River God also has stout elements on the female side of his pedigree. His dam Princess Morvi is a daughter of Graustark, an influence for stamina and a notable sire of broodmares. She won two races in France, at a mile and eleven furlongs, which was three fewer than her dam Silana, whose tally included the thirteen-furlong Prix de Royallieu. Silana's half-brother Barado was very much at home over long distances, winning the Group 2 Prix Gladiateur over three miles at Longchamp amongst other races. Besides River God and Pay The Butler, Princess Morvi has also produced the prolifically successful Little Current colt Progressive Slot. Her two-year-old of 1990, Father North (by Far North), is in training with Harwood but has still to be seen in public. River God himself remains relatively lightly raced on seven starts. He's yet to encounter a soft surface, and clearly handles firm ground well. *H. R. A. Cecil.*

RIVERHEAD (USA) 6 b.h. Riverman (USA) 131–Tertiary (USA) (Vaguely Noble 140) [1989 8g6 12g5 10v2 10g 10g 8g 1990 10m6] good-topped, attractive horse: has a quick action: winner in France: showed ability in Britain on first 4 outings in 1989: unsuited by modest gallop in Newmarket handicap in April: stays 1¼m: has form on firm going, but has run his best races over hurdles on an easy surface: usually wears bandages: very useful hurdler (suited by waiting tactics). *D. R. C. Elsworth.* —

RIVERILLON 2 ch.c. (May 1) Rousillon (USA) 133–Dance Lover's (FR) (Green Dancer (USA) 132) [1990 7m2] tall, lengthy colt: has plenty of scope: half-brother to French 9f and 1¼m winner Dadulas (by Thatching) and very useful 6f (at 2 yrs) to 10.5f winner Brave Dancer (by Pas de Seul): dam thrice-raced half-sister to St Leger winner Son of Love: 10 lengths second of 11, staying on well, to impressive Opera House in maiden at Leicester in October: showed a quick action: sure to improve, particularly over 1m. *J. W. Hills.* 75 p

RIVER NOMAD 3 b.f. Gorytus (USA) 132–Blue Rider (USA) (Wajima (USA)) [1989 NR 1990 7g3 8m* 8v5] 32,000Y: strong, sturdy filly: half-sister to French 1986 2-y-o 7f and 9f winner Voler La Nuit (by Melyno) and 4-y-o Cagnes-sur-Mer 1m winner Manardy (by Mendez): dam unraced half-sister to Cresta Rider: won £8,400 event at Ascot in May by length from Oriental Mystique, held up, tending to edge right then staying on very strongly final ½f despite flashing tail: 9 lengths fifth of 15 99 +

in Group 3 race at Milan 5 months later: should stay 1¼m: may well be capable of better. *P. F. I. Cole.*

RIVER PATROL   2 b.f. (Feb 6) Rousillon (USA) 133–Boathouse 116 (Habitat   **79** 134) [1990 7m³ 7m⁴] big, rangy, unfurnished filly: has scope: fifth foal: half-sister to smart middle-distance stayer Dry Dock (by High Line) and fair middle-distance maiden Head of The River (by Shirley Heights): dam stayed 1¼m, is half-sister to Bireme and high-class middle-distance stayer Buoy: fair form, staying on, behind Shamshir in maiden at Newmarket and Shadiyid in minor event (troublesome stalls) at Ascot in second half of season: will stay at least 1¼m: sure to win a race. *B. W. Hills.*

RIVER RHINE (USA)   2 br.c. (Mar 2) Riverman (USA) 131–Call The Queen   **80 p** (USA) (Hail To Reason) [1990 6m³] $200,000F: half-brother to ungenuine 3-y-o Empshott (by Graustark) and to several winners, including 1985 2-y-o 9f winner Shekana (by The Minstrel): dam 6f-winning daughter of champion 2-y-o filly Queen Empress: favourite but green, under 2 lengths third of 8, soon travelling comfortably after slow start then keeping on under hand riding, to Persianalli in maiden at Yarmouth in September: sure to improve. *H. R. A. Cecil.*

RIVERS RHAPSODY   3 b.f. Dominion 123–Trwyn Cilan 89 (Import 127) [1989   **104** 5m³ 6m² 5m³ 5m* 1990 5m* 5d⁴ 5g 5d* 5m³ 6m³ 6m 6m³ 5g* 6m 5m] smallish, good-quartered filly: useful sprinter: successful in good style in handicaps at Sandown in April and Ascot (£16,400 event) in June then put up best effort to win all-aged listed race at Doncaster in September: stays 6f: goes particularly well with some give in the ground: may well be best making wide challenge: has good turn of foot. *G. B. Balding.*

RIVER SUIR (USA)   2 ch.f. (Feb 18) Irish River (FR) 131–Viendra (USA) 113   **— p** (Raise A Native) [1990 7g] rather unfurnished filly: fourth reported foal: half-sister to a winner in North America by Sir Ivor: dam 7.6f winner suited by 1¼m and later successful in North America, is out of half-sister to dam of Nijinsky: bit backward and green, slowly away and beaten over 2f out in £14,900 event at York in August: moved poorly down. *B. W. Hills.*

RIVER TEST (USA)   4 b.c. Critique 126–River Valley (Riverman 131) [1989   **108** 10.5s⁴ 12m 10d⁵ 12.5d* 13d 12g 11.5g 1990 11d⁶ 15.5m² 14d 15g² 16g* 15.5m⁵ 20g*] second foal: dam French 10.5f winner, half-sister to dams of Lypharita and Belmez: ran in handicaps, winning at Deauville in August for second successive year, prior to contesting Ciga Prix Gladiateur at Longchamp in October: always travelling well and beat Chelsea Girl easily by 6 lengths in latter: suited by good test of stamina. *D. Smaga, France.*

RIVER TRAFFIC (USA)   2 ch.c. (Feb 28) Irish River (FR) 131–Bally Knockan   **109** (USA) (Exclusive Native (USA)) [1990 7g* 7d² 7g⁴ 6.5d³ 8.5f*] $37,000Y, resold $48,000Y: third foal: half-brother to 3-y-o Cut In Stone (by Assert) and Irish 6f and 1m winner To Die For (by Diesis): dam 6f stakes winner also placed at up to 8.5f in stakes, is out of a smart winner at up to 9f: very useful French colt: won minor event at Clairefontaine in August and Grade 3 Laurel Futurity (by a neck) at Laurel in October: in frame previous 2 starts in Prix de la Salamandre (over 3 lengths fourth to Hector Protector) at Longchamp and Prix Eclipse (close third to Crack Regiment) at Saint-Cloud: stays 8.5f: acts on firm and dead going. *J. E. Hammond, France.*

RIVERULLAH (USA)   3 br.c. Riverman (USA) 131–Mama Kali (USA) (Tom   **85** Rolfe) [1989 NR 1990 10f⁴ 10f*] $170,000Y: tall, leggy colt: has plenty of scope:

Doncaster Bloodstock Sales Scarbrough Stakes, Doncaster—
Rivers Rhapsody (rails) finishes strongly
to beat the two-year-old Never In The Red (checks) and Our Freddie (blinkers)

half-brother to several winners, one stakes placed: dam, smart winner at up to 1m, at her best at 4 yrs and 5 yrs: 8/1 on but still green after very promising debut at Newmarket, moved poorly down and struggled to win 4-runner maiden at Redcar in July: sold BBA (Italy) 16,000 gns Newmarket Autumn Sales. *L. Cumani.*

RIVER WAY (IRE)   2 b.f. (Apr 4) Soughaan (USA) 111–Eccentric Lady (London Bells (CAN) 109) [1990 6m 6m⁶ 5.8h⁴ 5f] IR 3,700F, 3,000Y: compact filly: first foal: dam half-sister to fairly useful miler Dr Bulasco: little worthwhile form, including in a seller. *C. J. Hill.*

RIVIERA MAGIC   3 ch.g. Niniski (USA) 125–Miss Beaulieu 106 (Northfields   89 (USA)) [1989 6m⁴ 6f² 7g⁴ 1990 8f³ 8g³ 10m 10f* 10m 12.5g* 10.8m² 12.3v⁵] compact gelding: moderate walker: shows a quick action: fairly useful performer: won 3-runner maiden at Carlisle (odds on) in September and minor event at Wolverhampton (making most and rallying well) in October: stays 1½m: acts on firm going, unsuited by heavy: sweating and edgy third outing: wore citation bridle last 3 starts: sold 40,000 gns Newmarket Autumn Sales. *G. Wragg.*

ROAD TO THE ISLE (IRE)   2 b.c. (Feb 4) Lomond (USA) 128–One Way   98 Street 119 (Habitat 134) [1990 6m² 7m² 8g* 9g] 30,000Y: angular colt: third foal: closely related to Irish 1¾m winner Street Opera (by Sadler's Wells) and 3-y-o Contraflow (by Rainbow Quest): dam (from good family) won Princess Royal Stakes: progressive colt: stayed on well to win 16-runner maiden at Kempton in September by ½ length: around 6 lengths eighth of 12 to Pistolet Bleu in Prix de Conde at Longchamp following month: will be suited by a test of stamina. *B. W. Hills.*

ROBBIE BURNS   4 br.c. Daring March 116–Gangawayhame 91 (Lochnager 132)   59 [1989 6v 7s⁵ 8s 10g 1990 11.7g 12m 10g⁶ 10s² a12g] workmanlike colt: quite modest form at best: appears suited by 1¼m: acts on soft going. *R. V. Smyth.*

ROBCHRIS   4 b. or br.c. Dunphy 124–Whispering Star 78 (Sound Track 132)   — [1989 6d³ 6f³ 6h⁴ 1990 6g 8m] leggy, close-coupled colt: quite modest maiden at best: soundly beaten in handicaps at 4 yrs: will probably stay 7f: sweating and edgy final start at 3 yrs: bandaged on reappearance: claimer ridden. *M. O'Neill.*

ROBELLATION (USA)   3 b.c. Robellino (USA) 127–Vexation (USA) (Vice   104 Regent (CAN)) [1989 5g² 6f* 6f 7f² 7f* 7m² 8d² 8m⁵ 7.3d² 1990 6g* 6m⁶ 7f 7g³ 7f⁶ 7m⁴ 8m⁶ a10g⁶] quite attractive colt: useful performer: won £7,300 event at Kempton in April: inconsistent afterwards, in frame in Group 3 event and £7,800 handicap at Newmarket: best form at up to 1m (stiff task at 1¼m): yet to race on very soft ground, acts on any other: twice below form when sweating. *G. Harwood.*

ROBERT DEAR (USA)   4 gr.c. Caro 133–Marketess (USA) (To Market) [1989   76 8g 7d 11.7m⁵ 10g³ 8f* 8h* 8f 8g³ 1990 8f4 10f² 12g⁵ 8f³ 8.3m* 8m 8.3m 8g 8m] rangy colt: modest handicapper: won at Windsor in July: ran moderately afterwards: ideally suited by 1m: acts on firm going: ran creditably when blinkered fourth outing: sold to join M. Tompkins' stable 17,500 gns Newmarket Autumn Sales. *P. F. I. Cole.*

ROBERTET (USA)   4 b.f. Roberto (USA) 131–Ethics (USA) (Nijinsky (CAN)   114 138) [1989 10d³ 10g* 12g³ 12g² 12.5m² 15.5g³ 1990 12d³ 15.5d³ 12g² 12d³ 12.5g² 12.5g* 12m³ 12.5g⁵ 15.5v] heavy-bodied filly: very useful performer: won 8-runner Grand Prix de Deauville Lancel by ¾ length from Theatre Critic: placed in pattern and listed events otherwise at 4 yrs until running creditably in Ciga Prix de Royallieu, then poorly in Prix Royal-Oak, both at Longchamp, on last 2 outings: stays 15.5f: yet to race on firm going, unsuited by heavy: splendidly consistent. *E. Lellouche, France.*

ROBERT'S REJECT (USA)   3 ch.f. Assert 134–Bold Sands (USA) (Wajima   — (USA)) [1989 NR 1990 16.2d⁵ 16g⁶] $100,000Y: workmanlike filly: fifth foal: sister to smart 2m and 19f winner Dam Busters and closely related to 1984 2-y-o 6f winner Allesheny (by Be My Guest): dam unraced half-sister to Riboboy: little promise in maidens: bandaged all round on debut: sold to join J. Czerpak 1,050 gns Newmarket September Sales. *Mrs L. Piggott.*

ROBERTY LEA   2 b.c. (Apr 22) Alleging (USA) 120–Rosy Lee (FR) (Le Haar   37 126) [1990 5m 7g] 3,400F, 5,600Y, 2,600 2-y-o: half-brother to several winners, including French middle-distance winner Grundylee (by Grundy) and inconsistent 1987 2-y-o 6f winner Warthill Girl (by Anfield): dam French 7.5f and 1½m winner: always behind in maiden auction events at Redcar and York in autumn. *T. Fairhurst.*

ROBINS RETURN   2 b.f. (Apr 24) Music Boy 124–Baidedones (Welsh Pageant   53 132) [1990 5f 6g 5f⁴ 6m⁶ a6g 8.2g 7f⁴ a7g⁶] 6,100Y: workmanlike filly: fourth live foal: half-sister to 3-y-o Busy Boy (by Dominion) and modest 1987 2-y-o 5f winner

Love Ballad (by Song: dam won twice in Italy at 3 yrs: plating-class maiden: best effort on all-weather final start: ran creditably in seller penultimate outing: may well stay 1m: trained first 2 outings by M. W. Easterby: reportedly sold 720 gns Doncaster October Sales. *Denys Smith.*

ROBINS SON 3 b.g. Krayyan 117–Fleam (Continuation 120) [1989 NR 1990 9m³ **49 +** 10.5g] IR 3,200F, 10,000Y: rather angular gelding: sixth foal: half-brother to Irish sprint winner God's Trust (by Green God) and an Irish 1m winner by Red Alert: dam won over 9f in Ireland: some promise in very slowly-run 6-runner auction event at Redcar in September, making most: 33/1, well beaten in competitive maiden at York. *J. G. FitzGerald.*

ROBORE (FR) 5 br.h. Zino 127–Mona Mou (FR) (Luthier 126) [1989 10.5v³ 12d* **116** 12m² 12d² 12g⁴ 12d² 12g⁶ 12m* 1990 12d* 12g⁵ 12d⁴ 12d⁴ 12m⁵ 12g 12g] angular horse: much improved as 4-y-o, successful at Longchamp in Prix d'Hedouville and Prix du Conseil de Paris and ran very well when sixth in Ciga Prix de l'Arc de Triomphe: not so good in 1990: landed the odds in first-named event in April, never able to challenge in other 2 on last 2 outings: best form at 1½m: yet to race on really firm going, acts on any other: heavily bandaged fifth outing, first for 3 months. *N. Pelat, France.*

ROCK BREAKER 2 b.c. (Feb 14) Green Ruby (USA) 104–Holloway Wonder 93 **64** (Swing Easy (USA) 126) [1990 5g a6g² a6g⁶ 5d 5m 5g² 5v] lengthy, good-quartered colt: has scope: moderate mover: second foal: half-brother to 3-y-o Stoneythorpewonder (by Smackover), 5f winner at 2 yrs: dam effective at 5f and stayed 1m: quite modest maiden: ran well in selling nursery penultimate start: stays 6f: seems unsuited by soft ground: headstrong. *B. A. McMahon.*

ROCK CITY 3 br.c. Ballad Rock 122–Rimosa's Pet 109 (Petingo 135) [1989 **120** 5s* 6f* 6f* 6g* 6m* 7g⁴ 6m² 1990 7g* 8f⁴ 7g² 8m² 7g* 6m³ 6.5g² 7.3g⁴]

The National Stud's two new stallions for 1991, Be My Chief and Rock City, had starkly contrasting fortunes in their second season. While Be My Chief made it to the track only once and failed to do himself justice, Rock City continued to tackle his varied tasks with enthusiasm and consistency until he was retired in the autumn with the exemplary record of seven wins, five of them in pattern races, and never having been out of the frame in fifteen starts. Unbounded enthusiasm wasn't enough to take Rock City right to the top, however. Game as he was he couldn't win a Group 1 race, and ended up, because of his outstanding consistency, as a yardstick by which to measure the best. Two-year-old racing in Britain in the summer of 1989 would have been the poorer without Rock City. He began his career with a string of five clear-cut victories, the last three in the Coventry Stakes, Anglia Television July Stakes and Scottish Equitable Gimcrack Stakes, and for a fair while

Van Geest Criterion Stakes, Newmarket—Rock City is too good for these; Aldbourne (left) comes second, ahead of Robellation

A. F. Budge (Equine) Ltd's "Rock City"

looked as though he might be the best around. But defeats behind Machiavellian in the Prix de la Salamandre—he finished fourth—and Balla Cove in the Tattersalls Middle Park Stakes cost him any chance of top billing at the end of the season; the compilers of the European Free Handicap put him on 9-0 along with Be My Chief, Elmaamul, Linamix and the filly Negligent. Rock City earned himself another crack at Machiavellian in the General Accident Two Thousand Guineas with a workmanlike front-running display on his seasonal reappearance in the Singer & Friedlander Greenham Stakes at Newbury: challenged from three furlongs out, he responded in typical fashion to win by a length from Montendre. Four and a half lengths fourth to shorter-priced stable-companion Tirol was Rock City's fate in the Guineas. A 14/1-shot, he showed up throughout and got the mile well, coming back at the third horse Anshan in the closing stages. From this point on, placing Rock City successfully became difficult for his connections. They explored several avenues—running under a penalty in Group 2 and Group 3 races, switching distances and even taking the bull by the horns again and trying Group 1 company again. At one time even a tilt at the Del Mar Derby was proposed. But though the colt continued to run well until finally his races seemed to catch up with him in the Gardner Merchant Hungerford Stakes at Newbury in August, he managed only one more victory. That came in the Van Geest Criterion Stakes over seven furlongs at Newmarket at the end of June, when he comfortably accounted for Aldbourne, Robellation and four others. A previous challenge for a Group 3 prize had ended in a narrow defeat by Funambule in the Prix du Palais Royal at Longchamp, while a subsequent one for a Group 2 in the Prix Maurice de Gheest at Deauville ended in a length defeat by Dead Certain who was receiving 9 lb. As for Group 1, it was a case of so near and yet so far. Only Shavian came between Rock City and that elusive prize in the St James's Palace Stakes at Royal Ascot. Rock City gave chase to the all-the-way winner up the straight and succeeded in halving the distance between them to a length and a half by the finish. Rock City came even closer to winning the Group 1 Carroll Foundation July Cup at Newmarket, when third to Royal Academy and Great Commotion. It was a little surprising to see him start favourite there against established sprinters in his first race over six furlongs since the Middle Park. As only to be expected though, he stuck to his task very gamely. Things never went smoothly for him. By halfway he was fractionally last of the nine runners, having been taken off his feet; shortly afterwards he received a bump as he began to improve position, then, just over a furlong from home, he found himself short of room. Nevertheless, he kept on to run the first two close, beaten only three quarters of a length and a neck.

	Ballad Rock (ch 1974)	Bold Lad (b 1964)	Bold Ruler
			Barn Pride
		True Rocket (gr 1967)	Roan Rocket
Rock City			True Course
(br.c. 1987)	Rimosa's Pet (b 1976)	Petingo (b 1965)	Petition
			Alcazar
		Rimosa (br 1960)	Mossborough
			Rosy Dolly

Rock City's below-par fourth to Norwich in the Hungerford Stakes signalled the end of his racing career. The National Stud bought a half share and is to stand him initially at fee of £6,000 with the usual October 1st concession. He's earned his place at stud through performance alone, and has an honest pedigree to back up his form. The dam Rimosa's Pet produced a good horse the year before Rock City in Kerrera (by Diesis), a speedy two-year-old who finished second in the One Thousand Guineas then went back to sprinting and came fourth in the July Cup. Rimosa's Pet was capable of more than useful form on her day at two years and three years; she won the Princess Elizabeth Stakes and Musidora Stakes at three before becoming disappointing (she started third favourite for the Oaks). The next dam Rimosa, suited by middle distances and soft ground, was out of a half-sister to the classic winners Dante and Sayajirao; she was half-sister herself to the dam of Track Spare, winner of the Middle Park Stakes and St James's Palace Stakes in the 'sixties and a very similar type to Rock City in ability, temperament and constitution. The compact, good-quartered Rock City, was effective at six furlongs to a mile, and he acted on any going. A more genuine and consistent individual would be difficult to find. *R. Hannon.*

ROCK FACE   3 b.f. Ballad Rock 122–Misty Halo 93 (High Top 131) [1989 7g a7g⁶   **77** a8g 1990 a 10g* 12.3f⁵ 12.5g 10g⁶ 10g⁴ 11d 12h* 14f* 12f* 14m⁴] leggy, workmanlike filly: fair handicapper: won at Lingfield in April, Brighton, Yarmouth and Brighton again (best effort, by 7 lengths) in August: well-backed favourite, bit below best at York final start: stays 1¾m: acts on hard ground, unsuited by dead: blinkered fifth and sixth starts. *Sir Mark Prescott.*

ROCK HOPPER   3 b.c. Shareef Dancer (USA) 135–Cormorant Wood 130 (Home   **116** Guard (USA) 129) [1989 8.2f⁵ 10g* 10g* 1990 10m² 11.5m*] well-made colt: has scope: has a fluent action: progressive colt: looking particularly well and wearing tongue strap, won 5-runner Calor Derby Trial at Lingfield by 2 lengths from Benzine, quickening to lead over 2f out and never seriously threatened: bit edgy, beaten length by Defensive Play in Guardian Classic Trial at Sandown 2 weeks earlier: will be very well suited by 1½m +: carries head bit high and has wandered markedly under pressure: co-favourite for Derby when reportedly sustained hairline fracture of cannon bone: remains in training. *M. R. Stoute.*

ROCKIN' ROSIE   2 b.f. (Mar 23) Song 132–Almarose 79 (Northfields (USA))   **59** [1990 a5g²] 4,500F, 7,600Y: first foal: dam 2-y-o 6f winner: beaten a short head in maiden at Lingfield in April, keeping on well after slow start and coming wide. *Dr J. D. Scargill.*

ROCK PULSE 4 ch.g. Ballad Rock 122–Muscadina (Major Portion 129) [1989 —
12.2d 8m 8f 10g 7.5m 1990 a7g] plain, sparely-made gelding: poor walker: moderate
mover: plater: stays 7.5f (pulled hard over 1¼m). *Ronald Thompson.*

ROCKRIDGE 3 b.g. Chief Singer 131–Croda Rossa (ITY) (Grey Sovereign 128§) 56
[1989 NR 1990 7f 8m 7g 10m 10g² 10m² 12g 12m³ 12m⁵] rather leggy, attractive
gelding: half-brother to several winners, including smart 5f to 1¼m winner Dancing
Rocks (by Green Dancer) and useful 1984 2-y-o 6f winner Red Rocks (by Grundy):
dam won 3 of 4 races in Italy and is half-sister to Italian Derby winner Cerreto:
plating-class maiden: suited by 1½m: edgy fourth start: gelded after final one. *G.
Wragg.*

ROCKY'S MATE 3 b.f. Young Man (FR) 73–Gold Spangle 97 (Klondyke Bill —
125) [1989 6g 1990 7f a12g 12m 10.1m 12f] workmanlike filly: little sign of ability: sold
out of J. Czerpak's stable 2,000 gns Ascot May Sales after second start, resold 775
gns Ascot December Sales. *W. T. Kemp.*

ROCTON NORTH (IRE) 2 ch.c. (Mar 25) Ballad Rock 122–Northern Scene 78 78
(Habitat 134) [1990 5m² 5m² 6d³ 6g* 7s] IR 7,600F, 31,000Y: compact colt: poor
mover: closely related to Irish 7f winner Star of The North (by Chief Singer) and
half-brother to a winner in Italy by Touching Wood: dam Irish 2-y-o 5f winner: kept
on well to win 17-runner maiden at Yarmouth in October: off course over 4 months
before third start week earlier: better suited by 6f than 5f: seems unsuited by soft
ground. *R. Hannon.*

RODEO STAR (USA) 4 ch.c. Nodouble (USA)–Roundup Rose (USA) (Minne- 69
sota Mac) [1989 10.6g⁵ 1990 11g³ 8.5d 11d* 12g 11.7g³ 12g³ 10m* 10.6s² 10.4d⁴]
workmanlike, plain colt: won handicap at Edinburgh in July and veterans race at
Ascot (favourite) in September: stays 1½m: acts on good to firm and soft going:
visored fourth and sixth outings: has been unruly in stalls: sold to join N. Tinkler's
stable 26,000 gns Newmarket Autumn Sales: winning novice hurdler in December.
J. H. M. Gosden.

ROGALSKA 3 b.f. Elegant Air 119–Chelsea Paperchase 73 (Thatching 131) [1989 — §
NR 1990 10g 10m⁵ 12g 10f⁵ 12m⁵] workmanlike filly: moderate mover: first foal: dam
maiden stayed 1m: little worthwhile form, looking ungenuine in seller fourth outing:
sold 400 gns Ascot November Sales. *R. Guest.*

ROGANY 2 br.f. (May 20) Lochnager 132–Jane Roy (Royalty 130) [1990 5m 5f 6f] —
third reported living foal: dam poor maiden: little worthwhile form in sellers: bolted
on intended debut: taken down early final 2 starts. *M. W. Easterby.*

ROGER DE BERKSTED (USA) 2 b.c. (Feb 28) Topsider (USA)–Liberty 97 p
Spirit (USA) (Graustark) [1990 6g* 7v*] $370,000Y: leggy, workmanlike colt:
fourth foal: half-brother to graded-stakes winner at up to 1½m Dawn's Curtsey (by
Far North): dam twice-raced half-sister to high-class 1m to 1¼m performer Mehmet: well-backed favourite, won 5-runner minor event at Chester by 2½ lengths

Calor Derby Trial Stakes, Lingfield—
Rock Hopper, the winner from Benzine looks on course for Epsom
before injury intervenes

from Maraakiz, travelling smoothly then staying on strongly: very green when winning York maiden earlier in October: will stay 1m: probably very useful colt in making. *J. H. M. Gosden.*

ROGERMEDE 4 b.g. Runnymede 123–Lenoushka (Lorenzaccio 130) [1989 NR — 1990 12m] half-brother to a winner in Norway: dam ran twice: saddle slipped and rider unseated in seller at Thirsk in May: backward and moved down poorly. *B. W. Murray.*

ROGER RAMJET (IRE) 2 b.c. (Apr 15) Law Society (USA) 130–Saraday **101** (Northfields (USA)) [1990 7m* 8d²] IR 3,200F, IR 42,000Y: third foal: half-brother to a winner in Germany by Commanche Run: dam Irish staying maiden: won 9-runner maiden at Leopardstown in July: short-head second of 6 to Approach The Bench in Juddmonte EBF Beresford Stakes at the Curragh in October: will stay 1¼m. *J. S. Bolger, Ireland.*

ROGER'S PAL 3 ch.c. Lir 82–Amberush 41 (No Rush) [1989 NR 1990 10f⁶ 8.3m] — leggy colt: second reported foal: brother to poor maiden/winning hurdler Lirchur: dam, plater on flat who stayed 1½m, won over hurdles: well beaten in maiden at Brighton and claimer at Windsor. *A. Moore.*

ROGERS PRINCESS 8 b.m. Owen Anthony 102–Ask For Roger (Menelek 114) — [1989 16.2d 1990 18f⁶] fairly useful staying hurdler: never able to challenge in handicap at Nottingham in May, only second run on flat since 1984: suited by extreme test of stamina. *M. Tate.*

ROGGAN HALL 4 br.f. Balidar 133–Star of The Arctic (Arctic Chevalier 112) — [1989 NR 1990 10.2f] workmanlike filly: always behind in late-season maidens as 2-y-o: reluctant then reared over in stalls and withdrawn under orders at Doncaster in March. *R. Earnshaw.*

ROI DE ROME (USA) 3 b.c. Time For A Change (USA)–Reve de Reine (USA) **112** 97 (Lyphard (USA) 132) [1989 8v* 8s* 1990 9.2s* 12m 10d⁶] tall, rather leggy, attractive colt: second foal: half-brother to fairly useful French 1m winner Rose de Thai (by Lear Fan): dam winner from 8.5f to 9.2f in France, out of French 1000 Guineas and Grand Prix de Saint-Cloud winner Riverqueen: sire won Grade 1 9f Flamingo Stakes: successful in newcomers event and listed race at Maisons-Laffitte late on at 2 yrs and in Prix de Guiche (by ¾ length from Slew The Slewor) at Longchamp in April: disappointed in Prix du Jockey-Club (looked tremendously well, wore tongue strap) at Chantilly and Grand Prix de Paris at Longchamp: should prove best at up to 1¼m: acts on heavy going. *Mme C. Head, France.*

ROLFESON 6 b.h. Rolfe (USA) 77–Do Something 77 (Pardao 120) [1989 10m⁴ **66** 10m² 9g* 10.6d⁵ 9m⁶ 11s 10g³ 8f 1990 10m³ 8.2m* 9.1m² 8f* 9g 8g 8m 8g 8.2d] sturdy, good-quartered horse: good mover: quite modest handicapper: won at Hamilton in July and Newmarket (invitation event) in August: lost his form after next outing: effective at 1m to 1¼m: acts on firm and dead going: blinkered twice: good mount for apprentice. *B. C. Morgan.*

ROLL A DOLLAR 4 b.g. Spin of A Coin 88–Handy Dancer 87 (Green God 128) **100** [1989 10g 10.1m* 10.1m³ 11.7m* 1990 12g 12m³ 16m⁴ 22d⁵ 12f³ 14g 12m* 11s] tall, workmanlike gelding: good mover: useful handicapper: won £7,600 event at Newmarket in October by head from Amelianne: slowly away and always well behind final outing: effective at 1½m and stays 2m: acts on firm going, probably unsuited by soft. *D. R. C. Elsworth.*

ROMAN FAN (IRE) 2 b.f. (Mar 15) Taufan (USA) 119–Crepe Myrtle 80 — (Crepello 136) [1990 5m] IR 12,500Y: small, sparely-made filly: sister to 5-y-o True Fan, placed in bumpers, and half-sister to several winners here and abroad, including useful 1976 2-y-o Ground Cover (by Huntercombe), later stakes winner at up to 1¼m in USA: dam 1m winner: green, soon struggling in maiden auction at Windsor in July: moved poorly down. *M. Bell.*

ROMANIAN (IRE) 2 ch.c. (Feb 28) Sallust 134–Cailin d'Oir (Roi Soleil 125) **66** [1990 6d⁵ 6m⁵ 6d⁶] IR 4,200Y: compact colt: fifth foal: half-brother to 3 winners in Ireland, including 2m winner Adapt (by Smoggy) and 1½m winner Gallant Gold (by Touch Paper): dam 5f winner (at 2 yrs) in Ireland: quite modest form in maidens: unruly stalls and withdrawn at Lingfield third intended start: will stay 7f. *A. R. Davison.*

ROMANOVNA 3 b.f. Mummy's Pet 125–Empress of Russia 79 (Royal Palace — 131) [1989 7g 6g 1990 8m 8m⁵ 7m 7g 7g] smallish, sparely-made filly: poor maiden: sweating and edgy final start. *T. Thomson Jones.*

ROMAN PROSE 5 ch.g. Sallust 134–Mothers Girl (Huntercombe 133) [1989 **116** 7.2g 6f 6m⁴ 1990 6g* 5.5v³ 6g* 6s² 6g³ 6d⁴ 6f*] workmanlike, sparely-made

Paul Green's "Roger Ramjet"

gelding: useful sprinter in Europe: won listed races at Evry in March and Baden-Baden in May: nearly 40/1, put up much improved effort in Grade 3 Laurel Dash at Laurel Park in October, accounting for eased Ron's Victory by neck: suited by 6f: best run on firm going: visored final start at 4 yrs. *J. Pease, France.*

ROMAN WALK 3 b.f. Petorius 117–Plum Bold 83 (Be My Guest (USA) 126) — [1989 6f4 6f2 6g2 6g* 6g 1990 5g 6m 7g] angular filly: fair winner at 2 yrs: not seen out until late-September in 1990, always behind facing very stiff tasks: may stay further than 6f. *Lord John FitzGerald.*

ROMANY MARSH (USA) 3 b.c. Lomond (USA) 128–Zinzara (USA) 119 (Stage — Door Johnny) [1989 NR 1990 12g] second foal: closely related to useful 1½m winner Zinsky (by Nijinsky): dam 6f and 1¼m winner: soundly beaten in apprentice maiden at Newmarket in June. *G. Wragg.*

RONALD IVOR 4 b.c. Bold Lad (IRE) 133–Lady Probus 70§ (Shantung 132) — [1989 10f6 12f5 10m 8m6 11d 8m* 7m 8.5g* 8g3 1990 10f 8m 12d6 8.2m 8g 8f] angular, medium-sized ex-Irish colt: poor mover: fourth foal: half-brother to modest 1986 2-y-o plater Galway Express (by Dunphy): dam, daughter of half-sister to top 1950 2-y-o Big Dipper, showed ability at 2 yrs but became disappointing: won handicaps at Phoenix Park and Galway as 3-y-o: well beaten in minor events and handicaps in 1990: best form at about 1m: acts on good to firm going. *C. F. C. Jackson.*

RON'S VICTORY (USA) 3 ch.c. General Holme (USA) 128–Tea And **129** Scandals (USA) (Key To The Kingdom (USA)) [1989 6g3 6.5g* 1990 8d5 7m2 5g* 5m2 5d2 6g* 6g5 6m* 6f2]

The champion Dayjur had no monopoly of spectacular performances in the sprints. One of his main rivals for the season's honours, Ron's Victory,

Prix de Ris Orangis, Evry—
Ron's Victory makes all for a comfortable win over Sharp N'Early and Whippet

stormed to a ten-length win in the Krug Diadem Stakes at Ascot in September, coming to head a fourteen-runner field on the bridle two furlongs out, extending his advantage to four lengths in the space of a furlong then drawing right away, just punched along until the rider dropped his hands approaching the line. A strong end-to-end gallop and the stiff Ascot finish no doubt accentuated the margin, as on some other memorable occasions there; even so, well-contested pattern races over six furlongs on a sound surface are seldom won by half that distance. Ron's Victory's closest pursuers were Northern Goddess, Tadwin and Polar Bird, three progressive fillies at the top of the sprint handicap with good recent form, some of it in listed or pattern company. They had every chance. Next came Pharaoh's Delight who was eased when beaten, well clear of the rest, notably Argentum and Dead Certain, both clearly below par. After this, the Laurel Dash should have been almost a formality for Ron's Victory. He'd been sent for the American Grade 3 turf race rather than take on Dayjur in the Prix de l'Abbaye, had favourable conditions for the attempt, and started 11/10 favourite to beat nine opponents. But that was to reckon without his jockey's mistaking the winning post when the colt had come from behind to lead inside the last furlong: Roman Prose and his rider Dettori kept going to snatch the prize on the line. There is very little doubt that Ron's Victory is a better sprinter than Roman Prose. We'll go further and say he is the one they all have to beat in 1991 now that Dayjur and Royal Academy have been retired. He may be less difficult to beat at five furlongs than six, but that is only speculation prompted by the excellence of his win in the Diadem. Ron's Victory has one top-class effort to his credit over five furlongs—a testing five at Ascot. The occasion was his British debut in the King's Stand Stakes, which he marked with second place behind Dayjur,

Krug Diadem Stakes, Ascot—a stunning performance from France's leading sprinter

J. S. Moss's "Ron's Victory"

beaten only two and a half lengths; he chased the winner from soon after the start, and in trying to close with him from the distance drew well clear of the rest. He'd been put back to sprinting after defeats in the early spring in listed races in France over a mile then seven furlongs, the latter of which had been his creditable second behind Machiavellian in the Prix Djebel. He'd made the best possible start as a sprinter with a length-and-a-half defeat of Nabeel Dancer in the five-furlong Prix de Saint-Georges at Longchamp in May but Nabeel Dancer, transformed in the blinkers, emphatically reversed the form in the Prix du Gros Chêne over the same distance at Chantilly three weeks prior to Royal Ascot. The experiment of running Ron's Victory over six after Royal Ascot also met with immediate success: he beat another British challenger Sharp N'Early by a length and a half in the Prix de Ris Orangis at Evry in July. However, defeat again followed, this time in the Ladbroke Sprint Cup at Haydock in September when he failed to run much of a race from the worst draw and finished a well-beaten fifth behind Dayjur.

			Star Kingdom
	General Holme (USA)	Noholme II	Oceana
	(ch 1979)	(ch 1956)	Count Fleet
Ron's Victory (USA)		Generals Sister	Cigar Maid
(ch.c. 1987)		(b 1960)	Bold Ruler
	Tea And	Key To The Kingdom	Key Bridge
	Scandals (USA)	(b 1970)	Jean-Pierre
	(b 1981)	Last Gossip	Gossip Time
		(b 1974)	

Ron's Victory, a useful winner over six and a half furlongs in the July of his two-year-old days, was worth a try over a mile on pedigree. His sire

767

General Holme showed high-class form at up to ten and a half furlongs in France, regularly gave the impression he'd stay further (though he finished only seventeenth of twenty-six to All Along in the Arc on his only attempt) and in his first crop had the Vermeille winner Indian Rose. The dam was quite speedy though, and gained her only win over six furlongs in a valuable handicap at Maisons-Laffitte as a three-year-old. Ron's Victory is her first foal. The next dam Last Gossip is a lightly-raced maiden racemare by the American stayer Jean-Pierre out of Gossip Time, winner of a six-furlong claimer as a three-year-old in the States.

Ron's Victory is quite an attractive colt, easily picked out by his broad blaze which gives the impression that he races with his head held high. It would seem unlikely that he'll be tried beyond six furlongs again. Like many of his generation he reached the end of three-year-old days without once encountering really soft going. His two runs at Ascot show he acts on good to soft and good to firm. Sometimes he is turned out wearing bandages behind; he has also worn a crossed noseband. *A. J. Falourd, France.*

ROOFING (IRE) 2 b.c. (Feb 13) Thatching 131–Joanne's Joy (Ballymore 123)   **85 p**
[1990 7m²] IR 85,000Y: quite attractive colt: fourth foal: dam Irish 7f and 1m winner: 4 lengths second of 12, going on well unable to challenge, to Peter Davies in maiden at Leicester in September: showed a quick action: sure to improve, and win a race. *B. W. Hills.*

ROOSTERS TIPPLE 4 b.g. Henbit (USA) 130–Amiel (Nonoalco (USA) 131)   **56**
[1989 10.6g 8g 8m 1990 a6g 10d 8m a6g⁶ a6g² a7g⁵ a7g] big, lengthy, angular gelding: plating-class maiden: should prove suited by 1m + : blinkered last 5 outings. *M. W. Easterby.*

ROPE TRICK 3 br.c. Indian King (USA) 128–Trickster 92 (Major Portion 129)   —
[1989 6f³ 7f² 7g⁶ 5m⁴ 6f² 6m⁵ 5g* 1990 5f 6g 6m 5.8f 8g 7f] leggy, lengthy, good-quartered colt: moderate mover: fair winner at 2 yrs: ran moderately in handicaps in first half of 1990, often slowly away: stays 6f: often blinkered or visored: edgy fifth start. *Mrs N. Macauley.*

ROSATEEN 2 br.f. (May 8) Teenoso (USA) 135–Red Roses (FR) (Roi Dagobert 128) [1990 10s] useful-looking filly: good walker: fifth foal: half-sister to 3 winners   —
abroad: dam won at up to 6f in France: tailed off in maiden at Nottingham in October. *R. T. Juckes.*

ROSCOES DINKY 3 br.f. Roscoe Blake 120–Minibus 77 (John Splendid 116)   —
[1989 NR 1990 7g 10.2h] leggy filly: sixth foal: dam won over 6f: on toes and showed nothing in maidens in May. *W. G. M. Turner.*

ROSCOE THE BRAVE 6 br.g. Roscoe Blake 120–My Plucky Lady 64 (Cash   —
And Courage 116) [1989 NR 1990 9s] leggy gelding: half-brother to 4 winners, including 7f winner Shipowner (by Quayside): dam won at up to 1m: apprentice ridden and on toes, tailed off in maiden claimer at Hamilton in April. *S. E. Kettlewell.*

ROSE ALTO 2 ch.f. (Apr 10) Adonijah 126–Rose Music 86 (Luthier 126) [1990   **67 p**
8g⁵] fifth foal: half-sister to 3 winners here and abroad, including fairly useful 6f (at 2 yrs) to 9.2f winner Milligan (by Tap On Wood) and fairly useful 7f (at 2 yrs) to 9f winner Jalmusique (by Jalmood): dam won at 7f and 1m: over 4 lengths fifth of 21, headway over 2f out and keeping on steadily, to Forbearance in maiden at Pontefract in October: sure to improve. *J. R. Fanshawe.*

ROSEATE LODGE 4 b.g. Habitat 134–Elegant Tern (USA) 102 (Sea Bird II   **90**
145) [1989 8s 8g* 9f² 8g* 8.2g* 8m 8s 8g² 1990 9g 8f² 8.2m 8f² 8.2s² 8.3m 9g 8g³ 8g* 8m* 8m2] compact, workmanlike gelding: fairly useful handicapper: in fine form in autumn, winning at Sandown and Ascot (£11,100 event gamely by head from Curtain Call) in September: stays 1m well: acts on any going: ran poorly when on toes on reappearance: trained first 6 starts by M. Tompkins. *R. W. Armstrong.*

ROSEATE TERN 4 b.f. Blakeney 126–Rosia Bay 102 (High Top 131) [1989 10g³   **117**
12m² 12f² 12g* 12f* 14.6s³ 1990 12m* 12g4 11.1g² 12s 12g³] strong, good-topped filly: good class as 3-y-o when trained by R. Hern: returned in excellent heart in spring and accounted for Ile de Nisky by 2 lengths in General Accident Jockey Club Stakes at Newmarket in May: looking really well on first run for 3 months, creditable second to Lord of The Field in strongly-run BonusPrint September Stakes at Kempton: favourite, 7¾ lengths third of 10 in Long Island Handicap at Belmont Park: should stay 1¾m: acts on firm going, probably unsuited by soft: blinkered in 1989: invariably held up. *L. M. Cumani.*

Peter M. Brant's "Roseate Tern"

ROSE BROCADE   2 b.f. (Apr 14) Primo Dominie 121–Blue Brocade 91 (Reform   —
132) [1990 6m 8g] second foal: half-sister to 3-y-o Catballou (by Tina's Pet): dam
10.6f winner, is half-sister to very smart Lockton: no show in large-field claimer at
Leicester (very backward, slowly away) and maiden at Yarmouth in October. *J. A. R.
Toller.*

ROSE CUT (USA)   3 ch.c. Diesis 133–Sweet Ramblin Rose (USA) (Turn-To)   —
[1989 NR 1990 8.3f 11.7m 10g⁵ 8g] brother to 4-y-o Two Worlds and half-brother to
several winners, including 1m stakes winner Sword Blade (by Damascus): dam,
stakes-placed winner at up to 6f, is half-sister to very smart Fleet Velvet: no
worthwhile form though has shown signs of ability: faced stiff task in handicap: sold
2,000 gns Newmarket Autumn Sales. *J. R. Fanshawe.*

ROSE D'ETOILE   2 b.f. (Mar 2) Jalmood (USA) 126–Angelic Appeal (Star   **49**
Appeal 133) [1990 5f⁵ 5m⁵ 5m 6d] sparely-made filly: fourth foal: half-sister to 1m
winner Just Mine (by Sparkler): dam ran once: poor form in maidens at Folkestone
and Lingfield: raced on disadvantageous part of track final outing: should be better
suited by 6f+ than 5f. *W. Carter.*

ROSE FESTIVAL   4 br.f. Ile de Bourbon (USA) 133–Vendemmia (Silly Season   —
127) [1989 10.2g⁶ 12.2g² 12g⁴ a12g⁴ 1990 a10g⁵] leggy, rather sparely-made filly:
easily best effort in maidens on debut: blinkered and facing stiff task, well beaten in
handicaps at Lingfield last 2 outings: may prove best at 1¼m. *R. J. O'Sullivan.*

ROSE GLEN   4 b.f. Lochnager 132–Phoenix Rose 85 (Frankincense 120) [1989   **75**
7g* 8s⁵ 6d⁴ 7m⁵ 7f² 7f² 7m a7g⁴ a8g 1990 8f⁶ 8g 7m 7g 6m⁶ 7m³ 6g 7d 8d 7m⁴ 7m]
big, workmanlike filly: has a rather round action: moderate handicapper: ideally suited
by 7f or 1m: acts on firm going: usually blinkered or visored, but wasn't last 2 starts.
A. Bailey.

ROSEHILL PARK   2 b.c. (Mar 28) Nishapour (FR) 125–Aquarula 88 (Dominion   —
123) [1990 5m 6d] 7,600Y, 9,600 2-y-o: small colt: moderate walker: second foal:

half-brother to 1½m winner To Be Fair (by Adonijah): dam 2-y-o 5f and 6f winner, is half-sister to 2 useful or better 2-y-o winners: last in maiden (very slowly away) at Wolverhampton and claimer at Goodwood. *D. Marks.*

ROSE OF HIGH LEGH   4 b.f. Martinmas 128–Halka (Daring March 116) [1989 — 7d* 6s* 6g 6f 7s⁵ 6g 6s⁵ 6g 1990 6m a8g 8v 7d] leggy, angular filly: moderate mover: plating-class winner (including for apprentice) in spring as 3-y-o: no form in 1990: stays 7f: used to go well with plenty of give in the ground: sometimes blinkered: often slowly away and gets behind: sold to join Mrs G. Reveley's stable 2,500 gns Doncaster November Sales. *J. Berry.*

ROSE OF TOUGET   3 b.f. Dreams To Reality (USA) 113–Loredana 64 (Grange   29 Melody) [1989 5f⁴ 5g 6m 1990 7m⁵ 7g⁶ 8h] small filly: poor mover: plater: should stay 1m: ran creditably for 7-lb claimer. *J. Pearce.*

ROSES HAVE THORNS   3 ch.f. Ela-Mana-Mou 132–Cienaga (Taboosh   64 (USA)) [1989 NR 1990 8m⁵ 10.6s 8.3f* 8g⁶ 9m] 5,000Y: leggy filly: has a rather round action: half-sister to several winners at up to 1¼m, including 5-y-o plater Seleucia (by Persian Bold): dam raced Irish middle-distance filly out of half-sister to smart 1m to 1½m performer Gift Wrapped, dam of Reach: won minor event at Windsor in August: easily better subsequent effort next time: worth another try over 1¼m. *C. F. Wall.*

ROSE'S PRIDE   4 b.f. Ballacashtal (CAN)–Tropingay (Cawston's Clown 113) — [1989 8m 10m 10.4m³ 10g 10g 1990 8g a12g] sturdy filly: poor maiden: tailed off in autumn, sweating and on toes second outing. *M. Dods.*

ROSGILL   4 ch.g. Mill Reef (USA) 141–Speedy Rose (On Your Mark 125) [1989   74 12d⁴ 12g 12d⁵ 10.5s⁴ 1990 14f⁴ 13.3m⁶ 11.5m* 11.5m⁴ 12f 11.5m⁴ 15g⁴ 13f² 12f³ 11.5m³ 14g⁴ 16f²] angular ex-French gelding: fourth foal: half-brother to a winner in Italy: dam won 6 times at up to 1¼m as 3-y-o in Ireland: dropped in class, won ladies race at Lingfield in June: in frame in handicaps after: stays 2m: acts on firm going: blinkered twice at 3 yrs: sweated fifth and sixth starts: has carried head high. *P. Mitchell.*

ROSGWEN   3 ch.f. Remainder Man 126§–Pamkins Hart (Pamroy 99) [1989 NR — 1990 12m 12.5g] close-coupled filly: first reported foal: dam well beaten on flat but winning staying hurdler: tailed off in maiden at Pontefract and seller (sweating, hampered early) at Wolverhampton. *J. P. Smith.*

ROSIETOES (USA)   2 b.f. (Feb 6) Master Willie 129–Desrose 74 (Godswalk   65 (USA) 130) [1990 6m² 5.8h² 6g 7d⁵] angular filly: fourth foal: dam thrice-raced here at 2 yrs, is half-sister to Irish 1000 Guineas runner-up Clover Princess: runner-up in minor event at Windsor and maiden auction at Bath in summer: should be suited by 7f: seems unsuited by an easy surface. *P. J. Makin.*

ROSILU   3 b.f. Norwick (USA) 120–Josilu (Caliban 123) [1989 NR 1990 11.7h³ 7f — 10m] angular filly: half-sister to 1986 2-y-o 5.8f seller winner Josie Smith (by Alias Smith) and several other winners here and abroad: dam of no account: bit backward, twice slowly away when well beaten in claimers. *R. J. Hodges.*

ROSTHERNE   8 ch.g. Crimson Beau 124–Correct Approach 77 (Right Tack 131) — [1989 NR 1990 13s] leggy, lengthy gelding: one-time modest handicapper: bandaged, ran poorly in April, only run on flat since 5 yrs: stays 1¾m: has seemed suited by give in the ground: suited by waiting tactics: often used to sweat and get on edge. *J. G. FitzGerald.*

ROSTOVOL   5 b.g. Vaigly Great 127–Emerin 85 (King Emperor (USA)) [1989   38 § 8.5f 9f 1990 8v 8g² 8m³] leggy gelding: moderate mover: poor form when placed in June handicaps: stays 1m: probably acts on any going: blinkered 3 times in 1988, finding nothing once headed last 2 occasions: visored last 3 outings. *D. H. Topley.*

ROSUDGEON   2 ch.c. (Apr 13) Undulate (USA)–April Rose (Wollow 132) [1990   36 5m 6g 7f 5.3h⁴] sparely-made, close-coupled colt: second reported foal: dam twice-raced granddaughter of Oaks second Maina: lowered in class, fourth of 7, having been outpaced, in seller at Brighton in August: should stay at least 7f. *W. G. R. Wightman.*

ROSY DIAMOND   4 ch.f. Jalmood (USA) 126–Sun Approach 84 (Sun Prince 128)   43 [1989 7.5g⁵ 6m³ 7f 6f 9m⁴ 11m 9.1f 6m* 6g 6f 1990 6m 7m⁵ 10.2f] angular filly: poor walker: poor handicapper: effective at 6f and probably stays 9f: best form on top-of-the-ground. *C. C. Elsey.*

ROSY SAKER   2 ch.f. (May 4) Absalom 128–Anoda (FR) (Amber Rama (USA)   52 133) [1990 5g⁵ 5m⁶ 5m³ 5f⁴ 5m⁶ 5v²] 6,400Y: smallish, workmanlike filly: poor walker: has a round action: sister to 3-y-o Apparel and useful 1985 2-y-o 5f winner

770

Sundeed and half-sister to 2 other winners, including 1988 2-y-o 5f to 1m winner Tanoda (by Tyrnavos): dam placed in Italy: plating-class maiden: will stay 6f: acts on any going. *W. G. M. Turner.*

ROTHERFIELD GREYS 8 b. or br.g. Mummy's Pet 125–Relicia (Relko 136) —
[1989 5m 6f 6f³ 6m³ 6m 6s 5m 1990 6m] strong, good-bodied gelding: carries plenty of condition: useful sprint handicapper at his best: bit backward only start at 8 yrs: best on a sound surface: good mount for apprentice: often sweats and gets on toes: best with waiting tactics. *M. McCormack.*

ROUCELLIST BAY 2 ch.g. (May 9) Rousillon (USA) 133–Cellist (USA) (Bag- —
dad) [1990 6m] 1,600Y: angular gelding: half-brother to several winners, including useful 1984 2-y-o 7f winner Concert Hall (by Monteverdi): dam, smart stakes winner at up to 1m, is half-sister to top-class Gay Fandango: green and better for race, slowly away, always behind and carried head awkwardly in maiden at Redcar in October. *S. E. Kettlewell.*

ROUND TRIP (IRE) 2 b.f. (Feb 23) Auction Ring (USA) 123–La Fortune (Le —
Haar 126) [1990 8g] rather unfurnished filly: sister to 3 winners, including very smart 7f and 1m winner Lucky Ring, and half-sister to useful 11f winner Latin Luck (by Homeric): dam placed over 1m in France at 2 yrs: bit backward, slowly away, tended to carry head awkwardly and always behind in maiden at Wolverhampton in October. *N. A. Graham.*

ROUSALA (IRE) 2 b.f. (Mar 26) Tender King 123–Fun (Jukebox 120) [1990 —
5.1m 6g] IR 2,500F, IR 2,000Y, 1,300 2-y-o: sparely-made filly: half-sister to several winners, including Irish sprint handicapper Life of The Party (by Wolverlife): dam, last on only outing, is half-sister to Record Run: little worthwhile form in sellers at Yarmouth and Nottingham in autumn. *J. D. Czerpak.*

ROUSILLON TO BE 3 b.c. Rousillon (USA) 133–Triple Bar 71 (Jimmy Reppin 70
131) [1989 NR 1990 11g² 12.3f³ 12f² 16f 10g⁵ a16g] 15,000Y: big, leggy colt: half-brother to fairly useful 1985 2-y-o 6f and 7f winner Colway Comet (by Formidable) and 2 winners abroad: dam won over 7.2f and stayed 1¼m: modest maiden: below best last 3 starts: should be suited by 1¾m, probably doesn't stay 2m: has carried head high and wandered under pressure: trained until penultimate start by J. Hudson. *J. D. Bethell.*

ROUSKI 3 b.g. Rousillon (USA) 133–Missy Baldski (USA) (Baldski (USA)) [1989 54 §
7g⁴ 7g 7m 6m² 6m 6g 1990 7f 8f³ 7h a8g⁵ 8m⁵ 7f 7f³ 7f 7m a6g³] angular, lengthy colt: moderate walker: has a long stride: quite modest maiden at best: probably stays 1m: best efforts on top-of-the-ground: sold to join J. Thomas 9,000 gns Ascot October Sales: inconsistent, difficult ride and one to be wary of. *J. W. Payne.*

ROUTE MARCH 11 ch.g. Queen's Hussar 124–Wide of The Mark 91 (Gulf Pearl —
117) [1989 10.1m 12m 12g 1990 16g 17.6m 18d] compact, round-barrelled gelding: of little account: visored first 2 starts. *P. A. Pritchard.*

ROUTILANTE 3 b.f. Rousillon (USA) 133–Danseuse Classique (CAN) (North- 93 §
ern Dancer) [1989 6g* 6m² 6m² 1990 8v⁵ 7m⁴ 8f 7m² 6g⁴ 7d²] workmanlike filly: good walker: capable of fairly useful form: second in £7,200 handicap (travelling smoothly to lead over 2f out then headed close home) at Sandown and 4-runner minor event at Ayr, clearly best efforts in 1990: should prove as effective at 6f as 7f: acts on good to firm ground and dead: probably ungenuine. *I. A. Balding.*

ROUTING 2 b.c. (May 1) Rousillon (USA) 133–Tura (Northfields (USA)) [1990 56
6g² 5f 7d⁴ 7m⁵ 6m] 11,500Y: rather angular colt: third foal: half-brother to 3-y-o Jagged Edge (by Sharpo), 5f winner at 2 yrs, and fair performer at up to 1m Young Turpin (by Young Generation): dam Irish 7f winner: plating-class maiden: ran badly at Folkestone final outing: stays 7f: best effort on dead ground. *M. Bell.*

ROUYAN 4 b.g. Akarad (FR) 130–Rosy Moon (FR) (Sheshoon 132) [1989 12m⁴ —
12g⁴ 14d* 15s⁶ 1990 14m] rangy, good-bodied gelding: fair winner (wandered) as 3-y-o: well beaten in handicap at Newmarket in April: stays 1¾m well: takes keen hold and will prove best with strong handling: fair hurdler. *R. Simpson.*

ROVIRIS 2 b.c. (Apr 18) Sir Ivor 135–Royal Caprice (USA) (Swaps) [1990 10.2s] —
big, rangy colt: brother to smart 1986 2-y-o 6f and 7f winner Genghiz, later successful at 1¼m, and to a winner in USA, and half-brother to 2 other winners: dam won at up to 1m: backward and green in minor event at Doncaster in November. *Mrs L. Piggott.*

ROWHEDGE 4 ch.c. Tolomeo 127–Strident Note 89 (The Minstrel (CAN) 135) —
[1989 NR 1990 8.3g] smallish, lengthy colt: 25/1 on only second outing on flat, not given hard race when ninth of 17 in seller at Windsor in August: winner of 2 selling hurdles shortly afterwards. *W. M. Perrin.*

771

ROYAL ACADEMY (USA)   3 b.c. Nijinsky (CAN) 138–Crimson Saint **130** (USA) (Crimson Satan) [1989 6g* 7g⁶ 1990 7g* 8m² 6m* 6g² 8g*]

England expected; Ireland delivered. Dayjur's unfortunate defeat in the Sprint on Breeders' Cup day, the nearest thing racing has to a world championship, is recounted elsewhere; but Royal Academy, Dayjur's closest rival for the top sprinting honours in Europe, provided the strong Anglo-Irish challenge with a victory in one of the other major events on the programme, the Breeders' Cup Mile. The versatile Royal Academy, winner of the Carroll Foundation July Cup at Newmarket and runner-up to Dayjur in the Ladbroke Sprint Cup at Haydock, started favourite for the Breeders' Cup Mile at Belmont Park in late-October despite reservations in some quarters about his being so effective at the longer trip. His only previous outing over a mile had been in the Airlie/Coolmore Irish Two Thousand Guineas in which he had gone down by a neck to the General Accident Two Thousand Guineas winner Tirol, edged out near the finish after looking full of running at the distance and quickening impressively to dispute the lead from just inside the final furlong. Royal Academy was one of four European challengers for the Breeders' Cup Mile—the Queen Elizabeth II Stakes winner Markofdistinction and the Prix Jacques le Marois first and fourth Priolo and Lady Winner were the others— while the home-trained runners included Steinlen, winner of the race the previous year, and the four-year-olds Expensive Decision and Who's To Pay who had fought out the finish of the Kelso Handicap in what was claimed, erroneously, as a world-record time over the course and distance three weeks earlier. Dropped to the rear as soon as the stalls opened and well back for most of the race, Royal Academy improved from sixth or seventh, half a dozen lengths behind the leaders, turning into the short straight and showed a dazzling turn of speed, brought to challenge on the outside. Responding gamely to the whip inside the final furlong, Royal Academy caught the 36/1-outsider Itsallgreektome in the shadow of the post, winning by a neck with the strong-finishing Priolo three quarters of a length further away third; Steinlen came fourth, followed by the long-time leader Expensive Decision, Who's To Pay, Markofdistinction and Lady Winner, a little over three lengths covering the first eight.

Royal Academy gave the Irish their first Breeders' Cup victory, adding a notable footnote to the brilliant career of his trainer. Vincent O'Brien's skill and judgement were clearly exhibited in his handling of Royal Academy as a three-year-old. Royal Academy was the most expensive yearling purchased at public auction in 1988—he cost 3,500,000 dollars—and he had a lot to live up

Carroll Foundation July Cup, Newmarket—
Royal Academy (noseband) copes well with the return to six furlongs;
Great Commotion (left), Rock City (hooped sleeves) and Magic Gleam (striped cap)
fill the places

*Breeders' Cup Mile, Belmont Park—Royal Academy (No. 1) and Piggott
pull off a remarkable win, just catching the grey Itsallgreektome;
Priolo (No. 2) just gets third ahead of the almost-hidden Steinlen and Expensive Decision;
No. 5 is Markofdistinction*

to. A disappointing performance when hot favourite for the Dewhurst on the second of two outings as a two-year-old left Royal Academy's halo askew and must have given his trainer and the numerous shareholders in Classic Thoroughbreds Plc, which owned forty per cent of the horse, plenty of food for thought over the winter. It was our view after the Dewhurst that Royal Academy would be seen to better advantage over longer distances, but there was much talk of his reverting to sprinting as a three-year-old. O'Brien, however, decided to aim Royal Academy initially at the Irish Two Thousand Guineas and tuned him up with a win in the Dermot McCalmont Tetrarch EBF Stakes over seven furlongs at the Curragh. Royal Academy ran well in the Irish Guineas, giving the finest performance of his career up to that time, but, as so often when a horse is beaten after looking to be going best, some thought they detected signs that Royal Academy had shirked the issue; he'd also been difficult when loaded up. Much worse was to follow when Royal Academy refused to enter the stalls on his next intended outing, in the St James's Palace Stakes at Royal Ascot. Was Royal Academy's temperament getting the better of him? The answer when it came, in the July Cup, was clear-cut. Royal Academy fully redeemed himself, giving no trouble at the start, put in first, and winning like a champion—in the absence of the side-lined Dayjur. In a race run at a cracking gallop, Royal Academy travelled smoothly from the start and was brought up on a tight rein after being held up near the back until halfway; he was clearly going much the best from two furlongs out and soon led when given his head inside the final furlong. Royal Academy's powerful finish was too much for the Cork And Orrery winner Great Commotion who was beaten three quarters of a length; the St James's Palace runner-up Rock City was a neck further behind in third. Royal Academy was again ridden from well behind in the Ladbroke Sprint Cup at Haydock on his next appearance. But this time he was up against Dayjur who consolidated his position as the best sprinter seen in Europe for some years with a one-and-a-half-length victory. Royal Academy again produced a first-class turn of finishing speed and was closing on the runaway Dayjur all the way to the line giving the impression he would have given the winner more to do had his jockey not encountered problems getting a clear run approaching the final furlong. With Dayjur out of the way, Royal Academy would have run out a most impressive winner: Pharaoh's Delight was five lengths further behind in third, three lengths ahead of fourth-placed Great Commotion in as strong a field as any all season for a sprint championship event. Royal Academy's regular jockey Reid missed the mount in the Breeders' Cup Mile

Classic Thoroughbreds Plc's "Royal Academy"

through injury, his place being taken by Piggott whose come-back in mid-October—five years after retiring from the saddle—took the racing world by surprise. Piggott's success on Royal Academy proved that being the wrong side of fifty need not necessarily be a hindrance to riding prowess: the popular Press had a field day!

		Nijinsky (CAN) (b 1967)	Northern Dancer (b 1961)	Nearctic
Royal Academy (USA) (b.c. 1987)				Natalma
			Flaming Page (b 1959)	Bull Page
				Flaring Top
		Crimson Saint (USA) (ch 1969)	Crimson Satan (ch 1959)	Spy Song
				Papila
			Bolero Rose (b 1958)	Bolero
				First Rose

The tall, lengthy, attractive Royal Academy—described by O'Brien as 'one of the best yearlings I've seen'—is to join another outstanding sprinter-miler Last Tycoon, winner of the Breeders' Cup Mile in 1986, at stud at Coolmore. Last Tycoon made a fine start to his career as a stallion, his first crop of two-year-olds winning more prize-money, world-wide, than any other European-based first-season sire. Royal Academy has excellent prospects of doing well at stud too. He has most of the attributes commercial breeders look for, including top-class form, outstanding conformation and a fine pedigree (his sire Nijinsky needs no introduction). The terms of Royal Academy's syndication placed a valuation on him of around IR £5,000,000 and he is to stand at IR 30,000 guineas, no foal, no fee, in 1991. Royal Academy's brother Encino and half-brother Pancho Villa (by Secretariat) are both at stud in North America. Most of Nijinsky's runners in Europe have been suited by middle distances but he has also sired Two Thousand Guineas winners in England, Ireland and France in a brilliant career. The very lightly-raced Encino gained his only success in a five-furlong maiden race at Hollywood Park and ran his best race when third in the six-furlong Hollywood Juvenile Championship Stakes. Like Nijinsky, Secretariat has been a general influence for stamina rather than speed, but Pancho Villa was a good-class sprinter-miler, winner of four stakes races from six furlongs to a mile including the Silver Screen Handicap and the Bay Shore Stakes, both Grade 2 events; he made a promising start to his career at stud with ten winners in his first crop of two-year-olds in 1990. Royal Academy's dam Crimson Saint was a sprinter, winner of seven of her eleven races from two to four years including the Hollywood Express Handicap, a five-and-a-half-furlong Grade 3 event, and the four-furlong Ballerina Stakes in which her time equalled the world record. Crimson Saint has bred five winners in all, the others being Terlingua (a sister to Pancho Villa) and Alydariel (by Alydar). Alydariel was a winner at up to eight and a half furlongs. Terlingua was rated 118, the third-best filly, in the 1978 Experimental Free Handicap and won seven of her seventeen races in three seasons' racing, including three graded stakes events from six furlongs to a mile as a two-year-old and one over seven as a three-year-old; Terlingua is the dam of two graded stakes winners including Storm Cat (by Storm Bird), runner-up in the Breeders' Cup Juvenile in 1985. Crimson Saint's two-year-old (by Secretariat), who fetched 650,000 dollars as a yearling, was in training with D. Wayne Lukas who paid the top price for a filly of 2,100,000 dollars at the Keeneland July Selected Sale for Crimson Saint's yearling by Secretariat. Terlingua and Pancho Villa were also trained by Lukas. Crimson Saint's sire Crimson Satan was another sprinter-miler; the average distance of races won by his progeny at three years and upwards was around seven furlongs. Crimson Saint's dam Bolero Rose won nine of her forty-five starts. Royal Academy, a quick-actioned colt with a brilliant turn of foot, did all his racing at distances from six furlongs to a mile and gave the impression he'd also have been fully effective over five furlongs. In a seven-race career he encountered only a sound surface. *M. V. O'Brien, Ireland.*

ROYAL ACCLAIM 5 ch.g. Tender King 123–Glimmer 58 (Hot Spark 126) [1989 7.6h² 7.6m² 8m⁶ 8m² 7.6f³ 7m⁶ 1990 7.6m² 7m³ 7.6g 8m 7m² 7.6f³ 7g* 7m² 7m² 8m* 8m 8d 7g³] sturdy gelding: carries condition: quite modest handicapper: has looked none too resolute, but in good heart in second half of season: won at Lingfield (apprentices) in August and Yarmouth in September: stays 1m: yet to race on soft going, acts on any other: usually blinkered or visored: has started slowly: often races with head high. *A. Hide.* **65**

ROYAL ARCHIVE (USA) 3 b.f. Shadeed (USA) 135–Round Tower 93 (High Top 131) [1989 6g⁴ 6m³ 8f⁵ 1990 10g⁶ 8g⁵] rangy, good-quartered filly: modest maiden at 2 yrs: should stay 1m: blinkered final start. *Major W. R. Hern.* **—**

ROYAL BEAR 8 gr.g. Rupert Bear 105–Queens Leap 54 (King's Leap 111) [1989 5s³ 5d 5d 6g⁴ 5f⁶ 5f 5f 5m 6m 1990 5f 5m 8f 7f 6m⁵ 8h 5m⁴ 5g⁶ 5g 6f 8.3m 6h 5m⁵] rangy gelding: poor handicapper judged on most form: best at sprint distances: acts on any going: ran poorly when blinkered: inconsistent. *K. O. Cunningham-Brown.* **29**

ROYAL DEQUEST (CAN) 4 b.c. Mill Reef (USA) 141–Regal Heiress 81 (English Prince 129) [1989 12g⁵ 12m³ 14f⁴ 11.7m² 1990 16.2m 12.5f⁵ 11g² 12m⁴ 11m⁴] compact, well-made colt: fair form in varied events as 3-y-o: well below his best in spring, including in seller: later a winner in Belgium: probably best short of 2m: gives impression not suited by firm going: disappointing. *N. Tinkler.* **52**

ROYAL BOROUGH 5 b.g. Bustino 136–Lady R B (USA) (Gun Shot) [1989 12m⁵ 12f⁶ 12m 12g³ 12.4g* 12g² 1990 12g* 12g⁴ 14g⁶ 12f] leggy gelding: has a quick action: fair handicapper: won in good style at Newmarket in April: sweating, badly hampered 2f out when fourth in quite valuable race at Epsom week later: suited by 1½m: best runs on good ground: bandaged off-hind first 3 starts: takes keen hold, and best held up: sold to join M. Naughton's stable 13,000 gns Doncaster August Sales. *J. L. Dunlop.* **84**

ROYAL BRINK (BEL) 3 ch.c. Ginger Brink (FR) 117–Royal Track 98 (Track Spare 125) [1989 a7g² 1990 a6g⁴ a7g³ a8g² a8g⁴ a7g*] good-quartered colt: quite modest form here, winning claimer at Lingfield in March: probably ideally suited by 7f: trained at 2 yrs by Allan Smith in Belgium when also winner over 7.5f. *M. J. Ryan.* **61**

ROYAL CHERUB (USA) 2 b.f. (Jan 9) Sovereign Dancer (USA)–Cherubim (USA) (Stevward) [1990 6m⁴ 6g 8d] $85,000Y: half-sister to minor winners in USA **42**

by Nodouble and Stalwart: dam minor winner, is half-sister to Diamond Prospect: poor form in maidens: blinkered final 2 outings: sold 4,100 gns Doncaster October Sales. *J. W. Watts.*

ROYAL DARTMOUTH (USA) 5 ch.g. Czaravich (USA)–Blushing Emy 60 (USA) (Blushing Groom (FR) 131) [1989 6v³ 7g³ 6f⁴ 6m 7.6m 6m 8f 1990 8m* 8f* 7g 8m² 10g⁴ 8m 8.3m* 8.3f⁴ 8g] tall, lengthy gelding: quite modest handicapper: successful at Warwick and Wolverhampton in April and Windsor in July: slowly away last 2 outings: stays 1¼m: acts on any going: usually wears severe bridle: finds little in front and is suited by exaggerated waiting tactics. *B. R. Millman.*

ROYAL DESIGN 3 b.c. Habitat 134–Gift Wrapped 116 (Wolver Hollow 126) — [1989 NR 1990 a8g a8g⁵] 40,000Y: neat colt: moderate mover: sixth foal: brother to modest sprint maiden Buthayna and half-brother to 1¼m seller winner Fusion (by Mill Reef), Royal Lodge winner Reach and useful but disappointing middle-distance maiden Wrapping (both by Kris): dam won Lingfield Oaks Trial but best at up to 1¼m: soundly beaten in maidens at Southwell: may do better over further: sold 2,300 gns Newmarket Autumn Sales. *M. R. Stoute.*

ROYAL DIGGER 4 ch.c. Sharpo 132–Canasta Girl 90 (Charlottesville 135) — [1989 6g 8f⁶ 8g⁵ 1990 7g 8g a8g] rather leggy, angular colt: quite modest maiden at best: behind in handicaps at 4 yrs: probably stays 1m: sold 3,500 gns Ascot September Sales: resold 1,600 gns Ascot November Sales. *J. P. Hudson.*

ROYAL ESTIMATE 4 br.g. Tender King 123–Nistona (Will Somers 114§) [1989 75 8g 6m² 6h² 7m* 8f* 9m⁵ 9g⁴ 10f⁶ 8m⁵ 8m⁴ 8g* 8s² 9g⁵ 1990 8.2s 8m 8m 8m³ a8g³ 9m 7g 8d² 8g] big, strong gelding: carries condition: keen walker: moderate mover: modest handicapper: suited by forcing tactics over 1m, and stays 9f: acts on any going: often blinkered. *M. W. Easterby.*

ROYAL FAN 7 br.g. Taufan (USA) 119–Miss Royal (King's Company 124) [1989 67 6d⁴ 5f⁴ 5m 5f⁵ 5m⁶ 5m⁴ 5m 5m 5.6g 6g³ 5d² 1990 a5g⁶ 5m 5d⁵ 5f⁴ 5g a5g a5g 5m⁶ 5f⁴ 5d⁴ 5d 6s] tall, good-quartered gelding: has a round action: quite modest handicapper nowadays: ideally suited by 5f and a bit of give in the ground: ran moderately when blinkered. *D. W. Chapman.*

ROYAL FI FI (USA) 3 b.f. Conquistador Cielo (USA)–Apple Betty (USA) (Best 86 Turn (USA)) [1989 5m* 6m* 6f* 6s⁴ 7g² 7g⁴ 1990 6g³ 5d 7m 8h 8s] leggy, quite good-topped filly: good third of 5, leading over 4f, in £7,200 event at Newmarket in May: well beaten in competitive handicaps (stiff tasks) and minor event here then handicap at Leopardstown: races keenly and has given impression will prove best at 6f: acts on firm going, possibly unsuited by a soft surface: trained until after fourth start by Mrs L. Piggott. *J. S. Bolger, Ireland.*

ROYAL GIRL 3 b.f. Kafu 120–Royal Aunt (Martinmas 128) [1989 NR 1990 7f] — 5,400Y: half-sister to 1986 2-y-o 5f seller winner Flag Bearer (by Runnett): dam modest Irish 2-y-o 6f winner: bandaged off-hind, in need of race in minor event at Thirsk in September. *Miss S. E. Hall.*

ROYAL HUNT 5 b.g. Mill Reef (USA) 141–Glass Slipper 100 (Relko 136) [1989 — 12g 10m³ 1990 a12g a16g a8g⁵ a10g⁶ 7f 12f 10m 11.5m 10h⁴] leggy, quite good-topped gelding: poor maiden: stays 1¼m: acts on firm going: blinkered or visored last 2 outings: sold 1,500 gns Ascot July Sales. *M. Madgwick.*

ROYAL HUNTER (USA) 3 b.c. Dr Carter (USA)–Royal Suite (Habitat 134) 76 § [1989 NR 1990 10m² 10g* 10g⁶ 10g² 13.3m 12g 10g] $30,000Y: leggy, good-topped colt: moderate mover: third foal: dam winner at 9f in Ireland later successful in USA: sire high-class 1m to 1¼m performer: impressive when winning moderately-run maiden at Nottingham in June: found nothing in handicaps last 3 starts: should stay 1½m: sweating and pulled hard fifth outing: one to be wary of. *J. L. Dunlop.*

ROYALIST (CAN) 4 b.c. Commemorate (USA)–Hangin Round (USA) (Stage 73 Door Johnny) [1989 8m⁵ 8f² 10g² 10m 1990 10.4d 12m³ 10g⁴ 8m² 8f² 8f³ 7d] strong, good sort: carries condition: modest maiden: stays 1½m, but at least as effective at 1m: acts on firm ground: visored or blinkered last 4 starts: looked unsatisfactory second outing, and isn't one to trust implicitly: sold 12,500 gns Newmarket Autumn Sales. *J. W. Watts.*

ROYAL MAC 3 br.c. Pas de Seul 133–Royal Wolff (Prince Tenderfoot (USA) 126) — [1989 8g 8d 1990 8.2g 12.2m 12h 10f⁵ 12m 10.2m 11m 10m 12.2d] rather leggy, good-topped colt: poor in all his paces: stays 1¼m: sold out of N. Tinkler's stable 1,600 gns Doncaster June Sales after sixth start. *D. Yeoman.*

ROYAL MARRIAGE 2 b.f. (May 6) King of Spain 121–Princess Story 64 59 (Prince de Galles 125) [1990 5f 6m 7m 8d 8.2d a8g a8g⁴] leggy filly: ninth foal: half-sister to several winners, including 6f winner Aquarian Prince (by Mansingh) and 1¼m and 1½m winner Kiki Star (by Some Hand): dam successful in sellers at around 1m: plating-class maiden: will probably stay beyond 1m: acts on dead ground. *M. D. I. Usher.*

ROYAL MAZI 3 b.f. Kings Lake (USA) 133–Seven Seas (FR) 78 (Riverman 58 (USA) 131) [1989 NR 1990 11.5g 12g⁵ 14g 14m³ 16f* 16s] angular, workmanlike filly: good walker: fifth foal: half-sister to 9f winner Soemba (both by General Assembly): dam won at 7f and 11f: odds on, won 3-runner claimer (claimed out of C. Wall's stable £10,059) at Redcar in August: tailed off in handicap 3 months later: stays 2m: claiming hurdle winner. *C. R. Beever.*

ROYAL PASSION 3 ch.f. Ahonoora 122–Courtesy Call (Northfields (USA)) 78 [1989 6g² 6m² 7m³ 8g² 8g⁶ 1990 8m⁶ 8g 8g 10f 10d* 10.2s* 9g³] lengthy, unfurnished filly: shows a quick action: comfortable winner of claimer (returned to form) at Goodwood and seller (6/5, bought in 20,500 gns) at Doncaster in October: should be suited by return to 1¼m, or more testing conditions over shorter: goes well on a soft surface. *M. A. Jarvis.*

ROYAL RESORT 3 b.f. King of Spain 121–Regency Brighton (Royal Palace 131) 42 [1989 6m⁵ 8m⁵ 7m 6g 1990 8f⁶ 10.2f⁴ 10.2f³ 10.2f³ 10.2f⁵ 10m 10.2f⁵ 8.2v³ a8g] leggy, angular filly: poor maiden: stays 10.2f: acts on firm going: races keenly: trained until after sixth start by R. Holder. *R. J. Hodges.*

ROYAL SCOTS GREYS 3 ch.f. Blazing Saddles (AUS)–Relicia (Relko 136) 38 [1989 a7g a8g⁶ 1990 8.5m³ 8f 6s⁶ 6f⁵ 6f⁵ a6g] small filly: poor mover: poor maiden: stays 8.5f: acts on any going: bandaged at 3 yrs: joined P. Mitchell. *J. Ringer.*

ROYAL SQUARE (CAN) 4 ch.c. Gregorian (USA) 115–Dance Crazy (USA) — (Foolish Pleasure (USA)) [1989 8s⁴ 10.1m² 12m³ 12f 13.3m 16.2m* 16f* 18g 14g³ 1990 16g] big, strong colt: quite useful winner (including for amateur) as 3-y-o: ran poorly in well-contested handicaps on 2 of his 3 subsequent outings: stays 2m: acts on firm going: suited by a galloping track: has sweated: useful hurdler as a juvenile. *G. Harwood.*

ROYAL STANDARD 3 b.c. Sadler's Wells (USA) 132–Princess Tiara 111 88 p (Crowned Prince (USA) 128) [1989 NR 1990 10m 12m⁵ 12g 11g² 16m* 14f⁵ 12m* 14d*] 340,000Y: rangy, attractive colt: closely related to smart French 7f to 1¼m winner What A Guest, Irish 4-y-o 2m winner Crowning Glory (both by Be My Guest) and very smart 10.4f winner Infantry (by Northfields), later stakes winner in USA, and half-brother to a winner: dam 2-y-o 7f winner, when appeared to stay 1¼m: won maiden at Lingfield in July and handicaps at Leicester and Haydock (rallied gamely) in September: will prove better at 1¾m + than shorter: acts on firm and dead going: visored after running in snatches and carrying head high fourth start: progressive. *J. Gosden.*

ROYAL STEEL 3 ch.g. Kings Lake (USA) 133–All Souls 96 (Saint Crespin III — 132) [1989 NR 1990 10.6d a14g] IR 5,000Y: half-brother to numerous winners here and abroad, including quite useful middle-distance handicapper Regal Steel (by Welsh Pageant): dam won twice at around 1¼m: behind in maiden and claimer in the autumn. *R. Hollinshead.*

ROYAL STING 4 b.g. Prince Bee 128–Dolly-Longlegs 74 (Majority Blue 126) — [1989 12s 12f 14g³ 1990 15.5f³] rather leggy gelding: blinkered, showed a modicum of ability in handicap at Folkestone in April: suited by test of stamina: sold 2,200 gns Ascot July Sales. *M. H. B. Robinson.*

ROYAL SUPREME 3 b.g. Another Realm 118–La Crima 63 (Runnymede 123) 44 [1989 5s 5s* 5f⁶ 1990 5d 5m 6g 6m 6m 10g 8.3m 8m⁵ 8.2s* 8d] leggy, close-coupled gelding: has a quick action: easily best efforts when successful, in apprentice selling handicap (bought in 6,000 gns) at Nottingham in October: should stay beyond 1m: seems to need soft ground: trained until after ninth start by G. Lewis. *L. Lungo.*

ROYAL TAFI 4 b.g. Tanfirion 110–Queen's Pet (Pall Mall 132) [1989 NR 1990 — a11g⁵ a11g] workmanlike gelding: poor form in modest company. *B. Richmond.*

ROYAL VERSE (FR) 3 b.c. Recitation (USA) 124–Sauce Royale (Royal Palace 87 d 131) [1989 5s 6m 7m* 7g 8f² 8g² 8f² 10g 1990 9m 11.5m² 10m 9m² 10m⁴ 8m 10f 10f] good-topped colt: fair performer: behind in handicaps last 3 starts, in valuable events first 2 occasions: may well stay 1½m: acts well on firm going: blinkered sixth start: sold to join D. Bell 20,000 gns Newmarket Autumn Sales. *P. A. Kelleway.*

ROYAL WARRANT (USA) 3 ch.g. Wavering Monarch (USA)–Gay Lady J 79 (USA) (Forli (ARG)) [1989 6m 6m⁵ 5g 8m⁶ 6s 1990 5m* 6g⁵ 5m² 5m⁵ 5m³ 5f² 5g 5m² 5m⁵] rangy, well-made gelding: moderate walker: good mover, with a long stride: fair handicapper: made all at Pontefract in April: will prove best over 5f: best efforts on top-of-the-ground: visored final start, blinkered previous 3: sold 18,000 gns Newmarket Autumn Sales. *J. W. Watts.*

ROY HOBBS 3 b.g. Glint of Gold 128–Glory of Hera 99 (Formidable (USA) 125) — [1989 6f⁴ 7m 6g 1990 10g 8m⁶ 8.3f 7m 6d 8.2v] strong gelding: poor walker: no worthwhile form (including in handicaps) since debut: should stay further than 6f: blinkered fifth start: sold to join K. Burke 1,800 gns Doncaster October Sales and gelded. *M. Brittain.*

ROZINANTE (USA) 3 ch.f. Sir Ivor 135–Quest (USA) 90§ (The Minstrel 80 (CAN) 135) [1989 NR 1990 10.6s⁶ 10m⁵ 12.5m* 14d] leggy filly: third foal: half-sister to useful 6f winner Bequest (by Sharpen Up) and disappointing maiden Hopeful Search (by Vaguely Noble): dam, 9f and 1¼m winner, is sister to high-class 1983 French 2-y-o Treizieme and half-sister to Gold Cup runner-up Eastern Mystic: sweating, won maiden at Wolverhampton in August by head from Sliprail: tailed off facing stiff task in handicap 8 weeks later: suited by 1½m: edgy last 2 starts: sold 17,000 gns Newmarket December Sales. *L. M. Cumani.*

RUADH ADHAR 4 b.f. Heroic Air 96–Rosemarkie 75 (Goldhill 125) [1989 8.2g⁴ — 7s⁶ 1990 a8g⁶ 8.2s 6f] lengthy filly: has shown signs of only a little ability. *J. S. Wilson.*

RUA D'ORO (USA) 2 b.f. (Mar 26) El Gran Senor (USA) 136–Thorough 115 76 p (Thatch (USA) 136) [1990 6m*] fourth foal: half-sister to fairly useful 7f winner Rah Wan (by Riverman): dam French 1m to 1½m winner: long odds-on winner of 8-runner maiden at Leopardstown in September: will stay 1m: likely to do good deal better. *M. V. O'Brien, Ireland.*

RUBDAN (USA) 3 gr.g. Lear Fan (USA) 130–Cindy Jennings (USA) (Silver — Series (USA)) [1989 NR 1990 10m] $40,000Y: well-made gelding: second foal: dam unraced half-sister to Grade 1 stakes winner Queen Lib: moved poorly to post and showed little in maiden at Newbury in May: sold to join G. Gracey 1,600 gns Newmarket Autumn Sales then gelded. *P. F. I. Cole.*

RUBICUND 3 b.c. Niniski (USA) 125–Rosananti 107 (Blushing Groom (FR) 131) 116 [1989 8.2d² 1990 14m² 14.8m* 14.6g⁴ 15g] strong, lengthy colt: fluent mover: easily won 3-runner maiden at Newmarket then put up smart performance, leading over 1¼m, when 7¾ lengths fourth of 8 to Snurge in St Leger at Doncaster 2½ months later: coupled favourite, ran poorly in Group 3 contest at Longchamp final start: should stay long distances. *J. L. Dunlop.*

RUBINKA 4 b.f. Bustino 136–Relkina (FR) 85 (Relkino 131) [1989 7d⁵ 6s 7.5d 28 8.2f 9f 10f 7f 6f 6g 1990 10f⁴ 14m² 12.3f 12g⁵ 12g 12m⁵ 12g 12h² 12m⁶ 12g a12g] leggy filly: poor handicapper: headstrong (has worn crossed noseband) and best short of 1¾m: acts on firm going: usually apprentice ridden. *R. Hollinshead.*

RUBY AZELLY 2 b.f. (Apr 4) Green Ruby (USA) 104–Azelly 77 (Pitskelly 122) 40 [1990 5s² 5d 5g⁵ 5g⁴ 5f 5m⁵ 5m] 6,400Y: lengthy, workmanlike filly: has a round action: first foal: dam placed over 5f at 2 yrs failed to train on: moderate plater: barely stays 5f: acts on good to firm ground and soft: sold 840 gns Doncaster September Sales. *J. Berry.*

RUBY JAYNE 2 b.f. (Mar 5) Green Ruby (USA) 104–Myna Tyna 85 (Blast 125) 48 [1990 5m 6g 6g⁶ 6g⁵ 5g* 5f³ 5m⁴ 5f 5.1m 5g 5v a5g] 4,400Y: small, leggy filly: has a quick action: half-sister to several winners here and abroad: dam won over 5f at 2 yrs: won seller at Wolverhampton by a short head from Meeson Gold: seems suited by 5f: seems unsuited by heavy ground: inconsistent. *A. Bailey.*

RUBY REALM 3 ch.f. Valiyar 129–Mai Pussy 91 (Realm 129) [1989 6g 1990 7g 47 d 7d⁵ 7d 8g³ 8f 6m 8m⁶ 12.5m a8g] lengthy, rather sparely-made filly: fair plater: well below form last 5 outings: should stay further than 1m: sold out of B. Hanbury's stable 5,000 gns Newmarket July Sales after fourth start. *A. P. James.*

RUBY SETTING 3 b.f. Gorytus (USA) 132–Sun Princess 130 (English Prince 91 129) [1989 6g⁵ 1990 10m² 10.2f⁴ 10.4m² 10m* 10m² 11.5g⁶ 10g⁴] rather sparely-made filly: fair performer: clearly best efforts in minor events at Salisbury and Sandown fifth and final starts: earlier won maiden at Sandown in July: may prove suited by more forcing tactics at 1¼m: usually wears crossed noseband: sold 12,000 gns Newmarket December Sales. *Major W. R. Hern.*

RUBY SHOES 4 b.f. Day Is Done 115–Very Seldom (Rarity 129) [1989 7s 8d⁴ 8g 43 10.6s 1990 a7g a11g a8g* 8f a7g a8g a11g⁵ a11g 10m³ 11v⁴] plain filly: has a quick action: won maiden at Southwell in March: other form as 4-y-o only in selling handicap penultimate outing: stayed 1¼m: sold 1,000 gns Doncaster November Sales in foal to Clantime. *R. Bastiman.*

RUBY SLIPPERS 3 ch.f. Stanford 121§–Tanzanite (Marino) [1989 NR 1990 a8g —
a8g] IR 2,800Y: half-sister to 1m seller winners Corofin Lass (by Junius) and Joy's
Toy (by Wolverlife) and to several winners abroad, including prolific French middle-
distance winner Sam's Turn (by Malicious): dam French 2-y-o 7f winner: no sign of
ability in maidens. *M. R. Channon.*

RUBY TIGER 3 gr.f. Ahonoora 122–Hayati 94 (Hotfoot 126) [1989 6g⁴ 7g* 8g* 114
1990 11.3d² 12d² 12d³ 12g⁵ 10g* 10s*] workmanlike filly: moderate walker:
progressed into smart performer, winning Premio Lydia Tesio at Rome by 7 lengths
from Cum Laude then E P Taylor Stakes at Woodbine, Canada, 2 weeks later by 5
lengths from Aldbourne: placed in pattern events at Chester, Milan and Longchamp
and about 7¾ lengths fifth of 6 to Hellenic in Aston Upthorpe Yorkshire Oaks at
York: stays 1½m: yet to race on top-of-the-ground. *P. F. I. Cole.*

RUDDA CASS 6 b.g. Rapid River 127–Glaven (Blakeney 126) [1989 12g 10f 1990 29
8f 8f 8.5g⁴ 10f 8f⁵ 10d³ 10m 8m 8.5f 12f⁴ 10g⁵ 11m 12g³ 12f⁵ 12m⁴ 8m 10m] smallish,
workmanlike gelding: poor handicapper: should stay 1¾m: acts on firm and dead
ground: blinkered 6 times. *Roy Robinson.*

RUDDA FLASH 6 b.m. General David–Palinode 98 (Pall Mall 132) [1989 8.5f —
12.3f 1990 9m⁵] sturdy, plain mare: poor mover: of little account. *Roy Robinson.*

RUDDA STAR 5 b.m. General David–Glaven (Blakeney 126) [1989 NR 1990 9f] —
lengthy, sparely-made mare: has a round action: third known foal: half-sister to
plating-class 1m and 1¼m winner Rudda Cass (by Rapid River): dam twice-raced on
flat: 200/1, tailed off in minor event at Ripon in April. *Roy Robinson.*

RUDDY CHEEK (USA) 3 b.c. Blushing Groom (FR) 131–Hail Maggie (USA) 86
(Hail To Reason) [1989 7s³ 8m⁴ 8g³ 1990 10m³ 10m⁴ 11.5g* 12m⁶] close-coupled,
sparely-made colt: shows knee action: fair form when winning minor event at
Lingfield in September: favourite and on toes, found little when last in handicap 12
days later: suited by 1½m, probably by give in the ground: has flashed tail: sold
11,000 gns Newmarket Autumn Sales. *J. L. Dunlop.*

RUDJIG (USA) 4 b.c. Secreto (USA) 128–Chic Belle (USA) (Mr Prospector 104
(USA)) [1989 9g⁶ 10.4m² 12m⁶ 1990 10.8m* 13.3m² 12g* 14.6d² 16s] good-topped,
attractive colt: first races for long time when winning maiden at Warwick in April

E. P. Taylor Stakes, Woodbine—
Ruby Tiger comes home well clear of Aldbourne

and minor event at Salisbury (by neck from Harefoot) in October: runner-up in listed race won by Sesame at Newbury and minor contest (losing place 6f out) won by Yalanoura at Doncaster: should stay 2m: acts on good to firm and dead going: likely to prove suited by galloping track. *J. Gosden.*

RUDRY PRINCESS 3 ro.f. Blazing Saddles (AUS)–Rudry Park 55 (Blue Cashmere 129) [1989 NR 1990 8g 6m a7g 6d 8m] 500F, 2,800Y: strong, lengthy filly: second foal: dam maiden stayed 1m: no sign of ability in sellers and claimers. *D. Haydn Jones.* —

RUDY'S FANTASY (USA) 3 b.c. Nureyev (USA) 131–Rainbow's Edge (USA) (Creme dela Creme) [1989 6m³ 7g³ 1990 10m³ 8g⁴ 8.5g* 8g] strong, angular, attractive colt: fairly useful form at Newmarket first 3 career starts, in 3-runner listed race on reappearance: landed odds of 7/2 on in maiden at Beverley in August but ran poorly in similar event and handicap (very edgy, raced freely) starts either side: probably stays 1¼m: one to be wary of. *L. Cumani.* **83 ?**

RUE DE FORT 2 gr.g. (Apr 25) Belfort (FR) 89–Royal Huntress (Royal Avenue 123) [1990 7m 8f 7g] leggy, close-coupled gelding: has a quick action: seventh reported foal: half-brother to 1½m winner Royal Craftsman (by Workboy): dam winning hurdler: soundly beaten in maidens and a median auction. *B. W. Murray.* **44**

RUE DU CIRQUE (IRE) 2 gr.f. (Mar 8) Godswalk (USA) 130–Ventimiglia (Bruni 132) [1990 6m a6g² 6f² 6m* 7h* 7m³ 8m³] leggy, sparely-made filly: third foal: half-sister to 3-y-o 7.6f and 9f winner Orvietto (by Try My Best): dam, raced only at 2 yrs, out of half-sister to Music Boy: ridden by 7-lb claimer, successful in nurseries at Yarmouth (by 5 lengths) in July and Thirsk (by a neck from Azureus) in August: stays 1m: blinkered in seller third start. *N. A. Callaghan.* **69**

RUGADAY 4 br.g. Milford 119–Relma (Relko 136) [1989 6f 7h³ 7m⁴ 8.3m⁶ 8f 8.3d 7.6m 1990 6m 7.6m 8.3m 8.3m] leggy, close-coupled gelding: plater: needs further than 6f and stays 1m: acts on hard going: ungenuine. *J. H. Baker.* — §

RUIZ MIGUEL 4 br.g. Precocious 126–Lakshmi 83 (Tribal Chief 125) [1989 8s⁵ 1990 8.3g 8.2d] strong, deep-girthed gelding: quite modest form at 2 yrs: lightly raced and no subsequent form: not bred to stay 1m. *L. G. Cottrell.* —

RULING PASSION 3 b.c. Bairn (USA) 126–Unbidden Melody (USA) (Chieftain II) [1989 6m* 1990 8m³ 8.2f² 7m] lengthy, quite attractive colt: good walker: moderate mover: won maiden at Nottingham in May at 2 yrs: fair form in valuable handicaps at Sandown and Haydock (looked somewhat reluctant) in the spring, then always behind in £71,900 handicap at Ascot in September: stays 1m: sold 10,000 gns Newmarket Autumn Sales. *M. R. Stoute.* **87**

RUM JOCKEY 3 b.c. Shack (USA) 118–Prairie Saint 74 (Welsh Saint 126) [1989 NR 1990 12f 10f a11g a11g] IR 2,500F, 1,000Y: leggy, plain colt: moderate mover: second living foal: dam, 2-y-o 5f winner, is half-sister to leading 1986 German 3-y-o filly Prairie Neba: no sign of ability, including in seller: visored last 2 starts. *P. J. Bevan.* —

RUN AND GUN (IRE) 2 b.c. (Jan 28) Lomond (USA) 128–Charming Life 88 (Habitat 134) [1990 6.5g* 7d³ 6.5d⁶ 5v*] 50,000F, 500,000 francs (approx £46,300) Y: third foal: closely related to 3-y-o 8.2f winner Saddle Bow (by Sadler's Wells): dam 4-y-o 7f winner: successful in newcomers race at Deauville in August and Prix du Petit-Couvert (by a nose from Luring with Lugana Beach 4½ lengths away in fourth) at Longchamp in October: evidently suited by 5f and heavy going. *R. Collet, France.* **111**

RUNAWAY LAD (IRE) 2 b.g. (May 11) Runnett 125–Kingston Rose (Tudor Music 131) [1990 6m⁴ 6m⁵ 6g* 6d] 13,000Y: good-topped gelding: sixth foal: half-brother to quite modest 1989 2-y-o 5f winner Hud (by Prince Tenderfoot) and 2 other winners, including fair 1985 2-y-o 5f winner King's Reef (by Main Reef): dam Irish 5f winner: favourite, won maiden at Ayr in July: had very stiff task in Racecall Gold Trophy at Redcar 3½ months later: races keenly. *G. A. Pritchard-Gordon.* **77**

RUNCIBLE CAT (USA) 4 b.c. J O Tobin (USA) 130–Beau Cougar (USA) (Cougar (CHI)) [1989 8d 6d 6f 7g 7m⁴ 7g⁶ 7m³ 7g 6f4 8f³ 8m² 6g⁵ 1990 8f 7.6m 7f a8g a12g a8g] small colt: moderate mover: modest maiden at best: no form at 4 yrs: stays 1m: acts on firm ground: occasionally sweats and gets on edge: has run tubed: trained until after third outing by C. Brittain. *B. J. McMath.* —

RUN DON'T FLY (USA) 4 b.c. Lear Fan (USA) 130–Gantlette (Run The Gantlet (USA)) [1989 10m³ 12m* 12f* 12m* 12m³ 1990 12m²] sturdy, quite attractive colt: carries condition: progressive handicapper as 3-y-o, on third and fourth outings winning valuable events at Goodwood and York: shaped as though retaining **96**

his ability when second to eased Pirate Army in 4-runner £12,500 race at Chepstow in July: stays 1½m well: acts on firm going: takes keen hold. *P. F. I. Cole.*

RUN FOR JOYCE 4 br.f. My Dad Tom (USA) 109–Assel Zawie (Sit In The Corner (USA)) [1989 5m 5m⁵ 5m 5m² 5m⁴ 5f 6f³ 5m 5f 5f 1990 6g 5f a5g 5d 5m a5g 5m 6g] smallish, close-coupled filly: carries plenty of condition: bad walker and moderate mover: poor maiden: best at 5f: acts on firm going: ridden by 7-lb claimer. *J. Balding.* —

RUN FOR NICK (FR) 2 b.g. (Feb 21) Nikos 124–Run For Juliet (USA) (Model Fool) [1990 8g 6g 6d³] 160,000 francs (approx £14,800) Y: good-topped gelding: half-brother to several minor winners in France: dam French maiden placed over 1m and 1¼m: plating-class form in maidens: caught eye all starts, particularly when over 8 lengths third of 17 to Samurai Gold at Folkestone in November, steadied start, headway over 1f out considerately handled then running on well: well worth another try beyond 6f: one to bear in mind in handicap company. *A. A. Scott.* 59 p

RUN FREE 5 b.g. Julio Mariner 127–Lucky Appeal 36 (Star Appeal 133) [1989 14s⁶ 12s* 12s² 16g a12g 1990 13s 16m⁵ a12g] smallish, leggy gelding: won handicap in spring as 4-y-o: well beaten last 5 starts: suited by forcing tactics at 1½m: best form on soft going: blinkered once at 3 yrs: trained until after second outing by R. Guest. *Pat Mitchell.* —

RUNHAM (IRE) 2 b.g. (Apr 5) Commanche Run 133–Imbrama (USA) (Imbros) [1990 7m 7.5f a7g 7g 8m* 8.2g 8m³ 9g 8.2d] IR 3,100Y, 5,800 2-y-o: leggy, useful-looking gelding: half-brother to several minor winners in USA: dam half-sister to good 7f to 8.5f winner Gummo and to Spearfish, dam of Gaily, King's Bishop and Empire Glory: quite modest performer: won selling nursery (no bid) at Leicester in September: good third of 30 in seller at Newmarket: will be suited by 1¼m: best efforts on good to firm ground: blinkered fifth to eighth starts: carries head high, and has looked an awkward ride: sold 1,200 gns Doncaster October Sales. *Pat Mitchell.* 65

RUN HIGH 7 b.g. Thatch (USA) 136–Fleet Noble (USA) (Vaguely Noble 140) [1989 12v⁵ 14s⁵ 14f* 12f⁵ 12m⁵ 14f² 14f³ 13m* 15f² 13g4 12g* 1990 14g 14m³ 12g² 13g4 14m* 12g³ 13g4 15g³ 14g³ 15.5f*] strong, medium-sized gelding: usually looks well: moderate mover: modest handicapper: won at Sandown in June and Folkestone (amateurs) in September: needs at least 1½m and stays 2m: acts on any going: good mount for inexperienced rider: splendidly tough, genuine and consistent. *P. Mitchell.* 71

RUN HOME 3 b.g. Homeboy 114–Chiparia 82 (Song 132) [1989 6m 6m 7f⁵ 7g⁵ a6g 1990 7m⁵ 6f⁶ 8f] small, close-coupled gelding: quite modest maiden: slow-starting fifth at Lingfield, best effort in handicaps: ridden by 7-lb claimer, ran poorly at Brighton final start (July): better at 7f than 6f. *R. Akehurst.* 55

RUNITAGAIN 3 b.g. Runnett 125–Staderas (Windjammer (USA)) [1989 NR 1990 6s 6m] IR 15,500Y, IR 11,500Y: third reported foal: brother to fair sprint winner My Pal Popeye and half-brother to a winner in Hong Kong: dam never ran: soundly beaten in maidens in early-summer. *K. B. McCauley.* —

RUN MILADY 2 b.f. (May 12) Blakeney 126–Bewitched 63 (African Sky 124) [1990 6d² 6d³] compact, workmanlike filly: fourth living foal: half-sister to modest sprinter Martinosky (by Martinmas): dam (stayed 1m) half-sister to Lucky Wednesday, high-class winner at up to 1¼m: plating-class form in maidens at Chester (green, pulled hard) and Leicester (had hard race) in October: will be suited by 7f. *M. Johnston.* 58

RUNNETT FOR CASH 4 b.f. Runnett 125–Melissa Claire (Camden Town 125) [1989 8g4 7.5d 8m² 8h⁵ 7m4 8m4 7m 8g* 8.2f 7g 10m³ 8f⁶ 10g4 12g³ 1990 12.5f 8m 11m 12g a12g a12g] small, workmanlike filly: moderate mover: poor winner as 3-y-o: no form in 1990, including in seller: stays 1½m: acts on good to firm going: sometimes blinkered: tends to carry head high and hang left: sold out of Mrs J. Ramsden's stable 1,100 gns Doncaster January Sales: trained first 5 starts by A. Potts: not genuine. *J. P. Leigh.* — §

RUNNING FLUSH 8 ch.g. Lord Gayle (USA) 124–Hidden Hand (USA) (Ribocco 129) [1989 10g 1990 a10g a13g² a12g] tall, lightly-made gelding: quite modest winner as 6-y-o: very lightly raced and little subsequent worthwhile form: best form at 1¼m: acts on any going: visored: has won for apprentice, but suited by strong handling. *P. Howling.* 32

RUNNING GLIMPSE (IRE) 2 br.f. (Feb 21) Runnett 125–One Last Glimpse 73 (Relko 136) [1990 5g² 5g* 5m⁵ 6m] 5,200Y: smallish filly: second foal: dam second from 8.2f to 10.6f: won maiden at Windsor in April: respectable fifth, running 61

as if in need of race, in nursery at Sandown over 4 months later: took keen hold final start: should stay 6f. *Miss B. Sanders.*

RUNNING SHADOW (IRE) 2 gr.g. (Feb 26) Kalaglow 132–Regal Flutter **67** (USA) (Beldale Flutter (USA) 130) [1990 8.2d⁴ 8.2s⁴] 6,200F, 15,500Y: first foal: dam never ran: quite modest form in autumn maidens at Haydock won by Paris of Troy and Red Rainbow: will stay 1¼m. *J. Etherington.*

RUNUN 4 br.c. Sharpo 132–Silent Movie (Shirley Heights 130) [1989 8m⁴ 7f² 7f⁵ **77** d 7m³ 8m⁴ 7m* 6g 1990 7g 7d 8.2m² 8.2v 16d³ a11g⁵ a11g⁴] lengthy, rather sparely-made colt: bad mover: quite useful winner at 3 yrs: easily best effort as 4-y-o in claimer on third outing: best form at 7f or 1m: acts on firm going: inconsistent. *N. Tinkler.*

RUNWAY ROMANCE (FR) 3 gr.c. Julius Caesar (FR) 115–Airstrip (Warpath **67** 113) [1989 7f³ 1990 8.2g* 9f⁵ 7g⁴ 7m 8h³] lengthy, angular colt: quite modest performer: won claimer at Nottingham in April, rallying well: stays 9f: acts on hard ground: sold out of P. Makin's stable 9,200 gns Newmarket July Sales after fourth start: winning hurdler. *P. J. Hobbs.*

RUPPLES 3 b.g. Muscatite 122–Miss Annie 73 (Scottish Rifle 127) [1989 6m a6g — a7g 1990 12.5g 14g a12g 11m⁴] leggy, workmanlike gelding: fourth of 8 in seller at Hamilton in August. *M. J. Ryan.*

RUSCINO 3 br.c. Rousillon (USA) 133–Eastern Shore 70 (Sun Prince 128) [1989 **97** 6d⁵ 1990 10f* 10m* 9g² 10f* 10m⁵ 10m 12s] finely-made, useful-looking colt: has a quick action: fairly useful form: favourite, won maiden at Folkestone in July, handicap at Lingfield in August and apprentice race at Chepstow in September: below form last 3 starts, in November Handicap at Doncaster final one: should stay 1½m: acts on firm going. *G. Harwood.*

RUSHANES 3 ch.c. Millfontaine 114–Saulonika 94 (Saulingo 122) [1989 6f 5m⁴ **49** 6f⁴ 5g⁵ a6g⁵ a5g* 1990 6m 5m 6f³ 6h 6m 6m⁵ 6m 6m 6d a7g] small, sturdy colt: shows traces of stringhalt: plating-class performer at 3 yrs: seems not to stay 7f: acts on firm going: blinkered seventh and eighth (ran creditably) starts: ran poorly when sweating and edgy: trained until after eighth outing by R. Hannon: inconsistent. *T. Casey.*

RUSHLUAN 6 gr.g. Kalaglow 132–Labista 116 (Crowned Prince (USA) 128) **66** [1989 8f² 10.2f 10.6m 12f⁴ 1990 10.8m* 12.5m* 12.2m² 11.7f⁴ 14f³ 10g⁵] leggy, good-topped gelding: has a quick action: quite modest handicapper: in very good form early in season, winning at Warwick and Wolverhampton: ran well in amateurs event final outing, first for 4 months: stays at least 12.5f: acts on firm going and is probably unsuited by soft surface: ran creditably in visor. *R. J. Hodges.*

RUSHMOOR 12 br.g. Queen's Hussar 124–Heathfield 99 (Hethersett 134) [1989 — NR 1990 12.3g 10f 15d] strong gelding: usually looks well: very lightly raced on flat nowadays, and well beaten in amateur events at 12 yrs: used to stay well: acts on any going. *R. E. Peacock.*

RUSHMORE (USA) 3 b.c. Mt Livermore (USA)–Super Act (USA) 71 (Native **103** Royalty (USA)) [1989 7f³ 6m* 6f³ 7m² 1990 7m 7.3g 8g 6m 7g 8g³ 6s⁶] rangy, angular colt: moderate walker: capable of useful form: showed little (including in pattern events) as 3-y-o until third of 9 to Two Left Feet in listed race at Newmarket in November, leading 6f: not entirely discredited in similar event at Doncaster week later: suited by 1m: acts on good to firm going: blinkered fourth start. *C. E. Brittain.*

RUSSIAN ADVENTURE (IRE) 2 b.c. (Apr 13) Petoski 135–Haskeir (Final **46** Straw 127) [1990 6g 7m 8d a6g] leggy colt: first foal: dam unraced daughter of half-sister to St Leger winner Athens Wood: poor maiden: needs further than 6f and should stay at least 1m. *D. J. G. Murray-Smith.*

RUSSIAN FRONTIER 3 gr.c. Nureyev (USA) 131–Lovelight 112 (Bleep-Bleep **86** 134) [1989 6d³ 1990 7g² 7.6d* 7m² 8d 8m 7m³ 7d⁶ 7m] lengthy, rather unfurnished colt: good walker: has quick action: fair performer: won maiden at Chester in May: inconsistent in handicaps: best short of 1m: acts on good to firm ground and dead: has worn net muzzle, including when blinkered (refused to settle, found nothing) final start: sweating and edgy fifth: may prove best with strong handling: sold only 2,000 gns Newmarket Autumn Sales. *B. W. Hills.*

RUSSIAN MINK (USA) 2 ch.f. (May 5) L'Emigrant (USA) 129–Furry Friend **79** (USA) (Bold Bidder) [1990 6m 6g² 7d³ 6s*] smallish, angular filly: fourth foal: dam lightly raced: co-favourite, won 17-runner nursery at Newbury in October by 2 lengths from Carn Maire: probably better suited by 6f than 7f: acts on soft going. *W. Hastings-Bass.*

RUSSIAN RED 3 ch.c. Kind of Hush 118–Green Diamond (Green God 128) **62**
[1989 5s 5g 6f⁶ 7m⁵ 7g³ 7f 7m³ 7m a8g 1990 12f⁶ 10f 10m⁶ 10m² 10g⁶ 10h 10g 10d
a12g a12g³ a13g² a13g⁴ a12g²] strong, lengthy colt: moderate mover: quite modest
handicapper, still a maiden: appeared to run very well in Lingfield maiden final start:
stays 13f: acts on good to firm ground: inconsistent. *W. G. R. Wightman.*

RUSTIMAN (IRE) 2 br.c. (Mar 18) Rusticaro (FR) 124–Sarsenet (Saritamer **72**
(USA) 130) [1990 6g 8d² a8g] 6,000Y, 3,400 2-y-o: fifth foal: dam of no account: 5
lengths second of 18 to El Dominio in maiden at Bath, best effort: ran moderately on
all-weather: much better suited by 1m than 6f. *M. J. Bolton.*

RUSTINO 4 ch.c. Bustino 136–Miss Britain (Tudor Melody 129) [1989 8s 8d⁶ **65**
8.5g⁵ 11f⁵ 12g 12.3g⁵ 9f 10.6d 1990 14.6f* 17m 16.2g³ 16g* 17.6m² 18m 17.4d 16g⁶
16.2s 18d] workmanlike colt: has a round action: won maiden at Doncaster in March
and moderately-run handicap at Nottingham in May: off course over 3 months after
sixth outing and didn't recapture his best form: should stay extreme distances: acts
on firm going: visored final start: trained first 7 outings by A. Robson, next 2 by D.
Dutton. *S. E. Kettlewell.*

RUST PROOF 3 gr.g. Rusticaro (FR) 124–Grecian Charter (Runnymede 123) —
[1989 7m 1990 12.5f 11.7f] workmanlike, angular gelding: bit backward, well beaten
in maidens. *M. Blanshard.*

RUTHERGLEN (IRE) 2 br.f. (Mar 19) Pitskelly 122–Miss Galwegian (Sand- **33**
ford Lad 133) [1990 6g 7m⁶ 6h 7d 10m] 3,000Y: small filly: third foal: dam placed over
6f at 2 yrs in Ireland: poor form in varied events, including a seller: seems to stay
1¼m: trained first 3 outings by M. Fetherston-Godley. *B. R. Millman.*

RUTH'S GAMBLE 2 b.g. (Feb 28) Kabour 80–Hilly's Daughter (Hillandale **73**
125) [1990 5g³ 6g* 5d* 6d⁶ 7s⁶] 2,000Y: leggy, lengthy gelding: third foal: dam no
form on flat or over hurdles: modest performer: successful in seller (no bid) at
Doncaster in June and nursery at Ayr in September: good sixth of 21 in nursery at
Doncaster final start: stays 7f. *D. W. Chapman.*

RYECOVE 2 ch.g. (Apr 11) Norwick (USA) 120–Niorkie (FR) (My Swallow 134) **68**
[1990 7g 5m² 6d⁴ 6g⁵] rangy gelding: has plenty of scope: sixth living foal:
half-brother to modest sprint winner Sandy Reef (by Main Reef) and a winner in
Yugoslavia: dam never ran: easily best effort second in maiden at Lingfield: pulled
hard next outing: should stay 7f. *R. J. O'Sullivan.*

RYEDALE LASS 2 ch.f. (May 23) Ballacashtal (CAN)–Mossy Girl (Ballymoss **33**
136) [1990 5f 5f² 5m⁵ 5m 5d 7.5g⁴ 7m 7g a7g⁵ 7g a8g] 1,100F, 1,700Y: small filly:
poor mover: half-sister to 2 winners, including 5f and 8.2f winner Winmoss (by
Windjammer), and a winner over hurdles: dam of little account: poor plater: better
suited by 7f+ than 5f: inconsistent: sold 700 gns Doncaster October Sales. *M.
Brittain.*

RYEWATER DREAM 2 b.f. (Apr 14) Touching Wood (USA) 127–Facetious 88 **72**
(Malicious) [1990 7m 7m² 8a] unfurnished filly: half-sister to several winners here
and abroad, including 3-y-o Facility Letter (by Superlative), 6f winner at 2 yrs, and
fairly useful 2-y-o 5f winner Bottesford Boy (by Record Token): dam disappointing
maiden: close second of 14, travelling well most of way, to Alsaaybah in maiden at
Chepstow: around 10 lengths seventh of 14 to Another Bob in minor event at
Newbury later in October: stays 1m. *D. R. C. Elsworth.*

S

SAAFEND 2 b.f. (May 11) Sayf El Arab (USA) 127–Gilt Star 92 (Star Appeal 133) **69**
[1990 6f⁶ 6m 6g² 6d⁴] 6,200Y: sparely-made filly: poor mover: third foal: dam 1½m
winner also disqualified 7f winner: quite modest maiden: well backed and ridden by
7-lb claimer, slow-starting fourth of 11, staying on well, in nursery at Newmarket in
October: will be better suited by 7f: may improve bit further. *J. Sutcliffe.*

SAALIB 7 b.g. Tyrnavos 129–Velvet Habit 89 (Habitat 134) [1989 6v 7m⁴ 7m 7g⁶ **31 §**
7m 6m⁴ 7m⁴ 7g⁵ 5m 8f 1990 a7g a5g 8m 7m⁴ 7.6m 7m³ 8g⁵ 7f 7f 10m 7m] sturdy
gelding: carries plenty of condition: poor maiden judged on most form: stays 1m:
acts on any going: has worn blinkers and visor: often claimer ridden: has carried
head high and isn't genuine. *Pat Mitchell.*

SABARAB 4 b.c. Sayf El Arab (USA) 127–Miss Speak Easy (USA) (Sea Bird II **66**
145) [1989 8s² 8d⁴ 8.5f⁴ 10.1m⁶ 12.3g³ 10m* 12f* 14f 12d³ 10f* 10g⁵ 11v 1990
10.8m⁵] compact colt: has a quick action: won 3 claimers as 3-y-o: sweating freely,

fair fifth in Warwick handicap in March: stays 1½m: acts on firm and dead going: blinkered last 3 starts at 3 yrs: sold 1,300 gns Newmarket September Sales. *M. R. Channon.*

SABINE'S GULL (USA) 3 br.f. Arctic Tern (USA) 126–Altesse de Loir (USA) — (Vaguely Noble 140) [1989 7g 1990 10m 12m 12m 12f6 10g] sturdy filly: poor walker: has a round action: behind, including in handicap: hung right throughout final start: sold 950 gns Ascot November Sales. *M. Blanshard.*

SABONIS (USA) 3 b.f. The Minstrel (CAN) 135–Journey (USA) (What A **60** Pleasure (USA)) [1989 6f* 7m5 6g6 1990 7v3 7m 7.5d5 6g 11g 8m 8m3 8g a8g] leggy filly: has a round action: quite modest performer: ran poorly last 2 outings: may prove ideally suited by 7f: acts on firm and dead going: visored fourth start: has sweated: sold 7,000 gns Newmarket December Sales. *Denys Smith.*

SABOTAGE (FR) 4 ch.c. Kris 135–Subject To Change (USA) (Buckpasser) **103** [1989 8g* 10.5f5 8f* 8m* 9g2 8g6 1990 7m4 8g 9g5 8g4] leggy, quite good-topped, attractive colt: easy walker: useful performer: creditable fourth in listed events at York (moved down moderately) in August and Newmarket (visored, one pace behind Two Left Feet) in November: stays 9f: yet to race on soft surface. *M. R. Stoute.*

SABOTEUR 6 ch.g. Pyjama Hunt 126–Frondia 76 (Parthia 132) [1989 7m 7g2 7g — 7g 1990 7g] lengthy, dipped-backed gelding: bad mover: poor handicapper: suited by 7f and a sound surface: blinkered once: inconsistent. *M. H. Tompkins.*

SACOSHE 3 b.f. Swing Easy (USA) 126–Just Irene 50 (Sagaro 133) [1989 5g 1990 — 8g 6g 10g 8.2g 11s 7v 7d] small, sparely-made filly: bad plater: often slowly away: visored final start. *M. P. Naughton.*

SACQUE 2 b.f. (Apr 13) Elegant Air 119–Embroideress 80 (Stanford 121§) [1990 **77** 6m5 5.3f2 5m* 5g] workmanlike filly: good walker: second foal: half-sister to 3-y-o 1m and 1¼m seller winner Tom Clapton (by Daring March): dam 5f to 7f winner: modest form: won maiden at Folkestone in October: respectable eighth in nursery at Newmarket: bred to stay further than 5f: tends to flash tail. *D. Morley.*

SACRED NUMBER (USA) 3 ch.c. Irish River (FR) 131–Disco Girl (FR) **89** (Green Dancer (USA) 132) [1989 NR 1990 11d3 10m4] rangy, rather sparely-made colt: fourth reported living foal: closely related to French 1m winner Fast Record (by Riverman) and half-brother to French 2-y-o 6.5f winner Femme de Nuit (by Cresta Rider): dam, French 1½m winner, is sister to Maximova and close relation to Vilikaia: evens, won 13-runner maiden at Newbury in May by 1½ lengths from Pashto: gave trouble in stalls: will stay 1½m: looked sure to improve. *H. R. A. Cecil.*

SADDLE BOW 3 b.f. Sadler's Wells (USA) 132–Charming Life 88 (Habitat 134) **87** [1989 6m 7g3 1990 7.6d3 8.2d* 10g5] leggy, workmanlike filly: has a rather round action: visored, won maiden at Haydock in July: 23/1, well beaten in Group 3 event at Deauville: should have stayed 1¼m: acted on dead going: stud in USA. *J. Gosden.*

SADDLERS' HALL (IRE) 2 b.c. (May 26) Sadler's Wells (USA) 132–Sunny **92 p** Valley (Val de Loir 133) [1990 7d5] half-brother to 3-y-o 1½m winner Sundar (by Darshaan) and 3 other winners, including Sun Princess (by English Prince) and smart 1m to 1¼m winner Dancing Shadow (by Dancer's Image): dam won at up to 1½m in France: heavily-backed favourite, around a length fifth of 11, keeping on well, to Junk Bond in valuable minor event at Newmarket in October: showed a quick action: sure to improve, particularly over longer distances, and win races. *M. R. Stoute.*

SADEEM (USA) 7 ch.h. Forli (ARG)–Miss Mazepah (USA) (Nijinsky (CAN) **108** 138) [1989 16f* 20f* 21f2 1990 14f* 20d 20f4] big, strong, workmanlike horse: carries plenty of condition: moderate walker and mover: good-class stayer at his best: successful in Gold Cup at Royal Ascot as 6-y-o for second successive season: won slowly-run minor event at Salisbury in May from Ashal: well below form after in Gold Cup and Goodwood Cup: suited by extreme test of stamina and a sound surface: usually sweated slightly and got a little on toes: wasn't the easiest of rides: tough and genuine: retired to Conkwell Grange Stud, Bath, fee £300 + £700 (Oct 1st). *G. Harwood.*

SAD EYED LADY (IRE) 2 b.f. (Feb 5) Ballad Rock 122–Moaning Low 85 **54** (Burglar 128) [1990 5g4 5f4 5m5 5m 5m] 8,200Y: small filly: half-sister to several winners here and abroad: dam 6f winner at 3 yrs: plating-class maiden: best effort second outing: very free to post penultimate start: sold 2,300 gns Newmarket Autumn Sales. *N. A. Graham.*

SAFA 2 b.f. (Apr 22) Shirley Heights 130–Beveridge (USA) 86 (Spectacular Bid **109 p** (USA)) [1990 6m* 8m2] 330,000Y: leggy, quite good-topped filly: very good walker:

Sheikh Ahmed Al-Maktoum's "Safa"

has plenty of scope: second foal: closely related to 3-y-o Between Time (by Elegant Air), 6f winner at 2 yrs: dam 2-y-o 7f winner, is out of half-sister to Formidable: second favourite but bit backward, impressive winner of 26-runner maiden at Nottingham, making all and quickening clear under 2f out to beat Sumonda 1½ lengths: 2 lengths second of 12, staying on well and finishing clear, to Shamshir in Brent Walker Fillies' Mile at Ascot later in September: will stay 1¼m: tail swisher: likely to improve further, and win more races. *A. A. Scott.*

SAFARI KEEPER 4 b.g. Longleat (USA) 109–Garden Party 111 (Reform 132) — [1989 7f a6g 1990 a7g a10g6] seems of little account. *M. J. Wilkinson.*

SAFAWAN 4 ch.c. Young Generation 129–Safita 117 (Habitat 134) [1989 7g **118** 7m* 8.2m* 8f* 1990 8m⁵ 7.2f* 8m* 8m⁵ 8m⁵ 7m⁵]

A graph of Safawan's record to date would show a steep, upward line protraying his virtual non-stop progression from Folkestone maiden race winner at two into one of the country's leading milers, a short peak depicting his stay at the top after his win in the Juddmonte Lockinge Stakes at Newbury, then a a sharp decline followed by a partial recovery. Safawan won the last three of his four races (all handicaps) as a three-year-old, his season ending early after he beat Serious Trouble a head in the Schweppes Golden Mile at Goodwood; and with a run under his belt as a four-year-old he coped comfortably with four opponents in the listed Fairey Group Spring Trophy at Haydock in May. Receiving weight from the three other four-year-olds, and backed down to odds on, Safawan quickened really well to draw four lengths clear of Just Three in the final furlong. Swinburn, who'd missed the ride at Haydock

Juddmonte Lockinge Stakes, Newbury—
Safawan quickens on from Distant Relative and Monsagem (No. 5)

when partnering Anshan in the Two Thousand Guineas, was back on board for
the Lockinge thirteen days later. Safawan looked to have plenty on his plate
against Markofdistinction and Magic Gleam who had beaten him in the
Trusthouse Forte Mile on his reappearance, and Distant Relative and Green
Line Express, both having their first run of the season. In many respects the
Lockinge proved an unsatisfactory race; Markofdistinction travelled like the
winner but found little once ridden along; Distant Relative stayed on well but
all too late after not having a clear passage two furlongs from home; and Green
Line Express refused to settle in pursuit of the long-time leader Magic Gleam.
Safawan went about his business in his usually reliable fashion, producing a
fine turn of foot to lead over a furlong out and immediately putting the issue
beyond doubt, accounting for Distant Relative by two lengths. It was a result
which made little sense at the end of the season as Distant Relative, Green
Line Express and Markofdistinction all went on to much better things, whilst
Safawan and Monsagem went back. Like Scottish Reel, Stoute's other recent
Lockinge winner, Safawan failed to add to his winning tally. Scottish Reel was
pulled out of the Queen Anne Stakes on the day because of the unsuitable
conditions and, with hindsight, connections must have wished they'd done the
same with Safawan. Another hard race on firm ground seemed to have a
detrimental effect on his form. Starting 7/4 favourite, he ran abysmally and
was afterwards reportedly found to have jarred himself up. He ended the
season with fifth placings in the Beefeater Gin Celebration Mile at Goodwood
and the Jameson Irish Whiskey Challenge Stakes at Newmarket both outings
preceded by around two months off the track, and while both runs were a big
improvement on the Queen Anne, they lacked the finishing burst that
characterized his best performances.

786

		Balidar	Will Somers
	Young Generation	(br 1966)	Violet Bank
	(b 1976)	Brig O'Doon	Shantung
Safawan		(ch 1967)	Tam O'Shanter
(ch.c. 1986)		Habitat	Sir Gaylord
	Safita	(b 1966)	Little Hut
	(gr 1977)	Safaya	Zeddaan
		(ro 1971)	Shiraza

Safawan is by Young Generation, the Lockinge winner of 1979, out of the Habitat mare Safita, who showed smart form at up to a mile and a quarter in France, running two of her best races when runner-up in the Poule d'Essai des Pouliches and the Prix Saint-Alary. Habitat was by a long way the most successful broodmare sire of the year in Europe, responsible for the winners of sixteen pattern races, twice as many as any other maternal grandsire. Safawan was bred by the Aga Khan who sold him after his final start at three. He is Safita's fourth and comfortably best foal following the 1984 two-year-old five-furlong winner Safka (by Irish River), the six-furlong winner Satiapour (by Blushing Groom), later successful twice in North America, and the seven-to nine-furlong winner Sadapour (by Auction Ring). Safita's fifth foal Sayyara (by Kris) landed the odds in a Newmarket maiden in May, while her sixth Saraposa (by Ahonoora) ran once late in the season. Her latest offspring are a colt by Darshaan and a filly by Doyoun. Safita is the first foal of the speedy juvenile Safaya, whose dam Shiraza won a mile-and-a-quarter maiden at Saint-Cloud. Safawan, a lengthy, robust colt, is suited by a mile and has shown his best form on top-of-the-ground; he's not run on anything else since his first outing as a three-year-old. He is to be trained in 1991 in France by John Hammond. *M. R. Stoute.*

SAFE 4 b.g. Kris 135–Carnival Dance 69 (Welsh Pageant 132) [1989 10h5 12.2m* — 14m 12m3 11.7m3 14m 12f5 1990 12f6 10f 10d] angular, close-coupled gelding: turns near-fore in: shows plenty of knee action: modest winner as 3-y-o: no worthwhile form in 1990, including in seller: suited by around 1½m: acts on good to firm going: trained until after second outing by P. Cole: winning selling hurdler in October: sold 1,900 gns Ascot December Sales. *J. Ffitch-Heyes.*

SAFE ARRIVAL (USA) 2 gr.f. (Mar 8) Shadeed (USA) 135–Flyingtrip (USA) 70 p (Vaguely Noble 140) [1990 7s5] closely related to smart 1¼m and 1½m winner Icona (by Green Dancer) and half-sister to several winners, including William Hill Futurity second Cock Robin (by Raise A Native): dam, successful at 3 yrs in Italy, is daughter of Molecomb and Lowther Stakes winner Flying Legs: weak 10/1-shot, around 7 lengths fifth of 22, soon in touch then staying on under hand riding final 2f, to Desert Sun in maiden at Doncaster in October: sure to improve. *M. R. Stoute.*

SAFETY (USA) 3 b.c. Topsider (USA)–Flare Pass (USA) (Buckpasser) [1989 67 6m 6f 1990 6m5 8f 9g* 8f2] lengthy colt: moderate mover: quite modest form: improved to win handicap at Wolverhampton in June by 5 lengths: should prove ideally suited by 1¼m: acts on firm ground: blinkered (best efforts) last 2 outings: sold 13,000 gns Newmarket July Sales: winning hurdler for J. White. *B. W. Hills.*

SAFFAAII (USA) 3 ch.c. Secreto (USA) 128 Somebody Noble (USA) (Vaguely 72 p Noble 140) [1989 NR 1990 10g4 10d2] 120,000Y: strong, compact colt: third foal: half-brother to 10.2f and 1½m winner Regency Fair (by Assert): dam, from family of Affirmed, never ran: running-on fourth to impressive Theatrical Charmer in maiden at Kempton: better for race, made most when ¾-length second of 3 to Mind The Step in Leicester minor event over 6 months later: should stay 1½m: stays in training, and can improve. *R. W. Armstrong.*

SAFFRON LACE 3 b.f. Rabdan 129–French Music (French Beige 127) [1989 — 5m4 5m 5.1f 7m 5.1m 8g 6m a6g a7g a8g 1990 8m 10f 8f] smallish, sparely-made filly: poor walker: poor plater: blinkered once: looks a difficult ride. *C. F. Wall.*

SAGACIOUS LADY (USA) 3 b. or br.f. Sagace (FR) 135–Feather Bow (USA) — (Gun Bow) [1989 NR 1990 10m6 12f] smallish, leggy filly: seventh foal: half-sister to 3 minor winners in USA: dam stakes winner at up to 9f in USA: always well behind in maidens at Sandown (virtually bolted to post, hung badly left leaving stalls) and Salisbury (pulled hard). *M. R. Channon.*

SAGAMAN (GER) 4 b.g. Solo Dancer (GER)–Scholastika (GER) (Alpenkonig 52 (GER)) [1989 10s6 12g 8.2s6 12h3 12f6 12h2 12f 10g 1990 12f4 14.8m3] plating-class maiden: stays 14.8f: possibly needs top-of-the-ground: virtually tailed off in visor at 2 yrs, often blinkered nowadays: winner over hurdles in November. *L. J. Codd.*

S'AGAPO 3 ch.f. Prince Ragusa 96–No Bello (Porto Bello 118) [1989 NR 1990 15g] — first foal: dam poor form, raced only at 3 yrs: 200/1, always behind in maiden claimer at Edinburgh in July. *J. Dooler.*

SAGAR ISLAND (USA) 3 b. or br.f. Sagace (FR) 135–Star River (FR) (Riverman (USA) 131) [1989 7f³ 1990 11.5g⁴ 12m⁶] close-coupled, angular, sparely-made filly: modest maiden: led over 1m when modest sixth at Beverley in June: should have stayed 1½m, at least: stud. *M. R. Stoute.* **75**

SAGE BRUSH 4 ch.f. Sagaro 133–Tentwort 79 (Shiny Tenth 120) [1989 11g 1990 14f⁴ 12f² 15m 16f] lengthy, dipped-backed filly: moderate mover: no worthwhile form, including in handicaps: sold 1,500 gns Doncaster October Sales. *C. W. C. Elsey.* —

SAGEBRUSH ROLLER 2 br.c. (Mar 29) Sharpo 132–Sunita (Owen Dudley 121) [1990 6d 5d 6d4] 8,000Y: rangy, unfurnished colt: first foal: dam unraced half-sister to Oaks-placed Suni and Media Luna: 33/1, over 10 lengths fourth of 18, travelling smoothly then keeping on not knocked about, to Reshift in maiden at Doncaster in November, easily best effort: will be better suited by 7f + : likely to do better at 3 yrs. *J. W. Watts.* **55 p**

SAHARA BALADEE (USA) 3 b.f. Shadeed (USA) 135–Splendid Girl (USA) (Golden Eagle (FR)) [1989 6f² 7m² 1990 8g³ 8g² 7m4] angular, sparely-made filly: has a roundish action: quite modest maiden: favourite, led 7f when second at Carlisle: poor fourth at Leicester in July: will stay beyond 1m: sweating last 2 starts. *M. R. Stoute.* **68**

SAHEL (IRE) 2 b.c. (May 17) Green Desert (USA) 127–Fremanche (FR) (Jim French (USA)) [1990 6g5] ninth foal: half-brother to several winners, notably very smart 1m to 1½m winner Free Guest (by Be My Guest) and useful 1¼m performer Fish 'N' Chips (by Rio Carmelo): dam won over 9f in Italy: weak in betting, over 4 lengths fifth of 17, chasing leaders and one pace, to Rocton North in maiden at Yarmouth in October: should improve. *J. H. M. Gosden.* **66 p**

SAIF CROWN (USA) 3 ch.c. Chief's Crown (USA)–Dimant Rose (USA) (Tromos 134) [1989 NR 1990 10g 8.2g⁵ 10.6d] first foal: dam unraced half-sister to Rainbow Quest: worthwhile form in maidens only when fifth at Hamilton: should stay middle distances: sold 1,400 gns Doncaster October Sales. *B. Hanbury.* **44**

SAI KUNG 4 gr.f. Nishapour (FR) 125–Languid (English Prince 129) [1989 7.5v 15g⁶ 7.5v³ 6.5s4 6g 11.2g 5g⁴ 5v⁵ 6.7g* 6.7g* 6.7g⁴ 1990 8f 5f 7.6m 6f] in frame in early-season sellers as 2-y-o when trained by N. Tinkler: then raced in Italy, winning twice at Livorno in 1989: behind in varied events in first half of 1990: bolted to post and withdrawn second intended outing. *Miss B. Sanders.* —

SAILOR BOY 4 b.c. Main Reef 126–Main Sail 104 (Blakeney 126) [1989 10.1m 12m* 13.1f³ 17.1f* 1990 16g 16d⁶ 14g 14m² 14m³ 17.1f³ 13.1h* 14g³ 16f⁵ 12d] smallish, quite attractive colt: easy mover, with a light action: fair handicapper: won 4-runner event at Bath in August, making most: stays 17f: acts on hard ground, possibly unsuited by soft surface: ran creditably in blinkers: best racing up with pace. *R. Akehurst.* **79**

SAILOR MILAN 3 ch.c. Pas de Seul 133–Sweet Home (Home Guard (USA) 129) [1989 6m 7f 7v 1990 7d 11m] leggy, sparely-made colt: poor maiden: edgy and fractious at start final outing. *N. Bycroft.* —

SAIL PAST (FR) 2 gr.g. (Feb 25) No Pass No Sale 120–All In White (FR) (Carwhite 127) [1990 5m⁵ 6m* 6g³ 7m⁶ 7s 6g 7g 7s] 160,000 francs (approx £15,400) Y: leggy, close-coupled gelding: first reported foal: dam French 10.5f winner, is half-sister to smart middle-distance winners Praise and Hard To Sing: modest performer: won 5-runner maiden at York in June: had stiff task when well beaten in valuable restricted event at Deauville fifth start: ran badly final outing: seems to stay 7f. *F. H. Lee.* **72**

SAINT BENE'T (IRE) 2 b.c. (Mar 13) Glenstal (USA) 118–Basilea (FR) (Frere Basile (FR) 129) [1990 6m³ 6h³ 6m 7m4 8m 7s] IR 4,200F, 20,000Y: workmanlike colt: third foal: closely related to very useful French 3-y-o Pont Aven (by Try My Best), 5f (at 2 yrs) and 6.5f winner, and half-brother to French 1m (at 2 yrs) and 1¼m winner Bigouden (by What A Guest): dam seemingly suited by 1½m in France: quite modest maiden: stays 7f: possibly unsuited by soft ground: races freely. *W. J. Pearce.* **64**

SAINT CALIGULA (IRE) 2 b.g. (Jan 22) Petorius 117–Saint Cynthia (Welsh Saint 126) [1990 7g² a6g* 6m 6d⁶ a7g*] IR 19,000Y: leggy gelding: fourth foal: **84**

half-brother 4-y-o Ski Nut (by Sharpo) and winners in Italy and Belgium: dam won over 1¾m and over hurdles in Ireland: fair performer: successful in 16-runner maiden and 12-runner claimer (by 10 lengths for 7-lb apprentice) at Southwell: ran well in nurseries in between: better suited by 7f than 6f. *M. Bell.*

SAINT CIEL (USA)   2 b.c. (Apr 10) Skywalker (USA)–Holy Tobin (USA) 83 (J O   **77** p
Tobin (USA) 130) [1990 7s²] 500,000 francs (approx £49,300) Y: first foal: dam half-sister to good American middle-distance performer Silver Supreme and to dam of Miesque: sire won Breeders' Cup Classic: bit backward and green, 6 lengths second of 22, pushed along vigorously 3f out and keeping on, to impressive Desert Sun in maiden at Doncaster in October: will be suited by 1¼m + : sure to improve. *A. A. Scott.*

SAINT NAVARRO   5 ch.m. Raga Navarro (ITY) 119–Saint Motunde 84 (Tyrant   **77**
(USA)) [1989 5f 6f⁶ 6f⁵ 5f* 5m⁴ᵈⁱˢ 5g* 5g* 5f² 5m 5g⁵ 5.6g 1990 5f³ 5g³ 5g* 5f⁶ 5f⁶ 5f⁴ 5m* a5g³ 5g⁵ 5d⁵ 5m⁶] rather leggy, plain, close-coupled mare: has a round action: modest handicapper: won at Chester (same race for second year running) in June and Pontefract (apprentice ridden) in August: best at 5f: probably acts on any going: best in blinkers: often starts slowly: sometimes hangs: sold to join C. Hill's stable 3,100 gns Doncaster November Sales. *B. A. McMahon.*

SAINT SYSTEMS   4 b.f. Uncle Pokey 116–Fire Mountain 87 (Dragonara Palace   **68**
(USA) 115) [1989 6m 6g 5f 5m 5h 5m³ 6f 5g 5m⁶ 1990 5m⁵ 5.8f* 5g⁵ 5f³ 5m⁵ 5.8h⁴ 5f³ 5g 5m 5.8f 5.3f 5g 5m* 5d³ 5.8d* a6g² a5g* a6g* a7g⁶] angular, sparely-made filly: modest handicapper: successful at Bath in June (making all), then in tremendous form in autumn, winning at Warwick (racing virtually alone) and Bath again in October and Lingfield (twice) in November: effective at 5f to 6f: acts on firm and dead going: below form in blinkers: has won for apprentice. *C. J. Hill.*

SAINT VENDING   2 br.c. (Apr 25) Grey Desire 115–Girdle Ness 56 (Pitskelly   **58**
122) [1990 5m 5v⁵ 5g 6g⁶ 6g² 7.5d* 7.5f 8.2s] 2,000Y: sparely-made colt: has a round action: first foal: dam 1m winner out of half-sister to smart fillies Flighting and Bonnie Isle: improved form when winning auction event at Beverley in June: faced very stiff task in nursery final start, first for over 3 months: better suited by 7.5f than shorter: possibly unsuited by firm ground: blinkered third outing. *M. Brittain.*

SAJJAYA (USA)   3 ch.f. Blushing Groom (FR) 131–Lady Cutlass (USA) (Cutlass   **97**
(USA)) [1989 7f² 7s* 7g⁶ 1990 8g 7m² 7f² 8m* 8m² 9.2g] leggy, attractive filly: good walker: fluent mover: fairly useful performer: won minor contest at Newmarket in August: beaten short head by Spring Daffodil in Group 3 event at the Curragh next start then not at all discredited, setting modest pace, in Group 2 contest (taken last and quietly to post) at Longchamp month later: stayed 1m: acted on any going: ridden up with or made pace: lacked turn of foot, but game: visits Unfuwain. *J. L. Dunlop.*

SAKIL (IRE)   2 b.c. (Feb 20) Vision (USA)–Sciambola (Great Nephew 126) [1990   **— p**
7s] 25,000Y: good-topped colt: third foal: half-brother to 3-y-o Corporate Member (by Exhibitioner) and a winner in Norway: dam ran in Italy without success: carrying condition and green, close up 5f in maiden at Lingfield in October: sure to improve. *C. J. Benstead.*

SAKURA DANCER   3 ch.f. Viking (USA)–Serenesse (Habat 127) [1989 5h⁶ 6g⁶   **—**
6f⁵ 5g 1990 a8g 9g 7m a8g] compact filly: moderate walker: poor handicapper. *J. M. Bradley.*

SALACITY   6 b.g. Sallust 134–Vera Van Fleet (Cracksman 111) [1989 NR 1990 10v   **—**
12s] close-coupled gelding: bad mover: lightly-raced maiden on flat: tailed off in autumn handicaps. *G. M. Moore.*

SALADAN KNIGHT   5 b.g. Dalsaan 125–Exciting Times (Windjammer (USA))   **72**
[1989 5m 5f a5g* a6g* 1990 a8g³ 6m⁵ 6m 6m 5m⁵] leggy, lengthy gelding: moderate mover: fairly useful from when winning 2 handicaps on all-weather late in 1989: easily best effort on turf as 5-y-o on second outing: slowly away and raced alone when visored final one (June): effective at 5f and 6f: best on a sound surface: has sweated, and often on toes: tends to wander. *J. G. FitzGerald.*

SALBYNG   2 b.c. (Mar 17) Night Shift (USA)–Hsian (Shantung 132) [1990 7m 7f⁶   **47**
7m 8.2d] 10,000Y, 11,000 2-y-o: strong colt: carries condition: has a quick action: fourth foal: half-brother to fair 3-y-o 7f winner Manalapan (by Superlative) and 4-y-o Princess Wu (by Sandhurst Prince): dam lightly-raced half-sister to smart 6f to 1m winner Bas Bleu and very useful middle-distance performer Primerello: poor form in varied events: stays 7f. *J. W. Hills.*

SALIC DANCE   2 b.c. (Apr 11) Shareef Dancer (USA) 135–Sandy Island 110 (Mill   **66** p
Reef (USA) 141) [1990 7m³ 8g 7m⁴] well-made, attractive colt: has scope: third foal:

half-brother to 2 animals by Lyphard, including 3-y-o Sardegna, winner at 7f (at 2 yrs) and 1¼m: dam won Pretty Polly Stakes and Lancashire Oaks, and is closely related to Slip Anchor: quite modest form in maidens: fourth of 12, staying on well despite flashing tail, at Warwick in October: will be suited by middle distances: looks sort to do better. *P. T. Walwyn.*

SALINAMAR 3 b.g. Muscatite 122–Bells of Ireland (Northfields (USA)) [1989 NR 1990 8m 9m 8m 12.5g 8.5g 10.2f⁵ 10m] IR 3,600F, 13,000Y: heavy-topped gelding: moderate mover: first foal: dam, unplaced on 5 starts in Ireland, is out of useful Irish 2-y-o 5f and 6f winner Phil's Fancy: no worthwhile form, including in selling handicap: bandaged first 3 starts, blinkered next 3: sold 850 gns Ascot November Sales. *G. Lewis.* —

SALINE 5 ch.m. Sallust 134–Silk Rein 107 (Shantung 132) [1989 17.1f 10m⁴ 11g 10.8m² 10f² 10.4m⁵ 12g⁶ 1990 a11g⁴ a11g⁴ a14g] angular, workmanlike mare: moderate mover: poor maiden: stays 11f: acts on firm going: usually blinkered: winner over hurdles in November with M. Pipe. *J. Mackie.* **38**

SALINGER 2 b.c. (Apr 5) Rousillon (USA) 133–Scholastika (GER) (Alpenkonig (GER)) [1990 7g 6m²] workmanlike colt: has scope: third known foal: half-brother to 3-y-o 11.5f winner Slipperose (by Persepolis): dam German bred: length second of 8, making most and keeping on well, to Persianalli in maiden at Yarmouth in September: should prove better suited by 7f: likely to improve again. *J. W. Hills.* **82 p**

SALLY ROUS 3 br.f. Rousillon (USA) 133–Sassalya (Sassafras (FR) 135) [1989 6g* 1990 7m⁴ 8m⁶ 10m⁶ 7f* 7m³ 7g² 7m* 8f²] **118**

The increasing success of British-trained horses abroad owes much to the speed and convenience of modern air travel. Just occasionally, however, accidents happen. Sally Rous, a tough, good-class filly at seven furlongs having had her final race of the season at Aqueduct, was on her return flight when she began to panic and struggle inside her box, sustaining injuries which led to her demise. Barely a week earlier Tate Gallery, who had been sold to stand at stud in Japan, had gone berserk in flight to Heathrow, and was found dead on arrival; such incidents thankfully have been rare. The very promising Sally Rous began her campaign as a three-year-old by lining up for Newmarket's Nell Gwyn Stakes which turned out to be a rather misleading trial for the Guineas. Heart of Joy beat In The Groove and Hasbah by a short head and the same, with Sally Rous, who looked backward and ran green early on, staying on well towards the finish after being outpaced when the principals quickened two furlongs out. Allowed to take her chance in the Guineas, she ran valiantly, caught one-paced once Salsabil and Heart of Joy went to the front, but kept on well during the closing stages. Any idea that a longer trip would suit Sally Rous, however, turned out to be wrong. She weakened significantly inside the final quarter mile of the ten-furlong William Hill Fillies Trial Stakes at Newbury, then reverted to seven furlongs for the Group 3 Jersey Stakes with the best possible outcome. Starting at 20/1, she was settled towards the rear as Norwich cut out the early running, but was able to weave her way through without much trouble to take the lead just inside the final furlong; once in front she gamely fended off the determined challenge of Bold Russian by a head. Having established herself over the distance, Sally Rous was kept to seven furlongs for her three remaining races in Britain, and with better luck she would have completed the season with more than two successes to her name. She was a most unfortunate loser in the listed Oak Tree Stakes at Goodwood at the end of July, being badly hampered when the tiring leader, Hasbah, drifted across her with a furlong to race, almost unseating Gary Carter; yet she rallied bravely and ran on to take third behind Alidiva. Six weeks later she was again denied, although on this occasion on merit, in the Group 3 Kiveton Park Stakes at Doncaster: having once more made steady headway from the rear, Sally Rous quickened approaching the furlong-pole, appearing to hold a narrow advantage over long-time leader Green Line Express as they entered the final hundred yards; however, Green Line Express rallied and got up by the narrowest of margins. Compensation for Sally Rous was forthcoming in the Group 2 Jameson Irish Whiskey Challenge Stakes at Newmarket. The 11/4 second favourite, she tracked the lead initially, went on with a quarter of a mile to race and ran on really strongly up the hill, as she had done on the course in the spring; and although Anshan,

Jersey Stakes, Ascot—
20/1-chance Sally Rous (noseband) holds off Bold Russian by a head;
also in the picture is Norwich

the 9/4 favourite, stumbled entering the Dip, the outcome wasn't materially
affected. At the beginning of November Sally Rous contested the Aqueduct
Budweiser Breeders' Cup, over a mile, and once more showed herself to be a
very tough filly with a game second, beaten three quarters of a length, to Fire
The Groom.

		Rousillon (USA) (b 1981)	Riverman (b 1969)	Never Bend River Lady
Sally Rous (br.f. 1987)			Belle Dorine (b or br 1977)	Marshua's Dancer Palsy Walsy
		Sassalya (b 1973)	Sassafras (b 1967)	Sheshoon Ruta
			Valya (b 1965)	Vandale II Lilya

Sally Rous, who was to have been kept in training as a four-year-old, was
the best of Rousillon's first crop, and a half-sister to five winners, all owned by
Sir Philip Oppenheimer and trained by Geoff Wragg; they included the 1986
Tote-Ebor second Chauve Souris (by Beldale Flutter), Assemblyman (by
General Assembly), who in 1985 won the Welsh Derby at Chepstow and was
second to Shardari in Ascot's Cumberland Lodge Stakes, and Bold Indian (by
Bold Lad (IRE)), a very useful colt at seven furlongs to a mile. Sally Rous
herself was probably best at seven; she raced most consistently once that had
been established. Usually held up to make most effective use of her turn of
foot, she acted on firm going and never encountered soft. *G. Wragg.*

SALLY'S PRINCE (IRE) 2 ch.g. (Apr 12) Prince Sabo 123–Sally Chase 101   **83**
(Sallust 134) [1990 5g³ 5m² 5f³ 6f² 6m⁵ a6g² a6g* 5m² 6m*] smallish, sparely-
made gelding: third foal: half-brother to 5f and 7f winner Sally's Son (by Beldale
Flutter): dam sprinter, ran only at 2 yrs: fair performer: made all in maiden at Southwell and claimer at Leicester in autumn: effective at 5f and 6f: blinkered or visored
final 7 starts: suitable mount for an apprentice. *W. A. O'Gorman.*

SALLY'S SON 4 b.g. Beldale Flutter (USA) 130–Sally Chase 101 (Sallust 134)   **65**
[1989 6f⁵ 7f 5.1m⁴ 6m a6g a6g⁴ a7g⁴ 1990 a7g* a7g³ a8g⁶ 6g³ 5m² 6m³ 6m⁶ 6g
5m⁶ 5.1f* 5m² a5g² 5m³] strong, good-bodied gelding: carries plenty of condition:
moderate walker: quite modest handicapper: won at Lingfield in January and
Yarmouth in August: ran well last 3 outings: stays 7f: acts on firm ground: effective
with or without blinkers or visor: ridden mostly by claimer nowadays: consistent.
W. A. O'Gorman.

SALLYS WON 6 b.g. Free State 125–Arbatina (Sallust 134) [1989 10.2g² 10g³   **41**
1990 10.2f 8f 10f⁵ 10m 10f³ 10f 8d 8g] rangy gelding: moderate mover: poor maiden:

broke out of stalls second intended outing: stays 1¼m: acts on firm going: has run well when sweating. *R. Curtis.*

SALMAN (USA) 4 b.c. Nain Bleu (FR)–H M S Pellinore (USA) (King Pellinore **77** (USA) 127) [1989 8.2m 8.5f² 8m* 1990 8f 8m⁶ 9m⁵ 10m⁴ 11d³ 9f] strong, good-topped colt: fair performer, only lightly raced: creditable third in handicap at Ayr in September: stays 11f: acts on any going: has run well when apprentice ridden. *S. G. Norton.*

SALMINO (IRE) 2 b.c. (Apr 16) Salmon Leap (USA) 131–Amina 80 (Brigadier **88** p Gerard 144) [1990 6m 8m* 7m*] 4,000F: closely related to a winner abroad by Dance In Time and half-brother to 2 winners, including 5-y-o 1¼m seller winner Khorevo (by Tyrnavos): dam 1¼m winner, is sister to Cheshire and Lancashire Oaks winner Princess Eboli: most progressive colt: dead-heated in maiden at Edinburgh then won 16-runner nursery at Redcar later in September: stays 1m: likely to progress again. *Mrs G. R. Reveley.*

SALMIYA 3 b.f. Superlative 118–The Firebird (Busted 134) [1989 7m⁶ 7m 1990 7f — a6g 7g] sturdy filly: plating-class maiden: soundly beaten as 3-y-o, in handicaps last 2 starts: may stay beyond 7f. *J. D. Czerpak.*

SALMONID 4 ch.c. Salmon Leap (USA) 131–Persian Polly 99 (Persian Bold 123) **71** [1989 10s⁶ 10g⁴ 7.6f⁵ 8f 7f² 10g* 10g* 1990 10g 8m⁵ 10m 10m⁴ 12m* 12m⁶ a12g² a12g*] sturdy, lengthy, rather dipped-backed colt: carries plenty of condition: won for amateur for third time in 17-runner event at Salisbury in June: below his best after, including when justifying favouritism in claimer at Southwell in December: effective at 1¼m and 1½m: acts on good to firm going. *P. F. I. Cole.*

SALMON PRINCE 4 ch.g. Salmon Leap (USA) 131–Princesse Anglaise **42** (Crepello 136) [1989 12d⁴ 12d⁵ 10g 1990 10h³ 14m⁶ 17.1f³ 16f³] workmanlike gelding: quite modest form at best: stays 17f: acts on firm and dead going: winning hurdler twice in August. *Miss B. Sanders.*

SALMON SPARKLE 3 ch.c. Salmon Leap (USA) 131–Sparkling Air (Malinow- **53** ski (USA) 123) [1989 a7g⁶ a8g⁴ 1990 a8g* a10g 8f⁴ 8h 7g] small colt: plating-class handicapper on his day: won maiden at Southwell in January: stays 1m well: visored final start, blinkered previously at 3 yrs: sold 3,600 gns Newmarket Autumn Sales, probably to Italy. *P. T. Walwyn.*

SALSABIL 3 b.f. Sadler's Wells (USA) 132–Flame of Tara 124 (Artaius **130** (USA) 129) [1989 6f* 7m² 8g* 1990 7.3d* 8m* 12d* 12g* 12m* 12g]

The flat-racing year provided more than its usual quota of stories for the front pages of the national newspapers. The latest season saw the first proven cases of 'nobbling' in Britain for over twenty years; the Aga Khan withdrew from British racing after his 1989 Oaks winner Aliysa became the first British classic winner to be disqualified following a positive dope-test; Pat Eddery became the first flat-race jockey to ride two hundred winners in a season in Britain since Gordon Richards thirty-eight years previously; Lester Piggott made a come-back to race-riding at the age of fifty-four. Would all the achievements of the season's best horses—which included a tip-top sprinter in Dayjur and a versatile top-class filly in Salsabil—had attracted publicity on the same scale! The performances of Dayjur and Salsabil greatly enriched the season and it wasn't surprising that the panel of journalists which decides

General Accident One Thousand Guineas, Newmarket—
Salsabil (striped cap) collars Heart of Joy; the pair have come clear of Negligent,
who in turn is clear of Free At Last (dark colours)

Gold Seal Oaks, Epsom — Salsabil has five lengths to spare;
Game Plan is a long-priced second in front of hard-ridden Knight's Baroness,
In The Groove (almost hidden) and Ahead (rails)

the official Horse of the Year award was almost equally divided between the pair. The result—Dayjur polled one more vote than Salsabil—was the closest since Charlottown pipped Sodium by a fraction in 1966 when the voters gave points to their six top horses in order of preference. Dayjur and Salsabil, both owned by the season's leading owner Sheikh Hamdan Al-Maktoum, virtually monopolised the latest poll, receiving twenty-seven of the thirty-two votes between them. Like most polls, however, the timing was probably critical and the fact that Dayjur's finest performances came in the second part of the season, and were fresher when the end-of-season voting took place, almost certainly helped to tip the balance. Salsabil's marvellous campaign included three classic victories, the last of them on July 1st—before Dayjur had even contested a Group 1 race (he went on to win the Keeneland Nunthorpe, the Ladbroke Sprint Cup and the Ciga Prix de l'Abbaye). Salsabil's assessment of 125 in the International Classification—lower than ten other three-year-olds—must have astounded those who voted for her. The Jockey Club doesn't permit publication during the season of its handicappers' assessments for horses above 120, but the handicapper responsible for assessing the middle-distance horses revealed in the *Racing Post* after Salsabil's final race that she was assessed at 131 and 'wouldn't be lowered on one disappointing performance'. The subsequent decision of the international panel of handicappers illustrates one of the upshots of 'handicapping by committee'.

To begin at the end with Salsabil. Her tenth of twenty-one placing in Europe's most prestigious all-aged middle-distance race, the Ciga Prix de l'Arc de Triomphe, was a disappointing finale to an illustrious career. It was the only defeat she suffered in a triumphant season which included victories in four Group 1 races, the General Accident One Thousand Guineas, the Gold Seal Oaks, the Budweiser Irish Derby and the Prix Vermeille. Salsabil's form made her the best European middle-distance three-year-old at weight-for-sex going into the Arc and she started a short-priced favourite on the French Tote, coupled in the betting with her pacemaker Albadr. Salsabil was fresh from her win in the Prix Vermeille over the course and distance three weeks earlier, though her margin of victory that day was only a neck and half a length over Miss Alleged and the fast-finishing In The Groove. Salsabil was never able to shake off the main pack after being sent into the lead halfway up the straight but seemed likely to come on for the run after her mid-season break. Salsabil looked well on Arc day, straighter and more muscled up than before the Vermeille, though she spoiled her appearance by sweating. Boxed in and squeezed for room on the long sweeping final turn, after being held up as usual, Salsabil produced little under pressure when a gap finally came, and Carson didn't knock her about once pursuit was futile. She finished over nine lengths behind the winner Saumarez, beaten by two other British-trained fillies Hellenic (eighth) and In The Groove (ninth, the only time in four meetings she finished ahead of Salsabil). 'She's given it all season but when I asked for more today, it wasn't there', reported Carson. 'I suppose we sought it once too often.' Salsabil's trainer Dunlop concurred: 'She wasn't the same filly we saw in the spring and summer'.

Salsabil was almost certainly past her best by Arc day. Her season had started in the Gainsborough Stud Fred Darling Stakes at Newbury in April and she'd been through a full programme of big races in the spring and early-summer. Salsabil won two of her three races as a two-year-old, including France's premier test for juvenile fillies the Prix Marcel Boussac. She lost no time in confirming her sound credentials for the General Accident One Thousand Guineas, looking better than ever when winning the Fred Darling most impressively by six lengths from Haunting Beauty, showing a fine turn of foot after being waited with. And afterwards Salsabil displaced the Nell Gwyn Stakes winner Heart of Joy as ante-post favourite for the One Thousand Guineas. The Nell Gwyn had produced a very close finish between Heart of Joy, In The Groove and Hasbah, all of whom were in the ten-horse Guineas line-up. Heart of Joy was Salsabil's main market rival on the day, Salsabil starting at 6/4 and Heart of Joy at 4/1, with the Rockfel Stakes winner Negligent (the winter favourite, making her first appearance of the season) at 11/2, Hasbah at 8/1 and In The Groove at 11/1 the only others shorter than 14/1. Salsabil and Heart of Joy dominated the finish, Salsabil getting the better of a battle-royal over the last two furlongs after Heart of Joy had appeared to be travelling the smoother running into the Dip; Salsabil gamely forged ahead, staying on strongly under pressure up the final hill to win by three quarters of a length. Negligent was third, five lengths behind Heart of Joy; In The Groove and Hasbah came eighth and tenth respectively. Salsabil's victory filled a gap in the record of her rider Carson who had been successful in every English classic bar the One Thousand Guineas; Salsabil's Oaks win gave him his fifteenth English classic victory, a score bettered only by eight jockeys.

Salsabil's trainer expressed doubts after the One Thousand Guineas about Salsabil's stamina and advised the public immediately after the race not to back her for the Oaks pending a firm decision. The shorter Prix de Diane (French Oaks) was mentioned as an alternative to Epsom, and there was even talk of keeping Salsabil to a mile, aimed at the Irish Guineas and the Coronation Stakes. Salsabil's pedigree provided plenty of encouragement for the view that she would stay a mile and a half. Her sire the versatile Sadler's Wells showed top-class form at the trip and her dam Flame of Tara, who made her name as a middle-distance performer, wasn't beaten far when eighth in the Irish St Leger. Salsabil became favourite in all the ante-post lists once her participation in the Gold Seal Oaks was confirmed—reportedly after 'considerable discussion'—but was eventually strongly challenged for favouritism by In The Groove. Salsabil didn't run between Newmarket and Epsom but In The Groove enhanced her reputation considerably with victories in the Tattersalls Musidora Stakes at York and the Goffs Irish One Thousand Guineas at the Curragh, where she beat odds-on Heart of Joy by three lengths. Salsabil and In The Groove started at 2/1 and 85/40 respectively but the anticipated duel didn't materialize. Salsabil turned the Oaks into a one-horse race, bursting into the lead two furlongs out after tracking the leaders Ahead and Knight's Baroness at Tattenham Corner and quickly drawing clear. Salsabil flashed her tail when Carson took the whip to her in the final furlong, but none of her rivals ever looked likely to land a blow. The 50/1-shot Game Plan stayed on strongly for second place, five lengths down; Knight's Baroness finished third, a length behind Game Plan and a head in front of In The Groove who was off the bridle from early in the straight and hard ridden (her rider received a two-day suspension for excessive use of the whip, Knight's Baroness' received a three-day suspension for a similar offence).

Another big disappointment in the Oaks field was the third favourite Kartajana, an impressive winner of the William Hill Fillies Trial at Newbury.

The stewards held an inquiry into Kartajana's running after she trailed in last, and ordered her to be doped-tested. Kartajana's owner the Aga Khan had led in the winner Aliysa twelve months earlier but the inquiry resulting from the discovery of hydroxycamphor, a metabolite of the prohibited substance camphor, in Aliysa's routine post-race sample had still not been held by the time the latest edition of the Oaks came to be run. The Disciplinary Committee of the Jockey Club finally began its hearing into the complex Aliysa case on July 16th. It had been postponed from May 21st after a request for an adjournment by Aliysa's connections who hadn't finished preparing their case. Part of the inquiry concerned with scientific evidence was put off until September when four days were set aside for it. But there was a further delay —to allow the Horseracing Forensic Laboratory at Newmarket to respond to 'significant new evidence' produced as a result of trials conducted on behalf of Aliysa's owner—and the case was finally concluded in November, fifteen months after the result of the routine test on Aliysa became known. After considering the evidence, the Disciplinary Committee disqualified Aliysa, awarding the 1989 Oaks to Snow Bride, with Roseate Tern second, Mamaluna third and Aliysa's stable-companion Knoosh fourth. Aliysa's trainer Stoute was found to be in breach of rule 53 and fined £200; in addition Stoute was ordered to pay the costs and expenses relating to the scientific and legal advisers employed. The committee was satisfied that the source of the hydroxycamphor was 'camphor contained in an unknown substance'. Connections of Aliysa maintained that the Horseracing Forensic Laboratory had failed to prove that the hydroxycamphor found in Aliysa was a metabolite of camphor, trials in North America reportedly having shown that hydroxycamphor could also be metabolised from borneol which is a normal constituent of feedstuffs and could be detected in horses bedded on wood shavings (wood shavings had been in use in the racecourse stables at Epsom). The Horseracing Forensic Laboratory maintained—after conducting its own trials—that the hydroxycamphor detected in Aliysa could not have come from her feed or bedding. The Aga Khan announced in December that he would have no more horses trained in Britain—about ninety were transferred to Ireland and France from Stoute and Cumani at around the turn of the year—until 'effective measures have been instituted to correct the flawed equine drug testing procedures and administration of the rules sanctioning the use of prohibited substances in racing in this country'. Whether the Aga Khan's dispute with the Jockey Club is to be continued in the law courts is not known at the time of writing but it raises the possibility of an enthralling legal wrangle and would be good news for all those who relish the prospect of the results of races being decided in the court room rather than on the racecourse!

Budweiser Irish Derby, the Curragh—Salsabil beats the colts

*Prix Vermeille, Longchamp—Salsabil holds on from Miss Alleged,
In The Groove, Wajd and Air de Rien*

To return to Salsabil. Her trainer said after the Oaks that he had always had misgivings about Salsabil's staying a mile and a half. 'Sheikh Hamdan thought she would and it was at his instigation that she ran in the Oaks', said Dunlop. Salsabil's primary target after the Oaks was announced as the Champion Stakes, a race sponsored by the owner's family, but it was soon decided that she would run in the interim in the Budweiser Irish Derby, her connections spurning the much easier and more conventional option of the Kildangan Stud Irish Oaks. The Irish Derby presented much the greatest challenge Salsabil had faced up to that time and provided a rare opportunity for a member of her sex to win a classic that is usually contested only by colts. Races such as the Two Thousand Guineas and the Derby in Britain and Ireland are nearly always a good deal harder to win than their counterparts for the fillies. Triptych provided a rare classic victory for a filly against the colts when successful in the Irish Two Thousand Guineas in 1985 (becoming the only winning filly in the history of the race); only two fillies—Sceptre in 1902 and Garden Path in 1944—have won the Two Thousand Guineas in England this century, and only three this century—Signorinetta (1908), Tagalie (1912) and Fifinella (1916)—have won the Derby. Salsabil's presence in the Irish Derby field provided the highspot of the season up to that time, setting up a fascinating clash with the first and second in the Derby, Quest For Fame and Blue Stag, and Quest For Fame's conqueror in the Chester Vase Belmez who had missed Epsom because of injury. Salsabil and Quest For Fame were last-minute entries, along with Quest For Fame's stable-companion Deploy, their owners paying IR £60,000 apiece at the supplementary entry deadline five days before the race. The three supplementary entries changed the complexion of the Irish Derby and proved none too popular among other owners whose horses had been entered in their two-year-old days. Robert Sangster, the owner of Blue Stag who would have vied for favouritism, complained that supplementary entry stages for big races provide an extra advantage to the small group of 'fabulously-rich owners'. Sheikh Hamdan and Khalid Abdulla (who owned both Quest For Fame and Deploy) were 'like two players in a poker game who suddenly come in to play for a big jackpot on the final hand after sitting it out all night'. Supplementary entry stages may not be popular with some but they can make a sizeable contribution to the prize-money pool and also enable good horses not entered at an early-closing date to take their place in a championship field. The quality of the Irish Derby field was boosted considerably by the supplementary entries; and no race benefited more during the season from having a supplementary clause than the Racing Post Trophy, the last big two-year-old race of the year in Britain, whose four eventual runners were all £18,000 supplementary nominations (there had been one hundred and twenty-nine entries at the original entry stage on April 4th). Salsabil and Deploy both fully justified the decision to supplement them for the Irish Derby, fighting out the finish clear of the rest. Salsabil again produced a fine turn of foot after being waited with and won, pushed out, by three quarters of a length after hitting the front inside the final furlong. The front-running Deploy kept on well and had four lengths (we made it nearer five) to spare over Belmez, with Blue Stag half a length further back and Quest For Fame (who started 5/4 favourite and returned injured) a neck away in fifth. The first five were all British-trained and Salsabil was the first filly to win the Irish Derby since 1900.

In view of the fighting policy pursued with Salsabil up to the Irish Derby it came as a surprise that her participation in the King George VI and Queen Elizabeth Diamond Stakes at Ascot at the end of July should have been the subject of so much uncertainty. Salsabil was at the top of her form and the King George seemed to provide a marvellous opportunity for her to end her spring and summer campaign in a blaze of glory. She'd have started favourite. But her owner wouldn't commit Salsabil as a definite runner at Ascot. She was trained for the race, continued to show her well-being at home, and appeared among fifteen five-day acceptors. But, after postponing a final decision until

Hamdan Al-Maktoum's "Salsabil"

the overnight stage, Sheikh Hamdan pulled her out. The state of the Ascot going—which was on the firm side—reportedly played some part in the deliberations of the owner and his advisers. It was surprising that fears were evidently entertained about conditions being 'too firm for her'. Salsabil had won under similar conditions in the One Thousand Guineas and went on to do the same in the Vermeille. She never encountered very soft ground in her nine-race career. Salsabil's absence from the field for the King George—won by Belmez from the older horses Old Vic and Assatis—was one of the disappointments of the season. British racegoers never saw her again.

		Northern Dancer	Nearctic
	Sadler's Wells (USA)	(b 1961)	Natalma
	(b 1981)	Fairy Bridge	Bold Reason
Salsabil		(b 1975)	Special
(b.f. 1987)		Artaius	Round Table
	Flame of Tara	(b 1974)	Stylish Pattern
	(b 1980)	Welsh Flame	Welsh Pageant
		(b 1973)	Electric Flash

Salsabil is an attractive filly, though she is rather lightly made and of only around medium size. She is a quick-actioned, fluent mover. Salsabil's sire the Irish Two Thousand Guineas and Eclipse winner Sadler's Wells finished second to In The Groove's sire Night Shift in the list of the season's leading stallions in Britain—Batshoof, Braashee, Dolpour and French-trained In The Wings were other pattern-race winners for him. Sadler's Wells is a son of Northern Dancer, who had to be put down in 1990. Northern Dancer was one of the most successful stallions in history and any number of his sons have made the grade at stud—including Be My Guest, Danzig, El Gran Senor, Lyphard, Night Shift, Nijinsky, Northern Baby, Northfields, Nureyev, Storm Bird and The Minstrel, all of whom have sired major winners in Europe. Northern Dancer's influence became so strong that by the mid-'eighties his stud fee had risen to around 900,000 dollars; his yearlings dominated the market and by the time reduced fertility brought retirement in 1987 he had sired more than fifty yearlings that had made a million dollars or more at public auction and had around one hundred and twenty sons at stud. The Northern Dancer dynasty will be a dominant force for many years to come and Sadler's Wells looks sure to play a big part in keeping it to the fore. Like Sadler's Wells—sire of a dual classic winner in Old Vic with his first crop—Salsabil's dam the Coronation Stakes and Pretty Polly Stakes winner Flame of Tara has been in the limelight in the past couple of seasons. Her first foal Nearctic Flame, a full sister to Salsabil, won twice at around a mile and a quarter as a three-year-old and came third in the mile-and-a-half Ribblesdale Stakes at Royal Ascot. Salsabil is Flame of Tara's second foal and her third is the most exciting prospect Marju (by Last Tycoon) who became ante-post favourite for the Two Thousand Guineas after trotting up on his only start in a minor event at York. Flame of Tara's half-sister Fruition has also done well at stud, producing the Jockey Club Cup winners Kneller and Great Marquess, the former also successful in the Doncaster Cup. Salsabil's grandam Welsh Flame, a daughter of a half-sister to the Derby winner Parthia, was a useful racemare, a winner four times at around a mile as a three-year-old. Salsabil begins her stud career in 1991 by visiting Nashwan. The resulting progeny will have plenty to live up to! *J. L. Dunlop.*

SALUTING WALTER (USA) 2 b.c. (Feb 21) Verbatim (USA)–Stage Hour   **77 p** (USA) (Stage Director (USA)) [1990 6m4] half-brother to several winners, including Proudest Hour (by Proudest Roman), stakes winner at up to 1m: dam minor winner at 3 yrs: sire good winner at up to 1¼m: 5 lengths fourth of 14 to Volksraad in maiden at Newmarket in November: will improve, particularly over further. *M. J. Ryan.*

SALWAN (USA) 2 ch.c. (Mar 28) Sagace (FR) 135–Sedra 116 (Nebbiolo 125)   **67** [1990 7g6 7s6] 10,500Y: leggy, quite attractive colt: third foal: half-brother to 3-y-o 7f winner Sherjamal (by Raise A Native) and Irish 7f and 1m winner Topper Up (by Sharpen Up): dam 6f (at 2 yrs) to 1¼m winner: bit backward, quite modest form in maidens at Folkestone and Doncaster (unable to quicken last 2f behind Desert Sun) in autumn: will be better suited by 1m+: sold 11,500 gns Newmarket Autumn Sales. *W. Jarvis.*

SAMAIN (USA)   3 ch.f. Caerleon (USA) 132–Samarta Dancer (USA) (Marshua's   —
Dancer (USA)) [1989 NR 1990 8m⁵ 10m³ 12.5m] $225,000F, IR 195,000Y: tall, leggy,
sparely-made filly: fourth foal: half-sister to fair 1m and 10.1f winner Knighted
Dancer (by The Minstrel) and French 1m winner Bid Dancer (by Spectacular Bid):
dam, best at 4 yrs, won 9 races at up to 1m, including in stakes company: poor form
in minor events then maiden: seems not to stay 1½m. *M. R. Stoute.*

SAMSOLOM   2 b.g. (Apr 8) Absalom 128–Norfolk Serenade 83 (Blakeney 126)   77
[1990 5s⁴ 5m* 5m³ 5g 5g⁵ 5f 6d 5m* 5g⁵] 7,200F, 15,000Y: strong, good-quartered
gelding: has round action: third foal: dam 11.7f winner: modest performer: made all
at Warwick in early-season maiden and nursery in October: ran moderately most
other starts: should be as effective at 6f as 5f: visored sixth start: sometimes hangs
left. *J. A. Glover.*

SAMSON-AGONISTES   4 b.c. Bold Fort 100–Hello Cuddles 99 (He Loves Me   68
120) [1989 5.8m 5f⁵ 5m² 6m 5.1m 5m 5.8h 5g 7.6m⁵ 8m 1990 a5g⁴ 5m* 5m a5g³ 5m*
5m² 5g⁴ 5m] leggy colt: moderate walker and poor mover: modest handicapper: won
at Windsor (making all impressively) in August and Pontefract (apprentices and
better effort) in September: suited by 5f: acts on good to firm going: apprentice
ridden. *B. A. McMahon.*

SAMSOVA   3 b.f. Shareef Dancer (USA) 135–Deadly Serious (USA) 113 (Queen's   105
Hussar 124) [1989 7m³ 7m³ 1990 8v* 8m⁴ 8g* 8.5d² 8g⁶ 8g⁴ 8m⁵ 8m 8m² 8v]
workmanlike filly: useful performer: won maiden at Ayr in April and listed race at
Rome in May: very good second, coming from towards rear, to Fire The Groom in
listed race at Ascot penultimate start: well beaten in Group 3 race at Milan 6 weeks
later: worth a try at 1¼m: acts on heavy going. *I. A. Balding.*

SAM THE MAN   3 b.g. Aragon 118–First Temptation (USA) 67 (Mr Leader   55
(USA)) [1989 6f 1990 8m 8f 9m 7g 10d⁶ 7d² a10g a7g⁵] rather sparely-made gelding:
plating-class form in handicaps at Folkestone and Lingfield sixth and final (blinkered, made most) starts: stays 7f: acts on dead going. *Miss B. Sanders.*

SAMURAI GOLD (USA)   2 b.c. (Mar 8) Golden Act (USA)–Taipan's Lady   83
(USA) (Bold Hour) [1990 5m⁵ 6f² 6m⁴ 6m⁴ 6d*] $14,500F, $37,000Y: rather leggy,
unfurnished colt: half-brother to 5 minor winners in North America: dam minor
winner at around 1m: sire top class at up to 13f: fair performer: favourite, made all in
17-runner maiden at Folkestone in November, beating Prince of The Sea by 5
lengths: will probably stay 7f: acts on firm and dead ground: blinkered final 4 starts:
races keenly: looked none too genuine third outing. *D. R. C. Elsworth.*

SANAWI   3 b.c. Glenstal (USA) 118–Russeting 76 (Mummy's Pet 125) [1989 6m⁴   62
5m⁵ 6m⁵ a6g 1990 a6g² a6g⁵ 6g 7f⁶ 8f* 7f* 7g 7m⁴ 8m³ 8m 8f 7m⁶ 8m⁶ 7g] strong,
attractive colt: has a round action: quite modest handicapper: led inside final 1f when
twice successful at Salisbury in May: well below form last 4 starts: will prove better
at 1m than 7f: goes well on firm ground: sold to join N. Twiston-Davies 8,000 gns
Ascot October Sales, and won selling hurdle. *C. J. Benstead.*

SAND CASTLE   9 ch.g. Tap On Wood 130–Pacific Sands (Sandford Lad 133)   46
[1989 10m⁶ 12f⁶ 12.4m⁴ 1990 10f² 10f⁴] compact, well-made gelding: poor handicapper: better suited by 1½m than 1¼m: acts on any going: used to wear blinkers:
band- aged at 9 yrs: suitable mount for inexperienced rider: winning hurdler/chaser.
M. J. Ryan.

SAND DAISY   3 b.f. Precocious 126–San Marguerite 80 (Blakeney 126) [1989 NR   —
1990 7m 8g⁵ 9g⁶ 10g 10m⁵ 10.2g 10.6v 10dj unfurnished filly: fifth foal: sister to
4-y-o Spanish Love and half-sister to Andartis (by Final Straw), useful 5f and 7f
winner as a 2-y-o in 1985 but later disappointing: dam, 1¼m winner, is half-sister to
St Leger second Zilos: little worthwhile form in varied events. *T. Thomson Jones.*

SANDFORD SPRINGS (USA)   3 b.f. Robellino (USA) 127–Tiger Scout   52
(USA) 86 (Silent Screen (USA)) [1989 6g 7f⁵ 1990 10g 14g 11.7m a12g⁵ 13.8m³ 11.7h²
11.7h* 12m⁵ 17.1m] good-bodied filly: plating-class performer: favourite, won
4-runner claimer (claimed out of I. Balding's stable £12,265) at Bath in August very
easily: seems to stay 13.8f: acts on hard going: blinkered (led 1m) fourth start,
visored last 5: bandaged final one. *J. D. Roberts.*

SANDHURST GODDESS   4 ch.f. Sandhurst Prince 128–Paradise Bird 94   103
(Sallust 134) [1989 7v² 8m 9g 7m⁴ 7f² 7.5m³ 7m² 7m* 7g* 8d⁵ 7d⁴ 6g* 7d 1990 6m²
6g⁵ 5m* 6m⁴ 6g 5g⁴ 6m⁵ 6g⁵ 5g 6g 7d] sturdy, angular filly: third living foal: sister
to Irish 7.9f to 9f winner Paradise Princess: dam 2-y-o 6f winner: won listed event at
Phoenix Park in May by 3 lengths from Duck And Dive, making all: always outpaced
in Group 3 race at Royal Ascot fifth outing, ran well in Tipperary listed contest on

next: best runs at 5f: occasionally blinkered, including final outing: useful at her best. *N. O'Callaghan, Ireland.*

SANDHURST TYPE (IRE) 2 ch.f. (Apr 22) Sandhurst Prince 128–Double   **48**
Type (Behistoun 131) [1990 6m⁵ 6g 6g² 7g⁴ 6f⁵ 6f⁵ 6m] 400Y: angular, sparely-made filly: has a round action: half-sister to middle-distance stayer Tender Type (by Prince Tenderfoot) and winners in Italy and France: dam unraced granddaughter of Meld: poor maiden: best effort penultimate start, despite hanging left: appears to stay 7f. *M. P. F. Murphy.*

SANDICLIFFE STAR 4 b.c. High Top 131–Georgina Park 88 (Silly Season   **88**
127) [1989 8.5g* 8.2g 8f* 8m⁴ 8.2d 1990 a10g*] workmanlike colt: has a rather round action: favourite, made all at Lingfield in February: stays 1¼m: acts on firm going. *B. W. Hills.*

SANDICLIFFE WAY (IRE) 2 ch.c. (Feb 15) Doulab (USA) 115–Plainsong   **81**
(FR) (Amen (FR)) [1990 5f⁵ 7g⁶ 6g³ 6f 8m 8.2d* a8g³] IR 10,000F, IR 15,000Y, resold 20,000Y: medium-sized, lengthy colt: half-brother to a winner in Italy: dam French 1½m winner, is half-sister to good-class 1979 French 2-y-o 7f and 7.5f winner Viteric and from family of Grey Dawn II: looked tremendously well when showing vastly improved form to win 20-runner nursery at Nottingham in October going away by 3 lengths from Tate Affair: respectable third in nursery at Lingfield after: will be suited by 1¼m: well suited by dead ground: not the easiest of rides. *B. W. Hills.*

SANDITTON PALACE 7 gr.g. Dragonara Palace (USA) 115–Petona (Mummy's   — §
Pet 125) [1989 5g 6f* 6f 6f⁵ 6m 6m⁴ 6g² 6m 7g 6m⁶ 1990 6s 6m⁶ 6g 6g a6g] tall gelding: carries plenty of condition: quite modest handicapper on his day: little form in first half of 1990: effective at 5f and 6f: unsuited by soft going, acts on any other: visored once: needs strong handling: trained until third outing by P. Felgate: has looked reluctant (definitely so when blinkered final start) and is unreliable. *J. Berry.*

SANDMOOR COTTON 4 b.c. Sayf El Arab (USA) 127–Dog's Bay (Tumble   **53**
Wind (USA)) [1989 5g⁵ 5s⁶ 5d⁵ 5f 6m 6m 6f 1990 5m⁶ 5m 6s⁵ 6f 6m 6m 6m³ 8f⁶] neat, good-quartered colt: plating-class handicapper on his day: stays 6f: probably acts on any going: blinkered 3 times at 4 yrs: sold 2,000 gns Doncaster August Sales: inconsistent. *G. M. Moore.*

SANDMOOR DENIM 3 b.g. Red Sunset 120–Holernzaye 93 (Sallust 134)   **54**
[1989 6g² 6h² 6m 5m a6g 1990 6f 7.5d⁵ a11g⁴ 8.5d* 8g a8g² a6g a7g 8m 8.5m 8m] close-coupled gelding: plating-class performer: won handicap at Beverley in June by short head, rallying well: below form last 5 starts: stays 1m well: acts on dead ground: blinkered twice at 2 yrs. *S. R. Bowring.*

SANDMOOR JACQUARD 3 ch.c. Noalto 120–Grand Opera 92 (Great Nephew   **55**
126) [1989 5d⁴ 6m 5f³ 7g 6g⁵ 7m⁵ 7f² 6g* 6g³ 7m 6g 1990 7m 7h 7d* 8m³ 7m² 8g 7f³dis 7d⁵] workmanlike, short-backed colt: plating-class handicapper: seems to go well at Catterick, winning in July: stays 1m: acts on firm and dead going: sometimes blinkered: lazy type, suited by strong handling. *M. H. Easterby.*

SANDSUMO 3 ch.g. Sandhurst Prince 128–Mursuma (Rarity 129) [1989 5m 6m   **37**
7m 5m 6f 1990 a8g 10d 8.3m 8.2m⁵] leggy, lengthy gelding: moderate mover: poor maiden: stays 1m: blinkered (ran well) final start. *M. H. Tompkins.*

SANDY STORM 3 ch.g. Lomond (USA) 128–Holly Deb (USA) (Xoda (USA))   —
[1989 NR 1990 a8g a10g 7g a5g a7g a8g⁶] 24,000F, 5,400Y: smallish, good-bodied gelding: second foal: half-brother to 1988 2-y-o sprint plater Ace Trouper (by Superlative): dam, 6f winner in USA, is half-sister to smart miler Top Socialite: little sign of ability: blinkered last 3 outings. *C. N. Williams.*

SANGLAMORE (USA) 3 ch.c. Sharpen Up 127–Ballinderry 112 (Irish   **126**
River (FR) 131) [1989 8g² 1990 10g* 10m² 10.5g* 12m*]
Old Vic, then Sanglamore: a second British-trained winner of the Prix du Jockey-Club Lancia came hot on the heels of the first. Their victories couldn't have been gained in more contrasting style, though each was most striking in its own way. Old Vic had been awe-inspiring in his display of front-running, quickening away on the final turn, whereas at the same point in the 1990 running Sanglamore was last of all, eleven in front of him. Sanglamore had taken a keen hold early on and was still travelling very strongly, but the next three furlongs would present a stern test of Sanglamore's ability to quicken and of his stamina to sustain his effort over a distance he'd never tried previously. And it looked a strong field before him: all bar the pacemaker

Mahshari had won earlier in the season; eight in the field on their previous starts; the same number were pattern or listed race winners; and three—in betting order Epervier Bleu, Theatrical Charmer and Roi de Rome—were unbeaten. It was the even-money favourite Epervier Bleu whom Eddery on Sanglamore tracked initially off the turn but as both horses improved their positions Sanglamore lost a couple of lengths looking for a way between the Derrinstown Stud Derby Trial winner Anvari and Roi de Rome (there was subsequently a stewards inquiry). Epervier Bleu, who'd had no such problems, wrenched the lead from the Hocquart winner Top Waltz approaching the final furlong but Sanglamore was now in full cry behind him, Eddery riding a typically forthright finish and getting a most willing response; the stamina doubts which had so influenced his tactics were quashed at the end of a truly-run race as Sanglamore stuck his neck out and got to Epervier Bleu in the last hundred yards to win by half a length. Erdelistan produced a renewed effort to finish the same distance back in third.

Sanglamore's triumph was the start of a near Derby-treble for Tree's successor at Beckhampton Roger Charlton, Quest For Fame winning at Epsom three days later and Deploy beating all but Salsabil at the Curragh. Racing is a game of swings and roundabouts, however, and that Irish run was the last we saw of any of the three. Sanglamore couldn't be worked properly at home because of the firm ground and suffered a number of 'niggling rather than serious' injuries. He and Quest For Fame underwent extensive tests at the Animal Health Trust to assess their injuries and to analyse, as far as was possible, whether they'd stand training as four-year-olds—particular attention in Sanglamore's case apparently being paid to his large feet—before it was announced that both would reappear in 1991. So Sanglamore didn't have the opportunity to progress, like for instance Epervier Bleu, in the second half of the season. He'd done so, relentlessly, up until the French Derby. Having failed to win a maiden on his one outing at two years, Sanglamore comfortably took a Leicester minor event on his reappearance before losing out to Anvari in the £7,400 May Stakes at Newmarket. Eddery apparently thought he'd

William Hill Dante Stakes, York —
the staying-on Sanglamore wins from Karinga Bay and Anshan

gone on too soon—entering the Dip—at Newmarket. Sanglamore's next stop, the William Hill Dante Stakes at York, saw a very different race altogether. Anshan was the only one of the seven runners to have graduated successfully to pattern company already—Raj Waki having disappointed in the Guineas, Karinga Bay having been well held in the Guardian Classic Trial—and was made an even-money chance, with Sanglamore the 11/2 second choice. Harried by Karinga Bay, Anshan had to set a very strong early pace to carry out his customary front-running tactics then was headed by Karinga Bay two and a half furlongs out and by Sanglamore approaching the last furlong. Separated by the width of over half the track initially (Karinga Bay had hung towards the stand side when his bit slipped), both principals stayed on strongly in a driving finish, Sanglamore the stronger to win by a length and a half.

	Sharpen Up (ch 1969)	Atan (ch 1961)	Native Dancer Mixed Marriage
		Rocchetta (ch 1961)	Rockefella Chambiges
Sanglamore (USA) (ch.c. 1987)			
	Ballinderry (ch 1981)	Irish River (ch 1976)	Riverman Irish Star
		Miss Manon (b 1970)	Bon Mot III Miss Molly

By a once-raced stallion standing at 100 guineas out of a disappointing maiden, Sanglamore's sire Sharpen Up is one of the sport's great success stories. After showing high-class form on the racecourse, he quickly established an even higher status at stud, so glaring that he was bought out of England to stand at Gainesway Farm, Kentucky. Sharpen Up was retired from stud duties in 1989 after getting just two mares in foal—Sanglamore is from his last full crop—but in Kris and Diesis he has established stallion sons to carry on the good work. For one who ended his racing career in the Nunthorpe Stakes, Sharpen Up has surprised with the effectiveness of some of his best progeny at a mile and a half (Pebbles, Trempolino and now Sanglamore). One of the first to illustrate Sharpen Up's stamina potential was Sanglamore's close relation Sharpman, a half-brother to Sanglamore's dam Ballinderry, who was second in the Poulains and Lupin then third in the Prix du Jockey-Club in which he suffered a career-ending injury. Miss Manon, the dam of Ballinderry and Sharpman, was fourth in Allez France's Prix de Diane; she has been barren as often as not but every foal she has produced has made an impact: following Sharpman came the Prix Hocquart winner Mot d'Or, the Gran Premio di Milano and Grosser Preis von Berlin winner Lydian, Ballinderry, the French listed winner Miss Summer and the very useful four-year-old handicapper Pride of Araby. Ballinderry didn't let the side down on the racecourse either, winning the Ribblesdale and reaching the frame in the Yorkshire Oaks and Vermeille. She slipped a foal by Mr Prospector to her first covering then, after Sanglamore, produced the as-yet unraced Balliasta (by Lyphard), a colt by Alydar and a filly by Lyphard. She visited Nureyev in 1990.

Prix du Jockey-Club Lancia, Chantilly—
Sanglamore shows acceleration and resolution after none too clear a run;
Epervier Bleu (centre) is second, strong-finishing Erdelistan (noseband) third
and Top Waltz (rails) fourth

Mr K. Abdulla's "Sanglamore"

Physically as well as from a form point of view, Sanglamore progressed noticeably well through his races in 1990; he's a good-topped colt with scope who carries plenty of condition. He's also a good walker and mover. One and a half miles suits Sanglamore well and he acts on good to firm ground. Incidentally, our representative at Chantilly was confident that the rain on French Derby day did not affect the good to firm ground significantly, and the time (only six tenths of a second outside Bering's course record) supports this view. *R. Charlton.*

SAN GRECO 3 b.g. Mandrake Major 122–Rich Lass (Broxted 120) [1989 6f³ 7g² 1990 7g] quite attractive, close-coupled gelding: modest maiden: favourite on first run for over 14 months, ran poorly only start in 1990: hung left final one at 2 yrs. *J. W. Watts.* —

SAN PIER NICETO 3 b.c. Norwick (USA) 120–Langton Herring (Nearly A Hand 115) [1989 7m⁶ 7g³ 6m a8g* a8g* a7g² 1990 8g⁴ 7.5d⁴ 10g⁴ 8g³ 8g 9f* 7f² 9s³ 10v] smallish, lengthy colt: moderate walker and mover: modest handicapper: 2/1 on, easy winner of 5-runner claimer at Hamilton in July: should stay 1¼m: acts on any going, with possible exception of heavy: inconsistent: not easiest of rides: trained until after seventh start by R. Boss: winning hurdler. *M. D. Hammond.* 72

SAN ROQUE 5 b.g. Aragon 118–Arch Sculptress 85 (Arch Sculptor 123) [1989 10s⁵ 8f 9.2f⁵ 8.2f 8m* 8.2g³ 8m⁴ 8m⁵ 10.2f* 10.6m 1990 10f 12g 10g 10m* 10.2f⁴ 10m 11m⁵ 10f 8f³ 10f⁴ 8g] sturdy, close-coupled gelding: moderate walker: has a quick action: plating-class handicapper: returned to form when winning apprentice race at Lingfield in June, leading post: ran creditably when in frame at Brighton (selling event first time) in autumn: effective at 1m and 1¼m: acts on firm going, unsuited by soft surface: has worn blinkers and visor, including last 5 starts: has looked a difficult ride: sold to join D. Wilson's stable 3,000 gns Newmarket Autumn Sales. *D. A. Wilson.* 56

SANS FRAIS   2 b.f. (Mar 21) Forzando 122–Shere Beauty 83 (Mummy's Pet 125)   **50**
[1990 5m³ 5m 6h³ 6f⁵ 5.3h⁵ 6m² 6g 6d 6m 5s³ a6g⁶] lengthy, sparely-made filly:
sixth foal: half-sister to untrustworthy 1m winner Colombiere (by Sallust): dam
2-y-o 5f winner became very temperamental: inconsistent plater: stays 6f: acts on
top-of-the-ground and soft: blinkered sixth outing: often finds little off bridle:
retained by trainer 1,400 gns Newmarket Autumn Sales. *R. J. R. Williams.*

SANTELLA BOBKES (USA)   5 b.h. Solford (USA) 127–Ambiente (USA)   —
(Tentam (USA)) [1989 12m 20f² 19f⁵ 18m⁴ 1990 16.2m] good-topped horse: fair
winner as 4-y-o: unable to dominate and ran moderately at Goodwood in May: suited
by extreme distances: acts on any going: blinkered last 4 outings: has won for
amateur: suited by forcing tactics: useful but inconsistent hurdler: sold to join J.
Birkett's stable 6,000 gns Ascot July Sales. *G. Harwood.*

SANTELLA PAL (USA)   9 b.g. Effervescing (USA)–Hempens Pal (USA)   —
(Hempen) [1989 12f 1990 10.2f 10.1g] workmanlike gelding: has been operated on for
wind infirmity: very lightly raced nowadays: stays 1½m: acts on hard and dead
going: suitable mount for inexperienced rider. *D. R. C. Elsworth.*

SAO PAULO (USA)   4 ch.c. El Gran Senor (USA) 136–Millingdale Lillie 119   **72**
(Tumble Wind (USA)) [1989 10g⁶ 10f² 10g² 10.2g⁵ 10.4m² 9.2m⁴ a12g⁴ a10g⁴ 1990 8f
10m 10m 10.1m² 10f* a12g 8f 10f 12m 12g⁴ 10g⁴ 10d* a12g³] rangy colt: has been
tubed: poor mover: successful in plating company at Folkestone in July (handicap,
bought in 7,200 gns) and November (no bid): stays 1½m: acts on firm and dead
going: below form for lady rider seventh outing: usually sweats and gets on edge:
has worn tongue strap: has found little off bridle. *C. N. Allen.*

SAPIEHA (IRE)   2 b.c. (Mar 26) Petorius 117–Sugarbird 82 (Star Appeal **115** p
133) [1990 6m⁵ 7m* 7.3g*]

First-season trainer James Fanshawe, previously assistant to Michael
Stoute, had his two-year-olds in great form in the autumn, and must be hopeful that Radwell and the Vodafone Horris Hill winner Sapieha in particular
among his colts can keep up the good work in the coming season. There isn't a
great deal to choose on form between the two—Radwell and Sapieha both won
a pattern race—but Sapieha, a good-bodied colt with plenty of scope, and
blessed with a particularly effective turn of foot, looks the better bet to
consolidate his progress. He is overpriced at 40/1 for the Two Thousand
Guineas at the time of writing.

Sapieha's season began at Newmarket in August. After a pipe-opener in
a six-furlong maiden when he wasn't fully wound up, Sapieha wasn't seen out
again until starting at 16/1 for a division of the Westley Stakes, over seven
furlongs of the Rowley Mile, in October. In a field of mostly newcomers
Sapieha's previous experience was put to good advantage: smartly away, then
steadying the pace, he had all his rivals in trouble when quickening under
three furlongs out and came home three and a half lengths to the good to
complete a double for his trainer following Environment Friend's success in
the other division earlier in the afternoon. Sapieha was one of the more
interesting runners in the Horris Hill at Newbury later in the month. It may
have looked a moderately-contested edition beforehand—none of the nine
runners had shown form approaching the level usually required to win, and
several looked exposed as just fairly useful sorts—but Sapieha had made such
progress since Newmarket that it was clear from early in the straight he was
easily the best horse in the field. Always travelling smoothly in sight of the
pace-setting Grove Aries, he responded immediately when asked to quicken
at the distance, drawing three or four lengths clear by the furlong pole, and
although he didn't increase his advantage through the final hundred yards he
was never in trouble and had four lengths and a neck to spare over the
Haydock winner Red Rainbow and the Gimcrack fourth Regal Sabre at the
post. The Horris Hill, often run on soft ground, has a patchy record as a guide
to future pattern-race form, but Sapieha was a mightily impressive winner:
the field overall, and Sapieha in particular, looked in tremendous condition,
the runners were well strung out and there could be no excuses on the score
of the ground.

Sapieha, who was bought at the Irish National Yearling Sales for 55,000
guineas, is a son of the good sprinter Petorius and first foal of the fair
two-year-old five-furlong winner Sugarbird. Most immediate members of the
family, who include Sugarbird's half-brother Cremation, a useful winner from

		Mummy's Pet	Sing Sing
	Petorius	(b 1968)	Money For Nothing
	(b 1981)	The Stork	Club House
Sapieha (IRE)		(b 1976)	Cryhelp
(b.c. Mar 26, 1988)		Star Appeal	Appiani II
	Sugarbird	(b 1970)	Sterna
	(ch 1983)	Sacred Ibis	Red God
		(b 1972)	The Veil

five furlongs to a mile, her half-sister Syboris, a fairly useful sprinting two-year-old in 1980, and, further back, such as the very useful 1969 two-year-old Red Velvet, a full sister to Sapieha's grandam Sacred Ibis, have had speed rather than stamina as their strong suit, and judged on his running at Newmarket and Newbury we should imagine that Sapieha, a good walker but less impressive in his faster paces, will be at his best at up to a mile. He has yet to encounter other than good or good to firm ground. *J. R. Fanshawe.*

SAPIENCE   4 ch.c. Niniski (USA) 125–Claretta (USA) 82 (Roberto (USA) 131) **117**
[1989 12m² 12f 14f* 14.6s² 16g² 15.5g6 1990 8m² 14g² 12m* 12m] leggy, rather angular colt: smart performer: well ridden (dictated pace) to win Princess of Wales's Stakes at Newmarket in July by ¾ length from Charmer: travelling best 3f out when ¾-length second to Braashee in Kosset Yorkshire Cup at York: looking really well, well beaten in King George VI and Queen Elizabeth Diamond Stakes at Ascot, and wasn't seen out again: will prove best at up to 1¾m: acts on any going: game and genuine: a credit to his trainer. *J. G. FitzGerald.*

SAPPHIRINE   3 b.f. Trojan Fen 118–By Surprise 68 (Young Generation 129)   **64**
[1989 NR 1990 a8g² a7g* 7g³ 8d* 7.5f² 8f* 8h³ 9f6 9f] IR 8,000Y: lengthy filly: first foal: dam 1m winner from family of Little Wolf: won maiden at Lingfield in February and claimers at Edinburgh and Pontefract in July: stays 1m: acts on hard and dead ground: blinkered final start: sold to join R. Whitaker 12,000 gns Newmarket Autumn Sales. *Sir Mark Prescott.*

SAPPHO COMET   4 b.c. Habitat 134–Sunbittern 112 (Sea Hawk II 131) [1989 8m   **91**
7.3m² 7f* 8f³ 7g a7g* 1990 a8g³ a8g* 8.2m 8m5 8f 10m5 8g] good-quartered, quite attractive colt: good walker: has a quick, rather round action: made all in 3-runner handicap at Southwell in January: ran poorly fifth (blinkered and edgy) and sixth outings, then off course 3 months and pulled up after breaking blood vessel on return: stays 1m: acts on firm going: sold 12,000 gns Newmarket Autumn Sales: rather moody. *J. L. Dunlop.*

SARABAH (IRE)   2 b.f. (Feb 21) Ela-Mana-Mou 132–Be Discreet (Junius (USA)   **66** p
124) [1990 6m6] IR 42,000F: first foal: dam, winner of 5 races at up to 7f in France, is half-sister to useful French 3-y-o 1m and 1¼m winner Theatre Critic: around 9 lengths sixth of 9, unable to quicken over 2f out and not knocked about unduly, to Shihama in maiden at Newmarket in November: should improve. *G. Harwood.*

SARAFIA   3 gr.f. Dalsaan 125–Safaya (FR) (Zeddaan 130) [1989 NR 1990 8f6 7d*   **91**
7d² 7d5] compact filly: fifth foal: closely related to smart French 7f and 1m winner Safita (by Habitat) and half-sister to useful French 5f winner Shayina (by Run The Gantlet): dam won twice at 5f at 2 yrs in France: won maiden at Lingfield in October: fairly useful efforts when headed post in £9,600 handicap at Redcar then fifth of 17 to The Caretaker in listed race at Leopardstown: will stay 1m. *L. M. Cumani.*

Princess of Wales's Stakes, Newmarket—
Sapience gets a fine tactical ride from Eddery in a slowly-run affair;
Charmer (centre) proves the only danger

SARAH CARTER 3 b.f. Reesh 117–Second Swallow 55 (My Swallow 134) [1989 —
5s* 6f³ 6f⁵ 5m a6g⁶ 1990 5s 5m 6g⁶ 9f 8.2v] leggy filly: fair plater at 2 yrs: behind in
non-selling handicaps then claimer (pulled hard) in 1990: stays 6f: blinkered, slowly
away and tended to hang second start: sold out of R. Stubbs's stable 2,000 gns
Newmarket July Sales after third. *A. P. James.*

SARAH'S INFLUENCE 4 b.g. Orchestra 118–Markon (On Your Mark 125) —
[1989 9v 9v² 6v 9f³ 7f⁵ 1990 10.6d a6g a11g] workmanlike ex-Irish gelding: brother
to useful 1984 Irish 2-y-o 7f winner Stramar and half-brother to 7f to 1m winner One
To Mark (by He Loves Me): dam unraced daughter of half-sister to Humble Duty:
placed in first half of 1989 in maiden at Tipperary and handicap at Mallow: no show in
claimers in Britain: stays 9f: acts on any going: wore martingale final start. *D. R.
Gandolfo.*

SARAPOSA (IRE) 2 ch.f. (May 28) Ahonoora 122–Safita 117 (Habitat 134) [1990 66 p
6g] lengthy, rather angular filly: sixth foal: half-sister to 5 winners, including smart
6f to 8.2f winner Safawan (by Young Generation) and useful 7f to 9f winner Sadapour
(by Auction Ring): dam smart at up to 1¼m in France: well backed, around 5 lengths
eighth of 17, ridden at halfway and keeping on, to West Riding in maiden at Newbury
in October: will improve, particularly at 7f + . *M. R. Stoute.*

SARATIN (USA) 2 ch.c. (Mar 22) Saratoga Six (USA)–Caline (USA) (Ack Ack 54
(USA)) [1990 8m⁶ 10.2s] $100,000Y: angular, rather unfurnished colt: has scope:
brother to a minor winner in USA and half-brother to minor stakes winner Shaugh-
nessy Road (by Irish River): dam won 6 races, including graded events at 7f and 8.5f:
plating-class form in minor events at Newmarket (not knocked about) and Doncaster in November: sold 10,500 gns Doncaster November Sales. *A. A. Scott.*

SARCITA 2 b.f. (Feb 20) Primo Dominie 121–Zinzi (Song 132) [1990 5g⁴ 5g² 5g⁵ 80 +
5m 6d*] 12,500Y: small, lengthy, good-topped filly: first foal: dam Irish 5f winner at
4 yrs, is from family of Kind of Hush and Sauceboat: improved filly: co-favourite,
won 17-runner nursery at Folkestone in November by 5 lengths, clear, from
Kalabridge: ran very well for inexperienced apprentice time before: better suited by
6f than 5f: acts on good to firm ground and dead: trained first 3 starts by J. Payne. *D.
R. C. Elsworth.*

SARDARMATI (FR) 2 b.c. (Apr 24) Lashkari 128–Shapaara 65 (Rheingold 137) 107
[1990 9g* 9s⁴] fifth foal: half-brother to 2 middle-distance winners in France,
including Shamirana (by Darshaan): dam in frame at 1½m, is half-sister to Shergar:
won 20-runner newcomers race at Evry in October by 2½ lengths: 2 lengths fourth
of 9 to Subotica in listed event there following month: will stay 1½m: potentially
very useful. *A. de Royer-Dupre, France.*

SARDEGNA 3 b.f. Pharly (FR) 130–Sandy Island 110 (Mill Reef (USA) 141) [1989 111
7g* 1990 10m* 10.5m² 12s] rangy, rather angular filly: has a round action: won
Crawley Warren Pretty Polly Stakes at Newmarket, taking keen hold and
quickening well from rear: 1½ lengths second to In The Groove in Tattersalls
Musidora Stakes at York, outpaced and hanging right over 2f out then staying on
well: well-backed favourite, remote last of 8 in St Simon Stakes at Newbury over 5
months later: should stay 1½m. *H. R. A. Cecil.*

SAREEN EXPRESS (IRE) 2 gr.c. (Apr 5) Siberian Express (USA) 125–Three —
Waves (Cure The Blues (USA)) [1990 5m 5m a6g 6m] IR 850Y: lengthy, plain colt:
first foal: dam half-sister to smart French 1987 2-y-o Harmless Albatross: well
beaten, including in sellers: blinkered final start. *K. G. Wingrove.*

SARHAN 4 ch.c. Ahonoora 122–Rosserk (Roan Rocket 128) [1989 8m⁴ 8.5f³ 7f 37
6f⁵ 6f⁶ 8g 6m 6f 6g⁴ a6g² 1990 a7g a7g 7d a5g 7m⁵] rangy colt: modest maiden at
best: backed at long odds, showed signs of retaining a little ability final outing:
unlikely to stay beyond 1m: acts on firm going: visored twice, blinkered once at 3
yrs: needs strong handling: trained until after fourth start by G. Blum: sold 9,200
gns Doncaster November Sales. *J. Pearce.*

SARIAH 2 ch.f. (Feb 26) Kris 135–Nouvelle Star (AUS) (Luskin Star (AUS)) [1990 87 p
6d²] rather leggy, unfurnished filly: second foal: dam won from 5f to 8.2f in Australia
and was champion older filly at 4 yrs: length second of 21, clear, to Fateful in maiden
at Doncaster in November, running on strongly near line: sure to improve, and win a
similar event at 7f or 1m. *Major W. R. Hern.*

SARNIA SOUND 5 ch.g. Music Boy 124–St Pauli Girl 114 (St Paddy 133) [1989 —
8g 10d⁴ 10f³ 10m 10.1m² 10g⁶ 13f³ 1990 a8g 11s] lengthy, angular gelding: has a quick
action: poor maiden: stays 13f: acts on firm and dead going: sometimes blinkered,
visored final outing: sweated last 2 starts at 4 yrs: has looked a difficult ride:
winning claiming hurdler in April: sold 1,350 gns Doncaster August Sales. *Mrs P. A.
Barker.*

Lord Howard de Walden's "Sardegna"

SARSAPARILLA (FR) 3 br.f. Shirley Heights 130 Sassika (GER) (Arratos **60**
(FR)) [1989 NR 1990 12f5 17.6m3 15d 16g] lengthy, angular filly: fourth known foal:
half-sister to fair 11f winner Harmonical (by Lyphard's Wish): dam, from good
German family, won in Germany: quite modest form in maidens: tailed off facing stiff
task in minor event then well beaten (took keen hold in blinkers) in handicap last 2
outings: sold 5,000 gns Newmarket December Sales. *J. W. Watts.*

SARSTA GRAI 2 b.f. (Apr 21) Blakeney 126–Horton Line 89 (High Line 125) **55**
[1990 5f 5g 6g3 7d4 7f 7m 8v a8g*] 1,600Y: workmanlike filly, second foal: dam 1½m
winner: plating-class performer: won 18-runner claimer at Southwell late in year by
1½ lengths: suited by 1m: unsuited by heavy going. *R. Earnshaw.*

SARUM 4 b.g. Tina's Pet 121–Contessa (HUN) (Peleid 125) [1989 6m* 5.8m 6f **56** d
6m5 a8g4 a7g6 a6g2 1990 a6g a6g* a6g6 a6g 6f 6f 7f 6g a6g a7g] tall, leggy, rather
narrow gelding: poor mover: poor handicapper: won at Lingfield in February: below
form after, off course over 4 months before ninth outing: effective at 6f and stays
1m: acts on good to firm going. *C. P. Wildman.*

SARYAN 7 b.g. Try My Best (USA) 130–High Fidelyty (FR) (Hautain 128) [1989 **67**
NR 1990 11.1m* 14m 11.7m 14g2 15.5f* 12m 16s] good-bodied gelding: quite modest
handicapper: successful at Kempton (landing gamble on first outing on flat since 3
yrs) in May and Folkestone (making all) in September: stays 2m: acts on firm going,
seems unsuited by soft: has run moderately in blinkers and for amateur: winning
hurdler in December. *B. J. Curley.*

SASAKI 3 b.c. Sadler's Wells (USA) 132–Sairshea (Simbir 130) [1989 7f* 1990 **102**
10m3 10.5g* 12m6] tall, quite attractive colt: impresses in appearance: useful per-

former: 11/8 on, won 4-runner minor event at York in May: travelled well long way when 6¾ lengths sixth of 8 to Private Tender in King Edward VII Stakes at Royal Ascot over 4 weeks later: may prove best at 1¼m: acts on firm going: found nothing and finished very tired on reappearance, and had tongue tied down afterwards. *M. R. Stoute.*

SASHTAL   3 ch.c. Ballacashtal (CAN)–Salala 83 (Connaught 130) [1989 7f² 7g   **70** 1990 6g⁵ 8f³ 7m a8g3³] strong, sturdy colt: quite modest maiden, not seen out after May: should stay beyond 1m: acts on firm going. *B. Hanbury.*

SASSY LASSY (IRE)   2 b.f. (Apr 21) Taufan (USA) 119–Miss Reasoning (USA)   **70 p** (Bold Reasoning (USA)) [1990 6g⁴] 16,000F, 56,000Y: leggy, close-coupled filly: eighth foal: half-sister to several winners, including 6f (at 2 yrs) and 1½m winner Realism (by Known Fact) and modest stayer Guessing (by Be My Guest): dam French sprint winner out of Poule d'Essai des Pouliches winner Pampered Miss: 3 lengths fourth of 17, staying on, to West Riding in maiden at Newbury in October: will improve. *W. Hastings-Bass.*

SATALITE BOY   2 ch.c. (May 2) Blazing Saddles (AUS)–Persiandale (Persian   **74** Bold 123) [1990 5f* 5f² 5m* 6g⁴ 5m⁴] 6,400Y: leggy, quite good-topped colt: has scope: quite good mover: first foal: dam unraced: successful in auction races at Ripon in April and Newmarket in May: modest fourth of 6 to Ayr Classic in minor event at York: sent to race in Italy, and finished 8 lengths fourth to Sir Basil in listed race at Milan in June. *J. Etherington.*

SATANIC DANCE (FR)   2 b.f. (Apr 30) Shareef Dancer (USA) 135–Satanella   **72** (GER) (Pentathlon) [1990 7m³ 6g⁵ 8g] rangy, useful-looking filly: ninth foal: half-sister to 2 pattern-placed winners in Germany and very useful 3-y-o Satin Wood (by Darshaan), successful at 7f (at 2 yrs) and 1¼m: dam, from good German family, won over 1¼m from 3 starts: around 4 lengths fifth of 26 to Zonda in maiden at Newbury, second and best effort: out of depth final start: should stay 1m. *C. E. Brittain.*

SATANIC PRINCE (IRE)   2 b.c. (Feb 6) Anita's Prince 126–Lady Ingrid (Tau-   **33** fan (USA) 119) [1990 5m 5m⁵ 5d 5g 6g 5f] 2,700Y: leggy colt, rather unfurnished: good whacker: first foal: dam unraced from family of Sparkler: poor plater: blinkered final start: sold 750 gns Doncaster August Sales. *C. Tinkler.*

SATIN LAKE (USA)   3 b.f. Well Decorated (USA)–Bunny Lake (Northern Baby   **57** (CAN) 127) [1989 6f⁴ 7f⁵ 7g 1990 8.2g 9s 8.5d 12m⁴ a11g³ a12g* a14g³ a11g⁵ a14g⁵ a12g⁶ a12g a14g⁵ a16g a12g²] smallish, workmanlike filly: plating-class handicapper: won at Southwell in July by 10 lengths: stays 1½m: acts on good to firm ground: blinkered fourth and twelfth outings: visored (well below form) final one. *S. G. Norton.*

SATIN LOVER   2 ch.g. (Feb 3) Tina's Pet 121–Canoodle 66 (Warpath 113) [1990   **—** 6m] 2,200F, 2,700 2-y-o: workmanlike gelding: fourth foal: half-brother to 1½m and 13f winner Pathero (by Godswalk) and a winner in Norway by Tender King: dam won from 1½m to 2m: burly, slowly away and virtually pulled up after 1f in seller at Lingfield. *A. R. Davison.*

SATIN POINTE   2 b.f. (Mar 26) Sadler's Wells (USA) 132–Jalapa (FR) 117 **110** (Luthier 126) [1990 7g** 8g³] eighth living foal: closely related to fair 9f winner Cairo Bay (by Lyphard) and half-sister to 3-y-o Princess Lucy (by Local Suitor) and several winners here and abroad, including useful 1¼m and 1½m winner Bahoor (by L'Enjoleur): dam smart at around 1¼m in France: won 8-runner maiden at the Curragh in September by 5 lengths from Next Episode: very close third of 8 to Masslama in Prix des Reservoirs at Longchamp in October: will stay 1½m. *M. Kauntze, Ireland.*

SATIN WOOD   3 b.c. Darshaan 133–Satanella (GER) (Pentathlon) [1989 7m² **117** 7m* 8m⁴ 8g² 1990 8g³ 10fwo 10m* 9.2g²] sturdy, useful-looking colt: smart form: walked over in Brighton minor event in April and won Group 3 Premio Emanuele Filiberto in Milan in May: good 1½ lengths second of 6 to Priolo in Prix Jean Prat at Longchamp later in month: should have proved better at 1¼m than 1m: sustained tendon injury: to stand at Fawley Stud, Wantage, fee £1,750 (Oct 1st). *H. R. A. Cecil.*

SATIS DANCER   3 br.f. Mashhor Dancer (USA)–Chrisanthy 81 (So Blessed 130)   **76** [1989 6m² 6m⁴ 6m² 7m² 7g* 7.3m³ 7g 7g⁵ 1990 8m² 8f* 8g³ 8m 10g⁵ 8g² 8f² 10g*] close-coupled filly: moderate walker: modest handicapper: won at Brighton in April and Nottingham (claimer) in June: will prove at least as effective returned to shorter: acts on firm ground: edgy fourth start: has run creditably for inexperienced apprentice: goes well with forcing tactics. *M. J. Ryan.*

SAUB (CAN) 3 ch.g. Shadeed (USA) 135–Overpraised (USA) (Raise A Native) **74**
[1989 NR 1990 7f³ 8g² 7d 8f² 6m* 6m³] 50,000Y: tall, useful-looking gelding:
half-brother to a winner in USA by Vice Regent: dam unraced half-sister to very
smart 6f to 1½m winner Proctor and daughter of sister to Bold Commander: won
handicap at Newmarket, making most: very good third in similar event there week
later in August: suited by 6f: acts on firm going: takes keen hold. *J. P. Hudson.*

SAUCY SAINT 3 b.g. Show-A-Leg 107–Stolen Halo 52 (Manacle 123) [1989 5h —
6f⁴ 5f 7f a6g 5g 1990 5g 8m 10m 6d a12g] leggy gelding: poor walker: plater:
blinkered 3 times, hanging left and none too keen on first occasion: also trained at 3
yrs by M. Johnston and P. Blockley. *M. B. James.*

SAUMAREZ 3 b. or br.c. Rainbow Quest (USA) 134–Fiesta Fun 105 (Welsh **132**
Pageant 132) [1989 7g⁴ 1990 8f* 8m* 10.4d² 10d* 10g 10d* 12g* 12g⁵]
Britain's challenge for Europe's richest race the Ciga Prix de l'Arc
de Triomphe was one of the strongest in the history of the event. British
stables were represented by a record eleven runners headed by three classic
winners—Salsabil, In The Groove and Snurge—and by Britain's leading
middle-distance three-year-old colt Belmez, the winner of the King George,
'Britain's Prix de l'Arc'. British-trained horses enjoyed a magnificent season
in France, earning the equivalent of around £2,000,000 in win and place
money and carrying off a string of top races, including the French Derby and
Oaks. The Ciga-sponsored programme on Arc day started with three British
winners, Zoman in the Prix du Rond-Point, Shadayid in the Prix Marcel
Boussac and Dayjur in the Prix de l'Abbaye. But there was a twist when the
Arc went to the French-trained expatriate Saumarez who had been sold out of
Cecil's stable earlier in the season. There was a further irony in that Sau-
marez takes his name from a nineteenth-century British naval commander,
later an admiral, who fought his greatest action when defeating a French-
Spanish fleet of fourteen off Cadiz in 1801 with only six ships. Defeat for
Saumarez the horse, a 45,000-guinea yearling, at the hands of Blue Stag in
the listed Dee Stakes at Chester in May—following clear-cut victories in a
maiden event at Ripon and a graduation race at Sandown—prompted owner
Charles St George to part with Saumarez for a reported 400,000 dollars
(around £240,000 at prevailing exchange rates). Ownership passed to a
partnership including the American Bruce McNall who transferred the horse
to the relatively modest string of the young French second-season trainer
Clement.
McNall had enjoyed a good deal of success with another horse purchased privately after the previous year's Chester meeting, the Chester Vase
runner-up Golden Pheasant who had gone on to win the Prix Niel (the race in
which Nashwan suffered his first defeat) and then firmly establish himself in
the top class on turf in the States where his victories in the latest season
included the Arlington Million in September. If reports are true, the sum paid
by McNall for Saumarez was half that which he paid for Golden Pheasant.
McNall didn't have long to wait for confirmation that he had struck another
good bargain with Saumarez. His new trainer supplemented him for the Grand
Prix de Paris Louis Vuitton at Longchamp at the end of June, a race worth the
equivalent of £155,200 to the winner. Cauthon had ridden Saumarez in all his
races in Britain and was again in the saddle at Longchamp where Saumarez
started fourth favourite behind the English and Irish Two Thousand Guineas
winner Tirol, the Prix Jean Prat winner Priolo and the disqualified Prix de

Grand Prix de Paris Louis Vuitton, Longchamp—
on his first appearance for his new stable Saumarez runs away from a field which includes
Priolo, Tirol, Candy Glen and Colour Chart

Diane runner-up Colour Chart. Cauthen had made plenty of use of Saumarez in his races as a three-year-old in Britain and he sent him on some way from home in the Grand Prix de Paris. Saumarez turned the race into a procession, galloping on in great style after opening up a clear lead early in the home straight. Ridden along all the way to the line, he had six lengths to spare over Priolo, with Tirol two lengths further away in third. A top-class performance in the Grand Prix de Paris was followed by a feeble one in the Phoenix Champion Stakes on his next outing ten weeks later; beaten at halfway, Saumarez trailed home over thirty lengths behind the winner Elmaamul. Cauthen reported that Saumarez might have swallowed his tongue and the colt was fitted with a tongue strap for the Prix du Prince d'Orange, one of the traditional Arc trials run at Longchamp in September. Cauthen had held up Saumarez in the Phoenix Champion Stakes and there was a return to more enterprising tactics in the Prix du Prince d'Orange, Mosse, partnering Saumarez for the first time, having him close up all the way and producing him to challenge the odds-on Creator for the lead early in the straight. Saumarez left his Phoenix Champion Stakes form a long way behind with a fluent two-length victory over the outsider Mister Riv with Creator a neck away in third, just in front of French Glory.

Saumarez started at 15/1 for the Prix de l'Arc on the French Tote. The five principal British-trained challengers were all at shorter odds—Salsabil (8/5 favourite coupled with her pacemaker Albadr), Belmez, the St Leger winner Snurge, In The Groove (winner of the Juddmonte International as well as the Irish One Thousand Guineas) and the Yorkshire Oaks winner Hellenic. Three of the home-trained contingent were also ahead of Saumarez in the betting—the Coronation Cup and Grand Prix de Saint-Cloud winner In The Wings, his improving stable-companion Antisaar (whom stable-jockey Asmussen chose in preference) and the Prix Lupin winner Epervier Bleu, second to British-trained Sanglamore in the Prix du Jockey-Club. Epervier Bleu was widely acknowledged as the best middle-distance three-year-old in France but he had been all out to beat Antisaar a head in his Prix de l'Arc trial the Prix Niel, after being off the course for over three months. The Arc field comprised eleven three-year-olds, four four-year-olds and six five-year-olds and was as representative as any that could have been assembled for a middle-distance race in Europe at the time (the Derby winners Quest For Fame and Sanglamore were side-lined through injury and the King George runner-up Old Vic had been retired). Saumarez hadn't been raced beyond a mile and a quarter before the Arc but the extra distance seemed unlikely to be to his disadvantage: he'd always given the impression he'd stay a mile and a half and both his sire and dam, the Arc winner Rainbow Quest and the Yorkshire Oaks third Fiesta Fun, had been suited by the distance. Mosse had said after the mile-and-a-quarter Prix du Prince d'Orange that he had no doubts that Saumarez would stay the Arc trip. Saumarez again had his tongue

Ciga Prix de l'Arc de Triomphe, Longchamp—
Saumarez lasts home by three quarters of a length from Epervier Bleu
with Snurge on his heels

tied down in the Arc, for which he was a supplementary entry at a cost equivalent to just under £30,000 (the Arc had originally closed on May 16th, six days after Saumarez had been beaten in the Dee Stakes).

The Prix de l'Arc provided its usual magnificent spectacle, the most abiding memory of which is a brilliant piece of race-riding by Mosse on the winner. French jockeys generally get a bad press in Britain—much is made, for example, of their supposed difficulties riding Epsom—but the best of the current crop of young French riders are a match for their counterparts anywhere in the world. Mosse rode Saumarez to perfection in the Arc, demonstrating first-class tactical appreciation. He had Saumarez in the first three from the start, in a good position to avoid the scrimmaging that often takes place in a big Arc field, and always with a clear passage to launch a challenge whenever he chose. The pace set by Albadr wasn't quite so strong as usual for an Arc and Mosse eased Saumarez past the pacemaker rounding the final turn and almost immediately set sail for home, dashing Saumarez into a good lead. The manoeuvre proved decisive: notwithstanding the element of surprise—the jockeys' maxim, evidently, is that it doesn't pay to go early at Longchamp—none of the chasing group was at first able to quicken with Saumarez who had opened up a gap of three or four lengths with about a furlong and a half left. Saumarez was coming back to his field in the final furlong and Epervier Bleu and Snurge, both staying on strongly, were overhauling him as the post was reached. Saumarez was all out to hold on by three quarters of a length and half a length. Mosse's tactics were a copybook example of making first run, often misleadingly described as 'getting' first run. He extracted everything from Saumarez, not by forceful riding, but by weighing up the situation and judging accurately the earliest moment at which he could unleash Saumarez's good turn of finishing speed so that he would still last home. Mosse will never ride a better race; it was testament to his opportunism that few good judges would have bet confidently on the result being the same a second time. Epervier Bleu and Snurge were followed home by In The Wings, nearer last than first turning for home, and the always-handy Belmez; British-trained horses filled six of the first ten places, the outsider Legal Case coming sixth, Hellenic eighth, In The Groove ninth and the disappointing Salsabil, never out of mid-division, tenth. Three-year-olds filled the first three places in the Arc for the first time since 1979 and In The Wings and Legal Case were the only older horses in the first eleven. Eddery, who rode In The Wings, described the Arc as 'one of the cleanest I've ridden in'. One of the few valid hard-luck stories concerned Antisaar who lost whatever chance he might have had when badly bumped by a weakening runner turning into the straight.

Saumarez's owner bought a share in Trempolino shortly before his victory in the 1987 Prix de l'Arc; and, like Trempolino, Saumarez was sent across the Atlantic afterwards to run in the Breeders' Cup Turf. He managed only fifth of eleven behind In The Wings, unable to emulate the splendid effort of Trempolino who had run North America's champion grass horse, the ex-European Theatrical, to half a length. Saumarez wasn't so good an Arc winner as Trempolino though they had similar racing characters, both being genuine, top-class middle-distance performers with a first-class turn of foot. Trempolino joined the glittering array of stallions at Gainesway Farm in Kentucky at the end of his three-year-old days; the rather leggy, quite attractive Saumarez starts his stud career at the Haras du Quesnay in France in 1991, the syndicate France Elevage having taken an option on the horse before the Arc.

		Blushing Groom	Red God
		(ch 1974)	Runaway Bride
	Rainbow Quest (USA)	I Will Follow	Herbager
	(b 1981)	(b 1975)	Where You Lead
Saumarez		Welsh Pageant	Tudor Melody
(b. or br.c. 1987)		(b 1966)	Picture Light
	Fiesta Fun	Antigua	Hyperion
	(br 1978)	(ch 1958)	Nassau

Saumarez, the Ever Ready Derby winner Quest For Fame and the Kildangan Stud Irish Oaks winner Knight's Baroness were all in of the first crop of Rainbow Quest who was awarded the Arc on the disqualification of Sagace after a close finish between the pair. Saumarez was one of the cheaper

B. McNall's "Saumarez"

yearlings from Rainbow Quest's first crop; he was sent up to the Newmarket Highflyer Sales in a small batch from the Heatherwold Stud near Newbury. As a British-bred, Saumarez did not qualify for the breeders' premiums available in each of the three races he won in France (for the Arc alone it was the equivalent of just over £62,000). Saumarez is the fourth foal of Heatherwold Stud's Fiesta Fun, a game and genuine racemare who finished third in the Hoover Fillies' Mile and won three races at a mile and a quarter before putting up easily her best effort when a close third to Condessa in the Yorkshire Oaks. Fiesta Fun is a full sister to the lightly-raced Anegada, the dam of the Gordon Stakes winner John French, and a half-sister to several winners, including the smart six- and seven-furlong performer Derrylin who is now a successful sire of jumpers. Fiesta Fun's first foal, a colt by Known Fact, died early but her second and third, the fillies Vivienda (by Known Fact) and Carnival Spirit (by Kris), were both winners, the former as a two-year-old over sprint distances and the latter a over a mile at three. Fiesta Fun had a colt by Top Ville, named Shrovetide, in 1988, lost her foal on a return visit to Rainbow Quest in 1989, had a colt by Mtoto in 1990 and is due to Shirley Heights in 1991. Fiesta Fun and Anegada (who was represented on the racecourse in the latest season by the mile-and-a-quarter winner Flamingo Pond) are both from a family that did very well for Lord and Lady Sefton before being acquired by Heatherwold Stud on the death of Lady Sefton. Antigua, the grandam of Saumarez, won the Galtres Stakes at York and is a daughter of the smart sprinter Nassau, who won five races as a two-year-old including the Hyde Park Stakes, the Princess

SAW

Stakes and the Doncaster Produce Stakes. Nassau produced numerous
winners in Britain, all named after islands in the Caribbean: the game and
consistent Andros followed in the footsteps of his dam by winning the
Doncaster Produce Stakes, and went on to win at up to ten furlongs; Cuba, the
dam of the useful stayer Fidel (now making his mark as a jumping stallion),
was useful at six and seven furlongs; St Lucia won the Coronation Stakes at
Royal Ascot and the Lancashire Oaks; St Lucia's sister St Kitts was quite a
useful staying handicapper; and Tobago was a useful stayer at his best and a
smart hurdler. Another daughter of Nassau, the unraced Bahama, bred the
dam of the Coventry Stakes winner Murrayfield. The victory of Saumarez in
the Arc might well have been toasted as a 'home win' but it may comfort some
that at least his antecedents on the dam's side are British through and
through! *N. Clement, France.*

SAUNDERS LASS 6 b.m. Hillandale 125–Portella 78 (Porto Bello 118) [1989   —
NR 1990 9g] lengthy mare: moderate mover: plating-class handicapper as 4-y-o:
bandaged only subsequent outing on flat, well beaten at Wolverhampton in May:
won selling hurdle later in month: stays 1¼m: acts on firm and dead going: has
sweated and got on edge. *P. J. Bevan.*

SAVAHRA SOUND 5 b.h. Song 132–Savahra 82 (Free State 125) [1989 6g 6f* 111
6g* 6f³ 6s* 7f³ 6s² 6m 6.5s* 7d² 6v⁴ 1990 6f² 6v* 5m 6m 7f* 6g⁴ 7g 6s] tall, rather
dipped-backed horse: has a round action: very useful performer: won listed event at
Milan in April and Federation Brewery Classic Lager Beeswing Stakes at Newcastle
(favourably drawn, comfortably by 3 lengths from Nicholas) in July: below form in
between and after in Group 3 events and listed contest: effective at 6f and 7f: acts on
any going. *R. Hannon.*

SAVANGA (USA) 2 b.g. (Apr 6) Secreto (USA) 128–Sun Sprite (USA) 51 p
(Graustark) [1990 7s a8g⁵] $100,000Y, resold 60,000Y: fifth foal: half-brother to a
minor winner in North America: dam sister to dam of Sunshine Forever: well-
beaten fifth of 12 in late-year maiden at Lingfield, second and better effort: will be
better suited by 1¼m +. *C. E. Brittain.*

SAVILLE WAY 3 ch.g. Gorytus (USA) 132–Claretta (USA) 82 (Roberto (USA) 46
131) [1989 6g⁶ 6m⁶ 7m 7g 7g 1990 9s 8.2g 10m 10m⁴ 10.6d⁵ 12g 10m² 12.5m³ 12g 9s]
strong, workmanlike gelding: keen walker: poor maiden: stays 1½m: acts on good to
firm ground and dead: has run well for inexperienced rider: retained 1,600 gns
Newmarket Autumn Sales. *W. J. Musson.*

SAVOUREUSE LADY 3 ch.f. Caerleon (USA) 132–Amazer (Mincio 127) [1989 111
8g² 1990 12d² 10.5g³ 10d* 10.5g⁵ 12.5g⁴ 10.5v*] 190,000Y: half-sister to numerous
winners, notably top-class middle-distance colt Mtoto (by Busted) and very useful
middle-distance fillies Button Up (also by Busted) and Astonished (by Connaught):
dam won over 6f at 2 yrs in France: won maiden at Deauville in August and Prix Fille
de l'Air at Saint-Cloud in October: narrowly-beaten fourth to Madame Dubois in
Prix de Royallieu at Longchamp: stays 12.5f: acts on heavy going. *A. Fabre, France.*

SAVOY FOREVER 2 b.c. (Mar 8) Bay Express 132–My Bushbaby 100 (Hul A 64
Hul 124) [1990 6g 5m³ 5s²] 9,000Y: strong, good-topped colt: has plenty of scope:
half-brother to several winners, including 4-y-o sprinter Letsbeonestaboutit (by
Petong) and fairly useful 1978 2-y-o 6f winner Bushwacker (by No Party): dam 2-y-o
5f winner, is half-sister to smart 2-y-o sprinter Panomark: quite modest form when
placed in maiden auctions at Redcar in September and Edinburgh (blinkered,
tending to carry head high and weakening noticeably) in October. *W. J. Pearce.*

SAVOY LADY 3 b.f. Noalto 120–Pure Perfection (So Blessed 130) [1989 NR 1990 45
8m⁴ a11g 12m] 4,600Y: workmanlike filly: second foal: dam, closely related to Irish
2000 Guineas winner Dara Monarch out of a half-sister to Intermezzo, showed little
worthwhile form: easily best effort in summer claimers on debut: should be suited
by further than 1m. *M. Bell.*

SAWAKI 3 br.f. Song 132–Roxy Hart (High Top 131) [1989 6g 1990 7.6d 8m³ 8m³ 71
8g³ 7f* 7d] tall, quite attractive filly: has a quick action: modest performer: odds on,
made all in 4-runner maiden at Redcar in August: stiff task in handicap 2½ months
later: will probably prove best at up to 1m: acts on firm ground: sold 12,000 gns
Newmarket Autumn Sales. *H. Thomson Jones.*

SAWSAN 3 b.f. Top Ville 129–Al Washl (USA) 79 (The Minstrel (CAN) 135) [1989 59
6g 1990 8f⁵ 10.2f 12.5m³ 17.6f 12m] lengthy, shallow-girthed, sparely-made filly:
plating-class maiden: stays 12.5f: acts on good to firm ground: edgy second start:
sold 3,000 gns Newmarket December Sales. *P. T. Walwyn.*

813

SAXBY STORM 3 ch.f. Northern Tempest (USA) 120–Rigton Sally (Joshua 129) 51
[1989 7f³ 8g 1990 8f 7m⁴ 8.2g 7f 13.8m⁴ 12g 10m³] sparely-made, plain filly:
moderate mover: plating-class maiden: stays 1¼m: acts on firm ground: ran well in
blinkers final start: twice refused to enter stalls after reappearance: trained until
after reappearance by Mrs R. Wharton: sold 860 gns Doncaster November Sales.
Mrs J. R. Ramsden.

SAXON COURT 4 b.g. Mummy's Game 120–Blickling 64 (Blakeney 126) [1989 68
8d 12.5f* 15.5f² 12f² 14f⁴ 17.1f⁶ 12m⁶ 12g 14f⁵ 12f 1990 12m⁵ 15.5f² 14g³ 13.8m* 12f³
17.1f² 16.2m⁵ 16m* 15.8g⁵ 20m⁶ 17.1f⁴] strong, good-bodied gelding: carries
condition: quite modest handicapper: sweating, won at Catterick (slowly-run race)
in April and Newcastle in June: not seen out in second half of year: stays well: acts
well on top-of-the-ground: usually blinkered. *K. M. Brassey.*

SAXONDALE 3 ch.g. Ballad Rock 122–Joanne's Joy (Ballymore 123) [1989 NR —
1990 6g] IR 1,300Y: lengthy, angular gelding: third foal: closely related to poor and
inconsistent maiden Persian Joy (by Persian Bold) and half-brother to a disappointing maiden by Salmon Leap: dam Irish 7f and 1m winner: always tailed off (moving
poorly) in claimer at Newcastle in October. *R. F. Marvin.*

SAXON LAD (USA) 4 b.g. Lear Fan (USA) 130–Presto Youth (USA) (Youth —
(USA) 135) [1989 7m⁴ 7f² 7m* 6f* 7.6f² 7d 1990 6m] angular colt: progressive form
in handicaps (winning 2) as 3-y-o until final start: below form only outing in 1990:
should stay 1m: acts on firm ground: tends to hang left and likely to prove best with
waiting tactics: sold to join G. Enright's stable 4,000 gns Newmarket July Sales. *Mrs
L. Piggott.*

SAY A PRAYER 3 ch.f. Sayf El Arab (USA) 127–Careless Flyer 66 (Malicious) 35
[1989 5m² 5m⁴ 6f³ 6g 1990 8v 11g⁴ 8.2g 8.2m 9m⁵ 10m 11m⁵ 8.2g] workmanlike filly:
plater: stays 11f: visored last 2 outings: often ridden by 7-lb claimer. *Denys Smith.*

SAYMORE 4 ch.g. Seymour Hicks (FR) 125–Huahinee (FR) 94 (Riverman (USA) —
131) [1989 8f² 10f³ 10m 8m* 8m 8.2d 8m 8d* 1990 8g] tall, leggy, close-coupled
gelding: fairly useful winner of handicaps as 3-y-o: ridden by 7-lb claimer, never
near to challenge only outing in 1990: effective at 1m and 1¼m: acts on firm and dead
ground: takes keen hold: has broken blood vessels over hurdles. *C. P. E. Brooks.*

SAYSANA 3 b.f. Sayf El Arab (USA) 127–Rosana Park 83 (Music Boy 124) [1989 57
5d 5.3m⁴ 5.3h* 6m⁶ 5f* 5.3h² 5f⁴ 5f⁴ 5.3f³ 1990 6f⁵ 5m 5.3h⁶ 7.6m⁵ 6f⁶ 7m⁵ 6f 6h
7h⁵ 6f 5f 7f* 6g⁶ a5g⁴ a7g⁵ a6g⁶] leggy, quite good-topped filly: keen walker:
plating-class handicapper: won selling event (no bid) at Brighton in October: ran
moderately previous 5 outings, fairly well next 3: effective at 6f and 7f: acts on hard
going. *A. Moore.*

SAYULITA 3 b.f. Habitat 134–Cheerful Heart (Petingo 135) [1989 NR 1990 67
10.4m⁴ 10g⁶ a12g² 12d⁴ a10g⁵ a12g⁴] 64,000Y: rangy, angular filly: half-sister to
fairly useful 1m and 1¼m winner Momtaaz (by Diesis) and 1¼m to 12.3f winner
Suluk (by Lypheor): dam, 1½m winner in Ireland, is half-sister to Gift Wrapped, dam
of Royal Lodge winner Reach: quite modest maiden: ran fairly well penultimate
(apprentice handicap) start, moderately when favourite on final one: stays 1½m. *J.
H. M. Gosden.*

SAYYAF'S LAD 5 ch.h. Sayyaf 121–Opinebo 82 (Nebbiolo 125) [1989 6d 5f⁵ 5g —
5g 7m 7g 1990 5m⁴ 5m⁶ 6g] small, good-quartered horse: poor handicapper: ran by
mistake (should have been stable-companion Cut Out) at Wolverhampton in July:
stays 6f: acts on good to firm and soft going: has worn severe bridle and been taken
down early: sold 820 gns Doncaster September Sales. *M. Brittain.*

SAYYARA 3 gr.f. Kris 135–Safita 117 (Habitat 134) [1989 NR 1990 7m⁵ 8g* 7f 8m] 81 +
small, lengthy, angular filly: moderate mover: fifth foal: half-sister to 4 winners,
including smart 6f to 8.2f winner Safawan (by Young Generation) and useful 7f to 9f
winner Sadapour (by Auction Ring): dam smart at up to 1¼m in France: 11/8 on,
smooth winner of maiden at Newmarket in May: stiff tasks when behind in Jersey
Stakes at Royal Ascot and £24,700 August handicap at York: stays 1m. *M. R. Stoute.*

SAY YOU WILL 6 b.g. Riboboy (USA) 124–Polita 86 (Constable 119) [1989 6d 6g 57
6g² 8.5d 7m* 7.5f* 7.6m* 7m⁵ 6m* 6f 7m 6s 7m 7g* 6g 7d² 1990 7.5d 7m 7g 7m 7g
6m 6g 7f 7d³ a7g a7g* a8g a7g²] robust gelding: carries condition: has a quick
action: successful 5 times in handicaps as 5-y-o: thoroughly disappointing for most
of 1990 and still well below his best when winning at Lingfield in December: best at
up to 1m: possibly unsuited by soft going nowadays, acts on any other: has worn
blinkers, usually visored: has looked unenthusiastic. *M. P. Naughton.*

SCALES OF JUSTICE 4 br.f. Final Straw 127–Foiled Again 110 (Bold Lad 85
(IRE) 133) [1989 10.6g 9g 10d a12g⁵ a12g* a12g 1990 10.8m³ 9g³ 11f² 9g* a12g 10m⁵

814

9m⁴ 9f* 8m* a10g²] big, rangy filly: much improved handicapper, winner at York (strongly-run ladies event) in May, Redcar in October and Newmarket in November: best form at up to 1¼m: acts on firm ground. *J. W. Hills.*

SCANDALIZE (IRE) 2 b.f. (Apr 6) Dalsaan 125–Dacani 118 (Polyfoto 124) 37 [1990 5m 6m⁶ 6g² 7m a7g] IR 4,400F, IR 7,500Y: leggy filly: poor mover: closely related to 1986 2-y-o 6f seller winner Fantine (by Hard Fought) and a winner abroad by Camden Town, and half-sister to a winner abroad: dam smart sprinter here won over 7f in USA, is sister to Valeriga: poor plater: should stay 7f: possibly unsuited by firm ground. *M. J. Fetherston-Godley.*

SCANTEC 2 b.f. (Apr 24) Trojan Fen 118–Instant Beauty (USA) (Pronto) [1990 5f 39 6m 6m⁴ 6f a8g] 6,000Y: neat filly: sister to 3-y-o Sapphire Symphony and half-sister to fair 9f winner Fulvio (by Full Out) and a winner in USA: dam unraced half-sister to both St Leger winner Boucher and the dam of outstanding racemare Numbered Account: poor form, including in a seller: ran badly when blinkered latest outing: should be suited by further than 6f: sold 480 gns Ascot December Sales. *M. J. Fetherston-Godley.*

SCARBA 2 b.g. (May 10) Skyliner 117–Looking For Gold (Goldfella 80) [1990 6d⁵] — workmanlike gelding: third foal: dam won over hurdles: backward, well beaten in 7-runner minor event at Doncaster in October. *D. T. Garraton.*

SCARED STIFF 2 b.f. (Apr 13) Electric 126–Petrify 71 (Air Trooper 115) [1990 51 7m 7m 7g] compact filly: first foal: dam lightly-raced 3-y-o 7f winner: poor form in maidens at Chepstow (2) and Newmarket: will be better suited by 1m +. *G. B. Balding.*

SCARLET EXPRESS 3 b.g. Precocious 126–Scarlet Slipper (Gay Mecene 54 (USA) 128) [1989 6m⁶ 7g 7g⁵ 1990 a10g⁵ a10g³ 9s² 10g 12d⁴ 11m² 10g⁶ 11g⁵ 12m⁶ 15.5f⁵] leggy gelding: poor walker: has a round action: plating-class maiden: stays 15.5f: acts on firm ground: blinkered 3 times: ran creditably for amateur final start: winning hurdler. *P. A. Kelleway.*

SCARLETT HOLLY 3 b.f. Red Sunset 120–Wilderness 88 (Martinmas 128) 81 [1989 6f* 6v 1990 5.8f⁴ 7d* 7m 7f⁶ 6g⁶ 6d] leggy, sparely-made filly: fair handicapper: well ridden to make all in £7,200 event at Epsom in June: soon pushed along in rear at Chester on final outing: unlikely to stay 1m: acts on any going: has run well when edgy. *P. J. Makin.*

SCARLET VEIL 4 b.f. Tyrnavos 129–Red Velvet 114 (Red God 128§) [1989 10m⁶ — 10h² 1990 12.2m 12m] plain, close-coupled filly: modest form at best: behind in handicap (stiff task) and maiden in spring: stays 1¼m. *W. Jarvis.*

SCATTER 3 b.c. Sharpo 132–Visitation 84 (Tarqogan 125) [1989 5f 6m* 6g* 6g 7g 98 1990 7m² 7.2g⁴ 7m⁴ 8m] good-topped colt: fairly useful handicapper: off course 5 months then good fourth in £7,700 event (took strong hold) at Haydock and £71,900 contest at Ascot: didn't get clear run final start: well worth another try at 1m: acts on good to firm ground: tends to hang. *G. Harwood.*

SCENIC 4 b.c. Sadler's Wells (USA) 132–Idyllic (USA) (Foolish Pleasure (USA)) 114 [1989 8f³ 10m* 10g 10g⁴ 12f 1990 9m⁴ 10m² 10m] rather leggy, useful-looking colt: keen walker: fluent mover, with a slightly round action: high class at his best, dead-heated with Prince of Dance in Dewhurst Stakes at Newmarket in 1988: best effort at 4 yrs second to Husyan in moderately-run Brigadier Gerard Stakes at Sandown: blinkered, tailed off in Prince of Wales's Stakes at Royal Ascot 3 weeks later: stayed 1¼m: acted on firm and dead going: best on galloping track: to stand at Coolmore Stud, Co. Tipperary, fee IR 6,000 gns (Oct 1st). *B. W. Hills.*

SCENIC DANCER 2 b.c. (May 2) Shareef Dancer (USA) 135–Bridestones 92 64 (Jan Ekels 122) [1990 6m 7g 8g 8m 7d] 25,000Y: compact colt: half-brother to 4 winners, notably smart 7f to 1¼m performer Lockton (by Moorestyle): dam, half-sister to high-class stayer Crash Course, won 4 times over middle distances: quite modest maiden, easily best effort third start: very slowly away final outing. *A. Hide.*

SCENTED GODDESS (IRE) 2 b.f. (Feb 6) Godswalk (USA) 130–Vivi (Welsh 54 Saint 126) [1990 5.8h² 5.3h³ 5s³ 7m* 7f⁶ a6g² a8g a6g] IR 2,100Y: close-coupled filly: fifth foal: half-sister to a winner in Holland: dam unraced: won 8-runner seller (retained 6,800 gns) at Lingfield in June by 1½ lengths: ran creditably in all-weather claimers late in year: stays 7f: trained first 5 outings by R. Hannon. *J. S. Moore.*

SCENT OF BATTLE 2 ch.c. (May 9) Rousillon (USA) 133–Light O'Battle 97 — p (Queen's Hussar 124) [1990 8g] 7,600Y: strong, lengthy colt: half-brother to 3-y-o Formidable Task (by Formidable), 10.2f winner Height O'Battle (by Shirley Heights) and fairly useful sprinter Lobbit (by Habitat): dam winner over 7f from 2 starts at 2 yrs, is sister to Highclere: over 13 lengths seventh of 8, never able to challenge, in minor event at Sandown in September: should improve. *M. J. Haynes.*

SCEPTRE HOUSE (IRE)   2 gr.f. (Feb 13) Hatim (USA) 121–Aerobic Dancer   32 §
(Bold Lad (IRE) 133) [1990 5g 5m⁴ 6m⁴ 5f 6m⁶ 6m 7m] IR 5,000F, 10,000Y, resold
4,300Y, 4,300 2-y-o: small filly: poor mover: second foal: dam unraced from family of
Ballad Rock: poor plater: on toes, mulish stalls and seemed reluctant to race when
last in nursery final start: blinkered and unruly in preliminaries fourth one: has
worn bandages: sometimes slowly away: not one to trust. *P. D. Evans.*

SCHWANTZ   2 b.g. (May 3) Exhibitioner 111–Hardirondo 93 (Hardicanute 130)   —
[1990 6g⁵ 6g 8.2m] strong, good-bodied gelding: half-brother to several winners,
including 3-y-o Hardiheroine (by Sandhurst Prince), 7f winner at 2 yrs, and smart
1¼m performer Belle Poitrine (by Dominion): dam game stayer: bit backward,
no show at Nottingham in 5-runner minor event (slowly away) and maidens. *J.
Wharton.*

SCORPIO LADY   3 ch.f. Vaigly Great 127–Buy G'S 60 (Blakeney 126) [1989 6m⁵   §§
6f² 6m⁶ 6g² 6m³ 7g⁶ 6v* a7g² 7g³ 1990 7m 8g a6g] sparely-made filly: has a round
action: modest winner at 2 yrs: refused to race in claimers last 2 outings in 1990:
should stay 1m: best form on an easy surface: visored on debut: usually sweats:
sometimes edgy and unruly in preliminaries: one to avoid. *G. Blum.*

SCOTCH IMP   6 ch.m. Imperial Fling (USA) 116–Bunduq 67 (Scottish Rifle 127)   56
[1989 6f 6m⁴ 6m⁶ 6g³ 6f⁵ 6f⁵ 6m 6m² 6m 6f⁴ 6g 7g a7g a8g a6g 1990 a7g⁶ a6g⁴ a7g⁵
6s 6f 6g 6g* 6m 6m 6s] workmanlike mare: usually dull in coat: ran by far her best
race for long time when winning apprentice handicap at Ripon in September, making
all on far rail: suited by 6f to 7f: acts on any going: sometimes blinkered. *D. W.
Chapman.*

SCOTONI   4 ch.c. Final Straw 127–Damiya (FR) (Direct Flight) [1989 8.3m 8m²   53
1990 9f 10.8m* 10.8f⁵ 12f³ 12m 8m⁵ 10.2m 10s 8d³ a7g] close-coupled, rather
sparely-made colt: plating-class handicapper: apprentice ridden, won at Warwick in
April: effective at 1m and stays 1½m: acts on firm and dead going: blinkered final
start: has got on edge: sold 2,300 gns Ascot December Sales: inconsistent. *R. J.
O'Sullivan.*

SCOTS LAW   3 b.c. Law Society (USA) 130–Tweedling (USA) (Sir Ivor 135) [1989   55
6m⁵ 7f* a8g⁶ 1990 a7g 7.5f 8m⁴ 10m⁴ 10f 8f a8g* a8g² a6g³] compact, quite
attractive colt: plating-class performer: on toes, made all in claimer at Lingfield in
October: ran creditably after: stays 1¼m: yet to race on soft surface: blinkered sixth
outing: has carried head awkwardly, appearing ungenerous second start: claimed
out of C. Brittain's stable £6,501 on fourth: seems best with forcing tactics. *R. J.
O'Sullivan.*

SCOTTISH CASTLE   2 ch.c. (Apr 18) Scottish Reel 123–Show Home 90 (Music   78
Boy 124) [1990 7g 7m³ 6d⁴ 7s* 7d* a7g* 7s⁵ a7g⁵] IR 13,000F, 21,000Y: strong colt:
moderate mover: first foal: dam 2-y-o 5f winner probably stayed 6f: much improved
towards end of season, winning nurseries at Doncaster, Leicester and Lingfield
within 8 days: ran moderately when blinkered final outing: will stay 1m: acts on soft
going: suitable mount for a claimer. *W. A. O'Gorman.*

SCOTTISH FLING   6 ch.g. Imperial Fling (USA) 116–Relicia (Relko 136) [1989   57
8f⁶ 9f* 8.2f³ 8f² 10f⁵ 12.3m⁵ 9f⁶ 10.2g⁵ 10.6d⁵ 8m² 9f³ 1990 10.6f* 10v 11f 10.6m]
workmanlike gelding: moderate mover: plating-class handicapper: led last stride in
apprentice race at Haydock in April, only form at 6 yrs: bandaged, pulled up feelingly
final outing, first for over 3 months: stays 1¼m: best form on top-of-the-ground: has
worn blinkers and visor, but not since 4 yrs: has won when sweating: excellent
mount for inexperienced rider: sold 1,000 gns Doncaster September Sales. *J. Berry.*

SCOTTISH JESTER (USA)   3 b.c. Northern Baby (CAN) 127–Foolish Lady   90
(USA) (Foolish Pleasure (USA)) [1989 NR 1990 9g* 8.2d 9m* 10m] $115,000Y:
lengthy, attractive colt: has a quick action: first foal: dam maiden half-sister to
Dancing Brave: won maiden at Ripon in July and moderately-run handicap at
Goodwood in September: tailed off in handicaps at Haydock and Newmarket: should
stay 1¼m: sold 25,000 gns Newmarket Autumn Sales, probably abroad. *G. Harwood.*

SCOTTISH REFORM   3 b.g. Night Shift (USA)–Molvitesse 75 (Molvedo 137)   66
[1989 6m² 6f³ 7m⁶ 8g⁴ 1990 6m 7m a7g² a7g⁴ 7g² 7m⁴ 7m² 10f³ 8m⁶] lengthy
gelding: moderate walker and mover: turns fore-feet in: quite modest maiden: at
least as effective over 7f as 1m: acts on good to firm ground: ran fairly well in
blinkers seventh start. *J. Berry.*

SCRABBLE MASTER   4 ch.g. Sunley Builds 102–Quorum's Diajem (Thesau-   —
ros 73) [1989 NR 1990 10.1g] leggy, narrow, plain gelding: first foal: dam unraced:
bandaged, tailed off in claimer at Windsor in April. *Miss L. Bower.*

SCRAVELS SARAN (IRE)   2 b.f. (Mar 20) Indian King (USA) 128–Persian   57
Royale 94 (Persian Bold 123) [1990 6g 7f³ 7f⁵] IR 9,000Y: sturdy filly: second foal:
dam won Irish Cambridgeshire: best effort third in maiden auction at Yarmouth in
July: didn't settle then flashed tail and looked irresolute in similar event at Redcar
following month: will stay 1m. *Dr J. D. Scargill.*

SCREEN SERENADE   2 b.f. (Feb 8) Nordance (USA)–Screenable (USA)   62
(Silent Screen (USA)) [1990 6g 6h³ 5d 6f² 6m⁴ 7.5m³ 6f² 5f² 6m⁴ 6m] IR 16,000Y:
leggy, workmanlike filly: second foal: half-sister to 1¼m winner Barrymore (by
Robellino): dam minor winner at around 1m in North America: quite modest maiden:
good running-on fourth in £18,100 nursery at Newmarket penultimate start: got
very upset before running moderately final outing: really needs further than 5f, and
stays 7f: acts on hard ground: blinkered and sweating sixth start: sold 4,600 gns
Newmarket Autumn Sales. *P. A. Kelleway.*

SCRIBBLING (USA)   3 br.f. Secretariat (USA)–Icy Pop (USA) (Icecapade   88
(USA)) [1989 NR 1990 7g 10.6d* 11.5g⁴ 10g* 10.6v 10.4v³] $160,000Y: strong filly:
turns off-fore in markedly: fourth reported foal: sister to 1986 French 2-y-o 5.5f
winner American Feeling, later successful in USA, and half-sister to 2 winners in
North America: dam successful at up to 9f at 3 yrs in USA and second in Grade 2 6f
contest at 2 yrs: won maiden (edgy) at Haydock in August and handicap at Newbury
in September: should stay 1½m: seems unsuited by heavy going. *J. H. M. Gosden.*

SCU'S LADY (IRE)   2 b.f. (Mar 7) Mazaad 106–Lydja 75 (Hethersett 134) [1990   47
5g³ 5g 6m³ 6g 6m 6g 6d 6m] IR 2,300F, 6,000Y: small, sturdy filly: half-sister to
numerous winners, including Troms (by Wollow), useful at up to 1¼m in France,
and 1m winner Hi-Hannah (by Red Sunset): dam stayed 1¼m: poor maiden: off
course 3 months after fifth outing: stays 6f: sold 2,100 gns Newmarket Autumn
Sales. *M. E. D. Francis.*

SEABEE   2 ch.c. (May 18) Adonijah 126–Fedra 81 (Grundy 137) [1990 7m 7f 7m   46
10s] small, stocky colt: first foal: dam stayer: well beaten in maidens: best effort
on debut: needed race final start, first for 3 months: twice slowly away. *K. O.
Cunningham-Brown.*

SEA CADET   2 ch.c. (Mar 4) Precocious 126–Sea Power 88 (Welsh Pageant 132)   68 p
[1990 7m⁶] stocky colt: first foal: dam maiden suited by 1¾m +, is half-sister to
smart 1¼m filly Upper Deck: carrying condition and very green, around 10 lengths
sixth of 16, slowly away then one pace from 2f out until eased final furlong, to
Sapieha in maiden at Newmarket in October: sure to improve. *Major W. R. Hern.*

SEA DEVIL   4 gr.g. Absalom 128–Miss Poinciana 78 (Averof 123) [1989 5g⁴ 6d²   71
7.5f⁴ 6m 5s 6s⁴ 6s 1990 6s* 6g 7.5d⁴ 7m³ 6g³ 6g⁵ 6s² 6s* 6s* 6s*] lengthy,
good-quartered gelding: moderate walker and mover: modest handicapper: won at
Hamilton in April, Ayr and Doncaster (rallying gamely) in October and Newcastle in
November: suited by 7f or stiff 6f: goes particularly well on soft going: sweating and
on toes third outing: consistent. *M. J. Camacho.*

SEA GODDESS   2 b.f. (Apr 28) Slip Anchor 136–Elysian 94 (Northfields (USA))   — p
[1990 7g] quite good-topped, angular filly: third foal: half-sister to 3-y-o winning
hurdler Olympian (by High Line) and 1m winner Circe (by Main Reef): dam 2-y-o 6f
winner seemed to stay 1½m, is from excellent family: prominent 5f, running better
than position suggests, in 20-runner maiden at Newmarket in November: should
improve. *W Jarvis.*

SEA LEVEL (FR)   2 b. or br.c. (Feb 19) Kind of Hush 118–Packet 89 (Royal   104 p
Palace 131) [1990 7m² 7m* 7g⁴ 8m*] rangy colt: has scope: eighth foal: closely
related to smart middle-distance stayer Capstan (by Welsh Pageant) and half-
brother to useful 1¼m winner Albacore (by Kris): dam, from family of Longboat,
won at up to 1¾m: most progressive colt: won 11-runner Bovis Autumn Stakes at
Ascot in October by a neck from Circus Light, always handy and staying on well,
despite carrying head high, to lead close to line: earlier comfortably landed odds in
maiden at Kempton, making all, and fourth of 9 to Radwell in Group 3 event at
Sandown: will be well suited by middle distances. *B. W. Hills.*

SEAL INDIGO (IRE)   2 b.f. (Feb 24) Glenstal (USA) 118–Simply Gorgeous   72
(Hello Gorgeous (USA) 128) [1990 5g⁶ 5m³ 8m⁶ 9g⁴ 8m⁴ 9m² 10g] IR 8,000Y, resold
72,000Y: workmanlike filly: moderate mover: first foal: dam unraced half-sister
to Give Thanks, family of Favoletta and Teenoso: modest maiden: ran well when
seventh of 9 in Newmarket listed event final outing: saddle slipped time before:
stays 1¼m. *R. Hannon.*

SEAMERE   7 b.g. Crofter (USA) 124–Whistling Waltz (Whistler 129) [1989 5f 6f   65
5m³ 5g⁵ 5g⁴ 5g 5g² 5m⁴ 5f* 5f² 5f³ 5g 1990 5g 5g 5g² 5f* 5f⁶ 5g³ 5m² 5f* 5m⁴ 5m³

$5g^3$ $5g^4$] workmanlike, deep-bodied gelding: carries plenty of condition: moderate mover: quite modest handicapper: won at Beverley in July and Carlisle in September: ran particularly well at Pontefract (not having clear run) and Newcastle (clear on far side having been badly bumped start) tenth and eleventh starts: ideally suited by stiff 5f: best form on a sound surface: has worn visor, usually blinkered nowadays: excellent mount for inexperienced rider. *B. R. Cambidge.*

SEA OF LOVE 2 b. or br.c. (Mar 17) Damister (USA) 123–Vexed Voter (Pontifex (USA)) [1990 6m $7f^4$ $7h^3$ $7m^6$ $7f^2$ 8m* 8f] 15,000F, 21,000Y: compact, good-bodied colt: sixth foal: half-brother to useful Italian sprinter Manoftheyear (by Sayf El Arab), 5f winner Silent Majority (by General Assembly) and a winner in Malaysia: dam useful 5f winner in Ireland: quite modest performer: narrowly won nursery at Yarmouth in September: ran moderately in similar event at Brighton after: better suited by 1m than shorter: tends to hang. *R. Guest.* 69

SE-AQ 5 b.g. Krayyan 117–Messie (Linacre 133) [1989 $7m^2$ 7m* 7.5m 7s 8s 7m $8.2d^3$ 8g 1990 8f $10.2m^2$ 10v 8m* $8.2f^6$ $8h^2$ 8m $11.5g^4$ 8f] leggy, lengthy gelding: has a quick action: quite modest handicapper: won amateurs event at Leicester in April: probably best short of 1½m: acts on hard and dead going: blinkered once: sold out of J. Wilson's stable 4,800 gns Ascot May Sales after fifth start. *C. L. Popham.* 62

SEARCHING STAR 2 b.f. (Apr 6) Rainbow Quest (USA) 134–Little White Star (Mill Reef (USA) 141) [1990 $6m^4$ $8.2v^5$] 40,000Y: close-coupled, quite attractive filly: half-sister to several winners, including very useful 7f and 1½m winner Beldale Star (by Beldale Flutter) and 1984 2-y-o 5f and 6f winner Bright Domino (by Dominion): dam poor daughter of half-sister to high-class miler Saintly Song: 20/1, green and on toes, over 10 lengths last of 4 to Crystal Gazing in £9,800 event at Ascot in September: bit edgy, well beaten in minor event at Haydock following month: should stay at least 1m. *P. T. Walwyn.* 63

SEARCY 2 b.g. (Feb 25) Good Times (ITY)–Fee 111 (Mandamus 120) [1990 7g 8g $7m^6$] workmanlike gelding: sour mover: sixth foal: half-brother to ungenuine 3-y-o 11.5f winner Bawbee (by Dunbeath) and 3 other winners, including 10.2f to 1½m winner Perk (by Jalmood) and fair stayer Franchise (by Warpath): dam thoroughly genuine 1¼m performer from stoutly-bred family: plating-class form, not at all knocked about, in maidens: will stay middle distances: likely to do better. *R. F. Johnson Houghton.* 55 p

SEASIDE MINSTREL 2 ch.c. (May 5) Song 132–Blackpool Belle 70 (The Brianstan 128) [1990 5m* $5f^4$ $6m^3$ $6d^5$ $6f^3$ $5f^3$ 5g $5m^3$ $5m^6$ 7f $a6g$] 9,200Y: leggy colt: first foal: dam sprinter: fair plater: won maiden at Warwick in May: mostly ran creditably (though not on all-weather) towards end of year: stays 7f: blinkered fifth and sixth starts: races very freely: sold out of J. Berry's stable 1,200 gns Doncaster October Sales before final outing. *C. J. Hill.* 54

SEA SIESTA 4 b.f. Vaigly Great 127–Janlarmar 69 (Habat 127) [1989 8f 1990 $10.2f$] leggy, workmanlike filly: well beaten in minor event and maiden. *Miss A. J. Whitfield.* —

SEATTLE BRAVE 3 b.g. Seattle Song (USA) 130–Oraston 115 (Morston (FR) 125) [1989 NR 1990 $14d^4$ $16.2d$ $13.6m^3$] 3,200Y, 23,000 2-y-o: rangy, good-topped gelding: has a round action: half-brother to modest 14.6f winner Rum Cay (by Our Native) and a winner in Italy: dam won 1¼m Premio Lydia Tesio and is half-sister to smart French 1m and 1¼m performer The Abbot: 14/1, best effort third of 8 to Spode's Blue in maiden at Redcar in October: will be suited by thorough test of stamina: gelded after final start. *G. Harwood.* 80

SEATTLE PRIDE (CAN) 4 b.g. Seattle Song (USA) 130–Minstrelsy (USA) (The Minstrel (CAN) 135) [1989 $10f^4$ $10.1g^4$ 8g 9m 12.2d 1990 $a12g^4$] leggy, quite attractive gelding: has a round action: poor handicapper: stays 1½m: edgy and blinkered fourth outing at 3 yrs: has worn tongue strap: winning hurdler in March: sold 1,300 gns Ascot November Sales. *M. H. Tompkins.* 45

SEA WAR (IRE) 2 ch.g. (May 2) Gorytus (USA) 132–Corinth Canal 77 (Troy 137) [1990 6m] second foal: dam once-raced sister to Helen Street: backward, under 6 lengths seventh of 15, keeping on steadily not knocked about, in maiden at Salisbury in June: looked sure to improve, but not seen out again. *Major W. R. Hern.* 70 p

SECOND STAR 2 b.f. (Mar 31) Final Straw 127–Appealing 49 (Star Appeal 133) [1990 $6d^6$ $6m^3$ $7m^6$ 6m* 6m $6d^3$ $5.8d^6$] 3,000F, 700Y: angular, rather leggy filly: first foal: dam 4-y-o 1¼m winner, is half-sister to fairly useful 1m to 12.2f winner Gifford: plating-class performer: made it up in 25-runner seller (no bid) at Redcar in September: will stay 1m: acts on good to firm ground and dead: sold 3,200 gns Newmarket Autumn Sales. *M. H. Tompkins.* 61

SECOND TO NONE 3 b.g. Superlative 118–Matinata (Dike (USA)) [1989 5f³   **60**
5m³ 5d⁶ 1990 5m³ 6f⁵ 5m² 5m² 5.8f²] strong gelding: quite modest maiden: second
in handicaps and seller (claimed to join D. Arbuthnot £6,250) in June: seems best at
5f: acts on firm ground: visored final start, blinkered previous two. *J. Berry.*

SECRETARY OF STATE 4 b.c. Alzao (USA) 117–Colonial Line (USA) 75   **97**
(Plenty Old (USA)) [1989 10s 8m* 8.2m³ 7f⁵ 8.3g 8m* 9g* 1990 8.2m³ 8m² 8f 10m]
strong, workmanlike colt: carries condition: good mover: quite useful performer:
ran well and reached a place in £6,600 handicap at Haydock and Group 2 event
(beaten nose) at Milan in spring: not seen out after July: suited by around 1m: acts
on firm going. *P. F. I. Cole.*

SECRET FOUR 4 b.g. My Top–Secret Top (African Sky 124) [1989 7v⁵ 7v⁶ 7v⁶   **57**
8m 12m³ 11d 11g⁵ 12g⁶ 12v⁵ 10d 1990 12.5f⁶ 6f⁶ 6m⁵ 10m³ 10m² 10m 10h⁵ 10m² 10f]
neat ex-Irish gelding: moderate mover: half-brother to 1984 2-y-o Irish 5f winner
Fringe of Heaven (by Godswalk): dam ran once: placed in handicaps at Lingfield in
June (twice, second for apprentices) and August: needs further than 6f and stays
1½m: acts on any going: blinkered last 2 starts: winner 4 times over hurdles in
autumn. *R. Akehurst.*

SECRET FREEDOM (USA) 2 b.f. (May 22) Secreto (USA) 128–Mary Biz   **87**
(USA) (T V Lark) [1990 6d³ 6g* 6m 7g 8m] 9,000Y: smallish, angular filly: closely
related to fair 1982 2-y-o 7f winner Ice Patrol (by Far North) and half-sister to
several winners, including Gimcrack winner Full Extent (by Full Out): dam unplaced 4 times, is half-sister to smart Terrible Tiger: favourite, won maiden auction
at Nottingham in June, leading on stand rail after 2f: bit backward, excellent seventh
of 12 to Shamshir in Brent Walker Fillies' Mile at Ascot: will stay 1¼m: may improve
again. *C. E. Brittain.*

SECRET HAUNT (USA) 2 ch.c. (May 26) Secreto (USA) 128–Royal Suite   **85 p**
(USA) (Herbager 136) [1990 8m*] $120,000Y: good-bodied colt: sixth foal: half-
brother to useful French 1m to 1¼m performer Trigger Finger (by Lyphard): dam
leading American 2-y-o filly of 1979 (stays mile to race) when stakes winner at up
to 6f: weak 10/1-shot and better for race, won 16-runner maiden at Redcar in October
by a neck from Stop Press, leading 1f out and running on well: moved moderately
down: sure to improve, particularly over further. *L. M. Cumani.*

SECRET HAZE 2 ch.f. (Apr 6) Absalom 128–Secret Gill 88 (Most Secret 119)   **80**
[1990 6m⁴ 6g² 6d*] 4,800Y: neat, sturdy filly: third foal: dam 7f performer later
successful in USA: favourite, won maiden auction at Catterick in July by 10 lengths
from Oliroan, leading 2f out: will stay 7f: looked to be progressing well, but not seen
out again. *Miss S. E. Hall.*

SECRETILLA (USA) 2 b.f. (Feb 13) Secreto (USA) 128–Satilla (FR) 118 (Tar-   **— p**
gowice (USA) 130) [1990 7f⁶] $130,000Y: medium-sized, close-coupled, sparely-
made filly: half-sister to a minor winner in North America and a winner in Sweden:
dam French 5.5f (at 2 yrs) to 1½m winner, is half-sister to dam of Saint Cyrien: weak
in market and green, 11 lengths sixth of 15, keeping on steadily under hand riding, to
Nunivak in maiden at Redcar in October: showed a moderate action: sure to
improve, particularly over further. *L. M. Cumani.*

SECRET INVESTMENT (USA) 2 b.c. (Mar 27) Secreto (USA) 128–Rephrase   **82**
(USA) (Affirmed (USA)) [1990 8m 8g⁴] 50,000Y: medium-sized, rather unfurnished
colt: has a very round action: third foal: half-brother to winner in USA by Kings
Lake: dam unraced daughter of Stewards' Cup winner Repetitious: around 6 lengths
fourth of 7, steadily outpaced last 2f, to Commendable in maiden at York in October:
sold 24,000 gns Newmarket Autumn Sales. *A. A. Scott.*

SECRET LIASON 4 b.g. Ballacashtal (CAN)–Midnight Mistress (Midsummer   **56**
Night II 117) [1989 7.5d 6f* 6f* 7m 7m* 6f 7m⁵ 7g⁴ 1990 a7g⁴ a8g³ a8g⁴ a7g a7g 7f
8m⁶] angular gelding: successful in 3 sellers in 1989: best efforts on all-weather as
4-y-o in non-selling handicaps on first 2 starts: ran moderately returned to turf, off
course almost 4 months before penultimate start: may prove best short of 1m: acts
on firm going: blinkered twice: has won for claimer. *W. G. M. Turner.*

SECRET SOCIETY 3 b. or br.c. Law Society (USA) 130–Shaara (FR) (Sanctus   **91**
II 132) [1989 8s 8.2d³ 8d 1990 8f* 10.6f⁵ 8m 8g² 8.5m 8m³ 12.3m* 12m⁴ 12m⁴ 12m*
12s⁶] big, deep-girthed colt: has scope: has a rather round action: won apprentice
maiden at Newcastle in April, 5-runner handicap at Ripon in August and £71,300
Festival Handicap (improved form to beat Ivory Way ¾ length) at Ascot in September: sweating and edgy, well-beaten sixth of 24 in November Handicap at
Doncaster: suited by 1½m: acts on firm ground. *M. J. Camacho.*

SECRET TALENT 2 b.g. (May 14) Grey Desire 115–Canty Day 87 (Canadel II —
126) [1990 7m 7f⁴ 7g] 3,000F, 5,000Y: leggy gelding: half-brother to 3 minor
winners here and abroad, including poor 13f winner Cantycroon (by Crooner): dam
2-y-o 5f winner: soundly beaten in maidens and a minor event. *P. Mitchell.*

SECRET WATERS 3 b.f. Pharly (FR) 130–Idle Waters 116 (Mill Reef (USA) 99
14 1) [1989 6g 7f⁶ 8g⁴ 1990 10g 12m³ 12.5g⁴ 14f⁵ 13.1m* 12.5m* 14f* 12m³ 14.6g⁶
12m] leggy, close-coupled filly: moderate mover: fairly useful performer: comfortable winner of handicaps at Bath and Wolverhampton in July then led final strides in
£7,500 handicap at Goodwood in August: faced stiff tasks after, good third to
Madiriya in listed race at York: should prove better at 1¾m than 1½m: goes well on
top-of-the-ground: usually held up: game. *R. F. Johnson Houghton.*

SEDAIR 2 b.c. (May 16) Green Desert (USA) 127–Double Celt 93 (Owen Dudley 94 +
12 l) [1990 6m* 7g* 7d] good-bodied colt: good walker and fluent mover: third foal:
half-brother to a winner in Sweden by Auction Ring: dam, from good family, suited
by 1½m: created very favourable impression when winning maiden at Ascot in July
by a head, clear, from Stone Mill: not so impressive in £14,900 event at York
following month, making all to beat Plan of Action by ¾ length: dropped away
quickly over 2f out (reportedly broke blood vessel) in Three Chimneys Dewhurst
Stakes at Newmarket: likely to be suited by 1m. *H. R. A. Cecil.*

SEDGY MEAD 2 b.g. (Apr 10) Myjinski (USA)–Miss Monroe 73 (Comedy Star 64
(USA) 12 l) [1990 8g 8.2s⁵ 10s] medium-sized, strong, angular gelding: first foal: dam
maiden, stayed 1¼m: fifth of 13, keeping on from rear, in maiden at Haydock in
October: carrying condition and well beaten other starts: should stay 1¼m. *P. J.
Jones.*

SEDUCTIVE SINGER (IRE) 2 b.c. (Mar 29) Dayeem (USA)–Inveigle 50
(Decoy Boy 129) [1990 6g⁴ 5m 6f³ 8g 6d] IR 2,100F, IR 4,000Y, 7,600 2-y-o: sturdy,
lengthy colt: second foal: dam ran twice: poor maiden: stays 6f: acts on firm and dead
ground. *R. Simpson.*

SEDUCTRESS 2 ch.f. (Mar 31) Known Fact (USA) 135–Much Too Risky 87 94
(Bustino 136) [1990 5m² 5m* 6g* 5m* 5f³ 6m⁵] small, unfurnished filly: has a quick
action: second foal: half-sister to 3-y-o 13f winner Boy Emperor (by Precocious):
dam 2-y-o 7.2f and 1m winner, is out of half-sister to very smart animals He Loves
Me and Wattlefield: fairly useful filly, successful in maiden at Sandown and £10,600
event (awarded race after being beaten on merit by Atlantic Flyer) at Newmarket in
June and Fairview New Homes Chesterfield Stakes (by ½ length from It's All
Academic) at latter course following month: beaten little more than a length when
fifth to Only Yours in 'Pacemaker Update' Lowther Stakes at York: stays 6f. *M. R.
Stoute.*

SEE ME DANCE (IRE) 2 b.f. (Apr 8) Niniski (USA) 125–Carnival Dance 69 —
(Welsh Pageant 132) [1990 7m a8g] smallish filly: sixth foal: half-sister to several
winners, including smart 5f to 8.2f winner Sarab (by Prince Tenderfoot) and 12.2f
winner Safe (by Kris): dam second over 1m and 1¼m: poor form in maidens at
Chepstow and Lingfield late in year. *P. F. I. Cole.*

SEENACHANCE 3 ch.f. King of Clubs 124–Masina (Current Coin 118) [1989 5d 55 d
7m⁵ 7m⁴ 7f⁵ 1990 a8g⁴ 7m⁵ 7m 10.6d 12m 12g] leggy, sparely-made filly: moderate
walker: plating-class maiden: below form after reappearance, in amateur handicaps
(facing very stiff tasks first 3) last 4 starts: should stay 1¼m: trained first 2 starts by
M. O'Neill. *D. Nicholson.*

SEE THE LIGHT 3 b.f. Relkino 131–Sun Worshipper (Sun Prince 128) [1989 6m —
8f 1990 14f⁵ 16s] leggy filly: little sign of ability on flat, in handicap final start:
winning hurdler. *Mrs V. A. Aconley.*

SELAAH 3 b.c. Rainbow Quest (USA) 134–Marwell 133 (Habitat 134) [1989 NR 100 p
1990 7g* 8m* 8f³] 110,000Y: leggy, sparely-made colt: third foal: half-brother to
high-class Caerwent (by Caerleon), effective from 5f to 1m: dam top-class sprinter
from good family: dead-heated in maiden at York and won 4-runner minor event
(readily by 1½ lengths from Bridal Toast) at Newbury in June: second favourite,
gave a lot of trouble at stalls, stayed on steadily from mid-division when 2½ lengths
fourth (promoted to third) of 16 in £64,400 Schweppes Golden Mile Handicap
(showed a quick, scratchy action) at Goodwood in August: stays 1m: looked very
useful performer in the making. *M. R. Stoute.*

SELDOM IN 4 ch.c. Mummy's Game 120–Pinzamber (Pinicola 113) [1989 8m 42
7m⁶ 8m 9fa 11g⁴ 1990 a11g* a11g a14g³ a14g⁵ a11g⁶] leggy, angular colt: won claimer
at Southwell in January, hanging left: off course 10 months before final outing:
seems to stay 1¾m: has swished tail. *J. Wharton.*

SELEUCIA 5 ch.m. Persian Bold 123–Cienaga (Tarboosh (USA)) [1989 NR 1990 **52**
10g 8f⁴ 8h⁶ 8f⁵ a8g⁵ 10.8m* 10.2g 12s³ 12.2m² 12m⁴ 12s] rather leggy, lengthy
mare: plater: ridden by 7-lb claimer, won for first time in handicap (no bid) at
Warwick in August: stays 1½m: acts on good to firm and soft going: has refused to
enter stalls, and was reluctant to race once at 3 yrs. *M. O'Neill.*

SELF EXPRESSION 2 b.c. (Mar 14) Homing 130–Subtlety (Grundy 137) [1990 **88**
7m* 7m² 7f⁴] leggy colt: has scope: second foal: half-brother to 3-y-o Intrigue (by
Mummy's Pet): dam half-sister to smart stayer Buttress and smart middle-distance
performer Dukedom: comfortably won maiden at Salisbury in June: better effort
½-length second of 6, quickening well from rear and running on strongly, to Bravefoot in Donnington Castle Stakes at Newbury following month: favourite, modest
fourth of 5 in Newmarket minor event: will be better suited by 1m +: carries head
high. *I. A. Balding.*

SELF IMPROVEMENT (USA) 4 b.c. Sharpen Up 127–Imaflash (USA) —
(Reviewer (USA)) [1989 11.5m⁴ 10f* 14m 1990 13v 16f] good-topped colt: modest
winner (ran in snatches) at 3 yrs: lightly raced and soundly beaten in subsequent
handicaps: suited by 1¼m: acts on firm going: found little when visored on debut. *N.
Tinkler.*

SELKIRK (USA) 2 ch.c. (Feb 19) Sharpen Up 127–Annie Edge 118 (Nebbiolo **108**
125) [1990 8m* 8g4] second foal: brother to fairly useful 3-y-o 16.2f winner Casual
Flash: dam 5f and 7f winner later successful at up to 11f in North America: 20/1, won
5-runner Country Lady Stardom Stakes at Goodwood in September by 4 lengths
from Balaat, leading over 2f out: ran well when over 5 lengths fourth of 5, keeping
on unable to challenge, to Hector Protector in Grand Criterium at Longchamp
following month: will stay 1¼m: useful. *I. A. Balding.*

SEMINOFF (FR) 4 b.g. In Fijar (USA) 121–Borjana (USA) (To The Quick —
(USA)) [1989 7m⁵ 10.1m 1990 9s 6v] close-coupled gelding: no sign of ability,
including in seller: blinkered final outing. *T. Craig.*

Mr George Strawbridge's "Selkirk"

SENOR POQUITO   2 b.g. (May 7) Primo Dominie 121–Poquito (Major Portion   **49** p
129) [1990 6d5 6f4 6m6] sturdy, good-quartered gelding: half-brother to several
winners, including very useful 6f and 1¼m winner Senorita Poquito (by Connaught):
dam won from 5f to 1¼m in Ireland: carrying condition, poor form in maidens at
Catterick and Pontefract: will probably be better suited by 7f: looks sort to do
better: retained by trainer 3,000 gns Doncaster September Sales. *Mrs J. R.
Ramsden.*

SENSIBLE DECISION (IRE)   2 b.g. (Apr 25) Reasonable (FR) 119–Lady   **40**
Monica (Irish Love 117) [1990 7.5m 8f 10s] IR 7,200Y: lengthy, rather angular
gelding: has scope: half-brother to Irish 9f winner Bushypark Lady (by Furry Glen):
dam unraced, from family of Juliette Marny and Julio Mariner: poor form in maidens,
including auctions: bit backward first 2 starts: seems to stay 1¼m. *T. D. Barron.*

SENTIMENTALITY (IRE)   2 b.c. (Apr 2) Reasonable (FR) 119–Good   **61**
Reliance (Good Bond 122) [1990 5m5 a5g3 a7g6 6m4 6m3 5m4 6m4 6m4 5g* 6d 5m4
5.8d] lengthy, good-quartered colt: carries condition: poor mover: half-brother to 3
winners, including fairly useful 5f to 1m winner Changabang and fairly useful 1981
2-y-o 5f and 6f winner Changatu (both by Touch Paper): dam never ran: useful
plater: won 20-runner nursery (no bid) at Wolverhampton in October: respectable
fourth in non-selling nursery there penultimate start: stays 6f: possibly unsuited by
a soft surface: blinkered last 4 starts. *K. T. Ivory.*

SEPTIEME CIEL (USA)   3 b.c. Seattle Slew (USA)–Maximova (FR) 121   **123**
(Green Dancer (USA) 131) [1989 6d5 7.5s* 8d4 7.5g* 7g* 1990 8d2 8f5 9.2g3
8d2 8g* 8g6 7g* 9f2]
    Septieme Ciel fared the worse of the two French challengers for the
General Accident Two Thousand Guineas at Newmarket. Looking well, he
came under pressure passing the two-furlong pole but kept on to finish fifth,
five lengths behind runner-up Machiavellian. But Septieme Ciel made the
better progress subsequently, showing form at least the equal of the horse
officially rated 9 lb his superior as a two-year-old. Placed efforts behind Priolo
in the Prix Jean Prat at Longchamp, eased close home having made most of
the running, and Boxing Day in the Prix de la Jonchere at Saint-Cloud, beaten
a short head, preceded a devastating success in the Prix Messidor at Maisons-
Laffitte in July. Ridden to lead approaching the final furlong Septieme Ciel
surged six lengths clear of River of Light and a very useful field by the line.
And Septieme Ciel finished his European career with his best performance
in winning the Group 1 Prix de la Foret at Longchamp in October. The Foret
has suffered slightly in competitiveness in the last two seasons for its re-
scheduling in mid- rather than late-October, but Septieme Ciel faced a worthy
opponent in Hungerford Stakes winner Norwich. Septieme Ciel justified
favouritism in workmanlike fashion. Always prominent, he took the front-
running Norwich's measure a furlong out and ran on well to score by two
lengths. On his only subsequent appearance Septieme Ciel was caught inside
the final furlong and beaten a head by the Breeders' Cup Mile runner-up
Itsallgreektome in the nine-furlong Hollywood Derby in November. He
reportedly remains in California to be trained by R. Mandella.

Prix de la Foret, Longchamp—Norwich does well to run Septieme Ciel to two lengths

John T. L. Jones's "Septieme Ciel"

Septieme Ciel (USA) (b.c. 1987)	Seattle Slew (USA) (b or br 1974)	Bold Reasoning (b or br 1968)	Boldnesian
			Reason To Earn
		My Charmer (b 1969)	Poker
			Fair Charmer
	Maximova (FR) (b 1980)	Green Dancer (b 1972)	Nijinsky
			Green Valley
		Baracala (ch 1972)	Swaps
			Seximee

Septieme Ciel is sure to attract support at stud. He's a good-looking, tall, though angular, son of Seattle Slew, whose progeny include young stallions such as Slew o'Gold and Slewpy. And he's well bred on the dam's side, too. Maximova reached a place in the French and Irish One Thousand Guineas prior to winning two pattern races over six furlongs in France. She's a half-sister to Prix d'Astarte winner Navratilovna and good sprinter/miler Vilikaia (both by Nureyev) out of useful miler Baracala. The next dam Seximee won twice over sprint distances in the States and also foaled Guineas winner Nonoalco and very smart middle-distance performer Stradavinsky. Septieme Ciel is a half-brother to two winners in France by Blushing Groom, namely the quite useful mile-and-a-quarter winner Balchaia and the promising two-year-old Maxigroom, successful in a seven-furlong maiden at Maisons-Laffitte in December. Septieme Ciel is effective at seven furlongs to nine furlongs. A short-actioned colt, he showed his best form in Europe on good ground—he ran only a fair race when second to Linamix in the Prix de Fontainebleau in April on good to soft and was below his best in the Prix de la Jonchere on similar ground at Saint-Cloud in June. *Mme C. Head, France.*

SEQUEL TWO 2 gr.c. (Apr 24) Nishapour (FR) 125–Roda Haxan 67 (Hunter-combe 133) [1990 7.5d 6g 7g² 7m² 6f⁶ 7m² 7f⁴ 8.2g⁴ 8m² 6s⁵ a7g a7g⁶] 8,000Y: neat   59 colt: ninth foal: half-brother to useful sprinter Novello (by Double Form): dam sister to high-class Pyjama Hunt: quite useful plater: suited by 7f: blinkered fourth and fifth starts: has run creditably for apprentice: sometimes races freely: has carried head high: fairly consistent. *J. Berry.*

SEREMO 4 gr.g. Morston (FR) 125–Serenata (Larrinaga 97) [1989 10s* 10v⁴ 10.6s 12g 10.6s⁴ 1990 a14g⁶ 8.3m 12f] leggy, sparely-made, angular gelding: quite modest handicapper at best: well beaten in 1990, in selling events last 2 outings: stays 1¼m: acts on good to firm and soft going: visored final start: sold out of Mrs N. Macauley's stable 2,700 gns Ascot May Sales after reappearance. *C. Holmes.* —

SERENADER (FR) 3 b.c. Ela-Mana-Mou 132–Seattle Serenade (USA) 82 (Seattle Slew (USA)) [1989 7m² 8.2g² 1990 11.7f⁴ 11.7f* 13.1h* 12g] tall colt: progressive form when winning maiden and handicap at Bath in May: co-favourite, struck into and severed tendons in King George V Handicap at Royal Ascot: should have stayed 1¾m: acted on hard ground: dead. *Major W. R. Hern.* 79

SERENIKI 3 b.f. Dublin Taxi–Highdrive (Ballymore 123) [1989 5f 5m⁵ 6f a6g⁵ a7g 1990 8m 7m 10f 8h⁶ a6g⁵] leggy, workmanlike filly: poor mover: plater: showed signs of retaining some ability in non-selling handicap final start, first for 7 months: best effort over 7f: twice bandaged behind: blinkered penultimate start: trained until after then by W. Wilson. *P. Mitchell.* —

SERENOSKI 2 b.g. (Apr 20) Petoski 135–Serenesse (Habat 127) [1990 6m 7f] leggy gelding: third foal: half-brother to 1¼m winner Towny Boy (by Camden Town) and 3-y-o Sakura Dancer (by Viking): dam listed winner in Italy: always behind in maidens at Salisbury (slowly away, showed knee action) and Brighton. *P. F. I. Cole.* —

SERGEANT MERYLL 6 b.g. Marching On 101–Mistress Meryll 61 (Tower Walk 130) [1989 7v 8f 1990 8m a7g⁶ 8g a8g⁶ 8m⁴ 8m a7g⁴ a8g 8d 7g³ a7g a8g a7g* a7g⁴] sturdy, quite attractive gelding: moderate mover: won 6-runner handicap at Lingfield in December, soon ridden along: effective at 7f and 1m: best form on an easy surface: visored once: bandaged first 3 starts in 1990: has won for apprentice. *P. Howling.* 52

SERIOUS HURRY 2 ch.c. (Mar 20) Forzando 122–Lady Bequick 81 (Sharpen Up 127) [1990 5f 5f² 5g² 5d³ a5g*] 10,500Y: strong, heavy-topped, sprint type: has plenty of scope: eighth foal: half-brother to 3-y-o Every One A Gem (by Nicholas Bill), useful sprinter Joytotheworld (by Young Generation) and sprint winner Kept Waiting (by Tanfirion): dam ran only at 2 yrs, winning at 5f: fair performer: odds on, won maiden at Lingfield in November by 6 lengths, making all: unsuited by a soft surface: may improve further. *Sir Mark Prescott.* 83

SERIOUS TIME 2 ch.c. (Mar 10) Good Times (ITY)–Milva 56 (Jellaby 124) [1990 7d a7g a7g³] 8,200Y, 21,000Y: leggy colt: second foal: half-brother to 3-y-o Miltiades (by Magic Mirror), modest 7f winner at 2 yrs: dam 6f winner: plating-class form in maidens at Yarmouth and Southwell: wore eyeshield and carried head high on final outing: will be better suited by 1m. *Sir Mark Prescott.* 57

SERIOUS TROUBLE 4 ch.c. Good Times (ITY)–Silly Woman (Silly Season 127) [1989 8g² 8s⁵ 7f* 7f* 7f² 8m² 8f² 8m* 7g⁴ 8g* 1990 10f² 8f* 7h* 9g 9m³ 8f] strong, good-topped colt: carries condition: won uncompetitive minor events at Brighton in spring, second hard held at 33/1-on from sole rival: well below form after, for lady rider first 2 occasions: best efforts at 1m: acts on any going: good mount for apprentice. *Sir Mark Prescott.* 98

SERLBY CONNECTION 5 ch.h. Crofthall 110–Well Connected (Bold And Free 118) [1989 10d 12f⁶ 12g⁵ 10m 8f 8.2g 8g 8.5f 7m 10.6d⁶ 8f* 8g* 8g 1990 7.5m⁶ 8f 7.5m 7f* 10d] big, lengthy horse: carries plenty of condition: has a slightly round action: plating-class handicapper on his day: worthwhile form in spring only when winning at Redcar in May: best at around 1m: acts on any going: not an easy ride: has swished tail under pressure: inconsistent. *S. R. Bowring.* 55

SESAME 5 b.m. Derrylin 115–Hot Spice (Hotfoot 126) [1989 10m 14f⁴ 12g⁵ 11f⁴ 12f* 12m³ 13.5g 10.2m² 14d⁵ 12m² 12v* 1990 12m 13.3m* 12d² 12g⁴ 12s⁶ 12f² 13.3g² 13.4g² 12m⁴ 12m⁴ 12d* 12s⁴ 12v*] strong, lengthy mare: carries condition: very useful performer: won listed events at Newbury in May and Bordeaux in November and EBF Blandford Stakes at the Curragh (making virtually all to beat Topanoora 2½ lengths) in October: ran creditably in good company seventh to tenth outings, behind The Wings in Prix Foy at Longchamp and Narwala in Princess Royal Stakes at Ascot last 2 occasions: suited by around 1½m: acts on any going, but particularly well on soft surface: takes strong hold and has worn a dropped noseband: splendidly tough and consistent: a credit to her trainer. *M. F. D. Morley.* 113

SET ASIDE (IRE) 2 b.c. (Mar 3) Petorius 117–Wollow Princess (Wollow 132) 72
[1990 5f³ 5f⁴ 6g a7g² a6g*] IR 7,000F, 15,500Y: rather leggy, attractive colt: half-brother to 1¼m seller winner Design Wise (by Prince Bee) and 3 winners abroad: dam third twice at 2 yrs in Ireland: blinkered, won 9-runner maiden at Lingfield late in year easily by 8 lengths: stays 7f. *D. R. C. Elsworth.*

SET THE STANDARDS (IRE) 2 b.g. (May 6) Mazaad 106–Jupiter Miss 76
(USA) (Hawaii) [1990 6g 6g³ 5f² 6g² 6m⁵ 5d⁵ 5s*] IR 6,500Y, 15,500 2-y-o: neat gelding: half-brother to a winner abroad by Prince Bee: dam ran once at 2 yrs in Ireland: modest performer: co-favourite, won 8-runner maiden auction at Edinburgh in October going away by 3 lengths from Savoy Forever: seems equally effective at 5f and 6f: probably acts on any going. *J. Berry.*

SEVENS ARE WILD 4 b.f. Petorius 117–Northern Glen (Northfields) (USA)) 40
[1989 8m 1990 a8g² a8g a8g4] leggy filly: slow-starting neck second of 8 in claimer at Lingfield in January, only sign of ability. *A. N. Lee.*

SEVEN SONS 3 b.g. Absalom 128–Archaic 65 (Relic) [1989 5s⁶ 5m* 6f⁶ 7m⁴ 6g —
5f⁵ 7g 6f 1990 7m 5m 8h⁶] small, close-coupled gelding: quite modest winner at 2 yrs: first form in handicaps when sixth in selling event at Bath: stays 7f: best form on top-of-the-ground: winning selling hurdler. *W. G. M. Turner.*

SEVERALS CLARE (IRE) 2 ch.f. (Apr 4) Tender King 123–Nutgrove 53
(Thatching 131) [1990 5f 5g⁵ 5m 6g 6g 6m² 5f] IR 500F, 1,000Y: sparely-made filly: has a sharp action: first foal: dam Irish maiden: over 2 lengths second of 10 to Gorinsky in seller at Goodwood, only worthwhile form: will be suited by 7f: sold 680 gns Doncaster September Sales. *F. Durr.*

SEVERALS PRINCESS 2 gr.f. (May 8) Formidable (USA) 125–Justicia 87 44
(Nonoalco (USA) 131) [1990 5f 5g 5g 5f³ 7m 6m 7f] 3,000Y: plain filly: poor mover: fifth foal: half-sister to 1m winner Justaglow (by Kalaglow) and 6f and 1m winner Crown Justice (by High Top): dam 2-y-o 5f winner, is half-sister to very useful 5f to 8.5f winner Royal Pinnacle: easily best effort staying-on third in maiden auction at Hamilton in July: should prove suited by further than 5f: sweating and very edgy penultimate start: withdrawn after throwing jockey and bolting eighth intended one: sold 600 gns Doncaster October Sales. *M. P. Naughton.*

SEXY MOVER 3 ch.g. Coquelin (USA) 121–Princess Sinna (Sun Prince 128) —
[1989 7g⁵ 8g⁶ 1990 10m] leggy gelding: lightly-raced maiden: should stay 1¼m. *J. P. Hudson.*

SHAADIN (USA) 3 ch.f. Sharpen Up 127–La Dolce 108 (Connaught 130) [1989 80
NR 1990 8m³ 8m³ 10.5g] close-coupled, angular filly: sister to Pebbles, closely related to 1989 maiden 3-y-o Ela Meem (by Kris) and half-sister to fair 1¼m winner Petradia (by Relkino): dam won twice over 1m and finished fifth in Oaks: fair maiden: should have stayed 1¼m: hung right second start, edged left third: stud. *L. M. Cumani.*

SHADAYID (USA) 2 gr.f. (Apr 10) Shadeed (USA) 135–Desirable 119 117 p
(Lord Gayle (USA) 124) [1990 6d* 7m* 8g*]

Shadayid had a lot to live up to when she made her debut at Ascot in late-June. She was out of a mare who wasn't far behind the best of her generation both at two and three years; was in the same ownership and stabled in the same yard as Salsabil, a filly who'd already won two classics and was to take another at the Curragh the following week; and, above all at this time, had an enormous home reputation which had already seen her supported at 66/1 and 33/1 for the 1991 One Thousand Guineas. When expectations run so high they

Prix Marcel Boussac, Longchamp—
Shadayid is the stable's third winner of this race in four years;
Caerlina (No. 10), Sha Tha (No. 4) and After The Sun can't match her turn of foot

seldom end up being fulfilled, but those who trusted the gallop reports and got involved with this gamble have every reason to feel satisfied. In a year in which good two-year-old fillies were thin on the ground, Shadayid stood out as one of the few with genuine classic potential. She won all her three starts without being stretched, and at Longchamp in October she signed off for the year with a striking performance in Europe's premier staying test for two-year-old fillies, the Prix Marcel Boussac.

The race in which Shadayid made her debut was the EBF Halifax Maiden Fillies Stakes over six furlongs. She looked slightly green and also a shade edgy beforehand, but after being backed from 5/2 to 13/8 she won in eye-catching style. The fact that none of the field had run before meant that it wasn't an easy race to assess. The timefigure was fast, though, and over the next couple of months the second, third and fourth, Futuh, Panchos Pearl and Jaffa Line all went on to prove themselves quite useful. Shadayid wasn't in action again until late-September, in the Kensington Palace Graduation Stakes back at Ascot. Apparently she pulled a shoulder muscle while being prepared for the Princess Margaret Stakes. Her trainer also felt she needed a tremendous amount of work during her recovery period, but if Shadayid was in any way ring-rusty after her lay-off, it certainly didn't show. This time she was faced with eight opponents. So Romantic, who'd won a Lingfield maiden in good style on her debut, looked the best of them on form; also in the line-up were a couple of impeccably-bred newcomers, namely Glint of Gold's half-sister Crystal Ring and the Cumani filly Shaima, a daughter of Shareef Dancer and the fillies' triple crown winner Oh So Sharp. Shadayid had far too much speed for all of them. As on her debut she took a strong hold under restraint early on. She had to be shaken up briefly to improve soon after halfway, but responded instantly, cruising through to lead approaching the distance and pulling away, with Carson sitting motionless, to beat Crystal Ring by three and a half lengths with Shaima close up in third. Despite the fact that the Guineas was over six months away and that she'd yet to prove herself in good company Shadayid continued to attract support for the first classic. The Coral firm alone had reportedly laid her to lose more than a quarter of a million pounds, a liability which prompted their representative to produce the memorable quote 'what can save us?' The brief answer to such a question was, and still is, plenty! The possibility of injury, loss of form or failure to train on is the bugbear of all ante-post bets on the classics, especially those made so far ahead.

Following the Boussac Shadayid's Guineas odds were even shorter. As it turned out the latest Boussac wasn't quite so strongly contested as some of its predecessors. Green Pola, probably the chief French hope following her wins at Saint-Cloud and in the Prix du Calvados at Deauville, was withdrawn on the morning of the race following a minor set-back. This left a field of nine. Shadayid was sent off a strong 5/3-on favourite to give her owner and trainer their third Boussac winner in four years following Salsabil and Ashayer; she was followed on 11/2 by the Fabre-trained Mr Prospector filly Sha Tha, who'd finished runner-up behind Magic Night in a tight finish to the Prix d'Aumale in September; Magic Night, reopposing on the same terms, started at 13/2 with the Prix d'Arenberg runner-up Polemic on 17/2 and the sole Irish challenger Jet Ski Lady among the outsiders on 28/1. As with so many races in France no-one seemed especially keen to go on, consequently Shadayid took a very strong hold and was soon close up in third behind Jet Ski Lady and the Prix d'Aumale fourth Joyeuse Marquise. The order remained that way until early in the straight, at which point the Irish filly began to find the pace more than she could cope with. Joyeuse Marquise took it up for a hundred yards or so, but it was clear Shadayid was still travelling well within herself. She edged right in behind the leader when just asked to quicken, then once straightened she accelerated in telling fashion, drawing clear entering the final furlong and being ridden out to maintain a two-length advantage to the line; Caerlina, who'd finished a close third in the Aumale, ran a splendid race for second considering how much she was set to do, while Sha Tha, a short head away in third, tracked the winner from a long way out but never looked like producing sufficient pace to trouble her. The Prix Marcel Boussac has an excellent record as a pointer to the classics. Recent winners of the Boussac have

Hamdan Al-Maktoum's "Shadayid"

included Triptych, Miesque, Midway Lady and Salsabil—the winners of no fewer than eight classics between them—so when an unbeaten filly wins the race in the style Shadayid did it's hardly surprising that bookmakers tread carefully. Shadayid is quoted at 3/1 at the time of writing with most firms for the One Thousand Guineas, which doesn't seem generous when you consider that Salsabil was available at 16/1 after beating a field of similar quality in the previous year's Boussac. Nevertheless, there's no doubting that Shadayid is already a very smart filly with a most effective turn of foot. More importantly, she's almost certainly capable of considerably better than she's needed to show so far, and provided she progresses along the right lines over the winter it'll take a very good filly to beat her at Newmarket on May 2nd.

Apparently Shadayid is regarded as a nervous type; she was edgy and on her toes at Longchamp and as a precautionary measure her trainer had her accompanied to the stalls by one of his staff. Her sire Shadeed was a highly strung colt who became very excitable in the preliminaries prior to his Guineas. He only scrambled home from Bairn that day, but at Ascot later in the year he proved himself one of the best milers of the 'eighties with a tremendously impressive defeat of Teleprompter and Zaizafon in the Queen Elizabeth II Stakes. Shadayid's a member of Shadeed's second crop. She's by far his best representative so far, but as yet he hasn't had enough runners to start drawing firm conclusions about his long-term prospects at stud. Shadayid's dam Desirable will be remembered by most people for her achievements as a two-year-old in 1983, when she won the Princess Margaret Stakes and the Cheveley Park. She didn't manage to get her head in front the following year, but she finished placed in several top contests—including the One Thousand Guineas and the Nassau Stakes—and after costing only IR 10,000 guineas as a yearling she was eventually sold to the Coolmore Stud for 1,000,000 guineas. Desirable was sold again in 1986 for 1,600,000 dollars to the Shadwell Estate Company. Her first foal by El Gran Senor died. Shadayid was produced the following year, while her two-year-old for 1991 is a colt by Blushing Groom. Desirable's dam Balidaress won three races in Ireland at up to a mile and a quarter and she also finished placed over hurdles. Her record as a broodmare bears the closest inspection. Besides Desirable, Balidaress is responsible for another Cheveley Park winner in Park Appeal, the Irish Oaks winner Alydaress and Nashamaa, who showed very useful form at up to a mile and a half in Ireland. Shadayid's third dam Innocence won twice over nine furlongs. She descends from The Veil, who produced several smart winners including the very speedy Miss Melody, dam of the Poule d'Essai des Pouliches winner Masarika.

		Nijinsky	Northern Dancer
	Shadeed (USA)	(b 1967)	Flaming Page
	(b 1982)	Continual	Damascus
Shadayid (USA)		(b or br 1976)	Continuation
(gr.f. Apr 10, 1988)		Lord Gayle	Sir Gaylord
	Desirable	(b 1965)	Sticky Case
	(gr 1981)	Balidaress	Balidar
		(gr 1973)	Innocence

What of Shadayid's stamina potential, then? Desirable stayed a mile and a quarter well as a three-year-old, and although Shadeed was never tried at that distance he was certainly bred to stay it. However, we think it likely that Shadayid will prove better over shorter. As we said earlier, she tends to take a very strong hold in the early part of her races; unless she learns to relax, a mile could well prove her optimum trip. Shadayid is a lengthy filly with scope. She seems to act on good to firm going and dead; it remains to be seen how she'll cope with ground that's very firm—she's not a particularly impressive mover in her slower paces. *J. L. Dunlop.*

SHADES OF JADE 2 gr.f. (May 4) General Wade 93–Gellifawr 80 (Saulingo 122) [1990 5f 5m] leggy, plain filly: has a very round action: fourth foal: half-sister to 8.3f seller winner Singing Gold (by Gold Claim), also winner in Belgium: dam best at 5f: soundly beaten in maidens at Salisbury and Newbury. *J. J. Bridger.* —

SHADES OF VERA 2 b.f. (May 23) Precocious 126–More Reliable (Morston (FR) 125) [1990 6f 5m6 5m 6m2 6g* 5g] angular, unfurnished filly: good walker: has quick action: fourth foal: half-sister to very useful 1984 5f and 6f winner Star Video (by Hittite Glory) and a winner in Belgium: dam never ran: improved form to win nursery at Pontefract in October: will probably stay 7f. *G. Lewis.* 76

SHADHA (USA) 2 ch.f. (Jan 26) Devil's Bag (USA)–Treizieme (USA) 121 (The Minstrel (CAN) 135) [1990 6f* 7f5 8d] $700,000Y: good-topped filly: has scope: first foal: dam French 1m to 1½m filly later successful in USA, is from good family: odds on, won maiden at Yarmouth in July: better effort over 5 lengths fifth of 6, keeping on never dangerous, to Trojan Crown in listed race at Newmarket: should stay 1m: seems unsuited by dead ground. *A. C. Stewart.* 77

SHADIDEEN (USA) 2 ch.c. (Feb 14) Shadeed (USA) 135–Allegretta 101 (Lombard (GER) 126) [1990 a8g5] 96,000Y: half-brother to 2 winners in France, including 3-y-o Irish Allegre (by Irish River), successful at 9f and 1¼m (at 2 yrs): dam 2-y-o 1m and 9f winner, stayed 1½m: favourite, always-prominent fifth of 11, beaten over a length, to Toshiba Comet Too in late-year maiden at Lingfield: should improve. *P. F. I. Cole.* 61 p

SHADOW BIRD 3 b.f. Martinmas 128–In The Shade 89 (Bustino 136) [1989 7m 7m 7g 1990 10m5 12g2 14g6 13g* 13.3g6 12g a12g5] leggy, workmanlike filly: moderate mover: quite modest performer: won 4-runner maiden auction race at Ayr in July: stiff tasks in handicaps afterwards: should prove best short of 1¾m: wandered under pressure second start. *G. A. Pritchard-Gordon.* 70

SHADOWLAND (IRE) 2 ch.g. (Mar 30) Be My Native (USA) 122–Sunland Park (Baragoi 115) [1990 7m a7g4 a6g 8d] IR 7,800F, IR 14,500Y: strong gelding: has scope: half-brother to several winners, including fairly useful middle-distance performer Gulfland (by Gulf Pearl): dam never ran: plating-class maiden: stays 1m. *G. A. Pritchard-Gordon.* 54

SHADOW THEM 2 gr.g. (May 31) Absalom 128–River Chimes 43 (Forlorn River 124) [1990 5m4 5m 5m 5m 8.2g] lengthy, rather dipped-backed gelding: moderate walker: seventh foal: brother to 3-y-o Star of The Sea, speedy 1984 2-y-o Absent Chimes and quite modest 1987 2-y-o Rapid Chimes: dam sister to high-class 47

Rapid River: poor form: has given impression something amiss: trained first 3 outings by W. Jarvis. *C. A. Dwyer.*

SHADY LEAF (IRE)   2 b.f. (May 8) Glint of Gold 128–Dancing Shadow 117   **56** p (Dancer's Image (USA)) [1990 8.2m4] sixth foal: half-sister to smart French 5f and 1m winner River Dancer (by Irish River) and 1986 French 2-y-o 7f winner Entracte (by Henbit): dam, half-sister to Sun Princess, smart over 1m and 1¼m: over 7 lengths fourth of 14 to Good Policy in minor event at Nottingham in September: will improve. *M. R. Stoute.*

SHADY PIMPERNEL   2 b.c. (May 21) Blakeney 126–Upanishad 85 (Amber   **38** Rama (USA) 133) [1990 8f 8.2g] 7,800Y: leggy colt: has scope: brother to useful 1¼m winner Goody Blake and half-brother to 1m winner Fenfire (by Trojan Fen) and middle-distance winner Diwali (by Great Nephew): dam 1¼m winner, is half-sister to smart sprinter Bas Bleu: poor form in maiden at Thirsk and seller at Nottingham: sold 2,200 gns Newmarket Autumn Sales. *Mrs J. R. Ramsden.*

SHAFFIC (FR)   3 b.c. Auction Ring (USA) 123–Tavella (FR) 98 (Petingo 135)   **78** [1989 NR 1990 10f5 10.1m* 12m2] rather angular, leggy colt: has a long stride: brother to very smart 5f to 1m winner Meis El-Reem and half-brother to 2 winners: dam beaten at 2 yrs when 6f winner: won minor event at Windsor in July: favourite, still green and ran in snatches when second of 6 in Goodwood handicap following month: stays 1½m: sold 8,600 gns Newmarket Autumn Sales. *D. R. C. Elsworth.*

SHAFOURI (IRE)   2 b.c. (Feb 19) Alzao (USA) 117–Sauntry (Ballad Rock 122)   **62** p [1990 6g4] IR 22,000F, 72,000Y: rather sparely-made colt: third foal: brother to fairly useful 5f (at 2 yrs) and 7.6f winner Bollin Zola: dam unraced daughter of half-sister to good French stayer El Badr: bandaged, over 4 lengths fourth of 16, racing keenly then keeping on, to Fancy Me in maiden at Newcastle in October: moved moderately down: should improve. *Mrs L. Piggott.*

SHAHI (USA)   2 ch.c. (Mar 10) Shahrastani (USA) 135–First Kiss 84 (Kris 135)   **85** P [1990 8m3] workmanlike colt: first foal: dam 1¼m winner, is half-sister to smart 1m winner Miller's Mate out of daughter of top-class middle-distance filly Pistol Packer: backward and very green, 3 lengths third of 14, soon prominent and staying on well under considerate ride last 2f, to Hilti's Hut in maiden at Newmarket in October: will stay 1¼m: sure to improve considerably, and win races. *H. R. A. Cecil.*

SHAHRIZA   3 br.f. Persian Bold 123–Amalee 57 (Troy 137) [1989 6d 6g 1990   — 13.3m 13.1m 10.8m] leggy, angular filly: has a round action: well beaten, including in selling handicap: sold 1,000 gns Ascot October Sales. *C. C. Elsey.*

SHAIKH SAFI   2 ch.c. (Apr 8) Claude Monet (USA) 121–Safidar 83 (Roan Rocket   — 128) [1990 6g 7m] close-coupled, angular colt: fifth reported living foal: half-brother to 1988 2-y-o 8.2f seller winner El Dalsad (by Dalsaan): dam won at 1m: well beaten in maidens at Nottingham and Warwick. *J. D. Czerpak.*

SHAIMA (USA)   2 b.f. (Mar 16) Shareef Dancer (USA) 135–Oh So Sharp   **101** p 131 (Kris 135) [1990 7m3 7.3s*]

The fillies triple crown winner Oh So Sharp has had two foals of racing age and both have won races; the second of them, Shaima, looks a very useful prospect. A sparely-made, angular filly, Shaima ran just twice at two, keeping on to be third to the subsequent Prix Marcel Boussac winner Shadayid in the Kensington Palace Graduation Stakes at Ascot in September before improving greatly to win the listed Woods Edge Radley Farm Stakes over an extended seven furlongs at Newbury in October. But for unseating her rider, getting loose and crashing into advertising boardings on the way to the start of a minor event at York in between, Shaima might never have run at Newbury; her injuries weren't serious, however, and she suffered no lasting effects, gaining a three-length victory over the Leicester maiden winner Brockette. Looking really well, Shaima, who started co-favourite for the six-runner event with the promising Leicester second Lupescu, travelled smoothly in a group of three along the far rail, quickened immediately when shaken up over a furlong out and kept on really well in the soft ground.

Oh So Sharp, whose first foal Ben Alisky (by Dunbeath) won over a mile in Ireland and whose third is by Blushing Groom, is a daughter of the Irish mile-and-a-quarter winner and excellent broodmare Oh So Fair; besides Oh So Sharp her numerous winners include the dual Nassau Stakes winner Roussalka (herself the dam of the smart sprinter Gayane), the One Thousand Guineas second Our Home, the Jersey Stakes winner Etienne Gerard and the

		Northern Dancer	Nearctic
	Shareef Dancer (USA)	(b 1961)	Natalma
	(b 1980)	Sweet Alliance	Sir Ivor
Shaima (USA)		(b 1974)	Mrs Peterkin
(b.f. Mar 16, 1988)		Kris	Sharpen Up
	Oh So Sharp	(ch 1976)	Doubly Sure
	(ch 1982)	Oh So Fair	Graustark
		(b 1967)	Chandelle

Ribblesdale third My Fair Niece. Oh So Fair is out of a half-sister to the very smart Prince Taj and a granddaughter of a full sister to Nasrullah. Shaima can fairly be expected to be suited by upwards of a mile and a quarter at three. So far the round-actioned Shaima has raced on good to firm ground and soft, both of which Oh So Sharp handled effectively when winning her three classics. Shaima may never become as good as her dam but she's certain to win more races and may well prove good enough for one of the minor classics, such as the Italian Oaks, in the event of her falling below classic standard in Britain. *L. M. Cumani.*

SHAKIRA BLEND   5 br.g. Royal Blend 117–High Seeker 54 (Hotfoot 126) [1989 NR 1990 a12g a12g] of no account: visored final outing: sold 1,900 gns Ascot June Sales. *R. Dickin.*   —

SHALAGEN   3 b.f. Lochnager 132–Hunslet 72 (Comedy Star (USA) 121) [1989 NR 1990 8.5m] 7,200Y: first foal: dam, 7.2f winner, is sister to useful 1m and 1¼m winner/smart hurdler Starfen: backward and very green when tailed off in claimer at Beverley in April. *M. H. Easterby.*   —

SHALFA (USA)   3 b.f. Riverman (USA) 131–Bon Gout (USA) (Dewan (USA)) [1989 NR 1990 7m6 10.5g4 10m3 10g5 12m5 9g 8.2d] 140,000Y: rangy, good sort: second foal: dam won 6 races in USA at up to 9f: modest maiden: deteriorated last 4 starts, hanging left and finding little, then slowly away in handicaps on last 2 of them: stays 1¼m: sold to join E. Incisa 3,200 gns Newmarket December Sales: one to be wary of. *A. A. Scott.*   71 d

SHALFORD (IRE)   2 ch.c. (Mar 18) Thatching 131–Enigma 87 (Ahonoora 122) [1990 6m 6m2 5m* 6m* 6f5 7m2 6g2 6g3] 70,000Y: strong colt, with scope: has a round action: first foal: dam maiden sprinter, best at 2 yrs, is sister to very useful Irish sprinter Princess Tracy: quite useful colt: successful in minor event at Chepstow and nursery (comfortably) at Windsor in July: best efforts when placed after, behind Time Gentlemen in Rokeby Farms Mill Reef Stakes at Newbury final start: effective at 6f and 7f. *R. Hannon.*   95

SHAMARZANA   3 b.f. Darshaan 133–Sharmeen (FR) (Val de Loir 133) [1989 NR 1990 10m 10f2] rangy, rather unfurnished filly: seventh foal: half-sister to 3 winners, notably Shergar (by Great Nephew) and Shernazar (by Busted): dam fairly useful French middle-distance winner: second favourite, made smooth headway to lead 1½f out and in process of making most promising debut before weakening quickly and collapsing soon after finish in maiden at Sandown in April: 11/8-on, beaten 10 lengths by sole opponent Mill Run in similar event at Yarmouth 3 months later and retired. *M. R. Stoute.*   ?

SHAMBO   3 b.c. Lafontaine (USA) 117–Lucky Appeal 36 (Star Appeal 133) [1989 6f5 6f6 7g 7g3 8.2d 10g6 1990 8.2s 11.7f2 11.5m3 12g 12.3m* 14f2 14g* 12m5 13.3g] strong, quite attractive colt: moderate walker and mover: fairly useful handicapper: won at Chester (made all) in July and York (£15,900 event) in August: ran moderately in £20,400 event at Newbury final outing: beaten by strongly-run race at 1¾m, and will stay further: appears best on sound surface: lacks turn of foot. *C. E. Brittain.*   91

SHAMIRANI   4 gr.g. Darshaan 133–Sharmada (FR) 113 (Zeddaan 130) [1989 8m* 11.5m2 10f2 1990 10f 8g 12s] leggy, good-topped gelding: useful winner as 3-y-o: lightly raced and no form in handicaps on flat in 1990: suited by middle distances: acts on firm going: has often flashed tail, and is difficult ride: wore crossed noseband on reappearance when trained by J. Johnson: winning hurdler. *G. M. Moore.*

SHAMPOO   3 ch.c. Sharpo 132–Wasslaweyeh (USA) 66 (Damascus (USA)) [1989 NR 1990 7m* 6g2 7m] leggy, quite good-topped colt: has quick action: first foal: dam stayed 1¼m: well backed, won maiden at Kempton in July: fairly useful performances when running-on second in minor event at Leicester and about 6 lengths ninth of 11 to Enharmonic in listed race (bit edgy, moved poorly down) at York: will prove best at up to 7f, possibly with give in the ground. *W. J. Haggas.*   95

SHAMSHAD 3 b.c. Darshaan 133–Shannfara (FR) (Zeddaan 130) [1989 NR 1990   **72** §
10g⁴ 12.2m⁴] leggy, close-coupled colt: fifth living foal: half-brother to fairly useful
10.4f winner Sharardoun (by Sharpen Up) and smart middle-distance performer
Shantaroun (by Green Dancer): dam very useful 1m to 9f winner in France: edgy,
running-on fourth of 22 in maiden at Kempton in June: favourite, below that form
and looked ungenuine in similar event at Catterick 5 weeks later: bandaged both
starts: sold 2,800 gns Newmarket Autumn Sales: one to be wary of. *M. R. Stoute.*

SHAMSHIR 2 ch.f. (Feb 21) Kris 135–Free Guest 125 (Be My Guest (USA)   **113** p
126) [1990 7m⁵ 7m* 8g² 8m*]
    Cumani and his retained jockey Dettori enjoyed a highly successful
partnership in the latest season. The trainer's final total of a hundred and
eight winners in Britain was by far his best, while the jockey became the first
teenager to ride a hundred winners in a British season since Piggott back in
1955. Naturally, there were also some set-backs along the way, and the
biggest came at the end of the year with the Aga Khan's decision to sever his
connection with British racing, depriving the yard of highly promising types
such as Sharifabad and also a number of impeccably-bred unraced horses.
However, there are plenty of interesting horses left for the coming season.
Snurge's half-brother Suomi, for example, looked a very useful prospect when
cruising home by ten lengths at Newcastle on his debut, while Island Universe was equally if not more impressive on his only start at Ascot. The
Rockfel winner Crystal Gazing is another who'll make her presence felt in
good company; and, last but by no means least, there's Shamshir, a really
progressive filly who put up an excellent performance on her final start to win
the Brent Walker Fillies' Mile at Ascot.
    The step up from seven furlongs to a mile proved instrumental in getting
the best out of Shamshir. On her debut in a maiden race at Newmarket in
August she was sent off at even money in a field of ten. She ran green and
never reached the front rank against more experienced rivals that day, but in

Brent Walker Fillies' Mile, Ascot—
Shamshir and Safa finish clear of Atlantic Flyer, Jaffa Line and the rest

Sheikh Mohammed's "Shamshir"

similar company over the same course and distance two weeks later she made
no mistake, leading two furlongs from home and running on strongly to hold
off the sustained challenge of the favourite Majmu by a head, the pair clear.
Majmu and Shamshir renewed rivalry in the May Hill Stakes at Doncaster in
September, both starting at 6/1 behind the 15/8 joint favourites Trojan Crown,
who'd won the Sweet Solera Stakes, and the Dancing Brave filly Joud, an
impressive winner of a minor event at Newmarket on her debut half an hour
after Shamshir had got off the mark. As at Newmarket it was clear from some
way out that Shamshir and Majmu would have the finish between them.
Indeed, the way the two of them quickened clear of their five opponents from
the distance was most impressive, and although Shamshir battled on tena-
ciously it was Majmu who prevailed this time by a short head. And so to Ascot
for the Brent Walker Fillies' Mile. Under its previous sponsorships by Green
Shield, Argos and Hoover the race had gradually grown in stature, producing
two Oaks winners in the last six runnings, and in 1990 it was upgraded to
Group 1 status. There were plenty of potentially smart fillies on view in the
field of twelve. The impressive Sandown maiden winner Third Watch was one
of them, and though she looked past her best for the season she started the
11/4 favourite. Shamshir and the Teachers Whiskey Prestige Stakes winner
Jaffa Line were next in the betting on 11/2, with Majmu a point longer and the
highly-regarded Nottingham winner Safa a 7/1-chance. Those who'd supported the favourite could have torn up their tickets early in the straight, at which
point she lost the lead and dropped away tamely. Majmu and then Glowing

Ardour took over briefly just under two out, but in the next hundred yards or so the complexion of the race altered dramatically. Shamshir, who'd tracked the leaders travelling strongly from the start, burst into the lead with a furlong and a half to run. Safa also showed a useful turn of foot despite edging right, but Shamshir held the upper hand throughout the final furlong, galloping on with great zest to win by two lengths with Atlantic Flyer a further three lengths away in third and Jaffa Line fourth. Majmu, who had also failed to take the eye in the paddock, ran well below her best in sixth. That turned out to be Shamshir's last race. She was due to run in the Racing Post Trophy at Doncaster but was withdrawn on the day because of the testing conditions.

			Sharpen Up	Atan
		Kris	(ch 1969)	Rocchetta
		(ch 1976)	Doubly Sure	Reliance II
Shamshir			(b 1971)	Soft Angels
(ch.f. Feb 21, 1988)			Be My Guest	Northern Dancer
	Free Guest	(ch 1974)	What A Treat
	(ch 1981)	Fremanche	Jim French
		(ch 1973)	La Manche

Shamshir, quite an attractive filly, was bred by the Fittocks Stud—which is run by the Cumani family—and she's extremely well related. Her sire Kris is one of Europe's most sought-after stallions, and besides Shamshir, the likes of Shavian, Rafha, Divine Danse and Shining Steel (in the USA) all represented him with distinction in 1990. Shamshir's dam will be instantly recognisable to anyone who followed the fortunes of this stable during the 'eighties. Free Guest, whose first live foal Shamshir is, was a high-class and admirably consistent performer at up to a mile and a half. In three seasons' racing she won nine of her fifteen starts, including the Sun Chariot Stakes twice, the Nassau Stakes, the Princess Royal Stakes and the Extel Handicap. Free Guest isn't the only Extel winner out of her dam. Fremanche, successful over nine furlongs in Italy on her only outing, also produced the 1985 winner Fish 'N' Chips. She's responsible for several other winners too, notably Fresh, a good middle-distance filly in Italy who produced the useful sprinter Be Fresh (by Free Guest's sire Be My Guest). Further back in the pedigree there's a South American connection. Shamshir's third dam La Manche was a fair performer in Argentina, and her grandam Cote d'Or was a high-class performer in the same country whose sixteen wins included the Argentine Oaks and the Gran Premio Carlos Pellegrini. According to her trainer Shamshir will be aimed at the One Thousand Guineas, for which she's quoted at around 16/1 as we go to press, and the Oaks. Although she's by no means short of pace we rather doubt she'll be speedy enough to win the Guineas, particularly if Shadayid is sent to Newmarket in top form. However, Shamshir could run well in that race, and once she goes beyond a mile she should come into her own. If Shamshir improves in the way that her dam did as a three-year-old there's every chance she'll develop into a leading contender for the Gold Seal Oaks. *L. M. Cumani.*

SHAMSHOM AL ARAB (IRE) 2 gr.c. (Mar 5) Glenstal (USA) 118–Love Locket (Levmoss 133) [1990 6d 7f6 7d 6g] IR 35,000Y: lengthy, angular colt: half-brother to quite useful 7f and 1m winner Allez Au Bon (by Glenstal) and 2 winning Irish middle-distance stayers, one by Taufan: dam once-raced half-sister to very smart sprinter Ballad Rock: plating-class maiden: blinkered first time, nineteenth of 20 in Cartier Million at Phoenix Park third start: trained first 2 by D. Murray-Smith. *W. Carter.* 57

SHAMYL 3 ch.g. Ahonoora 122–Salidar (Sallust 134) [1989 6f5 6f6 7f a7g a7g5 a6g 1990 a7g a6g2 5m5 5g6 6g 5g 6m5 5g3 5g3] small, lengthy gelding: plating-class maiden: seems best at sprint distances: acts on good to firm ground: trained until after reappearance (blinkered, ran moderately) by J. Dunlop: wore tongue strap seventh start: usually wears crossed noseband. *P. Mitchell.* 58

SHANAKEE 3 b.g. Wassl 125–Sheeog 80 (Reform 132) [1989 5s6 6f4 6h4 6m5 6f5 1990 a8g6] medium-sized gelding: plating-class form at best: blinkered once at 2 yrs. *D. Burchell.* —

SHANGHAI BREEZE 2 b.c. (May 4) Stanford 121§–Nanking 90 (Above Suspicion 127) [1990 6m 5m 5.8m 7m] 2,300Y, 4,800 2-y-o: tall, rather unfurnished —

colt: moderate walker and mover: half-brother to 3-y-o 7.5f seller winner Izzy Gunner (by Gunner B): dam suited by a good test of stamina: well beaten in varied events: sold 800 gns Newmarket Autumn Sales. *Mrs S. Armytage.*

SHANNON EXPRESS 3 gr.g. Magic Mirror 105–Tatisha (Habitat 134) [1989 6m⁴ 7m⁴ 6g a6g⁶ 1990 7g 7f 7g⁴ 7m⁵ 7d 8f³ 10f² 8f² 10g* 10f² 10d 8m a8g³ a10g² a11g²] leggy, angular, plain gelding: poor mover: modest performer: ridden by 7-lb claimer, won seller (bought in 9,500 gns) at Ripon in September: ran well when placed in handicaps and claimer afterwards: stays 11f: acts on firm going, unsuited by dead: blinkered sixth to eighth starts. *P. A. Kelleway.* **78**

SHANNON FLOOD 3 b.c. In Fijar (USA) 121–Gracious Girl (USA) (Forli (ARG)) [1989 NR 1990 7f³ 8f² 7m⁴] close-coupled colt: first foal: dam, French 2-y-o 6.5f winner, is half-sister to Prix de Diane Hermes winner Lady In Silver: quite modest form in maidens and minor event in the spring: sweating, very edgy and mulish to post second start: taken down early on third: races freely, but should be suited by further than 7f: wore tongue strap. *M. Moubarak.* **69**

SHARAGIL 3 b.g. Muscatite 122–Cameo Dancer (Jukebox 120) [1989 NR 1990 7f 6m 7g 5m³ 6g⁶ 5m⁶ 5.8f] 3,500F, 5,000Y, 6,000 2-y-o: strong, workmanlike gelding: fourth foal: dam ran 4 times at 2 yrs in Ireland: 50/1, easily best effort when third of 12 in handicap at Sandown in May: suited by 5f: visored final start: sold 950 gns Ascot October Sales. *S. Dow.* **51**

SHARBLASK 6 b.h. Sharpo 132–Blaskette 99 (Blast 125) [1989 8m 9g⁴ 11m 8.2d³ 8g a8g 1990 8.2m 8.2m 10d 8g 8v] leggy, quite good-topped horse: moderate mover: useful as 4-y-o: has lost his form completely: used to be suited by 1m and to go particularly well on a soft surface: usually blinkered or visored: reluctant to enter stalls fourth start. *T. Craig.* **—**

SHAREEF STAR 2 b.g. (May 21) Shareef Dancer (USA) 135–Ultra Vires 87 (High Line 125) [1990 7g 8m] leggy gelding: seventh foal: half-brother to several winners, including stayer Prince Sobur (by Jalmood) and Galtres Stakes winner Ulterior Motive (by Pyjama Hunt): dam winning stayer: no show in maidens at Wolverhampton and Chepstow: sold 650 gns Doncaster October Sales. *M. Blanshard.* **—**

SHARIFABAD (IRE) 2 b.c. (Apr 23) Darshaan 133–Safaya (FR) (Zeddaan 130) [1990 7m⁴ 8g*] **96 P**
Leading third-year stallion Darshaan was represented by a couple of very promising two-year-olds at the Cambridgeshire meeting in early-October. The filly Dartrey was one of them, justifying favouritism in most impressive fashion in the Oh So Sharp Stakes, and the other was the colt Sharifabad, who made his debut in division one of the Westley Maiden Stakes over seven furlongs two days earlier. The Westley Stakes has been used as a starting point for some good horses in the last few years, including Doyoun, Charmer, Old Vic and Observation Post. Significantly, it's also a race Cumani has won with Tolomeo and Pirate Army, and although Sharifabad didn't emulate that pair he ran with considerable promise, keeping on strongly despite being checked in his run, to finish a close fourth of eighteen behind the more experienced Environment Friend. The fact that Sharifabad started at 14/1 that day was understandable, as he looked green and in need of the race. He seemed much sharper when sent to contest the fifteen-runner Chesterton Maiden Stakes over a mile on the same course two weeks later and rewarded those who made him favourite by winning in fine style, leading on the bridle two furlongs out and forging clear under hands-and-heels riding up the hill to beat Peking Opera by two and a half lengths with the rest well strung out. Although the opposition wasn't exceptional, even by maiden standards, there was plenty to like about that performance, and bookmakers promptly introduced him into the ante-post market for the Ever Ready Derby at 33/1. If Sharifabad does prove good enough to contest a Derby it'll probably be at Chantilly or the Curragh. As a consequence of the Aliysa affair, his owner the Aga Khan decided to cut his connection with British racing in early-December; Sharifabad will be trained in Ireland by John Oxx for the 1991 season.

Sharifabad should stay a mile and a quarter as a three-year-old; whether he'll stay a mile and a half is more problematical. In his favour is the fact that he's by the Prix du Jockey-Club winner Darshaan, a horse who shaped as if he'd have had no problems staying a mile and three quarters given the chance

Sharifabad (IRE) (b.c. Apr 23, 1988)	Darshaan (br 1981)	Shirley Heights (b 1975)	Mill Reef Hardiemma
		Delsy (b or br 1972)	Abdos Kelty
	Safaya (FR) (ro 1971)	Zeddaan (gr 1965)	Grey Sovereign Vareta
		Shiraza (b 1966)	Twilight Alley But Lovely

and one who's already sired the likes of Aliysa, Hellenic, Narwala and Game Plan; there's also stamina on the female side of the pedigree in that Sharifabad's second dam Shiraza, successful at a mile and a quarter and second in the Prix Fille de l'Air, is by the Gold Cup winner Twilight Alley. However, closer up on the female side speed features more prominently. Sharifabad's dam Safaya won twice as a two-year-old in France over five furlongs. She's also produced the useful 1981 French two-year-old five-furlong performer Shayina (by Run The Gantlet), as well as the three-year-old seven-furlong winner Sarafia (by Dalsaan) and the Poule d'Essai des Pouliches and Prix Saint-Alary runner-up Safita (by Habitat). Whatever Sharifabad's optimum distance turns out to be, it's a fair bet he's got quite a bit of improvement in him. Not an especially handsome individual, he's well grown with plenty of scope for progress. *L. M. Cumani.*

SHARINSKI 3 ch.g. Niniski (USA) 125–Upanishad 85 (Amber Rama (USA) 133) 45
[1989 7f⁵ 7g³ 7.5f⁶ 7m 9g 1990 12f 12.3f 12.2m 15g² 15.3g² a12g] lengthy, angular gelding: plater: second at Edinburgh and Wolverhampton (claimed out of M. H. Easterby's stable £7,101) in June: off course 6 months before final start: suited by a test of stamina: blinkered last 5 starts (took keen hold first 2): never going well in visor final one at 2 yrs. *R. T. Juckes.*

SHARLIE'S WIMPY 11 ch.g. Tumble Wind (USA)–Sweet Sharlie 77 (Fighting 42
Charlie 127) [1989 6m² 6f⁶ 5f³ 7f⁴ 7m² 7m⁴ 7g³ 5f 8f⁶ 1990 5s 6f² 7.6m 7f³ a7g 6m 8m 7d] strong, attractive gelding: carries plenty of condition: good mover: poor handicapper: best at 6f or 7f: well suited by a sound surface: has worn blinkers: has won for apprentice: finds little and well served by waiting tactics. *W. J. Pearce.*

SHARON'S RABBIT 2 b.g. (Apr 10) Hotfoot 126–Loving Doll 72 (Godswalk 50
(USA) 130) [1990 a6g5 a7g] 8,800F, 5,500 (privately) Y: small gelding: moderate walker: second foal: brother to 3-y-o seller winner Ash Amour: dam stayed 7f: backward and ridden by apprentice when around 10 lengths fifth of 13 in claimer at Southwell: soundly beaten when well backed later in December. *R. J. Muddle.*

SHARPALTO 3 br.c. Noalto 120–Sharp Venita 84 (Sharp Edge 123) [1989 7.3g 82
5m 6m 5m³ 5m 5m³ 5g⁵ 6m⁴ 5f⁵ 1990 7f² 6m³ 6m³ 7g* 6m³ 6m² 7f⁴ 7.3g 6d 6g⁴ 6s] workmanlike colt: fair handicapper: impressive winner at Redcar in June: stays 7f well: acts on firm going, seems unsuited by soft: sometimes slowly away. *E. A. Wheeler.*

SHARP ANNE 3 gr.f. Belfort (FR) 89–Princess Sharpenup 63 (Lochnager 132) 74 §
[1989 5g* 5f* 5f² 5f 6m* 6f³ 6g³ 5m³ 6g³ 5g³ 6s⁵ 6v 1990 6m⁴ 6v⁵ 6f 5m² 5g² 5m* 5g* 5g⁴ 5g⁴ 5f⁴ 5m⁴ 6m 5m* 5m 6g* 6g 5g⁴] leggy, quite good-topped filly: has a quick action: modest performer: won claimers at Edinburgh, Sandown then Newcastle and handicap (ridden by 7-lb claimer seventh outing) at Carlisle: stays 6f when conditions aren't testing: blinkered thirteenth and fourteenth starts: changed hands 7,200 gns Doncaster October Sales: inconsistent and not one to rely on. *J. Berry.*

SHARP CHIEF 2 br.f. (Apr 28) Chief Singer 131–Sharp Castan 101 (Sharpen Up 71 p
127) [1990 5m³ 5m²] leggy, angular filly: sixth foal: half-sister to 5 winners (all at least quite useful), including good 3-y-o Dashing Blade (by Elegant Air), successful from 6f (at 2 yrs) to 1½m, and 1½m winner Belle Enfant (by Beldale Flutter): dam best at 2 yrs when 5f winner and placed in Hoover Fillies' Mile: bandaged near-hind, 2 lengths second of 14, soon close up but one pace, to Sacque in maiden at Folkestone in October: will be much better suited by 6f+: should improve further. *I. A. Balding.*

SHARP DREAM 2 ch.f. (Feb 20) Dominion 123–Sharp Jose (USA) (Sharpen Up 74
127) [1990 6m⁶ 6g² 7m³] leggy, useful-looking filly: has scope: second foal: dam won at up to 9f in USA: modest form in maidens, running well from disadvantageous draw final start: stays 7f. *Miss H. C. Knight.*

SHARPER BLUE 3 b.c. Sharpo 132–Riverlily (FR) (Green Dancer (USA) 132)   **78**
[1989 8v 1990 a8g² 10.2s a11g²] useful-looking colt: fair form: not seen out until
November as 3-y-o, when second of 13 in handicap at Southwell: stays 11f. *P. J.
Makin.*

SHARP GLITTERS 2 ch.c. (Mar 12) Crystal Glitters (USA) 127–Sharp Valley   —
(USA) (Sharpen Up 127) [1990 6m] good-quartered colt: first foal: dam ran once at 4
yrs: very green and coltish, always behind in maiden at Carlisle in June: wore tongue
strap. *M. Moubarak.*

SHARP GLOW 2 ch.g. (Feb 16) Reach 122–Jumra (Thatch (USA) 136) [1990 6g   **59**
5g⁴ 6f⁴ 7m⁶ 8.2g⁵ 8m* 10m 8d a8g] neat gelding: first foal: dam never ran: won
17-runner apprentice seller (retained 4,000 gns) at Warwick in October by 3½
lengths: not discredited on all-weather final start: suited by 1m: tends to sweat and
get on toes. *C. B. B. Booth.*

SHARP IMPOSTER (USA) 2 ch.c. (Feb 7) Diesis 133–Informatique   **95 P**
(USA) (Quack (USA)) [1990 7d*]
    What do Sally Rous, Sanglamore, Hellenic, Saumarez and Zilzal have in
common? The obvious answer is that they were or are excellent racehorses,
in all the winners of more than a dozen pattern races between them. However,
a somewhat less well known fact about them is that all five made their first
racecourse appearance not at Ascot or Newmarket but in the rather more
humble surroundings of Leicester. Indeed, Leicester now seems well established as a track where top trainers choose to introduce some of their more
promising performers, and the latest season proved no exception. Stoute
produced the high-class Kartajana to make a winning debut at the course in
the spring, while in the autumn he sent out the highly-regarded Opera House
to win a maiden race in the style of a colt destined for success at a much higher
level. The unbeaten Cherry Hinton winner Chicarica and the Racing Post
Trophy winner Peter Davies were two others who made a winning start to
their careers at Leicester, and another smart prospect turned up at the track's
last meeting of the season when Sharp Imposter won a minor event in eye-
catching fashion. The Pytchley Stakes was the final event on an eight-race
card which had featured three divisions of a maiden race, two divisions of an
uninspiring claimer plus a twenty-two-runner selling handicap, and a fair
proportion of an already-sparse crowd were on their way home as the field
went to post. Those who opted for a quick getaway probably missed seeing a
good horse in action. True, the opposition contained no world beaters, and
Sharp Imposter's rivals were reduced from four to three when Grain Lady
refused to budge as the stalls opened. Nevertheless, Melpomene had
recorded quite a useful timefigure in winning her only previous start, and the
way Sharp Imposter quickened to draw six lengths clear of her after taking
quite a while to realise what was required in the middle part of the race
suggests he has a bright future.

		Sharpen Up	Atan
	Diesis	(ch 1969)	Rocchetta
	(ch 1980)	Doubly Sure	Reliance II
Sharp Imposter (USA)		(b 1971)	Soft Angels
(ch.c. Feb 7, 1988)		Quack	T V Lark
	Informatique (USA)	(b 1969)	Quillon
	(b 1983)	Silver Bright	Barbizon
		(b 1963)	Silver Fog

    A rather leggy, attractive colt, Sharp Imposter cost 430,000 dollars as a
yearling. His sire Diesis owed his prominent position in the list of leading
sires in 1990 largely to the exploits of Elmaamul, but he was also represented
by a number of useful horses including Pharian, Madiriya, Ra'a and Keen
Hunter. Sharp Imposter is the first foal of Informatique, second over eleven
furlongs at Moulins-La-Marche from five starts. Her dam Silver Bright was a
very useful two-year-old in 1965, ending the year rated 11 lb inferior to
top-rated Buckpasser in the Experimental Free Handicap. She's also made a
significant impact at stud as the dam of Banquet Table, a high-class two-
year-old who later stayed eleven furlongs, State Dinner, a good winner at up
to a mile and a half, and the dam of the Prix de Minerve winner Gamberta.
Clearly, there's no lack of stamina in this family and as a three-year-old Sharp

Imposter ought to be suited by at least a mile and a quarter. With marked improvement certain he should pay to watch closely. *H. R. A. Cecil.*

SHARP INVITE 3 ch.f. Sharpo 132–Invitation 107 (Faberge II 121) [1989 5g 5d 1990 a7g a8g⁵] leggy filly: poor maiden. *J. M. P. Eustace.* —

SHARP MONEY 2 b.f. (Feb 19) Sharpo 132–Pennies To Pounds 80 (Ile de Bourbon (USA) 133) [1990 6m⁴ 6d³] second foal: half-sister to 3-y-o 7f winner Platinum Disc (by Song): dam, 8.5f winner, is half-sister to very useful 1978 2-y-o 5f winner Penny Blessing and daughter of sprinting half-sister to Mummy's Pet, Arch Sculptor and Parsimony: quite modest form in maidens at Newmarket (green and bit slowly away) and Folkestone in November: will probably be better suited by 7f. *D. R. C. Elsworth.* 65

SHARP MOVER 3 b.f. Sharpo 132–Matoa (USA) (Tom Rolfe) [1989 5s* 6f² 1990 5g⁵ 5.6g⁴ 5s] sparely-made filly: fairly useful performer: easily best effort as 3-y-o (not seen out until late-June) when fourth of 21 in Tote-Portland Handicap at Doncaster, keeping on well: slowly away and raced in unfavoured centre of track for Haydock minor event 4 weeks later: stays 6f: will prove best on an easy surface. *B. W. Hills.* 91

SHARP N' EARLY 4 b.c. Runnett 125–Irish Kick (Windjammer (USA)) [1989 7d⁵ 8v⁴ 8m 6m⁶ 6.5d³ 8s 7g⁶ 1990 6g³ 6f* 8g² 6m* 6g 6g² 6d⁵] rangy colt: moderate walker and mover: very useful performer: outpaced to halfway when winning 4-runner £7,100 event at Thirsk (odds on) in April and listed contest (quickening well to beat Afwaj 1½ lengths) at Lingfield in June: 42/1, very good second to Ron's Victory in Prix de Ris-Orangis at Evry, easily best subsequent effort: effective at 6f and stays 1m: acts on any going. *R. Hannon.* 110

SHARP N' EASY 3 b.f. Swing Easy (USA) 126–Dulcidene 71 (Behistoun 131) [1989 5m⁵ 5f² 6g⁴ 6g⁴ a7g a8g a7g⁶ 1990 5f⁴ 7m⁴ 8h⁴ 7d² 7d⁶ 7f⁵ 8h² 8f 8f⁶ 7f 8.2s] rather leggy, angular filly: inconsistent plater: ran moderately on all-weather: at least as effective over 7f as 1m: acts on firm and dead ground: sold 1,300 gns Newmarket Autumn Sales. *R. Hannon.* 50

SHARP N' SMOOTH 3 ch.c. Sharpo 132–Winning Look 71 (Relko 136) [1989 5d⁴ 5m² 5m 1990 7g 7g² 7m³ 7g 7g 6s⁵ 6d³ 7g⁴ a8g² 7d² a8g* a8g³] close-coupled colt: poor mover: modest performer: in good form late on, leading inside final 1f to justify favouritism in claimer at Lingfield in November: stays 1m: acts on dead ground: has run well for apprentice. *R. Hannon.* 75

SHARP REMINDER 6 b.h. Sharpo 132–Fallen Rose (Busted 134) [1989 6d² 6g² 7.2s³ 6m 6g 6d⁶ 1990 6m* 7m³ 6g 6g 6m 5d 6s] lengthy, quite attractive horse: carries plenty of condition: poor mover: useful performer who tends to be at his best in first half of season: won listed Severals Hotel Newmarket Abernant Stakes in April: ran poorly third to sixth outings, off course 2 months before fifth and sixth: effective at 7f, but probably better suited by 6f when conditions are testing: acts on soft going, unable to take much racing on top-of-the-ground: visored once: sold 20,000 gns Newmarket December Sales. *C. N. Williams.* 99

SHARP RUNNER (FR) 3 gr.g. Star Appeal 133–Assembly Day 66 (General Assembly (USA)) [1989 6f³ 6h⁶ 6m³ 7f⁶ 9g 8f a7g 1990 a8g⁵ a7g 6f 7.5d⁶ 8.5d⁶ a8g⁶ 6g 6m 8.5m 11m⁵ 8.2s 12d 12d a8g a10g] robust gelding: modest maiden at 2 yrs: well below form in 1990, including in sellers: unlikely to stay 1½m: blinkered first 4 outings: bought out of J. Dunlop's stable 3,600 gns Ascot February Sales: one to be wary of. *D. W. Chapman.* —

SHARP SALUTE (USA) 3 ch.g. Sharpen Up 127–Topolly (USA) (Turn-To) [1989 7g 8.2g⁴ 1990 7g² 9m² 9f4 8.5d 8g⁵ 8m* 8m² 9g] useful-looking gelding: fair performer: gelded then won maiden at York in September: ran poorly in handicap final start: effective over 1m and 9f: acts on firm going, possibly unsuited by dead: sweating and edgy most starts: sold 20,000 gns Newmarket Autumn Sales. *B. W. Hills.* 83

SHARP THISTLE 4 b.f. Sharpo 132–Marphousha (FR) (Shirley Heights 130) [1989 7.3s 8.5s 7f⁶ 7f² 7m⁵ 6m 7f⁶ 7g³ 8m 7s⁶ 8g⁴ a8g⁴ 1990 a10g³ a12g²] leggy, light-framed filly: turns near-fore out: moderate mover: quite modest handicapper: good second in apprentice event at Lingfield in January: stays 1½m: probably acts on any going: sometimes on toes. *W. J. Musson.* 69

SHARPTHORNE (USA) 2 ch.f. (Mar 17) Sharpen Up 127–Abeer (USA) 115 (Dewan (USA)) [1990 5g³ 5m⁵ 6g*] leggy, sparely-made filly: sixth foal: half-sister to 1½m winner Armourer (by Busted), 7f winner Nabeel (by Nodouble) and sprint winners Abaya (by Mr Prospector) and In Fact (by Known Fact): dam won 3 races at 84 p

5f at 2 yrs, including Flying Childers Stakes: on toes, dominated throughout towards stand side and ran on really well to win 24-runner maiden at Kempton in September shade comfortably by 2½ lengths from Sharp Dream: under 3 lengths third of 8 to Dominio in listed race at Newbury, easily better previous effort: at least as effective at 6f as 5f. *R. Charlton.*

SHARP TIMES   7 b.g. Faraway Times (USA) 123–Sharp Venita 84 (Sharp Edge   **60 d**
123) [1989 6s 6v⁶ 6d* 6f 6f 6m 6m⁶ 5g³ 6g 6d² 6m 1990 5g⁵ 7g⁵ 6g² 6d 6g 5g 6m 6m 6g⁶ 6m 6d 7g a6g] lengthy, shallow-girthed gelding: quite modest form in handicaps first 3 outings: below form after, in blinkers on last 2 outings: better suited by 6f than 5f, and stays 7f: acts on any going: often bandaged: has won for apprentice: wanders in front, and ideally suited by strong gallop and exaggerated waiting tactics. *W. J. Musson.*

SHARP TO OBLIGE   3 ch.g. Dublin Taxi–Please Oblige (Le Levanstell 122)   **54**
[1989 NR 1990 7f³ 7g 8.2g² 8d 10m 12d] 12,000Y: rather angular gelding: fifth living foal: half-brother to 3 winners, including fair 2-y-o 7f winner Lucky Crystal (by Main Reef) and Irish middle-distance winner David's Pleasure (by Welsh Saint): dam unraced half-sister to very useful Irish middle-distance performer Gargano: plating-class form when placed in maidens, coming from well behind and hanging over 1f out on second occasion: faced very stiff tasks next 2 starts: should stay 1¼m. *R. M. Whitaker.*

SHARP TRADITION (USA)   2 ro.f. (Mar 23) Sharpen Up 127–Nice Tradition   **65 p**
(ARG) (Search Tradition (USA)) [1990 6d³] $90,000Y: leggy filly: half-sister to a minor stakes winner at around 7f by Raise A Native: dam Grade 1 winner in Argentina later successful in USA: over 2 lengths third of 11, running on, to Wolf Hall in maiden at Lingfield in October: should improve. *I. A. Balding.*

SHARQUIN   3 b.c. Indian King (USA) 128–Lady of The Land 75 (Wollow 132)   **71**
[1989 7g 8d 1990 a8g 9s³ 12.3f⁴ 10d⁵ 11.7m² 11g⁵ 10g* 10f* 10f* 10f⁶] unfurnished, useful-looking colt: modest handicapper: in good form in the summer, successful at Leicester then twice (in space of 3 days) at Ayr: ran moderately final start and spoilt chance by hanging badly left on fifth: suited by 1¼m: acts on firm going. *M. Brittain.*

SHA THA (USA)   2 b. or br.f. (Mar 3) Mr Prospector (USA)–Savannah Dancer   **112**
(USA) (Northern Dancer (USA)) [1990 6.5g³ 7.5g* 8g² 8g³] big filly: has plenty of scope: second foal: dam won 6 races at up to 1¼m, including Grade 2 Del Mar Oaks, and is closely related to Geoffrey Freer winner Valinsky and half-sister to Oaks second Vals Girl, out of Oaks winner Valoris: very useful French filly: ran as Sabana on debut: won maiden at Deauville in August by ¾ length: placed in Prix d'Aumale (½-length second of 8 to Magic Night) and Prix Marcel Boussac (2 lengths third of 9 to Shadayid) at Longchamp in autumn: suited by 1m. *A. Fabre, France.*

SHATTERED DREAMS   3 ch.c. Sharpo 132–Only A Dream (FR) (Green   **86**
Dancer (USA) 132) [1989 5m⁴ 5m* 1990 6g⁴ 7d* 7d⁴ 7.6g³ 7g 7.6g 6d] strong, close-coupled colt: has a quick, moderate action: fair handicapper: favourite, won £7,600 event at Chester in May: ran poorly last 3 outings, sweating first occasion and blinkered on third: may well stay 1m: acts on good to firm ground and dead: sold 29,000 gns Newmarket Autumn Sales: clearly one to be wary of. *J. Gosden.*

SHAVIAN   3 b.c. Kris 135–Mixed Applause (USA) 101 (Nijinsky (CAN) 138) **125**
[1989 7g² 7m* 1990 8g³ 10m⁴ 8m* 8f³ 8m* 8m⁵]
When George Bernard Shaw's play Androcles and The Lion first opened at the St James's Theatre in 1913, financially supported by the renowned arts patron and racehorse owner Lord Howard de Walden, the response was varied. According to Shaw's biographer, Hesketh Pearson, a fair proportion of the theatre-going public considered the play blasphemous, and consequently they forbade their children to see it. After eight weeks the production was wound down. The well-named racehorse Shavian, owned by the present Lord Howard, also got off to a rather uncertain start in the latest season with a couple of training set-backs and a lack-lustre effort over a trip that we thought would suit him. However, such uncertainty proved short-lived. Shavian 'got his act together' during the summer and when the curtain came down on his racing career he'd emulated his sire Kris by winning both the St James's Palace Stakes and the Beefeater Gin Celebration Mile, formerly known as the Waterford Crystal Mile.

Despite the fact that he was beaten on his first two starts as a three-year-old, we didn't lose faith in Shavian. At that point he still impressed as a good horse in the making, probably over a mile and a quarter or more when allowed to force the pace. Shavian made his seasonal debut in the Craven Stakes at Newmarket in April when he finished a clear third of six behind the subsequent Guineas winner Tirol and Sure Sharp. That was a good effort considering he still looked green, but a lack of sparkle in his home work meant he missed the Guineas and was next seen out in the Predominate Stakes at Goodwood where he put up a rather disappointing effort. After taking a keen hold under restraint, Shavian made headway to lead with half a mile to run but he could never shake off his stable-companion Razeen, and close home he was also passed by Elmaamul and the maiden Silca An' Key. Shavian might well have needed that race after a lay-off—he certainly blew hard after it—and when interviewed a few days later his trainer seemed unsure what his optimum trip would be. Shavian's owner seemed keen to aim for the big races over a mile. The first opportunity came in the St James's Palace Stakes at Royal Ascot, and the step down in distance combined with the adoption of forcing tactics seemed to suit Shavian down to the ground. As usual, several of the main contenders for the race had made their presence felt at classic level, yet the 9/4 favourite was Lord Florey, a fast-improving colt who'd won the Heron Stakes easily and came from a stable in prime form. Anshan and Rock City, separated by half a length when third and fourth in Tirol's Guineas, were on 9/2 and 11/2 respectively, with the Irish Guineas runner-up Royal Academy on 4/1, the Dewhurst winner Dashing Blade on 10/1 and Shavian an 11/1-chance. Royal Academy had been troublesome at the stalls at the Curragh, and his refusal to enter them at Ascot inevitably robbed the race of some of its interest and significance. Even without Royal Academy against him Shavian did more than enough to prove himself a high-class miler. With Anshan and the Diomed Stakes winner Eton Lad in the line-up, a strongly-run race was always likely, and following a fast break it was Shavian, racing with plenty of enthusiasm, who took the field of eight along. Shavian was still travelling well within himself as the field turned for home, and when he quickened to open up a gap of two lengths early in the straight it proved decisive. Rock City chased the leader in typically resolute fashion in the final two furlongs, while Lord Florey produced a strong late run having been hemmed in with a lot to do as the race began in earnest. But none could get to grips with Shavian, who galloped on willingly under pressure to beat Rock City by a length and a half

St James's Palace Stakes, Ascot—Shavian emulates his sire in winning this race;
Rock City keeps on resolutely for second, just ahead of Lord Florey (No. 6)

Beefeater Gin Celebration Mile, Goodwood—another all-the-way win;
Lord Florey is third again, beaten by Candy Glen

with Lord Florey a short head away in third and the rest well back. According to Cecil, Shavian had really come to himself and developed physically in the lead-up to his Ascot win. He ran a cracking race, right up to form, when third of seven in Distant Relative's Sussex Stakes the following month, and another at least as good on his return to Goodwood for the Beefeater Gin Celebration Mile in August. Shavian was taken on by four opponents in the latter; Lord Florey, beaten at odds for a listed race at Lingfield on his latest start, was in the field again and on terms 6 lb better plenty were prepared to back him to reverse the Ascot form; the much-improved four-year-olds Safawan and Mirror Black were also present, while the outsider of the quintet was the Premio Parioli winner Candy Glen. The 5/2 favourite Shavian dominated his rivals from beginning to end. Smartly away again, he was soon four lengths clear of Lord Florey with the others, especially Safawan, strung out and off the bridle. Lord Florey managed to reduce the deficit to a couple of lengths early in the straight but he was all out to do so and Shavian was firmly in command from the distance, running on strongly to beat Candy Glen by a long-looking two and a half lengths and recording a timefigure of 1.25 fast (the equivalent to a timerating of 131), the best by a three-year-old miler all year. Shavian was due to end his career by running in the Queen Elizabeth II Stakes at Ascot and the Breeders' Cup Mile at Belmont Park. In the event he made only the first objective, performing a long way below his best in fifth of ten behind Markofdistinction. The tactics which had helped bring about his improvement over the last few months may have been overdone here.

Shavian (b.c. 1987)	Kris (ch 1976)	Sharpen Up (ch 1969)	Atan / Rocchetta
		Doubly Sure (b 1971)	Reliance II / Soft Angels
	Mixed Applause (USA) (b 1976)	Nijinsky (b 1967)	Northern Dancer / Flaming Page
		My Advantage (b 1966)	Princely Gift / My Game

Shavian has plenty to recommend him to breeders. Little needs to be said about his sire, other than that he continues to be one of the most influential stallions in Europe, while his dam, the useful five- and seven-furlong winner Mixed Applause, has also made a name for herself at stud. Shavian is her third foal by Kris, the others being Khandjar and Tempering, winners at

840

Lord Howard de Walden's "Shavian"

up to nine and eleven furlongs respectively. Mixed Applause produced the Gold Cup winner Paean when mated with Bustino, but after producing a dead foal from her 1987 mating with Green Desert and not being covered the following year it will be 1992 at the earliest before we see her next produce, a colt by Carmelite House. Mixed Applause is a half-sister to the dam of Be My Chief out of My Advantage, a two-year-old five-furlong winner. She in turn is a daughter of My Game, the grandam of Lord Seymour and Marwell and the great-grandam of another of Kris's best offspring, namely the Oaks winner Unite.

Shavian's record shows that he acted well on a firm surface; he never got a chance to race on ground with plenty of give. Physically, the strong-galloping Shavian was an imposing colt, lengthy and good bodied, who progressed really well. He'll be standing at the Brook Stud in Newmarket in 1991 at £8,000 with the October 1st concession. *H. R. A. Cecil.*

SHAWINIGA 4 b.f. Lyphard's Wish (FR) 124–Shining Bright (USA) (Bold Bidder) [1989 8g⁵ 8s 7m² 7m² 9f² 7m³ 7.5m⁶ 10f³ 8.2g² 8m 1990 10.2f 10f 8.2f 5s* 6f⁵ 8.2g* 12.3g⁶ 8.5g* 8.2g³ 10f⁵ 9g³ 9s⁴ 10.6d 6m⁴ a8g²] sparely-made filly: plating-class handicapper: successful at Hamilton in May (amateurs) and July: stays 1¼m: acts on any going: has sweated: consistent. *J. S. Wilson.* **54**

SHAWWAL (USA) 3 b. or br.c. Shirley Heights 130–Lady of Camelot (FR) (Bolkonski 134) [1989 NR 1990 10g 12m 13.8f* 12m] $325,000Y: lengthy, workman-like colt: has a quick action: fourth foal: half-brother to 2 winners in France, including Knighthood, later stakes winner at up to 9f in USA: dam 7f and 1m winner in France: 33/1, worthwhile form only when winning 6-runner claimer at Catterick **74**

841

in September, staying on to lead close home: sold out of J. Dunlop's stable 10,500 gns Newmarket September Sales after second outing. *J. Parkes.*

SHAY 5 b.g. Hays 120–Barefoot Contessa (Homeric 133) [1989 NR 1990 7g 6m a5g —
5d 7g 5s] leggy, rather sparely-made gelding: turns off-fore out: modest winner early as 3-y-o: no form in handicaps in 1990: suited by stiff 5f: acts on soft going: visored third start. *A. J. Chamberlain.*

SHEBA'S PAL 3 b.f. Claude Monet (USA) 121–Bread 'n Honey 51 (Goldhills **35**
Pride 105) [1989 5s 5d 1990 5m⁶ 6f 5f 5g 5f⁴ 5m⁶ 5. 1m 6g 7f] workmanlike filly: poor plater: best effort at 5f: visored twice: sometimes edgy: sold 920 gns Doncaster November Sales. *G. Blum.*

SHEDAD (USA) 2 ch.c. (Apr 11) Diesis 133–Love's Reward (Nonoalco (USA) **81**
131) [1990 6m³ 6f⁴ 7g³] $325,000Y: rangy colt: has a round action: third foal: brother to 3-y-o 6f winner Keen Hunter and half-brother to fair 1¾m winner Amoodi (by Forli): dam lightly-raced half-sister to high-class 1984 2-y-o Bassenthwaite: fair form in maidens: set very strong pace when third of 16 to Surrealist at Sandown final start: stays 7f: should win a race. *J. L. Dunlop.*

SHEEN CLEEN LAD 3 ch.c. On Your Mark 125–Mishcasu (Majority Blue 126) **47**
[1989 5f* 5m 6f⁶ 7.5m⁶ 8f⁴ 8.2s 8f a6g² a7g 1990 a7g³ a5g⁶] lengthy, rather angular colt: plating-class performer: stayed 1m: possibly unsuited by soft ground: visored last 2 starts at 2 yrs: raced keenly: dead. *Ronald Thompson.*

SHEER PRECOCITY 3 b.c. Precocious 126–Age of Elegance (Troy 137) [1989 **107**
6m* 6m* 7f⁴ 6m⁵ 7g 6g³ 1990 7m⁵ 7g 6f³ 6g 7m 7.6f* 8m³ 7m² 7m] strong, useful-looking colt: has a rather round action: useful performer: won £7,700 handicap at Chester in July: ran creditably next 2 starts, particularly so when second to Enharmonic in listed race at York: carrying plenty of condition, behind in £71,900 handicap at Ascot final start: should prove best at up to 7f: acts on firm going. *F. H. Lee.*

SHEERWIND 3 b.c. Shernazar 131–Windy Cheyenne (USA) (Tumble Wind —
(USA)) [1989 NR 1990 11.7m⁵ 10m⁵ 10.1m 10g] IR 21,000Y: sturdy, attractive colt: has a rather round action: sixth foal: half-brother to 3 winners, all successful as 2-y-o's, including useful 1983 6f winner Keep Tapping (by Tap On Wood): dam won 5 sprint races in USA, including stakes event at 2 yrs: no worthwhile form in maidens and handicap: sold to join J. White 1,500 gns Newmarket Autumn Sales. *J. P. Hudson.*

SHEIKH ALBADOU 2 b.c. (Apr 15) Green Desert (USA) 127–Sanctuary **66 p**
(Welsh Pageant 132) [1990 6g] 92,000Y: strong, good-bodied colt: fourth living foal: half-brother to 1987 Irish 2-y-o 5f winner Sawlah and 7f winner Assignment (both by Known Fact): dam unraced half-sister to Little Wolf and Smuggler: backward and green, shaped better than eighth-of-11 position suggests in maiden at Newmarket in October, soon travelling strongly with leaders after slow start then not at all knocked about final 2f: sure to improve. *A. A. Scott.*

SHEIKH PERCY 3 b.g. Busted 134–Sauhatz (GER) (Alpenkonig (GER)) [1989 —
NR 1990 a12g] seventh known foal: dam won at 3 yrs in Germany: 12/1, always behind in 10-runner maiden at Lingfield in December. *N. A. Callaghan.*

SHEIKH'S PET 4 b.c. Mummy's Pet 125–Parlais 101 (Pardao 120) [1989 5s³ 5s **51**
6m³ 6f* 7h² 6h⁴ 6m³ 6f⁶ 6g⁶ 6f 1990 7h 7f 7f⁶ 7m a6g] small colt: moderate walker: poor mover: quite modest winner at 3 yrs: below his best in 1990: stays 7f: acts on any going: usually wears blinkers or visor: sold to join Mrs J. Wonnacott's stable 1,700 gns Ascot September Sales. *J. P. Hudson.*

SHEILAS HILLCREST 4 b.c. Hotfoot 126–Be Honest 95 (Klairon 131) [1989 —
16.2f 1990 16m³] leggy, sparely-made colt: poor walker: first sign of ability when beaten 8 lengths by odds-on Nafzawa in 3-runner maiden at Newcastle in July. *N. Tinkler.*

SHEJRAH (USA) 3 b.f. Northjet 136–Bar J Gal (USA) (Key To The Mint (USA)) —
[1989 NR 1990 10g 7.6m⁶] rather leggy filly: second foal: dam, half-sister to French 1m winner later very smart American middle-distance stayer Properantes, second over 6f at 3 yrs in USA: well beaten in maidens in September: sold 1,600 gns Newmarket December Sales. *R. W. Armstrong.*

SHELEGAI 2 b.c. (Apr 19) Shernazar 131–Khandjar 77 (Kris 135) [1990 8m⁵] — **p**
second foal: half-brother to 3-y-o Tizona (by Pharly): dam 9f winner, is sister to Shavian and half-sister to Paean: over 11 lengths fifth of 11, considerably handled when beaten, to impressive Polish King in minor event at Newmarket in November: sure to improve. *H. R. A. Cecil.*

SHELLAC 4 b.c. What A Guest 119–Lacquer 118 (Shantung 132) [1989 10f* **109**
10.5m⁴ 10f* 11s* 9g 12v 1990 10f* 12g 10m⁵ 11s⁵ 10s²] sturdy, good sort: really good
walker: has a quick action: useful on his day: odds on, easy winner of 5-runner minor
event at Pontefract in April: nose second of 13 in Grade 3 Niagara Handicap at
Woodbine in September: rather disappointing in pattern events in between: stays
11f: acts on any going except possibly heavy. *L. M. Cumani.*

SHELTER 3 b.g. Teenoso (USA) 135–Safe House 81§ (Lyphard (USA) 132) [1989 —
5f 7m 1990 10m 12.4s 10d] robust gelding: poor maiden: sold 1,500 gns Ascot
December Sales. *R. J. R. Williams.*

SHEMALEYAH 3 b.f. Lomond (USA) 128–Burghclere 86 (Busted 134) [1989 7f **84**
1990 10.6s 14m* 17.6f²] lengthy, useful-looking filly: moderate mover: won 5-
runner maiden at Sandown in August, leading inside final 1f: persistently swished
tail when second in handicap at Wolverhampton 2 weeks later: should have proved
suited by thorough test of stamina: stud. *Major W. R. Hern.*

SHENTIT (FR) 2 b.f. (Mar 8) Shirley Heights 130–Porte des Lilas (FR) **56 p**
(Sharpman 124) [1990 8g 9m³] 700,000 francs (approx £64,800) Y: big, rangy filly:
second foal: half-sister to French 9f winner Port de Lanne (by Bellypha): dam
French 1¼m and 11f winner: weak in betting, over 7 lengths third of 5, outpaced
steadily final 3f, to Priceless Bond in maiden at Wolverhampton in October:
backward and green on debut: will stay 1½m: sort to do better at 3 yrs. *J. L. Dunlop.*

SHEPHERD'S SONG 2 b.c. (Apr 20) Elegant Air 119–Littleton Song 73 (Song **62**
132) [1990 5f 5g⁴ 5g³ 6g⁴ 5s 6m* 6g⁵ 6f² a6g² 6m* a6g³ 8m⁵] 5,000Y: strong,
compact colt: good walker and mover: half-brother to 3-y-o Indiana
Scarlett (by Blazing Saddles): dam 2-y-o 6f winner: useful plater: no bid after
winning at Doncaster in June and Ripon in August: stays 1m: blinkered final 7 starts:
often wears a tongue strap: usually on toes: tends to wander: sold 4,200 gns
Newmarket Autumn Sales. *W. J. Pearce.*

SHERIFF'S BAND 3 ch.g. Posse (USA) 130–Willis (FR) (Lyphard (USA) 132) **54**
[1989 5s³ 6m 1990 8f⁵ 8f³ 9f* 8.5d⁵] tall, leggy, sparely-made gelding: shows knee
action: evens, won seller (no bid) at Ripon in April: ran creditably in handicap
following month: stays 9f: probably acts on any going: lacks turn of foot and is suited
by forcing tactics. *M. H. Easterby.*

SHERJAMAL (USA) 3 ch.c. Raise A Native–Sedra 116 (Nebbiolo 125) [1989 **72**
NR 1990 6m⁵ 6f⁵ 7m 7f² 9g³ 8.5g⁵ a8g³ 7h² 7m* 7g 6d a7g] $110,000F: sturdy colt:
second foal: half-brother to Irish 7f and 1m winner Topper Up (by Sharpen Up): dam
6f (at 2 yrs) to 1¼m winner: modest performer: made all in maiden at Goodwood in
August: below form in handicap and claimers after: stays 9f: acts on hard ground:
bolted at start sixth outing: bandaged near-hind on seventh. *B. J. Curley.*

SHESLIKETHEWIND 2 b.f. (Apr 1) Shareef Dancer (USA) 135–Green Leaf **47**
(USA) 97 (Alydar (USA)) [1990 6m⁵ 6m⁵ 8m] second foal: sister to 3-y-o Lady In
Green: dam 2-y-o 6f winner, stayed 1¼m, is out of smart 5.5f to 11f winner Warfever:
poor maiden: seems to stay 1m: sold 4,000 gns Newmarket Autumn Sales. *M. R.
Stoute.*

SHE'S SMART 2 gr.f. (Apr 14) Absalom 128–Zeddenosa (Zeddaan 130) [1990 5f⁵ **77**
5m² 5m² 5g* 5m³ 5f⁴ 5f* 6g⁴] 7,400Y: small, workmanlike filly: ninth foal: half-
sister to winners in Belgium by Morston and Longleat: dam French middle-distance
winner: successful in maiden at Ripon in May and nursery (by 1½ lengths from
Spinechiller, showing much improved form) at Redcar in August: stays 6f: acts on
firm going: visored fourth and sixth starts. *M. H. Easterby.*

SHE'S THE TOPS 2 b.f. (Jan 23) Shernazar 131–Troytops 66 (Troy 137) [1990 **66 p**
8.2m³] second foal: half-sister to useful 1m winner Nayland (by Be My Guest): dam
1¼m winner, is half-sister to Most Welcome and daughter of Topsy, a half-sister to
Teenoso: over 2 lengths third of 14, staying on well having been outpaced 2f out, to
Good Policy in minor event at Nottingham in September: will be suited by middle
distances: sure to improve. *G. Wragg.*

SHEVAJI 4 br.g. Indian King (USA) 128–Brave Ivy 68 (Decoy Boy 129) [1989 NR **67**
1990 8.5g² 8.5g 8g 7.5d 9s] strong, workmanlike gelding: first foal: dam, sprint
maiden, is half-sister to smart miler Young Runaway: 7 lengths second to long
odds-on Song of Kings in slowly-run maiden at Beverley in May: dead. *Miss S. E.
Hall.*

SHEWHOMUSTBEOBEYED 3 ch.f. Miami Springs 121–Sleepline Promise — §
63 (Record Token 128) [1989 5d³ 5g 5m⁶ 5f 5m⁵ 1990 5g 5s 5g 5.8d] workmanlike
filly: poor and ungenuine maiden: twice visored. *A. W. Jones.*

SHEYRANN 3 b.c. Top Ville 129–Shaiyra (Relko 136) [1989 NR 1990 10m² **81**
11.5m² 14f² 12g] workmanlike colt: sixth foal: half-brother to 4 winners, including
smart miler Shaikiya (by Bold Lad (IRE)), useful 1987 2-y-o 8.2f winner Shehiyr (by
Hotfoot), winner in Italy in 1990, and very useful 1m and 1½m winner Shayraz (by
Darshaan): dam unraced half-sister to high-class French stayer Shafaraz: fair
maiden: will stay 2m: best efforts on top-of-the-ground: sold 17,000 gns Newmarket
Autumn Sales. *L. M. Cumani.*

SHEZNICE (IRE) 2 ch.f. (May 6) Try My Best (USA) 130–Miss Kate (FR) **58**
(Nonoalco (USA) 131) [1990 5m⁴ 6g] 18,000F: good-quartered filly: fourth foal:
closely related to 3-y-o 6f and 7f winner Glen Kate (by Glenstal) and half-sister to
1987 2-y-o 5f and 6f winner Tamarindo (by Touching Wood) and 1½m winner Ktolo
(by Tolomeo): dam French 1¼m winner, is half-sister to very smart stayer
Midshipman: over 5 lengths fourth of 7, slowly away then keeping on well under
hand riding, to Dome Lawel in maiden at Sandown in October: favourite, tailed off in
similar event at Folkestone: should be better suited by 6f than 5f. *Miss B. Sanders.*

SHIFTING BREEZE 3 ch.f. Night Shift (USA)–Easterly Wind 94 (Wind- **81**
jammer (USA)) [1989 7f 8m² 8g* a8g⁴ 1990 10f² 10s⁶ 10f* 10g* 10.1m³ 10f6 10f³
11.5m⁵] workmanlike filly: fair handicapper: won at Chepstow (claimer ridden) in
May and Yarmouth (on toes) in June: below form in £7,800 amateurs event final
start: stays 1¼m: acts on firm going, unsuited by soft: sold 7,200 gns Newmarket
Autumn Sales. *T. Thomson Jones.*

SHIFT SURPRISE (USA) 3 ch.f. Night Shift (USA)–Al-Burak (Silver Shark **64**
129) [1989 a7g⁴ 1990 a6g⁴ᵈⁱˢ a6g² a6g* 5f 8f 5f² 6h* 5m 5m] good-bodied filly: quite
modest at best: won handicaps at Lingfield in February and Brighton (made all,
edged right) in May: suited by 6f: acts on hard ground: has got on toes and sweated:
inconsistent. *R. V. Smyth.*

SHIHAMA (USA) 2 b.f. (Jan 31) Shadeed (USA) 135–Dubian 120 (High Line **88** p
125) [1990 6m*] first foal: dam winner from 7f (at 2 yrs) to 1½m, is half-sister to
Milverton and See You Then: favourite, won 9-runner maiden at Newmarket in
November by a short head from Repique, disputing lead, quickening 2f out and
running on well: will stay 1m: sure to improve. *A. A. Scott.*

SHIKARI KID 3 b.g. Kala Shikari 125–Muffet 75 (Matador 131) [1989 5g⁶ 6m⁶ **65** ?
7m 7m⁵ 8g⁴ a7g 1990 10.2f 7g⁵ 8.2s 7g⁴ 8g⁴ 10.4g² 12.2d³ 12.3f⁴ 10m 10f⁵ 10m⁶ 10m
10m⁴ 11v* 11d³] smallish, angular gelding: has a round action: quite modest
performer: easily best effort when winning seller (no bid) at Ayr in October, leading
6f out: probably stays 1½m: evidently needs very soft going: often visored or
blinkered, though not last 2 starts: has looked none too keen, and is somewhat
unreliable. *S. G. Norton.*

SHIKARI'S SON 3 br.c. Kala Shikari 125–Have Form (Haveroid 122) [1989 6m⁶ **79**
7g⁴ 6g 1990 5g⁵ 5g* 5.3h* 5.8f⁶ 5g² 5d 5f 5g⁵ 5d⁵] leggy colt: modest handicapper:
won at Wolverhampton and Brighton in May: suited by 5f: acts on hard ground and
dead: sweating on reappearance. *S. T. Harris.*

SHIKARI SUNSHINE 3 b.g. Kala Shikari 125–Sunshine Holyday 96 (Three —
Wishes 114) [1989 5g⁵ 6f⁴ 6f 6m 7m 1990 8.2g 11g 10f 13.8m] small, workmanlike
gelding: has a round action: no form, including in handicap and seller: visored fourth
start. *J. S. Wilson.*

SHILINSKI 3 b.c. Niniski (USA) 125–Sushila (Petingo 135) [1989 NR 1990 11m⁴ **68**
12.3m² 12.4m*] 98,000Y: lengthy colt: sixth foal: brother to top-class 1½m winner
former Petoski and half-brother to fairly useful Sanaabell (by Persepolis) and a
winner in Italy: dam, twice successful around 1m in France, is out of a sister to Val
de Loir: 9/1 on and looking very well, struggled to beat sole opponent Kalogy in
maiden at Newcastle in August: will be suited by further: sold 24,000 gns
Newmarket Autumn Sales. *L. Cumani.*

SHIMMERING SCARLET (IRE) 2 b.f. (Feb 6) Glint of Gold 128–Scarlet **68**
Slipper (Gay Mecene (USA) 128) [1990 7m⁴ 8f 7f] 18,000Y: close-coupled, well-
grown filly: second foal: half-sister to 3-y-o Scarlet Express (by Precocious): dam
French 1m winner, is half-sister to useful 7f and 1¼m winner Golden Braid: easily
best form in maidens when fourth of 17 at Newcastle: didn't handle turn at Thirsk
second start: should stay 1¼m. *T. D. Barron.*

SHIMMERING SEA 2 b.f. (Apr 21) Slip Anchor 136–Sushila (Petingo 135) **89**
[1990 5m* 7m* 7m⁴ 8m³] well-grown, close-coupled filly: seventh foal: half-sister
to several winners, notably top-class middle-distance performer Petoski (by
Niniski): dam winner twice at around 1m in France, is out of sister to Val de Loir: fair
performer: won maiden at Newbury (got loose twice) in June and £6,800 event at

Sandown (by a neck from Glowing Ardour) in July: over 2 lengths third to Glowing Ardour in pattern event at Leopardstown: will stay 1¼m. *Major W. R. Hern.*

SHINING JEWEL   3 b.c. Exhibitioner 111–Vaguely Jade (Corvaro (USA) 122)   **80**
[1989 7g 1990 7g4 8m a8g6 7h2 7m 7g 6m 9m5 8.2v4 8m* 8m3 9g a7g4 a8g* a10g* a8g2 a10g] strong, lengthy colt: moderate mover: fair performer: easy winner of claimer at Chepstow in October then narrowly in handicaps at Lingfield in November and December: stays 1¼m: acts on hard ground: blinkered once: bandaged third to eighth starts. *E. Eldin.*

SHINING SPEAR   3 b.f. Commanche Run 132–Golden Glint (Vitiges (FR) 132)   **69**
[1989 NR 1990 12g5 14d] 26,000Y: rangy filly: first foal: dam, slow maiden, is half-sister to smart middle-distance filly Moonlight Night and high-class middle-distance performer Main Reef: 14/1, ran on after slow start when fifth of 15 in maiden at Newbury in August: well beaten in similar event at Haydock 3 weeks later. *J. H. M. Gosden.*

SHINING WOOD   2 b.f. (Feb 12) Touching Wood (USA) 127–Nihad 76 (Alleged   **65**
(USA) 138) [1990 6m 7f 7m3 10s3] rather leggy, workmanlike filly: first foal: dam maiden suited by 1¼m, is out of half-sister to very smart sprinter/miler Clever Trick: quite modest maiden: stays 1¼m: acts on good to firm ground and soft. *B. Hanbury.*

SHINNEL WATER   4 b.c. Rolfe (USA) 77–Linda Dudley 81 (Owen Dudley 121)   —
[1989 11m 7m 8.2g5 7g 6s5 1990 6g 8d6 9g6 7m 8m 8.2v] workmanlike colt: poor maiden: easily best effort at 4 yrs on second outing: should stay further than 1m: possibly suited by an easy surface: sold privately 2,600 gns Doncaster November Sales. *J. M. Jefferson.*

SHIP OF GOLD   4 b.f. Glint of Gold 128–Sally Rose 92 (Sallust 134) [1989 10.1g4   **43**
12g3 10d 1990 10.2f 11s 9g 9g 10m 10m 12m6 10m3 8.5g 10f 10g] compact filly: moderate mover: modest form first 2 starts as 3-y-o, hanging on second: mostly disappointing in 1990: stays 1½m: blinkered twice: trained first 3 starts by P. Evans. *D. A. Wilson.*

SHOCKING   3 ch.f. Dunbeath (USA) 127–Time For Pleasure (Tower Walk 130)   **?**
[1989 NR 1990 a8g a8g] 4,600Y: third foal: dam twice-raced daughter of half-sister to Blushing Groom: successful 3 times over sprint distances in Austria, last occasion in early-September: prominent 5f in late-season claimers at Lingfield. *C. F. Wall.*

SHOCKING AFFAIR   3 ch.f. Electric 126–Bedspring 67 (Pyjama Hunt 126)   **32**
[1989 6g a6g 1990 8f 8f 8h 6m 6m 6f4 6f5 5m 7f] small, light-framed filly: poor handicapper: bred to stay at least 1m. *J. W. Payne.*

SHOEHORN   3 br.g. Prince Tenderfoot (USA) 126–Relkalim 102 (Relko 136)   **70**
[1989 7g 1990 8g 9m* 10f3 8d] sturdy, lengthy gelding: has a quick action: on toes and sweating, won claimer at Wolverhampton (claimed out of B. Hills's stable 15,000 gns and subsequently gelded) in May: easily better effort later in summer when third of 4 in minor event at Folkestone: better at 1¼m than shorter: acts on firm going. *R. W. Stubbs.*

SHOKA (FR)   2 gr.f. (Apr 2) Kaldoun (FR)–Sassika (GER) (Arratos (FR)) [1990   **55** p
7g] quite attractive filly: fifth foal: half-sister to 3-y-o Sarsaparilla (by Shirley Heights) and 11f winner Harmonical (by Lyphard's Wish): dam, from good German family, won in Germany: bit slowly away, held up and never placed to challenge or knocked about unduly in maiden at Newmarket in November: sure to improve over middle distances. *B. W. Hills.*

SHOOT TO KILL   3 ch.f. Posse (USA) 130–Sorata (FR) (Sodium 128) [1989 5g   **54**
6f3 1990 8f5 7h 7m5 7m6 6g 8.2g3 a8g3 10m4] leggy, sparely-made filly: plating-class maiden: favourite, pulled hard then ducked right and left 1f out when well below form in seller final start: stays 1m well: acts on firm ground: blinkered last 3 starts: has given trouble at stalls: has run creditably when sweating: not one to trust implicitly: joined D. Grissell. *J. G. FitzGerald.*

SHOREHAM MARINA   4 ch.f. Horage 124–Miss Duckins (Simbir 130) [1989   **52**
8m* 8m2 9.2f 10g 9m 1990 7h3 7m] leggy, good-topped filly: made virtually all to win maiden at Brighton in May, 1989: well below her best since next outing: stays 1m: acts on good to firm going. *P. D. Cundell.*

SHORT ENCOUNTER   3 b.g. Blakeney 126–Double Stitch 74 (Wolver Hollow   **59**
126) [1989 7g 7m 1990 10g4 a12g6 a12g] workmanlike gelding: has a quick action: quite modest form when fourth in claimer at Nottingham: twice never placed to challenge at Southwell in August: should stay 1½m. *D. T. Thom.*

SHORT SHOT 4 b.g. Young Generation 129–Blessed Damsel 99 (So Blessed 130) [1989 9s⁴ 10.1m² 10m⁵ 10.6s 10g 1990 10d] useful-looking gelding: no form in handicaps since second outing at 3 yrs: suited by 1¼m: best form on top-of-the-ground: sweating and on toes final outing at 3 yrs: lacks turn of foot. *R. Guest.*   —

SHORT STRAW 3 b.g. Thatching 131–Makeacurtsey (USA) (Herbager 136) [1989 7g 1990 7f⁵ 8.3f⁵ 7m⁴ 10.2f³ 12d 12g] sturdy, lengthy gelding: plating-class maiden: should prove suited by further than 7f: acts on firm ground: bandaged near-hind last 2 starts: sold 1,500 gns Newmarket Autumn Sales. *R. Hannon.*   —

SHOT STOPPER 2 gr.f. (Mar 1) Bellypha 130–Ideal Home 104 (Home Guard (USA) 129) [1990 5m³ 5m 7m 7f³ 7m⁵ 7.3g³ 7m] 30,000Y: unfurnished filly: good mover: third foal: half-sister to 3-y-o Dushenka (by Jalmood): dam 2-y-o 5f winner: modest maiden: ran poorly final start, awkward stalls time before: will stay 1m. *R. Hannon.*   73

SHOT WOOD 2 ch.c. (Apr 16) Crofthall 110–Squires Girl (Spanish Gold 101) [1990 6m 6m] 14,500Y: leggy, close-coupled colt: fifth reported foal: brother to fairly useful 5f to 7f winner Marcroft and half-brother to smart sprinter Jonacris (by Broxted): dam never ran: prominent around 4f in maidens at Folkestone and Pontefract: subsequently sold 920 gns Doncaster September Sales. *J. Berry.*   —

SHOUT AND SING (USA) 3 ch.c. The Minstrel (CAN) 135–Godetia (USA) 119 (Sir Ivor 135) [1989 7g⁵ 1990 8f³ 12g* 12g 12s 10s] strong, attractive colt: won listed race at Epsom in April: about 12¾ lengths ninth of 22 to Houmayoun in Derby Italiano (co-favourite) at Rome following month then soundly beaten in St Simon Stakes (wandered under pressure, 5 months later) at Newbury and Group 1 Premio Roma: stays 1½m: bought privately out of G. Harwood's stable after second start: useful. *M. A. Jarvis.*   103

SHOUT FORE 3 gr.g. Petong 126–Mavahra 93 (Mummy's Pet 125) [1989 5d⁶ 5s⁵ 6f* 6m 7m² 7g 5m⁵ 6g² 6m² 1990 6g⁵ 6m⁴ 5m 6m⁶ 6m* 5m 6m 7f 7g⁶ a6g³ 5m* 6g³ 5m 5g*] close-coupled, sparely-made gelding: fair performer on his day: comfortable winner of handicap at Windsor (sweating) in June and claimers at Sandown in September and Bath in October: stays 6f: acts on firm going: has run respectably for 7-lb claimer: ran moderately in blinkers on fourth start: sold 15,000 gns Newmarket Autumn Sales and gelded: inconsistent. *N. A. Callaghan.*   85

SHOUT OUT 3 b.c. Auction Ring (USA) 123–Manora (USA) (Stop The Music (USA)) [1989 6f³ 6m³ 1990 8m] rangy colt, rather dipped-backed: moderate mover: twice placed, drifting left, in fair company in May at 2 yrs: well beaten in September maiden on sole outing in 1990. *C. R. Nelson.*   —

SHOVEL 2 br.g. (May 2) Mummy's Game 120–Valley Farm 88 (Red God 128§) [1990 7s⁵ a8g a8g] 7,600Y: leggy gelding: brother to 3-y-o Into The Future and half-brother to several winners, including 1¼m to 15.8f winner Valls d'Andorra (by Free State), 1986 2-y-o 6f winner Margam (by African Sky) and jumper Cooch Behar (by Taj Dewan): dam won over 6f: slowly away and soundly beaten in maidens and a claimer at Lingfield: bandaged last 2 starts. *C. C. Elsey.*   —

SHOWACA 2 b.g. (Apr 11) Show-A-Leg 107–Elsaca (Ela-Mana-Mou 132) [1990 6m a7g] close-coupled gelding: first foal: dam unraced daughter of Yorkshire and Lancashire Oaks winner Busaca: soundly beaten in claimer at Leicester and maiden at Southwell. *R. F. Marvin.*   —

SHOWDOWN 4 ch.g. Final Straw 127–Sideshow 103 (Welsh Pageant 132) [1989 8.2v³ 10f 8m* 8m³ 8.3g* 8.3m³ 8d 1990 8f⁵ 10m 8f⁶ 10h⁵ 8h⁵ 12f] strong, heavy-bodied gelding: poor mover: quite modest handicapper: tailed off in ladies race final start: stays 1¼m: acts on hard ground, probably unsuited by soft: blinkered fourth outing: looked none too enthusiastic time before. *A. Moore.*   63

SHOWMANSHIP 3 b.g. Shernazar 131–Melodramatic 112 (Tudor Melody 129) [1989 7g 1990 8f 10.1g 10.6f² 10g 8.2s⁵ 11.5g 10d³ a12g² a10g] leggy, good-topped gelding: moderate mover: modest handicapper on his day: stays 1½m: acts on firm ground, possibly unsuited by very soft: has run well for an apprentice. *C. F. Wall.*   69

SHU FLY (NZ) 6 ch.g. Tom's Shu (USA)–Alycone (NZ) (Philoctetes 111) [1989 NR 1990 9g] workmanlike gelding: sweating freely, around 17 lengths eighth of 17 in ladies race at Kempton in June: fairly useful hurdler, winner of 2 handicaps in autumn. *Mrs S. Oliver.*   —

SHUTTLECOCK CORNER (USA) 4 b.c. Cresta Rider (USA) 124–Sweet Ellen (USA) (Vitriolic) [1989 6s* 5m 6f⁶ 5m² 5f⁴ 5m 6g⁵ 5m³ 1990 6g² 5f⁴ 5m² 5d] chunky, sprint type: carries plenty of condition: poor walker: moderate mover: useful sprinter: ran creditably first 3 outings at 4 yrs, in Palace House Stakes (fourth to Statoblest) at Newmarket and Compaq Computer EBF Ballyogan Stakes (fav-   106 ourite, didn't get clear run) at Leopardstown last 2 occasions: effective at 5f and 6f: best form on a sound surface: tough and consistent: sent to race in Australia. *P. S. Felgate.*

SHY MISTRESS 7 b.m. Cawston's Clown 113–Shy Talk 93 (Sharpen Up 127) 33 §
[1989 8m⁴ 6f* 7f 6g⁵ 8g⁵ 7f 1990 8.2s⁴ 8m⁶ 8g] smallish mare: moderate mover: poor on most form, but appeared to show vast improvement when winning amateurs handicap at Redcar as 6-y-o: seems to stay 1m and to act on any going: often slowly away: not one to trust. *G. A. Ham.*

SHYOUSHKA 4 ch.f. Shy Groom (USA)–Capsville (USA) (Cyane) [1989 8d⁴ 10f³ 91
10m* 10d 1990 10m 10f⁶ 10d 10s³] strong, lengthy filly: carries condition: has a quick action: useful winner as 3-y-o (finished lame final start): below her best in 1990, but showed she retains some ability when 6½ lengths third to Topanoora in quite valuable event at Leopardstown in November: should stay 1½m: easily best effort on good to firm going, though has won on soft: trained until after second start by H. Cecil. *P. Hill, Ireland.*

SIANEMA 2 ro.f. (Apr 29) Persian Bold 123–Seriema 72 (Petingo 135) [1990 6m] 62 p
50,000Y: half-sister to 3 winners, including very smart 1¼m and 1½m winner Infamy (by Shirley Heights): dam best at 1m, is half-sister to good staying filly High Hawk: around 10 lengths seventh of 9, slowly away and never near to challenge, to Shihama in maiden at Newmarket in November: sure to improve. *D. R. C. Elsworth.*

SIAN'S LADY 3 b.f. Dunbeath (USA) 127–Hawaiian Joss (USA) (Hawaii) [1989 58
5g 5g⁵ 5g⁴ 6m² 7f* 6m² 7m 1990 8m⁴ 7f⁶ 8.2g² 7m 8.3m³ 7f a8g 6d⁵] angular filly: plating-class performer: stays 1m: acts on firm and dead ground: has run moderately when blinkered (penultimate start) and for 7-lb claimer: bandaged third start: inconsistent. *D. Haydn Jones.*

SIBERIAN BREEZE 2 gr.c. (May 5) Siberian Express (USA) 125–Zepha 88 58 p
(Great Nephew 126) [1990 7g 7m] 18,000Y: leggy, workmanlike colt: has a quick action: sixth foal: half-brother to 3-y-o Zenella (by Precocious) and 4 winners, including smart 4-y-o 7f winner Fedoria (by Formidable) and 1987 2-y-o 1m winner Great Prospector (by Glint of Gold): dam won from 1m to 9.4f: around 8 lengths ninth of 13, slowly away and never dangerous, in maiden at Warwick in October: green on debut. *J. A. Glover.*

SIBERIAN FLOWER 2 gr.f. (Mar 28) Siberian Express (USA) 125–Rose of 61
The Sea (USA) 115 (The Minstrel (CAN) 135) [1990 5m⁴ 6m³ 6m³ 5m⁵ 5m 6m] leggy filly: has a round action: first foal: dam French sprinter: plating-class maiden: seems better suited by 6f than 5f: wore tongue strap first 2 outings: sold 4,300 gns Newmarket Autumn Sales. *M. Moubarak.*

SIBERIAN STEPPES 3 b. or br.f. Siberian Express (USA) 125–La Palma —
(Posse (USA) 130) [1989 5v 5s⁶ 5g 5f 6v 6g⁵ 1990 6g 7m 7.6m a8g 7f 6m] leggy filly: poor maiden: tailed off as 3-y-o except on fourth (led over 6f, hung right) outing: stays 1m: sold 1,900 gns Newmarket Autumn Sales. *P. Mitchell.*

SICILIAN SWING 5 b.g. Swing Easy (USA) 126–Mab (Morston (FR) 125) [1989 —
8f 9s 1990 a12g] big, workmanlike gelding: little sign of ability, including in seller. *W. Holden.*

SID THE MANAGER 2 b.c. (Mar 31) Tina's Pet 121–Breckland Lady 62 —
(Royalty 130) [1990 6m 6m 7s] lengthy colt: shows knee action: second foal: brother to 3-y-o Dancing May: dam 9f and 1¼m winner: well behind in maidens: off course 4 months after debut. *P. Howling.*

SIERRA D'OR 2 ch.f. (Apr 5) Never So Bold 135–Sacred Mountain 74 (Et Paddy 48
133) [1990 6m 5g⁵ 5g 6d] 22,000F: close-coupled, sparely-made filly: half-sister to several winners, including useful 1983 Irish 2-y-o 6f winner Mount Imperial (by Imperial Fling) and modest handicapper Welsh Pageantry (by Welsh Pageant), winner at up to 1¼m: dam sister to very smart 1m to 1¼m performer Calpurnius: poor maiden: raced on unfavoured part of track final outing: should be better suited by 6f than 5f: sold 800 gns Newmarket Autumn Sales. *R. Hannon.*

SIFTING GOLD (USA) 3 ch.c. Slew O'Gold (USA)–Repetitious 103 (North- 113
fields (USA)) [1989 6d⁴ 5d² 8d⁵ 7d³ 1990 8v* 10g* 10d 9g 9.7g] sixth foal: half-brother to very smart French middle-distance colt Sarhoob (by Alydar) and a winner in USA by J O Tobin: dam, sister to Nanticious, won Stewards' Cup and later stakes-placed winner in USA: won listed race at Maisons-Laffitte and Prix La Force (by head from Starstreak) at Longchamp in the spring: below form in Grand Prix de Paris, listed race and Prix Dollar: stays 1¼m: acts on heavy going. *A. Fabre, France.*

SIGAMA (USA) 4 ch.g. Stop The Music (USA)–Lady Speedwell (USA) (Secre- 88
tariat (USA)) [1989 5g² 5d³ 5g 5m³ 5m 5f 5m 5g 1990 5g 5m* 5f² 5m² 5s³ 5f* 5f² 5m* 5m a5g] sturdy, dipped-backed gelding: has a quick action: fairly useful handi-

capper: made all at Thirsk in May and Pontefract and Newcastle in July, on last 2 occasions (apprentice ridden) clear at halfway: very speedy: acts well on top-of-the-ground, unsuited by soft: blinkered once: much improved. *F. H. Lee.*

SIGGLESTHORNE 3 ch.f. Claude Monet (USA) 121–Le Levandoll 92 (Le — Levanstell 122) [1989 6f⁵ 5g⁵ 6f 5g 1990 7f 5f 6f a5g] close-coupled, sparely-made filly: turns off-fore in: has a round action: poor maiden: bred to be suited by 7f +: seems to need give in the ground. *B. Richmond.*

SIGNOR SASSIE (USA) 2 ch.c. (Mar 1) The Minstrel (CAN) 135–Sahsie — p (USA) (Forli (ARG)) [1990 7m] $210,000Y: half-brother to several winners, including useful 1984 American 2-y-o Easy Step (by Overskate): dam minor winner: steadied start, pushed along over 2f out but no significant headway in maiden at Newmarket in October: moved very well down: should improve. *G. Harwood.*

SIGN PEOPLE 4 ch.c. Sayyaf 121–Maura Paul (Bonne Noel 115) [1989 7m³ 8.2m 75 7m⁴ 8m² 8m⁵ 7m 7f⁴ 9g 1990 8f 8m 8.5f⁴ 7.6f² 8m a7g⁴] smallish, quite good-topped colt: poor mover: modest handicapper nowadays: stays 1m: acts on firm going: bandaged near-fore last 3 starts: wandered third outing: sold 2,000 gns Doncaster November Sales. *Dr J. D. Scargill.*

SIGN PERFORMER 3 ch.g. Longleat (USA) 109–Grandgirl (Mansingh (USA) — 120) [1989 NR 1990 12f] 6,000Y: third reported foal: dam unraced half-sister to Jimsun: always behind in claimer at Leicester: sold 1,900 gns Ascot May Sales. *Dr J. D. Scargill.*

SIGNSOFTHENINETIES (IRE) 2 b.c. (Apr 4) Red Sunset 120–Dominia 42 (Derring-Do 131) [1990 7g 7m⁵ 8.2m 8m 10s] IR 24,000Y: leggy, workmanlike colt: seventh foal: half-brother to 3 winners abroad: dam won at around 1m in USA: poor maiden: sold 1,850 gns Doncaster November Sales. *Dr J. D. Scargill.*

SIGWELL'S GOLD 3 b.f. Sonnen Gold 121–Manna Green (Bustino 136) [1989 62 6f² 7m² 7m⁵ 1990 10m 11.7m 8m 7.5g² 7g 8f* 8.2m⁵] tall, unfurnished filly: ridden by 7-lb claimer when easily best efforts on last 2 starts, winning seller (bought in 5,000 gns) at Chepstow in September: stays 1m: acts on firm going. *R. J. Holder.*

SIKESTON (USA) 4 b.c. Lear Fan (USA) 130–Small Timer (USA) (Ly- 124 phard (USA) 132) [1989 7d 8v* 12m 1990 8v* 8g 10g² 12g 10d 8v* 10s³ 8v*]
Italian-owned Sikeston may just as easily be Italian-trained judging by his record to date: he's managed at least one win in Group 1 company in Italy in each of his three seasons in training, has yet to break his duck outside Italy and on his two starts in Britain in the last two years has been tailed off. Sikeston's four races outside Italy as a four-year-old saw him taking on the best over a mile, a mile and a quarter and a mile and a half. In the Prix Jacques le Marois, Champion Stakes and Prix de l'Arc de Triomphe he finished in the rear and beat only seven home all told, but his run in the Phoenix Champion Stakes was a revelation. Rated a 66/1-chance in a field of eight, he was given a good tactical ride by Roberts in a moderately-run race, keeping close to the early leader Tanwi and being sent on over two furlongs out. Once headed by Elmaamul he stayed on gamely and pulled four lengths clear of Kostroma in going down by a length and a half to the favourite. It was obviously an improved effort, but his performances in the Arc and Champion Stakes suggested he'd been grossly flattered, though the trip was almost certainly too far at Longchamp and connections came up with the novel explanation that his girth had been too tight at Newmarket. In the testing conditions in which he revels Sikeston completed the season at the peak of his form. In the space of a fortnight in November he won the Premio Ribot at Rome easily by five lengths from the ex-English Irgaim, whom he'd also beaten in the Premio Natale di Roma back in April, finished third to Legal Case and Candy Glen in the Premio Roma, then became the first British-trained winner of the Premio Vittorio di Capua at Milan since it was granted Group 1 status in 1988 when he kept Candy Glen and Zoman at bay by three lengths and a neck. The Premio Vittorio di Capua had been due to take place a month earlier, but had to be rearranged after a strike by stable lads in Italy caused the meeting and several others in October to be lost. The strike, called in protest against revised pay and working conditions, proved a boon for connections of Sikeston for he hadn't been an intended runner on the original date.

Sikeston is from Lear Fan's first crop and is his best representative and only pattern winner in Europe. Lear Fan was retired to Gainesway Farm,

Mrs V. Gaucci Del Bono's "Sikeston"

		Lear Fan (USA) (b 1981)	Roberto (b 1969)	Hail To Reason Bramalea
Sikeston (USA) (b.c. 1986)			Wac (b 1969)	Lt Stevens Belthazar
	Small Timer (USA) (b 1980)	Lyphard (b 1969)	Northern Dancer Goofed
		Watch Fob (b or br 1965)	Tompion Pet Child

Kentucky in 1985. Unbeaten as a two-year-old and rated the third best juvenile behind El Gran Senor and Rainbow Quest, he'd shown high-class form over a mile at three when a four-length winner of the Prix Jacques le Marois at Deauville. Sikeston was his dam's third and last foal bred in the States before she was sent to New Zealand; the first was a winner in North America by Temperence Hill. The unraced Small Timer, half-sister to minor stakes winner Chime, is a daughter of Watch Fob, a winner of eleven of her fifty-six races over five seasons. A robust, heavy-topped colt, the type to always carry condition, Sikeston is effective at a mile and a mile and a quarter and revels in the mud. He didn't race on ground firmer than good at four years. If returning in the same form in which he ended the season, Sikeston should find a good race closer to home in 1991. *C. E. Brittain.*

SILCA AN' KEY 3 b.c. Commanche Run 133–Miss Silca Key 102 (Welsh Saint **105** d 126) [1989 6g⁶ 7g⁴ 1990 8g² 8m³ 10m³ 10m³ 10m³ 10g² 10.5g⁵] rangy, good-topped colt: impresses in appearance: good walker: capable of useful form, third of 6 in moderately-run Predominate Stakes (running on well from rear 4¾ lengths behind Razeen) at Goodwood third start: ran moderately in maidens afterwards: better at 1¼m than 1m: sold 38,000 gns Newmarket Autumn Sales: clearly one to be wary of. *D. R. C. Elsworth.*

SILCA SUPREME 4 b.g. Chief Singer 131–Miss Silca Key 102 (Welsh Saint 126) **100**
[1989 6m* 6f² 7f 6g² 7.3g 1990 6m⁵ 6m² 5m⁵ 6d 6m 6m 5m⁶ 5d] big, rangy, unfurnished gelding: usually looks really well: useful on his day, but is none too consistent: creditable sixth, soon off bridle, to Blyton Lad in listed race at Newmarket in October: stays 6f: acts on firm going: blinkered fifth and sixth starts: often bandaged and on toes: sold 17,500 gns Newmarket Autumn Sales. *D. R. C. Elsworth.*

SILENT GIRL 3 ch.f. Krayyan 117–Silent Pearl (USA) (Silent Screen (USA)) **75**
[1989 6m⁶ 8g⁶ 8m* 8s⁵ a7g 1990 8g 8g* 7d 11.7m³ 11.5m* 12m* 11.7m* 14m⁴ 12m] angular filly: modest performer: won seller (bought in 9,000 gns) at Leicester in June then claimer (tending to hang) at Sandown and handicaps at Kempton and Windsor in July: should stay 1¾m: acts on good to firm ground and soft: usually bandaged: needs plenty of driving: game. *N. A. Callaghan.*

SILENT LOCH 3 b.f. Lochnager 132–Keep Silent 83 (Balidar 133) [1989 a7g a6g —
1990 a6g a7g] angular filly: soundly beaten in Southwell claimers. *M. Johnston.*

SILENT PRINCESS 4 b.f. King of Spain 121–Silent Dancer 76 (Quiet Fling —
(USA) 116) [1989 10.1m 12f⁵ 14f 12m 17.1f⁴ 16f⁶ 1990 a14g⁶ a14g] neat filly: poor form at best: often blinkered or visored: winning selling hurdler. *J. L. Harris.*

SILENT STEPS 3 ch.c. Kind of Hush 118–On The Turn 87 (Manacle 123) [1989 —
6m 7m 1990 10f 10f] leggy, angular colt: never dangerous in maidens and selling handicap. *M. McCormack.*

SILICON BAVARIA (FR) 3 br.f. Procida (USA) 129–Siliciana 113 (Silly **110**
Season (USA) 127) [1989 6.5d² 7s⁵ 1990 8g⁴ 8d³ 8s⁶ 6g 7g³ 6g² 6d*] half-sister to 7 winners, including useful French 4-y-o 7.5f and 1m winner Silicon Lady (by Mille Balles) and French 1½m winner Silicon King (by Shirley Heights), and also to the dam of Risk Me: dam won Cambridgeshire: 24/1, led close home to prevail in very close finish for Prix de Seine-et-Oise at Maisons-Laffitte in September: ¾-length second to Flower Girl in Group 3 event at Baden-Baden 4 weeks earlier: seems best at 6f: acts on dead ground. *R. Collet, France.*

SILK DYNASTY 4 b.g. Prince Tenderfoot (USA) 126–Mountain Chase (Mount **61** d
Hagen (FR) 127) [1989 12d² 10g 8.5d 8g a10g⁶ 1990 a12g* a13g⁵ a12g a13g 10.6s 12.3g 8.5g 10.2f 12f a8g] small, compact gelding: turns near-fore out: moderate mover: won maiden at Lingfield in January: ran poorly in claimers and amateur events after: stays 1½m: pulled hard when blinkered: trained until after fourth outing by M. Francis: none too genuine. *R. Hollinshead.*

SILKEN LINES (USA) 3 b.f. Lines of Power (USA)–Bluebell 103 (Town Crier **59**
119) [1989 NR 1990 a8g* 8d 8m] leggy, workmanlike, rather angular filly: sixth foal: half-sister to fair 1m winner Mountain Bluebird (by Clever Trick), modest 9f and 1¼m winner Speedwell (by Grundy) and winners in Germany and USA: dam, out of half-sister to Queen's Hussar, ran only at 2 yrs when successful over 6f and 7.3f: won maiden at Southwell in January: off course 3 months then below that form in handicaps at Newbury (moved moderately down) and Doncaster: sold 2,500 gns Ascot October Sales. *N. A. Graham.*

SILKEN SAILED (USA) 2 b.c. (May 11) Gold Crest (USA) 120–Lady of **94** ?
Camelot (FR) (Bolkonski 134) [1990 5m⁴ 5d⁴ 5d⁵ 5m* 5m* 5m² 6f 5g 5d⁵] $15,000Y: lengthy, rather angular colt: good walker: half-brother to several winners in USA, one graded stakes-placed: dam, half-sister to numerous winners, won 7 times at up to 7f: fairly useful performer: made all in minor event at Beverley and nursery at Leicester in July: slowly away and appeared to take little interest penultimate outing, given reminders soon after start final one: best form at 5f: acts well on good to firm ground: blinkered final 6 starts. *W. A. O'Gorman.*

SILKEN WAGER 3 b.f. Beldale Flutter (USA) 130–Satin Box 73 (Jukebox 120) —
[1989 NR 1990 10g⁶] fifth foal: half-sister to a winner in Norway by Star Appeal and a minor winner by Gunner B at up to 9f in USA: dam middle-distance maiden, is granddaughter of Irish 1000 Guineas winner Black Satin: slow-starting last of 6 in maiden at Beverley in August. *N. A. Graham.*

SILK PETAL 4 b.f. Petorius 117–Salabella 64 (Sallust 134) [1989 7d³ 7f* 7s* 8g³ **103**
7d² 1990 8g 8g⁴ 8s* 8.5s⁶ 10.5v³] workmanlike filly: useful performer: won listed event at Cologne in September: had run very well when fourth to Thakib in similar race at Kempton earlier in month: suited by 1m: best form on an easy surface: visits Night Shift. *J. L. Dunlop.*

SILKS DOMINO 5 ch.g. Dominion 123–Bourgeonette 81 (Mummy's Pet 125) **47**
[1989 12s 12g 16m 12d⁶ 13s 12.2m 1990 a13g⁴ a16g² a14g³ a14g⁴ a14g a14g] rather plain gelding: has a long stride: poor handicapper: off course 10½ months before fifth outing, and tailed off on last: seems to stay 2m: best form on a soft surface:

sometimes blinkered or visored: best forcing the pace: sold out of M. Ryan's stable 1,600 gns Newmarket September Sales after fourth start: inconsistent. *O. O'Neill.*

SILK SLIPPERS (USA) 3 b.f. Nureyev (USA) 131–Nalee's Fantasy (USA) — (Graustark) [1989 7m* 8m* 1990 8m3] big, lengthy filly: gained second 2-y-o success in Hoover Fillies' Mile at Ascot by a head from Moon Cactus, staying on strongly to lead line: second favourite, 9 lengths third of 4 to Arousal in Newcastle minor event in June on only start in 1990, taking keen hold early: will stay 1¼m: sold to dissolve partnership $650,000 Keeneland January (1991) Sale. *B. W. Hills.*

SILKS PRINCESS 4 b.f. Prince Tenderfoot (USA) 126–Pitlessie 75 (Hook 66 Money 124) [1989 6s* 6s2 6s* 6m4 6g 6s 6m 6g 1990 a6g 6v 7m 7g 6g 6m6 a7g4 6g a7g5 a8g* 8.2m 6m* 6m 6m] lengthy, good-bodied filly: moderate mover: handicapper nowadays: won at Southwell and Lingfield in August: effective at 6f and stays 1m: acts on good to firm going, best efforts on soft: has been tried in blinkers and visor. *M. J. Ryan.*

SILKS VENTURE 5 br.h. Lochnager 132–Honey Thief 77 (Burglar 128) [1989 — a5g 1990 6s 5m 5d] rather leggy horse: poor mover: modest winner (including for apprentice) as 3-y-o: has lost his form: best form at 5f with give in the ground: blinkered once at 3 yrs: bandaged last 4 outings: sold 1,050 gns Doncaster May Sales. *P. A. Blockley.*

SILLARS STALKER (IRE) 2 b.g. (May 11) Stalker 121–Mittens (Run The 42 p Gantlet (USA)) [1990 5m 5f 5d 6d] 7,000Y: workmanlike gelding: half-brother to 1989 Irish 2-y-o 6f and 1m winner Teach Dha Mhile (by Kampala), very useful in Italy in 1990, staying handicapper Green Archer (by Hardgreen) and jumping winner Remittance Man (by Prince Regent): dam Irish bumpers and hurdles winner: never able to challenge in maidens at Catterick nor nursery (not at all knocked about) at Newmarket: probably capable of better over much further. *Mrs J. R. Ramsden.*

SILLERY (USA) 2 b.c. (Mar 19) Blushing Groom (FR) 131–Silvermine (FR) 124 108 p (Bellypha 130) [1990 8d4 8d2 8v* 8s*] second foal: half-brother to French 3-y-o Signorelli (by Cox's Ridge): dam French 1000 Guineas winner, is half-sister to Saint Cyrien out of very useful French 7.5f to 9f winner Sevres: much improved late in year, winning maiden at Maisons-Laffitte in November and listed Prix Herbager (by ¾ length) at Saint-Cloud in December: will stay 1¼m: acts well on heavy ground. *Mme C. Head, France.*

SILLY HABIT (USA) 4 b.f. Assert 134–Habitassa 100 (Habitat 134) [1989 65 11.7h6 12f2 10.1m2 12f2 1990 11.7g3 a14g 12g4 16g 15.3m3 14g5 17.6m2 18.1m2 17.6g3] workmanlike filly: moderate mover: quite modest maiden: stays 2¼m: acts on firm and dead going. *J. W. Hills.*

SILLY'S BROTHER 4 ch.g. Longleat (USA) 109–Scilly Isles 54 (Silly Season 45 127) [1989 7g 7v2 7m4 7f 9s 7g 1990 6s 7f4 7f 7m 6g 8.5g 7g 7.5f6 7f 8g 7.5m3 7d 8g a6g4 a6g4] heavy-topped gelding: one-time modest maiden: appeared to run by far his best race for long time in claimer at Southwell on penultimate outing, but was probably flattered: effective at 6f and 7f: acts on good to firm and heavy going. *N. Bycroft.*

SILVER AGE (USA) 4 b.c. Silver Hawk (USA) 123–Our Paige (USA) (Grand — Revival (USA)) [1989 a10g6 a14g6 1990 a12g6 a10g] no worthwhile form in varied events. *J. M. Bradley.*

SILVER BRAID (USA) 2 ch.f. (Feb 10) Miswaki (USA) 124–Chalice of Silver 83 p (USA) 74 (Graustark) [1990 6g 7g* 7g3] $21,000F, $70,000Y: leggy, angular filly: first foal: dam maiden stayed 17f: won maiden at Kempton in September by 2½ lengths going away from Crimson Conquest: well-backed favourite, over a length third of 15, keeping on despite poor run, to Fragrant Hill in minor event at Newbury: will stay 1m: likely to improve bit further, and win another race. *D. R. C. Elsworth.*

SILVER CONCORD 2 gr.c. (Apr 25) Absalom 128–Boarding House 73 (Shack 71 (USA) 118) [1990 6m 6g3 7v3 6s] 34,000 2-y-o: workmanlike colt: has scope: second foal: half-brother to a winner in Malaysia: dam best at 5f: best effort staying-on third to Emilia Romagna in maiden at Newcastle: should be suited by further than 6f: seems unsuited by soft ground. *J. M. P. Eustace.*

SILVERDALE FOX 3 ch.g. Sweet Monday 122–Its My Turn 80 (Palm Track 79 122) [1989 6m 7f6 7m 6m* 7m 6v* 1990 10v2 8.2s6 10.2m2 8.5m5 9g 9.1s4] angular, plain gelding: modest handicapper: off course 3 months (gelded) then well beaten last 2 starts: suited by 1¼m: acts on good to firm ground and heavy: has given trouble at stalls (edgy and coltish second start), once refusing to enter them: has run poorly when sweating and edgy: of doubtful temperament. *R. Hollinshead.*

SILVER DILEMMA (USA) 2 b.c. (Feb 18) The Minstrel (CAN) 135–Royal 78
Dilemma (USA) (Buckpasser) [1990 6m⁴ 6g³ 6g³] well-made colt: has a quick
action: brother to good sprinter Silver Fling and high-class 6f and 7f winner
Silverdip, closely related to 2 winners, including Imperial Fling (by Northern
Dancer), successful at up to 1½m, and half-brother to 3 other winners: dam stakes-
placed winner at up to 6f, is out of champion 1964 American 2-y-o filly Queen Empress: 2 lengths third of 17, edging left then hanging right and unable to quicken, to
West Riding at Newbury, final and best effort in maidens: will probably be better
suited by 7f. *I. A. Balding.*

SILVER HEELS 2 ch.c. (Apr 17) Capricorn Line 111–Balinese Dancer 54 —
(Moorestyle 137) [1990 6f⁴] first foal: dam lightly raced: tailed off in 4-runner claimer at Lingfield in July. *R. Hannon.*

SILVER HELLO 4 gr.g. Nishapour (FR) 125–Si (Ragusa 137) [1989 8g⁴ 10m —
12.4m³ 10.2f³ 10g³ 12g³ 12g 10v 12g* 1990 12.2m 11f 12m⁵] rather leggy, quite
good-topped gelding: good mover: showed improved form when winning claimer at
Edinburgh in November, 1989: failed to see out his races in spring, as though
something possibly amiss: stays 1½m: acts on firm going, possibly unsuited by
heavy. *P. S. Felgate.*

SILVER LODGE 3 ch.f. Homing 130–Silverhall (Sparkler 130) [1989 NR 1990 —
10m⁶] rather legggy filly: second foal: dam unraced half-sister to Swiss Maid: 50/1,
backward and moved poorly to post when well-beaten sixth of 7 in £7,400 event at
Newmarket in May. *A. Hide.*

SILVER ORE (FR) 3 ch.f. Silver Hawk (USA) 123–Forever Mary 81 (Red Alert 94
127) [1989 6m* 6g⁶ 1990 9f 6g⁵ 8f* 8f² 8m⁴ 9m] rather shallow-girthed, good-
quartered filly: fairly useful handicapper: won at Yarmouth in July: 33/1, disputed
lead 6f in Cambridgeshire Handicap at Newmarket final start: stays 1m well: acts on
firm going: ridden up with pace. *W. A. O'Gorman.*

SILVER OWL 4 gr.c. Daring March 116–Bird's Custard 80 (Birdbrook 116) [1989 99
7d 6g⁵ 6m 12h* 12f* 12f² 12f* 12h² 12h* 12g* 12g⁴ 1990 12g² 14g² 12m* 12d⁶ 12f*
16.2f³ 11.5m* 12m] leggy, close-coupled colt: useful handicapper: favourite, won at
Goodwood in May, Brighton (3-runner race) in June and Sandown (strongly-run
£7,800 amateurs event) in August: carrying plenty of condition, ran rare modest
race in £71,300 Ascot contest final outing: stays 1¾m: needs a sound surface: game
and consistent. *R. V. Smyth.*

SILVER PATROL 5 gr.g. Rusticaro (FR) 124–Goccia d'Oro (ITY) (Bolkonski —
134) [1989 10d⁴ 7.2s 12m 8m 8.2g 9g 11s 1990 a8g 8.2s] angular, sparely-made
gelding: won maiden at Sligo as 3-y-o: well beaten vast majority of subsequent
starts: stays 7f: acts on heavy going: blinkered final outing: taken early to post: sold
to join C. Popham's stable 2,900 gns Ascot July Sales. *A. P. Stringer.*

SILVER SALVER 3 b. or br.g. Known Fact (USA) 135–Sauceboat 120 (Con- —
naught 130) [1989 NR 1990 10f] angular gelding: sixth foal: half-brother to 5 winners,
notably useful 4-y-o Top-Boot (by High Top), successful at 1m, and smart 1m to 11f
winner Kind of Hush (by Welsh Pageant): dam won over 6f at 2 yrs and stayed 1¼m:
7/1, sweating and heavily bandaged, bolted to post then very slowly away and well
tailed off in maiden at Newmarket in August: subsequently gelded. *B. Hanbury.*

SILVER SHIFTER 3 b.f. Night Shift (USA)–The Silver Darling 75 (John —
Splendid 116) [1989 6g 1990 12f⁵ 12m 12m] angular filly: no sign of ability, including
in handicap: sold out of A. Stewart's stable 2,500 gns Doncaster August Sales after
second start. *Mrs A. Knight.*

SILVER SINGING (USA) 3 gr.f. Topsider (USA)–Early Rising (USA) (Grey 96
Dawn II 132) [1989 6m³ 6g⁵ 1990 5m* 7v⁵ 5.8h 7.3m 5.8m⁴ 5f* 5f* 5f* 5g* 5.6g 5m
5m] leggy, good-topped filly: progressed very well in justifying favouritism for
maiden at Wolverhampton and handicaps at Bath, Sandown, Goodwood and York:
never able to challenge in competitive handicaps last 3 outings, twice slowly away:
best at 5f: acts on firm going: probably best held up: blinkered (made most) fifth
start. *I. A. Balding.*

SILVER STICK 3 gr.g. Absalom 128–Queen's Parade (Sovereign Path 125) 43
[1989 6f 6f 6f 1990 8f⁴ 8g⁶ 9m⁴ a12g] leggy, rather angular gelding: plating-class
maiden at best: stays 9f: edgy final start, in July. *J. W. Watts.*

SILVER STONE BOY 2 gr.c. (Apr 12) Another Realm 118–Elkie Brooks 82 —
(Relkino 131) [1990 5m] 8,000F, 5,000Y: workmanlike, good-quartered colt: second
foal: brother to 1988 2-y-o 6f winner Dolly Bevan: dam second over 6f as 2-y-o,
didn't train on: backward, slowly away and always behind in maiden at Leicester in
April: showed a round action. *J. Balding.*

852

Falmouth Stakes (Handicap), York—fourth handicap win in a row for Silver Singing; behind there's little between Bold Lez, Ra'a (noseband) and Please Believe Me

SILVER SUSAN 4 gr.f. Ampney Prince 96–Pickwood Sue 74 (Right Boy 137) — [1989 NR 1990 a8g a5g a5g] small, close-coupled filly: of little account. *J. P. Leigh.*

SILVIE 3 b.f. Kind of Hush 118–Fallen Angel 88 (Quiet Fling (USA) 124) [1989 NR **66** 1990 12.5m3 14d 11.7f* 12m] rangy filly: second foal: half-sister to fair Irish 1987 2-y-o 6f winner Nations Spirit (by Thatching), later sent to USA: dam genuine stayer: favourite, easily made all in 5-runner maiden at Bath in September: disputed lead 1m when well beaten in apprentice handicap: shapes like a stayer: possibly unsuited by a soft surface: sold to join J. Baker 10,500 gns Newmarket Autumn Sales. *H. Candy.*

SIMASCALA 4 b.g. Electric 126–Elegida 93 (Habitat 134) [1989 8s 10s 12s 8m — 10f5 8.2m 10g5 1990 10h6 12m 18m] angular, workmanlike gelding: moderate mover: easily best effort as 3-y-o final start: tailed off in handicaps in first half of 1990: stays 1¼m: best form on a sound surface: often blinkered or visored: wore crossed noseband final outing. *W. Wilson.*

SIMMIE'S SPECIAL 2 b.f. (Jan 16) Precocious 126–Zalatia 97 (Music Boy 124) **70** [1990 5m2 5f2 5d2] 8,400Y: angular filly: first foal: dam 7f winner: modest form in auction events at Leicester and Ripon and maiden at Chester: speedy: carries head awkwardly, and tends to hang: unseated rider on way down at Chester: not seen out after May. *R. Hollinshead.*

SIMPLE TRUTH 3 b.f. Known Fact (USA) 135–Northern Ballerina 52 (Dance **68** In Time (CAN)) [1989 NR 1990 5m2 6g2 5s 5d a5g5] 10,000Y: small, lengthy filly: moderate walker and mover: first foal: dam won sellers at 7f and 8.2f: modest sprint maiden: seems not to act on a soft surface. *M. Johnston.*

SIMPLY BLUE 3 ch.f. Simply Great (FR) 122–Bluethroat 95 (Ballymore 123) — [1989 5.1f3 6h* 7m4 8f* 8f 1990 10f] modest winner at 2 yrs: ran as though something amiss final start as 2-y-o and again on only outing in 1990: should be suited by 1¼m. *M. Bell.*

SIMPLY DES 3 b.f. Simply Great (FR) 122–Kashida 68 (Green Dancer (USA) **52** 132) [1989 5h 5f4 6m 7g 6m 6f4 6m4 6m 6m4 6g 8m* 8g3 8.2s 1990 12f4 8m3 12f 10m 10m 12t- 9g 12f2 10f 12g a12g a13g] neat filly: has a round action: plating-class performer: easily best efforts in handicaps when second at Brighton, in ladies event on first occasion: stays 1½m: acts on firm going, possibly unsuited by soft: visored once at 2 yrs. *J. O'Donoghue.*

SIMPLY FIRST CLASS 4 b.g. Tower Walk 130–Duchy 99 (Rheingold 137) — [1989 12.2m 12f 10m 1990 8m] workmanlike gelding: lightly-raced maiden, well beaten since 2 yrs: should stay at least 1¼m: sweating and edgy only start in 1990. *W. J. Pearce.*

SIMPLY PERFECT 4 b.g. Wassl 125–Haneena 118 (Habitat 134) [1989 10s6 12f — 14m 9g 12g 14g3 1990 11s6] modest form at best: stays 1¾m: best efforts with give in the ground. *M. Johnston.*

SIMPLY SPIM 3 b.f. Simply Great (FR) 122–Spimpinina (Be My Guest (USA) **57** 126) [1989 6g 7m5 6f3 6v 1990 7f 8m 6m 7f5 10f3 10m 10m 10f3 12g 12d3] strong, good-topped filly: plating-class maiden: long-priced third at Brighton (twice) and Folkestone, only form in 1990: probably stays 1½m: acts on firm and dead going: edgy third outing. *W. G. R. Wightman.*

853

SIMPLY SWELL   4 br.g. Simply Great (FR) 122–Nelly Gail (Mount Hagen (FR) **54**
127) [1989 14f³ 16.2g 14m³ 14m⁴ 14f² 14m² 14m³ 14m 15.3f² 16f⁴ 15.8g⁵ a12g⁴ 1990
a13g 16.2m³ 14g⁵ 16.5m² 16g 16.2d³ 16.5m] small, leggy, close-coupled gelding:
good mover: plating-class maiden: very slowly away final outing: stays 2m: acts on
firm and dead going: often blinkered: finds little under pressure: sold 7,400 gns
Newmarket July Sales. *Lord John FitzGerald.*

SIMPLY THE BEST (IRE)   2 b.f. (Feb 27) Red Sunset 120–Miss Spencer **55**
(Imperial Fling (USA) 116) [1990 5f⁶ 5g²] 7,600Y: leggy, sparely-made filly: third
foal: half-sister to 11f and 2¼m winner Ejay Haitch (by Be My Native): dam unraced:
½-length second of 9 in maiden at Hamilton in May: not seen out again. *J. J. O'Neill.*

SINCERE BELIEF (IRE)   2 b.g. (Apr 7) Exhibitioner 111–Turkish Suspicion **—**
(Above Suspicion 127) [1990 6f³ a7g] IR 8,000Y: half-brother to Irish middle-
distance winner Geraldville (by Home Guard), later dam of very useful 5f to 7f
winner Fenny Rough, a winner abroad by Tudor Music and a winner over hurdles:
dam poor maiden: well beaten in 4-runner claimer at Lingfield and seller at Southwell. *M. J. Fetherston-Godley.*

SINCERELY YOURS   3 gr.f. Kind of Hush 118–Mallihouana 84 (Bustino 136) **—**
[1989 7f 1990 10g] lengthy, unfurnished filly: always behind in maiden and apprentice claimer. *R. Hollinshead.*

SINCLAIR BOY   4 b.c. Aragon 118–Amber Flyer 91 (Amber Rama (USA) 133) **71**
[1989 6d⁶ 8g⁶ 6m³ 6f² 7.6g⁵ 7.6f⁶ 9f² 9g 12.3m⁴ 8f 8.2f² 1990 10.8f* 8g⁴ 10m 10g²
10f⁴ 10f* 12f⁶ a12g* 10.2m* a10g] rather leggy, attractive colt: improved handicapper: won at Warwick in May, Redcar in August (apprentices), Lingfield in September and Bath (apprentices, clear 1f out then edging right) in October: stays 1½m:
acts on firm and dead going: usually apprentice ridden. *B. W. Hills.*

SINCLAIR LAD (IRE)   2 ch.c. Muscatite 122–Kitty Frisk 64 (Prince **61**
Tenderfoot (USA) 126) [1990 7m⁶ 6d²] IR 8,800Y: leggy, quite good-topped colt:
poor mover: third foal: dam suited by 1¼m: quite modest form behind Opera House
in maiden at Leicester (very green) and Jimlil in minor event at Doncaster (stayed
on well) in October: should prove better suited by 7f + than 6f. *R. Hollinshead.*

SINCLAIR PRINCE   3 ch.g. Local Suitor (USA) 128–Mothers Girl (Hunter- **51**
combe 133) [1989 6m 6g 1990 6f³ 7m⁴ 8m 7.6g 7g⁶ 8f³] light-framed gelding: plating-
class maiden: not seen out after fair third in apprentice claimer in July: stays 7f: has
run creditably when sweating and on toes: sold 2,000 gns Doncaster November
Sales. *R. Hollinshead.*

SINDEED (USA)   3 ch.c. Northern Baby (CAN) 127–Kit's Double (USA) (Spring **98**
Double) [1989 NR 1990 8g³ 8m² 8m⁴ 8g* 10g² 8d⁵ 10m 8m² 8d²] lengthy colt: has a
rather round action: brother to 1987 French 2-y-o 1m winner Double Wedge, later
successful in USA, and half-brother to 2 winners: dam won from 6f to 9f in USA,
including in graded stakes: 6/5 on, won maiden at Ayr in July: best efforts in minor
event at Ripon and apprentice race (made most, wandered and none too keen) at
Ascot fifth and eighth starts: stays 1¼m: may well prove best on an easy surface:
visored last 3 starts: sold 50,000 gns Newmarket Autumn Sales, probably abroad:
fairly useful but not one to trust implicitly. *P. T. Walwyn.*

SINGH HOLME   3 br.g. Mansingh (USA) 120–Ivy Holme (Silly Season 127) **65** d
[1989 5g 5d 5f 1990 5g² 5.3h² 5m 5f 7g a5g a5g⁵] leggy, lengthy, sparely-made
gelding: quite modest sprint maiden: showed little after second outing, hanging left
and looking reluctant in seller on fifth: blinkered fourth: sold out of P. Makin's
stable 2,300 gns Ascot September Sales after fifth. *S. T. Harris.*

SINGING DETECTIVE   3 gr.g. Absalom 128–Smoke Creek 67 (Habitat 134) **44**
[1989 5s³ 5g 5f² 6g⁶ 7g⁵ 7f⁶ 7g 7g 7g⁶ 1990 7f 10g 9f 10g 12g³ a14g² 16g 15v 9s a16g]
rangy, rather angular gelding: moderate walker: has a round action: poor maiden:
form in handicaps only when placed: stays 1¾m: acts on any going: blinkered twice:
bandaged seventh start. *M. Brittain.*

SINGING FOREVER   3 b. or br.f. Chief Singer 131–Manx Millenium 66 **—**
(Habitat 134) [1989 NR 1990 8m⁴ 10.1m⁶ 10m 9f 10g] strong, lengthy filly: has plenty
of scope: fifth foal: half-sister to 4-y-o maiden Northern Habit (by Sunken Leap):
dam placed at 1m at 3 yrs: sixth in maiden at Windsor in August: no subsequent
form, well-backed favourite in handicap fourth start: sold 3,600 gns Newmarket
Autumn Sales. *I. A. Balding.*

SINGING GOLD   4 b.g. Gold Claim 90–Gellifawr 80 (Saulingo 122) [1989 7f 6g **38**
a6g 1990 a8g a8g a8g⁴ 8m 10.1g 8.3g* 7f³ 8m 7m 8.2m 10f⁶ a8g] sturdy gelding:
moderate mover: winner twice in Belgium: best run in Britain when landing gamble

in selling handicap (bought in 4,900 gns) at Windsor in May: suited by 1m: visored last 7 starts: trained first 3 outings by R. Guest, next 3 by J. Pearce. *A. Hide.*

SINGING MISS 2 b.f. (May 3) Mansingh (USA) 120–Branston Express (Bay 35 Express 132) [1990 5g 6g⁴ a6g 6g⁵ 6f⁵] 3,300Y: lengthy, good-quartered filly: has a round action: second foal: half-sister to 3-y-o 6f winner Waltzing Weasel (by Nemorino): dam unraced half-sister to useful sprinter Tuxford Hideaway: poor plater: ran poorly at Southwell: worth another try at 5f: sold 700 gns Doncaster August Sales. *J. Berry.*

SINGING SARAH 2 b.f. (Mar 28) Mansingh (USA) 120–Fressingfield (Riboboy — (USA) 124) [1990 6m 5m 5m⁶] 1,200F: workmanlike filly: first foal: dam never ran: well beaten in maidens and minor event in summer. *J. D. Roberts.*

SINGING STAR 4 b.g. Crooner 119–Wild Jewel (Great Heron (USA) 126) [1989 79 5g 5d⁴ 5f³ 6g⁵ 6f⁶ 6h⁴ 6f 6f² 5m⁶ 5f 1990 6f* 5f³ 6m 5f⁶ 6m 6f⁵ 5f* 5m⁵ 5g² 5g 5f* 5m² 5m 5m⁴ 5s] close-coupled gelding: carries plenty of condition: won seller (retained 3,400 gns) at Pontefract in April then showed great zest to win handicaps easily at Thirsk in August and September: best form at 5f on top-of-the-ground: has worn blinkers, but not when successful: sometimes bandaged: much improved. *J. Balding.*

SINGING STREAM 4 b.f. Chief Singer 131–Sandstream 72 (Sandford Lad 133) 48 [1989 7f 6f⁵ 6f 1990 6m² 6g⁵ 7f 7m] rather leggy, good-topped filly: 33/1-second, keeping on well, at Kempton, best effort in handicaps in summer: should be as effective at 7f as 6f: blinkered final outing. *R. Hannon.*

SINGING (USA) 3 b.f. The Minstrel (CAN) 135–Social Column (USA) (Swoon's 91 Son) [1989 7f⁴ 1990 8.5d² 7m* 7f⁶] smallish, close-coupled, good-quartered filly: 5/4 on, won minor event at Kempton in June: favourite, looked temperamental in similar event at Chepstow 3 weeks later, finding little having been slowly away and hung left: stays 8.5f: to be trained by R. McAnally in USA. *B. W. Hills.*

SINGLE 8 gr.g. Jellaby 124–Miss Solo (Runnymede 123) [1989 8d 8g² 7.6f 8m — 8m⁴ 8g 8g⁵ 9g 8m a8g⁶ a10g⁵ 1990 9g⁵ 8m 7.6g 8f] leggy, sparely-made gelding: fair handicapper on his day in 1989: lightly raced and not so good at 8 yrs: effective at 7f to 9f: possibly ideally suited by an easy surface nowadays: occasionally bandaged: has won for apprentice: none too consistent. *W. G. R. Wightman.*

SINGLE FILE (USA) 2 ch.c. (Mar 30) Blushing Groom (FR) 131–Singletta 72 p (USA) 117 (Nodouble (USA)) [1990 7g 7m⁴ 8d²] smallish, workmanlike colt: first foal: dam won from 7f (at 2 yrs) to 10.5f, out of sister to high-class 1m to 1½m winner Critique: 7 lengths second of 9 to Fair Average in maiden at Salisbury in October: lacks turn of foot, and will be suited by 1¼m + : likely to progress again. *J. L. Dunlop.*

SING 'N SWING 2 b.g. (Apr 30) Chief Singer 131–Foston Bridge 68 (Relkino 61 d 131) [1990 5s³ 5m* 5d⁵ 5f 6m⁶ 5m⁶] 3,800Y: leggy, sparely-made gelding: good walker: third foal: half-brother to 1¼m winner Christmas Hols (by Young Generation): dam placed at 7f from 4 starts at 2 yrs: quite modest performer: easy winner of Pontefract maiden auction early in season: ran poorly after: should stay 6f: blinkered final 2 outings, finding little off bridle first occasion: hung badly right fourth start: one to have reservations about: sold 675 gns Ascot October Sales. *M. H. Easterby.*

SING OUT (FR) 2 b.c. (Mar 9) Auction Ring (USA) 123–Manora (USA) (Stop 83 The Music (USA)) [1990 6m⁴ 6g² a6g* 6m² 7m] quite good-topped colt: has a quick action: second foal: brother to 3-y-o Shout Out: dam unplaced in 2 starts in France: fair colt: won maiden at Southwell in September: very good second to Punch N'Run in nursery at Ascot: ran moderately in similar event there (mounted on track) after: should stay 7f. *C. R. Nelson.*

SING THE BLUES 6 b.g. Blue Cashmere 129–Pulcini 61 (Quartette 106) [1989 39 12g 16.5f³ 14f⁶ 16f* 16m² a16g⁶ a16g⁶ 1990 a16g³ 15.5f⁵ 17.1f⁵ a16g³ a16g] big, lengthy gelding: poor handicapper: ran well when third of 8 at Lingfield in November, first outing on flat for 6 months: should stay beyond 2m: acts on firm going: prolific winner over hurdles in handicaps in 1989/90. *C. J. Benstead.*

SIPSI FACH 2 br.f. (Apr 4) Prince Sabo 123–Miskin 58 (Star Appeal 133) [1990 81 6g³ 6g* 7m* 7f⁴ 7g* 8g⁴ 7.5g²] lengthy, rather sparely-made filly: third foal: half-sister to 1988 2-y-o 5f winner Kafkin (by Kafu): dam, placed over 1¼m at 3 yrs, is daughter of sister to Park Hill winner Quay Line: improved filly, first past post in claimer at Warwick, nurseries at Newmarket in July and York in August and Premio Novella (demoted after winning by 1¼ lengths) at Milan in September: good fourth to Majmu in May Hill Stakes at Doncaster: much better suited by 7f and 1m than 6f: possibly unsuited by very firm ground: suitable mount for a claimer. *M. Bell.*

SIRADAMI (IRE)   2 b.c. (Apr 28) Shardari 134–Damira (FR) (Pharly (FR) 130)   **32**
[1990 6g 7f 5m 8m⁶ 7d] 11,500Y, 6,600 2-y-o: leggy colt: second foal: dam unraced:
poor plater: will stay 1¼m: sold 1,100 gns Doncaster October Sales. *F. Durr.*

SIR ARTHUR HOBBS   3 b.g. Lyphard's Special (USA) 124–Song Grove 61   —
(Song 132) [1990 6m² 6f 6g⁶ 5g* 5d² 6g* 5m³ 5d³ 6g⁵ 6g 1990 8v⁵ 7f 7m 6m 6d 6d 8g
7d 6s 7d] lengthy, round-barrelled gelding: moderate mover: fairly useful winner at
2 yrs: generally well below form in 1990 though showed he retains some ability final
start: should prove best short of 1m: acts on dead ground: sometimes awkward at
stalls, refusing to enter them when blinkered intended fifth start: gelded after final
one. *F. H. Lee.*

SIR BANCROFT   2 b.c. (Feb 1) Chukaroo 103–State Romance 67 (Free State   **70**
125) [1990 6g4 5m* 7f5 6m 7m5 7d] 16,000Y: lengthy colt: moderate mover: third
reported living foal: brother to Stewards' Cup winner Very Adjacent and 12.5f seller
winner Strat's Legacy: dam won at 7f and 1m: modest performer: won maiden at
Pontefract in June: good fifth in nurseries at Goodwood and Newmarket: stays 7f:
seems unsuited by soft ground. *H. J. Collingridge.*

SIR BASIL (IRE)   2 b.c. (Feb 8) Double Schwartz 128–Ashbourne Lass   **83**
(Ashmore (FR) 125) [1990 5f* 5f3 5m5 5g* 5m* 5g 5m5 5g*] IR 14,000F: small,
well-made colt: good walker: third foal: dam never ran: successful in maiden at
Leicester in March, minor event (ridden by 7-lb claimer) at Windsor in May and
listed races at Milan in June and Rome in September: ran badly at Royal Ascot sixth
start: speedy. *M. Bell.*

SIR COSMO   4 b.c. Simply Great (FR) 122–Singing Away 66 (Welsh Pageant 132)   —
[1989 10m 14g3 14f6 1990 10.8m 8f 12.5f 11.7g 14m] compact, good-bodied ex-Irish
colt: moderate mover: seventh foal: half-brother to 1¾m winner Jazzy Lady (by
Persian Bold): dam, from excellent family, ran only at 2 yrs: of little account: pulled
up lame final outing: dead. *B. Stevens.*

SIR CROON   4 ch.g. Crooner 119–Sirette 42 (Great Nephew 126) [1989 7s6 10d6   —
a10g 1990 16d 8f 7m6 7g 10g] compact gelding: has a quick action: best effort in
Epsom maiden on first outing at 3 yrs: seems best at 7f. *L. G. Cottrell.*

SIR CRUSTY   8 br.g. Gunner B 126–Brazen (Cash And Courage 116) [1989 NR   —
1990 16m] sturdy, deep-bodied gelding: carries plenty of condition: plating-class
winner in 1988: never placed to challenge in handicap at Nottingham in September:
afterwards a winner over hurdles 3 times at Cheltenham: stays very well: best form
on flat on an easy surface, but unsuited by heavy going (has won on firm over
hurdles): good mount for apprentice. *R. J. Holder.*

SIREESH   3 b.g. Reesh 117–Record Lady (Record Token 128) [1989 5f4 5d 5f4 5f   —
6g 1990 a7g5 8.3m] leggy, sparely-made gelding: has a round action: plating-class
maiden: well beaten in selling events in summer as 3-y-o: stays 6f. *J. White.*

SIRGAME   4 b.c. Thatching 131–Vaunt (USA) (Hill Rise 127) [1989 8f 12g6 1990   —
7m] rather leggy, good-bodied colt: no worthwhile form: visored final start at 3 yrs.
Mrs N. Macauley.

SIR HARRY HARDMAN   2 b.c. (May 10) Doulab (USA) 115–Song Grove 61   **102**
(Song 132) [1990 5f4 5g* 5f2 5g* 5g2 5g2 5d2 6d* 6d] 21,000F, IR 38,000Y: strong,
good-quartered, sprint type: carries condition: moderate mover: half-brother to
3-y-o Sir Arthur Hobbs (by Lyphard's Special), fairly useful sprinter at 2 yrs, and
several other winners here and abroad: dam 4-y-o 5.8f winner in Ireland: useful
performer: won maiden at Edinburgh in July and nursery at Haydock in August:
improved further after, winning restricted IR £143,000 event at Phoenix Park:
below best when ninth of 19 in Racecall Gold Trophy at Redcar in October on final
start: stays 6f: acts on firm and dead ground: game and genuine. *F. H. Lee.*

SIRI   3 b.f. Horage 124–Starduster (Lucifer (USA)) [1989 NR 1990 12m a12g4 12m   **48**
11.5f2 12f5 14m] rather unfurnished filly: fifth living foal: half-sister to 3 winners,
including Irish pair 11f to 13f winner Pallasbeg (by Ballymore) and 8.5f to 14f winner
Pheopotstown (by Henbit): dam useful winner from 9f to 1½m in Ireland: form only
when second in strongly-run handicap at Lingfield: dead. *M. Bell.*

SIR NICK   3 gr.g. Sandhurst Prince 128–Silecia (Sky Gipsy 117) [1989 6m 8.2f4   **68**
8m4 8f4 8g a7g2 a7g2 a8g3 1990 9.1m2 a12g* 12m 11.7g 12m 11.5m6 12m4 a14g6]
leggy, lengthy, angular gelding: quite modest performer: won claimer at Lingfield in
April: made most and easily best effort in handicaps afterwards on seventh start:
stays 1½m: thrice blinkered: winning hurdler: may not be entirely genuine. *N. A.
Callaghan.*

SIR PETER LELY   3 b.g. Teenoso (USA) 135–Picture 98 (Lorenzaccio 130)   **67**
[1989 NR 1990 12g 10.6d4 13v* 12s] lengthy gelding with scope: sixth foal: half-

brother to several winners, including good sprinter Print (by Sharpo), successful in USA in 1990: dam, half-sister to Queen's Hussar, won over 6f at 2 yrs: 11/10 on, under pressure long way out when winning claimer (claimed out of W. Hastings-Bass' stable £14,516) at Ayr in October: well beaten in handicap 3 weeks later: will stay 1¾m: very slowly away on debut: winning hurdler. *M. D. Hammond.*

SIR RUFUS 4 ch.c. Thatching 131–La Melodie 77 (Silly Season 127) [1989 10g 9f 10g⁵ 10f⁴ a10g a11g³ a14g a12g³ 1990 a11g* a12g* a12g* a11g* a12g³ 12g] good-bodied, quite attractive colt: moderate mover: unbeaten in handicaps first 4 starts early in year, winning twice at Southwell and twice (apprentice event first occasion) at Lingfield: carrying plenty of condition, well beaten final outing (April): suited by around 1½m: acts on firm ground: blinkered 4 times, visored nowadays. *C. R. Nelson.* **83**

SIRSE 3 gr.f. Enchantment 115–Sea Farer Lake 74 (Gairloch 122) [1989 5d 5d 6m 6m³ 6f³ 6f⁴ 6f* 6f⁵ 6g* 5f³ 6f 7f⁶ a6g a6g a8g 1990 a7g⁴ 7.5f 6f 5f 7m 6f⁴ 6m 7f 6m⁶ 7h⁵ 7m 10f⁴ 8.2v 8m 8.2s] close-coupled, rather lightly-made filly: poor mover: inconsistent plater: probably stays 1m: acts on firm going: twice blinkered, once visored: bandaged on all-weather and last 2 starts: sold 2,100 gns Newmarket Autumn Sales. *M. D. I. Usher.* **41**

SIR TASKER 2 b.c. (Feb 1) Lidhame 109–Susie's Baby (Balidar 133) [1990 5d³ 5m 5.1g⁵] 20,000Y: compact, quite attractive colt: has a roundish action: third foal: half-brother to two 2-y-o 5f winners by Kafu: dam lightly raced: third of 6 in minor event at Chester in May: ran as if something amiss in maidens after. *A. Bailey.* **55**

SI SAWAT 3 ch.g. Superlative 118–Soft Chinook (USA) (Hitting Away) [1989 5g⁵ 6g² 6m 8.2f 7g 1990 a8g⁶ a5g⁵ 6m 8f² 8m* 8m⁵ 9f 8d] strong, deep-girthed gelding: carries condition: quite modest performer: won 20-runner handicap at Pontefract in September by 6 lengths: ran well next start, badly after: should stay beyond 1m: acts on good to firm going: wore crossed noseband, sweating and edgy fourth outing: visored 3 times: trained first 2 starts by S. Muldoon. *M. Avison.* **62**

SISTER CHABRIAS 5 b.m. Chabrias (FR) 103–Ginger Tart 87 (Swing Easy (USA) 126) [1989 7g⁶ 7f 7m³ 8f⁶ 1990 a12g 8m 8f 7g] lengthy mare: fair handicapper at best: no form in first half of 1990, including in selling company: stays 7f: acts on good to firm and soft going: sometimes visored: usually apprentice ridden: has started slowly: trained until after third start by M. Pipe. *R. W. Stubbs.* **—**

SISTER CHERYL 5 ch.m. Vaigly Great 127–Miss Merlin 79 (Manacle 123) [1989 10m 5f² 5f 7m² 7f 8f a7g 1990 a7g⁴ a7g 5m] tall, angular mare: moderate **39**

857

mover: poor performer: stays 7f: acts well on firm going: sweating final outing (June). *R. G. Frost.*

SISTER SAL 3 ch.f. Bairn (USA) 126–Mercy Cure 81 (No Mercy 126) [1989 5m 5m 5f 6f² 6m* 6g* 1990 6m 7m 8f 8.3m 8g⁴ 8g 9m⁴ 10m² 10d a8g⁵] lengthy filly: quite modest handicapper: form as 3-y-o only when in frame, pulling hard when short-priced favourite in seller eighth start: stays 1¼m: acts on firm ground: visored ninth start: often sweats and on toes. *J. Sutcliffe.* **59**

SIXOFUS (IRE) 2 b. or br.g. (Mar 3) Glenstal (USA) 118–Grace Darling (USA) (Vaguely Noble 140) [1990 6m² 5d⁴ 6m⁶ 6m* 5d⁶] 4,800F, 8,200Y: leggy, rather angular gelding: has a quick action: first foal: dam twice-raced daughter of half-sister to Sussex Stakes winner Ace of Aces: won maiden at Redcar in October: better form starts either side, beaten 11 lengths by Lycius in Newgate Stud Middle Park Stakes at Newmarket and 7 lengths by Snowy Owl in listed event at Doncaster: stays 6f. *R. Boss.* **87**

SIZZLING SAGA (IRE) 2 b. or br.c. (Mar 24) Horage 124–Alsazia (FR) (Bolkonski 134) [1990 5s⁵ a6g⁶ 5m* 5m* 5g³ 5f³ 5m² 6d*] IR 6,600Y, resold 5,600Y: sturdy, sprint type: poor mover: brother to a maiden and half-brother to Irish 3-y-o 7f winner Bunch of Jokers (by Montelimar) and Irish 1m winner Hazel Boy (by Rarity): dam won twice at 3 yrs in Italy: successful in maiden at Catterick in July, claimer (had simple task) at Edinburgh in August and minor event (by 3 lengths from Maraatib, showing much improved form) at Catterick again in October: seems better suited by 6f than 5f: acts on good to firm ground and dead: trained first 2 outings by P. Felgate. *J. Berry.* **103**

SKAZKA (USA) 4 b.f. Sir Ivor 135–Winter Words (USA) (Northern Dancer) [1989 8g 10.2m² 8f* 10m⁴ 10m² 10f6 12g 10m 1990 10.2f 10.8m 10m 10m⁴ 10m⁵ 12f* 10m⁵ 11.5m² 12f³ 10f³ 10.2m 12g⁶] sturdy, good-bodied filly: moderate mover, with a round action: modest handicapper: won ladies event at Beverley in July, making all and clear 4f out: stays 1½m: best form on top-of-the-ground: often ridden by 5-lb claimer: sold 82,000 gns Newmarket December Sales. *I. A. Balding.* **70**

SKERRYVORE 3 ch.f. Kalaglow 132–Highland Light 105 (Home Guard (USA) 129) [1989 NR 1990 8g³ 10f⁵ 10f³ 8m³ 8f 8g⁵ 8m² 11.5g] tall, leggy, lightly-made filly: fifth foal: half-sister to fair 6f and 1m winner Church Light, 1½m and Italian St Leger winner Welsh Guide (both by Caerleon) and a winner in Scandinavia by He Loves Me: dam sprinter: quite modest maiden: stays 1¼m: probably acts on firm going: very slowly away on debut: takes keen hold: sold 5,200 gns Newmarket December Sales. *W. Jarvis.* **66**

SKI CAPTAIN 6 b.g. Welsh Captain 113–Miss Nelski 84 (Most Secret 119) [1989 5f⁵ 5f⁵ 5f⁵ 5g² 6f⁴ 5g² 5m* 5g⁴ 5f⁵ 5g⁶ 5g⁴ 5m⁶ 5g 5m³ 5g* 5m 5m⁵ 5g² 5d 1990 5f⁴ 5f 5f 5m 5g 5m⁶ 5g⁶ 5m⁴ 5m² 5m⁶ 5m a5g 5m 5m 5f² 5m 5d 5m] strong, workmanlike gelding: usually looks well: moderate mover: fair handicapper: well-backed favourite, ran extremely well in attempt to win Gosforth Park Cup at New-castle for third successive season in June, caught close home by Superbrave: below form most starts after: suited by 5f: acts on any going: has worn blinkers and a visor, but since 1987: has won when sweating and for apprentice. *P. Howling.* **87**

SKIDADDLE (IRE) 2 b.g. (Apr 9) Kafu 120–La Mascotte 72 (Hotfoot 126) [1990 5m⁶ 5g 7g 6f 8.5m] 4,500Y, 5,000 2-y-o: smallish, sparely-made gelding: fourth reported foal: half-brother to a winner over hurdles in Ireland: dam won 8.5f seller: poor maiden: looked temperamental when blinkered penultimate outing. *J. S. Wainwright.* **—**

SKI DANCER 2 b.c. (May 1) Dancing Brave (USA) 140–Ski Sailing (USA) 115 (Royal Ski (USA)) [1990 8s] tall, rather angular colt: fourth foal: half-brother to 11.7f and 1½m winner Shareef Sailor (by Shareef Dancer): dam 7f and 1¼m winner also second in Lancashire Oaks: bit backward and green, slowly away but showed signs of ability in minor event at Newbury in October. *D. R. C. Elsworth.* **— p**

SKIFFLE 2 b.f. (Feb 18) Niniski (USA) 125–Fleet Girl (Habitat 134) [1990 7m] 41,000Y: lengthy, unfurnished filly: has scope: closely related to 2 winners by Ile de Bourbon, including Oaks and Irish Oaks second Bourbon Girl, and half-sister to 3 other winners: dam wide-margin winner of small races over 9f and 1½m in Ireland: green, slowly away, always behind and not knocked about in maiden at Leicester in October: will be suited by middle distances: likely to do better. *B. W. Hills.* **— p**

SKIPLAM WOOD 4 b.f. Cree Song 99–Mab (Morston (FR) 125) [1989 7m³ 7f³ 6f⁵ 9.1f⁴ 8f⁵ 1990 8m 7m] compact, plain filly: turns fore-feet in: plating-class maiden at best: stays 7f: wore crossed noseband final outing: not an easy ride. *D. Lee.* **—**

SKIPPER TO BILGE 3 b.g. Night Shift (USA)–Upper Deck 115 (Sun Prince 75 128) [1989 NR 1990 8.2s² 8v² 8.2g* 10.6d 10s⁵ 8g⁴] lengthy, rather angular gelding: modest form: off course nearly 5 months after making all to justify favouritism in apprentice maiden at Hamilton in May: probably stays 1¼m: acts on heavy going. *M. A. Jarvis.*

SKIP TRACER 2 b.g. (Feb 20) Balliol 125–Song To Singo 63 (Master Sing 109) 43 [1990 8g 7v⁵] close-coupled, angular gelding: second foal: brother to poor plater Swank Gilbert: dam 2-y-o 5f winner seemed to stay 1m: poor form in maidens. *J. Etherington.*

SKISURF 4 b.g. Niniski (USA) 125–Seasurf 106 (Seaepic (USA) 100) [1989 12m⁵ 69 11f 14m³ 13.3m⁵ 14.6s 1990 16g⁶ 17.6g⁴ 18.1m⁶ 16.5d] close-coupled, workmanlike gelding: fair maiden at best: respectable fourth in £7,400 handicap at Haydock in September, only form at 4 yrs: stays 2¼m: acts on good to firm going. *C. E. Brittain.*

SKOLERN 6 b.g. Lochnager 132–Piethorne 86 (Fine Blade (USA) 121) [1989 8.5d 66 8m² 7m 8.2d 1990 8f³ 8h 8f] rather leggy, good-topped gelding: quite modest handicapper: form in spring only on first outing: effective at 7f and 1m: acts on any going: tried in visor as 4-y-o, blinkered final outing: sometimes sweats: suitable mount for apprentice: has joined A. Harrison. *Mrs P. A. Barker.*

SKY CAT 6 b.g. Skyliner 117–Spring Kitten (Pitcairn 126) [1989 8g⁶ 8g² 8s⁴ 1990 — a12g a11g] leggy gelding: lightly-raced handicapper: still carrying condition, well beaten final outing: stays 1m: acts on good to firm and soft going: blinkered twice (setting strong gallop) at 5 yrs: sometimes sweats: seems best with strong handling. *M. H. Easterby.*

SKY CLOUD 4 ch.g. Formidable (USA) 125–Cloud Nine 97 (Skymaster 126) 77 [1989 7d² 7m 6m 7m⁶ 8f³ 7m² 7s 6f³ 7g² 7d* a6g³ 1990 6f 7f⁴ 7f 7g⁵ 6m² 6m* 6m 7.3g⁶ 6d³ 6s³ 6d* 6s] small, stocky gelding: modest handicapper: won at Pontefract in July and Chester in October: didn't get clear run final outing: ideally suited to 6f: acts on any going: trained until late sixth outing by W. Brooks. *R. Akehurst.*

SKY CONQUEROR (USA) 5 ch.h. Conquistador Cielo (USA)–Blushing — Cathy (USA) (Blushing Groom (FR) 131) [1989 10g 10f 10g³ 8f* 9m⁴ 10g 8m³ 10f 1990 10g 8f 8m 10g⁵ 8m⁶] sparely-made, rather angular horse: fairly useful winner as 4-y-o: generally well below his best in first half of 1990: better suited by 1m than 1¼m: acts on firm going: probably best when able to dominate: often wears crossed noseband and has tongue tied down: has been taken very quietly to post. *A. A. Scott.*

SKY DRAMA 2 ch.f. (Feb 27) All Systems Go 119–High Drama 90 (Hill Clown — (USA)) [1990 8m a6g 8.2d 6m] lengthy filly: eighth foal: half-sister to a winner in Hong Kong: dam stayed well: seems of little account: swerved badly at start when blinkered final outing. *J. P. Smith.*

SKY FIGHTER 3 b.f. Hard Fought 125–Sky Valley 101 (Skymaster 126) [1989 5d — 5f³ 6m 5m³ 7m⁴ 8g⁵ 1990 9m⁵ 12g 10.6f 13.8m 12m⁶ 12m a12g a11g⁶] leggy, sparely-made filly: moderate mover: poor maiden: blinkered, easily best effort in handicaps on fifth start: stays 1½m: acts on good to firm ground: changed hands 4,100 gns Doncaster February Sales, 1,350 gns Doncaster November Sales. *Capt. J. Wilson.*

SKY FOX (IRE) 2 br.f. (May 18) Glow (USA)–Stracomer Queen 106 (Prince — Tenderfoot (USA) 126) [1990 7m] IR 13,000F: strong, close-coupled filly: fourth foal: half-sister to 11f seller winner Victorious Prince (by Bold Lad): dam, winner over 7f (including at 2 yrs) and 1m, suited by middle distances and was third in Irish Guinness Oaks: backward in maiden at Leicester in October. *B. Hanbury.*

SKY SIGN (USA) 2 br.c. (Apr 8) Skywalker (USA)–Nurse Jo (USA) (J O Tobin 50 (USA) 130) [1990 7s a7g⁵ a7g⁴] second foal: half-brother to a winner in USA by Tantoul: dam twice-raced half-sister to Melodist: sire won 1¼m Breeders' Cup Classic: plating-class maiden: will probably be better suited by 1m +. *C. F. Wall.*

SKY SINGER 4 b.f. Kafu 120–Singalong Lass 63 (Bold Lad (IRE) 133) [1989 7d — 6g 1990 a6g a5g] workmanlike filly: poor maiden. *D. W. Chapman.*

SKY WATCHER 4 b.g. Skyliner 117–Holernzaye 93 (Sallust 134) [1989 7g⁶ 6v⁴ — 6v⁵ 8.2m 10f² 8h* 10f³ 11g⁴ 10m a8g 1990 8m 12f 12.5g 8m 8f 12s a12g] compact, workmanlike gelding: runner-up in sellers as 3-y-o, awarded second on technicality: showed nothing in 1990: stays 1¼m: acts on any going: blinkered fourth outing. *J. Dooler.*

SLADES HILL 3 b.c. Lochnager 132–Mephisto Waltz 98 (Dancer's Image 76 (USA)) [1989 5f⁴ 5g 1990 5f³ 6f* 5m 6m* 6g 6f] small, good-quartered colt: moderate mover: modest performer: made all in maiden at Pontefract in June and handicap at Hamilton in July: well beaten in handicaps last 2 outings: suited by 6f: acts on firm going. *Miss S. E. Hall.*

SLEEKBURN LADY 3 b.f. Rapid River 127–Sophia Western (Steel Heart 128) — [1989 5g⁴ 5g 1990 6m 5f a6g 5g 6f] stocky filly: no worthwhile form: blinkered last 2 starts, showing signs of ability (staying on) on first occasion. *R. O'Leary.*

SLEEPERS 6 br.m. Swing Easy (USA) 126–Jenny's Rocket (Roan Rocket 128) **81** [1989 5f 5f 5f4 5f² 5f 5f⁵ 6f 5f 5m⁶ 5m⁴ 5f⁴ 5m⁶ 5f⁴ 5f⁵ 1990 5g* 5d* 5f* 5m* 6g] lengthy, rather angular mare: poor mover: formerly unreliable, but much improved and unbeaten in handicaps on first 4 outings in 1990: successful twice at Tralee in last week of August and at Chepstow and Beverley in September: last of 12 in listed event at the Curragh: stayed 6f: acted on any going: tried in blinkers, but not after seventh start at 5 yrs: in foal to Carmelite House. *M. McDonagh, Ireland.*

SLEEPING CAR (FR) 2 b. or br.c. (Apr 6) Dunphy 124–Lorelta (FR) (Rose **105** Laurel 125) [1990 8d* 8m⁴] 180,000 francs (approx £16,700) Y: third foal: half-brother to French 7.5f winner Sarh (by Deep Roots): dam French 1m winner also successful over jumps: won newcomers race at Deauville in August by 8 lengths: under 2 lengths fourth to Beau Sultan in Prix La Rochette at Longchamp following month: will stay 1¼m: useful. *P. Bary, France.*

SLEEPLINE FANTASY 5 ch.g. Buzzards Bay 128§–Sleepline Princess 86 — (Royal Palace 131) [1989 6v 7s⁴ 7g² 8.2m⁵ 8f⁵ 7.6m⁵ 8m* 8.2d⁶ 7m 8m⁴ 8d 1990 8f 7f⁶ 9m 8f⁵] leggy, sparely-made gelding: fair winner as 4-y-o: below his best in 1990 (not seen out after July), tending to hang second and third outings: stays 1m: acts on any going: sometimes sweats, and has got on edge: trained until after third start by R. Holder. *M. R. Channon.*

SLEEPLINE PALACE 3 b.f. Homing 130–Sleepline Princess 86 (Royal Palace — 131) [1989 6f⁵ 5h* 5g 1990 8d 8g⁵ 10m⁴ 8m⁵ 10m 8f⁵ 10g 7m 7g 7.6m a10g⁶] lengthy, sparely-made filly: quite modest performer, who seemed to lose her form: may well prove best short of 1m: acts on hard ground: blinkered (raced freely in lead) eighth start: trained until after reappearance by R. Holder. *M. R. Channon.*

SLEEPLINE ROYALE 4 ch.g. Buzzards Bay 128§–Sleepline Princess 86 — (Royal Palace 131) [1989 6s³ 7d* 7g 7h 11m 10m⁴ 8h⁴ 8.2d⁵ 10.2f 1990 7.5m] leggy gelding: quite modest winner (sweating) early as 3-y-o: ran moderately at Beverley in March: winner 3 times over hurdles afterwards: stays 1¼m: acts on good to firm going and goes particularly well on a soft surface. *R. J. Holder.*

SLENDER 2 b.f. (Mar 10) Aragon 118–Handy Dancer 87 (Green God 128) [1990 **79** 6g³ 7m⁴ 6m² 6g² 6f² 6d⁶] workmanlike filly: moderate mover: sixth foal: half-sister to several winners, including 3-y-o Karinga Bay (by Ardross) and 1986 2-y-o 5f and 6f winner Mr Grumpy (by The Brianstan): dam 1¼m winner: modest maiden: good staying-on sixth to Imperfect Circle in listed race at Ayr: stays 7f: best form on dead ground: hung right final 1½f fourth outing. *Denys Smith.*

SLICK CHERRY 3 b.f. Noalto 120–Slick Chick 89 (Shiny Tenth 120) [1989 6m⁶ **70** 6g³ 7g 1990 10m 8f 8m 10m 10.1m* 10m² 9m³ 9g⁶ 10g] small, good-quartered filly: has a round action: modest performer: won seller (bought in 4,400 gns) at Windsor in July: stays 1¼m: acts on good to firm ground. *D. R. C. Elsworth.*

SLICK STYLE (USA) 2 b.f. (Feb 12) Barachois (CAN)–Delta Fly (USA) (Delta **50** Flag (USA)) [1990 5m⁶ 7m] lengthy filly: has scope: first reported foal: dam placed twice from 14 starts in USA: better effort sixth of 12, staying on well after slow start, in maiden at Beverley in September. *R. Hollinshead.*

SLIGHT INDULGENCE 3 br.c. Runnett 125–Bellagold (Rheingold 137) [1989 — 5s 5m 6m 1990 8m 6f⁵] compact, good-bodied colt: well beaten, including in seller: slowly away on 3 occasions. *L. J. Holt.*

SLIP-A-SNIP 3 b.f. Wolverlife 115–Stramenta (Thatching 131) [1989 6m 6m 5m **83** 1990 5m* 5f² 5m* 5f 5g⁵ 5f³ 5d² 5g³dis] lengthy, sparely-made filly: moderate mover: progressed into fair performer: won handicaps at Windsor (hanging left) and Lingfield (made all) in July: best at 5f: yet to race on soft going, acts on any other: has run well for apprentice. *R. Akehurst.*

SLIPPEROSE 3 gr.f. Persepolis (FR) 127–Scholastika (GER) (Alpenkonig **60** (GER)) [1989 6g⁶ 6g³ 6g² 1990 6g 8m 8g 6g 10f² 10g 10m⁵ 11.5g* a12g] sturdy filly: good walker: has a roundish action: quite modest handicapper: easily best 3-y-o efforts when placed at Yarmouth, winning 19-runner contest in October: stays 1½m: acts on firm going: usually held up in rear. *J. W. Hills.*

SLIPRAIL (USA) 3 b.f. Our Native (USA)–Oxslip 106 (Owen Dudley 121) [1989 **86** NR 1990 10g² 10m⁶ 12.5m² 10.2f* 10m] big, lengthy filly with scope: fourth foal:

sister to fair 1¼m winner Oxide and half-sister to fairly useful 1¼m and 1¾m winner Sixslip (by Diesis): dam, winner from 7f to 13f, is half-sister to very useful stayer Kambalda: 7/4 on, won 4-runner maiden at Bath in September: best effort when seventh of 16 in £8,400 handicap at Newmarket: should prove better at 1½m than 1¼m. *H. Candy.*

SLIPSALOM 2 gr.f. (Feb 4) Absalom 128–Let Slip 77 (Busted 134) [1990 a8g] 37 p
4,200F: small filly: half-sister to several winners, including fairly useful 1¼m winner Petit Roseanna (by Ile de Bourbon) and 1986 2-y-o 5f winner Susan Henchard (by Auction Ring): dam showed some ability at 2 yrs: carrying condition, slowly away and nearest at finish (tenth) in 16-runner maiden at Southwell late in year. *W. Carter.*

SLIP UP 10 b.g. Quiet Fling (USA) 124–Artemis 91 (King Emperor (USA)) [1989 30
18.8f 1990 16.5f4] winning hurdler: bandaged, showed he retains a little ability on flat in Folkestone handicap in July. *G. P. Enright.*

SLOE BERRY 4 b.f. Sharpo 132–Native Berry (FR) 76 (Ribero 126) [1989 6m 80
6m5 6f* 5f5 5f6 6m 6m2 5m2 6m3 5m 5d a5g2 1990 5f5 5g 5m 5m4 6m5 6g 5f3 6m6 5m* 5g6 5m* 5d] close-coupled, rather sparely-made filly: moderate walker and mover: fair handicapper: won at Kempton (well drawn and making most) in August and Ascot (ridden by 7-lb claimer, beating Almost Blue ¾ length in £16,800 event) in October: ran moderately in between: stays 6f: acts on firm going: blinkered ninth and tenth outings: tailed off at Chester once at 3 yrs. *C. E. Brittain.*

SLOW EXPOSURE 3 b.c. Pharly (FR) 130–Armure Bleue (FR) (Riverman 82
(USA) 131) [1989 8g4 8v 1990 12m* 14m3 11.5m 16.2f 13.3m] leggy, close-coupled colt: fair at best: won maiden at Newmarket in April, staying on steadily to lead close home: lost form in the summer: should stay beyond 1½m: visored last 2 starts. *M. R. Channon.*

SLY DREAMER 2 gr.c. (Apr 30) Dreams To Reality (USA) 113–River Vixen —
(Sagaro 133) [1990 a8g] 3,600Y: leggy colt: third foal: half-brother to Tongadin (by Petong), successful from 1m to 15.3f: dam lightly-raced daughter to half-sister to Oaks second Mabel: bit backward and on toes, slowly away and always behind in 17-runner maiden at Southwell late in year. *Mrs N. Macauley.*

SLY PROSPECT (USA) 2 ch.g. (Mar 22) Barachois (CAN)–Miss Sly (USA) —
(Diamond Prospect (USA)) [1990 7s] strong, lengthy gelding: second foal: brother to a minor winner in USA: dam never ran: slowly away and soon well behind in minor event at Doncaster in November. *R. Hollinshead.*

SMALL DOUBLE (IRE) 2 b.f. (May 18) Double Schwartz 128–Little Cynthia 55
76 (Wolver Hollow 126) [1990 6g 6m 5d* 6d a6g a6g5 a6g5] leggy filly: sixth foal: half-sister to several winners, including sprinter Hinari Video (by Sallust) and Irish 1¾m winner Saint Cynthia (by Welsh Saint): dam 1m winner: plating-class performer: won 4-runner claimer at Edinburgh by ½ length: stays 6f: sold 700 gns Ascot December Sales. *M. Johnston.*

SMALL FEE 5 ch.m. Blue Cashmere 129–Gay Picture 62 (Linacre 133) [1989 63
6d6 6g 6g2 6d 6s a7g3 a7g2 a7g a6g2 a6g4 a6g6 1990 a6g6 a6g2 a6g4 a6g3 a7g a5g* a7g* a7g4 5d5 6m 6g] angular, sparely-made mare: often unimpressive in appearance: poor mover: fairly consistent on all-weather, winning seller (bought in 4,600 gns) and handicap at Southwell in May: ran poorly on turf last 2 outings: effective at 5f and stays 7f: suited by an easy surface: suitable mount for apprentice: has been bandaged off-fore and visored. *M. Brittain.*

SMART BLADE 2 gr.c. (Mar 23) Elegant Air 119–Alsiba 68 (Northfields (USA)) 72
[1990 6m3 7m4] good-topped colt: has scope: first foal: dam staying daughter of half-sister to Irish 2000 Guineas winner Northern Treasure: beaten around 7 lengths in moderately-run £11,600 event at Newbury won by Anjiz and maiden at Sandown won by Hillzah in summer: will be better suited by 1m + . *I. A. Balding.*

SMARTIE LEE 3 ch.f. Dominion 123–Nosy Parker (FR) (Kashmir II 125) [1989 62
5d6 6m3 6m3 7f5 7m* 8.2f* 8f3 8f4 1990 10m3 10m3 12h2 11.7m5 11.5f 11.5g4 10f a12g* a13g a12g] small, close-coupled filly: keen walker: quite modest handicapper: on toes, won at Lingfield in November, leading inside last 1f: stays 1½m: acts on hard going: inconsistent. *P. F. I. Cole.*

SMART MAGICIAN (USA) 3 b.c. Clever Trick (USA)–Straight Edition (USA) 61
(Going Straight (USA)) [1989 NR 1990 8m 7g 8g5 8.5d4 8f 6f 10m3 12d] $120,000Y: angular colt: fifth foal: dam won 4 stakes races over 8.5f: quite modest maiden: stays 1¼m: acts on good to firm ground: sold 8,200 gns Newmarket Autumn Sales. *W. J. Haggas.*

SMART TURN 3 b.f. His Turn 82–Smashing Pet (Mummy's Pet 125) [1989 7g   54
1990 8.2m³ 8m⁵ 7f] leggy, close-coupled filly: quite modest form at best: very
slowly away and always struggling in handicap at Folkestone in July, final start:
ridden by 7-lb claimer first 3 starts. *G. A. Huffer.*

SMASH DANCE 2 b.c. (May 3) Mashhor Dancer (USA)–Solo Vacation (Pas de   65
Seul 133) [1990 6f⁶ 6g³ 5m⁶] leggy colt: first foal: dam granddaughter of 1000
Guineas and Oaks second Spree, the family of Juliette Marny and Julio Mariner:
easily best effort third of 21, staying on well, in minor event at Windsor in August:
will be suited by 7f: sold 3,600 gns Newmarket Autumn Sales. *D. R. C. Elsworth.*

SMASHER 2 b.f. (Feb 25) Simply Great (FR) 122–Star Face (African Sky 124)   42
[1990 7m 7d 6d] 3,700Y: rather sparely-made filly: seventh foal: sister to poor
maiden Zode and half-sister to 3 winners, including 3-y-o Lord of The Field (by
Jalmood), successful from 7f (at 2 yrs) to 11.1f, and 6f and 1m winner Torquemada (by
Try My Best): dam won over 10.5f in French Provinces: poor form in maidens, one
an auction: will probably be suited by 1m. *R. J. R. Williams.*

SMILES AHEAD 2 ch.c. (Mar 31) Primo Dominie 121–Baby's Smile 68 (Shirley   71
Heights 130) [1990 5f⁴ 6g 8f 6d⁴ 7m 7f² 7m⁶ 8d* a8g⁴ a8g] 9,600F, 7,200Y: third
foal: half-brother to 3-y-o Bold Patrick (by Never So Bold) and staying plater For A
While (by Pharly): dam suited by good test of stamina: wore net muzzle when
making all in 20-runner selling nursery (retained 5,500 gns) at Doncaster in
October: will be suited by 1¼m: acts on firm and dead ground: races keenly. *J.
Hetherton.*

SMILINGATSTRANGERS 2 b.f. (Apr 11) Macmillion 110–My Charade 79   41
(Cawston's Clown 113) [1990 6m 6g 9m⁴] small, rather sparely-made filly: first foal:
dam, 14f winner, is half-sister to very useful 6f to 7f performer Step Ahead: well
beaten in maidens. *Mrs Barbara Waring.*

SMILING SUN (IRE) 2 ch.g. (Jan 27) Thatching 131–Charites (Red God 128§)   92 ?
[1990 6g⁴ 6m⁴ 6d* 6m² 7g 8m⁴ 6g a6g⁴ a8g*] 18,000F, 54,000Y: sturdy gelding:
poor walker: half-brother to French 1¼m winner Imperial Import (by Imperial
Fling) and a winner in Denmark and Sweden: dam poor sister to top-class sprinter
Green God: ridden by 5-lb claimer, won 11-runner nursery at Lingfield late in year
by 8 lengths: earlier successful in maiden at Catterick: suited by 1m: blinkered
second start: unruly stalls fifth. *W. A. O'Gorman.*

SMOKE 4 gr.f. Rusticaro (FR) 124–Fire-Screen 92 (Roan Rocket 128) [1989 7v²   —
8.5m 12d⁵ 1990 12g 12h⁴] compact, rather angular ex-Irish filly: seventh foal:
half-sister to 3 winners here and abroad, including fairly useful 1981 2-y-o 7f winner
Marquessa d'Howfen (by Pitcairn): dam won over 1¼m: won maiden at Galway as
2-y-o: 10 lengths fourth of 13 in amateurs event at Thirsk in May: should stay at
least 1¼m: acts on heavy going: blinkered twice, including on reappearance: mulish
at stalls then and refused to enter them third intended outing. *J. Parkes.*

SMOKEY NATIVE (USA) 3 b.c. Our Native (USA)–Smokey Spender (USA)   79 §
(Bold Bidder) [1989 7m⁴ 7m² 7g 1990 8f² 10g⁵ 8f³ 7m³ a7g⁶ 8d 6f 7m³ 7f² 7h* 7m⁴
7f⁴ 7f⁶] well-made colt: modest performer: did little wrong when winning 4-runner
maiden at Brighton in August and ran well in handicaps next 2 starts: stays 1m: acts
on hard going: usually visored after fourth start: below form in blinkers third: not
one to trust. *C. R. Nelson.*

SMOOTH FINISH 3 b.g. Welsh Term 126–Chantry Pearl (Gulf Pearl 117) [1989   —
5m⁵ 5f 1990 7g 10m 12f³ 12f 12m] sparely-made gelding: poor performer: stays 1½m.
R. A. Harrison.

SMOOTH FLIGHT 4 ch.f. Sandhurst Prince 128–Female Mudwrestler   78
(Ahonoora 122) [1989 10m 10m 7m 8.2f³ 8f³ 8m* 7.5m² 8.2f⁶ 8m² 8g³ 8d³ 8f⁴ 1990
8.5f* 9g 7m⁴ 7.5m² 8f² 7.5d² 7m 8g* 7.5d³ 8m 7.5f² 8m 7.5g] angular, sparely-
made filly: fair handicapper: made all at Beverley (goes particularly well there) in
March and Edinburgh in June: ran poorly last 2 outings: suited by forcing tactics at
around 1m: acts on firm and dead going: blinkered once: usually wears bandages
behind: often gives trouble in preliminaries and is taken down early: possibly
unsuited by left-handed track: tough and genuine. *R. W. Stubbs.*

SMOOTH PERFORMANCE (USA) 2 b.c. (Feb 8) Seattle Slew (USA)–   95
Seasonal Pickup (USA) 108 (The Minstrel (CAN) 135) [1990 6g² 6g* 7m² 7m⁴ 7d²]
first foal: dam Irish filly best at 6f or 7f: odds-on winner of 7-runner maiden at
Phoenix Park in June: fourth of 8, unable to quicken final 1f, to Heart of Darkness in
GPA National Stakes at the Curragh in September: 4 lengths second to Kooyonga in
EBF Leopardstown Stakes in October: will probably stay at least 1m. *D. K. Weld,
Ireland.*

862

SMUGGLERS GOLD 2 b.f. (May 3) Gold Claim 90–Lareda 75 (Burglar 128) [1990 6m 7m 8m a6g] sparely-made filly: has a round action: third reported foal: dam stayed 6f: well beaten in sellers and a Lingfield claimer. *M. J. Bolton.* —

SMUTS 3 b.f. Local Suitor (USA) 128–Firework Party (USA) 115 (Roan Rocket 128) [1989 NR 1990 8m 8m 9g 8f³ 8.2d 8m⁵ 10m 10d] 6,400F: lengthy, quite good-topped filly: poor mover: half-sister to 1¼m winner Kalaparty and 1m to 11.7f winner Ghadbbaan (both by Kalaglow) and modest 1¼m winner Absolute Beginner (by Absalom): dam, very useful at up to 1m, is half-sister to good fillies Example, Amphora and Expansive: little worthwhile form: stays 1m: best efforts on top-of-the-ground: often sweating: blinkered final start. *J. F. Bottomley.* —

SNAFEE 3 b.g. Mummy's Pet 125–Miss Kuta Beach 91 (Bold Lad (IRE) 133) [1989 6f³ 6g 1990 6f³ 6s⁴ 8g 6f 6f² 5m 7f⁴ 7m] leggy gelding: quite modest maiden: needs further than 5f, and stays 7f: acts on any ground: blinkered fourth and sixth starts: inconsistent: sold 5,800 gns Newmarket Autumn Sales. *M. F. D. Morley.* 64

SNAKE EYE 5 b.g. Tina's Pet 121–Dingle Belle 72 (Dominion 123) [1989 9f 9f³ 10.8m 8.2f 1990 a11g⁶ a8g a8g 10.1g² 10.8f³ 11.7g 10m 15.3g* 14.8m⁵] smallish, sturdy gelding: moderate mover: apprentice ridden, easy winner of selling handicap (bought in 5,500 gns) at Wolverhampton in June: stays 15f: acts on any going: blinkered once: sometimes bandaged: has found little: inconsistent, and not one to trust. *J. Wharton.* 52 §

SNAP BACK 2 b.f. (Apr 5) Final Straw 127–Shalbee 93 (Tachypous 128) [1990 6g a6g] 500F: stocky filly: first foal: dam 2-y-o 5f winner: tailed off in Kempton maiden and Lingfield claimer. *S. Woodman.* —

SNAPPY DATE (USA) 4 ch.g. Blushing Groom (FR) 131–Mystery Mood (USA) (Night Invader (USA)) [1989 10s 8.5g² 1990 9f 10g] rather sparely-made, angular gelding: has a quick action: modest maiden at best: well beaten in handicaps in June: stays 8.5f: acts on good to firm going: visored twice, including reappearance. *K. A. Morgan.* —

SNAPPY SNAPS 4 ch.g. Tachypous 128–Pass The Hat 88 (High Hat 131) [1989 NR 1990 10m 17.6g] sturdy gelding: half-brother to several minor winners here and abroad, including moderate middle-distance winner Rhythmic Pastimes (by Dance In Time): dam stayed 11f: tailed off in claimers. *J. Akehurst.* —

SNAPSHOT BABY 6 br.m. Faraway Times (USA) 118–Firecat (Run The Gantlet (USA)) [1989 NR 1990 a8g a13g 7f] sparely-made mare: of little account: has worn blinkers and bandages: winning selling hurdler in November. *R. Voorspuy.* —

SNEEK 2 gr.g. (Mar 20) Belfort (FR) 89–Gold Duchess 53 (Sonnen Gold 121) [1990 5g] lengthy, angular gelding: first foal: dam 5f winner at 4 yrs: backward, tailed off in seller at Pontefract in June: withdrawn lame at start in Redcar maiden previous month. *M. W. Easterby.* —

SNIGGY 4 b.f. Belfort (FR) 89–Fircy Kim (CAN) (Cannonade (USA)) [1989 5f 6f⁴ 1990 a11g] leggy filly: poor and ungenuine maiden: visored once: has worn bandages. *D. W. Browne.* — §

SNO SERENADE 4 b.g. Song 132–When The Saints (Bay Express 132) [1989 7g 7.6f⁶ 8.5g* 9f* 10.2g 10h³ 10g³ 8.2f5 8f* 7f 1990 9g 7g 7.6d 9m 10g 8f* 8m⁶ 8h² 8h* 7f³ 8f* a8g* a7g² a8g* a8g³] tall, leggy, quite attractive gelding: has a quick action: goes well on switchback track, and made all or plenty of running when winning handicaps at Brighton in July, August and September and claimers at Lingfield in November and December (odds on): effective at 7f and stays 9f: acts well on very firm going, probably unsuited by heavy: below form in visor. *R. Boss.* 87

SNOW BLIZZARD 2 gr.c. (Mar 18) Petong 126–Southern Dynasty 81 (Gunner B 126) [1990 7s] workmanlike colt: has scope: second foal: dam best at 4 yrs, when suited by middle distances: bit backward, well behind in maiden at Lingfield in October. *S. Dow.* —

SNOW BUZZARD (USA) 3 ch.c. Arctic Tern (USA) 126–Hobby (Falcon 131) [1989 NR 1990 10.1m] $120,000Y: seventh reported foal: half-brother to 4 winners in Ireland, including 1½m and 2m winner Court Play (by Prince Regent) and useful 1978 2-y-o 5f winner Just A Game (by Tarboosh), later champion older female on grass at 4 yrs in USA when successful from 1m to 1¼m: dam 5f performer: backward and reluctant at stalls, virtually pulled up in minor event at Windsor: dead. *J. Gosden.* —

SNOWGIRL (IRE) 2 gr.f. (Mar 18) Mazaad 106–Rust Free 58 (Free State 125) [1990 5m² 5f² 5m² 6s 5d⁴] 25,000Y: well-grown, good-topped filly: has a quick action: third foal: half-sister to 3-y-o Glazerite (by Dunphy), 7f winner at 2 yrs later 56 effective at 13f, and a winner in Hong Kong: dam maiden stayed 1¼m, is half-sister to Petong: plating-class maiden: best efforts on top-of-the-ground: has run creditably for an apprentice. *J. Berry.*

SNOW PLOUGH (IRE) 2 b.f. (Feb 12) Niniski (USA) 125–River Dancer 118 **76 p** (Irish River (FR) 131) [1990 6m³] leggy filly: first foal: dam French 5f (at 2 yrs) and 1m winner is sister to River Dancer, the family of Sun Princess: promising 1½ lengths third of 11, keeping on well under hand riding, to Lominda in maiden at Yarmouth in September: will be better suited by 1m+: sure to improve. *M. R. Stoute.*

SNOW SHY 3 gr.f. Shy Groom (USA)–Snow Maid 90 (High Top 131) [1989 6m⁶ 6f — a6g 1990 a11g 12m⁶ 10g 10m 12m⁶ 12m 10f⁶] workmanlike filly: moderate mover: little sign of ability, including in seller. *Pat Mitchell.*

SNOWSPIN 3 b.f. Carwhite 127–Spin (High Top 131) [1989 7f 1990 10m³ 10g³ **75** 11.7m 12m³ 12h* 14g³ 16m⁴] smallish, close-coupled filly: good mover: modest performer: wearing crossed noseband, won maiden at Brighton in August: made most in handicaps after: stays 2m: acts on hard ground: edgy third and fourth (ran in snatches) starts, blinkered and sweating when running poorly first occasion: not an easy ride: sold 10,000 gns Newmarket Autumn Sales. *Major W. R. Hern.*

SNOW WONDER 4 gr.f. Music Boy 124–Grey Charter 58 (Runnymede 123) — [1989 6d⁴ 7s 6g 7h 6f⁵ 6m 6g a6g 1990 a8g⁴ a7g a7g 10f 8g] plain filly: has a rather round action: quite modest at best: mostly well below form since first outing at 3 yrs, including in sellers: probably doesn't stay 1m: best effort on a soft surface: sold 1,800 gns Ascot May Sales. *P. Howling.*

SNOWY OWL (USA) 2 b.c. (Apr 11) Storm Bird (CAN) 134–Nafees (USA) (Raja **107** Baba (USA)) [1990 6g³ 5d² 6m* 5d*] $300,000Y: medium-sized, sturdy colt: fourth foal: half-brother to a winner in South America: dam winner at up to 9f, is from family of champion mare Desert Vixen: visored first time, won listed Doncaster Stakes, showing much improved form, by 2½ lengths from Futuh, slowly away and covered up, headway 2f out and running on strongly: unimpressive winner of 2-runner minor event at Leicester earlier in October: had tongue tied down second and third outings. *M. R. Stoute.*

SNUGGLE 3 ch.f. Music Boy 124–Sinzinbra 112 (Royal Palace 131) [1989 5f⁴ 5h* **74 d** 6m² 5m 6m⁶ 6v 1990 6m⁵ 8m⁴ 8.2s² 7m 8.2s⁶ 11.5m 8g 7d 7d 6m 9g] lengthy, workmanlike filly: fair performer: below form after second in handicap at Haydock in June: suited by 1m: acts on any going, with possible exception of heavy: visored ninth and tenth starts. *M. H. Tompkins.*

SNURGE 3 ch.c. Ela-Mana-Mou 132–Finlandia (FR) (Faraway Son (USA) **130** 130) [1989 8m³ 10g² 10v² 1990 12d² 12g² 14.6g* 12g³]

Patience paid with Snurge. Firm ground for most of the 1990 turf season made training and running horses difficult, and plenty of those who did race in the first half weren't seen out later. Conversely, four of the five classics had been and gone before Snurge even made his reappearance; but he won the fifth and put up a second top-class performance three weeks later in the Arc, doing clearly the best of eleven British-trained challengers. Let's hope the elements and ground conditions allow this big, round-actioned colt to be seen out earlier and more frequently in 1991; now that he's a big name the Press will doubtless keep us regularly informed of his well-being. In the first half of the latest season, by contrast, virtually nothing was heard of Snurge. He was given a number of racecourse gallops but after a pulled muscle ruled out any chance of his going for the Prix du Jockey-Club, it was Derby challenger Zoman who attracted the publicity, with Snurge waiting in the wings. There should have been no mistaking that Snurge was a good horse, however, after his extraordinary run in France for the Group 1 Criterium de Saint-Cloud the previous November. 'I have never seen such an easy winner', said his trainer. 'He got left eight lengths and won by three', the rub coming when the stewards incredibly demoted him after an admittedly-major change of direction, despite his jockey's best efforts, in the last couple of furlongs. When Snurge finally did make his reappearance though, in the Churchill Stakes at Ascot on June 26th, there wasn't much fuss. The useful pair Lucky Guest and Middle Kingdom were the only ones in opposition yet Snurge started outsider of the three. The result was to take some believing at the end of the season as Middle Kingdom made most and beat Snurge by a head at level weights after Snurge had been the first to come under pressure, pushed along vigorously on

St Leger Stakes, Doncaster—a narrow yet decisive win for Snurge from Hellenic;
River God (third) is out to the left, Karinga Bay (sixth) on the rails behind

the turn before rallying gamely and losing on the nod. If the public interest in
that first run appeared subdued, it was almost non-existent for his next
outing, in the Great Voltigeur Stakes at York, where Snurge again started
outsider, this time at 22/1 in a field of five. He did seem to have a stiff task
though, receiving only 5 lb from the King George winner Belmez. But Snurge
was a revelation. He'd come on no end in the two months since his reappearance and he and Belmez needed a photo to separate them, Belmez getting
the verdict with fully eight lengths back to Karinga Bay, after Snurge had put
in a breathtaking run from last to first over two furlongs out, looking like the
winner.

The 1913 50/1-shot Night Hawk had been the last horse to win the St
Leger as a maiden but that technicality was now a pretty thin disguise for
Snurge's credentials in the two hundred and fourteenth running. Besides
Snurge who started at 7/2, the field included the favourite Hellenic, winner of
the Ribblesdale Stakes and Yorkshire Oaks, the very promising stayer River
God, Kneller's half-brother Great Marquess and a progressive colt in Hajade.
The Gordon Stakes winner Karinga Bay had something on his plate in
attempting to turn around the Voltigeur form and the inexperienced Rubicund
hadn't been out since June; the enigmatic Pier Damiani made no appeal
whatsoever. Rubicund cut out the early running and River God was pushed up
to take it off him early in the straight but the St Leger story really concerned
just two horses, Snurge and Hellenic. They had it between them from three
furlongs out where Snurge burst between the Sheikh Mohammed pair and
Hellenic challenged on the outside, and although still only a neck separated
them at the furlong pole, Snurge always had the edge. Using vigorous hands-
and-heels riding, Quinn never showed him the whip and having gone a length
and a half up with a hundred yards to go was able to ease Snurge a little close
home. River God was another four lengths back in third, followed by Rubicund, Great Marquess, Karinga Bay, Hajade and a remote Pier Damiani. It was
Quinn's and Cole's first British classic victory though, ironically, the colt is
not owned by the stable's chief patron Fahd Salman who has provided it with

so many good horses over the years. The St Leger-Arc double has never been completed by a three-year-old and it has seen some spectacular failures amongst those who've tried it. That's not surprising when one considers the stern test provided by the St Leger and the exceptionally competitive nature of the Arc, but there's no reason why a horse can't run well in both, as Snurge proved in his Arc, just over a length separating him from victory. Quinn had him in a good position entering the straight where Saumarez quickened into a decisive lead; Snurge couldn't respond immediately but made inroads into Saumarez's advantage in the last furlong, as did the runner-up Epervier Bleu, the first three finishing clear of a high-class field including In The Wings, Belmez, Legal Case, Hellenic, In The Groove and Salsabil.

Snurge's sire Ela-Mana-Mou, the best middle-distance horse trained in Britain in his day, remains at the Airlie Stud having been on the brink of a sale to Australia for a reported IR £2,000,000 in February. Antipodean interest in him was guaranteed after British exports Almaarad (Underwood Stakes, Caulfield Stakes and W. S. Cox Plate) and Natski (A.J.C. Metropolitan Handicap) had virtually doubled the number of Group 1/Grade 1 wins by Ela-Mana-Mou's progeny. His other Group 1 winners are Emmson, Sumayr and Eurobird, but Snurge is clearly the best. Snurge's dam Finlandia contested the Princess Elizabeth Stakes but quite why is something of a mystery as she failed to show any rateable form in that (finishing last of eight) or any of her seven starts, mostly in maidens. Before Snurge, she had had four living foals and two runners, the only one to make any impact being the Irish mile-and-a-half maiden winner and Irish Oaks fourth Faraway Pastures (by Northfields). Finlandia's 1988 produce Suomi (by Tate Gallery), however, was a runaway winner of a Newcastle maiden in November. He's followed by a Simply Great colt who made IR 150,000 guineas as a yearling at Goffs where Snurge fetched a final bid of IR 36,000 guineas in 1988. A colt by Pennine Walk was the result of Finlandia's 1989 mating. She may have made a slow start at stud but then so did her half-sister Musicienne who went on to produce Horage. This is a famous family, of course. Amongst Musical II's other offspring are the very useful French middle-distance filly Musique Royale and Master Guy, winner

Mr M. Arbib's "Snurge" (T. Quinn) goes to post at Doncaster

of the Prix Jean Prat and third in Nijinsky's Irish Derby. Musical II herself won the Prix du Rond-Point and is a daughter of the 1949 One Thousand Guineas and Oaks winner Musidora.

Snurge (ch.c. 1987)	Ela-Mana-Mou (b 1976)	Pitcairn (b 1971)	Petingo / Border Bounty
		Rose Bertin (ch 1970)	High Hat / Wide Awake
	Finlandia (FR) (b 1977)	Faraway Son (b 1967)	Ambiopoise / Locust Time
		Musical II (ch 1961)	Prince Chevalier / Musidora

Snurge is a big, strong, lengthy colt who stayed the extended one and three quarter miles of the St Leger well and is just as effective at a mile and a half. He's no out-and-out stayer, the label that's almost automatically been given to some St Leger winners. Ground conditions clearly are important to him, though; he shows a high knee action and demonstrated at Saint-Cloud that he goes well on heavy going. Snurge has shown some reluctance to enter the stalls but none at all once racing; he looked very keen to get on with things at Doncaster, taking a strong hold, and much more significantly, never flinched in some tough finishes. He is one to look forward to in 1991. *P. F. I. Cole.*

SO APT (IRE) 2 b.c. (Mar 28) Taufan (USA) 119–Anita's Princess (Miami 57 Springs 121) [1990 6m a6g 7m 8v³ 8.2s] IR 15,000F, 16,000Y: small, angular colt: has a round action: second foal: half-brother to Irish 3-y-o maiden Geht Schnell (by Fairy King): dam unraced half-sister to Anita's Prince: ridden by 7-lb claimer, staying-on third in nursery at Ayr: creditable seventh in similar event at Hamilton after: will stay 1¼m: best efforts with plenty of give in the ground. *M. H. Tompkins.*

SOBERING THOUGHTS 4 ch.g. Be My Guest (USA) 126–Soba 127 (Most — Secret 119) [1989 NR 1990 8.5d 7m⁵ 8g⁵ a8g 6m 6g 6m 6s 6d a6g] big gelding: second foal: half-brother to 7f and 1½m winner Gold Dust (by Golden Fleece): dam tough and consistent sprinter: poor maiden: blinkered eighth start: sold 1,800 gns Doncaster November Sales. *D. W. Chapman.*

SOBER MIND (USA) 3 b.g. Caro 133–Lolly Dolly 104 (Alleged (USA) 138) 98 [1989 7g² 7m* 1990 12g⁴ 12m³ 12g 12g 16.2f] angular, good-quartered gelding: fairly useful performer: in frame in listed race at Epsom and Prix Hocquart (took keen hold) at Longchamp: soundly beaten in Derby Italiano at Rome, Ever Ready Derby at Epsom and Queen's Vase (subsequently gelded) at Royal Ascot: should stay beyond 1½m: blinkered second and fourth starts: changed hands 85,000 gns Ascot February Sales: sold 31,000 gns Newmarket Autumn Sales. *P. A. Kelleway.*

SO BOLD 3 b.f. Never So Bold 135–Westonepaperchase (USA) (Accipiter (USA)) — [1989 NR 1990 7g 8f6 7g6 7m] 3,200F: workmanlike, deep-girthed filly: poor walker and mover: first foal: dam, raced only at 2 yrs, is out of half-sister to smart Prides Profile: plating-class form in maidens and claimer in the spring. *R. J. Holder.*

SOBRIETY 5 b.h. Noalcoholic (FR) 128–Sacred Mountain 74 (St Paddy 133) 52 [1989 8d⁵ 8f 10f 8m 10g 10m 8h² 10f 9m* 10g² 10.6d 7d* 1990 10.2f² 9f⁴ 10.8m⁴ 10m⁴ 7.6g*] leggy horse: plating-class handicapper: started slowly when winning amateurs event at Lingfield in June, leading post on stand side: stays 1¼m: acts on hard and dead going: excellent mount for inexperienced rider. *G. B. Balding.*

SO CAREFUL 7 br.h. Dalsaan 125–Miss Carefree 99 (Hill Clown (USA)) [1989 79 § 6d³ 6v⁵ 6s⁵ 7f 6f 6f² 6m 6g⁴ 6m⁶ 6s 6d 6m* 1990 6m* a6g² 6f 6m⁴ 6m⁴ 6h* 6d 6f 6m 6f⁴ 6d] lengthy, rather angular horse: usually looks very well: successful in handicaps at Catterick in March and Brighton (making virtually all) in May: well below best next 4 outings, then gave very temperamental display after 2-month absence final one, proving troublesome in stalls, swerving left leaving them and crashing through rail: suited by 6f: acts on any going: has won for lady: sometimes visored or blinkered: sold 2,200 gns Doncaster October Sales: one to treat with caution. *J. Berry.*

SOCIETY BALL 3 b.f. Law Society (USA) 130–Mariakova (USA) 84 (The 72 Minstrel (CAN) 135) [1989 8f⁴ 1990 11g⁴ a12g³ 12.4m a14g³ 14d² 15v² a12g*] workmanlike filly: modest handicapper: won at Southwell in November, always close up but running wide first turn: will stay 2m: acts on heavy going: didn't look entirely reliable fourth and fifth starts and blinkered after: sold N. Tinkler 3,600 gns Newmarket December Sales. *J. W. Watts.*

SOCKEM 3 b.g. Nordico (USA)–Floating Petal 90 (Wollow 132) [1989 6m⁶ 6f⁶ 6f⁶ 59 6h² 5m⁵ 6f³ 6f 5.3h⁴ 8.2f⁴ 8m 7d a6g⁴ a6g² a6g a6g a8g 1990 a6g⁵ a6g⁴ 7m² 7f* 7f*

7m³ 7g 7g⁶ 7m 7f 7m² 7m⁴ 7g 7m 7d* 7g] compact, rather sparely-made gelding: moderate mover: quite modest handicapper: led inside final 1f to win at Brighton (seller, bought in 5,200 gns) in April, Warwick in May and Catterick in October: best form at 7f: yet to race on soft ground, acts on any other: ran poorly when blinkered: has sweated: inconsistent. *C. N. Williams.*

SO DISCREET (USA)   2 b.c. (May 4) Secreto (USA) 128–I'll Be Around (USA)   **58** (Isgala) [1990 8g 8.2s⁶ 8d⁶] $67,000Y: smallish, workmanlike colt: closely related to fairly useful 8.5f and 9f winner Shafy (by Lyphard) and half-brother to a winner in USA: dam won 11 times at up to 1¼m, and is half-sister to dam of Cheveley Park winner Sookera: quite modest form in minor event at Newbury and maidens at Haydock and Leicester in autumn: will be better suited by 1¼m + . *J. W. Hills.*

SOFT CALL   2 br.f. (Feb 20) Ardross 134–Top Call 89 (High Top 131) [1990 8g   **72** 7d* 8s] small, lengthy filly: sixth foal: half-sister to several winners, including fair 1986 2-y-o 1m winner Salazie (by Ile de Bourbon) and fairly useful winner at up to 1m Coping (by Thatching): dam 2-y-o 7f and 1m winner, is half-sister to Final Straw and Achieved: won claimer at Edinburgh in October: seventh of 9 to Il Corsair in listed race at Turin in November: will stay 1¼m: sold out of N. Graham's stable 13,000 gns Newmarket Autumn Sales. *E. Schweigert, Italy.*

SOFT SHOE SHUFFLE   7 b.g. Hard Fought 125–Carroldance (FR) (Lyphard   — (USA) 132) [1989 11.1f⁴ 11.7m 12h⁴ 10h² 12f⁴ 1990 a10g] tall, leggy, close-coupled gelding: poor handicapper: suited by 1½m: acts on hard going: often apprentice ridden: has worn bandages. *Miss B. Sanders.*

SO GIFTED   4 b.f. Niniski (USA) 125–Maybe So 90 (So Blessed 130) [1989 5m   — 8.5f 7g³ 10m 8m 1990 a8g a13g 8m] angular filly: plating-class maiden at best: should be suited by further than 7f: hung right when blinkered final start at 3 yrs. *J. Norton.*

SOHRAB (IRE)   2 ch.c. (Apr 8) Shernazar 131–On Show 92 (Welsh Pageant 132)   **55 p** [1990 8d] leggy colt: has scope: moderate walker and mover: fifth foal: half-brother to 3-y-o Welney (by Habitat), very useful 6f winner at 2 yrs, and 2 other winners, including very useful miler Inchmurrin (by Lomond): dam 1¼m winner, is out of Park Hill winner African Dancer: bit backward and green, around 14 lengths seventh of 8, slowly away, ridden at halfway and fading from 2f out, in maiden at Leicester in October: looks sort to do better. *G. Wragg.*

SO KNOWLEDGEABLE   3 b.f. Night Shift (USA)–Sister Hannah 70 (Mon-   **53 d** seigneur (USA) 127) [1989 6s⁴ 1990 5f³ 5f⁵ 6m 6g⁴ 6g 6m 6f 6g⁶ 6d 7v⁴ 8d⁵ 5s] compact, good-quartered filly: poor mover: plating-class maiden at best: probably stays 7f and acts on any going: sold 1,800 gns Doncaster November Sales. *N. Tinkler.*

SOLAIA   2 ch.f. (Mar 12) Forzando 122–Tap The Line (Tap On Wood 130) [1990 6d   — 6g 6d] workmanlike filly: has a quick action: first foal: dam French middle-distance winner: bit backward, well beaten in maidens and a minor event: travelled well then weakened very quickly 2f out final start: sold 1,200 gns Newmarket Autumn Sales, resold 560 gns Ascot December Sales. *D. Morley.*

SOLA MIA   4 b.f. Tolomeo 127–Be My Sweet 78 (Galivanter 131) [1989 8g⁶ 11f   **62** 8.5m² 9g 10f 9f⁵ 8f 10s 8.2g 7m⁴ 1990 8f⁵ 9s 12f⁵ 6d a6g³ a8g a7g] lengthy filly: moderate mover: quite modest handicapper: best at up to 1m: probably acts on any going: blinkered twice (made running) at 3 yrs: often bandaged: has sweated badly: trained until after third start by W. Pearce: inconsistent. *S. R. Bowring.*

SOLAR GEM   3 b.g. Easter Topic–River Gem (Arctic Judge 94) [1989 NR 1990   — 10m] plain gelding: bad walker: fourth reported living foal: dam never ran: soon well tailed off in October seller. *M. J. Charles.*

SOLDE   2 ch.c. (Feb 13) Pharly (FR) 130–Quelle Chance 81 (General Assembly   **81** (USA)) [1990 6f² 6g² 7f* 7g⁴ 8.2g⁵] 26,000Y: angular, unfurnished colt: looks weak: second living foal: half-brother to useful 11f winner Ruddy Lucky (by Gorytus): dam Irish 5f winner at 2 yrs, is granddaughter of Oaks and 1000 Guineas winner Never Too Late: fair performer: won maiden at Ayr in July: ran well facing stiff tasks in £14,900 event at York (pulled hard then lost position at halfway) and minor contest at Haydock (tended to hang and carried head high) after: stays 1m: races keenly. *J. G. FitzGerald.*

SOLEIL DANCER (IRE)   2 b.c. (Mar 2) Fairy King (USA)–Cooliney Dancer   **71 p** (Dancer's Image (USA)) [1990 6m³ 7m⁵] IR 13,000F, 56,000Y: lengthy, good-quartered colt: has plenty of scope: sixth live foal: half-brother to quite useful 1983 2-y-o 6f winner Straw (by Thatch) and disqualified 1¼m seller winner Birmingham's Pride (by Indian King): dam Irish 2-y-o 5f winner: modest form, not unduly knocked about, at Ascot in maiden (green, hung right 1f out) and minor event over 3 months later: reared over at stalls at Newbury in between and withdrawn: looks sort to do better. *M. McCormack.*

SOLEIL EXPRESS 4 b.g. Bay Express 132–Peters Pleasure 70 (Jimsun 121) [1989 NR 1990 6g] fourth foal: half-brother to 1984 2-y-o 5f seller winner Steel Cavalier (by Dublin Taxi): dam showed form only at 2 yrs: well beaten in maiden at Nottingham in April: sold 2,500 gns Ascot May Sales: resold 1,200 gns Ascot July Sales. *J. D. Czerpak.* —

SOLEIL GRAND 3 b.g. Red Sunset 120–Becassine (El Gallo 122) [1989 6m3 6m 7g4 7g* 7m6 8f4 7g 1990 7g* 7d 7m2 7.6m3 7.6f6 8m 7g 7g 7.3g 8m6 7g] lengthy, robust gelding: carried condition: turned off-fore out: had a round action: fair handicapper: won at Epsom in April: broke leg at Newbury in October: best at 7f: acted on firm going, possibly unsuited to dead: dead. *M. McCormack.* 85

SOLEMN MELODY 3 b.g. Jalmood (USA) 126–Garganey (USA) (Quack (USA)) [1989 NR 1990 7f4 10.1m 8g] 3,100F, 8,000 3-y-o: big, angular gelding: second foal: dam never ran: well beaten in minor events and apprentice maiden. *A. Barrow.* —

SOLID (IRE) 2 b.c. (May 11) Glenstal (USA) 118–Reine de Chypre (FR) (Habitat 134) [1990 6m 6g 6d 6m a7g4 a8g a6g2 a7g] IR 6,500F, 9,200Y: leggy colt: eighth foal: half-brother to 2 French middle-distance winners by Forli and Shirley Heights: dam, French 6f and 7f winner, is half-sister to smart Beauvallon: plating-class maiden: best efforts on all-weather: stays 7f: ran moderately in visor on final start. *J. R. Jenkins.* 59

SOLID STEEL (IRE) 2 b.c. (Mar 28) Flash of Steel 120–Bonny Brae (Cure The Blues (USA)) [1990 a8g] first foal: dam ran 3 times in Ireland: tailed off from halfway in late-year maiden won by Wicked Things at Lingfield: wore eyeshield. *Mrs L. Piggott.* —

SOLINSKY 5 ch.m. Bali Dancer 107–Sailor's Sol (The Bo'sun 114) [1989 10.2m4 10m 1990 10.1g] sturdy, angular mare: sign of ability only on first of 3 outings: bandaged at 5 yrs. *Miss L. Bower.* —

SOLITARY REAPER 5 b.g. Valiyar 129–Fardella (ITY) (Molvedo 137) [1989 12f4 12f6 1990 a16g4 12f 16s] leggy gelding: poor maiden: should stay beyond 1½m: acts on firm going: sometimes visored or blinkered: usually claimer ridden: won selling hurdle in September. *C. R. Beever.* —

SOLO ARTIST 5 ch.g. Young Generation 129–Jubilee Song 71 (Song 132) [1989 9d 12v 10d* 10.4m* 11f 10f2 1990 10.4d] strong, rangy gelding: fair winner of spring handicaps as 4-y-o: bandaged, well beaten at Chester in October: suited by 1¼m: acts on any going: wears blinkers: often forces pace. *R. Simpson.* —

SOLO COURT 3 ch.f. King of Clubs 124–Mrs Tittlemouse (Nonoalco (USA) 131) [1989 6m2 6m5 6f3 1990 8f* 9f2 8m5 8f4 8f2 8m5] sparely-made filly: quite modest performer: led post in moderately-run maiden auction race at Thirsk in April: stays 9f: acts on firm going, yet to race on an easy surface: sometimes edgy and sweating. *Dr J. D. Scargill.* 63

SOLOMONS GIRL (NZ) 3 b.f. Babaroom (USA)–Henton Sylva (NZ) (Bellissimo (FR)) [1989 NR 1990 10.1g 10.1m a12g] leggy New Zealand-bred filly: well beaten in minor events and maiden. *J. R. Jenkins.* —

SOLOMONS NEPHEW 3 b.c. Absalom 128–Strawberry Fields 66 (Song 132) [1989 NR 1990 6m 6f* 7f 7m2] lengthy, rather sparely-made colt: third foal: half-brother to 1987 2-y-o 7f winner Lynsdale Boy and 1m seller winner Fille de Fraise (both by Mr Fluorocarbon): dam ran only at 2 yrs when 6f seller winner: favourite, won seller (bought in 17,000 gns) at Thirsk in April: led over 6f when second in handicap at Folkestone in July: better at 7f than 6f: slowly away first 2 outings. *Dr J. D. Scargill.* 60

SOLOMON'S SONG 4 b.g. Night Shift (USA)–Judeah 69 (Great Nephew 126) [1989 8m* 8.3m6 7g2 7m 6m6 6g* 7m 1990 a7g* a6g3 a6g* a6g3 a6g2 a7g 6f4 7g6 7.6d 6m3 6m5 6g4 6s* 6d 6m* 6g] strong, good-bodied gelding: hobdayed: moderate mover: fair handicapper: much improved, successful at Lingfield and Southwell early in year and at Haydock and Salisbury in June: suited by 6f: acted on any going: tough and genuine: dead. *M. Johnston.* 81

SO LONG BOYS (FR) 3 b.f. Beldale Flutter (USA) 130–Sweetly (FR) (Lyphard (USA) 132) [1989 5g3 5g2 6m 6g6 1990 7.5s 6v2 7g4 7v 6s5 5g5 8g 7f5 6g4 7d 10g 11.5g] 26,000Y: sparely-made filly: poor mover: sixth living foal: half-sister to 4 winners, including smart French 1987 2-y-o 6f and 7f winner Common Grounds and useful French 1m winner Lightning Fire (both by Kris): dam won 3 races at up to 9f in USA: ex-Italian maiden, formerly trained by D. Sasse: second at Milan in April: ?

ran 5 times here, twice looking none too keen: possibly best at up to 6f: acts on heavy going. *A. N. Lee.*

SOLWAY MIST 4 ch.f. Sagaro 133–Helewise 76 (Dance In Time (CAN)) [1989 **32** 12f 10g⁵ 12.2g 12g⁵ 18g 1990 13g² 13g⁵ 12d 12.3g 11m⁶ 15m 10m] small filly: poor maiden: little form after reappearance: stays 13f: visored third start, blinkered last 2: occasionally sweats. *R. A. Harrison.*

SOMBAT 3 b.c. Pal O Mine 96–Debitamer (Saritamer (USA) 130) [1989 NR 1990 — 8d 10d] small, plain colt: first reported foal: dam poor maiden: bandaged, tailed off in claimer and seller. *R. Guest.*

SOMEBODY 6 b.h. Bustino 136–Kashmir Lass 118 (Kashmir II 125) [1989 13v² — 16s⁴ 15.5s² 1990 14m] strong, stocky horse: carries condition: usually looks really well: poor mover: one-time modest handicapper: probably best at up to 1¾m: well suited by soft surface: doesn't find great deal and probably needs blinkers nowadays: winning hurdler in February. *J. White.*

SOMEONE BRAVE 2 b.c. (Feb 17) Commanche Run 133–Someone Special 105 **76** (Habitat 134) [1990 8f² 8.2d³ 9g⁵] 36,000Y: smallish, compact colt: first foal: dam 7f winner stayed 1m, is half-sister to top-class miler Milligram out of 1000 Guineas winner One In A Million: modest form in maidens and claimer (hampered 2f out, unable to recover and eased) in autumn: joined C. Horgan. *H. R. A. Cecil.*

SOMERSAULTING (IRE) 2 b.c. (Apr 28) Jester 119–Gwen Somers (Will **51** Somers 114§) [1990 6g 6g 6m³ 6m 5g³ 6d 5v⁴ 5g 6d⁴] IR 4,000Y, 3,400 2-y-o: tall, lengthy colt: seventh reported living foal: half-brother to fairly useful 6f winner Transflash (by Auction Ring): dam unraced half-sister to smart animals Cyprus and Right of The Line: poor maiden: stays 6f: suited by easy surface: usually blinkered. *A. R. Davison.*

SOMETHING QUICK (IRE) 2 b.c. (Apr 30) Mummy's Treasure 84–Artillery **56** Row (Pals Passage 115) [1990 5f 6m⁵ 7m³ 7g 6m 8m⁴ 7d²] IR 6,200Y: small colt: fifth foal: dam Irish maiden: plating-class maiden: ran well in sellers at Catterick and Warwick (apprentices) final 2 starts: probably ideally suited by 7f: acts on good to firm ground and dead. *R. Hannon.*

SONALTO 4 br.g. Noalto 120–Sanandrea (Upper Case (USA)) [1989 8g² 8s⁵ — 8.2s³ 8.5d 8m² 9m⁵ 9m 12m 1990 a8g] leggy, lengthy, quite attractive gelding: has a rather round action: quite modest maiden at best: has run poorly since fifth outing in 1989: suited by 1m: best form on top-of-the-ground: winning selling hurdler in May. *D. L. Williams.*

SONAR 4 b. or br.g. Pitskelly 122–Diana's Choice (Tudor Music 131) [1989 7g 8g **47 §** 12m 10m 10m 10m² 10f³ 12m⁶ 10g 12g 10g⁶ 1990 a13g² 14.6f⁶] leggy gelding: has a round action: capable of plating-class form but is temperamental: stays 13f: acts on good to firm going: blinkered last 6 outings in 1989: has sweated: one to treat with caution. *Pat Mitchell.*

SON ET LUMIERE 3 ch.f. Rainbow Quest (USA) 134–Soprano 112 (Kris 135) — [1989 NR 1990 7g 7.6d 7g 6g⁶] leggy, angular filly: first foal: dam winner at 7.6f and 1m: poor maiden: should be suited by at least 1m: joined D. Arbuthnot. *I. A. Balding.*

SONGLINES 2 b.f. (Feb 17) Night Shift (USA)–Donnas Dream 84 (Young **69** Generation 129) [1990 6d³ 5m³ 6g³ 6d² a5g*] 5,000 2-y-o: small, lengthy, angular filly: first foal: dam 1m winner, is half-sister to Town And Country: quite modest performer: made all in late-year maiden at Lingfield, beating Jess Rebec 4 lengths: stays 6f: acts on top-of-the-ground and dead. *R. V. Smyth.*

SONG OF GYMCRAK 3 b.f. Chief Singer 131–Dusty Letter (USA) 78 (Run **41** Dusty Run (USA)) [1989 5d 7g³ 8f 1990 8m 12g a8g⁴ 10.6f 11m a11g⁵ 11g³ a14g⁴] angular, workmanlike filly: plater: seems to stay 1¾m: needs give in the ground: blinkered last 7 outings: not an ideal mount for apprentice. *M. H. Easterby.*

SONG OF KINGS (CAN) 3 ch.c. The Minstrel (CAN) 135–Nabora (USA) **87** (Naskra (USA)) [1989 NR 1990 8m² 8.5g* 8.2m³] $100,000Y: leggy, rather sparelymade colt: has a round action: second foal: dam, winner twice at around 6f in USA, is half-sister to American Grade 2 9f winner Spanish Drums: easily landed odds in maiden at Beverley, making all: looked ill at ease on ground when third of 5 in minor event at Haydock later in May: will be suited by further: sold 6,600 gns Newmarket Autumn Sales. *M. R. Stoute.*

SONG OF SIXPENCE (USA) 6 b.g. The Minstrel (CAN) 135–Gliding By **110** (USA) [1989 12.3s² 11f⁵ 10.6d⁶ 1990 13v 10m* 10.2m⁴ 12m⁵ 10m* 10.5m 10f* 10m* 10f* 10.1g* 11.1g³ 10g⁵ 10d³] big, strong, close-coupled gelding: has a round action: vastly improved and in tremendous form in summer, winning handicaps at Newbury (ladies), Salisbury, Ayr (amateurs), Ascot (£11,350 event) and Goodwood (£22,500 Racal Chesterfield Cup) and listed contest at Windsor: good third to Lord of The Field in strongly-run BonusPrint September Stakes at Kempton: suited by middle distances: probably unsuited by heavy ground, acts on any other: best held up and suited by good gallop: tough and genuine: a credit to his trainer. *I. A. Balding.*

SONIC LORD 5 b.h. Final Straw 127–Lucent 117 (Irish Ball (FR) 127) [1989 12g 12m 10.1m* 10f 10f 10m 10h⁵ 10m* 10f 12m a11g 1990 12f 10g 10g 10g* 10f⁵ 11.7m a12g] strong horse: carries condition: poor mover: won handicap at Yarmouth in July, but is thoroughly unreliable and runs poorly more often than not: stays 1½m: yet to race on soft going, acts on any other: best visored or blinkered: best left alone. *R. Voorspuy.* **50 §**

SONIC SIGNAL 4 b.f. Trojan Fen 118–Danger Signal 106 (Red God 128§) [1989 8s 11m* 9m 12m 10d⁶ᵈⁱˢ 8m 11.7g² 12g* 10d² 14m 1990 a10g⁴ 9g⁶ 10g⁴ 10m⁴ 10m 12f⁴ 15.5f⁶ 12m a12g a12g⁶] small, sparely-made filly: poor handicapper: stays 1½m: acts on firm and dead going: inconsistent. *M. J. Haynes.* **55 d**

SONNY HILL LAD 7 ch.g. Celtic Cone 116–Honey Dipper (Golden Dipper 119) [1989 16.2m³ 1990 15d²] sturdy, workmanlike gelding: maiden on flat: 100/1, no chance with easy winner Pashto in amateurs race at Ayr in September: probably stays 2¼m: winning hurdler/novice chaser. *R. J. Holder.* **59**

SONSIE LAD 2 br.g. (Feb 20) Tickled Pink 114–Charlotte Amalie (No Mercy 126) [1990 6s⁶ 6m⁶ a6g 8m 10m] 1,300Y: leggy, quite good-topped gelding: third foal: half-brother to poor maiden Sonsie Mo (by Lighter): dam of little account: poor plater: seems to stay 1¼m: trained first 3 outings by J. Berry. *W. M. Perrin.* **35**

SOOTY TERN 3 br.c. Wassl 125–High Tern 93 (High Line 125) [1989 8s 6d 6g 1990 10.2f* 12m 8f⁴ 8m⁶ a10g] compact, quite attractive colt: plating-class handicapper: odds on, first worthwhile form when winning at Newcastle in April: fourth at Pontefract, leading 7f and easily best other effort: stays 1¼m: acts on firm ground: sometimes on toes, and has sweated: left J. W. Watts then sold out of J. Gosden's stable 3,800 gns Newmarket Autumn Sales after fourth start. *J. M. Bradley.* **50**

SOPHIA GARDENS 3 gr.f. Kalaglow 132–Mint Julep (Mill Reef (USA) 141) [1989 7m⁶ 1990 10.2f 11.7h⁴ 12m⁴ 14m⁴ 12f²] plain, angular filly: poor maiden: head second in apprentice selling handicap at Brighton in September, given hard race: withdrawn lame start at Southwell 2½ months later: should be suited by 1¾m+: pulled very hard in visor fourth outing: joined Pat Mitchell. *I. A. Balding.* **48**

SO RHYTHMICAL 6 b.g. Dance In Time (CAN)–So Lyrical 68 (So Blessed 130) [1989 5s 6f⁸ 6f* 7f* 8f 7.6m 1990 5f⁶ 5.8f³ 6g⁴ 6m⁵ 6m³ 6m 7g 7m² 6g* 6s² 5s⁴] sturdy gelding: fair handicapper: won £12,100 event at York in October despite drifting right: ran extremely well when in frame at Newbury (would have won had run started earlier) and Doncaster afterwards: stays 7f: acts on any going: sometimes sweats and gets on edge: bandaged off-hind: sometimes slowly away. *G. H. Eden.* **86**

SO ROMANTIC (IRE) 2 b.f. (Mar 30) Teenoso (USA) 135–Romara 105 (Bold Lad (IRE) 133) [1990 7m* 7m 7d²] leggy, close-coupled filly: seventh living foal: half-sister to 3-y-o Ile de Roma (by Ile de Bourbon), successful at 1m (at 2 yrs) and 10.6f, and to several other winners, including smart 6f and 1¼m winner Ela Romara (by Ela-Mana-Mou) and 1m and 1¼m winner Halstead (by Bustino): dam 7f and 1m winner: won maiden at Lingfield in September in quite good style by 2½ lengths from Good Policy: good second of 7, keeping on well, to Lilian Bayliss in minor event at Chester: will be better suited by 1m+. *G. Wragg.* **92 p**

SOUGHAAN'S PRIDE (IRE) 2 gr.f. (May 23) Soughaan (USA) 111–Divine Apsara (Godswalk (USA) 130) [1990 5g 5.8h a7g a7g] IR 1,200F, 6,200Y: leggy, sparely-made filly: has a round action: third foal: half-sister to 3-y-o Burslem Beau (by Burslem), 5f winner at 2 yrs: dam Irish 5f to 1m winner: little worthwhile form in varied events: off course 6 months after second outing. *R. A. Bennett.* **—**

SOUGHT OUT (IRE) 2 b.f. (Mar 17) Rainbow Quest (USA) 134–Edinburgh 117 (Charlottown 127) [1990 8m² 8g²] sixth foal: half-sister to several winners here and in France, including 7f and 14.6f winner Queen Helen (by Troy) and fairly useful 1½m winner Castle Peak (by Darshaan): dam, from family of Reform, stayed at around 1m at 2 yrs later stayed 10.5f: kept on well in autumn maidens won by Brockette at Leicester and Clare Heights at Yarmouth: will be well suited by 1¼m+: sure to improve again, and win a race. *M. R. Stoute.* **91 p**

SOUK (IRE) 2 b.f. (Apr 27) Ahonoora 122–Soumana (FR) (Pharly (FR) 130) [1990 **84 p** 6m⁴ 7f*] IR 105,000Y: fifth foal: half-sister to 3-y-o 1m and 1¼m winner Red Toto (by Habitat), Irish 1¼m winner Sharakou (by Tap On Wood) and 7.5f winner Tuxedo (by Persian Bold): dam unraced half-sister to Dumka, dam of Doyoun and Dafayna: odds on, won maiden at Brighton in October readily by 5 lengths from Ageetee: sure to improve further, and win another race or two. *L. M. Cumani.*

SOUL INTENT 2 b.f. (Feb 19) Lochnager 132–Tricky 66 (Song 132) [1990 5d 5f] — 1,150Y: sturdy filly: has plenty of scope: first foal: dam poor maiden best at 2 yrs: sister to smart sprinter Jester and useful 2-y-o Tricky Note: well beaten in maiden at Haydock and auction event (slowly away) at Carlisle in September. *W. Bentley.*

SOUND MUSIC 4 b.f. Music Boy 124–Kanvita (Home Guard (USA) 129) [1989 — 7g 7g a8g a6g a8g 1990 a7g a7g a12g 7m a7g⁵ a8g a8g 8d] angular, shallow-girthed filly: poor mover: little worthwhile form: blinkered fourth and fifth outings: has sweated: trained until after sixth start by R. Armstrong. *J. P. Leigh.*

SOUND OBSERVATION (USA) 2 ch.c. (Mar 28) The Minstrel (CAN) **57** 135–Thats The Reason (USA) (Bold Reason) [1990 6m 8g 9g] $50,000Y: compact, rather angular colt: fifth foal: brother to 3-y-o Desert Warbler: dam half-sister to Turf Classic winner Noble Fighter and Grand Prix d'Evry winner Vagaries: plating-class form in maidens and claimer (raced freely in blinkers) in autumn: sold 2,300 gns Newmarket Autumn Sales. *W. Haggas.*

SOUNDS CLASSICAL 3 ch.f. The Noble Player (USA) 126–Moon White **61** (Great White Way (USA)) [1989 NR 1990 8g 11f⁴ 12f⁶ 16f⁵ 12m⁵ 6f] IR 600 2-y-o: angular filly: half-sister to Irish middle-distance winners Penalty Kick (by Patch) and Northern Promise (by Viking): dam Irish sprinter successful at 2 yrs: ex-Irish maiden: soundly beaten in lady riders seller at Thirsk: stayed 1½m: blinkered penultimate start: trained until after then by J. Bolger: dead. *W. Storey.*

SOUPCON 4 b.f. King of Spain 121–Duck Soup 55 (Decoy Boy 129) [1989 7g⁵ **54** 1990 7g 7g 7g⁴ a10g a8g4] rather leggy filly: moderate walker: won maiden at Hamilton at 2 yrs: best effort since never-nearer fourth in claimer at Lingfield in December: stays 1m: acts on soft going: blinkered 3 out of last 4 outings. *Miss B. Sanders.*

SOUSON (IRE) 2 b.g. (Feb 27) Soughaan (USA) 111–Down The Line 74 **69** (Brigadier Gerard 144) [1990 6m³ 7f³ 6m 8d] IR 10,000F, 10,000Y: tall, unfurnished gelding: third foal: half-brother to 3-y-o Euchan Glen (by Wolverlife), successful at 6f (at 2 yrs) to 1½m: dam Irish 1½m winner, is out of close relation to More Light and half-sister to Shoot A Line: quite modest maiden: probably stays 1m. *R. M. Whitaker.*

SOUTARI 2 br.c. (May 11) Scorpio (FR) 127–Sousocks (Soueida 111) [1990 7m 7m — 8d] good-bodied colt: seventh known foal: dam seemed of no account over hurdles: always behind in maidens at Chepstow and Bath: backward first 2 starts. *M. McCormack.*

SOUTER'S HILL (USA) 3 b.c. Temperence Hill (USA)–Kissapotamus (USA) **63 ?** (Illustrious) [1989 NR 1990 7f 10.6f⁶ 12g 15.3m³ 16.2d³ 16g 15.8m⁵ 16m⁵ 15.3m 10f²] $37,000Y, IR 52,000Y: tall, leggy colt: half-brother to several winners, including fairly useful 1987 2-y-o 6f winner Margub (by Topsider), subsequently successful at 1¼m: dam won 2 stakes races over 1m: sire champion 3-y-o, successful in 1½m Belmont Stakes: quite modest maiden at best: stays 2m: acts on good to firm ground and dead: pulled hard for 7-lb claimer: visored final start: sold to join T. Craig 6,200 gns Newmarket Autumn Sales. *R. Hollinshead.*

SOUTH AUSTRALIA (CAN) 2 b.c. (Feb 23) Shadeed (USA) 135–Millicent **72** (USA) (Cornish Prince) [1990 7m⁴ 8.2d⁶] 210,000Y: sturdy, quite attractive colt: has a quick action: closely related to winners in Ireland and in USA, including useful 5f to 7f winner Western Symphony, and half-sister to several other winners, including smart sprinter Peterhof (by The Minstrel): dam unraced half-sister to Mill Reef: quite modest form behind Loki in maiden at Warwick (favourite) and Hip To Time in minor event at Nottingham later in October. *H. R. A. Cecil.*

SOUTH CROFTY (USA) 2 ch.g. (Feb 13) Imp Society (USA)–Pia's Estonia **69** (USA) (Nikoli 125) [1990 5f* 5f² 5m⁵ 5d⁴ 6d a6g⁴ 5s² a6g*] $15,000Y: strong, close-coupled gelding: has markedly round action: first foal: dam minor winner at around 6f in USA: sire best at 4 yrs when successful from 8.5f to 1¼m: won maiden at Doncaster in March and claimer at Lingfield in November: effective at 5f and 6f: acts on any going: sold out of W. O'Gorman's stable 3,200 gns Doncaster September Sales after sixth start. *M. Johnston.*

SOUTHEND SCALLYWAG 4 b.f. Tina's Pet 121–By The Lake 48 (Tyrant **44** (USA)) [1989 8.2m 8f⁵ 7f⁶ 8m* 8.2m 1990 11f³ 15m⁵] lengthy, sparely-made filly: has a round action: poor handicapper: stays 15f: acts on firm ground: winning hurdler (finished lame at Perth in August). *G. M. Moore.*

SOUTHERN BEAU (USA) 3 b.g. Dixieland Band (USA)–Love For Love — (USA) (Cornish Prince) [1989 6f⁵ 7g* 7m⁴ 8g⁶ 7.3m⁵ 1990 10v⁵ 10.6s] useful-looking gelding: fair winner at 2 yrs: moderate fifth at Ayr in April, keeping on from towards rear: stays 1¼m: blinkered last 2 starts at 2 yrs: gelded and joined S. Mellor: has suspect temperament. *C. R. Nelson.*

SOUTHERN SKY 5 b.m. Comedy Star (USA) 121–Starky's Pet (Mummy's Pet **85** 125) [1989 8d 7g⁴ 7g* 8m² 7g⁵ 8m³ 7f² 7m* 8f 1990 7g 8f 7f* 7m⁶] rather leggy, angular mare: fair handicapper: won £7,900 event at Goodwood (third success on track) in August: effective at 7f and 1m: acted on firm and dead going: game: in foal to Indian Ridge. *D. R. C. Elsworth.*

SOUTHROP 4 b.g. Auction Ring (USA) 123–Giovinezza (FR) (Roi Dagobert 128) — [1989 5s² 5s 6f 6f 7m 5m⁶ 6m 8.2g 1990 5m 8m 6m 6m⁵ 5d 8m] lengthy, quite attractive gelding: no worthwhile form at 4 yrs: stays 6f: acts on any going: bandaged near-hind last 2 starts: sold 1,900 gns Newmarket Autumn Sales. *M. Blanshard.*

SOUTH SHORE 3 b.f. Caerleon (USA) 132–Shore Line 107 (High Line 125) **102** [1989 NR 1990 8m⁴ 10g² 12d 10.1m* 12m⁴ 11.5g⁵ 14.6g 12m* a12g* a12g*] 130,000F, 440,000Y: leggy, workmanlike filly: moderate walker: third foal: half-sister to fair 11f winner Ahwak (by Shareef Dancer): dam, winner over 7f and fourth in Oaks, is sister to Park Hill winner Quay Line: made virtually all to win minor event at Windsor in July and handicaps at Chepstow in October and Lingfield (twice, best effort last time) in November: stays 1½m: seems to need top-of-the-ground on turf: sold T. Stack 50,000 gns Newmarket December Sales. *B. W. Hills.*

SOVEREIGN HEIGHTS 2 b.c. (Apr 16) Elegant Air 119–Blubella 86 (Balidar — 133) [1990 5v] 6,800Y: first living foal: dam sprinter: always behind in maiden at Ayr in April. *Denys Smith.*

SOVEREIGN HILL 3 ch.f. Dominion 123–Tuft Hill 92 (Grundy 137) [1989 5m — 5f⁶ 7f 6g 1990 6f 8g] sparely-made filly, slightly dipped-backed: poor maiden: should stay at least 1m: sweating badly, swished tail and looked temperamental final start at 2 yrs: sold to join R. Price's stable 875 gns Ascot July Sales: one to treat with caution. *M. H. Easterby.*

SOVEREIGN NICHE (IRE) 2 gr.c. (May 15) Nishapour (FR) 125–Sovereign — p Flash (FR) (Busted 134) [1990 6g 6d] 9,400Y: sturdy, lengthy colt: first foal: dam French middle-distance winner: showed signs of ability in maidens at Newcastle (backward, green, slowly away) and Doncaster (not knocked about) in autumn. *Mrs J. R. Ramsden.*

SOVEREIGN ROCKET (USA) 5 b.h. Sovereign Dancer (USA)–Jeffs Miss **80** Rocket (USA) (Jeff D) [1989 8m 8f 8m³ 10m⁵ 1990 8m² 8f 8m] strong, good-topped, quite attractive horse: moderate walker: has a quick action: fair performer: first run for 10 months, good second in amateurs race at Warwick in May: well beaten after in valuable handicaps: should stay 1¼m: acts on good to firm going: has won when sweating: sold 5,000 gns Newmarket September Sales. *G. Harwood.*

SOWETO (IRE) 2 b.g. (Mar 29) Katu 120–Golden Empress (Cavo Doro 124) **93** [1990 6m* 6m 6m* 7m² 8m³ 7d²] 7,400F, 14,000Y: leggy, good-topped gelding: has scope: half-brother to 1985 2-y-o 6f and 7f winner Feisty (by Pitskelly) and 2 winners abroad: dam lightly-raced granddaughter of 1000 Guineas winner Belle of All: fairly useful performer: successful in maiden at Doncaster in May and claimer (carried head high) at Newcastle in June: ran well in nurseries after, on final start second of 20, quickening really well but tending to carry head high, at Leicester: stays 1m: acts on good to firm ground and dead: likely to make useful handicapper. *G. A. Pritchard-Gordon.*

SPACE TRAVELLER (IRE) 2 ch.g. (Apr 15) Tate Gallery (USA) 117–Parlais — 101 (Pardao 120) [1990 6m] IR 28,000Y: smallish, workmanlike gelding: half-brother to numerous winners, including 3-y-o Chipandabit (by Mummy's Pet), 5f winner at 2 yrs, and several other sprint winners by same sire: dam sprinter: bit backward, slowly away and behind from halfway in maiden auction at Newbury in May: sold 950 gns Newmarket Autumn Sales. *J. Sutcliffe.*

SPANIARDS CLOSE 2 b.c. (Feb 12) King of Spain 121–Avon Belle 75 (Balidar **53** p 133) [1990 6g] compact, workmanlike colt: third foal: dam best at sprint distances:

bit backward and green, slowly away and always behind in maiden (moved poorly down) at Newbury in October. *P. J. Makin.*

SPANISH EMPIRE (USA)   3 b.c. El Gran Senor (USA) 136–Tea And Roses   81
(USA) (Fleet Nasrullah) [1989 8v4 1990 9g4 8.2d2 8m2] lengthy, rather angular colt: has a rather round action: moderate walker: fair form in listed race at Newmarket and maidens at Haydock and Ripon (odds on): uncertain to stay much further: sold 16,500 gns Newmarket Autumn Sales. *B. W. Hills.*

SPANISH ENVOY   3 br.g. King of Spain 121–Queen's Herald (King's Leap 111)   —
[1989 6m 5f 5m 7g a8g 1990 a10g a12g] tall gelding: of little account. *J. Akehurst.*

SPANISH HARLEM   4 b.g. King of Spain 121–Luscinia 73 (Sing Sing 134)   66 ?
[1989 5m 6f* 6g 1990 6g 6m3 6f4 5g 6h3 5f 5m 7m 7d 5s6] good-bodied gelding: quite modest handicapper: caught the eye final outing, staying on well from rear under tender handling: suited by 6f: probably acts on any going: sold out of W. Pearce's stable 4,000 gns Newmarket Autumn Sales after ninth start. *Mrs J. R. Ramsden.*

SPANISH HEART   5 b.m. King of Spain 121–Hearten (Hittite Glory 125) [1989   86
7g 8.5m 8f2 8g3 7f* 8m2 7.6m4 8f2 1990 8f5 9m2 8m* 7.6m2] medium-sized mare: fair handicapper: favourite, won at Chepstow in June: ran well at Lingfield 2 weeks later: effective at 7f to 9f: acts on firm going: consistent. *P. J. Makin.*

SPANISH LOVE   4 b. or br.f. Precocious 126–San Marguerite 80 (Blakeney 126)   38
[1989 7f2 7.3m 7f 7f6 a8g3 a8g6 a8g 1990 a10g 10f 8m 8m 8.3g4 8.3m2 8m3 10m 8f4 9g2 10d] close-coupled, workmanlike filly: poor mover: poor handicapper: stays 9f: acts on firm going: blinkered second to fifth outings: trained until after fifth by M. McCormack. *M. D. I. Usher.*

SPANISH REALM   3 b.f. King of Spain 121–Miss Realm 86 (Realm 129) [1989 5s   —
5d* 5f5 5d* 6f4 6g3 6m5 6g2 6g4 5m* 1990 5f 6g 5v 5m 5m 5g 6g 6m 6f 8g] small, sparely-made filly: quite modest handicapper at her best: below form after reappearance: stays 6f: acts on firm and dead going: tends to hang: sometimes bandaged: good mount for apprentice. *M. Brittain.*

SPANISH REEL   8 b.g. Gay Fandango (USA) 132–De Nada 79 (Ragusa 137)   —
[1989 10d 10.8m4 10.8m* 11.7m5 1990 a10g] good-bodied gelding: plating-class handicapper: pulled up (reportedly fractured knee) after 4f at Lingfield in January: stayed 11.7f: acted on any going: visored once: dead. *J. A. C. Edwards.*

SPANISH SERVANT   5 ch.g. Don 128–Please Oblige (Le Levanstell 122) [1989   58 +
NR 1990 14.6f2 16.2m] stocky, workmanlike gelding: modest maiden at best: co-favourite, always behind final outing (May): should be suited by 2m: best form with give in the ground. *R. Akehurst.*

SPANISH VERDICT   3 b.c. King of Spain 121–Counsel's Verdict (Firestreak   70
125) [1989 6f3 6f4 6g2 6g4 6v5 1990 7f4 7h 6f* 7g 6m4 8g 8f2 8.2d5 8m 7d] sturdy, good-quartered colt: has a round action: modest performer: landed odds in maiden at Carlisle in May: stays 1m: appears to act on any going, with exception of hard: visored 5 times. *Miss S. E. Hall.*

SPANISH WHISPER   3 b.g. Aragon 118–Whisper Gently 91 (Pitskelly 122)   49
[1989 6m 6f 6m5 6g a7g a7g 1990 10f6 8.3g3 8g4 7m6 7m5 7f 7f3 8m* 8m a8g4 a8g] medium-sized gelding: moderate mover: plating-class handicapper: claimed out of P. Makin's stable £6,051 third start: ran in non-selling events after, winning amateur riders race at Redcar in September: stays 1m: acts on firm ground: ran moderately in blinkers at 2 yrs: tends to hang. *J. R. Bostock.*

SPARE US ALL   6 b.g. Moorestyle 137–Second Generation 95 (Decoy Boy 129)   —
[1989 10s5 1990 6d] big, strong, workmanlike gelding: lightly-raced maiden: 5/1 from 12/1, soon had lot to do in handicap at Nottingham in October: suited by further than 6f. *B. J. Curley.*

SPARKLER GEBE   4 b.g. Be My Native (USA) 124–Siliferous (Sandy Creek   —
123) [1989 11.7m2 12f 10f4 13.3d 1990 a12g6 a13g6 12g 10.6s 8m] tall, leggy gelding: easily best effort on debut at 3 yrs: no form in handicaps at 4 yrs: blinkered 3 times: won claiming hurdle in November. *P. G. Bailey.*

SPARKLING NECTAR   3 b.f. Thatching 131–Baby Brew 123 (Green God 128)   52
[1989 6g 6m5 6g 1990 7m 6m2 7g] useful-looking filly: shows a fluent action: favourite, second of 6 in minor event at Folkestone in July: little other form, well backed in handicap on reappearance: not bred to stay much beyond 6f. *R. Hannon.*

SPARKLING WIT   8 b.m. Sparkler 130–Countess Walewski 85 (Brigadier   —
Gerard 144) [1989 NR 1990 11.7f] runner-up in point-to-point in March: bandaged and apprentice ridden at overweight, tailed off in handicap at Bath in May, only race on flat since 1986. *B. Palling.*

SPARK OF SUCCESS (USA) 2 b.f. (Mar 23) Topsider (USA)–Social Lesson **84** p
(USA) (Forum (USA)) [1990 6g*] $850,000Y: sister to Top Socialite and half-sister
to several other winners, notably 2000 Guineas second Exbourne (by Explodent):
dam sprint claimer winner: long odds on, won 10-runner maiden at Phoenix Park by
2½ lengths, coming clear towards line: will stay 7f: sure to improve. *D. K. Weld,
Ireland.*

SPEARMAN 3 b.c. Diesis 133–Oh So Bold (USA) (Better Bee) [1989 NR 1990 **92**
8m⁶ 10m⁵ 10g* 10f² 12.3g⁵ 10.2g 10m⁴] 185,000Y: lengthy, quite attractive colt: has
plenty of scope: half-brother to several winners, including 1988 2-y-o 6f winner
Hope And Glory (by Well Decorated): dam, minor winner in USA, is half-sister to
Law Society, Legal Bid and Strike Your Colors: led post in maiden at Kempton in
June: in frame in £8,000 events at Newmarket, clearly best efforts in handicaps:
stays 1¼m (didn't settle in moderately-run race at 1½m): swished tail fourth start:
has had difficulty handling turns. *J. R. Fanshawe.*

SPECIAL REQUEST 2 b.g. (Apr 9) Jalmood (USA) 126–Legal Sound 85 (Legal **42**
Eagle 126) [1990 a7g a6g 7m⁴ 7m 7g 8m 8m 10.6s] 15,500F, 15,000Y: small gelding:
third foal: half-brother to 3-y-o Brisas (by Vaigly Great), fairly useful 5f performer at
2 yrs: dam 6f winner: quite moderate plater: should stay 1m: possibly unsuited by
very soft ground: blinkered fifth and sixth starts, visored final one: has worn
bandages. *K. T. Ivory.*

SPECKLED BRAID (USA) 3 b.f. Miswaki (USA) 124–Petes Lucky Lady **—**
(USA) (Droll Roll) [1989 6g² 1990 8m] leggy, sparely-made filly: moderate walker:
second in maiden at Yarmouth at 2 yrs: fractured pelvis in similar event at York:
dead. *H. R. A. Cecil.*

SPECKYFOUREYES 7 b.m. Blue Cashmere 129–Sprightly Sprite 80 (Babur **—**
126) [1989 12m⁴ 16.2m⁶ 18f⁵ 1990 a14g] no form in varied events on flat: wears
bandages: sold 3,100 gns Ascot April Sales. *J. Pearce.*

SPENDING RECORD (USA) 3 ch.c. Topsider (USA)–Final Figure (USA) **107** p
(Super Concorde (USA)) [1989 NR 1990 10d² 10m* 11m* 10m* 11g*] third reported
foal: half-brother to minor Irish 8.5f winner Work That Way (by Czarvich): dam third
over 6f and 7f in Ireland, ran only at 2 yrs: not seen out until July then won 4 of his 5
races, namely maiden at Leopardstown then minor event at 2 listed races (by length
from Spinning the same distance from Topanoora 7 weeks later) at Phoenix Park:
will stay 1½m: may will prove capable of further improvement. *D. K. Weld, Ireland.*

SPENDOMANIA (USA) 3 b.f. Roberto (USA) 131–La Trinite (FR) 112 **113**
(Lyphard (USA) 132) [1989 7d⁵ 7m* 6d² 6g⁵ 8m⁴ 8m⁵ 1990 9.2d⁵ 10g³ 10.5d 9g* 8d
10g⁴ 10g² 10g* 12.5g² 10.5v] half-sister to several winners abroad, including Prix
Morny winners Seven Springs (by Irish River) and Regal State (by Affirmed): dam
won twice at around 6f at 2 yrs in France and is out of sister to Oaks winner Pia:
smart filly: successful in maiden at Saint-Cloud at 2 yrs and in minor event at
Maisons-Laffitte in July and listed race at Evry in September: second in Prix de la
Nonette and Prix de Royallieu at Longchamp seventh and ninth starts: stays 1½m:
possibly best on a sound surface. *J. Fellows, France.*

SPHINX 6 b.g. Auction Ring (USA) 123–The Yellow Girl 102 (Yellow God 129) **—**
[1989 10.8s² 8d² 10.8d 8g² 8.2g² 8v⁴ a11g⁴ a12g 1990 a11g⁴ a11g⁶ 10m 10.6s] lengthy,
robust gelding: poor handicapper: soundly beaten last 2 starts: stays 11f: probably
unsuited by firm going, acts on any other: blinkered once: has won for apprentice:
trained until after second outing by J. Jenkins. *J. R. Bostock.*

SPICA (USA) 3 b.f. Diesis 133–Giboulee Era (USA) (Giboulee (CAN)) [1989 6g³ **76** §
1990 7m³ 8m² 8f* 8f] leggy, angular filly: modest performer: won minor event at
Wolverhampton in July: refused to race in handicap following month: stays 1m: acts
on firm going: wandered under pressure second start: not one to trust. *R. Charlton.*

SPICE DANCER 2 b.f. (Mar 8) Mashhor Dancer (USA)–Saniette (Crystal **—**
Palace (FR) 132) [1990 8s] rangy, angular filly: third foal: half-sister to unreliable
13.1f winner Shoe Tapper (by Song): dam ran once in France: soon struggling in
minor event at Newbury in October: sold 3,600 gns Newmarket Autumn Sales. *I. A.
Balding.*

SPICE TRADER (IRE) 2 b.c. (Apr 25) Burslem 123–La Calera (Corvaro (USA) **84**
122) [1990 5g 6g² 6g* 7.5f² 6f³ 7g* 7.3g] IR 6,500F, 10,000Y: leggy, finely-made
colt: first reported foal: dam Irish 1¼m winner: fair performer: won maiden at Ripon
in June and listed race at Baden-Baden (by 2½ lengths from Candelaria) in August:
not entirely discredited in face of stiff task in Vodafone Horris Hill Stakes at
Newbury final outing: stays 7f. *T. Thomson Jones.*

SPIDER WOMAN   3 b.f. Touching Wood (USA) 127–Red Spider 78 (Red God   —
128§) [1989 6m⁶ 1990 11d 14g⁴ 16.2d a12g a14g] deep-girthed filly: moderate walker
and mover: well beaten in maidens and handicaps on flat: sold to join R. Whitaker
after winning selling hurdle. *K. O. Cunningham-Brown.*

SPINECHILLER   2 ro.g. (Apr 1) Grey Ghost 98–Swinging Gold 80 (Swing Easy   73
(USA) 126) [1990 5m² 5f³ 5f⁵ 5m* 5f² 5f² 5m] robust, attractive gelding: has scope:
first foal: dam sprinter: first run for over 3 months, apprentice-ridden winner of
maiden at Catterick in August: better efforts after when placed in nurseries:
speedy: hung right first 2 starts. *T. D. Barron.*

SPINNEYOVER   2 b.g. (Mar 8) Myjinski (USA)–Friendly Echo 61 (Reliance II   —
137) [1990 a6g 6f a6g 5.1m] 600Y: angular gelding: poor mover: second reported foal:
dam poor: little worthwhile form: sold 1,050 gns Doncaster September Sales. *J. L.
Harris.*

SPINNING   3 b. or br.g. Glint of Gold 128–Strathspey 105 (Jimmy Reppin 131) 107 §
[1989 8g* 8d³ 8m 1990 12g⁵ 10m³ 10m* 10.8m* 10f⁴ 12f² 10m² 10d 12g²] tall, rather
leggy, useful-looking gelding: good walker: easy mover: useful performer: favourite, had pacemaker when winning minor events at Pontefract and Warwick (made all
himself, then idled) in June: in frame, including 3 times in Ireland, in Group 2 events
then listed races: stays 1½m: acts on firm going, seems unsuited by a soft surface:
blinkered second start: has worn net muzzle: largely consistent but tends to hang
and is a difficult ride: gelded after final start: not one to trust. *I. A. Balding.*

SPIRIT AWAY   3 b.f. Dominion 123–Jove's Voodoo (USA) 74 (Northern Jove   54
(CAN)) [1989 6f 1990 8g 8m 10.2m 12d³ 12m 12.3g a8g 14m 12g 16.2m⁵ 12m⁵ 12d*
12d²] smallish, sparely-made filly: contested sellers last 3 starts, winning at Edinburgh (no bid) in October: claimed to join M. Pipe £6,001 next time: should stay
beyond 1½m: acts on good to firm ground and dead: ran moderately in blinkers sixth
start. *S. G. Norton.*

SPIRIT OF YOUTH   5 b.m. Kind of Hush 118–Bustle (Busted 134) [1989 NR   —
1990 a14g] sturdy mare: third foal: dam lightly raced and no form: bandaged, tailed
off in maiden at Southwell in June. *M. D. I. Usher.*

SPIRITUALIST   4 ch.c. Simply Great (FR) 122–Parima 72 (Pardao 120) [1989   66
12g² 12.3m 13.6f² 12g a16g² 1990 16.2d 15m⁵ 16m² 16m²] angular colt: has a long
stride: quite modest handicapper: stays 2m: acts well on top-of-the-ground: sold
3,000 gns Doncaster November Sales. *Dr J. D. Scargill.*

SPITFIRE   4 b.c. Shirley Heights 130–Home Fire 99 (Firestreak 125) [1989   92 §
10.2d* 12f³ 10f* 12m⁵ 10m³ 10g³ 9m⁵ 1990 10g 10f 9g 10m] medium-sized,
useful-looking colt: useful winner as 3-y-o: best effort in competitive handicaps in
spring when fifth to Starlet at Kempton: visored, ran poorly at same course (ladies
race) and Sandown (£35,800 handicap) last 2 outings: stays 1½m: acts on firm and
dead going: has sweated and got on edge: has hung, found little and looked a difficult
ride: sold 16,000 gns Newmarket Autumn Sales. *C. R. Nelson.*

SPITFIRE JUBILEE   4 b.c. Chief Singer 131–Altana 71 (Grundy 137) [1989 8d⁶   43
8s 8m 1990 a8g³ a13g³ 10f³ 9s³ 10f⁵ 10m² 11.5m 15.3g⁵] leggy, workmanlike colt:
carries plenty of condition: moderate mover: poor maiden: should stay at least 1½m:
acts on any going: blinkered last 3 outings: winning hurdler in October. *R. J. Hodges.*

SPITHEAD   2 b.c. (May 15) Shareef Dancer (USA) 135–Britannia's Rule 108   —
(Blakeney 126) [1990 7g] seventh foal: half-brother to several winners, including
useful middle-distance stayers Broken Wave (by Bustino), Guarde Royale (by Ile de
Bourbon) and Clifton Chapel (by High Line): dam Oaks third out of half-sister to
Vaguely Noble: backward and coltish, soon led after slow start, headed at halfway
and quickly tailed off in maiden at Salisbury in October. *H. Candy.*

SPITTIN MICK   6 b.g. The Brianstan 128–La Fille 58 (Crooner 119) [1989 5m 5m   42 §
6m³ 5f⁴ 6g³ 5f⁶ 5g⁴ 6h² 6m 6m 6f 6g 5f⁶ 7m³ a7g 1990 6f² 7f⁵ 6m 7m 6f⁴ 6g 6g]
lengthy, smallish gelding: carries condition: moderate mover: poor handicapper:
50/1, appearance to run excellent race on reappearance, but failed to reproduce that
effort: stays 7f: best on a sound surface: occasionally sweats: has run 31 times
without winning since 2 yrs. *G. M. Moore.*

SPITZABIT   6 br.g. Pitskelly 122–Marsabit (Martinmas 128) [1989 5d⁶ 6m 1990   49
a5g 6g 6m⁴ a6g² 6m] leggy gelding: moderate mover: plating-class handicapper:
poorly drawn, tailed off final outing: stays 6f: best form on an easy surface: sometimes on toes: bandaged after reappearance: inconsistent. *Pat Mitchell.*

SPLASHMAN (USA)   4 ch.c. Riverman 131–L'Extravagante (Le Fabuleux 133)   —
[1989 10.1g 10.1m⁴ 10.6g⁴ 10.6s² 12.4g 1990 12g 12d 16.2d⁶ 15.3g⁵ 14f⁴] big, lengthy,
angular colt: poor mover: fair maiden at 3 yrs: easily best effort in 1990 on fourth
outing (wandered): stays 15f: acts on soft going: very upset in stalls final outing at 3
yrs: none too resolute. *J. R. Jenkins.*

EBF Royal Whip Stakes, the Curragh—
Splash of Colour (right) makes ground on Ile de Nisky

SPLASH OF COLOUR 3 ch.c. Rainbow Quest (USA) 134–Cockade 104 **119**
(Derring-Do 131) [1989 NR 1990 10g* 12g* 10g⁶] IR 230,000Y: strong colt: sixth live
foal: half-brother to 4 winners, notably Old Vic (by Sadler's Wells) and smart Irish

Classic Thoroughbreds Plc's "Splash of Colour"

middle-distance filly Green Lucia (by Green Dancer): dam, 1m winner, is sister to High Top and Camden Town: successful at the Curragh in 24-runner maiden (13/8 on, sustained shin injury) in April and Group 3 EBF Royal Whip Stakes (making up a lot of ground final 2f to beat Ile de Nisky 1½ lengths) in August: didn't confirm that considerable promise when 10½ lengths sixth of 8 to Elmaamul in Phoenix Champion Stakes (edgy, showed a quick action), pulling hard then outpaced over 3f out: suited by 1½m. *M. V. O'Brien, Ireland.*

SPLENDID CHAP   3 br.c. Magnolia Lad 102–Splendid Girlie 75 (John Splendid — 116) [1989 NR 1990 10m⁵] close-coupled colt: fourth reported living foal: brother to poor plater/winning hurdler Splendid Magnolia: dam stayed 6f: 100/1 and ridden by 7-lb claimer, soon tailed off in minor event at Leicester in October: mulish at stalls. *Mrs H. Parrott.*

SPODE'S BLUE   3 b.f. Sadler's Wells (USA) 132–Wedgewood Blue (USA) 87   **91** (Sir Ivor 135) [1989 NR 1990 7m⁵ 10g² 7g² 8.5d³ 12d⁴ 10m² 10.6d³ 13.6m* 12.3v* 16.5d³] 49,000Y: rangy filly: good walker: moderate mover: closely related to 7f to 1m winner Minstrel Guest (by Be My Guest) and Bashayer (by Storm Bird), maiden here later successful in USA, both fairly useful: dam, 2-y-o 7f winner, is daughter of top-class filly Furl Sail and half-sister to dam of Green Line Express: fairly useful performer: favourite, made virtually all to win maiden at Redcar and minor event at Chester in October: stays 2m: yet to race on firm going, acts on heavy. *B. Hanbury.*

SPOFFORTH   3 b.g. Jalmood (USA) 126–Visible Form 99 (Formidable (USA)   **65** 125) [1989 7m 8m 8.2f 8s 1990 12f⁴ 12g⁴ 16.2d² 16g⁴ 14f4] quite modest maiden: gave impression would prove best short of 2m: acted on firm and dead ground: winning hurdler: dead. *G. A. Pritchard-Gordon.*

SPOOF   3 b.f. Precocious 126–Thimblerigger 62 (Sharpen Up 127) [1989 6g² 7g   **74** d 1990 8g⁴ 8g² 7.5d⁴ 8d⁴ 10f⁴ 10m⁴ 10m⁵] unfurnished filly: modest maiden: probably best at up to 1m: acts on dead going: blinkered and found little when running creditably third start: has taken keen hold: sold to join M. Hammond 4,300 gns Newmarket Autumn Sales. *W. Jarvis.*

SPORTING LASS   3 br.f. Blakeney 126–Audela 76 (Sovereign Path 125) [1989 — NR 1990 8m⁶ 10f³ 10.6d 8.2v] 2,200F, 4,200Y: lengthy, good-quartered filly: half-sister to some poor animals: dam lightly raced: well beaten in maidens then claimers, hanging third start. *P. A. Kelleway.*

SPORTING SIMON   5 ch.g. Vaigly Great 127–City Link Lass 92 (Double Jump   **81** 131) [1989 12f 10m 8g⁵ 7f³ 7f 7g⁶ 1990 6f² 6g² 6m* 6f* 7g* 6d 6m² 7m 6m 7m* 8d⁴ 7m 7.6v²] workmanlike, plain gelding: moderate mover: much improved, winner of handicaps at Lingfield, Salisbury and Epsom in first half of year and Goodwood (making all) in August: effective at 6f to 1m: acts on any going: has been tried in blinkers: genuine. *B. R. Millman.*

SPORTING WEDNESDAY   5 b.g. Martinmas 128–Philogyny 94 (Philip of   **48** Spain 126) [1989 8.3m 7.6m 1990 11.7g 11.1m⁶ 10m a8g 8f* 7m 8g a8g] leggy gelding: 25/1, ran easily best race for long time when winning apprentice handicap at Salisbury in August, getting up close home despite hanging right: tailed off in handicaps (first for amateurs) after: stays 1m: acts on firm going: has worn net muzzle: trained until after second outing by C. Horgan: best treated with caution. *K. O. Cunningham-Brown.*

SPORTS POST LADY (IRE)   2 ch.f. (Apr 22) M Double M (USA)–Pasadena   **67** Lady (Captain James 123) [1990 5f² 5f² 5m² 5g* 5g a6g] IR 1,000F, IR 2,100Y: angular, sparely-made filly: first foal: dam never ran: sire won from 6f to 9f: quite modest performer: made all in maiden auction at Goodwood in June: speedy: bandaged behind third outing: sold out of J. Berry's stable 3,100 gns Doncaster October Sales before final outing. *C. J. Hill.*

SPOT ON ANNIE   4 gr.f. Miami Springs 121–Hallo Rosie 67 (Swing Easy (USA)   — 126) [1989 6m 6m 5.3h³ 5f 5g* 6m⁴ 5f⁴ 1990 5m 6f 7f 7g 7.6g 6m] leggy filly: has quick action: plating-class handicapper: stays 7f: acts on hard and dead going. *M. Madgwick.*

SPRING DAFFODIL   3 b.f. Pharly (FR) 130–Daffodil Day (Welsh Pageant 132)   **97** [1989 7m 6f⁴ 6m⁵ 7m² 7m 6f⁴ 6m⁵ 10s⁴ 1990 7m 8g² 8g⁵ 7g* 7d* 7g 7m 7m* 7d* 8m*] 5,200Y: fourth foal: dam, twice-raced half-sister to Connaught: progressive filly: 14/1 outsider of 9, led post in Group 3 Mount Coote Stud EBF Matron Stakes at the Curragh final start, beating Sajjaya and Tafila by 2 short heads: earlier successful in handicaps at Tipperary and Limerick (£7,700 event) in May, Tipperary in July and Tralee in August: iron broke in listed race seventh start: seems suited by 1m: acts on good to firm ground and dead. *A. Leahy, Ireland.*

SPRING DRILL 3 ch.f. Blushing Scribe (USA) 107–Targuette (Targowice — (USA) 130) [1989 NR 1990 a7g a8g⁵] 5,800Y: fifth foal: half-sister to 3 winners abroad: dam poor plater: always behind in maidens at Lingfield in January. *D. J. G. Murray-Smith.*

SPRINGFIELD MATCH 5 b.m. Royal Match 117–Petoria 74 (Songedor 116) — [1989 8.5g 8f 8.5m 8m 8.5m⁶ 12.3m 11s 10f⁵ 12.5f a11g 1990 9m⁵] angular, sparely-made mare: has a round action: poor maiden: best at up to 1¼m: needs a sound surface: visored once at 3 yrs, blinkered final start in 1989: has worn severe bridle. *P. Wigham.*

SPRINGFIELD PARK 2 gr.c. (May 18) Belfort (FR) 89–Crimson Dawn — (Manado 130) [1990 5g 5f⁴ 5m] 5,000 (privately) Y: lengthy, rather shallow-girthed colt: has a roundish action: first foal: dam maiden probably stayed 6f: best effort fourth of 6, weakening quickly over 1f out, in maiden at Bath in June: flashed tail in seller on debut. *C. J. Hill.*

SPRING FORWARD 6 b.h. Double Form 130–Forward Princess (USA) 44 § (Forward Pass) [1989 18g⁵ 16s 18s³ 18.4m 19f4 15.8m³ 17.1h4 16g* 18.4f2 15.3m⁵ 16m⁴ 16.2f⁵ 1990 18.4d 17.6m* 14s 16g⁵ 15.8d⁶ 18.4f4 16.5f³ 16f4 16g4 17.6f⁵ 15.5f4] small, leggy horse: usually keeps well: poor handicapper: won at Wolverhampton in May: suited by a test of stamina: acts on any going: has worn blinkers, usually visored nowadays: has sweated and got on edge: tends to get behind: unreliable. *R. E. Peacock.*

SPRING HIGH 3 b.f. Miami Springs 121–High Voltage 82 (Electrify) [1989 5d⁵ — 5m³ 5f4 5m³ 6f* 5f² 5m² 6m 5f³ 5f 1990 5f 5g 6d 5g a7g a6g a8g] tall, leggy, lengthy filly: modest winner at 2 yrs: little form in handicaps and claimers in 1990: best form at 5f: acts on firm going: visored then blinkered (also twice at 2 yrs) last 2 starts: has been bandaged: possibly ungenuine. *K. T. Ivory.*

SPRING MORN (USA) 5 b.g. Alleged (USA) 138–Valenciennes (USA) 57 (Northern Dancer) [1989 10.2m³ 8.2g⁵ 1990 8g 8.2s 10g⁵ 12g* 12.3m⁴ 14m 10.6d] lengthy gelding: won (for first time) handicap at Beverley (hung badly right once in front) in July: suited by 1½m: blinkered fourth to sixth outings: often slowly away. *A. P. Stringer.*

SPRINGS WELCOME 4 b.f. Blakeney 126–Tomfoolery 73 (Silly Season 127) 78 [1989 10f 12f⁵ 11.5m 12.5f* 12f⁵ 14.8m⁵ 10.4m* 10g4 13.3m 12.2d³ 1990 12f 10g 12.3d 12m a12g* a12g* 12.3g² 14g 13d 12v4 a12g³ a12g4 a14g³] workmanlike filly: fair handicapper: successful twice at Southwell in August and showed herself as effective on turf when second at Ripon later in month: stays 1¾m: acts on good to firm and dead going: tends to get well behind: not the easiest of rides. *C. A. Cyzer.*

SPRING TERN (USA) 2 ch.c. (Jan 23) Arctic Tern (USA) 126–Date (USA) 69 (What Luck (USA)) [1990 8g 7m³ 10.2s] $100,000Y: sturdy colt: first foal: dam won at up to 1m: best effort over 2 lengths third of 22 to Il Corsair in maiden at Chepstow in October: soundly beaten but not at all knocked about in minor event at Doncaster after: should be suited by at least 1m: possibly unsuited by soft going. *G. Harwood.*

SPRING TO GLORY 3 b.c. Teenoso (USA) 135–English Spring (USA) 116 57 (Grey Dawn II 132) [1989 7g 1990 10m⁴ 10.8m⁵ 11.5f⁵ 12m* 14m 16m⁵] leggy, angular colt: good mover: plating-class performer: won claimer (claimed out of I. Balding's stable £10,250) at Salisbury in August: little worthwhile form otherwise: lacks turn of foot, and will prove suited by forcing tactics at 2m: in as pacemaker first 2 starts: blinkered second and third: flashes tail. *R. J. Hodges.*

SPRING TO LIGHT (USA) 2 ch.f. (Mar 12) Blushing Groom (FR) 131– 93 Holiday Dancer (USA) (Masked Dancer (USA)) [1990 7g² 7m* 7g²] $800,000Y: third foal: half-sister to winners in North America by General Assembly and Cure The Blues: dam minor stakes winner at up to 9f: Irish filly: odds on, won 8-runner maiden at the Curragh in September by 2 lengths: ½-length second of 6 to Isle of Glass in C L Weld EBF Park Stakes at Phoenix Park later in month: will stay at least 1m. *D. K. Weld, Ireland.*

SPRING TO THE TOP 3 b.c. Thatching 131–Queen of The Brush (Averof 123) 69 p [1989 NR 1990 8m 8m 7g4 6g 7g 7g*] 60,000Y: rather leggy colt: has a round action: sixth foal: closely related to quite useful 1985 Irish 2-y-o 8.5f winner Bristle (by Thatch) and half-brother to 3 other winners, including useful middle-distance stayer Princess Genista (by Ile de Bourbon): dam, Irish 1½m winner, is half-sister to Old Country: well-backed favourite, won handicap at Sandown in September, held up towards rear, switched 2f out then staying on strongly: capable of better, particularly when returned to 1m. *J. W. Payne.*

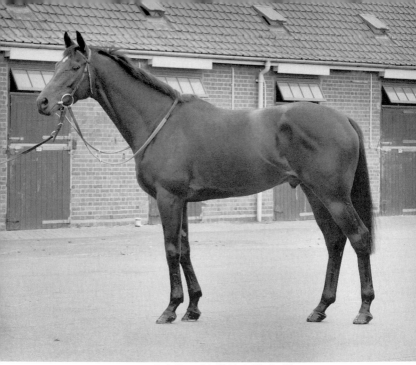

Lady Howard de Walden's "Spritsail"

SPRITSAIL   4 b.c. Kalaglow 132–Set Sail 64 (Alpenkonig (GER)) [1989 9s* 12f* **117**
12d³ 12f* 12f* 12m4 12m* 12v³ 1990 11d³ 12m* 12s³] tall, rather leggy colt: has a
quick action: not seen out until September: well-backed favourite, won listed event
at Newmarket following month by 2½ lengths, always going well, from Ahead:
weakened quite quickly final 1f when third to Down The Flag in St Simon Stakes at
Newbury: suited by 1½m: best form on top-of-the-ground: hung left on reappearance: smart. *H. R. A. Cecil.*

SPROUTING VENTURE   3 ch.f. Crooner 119–Two Diamonds (Double Jump   —
131) [1989 a7g a8g⁵ 1990 a10g a8g⁵ 11.5g 10d 10m 12d] sparely-made filly: plating-
class form at best: stays 1m: usually claimer ridden. *R. Curtis.*

SPURNED (USA)   3 b.f. Robellino (USA) 127–Refill 88 (Mill Reef (USA) 141)   **82**
[1989 6g³ 7m* 7g⁵ 8g⁶ 1990 8.5g² 11.3d 10g 10.1m³ 10m⁶ 10.1g 10g⁵ 11s⁶] lengthy,
rather angular filly: fair performer: stays 1¼m well: acts on good to firm ground:
raced very freely in lead when visored fifth outing. *I. A. Balding.*

SQUEAKY CLEAN   2 b.f. (Mar 18) Precocious 126–Clean Canasta 95 (Silly   —
Season 127) [1990 5f] 2,000F: good-bodied filly: half-sister to fairly useful 6f and
10.1f winner Knave of Trumps (by Great Nephew) and quite modest sprinter Lake
Onega (by Homing): dam 2-y-o 7f winner, is out of sister to Charlottown: backward,
edgy and on toes, slowly away and always behind in maiden at Ripon in April. *M. W.
Easterby.*

SQUIRSKY   4 b.c. Tina's Pet 121–Targos Delight (Targowice (USA) 130) [1989   —
6m 6f 6g 1990 a7g a8g] good-topped, workmanlike colt: carries condition: plating-
class form at best: has shown nothing since 2 yrs: has worn a visor: sold 1,350 gns
Ascot February Sales: possibly ungenuine. *R. Hollinshead.*

STACK ROCK 3 b.f. Ballad Rock 122–One Better 77 (Nebbiolo 125) [1989 NR 71
1990 7.2d 8s⁵ a8g* a7g] IR 1,200Y: robust filly: first foal: dam 1m to 10.1f winner:
20/1, first form in maidens when winning 16-runner event at Southwell in November
by 1½ lengths from Gaiety: ran moderatley in handicap there 2 weeks later: suited
by 1m. *E. J. Alston.*

STAGECRAFT 3 b.c. Sadler's Wells (USA) 132–Bella Colora 119 (Bellypha 130) **110** p
[1989 7d² 1990 10g³ 10.5g* 10g*] strong, lengthy colt: has plenty of scope: good
walker: second favourite, won 7-runner listed event at Newmarket in November in
very good style by ¾ length from Philharmonia, held up, quickening clear over 1f
out then eased last ½f: earlier successful in maiden (went down well, showing a
sharp action on first run for 4½ months) at York: will be well suited by 1½m: looked
really well last 2 starts: progressing extremely well, sure to win more races. *M. R.
Stoute.*

STAIRWAY TO HEAVEN (IRE) 2 b.f. (Mar 13) Godswalk (USA) 130– 74
Cathryn's Song (Prince Tenderfoot (USA) 126) [1990 6f* 7m² 6d² 7d* 7s a8g* a8g³
a8g*] IR 3,500F, 10,500Y: angular, sparely-made filly: second foal: half-sister to
4-y-o Katy's Lad (by Camden Town), successful at 5f (at 2 yrs) and 1m: dam never
ran: successful in sellers at Doncaster (bought out of R. J. R. Williams' stable 16,000
gns) in July and Catterick (no bid) in October and in claimers at Southwell in
November and December: will stay beyond 1m: acts on firm and dead going: suitable
ride for apprentice: genuine. *T. D. Barron.*

STAMFORD BRIDGE 2 b.c. (Apr 23) Dominion 123–Meadowbank 86 70
(Northfields (USA)) [1990 5f⁵ 6g⁵ 5m³ 5g² 6m⁶ 5m⁶ 6f 6d] 8,000F, 14,000Y: sturdy
colt: has a round action: first foal: dam 2-y-o 6f winner, is granddaughter of Sookera:
modest performer: won maiden at Haydock in May: ran poorly 3 of last 4 starts:
stays 6f. *M. Brittain.*

STANDING COUNT 4 ch.g. Stanford 121§–Barefoot Contessa (Homeric 133) 59
[1989 7s² 8g³ 7f² 8f⁶ 8g² 8.2g³ 8.2g 10.2g 1990 6s 8m³] leggy, angular gelding: good
mover: modest handicapper at best: effective at 7f and 1m: acted on any going: dead.
Mrs J. R. Ramsden.

STANDING ROOM ONLY 3 b.g. Stalwart (USA)–Mary Mary Mouse (USA) 69
(Valdez (USA)) [1989 7m⁴ 6m 7g 6f⁴ 1990 8m 8f³ 8m 8g⁵ 10f³ 12m⁵ 12m* 12m*
13.8d] strong, lengthy gelding: has a quick action: modest performer: won claimers
at Newmarket (made most, claimed out of H. Candy's stable £7,200) in August and
Leicester (gamely, claimed out of Mrs J. Ramsden's stable £9,059) in September:
should stay further than 1½m: acts on firm (possibly unsuited by dead) going:
blinkered 5 times, including when successful. *C. R. Beever.*

STANE STREET (IRE) 2 b.f. (Mar 29) Gorytus (USA) 132–Tumble Ria —
(Tumble Wind (USA)) [1990 a7g a8g⁶] 11,500Y: first foal: dam, winner in Belgium, is

*James Seymour Stakes, Newmarket—
fast-improving Stagecraft (left) wins easing up from Philharmonia*

sister to Cooliney Prince and half-sister to Kribensis: poor form in maiden and claimer at Southwell. *P. J. Makin.*

STANSTED FLYER 4 b.g. Rabdan 129–Maputo Princess (Raga Navarro (ITY) 119) [1989 7.5d[4] 8.2g[6] 7m 8g 9s 12g 1990 a8g a14g] small, sparely-made gelding: poor mover: plater: no form since first outing at 3 yrs: should be suited by further than 7.5f: suited by a soft surface: sometimes blinkered, visored final outing (tailed off). *J. F. Bottomley.* —

STANWAY 3 b.g. Sandhurst Prince 128–Spring Bride 57 (Auction Ring (USA) 123) [1989 6m 7m[3] 7m[2] 7h[5] 7m[4] 1990 10g 10f 8m[2] 9g[4] 11.7m[4] 12m[5] 10m[4]] strong, good-topped gelding: quite modest maiden: stays 1½m: best efforts on top-of-the-ground, and acts on hard: blinkered 4 times: races keenly: joined T. Casey. *R. Hannon.* **63**

STAPLEFORD LADY 2 ch.f. (May 17) Bairn (USA) 126–Marie Galante (FR) (King of The Castle (USA)) [1990 6g 7m 8d[5]] leggy, angular filly: has scope: half-sister to several minor winners in France: dam unraced half-sister to champion 1974 French 2-y-o Mariacci: quite modest maiden: easily best effort second start. *M. Johnston.* **65**

STAPLEFORD MANOR (USA) 3 br.c. Riverman (USA) 131–Round The Rosie (USA) (Cornish Prince) [1989 NR 1990 8m[2] 8m* 10.1m* 10m[2] 12g[4]] $700,000Y: tall, quite attractive colt: somewhat unfurnished: half-brother to several winners here and abroad, including very useful 7f and 1m performer Shmaireekh (by Super Concorde) and the dam of 1990 Grade 2 winner Jovial: dam 2-y-o 6f winner: landed odds in maiden at York in June and minor event at Windsor in July: good second in £7,800 event at Newbury, travelling strongly in lead then not finding as much as seemed likely final 1f: 11/8 on, weakened final 2f in listed race at Doncaster 8 weeks later: suited by 1¼m. *L. M. Cumani.* **104**

STAPLEFORD PARK (IRE) 2 b. or br.c. (Feb 24) Runnett 125–Spoons (Orchestra 118) [1990 a6g] IR 3,200F: dipped-backed colt: fourth foal: dam never ran: slowly away and always behind in seller at Southwell in July: sold 600 gns Doncaster October Sales. *J. Wharton.* —

STARA 3 b.f. Star Appeal 133–Saucy Flirt 102 (King's Troop 118) [1989 NR 1990 12m[5] 14f[6]] leggy, angular filly: sister to Prix de Diane winner Madam Gay and half-sister to 3 winners, including fairly useful 1¾m winner British (by Blakeney): dam stayed 6f: 25/1 and green, slow-starting fifth of 8 to Millionaire's Row at Newbury (showed a quick action), clearly better effort in maidens. *A. C. Stewart.* —

STARARCHY 4 b. or br.g. Starch Reduced 112–Good Sport (True Song 95) [1989 NR 1990 a11g] first reported foal: dam placed once in selling hurdle: always behind in claimer at Southwell in February. *G. H. Jones.* —

STAR BLAZE 3 b.f. Alzao (USA) 117–Space Mark (On Your Mark 125) [1989 6m 5m[4] 5g[6] 1990 5f 6f 8.3g] small filly: quite modest maiden: well beaten in 1990, in selling handicap last time: should stay beyond 5f. *M. J. Bolton.* —

STARCHY BELLE 3 b.f. Starch Reduced 112–Ty-With-Belle (Pamroy 99) [1989 5f* 6m 7f 1990 7m[4] 5f 6s 7g 6m 6m] dipped-backed, unfurnished filly: plater: easily best effort as 3-y-o on reappearance: should stay 7f. *B. Palling.* —

STARCHY COVE 3 br.f. Starch Reduced 112–Rosey Covert (Sahib 114) [1989 5g[6] 5d[6] 5f[2] 5m[5] 5g[5] 5f[5] 5f[3] 6m[3] 5f* 6g a5g[4] a6g[6] a5g[2] 1990 6m[6] 5m[5] 5m[5] 6g 5g[3] 6m* 6g 5f[3] 6f[2] 6m 6g 6g] leggy filly: plating-class handicapper: won at Chepstow in June: effective at 5f and 6f: probably best on top-of-the-ground: has sweated up: has run creditably for 7-lb claimer and when on toes. *R. Hollinshead.* **57**

STARCHYS IMAGE 2 b.c. (Apr 10) Starch Reduced 112–Mrs Dumbfounded (Adropejo 114) [1990 8.2m 6g[4] 7m[5]] compact colt: sixth foal: brother to a poor maiden and half-brother to 8.2f winner Baker's Double (by Rapid River): dam bad plater: quite modest maiden: probably stays 1m. *B. Palling.* **65**

STAR CONNECTION 2 b.f. (Mar 28) Faustus (USA) 118–Emerald Rocket 69 (Green God 128) [1990 5g[4] 5m[2] 5m[4] 5g[3] a5g[4]] 23,000Y: workmanlike, good-quartered filly: carries condition: has scope: moderate mover: sixth foal: half-sister to 4 winners, including 3-y-o Mademoiselle Chloe (by Night Shift), useful 5f winner at 2 yrs, and fair 1985 2-y-o Mandrake Madam (by Madrake Major): dam 1m winner: plating-class maiden: ran moderately in blinkers at Southwell final start. *J. Berry.* **55**

STAR EXHIBIT 3 ch.c. Exhibitioner 111–Star Bound (Crowned Prince (USA) 128) [1989 a8g 1990 a6g[6] a7g] workmanlike colt: well beaten in maiden and (slowly away) claimers: sold 680 gns Doncaster October Sales. *R. Hollinshead.* —

STAR GLORY   2 b.f. (Apr 1) Star Appeal 133–Rapid Glory 75 (Hittite Glory 125)   **44**
[1990 6m³ 5.8h 6g⁶ a7g² a6g a7g⁵] 4,000F, 625Y: small filly: second foal: dam 2-y-o
5f winner below form at 3 yrs: modest plater: better suited by 7f than shorter:
inconsistent. *P. A. Kelleway.*

STAR HILL   3 b.c. Star Appeal 133–Pook's Hill (High Top 131) [1989 5f² 6f* 6m²   **89**
6h* 6f* 6g* 6g⁶ 7.3d⁴ 1990 8g 8d⁴ 8f² 6m 6m 8m] strong, lengthy colt: shows a
quick action: fairly useful performer, not seen out after July: second in handicap at
Salisbury, best effort as 3-y-o: suited by 1m: acts on hard and dead ground: tends to
wander: genuine. *W. G. R. Wightman.*

ST ARILDA   3 b.f. Pas de Seul 133–St Isabel (Saint Crespin III 132) [1989 NR 1990   **—**
8f 10.4g⁴ 12f⁴ 16m] 3,200F: close-coupled filly: closely related to fair 12.3f winner
High Skies (by Shirley Heights) and half-sister to several winners here and abroad,
including smart 1m and 1¼m winner Pelorus (by High Top): dam won over 1m and
1¼m in France: quite modest maiden at best: soundly beaten facing very stiff task in
handicap: will be suited by further than 1½m: sold 2,000 gns Newmarket December
Sales. *H. Candy.*

STARK SOUTH (USA)   2 ch.c. (Apr 25) Dixieland Band (USA)–Miss Stark   **98**
(USA) (His Majesty) [1990 7m* 7g* 7d⁵ 7d⁵] IR 32,000Y: rangy colt: fluent mover:
first foal: dam minor winner at up to 1¼m in USA: useful Irish colt: won maiden at
Phoenix Park (heavily-backed favourite) in August and 17-runner minor event at
Kempton (quickening to lead 1½f out and running on well to beat Living Image 1½
lengths) in September: around 7 lengths fifth of 8, staying on having been outpaced
over 2f out, to Generous in Three Chimneys Dewhurst Stakes at Newmarket on
final start: will stay 1m. *Michael Kauntze, Ireland.*

STAR LEADER   3 b.f. Kafu 120–Sweet Relief 90 (Sweet Revenge 129) [1989 5f   **58**
5m⁶ 5m⁴ 5m⁴ 6d a6g 1990 6f⁶ 8m⁴ 6f⁵ 7g³ 7m* 8m 7m 8.2s] tall, short-backed filly:
moderate mover: plater: best effort when winning 22-runner handicap (no bid) at

Stark South Syndicate's "Stark South"

Newmarket in September: stays 7f: possibly unsuited by very firm going: suitable mount for apprentice, though sometimes slowly away. *R. Hollinshead.*

STARLET 4 b.f. Teenoso (USA) 135–Pas de Deux 80 (Nijinsky (CAN) 138) **119** [1989 11v 12d⁶ 1990 12g* 12s⁵ 10g* 10g* 10m* 10f² 10.5g* 10m²]

In terms of prize money won, the Queen recorded her best total as an owner-breeder in the latest season. This was due in no small part to the efforts of Starlet who made such great strides at four that she ended the year one of the leading older fillies in Europe at a mile and a quarter. Starlet's season can be divided into two. She was raced eight times in all and after her fourth start was sent to visit Sharrood. Fillies have been known to improve considerably when in foal—English Spring, Golden Flats, Minizen Lass and Sleepers are recent examples—and Starlet did the same. On her first start after being covered she trounced an admittedly below-par Theatrical Charmer by eight lengths in the listed Racal-Vodafone Stakes at Kempton in late-June then went on to finish an excellent runner-up to Kartajana in both the Vodafone Nassau Stakes and Sun Chariot Stakes. At Goodwood she kept on determinedly in the last quarter mile without ever quite getting on terms, eventually beaten two lengths but pulling four lengths clear of Moon Cactus; whilst at Newmarket, although undoubtedly flattered to finish within a length and a half of the winner—Kartajana was allowed to coast home in the last furlong having quickened at least six lengths clear entering the Dip—she again finished well clear of the remainder, this time headed by Filia Ardross. A comfortable two-and-a-half-length success in the Group 2 Team Trophy der Volksbanken und Raiffeisenbanken at Frankfurt was sandwiched between those efforts.

Starlet had begun the season very lightly raced. She'd shaped with a good deal of promise when unbeaten in two starts as a youngster, but had been very slow coming to hand at three and didn't reappear until late-season, finishing down the field in two handicaps. She regained winning ways as early as mid-February in 1990 though, in a minor event at Cagnes-sur-Mer, then finished a good fifth in a listed event there. On her French form Starlet was on a favourable handicap mark in the spring and took full advantage. Despite swerving left when in front a furlong out, she ran out a four-length winner of the Rosebery Handicap at Kempton in April and followed up under a penalty in the City And Suburban at Epsom, beating Hateel a couple of lengths.

		Youth	Ack Ack
	Teenoso (USA)	(b 1973)	Gazala II
	(b or br 1980)	Furioso	Ballymoss
Starlet		(b 1971)	Violetta III
(b.f. 1986)		Nijinsky	Northern Dancer
	Pas de Deux	(b 1967)	Flaming Page
	(ch 1974)	Example	Exbury
		(ch 1968)	Amicable

Starlet is the sixth foal of Pas de Deux, and one of three raced in Britain in the latest season. Starlet's three-year-old sister Once Upon A Time showed fair form over middle distances but, in marked contrast to Starlet, was possibly of unsatisfactory temperament. Their five-year-old half-brother Unknown Quantity (by Young Generation) had another good season, placed three times in valuable mile-and-a-quarter handicaps. Pas de Deux's other four foals of racing age have all been successful. They include the middle-distance stayer Insular (by Moulton), a winner ten times on the flat at up to two miles and also over hurdles and fences. Pas de Deux is now in foal to Unfuwain. A winner as a three-year-old over a mile and a quarter, she's a daughter of the Park Hill Stakes winner Example, who is a sister to the Ribblesdale Stakes winner Expansive. Amicable, Starlet's great-grandam, holds the distinction of winning the Nell Gwyn Stakes on her debut. From four other starts she managed to finish second in the Yorkshire Oaks. Starlet, a sparely-made filly, won over a mile and a half but showed easily her best form at a mile and a quarter on a sound surface. *W. Hastings-Bass.*

STARLIGHT FLYER 3 b.c. In Fijar (USA) 121–Nareen (USA) (The Minstrel **80** (CAN) 135) [1989 NR 1990 7g 8.2s⁴ 8g² 8m*dis 10.5m 10.1g 7g] workmanlike,

Westminster-Motor (Taxi) Insurance City And Suburban Handicap, Epsom—
Starlet defies her penalty, pulling away after being switched outside Hateel

good-bodied colt: carries condition: second foal: dam, ran twice in France, from family of Sauce Boat, Raja Baba and Gay Mecene: modest form: won maiden (disqualified after steroid test) at Pontefract in June, making virtually all: well beaten in handicaps (faced very stiff tasks) and minor event afterwards: takes keen hold and may prove best at up to 1m, though bred to stay 1¼m: blinkered except fourth and sixth starts. *M. Moubarak.*

STAR LORD 4 b.c. Lord Gayle (USA) 124–Crack of Light 95 (Salvo 129) [1989 **89** 11.7m² 12m² 14m* 11v² 1990 12m³ 14g 12m] angular, sparely-made colt: good mover with a long stride: fairly useful winner late as 3-y-o: shaped most promisingly in £6,700 handicap at York in July: ran poorly in Tote Ebor (co-favourite) and £7,600 handicap after: probably stays 1¾m: acts on good to firm and heavy going: takes keen hold. *A. C. Stewart.*

STAR NEWS 2 b.g. (Apr 12) Tremblant 112–Blakesware Saint 74 (Welsh Saint **45** 126) [1990 6m³ 6v⁴] 1,300Y: angular gelding: fourth live foal: half-brother to 6f winner Norton Melody (by Absalom): dam 5f winner: poor form in auction events at Pontefract and Ayr over 2 months later: withdrawn after failing to pull up after false start at Southwell in November: should stay 7f. *M. H. Tompkins.*

STAR OF ARAGON 2 b.c. (Mar 6) Aragon 118–Chart Climber (Song 132) [1990 **53** 5g 5m⁶ 5g² 5g² 5g³ 5d 5f⁵ 6h⁴ 6m 5g⁴ 7g 6m] 5,400F, 3,300Y: leggy colt: moderate mover: first foal: dam placed at 6f, is out of half-sister to Irish Oaks winner Celina: fair plater: stays 6f: blinkered final outing: has sweated up: has worn a tongue strap: inconsistent: sold 1,500 gns Doncaster October Sales. *Ronald Thompson.*

STAR OF FASHION 3 b.f. Comedy Star (USA) 121–Fashion Lover 70 (Shiny **—** Tenth 120) [1989 5f 5g 1990 9s 10g] close-coupled, good-topped filly: poor maiden: should stay 1m. *P. A. Blockley.*

STAR OF GDANSK (USA) 2 ch.c. (May 4) Danzig Connection (USA)–Star **99**
Empress (USA) (Disciplinarian) [1990 6g* 7g³ 8g²] $55,000Y: half-brother to 3
winners, including Grade 3 1m winner W D Jacks (by Matsadoon): dam minor stakes
winner at up to 7f: odds on, won 11-runner maiden at the Curragh in July: good
second to Misty Valley in Panasonic Smurfit EBF Futurity Stakes at the Curragh in
September: will stay 1¼m: fairly useful. *J. S. Bolger, Ireland.*

STAR OF THE FUTURE (USA) 3 b.f. El Gran Senor (USA) 136–Promising **100**
Girl (USA) (Youth (USA) 135) [1989 7f* 7.3v⁴ 1990 8.2m* 10m⁴ 9s³ 8m³] smallish,
angular filly: moderate mover: useful performer: most impressive winner of minor
event at Haydock in May: ran well in listed race (outpaced early) at Newbury, Prix
Chloe at Evry and listed event (favourite) at Leopardstown: stayed 1¼m: possibly
unsuited by heavy going: stud. *B. W. Hills.*

STAR OF THE GLEN 4 b.g. Glenstal (USA) 118–Bamstar 70 (Relko 136) [1989 —
8f 11m 13.3g 1990 16.5d] angular, lengthy gelding: little worthwhile form on flat:
should stay at least 1m: winning hurdler as juvenile. *C. A. Horgan.*

STAR OF THE SEA 3 gr.f. Absalom 128–River Chimes 43 (Forlorn River 124) —
[1989 5g 5m⁴ 6m 5s 1990 6m 5m 6g 8m 6m] small, lengthy filly: has a round action:
poor maiden: should prove suited by further than 5f: blinkered, taken down early
and gave trouble at stalls final start. *N. Chamberlain.*

STAR QUEST 3 b.c. Rainbow Quest (USA) 134–Sarah Siddons (FR) 122 (Le — p
Levanstell 122) [1989 NR 1990 12m⁶] half-brother to several winners here and
abroad, notably Irish Oaks winner Princess Pati (by Top Ville) and high-class
middle-distance performer Seymour Hicks (by Ballymore): dam won Irish 1000
Guineas and Yorkshire Oaks: 20/1 and green, about 10 lengths sixth of 8 to
Millionaire's Row in maiden at Newbury in July, held up taking keen hold then
wandering and one pace over 2f out. *R. Charlton.*

STARRLYN 4 ch.f. Star Appeal 133–Petingalyn (Petingo 135) [1989 8.5s 10.2m⁵ **42**
10f⁴ 12m⁵ 10m³ 9g 10g⁵ 1990 8g⁴ a10g³ 10.2f 9f 10.8m] tall, rather leggy filly: poor
maiden: best form over 1¼m: acts on firm going: sold 1,000 gns Newmarket September Sales. *S. Dow.*

STAR SHAREEF 4 b.c. Shareef Dancer (USA) 135–Anne Stuart (FR) (Bolkon- —
ski 134) [1989 12f⁵ 12m³ 1990 12m³ 11.7m] well-made colt: 3¼ lengths third in
Derby Italiano at Rome in May, 1989: ran poorly in 4-runner handicap at Doncaster
(keen to post, hung throughout straight) and minor event at Windsor in summer:
stays 1½m: acts on good to firm and soft going: looked unsuited by track at Lingfield
on reappearance at 3 yrs. *B. Hanbury.*

STARSTREAK 3 b.c. Comedy Star (USA) 121–Kochia 54 (Firestreak 125) [1989 **113**
6m⁶ 6g² 6m* 6m 7g* 1990 8v* 10m* 10g² 10m⁴ 12m² 10.6m³ 12g⁵ 10d⁶] rangy,
deep-girthed colt: easy mover: smart performer: won minor event at Ayr in April
and £9,100 contest at Ascot in May: very good second in Prix La Force at
Longchamp and Gordon Stakes at Goodwood: ran rather in snatches and tended to
hang on turn in Great Voltigeur Stakes at York penultimate start: stays 1½m: yet to
race on very firm going, acts on any other: game and consistent. *M. Johnston.*

STAR SYSTEM (IRE) 2 b.f. (Apr 14) Burslem 123–Wisdom To Know (Bay —
Express 132) [1990 6s] 3,500 (privately) Y: smallish, lengthy filly: third foal: dam
placed at 6f, only season to race: soundly beaten in maiden claimer at Hamilton in
November. *M. O'Neill.*

STAR TRACKER 3 br.f. Lochnager 132–Star Attention 91 (Northfields (USA)) —
[1989 6g 6g 1990 9g 5m 6f⁴ 6h⁶ 7f 6g⁶] small filly: poor form, including in handicaps:
may be ideally suited by 7f. *W. A. Stephenson.*

STATAJACK (IRE) 2 b.g. (May 10) King of Clubs 124–Statira 103 (Skymaster **73** p
126) [1990 a7g⁴ a8g*] IR 21,000Y: half-brother to 5 winners here and abroad,
notably good-class sprinter Statoblest (by Ahonoora): dam 5f winner at 2 yrs: half-
sister to smart sprinters Most Secret and Artaxerxes: short-priced favourite, won
7-runner maiden at Lingfield in December by 8 lengths from Twilight Flame: likely
to improve further. *D. R. C. Elsworth.*

STATE BANK 4 b.g. Kampala 120–Lily Bank 73 (Young Generation 129) [1989 —
9g 10g 12m⁶ 10m 12g² 11s 12g⁴ 1990 a12g a13g a10g⁵] rather leggy gelding: quite
modest maiden at best: well beaten in claimers and handicap at Lingfield late in
year: stays 1½m: best form on an easy surface: blinkered twice (including final
outing), visored once at 3 yrs. *A. Moore.*

STATE DANCER (USA) 3 b.c. El Gran Senor (USA) 136–Bimbo Sue (USA) **82**
(Our Michael (USA)) [1989 NR 1990 8m 8f 8f³ 8m* 7m 8m⁵] $825,000Y: angular,
lengthy colt: poor mover: fifth foal: half-brother to 3 winners in USA, including

useful 1985 2-y-o Danny's Keys (by Dewan Keys) and Grade 3 9f winner Do It Again Dan (by Mr Leader): dam successful in 5 sprint races in USA: won 4-runner maiden at Ripon in August: well beaten facing stiff tasks after: likely to prove best at around 1m. *M. Moubarak*.

STATE FLYER 2 ch.g. (Mar 25) Flying Tyke 90–Sunshine State (Roi Soleil 125) **68** [1990 6m² 7m³ 7f⁶] second foal: dam unraced: quite modest form, keeping on well, in maiden at Redcar and slowly-run minor event at York first 2 starts: ran moderately in visor after: ridden by 7-lb claimer. *G. R. Oldroyd*.

STATELY MARCH 2 b.f. (May 12) State Trooper 96–Musical Piece 91 (Song **64** 132) [1990 5.1m 6d³ 6m* 6m 6d⁶ 6d a5g⁶ a6g] very small filly: moderate mover: sister to 3-y-o Knight of Kirkton and half-sister to 1983 2-y-o 6f seller winner Dancing Orange (by Orange Bay) and a winner in Norway: dam best at sprint distances: made all in 10-runner seller (sold out of B. Hanbury's stable 6,000 gns) at Yarmouth, beating Mrs Barton 8 lengths: ran creditably first start on all-weather late in year: stays 6f: bandaged behind final start. *R. W. Stubbs*.

STATE OF AFFAIRS 3 b.c. Free State 125–Trigamy 112 (Tribal Chief 125) **78** d [1989 6g³ 6f⁴ 8d 1990 8f* 8m* 8m 7g 9g 8g] strong, sturdy colt: moderate mover: modest form at best: led 1f out and tended to idle when winning maiden auction race at Thirsk in April and moderately-run claimer (claimed out of R. Hollinshead's stable £22,000) at Warwick in May: well beaten in handicaps: stays 1m: best efforts on top-of-the-ground. *C. A. Horgan*.

STATION EXPRESS (IRE) 2 b.g. (Mar 10) Rusticaro (FR) 124–Vallee d'O **63** (FR) (Polyfoto 124) [1990 6g 6g⁵ 7g 7f 7f* 8.2g 7f³ 7d] IR 2,000Y, 1,000 2-y-o: smallish gelding: first foal: dam won at 9.2f in France: won claimer at Carlisle in September, showing vastly improved form: respectable staying-on third in seller at Redcar after: should stay 1m: acts well on firm ground. *R. Hollinshead*.

STATOBLEST 4 b.c. Ahonoora 122–Statira 103 (Skymaster 125) [1989 **120** 6g* 6m³ 6m² 5m* 5f² 5f* 5m³ 5g* 5g 1990 5f* 5m³ 5d 5f⁶ 5m² 6g 5g⁴]
Along with Nabeel Dancer and Tigani, Statoblest represented the best of the sprinters of 1989 kept in training. Each of their latest campaigns had its disappointments, and the trio managed just two wins between them. Statoblest's sole success came on his reappearance in the Palace House Stakes at Newmarket where, at a shade of odds on, he got the verdict over Boozy only by the narrowest of margins. The second and third (Blyton Lad) raced wide of the main body of the field against the stand rail, and Statoblest had to

Palace House Stakes, Newmarket—Statoblest (left) makes a winning reappearance, by the narrowest of margins from Boozy; Blyton Lad (centre) is a close third

Mr Richard L. Duchossois' "Statoblest"

overcome the disadvantage of racing with the slower group which was around three lengths down on Boozy at halfway. After seeming to falter a furlong out, he was driven out with hands and heels and prevailed on the nod. Appealing as the type to improve further at four, Statoblest looked a leading contender for top honours over five furlongs. That wasn't, however, taking into account Dayjur who, by that stage, had just a victory in a Nottingham minor event to his credit as a three-year-old. In five of his six remaining races Statoblest had no answer to Dayjur's phenomenal pace. He never finished any closer to Dayjur than the two and a half lengths he was beaten in the Sears Temple Stakes at Sandown later in May, but comfortably his best effort came in the Keeneland Nunthorpe Stakes at York, a race in which Dayjur lowered the course record by more than a second and produced one of the finest performances from a sprinter in many years. Statoblest went the pace set by Dayjur much more comfortably than any of the others and closed the gap to not much more than a length approaching the final furlong. When Dayjur hit top speed, however, Statoblest couldn't respond and he went down by four lengths, two in front of the third Pharaoh's Delight. He deserved to take the runner-up spot again in the Ciga Prix de l'Abbaye de Longchamp inasmuch as he chased Dayjur from the outset, but he couldn't quite sustain his effort and faded into fourth close home. On the two other occasions Statoblest took on Dayjur—in the King's Stand Stakes at Royal Ascot and the Ladbroke Sprint Cup at Haydock—ground conditions weren't ideal and he was beaten more than a dozen lengths.

Statoblest (b.c. 1986)	Ahonoora (ch 1975)	Lorenzaccio (ch 1965)	Klairon
			Phoenissa
		Helen Nichols (ch 1966)	Martial
			Quaker Girl
	Statira (b 1969)	Skymaster (ch 1958)	Golden Cloud
			Discipliner
		Parysatis (b 1960)	Darius
			Leidenschaft

Statoblest has been retired to the Brook Stud, Newmarket, where he'll stand at £3,000 with the October 1st concession. An attractive, strong-quartered colt with a quick action, he is one of six winners produced by the now-deceased Statira, whose eighth and final foal Statajack (by King of Clubs) got off the mark at the final all-weather meeting of the year at Lingfield. Statira's other winners include Ludova (by Right Tack), successful at six furlongs in France as a two-year-old and later a stakes-placed winner in America. A half-sister to smart sprinters Artaxerxes and Most Secret, Statira showed useful form over sprint distances at two but failed to train on. She's a daughter of the unraced Parysatis and granddaughter of Leidenschaft, a top-class winner in Germany. Statoblest, who often wore small bandages behind, was best at five furlongs on a sound surface. He sometimes found less off the bridle than seemed likely judged on the fluency with which he travelled through his races. *L. M. Cumani.*

STAUB 4 b.f. Konigsstuhl (GER)–Sauhatz (GER) (Alpenkonig (GER)) [1989 NR 1990 10m] small, sparely-made filly: poor form, including in sellers. *M. H. Tompkins.* —

STAUNCH RIVAL (USA) 3 b.g. Sir Ivor 135–Crystal Bright 75 (Bold Lad (IRE) 133) [1989 8.2g⁶ 8g³ 1990 10f⁶ a8g* 9g 10f* 10f 10f⁴ 8.2d] leggy, close-coupled gelding: shows knee action: modest performer: easily best 3-y-o efforts when successful in maiden (dead-heated) at Southwell in May and handicap at Yarmouth in July: suited by 1¼m: acts on firm going: raced freely in visor on reappearance: sold to join G. Thorner 6,000 gns Newmarket Autumn Sales: hung badly left and looked none too keen sixth start, and isn't one to trust. *J. Gosden.* 71 §

STAY AWAKE 4 ch.g. Anfield 117–Djimbaran Bay (Le Levanstell 122) [1989 6d 6m 7f⁵ 6m⁵ 8g 7f³ 1990 9s* 10.6v] rangy gelding: hobdayed: quite modest handicapper: apprentice ridden, won at Hamilton in May, hanging badly left last 1f: soundly beaten at Haydock nearly 5 months later: stays 9f: acts on any going: won 3 times over hurdles in 1989/90. *J. J. O'Neill.* 61

ST CADOC 5 ch.g. Caerleon (USA) 132–Melody (USA) 96 (Lord Gayle (USA) 124) [1989 8g⁶ 11m³ 12d⁴ 13s 17.6f² 13.8d a14g 1990 13v 12g 14g] sturdy, good-quartered gelding: one-time useful performer but has deteriorated considerably: seems to stay 17.6f: best form on an easy surface: disappointing. *W. Storey.* —

STEALTHY 3 ch.f. Kind of Hush 118–Misty Cat (USA) (Misty Flight) [1989 6f² 6f 6d 1990 8m² 8d⁵ a8g* a8g⁵] rangy filly: quite modest performer: made all in claimer at Lingfield in November: should stay beyond 1m: acts on firm going. *J. Akehurst.* 62

STEAM AHEAD 2 b.g. (Feb 22) All Systems Go 119–Mature (Welsh Pageant 132) [1990 5m² 6g⁴ 6f² 6m² 6m* 6d⁵ 6m³ 7m³ 7g] tall, leggy, close-coupled gelding: has a quick, fluent action: fourth living foal: brother to a plating-class maiden and half-brother to 1¼m seller winner Carbo Booster (by Good Times): dam, maiden, ran best race over 7f: fair performer: won maiden at Hamilton in August by 6 lengths from Heriz: better efforts after when placed in Newmarket nurseries: held up and never dangerous in mixed-aged event at latter course final start: stays 7f well: acts on good to firm ground and dead. *J. W. Watts.* 83

STEAMER DUCK (USA) 2 ch.c. (Jan 28) Bering 136–Lavender Mist (FR) 91 (Troy 137) [1990 7g⁴ 7.5g² 7.5g⁴ 8g⁴ 10g* 8v*] first foal: dam 7f and 1¼m winner, is half-sister to very useful 1984 French staying 2-y-o Hello Bill: very useful French colt: much improved late in year, winning minor event at Fontainebleu and Gran Criterium (by a short head from Akeem) at Milan: will stay 1½m: evidently suited by the mud. *Mme C. Head, France.* 113

STEEL CYGNET 7 gr.g. Taufan (USA) 119–Swan Girl (My Swanee 122) [1989 10d² 10s⁶ 10f⁶ 10.2h* 10g 1990 10.1g] small, light-framed gelding: won selling handicap at Bath in June, 1989: well beaten both subsequent outings: effective at 1¼m and 1½m: probably acts on any going: usually blinkered or visored: bandaged 2 of last 3 starts: sold 1,000 gns Ascot July Sales. *G. P. Enright.* —

STEEL DANCE 2 b.g. (Feb 26) Mashhor Dancer (USA)–Damaska (USA) — (Damascus (USA)) [1990 7g] workmanlike gelding: second foal: half-brother to 11f seller winner Taskalady (by Touching Wood): dam unraced: backward, slowly away and always behind in maiden at Sandown in September: went freely down. *M. Blanshard.*

STEEL RIVER 3 b.c. Be My Native (USA) 122–Oystons Propweekly 74 (Swing — Easy (USA) 126) [1989 6f 6g 1990 8m 10m6 12g 10d] big, angular colt: plating-class maiden: should stay beyond 6f: joined D. Dutton. *A. M. Robson.*

STEERFORTH (IRE) 2 b.c. (May 20) Lomond (USA) 128–Waffles 100 (Wollow 79 132) [1990 7f* 7m] 42,000F, 49,000Y: brother to 3-y-o Waffling and closely related to Irish 6f winner Great Shearwater (by Storm Bird): dam French 9f winner, is out of 1000 Guineas winner Night Off: won 5-runner maiden at Yarmouth in July: around 7 lengths eighth of 17, never able to challenge, in Tattersalls Tiffany Highflyer Stakes at Newmarket month later: will stay 1m. *A. C. Stewart.*

STELBY 6 ch.h. Stetchworth (USA) 120–Little Trilby 107 (Tyrant (USA)) [1989 66 7m6 6m6 7f3 6m2 6g3 6m5 6m4 7g2 8f6 7f5 8g 1990 7g4 6g 6m5 6g5 8.5f6 6h* 6m* 6m 6m 5f5 7m] small, quite well-made horse: good mover: modest handicapper: won at Carlisle in July and Pontefract in August: best at 6f or 7f: best on a sound surface: has run well when sweating: has hung and often got behind: sold 1,300 gns Doncaster November Sales. *O. Brennan.*

STELLA BIANCA (USA) 3 b.f. Vaguely Noble 140–Cahard (USA) (Lyphard 76 (USA) 132) [1989 6m2 7m4 7m3 1990 12g6 10.5g 8m 10d3 10m* 10f 10f5 12g] compact, workmanlike filly: shows traces of stringhalt: has a rather round action: modest performer: won handicap at Newbury in June: should stay beyond 1¼m: acts on good to firm ground: keen sort. *C. E. Brittain.*

STEPPEY LANE 5 b.m. Tachypous 128–Alpine Alice 94 (Abwah 118) [1989 8s 64 10d3 10.2g4 12f5 12m4 12.4m3 12d 12.3g4 13.8d* 12.4g3 14g4 1990 12f 13v5 13d 16g5 15v4 16.5d] leggy, workmanlike mare: has a round action: fair handicapper at 4 yrs: not so good in 1990, running as though something badly amiss and virtually pulled up final outing: should stay 2m: best efforts on an easy surface: has got on edge: has been mounted on track and taken down early: winning hurdler in January. *W. W. Haigh.*

STEREO (USA) 3 b.c. The Minstrel (CAN) 135–Silver In Flight (USA) (Silver 104 Series (USA)) [1989 8g2 1990 10m5 11.7f* 12m* 12g 12g3] strong, good-topped, attractive colt: has plenty of scope: progressive form when successful in May in maiden at Bath, appearing to run lazily in front, and £7,300 handicap at Newbury, leading well inside final 1f: well beaten in mid-division for Derby Italiano at Rome then third of 10 in listed race at Turin: will stay further: useful. *G. Harwood.*

STERLING BUCK (USA) 3 b.c. Buckfinder (USA)–Aged (USA) (Olden — Times) [1989 6d 7g 1990 10.1g 10m 12m a12g5 12m 10d a13g a12g] leggy, close-coupled colt: has a round action: no worthwhile form, including in handicaps. *M. D. I. Usher.*

STERVIAN 2 b.c. (May 3) Damister (USA) 123–Vian (USA) (Far Out East (USA)) 55 p [1990 6d6] 32,000Y: quite attractive colt: first foal: dam unraced half-sister to Optimistic Lass, herself dam of Golden Opinion: green, around 10 lengths sixth of 18, slowly away then staying on final 2f, to Reshift in maiden at Doncaster in November: sure to improve. *R. Charlton.*

STEVEN JOHN 3 b. or br.g. Carriage Way 107–Harmony Thyme 73 (Sing Sing — 134) [1989 8m 8g 1990 12f 15m] leggy gelding: plating-class maiden: well beaten in claimer and handicap late on as 3-y-o. *D. H. Topley.*

STEVE RACE 2 b.c. (Apr 11) Mansingh (USA) 120–My Music 68 (Sole Mio — (USA)) [1990 5m] 2,400F, 10,000Y: fourth foal: half-brother to 3-y-o Marsh's Law (by Kala Shikari) and 1m (at 2 yrs) and 12.3f winner Great Gusto (by Windjammer): dam 1m and 1¼m winner, is half-sister to Gunner B: broke a leg in maiden at Lingfield in May: dead. *T. Thomson Jones.*

ST GREGORY 2 b.g. (Mar 8) Ardross 134–Crymlyn 68 (Welsh Pageant 132) — [1990 7f5] sparely-made gelding: looks weak: second foal: dam maiden stayed 7f: backward, remote last of 5 in minor event at Doncaster in July. *M. H. Easterby.*

STIG 3 b.c. The Brianston 128–The Crying Game 55 (Manor Farm Boy 114) [1989 — 7m 7g 6d 5g 1990 7f 8.2m] leggy, sparely-made colt: turns fore-feet out: well beaten, including in handicap: unseated rider and bolted once at 2 yrs. *B. C. Morgan.*

ST NINIAN 4 ch.c. Ardross 134–Caergwrle 115 (Crepello 136) [1989 8s* 10.6s4 94 10.2f4 1990 12m6 10f 9f2 9m3 10m 8m* 8.2f3 8m 8g* 8d 8g] useful-looking colt:

usually impresses in appearance: improved as 4-y-o, winning handicaps at York in July and Doncaster (£11,900 contest) in September: badly hampered penultimate outing: suited by 1m to 9f: acts on any going: sometimes bandaged near-hind: game and genuine. *M. H. Easterby.*

STOCKAIR 4 ch.g. Air Trooper 115–Fair Nic (Romancero 100) [1989 6m⁵ 6f 6m a8g⁵ 1990 7g 8.2m] leggy, light-framed gelding: plating-class form at best: well beaten in handicaps in June. *F. J. O'Mahony.* —

STOCKTINA 3 ch.f. Tina's Pet 121–Mrewa (Runnymede 123) [1989 5f⁵ 1990 5h 5m 6g 5f 5d 5m 5g] smallish filly: no worthwhile form, including in handicaps: blinkered fourth start. *L. G. Cottrell.* —

STONE FLAKE (USA) 4 ch.g. Diesis 133–Wyandra (So Blessed 130) [1989 7d⁴ 8m 10.5f 8m⁵ 7.3g⁵ 7g 7m 1990 14g] neat gelding: useful at his best: 100/1, well beaten in Tote Ebor at York in August: stays 1m: acts on good to firm and dead going: below form when sweating: winning hurdler as juvenile: changed hands 32,000 gns Newmarket Autumn Sales. *P. A. Kelleway.* —

STONE FOREST 5 b. or br.g. Thatching 131–Senta's Girl (Averof 123) [1989 8g 8d 11.5g 12d 1990 11.7g 10d] strong, rangy gelding: has a quick action: lightly raced and little show since winning maiden as 3-y-o: stays 1m: acts on soft going. *Miss A. J. Whitfield.* —

STONELEIGH ABBEY (IRE) 2 b.c. (Mar 5) Sallust 134–Yellow Creek (Sandy Creek 123) [1990 5f⁴ 5g⁴ 5g⁴ 5m⁵ 5f⁵ 6d a6g² a6g a7g²] IR 5,000F: sturdy colt: has scope: carries condition: second foal: half-brother to 1989 2-y-o 7f winner Horrific (by Kafu): dam Irish maiden: quite modest performer: good second for 7-lb claimer to Dahlawise in maiden and Carrolls Marc in claimer at Southwell at end of year: seems suited by 7f. *R. Hollinshead.* 64

STONELEIGH STAR (IRE) 2 b.f. (May 10) Muscatite 122–Canebrake Lady (Formidable (USA) 125) [1990 5m 5f 5d⁶ 5g] 2,000 (privately) Y: close-coupled filly: first foal: dam poor daughter of half-sister to high-class stayer Almeira: soundly beaten in sellers. *J. Balding.* —

STONE MILL 2 b.c. (Feb 10) Caerleon (USA) 132–Miller's Creek (USA) 62 (Star de Naskra (USA)) [1990 6m² 6m* 6g² 7g³ 8m³] 100,000F: good-bodied, attractive 99

Sheikh Mohammed's "Stone Mill"

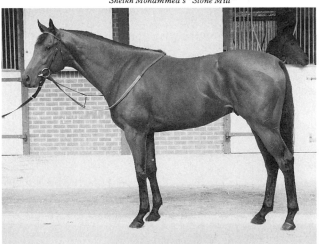

colt: good walker: has a fluent action: second foal: dam maiden suited by 1m, is out of half-sister to top Canadian colt Giboulee: progressive colt: sweating, placed in Laurent-Perrier Champagne Stakes at Doncaster and Royal Lodge William Hill Stakes (over 7 lengths third to Mujaazif) at Ascot final 2 starts: had simple task in Haydock maiden in August: suited by 1m. *B. W. Hills.*

STONE OR SCISSORS 3 ch.c. Ballad Rock 122–Take The Option (USA) (Bold Bidder) [1989 NR 1990 8m 6m2 6m6 6m* 6f2 7f3 7m 6g 6f2 6g5] big, rangy, good-bodied colt: has a rather round action: third foal: half-brother to Irish 7f and 1m winner Take The Honours (by Ahonoora): dam once-raced daughter of useful 1975 Irish 2-y-o Lace Curtain Lil: modest form: won minor event at Folkestone in July: should be suited by return to 7f: acts on firm going: ran moderately in blinkers eighth outing: rather inconsistent. *Mrs L. Piggott.* **73**

STONE RUN (IRE) 2 ch.c. (Apr 15) Commanche Run 133–Lake Tawa (Cure The Blues (USA)) [1990 7f 8f] 6,200F, 6,200Y: unfurnished colt: first foal: dam, poor Irish maiden, half-sister to useful miler Frax and useful staying hurdler Shell Burst: behind in claimer at Carlisle (slowly away) and maiden auction at Redcar (edgy) in autumn. *A. P. Stringer.* **—**

STONEYTHORPEWONDER 3 b.c. Smackover 107–Holloway Wonder 93 (Swing Easy (USA) 126) [1989 5d* 5d 5g* 6g 5g 1990 7d 6g 8.2v a5g6] lengthy colt: poor mover: modest winner at 2 yrs: well beaten in handicaps and claimers in 1990, off course 5 months after reappearance: likely to prove best at 5f. *P. A. Blockley.* **—**

STOP PRESS (USA) 2 b.f. (Apr 22) Sharpen Up 127–Glad Tidings (FR) 85 (Pharly (FR) 130) [1990 7m4 8m2] fifth foal: half-sister to 1¼m winner Settlement (by Irish River) and French 6f and 7f winner Arctic Swell (by Arctic Tern): dam 1¼m winner, is out of Irish 1000 Guineas winner Gaily: staying-on second of 16 to Secret Haunt in maiden at Redcar in October: will stay further: likely to improve again. *M. R. Stoute.* **79 p**

STORM AT NIGHT (USA) 2 b.c. (Jan 29) Storm Bird (CAN) 134–Nervous Pillow (USA) (Nervous Energy (USA)) [1990 6g2 6g3] IR 110,000Y: lengthy colt: half-brother to several winners in USA, including Breeders' Cup Juvenile Fillies third Fine Spirit (by Secretariat): dam sprinting sister to smart Nervous John, successful at up to 7f: well backed, on toes, ½-length third of 8, outpaced 2f out then going on well (and flashing tail) towards finish, to Majlood in listed race at Kempton in September: will stay 7f: sure to improve again, and win a race. *L. M. Cumani.* **92 p**

STORM FREE (USA) 4 b.g. Storm Bird (CAN) 134–No Designs (USA) 72 (Vaguely Noble 140) [1989 8s 8g5 10.6g6 10v 1990 8f 7g 6m 8.3m] rather leggy, angular gelding: fair maiden at best: behind in handicaps in 1990: should stay 1m: probably unsuited by soft going: visored third outing. *L. G. Cottrell.* **—**

STORM JIB 3 b.g. Elegant Air 119–Calvet 62 (Thatch (USA) 136) [1989 7f3 7g6 7g6 8.2g a7g6 a7g5 1990 a11g2 a10g3 a8g3 8f 8.2g 10.4d 10.6s 12m6 a11g 16.5m5] strong gelding: moderate mover: plating-class maiden: well behind last 4 starts, in handicaps first 3 of them: seems to stay 11f: sold out of J. Dunlop's stable 5,400 gns Ascot February Sales after third outing. *B. Preece.* **44**

STORM ORPHAN 3 ch.f. Ballacashtal (CAN)–Grandee Ann (USA) (Cyane) [1989 NR 1990 6f5 5m 7f4 6f4 8m a8g a12g6] lengthy, good-quartered filly: half-sister to 3 winners, including 1m winner Maris Quest (by Windjammer): dam won 6 times at up to 7f in USA: poor maiden: may prove best short of 1½m. *G. Lewis.* **—**

STORMY BELLE 3 ch.f. Tumble Wind (USA)–Never So Lovely 87 (Realm 129) [1989 5g2 5d3 5m* 5g6 5m 6g 1990 6m 5m3 5f4 5m 6g 5m 5m5] big, rather angular filly: moderate walker: fair performer: best form at 5f: acts on good to firm ground, hung right on very firm: sold 7,400 gns Ascot November Sales. *M. A. Jarvis.* **82**

ST PATRICK'S DAY 2 ch.g. (Mar 17) Night Shift (USA)–Princess Lieven (Royal Palace 131) [1990 6m3 6m5 6g 8m 10g] leggy, rather sparely-made gelding: very good mover: third living foal: half-brother to fair 11.5f winner Beau Ideal (by Brigadier Gerard): dam unraced daughter of sister to Brigadier Gerard: modest form in varied races: ran well in listed event at Kempton third start: pulled very hard in similar events after: should be suited by further than 6f: headstrong. *C. E. Brittain.* **75**

STRADBALLY MOUNT 2 gr.c. (Mar 22) Carwhite 127–Marymount (Mount Hagen (FR) 127) [1990 7m6 10s] 8,200Y: lengthy colt: has scope: fourth foal: half-brother to fair 1987 2-y-o 6f and 7f winner Belvedere Court (by Aragon): dam never ran: green, staying-on sixth of 14 in claimer at Salisbury in September: bit backward and never a factor in maiden at Nottingham. *M. McCormack.* **52**

STRADBROKE   3 b.c. Fairy King (USA)–Mattira (FR) (Rheffic (FR) 129) [1989   62
7m 1990 9m² 8g⁶ 10m³ a14g³] big, strong, lengthy colt: moderate mover: quite
modest maiden: placed in claimers and seller: stays 1¼m: claimed out of R. Boss's
stable £11,500 second start: winning selling hurdler: sold 2,500 gns Ascot December Sales. *J. Akehurst.*

STRAIGHTASANARROW   3 ch.g. Siberian Express (USA) 125–Blue Queen   —
54 (Majority Blue 126) [1989 NR 1990 7g 8.2m 11g⁶ 15g⁵] 11,000Y: smallish, angular
gelding: half-brother to several winners, including very useful middle-distance filly
Reprocolor (by Jimmy Reppin), dam of Colorspin, Bella Colora and Rappa Tap Tap:
dam half-sister to Sandford Lad: well beaten in maiden events, close up 1¾m in
claimer final start: bought to join Miss J. Barclay after winning selling hurdle. *C. W.
Thornton.*

STRAIGHT GOLD   5 ch.m. Vaigly Great 127–Merokette 83 (Blast 125) [1989   —
7s⁵ 8d⁶ 8m 8f² 8m² 8h⁶ 8f⁴ 9m⁶ 7s³ 10.2f² 12g² 1990 17.1f⁵] tall mare: quite modest
handicapper at 4 yrs: may prove best at up to 2m: acts on any going: visored 3 times
as 3-y-o: has started slowly, got long way behind and found little: won twice over
hurdles in spring. *G. A. Ham.*

STRAIGHT LACED (USA)   3 b. or br.g. Alleged (USA) 138–Swoonmist (USA)   —
(Never Bend) [1989 8v⁶ 1990 13.6m⁶] $250,000Y: lengthy, angular gelding: sixth
foal: half-brother to 2 winners in North America by Far North: dam unraced
daughter of sister to Swoons Son: well beaten in newcomers race at Maisons-
Laffitte (subsequently gelded) when trained by A. Fabre and maiden at Redcar year
later: sold to join J. Wainwright 5,000 gns Newmarket Autumn Sales. *N. A. Graham.*

STRAIGHT NO CHASER   2 b.g. (May 2) Norwick (USA) 120–Pepeke 78   61
(Mummy's Pet 125) [1990 7d 6g a6g⁶] 5,000F, 11,000Y: first foal: dam 7f winner:
quite modest maiden: best effort second start: ran moderately on all-weather: likely
to prove suited by further than 6f. *R. Boss.*

STRALDI (IRE)   2 br.c. (Mar 31) Ela-Mana-Mou 132–Cavurina 81§ (Cavo Doro   81 p
124) [1990 8d*] 48,000DM, IR 68,000Y: workmanlike colt: has scope: half-brother to 4
winners in Ireland, including middle-distance winner and hurdler Northern Oats (by
Oats): dam 1¼m winner, was temperamental: favourite but bit backward and green,
won 13-runner maiden at Leicester in October by ½ length from Chief Celebrity,
bustled along over 2f out and staying on: will be better suited by 1¼m +: sure to
improve. *H. R. A. Cecil.*

STRANGER STILL   3 b.f. Cragador 110–No Relation 94 (Klairon 131) [1989 6g   50
6g 1990 8m⁶ 10.2m 10m² 10g 10.1m⁶] leggy, sparely-made filly: has a quick action:
plating-class maiden: ridden by 7-lb claimer, clearly best effort when beaten short
head in claimer at Newmarket: stays 1¼m: trained until after third start by G.
Wragg: winning selling hurdler. *B. Stevens.*

STRANGER TO FEAR   3 ch.f. Never So Bold 135–Acadie (FR) 80 (Caracolero   —
(USA) 131) [1989 6g 1990 7g 10.1m] leggy, angular filly: no show in large-field
maidens then (moved moderately down) minor event. *R. F. Johnson Houghton.*

STRATFORD PONDS   5 b.h. High Top 131–Opinion 71 (Great Nephew 126)   —
[1989 14g² 16g⁴ 14m³ 12f* 12g³ 12m 1990 13.3g] big, angular horse: has a quick
action: fairly useful winner as 4-y-o: backed at long odds, ran poorly in valuable
handicap at Newbury in September: best at 1½m: best form on a sound surface:
lacks turn of foot and best ridden close to the pace: useful hurdler. *O. Sherwood.*

STRAT'S LEGACY   3 b.g. Chukaroo 103–State Romance 67 (Free State 125)   44
[1989 6g a6g 1990 a6g 7m 10f 12h⁵ 12.5m*] small, light-framed gelding: 33/1, first
form when winning 12-runner selling handicap (no bid) at Wolverhampton in October by a short head: suited by 1½m: has been bandaged behind. *D. W. P. Arbuthnot.*

STRAW BERET (USA)   2 ch.f. (Apr 25) Chief's Crown (USA)–Mostly Sunny   77
(CAN) (Sunny) [1990 7g⁴ 7s³] $100,000Y: rangy filly: has plenty of scope: half-sister
to several winners, notably Kentucky Derby winner Sunny's Halo (by Halo): dam
minor winner in North America: backed at long odds, highly promising fourth of 15,
held up in slowly-run race then quickening in great style over 1f out and running on
strongly under considerable ride, to Fragrant Hill in minor event at Newbury in
September: only third of 22, beaten 6 lengths, to Desert Sun in maiden at Doncaster
following month: will be better suited by 1m +. *J. H. M. Gosden.*

STRECKINSKI   2 ch.c. (May 2) Niniski (USA) 125–Princesse Timide (USA)   —
(Blushing Groom (FR) 131) [1990 8m] fourth foal: brother to very smart French
middle-distance colt Louis Cyphre: dam French 7.5f and 1¼m winner: bit backward
and visored, tailed off in maiden at Yarmouth in September. *R. Guest.*

STREET TALK 6 b.m. Beldale Flutter (USA) 130–Lusitanica 89 (Pieces of — Eight 128) [1989 NR 1990 14m] compact, quite attractive mare: poor maiden: sweating and backward, tailed off in Nottingham handicap in September: stays 1½m: acts on good to firm and dead going. *J. W. Payne.*

STRENGTH IN DEPTH (IRE) 2 b. or br.f. (May 8) Strong Gale 116–Second **49** Service (Red Regent 123) [1990 7d⁵ 7d⁵ 6d] workmanlike filly: second reported foal: dam behind in varied company: beaten at least 6 lengths in seller at Catterick and maidens at Edinburgh and Doncaster: should be suited by 1m + . *M. Johnston.*

STRIDE HOME 5 ch.m. Absalom 128–Another Treat 82 (Derring-Do 131) [1989 **52** 10.1m 12f 10h⁴ 12m⁴ 11.7m² 11.7m² 10f 9m 12f⁵ 1990 a10g a10g a16g⁶ 10f³ 10.8m³ 10. 1g* 11.5m⁵ 11.7m 10m] sturdy mare: has a quick action: won claimer at Windsor in April: off course 3 months after sixth outing, and ran poorly last 2: needs further than 9f and stays 1½m: seems to act on any going: usually blinkered or visored. *M. Madgwick.*

STRIDING EDGE 5 ch.g. Viking (USA)–Kospia (King Emperor (USA)) [1989 — 8s 9g 11m 8d⁴ 8g 9.5m⁴ 8s 8d 8s 1990 a8g⁶ 10f⁶ 10.1g] compact ex-Irish gelding: third foal: dam lightly-raced Irish maiden: well beaten in claimers and apprentice race before end of April: stays 9.5f: probably acts on any going: has been tried in blinkers: often apprentice ridden: winner 4 times over hurdles early in 1990/1. *J. R. Jenkins.*

STRIKE FIRE (IRE) 2 b.c. (Mar 6) Touching Wood (USA) 127–Ascot Strike **93** (USA) 85 (Mr Prospector (USA)) [1990 7.5f* 8g² 9g* 10g⁵] medium-sized, lengthy, quite attractive colt: second foal: half-brother to 3-y-o Thunderstorm (by Windwurf): dam 1¼m winner: fairly useful colt: successful in maiden at Beverley in July and nursery (by 3½ lengths from Green's Trilogy) at Sandown in September: modest fifth of 9, one pace final 3f, to Matahif in listed race at Newmarket: should stay at least 1¼m. *P. F. I. Cole.*

STRIKE FORCE 5 b. or br.g. Gorytus (USA) 132–Helaplane (USA) 68 (Super **102** Concorde (USA) 128) [1989 NR 1990 7m² 8g] well-made, attractive gelding: has a quickish action: won Schweppes Golden Mile (Handicap) at Goodwood in July, 1988: first race since reportedly spraining check ligament, 1½ lengths second to Monsagem in listed Leicestershire Stakes in April: ran as though something again amiss in valuable handicap at York under 3 weeks later: stays 1m: unsuited by soft going. *B. W. Hills.*

STRING PLAYER 8 ch.g. Orchestra 118–Ghana's Daughter 93 (Sallust 134) — [1989 18m 1990 a16g a14g] workmanlike, deep-girthed gelding: has a slightly round action: plating-class handicapper on flat, very lightly raced nowadays: stays 1½m: acts on any going: bandaged at 8 yrs: sometimes sweats: one-time useful hurdler. *F. H. Lee.*

STRIP CARTOON (IRE) 2 ch.g. (May 20) Tate Gallery (USA) 117–Reveal **51** (Pitskelly 122) [1990 6d 6m³ 7f 6m³ 6f⁶ 6m a5g a8g] 12,500Y: smallish, workmanlike gelding: closely related to 3-y-o Show And Tell (by Lomond) and fair 7f and 8.2f winner Hip Hip Hurry (by Glenstal): dam Irish 2-y-o 7f winner: fair plater: lost form towards end of year: should stay 7f: blinkered fourth and fifth outings: sold out of D. Morley's stable 2,900 gns Doncaster September Sales after fifth outing. *S. R. Bowring.*

STROBE LIGHT 3 b.g. Electric 126–Sequin Lady (Star Appeal 133) [1989 NR **44** 1990 13.3m 11.5m⁶ 10f 14f⁵ 15m 18d⁴] lengthy, good-topped gelding: first foal: dam unraced daughter of Oaks winner Scintillate, herself half-sister to Juliette Marny and Julio Mariner: poor maiden: suited by test of stamina: acts on firm and dead ground: blinkered (very slowly away) on debut: sold to join M. Pipe 8,200 gns Newmarket Autumn Sales. *J. A. R. Toller.*

ST ROBERT 3 b.c. Taufan (USA) 119–Sainthill (St Alphage 119) [1989 NR 1990 **61** 10f⁵ 12g 14d⁶ 14g 10g] 15,000Y: lengthy, quite good-topped colt: has a long, rather round stride: eighth reported foal: half-brother to 6f and 9f winner Knockglas (by Hardgreen): dam twice-raced sister to top sprinter Sandford Lad: quite modest maiden, disappointing after debut: seems not to stay 1½m: sold 10,000 gns Newmarket Autumn Sales. *C. E. Brittain.*

STROKE OF LUCK 3 br.f. Be My Native (USA) 122–Coup de Veine (FR) (Gift — Card (FR) 124) [1989 NR 1990 10.6f 12m 12f⁶] 17,000FR, 15,000Y: big, close-coupled filly: fifth foal: sister to quite modest maiden Seamrog and half-sister to very useful 7f and 1m winner Farajullah (by Jaazeiro): dam poor half-sister to smart French and American miler Tayyara: well beaten in maidens. *M. Bell.*

STUBBS ROAD 3 b.c. Blushing Scribe (USA) 107–Rheinza 66 (Rheingold 137) —
[1989 7g 8.5f 1990 10f⁶ 11.5g 7m] sturdy colt: poor mover: seems of little account:
blinkered second start. *R. Champion.*

STUFFY (IRE) 2 ch.g. (Apr 15) Doulab (USA) 115–Natural Sunshine (Manado —
130) [1990 6g 8f 8d] big, workmanlike gelding: tubed: has a long stride: fourth foal:
brother to fairly useful Irish 3-y-o Daawi, 5f winner at 2 yrs, and half-brother to Irish
1m and 9f winner Natural Lad (by Kafu): dam Irish 7f winner: well beaten in
maidens: sold 1,000 gns Doncaster November Sales. *M. W. Easterby.*

STUMBLE 6 ch.g. Sayyaf 121–Tumble Royal (Tumble Wind (USA)) [1989 NR **43**
1990 8g² 8.2m⁵] sturdy, workmanlike gelding: has a quick action: poor handicapper:
unlucky second at Ripon in July: favourite, reportedly returned lame in similar
event over week later: stays 1m: possibly unsuited by soft going, acts on any other:
bandaged at 6 yrs: winner 3 times over hurdles in 1989/90. *J. Mackie.*

ST VILLE 4 b.c. Top Ville 129–Dame Julian 84 (Blakeney 126) [1989 11.7d 12g **47**
15.3m³ 17.6g⁶ 16f⁵ 15.8g² a16g* a14g a16g⁵ 1990 16g⁴ 16m 14m⁴ a12g* 11.7g 12g²
a12g 15.3g⁶ 13.8d 16s] good-bodied colt: poor walker and moderate mover: poor
handicapper: won at Southwell in August: carried head high and tended to edge left
eighth outing: stays 2m: possibly needs a sound surface: has run moderately for
amateur: sold 7,000 gns Newmarket Autumn Sales. *J. D. Bethell.*

STYLISH GENT 3 br.g. Vitiges (FR) 132–Squire's Daughter (Bay Express 132) **84**
[1989 6g* 6g⁵ 7m* 1990 8f 9g⁶ 10g 7m⁶ 7d⁴] strong, lengthy gelding: fair performer:
easily best 3-y-o efforts in handicaps at Sandown and Redcar (£9,600 contest)
second and third starts: stays 9f: acts on good to firm ground and dead: headstrong
and found little when visored fourth start: sweating on reappearance: may be
unsatisfactory. *W. Hastings-Bass.*

STYLISH SENOR (USA) 2 ch.c. (Feb 15) El Gran Senor (USA) 136–Gladiolus **80**
(USA) (Watch Your Step) [1990 6m⁴ 7m² 7m⁶] 10,000Y: medium-sized, angular colt:
half-brother to useful French 6.5f and 7f winner Dramatis (by Spectacular Bid): dam
won 17 races in USA: fair maiden: sixth of 17, never able to challenge, to Flying
Brave in Tattersalls Tiffany Highflyer Stakes at Newmarket: will stay 1m: can win a
maiden. *J. R. Fanshawe.*

STYRIAN (USA) 2 b.c. (Mar 29) Storm Bird (CAN) 134–Vachti (FR) 114 — p
(Crystal Palace (FR) 132) [1990 7s] well-grown colt: second foal: dam French 1¼m
and 10.5f winner stayed 1½m: backward, held up and never knocked about in minor
event at Doncaster in November: sure to improve. *W. Jarvis.*

SUBSONIC (IRE) 2 b.c. (Jan 31) Be My Guest (USA) 126–Broken Wide (Busted **50**
134) [1990 7m⁴ 8g 8m] 44,000Y: big, good-bodied colt: has a round action: second
foal: dam Irish middle-distance maiden: soundly beaten in maidens, including a
4-runner event at Ascot: awkward stalls second start. *J. L. Dunlop.*

SUBTLE CHANGE (IRE) 2 b.f. (Apr 2) Law Society (USA) 130–Santa **87 p**
Luciana (GER) (Luciano) [1990 6m² 8m² 8.5m* 8m³ 8m⁵] 42,000Y: lengthy,
good-topped filly: half-sister to several winners, including Irish 1m and 13f winner
Walkyria and 11.7f and 1½m winner Sweet Alexandra (both by Lord Gayle): dam
2-y-o winner in Germany, from good family: odds on, made all in 4-runner maiden at
Beverley in September: fifth of 11, staying on having been set lot to do then had
poorish run, to Sea Level in listed race at Ascot: will be suited by 1¼m: should do
better. *G. Harwood.*

SUDDEN IMPACT 8 b.h. Be Friendly 130–False Evidence 53 (Connool 118) —
[1989 NR 1990 5f] lengthy, quite attractive horse: turns near-fore out: modest at
best: no form for long time; usually blinkered. *P. J. Arthur.*

SUDDEN VICTORY 6 ch.g. Kings Lake (USA) 133–Shebeen 124 (Saint **79**
Crespin III 132) [1989 13.3g⁵ 11s² 11s* 12v² 14g² 1990 20m 16g⁴ 13.4g⁶ 10d⁴ a14g]
tall, good-topped gelding: turned near-fore out: poor mover in slower paces: smart
performer (rated 115) at one time: long way below his best in varied events in 1990,
in Southwell claimer final outing: best form at up to 1¾m: best with plenty of give in
the ground: sold out of B. Hills's stable 10,500 gns Newmarket Autumn Sales after
fourth start: dead. *N. Tinkler.*

SUGAR THE PILL 3 b.g. Blue Cashmere 129–Maple Syrup 89 (Charlottown **43**
127) [1989 5s 5g³ 6f 7f⁵ 7f 8.2s a7g 1990 9.1m⁵ 12.3f 8g⁵ 9g⁵ 10g⁴] lengthy gelding:
moderate walker and mover: poor maiden: reportedly suffered eye injury on third
start: stayed 1¼m: dead. *T. Fairhurst.*

SUGEMAR 4 ch.g. Young Generation 129–Jade Ring 92 (Auction Ring (USA) **72**
123) [1989 NR 1990 7m 8f 10.6s 10m⁴ 9m³ 12g] big, strong gelding: poor walker and
mover: second foal: dam, second in Blue Seal Stakes at 2 yrs, stayed 1m: modest

maiden: stays 1¼m: acts on good to firm and soft going: bandaged third outing. *J. A. R. Toller.*

SUGO 3 ch.f. Prince Ragusa 96–Lucky Friend (Galivanter 131) [1989 5s 5m⁵ 1990 12.3m⁴ 12h⁵ 8f] lengthy, angular filly: of little account. *Ronald Thompson.* —

SUIVEZ MOI 6 ch.g. Pas de Seul 133–Reparata (Jukebox 120) [1989 14s² 21.6d 16g⁶ 18.4m 14.8m⁴ 14m⁵ 14m⁶ 15.3m* 15.3m⁵ a16g² a16g⁴ a16g⁵ 1990 a16g a14g* a14g 18f² 16.5m* 16g 17.6m³ a14g* 16m⁵ a18g⁴ 17.6f⁴ 15.3m 17.4d 16m* 15.3g³ 18d 16.5d a12g⁶ a16g a14g⁶] small, light-framed gelding: poor mover: poor handicapper: won at Southwell in February and May, Doncaster in between and Nottingham in September: stays well: acts on any going except possibly heavy: raced too freely when visored: suitable mount for apprentice: has sweated: reportedly broke blood vessel third start: genuine. *C. N. Allen.* **41**

SUKEY TAWDRY 4 gr.f. Wassl 125–Jenny Diver (USA) (Hatchet Man (USA)) [1989 7.5d⁵ 8h 10f⁴ 12m 12f² 8.5m* 18.1g⁴ 8.5f 10m 10f 1990 12.5f] leggy filly: winning plater at 3 yrs: stays 1½m: acts on firm going: visored twice at 3 yrs. *J. L. Spearing.*

SULA 2 br.f. (May 27) Sula Bula 109–Dusky Damsel 68 (Sahib 114) [1990 5m 5g a7g⁴] leggy, sparely-made filly: eighth foal: sister to 3-y-o Zulu Dancer: dam won over 6f at 3 yrs: little worthwhile form, including in a seller. *T. D. Barron.*

SULASTAR 2 gr.g. (Feb 15) Sulaafah (USA) 119–Bidula (Manacle 123) [1990 5f⁶ 5d³ 5f*] 5,400F, 6,000Y: lengthy gelding: has scope: moderate walker: half-brother to a winning plater and a winner in Austria: dam never ran: stayed on strongly to win maiden auction at Salisbury in May by 2½ lengths: hung left from halfway previous outing. *R. Hannon.* **69**

SULCIS 5 ch.g. Castle Keep 121–Skiboule (BEL) (Boulou) [1989 13f 12g 15s* 14g⁵ 15.5s 14s 15.5f³ 16.2m² 15.3m⁶ 12g⁵ 1990 13g 15g 14d² 17g² a14g] well-made gelding: has a fluent action: plating-class handicapper: stays 17f: seems to act on any going: blinkered third and fourth starts: trained early in each of last 3 seasons by C. Milbank in France: winning hurdler. *R. Hollinshead.* —

SULLI BOY (NOR) 5 b.g. Sparkling Boy 110–Lady Sullivan (Pitcairn 126) [1989 NR 1990 10f 6g 8f⁶ 11.7g] sturdy, workmanlike gelding: fourth foal: half-brother to 2 winners in Norway by Le Johnstan: dam lightly raced and well beaten on flat: winner 8 times in Scandinavia, including twice over 1m in Norway in 1989: never a threat in varied events on flat in Britain: winning hurdler in March. *Miss B. Sanders.* —

SULLY'S CHOICE (USA) 9 b.g. King Pellinore (USA) 127–Salute The Coates (USA) (Solar Salute (USA)) [1989 5m 6f 6m 6f⁵ 6h³ 6f* 5g⁶ 6m² 6m² 6m* 6f³ 6m* 6m² 5.6g 6s 6m 6g 6f 6g 5d a6g a6g⁵ a6g³ a6g 1990 a5g² a7g² a7g⁵ 5m 5f 6g 5m² 6d 6g 5m⁴ 5f⁶ 5m 6d] small, sturdy gelding: carries plenty of condition: usually looks very well: fairly useful handicapper at one time in 1989, but has deteriorated: best at 5f or 6f: acts on any going: visored 3 times: effective with or without blinkers: suitable mount for apprentice: suited by forcing tactics. *D. W. Chapman.* **62**

SULTANS GIFT 4 ch.f. Homing 130–Suzannah's Song (Song 132) [1989 6f⁶ 5m³ 6f 5.8h² 5g 6f 6f 6g 1990 a5g a5g⁶ a6g a7g a7g] small filly: poor mover: no longer of much account: blinkered twice, including final outing: has worn bandages: sold 680 gns Doncaster March Sales. *C. N. Allen.* —

SULTAN'S SON 4 b.c. Kings Lake (USA) 133–Get Ahead 58 (Silly Season 127) [1989 NR 1990 10f* 12m*] strong, good-bodied colt: has a round action: justified favouritism in apprentice events at Brighton in April and Ascot (handicap, in tremendous style by 10 lengths) in May: looked sure to improve, but wasn't seen out again: suited by 1½m: acts well on top-of-the-ground. *P. F. I. Cole.* **93 +**

SULUK (USA) 5 b.h. Lypheor 118–Cheerful Heart (Petingo 135) [1989 10s 10v 12.5g 12f 12g 12h* 12.3m* 16g6 12g³ 12.3m² 12h* 12f* 12m* 12f 12.2f 12f⁵ 12g 12g 1990 a12g* a16g³ a14g³ a12g² 13.8m³] dipped-backed, good-quartered horse: carries condition: won handicap at Southwell in January: best at 1½m: acts on hard going: goes well with forcing tactics: prolific winning hurdler at Southwell in 1989/90: genuine. *R. Hollinshead.* **63**

SUMAN 3 b.g. Remainder Man 126§–Camdamus 83 (Mandamus 120) [1989 5d 6f⁴ 6m⁶ 6m⁴ 6f 7m 8g 1990 6g 9g 7g 7.6m 8f a8g] small gelding: plater: should stay beyond 6f: twice wandered when blinkered: looks awkward ride: joined R. Lee. *L. J. Barratt.*

SUM MEDE 3 b.g. King Persian 107–Brun's Toy (FR) (Bruni 132) [1989 5m² 5m⁶ 6m 6f* 7f 8m 8m² 8f² 8f² 1990 10.8m⁶ 10.2f⁶ 9m 10.5g³ 12m] leggy, angular gelding: has a quick action: quite modest handicapper: mostly faced stiff tasks in **59**

1990, good third in selling event at York: suited by 1¼m: acts on firm going: sold 7,000 gns Newmarket Autumn Sales. *R. Hannon.*

SUMMER FASHION 5 b.m. Moorestyle 137–My Candy 81 (Lorenzaccio 130) [1989 8h² 8.5m 10m* 8f³ 10f* 10m* 9g 11v 1990 10m 10m* 11.5m² 10m] leggy mare: moderate mover: fair handicapper: won £7,400 event at Sandown in June: set too much to do next outing: stays 11.5f: acts well on top-of-the-ground, probably unsuited by soft: wears bandages behind: genuine. *D. R. C. Elsworth.*   **84**

SUMMERHILL SALLY 4 b.f. Dunbeath (USA) 127–Sharper Still (Sharpen Up 127) [1989 7s 8m 10m² 10.2h 8m 7h 1990 a11g⁵ 10.8m 12.5f⁶ 10.6f] medium-sized filly: plating-class maiden at best: below form since third outing at 3 yrs: best form at 1¼m: blinkered final outing: takes keen hold, and has found little. *P. Leach.*   **—**

SUMMER SANDS 2 ch.f. (Mar 14) Mummy's Game 120–Renira 60 (Relkino 131) [1990 5m 5m* 6g⁴ 5m 6s⁵] 5,000Y: lengthy filly: has scope: second foal: half-sister to 3-y-o Victoria Princess (by King of Spain): dam poor maiden: quite modest performer: won maiden at Windsor in July: ran well in nurseries afterwards: stays 6f. *D. R. C. Elsworth.*   **69**

SUMMERWOOD LADY 2 gr.f. (Apr 26) Godswalk (USA) 130–Nom de Plume 70 (Aureole 132) [1990 5g] rather leggy, sparely-made filly: half-sister to several winners, including useful French Gent (by Sassafras), 5f to 7f winner at 2 yrs who stayed 1½m: dam ran only at 2 yrs, winning over 7f: broke a leg in Wolverhampton maiden in May: dead. *R. J. Holder.*   **—**

SUM MUSIC 5 b.m. Music Boy 124–Sum Star 67 (Comedy Star (USA) 121) [1989 5m⁵ 5m⁶ 5m 5f 1990 a5g 5g a5g] leggy mare: has a round action: bad sprint maiden: sweating, edgy and very slowly away second outing: blinkered last. *J. S. Wainwright.*   **—**

SUMONDA 2 b.f. (Jan 23) Lomond (USA) 128–Soemba 86 (General Assembly (USA)) [1990 6m² 6m⁴ 7m*] strong, lengthy filly: has a quick action: first foal: dam 9f winner: best effort around 5 lengths fourth of 13, staying on well having been hampered at halfway, to Capricciosa in Tattersalls Cheveley Park Stakes at Newmarket: won maiden at Leicester later in October by short head from Lupescu, keeping on well despite swishing tail and carrying head high: should stay at least 1m. *G. Wragg.*   **100**

SUNBLINK 3 ch.f. Morston (FR) 125–Find The Sun 81 (Galivanter 131) [1989 NR 1990 12m] workmanlike filly: fourth foal: half-sister to quite modest 11f winner Calton Coleen (by Sagaro): dam, 7f winner at 2 yrs, stayed well and also won over hurdles: 100/1, always behind in maiden at Pontefract in September. *A. Smith.*   **—**

SUNBURST PRINCESS (IRE) 2 ch.f. (Mar 30) Tender King 123–Rhumb Line (Right Tack 131) [1990 6m 6m 8g] IR 400F, IR 6,200Y: smallish, angular filly: sixth reported foal: half-sister to 1984 2-y-o 5f seller winner The Copocabana Kid (by Ballad Rock): dam ran once: well beaten in maidens. *G. A. Huffer.*   **—**

SUNDANCE KID (USA) 3 b.c. Fappiano (USA) Gallanta (FR) 112 (Nureyev (USA) 131) [1989 6f* 6g 1990 7m* 8m³ 8m] angular, useful-looking colt: has scope: has a long, rather round stride: made all in 2-runner minor event at Goodwood in June: ran creditably in 4-runner minor contest (led 6f) at Newbury, as if something amiss in £24,700 handicap (second favourite) at York: should prove at least as effective returned to 7f: acts on firm going. *H. R. A. Cecil.*   **99**

SUNDAR 3 b.c. Darshaan 133–Sunny Valley (Val de Loir 133) [1989 NR 1990 10m 13.3m⁵ 12m* 13.3m6] strong, lengthy colt: has a rather round action: sixth foal: half-brother to Oaks and St Leger winner Sun Princess (by English Prince), about 1m to 1¼m winner Dancing Shadow (by Dancer's Image) and fairly useful 1½m winner Elevate (by Ela-Mana-Mou): dam won at up to 1½m in France: fair form: won maiden at Beverley in July: ridden along 7f out when well beaten in £11,500 handicap at Newbury 2 weeks later: will stay 1¾m: has plenty of scope. *L. M. Cumani.*   **87**

SUNDAY SPORT GEM 2 ch.f. (Feb 12) Lomond (USA) 128–Gemma Kaye 91 (Cure The Blues (USA)) [1990 6s² 6m 5d 8.2s 7d] 1,500Y: smallish, rather angular filly: first foal: dam maiden half-sister to Irish Oaks winner Olwyn: easily best effort, including in sellers, when second of 5 in maiden at Hamilton in May: should stay beyond 6f. *J. Berry.*   **42 d**

SUNDAY SPORT'S PET 3 b.f. Mummy's Pet 125–My Princess (King Emperor (USA)) [1989 5g⁴ 5m⁴ 6g⁴ 1990 6g⁶ 8m⁶ 7f 7g 7v] sparely-made filly: good walker: moderate mover: plating-class maiden: should stay 7f. *J. Berry.*   **—**

SUNDERLAND (USA) 3 b.g. Roberto (USA) 131–Sunny Bay (USA) (Northern Bay (USA)) [1989 NR 1990 10f² 10f⁴ 10.1m* 10.1m³] good-bodied gelding with   **86**

scope: modest mover: brother to very useful 1987 2-y-o 6f and 7f winner Suntrap and half-brother to winners abroad, including 1989 French 1½m winner Engulf (by Exceller): dam won 8 races at up to 8.5f: led post in minor event at Windsor in July: fair third (eased) in similar event there 2 weeks later: will be suited by 1½m. *R. Charlton.*

SUNFLOWER SEED 3 b.f. Mummy's Pet 125–Bright Sun (Mill Reef (USA) **60** 141) [1989 7f² 6g 1990 7m 8m⁶ 11m² 11.5g⁵ 10.2m⁵ 12g⁴ 11.5g⁶ a14g] lengthy, robust filly: quite modest maiden: will prove better at 1½m than 1¼m: acts on firm going: visored last 2 starts, running creditably first of them: ran fairly well for amateur: sold 6,600 gns Newmarket December Sales. *W. Hastings-Bass.*

SUNGROVE PRIDE 4 b.g. Chukaroo 103–Judann (Some Hand 119) [1989 7h 6h **34** 7m 6m 6m 5m 1990 6f⁶ 5f⁵ 5f 5m² a6g 5f 6m⁴ 8.3m 5m 6f⁶] leggy, lengthy gelding: bad mover: poor maiden: stays 6f: acts on firm going: blinkered 4 of last 5 outings: inconsistent. *E. A. Wheeler.*

SUNGROVE'S BEST 3 ch.g. Buzzards Bay 128§–Judann (Some Hand 119) **—** [1989 NR 1990 10f 7f⁶ 6m] lengthy gelding: second foal: half-brother to poor sprint maiden Sungrove Pride (by Chukaroo): dam half-sister to useful middle-distance stayer Woodlands Imp: well behind in maidens and minor event. *E. A. Wheeler.*

SUNIRAM 4 b. or br.f. Marching On 101–Wellington Bear (Dragonara Palace **—** (USA) 115) [1989 5m⁶ 7m 5g 5g 1990 5d] workmanlike filly: plating-class maiden at best: no form since first outing as 3-y-o: suited by sprint distances: tends to sweat and get on edge. *A. P. Stringer.*

SUNLEY SPARKLE 2 b.f. (Apr 19) Sunley Builds 102–Royal Darwin 69 (Royal **56 p** Palm 131) [1990 7g] leggy filly: looks weak: second reported foal: dam sprint plater: prominent 5f in large-field maiden at Newmarket in November: should improve. *M. R. Channon.*

SUNLIGHT EXPRESS 4 b.g. Homing 130–Princess Sunshine (Busted 134) **—** [1989 NR 1990 a14g⁶] lengthy gelding: first reported foal: dam, well beaten in modest company, is out of a half-sister to Double Jump and Royalty: second in NH Flat race in May: ridden by 7-lb claimer, tailed off in maiden at Southwell following month: sold 7,000 gns Doncaster August Sales. *Mrs L. Piggott.*

SUNNY DAVIS (USA) 2 ch.f. (Mar 20) Alydar (USA)–Goldie Hawn (USA) **71** (Northern Dancer) [1990 8g⁵ 7d² 7d*] $400,000Y: medium-sized, sparely-made filly: first foal: dam minor winner, is sister to Larida, dam of Magic of Life, and half-sister to Miss Oceana: modest performer: won maiden at Edinburgh in October by ½ length from Good Profile, staying on gamely: will stay 1¼m. *Sir Mark Prescott.*

SUNNYSIDE 3 ch.f. Doulab (USA) 115–Sunny Look 91 (Lombard (GER) 126) **—** [1989 5f² 5h² 5m³ 5m 6g 5g 1990 6m] leggy filly: plating-class maiden: ran poorly in claiming event in July: should stay 6f: tends to get on toes. *R. J. Hodges.*

SUN SCREEN 3 br.f. Caerleon (USA) 132–Hill Shade 116 (Hillary) [1989 NR **—** 1990 8m⁶ a8g 12d⁴ a8g] sparely-made filly: half-sister to numerous winners, including 1000 Guineas and Oaks winner Mysterious (by Crepello) and top-class 1976 2-y-o J O Tobin (by Never Bend), later Grade 1 8.5f and 1¼m winner in USA: dam 1m and 1¼m winner: quite modest maiden: off course over 4 months and below form after debut: soon struggling at Southwell, very slowly away on first occasion. *J. H. M. Gosden.*

SUNSET AGAIN 5 ch.g. Al Sirat (USA)–Noddy (Prince Hansel 118) [1989 NR **—** 1990 12f⁶] fifth foal: dam ran once: 50/1, tailed off in amateurs event at Newmarket in August: winning hurdler. *M. H. B. Robinson.*

SUNSET AND VINE 3 gr.g. Norwick (USA) 120–Starky's Pet (Mummy's Pet **—** 125) [1989 NR 1990 10m⁶ a12g⁴ a12g⁴ᵈⁱˢ 12m a13g] big, workmanlike gelding: poor mover: third foal: half-brother to 7f winner Southern Sky (by Comedy Star): dam behind in 4 starts on flat and over hurdles: little sign of ability in maidens then handicaps. *S. Dow.*

SUNSET DREAMS 3 b.c. Habitat 134–Pennyweight (Troy 137) [1989 NR 1990 **54** 8f 6g³ 7d] 30,000Y: good-bodied colt: second foal: half-brother to useful 6f and 7f winner Penny Candle (by Be My Guest): dam poor half-sister to Wassl: plating-class maiden: moved poorly down and reared leaving stalls on debut: should stay beyond 6f. *G. A. Huffer.*

SUNSET REINS FREE 5 b.h. Red Sunset 120–Free Rein (Sagaro 133) [1989 **60** 8s 12d⁵ 12g³ 10m 8.2g 12.3m 17.6g⁴ 17.4s 1990 12m² 12m a8g²] big, good-bodied horse: carries plenty of condition: moderate mover: quite modest handicapper: runner-up in amateur events in second half of year: stays 1½m: yet to show his best form on extremes of going: usually visored: withdrawn 3 times as 4-y-o, once after breaking blood vessel. *E. J. Alston.*

SUNSET ROSE 3 b.f. Shirley Heights 130–Rose Bowl (USA) 131 (Habitat 134) 57 [1989 7.3v 1990 8g 10g 12m* 11.7m 12m* 12f⁵ 12s 12m⁴ 12m³ 13.6d] small, workmanlike filly: has a quick action: plating-class handicapper: won at Chepstow in June, making all, and Hamilton in August, still in rear over 3f out: appeared to idle when very good third in apprentice race at Chepstow: better at 1½m than shorter: suited by top-of-the-ground: inconsistent. *I. A. Balding.*

SUNSET STREET (IRE) 2 b.c. (Mar 2) Bellypha 130–Sunset Reef (Mill Reef 86 (USA) 141) [1990 6d 7d* 7m³ 6m* 7g⁵ 8m⁵ 6m 7.3g] 26,000Y: workmanlike colt: has plenty of scope: good walker: has a quick action: second foal: half-brother to French 3-y-o 1½m winner Diagoras (by Caerleon): dam, maiden, should have been suited by middle distances: fair colt: successful in maiden in July and nursery (by ¾ length from Level Xing, making all) at Kempton in August: good fifth of 8 to Mujaazif in Royal Lodge William Hill Stakes at Ascot, best run in pattern company final 3 starts: probably better suited by 1m than shorter. *C. E. Brittain.*

SUN SURFER (FR) 2 ch.c. (Jan 20) R B Chesne 123–Sweet Cashmere (FR) 77 (Kashmir II 125) [1990 7m³ 6f³ 7s] 240,000 francs (approx £22,200) Y: rangy colt, shade unfurnished: third foal: half-brother to French 11f winner Crissa (by Vay-raan): dam French middle-distance winner: modest form when placed in maidens at Ascot (4 ran) and Newmarket: well beaten in valuable restricted race at Deauville: almost certainly needs further than 6f: looked weak, and is sort to need time. *H. R. A. Cecil.*

SUNWARD SOARING (USA) 3 b.f. Storm Bird (CAN) 134–Nell's Briquette 89 (USA) (Lanyon (USA)) [1989 NR 1990 8f³ 8g* 8m² 8m 8m*] rather angular filly: fourth reported foal: half-sister to high-class 1987 2-y-o 6f to 1m winner Sanquirico (by Lypheor) and very smart 1½m winner Love The Groom (by Blushing Groom): dam good-class performer at up to 1m in USA: fair form: won maiden at Edinburgh in June and handicap at Chepstow in October. *J. H. M. Gosden.*

SUNWIND 4 b.g. Windjammer (USA)–Mrewa (Runnymede 123) [1989 7s 7g 7f 6h 45 6m 6m⁶ 6f 6g² 1990 6f 6m 7.6m 7f⁶ 8m 8f] stocky gelding: poor maiden: form in handicaps at 4 yrs only on fourth outing (soon lost position): should stay 1m: acts on firm and dead going: inconsistent. *J. Sutcliffe.*

SUOMI (IRE) 2 b.c. (Mar 20) Tate Gallery (USA) 117–Finlandia (FR) (Far- 97 P away Son (USA) 130) [1990 7s*]
    Newcastle racecourse may be experiencing a lean time at present but it played host to an interesting two-year-old in Suomi, a half-brother to the St Leger winner Snurge, at its newly-inaugurated flat fixture in November, and those few spectators present witnessed a useful debut from a colt with a bright future over middle distances. Suomi started third favourite in a field of fifteen for what seemed just an ordinary northern seven-furlong maiden, though he had already been entered for the Irish Two Thousand Guineas and the Irish Derby, but so easily was he travelling three furlongs out that there was little doubt that he was going to win. One of a group of six who raced along the far rail, nearly always an advantage at Newcastle when the ground is soft, Suomi joined Mahong, quite a close fifth in a Newmarket maiden on his debut, two furlongs out, started to draw clear when pushed along half a furlong later and was five lengths in front inside the final furlong when Mahong, himself clear in second, was eased. At the line Suomi had been eased as well, but had ten lengths to spare, with Belsalaama, an eye-catching third under a considerate ride, staying on a further two lengths back. Though Suomi was flattered to win by so far his performance couldn't fail to impress, and his timefigure (equivalent to a timerating of 100) was one few two-year-olds achieve first time out. He might not be the most promising youngster in his stable—Island Universe is also there—but he's sure to improve a good deal, and he'll command respect in better company, particularly at a mile and a quarter or more.
    Suomi is from the first crop of the smart Irish two-year-old Tate Gallery, who died in 1990 in transit from Coolmore Stud to Heathrow from where he was due to be flown to Japan. A full brother to Sadler's Wells and Fairy King, and from the family of Nureyev and Thatch, Tate Gallery had made an auspicious start to his career as a stallion and figured among the leading first-

		Northern Dancer	Nearctic
	Tate Gallery (USA)	(b 1961)	Natalma
	(b 1983)	Fairy Bridge	Bold Reason
Suomi (IRE)		(b 1975)	Special
(b.c. Mar 20, 1988)		Faraway Son	Ambiopoise
	Finlandia (FR)	(b 1967)	Locust Time
	(b 1977)	Musical II	Prince Chevalier
		(ch 1961)	Musidora

season sires: his initial crop contained numerous individual winners and such useful performers as the Dewhurst third Surrealist, the Rockfel second Lee Artiste and the Irish sprinter Title Roll. Suomi was bought for 90,000 guineas at one of the Cartier sessions of the Irish National Yearling Sales; he is a three-parts brother to the 1987 Irish Oaks fourth Faraway Pastures (by Northfields) as well as a half-brother to Snurge (by Ela-Mana-Mou). His dam Finlandia is a half-sister to the Irish Derby third Master Glory and the very useful French middle-distance filly Musique Royale, and a granddaughter of the One Thousand Guineas and Oaks winner Musidora. Most of the better members of this successful family—who also include Horage, Homing, Heavenly Thought and Water Mill—needed a mile or more to show their best form, and Suomi looks sure to follow suit. His race at Newcastle was on soft ground; interestingly, Snurge acts well on heavy and has been kept clear of top-of-the-ground since his debut. *L. M. Cumani.*

SUPADUPA   3 ch.f. Superlative 118–Maysina 76 (Sheshoon 132) [1989 NR 1990   —
a8g⁵ a6g³ a8g a5g⁵ 10d a6g] 2,600F, 2,500Y, 4,500 2-y-o: fourth foal: half-sister to 6f seller winner Musical Rhapsody (by Music Boy): dam, placed over 7f and 1m at 2 yrs, is daughter of half-sister to high-class sprinter Moubariz: no worthwhile form, in seller on first run for 8 months penultimate start. *J. White.*

SUPER BAR   8 b.g. Le Bavard (FR) 125–Super Queen (Super Sam 124) [1989 NR   —
1990 16d5] second foal: dam placed over hurdles in Ireland: won 3 novice hurdles in 1987/8: well-beaten fifth of 9 in celebrity race at Sedgefield in November. *J. J. O'Neill.*

SUPER BENZ   4 ch.g. Hello Gorgeous (USA) 128–Investiture 62 (Welsh   87
Pageant 132) [1989 8.2s⁶ 10.6s 8.5d⁴ 8m⁴ 6f* 6m⁴ 6g³ 6m 5m 6g 1990 6m³ 5f⁶ 7m²
6g 6m⁶ 6g⁶ 7g* 7m* 7m² 7.6g 7d² 7m⁶ 7g 7d⁶ a5g³ a7g a7g4] leggy, lengthy gelding: has a roundish action: made all in seller (sold out of M. H. Easterby's stable £3,800) at Edinburgh in July and claimer at Catterick (claimed out of P. Monteith's stable £11,000) in August: also ran well when second in handicaps: ideally suited by 7f: acts on firm and dead going: occasionally visored: has won for apprentice: has looked none too genuine, but did little wrong at 4 yrs. *T. Fairhurst.*

SUPERBRAVE   4 b.c. Superlative 118–Tribal Feast 100 (Tribal Chief 125) [1989   82
7g 1990 6f* 6m⁴ 7m 7m⁴ 6m³ 5m*] strong, lengthy colt: won minor event at Folkestone in March and £12,100 Northern Rock Gosforth Park Cup (Handicap) at Newcastle in June: best at 6f or stiff 5f: has raced only a sound surface: raced freely and tended to wander third outing. *J. Etherington.*

SUPERCHIP   3 ch.c. Superlative 118–Crockfords Green 73 (Roan Rocket 128)   —
[1989 8f 7.5f 8f 1990 8f 8.2g] good-topped colt: poor maiden: sold 3,300 gns Doncaster September Sales. *J. Etherington.*

SUPER DEB   3 ch.f. Superlative 118–Debutina Park 87 (Averof 123) [1989 6m³   68
5f² 5m* 6g 1990 7g 5.8f 6m 7m 7f 6m* 6m⁴ 6f² 6g* 6m 6g 6g 6d⁶ a6g] good-topped filly: shows knee action: quite modest performer on her day: won claimer at Windsor in July and handicap (well-drawn favourite) at Hamilton in September: stays 6f: acts on firm going: bandaged behind fourth start: blinkered 4 times: sold 2,800 gns Newmarket December Sales. *B. Hanbury.*

SUPERENDO   2 ch.f. (Mar 1) Superlative 118–Moment In Time 91 (Without Fear   50 §
(FR) 128) [1990 5g⁴ 5m³ 7f⁴ 6m a8g] 12,500F: smallish, sparely-made filly: fourth foal: sister to 3-y-o 1m winner Superenfer: dam 7f winner at 2 yrs: best efforts when in frame in maidens at Chester and Wolverhampton first 2 starts: seemed reluctant to race at Southwell final outing. *D. Burchell.*

SUPERENFER   3 b.g. Superlative 118–Moment In Time 91 (Without Fear (FR)   74
128) [1989 6g³ 6m³ 6s² 6m 1990 8f³ 7d⁴ 7.6g 8m 8m*] strong, lengthy gelding: good mover: modest performer: visored, improved form to make all in moderately-run handicap at Pontefract in September: stays 1m: acts on any going: also visored once at 2 yrs: sometimes sweating and edgy: gelded after final start. *J. G. FitzGerald.*

SUPERETTA   3 ch.f. Superlative 118–Brown's Cay 71 (Formidable (USA) 125)   **61**
[1989 7g⁴ 6g⁵ 1990 8m³ 8m 8m² 8g 10g⁴ 11.7f² 10m* 10d² 10g⁶] angular, sparely-made filly: quite modest performer at best: looked reluctant once leading just inside final 1f when winning seller (sold out of J. Hills's stable 3,200 gns) at Leicester in October: second in similar event at Nottingham, easily better subsequent effort: probably stays 11.7f: acts on firm and dead ground: took good hold in blinkers fourth start: winning selling hurdler: not one to trust implicitly. *J. R. Jenkins.*

SUPERGLOW   3 ch.g. Kalaglow 132–Super Lady (Averof 123) [1989 NR 1990   **55**
10f⁶ 8.3f⁶ 8m 7d⁶ 8m] dipped-backed gelding: sixth foal: half-brother to 3 winners, including fair 6f and 1m winner Super Punk (by Hot Spark) and 1988 2-y-o 6f winner Super Morning (by Martinmas): dam ran 4 times at 2 yrs: plating-class maiden: should be suited by further than 7f: probably best on an easy surface: hung left final start: sold to join M. Madgwick 1,850 gns Ascot November Sales. *P. T. Walwyn.*

SUPER GUNNER   5 ch.g. Busted 134–Lunaria (USA) (Twist The Axe (USA))   **51**
[1989 11.7d 12d⁴ 1990 a13g* a12g* a13g 12.3d 12g⁵ 16g a12g a12g] lengthy gelding: poor mover: easy winner of claimers at Lingfield in February, making all in first: well beaten in handicaps after, off course 4½ months before final outing: stays 13f: acts on firm and dead going. *M. J. Fetherston-Godley.*

SUPER HEIGHTS   2 b.c. (Feb 21) Superlative 118–Shadha 57 (Shirley Heights   **79**
130) [1990 6m 5f* 6d 7s] 13,500Y: lengthy, useful-looking colt: has scope: second foal: half-brother to a winner in Italy: dam ran twice at 2 yrs: won maiden auction at Warwick in July by ½ length, soon behind and ridden along then headway to lead inside final 1f: very good eleventh of 19, never dangerous, in Racecall Gold Trophy at Redcar: should stay 7f: possibly unsuited by soft ground. *Miss A. J. Whitfield.*

SUPER LUNAR   6 gr.g. Kalaglow 132–Roxy Hart (High Top 131) [1989 7s⁵ 8g³   —
9.2f⁴ 8f 8m⁴ 8m² 9f* 8.5g⁵ 8m³ 8g³ 11v⁴ 10g² 1990 8f 11m] strong, close-coupled gelding: modest winner as 5-y-o: ran poorly in £7,900 handicap at Newbury in May, and not seen out again: stays 1¼m: seems not at his best on soft going, acts on any other: ran moderately in blinkers: often takes good hold. *L. G. Cottrell.*

SUPER MALT (IRE)   2 ch.f. (Mar 6) Milk of The Barley 115–Super Amber   **51**
(Yellow God 129) [1990 6g 7m 8m] IR 5,000Y: leggy, rather shallow-girthed filly: good walker: has rather round action: half-sister to several winners, including 1981 2-y-o 5f winner Super Natalie (by On Your Mark): dam never ran: poor form in maidens and a minor event: probably stays 1m. *R. Hannon.*

SUPER MORNING   4 b.c. Martinmas 128–Super Lady (Averof 123) [1989 8s   **54**
7s⁵ 8.5d 7g 7g²ᵈⁱˢ 7m 7m 7m⁴ 8f⁵ 8m 1990 8g 8g 7g² a8g⁴] tall, good-bodied colt: plating-class handicapper: slowly away and ridden throughout in amateurs race final outing: should stay 1¼m: acts on any going: blinkered or visored last 7 starts at 3 yrs. *G. B. Balding.*

SUPER ONE   3 b.g. Superlative 118–Josephine Gibney (High Top 131) [1989 5d   **77 d**
6m² 5f* 6f³ 5f4 7m 6g 6m* 6s 6m 7m 1990 a8g³ a8g* a7g* 9 1m⁶ 7f 7g 7g* 7g⁶ 7g 7m a7g³ 6m a8g² 7f³] compact gelding: moderate mover: modest handicapper: made most to win at Lingfield and Southwell in February and landed a gamble in seller (bought in 5,000 gns) at Catterick in June: rather headstrong, and should prove best at up to 1m: possibly unsuited by soft going: apprentice ridden: has won blinkered and when not: has worn a tongue strap: inconsistent. *T. D. Barron.*

SUPEROO   4 b.g. Superlative 118–Shirleen (Daring Display (USA) 129) [1989 7f⁶   **87**
10.1m 8f⁶ 7m* 7m* 7g* 7g 1990 7g 8f⁶ 8f⁶ 7.3g 7m] big, workmanlike gelding: has a rather round action: fair handicapper: good sixth (reportedly sustained knee injury) of 32, weakening final 1f, to Pontenuovo in Royal Hunt Cup at Royal Ascot: then off course 3 months and never able to challenge (carrying condition) both starts in September: ideally suited by 7f: acts on firm going. *J. Sutcliffe.*

SUPER SPACEMATE   2 gr.g. (Feb 18) Absalom 128–Stedham 84 (Jaazeiro   **75**
(USA) 127) [1990 5m³ 5f⁴ 5g² 5m³ 5m⁶ 6v² 6d⁴] 7,600F: compact, angular gelding: first foal: dam 2-y-o 6f winner: modest maiden: excellent second of 7, making most and battling on well, to Pesidanamich in nursery at Ayr penultimate start: ran badly at Chester after: stays 6f: acts well on heavy ground: retained 3,200 gns Doncaster October Sales. *J. Berry.*

SUPER STAFF (USA)   2 ch.f. (Mar 11) Secretariat (USA)–Prodigious (FR)   **85 p**
(Pharly (FR) 130) [1990 7m²] $160,000Y: quite attractive filly: third foal: half-sister to a winner by Blushing Groom at up to 1¼m: dam French 1m and 1¼m winner: backward and green, 1½ lengths second of 18, headway 2f out and keeping on well despite carrying head bit awkwardly, to Noble Destiny in maiden at Leicester in October: sure to improve, particularly over 1m + , and win a race. *B. W. Hills.*

SUP

SUPER TED   3 ch.g. Superlative 118–Gandoorah 90 (Record Token 128) [1989   —
NR 1990 6s 8.2v 8m 7g 8d⁵] 15,500Y: lengthy gelding: third foal: half-brother to
quite modest 1987 2-y-o 6f and 7f winner Axia (by Comedy Star) and 1990
Scandinavian 5f to 7f winner Intensive (by Superlative): dam 2-y-o 5f winner out of
half- sister to top-class sprinter Roman Warrior: 25/1, first sign of ability when
never-nearer fifth of 19 in selling handicap at Doncaster: stays 1m. *W. J. Musson.*

SUPERTOP   2 b. or br.c. (May 3) High Top 131–Myth 89 (Troy 137) [1990 7g 8g³]   89 p
IR 26,000Y: leggy, unfurnished colt: has scope: first foal: dam middle-distance
winner, is out of close relation to Wassl: around 3 lengths third of 7, making most of 6f,
to Commendable in maiden at York in October: may well improve again. *P. W.
Harris.*

SUPER TRIP   9 b.g. Windjammer (USA)–Esker Rose (Sunny Way 120) [1989 7f   58
8f⁴ 1990 7f 8f² 8f 7.6m 7m] well-made gelding: carries plenty of condition: poor
mover: modest winner as 7-y-o: 33/1, best effort for long time second in invitation
handicap (lady ridden) at Newmarket in August: best at around 1m: best form on a
sound surface: suited by waiting tactics: usually wears bandages. *M. J. Fetherston-
Godley.*

SUPER TRUCKER   7 b.g. Lochnager 132–The Haulier 53 (Pitskelly 122) [1989   —
8h 1990 10.2m 12.4f 8f⁴ 8m] leggy gelding: has a round action: poor handicapper:
stays 9f: used to go well on soft going: occasionally sweats: has won for apprentice:
inconsistent. *W. W. Haigh.*

SUPER VIRTUOSA   3 b.f. Wassl 125–Resolve (Reform 132) [1989 5s² 5g³ 5m⁴   47
6g⁶ 7m⁴ 8m⁵ 7g 1990 7g⁶ 7d 11.7m 12m⁵ 10d⁵ 10.6v 10g*] leggy, lengthy filly: poor
mover: plating-class performer: won claimer at Newmarket in November, strong
run to lead close home: stays 1¼m: acts on dead going: joined M. Pipe. *M. J. Haynes.*

SUPER ZOOM   4 ch.g. Ballad Rock 122–Ruby River (Red God 128§) [1989 NR   —
1990 5g 6d 6m] robust, lengthy, dipped-backed gelding: fairly useful 5f winner as
2-y-o: soundly beaten in handicaps in June: visored final outing. *M. R. Channon.*

SUPREME BLUES   4 b.c. Cure The Blues (USA)–Court Barns (USA) 101 (Riva   50
Ridge (USA)) [1989 8d 8g a8g⁴ a10g³ a8g 1990 a7g² a11g⁴ a8g⁵ a8g⁵ a7g* a7g⁶ a7g
8v a7g a5g] angular, sparely-made colt: moderate mover: made all in maiden at
Southwell in March: below form after, running poorly last 3 outings: best at 7f:
seems unsuited by heavy going: blinkered or visored: often claimer ridden: sold
1,150 gns Doncaster October Sales. *M. Brittain.*

SUPREME CHOICE (USA)   2 b.c. (Feb 6) Sovereign Dancer (USA)–Editor's   61 p
Choice (USA) (Sir Ivor 135) [1990 7m 7s] $75,000F, IR 250,000Y: leggy colt: has
scope: half-brother to 2 minor winners in North America: dam minor winner in
North America at up to 9f: green, 13 lengths seventh of 22, no impression from over
2f out, to Desert Sun in maiden at Doncaster in October: bit backward and slowly
away on debut: will be better suited by 1m + : likely to improve again. *B. W. Hills.*

SUPREME COURT   3 b.g. Yashgan 126–My Natalie 64 (Rheingold 137) [1989   54
5d⁴ 5f⁴ 6g 7.5g³ 7g 7m³ 7m 6m⁶ 10.6d a6g 1990 8.2f³ 7m 10g* 8m² 9m³ 13.8m⁶ a8g]
sparely-made gelding: plater: won at Ripon (no bid) in May, making most and staying on strongly: suited by 1¼m: acts on good to firm ground: visored 3 times at 2 yrs:
has given trouble at stalls: usually on toes: sold out of J. Johnson's stable 320 gns
Doncaster October Sales after sixth start. *M. Dods.*

SUPREME DANCER (FR)   3 b.g. Alzao (USA) 117–Supreme Solar (Royal   62
Captive 116) [1989 6g 1990 7f⁵ 8m* 8.2g⁵ 7f⁴ 8g 8g 8.3m² 8h³ 7f⁶ 8m⁴ 7d] quite
attractive gelding: modest performer: ridden by 5-lb claimer, won seller (bought in
11,000 gns) at Pontefract in April: should stay 1¼m: acts on hard going: trained until
after penultimate start by W. Jarvis: has joined N. Tinkler. *R. Akehurst.*

SUPREME DESIRE   2 gr.f. (Mar 21) Grey Desire 115–Fire Mountain 87   40
(Dragonara Palace (USA) 115) [1990 5m⁵ 5g 5m 6d⁴ 6m² 6m 5m 5v] leggy,
shallow-girthed filly: fourth foal: half-sister to fair sprinter Saint Systems (by Uncle
Pokey): dam 2-y-o 5f winner: poor maiden: better suited by 6f than 5f. *R. Akehurst.*

SUPRETTE   3 b.f. Superlative 118–Blaskette 99 (Blast 125) [1989 6g⁴ 1990 7m⁶   64
7m⁶ 7g⁴ 7.6g 7m] workmanlike filly: second modest maiden: ran poorly, facing stiffish
tasks, in handicaps last 2 outings: stays 7f. *J. W. Hills.*

SUPRISE ENVOY   2 b.c. (Apr 14) Grey Desire 115–Conrara 82 (Balidar 133)   61
[1990 5m⁴ 6m⁴ 6f⁶ 6m* 5m²] small, angular, good-quartered colt: third foal: half-
brother to 3-y-o Mistroma (by Absalom): dam sprinter: showed improved form to
win selling nursery (no bid) at Ripon in June: stayed 6f: bandaged first 2 starts and
last: dead. *M. Brittain.*

SURCOAT 3 b.c. Bustino 136–Mullet 75 (Star Appeal 133) [1989 6f 7f⁵ 8m⁵ 8.2g 76
a7g⁶ 1990 12.3f³ 12g* 11.5m² 16.2s⁵ 13.6g* 12.4m² 13g⁶ 12.3m* 14g 14d] small,
sturdy colt: carries condition: poor mover: modest handicapper: won at Carlisle in
May, Redcar in June and Ripon in August: may prove ideally suited by around 1¾m:
probably acts on any going: ran well in net muzzle once at 2 yrs: game and consistent: sold to join J. Baker 12,000 gns Newmarket Autumn Sales. *C. W. C. Elsey.*

SUREFOOT SILLARS 3 ch.g. Hotfoot 126–Make A Signal 76 (Royal Gunner 49 §
(USA)) [1989 7g 6f⁶ 6d⁶ 7g 1990 7f 8f 7m 8m⁶ 10.2m⁶ 12.2g³ 13m⁴ 12m 15.8m² 16m⁶]
neat gelding: plating-class maiden: stays 2m: acts on good to firm ground and dead:
has carried head high and wandered under pressure: blinkered seventh and eighth
starts: ran creditably for 7-lb claimer penultimate one: retained by trainer 5,000 gns
Doncaster August Sales: winning claiming hurdler: ungenuine. *Mrs J. R. Ramsden.*

SURENCHERE (FR) 2 b.g. (Feb 14) Maelstrom Lake 118–Pertinence (FR) 74
(Fiasco 119) [1990 8m⁵ 8.2d 8.2s³] 130,000 francs (approx £12,000) Y: first foal: dam
French 11f winner: ridden by 7-lb claimer, staying-on third of 13 to Port Sunlight in
maiden at Haydock in October, easily best effort: will stay 1¼m. *J. G. FitzGerald.*

SURE SHARP (USA) 3 b.c. Sharpen Up 127–Double Lock 104 (Home Guard 115
(USA) 129) [1989 6g⁵ 6g* 1990 8g² 8f] big, good-topped colt: has plenty of scope:
smart performer: backward, beaten short head by Tirol in Craven Stakes at
Newmarket, leading 2f out, edging right and no extra close home: 9/1, didn't confirm
that promise in 2000 Guineas there 16 days later, front rank long way and not given
hard race: may well stay beyond 1m: possibly unsuited by firm going. *B. W. Hills.*

SURE SIGN 2 b.f. (Mar 22) Sure Blade (USA) 128–Hyroglyph (USA) (Northern 54
Dancer) [1990 6f a6g³] leggy filly: fifth foal: half-sister to a winner in USA by Arts
And Letters: dam lightly-raced close relative of very smart 1¼m performer Upper
Nile and top-class filly at up to 1¼m De La Rose: ridden by claimer, third to Sally's
Prince in maiden at Southwell in September, better effort: will stay 7f. *B. W. Hills.*

SUREST DANCER (USA) 4 b.c. Green Dancer (USA) 132–Oopsie Daisy 61
(USA) (Dewan) [1989 7d 10m³ 10m 10.8f³ 12m 17.6m⁴ 16f⁴ 15.3f a12g⁶ 1990 16.2g⁴
18m⁵ 18m²] medium-sized, rather finely-made colt: has a fluent, slightly round
action: quite modest maiden: stays 2¼m: acts on firm going: blinkered last 3 starts
at 3 yrs. *Mrs P. A. Barker.*

SURE VICTORY (IRE) 2 ch.f. (Mar 31) Stalker 121–Ultra (Stanford 121§) —
[1990 6d] 13,500Y: second foal: dam maiden: soundly beaten in maiden at Folkestone in November. *P. T. Walwyn.*

SURPASSING 3 ch.f. Superlative 118–Catherine Howard 68 (Tower Walk 130) —
[1989 5f⁴ 6f² 5f⁴ 5f 7g* 7m⁵ 9g³ 8m 1990 8g⁶ 10d 8m 8g] lengthy, rather sparely-
made filly: has a fluent action: modest winner at 2 yrs: faced stiff tasks in 1990,
showing little last 3 outings: needs at least 7f and stays 9f: blinkered and edgy once
at 2 yrs. *C. E. Brittain.*

SURPRISE ATTACK 9 gr.g. Town Crier 119–Pearl Harbour (Martial 131) —
[1989 NR 1990 a8g a11g] strong, plain gelding: of no account. *E. Eldin.*

SURREALIST (IRE) 2 b.c. (Mar 1) Tate Gallery (USA) 117–Natuschka (Authi 107 p
123) [1990 6m 7g* 7d³] IR 30,000F, 64,000Y: strong, angular colt: has a quick
action: half-brother to winning Irish middle-distance stayers Newton John (by Head
For Heights) and Hanarch (by Dara Monarch): dam won from 9f to 2m in Ireland:
16/1 and carrying condition, won 16-runner maiden at Sandown in September by ¾
length from Jura: excellent third of 8, staying on well having been outpaced over 2f
out, to Generous in Three Chimneys Dewhurst Stakes at Newmarket following
month: will be well suited by 1m + : very much on the upgrade. *B. W. Hills.*

SURREY DANCER 2 b.c. (Apr 22) Shareef Dancer (USA) 135–Juliette Marny 57
123 (Blakeney 126) [1990 7m 8m 8m] 26,000Y: leggy, sparely-made colt: poor
mover: closely related to 1½m winner North Briton (by Northfields) and half-
brother to 2 other winners, including Pretty Polly winner Jolly Bay (by Mill Reef):
dam winner of Oaks and Irish Oaks, is sister to Julio Mariner and half-sister to
Scintillate: never dangerous, twice slowly away, in maidens at Newmarket twice
and Leicester: will stay 1¼m. *B. Hanbury.*

SURREY RACING 2 b.g. (Apr 11) Electric 126–Garnette Rose 74 (Floribunda 50 +
136) [1990 6f 6g 5m 5.8d] 14,000Y: neat gelding: half-brother to 4 winners here and
abroad, including fairly useful 1985 2-y-o 5f winner Camilla's Boy (by Faraway
Times): dam seemed to stay 1m: poor form: well backed after eye-catching run, last
in nursery at Bath final start: will be better suited by 7f + . *G. Lewis.*

SURSAS 3 b.g. Chief Singer 131–Dignified Air (FR) 70 (Wolver Hollow 126) [1989 —
6m⁴ 5m⁵ 6g 8.2s⁶ 7g 1990 10.2f] strong gelding: plating-class maiden at best: should

stay beyond 6f: looked ungenerous when blinkered once at 2 yrs: sold 6,000 gns Newmarket July Sales: resold 950 gns Newmarket Autumn Sales: one to be wary of. *J. G. FitzGerald.*

SURVEY 2 b.f. (Apr 26) Glint of Gold 128–Old Domesday Book 93 (High Top 131) **46** [1990 6s 7m 6m] workmanlike filly: has scope: first foal: dam 10.4f winner better at 1½m: poor form, including when blinkered in a seller final start: pulled hard previous outing. *G. A. Pritchard-Gordon.*

SUSAN HENCHARD 6 b.m. Auction Ring (USA) 123–Let Slip 77 (Busted 134) **—** [1989 10.2g³ 11v³ 11d 8f 10f 11f⁶ a11g 1990 a13g] rather angular, deep-girthed mare: moderate mover: poor performer: ran as though something amiss at Southwell in January: stays 11f: probably unsuited by firm going nowadays: occasionally blinkered or visored: has given trouble in preliminaries, and started slowly: sold 2,300 gns Doncaster March Sales: winning selling hurdler in December. *M. Avison.*

SUSANNA'S SECRET 3 b.c. Superlative 118–Queens Welcome 60 (North- **73** fields (USA)) [1989 6g 6g a6g 1990 6f⁵ 7f* 7m* 7m 7m* 7g] strong, close-coupled colt: keen walker: has a quick action: modest handicapper: led final 1f to win at Folkestone and Redcar (twice) in second half of season: ran poorly fourth and final starts: better at 7f than 6f: acts on firm going: seems rather lazy. *W. Carter.*

SUSAN'S REEF 5 b.g. Main Reef 126–Susan's Way (Red God 128§) [1989 5g 9f **38** 8m 8.3d 8f 6s² 1990 6f 6f 8m⁴ 6m⁵ a7g 6m] workmanlike gelding: has a long stride: poor maiden: stays 1m: acts on good to firm and soft going: tried in blinkers at 2 yrs: inconsistent. *J. M. Bradley.*

SUSHA 3 gr.f. Bay Express 132–Gem-May 71 (Mansingh (USA) 120) [1989 5d⁵ **—** 5f* 6m 5g³ 5g 1990 5d] neat filly: moderate mover: plating-class winner as 2-y-o: burly and mulish in paddock, last of 16 facing stiff task in handicap in September, 1990: likely to prove best at 5f: bandaged last 2 starts at 2 yrs. *A. M. Robson.*

SUSHI 2 gr.f. (Feb 15) Nishapour (FR) 125–Falaka 83 (Sparkler 130) [1990 8.2m **—** 8.2v] angular, unfurnished filly: second reported foal: half-sister to 3-y-o Sashimi (by Kind of Hush): dam 7f and 1m winner: always towards rear in minor events at Nottingham (ridden by 7-lb claimer, slowly away) and Haydock in autumn. *D. Morley.*

SUSPECT DEVICE 3 ch.g. Dublin Taxi–Kimstar 61 (Aureole 132) [1989 6g **—** 7.5f⁴ 8f⁶ 1990 7g 7d 9m⁶ 8.5f] smallish colt: poor maiden: mostly faced very stiff tasks in 1990: stays 7.5f: blinkered last 2 starts. *S. E. Kettlewell.*

SUSURRATION (USA) 3 b.f. Erins Isle 121–Grease 125 (Filiberto (USA) 123) **100** [1989 NR 1990 8g⁴ 10.5g⁶ 8s* 8v³] tall, angular filly: second foal: half-sister to fairly useful Italian 7.5f and 1m winner Squeaky Wheel (by Riverman): dam successful from 5f (as 2-y-o) to 1¼m in France, and later in USA: 4 lengths sixth of 12 to Stagecraft in maiden at York and easily landed odds in similar event at Newcastle in autumn: good third in Group 3 event at Milan: stays 1¼m: acts on heavy going. *J. H. M. Gosden.*

SUZY LORENZO 5 b. or br.m. Swing Easy (USA) 126–Love Beach 75 **—** (Lorenzaccio 130) [1989 a8g⁶ a10g 1990 a7g⁶ a7g] tall, leggy mare: lightly-raced maiden: best form at 1m: visored twice at 3 yrs, blinkered last 4 starts: sold privately 2,000 gns Ascot February Sales. *R. J. O'Sullivan.*

SVETLANA 2 b.f. (Feb 20) Darshaan 133–Belle Doche (FR) (Riverman (USA) **?** 131) [1990 8v*] fifth foal: half-sister to several winners, including French 5.5f to 1¼m winner Tamarinda (by Relkino), successful also in USA: dam French 5.5f and 7f winner at 2 yrs: won newcomers race at Saint-Cloud in November by a head: will stay 1¼m: sure to go on to better things. *A. de Royer-Dupre, France.*

SVETLANA PROSSER 2 b.f. (May 23) Welsh Captain 113–Balilyca (Balidar **41** 133) [1990 5g⁴ 6m⁵ 5f 5m² 5g⁵ 5d⁴] 800Y, resold 725Y: smallish, good-quartered filly: fourth live foal: dam plating class: quite modest plater: will prove better suited by 6f than 5f. *C. B. B. Booth.*

SWAGMAN (USA) 3 ch.g. Graustark–Mawgrit (USA) (Hoist The Flag (USA)) **53** [1989 NR 1990 7f 10m 10f² 14f⁵ 10f³ 14m⁵ a12g⁶ a12g*] $32,000, 320,000 francs (approx £29,300) Y: sparely-made gelding: good mover: fourth foal: dam minor winner at 2 yrs in USA, is half-sister to high-class 5f winner Raise A Cup: former plater: best efforts at Southwell last 2 starts, making all in handicap in November: suited by 1½m: sold out of P. Kelleway's stable 4,000 gns Ascot September Sales after sixth start. *J. L. Harris.*

SWAN WALK (IRE) 2 gr.c. (Jan 30) Godswalk (USA) 130–Garland Song (My **73** Swanee 122) [1990 6g 10s 7d³ 6d⁵] IR 4,000F, 16,000Y: close-coupled, quite good-topped colt: poor mover: half-brother to fairly useful 1981 2-y-o 6f winner Lala (by Welsh Saint): dam plating-class half-sister to Cajun and smart but moody sprinter Ubedizzy: best effort staying-on third to Sunny Davis in maiden at Edinburgh: backward previously, running better than position suggests second start: really needs further than 6f, and gives impression may prove best at around 1m. *Mrs N. Macauley.*

SWATTLING THOMAS 3 ch.g. Ballacashtal (CAN)–Princess Xenia (USA) — (Transworld (USA) 121) [1989 5g 5f 5m⁴ 6m³ 7f³ 6f² 6m* 6m 6g 6g 7d³ a6g³ a6g a7g 1990 a6g5] workmanlike gelding: winning plater at 2 yrs: seen out only once (in January) in 1990: best beyond 5f: blinkered 3 times at 2 yrs, visored once: has been taken down early: sometimes on toes. *J. Berry.*

SWEEP ALONG (IRE) 2 b.f. (Apr 12) Persian Bold 123–Bristle 96 (Thatch 67 (USA) 136) [1990 6m 6f⁶ 6.5g] 36,000Y: smallish filly: first foal: dam Irish 2-y-o 8.5f winner stayed 1½m, is out of half-sister to Old Country: fourteenth of 17, in touch 4f, in Tattersalls Tiffany Yorkshire Stakes at Doncaster, final and best effort: will be better suited by 7f + . *G. A. Pritchard-Gordon.*

SWEET AND SURE 5 gr.m. Known Fact (USA) 135–Fair Melys (FR) 81 (Welsh — Pageant 132) [1989 NR 1990 11.5m] sparely-made, close-coupled mare: has a round action: well beaten all 3 outings. *E. A. Wheeler.*

SWEET BAY 4 b.f. Sweet Monday 122–Moonlight Bay 53 (Palm Track 122) [1989 43 NR 1990 8g 7g 8m 12f 10.6d 8.2g⁴ 10m 12m] lengthy filly: first foal: dam won 1m seller and juvenile hurdle: 100/1, fourth to very easy winner Grey Owl in maiden at Hamilton in September: little other show, including in sellers: refused to enter stalls intended debut: sweated final start: sold 2,000 gns Doncaster November Sales. *M. P. Naughton.*

SWEET BUBBLES (IRE) 2 ch.f. (Mar 5) Dominion 123–Regal Decoy (Troy — 137) [1990 6d] angular filly: first foal: dam Irish 1½m winner, is half-sister to Knockando: bit backward, slowly away, ran green and never a threat in maiden at Leicester in June. *C. A. Cyzer.*

SWEET DECREE 2 ch.f. (Mar 19) Known Fact (USA) 135–Skiddaw (USA) — (Grey Dawn II 132) [1990 6g] 3,400F, 5,200Y: sparely-made filly: second foal: half-sister to 3-y-o 6f winner Lakeland Beauty (by Mummy's Pet): dam never ran: bit backward, hampered start and well behind from 2f out in maiden auction at Nottingham in June. *C. A. Cyzer.*

SWEET DESIRE 2 b. or br.f. (Apr 21) Grey Desire 115–Sweet Delilah (Hello 45 Gorgeous (USA) 128) [1990 5m 5g⁵ 5f⁴ 5s⁴ 6f⁴ 5m³ 5f⁴ a6g 5.3h⁵ 5.3h⁵ 5.1m⁴ 6m⁶] 3,000F, 400Y: leggy, light-framed filly: first foal: dam lightly raced: moderate plater: raced with head high penultimate start: stays 6f: acts on hard ground: usually ridden by 7-lb claimer: inconsistent: sent to Sweden. *C. N. Allen.*

SWEETEN GALE 4 ch.f. On Your Mark 125–Betty Bun (St Chad 120) [1989 5g — 10f 8.2g 1990 a6g] smallish, sparely-made filly: no longer of much account. *T. Kersey.*

SWEET GLEN 2 ch.c. (Apr 19) Glenstal (USA) 118–Quite Sweet 100 (Super Sam — 124) [1990 6m 6g 7g] 13,000Y: unfurnished colt: moderate walker: half-brother to several winners, including 1¼m winner Llanarmon (by Lochnager) and fairly useful 5f to 7f winner Lucky Man (by Manacle): dam best at up to 1¼m: well beaten in varied races: blinkered final start. *C. James.*

SWEETINGS PEARL 2 ro.f. (May 2) Domynsky 110–Nellie Bly 80 (Dragonara 51 Palace (USA) 115) [1990 5f 5g³ 5m⁴ 5t² a5g⁶ 5f⁵ 5m⁶ 5f] leggy non-thoroughbred filly: third foal: dam sprinter, successful at 2 yrs: plating-class performer: often visored: sometimes bandaged: inconsistent. *M. H. Easterby.*

SWEET 'N' LOW 3 b.c. Kampala 120–Karin Maria 86 (Double Jump 131) [1989 50 § a7g 1990 a8g³ a7g 8.5m 10f² 12m³ 10f 10f⁴] angular, rather sparely-made colt: plating-class maiden: may prove ideally suited by 1¼m: didn't run on on final start: one to treat with caution. *M. H. Tompkins.*

SWEET N' TWENTY 4 b.f. High Top 131–Royal Home 69 (Royal Palace 131) 65 [1989 8s² 8d 8m⁴ 10f 10h³ 12h⁵ 11.7m* 11.7m 12m⁴ 14f² 14m 13.8d 1990 10m⁴ 12f² 12h³ 14g³ 13.8m* 12g³ 11g⁶ 14d 12m²] cheaply bought, lengthy filly: moderate mover: quite modest handicapper: won at Catterick in May: good second in claimer (claimed to join M. Pipe's stable £10,652) at Newmarket final start: stays 1¾m: probably acts on any going: consistent: won over hurdles in December. *R. M. Whitaker.*

SWEET SHARPO 2 ch.f. (Feb 10) Sharpo 132–Tumble Judy (Tumble Wind — (USA)) [1990 5m 7g⁵ a6g] 14,500Y: sturdy, good-quartered filly: seventh foal: closely related to useful 6f and 7f winner Cutting Wind (by Sharpen Up): dam never ran: poor form: slow-starting favourite on second start: off course 5 months after: withdrawn after giving plenty of trouble in preliminaries once. *T. Casey.*

SWEET SOUL DREAM (USA)   2 b.f. (Apr 3) Conquistador Cielo (USA)–   **61**
Minstinguette (USA) (Boldnesian) [1990 5m3 8m5 9m4] $140,000Y: leggy filly: half-sister to several winners, including top-class sprinter Committed (by Hagley): dam ran once: quite modest form in varied events, including a listed race in Rome: pulled hard to post and in race when tailed-off last of 4 in Wolverhampton maiden in October. *P. F. I. Cole.*

SWEET TASSA   2 b.f. (Feb 12) Forzando 122–Granny's Bank 88 (Music Boy 124)   **40 p**
[1990 6d6 6d] 23,000Y: smallish, workmanlike filly: good walker: first foal: dam miler, best at 5 yrs: bit backward, sixth of 12, ridden at halfway and unable to quicken, in maiden at Leicester in October: held up and never placed to challenge under considerate ride in similar event at Doncaster following month: likely to do better. *C. F. Wall.*

SWEET VOILA   3 b.f. Sayyaf 121–Sweet Princess (Prince Regent (FR) 129)   **—**
[1989 5m6 1990 8.2g 8.2g] smallish, workmanlike filly: no sign of ability in minor event and claimers: blinkered final start. *R. A. Bennett.*

SWELL TIME (IRE)   2 b.f. (May 24) Sadler's Wells (USA) 132–Amata (USA)   **—**
(Nodouble (USA)) [1990 6m6 6d] 39,000Y: small, workmanlike filly: half-sister to several winners, including French 1m and 9.5f winner Grammene (by Grey Dawn II): dam French middle-distance winner later successful in USA, is half-sister to Princess Royal winner Trillionaire: ran very green and easily outpaced from halfway in 8-runner maiden at Ascot in October: never dangerous in similar race at Doncaster. *R. Hannon.*

SWERVIN MERVIN   2 ch.g. (Feb 15) Dominion 123–Brilliant Rosa 91 (Luthier   **53**
126) [1990 5m6 6g5 6f 7.5d a7g6 a8g6] 4,600Y: lengthy gelding: has scope: fourth foal: half-brother to fair 10.2f winner/winning hurdler Smart Performer (by Formidable) and Irish 9f winner Moose Malloy (by Try My Best): dam 7f and 1½m winner: plating-class maiden: ran creditably on all-weather final start: stays 1m. *D. Dutton.*

SWIFT ASCENT (USA)   8 b.g. Crow (FR) 134–Barely Flying (USA) (Fleet   **—**
Nasrullah) [1989 NR 1990 10.2f 14.8f4] leggy, short-backed gelding: quite modest maiden at best: extremely lightly raced on flat nowadays: suited by 1¾m: possibly unsuited by soft going, acts on any other: bandaged at 8 yrs. *A. Barrow.*

SWIFT ROMANCE (IRE)   2 ch.g. (Mar 24) Coquelin (USA) 121–Douschkina   **74**
86 (Dubassoff (USA)) [1990 5m3 5f4 6d4 6m5 5f3 5g3 6m4 6m] 7,800F: leggy, workmanlike gelding: moderate walker: fourth reported foal: dam 6f winner on only start at 2 yrs but no form at 3 yrs: modest maiden: easily best effort in nursery on penultimate start: better suited by 6f than 5f, and will stay 7f: acts well on top-of-the-ground. *B. R. Millman.*

SWIFT RUNNER   3 b.g. Runnett 125–Celeritas (Dominion 123) [1989 NR 1990   **—**
8m] first foal: dam, half-sister to Manor Farm Boy, showed little form in varied races: 50/1, tailed off in maiden at Warwick in April. *L. J. Holt.*

SWIFT SILVER   3 gr.c. Bairn (USA) 126–Asmalwi 61 (Averof 123) [1989 NR   **51**
1990 a8g5 a10g5 9s5 7.5d 7m 8m] leggy, sparely-made colt: first foal: dam maiden who eventually stayed 1¾m: plating-class form but has given impression capable of better: sweating and on toes final start, first for 3½ months: will be suited by return to further: retained by trainer 5,200 gns Doncaster March Sales after second start. *W. J. Musson.*

SWIFT STREAM   2 ch.f. (Mar 12) Chief Singer 131–Sandstream 72 (Sandford   **72**
Lad 133) [1990 6m5 7d 6d] lengthy, rather dipped-backed filly: has scope: seventh foal: half-sister to several winners here and abroad, including 3-y-o Between The Sticks (by Pharly), fair 5f winner at 2 yrs: dam 2-y-o 6f winner, is half-sister to Manado: modest maiden: best effort first start. *R. F. Johnson Houghton.*

SWIFT SWORD   2 gr.g. (Mar 31) Sayf El Arab (USA) 127–Lydiate 77 (Tower   **90**
Walk 130) [1990 5m 5g* 7.5f* 7g6 8m* 8g 8d] 4,200Y: leggy, quite good-topped gelding: moderate walker and mover: half-brother to winning stayer Snowy River (by Sagaro) and 11f winner/successful hurdler Impecuniosity (by Free State): dam 1¼m winner: fairly useful colt: successful at Beverley in maiden auction in May and auction in June and in nursery (by length, clear, from On Strike) at York in September: held up and not knocked about in nurseries at Doncaster and Redcar (impeded early on by loose horse) after: better suited by 1m than shorter. *Mrs G. R. Reveley.*

SWINGAWAY LADY 2 b.f. (May 23) Nomination 125–Partridge Brook 109 75
(Birdbrook 110) [1990 6m* 7m⁶ 6g⁶ 6d* 7m 7s] 10,000Y: lengthy, unfurnished filly:
seventh live foal: half-sister to 4 winners, including plater Topsoil (by Relkino),
successful from 1m to 1½m and also over hurdles: dam won from 5f to 1¼m: well
backed, won nursery at Ayr in September by a head from Time For The Blues,
having been last at halfway: dead-heated in maiden there in July: faced stiff tasks in
nurseries final 2 starts: seems to stay 7f: acts on good to firm ground and soft. *G.
Richards.*

SWING DANCER 3 br.f. Swing Easy (USA) 126–Four Lawns 77 (Forlorn River 59
124) [1989 NR 1990 7m² 6g⁴ 8g³ 7d³ 7m³ 6g⁵ 6g⁵ 6d*] 11,000 2-y-o: lengthy, rather
angular filly: moderate mover: fifth live foal: sister to 5-y-o miler Causley: dam 5f
winner: quite modest form, often in sellers: well drawn, won claimer at Nottingham
in October, edging right when ridden to lead 1f out: stays 7f: acts on good to firm
ground and dead: blinkered fourth and sixth outings: visored last 2: sold 4,500 gns
Newmarket Autumn Sales. *D. Morley.*

SWINGING BLUES 3 b.c. Cure The Blues (USA)–Lavender Dance 99 (Dance —
In Time (CAN)) [1989 NR 1990 8.2s 8f⁴ 8m⁶ 7d 8.2m] 5,000Y: lengthy, rather
sparely-made colt: fourth foal: half-brother to 1989 Italian 1¼m winner Danally (by
Ballymore): dam, fairly useful over 5f at 2 yrs, is out of half-sister to smart
Casabianca: plating-class form: never dangerous in handicap and claimer last 2
starts: stays 1m: moved badly down on debut: sold 580 gns Doncaster October
Sales. *M. Brittain.*

SWINGING MOLLY 6 br.m. Swing Easy (USA) 126–Molly Cockell (Wynkell —
88) [1989 NR 1990 10.1g 17.1d] leggy, light-bodied mare: well beaten in varied
company: trained until after reappearance by R. Brazington. *Mrs N. S. Sharpe.*

SWING IT HONEY 3 gr.g. Swing Easy (USA) 126–Pure Honey 94 (Don (ITY) 38
123) [1989 a8g 1990 a8g 10f 8h⁵ 7m⁶ 6m² 7g] angular gelding: poor walker and
mover: sixth reported foal: half-brother to 8.2f winner Honeyman (by Remainder
Man) and a winner in Belgium: dam 5f performer: plater: best effort over 6f. *F.
Jordan.*

SWING LUCKY 5 b.g. Swing Easy (USA) 126–Bounding (Forlorn River 124) 67
[1989 8g 7v 8f 6f³ 6m 6m³ 6g⁵ 5m³ 5f⁴ 5m 5.6g 5s 8s* 7g⁶ 8.2g a6g⁴ a8g 1990 8m
a8g* a8g* 8.3m 8m a7g 8g 10.4d a8g] rather leggy, workmanlike gelding: moderate
mover: modest handicapper on his day: successful twice on all-weather at Southwell
in summer: no form after, mainly on turf: threw jockey in paddock and withdrawn
second intended outing: stays 1m: acts on any going: effective with or without
blinkers: has won for apprentice: inconsistent. *K. T. Ivory.*

SWING NORTH 3 b.c. Night Shift (USA)–Run For Her Life 75 (Runnymede 71
123) [1989 5s⁴ 5m⁵ 5m⁴ 5f² 6f⁵ 5g² 5.8h² 6m⁶ 6g 6g⁵ 7d⁴ 5m* 5g³ a6g* 5g³ a5g⁶
a7g³ a7g² a5g* 1990 a6g³ a6g³ a6g* a5g³ a6g² 5f 6m 5d 5m 6m² 8g 5g 6g² 6f⁶ 6f³]
strong, dipped-backed colt: modest performer: made all in handicap at Lingfield in
January: claimed £6,205 in seller final start: stays 7f: possibly best on an easy
surface nowadays: effective with or without blinkers: has got on toes: game. *D. W.
Chapman.*

SWINGTIME BELLE 3 b.f. Swing Easy (USA) 126–Betbellof 65 (Averof 123) —
[1989 NR 1990 7m 10.2f⁶ 8.3m 10f 10h⁶] medium-sized filly: sixth foal: half-sister to
6f winner Laurenbel (by Dublin Taxi): dam 2-y-o 5f winner: no sign of ability on flati
winning hurdler. *M. P. Muggeridge.*

SWISS AFFAIR 3 ch.c. Private Account (USA)–Ten Cents A Kiss 85
(USA) (Key To The Mint (USA)) [1989 7m* 6m³ 6m⁴ 1990 8g 7f 7g 6m⁵ 7f]
attractive colt: shows a quick action: useful winner as 2-y-o: generally disappointing
in 1990 after £11,600 handicap on second outing: blinkered and slowly away when
tailed off in Jersey Stakes at Royal Ascot final start: stays 7f: acts on firm going:
visored (went very freely to post) fourth start. *A. A. Scott.*

SWISS BEAUTY 2 b.f. (May 4) Ballacashtal (CAN)–Cocked Hat Supreme 71 50
(Uncle Pokey 116) [1990 6m⁵ 6g⁵ 7f³ 7.5g⁵ 7.5m] 4,000Y: lengthy, good-quartered
filly: has a quick action: first foal: dam maiden stayer: plating-class performer: will
probably stay well: acts well on firm ground: consistent. *Miss S. E. Hall.*

SWORD BRIDGE 3 b.f. Broadsword (USA) 104–Tye Bridge (Idiot's Delight —
115) [1989 NR 1990 10.1g 10d⁵ 10.1m] lengthy, useful-looking filly: has scope: second
reported foal: sister to fair 1988 2-y-o 5f winner Broad Bridge: dam, once-raced over
hurdles, is out of sister to useful staying chaser Bentley Boy: no worthwhile form in
minor events: seems somewhat headstrong. *J. R. Jenkins.*

SWORD EXCALIBUR 3 b.g. Kings Lake (USA) 133–Etching 109 (Auction 72
Ring (USA) 123) [1989 NR 1990 10g⁶ 11.7m² 10.6d⁴ 12f* 12g] leggy gelding: sixth
foal: closely related to a winner in Germany and half-brother to fair 5f winner
Inscription (by Posse): dam won from 7f to 1¼m: modest form: sweating and edgy,
best effort to win claimer at Thirsk in September: stays 1½m: acts on firm going:
sold 20,000 gns Newmarket Autumn Sales, possibly abroad. *P. W. Harris.*

SWORDSMITH (USA) 3 b.c. Diesis 133–Lettre d'Amour (USA) (Caro 133) 105
[1989 7.3g 7g² 7g* 7m* 7g* 1990 7g⁴ 8f 7g 7m² 8g²] lengthy colt: usually looks
very well: has a round action: useful performer: off course nearly 5 months then
very good second to Rami in minor event at Warwick and Two Left Feet in listed
race (running on well) at Newmarket: stays 1m: acts on good to firm going: acted as
pacemaker in 2000 Guineas. *B. W. Hills.*

SYLVA HONDA 2 ch.c. (Mar 25) Adonijah 126–Wolverhants 79 (Wolver Hollow 93
126) [1990 5g³ 5m⁴ 6g* 5g² 6f³ 6g 6m] IR 23,000Y: leggy, lengthy colt: sixth foal:
closely related to fair stayer Breakout (by High Line) and half-brother to 1m winner
Test Case (by Busted): dam second over 6f on both starts, is half-sister to dam of
very smart middle-distance winner King's Island: fairly useful performer: won
Silver Seal Woodcote Stakes at Epsom in June by 2½ lengths from Level Xing: best
efforts after in Norfolk Stakes at Royal Ascot and Scottish Equitable Richmond
Stakes (4 lengths third to Mac's Imp) at Goodwood next 2 starts: favourite, ran
poorly in valuable restricted race in Ireland penultimate start: will stay 7f: yet to
race on soft ground, acts on any other. *C. E. Brittain.*

SYLVAN BREEZE 2 b.c. (Jan 29) Sulaafah (USA) 119–Langton Herring (Nearly 101
A Hand 115) [1990 6m⁶ 6g⁴ 6g² 6d] 3,500Y, 21,000 2-y-o: sturdy colt: has plenty of
scope: has a round action: fourth foal: half-brother to 3-y-o San Pier Niceto (by
Norwick), successful at 1m (at 2 yrs) and 9f and over hurdles, and quite moderate
1987 2-y-o 5f winner Sleep Easy (by Ballacashtal): dam unraced half-sister to very
smart Sylvan Barbarosa: useful maiden: good second of 7, running on well having
been set plenty to do, to Time Gentlemen in Rokeby Farms Mill Reef Stakes at
Newbury: ran poorly in Racecall Gold Trophy (wore crossed noseband) at Redcar
after: will be better suited by 7f: capable of winning a maiden. *P. Mitchell.*

SYLVAN SIROCCO 3 b.c. Known Fact (USA) 135–Juddmonte (Habitat 134) —
[1989 NR 1990 8m 10m⁶] 23,000F, 16,500Y: tall, useful-looking colt: first foal: dam
lightly raced from family of Caro: some signs of ability in minor event at Sandown
and maiden (bumped badly on turn) at Lingfield in the spring. *P. Mitchell.*

SYLVAN TEMPEST 4 b. or br.g. Strong Gale 116–Hedwige (African Sky 124) 76
[1989 6v* 7s² 8m 7.2g 6.3g 7g 7m 6v 7g⁶ 7d 1990 8f 7g² 6g⁵ 7g 8f 10m⁴ 8.3m³ 8m²
10f⁴ 9m⁵ 12g 11.5g 10d] leggy, useful-looking gelding: keen walker: poor mover:
generally disappointing since finishing second in Group 3 event at the Curragh in
spring as 3-y-o, and capable of only modest form nowadays: stays 1¼m: acts on firm
going, though easily best form on very soft: visored fifth start. *P. Mitchell.*

SYLVANUS (USA) 3 b.c. Chief's Crown (USA)–Sylvan's Girl (USA) (Restless 91
Native (USA)) [1989 NR 1990 8.2s³ 7g³ 10.6f* 10.1g² 12m] $245,000F: good sort:
good walker: half-brother to 3 winners in North America, notably Ride Sally (by
Raja Baba), stakes winner at up to 1¼m: dam won 9 races at up to 7f: fairly useful
performer: won 2-runner maiden at Haydock in August: second in Windsor minor
event, best effort: doesn't stay 1½m: possibly unsuited by soft going: sold A.
Falourd 37,000 gns Newmarket Autumn Sales. *L. Cumani.*

SYMPOSIUM IDOL (IRE) 2 b.f. (Apr 23) Gorytus (USA) 132–Estivalia —
(Persian Bold 123) [1990 7f⁶ 8f] 6,800Y: fourth foal: half-sister to 3-y-o 1¾m and 2m
winner Gippeswyck Lady (by Pas de Seul): dam, from family of Pampapaul, never
ran: poor form in maiden auctions at Doncaster (slowly away) and Redcar 3 months
later. *C. B. B. Booth.*

SYRING (FR) 3 ch.g. Sicyos (USA) 126–Lady Ring (Tachypous 128) [1989 6g 7m —
1990 6f 7d] sparely-made gelding: no worthwhile form in maidens: bandaged. *R.
Guest.*

SYRTOS 3 b.c. Shareef Dancer (USA) 135–Wayward Lass (USA) (Hail The 106
Pirates (USA) 126) [1989 7f² 10g⁴ 1990 12f³ 12m² 14m*] big, strong, lengthy colt:
useful form: 7/4 on, won 5-runner maiden at York in June, travelling strongly to lead
2f out then driven to hold stable-companion Rubicund by 1½ lengths: stays 1¾m:
sold to join H. Whiting only 2,600 gns Newmarket Autumn Sales. *J. L. Dunlop.*

SYSTEM TWO 3 ch.f. All Systems Go 119–Two's Up (Double Jump 131) [1989 —
NR 1990 8m⁵ 10g] workmanlike filly: fourth foal: half-sister to 10.5f seller winner
Bob-Double (by Import) and 1m to 1½m winner Burcroft (by Crofthall): dam never

ran: staying-on fifth in claimer (bandaged) at Doncaster, clearly better effort in the summer: sold 960 gns Doncaster November Sales. *R. M. Whitaker.*

T

TABDEA (USA) 3 b.f. Topsider (USA)–Madame Secretary (USA) (Secretariat **106** (USA)) [1989 6m³ 6m* 6g⁶ 6s* 6m 1990 8f⁴ 10g 8g* 9.2g³ 9g³ 10.5v] strong, sturdy filly: has a quick action: useful performer: won listed race at Doncaster in September: very good third (again always close up) to Colour Chart in moderately-run Ciga Prix de l'Opera at Longchamp and Raj Waki in Newmarket listed race: stayed 9.2f: acted on any going, with possible exception of heavy: visits Nashwan. *A. A. Scott.*

TABYAN (USA) 3 b.f. Topsider (USA)–Wink (USA) 101 (Forli (ARG)) [1989 5m⁵ **68** 5m⁵ 6g 1990 6m² 6f³ 6d⁵ 6m² 7g⁵ 6f*] workmanlike filly: has a quick action: quite modest performer: made all in 5-runner maiden at Folkestone in August despite hanging right last 1f: probably stayed 7f: acted on firm ground: visored second and third outings: visits Mtoto. *P. T. Walwyn.*

TACHYON PARK 8 b.h. Frimley Park 109–Frimley's Alana 73 (Lear Jet 123) **72** [1989 5g² 2s 5m 5f² 5g 5.8h³ 5g⁶ 5m⁴ 5m* 5f* 5g⁴ 5m 5m 5m⁶ 5f² 5m 5d 1990 5f 5m⁵ 5d 6m 5f 5m 5f] strong, good-quartered horse: fair winner as 7-y-o: below form in 1990 after second outing: speedy, and best at 5f: well suited by top-of-the-ground: usually blinkered or visored: has run well for apprentice, but has also hung under pressure. *P. J. Arthur.*

TACOMA HEIGHTS 4 b.g. Taufan (USA) 119–Good Relations (Be My Guest **71** (USA) 126) [1989 8g* 8g 10f³ 8.5g 10g 1990 a8g⁶ a8g a8g²] leggy gelding: moderate walker: ran well when second in handicap at Southwell in January: subsequently

Hamdan Al-Maktoum's "Tabdea"

Wynyard Classic Northumberland Sprint Trophy (Handicap), Newcastle—
Tadwin gets the better of a long-drawn-out duel with the grey Norton Challenger

gelded, and not seen out again: stays 1¼m: acts on firm and dead going: blinkered 5 of last 6 outings: has tended to hang: not one to trust implicitly. *B. A. McMahon.*

TADBIR 5 b.g. Try My Best (USA) 130–La Grange 79 (Habitat 134) [1989 10.2g 10s 10.1m⁶ 10f 11.7g⁶ 10.1m 12g 9s 1990 a10g 8f 10m⁶ 8m a8g] close-coupled, good-bodied gelding: one-time fair maiden: no worthwhile form for long time, and virtually refused to race last 2 outings: has pulled hard, and unlikely to stay 1½m: possibly unsuited by soft going: visored first 4 starts: occasionally sweats and gets on toes: sold out of W. Musson's stable 5,700 gns Doncaster January Sales after first outing: one to leave well alone. *M. C. Chapman.* §§

TADWIN 3 ch.f. Never So Bold 135–Songs Jest (Song 132) [1989 5g³ 5m* 5s² 1990 6m² 6m* 6m 6m* 5g² 6m³ 5v4] lengthy, good-quartered filly: useful sprinter: won £12,100 handicap at Newcastle in June and listed race at Newmarket in August: ran well in Group 3 contests won by Boozy at Phoenix Park and Ron's Victory at Ascot next 2 starts, fourth of 14 in similar event at Milan: stayed 6f: never raced on firm ground, probably acted on any other: visits Dayjur. *P. T. Walwyn.* 109

TAFFETA AND TULLE (USA) 4 ch.f. Nureyev (USA) 131–Miss Nymph (ARG) (Perugin (ARG)) [1989 8m⁶ 8m² 7.6m* 9.2g4 1990 8g² 8g² 8g² 8d* 8g* 9.2g⁵ 8g* 8s* 9f²] small, sparely-made filly: improved considerably in second half of year, successful in handicap at Deauville, listed races at Longchamp and Group 3 Prix Perth (leading 1f out and running on well to beat Zille 2½ lengths) at Saint-Cloud: beaten neck in Grade 1 Matriarch Stakes, Hollywood Park, final outing: will stay 1¼m: acts on any going: smart. *N. Clement, France.* 117

TAFFETA PIPKIN (USA) 2 ch.f. (Feb 22) Chief's Crown (USA)–Modiste (USA) (Sir Ivor 135) [1990 6f⁵ 8m] $325,000Y: well-made filly: has scope: half-sister —

910

to several winners, one minor stakes placed: dam unraced: poor form in maidens at Newmarket and Salisbury: to join H. Pantall in France. *L. M. Cumani.*

TAFFY JONES 11 br.g. Welsh Pageant 132–Shallow Stream 100 (Reliance II 137) [1989 12m 12h 1990 12m 10f 11.5m 12m 10m] big gelding: carries plenty of condition: no longer of much account on flat: has worn blinkers and visor (too keen): winning chaser. *M. McCormack.* —

TAFILA 4 ch.f. Adonijah 126–Brigata (Brigadier Gerard 144) [1989 8d² 10f² 10f* 8f⁶ 1990 8f³ 8m* 8f 8f* 7m 8m³] sturdy, good-topped filly: has a round action: led final 1f when winning £14,500 handicap at Sandown in May and moderately-run minor event at Ayr (by ¾ length from Performing Arts) in July: narrowly-beaten third to Spring Daffodil in Group 3 event at the Curragh final outing: suited by 1m: acted on firm and dead going: raced keenly and found little on occasions: in foal to Pharly. *W. Jarvis.* 101

TAGIO 10 b.g. Martinmas 128–Harford Belle 97 (Track Spare 125) [1989 8m⁶ 10.6g⁴ 1990 12.2m⁵ 12m] workmanlike gelding: poor handicapper: stays 1½m: possibly not at best on soft going, acts on any other: has won for apprentice. *M. Tate.* 44

TAILSPIN 5 b.g. Young Generation 129–Mumtaz Flyer (USA) (Al Hattab (USA)) [1989 12f 16.2m⁵ 16m 14g⁶ 14f 16m³ 1990 12f 14m⁴ 17.1f* 18m 20m 17.1f²] lengthy gelding: moderate mover: has looked ungenerous, but did little wrong (ridden by Pat Eddery) in 8-runner handicaps at Bath in May (beating Saxon Court ½ length) and June (second to Chucklestone): ran poorly in between: stays 17f: suited by a sound surface: sometimes blinkered: has got on edge: sold to join J. Roberts' stable 20,000 gns Newmarket July Sales: not one to trust. *B. W. Hills.* 76 §

TAJIKA 4 gr.f. Rusticaro (FR) 124–Taj Princess 88 (Taj Dewan 128) [1989 8m 10f 10f⁵ 9g⁶ 9g a11g* a11g⁵ 1990 a12g³ a12g³ a11g² a12g* 16g 14.8f] plain, angular filly: poor mover: won handicap at Southwell in March: ran poorly after, dropping herself out at halfway final outing: suited by 1½m: blinkered last 3 starts: sold 10,000 gns Newmarket July Sales. *J. L. Dunlop.* 70

TAJ VICTORY 3 ch.f. Final Straw 127–Taj Princess 88 (Taj Dewan 128) [1989 NR 1990 9m³ 10m⁴ 10g* 12m⁵] compact filly: good walker and mover: sixth living foal: half-sister to several winners, including very useful 1m to 15.5f winner Indian Queen (by Electric) and useful 6f winner Far Too Young (by Young Generation): dam won over 5f and 1m: quite modest form: won claimer Salisbury in October: ran creditably in apprentice handicap at Chepstow after: stays 1½m. *W. Hastings-Bass.* 68

TAKADDUM (USA) 2 ch.c. (Apr 29) Riverman (USA) 131–Lyphard's Holme (USA) (Lyphard (USA) 132) [1990 6m⁵ 6g 6d*] 1,400,000 francs (approx £129,600) Y: compact, robust colt: third foal: half-brother to French 3-y-o 1m and 9f winner Vijaya (by Lear Fan): dam French 8.5f and 9f winner, is out of Italian Oaks winner Carnauba, a half-sister to the dam of Salse: progressive colt: won 17-runner maiden at Folkestone in November by 1½ lengths: will be better suited by 7f +, and should stay at least 1¼m: likely to improve further. *P. T. Walwyn.* 76 p

TAKDEER 4 ch.g. Sharpo 132–Red Gloves 83 (Red God 128§) [1989 6v* 6s³ 7s⁶ 8m 8m⁴ 6s a8g* a8g⁴ 1990 a6g² a7g³ a7g² a7g⁴] leggy, rather sparely-made gelding: fairly useful winner as 3-y-o: stayed 1m: didn't race on firm going, probably acted on any other: blinkered first 2 starts: dead. *W. A. O'Gorman.* 68

TAKE A LIBERTY 5 ch.m. Aragon 118–Liberty Tree 96 (Dominion 123) [1989 NR 1990 a14g] plating-class winner as 3-y-o: only race on flat since, tailed off in claimer (reputedly lame) at Southwell in November: stays 8.5f: yet to race on soft going, acts on any other: has run well when sweating and on toes. *Miss S. J. Wilton.* —

TAKEALL 3 b.f. Another Realm 118–Cratloe (African Sky 124) [1989 5d³ 5d² 5f⁴ 5.3h² 5m² 5g* 5m* 5g 5m* 1990 5f 5d⁶ 5g⁴ 5g] rather leggy, unfurnished filly: quite modest winner at 2 yrs: below form in 1990: acts on good to firm ground and dead: didn't handle Brighton track. *B. A. McMahon.* —

TAKE EFFECT 6 b.g. Tap On Wood 130–Welsh Partner 91 (Welsh Saint 126) [1989 6v⁵ 6d³ 6f 6f 6f4 6f² 6m⁶ 7f⁶ 7.6m⁶ 6g⁵ 7f4 6m 7f 6s² a7g 1990 5f⁵ 6f⁵ 7f⁶ 5g⁵ 7m⁶] leggy, lightly-made gelding: tubed: moderate mover: poor handicapper: stays 7f: acts on any going: best in blinkers: suitable mount for apprentice: unsuited by sharp track: inconsistent. *M. Brittain.* 35

TAKE HEART 4 b.f. Electric 126–Hollow Heart 89 (Wolver Hollow 126) [1989 8.5m⁵ 10.2f⁵ 7m* 8g 1990 8f³ 10f* 7g² 8m⁵ 8f* 8m 10f4 8g* 10g⁴] workmanlike filly: fair handicapper: won at Salisbury in May (pulling hard) and July (making all) and Newbury (taken down early, racing alone until past halfway) in October: 33/1, good fourth, soon clear, to Stagecraft in Newmarket listed event final outing: stays 84

1¼m: acts on firm going: has worn severe bridle, but didn't last 7 outings: has got on edge: goes well fresh. *D. R. C. Elsworth.*

TAKE ISSUE   5 b.g. Absalom 128–Abstract 73 (French Beige 127) [1989 16s 14s⁴   — §
9m 14g 1990 14m⁵] well-made gelding: lightly raced nowadays: favourite and blinkered, soon off bridle and always behind in handicap at Nottingham in April: stays 1¾m: acts on any going: best left alone. *J. Sutcliffe.*

TAKENHALL   5 b.g. Pitskelly 122–Great Dora (Great Nephew 126) [1989 7d 8s   68 §
7m 8m 6f* 6f 6f⁵ 6m⁵ 7m⁴ 7m² 7m⁴ 7.3m⁴ 1990 7m⁴ 7g⁶ 8m³ 8g 6m 6g⁶ 6f 6m 7m⁴ 7m³ 7m³ 7m* 7g⁶ 7.3g⁴ 7m 7g 10d⁶] lengthy, workmanlike gelding: moderate mover: modest handicapper: led final strides to win at York in September: best form at 7f to 1m: acts on firm and dead going: has been tried in blinkers: usually gets behind, and is not an easy ride. *M. J. Fetherston-Godley.*

TAKE ONE   4 b.c. Teenoso (USA) 135–Old Kate 110 (Busted 134) [1989 12f⁴ 14g⁴   81
13s² 12g 1990 12f² 14g* 12m³] lengthy, robust colt: carries plenty of condition: moderate walker: poor mover in slower paces: showed improved form to win competitive handicap at Sandown in May, making most: ran creditably in £7,100 handicap at Newbury over month later: better suited by 1¾m than shorter, and will stay 2m: gives impression will prove best on ground easier than firm: sold to join P. Mitchell's stable 12,000 gns Newmarket Autumn Sales. *G. Wragg.*

TAKEOVER TALK (USA)   3 b.c. Conquistador Cielo (USA)–Love Words   —
(USA) (Gallant Romeo (USA)) [1989 8g 1990 12m⁴ 11.7f⁶ 15.3m⁶ 12m⁵ 14g 10.2f⁴] strong, lengthy colt: easy mover: plating-class form: probably stays 1¼m: blinkered last 3 starts: sold 7,500 gns Newmarket Autumn Sales. *G. Harwood.*

TAKE TWO   2 b.g. (Feb 20) Jupiter Island 126–Dancing Daughter 79 (Dance In   75
Time (CAN)) [1990 7f³ 7m⁵ 7g⁴ 8.2d 8m*] workmanlike gelding: second live foal: half-brother to 7f and 1m winner Handsome Hotfoot (by Hotfoot): dam 13.4f winner: modest performer: won 22-runner nursery at Warwick in October by a length: will be suited by 1¼m + : unsuited by dead ground. *R. F. Johnson Houghton.*

TALAB   5 b.g. Beldale Flutter (USA) 130–Glen Dancer 102 (Furry Glen 121) [1989   —
NR 1990 12f] leggy, quite good-topped gelding: modest maiden at 3 yrs: soon tailed off in handicap at Brighton in September, only subsequent outing on flat: stays 1¼m: acts on good to firm and heavy going. *J. V. Redmond.*

TALABAYRA   3 b.f. Darshaan 133–Takariyna (Grundy 137) [1989 7g³ 1990 12f²   88
12.2d* 12h² 12.3g⁶] small, sparely-made filly: fair form: odds on, won 4-runner maiden at Catterick in July: well beaten after, pulling hard and saddle slipped in handicap (ridden by 7-lb claimer, unimpressive in appearance) final start: stays 1½m: yet to race on soft ground, probably acts on any other: takes keen hold: sold 13,000 gns Newmarket December Sales. *M. R. Stoute.*

TALATON FLYER   4 b.g. Kala Shikari 125–Pertune (Hyperion's Curls) [1989   —
NR 1990 8m 10.8m] leggy, lengthy gelding: well beaten in varied events: taken down early final outing. *W. G. A. Brooks.*

TALIANNA   4 b.f. Kind of Hush 118–Friths Folly 62 (Good Bond 122) [1989 7g⁶   —
7.5d 8m 7m 7m⁶ 8.2f⁴ 7m 7.5m 6m 7g 1990 8m 10g⁶ 8m 7f 12f 10m 10m] small filly: carries condition: poor mover: plater: virtually no form at 4 yrs: stays 7f: acts on good to firm going: blinkered once: has been unruly on way down, mounted on track and taken to post early: sold 1,450 gns Doncaster October Sales. *J. Balding.*

TALISH   2 br.c. (Apr 17) Persian Bold 123–Baheejah (Northfields (USA)) [1990   61
6m⁶ 7g] rather leggy, quite attractive colt: third foal: half-brother to 3-y-o Beco-cious (by Precocious) and a winner abroad: dam lightly-raced half-sister to Irish Oaks winner Olwyn: quite modest maiden: better effort on first outing: should stay 1¼m. *C. E. Brittain.*

TALK OF GLORY   9 b.g. Hittite Glory 125–Fiddle-Faddle 85 (Silly Season 127)   —
[1989 8m⁴ 8m 8.3m 10h 8f a11g 1990 a10g a13g³ a8g] strong, rangy gelding: quite modest handicapper in 1988: no subsequent worthwhile form in varied contests, including sellers: stays 1¼m: used to be well suited by top-of-the-ground: blinkered at 9 yrs: has won for apprentice. *J. White.*

TALL MEASURE   4 b.g. High Top 131–Millimeter (USA) (Ribocco 129) [1989   36
10.6m 10f³ 12.4m⁵ 10g⁵ 12.4f* 12m⁵ 11m⁴ 12g² 12g 13s 12g 1990 13g 16.2d 13g 12g a12g a12g⁴ 15.3f⁵ 15m⁶ 16m 17.6g⁴ 15.8d] robust, round-barrelled gelding: modest handicapper at one time, but has deteriorated: seems to stay 17.6f: acts on firm going, probably unsuited by soft surface: often visored or blinkered: sold 2,800 gns Doncaster October Sales. *F. H. Lee.*

TALOS (IRE) 2 b.g. (May 19) Taufan (USA) 119–Jovial Josie (USA) (Sea Bird II 145) [1990 7m 7m] IR 8,800Y, resold 25,000Y: good sort: half-brother to several winners abroad: dam poor sister to high-class filly and good broodmare Kittiwake: plating-class form in maidens: sort to do better in time. *B. W. Hills.* **57 p**

TAMARPOUR (USA) 3 b.c. Sir Ivor 135–Tarsila (High Top 131) [1989 NR 1990 12m⁴ 12f² 11.5m² 10f⁶ 12g 12d⁶] big, useful-looking colt: third foal: half-brother to very smart 9f and 10.5f winner Torjoun (by Green Dancer) and winning hurdler Torkabar (by Vaguely Noble): dam, 1m and 9f winner in France, is sister to Top Ville: fair maiden: made most, claimed out of L. Cumani's stable £25,000 in Sandown claimer third start: below form in handicaps after: should be suited by 1¾m: joined M. Pipe. *L. J. Holt.* **77 d**

TAMBORA 3 b.f. Darshaan 133–Tameen (FR) (Pharly (FR) 130) [1989 7g 1990 10m* 11.5g] strong, deep-girthed, lengthy filly: second favourite, won 7-runner maiden at Beverley in September, quickening well 2f out but hanging right: 6/4 favourite, went down well but never travelling comfortably in Lingfield minor event: should stay 1½m. *L. M. Cumani.* **75**

TAMERTOWN LAD 9 b.g. Creetown 123–Gay Tamarind (Tamerlane 128) [1989 7.5m 8g 7f 1990 7g a8g] strong, quite attractive gelding: carries condition: no longer of much account on flat: slowly away when blinkered: has worn a tongue strap: sold 2,200 gns Doncaster September Sales. *A. W. Potts.* —

TAMI 5 ch.m. Miami Springs 121–Tenoria 82 (Mansingh (USA) 120) [1989 8.3m 1990 7m 8g 6m⁵] small, sturdy mare: poor plater: stays 6f: acts on any going: best in blinkers or visor: sweating only start at 4 yrs. *M. McCourt.* **30**

TAMISE 3 br.f. Dominion 123–Miss Thames 105 (Tower Walk 130) [1989 NR 1990 7m 7g² a7g⁴ 9g⁶] rather leggy, quite attractive filly: has rather round action: second foal: half-sister to fairly useful 6f winner Got Away (by Final Straw): dam useful performer at up to 1m: quite modest form: will stay 1¼m: wandered final start, in June: sold to join J. White 6,000 gns Newmarket Autumn Sales. *M. R. Stoute.* **63**

TAMONO DANCER (CAN) 3 b.c. Northern Dancer–Running Around (USA) (What A Pleasure) [1989 NR 1990 8m* 8m² 7d 8m 9g⁶ 8d a8g⁶] $800,000Y: work-manlike colt: fourth foal (third by Northern Dancer): dam, winner at up to 9f, is half-sister to high-class Full Out, successful at up to 1m: fair form: won £8,000 newcomers event at Newmarket in April: ran poorly in Southwell handicap, mostly faced stiff tasks in between: stays 9f: acts on good to firm ground: keen sort. *B. Hanbury.* **88**

TANAZEEM (IRE) 2 b.f. (May 14) Akarad (FR) 130–Takariyna (Grundy 137) [1990 8g³] small, sparely-made filly: second foal: half-sister to 3-y-o 1½m winner Talabayra (by Darshaan): dam French 1¼m winner, is half-sister to Top Ville: 10/1, around 7 lengths third of 13 to Melpomene in maiden at Wolverhampton in October: will stay 1¼m: sure to improve. *M. R. Stoute.* **63 p**

TANBURE 3 b.f. Law Society (USA) 130–Transit (Thatch (USA) 136) [1989 NR 1990 11.5g] IR 55,000Y: leggy filly: fourth foal: half-sister to 1¼m and 11f winner Shabby Doll (by Northfields): dam, half-sister to smart middle-distance colt Beauvallon, ran 3 times: 33/1 and ridden by 7-lb claimer, took keen hold when tailed off in maiden at Yarmouth in June. *B. Hanbury.* —

TANEGRUS 2 b.c. (Mar 1) Dunbeath (USA) 127–Tanagrea (Blakeney 126) [1990 7g³ 7m³ 7m] 50,000Y: compact, good-quartered colt: good walker: second foal; dam unraced sister to Irish Derby winner Tyrnavos and half-sister to several other high-class performers: fair maiden: not raced after July, and transferred to D. Elsworth: will be better suited by 1m+, and should stay 1½m. *J. W. Payne.* **81**

TANFEN 9 b.g. Tanfirion 110–Lady Mary (Sallust 134) [1989 6g 6m⁵ 6h³ 6f 5m⁴ 6f* 6h⁵ 6m 1990 5m 6g 5g⁵ 5g⁵ 6g] strong, workmanlike gelding: hobdayed: poor handicapper: best at sprint distances: acts on any going: has worn visor and blinkers, but not for some time: usually bandaged: suitable mount for apprentice: sometimes sweats: suited by forcing tactics. *T. Craig.* **38**

TANFIRION BAY (IRE) 2 b.c. (Apr 18) Whistling Deer 117–Alone All Alone (Tanfirion 110) [1990 6m 5m 7m⁵ a7g 7m 7g⁴ 7m a7g 6d a6g⁴ a7g² a7g] IR 3,200Y, 9,000 2-y-o: compact colt: has a round action: second foal: dam Irish maiden: quite modest maiden: best effort penultimate outing: suited by 7f: blinkered last 4 starts. *P. Mitchell.* **67**

TANFITH (CAN) 3 b.c. Chief's Crown (USA)–Foxy Olympia (USA) (Stage Door Johnny) [1989 7g* 8m* 1990 8g⁵ 8m⁵] rather sparely-made colt: useful performer: won maiden at Yarmouth and £7,100 event at Newbury as 2-y-o: not seen out again until late-September: good fifth to If Memory Serves in minor event at Newbury and **101**

Raj Waki in £11,600 contest at Newmarket: will stay 1¼m: stays in training. *R. W. Armstrong.*

TANGALOA (USA)   2 b.c. (Apr 29) Lyphard (USA) 132–Angel Island (USA)   **60**
(Cougar (CHI)) [1990 6f⁵ 7g 6m⁶ 6g] $400,000Y: neat, quite attractive colt: has a
powerful, round action: half-brother to several winners, including Sharrood (by
Caro), very smart performer from 6f to 1¼m in Europe later runner-up in Arlington
Million: dam very smart 2-y-o, winning graded stakes at 7f: quite modest maiden:
will be suited by 1m: sold 5,000 gns Doncaster November Sales. *M. R. Stoute.*

TANG DYNASTY   5 b.g. Artaius (USA) 129–Favant (Faberge II 121) [1989 NR   —
1990 6g 8f] seems of no account: blinkered once at 2 yrs and both starts in summer.
S. R. Bowring.

TANWI   3 br.f. Vision (USA)–Shine The Light (Home Guard (USA) 129) [1989 5v* **101**
5m² 6g³ 6d 6g⁵ 6g* 5d² 7d* 1990 7g 8g⁶ 8g 8g⁵ 12m⁵ 12g⁵ 10g⁵ 9m³ 11g⁴ 8d* 10d²]
useful performer: favourite, dead-heated for minor event at the Curragh in October:
ran well in Irish Oaks at the Curragh, Phoenix Champion Stakes and Group 3 event
at Leopardstown, fifth, seventh and eighth starts: probably stayed 1½m: never
raced on very firm ground, acted on any other: consistent: visits Riverman. *K. Prendergast, Ireland.*

TAPATCH (IRE)   2 b.c. (Feb 7) Thatching 131–Knees Up (USA) (Dancing   **87**
Champ (USA)) [1990 6m⁶ 7m* 7g⁴ 8g³] 13,500Y: compact colt: first foal: dam
unraced from family of Gorytus: fair performer: won 8-runner maiden at Sandown in
July by a short head, rallying gamely: ran well in quite useful company afterwards:
stays 1m. *J. M. P. Eustace.*

TAP DANCING   4 ch.g. Sallust 134–Amorak 85 (Wolver Hollow 126) [1989 7m   **45**
8.5f 8.2f³ 10m³ 10f 1990 10f⁴ 10m⁴ 12d] leggy gelding: has a round action: poor maiden: stays 1¼m: acts on firm going: apprentice ridden at 4 yrs: changed hands 2,200
gns Doncaster August Sales: winning selling hurdler in November. *M. O'Neill.*

TARANGA   7 b.g. Music Boy 124–Emblazon 91 (Wolver Hollow 126) [1989 8s*   **37**
8.2v⁶ 8d 8m³ 8g* 8.3m a6g⁴ a7g 1990 a8g 8g 8.2g³ a12g] strong, workmanlike
gelding: moderate mover: poor handicapper: suited by 1m: acts on any going: has
run creditably when visored: has worn bandages: has won for apprentice and when
sweating: has been taken down early: inconsistent. *J. White.*

TARA'S DELIGHT   3 b.f. Dunbeath (USA) 127–Tickton Bridge (Grundy 137)   **62**
[1989 6m³ 6m 8g 1990 9m³ 10g* 9f⁴ 11f³ 11m⁴ 11.7m 10f* 10g⁵ 11.5m 9f a10g]
deep-girthed filly: quite modest handicapper: successful at Nottingham in April and
in claimer (led 1m then rallied well) at Leicester in July: below form last 2 starts,
blinkered on first occasion: stays 11f: acts on firm going: sweating sixth start:
somewhat headstrong. *M. J. Ryan.*

TARA'S GIRL   3 b.f. Touching Wood (USA) 127–Esquire Lady (Be My Guest   **69**
(USA) 126) [1989 a6g 1990 a6g⁵ a7g⁵ a8g 6g² 6m* 6g 5d 8g³ 7m 6m 7m⁴ 6m 9m 5g³
5g²] small filly: modest handicapper: won £6,800 event at Newmarket in May: best
efforts after when in frame, soon outpaced last 2 starts: better suited by 6f than 5f,
and probably stays 1m: acts on good to firm ground: blinkered tenth and final starts:
hung left for 7-lb claimer on eleventh. *W. A. O'Gorman.*

TARATONG   4 b.f. Bold Fort 100–Lucinski (Malinowski (USA) 123) [1989 NR   —
1990 a6g a11g] small filly: behind all 4 starts. *K. White.*

TARDA   3 ch.f. Absalom 128–Ixia 91 (I Say 125) [1989 NR 1990 8m 10.4d 8m⁴ 7f⁴   **60**
7f⁶ 8f³ 10m 8.2g] angular, shallow-girthed filly: has a round action: half-sister to
several winners, including 1¼m to 13.8f winner Corn Lily (by Aragon) and useful 1m
and 1¼m performer Cardinal Flower (by Sharpen Up): dam very game winner at up
to 1½m: quite modest maiden: good third in moderately-run claimer (claimed out of
G. Pritchard-Gordon's stable £9,020) at Newmarket: well beaten in handicap and
claimer after: should be suited by further than 1m. *N. Tinkler.*

TARGA'S SECRET (USA)   2 b.f. (Apr 21) Secreto (USA) 128–Targa (USA)   **84**
(Cannonade (USA)) [1990 6f² 6.5g 6m* 7m 6d] 100,000Y: angular, rather sparely-
made filly: moderate mover: fourth reported living foal: closely related to French
provincial 9f and 10.5f winner Miss Evans (by Nijinsky): dam, from smart American
family, won 8.5f Santa Maria Handicap: fair performer: won 13-runner maiden at
Pontefract in September by 5 lengths: tenth of 19, keeping on, to Chipaya in Racecall
Gold Trophy at Redcar, final outing: should stay at least 1¼m: acts on good to firm
ground and dead. *J. H. M. Gosden.*

TARIKHANA   3 gr.f. Mouktar 129–Tremogia (FR) (Silver Shark 129) [1989 7g⁶ **107**
1990 10m* 10.5m³ 10m⁴ 12g* 13.4g* 12.5g⁶] lengthy, rather sparely-made filly:
good mover: won maiden at Lingfield in May, £11,100 handicap at Newbury in

August and listed race (beat Sesame ½ length) at Chester in September, on last 2 occasions making virtually all but not at strong pace: creditable sixth in Prix de Royallieu at Longchamp: stays 13.4f: takes keen hold: particularly mulish at stalls third and fourth outings: useful. *M. R. Stoute.*

TARISTEAC   10 ch.g. Be My Guest (USA) 126–Sans Culotte (FR) (Roi Dagobert   **34** 128) [1989 10m 12g 12.2m 7f 1990 a7g a8g a7g⁵ a8g⁴ a7g 10.2f] small, strong gelding: poor mover: poor handicapper: stays 1m: acts on hard and dead going: blinkered only occasionally nowadays: wears bandages: often gets well behind. *S. R. Bowring.*

TARLETON'S ROSE   2 b.f. (Apr 21) Ilium 121–Stately Gala (Gala Performance   **40** (USA)) [1990 5m⁴ 5m 7f⁵ 7g] small, short-backed filly: half-sister to 1¼m winner Tarleton's Oak (by Town Crier) and a winner in Barbados: dam never ran: poor maiden. *S. Dow.*

TARMON (IRE)   2 ch.c. (May 8) Whistling Deer 117–Royal Performance 57   **43** (Klairon 131) [1990 5f⁵ 5.8h³ 5f 5.8m 6f⁶ 6m a6g] IR 7,200Y: workmanlike colt: moderate mover: fourth foal: half-brother to a winner abroad: dam Irish 1m winner: poor maiden: stays 6f: has run creditably for 7-lb claimer: sometimes blinkered, usually bandaged. *K. M. Brassey.*

TARMON LASS   4 b.f. What A Guest 119–Turiana (USA) (Citation) [1989 10s⁶   — 12m⁶ 11f² 10f⁵ 12f³ 12m⁴ 11s 1990 7m 9s 10.2f 8m 5g] angular ex-Irish filly: half-sister to 2 winners, including stayer On Her Own (by Busted): dam, winner at up to 7f, half-sister to Kentucky Derby and Preakness Stakes winner Forward Pass: well beaten in spring in varied events, including sellers: needed further than 7f and stayed 11f: acted on firm going: occasionally blinkered: sold 1,200 gns Ascot May Sales: in foal to Risk Me. *J. Parkes.*

TARN PURE   5 ch.g. Blue Refrain 121–Sterling Kate (Sterling Bay (SWE)) [1989   — 11.5f⁵ 8f³ 12f² 10h* 12f⁵ 1990 12g] lengthy, workmanlike gelding: poor handicapper: stays 1½m: acts on hard going: visored or blinkered final 4 starts at 3 yrs. *P. Howling.*

TAROOM   3 b.c. Lomond (USA) 128–Gallic Pride (USA) (Key To The Kingdom   — (USA)) [1989 7m 1990 14g⁵] lengthy, good-quartered colt: moderate walker: has a round action: well beaten in maidens. *B. Hanbury.*

TAROUDANT   3 b.g. Pharly (FR) 130–Melbourne Miss (Chaparral (FR) 128)   **81** [1989 NR 1990 12.3v² 10.2s] rangy gelding: sixth foal: half-brother to French 1983 2-y-o 1m winner Danse du Norde (by Northfields): dam unraced close relation to Grand Prix de Paris winner Tennyson: 20/1, had hard race when second of 5 to Spode's Blue in minor event at Chester in October: ridden by 7-lb claimer: soundly beaten in Doncaster minor event following month. *R. Hollinshead.*

TAR'S HILL   9 gr.g. Hill Farmer–Tar's Tart (Rosyth 94) [1989 NR 1990 10s a12g]   — tall, workmanlike gelding: quite modest staying handicapper at best: well beaten at Lingfield in autumn, tailed off final 4f second outing (taken down early). *N. Kernick.*

TARTAN TINKER (IRE)   2 gr.c. (May 3) Godswalk (USA) 130–Travel Away   **65** 93 (Tachypous 128) [1990 7m 7m⁵ 8f 9g⁵ 7m 8g⁶ 9g] IR 7,200Y: leggy colt: moderate mover: second foal: dam 7f winner: quite modest maiden: seems best at 7f. *M. Brittain.*

TARTAR'S BOW   3 b.c. Gorytus (USA) 132–Sweet Eliane (Birdbrook 110) [1989   **67** 6g 1990 8.2m⁵ 10g 8.2d 8m* 8d 7d] lengthy, quite attractive colt: very good walker: quite modest performer: sweating, won claimer at Chepstow in October by short head: last in Doncaster handicaps afterwards, tenderly handled first occasion and blinkered second: stays 1m: seems to need a sound surface: joined R. Holder. *M. A. Jarvis.*

TARTIQUE TWIST (USA)   4 b.f. Arctic Tern (USA) 126–Professional Dance   **78** (USA) (Nijinsky (CAN) 138) [1989 8g 12g⁶ 12f⁵ a12g a16g⁵ 1990 a16g* a14g* a14g⁴ 18f] strong, rangy, attractive filly: has a quick action: won handicaps at Southwell in January: not raced after March: stayed 2m: sold 12,500 gns Newmarket December Sales in foal to Midyan. *J. L. Dunlop.*

TARVISIO   3 b.c. Northern Baby (CAN) 127–Bold And Bright (FR) (Bold Lad **112** (USA)) [1989 7.5d⁵ 8g³ 8d* 9m³ 1990 8d* 8v⁵ 10.5g² 10g⁵ 9d³ 10d 11g⁵ 10g⁶ 10v⁴ 10v* 10v³ 8v⁶] French colt from family of Assert and Bikala: won minor events at Maisons-Laffitte in March and November: very useful on his day, placed behind Epervier Bleu in Prix Lupin at Longchamp and Candy Glen in Prix Daphnis at Evry third and fifth outings: stays 10.5f: acts on heavy going: seems unreliable. *F. Boutin, France.*

TASHANITZA 3 b.f. Starch Reduced 112–Mrs Dumbfounded (Adropejo 114) [1989 5d 6f² 1990 a10g] lengthy, plain filly: poor form: easily best effort when second in claimer at Chepstow in July at 2 yrs: only outing in 1990 in December: should stay beyond 6f. *B. Palling.* —

TASKFORCE FIXED IT 3 b.g. Aragon 118–Broken Accent (Busted 134) [1989 5m 7f⁴ 7m² 8.2f 8f 1990 8g a7g] smallish, angular gelding: quite modest performer at 2 yrs: bandaged, tailed off in claimer and seller (blinkered) in May, 1990: has looked hard ride: sold privately 2,750 gns Doncaster November Sales. *Dr J. D. Scargill.* —

TASMIM 3 b.f. Be My Guest (USA) 126–Militia Girl (Rarity 129) [1989 NR 1990 8g 7d] 68,000Y: tall, sparely-made filly: first foal: dam once-raced half-sister to Kings Island and Bengal Fire and daughter of half-sister to very useful Tants: behind in autumn maidens, swishing tail second start: sold 1,400 gns Newmarket December Sales. *R. W. Armstrong.* —

TATE AFFAIR (IRE) 2 b.f. (Apr 11) Tate Gallery (USA) 117–Linda Dudley 81 (Owen Dudley 121) [1990 6m⁴ 8.2g* 8m² 8.2d²] IR 4,000F, 6,200Y: small, good-quartered filly: moderate mover: third living foal: half-sister to 3-y-o 1½m winner Hostess Quickly (by Hotfoot) and 4-y-o Shinnel Water (by Rolfe): dam lightly-raced half-sister to William Hill Futurity winner Count Pahlen: won 18-runner seller (retained 7,000 gns) at Nottingham in September easing up by 6 lengths: excellent second of 20, travelling smoothly most of way, to Sandicliffe Way in nursery at Nottingham following month final outing: may well prove as effective at 7f as 1m: easily best run on dead going: sold 8,500 gns Newmarket Autumn Sales. *A. N. Lee.* 78

TATWIJ (USA) 3 b.f. Topsider (USA)–Infantes (USA) (Exclusive Native (USA)) [1989 5g* 5s* 1990 8f³ 8g 6m³ 6s⁴ 5s³] leggy filly: moderate mover: fair performer: off course 4 months after third start, not discredited in minor events after: eighth of 14 in Poule d'Essai des Pouliches at Longchamp, and probably stayed 1m: needed an easy surface: visits Cadeaux Genereux. *H. Thomson Jones.* 85

TAUBER 6 b.g. Taufan (USA) 119–Our Bernie (Continuation 120) [1989 7v* 6d⁵ 7g* 7f⁴ 7f 7m 7m 7m 7g⁴ 8f³ 7m* a6g* a6g* a6g³ a8g² a8g 1990 a8g⁵ a7g⁵ 6v 7g² 7g³ 7m⁴ 7.6g² 7.6m³ 6f* 7f⁶ 6m⁵ 6m⁶ 6g* 6m 6m* 6m* 7m⁴ 6g⁵ 6s* a6g a6g²] rather leggy gelding: has a markedly round action: fairly useful handicapper: successful at Lingfield (has now won there 8 times) in July, August, September (twice) and October: effective at 6f and stays 1m: acts on any going: excellent mount for inexperienced rider: occasionally sweats: splendidly tough and consistent. *Pat Mitchell.* 87

TAULELA 3 b.f. Taufan (USA) 119–Balela (African Sky 124) [1989 5f² 5m⁴ 6g⁶ 1990 8.5d 8m 6g] leggy, unfurnished filly: quite modest maiden at 2 yrs: no show in 1990: sweating final start: trained until after first at 3 yrs by D. Elsworth: sold 1,100 gns Newmarket Autumn Sales. *E. Eldin.* —

TA WARDLE 6 ch.g. Import 127–Zephyr Lady 59 (Windjammer (USA)) [1989 12m³ a11g 1990 a12g⁵ 10f* 10f² 9f 12f 11.7g⁴ 17.1f⁴ 16g 12m 17.1d²] tall, leggy gelding: poor handicapper: won selling event (no bid) at Folkestone in March: effective at 1¼m and stays well: acts on firm and dead going: has got on edge: none too consistent. *M. J. Bolton.* 42

TAWJIH (USA) 3 b.c. Lyphard's Wish (FR) 124–Chop Towhee (USA) (Hatchet Man (USA)) [1989 6m⁶ 7.6m³ 1990 8g 8f³ 10m 8m] quite attractive colt: has round action: quite modest maiden: form at 3 yrs only when gambled-on third in handicap (ridden by 7-lb claimer) at Redcar: stays 1m: trained first 3 outings by R. Guest. *M. Madgwick.* —

TAYLORS CASTLE 3 b.f. Castle Keep 121–How Audacious (Hittite Glory 125) [1989 5m³ 6m 5m⁶ 7m 1990 6f⁴ 7m 7.5d³ 8h 7.6m 7d 7g⁵ 7m a8g 6d⁶] carries condition: poor and inconsistent plater: seems best at around 7f: acts on firm and dead going: visored fourth and fifth outings: headstrong and has carried head high: sold to join S. Cole 1,600 gns Newmarket Autumn Sales: one to be wary of. *E. Eldin.* 37 §

TAYLORS PRINCE 3 ch.c. Sandhurst Prince 128–Maiden's Dance 65 (Hotfoot 126) [1989 7g 8g 1990 10m⁵ 10g⁵ 9m⁴ 8d⁶ 7m* 7f² 8f 7m⁵ 7m 7.6d 8m³ 8d⁴] lengthy, angular colt: moderate mover: quite modest handicapper: won at Leicester in July despite hanging right: ran particularly well last 2 starts: stays 1m: acts on firm and dead going: visored last 7 starts, slowly away and sweating on fourth of them: refused to enter stalls intended reappearance: difficult ride, and none too genuine. *H. J. Collingridge.* 67

TAYLOR'S REALM 4 gr.f. Another Realm 118–Sweet Rosina 61 (Sweet **56** d
Revenge 129) [1989 8d⁴ 8.5d 8g 8m 8g⁵ 8m⁵ 11.5m* 12m 12g 14f 12g⁵ 12g 1990 10f²
12g 10.8m² 11.5g 10f⁵ 11.7m⁴ 12m³ 11.5m⁵ 10f 10f⁵ 12m] leggy, angular filly: has a
quick action: poor handicapper: stays 1½m: acts well on top-of-the-ground: inconsistent. *H. J. Collingridge.*

TEA AND HONEY 2 ch.f. (May 5) Night Shift (USA)–Tactless 91 (Romulus **—**
129) [1990 6d 5m a7g⁶ a6g] 2,100Y: sturdy filly: half-sister to several winners,
including very useful Padro (by Runnymede), successful at up to 7f: dam won at
1¼m: well beaten in maidens at Lingfield (3) and Warwick (auction event). *C. A.
Cyzer.*

TEACH DHA MHILE 3 b.c. Kampala 120–Mittens (Run The Gantlet (USA)) **113**
[1989 6f⁴ 8f* 6d* 8d* 1990 12g⁴ 8g² 8g³ 11g² 12g³ 12v² 10s⁵] very useful performer:
successful in maiden at Killarney, restricted event at Phoenix Park and Panasonic
Beresford EBF Futurity Stakes at the Curragh at 2 yrs: in frame in varied events in
Italy in 1990, in Group 1 contests won by Dashing Blade and Erdelistan at Milan fifth
and sixth starts: creditable 5 lengths fifth of 14 to Legal Case in Premio Roma: stays
1½m: seems to act on any going: consistent. *M. Berra, Italy.*

TEAMSTER 4 b.c. Known Fact (USA) 135–Rosetta Stone 89 (Guillaume **114**
Tell (USA) 121) [1989 12s* 12.3m⁴ 12f 14f* 14.8m² 17.6d* 18g 1990 16g⁴ 16m*
16m* 20d⁴ 16g 18g² 16m⁶]
   Ex-handicapper Teamster started clear favourite for the Gold Cup on the
strength of impressive wins in the Insulpak Sagaro EBF Stakes at Ascot and
the Mappin & Webb Henry II EBF Stakes at Sandown in May. His performance at Royal Ascot, though, was one of the disappointments of the race and
he could finish only fourth of the eleven runners, five and a half lengths behind
Ashal. He got the extra distance all right, for having been outpaced going into
the final turn he was coming back at the first three in the last furlong and
almost snatched third place. Teamster made three appearances subsequently;
on one of them, in the Doncaster Cup, he looked every bit as good as in the
spring, staying on strongly over the last quarter of a mile (having been held up
to the straight) to finish a neck second to Al Maheb. However, prior to that
he'd been pulled up after a mile or so, apparently having injured a foot, in a
listed race at York, and he ran poorly behind Great Marquess in the Jockey
Club Cup at Newmarket in October.

Mappin & Webb Henry II EBF Stakes, Sandown —
Teamster again looks a good staying prospect
as he wins very easily from Mountain Kingdom

A medium-sized, good-bodied colt, Teamster had indicated on his reappearance in a Kempton handicap that he was at least as good as ever and was stepped up to pattern company for the first time in the Sagaro Stakes for which he shared second favouritism with Double Dutch behind the 1988 Derby runner-up Glacial Storm, now trained in France. In a moderately-run contest Teamster was soon sent to the front and drew five lengths clear of the rest, headed by Thethingaboutitis, in the final furlong. The Henry II Stakes, a race in which Sadeem had run before each of his Gold Cup victories, was likewise chosen for Teamster as a stepping-stone to Royal Ascot. Favourite of six, Teamster this time tracked the leaders, moved up strongly early in the straight and quickened around ten lengths clear in a short time before being eased, crossing the line four ahead of Mountain Kingdom. At the time Teamster looked destined for top honours in the Cup races, but it wasn't to be and, like that of stable-mates Safawan, Dolpour and Heart of Joy, his season was one of anti-climax.

Teamster (b.c. 1986)	Known Fact (USA) (b 1977)	In Reality (b 1964)	Intentionally
			My Dear Girl
		Tamerett (b or br 1962)	Tim Tam
			Mixed Marriage
	Rosetta Stone (ch 1978)	Guillaume Tell (ch 1972)	Nashua
			La Dauphine
		Lady Clodagh (ch 1963)	Tyrone
			Chloris II

Known Fact is not usually associated with siring stayers, rather with milers like himself, notably Warning. Awarded the Two Thousand Guineas on the disqualification of Nureyev, Known Fact later won the Waterford Crystal Mile, the Kiveton Park Steel Stakes and the Queen Elizabeth II Stakes. The home-bred Teamster is one of only two horses Known Fact has sired to have

Mr Philip Newton's "Teamster"

won over a mile and three quarters-plus on the flat in Britain and Ireland, the other being the modest handicapper Real Moonshine; the dams of both were suited by a test of stamina. Teamster's dam Rosetta Stone made all in a mile-and-three-quarter maiden at Haydock in the mud. She produced two winners before Teamster, the better of them his full brother Blind Faith, successful over nine furlongs at two and awarded a quite valuable handicap at Newbury over an extended thirteen furlongs at three. Teamster's grandam Lady Clodagh, who holds the distinction of being placed in the Irish One Thousand Guineas on her only start, also produced the very useful Irish six-furlong and seven-furlong winner Columbanus, third to Jaazeiro in the Irish Two Thousand Guineas. Lady Clodagh's half-brothers Trouville and Arctic Sea were others to finish third in the Irish Two Thousand Guineas. Teamster, a good mover with a quick action, has won on very soft ground but has shown his best form under less testing conditions and acts on firm. He sweated on his last two starts, possibly unnerved by what affected him at York. As to his future, it's a matter of wait and see — he'd have a chance in the Cup races on his best form, but he couldn't be recommended on his last run. *M. R. Stoute.*

TEANARCO (IRE)   2 b.f. (Mar 9) Kafu 120–Lady Kasbah (Lord Gayle (USA)   **94**
124) [1990 5f³ 5.8m² 5.8h* 5m⁴ 6d* 6d²] 5,200Y, 3,200 2-y-o: leggy filly: half-sister to 1m winner Lady Donaro (by Ardoon) and Triumph Hurdle second Wahiba (by Tumble Wind): dam never ran: won maiden auction at Bath in July and nursery at Haydock in September: better suited by 6f than 5f: best form on a soft surface: genuine. *R. J. Holder.*

TEENOSO'S GIRL   2 b.f. (Apr 26) Teenoso (USA) 135–Mosso 81 (Ercolano   —
(USA) 118) [1990 6g 7g] 2,000Y: angular filly: fifth foal: half-sister to 3-y-o Agnes Dodd (by Homing) and 6f winner Mossy Rose (by King of Spain): dam 2-y-o 5.8f and 6f winner: of little account. *J. W. Payne.*

TEENY POP (IRE)   2 b.f. (Apr 10) Montekin 125–Gay Barbarella (Gay Fan-   —
dango (USA) 132) [1990 5f a5g⁵ 5m 5m 6d] small, deep-girthed filly: moderate walker: second foal: half-sister to winner in Austria: dam poor maiden here at 2 yrs won 3 times in Denmark as 3-y-o: seems of no account: bought out of D. Thom's stable 840 gns Newmarket July Sales after third start. *T. Kersey.*

TEES WHEELIE BIN   3 b.f. Balliol 125–Mead Lane (Ballymoss 136) [1989 NR   —
1990 10m] workmanlike filly: first reported foal: dam ran once: 50/1, backward, moved moderately down and showed nothing in maiden at Leicester in April. *Dr J. D. Scargill.*

TELEGRAPH CALLGIRL   3 b.f. Northern Tempest (USA) 120–Northgate   **67**
Lady 54 (Fordham (USA) 117) [1989 5f⁴ 5f⁴ 6m 6g a6g⁵ a8g² a7g² a8g² 1990 a8g² a8g* a7g⁴ a8g² a7g* a8g* a7g³ a8g² 8m 8.2s a8g] strong, compact filly: moderate mover: quite modest performer: in good form on the all-weather very early on, winning 3 Southwell claimers: suited by 1m: good mount for a claimer: bandaged final outing. *M. Brittain.*

TELEGRAPHTER (IRE)   2 b.c. (May 8) Drumalis 125–La Marne (USA)   —
(Nashua) [1990 5m 5g 5g⁶ a7g 7d] IR 2,100F, IR 3,000Y: small colt: half-brother to 3-y-o General Meeting (by General Assembly) and several winners, including fair 5f to 1m winner Akram (by Sandford Lad): dam lightly-raced half-sister to leading 2-y-o fillies Crimea II and Bravery: bad maiden: sold 620 gns Doncaster October Sales. *M. Brittain.*

TELEMACHUS   6 b.g. Runnett 125–Bee Hawk 87 (Sea Hawk II 131) [1989 NR   —
1990 a8g⁶] of little account on flat: blinkered 3 times: won twice over fences in 1989/90. *C. L. Popham.*

TELETRADER   9 ch.g. Nearly A Hand 115–Miss Saddler (St Paddy 133) [1989   **63**
10.2g² 10v 12d² 1990 12f³ 13.1h³ 10m* 10m⁶ 12m² 10f⁵ 10.2m⁶] workmanlike gelding: confirmed promise of reappearance when winning handicap at Nottingham in August: stays 1½m, but at least as effective at 1¼m: acts on firm going: has given trouble at stalls. *R. J. Hodges.*

TELLMEABOUTIT   2 b.g. (Mar 29) Blushing Scribe (USA) 107–Orchard Road   —
74 (Camden Town 125) [1990 6g 6f⁶ 5f a7g] 8,000 2-y-o: leggy, workmanlike gelding: fourth foal: brother to 4-y-o Red Pippin: dam placed at up to 7f at 2 yrs, only season to race: well beaten in maidens and a claimer: blinkered penultimate start. *Mrs N. Macauley.*

TELL NO LIES 3 b.f. High Line 125–No Cards 109 (No Mercy 126) [1989 NR **85**
1990 10m² 10m⁶ 10.6s⁴ 10.6d² 10.5g 8g³] angular, rather unfurnished filly: sister to
fair 1½m winner Line of Cards and half-sister to several other winners, including
fairly useful 7f and 1m winner Dabdoub (by Habat) and 4-y-o 1¼m performer Light
Hand (by Star Appeal): dam won at up to 1m: fair maiden: should be suited by return
to further than 1m: acts on good to firm ground and dead. *Lord John FitzGerald.*

TELLWRIGHT (IRE) 2 b.c. (Apr 17) Burslem 123–Travel Far 53 (Monseig- —
neur (USA) 127) [1990 6m⁶] IR 2,000F, IR 7,000Y, 8,200 2-y-o: close-coupled colt:
third living foal: dam maiden, is daughter of half-sister to top-class sprinter and
broodmare Stilvi: burly, dropped away over 2f out in 7-runner maiden at Newmarket
in July. *J. A. R. Toller.*

TEL QUEL (FR) 2 b. or br.c. (Feb 1) Akarad (FR) 130–Best Girl (Birdbrook 110) **103** p
[1990 8g*] brother to French 3-y-o Vue Ca Valiere, successful at 7.5f (at 2 yrs) and
1¼m: dam French sprinting sister to 1000 Guineas second Girl Friend: won
newcomers race at Longchamp in September by a nose, clear, from Exit To
Nowhere: will stay 1¼m. *A. Fabre, France.*

TELSTEAM (IRE) 2 ch.c. (Apr 8) King of Clubs 124–Ridge The Times (USA) —
78 (Riva Ridge (USA)) [1990 8g] 31,000Y: quite attractive colt: shade unfurnished:
third foal: half-brother to very useful 3-y-o sprinter Pharaoh's Delight (by Fairy
King) and ungenuine 1m winner Jumby Bay (by Thatching): dam 2-y-o 5f winner: bit
backward, slowly away and always behind in 15-runner maiden at Newmarket in
October. *W. Carter.*

TELYX 3 b.f. Mansingh (USA) 120–Spritely (Charlottown 127) [1989 NR 1990 7m⁶ —
7f] tall, sparely-made filly: fourth living foal: half-sister to 1986 2-y-o Irish 7f winner
Arabian Princess (by Taufan): dam plating-class maiden: sixth to Charming in minor
event at Salisbury: well beaten in claimer at same course nearly 2 months later: sold
1,150 gns Ascot November Sales. *P. J. Makin.*

TEMPERING 4 b.g. Kris 135–Mixed Applause (USA) 101 (Nijinsky (CAN) 138) **72**
[1989 9g 10f* 12f³ 11m² 1990 12m⁴ 14m⁴ 10.6m⁵ 7.5m 7m⁴ a8g² a7g a7g⁵ a11g* a8g⁵
a10g⁵ a14g⁵] strong, good-bodied gelding: has a powerful, round action: modest
handicapper: made all at Southwell in December: stays 1½m, but effective at much
shorter: acts on firm going: has often sweated and got on edge: sold out of W. Jarvis'
stable 9,200 gns Newmarket September Sales after fourth start: headstrong, and
has been taken down early. *D. W. Chapman.*

TEMPER TEMPER 3 b.f. Northern Tempest (USA) 120–Harriet Air 80 —
(Hardicanute 130) [1989 NR 1990 10g 13.8m⁶] workmanlike filly: half-sister to Txuri
(by Warpath), a winner at up to 9.5f in France: dam 2-y-o 1m winner: soundly beaten
in apprentice claimers in the summer. *P. A. Blockley.*

TEMPESTOSA 3 b.f. Northern Tempest (USA) 120–Lucky Candy 61 (Lucky —
Wednesday 124) [1989 7f6g 8g⁵ 1990 12.2m 12m] leggy filly: poor maiden: best form
at 1m: sold 820 gns Doncaster September Sales. *W. J. Pearce.*

TEMPORALE 4 ch.c. Horage 124–Traminer (Status Seeker) [1989 7s⁶ 6m 9f⁵ **57**
8g 10f 10g 12m³ 11g⁶ 1990 12m 10m a11g⁵ a14g⁵] close-coupled colt: moderate
walker: plating-class maiden: blinkered once: winning hurdler. *K. R. Burke.*

TEMPORAL POWER (USA) 3 b.c. Sharpen Up 127–Imperial Spirit (USA) **45**
(Never Bend) [1989 NR 1990 8m⁴] rather leggy, workmanlike colt: ninth foal:
half-brother to useful French 1m to 11f winner Lumineux (by Majestic Light) and
several winners in North America, including 9f Louisiana Derby second Native
Uproar (by Raise A Native): dam never ran: in need of race, fourth of 8 in maiden at
Pontefract in October, one pace final 2f: moved moderately down: sold only 800 gns
Newmarket December Sales. *J. H. M. Gosden.*

TENAYESTELIGN 2 gr.f. (Feb 1) Bellypha 130–Opale 117 (Busted 134) [1990 **72**
6f⁶ 7m 7d7* 6d 7d a7g³ 6d⁶] 4,600Y: workmanlike filly: turns fore-feet out: poor
mover: third foal: half-sister to 3-y-o 13.3f winner Pale Wine (by Rousillon): dam
won Irish St Leger at 4 yrs: won 18-runner maiden auction at Goodwood in October
by ½ length: good third in Lingfield nursery after: will be suited by 1m: acts on dead
ground: inconsistent. *D. Marks.*

TENDER ALI 5 b.h. Prince Tenderfoot (USA) 126–Vahila (Relko 136) [1989 NR —
1990 12g] smallish, sturdy horse: moderate mover: lightly raced and no form since 2
yrs. *N. Bycroft.*

TENDER BID 4 ch.g. Tender King 123–Princess Biddy 86 (Sun Prince 128) **68**
[1989 8.2s⁵ 7m⁴ 6m⁴ 7m* 7m² 7f 7g 1990 8f* 7f⁵ 9g 8.2m a8g⁵ 8m⁴ a8g a8g]
good-topped gelding: often doesn't take the eye: poor walker and mover: quite
modest handicapper: successful at Pontefract in April: suited by 1m: easily best

form on top-of-the-ground: hung left on fifth outing: mostly apprentice ridden: sold out of F. Lee's stable 1,600 gns Newmarket Autumn Sales after sixth start: inconsistent. *J. E. Long.*

TENDER CHARM 3 ch.g. Tumble Wind (USA)–Best Bidder 72 (Auction Ring (USA) 123) [1989 5f² 5m² a6g⁵ 1990 a5g* a5g⁶ 5m 5g 5m] smallish, sparely-made gelding: plating-class sprinter: won 4-runner claimer at Lingfield in January: off course 4½ months after second outing then well beaten in handicaps (sweating) and seller: trained until after fourth start by Mrs L. Piggott: sold 1,000 gns Doncaster September Sales. *R. Hollinshead.* — 51 d

TENDER DANCER (IRE) 2 ch.c. (Mar 28) Tender King 123–Exotic Dancer (Posse (USA) 130) [1990 5g⁶ 5d a6g 7g⁶ 7g⁶] IR 3,600Y, resold IR 2,400Y: leggy colt: first foal: dam ran 6 times in Ireland: poor plater: stays 7f: sold 610 gns Doncaster October Sales. *M. Brittain.* — 38

TENDER KISS (IRE) 2 b.f. (Apr 30) Tender King 123–Nordic Maid 84 (Vent du Nord) [1990 5f 5f⁶ 5.3h² 5m 5f 6h⁵ 5m 5m 5f³ 5m a5g⁵ a6g] IR 2,500F, 2,500Y: strong, plain filly: has a quick action: half-sister to Irish 1½m winner Ballinascreena (by Kampala): dam 1m winner: plating class: third of 8 to Precious Air at Bath: should stay 6f: sometimes bandaged behind. *R. A. Bennett.* — 51

TENDERLOIN 3 b.g. Tender King 123–Samkhya (Crocket 130) [1989 5g² 5s⁶ 5d⁴ 7m⁴ 7m² 6g 7f² 7d* 7g⁶ a6g⁵ a8g² 1990 8.2g 9f⁶ 8g³ 8m⁴ 8g² 8m* 8g² 9m³] leggy, close-coupled gelding: moderate mover: useful plater: won at Carlisle (no bid) in June: stays 9f: acts on firm and dead ground. *N. Tinkler.* — 64

TENDER MUSIC 2 ch.f. (May 8) Music Boy 124–Sobriquet (Roan Rocket 128) [1990 5m⁵ 5m³ 5f⁴ 5g] 6,000Y: workmanlike filly: has a round action: second foal: half-sister to 3-y-o Educated Rita (by The Brianstan): dam poor half-sister to very useful 1976 2-y-o 5f performer The Andrestan: poor maiden: in frame twice at Catterick: acts on firm going. *Miss L. C. Siddall.* — 48

TENDER REACH 2 b.f. (Apr 30) Reach 122–Betty's Bid (Auction Ring (USA) 123) [1990 5.3f⁵ 8m] 400Y: small filly: fourth foal: half-sister to 1986 2-y-o 6f seller winner The Chippenham Man (by Young Man) and 2 poor platers: dam poor daughter of half-sister to Royal Hunt Cup winner Picture Boy: soundly beaten in maiden auction at Brighton in April and apprentice seller (hit rail 3f out) at Warwick in October. *R. Voorspuy.* — —

TENDER SPOT (IRE) 2 b.f. (Apr 6) Tender King 123–Kalakan (Kalamoun 129) [1990 6g⁵ a6g] IR 5,400Y: fourth foal: half-sister to 1989 2-y-o 5f and 6f winner Crispy Duck (by Reasonable): dam, lightly raced, placed over 7.5f at 2 yrs in Ireland: beaten around 14 lengths in maidens at Folkestone and Lingfield (slowly away): sold 450 gns Ascot December Sales. *R. Hannon.* — 45

TENDER TILLY 4 b.f. Tender King 123–Nightly Dip (Wollow 132) [1989 5m 6m² a6g 1990 a6g 7m 5m 7d] leggy, quite good-topped filly: lightly-raced sprint maiden: no form at 4 yrs: has run in sellers: sold 720 gns Doncaster October Sales. *W. W. Haigh.* — —

TENDER TRAIL 3 ch.f. Tender King 123–Trail (Thatch (USA) 136) [1989 5v 5s 5f⁶ 5m² 5f⁴ 5f⁵ 5m⁴ 5g 5m 5m² 5f⁴ 1990 5m 6m 5.3h⁵ 5m⁴ 5m⁴ 5f⁶ 5.3h² 6m 6f 5.3f a6g] small, lengthy filly: has a round action: only poor form at 3 yrs: should stay 6f: acts on hard ground: sometimes sweating. *C. J. Denstead.* — 46

TENDER TYPE 7 b.g. Prince Tenderfoot (USA) 126–Double Type (Behistoun 131) [1989 13m⁵ 15f⁴ 12.3g⁵ 12f² 14f 1990 13v 12m⁴ 12.3d 14g* 16.1f⁵] strong, lengthy gelding: carries plenty of condition: moderate walker and mover: quite modest handicapper: won at Newmarket in May: bandaged, finished lame at same course nearly 2 months later: ideally suited by around 1¾m: acts on firm and dead going: good mount for inexperienced rider: has won when sweating: possibly unsuited by Chester track third outing. *R. M. Whitaker.* — 65

TENDER WHISPER 5 b.m. Tender King 123–Queens Message 93 (Town Crier 119) [1989 8h 5f a8g 1990 a6g a6g] sturdy, angular mare: poor maiden: blinkered final outing. *D. Burchell.* — —

TENDRESSE (IRE) 2 b.f. (Apr 19) Tender King 123–Velinowski (Malinowski (USA) 123) [1990 5m⁶ 5m 6m* 5f 6m⁴ 7m 6d 6m⁶] 2,600Y: workmanlike filly: second foal: dam unraced half-sister to smart Lord Helpus, successful from 5f to 1½m: moderate plater: won 8-runner event (no bid) at Lingfield in July: suited by 6f: below form on dead going: possibly a difficult ride. *R. J. Hodges.* — 47

TEN O'CLOCKS   2 b.f. (Apr 5) Domynsky 110–Mashin Time 73 (Palm Track   —
122) [1990 5m 5m] 1,000Y: fifth foal: half-sister to 3-y-o 1m seller winner Tiffin Time
(by Lochnager): dam 6f and 1m winner: of little account. *M. H. Easterby.*

TEODORICO   3 b.c. Simply Great (FR) 122–Tin Goddess (Petingo 135) [1989 NR   —
1990 10m⁶ a12g 11g] 12,000F, 11,000Y: half-brother to useful 1m winner Purchase-
paperchase (by Young Generation): dam placed over 9.5f in Ireland: well beaten in
maidens early on, 2 of them claimers: may be suited by return to 1¼m: sold to join
Miss K. George 2,600 gns Ascot June Sales. *M. A. Jarvis.*

TEQUILA GOLD   2 b.g. (Mar 16) Green Ruby (USA) 104–Diamante 83 (Spark-   **52**
ler 130) [1990 6g 6g 5s⁵] 6,800Y: rather angular gelding: fifth foal: half-brother to a
winner in Denmark: dam 2-y-o 7f seller winner: plating-class maiden: best effort
second outing: visored final one. *J. S. Wilson.*

TEREBRID   3 ch.c. Coquelin (USA) 121–Hone 79 (Sharpen Up 127) [1989 5d⁴ 6f³   —
6g 1990 a8g a10g] leggy, close-coupled colt: poor walker: plating-class maiden: faced
stiff tasks as 3-y-o, off course 7 months in between outings and showing nothing in
handicap on second of them: bred to stay 1m. *C. R. Nelson.*

TERIMON   4 gr.c. Bustino 136–Nicholas Grey 100 (Track Spare 125) [1989 **121**
7g² 8s² 10.4m³ 10m* 12g² 12f² 14.6s⁴ 1990 9m* 10m⁶ 10m³ 10m² 12m⁶ 10.5g⁴
10d]

    A well-received local success in the Group 3 Earl of Sefton Stakes in
April sent the Newmarket-trained Terimon off on a tour of British racing's
major theatres. As it turned out, he filled only a supporting role, but he showed himself still a good-class performer all the same, reaching the frame in the
Prince of Wales's Stakes at Royal Ascot, the Coral-Eclipse Stakes at Sandown
and the Juddmonte International Stakes at York. Terimon failed to show the
consistency one likes to see in a horse of his ability, occasionally forgetting
his lines, notably in the Brigadier Gerard Stakes at Sandown in May when he
started 6/5 favourite but trailed in last of the six behind Husyan. The modest
early pace seemed not to suit him. Terimon is at his best held up in a
strongly-run race, and can produce a good turn of foot. He'd shown as much in
the Earl of Sefton, quickening well to catch Citidancer on the post, having had
to wait for a run in the Dip. Terimon again had the race run to suit him in the
Prince of Wales's Stakes at Royal Ascot, where Relief Pitcher soon went
clear. Terimon was still well back early in the straight, but quickened to have
every chance inside the distance, and went down by just a short head and a
neck to Batshoof and Relief Pitcher in one of the best finishes of the meeting.
Terimon was involved in another stirring struggle in the Coral-Eclipse Stakes
at Sandown the following month, this time with the three-year-old Elmaamul.
The pair dominated the closing stages, pulling five lengths clear, but it was
Elmaamul who came out the better by half a length. Terimon's performance in
the Eclipse was the high point of his season, and he had just three more races.
He could finish only sixth of eleven in the King George at Ascot, beaten

Earl of Sefton EBF Stakes, Newmarket—
Terimon (grey) gets up on the line from Citidancer (rails);
Pirate Army is the horse between them

around nine lengths having met some interference approaching the straight, and he trailed in last of ten in the Dubai Champion Stakes at Newmarket in October, where he looked in need of the race having been off the course two months. In between, he was a highly creditable fourth in the Juddmonte International at York, where he met some scrimmaging about three furlongs out in going down by four and a half lengths to In The Groove, with Elmaamul and Batshoof second and third.

	Bustino	Busted	Crepello
	(b 1971)	(b 1963)	Sans Le Sou
Terimon		Ship Yard	Doutelle
(gr.c. 1986)		(ch 1963)	Paving Stone
	Nicholas Grey	Track Spare	Sound Track
	(gr 1976)	(b 1963)	Rosy Myth
		Rosy Morn	Roan Rocket
		(gr 1970)	Golden Pride

There's little to add to the pedigree details given about Terimon in *Racehorses of 1989*. His dam Nicholas Grey's three-year-old of 1990, the Dominion filly Nidomi, has so far proved only a plating-class maiden on the flat and over hurdles, while Axiaprepis (by Formidable), who'll be a three-year-old in 1991, was in training with Elsworth in 1990, but failed to appear. Nicholas Grey's first foal Young Nicholas has been busier of late, and won twice at around three miles over fences in 1989/90. Terimon has won only two of his nineteen races to date, but his prize-money haul for the latest season alone reached more than £100,000. The lion's share of it was earned in place money as it had been as a three-year-old when he picked up £111,000 in one go for finishing five lengths second to Nashwan in the Derby. His running there suggested a mile and a half suited him well, and that he'd stay further, but as a four-year-old he showed he's fully effective at around ten furlongs, as well as confirming that he's best on a sound surface. A medium-sized, good-topped colt, a good walker with a rather round action in his faster paces, he takes a keen hold. He reportedly stays in training. *C. E. Brittain.*

TERMINATOR 7 b.g. Tachypous 128–Petit Secret 64 (Petingo 135) [1989 NR —
1990 8f 10.4d 8g] rangy, robust gelding: carries plenty of condition: fair winner in 1987: showed signs of retaining ability third outing in spring, but didn't race again: suited by 9f to 1¼m: bandaged at 7 yrs: probably unsuited by Chester track second start: sold 7,200 gns Newmarket July Sales: resold 400 gns Ascot October Sales. *J. G. FitzGerald.*

TERNIMUS (USA) 3 ch.c. Arctic Tern (USA) 126–Lustrious (USA) (Delaware 80
Chief (USA)) [1989 8m 8g 1990 12f* 10.6s⁴ 12g 12.4m* 12f² 13.3m 14f² 12g* 12m 12d 12m⁵ 12s² 12g³] leggy, quite attractive colt: moderate mover: fair handicapper: won maiden at Carlisle in May and moderately-run races (led inside final 1f) at Newcastle in June and Beverley in August: well worth another try at 1¾m: acts on any going. *C. W. C. Elsey.*

TERRHARS (IRE) 2 b.c. (Apr 28) Anita's Prince 126–Clodianus (Bay Express 68
132) [1990 5m* 5m⁵ 6g³ 5m³ 5g 5m 5f] IR 2,200F: leggy colt: third foal: dam never ran: won seller (bought in 6,600 gns) at Warwick in April: ran well in varied races afterwards: best form at 5f: acts on firm going. *B. Palling.*

TESEKKUREDERIM 3 b. or br.g. Blazing Saddles (AUS)–Rhein Symphony 41
74 (Rheingold 137) [1989 7g 1990 12h 12.5g 12m⁴ 14m² 12m 12.5g] leggy, plain gelding: has no off-eye: plater: tailed off final start: better at 1¾m than 1½m: hooded on debut, usually fitted with eyecover: sold 1,250 gns Doncaster November Sales. *J. Pearce.*

TESORA 3 ch.f. Busted 134–Savahra 82 (Free State 125) [1989 7g⁴ 1990 12m* 12d 85
12m⁶ 13.4g⁵ 8g] good-bodied filly: fair form: won moderately-run maiden at Thirsk in May: contested Ribblesdale Stakes at Royal Ascot and listed races after, no extra over 1f out having quickened well when 7 lengths sixth of 12 (possibly in need of race, moved moderately down) to Madiriya at York: well worth a try at 1¼m: acts on good to firm ground. *W. Jarvis.*

TEST OF GOLD 2 b.f. (Mar 12) Glint of Gold 128–Fair Test 95 (Fair Season 120) 60
[1990 5m 6m⁶ 5d] workmanlike filly: second living foal: half-sister to a winner abroad: dam, raced mostly at sprint distances, is out of a fairly useful winner at up to 2m: quite modest maiden: easily best effort second start: should stay at least 7f. *I. A. Balding.*

Hamdan Al-Maktoum's "Thakib"

TETRADONNA (IRE)   2 b.f. (Feb 18) Teenoso (USA) 135–Miss Bali Beach 88   **87** P
(Nonoalco (USA) 131) [1990 7d³] 8,200Y: rangy filly: has plenty of scope: third foal:
dam 2-y-o 7f winner stayed 1¼m: bit backward and green, around a length third of
11, going on really well after being held up in slowly-run race, to Junk Bond in
valuable minor event at Newmarket in October: will stay 1¼m: sure to improve
considerably, and win races. *D. R. C. Elsworth.*

TEXAN CLAMOUR (FR)   2 b.c. (Jan 26) Vacarme (USA) 121–Texan Maid (FR)   **69**
(Targowice (USA) 130) [1990 7f² 7m 6m² 5.8h 6m² 6m 7f³ 6m⁴ a7g⁴ a6g³ a8g* a8g
a6g⁶] 9,800Y: small, rather unfurnished colt: closely related to French 1¼m winner
Godlike (by Bellypha) and half-brother to French 1m winner Doralie (by Carwhite):
dam unraced daughter of good French filly Tamoure II: quite modest performer:
narrow winner of late-year claimer at Lingfield: stays 1m: blinkered last 2 starts: has
run well for apprentice: has been bandaged off-hind. *R. Hannon.*

TEXAS BLUE   3 ch.f. Jalmood (USA) 126–Laurel Express 76 (Bay Express 132)   **37**
[1989 6m 6m⁵ 6g 7f⁵ 5v 6g³ 6g a6g a7g a7g 1990 a7g³ 6f⁴ 6m] small, angular filly:
plater: easily best 3-y-o effort on second start: should stay 7f: acts on firm going:
inconsistent: sold 1,400 gns Doncaster June Sales. *M. Brittain.*

THABEH   4 b.f. Shareef Dancer (USA) 135–Loveshine (USA) (Gallant Romeo   **38** §
(USA)) [1989 8m⁴ 7m⁶ a10g⁵ 1990 a12g a8g⁵ a8g² a10g a10g⁴ a8g² 8m³ 10h a8g a8g
8f⁶ 10f⁶ a8g] small filly: has a round action: appeared to run extremely well when
third of 7 in maiden at Sandown in July: well below that form after and looked
irresolute: probably best at 1m: has sweated and got on edge: unruly at start sixth
outing: sold 1,100 gns Ascot December Sales. *K. O. Cunningham-Brown.*

THAKIB (USA)   3 b.c. Sovereign Dancer (USA)–Eternal Queen (USA) (Fleet   **113**
Nasrullah) [1989 7m⁴ 1990 8f* 9g* 8d6 8m² 8f* 8g³ 8g*] lengthy, quite attractive
colt: modest walker: progressed into very useful performer: made all in maiden at

924

THE

Kempton and Wolverhampton minor event in May then always close up when winning £6,000 event at Goodwood in August and listed race at Kempton in September: subsequently joined T. Skiffington in USA, well beaten in Grade 3 Handicap and second in allowance race: stays 9f: acts on firm ground and dead: mulish and withdrawn intended reappearance: game. *J. Gosden.*

THANKYOU SPODE 2 ch.c. (May 2) Son of Shaka 119–Casanna 62 (Star **43** Appeal 133) [1990 5d 5d⁶ 5g⁵ a6g⁴ a6g 5g 5m a6g] small colt: first reported living foal: dam maiden stayed 13f: quite modest plater: no form after fourth outing: looked temperamentally unsatisfactory final one: stays 6f: tends to hang. *R. D. E. Woodhouse.*

THARSIS 5 ch.g. What A Guest 119–Grande Promesse (FR) (Sea Hawk II 131) — [1989 14.6g 1990 12.2d 14.6d] sparely-made gelding: quite modest maiden as 3-y-o: well beaten only 3 subsequent starts on flat: stays 2m: acts on firm going: usually blinkered at 3 yrs: winning hurdler. *W. Bentley.*

THATCH AND GOLD (IRE) 2 b.c. (Apr 7) Thatching 131–Tuck (Artaius — (USA) 129) [1990 6f 6f⁶] IR 58,000Y: small colt: third known foal (first 2 in USA): dam unraced: well beaten in fair company at Newmarket and Windsor in August. *J. Sutcliffe.*

THATCHENNE 5 b.m. Thatching 131–Enterprisor (Artaius (USA) 129) [1989 — NR 1990 8m 7g⁶ a6g 6m] leggy, lengthy mare: plating-class winner as 3-y-o: no worthwhile form, but showed signs of retaining some ability, in 1990: trained until after third outing by J. Glover: best at 6f to 7f: acts on firm going: blinkered or visored: often wanders. *M. W. Eckley.*

THATCHER'S DILEMMA 3 b.c. Final Straw 127–Crane Beach (High Top — 131) [1989 NR 1990 a7g 11.7m 10s 10d⁴ a13g] 5,200Y: workmanlike colt: second foal: half-brother to 1988 2-y-o 7f seller winner Cassibella (by Red Sunset): dam unraced: poor form, in sellers last 2 starts: may well prove best short of 1½m: reluctant at stalls and hung badly left for claimer on debut. *D. W. P. Arbuthnot.*

THAT'S THE ONE 4 br.g. Known Fact (USA) 135–Kesarini (USA) 87 (Singh **85** (USA)) [1989 7g 5m 6m⁵ 5m⁵ 6m 6s 5m 6g⁴ 5d 1990 6m 6m² 6d 7m² 7m a7g⁴ 6g³ 8m⁴ 6d⁶ 7m 6g 6s⁵] sturdy, close-coupled gelding: moderate walker: poor mover: fair performer: effective at 6f and stays 1m: has form on good to firm and soft going: too free in blinkers third start: has hung markedly on occasions: consistent. *J. Etherington.*

THEATRE CRITIC 3 b.c. Sadler's Wells (USA) 132–Querida (Habitat 134) **113** [1989 7d² 8s* 1990 10.5s² 12m⁴ 10g* 12.5g² 12m⁴] French colt out of half-sister to Chief Singer: won listed race at Deauville by head from Passing Sale and Goofalik: ran creditably in Grand Prix de Deauville Lancel and Prix Niel (edgy, found little) at Longchamp last 2 starts: stays 1½m: yet to race on very firm going, probably acts on any other. *A. Fabre, France.*

THEATRICAL CHARMER 3 b.c. Sadler's Wells (USA) 132–Very Charming **114** (USA) (Vaguely Noble 140) [1989 NR 1990 10g* 10m* 12m 10m² 9m 8m³ 9g²] 330,000Y: tall, attractive colt with scope: has a round action: half-brother to 5 winners in France, including 9f to 11f winner Very Nice (by Green Dancer) and 1m and 10.5f winner Charming Boy (by Habitat): dam, French 10.5f winner, is sister to Dahlia: highly-promising winner of maiden at Kempton in April and 3-runner listed Newmarket Stakes in May: very useful form after, including in Prix du Jockey-Club (edgy and sweating) at Chantilly and listed race (staying on well behind Raj Waki) at Newmarket third and final starts: may prove best at 1¼m: has given strong impression will prove suited by give in the ground: to join Brad McDonald in USA. *A. A. Scott.*

THE AUCTION BIDDER 3 b.c. Auction Ring (USA) 123–Stepping Gaily 79 **100** (Gay Fandango (USA) 132) [1989 NR 1990 6f³ 5s* 5d 6s³] robust, sprint type: good walker: fourth foal: half-brother to fair sprinter Dominuet (by Dominion) and a winner in Belgium: dam winning sprinter: 33/1, won minor event at Haydock in October by 2 lengths from Zanoni, always close up: easily better effort in listed races when third of 21 to Katies First at Doncaster, moderately drawn and hanging right: stays 6f: goes well on very soft going: progressive. *R. Hollinshead.*

THE BLUE BOY (IRE) 2 ch.c. (Feb 9) Tate Gallery (USA) 117–Blue Lookout **67** (Cure The Blues (USA)) [1990 7m 7g 7m 7m³] IR 14,500Y, 27,000Y: lengthy colt, rather unfurnished: first foal: dam lightly raced, from family of April Run: quite modest form: best effort third of 19, staying on well despite tending to hang, to Mutamarrid in maiden at Chepstow in October: will be suited by 1m +: may improve. *J. L. Dunlop.*

925

THE CAN CAN MAN 3 b.c. Daring March 116–Dawn Ditty 100 (Song 132) **77**
[1989 7g 6m⁵ 6f 1990 8g* 8.2g⁵ 8f* 8f* 8g² 8d 8d 7d* 7d] big, rangy colt: turns
fore-feet in: modest handicapper: won at Carlisle, Doncaster then Redcar (twice),
leading post in £9,600 contest penultimate start: inconsistent in second half of
season: stays 1m: acts on firm and dead going: gave lot of trouble at stalls second and
third outings: takes keen hold. *M. Johnston.*

THE CARETAKER 3 b.f. Caerleon (USA) 132–Go Feather Go (USA) (Go **103**
Marching (USA)) [1989 6g² 7g* 7g* 1990 8m* 8g⁴ 8g⁶ 8g² 10d⁴ 7d*] useful Irish
filly: short-priced favourite, won listed races at Leopardstown in May (below best)
and November: in frame in moderately-run Irish 1000 Guineas at the Curragh and
listed races at Phoenix Park: stays 1m: seems best on an easy surface: blinkered last
3 starts: sold 230,000 gns Newmarket December Sales to race in USA. *D. K. Weld,
Ireland.*

THE COTTAGE 5 ch.g. Thatching 131–Brave Lass 114 (Ridan (USA)) [1989 8d —
10f 8m 1990 7f 6f 7h 8m] small, dipped-backed gelding: little ability judged on most
runs: blinkered once: usually bandaged off-fore: mulish in preliminaries final outing.
D. Morris.

THE CUCKOO'S NEST 2 b.c. (Jan 29) Precocious 126–Troy Moon (Troy 137) **72 p**
[1990 8g 7d³] close-coupled colt: has scope: second foal: dam maiden stayed 1½m, is
out of half-sister to Sharpen Up: bit backward and green, over 9 lengths third of 5 to
impressive Sharp Imposter in minor event at Leicester in October, much better
effort: will improve further. *C. E. Brittain.*

THE DARA QUEEN 3 b.f. Dara Monarch 128–Ladyfish 79 (Pampapaul 121) **77**
[1989 8g 1990 8g 10h* 11m 10m 10f] workmanlike filly: has a rather round action:
modest form: won maiden at Brighton in May: easily best effort in handicaps on
penultimate start: well worth a try over 1½m: acts on hard ground: sold Horse
France 4,000 gns Newmarket December Sales. *M. A. Jarvis.*

THE DAWN TRADER (USA) 2 b.f. (Feb 15) Naskra (USA)–Dream Play **65**
(USA) (Blushing Groom (FR) 131) [1990 6m³ 5m³] $95,000Y: third foal: half-sister
to thrice-raced Arctic Play (by Arctic Tern), second here at 2 yrs in 1988: dam,
winner at up to 9f at 2 yrs, is half-sister to very useful American colt Irish Fighter:
sire reasonable influence for stamina: quite modest form in mid-season maidens at
Yarmouth and Chester (gave trouble stalls): withdrawn (appeared mulish at start) at
Carlisle in September: evidently somewhat temperamental. *M. A. Jarvis.*

THE DEVIL'S MUSIC 6 ch.g. Music Boy 124–Obergurgl 69 (Warpath 113) **55**
[1989 5g* 6d² 6v 6d 6.1f 6h⁶ 6m 6m 8.2m 6m⁴ 6m 5s⁵ 5g 6d 6s a6g 1990 5g 5g 7m*
7g⁶ 6f⁶ 6g 6g 7f⁵ 5g 6s 7d² a7g⁶ a7g⁵ a7g] robust gelding: carries plenty of
condition: turns fore-feet out: shows a quick action: plating-class handicapper on his
day: made all at Catterick in May: stays 7f: not at his best on soft going, acts on any
other: has worn blinkers and visor (almost bolted to post and tailed off):
inconsistent. *N. Bycroft.*

THE EAST ANGLIAN 4 ch.f. Sandhurst Prince 128–Vera Van Fleet (Cracks- —
man 111) [1989 12f⁵ 12m² 9m² 12g⁶ 12.5m* 10g 10d 1990 14g 11.7m⁵ 12f⁵] leggy,
close-coupled filly: won maiden at Thurles in September, 1989: stayed 1½m: acted
on firm going: blinkered once: trained at 3 yrs and on reappearance by D. Kinane:
dead. *P. J. Jones.*

THE FELTMAKER (IRE) 2 b.c. (Mar 3) Shernazar 131–Miss Siddons (Cure **74 p**
The Blues (USA)) [1990 7m⁵] 18,000Y: first foal: dam twice-raced half-sister to
Princess Pati and Seymour Hicks: over 6 lengths fifth of 14, running on, to Marcham
in maiden at Goodwood in September: sure to do better over further. *J. L. Dunlop.*

THE FINK SISTERS 7 ch.m. Tap On Wood 130–Mount Hala 74 (Mount Hagen —
(FR) 127) [1989 NR 1990 8v⁴ 11m⁴ 10f] leggy mare: poor handicapper: stays 1m: acts
on heavy going: has raced freely: winning/irresolute hurdler. *T. W. Cunningham.*

THE FIVE 2 b.c. (Mar 17) Doc Marten 104–Mivanwy (Welsh Saint 126) [1990 **39**
5.8f⁵ a6g 5f⁶] leggy colt: half-brother to a winner in USA: dam Irish maiden: quite
modest plater: blinkered final start. *D. Haydn Jones.*

THE GALVANIZER 2 b.g. (Jun 8) Castle Keep 121–Princess Log 78 (King Log —
115) [1990 8.5m 6d] 1,000Y: leggy gelding: has scope: closely related to very useful
French 9f to 11.5f winner Ragnel (by Ragstone) and half-brother to a winner in
Germany: dam miler and half-sister to Roi Soleil: soundly beaten at 7-runner
maiden at Beverley and 25-runner claimer (visored) at Goodwood: sold 1,150 gns
Doncaster October Sales. *R. Hollinshead.*

THE GOOFER 3 b.g. Be My Native (USA) 122–Siliferous (Sandy Creek 123) **83**
[1989 8s³ 8.2d⁵ 10g 1990 8.2s⁴ 10v⁴ 11g⁵ 9m 10.6d* 11d² 10.6v² 10.4v* 9g⁵] tall

gelding: has a round action: fair performer: in good form in handicaps in the autumn, winning at Haydock and Chester (£7,000 event, by 12 lengths): best at around 1¼m: very well suited by a soft surface. *A. P. Stringer.*

THE GROOVY KIPPER   2 b.f. (Mar 6) Hotfoot 126–Farandella 86 (English   32
Prince 129) [1990 6g 7d 6m³ a6g 6g a8g 8.2s] 3,000Y: sparely-made filly: has a round action: fifth live foal: dam 2-y-o 1m winner later successful in Italy: bad plater: dead. *R. Bastiman.*

THE HEALY   3 b.f. Blushing Scribe (USA) 107–Smitten 72 (Run The Gantlet   50 §
(USA)) [1989 5g 5v 1990 8m² 8.5m 12h* 12m 12.4m 13.8m⁵ 12f² a12g⁴ 11m³ 12f 12.5g 12d] lengthy, sparely-made filly: fair plater on her day: won at Thirsk (no bid) in May: should stay beyond 1½m: acts on hard ground: visored final start: thoroughly inconsistent. *R. M. Whitaker.*

THEHOOL (USA)   3 gr.c. Nureyev (USA) 131–Benouville (FR) (Caro 133) [1989   —
6f* 6m* 1990 8g 8f] unfurnished colt: fair winner at Goodwood and Chester at 2 yrs: faced stiff tasks and little promise in handicaps at Ripon (on toes, slowly away) and Newmarket (edged left) in summer as 3-y-o: should stay beyond 6f. *M. R. Stoute.*

THE HOUGH   9 b.g. Palm Track 122–Dunoon Twinkle (Dunoon Star 110) [1989   —
13.8d⁴ 16.2g* 15.8m³ 16m⁴ 1990 19f3] workmanlike gelding: poor handicapper: very lightly raced nowadays: suited by 2m: sometimes wears crossed noseband: often apprentice ridden: winning hurdler in September. *Mrs G. R. Reveley.*

THE ISLAND   3 ch.f. Bairn (USA) 126–Redhead 66 (Hotfoot 126) [1989 5d⁴ 5v*   —
5d⁶ 5m³ 7m³ 8m 8.5g⁶ 1990 7g 8g 8g 12m⁶] small, light-framed filly: moderate mover: modest winner at 2 yrs: well below form in handicap and claimers in first half of 1990: suited by 1m: acts on good to firm ground and heavy: sold 1,350 gns Ascot September Sales. *M. J. Haynes.*

THE JOLLYFRENCHMAN   2 br.g. (Mar 21) Macmillion 110–Willington   72
House (Comedy Star (USA) 121) [1990 7m 6d² 6g3] rangy gelding: has scope: fourth foal: dam ran once: modest maiden: best effort second outing: should stay 1m: acts well on dead ground. *Mrs Barbara Waring.*

THE JONES BOY (FR)   3 b.g. Top Ville 129–Rythmique (CAN) (The Minstrel   76
(CAN) 135) [1989 7f 8f 8.2s 1990 10m 8v 8.2g³ 10m⁴ 10m² 12s⁴ 10f² a8g* 9m] lengthy, rather angular gelding: modest performer: edgy, won maiden at Southwell in July, leading inside final 1f: below form in handicap month later: effective at 1m and 1¼m: acts on firm going. *D. Burchell.*

THE KINGS DAUGHTER   4 b.f. Indian King (USA) 128–Burnished (Formid-   78
able (USA) 125) [1989 5s⁴ 5.8m⁵ 6f* 5f² 5f* 6g² 5g² 6m 1990 5m⁴ 5.8h⁵ 5m² 6g 6m³ 6g 5m* 5.8f³ 6m³ 5d⁴ 6s a6g³ a7g] strong, rather plain filly: favourably drawn and blinkered, won handicap at Sandown in September: blinkered only other time, ran particularly well when sixth to Ra'a in listed event at Newmarket: stays 6f: acts on firm and dead going: has worn severe noseband: has been taken down early and very quietly: consistent. *P. F. I. Cole.*

THE LAST EMPRESS (IRE)   2 b.f. (Feb 6) Last Tycoon 131–Beijing (USA)   61
89 (Northjet 136) [1990 7m 8.2m⁶ 7m] workmanlike filly: moderate walker and mover: first foal: dam middle-distance stayer: half-sister to very smart stayer Protection Racket: quite modest maiden: best effort first outing: ran poorly, claimer ridden, final one. *P. F. I. Cole.*

THE LIGHTER SIDE   4 br.g. Comedy Star (USA) 121–Moberry 54 (Mossberry   52
97) [1989 8.2g³ 10v 8g 9s 1990 10.2f² 12.5m 8m 12h 11.7m] neat, good-bodied gelding: plating-class maiden: form at 4 yrs only on first outing: stays 1¼m: acts on firm going: prolific winning hurdler (mostly on all-weather) as juvenile. *B. Preece.*

THEMAAMEH (USA)   3 b.f. Riverman (USA) 131–Star Pastures 124 (North-   73
fields (USA)) [1989 NR 1990 8g² 8f4 12f5] 170,000Y: smallish, sparely-made filly: third foal: half-sister to quite useful middle-distance stayer Lord Justice (by Alleged) and useful Irish 7f to 13f winner Esprit d'Etoile (by Spectacular Bid): dam won at 6f to 1m, including in stakes company in USA, and second in 1¼m Sun Chariot Stakes: modest form: didn't fulfil promise of running-on second in maiden at Yarmouth in July: should prove suited by shorter than 1½m: probably unsuited by firm ground: sold 9,000 gns Newmarket December Sales. *A. C. Stewart.*

THE MAGUE   6 br.g. Bold Owl 101–Silvery Moon (Lorenzaccio 130) [1989 10m⁴   61
10.8m* 9f³ 10f² 10.8m⁶ 10.2m⁵ 9m 1990 10f 10s 10.8m³ 10m 10.8g* 10m* 10m 10.2f³ 10f⁶ 10.2m 12g 12f⁴ 13.8f5] neat gelding: quite modest handicapper: won at Warwick (for fifth time) in June and Pontefract in July: best at up to 1½m: acts on firm and dead going: often blinkered (also tried in hood): probably needs strong handling:

doesn't find much in front and goes well on tracks with short straights: none too reliable: sold 7,800 gns Newmarket Autumn Sales. *Miss L. C. Siddall.*

THE MARSHALLS LADY (IRE)   2 b.f. (May 8) Kafu 120–Miss Redmarshall   **71** 80 (Most Secret 119) [1990 5m⁴ 5f³ 5f⁴ 6m³ 6m²] IR 4,000F, 7,400Y: unfurnished filly: closely related to 7f winner Sequestrator (by African Sky) and half-sister to 3-y-o Granitton Bay (by Prince Tenderfoot), successful from 5f (at 2 yrs) to 1m, and sprinter Annaceramic (by Horage): dam best at 5f: modest maiden: best efforts in nurseries, third of 22 to Chipaya and second of 18 to Anxious Times at Folkestone: much better suited by 6f than 5f. *C. F. Wall.*

THE MIGHTY MAJOR   2 ch.c. (Feb 21) Noalto 120–Turtle Dove (Gyr (USA)   **44** 131) [1990 6g 6m 5g⁵ 6m 5f 5f 7m] small, plain colt: half-brother to numerous winners by Warpath, including useful middle-distance stayer Path of Peace and fair out-and-out stayer Path's Sister, and to 3-y-o Belfort Prince (by Belfort): dam ran once: poor maiden: best effort third outing: ran in sellers last 3: sometimes slowly away. *I. Campbell.*

THE MINDER (FR)   3 b. or br.g. Miller's Mate 116–Clarandal 80 (Young   **51** Generation 129) [1989 7m⁶ 1990 a10g⁴ a11g³] rather leggy gelding: first foal: dam 1m winner: first form in claimers when third of 14 at Southwell in December. *W. Hastings-Bass.*

THE NOBLE OAK (IRE)   2 ch.g. (Mar 21) The Noble Player (USA) 126–Sea   **—** Palace (Huntercombe 133) [1990 7m 7m 7d] IR 6,000F, 13,000Y: compact gelding: half-brother to a winner in Norway by Sparkling Boy: dam unraced: well beaten in large fields of maidens at Lingfield and Goodwood. *M. McCormack.*

THE OIL BARON   4 gr.g. Absalom 128–Ruby's Chance 71 (Charlottesville 135)   **42** [1989 10v 8g 10f² 12h² 11m 11.7m 12m⁵ 12h 1990 a10g 12f⁴ 10m⁶ 10.1m³ 12f⁶ 10d²] leggy gelding: poor maiden: ran well in seller final outing: stays 1½m well: acts on hard and dead going: trained first 2 starts by R. Akehurst. *R. P. C. Hoad.*

THE OLD FIRM (IRE)   2 ch.c. (Mar 11) Hatim (USA) 121–North Hut (North-   **92** fields (USA)) [1990 6d⁵ 5m* 5d 5d* 5m⁴ 6f³] IR 7,700F, 14,500Y: lengthy colt, rather unfurnished: moderate mover: half-brother to very smart 1985 2-y-o Dublin Lad (by Dublin Taxi): dam twice-raced daughter of very useful sprinting 2-y-o Whispering II: fairly useful performer: successful, claimer ridden, in minor events at Windsor in June and Catterick in July: ran creditably in listed race and Anglia Television July Stakes at Newmarket on successive days last 2 starts: equally effective at 5f and 6f: acts on firm and dead going. *N. A. Callaghan.*

THE PRINCESS OF SPEED   2 b.f. (Apr 23) Bay Express 132–La Jeunesse   **41** (Young Generation 129) [1990 5g⁴ 7g] 1,800Y: third foal: dam ran twice at 2 yrs: quite modest plater: not raced after July: sold 1,100 gns Doncaster November Sales. *C. W. Thornton.*

THE PRODIGAL   3 b.g. Aragon 118–Patois (I Say 125) [1989 7g⁵ 6f³ 8m a8g³   **41** 1990 8m 9m 12m 10m 10g 9g⁴ 10f] rangy gelding: modest maiden at 2 yrs: form in handicaps only when apprentice-ridden fourth at Kempton: stays 9f: possibly needs an easy surface: tended to carry head high on reappearance: sold to join P. Feilden 2,400 gns Newmarket Autumn Sales. *R. Hannon.*

THE PRUSSIAN (USA)   4 b.c. Danzig (USA)–Miss Secretariat (USA)   **104** (Secretariat (USA)) [1989 10g² 10m³ 12.4g* 1990 10f² 12f³ 10m] compact, rather angular colt: moderate mover: useful handicapper: put up best performance when third to Hateel in £14,900 Bessborough Stakes (Handicap) at Royal Ascot: better suited by 1½m than 1¼m: acts well on firm going: sold 12,500 gns Newmarket December Sales. *M. R. Stoute.*

THE REFRIGERATOR   6 b.g. Shirley Heights 130–Nip In The Air (USA) 114   **53 d** (Northern Dancer) [1989 14g⁵ 14m⁵ 14m⁵ 16m⁶ 16g⁴ 18g⁵ 1990 16m 16d³ 16.2m 15.3m 17.6f⁶ 16.2m⁵ 18d] rangy gelding: plating-class maiden: no form after reappearance: suited by good test of stamina: possibly suited by an easy surface nowadays (yet to show his form on very soft): best ridden close to pace: has seemed a difficult ride. *L. G. Cottrell.*

THERE YOU ARE   4 b.f. Kings Lake (USA) 133–Occupation (Homing 130)   **— §** [1989 8g² 10v 8d 8m⁶ 12m* 14f 14f 12h 12m⁵ 13.8g⁶ 1990 a14g a12g] workmanlike filly: no form since winning claimer in spring as 3-y-o: reluctant to race final outing: suited by 1½m: best efforts on a sound surface: blinkered once, visored once: has sweated and got on edge: sold 3,400 gns Doncaster January Sales: resold 1,400 gns Newmarket Autumn Sales: resold 400 gns Ascot December Sales: seems ungenuine. *C. C. Trietline.*

THE RIGHT TIME 5 b.g. King of Spain 121–Noddy Time 97 (Gratitude 130) 52
[1989 7.5g 7.5m 7f* 6m⁶ 6f⁴ 6g⁶ 6g* 6s³ 7g 1990 7f 5s³ 6f 6f³ 6g 7f⁴ 6m⁴ 6g⁵ 5m³ 6g
5d² 5s] robust gelding: plating-class handicapper: effective at 5f and stays 7f: acts on
any going: visored debut, usually blinkered. *J. Parkes.*

THE SCARLET DRAGON 4 b.f. Oats 126–Dragon Fire 67 (Dragonara Palace —
(USA) 115) [1989 9m⁶ 8m 1990 9f] seems of little account: sold 2,600 gns Doncaster
May Sales. *Mrs G. R. Reveley.*

THE SHANAHAN BAY 5 b.h. Hays 120–Tanala Bay (Sterling Bay (SWE)) 77
[1989 7m 7m³ 6g 5m³ 5f* 5m 6s⁴ a6g* a6g⁵ a6g* a6g* 1990 a6g* a6g⁶ a5g* a5g⁶
a6g⁵ 5m 5f² a5g 5m³ 5g a5g⁶ a6g 5.1m² 5d* 5g*] angular horse: poor walker: took
well to all-weather racing, winning claimers at Lingfield and Southwell early in year:
then in great form in autumn, winning handicaps at Haydock and York: effective at
5f and 6f: acts on any going: wears blinkers: tends to carry head high: goes well with
forcing tactics. *E. Eldin.*

THE SINGING MAN 4 b.c. Mansingh (USA) 120–Opalescent 71 (Gulf Pearl 43
117) [1989 NR 1990 6m 6d 5d 5g⁶ 5m* 5m 5m 5d⁴ 5s] lengthy, good-quartered colt:
carries condition: won handicap at Edinburgh in August: best at 5f: acts on good to
firm and dead going: inconsistent. *J. Balding.*

THE STAMP DEALER 7 b. or br.g. Runnett 125–Royal Meath 83 (Realm 129) —
[1989 5m⁵ 5m 6f 7.6m 5m 6m 5f 5m 1990 6s a5g] rangy gelding: no longer of much
account: has been tried in blinkers and visor. *A. W. Jones.*

THE SWAMP FOX 3 b.c. Mummy's Pet 125–River Maiden (FR) 86 (Riverman —
(USA) 131) [1989 5s 6f⁵ 1990 5g⁶ 5m 10.8f⁵ 8.3m] leggy colt: poor maiden: unlikely
to stay 10.8f: sold to join M. Bradley 1,200 gns Ascot November Sales. *K. M. Brassey.*

THE SWINGE 3 b.c. Thatching 131–Hi Gorgeous (Hello Gorgeous (USA) 128) —
[1989 6f⁵ 6g 1990 10.1g 11.7g 13.1h⁶ a14g 14m⁵] quite good-topped colt: plating-class
maiden: showed little in 1990: not bred to be suited by middle distances: blinkered
final start. *P. Mitchell.*

THETFORD FOREST 3 b.c. Blakeney 126–Leylandia 69 (Wolver Hollow 126) 106
[1989 7d² 7g* 8s⁵ 1990 10g⁵ 10g* 13g* 12m² 14f* 14g* 14g] 26,000Y: sixth reported
foal: half-brother to 1½m and 2m winner Hyokin (by Comedy Star) and 1987 2-y-o 5f
and 6f seller winner Instate (by Tower Walk): dam won over 2m at 4 yrs: useful
performer, successful in minor events at Gowran Park and the Curragh in May,
listed Curragh Cup (by 5 lengths from Cheering News) in July and minor contest
(9/4 on in 3-runner race) at Phoenix Park in August: led 1½m in Irish St Leger at the
Curragh: suited by 1¾m: probably acts on any going: blinkered in 1990, except for
fourth start: makes the running. *J. Oxx, Ireland.*

THETHINGABOUTITIS (USA) 5 gr.h. Fluorescent Light (USA)–Croquet 106
(USA) (Court Martial) [1989 12s 7m⁵ 12m 12f⁴ 16f* 16g* 10.1d 18g² 1990 12g 16m²
20g⁴ 20d³] lengthy, dipped-backed horse: has a round action: 20/1, showed improved form when third to Ashal in Gold Cup at Royal Ascot: in frame earlier in year
in Insulpak Sagaro EBF Stakes at Ascot and Prix du Cadran at Longchamp: suited by
extreme test of stamina: acts on firm and dead going: bandaged in front at 5 yrs:
splendidly game and genuine. *D. R. C. Elsworth.*

THE WADKIN 2 b.c. (May 16) Creetown 123–Thinkluckybelucky (Maystreak —
118) [1990 6g 7d] leggy colt: second foal: dam sprint plater: of little account. *A.
Smith.*

THE WEIR 3 ch.g. Salmon Leap (USA) 131–Galka 98 (Deep Diver 134) [1989 8g —
1990 7g 10f 12m 9m] smallish, stocky gelding: little sign of ability, in selling handicap
final start: mulish at stalls and bandaged first two. *A. N. Lee.*

THEY ALL FORGOT ME 3 b.g. Tender King 123–African Doll (African Sky 54
124) [1989 7m 7g 7f 1990 8m 10m 12m² 11.5g⁵ 14g 12f⁶] smallish, rather sparely-
made gelding: head second in claimer (went freely down) at Goodwood in June:
suited by 1½m: acts on good to firm ground: blinkered 3 times: winning selling
hurdler for T. Casey. *R. Hannon.*

THE YOMPER (FR) 8 ch.g. Arctic Tern (USA) 126–Grundylee (FR) (Grundy 50
137) [1989 12s⁵ 10g 1990 11.7g⁵] sturdy gelding: very lightly raced nowadays, but
showed he retains ability in handicap at Windsor in May: stays 1½m: suited by easy
surface: suited by forcing tactics: has won for amateur. *R. Curtis.*

THIBAAIN (USA) 2 b.c. (Mar 23) El Gran Senor (USA) 136–Catherine's Bet 75
(USA) (Grey Dawn II 132) [1990 8g² 8m⁶] $175,000F, $285,000Y: lengthy colt: has
scope: moderate walker: half-brother to 3-y-o 1m winner Blushing Bloom and a
winner in USA (both by Blushing Groom) and 2 minor winners in USA: dam Grade 2

9f winner at 4 yrs: modest form in maidens at Newcastle and Redcar (heavily-backed favourite) in October: will be suited by 1¼m + . *H Thomson Jones.*

THIMBALINA 4 ch.f. Salmon Leap (USA) 131–Maestretto 77 (Manado 130) 63
[1989 6m 7f⁶ 7g 9g⁵ a12g 1990 10.2f⁵ 11s³ 11g* 12f³ 10d⁵ 12d* 12g⁷ 10g* 11.5m*
12d² 12m³ 12d⁴ 10.6s] leggy, lightly-made filly: moderate walker: progressed well
as 4-y-o, winning maiden claimer at Hamilton in May and handicaps at Beverley (?)
and Yarmouth in summer: stays 1½m: not at her best on firm going, acts on any
other: apprentice ridden: often on toes: sold 10,500 gns Newmarket December
Sales: consistent. *S. G. Norton.*

THIN RED LINE 6 b. or br.g. Brigadier Gerard 144–Golden Keep 77 (Worden II 53 §
129) [1989 10m 10m 11.5f 11f* 10g² 11.7g⁴ a11g 1990 a12g⁴ a8g⁴ a10g⁶ 10f⁴ 10f³ 10.8m
10.1g 11.7m⁵ 10h² 11.5f² 10h* 10h² 12f² 10m⁵ 12f⁴ 10f*] leggy gelding: fair plater:
none too resolute, and goes particularly well on switchback track: won at Brighton
in August (no bid) and October (non-selling handicap): stays 1½m: acts well on hard
going: usually visored: often sweating and edgy: best waited with. *J. R. Jenkins.*

THIRD WATCH 2 b.f. (Mar 4) Slip Anchor 136–Triple First 117 (High Top 131) 78 p
[1990 7m* 8m] deep-girthed, attractive filly: half-sister to several winners,
including useful 6f and 1m winner Triagonal (by Formidable), Oaks third Three
Tails (by Blakeney) and 1000 Guineas and Oaks-placed Maysoon (by Shergar): dam
won from 5f to 1¼m: won 10-runner maiden at Sandown in August impressively by
2½ lengths, always close up and quickening in good style: heavily-backed favourite,
raced keenly when last of 12, weakening over 1f out, in Brent Walker Fillies' Mile at
Ascot following month: should stay at least 1¼m: had gone in her coat at Ascot, and
is worth another chance. *J. L. Dunlop.*

THIRTY FIRST 5 gr.g. Castle Keep 121–January (FR) (Sigebert 131) [1989 14s⁶ — §
18.4m 18f² 19f² 17.1f⁴ 18g 1990 14m 14.8m⁴ 12.2g⁵ 16.2f⁴ 17m⁶] lengthy, angular
gelding: has a quick action: fairly useful winner as 3-y-o, but retains little enthusiasm: blinkered, tailed off soon after halfway final outing: suited by test of stamina:
acts on firm going and is probably unsuited by soft: sold out of J. Dunlop's stable
8,800 gns Doncaster August Sales after fourth outing: resold 1,700 gns Doncaster
October Sales: not genuine. *B. McLean.*

THISONESFORALICE 2 b.g. (Mar 18) Lochnager 132–Bamdoro 54 (Cavo —
Doro 124) [1990 8.2s 7d] leggy gelding: first reported foal: dam 1m to 12.2f winner
out of fairly useful 5f performer Pat: always behind in maiden at Hamilton and seller
at Catterick. *W. J. Pearce.*

THOMAS LENG 5 ch.h. Homing 130–Fast Asleep (Hotfoot 126) [1989 8s 8.5d⁶ 66 §
8.2g 8.2g⁴ 8v 1990 8.2s 10v*] leggy, rather sparely-made horse: moderate mover:
25/1-winner of apprentice handicap at Ayr in April: stays 1¼m: goes particularly
well on heavy going: has worn blinkers and visor: has got on toes: usually makes
running at strong pace, but ridden with more restraint at Ayr: has looked reluctant,
and is unreliable. *M. Brittain.*

THOMPSON FLYER 3 b.g. Swing Easy (USA) 126–Off The Mark (On Your —
Mark 125) [1989 NR 1990 7g⁶ 10.1g 10.1m] 11,000Y: rangy gelding: has scope:
brother to 1983 2-y-o 5f and 6f winner Redhouse Charm and half-brother to 2
winners, including 1½m winner On Your Bridge (by Scottish Rifle): dam won over
1m in France: well beaten in maiden and minor events in the summer. *R. V. Smyth.*

THORESBY 3 ch.g. Thatching 131–Nana's Queen 86 (Brian (USA)) [1989 6g 6g —
1990 8m 8m 6s a8g a8g] small, workmanlike gelding: poor maiden: bred to stay
7f/1m: visored fourth start, blinkered previous 2: sold out of R. J. R. Williams' stable
1,500 gns Doncaster June Sales and gelded after third. *J. Norton.*

THORNBURY (IRE) 2 b.f. (Feb 15) Tender King 123–Glastonbury 73 (Grundy —
137) [1990 8g] medium-sized, angular filly: third foal: half-sister to quite modest
middle-distance handicapper Glastondale (by Beldale Flutter): dam 1½m winner, is
half-sister to smart 6f to 10.5f winner Church Parade and daughter of half-sister to
Highclere: 20/1, always behind in 13-runner maiden at Wolverhampton in October:
sold 900 gns Doncaster November Sales. *M. A. Jarvis.*

THORN GODDESS (IRE) 2 b.f. (Jan 18) Godswalk (USA) 130–La Tante —
(Bold Lad (IRE) 133) [1990 5m] IR 3,600Y: third foal: dam lightly-raced maiden:
chased leaders 3f in 13-runner claimer at Edinburgh in September. *P. A. Blockley.*

THORNY FLAT (IRE) 2 b.c. (May 24) Precocious 126–Top Bloom (Thatch 59
(USA) 136) [1990 5g² 5d* 5g³ 5f⁴ 5f⁴ 5f⁶ 5m 6v] 3,800Y: small, compact colt: carries
condition: moderate mover: first foal: dam (ran twice in Ireland) half-sister to very
useful Irish 5f to 7f winner Hegemony, later successful at 1m in USA: plating-class
performer: won apprentice maiden at Edinburgh in July: consistent until showing

little final outing: should stay 6f: seems unsuited by heavy ground: blinkered last 3 starts. *W. J. Pearce.*

THORNZEE   3 gr.f. Belfort (FR) 89–Trackally 95 (Track Spare 125) [1989 5f⁶ 5m⁶ 5m 5f 1990 5f⁴ 5m³ 5g 6f⁴ 5h 6m 5.8f⁴ 6m⁴ 6m⁴ 5m 7g⁴ 6f 6f 6m] leggy, lengthy filly: moderate walker and mover: plating-class maiden: below form last 5 starts: suited by 6f: acts on firm ground: has run creditably when on toes, and for apprentice. *J. J. Bridger.*   **50**

THOU FEEAL   3 b.f. Mr Fluorocarbon 126–Jose Collins 91 (Singing Bede 122)   —
[1989 5d 5g 6g 7f 1990 a8g] no worthwhile form, including in sellers: blinkered (tailed off in November maiden) only start in 1990: trained by M. W. Easterby at 2 yrs: bought 620 gns Doncaster February Sales. *D. Yeoman.*

THRILL   2 ch.f. (Jan 22) Good Times (ITY)–Naughty Party (Parthia 132) [1990 6g⁴ a7g³ 7g² 7f⁶ 7g 8m] stocky filly: carries condition: good walker: half-sister to 1m winner Bustellina (by Busted) and a winner in Italy by Mummy's Game: dam 7f winner in Ireland, is half-sister to Whistling Wind: plating-class maiden: stays 1m. *D. Haydn Jones.*   **52**

THRINTOFT   4 ch.g. Sandhurst Prince 128–Finlarrig (Thatching 131) [1989 7m⁴   —
6f 7m 6g² 6f² 8f⁶ 7.5m³ 8.2g 8.2f 7g⁴ 8m⁴ 8f² 8.2g³ 8g 1990 10.2m] leggy gelding: poor mover: fairly useful plater on his day: tailed off in non-selling apprentice handicap in October: stays 1m: acts on firm ground: not particularly consistent: sold out of T. Barron's stable 3,000 gns Doncaster August Sales. *A. Barrow.*

THUNDERBALL   3 gr.c. Kris 135–Southern Maid (USA) (Northern Dancer)   **70**
[1989 NR 1990 7g⁴ 7f⁶] lengthy colt: half-brother to several winners in France (at up to 10.5f) and Italy: dam unraced daughter of useful French 7f and 1m performer Midou: favourite, best effort when making all in minor event at Thirsk in September: probably unsuited by soft ground. *R. A. Cecil.*

THUNDER BUG (USA)   2 ch.f. (Mar 30) Secreto (USA) 128–Followevery-   **66**
rainbow (USA) (Mehmet (USA)) [1990 7m⁴ 7g⁴] 68,000Y: close-coupled filly: first foal: dam half-sister to champion 1985 2-y-o filly Family Style: fourth, keeping on, in maidens at Yarmouth (slowly away) and Kempton: should stay 1¼m. *B. Hanbury.*

THUNDERCLOUD   3 b.f. Electric 126–Set Free 90 (Worden II 129) [1989 NR   **70**
1990 9m⁶ 12f³] leggy filly: closely related to 7 winners by Blakeney, notably Julio Mariner and Juliette Marny, and half-sister to 2 other winners, including Scintillate (by Sparkler): dam won at 1m: wearing crossed noseband, 14½ lengths third of 7 to impressive Ahead in minor event at Salisbury in May: unruly in paddock: takes good hold, and needs to settle. *R. Charlton.*

THUNDERING   5 b.g. Persian Bold 123–Am Stretchin' (USA) (Ambiorix II 130)   **36**
[1989 7s 7.6m 6m 7m⁵ 8.5g 7m 12m 8.2d 8m 1990 a6g a7g⁵ a7g a8g⁵ 8.2s* 8m 10.6s 8.5g⁴ 8f⁵ 7f] lengthy gelding: has a running action: 33/1 and apprentice ridden, won (for first time) selling handicap (no bid) at Hamilton in May: stays 1m: possibly ideally suited by easy surface nowadays: blinkered once: retained by trainer 1,450 gns Doncaster January Sales. *A. W. Jones.*

TIA PERLITA (IRE)   2 ch.f. (Feb 15) Persian Bold 123–Militia Girl (Rarity 129)   **42**
[1990 6m⁵ 5m⁵ 5g] IR 46,000Y: lengthy filly: has scope: second foal: half-sister to 3-y-o Tasmim (by Be My Guest): dam once-raced half-sister to useful 1983 2-y-o 6f winner King's Island (by Persian Bold), later successful over middle distances in USA: poor form in maidens: dead. *F. H. Lee.*

TIBBY HEAD (IRE)   2 b.c. (Apr 3) Lyphard's Special (USA) 122–Deer Park   **65 p**
(FR) (Faraway Son (USA) 130) [1990 7m 7g⁵] 15,000F, 23,000Y: tall, angular colt: half-brother to 1988 2-y-o 7f winner Shalbood (by Runnett), later ungenuine, 1986 2-y-o 7.5f winner Museveni (by Kampala) and a winner in Italy: dam of little account in Ireland: quite modest form, not knocked about, in October maidens at Newmarket and Salisbury: will stay at least 1m: capable of better. *W. Jarvis.*

TIBER FLOW   2 b.c. (Mar 26) Damister (USA) 123–Roman River II (Bonconte di   **90**
Montefeltro) [1990 5f* 5m* 6m 6g*] 22,000F, 52,000Y: half-brother to 1982 Irish 2-y-o 5f winner Burrow Hill (by Godswalk) and a listed winner in Italy by Brigadier Gerard: dam won in Italy: progressive colt: won maiden at Sandown and 2-runner minor event at Newcastle in July, and 11-runner nursery (on disqualification of ½-length winner Jenufa) at Doncaster in September: will be suited by 7f +. *M. R. Stoute.*

TICKET TO PARADISE   2 b.f. (Apr 29) Daring March 116–Airlanka (Corvaro   —
(USA) 122) [1990 a7g⁵ 7f 6f⁶] small filly: first foal: dam poor half-sister to French 1000 Guineas third Speedy Girl: bad plater. *C. N. Williams.*

TICKHAM VIXEN (IRE)   2 b.f. (Jan 19) Heraldiste (USA) 121–Camden Dancer   54
(Camden Town 125) [1990 6m⁵ 6g²] IR 3,200F, IR 8,400Y: workmanlike filly: third
foal: half-sister to modest sprinter Resucada (by Red Sunset): dam Irish 9,5f winner:
4 lengths second of 16, keeping on steadily, to Penny Mint in maiden auction at
Leicester in July: will be better suited by 7f +. *J. D. Bethell.*

TICKLE TOUCH (USA)   3 b.f. Stop The Music (USA)–Abeesh (USA) 77   —
(Nijinsky (CAN) 138) [1989 7m* 8.2d⁵ 1990 8.5g 11.5m] workmanlike, good-
quartered filly: modest winner (ridden by 7-lb claimer, gave trouble at stalls) at 2
yrs: faced stiff tasks in handicaps, tailed off in May final start: stays 1m: sold 1,800
gns Newmarket Autumn Sales. *B. Hanbury.*

TIDDLY WINKS   3 b.g. Daring March 116–Party Game 70 (Red Alert 127) [1989   53
5m 6m 6g 5f⁶ 6f 6m⁴ 6g 1990 6f 7f 5m 6f² 7.6g 6m³] heavy-topped gelding: fair
plater: should stay 7f: acts on firm going: best with strong handling. *R. V. Smyth.*

TIDEMARK (USA)   3 b.c. Riverman (USA) 131–Remarkably (USA) (Prince   101
John) [1989 6g* 7g 1990 10g 10.2m* 12d* 12g⁵ 12m² 12m] lengthy, good-bodied colt:
has plenty of scope: moderate mover: useful handicapper: won at Newcastle and
Epsom in June: short-head second to Comstock in £8,100 event at York: favourite,
prominent until entering straight in £71,300 handicap at Ascot over month later:
stays 1½m: acts on good to firm ground and dead: worth another chance to confirm
excellent effort in strongly-run race at York. *L. M. Cumani.*

TIE BACK   4 b. or br.f. Tender King 123–Grattan Princess (Tumble Wind (USA))   —
[1989 10.2f 10g⁶ 11g 1990 a11g] quite good-topped filly: poor at best: has pulled hard,
and wore severe bridle only start at 4 yrs. *M. J. Camacho.*

TIEMPO   4 b.f. King of Spain 121–Noddy Time 97 (Gratitude 130) [1989 6m⁵ 6m⁵   50
7f 6d⁴ 5s⁵ 1990 6g⁴ 6m⁶ 5m] compact, workmanlike filly: plating-class maiden:
likely to prove best at 6f: acts on dead going. *M. H. Tompkins.*

TIFFANY DIAMOND   3 ch.f. Royal Palace 131–Friendly Echo 61 (Reliance II   —
137) [1989 NR 1990 7g⁵ 7.6m] sparely-made filly: first reported foal: dam poor: no
sign of ability in maidens at Lingfield: sold 600 gns Ascot December Sales. *M. J.
Haynes.*

TIFFIN TIME   3 b.f. Lochnager 132–Mashin Time 73 (Palm Track 122) [1989 5d³   52
5f 6g 5m⁶ 1990 6m 6f⁵ 7.5d³ 8g* 8g 6f⁶ 7.5g⁵ 10m 9g⁴ 10m⁶ 10m⁴ 8.2v] small,
workmanlike filly: moderate mover: plating-class handicapper: won at Ripon (no
bid) in June: stays 1¼m: best efforts on an easy surface: often blinkered. *M. H.
Easterby.*

TIGANI   4 b.c. Good Times (ITY)–She Who Dares (Bellypha 130) [1989 5f* 5g⁶   112 ?
5f² 5m⁴ 1990 5m² 5d 5f 6m 5g⁵] big, good-topped colt: carries condition: smart at his
best: good second to Dayjur in Sears Temple Stakes at Sandown in May, first outing
for 9 months: disappointing after in pattern and listed races: suited by 5f: goes
particularly well on firm going: often sweats nowadays, on toes fourth outing: has
joined C. Brittain. *G. Lewis.*

TIGER CLAW (USA)   4 b.g. Diamond Shoal 130–Tiger Scout (USA) 86 (Silent   68
Screen (USA)) [1989 8g⁵ 10.6m² 10g² 11m 11.7f⁴ a12g 1990 11s 9g⁶ 12f* 11.7g²
11.5m² 12g⁴ 12f* 12f³ 11.7m⁵ 10m⁵ 12g⁴ 10d] good-bodied gelding: modest handicapper: won at Brighton in April and June (3-runner event): ideally suited by 1½m:
best runs on a sound surface: best form without blinkers or visor. *R. J. Hodges.*

TIGER CUB (USA)   5 b.g. Robellino (USA) 127–Tiger Scout (USA) 86 (Silent   48
Screen (USA)) [1989 NR 1990 9m 11.7f³ 10f⁵ 9g 12.2f⁴ 10.6s] first foal: dam 2-y-o 7f
winner later successful over further in USA, is daughter of half-sister to high-class
6f to 8.5f winner Screen King: poor form: faced stiff tasks last 3 outings: stirrup
leather broke and rider unseated on debut: stays 1½m. *I. A. Balding.*

TIGER FLOWER   3 b.f. Sadler's Wells (USA) 132–Tigresse d'Amour (USA) 108   86
(Stage Door Johnny) [1989 NR 1990 10m* 12f³] 100,000Y: big, lengthy filly: moderate mover: first foal: dam, French 2-y-o 7f winner, is sister to high-class American
middle-distance stayer One On The Aisle: 3/1 on, won 16-runner maiden at
Leicester in April by length (well clear) from Afkar: weak favourite, 3 lengths third
of 4 to Hajade in slowly-run minor event at Newmarket nearly 3 months later,
looking to become unbalanced then one pace 2f out: should prove better at 1½m
than 1¼m: has plenty of scope. *H. R. A. Cecil.*

TIGER SHOOT   3 b.g. Indian King (USA) 128–Grand Occasion 63 (Great   63
Nephew 126) [1989 NR 1990 8.2m⁵ 10.2g⁶ 10f⁶ a12g*] workmanlike gelding: first
foal: plating-class maiden out of staying daughter of St Leger runner-up None
Nicer: 12/1, first worthwhile form to win 10-runner maiden at Lingfield in
December: seems suited by 1½m: trained first 3 starts by J. Shaw. *P. J. Feilden.*

TIGNANELLO   3 ch.g. Burslem 123–Ms Yvonne (Morston (FR) 125) [1989 6f⁵ **55**
6m 7m⁴ 7f 8f 1990 a10g² 10f⁶ 9f⁵ 9.1m] leggy gelding: plating-class maiden: second
in handicap at Lingfield in April, clearly best effort: stays 1¼m: possibly unsuited by
firm ground: has got on edge: trained until after second outing by G. Pritchard-
Gordon: winning hurdler. *M. D. Hammond.*

TIKVAH   3 b.f. Relkino 131–Tactless 91 (Romulus 129) [1989 NR 1990 8.2g 12m **38**
10g 9f⁵ 7.5g⁶ 8in] good-bodied filly: half-sister to 5 winners, including very useful
Padro (by Runnymede), a winner at up to 7f: dam won over 1¼m: plater: best effort
over 9f on firm going, when sweating. *Miss L. C. Siddall.*

TILSTONE LODGE   5 br.g. Sabiron (USA) 130–Sabirone (FR) (Iron Duke   —
(FR) 122) [1989 9g a11g⁴ a14g 1990 a11g a7g⁵ 9f⁵ 8v 9f] lengthy gelding: poor
maiden: ran poorly last 2 starts: stays 11f: wears blinkers or visor. *T. H. Caldwell.*

TILT TECH FLYER   5 b.g. Windjammer (USA)–Queen Kate 52 (Queen's   —
Hussar 124) [1989 7v³ 8g* 7.6f 7g 7m 7.6m 8f 1990 8f 8.2d] big, leggy, sparely-made
gelding: won handicap at Salisbury in spring as 4-y-o: well beaten last 5 outings, off
course 7 months between 2 in 1990: stays 1m: acts on heavy going and unsuited by
top-of-the-ground nowadays: occasionally sweats and gets on edge: winning hurdler
in 1989/90. *R. Akehurst.*

TIMBERLAND   3 gr.g. Hotfoot 126–Tanara 93 (Romulus 129) [1989 NR 1990   —
10m 10f] sturdy, lengthy gelding: brother to 3 winners, notably William Hill Futurity
winner Count Pahlen and fairly useful 1m and 1¼m winner Docksider: dam 1¼m
winner: well beaten in maidens at Newbury (moved poorly down) and Newmarket
(blinkered, bit edgy) in the summer: subsequently gelded. *A. C. Stewart.*

TIMBILYN (IRE)   2 ch.c. (Apr 3) Hatim (USA) 121–Vivungi (USA) (Exbury 138) **66**
[1990 6m⁴ 6s³ 6g 8m 8.2g* 8m 8.2d6] IR 9,500F, 8,600Y: rather sparely-made colt:
half-brother to several winners, including 1m and 9f winner Nail Don (by Don) and
fairly useful 1983 2-y-o 5f winner El Gazebo (by Tumble Wind), later successful at
up to 1m in USA: dam placed at around 7f in France and Ireland: visored first time,
won 19-runner seller (no bid) at Nottingham in September by 5 lengths: will stay
1¼m: inconsistent: sold 5,600 gns Newmarket Autumn Sales. *M. E. D. Francis.*

TIME FOR JOY   6 b.m. Good Times (ITY)–Cry of Joy 50 (Town Crier 119) [1989   —
7f 5f 7f 1990 a5g] lengthy, leggy mare: lightly raced: no form since first outing
(tended to hang left and carry head high) as 4-y-o: stays 6f: used to be well suited by
the mud. *Mrs N. Macauley.*

TIME FOR MISCHIEF (USA)   3 ch.f. Lyphard (USA) 132–Mischievously   —
(USA) (Decidedly) [1989 NR 1990 7m⁴ a8g] sixth reported foal: half-sister to Grade
1 8.5f Fantasy Stakes winner Rascal Lass (by Ack Ack): dam 4-y-o winner at around
1m from family of J O Tobin: well beaten in maidens at Newmarket and Southwell
(led 4f) in November: should stay 1m. *J. H. M. Gosden.*

TIME FOR THE BLUES (IRE)   2 b.c. (Feb 19) Wassl 125–Azurai 80 (Dance **86**
In Time (CAN)) [1990 5g* 5d³ 6m 6m⁵ 6g² 6d² 5v* 6d*] 13,000Y: leggy colt, rather
sparely-made: moderate mover: first foal: dam 10.2f winner, is half-sister to Wollow:
won maiden at Carlisle in April, and seller (no bid) at Ayr and claimer at Catterick in
October: better suited by 6f than 5f: needs an easy surface: races keenly: game and
genuine: sold 18,000 gns Newmarket Autumn Sales. *J. Berry.*

TIME GENTLEMEN   2 ch.c. (Mar 5) Night Shift (USA)–Final Orders **112** ?
(USA) (Prince John) [1990 6m* 6m² 6g* 6f⁴ 7m³ 6g* a8.5f⁵]
    Time Gentlemen married his best display of the season, in the Group 2
Rokeby Farms Mill Reef Stakes at Newbury in September, by swerving
sharply right inside the last furlong. Fortunately, he was far enough in front
not to do any damage, and, with the rails to help him, went on to beat Sylvan
Breeze by a length and a half, with Shalford two lengths away third. But for the
swerve, Time Gentlemen would probably have won by three lengths, perhaps
four; though whether even that evaluation of his performance would justify
his standing in the International Classification (only five English-trained colts
were placed above him) is another matter. Sylvan Breeze (rated at 114) was
subsequently 4 lb and twelve places *behind* Chipaya (112) in the Racecall Gold
Trophy at Redcar.
    Time Gentlemen's other performances represent something of a mixed
bag. On the credit side, he made a fight of it with Mac's Imp in the Kingsclere
Stakes at Newbury; easily accounted for some not very brilliant Irish two-
year-olds in a Group 3 race at the Curragh; and ran what was probably a pretty
fair race in the Breeders' Cup Juvenile over a mile at Belmont Park: however,

Rokeby Farms Mill Reef Stakes, Newbury—an unusual shot of the course.
The wide angle is necessary to get in Time Gentlemen, who swerves across to the rails,
and pursuers Sylvan Breeze (right), Shalford (centre) and Act of Diplomacy

he was properly shown up by Mac's Imp and Distinctly North (Sylva Honda was also ahead of him) in the Scottish Equitable Richmond Stakes at Goodwood; and Shalford, who was caught close home by Flying Brave, was in front of him every yard of the way in the Tattersalls Tiffany Highflyer Stakes over seven furlongs at Newmarket.

Had Time Gentlemen not run in the Breeders' Cup Juvenile, one might have been tempted to turn a blind eye to his breeding and suggest that the seven furlongs of the Highflyer Stakes was too far for him; but the distance won't wash as an excuse for his performance in the Richmond Stakes (possibly the firm ground was against him), and we have nothing at all to offer by way of an explanation for his sudden swerve in the Mill Reef. In any case, the practice of advancing reasons in explanation of failures or misdemeanours can sometimes be construed as a stubborn refusal to look the facts fully in the face—which in Time Gentlemen's case is that his record thus far doesn't square with that of an honest and consistent colt.

		Northern Dancer	Nearctic
	Night Shift (USA)	(b 1961)	Natalma
	(b 1980)	Ciboulette	Chop Chop
Time Gentlemen		(b 1961)	Windy Answer
(ch.c. Mar 5, 1988)		Prince John	Princequillo
	Final Orders (USA)	(ch 1953)	Not Afraid
	(ch 1967)	Battle Eve	Battlefield
		(ch 1957)	Evening Out

Time Gentlemen is a close-coupled colt, and an easy mover. He was bought most reasonably at 18,000 guineas as a yearling, his dam having already produced several winners, most notably the very useful Dike stayer Hans Brinker and the useful middle-distance performer Yard Bird, a son of Busted. His connections have good cause to look back upon his first season with considerable satisfaction, but whether they'll be quite so happy at the end of his next one, we wouldn't like to say. Apart from anything else, he is obviously going to have it all on in handicap company, and it is not anticipated that pattern events will be so easy to come by as he found them in 1990, in this country at least. *J. L. Dunlop.*

TIME GUARDIAN (USA)   3 ch.c. Devil's Bag (USA)–Times Are Tough (USA)   —
(Olden Times) [1989 NR 1990 10g⁶] $80,000Y: big, good-bodied colt: fifth foal: half-brother to 2 winners in USA: dam, 2-y-o 6f winner in USA, is half-sister to Frizette Stakes winner Bundler: very weak 13/2 and green, 13 lengths sixth of 15 to impressive Theatrical Charmer in maiden at Kempton in April, taking keen hold: should stay further: sold 3,200 gns Newmarket Autumn Sales. *H. R. A. Cecil.*

TIMELESS APPEAL (IRE)   2 b.f. (Apr 26) Alzao (USA) 117–Kazannka (FR)   44
(Wild Risk) [1990 5m⁵ 6d 7m⁵ a7g 7g] 11,000Y: smallish, sturdy filly: moderate walker: half-sister to several winners here and abroad, including 1½m winner Devil's Dyke (by Dike): dam once-raced granddaughter of top-class 1952 2-y-o Neemah: poor maiden: best effort third outing: stays 7f: sold 1,600 gns Newmarket Autumn Sales. *M. Bell.*

TIMELESS TIMES (USA)   2 ch.c. (Feb 18) Timeless Moment (USA)–   99
Lovely Hobo (USA) (Noholme II) [1990 5m* 5f* 5f* 5m* 5f* 6m² 6m* 5m*
5g* 6g* 6m* 6m* 7.3m* 6m* 7.5m* 6m² 5f* 6m³ 6m* 5m³ 8.5f]

America's National Museum of Racing and Hall of Fame celebrated its
fortieth anniversary in August. Sited at Saratoga Springs, New York, 'The
Hall'—as it's widely known—is a magnificent advertisement for the sport and
stands well with the professionals in American racing (all the living Hall of
Fame trainers and jockeys attended the lavish anniversary ceremonies). The
National Horseracing Museum at Newmarket has a growing collection of
racing art, historical objects and other memorabilia but, as yet, British racing
has no Hall of Fame. If it had, trainer Bill O'Gorman would be an automatic
qualifier. The O'Gorman-trained Provideo's achievement of equalling The
Bard's record of sixteen wins by a two-year-old, which had stood for ninety-
nine years, was remarkable—prompting *Racehorses of 1984* to record that 'if
the gap in time between The Bard's record and his is anything to go by we
shan't see their achievement equalled'. That O'Gorman should achieve the
same feat with Timeless Times only six years later is amazing. The remarkably tough and genuine Timeless Times reached the sixteen-mark on
September 4th—almost two months earlier than Provideo had done—in the
Timeform Futurity at Pontefract. Looking extremely well, as usual, and starting at 11/2 second favourite in a four-horse field, Timeless Times moved up to
challenge the front-running Allinson's Mate shortly after rounding the home
turn and, with no challenge coming from the disappointing odds-on Dominion
Gold, kept on in typically game style to get on top inside the final furlong,
earning a great reception. Timeless Times made his debut in early-April and
won fourteen of his first fifteen races, suffering his only defeat when 2/1-on at
Thirsk in May, the only occasion during the season that he wasn't ridden by
Alan Munro. Timeless Times reached the record without contesting either a
pattern race or a nursery, his trainer shrewdly taking advantage of the oppor-

Spindrifter Sprint Stakes, Pontefract—Timeless Times is an appropriate winner

tunities presented by the programme of minor conditions events available to two-year-olds (the racing programme is much more restrictive for horses in other age groups). Timeless Times won on eleven different courses, from Beverley to Wolverhampton, from Britain's most northerly flat course Edinburgh to Newbury, where he gained his most valuable victory in the £6,290 Strutt and Parker Stakes after winning at Windsor the previous evening. Timeless Times proved himself effective from five furlongs to seven and a half furlongs; he gained eight of his victories at the minimum distance but by the autumn he seemed better suited by seven furlongs or a stiff six (like Pontefract) and ran well below his best, fitted with blinkers for the only time 'to sharpen him up', when attempting to clinch the two-year-old record outright in a five-furlong event at York the day after the Timeform Futurity. Timeless Times's bid for a new record was thwarted by a knee injury which kept him off the course in the last part of the British season. He finished last of thirteen on his come-back, crossing the Atlantic for the Laurel Futurity in late-October. Timeless Times proved himself well suited by firm ground and, throughout the second hot British summer in a row which at times produced Mediterranean-like conditions, he never encountered a soft surface.

		Damascus	Sword Dancer
	Timeless	(b 1964)	Kerala
	Moment (USA)	Hour of Parting	Native Dancer
Timeless Times (USA)	(ch 1970)	(ch 1963)	Sweet Sorrow
(ch.c. Feb 18, 1988)		Noholme II	Star Kingdom
	Lovely Hobo (USA)	(ch 1956)	Oceana
	(ch 1977)	Always Lovely	Beau Gar
		(b 1962)	Eternal Great

The compact, good-quartered Timeless Times, a moderate mover in all his paces, was a 15,000-dollar yearling (purchased at the Keeneland September Sale where another of the stable's leading lights Mac's Imp was also bought cheaply). Timeless Times is by the middle-of-the-road American sire Timeless Moment, a smart sprinter who stayed seven furlongs; Lovely Hobo, the dam of Timeless Times, won at up to seven furlongs in the States where her only previous winner from four foals was the minor winner Fast Trick (by

Timeform Futurity, Pontefract—
win number sixteen, and the record is equalled with a very game display;
Allinson's Mate plays a full part in proceedings

Times of Wigan's "Timeless Times"

Clever Trick). Timeless Times is some way removed from the top class—he came last of three behind the comfortable winner Anjiz in the BonusPrint Champion Trophy at Ripon, the only race of listed status he contested—and he'll be difficult to place at three. He'll have to move on to handicaps unless he improves enough to have his sights raised to listed and pattern races. Either way Timeless Times is sure to find things very much tougher. Whatever the future holds, Timeless Times has already carved a niche for himself in British racing history, generating more interest and giving more pleasure to the race-going public than many a champion. *W. A. O'Gorman.*

TIME LINE (IRE) 2 ch.c. (Apr 6) Hadm (USA) 121–Up To You (Sallust 134) **106**
[1990 6g4 6m3 6g3 a7g 7f6* 8m5 6d4 7.6s* 8v4] IR 9,200Y: compact colt: has a quick action. fourth foal: half-brother to 7f and 1½m sellers winner Stisted Park (by Be My Native): dam ran once at 3 yrs in Ireland: progressive colt: won 16-runner maiden auction at Chepstow and 6-runner Burr Stakes at Lingfield in the autumn: excellent fourth in Group 1 Gran Criterium at Milan in November: stays 1m: acts on any going, but goes particularly well on soft or heavy: unseated rider leaving stalls fourth start: with L. d'Auria in Italy. *M. H. Tompkins.*

TIME LORD 2 ch.c. (May 6) Good Times (ITY)–Miss Trilli 89 (Ardoon 124) **49**
[1990 5g 6m 5m4 5f5 6m 6d] 4,400F, 6,200Y: strong colt: has scope: fifth foal: half-brother to 7f winner Twiller (by Noalcoholic) and 12.2f winner Princegate (by Absalom): dam 5f handicapper: poor maiden: best effort third start: suited by 5f. *L. J. Holt.*

TIME OF MY LIFE 2 b.f. (Feb 23) Good Times (ITY)–Stage Revue (Comedy **47**
Star (USA) 121) [1990 7g6 6m 7m5 6m4 5m a8g] 7,400Y: leggy filly: first foal: dam unraced sister to On Stage: poor maiden: stays 7f. *Denys Smith.*

TIME ON MY HANDS 4 ch.f. Warpath 113–Midsummer Madness 66 (Silly — Season 127) [1989 8g² 8.2m⁵ 13f⁵ 9f* 9f 1990 a10g 9g] leggy, sparely-made filly: winning plater as 3-y-o: stayed 9f: acted on firm going: winning hurdler in August: dead. *Mrs A. Knight.*

TIMES ARE HARD 6 b.g. Bay Express 132–Raffinrula 75 (Raffingora 130) 54 [1989 a10g³ 1990 a10g* a8g* a10g³ a10g 6g⁶ 8.2s] close-coupled gelding: much improved early in year, winning handicaps at Lingfield: not seen out after June: needs further than 6f and stays 1¼m: suitable mount for apprentice: winning hurdler in April. *D. Burchell.*

TIMES GOLD (USA) 3 b.g. Gold Stage (USA)–Snow Cone (USA) (It's Freez- — ing (USA)) [1989 NR 1990 a7g 6g 8d] $11,000Y, 2,500 2-y-o: first reported foal: dam won 5 sprint races in USA: showed little in seller and claimers: sold 880 gns Don- caster September Sales. *D. W. Chapman.*

TIME SHARE 5 b.g. Known Fact (USA) 135–Midsummertime (Midsummer 47 Night II 117) [1989 NR 1990 a6g a6g⁵ a6g] stocky, quite attractive gelding: carries condition: has a short, sharp action: extremely lightly raced nowadays: best at up to 1m: often used to wear a visor: inconsistent. *D. W. P. Arbuthnot.*

TIMID 3 ch.c. Never So Bold 135–Din Brown (USA) (Tom Rolfe) [1989 NR 1990 63 8g 6f³ 7f 8f³ 8m⁴ 10m²] leggy colt: bad mover: fifth foal: half-brother to 1½m seller winner La Castana (by Dunbeath): dam lightly-raced half-sister to top-class Ameri- can middle-distance colt Little Current: quite modest form: claimed to join M. Pipe £6,111 after moderately-run seller at Leicester final start: probably stays 1¼m: drifted left when blinkered fifth start: slowly away third. *W. J. Haggas.*

TIMIDE ESPION (FR) 4 b.g. Saint Cyrien (FR) 129–Wind Spring (FR) — (Baldric II 131) [1989 10s² 8m² 8d* 10d³ 9g 8g² 9.2g* 10m 1990 10d 12f⁴ 10.1g] big, rangy gelding: seventh foal: half-brother to 4 winners in France, including Wind Jet (by Tennyson), successful over 1¼m and 10.5f, and Classical Way (by Bellypha), 1m and 1¼m winner: dam, 5f winner at 2 yrs, ran 4 times: won maiden at Evry and listed race at Le Croise-Laroche as 3-y-o: set gallop when tailed off in listed events at Goodwood and Windsor (sweating, wore bar-bit) on 2 outings in Britain: stays 1¼m: trained until after reappearance by Mme C. Head. *D. R. C. Elsworth.*

TIMMINION 8 ch.g. Dominion 123–My Baby Love 61 (Sovereign Path 125) 67 [1989 NR 1990 16.2m² 17.4d 16.2s] smallish, lengthy gelding: has a round action: much improved in 1988: co-favourite, ran well when clear second, hanging right, in handicap at Goodwood in May: pulled up (as though something amiss) final outing: stays 16.5f: best form on sound surface: wears bandages: winning hurdler in April. *A. P. Stringer.*

TIMMY BOY 10 ch.g. Timolin (FR) 81–Cabarita (USA) 88 (First Landing) [1989 26 NR 1990 10.8m 12m³ 12m 10.2s] workmanlike gelding: carries condition: has a round action: retains only a modicum of ability. *J. P. Smith.*

TIMSOLO 7 ch.g. Remainder Man 126§–Miss Tehran 73 (Manacle 123) [1989 55 14s* 13v⁶ 12d⁵ 15g⁵ 13s⁶ 13.6f⁴ 15s 15g* a16g⁶ a14g³ 1990 a14g* a14g* a16g⁵] sturdy gelding: won handicaps at Southwell in January: stayed 15f: went particularly well on an easy surface: good mount for apprentice: best racing up with pace: dead. *G. P. Kelly.*

TIMUR'S KING 3 b.g. King of Spain 121–Timur's Daughter 103 (Tamerlane — 128) [1989 7g 1990 10.6d⁵ 14d 12g] big, lengthy gelding: showed signs of ability only when 12 lengths last of 5 to Scribbling in maiden at Haydock in August, outpaced from 3f out: faced stiff task in amateurs handicap final start: should stay at least 1½m: joined S. Mellor. *R. F. Johnson Houghton.*

TINA'S ANGEL 3 b.f. Martinmas 128–Tina's Magic (Carnival Night) [1989 5f — 7f⁵ 6g 1990 8g 10m 7f 6f 5.8f 7m 8m 7f] leggy, sparely-made filly: well beaten in varied company. *J. C. Fox.*

TINA'S GIRL 2 b.f. (May 16) Magic Mirror 105–Highland Beauty (High Line — 125) [1990 6g] second foal: dam well beaten: always towards rear in 18-runner maiden at Folkestone in October. *P. Howling.*

TINAS LAD 7 b.g. Jellaby 124–Arbatina (Sallust 134) [1989 12.2m 1990 12.5m⁴ 60 14.8m² 12g² 12m² 11.5m⁶ 12m⁵ 11.5m] big gelding: carries plenty of condition: has a round action: quite modest handicapper: ideally suited by 1½m: acts well on top-of- the-ground: has won for amateur: won novice chase in December. *J. A. C. Edwards.*

TINAZ 3 b.f. Homing 130–Claironcita 97 (Don Carlos) [1989 NR 1990 8m a10g] —
14,000Y: sister to fair middle-distance winner Castellita and half-sister to useful
7f winner Shabanaz (by Imperial Fling): dam middle-distance winner: behind in
maiden events at Yarmouth and Lingfield (claimer, prominent 6f) nearly 6 months
later. *H. J. Collingridge.*

TINCA (USA) 3 b.f. Alleged (USA) 138–Princess Toby (USA) (Tobin Bronze) 86
[1989 NR 1990 8f 10m* 9m² 12g] $75,000Y: strong, workmanlike filly: fifth named
foal: half-sister to fair 1¼m winner Dilman (by Riverman): dam very smart winner at
up to 9f: fair form in varied events: won maiden at Pontefract in August in good
style: should stay 1½m: very slowly into stride in apprentice race third start. *L.
Cumani.*

TIN HAT 4 b.g. Tina's Pet 121–Pretty Miss (So Blessed 130) [1989 NR 1990 7.6g —
6m⁵ 8m⁵ a8g 8f 8m 12g 10d] leggy gelding: poor mover: second foal: half-brother to
7f and 1¼m winner Follow The Drum (by Daring March): dam once-raced half-
sister to 3 winners, including useful 2-y-o Fair Parrot: poor form at best: visored,
tailed off in seller final outing. *J. D. Bethell.*

TINKERBIRD 3 b.f. Music Boy 124–Quaranta 83 (Hotfoot 126) [1989 6d³ 6g⁶ 76
1990 5f* 6m³ 6m⁶ 5m² 5.8m* 5f³] lengthy, angular filly: moderate mover: modest
sprinter: awarded maiden at Thirsk in May and won handicap at Bath in July: acts on
firm going: sold 4,000 gns Newmarket December Sales. *W. Jarvis.*

TINKINS WOOD 2 ch.c. (May 19) Vin St Benet 109–Anatolian Elf (Hittite Glory 83
125) [1990 5f³ 5f* 6m* 5m² 6m⁴ 6d] close-coupled, good-quartered colt: moderate
mover: fourth foal: half-brother to a winner in Italy: dam poor plater: fair performer:
successful early in the season in median auction and minor event (by 1½ lengths
from Timeless Times) at Thirsk: in frame later behind Balwa in listed race at
Sandown and Mac's Imp in Coventry Stakes at Royal Ascot: modest twelfth of 19 in
Racecall Gold Trophy at Redcar in October: stays 6f. *R. Boss.*

TINTAGEL CASTLE (IRE) 2 br.c. (Feb 11) Caerleon (USA) 132–Merlins — p
Charm (USA) 113 (Bold Bidder) [1990 6m] lengthy, angular colt: has scope: fifth foal:
closely related to 8.5f winner Island Charm (by Golden Fleece) and half-brother to
winners by Lomond (3-y-o Native Guile, 7f winner at 2 yrs) and Be My Guest: dam
won Jersey Stakes: 9/1, slowly into stride and always towards rear in 14-runner
maiden at Newmarket in November: showed a quick action: likely to do better. *B. W.
Hills.*

TIQUETEEN 3 b.f. Teenoso (USA) 135–Helvetique (FR) (Val de Loir 133) [1989 78
NR 1990 14m⁴ 14g² 16m³ 17.6m* 16.5d] lengthy, good-bodied filly: has round action:
half-sister to 3 winners, notably smart stayer Harly (by Pharly): dam won twice at
around 1¼m in France: favourite, won maiden at Wolverhampton in August: ran
well facing very stiff task in Doncaster handicap 2½ months later: stays well. *P.
Calver.*

TIROL 3 br.c. Thatching 131–Alpine Niece 87 (Great Nephew 126) [1989 127
6m³ 6m² 6g* 7.3d* 1990 8g* 8f* 8m* 10d³ 8m]
The steadily-expanding internationalism of racing, linked to the growth
in importance of richly-endowed races overseas such as the Breeders' Cup
series, means that success for a top horse in the races which constitute
Britain's 'classic pattern' is no longer paramount. The five classics continue
to catch the public's imagination and success still confers great prestige, but
there's much more to aim at nowadays, particularly in the last quarter of the
season. It used to be usual for potential classic horses to be campaigned in the
best races as two-year-olds—it nearly always paid to take the best two-year-
old form as a guide to the first four classics—but the modern trend seems to
be to forfeit the chance of winning the major two-year-old prizes with a good
horse to concentrate all efforts on an extended three-year-old campaign.
Valuable races in Europe, North America and elsewhere provide an enticing
international big-race programme which goes right through to late-autumn
and are realistic targets in an age of high-speed transport for the one-time
classic horse' who in former times would have completed arguably the most
important part of his three-year-old programme by mid-season. Recent Two
Thousand Guineas winners Shadeed and Dancing Brave were examples of
good horses lightly raced and steered clear of the top races as two-year-olds.
Both were considered way out of the ordinary at home and were prominent in
winter ante-post betting on the Guineas; and both ended their three-year-old

Charles Heidsieck Champagne Craven Stakes, Newmarket—
Tirol (right) gives 3 lb all round; the inexperienced Sure Sharp
hangs in towards the rails and is just caught;
Shavian (centre) comes third

campaign contesting events on the prestigious Breeders' Cup programme in November. The examples of Shadeed, Dancing Brave and another recent Guineas winner Nashwan—who took part only in a maiden race and a listed event at two—seem sure to be repeated.

There's sound reason, however, for continuing to think that the Two Thousand and One Thousand Guineas will still, more often than not, go to animals that have been good two-year-olds. When the Guineas are run, the turf season is barely six weeks old and, other things being equal, the races come too soon and are run over too sharp a distance for most of those that haven't shone as youngsters. It takes an outstanding horse—a Shadeed, a Dancing Brave or a Nashwan—to overcome relative inexperience to win the Two Thousand Guineas in a normal year. The first six home in the latest edition of the General Accident Two Thousand Guineas had all either won, or finished close up, in at least one of the major two-year-old events. The Guineas betting was dominated over the winter, and in the weeks immediately leading up to the race, by the unbeaten French-trained Machiavellian, widely regarded as the leading European two-year-old of 1989; Machiavellian, allotted 9-7 in the European Free Handicap, 5 lb clear, had won two of France's Group 1 races for two-year-olds, the Prix Morny and the Prix de la Salamandre, and had been warmed up in the Prix Djebel in April. Machiavellian's claims were seemingly strengthened further when his stable-companion Linamix (9-0 Free Handicap), rated some way behind Machiavellian at home, comfortably beat Septieme Ciel (8-12 FH) and Jade Robbery (9-2 FH) in the Prix de Fontainebleu at Longchamp six days after Machiavellian's victory at Maisons-Laffitte. Septieme Ciel, winner of the Prix Thomas Bryon and the Criterium de Maisons-Laffitte on his last two starts as a two-year-old, and the Grand Criterium winner Jade Robbery had been Two Thousand Guineas probables but, on the day, Septieme Ciel was the only other French-trained challenger to join Machiavellian. The Coventry Stakes, July Stakes and Gimcrack winner Rock City, who had lost his unbeaten record in the Prix de la Salamandre, but had recovered his best form when winning the Greenham at Newbury in April, and the unbeaten Elmaamul, winner of both his races at two (neither of them a pattern race) in impressive fashion, were the best two-year-olds in the Free Handicap rankings among the twelve home-trained runners; both had been given 9-0, the same mark as the unbeaten Racing Post Trophy winner Be My Chief who had been kept busily employed in his first season and, in our opinion, had done just enough to be entitled to marginal preference over Machiavellian in the European Free Handicap. Be My Chief eased in the ante-post lists as a result of rumours in the spring that he was working moderately, and it was announced some time beforehand that he wouldn't run in the Guineas. Others representing good two-year-old form, however, were: the Mill Reef Stakes winner Welney (8-10 FH); the Dewhurst winner Dashing Blade (8-9 FH), tackling the Guineas without a preliminary after a rushed preparation following injury; Anshan (8-8 FH), a close third, rallying well, in the Dewhurst and winner of the Ladbroke-sponsored race for the European Free Handicap in April, for which he had been the highest-weighted acceptor; and the Horris Hill winner Tirol (8-6 FH), a progressive two-year-old, and a stable-companion of Rock City.

Tirol was the only pattern-race winner in the field for the Charles Heidsieck Champagne Craven Stakes over the Guineas course and distance in April, a race which has proved the most conclusive Two Thousand Guineas trial in the last few years. Conceding 3 lb to each of his five opponents—and starting third favourite behind Nashwan's half-brother Mukddaam and Shavian who had had only three races between them as two-year-olds—Tirol followed in the footsteps of three of the five previous Two Thousand Guineas winners, Shadeed, Dancing Brave and Doyoun, by taking the Craven. We'd been none too impressed by Machiavellian at Maisons-Laffitte and regarded him as very poor value for the Guineas at 6/4; Tirol's victory—he ran on strongly, quickening after being waited with, to catch Sure Sharp in the last strides with Shavian and Mukddaam third and fourth—was the best trial we'd seen and the odds of 8/1 generally available after the Craven represented outstanding value at the time. However, trainer Hannon, although having a very high regard for Tirol, went on record as saying that the very firm going on Two Thousand Guineas day—May started with a heatwave—was more likely to favour Rock City. Tirol's odds lengthened and he started 9/1 joint fourth-favourite with Sure Sharp, behind the cramped Machiavellian (still 6/4 on the day), Anshan (6/1) and Now Listen (17/2) who had been impressive in two early-season minor races after being unraced at two. Elmaamul (12/1), Rock City (14/1) and Septieme Ciel (18/1) were the only others in the field to start at odds shorter than 20/1.

General Accident Two Thousand Guineas Stakes, Newmarket—
Tirol runs on strongly ahead of Machiavellian, Anshan and Rock City

Tirol beat Machiavellian by two lengths after both had been held up in a strongly-run race—the winning time of 1m 35.84sec surpassed the previous best electrically-timed record for the race—but there were excuses for Machiavellian. While Tirol's rider Kinane found an uninterrupted way through in a bunched field after being on the stand rail most of the way, Head ran into all sorts of trouble on Machiavellian, getting boxed in on the rails and then bumping the weakening Elmaamul (and also causing Welney to be checked slightly) when switching sharply right approaching the final furlong. Machiavellian produced a fine turn of foot but Tirol, driven out up the hill after being firmly ridden to lead over a furlong out, was holding Machiavellian's challenge in the last hundred yards, leaving little doubt in our minds at least that he was the better horse on the day under the conditions, though Machiavellian would have finished closer with a better run. Anshan, sent to the front soon after halfway, kept on for third, two lengths behind Machiavellian; Rock City, prominent throughout, was a further half a length away, followed by Septieme Ciel and Welney. The interference suffered by seventh-placed Elmaamul might have cost him a position or two but he wouldn't have reached the frame. The Newmarket stewards held an inquiry into the interference to Elmaamul, decided it had been accidental and allowed the placings to remain unaltered; had the stewards deemed Machiavellian's jockey guilty of careless riding—a view many thought would have been justified—the horse would compulsorily have been placed behind Elmaamul.

Tirol was the third Two Thousand Guineas winner saddled by Richard Hannon, following Mon Fils in 1973 and Don't Forget Me in 1987. Don't Forget Me won after being beaten three quarters of a length by the Guineas ante-post favourite Ajdal in the Craven Stakes, and held the record for the Two Thousand Guineas, covering the period since electrical timing was introduced in 1952, until it was bettered by Nashwan. Regular readers may be weary of reading that we don't regard a course-record time as having any particular significance. A record time usually means no more than conditions were ideal for the setting up of a fast time. What is important is the *time value* of any performance, which can be arrived at only after careful scientific study taking into account the conditions under which the time was recorded. The timefigures recorded by Don't Forget Me (0.80 fast), Nashwan (1.10 fast) and Tirol (1.10 fast) in the Two Thousand Guineas weren't out of the ordinary for Guineas winners (1.54 fast, by El Gran Senor, was the fastest timefigure recorded in the Two Thousand Guineas in the 'eighties).

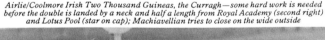

Airlie/Coolmore Irish Two Thousand Guineas, the Curragh—some hard work is needed before the double is landed by a neck and half a length from Royal Academy (second right) and Lotus Pool (star on cap); Machiavellian tries to close on the wide outside

Like Don't Forget Me, Tirol went on to complete the Anglo-Irish Two Thousand Guineas double, only the third colt to do so, Right Tack also having achieved the feat in 1969. Tirol was the sixth Two Thousand Guineas winner since Right Tack to attempt the double, High Top (1972), Nebbiolo (1977), To-Agori-Mou (1981) and Lomond (1983) having failed at the Curragh. Machiavellian was also sent over for the Airlie/Coolmore Irish Two Thousand Guineas which attracted a field of nine. None of the others that had run on Newmarket took on Tirol and Machiavellian who started at 5/4 and 9/4 respectively, with the highly-regarded O'Brien-trained Royal Academy at 4/1 the only other runner shorter than 14/1. With Kinane claimed for the unbeaten Lotus Pool, Eddery took the mount on Tirol at the Curragh and had him in front fully three furlongs out after a slow and muddling early pace. Tirol looked in danger of defeat as the patiently-ridden Royal Academy quickened to draw up to him inside the final furlong. But, showing the utmost gameness, Tirol came again under strong pressure to win by a neck, with Lotus Pool half a length away third, a short head in front of Machiavellian, whom Royal Academy's rider had cleverly kept hemmed in until he was ready to make his move. Less than three lengths covered the first six home, the 25/1-shot Mr Brooks and the 100/1-shot Bastille Day coming next.

Tirol's trainer had always believed Tirol would prove effective over a mile and a half in due course and Eddery was reportedly convinced after riding Tirol at the Curragh that the horse would be better suited by longer distances. There was talk at first of supplementing Tirol for the Budweiser Irish Derby —he hadn't been entered for Epsom (for which there was no supplementary entry stage)—but he eventually ran instead in the Grand Prix de Paris Louis Vuitton, run a week earlier over a mile and a quarter at Longchamp. Tirol managed only third behind the French-trained pair Saumarez and Priolo, beaten eight lengths by the winner, neither Hannon nor Eddery subscribing to the view that the defeat was due to Tirol's inability to stay. Tirol's next objective was the Juddmonte International at York's big August meeting where, with Eddery on Batshoof, Kinane was booked again. But Tirol was a surprising overnight withdrawal and was switched back to a mile for what turned out to be his final appearance, in the Queen Elizabeth II Stakes at Ascot in September. Tirol started favourite but ran well below his best in a very strong field; he looked in tremendous shape beforehand and almost bolted with Carson on the way to the start, but in the race he was soon being niggled along and came home eighth of ten as the four-year-olds Markofdistinction and Distant Relative fought out the finish clear of the rest. Tirol's saddle reportedly slipped but plans to run him in the Dubai Champion Stakes, announced before the Queen Elizabeth II Stakes, were soon abandoned and he was bought by Coolmore and syndicated at IR £27,500 a share. He will stand in 1991 at a fee of IR 7,500 guineas, no foal, no fee. The terms of Tirol's syndication placed a valuation on him of IR £1,100,000. It's a sign of the times that when Coolmore purchased Don't Forget Me for stud they paid IR £3,000,000. Tirol and Don't Forget Me are similar in many ways. In terms of racing merit, there was little or nothing between them and both were admirably game and genuine. Both stayed a mile well and acted well on top-of-the-ground. The major difference in racing character between them was in the riding tactics that suited them; Don't Forget Me was ideally suited by forcing the pace, Tirol was best waited with, to make the most of his good turn of foot.

		Thatch	Forli
	Thatching	(b 1970)	Thong
	(b 1975)	Abella	Abernant
Tirol		(ch 1968)	Darrica
(br.c. 1987)		Great Nephew	Honeyway
	Alpine Niece	(b 1963)	Sybil's Niece
	(b 1972)	Fragrant Morn	Mourne
		(ch 1966)	Alpine Scent

The tall, leggy Tirol hasn't the most fashionable of pedigrees—nor had Don't Forget Me—though his sire the top-class sprinter Thatching, also under the Coolmore banner, gets plenty of useful winners and there is good

Mr John Horgan's "Tirol"

demand for his yearlings. The average distance of races won by Thatching's progeny at three years and upwards is around seven and a half furlongs. Tirol is Thatching's first Group 1 winner in Europe; Thatching's daughter Fitzwilliam Place won the Grade 1 Gamely Handicap at Hollywood Park in 1989. Tirol was produced by Mrs Lennie Peacock's Manor House Stud which also bred the 1986 Kentucky Derby runner-up Bold Arrangement; the Manor House Stud is at Middleham and Tirol was the first Yorkshire-bred horse to win the Two Thousand Guineas for nearly a century. The two previous winners bred by Tirol's dam, the disappointing racemare Alpine Niece who was placed at up to a mile and a half, were both best at five furlongs: Relatively Sharp (by Sharpen Up) was a fair handicapper and Lady Donna (by Dominion) showed fairly useful form as a two-year-old when she was placed in the Molecomb. Tirol's grandam Fragrant Morn, who gained her only victory in a five-furlong maiden race at Folkestone as a two-year-old, bred numerous winners, notably Alpine Nephew, a very useful staying two-year-old (third in the Observer Gold Cup), and Minatzin who wasn't far behind the best two-year-olds of his year in France. Tirol's great grandam Alpine Scent was very useful as a two-year-old—runner-up in the Molecomb and the Lowther —but became bad at the gate; she was a sister to the One Thousand Guineas third Alpine Bloom (dam of the high-class mile- to mile-and-a-quarter performer Full of Hope). Alpine Scent and Alpine Bloom were daughters of the Cheveley Park Stakes runner-up Fragrant View, a half-sister to Airborne, the first post-war Derby winner. *R. Hannon.*

TISLAM 3 b.c. Formidable (USA) 125–Habutai 70 (Habitat 134) [1989 NR 1990 **62** 10m 10g 10g* 8.5g 10g] 9,800Y: quite attractive colt: turns off-fore out: first foal: dam maiden stayed 7f, is half-sister to Almaarad: bit coltish, form only when winner of moderately-run apprentice claimer at Nottingham in June: blinkered and edgy, tailed off in claimer final start: ridden by 7-lb claimer first 3 outings: sold to join M. Usher 8,600 gns Newmarket July Sales: not one to rely on. *B. Hanbury.*

TISSERAND (ITY) 5 gr.h. Nadjar (FR) 128–Tandina (ITY) (Claude (ITY)) **124** [1989 9g* 10v* 10g3 12m2 12m 12m 10s 1990 10.5s* 10v* 10s* 12g*] big, lengthy, good-bodied horse: good-class Italian runner, unbeaten on 4 outings in first half of year: contested Group 1 events on last 2 starts, beating Trioso 5 lengths in Premio Presidente della Republica at Rome and Rotatori 8 lengths in Gran Premio di Milano: stays 1½m: acts on good to firm and heavy going. *M. Vincis, Italy.*

TISWA (USA) 2 ch.f. (Mar 29) Lyphard (USA) 132–Happy Bride 116 (Royal **87** Match 117) [1990 6g 6g* 6m4 6m5] 105,000Y: third foal: dam smart Irish 6f (at 2 yrs) to 1¼m winner, also won in USA: made all in 5-runner minor event at Chester in September: ran well afterwards in minor event at Goodwood and nursery at Newmarket: should stay at least 1m. *B. Hanbury.*

TITE SPOT 3 ch.f. Muscatite 122–Luan Causca 70 (Pampapaul 121) [1989 5f3 5g3 **48** 6m 5f6 6m2 6m6 5m a6g* a5g 1990 7.5f 6f 6f 8m a7g* 7m 6s5 6m 7f 6d a6g a6g a6g a5g] narrow, workmanlike filly: turns off-fore in: fair plater: won at Southwell (bought in 3,500 gns) in May: easily best other effort in 1990 on seventh start: stays 7f: acts on soft going: blinkered once at 2 yrs: sometimes sweating and edgy. *N. Tinkler.*

TITLE ROLL (IRE) 2 ch.f. (Feb 2) Tate Gallery (USA) 117–Tough Lady 91 (Bay **84** Express 132) [1990 5g* 6g3 5g*] 31,000Y: angular, workmanlike filly: closely related to useful Irish 6f and 7f winner Northern Express (by Northern Guest) and half-sister to a winner in Spain: dam 2-y-o 6f winner: fairly useful filly: won maiden at Tipperary in August and minor event at Phoenix Park in September: 6 lengths third of 5 to Capricciosa in Group 3 event at Phoenix Park in between: should prove better suited by 6f than 5f. *T. Stack, Ireland.*

TIT WILLOW 8 b.g. He Loves Me 120–Willow Bird 74 (Weepers Boy 124) [1989 — § 8m6 7m3 7m3 1990 7g 8g] sparely-made gelding: poor handicapper: badly lame and virtually pulled up on second of 2 outings in first week of June: stays 1m: acts on any going: usually wears blinkers and bandages: often slowly away: best with strong handling: inconsistent and not one to trust. *T. Craig.*

TL QUARTER PINT 4 b.c. Prince Tenderfoot (USA) 126–Tumble Royal **38** (Tumble Wind (USA)) [1989 7f 8f5 1990 7f 7f 8m 8g 7h 10m 8f2 8m a8g] big, lengthy colt: little show in varied events except when second, wandering under pressure, in selling handicap at Bath in September: visored, stiff task final outing: stays 1m: blinkered fifth outing: resolution under suspicion. *M. J. Fetherston-Godley.*

TOBACCO ROAD 3 ch.g. Burslem 123–Ishtar (Dike (USA)) [1989 8g 8d a8g4 **56** a8g6 1990 a8g 10m 11.7m 8m 8f* 7m 8f] sparely-made gelding: plating-class handicapper: easily best effort as 3-y-o when winning selling event (bought in 4,400 gns) at Yarmouth in August: soon ridden along and carried head high penultimate outing: stays 1m: trained until after reappearance by R. Armstrong: sometimes bandaged: gelded after final outing: not one to rely on. *J. Akehurst.*

TO BE FAIR 3 ch.g. Adonijah 126–Aquarula 88 (Dominion 123) [1989 6f 8m6 8g **60** d 1990 12f* 12f6 10.2f3 12f 13. 1h3 12m6 12h 12f4 14m 12m 13v] workmanlike gelding: quite modest handicapper: won at Folkestone in March: ran poorly last 5 starts, twice making most: stays 13f: acts on hard ground, probably not on heavy: has run creditably for 7-lb claimer: visored eighth to tenth outings: retained by trainer 3,800 gns Newmarket Autumn Sales and gelded. *Dr J. D. Scargill.*

TOBERMORY BOY 13 b.g. Mummy's Pet 125–Penny Pincher 95 (Constable — 119) [1989 6.1f6 6m 6f5 6m 6m 7f 7f4 6m 6g3 6f4 6m 7f2 7m 7g 6g5 8g 1990 7m 6g 7m 7f] neat, strong gelding: carries plenty of condition: moderate mover: quite modest handicapper on his day: no form in 1990: stays 7f: best on a sound surface: visored once: often gets outpaced. *R. M. Whitaker.*

TOBY HENRY 2 b.c. (Feb 14) Jalmood (USA) 126–Wave Dancer 76 (Dance In **83** Time (CAN)) [1990 a6g 8f6 7f3 7.5m4 9g3] 10,000Y: sturdy colt: first foal: dam 11.7f winner, is sister to very useful middle-distance horse Sailor's Dance and half-sister to Longboat: fair maiden: easily best effort staying-on third in claimer at York on final appearance: suited by a good test of stamina. *Sir Mark Prescott.*

TOD 3 gr.c. Petorius 117–Mainly Dry (The Brianstan 128) [1989 6h2 6m2 6m* 6m4 **109** 6m2 6f* 5m 1990 6m* 6f6 6g5 6g 6m4 6d3 6g3 6g 5m2 5d3] good-topped colt: good

Hue-Williams Stakes, Newbury—Tod (No. 5) beats Dayjur

walker: has a quick action: won £8,000 event at Newbury in May by a head from
Dayjur: in frame in listed and pattern events: stays 6f: acts on firm and dead going:
out of depth when visored eighth start: never travelling well in blinkers final one at
2 yrs: sometimes on toes: tends to wander, and swerved left when leading 2f out
fifth outing: useful. *J. Berry.*

TODA   3 ch.f. Absalom 128–Lambay 88 (Lorenzaccio 130) [1989 6g 1990 5f6 8.5d   **53**
7m⁴ 7f⁴ 10f³ 8.2d 10m² 10m*] leggy, shallow-girthed filly: favourite, game winner of
moderately-run seller (sold to join M. Pipe 3,800 gns) at Leicester in September:
worth a try at 1½m: best efforts on top-of-the-ground: never going well in blinkers
sixth start. *R. F. Johnson Houghton.*

TODAY'S FANCY   2 b.g. (Feb 29) Today And Tomorrow 78–Fancy Pages 67   **54**
(Touch Paper 113) [1990 6g a6g⁴ a6g⁶ 6g 5f 5g⁶ a5g* 6d a5g] 4,600Y: tall, leggy
gelding: moderate mover: first foal: dam 2-y-o 5f seller winner: won 12-runner
nursery at Southwell, showing greatly improved form, by 5 lengths, making all: a
poor plater on other form: blinkered last 6 starts. *Pat Mitchell.*

TOKANDA   6 ch.g. Record Token 128–Andalucia 57 (Rheingold 137) [1989 14.8m   **—**
15.3m³ 12g² 16f5 12m5 12m6 1990 a5g* 12m5 12m6 1990 a13g⁴ 14m³ 16f5 16m] workmanlike gelding: has a
round action: bad handicapper: stays 2m: acts on any going: has worn blinkers, but
not for long time. *F. J. Yardley.*

TOLEDO BAY   2 b.f. (Feb 23) Flash of Steel 120–Silk Lady 97 (Tribal Chief 125)   **62**
[1990 5g 5g* 5g³ 5.8f* 6m³ 6f6 6g a6g² a7g a6g⁴] 27,000Y: sparely-made filly: keen
walker: moderate mover: half-sister to several winners, including sprinter Mzeff
(by Ahonoora) and 5f and 7f winner Mister Colin (by Lord Gayle): dam won three 5f
races at 2 yrs: modest performer: successful for 7-lb claimer in minor events
at Windsor in May and Bath in June: suited by 6f: blinkered last 2 outings. *R.
Hannon.*

TOLO   5 b.g. Bold Lad (IRE) 133–Thessaloniki 94 (Julio Mariner 127) [1989 6d 7s   **64**
7g 6f 6f* 6m⁴ 6m 5.6g 7m 7g 6f 1990 6f 6m 6m 8f4 8.3m⁴ 8f² 8g a6g] small, good-
topped gelding: usually looks well: good mover: modest winner as 4-y-o: easily best
efforts in 1990 on fourth and sixth (seller) outings: effective at 6f and stays 1m:
ideally suited by top-of-the-ground: ran poorly when blinkered: trained until after
fifth outing by W. Carter. *J. White.*

TOLOMENA   4 b.f. Tolomeo 127–Meg's Pride (Sparkler 130) [1989 8m 10.1m⁶ 7g   **48** d
12f³ 16f² 18g 1990 11.1m 11.5g 16f² 14g 12d5 12m 17.1d] lengthy, workmanlike filly:
poor maiden: looked unsatisfactory second outing: stays 2m: acts on firm ground:
has run in snatches: one to be wary of. *W. G. R. Wightman.*

TOMAHAWK   3 ch.c. Be My Guest (USA) 126–Siouan 78 (So Blessed 130) [1989   **71**
6s 1990 8g⁴ 10d² 12.3g* 14g 15d6] leggy, quite good-topped colt: modest form: won

946

moderately-run apprentice maiden at Ripon in June, always front rank and rallying strongly: soundly beaten in £15,900 handicap (moved moderately down, faced stiff task) and amateurs event (prominent 1½m) after: suited by 1½m: sold 17,000 gns Doncaster November Sales. *C. W. Thornton.*

TOM CLAPTON 3 b.g. Daring March 116–Embroideress 80 (Stanford 121§) [1989 7m 6g 8g 1990 7m³ 7h⁵ 8m 8h² 8f* 8f⁵ 9m⁴ 10f* 12h² 12f⁴ 12f³ 12m³ 10g] leggy gelding: poor walker and mover: won sellers (bought in 9,200 gns then 5,600 gns) at Brighton and Yarmouth in summer: usually visored but wasn't, travelling really well long way and giving impression would have gone close with clear run, eleventh and twelfth starts: stays 1½m: best efforts on top-of-the-ground, and acts on hard: tends to be on edge: is held up: bandaged behind last 2 outings: sold to join M. Pipe 11,000 gns Newmarket Autumn Sales. *D. Morley.* — 64

TOMMY ARR 4 b.g. Neltino 97–Promenade Concert (Tower Walk 130) [1989 NR 1990 a7g] no form in seller and claimer. *M. J. Wilkinson.* — —

TOMMY TARMAC (IRE) 2 b.c. (Apr 6) Fairy King (USA)–El-Glaka (Malinowski (USA) 123) [1990 a7g a6g⁵ 7g⁴ 8m] workmanlike colt: poor mover: half-brother to fair 1986 Irish 2-y-o 6f winner Seul Etoile (by Pas de Seul) and a winner in Italy: dam once-raced half-sister to very useful sprinter Pianissimo: moderate plater: stays 7f: visored last 2 starts, blinkered on debut: sold 720 gns Doncaster September Sales. *J. Mackie.* — 52 ?

TOM RUM 7 b.g. Liboi (USA) 76–Snow Rum (Quorum 126) [1989 8f⁶ 7f⁵ 7.5m* 8.2f 8m 1990 8m 7f 8m⁴ 8g 8m 8f] leggy gelding: poor walker: poor handicapper: best at around 1m: well suited by top-of-the-ground: sometimes sweats: good mount for inexperienced rider. *H. Candy.* — 35

TOM'S ARCTIC DREAM 2 b.f. (May 14) Oats 126–Tom's Nap Hand (Some Hand 119) [1990 7m 8m 7m] sturdy filly: first foal: dam poor on flat and over hurdles: poor form in quite modest company. *W. R. Williams.* — 46

TOM'S PROSPECT (USA) 2 ch.c. (May 10) Tank's Prospect (USA)–Snow Pearl (USA) (Boldnesian) [1990 6m 6d 6f⁵ a7g* 7f a8g 6m⁵] $23,000Y: leggy, quite good-topped colt: moderate mover: half-brother to a minor winner by Diamond Shoal: dam won at up to 1¼m: won 16-runner seller (bought in 4,100 gns) at Southwell in August by 10 lengths: should stay at least 1m: visored third outing. *C. R. Nelson.* — 71

TONGADIN 4 b.g. Petong 126–River Vixen (Sagaro 133) [1989 8.2v⁵ 8s* 8g² 8.2m⁴ 10.6m 9f 8g³ 8g² 8m 8.2g 8.2d 10g 9s⁵ 8.2g* 8g 8g 1990 8m 8f 12g* 12g⁴ 16.2d⁶ 12g⁶ 15.3m* 14m⁵ 14f³ 15.3m⁶ 13.8f⁶ 10.6s⁶ 13.8d* 12d³] sparely-made, angular gelding: plating-class handicapper: won at Beverley in May, Wolverhampton in July and Catterick in October: needs further than 1¼m and stays 15f: possibly not at his best on firm going, acts on any other: claimer ridden: has worn pricker near-side: not the easiest of rides. *M. J. O'Neill.* — 54

TONGUE TIED JOHNNY (USA) 4 b.c. Sir Ivor 135–Tongue Tied Muse (USA) (Stage Door Johnny) [1989 11f⁴ 11.5f 13.3d⁴ 14g⁵ 1990 12m² 16g 12g⁴ 14d 12.2m 18d] strong, chunky colt: quite modest maiden: wandered under pressure when second in handicap at Leicester in March, only form at 4 yrs: found nothing next outing: should stay beyond 13f: visored in 1990: sold 2,300 gns Newmarket Autumn Sales: one to avoid. *R. J. R. Williams.* — 63 d

TOO CONSPICUOUS (USA) 2 ch.c. (Feb 1) Miswaki (USA) 124–Petit Rond Point (USA) (Round Table) [1990 6g⁴ 6m* 7d⁴ 6dj IR 97,000Y. lengthy, attractive colt: brother to 3-y-o 7f and 1m winner Miss Tatting and half-brother to several winners in USA, including a minor stakes-placed winner at up to 9f by Nijinsky: dam, unplaced from 6 starts, is half-sister to dam of Lyphard's Wish: favourite, won 17-runner maiden at Goodwood in September: subsequently fourth of 20 to Rinka Das in Cartier Million at Phoenix Park and eighth of 19, staying on, to Chipaya in Racecall Gold Trophy at Redcar: will be well suited by 1m+: sure to improve further, and win more races. *A. C. Stewart.* — 98 p

TOO EAGER 4 b.g. Nishapour (FR) 125–Double Habit (Double Form 130) [1989 7m⁶ 8.2f 7f 7f* 7g² 6g* 7m² 6g⁶ 6g 7m³ 1990 8f 7m 6f 6d* 6g⁴ 5g³ a7g 6m 6m 7d 7m⁶ 7m 6s*] lengthy, dipped-backed gelding: returned to form when winning handicap at Catterick in July and seller (no bid) at Hamilton in November: stays 7f: probably suited by an easy surface nowadays: best in blinkers: usually bandaged near-hind: inconsistent. *M. W. Easterby.* — 61

TOO MUCH CHAMPAGNE (IRE) 2 b.f. (May 14) Kafu 120–Nadja 77 (Dancer's Image (USA)) [1990 6m⁵ 5f⁶ 6g 7g* 7f⁵ 8d 7m⁶ 8m] IR 3,700Y, 4,200 2-y-o: leggy filly: moderate walker: sixth foal: sister to 3-y-o Lady Emma and — 61

half-sister to 1988 2-y-o 5f winner Leg Before (by Runnett) and a winner abroad: dam won over 1m at 2 yrs: won 15-runner seller (no bid) at Thirsk in August: ran well in nursery next time, moderately afterwards: best form at 7f: acts on firm ground. *J. S. Wilson.*

TOOTSIE WOOTSIE 2 b.f. (Mar 9) Hotfoot 126–Hippona (Red God 128§) — [1990 5m⁶ 6g 7g] leggy filly: second reported foal: half-sister to a moderate plater: dam ran 3 times in Ireland: well beaten in maidens: gave lots of trouble going down or at stalls last 2 starts. *M. P. F. Murphy.*

TOOZAN TAK 4 b.g. Sadler's Wells (USA) 132–Calandra (USA) 114 (Sir Ivor — 135) [1989 NR 1990 11g] half-brother to useful Irish 1m winner Golden Temple (by Golden Fleece) and fair 1¾m winner Reef Lark (by Mill Reef): dam Irish 1m and 1¼m winner and fourth in Irish Oaks: tailed off throughout in maiden claimer at Hamilton in May: sold 3,700 gns Doncaster November Sales. *M. P. Naughton.*

TOPANOORA 3 b.c. Ahonoora 122–Topping Girl (Sea Hawk II 131) [1989 NR **111** p 1990 10g* 10g* 11g² 12d² 12v* 10s*] IR 125,000Y: half-brother to 4 winners, including Irish 6f to 1¼m winner Happy Bride (by Royal Match) and useful 1m winner Daring (by Bold Lad), both later successful in USA: dam never ran: very useful performer: not seen out until September, winning minor event at Phoenix Park, IR £49,200 restricted listed race at Fairyhouse then listed race and minor event (by 6 lengths from Victorious Deed) at Leopardstown: 2½ lengths second to Sesame in Blandford Stakes at the Curragh on fourth start: seems effective at 1¼m and 1½m: acts on heavy going: progressive. *J. S. Bolger, Ireland.*

TOPASANNAH 3 b.f. Commanche Run 133–Princess Tracy 111 (Ahonoora 122) **79** [1989 6g 6g⁵ 1990 6m 8g² 10d 8m* 8h* 8g⁵ 9m*] lengthy filly: modest performer: favourite, won handicaps at Ripon in July and Thirsk (edged left) in August and 28-runner claimer at Newmarket in November: well worth another try over 1¼m: seems to need a sound surface. *B. W. Hills.*

Mrs E. McMahon's "Topanoora"

Aster Racing Ltd's "Top Class"

TOP BERRY 3 b.f. High Top 131–Falcon Berry (FR) (Bustino 136) [1989 7m 8f2 **87** 1990 7m 7m3 8f* 8.2m* 9g5] close-coupled, good-bodied filly: progressive form: won handicaps at Doncaster in July and Haydock in August, in latter soon ridden along then quickening well, despite hanging left, to lead inside final 1f: should stay 1¼m: formerly rather headstrong. *L. Cumani.*

TOP-BOOT 4 b.c. High Top 131–Sauceboat 120 (Connaught 130) [1989 7g4 8s* **106** 8.2m2 8g2 10v2 1990 10m5 12d 10m 10d4 9g] lengthy, quite attractive colt: has a quick, sharp action: fifth to Batshoof in Tattersalls EBF Rogers Gold Cup Stakes at the Curragh in May: failed to reproduce that effort in Grand Prix d'Evry and listed events: stays 1¼m: yet to race on firm going, probably acts on any other: sold 35,000 gns Newmarket Autumn Sales. *J. L. Dunlop.*

TOP CLASS 5 b.h. High Top 131–Cassina 91 (Habitat 134) [1989 12s2 12s2 12f2 **114** 12g5 12m3 12g 12m6 1990 13.4d4 14g3 12g5] lengthy, good-topped horse: carries plenty of condition: grand walker: moderate mover: smart at his best: bandaged in front, in frame behind Braashee in slowly-run Ormonde EBF Stakes at Chester and Kosset Yorkshire Cup at York in spring: ran poorly in Hanson Coronation Cup at Epsom: appeared to act on any going: blinkered final start at 4 yrs: retired to stud. *C. E. Brittain.*

TOPCLIFFE 3 b.f. Top Ville 129–Sandford Lady 116 (Will Somers 114§) [1989 7m **57** 8.2f3 7g6 1990 8f 8f 10m 12.2m3 10m* 9m6] leggy, lightly-made filly: moderate mover: dropped in class, won seller (bought in 9,000 gns) at Pontefract in September, lame for short time afterwards: stays 1½m: acts on firm going: joined C. W. C. Elsey. *D. Morley.*

TOP COMPANY (FR) 3 b.g. Lomond (USA) 128–Highest (FR) (High Top 131) **57** [1989 7s 1990 8.2s 10g 10g a12g2 a14g 12m* 12m3] strong, lengthy gelding: led inside final 1f to win seller (bought in 9,000 gns) at Newmarket: withdrawn lame later in August: worth another try over further: acts on good to firm ground: blinkered fifth start: joined T. Caldwell. *P. A. Kelleway.*

TOP DREAM   5 br.h. High Top 131–Pleasant Dream 89 (Sharpen Up 127) [1989   **79**
8g 7d* 7.6f⁴ 7g 7m 7g 7m 1990 7f 7g 7.6m⁴ 6d] strong, close-coupled, attractive horse: good walker: has a quick, round action: reportedly chipped bone in knee final start as 3-y-o: fairly useful handicapper on his day, but unable to keep his form for long: easily best effort in first half of 1990 on third outing: suited by 7f: not suited by firm going and best run on dead. *M. A. Jarvis.*

TOPEKA EXPRESS (USA)   7 b.g. Topsider (USA)–Watch Out 99 (Blakeney   **59**
126) [1989 8g³ 8s 8f 8f⁴ 8.2f* 10.8f* 8m⁶ 8.2f² 8.2f⁴ 10f⁴ 8.2d³ 9m⁴ 1990 10.2m 10m⁵
10.8m 8m⁴ 8.2f* 9g⁶ 8f⁴ 8g³ 8.5g 8m³ 8.5f³ 8f⁴ 7.5g³ 8.2m² 8g 7.5m⁵ 8m 8m 8m] smallish, sturdy gelding: usually looks well: carries plenty of condition: moderate mover: quite modest handicapper: won amateurs event at Haydock in May: stays 10.8f: acts on firm going, not at his best on soft: effective with blinkers or without, visored sixteenth outing: suitable mount for inexperienced rider. *C. Tinkler.*

TOPGLOW   6 ro.g. Kalaglow 132–Lady Gaylass (USA) (Sir Gaylord) [1989 12g⁶   —
16s 12f 12f⁶ 14f 12.2g 8g a10g 1990 9f] lengthy gelding: poor mover: suffered hairline fracture of near-hind as 3-y-o and has enlarged joint: showed only sign of ability since winning maiden early in 1988 on final outing at 5 yrs: stays 1½m: acts on firm going: blinkered last 2 starts in 1989: sold 2,600 gns Newmarket July Sales. *W. J. Pearce.*

TOPHAMS   4 b. or br.c. Good Times (ITY)–Sun Lamp 76 (Pall Mall 132) [1989 6d   **72**
5g 6f⁵ 8m 8.2g⁶ 8f⁶ 6g² a6g⁴ a6g² a6g³ 1990 a6g* a5g a6g* a6g a6g] big colt: poor mover: won handicap (favourite) and claimer (making all) at Southwell in January: ran moderately there other 2 starts early in year: off course 10 months before final outing: suited by 6f. *R. Hollinshead.*

TOP IT ALL   2 b.c. (Feb 17) Song 132–National Dress 64 (Welsh Pageant 132)   **46**
[1990 6m 7m a8g a8g⁶] heavy-bodied colt: second foal: half-brother to Platinum Dancer (by Petorius), 6f winner at 2 yrs: dam, 12.2f winner, is out of half-sister to Connaught: poor form in maidens and a claimer, running best race on all-weather: gives impression will be suited by 1¼m. *M. J. Ryan.*

TOPKAPI   7 b.g. Beldale Flutter (USA) 130–Pithead 70 (High Top 131) [1989 NR   **48**
1990 a10g⁵] stocky, angular gelding: lightly-raced maiden on flat: stays 1½m: sold 2,400 gns Doncaster June Sales. *J. White.*

TOP LIVER   3 b.c. Lypheor 118–Tarop (USA) (Dr Fager) [1989 7g 1990 6s⁴ 7s 7d   **47**
7g⁶ 10d⁴] IR 140,000Y: brother to U.S. 4-y-o Lypheor's Love and half-brother to several winners, including very useful 1986 2-y-o 7f winner Tartuffe (by Golden Act): dam, winner over 6f at 3 yrs in USA, is sister to Amerrico, very useful performer at up to 1m in Britain later stakes winner in USA: poor ex-Irish maiden: nevernearer fourth of 13 in seller at Folkestone on first outing here: seems to stay 1¼m: trained until after fourth start (blinkered, off course over 5 months after) by D. K. Weld. *C. Weedon.* /

TOP OF THE BILL   3 b.c. Star Appeal 133–Cash Limit 62 (High Top 131) [1989   **74**
7m⁶ 7m⁵ 8g* 7g 1990 10g 11.7m³ 10f⁵ 10f⁵ 11.5m² 11.7g⁵ 10.6d³ 10.2g* 9s 9m⁶] small colt: has a long stride: modest handicapper: won at Doncaster in September: suited by 1¼m +: acts on firm and dead (possibly unsuited by very soft) going: has run creditably for 7-lb claimer. *N. A. Callaghan.*

TOP OF THE WORLD   3 b.c. Top Ville 129–Une Florentine (FR) (Pharly (FR)   **99**
130) [1989 7m³ 1990 8m² 8m 10.5g³ 12s⁶] tall colt: fairly useful maiden: not seen out until late-September as 3-y-o, ridden up with pace when placed at Yarmouth and (behind Stagecraft) at York: 33/1 and looking extremely well, led 1m in St Simon Stakes at Newbury final start: better at 1¼m than 1m. *C. E. Brittain.*

TOP ONE   5 ch.g. Sallust 134–Light Diamond (Florescence 120) [1989 9f 5f⁶ 7f   **67**
6f* 1990 5m³ 5m 7m² 8g] close-coupled, useful-looking gelding: quite modest handicapper: virtually pulled up and finished lame final outing: stays 7f: acts on any going: used to wear bandages: pulls hard. *C. J. Hill.*

TOP ROW   7 b.g. Beldale Flutter (USA) 130–Connaught Nymph 71 (Connaught   —
130) [1989 8.2d 8m a8g 1990 7g a8g] robust gelding: carries condition: poor walker and mover: poor maiden: bandaged, well beaten both starts in summer: best at 7f or 1m: well suited by the mud: sold 1,500 gns Doncaster October Sales. *A. W. Jones.*

TOP SCALE   4 b.g. Tower Walk 130–Singing High 87 (Julio Mariner 127) [1989   **45**
8m 8.2f⁶ 8m 8f² 1990 7.5d 8.2g² 8f⁴ 9.1m* 10m⁴ 8m² 8.5m⁶] good-topped gelding: won apprentice handicap at Newcastle in July: stays 9f: acts on firm ground: bandaged near-hind on reappearance: usually apprentice or amateur ridden. *C. Tinkler.*

TOP SHEREEK 2 b.c. (Mar 24) High Top 131–Shereeka 76 (Shergar 140) [1990   **73**
6f[4] 8m[4] 7m[2]] unfurnished colt: first foal: dam maiden placed at 6f and 7f, is half-sister to Irish Oaks fourth My Sister: progressive maiden: 1½ lengths second of 13, staying on well, to Loki at Warwick in October: will be suited by 1¼m: may improve further. *M. A. Jarvis.*

TOP SPINNER 2 ch.f. (Mar 28) Final Straw 127–Skiboule (BEL) (Boulou) [1990   **—**
6g 6g[5]] 6,800Y: sturdy filly: half-sister to several winners, including useful middle-distance fillies Rollrights and Rollfast (both by Ragstone): dam won in Belgium: beaten at least 10 lengths in mid-season maidens at Leicester and Chepstow. *D. Haydn Jones.*

TOP TERN 2 b.f. (Mar 29) Doulab (USA) 115–Golden Tern (FR) (Arctic Tern   **—**
(USA) 126) [1990 5g 5m 6m 5.1m 7m 6d] 7,800F, 2,000Y: small, dipped-backed filly: moderate mover: second foal: half-sister to bad 3-y-o Byker Lass (by Superlative): dam winner in Italy, is half-sister to Italian Derby winner Elgay: of little account: blinkered or visored third to fifth starts. *G. H. Eden.*

TOP VILLAIN 4 b.g. Top Ville 129–Swan Ann 84 (My Swanee 122) [1989 8g 10g[5]   **—**
1990 8f] rangy gelding: no worthwhile form: hung badly left final outing at 3 yrs. *Andrew Turnell.*

TOP WALTZ (FR) 3 b.c. Top Ville 129–Imperial Dancer 103 (Tudor Music 131) **119**
[1989 8v[4] 1990 11.5g* 11d[4] 12m* 12m[4] 10g] 300,000 francs (approx £27,400) Y: half-brother to French 1982 2-y-o 1¼m winner Sevruga and French 8.2f winner Ialdoa (both by Crystal Palace): dam Irish 9.5f winner at 2 yrs and French 9.2f and 1¼m winner at 3 yrs: won maiden at Maisons-Laffitte in March and Prix Hocquart at Longchamp in May: best effort when 3½ lengths fourth of 12 to Sanglamore in Prix du Jockey-Club (on toes) at Chantilly: stays 1½m: best form on top-of-the-ground: smart. *J-M. Beguigne, France.*

TORCELLO 3 b.c. Procida (USA) 129–Millieme 107 (Mill Reef (USA) 141) [1989   **99**
7g 1990 10.2h* 11.5m* 12g 14f[3] 12m[4] 13.8f[6]] attractive colt: has a quick action: won maiden at Bath in May and handicap (ran in snatches) at Lingfield in June: good narrowly-beaten third in quite valuable handicap at Goodwood, easily best effort after: odds on, well tailed off in claimer final start (reportedly broke down): stays 1¾m: possibly needs top-of-the-ground: changed hands 11,500 gns Ascot April Sales. *G. Harwood.*

TORCHON 2 b.c. (Feb 6) High Top 131–Cecilia Bianchi (FR) (Petingo 135) [1990   **81** P
8g[5]] rangy colt: has scope: fifth foal: brother to 1m winner Aigue and half-brother to 1m and 1¼m winner White-Wash (by Final Straw) and a winner in France by Blakeney: dam, winner in Italy, is half-sister to very smart 1m to 1½m filly Calderina: bit backward, shaped most promisingly when around 7 lengths fifth of 15 to Sharifabad in maiden at Newmarket in October, staying on in eye-catching style after being pushed along 2f out: will stay 1¼m: sure to improve considerably, and win races. *G. Wragg.*

TOREL (IRE) 2 b.c. (Apr 25) Glint of Gold 128–Henry's Secret 108 (Solinus 130)   **66**
[1990 7m 7h* 8m 8f[5]] smallish, quite attractive colt: fourth foal: dam, 5f and 6f winner at 2 yrs who didn't progress at 3 yrs, is out of very smart miler Katie Cecil: won 7-runner maiden at Brighton in August by a short head: should stay 1m: sold 14,000 gns Newmarket Autumn Sales. *J. L. Dunlop.*

TORGHIA 3 b.f. Taufan (USA) 119–Brave Louise 76 (Brave Shot) [1989 5f[5] 6f[2]   **75**
7f[4] 7m 1990 7f[5] 7m[5] 7.3m 7g[2] 8f[5] 7m[4] 9f* 8g[2] 8m 10d[0] a10g*] leggy, angular filly: has a round action: modest handicapper: won at Wolverhampton in September and Lingfield in December: will stay 1½m: acts on firm going: has run well for 7-lb claimer. *D. W. P. Arbuthnot.*

TORIUS 4 b.g. Petorius 117–Princess Martina 64 (English Prince 129) [1989 7s 6s   **47**
5s[5] 5.8m[4] 5f* 6f[6] 5f 5m* 5m 5.8f[4] 5f a6g[5] a6g[3] 1990 a7g[6] 6m 6f 6m[5] 5g[3] 5g 5m 5f 5.8h[5] 5.1f[4] 6m 5m[3] 6m 5m[5] 5f[3] 5.8f[5] 5m* 5.3f 5g 5d] lengthy gelding: moderate mover: favourably drawn, won claimer at Sandown in September: acted on any going: usually blinkered: none too resolute or consistent: dead. *R. Simpson.*

TORODIN (USA) 2 ch.c. (Mar 16) Northern Baby (CAN) 127–Bonnie And Gay   **66**
(USA) (Sir Gaylord) [1990 7m[4] 8d] $50,000Y: workmanlike colt: half-brother to numerous winners abroad, including smart French 7.5f and 1¼m winner Look Fast (by Little Current): dam, a leading 2-y-o filly of 1970 in USA, won at up to 1m at 3 yrs: quite modest form in maidens at Leicester and Bath (favourite) in the autumn: sold 31,000 gns Newmarket Autumn Sales. *G. Harwood.*

TORPEDOS LOS (FR) 2 b.c. (Apr 29) Baillamont (USA) 124–Artists Proof   **—** p
(USA) (Ribot 142) [1990 7s[4]] leggy, close-coupled colt: half-brother to at least 3

TOR

winners, including 1977 William Hill Futurity winner Dactylographer (by Secretariat) later successful over 1½m: dam stakes winner at up to 7f at 2 yrs and third in Kentucky Oaks: weak 9/2, around 11 lengths fourth of 14, not knocked about when beaten, to very easy winner Evasive Prince in maiden at Lingfield in October: will stay at least 1¼m: sure to improve. *H. R. A. Cecil.*

TORTIN (IRE) 2 b.f. (Mar 9) Auction Ring (USA) 123–Bernique (Hello **36** Gorgeous (USA) 128) [1990 7f 7m 7f a7g a8g] 4,800Y: second foal: half-sister to French 3-y-o Pas de Panique (by No Pass No Sale), successful 4 times at up to 1¼m: dam French 1m and 1¼m winner, is half-sister to good 1985 French 2-y-o stayer Bestebreuje: poor maiden: visored third outing. *J. Hetherton.*

TOSCANA 9 ch.m. Town And Country 124–Constanza 94 (Sun Prince 128) [1989 **21** 12f4 12.3m6 12m6 12m6 1990 a12g4 a16g6 a12g 12m 12f5 12f6 15.5f] of little account nowadays: has been tried in blinkers. *D. Marks.*

TO-SEVERALS (IRE) 2 b.g. (May 21) Horage 124–Sacred Ibis (Red God 128§) **40** [1990 6f 7m6 a6g] IR 9,500Y: smallish, angular gelding: has quick action: half-brother to 3-y-o Dovekie (by Ela-Mana-Mou), 7f winner at 2 yrs, and several other winners, all at up to 1m: dam short-running sister to very useful 1969 2-y-o Red Velvet: poor form in varied events: carried head high and hung right second start: wears blinkers: sold 2,500 gns Newmarket Autumn Sales. *B. Hanbury.*

TOSHIBA COMET 3 b.g. Noalto 120–Silk Lady 97 (Tribal Chief 125) [1989 5d5 **85** 5g3 5m3 6f2 7f4 7.5m 6g4 6g* 5s3 5g 1990 6m3 6m4 7m 5f 5f 6m* 6d* 5g a6g*] strong, sturdy gelding: moderate walker: fair performer: blinkered last 4 starts, winning claimers at Hamilton in August, Haydock in September and Southwell in December: suited by 6f: acts on good to firm ground and soft: sweating third start: has worn tongue strap. *W. J. Pearce.*

TOSHIBA COMET TOO (IRE) 2 ch.c. (Feb 25) Gorytus (USA) 132–No **64** Jargon (Nonoalco (USA) 131) [1990 6m 7m 7v6 7s a8g*] IR 12,500Y: third foal: half-brother to 3-y-o Caspian Talk (by Persian Bold) and a winner in Belgium by Ela-Mana-Mou: dam won twice at both 6f and 7f at 3 yrs in Ireland: 33/1, won 11-runner maiden at Lingfield by ½ length from Queen of Dreams: will probably stay 1¼m. *W. J. Pearce.*

TOSS OF THE COIN 3 ch.g. Rabdan 129–Cedees 48 (Habat 127) [1989 5g4 6g **40** 5f5 6g 6m2 6g* 6s 8.2f3 5m2 7g 7g a7g 1990 7m 6f6 6m 7g4 6m a6g 7m] sturdy gelding: modest winner at 2 yrs: has run poorly since placed in nurseries: needs further than 5f, and stays 1m: appears unsuited by soft ground: very slowly away in blinkers fifth start: sometimes hangs: joined P. Evans. *P. D. Evans.*

TOTAL SHAMBLES (IRE) 2 b.c. (Mar 7) Taufan (USA) 119–Home Bird **57 d** (Ragusa 137) [1990 a6g 6g 6g6 7f a7g 8m] IR 12,500Y, 10,000Y: smallish, angular colt: poor mover: half-brother to 4 winners in Ireland, including 8.5f and 1¼m winner Home And Dry (by Crash Course): dam lightly-raced half-sister to very useful middle-distance colt Pollerton: plating-class maiden: best effort third start: ran badly afterwards: should stay at least 1m. *J. S. Wainwright.*

TOTAL SPORT (USA) 2 b.f. (Jun 4) Taufan (USA) 119–Miss Habitat (Habitat **43** 134) [1990 7m 7m 6g 7m6] $3,400Y: leggy, angular filly: fifth foal: closely related to 3-y-o Blue Habit (by Cure The Blues) and half-sister to a winner in USA by General Assembly: dam won in Italy: poor form in maidens: trained debut by D. Browne. *R. Hannon.*

TOTEM (USA) 5 b.h. Al Nasr (FR) 126–Wooden (USA) (Time Tested (USA)) **102** [1989 NR 1990 7.2s 7m4 8g6 7v 8v] strong, good-bodied, attractive horse: smart winner as 3-y-o when trained by D. O'Brien: shaped as though retaining plenty of ability, having taken strong hold, in Warwick minor event and Newmarket listed race second and third outings: stays 1m: yet to race on firm going, seemingly unsuited by heavy nowadays: sold 22,000 gns Newmarket December Sales. *J. Gosden.*

TOTHAM 3 b.f. Shernazar 131–Susanna (USA) 81§ (Nijinsky (CAN) 138) [1989 7g **84** 7m3 7m2 7g 1990 10g 12f2 12.2g3 13.3m2 12.3m3 13.6m4 12g* 12g4] rangy, useful-looking filly: fair performer: won maiden at Pontefract in October, staying on strongly to lead close home: will be suited by 1¾m: acts on good to firm ground: has run creditably when sweating and edgy. *G. Wragg.*

TOUCH ABOVE 3 b.f. Shernazar 131–Touching Wood (USA) 127–B A Poundstretcher 82 **61** (Laser Light 118) [1989 8s2 8g3 10d 8m3 8.5f3 10f* 10g3 10.2f5 9g 10m4 12g6 10f5 10m6 1990 8.2s 10f3 10m* 10.2m4 10d6 10f 10d2 a12g2 10f* 10.2f2 10f2 10g6 10.2m3 12g4 10.2g2 10m* 10.5g6 10m] leggy colt: good mover: quite modest handicapper: successful at Beverley (has not won elsewhere) in April, July and September:

ideally suited by 1¼m: acts particularly well on sound surface: has run well when sweating: often given plenty to do: has gone freely to post: consistent. *T. D. Barron.*

TOUCH IN FLIGHT (IRE)   2 b.c. (Feb 14) Formidable (USA) 125–Tilia (ITY)   68
(Dschingis Khan) [1990 8g⁶ 7d 8d⁵] 19,000Y: strong, good-bodied colt: closely related to Italian Derby winner Tommy Way (by Thatch) and half-brother to a winner in Italy: dam won in Italy: quite modest maiden: best effort never-dangerous fifth of 18 at Bath in October: stays 1m. *J. L. Dunlop.*

TOUCHING STAR   5 b.g. Touching Wood (USA) 127–Beaufort Star 95 (Great   66
Nephew 126) [1989 8m* 10.6g* 10m 1990 10m* 9g 10.8m⁵ 10.2m 12m 17.1d⁶] leggy, good-topped gelding: has a quick action: fractured pedal bone final start at 4 yrs: quite modest handicapper: successful at Nottingham in April: may well prove best at up to 1¾m: acts on firm and dead going: blinkered twice at 3 yrs: sometimes sweats: good mount for inexperienced rider: has hung badly left: trained until after third start by F. Jordan. *P. J. Hobbs.*

TOUCHING TIMES   2 b.c. (Apr 22) Touching Wood 127–Pagan Deity 88   71
(Brigadier Gerard 144) [1990 5m a6g⁴ 6g⁵ 6g⁵ 7m 7g 8.2d³] 2,000Y: angular, sparely-made colt: fifth foal: half-brother to 1987 2-y-o 5f and 6f seller winner Lucky Grand (by Beldale Flutter), later successful over middle distances in Italy, and to a winner in Macau: dam won 3 times at around 1¼m: modest maiden: placed in 20-runner nursery at Nottingham in October, easily best effort: will be suited by 1¼m + : acts well on a soft surface: has worn bandages. *M. Brittain.*

TOUCHLIN PRIDE   4 b.g. Touch Boy 109–Lindrake's Pride (Mandrake Major   —
122) [1989 8f⁶ 7m⁵ 8g 7m⁴ 7m 1990 8f 8m 10d 7.5d 8.2g 8f 8.5g⁵ 6g] small gelding: quite modest maiden at best: little worthwhile form at 4 yrs: unseated rider and bolted second intended start: stays 1m: blinkered final outing: often sweats: has joined A. Harrison. *Miss L. C. Siddall.*

TOUCH 'N' PASS   2 ch.c. (Feb 3) Dominion 123–Hanglands (Bustino 136) [1990   —
6g 8m] 10,500Y: dipped-backed, lightly-made colt: first foal: dam lightly raced: always behind in late-season maidens at Newcastle and Redcar. *R. O'Leary.*

TOUCH OF BLUE   2 ch.c. (Mar 22) Ballacashtal (CAN)–Return To Tara   42
(Homing 130) [1990 5.3f³ 5g⁵ 5f] 6,200Y: leggy, workmanlike colt: first foal: dam well beaten: quite modest plater: not raced after June. *J. Berry.*

TOUCH OF DANGER   3 b.g. Gorytus (USA) 132–All Beige (Ballyciptic 122)   —
[1989 NR 1990 10m 10f 12h²] 16,000F, 13,000Y: strong, lengthy gelding: half-brother to 1½m winner Mukhuli (by Nonoalco) and 11f winner All Moss (by Prince Tenderfoot): dam unraced daughter of Yorkshire Oaks winner Feevagh and half-sister to dam of Levmoss, Sweet Mimosa and Le Moss: no worthwhile form in summer maidens: unseated rider on way down on debut, subsequently gelded. *C. A. Cyzer.*

TOUCH OF SPEED   6 b.g. Touch Paper 113–Maggie Mine 85 (Native Prince)   —
[1989 NR 1990 10.2f] strong-quartered, workmanlike gelding: poor maiden on flat: winning selling hurdler in October. *H. A. T. Whiting.*

TOUCH OF WHITE   4 ch.f. Song 132–Cayla (Tumble Wind (USA)) [1989 5g*   95
5f⁴ 1990 5m* 5g* 5m 5g⁶ 5d⁴] big, useful-looking filly: successful in handicaps at Doncaster (showing improved form, making most but hanging markedly left) and Newmarket (apprentice ridden) in May: chipped bone in knee later in month, and having only third race after when good fourth to Ra'a in listed race (blinkered) at Newmarket: speedy. *G. A. Huffer.*

TOUCH THE CLOUDS   3 b.f. Precocious 126–Siouxsie 90 (Warpath 113) [1989   53
5d 7s⁶ 7v⁵ 1990 8g 10g 12s 15d³ 16s] rather leggy, good-topped filly: moderate mover: plating-class maiden: probably stays 15f: acts on heavy going: has run well when on toes. *C. W. Thornton.*

TOUGH COOKIE   5 gr.g. Lochnager 132–Jovenita (High Top 131) [1989 11v⁴   —
1990 12.4f] big, rangy gelding: poor maiden: blinkered twice. *R. Allan.*

TOUGH OUT   6 b.g. Tumble Wind (USA)–Ragatina (Ragusa 137) [1989 NR 1990   —
8f 12h³ 12h⁴ 14.8f] heavy-topped gelding: poor mover: sixth living foal: half-brother to winning hurdler/chaser Unicol (by Manado): dam, placed over 1m, is half-sister to very useful sprinters Rollahead and Glenturret: apprentice ridden, soundly beaten in maidens (second 3-runner race) and handicap. *N. A. Smith.*

TOULAL   2 b.f. Taufan (USA) 119–Premiere Cuvee 109 (Formidable   61
(USA) 125) [1990 5d 5d³ 6d⁵ a5g a5g⁵] leggy filly: poor mover: first foal: dam sprinter, best at 4 yrs when sent to France: over 2 lengths third of 12, staying on well, to Access Holidays in maiden at Redcar, easily best effort. *M. Johnston.*

TOULON   2 b.c. (Apr 15) Top Ville 129–Green Rock (FR) 86 (Mill Reef (USA) 141)   ?
[1990 9g*] second living foal: half-brother to 1988 2-y-o 1m winner Greenovia (by
Ahonoora): dam middle-distance winner, is sister to smart French middle-distance
filly Green Reef and daughter of Prix Ganay winner Infra Green: won 8-runner
newcomers race at Longchamp in October by a neck: will stay 1½m: sure to do lot
better. *A. Fabre, France.*

TOUR EIFFEL   3 b.g. High Line 125–Gay France (FR) 91 (Sir Gaylord) [1989 NR   103 p
1990 12.2m* 12f*] 220,000Y: lengthy gelding: brother to very useful 1985 2-y-o 7f
winner Lucayan Princess and half-brother to fair 8.5f winner French Sonnet (by
Ballad Rock) and winners abroad: dam 2-y-o 6f winner: odds on, won maiden at
Catterick in June, making all, and 10-runner amateurs event (still bit green, by 10
lengths from Oshawa) at Newmarket in August, leading 2f out: looks sure to
improve. *H. R. A. Cecil.*

TOUSHTARI (USA)   4 b.g. Youth (USA) 135–Taduska (FR) (Daring Display   73
(USA) 129) [1989 10d* 10.6g5 1990 12.3g6 10m6 11g* 12g4 10.6g6] big, workmanlike
gelding: moderate walker and mover: won handicap at Ayr in July: withdrawn lame
at start previous intended outing: stays 1½m: best form on an easy surface: bandaged at 4 yrs. *M. F. D. Morley.*

TOWN CROWN (IRE)   2 ch.c. (Apr 17) King of Clubs 124–Apapa Port 80 (My   58 p
Swanee 122) [1990 5f5] IR 32,000F, IR 10,000Y: strong, lengthy colt: sixth foal:
half-brother to 3-y-o Rashita (by Alzao), 1988 Irish 2-y-o 6f winner Port Arms (by
Sandhurst Prince) and Irish 9f winner Papa Port (by Kampala): dam 5f mudlark: bit
backward and very green, fifth of 6, slowly away, in maiden at Sandown in July. *K. M.
Brassey.*

TOWN MEETING   6 ch.g. General Assembly (USA)–La Marne (USA) (Nashua)   —
[1989 10.2g* 10s* 8.2v 8d 10f4 10.6d3 10v3 1990 10.2f] close-coupled gelding:
plating-class winner (including for apprentice) in spring as 5-y-o: needed race only
start in 1990: suited by testing conditions at 1¼m and should stay further: not at his
best on firm going and acts well on soft: visored last 3 starts in 1988: occasionally
bandaged: sold 980 gns Doncaster October Sales. *M. Brittain.*

TOW-STAR'S LADY   4 b.f. On Your Mark 125–Miss Tehran 73 (Manacle 123)   38
[1989 7.5d 6m3 6f 8f 7m 6m5 6f* 6f 6f 5m3 6g 7m 5f3 6f 1990 6f a7g5 a7g 6f4 6m a6g]
sparely-made filly: winning plater as 3-y-o: form in 1990 only on fourth outing:
suited by 6f: acts on firm ground: visored or blinkered: has run well when sweating
and edgy: inconsistent. *J. Norton.*

TRACE OF IRONY (USA)   4 b. or br.f. Cannonade (USA)–Tracy L (USA)   —
(Bold Favorite (USA)) [1989 5f 6m 8.2f 6g5 a8g5 a10g a7g4 1990 a8g5 a12g5 a8g a8g6
10.2f a11g] quite good-topped filly: has a quick action: quite modest maiden at best,
but has deteriorated: bandaged, tailed off in handicap fifth outing, first for 8 months:
probably stays 1m: blinkered once: occasionally sweats: sold out of C. Wall's stable
3,400 gns Doncaster March Sales after fourth start. *Mrs A. Knight.*

TRACKBEE   2 ch.f. (Apr 11) Hotfoot 126–Trackally 95 (Track Spare 125) [1990   40
5m6 6m5 8.2g6 10.6s] 900F, 1,950Y: leggy, light-framed filly: has a roundish action:
closely related to a winner abroad by Free State and half-sister to 3-y-o Thornzee
(by Belfort): dam stayed 6f: poor plater: probably stays 1m: possibly unsuited by soft
ground. *C. James.*

TRACK MONARCH (USA)   2 b.c. (Mar 16) Track Barron (USA)–Coasting   103
Home (USA) (Coastal (USA)) [1990 6g* 6m* 8m 8g* 8m4 7.6s2] $12,000F,
$27,000Y: leggy, useful-looking colt: second foal: dam minor winner at 3 yrs in USA:
sire, stayed 9f, won 4 Grade 1 events: useful performer: successful in maiden at
Hamilton in June and nurseries at Pontefract in August and Doncaster in
September: excellent second to Time Lord in listed race at Lingfield in October: will
stay 1¼m: best form on an easy surface, and acts well on soft ground: blinkered or
visored last 3 starts. *S. G. Norton.*

TRACY'S PRINCE (IRE)   2 ch.g. (Mar 18) Be My Guest (USA) 126–Princess   68
Tracy 111 (Ahonoora 122) [1990 6m 7m3 8m5 8.2m5 7m] 26,000Y: leggy, sparely-
made gelding: moderate mover: second foal: half-brother to 3-y-o 1m and 9f winner
Topasannah (by Commanche Run): dam Irish sprinter: quite modest maiden: ran
badly (gave impression something amiss) on final start: stays 1m. *B. W. Hills.*

TRADE SECRET   3 b.c. Ela-Mana-Mou 132–For Your Eyes 85 (Gay Fandango   —
(USA) 132) [1989 NR 1990 10m 12m] 80,000F: compact colt: third foal: half-brother
to Scandinavian 7f to 9f winner Kifah (by Jalmood): dam 6f winner from family of
Washington D C International winner Providential and smart 1981 French 2-y-o filly

Play It Safe, also fourth in 1000 Guineas: no promise in minor event and maiden: sold 1,700 gns Newmarket Autumn Sales. *J. L. Dunlop.*

TRAFUL (USA) 3 b.c. Riverman (USA) 131–Wintergrace (USA) 80 (Northern **88** Dancer) [1989 NR 1990 9m³ 10.1m³ 10g² 12.3m² 12m³ 12.2d* 12g] $285,000Y: lengthy, well-made colt: has a quick action: brother to successful Irish jumper Blue Danube: dam, 1m winner at 3 yrs, is half-sister to top-class 1m to 1¼m winner Artaius: fair performer: won apprentice race at Catterick in October: made virtually all previous 3 starts, first past post (demoted having drifted left) at Beverley third start: ridden by 7-lb claimer, held up, pulled very hard and tended to drift right when running moderately in handicap final outing: will stay 1¾m. *M. R. Stoute.*

TRAINBLEU 2 b.c. (May 18) Siberian Express (USA) 125–Skyey 70 (Skymaster **74** § 126) [1990 6m³ 5.8m³ 6m* 6m 7g 7m] 5,200F, 10,000Y: strong colt: moderate mover: half-brother to 3-y-o Kinkajoo (by Precocious) and several winners, including very useful 1978 2-y-o Eyelet (by Sharpen Up) and 1986 2-y-o 1¼m winner Amadeus Rock (by Touching Wood): dam 6f winner: modest performer: won 16-runner maiden at Newbury in July by a short head: ran poorly next and final starts: stays 7f: one to be wary of. *R. F. Johnson Houghton.*

TRAINGLOT 3 ch.c. Dominion 123–Mary Green 81 (Sahib 114) [1989 6f 6m 7.5f² **107** 8.2s* 10g³ 1990 12.3d² 14f* 14g⁵ 16g* 18d* 16m²] compact colt: progressed into useful performer, successful in handicaps at Redcar in July and Newcastle and Newmarket (25-runner £52,000 Tote Cesarewitch, by 6 lengths from Further Flight well clear of remainder) in October: favourite, good second of 8 to Arzanni in listed event at last-named course, short of room over 2f out then running on well despite hanging left: suited by test of stamina: acts on any going: has run well for 7-lb claimer: should continue to give a good account of himself. *J. G. FitzGerald.*

TRALEE MAIDEN (IRE) 2 br.f. (May 11) Persian Bold 123–Tralee Falcon 82 **63** (Falcon 131) [1990 6g 5f* a7g] 2,800Y: leggy filly: sixth foal: half-sister to 3-y-o Falcon Blue (by Blue Cashmere) and 2 winners by Record Run, including 1984 2-y-o 5f winner Kenton's Girl: dam stayed 7f: blinkered, won 10-runner auction event at Carlisle in September by a short head from Pallium: slowly away and soon well behind in nursery (unseated rider at stalls) at Southwell 2 months later: should be at least as effective at 6f as 5f: sold 480 gns Ascot December Sales. *J. G. FitzGerald.*

TRANQUIL WATERS (USA) 4 ch.c. Diesis 133–Ebbing Tide (USA) (His **74** Majesty (USA)) [1989 10f² 10.2g³ 12.2g* 1990 12f 12m⁴ 14s 12g⁶] rather unfurnished

Tote Cesarewitch (Handicap), Newmarket—
six lengths separate Trainglot and Further Flight,
then there are ten more back to Clifton Chapel and Regal Reform

colt: has a rather round action: has shown signs of stringhalt: easily best efforts in handicaps as 4-y-o on second and final (backward following lay-off) outings: better at 1½m than 1¼m: possibly unsuited by soft going: won 3 times over hurdles in autumn. *N. Tinkler.*

TRANSATLANTICDREAM 2 b.c. (May 23) Fast Gold (USA)–Proud Miss (USA) (Semi-Pro) [1990 7g] leggy colt: half-brother to 3 winners in USA: dam unraced: sire, by Mr Prospector, seemed best at 9f or 1¼m: bit backward, lost touch from halfway in 21-runner maiden at Newbury in August. *I. A. Balding.* —

TRANSCRIBER (USA) 3 b.c. Transworld (USA) 121–Scrabbler (USA) (Verbatim (USA)) [1989 6f² 6m 7f 6g⁵ 8g⁵ a6g⁶ a7g² 1990 a6g² a6g4] angular, useful-looking colt: quite modest maiden: ridden by 7-lb claimer, ran at Southwell first 2 days in January: probably stays 1m: blinkered last 4 starts: joined W. Jarvis. *A. Bailey.* 61

TRANSCRIPT 2 b.f. (Mar 29) Transworld (USA)–Lawyer's Wave (USA) (Advocator) [1990 6m 8.2s²] strong, rangy filly: has plenty of scope: third reported foal: half-sister to 3-y-o 1m winner Regent's Inlet (by It's Freezing): dam minor 8.5f stakes winner, is sister to smart American colt Kirrary: carrying condition, 1½ lengths second of 13, good headway to lead briefly 1f out, to Port Sunlight in maiden at Haydock in October: will stay 1¼m. *C. E. Brittain.* 72

TRANSITIONAL 3 b.c. Dalsaan 125–Parkeen Princess (He Loves Me 120) [1989 6d 1990 8f² a8g³ 8m³ 8m² 8.2g* 9f* 10f⁴ 9g] good-topped colt: poor mover: fair performer: successful in July in maiden median auction event (odds on, by short head) at Hamilton, making most, and handicap at Redcar, leading 6f out: acts on firm going. *P. J. Makin.* 81

TRAVEL BYE 3 b.f. Miller's Mate 116–Travel Again 67 (Derrylin 115) [1989 6d⁵ 5f⁴ 6d 1990 10.2f⁵] angular filly: quite modest maiden: led 1m in handicap in May, 1990: should stay 1¼m: best effort on firm going: bandaged off-hind. *M. C. Pipe.* —

TRAVELLING BLUES (IRE) 2 gr.g. (Apr 18) Ballad Rock 122–Danielle Delight (Song 132) [1990 5f5m⁶5m*] 7,200F: leggy, quite good-topped gelding: has plenty of scope: fourth foal: half-brother to Irish 3-y-o 1½m winner Vision's Pride (by Vision) and a winner in USA: dam (showed some ability in USA) is sister to dam of Prince Sabo: won 11-runner seller (no bid) at Doncaster in May: should stay 6f. *Mrs J. R. Ramsden.* 59

TRAVELLING LIGHT 4 b.g. Electric 126–La Levantina (Le Levantell 122) [1989 6v⁵ 6d 7m 8g 12f* 11f* 12f* 12.3m⁵ 14g* 17.4s* 18g³ 1990 18f⁶ 14m² 18.4d* 20m 16m 18g 17.4d⁵ 18d⁶ 14s] good-topped gelding: moderate mover: progressive handicapper as 3-y-o: justified favouritism in £22,100 Ladbroke Chester Cup (Handicap) in May in tremendous style easing up by 6 lengths: apprentice ridden, creditable sixth to Trainglot in Tote Cesarewitch at Newmarket: tailed off in Group 3 race at Rome final outing: suited by good test of stamina and a soft surface: genuine. *Mrs J. R. Ramsden.* 95

TRAVELLING TRYST (USA) 4 ch.g. Pilgrim (USA) 108–King's Courtesan (USA) (Kauai King) [1989 8s³ 8m 10g 8m³ 10.1m³ 10m⁵ 14g³ 13.8g* 16m⁶ 13v² 1990 62

Ladbroke Chester Cup (Handicap), Chester—Travelling Light goes well on the ground, and wins very easily from Rambo Castle and Andorra (grey)

David Thompson's "Travelling Light"

12f⁶ 12m 10g 12g 13d⁵ 12m² 12g] angular, sparely-made gelding: moderate mover: easily best efforts in handicaps in 1990 on fifth and sixth (hanging left) outings: stays 13f: probably unsuited by firm going, acts on any other: takes keen hold, and pulled hard in visor: none too genuine. *W. J. Musson.*

TRAVEL MYTH   2 ch.f. (Apr 26) Bairn (USA) 126–Travel Legend 72 (Tap On Wood 130) [1990 6f 8g⁴ 7g⁴ 8d⁶] leggy, rather sparely-made filly: second living foal: dam 7f winner: quite modest maiden: stays 1m: carries head high, looks none too keen and is one to be wary of. *Mrs G. R. Reveley.*   **66 §**

TRAVEL NOON   2 b.f. (Feb 29) Scottish Reel 123–Lightning Gem (FR) (African Song 121) [1990 8.5m⁴ 6m] 3,200F: compact, workmanlike filly: moderate mover: second foal: dam lightly-raced daughter of half-sister to very smart 5f to 1m winner Lightning Label: well beaten in 4-runner maiden at Beverley and 25-runner seller at Redcar: sold 1,100 gns Doncaster October Sales. *Mrs G. R. Reveley.*   **—**

TRAVEL TOKEN   2 b.c. (Apr 20) Tina's Pet 121–Guiletta 63 (Runnymede 123) [1990 5m 6g 6d³] 10,500Y: lengthy, workmanlike colt: has a very round action: brother to fairly useful 1988 2-y-o 5f and 6f winner Paddy Chalk and half-brother to several winners, including middle-distance stayer Fiorenzo (by Filiberto): dam ran 3 times: third of 8 to easy winner Triviality in maiden at Goodwood in October: bit backward previously: may progress further. *L. J. Holt.*   **57 p**

TREACLE MINE   3 ch.g. (Apr 8) Ballacashtal (CAN)–Miss Anniversary (Tachypous 128) [1989 5m 6m 6f⁴ 6g a7g³ a6g a6g 1990 8v 7m 6s a8g a7g a7g 10g 8d] close-coupled gelding: poor mover: quite modest maiden at 2 yrs: well beaten as 3-y-o, including in sellers: suited by 7f: acts on firm going: has worn bandages: twice blinkered: gelded after final start. *Ronald Thompson.*   **—**

TREAD LIKA PRINCE   4 b.c. Prince Tenderfoot (USA) 126–Flat Refusal (USA) (Ribero 126) [1989 8.2s⁴ 11.7m 1990 10d 7m a6g⁴ 6d a5g a6g⁵ 5m² a6g³ 6m a6g a6g⁵] compact, workmanlike colt: moderate mover: poor at best nowadays: effective at 5f and stays 1m: has worn blinkers (including last 6 starts) and visor: bandaged off-hind last 2 outings: usually on toes, and sweated seventh outing: sold   **45**

out of J. Hudson's stable 2,500 gns Ascot April Sales before reappearance: a difficult ride, and not one to rely on. *R. D. E. Woodhouse.*

TREASURE COURT 3 b.g. Mummy's Treasure 84–Julia Too 93 (Golden — Horus 123) [1989 NR 1990 10m 8.2g] IR 1,800F, 3,800Y: tall, rather close-coupled gelding: half-brother to 3 winners here and abroad, including modest 1¼m winner Antique Seeker (by Status Seeker): dam best at 5f: poor form in maiden and claimer in the spring. *P. Burgoyne.*

TREATY STONE LADY 2 b.f. (Jun 5) Hotfoot 126–H R Micro 77 (High Award — 119) [1990 5m⁵ 6d 5g 5m⁶ 8m 5m] sturdy filly: second foal: dam sprinter: poor maiden. *M. P. F. Murphy.*

TREBLE EIGHT 3 ch.c. Kings Lake (USA) 133–Persian Polly 99 (Persian Bold **109** 123) [1989 8m* 1990 9g 10.1g* 12g⁴ 12g 10g³ 10.6m⁵ 8g⁵] strong, sturdy colt: very useful performer: made all in minor event at Windsor in May: ran well fourth to sixth starts in Ever Ready Derby at Epsom, Group 1 event at Munich and Group 3 contest won by Defensive Play at Haydock: somewhat headstrong, and likely to prove best with forcing tactics at 1¼m: acts on good to firm ground: taken down last and quietly final outing: changed hands after reappearance. *M. A. Jarvis.*

TREBLY 2 b.c. (Jan 31) Top Ville 129–Jeema 102 (Thatch (USA) 136) [1990 8.2s **60** 8d⁵ 10.2s⁵] IR 29,000F: tall colt: looked weak: second foal: half-brother to 3-y-o Mishab (by Local Suitor): dam, best at 2 yrs, won 3 times at 5f: plating-class form in fair company: probably stays 1¼m. *C. E. Brittain.*

TREBONKERS 6 b.g. Treboro (USA) 112–Sally Conkers (Roi Lear (FR) 126) — [1989 NR 1990 12g] good-bodied gelding: form on flat only when second in seller in 1987: stays 1m: visored 3 times: winning hurdler in 1989/90. *J. S. Wilson.*

TREE DANCE 7 br.m. Sonnen Gold 121–Tree Breeze 111 (Farm Walk 111) [1989 — NR 1990 10.6s] third foal: dam, very useful at 2 yrs, deteriorated but later showed fairly useful form at up to 3m over hurdles: 33/1, tailed off in claimer at Haydock in June. *D. Burchell.*

TREMBALINO 2 b.g. (Mar 31) Tremblant 112–Balinese 86 (Balidar 133) [1990 **75** 7m 7f⁵ 6g⁵] good-bodied, rather angular gelding: fourth foal: half-brother to 5f winner Bally Brave and a winner in Belgium (both by Daring March): dam suited by 7f: 50/1, 3 lengths fifth of 17, soon in touch and staying on well despite drifting left, to West Riding in maiden at Newbury in October: backward previously: should stay 7f. *R. V. Smyth.*

TRENDY AUCTIONEER (IRE) 2 b.g. (Apr 18) Mazaad 106–Trendy Princess **44** (Prince Tenderfoot (USA) 126) [1990 7m 6g 8f 8m 6d] IR 9,600Y: sturdy, lengthy gelding: first reported foal: dam unraced: poor form in maidens and nurseries: visored final start. *A. Hide.*

TRES AMIGOS 3 b.g. Norwick (USA) 120–Safeguard 77 (Wolver Hollow 126) — [1989 5m 5d 6m 7.5f 8f 7g 1990 8.2g 6g 6f] tall, good-bodied gelding: poor maiden: blinkered, swerved left stalls and prominent 4f before wandering and looking unsatisfactory under pressure in handicap last start: bred to stay middle distances: winning hurdler for R. Woodhouse. *D. W. Chapman.*

TRESSELLIO 2 b.f. (May 7) Blakeney 126–Ribaria (Ribero 126) [1990 5g 7g⁶ — 7.5g 7.5m 7d] 2,000Y: small filly: seventh live foal: dam ran twice: seems of little account. *J. Norton.*

TREVORS TREASURE 4 b.f. Roscoe Blake 120–Treasures Jubilee (Highland — Melody 112) [1989 NR 1990 12.2d a12g] quite good-topped filly: first foal: dam winning selling hurdler: always well behind in apprentice race at Catterick and claimer at Southwell. *F. H. Lee.*

TREVOSE 5 br.g. Penmarric (USA) 111–Belle Year (Quorum 126) [1989 8s 7m — 1990 11.7g 8f 8m] sparely-made gelding: poor form in varied company, including selling: probably suited by shorter than 1m. *A. W. Denson.*

TRIANGULATION 2 b.g. (May 9) Tremblant 112–Gangawayhame 91 (Loch- **56** nager 132) [1990 5m 8g 7f⁶ 7g] tall, unfurnished gelding: looks weak: fourth foal: half-brother to 3-y-o Guthrie Court, 5f sellers winner at 2 yrs, and to 5.8f winner Awa'wi'ye (both by Daring March): dam won over 6f at 2 yrs and stayed 7f: plating-class maiden: stays 1m. *R. V. Smyth.*

TRIBAL LADY 3 b.f. Absalom 128–Placid Pet 65 (Mummy's Pet 125) [1989 5d² **58** 5d⁴ 5d* 6f* 6f³ 5f⁵ 6m³ 6v 1990 7m 6m 6g 6m⁶ 7f³] sturdy filly: good mover: modest winner at 2 yrs: best efforts as 3-y-o in handicaps last 2 starts: stays 7f: acts on firm and dead going. *M. McCormack.*

TRIBAL MASCOT (USA) 5 b.g. Our Native (USA)–Little Lady Luck (USA) —
(Jacinto) [1989 11.7d 12f 1990 10m 11.5g 17.1d] tall, close-coupled gelding: quite
modest winner as 3-y-o: lightly raced and soundly beaten in subsequent handicaps
on flat: stays 1¼m: acts on good to firm going: blinkered twice at 2 yrs. *D. R. Gandolfo.*

TRIBUTE TO DAD 3 b.g. Aragon 118–Bourienne 58 (Bolkonski 134) [1989 5m⁶ 47
7g 1990 8m 7m⁶ 8v⁵ 12.5g² 10g 10.1m 10m³ 10m⁶ 15.3f] workmanlike gelding:
moderate mover: plater: stays 1½m: acts on good to firm ground and heavy: has
been bandaged. *D. Haydn Jones.*

TRICKY NUMBER (USA) 2 ch.c. (Mar 14) Phone Trick (USA)–Wrap It Up 45
(Mount Hagen (FR) 127) [1990 5g 6m⁵ 5m] IR 32,000Y: leggy, lengthy colt: fourth
foal: half-brother to 3-y-o Prost (by Raise A Cup) and very useful 1988 2-y-o 6f
winner Pure Genius (by Diesis): dam thrice-raced half-sister to Gift Wrapped, smart
winner at up to 1½m and dam of Royal Lodge winner Reach: sire smart sprinter:
poor form in modest company, best effort (catching eye running on under considerate handling) second start: not seen out after July. *J. D. Bethell.*

TRICOTRIC 3 br.f. Electric 126–Orpheline 76 (Thatch (USA) 136) [1989 8.2g 7g 38
1990 8m 10m 10.6s 10g 10g⁶ a14g 11m⁴ 12m] good-topped filly: poor maiden: should
be suited by further than 11f: joined G. Moore. *P. S. Felgate.*

TRICYCLING (IRE) 2 b.g. (May 15) Flash of Steel 120–Stradavari (Strada- 55
vinsky 121) [1990 a7g 7f⁴ 7f 8m] 10,000Y: leggy gelding, angular,
rather sparely-made: fourth foal: half-brother to a listed winner in Italy: dam French
maiden, placed from 6.5f to 1m: plating-class maiden: form only on second start:
should stay 1m. *J. Berry.*

TRIEMMA (IRE) 2 b.f. (Apr 21) M Double M (USA)–Suba (GER) (Limbo —
(GER)) [1990 6m 5m⁴ 6m] IR 5,400Y: second reported foal: dam placed in Germany:
sire 6f to 9f winner: poor form in sellers and a maiden: sold 1,600 gns Newmarket
Autumn Sales. *N. Tinkler.*

TRI FOLENE (FR) 4 b.f. Nebos (GER) 129–Jefty (FR) (Jefferson 129) [1989 11g —
11g³ 10.7g⁶ 12g² 1990 10.2f] angular ex-French filly: fourth foal: half-sister to 2
placed animals in France: dam placed over 15.5f in France: blinkered and sweating,
prominent to halfway in maiden at Doncaster in March: stays 1½m: fair front-
running hurdler, winner in November. *M. C. Pipe.*

TRIFOLIO 3 b.c. Touching Wood (USA) 127–Triple Reef (Mill Reef (USA) 141) 99
[1989 NR 1990 12.5f⁵ 14g* 12d 12d* 14f⁴ 14.8m* 16.2m³ 14d²] 50,000Y: rangy,
attractive colt: good mover, with a long stride: fourth foal: dam unraced daughter of
smart middle-distance filly Triple First and half-sister to Three Tails and Maysoon:
useful performer: successful in small fields for poor maiden (on toes, made all) at
Newmarket in May and handicaps at Haydock in July and Newmarket in August: ran
well in handicaps last 2 starts: suited by test of stamina: acts on firm and dead
ground. *H. R. A. Cecil.*

TRIGON 3 b.c. Kris 135–Triagonal 107 (Formidable (USA) 125) [1989 NR 1990 84
7m³ 8m² 10f* 10.1m³] 60,000Y: strong colt: carries condition: has a powerful, round
action: second foal: half-brother to fair 1988 2-y-o Trioso (by Teenoso), later 1m
winner in Italy: dam, 6f and 1m winner, is half-sister to Maysoon and Three Tails:
made all and stayed on strongly in maiden at Chepstow: again odds on, third in minor
event at Windsor later in July: needs forcing tactics over 1¼m and worth a try over
1½m. *P. T. Walwyn.*

TRINCOMALEE 3 ch.f. Electric 126–Copt Hall Princess 70 (Crowned Prince 42
(USA) 128) [1989 NR 1990 10f 12f⁵ 12g 12m³ 14g⁶ 12.3g 14d⁵] 5,400Y: rangy filly:
fifth foal: closely related to 1m and 1¼m winner Prince Merandi (by Blakeney) and
half-sister to 1¼m and 1½m winner Dovedon Lady (by Castle Keep) and 2 winners
in Italy: dam 7f winner: poor form: stays 1¾m: blinkered last 5 outings: tailed off for
lady rider: usually on toes: sold 6,000 gns Newmarket July Sales. *A. A. Scott.*

TRING PARK 4 b.g. Niniski (USA) 125–Habanna 107 (Habitat 134) [1989 10g 56
10m⁶ 15s 9m 12f² 18g 1990 a12g³ 12g 12f⁵ 11.7m⁶] big, leggy gelding: plating-class
maiden: claimed out of M. Tompkins' stable £7,202 on first outing: stays 1½m well:
acts on firm ground: not the easiest of rides: winning hurdler in August. *R. Curtis.*

TRIOMPHE MODEST 3 b.f. Petorius 117–Tinktura 92 (Pampapaul 121) [1989 54 d
5v² 5d³ 6g² 5d 7m⁴ 6f* 7f 6g⁶ 1990 6f³ 6g 7f⁵ 5g a5g⁵ 6f³ 6m a6g 7f 5m 6g] leggy
filly: plating-class performer: behind in handicaps last 5 outings: needs further than
5f, and stays 7f: acts on firm ground: successful for 7-lb claimer: blinkered final
outing: sold 1,500 gns Newmarket Autumn Sales. *C. A. Cyzer.*

TRIPLE BARREL (USA) 3 b.c. Sharpen Up 127–Galexcel (USA) (Exceller **66** (USA) 129) [1989 7g a8g⁶ 1990 a6g*] smallish, dipped-backed colt: apprentice ridden, won 4-runner maiden at Southwell in January: best effort at 6f. *N. A. Callaghan.*

TRIPLE SECRET (USA) 2 b.f. (May 2) Secreto (USA) 128–Queen's Banner **— p** (USA) (Hoist The Flag (USA)) [1990 7g] $140,000Y: strong, lengthy filly: has scope: half-sister to 2 winners in North America: dam showed a little ability: very backward, ridden about 3f out, hung left and soon weakened in 15-runner minor event at Newbury in September: should improve. *D. J. G. Murray-Smith.*

TRIPLE UNITE 2 ch.f. (Apr 23) Tina's Pet 121–Sussex Queen 82 (Music Boy **32** 124) [1990 5g⁵ 5m 6m⁶ 5m] 1,000F: workmanlike filly: has scope: third foal: dam 2-y-o 6f winner seemed to stay 1½m: well beaten in maidens and a minor event: unseated rider to post penultimate start: blinkered final one: sold 800 gns Doncaster November Sales. *J. White.*

TRIPLICATE 4 b.c. Mill Reef (USA) 141–Triple First 117 (High Top 131) [1989 **73** 9g 8s⁴ 8f 1990 8m⁴ 8m 9m⁵ 10.6v] small colt: best effort in face of stiff tasks in handicaps as 4-y-o on first outing: should be suited by further than 1m: acts on good to firm and soft going: bandaged near-fore at 3 yrs. *J. L. Dunlop.*

TRIP TO THE MOON 4 b.g. Red Sunset 120–Mile By Mile 92 (Milesian 125) **70 d** [1989 7g⁴ 8.2g² 8m⁵ 1990 a11g² a11g³ 8.2s 9s 10g 12g² 13g] lengthy gelding: plating-class handicapper: stays 1½m: inconsistent. *C. W. Thornton.*

TRIREME 3 ch.c. Rainbow Quest 134–Bireme 127 (Grundy 137) [1989 7g* **89** 1990 12g 10.1g³ 10m³ 14d³ 16.5d³] rangy colt: reportedly split pastern after winning maiden at Newmarket in July at 2 yrs: inconsistent in 1990, best effort in handicap at Newmarket fourth start: stays 1¾m: acts on dead going: sold to join J. White 22,500 gns Ascot November Sales. *Major W. R. Hern.*

TRISETTE 2 ch.f. (Mar 20) Adonijah 126–Canasta Girl 90 (Charlottesville 135) **61 p** [1990 8g⁴ 10s⁵] quite good-topped, useful-looking filly: half-sister to several winners, including quite useful 1975 2-y-o 7f winner Clean Canasta (by Silly Season) and Irish 1½m winner Mary's Mariner (by Julio Mariner): dam winner over 1¼m, is sister to Derby winner Charlottown: quite modest form, staying on, in late-season maidens at Wolverhampton and Nottingham: given great deal to do on latter: will stay well: likely to do better. *W. Jarvis.*

TRISTAN'S COMET 3 br.g. Sayf El Arab (USA) 127–Gleneagle 91 (Swing Easy **—** (USA) 126) [1989 7g a7g⁵ 1990 8m a8g³ 10.2f 8.3m 8m⁶ 10m] leggy gelding: quite modest form at best on the all-weather: little otherwise, in sellers last 3 starts: stays 1m: trained until after penultimate start by M. Jarvis. *J. L. Harris.*

TRISTIORUM 3 ch.g. Crofthall 110–Annie-Jo (Malicious) [1989 6g 1990 7.2d **69** 10.2s a8g³ a12g³ a11g] rangy gelding: modest performer: blinkered at Southwell last 3 starts, easily best efforts first 2 occasions, always behind in handicap on final outing: suited by 1½m. *J. Etherington.*

TRIUMPHAL SONG 3 ch.c. Caerleon (USA) 132–Zither 72 (Vienna 127) [1989 **67** 6m 7f³ 1990 8g 11g⁵ 11.5m* 12.2g⁴ 12.5m⁶ 12m] workmanlike colt: quite modest handicapper: ran moderately after winning at Lingfield in June: suited by 1½m: acts on firm ground: sweating last 4 starts: sold 15,500 gns Newmarket Autumn Sales. *B. W. Hills.*

TRIVIALITY 2 br.f. (Mar 12) Sharpo 132–Idle Days 80 (Hittite Glory 125) [1990 **98** 6g³ 6d* 6g* 5d⁵] leggy, quite good-topped filly: has scope: good mover: fourth live foal: half-sister to 7f winner Sunshine Coast (by Posse) and a winner in Malaysia by High Top: dam placed from 5f to 10.5f, is out of very useful middle-distance stayer Paresseuse: fairly useful performer: won maiden at Goodwood and 4-runner minor event (on toes) at York in October: heavily-backed favourite, not discredited when over 4 lengths fifth of 10, never able to challenge, to Snowy Owl in listed event at Doncaster later in the month: better suited by 6f than 5f. *J. H. M. Gosden.*

TRIXIE'S GUEST 3 gr.f. What A Guest 119–Winter Lady (Bonne Noel 115) **40** [1989 5m³ 6g 6f³ 7m⁶ 5m⁶ 7g⁴ 1990 9s 8f 8.5d 6g 10d⁴ 11m] IR 6,000Y: leggy, angular filly: poor maiden: broke leg at Hamilton in June: stayed 1¼m: acted on any going, with possible exception of soft: raced very freely when blinkered: visored fourth outing. *S. G. Norton.*

TROJAN CROWN (IRE) 2 b.f. (Mar 15) Trojan Fen 118–Crown Witness 95 **93** (Crowned Prince (USA) 128) [1990 7f* 7f* 8g³ 8m⁵] rangy filly: good walker: fourth foal: half-sister to 9f and 10.6f winner Oral Evidence (by Rusticaro): dam miler: won 4-runner maiden at Yarmouth and 6-runner Fay, Richwhite Sweet Solera Stakes at Newmarket, on each occasion quickening over 1f out and running on really well: ran creditably in May Hill Stakes at Doncaster and Brent Walker Fillies' Mile at Ascot: probably better suited by 1m than 7f. *G. Wragg.*

TROJAN DEBUT 4 b.g. Trojan Fen 118–Debutina Park 87 (Averof 123) [1989 **34**
7g² 6f 6h⁶ 6m 7g 7f⁵ a8g⁶ 1990 a10g³ a10g a10g a13g² 10f⁵ 12.5m² 12f⁴ 12.5g⁴ 16g a12g] robust gelding: carries plenty of condition: keen walker: poor mover: poor handicapper: claimed out of M. Ryan's stable £6,101.50 eighth outing: tailed off in face of stiff tasks last 2: suited by around 1½m: acts on firm going: blinkered once at 3 yrs. *R. T. Juckes.*

TROJAN EXCEL 3 b.f. Trojan Fen 118–War Ballad (FR) (Green Dancer (USA) **63 d**
132) [1989 5m 5m² 5f* 6m* 7.5f⁵ 7.5m³ 7f³ 7f* 7f* 6d 8.2f⁵ 1990 9m² 8.2g² 8.5m² 7h³ 8.2g⁵ 8m⁵ a8g 8.2m 9m 8d a12g a11g] strong, compact filly: carries condition: good mover: quite modest performer: deteriorated after staying-on third in handicap at Thirsk in May: should stay 1¼m: acts on firm ground: visored ninth and tenth starts: has hung right and found little. *C. Tinkler.*

TROJAN GENERAL 3 gr.c. Trojan Fen 118–Lady Regent (Wolver Hollow 126) **73**
[1989 6m⁴ 6g 1990 a7g* a7g* a6g* a7g²] smallish, workmanlike colt: modest performer: successful at Lingfield in 2-runner maiden and two 4-runner handicaps in January: ran fairly well following month: stays 7f. *D. J. G. Murray-Smith.*

TROJAN LANCER 4 b.c. Trojan Fen 118–Dunster's Cream 51 (Sharpen Up **66**
127) [1989 9g 10f 10m⁶ 12m 12g 10m³ 10v 9s⁴ 1990 11f* 10.2m³ 12m* 12.4m³ 11.5m³ 12m² 13.6d] sturdy, close-coupled colt: moderate walker and mover: quite modest handicapper: successful at Redcar and Leicester (led post) in May: stays 1½m: possibly needs top-of-the-ground: suited by waiting tactics. *Dr J. D. Scargill.*

TROJAN PLEASURE 3 br.f. Trojan Fen 118–Sweet Pleasure 88 (Sweet —
Revenge 129) [1989 8g 1990 10f³ 8m⁵ 10g a16g] leggy, lengthy filly: well beaten, including in handicaps: hung left second start: sold 1,100 gns Ascot December Sales. *D. J. G. Murray-Smith.*

TROJAN STEEL 3 gr.c. Bellypha 130–Troja (Troy 137) [1989 6m 6m 7g⁶ 6.3m —
6g 5g⁶ 6d 1990 7m 9f⁵ 12.4s] first foal: dam, showed a little ability in France, is daughter of Nell Gwyn winner Gently: plating-class ex-Irish maiden: well beaten in handicaps and Newcastle claimer (in November) as 3-y-o: trained until after penultimate start by M. O'Toole. *P. Liddle.*

TROJAN WAR 6 b.h. Troy 137–Sea Venture (FR) 98 (Diatome 132) [1989 NR —
1990 a13g] sturdy, smallish horse: poor maiden: stays 1¾m: acts on firm and dead going: twice visored and took very strong hold when tried in blinkers. *C. Spares.*

TROPICAL ACE 3 b.f. Final Straw 127–Rampage 93 (Busted 134) [1989 7g⁵ 8m **50**
8g 1990 12f 12m 14f³ 18m⁴ 18d³] strong, sturdy filly: has a quick action: 33/1, first worthwhile form when third of 17 in handicap at Nottingham in October, final outing: stays well: seems suited by a soft surface. *R. Voorspuy.*

TROPICAL ORCHID 2 b.f. (Feb 9) Nomination 125–Sister Hannah 70 (Mon- **42**
seigneur (USA) 127) [1990 6m 5m 5f⁶ 5m 5m] 5,000Y: small, stocky filly: third foal: half-sister to 3-y-o So Knowledgeable (by Night Shift): dam 5f winner, is daughter of half-sister to Mrs McArdy: poor maiden: best effort second start: should stay beyond 5f. *R. Voorspuy.*

TROPICO 7 ch.g. Hot Spark 126–Bella Canto 82 (Crooner 119) [1989 NR 1990 8f* **33**
8f⁶ 8m] workmanlike gelding: poor handicapper: first run on flat since 1987, won selling handicap (no bid) at Pontefract in July: started slowly both starts after: best at 1m: acts on any going: blinkered twice: wears bandages: occasionally sweats. *I. P. Wardle.*

TROUBLEWITHJACK 2 br.f. (Jan 30) Sulaafah (USA) 119–Babe In The Wood —
(Athens Wood 126) [1990 5m 6m 7d a7g] 1,250F, 5,000Y: smallish, workmanlike filly: half-sister to 5 winners, including Western Moxy (by Connaught), successful at up to 1½m: dam ran 3 times: soundly beaten in varied events. *W. Carter.*

TROUPE 2 b.c. (May 2) Sadler's Wells (USA) 132–Lovelight 112 (Bleep-Bleep **71**
134) [1990 6g² 6g⁵] lengthy colt: closely related to 3-y-o 7.6f winner Russian Frontier and very useful 1m and 9f winner Literati (both by Nureyev) and half-brother to several other winners, including very smart 6f to 1m winner Motavato (by Apalachee): dam very game sprinter: bit backward and weak in market, over 2 lengths third of 16, promoted to second, to Jimlil in minor event at Doncaster, staying on strongly when impeded final furlong: odds on, only fifth of 13 to Tumble Twist in maiden at Nottingham later in September: will be better suited by 7f+. *B. W. Hills.*

TR TOTO 2 b.g. (May 14) Final Straw 127–Trigamy 112 (Tribal Chief 125) [1990 — 6m] good-quartered gelding: half-brother to several winners, including 7f to 1¼m winner New Mexico (by Free State) and 7f winner Mango Manila (by Martinmas): dam 5f performer: last of 16 in maiden at Folkestone in October. *C. A. Horgan.*

TRUE BILL 3 b.c. Nicholas Bill 125–Cosset 56 (Comedy Star (USA) 121) [1989 — NR 1990 8g 10m⁵ 12g³ 11.5f⁶ 13.3g] rather close-coupled, good-bodied colt: moderate mover: fourth living foal: brother to 1¼m winner Billet: dam ran 3 times at 2 yrs: little worthwhile form, including in handicaps: sold 5,200 gns Newmarket Autumn Sales. *H. Candy.*

TRUE DIVIDEND (USA) 4 ch.c. Blushing Groom (FR) 131–Singing Rain 91 (USA) (Sensitivo) [1989 8g 1990 6f⁵ 9f⁴ 7.6d 10h* 8f 10m* 10f⁶ 10m⁶] good-topped colt: carries plenty of condition: won apprentice race at Brighton in May and handicap at Redcar (soon allowed to establish clear advantage) in July: didn't lead and ran moderately final outing: stays 1¼m: acts on hard going: ran poorly at Chester third outing: seems suited by forcing tactics. *L. M. Cumani.*

TRUE FLAIR 2 b.g. (Mar 3) Believe It (USA)–Willow Court (USA) (Little 63 d Current (USA)) [1990 5m⁴ 5g² 6g 5m⁵ 6m] 25,000Y: strong, close-coupled gelding: half-brother to several winners in USA: dam unplaced from 11 starts: easily best effort beaten head in maiden at Ripon in May: showed nothing in seller final start: should stay 6f: trained first 3 outings by P. Felgate. *J. Berry.*

TRUE GEORGE 3 ch.g. King of Clubs 124–Piculet 69 (Morston (FR) 125) [1989 — 5g⁶ 6g* 5f 6m 6v a8g 1990 10.2f⁵ 8.5g⁶] smallish, shallow-girthed gelding: moderate mover: only worthwhile form at 2 yrs when modest winner at Epsom in June: below that form in handicap and June claimer in 1990: should stay 1¼m. *J. D. Bethell.*

TRUE MARCH 2 br.g. (Mar 3) Daring March 116–Madam Muffin 77 (Sparkler 55 d 130) [1990 5m 5g 6m² 6f⁶ 6m⁶ 5m 6d 7d a7g a7g] neat gelding: carries condition: good walker: has a quick action: first foal: dam maiden sprinter: modest plater: best effort third start: ran mostly in non-sellers afterwards, usually showing little: best form at 6f: possibly unsuited by dead ground: blinkered final outing. *J. D. Bethell.*

TRUE OPTIMIST 3 b. or br.g. Try My Best (USA) 130–Lenticular 42 (Warpath 79 113) [1989 7d 1990 10g 6g 8d*ᵈⁱˢ 8m 12g 7m⁶ a8g 7d 8s 7d⁴ 10.2s] IR 27,000F, IR 42,000Y: smallish, good-quartered gelding: second foal: dam third in 1¼m seller from 3 starts at 3 yrs: favourite, first past post in 16-runner handicap at Gowran Park in May by neck, leading 1½f out but swerving left close home and disqualified: 33/1, apparently easily best effort but also hung left when narrowly-beaten fourth of 9 to Cosmic Princess in minor event at Leicester: stays 1m: acts on dead going: blinkered fourth, sixth and seventh starts: trained until after ninth by N. Meade. *R. Akehurst.*

TRULL 3 b.f. Lomond (USA) 128–Bird Point (USA) 87 (Alleged (USA) 138) [1989 — NR 1990 7m] 130,000Y: medium-sized, good-quartered filly: first foal: dam, 9f and 1¼m winner, is half-sister to smart 1989 1m to 10.5f winner Bex: visored and edgy, tailed-off last in maiden at Chepstow: moved moderately down: sold 3,700 gns Newmarket September Sales. *J. H. M. Gosden.*

TRUST DEED (USA) 2 ch.g. (Apr 2) Shadeed (USA) 135–Karelia (USA) 111 72 p (Sir Ivor 135) [1990 7g 7g³] well-made gelding: has scope: half-brother to ungenuine 1989 2-y-o Finette (by Northern Baby) and several winners, including French 1¼m winner Kia Real (by Irish River) and untrustworthy 1988 2-y-o 5f winner Dubrovnik (by L'Emigrant): dam 1m winner stayed 1½m, is out of half-sister to high-class sprinter Full Out: over 3 lengths third of 12, keeping on well, to River Consort in maiden at Salisbury in October: will be much better suited by 1m +: should improve further. *Major W. R. Hern.*

TRUTH ENDURES 2 b.f. (Mar 25) Absalom 128–Truth Will Out 82 (Blakeney 37 126) [1990 5f⁵ 5m] sixth foal: half-sister to 1m winner Dreyfus (by Derrylin): dam 5f-winning daughter of best 1974 2-y-o filly Cry of Truth: well beaten in maiden and seller at Lingfield in August: sold 1,800 gns Newmarket Autumn Sales. *Sir Mark Prescott.*

TRYING DAYS 3 b.c. Teenoso (USA) 135–April Days 75 (Silly Season 127) 78 [1989 7g⁵ 8f² 1990 11d 10f⁴ 11m] leggy, workmanlike colt: modest maiden: hung badly left, looking ill at ease on track, at Salisbury second start in first half of 1990: stays 11f: acts on firm ground: should prove best on left-handed track. *P. T. Walwyn.*

TRYING FOR GOLD (USA) 4 b.f. Northern Baby (CAN) 127–Expansive 111 (Exbury 138) [1989 12m* 12.5g* 12d² 1990 12f] big, leggy, quite attractive filly: progressive at 3 yrs, winning maiden at Salisbury and minor event (making all) at

Wolverhampton: backward and facing stiff task, well beaten in £27,900 handicap at Goodwood in August: should be suited by further. *Major W. R. Hern.*

TRY TRUST (USA) 4 ch.c. Vaguely Noble 140–Klepto (USA) (No Robbery) 97
[1989 NR 1990 11.7m⁴ 10m³ 10m* 12m⁴] lengthy, good-quartered ex-American colt: has a rather round action: brother to Estrapade, very smart French middle-distance winner later champion turf mare in USA, and half-brother to 4 winners, notably top-class American 5-y-o Criminal Type (by Alydar) and leading Italian miler Isopach (by Reviewer): dam smart stakes winner at up to 1m: made all in minor event at Nottingham in September, running on strongly to beat Regimental Arms 6 lengths: ran well when fourth to Spritsail in listed race at Newmarket over week later: stays 1½m. *C. E. Brittain.*

TSAR ALEXIS (USA) 2 br.c. (May 27) Topsider (USA)–Evening Silk (USA) —
(Damascus (USA)) [1990 6m 6m] $100,000F, 70,000Y: leggy colt: second foal: dam minor sprint winner at 4 yrs in USA: little sign of ability in fair company at Newmarket in August and Folkestone in October: sold 7,600 gns Newmarket Autumn Sales. *B. W. Hills.*

TSAR MAIDEN (USA) 3 ch.f. Nijinsky (CAN) 138–Optimistic Lass (USA) 117 60
(Mr Prospector (USA)) [1989 NR 1990 10d² 10.5g 10.7g² 10.7g² 12d²] second foal: half-sister to high-class miler Golden Opinion (by Slew O'Gold): dam won Musidora and Nassau Stakes: second in newcomers race (off course 4 months after) at Evry and maidens at Le Croise-Laroche (twice) and Folkestone: blinkered third and fifth starts: stud. *A. Fabre, France.*

TTAYWEN 3 br.f. Noalto 120–Scotch Thistle 73 (Sassafras (FR) 135) [1989 8g 9f³ —
a8g 1990 12m 11.5m⁶ 12f⁴ 16m 12f 11.7f⁵] angular, sparely-made filly: poor maiden: soundly beaten in handicaps and maidens as 3-y-o: best effort over 9f: blinkered fifth start: bandaged final one: refused to enter stalls once at 2 yrs: sold 875 gns Ascot November Sales. *J. A. Bennett.*

TUDOR ACE 3 b.g. Stanford 121§–Lusaka (Wolver Hollow 126) [1989 5.1m 6m 25
5.1f 5g 5f 6f 5m 1990 a5g⁴ 12f 9s 7m⁶ 7m 7.6m a7g] good-topped, rather dipped-backed gelding: has a quick action: plater: may prove best at around 1m. *Pat Mitchell.*

TUDOR BRAVE 3 b.g. Indian King (USA) 128–Stickpin 74 (Gulf Pearl 117) —
[1989 NR 1990 10f⁶ 11d 12f] 5,200Y: compact, angular gelding: brother to a French maiden and half-brother to several winners, including Italian 1000 Guineas winner Honey (by He Loves Me) and fair 6f to 11f winner African Pearl (by African Sky): dam placed over 5f and 7f at 2 yrs: well beaten in maidens and a claimer in the spring. *R. Simpson.*

TUDOR D'OR 7 br.m. Mister Tudor–Petit d'Or (Petit Instant) [1989 NR 1990 —
15.8g 10.8g] leggy, lightly-made mare: beaten some way in varied company. *R. Lee.*

TUDORGATEWAY 2 b.c. (Mar 30) Martinmas 128–Shikra (Sea Hawk II 131) —
[1990 6m] sixth reported living foal: half-brother to 11f to 2m winner Tudor Gate (by Tachypous) and 6f winner Croyland Pride (by Goldhills Pride): dam, from good staying family, placed over 1½m in Ireland: green, slowly away and always behind, tending to carry head high, in maiden at Newmarket in August. *M. H. Tompkins.*

TUDOR PRIDE 3 gr.f. Gold Claim 90–Gellifawr 80 (Saulingo 122) [1989 NR —
1990 a12g a8g⁶] third foal: sister to Belgian 2-y-o 6f and 7f winner Singing Gold, also successful in 1m seller here at 3 yrs: dam best at 5f: well beaten in summer maidens at Southwell. *S. R. Bowring.*

TUDOR ROMANCE 5 b g Aragon 118–Dovey (Welsh Pageant 132) [1989 NR 42
1990 12m* 14g] lengthy, angular gelding: has a round action: 12/1 from 20/1, won handicap at Leicester in March: reared stalls and ran poorly 3 weeks later: stays 1½m: acts on good to firm and dead going. *M. W. Eckley.*

TUFRAJ (USA) 2 ch.c. (Mar 26) Kris 135–Greenland Park 124 (Red God 128§) —
[1990 6m 7f⁵ 7m⁶] good-bodied colt: sixth foal: brother to good French 9.5f and 1¼m winner Fitnah and half-brother to a winner by Touching Wood: dam sprinter: plaiting-class form in summer maidens, once ridden by girl apprentice. *M. R. Stoute.*

TUGRA (FR) 2 b.f. (Apr 18) Baby Turk 120–Ramsar (Young Emperor 133) [1990 —
6g 8.2s] rather angular filly: fourth foal: half-sister to a prolific middle-distance winner in Holland by Dominion: dam Irish 1½m winner, is sister to Irish 1000 Guineas fourth Ararat: poor form in modest company at Windsor in August and Haydock in October. *C. James.*

TULFARRIS 3 b. or br.g. Glenstal (USA) 118–Trusted Maiden (Busted 134) 62
[1989 NR 1990 6s³ 9g 8g² 8.2d⁵ 7.2d⁴ 8v] 35,000F, IR 22,000Y: big, workmanlike gelding: moderate walker and mover: half-brother to several winners here and

abroad, including very useful 1987 2-y-o 7f winner Obeah (by Cure The Blues) and fair middle-distance stayer Trust The Irish (by Ile de Bourbon): dam placed at up to 1½m in Ireland: quite modest maiden: suited by 1m (pulled hard over 9f): acts on dead going. *D. Moffatt.*

TUMBLED BRIDE   4 b.f. Tumble Wind (USA)–Bridewell Belle (Saulingo 122)   —
[1989 7m 7m² 8g⁶ 8.5g 7g⁶ 8s⁴ 1990 a6g a11g a12g 10f 8.3g 8m] tall, leggy ex-Irish filly: third foal: dam won over 1m at 3 yrs in Ireland: little worthwhile form in first half of year, including in handicaps: stays 1m: acts on good to firm ground and soft: blinkered once at 3 yrs: sold 1,800 gns Ascot July Sales. *W. T. Kemp.*

TUMBLE TURN   3 ch.f. Ardross 134–Water Ballet 92 (Sir Gaylord) [1989 NR   —
1990 10.6d 11v 12.2d a11g] rather unfurnished filly: half-sister to 1983 Irish 2-y-o 5f winner Tomard (by Thatching): dam won over 7f at 2 yrs and stayed 1¼m: well beaten in claimers and seller. *M. H. Easterby.*

TUMBLE TWIST (IRE)   2 b.c. (Mar 31) Tumble Wind (USA)–Reshuffle   79
(Sassafras (FR) 135) [1990 7m⁵ 7m 6g* 6g] IR 20,000Y: leggy colt: good mover: half-brother to 3 winners in Ireland, all at 1m +, including stayer and hurdler Profligate (by Shack): dam never ran: made all, showing much improved form, in maiden at Nottingham in September, beating Benno by 5 lengths: well-backed favourite, ran moderately in nursery at York following month: should stay at least 7f: swerved stalls first 2 outings. *B. Hanbury.*

TUNED AUDITION   2 b.c. (May 27) Fit To Fight (USA)–Song Test (USA) (The   76
Minstrel (CAN) 135) [1990 6s 7.3m⁴ 7m³ 6f² 6d 7m 8.2g⁶ 7.6v³] 10,000Y: good-quartered colt: half-brother to winners in USA by Believe It and Alleged: dam winner at around 1m in USA: sire won from 6f to 1½m: modest maiden: best form at 6f or 7f: blinkered fourth and fifth starts: inconsistent: sold 14,500 gns Newmarket Autumn Sales. *C. E. Brittain.*

TUNEFUL CHARTER   3 gr.g. Song 132–Martin-Lavell Star 64 (Godswalk   39
(USA) 130) [1989 5m 5f⁶ 5m 6m 6g 5v a7g 1990 a6g⁶] quite good-topped gelding: poor maiden: best effort in claimer at Southwell only start in 1990: blinkered 4 times: often sweats and twice edgy: sold 650 gns Ascot February Sales. *T. Fairhurst.*

TUPGILL LASS   2 b.f. (Apr 12) Gabitat 119–Mizpah 71 (Lochnager 132) [1990 5f   —
6f] smallish, angular filly: third foal: dam 5f and 6f winner out of half-sister to Giacometti: well beaten in sellers. *S. E. Kettlewell.*

TUPPAT   2 ch.f. (May 6) Noalto 120–Stratch (FR) 71 (Thatch (USA) 136) [1990 6g³   41
6f⁶] 1,900Y: sparely-made filly: first foal: dam raced only at 6f: quite modest plater: sent to Norway. *G. A. Pritchard-Gordon.*

TUPPY (USA)   3 ch.f. Sharpen Up 127–Petradia 86 (Relkino 131) [1989 NR 1990   —
10g] IR 235,000Y: first foal: dam, 1¼m winner, is half-sister to top-class 1m to 1½m filly Pebbles (by Sharpen Up): 20/1, well-beaten seventh of 9 in maiden at Sandown in September. *C. R. Nelson.*

TURBOFAN (IRE)   2 b.c. (Apr 30) Taufan (USA) 119–Timinala 58 (Mansingh   75
(USA) 120) [1990 7m 7m⁵ 7g²] 14,000Y: close-coupled colt: third foal: half-brother to 3-y-o 1¼m winner Minimize (by Alzao): dam lightly-raced 5f performer, is half-sister to smart miler Pasticcio (by Taufan): best effort in maidens, 8 lengths second of 17, keeping on well, to Aghaadir at Salisbury in October: will stay 1m. *J. W. Hills.*

TURBO-R   2 ch.g. (Apr 3) Rabdan 129–Golderama (Golden Dipper 119) [1990 5m⁴   35
6g 5g 7m⁵ 5.8m 7m⁴ a7g 8m 10m 8d] 600Y: compact gelding: third foal: dam once-raced twin: poor plater: stays 6f: visored or blinkered last 6 starts: possibly ungenuine: sold 900 gns Ascot November Sales. *M. R. Channon.*

TURF DANCER   3 b.f. Anfield 117–Cachucha (Gay Fandango (USA) 132) [1989   44
NR 1990 6v 8.2g 8.2g⁴ 8.2m⁶ 8.2g 8.2m⁴ 8.2g 11s² 11v] 1,000 2-y-o: leggy, workmanlike filly: third foal: half-sister to plating-class 6f and 7f winner Supreme Optimist (by Absalom): dam poor granddaughter of Irish Oaks winner Aurabella: poor form: better at 11f than shorter: acts on soft ground: sweating and on toes sixth outing. *J. S. Wilson.*

TURGEON (USA)   4 gr.c. Caro 133–Reiko (Targowice (USA) 130) [1989 10s⁵ 113
12m⁶ 15d* 15g* 15d² 15m³ 15.5g² 1990 15.5f² 15.5d* 20g³ 20d⁵ 12s⁶ 12s³ 15.5v³] rather leggy colt: very useful stayer: evens, won Prix Vicomtesse Vigier at Longchamp in April by ¾ length from Mardonius: blinkered, moderate fifth to Ashal in Gold Cup at Royal Ascot, weakening final 2f: fair third, never able to challenge, to dead-heaters Braashee and Indian Queen in Prix Royal-Oak at Longchamp final outing: probably best at around 2m: acts on any going. *J. E. Pease, France.*

TURKISH DREAM 3 b. or br.g. Sayf El Arab (USA) 127–Thespian 76 (Ile de — Bourbon (USA) 133) [1989 NR 1990 a10g6 12d] 17,000Y: compact gelding: second foal: half-brother to 4-y-o 1½m and 13.8f winner Class Act (by Shirley Heights): dam 7f winner: backward, tailed off in maidens in November. *C. Holmes.*

TURKISH STAR (USA) 3 b.c. Blushing Groom (FR) 131–Perlee (FR) 122 66 (Margouillat (FR) 133) [1989 NR 1990 8.5d 8f 8m5] compact colt: fourth foal: half-brother to 3 winners, notably twice-raced Poule d'Essai des Pouliches winner Pearl Bracelet (by Lyphard): dam French 1m to 1½m winner: first worthwhile form when fifth in apprentice maiden at Yarmouth: edged right and wore tongue strap on debut: stays 1m. *M. Moubarak.*

TURKISH TOURIST 5 b.g. Busted 134–Kalazero 96 (Kalamoun 129) [1989 — 10.8m6 1990 10.2f] big, rangy gelding: lightly raced and little sign of ability: band-aged near-hind and slowly away only outing at 4 yrs. *D. T. Thom.*

TURKS HEAD TEN 2 b.g. (May 10) Domynsky 110–Oyster Gray 61 (Tanfirion 42 110) [1990 5m a6g 5m6 5v] 2,000Y: small gelding: first foal: dam maiden best at up to 6f: poor maiden: blinkered or visored last 2 outings. *W. G. M. Turner.*

TURMERIC 7 ch.g. Alias Smith (USA)–Hot Spice (Hotfoot 126) [1989 13.8d3 70 12g2 15.8m3 12m 15.8m* 13f3 15.8f* 15.8m* 14f3 14m4 12.2g2 13.8d3 1990 13.8m6 13.8m 14g 14g 14f3 14m3 14m 13.8f3 15.3g* 15.8d2 12g5 13.6d3 a16g5] leggy, sparely-made gelding: modest handicapper: successful at Wolverhampton in October: stays 2m: acts on any going: visored twice: bandaged behind: has a turn of foot and is held up: best with strong handling: has won 8 times at Catterick. *M. F. D. Morley.*

TUSKY 2 ch.c. (May 9) Prince Sabo 123–Butosky 71 (Busted 134) [1990 6f 6g a6g5 94 p 6g* 6g*] tall, good-topped colt: has plenty of scope: moderate walker: sixth foal: half-brother to 1m and 1¼m winner Sutosky (by Great Nephew) and 1m winner and Ebor second Bush Hill (by Beldale Flutter): dam middle-distance half-sister to very smart sprinter Crews Hill: showed much improved form last 2 starts, winning 20-runner maiden at Thirsk in August and 18-runner nursery (claimer ridden) at Haydock in September: gave trouble stalls and withdrawn under orders second outing: will stay 7f: likely to improve further, and make useful 3-y-o. *M. J. Camacho.*

TV PITCH (FR) 2 b.f. (Feb 7) Fast Topaze (USA) 128–Allatum (USA) 81 60 p (Alleged (USA) 138) [1990 7m] first reported foal: dam 2m winner: around 12 lengths seventh of 16, never better than mid-division, to Sapieha in maiden at Newmarket in October: should improve. *N. A. Graham.*

TWIGGERS 4 gr.g. Petong 126–Petulengra 98 (Mummy's Pet 125) [1989 8s 8d — 1990 10.1g] leggy, sparely-made gelding: no form in maidens or claimer. *J. H. Baker.*

TWILIGHT AGENDA (USA) 4 b.c. Devil's Bag (USA)–Grenzen (USA) 102 (Grenfall (USA)) [1989 8v* 8m 6.3m3 7m* 7g* 1990 7g* 8f 7m4 7m2 7g5] good-topped colt: carries plenty of condition: useful performer: 4-length winner of 5-runner minor event at Phoenix Park in May: in frame behind Norwich in listed races at Leopardstown and Phoenix Park: first home on disadvantageous far side in Royal Hunt Cup (Handicap) at Royal Ascot second outing: needs further than 6f, and stays 1m: acts on any going: blinkered last 2 starts. *D. K. Weld, Ireland.*

TWILIGHT FALLS 5 ch.g. Day Is Done 115–Grattan Princess (Tumble Wind — (USA)) [1989 7g 6d* 6g6 6g 1990 6s 6g 5d 6s] good-topped gelding: poor mover: no worthwhile form since landing gamble in selling handicap in April, 1989: suited by 6f: acts on dead going: gave trouble at stalls second outing. *M. J. Camacho.*

TWILIGHT FANTASY 4 b.f. Red Sunset 120–Imagination 91 (Reiko 136) 34 [1989 7m4 7f 7m 7.6m5 6f3 8f4 8m4 1990 7.6m 10g 8.3m* 8.3m 8h3 10f4 8f 15.3f 12m5] leggy, light-framed filly: plater: returned to form and won for first time in handicap (no bid) at Windsor in July: had stiff tasks last 2 outings: stays 1¼m: acts on hard ground: mulish at stalls fourth outing, slowly away next 2: sold 3,300 gns Newmarket Autumn Sales. *M. Blanshard.*

TWILIGHT FIESTA (IRE) 2 b.c. (Apr 22) Burslem 123–Caithness 78 64 (Connaught 130) [1990 5m4 5m3 6g2 5m5 7g 7f* 7g2 8m 7s4 8.2s] IR 6,800F, 10,500Y: smallish, workmanlike colt: good mover: sixth foal: half-brother to 9f to 1½m winner Firelight Fiesta (by Sallust): dam disappointing granddaughter of high-class filly Almeira: quite modest performer: won seller (retained 9,500 gns) at Wolverhampton in August after troubled run: best form at 7f: acts on any going: very slowly away final outing. *Mrs J. R. Ramsden.*

TWILIGHT FLAME (IRE) 2 ch.c. (Apr 26) Red Sunset 120–Fleur-de-Luce 56 (Tumble Wind (USA)) [1990 6g 6d 6d a8g a8g2] 13,500Y: rather leggy, close-coupled colt: second foal: half-brother to Irish 3-y-o Lady Be Magic (by Burslem), successful at 6f: dam Irish 9.5f winner: plating-class maiden: best effort on all-weather at Lingfield on final start: better suited by 1m than 6f: trained first 2 starts by D. Elsworth. *M. R. Channon.*

TWO BADGES (IRE) 2 ch.c. (May 26) Montekin 125–Lucy Lacerre 75 (Sallust 134) [1990 a6g a6g4] 2,800F: fifth living foal: half-brother to a good winner in Scandinavia and an Irish bumpers winner: dam lightly-raced half-sister to top-class French hurdler Hardatit: ridden by 7-lb claimer, over 3 lengths fourth of 16 in maiden at Southwell in September: will be better suited by 7f + . *R. J. Muddle.* **62**

TWO LEFT FEET 3 b.c. Petorius 117–Whitstar 93 (Whitstead 125) [1989 7m2 8f* 8.2g* 7g* 1990 8m2 7f2 11.5m2 10.5m 12f4 7.6v* 8g* 8s4] tall, lengthy colt: good walker: poor mover: off course over 3 months then put up useful performances to win £9,700 handicap at Chester (by 10 lengths) in October and listed race (by 2 lengths from Swordsmith) at Newmarket in November: fourth in listed race at Maisons-Laffitte on final start: best at around 1m (rather headstrong over further): seems best with give in the ground and goes extremely well on heavy: sweating and edgy before third intended start (spread plate): game. *Sir Mark Prescott.* **109**

TWO REALMS 4 b.f. Another Realm 118–Two Shots (Dom Racine (FR) 121) [1989 8g6 9f 8g 10g 10f2 12m 10f4 9f a8g 1990 8f 10.1m5 a11g] close-coupled, good-bodied filly: poor plater: appears to stay 1¼m: acts on any going: blinkered once at 3 yrs: has raced with head in air: takes keen hold and has worn pricker: sold 1,050 gns Ascot November Sales. *K. O. Cunningham-Brown.* **—**

TWOTIME BID 4 b.g. Taufan (USA) 119–Avebury Ring (Auction Ring (USA) 123) [1989 9g 9f6 8s* 8g2 8g* 1990 8f 10v 8f 8f* 7.5d* 8m3 8m3 8.2d3 8m 7m2 7m*] good-topped gelding: has a round action: successful in claimer at Pontefract in May and handicaps at Beverley in June and Newmarket (in good style) in October: suited by 7f to 1m: acts on any going: bandaged seventh start: consistent. *Miss S. E. Hall.* **78**

TWO TOTAL 5 b.g. Noalcoholic (FR) 128–Double Shuffle 103 (Tachypous 128) [1989 NR 1990 a10g a7g a8g] leggy, sparely-made gelding: poor maiden: visored second start. *S. Dow.* **—**

TYBURN LAD 3 gr.g. Belfort (FR) 89–Swing Is Back (Busted 134) [1989 5s 7g 7.5f6 8f 7g 6f 6g 1990 12m 15.3m 8g3 8f 8f 8.2g6 10.6v4 10d 9s2] lengthy, angular gelding: has a round action: plater: stays 1¼m: has form on firm going, but best as 3-y-o with some give: bandaged near-fore fourth start: visored last 7 outings: winning hurdler. *H. J. Collingridge.* **40**

TYBURN TREE 3 b.c. High Top 131–Catalpa 115 (Reform 132) [1989 8v* 1990 10g5 11.5m3 12m3 10m] strong, angular colt: has a rather round action: won maiden at Newbury as 2-y-o: 3½ lengths third of 4 to eased Pirate Army at Chepstow, weakening over 1f out, third and easily best effort in minor events: bit backward, tailed off in £8,300 handicap 3 months later: should be well suited by middle distances: sold 20,000 gns Newmarket Autumn Sales. *H. R. A. Cecil.* **90**

TYLERS WOOD 5 br.g. Homing 130–Beryl's Jewel 86 (Siliconn 121) [1989 5g 6h3 5.1m5 6m6 5g6 5f* 6h 1990 a6g4 a5g3 a5g4 5m3 5m 5f5] smallish, compact gelding: quite modest handicapper: not raced after July: stays 6f: yet to race on soft going, acts on any other: has run well when edgy and sweating. *S. Dow.* **60**

TYRIAN 3 b.f. Elegant Air 119–Character Builder 92 (African Sky 124) [1989 6g 7g 6g 1990 8f a8g 7g4 10.2f 6m2 10.6m 10.6g 8f3] leggy, lengthy filly: moderate mover: moderate plater: stays 1m: acts on firm going: has run well in blinkers: sold out of Sir Mark Prescott's stable 5,600 gns Newmarket July Sales after fifth start. *J. H. Baker.* **43**

TYRIAN BELLE 5 b.m. Enchantment 115–Chasten (Manacle 123) [1989 5s3 5f6 5g4 6f4 6g4 a6g2 a6g2 1990 6v 6m2 6m2 5g* 6m6 5m6 5m 6g5] strong-quartered, workmanlike mare: modest handicapper: didn't have to be at best to win claimer (claimed £10,000) at Goodwood in June: below form after, blinkered final outing: stays 6f: probably not at her best on firm going, acts on any other. *P. F. I. Cole.* **69**

TYRIAN PRINCE 3 b.g. Norwick (USA) 120–Chasten (Manacle 123) [1989 6f4 1990 a8g 7f 5f5 5g3 6m4 7g 7h6] leggy gelding: plating-class maiden: stays 6f: acts on firm going: blinkered third, fourth and sixth starts: often sweating. *P. F. I. Cole.* **50**

TYRIAN PURPLE (IRE) 2 b.c. (Apr 9) Wassl 125–Sabrine (Mount Hagen (FR) 127) [1990 6f5 6m5 8m2 10s5] IR 6,200F: leggy colt: half-brother to 1986 Irish 2-y-o 6f winner Solany (by Encino): dam Irish middle-distance performer from family of Slip Anchor: 33/1, 1½ lengths second of 13, leading halfway and keeping on well, to Orujo in maiden at Leicester in October, first run for 2 months and easily best effort: should stay 1¼m. *R. Hollinshead.* **77**

TYRNIPPY 4 b.c. Tyrnavos 129–Floral 82 (Floribunda 136) [1989 7g⁴ 7g* 6s² **58** 7g⁶ 8d* 8.5d⁵ 7f 7f⁶ 8.2g 8m 8.2g 8.2d 7g 7g 1990 8.2g a11g² a11g⁴ 9g a11g* 8.2d 10v⁴ a12g⁵ 8d⁴ a12g a11g⁶] smallish, sparely-made colt: moderate mover: won seller (bought in 4,200 gns, apprentice ridden) at Southwell in September: finds 1m on short side nowadays, and probably stays 1½m: suited by an easy surface: wore bandage off-hind towards end of season (also near-fore final outing). *M. Brittain.*

TYRONE BRIDGE 4 b.g. Kings Lake (USA) 133–Rhein Bridge 107 (Rheingold **110** 137) [1989 10v* 14m* 16f 14m* 12m² 14d² 12s³ 1990 12d* 20d² 16g² 14g⁴] leggy, angular gelding: very useful stayer: in frame in Irish St Leger at the Curragh for last 2 seasons, blinkered when fourth to Ibn Bey in September: had beaten Sesame 2½ lengths in moderately-run minor event at Beverley and finished second to Ashal, battling on gamely, in Gold Cup at Royal Ascot in June: suited by test of stamina: goes very well on a soft surface: tough: good novice hurdler. *M. C. Pipe.*

TYRWHITT TRYST (IRE) 2 b.g. (Feb 11) Prince Regent (FR) 129–White — Goddess 65 (Red God 128§) [1990 6f 5m⁵ a8g] IR 2,800Y, 5,400 2-y-o: small, stocky gelding: poor mover: half-brother to quite moderate middle-distance performer China God (by Cumshaw), winning sprinter Manx God (by Welsh Saint) and a winner abroad: dam stayed 1m: bit backward, soundly beaten in varied races. *D. W. Chapman.*

U

ULURU (IRE) 2 b.c. (Feb 23) Kris 135–Mountain Lodge 120 (Blakeney 126) **61** p [1990 7g⁵] 75,000Y: fourth foal: half-brother to 1¼m winner Turbine Blade (by Kings Lake): dam winner of Cesarewitch and Irish St Leger: 20/1, ran green when 14 lengths fifth of 17 to Aghaadir in maiden at Salisbury in October: sure to do better. *B. W. Hills.*

UNANIMOUS (IRE) 2 b.c. (May 2) Fairy King (USA)–Consensus (Majority **86** Blue 126) [1990 6m³ 6m* 6m² 6g⁴ 6m³] IR 6,600F, 56,000Y: close-coupled colt: moderate mover: half-brother to several winners, including very smart 1m to 1¼m horse Princes Gate (by Realm) and good Italian winner Mispy (by Pall Mall): dam Irish 2-y-o 6f winner, is half-sister to very smart miler Pally: fair performer: won maiden at Ripon in July: twice ran very well in nurseries afterwards: will stay 7f. *A. C. Stewart.*

UNASSUMING 2 ch.g. (May 28) Vaigly Great 127–Petard 112 (Mummy's Pet **44** 125) [1990 5g⁵ 6m 5m 8.2g 6d] 7,200Y, 10,500 2-y-o: workmanlike gelding: half-brother to 1m and 9f winner Boy Jamie (by Nicholas Bill) and 2 winners by Monsanto, including quite useful 1983 2-y-o sprinter Stanley The Baron: dam won five 5f races: poor maiden: best effort first outing. *Mrs J. R. Ramsden.*

UNCERTAIN 2 ch.c. (Mar 29) Noalto 120–Paridance (Doudance 99) [1990 7s 7s] — sixth foal: half-brother to 6f winner Pine Hawk (by Algora): dam of no account: well beaten in maidens at Doncaster (green, slowly away) and Newcastle (in touch 4f on favoured side) in autumn. *M. Johnston.*

UNCERTAIN DATE 3 b.f. Habitat 134–Sooner Or Later (Sheshoon 132) [1989 — NR 1990 7m] IR 60,000Y: big, rather leggy filly: closely related to 6f and 7f winner Soon To Be (by Hot Spark) and half-sister to several winners, including fairly useful stayer Sunny Look (by Lombard): dam lightly-raced half-sister to Oaks-placed Suni and Media Luna: 40/1, last of 9 in maiden at Newmarket in April: moved well to post. *B. W. Hills.*

UNCLE BOBBY 3 ch.g. King Persian 107–Honi Soit (Above Suspicion 127) — [1989 6m 7g² 1990 10m] close-coupled, sparely-made gelding: has a quick action: second of 4 in minor event at Wolverhampton in July at 2 yrs: bandaged, hampered when well behind in August claimer (moved moderately down) only start in 1990: will be suited by further than 7f. *Miss S. J. Wilton.*

UNCLE ERNIE 5 b.g. Uncle Pokey 116–Ladyfold 60 (Never Dwell 89) [1989 — 10.2g 12.3s³ 10s² 12d³ 12.3f² 14g 1990 12g] leggy, workmanlike gelding: has a round action: modest handicapper at 4 yrs: best at 1¼m to 1½m: acts on any going: leading novice chaser. *J. G. FitzGerald.*

UNDERTONES 3 b.f. Song 132–Tattle 61 (St Paddy 133) [1989 5m⁵ 5f³ 5g⁶ 5d **43** 6g 5g a6g⁴ 1990 5m 8m 6s 5g⁶ a5g² a5g 5d 5m a6g 5g 5.1m 5m 5d 5g a6g] rather leggy filly: poor maiden: easily best 3-y-o efforts at Southwell fifth and sixth starts: stays 6f: has run well for 7-lb claimer: blinkered 9 times (also hooded final start) in 1990 but seems best without: sold 775 gns Ascot November Sales. *J. A. Glover.*

UNEX-PLAINED 7 b.g. Last Fandango 125–Miss Pinkerton (Above Suspicion — 127) [1989 NR 1990 13s] rather angular gelding: quite modest handicapper as 3-y-o: never near to challenge at Hamilton in April, only subsequent outing on flat: best form at around 1m: possibly unsuited by firm going: sometimes used to wear blinkers: fair hurdler/chaser at his best. *G. M. Moore.*

UNINVITED 3 b.f. Be My Guest (USA) 126–Fai La Bella (USA) 85 (Fifth Marine 73 (USA)) [1989 NR 1990 8g 10m² 8s²] leggy, angular filly: third foal: dam out of unraced half-sister to smart filly Kootenai, showed much improved form at 4 yrs, winning 4 times at 1¼m: modest form: second in claimer at Goodwood and maiden (made most) at Newcastle in the autumn: seems suited by 1¼m: sold 5,600 gns Newmarket December Sales. *Pat Mitchell.*

UNKNOWN QUANTITY 5 b.g. Young Generation 129–Pas de Deux 80 107 (Nijinsky (CAN) 138) [1989 7.6f* 10g* 10s* 12f⁶ 1990 10g 10m 10m² 10f³ 10g² 9m] leggy, quite attractive gelding: useful performer: ran very well when second in valuable handicaps won by Song of Sixpence at Ascot and Lord of Tusmore, leading still virtually 1½f out, at Newbury: stayed 1¼m: possibly unsuited by very firm going, acted on any other: genuine: dead. *W. Hastings-Bass.*

UNPAID MEMBER 6 b.g. Moorestyle 137–Sunningdale Queen 88 (Gay Fan- — dango (USA) 132) [1989 10.2g⁶ 1990 a14g⁴ 16.5m⁶] smallish, workmanlike gelding: has a round action: won maiden at Galway at 4 yrs: well beaten in handicaps in 1990: stays 1½m: acts on dead going, but probably not at best on very soft: winning hurdler in April: changed hands 9,600 gns Ascot September Sales. *P. A. Blockley.*

UNTITLED (USA) 3 br.c. Far Out East (USA)–Majestic Gina (USA) (Ambio- 63 poise) [1989 NR 1990 a8g⁴ 10g a11g² a12g] $16,000Y: seventh foal: half-brother to several minor winners in USA: dam won at up to 9f: quite modest maiden: staying-on second in claimer at Southwell in November: off course over 7 months after debut: should stay 1½m. *J. W. Hills.*

UNVEILED 2 ch.f. (Jan 26) Sayf El Arab (USA) 127–Collegian 90 (Stanford 121§) 72 [1990 6m³ 5f* 5d⁶ 6g 5m⁵] 14,000Y: good-quartered filly: second foal: sister to modest 6f (at 2 yrs) to 1½m winner South Sands: dam 6f and 1m winner: won maiden at Salisbury in May: sweating, ran poorly after in valuable events and a nursery: trained first 4 starts by M. McCormack. *R. J. Hodges.*

UNWANTED TREASURE (USA) 2 b.f. (May 14) Cozzene (USA)–When And 66 If (USA) (Dr Fager) [1990 5m³ 5m* 5m 5m 6d] $15,000Y: lengthy, good-quartered filly: half-sister to several winners in USA, including Machalstua (by Stage Door Johnny), successful at up to 9f, including in minor stakes: dam won at up to 7f: quite modest performer: odds on, won maiden at Ripon in August: ran well in nursery at Warwick penultimate start: should be better suited by 6f than 5f: seems unsuited by softish ground: sold 5,200 gns Newmarket December Sales. *J. Etherington.*

UP-A-POINT 5 gr.g. Rusticaro (FR) 124–Malmsey (Jukebox 120) [1989 NR 1990 47 12m³ 10m³ 12f 10s² 8f³ 11d⁵ 9s] tall gelding: poor handicapper: headstrong, and should prove best at up to 1¼m: seems to act on any going: has worn crossed noseband: a difficult ride, and isn't entirely genuine. *F. H. Lee.*

UPPER CIRCLE 3 b.f. Shirley Heights 130–Odeon 114 (Royal And Regal (USA)) — [1989 NR 1990 10.6d 12g] fifth live foal: sister to 1987 2-y-o 7f winner Shirley Superstar and half-sister to useful 7f winner Moviegoer (by Pharly) and useful sprinter Si Signor (by Habitat): dam very useful at up to 1¾m: no worthwhile form in autumn maiden and minor event. *L. Cumani.*

UP THAT DRIVE 2 gr.g. (Feb 5) Kalaglow 132–Vitry 48 (Vitiges (FR) 132) 52 [1990 6m a8g] 9,000F: leggy, rather angular gelding: first foal: dam, stayed 1½m, is half-sister to very useful 6f and 1¼m winner Homeboy: backward and green, around 9 lengths eighth of 17, staying on well, at Leicester, first and better effort in autumn claimers. *M. H. Tompkins.*

UP THE LADDER 6 gr.g. Taufan (USA) 119–Magnesia (Upper Case (USA)) — [1989 NR 1990 8.2s] workmanlike, close-coupled gelding: moderate mover: very lightly raced on flat nowadays: stays 1m: blinkered once. *D. J. Wintle.*

UP THE WAGON 3 ch.c. Formidable (USA) 125–Skiboule (BEL) (Boulou) 43 d [1989 8m a8g 1990 a10g a10g² a10g⁵ a10g⁵ 12f 12f⁶ 12.2m 11g 12g 10g] small, workmanlike colt: poor walker and mover: poor maiden: second in claimer at Lingfield, easily best effort: stays 1¼m: blinkered fourth start. *C. N. Allen.*

UPTON PARK 5 br.g. High Top 131–Polly Packer 81 (Reform 132) [1989 12m⁵ 73 14g³ 16.1g⁴ 17.4s³ 16.2d³ 18g 1990 12f³ 14m 18.4d 16m³ 18d] leggy, good-topped gelding: easy mover: modest handicapper: first run for 4½ months, good third at

Nottingham in September: stays well: probably acts on any going: often wears crossed noseband: trained until after third start by J. W. Watts: winning novice hurdler. *J. R. Fanshawe.*

UPWARD TREND   4 ch.f. Salmon Leap (USA) 131–Ivory Home (FR) (Home **101** Guard (USA) 129) [1989 9v² 10s* 10d* 10g² 10m⁵ 8g* 8g² 8g² 9g* 8g* 9.2g 1990 8f 8g³ 10g 8m 14g] good-bodied filly: very useful winner as 3-y-o, including Group 3 Mount Coote Stud EBF Matron Stakes at the Curragh: little form in 1990 apart from third to Esprit d'Etoile in Group 3 race at the Curragh: last of 24 in Lincoln Handicap at Doncaster almost 3 months earlier: suited by 1m: best on an easy surface. *J. S. Bolger, Ireland.*

URFAN   3 br.c. Valiyar 129–Nafla (FR) (Arctic Tern (USA) 126) [1989 5f⁵ 5f⁴ 6m⁵   — §
1990 6f 5d a8g 5m 5g 7.6m 5f 10m 5g 6d] smallish, rather sparely-made colt: poor maiden: bred to stay 1m: acts on dead going: visored once: often edgy: temperamental. *K. White.*

URRAY ON HARRY   6 b.g. Anfield 117–Noorina (Royal And Regal (USA)) [1989 **67** 8s 8d 8d 7f⁴ 8.2g* 7.6m⁴ 8m* 8.2g² 8.2d² 9f⁶ 10.6s⁵ 8v² 8g a8g⁵ 1990 8.2s 10v⁵ 8f* 9g⁵] smallish, workmanlike gelding: poor mover: quite modest handicapper: edgy, won at Ripon in April: ran well following month: should prove as effective at 1¼m as 1m: acts on any going: has won for apprentice: tends to idle, and suited by exaggerated waiting tactics. *R. Hollinshead.*

USA DOLLAR   3 b.c. Gabitat 119–Burglars Girl 63 (Burglar 128) [1989 6g 7m 8g **87** 1990 a10g⁴ 12g⁴ 10g⁵ 8g² 8m* 8m* 8m⁴ 8m⁶ a8g² 8m³ 9m 8m] big, strong colt: fair handicapper: led inside final 1f to win at Goodwood in June (very slowly away, seemed reluctant to race) and Newmarket (£15,400 event, started 33/1) in July: ran well in valuable events next 4 starts, poorly when sweating and edgy at Ascot on final one: goes well in strongly-run race at 1m, and should stay further: acts on good to firm ground: blinkered (usually) or visored after fourth start: difficult ride. *B. Gubby.*

USAYLAH   3 ch.f. Siberian Express (USA) 125–Nawara 75 (Welsh Pageant 132) **98** [1989 7m 8g 6g² 1990 9f 9g* 10m* 10m 10.6m* 10g⁶ 10g] lengthy, sturdy filly: fairly useful performer: won handicaps at Goodwood in June (2, jinking right 1½f out first occasion), Haydock in August and Sandown (made all) in September: ran poorly starts in between and behind in Longchamp listed race final outing: stays 10.6f: acts on good to firm ground. *J. L. Dunlop.*

USHBA (FR)   2 b.f. (Mar 24) Head For Heights 125–Uruguay (GER) 67 (Thatch **70 p** (USA) 136) [1990 6g 6m⁴] 3,200Y: compact filly: moderate walker: first foal: dam lightly-raced half-sister to 2 pattern winners in Germany: bit backward, over 8 lengths fourth of 7, weakening approaching final 1f, to Lee Artiste in minor event at Salisbury in September: sure to improve again. *M. D. I. Usher.*

V

VAGADOR (CAN)   7 ch.g. Vaguely Noble 140 Louisador (Indian Hemp 124) **78** [1989 NR 1990 16.2d³ 16m³ 16m⁴] close-coupled, good-bodied gelding: has a round action: fair handicapper: stays 2m: possibly unsuited by extremes of going: often sweats, freely so on first outing (pulled hard): has won for amateur: smart hurdler at his best. *G. Harwood.*

VAGUE DANCER   4 b.g. Vaigly Great 127–Step You Gaily 71 (King's Company **73 d** 124) [1989 6m* 6m³ 7f6m⁶ 6m⁶ 7m 1990 7f 8h 6m 7g⁵ 8.2d⁶ 8m 8d 7m 9.1s⁶] leggy, rather angular gelding: has a powerful, roundish action: fairly useful winner as 3-y-o: not so good in 1990 and ran poorly last 3 outings, blinkered first 2 occasions: seems to stay 1m: acts on good to firm and dead going: sometimes sweats, and has got on toes: none too consistent. *E. Weymes.*

VAGUE DISCRETION   5 b.g. Vaigly Great 127–Discreet 104 (Jukebox 120)   —
[1989 7d⁴ 8s 7m 6g⁶ 7g 1990 8.2m] strong, sturdy gelding: carries condition: moderate walker and mover: chipped bone in knee only start at 3 yrs: lightly raced and no form since first outing in 1989: suited by 7f: possibly needs a soft surface nowadays: bandaged and slowly away only start at 5 yrs. *R. J. R. Williams.*

VAGUE NANCY (IRE)   2 b.f. (Feb 19) Mazaad 106–Noble Nancy (Royal And   —
Regal (USA)) [1990 5m] 2,400Y: fourth foal: half-sister to 1m seller winner Dusky Nancy and a winner in Norway (both by Red Sunset): dam Irish 1¾m winner: unfavourably drawn in Lingfield seller in August. *C. J. Hill.*

VAGUE SHOT 7 ch.h. Vaigly Great 127–Cease Fire 112 (Martial 131) [1989 8g⁵ **95** 8d 7.2s 8m² 8f 8g⁴ 8s⁴ 8.5s⁵ 8g 1990 8g 8m⁶ 9.2g 8.5g⁵ 8m 8g² 7.2g 9m 7.6v] smallish, useful sort: usually looked well: has a quick action: useful at his best: creditable 5 lengths second to Just Three in listed race at the Curragh in July: faced very stiff tasks in pattern events previous 4 outings: stayed 9f: went particularly well with give in the ground, though seemingly unsuited by heavy going: blinkered once: sometimes wore bandages: retired to Benson Stud, Colchester, fee £700 (Oct 1st). *C. E. Brittain.*

VAIG APPEAL 3 b.c. Star Appeal 133–Dervaig 90 (Derring-Do 131) [1989 6g **75** 1990 6m² 5h⁴ 6m a8g⁶ 8g⁵] sparely-made, angular colt: has a quick action: modest performer: stays 1m: ran well for 7-lb claimer on reappearance: sold 6,000 gns Newmarket Autumn Sales. *M. R. Stoute.*

VAIGLY BLAZED 6 ch.g. Vaigly Great 127–Monkey Tricks 85 (Saint Crespin **34** III 132) [1989 14.6g 16g 14f 11.7m 11.7m 14m 16f 1990 18f⁴ 16.5m³ 16g² 16.5m 17. 1f⁵] workmanlike gelding: poor maiden: stays 2¼m: wore crossed noseband at 6 yrs: winning hurdler in August. *C. A. Horgan.*

VAIGLY PERCEPTIVE 4 b.c. Vaigly Great 127–Ash Gayle 49 (Lord Gayle — (USA) 124) [1989 10s 7d⁶ 6m² 6m 6m 8.3m 6m 6g 6g² 1990 8m 8.3g⁶ 10.1m] smallish colt: poor mover: poor maiden: best efforts at 6f, but at 4 yrs ran as though he should stay 1m: acts on good to firm and soft going: blinkered last 4 outings. *B. Stevens.*

VAIN GLORY (USA) 5 b.g. Sir Ivor 135–Eyeliner (USA) (Raise A Native) [1989 — NR 1990 10g⁴] won 3 times in selling company over hurdles in autumn: 50/1 on only second start on flat, 11½ lengths fourth of 6 in maiden at Beverley in August. *G. M. Moore.*

VAIN PRINCE 3 b.c. Sandhurst Prince 128–Vain Deb 66 (Gay Fandango (USA) **64** 132) [1989 8.2g 8.2g 10g 1990 9s 10.2f⁴ 12s⁶ 10g⁴ 11.5g² 12.3f* 16d] rangy colt: quite modest performer: won slowly-run 4-runner maiden claimer at Chester in July: ran as though something amiss at same course over 3 months later: will stay 1¾m: acts on any going: winning hurdler. *N. Tinkler.*

VAIN SEARCH (USA) 3 gr.f. Vigors (USA)–Hunt The Thimble (USA) 86 **57** (Turn And Count (USA)) [1989 7g⁶ 10g 1990 9m⁵ 8g 6g 7h⁵ 10g] rangy filly: quite modest form at best, little after reappearance: should prove suited by 9f +: acts on good to firm going: hung badly left and looked unsatisfactory third start: sold 5,200 gns Newmarket Autumn Sales. *M. A. Jarvis.*

VAIRAGYA (FR) 3 gr.c. Mendez (FR) 128–Exigence (USA) (Exclusive Native — (USA)) [1989 NR 1990 8m 11f³ 10m⁶ 11.5g 12d 10d a12g] 180,000 francs (£16,500 approx) Y: leggy, angular colt: moderate walker: fourth foal: half-brother to French provincial 1¼m winner Melygence (by Melyno) and modest maiden Azriell (by Lichine): dam, half-sister to Sportin' Life, ran twice in France: little worthwhile form, in mid-division facing stiff task for Southwell handicap final start: trained until after third by R. Guest. *A. Hide.*

VALATCH 2 ch.c. (Apr 17) Valiyar 129–Love Match (USA) (Affiliate (USA)) [1990 — 8g] IR 8,200F, 6,200Y: big, strong, lengthy colt: third foal: half-brother to bumpers winner Ard T'Match and 11f and 12.2f winner Burgoyne (both by Ardross): dam ran twice: burly and green, well beaten in maiden at Newmarket in October. *Pat Mitchell.*

VALCENA 3 ch.f. Glint of Gold 128–Baltimore Belle 95 (Bold Lad (IRE) 133) **49** [1989 6g 7g 1990 8g⁴ 10g⁵ 9m] sturdy filly: plating-class form: faced stiff task in ladies event final start: should stay beyond 1m: edgy on reappearance: sold 5,400 gns Newmarket July Sales. *W. Jarvis.*

VAL DES BOIS (FR) 4 gr.c. Bellypha 130–Vallee des Fleurs 116 (Captain's Gig **119** (USA)) [1989 9.2s* 10m* 8g 9.7m³ 8v³ 1990 8g* 8g* 9.2g² 8d³ 8g⁴ 8g⁴ 8s⁵] good-class colt: successful at Saint-Cloud in spring in Prix Edmond Blanc by 2 lengths from Mister Sicy and Prix du Muguet by ¾ length from Lady Winner: ran very well when ½-length second to Creator in Prix d'Ispahan at Longchamp: performed with credit next 3 outings, on middle one fourth to Distant Relative in Emirates Prix du Moulin de Longchamp: effective at 1m to 1¼m: yet to race on firm going, acts on any other. *Mme C. Head, France.*

VAL DI SUGA (IRE) 2 gr.f. (Feb 26) Vision (USA)–Weapon (Prince Ippi (GER)) — [1990 6m 6m 6m 7f] IR 2,800Y: leggy filly: fifth foal: dam half-sister to leading 1980 German 3-y-o Wauthi: behind in maidens and minor events. *E. A. Wheeler.*

VALIANT DASH 4 b.g. Valiyar 129–Dame Ashfield 90 (Grundy 137) [1989 10f — 8.2m⁶ 12m⁶ 10f 12f³ 12m⁶ 13.8g² 16.2m⁵ 1990 15.8d] workmanlike gelding: has a round action: appeared to put up easily best effort since 2 yrs when second in seller at Catterick in August, 1989: lacks turn of foot, and should stay well: often blinkered or visored at 3 yrs: sometimes claimer ridden: winning hurdler. *S. E. Kettlewell.*

VALIANT HOPE 3 ch.f. Valiyar 129–Lucky Fingers 81 (Hotfoot 126) [1989 6g⁵ 1990 7.6d⁵ 8g³ 8m] angular, workmanlike filly: moderate mover: quite modest maiden: will be suited by further: possibly needs an easy surface: sold 1,100 gns Newmarket Autumn Sales. *T. Thomson Jones.* **62**

VALIANT RED 4 ch.c. Blushing Scribe (USA) 107–Corvelle (Reliance II 137) [1989 8g 7h 6f⁵ 7m 6f³ 7m* 7.5f⁵ 7g 1990 a8g² a8g² a8g² a10g* a10g* 8.2s a10g⁵ 8m⁵ 8g] good-topped colt: quite modest handicapper: ran well on all-weather at Lingfield early in year, winning in February and March: didn't reproduce those efforts back on turf: stays 1¼m: acts on firm ground, seems unsuited by soft: visored once at 3 yrs. *D. J. G. Murray-Smith.* **62**

VALIANT SAINT 5 b.h. Welsh Saint 126–Corvelle (Reliance II 137) [1989 7v 6f a6g a6g 1990 a6g³ a8g⁴ a6g² a8g³ a7g⁴ a7g³ a6g⁶ a7g 7m a6g a7g* 7m 8.2m a6g*] good-bodied horse: bad mover: plating-class handicapper: seems best on all-weather and won at Southwell in August and September: best form at 6f to 7f: blinkered once at 3 yrs: none too easy a ride. *D. J. G. Murray-Smith.* **49**

VALIANT VICAR 3 b.g. Belfort (FR) 89–Shagra (Sallust 134) [1989 6m³ 6g⁶ 8.2s³ 7m 1990 8.2s a8g* 8g 9m] sparely-made, rather angular gelding: quite modest performer: ran poorly after winning seller (no bid) at Ayr in June by short head: suited by 1m: acts on good to firm ground and soft. *C. W. Thornton.* **59**

VALIANT WARRIOR 2 br.g. (Mar 27) Valiyar 129–Jouvencelle 68 (Rusticaro (FR) 124) [1990 7m 7g⁶ 8d⁶] 16,000Y: workmanlike gelding: second foal: half-brother to 3-y-o Land Afar (by Dominion) winner over 6f (at 2 yrs) and 9f: dam maiden, placed at up to 14.7f: plating-class form in maidens: sixth of 8, squeezed start, held up then staying on not knocked about, to Peking Opera at Leicester final start: will be better suited by 1¼m +: bandaged near-hind, and unruly stalls, second start. *H. Candy.* **58**

VALIANT WORDS 3 br.g. Valiyar 129–Wild Words 76 (Galivanter 131) [1989 7g 8f⁵ 8g 1990 7m⁶ 8f³ 7m* 7.6f⁴ 7g 7g 10g] leggy gelding: plating-class performer: made virtually all to win moderately-run handicap at Sandown in July, rallying well: may well stay beyond 1m: acts on firm going: bandaged near-fore final start. *R. Akehurst.* **57**

VALID POINT 2 b.c. (Feb 23) Valiyar 129–Arianna Aldini (Habitat 134) [1990 5f³ 6s* 7g³ 7g 8m 6d 8v⁴ 7.6v² 7s] 4,200Y: useful-looking colt: good walker: third foal: half-brother to fairly useful 6f and 1m winner Langtry Lady (by Pas de Seul): dam never ran: modest performer: made all in maiden at Haydock in June: very good second in nursery at Chester: ran moderately only subsequent start: stays 1m: acts well on very soft ground: sweating and edgy fourth outing: has carried head awkwardly. *M. Brittain.* **77**

VALIRA (USA) 3 ch.f. Nijinsky (CAN) 138–Condessa 121 (Condorcet (FR)) [1989 7m² 1990 10.5g³ 12m³ 10.5m² 10.6d 7d² a8g*] big, well-made filly: has plenty of scope: has a rather round action: fair performer: comfortably landed odds in maiden at Southwell in November: should stay 1½m: acts on good to firm ground. *B. W. Hills.* **81**

VALLANCE 2 b.c. (Mar 18) Top Ville 129–Kindjal 84 (Kris 135) [1990 6m³] robust colt: has plenty of scope: second foal: half-brother to 3-y-o Marian Evans (by Dominion): dam 1m winner from 3 starts is out of Yorkshire Oaks and Nassau Stakes winner Connaught Bridge: bit backward, over 4 lengths third of 6, staying on having run green, to Jimmy Barnie in maiden at Lingfield in June: looked sure to improve, particularly over further, but not seen out again. *P. W. Harris.* **70 p**

VALLAURIS 2 b.f. (Apr 7) Faustus (USA) 118–Valeur (Val de Loir 133) [1990 7g] 11,000Y: rangy filly: has scope: half-sister to several winners, including 1m and 9f winner Make Your Bid (by Auction Ring): dam second over 10.5f in France: 33/1 and green, around 6 lengths eighth of 20, going on well after slow start, to Campestral in maiden at Newmarket in November: sure to improve. *D. R. C. Elsworth.* **67 p**

VALLDEMOSA 4 ch.f. Music Boy 124–Astral Suite 82 (On Your Mark 125) [1989 5f 5f⁴ 5m 5f* 5g 5g⁴ 5m³ 5f 5f⁶ 5g⁵ 1990 5f⁵ 5m 5m⁶ 5m 5m* 5g 5m* 5g⁶ 5g⁶ 5m⁵ 6h⁵ 6g⁴ 5f 5m] compact filly: has a quick action: quite modest handicapper: won at Warwick (for second time) in June: far superior to rival in match at Catterick earlier in month: ran creditably in blinkers tenth start: best at 5f: acted on firm and dead going: suitable mount for 7-lb claimer: often went freely to post: in foal to Risk Me. *J. Berry.* **66**

VALLEY MILLS 10 ch.g. Red Alert 127–Haunting 79 (Lord Gayle (USA) 124) **37**
[1989 NR 1990 5g 6g a7g 6g 6f 6g⁵ 6g⁶] lengthy, strong gelding: one-time quite
useful handicapper: retains only a little ability: ideally suited by 7f or testing 6f:
needs give in the ground and used to go very well in the mud: has worn blinkers: has
sweated and got on edge: suited by strong handling and good gallop. *T. D. Barron.*

VALOUROUS 3 b.f. Bold Lad (IRE) 133–Midsummer Madness 66 (Silly Season —
127) [1989 6f 1990 a7g] leggy filly: well beaten in maidens. *M. A. Jarvis.*

VALTAKI 5 b.g. Valiyar 129–Taqa 85 (Blakeney 126) [1989 12.4g⁴ a10g 1990 —
10.2f⁶] small gelding: bad mover: fair winner at 2 yrs, very lightly raced on flat
nowadays: should stay 1½m: best effort on a soft surface (has won on hard over
hurdles). *L. J. Codd.*

VA LUTE (FR) 6 b.g. No Lute (FR) 129–Viverba (FR) (Sanctus II 132) [1989 12g **34**
8.2d 9s 1990 10.2f 10m⁵] leggy, lightly-made gelding: has a round action: improved
hurdler in 1989/90: evidently only poor on flat: lost plenty of ground at start both
outings in spring. *R. J. Holder.*

VANDA'S GIRL 2 b.f. (Jan 24) Noalto 120–Concorde Lady 66 (Hotfoot 126) **57**
[1990 a7g a8g a7g³ a7g a8g] 3,000 2-y-o: sparely-made filly: half-sister to several
winners here and abroad, including fairly useful 1m to 13.3f winner General Concorde (by Radetzky): dam showed little on flat or over hurdles: plating-class maiden:
stays 7f. *A. Bailey.*

VANIE 3 b.f. Niniski (USA) 125–Vadrouille (USA) 111 (Foolish Pleasure (USA)) **75**
[1989 NR 1990 12m⁵ 11g* 12.4m⁶ 13m* 15m² 16m] leggy, rather angular filly:
moderate mover: third foal: half-sister to 1½m seller winner Vagog (by Glint of
Gold), later fair hurdler: dam, from good family, won over 1m and 1¼m: modest
performer: set pace when justifying favouritism at Hamilton in 3-runner maiden in
June and handicap in July: stays 15f. *P. Calver.*

VANISKI 3 b.g. Niniski (USA) 125–Voltigeuse (USA) (Filiberto (USA) 123) [1989 —
NR 1990 10m 10g⁶ 12.2d] leggy gelding: sixth foal: half-brother to 1¼m winner Volte
Face (by Blakeney) and 3 other winners: dam unraced daughter of sister to Valoris
and half-sister to Val de Loir: 33/1, well beaten in claimers. *Mrs Barbara Waring.*

VANNOZZA 2 ch.f. (Jan 24) Kris 135–Vilikaia (USA) 125 (Nureyev (USA) 131) **58**
[1990 5m⁴ 6m] leggy, close-coupled filly: second foal: sister to 3-y-o Villeroi, winner
over 5f (at 2 yrs) to 1m: dam effective from 5f to 1m, is half-sister to good filly at up to
1m Maximova and daughter of half-sister to 2000 Guineas winner Nonoalco: around
8 lengths fourth of 13, finishing strongly having been well behind and green, to
Maraatib in minor event at Bath: well backed, soon pushed along, lost place 2f out
and eased considerably in maiden at Redcar later in October. *M. R. Stoute.*

VANROY 6 b.g. Formidable (USA) 125–Princess Tavi (Sea Hawk II 131) [1989 8s **86**
7.6m 7m² 7g² 8.5m⁶ 8f 8f⁶ 8f⁴ 8g a10g a8g* a8g 1990 8f⁴ 7g⁴ 7m 7g 7g² 7.6m⁵ 8.3m⁵
11.7m⁵ 8g³ 8g⁵ 9m a8g⁶ a8g² a8g* a7g*] sturdy gelding: carries plenty of condition:
has a rather round action: visored when winning handicaps at Lingfield in
December: suited by 7f to 1m: best recent form on good ground on turf or on
all-weather: went freely to post and hung badly left sixth outing. *J. R. Jenkins.*

VAN WINKLE 3 b.g. Jalmood (USA) 126–Daydreamer 78 (Star Gazer 123) [1989 —
NR 1990 6d 7g 8g 10m 10g 10g⁶] 7,000Y: half-brother to numerous winners here and
abroad, including 1988 2-y-o 5f winner Taylors Appeal (by Star Appeal), successful 3
times over 1m in Italy in 1990, and 1¼m winner Queen Mathilda (by Castle Keep):
dam won 1m seller: sixth of 12 in claimer at the Curragh in June: ran in Epsom
maiden time before: dead. *Kevin Connolly, Ireland.*

VARNISH 3 ch.f. Final Straw 127–Rainbow's End 83 (My Swallow 134) [1989 7g² —
7m* 8g⁴ 1990 7m 8m] unfurnished filly: good walker and mover: fair winner at 2 yrs:
facing stiff tasks, below form in valuable handicaps at Newmarket in July, 1990: bred
to stay 1m. *W. Hastings-Bass.*

VASSILEVA (IRE) 2 ch.g. (May 14) Gorytus (USA) 132–Belle Epoque 64 **84**
(Habitat 134) [1990 6g* 5g⁶ 5g³ 6m⁴ 7m⁵ 7m] small, good-quartered gelding:
second foal: half-brother to Irish 3-y-o Aminata (by Glenstal), fairly useful 5f and 6f
winner at 2 yrs: dam stayed 7f, is sister to top-class sprinter Double Form and
half-sister to smart middle-distance filly Scimitarra: won early-season maiden at
Fairyhouse by 6 lengths: in frame afterwards in small-field minor events at Bellewstown and Gowran Park: never able to challenge in Norfolk Stakes at Royal Ascot
second outing or in GPA National Stakes at the Curragh on final one: stays 7f. *J. S.
Bolger, Ireland.*

VA TOUJOURS 3 b.f. Alzao (USA) 117–French Princess 94 (Prince Regent (FR) **101**
129) [1989 6g* 7g* 7g³ 1990 9m* 9.2g] strong, workmanlike filly: suffered knee

972

injury final start at 2 yrs: 20/1 and carrying condition on first run for over 10 months, returned with useful performance to win listed race at York in September by ¾ length from Message Pad, leading inside final 1f: second favourite, not discredited when one-paced ninth of 14 in moderately-run Prix de l'Opera at Longchamp month later: should stay 1¼m. *H. J. Collingridge.*

VA UTU 2 b.c. (Apr 15) Balliol 125–Flame 49 (Firestreak 125) [1990 6g 7m⁶ 10g] 65 p small, angular colt: third foal: dam second in 7f seller at 2 yrs, only season to race, is sister to middle-distance performer Ridgefield: late progress in maidens at York and Chepstow in October: soundly beaten in listed race at Newmarket final start: likely to do better back at shorter. *M. R. Channon.*

VAX LADY 3 ch.f. Millfontaine 114–Opinebo 82 (Nebbiolo 125) [1989 5d² 5m* 98 5m* 6g² 6g³ 6g 1990 6g⁶ 6f⁴ 5d 5m² 5m⁶ 5f³ 6g* 5g 6g* 6d 6d⁴] small, rather lightly-made filly: fairly useful sprinter: won minor event (made all) at Leicester in August and listed race (soon under pressure but always close up) at Phoenix Park in September: ran badly in Ayr Gold Cup and Goodwood minor event last 2 starts: will prove suited by 6f or stiff 5f: acts on good to firm ground. *J. L. Spearing.*

VAX PRINCESS (IRE) 2 br.f. (Apr 12) Jester 119–Cape of Storms (Fordham 50 (USA) 117) [1990 5f⁶ 5g³ 5m⁴ 5f 6d 6d] 3,000 (privately) Y: workmanlike filly: keen walker: second foal: half-sister to 3-y-o Hannah's Choice (by Kampala): dam, raced only at 2 yrs, out of staying half-sister to top-class sprinter Sandford Lad: poor maiden: should stay 6f: best form on a sound surface. *J. L. Spearing.*

VAYRUA (FR) 5 ch.g. Vayrann 129–Nabua (FR) (Le Fabuleux 133) [1989 NR 84 + 1990 12g⁵] big, good-topped gelding: fairly useful as 3-y-o, winner of amateurs race at Newmarket: burly, shaped well in handicap at same course in November: stays 1½m: probably acts on any going: leading juvenile hurdler in 1988/9 (has run only twice since). *G. Harwood.*

VEE M DOUBLEYOU 2 b.c. (Mar 16) Crofthall 110–Jamshera (Tender King — 123) [1990 7m] 1,000F: first foal: dam unraced twin: tailed off in seller at Wolverhampton in July. *B. Preece.*

VELOCE (IRE) 2 b.c. (Apr 19) Kafu 120–Joanns Goddess (Godswalk (USA) 130) 67 [1990 6m⁶ a6g 5f 6d³ 5m⁴] IR 3,500F, 8,200Y: first foal: dam Irish maiden: easily best effort staying-on third in maiden at Ayr in September: needs further than 5f, and will probably stay 7f. *A. Bailey.*

VELVET PEAK 2 ch.f. (May 21) Superlative 118–Velvet Pigeon 70 (Homing — 130) [1990 6d 7m 7s] 8,800F, 6,000Y: close-coupled, good-quartered filly: second foal: dam lightly-raced half-sister to useful middle-distance performer Heighten and daughter of half-sister to Final Straw and Achieved: tailed off in maidens. *S. T. Harris.*

VELVET PEARL 7 ch.m. Record Token 128–Pearlinda (Gulf Pearl 117) [1989 — NR 1990 13s] strong, lengthy mare: winning plater over 1¼m as 5-y-o: visored, never dangerous in handicap at Hamilton in April: best form in blinkers. *I. Semple.*

VENDREDI TREIZE 7 b. or br.g. Lucky Wednesday 124–Angel Row 96 42 (Prince Regent (FR) 129) [1989 8v⁶ 8m 7f 7m 6g 7f 1990 a5g⁴ 6g⁶ a7g² a8g⁴ a5g* a7g⁶] tall gelding: bad mover: poor handicapper: won at Southwell in July, switched to race alone far side: ran moderately week later: stays 7f: acts on firm and dead going: sometimes blinkered: apprentice ridden at 7 yrs: wandered second start. *S. R. Bowring.*

VENICE IN PERIL (IRE) 3 ch.g. (Apr 11) Lomond (USA) 128–Rising Tide 101 — (Red Alert 127) [1990 6m 6d] IR 17,000Y: workmanlike gelding: closely related to fairly useful Irish sprinter Northern Tide (by North Pole) and half-brother to winners in France and Malaysia: dam 2-y-o 5f winner didn't train on, is half-sister to useful 1983 Irish 2-y-o King Persian: prominent to halfway in maiden at Hamilton and minor event at Ayr. *M. Johnston.*

VENT DE MER 4 b.g. Tumble Wind (USA)–Ocean Boulevard (Pitskelly 122) — [1989 5s² 5f 1990 a5g 7g] strong, lengthy, good-quartered gelding: second in handicap at Sandown early as 3-y-o: very lightly raced and well beaten since: easily best form over 5f on soft ground. *J. Akehurst.*

VENTURIST (USA) 3 b.c. Al Nasr (FR) 126–Sleek Lassie (USA) (Northern 91 Prospect (USA)) [1989 NR 1990 7m 10m³ 10.4m* 10g 11.5m* 11.7m² 12v³ 12.3v⁴] $70,000Y: big, good-topped colt: third foal: dam unraced daughter of half-sister to very useful 7f winner Alquoz: fairly useful performer: won maiden at Chester in July and 5-runner handicap at Yarmouth in September: stays 1½m well: acts on good to firm ground, not heavy: usually makes the running: joined N. Henderson. *J. Gosden.*

VENT-X-FLYER 2 gr.c. (Mar 21) Carwhite 127–Sophistication (Morston (FR) 125) [1990 a7g] first foal: dam unraced: slowly away and always behind in late-year maiden at Southwell. *W. J. Pearce.* —

VENUS OBSERVED 2 ch.f. (May 22) Sharpo 132–Fair And Wise 75 (High Line 125) [1990 5m⁴ 7m* 7m⁶] 9,800Y: leggy, rather angular filly: second foal: sister to 3-y-o Musical Note: dam suited by 1¾m: won moderately-run maiden at Salisbury: creditable sixth of 9, off bridle at halfway, to Shadayid in minor event at Ascot later in September: will stay 1m. *H. Candy.* 73

VERBARIUM (USA) 10 br.g. Verbatim (USA)–Havre (Mister Gus) [1989 8g⁵ 8g 8v² 10s⁴ 10m⁵ 10f* 12h³ 12.3m⁴ 10.8m* 11s 1990 10.2f 10m 8m⁶ 10s 10f] close-coupled, workmanlike gelding: winning plater (including for apprentice) as 9-y-o: never near to challenge most starts in spring, often slowly away: best at up to 1¼m: acts on any going. *Mrs J. R. Ramsden.* —

VERDANT BOY 7 br.g. Green Dancer (USA) 132–Favorite Prospect (USA) (Mr Prospector (USA)) [1989 8g 6d 6.1f⁴ 6f 6g⁶ 6f 6g* 6m 7g⁶ 6m a8g* a7g* 1990 8f 8f 8g⁵ 8.2g⁴ 8m 8m a7g⁵ 7m⁴ 7g⁴ 8g 6g² 7d a8g a7g a7g³] quite attractive gelding: carries condition: moderate walker: quite modest handicapper: effective at 6f and stays 1m: best form on a sound surface: good mount for apprentice. *K. B. McCauley.* 61

VERDEUSE (FR) 3 ch.f. Arctic Tern (USA) 126–Toujours Vert 73 (Northfields (USA)) [1989 5m⁵ 7g 7m² 1990 8g⁵ 8g⁴ a7g³ 7d² 7g³ 8f⁵ 9f⁵ a10g* a10g³] sparely-made, angular filly: moderate mover: modest performer: won maiden at Lingfield in November: worth a try at 1½m: acts on firm and dead going: consistent: sold 10,500 gns Newmarket December Sales. *B. W. Hills.* 73

VERICA (USA) 2 ch.f. (Feb 15) Diesis 133–Verria (USA) 118 (Blushing Groom (FR) 131) [1990 7v*] first foal: dam French 1m and 9f winner out of a useful winner at up to 1½m: won 14-runner newcomers race at Maisons-Laffitte in November by ¾ length: sure to do better, particularly over 1m + . *F. Boutin, France.* ?

VERMONT MAGIC 2 b.g. (Apr 20) Elegant Air 119–Jove's Voodoo (USA) 74 (Northern Jove (CAN)) [1990 7g 7g 7g a8g⁶] 24,000Y: lengthy gelding: has scope: third foal: half-brother to 1m winner and hurdler Zamore and 3-y-o 1½m seller winner Spirit Away (both by Dominion): dam 6f winner: plating-class maiden: probably stays 1m. *W. Hastings-Bass.* 55

VERRE BLEU (FR) 3 ch.c. Crystal Glitters (USA) 127–Victory Tune (FR) (Dr Fager (USA)) [1989 7g² 8m⁴ 1990 10d³ 10.5g* 10m²] half-brother to several winners, including French 11.5f to 15f winner Vlassova (by Green Dancer): dam lightly-raced French 11f winner: won maiden at Longchamp in May: 3 lengths second to Dashing Blade in Prix Eugene Adam at Saint-Cloud 2 months later but not seen out again. *A. Fabre, France.* 108

VERRO (USA) 3 ch.c. Irish River (FR) 131–Royal Rafale (USA) (Reneged) [1989 7m² 1990 8m 10f 10m 7g⁵ 7m 8g] sturdy colt: quite modest form in maiden in June at 2 yrs: best effort since when staying-on fifth in handicap at Wolverhampton in July: bred to stay beyond 7f: sold out of G. Harwood's stable before final start 8,200 gns Newmarket Autumn Sales. *J. A. Bennett.* —

VERSAILLES ROAD (USA) 7 b.h. Blushing Groom (FR) 131–Lucinda Lea (USA) (Best Turn (USA)) [1989 12m⁴ 11.7m⁵ 10m³ 12m² 12.8m* 12m* 12m² 12f 12m* 12.3g⁶ 12m⁴ 10m⁴ 1990 10.1g⁵ 11.5m² 12g 16m⁵ 12m] strong, angular horse: carries condition: easy mover: has had operations for soft palate: fair winner as 6-y-o: below his best in 1990, running poorly final outing: then sent to join P. Bruen in Ireland: suited by 1½m and top-of-the-ground: has worn blinkers: bandaged on reappearance: good mount for inexperienced rider: usually has tongue tied down: races up with pace. *Mrs L. Piggott.* 69

VERTEX 2 c. (Feb 13) Shirley Heights 130–Rockfest (USA) 104 (Stage Door Johnny) [1990 7s] fourth foal: half-brother to useful French 1m winner Best Rock (by Try My Best) and a winner in Belgium: dam 2-y-o 7f and 1m winner stayed 1½m, is out of half-sister to very smart Glen Strae: showed signs of ability in maiden at Doncaster in November. *R. Charlton.* — p

VERY ADJACENT 5 b.h. Chukaroo 103–State Romance 67 (Free State 125) [1989 5s 5m 6m 5.8h⁵ 6f⁵ 6f⁴ 6f* 6h³ 1990 6m⁵ 6d 6d 6m⁴ 6m 6m 6m 7.6m 6d] leggy, lengthy horse: has a quick action: fair handicapper: ran well in competitive events at Newbury and Salisbury first and fourth starts, only form at 5 yrs: suited by 6f and top-of-the-ground: usually visored or blinkered (wasn't last 2 outings): sold 5,000 gns Newmarket Autumn Sales. *L. G. Cottrell.* 86 d

VERY DICEY 2 b.g. (Mar 29) Tremblant 112–Party Game 70 (Red Alert 127) [1990 5m⁵ 6m⁵ 6m⁵ 6g⁵ 5m* 5m 5m⁴ 5.8d²] strong, workmanlike gelding: second 76

foal: half-brother to 3-y-o Tiddly Winks (by Daring March): dam 6f winner stayed 7f: made all, showing much improved form, in maiden at Lingfield in September: ran well in nurseries final 2 starts: keen sort, likely to prove best at sprint distances: acts on good to firm ground and dead. *R. V. Smyth.*

VESTAL BELL 3 b.f. Shirley Heights 130–Vestal Virgin (USA) 91 (Hail To — §
Reason) [1989 NR 1990 10.2f³ 11.7m³ 12.5m⁶] leggy, angular filly: sixth foal: sister to 4-y-o Vestal Hills and closely related to 2 winners by Mill Reef, including 10.6f winner Tiber Creek, and useful but disappointing maiden Nonesuch Bay (also by Mill Reef): dam 1m and 1½m winner out of half-sister to Irish classic winners Reindeer, Santa Tina and Atherstone Wood: disappointing maiden: should stay 1½m: didn't look keen final start and is one to treat with caution. *I. A. Balding.*

VESTAL HILLS 4 b.g. Shirley Heights 130–Vestal Virgin (USA) 91 (Hail To —
Reason) [1989 NR 1990 11s 12m⁵ 16m 16m⁶ 12m 10f⁵] rangy gelding: fair form as 2-y-o: showed he'd retained some ability in amateurs handicap at Salisbury (sweating) on second outing: ran poorly after: should prove suited by 1¼m + : reportedly broke blood vessel on reappearance: sold 4,800 gns Newmarket Autumn Sales. *I. A. Balding.*

VESTIGE 3 ch.c. Remainder Man 126§–Starchy (Crisp And Even 116) [1989 7.5f 69
7m 8.2g⁴ 10g 1990 a8g² a8g³ a8g 12f⁶ 12.2m* 12m* 12.2m² 12.5g⁵ 13.8m* 16g⁵ 15.3f²] workmanlike colt: good mover: very useful plater: twice no bid then bought in 6,400 gns when winning at Catterick in April, Thirsk in May and Catterick in August: claimed to join J. O'Shea £7,359 final start: stays well: acts on firm ground: visored last 7 starts: suited by forcing tactics: sometimes on toes: game. *R. Hollinshead.*

VICEROY 3 b.g. Indian King (USA) 128–Bold Polly 67 (Bold Lad (IRE) 133) [1989 90
5g* 5m* 6f² 5d* 5m⁵ 1990 5d² 5d⁶ 5g 5d 6m⁵ 5g 5m] strong, well-made gelding: fairly useful performer: stays 6f: yet to race on soft going, has form on any other: blinkered last 3 starts, taking strong hold and finding nothing on second of them: has been slowly away: wears crossed noseband: often unimpressive in appearance. *W. J. Pearce.*

VICEROY AGAIN 5 ch.g. Krayyan 117–Regal Step 101 (Ribero 126) [1989 10.1m —
1990 11.7g 7f 8.2m] angular gelding: of little account: has been visored and blinkered. *T. Casey.*

VICEROY EXPRESS 3 ch.f. Jalmood (USA) 126–Viceroy Princess 65 56
(Godswalk (USA) 130) [1989 6m 5f⁵ 5f 6g 7g a7g a7g 1990 8m 10m 11.7m⁶ 10g² a12g³ a8g⁶ 10f* 10f 10g a10g] good-topped filly: carries condition: plating-class form: won handicap at Folkestone in August, soon leading and clear over 2f out: well below form after, blinkered when bit backward final start: suited by 1¼m: acts on firm ground. *J. R. Jenkins.*

VICEROY GEM (IRE) 2 ch.c. (Mar 27) Sallust 134–Gang Plank 84 (Tower 60
Walk 130) [1990 6m 8g 7g 7g a7g] 11,500F, 17,500Y: leggy, workmanlike colt: has a round action: half brother to 2 winners, including useful 1982 Irish sprinting 2-y-o Sweet Emma (by Welsh Saint): dam disappointing after 2 yrs, is half-sister to chaser Katmandu: quite modest maiden: ran well before form on all-weather: best effort at 1m. *R. Hannon.*

VICEROY JESTER 5 br.g. Jester 119–Midnight Patrol (Ashmore (FR) 125) 68
[1989 6s² 7v² 7d 7g⁵ 7f 8f 7g 7g 1990 8f² 8f⁴ 8f 9g 7f 8m⁵ 10g 10g³ 10f² 12m² 10g³ 12m³ 10.2m³ 10d² 12.2m* 12m² 12d⁴] leggy gelding: moderate mover: quite modest handicapper: co-favourite, won apprentice race at Warwick in October: stays 1½m: acts on any going: has worn blinkers, but not for long time: often sweats, and has got on edge: suitable mount for inexperienced rider: tough: won twice over hurdles in autumn. *R. J. Holder.*

VICEROY MAJOR 7 ch.g. Bay Express 132–Lady Marmalade (Hotfoot 126) —
[1989 12m 1990 a12g] good-bodied gelding: winning plater as 5-y-o: tailed off only 2 subsequent starts: stays 1½m: acts on any going: blinkered twice. *N. B. Thomson.*

VICKENDA 5 ch.m. Giacometti 130–Phlox 101 (Floriana 106) [1989 6g 6m 7m² 29
7f⁵ 7.6h 8.3g³ 8g⁶ 7m* 7m 7g⁵ 1990 6f 7.6m⁴ 7m 7m] angular, sparely-made mare: poor mover: poor handicapper: suited by about 7f: acts on any going: often visored: often slowly away: changed hands 1,900 gns Doncaster March Sales. *C. N. Allen.*

VICKI-VICKI VEE 5 ch.m. Busted Fiddle 90–Olymena (Royalty 130) [1989 10f —
6f 10.1m 8f 1990 10.8m] lightly-made mare: moderate mover: of little account. *J. M. Bradley.*

VICTORIA PRINCESS 3 b.f. King of Spain 121–Renira 60 (Relkino 131) [1989 55
6g 6g 1990 6m⁵ 6d⁶ 5m 5m⁶ 6m 6g 5m] compact, workmanlike filly: poor mover:

plating-class maiden: form only in handicap (set plenty to do) at Salisbury fourth start: should stay 6f: looked ill at ease on Epsom track: bandaged on reappearance. *C. C. Elsey.*

VICTORIA ROAD (IRE) 2 b.g. (Feb 29) Runnett 125–That's Swiss (Thatching 131) [1990 6g 6d³ 5d 6d] 16,500Y: lengthy, workmanlike gelding: has a quick action: second foal: dam ran once at 4 yrs in Ireland: quite modest form: caught eye in maiden at Doncaster final start, held up, several positions, very considerably handled then finishing really well: will stay 7f: should do better. *M. H. Easterby.*   **63** p

VICTORIA'S DELIGHT 3 br.f. Idiot's Delight 115–Hasty Dawn 80 (Dawn Review 105) [1989 NR 1990 10m 12.2f] plain, angular filly: third reported foal: dam middle-distance maiden: gave trouble at stalls and tailed off in maidens. *K. S. Bridgwater.*   —

VICTORIOUS DEED (USA) 3 ch.c. Roberto (USA) 131–Golden Highlights (USA) (Secretariat (USA)) [1989 NR 1990 8g* 10.5m⁴ 10d²] $500,000Y: fourth foal: brother to once-raced 1989 3-y-o Rozala and half-brother to 2 winners in USA, including fairly useful 1987 2-y-o 6f winner here Fariedah (by Topsider): dam stakes winner at up to 1m: won maiden at the Curragh in May: 2½ lengths last of 4, held up and never able to challenge, edging left, to Emperor Fountain in listed race (favourite but bit coltish, moved poorly down) at York then 6 lengths second to Topanoora in IR £6,900 event at Leopardstown 5 months later: better at 1¼m than 1m. *T. Stack, Ireland.*   **94**

VICTORIOUS PRINCE 3 b.c. Bold Lad (IRE) 133–Stracomer Queen 106 (Prince Tenderfoot (USA) 126) [1989 NR 1990 8f 8g 7g 8d a8g⁴ 7f⁶ 7m 7m 8f⁴ 8f⁵ 10m 11m* 10d⁵] IR 18,000Y: good-topped colt: poor walker: third foal: half-brother to lightly-raced maiden Gometra (by Lomond): dam winner over 7f and 1m in Ireland and third in Irish Oaks: plater: won handicap (no bid, settled well) at Redcar in October: should prove best at middle distances: acts on firm and dead going: visored tenth and eleventh (headstrong) outings: not an easy ride and has looked ungenuine: sold to join R. Lee 7,000 gns Newmarket Autumn Sales. *Sir Mark Prescott.*   **39**

VICTORY PIPER (USA) 3 ch.c. Nijinsky (CAN) 138–Arisen (USA) (Mr Prospector (USA)) [1989 7g⁴ 8s* 1990 10m⁶ 8m² 9g⁴ 12g⁵] rather leggy, good-topped colt: won Juddmonte EBF Beresford Stakes at the Curragh at 2 yrs: well-beaten last of 6 in Guardian Classic Trial at Sandown then second of 4 in minor event (sweating) at Newcastle, easily best efforts as 3-y-o: should be suited by middle distances: acts on good to firm ground and soft. *M. A. Jarvis.*   **91**

VICTORY TORCH (CAN) 5 b.g. Majestic Light (USA)–Victory Songster (USA) (Stratus 122) [1989 13.8d 11g³ 12m 13f⁶ 12m 8g² 9f⁵ 9g 12g 9s 1990 8.2s* 8v⁶ 8m² 10s 8.2s 11d⁶ 8g 7d] close-coupled gelding: hobdayed: moderate mover: 33/1-winner of 18-runner selling handicap (no bid) at Hamilton in April: ran moderately last 4 outings, off course nearly 4 months before final one: effective at 1m and stays 1½m: acts on good to firm and soft going. *K. B. McCauley.*   **37**

VIDEO DEALER 2 b.g. (May 18) Aragon 118–Ginnies Pet 106 (Compensation 127) [1990 6m] leggy, rather sparely-made gelding: half-brother to a winning plater: dam sprinter: bit backward, slowly away and little chance from halfway in maiden at Windsor in August. *C. A. Horgan.*   —

VIENTO (FR) 2 ch.c. (Feb 2) Vacarme (USA) 121–Force Nine (FR) (Luthier 126) [1990 7m] 190,000 francs (approx £17,600) Y: rather leggy, workmanlike colt: third reported foal: half-brother to a winning hurdler in France: dam, French 1½m winner, is half-sister to dam of Saint Estephe: bit backward, never able to challenge in maiden at Newmarket in October: dead. *P. A. Kelleway.*   —

VIGANO (USA) 4 ch.g. Lyphard (USA) 132–Pasadoble (USA) (Prove Out (USA)) [1989 8m 8m 8m 1990 11.1m a11g] medium-sized gelding: easily best effort in maidens as 3-y-o on second start: tailed off in handicaps in summer: has joined M. Pipe and won selling hurdle. *J. R. Jenkins.*   —

VIGLA 3 gr.f. Siberian Express (USA) 125–Egnoussa 76 (Swing Easy (USA) 126) [1989 NR 1990 8m] fourth foal: half-sister to Italian 4-y-o 1m winner Enoussian Breeze (by Formidable): dam, half-sister to very smart Devon Ditty, won over 7f: never dangerous in maiden at Yarmouth in June. *C. E. Brittain.*   —

VIKING LADY 2 b.f. (Mar 6) Music Boy 124–Frozen Asset (FR) (Northern Treat (USA)) [1990 7m 5v] lengthy filly: second living foal: dam lightly raced, from family of El Badr and Poachers Moon: always behind in sellers at Newmarket (backward, slowly away) and Ayr over 2 months later: subsequently sold 800 gns Newmarket Autumn Sales, resold 550 gns Ascot December Sales. *M. H. Tompkins.*   —

VILANIKA (FR)   4 b.f. Top Ville 129–Kamanika (FR) (Amber Rama (USA) 133)   77
[1989 8v² 9g⁵ 11.5m 8m⁴ 7m² 9m⁴ 7.6m² 8m² 8g 1990 8f² 8g 7m 8f⁵ 8.2m⁶ 8g* 9m]
tall, leggy filly: modest handicapper: won (for first time) at Salisbury in August:
suited by 1m: acts on any going: has run well when sweating and on edge: often pulls
hard: sold to join W. Holden's stable 3,000 gns Newmarket December Sales. *C. E.
Brittain.*

VILANY   2 b.f. (Apr 21) Never So Bold 135–Bellagio 68 (Busted 134) [1990 6d⁴ 6m   66
6g⁶] 23,000Y: angular, unfurnished filly: has a roundish action: third foal: half-sister
to 3-y-o Arany (by Precocious), successful at 6f (at 2 yrs) and 1m, and 1988 2-y-o
winner Slice (by Sharpo): dam 1¼m winner, stayed 1½m: quite modest form in
varied events, including Tattersalls Cheveley Park Stakes at Newmarket: will
probably be better suited by 7f. *M. H. Tompkins.*

VILCOE BAY   3 b.c. Roscoe Blake 120–Vilmainder 78 (Remainder 106) [1989 NR   —
1990 6g 5m 6f 8.2v⁵ 8m] workmanlike colt with scope: half-brother to successful 6f
to 1¼m plater Whangarei (by Gold Rod): dam won over 5f at 2 yrs: no worthwhile
form, in claimer and handicap last 2 starts. *B. A. McMahon.*

VILLA BIANCA   4 b.f. Mummy's Game 120–Belinda (Ragusa 137) [1989 6s³ 8.2s   —
9m 7f 9m⁵ 8m 8f 9s* 1990 11s⁵ 12g a12g 11d 12s a6g a6g a8g⁵ a12g] angular,
sparely-made filly: poor walker, turns fore-feet in: moderate mover: quite modest
winner late in 1989: little form as 4-y-o: needs further than 6f and stays 11f: needs
the mud: blinkered twice at 3 yrs: often ridden by 7-lb claimer: trained first 3 starts
by N. Graham. *S. T. Harris.*

VILLAGE PET   2 b.c. (Apr 2) Tina's Pet 121–Village Lass (No Mercy 126) [1990   62
5d⁴ 5f² 5f* 6g 5d 5m³ 5m⁶ 5f 5.3f⁵ 5.8d a7g] 1,600F, 4,200Y: leggy, angular, plain
colt: has a round action: half-brother to 1m and 1¼m winner Sunapa's Owlet (by
Derrylin): dam never ran: made all in maiden at Bath in May: well below form last 3
outings: may prove best at 5f: seems suited by firm ground: sweating seventh start.
R. A. Bennett.

VILLEROI   3 ch.c. Kris 135–Vilikaia (USA) 125 (Nureyev (USA) 131) [1989 6g   104
5g* 1990 7m³ 8d 7f* 8m* 7.3g 7.6v] lengthy, angular colt: useful handicapper: made
virtually all to win at Newcastle in July and Ripon (£8,200 event, by short head) in
August: well beaten last 2 starts: should prove best at up to 1m: acts on firm going,
not heavy: on toes final start: sold 48,000 gns Newmarket Autumn Sales to race in
Italy. *G. Harwood.*

VINEGAR BOB   3 b.g. Blushing Scribe (USA) 107–Gentle Gypsy 94 (Junius   —
(USA) 124) [1989 5s 1990 9g 8m 7d a12g a8g] strong, workmanlike gelding: no
worthwhile form, including in claimers: dead. *M. W. Easterby.*

VINTAGE   5 b.g. Noalcoholic (FR) 128–Good To Follow 82 (Wollow 132) [1989   85
10s 10f³ 12m² 10m² 10f* 11.7g* 11.7m* 12m* 11.7d⁴ 12f² 1990 12m³ 12g⁴ 12f 11.7m²
11.7m³ 12g⁴ 12g 12d³] strong, lengthy gelding: has round action: fair handicapper:
ran well fourth to sixth outings, hanging left and demoted second of them: better at
1½m than 1¼m: acts on firm and dead going: has worn crossed noseband, but didn't
at 5 yrs: sometimes sweats and gets on toes: usually held up. *Major W. R. Hern.*

VINTAGE ONLY   2 b.c. (Mar 5) Sayf El Arab (USA) 127–Bias 108 (Royal   108
Prerogative 119) [1990 5f* 5f³ 5d⁴ 5d* 5d² 6m* 6f* 6g² 5g* 5g³ 5m³ 6d⁴] 16,500Y:
close-coupled, quite good-bodied colt: quite good mover: half-brother to maidens by
Young Generation (quite modest miler Prejudice) and Free State: dam won from 7f
to 10.4f: useful colt: successful in maiden at Haydock in April and minor events at
Beverley, Catterick, Thirsk in summer and Ripon in September: placed 3 times in
pattern company too, very good third to Mujadil in Cornwallis Stakes at Ascot
penultimate start: stays 6f: possibly ideally suited by a sound surface: tends to hang:
usually looks really well. *M. H. Easterby.*

VINTAGE PORT (USA)   8 b.g. Blood Royal (USA) 129–Port Au Pass (USA)   64
(Pass (USA)) [1989 12f a14g² a16g² a14g² 1990 a12g⁵ a16g*] leggy gelding: favourite, won handicap at Lingfield in February: stays 2m: acts on firm going: sold 1,000
gns Ascot June Sales. *R. Akehurst.*

VINTAGE TYPE   3 b.g. Import 127–Marock Morley 59 (Most Secret 119) [1989   74
5m² 5m² 5m³ 1990 5m⁶ 7m³ a7g 7d⁴ 6m⁴ 7m² 7m* 7m⁶ 7d 6s a7g a6g] strong,
workmanlike gelding: modest performer: won handicap at Catterick in August:
better at 7f than 6f: acts well on good to firm going: blinkered tenth and eleventh
starts: mulish beforehand, found little on them: rather headstrong, and has worn a
crossed noseband: taken down early: sold out of J. W. Watts's stable 5,000 gns
Doncaster November Sales after eleventh start. *D. W. Chapman.*

VINTON VA   5 b.m. Crofter (USA) 124–Bold Flirt (USA) (Bold Ruler) [1989 10s   53
10d 9g⁶ 10.6d 12d 9g* 8s 1990 10.2f 10.1g 10.8f 9g 12m a10g⁵] rather leggy,
close-coupled mare: plating-class winner as 4-y-o: show in 1990 only on final outing:
stays 1¼m: suited by give in the ground: has won for apprentice: has given trouble
at stalls (withdrawn once): sold out of Capt. J. Wilson's stable 4,600 gns Doncaster
September Sales after fifth start. *R. A. Bennett.*

VIRELAI   3 ch.f. Kris 135–Lyric Dance 106 (Lyphard (USA) 132) [1989 NR 1990   72
11.5g⁵ 12g² 12.3m*] 150,000Y: rangy, rather plain filly: fifth living foal: sister to
lightly-raced maiden Dancing Crystal and half-sister to fairly useful 1¼m winner
Laabas (by Ile de Bourbon), 1m and 1½m winner Librate (by Mill Reef) and 7f winner
Zeffirella (by Known Fact): dam won Free Handicap: 11/4 on, made all in 4-runner
maiden at Ripon in July: pulled hard previously: should have stayed further: stud. *H.
R. A. Cecil.*

VIRGINIA STOCK   2 b.f. (May 4) Swing Easy (USA) 126–Only Miranda 57   —
(Typhoon 125) [1990 7m⁵ 7m 7d 6m] 400Y: angular, workmanlike filly: third reported living foal: half-sister to 3-y-o Relkoni (by Relkino): dam, plater, stayed 1m: well
beaten in claimers and a maiden auction. *Dr J. D. Scargill.*

VIRKON   3 ch.g. King Persian 107–Beyond The Rainbow (Royal Palace 131) [1989   47
5.3g⁶ 5f³ 5m⁴ 5f² 5.1m³ 7f² 7m 6m 1990 7m² 7g⁴ 7m a7g⁵ 7f⁵ 7m³ 7m 7h] leggy,
sparely-made gelding: moderate walker: quite modest plater: ran poorly last 2 starts
(July), awkward to post on first occasion: well below form on all-weather: stays 7f:
acts on firm going: has run well when on toes. *Mrs N. Macauley.*

VISAGE   3 b.f. Vision (USA)–Be Tuneful 130 (Be Friendly 130) [1989 7m 8g³ 1990   75
10g 10.6s 10m* 10m³ 11m⁴ 11.7m⁶ 10.6g* 10g 10.6v 12s⁶ 9g] big, strong, lengthy
filly: poor mover: modest performer: made all in claimers at Newbury in June and
Haydock (£10,500 event) in September: well beaten in handicaps last 3 starts:
should be suited by further than 1¼m: acts on good to firm ground, ran poorly on
soft: has run creditably when on toes. *D. W. P. Arbuthnot.*

VISION OF FREEDOM (IRE)   2 b.g. (Mar 21) Vision (USA)–Captive   38
Audience (Bold Lad (IRE) 133) [1990 5m 7m 5f 6m 6d 10m⁵] IR 7,500F, IR 11,000Y:
neat gelding: moderate walker: third foal: half-brother to Irish 3-y-o 7f winner Two
Magpies (by Doulab): dam never ran: poor plater: badly drawn when blinkered
penultimate outing: seems to stay 1¼m. *S. T. Harris.*

VISION OF INDIA   3 b.f. Vision (USA)–Flying Bid 71 (Auction Ring (USA) 123)   73
[1989 7f⁴ 1990 8m 8m 8f 7g* 8g 6m] workmanlike filly: worthwhile form as 3-y-o
only when winning 6-runner maiden at Lingfield in August: led 6f in handicap next
start: seems suited by 7f. *P. T. Walwyn.*

VISION OF WONDER   6 b.g. Tyrnavos 129–Valeur (Val de Loir 133) [1989   29
16m 17.1f* 14.8f⁴ 1990 12.5m 18f 17.1f⁴ 16g⁵ 16.5f⁵] angular gelding: good mover:
poor handicapper: suited by a test of stamina: acts on any going: has won for apprentice: winning hurdler. *J. S. King.*

VISUAL STAR   4 b.g. Vision (USA)–Eternal Tam (USA) (Tentam (USA)) [1989   29
8.5f⁴ 10f 11m³ 10m³ 10g 10m⁶ 10m 8.2f⁵ 8.2g 8s a8g² 8g 1990 10g⁵ 8m 8f⁶ 7f]
good-topped gelding: poor walker: poor maiden: probably best at around 1m: acts on
firm going, probably unsuited by soft: sometimes blinkered. *R. O'Leary.*

VITAL CLUE (USA)   3 b.g. Alleged (USA) 138–Where You Lead (USA) 120   88
(Raise A Native) [1989 8.2g 1990 10.6s² 10.1m²] lengthy gelding: has scope: fair
form in June as 3-y-o in maiden (green, running on strongly) at Haydock and minor
event (showed a quick action) at Windsor: will stay 1½m: gelded after final start. *J.
L. Dunlop.*

VITALITY   4 b.f. Young Generation 129–Blaze of Glory 92 (Queen's Hussar 124)   81
[1989 8d⁵ 10m⁵ 10g⁵ 9m 8g³ 9g⁵ 1990 8f⁴ 8g 8m³ 8m] big, rangy filly: keen walker:
has a good, easy action: fair performer: ran moderately in blinkers final outing
(June): stays 9f: acts on good to firm and dead going: races keenly. *I. A. Balding.*

VITAL WITNESS (CAN)   3 b.g. Val de L'Orne (FR) 130–Friendly Witness   —
(USA) (Northern Dancer) [1989 NR 1990 11.7f⁵ 12f³] $72,000Y: tall, good-topped
gelding: ninth foal: brother to smart stayer Valuable Witness and half-brother to 4
winners, including useful Canadian stakes winner Leading Witness (by Mr Leader),
successful at up to 1¼m: dam won over 1m: beaten 9 lengths in maiden at Bath
(didn't handle bend) and further in similar event at Brighton (hung left under
pressure) when seemed quite headstrong: sold to join K. Morgan 12,500 gns
Newmarket July Sales and gelded. *R. Charlton.*

VITE VITE   4 ch.g. Kind of Hush 118–Swiftacre (Bay Express 132) [1989 7d 7s³   —
8f⁴ 7f 7m* 7m⁵ 8.5g³ 8f³ a10g* a8g⁵ 1990 a10g a8g] strong, workmanlike gelding:

won handicaps at Salisbury and Lingfield as 3-y-o: ran poorly at latter in apprentice event in February and claimer 10 months later: better suited by 1¼m than shorter: acts on firm ground: sold 1,900 gns Ascot December Sales. *J. Sutcliffe.*

VITTORIA GLENN 2 b.f. (Mar 17) Town And Country 124–Ganadora (Good 50 Times (ITY)) [1990 5m³ 5m³ 5s 5f³ 7f³ 6m 8m⁶] 1,200Y: unfurnished filly: first foal: dam unraced: fair plater: should stay 1m. *R. J. Holder.*

VOGOS ANGEL 3 b.f. Song 132–Lovage (Linacre 133) [1989 7f³ 7f⁴ 8g⁵ 1990 8f⁶ 48 8f 8g* 8.2g³] leggy filly: moderate mover: poor performer: favourite, won claimer at Carlisle in May: stays 1m: acts on firm going: has wandered under pressure. *Sir Mark Prescott.*

VOLCALMEH 2 br.f. (Feb 14) Lidhame 109–Capel Curig 74 (Welsh Pageant 132) 60 p [1990 6m⁶ a6g²] well-grown, useful-looking filly: first foal: dam 2-y-o 1¼m winner: staying-on second of 16 to Saint Caligula in maiden at Southwell in August: green and slowly away on debut: will improve again, particularly at 7f. *P. T. Walwyn.*

VOLCANIC DANCER (USA) 4 b.g. Northern Baby (CAN) 127–Salva (USA) ? (Secretariat (USA)) [1989 10.5d 11g² 10d² 12d⁶ 10.5d⁴ 1990 9.1g⁵ 14g* 14g* 12.5g* 11g* 12.5g 10g] workmanlike gelding: second foal: brother to minor winner in France: dam unraced half-sister to Del Mar Oaks winner Savannah Dancer: won 4 times in French Provinces in summer, twice in amateur events: one pace in similar contest at Sandown in September: stays 1¾m: trained until after sixth outing by J. Hammond. *G. A. Pritchard-Gordon.*

VOLKSRAAD 2 b.c. (Feb 5) Green Desert (USA) 127–Celtic Assembly (USA) 95 90 P (Secretariat (USA)) [1990 6m*] powerful, good-bodied colt: third foal: half-brother to 4-y-o Prefabricate (by Kings Lake) and 1m winner In Vision (by Bellypha): dam 10.6f winner, is daughter of Welsh Garden, top 2-y-o filly in Ireland in 1975: heavily-backed odds-on shot, won 14-runner maiden at Newmarket in November in good style by 4 lengths from Bowden Boy, soon prominent after slow start, leading around 2f out and pushed clear: has plenty of scope, and is sure to improve considerably and win more races. *H. R. A. Cecil.*

VOLPEDO (USA) 3 ch.c. Secreto (USA) 128–Votre Altesse (FR) 122 — (Riverman (USA) 131) [1989 NR 1990 10.1m⁴ 10g⁵ 10.6d 16d³] 220,000Y: well-made colt: has round action: third foal: dam good-class winner at up to 10.5f in France and half-sister to very smart middle-distance horse Dragoon: no worthwhile form, but showed signs of ability in handicap at Chester final start: shapes like dyed-in-the-wool stayer: sold to join R. Manning 7,200 gns Newmarket Autumn Sales. *N. A. Graham.*

VOLTA (USA) 3 b.c. Nureyev (USA) 131–Ivory Lady (USA) (Sir Ivor 135) [1989 — NR 1990 8f] $300,000Y: first foal: dam minor winner at around 1m, is half-sister to very smart 1976 American 2-y-o Mrs Warren, Grade 1 winner at 6f and 7f: second favourite, chased leaders 5f in 20-runner maiden at Kempton in May: sold 3,200 gns Newmarket Autumn Sales. *M. R. Stoute.*

VORIANS TIME 2 ch.c. (Apr 30) Vencedor 79–Hunu (Hul A Hul 124) [1990 5m — 6g a7g 8.2s] leggy, sparely-made colt: fifth reported foal: half-brother to winning chaser Snap Tin (by Jimmy Reppin): dam poor on flat: soundly beaten in maidens. *E. J. Alston.*

VOSTOK (IRE) 2 ch.f. (May 3) The Noble Player (USA) 126–The Flying Sputnik — (Touch Paper 113) [1990 7m 10s 8g] workmanlike filly: has scope: fourth foal: half-sister to 3-y-o Bodge (by Horage) and 1988 2-y-o 5f winner Sam's Choice (by Kampala): dam Irish 2-y-o 5f winner: bit backward, behind in autumn maidens: slowly away on debut. *G. A. Pritchard-Gordon.*

VOTE IN FAVOUR 3 b.f. General Assembly (USA)–Favoridge (USA) 122 (Riva 73 Ridge (USA)) [1989 6g² 1990 7f² 6g³ 6m⁴ 7m 7m 8m* 8d*] close-coupled filly: modest performer: made all in maiden at Pontefract and minor event at Edinburgh in October: moved moderately down and tended to hang fourth start: stays 1m: best efforts on an easy surface. *G. Wragg.*

VUCHTERBACHER 4 b.c. Longleat (USA) 109–Queensbury Star 76 (Wishing 39 Star 117) [1989 10g 7.5g 8g⁶ 7m 7g 1990 a7g⁵ a7g⁶ a7g²] leggy, close-coupled colt: has a round action: poor form at best: stays 7f: tailed off when visored: sometimes bandaged. *P. F. Tulk.*

VUE CAVALIERE (FR) 3 b.f. Akarad (FR) 130–Best Girl 108 (Birdbrook 110) 117 [1989 7.5d³ 7.5d⁴ 1990 10s³ 10.5g² 10.5d⁵ 10g* 12m 9.7g] 340,000 francs (£31,110) Y: leggy, sparely-made filly with a markedly round action: fifth foal: half-sister to Irish 1½m winner Fast N' Fabulous (by Le Fabuleux) and a winner in Italy: dam, French 6.5f winner at 3 yrs, is sister to high-class sprinter and 1000 Guineas second

Girl Friend: won maiden at Deauville as 2-y-o: always front rank when good fifth in Prix de Diane Hermes at Chantilly then winning Prix de Psyche at Deauville: disputed lead over 1¼m in Prix Vermeille at Longchamp penultimate start: best at up to 10.5f: acts on dead ground. *J-M. Beguigne, France.*

W

WAAD (IRE)   2 ch.c. (Mar 29) Milk of The Barley 115–Serena Maria 63 (Dublin   65
Taxi) [1990 5g³ 5f³ 6m⁵ 6g⁵ a6g² a5g³ a6g* 5m* 6m³ 6m* 6m* 6m 7.3g a7g⁵]
leggy, sparely-made colt: moderate mover: first foal: dam won 6f seller: modest
performer: successful in sellers at Southwell (no bid) in June and Folkestone
(bought in 4,200 gns) in July and in nurseries at Nottingham and Catterick in
August: better suited by 6f than 5f: blinkered fourth outing: suitable mount for
apprentice. *N. A. Callaghan.*

WAAFI   8 b.g. Wolver Hollow 126–Geraldville (Lord Gayle (USA) 124) [1989 14f   —
16f⁴ 15.3f⁴ 12f⁵ 14m⁵ 1990 a16g] lengthy gelding: poor handicapper: barely stayed
2m: acted on firm and dead going: suitable mount for inexperienced rider: winning
hurdler: dead. *K. C. Bailey.*

WAATHIG   3 ch.c. Sharpen Up 127–Clunk Click 72 (Star Appeal 133) [1989 NR   88
1990 7g 8m⁵ 10.5g² 9f* 10g] 230,000Y: lengthy, good sort: second foal: dam maiden
suited by middle distances: 5/4 on, won maiden at Redcar in May: 3 lengths second
of 4 to odds-on Sasaki in minor event at York: broke leg in similar contest at
Goodwood: stayed 10.5f: dead. *A. A. Scott.*

WACE (USA)   3 b.c. Nijinsky (CAN) 138–La Mesa (USA) (Round Table) [1989 8f⁴   82
1990 11f* 12m 13.3m] rangy colt: won maiden at Redcar in May, staying on gamely:
beaten long way, held up and never able to challenge, in handicaps at Newbury in the
summer: should stay 1½m: sold 9,800 gns Newmarket September Sales. *M. R.
Stoute.*

WAFFLING   3 b.f. Lomond (USA) 128–Waffles 100 (Wollow 132) [1989 NR 1990   68
7m³ 6m⁵ 8d 8g³ 7m 7m 9f² 10d⁴ 10d a8g³] 52,000Y, 60,000Y: closely related to

Prix Minerve, Evry—
Wajd lands the odds in this Group 3 event, from Echoes (No. 9),
Vanya and Passagere du Soir

Sheikh Mohammed's "Wajd"

winning hurdler Iveagh House (by Be My Guest) and Irish 6f winner Great Sheerwater (by Storm Bird): dam Irish 9f winner out of 1000 Guineas winner Night Off: modest Irish maiden: creditable staying-on third at Lingfield in November final start: probably stays 1¼m: yet to race on very soft ground, acts on any other: blinkered fourth, fifth and eighth outings: sold 7,000 gns Newmarket December Sales. *T. Stack, Ireland.*

WAIKANINI 3 b.f. Mummy's Pet 125–Harmonise 113 (Reliance II 137) [1989 NR 1990 a8g 10m3] 9,000F, 16,500Y: leggy filly: tenth foal: half-sister to several winners abroad: dam stayed 1½m: pulled hard when staying-on third of 9 in claimer (went freely down) at Sandown: sold 8,800 gns Newmarket July Sales. *W. J. Musson.* **53**

WAJD (USA) 3 ch.f. Northern Dancer (CAN)–Dahlia (USA) 135 (Vaguely Noble 140) [1989 NR 1990 10.5v* 10.5g* 12g* 12g3 12m4 12f] 1,300,000Y: rangy filly: ninth foal: closely related to good middle-distance colt Dahar (by Lyphard) and half-sister to 4 winners, notably smart French 1¼m and 15f winner Rivlia (by Riverman), later high class in USA: dam brilliant and tough middle-distance mare: short-priced favourite, won maiden at Maisons-Laffitte, listed race at Longchamp and Prix Minerve at Evry: beaten about 1½ lengths behind Hellenic in Aston Upthorpe Yorkshire Oaks (sweating and edgy) at York and Salsabil in Prix Vermeille at Longchamp: below-form favourite for Grade 1 event at Santa Anita final start: stays 1½m well: takes time to quicken: very smart. *A. Fabre, France.* **121**

WAJNA (USA) 3 b.f. Nureyev (USA) 131–Wind Spirit (USA) (Round Table) [1989 7g* 8g6 1990 11.3d3 14m* 16g3] workmanlike, quite attractive filly: impressed in condition: won 4-runner listed race at York in July by 6 lengths from Alphabel, leading 6f out and running on strongly: set too strong a pace in similar event at same course over 5 weeks later: possibly unsuited by dead ground: stud. *H. R. A. Cecil.* **105**

WAKASHAN 2 b.c. (Jan 30) Dancing Brave (USA) 140–Lady Moon 101 (Mill Reef **86 p**
(USA) 141) [1990 8s³] lengthy, rather angular colt: has scope: fourth foal: half-
brother to 3 winners, including 3-y-o Moon Cactus, successful at 7f (at 2 yrs) and
1¼m, and useful 7f (at 2 yrs) to 8.5f winner in Britain Shining Steel (both by Kris):
dam middle-distance winner, is out of half-sister to Main Reef: well backed, over 2
lengths third of 14, travelling well, leading briefly under 2f out then not knocked
about when beaten, to Another Bob in maiden at Newbury in October: will stay
1¼m: sure to improve, and win a race or two. *H. R. A. Cecil.*

WAKE UP 3 ch.c. Night Shift (USA)–Astonishing (Jolly Good 122) [1989 5g³ 5f* **64**
6m³ 6h 7m⁵ 8m 7g 1990 7g 7f 10m* 11.7m 10g⁶ 12d 12m 12.2d 12d⁶] sturdy colt: has a
long stride: quite modest but unreliable handicapper: little 3-y-o form apart from
when 33/1-winner of slowly-run event at Goodwood in June, leading post: best effort
at 1¼m, but shapes as though worth a try at 1¾m: acts on good to firm ground: has
worn tongue strap: sold to join R. O'Leary 11,000 gns Newmarket Autumn Sales. *J.
M. P. Eustace.*

WAKI GOLD (USA) 3 ch.c. Miswaki (USA) 124–Sainte Croix (USA) (Nijinsky **82**
(CAN) 138) [1989 6f² 6g 8m² 7g 1990 8m⁶ 10g⁴ 8m² 8m³ 8f² 8f⁶ 9m* 12g 9m] rangy
colt: good mover with a long stride: fair performer: 6/4 on, made all in 5-runner
maiden at Redcar in August: behind in Group 1 event at Milan and Cambridgeshire
Handicap at Newmarket after: keen sort, may prove best short of 1¼m: acts well on
firm going: goes well with forcing tactics: sometimes sweats. *P. A. Kelleway.*

WALAYAH 3 b.f. Wassl 125–Maybe So 90 (So Blessed 130) [1989 NR 1990 7g 7m **—**
7m 11.7m 7m] 27,000Y: tall, workmanlike filly: sixth foal: half-sister to 3 winners
here and abroad, including quite useful sprinters Que Sera (by Music Boy) and So
Kind (by Kind of Hush): dam, half-sister to smart sprinter Chapel Cottage, won over
5f and 6f: little worthwhile form, pulling hard in 11.7f handicap: reluctant to go down
and wandered under pressure second outing: sold 3,100 gns Ascot October Sales. *C.
J. Benstead.*

WALEEF 2 b.g. (Jan 17) Persian Bold 123–Henaadi 64 (Affirmed (USA)) [1990 7f³ **68**
7g* 8g] good-topped gelding: has scope: first foal: dam lightly-raced maiden, stayed
1m: made virtually all and stayed on strongly in claimer (claimed out of B. Hanbury's
stable £12,250) at Leicester in August: not discredited when ninth in Doncaster
nursery: probably stays 1m: has thrice been withdrawn at start, twice after bolting:
taken down early final outing. *M. J. Fetherston-Godley.*

WALIM (USA) 2 ch.c. (Mar 3) Nijinsky (CAN) 138–Splendid Girl (USA) (Golden **96 p**
Eagle (FR) [1990 7f⁵ 8g² 10s* 10g²] big, rangy colt: has plenty of scope: sixth foal:
brother to fair maiden Jadeer (stayed 1¼m) and closely related to 3 winners, including top-class French 1m and 9f winner Thrill Show (by Northern Baby), later good
winner in USA: dam won at up to 1m: most progressive colt: odds on, won maiden at
Nottingham in October by 3½ lengths from Dance Partout, value for more than
twice winning margin: well backed, ¾-length second of 9, keeping on well, to
Matahif in listed race at Newmarket following month: suited by 1¼m: acts well on
soft ground: likely to make a useful handicapper. *M. R. Stoute.*

WALKERN WITCH 3 b.f. Dunbeath (USA) 127–Emblazon 91 (Wolver Hollow **—**
126) [1989 6m⁵ 7m 7m 6g* 6g 8s 7d³ a8g 1990 7g 7d 7g 12g 6d] big, strong,
workmanlike filly: carries condition: modest winner at 2 yrs: little other form: stays
7f: acts on dead going: visored 3 times: sold 700 gns Ascot December Sales. *D. T.
Thom.*

WALKERWAY BOY 3 b.c. Muscatite 122–Hadala (Le Levanstell 122) [1989 **—**
7m⁵ 7g 7h⁴ 8g⁶ 8f 1990 9m a12g 16m 12m⁵ 10m a8g] workmanlike, dipped-backed
colt: moderate mover: plating-class form at 2 yrs: little in 1990, mostly in amateur
handicaps: should stay at least 1¼m: blinkered last 5 (seemed reluctant to race first
occasion, pulled hard second) starts and once at 2 yrs. *A. Bailey.*

WALKING SAINT 3 b.f. Godswalk (USA) 130–Saintly Tune (Welsh Saint 126) **73**
[1989 6g 7g* 7m² 7g 1990 8f² 8.5g* 8m³ 8f⁴ 7d⁵ 7g 7.6m⁶ 8m⁴ 7g a8g³ a8g* a8g
a10g] close-coupled filly: modest handicapper: won at Epsom in April and Lingfield
(claimer) in December: stays 8.5f: acts on firm ground: has run creditably for 7-lb
claimer. *R. Hannon.*

WALK UP THE MALL 3 gr.f. Godswalk (USA) 130–Pall Nan 86 (Pall Mall 132) **—**
[1989 NR 1990 a8g³ a6g⁶] IR 3,400Y: half-sister to numerous winners here and
abroad, including useful Irish 1¼m winner Domino's Nurse (by Dom Racine), also
successful at 7f at 2 yrs and in USA, and fairly useful 1979 2-y-o 7f winner Appleby
Park (by Bay Express): dam best at 5f: no worthwhile form in maidens at Lingfield in
January: sold 1,200 gns Ascot July Sales. *R. Hannon.*

WALK WELL   3 b.f. Sadler's Wells (USA) 132–Walkyria (Lord Gayle (USA) 124)   ?
[1989 8f³ 1990 8m⁶ 10g 8.5g⁵ 8.5v 10v] tall, leggy, quite attractive filly: quite modest
form at Wolverhampton at 2 yrs, easily better effort in maidens here when trained
by B. Hanbury: off course 3½ months before appearing in Italy, in Group 2 event on
first start there: bred to be suited by middle distances. *O. Pessi, Italy.*

WALLANGRIFF   2 ch.g. (Feb 14) Noalto 120–Concern 63 (Brigadier Gerard   60
144) [1990 7g 7m⁶ 6m 8m] 6,000Y: strong, lengthy gelding: seventh foal: half-
brother to 1984 2-y-o 5f winner Diami (by Swing Easy), 14.7f winner Prince Henry
(by Whitstead) and a winner in Norway: dam won over 9.4f: quite modest maiden at
best: ran badly in seller final outing: should be suited by 1m. *N. A. Callaghan.*

WALLED GARDEN   2 ch.g. (Mar 18) Dominion 123–Last Cutting (Final Straw   —
127) [1990 7s a8g] 5,400Y: tall, plain gelding: first foal: dam unraced half-sister to St
Leger winner Cut Above and Irish 2000 Guineas winner Sharp Edge: backward,
soundly beaten in Lingfield maidens. *A. Moore.*

WALLINGFEN LANE   3 b.g. Lochnager 132–On A Bit 66 (Mummy's Pet 125)   80
[1989 NR 1990 8.5g⁵ 8.5d* 8.5m 8m⁴ 8g 8g* 8d 8g³ 8g] neat gelding: eighth foal:
half-brother to 7f to 9f winner Bit of A State (by Free State) and fair 9f and 1¼m
winner White Sapphire (by Sparkler): dam placed at up to 11f: won maiden (33/1,
hung right) at Beverley in June and handicap at Doncaster in September: stays 8.5f
well: acts on dead going: bandaged near-hind fourth to eighth starts: idled markedly
in front penultimate start, failed to settle final one, and is not an easy ride: may
prove best chasing pace and with delayed challenge. *J. G. FitzGerald.*

WALL STREET SLUMP   4 gr.g. Belfort (FR) 89–Running Dancer (FR)   32 §
(Dancer's Image (USA)) [1989 6f⁵ 7m 7m 8f 6f⁴ 5m 9f 7m⁵ 7.5m 8.2g 12g 12m⁶ 1990
8.2s 6v⁶ 7m⁵ 5g⁶ 5g] leggy gelding: poor maiden and has looked temperamentally
unsatisfactory: blinkered and visored twice: sold 1,600 gns Doncaster June Sales:
resold 1,000 gns Doncaster November Sales. *P. Monteith.*

WALTER STREET   5 b.g. Lochnager 132–Shady Desire 88 (Meldrum 112)   —
[1989 NR 1990 8.5m] big, workmanlike gelding: fourth foal: half-brother to two 6f
winners, including Ben Jarrow (by Roman Warrior), also successful over 7f: dam
won from 5f to 1m: 100/1, backward and taken quietly to post, took keen hold when
tailed off in maiden at Beverley in April. *D. W. Chapman.*

WALTZING HOME   3 b.c. Habitat 134–State Ball 61 (Dance In Time (CAN))   70
[1989 6m³ 1990 7.6d 8m⁵ 10g 7.2d 8m⁵ 8m⁵ 8d²] lengthy, robust colt: quite modest
form: didn't find much when second in claimer at Leicester: probably stays 1m: yet
to race on extremes of going: sometimes sweating, on toes fourth start: ran as if
something amiss first 3: sold 6,600 gns Newmarket Autumn Sales: may be unsatisfactory. *R. F. Johnson Houghton.*

WALTZING WEASEL   3 b.f. Nemorino (USA) 81–Branston Express (Bay   44 §
Express 132) [1989 5s² 5d 5m 7g a7g a7g 1990 a6g* a5g⁶ a6g⁶ a5g⁶] leggy filly: poor
mover: made all in claimer at Southwell in January: tailed off in handicaps after:
stays 6f: blinkered last 2 starts: sold 1,500 gns Ascot April Sales: clearly one to
avoid. *J. Wharton.*

WALTZ ON AIR   4 b.f. Doc Marten 104–Young Romance (King's Troop 118)   —
[1989 6d 6d* 8f 8g 7g 7g 8v⁵ 7g 1990 9f 8m a8g 8m 9g 10.6d 8.2v] compact filly: poor
walker: has a roundish action: fair winner early as 3-y-o: has lost her form: best form
at 6f (should stay 1m): used to go well on a soft surface: visored last 2 starts,
bandaged near-hind first time. *C. Tinkler.*

WANDA   3 b.f. Taufan (USA) 119–Pitaka (Pitskelly 133) [1989 5s² 5g* 5f² 5f² 6g⁵   72
6d 5g² 1990 5f² 5v² 5d 7m⁴ 7m 5m² 5g⁴ 6m 5g 5g* 5m] close-coupled,
angular filly: moderate walker: modest handicapper: won at Ripon in August by a
head: best at 5f: acts on any going: blinkered: has had tongue tied down: has sweated
up and got on edge: should prove best with strong handling. *M. W. Easterby.*

WANDA'S DREAM (USA)   2 ch.f. (Feb 17) Miswaki (USA) 124–Halo Reply   65
(CAN) (Halo (USA)) [1990 5m³ 6f² 5f²] $72,000Y: good-bodied filly: fourth reported
foal: closely related to a winner in North America by Conquistador Cielo: dam won
at up to 9f: well backed, quite modest form in maidens at Newbury, Goodwood and
Lingfield: likely to prove better suited by 6f than 5f. *D. J. G. Murray-Smith.*

WANE'S SECRET (IRE)   2 b.c. (Apr 12) Horage 124–Zestino (Shack (USA)   42
118) [1990 5m 5m⁴ 6g⁶ 6m 7f 5s⁵ a5g a7g] IR 4,000Y, 2,500 2-y-o: small, sturdy colt:
first foal: dam unraced half-sister to Ginevra: modest plater: should stay beyond 5f.
K. B. McCauley.

WAR BEAT   2 b.c. (May 6) Wolver Heights 99–Branitska (Mummy's Pet 125)   57
[1990 7f⁵ 8m 8m 10.2s] strong, sturdy colt: has a quick action: second foal: half-

brother to 3-y-o Call To Arms (by North Briton), 6f and 7.5f winner at 2 yrs: dam poor maiden from family of Dominion: quite modest form in maidens and minor events: pulled very hard final start. *C. E. Brittain.*

WARM FEELING 3 b.c. Kalaglow 132–Height of Passion (Shirley Heights 130) 97
[1989 7g 1990 a10g* a10g* 11g² 12.3d* 12m⁴ 16.2f⁴] lengthy, workmanlike colt: has quick action: progressed well and very easily justified favouritism in maiden at Lingfield in January and handicaps at Lingfield in March and Chester (£7,100 event) in May: below-form fourth in £7,300 handicap at Newbury and Queen's Vase at Royal Ascot: should stay beyond 1½m: needs an easy surface. *B. W. Hills.*

WARM WINTER 4 gr.f. Kalaglow 132–Fair Head 87 (High Line 125) [1989 7f 7f⁵ —
1990 14.6f 10.2f] rangy, rather angular filly: lightly-raced maiden: should stay 1¼m: bandaged final outing: winning hurdler in March: sold out of R. Curtis' stable 5,500 gns Ascot June Sales after reappearance. *J. H. Baker.*

WARRIOR PRINCE 2 b.c. (Apr 13) Prince Sabo 123–Choral Park (Music Boy 62
124) [1990 5d⁵ 5m⁴ 5f⁵ 6g 5m* 5m 5v⁶ 6d] 7,400Y: sturdy, lengthy colt: poor walker: first foal: dam poor maiden: quite modest performer: won Redcar nursery in September: ran well when fourteenth of 19 in Racecall Gold Trophy at Redcar final start: stays 6f: possibly unsuited by heavy ground, acts on any other. *R. M. Whitaker.*

WASHITA 3 b.f. Valiyar 129–Ardneasken 84 (Right Royal V 135) [1989 7v 1990 8g 46
8g 11g⁴ 12g 15v] workmanlike filly: poor maiden: form only when fourth in handicap at Hamilton in July: should be suited by further than 11f. *C. W. Thornton.*

WASNAH (USA) 3 b.f. Nijinsky (CAN) 138–Highest Trump (USA) 112 (Bold 96
Bidder) [1989 7g² 1990 8g⁴ 10m² 10m⁴ 11.5g⁶ 10.5g²] rangy filly: fairly useful performer: outpaced towards rear then stayed on very well when second to Sardegna in listed race at Newmarket in May: ridden up with pace when in frame in similar event at Newbury and maiden (sweating and very edgy on first run for 4 months) at York after: should have stayed 1½m: visits Riverman. *J. L. Dunlop.*

WASPY (IRE) 2 b.f. (Mar 6) Horage 124–Persian Caprice (Persian Bold 123) 40
[1990 5m⁴ 5g⁶ 6g] IR 3,200Y: angular filly: first foal: dam Irish 4-y-o 1¾m winner: best effort in 6-runner maiden at Catterick on debut: well beaten after in sellers. *M. H. Easterby.*

WASSELNI 4 br.g. Wassl 125–Monongelia 98 (Welsh Pageant 132) [1989 8h⁵ —
12h⁴ 14g² 1990 16.2m] angular, sparely-made gelding: moderate mover: fair form when second in Nottingham maiden in July, 1989: should be suited by good test of stamina: best run on good ground: blinkered only outing (well beaten) at 4 yrs: sold 1,600 gns Ascot November Sales. *K. A. Morgan.*

WASSIFA 2 b.f. (Jan 27) Sure Blade (USA) 128–Rye Tops 97 (Ile de Bourbon — p
(USA) 133) [1990 6d] close-coupled, deep-girthed filly: second foal: half-sister to 3-y-o Minsayah (by Electric): dam 10.5f winner stayed 1½m, is half-sister to Most Welcome and daughter of Topsy, smart winner at up to 1¼m: backward and very green, prominent 4f then considerably handled in 8-runner maiden at Ascot in June: should do better. *B. Hanbury.*

WASSL PORT 4 b.c. Wassl 125–Sea Port (Averof 123) [1989 7g³ 8.2m⁴ 8.5m* 103
8g* 8d⁵ 1990 8g* 7.6d² 10g³ 7m 7.6g³ 7.3g²] tall, attractive colt: good mover: useful handicapper: showed improved form when winning £11,500 event at Newbury in April and would have won at Chester over 2 weeks later granted clear run: ran well at same courses last 2 outings: stays 8.5f: best form on an easy surface: sweating fourth (also on toes) and fifth starts: sent to race in Saudi Arabia. *B. W. Hills.*

WATCH IT MATEY 2 b.g. (Feb 20) Tina's Pet 121–Mouletta (Moulton 128) 70 p
[1990 8g⁶] workmanlike gelding: second foal: dam, unplaced on both starts, is half-sister to Furioso and Favoletta: bit backward, around 6 lengths sixth of 21, staying on despite being hampered inside final furlong, to Forbearance in maiden at Pontefract in October: will improve. *D. Morley.*

WATCH TOWER BAY (IRE) 2 ch.c. (May 4) Kings Lake (USA) 133–Noon 46
Bells (Ballymore 123) [1990 7f 7f⁵] 5,000Y: close-coupled filly: second foal: dam Irish middle-distance winner: over 6 lengths fifth of 8, leading around 5f, in maiden auction at Yarmouth in July: slowly away and not at all knocked about on debut: will be better suited by 1m. *R. Boss.*

WATER CANNON 9 b.g. Gunner B 126–Awash (Busted 134) [1989 21.6d⁴ 18s —
17.6f³ 18f 18h 20.4g³ 1990 15m 16m 16.2s] compact gelding: poor handicapper: no form in autumn: out-and-out stayer: has worn a visor: often wears a tongue strap: inconsistent. *F. H. Lee.*

WATER GOD 3 b.c. Dominion 123–Silent Pool 68 (Relkino 131) [1989 6g 1990 8g **58** a8g 9g2 9g* 10f* 10m 12g 12f] smallish, quite attractive colt: has a quick action: plating-class performer: won handicaps at Redcar in June and Brighton in July: faced stiff tasks last 2 starts: should stay 1½m: sold 7,400 gns Newmarket Autumn Sales. *R. F. Johnson Houghton.*

WATERLOW PARK 8 ch.g. Wollow 132–Caraquenga (USA) 92 (Cyane) [1989 **76** 10.2g3 12g3 12m* 12f2 12f* 12h* 12h* 12m2 12f* 11d 12d 10.6m 1990 10m3 12.2m 12m 11.5m4 8m* 12.3g3 10m2] big gelding: good mover: modest handicapper: an excellent mount for inexperienced rider, and won amateurs event at Goodwood in June: evidently effective at 1m in strongly-run race and stays well: suited by a sound surface: has broken blood vessels: genuine. *I. A. Balding.*

WATERMILL LAD 3 b.g. Reesh 117–Absalom 60 (Absalom 128) [1989 NR 1990 — 8g] 5,200Y: small, sturdy gelding: first foal: dam 9f winner: bandaged and burly, tailed off in June seller: sold 1,050 gns Newmarket July Sales. *J. Ringer.*

WATERTIGHT (USA) 5 b.g. Affirmed (USA)–Brookward (USA) (Stevward) — [1989 NR 1990 13s4] leggy, angular, sparely-made gelding: has a round action: fair winner as 3-y-o: well-beaten fourth in Hamilton handicap in April: should stay 2m: best form on a soft surface: blinkered when withdrawn lame once at 3 yrs: winning hurdler in 1989/90. *G. M. Moore.*

WATER WELL 3 b.f. Sadler's Wells (USA) 132–Soba 127 (Most Secret 119) **96** [1989 6g4 6m6 6g 6m 8f3 7g3 1990 7m6 7.6d* 8m4 8f6 8g 6s] workmanlike, good-quartered filly: fairly useful performer: won maiden at Chester in May: out of depth next 2 starts, running very well on first occasion: off course 3 months then front rank 6f when about 5 lengths seventh of 9 to Tabdea in listed race at Doncaster penultimate start: probably needs further than 6f, and stays 1m: may well prove best on an easy surface. *C. E. Brittain.*

WATSON HOUSE 2 b.g. (Mar 13) Palm Track 122–Maydrum 50 (Meldrum 112) **42** [1990 5m 6g 6g 6d4] big gelding: moderate mover: first foal: dam lightly-raced maiden: bit burly on first run for 3½ months, 17 lengths fourth of 7 to Jimlil in minor event at Doncaster in October: little worthwhile form previously, including in a seller. *J. Balding.*

WATTLE SYKE 3 ch.g. King Persian 107–Sandforgold (Sandford Lad 133) [1989 **44** NR 1990 10.2f 8f 8g6 8.2g4 7m 8.2m2dis 8f3 7.5g] IR 5,500Y: leggy gelding: second foal: dam Irish 4-y-o 9f winner: poor handicapper: best at around 1m: best effort on firm going: hung left sixth start: twice slowly away: sold to join L. Lungo 4,700 gns Doncaster November Sales. *C. Tinkler.*

WATTO (IRE) 2 b.c. (Apr 29) Mazaad 106–Jolie Brise (Tumble Wind (USA)) **41** [1990 5f 5m 5f4 5d 6f] IR 2,400F, 6,000Y: compact colt: has a round action: fifth foal: half-brother to quite modest 5f winner First Fastnet (by Ahonoora) and a winner in Denmark: dam unraced daughter of half-sister to Swing Easy: poor plater: best effort third outing: sold 800 gns Doncaster September Sales. *Ronald Thompson.*

WAVE MASTER 3 b.g. Chief Singer 131–Sea Fret 96 (Habat 127) [1989 5.1m* **72** 6m2 5g 6f5 8f5 7g 1990 6m3 6f 6m2] sturdy, close-coupled gelding: has a roundish action: modest performer: should stay further than 6f: possibly unsuited by very firm ground: blinkered final outing at 2 yrs: sold to join J. S. Wilson 6,500 gns Newmarket Autumn Sales. *G. A. Pritchard-Gordon.*

WAVERLEY GIRL 4 b.f. Seymour Hicks (FR) 125–Iamstopped (Furry Glen — 121) [1989 8s 12m5 14t6 8f 9f 12m 12g 1990 16g 16m 16.5m] sparely-made filly: poor mover: little sign of ability on flat: sweating final start: winning but ungenuine selling hurdler. *J. S. Wainwright.*

WAVERLEY STAR 5 br.g. Pitskelly 120–Quelle Blague (Red God 128§) [1989 **60** 5g3 5g4 6v 6.1f5 7.5g 5f* 6m 6f4 5f 5m 5f4 6f5 8m 6m3 6f 6g4 7m 1990 a6g4 a6g3 a6g6 5f3 6f 5f3 5g 5m5 6m 5f4 6f4 6g a5g* 5m2 a5g5 6f3 5f2 6m 5m3 6f3 6g 6g 5m* 5m4 5g] big, workmanlike gelding: poor mover: quite modest handicapper: won at Southwell in July and Salisbury in September: best at sprint distances: ideally suited by top-of-the-ground: often blinkered (has been tried in visor): has sweated, and often gets on toes: ideally needs strong handling. *J. S. Wainwright.*

WAY OFF BEAT (IRE) 2 br.g. (Feb 5) Ballad Rock 122–Astral Way (Hotfoot — 126) [1990 7m 10.2s] IR 8,700Y, resold IR 13,000Y: heavy-bodied gelding: fifth foal: half-brother to 2 winners in Ireland, including 11f winner Gemini Way (by Pas de Seul): dam French 2-y-o 1m winner: always behind in maiden auction (coltish and very green) at Leicester and minor event at Doncaster in autumn: sold 940 gns Doncaster November Sales. *Dr J. D. Scargill.*

WAYPOST 2 b. or br.g. (Feb 27) Belfort (FR) 89–Golden Slade 70 (Octavo (USA) 115) [1990 7m 6g] 1,900Y: good-bodied gelding: has scope: first foal: dam 7f and 1m winner: soundly beaten in maidens at Lingfield and Yarmouth. *A. Hide.*

WEAREAGRANDMOTHER 3 b.f. Prince Tenderfoot (USA) 126–Lady **50** Bettina (Bustino 136) [1989 6g 6m 7m⁶ 8m* 9g 7g 1990 8g 11m 10m³ 12.5g* 12.5m² 10f⁵ 12v] workmanlike filly: plating-class performer: won claimer (claimed out of P. Calver's stable £8,020) at Wolverhampton in July: stays 1½m well: possibly unsuited by extremes of going: bandaged behind second to fourth starts. *B. A. McMahon.*

WEAR VALLEY (IRE) 2 b.f. (Apr 1) Sandhurst Prince 128–North North West **44** (Northfields (USA)) [1990 5m⁶ 7g³ 6m⁵ 6m 7f 8.2s] IR 3,000Y: leggy filly: moderate walker: half-sister to 8.5f winner Watendlath (by Skyliner): dam never ran: plater: easily best effort third in non-selling maiden (hung left) at Edinburgh: should stay 1m: sold 700 gns Doncaster October Sales. *Denys Smith.*

WEDDING BOUQUET 3 b.f. Kings Lake (USA) 133–Doff The Derby (USA) **106** (Master Derby (USA)) [1989 6g* 6d³ 6g³ 7g² 5d* 7g* 1990 7g* 8g⁵ 8g 8d³] useful Irish filly: led close home to land odds in listed race at the Curragh in April: best efforts in Poule d'Essai des Pouliches at Longchamp and 4-runner Phoenix International Stakes (never able to challenge, 3¾ lengths behind Zoman), below form in Irish 1000 Guineas at the Curragh in between: better at 1m than shorter: sent to USA, winning over 1m at Del Mar in August. *M. V. O'Brien, Ireland.*

WEDDING DAY (DEN) 4 gr.f. Honduras (GER)–Ramlosa (DEN) (Belmont (FR)) [1989 NR 1990 8m⁶ 8g 6g 7f] plain, angular filly: successful once over 5.5f from 9 starts in Sweden in 1989: no show here as 4-y-o, including in selling handicap. *W. J. Pearce.*

WEDNESDAYS AUCTION (IRE) 2 b.c. (Apr 13) Mazaad 106–Happy Always 48 (Lucky Wednesday 124) [1990 6g] IR 700Y: workmanlike colt: fourth foal: dam ran twice: burly and green, around 11 lengths eighth of 11, slowly away and

Mrs M. V. O'Brien's "Wedding Bouquet"

never dangerous, in maiden auction at Pontefract in June: looked sure to improve, but not seen out again. *B. Hanbury.*

WEEKDAY CROSS (IRE) 2 b.c. (Mar 26) Taufan (USA) 119–Isoldes Tower (Balliol 125) [1990 6g 6d a7g] IR 13,500F, IR 38,000Y: good-topped colt: has scope: third foal: half-brother to French 3-y-o Alah Kareem (by Alzao), 7.2f winner at 2 yrs: dam Irish stayer, also won over hurdles: poor form in maidens. *W. Jarvis.* — 44

WEEKENDER 3 ch.f. Mummy's Game 120–Antique Bloom 101 (Sterling Bay (SWE)) [1989 6m⁴ 6m⁴ 7f 1990 9m] workmanlike filly: poor plater: tailed off in claimer on only start at 3 yrs: suited by 7f. *M. J. Charles.* —

WEEK ST MARY 4 gr.f. Warpath 113–Sophia Western (Steel Heart 128) [1989 7s 10m 10.2h 9g 8m 8f⁵ 8f* 10.2f 8f 8.2g 1990 10f 8.3g 8.3m 8h* 10.8m⁶ 8f⁴ 8f] sturdy filly: carries condition: moderate mover: plater: won handicap at Bath (second course success, bought in 3,500 gns) in August: suited by 1m: acts on hard going: trained on reappearance by C. Hill: sold 1,200 gns Ascot December Sales: inconsistent. *R. J. Hodges.* 30

WELCOMING ARMS 3 b.f. Free State 125–The Guzzler 69 (Behistoun 131) [1989 NR 1990 10.6s 10m⁵ 14f⁶ 12.2m² 12.5m⁵ 12d 15v 13.6d] angular, workmanlike filly: half-sister to several winners, including stayer and winning jumper King's College Boy (by Andrea Mantegna): dam won 6f seller: quite modest maiden: mostly faced stiff tasks in handicaps: should stay beyond 1½m: acts on good to firm going. *P. Calver.* 65

WELD 4 ch.c. Kalaglow 132–Meliora 73 (Crowned Prince (USA) 128) [1989 10s⁴ 14m* 16f* 16f* 18g* 16g* 1990 20d 14m³] big, rather leggy, useful-looking colt: has a round action: unbeaten over 1¾m or further as 3-y-o, including in Doncaster Cup and Jockey Club Cup at Newmarket: then suffered leg trouble, and well beaten (bandaged in front) in Gold Cup (tongue tied down) at Royal Ascot and listed race (finished lame) at York in summer: suited by test of stamina: acted on firm going: took strong hold: to stand at Blakeley Stud, Shrewsbury. *W. Jarvis.* —

WELL AND TRULY 3 b.f. Rousillon (USA) 133–Altana 71 (Grundy 137) [1989 NR 1990 10m⁶ 10g 10.1m 11.5f⁴ 11.7m 10s⁴ a12g] 2,100Y, 10,500 2-y-o: leggy, unfurnished filly: second foal: half-sister to 4-y-o Spitfire Jubilee (by Chief Singer): dam 1½m and 1¾m winner: quite modest maiden: stays 11.5f: acts on any going: ran moderately on all-weather. *C. C. Elsey.* 57

WELL FURNISHED 3 ch.c. Salmon Leap (USA) 131–Mimicry (Thatch (USA) 136) [1989 6m 7g⁴ 7g 1990 8g* 9f* 8g* 9m⁵ 8m 8g⁶ 9m a10g² a10g³ a10g⁵] rangy colt: fair handicapper: progressive form in winning at Kempton in April, May and June: easily best subsequent efforts, running very well, when placed at Lingfield: stays 1¼m: acts on firm going: has run moderately for lady rider: below form sweating fourth and sixth starts. *A. A. Scott.* 89

WELL LOG 2 br.f. (Mar 21) Reach 122–Cachucha (Gay Fandango (USA) 132) [1990 6g 6m 6m 8.2g²] leggy filly: moderate mover: third foal: half-sister to 6f and 7f winner Supreme Optimist (by Absalom) and poor maiden Spanish Lake (by King of Spain): dam well-beaten granddaughter of Irish Oaks winner Aurabella: easily best effort 6 lengths second of 18, staying on never dangerous, to Tate Affair in seller (on toes, awkward stalls) at Nottingham in September: will stay 1¼m: bandaged behind second and third starts. *B. Stevens.* 50

WELLOW WINE (USA) 5 b.g. Sensitive Prince (USA)–Tempting Lady (USA) (L'Enjoleur (CAN)) [1989 5s a6g 1990 a6g a7g 6m] tall, leggy, lengthy gelding: lightly-raced maiden: stays 6f: probably acts on any going: blinkered and visored once: often bandaged. *R. A. Bennett.* —

WELLSY LAD (USA) 3 ch.c. El Baba (USA)–Iwishiknew (USA) (Damascus (USA)) [1989 9g a6g⁵ a6g² a7g* a8g² 1990 a7g² a8g³ a7g* a6g² a6g* a7g* a7g² a8g³ a7g³ 6f 6m 6g⁵ 6m⁵ 6f⁶ 7g 6m 6g² 6d⁶ 6f 8d* 6s³ a6g³ a6g⁶] leggy, angular colt: moderate walker: quite modest handicapper: successful at Southwell (twice, first of them a claimer) and Lingfield early on: inconsistent on turf, below best when winning claimer at Leicester in October: effective at 6f to 1m: probably best with give in the ground: blinkered on debut: usually claimer ridden: has given trouble in preliminaries and been slowly away. *D. W. Chapman.* 72

WELNEY 3 b. or br.g. Habitat 134–On Show 92 (Welsh Pageant 132) [1989 6m⁴ 6g* 6m* 7g⁴ 1990 7g⁶ 8f⁶] close-coupled gelding: has a quick action: very useful performer, successful in Mill Reef Stakes at Newbury as 2-y-o: never able to challenge in smart company since, best effort when about 7 lengths sixth of 14 to Tirol in 2000 Guineas (blinkered, went very freely to post) at Newmarket final start, 112 soon off bridle in rear, not getting best of runs then staying on steadily: subsequently gelded: stays 1m: acts on firm going: bandaged on reappearance. *G. Wragg.*

WELSH FLUTE 4 b.f. Welsh Captain 113–Spanish Flute 55 (Philip of Spain 126) — [1989 8g 5s 6s 6f 6f 8f 1990 a11g] workmanlike, sparely-made filly: no form since 2 yrs: probably doesn't stay 1m: blinkered final start at 3 yrs. *R. Thompson.*

WELSH GOVERNOR 4 b.g. Welsh Term 126–The Way She Moves (North — Stoke 130) [1989 10m 1990 8g a11g] leggy gelding: made all in claimer as 2-y-o: very lightly raced and no subsequent form: should stay beyond 7f. *E. H. Owen jun.*

WELSHMAN 4 ch.g. Final Straw 127–Joie de Galles 72 (Welsh Pageant 132) — [1989 8s⁶ 12v* 12g 12s 1990 12d 16.2s] close-coupled, workmanlike gelding: modest winner of claimer early as 3-y-o: burly, tailed off in Haydock handicaps in autumn: suited by 1½m: goes well in the mud: winning hurdler. *M. Blanshard.*

WELSH PAGEANTRY 7 b.m. Welsh Pageant 132–Sacred Mountain 74 (St — Paddy 133) [1989 10h⁵ 9m 10f⁶ 8f 1990 10f 8h 10m 10.6d 10m] lengthy, quite attractive mare: quite modest winner as 5-y-o: form after only on first outing in 1989: better suited by 1¼m than 1m: didn't show her best form on soft going, acted on any other: blinkered once: won for apprentice: in foal to Primo Dominie. *R. Hollinshead.*

WELSH SECRET 2 b.f. (May 17) Welsh Captain 113–Bridge of Gold 68 (Balidar 56 133) [1990 5m 6d 5m 5m² 6g² 6d] 2,000Y: workmanlike filly: has scope: poor mover: first foal: dam 5f winner: plating-class form when runner-up in nurseries at Wolverhampton and Pontefract: found little off bridle in all-aged seller third start: gives impression will prove best at 5f: races keenly. *Mrs J. R. Ramsden.*

WELSH SIREN 4 b.f. Welsh Saint 126–Kalonji (Red Alert 127) [1989 8f 7f⁴ 7m⁵ 65 7g² 6f⁵ 8f² 10.2g 10s⁴ 9m⁴ 9f⁴ 10f⁴ 1990 8h* 10g 10g³ 8m² 10f 8.3m⁵ 8h⁵ 10g⁴ 10.2m⁴ 8d] workmanlike filly: keen walker: moderate mover: won (for first time) handicap at Bath in May: stays 1¼m: acts on hard going: has edged right: occasionally sweats. *D. R. C. Elsworth.*

WELSH SONNET 2 b.f. (Mar 2) Welsh Captain 113–Black Symphony 70 — (Grisaille 115) [1990 6g 6d] 1,250Y: small, sparely-made filly: fifth foal: dam won 6f seller: no worthwhile form in maidens at Kempton and Lingfield. *R. Akehurst.*

WENDOVER LADY 2 b.f. (May 12) Alleging (USA) 120–Flight Feathers (USA) 62 (Ribocco 129) [1990 6m 7f⁶ 6f² 6m* 6m 8.2g⁴ 6d⁴] 2,100Y: close-coupled filly: half-sister to 1981 2-y-o 5f winner Sam-Bam (by Shiny Tenth) and a winner abroad: dam poor half-sister to champion American mare Old Hat: quite modest performer: rallied really well to win seller (bought in 8,500 gns) at Goodwood in August: best form at 6f: acts on firm and dead ground: looks a difficult ride: none too consistent: sold 6,800 gns Newmarket Autumn Sales. *S. Dow.*

WESAYEM 3 b.f. Shirley Heights 130–Capital Risk 82 (Bustino 136) [1989 NR 66 1990 14g⁵ 14f²] angular filly: first foal: dam 1m winner out of half-sister to very smart colts Lord Gayle and Never Return: staying-on second of 6 to Bestow in maiden at Yarmouth in August: sold 4,000 gns Newmarket Autumn Sales. *A. C. Stewart.*

WESSEX 8 b.h. Free State 125–Bonandra 82 (Andrea Mantegna) [1989 13v⁵ 13v⁴ 47 13f⁵ 16.5g⁴ 13m 20.4g² 15s⁶ 1990 13v 18m⁴ 13g 16.5m 20.4m² 18g] strong horse: shows traces of stringhalt: poor handicapper: out-and-out stayer: acts on any going: effective with blinkers or without: good mount for apprentice. *N. Tinkler.*

WEST BECK 4 ch.f. Mr Fluorocarbon 126–Hod On 67 (Decoy Boy 129) [1989 52 7.5d* 7g* 7m* 7.6f 7d a7g 1990 7m 7g 7.5m⁴ 8.2d 7d⁵ 8d*] lengthy, rather angular filly: turns fore-feet in: won selling handicap at Doncaster (bought in 4,000 gns) in November: stays 1m: possibly unsuited by firm going, acts on any other: sometimes bandaged behind. *M. J. Camacho.*

WESTERN ACE (IRE) 2 ch.c. (May 9) On Your Mark 125–Galva (Gulf Pearl 62 117) [1990 7m 7g a8g² a7g a8g] IR 8,600Y, 10,500 2-y-o: sturdy colt: sixth foal: half-brother to a winner in Italy: dam won over 1½m and 1¾m in Ireland: 1½ lengths second of 10 to Moving Out in late-year maiden at Southwell, easily best effort: will stay 1¼m. *J. M. P. Eustace.*

WESTERN DANCER 9 b.g. Free State 125–Polyandrist 92 (Polic 126) [1989 63 16s⁴ 12v⁴ 14f⁴ 16m⁵ 14g 16.2d* 1990 a14g³ 14m⁵] lengthy gelding: usually looks well: good mover: quite modest handicapper: not raced after April: suited by good test of stamina: acts on any going: has started slowly: well served by strong gallop. *C. A. Horgan.*

WESTERN DYNASTY 4 ch.g. Hotfoot 126–Northern Dynasty 65 (Breeders   85
Dream 116) [1989 12g⁴ 14f⁴ 1990 12g³ 14m⁵ 12m⁴ 14g² 12f² 11.5d* 12m* 12g* 12d*
13.3g⁴ 12m 12g⁶ 12s⁵] big, lengthy gelding: moderate mover: progressed very well
in summer, winning amateurs maiden at Yarmouth (setting slow pace) and
handicaps at Leicester (twice) and Haydock: stays 1¾m: probably acts on any going:
game, and a credit to his trainer. *M. J. Ryan.*

WESTERN GUN (USA) 5 b.h. Lypheor 118–Fandangerina (USA) (Grey Dawn   —
II 132) [1989 8g⁵ 1990 8g 6m] lengthy, good-bodied horse: has a sharp action: useful
at his best, but very lightly raced nowadays: always behind in Group 3 event at
Baden-Baden and handicap at Pontefract at 5 yrs: stays 8.5f: acts on firm and dead
going. *Mrs L. Piggott.*

WESTERN LOCH 3 b.f. Reesh 117–Westerlake (Blakeney 126) [1989 NR 1990   64
7.6d 6g 10.1m 6 a8g 10m² 9f⁵ 10f* 10d⁴ 8m 8d 10d] strong, workmanlike filly: carries
condition: first foal: dam twice-raced half-sister to good 1975 2-y-o 5f performer
Western Jewel and Queen Anne winner Mr Fluorocarbon: quite modest performer:
favourite, easily made all in seller (sold out of R. Boss's stable 4,800 gns) at
Folkestone in September: ran poorly last 2 starts: suited by 1¼m: acts on firm
going. *R. J. Hodges.*

WESTERN MUSIC 3 ch.f. Music Boy 124–Tripolitaine (FR) (Nonoalco (USA)   67
131) [1989 5f* 5m³ 6m⁵ 5s⁴ 5s⁴ 5s² 5g³ 7d 1990 7v⁴ 6m⁴ 7d² 7g⁵ 7m³ 8f⁵ 8.2d⁴ 6m³
7m⁴ 7d⁴ 7g 8d⁴] compact, workmanlike filly: quite modest performer: may prove
ideally suited by 1m: acts on any going: sold 3,700 gns Newmarket December Sales:
unreliable. *J. S. Wilson.*

WESTERN OCEAN 3 ch.c. Pharly (FR) 130–Pretty Pol 102 (Final Straw 127)   93
[1989 7m² 7m* 8g⁴ 1990 10f⁵ 12m 10.2g² 10m] lengthy colt: fairly useful performer:
good second in £8,600 handicap at Doncaster in September: ran in snatches final
start: should stay 1½m: acts on firm going: sold 18,000 gns Newmarket Autumn
Sales, probably to Italy. *M. R. Stoute.*

WESTERN SECRET 3 br.g. Kind of Hush 118–My Ginny 83 (Palestine 133)   —
[1989 6s 1990 12f⁵ 11v 12d] well-made gelding: well beaten, including in sellers:
retained by trainer 940 gns Doncaster November Sales. *J. S. Wilson.*

WESTERN WOLF 5 ch.h. Wolverlife 115–Sweet Kate (Slippered 103) [1989 8v   81
10f⁴ 8f⁵ 8.5g 10m⁴ 12g 8.3m⁵ 8.5f* 8g* 8m 8d 1990 8f 9g⁴ 8f³ 7m² 7.6m 8m² 8f 8.2s
8.2f⁴ 8g 8m⁶ 9m] plain horse: usually looks well: fair handicapper: best at around
1m: goes particularly well on top-of-the-ground: ran poorly in blinkers: bandaged
behind penultimate start: has broken blood vessel over hurdles: has joined C.
Popham. *W. Carter.*

WESTFIELD MOVES (IRE) 2 b.c. (Mar 24) Montelimar (USA) 122–   82
Rathcoffey Daisy (Pampapaul 121) [1990 7f² 7.5g* 8.2g³ 7g² 8d* 7s] IR 4,200F,
4,200Y: leggy, lengthy colt, rather unfurnished: third foal: dam never ran: fair
performer: successful, staying on strongly, in maiden auction at Beverley in August
and nursery (by a neck) at Redcar in October: will be suited by 1¼m: acts on firm
and dead (possibly unsuited by soft) ground: game and genuine. *H. J. Collingridge.*

WESTGATE ROCK 3 b.c. Jalmood (USA) 126–Westgate Sovereign 89 (Sove-   74
reign Path 125) [1989 7g⁶ 1990 8f 8.5g 10m* 10g 10f⁴ 10.6m³ 12m⁵ 9m] quite
attractive colt: has quick action: modest performer: won claimer at Sandown in
June: should stay further than 10.6f: best effort on good to firm ground: bandaged
off-fore fifth start: inconsistent. sold 14,000 gns Newmarket Autumn Sales. *L. M.
Cumani.*

WESTHOLME (USA) 2 ch.c. (Apr 25) Lyphard's Wish (FR) 124–Shroud (USA)   82
(Vaguely Noble 140) [1990 5f² 6g 7m* 7g* 8d²] 14,500Y: lengthy colt: has scope:
second foal: dam unraced half-sister to Grade 1 9f winner Adept: fair performer:
much improved in autumn final 3 starts, winning maiden at Redcar and nursery
(gamely by a short head from Worldbeta) at York then second under very hard ride
in nursery at Redcar: will stay 1¼m: acts on good to firm ground and dead. *M. H.
Easterby.*

WEST RIDING (USA) 2 b.c. (Feb 2) Topsider (USA)–Kashie West (USA) (Sir   83 p
Ivor 135) [1990 6g*] $375,000Y: smallish, angular colt: first foal: dam won at up to 9f
in USA after being placed in France: well-backed favourite but green, made all in
17-runner maiden at Newbury in October, shaken up 2f out then staying on strongly:
will stay 1m: sure to improve. *J. H. M. Gosden.*

WEST WITH THE WIND 3 b. or br.g. Glint of Gold 128–Mighty Fly 117   67
(Comedy Star (USA) 121) [1989 8m 8v⁶ 1990 10m⁴ 11.5m* 13.3m 12f⁴ 12m⁵ 10g]
leggy, workmanlike colt: quite modest at best: won maiden at Lingfield in June,

making most and rallying gamely: well beaten in handicaps and amateurs event after: will prove suited by 1½m+: sold 25,000 gns Newmarket Autumn Sales. *I. A. Balding.*

WESTWOOD HOPE 2 ch.c. (Apr 17) Ballacashtal (CAN)–Jenny's Rocket 90 — (Roan Rocket 128) [1990 6m 6f a8g] 1,550 2-y-o: tall, leggy colt: fifth foal: half-brother to 5f winner Sleepers (by Swing Easy) and 3-y-o Wild Sage (by Noalto): dam 2-y-o 6f winner also won over hurdles: soundly beaten in minor events and a maiden (sweating and on toes). *A. Moore.*

WHASSAT 6 b.g. Saher 115–Whisht (Raise You Ten 125) [1989 12f 14g² 16f⁵ 16g 14g³ 16g² 12m* 1990 9g 9m 10.1m 16m] smallish, good-topped ex-Irish gelding: carries plenty of condition: first foal: dam Irish 1½m winner: odds on, won 4-runner handicap at Tramore as 5-y-o: well beaten in varied events in summer: suited by 1½m+: acts on any going: usually apprentice or amateur ridden: sold out of P. Mullins' stable 3,600 gns Doncaster January Sales. *J. D. J. Davies.*

WHAT A CARD 2 b.f. (May 19) Myjinski (USA)–Ventrex 95 (Henry The 42 Seventh 125) [1990 5m⁶ 5g 5g² 6g 7g a8g⁶] unfurnished filly: sixth foal: half-sister to 1986 2-y-o 6f winner Dohty Baby (by Hittite Glory) and a winner in Sweden: dam 1¾m and 2m winner: sire by Niniski: quite modest plater: should stay 1m. *Denys Smith.*

WHATANICE SUPRISE 2 b.c. (Mar 9) Norwick (USA) 120–Lady Spey 55 (Sir — Gaylord) [1990 a7g] 700Y: rather dipped-backed colt: third foal: dam maiden suited by 1½m: bit backward and slowly away in seller at Southwell in August. *J. D. Czerpak.*

WHAT A SAVE 3 b.f. Law Society (USA) 130–Merriment (Kings Lake (USA) — 133) [1989 6m 6g³ 1990 10m 10g 8g] leggy filly: has a rather round action: plating-class maiden: behind in 1990, in handicaps last 2 starts: should be well suited by 7f+: edgy on reappearance: flashed tail final start at 2 yrs. *R. Hannon.*

WHAT A SHOW OFF (IRE) 2 ch.g. (Mar 10) Exhibitioner 111–Berserk 68 62 (Romulus 129) [1990 5f³ 5f 5g⁵ 7f⁴ 8m 8.5m⁴ 8.2s* 8m 8d 8.2s] 6,200Y: sparely-made gelding: half-brother to several winners here and abroad, including useful 1m and 1¼m winner Kazankina (by Malinowski): dam 2-y-o 5f winner out of a very speedy but temperamental mare: useful plater: won nursery (no bid) at Hamilton in September: ran moderately after: suited by a test of stamina: acts very well on soft ground: sold 1,600 gns Doncaster November Sales. *R. M. Whitaker.*

WHAT HAPPENS NEXT 3 ch.c. Lucky Wednesday 124–Delayed Action 113 — (Jolly Jet 111) [1989 5f³ 5h⁶ 7f a6g 1990 a6g] poor form, including in sellers: sold 1,250 gns Doncaster February Sales. *Ronald Thompson.*

WHEELS OF WEETMAN 3 b.c. Stanford 121§–Miss Legend (USA) (Bold — Legend) [1989 NR 1990 8g⁵ 8.2m⁶ 6g] IR 4,600Y: heavy-topped colt: has plenty of scope: closely related to useful 1978 Irish 2-y-o 5f winner Devilish (by Red God) and half-brother to several winners: dam won twice over 6f in USA: burly, well beaten in maiden, minor event and claimer. *B. A. McMahon.*

WHENTHETIDETURNS 2 b.f. (Jan 24) Aragon 118–Swaynes Lady 76 (St 39 Alphage 119) [1990 5f 6g 6f³ 6g³ 7f 7f] small filly: good walker: half-sister to moderate 1982 2-y-o 6f winner Leadenhall Lad (by Comedy Star): dam 2-y-o 5f winner: poor plater: best form at 6f: blinkered final 3 starts: looks a difficult ride: possibly ungenuine: sold 700 gns Newmarket September Sales: resold 850 gns Doncaster November Sales. *R. Hannon.*

WHERE'S CAROL 2 gr.f. (Feb 5) Anfield 117–Ludovica (Bustino 136) [1990 67 5m⁶ 5f⁶ 5m² 5m 5f⁵ 5d³ a6g* a6g* a8g² 6g 7g 8m a6g³ a6g* a6g⁴] 2,000Y: lengthy, leggy filly: first foal: dam unraced daughter of Ebor second Lorelene: modest filly: successful in seller (retained 5,000 gns), nursery and 2 claimers at Southwell: stays 1m: acts particularly well on all-weather: blinkered sixth start: has been unruly at stalls: has worn a tongue strap: claimed out of M. W. Easterby's stable £7,201 tenth start. *C. N. Allen.*

WHERE'S THE MONEY 4 b.f. Lochnager 132–Balearica 90 (Bustino 136) 49 [1989 5s³ 5g 5d 6s 5m 5d 1990 5d 5g⁵ 5g 6d⁴ 6s 5s a6g a5g] sturdy, workmanlike filly: poor handicapper at best nowadays: well beaten on all-weather last 2 outings: stays 6f: acts on soft going: blinkered sixth and final outings: sweating and wandered under pressure third start: sold 950 gns Ascot December Sales. *M. J. Fetherston-Godley.*

WHIMBREL 2 b.f. (Jan 14) Dara Monarch 128–Lola Sharp (Sharpen Up 127) 54 [1990 5f 7g² 7.5g³ 7m² 7.5g³ 8.5m*] IR 7,000Y: lengthy filly: fourth foal: half-sister to 3-y-o Dawson City (by Glint of Gold), winner over 6f (at 2 yrs) and 1¼m and over hurdles, and 6f winner Rocquaine (by Ballad Rock): dam won in Italy at 3 yrs: plating-class performer: won selling nursery (no bid) at Beverley in September: will stay 1¼m: hung and didn't run on when visored fourth outing. *M. H. Easterby.*

WHIPPER IN 6 b.g. Bay Express 132–Whip Finish 77 (Be Friendly 130) [1989 6f 5f⁴ 6f 6g 5m⁶ 5m⁵ 6m² 6g 5d 1990 6m⁶ 5f 6g³ a6g³ 6g 7g a7g 6g a7g⁴ a8g] tall, good-topped gelding: carries plenty of condition: poor mover: very useful at his best, but has deteriorated considerably: stays 7f: best form on a sound surface: blinkered 5 times, visored once: often slowly away: has worn crossed noseband: sold out of J. Etherington's stable 1,550 gns Doncaster November Sales after ninth start: not to be trusted. *Mrs N. Macauley.* **55 §**

WHIPPERS DELIGHT (IRE) 2 ch.g. (Apr 22) King Persian 107–Crashing Juno (Crash Course 128) [1990 5g⁵ 6f³ 7g* 7m* 7f 7g 7f⁴ 7g a8g⁶] 800Y: leggy gelding: brother to 4-y-o Jupiter Girl and half-brother to winning jumper Macroom (by Furry Glen) and a winner in Norway: dam never ran: made all in sellers at Carlisle (bought in 4,500 gns) in June and Wolverhampton (retained 7,000 gns) in July: ran creditably on all-weather final start: stays 1m: bought out of J. Berry's stable 4,500 gns Doncaster October Sales after eighth appearance. *T. D. Barron.* **58**

WHIPPET 6 b.h. Sparkler 130–St Louis Sue (FR) 79 (Nonoalco (USA) 131) [1989 5g* 6.5g⁴ 6s⁴ 6s* 5m⁶ 5g⁵ 5m* 6d² 5f⁵ 5g² 6g⁴ 5g⁶ 5g⁴ 1990 5.5v² 5g⁵ 5m⁴ 6g* 6g³ 6.5g⁴ 6d 5g³ 5v⁵ 5v] lengthy, good-quartered horse: bad walker and moderate mover: useful performer: won listed event at Evry in June: ran creditably behind Ron's Victory in Prix de Ris-Orangis at same course and Dead Certain in Prix Maurice de Gheest at Deauville next 2 outings: unseated rider at stalls and had to be withdrawn from Ciga Prix de l'Abbaye de Longchamp ninth intended start: suited by sprint distances: acts on any going: has worn visor, usually blinkered nowadays. *J. E. Hammond, France.* **106**

WHISPERING SEA 3 b.f. Bustino 136–Sound of The Sea 91 (Windjammer (USA)) [1989 8g 1990 8g] unfurnished filly: showed ability in maiden on debut, none on only start in 1990. *N. A. Graham.* **—**

WHISTLING GALE 3 ch.f. Whistling Deer 117–Velpol (Polyfoto 124) [1989 6f 5f 6m⁴ 7m⁵ 7d 6s⁶ 1990 8m] small filly: plater: backward, faced stiff task only start in 1990: should stay 1m: acts on soft going. *D. Burchell.* **—**

WHITCOMBE PRINCE 3 b.c. Anita's Prince 126–Hello Stranger (Milesian 125) [1989 5m 5h⁵ 6m 5.8f⁵ 5f 8f 1990 6m 6g⁴ 6f⁵ 7h³ a8g] small colt: has a quick action: plating-class sprinter at best: possibly suited by give in the ground: dead. *R. Akehurst.* **42**

WHITCOMBE WARRIOR 4 b.g. Tina's Pet 121–Minuetto 59 (Roan Rocket 128) [1989 7s 1990 7m 6f 8.3m 8g] smallish gelding: lightly-raced maiden: showed signs of ability final outing: shapes as though he should be suited by 1¼m: has worn crossed noseband. *R. Akehurst.* **47**

WHITEHAVEN 3 b.f. Top Ville 129–White Star Line (USA) (Northern Dancer) [1989 8g* 1990 10.5g² 10.5d² 12d* 12d² 13.5d* 14.6g³] seventh foal: half-sister to 5 winners, including 1988 2-y-o 6f winner Lustre (by Halo) and useful 1985 2-y-o 7f winner Native Wizard (by In Reality), later successful in USA: dam won 3 Grade 1 events at 8.5f to 1¼m at 3 yrs in USA: successful in maiden at Saint-Cloud at 2 yrs, listed race at Chantilly in June and Prix de Pomone (led close home to beat Tycana a length) at Deauville: fair third to Madame Dubois in Park Hill Stakes at Doncaster, tending to hang and never dangerous: stays 13.5f: tail swisher: stud. *A. Fabre.* **116**

WHITE JASMIN 4 ch.f. Jalmood (USA) 126–Willowbed 66 (Wollow 132) [1989 12.2m³ 12f 12m⁵ 12.2m⁴ 16f* 19f³ 16m⁵ 1990 13.8m 16.5m 16g 13.8m⁶ 16m⁴ 18m⁵ 16m³ 16.5g⁴ a14g⁵ 16f⁴] angular filly: poor handicapper: stays 19f: best efforts on top-of-the-ground: has looked none too keen: sold to join J. Parkes's stable 5,000 gns Doncaster September Sales: winning hurdler in October. *C. W. Thornton.* **35**

WHITE RIVER 4 ch.c. Pharly (FR) 130–Regain 86 (Relko 136) [1989 6d 8.2s 8g 9f⁶ 12m² 17.6m⁵ 12g a16g 1990 12.5f³ 12m 13m⁷ 15.3g* 15.3m⁴ 15.3f* 17.6f⁵ 14m² 14d] smallish, lengthy colt: poor mover: plating-class handicapper: won at Wolverhampton in July: stays 15.3f: acts on firm ground: won twice over hurdles in March. *D. Haydn Jones.* **56**

WHITE SAPPHIRE 5 b.h. Sparkler 130–On A Bit 66 (Mummy's Pet 125) [1989 9m⁶ 9g³ 10.2m³ 10m* 9f 10.6m 9g 1990 9f 4m 10.2m⁵ 10g² 10.2m 10m⁶] good-topped horse: moderate mover: modest handicapper: refused to enter stalls third intended outing, reluctant at them next time: ran moderately last 2 starts: suited by around 1¼m: possibly suited by easy surface nowadays: wandered and found little when blinkered: has worn tongue strap: difficult ride. *J. G. FitzGerald.* **68**

WHITE SQUIRREL 3 b.f. Noalto 120–Lovely Lassie (Connaught 130) [1989 6f — 5m⁶ 7m⁶ 1990 6f 10m 10f a7g⁶ 7g 7m] angular, dipped-backed filly: plater: little form in 1990: should stay at least 1m: blinkered last 4 starts: sold 1,100 gns Newmarket September Sales. *W. Carter.*

WHITESVILLE (IRE) 2 b.f. (Mar 22) Top Ville 129–White Star Line (USA) **84 p** (Northern Dancer) [1990 6.3g 6m² 6d*] eighth foal: sister to smart French middle-distance 3-y-o Whitehaven and half-sister to 5 other winners, 3 of them fairly useful, including 1m winner Urjwan (by Seattle Slew) and 1987 2-y-o 6f winner Lustre (by Halo): dam won Kentucky Oaks: progressive form in maidens, winning one at Punchestown in October by 6 lengths: will be well suited by 1m + : will do better. *M. Kauntze, Ireland.*

WHITEWEBB 3 br.g. Carwhite 127–Mrs Webb (Sonnen Gold 121) [1989 5s⁶ 5g⁶ — 6m 6v 8g 1990 8f 7h 8g 7f 10m 11m] leggy, sparely-made gelding: moderate mover: poor maiden. *B. W. Murray.*

WHITTINGHAM VALE 7 b.m. Sagaro 133–Whittingham Fair (Welsh Pageant — 132) [1989 NR 1990 a16g a12g a8g] small, lightly-made mare: of little account: blinkered once. *M. C. Chapman.*

WHITTON LAD (IRE) 2 b.c. (Jan 23) Anita's Prince 126–Shuckran Habibi **65** (Thatching 131) [1990 5m³ 5f 5m⁵ a6g³] IR 5,000F, IR 7,800Y, 1,000 2-y-o: lengthy, workmanlike colt: moderate mover: second living foal: dam ran once at 3 yrs in Ireland: over 2 lengths third of 9, leading 5f, in maiden at Lingfield in November, easily best effort: ran badly in blinkers fourth start. *R. Akehurst.*

WHITWORTH GREY 2 gr.g. (May 28) Marching On 101–Grey Morley 78 **55** (Pongee 106) [1990 5m⁶ 6f⁶ 6m³ 7f⁵ 7d⁴] rather leggy, medium-sized gelding: third reported foal: half-brother to 3-y-o 6f winner Grey Tudor (by Import): dam placed at 5f at 2 yrs, won over hurdles: plating-class performer: will probably stay 1m: acts on firm and dead ground. *G. M. Moore.*

WHO'S TEF (IRE) 2 b.g. (May 16) Muscatite 122–Eternal Optimist (Relko 136) **56** [1990 5f⁴ 5f* 6g⁴ 7.5f 7f⁵ 5f³ 6m² 6m 6g 5m⁵ 6g a6g] rather leggy, close-coupled gelding: third foal: brother to a winner in Macau: dam never ran: plating-class form in varied races: won weak maiden at Redcar in May: really needs further than 5f, and stays 7f: acts on firm ground, and may be unsuited by an easy surface: blinkered tenth and final starts: inconsistent. *M. H. Easterby.*

WHO'S ZOOMIN' WHO 6 b. or br.m. Kind of Hush 118–Miss Twomey (Will — Somers 114§) [1989 NR 1990 8.5m] tall, good-bodied mare: winning plater as 3-y-o: no form in subsequent non-selling handicaps: bandaged and backward only start in 1990: stays 7.5f: acts on firm going: tailed off when blinkered: bought 1,600 gns Doncaster August Sales. *G. P. Kelly.*

WHO WAS THAT 3 ch.g. Crofthall 110–Petriva (Mummy's Pet 125) [1989 NR — 1990 8m 12f⁵] 1,000Y: rather leggy, workmanlike gelding: second foal: dam unraced: tailed off in auction events. *R. M. Whitaker.*

WICKED FOLLY 3 ch.f. Exhibitioner 111–Glencoe Lights 98 (Laser Light 118) **102** [1989 5g 5g² 5g 5g² 1990 5d* 5g 5m⁵ 6m 6g* 5m* 5g³ 6g 5g 6g] IR 6,200Y: fourth foal: dam Irish sprinter: useful performer: won maiden at Navan in April, minor event at Phoenix Park in May and Group 3 Compaq Computer EBF Ballyogan Stakes (beat Shuttlecock Corner 1½ lengths) at Leopardstown in June: creditable third to Dancing Music at Tipperary, best effort in listed races after: best form at 5f: yet to race on extremes of going: sold 26,000 gns Newmarket December Sales. *K. Prendergast, Ireland.*

WICKED THINGS (FR) 2 b.c. (Jan 27) Vayrann 133–Daffodil Walk 91 (Furry **83 p** Glen 121) [1990 a8g*] 7,200Y: second foal: half-brother to French 10.5f winner Akasha (by Akarad): dam Irish 2-y-o 8.5f winner: well-backed 11/4-shot, won late-year maiden at Lingfield by a length after slow start: will improve, and looks quite useful 3-y-o in making. *D. R. C. Elsworth.*

WICK POUND 4 b.c. Niniski (USA) 125–Hors Serie (USA) 103 (Vaguely Noble — 140) [1989 10.1m⁶ 10m 12.2m* 1990 12.5m 12.2m 12f 13.1h⁴ 14g] small, lightly-made colt: poor mover: modest winner as 3-y-o: well beaten in handicaps in 1990: stays strong early pace when blinkered final outing: stays 1½m: bandaged near-hind second outing. *J. A. B. Old.*

WIDYAN (USA) 2 b.c. (Jan 29) Fappiano (USA)–Hotel Street (USA) 93 (Alleged **105** (USA) 138) [1990 7.3m³ 7f* 8g³ 10s⁴ 10v³] rangy, good sort: has scope: first foal: dam lightly-raced 1½m winner, is half-sister to smart stakes winners Royal And Regal and Regal And Royal: useful performer: made all in maiden at Chester in July: better efforts after when fourth (hampered) to Pistolet Bleu in Criterium de

Saint-Cloud and narrowly-beaten third in Group 2 event at Rome: seems suited by 1¼m: acts on any going but goes particularly well on soft or heavy: keen sort: bandaged off-fore on debut. *P. F. I. Cole.*

WIGWAM BLEU 3 b.c. Lomond (USA) 128–Warsaw (FR) (Bon Mot III 132) [1989 NR 1990 15g] sixth foal: half-brother to several winners, notably high-class 1985 French 3-y-o 1½m winner Walensee (by Troy) and French 4-y-o 10.5f and 1½m winner Wall Street Wonder (by Simply Great): dam ran 3 times in France, winning twice at up to 13f, and is half-sister to Waya and Warfever, top-class performers in USA: well behind in maiden claimer at Edinburgh: sold to join J. Baker 1,550 gns Newmarket July Sales. *K. A. Morgan.* —

WILD AND LOOSE 2 b.c. (Mar 9) Precocious 126–Regain 86 (Relko 136) [1990 5m] 14,500F, 12,500Y: big, workmanlike colt: fifth foal: half-brother to 3-y-o Gentle Gain (by Final Straw) and 3 winners here and abroad, including 1986 2-y-o 7f winner Counter Attack (by Nishapour) and stayer White River (by Pharly): dam 1½m winner: burly and green, slowly away and behind until late progress in maiden at Windsor in July: looked sure to improve, particularly over further, but not seen out again. *D. R. C. Elsworth.* —

WILD COINCIDENCE 2 ch.g. (Apr 19) Faustus (USA) 118–Wild Rosie 66 (Warpath 113) [1990 5m⁶ 5m 8m 10m] small, plain gelding: fourth foal: dam staying half-sister to Derby third Mount Athos and smart sprinter John Splendid: poor plater: off course 5 months after second start: blinkered final outing: sold 1,150 gns Doncaster November Sales. *J. Wharton.* 36

WILD DANCER 3 br.g. Gorytus (USA) 132–Rosserk (Roan Rocket 128) [1989 6m* 7g³ 7m⁴ 7f4 1990 8.5m 10d 13.8d 8h⁴] good-topped gelding: good mover with long stride: quite modest winner at 2 yrs: no form in claimers and handicaps in 1990, and showed signs of temperament: stays 7f: visored third start: sold to join J. D. Thomas 1,500 gns Doncaster August Sales. *C. Tinkler.* —

WILD ONE 3 gr.f. Nordico (USA)–To Oneiro 69 (Absalom 128) [1989 NR 1990 a6g 7.5f 5m] small filly: second foal: half-sister to 1989 Norwegian winner Shy Yappy (by Mourtazam): dam 5f and 6f winner: no promise, including in seller. *R. J. R. Williams.* —

WILD PROSPECT 2 b.c. (May 29) Homing 130–Cappuccilli 111 (Lorenzaccio 130) [1990 6g* 6f5 6g] 8,000Y: smallish, good-quartered colt: has a quick action: seventh foal: brother to 1984 2-y-o 6f winner Vie Parisienne and half-brother to 3 other winners, including useful 1983 2-y-o 7f winner Falstaff (by Town And Country): dam very useful staying 2-y-o didn't train on: quite modest form: won maiden at Carlisle in May: ran respectably plater in nursery at Hamilton and seller at York: will probably be better suited by 7f +. *C. Tinkler.* 62

WILD WALTZ (USA) 2 b.c. (Feb 23) Wild Again (USA)–Waltz Me Sue (USA) (Olden Times) [1990 7m 8m] $80,000Y: workmanlike colt: half-brother to several minor winners in North America: dam winner at up to 7f, is half-sister to good 8.5f to 1¼m performer Imp Society: sire won 1¼m Breeders' Cup Classic: burly, plating-class form in maidens at Newmarket and Redcar: sold 8,200 gns Newmarket Autumn Sales. *M. A. Jarvis.* 56

WILL 3 gr.g. Tender King 123–Fine Flame (Le Prince 98) [1989 NR 1990 6v 7g a7g⁶ 8g] 5,200Y: angular gelding: moderate mover: fourth foal: half-brother to 3 winners, including Irish 1½m winner Fuego Del Amor (by Ahonoora) and fair 6f and 7f winner Battleaxe (by Kampala): dam modest Irish maiden placed twice at 2 yrs: no form, in selling handicap final start: sold 900 gns Doncaster November Sales. *C. W. Thornton.* —

WILLBUTWHEN 3 ch.c. Nicholas Bill 125–Henceforth 58 (Full of Hope 125) [1989 5s* 5m⁴ 5g² 1990 6g 6m5 7d6 6m6 5m 6g4 6d2 6s*] neat, good-quartered colt: good walker: fair handicapper: game winner of 24-runner race at Haydock in October, leading close home: stays 7f: goes well with plenty of give in the ground: below form in apprentice contest: sold 40,000 gns Newmarket Autumn Sales, probably to race in Italy. *H. Candy.* 89

WILLESDON (USA) 6 ch.h. Master Willie 129–Dona Maya (USA) (Reviewer (USA)) [1989 NR 1990 12f4 8g 8m] angular horse: hobdayed: won Group races prior to winning in French Provinces (blinkered) as 3-y-o: has deteriorated considerably: stays 11f: probably unsuited by soft going, acts on any other: bandaged at 6 yrs. *A. Barrow.* —

WILLFY (USA) 3 ch.c. Diesis 133–Little Mandy (USA) (Little Current (USA)) [1989 NR 1990 8.2g] $50,000Y: first foal: dam minor 2-y-o winner in North America: —

last of 12 in maiden at Hamilton in September: sold 1,900 gns Newmarket Autumn Sales. *B. Hanbury.*

WILL HE OR WONT HE (IRE)   2 b.c. (Jan 26) The Noble Player (USA)   71
126–Dusty Highway (High Top 131) [1990 5m⁶ 6s⁶ 7m a6g a6g⁶ 7d 8.2s 10.2s a8g²]
IR 6,900F, IR 10,000Y: sturdy, quite attractive colt: has a round action: first foal:
dam never ran: gambled-on second of 12 to Stairway To Heaven in claimer (visored) at Southwell, easily best effort: stays 1m well: trained first 5 outings by M.
McCormack. *C. N. Allen.*

WILLIAM BUNTER (IRE)   2 ch.g. (Apr 30) Horage 124–Alldyke (Klondyke   —
Bill 125) [1990 5m 6g 6m a7g] 1,000Y: small, sturdy gelding: poor mover: related to
3-y-o Pure Energy and half-brother to several winners, including fairly useful 1¼m
performer Lady Justice (by Status Seeker): dam closely related to Italian 1000
Guineas winner Alea II: seems of little account: sold 575 gns Ascot December Sales.
P. Howling.

WILLIAM CLITO (USA)   3 b. or br.g. Vaguely Noble 140–Pretty Pretender   —
(USA) (Quack (USA)) [1989 NR 1990 10.1m 11.5d³ 15.8m] $200,000Y: fifth foal:
brother to very useful 1m to 1½m winner Perkin Warbeck and half-brother to 2
winners in USA, including 1m stakes winner Kafiristan (by Key To The Mint): dam,
from good family, won 3 races at up to 6f from 4 starts: well beaten in minor event
and maidens: sold 2,500 gns Newmarket Autumn Sales and gelded. *J. Gosden.*

WILLIAM FOUR   5 b.g. Nicholas Bill 125–Henceforth 58 (Full of Hope 125)   73
[1989 8m³ 10f⁵ 10m* 10.2g² 10g³ a10g⁶ 1990 10.8m 10f 10g² 10m⁴ 11.7m² 12m⁶
12m* 12m² 12m² 12g*] leggy, quite good-topped gelding: modest handicapper: won
apprentice events at Chepstow in August and York in October: stays 1½m: yet to
race on soft going, acts on any other: wandered under pressure last 2 starts: has won
when sweating: sold 21,000 gns Newmarket Autumn Sales. *H. Candy.*

WILLIE MCGARR (USA)   5 ch.g. Master Willie 129–Pay T V (USA) (T V   —
Commercial (USA)) [1989 8.3m 1990 a12g⁵ a11g⁶ a12g] medium-sized gelding: no
sign of ability. *B. Palling.*

WILLILOV   4 ch.g. Rabdan 129–Miss Love 58 (Ragstone 128) [1989 7m⁵ 8.5f⁵   —
10f³ 10m 8f⁴ 10m 1990 17.6g] leggy gelding: little worthwhile form, including in
handicaps: should stay beyond 1m: has looked ill at ease on firm going. *H. A. T.
Whiting.*

WILLOW GORGE   7 ch.g. Hello Gorgeous (USA) 128–Willowy (Mourne 126)   —
[1989 15.5f 1990 12m] tall, quite attractive gelding: poor maiden: stayed 13f:
probably acted on any going: tailed off in blinkers: dead. *Miss B. Sanders.*

WILL PLASI   2 b.c. (Mar 10) Elegant Air 119–Miss Plasi 86 (Free State 125)   48
[1990 a6g⁵ 5.1m³ 6g 5f] good-bodied colt: has scope: third foal: half-brother to 1988
2-y-o sprint plater Dom Plasi (by Dominion) and a winner in Denmark: dam 5f and 6f
winner at 2 yrs, only season to race: best effort third of 7 in seller at Yarmouth:
should be suited by further than 5f. *Sir Mark Prescott.*

WILVICK   3 ch.g. Gabitat 119–Pas de Chat (Relko 136) [1989 5h⁵ 6m³ 5m³ 5.3h*   62
6g⁶ 1990 6g 5.3h⁴ 5m 8.3m⁶ 7h* 7f⁴ 8m³ 8f 8m] compact gelding: moderate mover:
quite modest performer: won claimer at Brighton in August: stays 1m: acts on hard
going: sold 5,400 gns Newmarket Autumn Sales. *R. Akehurst.*

WIMBORNE   5 ro.h. What A Guest 119–Khadija 69 (Habat 127) [1989 8.2v³ 10d   —
12.5f 8.2f 8h* 8f* 9m² 11f² 10f⁵ 8.2d 1990 8g 8.5f⁵ 10.2g 10d 12s] lengthy, rather
angular horse: has round action: winning plater as 4-y-o: facing stiff tasks, well
beaten in non-sellers and claimer in 1990: stays 11f, at least in slowly-run race: acts
on any going: wore crossed noseband final outing: taken quietly to post: winning
selling hurdler in October. *R. Bastiman.*

WINDATUM   5 gr.g. Windjammer (USA)–Raffinata (Raffingora 130) [1989 6s 7g   49 §
7.6m³ 9m⁵ 8m⁵ 7.6f* 8m 7.6f² 8g⁴ 8m 7.6m² 7.6m 1990 a8g 7f⁴ 8f 7g⁴dis 7m 7m 8.2v
8m 10g] tall, sparely-made gelding: poor mover: has gained 2 of his 4 wins at
Lingfield: first run for 6½ months, fourth in handicap at Leicester in July: little form
after, wandering and demoted fourth outing: stays 9f: acts on any going: has worn
blinkers and visor, but not when successful: usually bandaged: has won for
apprentice: of unsatisfactory temperament. *Mrs N. Macauley.*

WINDBOUND LASS   7 ch.m. Crofter (USA) 124–Nevilles Cross (USA) 67   57
(Nodouble (USA)) [1989 12g⁵ 12g³ 11.5f³ 17.1h² 13.1h² 12f² 12m 1990 12m⁵ 11.5m
17.1f* 15.3m 17.1m³] leggy, plain mare: plating-class handicapper: won at Bath in
July: stays 17f: acts very well on top-of-the-ground: consistent. *R. J. Holder.*

WINDMILL PRINCESS 3 b.f. Gorytus (USA) 132–Cley 85 (Exbury 138) [1989   55
NR 1990 8f² 10m⁶ 11g³ 7m 7d] 17,000Y: lengthy filly: moderate mover: half-sister to
3 winners, including fair 1½m and 13.3f winner Bodham (by Bustino): dam, 1½m
winner, is half-sister to Blakeney and Morston: plating-class maiden: will be suited
by return to 1¼m, at least: has flashed tail and wandered under pressure: trained
first 3 outings by M. Jarvis. *G. H. Eden.*

WINDSOR PARK (USA) 4 br.c. Bold Forbes (USA)–Round Tower 93 (High   69
Top 131) [1989 5g 7h⁵ 8m³ 10m² 12g 10g⁴ 10g* 10g² a12g* a12g* a12g² 1990 10m⁴
9m⁴ 10m⁵ 11.5g⁵ 10f⁵ a12g a10g⁴ a10g⁶] leggy, quite attractive colt: good walker:
modest handicapper: stays 1½m: acts on good to firm going: has won for apprentice:
blinkered last 2 starts. *R. J. O'Sullivan.*

WINDWARD ARIOM 4 ch.g. Pas de Seul 133–Deja Vu (FR) (Be My Guest   41
(USA) 126) [1989 9f 8h 8m 8g 12.2m⁵ 1990 13.8m⁴ 13.8m² 15.8g⁶ 15m⁶ 15.8m³ 12h⁵
12f⁶ 13.8f 13.8d⁶] leggy, close-coupled gelding: has a roundish action: poor handicapper: stays 1¾m: acts on good to firm and dead going: blinkered once: winner
over hurdles. *D. H. Topley.*

WINDY HOWE 3 b.g. Comedy Star (USA) 121–Kenton's Girl 86 (Record Token   53
128) [1989 6m 5g 6m 7m 7g⁵ 8g 1990 10d 10f⁶ 8.5m⁴ 10d 9s a12g⁵] ex-Irish gelding:
first foal: dam, raced only at 2 yrs, won both starts at 5f: plating-class maiden: ridden
by 7-lb claimer, below best in claimer at Southwell in December, well behind early
on: should stay 1½m: sometimes blinkered: trained until after fifth outing by J.
Canty. *J. G. FitzGerald.*

WING PARK 6 ch.h. Golden Dipper 119–Puente Primera 90 (Primera 131) [1989   97
6m 6f 1990 6g 7.6m 6m 7m⁶ 6s² 6s⁴ a6g²] strong, lengthy horse: useful as 4-y-o:
showed he retains most of his ability in listed race at Doncaster and handicap at
Southwell last 2 outings: effective at 5f and has won over 7f: acts on any going:
blinkered second start: suited by forcing tactics: trained first 2 starts by T. Jones. *J.
Pearce.*

WINGS OF FREEDOM (IRE) 2 b.g. (May 11) Fairy King (USA)–Wingau   85
(FR) (Hard To Beat 132) [1990 7m 8f 8d³ 9g* 10.2s²] 21,000Y: rangy gelding: has
scope: seventh foal: closely related to plating-class stayer Be My Wings (by Be My
Guest) and half-brother to a winner in Germany: dam middle-distance handicapper:
heavily-backed favourite, won claimer at York in October, swerving left when in
front 2f out: blinkered, good second, edging left, to Knifebox in minor event at
Doncaster following month: suited by a test of stamina: acts well on soft ground:
improving sort. *G. Lewis.*

WINTERHALTER 3 b.c. Busted 134–Winter Queen 60 (Welsh Pageant 132)   —
[1989 NR 1990 14g 14g 14f⁴] strong, rangy colt: third living foal: half-brother to very
useful 1m and 1¼m winner Main Objective (by Main Reef): dam won over 13f at 4 yrs
in Ireland: no promise in maidens. *L. M. Cumani.*

WINTER PEARL 2 gr.f. (Apr 30) Kenmare (FR) 125–Crillion (USA) (L'Enjoleur   —
(CAN) [1990 6m⁶] first foal: dam unraced half-sister to Allez France, is out of high-
class 2-y-o Priceless Gem, a half-sister to champion American filly Affectionately:
tailed off from halfway in 6-runner maiden at Newmarket in November. *R. Hannon.*

WISE FRIEND (USA) 2 b.c. (Mar 21) Sagace (FR) 135–Swalthee (FR) (Sword   —
Dancer (USA)) [1990 7g] IR 55,000F: good sort: half-brother to several winners,
including very useful 7f (at 2 yrs) and 1¼m winner Tralthee (by Tromos): dam
French 10.5f winner: very green, around 13 lengths eighth of 12 in maiden at
Salisbury in October: sold 1,600 gns Ascot November Sales. *P. F. I. Cole.*

WISH OF LUCK (USA) 2 ch.f. (Feb 5) Diesis 133–Kesar Queen (USA) 117   80
(Nashua) [1990 6m² 6d² 7d³ 6m⁴] unfurnished filly: has a roundish action: half-
sister to fair 1m winner Majestic Ace (by Majestic Light) and 1¾m winner Kesarini (by Singh): dam won Coronation Stakes and third in 1000 Guineas:
modest maiden: stays 7f: acts on good to firm ground and dead. *H. Thomson Jones.*

WISH QUICK (CAN) 3 br.f. Lyphard's Wish (FR) 124–Quicksand (USA) (Mill   52
Reef (USA) 141) [1989 NR 1990 10g 10m⁶ 10f 11.5f³] $65,000Y: rather sparely-made
filly: half-sister to several winners, including fair 7f and 1m winner Ampersand (by
Stop The Music): dam once-raced half-sister to smart 1m and 1½m winner Leap
Lively, dam of Forest Flower: plating-class maiden: should stay 1½m: edgy third
start: sold 3,000 gns Newmarket December Sales. *W. J. Haggas.*

WITH GUSTO 3 b.c. Taufan (USA) 119–Finesse 87 (Miralgo 130) [1989 7m 7g   47
1990 10g 10m 11.7m⁴ a12g a12g⁵ 12d⁵ a13g³ a13g³ a12g⁶] good-topped colt: plating-
class maiden: moderate third in handicaps at Lingfield: may stay 1¾m: sometimes
bandaged: wore tongue strap fifth start. *K. O. Cunningham-Brown.*

WITHIN REASON 3 ch.f. Reasonable (FR) 119–Nom de Plume 70 (Aureole — 132) [1989 6m⁶ 5m 5g 6g 1990 7f 8.2g 10d 10m 10m⁶ a12g⁵ a11g] lengthy, sparely-made filly: poor mover: of little account: sold 1,000 gns Ascot November Sales. *P. S. Felgate.*

WITHOUT EQUAL (USA) 3 ch.c. Sharpen Up 127–Key Tothe Minstrel 74 (USA) 108 (The Minstrel (CAN) 135) [1989 6m⁶ 8g⁴ 1990 8f² 9f⁶ 8g² 10d² 11.7m⁴ 8m 10g] compact colt: moderate mover: modest maiden: below form last 3 starts: should prove better at 1¼m than shorter: yet to race on soft going, acts on any other: visored fifth start: bandaged final one: tongue tied down fourth and fifth: sold out of M. Stoute's stable 16,000 gns Newmarket July Sales after latter. *M. Madgwick.*

WITNESS BOX (USA) 3 b.c. Lyphard (USA) 132–Excellent Alibi (USA) 83 + (Exceller (USA) 129) [1989 NR 1990 10g 10f* 12m] rangy, workmanlike colt with scope: first reported foal: dam, French 1¼m to 1½m winner, is closely related to Dahlia: co-favourite but still green, won 7-runner maiden at Ripon in April: well-beaten last of 7, facing stiff task, in £14,800 York handicap over 4 months later. *J. H. M. Gosden.*

WIZZARD MAGIC 7 ch.h. Ahonoora 122–Siofra Beag (Steel Heart 128) [1989 58 8g 9d⁵ 10f⁶ 9.2f 9m 8m² 10m⁵ 10g⁴ 7s a8g* a10g⁶ 1990 7.6m 9m⁶ 10m* 10f⁴ 10.2f³ a8g 9m³ 10m 10f⁴ 10f a8g² a8g³] good-topped horse: poor mover: won amateurs handicap at Folkestone in July: stays 1¼m: acts on firm going and possibly unsuited by soft: best blinkered or visored: suitable mount for inexperienced rider: sometimes sweats. *M. J. Haynes.*

WOLD GUEST (IRE) 2 b.c. (Mar 10) Kafu 120–Opera Guest (Be My Guest — (USA) 126) [1990 5f 6f 5v] 8,400Y: lengthy, workmanlike colt: good walker and mover: first foal: dam never ran: little worthwhile form in varied events: blinkered in a seller final start. *J. Etherington.*

WOLFGANG 3 ch.g. Music Boy 124–Hello Honey 105 (Crepello 136) [1989 NR — 1990 10m 12f a12g 8m] 11,500Y: leggy gelding: moderate mover: half-brother to 5 winners, including quite useful middle-distance performers Positive (by Posse) and Concert Hall (by Connaught): dam won 4 times at up to 1½m: no show in varied company, blinkered and carrying head high in handicap: sold 3,100 gns Newmarket Autumn Sales. *M. H. Tompkins.*

WOLF HALL (IRE) 2 b.c. (May 18) Green Desert (USA) 127–Lady Seymour 88 109 (Tudor Melody 129) [1990 6m⁴ 6f² 6m² 5f² 6d* 6d³] IR 65,000Y: angular colt: moderate mover: half-brother to 6 winners, including top-class sprinter Marwell and Mill Reef Stakes winner Lord Seymour (both by Habitat) and useful middle-distance colt Lord Grundy (by Grundy): dam, successful over 5f on only 2 starts, is out of half-sister to Eclipse winner Arctic Explorer: fair performer: very easy winner of modest maiden at Lingfield in October: will stay 7f: acts on firm and dead ground: races freely: consistent. *M. R. Stoute.*

WOLVER GOLD 3 b.f. Wolverlife 115–Mahele (USA) (Hawaii) [1989 6f 6g 5f² 62 5.8f² 5f* 6g 5f 1990 6f 5g 6m 8m 5f⁵ 5.8h] tall, leggy filly: modest winner at 2 yrs: best effort in 1990 penultimate start, soon outpaced: best form at 5f: acts on firm going: sometimes troublesome at stalls, and very mulish to post on reappearance. *J. D. Roberts.*

WONDERMENT 3 b.f. Mummy's Pet 125–Baffle 87 (Petingo 135) [1989 7f 1990 72 ? 10.1g⁴ 8g a12g³ a8g] leggy, lengthy filly: modest maiden: form only when fourth in minor event at Windsor in August: should stay 1½m: looked irresolute penultimate start: blinkered final one. *Lady Herries.*

WOODCOCK WONDER 3 ch.g. Royal Vulcan 83–Deandar (Communication 51 119) [1989 6m 7m 6g a8g⁶ a7g⁴ a7g 1990 12f³ a12g⁴ 12.2m⁴ 12g⁶ 11.5m⁴ a12g² 12m²] rather sparely-made gelding: plating class on most form: blinkered and claimer ridden when second in handicap at Southwell and seller at Newmarket: will stay beyond 1½m: best turf efforts on top-of-the-ground: has run creditably when sweating. *J. R. Jenkins.*

WOODHEAD 3 br.f. Touching Wood (USA) 127–Ravenshead (Charlottown 127) — [1989 NR 1990 14g] leggy filly: half-sister to 3 winners, including 1½f winner Kenilworth Castle (by Dunbeath) and very useful 1981 staying 2-y-o Ashenden (by Blakeney): dam poor half-sister to very smart sprinter Nevermore: very green, always behind in maiden at Nottingham in July: joined M. W. Easterby. *A. C. Stewart.*

WOODHOOPOE 4 ch.f. Touching Wood (USA) 127–Good Try 92 (Good Bond 66 122) [1989 10g 12.2m 10.2h⁵ 8m⁵ 7m 7s⁶ 8.2g² a11g a11g* 1990 a12g* a12g*] rather sparely-made filly: apprentice ridden, successful at Southwell in 2 handicaps in

January: would have stayed beyond 1½m: sometimes sweated and got on edge: dead. *C. J. Bell.*

WOODLANDS CROWN 7 ch.g. Milford 119–Town Girl 99 (Town Crier 119) — [1989 11.7d³ 11.7m 8.5g⁶ 1990 12g] leggy, quite good-topped gelding: poor handicapper: virtually pulled up only start at 7 yrs: stays 1½m: acts on good to firm and dead going. *D. C. Tucker.*

WOODLANDS GREY 4 gr.g. Nishapour (FR) 125–Topling 85 (High Top 131) — [1989 7g 8d 8g 8f 1990 8m 8m a10g] close-coupled, workmanlike gelding: of little account: has worn bandages behind. *P. A. Pritchard.*

WOODLAND STEPS 4 ch.f. Bold Owl 101–Sweet Minuet (Setay 105) [1989 NR — 1990 10m 11f⁴] small, workmanlike filly: has a quick action: fair winner as 2-y-o: well beaten in handicaps at 4 yrs: best at 7f: yet to race on an easy surface. *Miss L. C. Siddall.*

WOODMAN'S MOUNT (USA) 2 b.c. (Mar 16) Woodman (USA) 126–Tenta- 102 mount (USA) (Tentam (USA)) [1990 6f* 7g³ 7f* 7d 9f] IR 105,000Y: angular, quite attractive colt: third foal: half-brother to a winner in USA by Northern Prospect: dam minor winner in USA: useful colt: successful in maiden (pulled hard) at Newmarket in August and minor event (readily made all by 2½ lengths from Obligation) at Folkestone in September: favourite, never able to challenge in Cartier Million at Phoenix Park then seventh in Grade 3 event at Aqueduct in October: best form at 7f on firm ground. *L. M. Cumani.*

WOODSIDE HEATH 3 ch.c. King Persian 107–Saga's Humour 61 (Bustino 67 136) [1989 6h³ 5f³ 7h³ 6g³ a7g* a8g³ 1990 7g 7.6m² 8m⁶ 7h⁵ 8f⁶ 8m² 7h 7g 7.6d⁶ 8m⁶] neat colt: has a round action: quite modest handicapper: stays 1m: acts on good to firm ground and dead: has worn bandages: hung left when running well for apprentice sixth outing: joined J. S. Moore: inconsistent. *R. Hannon.*

WOODSTOCK LODGE (USA) 2 ch.c. (Apr 29) Lyphard's Wish (FR) 124– 57 Renaissance Queen (USA) (Elocutionist (USA)) [1990 6f⁴ 7m 6m⁶ 8f] $5,000F, IR 6,200Y: strong, workmanlike colt: good walker: second foal: dam ran 4 times: plating-class maiden at best: should stay 7f. *D. H. Topley.*

WOODURATHER 4 br.g. Touching Wood (USA) 127–Rather Warm 103 (Tribal 71 Chief 125) [1989 8g² 8f⁴ 1990 12d⁵ 12m 10m* 10.4d*] small, light-framed gelding: moderate walker: successful in handicaps at Chepstow (edging left) in July and Chester (impressively) in October: keen sort, better suited by 1¼m than 1½m: acts on good to firm going, but clearly goes particularly well on dead: wore crossed noseband last 3 starts: seems to need strong handling. *M. C. Pipe.*

WOODY EXPRESS 2 b.g. (May 6) Today And Tomorrow 78–Dewberry 68 44 (Bay Express 132) [1990 5g² 5g 5m³ a6g³ 5f⁶ 5m] 780Y: workmanlike gelding: moderate walker: half-brother to 2 winners by Monsanto, including 1985 2-y-o 5f winner Monstrosa, and a winner in Macau: dam 6f winner: poor maiden: best efforts at Catterick: looked difficult ride in blinkers penultimate outing: better form at 5f. *M. W. Ellerby.*

WOOLAW BOY 2 b.c. (May 2) Enchantment 115–Lightening Blue (Roan Rocket 40 128) [1990 6g⁶ 7m⁶ 7g] 5,000Y: compact colt: third foal: dam never ran: poor form, including in seller (edged left) at Thirsk: slowly away on debut. *J. S. Haldane.*

WOOLAW LASS (USA) 2 b.f. (May 27) Full Extent (USA) 113–Current River — (USA) (Little Current (USA)) [1990 5m 5g] smallish, workmanlike filly: second foal: dam minor winner at 3 yrs in North America: always behind in claimers at Hamilton (backward and very green) and Edinburgh in June. *J. S. Haldane.*

WOOLSTONE LAD 2 b.c. (Apr 29) Today And Tomorrow 78–Be Cool (Relkino — 131) [1990 6m 6m] leggy colt: first foal: dam (ran once over hurdles) daughter of half-sister to Derby Italiano winner Appiani II: always behind in sellers at Goodwood and Lingfield. *P. Burgoyne.*

WOOLY RAGS 4 ch.f. Raga Navarro (ITY) 119–Woolcana 71 (Some Hand 119) — [1989 8d 6g 7m 6m 1990 a7g 8m] close-coupled filly: poor walker and mover: won seller at 2 yrs: well beaten subsequently: bandaged near-hind final outing: sold 925 gns Ascot July Sales. *P. A. Pritchard.*

WORK ON AIR 4 ch.g. Doc Marten 104–Set To Work (Workboy 123) [1989 5m³ — 5f 5f 5f 6f² 6m 6g 6g⁴ 6m⁴ 8f³ 7g 6g a6g⁴ 1990 a7g⁴ a7g a6g] plain, angular gelding: has a quick action: poor handicapper: below form all 3 starts early in year: should prove as effective over 7f as 1m: acts on firm going: visored once, blinkered 3 times. *W. A. O'Gorman.*

WORLDBETA (IRE)   2 ch.c. (Feb 22) Hatim (USA) 121–Celestial Star 108 (So   76
Blessed 130) [1990 6g 6m 5m⁴ 8m 7m² 7g² 7.6v* 8.2s] 13,500Y: lengthy,
good-bodied colt: good walker: moderate mover: half-brother to several winners,
including quite useful Irish 1½m winner Royal Counsellor (by Gunner B) and 9f
winner Main Hand (by Main Reef): dam 2-y-o 5f and 6f winner: improved colt: won
nursery at Chester in October by 1½ lengths, making most and staying on gamely,
from Valid Point: ran poorly after: stays 1m: yet to race on firm ground, acts on any
other: blinkered final 4 starts. *J. W. Watts.*

WORLD'S CREATION (USA)   2 b.c. (Jan 29) Cormorant (USA)–Worlds Fair   65 +
(USA) (Our Hero (USA)) [1990 5m³ 6s 6g⁶ 8m⁴] $50,000F, IR 66,000Y: smallish
colt: half-brother to 2 minor winners in USA: dam once-raced half-sister to Super
Asset, Bates Motel and Hatim: sire won from 6f to 9f: progressive maiden: ran
exceptionally good race and gave strong impression would have gone very close
better placed early on in nursery at Pontefract in September: suited by 1m. *B. W.
Hills.*

WORLDSPORTFLYER   4 b.g. Hays 120–Arabian Pearl (Deep Diver 134)   —
[1989 9g 12s 12f² 12m 12m⁴ 15.3g 10g 1990 a12g a8g a8g] rangy, angular gelding:
modest plater at best: stays 1½m: acts on firm going: blinkered once at 2 yrs:
untrustworthy hurdler. *M. C. Chapman.*

WORTH OF MELTHAM   3 ch.g. What A Guest 119–Corofin (USA) (Key To   —
The Kingdom (USA)) [1989 NR 1990 11m 12.2m⁵ 12.5g⁴ 18d 11d⁵] 9,200Y: big, plain
gelding: first foal: dam thrice-raced in Ireland: poor maiden. *Miss L. C. Siddall.*

WOTAMISTAKATOMAKA   2 ch.g. (Mar 30) Crofthall 110–Redgrave Design   41
77 (Nebbiolo 125) [1990 5m 8.5m⁵ 8.2g 10m 7d] lengthy, angular gelding: third foal:
brother to 3-y-o First Bid and 1987 2-y-o 5f seller winner Arroganza: dam 2-y-o 5f
winner: quite modest plater: visored then blinkered final 2 starts: reluctant to enter
stalls second outing. *R. M. Whitaker.*

WOTAMONA   2 b.f. (May 17) Another Realm 118–Meadow Wood (Meadow Court   56
129) [1990 5m⁵ 7g⁵ 6g 8m 7g 10m² 10s 10.2s] 620F, 2,700Y: leggy, sparely-made
filly: half-sister to quite modest 1978 2-y-o 5f winner Betbellof (by Averof) and 2
winners abroad: dam never ran: easily best effort staying-on second of 18 to Long
Furlong in selling nursery at Leicester: suited by 1¼m, possibly by sound surface.
B. Palling.

WRETHAM HOUSE   2 b.c. (Mar 26) Bellypha 130–Hayley Warren (Habitat   76 §
134) [1990 7m⁶ 8g³ 10s⁶] sturdy colt: fifth foal: half-brother to 1m and 1¼m winner
Wretham (by Henbit), fair 1988 2-y-o 8.2f winner West Wretham (by Dominion) and
a winner in Italy: dam Irish 9f winner: visored, easily best effort staying-on third in
minor event at Wolverhampton: looked ungenuine when blinkered after: carries
head high: one to be wary of: sold 7,500 gns Newmarket Autumn Sales. *M. R. Stoute.*

WRYBILL   3 b.c. Sharpo 132–Wryneck 89 (Niniski (USA) 125) [1989 6m⁴ 6g³ **100** p
1990 6g² 6m 7d* 8m* 8g 7.2g* 7d*] close-coupled, useful-looking colt: carries
condition: grand walker: progressed into useful handicapper, winning at Leicester
(£6,300 event) in June, Chepstow in July and Haydock (£17,700 event) and Ayr
(soon outpaced, led post) in September: stays 1m: acts on good to firm ground and
dead: usually held up: can continue to give good account of himself. *R. Charlton.*

Philip Cornes Nickel Alloys Handicap, Ayr — Wrybill (far side) gets up to pip Ashdren

WSOM (IRE) 2 b.c. (Mar 22) Tate Gallery (USA) 117–April Bride (USA) (Run **66**
The Gantlet (USA)) [1990 7g⁵ 6d 6g 6d² 7d] IR 15,500F, 29,000Y: lengthy colt:
second foal: dam well beaten: quite modest maiden: will probably stay at least 1m:
acts on dead ground: inconsistent. *M. O'Neill.*

WYCLIFFE 2 ch.g. (Apr 4) Dunbeath (USA) 127–Blakewood 75 (Blakeney 126) **51**
[1990 6g 5g³ 7m⁵ 6f⁴ 6m 6g 7m] 1,700F, 2,600Y: workmanlike gelding: moderate
mover: seventh live foal: half-brother to 3 winners, including 16.5f winner Jai-Alai
(by Grundy): dam winning stayer: poor maiden: showed nothing final 3 starts: will
stay beyond 7f. *Denys Smith.*

WYKEHAMIST 7 ch.g. Blue Refrain 121–Flying Portion 72 (Major Portion 129) —
[1989 9d⁴ 9v⁵ 8g a10g⁴ a12g a10g a12g² 1990 a10g] rangy gelding: carries plenty of
condition: moderate mover: quite modest handicapper at 6 yrs: stays 1½m: acts on
any going: has won for apprentice: occasionally sweats: usually held up: sold 820
gns Newmarket Autumn Sales. *C. J. Benstead.*

WYLAM 3 b.g. What A Guest 119–Wish You Wow (Wolver Hollow 126) [1989 7m⁴ —
1990 8.5m 12s⁵ 8g 10f] lengthy, rather sparely-made gelding: disappointing maiden:
should stay 1¼m. *M. H. Tompkins.*

X

XAFU XAFU 4 b.c. Kafu 120–On The Road (On Your Mark 125) [1989 6m 8h³ **66**
7.5f² 8m³ 6m² 6m² 6g 6s 6g 8g 1990 a7g 7.6m² 7m⁶ 7f⁵ 8f* 8.5f* 8.2m 8g 8g]
tall, good-topped colt: moderate mover: quite modest performer: rallied when
winner of selling handicap (bought in 4,400 gns) at Yarmouth and claimers at
Beverley in summer: below form after, seeming to lose his action final 1f next
outing: stays 8.5f: acts on any going: has worn blinkers and visor, but didn't in 1990.
M. H. Tompkins.

XAI-TANG 3 gr.g. Petong 126–Northern Dynasty 65 (Breeders Dream 116) [1989 **49**
5m⁶ 5m 7m 7m⁵ 6g 1990 8m⁶ 10f 12.5g 9m³ 10g 10g 8g⁴ 9f³ 8.2d* 9g 8m 8m]
close-coupled gelding: plating-class performer at best: won claimer at Haydock in
August, taking good hold and always close up: stays 9f: acts on dead ground: very
edgy fifth start. *K. White.*

XALISCO (USA) 2 b.c. (Mar 26) Shahrastani (USA) 135–Irlanda (USA) (Tom **57 p**
Rolfe) [1990 8.2d] IR 26,000Y: third foal: dam unraced half-sister to dam of Shadeed
(by Nijinsky): backward, moderate headway 2f out but never able to challenge in
minor event at Nottingham in October: should improve. *B. Hanbury.*

XEROMEDE 6 b.g. Runnymede 123–Nervous Cough (New Linacre 82) [1989 5f —
10m⁶ a10g 1990 5g 8f⁶ 7f] non-thoroughbred gelding: showed signs of a modicum of
ability second outing: wears bandage on off-hind. *N. Kernick.*

XHAI 8 b.g. Brave Shot–Wild Thyme 63 (Galivanter 131) [1989 8g 8f⁴ 8m 8m² 8m⁶ **55**
8f 8g⁶ 10m² 10m⁶ 8f 8f⁴ 8.2g 1990 10.2f⁴ 10.8m⁴ 9f 12.2m* 12f² 16f⁵ 14f⁶ 12g³ 12m⁶]
angular, workmanlike gelding: plating-class handicapper: carrying 6 lb overweight,
won at Warwick in April in very close finish: seems to stay 2m: acts on any going:
usually wears blinkers: bandaged: suitable mount for apprentice: winning hurdler in
June. *R. Simpson.*

Y

YAAZI 3 b.c. Mummy's Pet 125–Ica (Great Nephew 126) [1989 6m* 1990 7m 6m **75**
9m⁵ 8d 6f⁵ 5m* 5g 5g 5s] attractive colt: suffered knee injury when making all in
minor event at Newmarket in August at 2 yrs: easily best effort in handicaps (faced
stiff tasks early on) when winning at Newmarket in August: seemed best at sprint
distances on top-of-the-ground: sweating and edgy fifth outing: retired. *A. C.
Stewart.*

YAHALABEAK 3 b. or br.c. Glint of Gold 128–Spring Rose (Blakeney 126) [1989 —
8m 8g 1990 12f4] sturdy colt: no worthwhile form in maidens: sold 1,900 gns
Newmarket July Sales. *B. Hanbury.*

YAHEEB 6 b.h. Alleged (USA) 138–Rissa (USA) (Nijinsky (CAN) 138) —
[1989 NR 1990 12s] strong, sturdy horse: fair winner in 1988: carrying plenty of
condition, tailed off final 5f in handicap at Doncaster in October: better suited by

1¼m than 1m: probably acts on any going: occasionally sweats: successful novice hurdler in 1989/90. *M. W. Easterby.*

YAJIB (USA) 3 b.c. El Gran Senor (USA) 136–Chocolate Puff (USA) (Hawaii) 79
[1989 7m 8.2g 1990 10g⁴ 12m⁴ 13.1h⁵ 14f⁴ 16.2s* 16.2d⁴ 16f* 17.6f 16m] good-topped, quite attractive colt: moderate walker: modest handicapper: won moderately-run races at Haydock in June and Thirsk (idling) in August: wearing tongue strap, well behind final start: stays very well: acts on any going, with probable exception of hard: sometimes coltish: has run in snatches: sold A. Falourd 32,000 gns Newmarket Autumn Sales. *J. L. Dunlop.*

YAKITORI 2 b.c. (May 6) Petoski 135–Epithet 105 (Mill Reef (USA) 141) [1990   — p
7m] 25,000Y: fourth foal: half-brother to fairly useful 9.2f and 10.8f winner Sugar Plum Fairy (by Sadler's Wells): dam 5f and 6f winner stayed 1½m, is half-sister to smart 6f and 7f performer Columnist: slowly away and always behind in minor event at York in September: should improve. *Sir Mark Prescott.*

YALANOURA 3 b.f. Lashkari 128–Yashina (FR) (Tennyson (FR) 124) [1989 NR   96
1990 8g⁴ 10f* 10f² 12m³ 12s* 14.6d*] leggy, unfurnished filly: third foal: half-sister to quite useful 6f and 1m winner Yalciyna (by Nishapour), later stayed 1¼m: dam won over 10.5f at 3 yrs in France: successful in maiden at Lingfield in July, handicap at Doncaster in October and minor event (well-backed favourite, made all to beat Rudjig ¾ length) at Doncaster in November: stays 14.6f: acts on any going. *L. M. Cumani.*

YAMRAH 6 b.m. Milford 119–Silojoka 95 (Home Guard (USA) 129) [1989 10m²   —
11.5g⁴ 10m⁴ 10f³ 12h⁶ 1990 7.6f⁵ 11.5m³ 11.5m 12m⁵] lengthy mare: quite modest handicapper as 5-y-o: little form in summer: stays 1½m: acts on hard and dead going: good mount for apprentice. *Miss B. Sanders.*

YANKEE FLYER 3 b.f. Henbit (USA) 130–Yankee Special 60 (Bold Lad (IRE)   72
133) [1989 NR 1990 7g³ 8g³ 7m³ 8g² 7.6m² 7d³ 8m] first foal: dam plating-class maiden: modest maiden: stumbled and unseated rider final start: stays 1m: acts on good to firm ground: has run well when edgy. *W. Hastings-Bass.*

YANKEE TRADER 3 b.f. Stanford 121§–Amboselli 73 (Raga Navarro (ITY) 119)   36
[1989 5f 6f 6g 1990 a7g* 8f⁴ 8.3m] rather unfurnished filly: poor plater: won at Southwell in May: stays 1m: acts on firm ground: sold 6,400 gns Newmarket July Sales. *Sir Mark Prescott.*

YARRA GLEN 3 ch.f. Known Fact (USA) 135–Sloane Ranger 84 (Sharpen Up   59
127) [1989 8m³ 8f² 8.5f² 1990 7g⁶ 10f² 10.2f² 9m 10g] lengthy filly: quite modest maiden: below form after finishing second at Brighton and Bath, on latter running very wide on turn: may stay 1½m: visored, claimed out of C. Nelson's stable £5,110 penultimate start: reared stalls final one: tail flasher. *M. P. Muggeridge.*

YARRAMAN 3 b.g. Ya Zaman (USA) 122–Isa (Dance In Time (CAN)) [1989 6s 6g   —
a8g⁶ a6g⁶ a7g³ 1990 8m 6m 7f 7m] leggy gelding: plater: below form in 1990: best effort over 7f: very slowly away second outing: blinkered final one: sold 1,550 gns Ascot May Sales. *R. Hollinshead.*

YASLOU 3 ch.g. Yashgan 126–Lough Graney (Sallust 134) [1989 5f⁶ 6m⁴ 6m⁴ 7f⁶   —
1990 10v 8.2g 10.6s 8g] good-quartered gelding: poor mover: quite modest maiden: behind in handicaps and claimer as 3-y-o: should stay 1¼m. *M. E. D. Francis.*

YASMEEN VALLEY (USA) 2 b.f. (Feb 17) Danzig Connection (USA)–   76 p
Friendly Circle (USA) (Round Table) [1990 6m² 7m³] $400,000Y: tall, rangy, rather angular filly: half-sister to several winners, including smart 6f to 1½m winner Ginistrelli (by Hoist The Flag): dam, smart stakes winner at 2 yrs, won at up to 9f: sire won Belmont Stakes: edgy, 3 lengths third of 9, leading over 5f, to Sumonda in maiden at Leicester in October: will probably improve again. *A. C. Stewart.*

YEARSLEY 4 b.g. Anfield 117–Mantina (Bustino 136) [1989 8m 7m 7f* 7.5f* 8f*   93
8.2d⁵ 1990 7f⁴ 8h* 7.5d⁵ 7m* 8f 8m 8g] rangy gelding: usually dull in coat: good walker and mover: quite useful handicapper: successful in quite valuable events at Thirsk (heavily-backed favourite, showing improved form) in May and Newcastle (rallying gamely) in June: well beaten last 3 outings: effective at 7f to 1m: suited by top-of-the-ground: suited by forcing tactics: has won when sweating. *M. H. Easterby.*

YELLOW BEAR 8 ch.g. Gold Form 108–Dumb Kathy (Dumbarnie 125) [1989   —
NR 1990 a8g 8.5g a8g 6g] leggy gelding: fairly useful plater at one time: well beaten at 8 yrs: stays 7f: acts on heavy going: blinkered last 2 outings: has worn a hood: usually sweats: sold 940 gns Doncaster October Sales. *J. Parkes.*

YELLOW METAL   3 b.c. Reesh 117–Madame Decoy 67 (Decoy Boy 129) [1989   —
NR 1990 7m 7h] leggy colt: half-brother to a winner in Norway: dam winning
sprinter: always behind in minor event and seller. *A. W. Denson.*

YEMANJA (USA)   3 b.f. Alleged (USA) 138–Korveya (USA) (Riverman (USA)   —
131) [1989 NR 1990 10.1m 10.1m 12g] sturdy, useful-looking filly: first foal: dam,
French 1m and 9f winner, is half-sister to high-class sprinter Proskona out of 1000
Guineas runner-up Konafa, herself half-sister to top-class middle-distance filly
Awaasif: no worthwhile form in minor event and maidens, though did show signs of
ability. *R. Charlton.*

YEOMAN BID   3 b.g. Longleat (USA) 109–Bounding (Forlorn River 124) [1989   74
5s 5f5 8.2d a6g a7g3 a8g2 1990 a7g3 6f a8g2 8g a7g2 a7g3 7m a8g5 7g a8g4 a7g2 a7g3
a7g5] big, angular gelding: has a roundish action: modest maiden: visored, ran
moderately in Lingfield handicap final outing: blinkered, ran well in similar events
previous 2 starts: seems best at 7f on all-weather. *K. T. Ivory.*

YEOMAN BOUND   2 b.c. (Mar 11) Norwick (USA) 120–Bounding (Forlorn   —
River 124) [1990 5m] workmanlike colt: has scope: good walker: sixth living foal:
half-brother to 3-y-o Yeoman Bid (by Longleat) and several winners, including
sprinter Pendor Dancer (by Piaffer): dam never ran: backward and green in minor
event at Windsor in June. *K. T. Ivory.*

YEOMAN FORCE   4 b.g. Crofter (USA) 124–High Voltage 82 (Electrify) [1989   67
6s3 5g 6d4 6m6 6f 8m6 6m 6d 5d a6g3 5d a6g2 a6g2 a7g2 1990 a6g 6f6 5g 5d5 6m 6g*
6m6 6g 6m] tall, angular gelding: has a long stride: quite modest handicapper: 25/1
and having first race for new trainer (formerly with K. Ivory), won 26-runner event
at Nottingham in June, making most on far rail: ran poorly final outing: ideally suited
by 6f: probably acts on any going: has worn blinkers, often visored: sold to join M.
Bradley's stable 1,500 gns Newmarket Autumn Sales. *M. Bell.*

YERIF NOGARD   4 b. or br.f. Don 128–Firey Dragon (Tarboosh (USA)) [1989   —
8g5 1990 a7g a11g6 8.2s] rangy, rather leggy filly: showed promise on debut: well
beaten in maidens (first claimer) and selling handicap early in year: has worn bandages. *R. W. Stubbs.*

YES   2 b.f. (Jan 27) Blakeney 126–Arrapata (Thatching 131) [1990 a7g 6f6 5f3 5m2   72
5m2 6g6 6d 5g3 5d3] 5,600Y: compact filly: moderate mover: fourth reported foal:
half-sister to leading 1988 Scandinavian 2-y-o Henry Light (by Salmon Leap): dam
unraced: modest maiden: should be suited by further than 5f: acts on good to firm
ground and dead: visored seventh start: usually ridden by claimer: often slowly
away. *D. T. Thom.*

YESICAN   4 gr.c. Kalaglow 132–Geoffrey's Sister 102 (Sparkler 130) [1989 7g4   60
1990 8.3m2 a11g4 a12g5] lengthy, workmanlike colt: very lightly raced, but has
shown quite modest form in varied events: should stay beyond 1½m: often bandaged: ran in snatches second start: bought 1,300 gns Doncaster March Sales before
reappearance. *T. Thomson Jones.*

YET   5 gr.m. Last Fandango 125–Rana of Coombe (Moulton 128) [1989 12g 10m 12g   —
10m4 12g 12.2f6 1990 a11g a11g a11g] workmanlike mare: has a quick action: poor handicapper: form since 3 yrs only on fourth outing (demoted) in 1989: suited by 1¼m:
acts on firm going: blinkered once at 3 yrs and once (sweating, edgy and mulish at
stalls) as 4-y-o: has started slowly: sometimes wanders and not the easiest of rides:
sold 1,500 gns Ascot April Sales: resold 625 gns Ascot December Sales. *M. J. Ryan.*

YONGE TENDER   3 b.f. Tender King 123–St Clair Star (Sallust 134) [1989 5m6   68
5g 6g5 a5g3 a5g4 1990 5f5 5g4 5d6 6s6 6m3 7m3 6f2 a7g2 6m* 6m3 6d2 6g* 6f a6g5]
small, close-coupled filly: carries condition: moderate walker and mover: quite
modest performer: blinkered and usually claimer ridden since ninth start, winning
seller (no bid) at Newcastle in August and claimer on same course in October: well
below form last 2 outings: suited by 6f: acts on firm and dead going. *J. Wharton.*

YORKSHIRE HOLLY   7 br.g. Bivouac 114–Holly Doon (Doon 124) [1989 10g   75
10m 14f4 15f* 16f4 16.2m2 19f2 16.2m* 18m5 1990 16f6 16f* 18d] smallish,
workmanlike gelding: best effort on flat on first run for over 5 months when winning
handicap at Redcar in October: suited by 2m: acts on firm going: usually ridden by
claimer: held up, and has turn of foot: much improved hurdler. *Mrs G. R. Reveley.*

YOU ARE A STAR   4 b.g. Persian Bold 123–Flinging Star (USA) (Northern   83
Fling (USA)) [1989 7d 7s3 8g* 7.6f3 7g* 7f2 8f2 7h 8d 1990 10m 8m* 8f 8g6 8m* 7m
8m6 8f 9m4 8g 8m* 8g5] big, rangy gelding: carries condition: usually looks well:
fair handicapper: successful at Pontefract (showing improved form) and Newcastle in June and Bath in October: suited by 1m: best form on sound surface:

Bradford & Bingley Handicap, York —
You Missed Me (left) and Pontenuovo both had a notable season
in this type of event

ran moderately in visor: trained until after reappearance by R. Hannon. *M. H. Tompkins.*

YOUGOTIT 4 b.f. Orange Reef 90–Costerini 70 (Soderini 123) [1989 NR 1990 9f a14g⁵ 9g] angular filly: seventh reported living foal: half-sister to 2 winners, including Irish 1m and 9f winner Hard About (by Right Tack): dam, 1m winner, is half-sister to Record Token: won NH Flat race at Bangor in March: well beaten in lady riders seller and maidens in summer. *R. O'Leary.* —

YOU JEST 3 b.g. Comedy Star (USA) 121–Paradise Straits 65 (Derrylin 115) [1989 NR 1990 10f 12f 12m] compact gelding: first foal: dam 2m winner also successful over hurdles: tailed off in maidens and claimer, flashing tail second start: blinkered final one. *S. Woodman.* —

YOU KNOW THE RULES 3 b.f. Castle Keep 121–Falls of Lora 107 (Scottish Rifle 127) [1989 6f 7f⁵ 6m⁴ 8f⁴ 8g⁴ 8.2f* 7f³ 8f³ 1990 8.5g 7m³ 7f⁵ 8m* 7g⁴ 9g* 12g 8g* 8m 9g] sparely-made filly: has a quick action: modest handicapper: successful in late-summer at Kempton and Sandown (twice), having to be switched with plenty to do over 1f out both occasions at Sandown: ran moderately last 2 outings: will stay 1¼m: acts on firm going: has turn of foot, and is usually held up towards rear. *M. R. Channon.* 79

YOU MISSED ME 4 b.c. Known Fact (USA) 135–Milk And Honey 102 (So Blessed 130) [1989 6s² 7g³ 8f⁵ 7f³ 8m* 8g* 8.3g⁶ 9g⁵ 9g 1990 7m* 8m⁵ 8f 8m* 8f 8m* 8g 7m⁵ 9m] angular colt: has a quick action: fairly useful handicapper: generally in very good form as 4-y-o, successful at Kempton in May, Sandown (£27,000 event) in July and York (£24,700 Bradford & Bingley Handicap by head from Pontenuovo) in August: stays 9f: acts on any going: sold 72,000 gns Newmarket Autumn Sales. *D. W. P. Arbuthnot.* 96

YOUNG BENZ 6 ch.g. Young Generation 129–Cavalier's Blush (King's Troop 118) [1989 12d⁴ 12.3f⁴ 11s 12s 10g 1990 13d⁶ 12d³ 12v⁵ 13.6d*] workmanlike gelding: usually dull in coat: moderate mover: quite modest handicapper: well-backed favour- ite and visored first time, confirmed promise shown earlier in autumn when winning at Redcar in October, tending to edge left once in front: stays 13.6f: 63

probably acts on any going: best blinkered or visored: best covered up: promising novice chaser. *M. H. Easterby.*

YOUNG BILL   3 ch.g. Nicholas Bill 125–Lingdale Lady 66 (Sandford Lad 133)   —
[1989 NR 1990 8f 8.2d 6g] close-coupled gelding: fourth living foal: dam stayed 6f: behind in claimers, very much on toes and slowly away on debut: joined A. James. *Mrs J. R. Ramsden.*

YOUNG BUSTER (IRE)   2 b.c. (Mar 13) Teenoso (USA) 135–Bustara 92   79
(Busted 134) [1990 7g² 7g²] rather angular colt: first foal: dam 2-y-o 6f winner stayed 10.2f, is daughter of Romara: second behind Dawning Street in maiden at Salisbury and Full of Pluck in median auction at York in October: will be well suited by middle distances: sure to win a race. *G. Wragg.*

YOUNG CHRISTOS   3 b.c. Sayf El Arab (USA) 127–Pahaska 86 (Wolver Hollow   —
126) [1989 6d 6g 6g 1990 a10g⁶] leggy colt: well beaten in maidens and a handicap: took keen hold and carried head rather awkwardly only start in 1990. *C. N. Allen.*

YOUNG COMMANDER   6 br.g. Bustino 136–Bombshell 76 (Le Levanstell   64
122) [1989 8g³ 8d³ 8f³ 8m⁵ 9f² 7m² 12m⁵ 8f⁶ 8g² 8.2f* 8.2f* 8m⁶ 8.2g 8.5f⁴ 8f* 8g 8g 1990 8f⁶ 8f⁴ 9g⁴ 8f⁵ 8g* 8m³ 8m 9m 8f³ 8.5m] lengthy gelding: hobdayed: quite modest handicapper: often finds little off bridle, but did little wrong when winning at Edinburgh in June: effective at 7f to 9f: possibly unsuited by soft going, acts on any other: wears visor: best with waiting tactics: none too resolute. *M. P. Naughton.*

YOUNG DUKE (IRE)   2 gr.c. (Mar 19) Double Schwartz 128–Princess Pamela   55 p
70 (Dragonara Palace (USA) 115) [1990 6m] IR 3,000Y: first foal: dam, 5f winner at 2 yrs and stayed 7f, failed to train on: over 9 lengths eighth of 17, shaping well over 4f after slow start, in maiden at Goodwood in September: sure to improve. *M. D. I. Usher.*

YOUNG FACT   5 b.g. Known Fact (USA) 135–Yelming 76 (Thatch (USA) 136)   74
[1989 NR 1990 10.1g³ 11.5m* 11.5m⁵ 10.6s⁴ 10.6s⁵ 10.6m² 10.6g⁵ 12g⁴] sturdy, compact gelding: fourth foal: half-brother to 1983 2-y-o 1m winner Feasibility Study (by Welsh Pageant), later successful in USA, and modest 1¼m winner Follow The Band (by Dance In Time): dam, placed at up to 7f, is half-sister to high-class 1984 sprinting 2-y-o Bassenthwaite: successful at 2 yrs and 3 yrs in Germany: claimed out of D. Elsworth's stable £6,562 first outing (bandaged) on flat in Britain: won claimer at Lingfield in May: stays 11.5f: possibly ideally suited by top-of-the-ground. *J. H. Baker.*

YOUNG GEORGE   3 b.g. Camden Town 125–Young Grace (Young Emperor   62
133) [1989 6f 7g 7f⁶ 6f 1990 5s⁴ 8f* 7f⁵ 7g 9m* 10.6m⁵ 10.2m 8g² 9s 9f] good-topped, close-coupled gelding: quite modest performer: won sellers at Ripon (handicap, no bid) in April and Hamilton (on toes, bought in 9,000 gns) in July: stays 10.6f: acts on firm ground, possibly unsuited by soft: trained until after fourth start by M. Naughton. *M. Dods.*

YOUNG GERARD   5 ch.g. Brigadier Gerard 144–Eastern Queen (Sharpen Up   —
127) [1989 NR 1990 a5g a8g 10.2f 16.2m 21.6m a12g] leggy, angular gelding: has a round action: of little account on flat: visored fourth outing: winning selling hurdler in May. *M. C. Chapman.*

YOUNG INCA   12 gr.g. Young Emperor 133–Sunny Eyes (Reliance II 137) [1989   —
7g 6f 6f² 7g 6f² 6m 6m⁴ 6m* 6f⁶ 5m⁵ 6m⁵ 6s⁴ 5m 6g 1990 6f 6f 5g 6g 5s 6f 6f⁶ 6g 7m⁶] big, strong gelding: good mover: fair winner in 1989: no worthwhile form as 12-y o, including in claimer: best at 6f: acts on any going: has won in blinkers, but better without: sometimes bandaged behind in 1990: often starts slowly: sold out of G. Cottrell's stable 6,200 gns Ascot February Sales before reappearance. *R. W. Stubbs.*

YOUNG INDIA   3 br.f. Indian King 128–Marfisa (Green God 128) [1989 5g   61
5g² 6m* 5g* 5m² 1990 6m 5f⁵ 6f 6m 5g 5m 5m 6g⁴ 6f 8.2s³ 8d³] big, workmanlike filly: inconsistent handicapper: probably stays 1m: probably acts on any going: blinkered sixth outing: bandaged occasionally: changed hands 1,500 gns Doncaster September Sales: sold to join D. Burchell 1,600 gns Doncaster November Sales. *T. D. Barron.*

YOUNG JAMES   2 ch.g. (May 27) Hotfoot 126–Deep Lady 78 (Deep Diver 134)   —
[1990 7f 6d] 4,200F, 5,200Y: half-brother to 1986 2-y-o 6f winner Green's Herring (by Mansingh) and 1984 2-y-o 6f winner and fair hurdler Ballyarry (by Balliol): dam 2-y-o 5f winner: prominent to 2f out in maidens at Chepstow (auction event) and Goodwood in autumn. *B. R. Millman.*

YOUNG JASON   7 ch.g. Star Appeal 133–Smarten Up 119 (Sharpen Up 127)   77
[1989 10.2g 7.6m* 8m* 8.2m⁶ 8m⁵ 8m⁵ 8.5m* 8m² 8.2d⁴ 8m⁴ 7.6m² 8.5f 8g 1990

10f⁵ 7.5m 8.2m⁴ 7.5d² 8m² 8g⁵ 10f⁵ 10f⁴ 8m⁵ 8g* 9m 8.5m* 8m 7d] small, good-bodied gelding: moderate mover: modest handicapper: won at Thirsk and Beverley in September: ideally suited by strong gallop at around 1m: acts on any going: blinkered once: goes well with extreme waiting tactics and on a turning track: tends to carry head high: tough. *F. H. Lee.*

YOUNG JAZZ 4 b.c. Young Generation 129–River Music (Riverman (USA) 131) 95 [1989 7d⁶ 1990 8m² 9.1f* 8g 8d* 8g³ 8v] big, close-coupled, attractive colt: split pastern on debut at 3 yrs: won 3-runner maiden (odds on) at Newcastle in July and 29-runner handicap at Newmarket (putting up a quite useful performance under 10-0) in October: should prove as effective at 9f as 1m: sold out of G. Harwood's stable to race in Italy 30,000 gns Newmarket Autumn Sales after fifth start. *E. Pistoletti, Italy.*

YOUNG MOTHER (FR) 4 b.f. Youth (USA) 135–Santa Tina 123 (Santa Claus 114 133) [1989 10.7g* 12s* 12g* 12g* 13.5g³ 12d* 12g⁴ 1990 10f³ 10.5d⁵ 12d⁶] French filly: developed into high-class performer as 3-y-o, on last 2 outings winning Prix Vermeille and finishing fourth in Prix de l'Arc de Triomphe, both at Longchamp: failed to recapture her form in 1990 and not seen out after middle of June: stays 13.5f: acts on soft going. *J-M. Beguigne, France.*

YOUNG PITT (IRE) 2 b.g. (Apr 22) Pitskelly 122–Magloire (FR) (Sir Gaylord) — [1990 8g 8.2s 10s] IR 4,600F, IR 8,500Y: quite good-topped gelding: half-brother to a minor 1½m winner in France by Touching Wood: dam lightly raced: slowly away and always behind in maidens. *T. M. Jones.*

YOUNG SHADOWFAX 3 gr.c. Absalom 128–Miss Twiggy 80 (Tycoon II) 80 [1989 NR 1990 5m⁴ 5m⁴ 6m² 5d 5m 6f*] 5,400F, 7,000Y: sturdy, good-quartered colt: fourth foal: dam 5f winner at 2 yrs: fair form second and third starts: 11/10 on, made most to win 4-runner maiden at Hamilton in July: suited by 6f: retained by trainer 14,500 gns Doncaster November Sales. *C. N. Allen.*

YOUNG TEARAWAY 5 br.m. Young Generation 129–Chiparia 82 (Song 132) — [1989 5s 6f² 6m 5f 6s⁶ 6m² 6g² 6g 6d 1990 7m 6m 6m⁵ 6m 6d⁵] good-quartered mare: appeared to run well in face of stiff task in Newmarket listed event on third outing: no worthwhile form otherwise as 5-y-o in handicaps and minor event: suited by 6f: acts on any going: visored (below form) final start at 4 yrs. *R. Boss.*

YOUNG WHISTLER 2 b.c. (Apr 26) Wassl 125–Rayhaan 83 (Kings Lake (USA) 59 133) [1990 5m 5m⁵ 6g⁶ 6m² 7g 7f 6m 6d 6m 6m³] IR 7,500Y, 7,000 2-y-o: leggy, lengthy colt: first foal: dam 5f and 6f winner: plating-class maiden: should be well suited by 7f: best form on good to firm ground: blinkered or visored final 2 starts. *P. Mitchell.*

YSATIROUS 3 gr.c. Ahonoora 122–Amalancher (USA) 85 (Alleged (USA) 138) 91 [1989 7g² 1990 8.5g* 7.6m⁶ 8.5m 6m* 6g 6m] big, lengthy colt: made most to win maiden at Beverley in May then ran on strongly from rear to win £8,900 handicap at Ascot in July: well beaten in quite valuable handicaps last 2 outings: headstrong and seems better at 6f than further: wears citation bridle nowadays: sold 8,500 gns Newmarket Autumn Sales. *M. R. Stoute.*

YUFFROUW ANN 5 b.m. Tyrnavos 129–Recline 70 (Wollow 132) [1989 9f 1990 — a7g] small mare: won 3 races (2 sellers) as 2-y-o: has deteriorated, and is very lightly raced nowadays: best form in visor, blinkered only start in 1990: sold 2,000 gns Ascot April Sales. *K. G. Wingrove.*

YUKOSAN 3 ch.f. Absalom 128–K-Sera 95 (Lord Gayle (USA) 124) [1989 5g* 6g 63 a6g² a6g* a5g³ a8g⁵ 1990 a6g* a6g³ a6g⁵ 6m⁵ 6v* 7.5g⁶ 7g 6g⁵ a6g a6g⁶ a6g a7g] lengthy filly: quite modest performer: won claimer at Southwell in January and seller (no bid) at Ayr in April: off course 3½ months then below form after eighth start: should stay beyond 6f: acts on heavy going: sweating and edgy sixth start. *Ronald Thompson.*

Z

ZABARRJAD (USA) 3 b.f. Northern Dancer–Smooth Bore (USA) (His Majesty 72 (USA)) [1989 8g⁶ 1990 11.5g 14g³ 15.8m* 16f² 16m] sturdy filly: moderate mover: modest performer: won maiden at Catterick in July: suited by test of stamina: acts on firm going: sold 76,000 gns Newmarket December Sales. *M. R. Stoute.*

ZAFIRO 4 br.g. Starch Reduced 112–Miss Admington 71 (Double Jump 131) [1989 30 5m 6m⁴ 6m 5m⁵ 5f² 5g 5f⁴ 7m 6f 5f 8f 5g⁴ 1990 5m 5s 5m⁵ a8g a6g² a5g 7.6m 7m a6g⁵ 6g 5m a6g] sturdy gelding: moderate mover: poor maiden: stays 6f: acts on firm going: sweating fourth outing, and has got on toes: has looked none too keen. *B. Preece.*

ZAFOD 3 b.c. Silly Prices 110–Coatham 81 (Divine Gift 127) [1989 5g 5g 7m 1990 — 5f 8g] small colt: poor mover: of no account. *B. Preece.*

ZAFRA 2 b.f. (Mar 11) Dunbeath (USA) 127–White's Ferry (Northfields (USA)) 48 [1990 6s 6g 7g⁴ 7f 8m 8m 8d] 5,800Y: neat filly: has a round action: second foal: half-sister to 3-y-o Gilt Banner (by Ballad Rock): dam Irish 2-y-o 6f winner from family of My Swallow: poor maiden: has run in sellers: should stay 1m: sold out of C. W. C. Elsey's stable 1,600 gns Ascot October Sales before final outing. *C. A. Horgan.*

ZAMANAYN (IRE) 2 gr.c. (Mar 24) Mouktar 129–Zariya (USA) 88 (Blushing 73 p Groom (FR) 131) [1990 8m⁶] medium-sized, quite good-topped colt: third foal: half-brother to smart 7f winner Zayyani (by Darshaan) and 1¼m winner Zerzaya (by Beldale Flutter): dam 7f winner at 2 yrs, is granddaughter of Petite Etoile: 8 lengths sixth of 14, travelling quite well behind leaders 6f, to Hilti's Hut in maiden at Newmarket in October: sure to improve and win a similar event. *L. M. Cumani.*

ZAMBOANGA 3 br.f. Blazing Saddles (AUS)–Maid of The Manor (Hotfoot 126) 42 [1989 5f 1990 7g 8.2g 10.2m⁴ 9m⁴ 13.8d³ 9.1m 7.5g 11m⁵ 10m] big, workmanlike filly: poor performer: stays 11f: acts on good to firm ground: ran moderately in visor final start: slowly away and looked reluctant on sixth: sold 1,600 gns Doncaster November Sales. *M. J. Camacho.*

ZAMIL (USA) 5 b.g. Lyphard (USA) 132–Wayward Lass (USA) (Hail The Pirates — (USA) 126) [1989 NR 1990 14.6d] third foal: half-brother to a minor winner by In Reality: dam best 3-y-o filly in USA in 1981, winning 7 races including CCA Oaks: one-time fair hurdler: 66/1, well beaten in minor event at Doncaster in November. *K. R. Burke.*

ZAMINA 2 b.f. (Feb 18) Sayf El Arab (USA) 127–Scotch Thistle 73 (Sassafras (FR) 45 135) [1990 5f⁵ 6m⁶ 7f³ a7g⁴ 7m⁶ 7g 7m] 3,200Y: sparely-made filly: moderate mover: half-sister to 3-y-o Ttaywen (by Noalto), modest 1m to 10.4f winner Flying Scotsman (by Tower Walk) and 7f winner Scotch Rocket (by Roan Rocket): dam placed at up to 1½m: moderate plater: will stay 1m: acts on firm ground: sold 740 gns Newmarket September Sales. *C. N. Allen.*

ZAMMAH 3 b.f. Jalmood (USA) 126–Petrol 73 (Troy 137) [1989 6f⁴ 8m⁴ 7m³ 8.2f² 77 1990 8.5g⁶ 8g² 8m 8h³ 8m* 8f⁴ 9m* 10.6v] compact filly: modest performer: won apprentice maiden at Yarmouth in August and handicap at Redcar (comfortably) in September: should stay 1¼m: acts on hard ground: apprentice ridden last 2 starts: sold 4,200 gns Newmarket December Sales. *P. T. Walwyn.*

ZANDRIL 2 b.c. (Mar 8) Forzando 122–Champ d'Avril 89 (Northfields (USA)) 97 [1990 6m 6m⁴ 5m* 5m* 5g* 5g] 66,000Y: lengthy, good-topped colt: poor mover: fifth live foal: half-brother to very useful sprinter Superpower (by Superlative) and 1987 2-y-o 5f winner Florentynna Bay (by Aragon): dam 5f winner seemed to stay 7f, is out of half-sister to Music Boy: fairly useful colt: won maiden at Windsor and nurseries at Goodwood (gamely) in July and Chester (by 1½ lengths from Gorinsky) in August: ran poorly final start: suited by 5f. *R. Hannon.*

ZANOBA 3 ch.f. Precocious 126–Zanubia 81 (Nonoalco (USA) 131) [1989 6g 5m — 5m⁵ 5m³ 5f 1990 8.2f 7f 6g⁶ 8m⁶ 8g 7.5f 8m] workmanlike filly: plating-class maiden: blinkered and sweating final start: bandaged on reappearance: sold 1,300 gns Doncaster October Sales. *F. Durr.*

ZANONI 3 b.c. Mummy's Pet 125–Princely Maid 71 (King's Troop 118) [1989 6m² 98 6d² 1990 6m* 6g⁴ 5m⁵ 5m⁴ 5d* 6d 5s² 5d] leggy, quite attractive colt: has rather round action: fairly useful performer: narrow winner of Newmarket maiden (odds on, on toes) in April and handicap at Haydock in September: best efforts over 5f on a soft surface: has sometimes found little off bridle: wore brush pricker off-side on final start. *M. A. Jarvis.*

ZARAKAI 4 b.f. Move Off 112–Ribera (Ribston 104) [1989 NR 1990 6v 5g 6m 7d] — lengthy, dipped-backed filly: poor mover: fifth foal: sister to 2 bad animals: dam pulled up in hurdle race: of little account: sold 1,000 gns Doncaster August Sales. *N. Chamberlain.*

ZARISSA (USA) 2 b.f. (Mar 4) Lyphard (USA) 132–I Want To Be (USA) 116 — p (Roberto (USA) 131) [1990 6d⁵] leggy filly: first foal: dam winner from 7f (at 2 yrs) to 14.5f, from very good family: better for race and very green, moderate progress around halfway then no extra in maiden at Goodwood in October: sure to improve. *J. L. Dunlop.*

ZARNA 3 ro.f. Shernazar 131–Zahra (Habitat 134) [1989 7m² 7g³ 6g 1990 8m* 8g **71** §
7d 9f³] compact, workmanlike filly: moderate mover: modest handicapper: won at
Doncaster in May: easily best effort as well-backed favourite after when third at
Redcar in July, but found little under pressure: should stay 1¼m: acts on firm going:
one to treat with caution. *M. R. Stoute.*

ZARTOTA (USA) 4 ch.f. Assert 134–Literary Lark (USA) (Arts And Letters **120**
(USA)) [1989 10g⁶ 12d⁶ 10.5s⁵ 1990 12d* 10.5d⁶ 12d² 12g³ 13.5d⁵ 12m² 12g] strong,
rangy filly: fifth foal: half-sister to a minor winner in USA by Mr Prospector: dam,
minor winner at up to 9f in USA, is half-sister to very smart American filly Sea Saga:
much improved as 4-y-o: won 120,000-franc event at Saint-Cloud in March: placed
behind In The Wings, showing smart form, in Grand Prix de Saint-Cloud and Prix
Foy at Longchamp on fourth and sixth outings: 33/1, prominent until 2f out in Ciga
Prix de l'Arc de Triomphe at Longchamp final one: suited by 1½m: acts on good to
firm and dead going. *A. Spanu, France.*

ZARYA 3 b.f. Shelter Half (USA)–Ice Blue (Cure The Blues (USA)) [1989 NR 1990 —
7f] IR 5,200Y: first foal: dam lightly-raced daughter of Nell Gwyn winner and 1000
Guineas/Oaks second Freeze The Secret: sire won from 6f to 7f: 16/1, never
dangerous in claimer at Newmarket in August: joined W. Perrin. *W. M. Perrin.*

ZAXIS 2 ch.f. (Mar 21) Noalto 120–La Pirouette (USA) 73 (Kennedy Road (CAN)) **56**
[1990 8g 8.2v⁶ 8d] tall, lengthy, unfurnished filly: fourth foal: half-sister to 3-y-o
Plie (by Superlative), modest 5.8f winner at 2 yrs, and a winner in Germany: dam
7f winner: easily best effort around 10 lengths ninth of 18, prominent to 2f out, in
maiden at Bath final start. *D. W. P. Arbuthnot.*

ZENELLA 3 b.f. Precocious 126–Zepha 88 (Great Nephew 126) [1989 7g 1990 —
8.2g 9m] rangy, workmanlike filly: has quick action: no show in maiden and claimers: swished tail repeatedly in preliminaries final start: sold 2,700 gns Newmarket
July Sales. *W. Jarvis.*

ZENISKA (USA) 2 b.c. (Feb 5) Cozzene (USA)–Istiska (FR) (Irish River (FR) —
131) [1990 7s 7s a7g] $15,000Y: big, rangy colt: third foal: half-brother to 2 winning
2-y-o stayers in France: dam French maiden: sire won Breeders' Cup Mile: poor
form in maidens, best effort final start. *S. G. Norton.*

ZEPHYR FIRE 2 ch.c. (Mar 12) Hotfoot 126–Delta Wind 72 (Tumble Wind —
(USA)) [1990 5m 5f 5f 6g 6g 7f] 1,100Y: compact colt: poor walker: first foal: dam
best at 2 yrs: bad plater: raced freely in blinkers fourth outing. *G. Blum.*

ZEPHYR NIGHTS (USA) 3 b.g. Grey Dawn II 132–Vaslava (Habitat 134) —
[1989 7g 7g 1990 10f⁶ 12.5g⁵ 13.8m 14m 12f] leggy, angular gelding: form only when
fifth in handicap at Wolverhampton in May: suited by 1½m: trained until after fourth
start by I. Campbell: of suspect temperament. *A. Hide.*

ZEPPEKI (IRE) 2 b.c. (Feb 15) Taufan (USA) 119–Avital (Pitskelly 122) [1990 **66**
5f⁴ 6m² 6m⁴ 6f³ 6s² 7m⁶ 6d] 14,000Y: lengthy, good-quartered colt: has scope: first
foal: dam never ran: quite modest performer, in frame in varied company: ran
moderately in blinkers final start: should stay 7f: seems well suited by soft ground:
sold to join D. Chapman's stable 5,200 gns Doncaster September Sales. *J. Berry.*

ZERMANSKY (IRE) 2 b.g. (Mar 23) Camden Town 125–Middle Verde (USA) **72**
(Sham (USA)) [1990 5g² 5g* 6m³ 5f⁶ 6d* 6g² 6m* 6m⁶] IR 6,200Y: workmanlike
gelding: shows knee action: third foal: half-brother to 2 winners in Belgium: dam
Irish maiden: modest performer: successful in maiden at Hamilton in May and
claimers at Haydock and Hamilton (looking none too keen but showing improved
form) in July: twice gave impression something amiss, including when also rearing
stalls final start: better suited by 6f than 5f: acts on good to firm ground and dead. *C.
Tinkler.*

ZERO TIME 3 br.f. Alzao (USA) 117–Queen of Time (USA) (Roi Dagobert 128) **50**
[1989 5s³ 6f³ 6g 1990 8m 10f⁵ 10m 7m* 7f 8.2m³] compact, good-bodied filly: has a
roundish action: plating-class handicapper: won at Doncaster in June, making most
and rallying: stays 1¼m: acts on firm going: blinkered last 3 starts: sold 3,900 gns
Newmarket Autumn Sales. *P. F. I. Cole.*

ZHIVAGO'S PASSION 3 gr.f. Another Realm 118–Crystal Gael 79 (Sparkler —
130) [1989 5g² 5m⁶ 5m⁵ 5g 1990 7f 8g 6m 6g⁶ 6f³] workmanlike filly: plating-class
maiden: showed little in 1990: may prove suited by further than 5f: visored final
start: sold to join J. Ringer 1,600 gns Newmarket September Sales. *J. Bridger.*

ZIGAURA (USA) 2 b.f. (May 2) Ziggy's Boy (USA)–Our Feast (USA) (Banquet **95**
Table (USA)) [1990 5m² 6m² 6m³ 6m⁴ 6m³ 6m⁶] $20,000Y: lengthy, quite
attractive filly: has a quick action: half-sister to 2 minor winners in USA: dam
twice-raced half-sister to Our Native: sire (by Danzig) won from 5f to 7f: fairly

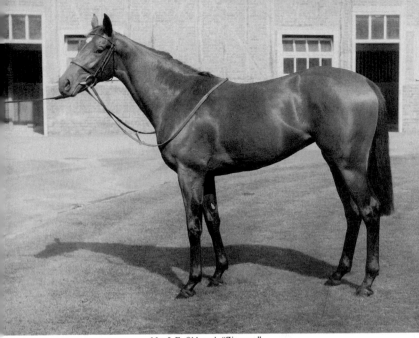

Mrs J. E. Ohlsson's "Zigaura"

useful maiden: beaten little more than a length in pattern events on 3 occasions, final one Moyglare Stud Stakes at the Curragh won by Capricciosa penultimate start: creditable sixth to same filly in Tattersalls Cheveley Park Stakes at Newmarket: will probably stay 7f: has a turn of foot, and is usually held up: hung badly right when below form third outing. *D. R. C. Elsworth.*

ZINBAQ 4 ch.c. Ahonoora 122–Zaiyundeen (FR) (Exbury 138) [1989 6d 6m 7g 6m **43**
6g 7g 1990 a6g 6m a7g² a7g⁴ 6d 6m³ 7m⁴ 7f⁵ 7m⁵ 7m⁴ 7g⁴ 6m⁴ 6g² 7g⁶ a6g⁵] quite attractive colt: moderate mover: poor handicapper: stays 7f: acts on good to firm going: suitable mount for inexperienced rider. *C. J. Benstead.*

ZINGER 2 b.c. (Jan 26) Lucky Wednesday 124–Starkist 81 (So Blessed 130) [1990 **55**
a7g* 6g a6g⁵ 8.2s] leggy, quite good-topped colt. brother to 1988 2-y-o 5f winner MCA Lucky Star and 6f and 7f winner Lucky Starkist, and half-brother to fair miler Star of A Gunner (by Gunner B): dam 2-y-o 5f winner: won seller (no bid) at Southwell in August: ran moderately after, including in selling nursery. *W. J. Pearce.*

ZIO PEPPINO 9 ch.g. Thatch (USA) 136–Victorian Habit 101 (Habitat 134) [1989 **—**
8g 8.5d 8m 8.2f⁶ 8m 8m 7g 10.8m 8f 10f a12g 1990 a11g a16g] sturdy gelding: poor handicapper: stays 9f: unsuited by soft going and used to act well on top-of-the-ground: blinkered 5 times: has worn bandages. *J. P. Smith.*

ZIPPERTI DO 4 ch.f. Precocious 126–Doobie Do 106 (Derring-Do 131) [1989 7g **—**
a8g* 1990 a8g⁵] deep-girthed filly: won maiden at Southwell (reluctant at stalls) in December, 1989, only form from 3 outings. *P. J. Makin.*

ZISKA (USA) 2 gr.f. (Apr 18) Danzig (USA)–Heavenly Cause (USA) (Grey Dawn **75** P
II 132) [1990 7g³] $600,000Y: big, lengthy, good-topped filly: has plenty of scope: half-sister to 3 winners in North America: dam champion 2-y-o later won Kentucky Oaks and Acorn Stakes: favourite but very green, 3 lengths third of 20, soon in touch

after slow start and going on well under considerate ride, to Campestral in maiden at Newmarket in November: sure to improve considerably, and win races. *H. R. A. Cecil.*

ZIZANIA 3 ch.f. Ahonoora 122–Bolkonskina (Balidar 133) [1989 6g 6g 7f⁶ 6g⁴ 6g⁶ 1990 8f⁴ 7m² 8.5d⁶ 7g² 7h⁴ 9g 8g* 8m⁶] quite good-topped filly: shows knee action: modest performer: 20/1 and ridden by 7-lb claimer, won handicap at Wolverhampton in October, making most and rallying well: stayed 1m: probably best with give in the ground: stud. *C. E. Brittain.*   73

ZIZI JEAN MAIRE 3 ch.f. Chief Singer 131–Ring Lady 98 (Thatch (USA) 136) [1989 NR 1990 10m 7f 8.2m 12.5g 10.5g] 4,500Y: big, rather leggy, workmanlike filly: fifth live foal: half-sister to useful 6f and 7f winner Bel Byou (by Try My Best) and a winner in Canada by General Assembly: dam 5f and 1m winner: hung badly and no worthwhile form, including in sellers: blinkered final start: sold 2,500 gns Newmarket Autumn Sales: one to avoid. *D. Morley.*   — §

ZLOTY 2 b.c. (Mar 7) Elegant Air 119–Chase Paperchase 79 (Malinowski (USA) 123) [1990 5m⁴ 5m³ 6h² 6f² 5g⁶ 6m² 6f*] 1,000Y: smallish, sturdy colt: first foal: dam maiden stayed 6f: modest performer: won maiden at Newcastle in July: will stay 7f: acts on hard ground. *W. Jarvis.*   80

ZODE 4 b.g. Simply Great (FR) 122–Star Face (African Sky 124) [1989 7d 1990 8f 8m 8m 6g⁶ 7g] good-topped, attractive gelding: lightly-raced maiden: show as 4-y-o only on fourth outing: has been taken down early. *J. S. Wilson.*   —

ZODIAC BOY 5 b.g. Monseigneur (USA) 124–Hannie Caulder (Workboy 123) [1989 10s 12.5f 12m 12h 1990 10.2f 7f⁵] close-coupled, workmanlike gelding: of little account: wears bandages behind: sold 600 gns Ascot July Sales. *J. Pearce.*   —

ZOLLY'S TREASURE 2 b.g. (Mar 22) Sayf El Arab (USA) 127–Gleneagle 91 (Swing Easy (USA) 126) [1990 5f⁶ 5f a6g a6g 6g 8m] 4,800F, 16,500Y: lengthy, good-bodied gelding: brother to 3-y-o Tristan's Comet and half-brother to a winner in Italy by Coquelin: dam 5f and 6f winner: little worthwhile form in varied events: blinkered final 2 (had very stiff task second one) starts. *M. W. Easterby.*   —

ZOMAN (USA) 3 ch.c. Affirmed (USA)–A Little Affection (USA) (King 119 Emperor (USA)) [1989 7m* 1990 8m² 12g 8d* 8f⁵ 8g* 8v³]
    Zoman had things against him in two outings in Britain in 1990. The trip proved too far in the Ever Ready Derby—in third place and poised to challenge two furlongs out, Zoman soon weakened to finish over nine lengths seventh of eighteen behind Quest For Fame; and he seemed unsuited by the very firm ground when a modest fifth to Distant Relative in the Sussex Stakes at Goodwood. On the form he showed abroad, Zoman was fully entitled to his place in both fields. He started third favourite at Epsom, having finished an excellent length-and-a-half second to Linamix in the Dubai Poule d'Essai des Poulains at Longchamp in May on only his second appearance. Dropped slightly in class subsequently and ridden from the front, two hard-fought wins in Group 2 company ranked Zoman not too far behind some of the best three-year-old milers in Europe. He got the better of the other supplementary entry Distant Relative—opposing on terms considerably worse than at Goodwood three weeks later—in the four-runner Phoenix International Stakes at Phoenix Park in July. Though narrowly headed in the final furlong, Zoman fought back to regain a three-quarter-length advantage by the line. He was again tested to the full in the Ciga Prix du Rond-Point at Longchamp in October. Though the favourite, Poule d'Essai des Pouliches winner Houseproud, failed to do herself justice, it took a game performance from Zoman to beat Honor Rajana and Fils Unique, each receiving 5 lb, by a length and the same; he had the field on the stretch well before the home turn and responded well to pressure in the straight.

		Affirmed (USA) (ch 1975)	Exclusive Native (ch 1965)	Raise A Native
Zoman (USA) (ch.c. 1987)				Exclusive
			Won't Tell You (b 1962)	Crafty Admiral
				Scarlet Ribbon
		A Little Affection (USA) (ch 1977)	King Emperor (b 1966)	Bold Ruler
				Irish Jay
			Chicken Little (b 1966)	Olympia
				Dashing By

    Zoman runs as though a mile won't prove the limit of his stamina. Though Affirmed is the sire of Irish One Thousand Guineas winner Trusted

Partner and smart French miler Regal State, the average winning distance at three years and upwards of his progeny in Britain and Ireland is around a mile and a quarter, and he's known more in Europe through middle-distance performers such as Bint Pasha and Claude Monet. However, the dam A Little Affection was a smart sprinter, who gained her most notable success in the six-furlong Miss Prosperity Handicap at Meadowlands. She's a half-sister to several winners, including smart two-year-old Spanish Way, out of an unraced daughter of multiple winner Dashing By. Easily the pick of A Little Affection's three previous foals was Zoman's close relation Love And Affection (by Exclusive Era), runner-up in the Grade 1 Spinaway Stakes at two years and successful in the Sorority Breeders Cup at around a mile in 1989. A good family, then, and Zoman fetched 300,000 dollars as a yearling at Fasig Tipton, the highest price paid at public auction for one of Affirmed's seventh crop. He remains in training and should recoup more of his purchase price in 1991, particularly if, as seems likely, he has further starts on the Continent. A tall, lengthy though rather sparely-made colt, Zoman is still relatively lightly raced. Though he'll need to improve to challenge the best at a mile, he could be an interesting prospect campaigned over nine furlongs or a mile and a quarter. Zoman acts on any going with the possible exception of very firm—he ran right up to his best on heavy when third to Sikeston in the Premio Vittorio di Capua at Milan in November. *P. F. I. Cole.*

ZONDA 2 br.f. (Apr 24) Fabulous Dancer (USA) 124 Oh So Hot (Habitat 134) **100 p**
[1990 6m³ 6g* 6m⁵] leggy, close-coupled filly: good mover: second foal: half-sister to 3-y-o Fancy Dress (by Local Suitor): dam unraced sister to Roussalka and Our Home and half-sister to Oh So Sharp: made all in 26-runner maiden at Newbury in August, quickening 2f out and running on strongly to win by 1½ lengths from Lilian Bayliss: excellent fifth of 11, keeping on well, to Capricciosa in Tattersalls Cheveley Park Stakes at Newmarket: will be better suited by 7f: likely to improve further. *P. F. I. Cole.*

ZONINA (IRE) 2 br.f. (Apr 5) Runnett 125–Captivate 79 (Mansingh (USA) 120) **54**
[1990 5g⁵ 5f⁴ 5m² 6m⁴ 5m³ 5m 6m] 12,000Y: well-made filly: third foal: half-sister to a winner in Denmark: dam 5f winner from speedy family: plating-class maiden: better suited by 6f than 5f: sold 3,500 gns Ascot November Sales. *R. Hannon.*

ZUBROVKA (FR) 3 b.c. Law Society (USA) 130–Czar's Bride (USA) 78 **89**
(Northern Dancer) [1989 7g⁴ 1990 8f⁵ 10.1g² 10.1g² 12g 12g⁴] medium-sized, attractive colt: fair form here, second in Windsor minor events: well beaten in Derby Italiano at Rome then fourth of 10 in listed race at Turin: may prove best at around 1¼m: best efforts with give in the ground: swished tail persistently in paddock second start: changed hands before fourth start: trained until after fourth by R. Charlton. *O. Pessi, Italy.*

ZULU DANCER 3 b.f. Sula Bula 109–Dusky Damsel 68 (Sahib 114) [1989 NR **—**
1990 8m 9m 8f 8m] sparely-made filly: seventh foal: dam won over 6f at 3 yrs: well beaten in claimers and seller: joined J. King. *R. J. Holder.*

BATTLE OF THE SEXES IN CURRAGH SHOWDOWN

Salsabil to silence colts

SATURDAY MORNING'S ODDS ON FAVOURITE!

Ireland's International Racing and Bloodstock Weekly

The Irish Field
11-15, D'Olier Street, Dublin 2, Ireland
Telephone: Dublin 6792022. Fax: Dublin 6793029

TIMEFORM CHAMPIONS OF 1990

HORSE OF THE YEAR
BEST SPRINTER
(RATED AT 137)

DAYJUR (USA)
3 br.c. Danzig–Gold Beauty (Mr Prospector)
Owner Hamdan Al-Maktoum   Trainer R. Hern

BEST TWO-YEAR-OLD COLT (RATED AT 122p)

HECTOR PROTECTOR (USA)
2 ch.c. Woodman–Korveya (Riverman)
Owner Mr S. S. Niarchos   Trainer F. Boutin

BEST TWO-YEAR-OLD FILLY (RATED AT 117p)

SHADAYID (USA)
2 gr.f. Shadeed–Desirable (Lord Gayle)
Owner Hamdan Al-Maktoum   Trainer J. Dunlop

BEST MILERS (RATED AT 130)

MARKOFDISTINCTION
4 b. or br.c. Known Fact–Ghislaine (Icecapade)
Owner Mr G. Leigh   Trainer L. Cumani

ROYAL ACADEMY (USA)
3 b.c. Nijinsky–Crimson Saint (Crimson Satan)
Owner Classic Thoroughbreds Plc   Trainer V. O'Brien

BEST MIDDLE DISTANCE HORSE (RATED AT 132)

SAUMAREZ
3 b. or br.c. Rainbow Quest–Fiesta Fun (Welsh Pageant)
Owner Mr B. McNall   Trainer N. Clement

BEST STAYER (RATED AT 130)

SNURGE
3 ch.c. Ela-Mana-Mou–Finlandia (Faraway Son)
Owner Mr M. Arbib   Trainer P. Cole

THE TIMEFORM 'TOP HUNDRED'

Here are listed the 'Top 100' two-year-olds, three-year-olds and older horses in the annual.

Two-Year-Olds

122p	Hector Protector
121p	Exit To Nowhere
120p	Mukaddamah
120p	Peter Davies
119	Ganges
119	Mujadil
118p	Pistolet Bleu
118	Mujtahid
117p	Shadayid
116p	Lycius
116	Chipaya
116	Mac's Imp
116	Masterclass
116	Mujaazif
115p	Sapieha
115	Crack Regiment
115	Distinctly North
115	Generous
114	Booming
114	Divine Danse
113p	Capricciosa
113p	Shamshir
113	Akeem
113	Bog Trotter
113	Steamer Duck
112p	Island Universe
112p	Radwell
112	Bufalino
112	Caerlina
112	Sha Tha
112?	Time Gentlemen
111p	Imperfect Circle
111	Alnaab
111	Masslama
111	Pigeon Voyageur
111	Run And Gun
110p	Majlood
110p	Marcham
110	After The Sun
110	As Que To
110	Beau Sultan
110	Reason To Trick
110	Satin Pointe
109p	Brockette
109p	Green Pola
109p	Safa
109	River Traffic
108p	Jahafil
108p	Sillery
108	Clark Store
108	Clifton Charlie
108	Danseuse du Soir
108	Joyeuse Marquise
108	Line Engaged
108	Selkirk
108	Vintage Only
107P	Dartrey
107p	Surrealist
107	Danzante

107	Eternity Star
107	Gipsy Fiddler
107	Magic Night
107	Rinka Das
107	Sardarmati
107	Snowy Owl
106p	Heart of Darkness
106	Acteur Francais
106	Fortune's Wheel
106	Jet Ski Lady
106	Time Line
105	Heard A Whisper
105	Majmu
105	Malvernico
105	Red Rainbow
105	Sleeping Car
105	Widyan
104p	Crystal Gazing
104p	Misty Valley
104p	Regal Sabre
104p	Sea Level
104 +	Anjiz
104	Alexandra Fair
104	Lee Artiste
104	Polemic
104?	Half A Tick
103p	Circus Light
103p	Tel Quel
103	Dominion Gold
103	Full of Pluck
103	Prodigal Blues
103	Sizzling Saga
103	Track Monarch
102p	Chicarica
102p	Junk Bond
102	Caerdydd
102	Golden Mintage
102	Jimmy Barnie
102	Sir Harry Hardman
102	Woodman's Mount
101p	Gentle Aria
101p	Shaima
101	Almendares
101	Approach The Bench
101	Democratic
101	Flying Brave
101	Kooyonga
101	Miss The Point
101	Noora Park
101	Punch N'Run
101	Roger Ramjet
101	Sylvan Breeze

Three-Year-Olds

137	Dayjur
132	Saumarez
131	Belmez
131	Deploy
131	Epervier Bleu

130	Royal Academy
130	Salsabil
130	Snurge
129	Ron's Victory
127	In The Groove
127	Linamix
127	Priolo
127	Quest For Fame
127	Tirol
126	Sanglamore
125	Elmaamul
125	Hellenic
125	Shavian
124	Erdelistan
123p	Miss Alleged
123	Kartajana
123	Machiavellian
123	Rafha
123	Septieme Ciel
123§	Dead Certain
122	Colour Chart
121p	Antisaar
121p	River God
121	Blue Stag
121	Chimes of Freedom
121	Madame Dubois
121	Wajid
120	Air de Rien
120	Candy Glen
120	Narwala
120	Rock City
120?	Heart of Joy
119	Anshan
119	Madiriya
119	Passing Sale
119	Splash of Colour
119	Top Waltz
119	Zoman
119?	Lord Florey
118	Agent Bleu
118	Defensive Play
118	Funambule
118	Game Plan
118	Moon Cactus
118	Norwich
118	Panoramic
118	Sally Rous
117	Applecross
117	Dr Somerville
117	Satin Wood
117	Vue Cavaliere
116	Argentum
116	Down The Flag
116	Knight's Baroness
116	North Col
116	Pole Position
116	Rock Hopper
116	Rubicund
116	Whitehaven
116?	In Excess
116?	Private Tender

TIMEFORM COMPUTER TIMEFIGURES

Timefigures measure the performance of horses not on their form one against another but in terms of time, in seconds (per five furlongs) faster or slower than a certain fixed standard. The following tables show the best timefigure recorded by the leading horses — judged on time — in each category in 1990. Next to the timefigure is the equivalent timerating in pounds, directly comparable with the Timeform Ratings in this annual volume.

TWO-YEAR-OLDS

1	MUJTAHID	−0.84	121
2	MUJADIL	−0.84	121
3	MUJAAZIF	−0.75	119
4	CHIPAYA	−0.68	117
5	LYCIUS	−0.56	114
6	SELKIRK	−0.53	113
7	MAC'S IMP	−0.51	113
8	DISTINCTLY NORTH	−0.49	112
9	JAHAFIL	−0.40	110
10	IMPERFECT CIRCLE	−0.37	109
11	CAPRICCIOSA	−0.37	109
12	RADWELL	−0.32	108
13	GENEROUS	−0.30	108
14	MAJLOOD	−0.29	107
15	SAPIEHA	−0.29	107
16	CLIFTON CHARLIE	−0.28	107
17	ALNAAB	−0.27	107
18	VINTAGE ONLY	−0.26	107
19	TRACK MONARCH	−0.25	106
20	SNOWY OWL	−0.25	106
21	AGHAADIR	−0.25	106
22	JIMMY BARNIE	−0.23	106
23	SHADAYID	−0.22	106
24	GENTLE ARIA	−0.22	106
25	BOG TROTTER	−0.21	105
26	PUNCH N' RUN	−0.18	105
27	DOMINION GOLD	−0.16	104
28	KNIFEBOX	−0.16	104
29	POETS COVE	−0.15	104
30	BALAAT	−0.13	103

THREE-YEAR-OLD SPRINTERS

1	DAYJUR	−1.69	142
2	ROYAL ACADEMY	−1.06	127
3	RONS VICTORY	−0.95	124
4	POLAR BIRD	−0.93	123
5	REFERENCE LIGHT	−0.62	116
6	PHARAOHS DELIGHT	−0.61	115
7	TADWIN	−0.58	115
8	DUCK AND DIVE	−0.53	113
9	ARGENTUM	−0.49	112
10	NORTON CHALLENGER	−0.33	108

THREE-YEAR-OLD MILERS

1	SHAVIAN	−1.25	131
2	TIROL	−1.10	128
3	CANDY GLEN	−1.00	125
4	NORWICH	−0.99	125
5	MACHIAVELLIAN	−0.90	123
6	SALSABIL	−0.86	122
7	HEART OF JOY	−0.79	120
8	SALLY ROUS	−0.75	119
9	THEATRICAL CHARMER	−0.71	118
10	ANSHAN	−0.70	118

THREE-YEAR-OLD MIDDLE DISTANCE

1	KARTAJANA	−1.05	126
2	BELMEZ	−1.04	126
3	QUEST FOR FAME	−0.95	124
4	ELMAAMUL	−0.85	121
5	LORD OF THE FIELD	−0.79	120
6	SALSABIL	−0.76	119
7	BLUE STAG	−0.75	119
8	SANGLAMORE	−0.70	118
9	APPLECROSS	−0.69	117
10	SAUMAREZ	−0.66	117

THREE-YEAR-OLD STAYERS

1	RIVER GOD	−0.68	117
2	PARTING MOMENT	−0.50	113
3	GREAT MARQUESS	−0.47	112
4	TRAINGLOT	−0.43	111
5	SNURGE	−0.40	110
6	LUCKY MOON	−0.34	109
7	MADAME DUBOIS	−0.29	107
8	HELLENIC	−0.24	106
9	TRIFOLIO	−0.19	105
10	APPLECROSS	−0.15	104

OLDER HORSE
SPRINTERS

1	STATOBLEST	−1.10	128
2	SAVAHRA SOUND	−0.67	117
3	CAROLS TREASURE	−0.52	113
4	GREAT COMMOTION	−0.49	112
5	LUGANA BEACH	−0.49	112
6	MR NICKERSON	−0.48	112
7	MACS FIGHTER	−0.46	112
8	NICHOLAS	−0.44	111
9	OUR FREDDIE	−0.41	110
10	BLYTON LAD	−0.41	110

OLDER HORSE
MILERS

1	MARKOF-DISTINCTION	−1.30	133
2	DISTANT RELATIVE	−1.20	130
3	GREEN LINE EXPRESS	−1.12	128
4	MIRROR BLACK	−1.06	127
5	LANDYAP	−0.71	118
6	PRIDE OF ARABY	−0.59	115
7	FEDORIA	−0.58	115
8	SAFAWAN	−0.58	115
9	CITIDANCER	−0.55	114
10	MAGIC GLEAM	−0.53	113

OLDER HORSE
MIDDLE DISTANCE

1	BRUSH ASIDE	−1.10	128
2	OLD VIC	−1.07	127
3	IN THE WINGS	−1.00	125
4	ASSATIS	−0.96	124
5	STARLET	−0.92	123
6	OBSERVATION POST	−0.90	123
7	TERIMON	−0.86	122
8	ROSEATE TERN	−0.81	120
9	CACOETHES	−0.80	120
10	IBN BEY	−0.76	119

OLDER HORSE
STAYERS

1	NOBLE SAVAGE	−0.77	119
2	TEAMSTER	−0.68	117
3	MOUNTAIN KINGDOM	−0.56	114
4	CHELSEA GIRL	−0.38	110
5	FURTHER FLIGHT	−0.35	109
6	BRAASHEE	−0.30	108
7	DOUBLE DUTCH	−0.28	107
8	SADEEM	−0.27	107
9	SAPIENCE	−0.26	107
10	ECRAN	−0.16	104

1990 STATISTICS

The following tables show the leading owners, trainers, breeders, jockeys, horses and sires of winners during the 1990 turf season, under Jockey Club Rules. The tables are reproduced by permission of *The Sporting Life.*

	OWNERS	Horses	Races Won	Stakes £
1.	Hamdan Al-Maktoum	76	127	1,536,815
2.	Sheikh Mohammed	122	176	1,498,195
3.	K. Abdulla	46	61	690,997
4.	Brian Cooper	1	3	459,117
5.	R. E. Sangster	24	41	347,753
6.	Maktoum Al-Maktoum	19	28	346,385
7.	H. H. Aga Khan	20	37	313,281
8.	Gerald Leigh	3	5	294,515
9.	C. A. B. St George	9	14	238,678
10.	Lord Howard de Walden	8	10	214,033
11.	Wafic Said	5	7	199,610
12.	Fahd Salman	17	23	195,107

	TRAINERS	Horses	Races Won	Stakes £
1.	H. R. A. Cecil	68	111	1,519,864
2.	L. M. Cumani	69	109	1,008,843
3.	M. R. Stoute	55	78	803,675
4.	D. R. C. Elsworth	30	41	780,890
5.	B. W. Hills	67	106	747,499
6.	R. Hannon	45	69	653,526
7.	J. L. Dunlop	49	74	626,805
8.	R. Charlton	26	37	614,707
9.	W. R. Hern	19	30	502,902
10.	G. Harwood	47	69	457,715
11.	P. F. I. Cole	37	49	446,230
12.	J. Berry	66	127	397,274

	BREEDERS	Horses	Races Won	Stakes £
1.	Juddmonte Farms	20	40	615,115
2.	J. Macdonald-Buchanan	1	3	459,117
3.	Kilfrush Stud	5	7	411,973
4.	Darley Stud Management	8	13	404,987
5.	H. H. Aga Khan	23	47	386,915
6.	Gerald Leigh	6	9	307,695
7.	Barronstown Stud	13	19	288,320
8.	Georgia E. Hofmann	1	5	243,370
9.	Sheikh Mohammed	22	34	232,735
10.	Flaxman Holdings Ltd	11	15	215,277
11.	Swettenham Stud	30	46	204,092
12.	Lord Howard de Walden	7	9	202,385

	JOCKEYS	1st	2nd	3rd	Unpl	Total Mts	Per Cent
1.	Pat Eddery	209	133	90	459	891	23.5

		1st	2nd	3rd	Unpl	Total Mts	Per Cent
2.	W. Carson	187	131	102	485	905	20.7
3.	S. Cauthen	142	78	73	332	625	22.7
4.	L. Dettori	140	83	74	399	696	20.1
5.	M. Roberts	128	113	117	500	858	14.9
6.	W. R. Swinburn	112	119	108	397	736	15.2
7.	R. Cochrane	109	100	97	519	825	13.2
8.	A. Munro	94	58	58	409	619	15.2
9.	K. Darley	82	83	71	370	606	13.5
10.	D. McKeown	78	86	61	491	716	10.9
11.	G. Duffield	75	70	56	472	673	11.1
12.	G. Carter	73	81	55	367	576	12.7

HORSES

		Races Won	Stakes £
1.	In The Groove 3 b.f. Night Shift–Pine Ridge	3	459,117
2.	Belmez 3 b.c. El Gran Senor–Grace Note	4	367,321
3.	Quest For Fame 3 b.c. Rainbow Quest–Aryenne	2	359,272
4.	Markofdistinction 4 b. or br.c. Known Fact–Ghislaine	3	290,061
5.	Dayjur 3 br.c. Danzig–Gold Beauty	5	243,370
6.	Salsabil 3 b.f. Sadler's Wells–Flame of Tara	3	234,750
7.	Peter Davies 2 ch.c. Bering–French Flick	3	176,263
8.	Elmaamul 3 ch.c. Diesis–Modena	2	167,876
9.	Shavian 3 b.c. Kris–Mixed Applause	2	162,973
10.	Snurge 3 ch.c. Ela-Mana-Mou–Finlandia	1	151,938
11.	Chimes of Freedom 3 ch.f. Private Account–Aviance	2	145,848
12.	Hellenic 3 b.f. Darshaan–Grecian Sea	3	144,587

SIRES OF WINNERS

		Horses	Races Won	Stakes £
1.	Night Shift (1980) by Northern Dancer	17	32	620,417
2.	Sadler's Wells (1981) by Northern Dancer	25	36	602,877
3.	Known Fact (1977) by In Reality	14	23	467,339
4.	El Gran Senor (1981) by Northern Dancer	10	17	431,610
5.	Rainbow Quest (1981) by Blushing Groom	12	18	418,576
6.	Kris (1976) by Sharpen Up	18	29	395,294
7.	Diesis (1980) by Sharpen Up	20	29	343,027
8.	Danzig (1977) by Northern Dancer	11	21	327,461
9.	Caerleon (1980) by Nijinsky	17	31	253,300
10.	Touching Wood (1979) by Roberto	14	26	250,566
11.	Darshaan (1981) by Shirley Heights	10	17	237,220
12.	Aragon (1980) by Mummy's Pet	16	23	218,188

ETALONS
1991

- **Stallion review**
- **Racing and Breeding Chronicles**
- **Statistics and Results of the main sales of the year**
- **Results of the 1990 Group Races**
- **Register of all stallions standing in France in 1990**

NAME ....

ADDRESS ....

TOWN ....

COUNTRY ....

would like to receive (   ) copy(ies) of ETALONS 1991
at the unit price of 150 FF + 50 FF for p & p

Kindly complete and mail to:
ETALONS, 6 rond-point des Champs-Elysées, 75008 Paris, France
Tel: (1) 43 59 94 14   Telex: 648 665 Etalons   Fax: 42 25 44 25

☐ attached payment by cheque in Fr. Francs at the order of **ETALONS**
☐ wishes to pay by charge card
☐ Visa   ☐ Mastercard

Card number ....

Expiration date ....   Signature

THE FREE HANDICAPS

TWO-YEAR-OLDS

The following are the weights allotted in the Ladbroke European Free Handicap published on 17th January. The race is to be run over seven furlongs at Newmarket on 17th April, 1991.

	st	lb		st	lb		st	lb
Hector Protector	9	7	Line Engaged	8	7	Storm At Night	8	2
Mujtahid	9	4	Majmu	8	7	Zigaura	8	2
Exit To Nowhere	9	3	Run And Gun	8	7	Arokat	8	1
Lycius	9	1	Satin Pointe	8	7	Ausherra	8	1
Mac's Imp	9	1	Surrealist	8	7	Balaat	8	1
Masterclass	9	1	Vintage Only	8	7	Caerdydd	8	1
Pistolet Bleu	9	1	Cloche d'Or	8	6	Desert Sun	8	1
Shadayid	9	1	Joyeuse Marquise	8	6	Fennel	8	1
Generous	9	0	Marju	8	6	Heart of Darkness	8	1
Shamshir	9	0	Misil	8	6	Hip To Time	8	1
Bog Trotter	8	13	Sleeping Car	8	6	Matahif	8	1
Booming	8	13	Balleroy	8	5	Prince Russanor	8	1
Distinctly North	8	13	Belle Bleue	8	5	Red Rainbow	8	1
Ganges	8	12	Bravefoot	8	5	Regal Sabre	8	1
Time Gentlemen	8	12	Crystal Gazing	8	5	Sedair	8	1
Capricciosa	8	11	Danzante	8	5	Stark South	8	1
Mujaazif	8	11	Democratic	8	5	Sumonda	8	1
Mukaddamah	8	11	Dominion Gold	8	5	Time Line	8	1
Peter Davies	8	11	Gipsy Fiddler	8	5	Timeless Times	8	1
Beau Sultan	8	10	Hello Pink	8	5	Trojan Crown	8	1
Caerlina	8	10	Jahafil	8	5	Widyan	8	1
Crack Regiment	8	10	Magic Night	8	5	Zonda	8	1
Majlood	8	10	Marcham	8	5	Environment Friend	8	0
Reason To Trick	8	10	Misty Valley	8	5	Full of Pluck	8	0
Safa	8	10	On Tiptoes	8	5	Glowing Ardour	8	0
Sha Tha	8	10	Only Yours	8	5	Golden Birch	8	0
As Que To	8	9	Sea Level	8	5	Heard A Whisper	8	0
Chicarica	8	9	Shalford	8	5	Jameelaty	8	0
Imperfect Circle	8	9	Snowy Owl	8	5	Junk Bond	8	0
Masslama	8	9	Tycoon's Drama	8	5	Lilian Bayliss	8	0
Mujadil	8	9	Aimaam	8	4	Polish Patriot	8	0
Pigeon Voyageur	8	9	Circus Light	8	4	Seductress	8	0
Radwell	8	9	Dangora	8	4	Self Expression	8	0
River Traffic	8	9	Half A Tick	8	4	Shimmering Sea	8	0
Sapieha	8	9	Lee Artiste	8	4	Stone Mill	8	0
Selkirk	8	9	Sylva Honda	8	4	Walim	8	0
Sylvan Breeze	8	8	Jimmy Barnie	8	3	Commendable	7	13
After The Sun	8	8	Nazoo	8	3	Corrupt	7	13
Alnaab	8	8	Poets Cove	8	3	Flying Down To Rio	7	13
Danseuse du Soir	8	8	Sharifabad	8	3	Green's Ferneley	7	13
Divine Danse	8	8	Act of Diplomacy	8	2	Grove Aries	7	13
Eternity Star	8	8	Andrassy	8	2	Hot Desert	7	13
Gramy Award	8	8	Atlantic Flyer	8	2	Marcus Thorpe	7	13
Hokusai	8	8	Big Blow	8	2	Ocean Air	7	13
Steamer Duck	8	8	Bold Nephew	8	2	Plan of Action	7	13
Acteur Francais	8	7	Clifton Charlie	8	2	Punch N'Run	7	13
Akeem	8	7	Dartrey	8	2	Shaima	7	13
Anjiz	8	7	Jaffa Line	8	2	Shedad	7	13
Chipaya	8	7	Mohawk Chief	8	2	The Old Firm	7	13
Flying Brave	8	7	Mystiko	8	2	Track Monarch	7	13
Green Pola	8	7	Roger de Berksted	8	2	Woodman's Mount	7	13

THREE-YEAR-OLDS

5 furlongs plus
133 Dayjur
129 Ron's Victory
119 Dead Certain
119 Rock City
118 Argentum
112 Duck And Dive
112 Haunting Beauty
112 Pharaoh's Delight
111 Keen Hunter
111 La Grange Music
110 Northern Goddess
110 Polar Bird
109 Night At Sea
109 Tod
108 Dancing Music
108 Flower Girl
108 Tadwin
107 Boozy
106 Reference Light
105 Case Law
105 Mademoiselle Chloe
105 Ra'a
104 Montendre
103 Kadim
103 Rivers Rhapsody
102 Centerland
102 Childrey
102 Elbio
101 Katzakeena
100 Cullinan

7 furlongs plus
129 Royal Academy
127 Linamix
125 Tirol
124 Ch's of Freedom
122 Shavian
121 Candy Glen
121 Machiavellian
117 Anshan
117 Norwich
117 Satin Wood
116 Lord Florey
114 Bold Russian
114 Fire The Groom
113 Hasbah
113 Heart of Joy
113 In Excess
113 Maximilian

113 Sally Rous
112 Theatrical Charmer
111 Arousal
110 Book The Band
110 Gharam
110 Mukddaam
110 Raj Waki
110 Rami
110 Thakib
109 Enharmonic
109 London Pride
109 Qui Danzig
109 Tabdea
108 Batzushka
108 Message Pad
107 Alidiva
107 Arpero
107 Now Listen
107 Palace Street
107 Sure Sharp
106 Eton Lad
106 Lifewatch Vision
106 Rasan
106 Two Left Feet
106 Va Toujours
105 El Paso
105 Marienski
104 Croupier
104 Glen Kate
104 Negligent
104 Risen Moon
103 Daarik
103 Quavering
103 Sheer Precocity
102 Call To Arms
102 Field Glass
102 Line of Thunder
102 Osario
102 Selaah
101 Swordsmith
100 Akamantis
100 Alwathba
100 Free Thinker
100 Lord Charmer
100 Model Village
100 Mutah
100 Robellation
100 Sajjaya
100 Star of The Future
100 Sundance Kid
100 Villeroi

9½ furlongs plus
130 Saumarez
126 In The Groove
125 Elmaamul
120 Rafha
116 Missionary Ridge
116 Moon Cactus
114 Ruby Tiger
111 Anvari
111 Native Twine
111 Noble Patriarch
111 Razeen (USA)
110 Sardegna
110 Treble Eight
107 Stapleford Manor
106 Baylis
106 Stagecraft
105 Halston Prince
105 Spinning
103 Cameo Performance
103 Lucky Guest
102 Berry's Dream
102 Bridal Toast
102 Cum Laude
102 Rakeen
102 Red Toto
101 Aromatic
101 Escrime
101 Fearless Revival
101 Mill Run
100 Dress Parade

11 furlongs plus
132 Saumarez
131 Belmez
129 Snurge
125 Salsabil
124 Deploy
123 Hellenic
123 Quest For Fame
123 Sanglamore
121 Kartajana
120 Wajd
118 Madiriya
117 Blue Stag
117 Defensive Play
116 Madame Dubois
114 Narwala
113 Game Plan
113 Karinga Bay
113 Pharian
112 Down The Flag

112 Knight's Baroness
112 Whitehaven
111 Cruising Height
111 Ivrea
111 Private Tender
111 Rock Hopper
111 Starstreak
110 Hajade
110 Kaheel
109 Air Music
109 Duke of Paducah
109 Lord of The Field
108 Marquetry
108 Pier Damiani
106 Ahead
106 Azzaam
106 Tarikhana
105 Admiral Byng
104 Curia Regis
104 Sasaki
103 Tour Eiffel
102 Cleonte
102 Great Heights
102 Stereo
101 Chirrup
101 Secret Waters
100 Circus Feathers
100 Emperor Fountain
100 Ijtihaad
100 Lift And Load

14 furlongs plus
123 Snurge
116 River God
112 Applecross
112 Great Marquess
112 Rubicund
110 Wajna
107 Lucky Moon
106 Arzanni
105 Beauchamp Express
105 Criminal Law
104 Greenham
104 Parting Moment
102 Crack
102 Judicial Hero
101 Kasayid
101 Trainglot
100 Syrtos

FOUR-YEAR-OLDS AND UPWARDS

5 furlongs plus
120 Great Commotion
119 Statoblest
116 Lugana Beach
112 Savahra Sound
112 Sharp N'Early
110 A Prayer For Wings

110 Blyton Lad
110 Carol's Treasure
108 Afwaj
107 Tigani
106 Mac's Fighter
105 Shuttlecock Corner
102 Paley Prince
102 Sharp Reminder

101 Be Fresh
101 Nicholas
101 Our Freddie

7 furlongs plus
128 Markof-distinction
127 Distant Relative

124 Green Line Express
120 Safawan
119 Citidancer
114 Mirror Black
114 Monsagem
112 Aldbourne
111 Magic Gleam
109 Filia Ardross

107 Princess Accord	115 Starlet	118 Brush Aside	100 Hateel
105 Just Three	114 Eradicate	118 Sapience	
104 Pride of Araby	114 Pirate Army	117 Charmer	**14 furlongs plus**
103 Fedoria	113 Shellac	116 Per Quod	117 Braashee
102 Power Take Off	112 Husyan	115 Ile de Nisky	114 Top Class
102 Strike Force	111 Scenic	115 Observation Post	112 Ashal
101 Grand Blush	110 Landyap	114 Michelozzo	111 Al Maheb
100 Light of Morn	109 Alphabel	113 Roseate Tern	110 Teamster
100 Pelorus	105 Alcando	113 Tyrone Bridge	109 Dance Spectrum
100 Wassl Port	105 Song of Sixpence	112 Artic Envoy	108 Thething-
	101 Try Trust	111 Mountain	aboutitis
9½ furlongs plus	100 If Memory	Kingdom	106 Sadeem
125 Legal Case	Serves	111 Spritsail	105 Chelsea Girl
124 Ibn Bey		110 Sesame	104 Cossack Guard
120 Batshoof	**11 furlongs plus**	109 Albadr	104 Weld
119 Terimon	130 Old Vic	104 My Lamb	103 Mill Pond
117 Dolpour	127 In The Wings	103 Rudjig	100 Ecran
117 Relief Pitcher	126 Assatis	102 Bold Fox	100 Noble Savage
115 Ile de Chypre	123 Cacoethes	101 The Prussian	100 Regal Reform

INTERNATIONAL CLASSIFICATIONS

The following were published for information only on 17th January, 1991. The figure allotted to each horse is that which the Official Handicappers, having regard to previous Classifications, consider to represent its overall racing merit. Horses racing over different distances and being top rated, are credited with those performances by inclusion in the appropriate division.

TWO-YEAR-OLDS

126 Hector Protector	115 Crack Regiment	113 Divine Danse	111 Misil
123 Mujtahid	115 Majlood	113 Eternity Star	111 Sleeping Car
122 Exit To Nowhere	115 Reason To Trick	113 Gramy Award	110 Balleroy
120 Lycius	115 Safa	113 Hokusai	110 Belle Bleue
120 Mac's Imp	115 Sha Tha	113 Steamer Duck	110 Bravefoot
120 Masterclass	114 As Que To	112 Acteur Francais	110 Crystal Gazing
120 Pistolet Bleu	114 Chicarica	112 Akeem	110 Danzante
120 Shadayid	114 Imperfect Circle	112 Anjiz	110 Democratic
119 Generous	114 Masslama	112 Chipaya	110 Dominion Gold
119 Shamshir	114 Mujadil	112 Flying Brave	110 Gipsy Fiddler
118 Bog Trotter	114 Pigeon	112 Green Pola	110 Hello Pink
118 Booming	Voyageur	112 Line Engaged	110 Jahafil
118 Distinctly North	114 Radwell	112 Majmu	110 Magic Night
117 Canges	114 River Traffic	112 Run And Gun	110 Marcham
117 Time Gentlemen	114 Sapieha	112 Satin Pointe	110 Misty Valley
116 Capricciosa	114 Selkirk	112 Surrealist	110 On Tiptoes
116 Mujaazif	114 Sylvan Breeze	112 Vintage Only	110 Only Yours
116 Mukaddamah	113 After The Sun	111 Cloche d'Or	110 Sea Level
116 Peter Davies	113 Alnaab	111 Joyeuse	110 Shalford
115 Beau Sultan	113 Danseuse	Marquise	110 Snowy Owl
115 Caerlina	du Soir	111 Marju	110 Tycoon's Drama

THREE-YEAR-OLDS

5 furlongs plus	116 Pole Position	111 Keen Hunter	**7 furlongs plus**
133 Dayjur	112 Duck And Dive	111 La Grange Music	129 Royal
129 Ron's Victory	112 Haunting	110 Dictator's Song	Academy
119 Dead Certain	Beauty	110 Northern	128 Priolo
119 Rock City	112 Pharaoh's	Goddess	127 Linamix
118 Argentum	Delight	110 Polar Bird	125 Tirol

124 Chimes of Freedom	110 Last Midnight	110 Filago	115 Splash of Colour
122 Shavian	110 Mukddaam	110 Sardegna	114 Atoll
121 Candy Glen	110 Polar Falcon	110 Sifting Gold	114 Narwala
121 Machiavellian	110 Raj Waki	110 Spendomania	114 Rotatori
121 Septieme Ciel	110 Rami	110 Tarvisio	113 Game Plan
120 Zoman	110 River of Light	110 The Tender Tr'k	113 Karinga Bay
118 Funambule	110 Thakib	110 Treble Eight	113 Pharian
117 Anshan	110 Vijaya		112 Down The Flag
117 Norwich	110 Welney	**11 furlongs plus**	112 Indica
117 Satin Wood		132 Saumarez	112 Knight's Baroness
116 Lord Florey	**9½ furlongs plus**	131 Belmez	112 Peinture Bleue
115 Houseproud	130 Saumarez	130 Epervier Bleu	112 Theatre Critic
114 Bold Russian	126 In The Groove	129 Snurge	112 Whitehaven
114 Fire The Groom	125 Elmaamul	125 Salsabil	111 Cruising Height
114 Qirmazi	120 Rafha	124 Deploy	111 Ivrea
113 Gaelic Bird	119 Air de Rien	123 Hellenic	111 Private Tender
113 Hasbah	119 Colour Chart	123 Quest For Fame	111 Rock Hopper
113 Heart of Joy	116 Missionary Ridge	123 Sanglamore	111 Starstreak
113 Honor Rajana	116 Moon Cactus	122 Erdelistan	111 Teach Dha Mhile
113 In Excess	115 Agent Bleu	122 Miss Alleged	110 Hajade
113 Maximilian	115 Vue Cavaliere	121 Kartajana	110 Intimiste
113 Sally Rous	114 Guiza	120 Wajd	110 Kaheel
112 Jade Robbery	114 Louve Bleue	119 Antisaar	110 Mandelbaum
112 Theatrical Charmer	114 Ruby Tiger	118 Go And Go	
111 Arousal	113 Free At Last	118 Madiriya	**14 furlongs plus**
111 Fils Unique	112 Dr Somerville	117 Blue Stag	123 Snurge
111 Pont Aven	112 Prudent Manner	117 Defensive Play	116 River God
111 Roi de Rome	111 Anvari	117 Passing Sale	112 Applecross
110 Book The Band	111 Dear Doctor	116 Houmayoun	112 Comte du Bourg
110 Boxing Day	111 Lotus Pool	116 Madame Dubois	112 Great Marquess
110 Daisy Dance	111 Native Twine	116 Panoramic	112 Rubicund
110 Gharam	111 Noble Patriarch	116 Top Waltz	110 North Col
	111 Razeen (USA)	116 Vanya	110 Wajna
	110 Catherine Parr	115 Dashing Blade	

FOUR-YEAR-OLDS AND UPWARDS

5 furlongs plus	115 Mister Sicy	111 Mansonnien	115 Robore
120 Great Commotion	114 Mirror Black	111 Muroto	114 Carroll House
119 Statoblest	114 Monsagem	111 Scenic	114 Michelozzo
116 Lugana Beach	114 Zille	111 Sir Felix	114 Silvestro
116 Nabeel Dancer	112 Aldbourne	110 Deliorman	114 Tempeltanz
112 Savahra Sound	112 Bin Shaddad	110 Landyap	113 Roseate Tern
112 Sharp N'Early	112 Kostroma	110 Petrullo	113 Tyrone Bridge
111 Nityo	112 Ocean Falls	110 Twist King	112 Artic Envoy
111 Or Acier	112 Philippi	110 Yellow King	111 Mountain Kingdom
111 Roman Prose	111 Magic Gleam		111 Spritsail
110 A Prayer For Wings	110 Elementary	**11 furlongs plus**	110 Robertet
110 Blyton Lad		130 Old Vic	110 Sesame
110 Carol's Treasure	**9½ furlongs plus**	127 In The Wings	
	125 Legal Case	126 Assatis	**14 furlongs plus**
7 furlongs plus	124 Ibn Bey	126 Tisserand	117 Braashee
128 Markof-distinction	123 Creator	123 Cacoethes	114 Top Class
127 Distant Relative	120 Batshoof	122 Mondrian	112 Ashal
124 Green Line Express	119 Terimon	119 Ode	112 River Test
121 Sikeston	117 Dolpour	118 Brush Aside	112 Turgeon
120 Lady Winner	117 Relief Pitcher	118 Sapience	111 Al Maheb
120 Safawan	117 Turfkonig	117 Charmer	111 Mr Pintips
119 Citidancer	115 Ile de Chypre	117 Lights Out	110 Indian Queen
117 Taffeta And Tulle	115 Starlet	116 French Glory	110 Mardonius
117 Val des Bois	114 Eradicate	116 Gasson	110 Mercalle
	114 Mister Riv	116 Per Quod	110 Teamster
	114 Pirate Army	116 Zartota	
	113 Shellac	115 Ile de Nisky	
	112 Braiswick	115 Louis Cyphre	
	112 Husyan	115 Observation Post	
	112 Young Mother		

SELECTED BIG RACES 1990

Prize money for racing abroad has been converted to £ Sterling at the exchange rate current at the time of the race. The figures are correct to the nearest £.

1   LANES END JOHN   1½m
PORTER EBF STAKES
(Gr 3)
£25,815   Newbury   21 April
  Brush Aside (USA) 4-8-10
    SCauthen 1
  Albadr (USA) 5-8-11
    BMarcus 8.2
  Charmer 5-8-11
    MRoberts sh.3
  Ile de Nisky 4-8-10
    PatEddery ½.4
  Per Quod (USA) 5-8-11
    BRaymond 3.5
  Artic Envoy (USA) 4-8-10
    RCochrane 7.6
  Husyan (USA) 4-8-10
    WCarson 10.7
  Thethingaboutitis (USA) 5-8-11
    JWilliams ¾.8
  Jehol 4-8-10 GCarter nk.9
  Shellac 4-8-10
    LDettori 7.10
  Indian Queen 5-8-11
    WNewnes 1.11
9/2 BRUSH ASIDE, 5/1 Per Quod, Shellac, 6/1 Charmer, Ile de Nisky, 8/1 Husyan, 14/1 Artic Envoy, Jehol, 16/1 Albadr, 33/1 Indian Queen, 50/1 Thethingaboutitis
  Sheikh Mohammed (H. R. A. Cecil) 11ran 2m33.73 (Good to Soft)

2   GORDON RICHARDS   1¼m
EBF STAKES
(Gr 3)
£22,518   Sandown   28 April
  Dolpour 4-8-10
    WRSwinburn 1
  Ile de Chypre 5-9-3
    AClark nk.2
  Batshoof 4-8-10
    PatEddery nk.3
  Observation Post 4-8-10
    MHills ¾.4
  Relief Pitcher 4-8-10
    GBaxter 2½.5
  Filia Ardross 4-8-12
    MRoberts 3.6
  Monastery 4-8-10
    WCarson 10.7
  Gold Minories 6-8-10
    AMcGlone ½.8
7/4 Ile de Chypre, 5/2 DOLPOUR, 11/2 Batshoof, 6/1 Observation Post, 9/1 Filia Ardross, 16/1 Relief Pitcher, 20/1 Monastery, 100/1 Gold Minories
  H. H. Aga Khan (M. R. Stoute) 8ran 2m05.24 (Good to Firm)

3   PRIX GANAY   1¼m 110y
(Gr 1)
£53,648   Longchamp   29 April
  Creator 4-9-2 CAsmussen 1
  In The Wings 4-9-2
    PatEddery 2½.2
  Ibn Bey 6-9-2 TQuinn 2½.3
  Petrullo 5-9-2
    WRSwinburn 1½.4
  Young Mother (Fr) 4-8-13
    ELegrix snk.5
  Passionaria (Fr) 4-8-13
    GDubroeucq 2.6
  Porter Rhodes (USA) 4-9-2
    SCauthen 8.7
  Old Maestro (USA) 6-9-2
    MO'Callaghan snk.8
  Mansonnien (Fr) 6-9-2
    DBoeuf 15.9
  Emmson 5-9-2 ALequeux ... 3.10
3/10 CREATOR and In The Wings, 31/10 Young Mother, 82/10 Ibn Bey, 13/1 Porter Rhodes, 14/1 Mansonnien, 29/1 Passionaria, 31/1 Petrullo, 32/1 Emmson, 61/1 Old Maestro
  Sheikh Mohammed (A. Fabre) 10ran 2m13.00 (Good to Soft)

4   GENERAL ACCIDENT   1m
1000 GUINEAS STAKES
(Gr 1) (3y f)
£110,493   Newmarket   3 May
  Salsabil 9-0 WCarson 1
  Heart of Joy (USA) 9-0
    WRSwinburn ¾.2
  Negligent 9-0 PatEddery 5.3
  Free At Last 9-0 AClark 3.4
  Palace Street (USA) 9-0
    JWilliams 6.5
  Sally Rous 9-0 GCarter ½.6
  Ra'a (USA) 9-0 GDuffield 6.7
  In The Groove 9-0
    SCauthen ½.8
  Lakeland Beauty 9-0
    WNewnes 5.9
  Hasbah 9-0 RHills ½.10
6/4 SALSABIL, 4/1 Heart of Joy, 11/2 Negligent, 8/1 Hasbah, 11/1 In The Groove, 14/1 Sally Rous, 16/1 Free At Last, 50/1 Ra'a, 100/1 Lakeland Beauty, Palace Street,
  Hamdan Al-Maktoum (J. L. Dunlop) 10ran 1m38.06 (Good to Firm)

5   GENERAL ACCIDENT   1m
2000 GUINEAS STAKES
(Gr 1) (3y c + f)
£106,491   Newmarket   5 May
  Tirol 9-0 MJKinane 1

Machiavellian (USA) 9-0
FHead **2.2**
Anshan 9-0 WRSwinburn **2.3**
Rock City 9-0 BRaymond ... ½.4
Septieme Ciel (USA) 9-0
GGuignard 2½.5
Welney 9-0 (b) GCarter hd.6
Elmaamul (USA) 9-0
WCarson 2½.7
Sure Sharp (USA) 9-0
SCauthen hd.8
Now Listen (USA) 9-0
PatEddery sh.9
Rami (USA) 9-0 MRoberts .. 1.10
Lord of The Field 9-0
GDuffield 2½.11
Dashing Blade 9-0
JMatthias 5.12
Raj Waki (USA) 9-0
RCochrane ½.13
Swordsmith (USA) 9-0
WRyan 14
6/4 Machiavellian, 6/1 Anshan, 17/2 Now
Listen, 9/1 Sure Sharp, TIROL, 12/1
Elmaamul, 14/1 Rock City, 18/1 Septieme
Ciel, 20/1 Raj Waki, 25/1 Dashing Blade,
33/1 Rami, 50/1 Lord of The Field, 66/1
Welney, 250/1 Swordsmith
John Horgan (R. Hannon) 14ran
1m35.84 (Firm)

6   DUBAI POULE D'ESSAI   1m
    DES POULAINS (Gr 1)
    (3y c)
£108,342   Longchamp   6 May
Linamix (Fr) 9-2 FHead **1**
Zoman (USA) 9-2
TQuinn 1½.2
Funambule (USA) 9-2
GGuignard 3.3
Book The Band 9-2
PatEddery 2.4
Jade Robbery (USA) 9-2
CAsmussen 1.5
Honor Rajana (USA) 9-2
ELegrix snk.6
Reinstate (Fr) 9-2
CPiccioni 10.7
Evens LINAMIX, 16/10 Jade
Robbery, 63/10 Book The Band, 76/10
Funambule, 12/1 Zoman, 22/1 Honor
Rajana
J.-L. Lagardere (F. Boutin) 7ran
1m35.90 (Good to Firm)

7   DALHAM CHESTER   1½m65y
    VASE (Gr 3) (3y)
£24,771   Chester   8 May
Belmez (USA) 8-11
SCauthen **1**
Quest For Fame 8-11
PatEddery 1.2
Missionary Ridge 8-11
WCarson 10.3
8/13 BELMEZ, 10/3 Quest For Fame, 4/1
Missionary Ridge

Sheikh Mohammed (H. R. A. Cecil)
3ran 2m41.42 (Good to Soft)

8   DUBAI POULE D'ESSAI   1m
    DES POULICHES (Gr 1)
    (3y f)
£97,087   Longchamp   13 May
Houseproud (USA) 9-2
PatEddery **1**
Pont Aven 9-2 ALequeux 2.2
Gharam (USA) 9-2
MRoberts ½.3
Cydalia (USA) 9-2 GMosse . ¾.4
Wedding Bouquet 9-2
JReid hd.5
Pharaoh's Delight 9-2
CAsmussen 2.6
Be Grise 9-2
ESaint-Martin ¾.7
Tatwij (USA) 9-2 RHills ¾.8
Sharp Sass (USA) 9-2
ASCruz ½.9
Slinkee (Can) 9-2
GDubroeucq hd.10
Golden Era (USA) 9-2
ELegrix 0
Princess Taufan 9-2 AMunro ... 0
Sous Entendu (USA) 9-2
FHead 0
Zinarelle (Fr) 9-2 AGibert 0
9/10 HOUSEPROUD, 54/10 Cydalia,
61/10 Wedding Bouquet, 82/10
Pharaoh's Delight, 97/10 Be Grise and
Pont Aven, 11/1 Gharam and Tatwij, 12/1
Sharp Sass, 13/1 Sous Entendu, 16/1
Slinkee, 17/1 Golden Era, 21/1 Zinarelle,
68/1 Princess Taufan
K. Abdulla (A. Fabre) 14ran 1m38.50
(Good)

9   WILLIAM HILL   1¼m 110y
    DANTE STAKES (Gr 2)
    (3y)
£75,600   York   16 May
Sanglamore (USA) 9-0
PatEddery **1**
Karinga Bay 9-0 BRouse 1½.2
5³ **Anshan** 9-0 WRSwinburn 1½.3
Laxey Bay 9-0 SCauthen .. 2½.4
Ridgepoint 9-0 MRoberts ... 10.5
Dorset Duke 9-0
CAsmussen 1½.6
5 Raj Waki (USA) 9-0
RCochrane 3.7
Evens Anshan, 11/2 SANGLAMORE, 6/1
Dorset Duke, 7/1 Raj Waki, 16/1 Karinga
Bay, 20/1 Laxey Bay, 40/1 Ridgepoint
K. Abdulla (R. Charlton) 7ran 2m09.18
(Good)

10   KOSSET YORKSHIRE   1¾m
    CUP (Gr 2)
£47,223   York   17 May
Braashee 4-8-9 MRoberts **1**
Sapience 4-8-9
PatEddery ¾.2

Top Class 5-8-12 BMarcus .. **4.3**
1²   Albadr (USA) 5-8-9
    WCarson 3.4
  Noble Savage 4-8-9
    RCochrane 2½.5
  Androbote (Fr) 4-8-9
    WNewnes 20.6

11/8 BRAASHEE, 3/1 Sapience, 7/2 Noble Savage, 12/1 Albadr, Top Class, 100/1 Androbote
  Maktoum Al-Maktoum (A. C. Stewart) 6ran 2m56.79 (Good)

---

11   JUDDMONTE   1m
    LOCKINGE STAKES
    (Gr 2)
£32,922   Newbury   18 May
  Safawan 4-9-0 WRSwinburn . **1**
  Distant Relative 4-9-3
    MHills 2.2
  Monsagem (USA) 4-9-0
    SCauthen ¾.3
  Markofdistinction 4-9-3
    LDettori 1.4
  Magic Gleam (USA) 4-9-0
    PatEddery sh.5
  Green Line Express (USA) 4-9-0
    RCochrane 1½.6

6/4 Markofdistinction, 9/2 Distant Relative, 5/1 SAFAWAN, 6/1 Green Line Express, 8/1 Magic Gleam, 10/1 Monsagem
  Mrs David Thompson (M. R. Stoute) 6ran 1m36.42 (Good to Firm)

---

12   AIRLIE/COOLMORE   1m
    IRISH 2000 GUINEAS
    (Gr 1) (3y c + f)
£130,485   Curragh   19 May
5*   **Tirol** 9-0 PatEddery **1**
  Royal Academy (USA) 9-0
    JReid nk.2
  Lotus Pool (USA) 9-0
    MJKinane ½.3
5²   Machiavellian (USA) 9-0
    FHead sh.4
  Mr Brooks 9-0 PShanahan 1.5
  Bastille Day 9-0 SCraine ½.6
  Noble Patriarch 9-0
    LDettori 2.7
  Legal Verdict 9-0
    CRoche 2.8
  Dickens Lane 9-0
    PVGilson 25.9

5/4 TIROL, 9/4 Machiavellian, 4/1 Royal Academy, 14/1 Lotus Pool, 25/1 Mr Brooks, 33/1 Legal Verdict, 40/1 Noble Patriarch, 100/1 Bastille Day, 200/1 Dickens Lane
  John Horgan (R. Hannon) 9ran 1m39.20 (Good to Firm)

---

13   GOFFS IRISH 1000   1m
    GUINEAS (Gr 1) (3y f)
£121,238   Curragh   26 May
4   **In The Groove** 9-0 SCauthen **1**

4²   **Heart of Joy (USA)** 9-0
    WRSwinburn 3.2
  Performing Arts 9-0
    MHills ½.3
  The Caretaker 9-0
    MJKinane 1.4
  Lady of Vision 9-0
    DGillespie sh.5
  Aminata 9-0 CRoche 1.6
8   Wedding Bouquet 9-0
    JReid ¾.7
  Tanwi 9-0 WHarris 5.8
  Ring of Light 9-0
    PShanahan 1½.9
  Annie Laurie 9-0
    PVGilson sh.10
  Needy Thatch 9-0
    KJManning 7.11
  Habira 9-0 SCraine sh.12

4/6 Heart of Joy, 5/1 IN THE GROOVE, 7/1 The Caretaker, Wedding Bouquet, 20/1 Aminata, 25/1 Performing Arts, 40/1 Ring of Light, Tanwi, 50/1 Annie Laurie, 100/1 Lady of Vision, Needy Thatch, 150/1 Habira
  Brian Cooper (D. R. C. Elsworth) 12ran 1m41.30 (Good)

---

14   PRIX JEAN PRAT (Gr 1) 1m1f55y
    (3y c + f)
£52,521   Longchamp   27 May
  Priolo (USA) 9-2 GMosse **1**
  Satin Wood 9-2
    SCauthen 1½.2
5   **Septieme Ciel (USA)** 9-2
    FHead 1½.3
  Polar Falcon (USA) 9-2
    ELegrix 2.4
6   Jade Robbery (USA) 9-2
    CAsmussen ¾.5
  Agent Bleu (Fr) 9-2
    DBoeuf 1½.6

19/10 Septieme Ciel, 26/10 Jade Robbery, PRIOLO, 38/10 Satin Wood, 10/1 Polar Falcon, 108/10 Agent Bleu
  Ecurie Skymarc Farm (F. Boutin) 6ran 1m53.70 (Good)

---

15   PRIX D'ISPAHAN (Gr 1) 1m1f55y
£52,521   Longchamp   27 May
3*   **Creator** 4-9-2
    CAsmussen **1**
  Val des Bois (Fr) 4-9-2
    GGuignard ½.2
  Citidancer 4-9-2
    SCauthen nk.3
  Louis Cyphre 4-9-2 FHead . ¾.4
  Lady Winner (Fr) 4-8-13
    ELegrix ¾.5
2²   Ile de Chypre 5-9-2 AClark ... 8.6
3   Mansonnien (Fr) 6-9-2
    DBoeuf 2.7
  Vague Shot 7-9-2 ALequeux . 1.8
2   Gold Minories 6-9-2
    AMcGlone 15.9

3/10 CREATOR, 51/10 Gold Minories

and Ile de Chypre, 79/10 Val des Bois, 13/1 Citidancer, Lady Winner, 22/1 Louis Cyphre, 25/1 Mansonnien, 92/1 Vague Shot

Sheikh Mohammed (A. Fabre) 9ran 1m51.50 (Good)

16	SEARS TEMPLE STAKES (Gr 2)		5f
£32,382	Sandown		28 May
	Dayjur (USA) 3-8-8		
	WCarson	....	1
	Tigani 4-9-3 CAsmussen	.....	2.2
	Statoblest 4-9-3		
	LDettori	....	½.3
	Blyton Lad 4-9-3		
	SWebster	....	nk.4
	Paley Prince (USA) 4-9-3		
	BRouse	....	3.5
	Lugana Beach 4-9-3		
	SCauthen	....	2.6
	Nabeel Dancer (USA) 5-9-3		
	PatEddery	....	1½.7
	Savahra Sound 5-9-3		
	WRSwinburn	....	¾.8

9/4 Statoblest, 10/3 Lugana Beach, 5/1 Nabeel Dancer, Tigani, 11/2 DAYJUR, 12/1 Blyton Lad, 20/1 Savahra Sound, 66/1 Paley Prince

Hamdan Al-Maktoum (Major W. R. Hern) 8ran 1m01.89 (Good to Firm)

17	PRIX DU JOCKEY-CLUB LANCIA (Gr 1) (3y c + f)		1½m
£260,417	Chantilly		3 June
9*	**Sanglamore (USA)** 9-2		
	PatEddery	....	1
	Epervier Bleu 9-2		
	DBoeuf	....	½.2
	Erdelistan (Fr) 9-2		
	ASCruz	....	½.3
	Top Waltz (Fr) 9-2		
	ELegrix	....	2½.4
	Panoramic 9-2		
	CAsmussen	....	hd.5
	Passing Sale (Fr) 9-2		
	GGuignard	....	2½.6
	Theatrical Charmer 9-2		
	WCarson	....	¾.7
	Blash (USA) 9-2		
	WMongil	....	8.8
	Roi de Rome (USA) 9-2		
	FHead	....	6.9
	Mahshari 9-2 PCoppin	....	2.10
	Anvari 9-2 MRoberts	....	½.11
	Intimiste (USA) 9-2		
	GMosse	....	20.12

Evens Epervier Bleu, 9/2 Theatrical Charmer, 58/10 Anvari and Panoramic, 95/10 SANGLAMORE, 12/1 Top Waltz, 13/1 Erdelistan and Mahshari, 14/1 Roi de Rome, 17/1 Intimiste, Passing Sale, 28/1 Blash

K. Abdulla (R. Charlton) 12ran 2m24.70 (Good to Firm)

18	PRIX DU GROS-CHENE (Gr 2) (3y + c + f)		5f
£32,195	Chantilly		3 June
16	**Nabeel Dancer (USA)** 5-9-2		
	PatEddery	....	1
	Ron's Victory (USA) 3-8-13		
	ASCruz	....	5.2
	Luring (USA) 3-8-6		
	AGibert	....	1½.3
	Whippet 6-9-2 CAsmussen	...	1.4
	Zanoni 3-8-6 BRaymond	....	5.5
	Company (USA) 3-8-6		
	GGuignard	....	5.6
	Hinari Televideo 4-8-9		
	RPElliott	....	2.7
	Green's Picture 6-8-13		
	OLarsen	....	½.8

7/5 Ron's Victory, 29/10 Whippet, 31/10 NABEEL DANCER, 84/10 Zanoni, 11/1 Green's Picture, 12/1 Company, 14/1 Luring, 31/1 Hinari Televideo

Maktoum Al-Maktoum (A. A. Scott) 8ran 58.80secs (Good To Firm)

19	EVER READY DERBY (Gr 1) (3y c + f)		1½m
£355,000	Epsom		6 June
7²	**Quest For Fame** 9-0		
	PatEddery	....	1
	Blue Stag 9-0 CAsmussen	...	3.2
5	**Elmaamul (USA)** 9-0		
	WCarson	....	1½.3
	Kaheel (USA) 9-0		
	MRoberts	....	2½.4
9²	Karinga Bay 9-0 BRouse	......	2.5
	Duke of Paducah (USA) 9-0		
	RCochrane	....	hd.6
6²	Zoman (USA) 9-0 TQuinn	...	hd.7
	Treble Eight 9-0		
	BRaymond	....	nk.8
6*	Linamix (Fr) 9-0 GMosse	..	1½.9
7³	Missionary Ridge 9-0		
	MHills	....	10.10
	Digression (USA) 9-0		
	WRSwinburn	....	¾.11
	Sober Mind (USA) 9-0		
	AMunro	....	1½.12
	Bookcase 9-0 JWilliams	...	1½.13
	Razeen (USA) 9-0		
	SCauthen	....	1½.14
12	Bastille Day 9-0 SCraine	..	hd.15
	River God (USA) 9-0		
	MJKinane	....	3.16
	Aromatic 9-0 AClark	....	12.17
12	Mr Brooks 9-0		
	PShanahan	....	3.18

9/2 Razeen, 11/2 Linamix, 6/1 Zoman, 7/1 QUEST FOR FAME, 8/1 Blue Stag, 10/1 Elmaamul, 14/1 Digression, Duke of Paducah, Karinga Bay, 28/1 River God, 33/1 Kaheel, 50/1 Missionary Ridge, 66/1 Mr Brooks, Treble Eight, 100/1 Aromatic, Bastille Day, 150/1, Bookcase, Sober Mind

K. Abdulla (R. Charlton) 18ran 2m37.26 (Good)

| 20 | HANSON CORONATION CUP (Gr 1) | 1½m |
| £81,045 | Epsom | 7 June |

3²	**In The Wings** 4-9-0	
	CAsmussen 1	
2	**Observation Post** 4-9-0	
	WCarson 1½.2	
3³	**Ibn Bey** 6-9-0 TQuinn 1½.3	
	Roseate Tern 4-8-11	
	LDettori 15.4	
10³	Top Class 5-9-0 BMarcus ... 15.5	
	Mondrian (Ger) 4-9-0	
	SCauthen 30.6	

15/8 IN THE WINGS, 5/2 Roseate Tern, 5/1 Ibn Bey, Observation Post, 16/1 Mondrian, Top Class
Sheikh Mohammed (A. Fabre) 6ran
2m36.43 (Good)

| 21 | GOLD SEAL OAKS (Gr 1) (3y f) | 1½m |
| £101,475 | Epsom | 9 June |

4*	**Salsabil** 9-0 WCarson 1	
	Game Plan 9-0 BMarcus 5.2	
	Knight's Baroness 9-0	
	TQuinn 1.3	
13*	In The Groove 9-0	
	CAsmussen hd.4	
	Ahead 9-0 RCochrane 1½.5	
	Cameo Performance (USA) 9-0	
	PatEddery 12.6	
8³	Gharam (USA) 9-0	
	MRoberts 20.7	
	Kartajana 9-0 WRSwinburn 2½.8	

2/1 SALSABIL, 85/40 In The Groove, 7/2 Kartajana, 12/1 Gharam, 16/1 Ahead, Knight's Baroness, 25/1 Cameo Performance, 50/1 Game Plan
Hamdan Al-Maktoum (J. L. Dunlop)
8ran 2m38.70 (Good to Soft)

| 22 | PRIX DE DIANE HERMES (Gr 1) (3y f) | 1¼m110y |
| £145,833 | Chantilly | 10 June |

	Rafha 9-2 WCarson 1	
	Moon Cactus 9-2	
	SCauthen 2	
	Air de Rien 9-2 ABadel sh.3	
	Colour Chart (USA) 9-2	
	CAsmussen 4	
	Vue Cavaliere (Fr) 9-2	
	ELegrix sh.5	
	Guiza (USA) 9-2	
	GDubroeucq sh.6	
	Atoll 9-2 GWMoore ¾.7	
	Noble Ballerina 9-2	
	ALequeux ¾.8	
8*	Houseproud (USA) 9-2	
	PatEddery ½.9	
	Spendomania (USA) 9-2	
	ASCruz sh.10	
	Appealing Missy (USA) 9-2	
	WMongil 2.11	
	Ivor Jewel (USA) 9-2	
	DBoeuf ½.12	

Gold Quest (Fr) 9-2
GMosse 4.13
Helen's Guest 9-2 GCarter . 3.14

Colour Chart finished second, ½ length behind Rafha and 2 lengths ahead of Moon Cactus, but was demoted to fourth for causing interference to Air de Rien. Air de Rien was promoted a place to third.

24/10 Air de Rien, 3/1 Colour Chart and Helen's Guest and Moon Cactus, 42/10 Houseproud, 52/10 Atoll, 9/1 RAFHA, 11/1 Guiza, 26/1 Gold Quest, 27/1 Spendomania, 29/1 Ivor Jewel, Vue Cavaliere, 32/1 Appealing Missy, 42/1 Noble Ballerina
Prince A. Faisal (H. R. A. Cecil) 14ran
2m11.70 (Good to Soft)

| 23 | QUEEN ANNE STAKES (Gr 2) | 1m |
| £51,861 | Ascot | 19 June |

11	**Markofdistinction** 4-9-5	
	LDettori 1	
	Mirror Black 4-9-2	
	BRaymond nk.2	
11²	**Distant Relative** 4-9-5	
	MHills 5.3	
11	Magic Gleam (USA) 4-9-2	
	PatEddery ¾.4	
11*	Safawan 4-9-5	
	WRSwinburn 20.5	
	Aldbourne 4-8-13	
	PaulEddery ¾.6	
	Lunar Mover (USA) 4-9-2	
	JReid 2½.7	
15	Vague Shot 7-9-2 BMarcus ... 6.8	
11³	Monsagem (USA) 4-9-2	
	SCauthen 9	

7/4 Safawan, 9/4 Distant Relative, 7/1 MARKOFDISTINCTION, 11/1 Magic Gleam, Monsagem, 16/1 Aldbourne, 20/1 Mirror Black, 50/1 Lunar Mover, 150/1 Vague Shot
Gerald Leigh (L. M. Cumani) 9ran
1m39.68 (Good to Firm)

| 24 | PRINCE OF WALES'S STAKES (Gr 2) | 1¼m |
| £56,894 | Ascot | 19 June |

2³	**Batshoof** 4-9-5 PatEddery 1	
2	**Relief Pitcher** 4-9-3	
	SCauthen sh.2	
	Terimon 4-9-3 MRoberts .. nk.3	
	Legal Case 4-9-7	
	LDettori 2½.4	
2*	Dolpour 4-9-3	
	WRSwinburn 1½.5	
	Alcando 4-9-0 MJKinane ¾.6	
	Pelorus 5-9-3 BRouse 8.7	
	Scenic 4-9-3 MHills 8.8	

2/1 BATSHOOF, 7/2 Dolpour, Legal Case, 10/1 Relief Pitcher, 11/1 Scenic, 14/1 Terimon, 20/1 Pelorus, 33/1 Alcando
Muttar Salem (B. Hanbury) 8ran
2m06.72 (Good to Firm)

25 ST JAMES'S PALACE 1m
STAKES (Gr 1) (3y c + f)
£112,383 Ascot 19 June
Shavian 9-0 SCauthen **1**
5 **Rock City** 9-0 WCarson ... 1½.2
Lord Florey (USA) 9-0
LDettori sh.3
5 Dashing Blade 9-0
JMatthias 5.4
6 Book The Band 9-0
BRaymond 4.5
Call To Arms 9-0
MRoberts nk.6
9[3] Anshan 9-0 PatEddery nk.7
Eton Lad 9-0 MJKinane 25.8

9/4 Lord Florey, 9/2 Anshan, 11/2 Rock
City, 10/1 Dashing Blade, 11/1
SHAVIAN, 20/1 Eton Lad, 33/1 Book
The Band, 40/1 Call To Arms
Lord Howard de Walden (H. R. A.
Cecil) 8ran 1m41.52 (Good to Firm)

26 CORONATION STAKES 1m
(Gr 1) (3y f)
£102,438 Ascot 20 June
Chimes of Freedom (USA) 9-0
SCauthen **1**
4 **Hasbah** 9-0 RHills 5.2
13[2] **Heart of Joy (USA)** 9-0
WRSwinburn 1½.3
Mais Oui (USA) 9-0
GMosse 1½.4
8 Pharaoh's Delight 9-0
PatEddery 7.5
Water Well 9-0 MRoberts .. 1½.6
Model Village 9-0 MHills sh.7

11/8 Heart of Joy, 4/1 Pharaoh's Delight,
9/2 Hasbah, 11/2 CHIMES OF
FREEDOM, 12/1 Mais Oui, 33/1 Model
Village, Water Well
S. S. Niarchos (H. R. A. Cecil) 7ran
1m41.29 (Firm)

27 CORK AND ORRERY 6f
STAKES (Gr 3)
£34,308 Ascot 21 June
Great Commotion (USA) 4-9-0
PatEddery **1**
Dead Certain 3-8-10
SCauthen hd.2
La Grange Music 3-8-2
MWigham 1½.3
Haunting Beauty (USA) 3-8-3
MRoberts 1.4
Tod 3-8-2 AMunro hd.5
Childrey (USA) 3-8-2
AClark 2.6
Montendre 3-8-2 LDettori . sh.7
Afwaj (USA) 4-8-10
WCarson 4.8
Sheer Precocity 3-8-2
GCarter 3.9
Polar Bird 3-8-3 MHills ... 1½.10
Green's Canaletto (USA) 4-8-10
RCochrane 4.11

Flower Girl 3-8-0
BMarcus ¾.12
Sloe Berry 4-8-7 JReid 1.13
Sandhurst Goddess 4-8-7
MJKinane ½.14
Sharp Reminder 6-8-10
TWilliams 6.15
8[2] Pont Aven 3-7-13
PaulEddery ¾.16
Sharp N' Early 4-9-4
BRaymond 1.17

7/2 Pont Aven, 5/1 GREAT
COMMOTION, 13/2 Montendre, 9/1
Dead Certain, 10/1 Haunting Beauty,
11/1 Afwaj, 12/1 Flower Girl, La Grange
Music, 16/1 Polar Bird, 20/1 Sharp
N'Early, Tod, 25/1 Childrey, Sandhurst
Goddess, 33/1 Green's Canaletto, 50/1
Sharp Reminder, Sheer Precocity, 66/1
Sloe Berry
Maktoum Al-Maktoum (A. A. Scott)
17ran 1m14.42 (Good)

28 GOLD CUP (Gr 1) 2½m
£83,501 Ascot 21 June
Ashal 4-9-0 RHills **1**
Tyrone Bridge 4-9-0
PShanahan 4.2
1 **Thethingaboutitis (USA)**
5-9-2 PatEddery 1½.3
Teamster 4-9-0
WRSwinburn sh.4
Turgeon (USA) 4-9-0
ASCruz 2.5
Cossack Guard 4-9-0
MRoberts 30.6
Mountain Kingdom (USA) 6-9-2
BMarcus 1½.7
Sadeem (USA) 7-9-2
RCochrane 7.8
Chelsea Girl 4-8-11
BRaymond 9
Weld 4-9-0 SCauthen 10
10 Noble Savage 4-9-0 AClark 11

13/8 Teamster, 5/1 Sadeem, Weld, 7/1
Tyrone Bridge, 14/1 ASHAL, 16/1
Turgeon, 20/1 Thethingaboutitis, 33/1
Chelsea Girl, Cossack Guard,
Mountain Kingdom, 66/1 Noble Savage
Hamdan Al-Maktoum (H. Thomson
Jones) 11ran 4m28.58 (Good to Soft)

29 HARDWICKE STAKES 1½m
(Gr 2)
£59,621 Ascot 22 June
Assatis (USA) 5-9-0
RCochrane **1**
1 **Ile de Nisky** 4-8-9
GCarter ¾.2
Old Vic 4-9-0 SCauthen 10.3
1[3] Charmer 5-8-9 BMarcus 1½.4
1 Husyan 4-8-9
WCarson 1½.5
Michelozzo (USA) 4-9-0
PatEddery 2.6
Carroll House 5-9-0
MJKinane 5.7

1028

4/5 Old Vic, 4/1 Michelozzo, 11/2 Carroll House, 8/1 Husyan, 25/1 Charmer, 50/1 ASSATIS, Ile de Nisky
S. Harada (G. Harwood) 7ran 2m32.53 (Good to Soft)

30 KING'S STAND STAKES (Gr 2) 5f
£57,343 Ascot 22 June

16* **Dayjur (USA)** 3-8-10 WCarson ... 1
18² **Ron's Victory (USA)** 3-8-10 ASCruz ... 2½.2
16 **Lugana Beach** 4-9-3 SCauthen ... 6.3
Poyle George 5-9-3 JWilliams ... nk.4
Mademoiselle Chloe 3-8-7 MRoberts ... nk.5
Dancing Music 3-8-10 DeanMcKeown ... 1½.6
16³ Statoblest 4-9-3 LDettori ... 2.7
Boozy 3-8-7 RFox ... ¾.8
16 Paley Prince (USA) 4-9-3 MJKinane ... nk.9
18 Hinari Televideo 4-9-0 RPElliott ... hd.10
18* Nabeel Dancer (USA) 5-9-3 PatEddery ... nk.11
16² Tigani 4-9-3 RCochrane .. 1½.12
Argentum 3-8-10 JReid ... 2½.13
Shuttlecock Corner (USA) 4-9-3 WRSwinburn ... 2.14
In The Papers 3-8-7 MWigham ... 15

4/1 Nabeel Dancer, 9/2 Tigani, 11/2 DAYJUR, 7/1 Argentum, 8/1 Lugana Beach, 10/1 Mademoiselle Chloe, 11/1 Statoblest, 14/1 Ron's Victory, 20/1 Poyle George, 25/1 Boozy, 33/1 In The Papers, Shuttlecock Corner, 50/1 Paley Prince, 66/1 Dancing Music, 100/1 Hinari Televideo
Hamdan Al-Maktoum (Major W. R. Hern) 15ran 1m01.96 (Good to Soft)

31 GRAND PRIX DE PARIS LOUIS VUITTON (Gr 1) (3y c + f) 1¼m
£155,280 Longchamp 24 June

Saumarez 9-2 SCauthen ... 1
14* **Priolo (USA)** 9-2 GMosse ... 6.2
12* **Tirol** 9-2 PatEddery ... 2.3
Candy Glen 9-2 ASCruz ... 1.4
disq 22² Colour Chart (USA) 8-13 CAsmussen ... nk.5
17 Roi de Rome (USA) 9-2 FHead ... 1.6
Boxing Day (Fr) 9-2 DBoeuf . 3.7
Sifting Gold (USA) 9-2 ELegrix ... 8.8

11/10 Tirol, 38/10 Priolo, 47/10 Colour Chart, 5/1 SAUMAREZ, 73/10 Roi de Rome, 16/1 Sifting Gold, 20/1 Boxing Day, 30/1 Candy Glen
B. McNall (N. Clement) 8ran 2m07.50 (Good to Soft)

32 BUDWEISER IRISH DERBY (Gr 1) (3y c + f) 1½m
£339,352 Curragh 1 July

21* **Salsabil** 8-11 WCarson ... 1
Deploy 9-0 WRSwinburn ... ¾.2
7* **Belmez (USA)** 9-0 SCauthen ... 4.3
19² Blue Stag 9-0 MJKinane ... ½.4
19* Quest For Fame 9-0 PatEddery ... nk.5
Super Flame (Can) 9-0 CRoche ... 2½.6
Emperor Chang (USA) 9-0 SCraine ... ½.7
19 Kaheel (USA) 9-0 MRoberts ... 1½.8
Alterezza (USA) 9-0 WFHarris ... 20.9

5/4 Quest For Fame, 11/4 SALSABIL, 4/1 Belmez, 5/1 Blue Stag, 16/1 Deploy, 20/1 Kaheel, 150/1 Super Flame, 300/1 Alterezza, Emperor Chang
Hamdan Al-Maktoum (J. L. Dunlop) 9ran 2m33.54 (Good)

33 GRAND PRIX DE SAINT-CLOUD (Gr 1) (3y + c + f) 1½m
£176,646 Saint-Cloud 1 July

20* **In The Wings** 4-9-8 CAsmussen ... 1
Ode (USA) 4-9-5 DBoeuf 1½.2
Zartota (USA) 4-9-5 TJarnet ... ¾.3
29 Carroll House 5-9-8 RCochrane ... 2½.4
Air Music (Fr) 3-8-9 BMarcus ... ¾.5
22³ Air de Rien 3-8-6 ABadel ... 2.6
3 Passionaria (Fr) 4-9-5 GMosse ... 1½.7
Srivijaya 3-8-9 PBodin ... 4.8

3/10 IN THE WINGS and Srivijaya, 4/1 Air de Rien, 29/4 Ode, 15/2 Carroll House, 26/1 Zartota, 31/1 Air Music, Passionaria
Sheikh Mohammed (A. Fabre) 8ran 2m29.60 (Good)

34 CORAL-ECLIPSE STAKES (Gr 1) 1¼m
£157,056 Sandown 7 July

19³ **Elmaamul (USA)** 3-8-10 WCarson ... 1
24³ **Terimon** 4-9-7 MRoberts .. ½.2
15 **Ile de Chypre** 5-9-7 AClark . 5.3
24² Relief Pitcher 4-9-7 RCochrane ... ¾.4
19 Razeen (USA) 3-8-10 SCauthen ... ¾.5
15* Creator 4-9-7 CAsmussen ... 2.6

25   Call To Arms 3-8-10
BMarcus 4.7

5/6 Creator, 11/2 Razeen, 13/2 ELMAAMUL, 9/1 Relief Pitcher, Terimon, 10/1 Ile de Chypre, 100/1 Call To Arms
    Hamdan Al-Maktoum (Major W. R. Hern) 7ran 2m04.63 (Good to Firm)

35   EBF PHOENIX   1m
    INTERNATIONAL
    STAKES (Gr 2)
£21,147   Phoenix Park   7 July
19   **Zoman (USA)** 3-8-7 TQuinn .. 1
23[3]   **Distant Relative** 4-9-11
    MHills ¾.2
13   **Wedding Bouquet** 3-8-4
    DGillespie 3.3
    Contract Law (USA) 3-8-11
    MJKinane 5.4

5/4 ZOMAN, 7/4 Distant Relative, 5/1 Wedding Bouquet, 8/1 Contract Law
    Fahd Salman (P. F. I. Cole) 4ran 1m39.70 (Good to Soft)

36   PRINCESS OF WALES'S   1½m
    STAKES (Gr 2)
£48,138   Newmarket   10 July
10[2]   **Sapience** 4-9-0 PatEddery 1
29   **Charmer** 5-9-0 MRoberts .. ¾.2
29*   **Assatis (USA)** 5-9-5
    RCochrane 2½.3
29[2]   Ile de Nisky 4-9-0 GCarter 1½.4
24   Legal Case 4-9-5 LDettori .. hd.5
1   Artic Envoy (USA) 4-9-0
    AMunro sh.6
    Private Tender 3-8-4
    WRyan 1.7

7/4 Legal Case, 5/2 Private Tender, 11/2 SAPIENCE, 13/2 Assatis, 11/1 Ile de Nisky, 20/1 Charmer, 50/1 Artic Envoy
    W. H. O'Gorman (J. G. FitzGerald) 7ran 2m34.96 (Good to Firm)

37   ANGLIA TELEVISION   6f
    JULY STAKES (Gr 3)
    (2y c + g)
£21,384   Newmarket   11 July
    Mujtahid (USA) 8-10
    WCarson 1
    Mac's Imp (USA) 9-1
    AMunro 7.2
    The Old Firm (Ire) 8-10
    LDettori 1½.3
    Bold Nephew 8-10
    PatEddery nk.4

5/4 Mac's Imp, 2/1 MUJTAHID, 11/4 Bold Nephew, 16/1 The Old Firm
    Hamdan Al-Maktoum (R. W. Armstrong) 4ran 1m10.61 (Firm)

38   CARROLL   6f
    FOUNDATION JULY
    CUP (Gr 1)
£103,132   Newmarket   12 July
12[2]   **Royal Academy (USA)** 3-8-13
    JReid 1

27*   **Great Commotion (USA)** 4-9-6
    BRaymond ¾.2
25[2]   **Rock City** 3-8-13
    WCarson nk.3
23   Magic Gleam (USA) 4-9-3
    PaulEddery 3.4
    Keen Hunter (USA) 3-8-13
    WRSwinburn ¾.5
27[2]   Dead Certain 3-8-10
    SCauthen 7.6
30[3]   Lugana Beach 4-9-6
    LDettori 2.7
26   Pharaoh's Delight 3-8-10
    RCochrane 8.8
30   Nabeel Dancer (USA) 5-9-6
    PatEddery nk.9

11/4 Rock City, 3/1 Dead Certain, 4/1 Keen Hunter, 13/2 Nabeel Dancer, 7/1 ROYAL ACADEMY, 16/1 Great Commotion, 20/1 Magic Gleam, 33/1 Lugana Beach, Pharaoh's Delight
    Classic Thoroughbreds Plc (M. V. O'Brien) 9ran 1m11.46 (Good to Firm)

39   KILDANGAN STUD   1½m
    IRISH OAKS (Gr 1) (3y f)
£118,378   Curragh   14 July
21[3]   **Knight's Baroness** 9-0
    TQuinn 1
22   **Atoll** 9-0 GMoore nk.2
    Assertion 9-0 DGillespie . nk.3
    Crockadore (USA) 9-0
    MJKinane 1.4
13   Tanwi 9-0 WHarris nk.5
    Cosmic Princess 9-0
    PShanahan 1.6
    Pharian (USA) 9-0
    BMarcus ¾.7
    Walliser 9-0 PVGilson 1.8
    Rosati (USA) 9-0 RQuinton ½.9
13   Annie Laurie 9-0 CRoche ... 3.10

13/8 KNIGHT'S BARONESS, 3/1 Pharian, 5/1 Atoll, 6/1 Crockadore, 10/1 Cosmic Princess, 12/1 Rosati, 20/1 Tanwi, 25/1 Annie Laurie, 50/1 Assertion, 100/1 Walliser
    Fahd Salman (P. F. I. Cole) 10ran 2m32.89 (Hand Timed) (Good to Firm)

40   KING GEORGE VI AND   1½m
    QUEEN ELIZABETH
    DIAMOND STAKES
    (Gr 1)
£284,715   Ascot   28 July
32[3]   **Belmez (USA)** 3-8-9
    MJKinane 1
29[3]   **Old Vic** 4-9-7 SCauthen nk.2
36[3]   **Assatis (USA)** 5-9-7
    MShibata 1½.3
    Cacoethes (USA) 4-9-7
    RCochrane 5.4
33*   In The Wings 4-9-7
    CAsmussen 1.5
34[2]   Terimon 4-9-7 MRoberts .. 1½.6
36[2]   Charmer 5-9-7
    WRSwinburn nk.7

29   Husyan (USA) 4-9-7
        WCarson 15.8
36*   Sapience 4-9-7 PatEddery .. 10.9
36   Legal Case 4-9-7
        LDettori hd.10
    Limeburn 4-9-7
        AMcGlone 11

3/1 In The Wings, 4/1 Old Vic, 11/2
Cacoethes, 15/2 BELMEZ, Terimon, 8/1
Sapience, 14/1 Legal Case, 16/1 Assatis,
Husyan, 25/1 Charmer, 200/1 Limeburn
    Sheikh Mohammed (H. R. A. Cecil)
11ran 2m30.76 (Good to Firm)

41   SUSSEX STAKES (Gr 1)   1m
£132,750   Goodwood   1 August
35² **Distant Relative** 4-9-7
        WCarson 1
11   **Green Line Express (USA)**
        4-9-7 SCauthen ½.2
25*   **Shavian** 3-9-0 SCauthen 1.3
38² Great Commotion (USA) 4-9-7
        PatEddery 7.4
35*   Zoman (USA) 3-9-0
        TQuinn 1½.5
    Lord Charmer (USA) 3-9-0
        WRSwinburn 2½.6
34   Call To Arms 3-9-0
        LDettori 12.7

100/30 Shavian, 7/2 Green Line Express,
4/1 DISTANT RELATIVE, 5/1 Zoman,
7/1 Lord Charmer, 15/2 Great
Commotion, 50/1 Call To Arms
    Wafic Said (B. W. Hills) 7ran 1m36.06
(Firm)

42   KING GEORGE STAKES   5f
    (Gr 3)
£20,646   Goodwood   2 August
30   **Argentum** 3-9-0 JReid 1
16   **Blyton Lad** 4-9-0
        SWebster 1½.2
30   **Dancing Music** 3-8-9
        GCarter dh.2
    Hana Marie 3-8-6
        BRaymond nk.4
27   Afwaj (USA) 4-9-0
        WCarson sh.5
30   Statoblest 4-9-5
        RCochrane sh.6
30   Boozy 3-8-6 RFox nk.7
    Barrys Gamble 4-9-0
        TQuinn 2½.8
    Carol's Treasure 6-9-0
        MHills hd.9
30   Tigani 3-8-6 PatEddery 10
    Night At Sea 3-8-6 LDettori ... 11
    Jondebe Boy 6-9-0 ACulhane . 12
    Retiring Imp (USA) 3-9-0
        AMunro 13
30   Poyle George 5-9-0
        SCauthen 14

4/1 ARGENTUM, 5/1 Night At Sea, 11/2
Tigani, 7/1 Boozy, 9/1 Statoblest, 10/1
Carol's Treasure, 16/1 Blyton Lad, Poyle
George, 25/1 Jondebe Boy, Retiring Imp,

28/1 Dancing Music, 33/1 Barrys
Gamble, Hana Marie
    K. F. Khan (L. J. Holt) 14ran 57.02secs
(Firm)

43   VODAFONE NASSAU   1¼m
    STAKES (Gr 2) (3y + f)
£54,070   Goodwood   4 August
21   **Kartajana** 3-8-6
        WRSwinburn 1
    Starlet 4-9-1 PatEddery 2.2
22² **Moon Cactus** 3-8-7
        SCauthen 4.3
    Mamaluna 4-9-1
        RCochrane 1½.4
24   Alcando 4-9-1 TQuinn 5.5
    Shyoushka 4-9-1 WCarson .. 15.6

5/4 Moon Cactus, 9/4 Scarlet, 11/2
KARTAJANA, 12/1 Mamaluna, 25/1
Alcando, Shyoushka
    H. H. Aga Khan (M. R. Stoute) 6ran
2m04.96 (Firm)

44   PRIX MAURICE DE   6f110y
    GHEEST (Gr 2)
£30,709   Deauville   5 August
38   **Dead Certain** 3-8-4
        CAsmussen 1
38³ **Rock City** 3-8-13
        BRaymond 1.2
    Pole Position 3-8-7
        DBoeuf sh.3
18   Whippet 6-8-11
        GDubroeucq 5.4
12   Machiavellian (USA) 3-8-7
        FHead ½.5

1/2 Machiavellian, 3/1 Rock City, 34/10
DEAD CERTAIN, 10/1 Pole Position,
13/1 Whippet
    G. G. Marten (D. R. C. Elsworth) 5ran
1m19.60 (Good)

45   HEINZ 57 PHOENIX   6f
    STAKES (Gr 1) (2y c + f)
£95,270   Phoenix Park   12 August
37² **Mac's Imp (USA)** 9-0
        AMunro 1
    Distinctly North (USA) 9-0
        JCarroll ...,.................. nk.2
    Gipsy Fiddler 9-0
        BRaymond 3.3
    Noora Park (Ire) 8-11
        WJSupple 1.4
    Inishdalla (Ire) 8-11
        MJKinane 1½.5
    On Tiptoes 8-11
        DeanMcKeown nk.6
    Karens Keeper (Ire) 9-0
        JKManning ¾.7
    Brentsville (USA) 8-11
        WFHarris 1½.8
    Downeaster Alexa (USA) 8-11
        GCurran 1½.9
    Capricciosa (Ire) 8-11
        JReid 1.10

Panchos Pearl (USA) 8-11
TQuinn ½.11
Torque 9-0 DGillespie hd.12
Barry's Run (Ire) 9-0 LFay . 7.13

Evens MAC'S IMP, 5/1 Capriciosa,
Distinctly North, 7/1 On Tiptoes, 8/1
Gipsy Fiddler, 12/1 Inishdalla, 14/1
Panchos Pearl, 20/1 Brentsville, Noora
Park, 50/1 Downeaster Alexa, Torque,
66/1 Karens Keeper, 300/1 Barry's Run
  Tamdown Ltd (W. A. O'Gorman)
13ran 1m09.90 (Good to Firm)

46	PRIX DU HARAS DE	1m
	FRESNAY-LE-BUFFARD	
	JACQUES LE MAROIS	
	(Gr 1)	
£100,301	Deauville	12 August

31² **Priolo (USA)** 3-8-9
ALequeux 1
19 **Linamix (FR)** 3-8-9
GMosse ½.2
41* **Distant Relative (Ire)** 4-9-2
PatEddery nk.3
15 Lady Winner (Fr) 4-8-13
ELegrix ½.4
31 Candy Glen (Ire) 3-8-9
ASCruz 1.5
14³ Septieme Ciel (USA) 3-8-9
FHead 1½.6
26* Chimes of Freedom (USA) 3-8-7
SCauthen 2.7
Sikeston (USA) 4-9-2
MRoberts 4.8
41² Green Line Express (USA) 4-9-2
CAsmussen 2.9
6 Reinstate (Fr) 3-8-9
DBoeuf dist.10

2 1/10 Chimes of Freedom, 42/10 Green
Line Express, 44/10 Distant Relative,
5/1 Linamix and Reinstate, 64/10
Septieme Ciel, 87/10 Lady Winner,
113/10 PRIOLO, 135/10 Candy Glen, 48/1
Sikeston
  Ecurie Skymarc Farm (F. Boutin)
10ran 1m38.20 (Good)

47	WALMAC	1m5f60y
	INTERNATIONAL	
	GEOFFREY FREER	
	STAKES (Gr 2)	
£41,837	Newbury	18 August

40 **Charmer** 5-9-2 LDettori 1
Sesame 5-8-13
WRSwinburn 2½.2
28 **Mountain Kingdom (USA)**
6-9-5 SCauthen 1.3
40³ Assatis (USA) 5-9-8
RCochrane 2.4
Ijtihaad (USA) 3-8-5
WCarson 20.5

13/8 Assatis, 11/4 Ijtihaad, 4/1
CHARMER, 5/1 Mountain Kingdom,
12/1 Sesame
  The Dowager Lady Beaverbrook (C.
E. Brittain) 5ran 2m55.24 (Good to
Firm)

48	JUDDMONTE	1¼m 110y
	INTERNATIONAL	
	STAKES (Gr 1)	
£180,338	York	21 August

21 **In The Groove** 3-8-9
SCauthen 1
34* **Elmaamul (USA)** 3-8-12
WCarson 1½.2
24* **Batshoof** 4-9-6
PatEddery 2½.3
40 Terimon 4-9-6
MRoberts ½.4
24 Dolpour 4-9-6
WRSwinburn ¾.5
19 Missionary Ridge 3-8-12
MJKinane 5.6
4³ Negligent 3-8-9 MHills 7.7
34 Relief Pitcher 4-9-6
LDettori hd.8
25 Dashing Blade 3-8-12
RCochrane 2.9

5/2 Batshoof, 7/2 Elmaamul, 4/1 IN
THE GROOVE, 13/2 Dolpour, 11/1
Terimon, 14/1 Dashing Blade, 16/1
Negligent, Relief Pitcher, 33/1
Missionary Ridge
  Brian Cooper (D. R. C. Elsworth)
9ran 2m08.77 (Good)

49	GREAT VOLTIGEUR	1½m
	STAKES (Gr 2)	
	(3y c + g)	
£50,895	York	21 August

40* **Belmez (USA)** 9-0
SCauthen 1
Snurge 8-9 TQuinn hd.2
19 **Karinga Bay** 8-9
BRouse 8.3
32 Blue Stag 8-9 WCarson ¾.4
Starstreak 8-9
WRSwinburn 8.5

1/2 BELMEZ, 9/2 Blue Stag, 13/2
Karinga Bay, 14/1 Starstreak, 22/1
Snurge
  Sheikh Mohammed (H. R. A. Cecil)
5ran 2m30.29 (Good)

50	ASTON UPTHORPE	1½m
	YORKSHIRE OAKS	
	(Gr 1) (3y f)	
£76,423	York	22 August

Hellenic 9-0 WCarson 1
43* **Kartajana** 9-0
WRSwinburn 1½.2
Wajd (USA) 9-0
CAsmussen hd.3
Cruising Height 9-0
PatEddery 6.4
Ruby Tiger 9-0 TQuinn sh.5
21² Game Plan 9-0
MRoberts 10.6

15/8 Kartajana, 100/30 HELLENIC, 7/2
Wajd, 5/1 Game Plan, 15/2 Cruising
Height, 33/1 Ruby Tiger
  Lord Weinstock (M. R. Stoute) 6ran
2m28.14 (Good)

51 KEENELAND NUNTHORPE STAKES 5f
(Gr 1)
£72,552   York   23 August

30*	Dayjur (USA) 3-9-3	
	WCarson	1
42	Statoblest 4-9-6 LDettori ...	4.2
38	Pharaoh's Delight 3-9-0	
	RCochrane	2.3
42*	Argentum 3-9-3 JReid	1½.4
42	Carol's Treasure 6-9-6	
	MHills	hd.5
38	Lugana Beach 4-9-6	
	SCauthen	nk.6
	Mr Nickerson (USA) 4-9-6	
	CAsmussen	sh.7
d-h 42²	Blyton Lad 4-9-6 SWebster ..	4.8
42	Poyle George 5-9-6	
	PatEddery	7.9

8/11 DAYJUR, 11/4 Argentum, 14/1 Statoblest, 18/1 Mr Nickerson, 20/1 Lugana Beach, 33/1 Carol's Treasure, 40/1 Blyton Lad, 50/1 Poyle George
Hamdan Al-Maktoum (Major W. R. Hern) 9ran 56.16 (Good to Firm)

52 BEEFEATER GIN CELEBRATION MILE 1m
(Gr 2)
£50,590   Goodwood   25 August

41³	Shavian 3-9-0 SCauthen	1
46	Candy Glen 3-9-0	
	RCochrane	2½.2
25³	Lord Florey (USA) 3-8-8	
	LDettori	2.3
23²	Mirror Black 4-9-0	
	TQuinn	1½.4
23	Safawan 4-9-3	
	WRSwinburn	sh.5

5/2 SHAVIAN, 11/4 Lord Florey, 3/1 Mirror Black, 7/2 Safawan, 9/1 Candy Glen
Lord Howard de Walden (H. R. A. Cecil) 5ran 1m37.05 (Good to Firm)

53 GROSSER PREIS VON BADEN 1½m
(Gr 1)
£82,781   Baden-Baden   2 September

20	Mondrian (GER) 4-9-6	
	MHofer	1
20³	Ibn Bey 6-9-6 TQuinn	1.2
1	Per Quod (USA) 5-9-6	
	RCochrane	1¾.3
	Turfkonig 4-9-6	
	GBocskai	2½.4
	Silvestro 5-9-6	
	DRichardson	1½.5
28	Turgeon (USA) 4-9-6 ACruz .	1.6
	Buenos 3-8-9 MRimmer	nk.7
	Comte du Bourg (Fr) 3-8-9	
	AGibert	8
48	Dolpour 4-9-6 WSwinburn	9

14/10 Ibn Bey, 32/10 Turfkonig, 43/10 MONDRIAN, 59/10 Dolpour, 69/10 Comte du Bourg, 16/1 Turgeon, 24/1 Silvestro, 32/1 Buenos, 34/1 Per Quod
S. Hanse (V. Stoltefuss) 9ran 2m34.60 (Soft)

54 PHOENIX CHAMPION STAKES 1¼m
(Gr 1)
£121,943   Pheonix Park   2 September

48²	Elmaamul (USA) 3-8-11	
	WCarson	1
46	Sikeston (USA) 4-9-6	
	MRoberts	1½.2
	Kostroma 4-9-3 SCraine	4.3
48³	Batshoof 4-9-6	
	BRaymond	½.4
39	Tanwi 3-8-8 WFHarris	1½.5
	Splash of Colour 3-8-11	
	JReid	3.6
31*	Saumarez 3-8-11	
	SCauthen	20.7
	Old Talka River 3-8-11	
	DGillespie	8

2/1 ELMAAMUL, 5/2 Saumarez, 7/2 Batshoof, 4/1 Splash of Colour, 11/1 Kostroma, 66/1 Sikeston, 100/1 Tanwi, 200/1 Old Talka River
Hamdan Al-Maktoum (Major W. R. Hern) 8ran 2m02.90 (Good)

55 EMIRATES PRIX DU MOULIN DE LONGCHAMP 1m
(Gr 1)
£88,670   Longchamp   2 September

46³	Distant Relative 4-9-2	
	PatEddery	1
46²	Linamix (Fr) 3-8-12	
	GMosse	sh.2
46*	Priolo (USA) 3-8-12	
	ALequeux	¾.3
15²	Val des Bois (Fr) 4-9-2	
	GGuignard	4.4
44³	Pole Position 3-8-12	
	DBoeuf	nk.5
46	Reinstate (Fr) 3-8-12	
	CPiccioni	dist.6

6/5 Linamix and Reinstate, 26/10 DISTANT RELATIVE, Priolo, 69/10 Val des Bois, 21/2 Pole Position
Wafic Said (B. W. Hills) 6ran 1m38.30 (Good)

56 LADBROKE SPRINT CUP 6f
(Gr 1)
£77,597   Haydock   8 September

51*	Dayjur (USA) 3-9-6	
	WCarson	1
38*	Royal Academy (USA) 3-9-6	
	JReid	1½.2
51³	Pharaoh's Delight 3-9-3	
	MRoberts	5.3
41	Great Commotion (USA) 4-9-9	
	BRaymond	3.4
30²	Ron's Victory (USA) 3-9-6	
	ASCruz	3.5
	Duck And Dive 3-9-6	
	WRyan	2.6

51² Statoblest 4-9-9 LDettori ... sh.7
27 Tod 3-9-6 TQuinn hd.8
44* Dead Certain 3-9-3
AMunro 30.9
1/2 DAYJUR, 11/2 Royal Academy, 13/2 Dead Certain, 16/1 Great Commotion, Ron's Victory, 25/1 Pharaoh's Delight, Statoblest, 66/1 Duck And Dive, Tod
Hamdan Al-Maktoum (Major W. R. Hern) 9ran 1m12.50 (Good)

57 PRIX DE LA   7f
SALAMANDRE (Gr 1)
(2y)
£55,739 Longchamp 9 September
Hector Protector (USA) 8-11
FHead 1
Lycius (USA) 8-11
CAsmussen 1.2
Booming (Fr) 8-11
ALequeux ½.3
River Traffic (USA) 8-11
ELegrix 2.4
Belle Bleue 8-8 DBoeuf ½.5
Hello Pink (Fr) 8-11 ABadel . 2.6
Mousquetaire (USA) 8-11
GMosse 10.7
3/5 HECTOR PROTECTOR and Mousquetaire, 3/1 Lycius, 57/10 Booming, 13/2 Hello Pink, 12/1 Belle Bleue, 16/1 River Traffic
S. S. Niarchos (F. Boutin) 7ran 1m20.80 (Good)

58 FLYING CHILDERS   5f
STAKES (Gr 2) (2y)
£27,015 Doncaster 15 September
45² **Distinctly North (USA)**
8-11 PatEddery 1
Mujadil (USA) 8-11
WCarson 1½.2
Vintage Only 8-11
KDarley ¾.3
Line Engaged (USA) 9-2
SCauthen nk.4
Dominio (Ire) 8-6
WRSwinburn 1½.5
Poets Cove 9-2 WNewnes ... 7.6
6/4 DISTINCTLY NORTH, 5/2 Mujadil, 6/1 Line Engaged, 7/1 Vintage Only, 9/1 Dominio, 14/1 Poets Cove
R. E. Sangster (J. Berry) 6ran 1m00.23 (Good)

59 2 14TH ST LEGER   1¾m 127y
STAKES (Gr 1) (3y c + f)
£151,938 Doncaster 15 September
49² **Snurge** 9-0 TQuinn 1
50* **Hellenic** 8-11
WRSwinburn ¾.2
19 **River God (USA)** 9-0
SCauthen 4.3
Rubicund 9-0 WCarson 3.4
Great Marquess 9-0
PatEddery ½.5
49³ Karinga Bay 9-0 BRouse 1.6

Hajade 9-0 LDettori 7.7
Pier Damiani (USA) 9-0
MRoberts 25.8
2/1 Hellenic, 10/3 River God, 7/2 SNURGE, 9/1 Hajade, 11/1 Great Marquess, Karinga Bay, 16/1 Rubicund, 100/1 Pier Damiani
M. Arbib (P. F. I. Cole) 8ran 3m08.78 (Good)

60 PRIX NIEL (Gr 2)   1½m
(3y c + f)
£43,925 Longchamp 16 September
17² **Epervier Bleu** 9-2 DBoeuf 1
Antisaar (USA) 9-2
CAsmussen hd.2
17 **Passing Sale (Fr)** 9-2
DBouland 1.3
Theatre Critic 9-2
PatEddery 3.4
Heraut Bleu Fonce 9-2
WMongil 8.5
2/5 EPERVIER BLEU and Heraut Bleu Fonce, 13/10 Antisaar and Theatre Critic, 53/10 Passing Sale
D. Wildenstein (E. Lellouche) 5ran 2m32.00 (Good to Firm)

61 PRIX VERMEILLE (Gr 1) 1½m
(3y f)
£79,171 Longchamp 16 September
32* **Salsabil** 9-2 WCarson 1
Miss Alleged (USA) 9-2
DBoeuf nk.2
48* **In The Groove** 9-2
SCauthen ½.3
50³ **Wajd (USA)** 9-2
CAmussen ½.4
33 Air de Rien 9-2 ABadel ½.5
Madiriya (Ire) 9-2
LDettori nk.6
Vanya (Ire) 9-2
GMosse ¾.7
22 Vue Cavaliere (Fr) 9-2
ELegrix ½.8
La Belle France (Ire) 9-2
PBodin dist.9
2/5 SALSABIL, 54/10 Wajd and La Belle France, 77/10 Air de Rien, 78/10 Miss Alleged, 9/1 In The Groove, 13/1 Madiriya, 29/1 Vue Cavaliere, 42/1 Vanya
Hamdan Al-Maktoum (J. Dunlop) 9ran 2m29.60 (Good to Firm)

62 PRIX FOY (Gr 3)   1½m
(4y + c + f)
£21,276 Longchamp 16 September
40 **In The Wings** 4-9-2
PatEddery 1
33³ Zartota (USA) 4-8-13
TJarnet ½.2
Robertet (USA) 4-8-13
DBoeuf 3.3
47² Sesame 4-8-13
WRSwinburn nk.4

1034

Robore (Fr) 5-9-2 AGibert . 1½.5
2/5 IN THE WINGS, 26/10 Robertet, 6/1 Robore, 78/10 Sesame, 14/1 Zartota
 Sheikh Mohammed (A. Fabre) 5ran 2m31.30 (Good to Firm)

63   JEFFERSON SMURFIT   1¾m
      MEMORIAL IRISH
      ST LEGER (Gr 1)
£88,091   Curragh   22 September
53²   **Ibn Bey** 6-9-8 TRQuinn 1
      Mr Pintips 6-9-8
       DGillespie 1.2
10*   **Braashee** 4-9-8 MRoberts .. 3.3
28²   Tyrone Bridge 4-9-8
       PShanahan sh.4
53³   Per Quod (USA) 5-9-8
       BRaymond 3.5
      Glowing Star 4-9-8 JReid ... 1½.6
      Thetford Forest 3-8-12
       RQuinton 2½.7
      Northern Pet 3-8-9
       WFHarris 2.8
39   Annie Laurie 3-8-9
       CRoche 15.9
      Rare Holiday 4-9-8
       MJKinane 10
29   Michelozzo (USA) 4-9-8
       SCauthen 11
      Upward Trend 4-9-5 SCraine . 12
5/4 Michelozzo, 5/1 Braashee, IBN BEY, 13/2 Tyrone Bridge, 10/1 Thetford Forest, 12/1 Per Quod, 20/1 Glowing Star, 25/1 Mr Pintips, Northern Pet, Rare Holiday, Upward Trend, 33/1 Annie Laurie
 Fahd Salman (P. F. I. Cole) 12ran 3m00.60 (Good)

64   PRIX DU PRINCE   1¼m
      D'ORANGE (Gr 3)
£24,421   Longchamp   23 September
54   Saumarez 3-9-2 GMosse 1
      Mister Riv (Fr) 5-9-2
       TJarnet 2.2
34   Creator 4-9-6
       CAsmussen nk.3
      French Glory 4-9-4
       ALequeux sh.4
15   Mansonnien (Fr) 6-9-2
       ELegrix 10.5
      Nosferatu (Can) 4-9-0
       WMongil 10.6
7/10 Creator, 6/5 Nosferatu and SAUMAREZ, 7/1 French Glory, 10/1 Mister Riv, 15/1 Mansonnien
 B. McNall (N. Clement) 6ran 2m11.50 (Soft)

65   HOOVER   1½m
      CUMBERLAND LODGE
      STAKES (Gr 3)
£34,350   Ascot   27 September
36   Ile de Nisky 4-9-0 GCarter 1
40   Cacoethes (USA) 4-9-5
       RCochrane ½.2

Alphabel 4-9-0 MRoberts 5.3
40   Limeburn 4-9-0 AClark nk.4
5   Lord of The Field 3-8-9
       WNewnes 20.5
10   Albadr (USA) 5-9-0
       WCarson 2.6
47³   Mountain Kingdom 6-9-5
       SCauthen 2½.7
13/8 Cacoethes, 3/1 Lord of The Field, 5/1 Alphabel, 6/1 Albadr, 7/1 ILE DE NISKY, 25/1 Mountain Kingdom, 100/1 Limeburn
 H. H. Prince Yazid Saud (G. A. Huffer) 7ran 2m31.04 (Good to Firm)

66   ROYAL LODGE   1m
      WILLIAM HILL STAKES
      (Gr 2) (2y c + g)
£71,478   Ascot   29 September
      Mujaazif (USA) 8-10
       WRSwinburn 1
      Jahafil 8-10 WCarson 3½.2
      Stone Mill 8-10 SCauthen ... 4.3
      Hailsham (Can) 8-10
       MRoberts 3½.4
      Sunset Street (Ire) 8-10
       FCoetzee 2½.5
      Prodigal Blues (USA) 8-10
       MHills 4.6
      Green Turban 8-10
       PatEddery 5.7
      Peleng (Ire) 8-10 LDettori ... 8.8
11/8 Jahafil, 11/2 Green Turban, MUJAAZIF, 6/1 Prodigal Blues, 7/1 Stone Mill, 33/1 Hailsham, Peleng, 40/1 Sunset Street
 Maktoum Al-Maktoum (M. R. Stoute) 8ran 1m41.53 (Good to Firm)

67   QUEEN ELIZABETH II   1m
      STAKES (Gr 1)
£206,538   Ascot   29 September
23*   **Markofdistinction** 4-9-4
       LDettori 1
55²   **Distant Relative** 4-9-4
       PatEddery 1.2
46   Green Line Express (USA)
       4-9-4 WRSwinburn 8.3
      Croupier 3-9-0 FCoetzee 5.4
52*   Shavian 3-9-0 3Cauthen .., 2½.5
55²   Linamix (Fr) 3-9-0 FHead 4.6
52²   Candy Glen 3-9-0
       RCochrane ¾.7
31³   Tirol 3-9-0 WCarson ½.8
15³   Citidancer 4-9-4 WRyan ¾.9
41   Call To Arms 3-9-0
       MRoberts 1½.10
7/2 Tirol, 4/1 Shavian, 9/2 Distant Relative, 5/1 Linamix, 6/1 MARKOFDISTINCTION, 11/1 Green Line Express, 20/1 Citidancer, 25/1 Candy Glen, 100/1 Call To Arms, 200/1 Croupier
 Gerald Leigh (L. M. Cumani) 10ran 1m39.70 (Good to Firm)

68   **BRENT WALKER**   1m
      FILLIES' MILE (Gr 1) (2y)
£101,025   Ascot   29 September

Shamshir 8-10 LDettori **1**
Safa 8-10 BRaymond 2.2
Atlantic Flyer (USA) 8-10
    MRoberts 5.3
Jaffa Line 8-10 SCauthen ¾.4
Trojan Crown (Ire) 8-10
    AMunro 1½.5
Majmu (USA) 8-10 WCarson   2.6
Secret Freedom (USA) 8-10
    FCoetzee nk.7
Glowing Ardour 8-10
    WRSwinburn sh.8
Desert Gem 8-10
    DeanMcKeown nk.9
Ausherra (USA) 8-10
    TQuinn 2.10
Lofty Lady (Ire) 8-10
    MHills nk.11
Third Watch 8-10
    PatEddery 12

11/4 Third Watch, 11/2 Jaffa Line, SHAMSHIR, 13/2 Majmu, 7/1 Safa, 17/2 Ausherra, 9/1 Glowing Ardour, 14/1 Lofty Lady, 20/1 Atlantic Flyer, Trojan Crown, 100/1 Desert Gem, Secret Freedom
    Sheikh Mohammed (L. M. Cumani) 12ran 1m43.27 (Good to Firm)

69   **KRUG DIADEM STAKES**   6f
      (Gr 3)
£53,928   Ascot   29 September

56   **Ron's Victory (USA)** 3-8-11
    FHead **1**
    Northern Goddess 3-8-8
    RCochrane 10.2
    Tadwin 3-8-8 AMunro ¾.3
27   Polar Bird 3-8-8 MHills nk.4
56³   Pharaoh's Delight 3-8-8
    MRoberts 3.5
51   Argentum 3-8-11 PatEddery   5.6
    Rivers Rhapsody 3-8-8
    JWilliams ¾.7
    Rushmore (USA) 3-8-11
    TQuinn nk.8
    Alo Ez 4-8-11 WNewnes ½.9
42   Afwaj (USA) 4-9-0
    WCarson ½.10
    Be Fresh 4-9-0 LDettori 3.11
56   Dead Certain 3-8-12
    SCauthen 1.12
    Centerland (USA) 3-8-11
    WRSwinburn ½.13
27   Flower Girl 3-8-8
    FCoetzee 2.14

4/1 Argentum, 5/1 Polar Bird, 13/2 RON'S VICTORY, 7/1 Dead Certain, 8/1 Pharaoh's Delight, 10/1 Tadwin, 11/1 Northern Goddess, 14/1 Rivers Rhapsody, 16/1 Be Fresh, 20/1 Afwaj, Flower Girl, 66/1 Centerland, 100/1 Alo Ez, Rushmore
    J. S. Moss (A. J. Falourd) 14ran 1m 12.66 (Good to Firm)

70   **TATTERSALLS**   6f
      CHEVELEY PARK
      STAKES (Gr 1) (2y f)
£94,934   Newmarket   3 October

45   **Capricciosa (Ire)** 8-11
    JReid **1**
    Imperfect Circle (USA) 8-11
    PatEddery ¾.2
    Divine Danse (Fr) 8-11
    FHead 2½.3
    Sumonda 8-11 GCarter 1½.4
    Zonda 8-11 TQuinn sh.5
    Zigaura (USA) 8-11
    SCauthen 1½.6
45   Panchos Pearl (USA) 8-11
    LDettori hd.7
    Himiko (Ire) 8-11
    MShibata 3½.8
    Only Yours 8-11 WCarson   2½.9
    Ivory Bride 8-11 NDay 1½.10
    Vilany 8-11 MHills 5.11

9/4 Divine Danse, 5/2 Imperfect Circle, 7/1 CAPRICCIOSA, 9/1 Only Yours, Sumonda, 12/1 Zonda, 14/1 Zigaura, 25/1 Himiko, 33/1 Ivory Bride, Panchos Pearl, 100/1 Vilany
    R. E. Sangster (M. V. O'Brien) 11ran 1m 12.23 (Good to Firm)

71   **NEWGATE STUD**   6f
      MIDDLE PARK STAKES
      (Gr 1) (2y c)
£78,566   Newmarket   4 October

57²   **Lycius (USA)** 9-0
    CAsmussen **1**
58*   **Distinctly North (USA)** 9-0
    PatEddery ½.2
    Majlood (USA) 9-0
    WRSwinburn 1½.3
37   Bold Nephew 9-0 WCarson ... 4.4
    Polish Patriot (USA) 9-0
    RCochrane 1.5
    Sixofus (Ire) 9-0 LDettori 4.6
    Sylva Honda 9-0 MRoberts . sh.7
    Don't Give Up 9-0
    GDuffield 6.8
66   Sunset Street (Ire) 9-0
    SCauthen nk.9

13/8 LYCIUS, 5/2 Distinctly North, 10/3 Majlood, 16/1 Polish Patriot, 20/1 Sylva Honda, 25/1 Bold Nephew, 33/1 Sunset Street, 66/1 Sixofus, 200/1 Don't Give Up
    Sheikh Mohammed (A. Fabre) 9ran 1m 10.14 (Good to Firm)

72   **CHEVELEY PARK STUD**   1¼m
      SUN CHARIOT STAKES
      (Gr 2) (3y + f + m)
£43,782   Newmarket   6 October

50²   **Kartajana** 3-8-11
    WRSwinburn **1**
43²   **Starlet** 4-9-3 SCauthen ... 1½.2
2   **Filia Ardross** 4-9-3
    MRoberts 6.3
    Line of Thunder (USA) 3-8-8
    LDettori 1½.4

43   Mamaluna (USA) 4-9-3
      AClark ½.5
      Arpero 3-8-8 GDuffield 3½.6
      Bex (USA) 4-9-0
      BCrossley dist.7
11/10 KARTAJANA, 4/1 Starlet, 11/2 Filia
Ardross, 7/1 Line of Thunder, 12/1
Arpero, 33/1 Bex, Mamaluna
   H. H. Aga Khan (M. R. Stoute) 7ran
2m03.05 (Good to Firm)

73   JOCKEY CLUB CUP   2m
      (Gr 3)
£25,476   Newmarket   6 October
59   **Great Marquess** 3-8-3
      LDettori 1
      Dance Spectrum (USA) 4-9-0
      AClark ¾.2
28*   **Ashal** 4-9-7 RHills 8.3
      Al Maheb (USA) 4-9-5
      MRoberts 10.4
      Regal Reform 7-9-0
      DeanMcKeown 7.5
28   Teamster 4-9-3
      WRSwinburn 15.6
      Jurran 5-9-0 NCarlisle dist.7
5/2 Teamster, 11/4 Al Maheb, 3/1
GREAT MARQUESS, 8/1 Dance
Spectrum, 11/1 Ashal, 12/1 Regal Reform,
66/1 Jurran
   C. A. B. St George (H. R. A. Cecil) 7ran
3m21.52 (Good to Firm)

74   CIGA GRAND   1m
      CRITERIUM (Gr 1)
      (2y c + f)
£119,166   Longchamp   6 October
57*   **Hector Protector (USA)** 8-11
      FHead 1
      Masterclass (USA) 8-11
      PatEddery 2½.2
      Beau Sultan (USA) 8-11
      CAsmussen 2½.3
      Selkirk (USA) 8-11 JReid ¾.4
57   Mousquetaire (USA) 8-11
      GMosse 20.5
4/5 HECTOR PROTECTOR and
Mousquetaire, 18/10 Beau Sultan, 33/10
Masterclass, 42/10 Selkirk
   S. S. Niarchos (F. Boutin) 5ran
1m41.10 (Good)

75   CIGA PRIX DE   1½m 110y
      ROYALLIEU (Gr 2)
      (3y + f + m)
£37,860   Longchamp   6 October
      Madame Dubois 3-9-1
      PatEddery 1
22   **Spendomania (USA)** 3-8-8
      GGuignard snk.2
      Echoes (Fr) 3-8-8 FHead . nk.3
      Savoureuse Lady 3-8-8
      CAsmussen ½.4
62³   Robertet (USA) 4-9-6
      DBoeuf nk.5

      Tarikhana 3-8-8
      PaulEddery 2½.6
      Franc Argument (USA) 4-9-0
      MdeSmyter 1.7
      Tycana (Fr) 5-9-0 GMosse ... 1.8
9/10   MADAME   DUBOIS,   44/10
Robertet,   46/10   Tarikhana,   9/1
Savoureuse Lady, 12/1 Spendomania,
14/1 Franc Argument, 17/1 Tycana, 20/1
Echoes
   Cliveden Stud (H. R. A. Cecil) 8ran
2m42.60 (Good)

76   TURF CLASSIC   1½m
      INVITATIONAL (Gr 1)
£185,567   Belmont Park   7 October
65²   **Cacoethes** 4-9-0 RCochrane . 1
      Alwuhush 5-9-0 JSantos . 1½.2
      With Approval (CAN) 4-9-0
      CPerret ns.3
      El Senor 6-9-0 ACordero .. 2¾.4
      Shy Tom 4-9-0 CAntley 2.5
      Fast 'N' Gold 4-9-0 JBailey . nk.6
12/10   With   Approval,   19/10
CACOETHES, 44/10 El Senor, 88/10
Shy Tom, 93/10 Alwuhush, 247/10 Fast
'N' Gold
   Lady Harrison (G. Harwood) 6ran
2m25.00 (Firm)

77   PRIX MARCEL   1m
      BOUSSAC (Gr 1) (2y f)
£79,444   Longchamp   7 October
      Shadayid (USA) 8-9
      WCarson 1
      Caerlina (Ire) 8-9
      ELegrix 2.2
      Sha Tha (USA) 8-9
      CAsmussen sh.3
      After The Sun (USA) 8-9
      GMosse 1.4
      Joyeuse Marquise (Ire) 8-9
      LDettori 1.5
      Magic Night (Fr) 8-9
      DBoeuf ½.6
      Jet Ski Lady (USA) 8-9
      CRoche nk.7
      Alexandra Fair (USA) 8-9
      FHead 1.8
      Polemic (USA) 8-9
      PatEddery sh.9
3/5 SHADAYID, 11/2 Sha Tha, 13/2
Magic Night, 17/2 Polemic, 12/1 After
The Sun, 23/1 Alexandra Fair, 28/1 Jet
Ski Lady, 29/1 Caerlina, 38/1 Joyeuse
Marquise
   Hamdan Al-Maktoum (J. Dunlop) 9ran
1m40.70 (Good)

78   CIGA PRIX DE   5f
      L'ABBAYE DE
      LONGCHAMP (Gr 1)
£69,514   Longchamp   7 October
56*   **Dayjur (USA)** 3-9-11
      WCarson 1

1037

51	**Lugana Beach** 4-9-11	
	SCauthen 2.2
69	**Pharaoh's Delight** 3-9-8	
	MRoberts ¾.3
56	Statoblest 4-9-11 LDettori . sh.4
42	Boozy 3-9-8 RFox 5.5
	Touch of White 4-9-8
	GCarter 1½.6

1/10 DAYJUR, 93/10 Boozy, 11/1 Statoblest, 14/1 Pharaoh's Delight, 17/1 Lugana Beach, 29/1 Touch of White
Hamdan Al-Maktoum (Major W. R. Hern) 6ran 58.70secs (Good)

79	CIGA PRIX DE L'ARC DE	1½m
	TRIOMPHE (Gr 1)
	(3y+ c+f)

£496,525   Longchamp   7 October

64*	**Saumarez** 3-8-11 GMosse 1
60*	**Epervier Bleu** 3-8-11	
	DBoeuf ¾.2
59*	**Snurge** 3-8-11 TQuinn ½.3
62*	In The Wings 4-9-4	
	PatEddery 2.4
49*	Belmez (USA) 3-8-11	
	SCauthen 1½.5
40	Legal Case 4-9-4 LDettori 1.6
17³	Erdelistan (Fr) 3-8-11	
	ASCruz snk.7
59²	Hellenic 3-8-8 WRSwinburn . 1.8
61³	In The Groove 3-8-8 RFox 2.9
61*	Salsabil 3-8-8 WCarson sh.10
60²	Antisaar (USA) 3-8-11	
	CAsmussen sh.11
47	Assatis (USA) 5-9-4	
	MShibata ½.12
62	Robore 5-9-4 FHead nk.13
47*	Charmer 5-9-4 FCoetzee .. ¾.14
64²	Mister Riv (Fr) 5-9-4	
	GGuignard ½.15
62²	Zartota (USA) 4-9-1	
	TJarnet nk.16
22	Guiza (USA) 3-8-8	
	ELegrix ¾.17
54²	Sikeston (USA) 5-9-4	
	MRoberts 1.18
65*	Ile de Nisky 4-9-4 GCarter . 8.19
65	Albadr (USA) 5-9-4	
	RHills 20.20
	Abyad 3-8-11 WMongil ... dist.21

8/5 Albadr and Salsabil, 37/10 Antisaar and Belmez and In The Wings, 5/1 Epervier Bleu, 15/2 Snurge, 25/2 In The Groove, 14/1 Hellenic, 15/1 SAUMAREZ, 22/1 Abyad and Erdelistan, 30/1 Assatis, 33/1 Mister Riv, Zartota, 46/1 Legal Case, 70/1 Robore, 74/1 Ile de Nisky, Sikeston, 83/1 Guiza, 89/1 Charmer
B. McNall (N. Clement) 21ran 2m29.80(Good)

| 80 | CIGA PRIX DE | 1m 1f55y |
| | L'OPERA (Gr 2) (3 + 4y f) |

£53,084   Longchamp   7 October

| 31 | **Colour Chart (USA)** 3-8-11 | |
| | CAsmussen .... 1 |

46	**Lady Winner (Fr)** 4-9-4	
	ELegrix 2.2
	Tabdea (USA) 3-8-9	
	WCarson 1½.3
	Karlafsha 3-8-9 ASCruz ¾.4
	Taffeta And Tulle (USA) 4-8-13
	PatEddery sh.5
26³	Heart of Joy (USA) 3-8-11	
	WRSwinburn dh.5
	Gaelic Bird (Fr) 3-8-13	
	WMongil 1.7
	Well Known (Ger) 3-8-9	
	TQuinn 1.8
	Va Toujours 3-8-9	
	MRimmer nk.9
	Sajjaya (USA) 3-8-9	
	LDettori 1½.10
	Miss Matho (Fr) 3-8-9	
	LAuriemma ¾.11
	Caprarola (Fr) 3-8-11	
	GMosse ¾.12
26	Mais Oui (USA) 3-8-9	
	FHead ¾.13
	Sorceress (Fr) 3-8-9	
	GDubroeucq 3.14

7/5 COLOUR CHART and Taffeta And Tulle, 3/1 Va Toujours, 4/1 Heart of Joy, 6/1 Lady Winner, 13/2 Sajjaya and Tabdea, 17/2 Karlafsha, 28/1 Caprarola, 44/1 Mais Oui, 48/1 Well Known, 51/1 Gaelic Bird, 79/1 Sorceress, 109/1 Miss Matho
Sheikh Mohammed (A. Fabre) 14ran 1m54.60 (Good)

| 81 | CORNWALLIS STAKES | 5f |
| | (Gr 3) (2y) |

£26,866   Ascot   13 October

58²	**Mujadil (USA)** 8-13	
	SCauthen 1
	Clifton Charlie (USA) 8-13	
	PaulEddery 3½.2
58³	**Vintage Only** 8-13	
	JCarroll sh.3
	Fiorentia 8-8 CRutter 3.4
	Never In The Red 8-13	
	AClark 3.5
	Rio Tejo (USA) 8-8	
	GCarter ¾.6
58	Poets Cove 9-2 WNewnes 5.7
	Bit of A Lark 8-13 SPerks ... sh.8
	Jimmy Barnie 9-5	
	PatEddery 2.9
	Maria Cappuccini 8-8	
	RCochrane 2.10
	Racketeer (Ire) 8-8	
	DHolland nk.11

9/4 MUJADIL, 5/1 Jimmy Barnie, Vintage Only, 7/1 Clifton Charlie, 10/1 Rio Tejo, 11/1 Never In The Red, 14/1 Poets Cove, 16/1 Bit of A Lark, 33/1 Racketeer, 50/1 Maria Cappuccini, 100/1 Fiorentia
Hamdan Al-Maktoum (R. W. Armstrong) 11ran 1m00.29 (Good to Firm)

82   PRIX DE LA FORET   7f
(Gr 1) (2y + c + f)
£60,823   Longchamp   14 October
46   **Septieme Ciel (USA) 3-9-11**
    FHead 1
    Norwich 3-9-11 MHills 2.2
    Philippi (Fr) 4-9-13
      ELegrix 2½.3
    Ernani 3-9-11 WMongil 1½.4
55   **Pole Position** 3-9-11
    DBoeuf ¾.5
27   **Pont Aven** 3-9-8
    CAsmussen nk.6
8   **Cydalia (USA)** 3-9-8
    GMosse ½.7
    Silicon Lady (Fr) 4-9-10
      MdeSmyter 1½.8
6[3]   **Funambule (USA)** 3-9-11
    GGuignard 5.9
    Ocean Falls 4-9-13
      ABadel 2½.10

17/10 SEPTIEME CIEL, 26/10 Norwich,
5/1 Philippi, 61/10 Funambule, 72/10
Ernani and Pont Aven, 81/10 Ocean
Falls, 13/1 Pole Position, 20/1 Cydalia,
24/1 Silicon Lady
  J. T. L. Jones (Mme C. Head) 10ran
1m 19.40 (Good)

83   PRIX THOMAS BYRON   7f110y
(Gr 3) (2y c + f)
£27,645   Saint-Cloud   16 October
    Exit To Nowhere (USA) 8-9
    FHead 1
    Reason To Trick (USA) 8-9
      ELegrix 5.2
    As Que To 8-9 DBoeuf 1½.3
    Zanadiyka 8-6 WMongil ½.4
57[3]   **Booming** 8-11 ABadel ns.5
    Platinum Pleasure (USA) 8-9
      GMosse 2.6
    Only Seule (USA) 8-6
      ODoleuze 1.7
    Orage Noir (USA) 8-9
      MPhilpperon ¾.8
    Northern Winter 8-9
      MdeSmyter 6.9

2/1 Booming, 11/4 Reason To Trick,
43/10 EXIT TO NOWHERE, 9/2
Zanadiyka, 7/1 As Que To, 9/1 Orage
Noir, 21/1 Only Seule, 25/1 Platinum
Pleasure, 89/1 Northern Winter
  S. S. Niarchos (F. Boutin) 9ran
1m34.20 (Good to Soft)

84   THREE CHIMNEYS   7f
DEWHURST STAKES
(Gr 1) (2y)
£117,609   Newmarket   19 October
    Generous (Ire) 9-0 TQuinn .. 1
    Bog Trotter (USA) 9-0
      NDay ¾.2
    Surrealist (Ire) 9-0
      LPiggott 2½.3
37*   Mujtahid (USA) 9-0
    WCarson 2.4

    Stark South (USA) 9-0
      WRSwinburn 2.5
    Anjiz (USA) 9-0 PatEddery ... 8.6
    Kohinoor (Ire) 9-0
      MRoberts 12.7
    Sedair 9-0 SCauthen 15.8

4/5 Mujtahid, 4/1 Anjiz, 13/2 Sedair, 8/1
Bog Trotter, 16/1 Surrealist, 25/1 Stark
South,   50/1   GENEROUS,   100/1
Kohinoor
  Fahd Salman (P. F. I. Cole) 8ran
1m28.43 (Good to Soft)

85   DUBAI CHAMPION   1¼m
STAKES (Gr 1)
£255,100   Newmarket   20 October
79   **In The Groove** 3-8-9
    SCauthen 1
67   **Linamix (Fr)** 3-8-12
    FHead 1½.2
79   **Legal Case** 4-9-3
    LDettori ¾.3
54*   Elmaamul (USA) 3-8-12
    WCarson 3½.4
72[3]   Filia Ardross 4-9-0
    MRoberts 5.5
72*   Kartajana 3-8-9
    WRSwinburn hd.6
17   Anvari 3-8-12 RCochrane 7.7
79   Sikeston (USA) 4-9-3
    LPiggott 15.8
79   Albadr (USA) 5-9-3
    JWilliams 8.9
48   Terimon 4-9-3 PatEddery   ¾.10

13/8 Kartajana, 9/2 IN THE GROOVE,
5/1 Elmaamul, 6/1 Legal Case, 12/1
Terimon, 14/1 Linamix, 20/1 Sikeston,
33/1 Filia Ardross, 66/1 Anvari, 200/1
Albadr
  Brian Cooper (D. R. C. Elsworth)
10ran 2m05.67 (Good to Soft)

86   PRIX DU CONSEIL DE   1½m
PARIS (Gr 2)
£37,136   Longchamp   21 October
60[3]   **Passing Sale** 3-8-9 GMosse .. 1
17   **Panoramic** 3-8-9
    CAsmussen s.nk.2
    Gasson 4-8-13 JBoisnard ... hd.3
75[3]   Echoes 3-8-6 FHead 1½.4
    Pirate Army (USA) 4-8-13
      MJKinane 2.5
    Wall Street Wonder 4-8-13
      ELegrix s.hd.6
79   Robore 5-9-4 WMongil s.nk.7
    Marquinor 3-8-7 ABadel 6.8

11/10 PASSING SALE, 9/5 Panoramic
and Pirate Army, 59/10 Gasson, 64/10
Robore, 15/1 Wall Street Wonder, 18/1
Echoes, 25/1 Marquinor
  A. Boutboul (B. Secly) 8ran 2m35.80
(Good)

87   LAUREL DASH (Gr 3)   6f
£66,667   Laurel Park   21 October
    Roman Prose 5-8-8 LDettori   1

69* **Ron's Victory (USA)** 3-8-7
JSantos nk.2
My Frenchman (USA) 5-8-8
DMiller 3.3
Brave Adventure 3-8-8
WMcCauley hd.4
Fourstardave 5-8-10
MSmith hd.5
Weldnaas 4-8-10
PatEddery nk.6
Kohen Witha K 5-8-8
CBlack hd.7
51 Carol's Treasure 6-8-8
RHills 2.8
Diamonds Galore 5-8-8
CPerret 3.9
Philippa Rush (AUS) 4-8-5
MNorris 1.10

11/10 Ron's Victory, 34/10 Fourstardave, 69/10 Weldnaas, 72/10 My Frenchman, 133/10 Diamonds Galore, 143/10 Philippa Rush, 2 15/10 Kohen Witha K, 223/10 Brave Adventure, 393/10 ROMAN PROSE, 666/10 Carol's Treasure
H. C. Seymour (J. Pease) 10ran 1m09.40 (Firm)

88 VODAFONE HORRIS 7f60y
HILL STAKES (Gr 3)
(2y c + g)
£25,196 Newbury 25 October
Sapieha (Ire) 8-12
WRSwinburn 1
Red Rainbow 8-12
BRaymond 4.2
Regal Sabre (USA) 8-12
MJKinane nk.3
Grove Aries (Ire) 8-12
RCochrane 2½.4
Bold Bostonian (Fr) 8-12
CRutter 4.5
El Dinero (Ire) 8-12
LPiggott 4.6
Spice Trader (Ire) 9-1
SWhitworth 1½.7
First Success (Ire) 8-12
MRoberts 1.8
71 Sunset Street (Ire) 8-12
PatEddery 9

5/2 SAPIEHA, 10/3 Regal Sabre, 5/1 Red Rainbow, 6/1 El Dinero, 10/1 Grove Aries, 14/1 Bold Bostonian, 16/1 First Success, Sunset Street, 20/1 Spice Trader
Baron G. De Geer (J. R. Fanshawe) 9ran 1m32.13 (Good)

89 CRITERIUM DE 7f
MAISONS-LAFFITTE
(Gr 2) (2y c + f)
£39,949 Maisons-Laffitte 26 October
Ganges (USA) 8-9 ELegrix ... 1
Crack Regiment (USA) 8-12
GGuignard 3.2
74² **Divine Danse** 8-9 FHead 2.3

74² Masterclass (USA) 8-9
PatEddery 2.4
Ski Chief (USA) 8-9
CAsmussen hd.5
57 Hello Pink 8-9 ABadel nk.6
Dynamique 8-9 WMongil 3.7
King of Valois 8-9 YTalamo .. 6.8
Red Coat 8-9 DBoeuf 8.9

7/10 Masterclass, 11/2 Divine Danse, King of Valois, Red Coat, 9/1 Hello Pink, Ski Chief, 12/1 Dynamique, 14/1 GANGES, 15/1 Crack Regiment
A. Paulson (F. Boutin) 9ran 1m25.90 (Soft)

90 RACING POST TROPHY 1m
(Gr 1) (2y c + f)
£159,163 Doncaster 27 October
Peter Davies (USA) 9-0
SCauthen 1
Mukaddamah (USA) 9-0
RHills sh.2
Marcham (Ire) 9-0 MHills .. 4.3
66* Mujaazif (USA) 9-0
WRSwinburn 15.4

2/1 Mujaazif, PETER DAVIES, 10/3 Mukaddamah, 6/1 Marcham
C. A. B. St George (H. R. A. Cecil) 4ran 1m46.00 (Soft)

91 BREEDERS' CUP 6f (Dirt)
SPRINT (Grade 1)
£279,503 Belmont Park 27 October
Safely Kept (USA) 4-8-11
CPerret 1
78* **Dayjur (USA)** 3-8-11
WCarson nk.2
Black Tie Affair 4-9-0
LPincayJnr 4.3
Adjudicating (USA) 3-8-11
HKawachi 2¼.4
Prospectors Gamble (USA) 5-9-0
GStevens ns.5
Dancing Spree (USA) 5-9-0
ACorderoJnr nk.6
Dargai (Can) 4-9-0
BSwatuk 2¼.7
Corwyn Bay 4-9-0
EDelahoussaye ¾.8
Senor Speedy (USA) 3-8-11
WHMcCauley ns.9
Carson City (USA) 3-8-11
JBailey 4½.10
Glitterman (USA) 5-9-0
WGuerra 6½.11
Potentiality (USA) 4-9-0
PDay hd.12
51 Mr Nickerson (USA) 4-9-0
CAntley .... f
Shaker Knit (USA) 5-9-0
JASantos .... bd

2/1 Corwyn Bay, Dayjur, 9/2 Dancing Spree, 7/1 Mr Nickerson, 9/1 Carson City, Senor Speedy, 122/10 SAFELY KEPT, 20/1 Glitterman, 22/1 Prospectors Gamble, 38/1 Adjudicating,

53/1 Black Tie Affair, 80/1 Potentiality, 87/1 Shaker Knit, 149/1 Dargai
Jayeff B Stable (A. Goldberg) 14ran 1m09.61 (Fast)

92	BREEDERS' CUP MILE (Grade 1)	1m

£279,503   Belmont Park   27 October

56[2]	**Royal Academy (USA)** 3-8-10	
	LPiggott	1
	Itsallgreektome (USA) 3-8-10	
	CNakatani	nk.2
55[3]	Priolo (USA) 3-8-10	
	CAsmussen	¾.3
	Steinlen 7-9-0 JASantos	½.4
	Expensive Decision (USA) 4-9-0	
	J-LSamyn	hd.5
	Who's To Pay (USA) 4-9-0	
	JBailey	½.6
67*	Markofdistinction 4-9-0	
	LDettori	½.7
80[2]	Lady Winner (Fr) 4-8-11	
	KDesormeaux	½.8
	Jalaajel (USA) 6-9-0 PDay .	3¾.9
	Go Dutch (USA) 3-8-10	
	EDelahoussaye	1.10
	Shot Gun Scott (USA) 3-8-10	
	KClark	6.11
	Great Normand (USA) 5-9-0	
	CLopez	2.12
	Colway Rally 6-9-0	
	CMcCarron	2¾.13

5/2 ROYAL ACADEMY, 7/2 Who's To Pay, 9/2 Priolo, Steinlen, 7/1 Markofdistinction, 12/1 Lady Winner, 16/1 Expensive Decision, 31/1 Great Normand, 35/1 Shot Gun Scott, 36/1 Itsallgreektome, 41/1 Jalaajel, 48/1 Go Dutch, 113/1 Colway Rally
Classic Thoroughbreds (M. V. O'Brien) 13ran 1m35.24 (Good)

93	BREEDERS' CUP TURF (Grade 1)	1½m

£559,006   Belmont Park   27 October

79	**In The Wings** 4-9-0	
	GStevens	1
76[3]	With Approval (Can) 4-9-0	
	CPerret	½.2
76	El Senor (USA) 6-9-0	
	ACorderoJnr	1½.3
76[2]	Alwuhush (USA) 5-9-0	
	JASantos	2½.4
79*	Saumarez 3-8-9 GMosse ..	6½.5
	Colchis Island 6-9-0	
	JGChavez	3.6
64	French Glory 4-9-0	
	PatEddery	1.7
	Pleasant Tap (USA) 3-8-9	
	JBailey	¾.8
76*	Cacoethes (USA) 4-9-0	
	RCochrane	8½.9
76	Shy Tom (USA) 4-9-0	
	CMcCarron	½.10
	Sky Classic (Can) 3-8-10	
	SHawley	1¼.11

9/5 French Glory and IN THE WINGS, 5/2 Saumarez, 5/1 Cacoethes, 6/1 With Approval, 10/1 Pleasant Tap, 13/1 El Senor, 14/1 Colchis Island, 20/1 Alwuhush, 36/1 Shy Tom, 38/1 Sky Classic
Sheikh Mohammed (A. Fabre) 11ran 2m29.61 (Good)

94	BREEDERS' CUP CLASSIC (Grade 1)	1¼m (Dirt)

£838,509   Belmont Park   27 October

	Unbridled (USA) 3-8-9	
	PDay	1
63*	Ibn Bey 6-9-0 TQuinn	1.2
	Thirty Six Red (USA) 3-8-9	
	MSmith	1.3
	Lively One (USA) 5-9-0	
	ASolis	ns.4
	De Roche (USA) 4-9-0	
	ACorderoJnr	4.5
	Izvestia (Can) 3-8-9	
	RRomero	4.6
	Opening Verse (USA) 4-9-0	
	CMcCarron	1½.7
	Rhythm (USA) 3-8-9	
	CPerret	2.8
	Mi Selecto (USA) 5-9-0	
	JASantos	1½.9
	Beau Genius (Can) 5-9-0	
	RDLopez	1.10
	Flying Continental (USA) 4-9-0	
	CBlack	9.11
	Dispersal (USA) 4-9-0	
	EDelahoussaye	2½.12
	Home At Last (USA) 3-8-10	
	JBailey	pu
	Go And Go 3-8-10	
	MJKinane	pu

5/2 Rhythm, 9/2 Flying Continental, 5/1 Izvestia, 6/1 Go And Go, Home At Last, UNBRIDLED, 8/1 Dispersal, 19/1 De Roche, Lively One, 23/1 Opening Verse, 29/1 Thirty Six Red, Ibn Bey, 44/1 Beau Genius, 85/1 Mi Selecto
Frances A. Genter Stable (C. Nafzger) 14ran 2m02.36 (Fast)

95	PRIX ROYAL-OAK (Gr 1)	1m7f110y

£31,964   Longchamp   28 October

63[3]	**Braashee** 4-9-3 MRoberts	1
1	Indian Queen 5-9-0	
	WRSwinburn	dh.1
53	Turgeon (USA) 4-9-3	
	CAsmussen	6.3
63	Michelozzo (USA) 4-9-3	
	SCauthen	2.4
53	Comte du Bourg (Fr) 3-8-11	
	WMongil	2.5
	Nil Bleu 3-8-11	
	ELegrix	3.6
75	Robertet (USA) 4-9-0	
	DBoeuf	10.7
	Glorify (USA) 3-8-11	
	FHead	20.8

Ruling (USA) 4-9-3
BRaymond 8.9
Trick Tern (USA) 3-8-11
GGuignard 8.10
36   Private Tender 3-8-11
WRyan 1½.11

22/10 Nil Bleu, 22/10 Robertet, 26/10 BRAASHEE, 48/10 Turgeon, 49/10 Comte du Bourg, 59/10 Michelozzo, 19/1 Glorify, 2 1/1 Trick Tern, 24/1 INDIAN QUEEN, 28/1 Private Tender, 4 1/1 Ruling

Braashee: Maktoum Al-Maktoum (A. C. Stewart)
Indian Queen: Sir G. Brunton (W. Hastings-Bass)
11ran 3m38.40 (Heavy)

96	RACECALL GOLD	6f
	TROPHY (2y)	
£99,966	Redcar	30 October

Chipaya 8-5 WCarson 1
71² **Distinctly North (USA)** 8-5
PatEddery 5.2
Punch N'Run 8-10
BRouse 1½.3
81³ Vintage Only 8-1 JLowe 1.4
70   Only Yours 8-6
BRaymond sh.5
Dominion Gold 8-1
KDarley ¾.6
Desert Splendour 9-0
LPiggott ¾.7
Too Conspicuous (USA) 9-0
MRoberts nk.8
Sir Harry Hardman 8-10
DeanMcKeown 1.9
Targa's Secret (USA) 8-9
WRyan ¾.10
Super Heights 8-7
GBaxter 1.11
Tinkins Wood 7-12
GHind 3½.12
Sylvan Breeze 8-1
GDuffield 1½.13
Warrior Prince 8-4
ACulhane nk.14
Highland Magic (Ire) 8-1
RHills hd.15
Azureus (Ire) 8-4
JKFanning 2.16
Small Double (Ire) 8-2
RPElliott sh.17
Runaway Lad (Ire) 8-4
SWhitworth 1½.18
Highland Spirit 7-13
JQuinn 19

5/2 Distinctly North, 7/1 CHIPAYA, 8/1 Vintage Only, 9/1 Dominion Gold, 10/1 Punch N'Run, Sylvan Breeze, 12/1 Desert Splendour, Only Yours, Tinkins Wood, Too Conspicuous, 16/1 Sir Harry Hardman, 50/1 Azureus, Highland Spirit, Runaway Lad, Targa's Secret, 100/1 Highland Magic, Small Double, Super Heights, Warrior Prince
G. Algranti (J. R. Fanshawe) 19ran 1m 11.20 (Good to Soft)

97	CRITERIUM DE	1¼m
	SAINT-CLOUD	
	(Gr 1) (2y c + f)	
£54,568	Saint-Cloud	4 November

Pistolet Bleu (Ire) 8-11
DBoeuf 1
Pigeon Voyageur (Ire) 8-11
CAsmussen 4.2
Fortune's Wheel (Ire) 8-11
ELegrix 2½.3
Widyan (USA) 8-11 TQuinn .. 2.4
Bormio (Fr) 8-11 GMosse 6.5
Clark Store (Fr) 8-11
LPiggott 4.6
One To Two (Fr) 8-11
FHead hd.7
Golden Mintage (USA) 8-11
MJKinane 1½.8
Approach The Bench (Ire) 8-11
PatEddery snk.9

7/10 PISTOLET BLEU, 58/10 Pigeon Voyageur, 6 1/10 Approach The Bench, 64/10 Clark Store, 77/10 Bormio and One To Two, 16/1 Fortune's Wheel, 22/1 Golden Mintage, 29/1 Widyan
D. Wildenstein (E. Lellouche) 9ran 2m 17.80 (Soft)

98	PREMIO ROMA	1¼m
	(Gr 1)	
£115,116	Rome	10 November

85³ **Legal Case** 4-8-12 LDettori .. 1
67   **Candy Glen** 3-8-11 NDay 2.2
85   **Sikeston (USA)** 4-8-12
MRoberts 1½.3
Muroto (Ity) 4-8-12
GMosse 1½.4
Teach Dha Mhile 3-8-11
LSorrentino snk.5
12   Noble Patriarch 3-8-11
WCarson ns.6
Heart of Groom (USA) 4-8-12
MJKinane 12.7
Theresa Moreau (Ity) 3-8-8
VPanici 2.8
Jung (Ity) 6-8-12 FJovine nk.9
Benzine (USA) 3-8-11
GDettori nk.10
Eterea Leap 3-8-8
EJerome 3.11
Malthus (Fr) 3-8-11
MLatorre hd.12
Shout And Sing (USA) 3-8-11
PaulEddery 1½.13
9   Ridgepoint 3-8-11
BJovine 12.14

16/10 LEGAL CASE, 39/10 Heart of Groom and Sikeston, 72/10 Benzine and Candy Glen and Shout And Sing, 142/10 Noble Patriarch, 170/10 Teach Dha Mhile, 192/10 Muroto, 207/10 Jung, 463/10 Ridgepoint, 474/10 Eterea Leap, 508/10 Theresa Moreau, 582/10 Malthus
Sir G. White (L. Cumani) 14ran 2m 02.30 (Soft)

99   PREMIO   1m
VITTORIO DI
CAPUA (Gr 1)
£59,784   Milan   16 November

98³   **Sikeston (USA) 4-8-11**
     MRoberts 1
98²   **Candy Glen** 3-8-11 NDay 3.2
41   **Zoman (USA)** 3-8-11
     TQuinn nk.3
     Zille (Ger) 5-8-11
     PSchiergen 2.4
     My Robert 3-8-11 SDettori . hd.5
     Goofalik (USA) 3-8-11
     GGuignard 1.6
     Venecuela (USA) 4-8-11
     MLeroy ½.7
     Totem (USA) 5-8-11
     GCarter nk.8
     Glen Jordan 4-8-11
     LSorrentino 4½.9
     Irgaim 5-8-11 LPiggott 1.10
82   Ocean Falls 4-8-11
     ABadel 1½.11
     Hello Vaigly 5-8-11
     VMezzatesta 5.12
     Capolago 3-8-11 MBucci 2.13
     Toskano (Pol) 4-8-11
     AMarcialis 2.14
     Young Jazz 4-8-11
     JHeloury dist.15

24/10 Zoman, 47/10 SIKESTON, 66/10
Candy Glen, 67/10 Zille, 11/1 Goofalik,
135/10 Irgaim, 162/10 My Robert, 169/10
Glen Jordan, 193/10 Ocean Falls, 202/10
Capolago, 488/10 Young Jazz, 525/10
Venecuela, 779/10 Hello Vaigly, 1073/10
Totem, 1123/10 Toskano
   Allevamento White Star (C. Brittain)
15ran 1m44.10 (Heavy)

---

100   JAPAN CUP (Gr 1)   1½m
£572,000   Tokyo   25 November
     Better Loosen Up (Aus) 5-8-13
     MClarke 1
33²   **Ode (USA)** 4-8-9 DBoeuf .. hd.2
93   **Cacoethes (USA)** 4-8-13
     RCochrane hd.3
     White Stone 3-8-9
     MShibata 1¼.4
93   Alwuhush (USA) 5-8-13
     JSantos nk.5
     Yaeno Muteki 5-8-13
     YOkabe 1¾.6
79   Belmez (USA) 3-8-9
     SCauthen 1½.7
94²   Ibn Bey 6-8-13 HKawazu hd.8
93   French Glory 4-8-13
     PatEddery hd.9
     Stylish Century (Aus) 4-8-13
     KMoses nk.10
     Oguri Cap 5-8-13
     SMasuzawa ns.11
     Petite Ile 4-8-9 CBlack 2½.12
     Osaichi George 4-8-13
     KMaruyama 1¼.13
     Phantom Breeze 4-8-13
     JulieKrone 6.14
     George Monarch 5-8-13
     FMatoba 1¼.15

48/10 Belmez, 52/10 BETTER
LOOSEN UP, 63/10 Cacoethes, Oguri
Cap, 69/10 White Stone, 74/10 Petite
Ile, 104/10 Alwuhush, 13/1 Yaeno
Muteki, 14/1 Ode, 15/1 Osaichi George,
17/1 Ibn Bey, 18/1 Stylish Century, 22/1
French Glory, Phantom Breeze, 76/1
George Monarch
   G. Farrah (D. Hayes) 15ran 2m23.20
(Firm)

INDEX TO
SELECTED BIG RACES

1046

TRAINERS

The figures in brackets are the number of winners each trainer has had on the flat (turf and all-weather) in Britain over the past five years from 1986 to 1990 inclusive. Quarters and telephone numbers are given.

Aconley, Mrs V. A. (—:—:—:—:0)
Westow
Whitwell-on-the-Hill (0653 81) 594 and
Malton (0653) 695042 (home)
Akehurst, J. (—:—:—:—:4) Epsom
Epsom (03727) 23638
Akehurst, R. P. J. (16:27:25:33:34)
Whitcombe
Dorchester (0305) 260724
Allan, A. R. (0:1:1:1:1)
Cornhill-on-Tweed
Crookham (089082) 581
Allen, C. N. (—:2:7:8:19) Newmarket
Newmarket (0638) 667870 and 76767
and mobilephone (0831) 349629
Alston, E. J. (1:1:10:1:6) Preston
Longton (0772) 612120
Arbuthnot, D. W. P. (8:17:3:10:20)
Newbury Newbury (0635) 578427
Armstrong, R. W. (31:25:36:21:26)
Newmarket
Newmarket (0638) 663333 or 663334
Armytage, Mrs S. (—:—:—:0:1:1)
Malmesbury (0638) 238
Arthur, P. J. (2:4:5:6:2) Abingdon
Abingdon (0235) 850669
Austin, C. A. (3:0:0:1:0) Wokingham
Wokingham (0734) 786 425
Austin, Mrs S. M. (—:—:—:—:0)
Malton
Burythorpe (065385) 200
Avison, M. (—:—:1:0:4) Nawton
Helmsley (0439) 71672

Bailey, A. (19:30:21:12:10) Newmarket
Newmarket (0638) 661537
Bailey, K. C. (1:0:0:1:0) Lambourn
Lambourn (0488) 71483
Bailey, P. G. (1:2:2:0:0) Salisbury
Amesbury (0980) 622964 (home) and
622682 (office)
Baker, J. H. (0:0:2:0:3)
Tiverton (03985) 317 and
mobilephone (0831) 500767
Balding, G. B. (13:13:7:15:18) Weyhill
Weyhill (026 477) 2278
Balding, I. A. (48:31:43:41:48)
Kingsclere
Kingsclere (0635) 298210
Balding, J. (—:1:2:5:7) Doncaster
Doncaster (0302) 710096 and
Retford (0777) 818407 (stable)
Barker, Mrs P. A. (—:—:—:—:0)
Wetherby Wetherby (0937) 62151
Barons, D. H. (0:0:0:0:0) Kingsbridge
Kingsbridge (0548) 550326 and 550411
Barratt, L. J. (2:0:4:0:0) Oswestry
Queens Head (069 188) 209
Barron, T. D. (13:19:18:24:58) Thirsk
Thirsk (0845) 587 435

Barrow, A. K. (0:—:—:0:0) Bridgwater
Bridgwater (0278) 732522
Barwell, C. R. (—:—:—:—:0)
Tiverton (03985) 537 and 224
Bastiman, R. (—:1:3:7:12) Wetherby
Wetherby (0937) 63050
Beaumont, P. (—:—:0:0:0) Brandsby
Brandsby (03475) 208
Beever, C. R. (—:—:—:0:1) Doncaster
Doncaster (0302) 725939
Bell, C. J. (—:0:0:1:2) Doncaster
Cleckheaton (0274) 872715 and
carphone (0836) 273153 and
(0302) 350774
Bell, M. L. W. (—:—:—:18:21)
Newmarket
Newmarket (0638) 666567
Bennett, J. A. (—:0:0:0:0) Sparsholt
Childrey (023559) 635
Bennett, R. A. (—:—:0:1:4)
Maidenhead
Maidenhead (0628) 30290
Benstead, C. J. (14:12:14:9:6) Epsom
Ashtead (037 22) 73152
Bentley, W. (1:8:0:1:1) Middleham
Wensleydale (0969) 22289
Berry, J. (21:31:70:92:127) Lancaster
Forton (0524) 791179
Bethell, J. D. W. (6:2:4:11:10) Didcot
Abingdon (0235) 834333
Bevan, P. J. (2:4:0:0:0) Kingstone
Dapple Heath (0889) 500647 (yard) or
500670 (home)
Bill, T. T. (0:1:0:0:0) Ashby-de-la-Zouch
Ashby-de-la-Zouch (0530) 415881
Bishop, K. S. (0:0:0:0:0) Bridgwater
Spaxton (027867) 437
Blanshard, M. T. W. (4:5:3:8:5)
Lambourn Lambourn (0488) 71091
Blockley, P. A. (0:0:3:2:3) Catwick
Hornsea (0964) 542583 (home) and
562440 (stable)
Blum, G. (8:2:3:1:2) Newmarket
Newmarket (0638) 713916
Bolton, M. J. (3:0:0:0:2) East Grinstead
Shrewton (0980) 621059
Booth, C. B. B. (5:6:7:4:4) Flaxton
Whitwell-on-the-Hill (065 381) 586
Bosley, J. R. (2:1:0:0:0) Bampton
Bampton Castle (0993) 850 212
Boss, R. (21:19:23:23:36) Newmarket
Newmarket (0638) 661335
Bostock, J. R. (—:—:—:—:1) Swaffham
Kings Lynn (0553) 765231
Bottomley, J. F. (—:—:—:4:5) Malton
Malton (0653) 694597 (stable)
Bower, Miss L. J. (2:0:0:0:0) Alresford
Bramdean (096 279) 552
Bowring, S. R. (0:2:7:2:4) Mansfield
Mansfield (0623) 822451

1047

Bradley, J. M. (0:2:2:1:4) Chepstow
Chepstow (0291) 622486
Bradstock, M. F. (—:—:0:0:0) East
Garston
Great Shefford (048839) 8801
Brassey, K. M. (17:14:16:13:14)
Lambourn Lambourn (0488) 71508
Bravery, C. V. (—:—:0:1:0) Jevington
Polegate (03212) 3662
Brazington, R. G. (0:0:0:0:0)
Redmarley, Glos.
Staunton Court (045 284) 384
Brennan, O. (1:1:2:0:2) Newark
Caunton (063 686) 332
Bridger, J. J. (0:0:0:0:2) Chichester
Liphook (0428) 722528
Bridgwater, K. S. (2:0:1:0:0) Solihull
Lapworth (05643) 2895
Brittain, C. E. (39:38:40:36:42)
Newmarket
Newmarket (0638) 663739 and 664347
Brittain, M. A. (24:57:44:26:27)
Warthill Stamford Bridge (0759) 71472
Brooks, C. P. E. (—:—:—:0:1:0)
Lambourn
Lambourn (0488) 72077 (office) and
72909 (home)
Burchell, W. D. (0:0:0:1:7) Ebbw Vale
Ebbw Vale (0495) 302551
Burgoyne, P. V. J. P. (0:3:0:0:0)
Sparsholt Childrey (023 559) 688
Burke, K. R. (—:—:—:—:0) Barnby
Fenton Claypole (0636) 84522 (home)
and 84750 and carphone (0860) 744172
Butler, P. (1:0:0:0:0) Lewes
Plumpton (0273) 890124
Bycroft, N. (6:10:10:2:2) Brandsby
Brandsby (034 75) 641

Caldwell, T. H. (—:—:—:0:0)
Warrington Arley (0565) 777275
Callaghan, N. A. (25:20:27:32:31)
Newmarket
Newmarket (0638) 664040
Calver, P. (9:7:7:7:18) Ripon
Ripon (0765) 700313
Camacho, M. J. C. (6:6:8:12:20) Malton
Malton (0653) 694901
Cambidge, B. R. (1:0:2:1:2) Shifnal
Weston-under-Lizard (095 276) 249
Campbell, I. (—:1:4:3:7) Newmarket
Newmarket (0638) 660829
Candy, H. D. N. B. (27:33:20:16:23)
Wantage Uffington (036 782) 276
Carter, W. Y. (—:—:2:23:20)
Leatherhead
Leatherhead (0372) 377209
Casey, W. T. (2:1:3:1:4) Lambourn
Lambourn (0488) 73004
Cecil, H. R. A. (115:180:112:117:111)
Newmarket
Newmarket (0638) 662192 or
662387 (home)
Chamberlain, A. J. (—:—:—:—:0)
Swindon Cirencester (0285) 861347
Chamberlain, N. (0:1:0:0:0)
West Auckland
Bishop Auckland (0388) 832 465

Champion, R. (0:0:0:1:0) Newmarket
Newmarket (0638) 666546
Channon, M. R. (—:—:—:—:16)
Lambourn (0264) 810225 and
(0488) 71149 (stable)
Chapman, D. W. (14:13:36:29:22)
Stillington Easingwold (0347) 21683
Chapman, M. C. (1:0:0:0:1)
Market Rasen
Market Rasen (0673) 843663
Charles, M. J. (—:0:0:0:1) Warwick
Warwick (0926) 493878
Charlton, J. I. A. (0:0:0:0:0) Stocksfield
Stocksfield (0661) 843 247
Charlton, R. J. (—:—:—:—:37)
Beckhampton (06723) 533 (office) and
330 (home)
Christian, S. P. L. (0:1:1:0:0)
Kinnersley
Severn Stoke (090567) 233
Clay, W. (0:0:0:0:0) Fulford
Stoke-on-Trent (0782) 392 131
Codd, L. J. (—:—:—:3:0) Redditch
Inkberrow (0386) 793263
Cole, P. F. I. (64:55:43:51:53)
Whatcombe
Chaddleworth (04882) 433 or 434
Collingridge, H. J. (4:6:7:12:7)
Newmarket
Newmarket (0638) 665454
Cottrell, L. G. (8:23:19:12:4)
Cullompton
Kentisbeare (088 46) 320
Craig, T. (4:6:1:4:1) Dunbar
Dunbar (0368) 62583
Cumani, L. M. (67:83:73:88: 109)
Newmarket
Newmarket (0638) 665432
Cundell, P. D. (13:8:5:1:0) Newbury
Newbury (0635) 578267
Cunningham, T. W. (—:0:0:0:0)
Northallerton
East Harlsey (060982) 695
Cunningham-Brown, K. O. (0:1:0:7:4)
Stockbridge
Andover (0264) 781611
Curley, B. J. (—:0:1:0:3) Newmarket
Stetchworth (063850) 8251
Curtis, R. (—:—:3:3:4)
Epsom (0372) 277645
Cyzer, C. A. (—:—:—:14:9) Horsham
Southwater (0403) 730455
Czerpak, J. D. (—:—:—:0:2) Farnham
Frensham (Surrey) (025125) 3505

Davies, J. D. J. (0:2:0:0:0) Dymchurch
Folkestone (0303) 874089
Davison, A. R. (1:0:2:0:0) Caterham
Caterham (0883) 44523
Denson, A. W. (—:0:0:1:0) Epsom
Epsom (03727) 29398
Dickin, R. (0:0:0:0:1) Dymock
Dymock (053185) 644
Dooler, J. (—:—:—:0:0) Goole
Goole (0405) 861903
Dow, S. L. (3:0:6:7:5) Guildford
Epsom (03727) 21490 (stable) and
Ashtead (03722) 75878 (home)

Dunlop, J. L. (106:61:66:66:78) Arundel
  Arundel (0903) 882 194 (office) or
  882 106 (home)
Durr, F. (4:10:2:10:5) Newmarket
  Newmarket (0638) 730030
Dutton, D. (—:—:—:—:0) Malton
  North Grimston (09446) 364
Dwyer, C. A. (—:—:—:—:0)
  Malton (09442) 8894

Earnshaw, R. (—:0:0:3:4) Harrogate
  Harrogate (0423) 567790
Easterby, M. H. (49:68:64:57:61)
  Malton
  Kirby Misperton (065 386) 566
Easterby, M. W. (33:12:25:19:25)
  Sheriff Hutton
  Sheriff Hutton (03477) 368
Eckley, M. W. (4:5:4:1:1) Ludlow
  Brimfield (058 472) 372
Eckley, R. J. (—:—:—:—:0) Kington
  Lyonshall (05448) 216
Eden, G. H. (—:—:—:—:2) Newmarket
  Newmarket (0638) 667938
Edwards, J. A. C. (1:5:6:1:0)
  Ross-on-Wye
  Harewood End (098987) 259 and
  639 (home)
Eldin, E. (17:6:10:10:10) Newmarket
  Newmarket (0638) 662036 or
  663 217
Ellerby, M. W. (0:0:0:1:0) Pickering
  Pickering (0751) 74092
Ellison, B. (—:—:—:—:0) Burythorpe
  Malton (0653) 600 158
Elsey, C. C. (—:—:—:3:8) Lambourn
  Lambourn (0488) 71 242
Elsey, C. W. C. (7:13:10:10:9) Malton
  Malton (0653) 693 149
Elsworth, D. R. C. (31:31:28:35:44)
  Fordingbridge
  Rockbourne (07253) 220 (home) or
  528 (office)
Enright, G. P. (—:—:0:1:0)
  Haywards Heath
  Lewes (0273) 479 183
Etherington, J. (16:11:11:18:17) Malton
  Malton (0653) 692842
Eustace, J. M. P. (—:—:—:0:6)
  Newmarket
  Newmarket (0638) 664277
Evans, P. D. (—:—:—:0:0) Welshpool
  Trewern (093874) 288

Fairhurst, T. (16:8:10:11:12) Middleham
  Wensleydale (0969) 23362
Fanshawe, J. R. (—:—:—:0:18)
  Newmarket
  Newmarket (0638) 660 153 and 664525
Feilden, P. J. (2:0:1:7:6) Newmarket
  Exning (063877) 637
Felgate, P. S. (11:8:17:12:10)
  Melton Mowbray
  Melton Mowbray (0664) 812019
Fetherston-Godley, M. J. (9:6:10:2:7)
  East Ilsley   East Ilsley (063 528) 250
Ffitch-Heyes, J. R. (0:2:0:0:1) Lewes
  Brighton (0273) 480804

Fisher, R. F. (2:4:2:1:0) Ulverston
  Ulverston (0229) 55664 and
  558 19 (office)
FitzGerald, J. G. (17:7:20:22:21)
  Malton   Malton (0653) 692718
FitzGerald, Lord J. (11:11:9:11:5)
  Newmarket
  Newmarket (0638) 660605
Forsey, B. (0:0:1:0:0) Crowcombe
  Crowcombe (098 48) 270
Forster, T. A. (0:0:0:0:0)
  Letcombe Bassett
  Wantage (023 57) 3092
Fox, J. C. (2:0:1:3:2) Amesbury
  Shrewton (0980) 620 861
Francis, M. E. D. (7:8:8:4:3) Lambourn
  Lambourn (0488) 71700
Francis, R. B. (0:0:0:0:0) Malpas
  Tilston (0829) 250208 (office) and
  250515 (home)
Frost, R. G. (0:1:0:0:0) Buckfastleigh
  Buckfastleigh (03644) 2267

Gandolfo, D. R. (0:0:0:0:0) Wantage
  Wantage (023 57) 3242
Garraton, D. T. (—:—:—:—:0)
Gaselee, N. A. D. C. (0:1:3:2:0)
  Lambourn   Lambourn (0488) 71503
Gifford, J. T. (0:0:0:0:3)
  Findon (0903) 872226
Glover, J. A. (3:8:12:3:5) Worksop
  Worksop (0909) 475962 or
  475425 (stable)
Gosden, J. H. M. (—:—:—:28:87)
  Newmarket
  Newmarket (0638) 669944
Gracey, G. G. (1:0:0:0:0) Winkfield
  Winkfield Row (0344) 890461
Graham, N. A. (—:—:11:—:6)
  Newmarket
  Newmarket (0638) 665202 (office) and
  667851 (home)
Grissell, D. M. (0:0:—:0:0) Heathfield
  Brightling (042 482) 241
Gubby, B. (0:0:1:0:7) Bagshot
  Bagshot (0276) 63282 and
  71030 (evenings)
Guest, R. (—:—:—:7:7) Newmarket
  Newmarket (0638) 661508

Haggas, W. J. (0:17:14:16:21)
  Newmarket
  Newmarket (0638) 667013
Haigh, W. W. (7:7:3:3:5) Malton
  Malton (0653) 694428
Haine, Mrs D. E. S. (—:—:0:1:0)
  Newmarket   Exning (063877) 719
Haldane, J. S. (1:1:1:0:0) Kelso
  Kelso (0573) 24956
Hall, Miss P. J. (—:—:—:—:0)
  Grantham   Grantham (0476) 860891
Hall, Miss S. E. (12:9:7:6:12)
  Middleham
  Wensleydale (0969) 40223
Hallett, T. B. (4:0:0:0:0) Saltash
  Saltash (0752) 846829
Ham, G. A. (—:—:—:—:0) Axbridge
  Edingworth (0934) 750331

1049

Hammond, M. D. (—:—:—:—:5)
Middleham
Wensleydale (0969) 40228
Hanbury, B. (24:31:40:42:36)
Newmarket
Newmarket (0638) 663193 (stable) and
Wickhambrook (0440) 820396 (home)
Hannon, R. M. (56:33:43:55:73)
Marlborough
Collingbourne Ducis (0264) 850254
Harris, J. L. (0:0:0:0:6)
Melton Mowbray
Harby (0949) 60671
Harris, P. W. (0:0:0:2:8) Berkhamsted
Hemel Hempstead (0442) 842 480
Harris, S. T. (0:0:0:0:2) Amersham
Chesham (0494) 715446
Harrison, R. A. (—:—:—:—:7)
Middleham
Wensleydale (0969) 23788
Harwood, G. (112:67:73:109:69)
Pulborough
Pulborough (079 82) 3011 or 3012
Hastings-Bass, W. E. R. H.
(30:15:31:26:20)
West Ilsley (0635) 28747 or
28725 (stable)
Haynes, M. J. (5:10:11:6:9) Epsom
Burgh Heath (073 73) 51140
Hayward, P. A. (—:2:0:1:1) Netheravon
Netheravon (0980) 70585
Henderson, N. J. (0:0:0:0:0) Lambourn
Lambourn (0488) 72259
Hern, W. R. (45:36:30:45:30) Lambourn
Herries, Lady (2:6:6:9:4) Arundel
Patching (090674) 421
Hetherton, J. (—:—:—:2:4) Malton
Malton (0653) 696778
Hide, A. G. (9:8:8:11:10) Newmarket
Newmarket (0638) 662063
Hill, C. J. (3:2:5:3:11) Barnstaple
Barnstaple (0271) 42048
Hills, B. W. (55:96:93:73:113)
Marlborough
Marlborough (0672) 514901 (office)
and 514871 (home)
Hills, J. W. (—:13:14:16:28) Lambourn
Lambourn (0488) 71548
Hoad, R. P. C. (1:0:1:0:2) Lewes
Brighton (0273) 477124
Hobbs, P. J. (0:0:0:0:0) Watchet
Washford (0984) 40366
Hodges, R. J. (5:2:8:12:25)
Somerton
Charlton Mackrell (045822) 3922
Holden, W. (6:5:4:3:1) Newmarket
Exning (063 877) 384
Holder, R. J. (8:13:8:17:16) Portbury
Pill (027 581) 2192 and 4185
Hollinshead, R. (28:28:33:30:41) Upper
Longdon
Armitage (0543) 490298 and
490490
Holmes, C. J. (0:0:0:0:0)
Gerrards Cross
Chalfont St Giles (02407) 5964
Holt, L. J. (9:9:6:13:6) Tunworth
Basingstoke (0256) 463376

Horgan, C. A. (15:1:6:9:3) Billingbear
Winkfield Row (0344) 425382
Houghton, R. F. J. (34:26:36:24:25)
Blewbury
Blewbury (0235) 850480
Howling, P. (—:5:9:5:6)
Brook (0428) 794065 (stable)
Hudson, J. P. (—:—:—:10:5) Lambourn
Lambourn (0488) 71485
Huffer, G. A. (17:23:12:16:21)
Newmarket
Newmarket (0638) 667997

Incisa, D. E. (1:1:2:0:2) Leyburn
Wensleydale (0969) 40653
Ivory, K. T. (9:18:7:7:7)
Radlett (0923) 855337

Jackson, C. F. C. (0:3:2:0:0) Malvern
Malvern (0886) 880463
James, A. P. (0:0:0:0:0)
(0885) 410240
James, C. J. (1:4:6:1:1) Newbury
Great Shefford (048 839) 280
James, M. B. C. (1:0:2:0:0) Whitchurch
Whitchurch (0948) 4067
Jarvis, M. A. (30:19:31:28:28)
Newmarket
Newmarket (0638) 661702 and 662519
Jarvis, W. (16:27:26:32:31) Newmarket
Newmarket (0638) 669873 (office) or
662677 (home)
Jefferson, J. M. (2:5:4:1:0) Malton
Malton (0653) 697225
Jenkins, J. R. (1:8:15:10:13) Royston
Royston (0763) 241141 (office) and
246611 (home)
Jermy, D. C. (0:0:0:0:0) Warminster
Warminster (0985) 213155
Johnson, J. H. (0:0:0:0:1)
Bishop Auckland
Bishop Auckland (0388) 762113 and
730872
Johnston, M. S. (—:1:5:15:28)
Middleham
Wensleydale (0969) 22237
Jones, A. W. (1:1:0:1:1) Oswestry
Oswestry (0691) 659 720
Jones, D. H. (13:4:6:3:7) Pontypridd
Pontypridd (0443) 202515
Jones, Mrs G. E. (—:—:0:0:0)
Upton-on-Severn
Upton-on-Severn (06846) 2691
Jones, G. H. (—:0:0:0:0) Tenbury Wells
Leysters (056887) 676 and
305 (stable)
Jones, H. Thomson (43:30:41:37:34)
Newmarket
Newmarket (0638) 664884
Jones, P. J. (0:0:0:0:0) Marlborough
Lockeridge (067286) 427
Jones, T. M. (0:0:4:0:2) Guildford
Shere (048 641) 2604
Jones, T. Thomson (—:—:—:7:8)
Lambourn
Lambourn (0488) 71596 and 72933
Jordan, F. T. J. (1:3:1:3:1) Leominster
Steens Bridge (056 882) 281

1050

Juckes, R. T. (0:0:0:0:0)
 Abberley (Worcs)
 Great Witley (0299) 896471

Kelleway, P. A. (18:12:16:13:8)
 Newmarket
 Newmarket (0638) 661461
Kelly, G. P. (—:0:0:0:0) Sheriff Hutton
 Sheriff Hutton (03477) 518
Kemp, W. T. (1:0:0:0:0) Ashford (Kent)
 Ashford (0233) 72525
Kernick, N. (0:0:0:0:0)
 Kingsteignton (0364) 42755
Kersey, T. (0:0:0:1:0) West Melton
 Rotherham (0709) 873166
Kettlewell, S. E. (—:1:0:0:1)
 Middleham
 Wensleydale (0969) 40295
King, Mrs A. L. M. (1:3:0:0:1)
 Stratford-on-Avon
 Stratford-on-Avon (0789) 205087
King, J. S. (1:2:0:4:2) Swindon
 Broad Hinton (0793) 731481
King, R. V. C. (—:—:—:—:0) Exning
Knight, Mrs A. J. (—:0:0:0:0)
 Cullompton
 Hemyock (0823) 680959
Knight, Miss H. C. (—:—:—:—:0)
 Wantage
 East Hendred (0235) 833535

Leach, M. R. (0:0:1:0:0) Newark
 Fenton Claypole (0636) 626518
Leach, P. S. (—:—:—:0:1) Taunton
 Bishop's Lydeard (0823) 433249
Leadbetter, S. J. (0:0:0:0:0) Ladykirk
 Berwick-upon-Tweed (0289) 382519
Lee, A. N. (—:—:2:8:7) Newmarket
 Newmarket (0638) 662734 (home) and
 669783 (stable)
Lee, D. (0:0:0:0:0) Pickering
 Pickering (0751) 32425
Lee, F. H. (—:2:8:27:25) Wilmslow
 Wilmslow (0625) 529672 and
 533250 (stud)
Lee, R. A. (—:0:0:0:0) Presteigne
 Presteigne (0544) 267672 and
 mobilephone (0836) 537145
Leigh, J. P. (0:3:3:1:4)
 Willoughton (Lincs)
 Hemswell (042 773) 210
Lewis, G. (25:25:32:23:26) Epsom
 Ashtead (037 22) 77662 or
 77366
Liddle, P. (—:—:—:0:0)
 Chester-le-Street
 Wearside 091-410-2072
Long, J. E. (0:1:0:0:0) Plumpton
 Plumpton (0273) 890244
Lungo, L. (—:—:—:—:0)
 Carrutherstown (0387) 84691

Macauley, Mrs N. J. (4:7:6:14:24)
 Sproxton
 Grantham (0476) 860578 and
 860090 (office)
Mackie, W. J. W. (1:0:9:6:8) Derby
 Sudbury (028378) 604

Madgwick, M. J. (2:1:2:3:5) Denmead
 Horndean (0705) 258313
Makin, P. J. (19:18:24:29:27)
 Ogbourne Maisey
 Marlborough (0672) 512973
Manning, R. J. (—:—:—:—:0)
 Winterbourne (Avon)
 Winterbourne (0454) 773274
Marks, D. (3:3:1:2:1) Lambourn
 Lambourn (0488) 71767
Marvin, R. F. (—:—:—:—:0) Newark
 Mansfield (0623) 822714
McCain, D. (0:0:0:0:0) Southport
 Cholmondeley (0829) 720352
McCauley, K. B. (—:—:—:—:6)
 Melsonby
 Darlington (0325) 718008
McConnochie, J. C. (—:—:—:0:0)
 Stratford-on-Avon
 Alderminster (078987) 607
McCormack, M. (16:7:4:12:5) Wantage
 Childrey (023 559) 433
McCourt, M. (8:4:1:3:2)
 Letcombe Regis
 Wantage (023 57) 4456
McGovern, T. P. (—:—:—:—:0)
 Lambourn (0488) 72999
McLean, B. (0:0:0:0:0) Morpeth
 Morpeth (0670) 787478 and
 787314 (home)
McMahon, B. A. (8:6:20:21:22)
 Tamworth   Tamworth (0827) 62901
McMath, B. J. (—:—:—:—:0)
 Timworth   Culford (028484) 439
Mellor, S. T. E. (8:3:2:2:0) Wanborough
 Swindon (0793) 790230
Millman, B. R. (—:—:—:—:12)
 Cullompton (0884) 6620 and
 carphone (0860) 661854
Mitchell, N. R. (0:0:0:0:0)
 Piddletrenthide
 Cerne Abbas (03003) 651
Mitchell, P. (9:5:12:15:13) Epsom
 Ashtead (037 22) 73729
Mitchell, P. (Pat) K. (4:6:2:6:11)
 Newmarket
 Newmarket (0638) 660013
Moffatt, D. (3:2:0:2:1) Cartmel
 Cartmel (05395) 36689
Monteith, P. (1:2:3:1:2) Rosewell
 Edinburgh (031-440) 2309
Moore, A. (5.1.0:4:3) Woodingdean
 Brighton (0273) 681679
Moore, G. M. (10:18:12:18:10)
 Middleham
 Wensleydale (0969) 23823
Moore, J. S. (—:—:—:—:0) Thruxton
Morgan, B. C. (1:6:6:3:2)
 Barton-under-Needwood
 Hoar Cross (028 375) 304
Morgan, K. A. (0:0:0:0:0)
 Waltham-on-the-Wolds
 Waltham-on-the-Wolds (066478) 711
Morley, M. F. D. (16:19:30:26:25)
 Newmarket
 Newmarket (0638) 667175
Morrill, D. (—:—:—:—:0)
 Market Rasen (077587) 444

Morris, D. (—:—:—:—:2) Newmarket
Newmarket (0638) 667959
Moubarak, M. Y. (—:—:1:1:15)
Newmarket
Newmarket (0638) 666553
Muddle, R. J. (—:—:—:—:0)
Newark (0636) 814481
Muggeridge, M. P. (—:—:—:—:1)
Marlborough
Collingbourne Ducis (0264) 850652
Mulhall, J. L. (2:0:0:0:0) York
York (0904) 706321
Murphy, M. P. F. (—:—:—:—:0:0)
Bury St Edmunds
Culford (028484) 8980 and
Newmarket (0638) 665328
Murray, B. W. (—:—:—:—:0) Malton
Malton (0653) 692879
Murray-Smith, D. J. G. (4:2:9:8:9)
Upper Lambourn
Lambourn (0488) 71041
Musson, W. J. (21:14:10:6:4)
Newmarket
Newmarket (0638) 663371

Naughton, M. P. (3:7:8:19:12)
Richmond (N Yorks)
Richmond (0748) 2803
Nelson, C. R. (26:26:22:19:30)
Lambourn
Lambourn (0488) 71391
Nicholson, D. (1:0:0:0:0) Condicote
Cotswold (045 1) 30417
Norton, J. (0:0:2:0:0) Barnsley
Barnsley (0226) 387633
Norton, S. G. (21:33:33:11:20) Barnsley
Wakefield (0924) 830450 and
830406 (office)

O'Donoghue, J. (0:0:0:0:0) Reigate
Reigate (073 72) 45241
O'Gorman, W. A. (20:10:24:10:51)
Newmarket
Newmarket (0638) 663330
Old, J. A. B. (0:1:1:0:1) Ditcheat
Ditcheat (074986) 656 and
carphone (0836) 721459
Oldroyd, G. R. (3:1:2:0:1) Malton
Malton (0653) 695991 (home) and
Burythorpe (065385) 224 (stable)
O'Leary, R. M. (—:0:1:2:0) Malton
Kirby Misperton (065386) 684 and 404
Oliver, Mrs S. (1:1:0:1:0) Himley
Wombourne (0902) 892648 (stable)
and 892017 (home)
O'Mahony, F. J. (—:—:—:—:0)
Dormansland
Lingfield (0342) 833278
O'Neill, J. J. (0:0:1:0:8) Penrith
Skelton (08534) 555
O'Neill, M. J. (—:—:—:9:12) Lydiate
Liverpool 051-531 9616 (office),
6887 (home) and 526 9115 (evening)
O'Neill, O. (0:0:1:0:2) Cheltenham
Bishops Cleeve (024 267) 3275
O'Shea, J. G. M. (—:0:0:0:0)
Kidderminster
Kidderminster (0562) 823160

O'Sullivan, R. J. (—:—:0:7:6) Bognor
Pagham (02432) 67563
Owen, E. H. (0:0:0:1:0) Denbigh
Llandyrnog (08244) 264 and 356

Palling, B. (2:1:1:4:4) Cowbridge
Cowbridge (044 63) 2089
Parker, C. (0:0:0:0:0) Lockerbie
Kettleholme (05765) 232
Parkes, J. E. (0:0:1:6:2) Malton
Malton (0653) 697570
Parrott, Mrs H. K. (—:—:—:—:0)
Deerhurst
Tewkesbury (0684) 292214
Payne, J. W. (2:9:9:5:4) Newmarket
Newmarket (0638) 668675
Payne, S. G. (—:—:—:—:0) Carlisle
Aspatria (06973) 20010
Peacock, R. E. (2:0:2:3:1) Tarporley
Tarporley (0829) 732716
Pearce, J. N. (—:3:3:5:13) Newmarket
Newmarket (0638) 664669
Pearce, W. J. (7:8:18:24:21) Hambleton
Thirsk (0845) 597373
Perrin, W. M. (—:—:—:—:0)
Buntingford   Barkway (076 384) 8113
Piggott, Mrs S. E. (—:1:17:34:13)
Newmarket
Newmarket (0638) 662584
Pipe, M. C. (4:16:5:2:10)
Wellington (Somerset)
Craddock (0884) 840715
Pitman, Mrs J. S. (0:0:2:2:1) Lambourn
Lambourn (0488) 71714
Popham, C. L. (—:0:0:0:0)
Bishop's Lydeard
Bishop's Lydeard (0823) 432769
Potts, A. W. (1:0:0:0:0)
Barton-on-Humber
Saxby All Saints (065 26 1) 750
Preece, W. G. (0:1:2:0:0) Telford
Uppington (095 286) 249
Prescott, Sir Mark (39:26:34:40;48)
Newmarket
Newmarket (0638) 662117
Price, G. H. (5:1:10:1:1) Leominster
Steens Bridge (056 882) 235
Pritchard-Gordon, G. A.
(37:35:20:16:18) Newmarket
Newmarket (0638) 662824
Pritchard, P. A. (—:—:0:0:0)
Shipston-on-Stour
Tysoe (029588) 689

Radbourne, Miss D. J. (—:—:—:—:0)
Droitwich (029923) 301
Ramsden, Mrs L. E. (—:11:14:32:26)
Sandhutton   Thirsk (0845) 587226
Redmond, J. V. (—:—:—:—:0)
Guildford
Guildford (0483) 892233
Rees, Miss G. M. (—:—:—:—:0)
Scunthorpe
Scunthorpe (0724) 863347
Reveley, Mrs M. (6:20:12:15:15)
Saltburn (0287) 50456
Richards, G. W. (0:1:1:0:2) Greystoke
Greystoke (085 33) 392

Richmond, B. A. (0:1:0:0:0) Wellingore
  Lincoln (0522) 8 10578
Ringer, D. J. (—:—:0:0:0) Newmarket
  Newmarket (0638) 662653 and
  66602 1 (home)
Roberts, J. D. (0:0:0:1:0) Tiverton
  Bampton (0398) 3 1626
Robinson, M. H. B. (—:1:0:0:0)
  Wantage Wantage (0235) 835050
Robinson, W. R. (0:0:0:0:0)
  Scarborough
  Scarborough (0723) 862 162
Roe, C. G. A. M. (—:0:0:0:0) Chalford
  Brimscombe (0453) 885487
Ryan, M. J. (33:29:22: 13:32)
  Newmarket
  Newmarket (0638) 664 172

Sanders, Miss B. V. J. (1:5:14:7:4)
  Epsom Ashtead (03722) 78453
Scargill, Dr J. D. (—:—:9:8: 18)
  Newmarket
  Newmarket (0638) 663254
Scott, A. A. (—:—:—:24:29)
  Newmarket
  Newmarket (0638) 66 1998
Scudamore, M. J. (0:0:0:0:0)
  Hoarwithy Carey (043 270) 253
Sharpe, Mrs N. S. A. (—:0:0:0:0)
  Leominster
  Leominster (0568) 2673
Shaw, J. R. (6:4:1:2:2) Newmarket
  Newmarket (0638) 66 1680
Sherwood, O. M. C. (0:0:2:0:0)
  Upper Lambourn
  Lambourn (0488) 7 14 11
Sherwood, S. E. H. (—:—:—:—:0)
  East Ilsley (063528) 678
Siddall, Miss L. C. (7:2:9:8:4) York
  Appleton Roebuck (090 484) 29 1
Simpson, R. (14: 14:8:7:6)
  Upper Lambourn
  Lambourn (0488) 72688
Smart, D. (0:0:0:0:0) Lambourn
  Lambourn (0488) 7 1632
Smith, A. (1:1:3:1:1) Beverley
  Beverley (0482) 882520
Smith, D. (20: 16: 14: 15:8)
  Bishop Auckland
  Bishop Auckland (0388) 603317 and
  606 180
Smith, J. P. (0:2:0:1:0) Rugeley
  Burntwood (054 36) 6587
Smith, N. A. (—:—:—:—:0) Evesham
  Evesham (0386) 860 13 1
Smyth, R. V. (9:6: 12: 10: 1 1) Epsom
  Epsom (037 27) 20053
Spearing, J. L. (5:5:3:8: 13) Alcester
  Bidford-on-Avon (0789) 772639
Stephenson, W. A. (4:1:0:0:0)
  Bishop Auckland
  Rushyford (0388) 7202 13 and
  720432 (hostel)
Stevens, B. (7:1:0:2:0) Winchester
  Winchester (0962) 883030
Stewart, A. C. (26:37:40:30:4 1)
  Newmarket
  Newmarket (0638) 667323

Storey, W. L. (3:1:0:0:0) Consett
  Edmundbyers (0207) 55259
Stoute, M. R. (76: 105:99: 116:78)
  Newmarket
  Newmarket (0638) 66380 1
Stringer, A. P. (—:—:—:2:5)
  Carlton Husthwaite
  Thirsk (0845) 40 1329
Stubbs, R. W. (10:9: 12:8:9) Newmarket
  Newmarket (0638) 560014
Sutcliffe, J. R. E. (16: 13: 12: 18: 17)
  Epsom Ashtead (037 22) 72825

Tate, F. M. (0:0:0:0:0) Kidderminster
  Chaddesley Corbett (056 283) 243
Thom, D. T. (7: 12: 10:6: 11) Newmarket
  Exning (063 877) 288
Thompson, R. (0:2:0:4: 1) Grantham
  Castle Bytham (0780) 4 108 12
Thompson, Ronald (6:8:7:5:7)
  Doncaster
  Doncaster (0302) 842 857, 845904 and
  840 174
Thompson, V. (0:0:0:0:0) Alnwick
  Embleton (066 576) 272
Thorne, Miss J. C. (0:0:0:1:0)
  Bridgwater
  Holford (027 874) 588
Thornton, C. W. (5: 14: 15: 12: 12)
  Middleham
  Wensleydale (0969) 23350
Tinkler, C. H. (2 1:3 1:24:35:29) Malton
  Malton (0653) 69598 1
Tinkler, N. D. (30:3 1:24:24: 17) Malton
  Burythorpe (065385) 245 and 5 12
Toller, J. A. R. (7: 15:6:7:7) Newmarket
  Newmarket (0638) 668503
Tompkins, M. H. (19:24: 16:44:46)
  Newmarket
  Newmarket (0638) 66 1434
Topley, D. H. (—:—:—:1:0) Esh
  Wearside 091-373 5460 (office) and
  03 12 (home) and 091-384 0989
Trietline, C. C. (0:0:0:0:0)
  Welford-on-Avon
  Stratford-on-Avon (0789) 750 294
Tucker, D. C. (2:0:0:0:0) Frome
  Frome (0373) 62383
Tucker, D. R. (0:1:0:0:0) Cullompton
  Hemyock (0823) 680 159
Turnell, A. (1:1:2:4:2) East Hendred
  East Hendred (0235 833) 297
Turner, W. G. (0:—:0:0:0) Tavistock
  Mary Tavy (082 28 1) 237
Turner, W. (Bill) G. M. (1:5:3:6:2)
  Corton Denham
  Corton Denham (096322) 523
Twiston-Davies, N. A. (—:—:—:0:0)
  Cheltenham
  Guiting Power (045 15) 278

Usher, M. D. I. (16: 15:8: 14: 12)
  East Garston
  Lambourn (0488) 398953/4 (office)
  and 7 1307 (home)

Voorspuy, R. (2:3:2:0: 1) Polegate
  Polegate (032 12) 7 133

1053

Wainwright, J. S. (—:2:2:4:3) Malton
Burythorpe (065385) 537
Wall, C. F. (—:9:13:9:15) Newmarket
Newmarket (0638) 66 1999
Walwyn, P. T. (43:36:30:36:48)
Lambourn   Lambourn (0488) 7 1347
Wardle, I. P. (0:0:1:0:1) Newmarket
Newmarket (0638) 666388
Waring, Mrs B. H. (1:0:2:1:5)
Malmesbury (0225) 742044
Watson, F. (0:0:0:1:0) Sedgefield
Sedgefield (0740) 20582
Watts, J. W. (24:32:23:25:27)
Richmond   Richmond (0748) 850444
Weaver, R. J. (—:0:—:0:0) Leicester
Markfield (0530) 243 105
Webber, J. H. (0:0:0:0:0) Banbury
Cropredy (0295) 750226 and
750466 (stable) and
mobilephone (0836) 580 129
Weedon, C. V. (—:—:—:—:0)
Chiddingfold
Wormley (0428) 683344
Weymes, E. (5:4:10:6:5) Leyburn
Wensleydale (0969) 40229
Wharton, J. (—:—:9:13:15)
Melton Mowbray
Melton Mowbray (0664) 78334
(stable) and 65225 (home)
Wheeler, E. A. (0:3:4:2:7) Lambourn
Lambourn (0488) 7 1650
Whitaker, R. M. (27:33:49:29:36)
Wetherby
Leeds (0532) 892265 and
Wetherby (0937) 62 122
White, J. R. (—:—:0:5:2) Wendover
Wendover (0296) 623387
White, K. B. (0:2:1:0:1) Craven Arms
Munslow (058 476) 200
Whitfield, Miss A. J. (—:—:—:0:4)
Lambourn   Lambourn (0488) 72342
Whiting, H. A. T. (4:1:—:—:0)
Broadway
Broadway (0386) 858489 and 852569
Wigham, P. (2:0:0:0:1) Malton
Rillington (094 42) 332
Wightman, W. G. R. (3:7:3:8:3) Upham
Bishop's Waltham (0489) 892565
Wildman, C. P. (0:3:1:3:3) Salisbury
Durrington Walls (0980) 52226
Wilkinson, B. E. (0:0:0:0:0) Middleham
Wensleydale (0969) 23385
Wilkinson, M. J. (0:0:0:0:0)
Chipping Warden
Chipping Warden (029586) 7 13
Williams, C. N. (1:1:1:2;4) Newmarket
Newmarket (0638) 665 116
Williams, D. L. (0:0:0:0:0) Peasemore
Newbury (0635) 248969 and
mobilephone (0836) 547894

Williams, R. J. R. (25:26:18:17:15)
Newmarket
Newmarket (0638) 663 2 18
Williams, W.R. (0:0:0:—:0) Idestone
Exeter (0392) 8 1558
Wilson, A. J. (0:0:0:0:0) Cheltenham
Cheltenham (0242) 244 7 13
Wilson, D. A. (1:9:7:15:19) Headley
Ashtead (03722) 78327 (office) and
73839 (home)
Wilson, Capt. J. H. (8:5:11:8:7) Preston
Hesketh Bank (0772) 8 12780
Wilson, J. S. (13:7:8:13:22) Ayr
Ayr (0292) 266232
Wilson, W. T. J. (—:—:2:0:0)
Newmarket
Newmarket (0638) 66 1393
Wilton, Miss S. J. (—:—:0:0:0)
Stoke-on-Trent
Stoke-on-Trent (0782) 550861
Wingrove, K. G. (—:—:—:0:0) Rugby
Southam (092 681) 3958
Wintle, D. J. (0:1:0:0:0)
Westbury-on-Severn
Westbury-on-Severn (045 276) 459
and 825
Wise, B. J. (2:0:0:0:0) Polegate
Polegate (032 12) 333 1 and 2505
Woodhouse, R. D. E. (4:0:0:0:0) York
Whitwell-on-the-Hill (065 38 1) 637
Woodman, S. (—:2:0:0:0) Chichester
Chichester (0243) 527 136
Wragg, G. (32:27:31:25:32) Newmarket
Newmarket (0638) 662328

Yardley, F. J. (1:1:1:1:1) Ombersley
Worcester (0905) 620477
Yeoman, D. (0:1:0:0:0)
Sherburn (N Yorks)
Sherburn (0944) 70088

The following relinquished their licence
during the season

Brooks, W. G. A. (2:5:4:5:1)
Dods, R. W. the late (—:—:—:—:1)
Morris, W. G. (0:0:0:0:0)
Robson, A. M. (2:1:3:5:2)
Salmon, P. (—:—:—:—:0)
Semple, I. (—:—:—:0:0)
Spares, C. W. (0:3:2:0:0)
Wharton, Mrs V. R. T. (—:—:—:0:0)

The following had their licence
withdrawn

Browne, D. W. P. (—:—:—:—:0)
Muldoon, S. J. (—:1:9:4:0)

1054

JOCKEYS

The figures in brackets show the number of winners each jockey has ridden on the flat (turf and all-weather) in Britain during the past five years from 1986 to 1990 inclusive. Also included are telephone numbers and riding weights.

Elliott, R. P. (8:8:10:19:22) 8   0
Wensleydale (0969) 22884

Fahey, R. A. (—:—:—:—:0) 9   0
York (0904) 6472 13 (agent) and
Kirby Misperton (065386) 635 and
mobilephone (0836) 567580

Fallon, K. F. (—:—:31:28:39) 8   1
York (0904) 6472 13 (agent) and
Malton (0653) 693087 (home)

Fox, R. D. S. (9:20:16:11:6) 7   7
Newmarket (0638) 778 188 and
Peterborough (0733) 263816 (agent)

Giles, M. A. (3:3:3:4:12) 7   7
(0904) 6472 13 (agent)

Guest, E. J. (15:0:—:1:5) 8   7
Newmarket (0638) 721183 and
(0253) 8 12 194 (agent)

Hill, P. D. (4:10:0:—:0) 7   7
Cannock (05435) 78213 and
c/o Tamworth (0827) 62901

Hills, M. P. (40:75:76:77:61) 8   0
Newmarket (0638) 750379 and
75 1421 (agent)

Hills, R. J. (42:46:52:63:56) 8   0
Newmarket (0638) 750379 and
75 1421 (agent)

Hindley, M. G. (3:2:0:1:0) 8   6
Malton (0653) 693628

Hodgson, K. (19:4:10:5:4) 8   6
Malton (0653) 696651

Hood, W. (0:2:1:4:7) 8   5
Newmarket (0638) 778366

Horsfall, S. S. (1:3:0:0:3) 8   3
c/o Doncaster (0302) 7 10096

Howe, N. J. (12:7:5:4:8) 8   0
Wantage (02357) 68227 (home) and
69742 (office)

Johnson, E. (—:5:10:4:4) 7   8
Cirencester (0285) 655020

Keightley, S. L. (4:4:3:6:0) 8   11
Newmarket (0638) 666070

Kinane, M. J. (—:—:—:—:3) 8   4
(0903) 882 194 and
724756 (agent)

King, G. N. (7:5:0:0:0) 7   10
Newmarket (0638) 668 163

Lang, T. L. (3:0:0:1:0) 8   0
Kentisbeare (08846) 4 19

Lappin, R. T. (3:13:6:4:22) 7   12
(0372) 724018 and
mobilephone (0860) 394890

Lowe, J. J. (38:60:4 1:36:45) 7   8
(0904) 70887 1 (home) and
mobilephone (0860) 244284 or
(0609) 74824 1 (agent) and
mobilephone (0836) 229366

Mackay, A. (47:2 1:36: 10: 14) 7   8
Newmarket (0638) 662036 and
(agent) mobilephone (0831) 349630

Marcus, B. (—:—:—:—:16) 7   12
(0353) 723034 (home) and
07 1-407 6805 (agent)

Matthias, J. J. (14:11:7:22:9) 8   6
Kingsclere (0635) 298423 and
(0831) 208276

McAndrew, M. A. (0:0:0:0:0) 7   13

McGhin, R. (0:0:1:2:1) 8   3
Newmarket (0638) 660920

McGlone, A. D. (28:9:16:15:25) ... 7   12
Andover (0264) 79042 1 and
carphone (0836) 242788 and
(agent) Harrogate (0423) 87 1624 or
mobilephone (0836) 60 1850

McKay, D. J. (6:9:5:3:3) 7   8
Lambourn (0488) 684993 and
carphone (0860) 889007

McKeown, D. R.
(21:20:59:86:87) 8   2
South Milford (0977) 681247 and
mobilephone (0860) 685439 and
(agent) 07 1-3537440 ext. 3094 or
(0306) 8883 18

McKeown, T. P. (—:—:—:0:1) 7   9
Newmarket (0638) 66 1589

Mellor, Miss. A. D. (3:9:11:7:3) ... 7   7
Swindon (0793) 790230 and
carphone (0836) 278602

Mercer, A. (4:6:2:5:3) 7   10
Richmond (0748) 8 11103 and
Rillington (09442) 4 19 and
8879 (agent)

Miller, D. (—:—:—:—:2) 7   12
Newmarket (0638) 667624

Morris, Mrs C. L. (0:1:0:—:1) 8   8
Brighton (0273) 68 1679

Morris, S. D. (2:2:7:2: 1) 8   0
Malton (0653) 692098

Morse, R. R. (10:10:2:4:9) 7   10
08 1904 8927 (agent)

Munro, A. K. (0:6:33:38:95) 7   12
mobilephone (0831) 364757 and
(home) 076389 and
(agent) 07 1-222 2867 and
mobilephone (0831) 3 10505

Murray, J. G. (0:0:4:3:0) 8   4
c/o Southwater (0403) 730255 and
Rillington (09442) 4 19 and
8879 (agent)

Newnes, W. A. P.
(15:48:44:40:53) 8   2
(02357) 68 168 (home) and
(agent) 08 1-674 3673 and
(0271) 8838 13 and
mobilephone (0831) 235560

Nicholls, D. (38:33:32:28:26) 8   6
Easingwold (0347) 23094,
mobilephone (0831) 238088 and
York (0904) 6472 13 (agent)

Nutter, C. (2:2:1:2:5) 8   0
Newmarket (0638) 668 153

Peate, Mrs A. J. (—:—:—:—:2) ... 7   8

Perks, S. J. (19:18:18:34:29) 8   5
Armitage (0543) 49 1594

Piggott, L. K. (—:—:—:—:3) 8   7
Newmarket (0638) 662584

1056

Procter, B. T. (0:2:2:4:1) 8   3
East Ilsley (063528) 596
Proud, A. (6:10:12:7:4) 7   10
Bingham (0949) 43350 (home) and
50099 (office)

Quinn, J. A. (12:14:23:19:31) 7   7
Newmarket (0638) 730445
mobilephone (0831) 32 18 13 and
York (0904) 6472 13 (agent)
Quinn, T. R. (69:55:46:63:90) 8   2
Lambourn (0488) 72576 (home) and
carphone (0860) 287 172

Rate, C. (0:4:9:0:0) 8   0
Newmarket (0638) 66 1777
Raymond, B. H.
(—:45:77:66:75) 8   5
Newmarket (0638) 730387 (home) and
66643 1 (agent)
Raymont, S. J. (0:2:1:1:5) 8   2
Avebury (06723) 573
Reid, J. A. (60:81:79:84:67) 8   6
(0793) 522359 (agent)
Roberts, M. L.
(42:74:12 1:107:128) 7   13
Newmarket (0638) 66 1026 (home) and
East Ilsley (063528) 33 1 (agent)
Rogers, T. (—:—:—:—:0) 8   7
(0635) 64853
Rouse, B. A. (34:50:51:56:36) 8   2
Rusper (0293) 87 1547
Rutter, C. L. P. (30:27:15:14:28) . 7   10
Uffington (036 782) 276 (office),
Wantage (02357) 65263 (home),
(0836) 760769 (mobile)
Ryan, W. (56:69:58:49:59) 8   2
Harrogate (0423) 87 1624 or
mobilephone (0836) 60 1850 (agent)
and Newmarket (0638) 7 17236 (home)

Sedgwick, P. (—:—:—:0:3) 8   2
c/o Stamford Bridge (0759) 7 1472
Sexton, G. C. (8:6:1:0:0) 8   4
Newmarket (0638) 660252 (home)
Shoults, A. F. (22:11:4:4·7) 7   12
Newmarket (0638) 73037 1 and
(0932) 243913 or
carphone (0860) 234342 (agent)
Sidebottom, R. (0:—:—:—:1) 8   7
Newmarket (0638) 6667 11
Smith, V. (1:1:3:0:1) 8   6
Newmarket (0638) 668972
Sofley, J. A. (—:—:—:—:0) 7   10
Newmarket (0638) 66 1331
Street, R. (5:8:6:3:0) 7   8
Lambourn (0488) 714 12 and 7 1548
Struthers, P. A. (0:0:—:—:0) 8   4
Newmarket (0638) 665844

Swinburn, W. R. J.
(83:92:88:93:1 12) 8   6
Wickhambrook (0440) 820277 (home)
and Newmarket (0638) 6608 11 and
660258 (agent)

Taylor, C. (0:—:—:—:0) 7   10
c/o Newmarket (0638) 665454
Tebbutt, M. J. (2:0:2:8:23) 8   4
Newmarket (0638) 666625 (home) and
(agent) Harrogate (0423) 87 1624 or
mobilephone (0836) 60 1850
Thomas, M. L. (7:—:7:0:0) 7   7
Newmarket (0638) 666 187 and
663646 (agent)
Tinkler, Mrs K. A.
(18:2 1:16:12:13) 7   7
Burythorpe (065385) 245 and 5 12

Walsh, M. P. (—:—:—:1:2:4) 7   11
c/o Melton Mowbray (0664) 65225
Webster, S. G. (8:3:19:23:19) 8   1
(0904) 608458
Wernham, R. A. (12:3:12:6:7) 8   3
Abingdon (0235) 833754
Wharton, W. J. (3:0:0:1:0) 8   6
Newmarket (0638) 702808
Whitehall, A. J. (1:3:8:0:0) 7   11
Kingsclere (0635) 298598 and
Epsom (03727) 240 18 (agent)
Whitworth, S. J.
(28:22:31:24:34) 8   0
Marlborough (0672) 4096 1 (home),
carphone (0860) 676696 and
(agent) (0932) 2439 13 and
(0860) 234342 (mobile)
Wigham, C. (—:—:—:—:0) 7   10
Rillington (09442) 332
Wigham, M. (32:28:23:33:27) 8   2
York (0904) 488008 and
carphone (0831) 456426
Williams, D. J. (9:6:3:3:0) 7   10
Richmond (0748) 5640 (agent)
Williams, J. A. N.
(14:15:25:35:62) 8   3
Badminton (04542 1) 622 and
carphone (0836) 520252
Williams, T. L. (50:53:28:38:27) .. 7   10
Lambourn (0488) 72734 (home) and
carphone (0860) 589885
Wood, M. (15:10:1:2:1) 8   0

The following relinquished their licence
during the season

Bloomfield, P. S. (3:12:14:11:1)
Fry, M. J. (22:13:15:13:3)
Ryan, M. J. (—:—:—:1:0)

APPRENTICES

The following list shows the employer and riding weight of every apprentice who has ridden a winner and holds a current licence to ride on the flat, and the number of winners he or she has ridden in Britain, wins in apprentice races being recorded separately.

Armes, Miss A. C. (7) 1 + 4 ap 7   0
  (H. Candy)
Arrowsmith, F. P. (7) 3 + 8 ap 8   5
  (I. Balding)
Avery, C. M. (7) 3 + 2 ap 7   7
  (L. Holt)

Balding, Miss Claire (7) 1 ap 7   0
  (J. Balding)
Bastiman, H. J. (7) 1 7   7
  (R. Bastiman)
Bates, A. (7) 1 7   7
  (P. Kelleway)
  Newmarket (0638) 560464 and
  mobilephone (0831) 390708
Beeching, Miss K. F. (7) 2 7   7
  (S. Bowring)
Bentley, E. (7) 2 + 1 ap 7 12
  (M. Morley)
Biggs, D. D. (5) 21 + 11 ap 7   7
  (M. Jarvis)
  (0860) 766903 or (0323) 2 1877 (agent)
Biggs, Miss D. D. M. (7) 1 ap 7   7
  (P. Howling)
Birch, J. (7) 2 + 2 ap 7   3
  (M. O'Neill) 061-439 9023 (agent)
Bray, V. (7) 1 ap 7 10
  (M. Stoute)
Brislen, P. (7) 1 .... 7 12
  (H. Candy)
Brownsword, K. (7) 3 .... 7 11
  (T. Fairhurst)

Cairns, S. (7) 3 ap 7 10
  (W. Carter)

Dalton, P. J. (7) 6 + 1 ap 7   0
  (D. Smith) York (0904) 6472 13 (agent)
D'Arcy, D. J. (7) 4 ap 7   7
  (J. Gosden)
Davies, L. (7) 1 + 1 ap 7   6
  (C. Nelson)
Davies, S. G. (7) 2 ap 7   8
  (H. Cecil)
Deering, M. V. (7) 1 + 4 ap 7 12
  (J. FitzGerald)
Denaro, Mark (7) 1 ap 7   6
  (R. Hannon)
Denaro, M. J. (7) 1 + 3 ap 8   7
  (C. Allen)
Dobbin, A. G. (7) 2 + 2 ap 8   0
  (J. O'Neill)
Doyle, B. (7) 4 + 1 ap 6   5
  (C. Brittain)
Drowne, S. J. (7) 1 + 1 ap 7 10
  (R. Holder)

Fanning, J. K. (5) 15 + 2 ap 7   4
  (T. Fairhurst)
Forster, G. (7) 4 + 3 ap 7 12
  (J. Etherington)
Fortune, J. J. 77 + 7 ap 7 10
  (M. O'Neill)

  Coxwold (03476) 482 or
  carphone (0836) 326084 (agent)
Foster, G. N. (7) 3 + 11 ap 7   9
  (Lady Herries)

Garth, A. R. (7) 1 ap 7   0
  (R. Hollinshead)
Gibbs, D. (7) 1 + 1 ap 7 12
  (R. Hannon)
Gibson, D. R. 77 + 24 ap 7   9
  (W. Hastings-Bass)
  (0235) 835 184 and
  mobilephone (0831) 103354 and
  (0635) 28747 (office)
Giles, S. M. (7) 4 + 7 ap 7 12
  (J. Berry)
Greaves, Miss A. A. (3)
  50 + 2 ap 8   3
  (T. Barron)
Gwilliams, N. L. (5) 16 + 1 ap 7   3
  (M. Ryan)
  Newmarket (0638) 668484 (agent)

Hall, N. V. (7) 1 + 1 ap 7 10
  (G. Wragg)
Harper, Miss A. M. (7) 4 + 4 ap 7 12
  (R. Williams)
Haworth, S. M. (7) 2 + 4 ap 7   7
  (J. Berry)
Hillis, R. P. (3) 56 + 2 ap 7 13
  (B. McMahon)
  Newmarket (0638) 660767 (home)
  carphone (0831) 236748 and
  (agent) Peterborough (0733) 263816
Hind, G. E. P. (3) 65 + 8 ap 7   6
  (R. Hollinshead)
Hodgson, C. A. (5) 12 + 8 ap 7 10
  (M. Tompkins)
  Newmarket (0638) 66 1434 and
  (agent) (09442) 4 19
Holland, D. P. (5) 26 + 4 ap 7   4
  (B. Hills)
Houston, Miss J. (7) 3 + 7 ap 7   0
  (J. Toller)
  061-439 9023 (agent)
Hunt, M. R. (7) 2 ap 7 10
  (G. Balding)
Hunter, J. J. (7) 2 + 2 ap 7   0
  (D. Elsworth)
Husband, E. L. (7) 2 ap 7   2
  (R. Hollinshead)
Husband, G. I. (5) 29 + 9 ap 7   7
  (R. Hollinshead)

Johnson, P. A. (7) 1 ap 8   0
  (C. Booth)

Kennedy, N. A. (5) 11 7   5
  (G. Moore)
  York (0904) 6472 13 (agent)

Lanigan, S. (7) 1 ap 7   7
  (L. Cumani)

1991 FLAT RACING FIXTURES

(a)   Denotes All-Weather meeting
* Denotes evening meeting

March

1 Fri.	Southwell (a)
2 Sat.	Lingfield (a)
5 Tue.	Lingfield (a)
8 Fri.	Southwell (a)
9 Sat.	Lingfield (a)
12 Tue.	Lingfield (a)
16 Sat.	Southwell (a)
20 Wed.	Southwell (a)
21 Thu.	Doncaster
22 Fri.	Doncaster
23 Sat.	Doncaster, Lingfield (a)
25 Mon.	Folkestone, Leicester
26 Tue.	Leicester
27 Wed.	Catterick
28 Thu.	Brighton
30 Sat.	Haydock, Kempton, Newcastle

April

1 Mon.	Kempton, Newcastle, Nottingham, Warwick
2 Tue.	Warwick
3 Wed.	Hamilton
4 Thu.	Brighton
5 Fri.	Kempton
6 Sat.	Lingfield (a)
8 Mon.	Newcastle, Wolverhampton
9 Tue.	Pontefract, Wolverhampton
10 Wed.	Ripon
11 Thu.	Ripon
12 Fri.	Beverley
13 Sat.	Beverley, Warwick
15 Mon.	Edinburgh, Folkestone, Nottingham
16 Tue.	Newmarket
17 Wed.	Ayr, Newmarket, Pontefract
18 Thu.	Ayr, Newmarket
19 Fri.	Newbury, Thirsk
20 Sat.	Newbury, Thirsk
22 Mon.	Brighton, Hamilton
23 Tue.	Kempton
24 Wed.	Catterick, Kempton
25 Thu.	Beverley
26 Fri.	Carlisle, Sandown
27 Sat.	Leicester, Ripon, Sandown (mixed)
29 Mon.	Pontefract, Windsor*, Wolverhampton
30 Tue.	Bath, Nottingham

May

1 Wed.	Ascot
2 Thu.	Newmarket, Redcar, Salisbury
3 Fri.	Hamilton, Newmarket
4 Sat.	Haydock, Newmarket, Thirsk
6 Mon.	Doncaster, Haydock (mixed), Kempton, Warwick
7 Tue.	Chester, Salisbury
8 Wed.	Chester, Salisbury, Sandown*
9 Thu.	Brighton, Carlisle, Chester
10 Fri.	Beverley, Carlisle, Lingfield

11 Sat.	Bath, Beverley, Lingfield, Newmarket
13 Mon.	Edinburgh, Windsor*, Wolverhampton
14 Tue.	Nottingham*, York
15 Wed.	Kempton*, York
16 Thu.	York
17 Fri.	Newbury, Newmarket, Thirsk
18 Sat.	Hamilton*, Lingfield*, Newbury, Southwell*, Thirsk
20 Mon.	Bath, Folkestone, Hamilton, Wolverhampton
21 Tue.	Beverley, Goodwood
22 Wed.	Goodwood
23 Thu.	Catterick, Goodwood
24 Fri.	Haydock, Pontefract*
25 Sat.	Doncaster, Haydock, Kempton, Lingfield*, Southwell*, Warwick*
27 Mon.	Chepstow, Doncaster, Leicester, Redcar, Sandown
28 Tue.	Leicester, Redcar, Sandown*
29 Wed.	Brighton, Ripon*
30 Thu.	Brighton, Carlisle
31 Fri.	Goodwood*, Hamilton, Newcastle, Nottingham

June

1 Sat.	Edinburgh, Lingfield
3 Mon.	Edinburgh*, Leicester, Redcar
4 Tue.	Folkestone, Yarmouth
5 Wed.	Beverley*, Epsom, Yarmouth
6 Thu.	Beverley, Epsom,
7 Fri.	Catterick, Epsom, Goodwood*, Haydock*, Southwell
8 Sat.	Carlisle*, Catterick, Epsom, Haydock, Leicester*
10 Mon.	Brighton*, Nottingham, Pontefract
11 Tue.	Pontefract, Salisbury
12 Wed.	Beverley, Hamilton*, Kempton*, Newbury
13 Thu.	Chepstow*, Hamilton, Newbury
14 Fri.	Doncaster*, Goodwood*, Sandown, Southwell, York
15 Sat.	Bath, Lingfield*, Nottingham*, Sandown, York
17 Mon.	Brighton, Edinburgh, Windsor*, Wolverhampton*
18 Tue.	Royal Ascot, Thirsk
19 Wed.	Ripon, Royal Ascot
20 Thu.	Ripon, Royal Ascot
21 Fri.	Ayr, Redcar, Royal Ascot, Southwell*
22 Sat.	Ascot, Ayr, Lingfield*, Redcar, Warwick*
24 Mon.	Edinburgh, Nottingham, Windsor*
25 Tue.	Brighton, Newbury*, Yarmouth
26 Wed.	Carlisle, Chester*, Kempton*, Salisbury

27 Thu.	Carlisle, Salisbury
28 Fri.	Bath*, Doncaster, Goodwood*, Lingfield, Newcastle*, Newmarket
29 Sat.	Chepstow, Doncaster*, Lingfield*, Newcastle, Newmarket, Warwick*

July

1 Mon.	Edinburgh, Pontefract, Windsor*, Wolverhampton*
2 Tue.	Chepstow, Folkestone
3 Wed.	Catterick*, Warwick, Yarmouth
4 Thu.	Brighton*, Catterick, Haydock*, Yarmouth
5 Fri.	Beverley*, Haydock, Sandown, Southwell
6 Sat.	Bath, Beverley, Haydock, Nottingham*, Sandown
8 Mon.	Edinburgh, Leicester, Ripon*, Windsor*
9 Tue.	Newmarket, Pontefract
10 Wed.	Bath, Kempton*, Newmarket, Redcar*
11 Thu.	Chepstow*, Hamilton*, Kempton, Newmarket
12 Fri.	Chester*, Hamilton*, Lingfield, Warwick, York
13 Sat.	Ayr, Chester, Lingfield, Salisbury, Southwell*, York
15 Mon.	Ayr, Beverley*, Windsor*, Wolverhampton
16 Tue.	Ayr, Beverley, Folkestone*, Leicester*
17 Wed.	Catterick, Hamilton, Sandown*, Yarmouth*
18 Thu.	Catterick, Chepstow*, Hamilton*, Sandown
19 Fri.	Ayr, Newbury, Newmarket*, Thirsk
20 Sat.	Ayr, Lingfield*, Newbury, Newmarket, Ripon, Southwell*
22 Mon.	Ayr, Bath, Nottingham*, Windsor*
23 Tue.	Folkestone, Redcar,
24 Wed.	Doncaster, Redcar*, Sandown*, Yarmouth
25 Thu.	Brighton, Doncaster*, Yarmouth
26 Fri.	Ascot, Carlisle, Pontefract*, Yarmouth
27 Sat.	Ascot, Hamilton, Newcastle, Southwell*, Warwick*
29 Mon.	Lingfield, Newcastle, Windsor*, Wolverhampton*
30 Tue.	Beverley, Goodwood, Leicester*
31 Wed.	Catterick, Goodwood, Southwell*

August

1 Thu.	Goodwood, Yarmouth
2 Fri.	Edinburgh*, Goodwood, Newmarket*, Thirsk
3 Sat.	Goodwood, Newmarket, Thirsk, Windsor*
5 Mon.	Nottingham*, Ripon

6 Tue.	Brighton, Nottingham*, Redcar
7 Wed.	Brighton, Kempton*, Pontefract
8 Thu.	Brighton, Pontefract
9 Fri.	Haydock*, Newmarket*, Redcar
10 Sat.	Haydock, Lingfield*, Newmarket, Redcar, Southwell*
12 Mon.	Leicester*, Thirsk*, Windsor
13 Tue.	Bath, Catterick*, Yarmouth
14 Wed.	Beverley, Folkestone, Salisbury, Southwell
15 Thu.	Beverley, Salisbury, Southwell
16 Fri.	Haydock*, Newbury, Southwell
17 Sat.	Lingfield*, Newbury, Ripon, Wolverhampton*
19 Mon.	Hamilton, Windsor
20 Tue.	Folkestone, York
21 Wed.	Yarmouth, York
22 Thu.	Salisbury*, Yarmouth, York
23 Fri.	Goodwood, Newmarket
24 Sat.	Goodwood, Newcastle, Newmarket, Windsor*
26 Mon.	Chepstow, Newcastle, Ripon, Sandown, Warwick, Wolverhampton
27 Tue.	Ripon
28 Wed.	Brighton, Redcar
29 Thu.	Lingfield
30 Fri.	Chester, Sandown, Thirsk
31 Sat.	Chester, Ripon, Sandown

September

2 Mon.	Nottingham
3 Tue.	Brighton, Pontefract
4 Wed.	York
5 Thu.	Salisbury, York
6 Fri.	Haydock, Kempton
7 Sat.	Haydock, Kempton, Southwell, Thirsk
9 Mon.	Hamilton, Wolverhampton
10 Tue.	Carlisle, Leicester, Lingfield
11 Wed.	Doncaster
12 Thu.	Doncaster, Folkestone
13 Fri.	Doncaster, Goodwood
14 Sat.	Chepstow, Doncaster, Goodwood
16 Mon.	Bath, Edinburgh, Leicester
17 Tue.	Sandown, Yarmouth
18 Wed.	Ayr, Beverley, Sandown, Yarmouth
19 Thu.	Ayr, Beverley, Lingfield, Yarmouth
20 Fri.	Ayr, Newbury, Southwell
21 Sat.	Ayr, Catterick, Newbury
23 Mon.	Folkestone, Nottingham, Pontefract
24 Tue.	Kempton, Nottingham
25 Wed.	Brighton
26 Thu.	Ascot
27 Fri.	Ascot, Haydock, Redcar
28 Sat.	Ascot, Haydock, Redcar
30 Mon.	Bath, Hamilton, Wolverhampton

October

| 1 Tue. | Brighton, Newcastle, Wolverhampton |
| 2 Wed. | Newmarket, Salisbury |

3 Thu.	Lingfield, Newmarket
4 Fri.	Goodwood, Newmarket
5 Sat.	Goodwood, Newmarket
7 Mon.	Pontefract, Warwick
8 Tue.	Folkestone, Redcar, Warwick
9 Wed.	Haydock, York
10 Thu.	Haydock, York
11 Fri.	Ascot
12 Sat.	Ascot, York
14 Mon.	Ayr, Leicester
15 Tue.	Ayr, Chepstow, Leicester
16 Wed.	Redcar, Wolverhampton
17 Thu.	Newmarket
18 Fri.	Catterick, Newmarket
19 Sat.	Catterick, Newmarket
21 Mon.	Folkestone, Nottingham
22 Tue.	Chepstow, Chester, Nottingham
23 Wed.	Chester, Edinburgh
24 Thu.	Newbury, Pontefract
25 Fri.	Doncaster
26 Sat.	Doncaster, Newbury
28 Mon.	Bath, Leicester, Lingfield
29 Tue.	Leicester, Redcar, Salisbury
30 Wed.	Yarmouth
31 Thu.	Newmarket

November

1 Fri.	Newmarket
2 Sat.	Newmarket
4 Mon.	Newcastle
5 Tue.	Hamilton
7 Thu.	Edinburgh, Lingfield (a)
8 Fri.	Doncaster
9 Sat.	Doncaster
11 Mon.	Folkestone
12 Tue.	Southwell (a)
14 Thu.	Lingfield (a)
19 Tue.	Southwell (a)
28 Thu.	Lingfield (a)
29 Fri.	Southwell (a)

December

4 Wed.	Southwell (a)
5 Thu.	Lingfield (a)
12 Thu.	Southwell (a)
14 Sat.	Lingfield (a)
17 Tue.	Southwell (a)
18 Wed.	Lingfield (a)
27 Fri.	Lingfield (a)
28 Sat.	Southwell (a)

ERRATA & ADDENDA

'RACEHORSES OF 1989'

Aminata	rated at 98
Belmez (USA)	Page 112 Classic Fame is by Nijinsky
Be My Chief (USA)	Lord Seymour stayed 7f
Calabali	Bedhead, not Bedfellow
Commanche Nation	*Time* Domain
Deficit (USA)	dam won at up to 1¼m
Eventide	trainer, A. Hide
Exchange Fayre	first foal: dam never ran
Katsina (USA)	Newmarket, not Leicester
Lochross	*second* foal
Lord Glen	Catterick *and Ayr* in July
Mansonnien (Fr)	also won Grand Prix de Marseille in November (10g*)
Middle Kingdom (USA)	dam also won over 1m
Page 653	The photograph is of Fanatical winning the Coral Line Handicap at Newcastle
Royal Academy (USA)	won at the Curragh, not Phoenix Park
Septieme Ciel (USA)	additional form figure at end, 7g*
Snurge	2nd paragraph — Master *Guy*

SWING IT HONEY 2 gr.c. Swing Easy (USA)–Pure Honey 94 (Don (Ity) 123) —
[1989 a8g] sixth reported foal: half-brother to a winner in Belgium by High Line
and 8.2f winner Honeyman (by Remainder Man), also successful jumper: dam 5f
performer: always behind in maiden at Southwell (ran green). *F. Jordan*

Tiempo	sister to fair plater The Right Time
Topcliffe	third to Idle Chat
Index to photographs	Moyglare Stud Stakes Page 191

'RACEHORSES OF 1988'

Dancing Dissident (USA)	second foal: half-brother to a winner in Japan by Assert
Page 974	The official time for the Prix de l'Arc de Triomphe was 2m 27.30 secs

CHARACTERISTICS OF RACECOURSES

ASCOT—The Ascot round course is a right-handed, triangular circuit of 1m 6f and 34 yds, with a run-in of 2½f. There is a straight mile course, over which the Royal Hunt Cup is run, and the Old mile course which joins the round course in Swinley Bottom. All races shorter than a mile are decided on the straight course. From the 1½-mile starting gate the round course runs downhill to the bend in Swinley Bottom, where it is level, then rises steadily to the turn into the straight, from where it is uphill until less than a furlong from the winning post, the last hundred yards being more or less level. The straight mile is slightly downhill from the start and then rises to the 5f gate, after which there is a slight fall before the junction with the round course. Despite the downhill run into Swinley Bottom and the relatively short run-in from the final turn, the Ascot course is galloping in character; the turns are easy, there are no minor surface undulations to throw a long-striding horse off balance, and all races are very much against the collar over the last half-mile. The course is, in fact, quite a testing one, and very much so in soft going, when there is a heavy premium on stamina. In such circumstances races over 2 miles to 2¾ miles are very severe tests.
DRAW: The draw seems of little consequence nowadays.

AYR—The Ayr round course is a left-handed, oval track, about twelve furlongs in extent, with a run-in of half a mile. Eleven-furlong races start on a chute, which joins the round course after about a furlong. There is a straight six-furlong course of considerable width. The course is relatively flat, but there are gentle undulations throughout, perhaps more marked in the straight. It has a good surface and well-graded turns, and is a fine and very fair track, on the whole galloping in character.
DRAW: On the straight course a low draw is an advantage in big fields, particularly when the ground is soft.

BATH—The Bath round course is a left-handed, oval track, just over a mile and a half in extent, with a run-in of nearly half a mile. There is an extension for races over five furlongs and five furlongs and 167 yards. The run-in bends to the left, and is on the rise all the way. The mile and the mile-and-a-quarter courses have been designed to give over a quarter of a mile straight at the start, and the track generally is galloping rather than sharp.
DRAW: The draw seems of little consequence nowadays.

BEVERLEY—The Beverley round course is a right-handed, oval track, just over a mile and three furlongs in extent, with a run-in of two and a half furlongs. The five-furlong track bends right at halfway. The general galloping nature of the track is modified by the downhill turn into the straight and the relatively short run-in. The five-furlong course is on the rise throughout, and so is rather testing even in normal conditions; in soft going it takes some getting, particularly for two-year-olds early in the season.
DRAW: High numbers have an advantage over the five-furlong course.

BRIGHTON—The Brighton course takes the shape of an extended 'U' and is 1½ miles in length. The first three furlongs are uphill, following which there is a slight descent followed by a slight rise to about four furlongs from home; the track then runs more sharply downhill until a quarter of a mile out, from where it rises to the last hundred yards, the finish being level. The run-in is about 3½ furlongs, and there is no straight course. This is essentially a sharp track. While the turns are easy enough, the pronounced gradients make Brighton an unsuitable course for big, long-striding horses, resolute gallopers or round-actioned horses. Handy, medium-sized, fluent movers, and quick-actioned horses are much more at home on the course. There are no opportunities for long-distance plodders at Brighton.
DRAW: In sprint races a low number is advantageous, and speed out of the gate even more so.

CARLISLE—Carlisle is a right-handed, pear-shaped course, just over a mile and a half in extent, with a run-in of a little more than three furlongs. The six-furlong course, of which the five-furlong course is a part, the mile course, and the mile-and-a-half course start on three separate off-shoot extensions. For the first three furlongs or so the course runs downhill, then rises for a short distance, levelling out just beyond the mile post. From there until the turn into the straight the course is flat, apart from minor undulations. The six-furlong course, which bears right soon after the start, and again at the turn into the straight, is level for two furlongs, then rises fairly steeply until the distance, from which point it is practically level. The track is galloping in character, and the six-furlong course is a stiff test of stamina for a two-year-old.

DRAW: High numbers have an advantage which is more marked in the shorter races.

CATTERICK—The Catterick round course is a left-handed, oval track, measuring one mile and 180 yards, with a run-in of three furlongs. The five-furlong course bears left before and at the junction with the round course. From the seven-furlong starting gate the round course is downhill almost all the way, and there is a sharp turn on the falling gradient into the straight. The five-furlong course is downhill throughout, quite steeply to start with, and less so thereafter. Catterick is an exceedingly sharp track with pronounced undulations of surface, and it is therefore an impossible course for a big, long-striding animal. Experience of the track counts for a great deal, and jockeyship is of the utmost importance.

DRAW: A low number gives a slight advantage over five furlongs, but in races over six furlongs and seven furlongs a slow beginner on the inside is almost certain to be cut off.

CHEPSTOW—The Chepstow round course is a left-handed, oval track, about two miles in extent, with a run-in of five furlongs. There is a straight mile course, over which all races up to a mile are run. The round course has well-marked undulations, and the straight course is generally downhill and level alternately as far as the run-in, thereafter rising sharply for over two furlongs, and then gradually levelling out to the winning post. Notwithstanding the long run-in and general rise over the last five furlongs, this is not an ideal galloping track because of the changing gradients.

DRAW: Of little consequence nowadays.

CHESTER—Chester is a left-handed, circular course, only a few yards over a mile round, the smallest circuit of any flat-race course in Great Britain. It is quite flat and on the turn almost throughout, and although the run-in is nearly straight, it is less than two furlongs in length. Apart from extreme distance events, such as the Chester Cup and other 2¼m races, the course is against the long-striding, resolute galloper and greatly favours the handy, medium-sized, sharp-actioned horse.

DRAW: Given a good start, the draw is of little consequence. A slow start is virtually impossible to overcome in sprint races.

DONCASTER—Doncaster is a left-handed, pear-shaped course, over 15 furlongs round and quite flat, except for a slight hill about 1¼ miles from the finish. There is a perfectly straight mile, and a round mile starting on an off-shoot of the round course. The run-in from the turn is about 4½ furlongs. This is one of the fairest courses in the country, but its flat surface and great width, its sweeping turn into the straight, and long run-in, make it galloping in character, and ideal for the big, long-striding stayer.

DRAW: The draw is of no importance on the round course. On the straight course high numbers have an advantage, particularly in big fields.

EDINBURGH—The Edinburgh round course is a right-handed oval track, nearly a mile and a quarter in extent, with a run-in of half a mile. There is a straight five-furlong course. The track is flat, with slight undulations and a gentle rise from the distance to the winning post. The turns at the top end of the course and into the straight are very sharp, and handiness and adaptability to negotiate the bends is of the utmost importance. The big, long-striding, cumbersome horse is at a distinct disadvantage on the round track, especially in races at up to a mile and three furlongs, but to a lesser extent in races over longer distances.

DRAW: Over five furlongs low numbers have a considerable advantage when the stalls are on the stand side and high numbers have a slight advantage when the stalls are on the far side. High numbers have an advantage in seven-furlong and mile races.

EPSOM—Epsom is a left-handed, U-shaped course, 1½ miles in extent. The Derby course is decidedly uphill for the first half-mile, level for nearly two furlongs and

FLAT RACING FIXTURES 1991

MARCH
30th Sat.
Beamish Handicap; Field Marshal Stakes.

MAY
4th Sat.
Fairey Spring Trophy.

6th Mon. Mixed
Swinton Insurance Hurdle.

24th & 25th Fri. & Sat.
Be Friendly Handicap (Friday); Tote Credit Silver Bowl, Sandy Lane Stakes (Saturday).

JUNE
7th & 8th Fri. (Eve) & Sat.
Burtonwood Brewery Handicap (Friday); John of Gaunt Stakes (Saturday).

JULY
4th, 5th & 6th Thur. (Eve), Fri. & Sat.
July Trophy (Thursday); Johnny Osborne Handicap (Friday); Lancashire Oaks, Old Newton Cup, Cock of the North Stakes (Saturday).

AUGUST
9th & 10th Fri. (Eve) & Sat.
Manchester Evening News Handicap (Friday); Burtonwood Brewery Rose of Lancaster Stakes, Coral Bookmakers Handicap (Saturday).

16th Fri. (Eve)
Claude Harrison Handicap.

SEPTEMBER
6th & 7th Fri. & Sat.
Castle Casinos Handicap (Friday); Ladbroke Sprint Cup (Saturday).

27th & 28th Fri. & Sat.
Stanley Leisure Dream Mile (Friday);

OCTOBER
9th & 10th Wed. & Thur.
Fonseca Port Handicap (Wednesday); Henriot Blanc de Blancs Handicap (Thursday).

N.B. The details given above are correct at the time of going to press, but factors outside the control of the Haydock Park Executive may result in alterations having to be made.

For enquiries and special group prices please contact:
HAYDOCK PARK RACECOURSE, NEWTON-LE-WILLOWS,
MERSEYSIDE WA12 0HQ
Phone: Ashton-in-Makerfield (0942) 725963

HAYDOCK PARK .... *LEADING THE FIELD*

then quite sharply downhill round the bend to Tattenham Corner and all the way up the straight until approaching the final furlong, from where there is a fairish rise to the winning post. The run-in is less than four furlongs. The 7f and 6f courses start on tangential extensions. The 5f course is quite straight and sharply downhill to the junction with the round course. Races over 1½ miles can be testing if the pace over the first uphill four furlongs is strong, as it frequently is in the Derby. Otherwise the track is not really testing in itself, and races up to 8½ furlongs are very sharp indeed, the sprint courses being the fastest in the world. Owing to its bends and pronounced downhill gradients, Epsom favours the handy, fluent-actioned, medium-sized horse: big horses sometimes handle the course well enough, but cumbersome horses, long-striding gallopers, or those with pronounced 'knee-action' are not suited by it and are frequently quite unable to act upon it, especially when the going is firm or hard. Any hesitation at the start or slowness into stride results in considerable loss of ground over the first furlong in sprint races. For this reason Epsom is no course for a green and inexperienced two-year-old, slow to realise what is required.

DRAW: Nowadays a high draw is a considerable advantage over five furlongs and a slight advantage over six. A low number is an advantage over distances of seven furlongs to a mile and a quarter. A quick start is desirable at up to seven furlongs at least.

FOLKESTONE—The Folkestone round course is a right-handed, pear-shaped track, about ten and a half furlongs in extent, with a run-in of two and a half furlongs. There is a straight six-furlong course. The course is undulating, with the last part slightly on the rise, but notwithstanding its width, the easy turns, and the uphill finish, it is by no means a galloping track.

DRAW: No advantage on the straight course. Middle to high numbers have a slight advantage over seven furlongs. High numbers seem to have an advantage over a mile and a quarter and a mile and a half.

GOODWOOD—The Goodwood track consists of a nearly straight six-furlong course, with a triangular right-handed loop circuit. The Goodwood Cup, run over two and a half miles nowadays, starts near the winning post: the horses run the reverse way of the straight, branch left at the first or lower bend, go right-handed round the loop and return to the straight course via the top bend. Races over two miles, one and three quarter miles and one and a half miles are also run on this course. Over distances between seven furlongs and a mile and a quarter all running is done in the direction of the finish, with all but the mile and a quarter races using the lower bend. Although there is a five-furlong run-in from the top bend, the turns and, more specially, the pronounced downhill gradients from the turn, make Goodwood essentially a sharp track, favouring the active, handy, fluent-mover rather than the big, long-striding horse. This is of lesser importance in long-distance races, where the emphasis is on sound stamina, and of great importance in the shorter-distance races, particularly in sprints and especially when the going is on top. The five-furlong course is one of the fastest in the country.

DRAW: A low number is regarded as advantageous in sprint races when the ground is soft. Alacrity out of the gate is certainly of importance in five-furlong races.

HAMILTON—The Hamilton track is a perfectly straight six-furlong course, with a pear-shaped, right-handed loop, the whole being a mile and five furlongs in extent from a start in front of the stands, round the loop and back to the winning post. The run-in is five furlongs. The turns are very easy, and the course is undulating for the most part, but just over three furlongs from the winning post there are steep gradients into and out of a pronounced hollow, followed by a severe hill to the finish.

DRAW: Middle to high numbers have an advantage in races over the straight course.

HAYDOCK PARK—Haydock Park is a left-handed, oval-shaped course, about thirteen furlongs round, with a run-in of 4½ furlongs, and a straight 6-furlong course. The alternative 6-furlong course and all races of 1½ miles start on tangential extensions to the round course. Haydock is rather galloping in character.

DRAW: When conditions are testing there is a considerable advantage in racing close to the stand rail in the straight. Whatever the conditions, in races over 7 furlongs and a mile a good start and a handy position on the home turn are important.

KEMPTON—Kempton is a right-handed, triangular course, just over 13 furlongs round. The ten-furlong Jubilee Course starts on an extension to the round course. Sprint races are run over a separate diagonal course. The Kempton track is perfectly flat with normal characteristics, being neither a sharp track nor a galloping one.
DRAW: On the sprint course a draw near the rails is advantageous when the ground is soft; when the stalls are placed on the far side a high draw is an enormous advantage nowadays whatever the going.

LEICESTER—The Leicester round course is a right-handed, oval track, about a mile and three quarters in extent, with a run-in of four and a half furlongs. The straight mile course, on which all races of up to a mile are run, is mainly downhill to halfway, then rises gradually for over two furlongs, finishing on the level. The course is well-drained, the bends into the straight and beyond the winning post have been eased and cambered, and the track is galloping. For two-year-olds early in the season it poses quite a test of stamina.
DRAW: Low numbers have an advantage in races at up to a mile and the advantage seems to be more marked when the going is on the soft side.

LINGFIELD (Turf)—The Lingfield Park round course is a left-handed loop, which intersects the straight of seven furlongs and 140 yards nearly half a mile out. For nearly half its length the round course is quite flat, then rises with easy gradients to the summit of a slight hill, after which there is a downhill turn to the straight. The straight course has a considerable downhill gradient to halfway, and is slightly downhill for the rest of the way. The straight course is very easy, and the track as a whole is sharp, putting a premium on speed and adaptability, and making relatively small demands upon stamina, though this does not, of course, apply to races over two miles. The mile and a half course, over which the Derby Trial is run, bears quite close resemblance to the Epsom Derby course.
DRAW: On the straight course high numbers have a big advantage, the higher the number the bigger the advantage.

LINGFIELD (All-Weather)—The all-weather track is laid out inside the turf track, following much the same line in the straight and the back straight then turning sharply for home at the top corner, so that it is only a mile and a quarter in extent, a chute in the straight providing a thirteen-furlong start. There is no straight sprint course, the fields at five furlongs and six furlongs having two bends to negotiate. The surface is Equitrack, whereas Southwell's is Fibresand.
DRAW: Insufficient data available yet.

NEWBURY—The Newbury round course is a left-handed, oval track, about a mile and seven furlongs in extent, with a run-in of nearly five furlongs. There is a straight mile course, which is slightly undulating throughout. Races on the round mile and over the extended seven furlongs start on an extension from the round course. Notwithstanding the undulations this is a good galloping track.
DRAW: A high number used to be a fairly considerable advantage over the straight course, but since the narrowing of the track the advantage seems to have disappeared.

NEWCASTLE—Newcastle is a left-handed, oval-shaped course of a mile and six furlongs in circumference. There is also a straight course, over which all races of seven furlongs or less are run. The course is decidedly galloping in character, and a steady climb from the turn into the straight makes Newcastle a testing track, particularly for two-year-olds early in the season. Ability to see the journey out thoroughly is most important.
DRAW: On the straight course, the softer the ground the bigger the advantage the lower numbers enjoy. On a sound surface, horses racing up the middle seem to be at a disadvantage with those racing towards either rail.

NEWMARKET ROWLEY MILE COURSE—The Cesarewitch course is two and a quarter miles in extent, with a right-handed bend after a mile, the last mile and a quarter being the straight Across the Flat. From the Cesarewitch start the course runs generally downhill to a sharp rise just before the turn. There are undulations throughout the first mile of the straight, then the course runs downhill for a furlong to the Dip, and uphill for the last furlong to the winning post. This is an exceedingly wide, galloping track, without minor irregularities of surface, so it is ideal for the big, long-striding horse, except for the descent into the Dip, which is more than counterbalanced by the final hill.

DRAW: Little advantage normally, but in big fields low numbers have been favoured recently.

NEWMARKET SUMMER COURSE—The Newmarket Summer Course is two miles and twenty-four yards in extent, with a right-handed bend at halfway, the first mile being part of the Cesarewitch course, and the last the straight Bunbury Mile. The course runs generally downhill to a sharp rise just before the turn. There are undulations for the first three quarters of a mile of the straight, then the course runs downhill for a furlong to a dip and uphill for the last furlong to the winning post. This is an exceedingly wide, galloping track, ideal for the big, long-striding horse, except for the descent into the dip, which is more than counterbalanced by the final hill.
DRAW: The draw confers little advantage.

NOTTINGHAM—The Nottingham round course is a left-handed, oval track, about a mile and a half in extent, with a run-in of four and a half furlongs. There is a straight 6f course, but no longer a straight mile. The course is flat and the turns are easy.
DRAW: In sprints when the stalls are placed on the stand side high numbers have a clear advantage, increasing as the ground softens. With the stalls on the far side low numbers are preferred.

PONTEFRACT—Pontefract is a left-handed, oval track, about two miles in extent. There is no straight course, and the run-in is only just over two furlongs. There are considerable gradients and a testing hill over the last three furlongs. The undulations, the sharp bend into the straight, and the short run-in disqualify it from being described as a galloping track, but there is a premium on stamina.
DRAW: A low number is advantageous particularly over five furlongs but it becomes a decided disadvantage if a horse fails to jump off well.

REDCAR—Redcar is a narrow, left-handed, oval track, about a mile and three quarters in extent, with a run-in of five furlongs, which is part of the straight mile course. The course is perfectly flat with normal characteristics, and provides an excellent gallop.
DRAW: Middle to high numbers have a big advantage on the straight course.

RIPON—The Ripon course is a right-handed, oval circuit of 13 furlongs, with a run-in of 5f, and a straight 6f course. Owing to the rather cramped bends and the surface undulations in the straight, the Ripon track is rather sharp in character.
DRAW: On the straight course the draw is of no importance but in races on the mile course, horses drawn in the high numbers seem to have an advantage.

SALISBURY—The Salisbury track is a right-handed loop course, with a run-in of seven furlongs, which, however, is not straight, for the mile course, of which it is a part, has a right-handed elbow after three furlongs. For races over a mile and three quarters horses start opposite the Club Enclosure, and running away from the stands, bear to the left, and go round the loop. The course, which is uphill throughout the last half-mile, is galloping and rather testing.
DRAW: Low numbers are favoured in sprints when the going is soft.

SANDOWN—Sandown is a right-handed, oval-shaped course of 13 furlongs, with a straight run-in of 4f. There is a separate straight course which runs across the main circuit over which all 5f races are decided. From the 1¼m starting gate, the Eclipse Stakes course, the track is level to the turn into the straight, from where it is uphill until less than a furlong from the winning post, the last hundred yards being more or less level. The 5f track is perfectly straight and rises steadily throughout. Apart from the minor gradients between the main winning post and the 1¼m starting gate, there are no undulations to throw a long-striding horse off balance, and all races over the round course are very much against the collar from the turn into the straight. The course is, in fact, a testing one, and over all distances the ability to see the trip out well is of the utmost importance.
DRAW: On the five-furlong course high numbers have a considerable advantage in big fields when the ground is soft, and high numbers are favoured when the stalls are placed on the far side whatever the ground. Low numbers are favoured when the stalls are on the stand side.

SOUTHWELL—The left-handed course is laid out in a tight, level, mile-and-a-quarter oval, a spur to the three-furlong run-in providing a straight five furlongs.

York
1991 Fixtures
Great Races Great Racing

MAY
TUESDAY 14th●WEDNESDAY 15th●THURSDAY 16th

JUNE
FRIDAY 14th●SATURDAY 15th

JULY
FRIDAY 12th●SATURDAY 13th

AUGUST
TUESDAY 20th●WEDNESDAY 21st●THURSDAY 22nd

SEPTEMBER
WEDNESDAY 4th●THURSDAY 5th

OCTOBER
WEDNESDAY 9th●THURSDAY 10th●SATURDAY 12th

Fifteen Days Racing●Over £2,000,000 Prize Money

See it Live . . .

York Races

York Race Committee, The Racecourse, York YO2 1EX
Telephone: (0904) 620911   Fax: (0904) 611071

There are two types of surface, the all-weather track on the outside of the turf track. The all-weather surface is Fibresand, whereas Lingfield's is Equitrack.
DRAW: Insufficient data available yet.

THIRSK—The Thirsk round course is a left-handed, oval track, just over a mile and a quarter in extent, with a run-in of half a mile. There is a straight six-furlong course, which is slightly undulating throughout. The round course itself is almost perfectly flat, but though the turns are relatively easy and the ground well levelled all round, the track is on the sharp side and by no means ideal for a horse that requires time to settle down, and time and space to get down to work in the straight.
DRAW: High numbers have a big advantage on the straight course.

WARWICK—Warwick is a broad, left-handed, oval track, just over a mile and three quarters in extent, with a run-in of about three and a half furlongs. There is no straight course, the five-furlong course having a left-hand elbow at the junction with the round course. Mile races start on an extension from the round course, the first four and a half furlongs being perfectly straight. This is a sharp track, with the emphasis on speed and adaptability rather than stamina. The laboured galloper is at a disadvantage, especially in races at up to a mile.
DRAW: A high number is advantageous in races up to a mile when the ground is soft, but a quick beginning is also important.

WINDSOR—Windsor racecourse, laid out in the form of a figure eight, is 12½ furlongs in extent. In races of around 1½ miles both left-handed and right-handed turns are met. The last five furlongs of the course are straight, except for a slight bend to the right three furlongs from the finish. The six-furlong start is now on an extension of the straight. Although perfectly flat throughout, the bends make this track rather sharp in character. However, as there is a nearly straight 5f run-in the relative sharpness of the track is of no consequence in the longer races. Big, long-striding horses which normally require a more galloping course are at little or no disadvantage over these trips.
DRAW: No material advantage.

WOLVERHAMPTON—The Wolverhampton round course is a left-handed, pear-shaped or triangular track, just over a mile and a half in extent, with a run-in of five furlongs. There is a straight course of five furlongs. The course is level throughout, with normal characteristics.
DRAW: The draw confers no advantage.

YARMOUTH—The Yarmouth round course is a narrow, left-handed, oval track, about thirteen furlongs in extent, with a run-in of five furlongs. There is a straight mile course. Apart from a slight fall just before the run-in, the track is perfectly flat, with normal characteristics.
DRAW: Middle to high numbers have an advantage on the straight course.

YORK—York is a left-handed, U-shaped course, 2 miles in extent, and quite flat throughout. There is also a perfectly flat straight course, over which all 5f and 6f races are run. 7f races start on a spur which joins the round course after about two furlongs. The run-in from the turn is nearly 5 furlongs. This is one of the best courses in the country, of great width throughout and with a sweeping turn into the long straight. The entire absence of surface undulations makes it ideal for a long-striding, resolute galloper, but it is really a splendid track, bestowing no great favour on any type of horse.
DRAW: In 1989 low numbers had a marked advantage, particularly when the ground was on the soft side, but that seemed to have disappeared in the latest season.

LONDON THOROUGHBRED SERVICES LTD.

Purchases · Sales · Shares · Nominations
Stallion Management · Valuations · Transport · Insurance

1991 STALLION FEES

FORZANDO	£3,000	N.F.N.F. October 1st
KRIS	£35,000 +	£35,000 October 1st
PHARLY	£5,000	N.F.N.F. October 1st
ROBELLINO	£5,000	N.F.N.F. October 1st
SHARPO	£6,000	N.F.N.F. October 1st
SHARROOD	£5,000	N.F.N.F. October 1st
SHAVIAN	£8,000	N.F.N.F. October 1st
SLIP ANCHOR	£20,000	N.F.N.F. October 1st

APPROVED MARES ONLY
All nominations subject to availability

Enquiries to
LONDON THOROUGHBRED SERVICES LTD.,
44 St Leonard's Terrace, London SW3 4QH.
Telephone: 071-351-2181. Fax: 071-352-8958.
Telex: 916950 LONTSL G.

At Thornton Stud, Thornton-le-Street, Thirsk

KRIS

Chesnut, 1976, by **SHARPEN UP** out of **DOUBLY SURE,** by RELIANCE II

CHAMPION EUROPEAN MILER
CHAMPION SIRE
Sire of 3 Group 1 Winners in 1990
SHAVIAN (St James's Palace Stakes)
SHAMSHIR (Brent Walker Fillies Mile)
RAFHA (Prix de Diane Hermes)
KRIS has now sired 9 Group 1 Winners

Enquiries to: **LONDON THOROUGHBRED SERVICES LTD.,**
44 St Leonard's Terrace, London SW3 4QH.
Telephone: 071-351-2181. Fax: 071-352-8958. Telex: 916950 LONTSL G.
or John Day, **THORNTON STUD,** Thornton-le-Street, Thirsk, Yorkshire.
Telephone: (0845) 522522.

Standing at Woodland Stud, Newmarket

PHARLY

Multiple Group 1 winning son of LYPHARD

From his first 9 crops sire of 51% Winners to Foals

THE LEADING SIRE STANDING IN ENGLAND in 1990
(by number of Individual Winners)

Fee: £5,000 N.F.N.F. Oct. 1st

Standing at Woodland Stud, Newmarket

SHARPO

Chesnut, 1977, by Sharpen Up - Moiety Bird, by Falcon

Champion European Sprinter 1981/2

1986 **LEADING FIRST SEASON SIRE**

1987 Sire of dual Group 1 winner **RISK ME,** winner of Grand Prix de Paris **Gr.1,** Prix Jean Prat Ecurie Fustok **Gr.1**

1988 Sire of 27 individual winners of 39 races and £264,661 incl. **SWs SHARP GAIN, SHARP JUSTICE, SHARP REMINDER**

1989 Sire of 35 individual winners of 50 races and £338,463 including 2-y-old Group winner **POLE POSITION** and 10 individual 2-y-old winners.

1990 Sire of 32 individual winners of 54 races and £385,650 including **POLE POSITION** (Prix de Meautry **Gr.3**) and **SW SHARP REMINDER**

Fee: £6,000 N.F.N.F. Oct. 1st

Enquiries to: **LONDON THOROUGHBRED SERVICES LTD.,**
44 St Leonard's Terrace, London SW3 4QH.
Telephone: 071-351-2181. Fax: 071-352-8958. Telex: 916950 LONTSL G.

Standing at Highclere Stud, Nr. Newbury, Berkshire.

SHARROOD

Grey 1983, 16h.1in., by **CARO** ex **ANGEL ISLAND** by **COUGAR II**
Winner of 7 races from 2-4 years and £355,193

Won 4 consecutive races 6-7F at 2

Classic-placed at 3

Dual **Gr.2** winner in USA at 4

EXCELLENT OUTCROSS FOR
NORTHERN DANCER MARES

First Runners 1991

Fee: £5,000 N.F.N.F. Oct. 1st

Enquiries to: **LONDON THOROUGHBRED SERVICES LTD.,**
44 St Leonard's Terrace, London SW3 4QH.
Telephone: 071-351-2181. Fax: 071-352-8958. Telex: 916950 LONTSL G.
or **HIGHCLERE STUD,** Highclere, Newbury, Berks RG15 9LT.
Tel: (0635) 253212.

Retiring to Brook Stud in 1991

SHAVIAN

bay 1987, by Kris - Mixed Applause by Nijinsky

GROUP 1 WINNER BY KRIS

Winner of

St James's Palace Stakes **Gr.1** at Royal Ascot in 1990

Fee: £8,000 October 1st NFNF (Limited to 48 mares)

132 Timeform Black Book, 20th October 1990

"lengthy, good-bodied colt: strong-galloping type,
with powerful action…high-class performer"

Standing at Plantation Stud

SLIP ANCHOR

Bay 1982 by **SHIRLEY HEIGHTS** out of **SAYONARA**, by **BIRKHAHN**

CHAMPION EUROPEAN 3-YEAR-OLD OF 1985

WON Ever Ready Derby **Gr.1** by 7 lengths.

Successful First Crop Sire in 1990 with 4 winners of 5 races including **SHIMMERING SEA** (also 3rd Silken Glider Stakes **Gr.3**), **THIRD WATCH** and **WALEWSKAIA** (in France).

Fee £20,000 N.F.N.F. Oct 1st

Enquiries to: **LONDON THOROUGHBRED SERVICES LTD.,**
44 St Leonard's Terrace, London SW3 4QH.
Telephone: 071-351-2181. Fax: 071-352-8958. Telex: 916950 LONTSL G.
Leslie Harrison, **PLANTATION STUD,** Exning, Newmarket, Suffolk.
Telephone: Exning (063877) 341

1081

BBA

STALLIONS FOR 1991

ARAGON
(1980 by Mummy's Pet)
LAVINGTON STUD

BALIDAR
(1966 by Will Somers)
MEDDLER STUD

 BE MY CHIEF (USA)
(1987 by Chief's Crown)
THE NATIONAL STUD

BUSTINO
(1971 by Busted)
WOLFERTON STUD

 CHARMER
(1985 by Be My Guest)
BARTON STUD

CHIEF SINGER
(1981 by Ballad Rock)
SIDE HILL STUD

CHILIBANG
(1984 by Formidable)
THE NATIONAL STUD

DAMISTER (USA)
(1982 by Mr Prospector)
WOODDITTON STUD

 DASHING BLADE
(1987 by Elegant Air)
LITTLETON STUD

 DISTANT RELATIVE
(1986 by Habitat)
WHITSBURY MANOR STUD

DOMYNSKY
(1980 by Dominion)
EASTHORPE HALL STUD

DREAMS TO REALITY (USA)
(1982 by Lyphard)
WOOD FARM STUD

FAUSTUS (USA)
(1983 by Robellino)
FAWLEY STUD

HADEER
(1982 by General Assembly)
STETCHWORTH PARK STUD

HUBBLY BUBBLY (USA)
(1985 by Mr Prospector)
BELLMOR STUD

INSAN (USA)
(1985 by Our Native)
SLEDMERE STUD

JALMOOD (USA)
(1979 by Blushing Groom)
THE NATIONAL STUD

KALAGLOW
(1978 by Kalamoun)
BROOK STUD

K-BATTERY
(1981 by Gunner B)
CHESTERS STUD

LOCHNAGER
(1972 by Dumbarnie)
TICKLERTON STUD

MAZILIER (USA)
(1984 by Lyphard)
THE BARLEYTHORPE STUD

MIDYAN (USA)
(1984 by Miswaki)
WHITSBURY MANOR STUD

MINSTER SON
(1985 by Niniski)
LONGHOLES STUD

MOST WELCOME
(1984 by Be My Guest)
MEDDLER STUD

NIGHT SHIFT (USA)
(1980 by Northern Dancer)
BARTON STUD

NINISKI (USA)
(1976 by Nijinsky)
LANWADES STUD

NOMINATION
(1983 by Dominion)
LIMESTONE STUD

NORTHERN STATE (USA)
(1985 by Northern Dancer)
THE BARLEYTHORPE STUD

PETONG
(1980 by Mansingh)
THE BARLEYTHORPE STUD

PETOSKI
(1982 by Niniski)
THE NATIONAL STUD

PRECOCIOUS
(1981 by Mummy's Pet)
GOOSEMOOR STUD

REPRIMAND
(1985 by Mummy's Pet)
THE NATIONAL STUD

 ROCK CITY
(1987 by Ballad Rock)
THE NATIONAL STUD

SATIN WOOD
(1987 by Darshaan)
FAWLEY STUD

SAYF EL ARAB (USA)
(1980 by Drone)
WOODDITTON STUD

SHIRLEY HEIGHTS
(1975 by Mill Reef)
SANDRINGHAM STUD

SIZZLING MELODY
(1984 by Song)
GAZELEY STUD

SUPERLATIVE
(1981 by Nebbiolo)
WOODDITTON STUD

WAKI RIVER (USA) _NEW_
(1985 by Miswaki)
SLEDMERE STUD

WARRSHAN (USA) _NEW_
(1986 by Northern Dancer)
LAVINGTON STUD

ZALAZL (USA) _NEW_
(1986 by Roberto)
THE HALL STUD

For further details of nomination fees and availability
please contact **Simon Morley** or **Martin Percival**,
BBA Stallion Department on **(0638) 665021**

The BRITISH
BLOODSTOCK AGENCY plc

Queensberry House, High Street, Newmarket, Suffolk CB8 9BT
Tel: (0638) 665021   Fax: (0638) 660283   Telex: 817157 BBA NKT G
also at: 1 Chapel View, High Street, Lambourn, Berks RG16 7XL
Tel: (0488) 73111   Fax: (0488) 71219

COOLMORE STALLIONS FOR 1991

AL HAREB (El Gran Senor - Icing)

ALZAO (Lyphard - Lady Rebecca)

BE MY GUEST (Northern Dancer - What a Treat)

BLUEBIRD (Storm Bird - Ivory Dawn)

CAERLEON (Nijinsky - Foreseer)

COMMANCHE RUN (Run the Gantlet - Volley)

DANEHILL (Danzig - Razyana)

DON'T FORGET ME (Ahonoora - African Doll)

GALLIC LEAGUE (Welsh Saint - Red Rose Bowl)

GLENSTAL (Northern Dancer - Cloonlara)

COOLMORE

CONTACT: **COOLMORE STUD**, FETHARD, CO. TIPPERARY, IRELAND.
TEL: 353-52-31298. TELEX: 80695. FAX: 353-52-31382.
BOB LANIGAN: 353-52-31298. **CHRISTY GRASSICK:** 353-52-31313.

HIGH ESTATE (Shirley Heights - Regal Beauty)

LAST TYCOON (Try My Best - Mill Princess)

LAW SOCIETY (Alleged - Bold Bikini)

PERSIAN HEIGHTS (Persian Bold - Ready & Willing)

ROYAL ACADEMY (Nijinsky - Crimson Saint)

SADLER'S WELLS (Northern Dancer - Fairy Bridge)

SALMON LEAP (Northern Dancer - Fish Bar)

SCENIC (Sadler's Wells - Idyllic)

THATCHING (Thatch - Abella)

TIROL (Thatching - Alpine Niece)

TRY MY BEST (Northern Dancer - Sex Appeal)

WAAJIB (Try My Best - Coryana)

PAUL SHANAHAN: 353-52-31298/353-52-31645 (HOME). TOM GAFFNEY: 353-25-31966.
DAVID MAGNIER: 353-25-31966/31689/31465 (HOME),
OR JOE HERNON: 353-25-31966/31689 OR 353-22-26275 (HOME).

ᴄAirlie — *SIRES FOR 1991*

FEES: Ir. Gns N.F.N.F.
1st Oct. terms

BALLAD ROCK

6,500

Champion Sprinter, 9th Leading Sire standing in Ireland in 1990 with **14** winners of **28** races, **£280,000**, incl. **ROCK CITY** (**Gr. 3** Greenham S and **Gr. 3** Criterion Stakes; placed **Gr. 1** 2000 Guineas, **Gr. 1** St. James's Palace Stakes, **Gr. 1** July Cup, etc.), **BALLA COVE** (Stakes winner in U.S.A.), **TREBLE HOOK** (good 2-y-o winner and **LR**-placed in Ireland), **MISS ALESSIA**, **BOLD FOX** and **6 individual 2-y-o winners** in 1990. 22 yearlings averaged **27,331 gns** in 1990.

ELA MANA MOU

10,000

European Champion. **A leading European Sire** — with Classic winners **SNURGE** (**Gr. 1** St Leger, and third **Gr.1** Prix de l'Arc de Triomphe 1990), **TRIVIAL PURSUIT** (**Gr. 2** Swedish Derby, £50,000), and **EUROBIRD; Gr.1** winners **ALMAARAD, EMMSON, SUMAYR** and **NATSKI; Gr.2** winners **FAIR OF THE FURZE, ELA ROMARA, GRECIAN URN**, etc. 20 yearlings averaged **18,936 gns** in 1990.

GLOW

7,000

Grade 2 winning Miler by **NORTHERN DANCER.** Closely related to leading sire **Caerleon** and Group sire **Vision**. GLOW's first crop winners include **NORTHERN GLOW** (also stakes-placed in Orby S, at Leopardstown) **GLOW LAMP** (also stakes placed) and **BETTINA DA CASERTA**. Yearlings have made up to **120,000 gns** at Newmarket.

KING OF CLUBS

4,000

Group 1 winning Miler by **MILL REEF**. Won 10 races, over £¼ million. Sire of stakes winners in 1989 and 1990 with just two crops of racing age — **GRAND MORNING** — **LR** Marble Hill EBF S, Curragh, 1990. **KAA** — **LR** Criterium Varesino at 2, 1990. **CLOONCARA** — **LR** Criterium Nazionale, **LR** Premio Vittorio Crespi at 2, 1989; also winner in 1990 and **LR**-placed. **QUEENEMARA** — 5 wins incl. **LR** Grand Criterium de Bordeaux. Sire of **11 ind. 2-y-o winners** in 1990.

SALT DOME

3,500

Group 2 winning sprinter by **Nashwan's** sire **BLUSHING GROOM**. Brother in blood to top U.S. sprinter and 1990 **Gr. 1** sire **MT. LIVERMORE** (sire of **Housebuster**, 10 Gr and stakes wins at 2 and 3 years, etc.). **First crop are yearlings in 1991**.

STANDAAN

3,000

Brilliant sprinter — **Gr. 3** Palace House S. (beating Sharpo by over 3 lengths), **LR** Stewards' Cup, etc. **Champion First Crop sire in New Zealand**. Group and Classic sire there. First Irish crop yearlings have averaged more than twice his stud fee and made up to **14,500 gns**.

ᴄAirlie

Airlie Stud, Lucan, Co. Dublin.
Tel: 010 353 1 6280267/6281548. Fax 1 6283109.